SONG INDEX

An Index To More Than 12000 Songs
In 177 Song Collections
Comprising 262 Volumes

AND SUPPLEMENT, 1934

EDITED BY
MINNIE EARL SEARS

ASSISTED BY
PHYLLIS CRAWFORD

Two Volumes in One

THE SHOE STRING PRESS, INC.
1966

Originally issued as part of STANDARD CATALOG
SERIES by The H. W. Wilson Company. SONG
INDEX first published 1926. SONG INDEX SUPPLE-
MENT first published 1934.

Reprinted 1966 by arrangement with
The H. W. Wilson Company

Library of Congress Catalog Card Number: 66–25185
Printed in the United States of America

PUBLISHER'S NOTE:

This volume is a facsimile reproduction of both the SONG INDEX and SONG INDEX SUPPLEMENT, originally published as two separate volumes. The former covers pages i-xxxviii, 1–648 and the latter covers pages i-xl, 1–366. The only change is the deletion of the "Directory of Publishers" due to its outdated information.

SONG INDEX

AN INDEX TO MORE THAN 12000 SONGS

IN 177 SONG COLLECTIONS
COMPRISING 262 VOLUMES

PREFACE

At the Swampscott meeting of the American Library Association in 1921, the undersigned suggested that the A.L.A. undertake the publication of a S o n g I n d e x. The Executive Board, however, had ruled that the A.L.A. should not publish a work which might be issued profitably by a regular publisher. Mr. H. W. Wilson was then asked to consider publishing such a book, and he took the matter under advisement. Previous to the Detroit meeting of 1922, Mrs. Jennie T. Jennings, chairman of the Catalog Section, had sent to some thirty libraries a comprehensive questionnaire on the subject, accompanied by a list of 125 collections, which the libraries were asked to check for those they would wish indexed. The answers were tabulated and the results presented to the Catalog Section at Detroit by Mrs. Jennings. Mr. Wilson then announced that The H. W. Wilson Company had decided to publish the I n d e x. At the meeting of the Catalog Section in 1923, the undersigned was appointed chairman of the A.L.A. Committee on S o n g I n d e x. The chairman then appointed the following as members of the committee: Miss Emily E. Child, Brooklyn Public Library; Mr. Julius Mattfeld, New York Public Library; Miss Dorothy Lawton, New York Public Library; Miss Isadore Gilbert Mudge, Columbia University Library; Miss Catherine Van Dyne, Newark Free Public Library. The committee represents both the general reference worker and the specialist in music in public libraries. Early in 1924 the answers to the 1922 questionnaire and the checked lists were turned over to the editor and furnished a starting point for the I n d e x. The committee as a whole and the members individually were frequently consulted by the editor during the process of compilation, approved decisions of the editor from time to time, and kept in touch with the progress of the work.

The S o n g I n d e x is a reference book long needed by every public library. The committee rejoice at its publication, extend thanks to the editor and the publishers for their careful work, and commend the I n d e x to the library world.

Franklin F. Hopper.

June 14, 1926

INTRODUCTION

As the interest in music collections in libraries has constantly increased, the need of an index to songs has been so much felt that a number of libraries have made their own indexes. The present work, which indexes 177 collections in 262 volumes, results from this need on the part of many libraries. More than 12000 songs are included.

In using this I n d e x it is essential to bear in mind the fact that it is an index made from the collections themselves and not a comprehensive dictionary of songs. In other words, in the main the information *as given in the books themselves* forms the basis of the work. It does not pretend to be a court of last resort to settle disputed points about the history, authorship, etc. of the songs. When it is considered that the work includes over 12000 songs in many languages, and at least 3500 names of composers and authors, it will readily be seen that it was impossible (even if desirable) to do the research work that would have been necessary in order to verify all entries. That is work for the music specialist with unlimited time at his disposal. Some of the collections indexed were compiled and edited much more carefully than others and doubtless many mistakes occurring in the less carefully made books have been copied here. When mistakes were evident they were corrected but of course no attempt could be made to check the accuracy of each item. When conflicting information about a song was given in different collections, the entry has been made in accordance with the weight of evidence. As the work developed, it was found that a considerable amount of verification and investigation was necessary to obtain reasonably satisfactory entries. Sometimes when a song has been variously attributed to different composers it has seemed necessary to give this information in the main entry as a guide to those who may look for it under various composers (e.g. "Drink to me only with thine eyes." Attributed to R. Mellish; wrongly attributed to Mozart). Necessary references have then been made to the proper entry.

Scope. The standard collections of songs by various composers which have been found most useful in the medium sized public library have been included. In a small or medium sized library this should be a fairly complete index to the library's resources within the field covered, and in the large libraries it will serve as a "first aid." While the desirability of including as many songs as possible was realized, to have included all existing song collections (as was suggested by a few libraries) was impracticable because the resulting size and expense would have put the I n d e x beyond the reach of the smaller libraries, where this help is much needed. Some few out of print and likewise a few unusual collections have been included and the impossibility of including more of the latter is regretted. These should add greatly to the usefulness of the I n d e x even in small libraries where these collections are not to be found. If the librarian is thus able to locate a desired song in a particular book not in the library, it is always possible to write to a large library which has the book and have the item copied from that book.

Selection of Titles Included. The selection of the 177 collections (in 262 volumes) included is based on lists voted on by the following libraries: Public libraries of Baltimore; Boston; Brooklyn; Chicago; Cincinnati; Cleveland; Denver; Detroit; Evanston, Ill.; Haverhill, Mass.; Los Angeles; Louisville, Ky.; Minneapolis; New York; Newark; Omaha, Neb.; Providence, R. I.; St. Louis; St. Paul; San Diego; Seattle; Springfield, Mass.; Tacoma, Wash.; Wilmington, Del.; other libraries: Eastman School of Music, University of Rochester, Rochester, N.Y.; Library of Congress; Newberry Library, Chicago; Peabody Institute, Baltimore. In taking up the work in 1924 the editor started with the lists sent out in 1922 by Mrs. Jennie Thornburg Jennings, at that time chairman of the A.L.A. Catalog Section. In 1924 a revised and much enlarged list of 219 titles of collections was sent to 31 libraries of various sizes and from the returns the collections to be indexed were selected. In order to include some of the newer collections, a short supplementary list was sent out late in 1925. With the advice of our collaborators, 50 collections have been selected from the total number for first purchase in smaller libraries and these are marked with a star in the Classified List of Collections Indexed.

Classes of Songs Excluded. In order to keep the size of the I n d e x within reasonable bounds it was necessary to limit not only the number of collections included but also the type of collection, hence it was decided to exclude the following: (1) Collections of individual composers. The best known songs are in the general collections and the others are comparatively easy to find in the collections themselves. The original plan to give a preliminary list of best editions of collections of individual composers recommended to medium sized libraries was abandoned when it was found that such a list would be confined to the publications of about six of the leading music publishers in the United States and England. (2) Hymn books. The several hundred hymns included in the general collections indexed are of course included. There is the Julian Dictionary of Hymnology, and, as one library said, "Let Julian do it." The hymn books themselves are usually well indexed under author, composer, title, tune and first line. (3) Collections of folk dances and singing games, and most collections of children's songs. A selection of these will be found in the Quigley Index to Kindergarten Songs. Those found in the general collections indexed we have included. (4) Collections published in foreign countries other than Great Britain, except one German collection (Erk's Deutscher Liederschatz). (5) Collections with words only. (6) Collections with words and tune but without instrumental setting have usually been excluded, but a few such have been included because of their importance.

Entries. Entries will be found under *title* (the main entry), *composer*, and *author* of the words. *References from first line to title* are also included.

(1) TITLE ENTRY. This is the main entry and the place where the fullest information is given. It is the only place where the symbol for the collection in which the song is located is given. References to this main title entry have been made (a) from alternate titles, from different titles in different collections, from all translations of a title, when entry is in the original language, and from the original titles in those languages (such as Russian) where the main entry is under an English title; (b) from first lines both in original and translation and, in a few

cases, from first line of chorus. The reader is thus directed to the place where the fullest information is to be found. Under the main title entry will be found listed all variations in title in different collections. Entries for these are indented under the main title entry, and for the sake of clearness the main title has been repeated here when it is used in the copies noted. The title entry gives: (a) title, followed by alternate titles in parenthesis. Often the first line is given in parenthesis, especially when necessary to distinguish between songs with same or similar titles (e.g. Abschied); (b) name of composer, when given. This has occasionally been supplied. If no composer is given, "Folk air" or some other descriptive term is often given, or name of the setting, following in this respect the usage of the collections; (c) name of author, when known, preceded by "Words by"; (d) language abbreviations for foreign songs; (e) symbols for collections in which the song is to be found. In many cases the title and first line are identical. Occasionally, even when title of song is used in the collection, the first line, followed by title, has been used as the main entry in order to bring different settings of a poem together and in such cases the user of the I n d e x will need to look in the collection indexed under both in order to find the song.

(2) COMPOSER ENTRY. Composers' names are printed in boldface roman type. Under the name are given titles of songs. When the same air has been used for two songs, a note to this effect is added to the second. If a song is known to be from an opera or oratorio this information is added. In cases where a composer is also author of words, that information is usually given in title entry only. When a man is composer of some songs, and author, or composer and author, of others these titles are separated. Probably this division is not always accurate, as it has usually been made from the information given in the collections, which vary greatly in the amount and accuracy of their information. Obvious mistakes of composer for author and vice versa have been corrected.

(3) AUTHOR ENTRY. Authors' names are printed in boldface italics to distinguish them from composers, which are in roman. After the title of the poem is given composer's name. When there is another setting of the same song entered under a translated title, this is noted. If composer's name is not known a descriptive phrase (such as "French air") is used. These author entries have been included because various collaborators have emphasized their importance in general reference work as distinct from the special reference work of the music library. In some of the collections indexed, translators are sometimes given as authors, and, while we have corrected many such errors, doubtless there are others which have not been discovered.

(4) FIRST LINE REFERENCES. The first line is always given in quotation marks, even when it is also the title. Where the title differs from first line, references have been made from first line to title, including references from first lines in all translations as well as in the original. Where one or two words only of first line are used as title, reference from the entire first line has sometimes been made when the two alphabet rather far apart. These first line entries often proved very useful in bringing together copies of a song appearing in different collections under such widely divergent titles that their identity was not at first discovered. Reference from the first line of the chorus has not ordinarily been made, but in some exceptional cases, where a song is better known by the

first line of the chorus, reference has been made from it (e.g. For a' that, an' a' that. See "Tho' women's minds like winter winds," by Burns).

Arrangement. In the main the arrangement is strictly alphabetical. The Rules for Filing Cards of the Carnegie Library of Pittsburgh, which are now used in many libraries, have been followed in the main. The whole question of arrangement has presented difficulties because of the title and first-line entries in so many languages, but the aim has been to present a usable and convenient arrangement rather than a scholarly one. Articles are always retained at the beginning of title and first line but the articles are disregarded in the arrangement. In such entries the title is alphabeted by the word following the article and this word is printed in boldface. In some of the less familiar languages, where the articles will not be recognized by the ordinary person, this practice may be questioned but it seemed better to apply the same rule to all. Abbreviations are arranged as if spelled in full. Contractions are arranged as one word, e.g. Who'd is filed as Whod. Elisions are arranged as printed and are treated as part of the following words, e.g. C'est is filed as Cest. In hyphened words the hyphen is disregarded and the words are arranged as separate words. An exception is made where the hyphen is really part of the word (e.g. a-nutting, a-roving) and in American Indian names. Modified vowels in German, in the Scandinavian languages, etc., are written as they occur and are arranged as one letter unless written as two (e.g. Goethe). To facilitate quick use the many titles beginning O and Oh have been filed together, under O. This same rule has been applied in a few other cases.

Language of Entry. Foreign songs are entered under the title in the original language when it is given in the collection indexed, with the exception of the languages noted below. When none of the collections indexed gives the original title or words then the entry is under the English title, with reference from the original title. Songs in the following languages, many of which do not use the Latin alphabet, are entered under the English title unless the original title is much better known (e.g. Aloha oe; Kimi ga yo).

(a) African languages
(b) Albanian
(c) American Indian languages
(d) Eskimo
(e) Finno-Ugrian languages, including Esthonian, Finnish, Hungarian, Lappish
(f) Greek, Modern
(g) Oriental languages, including Armenian, Arabic, Chinese, Hebrew, Indic languages (languages of India), Japanese, Persian, Turkish; also Fijian language and Polynesian languages (including Hawaiian)
(h) Russian and other Slavic languages and Lithuanian-Lettish, including Bohemian, Bulgarian, Lettish, Lithuanian, Polish, Russian, Serbo-Croatian, Slovak, Slovenian
(i) Yiddish

The decision to enter under the title in the original language was made in accordance with the preference of the majority of the libraries consulted.

Transliteration. All titles are given in the Latin alphabet. Titles in languages employing other alphabets (e.g. Russian) have been transliterated when necessary. This will probably meet the needs of most libraries using the I n d e x. When we have done the transliterating, the Library of Congress system has been followed but when the collections themselves contained the title in transliteration we have used it as given, regardless of the fact that different systems have been used by the various editors. Only one collection indexed (Botsford, Folk Songs of Many Peoples) contains text in the original characters. In the main title entries, where the languages of a song are indicated, no distinction has been made between this collection and those which contain transliterated text.

Language Abbreviations. The language or languages of the text of a song are indicated in the main title entry by a language abbreviation which precedes the location symbol. For example, "Casta diva, che inargenti." Bellini. e.i. PP, contains words in both English and Italian. No language abbreviation is given for songs in the English language, when this is the original language of the song. Doubtless some songs which have been regarded as English, because so given in the collection indexed, are in reality translations into English. Many such cases have been caught, and the correct information supplied. Under a language are included all songs in dialects of that language.

Airs. The I n d e x is an index of songs and not of airs, but for hymns included it has often been necessary to make a reference from the name of the tune, as hymns are frequently known by that rather than by title. For convenience the name of the tune is then given as an alternate title in the title entry.

Variants. In obvious cases the variants of songs have been noted but it has not been feasible to do this in all cases. Versions of a folk song will usually be found entered under the main title entry (e.g. Barbara Allen). In the case of folk songs (including negro spirituals) which occur in several collections indexed, it is safe to assume that minor variations occur, but these we have disregarded unless they are distinct enough to be regarded as different versions. In the case of several chanteys with the same title, the variations are of such a character that they have not been grouped under one entry but each has been given its own entry, with notes as to variants (e.g. A-roving; Blow the man down).

Subjects. It was originally suggested that a classified list be added, arranged under a few subjects such as Christmas songs, Folk songs, Shakespeare songs, etc. Limitations as to size made it necessary to choose between (1) indexing as many collections as possible, or (2) cutting down the number of collections in order to include this feature. The A.L.A. S o n g I n d e x Committee and the majority of libraries consulted agreed that it was more essential to include as many collections as possible. However, anyone looking for subjects will not find them lacking. Under Shakespeare's name will be found all Shakespeare songs. The Classified List of Collections Indexed is arranged by subject and this should be a help and convenience in reference work. Folk songs, which are probably more often called for to illustrate the music of different countries rather than as individual titles, will be found in the section of the list entitled "National and Folk Songs" and its country subdivisions. Collections of this kind which are general in scope (e.g. Elson's Folk Songs of Many Nations) have annotations giving a classification of the contents by country. Collections in the section called "General" have similar notes, classifying the contents of each volume.

Voice. When voice is specified in the title of the collection, this information is given after the title in the Classified List of Collections Indexed.

Uses. In its field this I n d e x should be as useful to libraries as is the well known Granger Index to Poetry and Recitations. Its usefulness in the music department of a library in finding words and music of a wanted song need not be dwelt on. General reference workers and those who do work with schools will find a valuable feature in the entries under the authors of words, which show what poems of individual authors have been set to music. In giving them, the I n d e x follows the precedent set by the Catalogue of the Allen A. Brown Collection of Music in the Boston Public Library. It will likewise supplement Granger to those looking for foreign poems, for it will serve as a first line and title index to many poems from foreign languages, both in the original and in translation. With the increasing interest in music collections in libraries and with the scarcity of aids in the selection of this material, libraries should find the list of collections indexed, which has been carefully selected, a timely aid as a buying list. A number of libraries have already used it for that purpose. All publishers of music should find it a valuable tool.

Acknowledgements. The editor wishes to express her thanks to the libraries which cooperated in answering questionnaires, in checking lists of titles to be included, and in giving advice at various times. To all members of the A.L.A. Committee on the S o n g I n d e x the editor extends grateful thanks for help and advice. The resources of the Music Division of the New York Public Library have been much used and Miss Dorothy Lawton, head of the Music Library of the Circulation Department, and Mr. Julius Mattfeld, formerly acting chief of the Music Division, have given freely of their time. Special acknowledgement is made to the reference staff of the Columbia University Library for help on many points. The service rendered by Mrs. Jennie Thornburg Jennings, who sent out the first questionnaire on the subject and thus paved the way for this I n d e x, should also receive special mention. The devoted service of Phyllis Crawford has contributed largely to the making of the I n d e x. She is responsible for all of the detailed work of the indexing, and also for seeing the work through the press. The editor extends hearty thanks to her for her able assistance in all parts of the work. Grateful acknowledgment is made to Eva Cotter for careful proofreading.

Thanks are due to the publishers who, with one exception, generously gave us copies of their books which are included in the I n d e x. In this exceptional case the books which were considered of first importance by cooperating libraries were purchased.

The editor will be grateful for notices of any mistakes which may be discovered by users of this work. It is realized that errors occur, but those familiar with the peculiarities and inconsistencies of the class of books indexed will understand the difficulty of producing an index free from errors.

MINNIE EARL SEARS.

July, 1926

Contents

Classified List of Collections Indexed xiii

Key to Symbols for Collections Indexed........ xxix

Key to Language Abbreviations xxxiii

Key to Miscellaneous Abbreviations xxxiii

Directions for Use xxxiv

Song Index 1-648

Classified List of Collections Indexed

Titles starred are recommended for first purchase
Unless otherwise indicated, collections contain piano accompaniment
When a collection is issued in two editions, high voice and low voice, this is specified
All prices are subject to change

Arrangement

General p. xiii
National and Folk Songs p. xviii
   A. General Collections p. xviii
   B. Collections by Nationality p. xx

American, including Indian and Negro p. xx
Danish. See Scandinavian
Dutch p. xxi
English p. xxi
French p. xxii
German p. xxiii
Hawaiian p. xxiii
Irish p. xxiii
Italian p. xxiii
Japanese p. xxiv

Mexican and South American p. xxiv
Norwegian. See Scandinavian
Russian p. xxiv
Scandinavian p. xxv
Scottish p. xxv
South American. See Mexican and South American
Spanish p. xxv
Swedish. See Scandinavian
Welsh p. xxv

Yiddish p. xxv

Chanteys p. xxv
Christmas Carols p. xxvi
Sacred Songs p. xxvi
School and College Songs p. xxvii

GENERAL COLLECTIONS

Album of bass songs. 4v G. Schirmer c1888-94 pa ea $1.25; cl ea $2.75
English; and French, German, Italian with English translations
Contents: v1, 21 songs by Beethoven, Esser, Gounod, Henrion, Kreutzer, Löhr, Lortzing, Loewe, Mozart, Nessler, Roeckel, Rodney, Schubert, Schumann, Vogrich,
v2, 21 songs by Brüll, Carissimi, Graben-Hoffmann, Gumbert, Hatton, King, Kreutzer, Lassen, Mattei, Mendelssohn, Meyerbeer, Pinsuti, Randegger, Reissiger, Schäffer, Vogrich, Watson, Widor
v3, 21 songs by Alquen, Binder, Dorn, Gailhard, Hartmann, Hölzel, Kleffel, Lassen, Mariani, Marschner, Matys, Massenet, Mattei, Pfeil, Reissiger, Schubert, Shield, Vogrich, Wallnöfer, Weidt, Wurda
v4, 18 songs by Gounod, Jude, Lachner, Lindpaintner, Loewe, Lortzing, Mendelssohn, Mililotti, Moszkowski, Nicolai, Proch, Pressel, Ries, Sieber, Slansky, Spohr, Tschaikowsky, Weidt

*Bacon, Mrs Mary Schell (Hoke), ed. Songs every child should know. Grosset c1906 cl $1
English only, no accompaniments
Contents: 58 songs of sentiment; 10 songs of war; 10 national hymns; 7 songs of patriotism; 3 military nonsense songs; 7 Shakespeare songs; 31 miscellaneous songs

Baritone songs. 2v Boosey 1921 pa ea $1.50
English; and French, German, Italian with English translations
Contents: v1, 47 songs; v2, 39 songs

Bass songs. 2v Boosey 1924 pa ea $1.50
English; and French, German, Italian with English translations
Contents: v1, 41 songs; v2, 36 songs

Bispham, David, ed. Celebrated recital songs. Presser 1919 pa $2
English only, except some French with English translations
Contents: 14 songs for men; 15 songs for women; 15 songs for either men or women

*Bispham, David, ed. The David Bispham treasury of song. Winston 1920 cl $1.50; school ed $1
Cover title: David Bispham song book
English only
Contents: 25 songs from the operas Aida, Carmen, The damnation of Faust, The daughter of the regiment, Don Giovanni, Faust, The freeshooter, Jocelyn, Lucia of Lammermoor, Lucrezia Borgia, Martha, The Puritans, Rigoletto, Rinaldo, Samson and Delilah, Semela, Tales of Hoffmann, The troubadour, and William Tell; 51 miscellaneous songs; 19 popular and folk songs; 16 patriotic songs; 16 rounds, catches, and canons; 17 sacred songs; 32 hymns

*Boy scout song book; comp. and ed. for the Boy scouts of America. Birchard ₍pref.
1920₎ pa 40c
English only
Contents: 3 songs of achievement; 12 songs of animals; 13 songs of cheerfulness; 3 Christmas
songs; 1 song of cleanliness; 9 songs of comradeship; 4 songs of courage; 28 songs of devotion;
8 evening songs; 7 songs of the flag; 7 songs of freedom; 8 songs of friendship; 4 songs of gen-
erosity; 1 song of health; 6 songs of helpfulness; 6 songs of home; 46 songs of humor; 4 songs
of imitation; 6 songs of kindness; 2 songs of law and order; 3 songs for male voices; 14 march
songs; 2 mess songs; 4 morning songs; 7 narrative songs; 17 nature songs; 17 patriotic songs; 11
precept songs; 5 songs of resolution; 8 rounds; 45 scouting songs; 9 sea songs; 13 songs of sentiment;
3 spirituals; 10 stunt songs
The book contains also the words of a few well known songs without music; these are omitted
from the Song Index

Buck, Percy Carter, ed. Oxford song book. Oxford univ. press 1919 cl $2.50
Contents: 128 songs, English and a few Latin not translated

Cartwright, Harriet Garton, ed. Song treasury. Macmillan 1920 cl $1.80
English only, except a few French with English translations, and a few Latin not translated
Contents: 15 patriotic songs; 6 student songs; 41 hymns and carols; 7 American songs; 3 Bo-
hemian songs; 6 English songs; 4 French songs; 2 Hebrew songs; 1 Icelandic song; 4 Irish songs; 6
Italian songs; 4 Russian songs; 6 Scotch songs; 1 Spanish song; 4 Swedish songs; 3 Welsh songs

Classic baritone and bass songs. Ditson c1888 pa $1.50
English; and French, German, Italian with English translations
Contents: 33 songs by Abt, Bendel, Bizet, Bonheur, Denza, Eayrs, Gordigiani, Götze, Graben-
Hoffmann, Jensen, Löhr, Mattei, Meyer-Helmund, Moir, Molloy, Nessler, Osgood, Pinsuti, Ries,
Roeckel, Schumann, Spohr, Temple, A. G. Thomas, Wagner, M. Watson, Weidt

Contralto songs. 2v Boosey n.d. pa ea $1.50
English; and French, German, Italian with English translations
Contents: v1, 50 songs; v2, 40 songs

Culp, Julia, comp. My favorite songs. 2v Ditson 1916 high, low pa ea $2
Words in the original language with English translations, except the Norwegian and Russian
songs, which have words in German and English
Contents: v1, 4 American songs; 2 Dutch songs; 4 English songs; 21 German songs; 3 Irish songs
v2, 4 American songs; 6 French songs; 17 German songs; 2 Norwegian songs; 2 Russian songs

*Davison, Archibald Thompson, and Surette, Thomas Whitney, eds. Home & com-
munity song-book. (The Concord series) E. C. Schirmer c1921 pa $1
English only
Contents: 57 patriotic songs, hymns, Christmas carols, folk songs, etc.

*Encore songs. (The O. D. music series) Ditson 1910 high, low pa $1
English; and French, German with English translations
Contents: 3 old songs and 18 songs by Barnard, Brackett, Burnham, Ferrari, Fontenailles, Götze,
Hadley, Hahn, V. Harris, Hook, Lowitz, Mawson-Marks, T. Morley, Ostlere, E. Purcell, Reichardt,
Rich, Thomé

Family music book; a collection of two hundred and fifty-two pieces of piano and
vocal music of moderate difficulty, selected from the works of classic and modern
composers and including many old favorites, universally known. G. Schirmer
c1914 cl $4
English; and French, German, Italian, Norwegian with English translations
Contents: 27 ballads; 7 convivial songs; 8 plantation songs; 8 French children's songs; 20 English children's songs; 10 sacred songs; 9 patriotic songs; national songs of Belgium, England, France,
Ireland, Norway, Russia, Scotland; 12 hymns; 14 vocal duets
The book contains also piano selections without words; these are omitted from the Song Index

Farrar, Geraldine, comp. My favorite songs. Ditson c1916 high, low pa $2
English; and French, German, Italian, Swedish with English translations
Contents: 34 songs by Arensky, Beethoven, Berlioz, Bleichmann, Franz, C. Gluck, Gretchaninoff,
Grieg, Loewe, Moussorgsky, Rubinstein, Schubert, Schumann, Sibelius, Sinding, Tchaikovsky

*Finck, Henry Theophilus, ed. Fifty master-songs by twenty composers. (The musi-
cians library) Ditson c1903 high, low pa $2.50; cl $3.50
English; and French, German with English translations
Songs by Beethoven, Brahms, Chopin, Cornelius, Dvořák, Franz, Godard, Grieg, Jensen, Liszt,
MacDowell, Massenet, Mozart, Paderewski, Rubinstein, Schubert, Schumann, R. Strauss, Tchaikovsky,
Wagner

*Finck, Henry Theophilus, ed. One hundred songs by ten masters. (The musicians
library) 2v Ditson c1917 high, low pa ea $2.50; cl ea $3.50
French, German with English translations
Contents: v1, 10 songs each by Franz, Jensen, Rubinstein, Schubert, Schumann; v2, 10 songs each
by Brahms, Grieg, R. Strauss, Tchaikovsky, Wolf

Finck, Henry Theophilus, and Bentley, Alys E., eds. Thirty sterling songs by the
great masters. Allyn and Bacon 1906 cl $1.40
English only
Songs by Brahms, Chopin, Franz, Grieg, Jensen, Liszt, MacDowell, Mendelssohn, Rubinstein,
Schubert, and Schumann

Franklin square song collection; selected by J. P. McCaskey. 8v Harper 1881-91 cl
o.p. 1926
Contents: 200 songs in each volume, English; and a few German, French, Italian with English
translations

Gluck, Alma, comp. My favorite songs. Ditson c1917 high, low pa $2
English; French, German, Spanish with English translations
Contents: 31 songs by T. A. Arne, Bach, Beethoven, Brahms, Debussy, Dichmont, W. A. Fisher,
Sanchez Fuentes, Gretchaninoff, Händel, Haydn, Loewe, Massenet, Mendelssohn, Moussorgsky, Mo-
zart, Paladilhe, Rachmaninoff, Rimsky-Korsakoff, Rubinstein, Schubert, Schumann, Spohr, Tiersot

*Heart songs dear to the American people, and by them contributed in the search for treasured songs initiated by the National magazine. Chapple pub. co. c1909 cl $1.50; de luxe ed $3.50
> English only, except 2 Latin not translated
> Contents: 54 patriotic songs; 47 sea songs; 48 lullabies and children's songs; 48 songs that have been popular as dance music; 54 negro melodies and minstrel songs; 57 sacred songs, revival hymns, etc.; 80 love songs; 51 songs of the great masters in operas, operettas, oratorios, etc.; 98 concerts, solos and quartettes; 48 college and fraternal songs

Home songs; a collection of favorite songs, hymns and rounds for the fireside. Ditson 1906 pa $1
> English only
> Contents: 14 patriotic songs; 27 hymns; 11 rounds; 101 miscellaneous songs

*Johnson, Charles W., ed. Songs of the nation. Silver c1912 bds 96c
> English only
> Contents: 131 patriotic and national songs, college and home songs, occasional and devotional songs

*Johnson, Clifton, ed. Songs every one should know. American book co. c1908 cl 72c
> English only
> Contents: 6 national hymns; 7 songs of patriotism; 9 war songs; 16 Scotch songs; 22 childhood songs; 22 songs with a moral; 11 ballads; 8 songs of romance; 24 nature songs; 7 songs of the sea; 18 songs of sentiment; 4 rounds; 9 college songs; 11 minstrel and plantation songs; 15 slave hymns; 13 religious songs

*Johnson, Helen Kendrick, ed. Our familiar songs and those who made them. Holt 1909 cl $5
> English only
> Contents: 15 songs of reminiscence; 15 songs of home; 15 songs of exile; 30 songs of the sea; 8 songs of nature; 47 songs of sentiment; 36 songs of hopeless love; 50 songs of happy love; 13 convivial songs; 10 political songs; 46 martial and patriotic songs; 24 moral and religious songs

*Krehbiel, Henry Edward, ed. Famous songs. 4v Church 1912 pa ea $1.50
> English; and French, German, Italian, Norwegian with English translations
> Contents: v1, soprano, 68 songs; v2, alto, 69 songs; v3, tenor, 65 songs; v4, bass, 53 songs

*Krehbiel, Henry Edward, ed. Songs from the operas. (The musicians library) 5v Ditson c1907-11 pa ea $2.50; cl ea $3.50
> English; and French, German, Italian with English translations
> Contents: v1, for soprano, 22 songs from the operas Alceste, Carmen, Don Giovanni, Euryanthe, Faust, Les fêtes vénitiennes, Fidelio, Der freischütz, Griselda, Hippolyte et Aricie, Lakmé, Lucia di Lammermoor, Mignon, Norma, Otello, Le pardon de Plöermel, La perle du Brésil, Semiramide, La serva padrona, La sonnambula, La traviata
> v2, for mezzo-soprano, 30 songs from the operas Arianna, Astarto, Un ballo in maschera, Il barbiere de Siviglia, I Capuleti ed i Montecchi, Carmen, Céphale et Procris, Le domino noir, Don Carlo, Euryanthe, Faust, La favorita, Giasone, Giulietta e Romeo, Hérodiade, Les Huguenots, Mignon, Le nozze di Figaro, Paul et Virginie, La reine de Saba, Rienzi, Rinaldo, Samson et Dalila, Sapho, La Semiramide riconosciuta
> v3, for alto, 29 songs from the operas Alcina, Amadigi, Amadis, Arodiant, Un ballo in maschera, Cenerentola, Cinq mars, La clemenza di Tito, Demofoonte, Dido and Aeneas, Donna Caritea, Faust, La Gioconda, Jean de Nivelle, Lucrezia Borgia, Martha, Mignon, Mitrane, Nadeshda, Orfeo ed Euridice, Paride ed Elena, Le prophète, Russlan and Ludmilla, Semiramide, Tancredi, Tigrane
> v4, for tenor, 29 songs from the operas L'Africaine, Aida, Alessandro nell' Indie, Carmen, Cavalleria rusticana, La dame blanches, Don Giovanni, L'elisir d'amore, Enrico, Euryanthe, Faust, Fidelio, La Gioconda, Guillaume Tell, The Indian queen, Iphigénie en Tauride, Joseph, Lohengrin, Manon, Il matrimonio segreto, Die meistersinger, Mignon, Oberon, La reine de Saba, Rienzi, Roméo et Juliette, Telemacco, Il trovatore, Die Walküre
> v5, for baritone and bass, 27 songs from the operas Acis and Galatea, Agrippina, Ariodant, Un ballo in maschera, Les deux journées, Don Giovanni, Esmeralda, Eugene Onegin, Euryanthe, Giamina e Bernardone, La Gioconda, Hans Heiling, Die heimkehr aus der fremde, Hérodiade, Iphigénie en Aulide, Jean de Paris, Jessonda, Le jolie fille de Perth, La Juive, Il maestro di musica, Mefistofele, Le pardon de Plöermel, Philémon et Baucis, La sonnambula, Die zauberflöte

Levermore, Charles Herbert, ed. The abridged academy song-book. rev ed Ginn c1918 cl $1.24
> English only
> Contents: 57 patriotic and national songs; 66 school and college songs; 104 familiar songs; 112 songs of devotion; 1 Arbor day song; 6 rounds

MacConnell, Marie Florence, ed. Standard songs and choruses for high schools. American book co. c1908 cl $1.20
> Contents: 99 miscellaneous songs; English, and French, German and English translations

Marzo, Eduardo, ed. Coloratura album for soprano. Ditson 1909 pa $2
> French, Italian with English translations
> Contents: 22 arias from the operas Un ballo in maschera, Les deux avares, Les fêtes vénitiennes, Il flauto magico, Les Huguenots, Lakmé, Linda di Chamounix, Lucia di Lammermoor, Manon, Mefistofele, Mignon, Le pardon de Plöermel, Partenope, Les pêcheurs de perles, La perle du Brésil; I Puritani, Rigoletto, Roméo et Juliette, Semiramide, La sonnambula, La traviata, I vespri Siciliani

Mezzo-soprano songs. 2v Boosey n.d. pa ea $1.50
> English; and French, German, Italian with English translations
> Contents: v1, 47 songs; v2, 37 songs

Modern song favorites. (Schirmer's household music books) 2v G. Schirmer c1882
high, low pa ea 75c
English; and French, German with English translations
Contents: v1, 25 songs by Bendel, Blumenthal, Bradsky, Cowen, De Koven, Delbrück, Fontenailles, Godard, Hahn, Hardelot, Hawley, Hervey, Horrocks, Nevin, Somerset, Somervell, Strelezki, A. G. Thomas, Tosti, M. K. Wood
v2, 22 songs by Abt, Behrend, De Koven, Götze, Gregh, Hawley, Hildach, Jüngst, Kjerulf, Marzials, Molloy, Moncrieff, Needham, Rodney, Somerset, Sullivan, Temple, A. G. Thomas, Tosti, Wakefield, H. L. Wilson

Neitzel, Otto, ed. Gems of antiquity. Church c1909 pa $1.50
Contents: 39 songs, English, and French, German, Italian with English translations, covering a period from 1240 to 1786

Noble, Gilbert Clifford, ed. The most popular home songs. new and enl ed Hinds, Hayden and Eldredge c1913 pa 75c; cl $1.12
Patriotic songs of foreign nations have words in the original with English translations
Contents: 140 home songs of the United States, and patriotic songs of England, France, Hawaii, Holland, Ireland, Italy, Poland, Russia, Scotland, Spain, Sweden, Switzerland and Wales

Noble, Gilbert Clifford, ed. The most popular love songs. Hinds, Hayden and Eldredge c1906 pa 75c
Contents: 84 songs, English only

Noble, Gilbert Clifford, ed. The most popular songs for every occasion. Hinds, Hayden and Eldredge 1912 pa 75c; cl $1.12
English only, except 18 songs of other nations, which have words in the original with English translations
Contents: 6 songs for New Year's; 5 songs for Easter; 4 songs for Labor day; 6 songs for Lincoln's birthday; 5 songs for Arbor day; 3 songs for Hallowe'en; 4 songs for St Valentine's day; 7 songs for Memorial day; 2 songs for Columbus day; 7 songs for Washington's birthday; 5 songs for Flag day; 7 songs for Thanksgiving; 3 songs for St Patrick's day; 7 songs for the Fourth of July; 8 songs for Christmas; 5 morning and evening songs; 16 songs of the months; 11 songs of the seasons; 16 songs for children's entertainments; 17 songs for social gatherings; 8 songs for partings and farewells; 8 songs for home comings; 16 songs for devotional exercises; 25 songs for schools and colleges; 7 songs for commencement exercises; 7 songs for reunions; 6 songs for conventions; 18 songs of other nations

One hundred and one best songs. rev ed Cable co. c1925 pa 10c
Old favorites, hymns, patriotic songs, college songs, English only

Opera songs. 4v Church 1901 pa ea $1.50
Contents: v1, soprano, 32 songs; v2, alto, 35 songs; v3, tenor, 35 songs; v4, bass, 33 songs
French, German, Italian with English translations, from the operas Aben Hamet, L'Africaine, Aida, Alceste, L'amico Fritz, Attila, Un ballo in maschera, Il barbiere di Siviglia, Carmen, Cavalleria rusticana, Le Cid, Cinq Mars, Dinorah, Don Carlo, Don Giovanni, L'elisir d'amore, Ernani, Esmeralda, Der freischütz, Galathée, Gil Blas, La Gioconda, Il Guarany, Hamlet, Herodiade, Jean de Neville, Jocelyn, La jolie fille de Perth, Lakmé, Lohengrin, I Lombardi, Lucia di Lammermoor, Lucrezia Borgia, Manon, Martha, Mefistofele, Der meistersinger, Mignon, Mitrane, Nabucodonosor, Nadeschda, Le nozze di Figaro, Oberon, Orfeo, Osteria, Otello, Paul et Virginia, La perle du Brésil, Philémon et Baucis, Polyeucte, Il profeta, Reginella, La reine de Saba, Rienzi, Rigoletto, Rinaldo, Roberto il diavolo, Le roi de Lahore, Romeo and Juliet, Samson et Delila, Sappho, Semiramide, La sonnambula, Tannhäuser, La traviata, Der trompeter von Säkkingen, Il trovatore, Gli Ugonotti, Le Villi

Parker, Horatio William, ed. German, French and Italian song classics. 4v Church 1912 pa ea $1.50
Cover title: Song classics
German, French, Italian with English translations
Contents: v1, soprano, 51 songs; v2, alto, 54 songs; v3, tenor, 51 songs; v4, bass, 49 songs

Pittmann, Josiah, ed. Prima donna's album; a collection of 41 celebrated cavatinas and arias. v1 G. Schirmer n.d. pa $2; cl $3.50
Italian with English translations
Only iv published
Cavatinas and arias from the operas Un ballo in maschera, Il barbiere di Siviglia, Beatrice di Tenda, Bianca e Falliero, Il castello di Kenilworth, Don Giovani, Dinorah, La donna del Lago, Ernani, Il flauto magico, Der freischütz, La figlia del reggimento, La favorita, Faust, La gazza ladra, Linda di Chamounix, Lucia di Lammermoor, Lucrezia Borgia, Norma, Le nozze di Figaro, Otello, I Puritani, La prigione d'Edimburgo, Roberto il diavolo, Rigoletto, Semiramide, La sonnambula, Il trovatore, La traviata, I vespri Siciliani, Zelmira

Potter, Frank Hunter, ed. Old song favorites; twenty-four songs for a medium voice. (Schirmer's household music books) G. Schirmer n.d. pa 75c
Familiar songs, English only

Scottish students' song book. Bayley and Ferguson n.d. pa 3s; cl 4s6d
English; and a few French, Gaelic, German and Norwegian, not always translated
Contents: 30 songs of the gown; 17 songs of the nations; 19 soldier-songs and sea-songs; 18 songs of love; 20 songs of revelry; 40 divers ditties; 17 plantation songs; 6 songs for auld lang syne; 13 songs of the universities

Song miscellany. 4v G. Schirmer c1902 pa ea $1.25; cl ea $2.75
English; and French, German, Italian with English translations
Contents: v1, for soprano, 25 songs by Becker, Bohm, Brahms, Burleigh, Cantor, Cesek, Chaminade, Chopin, Faning, Franz, Gray, Hawley, Hildach, Jouberti, Koss, Lehmann, Lemaire, Meyer, Meyerbeer, Meyer-Helmund, Purcell, Somerset, A. G. Thomas, Tosti
v2, for alto, 28 songs by Beethoven, Bendel, Brahms, Burleigh, Cantor, Chaminade, Cowen, Dessauer, S. C. Foster, Franz, Gray, Grieg, Hahn, Hardelot, Haydn, Henschel, Hervey, Hildach, Horrocks, Kjerulf, Lalo, Nevin, Proch, Quaranta, Saint-Saëns, Thomé, Wickede

v3, for tenor, 22 songs by T. A. Arne, Blumenthal, Bohm, Burleigh, Cantor, Denza, Fitzenhagen, Gall, Gastaldon, Gounod, Gray, Hawley, Massenet, Slansky, Slaughter, Spicker, Sullivan, A. G. Thomas, Thomé, Tosti, Wakefield

v4, for bass, 27 songs by Bizet, Blumenthal, Bonheur, Burleigh, Cantor, Cavallo, Clay, Denza, Dvořák, Flégier, Fontenailles, Franz, Graben-Hoffmann, Hawley, Levi, Mackenzie, Molloy, Pressel, Radecke, Rodney, Sarjeant, Somervell, Stainer, Stanford, White

Soprano songs. 2v Boosey n.d. pa ea $1.50
English; and French, German, Italian with English translations
Contents: v1, 43 songs; v2, 32 songs

Spicker, Max, ed. Obbligato-songs; a collection of songs with accompaniment of piano and violin (or violoncello). 2v G. Schirmer c1905 pa ea $1.50; cl ea $3
English; and French, German, Italian with English translations
Contents: v1, 19 songs for high voice, by Bedford, Braga, Claus, Dancla, Denza, Godard, Goltermann, Gounod, Hollmann, Leroux, Massenet, Mattei, Mertens, Muratori, Reinecke, Vogrich, Weil
v2, 18 songs for low voice, by Berlioz, Dancla, Degele, Denza, Flégier, Godard, Goodeve, Gueroult, Hardelot, Hollmann, Kücken, Lucantoni, Marrei, Massenet, Robaudi, Zech

Spicker, Max, ed. Operatic anthology; celebrated arias selected from operas by old and modern composers. 5v G. Schirmer c1903-04 pa ea $1.50; cl ea $3
English; and French, German, Italian with English translations
Contents: v1, 43 songs from the operas Acanthe et Céphise, Acis and Galathea, Aida, Alceste, Carmen, Le Cid, La clemenza di Tito, Les deux avares, Dimitri, Don Carlo, Etienne Marcel, La fée aux roses, La fiancée d'Abydos, Fidelio, Der fliegende Holländer, La forza del destino, Der freischütz, Il Guarany, Hérodiade, Les Huguenots, Jeanne D'Arc, La Juive, Lohengrin, Mignon, Mireille, Le nozze di Figaro, Oberon, Orfeo, Osteria, Otello, Les pêcheurs de perles, Philémon et Baucis, La reine de Saba, Le roi et le fermier, Roméo et Juliette, Les saisons, Tannhäuser, Tristan und Isolde
v2, 39 songs from the operas Alcina, Amadis, Anna Bolena, Carmen, La cenerentola, Charles VI, Cinq-Mars, La donna del lago, Don Sebastiano, Faust, La favorita, Gil Blas, La Gioconda, Giulietta e Romeo, Il giuramento, Lucrezia Borgia, Maria Rohan, Medea, Mignon, Mitrane, Nadeschda, Orfeo, Le prophète, La reine de Chypre, Rienzi, Rinaldo, Le roi de Lahore, Samson et Dalila, Sapho, Scipione, Semiramide, Serse, Tancredi
v3, 40 songs from the operas L'Africaine, Aida, L'amant jaloux, Carmen, Cavalleria rusticana, Le Cid, Dardanus, Don Giovanni, Don Pasquale, I due Foscari, Euryanthe, Faust, La favorita, Der freischütz, La Gioconda, Hérodiade, Les Huguenots, Jocelyn, Joseph en Égypte, Lakmé, Lohengrin, Macbeth, Martha, Die meistersinger, Mignon, La muette de Portici, Polyeucte, Reginella, La reine de Saba, Rienzi, Le roi d'Ys, Salvator Rosa, Sapho, Il trovatore, Die Walküre, Die zauberflöte, Zémire et Azor
v4, 37 songs from the operas L'Africaine, Ariodant, Attila, Un ballo in maschera, Carmen, Cavalleria rusticana, Le déserteur, Don Carlo, Don Giovanni, Don Sebastiano, Euryanthe, Faust, Der fliegende Holländer, La Gioconda, Das goldene kreuz, Il Guarany, Guillaume Tell, Hamlet, Hans Heiling, Henry VIII, Hérodiade, Lucia di Lammermoor, Macbeth, Maria di Rudenz, Orfeo, Le pardon de Ploërmel, Parsifal, Richard Coeur de Lion, Rigoletto, Le roi de Lahore, Le siège de Corinthe, Tannhäuser, Der trompeter von Säkkingen, Il trovatore
v5, 40 songs from the operas Agrippina, Le chalet, Dardanus, Don Carlo, Don Giovanni, L'ebreo, Ernani, L'étoile du nord, Faust, La favorita, Der freischütz, La Gioconda, Herculanum, Iphigénie en Tauride, La jolie fille de Perth, La Juive, Lucrezia Borgia, Die lustingen weiber von Windsor, Macbeth, Il maestro di musica, Martha, Die meistersinger, Mignon, Nabucodonosor, Le nozze di Figaro, Le pardon de Ploërmel, Philémon et Baucis, La reine de Saba, Robert Bruce, Robert le diable, Sardanapale, La selva incantata, Simone Boccanegra, I vespri Siciliani, Die Walküre, Die zauberflöte

Tenor songs. Boosey n.d. pa $1.50
Contents: 44 songs, English; and French, German, Italian with English translations

*Tomlins, William Lawrence, ed. Laurel song book; for advanced classes in schools, academies, choral societies, etc. (Laurel music series) Birchard c1901 bds $1.50
English only
Contents: 90 songs and choruses; 77 folk songs and hymns

Twice 55 community songs. 2v Birchard c1919-23 no.1, vocal ed pa 15c; bds 30c; complete ed (voice and piano) 75c; no. 2, vocal ed pa 25c; bds 45c; complete ed (voice and piano) $1
English only, except some Latin with English translations
Contents: No. 1, The brown book: 93 songs; no. 2, The green book: 125 songs
Both volumes contain also the words of some well-known songs, without music; these are omitted from the Song Index
Previous editions had the titles: 18 community songs (1913); 55 community songs (1917); Twice 55 community songs (1919)

Wier, Albert E., ed. The American home music album. Appleton c1915 cl $5
English; a few German with English translations; and national songs with words in the original with English translations
Contents: 8 vocal duets; 26 songs from the operas Aida, Bohemian girl, Carmen, Cavalleria rusticana, L'éclair, Erminie, Faust, Il trovatore, Incognito, Jocelyn, Maritana, Martha, Merry widow, Mignon, Pinafore, Rigoletto, Samson and Delilah, Tannhäuser, and Trumpeter of Säkkingen; 17 sacred songs; 21 hymns; 15 standard love songs; 33 old-fashioned love songs; 11 songs of home; 6 songs for children; 20 kindergarten and nursery songs; 16 songs of the South; 19 college songs; 10 American patriotic songs; national songs of Austria, Belgium, Canada, Denmark, England, France, Germany, Holland, Hungary, Ireland, Italy, Japan, Norway, Poland, Russia, Scotland, Serbia, Spain, Sweden, Switzerland, Transvaal, Wales
The book contains also piano music without words; this is omitted from the Song Index

*Wier, Albert E., ed. Ballads the whole world sings. Appleton c1917 pa $1.25
Contents: 149 songs, English only
The contents of this volume are identical with the contents of v4 of "Everyman's music library," formerly published by Appleton. Indexing arrangement and binding are different

*Wier, Albert E., ed. The book of a thousand songs. Mumil pub. co. c1918 pa $2;
cl $3
> English only, except 3 college songs in Latin, and a few national songs in the original with Eng-
> lish translations
>> Contents: 124 home songs; 226 sentimental songs; 82 songs from the operas Beggar student,
>> Bohemian girl, Carmen, Cavalleria rusticana, Chimes of Normandy, Daughter of the regiment,
>> L'éclair, Erminie, Faust, Fra Diavolo, Der freischütz, Giroflé-girofla, Grand duchess, Hansel and
>> Gretel, Incognito, Jocelyn, Lohengrin, Lucia di Lammermoor, Lucrezia Borgia, Magic flute, Maritana,
>> Martha, Mascot, Merry widow, Mikado, Olivette, Patience, Pinafore, Queen's lace handkerchief,
>> Rigoletto, Samson et Dalilah, La sonnambula, Tales of Hoffman, Tannhäuser, Il trovatore, Trumpeter
>> of Säkkingen, Tyroleans, and Waltz dream; 44 sacred songs; 99 hymns; 123 children's songs; 74
>> southern songs; 77 college songs; 29 sea songs; 9 rounds; 56 patriotic songs; 1 Belgian song; 3
>> Canadian songs; 1 Danish song; 11 English songs; 2 French songs; 1 Dutch song, 16 Irish songs;
>> 2 Italian songs; 1 Japanese song; 1 song of New Zealand; 1 Norwegian song; 1 Polish song; 1
>> Portuguese song; 1 Russian song; 9 Scottish songs; 1 Serbian song; 1 Spanish song; 1 Swedish
>> song; 1 Swiss song; 1 song of Transvaal; 1 Welsh song

Wier, Albert E., ed. Love songs the whole world sings. Appleton c1916 pa $1.25
> English only
>> Contents: 21 American songs; 3 Austrian songs; 3 Bohemian songs; 2 Danish songs; 4 Dutch
>> songs; 40 English songs; 12 French songs; 27 German songs; 1 Greek song; 4 Hawaiian songs; 4
>> Hungarian songs; 13 Irish songs; 11 Italian songs; 2 Norwegian songs; 3 Polish songs; 4 Russian
>> songs; 19 Scotch songs; 1 Serbian song; 7 Spanish songs; 4 Swedish songs; 1 Swiss song; 7 Welsh
>> songs
> The contents of this volume are identical with the contents of v7 of "Everyman's music library,"
> formerly published by Appleton. Indexing arrangement and binding are different

Wier, Albert E., ed. Songs the children love to sing. Appleton 1916 pa $1.25
> English only
>> Contents: 22 song games; 22 lullabies and cradle songs; 7 flower songs; 60 nursery rhymes and
>> songs; 17 songs of home; 14 songs for little girls; 20 songs for little boys; 8 folk songs; 17 animal
>> songs; 32 work and play songs; 19 songs of the months and seasons; 14 bird songs; 11 nature
>> songs; 34 sacred songs and hymns; 11 Christmas songs; 10 songs of our country

*Wier, Albert E., ed. Songs the whole world sings. Appleton c1915 pa $1.25
> English only, except national songs, which have words in the original with English translations
>> Contents: 20 home songs; 37 sentimental songs; 22 operatic songs; 18 southern songs; 24 chil-
>> dren's songs; 11 sacred songs; 25 hymns; 28 college songs; 15 American patriotic songs; 16 national
>> songs of other nations
> The contents of this volume are identical with the contents of v10 of "Everyman's music library,"
> formerly published by Appleton. Indexing arrangement and binding are different

NATIONAL AND FOLK SONGS
GENERAL

*Bantock, Granville Ransome, ed. One hundred folk-songs of all nations. (The musicians library) Ditson c1911 pa $2.50; cl $3.50
> Words in the original languages with English translations. Only a transliterated text is given
> for languages not using Latin alphabet
>> Contents: 2 minnesingers' songs; 2 troubadour songs; 1 Algerian song; 2 American Indian songs;
>> 1 Arabian song; 1 Austrian song; 1 Bohemian song; 1 Bosnian song; 1 Bulgarian song; 1 Chinese
>> song; 2 Danish songs; 2 Dutch songs; 1 East Indian song; 2 Egyptian songs; 4 English songs; 1
>> Finnish song; 4 French songs; 11 German songs; 1 Greek song; 2 Hungarian songs; 1 Icelandic
>> song; 4 Irish songs; 4 Italian songs; 2 Japanese songs; 1 Lapp song; 1 Lithuanian song; 1 Manx
>> song; 1 Moroccan song; 3 Norwegian songs; 2 Persian songs; 2 Polish songs; 2 Portuguese songs;
>> 6 Russian songs; 4 Scottish songs; 1 Serbian song; 3 Spanish songs; 1 Styrian song; 3 Swedish
>> songs; 2 Swiss songs; 2 Syrian songs; 1 Tripolitan song; 1 Tunisian song; 1 Turkish song; 2
>> Tyrolese songs; 3 United States songs; 3 Welsh songs

*Bantock, Granville Ransome, ed. Sixty patriotic songs of all nations. (The musicians
library) Ditson c1913 pa $2.50; cl $3.50
> Words in the original languages with English translations. Only a transliterated text is given for
> languages not using Latin alphabet
>> Contents: 1 Argentine song; 1 Austrian song; 1 Belgian song; 1 Brazilian song; 1 Bulgarian
>> song; 2 Canadian songs; 3 Danish songs; 1 Dutch song; 1 Egyptian song; 5 English songs; 1
>> Finnish song; 5 French songs; 3 German songs; 2 Greek songs; 2 Hebrew songs; 1 Hungarian
>> song; 1 Icelandic song; 3 Irish songs; 1 Italian song; 2 Japanese songs; 1 Mexican song; 2 Nor-
>> wegian songs; 2 Polish songs; 1 Portuguese song; 1 Rumanian song; 1 Russian song; 2 Scottish songs;
>> 1 Serbian song; 1 South African republic song; 2 Spanish songs; 2 Swedish songs; 1 Turkish song;
>> 3 United States songs; 1 Welsh song

*Botsford, Florence Hudson, ed. Folk songs of many peoples; with English versions
by American poets. 2v Womans press 1921-22 v1, pa $2.75; cl $3.25; v2, pa $3.50;
cl $4
> All words in the original with English translations by American poets. The text for languages
> not using Latin alphabet is in the original characters
>> Contents: v1, 1 Bosnian song; 9 Bulgarian songs; 1 Carniolan song; 5 Croatian songs; 14 Czech
>> songs; 2 Dalmatian songs; 5 Esthonian songs; 11 Finnish songs; 1 Herzegovinian song; 1 Istrian
>> song; 3 Latvian songs; 7 Lithuanian songs; 2 Macedonian songs; 1 Montenegran song; 24 Polish
>> songs; 27 Russian and Ukrainian songs; 8 Serbian songs; 7 Slovakian songs; 3 Slavonian songs;
>> 4 Slovenian songs
>> v2, 2 African songs; 3 Albanian songs; 8 Armenian songs; 3 Austrian songs; 4 Belgian songs; 6
>> Chinese songs; 7 Danish songs; 6 French Canadian songs; 7 German songs; 9 Greek songs; 4 songs
>> of India; 6 Irish songs; 29 Italian songs; 11 Japanese songs; 9 Jewish songs; 6 Latin American
>> songs; 11 Mexican songs; 7 Norwegian songs; 10 Portuguese songs; 11 Rumanian songs; 4 Scottish
>> songs; 7 Swedish songs; 5 Swiss songs; 9 Syrian songs; 36 United States songs, comprising 4 mis-
>> cellaneous songs, 3 cowboy songs, 9 Indian songs, 6 Kentucky songs, 10 negro songs, 2 creole songs,
>> 2 Hawaiian songs; 1 Welsh song

*Brown, James Duff, and Moffat, Alfred, eds. Characteristic songs and dances of all nations. Bayley and Ferguson 1901 pa 5s
  English only
  Contents: 1 Algerian song; 1 Arabian song; 1 Armenian song; 1 Austrian song; 1 Basque song; 1 Belgian song; 2 Bohemian songs; 1 Bolivian song; 1 Breton song; 1 Bulgarian song; 3 Canadian songs; 1 Chilean song; 2 Chinese songs; 4 Danish songs; 2 Dutch songs; 1 Egyptian song; 10 English songs; 1 Eskimo song; 1 Fiji song; 1 Finnish song; 1 Flemish song; 6 French songs; 9 German songs; 2 Greek songs; 1 Hawaiian song; 1 Hebrew song; 1 Hottentot song; 3 Hungarian songs; 1 Icelandic song; 5 songs of India; 8 Irish songs; 5 Italian songs; 2 Japanese songs; 1 Javanese song; 1 Lapp song; 1 Lithuanian song; 1 Malagasy song; 1 Mexican song; 1 Moorish song; 1 Moravian song; 1 song from New Zealand; 3 Norwegian songs; 2 Persian songs; 3 Polish songs; 1 Portuguese song; 2 Rumanian songs; 5 Russian songs; 10 Scottish songs; 1 Serbian song; 1 Siamese song; 3 South African songs; 2 Spanish songs; 3 Swedish songs; 1 Swiss song; 1 Tunisian song; 1 Turkish song; 1 Tyrolean song; 6 songs of the United States; 9 Welsh songs
  The book contains also scores for piano without words; these are omitted from the S o n g
  I n d e x

Davison, Archibald Thompson, and Surette, Thomas Whitney, eds. 140 folk-songs. (The Concord series) new and rev ed E. C. Schirmer c1921 students ed (words and music) cl 65c; teachers ed (words, music and piano accompaniment) cl $2
  English, French, Latin. The French songs have also English words, but these are not always translations from the French

*Elson, Louis Charles, ed. Folk songs of many nations. Church. c1905 pa $1.10
  English; and Dutch, French, German, Italian, Norwegian, Spanish with English translations; some songs in English translation only
  Contents: 9 American songs; 4 Austrian songs; 3 Bohemian songs; 1 Castilian song; 2 Canadian songs; 9 English songs; 7 French songs; 9 German songs; 12 Irish songs; 4 Italian songs; 3 Norwegian songs; 1 Netherlands song; 1 Polish song; 5 Russian songs; 10 Scotch songs; 2 Slavonic songs; 3 Swedish songs; 1 Swiss song; 1 Welsh song

Gilbert, Henry Franklin Belknap, ed. One hundred folk-songs from many countries. (Laurel music series) Birchard 1910 pa $1.25
  English only
  Contents: 7 American songs; 2 Bohemian songs; 1 Chinese song; 1 Croatian song; 3 Danish songs; 10 English songs; 8 French songs; 9 German songs; 2 Hungarian songs; 8 Irish songs; 8 Italian songs; 1 Manx song; 3 Norwegian songs; 2 Polish songs; 1 Portuguese song; 10 Russian songs; 8 Scottish songs; 5 Spanish songs; 3 Swedish songs; 4 Welsh songs; 5 sea songs

Kappey, J. A., ed. Songs of eastern Europe. Boosey n.d. pa $2
  English only
  Contents: 34 Austrian songs; 23 Hungarian songs; 18 Bohemian songs; 7 Serbian songs; 8 Swiss songs; 4 Turkish songs; 5 Greek songs

Most popular songs of patriotism. Hinds, Hayden and Eldredge. c1916 pa 75c
  Generally in the original language with English translations. Only a transliterated text is given for languages not using the Latin alphabet
  Contents: 92 patriotic songs of the United States, and national songs of Argentina, Australia, Belgium, Brazil, Bulgaria, Canada, Chile, Cuba, Denmark, Ecuador, Egypt, England, Finland, France, Greece, Guatemala, Hawaii, Holland, Ireland, Italy, Japan, Mexico, New Zealand, Norway, Poland, Portugal, Roumania, Russia, Scotland, Serbia, Spain, Sweden, Switzerland, Turkey, Venezuela, and Wales
  The book contains also many songs without words; these are omitted from the S o n g I n d e x

National anthems of the allies. G. Schirmer 1917 pa 25c
  Words in the original language with English translations. Only a transliterated text is given for languages not using the Latin alphabet
  National anthems of Belgium, Cuba, France, Great Britain, Italy, Japan, Portugal, Rumania, Russia, Serbia, the United States

Sembrich, Marcella, comp. My favorite folk songs. Ditson c1918 high, low pa $2
  Words generally in the original language with English translations. Only a transliterated text is given for languages not using the Latin alphabet
  Contents: 2 American Indian songs; 1 American negro song; 2 Austrian songs; 2 Bohemian songs; 1 Bosnian song; 1 Bulgarian song; 1 Canadian song; 1 Chinese song; 3 English songs; 4 French songs; 5 German songs; 1 Greek song; 1 Hungarian song; 2 Irish songs; 7 Italian songs; 2 Norwegian songs; 3 Polish songs; 4 Russian songs; 3 Ruthenian songs; 3 Scottish songs; 1 Serbian song; 4 Swedish songs; 3 Spanish songs; 1 Syrian song; 1 Turkish song

*Sousa, John Philip, ed. National, patriotic and typical airs of all lands. C. Fischer c1890 cl $1.50
  Words generally in the original language with English translations. Only a transliterated text is given for languages not using the Latin alphabet. The book contains also many songs without words; these are omitted from the S o n g I n d e x
  Contents: 6 American songs; 5 American Indian songs from tribes of the Cherokee, Dakota, Iowa, Iroquois and Vancouver Indians; 1 Argentine song; 1 Armenian song; 1 Australian song; 3 Austrian songs; 1 Bohemian song; 1 Bosnian song; 1 Brazilian song; 1 Canadian song; 1 Carinthian song; 1 Carniolan song; 1 Costa Rican song; 2 Croatian songs; 1 Cuban song; 1 Dalecarlian song; 5 Danish songs; 4 Dutch songs; 1 Ecuadorian song; 3 English songs; 3 Eskimo songs; 1 Fiji song; 3 Finnish songs; 5 French songs; 6 German songs; 1 Greek song; 1 Guatemalan song; 1 Hawaiian song; 1 Hungarian song; 4 Irish songs; 1 Istrian song; 3 Italian songs; 1 Japanese song; 1 Lapp song; 1 Liberian song; 1 Lithuanian song; 1 song of Marianna island; 1 Montenegran song; 1 song of New Zealand; 1 Norwegian song; 1 song of Orange free state; 1 Peruvian song; 1 Polish song; 1 Rumanian song; 3 Russian songs; 1 Salvadorean song; 1 Samoan song; 1 song of San Domingo; 1 song of San Marino; 3 Scottish songs; 1 Serbian song; 1 Silesian song; 1 Slavonian song; 1 Spanish song; 1 Styrian song; 1 Swedish song; 3 Swiss songs; 1 Turkish songs; 1 Trieste song; 1 Tyrolese song; 1 Uruguayan song; 1 Venezuelan song; 1 Welsh song

Whitehead, Ralph Radcliffe, ed. Folk-songs of Eastern Europe. Ditson c1912 pa $1.50
  English only. Words are all either rewritten or based upon free translations from the original
  Contents: 2 Bohemian songs; 1 Bosnian song; 5 Croatian songs; 2 Dalmatian songs; 2 Finnish songs; 4 Greek songs; 1 Herzegovinian song; 6 Hungarian songs; 1 Lithuanian song; 3 Polish songs; 11 Russian songs; 9 Ruthenian songs; 2 Serbian songs; 1 Slavonian song

World's collection of patriotic songs and airs of the different nations.   Ditson 1903
   pa $1
   Usually in the original language with English translations; some in English only. Only a trans-
   literated text is given for languages not using the Latin alphabet
   Contents: 53 patriotic songs of America, Argentine republic, Austria, Belgium, Bolvia, Chili,
   China, Denmark, England, Finland, France, Germany, Greece, Guatemala, Holland, Ireland, Italy,
   Japan, Mexico, Norway, Peru, Poland, Portugal, Russia, Scotland, Spain, Sweden, Switzerland,
   Turkey, United States of Brazil, Wales

AMERICAN

a. General

*Anthology of American song. G. Schirmer 1911 high, low pa $1.50; cl $3
   Contents: 25 songs by Bartlett, Cadman, Chadwick, Coombs, De Koven, Hadley, V. Harris,
   Hawley, Homer, Johns, La Forge, MacDowell, Mack, Neidlinger, A. Nevin, H. Parker, J. H.
   Rogers, W. L. Rogers, Salter, Shelley, W. G. Smith, Thayer, H. Ware, Whiting, Woodman

Campbell, Mrs Olive Dame, and Sharp, Cecil James, eds. English folk songs from
   the southern Appalachians. Putnam 1917 cl o.p. 1926
   Contents: 122 songs and variants
   The book contains also fragments of songs; these are omitted from the S o n g I n d e x

*Hughes, Rupert, ed. Songs by thirty Americans. (The musicians library) Ditson
   c1909 high, low pa $2.50; cl $3.50
   Contents: 30 songs by Baltzell, H. N. Bartlett, Buck, Bullard, Clough-Leighter, De Koven, Farwell,
   W. A. Fisher, A. N. Foerster, H. F. Gilbert, Goldmark, Hadley, V. Harris, Huss, Hyatt, Johns, Loomis,
   Manney, J. P. Marshall, E. Nevin, H. A. Norris, N. C. Page, J. K. Paine, Pasmore, J. R. Rogers,
   Shelley, D. S. Smith, G. Smith, W. G. Smith, R. H. Warren

Lawrence, William M., and Blackman, Orlando, eds. Riverside song book; containing
   classic American poems set to standard music. (Riverside literature series)
   Houghton c1893 bds 56c
   Contents: 19 patriotic songs; 7 songs of labor; 17 songs of home and childhood; 18 songs of affection; 10 songs of bereavement; 23 songs of nature and seasons; 28 hymns and ethical songs; 6 songs
   of Election day; 13 songs of the Fourth of July; 9 songs of Washington's birthday; 16 songs for
   birthdays of Lincoln, Grant, and other eminent Americans; 10 songs of Memorial day; 6 songs of
   Arbor day; 11 songs of Thanksgiving day and autumn festival; 13 songs of Christmas and New
   Year's day; 4 songs of Indians

Lomax, John Avery, ed. Cowboy songs and other frontier ballads. Macmillan c1916
   cl $2; Seventy-five cent lib. 75c
   Contents: 18 songs. The book includes also many poems without music; these are omitted from
   the S o n g I n d e x

*Sharp, Cecil James, ed. American-English folk-songs; collected in the Southern
   Appalachians. 1st series G. Schirmer c1918 pa $1.50
   Contents: 6 old ballads and 6 folk songs
   Only 1st series published

Sturgis, Edith Barnes, ed. Songs from the hills of Vermont; music edited and arranged by Robert Hughes. G. Schirmer c1919 pa $2
   Contents: 13 folk songs

*Wyman, Loraine, ed. Lonesome tunes; folk songs from the Kentucky mountains;
   the words collected and edited by Loraine Wyman; the pianoforte accompaniment
   by Howard Brockway. v1 H. W. Gray c1916 pa $1.50; bds $2
   Only iv published
   Contents: 25 folk songs and ballads of English origin

Wyman, Loraine, ed. Twenty Kentucky mountain songs; the words collected by
   Loraine Wyman; the melodies collected and piano accompaniments added by
   Howard Brockway. Ditson c1920 pa $1.50
   Contents: 20 folk songs and ballads of English origin

b. Indian

Burton, Frederick Russell, ed. American primitive music. Moffat 1909 cl o.p. 1926
   Contents: 57 American Indian songs, in English translation only or in Indian with English
   translation
   The book contains also many airs without words, and some fragments of both words and music;
   these are omitted from the S o n g I n d e x

*Cadman, Charles Wakefield. Four American Indian songs: founded upon tribal melodies. White-Smith 1909 high, low pa $1
   English only

Fletcher, Alice Cunningham, ed. Indian games and dances with native songs; arr from
   American Indian ceremonials and sports. Birchard 1915 cl $2
   Contents: 29 songs, no accompaniments, English only. The book contains also poems without
   music; these are omitted from the S o n g I n d e x

Fletcher, Alice Cunningham, ed. Indian story and song from North America. Small
   c1900 cl $1.50
   Contents: 24 songs. English, Indian and Indian with English translations

Lieurance, Thurlow. Nine Indian songs. Presser c1913 pa $1.50
   English only, founded on American Indian tribal melodies and themes

Lieurance, Thurlow. Songs of the North American Indians. Presser c1920 pa $1.50
   Contents: 9 songs, English only, founded on Indian tribal melodies and themes

c. Negro

Bond, Mrs Carrie (Jacobs), comp. Old melodies of the south; transcribed by Mary Gillen and Oliver Chalifoux. Boston music co. c1918 pa $1.25
Contents: 10 negro spirituals

Burleigh, Henry Thacker. Plantation melodies old and new; words by R. E. Phillips, J. E. Campbell, P. L. Dunbar; music composed or transcribed and adapted by H. T. Burleigh. G. Schirmer 1901 pa $1
Contents: 5 negro spirituals arranged, 2 original songs by Burleigh

Burlin, Natalie Curtis, ed. Negro folk-songs. (Hampton series) 4v G. Schirmer c1918-19 pa ea 50c
Contents: v1, 4 spirituals; v2, 4 spirituals; v3, 4 work songs; v4, 7 work and play songs
Arranged for vocal quartette

Dann, Hollis, ed. Fifty-eight spirituals for choral use; harmonized by Harvey Worthington Loomis. Birchard c1924 pa $1
Contents: 58 negro spirituals

Hampton, Va. Normal and agricultural institute. Religious folk songs of the negro; arr from the original edition by Thomas P. Fenner. Hampton institute press c1909 cl $1
Contents: 79 negro spirituals

*__Johnson,__ James Weldon, ed. The book of American negro spirituals. Viking press 1925 cl $3.50
Contents: 62 negro spirituals

Jubilee and plantation songs; characteristic favorites, as sung by the Hampton students, jubilee singers, Fisk university students, and other concert companies. Ditson c1887 pa 50c
Contents: 104 negro spirituals

*__Krehbiel,__ Henry Edward, ed. Afro-American folk songs; a study in racial and national music. G. Schirmer. c1914 cl $2
The creole songs are in creole patois, generally with English translations; the Breton and Welsh songs are in the original languages with English translations
Contents: 3 slave songs; 31 spirituals; 2 folk songs; 13 negro creole songs; 1 Breton folk song; 1 Welsh folk song

Noble, Gilbert Clifford, ed. The most popular plantation songs. Hinds, Hayden and Eldredge c1911 pa 75c
Contents: 110 southern songs, including some spirituals

DUTCH

Bos, Coenraad, ed. Dutch folk-songs. G. Schirmer c1917 pa 75c
Contents: 10 songs, Dutch with English translations

ENGLISH

*__Bantock,__ Granville Ransome, ed. One hundred songs of England. (The musicians library) Ditson c1914 high, low pa $2.50; cl $3.50
Contents: 31 traditional songs; 10 county songs; 59 songs by T. A. Arne, Benet, Bishop, Blow, Braham, Byrd, Campion, Davy, C. Dibdin, Dowland, T. Ford, Gibbons, Hook, Horn, Humfrey, W. Jackson, R. Johnson, H. Lawes, W. Lawes, Leveridge, T. Linley, Locke, Mellish, Morley, H. Purcell, Rosseter, Savile, R. J. S. Stevens, Wade, Weelkes, Wilbye

Baring-Gould, Sabine, ed. English minstrelsie; a national monument of English song; the airs arr by H. Fleetwood Sheppard, F. W. Bussell and W. H. Hopkinson. 8v T. C. and E. C. Jack n.d. cl o.p. 1926
Contents: v1, 40 songs; v2, 45 songs; v3, 37 songs; v4, 40 songs; v5, 40 songs; v6, 48 songs; v7, 45 songs; v8, 51 songs
English songs from the earliest times through the 18th century

Baring-Gould, Sabine, Sheppard, Henry Fleetwood, and Bussell, F. W., eds. Songs of the west. new and rev ed Methuen n.d. bds 10s6d
Contents: 121 folk songs of Devon and Cornwall

Chappell, William, ed. Old English popular music. New edition with a preface and notes, and the earlier examples entirely revised by H. Ellis Wooldridge. 2v Chappell and co. 1893 cl o.p. 1926
Contents: v1, 94 songs; v2, 83 songs
English songs from the earliest times through the 18th century. The book contains also many airs without words, and fragments of both words and music; these are omitted from the S o n g I n d e x

Duncan, Edmondstoune, ed. The minstrelsy of England. 2v Augener ₍pref. 1905-09₎ pa ea 4s; cl ea 6s
Contents: v1, 220 songs; v2, 200 songs

Farnsworth, Charles Hubert, and Sharp, Cecil James, eds. Folk-songs, chanteys and singing games. H. W. Gray n.d. bds $1
Contents: 33 English folk songs; 7 singing games; 9 chanteys

Hatton, John Liptrot, and Faning, Eaton, eds. The songs of England. 3v Boosey n.d. pa ea $2
  Contents: v1, 274 songs; v2, 281 songs; v3, 281 songs

Jackson, Vincent, ed. English melodies from the 13th to the 18th century. Dent 1910 cl 9s6d
  Contents: 100 songs

Kimmins, Mrs Grace Thyrza (Hannan), ed. Songs from the plays of William Shakespeare; with dances as sung and danced by the Bermondsey guild of play with incidental music; the pianoforte accompaniments by Richard Chanter. Novello ₍pref. 1911₎ bds $3.75
  Contents: 22 of the best known settings of 16 Shakespeare songs
  The book contains also directions for children's dances, with both traditional and modern music; these are omitted from the S o n g I n d e x

Moffat, Alfred, and Kidson, Frank, eds. English songs of the Georgian period. Bayley and Ferguson n.d. pa 5s; cl 8s
  Contents: 200 songs, 1760-1820

Moffat, Alfred, and Kidson, Frank, eds. The minstrelsy of England. Bayley and Ferguson 1901 pa 3s; cl 5s6d
  Contents: 200 songs, 16th to 18th century

Potter, Frank Hunter, ed. Reliquary of English song. 2v G. Schirmer c1915-16 pa ea $1.25
  Contents: v1, 52 songs covering a period from 1250 to 1700; v2, 54 songs, 1700-1800

Sharp, Cecil James, ed. English folk songs; songs and ballads. 2v Novello n.d. cl ea $6.75
  Contents: v1, 16 ballads, 34 folk songs; v2, 16 ballads, 29 folk songs, 5 accumulative folk songs

Sharp, Cecil James, ed. Folk-songs of England. 5v Novello c1908-12 pa v1,4 ea 4s; v2,3,5, ea 4s6d
  Contents: v1, 16 folk songs from Dorset; v2, 6 folk songs from Essex, 7 from Norfolk, 2 from Cambridgeshire; v3, 16 folk songs from Hampshire; v4, 3 folk songs from Worcestershire, 3 from Warwickshire, 2 from Oxfordshire, 1 from Gloucestershire, 1 from Berkshire, 1 from Devonshire, 1 from Cambridgeshire; v5, 15 folk songs from Sussex

*****Sharp**, Cecil James, ed. One hundred English folksongs. (The musicians library) Ditson c1916 pa $2.50; cl $3.50
  Contents: 29 folk ballads; 66 folk songs; 5 accumulative folk songs

*****Vincent**, Charles John, ed. Fifty Shakspere songs. (The musicians library) Ditson c1906 high, low pa $2.50; cl $3.50
  Contents: 7 songs mentioned by Shakespeare in his plays; 7 songs possibly sung in the original performances; 21 settings composed since Shakespeare's time to the middle of the 19th century; 15 recent settings

FRENCH

Barbeau, Marius, and Sapir, Edward, eds. Folk songs of French Canada. Yale univ. press 1925 cl $4
  Contents: 41 songs, French with English translations
  No accompaniments

Calvé, Emma, comp. My favorite French songs. 2v Ditson c1915 high, low pa ea $2
  French with English translations
  Contents: v1, 2 folk songs; 25 songs by Bemberg, Bérat, Bizet, Chausson, Dalayrac, David, Debussy, Delibes, Duparc, Fauré, Franck, Godard, Niedermeyer
  v2, 2 folk songs; 23 songs by Gounod, Hahn, Indy, Lalo, Marie Antoinette, Massenet, Méhul, Saint-Saëns

Dickinson, Clarence, and Dickinson, Helen Adell (Snyder), eds. Troubadour songs. H. W. Gray c1920 bds $3
  Contents: 6 songs, English only

Ferrari, Gustave, ed. Ten folk-songs of Alsace, Lorraine and Champagne. G. Schirmer c1919 pa $1.25
  Contents: 4 songs from Alsace, 4 from Lorraine, 2 from Champagne; French with English translations

*****Hale**, Philip, ed. Modern French songs. 2v Ditson c1904 high, low pa ea $2.50; cl ea $3.50
  French with English translations
  Contents: v1, 30 songs by Bemberg, Berlioz, Bizet, Blanc, Bouval, Bréville, Chaminade, Chausson, Chrétien, Coquard, Debussy, Delibes, Duparc, Fauré, Ferrari, Fontenailles, Franck
  v2, 30 songs by Georges, Godard, Gounod, Hahn, Holmès, Hüe, Indy, Lalo, Lemaire, Leroux, Massenet, Paladilhe, Pessard, Pierné, Ropartz, Rothschild, Saint-Saëns, Thomas, Thomé, Widor

*****Spicker**, Max, ed. Anthology of modern French song; a collection of thirty-nine songs with piano accompaniment by modern French composers. G. Schirmer c1912 high, low pa $1.50; cl (Golden treasury ed) $3
  French with English translations
  Songs by Bachelet, Bizet, Bruneau, Chausson, Coquard, Debussy, Delibes, Duparc, Fauré, Franck, Hüe, Indy, Lalo, Lekeu, Leroux, Massenet, Paladilhe, Pierné, Saint-Saëns, Vidal, Widor

Tiersot, Julien, ed. Forty-four French folk songs and variants from Canada, Normandy, and Brittany. (Songs of the people) G. Schirmer c1910 pa $1; cl $2.50
     French with English translations. The book contains also some fragments of songs; these are omitted from the S o n g I n d e x

*Tiersot, Julien, ed. Sixty folksongs of France. (The musicians library) Ditson c1915 pa $2.50; cl $3.50
     French with English translations

Wekerlin, Jean Baptiste, ed. Bergerettes; romances and songs of the eighteenth century. Ditson 1913 pa $1.25
     Contents: 20 songs, French with English translations

GERMAN

Erk, Ludwig Christian, ed. Deutscher liederschatz; eine auswahl der beliebtesten volks-, vaterlands-, soldaten-, jäger-, studenten- & weihnachtslieder. 3v Peters n.d. pa ea $2.25; cl ea $2.50
     German only
     Contents: v1, 250 songs; v2, 200 songs; v3, 200 songs

Gerhardt, Elena, comp. My favorite German songs. Ditson c1915 high, low pa $2
     German with English translations
     Contents: 31 songs by Beethoven, Brahms, Franz, Jensen, Liszt, Schubert, Schumann, R. Strauss, Wolf

*Spicker, Max, ed. Songs of Germany; eighty-one German folk- and popular songs. (Songs of the people) G. Schirmer c1904 pa $1.25; cl $2.75
     German with English translations

HAWAIIAN

Hopkins, Charles A. K., ed. Aloha collection of Hawaiian songs. Wall, Nichols co. 1901 pa $1.50
     Contents: 43 songs, English only, Hawaiian only, and Hawaiian with English translations

IRISH

*Fisher, William Arms, ed. Sixty Irish songs. (The musicians library) Ditson c1915 high, low pa $2.50; cl $3.50
     Traditional songs, and modern poems set to old airs; English only

Joyce, Patrick Weston, ed. Old Irish folk music and songs. Longmans 1909 cl o.p. 1926
     English, and Irish with English translations
     Contents: 120 songs, no accompaniments. The book contains also many airs without words, and some fragments of both words and music; these are omitted from the S o n g I n d e x

Moffat, Alfred, ed. The minstrelsy of Ireland. 4th ed Augener n.d. pa 4s; cl 6s
     Contents: 200 songs, English only

Moore, Thomas. Irish melodies; with symphonies and accompaniments by various eminent authors. rev and enl ed Ditson 1893 pa $1.50
     Contents: 47 settings of Moore's poems, both traditional airs and more recent compositions

Page, Nathaniel Clifford, ed. Irish songs; a collection of airs old and new. Ditson 1907 pa $1
     Contents: 68 Irish traditional songs and songs of more recent composition, English only

ITALIAN

Favilli, Mario, ed. Echoes of Naples; thirty Neapolitan songs. Ditson 1909 pa $1.50
     Contents: 30 songs, traditional and modern, Italian with English translations. In a few cases only, the words are given in the Neapolitan dialect

*Floridia, Pietro, ed. Early Italian songs and airs. (The musicians library) 2v Ditson c1923-24 high, low pa ea $2.50; cl ea $3.50
     Italian with English translations, covering a period from the 16th to the beginning of the 19th century
     Contents: v1, 40 songs by G. M. Bononcini, Caccini, Carissimi, Cavalli, Cesti, Falconieri, Frescobaldi, Gaffi, Gagliano, Legrenzi, Mazzaferrata, Monteverde, Peri, Quagliati, Rontani, Salvator Rosa, Strozzi, Tenaglia
     v2, 40 songs by Bencini, G. B. Bononcini, Caldara, D'Astorga, Durante, Fedeli, Gasparini, Giordani, Leo, Lotti, Mancini, Marcello, Paisiello, Pergolesi, Perti, Provenzale, Salvator Rosa, Scarlatti, Secchi, Steffani, Stradella, Torelli, Supriani, Traetta, Vivaldi

Marzo, Eduardo, ed. Neapolitan songs; nineteen folk- and popular songs. (Songs of the people) G. Schirmer c1905 pa $1
     Italian with English translations

*Marzo, Eduardo, ed. Songs of Italy; sixty-five Tuscan, Florentine, Lombardian and other Italian folk- and popular songs. (Songs of the people) G. Schirmer c1904 pa $1; cl $2.50
Italian with English translations
Contents: 5 Abruzzian songs; 3 Calabrian songs; 1 Istrian song; 8 Lombardian songs; 18 Neapolitan songs; 2 Piedmontese songs; 5 Roman songs; 4 Romanesca songs; 9 Sicilian songs; 7 Tuscan songs; 4 Venetian songs

Parisotti, Alessandro, ed. Anthology of Italian song. (Schirmer's library of musical classics, v290) 2v G. Schirmer 1894 pa ea $2; cl ea $3.50
Italian with English translations
Contents: v1, 29 songs by G. M. Bononcini, Caldara, Carissimi, Cesti, C. Gluck, Händel, Jomelli, Legrenzi, Lotti, Marcello, Martini, Paisiello, Pergolesi, Piccinni, A. Scarlatti, D. Scarlatti, Traetta, Vivaldi
v2, 30 songs by Bassani, G. B. Bononcini, Caccini, Cavalli, Cesti, Del Leuto, De Luca, Durante, Falconieri, Fasolo, Gasparini, Giordani, Marcello, Monteverde, Paradies, Piccinni, Rontani, Sarri, Scarlatti, Stradella, Tenaglia

JAPANESE

Ross, Gertrude. Art songs of Japan (Yamata Shirabe); traditional Japanese themes and poems. White-Smith ⌊pref. 1917⌋ high, low pa $1
Contents: 6 songs, some English only and some Japanese (transliterated) with English translations

Yamada, Kôsçak. Japanese folk songs for voice & piano; the music transcribed from the original version and modernized. C. Fischer n.d. pa $1.25
On cover, Book 1. Only 1v published
Contents: 6 songs, Japanese (transliterated) with English translations

MEXICAN AND SOUTH AMERICAN

*Hague, Eleanor, ed. Folk songs from Mexico and South America. H. W. Gray c1914 pa $1
Contents: 12 songs, Spanish with English translations

Hague, Eleanor, ed. Spanish-American folk-songs. (Memoirs of the American folk-lore society, vX) Stechert 1917 cl $3.50
Contents: 89 songs, no accompaniments, Spanish with English translations
The book contains also many airs without words; these are omitted from the S o n g I n d e x

Luce, Allena, ed. Canciones populares. Silver c1921 bds $1.28
Spanish only
Contents: 28 songs of Porto Rico; 12 songs of Cuba, Spain and Mexico; 13 patriotic songs translated from other languages; 22 old folk songs and game-songs

Lummis, Charles Fletcher, ed. Spanish songs of old California; pianoforte accompaniments by Arthur Farwell. C. F. Lummis c1923 pa $1.50
Contents: 14 songs, Spanish with English translations

RUSSIAN

*Newman, Ernest, ed. Modern Russian songs. (The musicians library) 2v Ditson c1921 high, low pa ea $2.50; cl ea $3.50
French, German, English translations only
Contents: v1, 52 songs by Alpheraky, Arensky, Bagrinofski, Balakireff, Borodine, Bleichmann, Cui, Dargomijsky, Glière, Glinka, Gretchaninoff, Ippolitoff-Ivanoff, Jacobson, Kalinnikoff, Kopyloff, Korestschenko, Liapounoff, Medtner, Moussorgsky
v2, 50 songs by Moussorgsky, Rachmaninoff, Rimsky-Korsakoff, Rubinstein, Sachnofsky, Sokoloff, Stravinsky, Taneieff, Tchaikovsky, Tcherepnin, Tiniakoff, Vassilenko, Wihtol

Newmarch, Rosa, ed. The Russian song books. 4v Chester n.d. pa ea 3s
English and French translations only
Contents: Songs for a soprano voice: v1, 6 songs; v2, 6 songs; songs for a bass voice: v1, 7 songs; v2, 7 songs

*Schindler, Kurt, ed. A century of Russian song from Glinka to Rachmaninoff. (Golden treasury of music, VXXVI) G. Schirmer c1911 pa $2; cl $3.50
French, German, English translations only
Contents: 50 songs by Arensky, Balakirew, Borodine, Cui, Dargomijsky, Glazunoff, Glinka, Moussorgsky, Rachmaninoff, Rimsky-Korsakow, Rubinstein, Tschaikowsky

Schindler, Kurt, ed. Masters of Russian song. 2v G. Schirmer c1917 pa ea $2.50; cl ea $4
English translations only
Contents: v1, 25 songs by Moussorgsky; v2, 25 songs by Balakireff, Borodine, Gretchaninoff, Rachmaninoff, Rimsky-Korsakoff, Tchaikovsky

Schindler, Kurt, ed. Sixty Russian folk-songs for one voice. 3v G. Schirmer. c1918-19 pa ea $1.50
Contents: v1-3, each 20 songs, English translations only

SCANDINAVIAN

Hägg, Gustaf, ed. Songs of Sweden; eighty-seven Swedish folk- and popular songs. (Songs of the people) G. Schirmer c1909 pa $1.50; cl $3
Swedish with English translations

Kappey, J. A., ed. Songs of Scandinavia and northern Europe. Boosey n.d. pa $2
English only
Contents: 24 Russian songs; 5 Polish songs; 2 Lithuanian songs; 2 Finnish songs; 23 Swedish songs; 4 Norwegian songs; 11 Danish songs; 13 Dutch songs

Moore, Mrs Aubertine Woodward, and Anderson, Rasmus Bjorn, eds. The Norway music album. Ditson 1909 pa $2
Norwegian, generally with English translations
Part 1: 77 folk songs; part 2: 26 songs by Backer-Gröndahl, Bull, Grieg, H. Kjerulf, Nordraak, Reissiger, Svendsen
The book contains also many folk dances without words; these are omitted from the Song Index

Stub, Mrs Valborg Hovind, ed. Songs from the north; representative songs of Norway, Sweden, and Denmark. Ditson 1907 pa $1.50
Danish, Norwegian, Swedish with English translations
Contents: 53 songs by Ahnfeldt, Backer-Gröndahl, Berg, Bull, Collan, Egeberg, Gade, Grieg, Hartmann, Heise, H. Kjerulf, Lange-Müller, Lassen, Lie, A. F. Lindblad, O. Lindblad, Nordraak, Olsen, Rosenfeld, Rung, Selmer, Sinding, Sjögren, Söderberg, Söderman, Svendsen, Thrane, Warmuth

***Werrenrath,** Reinald, ed. Modern Scandinavian songs. (The musicians library) v1 Ditson c1925 high, low pa $2.50; cl $3.50
Danish, Finnish, Norwegian, Swedish with English translations
Contents: v1, 50 songs by Alfvén, Alnaes, Backer-Gröndahl, Beckman, Beyer, Börresen, Bull, Elling, Gade, Grieg, Hallén, Hallström, Halvorsen, Hartmann, Heise, Holter, Järnefelt, Jordan, C. Kjerulf, H. Kjerulf

SCOTTISH

Burns, Robert. Songs of Burns. centenary ed new and rev Bayley and Ferguson n.d. pa $2; cl $3.75
Contents: 106 songs

Burns, Robert. The songs of Robert Burns; with bibliography, historical notes, and glossary by James C. Dick. Frowde 1903 cl o.p. 1926
Contents: 351 songs, no accompaniments
The book contains also many songs without music; these are omitted from the Song Index

***Hopekirk,** Helen, ed. Seventy Scottish songs. (The musicians library) Ditson c1905 high, low pa $2.50; cl $3.50
Celtic and Saxon folk songs from Scotland; English only

Moffat, Alfred, ed. The minstrelsy of Scotland. 4th ed Augener n.d. pa 4s; cl 6s
Contents: 200 songs, English only

Pittmann, Josiah, and Brown, Colin, eds. The songs of Scotland. 2v Boosey n.d. pa ea $2
English only
Contents: v1, 190 songs; v2, 151 songs

SPANISH

Sturgis, M. H., and Blake, W. P., eds. Songs of the Pyrenees. A. P. Schmidt co. c1918 pa $1.50
Contents: 10 folk songs, Spanish or French with English translations

For additional Spanish songs see Mexican and South American

WELSH

Moffat, Alfred, ed. The minstrelsy of Wales. Augener ₁pref. 1906₁ pa 4s; cl 6s
Contents: 151 songs, English only

YIDDISH

Gideon, Constance, and Gideon, Henry, eds. From the cradle to the chuppe. 2v A. P. Schmidt co. 1923 pa ea $1
Yiddish (transliterated) with English translations
Contents: v1, 5 childhood songs; 3 love songs; v2, 3 songs of meditation; 4 festival and wedding songs

CHANTEYS

***Colcord,** Joanna Carver, ed. Roll and go; songs of American sailormen. Bobbs-Merrill c1924 bds $5
Contents: 5 short-drag chanteys; 25 halyard chanteys; 25 windlass or capstan chanteys; 31 forecastle songs
No accompaniments. The book contains also fragments of songs; these are omitted from the Song Index

King, Stanton Henry, ed. King's book of chanties. Ditson 1918 pa 25c
Contents: 11 long drag chanties; 4 short drag chanties; 7 capstan chanties; 2 pumping chanties; 4 old sea songs

Sharp, Cecil James, ed. English folk-chanteys. Wessex press 1914 pa 5s
Contents: 60 chanteys

Smith, Laura Alexandrine. The music of the waters; a collection of the sailors' chanties, or working songs of the sea, of all maritime nations; boatmen's, fishermen's and rowing songs, and water legends. Kegan Paul 1888 cl o.p. 1926
Words generally in the original language with English translations. Only a transliterated text is given for languages not using the Latin alphabet. The book has also many airs without words, and fragments of both words and music; these are omitted from the Song Index
Contents: 44 English and American chanties; 11 keelmen's and fishermen's songs and Tyneside ballads; 4 Canadian boat songs; 2 Chinese songs; 1 Creole song; 2 Dutch sailors' and herring-fishers' songs; 15 French sailors' and boatmen's songs; 4 Gaelic boat songs; 5 German sailors' songs; 1 Hebrew song; 3 East Indian water-songs; 2 Italian sailors' songs; 4 Japanese sailors' songs; 4 Neapolitan fishermen's songs; 3 Nile boatmen's chants; 1 Russian sailors' song; 2 Samoan songs; 9 Scandinavian sea songs; 3 Scotch songs; 1 Tongese song; 1 Venetian gondoliers' song

CHRISTMAS CAROLS

Bramley, Henry Ramsden, and Stainer, Sir John, eds. Christmas carols new and old. Novello n.d. cl $3
Contents: 70 songs, English only

*****Dann**, Hollis, ed. Christmas carols and hymns for school and choir. American book co. c1910 cl 80c
Contents: 43 songs, English only

Davis, Katherine Wallace, ed. Christmas songs of many nations; a musical entertainment for children. C. F. Summy co. 1899 pa 25c
Contents: 23 songs, English, American Indian without English translation, and Bohemian, Danish, German, Italian, Norwegian and Swedish with English translations
The book contains also poems and other material for a Christmas entertainment; these are omitted from the Song Index

*****Hutchins**, Charles Lewis, ed. Carols old and carols new; for use at Christmas and other seasons of the Christian year. Parish choir c1916 cl $5
English only, except 1 song in Flemish, 1 in French, 1 in German, and 3 in Latin, without English translations
Contents: 525 carols for Christmas and Epiphany; 215 Easter songs; 11 songs for Ascension and Whitsun-tide; 38 harvest songs; 28 songs for children's day and flower services

McCaskey, J. P., ed. Christmas in song, sketch, and story. Harper c1890 cl o.p. 1926
Contents: 272 songs, English, and some German with English translations

Marzo, Eduardo, ed. Fifty Christmas carols of all nations. Willis music co. c1923 pa 75c
English only
Contents: 1 Alsatian song; 1 Austrian song; 2 Bohemian songs; 1 Danish song; 3 Dutch songs; 12 English songs; 11 French songs; 5 German songs; 4 Italian and Latin songs; 1 Polish song; 2 Portuguese songs; 1 Russian song; 5 Spanish songs; 1 Swedish song

Walter, Lavinia Edna, ed. Christmas carols; old English carols for Christmas and other festivals; harmonised by Lucy E. Broadwood. Macmillan c1922 cl $2
Contents: 28 carols, mostly for Christmas

SACRED SONGS

Henderson, William James, ed. Sacred songs. 4v Church 1903 pa ea $1.50
English; and French, German, Latin with English translations
Contents: v1, soprano, 58 songs; v2, alto, 54 songs; v3, tenor, 53 songs; v4, bass, 56 songs

*****Oratorio** songs. 4v Church c1900 pa ea $1.50
Contents: v1, soprano, 40 songs; v2, alto, 39 songs; v3, tenor, 39 songs; v4, bass, 41 songs
English, and a few Latin with English translations, from the oratories Abraham, Calvary, Christ on the Mount of Olives, Christmas oratorio, Christus, Creation, Crucifixion, The daughter of Jairus, Deborah, Eli, Elijah, The fall of Babylon, Hercules, The holy city, Israel in Egypt, Jephtha (Händel), Joseph, Joshua, Judas Maccabaeus, The light of the world, The Lord is King, Mary Magdalen, The Messiah, Naaman, Occasional oratorio, Ode for St Cecilia's day, Paradise lost, The St John Passion, The St Matthew Passion, Rebekah, Requiem, The rose of Sharon, Ruth, St Elizabeth, St Ludmila, St Paul, St Peter, Samson, Samson and Delilah, Saul, The seasons, Solomon, Stabat Mater, Susanna, Theodora, The woman of Samaria

Spicker, Max, ed. Anthology of sacred song. 4v G. Schirmer c1902 pa ea $1.50; cl ea $3
English only
Contents: v1, soprano, 56 songs from Abraham, Alexander Balus, Calvary, Creation, Destruction of Jerusalem, Eli, Elijah, Engedi, Golden legend, Harvest cantata, Hercules, Holy city, Jephtha (Händel), Jephthah and his daughter, Joshua, Judas Maccabaeus, Judith, Light of the world, Mary Magdalen, Messiah, Moses, My spirit was in heaviness, Ode to St Cecilia's day, Paradise lost, Pentecost cantata, Resurrection of Lazarus, Samson, Saul, Seasons, Seven last words, St John's eve, St Paul, St Peter, Susanna, Ten virgins
v2, alto, 60 songs from Athalia, Christmas eve, Christmas oratorio, Christus, Constantin, Deborah, Eli, Elijah, Fall of Jerusalem, Gethsemane, Heavens declare, Hercules, Holy city, Israel in Egypt, Jephtha (Händel), Joshua, Judas Maccabaeus, Judith, Light of the world, Messiah, Miracle of Nain, Prodigal son, Rose of Sharon, Ruth (Cowen), Ruth (Gaul), Samson, Saul, Solomon, Star of Bethlehem, St Cecilia, St Ludmilla, St Paul, St Peter, Susanna, Ten virgins, Theodora, Woman of Samaria, World's end

v3, tenor, 61 songs from Abraham, Athalia, Christmas oratorio, Creation, Crucifixion, Daughter of Jairus, Destruction of Jerusalem, Elijah, Engedi, Fall of Babylon, Harvest cantata, Hercules, Holy city, Hymn of praise, Jephtha (Händel), Jephtha and his daughter, Judas Maccabaeus, Judith, Light of the world, Messiah, Occasional oratorio, Prodigal son, Rebekah, Resurrection of Lazarus, Ruth (Cowen), St Cecilia, St Paul, Samson, Seasons, Seed-time and harvest, Seven last words, Susanna, Ten virgins, Tobias, Woman of Samaria

v4, bass, 58 songs from Abraham, Burial of Christ, Calvary, Christmas oratorio, Creation, Deborah, Destruction of Jerusalem, Elijah, Fall of Jerusalem, Judas Maccabaeus, Light of the world, Mary Magdalen, Messiah, Moses, Nativity, Occasional oratorio, Paradise lost, Passion, Rebekah, Rose of Sharon, Ruth (Gaul), St Ludmilla, St Paul, St Peter, Samson, Saul, Seasons, Seven last words, World's end

Wier, Albert E., ed. Sacred music the whole world loves. Appleton c1916 pa $1.25
English only, except some Latin with English translations
Contents: 27 sacred songs; 74 hymns
The book contains also piano scores without words; these are omitted from the S o n g I n d e x

SCHOOL AND COLLEGE SONGS

Chamberlain, David Blaisdell, and Harrington, Karl Pomeroy, eds. Songs of all the colleges. Hinds, Hayden and Eldredge 1903 cl o.p. 1926
Contents: 300 songs from colleges and universities of the United States

Columbia university songs; comp. by William Ballou Donnell, Russell Pratt Hoyt, Jr., Leonard Gordon McAneny, and Gilbert Oakley Ward. Ditson 1904 cl $2
Contents: 67 songs, English only, except 2 Latin without translations and 1 German with English translation

Most popular college songs. rev ed Hinds, Hayden and Eldredge c1906 pa 75c
English only, except a few Latin songs without translations
Contents: 99 student songs, and 1 song each from the universities of California, Chicago, Columbia, Cornell, Denver, Harvard, Illinois, Johns Hopkins, Leland Stanford, Michigan, Minnesota, Nebraska, New York, Northwestern, Ohio State, Pennsylvania, Princeton, Syracuse, Western Reserve, Wisconsin, and Yale

*****Waite,** Henry Randall, comp. College songs; a collection of the most popular songs of the colleges of America. new and enl ed Ditson 1918 pa $1
Contents: 118 songs, English only, except 1 Latin without translation

Key to Symbols for Collections Indexed

AA   Anthology of American song. G. Schirmer 1911

AB 1-4   Album of bass songs. 4v G. Schirmer c1888-94

BA   Burton, F. R. American primitive music. Moffat 1909

BAS 1-2   Baritone songs. 2v Boosey 1921

BC   Bispham, D. S. Celebrated recital songs. Presser 1919

BD   Bispham, D. S. The David Bispham treasury of song. Winston 1920

BDF   Bos, C. V. Dutch folk-songs. G. Schirmer c1917

BE 1-8   Baring-Gould, S. English minstrelsie. 8v T. C. and E. C. Jack n.d.

BF 1-2   Botsford, F. H. Folk songs of many peoples. 2v Womans press 1921-22

BFS   Barbeau, M., and Sapir, E. Folk songs of French Canada. Yale univ. press 1925

BMC   Brown, J. D., and Moffat, A. Characteristic songs and dances of all nations. Bayley and Ferguson 1901

BN 1-4   Burlin, N. C. Negro folk-songs. 4v G. Schirmer c1918-19

BO   Bantock, G. R. One hundred folksongs of all nations. Ditson c1911

BOH   Bantock, G. R. One hundred songs of England. Ditson c1914

BOM   Bond, C. J. Old melodies of the south. Boston music co. c1918

BOS   Buck, P. C. Oxford song book. Oxford univ. press 1919

BP   Burleigh, H. T. Plantation melodies old and new. G. Schirmer 1901

BS 1-2   Bass songs. 2v Boosey 1924

BSB   Burns, R. Songs of Burns. Centenary rev ed Bayley and Ferguson n.d.

BSC   Bramley, H. R., and Stainer, J. Christmas carols. Novello n.d.

BSE   Bacon, M. S. H. Songs every child should know. Grosset 1906

BSP   Bantock, G. R. Sixty patriotic songs of all nations. Ditson c1913

BSR   Burns, R. The songs of Robert Burns; ed. by J. C. Dick. Frowde 1903

BSS   Boy scout song book. Birchard [pref. 1920]

BSW   Baring-Gould, S., Sheppard, H. F., and Bussell, F. W. Songs of the west. new and rev ed Methuen n.d.

CB   Classic baritone and bass songs. Ditson c1888

CF   Cadman, C. W. Four American Indian songs. White-Smith 1909

CHS   Chamberlain, D. B., and Harrington, K. P. Songs of all the colleges. Hinds, Hayden and Eldredge 1903

CM 1-2   Calvé, E. My favorite French songs. 2v Ditson 1915

CMF 1-2   Culp, J. My favorite songs. 2v Ditson 1916

CO 1-2   Chappell, W. Old English popular music. new ed 2v Chappell and co. 1893

CR   Colcord, J. C. Roll and go. Bobbs-Merrill c1924

CS 1-2   Contralto songs. 2v Boosey n.d.

CSE   Campbell, O. D., and Sharp, C. J. English folk songs from the southern Appalachians. Putnam 1917

CST   Cartwright, H. G. Song treasury. Macmillan 1920

CU   Columbia university songs. Ditson 1904

DC   Dann, H. Christmas carols and hymns for school and choir. American book co. c1910

DCS   Davis, K. W. Christmas songs of many nations. C. F. Summy co. 1899

DF   Dann, H. Fifty-eight spirituals for choral use. Birchard c1924

DM 1-2   Duncan, E. The minstrelsy of England. 2v Augener [pref. 1905-09]

DO   Davison, A. T., and Surette, T. W. 140 folk-songs. new and rev ed E. C. Schirmer c1921

DSH   Davison, A. T., and Surette, T. W. Home & community songbook. E. C. Schirmer c1921

DT   Dickinson, C., and Dickinson, H. A. S. Troubadour songs. H. W. Gray c1920

ED 1-3   Erk, L. C. Deutscher liederschatz. 3v Peters n.d.

EF   Elson, L. C. Folk songs of many nations. Church c1905

ES   Encore songs. Ditson 1910

FE   Favilli, M. Echoes of Naples. Ditson 1909

FEI 1-2   Floridia, P. Early Italian songs and airs. 2v Ditson c1923-24

FF   Finck, H. T. Fifty mastersongs by twenty composers. Ditson c1903

FI   Fletcher, A. C. Indian games and dances with native songs. Birchard 1915

FIS   Fletcher, A. C. Indian story and song from North America. Small c1900

FM   Farrar, G. My favorite songs. Ditson c1916

FMB   The family music book. G. Schirmer c1914

FO 1-2   Finck, H. T. One hundred songs by ten masters. 2v Ditson c1917

FSF   Farnsworth, C. H., and Sharp, C. J. Folk-songs, chanteys and singing games. H. W. Gray n.d.

FSI   Fisher, W. A. Sixty Irish songs. Ditson c1915

FSS 1-8   Franklin square song collection. 8v Harper 1881-91

FTF   Ferrari, G. Ten folk-songs from Alsace, Lorraine and Champagne. G. Schirmer c1919

FTS   Finck, H. T., and Bentley, A. E. Thirty sterling songs by the great masters. Allyn and Bacon 1906

GF 1-2   Gideon, C., and Gideon, H. From the cradle to the chuppe. 2v A. P. Schmidt 1923

GM   Gerhardt, E. My favorite German songs. Ditson c1915

GMF   Gluck, A. My favorite songs. Ditson c1917

GO   Gilbert, H. F. B. One hundred folk-songs from many countries. Birchard 1910

HA   Hopkins, C. A. K. Aloha collection of Hawaiian songs. Wall, Nichols co. 1901

HC   Hutchins, C. L. Carols old and carols new. Parish choir c1916

HF   Hague, E. Folk songs from Mexico and South America. H. W. Gray c1914

HM 1-2   Hale, P. Modern French songs. 2v Ditson c1904

HR   Hampton, Va. Normal and agricultural institute. Religious folk songs of the negro; arr. by T. P. Fenner. Hampton institute press c1909

HS   Hague, E. Spanish-American folk-songs. Stechert 1917

HSC   Home songs; a collection of favorite songs, etc. Ditson 1906

HSD   Heart songs dear to the American people. Chapple pub. co. c1909

HSE 1-3   Hatton, J. L., and Faning, E. The songs of England. 3v Boosey n.d.

HSOS   Hägg, G. Songs of Sweden. G. Schirmer c1909

HSS 1-4   Henderson, W. J. Sacred songs. 4v Church 1903

HSSS   Hopekirk, H. Seventy Scottish songs. Ditson c1905

HST   Hughes, R. Songs by thirty Americans. Ditson c1904

JB   Johnson, J. W. The book of American negro spirituals. Viking press 1925

JE   Jackson, V. English melodies from the 13th to the 18th century. Dent 1910

JO   Johnson, H. K. Our familiar songs and those who made them. Holt 1909

JOI   Joyce, P. W. Old Irish folk music and songs. Longmans 1909

JP   Jubilee and plantation songs. Ditson c1887

JS   Johnson, C. W. Songs of the nation. Silver 1912

JSE   Johnson, C. Songs every one should know. American book co. 1908

KA   Krehbiel, H. E. Afro-American folksongs. G. Schirmer c1914

KB   King, S. H. King's book of chanties. Ditson 1918

KF 1-4   Krehbiel, H. E. Famous songs. 4v Church 1902

KS 1-5   Krehbiel, H. E. Songs from the operas. 5v Ditson c1907-11

KSE   Kappey, J. A. Songs of eastern Europe. Boosey n.d.

KSN   Kappey, J. A. Songs of Scandinavia and northern Europe. Boosey n.d.

KSS   Kimmins, G. T. H. Songs from the plays of William Shakespeare. Novello [pref. 1911]

LA   Levermore, C. H. The abridged academy song-book. rev ed Ginn 1918

LBR   Lawrence, W. M., and Blackman, O. Riverside song book. Houghton c1893

LC   Lomax, J. A. Cowboy songs. Macmillan c1916

LCP   Luce, A. Canciones populares Silver c1921

LN   Lieurance, T. Nine Indian songs. Presser c1913

LS   Lieurance, T. Songs of the North American Indian. Presser c1920

LSS   Lummis, C. F. Spanish songs of old California. C. F. Lummis c1923

MAN   Moore, A. W., and Anderson, R. B. The Norway music album. Ditson 1909

MC   Marzo, E. Coloratura album for soprano. Ditson 1909

MCS   McCaskey, J. P. Christmas in song, sketch, and story. Harper c1890

ME   Moffat, A., and Kidson, F. English songs of the Georgian period. Bayley and Ferguson n.d.

MF   Marzo, E. Fifty Christmas carols of all nations. Willis music co. 1923

MI   Moore, T. Irish melodies. rev and enl ed Ditson 1893

MM   Moffat, A., and Kidson, F. The minstrelsy of England. Bayley and Ferguson 1901

MMI   Moffat, A. The minstrelsy of Ireland. 4th ed Augener n.d.

MMS   Moffat, A. The minstrelsy of Scotland. 4th ed Augener n.d.

MMW   Moffat, A. The minstrelsy of Wales. Augener ⌊pref. 1906⌉

MN   Marzo, E. Neapolitan songs. G. Schirmer c1905

MP   The most popular songs of patriotism. Hinds, Hayden and Eldredge c1916

MPC   The most popular college songs. rev ed Hinds, Hayden and Eldredge c1906

MS   MacConnell, M. F. Standard songs and choruses for high schools. American book co. c1908

MSF 1-2   Modern song favorites. 2v G. Schirmer c1882

MSI   Marzo, E. Songs of Italy. G. Schirmer c1904

MSS 1-2   Mezzo-soprano songs. 2v Boosey n.d.

NA   National anthems of the allies. G. Schirmer 1917

NG   Neitzel, O. Gems of antiquity. Church c1909

NM 1-2   Newman, E. Modern Russian songs. 2v Ditson c1921

NMH   Noble, G. C. The most popular home songs. new and enl ed Hinds, Hayden and Eldredge c1913

NML   Noble, G. C. The most popular love songs. Hinds, Hayden and Eldredge c1906

NMP   Noble, G. C. The most popular plantation songs. Hinds, Hayden and Eldredge c1911

NMS   Noble, G. C. The most popular songs for every occasion. Hinds, Hayden and Eldredge 1912

NR 1-4   Newmarch, R. The Russian song books. 4v Chester n.d.

OH   The one hundred and one best songs. rev ed Cable co. c1925

OPS 1-4   Opera songs. 4v Church 1901

OS 1-4   Oratorio songs. 4v Church c1900

PA 1-2   Parisotti, A. Anthology of Italian song. 2v G. Schirmer 1894

PG 1-4   Parker, H. W. German, French and Italian song classics. 4v Church 1912

PI   Page, N. C. Irish songs. Ditson 1907

PO   Potter, F. H. Old song favorites. G. Schirmer n.d.

PP   Pittmann, J. Prima donna's album. VI G. Schirmer n.d.

PR 1-2   Potter, F. H. Reliquary of English song. 2v G. Schirmer c1915-16

PS 1-2   Pittmann, J., and Brown, C. The songs of Scotland. 2v Boosey n.d.

RAS   Ross, G. Art songs of Japan. White-Smith ⌊pref. 1917⌉

SA   Sharp, C. J. American-English folk-songs. 1st series G. Schirmer c1918

SAM   Spicker, M. Anthology of modern French song. G. Schirmer c1912

SAS 1-4   Spicker, M. Anthology of sacred song. 4v G. Schirmer c1902

SC   Schindler, K. A century of Russian song from Glinka to Rachmaninoff. G. Schirmer c1911

SE   Sharp, C. J. English folk-chanteys. Wessex press 1914

SEF 1-2   Sharp, C. J. English folk songs. 2v Novello n.d.

SF 1-5   Sharp, C. J. Folk-songs of England. 5v Novello c1908-12

SM 1-4   Song miscellany. 4v G. Schirmer c1902

SMF   Sembrich, M. My favorite folk songs. Ditson c1918

SMR 1-2   Schindler, K. Masters of Russian song. 2v G. Schirmer c1917

SMW   Smith, L. A. The music of the waters. Kegan Paul 1888

SN   Sousa, J. P. National, patriotic and typical airs of all lands. C. Fischer c1890

SO   Sharp, C. J. One hundred English folksongs. Ditson c1916

SOA 1-5   Spicker, M. Operatic anthology. 5v G. Schirmer c1903-04

SOS 1-2   Spicker, M. Obbligato-songs. 2v G. Schirmer c1905

SS 1-2   Soprano songs. 2v Boosey n.d.

SSG   Spicker, M. Songs of Germany. G. Schirmer c1904

SSH   Sturgis, E. B. Songs from the hills of Vermont; music ed. and arr. by R. Hughes. G. Schirmer c1919

SSN   Stub, V. H. Songs from the north. Ditson 1907

SSP   Sturgis, M. H., and Blake, W. P. Songs of the Pyrenees. A. P. Schmidt co. c1918

SSR 1-3   Schindler, K. Sixty Russian folk-songs for one voice. 3v G. Schirmer c1918-19

SSS   The Scottish students' song book. Bayley and Ferguson n.d.

TF	Tiersot, J. Forty-four French folk-song and variants from Canada, Normandy, and Brittany. G. Schirmer c1910		WCP	The world's collection of patriotic songs and airs of the different nations. Ditson 1903
TFC 1-2	Twice 55 community songs. 2v Birchard c1919-23		WF	Whitehead, R. R. Folk-songs of Eastern Europe. Ditson c1912
TL	Tomlins, W. L. Laurel song book. Birchard c1901		WL	Wier, A. E. Love songs the whole world sings. Appleton c1916
TS	Tenor songs. Boosey n.d.		WLT	Wyman, L. Lonesome tunes; accompaniment by H. Brockway. vi H. W. Gray c1916
TSF	Tiersot, J. Sixty folksongs of France. Ditson c1915		WM 1	Werrenrath, R. Modern Scandinavian songs. vi Ditson c1925
VFS	Vincent, C. J. Fifty Shakspere songs. Ditson c1906			
WA	Wier, A. E. The American home music album. Appleton c1915		WS	Wier, A. E. Sacred music the whole world loves. Appleton c1916
WB	Wekerlin, J. B. Bergerettes. Ditson 1913		WSC	Wier, A. E. Songs the children love to sing. Appleton c1916
WBT	Wier, A. E. The book of a thousand songs. Mumil pub. co. c1918		WSW	Wier, A. E. Songs the whole world sings. Appleton c1915
WBW	Wier, A. E. Ballads the whole world sings. Appleton c1917		WT	Wyman, L. Twenty Kentucky mountain songs; accompaniments by H. Brockway. Ditson c1920
WC	Waite, H. R. College songs. new and enl ed Ditson 1918			
WCC	Walter, L. E. Christmas carols. Macmillan c1922		YJ	Yamada, K. Japanese folk songs for voice & piano. C. Fischer n.d.

Key to Language Abbreviations

a.	Armenian	ind.	Indic languages (languages of India)
af.	African languages	ir.	Irish
al.	Albanian	j.	Japanese
ar.	Arabic	l.	Latin
b.	Bulgarian	la.	Lappish
bo.	Bohemian	le.	Lettish
br.	Breton	li.	Lithuanian
c.	Chinese	n.	Norwegian
d.	Dutch	p.	Polish
da.	Danish	pe.	Persian
e.	English (used only for English translations)	po.	Portuguese
		pol.	Polynesian languages, except Hawaiian
es.	Esthonian		
esk.	Eskimo	pr.	Provençal
f.	French, including dialects	r.	Russian, including Ruthenian
fi.	Finnish	ru.	Rumanian
fij.	Fijian	s.	Spanish
fl.	Flemish	se.	Serbo-Croatian, including the languages of Bosnia, Croatia, Dalmatia, Herzegovina, Macedonia, Montenegro, Serbia, Slavonia, and some isles of the Adriatic
g.	German, including dialects		
ga.	Gaelic		
gr.	Greek, Modern		
h.	Hawaiian		
he.	Hebrew	sl.	Slovak
hu.	Hungarian	slo.	Slovenian
i.	Italian, including dialects	t.	Turkish
ic.	Icelandic, Modern	w.	Welsh
in.	Indian, American, including all languages	y.	Yiddish

Key to Miscellaneous Abbreviations

arr.	arranged	n.d.	no date
bds.	boards	o.p.	out of print
cl.	cloth	pa.	paper
comp.	compiled, compiler	pref.	preface
ea.	each	pseud.	pseudonym
ed.	edited, edition, editor	rev.	revised
enl.	enlarged	tr.	translation
jt. auth.	joint author	v.	volume, -s
jt. comp.	joint compiler		

DIRECTIONS FOR USE

The *title entry* is the main entry and gives the fullest information, including name of composer, of author of words, abbreviation for language of song, symbols for collections in which the song is to be found. An example follows:

> La **chevelure** (Her hair)   A. C. Debussy.
> Words by P. Louÿs.   e.f.   CM 1—
> SAM

If entry under composer, author, alternate title, or first line is consulted first, the title entry should then be consulted for fuller information.

Under the title, entry, indented, are listed all variations of title in different collections. An example follows:

> **Auf** dem meere ("On ocean's breast")   R.
> Franz.   Words by Heine.   e.g.
> PG 4
> "Das meer hat seine perlen" ("The sea
> its pearls possesses")   e.g.   GM

The symbols indicating the collections in which a song may be found are given in title entry only.

Foreign songs are entered under title in the original language, with the exception of some of the less well known languages. For list of these see the Introduction, p. viii.

The language or languages of the text of a song are indicated for all songs where the original is not English by a language abbreviation in the title entry.

Entries for composers are printed in boldface roman (e.g. **Beethoven, Ludwig van**).

Entries for authors are printed in boldface italics (e.g. *Burns, Robert*).

First lines are given in quotation marks, even when used as title.

SONG INDEX

The **A.** and M. college song. Oklahoma agricultural and mechanical college song. A. C. Scott. CHS

"A B C D E F G H I J K L M N O P Q R S and T U V W (Double U) and X Y Z. Now I've said my A.B.C." See The alphabet

"A B C D E F G, H I K L M N O P, Q R S T U V W, Q R S T U V W, X̆ X Yps'lon Z, o weh! kann's ja nicht lernen das A-B-C." See Der dorf-schulmeister

"A B C D, wenn ich dich seh." See Liebes-A-B-C (Pohlenz)

"A, B, C, tumble down D." WBT—WSC

A ba'al eglah lied. See A teamster's complaint

A cantar a una niña. Folk song from Costa Rica. e.s. HS

"A chiad Oidhche dhe'n Challuin." See Na gillean mo rùin

A chushla gal mochree ("I think of you") See Acushla gal machree

A chushla gal mochree ("When first into this town I came."—Thou fair pulse of my heart) Irish folk song. e. JOI

"A core a core." See Raziella

"A, dass's im wald finst'r is." See Liebes-kummer

A.E., pseud. See Russell, George William

"'A' is the maid of winning charm." See A demonstration (Jones)

"A Ischia no nce so tanta ventaglie" ("In Ischia there are not so many fans") Neapolitan song. e.i. MSI

"A jänta å ja" ("The maiden and I") Swedish folk song. Words by F. A. Dahlgren. e.sw. HSOS

"A la claire fontaine" ("By the clear fountain") Canadian folk song. e.f. TF

—1st variant. e.f. TF
—2d variant. e.f. TF
Variant of: "En revenant de noces"

"A la fiera de Mast' Andrea." See La fiera de Mast' Andrea

A la fontaine (At the well, oh) French Canadian folk song. e.f. BFS

A la guerra (Off to the war) Italian folk song. e. GO

"A la luz de la luna." Folk song from lower California. e.s. HS

"A la puerta del cielo venden zapatos." See Dodo

"A la vívora, vívora del amor." See La puerta de Alcalá

"A l'heure où notre esprit moins fier." See Les trois prières (Paladilhe)

A loha kuu lei pika ke. See Remember be sure and be there (Hopkins)

A Lucette (To Lucette) G. Pierné. Words by H. Gautier-Villars. e.f. SAM

"A ma main droite j'ai un rosier" ("With care I tend my rosebush gay") French folk song. e.f. TSF

"A mezzanotte in punto." See Gli scar-riolanti

A mi madre. J. Betinoti (music and words) s. LCP

"A morìre" ("Ah, to perish") G. Carris-simi. e.i. FEI 1

A my proso sìeìali, sìeìali. See The sow-ing of the millet

A Nina (To Nina) Venetian folk song. e.i. MSI

"A nos pieds les flots chantent dans les roseaux." See "Gelb rollt mir zu füs-sen" (Rubinstein)

"A orillas de una fuente." See La zagala

"A Paris y-a-t une brune, qu'est bell' comm' le jour." See La brune et le brigand

"A Parthenay il y avait." See La fille de Parthenay

A peine au sortir de l'enfance. For Ger-man translation see Joseph (Méhul)

A quoi bon l'économie (While there are such things as dice) Massenet. e.f. OPS 4

"A roro mi nena, a roro mi sol." See Arrullo (Argentine version)

"A Saint-Malo, beau port de mer." Can-adian sea song. e.f. SMW

"A Saint-Malo" (At Saint-Malo) e.f. BFS

"A Serpina penserete" ("On Serpina think with pleasure") G. B. Pergolesi. e.i. FEI 2—KS 1

"A susida." See My neighbor

A tanto amor. G. Donizetti. e.i. SOA 5

"A te l'estremo addio." See Il lacerato spirito (Verdi)

"A' the lads o' Thornie-bank." Air: Ruffian's rant. Words by R. Burns. BSR

"A the syghes yt cu from my hart." See "Ah! the sighs" (Cornysshe)

A toi mon coeur (My heart to thee) C. Gounod. [Words by H. Heine. Tr of Auf dem meere] e.f. SOS 1

A travers champs, l'hiver. See Through the fields in winter (Sokolov)

"A un niño ciegocito" ("Unto a poor blind lover") Bolero. e.s. BO

"A Úna bán, a bláit na n-dlaoi ómrac." See Úna bán

"A vill int' du, så vill fäll ja" ("Well, if you won't, why then I will") Swedish folk song. e.sw. HSOS

"**Aa** Dalebu hadde ei festarmöj bold."
See Dalebu Jonson

"**Aa** denne vise har ingen ende" ("This song of mine is without an ending") Norse folk song. e.n. MAN

"**Aa** kjöre vatten aa kjöre ve" ("Come haul the water and haul the wood") Norse folk song. e.n. MAN

"**Aa** kjøre vatten aa kjøre ve'" ("O fetch the water") e.n. BF 2

"**Aa** Ola, Ola, min eigen onge" ("Oh, Ole, Ole, I loved you dearly") Norse folk song. e.n. MAN

"**Aa** Ola, Ola" ("Ah, Ola, Ola") e.n. BF 2

"**Aa** ormekongen kom seg riandes i gaar med de vivit va saa ungt." See Solfager ag ormekongen

"**Aa** skamme dig, sunev, du svar' ikkje mej." See Kau fra Hallingdalen

Aa skynn dej, aa straev saa. See "Go javten"

"**Aa** vil du hava meg te aa kveda" ("Now if you want me to sing a ditty") Norse folk song. e.n. MAN

Aagots fjeldsang (Aagot's moutain song) Norse folk song. Words by H. A. Bjerregaard. e.n. MAN

Aagot's mountain song. See Aagots fjeldsang

Aarestrup, Emil
Ångest (Alfvén)
Blicken (Alfvén)

Die **Aargauer** lieben ("Im Ärgäu sind zweu liebi") Schweizerishes volkslied. g. ED 3
Die heimkehr (The home-coming.— "Im Aergäu sind zweu liebi."—"In Aargau dwelt two sweethearts") e.g. BO

Aasen, Ivar
"Millom bakkar og berg utmed havet" (Norse air)

Abandoned. Norwegian song. e. KSN

The **abbot** of Canterbury, Air: The king and Lord Abbott. DM 2

Abdul, the Bulbul Ameer. College song. SSS
Variants: Abdulla Bul-Bul Ameer; Ivan Skizavitzky Skivar

Abdulla Bul-Bul Ameer. College song. CU
Variants: Abdul, the Bulbul Ameer; Ivan Skizavitzky Skivar

A **begging** we will go. 17th century song. Words attributed to R. Brome. CO 2
The jovial beggar. MM

"Der **abend** hüllt das schöne land in immer schwärzeres gewand." See Abendlied (Fink)

"**Abend** ist's, die sonne ist verschwunden." See Abendempfindung (Mozart)

"Der **abend** schaut durch's fensterlein." See Wiegenlied (Ries)

"Der **abend** schleiert flur und hain in traulich holde dämmrung ein." See Am sommerabend (Spazier)

"Das **abend** sinkt, kein sternlein blinkt." See Schutz (Bergt)

"**Abend** wie milde! sonne wie roth." See Vom Monte Pincio (Grieg)

"**Abend** wird es wieder." See Abendlied (Rinck)

Die **abenddämmerung** ("Seht, die sonne sinkt") H. G. Nägeli. Words by E. Anschütz. g. ED 3

Abendempfindung (Evening thoughts) W. A. Mozart. e.g. NG

Abendlied ("Der abend hüllt das schöne land") G. W. Fink (music and words) g. ED 2

Abendlied ("Abend wird es wieder") C. H. Rinck. Words by H. Hoffmann von Fallersleben. g. ED 3

Abendlied ("Abend wird es wieder."—Even song) F. von Wickede. [Words by H. Hoffmann von Fallersleben] e.g. SM 2

Abendlied ("Dankt dem Herrn") J. H. Rolle. Words by Kurze. g. ED 2

Abendlied ("Der mond ist aufgegangen") J. A. P. Schulz. Words by M. Claudius. g. ED 1—ED 2

Abendlied ("Das tagewerk ist abgetan") K. F. Zelter. Words by J. H. Voss. g. ED 3

Abendlied ("Unter allen wipfeln"). F. Kuhlau. Words after Goethe [adapted from "Über allen gipfeln ist ruh"] g. ED 2

Abendlied froher landleute ("Kühl und labend") F. L. Seidel. Words by F. Voigt. g. ED 3

Abendlied, wenn man aus dem wirtshaus geht ("Jetzt schwingen wir den hut") A. Methfessel. Words by J. P. Hebel. g. ED 2

Abendruhe ("Wie herrlich sind die abendstunden") W. A. Mozart. g. ED 3

"Des **abends** rosen sind abgeblüht." See entry under Des

Abercrombie, Beatrice
"If my mistress hide her face" (Hatton)
The pilgrim (Maybrick)

Aberle, J.
Saludemos la patria
Salute our country. See Saludemos la patria

"**Abide** with me! fast falls the eventide" (Berlin) Mendelssohn. Words by H. F. Lyte. FSS 3

"**Abide** with me! fast falls the eventide." W. H. Monk. Words by H. F. Lyte. BSS— FSS 1—HSD— LA—NMH —NMS— OH— TFC 2—WA— WBT—WS—WSC—WSW
"Abide with me" (Eventide) BD— FMB—HSC—JS

"**Abide** with me then will I fear not." See "Bist du bei mir" (Bach)

"**About** my beloved idol." See "Intorno all' idol mio" (Cesti)

"**About** the sweet bag of a bee." H. Lawes. PR 1

"Above on the hillside yonder." See Das mühlrad

"Above our union, broad and wide." See Our banner (Wilhelm)

"Above the grave of warrior brave." See Hail, Beloit (Olds)

Above the mountains. See Wanderers nachtlied (Schubert)

Abreise ("So hab ich denn die stadt verlassen") C. Kreutzer. Words by L. Uhland. g. ED 2

"Abroad as I was walking, and a-walking alone." See High Germany

"Abroad as I was walking down by a riverside." See The Irish girl (Hampshire version)

"Abroad as I was walking down by some greenwood side." Folk song from Hampshire. SF 3

"Abroad as I was walking one morning in the spring." See Bedlam

"Abroad we must wander." Composer unknown. Words by J. Love. BE 5

"Abscheulicher! wo eilst du hin" ("Thou monstrous fiend") L. van Beethoven. e.g. SOA 1

"Abscheulicher, wo eilst du hin" ("Accursed one, where leads thy haste") e.g. KS 1

Abschied ("Als wir beiden."—Parting) J. N. Cavallo. Words by P. Heyse. e.g. SM 4

Abschied ("Bemooster bursche") A. Methfessel. Words by G. Schwab. g. ED 1

Abschied ("Liebchen ade") Folk air. Words after a folk song: Schätzchen, ade. g. ED 1. e. only BSE

Abschied (Farewell) e.g. SSG

Abschied ("Muss i denn") Suabian folk song. Words after an old folk song by H. Wagner (pseud. Wergan) g. ED 1

Abschied (Departure) e.g. SSG

Departure. e. BSE

"Muss i denn" ("Must I go") e.g. BO—SMF

Muss i denn zum städtele 'naus (Must I then go afar from the town) e.g. EF

Parting. e. WL

When I come. e.g. FSS 5—WBT

Abschied ("So leb' denn wohl") W. Müller. Words by F. Raimund. g. ED 1. e. only MS

Abschied (Departure) e.g. SSG

Abschied ("Was klinget") Folk air. Words by Uhland. g. ED 2—ED 3

Abschied ("Wenn die schwalben heimwärts ziehn") F. Abt. Words by C. Herlossssohn. g. ED 1

"Wenn die schwalben heimwärts zieh'n" ("When the swallows homeward fly") e.g. SSG

"When the swallows homeward fly." e. FSS 1—HSC—HSD—NMH—NML— WA—WBT—WL—WSC—WSW

Abschied vom dirndel ("Von meinem bergli muss i scheiden") Schweizerisches volkslied. g. ED 1

Abschied vom dirndel (Farewell to the sweetheart) e.g. SSG

Abschied vom dirndel ("From these dear mountains."—"Von meinem bergli") e.g. BO

The Switzer's farewell. e.g. EF. e. only FSS 3—HSD—WBT

Abschied vom walde. For English translation see Farewell to the forest (Mendelssohn)

Abschiedsabend ("Traurig sehen wir uns an") F. W. Weiss. Words by J. M. Miller. g. ED 3

Abschiedslied ("Auf, auf, ihr brüder") C. F. D. Schubart (music and words) g. ED 2

Absence ("Ah, whither, my Mary") Pastoral. J. Hook. Words by E. Le Strange. ME

Absence ("Reviens, reviens ma bien aimée") H. Berlioz. Words by T. Gautier. e.f. FM—MSS 1

Absent friends and you, Mary. Spicer. MP

Abt, Franz

Abschied

Alma mater—Lake Erie

"Ave Maria"

Basseti. See A faithful heart

Birdie in the cradle

"Blissful dreams come stealing o'er me"

"The day-star is shining"

Embarrassment. See Verlegenheit

An evening song

A faithful heart

"Far over the stars there is rest." See "Über den sternen ist ruh"

"The flow'rets close at eve, my love"

"For the blessings that surround me." See My native land

"Fragant air"

Good night

Good-night, sweet child. See Gute nacht, du mein herziges kind

"Guardian mother"

Gute nacht, du mein herziges kind

He giveth His beloved sleep

Home so blest

I hear the robin sing. See Rothkehlchen

"Jesus, Lover of my soul"

Kathleen aroon

The lake

A midsummer song

My native land

"Nearer, my God, to Thee"

Night and day love

"Not a sparrow falleth"

"O Lord, most holy." See "Ave Maria"

"O ye tears" (Tr of Rinnt, ihr thränen)

Our fatherland

Our native land. See Our fatherland

"Over the stars there is rest." See "Über den sternen ist ruh"

Abt, Franz —*Continued*
The postilion
The quiet night
"Ring on, ye bells"
Rothkehlchen
Serenade. See "The flow'rets close at eve, my love"
Serenade. See "Wenn die nacht mit ihrem schleier"
"Still is the night, still is the night"
Sunday morning
"There is hovering about me"
"Über den sternen ist ruh"
Verlegenheit
"Wenn die nacht mit ihren schleier"
"Wenn die schwalben heimwärts zieh'n." See Abschied
"When the night in dusky shadows." See "Wenn die nacht mit ihrem schleier"
"When the swallows homeward fly." See Abschied

Acadian boatmen's song. Negro folk song from New Orleans. f. KA

"**Accours,** voyageur, accours, c'est la nuit." See The sea-queen (Borodin)

"**Accursed** one, where leads thy haste." See "Abscheulicher, wo eilst du hin" (Beethoven)

"**Accuse** me not." Scottish air. Words by R. Tannahill. PS 2

"**Ach!** die qualen." See "Ah! the torment" (Paderewski)

"**Ach,** dürft' als sonne droben ich scheinen." See The maiden's wish (Chopin)

"**Ach** Gott, das drückt das herz mir ab." See Herzensbeklemmung (Thümmel)

Ach ich fühls. For English and Italian translations see "Ah! lo so" (Mozart)

"**Ach** lieb, ich muss nun scheiden" ("Dear love, I now must leave thee") R. Strauss. Words by F. Dahn. FO 2

"**Ach,** mädchen, nur einen blick." See Der liebe seligkeit

"**Ach** není tu není." See All joy is gone

"**Ach!** so fromm." F. von Flotow. e.g. SOA 3
"Ah! so pure, ah! so bright." e. FSS 3—HSD—WA—WBT—WSW
"M'appari tutt' amor." e.i. OPS 3

"**Ach,** um deine feuchten schwingen." See Suleika (Mendelssohn)

"**Ach** umsonst auf aller länder karten." See Echtes glück (Kempt)

"**Ach,** Värmeland, du sköna." See Vermeland

"**Ach,** was ist leben doch so schwer." See Sei still! (Raff)

"**Ach** wenn ich doch ein immchen wär" ("Ah! were I but a little bee") R. Franz. Words by K. W. Osterwald. e.g. FM

"**Ach** wenn mutter Wolga." See "Ah, if mother Volga" (Cui)

"**Ach!** wer bringt die schönen tage." See Erster verlust (Medtner)

"**Ach,** wie flieht das leben so geschwind." A. André. Words by K. Rudolphi. g. ED 3

"**Ach!** wie ist's möglich dann." See Treue liebe (Kücken)

"**Ach,** wie so bald verhallet der reigen" (Autumn song) F. Mendelssohn. Words by Klingeman. e.g. MS

"**Ach!** zéléna grusha." See The bride's farewell

"**Ack!** i Arkadien äfven jag har varit" ("Ah! in Arcadia I too once did wander") G. Wennerberg (music and words) e.sw. HSOS

"**Ack** Vermeland, du sköna." See Vermeland

"**Acordemos** nuestras." See Flores a María (Gonzáles)

"**Across** the bridge, O come" (El-debkah) Syrian folk song. ar.e. BF 2

"**Across** the eastern hill-tops." J. R. Fairlamb. HC

"**Across** the fertile prairies of dear old Illinois." See Tribute to Wesleyan (Smedley)

Across the Niemen ("Za Niemen") Polish song. e.p. BF 1

"**Across** the sea, came the Sinclair brave." See "Hr. Sinklar"

Across the western ocean ("I wisht I was in London town") Chantey. SMW

Across the western ocean ("Oh, the times are hard") Capstan chantey. CR

Action song. A. S. Gatty. WSC

Acuirle mo criode créad ian gruaim ort. For English translation see Pulse of my heart

Acushla gal machree ("I think of you by day, my love."—Thou fair pulse of my heart) Irish folk song. e. JOI

Acushla gal machree ("When first into this town I came") See A chushla gal mochree

Ad perennis vitae fontem. For English translation see "On the fount of life eternal"

Adam de la Halle
"I have here a little cake." See "J'ai encor un tel paté"
"J'ai encor un tel paté"
"Robin loves me"

Adam, Adolphe Charles
Cantique de Noël
Christmas song. See Cantique de Noël
Noël. See Cantique de Noël
"O holy night." See Cantique de Noël
Vallons de l'Helvétie (from Le chalet)

Adam, Jean
There's nae luck about the house (Scottish air) Authorship uncertain

"**Adamastor,** re dell'onde profonde." See "Adamastor, roi des vagues profondes" (Meyerbeer)

"Adamastor, roi des vagues profondes." G. Meyerbeer. e.f.i. SOA 4

"Adamastor, roi des vagues profondes" ("King Adamastor, the ruler of ocean") e.f. OPS 4

Adamei,
To my mother (Bradsky)

Adams, Arthur
"Dance with me" (Harrington)

Adams, Mrs Carrie Belle (Wilson)
"Fare thee well, lovely year"
Summer parting hymn

Adams, Lloyd
          Composer
I doubt it
"Jolly golfing weather"
          Author
"Old college chum" (Composer unknown

Adams, Rosamund W.
The pale white rose (Composer unknown)

Adams, Mrs Sarah (Flower)
"Nearer, my God, to Thee" (music by Abt; Herron; Mason; Sullivan; also unknown composer)

Adams, Stephen, pseud. See Maybrick, Michael

Adams, Thomas
"In the hallowed manger"

Adams, W. T.
"How sad mid the sunshine" (Old air) Authorship uncertain

Adams, William T.
"Peace to the brave"

Adams and liberty. Air: Anacreon in heaven. Words by R. T. Paine. JO

Adderley, R. E.
"In the hallowed manger" (Adams)

Addio a Napole ("Addio mia bella Napoli." —Addio a Napoli.—Farewell to Naples) Neapolitan song. e.i. FE

Addio a Napole ("Nce simmo a la partenza."—Farewell to Napoli) Neapolitan song. Words by D. Bolognese. e.i. MN
The boatman's farewell to Naples. e.i. SMW
Napole mio ("È pronta la partenza."— My Naples.—Addio a Napoli.— Farewell to Naples) e.i. FE

L'addio del voluntario (The volunteer's farewell) Florentine patriotic song. e.i. MSI—SN

"Addio mia bella, addio." See L'addio del voluntario

"Addio mia bella Napoli." See Addio a Napole

Addison, Joseph
Creation (Haydn)
"Oh! the charming month of May" (Composer unknown)
"The spacious firmament on high" (music by Haydn; also unknown composer)
These see his wonders in the deep (Franc)
"Was ever nymph like Rosamond" (Arne)

"When all Thy mercies" (Händel)
"While we shed a tear" (Composer unknown)

Address. See Pogner's anrede (Wagner)

Ade du lieber tannenwald. For English translation see "Farewell, O joyous, sunny grove" (Esser)

Adelaïde ("Einsam wandelt dein freund") L. van Beethoven. Words by F. von Matthisson. e.g. CMF 1—FF—KF 3 —PG 3—TS

Adelaide ("Einsam wandelt dein freund") K. P. E. Pilz. Words by F. von Matthison. g. ED 3

Adelina, the Yale Boola girl. See Boola song (Hirsh)

Adelphi school song. LA

Adenis, Eugène, pseud. See Colombeau, Eugène Félix Adenis de

Adeste, coelitum chori. 13th century air. Words by N. Le Tourneaux. e. HC

"Adeste fideles." Attributed to J. Reading. 1. FSS 6—MCS. e. only CST—LA
"Adeste fideles" ("O come all ye faithful") e.l. BSS—DO. e. only DC—FMB—HC—MF—WS
"Come, all ye faithful." e.l. HSD. e. only FSS 1—MCS
"O come, all ye faithful." e. NMS— TFC 1—WA—WBT—WSW
"Oh, come, all ye faithful" (Portuguese hymn) BD—TL

The adieu ("Dear love, adieu") FSS 6

Adieu ("Io ti lascio, o cara, addio") Mozart. e.i. CS 1

L'adieu ("One kind kiss before we part") G. Jackson. BE 8

Adieu ("We've trod one road") See Parting (Ippolitov-Ivanov)

"Adieu! a heart-warm, fond adieu." Air: Good night and joy be wi' you a'. Words by R. Burns. BSR

"Adieu, adieu, fair Annie, he did say." See Fair Annie

"Adieu, adieu, my only life." See The soldier's adieu (Dibdin)

Adieu, belle France (Adieu, fair France) L. Niedermeyer. e.f. CM 1

"Adieu, chère Louise." P. A. Monsigny. e.f. SOA 4

"Adieu, dear land, with beauty teeming." See Abschied vom dirndel

"Adieu, Dundee." Scottish air: Adew, Dundee. Words by C. Neaves. HSSS—MMS—PS 2

Adieu, fair France. See Adieu, belle France (Niedermeyer)

Adieu, forêts. P. I. Tschaikowsky. e.f. SOA 1

Adieu my love (Adios ke aloha) C. K. Hopkins. e.h. HA

"Adieu, my native land, adieu." Chandler. BE 3

"Adieu, my native land, adieu." Labitzky. FSS 3

"Adieu, thou dear land." See Adieu to Cambria

"Adieu! 'tis love's last greeting." See
The last greeting (Schubert)
Adieu to Cambria ("Adieu, thou dear land")
Air: Llandovery. Words by M. S.
Lawrence. MMW
"Adieu to delight." J. G. Graeff. Words
by Mrs F. Plowden. HSE 3
Adieu to old England. Folk song. BE 6
"Adieu to the village delights." Baildon.
Words by Littleton. BE 6
Les adieux des amants (Lovers' farewell)
French Canadian folk song. e.f. BFS
Un adios. Mexican folk song. e.s. HS
"Adios, adios, amores" ("Farewell, O love,
forever") Spanish American song. e.s.
LSS
Adios ke aloha. See Adieu my love
(Hopkins)
Adlam, F.
"Angels bright, their pinions folding"
Der adler. See The eagle (Arenski)
"Ein adler sass auf felsgestein." See The
eagle (Arenski)
Admiral Benbow ("Come all you seamen
bold") Folk song. FSF—SEF 2—SO
Admiral Benbow ("O we sailed to Vir-
ginia") 18th century song. CO 2—
DM 1—MM
"Adonde irá veloz y fatigada." See La
golondrina (Serradell)
"Adorables aveux, qu'on ne peut trop en-
tendre." See Les premiers aveux
(Dancla)
Adore and quiet be. See "Le ciel a visité
la terre" (Gounod)
"Adown the stairway bounding." See
Niemand hat's geseh'n (Loewe)
"Adown winding Nith I did wander." Air:
The muckin o' Geordy's byre. Words
by R. Burns. BSR
Adrian, J. V.
Entschluss (Lindpaintner)
"The advent of our King." See Thy
King cometh (Nägeli)
Advice. Old French song. e. BC
Advice to lovers (U vorot batiūshkinykh)
Russian folk song. e. SSR 2
Advice to the fair sex. Composer un-
known. BE 6
"Adzooks! che's went the other day to Lon-
don town." See Bartholomew fair
"Ae fond kiss." Old Highland air.
Word by R. Burns. SSS
"Ae fond kiss." Air: Rory Dall's port.
Words by R. Burns. BSR—MMS—
PS 1
"Ae fond kiss." Composer unknown. Words
by R. Burns. BSB—FSS 8—JO
"Ae nicht i' the gloaming." Scottish air.
Words by Hogg. PS 2
"Aennchen von Tharau." See "Ännchen
von Tharau" (Silcher)
"Af hjärtat jag dig älskar" ("As long as
life endureth") Swedish folk song.
e.sw. HSOS
Afar ("Wehe dem fliehenden welt") See
In der ferne (Schubert)

Afar ("Wind! dost thou kiss") Lind-
blad. e. KSN
"Afar from sweet Nanette." See Nanette
"Afar in the forest, on sunny lea." See
Song of my dear
"Afar in the ocean sinketh the sun." See
Lied maritime (Indy)
"Afar in the sea the sun's going down."
See Lied maritime (Indy)
Afar in the wide world they wandered.
See Marsk Stigs døttre
"Afar we live from toil and care." See
Bohemian gipsy song
"Affanni del pensier" ("O agonies of
thought") G. F. Händel. e.i. PA 1
"Affanni del pensier" ("Ye pangs of
anxious thought") e.i. SS 2
"Afield, charming the sight." See "Y-a
rien de si charmant" (La bergère aux
champs); "Y-a rien de si charmant"
(La vie de la bergère)
Afloat. See Im kahne (Grieg)
"Af'n veg." See "On the way stands a
tree"
"Aften hae I play'd at the cards and the
dice." Air: The rantin laddie. Words
by R. Burns. BSR
Aftenstemning. See "Prinsessen sad höjt
i sit jomfrubur" (Kjerulf)
After. L. Diehl. FSS 7—JSE
After a dream. See Après un rêve
(Fauré)
After many roving years. C. E. Horn.
Words by T. H. Bayly. FSS 3
"After showers, the tranquil sun." See
After (Diehl)
After the battle ("He met his death") P.
Moussorgsky. Words by A. Golen-
ishtcheff-Kutoozoff. e. SMR 1
After the battle ("Night closed around")
Air: The fair bosom. Words by T.
Moore. JO—MI
"After the day has sung its song of sor-
row." See Afterwards (Mullen)
"After the pangs." J. E. Gailliard. BE 8
After years (Menyá tui v'tolpyé nye
ōōznála) M. P. Moussorgsky. Words
by A. Golenishtcheff-Kutoozoff. e.
SMR 1
Afternoon in February. J. Hullah. Words
by H. W. Longfellow. LBR
Afterwards. J. Mullen. Words by M.
Mark-Lemon. HSD—WA—WBT—
WL
Afton water ("Flow gently, sweet Afton")
Scottish air: Afton water. Words
by R. Burns. MMS—PS 1
"Flow gently, sweet Afton." BSR
Afton water ("Flow gently, sweet Afton")
Old Scottish air. Words by R. Burns.
HSSS—JO—NG
Afton water ("Flow gently, sweet Afton")
A. Hume. Words by R. Burns. BSB
Afton water ("Flow gently, sweet Afton")
J. E. Spilman. Words by R.
Burns. JO
"Flow gently, sweet Afton." BD—
FSS 2— HSC— HSD— NMH—
TFC 1—WBT—WL

Afzelius, Arvid August
Neckens polska (Swedish air)
Again and again. See For once again (Kalakaua)
"**Again** my heart beats time their measure." See Spring (Alferakiï)
"**Again** rejoicing nature sees." Air: Jockey's gray breeks. Words by R. Burns. BSR
"**Again** the balmy breezes play." See Frühlingsglaube (Ries); Frühlingsglaube (Schubert)
"**Again** the fertile land a goodly harvest yields." See Harvest song (Marshall)
"**Again** the morn of gladness." J. Stainer. Words by J. Ellerton. HC
"**Again** the trailing forest-moss." See Christmas green (Coles)
"**Again** we come this day to greet." See Arbor day (Jones)
"**Against** the strand beats wild the flood." See Disappointed expectation (Lindblad)
The **age** of progress. J. Hutchinson. FSS 8
The **aged** lover. See "In youth when I did love"
"**Aggio** visto na figliola." See La Carolina
Agnes. See "O Angenietje"
"**Agnus** Dei" (O lamb of God) G. Bizet. e.l. HSS 1—HSS 2—HSS 3—HSS 4
L'**Aguignolé** (New Year's day) Canadian folk song. e.f. TF
Aguinaldo ("Si me dan pasteles") s. LCP
"**Ah!** ah! ma gazelle." See Ma gazelle
Ah, ah, zunyenyu, ah, ah, zunyenyu. See "By the cradle of Yankele"
"**Ah!** all is lost, indeed." See Ô souverain, ô juge, ô père (Massenet)
"**Ah!** all peace is lost unto me." See Peace (Varlamov)
"**Ah!** Betty, deep within my heart." See Courting (Lindblad)
"**Ah,** birdie, be thou ever so poor." See The beggar-boy
"**Ah!** ça ira" ("Ah, it will go") Old dance: Carillon national de Bécourt. e.f. BSP
"**Ah!** c'était un riche marchand." See La fille vendue au diable
Ah! che la morte ognora. For English translation see "Ah! I have sighed to rest me" (Verdi)
"**Ah!** che oscurità." See Della vita in sull' aurora (Beethoven)
"**Ah!** che questi avventurieri." See "Solche hergelauf' ne laffen" (Mozart)
"**Ah!** che voglio trionfare." See "Ha! wie will ich triumphiren" (Mozart)
"**Ah,** Chloris, since it may not be." Air: Major Graham. Words by R. Burns. BSR
"**Ah,** come, nor linger more." See "Deh vieni, non tardar" (Mozart)
"**Ah** come, weary one, make haste, it is eve." See The sea-queen (Borodin)

"**Ah,** comment, mon Dieu, vivre ainsi tout seul." See The laborer's plaint (Kopylov)
"**Ah!** could we but fathom the mighty deep." See The mighty deep (Jude)
"**Ah!** could you possibly know." T. Linley. ME
"**Ah!** County Guy, the hour is nigh." See County Guy (Old English air); County Guy (Bishop)
"**Ah,** cruel, ruthless fate." H. Purcell. DM 2
"**Ah,** dear friends, these moments fair." See Good night (Offenbach)
"**Ah,** dear one, hold me closer." See Ångest (Alfvén)
Ah! depart, image fair. See Ah! fuyez, douce image (Massenet)
"**Ah!** do not let thy face pretend." See "Deh! non voler costringere" (Donizetti)
"**Ah,** don't be sorrowful, darling." See Don't be sorrowful, darling (Webster)
"**Ah,** don't kill me." See "No me mates"
"**Ah!** è strano poter il viso suo veder." See "Ah! je ris de me voir" (Gounod)
"**Ah!** fair spring of days now gone by." See Élégie (Massenet)
Ah! fairest sun, arise. See Ah! lève-toi, soleil (Gounod)
"**Ah,** far in the field." See The garland
"**Ah** figliuol! mio figliuol." See "Ah! mon fils" (Meyerbeer)
"**Ah!** fisherboy, thy bait be throwing." See Pescator, affonda l'esca (Ponchielli)
"**Ah!** fly me not, sweet hope of vengeance swift and certain." See Asile héréditaire (Rossini)
"**Ah,** fly my gondolier." See The carnival of Venice
"**Ah,** for to-night I am queen of the fairies." See Je suis Titania (Thomas)
"**Ah!** for wings to soar." Jullien. FSS 3 —WBT
"**Ah,** fors' è lui." Verdi. e.i. OPS 1 —PP

Ah, fors' è lui (Ah! was it he) e.i. KS 1—MC

"**Ah** friends and comrades all." See Canto del carcerato
Ah! fuyez, douce image (Ah! depart, image fair) J. Massenet. e.f. KS 4
"Je suis seul" (I am alone) e.f. OPS 3
"**Ah!** give me back that heart of thine." See "Ah! rendimi" (Rossi)
"**Ah!** give me back thy heart." See "Ah! rendimi" (Rossi)
"**Ah!** give to me." See "Ah! rendimi" (Rossi)
"**Ah!** glad are the children of Egypt of old." See Khedival hymn
"**Ah!** gloomy the forest is." See Love's sorrow
"**Ah,** good evening, fair maiden." See Vergebliches ständchen (Brahms)
"**Ah!** great is our good fortune." See Ai! la bono fortuno

Ah, ha, ha, little cap so round. See "Mon père a fait bâtir maison" (Va, va, va p'tit bonnet tout rond)

"Ah, haughty youth, O thou slayer of wild deer." See La solitaire (Saint-Saëns)

"Ah! here come the Yankees." See "Ay! vienen los Yankees"

"Ah hey they hey, ah hey they hey." See Pu-in game song

"Ah, ho! heart of mine." See Laughing water

"Ah, how enchanting a sight." See Plus blanche que la blanche hermine (Meyerbeer)

"Ah! how it hurts! and oh, how sad my heart is." See Little Snowflake's arietta (Rimskiï-Korsakov)

Ah, how precious is my wreath so charming. See "How I love to gaze" (Nape)

"Ah! how sweet are the cooling breeze, and the blooming trees." See Musidora (Croft)

"Ah! I am tardy, and therefore at our dear place of trysting." See O luce di quest' anima (Donizetti)

"Ah! I feel how all hath vanish'd." See "Ah! lo so" (Mozart)

"Ah! I have sighed to rest me." G. Verdi. [Tr of Ah! che la morte ognora]   e. FSS 3—HSD— NML—WA— WBT— WL—WSW

"Ah! I love thee, idolize thee." See "Yo te amo, idolatro"

"Ah I wonder where thou art dear." See Sweet violet (Hopkins)

"Ah! if I could but see her." See More and more (Seifert)

"Ah, if mother Volga" ("Ach, wenn mutter Wolga") C. Cui.   Words from the Russian of A. Tolstoi.   e.g. NM 1

"Ah! if my charms again were glowing." See "Ah! si je redevenais" (Gounod)

Ah! if thou sleepest, wake, my love.   See Ah! se tu dormi (Vaccai)

"Ah, if thou still art sleeping." See Posate, dormite (Bassani)

"Ah! in Arcadia I too once did wander." See "Ack! i Arkadien äfven jag har varit" (Wennerberg)

"Ah! in my fairy dream I'd revel." See "Ah! je veux vivre" (Gounod)

"Ah! in our still and mournful meadow." See Chorus of mourners (Gluck)

"Ah! it is hard to say." See Treue liebe (Kücken)

"Ah! it was gay, night and day." See Fiddle and I (Goodeve)

"Ah, it was Paloma, little dove." See La paloma cuencana

"Ah, it will go." See "Ah! ça ira"

"Ah! je li gdje koja." See Mournful love

"Ah! je ris de me voir" ("Ah! the joy past compare."—Jewel song) C. F. Gounod.   e.f.   KS 1

È strano poter il viso suo veder.   e.i. PP

"Ah! je veux vivre."   C. Gounod.   e.f. SOA 1

"Ah! je veux vivre" (Like a vision) e.f.   MC

Je veux vivre dans ce rêve (Song, jest, perfume and dances)   e.f.   OPS 1

Waltz song.   e.f.   MSS 2—SS 2

"Ah Kathrin, pretty Kathrin." See "Catina bellina"

"Ah, kindly star" ("Du trauter stern") M. I. Glinka.   Words after Pushkin. e.g.   SC

Ah, la paterna mano.   G. Verdi.   e.i. SOA 3

"Ah! lassie never angry be."   Carinthian song.   e.   KSE

Ah! lève-toi, soleil (Ah! fairest sun, arise) C. F. Gounod.   e.f.   KS 4

L'amour! oui, son ardeur a troublé ('Tis love, ah! 'tis love)   e.f. OPS 3

"Ah, light no garish lamp." See The hour of dreams (Arenski)

"Ah! like a vision fair and golden." See "Ah! je veux vivre" (Gounod)

"Ah! like the green pear-tree." See The bride's farewell

"Ah! linden standing in the dale." See Die linde im thal

"Ah, little girl, don't you cry." See Little girl, don't you cry

"Ah! lo conosco. Il mulino." See Vi ravviso, O luoghi ameni (Bellini)

"Ah! lo so."   Mozart. [Tr of Ach ich fühls]   e.i.   PP

"Ah, longing! my tears ebb and flow like the swift waves." See Longing (Vassilenko)

"Ah, love is but a child." See L'amour s'envole

"Ah! love, thou art a wilful bird." See Habanera (Bizet)

"Ah! lulled by visions pure and tender." See "Ah! je veux vivre" (Gounod)

"Ah Magdalen beware! beware." See Warnung (Meyer-Helmund)

Ah! malgré moi.   C. W. von Gluck.   e.f. SOA 1

Ah! Marì! ah! Marì.   See Maria, Marì (Capua)

"Ah, Marì, give an ear one moment." See Judas (Massenet)

"Ah me! I am lost and forlorn." See Well-a-day! lack-a-day (Storace)

Ah me! too many deaths.   H. Purcell. DM 2

"Ah! mio cor" ("Ah, poor heart") G. F. Händel.   e.i.   PA 1

"Ah! mon fils" ("Ah! my son")   e.f. KS 3 —SOA 2

"Ah figliuol! mio figliuol" ("Ah, my son, dearest son")   e.i.   OPS 2

"Ah! mon remords te venge" ("Ah! now I feel the burden")   G. Meyerbeer. e.f.   KS 5—SOA 4

"Sei vendicata assai" ("Ah! now I feel the burden")   e.i.   OPS 4

"Ah! must ye fade."   See "Ah! non credea mirarti" (Bellini)

"**Ah**! my child, my dear, think how sweet it were." See L'invitation au voyage (Duparc)

"**Ah**! my darling, when once we marry." See "Bella mia" (Pergolesi)

"**Ah,** my fate is bitter; sad my lot." See The conscript's return

"**Ah** my love is from fair Castilla." See Linda mia

"**Ah,** my passion by him, by him ungrateful." See Ma la sola, ohimè! son io (Bellini)

Ah! my sad song dies away. Lindblad. e. KSN—WL

"**Ah**! my son." See "Ah! mon fils" (Meyerbeer)

"**Ah**! my soul." Bach. e. OS 3

"**Ah**! ne repousse pas." See Repentir (Gounod)

Ah! non avea più lagrime. G. Donizetti. e.i. SOA 4

"**Ah,** non chiamarmi" ("Deem not my heart ungrateful") C. W. Gluck. e.i. KS 4

"**Ah**! non credea mirarti" ("Yes, time with fate e'er striving") V. Bellini. e.i. OPS 1—PP

"**Ah**! non credea mirarti" ("Ah! must ye fade")   e.i. KS 1—MC

"**Ah**! non giunge" ("Do not mingle") V. Bellini. e.i. OPS 1—PP

"**Ah**! non giunge" ("Oh, recall not") e.i. KS 1—MC

"**Ah,** not with God's thunder." M. Moussorgsky. Words from the Russian of A. K. Tolstoi. e. NM 1

"**Ah**! now I feel the burden." See "Ah! mon remords te venge" (Meyerbeer)

Ah of thee I'm ever thinking. See Sweet violet (Hopkins)

"**Ah,** Ola, Ola." See "Aa Ola, Ola, min eigen onge"

"**Ah**! once I had a fatherland so fair." See Es war ein traum (Lassen)

"**Ah**! once when I was a very little maid." T. Attwood. Words by S. Birch. ME

Ah! parea che per incanto. C. Donizetti. e.i. SOA 2

"**Ah**! perchè non posso odiarti" ("Still so gently o'er me stealing") V. Bellini. e.i. FSS 5

"**Ah**! pescator." See Pescator, affonda l'esca (Ponchielli)

"**Ah,** pilot! dangers often met." See The pilot (Nelson)

"**Ah** poor heart, and I must see thee." See "Il pensier stà negli oggetti" (Haydn)

"**Ah,** poor heart! he scorns thy love." See "Ah! mio cor" (Händel)

"**Ah**! pour ce soir je suis reine des fées." See Je suis Titania (Thomas)

"**Ah,** Psyche, nature knows, knows how to make me jealous." See Psyché (Paladilhe)

"**Ah,** Psyche, vex'd am I." See Psyché (Paladilhe)

"**Ah** quanto è vero" ("Cupid can never") M. Cesti. e.i. FEI 1

Ah! quel giorno (Live this day) G. Rossini. e.i. KS 3—OPS 2

"**Ah**! quel spectacle enchanteur." See Plus blanche que la blanche hermine (Meyerbeer)

Ah! qui me passera le bois. See L'occasion manquée

"**Ah**! rendimi" ("Ah! give me back that heart of thine") Attributed to F. Rossi. e.i. SOA 2

"**Ah**! rendimi" ("Ah! give me back thy heart")   e.i.   KS 3

"**Ah**! rendimi" ("Ah! give to me") e.i. OPS 2

"**Ah**! rendimi" ("Give back the heart you stole from me") e.i. CS 1

"**Ah**! sad indeed my heart." See "Nur wer die sehnsucht kennt" (Tchaikovsky)

Ah, say but yes. See Dimme 'na vota sì (Scalisi)

Ah! se intorno a quest' urna funesta. For English translation see Chorus of mourners (Gluck)

Ah! se tu dormi. N. Vaccai. e.i. SOA 2

Ah! se tu dormi, svegliati (Ah! if thou sleepest, wake, my love)   e.i. KS 2

"**Ah** se tu dormi ancora." See Posate, dormite (Bassani)

"**Ah** search the world over, home is best." See Her hjemme

"**Ah**! see the old pear-tree." See The bride's farewell

"**Ah**! s'estinto ancor mi vuoi" ("Ah, since vainly I now implore thee") G. S. Mercadante. e.i. KS 3

"**Ah,** shepherds, leave your crooks." See "Quittez, pasteurs, vos brebis, vos houlettes"

"**Ah** sì, ben mio; coll'essere io tuo" ("Yes, now thou art") G. Verdi. e.i. OPS 3

"**Ah** sì, ben mio" ("O come, let links eternal') e.i. KS 4—SOA 3

"**Ah**! si je redevenais." C. Gounod. e.f. SOA 1

"**Ah**! s'il est dans votre village" (Chanson de Florian.—Florian's song) B. Godard. Words by J. P. C. de Florian. e.f. CM 1—FF—FMB —KF 1—KF 2—MSF 1

Florian's song. e. BD—WA—WL

"**Ah**! s'il est dans votre village" (C'est mon ami.—He is my love) Marie Antoinette (really Maria Charlotte Amelia) Words by J. P. C. de Florian. e.f. CM 2

"**Ah,** si j'étais la rose." See Like the rosebud (La Forge)

"**Ah,** since vainly I now imlore thee." See "Ah! s'estinto ancor mi vuoi" (Mercadante)

"**Ah**! Ski-bi-bi-la, tell me true." See Indian spring bird (Lieurance)

"**Ah**! so pure." See "Ach! so fromm" (Flotow)

"**Ah!** son vergin vezzosa." See Son vergin vezzosa (Bellini)

"**Ah!** song, jest, perfume and dances." See "Ah! je veux vivre" (Gounod)

"**Ah!** stay; ah! turn." J. Eccles. Words by W. Congreve. DM 1

"**Ah,** stay with me, my lovely boy, ah, stay." See The little fish's song (Arenski)

"**Ah,** Suzette, Suzette." See Suzette

"**Ah,** sweet angels, let him dream." See Tristram and Iseult (Foerster)

"**Ah,** sweet Kitty Neil, rise up from your wheel." See Kitty Neil

"**Ah!** sweet my love." See "Wie bist du, meine königin" (Brahms)

"**Ah,** tardai troppo e al nostro favorito convegno." See O luce di quest' anima (Donizetti)

"**Ah!** tell me if you ever meet him." See "Ah! s'il est dans votre village" (Godard)

Ah! tell me why. A. Warlamoff. e. KSN—WBT—WL

"**Ah** the bully boat is coming." See The bully boat

"**Ah!** the eventide's returning." See To rest I call ye lambkins all

"**Ah,** the ice upon the river." See Bulgăraş

"**Ah!** the joy past compare." See "Ah! je ris de me voir" (Gounod)

"**Ah!** the sighs." 15th century song. Composer unknown. BOH—CO 1—MM

"**Ah!** the syghes." DM 1—PR 1

"**Ah!** the sighs." 15th century song. W. Cornysshe, jr. CO 1

Ah! the time is long. See Den bergtagna

Ah! the torment ("Ach! die qualen") I. J. Paderewski. Words by A. Mickiewicz. e.g. FF

"**Ah,** the world asks vexing questions." See The old, old questions

"**Ah!** then when health is glowing." See Journeyman's song (Hillebrand)

Ah! 'tis a dream. See Es war ein traum (Lassen)

"**Ah,** 'tis not the raging winter wind." See The Tartar host

"**Ah!** 'tis the voice of angel bright." See "Voce di donna" (Ponchielli)

"**Ah!** 'tis thou, I know the gleaming." See Hymn of freedom (Manzaros)

"**Ah,** 'tis too late now, perhaps e'en waited here." See O luce di quest' anima (Donizetti)

"**Ah!** 'tis wonderful to feel what thy words impart." See "Wie berührt mich wundersam" (Bendel)

"**Ah,** to perish." See "A morìre" (Carissimi)

"**Ah!** toi, belle hirondelle, qui vole ici." See L'hirondelle, messagère de l'amour

"**Ah!** tout est bien fini." See Ô souverain, ô juge, ô père (Massenet)

"**Ah!** turn me not away." See Repentir (Gounod)

"**Ah!** 'twas a time of happiness." See "Wohl war es eine seligkeit" (Witt)

"**Ah,** twine no blossoms" ("O, winde keine duft'ge blüte") R. Glière. Words from the Russian of D. Rathaus. e.g. NM 1

"**Ah!** vous dirai-je, maman." Old French song. f. DO

Ah! was it he. See Ah, fors' è lui (Verdi)

"**Ah!** weep no more." Tschaikovsky. e. BS 1

Ah, well-a-day. 18th century song, attributed to S. Howard. ME

Ah, well-a-day, my poor heart. W. Shield. Words by T. Holcroft. ME

"**Ah!** were I but a little bee." See "Ach wenn ich doch ein immchen wär'" (Franz)

"**Ah!** what a rapturous thought." See 'Tis God who ordains me (Concone)

"**Ah!** what darkness here." See In des lebens frühlingstagen (Beethoven)

"**Ah,** what has life for him in store." See Sei still (Raff)

"**Ah!** what joy past compare, these jewels bright to wear." See "Ah! je ris de me voir" (Gounod)

"**Ah,** what makes the forest dark." See Liebeskummer

Ah, when, love. See Adieu my love (Hopkins)

"**Ah,** when my love was here." See Den långa dagen (Kjerulf)

"**Ah!** when quick flashing fell on me." See Ohé! mamma (Tosti)

"**Ah,** whither, my Mary, ah, whither art fled." See Absence (Hook)

"**Ah,** who once wore a fine bonnet." See "Ak, hvem der havde en hue" (Heise)

Ah, who will lead me thro' the wood. See L'occasion manquée

"**Ah,** who'll bring me back those fairest." See Erster verlust (Medtner)

Ah, why? ay, ay. See Mån tro? jo, jo (Lindblad)

"**Ah!** why let me ever languish." See "Deh più a me non v'ascondete" (Bononcini)

"**Ah,** why will my dear little child be so cross." Words by J. Taylor. FSS 6

"**Ah,** wide-wing'd seagull." See The seagull

"**Ah!** with joy my heart is bounding." See Son vergin vezzosa (Bellini)

"**Ah!** your eyes! what there is in them I can't tell." See Cartarì! Cartarì (Luca)

"**Aha!** hi-a-ha." See Indian song

Ahea, oe. See Adieu my love (Hopkins)

"**Ahi,** meschina pastorella." See La pastorella

Ahi, troppo è duro ("Alas, all too harsh and ruthless") C. Monteverde. e.i. FEI 1

"**Ahimè!** dove trascorsi." See "Che farò senza Euridice" (Gluck)

"**Ahlan** biman kad zār." See Welcome song

Ahlborn, Ida A.
Baker university hymn (Hatton)

Ahlstrom,
"Love smiles no more"
"Ahmbaygewaydo chewah." See Parting
Ahnfeldt, Oscar
Hvad fattas dig
The light of the world. See Hvad
fattas dig
Ahrem, Jacques
"J'ai perdu celle" (Henri III?)
A-hunting we will go. 18th century air,
attributed to Arne. Words by H.
Fielding. BOS—CO 2—DM 1—GO
—HSE 1—SSS
"The dusky night rides down the sky."
MM
"Ahyah! nenemoshaynon deguishid." See
Waubunosa's longing
Ai! la bono fortuno ("Ah! great is our good
fortune") Noël provençal. e. MF
Ai nostri monti ritorneremo. For English
translation see "Home to our moun-
tains" (Verdi)
Aĭ vo polĭe lipen'ka. See The garland
Aia i ka nu'a kapalaila. See "The ground
is strewn" (Leleihoku)
"Aia kuu lei i mailehuna." See "My
wreath of lehua" (Nape)
"Aid a sailor, kind sirs, who once made it
his glory." See The disabled seaman
(Dignum)
Aïdé, Hamilton
Composer and author
Dance on forever
The Danube river
Author
The blushing maple tree (McCaskey)
The maid of the mill (Maybrick)
Aikendrum ("A wooer cam' to our town")
Scottish air. Words by A. Cunning-
ham. MMS
Aikman, James H.
"Touch not the cup" (Bayly)
"Ailie bain o' the glen." See Eilidh bhàn
Ainahau. See Princess Kaiulani's home
(Likelike)
"Aine, dé, trois, Caroline." See Caroline
Ainger, Arthur Campbell
Carmen Etonense (Barnby)
Vale (Barnby)
"Ainsi qu'une jeune beauté." See Le lever
de la lune (Saint-Saëns)
"Ainsi, toujours poussés ver de nouveaux
rivages." See Le lac (Niedermeyer)
Ainslie, Hew
The ingle side (Wiesenthal)
Ain't goin' study war no more. Negro
song. BF 2
Aint that a pity, Lord, sin and a shame.
See "Don't call the roll"
Aïnte. See "Sleep, my child, my pretty
one"
Air de Nicolette ("Heart of hearts") A. E.
M. Grétry. e.f. NG
Air du tambour major (The drum-major's
song) A. Thomas. e.f. BS 1
"L'air est embaumé." See Nuit d'Espagne
(Massenet)
Air of Salomé. See Il est doux, il est bon
(Massenet)

Air of the queen of Shemakhá. See Hymn
to the sun (Rimskii-Korsakov)
"Aissera, Nanninè, me ne sagliette." See
Funiculì-funiculà (Denza)
"Aizaje l'uocchie 'ncielo." See Canzone
di Somma
"Aja. Ajaja adlenoipa." See Summer song
"Aje tradettore." See La romanella
"Ak, hvem der havde en hue" ("Ah, who
once wore a fine bonnet") P. Heise.
Words by H. Drachmann. da.e. WM 1
Akahi hoi. See For once again (Kalakaua)
Akeroyd, Samuel
"As May in all her youthful dress"
Russell's triumph
Akers, Mrs Elizabeth (Chase) See Allen,
Mrs Elizabeth (Chase) Akers
Akh po mostu mostu. See The village
Don Juan
Akh, talan li moĭ, talan. See The con-
script's return
Akh ty Khrist'ka, Khrist'ka chernen'kafâ.
See The impish little girl
"Akh ty nochka, nochen'ka." See Night
Akh ty pole moe. See The slain Cossack
Akh ulitsa, ulitsa shirokaĭâ. See Little
Yashka
Akh! zelena grusha v sadu shataetsĭâ. See
The bride's farewell
"Ako se zhenish." See Donna
"Al combate corred, Bayameses." See
Himno Bayamés (Figueredo)
"Al die daar zegt: De reus die komt." See
La chanson du reuze
"Al furor d'avversa sorte." See Senza
timore (Sieber)
"Al mio ciel m'ha tolto il fato." See Pa-
tria (Mattei)
Al nome tuo temuto. V. Righini. e.i.
SOA 5
"Al pie de la cruz del valle." See La cruz
del valle
"Al silencio de la media noche." See Media
noche
Ke ala kai hiki mai. See Wreath of carna-
tions (Hopkins)
Alabama. Halliard chantey. CR
Alabiev, Aleksandr Nikolaevich
Die nachtigall. See "Nightingale, oh
nightingale"
"Nightingale, oh nightingale"
Alack-a-day. See Hai luli (Coquard)
Aladdin. V. Bellini. Words by J. R.
Lowell. LA
Aladdin (Castles in Spain) FSS 6
Castles in Spain. WBT
The Alamo trail. See The old Chisholm
trail
"Alas! alas! when charming Sylvia's gone."
See Alas! when charming Sylvia's gone
"Alas, all too harsh and ruthless." See Ahi,
troppo è duro (Monteverdi)
"Alas and alas, that there is not a fairy-
fog on the roads." See "Mo chreach
a's mo dhiachairt"
"Alas by what mene may I make ye to
know." See All a green willow

"**Alas!** for the days that are gone." J. Percy. BE 5

"**Alas,** my love, ye do me wrong." See Greensleeves

"**Alas!** my love's enlisted." See The white cockade

"**Alas,** poor lonely heart." See Le vallon (Gounod)

"**Alas!** that I cam' o'er the muir." Old Scottish song. PS 2

"**Alas!** we are entering upon our voyage." See Tongese water-song

Alas! when charming Sylvia's gone. D. Purcell. DM 2

"**Alas,** when my dear love is near me." See Le départ du soldat

"**Alas!** why hast thou left me." See "Che farò senza Euridice" (Gluck)

Alasdair Mac Mhaighstir Alasdair. See MacDonald, Alexander

Alau, Jack
One, two, three, four

Alaw, Owain. See Owen, John

Albaÿdé. C. M. Widor. Words by V. Hugo. e.f. SAM

"**Albero,** ti teneva tanto caro." See Canzonetta di campagnuolo

Albert, Heinrich
Im frühling

Albuquerque, Medeiros e. See Medeiros e Albuquerque

Alburn, W. H.
Dear old Reserve (Composer unknown)

Alcott, Louisa May
"O the beautiful old story" (Ryley)

Alderson, Mrs Eliza Sibbald (Dykes)
In terra pax (Dykes)

Aldighieri,
Il bacio (Arditi)

Aldrich, Thomas Bailey
Cradle song (De Koven)
For ever and a day (Mack)
Kriss Kringle (Old air)

Alecsandri, Basile. See Alexandri, Vasile

Alexander, Mrs Cecil Frances (Humphreys)
"Once in Bethlehem of Judah" (music by Dugard; Kettle; Maunder; Stanford)
"Once in royal David's city" (Gauntlett)
"Saw ye never in the twilight" (music by Mozart; Tours; also unknown composer)
"There is a green hill far away" (music by Gounod; Willis)

Alexander, James I.
"Ostera! spirit of spring-time"

Alexandri, Vasile
"Tracascâ regele" (Hübsch)

Alexis, Wilibald, pseud.
Walpurgisnacht (Loewe)

Alferakii, Achilles Nikolaevich
The bouquet
The song of songs
Spring
"When leaves are falling sere"

Alfio's entrance-song. See "Il cavallo scalpita" (Mascagni)

Alford, Henry
Alleluia (Barnby)
"Come ye thankful people, come" (Elvey)
"Ten thousand times ten thousand" (Dykes)

Alfvén, Hugo
Ångest
Anguish. See Ångest
Black roses. See Svarta rosor
Blicken
The look. See Blicken
Svarta rosor
Tristi amori. See Svarta rosor

Algerian song. See "Remain love"

"**Ali!** alo." French chantey. e.f. SMW

Alibieff, Alexander Nicholaevitch. See Alabiev, Aleksandr Nikolaevich

Alice Gray. Mrs P. Millard. Words by W. Mee. FSS 6—HSE 1

Alice, where art thou. J. Ascher. Words by W. Guernsey. FSS 3—HSC—HSD —NMH— NML— TS— WA— WBT— WL—WSW

Alie bain o' the glen, bonnie lassie, winsome lassie. See Eilidh bhàn

"**Alike** are life and death." C. H. Rinck. Words by H. W. Longfellow. LBR

Alinde (Alinda) F. Schubert. Words by F. Roehlitz. e.g. FM

All a green willow. 16th century song. Words by J. Heywood. CO 1

"**All'** abend bevor ich zur ruhe geh'." See Gute nacht, du mein herziges kind (Abt)

"**All'** acquisto di gloria" ("To achieve all the glamor of glory") A. Scarlatti. e.i. KS 3
"**All'** acquisto di gloria" ("To win glory") e.i. PA 2

"**All,** all the livelong day." See Des mädchens klage

All alone. See Mutterseelenallein

"**All** alone by the waves under the starry skies." See Extase (Gueroult)

All among the barley. E. Stirling. FSS 5

"**All** are sleeping, sweet, but now." See "Alle gingen, herz, zur ruh" (Wolf)

"**All'** armi! all' armi! si scopron le tombe, si levano i morti." See Inno di guerra dei cacciatori delle Alpi (Olivieri)

"**All** around the cobbler's bench." See Pop! goes the weasel

All at rest, my sweet, but thee. See "Alle gingen, herz, zur ruh" (Wolf)

All birds follow me. Ojibway Indian song. in. BA

"**All** by the shady greenwood tree." G. Rossini. FSS 5

"**All** children are on Christmas eve." HC

"**All** day I have tried to be spinning in vain." See Maggie's welcome (Barnard)

"**All** day long o'er the ocean I fly." See Song of the sea-gull

"**All** day on the prairie in the saddle I ride." See The cowboy

"**All** down the quay the ships so tall." See Les berceaux (Faure)

"**All** embalmed the air." See Nuit d'Espagne (Massenet)

All for the sake of California. R. W. Tully. Words by M. H. Schwartz and R. W. Tully. CHS—MPC

"**All** for thee, all for thee, azure Tar." See Tar (Vassilenko)

"**All** forward! all forward! all forward to battle." See Inno di guerra dei cacciatori delle Alpi (Olivieri)

"**All** forward to battle the trumpets are crying." See Hurrah for our banner (Custance)

"**All** glory, laud, and honor." See Glory, laud, and honor (Teschner)

All God's chillun got wings. Negro spiritual. JB
Going to shout all over God's heav'n. HR

"**All** Grenada deeply slumbers." See Don Juan's serenade (Tchaikovsky)

"**All** Grenada lieth sleeping." See Don Juan's serenade (Tchaikovsky)

"**All** hail! all hail to the natal day." E. H. Thorne. Words by S. C. Clarke. HC

"**All** hail, beloved fatherland." See Columbia, hail (Custance)

"**All** hail! bright was the dawning." See Sing, joyously sing

"**All** hail! far away, so the glad bells all say." See The glad bells all say (Crowe)

"**All** hail! gone is our night." See Forevermore (Wellings)

"**All** hail, Liberia, hail." National song. O. Luca. SN

"**All** hail! ring the bells." See Lo! now he is come

"**All** hail, San Giusto." See "Viva San Giusto" (Sinico)

"**All** hail! the bells are ringing." See Over the happy town (Auber)

"**All** hail the college on the hill." See The college on the hill

"**All** hail the gladsome Easter morn." B. Briggs. HC

"**All** hail the gladsome Easter morn." H. E. Earle. HC

"**All** hail the power of Jesus' name" (Coronation) Old air. [Words by E. Perronet] LA

"**All** hail the power of Jesus' name." O. Holden. Words by E. Perronet. NMH—NMS—WBT—WS
"All hail the power of Jesus' name" (Coronation) BD—FSS 2—FSS 8 —HSC—TL

All hail, thou Bethlehem. MCS

All hail, thou dwelling. See Salut! demeure chaste et pure (Gounod)

"**All** hail to the days." See Drive the cold winter away

"**All** hail to the friendship." See Bavarian yodel

"**All** hail to thee, Cambria." Air: Llwyn on, or, The ash grove. Words by Talhaiarn. MMW

"**All** hail to thee, fair Western." Western college song. M. M. Charlton. Words by M. E. Hart. CHS

"**All** hail, ye merry folk to-day." G. F. Terry. Words by H. G. Rosedale. HC

"**All** hayle to the dayes." See Drive the cold winter away

All I want, all I want. See A little more faith in Jesus

"**All** in a delicious port." See La barquillera

"**All** in a garden green." 16th century song. Composer unknown. CO 1 —DM 1—MM

"**All** in a garden green." 16th century song. W. Byrd. CO 1

"**All** in a morning very fair." See The duke's hunt

"**All** in a wood." See The tree in the wood

"**All** in the dim forest." See "I villande skogen" (Randel)

"**All** in the downs the fleet was moor'd." See Black-eyed Susan (Leveridge)

"**All** in the merry month of May." See Barbara Allen (Kentucky version; Carmen, N.C. version)

"**All** in the month, the month of May." See Barbara Allen (Tenessee version)

All in the morning early, O. Irish air. Words by K. T. Hinkson. FSI

"**All** in vain, O my beloved." See "Vainement, ma bien-aimée" (Lalo)

"**All** into service let us sing merrily together." See Going to church

"**All** is bright and cheerful round us." W. H. Walter. Words by J. M. Neale. HC

"**All** is quiet." A. H. Rosewig. HSD

"**All** is still and restful now." See Sleep, baby dear (Tauwitz)

"**All** is still in sweetest rest." See "Alles still in süsser ruh" (Kücken)

"**All** is yet tranquil, dawn is drifting in." See What would I do for my queen (Thomas)

"**All** joy flies from my heart." See "Nel cor più non mi sento" (Paisiello)

All joy is gone ("Ach není tu není") Czech folk song. bo.e. BF 1
Lament (Stesk) bo.e. SMF

"**All** jubilant with psalm and hymn." J. F. Bridge. Words by F. W. Farrar. HC

"**All**' mein gedanken, mein herz und mein sinn" ("All of the thoughts in my heart and my mind") R. Strauss. Words by F. Dahn. e.g. FO 2

"**All** minstrels sing thy fame." See Mentra, Gwen

"**All** my heart this night rejoices." J. Booth. Words by P. Gerhardt. Tr of Fröhlich soll mein herze springen. e. HC

"All my heart this night rejoices." A. Esmond. Words by P. Gerhardt. Tr of Fröhlich soll mein herze springen. e. HC

"All my heart this night rejoices." F. C. Maker. Words by P. Gerhardt. Tr of Fröhlich soll mein herze springen. e. HC

"All my heart this night rejoices." H. W. Parker. Words by P. Gerhardt. Tr of Fröhlich soll mein herze springen. e. HC

"All my pass'd life." J. Blow. Words by Rochester. DM 1

"All my silver and gold." Russian folk air. Words by D. Radford. WF

"All my strength hath fled away." F. Hiller. e. SAS 3

"All my tears." Bach. e. OS 2

"All night thro' thy slumbers." See Farewell forever (Connelly)

All of a row. Folk song. BE 2

"All of anguish most unsparing." See "Ogni pena più spietata" (Pergolesi)

"All of the thoughts in my heart and my mind." See "All' mein gedanken, mein herz und mein sinn" (Strauss)

"All on a misty morning." Old English air. Words by T. D'Urfey. BE 7

"All on one summer's evening." See The grey cock

"All our laddies love shooting." See The Tyrolese maiden

"All padded and muffled." See The thatcher

"All people that on earth do dwell." See Old hundred (Franc)

"All praise to Thee" (Leyden) Costello. Words by M. Luther. ᵗTr of Gelobet seis tu Jesu Christᵗ e. MCS

All pull together. ᵗA. Drummondᵗ Words by P. Hastings. BSS

"All quiet along the Potomac." J. Dayton. Words by E. Beers. JO—WBT

All round my hat (" 'Twas a-going of my rounds") J. Valentine. Words by J. Hansell. FSS 8

"All round my hat I will wear the green willow." Irish folk song. JOI

All saints (Cutler) See "As shadows cast by cloud and sun"; "The Son of God goes forth to war"

"All silver the roofs." Scotch air. MCS

All souls' day. E. Lassen. Words by H. von Gilm. ᵗTr of Allerseelenᵗ e. BC—WBT—WL

All souls' day. For words in the original with a different air see Allerseelen (Strauss)

All that glitters. J. L. Roeckel. Words by F. E. Weatherly. FSS 8

"All that springeth from the sod." See Invocation

"All that wondrous Christmas night." See Noite de Natal

"All the bells bring far-off word." See "Alle klokker bringer fjaernt" (Kjerulf)

"All the bells, the little bells." M. Bagrinofski. Words by Ckitaltz. e. NM 1

"All the birds so gaily sing." See Welcome to spring

"All the brave boys under canvas are sleeping." See The sweet little man

"All the earth is deck'd in glory." See Autumn glory

"All the lassies of Camacha." See "As meninas de Camacha"

"All the livelong night." See I think on thee

"All the night and all the day." Russian folk air. Words by D. Radford. WF

"All the night was dark and dreary." Polish folk air. Words by R. R. Whitehead. WF

"All the notes of all the earth make one great song." Hungarian folk air. Words by J. Russell. WF

All the saints adore Thee. See "Holy, holy, holy! Lord God Almighty" (Dykes)

"All the skies to-night sing o'er us." German air. Words by J. O'Connor. HC

"All the trees they are so high." See The trees they do grow high

"All the winter long the trees are bare." See Winter

All the world am dark and dreary. See Old folks at home

"All the world around I'm straying." See Ubi bene, ibi patria

All things love thee, so do I. C. E. Horn. FSS 8—HSE 2

"All this night bright angels sing." J. T. Field. Words by W. Austin. HC

"All this night bright angels sing." F. Fruttchey. Words by W. Austin. HC

"All this night bright angels sing." A. S. Sullivan. Words by W. Austin. HC

Carol for Christmas day. BSC—DC Christmas carol. JS

"All those who cry: The giant comes." See La chanson du reuze

"All thoughts within my heart that dwell." Chant d'amour. e. DT

All through the night. See Ar hyd y nos (Owen)

"All thy wonders are far beyond telling." See Waters of Punalau (Nape)

"All together, all together." G. F. Root. FSS 1

"All together let us sing." See Let us sing

"All under the stars, and beneath the green tree." See The blue flame

"All who hear what I say." See C'est la princesse de Navarre (Boieldieu)

All who labor. Words by C. F. Orne. NMS

"All who of Britons bear the name." See Freedom's contribution (Dibdin)

"All who sing." Round. T. Goodban. BD

"**All** will hail the joyous day." S. Storace. Words by J. Cobb. ME

"**All** worldly shapes shall melt in gloom." See The last man (Callcott)

"**All** ye that labor, come to me." See Come unto me (Dvořák)

"**All** ye that love to hear music perform'd in air." See Brixham town

"**All** ye who would wish to succeed with a lass." See As sure as a gun (Arne)

"**All** yields to your charm so sweet." See "Tout cède à vos doux appas" (Colasse)

"**All** you that cry O hone O hone." See Essex's last good night

"**All** you that love a bit of fun." See The tythe pig

"**All** you who roam, both young and old." See Bridgewater fair

"**All** your shades." See "Bois épais, redouble ton ombre" (Lully)

"**Allá** en el campo muy a la orilla." See La casita

Alla fontana (By the spring) Sicilian song. e.i. MSI

"**Alla** mente confusa." See Preghiera (Tosti)

Alla stella confidente ("Bright star of love") V. Robaudi. e.i. SOS 2

"**Alla** Trinità beata" ("Unto Thee, blest Trinity") 15th century song. e.i. NG

Allan, Robert
Put off, and row wi' speed (Highland boat air)

Allan water. See The banks of Allan water

"**Allant** m'y promener." See Au bois rossignolet

Alle, die ihr Gott zu ehren. For English translation see "Would'st thou magnify the story" (Ebeling)

"**Alle** gingen, herz, zur ruh" (All at rest, my sweet, but thee) H. Wolf. e.g. PG 2

Alle jahre wieder ("As each happy Christmas") J. C. Rinck. [Words by W. Hey] e. MF

"**Alle** jahre wieder." F. Silcher. Words by W. Hey. g. ED 1
Christmas song. e. WBT—WSC

"**Alle** klokker bringer fjaernt" ("All the bells bring far-off word") C. Kjerulf. Words by H. Drachmann. da.e. WM 1

Alleluia ("Let us all in concert") Ancient air, arr by J. Barnby. Words by H. Alford. TL

Alleluia ("Lord of every land") A. Lowe. LA

"**Alleluia!** alleluia! alleluia! a great and mighty wonder." See Our Christmas festal

"**Alleluia!** alleluia! alleluia! now all the bells are ringing." See Now all the bells are ringing (Dykes)

"**Alleluia,** alleluia, alleluia! O Zion, that bringest good tidings." See O Zion, that bringest good tidings (Stainer)

"**Alleluia!** alleluia! alleluia! risen Lord." See Alleluia! risen Lord (Wilson)

"**Alleluia!** alleluia! alleluia! the strife is o'er, the battle done." See The strife is o'er: The battle done (Palestrina)

"**Alleluia!** alleluia! hearts to heav'n and voices raise." F. Westlake. Words by C. Wordsworth. HC

"**Alleluia!** alleluia. The crown is on the victor's brow." See The crown is on the victor's brow (Field)

"**Alleluia!** King victorious." S. C. Umlauf (music and words) HC

Allelúia lubvee. See The hallelujah of love (Musorgskiï)

Alleluia! risen Lord. H. Wilson. HC

"**Alleulia!** sing the triumph." A. H. Brown. Words by E. M. Dawson. HC

Allen, Alice E.
An autumn lullaby (Fearis)

Allen, Mrs Elizabeth (Chase) Akers
Because he loved you so (Dempster)
Rock me to sleep (music by Leslie; Mueller)
Singing in the rain (Haydn)

Allen, George Benjamin
None can tell
When you and I were young

Allen, George Nelson
"Let worldly minds the world pursue" Maitland. See "Let worldly minds the world pursue"; "Must Jesus bear the cross alone"
"Must Jesus bear the cross alone" (same air as "Let worldly minds the world pursue")

Allen, Henry Robinson
"Maid of Athens"

Allen, Ira
Entreaty (Smith)

Allen, T. H.
Good-bye, my lover, good-bye (words and music)
Good-bye, my lover, good-bye (words with old American air)

Allen, Thomas
Memorial hymn

"**Aller** berge gipfel ruh'n in dunkler nacht." See Wanderers nachtlied (Rubinstein)

Allerseelen (All souls' day) R. Strauss. Words by H. von Gilm. e.g. FO 2 —GM—PG 4

Allerseelen. For English translation with a different air see All souls' day (Lassen)

Alles ist hin ("O du lieber Augustin") Volkslied. g. ED 1
Alles ist hin (Everything's gone) e.g. SSG
Everything's gone. e. BSE
"O du lieber Augustin." g. WA— WBT—WSW
"O du lieber Augustin" ("O thou dearest maiden mine") e.g. BO

"**Alles** liebt und paart sich wieder."   See Frühlingsempfindung (Sterkel)

"**Alles** schläft."   See "Slumber reigns" (Grechaninov)

"**Alles** schweige! jeder neige ernsten tönen nur sein ohr."   See Weihelied

"**Alles** still in süsser ruh" (The slumber-song) F. Kücken.   e.g.   FSS 2 Slumber song.   e.   JSE—WBT—WSC

Alles um liebe ("Was ist es") J. R. Zumsteeg.   Words by L. T. Kosegarten.   g.   ED 2

Allingham, John Till
"Far, far from me my lover flies" (King)

Allingham, William
The bird song (Composer unknown)
"I once was a guest at a nobleman's wedding" (Irish air)
Lovely Mary Donnelly (Barker)
Robin Redbreast (German air)

Allister MacAllister.   Scottish air. Words by J. Hogg.   PS 1

Allitsen, Frances
An old English love song
A song of Thanksgiving

Die **Allmacht** (The Almighty) F. Schubert. Words by J. L. Pyrker.   e.g.   PG 1 —PG 2.   e. only FTS

"**Allmächt'ge** Jungfrau."   See Gebet der Elisabeth (Wagner)

"**Allmächt'ger** Vater" ("Almighty Father." —Prayer) R. Wagner.   e.g.   KS 4— OPS 3—SOA 3

"**Allons,** enfants de la patrie."   See La Marseillaise (Rouget de Lisle)

"**Allons,** mes deux p'tits enfants."   See Briolage

"**Allons-y,** bell', nous promener."   See Le méchant guillon

"**Alls** ingen flicka laster ja" ("No maiden I should e'er refuse") Swedish folk song. e.sw.   HSOS

All's one to Jack.   Dibdin.   HSE 2

"**All's** the same to me."   See "'s ist mir alles eins" (Fuss?)

All's well.   J. Braham.   Words by T. Dibdin.   BE 3—FSS 8—JO

"**Allt** under himmelens fäste."   See Sorgen

Alma Andaluza.   R. Gómez.   Words by O. Vellido.   s.   LCP

"**Alma** del core" ("Heart of my own heart") A. Caldara.   e.i.   FEI 2

"**Alma** mater."   H. Oakeley.   Words by D. Maclagan.   1.   SSS

Alma mater.   Amherst university song. CHS

Alma mater.   Brown university song. CHS

Alma mater.   Colby college song.   W. C. Crawford.   Words by B. R. Willis.   CHS

Alma mater.   Colgate university song. CHS

Alma mater.   Cornell university song. Air: Annie Lisle.   Words by C. K. Urguhart.   CHS— LA— MPC— NMS
"Far above Cayuga's waters."   JS

Alma mater.   Greenville college song. Air: Annie Lisle.   Words by W. A. Joy.   CHS

Alma mater.   Lake Erie college song. Arr from Abt.   Words by F. P. Treat. CHS

Alma mater.   Lehigh university song. Words by C. K. Urguhart.   CHS

Alma mater.   Muhlenberg university song.   E. H. Kistler.   CHS

Alma mater.   Ohio state university song. R. P. Smith (music and words)   CHS

Alma mater.   Ohio Wesleyan university song.   Words by R. T. Stevenson. CHS

Alma mater.   Swarthmore college song. Air: Annie Lisle.   Words by E. J. Taylor.   CHS

Alma mater.   Syracuse university song. Air: Annie Lisle.   Words by J. W. Stevens.   CHS—MFC

Alma mater.   University of Chicago song. Words by E. H. Lewis.   CHS—MPC —NMS

Alma mater.   University of Illinois song. Air: Annie Lisle.   MPC—NMS

Alma mater.   University of North Dakota song. Air: Austrian hymn. Words by J. Macnie.   CHS

Alma mater.   University of Wisconsin song.   Words by W. T. Arndt.   CHS —MPC—NMS

Alma mater.   Vassar college song.   CHS

Alma mater.   Yale university song.   T. G. Shepard.   Words by J. K. Lombard.   CHS

"**Alma** mater, alma mater ich can sprech-a." See Ich can sprech-a

Alma mater, O.   As sung at Yale.   WBT —WC

"**Alma** mater, te canamus."   See "Alma mater" (Oakeley)

"**Alma** mater, tried and true."   See Noble Dickinsonia

"**Almen** fanciulla ascoltami."   See Che t'ho fatto

Almendros,
Marcha real (Spanish air)

Almers, Hermann
Feldeinsamkeit (Brahms)

The **Almighty.**   See Die Allmacht (Schubert)

"**Almighty** Father."   See "Allmächt'ger Vater" (Wagner)

"**Almighty** God of Israel."   Spohr.   e. OS 4

"**Almighty** powers."   See "Gerechter Gott" (Wagner)

The **almond** tree.   See Der nussbaum (Schumann)

Alnaes, Eyvind
Jul
Sol
Sunlight. See Sol
Yuletide. See Jul
"Aloha au oka lau o kapaa ea." See "My love to thee" (Nape)
Ke aloha ihiki mai. See Flower of my heart (Hopkins)
"Aloha no paha oe." See The he-i blossom (Hopkins)
Aloha oe. Hawaiian song. Liliuokalani. e.h. BD—BF 2—MP—NMH—NMS. e. only BSS—TFC 1
Aloha oe (Farewell to thee) e.h. HA
Aloha oe (Hawaiian farewell song) e. WBT—WL
Hawaiian farewell song. e. WA
"Aloha to thee, flow'r hinahina." See For once again (Kalakaua)
"Aloha wale, pua hinahina." See For once again (Kalakaua)
"Aloha wale pua violeta." See Violeta (Hopkins)
Alone. See Sonntagslied (Mendelssohn)
"Alone as I walked on a fair summer morning." See Sighile ni Ghadhra
"Alone I lean, and sing my lay." See Deign my voice to hear
"Alone I went one day." See Au bois rossignolet
"Alone in crowds we wander on." Air: Shule aroon. Words by T. Moore. MI
"Alone in my prison so narrow and dark." See The captive (Grechaninov)
"Alone in the dusk at his door he stands." See The old guard (Rodney)
"Alone on the banks of the dark rolling Danube." See The wounded Hussar (Hewitt)
"Alone upon the mountain height." See The brave sentinel (Rodney)
"Along the meadow-path I stray." See Lauf der welt (Greig)
Alouette. French-Canadian folk song. f. BSS—TFC 2
Alouette (The lark) e.f. EF
Der alpenhirt ("Dort hoch auf der Alpe") Oesterreichische volksweise. Words by Hoffmann von Fallersleben. g. ED 3
The alphabet ("A B C D E F G") Old French air: Ah! vous dirai-je, maman. DO
The alphabet ("A B C D E F G") See Der dorfschulmeister
Alpheraky, Achilles Nikolaievitch. See Alferakiï, Achilles Nikolaevich
The Alpine horn. Rimbault. Words by Malibran. FSS 1
Alpine peace. Styrian song. e. KSE
The Alpine rose. Swiss song. e. KSE
"Alpuchariens gold'ne streifen." See Don Juan's serenade (Tchaikovsky)

"Als büblein klein an der mutter brust" ("When that I was and a tiny boy") Drinking song. O. Nicolai. [Words by Shakespeare. Tr of "When that I was a little tiny boy"] e.g. SOA 5
"Als büblein klein an der mutter brust" ("A weanling small on my mother's breast") e.g. AB 4
"Als der grossvater die grossmutter nahm." See Das grossvaterlied
"Als die alte mutter." See "Songs my mother taught me" (Dvořák)
"Als die Preussen marschierten vor Prag." See Die Prager schlacht
"Als die Römer frech geworden." See Die Teutoburger schlacht
"Als ich auf meiner bleiche." J.A. Hiller. Words by C. F. Weisse. g. ED 1
"Als ich das erste veilchen erblickt." See Das erste veilchen (Mendelssohn)
"Als ich ein junggeselle war." See Der tod von Basel
"Als ich noch im flügelkleide." See Dauernde liebe (Mozart)
"Als mein schönster tag begann." Russian folk song. g. ED 3
"Als Noah aus dem kasten war." See Noah (Reissiger)
"Als wir beiden mussten scheiden." See Abschied (Cavallo)
"Als wir jüngst in Regensburg waren." See Fräulein Kunigund
"Alsati! là, tuo figlio a te concedo riveder." See Eri tu che nacchiavi (Verdi)
"Alt Heidelberg, du feine" ("Old Heidelberg, the splendid") A. Jensen. e.g. KF 4
"Alt laegger for din fod jeg ned." See My heart and lute (Kjerulf)
"Der alte Barbarossa, der Kaiser Friederich." See Barbarossa (Gersbach)
Alte freundschaft, alter wein ("Unsre freundschaft zu erneuen") J. André. Words by C. F. Bretzner. g. ED 3
Das alte Guggisberger lied (The old Guggisberg song) Swiss song. e.g. BF 2
"Das alte jahr vergangen ist." L. Erk. Words by H. Hoffmann von Fallersleben. g. ED 3
Di alte kashyeh. See The old, old questions
Alte laute, I ("Why are you ill and drooping") R. Schumann. Words by J. Kerner. e.g. GM
Alte laute, II (Bygone pleasures) R. Schumann. Words by J. Kerner. e.g. GM
Die alte mutter. See Gamle mor (Grieg)
Der alte reiter und sein mantel ("Schier dreissig jahre bist du alt") Volksweise. Words by C. von Holtei. g. ED 1
"Alter'd seems the world." See Heimweh (Wolf)
Altes studentisches tafellied. See Edite, bibite

"**Although** a daughter good am I."   See
  The wedding dance
"**Altho'** a fate unkindly hath not smiled on
  my wooing."   See Col raggio placido
  (Händel)
"**Although** I be but a country lass."   See
  A country lass
"**Although** Knox is on the prairie."   See
  The purple and the gold (Knox col-
  lege)
"**Altho'** my back be at the wa'."   Air: The
  job of journey work.   Words by R.
  Burns.   BSR
"**Altho'** my bed were in yon muir."   Air:
  Galla water.   Words by R. Burns.
  BSR
"**Although** my house be not with God."
  Costa.   OS 4
"**Altho'** thou maun never be mine."   See
  Here's a health to ane I lo'e dear
"**Altho'** unkindly Fortune fail'd to smile on
  my wishes."   See Col raggio placido
  (Händel)
"**Although** Yale has always favored the
  violet's dark blue."   See The orange
  and the black—Princeton (Schackel-
  ton)
"**Although** you enjoy a lover, learn to your
  sorrow."   See "Aunque ames"
"**Although** you see me going along so."
  See O redeemed
"**L'altra** notte in fondo al mare" ("In the
  night my babe was taken")   A.
  Boito (music and words)   e.i.
  MC
  "L'altra notte in fondo al mare" ("Last
  night in the deep, deep sea")   e.i.
  OPS 1
Alumni song.   Columbia university song.
  Stephen C. Foster.   Words by G. W.
  Carryl.   CU
Alvarez, Rafael
  Guatemala, around thy free banner. See
  Guatemala, en tu limpia bandera
  Guatemala, en tu limpia bandera (same
  air as Himno nacional de Guate-
  mala)
  Himno nacional de Guatemala
  National hymn of Guatemala.   See
  Himno nacional de Guatemala
"**Alzati!** là, tuo figlio a te concedo riveder."
  See Eri tu che macchiavi (Verdi)
"**Am** brunnen vor dem tore."   See Der
  lindenbaum (Schubert)
"**Am** danat ti mae son."   See Mentra,
  Gwen
"**Am** frischgeschnitt'nen wanderstab."   See
  Fussreise (Wolf)
"**Am** gewaltigen meer in der mitternacht."
  See Thurmwächters lied (Weidt)
"**Am** heiligen abend vorm osterfest."   See
  Die verlassene (Fink)
"**Am** I a soldier of the cross."   See Sol-
  dier of the cross (Arne)
Am I not fondly thine own.   See "Du,
  du, liegst mir in herzen"
"**Am** I the doctor you wished for to see."
  Donegal song.   JOI

"**Am** kreuzweg, da lausche ich."   See Die
  zigeunerin (Wolf)
Am Rhein und beim wein.   F. Ries.
  Words by E. Ritterhaus.   g. KF 3
  —PG 4
  Am Rhein und beim wein (Rhine-wine
  song)   e.g.   AB 4
Am schönsten sommerabend war's (A sum-
  mer evening in Norway) Grieg.
  Words by J. Paulsen.   e.   FTS
  Summer evening.   e.   BD
Am sommerabend ("Der abend schleiert")
  C. Spazier.   Words by F. von Matthis-
  son.   g.   ED 2
"**Am** stillen herd" ("By silent hearth") R.
  Wagner.   e.g.   SOA 3
Am Sylvester-abend ("Des jahres letzte
  stunde")   J. A. P. Schulz.   Words by
  J. H. Voss.   g.   ED 1
"**Am** ufer des flusses, des Manzanares"
  ("Where flows the bright river")
  A. Jensen.   Words from an anony-
  mous Spanish poet.   e.g.   CMF 1
  —FO 1—GM
  "Am ufer des flusses des Manzanares"
  (By Manzanares)   e.g.   PG 2
"**Am** wiesenhügel schlummert' ich."   See
  The dream (Rubinstein)
"**Amanda's** fair, by all confessed."   18th
  century song.   ME
"**Amang** the trees, where humming bees."
  Air: The king of France he rade a
  race.   Words by R. Burns.   BSR
"**Amanheceu** finalmente."   See Hymno
  nacional (Brazil)
"**Amapolita** morada" (Little purple poppy)
  Mexican song.   e.s.   BF 2
"**Amarantha** sweet and fair."   H. Lawes.
  Words by R. Lovelace.   DM 2
"**L'amant** des fleurs, le rossignol."   See
  Song of Zuleika (Rimskiï-Korsakov)
"**Amarilli**, mia bella" ("Amarilli, my fair
  one") G. Caccini.   e.i.   PA 2
  Amarilli.   e.i.   KF 2—PG 1—PG 2
  —PG 3
  Amarilli (Amaryllis)   e.i.   FEI 1
  "Amarilli, mia bella" ("Tell me, fair
  Amarillis")   e.i.   KS 2
  Amaryllis.   e.i.   MSS 2—SS 2
Amarillis ("Amarillis told her swain") 17th
  century song.   CO 2
Amaryllis ("Tu crois ô beau soleil") Louis
  XIII (music and words)   e.f.   EF
A-maying.   Air: Sellenger's round. DM 2
"**Amaz'd** to find the foe so near." Händel.
  MSS 2
"**Ambaygewaydo** chewahdebahbun."   See
  Parting
Amber.   See Rav (Sinding)
"**Ambos** a dos."   See Matarile
Ambrose, Robert Steele
  "One sweetly solemn thought"
Ambrosius
  "Sing God praises"
Ambrosius, Johanna.   See Voigt, Frau
  Johanna (Ambrosius)
Am Bühl, Johann Ludwig
  An den mond (Auberlen)

"L'âme évaporée et souffrante." See Romance (Debussy)

"Ameime mi, Dona Lombarda." See Dona Lombarda (Piedmontese version)

"Ameme mei, O Donna Lombarda." See Dona Lombarda (Istrian version)

America ("God bless our native land") Words by T. Dwight. FSS 1

America ("My country, 'tis of thee") Attributed to H. Carey. Words by S. F. Smith. BD—BMC—BSE—BSS—CST—DO— DSH— FMB—HSC—HSD— JO—JS—JSE— LA —MP—MS— NMH— NMS—OH—TFC 1—TL—WA—WBT—WCP—WSC—WSW. s. only LCP

"My country, 'tis of thee." LBR—SN

National hymn. FSS 1

America ("My country, 'tis of thee") J. J. McCabe. Words by S. F. Smith. MP

America: fugitive stanza ("Lord, let war's tempests cease") Attributed to H. Carey. Words by Longfellow. BSE

America! all hail to thee. See United (Mercer)

"America! America! dear land of liberty." See Hymn of the adoption (Lemmel)

America for me. M. S. Mercer. Words by H. Van Dyke. MP

"America, our mother fair." See United (Mercer)

"America, so proud and free." See Long live, long live America (Pontius)

America, the beautiful. S. A. Ward. Words by K. L. Bates. BSS—CST—DSH—LA—TFC 1

America the beautiful (Materna) OH

American cradle-song. See "Rock-a-bye, baby"

The American eagle. A. M. Foerster. Words by A. Coll. MP—NMS

The American flag. J. W. Tufts. Words by J. R. Drake. JS

"An American frigate, the Richard by name." See Paul Jones

The American hymn ("Speed our republic") M. Keller (music and words) HSC—WCP

Hail to our flag. LA

Keller's American hymn. FSS 4—HSD—MP—WBT

"Speed our republic." BD

The American war. Political ballad (unfinished) Scottish air: The black watch. Words by Burns. PS 2

"When Guilford good our pilot stood." BSR

Ames, Francis
Bow! wow
The contented camel
My old horse-blanket pin
The patteran
Sailor's home song

Amici. College song. Air: Annie Lisle. CHS—CU— LA—MPC—NMS— SSS—WBT

"Amici, amici, chi'n Palermu jiti." See Canto del carcerato

Amid roses. See Millom rosor (Beyer)

"Amid the boughs of an old pine tree." See The pine tree swing

"Amid the cotillion, confusing." See At the ball (Tchaikovsky)

"Amid the greenwood." Thalberg. FSS 4—JSE

"Amid the silence" ("Wśród nocnej ciszy") Polish carol. e.p. BF 1

"Amid the woods and heather." See Jägerleben

"Amidst the myrtles." J. Battishill. Words by R. Herrick. DM 2

"Amidst the myrtles." H. Lawes. [Words by R. Herrick] MM

Amina's song (Song of a Burmese girl) Song from India. Words by R. Tagore. e. BF 2

Aminte ("Fair Aminta") Bergerette. e.f. WB

"Amo, amas, I love a lass." Air: The frog and the mouse, arr by S. Arnold. Words by J. O'Keeffe. BE 1—BOS —DM 2—HSE 2—ME—SSS

"Among our ancient mountains." See God bless the prince of Wales (Richards)

"Among the lilies." A. Czibulka. Words by H. B. Farnie. WBT—WBW

Among the new-mown hay. Folk song. BSW

Variant of: The new-mown hay

"Among the things that linger yet." See Minuet (Tanieev)

"Among the winter's happy days." See St Valentine's day

"Among wild weeds and earth." See Violen (Svendsen)

"Amor, amor, non dormir più." See Amor dormiglione (Strozzi)

Amor dormiglione (Love sleeping) B. Strozzi. e.i. FEI 1

"Amor misterioso agello." See Habanera (Bizet)

Amore ("E puoi se barbara."—Love) G. Lucantoni. Words by A. de Lauzieres. e.i. SOS 2

Amore ("T'amo perchè sei bella."—Love) G. Muratori. e.i. SOS 1

L'amour (Love) B. Godard. Words by R. Harel. e.f. HM 2

"L'amour est un enfant." See L'amour s'envole

"L'amour est un oiseau rebelle." See Habanera (Bizet)

"L'amour! l'amour! oui, son ardeur a troublé tout mon être." See Ah! lève-toi, soleil (Gounod)

"L'amour ne trouble point mon coeur." See Chanson à danser

"Amour, que veux-tu de moi." G. B. Lully. e.f. SOA 2

L'amour s'envole ("Ah, love is but a child") Bergerette. e.f. WB

Amour, viens aider.   C. Saint-Saëns.   e.f.
SOA 2
Amour! viens aider (Dear love! thine
aid)   e.f.   OS 2
Amour! viens aider (O love, lend thine
aid)   e.f.   KS 2
"Amoureux, amoureuses, suivez moi."   See
L'appel du printemps (Holmès)
"Ampeli mou, palĕampelo."   See The
vineyard and its master
Amthor, Eduard
"Wenn ich einmal der Herrgott wär' "
(Binder)
"Amuri, amuri" (Love! love) Sicilian boat-
man's song.   i.   SMW
"Amuri, amuri" ("O love! O love")
e.i.   MSI
Amyntor's well-a-day.   J. Eccles.   Words
by H. Hughes.   MM
"An' a howdy, howdy, brother."   See
Howdy
"An Alexis send ich dich."   See Der rose
sendung (Himmel)
"An Celia's baum, in stiller nacht."   See
"By Celia's arbor" (Mendelssohn)
An' Charlie, he's my darling.   See O
Charlie is my darling (Additional words
by Burns)
"An dem schönsten frühlingsmorgen."   See
Die bekehrte schäferin (Cimarosa)
An den frühling ("Willkommen, schöner
jüngling") J. F. Reichardt.   Words by
F. von Schiller.   g.   ED 3
An den mond ("Füllest wie der busch und
tal") J. G. D. Gackstatter.   Words
by Goethe.   g.   ED 3
An den mond ("Füllest wie der busch und
tal") G. F. Zelter.   Words by Goethe.
g.   ED 2
An den mond ("Guter mond, du gehst so
stille") German folk song.   g.
ED 1
An den mond (To the moon)   e.g.
SSG
An den mond ("Willkommen, lieber mon-
denschein") S. G. Auberlen.   Words
by J. L. Am Buhl.   g.   ED 2
"An den Rhein, an den Rhein."   See
Warnung vor dem Rhein   (Pöthko)
An den schlaf.   See To sleep (Tchaikov-
sky)
An den sonnenschein ("Oh, fair sunshine")
R. Schumann.   Words by R.
Reinick.   e.g.   MS
An den sonnenschein ("O sunny
beam")   e.g.   KF 1—KF 2
An den sonnenschein (O sunshine)
e.   FTS
"An der Bretagne strande."   See Saved
from the storm (Barry)
"An der quelle sass der knabe."   See Der
jüngling am bache
"An der Salle hellem strande."   See Ru-
delsburg (Fesca)
An der Weser (By the river) G. Pressel.
Words by F. Dingelstedt.   e.g.   SM 4

An die abendsonne ("Goldne abendsonne")
H. G. Nägeli.   Words by B.
Urner.   g.   ED 3
Sunset song.   e.   WSC
An die freude   ("Freude, schöner Götter-
funken")   Composer   unknown.
Words by F. Schiller.   g.   ED 1
An die freundschaft ("In stiller wehmut")
J. Haydn.   Words by Küttner.   g.
ED 2
An die glocke ("Glocke, du klingst fröh-
lich")   F. E. Fesca.   Words by A.
Schreiber.   g.   ED 2
An die hoffnung (To hope) Beethoven.
e.g.   HSS 3
An die musik (To music) F. Schubert.
Words by Schober.   e.g.   CS 1—
KF 2—PG 1
An die wankelmütige ("Dir folgen meine
tränen")   J. A. P. Schulz.   Words by
J. T. Hermes.   g.   ED 2
"An dir allein, an dir hab' ich gesündigt."
See Busslied (Beethoven)
An eine Aeolsharfe (To an Aeolian harp)
J. Brahms.   Words by E. Mörike.
e.g.   GM—PG 1
An einem bache.   See Langs en å (Grieg)
"An einem sonnigen morgen."   See
Glockengeläute (Hölzel)
An Emma ("Weit in nebelgrauer ferne")
K. F. Zelter.   Words by F. von Schil-
ler   g.   ED 3
"L'an fuit vers son déclin."   See Pensée
d'automne (Massenet)
"An hor du liden baadsmand."   See Op-
sang
"An' I couldn't hear nobody pray."   See I
couldn't hear nobody pray
"An jedem abend geh' ich aus."   See Lauf
der welt (Grieg)
"An jenem tag" ("Upon the day") H.
Marschner.   e.g.   SOA 4
"An jenem tag" ("Upon that day")
e.g.   AB 3—KS 5
An junge spröde schönen.   See "Ich sah
ein röschen am wege stehn" (Methfes-
sel)
"An meines vaters hügel."   See Das land-
mädchen (Harder)
An Mignon ("Über tal und fluss")   K. F.
Zelter.   Words by Goethe.   g.   ED 2
An' O, for ane-an'-twenty, Tam.   Air: The
moudiewort.   Words by R. Burns.
BSB
And oh! for ane-and-twenty, Tam.
PS 1
"They snool me sair, and haud me
down."   Air: BSR
An' O my Eppie, my jewel, my Eppie.
See "By love and by beauty"
"An somebody were come again."   Air:
Carl, an the king come.   Words by
R. Burns.   BSR
"An thou wert mine ain thing."   Scottish
air.   Words by Ramsay.   PS 2
An' we'll all rise togedder.   See Four and
twenty elders
An ye had been whare I hae been.   See
"Whare hae ye been sae braw, lad"

"**Ana** bekorenu." See "Give ear, O Lord"

Aná, kak póldyen, kharashá. See "As fair is she as noonday-light" (Rachmaninov)

Anacreon
"Fill me a bowl" (Corfe)
Pleasant old age (Wynne)

Anakreon's grab (Anacreon's grave) H. Wolf. Words by Goethe. e.g. PG 4

Anastoseōs hemera. For English translation see "The day of resurrection" (Oliver); "The day of resurrection" (Vibbert)

Anatolius
Our Christmas festal (Composer unknown. Tr of Mega kai paradoxon thagma)

Ance crowdie, twice crowdie. See "O, that I had ne'er been married"

"**Ance** mair I hail thee, thou gloomy December." Air: Thro' the lang moor. Words by R. Burns. BSR

"**Anchor** in the Lord." Negro spiritual. DF

Anchored. M. Watson. Words by S. K. Cowan. AB 2—CB

The **anchor's** weighed. J. Braham. Words by S. J. Arnold. DM 1— FSS 8—HSE 1

The **anchorsmiths.** Dibdin (music and words) HSE 1

Ancient bourrée from Auvergne. See Bourée du Mont Doré

Ancient chant of the Taborites. Bohemian folk air. Words from J. Ziska. e. GO

Ancient lullaby. See "Sweet babe, a golden cradle holds thee"

Ancient march from Dalecarlia. See "Mandom, mod och morske män"

"**Ancient** of days." J. A. Jeffery. Words by W. C. Doane. CST

"An **ancient** story I'll tell you anon." See The abbot of Canterbury

"**And** are ye sure the news is true." See There's nae luck about the house

"**And** by day and by night I fare." See Martha's song (Musorgskiï)

"**And** did you not hear of a jolly young waterman." See The jolly young waterman (Dibdin)

"**And** doth not a meeting like this make amends." See The meeting

"**And** he journey'd with companions." F. Mendelssohn. e. SAS 2
Also in But the Lord is mindful of his own (Mendelssohn) CS 1—OS 2

"**And** God created man." J. Haydn. e. OS 3—SAS 3
Also in "In native worth and honour clad" (Haydn) TS

"**And** God said, let the earth bring forth grass." J. Haydn. e. OS 1— SAS 1—SAS 4
Also in With verdure clad the fields appear (Haydn) MSS 2

"**And** God said: Let the waters bring forth abundantly." J. Haydn. e. OS 1 —SAS 1

"**And** God said, let the waters under the heaven." J. Haydn. e. OS 4— SAS 4

"**And** has she then fail'd in her truth." H. R. Bishop. HSE 2

"**And** he said: All the night have I dreamed." See La chevelure (Debussy)

"**And** I aint got weary yet." See I aint got weary yet

And I will die in the field. See We'll die in the field

And I'll kiss thee yet. See "Ilk care and fear, when thou art near"

"**And** it was Olaf Trygvason." See Olaf Trygvason (Grieg)

"**And** Job's grief was very great, very great." See Where the wicked cease from troubling (Parker)

"**And** let me the canakin clink." H. W. Loomis. Words by W. Shakspere. VFS

"**And** lo! the star, which they saw in the east." See Star of glory brightly streaming (Garnett)

"**And** many thousand ducats." See "Och många tusen kroner" (Hallén)

And maun I still on Menie doat. See "Again rejoicing nature sees"

And my wife is nagging. See A teamster's complaint

And oh! for ane-and-twenty, Tam. See An' O, for ane-an'-twenty, Tam

"**And** she says true, the bond is riven." See O vision entrancing (Thomas)

"**And** so, my lord, you'd fain dance a measure." See "Se vuol ballare, signor contino" (Mozart)

"**And** so, when evening shadows creep." See When I wake (Watts)

"**And** that potion prevail'd to produce such a vision." See Vision fugitive (Massenet)

"**And** the kaiser he sat in his castle so high." See Ved ankerhioning

"**And** the Lord looked down from heaven." e. Molique. OS 2

And then—. E. S. Hosmer. Words by G. C. Gow. CHS

"**And** there goes the bull; look out there." See El toro y el ranchero

"**And** they calls me Hanging Johnny." See Hanging Johnny

"**And** this potion could bring such a vision before me." See Vision fugitive (Massenet)

"**And** tho' a cloud o'erspread yon heaven." See "Und ob die wolke" (Weber)

"**And** thou appear'st, O fairest star of heaven." See O du mein holder abendstern (Wagner)

"**And** thou I lov'd art gone." See Yesterday (Blockley)

And we're a' noddin', nid, nid, noddin. See We're a' noddin'

"And what of Christmas day."   See What of Christmas day

"And why should not that land rejoice." See The glad new day

"And will he not come again."   Traditional air.   Words by Shakespeare. DM 1

And wouldst thou thus have sullied.   See Eri tu che macchiavi (Verdi)

"And ye shall walk in silk attire."   English air.   Words by S. Blamire. PS 1

"And ye shall walk in silk attire."   Scottish air: The siller crown.   Words by S. Blamire.   JO—PS 1

"And yet, I know I love her."   See Bella del tuo sorriso (Braga)

Ändå ("As yet") W. Lagercrantz.   Words by C. W. Böttiger.   e.sw.   HSOS

Andenken.   See "Ich denk dein, wenn durch den hain" (Beethoven)

"Anders wird die welt."   See Heimweh (Wolf)

Andersen, Hans Christian
    "Child Jesus came to earth this day" (Gade.   Tr of Barn Jesus i en krybbe lad)
    En digters sidste sang (Grieg)
    "Hun er saa hvid" (Grieg)
    "I himlen" (Selmer)
    Jeg elsker dig (Grieg)
    Martsviolerne (Gade)
    The nightingale (Molloy)
    Punchinello (Molloy)
    Der soldat (Silcher)
    Vandring i skoven (Grieg)

Anderson,
    Christmas aftermath

Anderson, Alexander
    Cuddle doon (Composer unknown)

Anderson, C. S.
    Song of the "O. W. U."   (O'Kane)

Anderson, Mrs J. W.
    "Come forth and bring your garlands" (music by Kotschmar; Ulmann)

Anderson, John
    A prayer

André, Anton
    "Ach, wie flieht das leben so geschwind"
    Ewiger wechsel
    Das geständnis
    Heutzutage
    Wiegenlied

André, Johann
    Alte freundschaft, alter wein (from Das wütende heer)
    For an autumn festival
    Rheinweinlied
    "Süsse, heilige natur"

Andreas Hofer ("Zu Mantua in banden") Tyrolean national song.   Words by J. Mosen.   e.g.   SN.   e. only FSS 6. g. only ED 1

Andrew, Saint, of Crete
    "Christian! dost thou see them" (Dykes. Tr of Oy gar Blepeis tarattontas)

"Andrew Rose."   Forecastle song.   CR

Andrews, Bond
    The nipper's lullaby
    The toddler's lullaby.   See The nipper's lullaby

Andrews, Joseph Warren
    "Hallelujah, raise the song"

Andulko ("Andulko, mé díte") Czech folk song.   bo.e.   BF 1

The **angel** (Der engel) A. Rubinstein. e.g. FMB

The **angel** and the shepherds ("Awake, ye shepherds, instantly") French Flanders song.   e.   HC—MF

The **angel** and the shepherds ("Now rise up, ye shepherds") E. H. Thorne. BSC—HC

Angel de mis amores.   Mexican folk song. e.s.   HS

"Angel fair with golden hair."   See "Angiolin dal biondo crin" (Liszt)

"The angel Gabriel."   Traditional Devonshire air.   BSC

Angel Gabriel ("Oh! my soul")   J. E. Stewart.   WBT—WC

"Angel hosts in bright array."   G. P. Grantham (music and words)   HC

"Angel of light, whom once I cherish'd." See "Spirto gentil" (Donizetti)

"Angel of peace."   M. Keller.   Words by O. W. Holmes.   FSS 4—LA—LBR—WCP

"An angel through heaven flew swift as the light."   See The angel (Rubinstein)

The **angel** trio.   See "Lift thine eyes, O lift thine eyes" (Mendelssohn)

"Angel voices."   A. S. Sullivan.   Words by F. Pott.   LA

"Angelehnt an die epheuwand dieser alten terrasse."   See An eine Aeolsharfe (Brahms)

Angelic songs are swelling.   See "Hark! hark! my soul" (Armstrong)

Angelina Baker.   S. C. Foster (music and words)   NMP—WBT

"Angels above on Advent morn."   See The Christ child (Cornelius)

"Angels bright, their pinions folding."   F. Adlam.   HC

"Angels come, on joyous pinion."   See Adeste, coelitum chori

"Angels ever bright and fair."   Händel. FSS 2—HSD—JSE—MSS 1—OS 1— SS 1—WBT

"Angels, from the realms of glory" (Regent square) H. Smart.   Words by J. Montgomery.   DC
    Come and worship.   FSS 6—MCS

The **angel's** greeting.   Salzburger sacred song.   e.   KSE

Angels meet me at de cross-roads.   W. S. Hays.   WBT

"The angels sat in the garden-tomb." Easter carol.   HC

Angel's serenade.   See La serenata (Braga)

"The angels sing around the stall."   J. M. Haydn.   HC

The **angels'** song ("Glory to God in the highest") G. B. Pergolesi.   DSH

The **angel's** song ("Last night") See "Last night as I lay sleeping" (Vincent)

"The **angels'** songs this joyful day." A. Redhead. HC

Angels waiting at the door. Negro spiritual. JP

"**Angels** we have heard on high." See Bergers, pour qui cette fête

The **angels'** whisper ("A baby was sleeping, its mother was weeping") Air: Mary, do you fancy me. Words by S. Lover. JO—MMI

Angelus ad Virginem. 13th century air. Words from the Latin. e. HC

"**Anger** is welling." A. Rubinstein. e. SAS 4

"From my soul's depths." e. OS 4

Anges du paradis. C. Gounod. e.f. SOA 3

Ångest (Anguish) H. Alfvén. Words by E. Aarestrup. da.e. WM 1

"**Angiol** d'amor il cor che geme." See "Spirto gentil" (Donizetti)

"**Angiolin** dal biondo crin" ("Angel fair with golden hair") F. Liszt. Words by C. Bocella. e.i. CMF 1

The **angler.** Irish folk song. JOI

The **angler's** song. H. Lawes. Words attributed to J. Chalkhill. MM

The **angry** father-in-law (Kak u nashikh u vorot) Russian folk song. e. SSR 3

"**Angry** words." Childhood song. FSS 3—WBT

Anguish. See Ångest (Alfvén)

"**Anguish** of mind, sadness, too, leaves me." See "Plus de dépit, plus de tristesse" (Grétry)

Angus Macdonald. J. L. Roeckel. Words by F. E. Weatherly. FSS 8

"**Angutivum** taina taunane taina." See The returned hunter

"**Anička** mlynárova." See Annie, the miller's daughter

Anketell, John
"Ring out, sweet Easter bells, ring out" (words and music)
"Ring out, sweet Easter bells, ring out" (words with music by Blaikie)

Anna song. See "Was ist denn heut' wohl fuer ein tag" (Genée)

"**Anna,** thy charms my bosom fire." J. Oswald. Words by R. Burns. BSR

"**Ännchen** von Tharau." F. Silcher. Words by S. Dach. g. ED 1
"Ännchen von Tharau" ("Annie of Tharau") e.g. BO—SSG
"Annie of Tharau." e. BSE

L'**anneau** d'argent (The silver ring) C. Chaminade. Words by R. Gérard. e.f. PG 2
The silver ring. e.f. BC

Annie dear ("Our mountain brooks were rushing") Irish air: Maids in May. Words by T. Davis. MMI

Annie Laurie. Lady John Scott. Words by W. Douglas of Finland. BD—BO—BOS—BSE— CHS— EF— FSS 1—HSC—HSD—JO—JS—JSE

—LA—MP— MPC—NMH— NML —NMS—OH—PS 1—TFC 1—TL —WA—WBT— WC—WL—WSW

Annie Laurie ("Maxwellton braes are bonnie") HSSS—NMS—SMF

Annie Laurie ("Maxwelton's braes are bonnie") MS

Annie Lisle. H. S. Thompson. HSD—WBT

"**Annie** of Tharau." See "Ännchen von Tharau" (Silcher)

Annie, the miller's daughter ("Anička mlynárova") Slovak folk song. e.sl. BF 1

Annie wept. Old Serbian song. e. KSE—WL

Annie's tryst. Words by W. E. Aytoun. FSS 6

"**Another** hand is beck'ning us." See Gone (Stein)

"**Another** little hour I begged" ("Ich wollt' ein wenig mit dir plaudern") A. Grechaninov. Words from the Russian of A. Pleschtschejeff. e.g. NM 1

Anschütz, Ernst
Die abenddämmerung (Nägeli)
Warnung (Volksweise)

Answer to Kate Kearney. See Kate Kearney, Answer to

Answers. See "Do you think of the days" (Blumenthal)

An **ante-bellum** sermon. Air: Joshua fit de battl' ob Jerico, arr by H. T. Burleigh. Words by P. L. Dunbar. BP —SM 4

Antheunis,
Wiegeliedje (Rennes)

Antioch. See "Joy to the world" (Händel)

Antonia ("Mme voglio i a'nzo rare") See La ricciolella

Antonia ("T'aje fatta la gonnella, Antonia") Neapolitan song. e.i. MSI

A **nutting** we will go. Folk song. BSW

Ao menino Jesus (To the child Jesus) Portuguese song. e.po. BF 2

Aohe lua. See "Wrapt in verdure" (Hopkins)

Aoleo. Rumanian song. e.ru. BF 2

Aooah. Love song from the Red Willow pueblos. T. Lieurance. e. LN

Der **apfelgarten** (The apple orchard) A. F. Lindblad. e.g. EF

Apolloni, Giovanni
Fu Dio che disse (from L'ebreo)

L'**appel** du printemps (The call of spring) A. Holmès. e.f. KF 2—PG 2

The **apple** orchard. See Der apfelgarten (Lindblad)

The **apple-tree** house. German air. Words by R. Compton. DO

"The **apple-tree** is cover'd with blossoms of pink." See The apple-tree house

"The **apple-trees** grow in the orchard fair." See Der apfelgarten (Lindblad)

Appleby, M. E. J.
"Little birds are singing" (Naylor)

Apprehension. Ojibway Indian song. in. BA

Approach to the tree. Omaha Indian air. e. FI

"Apra il suo verde seno" ("Open your hearts") P. Quagliati. e.i. FEI 1

"Après des siècles d'esclavage." See La Brabançonne (Campenhout)

Après un rêve (After a dream) G. Fauré. Words from the Tuscan of R. Bussine. e.f. SAM

April ("April, April, laugh thy girlish laughter") J. H. Densmore. Words by W. Watson. CMF 1

April ("April, April, laugh thy girlish laughter") V. Harris. Words by W. Watson. AA

April vacation. English air. Words by J. Erwin. DO

April weather. J. H. Rogers. Words by E. P. Clarke. CMF 2—HST

Aprile. See Au printemps (Gounod)

"April's just a little child." See Song of April (Fairlamb)

"Apritio finestretta." See Maria, Marì (Capua)

Apukhtin, Aleksieĭ Nikolaevich
He truly loved me so (Tchaikovsky)
"Whether day dawns" (Tchaikovsky)

"Aquéros mountagnos" ("High the craggy mountains") Béarnese song. Attributed to Gaston Phébus ſcomte de Foixı e.f. TSF

"Aquí está la piedra lisa." See Las mananitas

"Är det ödsligt ock mörkt och kallt i ditt hjertas hus." See Hvad fattas dig (Ahnfeldt)

Ar hyd y nos (All through the night) D. Owen. Words from the Welsh. e.w. BO
All through the night. e. BAS 1— BC— BD— BOS— BSE— CS 1— CST—DO—DSH— EF—GO— JS —KF 1—KF 2—KF 3—KF 4—MS —OH—TFC 1—TL—WBT—WL
Welsh lullaby. Words adapted. WSC

"Ar rah! Mrs McSorley had fine purty twins." See McSorley's twins (Phillips)

Arabian melody (Arábskaya melódia) A. Borodine (music and words) e. SMR 2

Arabian song. See "Schön blinkt's aus allen sternen" (Vogrich)

Arábskaya melódia. See Arabian melody (Borodin)

Araby's daughter. E.ɾɦ Kiallmark. Words by T. Moore. FSS 5—JO—WBT

"Aràpete, fenesta." See Maria, Marì (Capua)

Araya, Jose
The pearl. See La perla (attributed)
La perla (attributed)

Arbor day. W. H. Jones. Words by S. S. Short. NMS

An **Arbor** day song ("Is this a time") J. L. Molloy. Words by W. C. Bryant. FSS 8

Arbor day song ("Joy for the sturdy trees") See "Joy for the sturdy trees" (Oliver)

Arcadelt, Jacob
"Ave Maria"
"O Savior, Lord of heaven." See "Ave Maria"

The **arch** denial. T. A. Arne. MM

Die **arche** Noah ("Das essen, nicht das trinken") F. Schneider. Words by W. Müller. g. ED 2

Archibald Douglas. C. Loewe. e.g. KF 4

Ardeleanca (The Ardelean woman) Rumanian song. e.ru. BF 2

Arditi, Luigi
Il bacio
The banks of the Lee
The dream of home. See Il bacio
"Let me love thee"
The stirrup cup

"Are there tidings." H. R. Bishop. FSS 4—JO

"Are you sleeping? are you sleeping? brother John! brother John." See Mingled melodies

"Are you sleeping, are you sleeping, friar John." See "Frère Jacques"

"Are you the doctor they sent for me here." See The brown girl (Virginia version)

Arenski, Anton Stepanovich
Der adler. See The eagle
Berceuse
"Deep hidden in my heart"
The eagle
Fischleins lied. See The little fish's song
L'heure du rêve. See The hour of dreams
The hour of dreams
In halbschlaf. See Revery
"In meinem herzchen." See "Deep hidden in my heart"
The little fish's song
Les loups. See The wolves
La poésie. See The spirit of poesy
Revery
Song of the little fish. See The little fish's song
The spirit of poesy
The wolves

The **Arethusa.** Old air, attributed to W. Shield and to O'Carolan. Words by P. Hoare. BE 3—BOS—HSE 1—JO —ME

"Arev tur-vu-rov ye-lav." See O my love, my plane-tree

Arguing the bargain. Negro song. BF 2

"Argyle is my name." See Bannocks o' barley-meal

"Ari im sokhag, togh bardez merin." See "Come, O nightingale"

"Ari Manan." See Come, Mannan

Aria of Rudolph. See "Gentle maiden" (Bellini)

Aria Oksánui. See Oxana's song (Rim-skiĭ-Korsakov)

Ariel. Words by S. Medley. HSD

Ariel's song. See "Where the bee sucks" (Arne)

Ariette ("Were I sunshine, I should come") P. Vidal. Words by P. Collin. e.f. SAM

Arikoto
Fuji (Ross)

Arioso from 100th psalm. See "Erkennet, erkennt, dass der Herr ist Gott" (Jadassohn)

"Arise, and hail the sacred day." A. H. Brown. BSC

"Arise, arise, sweet messenger of morn." See Arise, sweet messenger of morn (Arne)

"Arise, arise, the morning bells." E. Moss. Words by H. R. Haweis. HC

"Arise! arise! tread lightly, my sweet." See Ständchen (Strauss)

"Arise, arise, ye subterranean winds." See Arise, ye subterranean winds (Purcell)

"Arise, arise, you drowsy maiden." Folk song. SEF 1—SO

"Arise, fair maid." Old English song. DM 2

"Arise from thy slumbers." Irish air: The old Truigha. Words from the Irish. e. MMI

Arise! He calleth thee. J. L. Roeckel. Words by M. Mark-Lemon. HSS 4

"Arise, my soul." L. Edson. Words by C. Wesley. HSD

"Arise, O Lord." Costa. OS 4

Arise, sweet messenger of morn. Arne. Words by Thompson and Mallet. BE 8

"Arise, ye children." See La Marseillaise (Rouget de Lisle)

Arise, ye subterranean winds. Purcell. BAS 2—BS 2—HSE 3—PR 1

"Ark of freedom! glory's dwelling." See Columbia, God preserve thee free (Haydn)

The Arkansaw traveler. Old American air. Words by D. Stevens. BSS—TFC 2

Arkwright, Mrs Mary Anne (Browne) See Browne, Mary Anne

Arlberg, Frits
Fond fancy. See Svärmeri
Svärmeri (Tr of "Mit deinen blauen augen")

Arlington (Arne) See My title clear; "Salvation! oh, the joyful sound"; Soldier of the cross

Arm, arm, ye brave. Händel. OS 4
Arm, ye brave. SAS 4

"Arm und klein ist meine hütte." See Zufriedenheit (Wolf)

"Lé z'armaillis dei Colombettè." See Ranz des vaches

Der arme Thoms ("Thoms sass am hallenden see") K. F. Zelter. Words by J. Falk. g. ED 2

Armida. See Lascia ch'io pianga (Händel)

Armitage, M. Theresa
The country's call (same air as The watchword)
The watchword

Arms are strong and hearts are true. Words by J. B. Phillips. FSS 4

Armstrong, J. M.
Angelic songs are swelling. See "Hark! hark! my soul"
"Hark! hark! my soul"

Armstrong, W. A. A.
Moriar, Melpomene (Glover)

Armstrong, W. D.
"We sing to-day our Easter hymn"

The army and navy of Britain. Early 19th century song. ME

Army hymn ("God of all nations") A. T. von Lwoff. Words by O. W. Holmes. JSE

Army hymn ("O Lord of hosts") H. K. Oliver. Words by O. W. Holmes. LA

"The army is gath'ring from near and from far." See Marching along (Bradbury)

Army of the Yankees. Lorraine folk air. Words by H. H. Harbour. DSH

Arndt, Ernst Moritz
Composer and author
Das feuerlied
Trinklied
Author
Bundeslied (Hanitsch)
Des Deutschen vaterland (Reichardt)
Deutscher trost (Berner)
Der feste mann (Nägeli)
Gebet an den heiligen Christ (Siegert)
"Der knabe Robert" (Methfessel)
Das lied vom feldmarschall (Volksweise)
Sonne, mond und sterne (Volksweise)
Vaterlandslied (Methfessel)

Arndt, W. T.
Alma mater—Wisconsin (Composer unknown)

Arne, Michael
"Care flies from the lad that is merry" (from Cymon)
"Come, come, my good shepherds"
Homeward bound
The lass with the delicate air
Sweet passion of love (from Cymon)
"Sweet Poll of Plymouth" (from The positive man)
"The topsails shiver in the wind"

Arne, Thomas Augustine
A-hunting we will go (attributed)
"All ye who would wish to succeed with a lass." See As sure as a gun
"Amanda's fair, by all confessed" (attributed)
The arch denial
Ariel's song. See "Where the bee sucks"
Arise, sweet messenger of morn (from Alfred)
Arlington. See My title clear; "Salvation! oh, the joyful sound"; Soldier of the cross

Arne, Thomas Augustine—*Continued*

As sure as a gun (from Thomas & Sally)

"Blow, blow, thou winter wind"

"By dimpled brook" (from Comus)

"By the gaily circling glass"

"Cast, my love, thine eyes around." See Damon and Florella

"Come, haste to the wedding" (attributed)

The cuckoo song. See "When daisies pied, and violets blue"

Damon and Florella (from The harlequin sorcerer)

"Decrepit winter limps away." See Ode to spring

"The echoing horn" (from Thomas & Sally)

"Fair Hebe" (attributed)

The faithful lover

"Fresh and strong the breeze is blowing"

Haste to the wedding. See "Come, haste to the wedding" (attributed)

"Honest lover"

"How happy a state does the miller possess" (attributed)

"In infancy" (from Artaxerxes)

The lass with the delicate air (wrongly attributed) See Arne, M. The lass with the delicate air

Lotharia

The maiden's complaint

"My banks they are furnished with bees"

My dog and my gun (wrongly attributed) See Baildon, J. "Let gay ones and great"

My title clear

Now Phoebus sinketh in the west

"O Thou, who by a star"

Ode to spring

The owl

Peggy

"Phillis, we don't grieve"

The retort

Rule, Britannia (from Alfred)

Sally

"Salvation! oh, the joyful sound" (same air as My title clear)

"Sigh no more, ladies"

Soldier of the cross (same air as My title clear)

"The soldier tired of war's alarms"

Spring. See "When daisies pied, and violets blue"

Strephon of the hill

"Sure Sally is the loveliest lass"

Sweet Nan of the vale

"Tell me where is fancy bred"

"This cold flinty heart" (from Cymon)

"Thou soft-flowing Avon"

"Under the greenwood tree, who loves to lie with me"

"Was ever nymph like Rosamond" (from Rosamond)

"Water parted from the sea" (from Artaxerxes)

The way to keep him

We all love a pretty girl under the rose

"When daisies pied, and violets blue"

"When forced from dear Hebe to go"

When I was a young one (from Thomas & Sally)

"When icicles hang by the wall." See The owl

When the heart is at ease (from The sacrifice of Iphigenia)

"Where the bee sucks"

"While you here do snoring lie" (attributed)

"Why so pale and wan"

"Ye fair, possest of ev'ry charm." See The way to keep him

Arnes sang (Arne's song)   P. A. Heise. Words by B. Bjørnson.   e.n.   SSN

Arnim, Ludwig Achim, freiherr von

Kriegslied des maies (Reichardt)

Arnold, Charles O.

"Awake! awake! glad voices make"

"Welcome happy morning" (Tr of Salve, festa dies)

Arnold, F.

"Haste thee, nymph"

Arnold, George Benjamin

"Hark, what mean those holy voices"

Arnold, Matthew

Tristram and Iseult (Foerster)

Arnold, Maurice

A Canadian boat song

Arnold, Samuel

"Amo, amas, I love a lass": traditional air arranged (from The agreeable surprise)

The Cheshire chambermaid (from Turk and no Turk)

"Faint and wearily."   See The way-worn traveller

"Flow, thou regal purple stream" (from The castle of Andalusia)

Galloping dreary dun (from The castle of Andalusia)

Hark! when the trumpet now calls you to arms (from The genius of nonsense)

The invincible Armado (from The siege of Curzola)

Jonathan (from Turk and no Turk)

Lira, lira, la

Little Sally's wooden ware (from The shipwreck)

"Little thinks the townsman's wife." See Lira, lira, la

The poor little gipsy (from The review)

The Spanish Armada

The star-spangled banner (same air as "To Anacreon in heaven"; wrongly attributed)   See Smith, J. S. The star-spangled banner

"To Anacreon in heaven"   (wrongly attributed)   See Smith, J. S. "To Anacreon in heaven"

The way-worn traveller

Arnold, Samuel James

The anchor's weighed (Braham)

The death of Nelson (Braham)

Jockey (Composer unknown)

Arnold, Samuel James—*Continued*
Little Sally's wooden ware (Arnold)
"Rest, my child" (Bishop)
Tom Steady (King)
A-rolling my bowl. See En roulant ma boule
Around our blazing fires. S. Nelson. MCS
Around the hearth. Air: Auld lang syne. Words by G. Howland. LBR
Around the lodge. See Wa-wan wa-an
Around the May-pole. Words by R. I. Halsey. NMS
"Around the throne of God." F. Peel. Words by J. M. Neale. HC
"Arouse thyself, companion of my shame." See Durch dich musst' ich verlieren (Wagner)
A-roving ("At number three Old England square") Chantey. MPC—SSS—WBT—WC
For variants see following songs of the same title
A-roving ("In Amsterdam there lived a maid") Capstan chantey. KB
"In Amsterdam there dwelt a maid." DM 2
A roving ("In Amsterdam there lived a maid") Capstan chantey. CR
A-roving ("In Plymouth town there lived a maid") Chantey. CST—FSF—SE
El arpa triste. German air. Words by T. Moore. [Tr of My harp has one unchanging theme] s. LCP
"Arrah! Mrs McSorley had fine purty twins." See McSorley's twins (Phillips)
Arras, Pierre Moniot d'. See Moniot d'Arras, Pierre
"Arrêtons-nous ici." See Vallons de l'Helvétie (Adam)
The arrow and the song. Balfe. Words by Longfellow. CS 1—DM 1—HSE 1 —JO
"Arroz con leche." Porto Rican song. s. LCP
Arrullo. Argentine version. e.s. HS —Chilian version. e.s. HS
Arshalouise. See Daybreak
"Art thou poor, yet hast thou golden slumbers." See Sweet content (Smith)
"Art thou sleeping, fair one." See Dormi, bella, dormi tu (Bassani)
"Art thou weary? and sad and dark is thy troubled breast." See Hvad fattas dig (Ahnfeldt)
"Art thou weary, art thou languid" (Stephanos) H. W. Baker. [Tr of Kopon te kai kamaton] e. TL
"Art thou weary, art thou languid." E. W. Bullinger. [Tr of Kopon te kai kamaton] e. LA
"Art thou weary, art thou languid." J. H. Hopkins. [Tr of Kopon te kai kamaton] e. FSS 5—LA
"Art thou weary, toiling wand'rer." See Until the day breaks (Gounod)

Arthur, Clarence
Composer and author
My gentle village maid
My trusty trot
The old college clock in the tower
Author
"Jolly golfing weather" (Adams)
Upidee (Composer unknown)
Wouldn't you (Shepard)
Arthur, J. C.
Vive Purdue
Arthur-a-Bland. Air: Hey down, a-down. DM 2
Arthur Le Bride. English folk song. BSW
Arthur MacBride. Irish folk song. JOI
Artillery song. U.S. army song. BSS
Caisson song. DSH
"As a beam o'er the face of the waters." Irish air: The young man's dream. Words by T. Moore. MI—MMI
"As a bird in prison pining." See Be still my heart
"As a jolly young ploughboy was viewing his land." See The ploughboy
"As a lady was walking down by the sea side." See The drowned sailor
"As a little child." C. M. von Weber. HSC—WBT—WSC
"As a little child" (Seymour) FSS 1
"As a marvelous mission of soul to soul." See Reverie (Hahn)
"As a sunbeam at morn." See "Come raggio di sol" (Caldara)
"As a twig trembles, which a bird." See She came and went
"As att noone Dulcina rested." See Dulcina
"As back from work the drover comes." See La chanson du bouvier
"As beauteous as Flora." See Norah, the pride of Kildare (Parry)
"As beautiful Kitty one morning was tripping." See Kitty of Coleraine
"As beautiful Nancy was a-walking one day." See Beautiful Nancy
As cold as the snows ("The mountains are robed") Air: Calenig, or, New Year's gift. Words by L. S. Jast. MMW
"As 'cross the fields the other morn." See Be quick, for I'm in haste
"As Dolly sat milking." Folk song. BE 1
"As down in the meadows I chanced to pass." 18th century song. CO 2—DM 2—MM
"As down in the sunless retreats." J. Haydn. Words by T. Moore. WBT
"As down in the sunless retreats" (Down in the sunless retreats) O. Shaw. Words by T. Moore. JO
"As down the burn they took their way." Air: Down the burn, Davie. Words by R. Burns. BSR
"As dreaming by the fire I sat." See Heigh-ho, the holly (Crawford)
"As droops the ivy, rudely torn." See Ce que je suis sans toi (Gounod)

"**As** each happy Christmas." See "Alle jahre wieder" (Rinck)

"**As** fair is she as noonday-light" (Aná, kak póldyen, kharashá) S. Rachmaninoff. Words by N. Minsky. e. SMR 2

"**As** falls the moonlight gently." See "Où va la jeune Indoue" (Delibes)

"**As** freshmen first we came to college." See A college medley

"**As** freshmen first we come to Yale." See Eli Yale

"**As** from Newcastle I did pass." See Cavalilly man

"**As** he was a-riding." See Sweet Kitty

"**As** I abroad was walking by the breaking of the day." See The carman's whistle

"**As** I cam' doon the Sandgate." See The keel row

"**As** I cam down by yon castle wa'." Air: As I cam down, etc. Words by R. Burns. BSR

"**As** I cam down the banks o' Nith." Air: The black watch. Words by R. Burns. BSR

"**As** I came back from beautiful Rochelle." See "En revenant de la joli' Rochelle"

"**As** I came down the Bowery." See Can't you dance the polka

"**As** I came down the Canon gate." See The keel row

"**As** I came o'er the Cairney mount." Air: The Highland lassie. Words by R. Burns. BSR

"**As** I came thro' Sandgate." See The keel row

"**As** I came through the north countrie." See York! York for my money

"**As** I crossed over London's bridge." See Geordie (Swannanoah, N.C. version)

"**As** I gaed down the water-side." Air: Ca' the yowes. Words by R. Burns. BSR

"**As** I gaed o'er the Highland hills." See Peggy Bawn

"**As** I grew up in Boston." See The Sheffield apprentice (Allanstand, N.C. version)

"**As** I lay me, weary, down to rest." See Evening prayer

"**As** I lay on my bed on a night." Air: Go from my window, love, do. Words attributed to R. Burns. BSR

"**As** I look'd over the castle wall." See Lord Thomas of Winesberry

"**As** I roam'd out one morning." See At dawning of the day

"**As** I rose on Sunday morning." See The shepherd's call

"**As** I roved out on a summer's morning, a speculating most curiously." See The colleen rue

"**As** I roved out on a summer's morning down by the banks of Blackwater side." See Castlehyde

"**As** I roved out one morning down by a river side." See The angler

"**As** I rummag'd thro' the attic." See My trundle-bed (Baker)

"**As** I sat on a sunny bank." WCC

"**As** I saw fair Clora walk." G. Hayden. Words by E. Waller. BE 6

"**As** I stood by yon roofless tower." Air: Cumnock psalms. Words by R. Burns. BSR

"**As** I strayed from my cot at the close of the day." See Roll on, silver moon

"**As** I to war did go." See A soldier brave (Hornemann)

"**As** I trudged on at ten at night." See Northern Nancy

"**As** I walk'd forth one summer's day, to view the meadows sweet and gay." See A forsaken lover's complaint (Johnson)

"**As** I walked forth one summer's morn hard by a river side." See The new-mown hay

"**As** I walked out in the streets of Laredo." See The cowboy's lament

"**As** I walked out last Sunday night." See I seen her at de window

"**As** I walked out one cool summer morning." See George Reilly (Black Mountain, N.C. version)

"**As** I walk'd out one day, one day." See Death and the lady

"**As** I walked out one evening down by a river side." See The Irish girl (Irish version)

"**As** I walked out one fine morning." See Heave away, my Johnny

"**As** I walked out one fine summers morning." See Tarry Trowsers

"**As** I walk'd out one May morning down by the riverside." See The bold fisherman

"**As** I walked out one May morning for to hear the pretty birds sing sweet." Kentucky mountain song. WT

"**As** I walk'd out one May morning, one May morning so early, I overtook a handsome maid." See I'm seventeen come Sunday

"**As** I walked out one May morning, one May morning so early, I there espied a fair pretty maid." See On a May morning so early

"**As** I walked out one May morning, one May morning, as it happened to be." Folk song from Dorset. SF 1

"**As** I walked out one May morning, so early in the spring." Essex folk song. SF 2
Variant: The false young man

"**As** I walked out one morn betime." See Among the new-mown hay

"**As** I walk'd out one morning fair." See Jack the sailor

"**As** I walked out one morning fine." See Heave away, my Johnny

"**As** I walked out one morning in spring." See The false young man (Flag Pond, Tenn. version no. 2)

"**As** I walked out one summer's morning." See George Reilly (Hot Springs, N.C. version)

"As I walked over London bridge." See Geordie (Cambridgeshire version)

"As I walked through the meadows." Folk song: 1st version. SEF 1—SO —2d version. SEF 1—SO

"As I walk'd through the pleasant grove." See The inquisitive lover

"As I wandered 'neath the stars." See Strambotto

"As I was a-riding to Brimbledon fair." See Brimbledon fair

"As I was a-walking down by the sea-shore." See The drowned lover (Devon version)

"As I was a-walking down in Stokes bay." See The drowned lover (Hampshire version)

"As I was a-walking down Paradise street." See Blow the man down

"As I was a-walking down Watchet Swayne street." See The Watchet sailor

"As I was a-walking for my recreation." See Blackbirds and thrushes

"As I was a-walking for pleasure one day." See The little Mohee

"As I was a-walking one midsummer morning." See The sweet primeroses

"As I was a-walking one morning for pleasure." See Whoopee ti yi yo, git along little dogies

"As I was a-walking one morning in May, enjoying the sunshine, all careless and gay." See Cupid's trick

"As I was a-walking one morning in May, I heard a young damsel to sigh and to say." See Timothy

"As I was a-walking one morning in May, to hear the birds whistle, see lambkins at play." See Green bushes (Devon version)

"As I was a-walking one morning in spring, for to hear the birds whistle and the nightingales sing." See Green bushes

"As I was a-walking one morning in spring, I heard a pretty ploughboy." See The pretty ploughboy (Yorkshire version)

"As I went a-walking one morning in spring, to hear the birds whistle, and nightingales sing, I heard a fair lady a-making great moan." See I'm a poor stranger and far from my own

"As I was a-walking one morning in spring, to hear the birds whistle and the nightingale sing, I heard a fair damsel, so sweetly sang she." See The sign of the Bonny Blue Bell

"As I was a-walking one morning in spring to hear the small birds whistle and the nightingales sing, I heard a fair maid making sorrowful moan." See The happy stranger

"As I was a-walking one morning in the spring I heard a pretty damsel most sweetly to sing." See The lark in the morning

"As I was a-walking one morning in the spring, I met a young damsel, so sweetly she did sing." See The lark in the morn

"As I was a-walking one morning so fair." See Down among the banks of roses

"As I was going down Paradise street." See Blow the man down

"As I was going out one day, down by the Clarence dock." See Heave away, my Johnny

"As I was going to Banbury." Folk song from Berkshire. FSF

"As I was going to Derby, sir, 'twas on a summer's day." See The Derby ram (Derbyshire county song)

"As I was going to Derby, 'twas on a market day." See Derby ram (Forecastle song)

"As I was going to Strawberry fair." See Strawberry fair

"As I was lumbering down the streets of bully London town." See O you Santy

"As I was walking all alone." See Lull me beyond thee

"As I was walking by yon river-side." See He's dear to me tho' he's far frae me

"As I was walking down Lime street." See Hoodah-day

"As I was walking down the street." See Rig-a-jig

"As I was walking through the shade." See Les adieux des amants

"As I was walking up the street." Air: Mally's meek, Mally's sweet. Words by R. Burns. BSR

"As I went a-walking all by the seashore." See The Little Mohee

"As I went a-walking one morning in June." See The mantle so green

"As I went down the valley to pray." See Down in the valley

"As I went down to Nottiman town." See Fair Nottiman town

"As I went lumbrin' down de street." See Buffalo gals

"As I went out ae May morning." Air: As I went out. Words by R. Burns. BSR

"As I went out one May morning, one May morning betime." See Searching for lambs

"As I went over London's bridge." See Geordie (Hot Springs, N.C. version)

"As I went to Walsingham." See Walsingham

As I'd nothing else to do. J. L. Hatton. Words by H. Fry. FSS 5—JSE

"As it fell on a holiday." See John Dory

"As it fell on a holy day." See John Dory

"As it fell out on a long summer's day." See Fair Margaret and sweet William (English version)

"As it fell out one May morning." See The holy well

"As it fell out upon a day." See Dives and Lazarus

"**As** it fell upon a day." H. R. Bishop. Words by Shakespeare. BE 7

"**As** it fell upon a holy day." See John Dory

"**As** Jacob with travel was weary one day." See Jacob's ladder

"**As** Jan was hurrying down the glade." See The barley straw

"**As** Johnny walked out." Folk song. BSW

"**As** Joseph and Mary were a-walking the green." See The cherry-tree carol (Big Laurel, N.C. version)

"**As** Joseph was a-walking." Traditional Somersetshire song. MCS—WCC

"**As** Joseph was a walking" (Joseph and the angel) R. R. Terry. Traditional Somersetshire words. HC

"**As** Kathleen fair beyond compare." See The banks of the daisies

"**As** Lady Marg'ret was a-going to bed." See Young hunting (Virginia version)

"**As** late by a sodger I chanced to pass." Air: I'll mak you be fain to follow me. Words by R. Burns. BSR

"**As** lately we watched." Austrian carol. e. MF

"**As** long as life endureth." See "Af hjärtat jag dig älskar"

"**As** Mary walked in the garden green." G. P. Grantham (music and words) HC

"**As** Mary walked in the garden green." R. F. Smith. Words by G. P. Grantham. HC

"**As** May in all her youthful dress." S. Akeroyde. MM

"**As** me and my marrow was ganning to wark." See The collier's rant

"**As** my dear old mother." See "Songs my mother taught me" (Dvořák)

"**As** on the swelling wave." See "Come raggio di sol" (Caldara)

"**As** on you I am gazing." See Dreaming of you

"**As** once I sat beneath a shade." See Strephon of the hill (Arne)

"**As** one who is lovely and young." See Le lever de la lune (Saint-Saëns)

As pants the hart. F. Mendelssohn-Bartholdy. ɪTr of Meine seele dürstet nach Gottɪ e. JSE Consolation. e. LA

"**As** pretty Polly Oliver." See Pretty Polly Oliver

"**As** rays of setting sun." See "Come raggio di sol" (Caldara)

"**As** shadows cast by cloud and sun" (All saints) H. S. Cutler. Words by W. C. Bryant. LA

"**As** she was sitting in her dower room." See Fair Margaret and sweet William (Allanstand, N.C. version)

"**As** silent night is descending." See Le soir (Gounod)

"**As** slow our ship her foamy track." Air: The girl I left behind me, or, Brighton camp. Words by T. Moore. MI—MMI

"**As** Sparabella pensive lay." See Sparabella's complaint

As sure as a gun ("All ye who would wish to succeed with a lass") T. A. Arne. Words by I. Bickerstaffe. ME

"**As** swift as passing fancy." See Le roitelet (Paladilhe)

"**As** the blackbird in the spring." See Aura Lee

"**As** the dove her flight is winging o'er the valley." See The blue dove

"**As** the golden stars." German air. FSS 5

"**As** the moon shone bright and fair." See Hare and hunter

"**As** the rose is overtaken." See The disappointed suitors

"**As** the savage hawk pursueth." See A maiden's revenge

As the star. See "Somι stjärnan uppå himmelen så klar"

"**As** the story is related." See Dutch dolls (Ostlere)

"**As** the voyager turns with a love-longing gaze." See Graduation song

"**As** the wild rose am I." See The song of Solomon (Musorgskii)

As the wind blows. R. Genée. FSS 8

"**As** those who seek the break of day." R. F. Smith. Words by W. C. Dix. HC

"**As** Thou wilt, Father." C. L. Williams. SAS 2

"**As** tippling John was jogging on." See Tippling John

"**As** vanquished Erin." Air: The Boyne water. Words by T. Moore. MI

"**As** we lay on an afternoon." See Russian song used for heaving the anchor

"**As** we marched down thro' Ivory." See Pretty Peggy O (North Carolina version)

"**As** we marched down to Fernario." See Pretty Peggy O (Kentucky version)

"**As** we parted, tear-drops started." See Abschied (Cavallo)

"**As** we row." G. Rossini. BD

"**As** we sailed from the downs." Irish folk song. JOI

"**As** when a lamb confiding." See "Sen corre l'agnelletta" (Sarro)

As when the dove laments her love. G. F. Händel. SOA 1

"**As** when the softly blushing rose." See Mild Mabel Kelly

As when the traveler. W. B. Bradbury. Words by J. Newton. FSS 7

"**As** William crossed the briny ocean." See William Hall

"**As** with gladness men of old." H. W. Davies. Words by W. C. Dix. HC

"**As** with gladness men of old." Arr from C. Kocher. Words by W. C. Dix. DC—HC

"**As** with gladness men of old." W. H. Monk. Words by W. C. Dix. FSS 7

"**As** with gladness men of old" (With gladness men of old) MCS

"**As** with gladness men of old." A. Russell. Words by W. C. Dix. BD

"**As** yet, as yet, the sky may be gray and the ground may be wet." See Ändå (Lagercrantz)

"**As** young Johnny walked out on a fair dewy morn." See Searching for young lambs

"**As** young Rory and Moreen were talking." See Móirín ni Chealla

Ascher, Joseph
Alice, where art thou

"**A**-schooling I went as a boy to a dame." See Marigold lane

"**Asco** Giannetta ti vouesti lougar." See La Savoyarde

A-scouting. Air: A-roving. Words by S. Rowe. BSS

Ascribe unto the Lord worship and power. A. R. Gaul. SAS 3

"The **ash** grove." See Llwyn on

Ashes of roses. M. K. Wood. Words by E. Goodale. MSF 1

Ashes of roses. R. H. Woodman. Words by E. Goodale. AA

Ashley, John
"Poor Joe, the marine"

Así canto mis amores. J. Pericás. Words by F. M. Bernier. s. LCP

"**Así** cual mueren en occidente los tibios rayos del astro rey." See Carmela

"**Aside** dark sorrow laying." See "Serena i vaghi rai" (Rossini)

Asile héréditaire (Dear home, where dwelt my father) G. Rossini. e.f. KS 4

"**Ask** if yon damask rose be sweet." See "Frag' ob die rose" (Händel)

"**Ask** me not why my heart with fond emotion." See Child of the regiment (Donizetti)

"**Ask** me why I send you here." See The primrose (Lawes)

"**Asleep** in their shady beds." See A night in the woods

Asōmen pantes laoi. For English translations see "Come, ye faithful, raise the strain" (Flemish air) ;"Come, ye faithful, raise the strain" (Sullivan)

Aspiration. See "Saviour, blessed Saviour! listen while we sing" (Dykes)

Der **Asra** (The Asra) C. Loewe. Words by H. Heine. e.g. CMF 1

Der **Asra** (The Asra) A. Rubinstein. Words by H. Heine. e.g. FF—FO 1—KF 2—KF 4—NM 2—SS 1. e. only FTS

"**Assisa** a piè d'un salice." Rossini. e.i. PP

"**Assist** me, ev'ry tuneful bard." See Nanny of the hill (Worgan)

Astol, Félix
Borinquen
La Borinqueña

Astorga, Emanuele, barone d'
"I am seeking in every valley." See "Vo' cercande in queste valli"
"Morir vogl'io"
"O death, receive me." See "Morir vogl'io"

"That I might die." See "Morir vogl'io"

"Vo' cercande in queste valli"

"**Astri!** mi Astri" ("Astri! my Astri") Norse song. Words by H. Hanson. e.n. MAN

"**Astro** d'amore ch'in ciel mi segui nel tuo viaggio." See Alla stella confidente (Robaudi)

"**At** Boleyvogue, as the sun was setting." See Father Murphy of the county Wexford

"**At** court a serving maiden." See Liten Karin

"**At** crossways I listen." See Die zigeunerin (Wolf)

"**At** dawn Aurora gaily breaks." See The mellow horn (Jones)

"**At** dawn I rise with weeping eyes." See Song to the chief

At dawning of the day. Irish air. Words by K. T. Hinkson. FSI

"**At** dead of night, when all is still." E. J. Hopkins. HC

"**At** dreary midnight's cheerless hour." See Larboard watch (Williams)

"**At** early dawn from humble cot." T. Attwood. Words by S. Birch. PR 2

"**At** early dawn I once had been." See The dawning of the day

"**At** Easter morn the lark ascending." J. Knecht. Words by E. Geibel. e. HC

"**At** eve alone among the trees." See The hour of rest (Roeckel)

At evening-time. Sporle. Words by C. M. Steadman. FSS 4—WBT

"**At** ev'ning, when I go to bed." See Daisies (Hawley)

"**At** evening, when off to my rest I go." See Gute nacht, du mein herziges kind (Abt)

"**At** ev'ning when the cricket calls along the grassy lane." See Trainona

At happy Easter time. Reinecke. Words by L. E. Richards. HC

"**At** home in our Tyrolese land." Tyrolese song. e. KSE

At honor's glorious call. See "Oh, give me but my Arab steed" (Sullivan)

"**At** last am I alone." See Plus grand, dans son obscurité (Gounod)

"**At** last from Aries rolls the sun." See With joy the impatient husbandman (Haydn)

"**At** last has dawn'd that bright morning." See Hymno nacional (Brazil)

"**At** last hope's cheering ray." See "Bel raggio lusinghier" (Rossini)

"**At** last I see once more the hills and valleys." See Auf der reise zur heimath (Grieg)

"**At** last on Brazil rose the dawning." See Hymno nacional (Brazil)

"**At** last the bounteous sun." Haydn. e. OS 4—SAS 4

"**At** Lauterbach." See Zu Lauterbach

"**At** Mont Parnasse there lived a lass." See La fille de Parthenay

At Monte Pincio. See Vom Monte Pincio (Grieg)

"At morning the maiden went to matin-song one day." See Den bergtagna

"At my command let your weapons be lower'd." See La gloire et la fortune (Rossini)

At my cradle. See Vor meiner wiege (Schubert)

At my love's window. See "Vor lieb-chens fenster"

"At night, by moonlight, on the plain." See There lives a lass upon the green

"At noon we traversed together." See Noon and eve

"At number three Old England square." See A-roving

At parting ("Breaks now, breaks now my heart."—"Caṇte másica") Dakota Indian song. e.in. BF 2

At parting ("O my love's bright eyes."—Razstanak) Slavonian folk song. e.se. BF 1

At parting ("The sweetest flow'r that blows") J. H. Rogers. Words by F. Peterson. AA

At parting ("Unspoken words at parting") E. MacDowell (music and words) CU

At Pierrot's door. See "Au clair de la lune"

"At Polwarth on the green." Scottish air. Words attributed to A. Ramsay. MMS

"At Polwart on the green." PS 2

"At Saint-Malo." See "A Saint-Malo, beau port de mer"

"At Saratoff and Tzaritzine." See Ukranian song

At sea. See Tilsjös (Backer-Gröndahl)

"At setting day and rising morn." Air: Pe cawn i hon, or, Could I have this one. MMW

"At sixteen years of age." See Pat Malloy

At the ball ("Inmitten des balles") P. I. Tchaikovsky. Words by A. Tolstoi. e.g. CMF 2—SC

"At the baron of Mowbray's gate was seen." See He loves, and rides away (Horn)

At the brookside. See Langs en å (Grieg)

"At the city's western portal." See The land beyond (Pinsuti)

"At the cosy hearth" ("Aufen pripatshaķ") M. Warshavsky. e.y. BF 2

"At the early Easter morn." J. A. Johnson. HC

"At the fair of Mast' Andrea." See La fiera de Mast' Andrea

At the ferry. M. Wellings. Words by F. E. Weatherly. FSS 6

"At the foot of Newry mountain." See Newry mountain

At the forge. See Der schmied (Brahms)

At the hop. E. Carter. CHS

"At the loud cry of war all assemble." See Himno nacional de Mejico (Nunó)

At the making of the hay. L. Lehmann. Words by S. M. Peck. SM 1—WBW

"At the mid hour of night." Air: Molly, my dear. Words by T. Moore. MI

At the nightingale's. See Im wald bei der amsel

"At the peaceful midnight hour." See The wolf (Shield)

"At the rosy sunset hour." See Die bekehrte (Wolf)

At the setting of the sun. Folk song. BSW

"At the sign of the Whale in Askalon." See Jonas

At the smithy. See "Au bruit des lourds marteaux d'airain" (Gounod)

At the spinning wheel (Prząśniczka) S. Moniuszko. e.p. BF 1

At the spring ("Kur tas saltinelis") Lithuanian folk song. e.li. BF 1

At the well, oh. See À la fontaine

At the window. A. Warlamoff. e. KSN

"At the yellow boreen." Irish song. e. MMI

At twilight ("'Tis twilight, and the heat of day") A. Tiniakoff. Words from the Russian of A. Tolstoi. e. NM 2

At twilight ("The twilight shades, fast descending") LA

"At Willie's wedding on the green." See Jenny dang the weaver (Gardner)

"At Winchester was a wedding." See The king's jig

"At Yuletide, so the story tells." See The Christ-Child

Atá-a-kut game song. Indian song. in. FI

"Atá cailín deas am crád." See Péarla an brollaig báin

Atherton, Percy Lee
"Sing we now our hymns of gladness"

The Athole gathering. Scottish song. PS 2

Atkinson, R. H.
Song of the bobolink

Atkinson, R. W.
Floating 'mid the lilies
I am thinking, love, of thee

Atkyns, B. K.
"Carol we the blessing"

El atole (The gruel) Mexican song. e.s. BF 2
Jarabe. e.s. HS

"An atom is a little thing." See A parody song

"Atra procella travolge il mar." See Odi tu (Mattei)

Atri, Raffaele d'
Chi sa
Who knows. See Chi sa

"Attend, you feeling Christians." See Execution song

Atterbury, Luffman
Harvest home (from Mago and Dago)
"Pretty maidens, pretty maidens"

Attwood, Thomas
"Ah! once when I was a very little maid" (from Fast asleep)
"At early dawn from humble cot"
The cold wave my love lies under
The soldier's dream

Atwood, M.
"Upon a lowly manger"

Au bois rossignolet (The nightingale) French folk song. e.f. TSF

"Au bruit des lourds marteaux d'airain" (Vulcan's song) C. Gounod. e.f. BAS 1—BS 1—SOA 5

"Au bruit des lourds marteaux" ("The sparks fly thro' the smithy door") e.f. OPS 4

"Au bruit des lourds marteaux" ("To clang of brazen hammer's blow") e.f. KS 5

"Au bruit des lourds marteaux d'airain" (Vulcan's song.—At the smithy) e.f. AB 4

"Au clair de la lune." Words by Lully. f. FMB

At Pierrot's door. e. WBT

"Au clair de la lune" (By moonlight) e. BSE

"Au clair de la lune" ("Good Pierrot") e.f. DO

"In the silver moonlight." e. CST

"Au Corsaire qui courts au bord." See La Corsairienne

"Au loin, dans la mer." See Lied maritime (Indy)

"Au milieu des platanes." See Havanaise (Paladilhe)

Au printemps (Love in spring) C. Gounod. Words by J. Barbier. e.f. CS 2 —MSS 2—SS 2

Au printemps (To spring) e.f. CM 2 —HM 2

Au printemps (To spring.—Aprile) e.f.i. KF 1

To spring. e. BD

"Au royaume du vin et des roses." See Come to the realm of roses and wine (Rimskiï-Korsakov)

"Au sein des nuits tout dort." See Sérénade (Pierné)

Aubade. See Vainement, ma bien-aimée (Lalo)

Auber, Daniel François Esprit
"Away! away! the moon and stars are shining"
Boat song
Christmas vesper hymn
Come away to the fields
"Du pauvre seul ami" (from La muette de Portici)
Fairies' song. See The noontide ray
Fishermen's chorus (from La muette de Portici)
Flame of love. See Flamme vengeresse
Flamme vengeresse (from Le domino noir)
"Hark! o'er the stilly lake" (from La muette de Portici)
"Night sinks on the wave"

The noontide ray
Oh! sister dear. See "Pourquoi pleurer? pourquoi pleurer"
"On yonder rock reclining" (from Fra Diavolo. Tr of Voyez sur cette roche)
Over the happy town
La Parisienne
"Pourquoi pleurer? pourquoi pleurer" (from Masaniello)
The sail-boat (same air as Boat song)
Slumber song. See "Du pauvre seul ami"
We hail thee, glad springtime
With every golden string
"Young Agnes" (from Fra Diavolo)

Auber, Harriet
Bright was the star (Bradbury)
"With joy we hail the sacred day" (Kingsley)

Auberlen, Samuel Gottlob
An den mond

"Auch kleine dinge" ("E'en little things") H. Wolf. Words from a Tuscan popular song. e.g. FO 2

Audran, Edmond
Bob up serenely (from Olivette)
The gobble duet (from La mascotte)
The torpedo and the whale (from Olivette)
Waltz song

"Auf, auf, ihr brüder, und seid froh." Words by C. J. Wagenseil. g. ED 1

"Auf, auf, ihr brüder und seid stark." See Abschiedslied (Schubart)

"Auf, auf, wer deutsche freiheit liebet." See Kriegslied (Zumsteeg)

"Auf, auf! zum fröhlichen jagen." See Jägerlied

"Auf dem berge da weht der wind" ("On the mountain") German song. e.g. BF 2

"Auf dem berge dort oben, da wehet der wind." K. von Burgwedel. Words by C. A. Tiedge. g. ED 3

"Auf dem grünen balcon" ("From her balcony green") H. Wolf. Words from an anonymous Spanish poet. e.g. FO 2

Auf dem meere ("On ocean's breast") R. Franz. Words by Heine. e.g. PG 4

"Das meer hat seine perlen" ("The sea its pearls possesses") e.g. GM

Auf dem meere. For French and English translations with a different air see A toi mon coeur (Gounod)

"Auf dem rasen im walde." See Waldeslied (Kreutzer)

Auf dem wasser zu singen (To be sung on the water) F. Schubert. Words by F. L. Stollberg. e.g. CMF 2 —GM—KF 1

Auf dem wasser zu singen (Evening boat-song) e.g. CS 1

Auf der alm. J. N. freiherr von Poissl. g. ED 2

"Auf der alma" ("On the alma") e.g. BO

Auf der reise zur heimath (On the journey home) E. Grieg.   Words by A. O. Vinje.   e.g.   FO 2
Auf der reise zur heimath (On the way home)   e.   FTS
Auf der wanderung.   See Nur in Deutschland (Hoffmann von Fallersleben)
Auf die schlacht bei Torgau ("Schwerin der hat uns kommandiert")   Air: Franzosen habn'ne schanz gebaut.   Words by K. von Holtei.   g.   ED 2
Auf ein altes bild (To an ancient picture) H. Wolf.   Words by E. Mörike.   e.g.   PG 3
"Auf einen totenacker hat mich mein weg gebracht."   See Das wirthshaus (Schubert)
Auf einer herbstreise.   See Schutz (Bergt)
"Auf einsamer höhe erstarrt und verlassen."   See The pine-tree (Balakirev)
Auf ewig mein.   See For ever mine (Cantor)
"Auf ferner fremder aue da liegt ein todter soldat."   See Der todte soldat (Esser)
"Auf flügeln des gesanges" ("On wings of music") F. Mendelssohn.   Words by Heine.   e.g.   KF 1—PG 3—PG 4
"Auf flügeln des gesanges" ("On wings of music."—"On song's bright pinions")   e.g.   CMF 1
"Auf flügeln des gesanges" ("On wings of song")   e.g.   BAS 1—MS—TS
"Auf geht der tag, mit feur'gem geschoss." See God morgen (Grieg)
"Auf, ihr meine deutschen brüder."   18th century song.   Words by J. M. Miller.   g.   ED 2
"Auf, matrosen, die anker gelichtet."   See Matrosenlied (Pohlenz)
Auf Scharnhorsts tod ("In dem wilden kriegestanze")   Air: Prinz Eugen der edle ritter.   Words by M. von Schenkendorf.   g.   ED 2
Auf, schicke sich.   For English translation see "Come tune your heart" (Ouseley)
"Auf Schlesiens bergen, da wächst ein wein."   See Der schlesische zecher und der teufel (Reissiger)
Auf wiedersehn ("Es ist bestimmt")   See "Es ist bestimmt in Gottes rath" (Mendelssohn)
"Auf wiederseh'n! she murmur'd softly." See "Auf wiederseh'n! so sprachst du leise" (Nevin)
"Auf wiederseh'n! so sprachst du leise." A. Nevin.   Words by R. Dietrich.   e.g.   AA
"Aufen pripatshak."   See "At the cosy hearth" (Warshawski)
Aufenthalt (My abode) F. Schubert.   Words by L. Rellstab.   e.g.   FF—FO 1
Aufenthalt (My last abode)   e.g.   BS 2

"Auferstehn, ja auferstehn wirst du."   See Die auferstehung (Graun)
Die **auferstehung** ("Auferstehn, ja auferstehn") K. H. Graun.   Words by F. G. Klopstock.   g.   ED 1—ED 3
Aufgegebene liebe ("Hier unten im schatte")   Schweizerisches volkslied.   g. ED 3
"Auf'm berg steht a schloss."   Baierisches volkslied.   g.   ED 3
Auf'm berg steht a schloss ("On the hill stands a tower."—Bavarian song)   e.   BMC
"On the hill stands a tower."   e.   JSE
Aufmunterung zur freude ("Wer wollte sich mit grillen plagen")   Composer unknown.   Words by L. H. C. Hölty.   g.   ED 1
Aufmunterung zur freude ("Wer wollte sich mit grillen plagen")   J. F. Reichardt.   Words by L. H. C. Hölty.   g.   ED 3
Aufträge (Messages) R. Schumann.   Words by C. L'Égru.   e.g.   KF 1
"Die augen schliessen sich vom schlummer leicht getrübet."   See Revery (Arenski)
Augier, Émile
Ô jours heureux (Gounod)
Ô ma lyre immortelle (Gounod)
August, E. F.
Turnlied (Volksweise)
August ("Green in the valley")   W. B. Olds.   Words by J. L. Shroy.   NMS
"August the last 'twas we did see."   See Le combat naval
"Auhea la o Anoi."   See Sweet violet (Hopkins)
"Auhea o Moani ke ala."   See My sweet (Leleiohoku)
"Auhea wale ana oe."   See Gardenia flower (Nape)
The **auld** hoose.   Scottish air.   Words by Nairne.   PS 2
Auld Joe Nicolson's bonnie Nannie.   Scottish air.   Words by J. Hogg.   PS 1
Auld King Coul.   Ancient Scottish song.   PS 2
Variant: "Old King Cole"
Auld lang syne ("Should auld acquaintance be forgot")   Original Scottish air.   Words partly rewritten by R. Burns.   BSR
Auld lang syne ("Should auld acquaintance be forgot")   Air: I fee'd a lad at Michaelmas.   Words partly rewritten by R. Burns.   BAS 1—BD— BMC— BOS— BS 1—BSB—BSE— BSP— CST— DO— EF—FSS 1—GO—HSC—HSD— HSSS—JO—JS—JSE— LA—MP— MMS—MPC—NMH—NMS—OH—PS 1—SSS—TFC 1—TS—WA—WBT—WC—WSC—WSW
"Should auld acquaintance be forgot."   BSR
"The auld man."   Scottish song.   PS 2
"The auld man's mare's dead."   Air: The auld man's mare's dead.   Words altered by R. Burns.   BSR

Auld Rob Morris. Scottish air. Words by Burns. BSB—PS 1 "There's auld Rob Morris that wons in yon glen." BSR

Auld Robin Gray ("Young Jamie lo'ed me weel") Air: The bridegroom grat. Words by A. L. Barnard. BSE—HSD—JO—PS 1

Auld Robin Gray ("Young Jamie lo'ed me weel") W. Leeves. Words by A. L. Barnard. CS 1—FSS 3—HSSS—JO—MMS—PS 1

Auld Robin Gray: sequel ("The winter was come") [Air: The bridegroom grat] Words by A. L. Barnard. JO

Auld Santa Claus. Ancient Scotch song. DCS

"Aunque ames." Folk song from Spain and Spanish America. e.s. HS

Aunt Jemima's plaster ("Aunt Jemima she was old") FSS 8

Aunt Jemima's plaster ("Last time I met my wife") Short drag chantey. Air: Johnny Boker. CR

Aunt Leah's song. Kentucky song. BF 2

Auprès de ma blonde (Near my own blonde sweetheart) French folk song. e.f. TSF

Aura Lee. HSD—MPC—NMH—NML—WBT

Aurelia. See "The church's one foundation" (Wesley)

Aurora coelum purpurat. For English translation see "The morning purples all the sky"

Aurora lucis rutilat. For English translation see "Heaven with rosy morn is glowing" (Higinbotham)

"Aurore Pradère." Negro creole folk song. e.f. KA

"Aus dem walde tritt die nacht." See Die nacht (Strauss)

"Aus der heimath hinter den blitzen roth." See In der fremde (Schumann)

"Aus der jugendzeit." L. Erk. Words by F. Rückert. g. ED 3

"Aus der jugendzeit" (From youth's happy day) R. Radecke. Words by F. Rückert. e.g. SM 4 "Aus der jugendzeit" (The swallows' song) e.g. KF 3—KF 4 The days of youth. e. WBT

"Aus feuer ist der geist geschaffen." See Das feuerlied (Arndt)

"Aus meinen grossen schmerzen" ("Born of a pain undying") R. Franz. Words by H. Heine. e.g. SM 1 "Aus meinen grossen schmerzen" ("From grief I cannot measure") e.g. KF 4—PG 2 "Aus meinen grossen schmerzen" ("Out of my soul's great sadness") e.g. CMF 1—FO 1

"Aus meinen tränen spriessen" (Tears and sighs) Schumann. e.g. BS 2

"Aus tiefer nacht ein brausen zieht." See Lied des alten im bart (Löffler)

Die **auserwählte** ("Mädele, ruck") Swabian folk song. g. ED 1 Die auserwählte (The chosen one) e.g. SSG

Austin, Adam "For lack of gold" (Scottish air)

Austin, William
Composer
"Sleep, holy Babe"
Author
"All this night bright angels sing" (music by Field; Fruttchey; Sullivan)
"We sing to-day our Easter hymn" (Armstrong)

Austrian hymn (Haydn) See Columbia, God preserve Thee free; Deutschland über alles; "Gott erhalte Franz den kaiser"; "Land of greatness! home of glory"; "Lord, with glowing heart I'd praise Thee"; Our country; "Praise the Lord! ye heavens, adore Him"; Stand, Columbia

Austrian national hymn. See "Gott erhalte Franz den kaiser" (Haydn)

"Author of all my joys." See "O del mio dolce ardor" (Gluck)

"Autiko mai na." Fiji song. e.fij. SN

Autolycus' song. See "Lawn as white as driven snow" (Greenhill); "Lawn, as white as driven snow" (Linley)

"Autrefois le rat de ville." See Le rat de ville et le rat des champs

"L'autrier par la matinée" ("Early strolling at my leisure") Count Thibaut of Champagne, king of Navarre. e.f. BO L'autr'ier par la matinée ("T'other morning very early") e. BMC

Autumn ("From the branches dead leaves sever") Hungarian song. e. KSE—WL

Autumn ("Nebel brauen") See Herbstgang (Jordan)

Autumn ("Somrens dage svinder") See Höst (Beyer)

Autumn dreaming. F. Weiland. Words by B. Taylor. FSS 4

Autumn glory. Russian folk air. Words by R. R. Whitehead. WF

"Autumn leaves." Words by C. Dickens. FSS 5

An **autumn** lullaby. J. S. Fearis. Words by A. E. Allen. OH

Autumn melody (Chant d'automne) A. Koreshchenko. Words by D. Rathaus. e.f. NR 2

Autumn song ("Ach, wie so bald") See "Ach, wie so bald verhallet der reigen" (Mendelssohn)

Autumn song ("From the boughs o'erhead") Bohemian folk air. Words by J. Irwin. DO

Autumn song ("Oh, little bird upon the tree") A. S. Gatty. WSC

Autumn thought. See Pensée d'automne (Massenet)

"Autumn winds at our casement are beating." See Autumn melody (Koreshchenko)

Autumnal gale. See Herbststurm (Grieg)

Autumn's glory. C. W. Johnson (music and words) JS

Aux armes, citoyens. See La Marseillaise (Rouget de Lisle)

Aux champignons. See Gathering mushrooms (Musorgskiĭ)

"Aux échos des bois" ("In the shady woods") Air romanesque. e.f. NG

"Aux troupes du sultan." See Promesse de mon avenir (Massenet)

"Avant de quitter ces lieux" ("Even bravest heart may swell") C. Gounod. e.f. OPS 4—SOA 4

    "Even bravest heart may swell." e. WBT

    Loving smile of sister kind ("Dio possente, dio d'amor") e.i. BAS 2

"Ave, ave Maria! gratia plena." See "Ave Maria" (Chérubini)

"Ave, ave, verum corpus." See Ave verum (Mozart)

Ave Jesu Deus. For English translation see "Jesu, hail! O God most holy" (Stainer)

"Ave Maria" ("O Lord, most holy") F. Abt. e.l. HSS 1

"Ave Maria" ("O Savior, Lord of heaven") J. Arcadelt. e.l. HSS 1

"Ave Maria" ("Holy, holy, Lord God of hosts") L. Cherubini. e.l. HSS 1

"Ave Maria" ("Ave Maria, Thou happy Mother") C. Gounod, arr from Bach. e.l. FSS 7—MCS—WBT —WS. e. only WA—WSW

    "Ave Maria" ("Father eternal."—Evening meditation) e.l. MSS 1

    "Ave Maria" ("Father in heaven") e.l. HSS 2

"Ave Maria" ("O blessed Savior") L. Luzzi. e.i. HSS 2—PG 2

    "Ave Maria" ("Sing hallelujah with glad rejoicing") e.i. HSS 1

"Ave Maria" ("Ave Maria, hear my cry") P. Mascagni. Words by P. Mazzoni. e.i. FMB. e. only WA—WBT— WS—WSW

Ave Maria ("See, now the dusk is falling") J. Raff. e.g. MSS 2

"Ave Maria," no. 1 ("Father in heaven") C. Saint-Saëns. e.l. HSS 1—HSS 2

"Ave Maria," no. 2 ("Father in heaven") C. Saint-Saëns. e.l. HSS 3—HSS 4

"Ave Maria" ("Ave Maria! Maiden mild") F. Schubert. Words by W. Scott. e.g. SS 1. e. only FMB—FSS 7—MCS

    Ave Maria (Hymne an die Jungfrau) e.g.l. CMF 2—FO 1

    Ave Marie. e.g. PG 1

"Ave Maria" ("Hail, Mary, hail") G. Verdi. e.i. KS 1—SOA 1

    "Ave Maria" ("Hail to thee, Mary") e.i. OPS 1

"Ave Sanctissima, we lift our souls to thee." See Evening song to the Virgin♦

Ave verum ("Jesu, word of God incarnate") Mozart. e.l. HSS 2—HSS 4

"Avec tes yeux, Mignonne." See "Mit deinen blauen augen" (Lassen)

Avec une rose. See Like the rosebud (La Forge)

"Avenging and bright." Irish air: Cruachan na Feinne, Crooghan a Venee, or, Mount of the Fenians. Words by T. Moore. FSI—GO—MI—MMI—PI

"Avenging God." See "Gerechter Gott" (Wagner)

Averhill, Sara

    Holyoke (German air)

"Avete pure un pallido visino." See Bianchina (Gordigiani)

Avon. See "God moves in a mysterious way"; Sweet will of God; "There's nothing bright, above, below"

The avowal. J. Eccles. DM 2

L'avvelenato (The poisoned lover) Lombardian folk song. e.i. MSI

"Aw! come now, I'll sing you a song." See The silly old man

Awa, Whigs, awa. Old Scottish song, with additional words by R. Burns. BSB—BOS—MMS—PS 1

    "Our thrissles flourish'd fresh and fair." BSR

Awa wi' your belles and your beauties. See "Adown winding Nith I did wander"

"Awa wi' your witchcraft o' beauty's alarms." Air: Balin a mone. Words by R. Burns. BSR

Awaiaulu. See "The remembrance of our last meeting" (Hopkins)

"Awaiting, awaiting you." See Waiting

"Awake, arise, good Christians." F. Schilling. HC

"Awake! awake." Folk song: Allanstand, N.C. version. CSE

    —Alleghany, N.C. version. CSE

    —Black Mountain, N.C. version. CSE Variants: "O who is that that raps at my window"; The shining dagger

"Awake! awake! and softly arise." See Ständchen (Strauss)

"Awake! awake! glad voices make." C. O. Arnold. Words by W. W. Newton. HC

"Awake, awake, O come with me." See Wandering in the woods (Grieg)

"Awake! awake! 'tis Easter morn." J. H. Hopkins (music and words) HC

"Awake, awake, you drowsy sleeper, awake and listen unto me." See The shining dagger

"Awake! awake! you drowsy sleeper, awake! awake! it's almost day; how can you lie and sleep and slumber." See "Awake! awake" (Allanstand, N.C. version)

"Awake! awake! you drowsy sleeper, awake! awake! it's almost day; who's there? who's there at my doors and windows." See "Awake! awake" (Alleghany, N.C. version)

"Awake from sleep and dreaming." Round. C. Schultz. FSS 6

"Awake from sweetest slumber." See Morning song

"Awake, glad soul! awake, awake." W. A. Smith. HC

"Awake, my soul, and with the sun." Round. FSS 3

"Awake, my soul, and with the sun" (Ward) Scotch air. FSS 4

"Awake, my soul, stretch every nerve." G. F. Händel. Words by P. Doddridge. FSS 4—TL

"Awake, Saturnia." G. F. Händel. Words by Congreve. CS 2

"Awake, sweet love." J. Dowland. BE 4 —BOH—DM 2—PR 1

"Awake thee, my lady-love." See The call

"Awake, ye drowsy maids, awake." See The morning-break

"Awake, ye drowsy swains, awake." See The morning-break

"Awake, ye pretty maids, awake." See May-day carol

"Awake, ye shepherds, instantly." See The angel and the shepherds

"A-walking, a-talking, a-walking went I." See The cuckoo

"Away, away, along our crystal path." See Skaters' song (Schumann)

"Away, away, away, away! the woodlands fair invite." See Hunting song (Weber)

"Away, away, dark clouds, away." Indian air. e. FI

"Away! away! the moon and stars are shining." Auber. FSS 1

"Away, away, to the mountain's brow." See Away to the mountain's brow (Lee)

Away down souf. S. C. Foster (music and words) NMP—WBT

"Away down south on the old Swanee." See Boola song (Hirsh)

"Away down south where I was born." See A long time ago

"Away from Mississippi's vale." See The rose of Alabama

"Away, haul away." See Haul away, Joe

"Away in a manger." Composer unknown. Words by M. Luther. e. MF

"Away in a manger" (Cradle hymn) J. B. Herbert. ₁Words by M. Luther₁ e. OH

"Away in a manger." J. E. Spilman. Words by M. Luther. e. HC Cradle hymn. e. DC

"Away now, joyful riding." F. Kücken. e. FSS 5

"Away the night is balmy." See Mandolinata (Paladilhe)

Away to school. German air. FSS 2

Away to the mountain's brow. A. Lee. HSE 1

Away to the mountain. FSS 7

"Away to the sport in the greenwood." See Chant du chasseur (Meyerbeer)

"Away up in the tower." See The bells

"Away, way down on the old Swanee." See Boola song (Hirsh)

"Away with bondage long enthralling." See La Brabançonne (Campenhout)

"Away! with loyal hearts." J. B. Gray (music and words) HC

"Away with melancholy." W. Mozart. FSS 6—WBT

"Away with these self-loving lads." J. Dowland. Words by F. Greville (Lord Brooke) BE 6—DM 2

"Away, ye gay landscapes." Scottish air: Lochnagarr. Words by Byron. PS 2

"Awful, pleasing being, say." G. F. Händel. SAS 2

The awful wedding. Folk song from Georgia. CSE

The awkward ballad. See Den bakvende visa

"Awn i hela'r ysgyfarnog." See Hela'r 'sgyvarnog

"Ay me! what shall I do." Old English air. BE 7

"Ay, said de black-bird to de crow." See De black-bird an' de crow

"Ay! se fué mi Palomita." See La paloma cuencana

"Ay! sin tu amor, moriré, sí, mujer." See Mi sueño

"Ay, tear the tattered ensign down." See Old Ironsides (German air); Old Ironsides (Klein); Old Ironsides (Lardner)

"Ay, this land her sons and daughters." See "Ja vi elsker dette landet" (Nordraak)

"Ay! vienen los Yankees." Folk song from southern California. e.s. HS

Ay wakin' O. Scottish air. Old song with words altered by R. Burns. BSB—MMS

Aye wakin', O. HSSS—PS 1

Aye waukin', O. SSS

"Simmer's a pleasant time." BSR

"Ay, ye warriors! the Saracenic hydra." See Fu Dio che disse (Apolloni)

Aye sure ("I hear people say") Welsh air. Words by J. Parry. MMW

Aye wakin O. See Ay wakin' O

"Aye yo-o, aye yo-o, I thought I heard our captain say." See Good morning, ladies all

"Ayer me dijistes que hoy." See Cruel Caramba

Aylward, Florence
    Mavourneen

Ayo po. Dakota Indian song. G. Dowanna (music and words) e.in. BF 2

"Ayquanahquog peah bedahgo jing." See Her shadow

"Ayquayquogningah dejah min." See Red blanket

Ayton, Sir Robert
    "I do confess thou'rt smooth and fair" (Lawes) Authorship uncertain

Aytoun, William Edmondstoune
    Annie's tryst (Composer unknown)
    The old Scottish cavalier (Old air)

"**Az** yshir Moshe." See Song of Moses or Miriam

Azmon (Glaser) See "Oh, for a thousand tongues"; "Once more, my soul"

B

Ba-be-bi-bo-bu. CHS—WBT—WC

"**Baa!** baa! black sheep." Nursery song. FSS 4—WA—WBT—WSC—WSW

Baadn-laatt ("Bissam, bissam baadne."—Lullaby) Norse folk song. e.n. MAN

Baadn laatt ("Brumbraskön i bumba."—A humorous lullaby) Norse folk song. e.n. MAN

Baadsmands hus, krusnusidus. See De tre skalke

"The **Babe** in Beth'lem's manger laid." See The Babe of Bethlehem

"A **Babe** is born, all of a Maid." Ancient air. 15th century words. BSC—HC

"A **Babe** is born in Bethlehem." 15th century air. Tr of Puer natus in Bethlehem. e. HC

The **Babe** of Bethlehem. Traditional song. BSC—MCS—MF

Baby Bunting. HSD—WBT—WSC

"**Baby** bye, here's a fly." G. B. Loomis. Words by T. Tilton. FSS 1—JSE—WSC

Baby Charley. Old college air. Words by S. Lanier. LBR

"**Baby** is a sailor boy." See Swing, cradle swing (Cooper)

Baby mine. A. Johnston. Words by C. Mackay. HSD—MP—WBT

"**Baby** owlet, purple owlet." See Tecolotito

"**Baby,** sleep! shadows creep." See Cradle song of soldier's wife

"A **baby** was sleeping." See The angel's whisper

Babylon ("Our harps were tun'd") M. Watson. FMB—HSS 3—HSS 4

Babylon is fallen. H. C. Work (music and words) NMP—WBT

Babylon's fallin'. Negro spiritual. HR

Baby's night. MCS—WBT

Baby's ring. English air. Words by P. Cary. LBR

Bacchanal. F. Chopin. e. KF 4

"**Bacchus,** Iacchus." H. Lawes. Words by A. Tounshend. JE

Bach, Johann Sebastian
"Abide with me." See "Bist du bei mir"
"Ah! my soul" (from Passionsmusik nach dem Evangelisten Johannis)
"All my tears" (from Passionsmusik nach dem Evangelisten Matthäus)
"Ave Maria." See Gounod, C. F. "Ave Maria"

"Before the Father our Redeemer falling" (from Passionsmusik nach dem Evangelisten Matthäus)
"Bist du bei mir"
"Break forth, O beauteous heavenly light" (from Weihnachts-oratorium)
"Bring me cross and cup" (from Passionsmusik nach dem Evangelisten Matthäus)
Chorale. See "Commit thy ways, O Lord"
"Commit thy ways, O Lord" (from Passionsmusik nach dem Evangelisten Matthäus)
"Consider, O my soul" (from Passionsmusik nach dem Evangelisten Johannis)
"Depart! enough, my treasure I retain" (from Weihnachts-oratorium)
"Endure! endure" (from Passionsmusik nach dem Evangelisten Matthäus)
"Forget-me-not." See "Vergiss mein nicht, vergiss mein nicht"
"From ill do Thou defend me"
"Give me Jesus, I implore ye" (from Passionsmusik nach dem Evangelisten Matthäus)
Gladly God exalt, rejoicing. See Jauchzet Gott in allen landen
"Haste, ye shepherds" (from Weinachts-oratorium)
"I follow Thee also" (from Passionsmusik nach dem Evangelisten Johannis)
I wrestle and pray
"If Thy disciples" (from Passionsmusik nach dem Evangelisten Matthäus)
"It is finished" (from Passionsmusik nach dem Evangelisten Johannis)
Jauchzet Gott in allen landen
"Lord, can it be" (from Passionsmusik nach dem Evangelisten Matthäus)
"Mein gläubiges herze frohlocke"
"Mighty Lord, and King all glorious" (from Weihnachts-oratorium)
"My heart ever faithful, sing praises." See "Mein gläubiges herze frohlocke"
"Now let every tongue adore Thee." See Sleepers, wake
Nuremberg. See "Praise to God, immortal praise"; "Songs of praise"
"O Lord, my darken'd heart enlighten" (from Weihnachts-oratorium)
"O Lord, thy love unbounded" (from Passionsmusik nach dem Evangelisten Matthäus)
"O sacred Head! once wounded" (Tr of Salve caput cruentatum)
"Only bleed, tender heart" (from Passionsmusik nach dem Evangelisten Matthäus)
Passion chorale. See "O sacred Head! once wounded"
"Penitence, fearful pain" (from Passionsmusik nach dem Evangelisten Matthäus)
"Praise to God, immortal praise"

Bach, Johann Sebastian—*Continued*
  "Prepare thyself, Zion" (from Weih-
    nachts-oratorium)
  "See now the bridegroom" (from Weih-
    nachts-oratorium)
  "Sighing, weeping, sorrow, need"
  Sleepers, wake
  "Slumber, beloved, and take thy re-
    pose" (from Weihnachts-orator-
    ium)
  "Songs of praise" (same air as "Praise
    to God, immortal praise")
  " 'Tis Thee I would be praising" (from
    Weihnachts-oratorium)
  Venetian boatmen's song
  "Vergiss mein nicht, vergiss mein
    nicht"
  "What tongue can tell Thy greatness,
    Lord"
  "Whate'er may vex or grieve thee"
  "Ye foes of man, your might is shaken"
    (from Weihnachts-oratorium)
Bach, Wilhelm Friedmann
  "Kein hälmlein wächst auf erden"
  "Soft dews from heaven falling." See
    "Kein hälmlein wächst auf erden"
Bachelet, Alfred
  Chère nuit
  Dearest night.   See Chère nuit
Das bächlein.   See The brook (Bleikh-
    man)
Bachmetieff, Nicholas Ivanovitch.   See
  Bakhmetiev, Nikolaï Ivanovich
Il bacio (The dream of home) L. Arditi.
  Words by Aldighieri.   e.i.   SS 2
"Back from the wedding coming."   See
  "En revenant de noces"
"Back in the time when my grandfather
  wed."   See Das grossvaterlied
"Back of father's cottage."   See "Derrièr'
  chez mon père, vole, mon coeur, vole"
"Back to a happy day."   See "Torna ai
  felici dì" (Puccini)
Back to the army again.   G. F. Cobb.
  Words by R. Kipling.   SSS
"Back yonder at my father's."   See Le
  prisonnier de Holland (Breton version)
Backer-Gröndahl, fru Agathe Ursula
  At sea.   See Tilsjös
  Late.   See Sildig
  Lind
  The linden.   See Lind
  "Now sleeps the wave."   See "Nu
    somnar vågen"
  "Nu somnar vågen"
  Sildig
  Tilsjös
  When the linden's in flower.   See
    Lind
Backer-Lunde, Johan
  Genrebillede
  Idyl.   See Genrebillede
  Laengsel
  Longing.   See Laengsel
Backus, B. E.
  Raise the song for Easter
"Backward and forward under the moon."
  See Song of the sea (Eayrs)

"A backward glance across the billows."
  See Epilog (Grieg)
"Backward, turn backward, oh, time in
  your flight."   See Rock me to sleep
  (Leslie); Rock me to sleep (Mueller)
Bacon, Leonard
  God be with us (Hatton)
Bada bene.   See Statt' attiente
The baffled knight.   17th century song.
  CO 2
The bag-pipes ("Hrály dudy") Czech folk
  song.   bo.e.   BF 1
Baggesen, Jens Emanuel
  "Seit vater Noah in becher goss" (Ger-
    man folk air)
Bagrinovskiï, M.
  "All the bells, the little bells"
Baildon, Joseph
  "Adieu to the village delights"
  "From the east breaks the morn"
  "Let gay ones and great" (from Love
    in a village)
  "When I drain the rosy bowl"
The bailiff's daughter of Islington.   17th
  century air: The jolly Pindar.   BE 1
  —BOH—BOS—CO 2—CS 1—DM 1
  —HSE 1—MM—MSS 1—SS 1
  —Somerset version.   SEF 2
  Variant: The maid of Islington
Baillie, Lady Grizel (Hume)
  Were na my heart licht I wad dee
    (Scottish air)
Baillie, Joanna
  The blackcock (Welsh air)
  The maid of Llanwellyn (Welsh air)
  "The morning air plays on my face"
    (Welsh air)
  "O swiftly glides the bonnie boat"
    (Scottish air)
  "O welcome bat and owlet gray"
    (Welsh air)
  The robbers (Parker)
  Woo'd and married and a' (Scottish
    air)
Bainbridge, Leslie
  "Whilst Bethlehem's shepherds kept
    their flocks" (Smith)
"The bairnies cuddle doon at night."   See
  Cuddle doon
"The bairns gat out."   See The deuks
  dang ow're my daddie
"Baja esos ojos."   Mexican folk song.
  e.s.   HS
Baker, Annette
  For ever mine (Cantor)
  "Sleep on, sleep on, my beloved one"
    (Cantor)
Baker, C. S.
  Gems and flowers of rich perfume
Baker, Sir Henry Williams, bart.
                Composer
  "Art thou weary, art thou languid" (Tr
    of Kopon te kai kamaton)
  Stephanos.   See "Art thou weary, art
    thou languid"
                Author
  "The King of love my Shepherd is"
    (music by Dykes; Gounod)

Baker, J. G.
  My trundle-bed
Baker, John C.
  Old Granite state (wrongly attributed)
    See Hutchinson, J. J. Old Granite
    state
Baker, Thomas
  How happy we have been
Baker, W. C.
  "Hark! I hear an angel sing" (Shrival)
Baker university hymn. J. Hatton.
  Words by I. A. Ahlborn. CHS
Bakewell, John
  "Hail, Thou once despised Jesus"
    (Spanish air)
Bakhmetiev, Nikolaĭ Ivanovich
  The Cossack's lullaby
  The Jamschick's complaint
Den bakvende visa (The awkward ballad)
  Norse folk song. e.n. MAN
Balakirev, Miliĭ Aleksĭeevich
  "Burning out is the sunset's red flame"
  The call of freedom
  The desert
  Der fichtenbaum. See The pine-tree
  Invocation. See To Russia
  Mnye li molodsu razoodálomu. See
    The call of freedom
  Nachtstück. See Nocturne
  Nocturne
  "Oh come to me when breezes stir"
  The pine-tree
  To Russia
  "Viens près de moi." See "Oh come
    to me when breezes stir"
  Zapyévka. See To Russia
Balance a straw. J. Oswald. BE 8
"Bald gras' ich am Neckar." See Das
  ringlein
"Bald ist der nacht ein end' gemacht." See
  Morgen-hymne (Henschel)
"Bald prangt, den morgen zu verkünden."
  W. A. Mozart. Words by E. Schik-
  aneder. g. ED 2
Baldwin, Henry R.
  "Rejoice to-day with glad accord"
    (Southwick)
Baldwin, L. E.
  A parody song (Composer unknown)
Il balen del suo sorriso. G. Verdi. e.i.
  SOA 4
  Il balen del suo sorriso (Bright her
    smiles) e.i. OPS 4
  Tempest of the heart. e.i. HSD.
    e. only FSS 6—WA
Balfe, Michael William
  The arrow and the song
  Brightest of golden days
  "Come into the garden, Maud"
  "Come with the gipsy bride"
  Couldst thou but know
  "The dawn is breaking"
  "Ever be happy" (from The enchan-
    tress)
  Fair land of Poland (from The Bohe-
    mian girl)
  "From rushy beds of silver Nile" (from
    Keolanthe)
  Gipsy song (from The Bohemian girl)

  Good night, good night, beloved
  "The green trees whispered low and
    mild"
  "Happy and light" (from The Bohe-
    mian girl)
  "The heart bowed down" (from The
    Bohemian girl)
  "Her gentle voice"
  "I dreamt that I dwelt in marble halls"
    (from The Bohemian girl)
  "In this old chair my father sat" (from
    The maid of honor)
  Killarney
  "Let Erin remember the days of old"
  "The light of other days"
  "Norah darling"
  "Oh, the land that we love"
  "The peace of the valley"
  Pirates' chorus
  Pity one in childhood torn (from The
    Bohemian girl)
  The power of love (from Satanella)
  The scarlet and black (same air as
    Silver and gold)
  Scarlet and cream (same air as Silver
    and gold)
  "See at your feet" (from The Bohemi-
    an girl)
  Serenade. See "Stars of the summer
    night"
  Si tu savais. See Couldst thou but
    know
  Silver and gold
  "A soldier's life has seen of strife"
  Starlight is streaming (from The siege
    of Rochelle)
  "Stars of the summer night"
  Then you'll remember me (from The
    Bohemian girl)
  "They tell me thou'rt the favour'd
    guest" (from The seige of Ro-
    chelle)
  Vive le roi
  We may be happy yet (from The
    daughter of St Mark)
  "When other lips." See Then you'll
    remember me
  The yellow and blue
Balfour, Mary
  "The dew each trembling leaf en-
    wreath'd" (Irish air)
Ball, Edward. See Fitzball, Edward
Ball, William
  Dear native home (Composer un-
    known)
  Light o' love (16th century air)
  The vine-dressers' song (Weber)
The ballad of John Dory. See John Dory
A ballad of the Boston tea party. Air:
  Yankee Doodle. Words by O. W.
  Holmes. LBR
Ballantine, James
  Castles in the air (Composer unknown)
  Ilka blade of grass (Wilson)
Ballatine, W. G.
  "God save America! here may all
    races" (Lvov)
De ballet of de boll weevil. Texas song.
  BF 2

Ballinamona Oro ("With my Ballinamona Oro") Irish folk song.   JOI

Ballinamona Oro ("You know I'm your priest") Irish air: Ballinamona. Words by J. O'Reefe (i.e. O'Keeffe)   MMI

Ballindown braes.   Ulster air.   JOI

Ballmont, Konstantin.   See Balmont, Konstantin

Ballou, Harry J.
"Don't forget dar's a weddin' to-night"

Balm in Gilead ("Sometimes I feel discouraged") Negro spiritual.   DF

Balm of Gilead ("Massa lov'd his good old Jamaica") H. T. Bryant.   WBT

Balmont, Konstantin
Longing (Vassilenko)
"O my beloved one" (Vassilenko)
The siren (Grechaninov)

"The balmy breeze is softly sighing."   See Sérénade à Juanita (Jouberti)

Baloo, baloo, my wee, wee thing.   See Scotch cradle-song

"Baloo, my boy" (Lady Ann Bothwell's lament) 17th century song.   PS 2

"Balooloo, my lammie."   Scottish air. Words by C. Nairne.   HSSS

Baltzell, Winton James
"Thou art mine, thou art mine"

Bán-cnoic Éireann óg (The fair hills of Eire O) Irish folk song.   e.ir.   BF 2

De band o' Gideon.   See Gideon's band

La bandera de franjas y estrellas.   See The star-spangled banner (Smith)

"Die bange nacht ist nun herum."   See Reiterlied (Lyra)

Bange trauer.   For English and Italian translations see "Esser mesto" (Flotow)

"Banging of the hammer."   See Music of labor

"Bangry Rewey a-courting did ride."   See Sir Lionel (North Carolina version)

"Banish thy sorrow."   G. F. Händel.   e. BD

Banished.   Ojibway Indian song.   e. BA

Banister, John
"Come unto these yellow sands"
"Full fathom five"
"He that is a clear cavalier"

The banks of Allan water.   Traditional air, arr by C. E. Horn.   Words by M. G. Lewis.   BE 6—BOS—CS 1—FSS 6—HSE 1—MSS 1—PO—SS 1—WBT—WL

Allan water.   JO
"On the banks of Allan water."   DM 1 —ME

The banks of Glenoe.   Irish folk song. JOI

The banks of Newfoundland.   Forecastle song.   CR

The banks of the blue Moselle.   G. H. Rodwell.   HSE 2

The banks of the daisies.   Old Irish air. Words by A. P. Graves.   PI

The banks of the Dee.   Vermont song. SSH

The banks of the Devon.   Scottish air: Bhannerach dhon na chri.   Words by Burns.   PS 2

The banks of the Don (Po nad Dónom sad tzvyetyót) M. P. Moussorgsky.   Words by Koltzóff.   e.   SMR 1

The banks of the Lee.   L. Arditi.   FSS 8

The banks of the roses.   Irish folk song. JOI

The banner-bearer's death.   See La mort du porte-enseigne

Bannocks o' barley-meal   ("Argyle is my name") Old ballad modified by A. Boswell.   MMS
"Argyle is my name."   PS 2

Bannocks o' bear-meal.   Jacobite song. Air: The Killogie.   Words by R. Burns.   MMS—PS 2
"Wha in a brulzie."   BSR

Banville, Théodore Faullain de
"Nuit d'étoiles" (Widor)

Baptizing hymn.   Negro folk song from Kentucky.   KA

Bara Fostus dream.   See The shepherd's joy

Barbara Allen ("In Scarlet town where I was born") English folk song. BOH—BOS—CS 1—DM 1—HSD—HSE 1—JE—PR 1—SMF—WL

Barbara Allan ("In Scarlet town where I was born")   JO

Barbara Allan ("It was in about the Mart'mas time") Scottish version. JO—PS 1

Barbara Allen ("All in the merry month of May") Kentucky version no. 1.   BF 2—WLT

Barbara Allen ("All in the merry month of May") Carmen, N.C. version.   CSE

Barbara Allen ("All in the month, the month of May") Tennessee version.   CSE

Barbara Allen ("In yonders town where I was born") Chicopee co., Ga. version no. 1.   CSE

Barbara Allen ("One cold and cloudy day") Chicopee co., Ga. version no. 2.   CSE

Barbara Allen ("Sweet William was down") Hot Springs, N.C. version CSE

Barbara Allen ("'Twas in the merry month of May") Habersham co., Ga. version.   CSE

Barbara Allen ("'Twas in the merry month of May") Kentucky version no. 2.   CSE

Barbara Allen's cruelty ("In Scarlet town, where I was born")   MM

Barbara Ellen ("In Scotland I was born and bred")   SEF 1—SO

"Le barbare tribù."   See Promesse de mon avenir (Massenet)

Barbarossa ("Der alte Barbarossa") J. Gersbach.   Words by F. Rückert.   g. ED 2

Barbauld, Mrs Anna Letitia (Aikin)
"Come, said Jesus' gentle voice" (Schnyder)
"Praise to God, immortal praise" (music by Bach; Elvey; Kochner; Mason; Pleyel)
The **barberry** (Kalina) J. Komorowski. e.p.   BF 1
Barbier, Jules
Au printemps (Gounod)
Medjé (Gounod)
Noël (Gounod)
See also Carré, Michel, ·jt. auth.
Barbour, Mrs J. H.
"Ring out, ye throbbing stars of night"
Barcarola veneziana (Venetian barcarole) Old Venezian air.   e.i.   NG
Barcarolle ("Belle nuit")   See "Belle nuit" (Offenbach)
Barcarolle ("Come, maiden, come")   See Come to the sea (Roberti)
Barcarolle ("Dites, la jeune belle")   See "Dites, la jeune belle" (Gounod)
Barcarolle ("Nymphes attentives")   See "Nymphes attentives" (Gounod)
Barcarolle ("Silent now")   See "Silent now the drowsy bird" (Offenbach)
Barcarolle ("Sul mare luccica")   See Santa Lucia
Barcarolle ("Waves, oh! cease") Kalliwoda. e.   KSE
La **barchetta** (The little boat) Tuscan song.   e.i.   MSI
Barclay, B. S.
"Come, oh! come with me, the moon is beaming" (Italian air)
Bard, Andreas
Like the rosebud (La Forge)
Bard of Thomond, pseud.   See Hogan, Michael
"The **bard** to Bala journey'd home."   See The bard's visit
The **bard's** lament ("I think upon the lighted halls") Air: Prydain's lament. Words by C. B. Wilson.   MMW
The **bard's** love.   Welsh folk song.   WL
The **bard's** visit ("The bard to Bala journey'd home") Welsh air.   Words from the Welsh of Tegid.   e. MMW
The **barefoot** boy.   C. Johns.   Words by Whittier.   TL
Bargiel, Woldemar
May-bells
Baring-Gould, Sabine
"Britannia's sons, rejoice" (Old English air)
A country dance (Folk air)
"The fields are white to harvest" (Sheppard)
"From thee to me she·turns her eyes" (Old English air)
"Joan's placket is torn" (Old English air)
The last of the singers (Folk air)
The merry haymakers (Folk air)
"The night her blackest sables wore" (Farmer)
"Now the day is over"   (Barnby)
Old Adam the poacher (Folk air)

"Onward, Christian soldiers" (Sullivan)
Plymouth sound (Folk air)
"Sleep, my Saviour, sleep" (Bohemian air)
"The song of the heavenly harvest home"   (Skeffington)
The song of the moor (Folk air)
"The winds were wailing" (Composer unknown)
Barker, George A.
Dublin bay
"I'm leaving thee"
The manly heart.   See "Shall I, wasting in despair"
"Ring out, O bells, ring silver-sweet"
"Shall I, wasting in despair"
"The time of the singing of birds" (same air as Dublin bay)
"Where are the friends of my youth"
The white squall
"Why do summer roses fade"
Barker, Nathan
The graves of a household
The tempest.   See "We were crowded in the cabin"
"We were crowded in the cabin"
Where are those dreamers now.   See The graves of a household
Barker, T. T.
Cradle song of soldier's wife (Composer unknown)
Barker, Theodore T.
Lovely Mary Donnelly
The **Barkshire** tragedy.   Berkshire county song.   BOH
The **barley-mow** ("O I will drink out of the nipperkin, boys") Folk song.   SEF 2 —SO
The **barley** mow ("We'll drink it out of the nut-brown bowl") Folk song.   BOH— DM 2—MM
The **barley** raking.   Folk song.   BSW
The **barley** straw.   Folk song.   BSW
"**Barley's** rare and so is rye."   See Rare the barley, rare the rye, rare the wheat
Barmby, J.
"Good people, give ear" (Swire)
"Et **Barn** er fodt i Bethlehem" (Danish Christmas song) da.e.   DCS
Barn Jesus i en krybbe lad.   For English translation see "Child Jesus came to earth this day" (Gade)
Barnard, Lady Ann (Lindsay)
Auld Robin Gray (Scottish air; also music by Leeves)
Auld Robin Gray: sequel (Scottish air)
Barnard, C.
The gap in the hedge
Barnard, Mrs Charles.   See Barnard, Mrs Charlotte (Alington)
Barnard, Mrs Charlotte (Alington)
Composer
"Come back to Erin"
Dreamland
Drifting
First Christmas gifts
Five o'clock in the morning

Barnard, Mrs C. A.—Composer—*Cont.*
"Hail and farewell."   See Parting
    graduation song
"Jesus, tender Shepherd, hear me"
Little bird on the green tree
"Little by little"
Maggie's secret
Maggie's welcome
"Oh, mother, take the wheel away"
Once upon a time
Parting graduation song
Silver chimes
"Strangers yet"
Under the holly bough
"When all the world is young"
Ye sons of the nation
You and I
            Composer and author
"I cannot sing the old songs"
"Take back the heart"
We'd better bide a wee
Won't you tell me why, Robin
            Author
The blue Alsatian mountains (May-
    brick)
Hope (Benedict)
"I am content" (Sainton-Dolby)
Barnard, D'Auvergne
Bid me to love
Barnard, F. C.
The tar's farewell (Maybrick)
Barnby, Sir Joseph
Alleluia: ancient air arranged
Carmen Etonense
A cradle-song of the blessed Virgin.
    See "The Virgin stills the crying"
Crossing the bar
"The daughters of the city"   (from
    Rebekah)
Dawn
"The day is gently sinking to a close"
"Fair Luna"
"Holy night! peaceful night" (Tr of
    Die heilige nacht)
"How gentle God's commands"
"Like silver lamps"
"May, the maiden" (same air as "Sweet
    and low")
Morning song
"Now the day is over"
"O Babe! in manger lying"
"O Lord, God of my master" (from
    Rebekah
"O paradise, O paradise"
"O sing a song of Bethlehem"
"O ye that love the Lord" (from The
    Lord is King)
Paradise.   See "O paradise"
St Gregory.   See "Ye holy angels
    bright"
Silent night.   See "Holy night! peace-
    ful night"
"The soft southern breeze plays
    around" (from Rebekah)
"Still, still with Thee"
The story of the Shepherd
"Sweet and low"
A thousand leagues away
" 'Twas in the winter cold"

Vale
"The Virgin stills the crying"
"We march, we march"
"When I view the Mother holding" (Tr
    of Parvum quando cerno Deum)
"With overflowing heart, O Lord"
    (from Rebekah)
"Ye holy angels bright"
Barnes, Paul
Good old blue and white will fix you
Barnett, John
The burial of Sir John Moore
"Little Fay, pretty Fay"
"Maid of Athens"
"Oh! for those old familiar friends"
Rise, gentle moon (from Charles XII)
Barnett, John Francis
"The shepherds went their hasty way"
Barnett, R.
Dreaming golden dreams (Scuderi)
Barney Brallaghan's courtship (" 'Twas on
    a windy night") Irish air: Blewitt's jig.
    Words by J. Blewitt.   MMI
Barney Buntline.   Old English air.
    Words by W. Pitt.   FSS 8—JO—
    WBT
Barney O'Hea ("Now let me alone, though
    I know you won't") S. Lover (music
    and words)   FSI—MMI—PI
The **barnyard** song.   Kentucky moun-
    tain folk song.   TFC 2—WLT
    Variant: The farmyard
La **barquillera** (The girl and the wherry)
    Spanish-American song.   e.s.   LSS
A **barquinha** (The little boat) Portuguese
    song.   e.po.   BF 2
Barr, James
"Thou bonnie wood of Craigielea"
Barratt, W. Augustus
Goldthred's song
"A mile an' a bittock"
"Shon Campbell"
Barrett, John
Burton ale
The country fair
"Ianthe the lovely"
"In the pleasant month of May."   See
    The country fair
"No cold approach, no alter'd mien"
    (same air as Ianthe the lovely)
The pilgrim
Barrows, O. R.
Swinging 'neath the old apple-tree
Barry, Mrs Ann Spranger (Street)   See
    Crawford, Mrs Ann Spranger (Street)
    Barry
Barry, Charles Ainslie
"Easter day hath dawned again"
"It is a day of gladness"
Barry, Edward
"Bread to pilgrims given"
Come unto me
The good Shepherd
O esca viatorum.   See "Bread to pil-
    grims given"
L'ombra della croce.   See The shad-
    ow of the cross
Savèd from the storm
The shadow of the cross

Barry, Edward—*Continued*
Song of the old bell
Thy will be done
Barry, Michael Joseph
Saint Patrick's day (Irish folk air)
Bartalus, Stephan
"Seprik a Váradi utczát."   See Vára-
di's highways (attributed)
Váradi's highways (attributed)
Barthe, Grat Norbert
Ô nuit, qui me couvre (from La fiancée
d'Abydos)
Bartholomew, William
Damascus (Costa)
Liebe ist die zarte blüthe (Spohr)
"Lord, at all times I will bless Thee"
(Mendelssohn)
"O könnt' ich fliegen wie tauben dahin"
(Mendelssohn)
Bartholomew fair (The Dutchwoman's
jigg)   17th century song.   CO 2
Bartlett, B. T.
The royal purple
Bartlett, Homer Newton
Highland Mary
"Look not upon me with thine eyes"
Bartlett, Kate
"In the country nigh to Bethlehem"
(Hine)
Bartolillo.   Costa Rican folk song.   e.s.
HS
Barton, Gerard
"It was a lover and his lass"
Barton, J. F.
"Holy Bible, book divine"
Bas, William.   See Basse, William
Basque serenade.   See Sérénade basque
Bassani, Giovanni Battista
"Art thou sleeping, fair one."   See
Dormi, bella, dormi tu
Dormi, bella, dormi tu (from La se-
renata)
Mourn with temerity.   See Seguita a
piangere
Posate, dormite (from La serenata)
Seguita a piangere (from L'amante
placata)
Sleep on, then.   See Posate, dormite
Basse, William
The hunter in his career (Composer un-
known)
Mad Tom (Coperario)
Basse's career.   See The hunter in his
career
Basseti.   See A faithful heart (Abt)
Bassford, W. R.
"Can a little child, like me"
La Bastringue.   French Canadian song.
e.f.   BF 2
Bate, Henry.   See Dudley, Sir Henry
Bate, bart.
Bates, Arlo
When Allah spoke (Fisher)
Bates, Charlotte Fiske.   See Rogé, Mme
Charlotte Fiske (Bates)
Bates, David
"Speak gently—it is better far" (Wal-
lace)

Bates, Katharine Lee
America the beautiful (Ward)
Batlle, Ramon Carnicer y.   See Carnicer
y Batlle, Ramon
Battell, Edith
"Speed up" (Fairfax)
Batterson, Hermon G.
Composer
"O Holy Church, but yester-night"
Author
"Bright Easter day" (Brown)
"Ring on, ye joyous Christmas bells"
(music by Brown; Wilson)
"Batti, batti" ("Chide me, if thou wilt")
W. A. Mozart.   e.i.   PP
"Batti, batti" ("Chide, oh, chide me")
e.i.   KS 1
Batti il tacco, la punta, il pie.   See "Sul
mare torbido"
Battishill, Jonathan
"Amidst the myrtles"
"Come here, fellow servant" (from
High life below stairs)
Kate of Aberdeen
Laus Deo
"The silver moon's enamour'd beam."
See Kate of Aberdeen
The battle eve.   Air: Cruiskeen lawn.
Words by T. Moore.   FSS 4
Song of the battle eve ("To-morrow,
comrade, we")   MI
Battle-cry of freedom ("Der Gott der eisen
wachsen liess'")   See Vaterlandslied
(Methfessel)
The battle cry of freedom ("Yes, we'll rally
round the flag")   G. F. Root (mu-
sic and words)   BD—HSD—MP—
NMH—NMS— OH— TFC 1—WA—
WBT—WSW
The battle hymn of the republic ("Mine
eyes have seen the glory") Air: John
Brown's body, arr by W. Steffe. Words
by J. W. Howe.   BD—BMC—BOS—
BSE— CST— DSH— EF— FMB—
FSS 2— HSC— HSD— JS— JSE—
LA—LBR—MP—NMH— NMS—OH
TL— WA—WBT—WSW
Battle of Agincourt.   See Deo gratias
The battle of Harlem heights.   Words by
G. O. Ward.   CU
The battle of Killiecrankie.   Scottish
song.   PS 2
The battle of St Cast.   See Emgann Sant-
Kast
Battle of the Baltic.   C. H. Purday.
Words by Campbell.   JO
The battle of the Boyne.   See The Boyne
water
Battle prayer.   See Gebet während der
schlacht (Himmel)
Battle-song.   Silcher.   e.   BSE
Baudelaire, Charles Pierre
Harmonie du soir (Debussy)
L'invitation au voyage (Duparc)
La mort des amants (Debussy)
La vie antérieure (Duparc)
"Der bauer schwankt beim stillestehn."
See Hunger song (Cui)

Baum, M. Louise
  Dance and sing (Wilson)
  The gipsy forge (Hungarian air)
  Trainona (Irish air)
  The wild boy (Irish air)
Der **baum** im Odenwald ("Es steht ein baum") Volkesweise after J. F. Reichardt. g. ED 1
Der **baum** im Odenwald. For English translation with a different air see The tree of Odenwald
Bavarian song ("Auf'm berg")   See "Auf'm berg steht a schloss"
Bavarian song ("O wind in the tree tops") See Vom scheib'nschiessen
Bavarian yodel ("All hail to the friendship") e. CHS—MPC—WBT
Bavarian yodle ("Down the mountain side") See The waterfall
Baxter, Richard
  "Ye holy angels bright" (Barnby)
Baxter. See "Thy way, not mine, O Lord" (Burnap)
Bay, Rudolph
  The Dannebrog
  "Denmark, by whose verdant strand"
The **bay** of Biscay. J. Davy. Words by A. Cherry. BE 1—BOH—BOS—DM 1—HSE 1—JO—ME—PR 2—TS —WBT
La **Bayamesa.** Song of the Guarachas. e.s. MP—SN
Bayerisches bierlied ("Das jahr ist gut") Volkslied. g. ED 2
Bayly, Thomas Haynes

Composer

  Lays of a minstrel. See "Oh! 'tis the melody"
  "Oh! 'tis the melody"
  Romeo and Juliet (same air as Long, long ago)
  "Shed not a tear" (same air as Long, long ago)
  Song of praise (same air as "Gaily the troubadour")
  "Touch not the cup" (same air as Long, long ago)

Composer and author

  "Fly away, pretty moth"
  "Gaily the troubadour"
  Lang', lang' ist's her. See Long, long ago
  The long ago. See Long, long ago
  Long, long ago
  "We met, 'twas in a crowd"

Author

  After many roving years (Horn)
  "Come where the aspens quiver" (Lee)
  "Deck not with gems" (Turnbull)
  Erin is my home (German air)
  "Give that wreath to me" (Felton)
  "I'd be a butterfly" (Bayly)
  "I'll be no submissive wife" (Lee)
  I'm saddest when I sing (Bishop)
  Isle of beauty (music by Rawlings; Whitmore)
  Mistletoe bough (Bishop)

  "Of what is the old man thinking" (Knight)
  "Oh no, we never mention her" (Bishop)
  The pilot (Nelson)
  "The rose that all are praising" (Loder)
  "She wore a wreath of roses" (Knight)
  The soldier's tear (Lee)
  Spanish serenade (Lee)
  When green leaves come again (Bishop)
Bayly, Mrs Thomas Haynes
  "I'd be a butterfly"
"**Bayon, baï, baï, bayon, baï, baï.**" See Cradle song of the poor (Musorgskiĭ)
"**Bayzhig** equayzess ne me negonun." See Wedding song
Bazot, Eugène
  "Vous dansez, Marquise" (Lemaire)
Bdellium. See "Saw ye my Saviour"
"**Be a god and hold me with a charm.**" See Lov'd by thee (Cantor)
"**Be aisy an' list to a chune.**" See Tim, the dragoon (Stanford)
"**Be content with what you have.**" See Song of sunshine
"**Be greeted, ye ladies.**" See "Vaer hilset, i damer" (Grieg)
"**Be handy in the morning.**" See Round the corner, Sally
"**Be hushed, my dear, thy mother's near.**" Slumber song. FSS 6
Be kind to the loved ones at home. I. B. Woodbury (music and words) FSS 3 —HSC— HSD— NMH— WBT—WSC —WSW
Be lordly, Willy, be lordly. Northumbrian ballad. BE 7
"**Be** merry, Christian men, and sing." See Happy Christmas morning (Simper)
"**Be** mine, dear maid." H. R. Bishop. FSS 7
"**Be** not alarm'd, thou gallant stranger." See Infelice sconsolata (Mozart)
"**Be** not so coy." See "Thu' nicht so spröde, schönes kind" (Rubinstein)
"**Be** of good comfort." Cowen. OS 1
"**Be** prepared! zing-a-zing." See The scouts international chorus
Be quick, for I'm in haste. 18th century song. ME
Be still. See Sei still (Raff)
Be still my heart (Miruj, miruj, srce moje) Croatian folk song. e.se. BF 1
"**Be** still my puuwai." See Sweet lei Lehua (Kalakaua)
"**Be** still, O thrush." See Trasten i höstkvällen (Wennerberg)
Be-thae wa-an. See Laughing water
"**Be** thou faithful unto death." Mendelssohn. e. OS 3—SAS 3—TS
"**Be** Thou, O God, exalted high." See Old hundred (Franc)
"**Be** thou twined, O hedgerow of willow." See "Come and twine the slim boughs"
"**Be** thou welcome, dear friend." See "Ti riveggo, Fanny" (Donizetti)

Be true to me fair one. See Sweet lei Lehua (Kalakaua)

Be we merry in this feast. See "In Bethlehem, that noble place" (Ouseley)

Beach, John
Stillness of night

Beale, Thomas Willert
The bells of Aberdovey (Welsh air)
"Let me love thee" (Arditi)
"The old year is dying" (Welsh carol)

Beale, William
Brutus

"**Beam** from yonder star." Serenade. F. F. Bullard. Words by W. P. Foster. HST

Beamish, Florence
"Sleep on, for I know 'tis of me you are dreaming" (Irish air)

Bear a lily in thy hand. Words by H. W. Longfellow. FSS 7—LA

"**Bear** the love of my heart to my land far away." See Bán-cnoic Éireann óg

"The **bear** went over the mountain." BSS —TFC 1

"**Beasts** of the forest." See "Fere selvagge" (Caccini)

"**Beats** there a heart on earth sincere." FSS 4

"Le **beau** galant" ("The gallant soldier") Folk song from Lorraine. e.f. FTF

"**Beau** page! ah! mon beau page." See "Malbrough s'en va-t-en guerre"

Beau soir (Evening fair) C. Debussy. Words by P. Bourget. e.f. SAM

Le **beau** vaisseau (The gallant ship) Pyrenean song. e.f. SSP

"**Beauing**, belleing, dancing, drinking." See The rakes of Mallow

Beaumont, Francis, and Fletcher, John
"Better music ne'er was known" (Douty)
"Take, O take those lips away" (music by Gaillard; Wilson) See Shakespeare, W. "Take, O take those lips away" (music by Gaillard; Wilson)

"**Beauteous** are the flowers of earth." J. Stainer. Words by W. C. Dix. HC

"**Beauteous** land, to thy glory we proudly sing." See Guatemala, en tu limpia bandera (Alvarez)

"**Beautiful** and wide are the green fields of Erin." See The fair hills of holy Ireland

Beautiful bells ("On the breeze") E. O. Lyte. FSS 6—JSE—MCS—WBT

"**Beautiful** bells! O beautiful bells." Words by G. Cooper. HSD

"**Beautiful** blossom, art thou again." See Primula veris (Kleffel)

"A **beautiful** damsel of fame and renown." See The Enniskillen dragoon

The **beautiful** day. D. Hime. FSS 8

"**Beautiful** dreamer." S. C. Foster. HSD —WBT—WL

"**Beautiful** faces." Words by D. Swing. FSS 3

"**Beautiful** girl, come walk with me." See Le méchant guillon

"**Beautiful** isle of the sea." J. R. Thomas. Words by G. Cooper. HSD

Beautiful Istria. See Oll Istria (Georgieri)

The **beautiful** little vale of Araglin. See Glounthaun Araglin eeving

The **beautiful** maid. Braham. HSE 2

Beautiful Minka. Russian folk song. e. FSS 6—JSE
A Russian melody. e. BSE
"Schöne Minka" (Der Kosak und sein mädchen) g. ED 1

Beautiful Nancy. Folk song from Hampshire. SF 3

Beautiful nose (Und' e bukur) Albanian song. al.e. BF 2

The **beautiful** Rhine. German song. e. FSS 7

"**Beautiful** sea, beautiful sea, oh how I love on thy bosom to rove." Children's song. FSS 8—WBT

"**Beautiful** sea! beautiful sea! on thy calm bosom ever I'd be." E. Ransford. FSS 3

"**Beautiful** spring-time." Verdi. FSS 2

"**Beautiful** star in heaven so bright." S. M. Sayles. HSD—WBT

"**Beautiful** Venice." J. P. Knight. Words by J. E. Carpenter. FSS 2

"**Beautiful** Waipio" ("Maikai Waipio") Likelike. e.h. HA

"**Beauty** and Love." H. Lawes. PR 1

Beauty in eclipse. W. Lawes. MM

Beauty's eyes. F. P. Tosti. Words by F. E. Weatherly. CU—KF 3—MSF 1 —NML—WA—WBT—WL

The **beaver** hunt. Cycle of four Ojibway Indian songs. e.in. BA

Because he loved you so. W. R. Dempster. Words by E. Akers. FSS 7

"**Because** I love you, dear." C. B. Hawley. Words by W. H. Stanton. MSF 1

"**Because** she had a foretop." See Haul on the bow-line

Because you're you. V. Herbert. Words by H. Blossom. HSD

Beck, R. H.
The nightingale and the rose (Hawley)

Beckel, George W.
My little valley home

Beckel, James Cox
Old easy-chair by the fire

Becker, Niklas
Der deutsche Rhein (Kunze)

Becker, Reinhold
Frühlingszeit. See "Wenn der frühling auf die berge steigt"
Spring-time. See "Wenn der frühling auf die berge steigt"
Springtide. See "Wenn der frühling auf die berge steigt"
"Wenn der frühling auf die berge steigt"

Becker, Wilhelm Gottlieb
Composer
The fortune in the daisy (same air as Sommer-abendlied)
Sommer-abendlied
Welcome, fair evening.   See Sommer-abendlied
Author
Frühlingsempfindung (Sterkel)
Das geständnis (André)

Becket, Thomas à
Composer
"Britannia, the pride of the ocean" (same air as Columbia, the gem of the ocean)
The red, white and blue ("Britannia, the pride")   See "Britannia, the pride of the ocean"
Composer and author
Columbia, the gem of the ocean
The red, white and blue ("O Columbia, the gem")   See Columbia, the gem of the ocean

Beckman, Bror
En låt i tri toner
Three promises.   See Tre löften
Tre löften
A tune in three keys.   See En låt i tri toner

Bed-time ("The evening is coming") WBT —WSC
The **bed-time** song ("Saw a crow") Kentucky mountain song.   WLT
A **bed-time** song ("Sway to and fro") E. W. Nevin.   Words by L. D. Rice. HST

"**Bedda**, palchi tanti peni."   See Cantu di janna

"**'s beddleweibl** woll kîarfirt'n gehn."   See 's lied vom Wiener beddlmandl

Beddome, Benjamin
"Heirs of unending life" (Nägeli)

Bede, Cuthbert, pseud.   See Bradley, Edward

Bedenklichkeiten ("Grad aus dem wirtshaus") Spanish air: La madrilena. Words by H. von Mühler.   g.   ED 1

Bedford, Herbert
Three shadows

Bedford, Mrs Liza (Lehmann)   See Lehmann, Liza

Bedingfield, W.
True happiness (18th century air)

Bedlam.   Folk song.   SEF 1—SO
Variant: Bedlam city

Bedlam city.   Folk song from Hampshire. SF 3
Variant: Bedlam

Bedouin love song.   C. Pinsuti.   Words by B. Taylor.   AB 2—CB—FSS 6

"**Bedwas** hills, the voice of sorrow."   See Lament

The **bee.**   See "To heal the smart a bee had made" (18th century song)

The **bee** and the pup.   BSS

"The **bee** is to come and the bee is to hum."   See Amina's song

The **bee** proffers honey but bears a sting (Tink a tink)   C. Dibdin, junr. HSE 2

"**Been** a-lis'nin' all de night long."   See Hard trials

Been a listening ("Some say that John the Baptist") Negro spiritual.   JP
Variant of: "I've been a-list'ning all de night long"

"**Been** here since de early morn."   See Get away from dis co'nfiel'

"**Been** praying for the sinner so long."   See I ain't got weary yet

Beer waltz.   Heidelberg song.   e.   WBT

Beers, Mrs Ethelinda (Eliot)
"All quiet along the Potomac" (Dayton)

"**Bees** are all humming."   See Summer is coming (Cooke)

Beethoven, Ludwig van
"Abscheulicher! wo eilst du hin" (from Fidelio)
"Accursed one, where leads thy haste." See "Abscheulicher, wo eilst du hin"
Adelaïde
An die hoffnung
Andenken.   See "Ich denke dein, wenn durch den hain"
Das blümchen wunderhold
Busslied
Christ on the Mount of Olives (from Christus am Ölberge)
Concord hymn
Creation's hymn.   See Die ehre Gottes aus der natur
Death.   See Vom tode
Della vita in sull' aurora (from Fidelio)
Die ehre Gottes aus der natur
Evening
Faithfu' Johnnie: Scottish air arranged
The farewell
"Freudvoll und leidvoll"
Gesang der mönche
Das glück der freundschaft
"God is love; His mercy brightens"
"Good friend, for Jesus' sake forbear" (same air as "In questa tomba oscura")
"Gott, deine gute reicht"
The happiness of friendship.   See Das glück der freundschaft
"Hark! my soul"
"The heavens declare His glory."   See Die ehre Gottes aus der natur
"The heavens resound."   See Die ehre Gottes aus der natur
I love thee.   See "Ich liebe dich, so wie du mich"
"Ich denke dein, wenn durch den hain"
"Ich liebe dich, so wie du mich"
In des lebens frühlingstagen (from Fidelio)
In life's day of springtime beauty.   See In des lebens frühlingstagen
In my spring of life.   See Della vita in sull' aurora
"In questa tomba oscura"

Beethoven, Ludwig van—*Continued*
"In this sepulchral darkness."   See "In questa tomba oscura"
"Joyful and mournful."   See "Freudvoll und leidvoll"
"Kennst du das land"
The kiss.   See Der kuss
"Knowst thou the land."   See "Kennst du das land"
Der kuss
Larghetto (from 2d symphony)
"Life is passing fast away"
"Like morning"
"Lord! who dost see our heavy grief"
"Loud strike the sounding strings"
The man of his word
"Mark yonder tomb."   See "In questa tomba oscura"
Marmotte
Mignon.   See "Kennst du das land"
Mit einem gemalten band
Morning hymn
My faithful Johnny.   See Faithfu' Johnnie: Scottish air arranged
Nähe des geliebten
Nature's adoration.   See Die ehre Gottes aus der natur
"Now with creation's morning song" (Tr of Lux ecce surgit aurea)
"O how kindly hast Thou led me"
"O Jehovah, hear! oh hear me" (from Engedi)
"Oh! my heart is sore within me" (from Engedi)
Ode for Washington's birthday
Open, Lord, my inward ear
Opferlied
The pleasure of melancholy.   See Wonne der wehmuth
The power of God
The praise of God.   See Die ehre Gottes aus der natur
"Praise, praise ye Jehovah's goodness" (from Engedi)
Rapture of melancholy.   See Wonne der wehmuth
Remembrance.   See "Ich denke dein, wenn durch den hain"
Sardis.   See "God is love; His mercy brightens"
The scale
A song of penitence.   See Busslied
"Sweetly sleep"
"Those evening bells" (attributed)
To hope.   See An die hoffnung
"To Thee, my God."   See "Gott, deine güte reicht"
To-day and to-morrow
Das treue Johnie.   See Faithfu' Johnnie: Scottish air arranged
Vom tode
"What sorrow pierceth the righteous David's heart" (from Engedi)
With a painted ribbon.   See Mit einem gemalten band
Wonne der wehmuth
The beetle (Le hanneton)   M. Moussorgsky (music and words)   e.   SC

Beevor, M. L.
The bride's farewell (Williams)
Befiehl du deine wege.   For English translation see "Give to the winds"
"**Before** Jehovah's awful throne."   F. M. A. Venua.   Words by I. Watts. WBT—WS
"**Before** my eyes beheld him."   See "Wie nahte mir der schlummer" (Weber)
"**Before** my window."   S. Rachmaninoff. Words from the Russian of G. Galina. e.   NM 2—SC
Before the battle ("By the hope within us springing")   Air: The fairy queen. Words by T. Moore.   MI
Before the battle ("Kahkeenah wahweengay") Ojibway Indian song.   e.in. BA
"**Before** the Father our Redeemer falling." Bach.   e.   OS 4
"**Before** the gates a fountain."   See Der lindenbaum (Schubert)
"**Before** the Lord we bow."   See God reigns (Mendelssohn)
"**Before** the sun rose at yester dawn."   See Pulse of my heart
Begegnung (The encounter)   H. Wolf. Words by E. Mörike.   e.g.   GM
The **beggar.**   Folk song from Exmoor. SEF 2—SO
The **beggar-boy.**   See Tiggargossen
The **beggar girl.**   18th century song.   H. Piercy.   JO—ME
   "Over the mountain."   FSS 6
"A **beggar** man laid himself down to sleep." See Rumsty ho
The **beggar's** blessing (Da pomianet Gospodi.—Stikh nishchikh) Russian folk song.   e.   SSR 2
Beggar's song (Chant du mendiant) J. Wihtol.   Words from the Russian of Vieting.   e.f.   NM 2
"**Begli** occhi, io non mi pento" ("I yielded without repenting")   J. A. Perti.   e.i. FEI 2
"**Begli** occhi, mercè"   ("Have mercy, dark eyes")   A. F. Tenaglia.   e.i. FEI 1
"**Beglückt,** beglückt, wer die geliebte findet."   See Seligkeit der liebe (Schulz)
Beglückt dorf nun dich.   For English translation see Pilgrims' chorus (Wagner)
"**Begone!** dull care."   17th century air: The queen's jig.   BE 6—BOH—DM 1 —HSE 1—JO—MM—TFC 2—WBT
"**Behind** him lay the gray Azores."   See Columbus
"**Behind** our cabin's a little lake."   See En roulant ma boule
"**Behind** our home there is a pond."   See Le canard blanc
"**Behind** yon hills where Lugar flows." See My Nannie, O
"**Behold** a little Child."   R. Brown-Borthwick.   Words by W. W. How.   HC

"Behold a little, tender Babe." See New Prince, new pomp (Scotch air); New Prince, new pomp (Steggall)

"Behold! a Virgin shall conceive." Händel. OS 2—SAS 2

"Behold above the clear horizon mounting." See Funicoli-funicola (Sailing o'er a summer sea) (Denza)

"Behold, along the dewy grass." F. J. Haydn. e. OS 4—SAS 4

"Behold him, O crag of the mountain." See The American eagle (Foerster)

"Behold, how brightly breaks the morning." See Fishermen's chorus (Auber)

"Behold I am a village lass." S. Storace. Words by P. Hoare. BE 5

Behold! I stand at the door. W. H. Jude. Words by L. Morrison. HSS 3—HSS 4

"Behold, I tell you a mystery." G. F. Händel. SAS 4

"Behold, my love, how green the groves." Scottish air: Doun the burn, Davie. Words by R. Burns. PS 2

"Behold, my love, how green the groves." M. Lock. Words by R. Burns. BSR

Behold that star. T. W. Talley (music and words) BF 2

"Behold, the blushing red roses marry, my darling." See Le mariage des roses (Franck)

"Behold the brilliant sun in all its splendor." See 'O sole mio (Capua)

"Behold the gifts we are bringing, ladoo, ladoo." See Wedding-day song

"Behold the hour, the boat arrive." Air: Oran Gaoil. Words by R. Burns. BSB—BSR

"Behold, the house of God is with men." J. Raff. e. SAS 2

"Behold! the Lord hath done great things for us." See Miriam's song of triumph (Reinecke)

"Behold the monarch of the woods." See Monarch of the woods (Cherry)

"Behold the night is waning." See Adieu, belle France (Niedermeyer)

"Behold the sabre of my father." See The sabre song (Offenbach)

"Behold, the time is come." See Harmonie du soir (Debussy)

Behold thy King. Words by I. Watts. MCS

"Behold, thy King draws near the city gates." See Jerusalem (Parker)

Behold Titania. See Je suis Titania (Thomas)

Behrend, Arthur Henry
Daddy
The gift
"My friend! my friend"

"Bei dem glanz der abendröthe." See Die bekehrte (Wolf)

Bei der wiege (Cradle song) Mendelssohn. Words by Klingemann. e.g. CS 2

"Bei einem wirte wundermild." See Einkehr (Gersbach); Einkehr (Schnyder von Wartensee)

Bei sonnenuntergang ("Fahr wohl! o goldne sonne") J. F. Reichardt. Words by F. Rückert. g. ED 3

Die beiden grenadiere (Les deux grenadiers.—The two grenadiers) R. Schumann. Words by H. Heine. e.f.g. KF 4—PG 4
Die beiden grenadiere (The two grenadiers) e.f.g. AB 1—FO 1.
e.g. only BAS 1—CB—MS
The two grenadiers. e. BC—BD—TL

Die beiden grenadiere. For French and English translations with a different air see Les deux grenadiers (Wagner)

Beim ausmarsch ("Brüder, brüder, jetzt geht's in den krieg") Volkslied aus Franken. g. ED 3

Beim liebchen zu haus (With my loved one at home) Pfeil. e.g. MS

Beim mondenschein ("Gestern beim mondenschein") Volkslied aus Österreich-Schlesien. g. ED 3

Beim rheinwein ("Vom flaschenhaupt den pfropfen fort") H. Gilbert. Words by E. Ritterhaus. g. ED 3

"Being young like myself." See Ballindown braes

"Beir beannact om' croide go tir na n-Éirreann." See Bán-cnoic Éireann óg

Beirly, Alfred
"O weary feet"

"Bejahkah nindegobun." See Midnight tryst

"Bejeenug ningahbedugweshing." See Waiting

Die bekehrte (The elfin's song) H. Wolf. e.g. PG 1

Die bekehrte schäferin ("An dem schönsten frühlingsmorgen") D. Cimarosa. Words by Goethe. g. ED 2

Beketov, Kath.
Lilacs (Rachmaninov)

"Bekränzt mit laub den lieben vollen becher." See Rheinweinlied (André)

"Bel raggio lusinghier" ("Here hope's consoling ray") Rossini. e.i. OPS 1—PP
"Bel raggio lusinghier" ("At last hope's cheering ray") e.i. KS 1—MC

Belanger,
Judith (Concone)
'Tis God who ordains me (Concone)

Belcher, W. T.
"Hark! sweet angel voices singing"

Belén. See Bethlehem (Gounod)

"Believe me, if all those endearing young charms." Air: My lodging is on the cold ground, arr by J. Stevenson. Words by T. Moore. BD—BSE— DSH— FSI— HSC—HSD — JS— MI— NMH— OH— PI—SMF—TFC 1—TS— WA—WBT—WL—WSW
Those endearing young charms. FSS 1—LA—NML

"Believe me not." N. Rimsky-Korsakoff. Words from the Russian of A. Tolstoi. e. NM 2

The **bell.** See La cloche (Saint-Saëns)

"The **bell** doth toll." Round. BD—BSS—FSS 1—HSC— JSE—NMS—OH —TFC 1—WBT

The **bell** is ringing. Round. F. Silcher. FSS 2—HSC—WBT

The **bell-man.** N. Douty. Words by R. Herrick. TL

The **bell** ringer. W. V. Wallace. Words by J. Oxenford. BAS 1—BS 1

The **bell** ringing. Folk song. BSW

"La **bell'** s'est endormi'." See Blanche comme la neige

"La **bell'** si nous étiom' dadans" ("My dear, if we were wandering") Normandy folk song. e.f. SMF

Bell-tones. See Glockengeläute (Hölzel)

Bella, adorata incognita. S. Mercadante. e.i. SOA 2

Bella del tuo sorriso. G. Braga. e.i. SOA 3

Bella del suo sorriso (Fair in her grace so loving) e.i. OPS 3

"**Bella** es la vida." See Laura y Georgina (Campos)

"**Bella** mia" ("Ah! my darling") G. Pergolesi. e.i. SOA 5

"Bella mia" ("O thou loveliest") e.i. KS 5

Bella morettina, tu non senti. See "Guarda la luna"

"**Bella** patria, tu gloria cantamos." See Guatemala, en tu limpia bandera (Alvarez)

"**Bella** porta di rubini" ("Ruby portal, fair, beguiling") A. Falconieri. e.i. FEI 1

"**Bella** ragazza dalla treccia bionda." See La treccia bionda

"**Bella** siccome un angelo." See Serenata

Bellamy, Claxson
Lullaby (Jakobowski)

Bellamy, W. H.
Come unto me (Bliss)
Eulalie (Hobbs)
The lady of the lea (Smart)
"Little Fay, pretty Fay" (Barnett)
"Martin, the man-at-arms" (Loder)
Philip the falconer (Loder)
Simon the cellarer (Hatton)

Bellamy, W. T.
"Through the wood, through the wood" (Horn)

La **belle** au rosier blanc (The fair maid of the white-rose tree) French folk song. e.f. TSF

"La **belle** étoile tombe de son brillant séjour." See Lied (Mertens)

La **belle** Françoise (Pretty Fanny) French Canadian song. e.f. BF 2

Belle Mahone. J. H. McNaughton HSD —WBT

"**Belle** nuit" (O lovely night.—Barcarolle) J. Offenbach. e.f. FMB—PO
"Lovely night." e. BD—WA—WBT—WL—WSW

"La **belle** table est mise" ("Beneath the verdant arbor") Old Provençal Noël. Words by F. Mistral. e.f. CM 1

Belleau, Remi
The pearl (15th century chanson)

Bellini, Vincenzo
"Ah! must ye fade." See "Ah! non credea mirarti"
"Ah! non credea mirarti" (from La sonnambula)
"Ah! non giunge" (from La sonnambula)
"Ah! perchè non posso odiarti"
Aladdin
Aria of Rudolph. See "Gentle maiden"
"Care compagne" (from La sonnambula)
"Casta diva, che inargenti" (from Norma)
Castles in Spain. See Aladdin
"Chaste enchantress." See "Casta diva, che inargenti"
Christmas dawn
Christmas treasures
Christmas waits
"Come per me sereno" (from La sonnambula)
"Come to the home of boyhood's love"
"Do not mingle." See "Ah! non giunge"
The first violets (same air as Aladdin)
Flowers for the brave
"Gentle maiden, those eyes remind me" (from La sonnambula. Tr of Tu non sai in quel begli occhi)
"The Hindoo girl"
The hour of parting
"I am a glad maiden." See Son vergin vezzosa
"I come, I come! ye have called me long"
"If Ser Romeo thy son's life ended." See "Se Romeo tuccise un figlio"
"If thou hast crushed a flower"
"In mia man alfin tu sei" (from Norma)
Ma la sola, ohimè! son io (from Beatrice di Tenda)
"Oh! gladly now we hail thee"
"Oh! mie fedeli" (from Beatrice di Tenda)
"Oh, my bravest and best" (from I Capuleti ed i Montecchi)
Oh! recall not. See "Ah! non giunge"
O remembrance of scenes long vanished. See Vi ravviso, O luoghi ameni
"O rendete mi la speme" (from I Puritani)
"On to the field"
"One by one"
"Quì la voce" (from I Puritani)
"Se Romeo tuccise un figlio" (from I Capuleti ed i Montecchi)
Serenade
"Sing the holly"
Son vergin vezzosa (from I Puritani)
"Sound ye the trumpet" (from I Puritani. Tr of Suoni la tromba)
"Sovra il sen" (from La sonnambula)

Bellini, Vincenzo—*Continued*
"Still so gently o'er me stealing." See "Ah! perchè non posso odiarti"
"Those evening bells"
Vi ravviso, O luoghi ameni (from La sonnambula)
"Where are now the hopes I cherished." See "In mia man alfin tu sei"
"Yes, time with fate e'er striving." See "Ah! non credea mirarti"
"Bellísima trigueña." See La Borinqueña (Astol)
Bellman, Karl Mikael
A butterfly at Haga. See "Fjäriln vingad syns på Haga"
"Fjäriln vingad syns på Haga"
Bellmann, Karl Gottlieb
The fatherland. See "Where is the true man's fatherland"
"Where is the true man's fatherland"
The bellringer's daughter. See Des glockenthürmers töchterlein (Loewe)
The bells ("Away up in the tower") French folk air. Words by J. Erwin. DO
The bells ("Cloques, sonez") See Les cloques
The bells ("Les feuilles s'ouvraient") See Les cloches (Debussy)
The bells ("Hear the sledges with the bells") A. Foote. Words by E. A. Poe. TL
The bells ("I heard the bells") See "I heard the bells on Christmas day" (Hatton)
Bells across the snow. See "O Christmas, merry Christmas" (Lassen)
"The bells are ringing glad and sweet." D. E. Hervey. HC
"The bells are ringing joyfully." G. E. Oliver. HC
The bells of Aberdovey ("In the peaceful ev'ning time") Welsh air. Words by W. Maynard. FSS 7—SS 1
The bells of Aberdovey ("Listen to the joyous bells") Air: Clychan Aberdyfi. Words by Talhaiarn (J. Jones) MMW
The bells of Novgorod (Zvonili zvony v Novgorodîe) Russian folk song. e. SSR 1
The bells of Saint Michael's tower. W. Knyvett. MS
The bells of Seville. W. H. Jude. WBW
The bells of Shandon ("With deep affection") Irish air: The groves of Blarney. Words by F. Mahony (Father Prout) MMI—PI—WBT
Bells of Shandon (The River Lee) FSS 3
Beloved Columbia. F. Ries. Words by F. W. Root. PG 4
"Beloved, it was April weather." See April weather (Rogers)
"Beloved, know'st thou how sweet." See Le mariage des roses (Franck)

Bemberg, Herman
Chant hindou
Hindoo song. See Chant hindou
Venetian song (Tr of Chant vénitien)
"Bemooster bursche zieh ich aus." See Abschied (Methfessel)
"Ben Backstay." SSS
Ben Block the veteran. Collins (music and words) ME
Ben Bolt ("Oh! don't you remember sweet Alice") German air, arr by N. Kneass. Words by T. D. English. BSE—FSS 5—HSC—HSD—JO—LBR—MP— NMH— OH——WA—WBT—WL—WSW
Sweet Alice, Ben Bolt. JS
Benbow, the brother tar. 18th century song. CO 2
"Come all you sailors bold." DM 2
Bencini, Pietro Paolo
"E'er will I sigh." See "Tanto sospirerò"
"Tanto sospirerò"
"Bend, lovely bud." See "Neig', schöne knospe" (Rubinstein)
Bendel, Franz
Heart throbs. See "Wie berührt mich wundersam"
"Wie berührt mich wundersam"
"Wondrous is the power." See "Wie berührt mich wundersam"
Bendemeer's stream. Irish air. Words by T. Moore. BF 2—DSH
"Bendin' knees a-achin'." See O'er the crossing
The bending branch ("To me vîeter vîetku klonit") Ukrainian song. e.r. BF 1
'O bene antico (Lost happiness) E. Nutile. Words by F. Russo. e.i. MN
"Beneath a green shade." Scottish air: The braes o' Ballendyne. Words by T. Blacklock. PS 2
"Beneath our barque the green waters are gliding." See Le Nil (Leroux)
Beneath the branches. See Sous les branches (Hardelot)
"Beneath the cypress' gloomy shade." G. F. Händel. SAS 1
"Beneath the moonlight and the snow." See My birthday (Reichardt)
"Beneath the oak." Serbian song. e. KSE
"Beneath the pines my dearie, O." See Lullaby
"Beneath the ramparts of Béthula." See Judith (Concone)
"Beneath the sky there does not blow." See Song of my dear
"Beneath the trees together." See Love, I will love you ever (Bucalossi)
"Beneath the verdant arbor." See "La belle table est mise"
"Beneath the white-rose tree." See La belle au rosier blanc
"Beneath thy windows I am serenading." See Ipiddinisca sutta li to' finestri
"Beneath your balcony." See Serenata ("Son soto")

"Benedeit die sel'ge mutter" ("Blessed be the tender mother") H. Wolf. Words from an Italian popular song. e.g. CMF 2

Benedicamus Domino. C. Vincent. Words from the German. e. HC

Bénédict, Jean
　Le furet du bois joli (Onfroy de Bréville)

Benedict, Sir Julius
　"By the sad sea waves" (from The brides of Venice)
　"Eily mavourneen" (from The lily of Killarney)
　"Father, whose blessing we entreat" (from St Cecilia)
　He giveth His beloved sleep
　Hope
　How great, O Lord, is Thy goodness (from St Peter)
　"I mourn as a dove" (from St Peter)
　"The Lord is very pitiful" (from St Peter)
　"O house of Jacob" (from St Peter)
　"O Thou afflicted" (from St Peter)
　"On the mountains, when our toil is done"
　Rage, thou angry storm
　"A wondrous change my spirit doth surprise" (from St Cecilia)

The **benediction** ("Del nostro sangue nata") See La benedizione (Gordigiani)

Benediction ("My blessing rest on ye, O woods") P. Tchaikovsky. Words by A. Tolstoi. e.f. NR 2

Benediction ("Spirit of God") See "Spirit of God" (Hopkins)

La **benedizione** (The benediction) Biblical romance. L. Gordigiani. Words by E. Frullani. e.i. CB

Beneken, Friedrich Burchard
　"Wie sie so sanft ruhn"

"Beneseug hey newegewego." See "All birds follow me"

Benet, John. See Bennet, John

Benjamin, Park
　The old sexton (Russell)

Bennet, John
　"My mistress is as fair as fine"
　"Weep, O mine eyes"

Bennett, Henry, and Toleken, of Cork
　"Saint Patrick was a gentleman" (Irish air)

Bennett, Henry Holcomb
　The flag goes by (Foote)

Bennett, Joseph
　"Three kings once lived" (Cowen)

Bennett, Sanford Fillmore
　The sweet by and by (Webster)

Bennett, William Cox
　A thousand leagues away (Barnby)

Bennett, Sir William Sterndale
　The better land
　"Dawn, gentle flower"
　Gentle Zephyr"
　"His salvation is nigh them that fear him" (from The woman of Samaria)
　I will love Thee, O Lord (from The woman of Samaria)
　"Jesus answered" (from The woman of Samaria)
　Long is the night. See To Chloe in sickness
　Maienthau
　May dew. See Maienthau
　"O Lord, Thou hast searched me out" (from The woman of Samaria)
　"O'er the woodlands." See Maienthau
　"Sing, maiden, sing"
　"Sing, mädchen, sing." See "Sing, maiden, sing"
　To Chloe in sickness
　"Whosoever drinketh" (from The woman of Samaria)

Benny Havens, oh. West Point military academy song. CHS—MP

Bensel, Joseph
　"In heavenly love abiding"
　"The shadows of the evening hours"

Benson, J. Allanson
　"A song of spring once more we sing"

Benson, Louis Fitzgerald
　"O sing a song of Bethlehem" (Barnby)

Benyon, V. B. Crowther-. See Crowther-Benyon, V. B.

Benzon, Otto
　Eros (Grieg)
　Sieh dich vor (Grieg)

"Beppe then also loves." See "Ed anche Beppe amò" (Mascagni)

Béranger, Pierre Jean de
　Le roi d'Yvetot (French air)

Béranger's Lisette. See Souvenirs de Lisette (Bérat)

Bérat, Frédéric
　Béranger's Lisette. See Souvenirs de Lisette
　Ma Normandie
　My Normandy. See Ma Normandie
　Souvenirs de Lisette
　"When gloomy winter takes his flight." See Ma Normandie

Les **berceaux** (The cradles) G. Fauré. Words by A. Sully-Prudhomme. e.f. CM 1—HM 1—SAM

Berceuse ("Dans le bois") See "Dans le bois à ma voix" (Massé)

Berceuse ("De son coeur") See "De son coeur j'ai calmé la fièvre" (Thomas)

Berceuse ("Now stillness and dusk") A. Arensky. Words by Tsepkinoi-Kupernik. e.f. NR 3

Berceuse ("Ô petits enfants."—Lullaby) J. G. Ropartz. Words by H. Lucas. e.f. HM 2

Berceuse ("Sleep, my baby") See Cradle-song (Grechaninov)

Berceuse de Yerómushka. See Cradle-song of the poor (Musorgskiĭ)

La **berceuse** du pauvre. See Cradle-song of the poor (Musorgskiĭ)

Berceuse du paysan. See Peasant cradle-song (Musorgskiĭ)

Berg, Isak Albert
Herdegossen
The herdsman's song. See Herde-
gossen
Berg, Philip
Der hirt
Bergen, John Tallmadge
Take my love to Rosalie (Dickhaut)
Bergen op Zoom. Old Dutch war song.
d.e. BSP
Bergen-op-Zoom (Dutch war song.—
"Bergen, thou sturdy and bravest of
towns") e. BMC
Berger, H.
Hawaiian national song. See Our na-
tive land
"Hawaii ponoi." See Our native
land
Our native land
Berger, Ludwig
Die erscheinung
Herbstlied
"In einem kühlen grunde"
Das zerbrochene ringlein. See "In
einem kühlen grunde"
La bergère. See "Il était un' bergère"
La bergère à confesse (The repentant shep-
herdess) French Canadian folk
song. e.f. BFS
Variant of: "Il était un' bergère"
La bergère aux champs. See "Y-a rien
de si charmant"
La bergère de France et le roi d'Angleterre
(The French shepherdess and the king
of England) Norman folk song. e.f.
TF
"Bergère légère" ("Oh, shepherdess fickle")
Bergerette. e.f. WB
"Bergère légère" (Fickle shepherdess)
e.f. PG 3
La bergère muette (The dumb shepherd-
ess) French Canadian folk song. e.f.
BFS
Bergers, pour qui cette fête ("Angels we
have heard on high") Ancient Noël.
e. MF
"Angels we have heard." e. HC
Bergh, Arthur
Red, white and blue
Bergmannslied ("Glück auf") Volkslied aus
dem Odenwald. g. ED 3
Bergsøe, Vilhelm Jørgen
Lind (Backer-Gröndahl)
Bergt, August
Auf einer herbstreise. See Schutz
Beruf zur freude
Schutz
Den bergtagna (The mountain captive)
Swedish song. e.sw. BF 2
Den bergtagna (The mountain-king)
e.sw. HSOS
Bériot, Charles Auguste de
The bluebird
**Bériot, Mme Maria Félicita (Garcia)
Malibran.** See Malibran, Mme Maria
Félicita (Garcia)

Berlin (Mendelssohn) See "Abide with
me! fast falls the eventide"; As pants
the hart; "Sleep, noble hearts"; "Still,
still with Thee"
Berlioz, Hector
Absence
La captive
"Dites, la jeune belle"
For liberty
L'île inconnue. See "Dites, la jeune
belle"
Love in May. See Villanelle
Le spectre de la rose
The spirit of the rose. See Le spectre
de la rose
The undiscovered country. See
"Dites, la jeune belle"
Villanelle
Berls, Johann Rudolf
"Spinne, mägdlein, spinne, so wachsen
dir die sinne"
Spinnerlied. See "Spinne, mägdlein,
spinne, so wachsen dir die sinne"
Bernard de Clairvaux, Saint
"Jesus! the very thought of Thee" (mu-
sic by Dykes; Rossini. Tr of Jesu
dulcis memoria)
"O sacred Head! once wounded"
(Greek air; also music by Bach. Tr
of Salve caput cruentatum)
Bernard de Cluny
"Brief life is here our portion" (Herron.
Tr of Hic breve vivitur)
"For thee, O dear, dear country" (mu-
sic by Herron; Oliver. Tr of O
bona, lumina sobria te speculantur)
"Jerusalem the golden" (Ewing. Tr
of Urbs Syon aurea)
"The world is very evil" (Herron. Tr
of Hora novissima)
Bernard de Ventadour
"Lo! now I bid farewell to Ventadorn"
Berner, Friedrich Wilhelm
Deutscher trost
Frühlings-ankunft
Der spaziergang (same air as Früh-
lingsankunft)
Bernier, Féliz Matos
Así canto mis amores (Pericás)
Puesta de sol (Pericás)
Berridge, Arthur
Ye bells of Christmas time
Berry, Arthur
"Home of the happy and free" (Pease)
Berry, Richard James Arthur
The examiner's song (Lutz)
A medical medley (Lowe)
Beruf zur freude ("Zu des lebens freuden")
A. Bergt. Words by F. von Kopken.
g. ED 3
Die beruhigte (Reassured) Austrian folk
song. e.g. SMF
"Wenn i håld frua afsteh." g. ED 1
Beschnitt, J.
Cottage fair. See Hüttelein
Hüttelein
"Beside a green meadow." S. Glover.
FSS 8

"Beside a weeping willow-tree." See "Assisa a piè d'un salice" (Rossini)

"Beside my campfire's flaring light." See The beaver hunt

"Beside the clear river, the Manzanares." See "Am ufer des flusses des Manzanares" (Jensen)

"Beside the lake of Thun." Modern Swiss ballad. J. G. A. Thiele. e. KSE

"Beside the mill." Gluck. e. FSS 1 —LA

"Beside the old mill-stream we stand." See How happy we have been (Baker)

"Beside the old stone fountain." See Der lindenbaum (Schubert)

"Beside the rolling ocean." See The bonny bunch of roses

"Beside the stream a maiden fair." See Old Dutch song

"Beside the stream and forest tree." See The barberry (Komorowski)

Besly, E. A. H.
"Joyful tidings of a Saviour" (Sullivan)

Bessie Bell and Mary Gray. Scottish air. Words by Ramsay. PS 2

"Bessy's beauties shine sae bright." See Bonny Bessy

"Best beloved, I must say sad farewell tomorrow." See Lebewohl (Silcher)

Best of all. F. Moir (music and words) CB

The best of holidays. Christmas song. MCS

"Das beste bier im ganzen nest." See Margreth am thore (Jensen)

Bestikkelse (Captured) S. Lie. Words by T. Caspari. e.n. SSN

Die betende ("Laura betet") F. W. Rust. Words by F. von Matthisson. g. ED 3

Die betende ("Laura betet") K. F. Zelter. Words by F. von Matthisson. g. ED 2

Bethany. See "Nearer, my God, to thee" (Mason)

Bethlehem (The shepherds' nativity hymn) C. Gounod. Words by H. Farnie. DC
Belén. s. LCP
"Cradled all lowly." FSS 6—HC— MCS

"Bethlehem calls you, waken, O shepherds." See Chirstmas carol

Bethlehem land. T. T. Noble. Words by C. W. Stubbs. HC

The Bethlehem shepherd-boy's tale. W. H. Havergal (music and words) HC

"Bethörte! die an meine liebe glaubt" ("Insensate! to believe that I can love") C. M. von Weber. e.g. KS 2

Bethune, George Washington
"Joy and gladness" (Lissant)

Betinoti, José
A mi madre

"Betray Vincent! shall I my very reason banish." See Mon coeur ne peut changer (Gounod)

Betrayal ("Mein lied ist klein") See Untreu (Cornelius)

Betrayal ("Die rosen, deine schwestern") See Verrath (Zech)

"Betray'd! betray'd." M. Blumner. e. SAS 4

Betsy. Folk song from North Carolina. CSE

The better land. Arkwright. Words by F. Hemans. FSS 6—JO

The better land. W. S. Bennett. Words by F. Hemans. HSE 3

The better land. F. H. Cowen. Words by F. Hemans. WS

"Better music ne'er was known." N. Douty. Words by Beaumont and Fletcher. TL

The better wish. H. Russell. FSS 2— JSE
Robin Ruff. HSD

Betterton, Thomas
"What shall I do, to show how much I love her" (Purcell) Authorship uncertain

Betty and her ducks. Folk song from Dorset. SF 1

Betty Anne. Folk song from North Carolina. CSE

Betty Brown. 18th century song. ME

"Between the darkness and the morn." See Hark! the angel sound

"Between us twain were woven tender ties." See "Un doux lien" (Delbrück)

Beulah land. J. R. Sweney. Words by E. Page or E. P. Stites. FSS 2—JSE

Beuler, J.
Tea in the arbor

Bevacqua Lombardo, L.
Donna Clara (Gastaldon)

Beverly, Mike
"Go, pretty rose" (Marzials)

Beware. J. L. Hatton. Words by H. W. Longfellow. BD

Beyer, Frantz Discke Cappelen
Amid roses. See Millom rosor
Autumn. See Höst
Höst
Millom rosor

"Beyond the city gateway." See Der lindenbaum (Schubert)

"Beyond the starry skies." F. O. Marvin. HC

Beyond the wood ("Tuonne taakse metsämaan") Finnish folk song. e.fi. BF 1

"A bhean-a'-tighe shéimh cuir a déirc amach cun a doill." See An cailín deas ruadh

Bianchi, Francesco
Der liebende. See Vien qua Dorina bella
Vien qua Dorina bella

La Bianchina (Bianchina) L. Gordigiani. e.i. MSI

Bianco, H. Lo.
The Christmas message

Bibabutzemann. e.g. FSS 5. e. only JSE—WBT—WSC

Bickerstaffe, Issac
　　As sure as a gun (Arne)
　　"The echoing horn" (Arne)
　　"Hope, thou nurse of young desire"
　　　　(Weldon)
　　"Let gay ones and great" (Baildon)
　　　　Authorship uncertain
　　When I was a young one (Arne)

Bickersteth, Edward Henry
　　"Thine, Lord, are the blessings of for-
　　　　est and field" (Vincent)

"**Bid** me discourse." H. R. Bishop.
　　Words by W. Shakespeare. BOH—
　　HSE 1—MSS 1—SS 1—VFS

Bid me good-bye. F. P. Tosti. Words
　　by F. E. Weatherly. FSS 5—HSC—
　　NML—WBT—WL—WSW

"**Bid** me to live." J. L. Hatton. Words
　　by R. Herrick. PO—WBW
　　To Anthea. BAS 1—BE 8—HSE 1
　　　　—SSS

"**Bid** me to live." H. Lawes. Words by
　　R. Herrick. BOH
　　"Bid me but live." DM 1
　　Love's votary. MM

Bid me to love. D. Barnard. Words
　　by C. Bingham. WBW

Bid the day be born. A. Randegger.
　　Words by A. C. Swinburne. MCS

"**Bid** yonder rushing river." See "Potrà
　　lasciare il rio" (Supriani)

Bide ye yet. Scottish song. PS 1
　　Byde ye yet ("Gin I had a wee
　　　　house") MMS

Biedermann, E. J.
　　A Vassar chant

Bĭelolitsa, kruglolitsa. See The love-
　　spell

Biely, A.
　　A poet's epitaph (Medtner)

Bier, bier und wein ("Warum sollt im leben
　　ich") Composer and author of words
　　unknown. g. ED 1

Bierlala. College song. CU

Big fat mouse lives in the house. See De
　　tre skalke

Biggs, Edward
　　The Hindustani girl's lament

"The **billet-doux.**" W. Shield. Words
　　by O'Keeffe. ME

Billy boy. Old American air. Boy scout
　　words by G. Kilburn. BSS

Billy boy. For traditional words see My
　　boy Willie

Billy Byrne of Ballymanus. Irish folk
　　song. JOI

Billy Magee, Magaw. See Crow song

"**Bim** was a bull-pup who hadn't any sense."
　　See Bow! wow (Ames)

"**Bin** der kleine tambour veit." See Der
　　kleine tambour (Pohlenz)

"**Bin** ich im wald ferne von dir." See Der
　　hirt (Berg)

"**Bind'** auf dein haar." See "My mother
　　bids me bind my hair" (Haydn)

Binder, Karl
　　"If power divine for once were mine."
　　　　See "Wenn ich einmal der Herr-
　　　　gott wär'"
　　"Wenn ich einmal der Herrgott wär'"

Bingen on the Rhine. J. Hutchinson.
　　Words by C. Norton. JO

Bingham, G. Clifton
　　Bid me to love (Barnard)
　　Dear heart (Mattei)
　　The dear home-land (Slaughter)
　　The good Shepherd (Barry)
　　In old Madrid (Trotter)
　　Jack at sea (Roeckel)
　　Leonore (Trotter)
　　Love's old, sweet song (Molloy)
　　The mission of a rose (Cowen)
　　Morning song (Barnby)
　　Rosemonde (Chaminade)
　　Sion (Rodney)

Bingo ("Here's to B. S. A.") Boy scout
　　song. Words by J. Vinton. BSS

Bingo ("Here's to Columbia college")
　　CU

Bingo ("Here's to good old Yale") March-
　　ing or street song. CHS—NMS—WC

Bingo ("Here's to Rensselaer") MPC
　　—WBT

Bingo ("The miller's big dog") As sung
　　at Brown. WC

"Die **Binschgauer** wollten wallfahrten
　　gehn." See Die Pinzgauer wallfahrt

Binzer, August, freiherr von
　　　　Composer and author
　　"Stosst an! (Jena) soll leben"
　　　　　　Author
　　"Wir hatten gebauet ein stattliches
　　　　haus" (Thüringische volksweise)

Biondina. F. N. Löhr. Words by F.
　　E. Weatherly. CB

"La **biondina** di Voghera" (The fair maid
　　of Voghera) Lombardian song. e.i.
　　MSI

Birch, Samuel
　　"Ah! once when I was a very little
　　　　maid" (Attwood)
　　"At early dawn from humble cot"
　　　　(Attwood)

The **birch** in the meadow (Vo polě be-
　　reza stoǐala) Russian folk song.
　　e. SSR 2
　　The birch tree ("Vo polě bereza
　　　　stoǐala") e.r. BF 1

The **birch-tree** ("Hvi staaer du saa een-
　　som") See Birken (Gade)

"**Birch** tree white stood in the shady forest
　　green." See Woe is me

Birche, William
　　Come o'er the bourne, Bessy (Compo-
　　　　ser unknown)

The **birchen** brand (Luchinushka) Russian
　　song. e.r. BF 1
　　The birchwood splinter (Luchinush-
　　　　ka) e. SSR 2

"**Birches** now are yellow turning." See
　　October (Custance)

"**Birchrids** booming, booming." See
　　Baadn laatt

The **birchwood** splinter.   See The birchen brand

"**Bird** and blossom."   A. A. Wild.   HC

The **bird** and the rose.   A. E. Horrocks. Words by R. S. Hichens.   FMB—MSF 1—SM 2—WBW

"The **bird** let loose."   Air: Devotion. Words by T. Moore.   FSS 1—JSE—LA

"The **bird** let loose"   (The carrier bird) S. Bruce.   Words by T. Moore.   JO

The **bird** of hope.   R. G. Cole.   Words by C. Swain.   BD

"**Bird** of the forest."   G. Verdi.   Words by G. Linley.   FSS 3

"**Bird** of the greenwood."   G. Verdi. FSS 7

"**Bird** of the wilderness"   (The sky-lark) Composer unknown.   Words by the Ettrick shepherd.   FSS 7

"**Bird** of the wilderness"   (The skylark) Scottish air.   Words by the Ettrick shepherd.   PS 2

"**Bird** of the wilderness."   J. Blewitt. Words by the Ettrick shepherd. HSE 2

"A **bird** once sang on the linden tree." See Fågelns visa (Söderberg)

"A **bird** sang out from the linden tree." See Fågelns visa (Söderberg)

The **bird** song.   Folk song: North Carolina version.   CSE
—Vermont version.   CSE
Birds' courting song.   Vermont version.   SSH

The **bird** song ("My bird, my bird, why go, my pet")   Words by Allingham. FSS 1

The **bird** song ("The winter is over") Carol for Easter.   J. D. Herron. Words by A. C. Coxe.   LA

Birdie in the cradle.   F. Abt.   FSS 3—JSE

"**Birdie** sweet."   FSS 7

"**Birdie**, tho' poor, a poor little thing." See Tiggargossen

The **birdies'** maiden-friend.   See La fille aux oiseaux   (Dancla)

The **birdling**.   See L'oiselet   (Chopin)

"**Birdling**, why sing in the forest wide." See Jenny Lind's bird song

"**Birds** are in the woodland."   Kindergarten song.   FSS 2

"The **birds** are singing on the trees."   H. L. Jenner.   HC

"**Birds** blithely sing now."   See Nära (Lindblad)

Bird's courting song.   See The bird song (Vermont version)

"**Birds** in the night."   A. Sullivan. Words by L. H. Lewin.   FSS 5—HSD—JSE

"**Birds** in the night"   (Lullaby) LA—MSS 1

"The **birds** must know."   Arbor day song. Words by H. Hunt.   FSS 5

The **bird's** nest   ("A briery lane where wild-birds sing")   Words by H. Thomas.   FSS 7

The **bird's** nest ("Ho-o ha-re ha-re ha-re." —Song of the bird's nest)   Pawnee Indian song.   in.   FIS

Birds of a feather.   E. Jakobowski. WBT

"The **birds** sleeping gently."   See Alice, where art thou   (Ascher)

The **bird's** song.   See Fågelns visa (Söderberg)

Birge, G. R.
Cornell   (Composer unknown)

Birken   (The birch-tree)   N. W. Gade. Words by C. Hauch.   da.e.   WM 1

Birkhead, Matthew
The freemason's health   (17th century air; also Welsh air)

The **birks** of Aberfeldy.   Scottish air. Words by R. Burns.   BSB—JO—PS 1
The birks o' Aberfeldy   (Bonnie lassie, will ye go)   MMS
"Now simmer blinks on flow'ry braes." BSR

The **birks** of Invermay.   Scottish air. Words by D. Mallet.   PS 1

The **birth** of Christ   ("How still the earth")   See La naissance du Christ

The **birth** of Christ ("The time draws near")   A. Reichardt.   Words by A. Tennyson.   MCS

The **birth** of the harp.   See "'Tis believed that this harp" (Tanieev)

The **birthday** of a King ("The flow'rs so fair have faded")   Guglielmo.   Words by H. Martin.   MCS

The **birthday** of a King ("In the little village of Bethlehem")   W. H. Neidlinger. DC

Biscardi, L.
Lu carcerato p'ammore
Il carcerato per amore.   See Lu carcerato p'ammore
Chelle che tu me dice
Love's prisoner.   See Lu carcerato p'ammore
"Quello che tu mi dici."   See Chelle che tu me dice
"What thou of me requirest."   See Chelle che tu me dice

Bishop, Sir Henry Rowley
"Ah! County Guy."   See County Guy
"And has she then fail'd in her truth"
"Are there tidings"
"As it fell upon a day"
"Be mine, dear maid"
"Bid me discourse"
The bloom is on the rye.   See When the bloom is on the rye
"By the simplicity of Venus' doves"
Chime again, beautiful bells
"Come live with me, and be my love"
"Come, my gallant soldier, come"
County Guy
The dashing white sergeant
Every bullet has its billet
"Hail to the chief"

Bishop, Sir Henry Rowley —*Continued*
   "Hogar, por ti suspiro."   See Home,
      sweet home
   Home, love and liberty
   Home, sweet home (from Clari)
   I'm saddest when I sing
   "Little Love is a mischievous boy"
   "Lo! here the gentle lark"
   Love has eyes
   The mistletoe bough
   "My boat is on the shore"
   My heart and lute
   "My pretty Jane."   See When the
      bloom is on the rye
   "Oh! firm as oak"
   "Oh no, we never mention her"
   "Oh! where do fairies hide their heads."
      See When green leaves come again
   The pilgrim of love
   Pretty mocking bird
   "Rest, my child"
   "Should he upbraid"
   The sun o'er the mountain
   "Take, oh! take those lips away"
   "Tell me, my heart"
   "'Tis when to sleep"
   To Greece we give our shining blades
   "'Twas clear and cold"
   When green leaves come again
   When the bloom is on the rye
Bishop Butler of Kilçash.   Air: Seoladh
   na n-gamhan.   JOI
Bispham, David Scull
   "Come from the prairies" (Verdi)
   "Now are flown the shades of night"
      (Weber)
   A wealthy lord (Haydn)
"Bissam, bissam baadne."   See Baadn-
   laatt
Bissell, A. D.
   The ghost-dance
Bist du ("Soft as the zephyr") Liszt.
   Words by Metschersky.   e.g. MSS 2
   —SS 2
"Bist du bei mir" ("Abide with me") J. S.
   Bach.   e.g.   NG—PG 3
Biterolf (In the camp of Akkon, 1190.—Im
   lager von Akkon, 1190)   H. Wolf.
   Words by J. V. von Scheffel.   **e.g.**
   FO 2
Bitte ("Dearest heart")   For English
   translation see Entreaty (Bohm)
Bitte ("Weil' auf mir."—Request) R. Franz.
   Words by N. Lenau.   e.g.   FF—FO 1.
   e. only FTS
"Bitter sadness and sorrow."   See Sad-
   ness (Saint-Saëns)
Bizet, Georges
   "Agnus Dei"
   "L'amour est un oiseau rebelle."   See
      Habanera
   Castanet song (from Carmen)
   Chanson du toréador (from Carmen)
   "Close by the walls of Sevilla."   See
      Séguédille
   "Con voi ber."   See Chanson du to-
      réador
   "De mon amie, fleur endormie" (from
      Les pêcheurs de perles)

"La fleur que tu m'avais jetée" (from
    Carmen)
Habanera (from Carmen)
"Here's to you."   See Chanson du
    toréador
I say that by fear I'm not haunted.
    See Je dis que rien ne m'épouvante
I vow that nothing shall prevent me.
    See Je dis que rien ne m'épouvante
"If you love me" (from Carmen.   Tr
    of Si tu m'aimes, Carmen)
"In the woods."   See Vieille chanson
Je dis que rien ne m'épouvante (from
    Carmen)
"Love is like a wild bird rebelling."
    See Habanera
"Ma vie a son secret"
"Me voilà seule dans la nuit" (from Les
    pêcheurs de perles)
"Now a toast! your own I will make
    me."   See Chanson du toréador
"Ô Dieu Brahma" (from Les pêcheurs
    de perles)
"O God of light."   See "Ô Dieu Brah-
    ma"
O lamb of God.   See "Agnus Dei"
"Of my beloved, flower that dreams."
    See "De mon amie, fleur endormie"
Pastorale
"Près des remparts de Séville."   See
    Séguédille
"Quand la flamme de l'amour"   (from
    La jolie fille de Perth)
"A secret tell I thee."   See "Ma vie
    a son secret"
Séguédille (from Carmen)
Sérénade.   See "De mon amie, fleur
    endormie"
A song of the woods.   See Vieille
    chanson
"This flower you gave to me." See "La
    fleur que tu m'avais jetée"
"This flower you threw to me."   See
    "La fleur que tu m'avais jetée"
Toreador song.   See Chanson du to-
    réador
Vielle chanson
"Votre toast, je peux vous rendre."
    See Chanson du toréador
"When the flame of love."   See
    "Quand la flamme de l'amour"

Bjerregaard, Henrik Anker
   Aagots fjeldsang (Norse folk air)
   Norsk fjeldsang (Thrane)
   "Sönner af Norge" (Blom)
Björneborgarne's march (Finnish hymn)
   e.   BSE
Bjørnson, Bjørnstjerne
   Arnes sang (Heise)
   "Der ligger et land" (Nordraak)
   Erstes begegnen (Grieg)
   Det förste möde (Grieg)
   God morgen (Grieg)
   "Ingerid Sletten" (Söderman)
   "Ja, vi elsker dette landet" (Nordraak)
   Jngrids vise (Kjerulf)
   Killebukken (Nordraak)
   Landkjending (Grieg)

Bjørnson, Bjørnstjerne—*Continued*
Olaf Trygvason (music by Grieg; Reissiger)
Over de höje fjelde (music by Kjerulf; Nordraak)
"Prinsessen sad höjt i sit jomfrubur" (music by Grieg; Kjerulf)
En solskins dag (Nordraak)
Sövnen (music by Kjerulf; Reissiger)
Synnöves sang (Kjerulf)
"Tak for dit råd" (Grieg)
Tonen (Nordraak)
Traeet (Nordraak)
The tree (Composer unknown. Tr of Traeet)
Vom Monte Pincio (Grieg)

Black, J. C.
" 'Twas in the winter cold" (Barnby)
"Black as a pall o'er us." See Der seeräuber (Gumbert)
The **Black** Ball line ("I served my time") Halliard chantey. CR
The **Black** Ball line ("In Tapscott's line") Capstan chantey. SE
De **black-bird** an' de crow. Air: We will go er-pickin' up cohn, arr by H. T. Burleigh. Words by R. E. Phillips. BP
The **black** decree ("Let Christians all") Traditional song. BSC
—Shropshire version. WCC
Black-eyed Susan. R. Leveridge. Words by J. Gay. BE 2—BOH—DM 1 —HSE 1—JO—MM—PR 2—WBT
Sweet William's farewell to black-ey'd Susan. CO 2
Black is the colour. Folk song from North Carolina. CSE
"**Black** is the night on every hill." See The kleftman (Seiller)
Black roses. See Svarta rosor (Alfvén)
Black solven. Hunting song. MM
"Last Valentine's day." DM 2
"**Black** swans." See "Svarta svanor" (Hallström)
The **blackbird** ("Oh, siren, whose song from the thicket") Air: Y fwyalchen, or, The blackbird. Words by C. M. Oliver. MMW
The **blackbird** ("On a fair summer's morning") Irish folk song. JOI
The **blackbird** (" 'Twas on a bank") J. Hook. Words by Upton. ME
The **blackbird** ("The valley rings") FSS 6
The **blackbird** in the bush. Folk song. BSW
Blackbirds and thrushes. Folk song. SEF 1—SO
The **blackcock** ("Good-morrow to thy sable beak") Air: Ton y ceiliog dhu, or, The note of the blackcock. Words by J. Baillie. MMW

Blackie, John Stuart
Capped and doctored and a' (Scottish air)
Concerning I and non-I (German air)
Give a fee (Old air)
"Sam'el Sumph" (Scottish air)

Blacklock, Thomas
"Beneath a green shade" (Scottish air)
The **blacksmith** ("Harsh my singing sounds to you."—Le forgeron) T. Koeneman. Words by Skitaletz. e.f. NR 1
The **blacksmith** ("Ich hör' mein schatz") See Der schmied (Brahms)
The **blacksmith** ("Oh! the blacksmith's a fine sturdy fellow") W. A. Mozart. BSE—WBT

Blaikie, James
"Let the merry church bells ring"
"Ring out, sweet Easter bells, ring out"

Blake, J. V.
Waking or sleeping (Composer unknown)
Waking or sleeping: Christmas version (Composer unknown)

Blake, William
The lamb (Chadwick)
"My silks and fine array" (Traditional air)
The piper (Gilchrist)

Blamire, Susanna
"And ye shall walk in silk attire" (English air; also Scottish air)
The waefu' heart (Scottish air)
"What ails this heart o' mine" (Scottish air)

Blamphin, Charles
Brahmin love song
"Just touch the harp gently"
Little Maggie May
"When the corn is waving"

Blanc, Claudius
Parfum de fleur
Perfume of a flower. See Parfum de fleur

"Las **blancas** flores." Folk song from southern California. e.s. HS

Blanchard, E. L.
Song of the hop-pickers (Philp)

Blanchard, G. F.
"God of our boyhood" (same air as "God of our fathers, known of old")
"God of our fathers, known of old"

Blanche Alpen. S. Glover. Words by C. Jefferys. HSD
Song of Blanche Alpen. FSS 3
Blanche comme la neige (White as the snow) French Canadian folk song. e.f. BFS

Blanchecotte, Mme Augustine Malvine
Le fidèle coeur (Vidal)
Le sais-tu bien (Pierné)

Bland, Dora. See Jordan, Mrs Dorothea (Bland)

Bland, James A.
"Carry me back to old Virginny"
De golden wedding
In the morning by the bright light
Oh, dem golden slippers
"**Bland** as the morning breath of June." See A dream of summer
"**Blandt** alle lande" ("Of all the lands") B. M. Hansen. Words by O. Vig. e.n. MAN

The **blanket.** See The weaver (Lieurance)

Blanket fair. Air: Packington's pound. DM 2

Blaris moor. Irish folk song. JOI

Blasco, Eusebio
La perla (Araya?)

Le **blasphemateur** châtié (The blasphemer chastised) French Canadian folk song. e.f. BFS

The **blasphemer** chastised. See Le blasphemateur châtié

"The **blasted,** bloomin' spider." See The spider and the scout

The **blatherskite.** Irish air. Words by A. Stringer. FSI

Blau, Édouard. See Philippe, Adolphe, jt. auth.

"Die **blauen** frühlingsaugen" ("The eyes of spring so azure") F. Ries. Words by H. Heine. e.g. PG 2

"Die **blauen** frühlingsaugen" ("The spring's blue eyes") A. Rubinstein. Words by H. Heine. e.g. GMF

"**Blaw** the wind southerly." Scotch song. SMW

Bleib bei mir (Stay, my darling, stay) A. Reichardt. e.g. FSS 5

Bleikhman, Julius Ivanovich
Das bächlein. See The brook
The brook
Le convoi. See The convoy
The convoy
Liebe. See Love
Love
"Wenn ich in deine augen seh' "
"When gazing in thine eyes." See "Wenn ich in deine augen seh' "

Blémont, Émile
Parfum de fleur (Blanc)

"**Bless** our land with gladness." See Hungarian national hymn (Erkel)

"**Blessed** are the pure in heart." H. Mitchell. BSS

"**Blessed** be that maid Marie." Old English Christmas carol. HC

"**Blessed** be the tender mother." See "Benedeit die sel'ge mutter" (Wolf)

The **blessed** Birth. H. W. Davies. Words by G. Wither. HC

The **blessed** country. F. H. Himmel. ₁Words by E. K. Mills₁ FSS 6

Blessed is He that cometh. See "Salve Maria" (Mercadante)

"**Blessed** night, when Bethlehem's plain." J. W. Sidebotham. Words by H. Bonar. HC

"**Blessed!** O blessed, blessed is He." See "Salve Maria" (Mercadante)

"**Blessed** Saviour, Thee I love." Words by G. Duffield. WBT—WS

"**Blessed** Virgin, behold I kneel before Thee." See Ogni Sabato avrete il lume acceso (Gordigiani)

"**Blessings** on thee, little man." See The barefoot boy (Johns)

"**Blest** be the tie that binds." H. G. Nägeli. Words by J. Fawcett. WBT

"Blest be the tie that binds" (Dennis) FSS 5—MCS

Blest symbol of blest name. B. Briggs. Words by G. W. Cloak. FSS 3

Blewitt, Jonas
The lass of Humberside

Blewitt, Jonathan
Barney Brallaghan's courtship
"Bird of the wilderness"
The cork leg

"**Blick'** ich umher" (Wolfram's address) R. Wagner. e.g. SOA 4

"Ein **blick** von deinen augen in die meinen." See Die liebende schreibt (Mendelssohn)

"Ein **blick** zurück noch von der schwelle." See Epilog (Grieg)

Blicken (The look) H. Alfvén. Words by E. Aarestrup. da.e. WM 1

"**Blight** shall ne'er come to thee, field beloved." See Field beloved (Rachmaninov)

De **blin'** man stood on de road an' cried. Negro spiritual. JB

The **blind** beggar of Bethnal green ("It was a blind beggar had long lost his sight") Rogers. CO 2

The **blind** beggar of Bethnal green ("It's of a blind beggar who'd lost his sight") Folk song: Somerset version. SEF 2

The **blind** boy. C. J. Stanley. Words by C. Cibber. DM 2

The **blind** girl's song. See "Voce di donna" (Ponchielli)

Blind man's buff. See Blinde kuh (Brahms)

Blinde kuh (Blind man's buff) J. Brahms. Words from the Italian. e.g. GM

"**Blink** o'er the burn, sweet Betty." Scottish song. MMS

Bliss, Mrs Maria (Lindsay)
The bridge
Carol, carol, Christians
Come unto me
Far away
My laddie far away
Tired, so tired
Too late, too late

Bliss, Philip Paul
Little birdie in the tree
Now

Bliss. See Seligkeit (Meyer)

"The **bliss** of that first meeting." See Erstes begegnen (Grieg)

"**Blissful** dreams come stealing o'er me." F. Abt. WBT

"The **blithe** birds are singing." Air: Ton y fammaeth, or, Difyrwch gwyr dyfi. Words by C. B. Wilson. MMW

"**Blithely** from the moated churchyard." R. F. Smith. HC

"The **blithest** bird that sings in May." See Ah, well-a-day (Howard)

Block, Alexander. See Blok, Aleksandr Aleksandrovich

Block island song. GO

Blockley, John
The Englishman
"Hearts and homes"
"I remember, I remember the house where I was born"

Blockley, John —*Continued*
  List to the convent bells
  "Love not! love not"
  "The moon is beaming o'er the lake"
  " 'Tis lone on the waters"
  Yesterday
Blodgett, B. C.
  "Fair Smith"
Blödigkeit ("Warum blickt doch so verstohlen") Composer and author of words unknown. g. ED 1
Blok, Aleksandr Aleksandrovich
  A maiden sang (Vassilenko)
  Palm branches (Grechaninov)
Blom, Christian
  "Children of Norway." See "Sönner af Norge"
  "Minstrel, awaken." See "Sönner af Norge"
  National song of Norway. See "Sönner af Norge"
  Den norske nationalsang. See "Sönner af Norge"
  "Sönner af Norge"
Blomman bland blommorna (The flower among flowers) Swedish folk song. e.sw. HSOS
Blondel's lied ("Spähend nach dem eisengitter."—Blondel's song) R. Schumann. Words by J. G. Seidl. e.g. KF 3—PG 3
Blondel's song ("One day a burning fever") Composer unknown. e. BSE
Blondel's song ("Spähend nach dem eisengitter") See Blondel's lied (Schumann)
"Blood, O Maritza." See "Join, O Maritza"
The bloom is on the rye. See When the bloom is on the rye (Bishop)
"Bloom my little bud of rosemary." See Rosemary (Polish song)
"Bloom, my tiny violet." WSC
Bloom on, my roses. F. H. Cowen. Words by R. E. Francillon. FSS 8
Bloomfield, Robert
  Old Ringwood (Hawes)
"Blooming May." See "Blüten mai" (Gluck)
"Blooming youth, sing the song." See Cold water song (Lee)
Blossom, Henry Martyn
  Because you're you (Herbert)
"Blossom, little bud." See Mugur, mugurel
The blossom of the year. Air: Gathering peascods. Words by J. A. Wade. MM
Blossom time. Irish folk song. Words by M. E. Dodge. JSE
Blow, John
  "All my pass'd life"
  "It is not that I love you less"
  The self banished. See "It is not that I love you less"
  "Since the spring comes on"
  "Tell me no more, no more you love"
  "We all to conqu'ring beauty bow"

Blow away the morning dew. Folk song. FSF—SEF 2—SO
"Blow away ye morning breezes." Folk song. BSW
"Blow, blow, thou winter wind." T. A. Arne. Words by W. Shakespeare. BE 8—BOH—DM 1—HSE 1—JE—KSS—ME—PR 2
"Blow, blow, thou winter wind." W. A. Fisher. Words by W. Shakespeare. VFS
"Blow, blow, thou winter wind." J. Sarjeant. Words by W. Shakespeare. SM 4
"Blow, blow, thou winter wind." A. Whiting. Words by W. Shakespeare. TL
Blow, boys, blow ("Blow, my bullies, I long to hear you") Hoisting chantey. HSD—WBT
  For variants see following songs of similar title; also "A Yankee ship"
Blow, boys, blow ("A Yankee ship came down the river") Halliard chantey. CR
Blow, boys, blow ("A Yankee ship came down the river") Long drag chantey. KB
"Blow, boys, come blow together." Pulling chantey. SE
Blow, bugle, blow. W. H. Neidlinger. Words by A. Tennyson. TL
"Blow high, blow low, let tempests tear." Dibdin (music and words) BOH—DM 1—HSE 1—JE—PR 2
"Blow high, blow low, O wind from the west." See The wind from the west
"Blow, my bullies, I long to hear you." See Blow, boys, blow
"Blow the man down." Chantey. SMW
  For variants see following songs of same title
Blow the man down ("As I was a-walking") Halliard chantey. CR
Blow the man down ("As I was a-walking") Hoisting chantey. HSD—WBT
Blow the man down ("As I was going") Chantey. SSS
Blow the man down ("Come all ye young fellows") Chantey. BSS—CR—TFC 1
Blow the man down ("I'm a true English sailor") Hauling chantey. SMW
Blow the man down ("Oh, blow the man down") Halliard chantey. CR
Blow the man down ("Oh, blow the man down") Long drag chantey. KB
"Blow thy horn, hunter." W. Cornish (music and words) CO 1—DM 1—JE
"Blow thy horn, hunter." Traditional air. [Words by W. Cornish] CO 1
"Blow, ye northern winds." See Winter
Blow, ye winds ("'Tis advertised") Forecastle song. CR
Blow ye winds, heigh-ho. See "A capital ship"
"The blude red rose at Yule may blaw." Air: To daunton me. Words by R. Burns. BSB—BSR—PS 1

"Blue against the bluer heavens." See Listening angels (Cowen)

The blue Alsatian mountains. S. Adams. Words by Claribel. FSS 2—HSD— NML— PO— WA— WBT— WL— WSW

The blue and the gray. P. Dresser. MP

The blue and the tan. Sea-scout song. BSS

The blue-bell of Scotland ("Of all flowers") Jordan (same air as The blue bells of Scotland) HSC—JS

The blue bells of Scotland ("O where, tell me where") Jordan. Words by A. M. Grant. Original version of words. HSC—HSD— HSSS—JO —MS—PS 1—WL—WSC— WSW —Altered version of words. BOS— FSS 1—JO— JSE— LA— MMS— MP—NMH—NMS—TFC 2—WA— WBT

Des mädchens klage ("Hinaus, ach hinaus") g. ED 3

The blue bird. See The bluebird (Bériot)

Blue bonnets over the border. Scotch patriotic song. Words by W. Scott. JO—PS 1—SN

The blue dove (Vyletala golubina) Russian folk song. e. SSR 1

The blue-eyed lassie ("I gaed a waefu' gate yestreen") R. Riddell. Words by R. Burns. BSB "I gaed a waefu' gate yestreen." BSR —PS 1

Blue-eyed Mary. German air. Author of words unknown. FSS 2—JO— WBT

The blue flame. Folk song. Modern words. BSW

"Blue is the ocean, changeless and boundless." See Sadko's song of glorification (Rimskiï-Korsakov)

"Blue is the sky." See Punchinello (Tchaikovsky)

The blue Juniata. M. D. Sullivan (music and words) FSS 3—HSC— HSD—JO—JSE—WBT

The blue kerchief. Folk song. BSW

Blue muslin. Folk song. BSW

"Blue waves are sparkling." G. Verdi. Words by U. Fairweather. BD

The bluebird. C. A. de Bériot. JSE— WBT—WSC The blue bird. FSS 1

"Blühe, liebes veilchen." See Der knabe an das veilchen (Schulz)

Blüher, Johann August Grabgesang

"Ein blümchen schön, doch unbekannt." See Das wunderblümchen

Das blümchen wunderhold ("Es bluht ein blümchen irgendwo") L. van Beethoven. Words by G. A. Burger. g. ED 2

Die blume der blumen ("Es blüht eine schöne blume") L. Reichardt. Words by P. O. Runge. g. ED 3

"Die blume die an baches rand." See Das vergissmeinnicht (Suppé)

"Die blümelein sie schlafen." See Sandmännchen

's blümeli ("Han anem ort e blümeli g'seh'") Schweizerisches volkslied. G. J. Kuhn (music and words) g. ED 3

Der blumenkranz. See "By Celia's arbor" (Mendelssohn)

Blumentag ("Des jahres ganze blumenzeit") Volksweise. Words by W. Smets. g. ED 3

Blumenthal, Jacques Answers. See "Do you think of the days" The children's kingdom "Depth of mercy" "Do you think of the days" Life Mary at the tomb Sunshine and rain Venetian boat song

Blumner, Martin "Betray'd! betray'd" (from Der fall Jerusalems) "Despoiled is thy crown of honor" (from Der fall Jerusalems) "My warning heed" (from Der fall Jerusalems) Thine, O Savior, is love unending (from Der fall Jerusalems) "Thou sittest on Thy judgment-seat" (from Der fall Jerusalems) "Unfaithful heart" (from Der fall Jerusalems)

Blunt, Henry "Now join we all with holy mirth" (Stainer)

The blushing maple tree. J. P. McCaskey. Words by H. Aïdé. FSS 6—LA

"Blüten mai" ("Blooming May") C. von Gluck. e.g. MS

Blüthgen, Viktor Strampelchen (Hildach)

Blythe, blythe, and merry was she. Air: Andro and his cutty gun. Words by R. Burns. BSB—HSSS—MMS —PS 1 "By Oughtertyre grows the aik." BSR

"Blythe hae I been on yon hill." Air: The Quaker's wife. Words by R. Burns. BSR

"Blythesome may I see thee." See The rural queen

Boanerges. Mexican folk song. e.s. HS

Boardman, Mrs Sophie Smith The purple and the gold (Elmira college song)

The boar's head carol. Traditional English air. CST—JE—MCS—TFC 2— WCC

"A boat! a boat! haste to the ferry." Round. BD

"A boat, a boat to cross the ferry." See The ferry

The **boat** song ("On we are floating") Weber. FSS 1—LA—WBT—WSC

Boat song ("Our hearts with joy are bounding") D. F. E. Auber. JSE

Boat song ("Row, row, gently row") F.
H. Cowen. Words by E. Oxenford.
BD—MS

Boat song ("With the Loorgeen")   See
Leis an Lurgainn

Boat to cross the ferry.   See The ferry

The **boatie** rows.   Composer unknown.
Words attributed to J. Ewen. JO
—PS 1
"O weel may the boatie row." MMS

The **boatman.**   See Fhir a bhàta

"De **boatman** dance."   See De boatmen's
dance (Smith)

The **boatman** of Kinsale ("His kiss is sweet,
his word is kind") Irish air: An cota
caol. Words by T. Davis. MMI

The **boatman's** farewell to Naples.   See
Addio a Napole

Boatman's return. N. J. Sporle. FSS 3

"The **boatmen** are calling, Stali! Stali." See
Venetian boat song (Blumenthal)

De **boatmen's** dance. D. D. Smith. HSD
"De boatman dance." JSE

"The **boats** are pushing from the shore."
See Good-bye, my little lady (Macy)

The **boatsman** and the chest. Folk song
from North Carolina. CSE

The **boatswain's** story. J. L. Molloy.
Words by F. E. Weatherly. FSS 7

Bob up serenely. E. Audran. e. WBT

Bobbie Shaftoe ("Bobbie Shaftoe's one
year old") English air. Words by
H. H. Harbour. DO

Bobby Shafto ("Bobby Shafto's gone to
sea") Traditional air. Words from
Mother Goose. TFC 2

Bobby Shafto ("Bobby Shafto's gone to
sea") Composer unknown. Words
from Mother Goose. WSC

Boberfeld, Martin Opitz von.   See Opitz
von Boberfeld, Martin

La **boca** de Pepita (Pepita's mouth) Pyrenean song. e.s. SSP

Bocella, Cesare, marchese
"Angiolin dal biondo crin" (Liszt)

Bochsa, Robert Nicholas Charles
Happy Bayadere

Boddien, G. von
"Es blinkt der thau" (Rubinstein)

Bodenstedt, Friedrich Martin von
Es hat die rose sich beklagt (Franz)
"Gelb rollt mir zu füssen" (Rubinstein)
"Ich fühle deinen odem" (Rubinstein)
"Mein herz schmückt sich mit dir"
(Rubinstein)
"Neig', schöne knospe" (Rubinstein)
"Nicht mit engeln" (Rubinstein)
"Seh' ich deine kleinen füsschen an"
(Rubinstein)
Spring song (Weil. Tr of "Wenn der
frühling auf die berge steigt")
"Thu' nicht so spröde, schönes kind"
(Rubinstein)
Ein traum (Grieg)

"Wenn der frühling auf die berge
steigt" (music by Becker; Coenen.
For music by Weil see Spring
song)

The **bodyguardsman** and King Eric. See
Lifdrabanten och kung Erik (Lindblad)

"**Boer** jeg paa det höje fjeld" ("Dwell I
on the lofty mount") Norse folk
song. Words by J. N. Brun. e.n.
MAN

Boer national volkslied. See "Kent gij
dat volk vol heldenmoed" (Rees)

Bohemian Christmas carol ("Narodil se
Kristus Pán") 15th century song.
bo.e. BF 1

Bohemian gipsy song. FSS 7

The **Bohemian** maid ("I'm a sweet Bohemian maid") Bohemian folk song. Air:
Otbytý Pisăr. e. BMC

Bohm, Karl
"Calm as the night." See "Still wie
die nacht, tief wie das meer, soll
deine liebe sein"
Entreaty (Tr of Bitte)
"In a year." See "Ueber's jahr"
Der schwur
"Silent as night." See "Still wie die
nacht, tief wie das meer, soll deine
liebe sein"
"Still as the night." See "Still wie
die nacht, tief wie das meer, soll
deine liebe sein"
"Still wie die nacht, tief wie das meer,
soll deine liebe sein"
"Ueber's jahr"
The vow. See Der schwur

"**Bohn** is to the neophyte in arts." See
The pocket Gray (Newton)

Bohunkus. HSD—MPC—WBT—WC

Boie, Heinrich Christian
Die Lore am tore (Composer unknown)

Boieldieu, François Adrien
C'est la princesse de Navarre (from
Jean de Paris)
Come, thou gracious beauty. See
Viens, gentille dame
Of fair Navarre the princess royal. See
C'est la princesse de Navarre
Viens, gentille dame (from La dame
blanche)

"**Bois,** champs et plaine s'allongent déserts."
See Trepak (Musorgskii)

"**Bois** épais, redouble ton ombre" ("Gloomy
woods, in darkness receive me")
J. B. de Lully. e.f. KS 3
"Bois épais" ("All your shades") e.f.
BAS 2—BS 2

"**Bois** frissonnants, ciel étoilé." See Chanson perpetuelle (Chausson)

Bois-Gontier, Adam
Les premiers aveux (Dancla)

Boito, Arrigo
"L'altra notte in fondo al mare" (from
Mefistofele)
"Dai campi" (from Mefistofele)
"From the fields." See "Dai campi"
"I am the spirit who denieth." See
"Son lo spirito che nega"

Boito, Arrigo—*Continued*
"In the night my babe was taken."
See "L'altra notte in fondo al mare"
"Last night in the deep, deep sea." See
"L'altra notte in fondo al mare"
"Son lo spirito che nega" (from Mefistofele)
"**Boje** tsaria khrani." See Russian national hymn (Lvov)
"**Bolan** mi leži Kara Mustafa." See "Kara Mustafa"
"**Bold** Arder went forth one summer morning." See Robin Hood and the tanner
"**Bold** be your stroke, swift as the light." See Hearts of oak (Campana)
Bold Captain Freney. Irish folk song. JOI
The **bold** dragoon. Folk song. BSW
"**Bold** Dunkins was as fine a mason." See Lamkin (North Carolina version)
The **bold** fisherman ("As I walk'd out") Folk song. SEF 2—SO
The **bold** fisherman ("There once was a bold fisherman") G. W. Hunt (music and words) WBT—WC
"**Bold** General Wolfe." Folk song from Sussex. SF 5
The **bold** Hussar. Hungarian song. e. KSE
"**Bold** Jack, the sailor, here I come." See In every port a wife (Dibdin)
"**Bold** Nelson's praise." Folk song from Worcestershire. SEF 2—SF 4—SO
The **bold** Princess Royal. Folk song from Norfolk. SF 2
"A **bold** young farmer." Folk song from Essex. SF 2
Bolero ("Cuando los matadores") Pyrenean song. e.s. SSP
Bolero ("Domani, domani") See Domani, o me felice (Lillo)
Bolero castellano ("Se piensas enganarme." —"Think not thou canst deceive me") Spanish folk song. e.s. SMF
Bolero castellano (Castilian bolero) e.s. EF
Bolognese, Domenico
Addio a Napole (Neapolitan air)
Napole mio (Neapolitan air)
Bonar, Horatius
"Blessed night, when Bethlehem's plain" (Sidebotham)
"Come and hear the grand old story" (Saxton)
"Come unto me, all ye that labor" (Coenen)
"A few more years shall roll" (Hayne)
"I heard the voice of Jesus say" (music by Dykes; Wild)
Jesus is mine (Perkins)
The peaceful fold (Zundel)
"Thy way, not mine, O Lord" (Burnap)
"When the weary, seeking rest" (Stainer)
"Where the faded flower" (Composer unknown)

Bonden i bryllaupsgarden (The peasant at the wedding) Norse folk song. Words by N. P. Heyberg. e.n. MAN
The **bondmaid**. See L'esclave (Lalo)
The **bonds** of love. W. H. Jones. CHS
Boney. Short drag chantey. CR
For variants see songs of similar title, as "Boney was a warrior"; Bonny; "Bonny was a warrior"; "Oh, Boney was a warrior"
"**Boney** was a warrior." Long drag chantey. KB
Bonheur, Theo.
The clang of the hammer
The red scarf
"Le **bonheur** est chose légère" ("Happiness is a thing of changes") C. Saint-Saëns. Words by J. Barbier and M. Carré. e.f. PG 1
"**Bonjour, Suzon**" ("Good-morning, Sue") L. Delibes. Words by A. de Musset. e.f. SAM
"**Bonjour, Suzon**" ("Good-day, Susanne") e.f. PG 3—PG 4
"**Bonjour, Suzon**" ("Good morning, Claire") E. Pessard. Words by A. de Musset. e.f. HM 2
La **bonne** aventure. Old French song. f. DO
Bonne nuit (Sweet good-night) J. Massenet. Words by C. Distel. e.f. KF 1—KF 2—KF 3—PG 1
"**Bonne** Sainte Anne, grande Sainte" (Hymn to Saint Anne) French fishermen's song. e.f. SMW
Bonnie. See Bring back my Bonnie to me
The **bonnie** banks of Loch Lomond. See Loch Lomond
Bonnie bell ("The smiling spring") Scottish border air. Words by Burns. MMS
"The smiling spring comes ir rejoicing." BSR—PS 2
"**Bonnie** Bessie Lee." Scottish air. Words by R. Nicoll. PS 2
The **bonnie** blue flag. H. Macarthy. Words by A. Chambers-Ketchum. BSE—FSS 6—HSD—JSE—WBT
"The **bonnie**, bonnie bairn, who sits poking in the aes." See Castles in the air
The **bonnie** breast-knots. Scottish song. PS 2
The **bonnie** brier-bush. See "There grew a bonnie brier-bush at our ha' door"; "There grows a bonnie brier-bush in oor kail-yaird, and white are the blossoms on't"
Bonnie Charlie. Atributed to N. Gow. Words by Nairne. FSS 1—JSE—WBT
"Bonnie Charlie's now awa." BOS
Will ye no come back again. PS 2
Will ye no more back again. SSS

Bonnie Doon. J. Millar. Words by R. Burns. BSE—FSS 1—JO—JSE—TFC 2—WBT—WL
"Ye banks and braes." BOS—BSB—BSR—CS 1—HSSS—MMS—PS 1—SSS

Bonnie Dundee ("To the lords o' convention") Attributed to C. Sainton-Dolby. Words by W. Scott. BOS—BS 1—DSH—EF—FSS 6—GO— HSD—JO LA—MMS—PS 1—SN—WBT

Bonnie Georgie Campbell ("Hie upon Hielands and laigh upon Tay") Scottish song. MMS

"Bonnie hills of heather." A. F. Harrison. Words by J. Selwyn. ·FSS 3

The bonnie house o' Airlie ("It fell on a day") Old Scottish ballad. MMS—PS 1

Bonnie Jean. See "There was a lass and she was fair"

Bonnie lad and gentle lassie. Scottish song. FSS 3

Bonnie laddie, Highland laddie. Air: Highland laddie. Words by C. Walker. PS 1
"Where ha'e ye been a' the day." MMS

The bonnie lass o' Ballochmyle. See "'Twas even—dewy fields were green" (Jackson)

Bonnie lassie, will ye go. See The birks of Aberfeldy

Bonnie Lizzie Baillie. Scottish song. PS 2

Bonnie wee thing. Air: The bonnie wee thing. Words by R. Burns. BSB—MMS—PS 1
"Wishfully I look and languish." BSR

Bonnières, Robert de
Madrigal dans le style ancien (Indy)
Le manoir de Rosemonde (Duparc)

"The bonniest lad that e'er I saw." Air: The Highland laddie. Words by R. Burns. BSR

Bonny ("Oh, Bonny was a warrior") Hauling chantey. SMW
For variants see songs of similar title, as Boney; "Boney was a warrior"; "Bonny was a warrior"; "Oh, Boney was a warrior"

Bonny Bessy. Scottish air. Words by A. Ramsay. PS 2

The bonny bird. Folk song. BSW

The bonny bunch of roses. Folk song. BSW

Bonny Eloise. J. R. Thomas. Words by C. W. Elliott. TFC 1—WBT—WL
Bonny Eloise, the belle of the Mohawk vale. HSD

"The bonny gray-eyed morn." Attributed to J. Clark. BE 2—DM 2—MM

The bonny keel laddie. Air: The bonny pit laddie. SMW

The bonny lighter-boy. Folk song. SEF 1—SO

The bonny milkmaid. See "Ye nymphs and sylvan gods"

Bonny Nell. Old English air. Modern words by H. F. Sheppard. BE 8

"Bonny Peggy Ramsay that any man may see." See Peg o' Ramsay

The bonny sailor. J. Hook. ME

"Bonny was a warrior." Pulling chantey. SE
For variants see songs of similar title, as Boney; "Boney was a warrior"; Bonny; "Oh, Boney was a warrior"

Bononcini, Giovanni Battista
"L'esperto nocchiero" (from Astarto)
"Eyes so tender." See "Per la gloria d'adorarvi"
"For the love my heart doth prize." See "Per la gloria d'adorarvi"
"If where a wound is." See "Se mai vien tocca"
"Love leads to battle." See "Pupille nere"
"Per la gloria d'adorarvi" (from Griselda)
"Proud and peerless." See "Per la gloria d'adorarvi"
"Pupille nere"
"Se mai vien tocca" (from Calpurnia)
"Since 'tis glory to adore you." See "Per la gloria d'adorarvi"
"Though I only bow before you." See "Per la gloria d'adorarvi"
"Vado ben spesso congiando loco" (attributed; attributed also to Salvator Rosa)
"The wise sailor steering." See "L'esperto nocchiero"

Bononcini, Giovanni Maria
"Ah! why let me ever languish." See "Deh più a me non v'ascondete"
"Deh più a me non v'ascondete"
"Have pity, my beloved." See "Pietà, mio caro bene"
"Oh, those charming lights." See "Deh più a me non v'ascondete"
"Pietà, mio caro bene"

"Bonsoir le maître la maîtresse." See L'Aguignolé

De boodschap van Maria (The message of Mary) Dutch song. d.e. BDF

"De book of revelation God to us revealed." See Going to heaven

Boola song ("Away, way down."—Adelina, the Yale Boola girl) A. M. Hirsh. OH—WC
Adelina, the Yale Boola girl. CHS

Boola song ("Well, here we are") Yale athletic version. A. M. Hirsh. OH—WC
Yale Boola song. CHS—MPC

Boosey, William
Come to me (Denza)
"Over the heather" (Moir)
"Sweet are the charms of her I love" (Leveridge)

Booth, Josiah
    "All my heart this night rejoices" (Tr of Fröhlich soll mein herze springen)
    "O little town of Bethlehem"
    "Once o'er the fields of Bethlehem"
    "Pansies, lilies, roses"
    "A song of spring once more we sing"
    "The spring-tide hour"
    "When wilt Thou save the people"
The **bootmaker.**   See Sapateia

Boott, Francis
    The sands o' Dee
The **border** widow's lament ("My love he built me a bonnie bower") Traditional Scottish song. BMC
    "My love built me a bonnie bouir." MMS

Bordèse, Luigi
    David chantant devant Saül
    David singing before Saul. See David chantant devant Saül

Bordèse, Stéphan
    Simple aveu (Thomé)
Borel, G.
    Lou nouvè di pescaire
    Lou revestidon
La **Borinquen** ("Borinquen, la isla") E. S. de Fuentes. Words by F. G. Marin. s. LCP
Borinquen ("La tierra de Borinquen") F. Astol. Words by M. Fernández Juncos. s. LCP
La **Borinqueña** ("Bellísima trigueña") F. Astol (music and words) s. LCP
"**Borinqueños** marchemos adelante." See La canción del soldado (Pujals)
Borland, J. E.
    "Love came down at Christmas"
"**Born** amid the rugged wildwood." See "Nasce al bosco" (Händel)
"**Born** but to labor in sorrow." See Non più mesta accanto al fuoco (Rossini)
"**Born** of a pain undying." See "Aus meinen grossen schmerzen" (Franz)
Born of Maiden fair. See "Christ is born of Maiden fair" (Gauntlett)
"**Born** of the midnight cold." See Croon of the dew (Gilbert)
"**Born** on the summit of a lofty mountain." See Boanerges
"**Borne** on the breeze a martial strain." See Soldier's departure for foreign service
"**Borne** on the mirror of clear flowing waters." See Auf dem wasser zu singen (Schubert)
"**Borne** on wings of song away." See Die lerche (Rubinstein)
Bornemann, Wilhelm
    Jägerleben (Folk air)
Bornhardt, Johann Heinrich Carl
    Sehnsucht
    Zitherbubens morgenlied
Borodin, Aleksandr Porfir'evich
    Arabian melody
    Arábskaya melódia. See Arabian melody
    Chanson de la forêt sombre. See Song of the dark forest

    A dissonance
    The fair garden
    The false note. See A dissonance
    Fleurs d'amour. See Flowers of love
    Flowers of love
    A lament
    "Lentement baissa le jour." See "Slowly the daylight departs"
    La mer. See The sea
    "Mon chant est amer et sauvage." See "My songs are envenomed and bitter"
    "My songs are envenomed and bitter" (Tr of Vergiftet sind meine lieder)
    La princesse endormie. See The sleeping princess
    La reine de la mer. See The sea-queen
    The sea
    The sea-queen
    The sleeping beauty. See The sleeping princess
    The sleeping princess
    "Slowly the daylight departs" (from Prince Igor)
    Song of the dark forest
Børresen, Hakon
    "Hvis du har varme tanker"
    "If you have kindly feelings." See "Hvis du har varme tanker"
    Landscape. See Landskab
    Landskab
Borrow, W.
    "In the early morning, early"
    "Ring out, ring out a joyful peal"
    "Slowly fall the snow-flakes"
Borte (Gone) E. Grieg. Words by H. Ibsen. e.n. WM 1
Borthwick, R. Brown-. See Brown-Borthwick, R.
Bortñánskiĭ, Dmitriĭ Stepanovich
    Glory to the Lord in Zion
    "Kol' slaven." See Glory to the Lord in Zion
    Vesper hymn
Der **böse bach** ("Du bach mit den silbernen wellen") Volksweise. Words by H. Hoffmann von Fallersleben. g. ED 3
"**Bòshe** zaria chrani." See Russian national hymn (Lvov)
"**Boss** is callin', (huh!)." See Hammerin' song
Bossetti, Carlo
    "Would I were with thee"
Boston ("From Boston harbor we set sail") Forecastle song. CR
The **Boston** come-all-ye (The fishes) Forecastle song. CR
Boswell, Sir Alexander, bart.
    "Argyle is my name" (Scottish air)
    Conway castle (Welsh air)
    Cornish May song (Old Cornish air)
    "Good night and joy be wi' ye a'" (Scottish air)
    "I'll ha'e my coat o' gude snuff-brown" (Scottish air)
    Jenny dang the weaver (Gardner)
    Jenny's bawbee (Scottish air)

Botany bay.   Folk song: English version. SEF 2—SO
—Vermont version.   SSH
The botany class.   Edinburgh university song.   Air: Kate Dalrymple.   SSS
"Both sexes give ear."   Folk song. BSW
Botschaft (The message)   J. Brahms.   e.g. BAS 2
Böttcher, Dorothea
"Ueber's jahr" (Bohm)
Böttiger, Karl Wilhelm
Ändå (Lagercrantz)
Kväll och frid (Geijer)
Boucher, J. B.
"Simple carollers are we"
Boucicault, Aubrey
"I plucked a quill from Cupid's wing" (Hadley)
Boucicault, Dion
Pat Malloy (Composer unknown)
The wearing of the green (Irish air)   Additional words
Boulter, Ben C.
The crib and the cross (Boulter)
Boulter, Bertha C.
The crib and the cross
Boulton, Harold
The gentle maiden (Old Irish air)
Pretty Polly Oliver (Old English air)
Skye boat song (Scottish air)
"Bound prentice to a waterman."   J. Sanderson.   Words by W. Cross. BE 6
Bound with chains.   See Serenata ("Bella siccome")
"Bounding billows, cease your motion."   Words by M. D. Robinson. FSS 2—JO
The bouquet.   A. Alpheraky.   Words after Hafiz.   e. NM 1
Bourdillon, Francis William
Farewell (Hadley)
"The night has a thousand eyes" (music by Hanlyn; Olds)
Bourée du Mont Doré (Ancient bourrée from Auvergne) French song.   e. GO
Les bourgeois de Chastres.   For English translation see "The good men all of Chastres"
Bourges,
Le retour des promis (Dessauer)
Bourget, Paul
Beau soir (Debussy)
Les cloches (Debussy)
Romance (Debussy)
Bourne, William St Hill
"The sower went forth sowing" (Bridge)
Bouval, Jules Henri
The clouds.   See Les nuages
Fleur messagère
A flower message.   For Fleur messagère
Les nuages
Bow! wow ("Bim was a bull-pup")   F. Ames.   Words by A. Guiterman. BSS
Bow-wow-wow ("When I first came down")   Rutgers college song.   L. Bragdon. CHS

"Bow'd the rose with her burden."   See I seraljens lustgard (Sjögren)
Bowdoin beata.   Bowdoin college song. CHS
Bowen, Craufurd Townshend
"Sing we merry Christmas"
Bowen, E. E.
"Forty years on" (Farmer)
The bowld sojer boy.   S. Lover (music and words)   FSS 7—HSD—JO— MP— WBT
Bowline chanty.   Norwegian sea song.   e.n. SMW
Bownes, J.
"Hearken to the thankful reapers" (Smith)
"Twine the Easter garland" (Lissant)
Bowring, Sir John
"God is love; His mercy brightens" (music by Beethoven; Conkey)
"Watchman, tell us of the night" (music by Mason; Parry)
While to Bethl'em going (Rousseau)
The boy and the cuckoo. WSC
The cuckoo. FSS 6
"Boy, I adore you, my golden laddie."   See Ráda song
"A Boy is born in Bethlehem."   German air.   Tr of Puer natus in Bethlehem.   e. HC
"A Boy-scout hiked with careless stride."   See Three good turns
Boy scout march.   M. S. Morison (music and words) OH
The Boy scouts.   Arr from F. von Suppé.   Words by D. Stevens. BSS
The boy with the magic horn.   See Der knabe mit dem wunderhorn (Schumann)
Boyce, William
Heart of oak
The silent lover
"Softly rise, O southern breeze" (from Solomon)
"Tell me, lovely shepherd" (from Solomon)
"Tell me no more I am deceived"
"Tho' Chloe's out of fashion"
"When Orpheus went down"
Boye, Caspar Johannes
Sang for Danske (Weyse)
The Boyne water.   Irish folk song. JOI
The battle of the Boyne ("July the first in Oldbridge town") MMI
"Boys and girls come, let us all go."   See Sapateia
"Boys and girls come out today."   See Haymaking song
"The boys and girls went a-huckleberry hunting."   See Huckleberry hunting
The boy's dream.   W. H. Monk. BSC
The boys of Mullaghbawn.   Irish folk song. JOI
"Boże! coś Polske."   See God for Poland (Kurpinski)
"Boże prar de ti što spase."   See Serbian national anthem (Jenko)

La Brabançonne. Belgian national anthem. F. Campenhout. Words by L. Dechez, surnamed Jenneval. e.f. FMB— MP—NA— WA— WBT—WSW. e. only BD—BMC —CST
La Brabançonne ("Who'd have believed such self-willed daring") e.f. BSP

Bracken, Thomas
God defend New Zealand (Woods)

Brackett, Frank Herbert
Proposal

Bradbury, William Batchelder
As when the traveler
Bright was the star
"Chide mildly the erring"
"He leadeth me"
"Just as I am" (same air as As when the traveler)
Marching along
My own native land
"Rally 'round the flag"
"Sweet hour of prayer"
To Thy cradle throne

Bradley, Arthur
The morning-break (English air)
The slighted swain (Composer unknown)
Colin's request (Monro)

Bradley, Edward
Joyful tidings (Verdi)
Shepherds in the field (Verdi)

Bradley, William Aspenwall
Van Am (Composer unknown)

Bradsky, Wenzel Theodor
Du bist mein all'
Meiner mutter. See To my mother
Thou art mine all. See Du bist mein all'
To my mother

Brady, Nicholas. See Tate, Nahum, jt. auth.

The **braes** aboon Bonaw. Scottish air. Words by W. Gilfillan. PS 1
The **braes** o' Balquhidder. R. A. Smith. Words by R. Tannahill. JO—PS 1
The braes o' Balquither. FSS 3
The **braes** o' Gleniffer. Scottish air: Bonnie Dundee. Words by R. Tannahill. FSS 7—JO—PS 2
The **braes** of Mar. Scottish air. Words by A. Laing. PS 2
The **braes** of Yarrow ("Busk ye, busk ye, my bonnie, bonnie wife") Scottish air. Words by Hamilton. PS 1
"The **braes** they are aflame with whin." See Bright darling of my heart

Braga, Gaetano
Angel's serenade. See La serenata
Bella del sorriso (from Reginella)
Fair in her grace so loving. See Bella del sorriso
La serenata

Bragdon, Loren
Bow-wow-wow

Braham, Dave
Paddy Duffy's cart

Braham, John
All's well (from The English fleet)
The anchor's weighed
The beautiful maid
The death of Nelson (from The Americans)
"Is there a heart that never lov'd"
"No more by sorrow"
The origin of gunpowder
"Said a smile to a tear"
'Tis but fancy's sketch
"When Vulcan forged the bolts of Jove." See The origin of gunpowder

"**Brahma, Dieu des croyants.**" See Chant hindou (Bemberg)
"**Brahma** divine! O Lord whom creation confesses." See "Ô Dieu Brahma" (Bizet)
"**Brahma, God of the Hind.**" See Chant hindou (Bemberg)
"**Brahma, thou mighty god.**" See Chant hindou (Bemberg)
Brahmin love song. C. Blamphin. FSS 4

Brahms, Johannes
"Ah! sweet my love." See "Wie bist du, meine königin"
An eine Aeolsharfe
At the forge. See Der schmied
The blacksmith. See Der schmied
Blind man's buff. See Blinde kuh
Blinde kuh
Botschaft
By the window. See Vor dem fenster
Cradle song. See Wiegenlied
The disappointed serenader. See Vergebliches ständchen
"E'en in slumber do I languish." See "Immer leiser wird mein schlummer"
Eternal love. See Von ewiger liebe
Feldeinsamkeit
"Grant me but one single smile, love." See "Wenn du nur zuweilen lächelst"
A hasty vow. See Vorschneller schwur
"How fair art thou, my lovely queen." See "Wie bist du, meine königin"
"I said, I will forget thee." See "Nicht mehr zu dir zu gehen"
"Immer leiser wird mein schlummer"
"In summer fields." See Feldeinsamkeit
"Lighter far is now my slumber." See "Immer leiser wird mein schlummer"
"Like a blossoming lilac." See "Meine liebe ist grün"
The little dustman. See Sandmännchen: folk air arranged
Love song. See Minnelied
Love triumphant. See Von ewiger liebe
Lullaby. See Wiegenlied
"Lullaby, and good-night." See Wiegenlied
Die mainacht
"Meine liebe ist grün"

Brahms, Johannes —*Continued*
The message. See Botschaft
Minnelied
My heart is in bloom. See "Meine liebe ist grün"
My queen. See "Wie bist du, meine königin"
Nachtigall
"Nicht mehr zu dir zu gehen"
A night in May. See Die mainacht
Nightingale. See Nachtigall
"Ruhe, süssliebchen"
Sandmännchen: folk air arranged
Sandyman. See Sandmännchen: folk air arranged
Sapphic ode. See Sapphische ode
Sapphische ode
Der schmied
Die schwälble
Serenade. See Ständchen
Slumber song ("Hush-a-by and good-night")
Slumber-song ("Ruhe, süssliebchen") See "Ruhe, süssliebchen"
Sonntag
Ständchen
Summer dreams. See Feldeinsamkeit
Sunday. See Sonntag
The swallow. See Die schwälble
"A thought like music." See "Wie melodien zieht es mir"
To an Aeolian harp. See An eine Aeolsharfe
The vain suit. See Vergebliches ständchen
Vergebliches ständchen
Von ewiger liebe
Vor dem fenster
Vorschneller schwur
"Wenn du nur zuweilen lächelst"
"Wie bist du, meine königin"
"Wie melodien zieht es mir"
Wiegenlied
Braley, Berton
"Casey Jones" (Newton)
Co-ca-che-lunk (College air)
One of a jolly crew (Composer unknown)
The parlor scout (College air)
Scout marching song (Old English air)
Tramp, tramp, tramp (Root)
Bramley, Henry Ramsden
"The great God of heaven" (Traditional air no. 1; traditional air no. 2)
Branch, Anna Hempstead
The first violets (Bellini)
Brand, Charles A.
Don't I though
Brandreth, Henry
Truth in absence (Harper)
Brandts-Buys, Jan
Petrus klage
The remorse of Peter. See Petrus klage
Brassier, Joseph von
Schifferlied (Italian air)
Braun, Albert
The river's message
Braun, Anton
Mutterseelenallein

Brautjungfernlied ("Wir winden dir den jungfernkranz") C. M. von Weber. Words by F. Kind. g. ED 1
Brautlied. For English translation see Bridal chorus (Wagner)
"Brave grenadiers rejoice." H. Carey. DM 2—MM
"Brave Llewelyn turn'd and sigh'd." See The departure of the king
Brave Lord Willoughby. See Lord Willoughby (Byrd)
Brave men of Kent. R. Leveridge. Words by T. D'Urfey. BE 7
The man of Kent. CO 2
"Brave my bark set sail." See Tölf synir
"Brave of heart and warriors bold." See "Mandom, mod och morske män"
The brave old oak. E. J. Loder. Words by H. F. Chorley. BAS 1—BE 3—BS 1—DM 1—FSS 2—HSE 3—JO—WBT
Brave Prancer! gay Dasher. See "A funny old fellow" (Brown)
The brave sentinel. P. Rodney. Words by H. Vaughan. AB 1
"Bravely chime, O Easter bells." J. R. Higinbotham. Words by E. Claxton. HC
"Bravely sails my bark." See Tölf synir
The bravest. Ojibway Indan song. in. BA
"Braw, braw lads on Yarrow braes." See Gala water
Bread and butter. R. A. Christison. Words by J. S. Clouston. SSS
"Bread of the world." Words by R. Heber. FSS 4
"Bread to pilgrims given." O. Barri. Tr of O esca viatorum. e. FSS 6
"Break, break, break." W. R. Dempster. Words by A. Tennyson. FSS 3—HSD—JO—WBT
"Break forth, O beauteous heavenly light." J. S. Bach. e. CST
The breaking of the day ("The sun is on the mountain") C. Horn. HSE 2
"The breaking waves dashed high." See Landing of the Pilgrims (Browne)
"Breaks now, breaks now my heart." See At parting
"Breaks the joyful Easter dawn." German air. Words by L. Larcom. HC
"Breaks the joyful Easter dawn." H. G. Gilmore. Words by L. Larcom. HC
The breath of Allah. J. F. Cooke (music and words) BC
"Breath of hawthorne, scent of rose." See The homeward way
"A breath of spring." See "Wie lenzeshauch" (Jensen)
"Breathe balmy airs, ye fragrant flow'rs." See Precious lives (Marshall)
"Breathe on me, breath of God." J. E. Sweetser. Words by E. Hatch. LA
Breathings of spring. Weber. Words by F. Hemans. FSS 2

"**Brede** sejl over Nordsjö gaar." See Olaf Trygvason (Reissiger)

The **breeze**. See La brise (Saint-Saëns)

The **breeze** from home. German air. FSS 3

"**Breeze** of my native city." See Dal più remoto esilio (Verdi)

"A **breeze** plays 'round yon mountain peak." See Petites roses (Cesek)

"The **breeze** was fresh, the ship in stays." See The token (Dibdin)

"**Breezes** from Waban blow gently." See Crew song (Kellogg)

Breezes of other days. See Brises d'autrefois (Hüe)

"**Breit** über mein haupt dein schwarzes haar" ("Thy wonderful eyes my heart inspire") R. Strauss. Words by A. F. von Schack. e.g. CMF 2—FO 2 —GM

Bremner, Robert L.
The student song (Maxfield)

Brennan on the moor. Folk song: English version. CST—FSF
—Irish version. JOI

Brentano, Clemens
"Ich wollt ein sträusslein binden" (Reichardt)
Lorelei (Erk)
"Nach Sevilla" (Reichardt)
Der spinnerin nachtlied (Reichardt)

"**Bretherin**, a long time I lived in sin." See A few more years

Breton, Nicholas
"In the merry month of May" (Wilson)
Phillida and Corydon (Wilson)

Breton sailors' litany. See Er re goli

Brett, Jesse
"Over all the land is glowing" (Brown)
"Sweet Child divine" (Brown)

Bretzner, Christoph Friedrich
Alte freundschaft, alter wein (André)
"Vivat Bacchus" (Composer unknown)
"Wer ein liebchen hat gefunden" (Mozart)

Bréville, Pierre Eugène Onfroy de. See Onfroy de Bréville, Pierre Eugène

Brewer, Alfred Herbert
"I heard the bells on Christmas day"

"**Brewing** mists the lake enshroud." See Herbstgang (Jordan)

"**Brezza** del suol natio." See Dal più remoto esilio (Verdi)

Bridal chorus. R. Wagner. [Tr of Brautlied] e. FSS 3—HSD—OH—TFC 2 —WBT

The **bridal** of Andalla. Arkwright. Words by J. G. Lockhart. JO

A **bridal** party on the Hardanger fjord. See Brudefaerden i Hardanger (Kjerulf)

Bride, Richard
"Hark! hark! the joy-inspiring horn." See The joy-inspiring horn
The joy-inspiring horn

The **bride** bells. J. L. Roeckel. Words by F. E. Weatherly. FSS 3—JSE

"The **bride** she cam' out o' the byre." See Woo'd and married and a'

Brideen ban mo store ("I am a wand'ring minstrel man") Attributed to O'Carolan. Words by E. Walsh. MMI

The **bridegroom's** plea (Kak po sadiku, sadiku) Russian folk song. e. SSR 2
"In the shade of the garden strolling" ("Kak po sadeku") e.r. BO

The **bride's** farewell ("Ah! like the green pear-tree."—Akh! zelena grusha v sadu shataetsîa) Russian folk song. e. SSR 1
"Ah! see the old pear-tree" (Zéléna grusha) e.r. BO—SMF

The **bride's** farewell ("Farewell, mother! tears are streaming") T. Williams. Words by M. L. Beevor. FSS 8

The **bride's** farewell ("Yonder fragrant marjoram") Lithuanian daina. e. KSN—SN

The **bride's** song. See Lied der braut (Schumann)

A **bride's** sorrow. Bohemian song. e. KSE

Bridge, Mrs Elizabeth (Stirling) See Stirling, Elizabeth

Bridge, J. C.
"The shepherds had an angel"

Bridge, Sir John Frederick
"All jubilant with psalm and hymn"
Child divine
"In sorrow and in want"
"Joy, ye people, great and small"
Legends of the Infancy
The morning star
"Past is Lenten sadness"
"The sower went forth sowing"
Welcome be our heavenly King

The **bridge**. M. Lindsay. Words by H. W. Longfellow. FSS 3—HSC—LBR —NMH—WBT

Bridgeman, J.
Old Christmas (Romer)

Bridges, Matthew
"Crown Him with many crowns" (Elvey)
"Rise, glorious Conqueror" (Giardini)

Bridgwater fair. Folk song. SEF 2— SO

"**Brief** life is here our portion." J. D. Herron. Words by Bernard of Cluny. [Tr of Hic breve vivitur] e. LA

Brien the brave. Air: Molly Macalpin. Words by T. Moore. CO—TL
"Remember the glories of Brien the brave." MI—MMI—PI

The **briery** bush. Folk song. SEF 2— SO
Variants: The hangman's song; The maid freed from the gallows

"A **briery** lane where wild-birds sing." See The bird's nest

Briesewitz,
Fiducit

Le **brig** black. f. SMW

Briggs, Bowness
"All hail the gladsome Easter morn"
Blest symbol of blest name
"Come, ye, lift your joyous voices"
"Fare thee well, love, fare thee well"

Briggs, T. F.
Jordan am a hard road to trabbel

Bright, William
"Once again, O blessed time" (music by Dykes; Sullivan)

"Bright angel hosts are heard on high." Cornish air. HC

"Bright beams array the fields at dawn." See The Westmorland hunt

"Bright chanticleer proclaims the dawn." See Old Towler (Shield)

"Bright college years." Yale university song. C. Wilhelm. Words by H. S. Durand. CHS—NMS
Dear old Yale. MPC

Bright darling of my heart (A mhuirnin geal mo chroidhe) Irish air. Words by S. MacManus. FSI

"Bright Easter day." A. H. Brown. Words by H. G. Batterson. HC

"Bright Easter skies." G. W. Marston. Words by A. Burgess. HC

"Bright fairies by Glengariff's bay." See The invocation

Bright her smiles. See Il baien del suo sorriso (Verdi)

"Bright in the east are the clouds of the dawning." See Morning (Tchaikovsky)

"Bright is the sun on the ocean" (Sicilian song) e. BMC

"Bright morning, hail." German song. e. FSS 4

"Bright Phoebus." J. Hook. NG

"Bright red is the sun." See The flower of Finae

"The bright red sun in ocean slept." See Danish love song

"The bright, rosy morning." FSS 2— WBT

Bright sparkles in de churchyard. Negro spiritual. HR
Bright sparkles in the churchyard. JP

Bright star of hope. See "Call me thine own" (Halévy)

"Bright star of love." See Alla stella confidente (Robaudi)

"Bright star of night." L. Spohr. e. CB

"The bright stars fade." See Good-bye, sweetheart, good-bye (Hatton)

"The bright stars of night on thy dark waters shine." See The beautiful Rhine

"Bright sun! before whose glorious ray" (Irish war song) Air: The merchant's daughter. Words by E. Walsh. BMC —MMI

"Bright was the guiding star that led." See Bright was the star (Bradbury)

"Bright was the morning." 18th century air. MM

Bright was the star. W. B. Bradbury. Words by H. Auber. MCS

"Brightest and best." K. S. Chittenden. Words by R. Heber. JS

"Brightest and best." J. P. Harding. Words by R. Heber. HC

"Brightest and best." G. Kiallmark. Words by R. Heber. MCS

"Brightest and best." F. Mendelssohn. [Words by R. Heber] WBT—WS

"Brightest and best." S. Webbe. Words by R. Heber. FSS 3 — MCS—WBT

The brightest angel. See Der schönste engel (Graben-Hoffmann)

Brightest of golden days. M. W. Balfe. Words by C. Wallace. MCS

"Brightly, brightly gleam the sparkling rills." Haydn. e. FSS 2

"Brightly dawns upon me." See Il bacio (Arditi)

"Brightly glows the morning star." Mercadante. FSS 3

"Brightly speed the hours o'er the hunter's way." See Swiss hunter

"Brightly the silver star shines o'er the ocean." See Santa Lucia

"Brightly the stars are shining." See "Schön blinkt's aus allen sternen" (Vogrich)

Brighton camp. See The girl I left behind me

Brimbledon fair (Young Ramble-away) Folk song. SEF 2—SO

Brindisi ("Libiamo, libiamo") See Libiamo ne' lieti calici (Verdi)

Brindisi ("Sa couleur est blonde") See "Sa couleur est blonde et vermeille" (Massé)

Brindisi ("Il segreto per esser felici") See "Il segreto per esser felici" (Donizetti)

Brindley, G. W.
Good news we bring and peace (Simper)
"Sweetest music, softly stealing" (Simper)
"What do they say, these bells to me" (Simper)
"Wheat and barley bright with sunshine" (Simper)

"Bring a torch, Jeannette, Isabella." Old French carol. Words attributed to Saboly. e. DO—DSH

Bring back my Bonnie to me. H. J. Fuller (music and words) WC
Bonnie. HSD
"My Bonnie." CHS— JSE— MPC— NMH— OH— SSS— WA— WBT —WSW

"Bring back my comfort." E. Colman. Words by C. Cotton. DM 2

"Bring flowers." Air: Musette di Nina. Words by F. Hemans. FSS 4—JO

Bring me, boy, a bowl of wine. Hook. Words by Upton. HSE 2

"Bring me cross and cup." Bach. e. OS 4

"Bring the good old bugle, boys." See Marching through Georgia (Work)

Bring the wagon home, John. College song. CU—TFC 2—WC

"Bring the wreath of rich lehua." See A wreath for Princess Kaiulani (Hopkins)
"Bring them to the Master." G. C. E. Ryley. HC
"Bringt mir blut der edlen reben." See Trinklied (Arndt)
Briolage (Song of the laborers of Berri) French folk song. e.f. TSF
La brise (The breeze) C. Saint-Saëns. e.f. PG 2
"La brise douce a caressé." See Petites roses (Cesek)
"La brise souffle parfumée." See Sérénade à Juanita (Jouberti)
Brises d'autrefois (Breezes of other days) G. Hüe. Words by H. Gauthier-Villars. e.f. SAM
Brises d'autrefois (Memories of yore) e.f. HM 2
The brisk young bachelor. Folk song. SEF 2—SO
The brisk young lover. Folk song: Georgia version. CSE
—North Carolina version. CSE
"A brisk young sailor." Folk song. SEF 2—SO
"Britannia, the pride of the ocean" (The red, white and blue) [T. à Becket] SSS
"Britannia's sons at sea." W. Reeve. Words by E. Knight. ME
"Britannia's sons, rejoice." English patriotic song of 1758. Modern words by S. Baring-Gould. BE 8
The British grenadiers. 16th century air: Sir Edward Nowell's delight. BE 2 —BOH—BOS—BSP— CST—DM 1— GO—HSD—HSE 1—MM—PR 1—SSS WBT
The British national anthem. See God save the king (Carey)
"Britons, raise your banners high." Air: Ymdawiad y brenin, or, The departure of the king. Words by Talhaiarn. MMW
Britons, strike home. Chantey. SMW
"Britons, where." Patriotic song of 1738. BE 7
Briussov, W.
Snowflakes (Grechaninov)
Brixham town. Folk song. BSW
Brizeux, Charles
La procession (Franck)
"Broad the fields about her lying." See Vive Purdue (Arthur)
Brock, Mad.
Wiegenlied (Mozart)
Brodie-Innes, J. W.
Lasses of Scotland (Irish air)
"Broke! broke! broke." W. H. Jones. CHS
The broken flower. See Fleur jetée (Fauré)
Broken is my violin ("Eltörött a hegedüm") P. Danko. e.hu. BF 1
The broken pitcher. H. Pontet. WBW

The broken ring. See "In einem kühlen grunde" (Folk air); "In einem kühlen grunde" (Glück)
A broken song. Irish air. Words by M. O'Neill. FSI
The broken token. Folk song: Devon version. BSW
—Allanstand, N.C. version no. 1. CSE
—Allanstand, N.C. version no. 2. CSE
—Black Mountain, N.C. version. CSE
—Hot Springs, N.C. version. CSE
Variant: The sweet-heart in the army
Brome, Richard
A-begging we will go (17th century air) Authorship uncertain
The brook. Composer unknown. Words by Tennyson. JO
[The brook] Song of the brook. G. D. Wilson. [Words by Tennyson] FSS 2—JSE
The brook ("Thro' meadows, flowing swift and clear."—Das bächlein) J. Bleichmann. Words from the Russian of I. Gumeneva. e.g. FM
"The brook was all a-riot." See La zagala
Brooke, Fulke Greville, 1st baron
"Away with these self-loving lads" (Dowland)
Brooke, Stopford Augustus
"Let the whole creation cry" (Elvey)
The spring of love (Hyatt)
Brooke, William Thomas
"Come ye, with the angels sing" (Brown)
Brooks, Charles Timothy, and Dwight, John Sullivan
"God bless our native land! firm may she ever stand" (Carey)
Brooks, Helen
Three cheers for T. A. and P. U. (Old air)
Brooks, Phillips
Everywhere, everywhere, Christmas tonight (Redner)
"God hath sent His angels" (Parker)
"O little town of Bethlehem" (music by Booth; Burdett; Custance; Redner)
The brookside. J. Hine. Words by R. M. Milnes (Lord Houghton) FSS 4 —JO
"The broom bloomed so fresh and so fair." See She lives in the valley below (Hook)
Broom, green broom. Traditional song. MM
Variant of: Green broom
The broom o' the Cowdenknowes. See The brume o' the Cowdenknowes
Brooman, Hanna
Norrländingens hemlängtan
The Northlander's longing for home. See Norrländingens hemlängtan
Brorson, Etter
"Den yndigste rose" (Danish air)
"Brothe' Andrew, whey you bin when de dry weathe' come." See Opon de rock

Brother and I. FSS 6

"Brother come and dance with me." See The dancing lesson (Humperdinck)

Brother Green (The dying soldier) Kentucky mountain song. WLT

"Brother so fine." See "Bruderlein fein" (Drechsler)

"Brother, tell me of the battle." G. F. Root. Words by T. Manahan. HSD —WBT

"Brother, thou and I." See Wiegenlied

"Brother, thou art gone before us." See The weary are at rest

"Brother, won't you pray for me." See Nobody knows de trouble I see

Brotherhood. See Brüderschaft

"Brothers, circle round in chorus." See "Brüder, lagert euch im kreise"

Brothers, don't get weary. Negro spiritual. DF

"Brothers, Poland is in need." See Polish national song (Oginski?)

"Brothers up, swift arise." See War song

"Brothers, will you pray for me." See Nobody knows de trouble I see

"Brothers, you oughter had a been there." See Roll, Jordan, roll

"Brought up I was in Lincolnshire." See Botany bay (Vermont version)

Brown, Abbie Farwell
Sailing at Napoli (Italian air)
The sprig of thyme (Folk air)

Brown, Arthur Henry
"Alleluia! sing the triumph"
"Arise, and hail the sacred day"
"Bright Easter day"
Carol for New Year's day
"Carol we joyfully"
Christmas night
"Come ye, with the angels sing"
"Easter flowers and dressing"
"Easter flowers are blooming bright"
"Fields of gold are glowing"
"God is gone up"
"Hail! all hail this brightest morning"
"Hallelujah! raise the song"
"He is risen from the dead"
"If angels sung our Saviour's birth"
"A little Child is born to-night"
"Now lift the carol, men and maids"
"Now, prithee, minstrel, tell to me"
"O sing we a carol"
"The old year now away has fled"
"On Christmas night true Christians sing"
"On the eve before the Sabbath"
"Over all the land is glowing"
"Ring on, ye joyous Christmas bells"
"Ring the bells, the Christmas bells"
"See, the morning fair and bright"
"The shepherds amazed"
"Soft falls the snow"
"Sweet Child divine"
"When Christ was born of Mary free" (Tr of Christo paremus canticam, excelsis gloria)

Brown, Arthur Lawrence
"Glad light"

Brown, Ella W.
"Come, let us sing a merry song" (Composer unknown)

Brown, Francis H.
"A funny old fellow"
Trancadillo

Brown, I. L.
"Silent now the drowsy bird" (Offenbach)

Brown, J. H.
Faded flowers (Power)

Brown, Jessie Christian
Old Butler (Composer unknown)

Brown, M. O.
"Ring, bells, ring"

Brown, Margaret Coote
"Under the stars one holy night"

Brown, R. E.
The knights of the golden O (Scott)

Brown, T. E.
"Three kings from out the Orient" (Gill)

Brown, Theron
Song of Columbus day (Haydn)

Brown, W. C.
A hundred years to come

Brown-Borthwick, R.
"Behold a little Child"
"There came a little Child to earth"

The brown bride. See Lord Thomas and fair Ellinor (Kentucky version)

The brown girl. Folk song: Allanstand, N.C. version no. 1. CSE
—Allanstand, N.C. version no. 2. CSE
—Alleghany, N.C. version. CSE
—Big Laurel, N.C. version. CSE
—Virginia version. CSE

The brown hair'd maiden. See Ho-ro mo nighean donn, bhòidheach

The brown lad. See An gille donn

Browne, Felicia Dorothea. See Hemans, Mrs Felicia Dorothea (Browne)

Browne, M. A.
"How I love to look on the fresh green moss" (Welsh air)
"The waters! the waters" (Welsh air)

Browne, Mary Anne
The better land
"The breaking waves dash high." See Landing of the Pilgrims
The bridal of Andalla
The captive knight
Landing of the Pilgrims
The messenger bird
The Pilgrim fathers. See Landing of the Pilgrims
Plymouth rock. See Landing of the Pilgrims
Treasures of the deep
Tyrolese evening hymn

Browne, M. E.
"Shepherds night-watch keeping" (Deffell)

Brownell, H. H.
John Brown's body (Old air)

Browning, Mrs Elizabeth (Barrett)
"How do I love thee" (music by Hadley; White)

Browning, F.
Sing tangent, co-tangent (Amherst college song)
Browning, Robert
Lov'd by thee (Cantor)
Rabbi Ben Erza (Hadley)
Browning ("The leaves be green") See "The leaves be green"
Bruce, John
"But warily tent when ye come to court me." See O whistle, an' I'll come to you, my lad (attributed)
"First when Maggie was my care." See Whistle o'er the lave o't
O whistle, an' I'll come to you, my lad (attributed)
Whistle o'er the lave o't
Bruce, Michael
"How happy is the child who hears" (Composer unknown)
Bruce, Silas
"The bird let loose"
The carrier bird. See "The bird let loose"
Bruce, V.
In the tomb (Vassilenko)
Bruce to his men at Bannockburn. See "Scots wha hae wi' Wallace bled"
Bruce's address. See "Scots wha hae wi' Wallace bled"
Bruch, Max
Hymnus
Thou only canst give peace. See Hymnus
Bruchmann,
Im haine (Schubert)
Bruck, M. See Bruce, Michael
Brudefaerden i Hardanger (A bridal party on the Hardanger fjord) H. Kjerulf. Words by A. Munch. e.n. MAN
"Brüder, brüder, jetzt geht's in den krieg." See Beim ausmarsch
"Brüder, das ist deutscher wein." See Rheinweinlied (Silcher)
"Brüder, lagert euch im kreise." Studentenlied. g. ED 1
"Brüder, lagert euch im kreise" ("Brothers circle round in chorus") e.g. SSS
"Brüder, reicht die hand zum bunde." See Bundeslied (Mozart)
"Brüder, zu dem festlichen gelage." See Zu festgelagen
Brüderchen, komm tanz' mit mir. For English translation see The dancing lesson (Humperdinck)
"Brüderlein fein." J. Drechsler. Words by F. Raimund. g. ED 1
"Brother so fine." e. WBT—WSC
"Brüderlein fein" ("Brother so fine") e. FSS 2
"Brüderlein fein" ("Eh! my dear lad") e.g. SSG
Brüderschaft ("Im krug zum grünen kranze") Volkesweise: Ich stand auf hohem berge. Words by W. Müller. g. ED 1
Brüderschaft (Brotherhood) e.g. SSG

Brüll, Ignaz
"How times have changed." See "Wie anders war es"
"Wie anders war es" (from Das goldene kreuz)
"Brumbraskön i bumba." See Baadn laatt
The brume o' the Cowdenknowes ("How blythe the ilk morn was I to see") Scottish song. MMS
The broom o' the Cowdenknowes. PS 1
"La brume plane sur les monts de l'Érivan." See On the Georgian hills (Rimskii-Korsakov)
Brun, frau Friederike (Münter)
Freude in unschuld (Schulz)
Liebe in allem (Schulz)
Brun, Johan Nordahl
"Boer jeg paa det hoje fjeld" (Norse folk air)
"For Norge, kjaempers fodeland" (Grétry)
La brune et le brigand (The brunette and the brigand) French Canadian folk song. BFS
Bruneau, Alfred
The gay vagabond. See L'heureux vagabond
L'heureux vagabond
The brunette. See La Moraschina
The brunette and the brigand. See La brune et le brigand
Bruni, Pier Francesco Caletti-. See Cavalli, Francesco
Brunonia. Brown university song. L. B. Marshall. Words by E. O. Silver. CHS
Brüssoff, W. See Briussov, W.
Bruton, J.
"Happy land! happy land" (Rimbault)
Bruton town. Folk song. SEF 1—SO
Brutus. W. Beale. Words by W. Smith. BE 4
Bryant, H. T.
Balm of Gilead
Bryant, William Cullen
An Arbor day song (Molloy)
"As shadows cast by cloud and sun" (Cutler)
The hunter's serenade (German air)
The Indian girl's lament (Mendelssohn)
Our country's call (German air)
To the fringed gentian (Lang)
Bryce, Catherine T.
The watchword (Armitage)
"Bubbling and splashing." Round. BD
Bucalossi, Procida
Love, I will love you ever
Buck, Dudley
In thy dreams
Buckhurst, Charles Sackville, lord. See Dorset, Charles Sackville, 6th earl of
Buckley, Frederick
Kiss me quick and go
Buckley, R. Bishop
Wait for the wagon

Das **bucklige** männlein ("Will ich in mein gärtlein gehn") Volkslied.   g. ED 3

Bucks a-hunting go.   Composer and author of words unknown.   MM
The Cheshire hunt.   DM 2
Variant: Sweet Tally-ho

Buddhist chant (Imayo)   Japanese folk song.   e.j.   YJ

"The **buds** are bursting on the trees."   R. H. Clouston, jr.   Words by M. G. Osgood.   HC

Buffalo gals.   HSD

"The **bugler** paced thro' the driving snow."   Arr from Pinsuti.   JS

"**Build** thee more stately mansions."   A. Farwell.   Words by O. W. Holmes. TL

"**Bula** sobi Marusîa."   See Petrus

Bulfinch, Maria H.
"Now we bring our Christmas treasures" (Gurney)

Bulgăraş (Ice upon the river)   Rumanian song.   e.ru.   BF 2

Bulgarian song.   See "Fare thee well, old world"

Bull, John
God save the king: old version (attributed)

Bull, Ole Borneman
The chalet girl's Sunday.   See Saetergjentens söndag
The herdgirl's Sunday.   See Saetergjentens söndag
"I ensomme stunde"
In lonely moments.   See "I ensomme stunde"
Saetergjentens söndag

The **bull** and the cowboy.   See El toro y el ranchero

The **bull-dog** on the bank.   College song. TFC 1
The bulldog.   CHS—HSD—MPC—OH—WBT—WC

Bullard, Frederick Field
"Beam from yonder star"
The pigtail
A stein song
"Sweet and clear the birds are singing"

Bullinger, Ethelbert William
"Art thou weary, art thou languid" (Tr of Kopon te kai kamaton)
"The stars are shining bright and clear"

Bulloch, John Malcolm
A mathematic monody (Newton)
Our noble selves (Newton)
The pocket Gray (Newton)
The student and his bow-wow (Tabrar)
The sunniest season of life (Kirby)

The **bully** boat.   Capstan chantey.   SE

Bully in the alley.   Pulling chantey.   SE

"A **bully** ship and a bully crew."   See Sacramento

Bulwer-Lytton, Edward George Earle Lytton.   See Lytton, Edward George Earle Lytton Bulwer-Lytton, 1st baron

Bulwer-Lytton, Edward Robert Lytton.   See Lytton, Edward Robert Bulwer-Lytton, 1st earl of

Bumpers, Squire Jones ("Ye good fellows all")   O'Carolan.   Words attributed to A. Dawson.   MMI

The **bumpkin**.   See El payo

A **bunch** of cowslips.   See "Polly and I" (Wakefield)

Bundesfeier ("Wo zur frohen feierstund")   Composer and author of words unknown.   g.   ED 1

Bundeslied ("Brüder, reicht die hand")   W. A. Mozart.   Author of words unknown.   g.   ED 1—ED 3

Bundeslied ("In allen guten stunden")   J. F. Reichardt.   Words by W. von Goethe.   e.   ED 1

Bundeslied ("Sind wir vereint")   G. F. Hanitsch.   Words by E. M. Arndt.   g. ED 1

Bundeslied ("Wo mut und kraft")   French air: Brûlant d'amour.   Words by C. Hinkel.   g.   ED 1

Bunker hill.   H. L. Tuckerman.   Words by J. B. Taylor.   HSD—WBT

Bunn, Alfred
"The heart bowed down" (Balfe)
"I dreamt that I dwelt in marble halls" (Balfe)
"The light of other days" (Balfe)
"Scenes that are brightest" (Wallace)
Then you'll remember me (Balfe)
We may be happy yet (Balfe)

Bunnett, Edward
"Carol, sweetly carol, a Saviour born today"
Joyful is the morn.   See "Once again the olden story"
"O wonderful the tidings"
"Once again the olden story"
"The stars are shining bright and clear"

"**Bunt** sind schon die wälder."   See Herbstlied (Reichardt)

Buononcini, Giovanni Maria.   See Bononcini, Giovanni Maria

Burdett, George Albert
"O little town of Bethlehem"

Burdette, Robert Jones
"Rock-a-bye, baby" (Old lullaby)

Bürger, Gottfried August
Das blümchen wunderhold (Beethoven)
Liebeszauber (Schulz)
Die trennung (Rousseau)
Wilhelm (Schulz)

Burgess, Alexander
"Bright Easter skies" (Marston)

Burgoyne, John
The dashing white sergeant (Bishop)

Burgwedel, Karl von
"Auf dem berge dort oben, da wehet der wind"

Buri, Christian von
Jünglings weihe (Student air)

The **burial** of Sir John Moore.   J. Barnett.   Words by C. Wolfe.   JO

The **burial** of the robin.   A. S. Gatty. WSC

Buriâno.   Bulgarian folk dance.   b.e.
BF 1

Burleigh, Henry Thacker
An ante-bellum sermon: negro spiritual
arranged
De black-bird an' de crow: negro spir-
itual arranged
The Danville chariot: negro spiritual ar-
ranged
"Ma Lawd's a-writin' down time":
negro spiritual arranged
My Merlindy Brown
Negro lullaby
When de debble comes 'round: negro
spiritual arranged

"**Burly**, dozing humble-bee."   See The
humble-bee (German air); The humble
bee (Neidlinger)

Burn, minstrel
"When Phoebus bright"

Burnap, Uziah Christopher
Baxter.   See "Thy way, not mine, O
Lord"
"Thy way, not mine, O Lord"

Burney, Agnes
"Ring the bells, the Christmas bells"
(music by Brown; Dean; Erskine;
Oake)

Burnham, Charles S.
The moon's lullaby

Burnham, Mrs Clara Louise (Root)
Funiculi-funicola (Sailing o'er a summer sea)   (Denza)

"**Burning** heart and bold."   See A song of
the great adventure

"**Burning** out is the sunset's red flame."
M. Balakireff.   Words from the Russian of V. Kulchinsky.   e.   NM 1

Burns, Robert
"A' the lads o' Thornie-bank"   (Scot-
tish air)
"Adieu! a heart-warm, fond adieu"
(Scottish air)
"Adown winding Nith I did wander"
(Scottish air)
"Ae fond kiss" (Old Highland air; air:
Rory Dall's port; also music by un-
known composer)
"Aften hae I play'd at the cards and
the dice"   (Scottish air)
Afton water (Old Scottish air; air:
Afton water;   also music by
Hume;   Spilman)
"Again rejoicing nature sees" (Scottish
air)
"Ah, Chloris, since it may not be"
(Scottish air)
"Altho' my back be at the wa'" (Scot-
tish air)
"Altho' my bed were in yon muir"
(Scottish air)
"Amang the trees, where humming
bees"   (Scottish air)
The American war (Scottish air)
An' O, for ane-an'-twenty, Tam (Scot-
tish air)
"An somebody were come again" (Scot-
tish air)

"Ance mair I hail thee, thou gloomy
December" (Scottish air)
"Anna, thy charms my bosom fire"
(Oswald)
"As down the burn they took their
way" (Scottish air)
"As I cam down by yon castle wa'"
(Scottish air)
"As I cam down the banks o' Nith"
(Scottish air)
"As I came o'er the Cairney mount"
(Scottish air)
"As I gaed down the water-side" (Scot-
tish air)
"As I lay on my bed on a night" (Scot-
tish air)   Authorship uncertain
"As I stood by yon roofless tower"
(Scottish air)
"As I was walking up the street"
(Scottish air)
"As I went out ae May morning"
(Scottish air)
"As late by a sodger I chanced to pass"
(Scottish air)
Auld lang syne (Original Scottish air;
also air: I fee'd a lad at Michael-
mas)
"The auld man's mare's dead"   (Scot-
tish air)
Auld Rob Morris (Scottish air)
Awa, Whigs, awa (Old Scottish air)
"Awa wi' your witchcraft o' beauty's
alarms" (Scottish air)
Ay wakin', O (Scottish air)
Bannocks o' bear meal (Scottish air)
"Behold, my love, how green the
groves" (Scottish air;   also music
by Locke)
"Behold the hour, the boat arrive"
(Scottish air)
The birks of Aberfeldy (Scottish air)
"The blude red rose at Yule may blaw"
(Scottish air)
The blue-eyed lassie (Riddell)
Blythe, blythe, and merry was she
(Scottish air)
"Blythe hae I been on yon hill" (Scot-
tish air)
Bonnie bell (Scottish air)
Bonnie Doon (Miller)
Bonnie wee thing (Scottish air)
"The bonniest lad that e'er I saw"
(Scottish air)
"But lately seen in gladsome green"
(East Indian air)
"By Allan stream I chanc'd to rove"
(Scottish air)
"By love and by beauty"   (Scottish
air)
Ca' the yowes to the knowes (Scottish
air)
The Campbells are comin' (Old Scot-
tish air)
"Can I cease to care" (Scottish air)
The captain's lady (Scottish air)
"The Catrine woods were yellow seen"
(Masterton)
"Cauld is the e'enin blast" (Scottish
air)

Burns, Robert —*Continued*

"Clarinda, mistress of my soul" (Schet-ky)

Cock up your beaver (Scottish air)

"The collier has a 'dochter" (Scottish air)

"Come boat me o'er, come row me o'er" (Scottish air: O'er the water to Charlie; also Scottish air: Over the water to Charlie)

"Come, bumpers high! express your joy" (Scottish air)

"Come, let me take thee to my breast" (Scottish air)

"Come under my plaidie" (Scottish air)

Comin' thro' the rye (Old Scottish air)

"Comin thro' the rye, poor body" (Scottish air)

"Contented wi' little" (Air: Lumps of pudding; air: The wee, wee man)

"The cooper of Cuddie came here awa" (Scottish air)

Corn rigs are bonnie (Scottish air)

Craigie-burn wood (Scottish air)

Dainty Davie (Scottish air)

"The day returns, my bosom burns" (Riddell)

The deil's awa' wi' the exciseman (Scottish air)

"Deluded swain, the pleasure" (Scottish air)

The deuks dang ow're my daddie (Scottish air)

"Dire was the hate at old Harlaw" (Scottish air)

"Does haughty Gaul invasion threat" (Scottish air)

The dream (Scottish air)

"Duncan Gray cam' here to woo" (Scottish air)

"Fareweel to a' our Scottish fame" (Scottish air)

"Farewell, thou stream" (Air: Alace yat I came owr the moor; air: Nannie's to the greenwood gone)

"Farewell, ye dungeons dark and strong" (Scottish air)

"Fate gave the word—the arrow sped" (Scottish air)

Fine flowers in the valley (Scottish air)

"For thee is laughing nature gay'" (Scottish air)

"Forlorn my love, no comfort near" (Scottish air)

"Frae the friends and land I love" (Scottish air)

"From thee, Eliza I must go" (Air: Donald; air: Gilderoy)

"Fy, let us a' to Kirkcudbright" (Scottish air)

"Gae bring to me a pint o' wine" (Scottish air; also music by Oswald)

Gala water (Scottish air)

The gallant weaver (Scottish air)

"Gane is the day" (Scottish air)

"Gat ye me, O, gat ye me" (Scottish air)

"The gloomy night is gath'ring fast" (Scottish air)

Green grow the rashes, O (Scottish air)

"Guide'en to you, kimmer, and how do you do" (Scottish air)

Guidwife, count the lawin (Scottish air)

"Had I a cave" (Scottish air)

"Had I the wyte" (Scottish air)

"He clench'd his pamphlets in his fist" (Scottish air)

"The heather was blooming" (Scottish air)

"Hee balou, my sweet wee Donald" (Scottish air)

"Her daddie forbad, her minnie forbad" (Scottish air)

Here's a health to ane I lo'e dear (Scottish air)

"Here's a health to them that's awa'" (Scottish air)

"Here's to thy health, my bonie lass" (Scottish air)

Hey, ca' thro' (Scottish air)

"Hey, the dusty miller" (Scottish air)

Highland cradle song (Schumann)

"A Highland lad my love was born" (Air: O, an ye were dead, guidman; air: The white cockade)

Highland Mary (Scottish air; also music by Bartlett)

The Highland widow's lament (Scottish air)

"How can my poor heart be glad" (Scottish air)

"How cruel are the parents" (Scottish air)

"How lang and dreary is the night" (Scottish air)

"How pleasant the banks" (Air: Bhannerach dhon na chrie; air: The maids of Arrochar)

"I am a bard" (Scottish air)

"I am a son of Mars" (Scottish air)

"I coft a stane o' haslock woo" (Scottish air)

"I do confess thou art sae fair" (Scottish air)

"I fee'd a man at Martinmas" (Scottish air)

"I gaed up to Dunse" (Scottish air)

"I had sax owsen in a pleugh" (Scottish air)

"I hae a wife o' my ain" (Scottish air)

"I hae been at Crookieden" (Scottish air)

I love my love in secret (Scottish air)

"I never saw a fairer" (Scottish air)

"I once was a maid tho' I cannot tell when" (Scottish air)

"I sing of a whistle" (Riddell?)

"I wish I war where Eelin lies" (Air: Fair Helen of Kirkconnel; air: Where Helen lies)

"If thou should ask my love" (Scottish air)

"Ilk care and fear, when thou art near" (Scottish air)

I'm owre young to marry yet (Scottish air)

Burns, Robert—*Continued*

"In comin by the brig o' Dye" (Scottish air)

"In Mauchline there dwells six proper young belles" (Scottish air)

"In simmer, when the hay was mawn" (Scottish air)

"Is this thy plighted, fond regard" (Scottish air)

"It is na, Jean, thy bonnie face" (Scottish air; also music by Oswald)

"It was a' for our rightfu' king" (Scottish air)

"It was in sweet Senegal" (Scottish air)

"It was the charming month of May" (Scottish air)

"It's now the day is dawin" (Scottish air)

"It's up wi' the Souters o' Selkirk" (Scottish air)

"Jockie's ta'en the parting kiss" (Scottish air)

"John Anderson my jo, John" (Watson)

Kellyburnbraes (Scottish air)

"Ken ye ought o' Captain Grose" (Scottish air)

"The laddies by the banks o' Nith" (Scottish air)

Lady Mary Ann (Scottish air)

"Landlady, count the lawin" (Scottish air)

"Lang hae we parted been" (Scottish air)

The lass of Ecclefechan (Scottish air)

"Lassie, lend me your braw hemp heckle" (Scottish air)

Lassie wi' the lint-white locks (Scottish air)

"Last May a braw wooer" (Scottish air)

"The lazy mist hangs from the hill" (Scottish air)

The lea rig (Scottish air; also music by Reid)

Leezie Lindsay (Scottish air)

Let loove sparkle in her e'e (Scottish air)

"Let me ryke up to dight that tear" (Scottish air)

"Let not woman e'er complain" (Scottish air)

Logan braes (Scottish air)

Lord Gregory (Ancient Galloway air)

"Loud blaw the frosty breezes" (Scottish air)

"Louis, what reck I by thee" (Scottish air)

"The lovely lass of Inverness" (Oswald)

Lovely Polly Stewart (Scottish air)

McPherson's farewell (Scottish air)

A man's a man for a' that (Scottish air)

"Mark yonder pomp of costly fashion" (Scottish air)

"Musing on the roaring ocean" (Gaelic air)

My ain kind dearie, O (Scottish air)

"My bonie lass, I work in brass" (Scottish air)

"My daddie was a fiddler fine" (Scottish air)

"My father was a farmer" (Scottish air)

"My Harry was a gallant gay" (Scottish air)

"My heart is a-breaking, dear tittie" (Air: The muckin' o' Geordie's byre; air: Tam Glen)

"My heart is sair—I darena tell" (Air: For the sake o' somebody; air: The Highland watch's farewell)

"My heart is wae, and unco wae" (Scottish air)

"My heart was ance as blythe and free" (Scottish air)

"My heart's in the Highlands" (German folk air; air: Cro challin; air: The musket salute; air: Portmore; also music by Courtney; Jensen)

My jo Janet (Scottish air)

"My lord a-hunting he is gane" (Greig)

"My love she's but a lassie yet, my love she's but a lassie yet" (Scottish air)

"My love was born in Aberdeen" (Scottish air)

"My luve is like a red, red rose" (Air: Low down in the broom; air: Major Graham; also music by Garrett; Schumann)

My Nannie, O (Scottish air)

"My Peggy's face, my Peggy's form" (Scottish air)

My spouse, Nancy (Scottish air)

My tocher's the jewel (Scottish air)

"My wife's a winsome wee thing" (Scottish air)

"Nae birdies sang the mirky hour" (Scottish air)

"Nae gentle dames, tho' ne'er sae fair" (Scottish air)

"Near Edinburgh was a young son born" (Scottish air)

"No churchman am I for to rail and to write" (Scottish air)

"No cold approach, no alter'd mien" (Barrett)

"The noble Maxwells and their powers" (Riddell)

"Now in her green mantle blythe nature arrays" (Air: My Nannie's awa'; air: There are few good fellows when Jamie's awa')

"Now nature hangs her mantle green" (Scottish air)

"Now westlin winds and slaught'ring guns" (Scottish air)

"Oh, aye my wife she dang me" (Scottish air)

"O bonnie was yon rosy brier" (Air: I wish my love were in a mire; air: Laggan burn; air: The wee, wee man)

"O, cam ye here the fight to shun" (Scottish air)

Burns, Robert —*Continued*

O Charlie is my darling (Jacobite air)

"O dear minny, what shall I do" (Scottish air)

"O, Donald Couper and his man" (Scottish air)   Authorship uncertain

"O, for my ain king, quo' gude Wallace" (Scottish air)

"O, Galloway Tam cam here to woo" (Scottish air)

"O heard ye of a silly harper" (Scottish air)

"O, how can I be blythe and glad" (Scottish air)

"O, how shall I, unskilfu', try" (Scottish air)

"O, I am come to the low countrie" (Scottish air)

"O, I forbid you maidens a'" (Scottish air)

"O, ken ye what Meg o' the mill has gotten" (Air: O bonie lass, will ye lie in a barrack;   air: O ken ye what Meg)

"O Kenmure's on and awa', Willie" (Scottish air)

"O lassie, art thou sleeping yet" (Air: Let me in this ae nicht;   air: Will ye lend me your loom, lass)

"O lassie, art thou sleeping yet": Her answer (Air: Let me in this ae nicht)

O lay thy loof in mine, lass (Scottish air)

"O, leave novéls, ye mauchline belles" (Scottish air)

"O, leeze me on my spinnin-wheel" (Scottish air)

"O luve will venture in" (Scottish air)

"O, Mary, at thy window be" (Air: Duncan Davison;   air: The miller)

"O May, thy morn was ne'er so sweet" (Air: O May, thy morn;   air: The rashes)

"O merry hae I been teethin a heckle" (Scottish air)

"O, open the door" (Irish air;   Scottish air)

"O Philly, happy be that day" (Scottish air)

"O, poortith cauld" (Air: Cauld kail;   air: I had a horse)

"Oh, raging fortune's withering blast" (Scottish air)

"O saw ye bonnie Lesley" (Scottish air)

"O, saw ye my dear, my Philly" (Scottish air)

"O, saw ye my dearie, my Eppie McNab" (Scottish air)

"O, some will court and compliment" (Scottish air)

"O, stay, sweet warbling woodlark, stay" (Scottish air)

"O, steer her up" (Scottish air)

"O, that I had ne'er been married" (Scottish air)

O this is no my ain lassie (Scottish air)

"O thou pale orb that silent shines" (Scottish air)

"O Tibbie, I ha'e seen the day" (Scottish air)

O wat ye wha's in yon toun (Scottish air)

"O were I on Parnassus hill" (Oswald)

"O were my love yon lilac fair" (Air: Gin my love were yon red rose; air: Hughie Graham)

"O wert thou in the cauld blast" (Scottish air;   air: Lenox love to Blantyre;   also music by Mendelssohn)

"O wha is she that lo'es me" (Scottish air)

"O, wha my babie-clouts will buy" (Scottish air)

"O, wha will to Saint Stephen's house" (Scottish air)

"O, whar gat ye that hauver-meal bannock" (Scottish air)

"O, when she cam ben, she bobbed fu' law" (Scottish air)

"O, where hae ye been Lord Ronald, my son" (Scottish air)

"O whistle, and I'll come to you, my lad" (Bruce?)

"O Willie brew'd a peck o' maut" (music by Masterton; Shore)

"O, wilt thou go wi' me, sweet Tibbie Dunbar" (McGill?)

"Of a' the airts the wind can blaw" (Marshall)

"On a bank of flowers in a summer day" (Gaillard)

"On Cessnock banks" (Air: The butcher boy;   air: The cardin o't)

"One night as I did wander" (Scottish air)

"Orthodox! orthodox! wha believe in John Knox" (Scottish air)

"Our lords are to the mountains gane" (Scottish air)

"Our young lady's a huntin gane" (Scottish air)

"Out over the Forth, I look to the north" (Gow)

"Peg Nicholson was a good bay mare" (Scottish air)

Phillis the fair (Scottish air)

"The ploughman, he's a bonie lad" (Scottish air)

"Powers celestial" (Scottish air)

Rattlin' roarin' Willie (Scottish air)

"Raving winds around her blowing" (Scottish air)

"Rob Roy from the Highlands cam" (Scottish air)

"Rob Roy was my father ca'd" (Scottish air)

"The robin cam to the wren's nest" (Scottish air)

"A rosebud by my early walk" (Scottish air;   also music by Sillar)

Sae far awa' (Scottish air)

Burns, Robert —*Continued*

"Sae flaxen were her ringlets" (Scottish air)
"Scots, wha ha'e wi' Wallace bled" (Scottish air)
Scottish wedding (Scottish air)
"See the smoking bowl before us" (Scottish air)
"Sensibility how charming" (Scottish air)
"She play'd the loon or she was married" (Scottish air)
"She's fair and fause that causes my smart" (Scottish air)
Sic a wife as Willie had (Scottish air)
"Sir John Cope trode the north right far" (Scottish air)
"Sir Wisdom's a fool when he's fou" (Scottish air)
"Sleepst thou or wak'st thou" (Scottish air)
"The small birds rejoice" (Scottish air)
The soldier's return (Scottish air)
The song of death (Scottish air)
"Stay, my charmer, can you leave me" (Gaelic air)
"The sun he is sunk in the west" (Scottish air)
"Sweet are the banks—the banks o' Doon" (Scottish air)
"The taylor fell thro' the bed" (Scottish air)
"The taylor he cam here to sew" (Scottish air)
"The Thames flows proudly to the sea" (Scottish air)
"Their groves o' sweet myrtle" (Scottish air)
Theniel Menzie's bonnie Mary (Scottish air)
"There grows a bonie brier-bush in our kail-yard, there grows a bonie brier-bush in our kail-yard" (Scottish air)
"There liv'd a man in yonder glen" (Scottish air)
"There was a battle in the north" (Scottish air)
"There was a bonie lass" (Scottish air)
"There was a lad was born in Kyle" (Air: Dainty Davie; air: O gin ye were daid, guidman)
"There was a lass and she was fair" (Air: Bonnie Jean; air: Willie was a wanton wag)
"There was a lass, they ca'd her Meg" (Scottish air)
"There was a wife wonn'd in Cockpen" (Scottish air)
"There was five carlins in the south" (Scottish air)
"There was on a time" (Scottish air)
"There was three kings into the east" (Scottish air)
There'll never be peace till Jamie comes hame (Scottish air)
"There's a youth in this city" (Gow)
"There's cauld kail in Aberdeen" (Scottish air)

"There's nane shall ken, there's nane can guess" (Scottish air)
"There's news, lasses, news" (Scottish air)
"There's sax eggs in the pan, gudeman" (Scottish air)
"Thickest night, surround my dwelling" (Masterton)
"Thine am I, my faithful fair" (Scottish air; also music by Whitaker)
"Tho' cruel fate should bid us part" (Air: The northern lass; air: She rose and let me in)
"Tho' women's minds like winter winds" (Scottish air)
"Thou hast left me ever, Jamie" (Scottish air)
"Thou ling'ring star with less'ning ray" (Scottish air; also music by Oswald)
The tither morn (Highland air)
To Chloe in sickness (Bennett)
The trogger (Scottish air)
"True-hearted was he" (Scottish air)
"Turn again, thou fair Eliza" (Gaelic air)
"Twa bonie lads were Sandy and Jockie" (Scottish air)
"'Twas even—the dewy fields were green" (Scottish air)
"'Twas in the seventeen hunder year" (Scottish air)
"'Twas na her bonie blue e'e was my ruin" (Scottish air)
"'Twas past one o'clock" (Scottish air)
Up in the morning early (Scottish air)
"Wae is my heart" (Scottish air)
Wandering Willie (Scottish air)
"Wantonness for evermair" (Scottish air)
"Weary fa' you, Duncan Gray" (Scottish air)
The weary pund o' tow (Scottish air)
"Wee Willie Gray" (Scottish air)
"Wha in a brulzie" (Scottish air)
"Wha is that at my bower-door" (Scottish air)
"Wham will we send to London town" (Scottish air)
"Whare are you gaun, my bonie lass" (Scottish air)
"Whare hae ye been sae braw, lad" (Scottish air)
"Whare live ye, my bonie lass" (Scottish air)
"What can a young lassie" (Scottish air)
"What merriment has taen the Whigs" (Scottish air)
"What will I do gin my hoggie die" (Scottish air)
"When chill November's surly blast" (Scottish air)
"When first I came to Stewart Kyle" (Scottish air)
"When first my brave Johnie lad" (Scottish air)
"When Januar' wind was blawin cauld" (Scottish air)

Burns, Robert—Continued
"When we gaed to the braes o' Mar" (Scottish air)
"Where are the joys I hae met in the morning" (Scottish air)
"Where, braving angry winter's storms" (Gow)
Whistle o'er the lave o't (Bruce)
"Why, why tell thy lover" (Scottish air)
"Will ye go to the Indies, my Mary" (Scottish air)
"Willie Wastle dwalt on Tweed" (Scottish air)
"Wilt thou be my dearie" (Scottish air)
"The winter it is past" (Scottish air)
"The wintry west extends his blast" (Scottish air)
"Ye flowery banks o' bonie Doon" (Scottish air)
"Ye gallants bright, I rede you right" (Masterton)
"Ye Jacobites by name" (Scottish air)
"Ye sons of old Killie" (Scottish air)
"Yestreen I had a pint o' wine" (Scottish air)
"Yestreen I met you on the moor" (Scottish air)
"Yon wild mossy mountains" (Oswald)
"Young Jamie, pride of a' the plain" (Scottish air)
"Young Jockie was the blythest lad" (Scottish air)
"Young Peggy blooms our boniest lass" (Air: Loch Eroch Side; air: Peggie, I must love thee)
"Your friendship much can make me blest" (Scottish air)
"You're welcome to despots, Dumourier" (Scottish air)

Burnside, Helen M.
"Moonlight and music" (Pinsuti)
An old garden (Temple)
Tired, so tired (Bliss)

Burroughs, John
My own shall come to me (Foster)

Burroughs, Ole
The red and the black (Old air)

"**Burschen,** heraus." Composer and author of words unknown. g. ED 1

Burschenlust ("Der mai ist gekommen") J. W. Lyra. Words by E. Geibel. g. ED 1

Burschenlust (Student delight) e.g. SSG

Burton, Henry
"In the secret of His presence I am kept from strife of tongues" (Oliver)

Burton, Richard Eugene
The children's voices (Alpine air)

Burton ale. J. Barrett. BE 5

"**Bury** me, for love and pity." Air: The queen's dream. Words from the Welsh. e. MMW

"**Bury** my Bible at my head." See Sir Hugh

Busch, Carl
"Orpheus with his lute"
"Under the greenwood tree, who loves to lie with me"

Bush, Bertha Evangeline
Harvest home song (Olds)
Memorial day song (Olds)
Thanksgiving hymn (Olds)

The **bush** aboon Traquair ("Hear me, ye nymphs, and every swain") Scottish air. Words by R. Crawford; wrongly attributed to W. Crawford. JO—MMS —PS 1

Bushes and briars. Folk song from Essex. SF 2

"**Busk** ye, busk ye, my bonnie, bonnie wife." See The braes of Yarrow

Bussine, Romain
Après un rêve (Fauré)

Busslied (A song of penitence) Beethoven. Words by Gellert. e.g. HSS 1— HSS 2—PG 2

"**Busy,** curious, thirsty fly." Greene. Words by W. Oldys. DM 1—JE

"The **busy** lark." G. W. Chadwick. Words by G. Chaucer. TL

"**But** are you sure the news is true" See There's nae luck about the house

"**But** black is the colour of my true love's hair." See Black is the colour

But He ain't comin' here t' die no mo'. See Jesus ain't comin' here t' die no mo'

But I care not what others may say. See Rosalie

"**But** lately seen in gladsome green." East Indian air. Words by R. Burns. BSR

"**But** oh! what art can teach." Händel. OS 1

"**But** the Lord is mindful of His own." F. Mendelssohn. e. BD—CS 1—FSS 2 —JS—JSE—OS 2—SAS 2—WS

"**But** warily tent when ye come to court me." See O whistle an' I'll come to you, my lad (Bruce?)

But when morning dawneth. A. Randegger. Words by F. R. Havergal. JS

"**Sadly** bend the flowers." FSS 4

"**But** when young Suse came to knew this." See The two brothers (Mount Fair, Va. version no. 2)

"**But** who is this? tremendous to behold." Händel. SAS 2

"**But** who may abide the day of His coming." Händel. OS 4—SAS 4

Butler,
Rosalinda

Butler, Samuel
The clear cavalier (Banister) Authorship uncertain

Butter-week (Maslíanitsa) Russian folk song. e. SSR 3

The **buttercup** test. FSS 7

"**Buttercups** and daisies." WBT—WSC

"**Buttercups** ev'ry one bright." See The buttercup test

Butterfield, James Austin
When you and I were young, Maggie

Butterflies ("Les papillons couleur de neige") See Les papillons (Chausson)

Butterflies ("What pretty wings you flutter") French folk air: Giroflé, girofla. Words by N. H. Dole. DO

Butterfly (Chō-chō) G. Ross. e.j. RAS

A butterfly at Haga. See "Fjäriln vingad syns på Haga" (Bellman)

"Butterfly, butterfly light upon a naleaf, pray." See Butterfly (Ross)

Butterfly in April. See Citronenfalter im april (Wolf)

Butterfly love. See "Es el amor mariposa"

"The butterfly the candle seeks." See "Le papillon suit la chandelle"

"Butterfly white would light here." See Trippole, trappole

The butterfly's ball. WSC

"The butterfly's fallen in love with the rose." See "Der schmetterling ist in die rose verliebt" (Franz)

Butterworth, Hezekiah
The school-house and the flag (Southwick)

Button, E.
The girl of the seasons (Sanderson)

Button, Henry Elliott
"The fishers sat within their boat"
"Hark! the angels bright are singing"

The buxom matron. See The song of Khívria (Musorgskiï)

Buy a broom. Air: Lieber Augustin, attributed to A. Lee. HSD—JO—WA—WBT—WSC—WSW
"From Teutschland I come." BE 3

Buy braw troggin frae the banks o' Dee. See The trogger.

Buy my dainty beans. Round. BD

Buy my roses. J. T. Norton. FSS 7

Buy my strawberries. C. Howard. FSS 4

"By a bancke as I lay, musing on a thing that was past and gone, hey how." See "By a bank as I lay" (2d version)

"By a bancke as I lay musying mysylfe alone hey how." See "By a bank as I lay" (1st version)

"By a bank as I lay." 15th century song. 1st version. BOH—CO 1—JE —2d version. CO 1

By a new-made grave. S. Rachmaninoff. Words from the Russian of S. Nadson. e. NM 2

"By Allan stream I chanc'd to rove." Air: Allan water. Words by R. Burns. BSR

By an' by ("I know my robes") Negro spiritual. JB

By-and-by. DF

"By Anchtertyre there grows the aik." See Blythe, blythe and merry was she

By and by ("A little blithesome merry lass") J. Hook. Words by Upton. ME

By and by we'll all go down. See Down in the valley

"By Auchtertyre there grows the aik." See Blythe, blythe and merry was she

"By-bye, by-bye! by-bye, by-bye! lower than the humble wayside flow'r." See Cradle-song of the poor (Musorgskiï)

"By-bye, by-bye, sleep, my pretty boy." See Peasant cradle-song (Musorgskiï)

"By Celia's arbor." F. Mendelssohn. Words by T. Moore. BC—BD
The garland (Der blumenkranz) e.g. TS

"By chance it was." Folk song. BSW

"By cool Siloam's shady rill." Words by R. Heber. FSS 1—JS

"By day, when I am working." See "Om dagen vid mitt arbete"

"By daytime at my work." See "Om dagen vid mitt arbete"

"By dimpled brook." T. A. Arne. Words from Milton. DM 1—HSE 2—JE—ME—PR 2

"By force I am fixed." See Light o' love

"By Galilee's calm waters, on a day." See Come unto me (Bliss)

"By Killarney's lakes and fells." See Killarney (Balfe)

"By Logan's streams that run sae deep." See Logan water

"By love and by beauty." Air: Eppie Adair. Words by R. Burns. BSR

By Manzanares. See "Am ufer des flusses des Manzanares" (Jensen)

By moonlight. See "Au clair de la lune"

"By my love's window here." See "Vor liebchens fenster"

"By Ochtertyre grows the aik." See Blythe, blythe and merry was she

"By Oughtertyre grows the aik." See Blythe, blythe, and merry was she

"By road and river, country-side and town." See Fiddle and I (Goodeve)

"By St Gille, hasten on." See Les pas d'armes du roi Jean (Saint-Saëns)

"By silent hearth." See "Am stillen herd" (Wagner)

"By snow-fields encompass'd alone stands a pine-tree." See The pine-tree (Balakirev)

"By that lake, whose gloomy shore." Air: The brown Irish girl. Words by T. Moore. MI

"By the blue Alsatian mountains." See The blue Alsatian mountains (Maybrick)

By the blue sea. H. Smart. Words by F. Enoch. FSS 6

"By the bridge" (Wozli ryczki wozli mosta) Russian dumka. e. SMF

By the clear fountain. See "A la claire fontaine"

"By the cradle of Yankele" ("Unter Yankele's vigele") Jewish folk song. e.y. GF 1

"By the Danube do I wander." See The old lover and the new

"By the dark waves of the rolling sea." See O, take me back to Switzerland (Norton)

"By the Don a flow'ry lane."   See The banks of the Don (Musorgskiï)

"By the Feal's wave benighted."   See Desmond's song

By the fireside (U kamina)   Modern Russian gypsy song.   e.r.   BF 1

"By the gaily circling glass."   Arne. Words by Milton.   DM 1—HSE 2

"By the glimmering moonlight first I saw thee."   See "À la luz de la luna"

"By the glories of earth, sea and sky."   See Power and love (Gounod)

"By the hatchet wounded."   See The wounded birch (Grechaninov)

"By the hope within us springing."   See Before the battle

By the lake ("Z tamtej strony jezioreczka") Polish folk song.   e.p.   BF 1

"By the lakes of Killarney."   Irish air. Words by A. P. Graves.   FSI

"By the lore of ages far."   See The enchantress (Hatton)

"By the old Moulmein pagoda."   See On the road to Mandalay (Trevannion)

By the path.   See Par le sentier (Dubois)

"By the quiet water gleaming."   See Das vergissmeinnicht (Himmel)

By the river.   See An der Weser (Pressel)

"By the rude bridge that arched the flood." See Concord hymn (Beethoven)

"By the sad sea waves."   J. Benedict. FSS 2—HSC—HSD—HSE 2—WBT

By the sea shore (Serenade)   N. W. Gade. e.   KSN

"By the simplicity of Venus' doves."   H. R. Bishop.   Words by Shakespeare. DM 1—HSE 3

By the spring.   See Alla fontana

"By the stream so pure and clear."   See Song of the isle of Saint Kilda

"By the thorny way of sorrow."   G. E. Oliver.   HC

"By the tomb of Grant the hero."   See Morningside

"By the vineyard a garden grows."   See The bridegroom's plea

"By the voice of her cannon alarming." See Mourir pour la patrie

By the water.   M. Moussorgsky.   Words by A. Golenistchew-Koutouzow.   e. SC

By the waters of Minnetonka.   Indian love song.   T. Lieurance.   Words by J. M. Cavanass.   LS

By the weeping waters.   Indian song.   T. Lieurance.   LS

"By the well before the doorway."   See Der lindenbaum (Schubert)

By the window ("Soll sich der mond") See Vor dem fenster (Brahms)

By the window ("To the window I rushed." —Rastvoríl ya oknó)   P. I. Tchaikovsky.   e.   SMR 2

"By the window one youth now is standing."   See Good advice

"By those eyes."   H. Leander.   BE 5

By Thy Christmas cheer.   MCS

"By thy rivers gently flowing."   See Illinois (Old air); Illinois (Jones)

"By t'side of a brig."   See The Yorkshire man (Reeve)

"By Varennes going carelessly."   See Je ne suis pas si vilaine

"By weeping waters, here will I mourn." See By the weeping waters (Lieurance)

"By what trouble profound now am I overtaken."   See Nuit resplendissante (Gounod)

"By what troubled unrest am I now overtaken."   See Nuit resplendissante (Gounod)

"By yon bonnie banks."   See Loch Lomond

"By yon castle wa', at the close of the day." See There'll never be peace till Jamie comes hame

"By Ystwyth I number my sheep."   See Nel Pugh

Byde ye yet.   See Bide ye yet

"Bye, baby Bunting, daddy's gone a-hunting."   See Baby Bunting

"Bye, bye, drowsiness o'ertaking."   See Lullaby (Jakobowski)

Bye, bye, my darling! sleep to de rattle ob de bones.   See Dolcy Jones (Foster)

"Bye-lo, baby, bye-lo, baby, bye-lo, baby." Nursery song.   FSS 7

"Bye-lo, baby, by-lo, bye; hush, my little fawn so shy."   See Cradle song (Rimskiï-Korsakov)

"Bye-low, bye, bye, bye-low, bye, bye, lower than the tiniest green grass-blade." See Cradle-song of the poor (Musorgskiï)

"Bye, O Baby Bunting, daddy's gone a hunting."   See Baby Bunting

"Bygone days."   See "Jours passés" (Delibes)

Bygone pleasures.   See Alte laute, II (Schumann)

Byrd, William
"All in a garden green"
Brave Lord Willoughby.   See Lord Willoughby
"Fortune, my foe"
"From heavenly maid"
"I thought that love had been a boy" Lord Willoughby
"Malt's come down"
"My mind to me a kingdom is"
"O, dear life"
"O mistress mine": traditional air arranged

Byrom, John
"Christians, awake" (Old English air; also music by Wainwright)

Byron, George Gordon Noel Byron, 6th baron
"Away, ye gay landscapes" (Scottish air)
"Farewell if ever fondest prayer" (Wesley)
Jephtha's daughter (Hebrew air)
"The kiss, dear maid" (Jausen)
"Maid of Athens" (music by Allen; Barnett; Nathan)
"My boat is on the shore" (Bishop)
"There be none of beauty's daughters" (Mendelssohn)
"We sate down and wept by the waters" (Wesley)

Byron lay dreaming.   Harrow school song.   LA

C

"Ça ça geschmauset." See Edite, bibite

Ca' the yowes to the knowes. Scottish air. Words by R. Burns. BSB—MMS
  Ca' the ewes to the knowes. PS 1
  "Hark the mavis' e'ening sang." BSR

La cabaña (The cabin) Latin American song. e.s. BF 2

The cabin boy. W. H. Ware. Words by T. Dibdin. BE 5

Caccini, Giulio
  "Amarilli, mia bella"
  "Amarilli, my fair one." See "Amarilli, mia bella"
  Amaryllis. See "Amarilli, mia bella"
  "Beasts of the forest." See "Fere selvagge"
  "Fere selvagge"
  "Tell me, fair Amarillis." See "Amarilli, mia bella"
  "Thou that hast wings for flying." See "Tu, ch'hai le penne, amore"
  "Tu, ch'hai le penne, amore"
  "Wild woodland creatures." See "Fere selvagge"

"Cachés dans cet asile." See Oh, ne t'éveille pas encor (Godard)

La cachucha. Spanish dance. s. LCP. e. only GO—WL
  La cachuca (Castanets are sounding) e. FSS 6—HSD

"Cade la sera" ("Shadows of evening") L. Mililotti. e.i. PG 1—PG 2

Cadlef gwyr Morganwg. See The war-song of the men of Glamorgan

Cadman, Charles Wakefield
  "Far off I hear a lover's flute"
  "From the land of the sky-blue water"
  "The moon drops low"
  A moonlight song
  "The white dawn is stealing"

"Caelia thy bright angel's face." See The The celestial mistress (Lawes)

Cagaran Gaolach ("Hush ye, my bairnie") Old Gaelic (Lochaber) lullaby. e. HSSS
  Cagaranan Gaolach ("Hush ye, my bairnie") e. MMS

"A cage all of gold was hanging." See La jaula de oro

Caidil gu lo. For English translations see "O hush thee, my babie" (Jensen); "O hush thee, my babie" (Sullivan); "Oh, hush thee, my babie" (Whitaker)

The cailín deas ("The gold rain of eve was descending") Irish air: Cailín deas g-cruidadh na mbo, or, The pretty girl milking the cow. Words by G. Sigerson. e. MMI

An cailín deas ruadh (The colleen dhas rue. —The pretty red girl) Irish folk song. e. JOI

Caisson song. See Artillery song

Cakes and ale. D. Lowe. Words by A. S. Walker. SSS

La Calavresella (The Calabrian maiden) Calabrian song. e.i. MSI

Caldara, Antonio
  "Alma del core"
  "As a sunbeam at morn." See "Come raggio di sol"
  "As on the swelling wave." See "Come raggio di sol"
  "As rays of setting sun." See "Come raggio di sol"
  "Come raggio di sol"
  "Friendly forest." See "Selve amiche, ombrose piante"
  "Heart of my own heart." See "Alma del core"
  "Kindly forest." See "Selve amiche, ombrose piante"
  "Like the sun's golden ray." See "Come raggio di sol"
  "Sebben, crudele"
  "Selve amiche, ombrose piante"
  "Tho' not deserving." See "Sebben, crudele"

Caldwell, W. W.
  Harvest song (Marshall)
  "My native land! what words can be" (Marshall)
  Washington (Marshall)
  Winter (Marshall)

Caleb Quotem. Shield. Words by G. Colman. BE 4

Calendar song. WSC

Caletti-Bruni, Pier Francesco. See Cavalli, Francesco

Caliban's song ("No more dams I'll make for fish") J. C. Smith. Words by W. Shakespeare. VFS

Calino casturame (Colleen oge astore) 16th century English song. CO 1

Calkin, John Baptiste
  "Fling out the banner: let it float"
  "Let music break on this blest morn"

Call, Leonhard von
  "Viel tausend sterne prangen"

The call ("Awake thee, my lady-love") Air: Per alaw, or, Sweet Richard. Words by G. Darley. MMW

"Call all hands to man the capstan." See Rolling home

"A call I hear! Hark! soft the tones and weak." Indian ritual air. FI

Call me back. L. Denza. Words by F. E. Weatherly. WBW

"Call me pet names." C. Jarvis. Words by Osgood. FSS 7—HSD

"Call me thine own" (Bright star of hope) J. Halévy. [Tr of Quand de la nuit] e. FSS 5—WA—WBT—WL—WSW

The call of freedom (Mnye li molodsú razoodálomu) M. Balakireff. Words by Koltsoff. e. SMR 2

The call of spring. See L'appel du printemps (Holmès)

Call to worship ("Yisroel, am kdeishim")
Jewish folk song. e.y. GF 1

Callanan, Jeremiah John
Farewell (Irish air)
"The night was still" (Irish air)

Callcott, John George
"Love wakes and weeps"

Callcott, John Wall
The fairies
"Friend of the brave"
The May fly
That day the world shall see
"Ye mariners of England"

Callcott, William Hutchins
The last man

La calle de la paloma (The street called
     Dove street)   Mexican folk song.
     e.s.   HF
"Como nací en la calle."   e.s.   HS

Caller herrin'.   Attributed to N. Gow.
Words by C. Nairne.   BF 2—BOS—
CS 1—CST—FSS 3—JO—PS 1—SMW

"**Call'st** thou, my fatherland."   See "Rufst
du, mein vaterland"

"**Calm** as the night, deep as the sea, oh!
son of man."   See "Still wie die
nacht, tief wie das meer, o mensch,
muss deine liebe sein" (Götze)

"**Calm** as the night, deep as the sea, should
be thy love."   See "Still wie die
nacht, tief wie das meer, soll deine
liebe sein" (Bohm)

"**Calm** is the lake."   See "Still ruht der
see" (Pfeil)

"**Calm** me, calm me, calm me."   See Pace,
pace, mio Dio (Verdi)

"**Calm** o'er the ocean blue."   See Santa
Lucia

"**Calm** on the listening ear of night."
Traditional air.   Words by E. H.
Sears. DC

"**Calm** on the listening ear of night."   J.
B. Dykes.   Words by E. H.
Sears. FSS 1
Calm on the ear of night. MCS

"**Calm** on the listening ear of night."   E.
J. Hopkins.   Words by E. H. Sears.
HC

"**Calm** the sun sets o'er the hills of Caer-
narvon."   See Morva Rhuddlan

"**Calm** thy sorrow, dear mother."   See
Rend'il sereno al ciglio (Händel)

"**Calm** was the hallowed night."   See
Calm was the night (Sullivan)

Calm was the night.   A. S. Sullivan.
Words by C. Elliott. MCS

Calm'd by her gentle, tender sway.   See
De' miei bollenti spiriti (Verdi)

"**Calmly** on sombre wings."   See "Regnava
nel silenzio" (Donizetti)

Le **Calvaire**.   See "There is a green hill
far away" (Gounod)

Calvary ("Ev'ry time I think about Jesus")
Negro spiritual. JB

Calvary ("Rest, rest to the weary")   P.
Rodney.   Words by H. Vaughan.
AB 1—FMB—HSS 1—HSS 2—HSS 4
—WA—WBT—WS

Calvé, Emma
"Va loin"

"**Cam**' ye by Athol."   Scottish air.
Words by J. Hogg. HSSS—PS 1

"**Came** a birdie a-flying."   See Frohe
botschaft (Müller)

"**Came** th' archangel to the Maid."   See
Angelus ad Virginem

"**Came** to the wedding."   See The uninvited aunt

"**Came** you not from Newcastle."   See
Newcastle

Campana, Fabio
"Come where the sunlight"
"Dal profondo dell' obblio"
"Dammi ch'io libi l'alito"
"A day, a day of glory"
"From the depths."   See "Dal pro-
fondo dell' obblio"
Glory of Christmas.   See "A day, a
day of glory"
Hearts of oak
I live and love thee.   See "Dammi
ch'io libi l'alito"
Joy must reign to-night
The mahogany tree
"Only to see thee"
The scout
Somewhere
Speak to me

Campbell, Alexander
"Holy was that night so fair" (Hollins)
The rural queen (Gaelic air)

Campbell, J.
The college gown (German air)

Campbell, James Edwin
My Merlindy Brown (Burleigh)
Negro lullaby (Burleigh)

Campbell, John Francis
Is toigh leam a' Ghaidhealtachd

Campbell, Joseph
"I love the din of beating drums"
     (Limerick air)
The ninepenny fidil (Irish air)

Campbell, Lewis
Carmen seculare (Oakeley)

Campbell, Mary Maxwell
The march of the Cameron men (Old
     air)

Campbell, Thomas
Battle of the Baltic (Purday)
The exile of Erin (Irish air)
"Friend of the brave" (Callcott)
Glenara (Scottish air)
The last man (Callcott)
Lord Ullin's daughter (Thomson)
The soldier's dream (Attwood)
"When Jordan hushed" (Phelps)
The wounded Hussar (Hewitt)
"Ye mariners of England" (music by
     Callcott; Pierson)

Campbell, W. W.
Joy must reign to-night (Campana)

The **Campbells** are comin'. Scottish national song. Words by R. Burns. BOS— BSE— EF—GO— HSSS— JO— LA— MMS— PS 1—WA— WCP—WSW

The Campbells are coming. FSS 5— HSC—HSD—JSE—WBT

"Upon the Lomonds I lay, I lay." BSR

Campenhout, François van
La Brabançonne
"Who'd believe this arbitrary deed." See La Brabançonne
"Who'd have believed such self-willed daring." See La Brabançonne

Campion, Thomas
Composer and author
"Move now with measured sound"
"Never weather-beaten sail"
"Now hath Flora robb'd her bow'rs"
"Shall I come, sweete love, to thee"
"There is a garden in her face"
Author
"If she forsake me" (Rosseter)
"O sweet delight" (17th century air)
"Though you are young" (17th century air)
"Triumph now with joy and mirth" (Giles)
"What if a day, or a month, or a year" (17th century air)

"**Campmeeting** down in the wilderness." See There's a meeting here to-night

Campo, Armand. See Ocampo, Armand

Campos, Juan Morell
El huérfano
Laura y Georgina

Campra, André
"Charmant papillon"
"Graceful butterfly." See "Charmant papillon"

De **Camptown** races. S. C. Foster (music and words) BOS—BSE—CR —HSD—NMP—SSS—WBT

De Camptown races (Gwine to run all night) FMB

"**Can** a little child, like me." W. R. Bassford. Words by M. M. Dodge. OH

"**Can** I believe it." See O mio Fernando (Donizetti)

"**Can** I cease to care." Air: Ay, waukin, O. Words by R. Burns. BSR

"**Can** it be so awfully bad." See Fantaisie aux divins mensonges (Delibes)

"**Can** nothing, sir, move you." See Lovely Nancy

"**Can** we weep for thee." See Ombra mai fu (Händel)

"**Can** you now leave me." Composer unknown. BE 7

Canadian boat song. Canadian air. Words by T. Moore. FSS 4—JO— LA—WBT

A **Canadian** boat song. M. Arnold. Words by T. Moore. TL

"Un **Canadien** errant" (A wandering Canadian) Canadian folk song. Air: La chanson des métamorphoses. e.f. TF

Le **canard** blanc (The white duck) Canadian folk song. e.f. TF
—Variant. e.f. TF
V'là l'bon vent. e.f. SMW
V'là l'bon vent ("Here's good wind."— French Canadian song) e. BMC

Le **canari.** See The canary (Tchaikovsky)

The **canary** (Der kanarienvogel) P. I. Tchaikovsky. Words from the Russian of Mey. e.g. FO 2— NM 2

The canary (Le canari) e.f. SC

Canas, Juan J.
Saludemos la patria (Aberle)

Canção do figueiral (Song of the fig-tree orchard) 13th century troubadour song. e.po. BO

Canción de cuna. Porto Rican song. s. LCP

Canción de la mañana. M. G. Tavárez. Words by M. Fernández Juncos. s. LCP

Cancion de maja (May song) Andalusian song. e.s. BO—SMF

La **canción** del soldado. E. Pujals. s. LCP

Cancion patriotica (Patriotic song) Mexican song. e.s. BSP
Patriotic song. e.s. MP

Cane, Melville Henry
To stand by thee, Columbia (Erskine)

Canfield, Hattie G.
His favorite flower (Lowitz)

"**Cangia,** cangia tue voglie" ("Change, O change thy fond wishes") G. B. Fasolo. e.i. PA 2

"**Cangiò** d'aspetto" ("How changed the vision") Händel. e.i. CS 1

Le **Canigou** (The Canigou) Song of the southern Pyrenees. e.f. TSF

Canitz, Friedrich Rudolf Ludwig, freiherr von
"Come, my soul, thou must be waking" (Hodges. Tr of Seele du musst munter werden)

"A **canner,** exceedingly canny." See Limericks

Cannibalee. M. A. Taylor. SSS

Canny-Soogagh. See An ceannuighe Sugach

Canoe song (Indian love) T. Lieurance. LS

Canonbury. See "Forth in Thy name, O Lord, I go" (Schumann)

"**Canst** thou believe I could forget." See Que je t'oublie (Chrétien)

"**Canst** thou believe love could deceive." See "Caro mio ben" (Giordani)

Canst thou leave me thus, my Katie. See "Is this thy plighted, fond regard"

El **cant** des aucels (The song of the birds) Catalan carol. e. MF

Can't you dance the polka. Capstan chantey. Air: Laddy Doolan. CR

Can't you live humble. Negro spiritual. DF

Cantata a Dom Miguel I. See Dom Miguel

"**Cante**, cante, fiette" ("O sing, fair maid")
Italian song. e.i.   BF 2
"**Cante** maśica."   See At parting
Canti, ridi, dormi.   See Chantez riez et
dormez (Gounod)
Canticum in alman matrem Abredonensem.
Aberdeen university song.   Words by
W. D. Geddes.   e.l.   SSS
Cantique de Noël.   A. Adam.   Words by
M. Cappeau.   e.   DC—TFC 1
Cantique de Noël (Christmas song)
e.   FSS 5—HSS 1—HSS 2—HSS 3
—HSS 4—PG 3
Christmas song.   e.   WBT
Noël.   e.f.   TS
Noël ("O holy night")   e.   HC
"O, holy night."   e.   BD
Cantique du Trappiste (Song of the Trap-
pist)   G. Meyerbeer.   e.f.   AB 2
Canto de' contadini Etnei (Song of the
peasants from Etna)   Sicilian song.
e.i.   MSI
El **canto** de la madre ("Duerme pronto")
Lullaby.   s.   LCP
Canto del carcerato (Song of the prisoner)
Sicilian song.   e.i.   MSI
Canto pel Natale.   C. Moderati (music
and words)   e.i.   DCS
Cantor, Otto
Auf ewig mein.   See For ever mine
For ever mine
Lov'd by thee
"Oh fair, oh sweet" (Tr of "Du bist
wie eine blume")
Rose-tide.   See Die rosen kommen
Die rosen kommen
"Sleep on, sleep on, my beloved one"
Cantu di janna (Why wound me)   Sar-
dinian song.   e.i.   BF 2
"**Canyons** cold! aeons old."   See From
Ghost Dance canyon (Lieurance)
Canzone del rabbino (Song of the rabbi)
Mascagni.   e.i.   OPS 4
Canzone di Natale (Christmas lullaby)
Italian song.   e.i.   BF 2
Canzone di Somma (Song from Somma)
Neapolitan song.   e.i.   MSI
Canzone d'i zampognari (Song of the bag-
pipers)   Neapolitan carol.   e.i.
MSI
Song of the bagpipers ("When Christ
our Lord was born")   e.   BSE
Song of the bagpipers ("When Christ
was born on earth")   e.   MF
Canzone marinaresca.   See Luna nova
(Costa)
Canzonetta ("O never lay me")   B. Zo-
lotariev.   Words by Tioutchev.   e.f.
NR 3
Canzonetta ("War schöner als")   See
Canzonette (Loewe)
Canzonetta di campagnuolo (Peasant's
song)   Italian folk song from the Ro-
magna.   e.i.   MSI—SMF
Canzonette ("War schöner als."—Canzo-
netta)   C. Loewe.   Words by J. W.
von Goethe.   e.g.   GMF
Canzuna di li carriteri (Song of the wagon-
ers)   Sicilian song.   e.i.   MSI

Cape Cod chantey.   BF 2
Capellina, Domenico
Invocazione a Dio (Mariani)
Capes, Bernard
Serenade (Smart)
"A **capital** ship."   Air: Ten thousand miles
away.   [Words by C. E. Carryl]   SSS
"A **capital** ship."   Old English air.
Words by C. E. Carryl.   BSS—
CST
Blow, ye winds, heigh-ho.   CHS—
MPC—WBT
"**Cap'n**, go side-track yo' train."   See
Chickahanka
El **capotin** (The rain song)   Spanish-
American song.   e.s.   LSS
Cappeau, M.
Cantique de Noël (Adam)
Capped and doctored and a'.   Air: Woo'd
and married and a'.   Words by J. S.
Blackie.   SSS
Captain Bover.   Scottish press gang song.
SMW
Captain Grant.   Folk song from Sussex.
SF 5
Captain Jinks.   HSD—WBT
Captain Kidd.   Forecastle song.   Air:
Samuel Hall.   CR—JO
Variant: Kidd's lament
Captain Morgan's march.   See Rhyvel-
gyrch Cadpen Morgan
Captain Thompson.   Irish folk song.
JOI
The **captain** with the smart cockade ("On
Entick's green meadows")   J. Hook.
ME
The **captain's** apprentice.   Folk song from
Norfolk.   SF 2
The **captain's** daughter.   See "We were
crowded in the cabin" (Woodbury)
The **captain's** lady.   Scottish air.   Words
by R. Burns.   BSB
"When the drums do beat."   BSR
Le **captif**.   See The captive (Grechani-
nov)
The **captive** ("Alone in my prison."—Le
captif)   A. Gretchaninoff.   Words
by Puschkin.   e.f.   NM 1
The **captive** ("Captive, et peut-être ou-
bliée")   See L'esclave (Lalo)
La **captive** ("Si je n'étais captive")   H.
Berlioz.   Words by V. Hugo.   e.f.
SOS 2
The **captive** admiral.   See Der gefangene
admiral (Lassen)
"A **captive** and forgotten, ill-fated."   See
L'esclave (Lalo)
"A **captive**, and perchance unremember'd."
See L'esclave (Lalo)
"**Captive**, et peut-être oubliée."   See L'es-
clave (Lalo)
The **captive** knight.   Arkwright.   Words
by Hemans.   JO
The **captive** maiden (Ty vzoidi, solntse
krasnoe)   Russian folk song.   e.
SSR 3
Captured.   See Bestikkelse (Lie)

Capua, Eduardo di
 Ah! Marì! ah! Marì. See Maria, Marì
 Maria, Marì
 Marie, ah, Marie. See Maria, Marì
 My sun. See 'O sole mio
 My sunshine. See 'O sole mio
 Serenade of the roses. See 'A sere-
  nata d' 'e rrose
 'A serenata d' 'e rrose
 'O sole mio
La Capuana (The girl from Capua) Nea-
  politan song. e.i. MSI
Capurro, G.
 'O sole mio (Capua)
"Cara mamma, io sono malata" (Dearest
  mother, I am ill) Italian song. e.i.
  BF 2
"Cara sposa, amante cara" ("Wife beloved")
  G. F. Händel. e.i. SOA 2
 "Cara sposa" ("Dearest consort") e.i.
  CS 2
"Cara sposa! Euridice." See "Che farò
  senza Euridice" (Gluck)
Caraid nan Gaidheal. See MacLeod, Nor-
  man
Carbery, Ethna, pseud. See MacManus,
  Mrs Anna (Johnston)
Lu carcerato p'ammore (Il carcerato per
  amore.—Love's prisoner) L. Biscardi.
  Words by A. Migliorato. e.i. FE
Lu cardillo (Il cardello.—The goldfinch) P.
  Labriola. e.i. FE
 Lu cardillo (The goldfinch) e.i. MN
 The **cardin** o't, the spinnin o't. See "I
  coft a stane o' haslock woo"
"Care compagne." Bellini. e.i. PP
"Care flies from the lad that is merry." M.
  Arne. Words by D. Garrick. BE 5
  —ME
"Care, thou canker of our joys." J. Garth.
  Words by Grant. CO 2—DM 2
"Careless of love." See The surprise
  (Lawes)
"Caressing mine idol's pillow." See "In-
  torno all'idol mio" (Cesti)
Carew, Thomas
 "Mark how the blushful morn"
  (Charles I)
 Unfading beauty (Lawes)
Carey, George Saville
  Composer
 The lovers' controversy
  Author
 The disconsolate sailor (Hook)
Carey, Henry
  Composer
 America (same air as God save the
  king; attributed)
 America: fugitive stanza (same air as
  God save the king; attributed)
 "Brave grenadiers, rejoice"
 "Daughter, you're too young" (from
  Nancy)
 "Divinest fair"
 "Flocks are sporting"
 "God bless our native land! firm may
  she ever stand" (same air as God
  save the king; attributed)
 God save the king (attributed)

"Hail thou, whose victor's crown." See
 "Heil dir im siegerkranz" (attribu-
 ted)
The happy beggars (attributed)
"Heil dir im siegerkranz" (same air as
 God save the king; attributed)
"Heil, unserm könig, heil" (same air
 as God save the king; attributed)
"Here's to thee, my boy"
The honest Yorkshireman
"The hounds are all out"
The merry Gregorians
The modern beau (from The honest
 Yorkshireman)
"My country, 'tis of thee." See
 America (attributed)
"Now away, my brave boys" (attribut-
 ed)
"Of all the girls that are so smart."
 See Sally in our alley
A pastoral. See "Flocks are sporting"
The plausible lover
Roger's courtship
Sally in our alley
Sally Sweetbread
"Saw you the nymph"
Spring. See "Flocks are sporting"
"Though beauty like the rose"
  Author
Sally in our alley (Old English air;
 also music by author)
Caribou dance. Ojibway Indian song. 2
 airs. in. BA
Carissimi, Giacomo
 "A morìre"
 "Ah, to perish." See "A morìre"
 Deh, contentatevi
 "Filli, non t'amo più"
 "I triumph! I triumph." See Vittoria,
  mio core
 "No, no, hope has perished." See
  "No, no, non si speri"
 "No, no, mio core"
 "No, no, non si speri"
 "Phyllis no more I love." See "Filli,
  non t'amo più"
 Pray, let me, suffering. See Deh, con-
  tentatevi
 Victorious my heart is. See Vittoria,
  mio core
 Vittoria, mio core
 "Vittoria! vittoria." See Vittoria,
  mio core
 "Yield not, my heart." See "No, no,
  mio core"
Carl, and the king come. See "An some-
  body were come again"
"Carl Johan." National song of Sweden.
  J. Du Puy. Words by H. A. Kull-
  berg. e.sw. BSP
 "Charles John, our brave King." e.sw.
  MP—NMS—WBT. e. only JS—
  KSN
 "Charles John, our brave king."
  (Swedish national hymn) e.sw.
  NMH
 "Karl John" ("Karl John, our great
  king") e. BMC
 Swedish national air. e. LA
 Swedish national song. e.sw. WA

The **carles** o' Dysart.   See Hey, ca' thro'
Carleton, Mrs C. J.
  The song of Australia (Linger)
Carleton spelling song.   Carleton college
  song. Words by G. Huntington. CHS
Carlyle, Alexander
  "O, wha's at the window, wha, wha"
  (Smith)
La **Carmagnole.**   Italian air. e.f. BSP
The **carman's** whistle.   Old song.   BOH
Carmarthen bells (How oft to mind I call)
  Air: The days that won't return.
  Words by Ieuan Dhu.   MMW
Carmè.   Canto sorrentino.   G. B. de Cur-
  tis.   e.i.   FE.   e. only CST—
  WBT—WL
  Carmela.   e.i.   MN
Carmela ("Así cual mueren")   Mexican
  folk song.   e.s.   HS
Carmela ("Fore mura nce sta")   See
  Carmè. (Curtis)
Carmen Carthusianum.   Charterhouse
  school song. W. Horsley.   1. BOS
Carmen de Lalages agna.   S. Winner.
  Words by J. D. Symon.   1.   SSS
Carmen Etonense.   J. Barnby.   Words
  by A. C. Ainger.   1.   BOS
Carmen seculare (A song of centuries) St
  Andrews university song. H. Oake-
  ley.   Words by L. Campbell.   e.l.
  SSS
Carmeña ("Dance and song make glad the
  night")   H. L. Wilson.   Words by
  E. Walton. MSF 2
Carmeña ("Dance, play, sing, sorrow dis-
  dain."—Dance and sing)   H. L. Wil-
  son. Words by M. L. Baum. TFC 2
Carmichael, Mary
  A May song
  Mowing the hay
Carnicer y Batlle, Ramon
  Causion nacional chilena.   See Dulce
  patria
  Chilean national hymn.   See Dulce
  patria
  Dulce patria
  National anthem of Chili.   See Dulce
  patria
The **carnival** of Venice ("Ah, fly my gon-
  dolier")   18th century Neapolitan folk
  air: La ricciolella, or, Carnival of Ven-
  ice.   e.   BD
Carnival of Venice ("Oh, come to me")
  18th century Neapolitan folk air:
  La ricciolella, or, Carnival of Ven-
  ice. Words by T. Moore. WBT
  "Oh, come to me."   BO
  "Oh, come to me when daylight sets"
  (Venetian song) BMC
"**Caro** cibus, sanguis potus" ("Lord at all
  times I will bless Thee")   Mendelssohn.   e.l.   HSS 3
  "Lord, at all times I will bless Thee."
  e.   HSS 4
"**Caro** laccio, dolce nodo" ("Dainty meshes,
  net enticeful") F. Gasparini.   e.i.
  PA 2

"**Caro** mio ben" ("Canst thou believe") G.
  Giordani.   e.i.   KS 3
"Caro mio ben" ("Darling, my own")
  e.i.   KF 4—PG 3—PG 4
"Caro mio ben" ("My dearest love")
  e.i.   FEI 2
"Caro mio ben" ("Thou, all my bliss")
  e.i.   PA 2
"Caro mio ben" ("Turn once again")
  e.i.   CS 1
Caro nome.   Verdi.   e.i.   OPS 1—PP.
  e. only WBT
  Caro nome (Dearest name)   e.i.   MC
Carol, brothers, carol (A Christmas carol)
  A. F. M. Custance.   [Words by W. A.
  Muhlenberg]   NMS
Carol, brothers, carol.   W. A. Muhlenberg
  (music and words)   FSS 3—HC—JSE
  —MCS
"**Carol,** but in gladness."   See Carol,
  brothers, carol (Muhlenberg)
"**Carol,** but with gladness."   See Carol,
  brothers, carol (Custance)
Carol, carol, Christians.   Composer un-
  known. Words by A. C. Coxe. FSS 7
  —MCS—WS
Carol, carol, Christians.   M. Lindsay
  Bliss.   Words by A. C. Coxe.   HC
Carol, carol, Christians.   R. F. Smith.
  Words by A. C. Coxe.   HC
"**Carol,** carol, Easter morn."   A. Russell.
  Words by H. S. Lee.   BD
"**Carol!** carol joyfully."   C. Simper.
  Words by A. S. Woods.   HC
"**Carol,** children carol, carol joyfully." Old
  English song.   WSC
Carol, children, carol gladly.   See Lo!
  now he is come
"**Carol,** Christian children."   A. Moffat.
  Words by H. W. Selby.   HC
Carol for Christmas day.   See "All this
  night bright angels sing" (Sullivan)
Carol for Christmas eve ("Listen, lord-
  lings")   See "Listen, lordlings, unto
  me" (Gascon air); "Listen, lordlings,
  unto me" (Ouseley)
A **carol** for Christmas eve ("The Lord at
  first")   See "The Lord at first did
  Adam make"
Carol for Christmas eve ("The sun sets
  brightly")   Words by R. Herrick.
  MCS
Carol for New Year's day.   A. H. Brown.
  BSC
  "The old year now away has fled." HC
A **carol** for Twelfth day.   WCC
Carol of the birds.   See Nouël des ausèls
Carol of the flowers ("Come with us, sweet
  flowers")   Carol from Bas-Quercy.
  Tr of Nouël de las flous.   e.   DC—
  HC—MF—TL
"**Carol,** sweetly carol, a Saviour born to-
  day."   E. Bunnett.   Words by F.
  Crosby.   HC
"**Carol,** sweetly carol, a Saviour born to-
  day."   T. E. Perkins.   Words by F.
  Crosby.   HC

"**Carol**, sweetly carol; raise your voices high." W. Sharrot. HC

"**Carol** we high, carol we low." A. Redhead. HC

"**Carol** we joyfully." A. H. Brown. Words by S. C. Clarke. HC

"**Carol** we the blessing." B. K. Atkyns. HC

Carolan, Turlogh. See O'Carolan, Turlogh

La **Carolina** ("Aggio visto na figliola."— Caroline) Neapolitan song. e.i. MSI—SMW

La **Carolina** ("Carolina, de mi vida") M. Pablo Andraca. Words by J. C. Martinez. s. LCP

"**Carolina,** de mi vida." See La Carolina (Pablo Andraca)

Caroline ("Aggio visto na figliola") See La Carolina

Caroline ("Aine, dé, trois, Caroline") Negro creole folk song. e.f. KA

"**Carolling,** carolling all thro' the night." C. Simper. Words by T. D. Hyde. HC

Carousal. Ojibway Indian song. e.in. BA

Carpani, Guiseppe
   "In questa tomba oscura" (Beethoven)

Carpenter, Joseph Edwards
   "Beautiful Venice" (Knight)
   "Do they think of me at home" (Glover)
   A faithful heart (Abt)
   The good-bye at the door (Glover)
   Her bright smile haunts me still (Wrighton)
   "In the starlight" (Glover)
   Light of the world (Hatton)
   Little Sunbeam (Farmer)
   "Oh! for those old familiar friends" (Barnett)
   The old familiar place (Glover)
   "Over the waves we float" (Glover)
   "Sunshine and cloud" (Glover)
   "What are the wild waves saying" (Glover)
   "When gentle winds" (Schumann)
   When the soft twilight (Schumann)

El **carpintero.** See Ris, ras

Carré, Michel
   Chanson de la sorcière (Gounod)
   Chant provençal (Massenet)
   "De mon amie, fleur endormie" (Bizet)
   "Ô légère hirondelle" (Gounod)
   "Si les filles d'Arles" (Gounod)
   Le soir (Thomas)

Carré, Michel, and Barbier, Jules
   "Le bonheur est chose légère" (Saint-Saëns)
   Je suis Titania (Thomas)

Carreris, P.
   Ho gerō-Demōs. See Old Demos and his rifle
   Old Demos and his rifle

Carried off to sea. See "Isabeau se promène"

The **carrier** bird. See "The bird let loose" (Bruce)

The **carrier** dove. D. Johnson. FSS 2— HSD—JO—WBT

The **carrier** pigeon. Irish air. Words by J. G. Percival. JO

The **carrion** crow. Folk song from North Carolina. CSE

Carrott, Liversey
   "O'er Bethlehem's hill, in time of old"

"**Carry** me back to old Virginny." J. Bland. HSD

Carry me back to old Virginny ("On the floating scow of old Virginny") E. P. Christy (music and words) NMP— WA—WBT—WSW

Carryl, Charles Edward
   "A capital ship" (Old English air; also music by unknown composer)

Carryl, Guy Wetmore
   Alumni song (Foster)
   Evening on the campus (Composer unknown)
   The glorious Sophomore class (Irish air)
   A knot of white and blue (Woodruff)

Carter, E. T.
   Mary's little wise man

Carter, Elizabeth
   "The solitary bird of night" (Composer unknown)

Carter, Ernest
   At the hop
   Steps song

Carter, Florence L.
   Weary (Gabriel)

Carter, Thomas
   "O Nannie, wilt thou gang wi' me"
   "Stand to your guns"

Cartwright,
   To a lady weeping (Lawes)

"**Carulì,** cu st'uocchie doce, nire, nire." See Oje Carulì (Costi)

"**Carv'd** upon my inmost heart." See Caro nome (Verdi)

Carve dat possum. S. Lucas (music and words) NMP—WBT—WC

Cary, Alice
   Don't be sorrowful, darling (Webster)
   Idle (Seidel)
   The little house on the hill (Schubert)
   November (Hutchinson)
   "There is hovering about me" (Abt)
   To mother Fairie (Scottish air)

Cary, Phoebe
   Baby's ring (English air)
   Faithful (Mozart)
   The fortune in the daisy (Becker)
   Hark! the angel choir (Composer unknown)
   In absence (Haydn)
   "One sweetly solemn thought" (music by Ambrose; Weber; also unknown composer)
   Ready (Composer unknown)

"**Casey** Jones." Boy scout song. E. Newton. Words by B. Braley. BSS

La **casita.** Folk song from central Mexico. e.s. HS

Caspari, Theodor
   Bestikkelse (Lie)

Casson, Margaret
   The cuckoo
"Cast, my love, thine eyes around." See Damon and Florella (Arne)
"Cast thy bread on the waters." J. L. Roeckel. Words by M. Mark-Lemon. FSS 6—HSS 2—JSE
"Cast thy burden on the Lord." F. Mendelssohn. e. FSS 6—WBT
"Cast your caps and cares away." J. Wilson. Words by J. Fletcher. JE
"Casta diva, che inargenti" ("Goddess fairest") Bellini. e.i. PP
   "Casta diva, che inargenti" ("Chaste enchantress") e.i. KS 1
Castanet song. G. Bizet. WBT
Castanets are sounding. See La cachuca
Castilian bolero. See Bolero castellano
Castlehyde. Irish folk song. JOI
Castles in Spain. See Aladdin (Bellini)
Castles in the air ("The bonnie, bonnie bairn") Composer unknown. Words by J. Ballantine. JO
Castles in the air ("Spring's bright sunlit time") Greek folk air. Words by R. R. Whitehead. WF
Caswall, Edward
   "Gently falls the winter snow" (Irons)
   "See amid the winter's snow" (French carol; also music by Gollmick; Goss; Hatton; Smith)
   "Sleep, holy Babe" (Ancient air; also music by Austin; Custance; Dykes; Field; Partridge; also unknown composer)
La **Catanzarese** (The maid of Catanzaro) Calabrian song. e.i. MSI
Catarì! Catarì (Catari! Catari) L. de Luca. Words by F. Feola. e.i. MN
"Catarina, while you play at sleeping." See "Vous qui faites l'endormie" (Gounod)
"Catarina, while you sham asleep." See "Vous qui faites l'endormie" (Gounod)
Catch him and hold him. See Oi, alas, a robber
Cate, A. ten
   To stay at home is best
"Caterpillar! caterpillar." Russian folk air. Words by H. H. Harbour. DO
"Catina bellina" ("Catina, my sweetheart") Venetian folk song. e.i. SMF
   "Catina bellina" (Pretty Kathrin) e.i. MSI
"The **Catrine** woods were yellow seen." A. Masterton. Words by R. Burns. BSR
"The **cattle** from the kraal have strayed." (Hottentot song) e. BMC
Cauffman, Frank G.
   "Have you seen but a bright lily grow" Love song. See "Have you seen but a bright lily grow"
   Wind and sea
"Cauld blaws the wind." See Up in the morning early
"Cauld is the e'enin blast." Air: Peggy Ramsay. Words by R. Burns. BSR

Cauld kail in Aberdeen. See "There's cauld kail in Aberdeen"
Causion nacional chilena. See Dulce patria (Carnicer y Batlle)
Cavalilly man. 17th century song. CO 2
Cavalli, Francesco
   "Delizie contente, che l'alma beate" (from Giasone)
   "Dell' antro magico"
   "Dolce Amor, bendato dio"
   "Donzelle, fuggite"
   "Gates of gloom." See "Dell' antro magico"
   "God of love, fair blindfold Cupid." See "Dolce Amor, bendato dio"
   "Many and sweet the raptures." See "Troppo soavi i gusti"
   "O exquisite pleasures." See Delizie contente, che l'alma beate"
   "Oh, hasten, ye maidens." See "Donzelle, fuggite"
   "Troppo soavi i gusti"
   "Ye blisses, that ravish." See "Delizie contente, che l'alma beate
Cavallo, Johann N.
   Abschied
   Parting. See Abschied
"Il **cavallo** scalpita" (Alfio's entrance-song) P. Mascagni. e.i. SOA 4
Cavalry song. See Reiterlied (Zahn)
Cavanass, J. M.
   By the waters of Minnetonka (Lieurance)
Cavendish, Georgiana, duchess of Devonshire. See Devonshire, Georgiana Cavendish, duchess of
Cawein, Madison Julius
   Under the stars and stripes (Converse)
Cawood, John
   "Hark! what mean those holy voices" (music by Arnold; Geer; Gilbert; Pearce)
Cazalis, Henri
   Chanson triste (Duparc)
   Extase (Duparc)
"Ce breuvage pourrait me donner un tel rêve." See Vision fugitive (Massenet)
"Ce matin me suis levé" ("It was early that I woke") French folk song. e.f. TSF
Ce que je suis sans toi (Without thee) Gounod. Words by L. de Peyre. e.f. CS 2—MSS 2—SS 2
"Ce qu'est le lierre sans l'orneau." See Ce que je suis sans toi (Gounod)
"Ce sont les fill's d'un cantinier." See Le cotillon racheté
"Cé ti manmaille-là." See Loéma tombé
An **ceannuighe** Sugach (Canny-Soogagh.—The jolly pedlar) Irish folk song. e. JOI
"Cease, cease to think." See Summer studies (Hutchinson)
Cease my heart from wounding. See "O cessate di piagarmi" (Scarlatti)
"Cease, oh, cease my heart from wounding." See "O cessate di piagarmi" (Scarlatti)

"Cease, oh maiden." See "O cessate di piagarmi" (Scarlatti)

"Cease, O my sad soul." H. Purcell. Words by C. Webbe. DM 2—JE—PR 1

"Cease, rude Boreas, blust'ring railer." See The storm

"Cease, sorrows, now." T. Weelkes. BOH

"Cease to torment." See "O cessate di piagarmi" (Scarlatti)

"Cease your funning." 18th century air. Words by J. Gay. BE 4—CO 2—DM 1 —HSE 1—MM

Cécilia. See "Mon pèr' n'avait fille que moi"

Cedant justi signa luctus. For English translation see "Far be sorrow, tears, and sighing" (Hodges)

"The cedar of Lebanon." Old air. Words by R. F. Littledale. HC

Cedit hyems eminus. For English translation see "Winter-tide hath past away"

"Celamina, of my heart." Pepusch. Words by J. Dryden. DM 2

"Celebrate this festival." H. Purcell. BE 4

Celeste Aida. Verdi. e.i. OPS 3— SOA 3
　　Celeste Aida (Heavenly Aida) e.i. KS 4. e. only WA
　　"Heav'nly Aïda." e. WL

The celestial mistress ("Caelia thy bright angel's face") ·H. Lawes. Words by Earl of Winchilsea. JE

"Celia, let not pride undo you." J. Weldon. PR 2

Celia's invitation ("The earth is clothed in cheerful green") 18th century song. ME

Los celos de Carolina. Folk song from southern California. e.s. HS

"Celui dont la parole efface toutes peines." See Il est doux, il est bon (Massenet)

Cennick, John
　　"Children of the heavenly King" (Malan)
　　"Jesus, my all, to heaven is gone" (Coles)

Centennial hymn. J. K. Paine. Words by J. G. Whittier. LBR

The centipede and the frog. W. H. Jones. CHS

"C'era un re, un re di Thulé." See Le roi de Thule (Gounod)

C'era una volta un principe. A. C. Gomes. e.i. SOA 1

"Un certo non so che" ("Some one, I know not who") A. Vivaldi e.i. FEI 2

"Un certo non so che" ("There's one, I know him not") e.i. PA 1

"Ces montagnes qui sont tant hautes." See "Aqueros mountagnos" (Foix)

Cesek, Hans A.
　　Petites roses
　　Sweet wild roses. See Petites roses
　　Wild roses. See Petites roses

"C'est à la port' d'un cabaret." See La femme avare et le crucifix

"C'est des contrebandiers la refuge ordinaire." See Je dis que rien ne m'épouvante (Bizet)

"C'est en vain que j'ai cru me soustraire au remords." See Je t'implore, ô mon frère (Thomas)

"C'est ici que le beau Céphale." See Naissantes fleurs (Grétry)

"C'est la belle Françoise, lon gai." See La belle Françoise

"C'est la fille d'un geôlier." See Le prisonnier et la fille du geôlier

"C'est la fille d'un prince." See La princesse et le bourreau

C'est la princesse de Navarre (Of fair Navarre the princess royal) F. A. Boieldieu. e.f. KS 5

"C'est la vieille qui est ma douce (amie)." See "Ann hini gouz"

"C'est l'automne qui frappe à nos portes." See Autumn melody (Koreshchenko)

"C'est le prince d'Orange." See Le prince d'Orange

"C'est le roi Dagobert." See Le roi Dagobert

"C'est moi, j'ai tout brisé." See Me voici dans son boudoir (Thomas)

C'est mon ami. See "Ah! s'il est dans votre village" (Maria Charlotte Amelia)

"C'est passant par Varennes." See Je ne suis pas si vilaine

"C'est un garçon vive-la-joie." See Le retour funeste

"C'est une fleur, fleur des prairies." See Rose de Provence

Cesti, Marc' Antonio
　　"About my beloved idol." See "Intorno all'idol mio"
　　"Ah! quanto è vero" (from Il pomo d'oro)
　　"Caressing mine idol's pillow." See "Intorno all'idol mio"
　　"Che angoscia, che affanno" (from Il pomo d'oro)
　　"Cupid can never." See "Ah! quanto è vero"
　　"E dove t'aggiri" (from Il pomo d'oro)
　　"Intorno all'idol mio" (from Orontea)
　　"O del ben che acquisterò" (from Il pomo d'oro)
　　"Oh, whither art roaming." See "E dove t'aggiri"
　　'Round thee, my idol. See "Intorno all'idol mio"
　　"Soon I'll own riches divine." See "O del ben che acquisterò"
　　"Tu mancavi a tormentarmi"
　　"Wilt no longer thou torment me." See "Tu mancavi a tormentarmi"
　　"With torments overpowering." See "Che angoscia, che affanno"

"Cet étang qui s'étend." See Menuet d'Exaudet (Exaudet)

"C'était la fill' d'un roi français." See La princesse de France mariée à un Anglais (Norman version)

"C'était un chasseron, un chasseur de gibier." See L'occasion manquée (Canadian version)

Cette aimable tourterelle (This lovely turtle-dove) French Canadian folk song. e.f. BFS

"Ceux qui diront: Le reus il vient." See La chanson du reuze

Chadwick, George Whitefield
"The busy lark"
In my beloved's eyes
The lamb
"Land of our hearts"
"The stormy evening"

Chadwick, John White
"Now sing we a song for the harvest" (Reay)

Chaffee, A. G.
A health to all good fellows

Chaikovskiĭ, Petr Il'ich. See Tchaikovsky, Peter Ilyich

"Chairs to mend, old chairs to mend." Round. FSS 7—HSC—TFC 2—WBT

The chalet girl's Sunday. See Saetergjentens söndag (Bull)

Chalkhill, John
The angler's song (Lawes) Authorship uncertain

Challinor, F. A.
"Ring, ring the bells"

"Chałupeczka niska, ojciec matkę ściska." See The tiny hut

Chalvey. See "A few more years shall roll"; Glory begun below (Hayne)

Chamarrita (The Chamarrita) Song from the Azores. e.po. BF 2

Chamberlain, C. H.
Illinois (Old air; also music by Jones)

Chambers-Ketchum, Mrs Annie. See Ketchum, Mrs Annie (Chambers)

Chaminade, Cécile Louise Stéphanie
L'anneau d'argent
Chanson slave
"If thou shouldst tell me." See "Tu me dirais"
Ritournelle
Rosemonde
"Si j'étais jardinier"
The silver ring. See L'anneau d'argent
Slav song. See Chanson slave
"Tu me dirais"
"Were I gardener." See "Si j'étais jardinier"

Chamisso, Adelbert von
"Er, der herrlichste von allen" (Schumann)
The pigtail (Bullard)
Verrathene liebe (Schumann)

Champlain. University of Vermont song. C. S. Putnam. Words by C. W. Fisher. CHS

Champneys, Frank
"Come let us all sweet carols sing"

Champs paternels. E. N. Méhul. e.f. SOA 3
"Vainement Pharaon" ("Vainly Pharaoh attempts") e.f. KS 4

Chancellor Inglis. Edinburgh university song. Air: Kate Dalrymple. Words by D. Maclagan. SSS

Chandler,
"Adieu, my native land, adieu"

"Change, O change thy fond wishes." See "Cangia, cangia tue voglie" (Fasolo)

A change of mind. See Le changement

Le changement (A change of mind) French Canadian song. e.f. BF 2

Chanson à boire. See "Ma bouteille m'est fidèle"

Chanson à danser ("I sigh of love") Old French air. e.f. NG

Chanson bachique ("O vin, dissipe la tristesse") A. Thomas. e.f. SOA 4

Chanson d'amour (Love-song) J. Hollman. Words by C. Grandmougin. e.f. SOS 1—SOS 2

Chanson de berger (Shepherd song) Canadian folk song. e.f. TF

Chanson de Florian. See "Ah! s'il est dans votre village" (Godard)

Chanson de la forêt sombre. See Song of the dark forest (Borodin)

La chanson de la mariée (Song of the bride) French folk song. e.f. TSF

Chanson de la sorcière ("Now's the time to love") Gounod. Words by M. Carré. e.f. CS 1

La chanson de l'alouette (The lark's song) E. Lalo. Words by V. de Laprade. e.f. SAM

La chanson de Malbrough. See "Malbrough s'en va-t-en guerre"

Chanson de matelots. Provençal sailors' song. e.f. SMW

La chanson de Renaud (The song of Renaud) French folk song. e.f. TSF

Chanson de Zuleika. See Song of Zuleika (Rimskiĭ-Korsakov)

Chanson d'enfant. See A child's song (Musorgskiĭ)

La chanson des mensonges (The song of lies) Canadian folk song. e.f. BFS—TF

La chanson des métamorphoses (The song of transformations) Folk song:
Breton version. e.f. TF
—Canadian version. e.f. TF

Chanson des rues. See "'Neath the shadow of a tree"

La chanson du bouvier (The drover's song) Song of Gascony. e.f. TSF

La chanson du reuze (Song of the giant) Flemish song. e.f.fl. TSF

Chanson du toréador (Toréador song) G. Bizet. e.f. SM 4
Chanson du toréador ("Votre toast, je peux vous le rendre") e.f. SOA 4
Toreador song. e. WA—WBT
Toreador's song. e. BD
Toreador's song ("Here's to you."—"Con voi ber") e.i. CB
"Votre toast, je peux vous le rendre" ("Now a toast! your own I will make me."—Toréador song) e.f. OPS 4

Chanson hebraïque. See Hebrew love-song (Rimskiï-Korsakov)

Chanson indoue. See A song of India (Rimskiï-Korsakov)

Chanson mauresque. See Soleïma

Chanson perpétuelle (The eternal song) E. Chausson. Words by C. Cros. e.f. CM 1

Chanson slave (Slav song) C. Chaminade. Words by P. Ginisty. e.f. PG 2

Chanson triste (A song of sorrow) H. Duparc. Words by J. Lahor. e.f. SAM

Chant d'automne. See Autumn melody (Koreshchenko)

Chant de Marthe. See Martha's song (Musorgskiï)

Chant de quête de l'Alsace. Alsatian traditional air. e.f. TSF

Chant du chasseur (Le jour est levé) G. Meyerbeer. e.f. SOA 5

Le chant du départ (Song of departure) War hymn. É. N. Méhul. Words by M. J. Chénier. e.f. CM 2

Le chant du départ (The departure of the patriots) e.f. SN

Chant du mendiant. See Beggar's song (Wihtol)

Chant hindou (Hindoo song) H. Bemberg. Words by A. Ocampo. e.f. CM 1—HM 1—PG 1—PG 2

Chant of Breton peasants. Naumann. Words by L. C. Redden. MCS

The chant of the Girondins. See Mourir pour la patrie

Chant of the "Short ags." College song. CHS

Chant provençal (Provence song) J. Massenet. Words by M. Carré. e.f. HM 2

Chant vénitien. For English translation see Venetian song (Bemberg)

"Chante qui voudra les attraits." See La charmante Marguerite

Chanter, mignonne, Cécilia. See "Mon pèr' n'avait fille que moi" (Si mon papa le savait)

"Chantez pipeaux." See The reapers (Vassilenko)

Chantez riez et dormez (Sing, smile and slumber) C. Gounod. Words by V. Hugo. e.f. PG 1—PG 4

Chantez, riez, dormez (Sing, smile, slumber) e. BSE

Sérénade ("Quand tu chantes") e.f. CM 2—CS 1—MSS 1—SS 1

Serenade ("When thou'rt cradled") e. WL

Sing, smile, slumber. e. JSE—WBT

Sing, smile, slumber (Canti, ridi, dormi) e.f. FSS 6—HSD

Chantons! bargiés, Noué, Noué ("Shepherds, shake off your drowsy sleep") Besançon carol. e. MF

Chantons, bergers, Noël, Noël. e. DC

"Shepherds, shake off your drowsy sleep." e. HC

Chantons, je vous en prie. For English translation see "Now sing we all full sweetly"

Chantons les amours de Jean (I sing of the love of Jean) Bergerette. e.f. WB

"Chantons pour passer le temps." See La fille matelot

The chapel ("See yon chapel on the hill") Words by Uhland. e. FSS 2

The chapel ("What gleams so bright") Kreutzer. e. LA

"What beams so bright." e. WC

Chapin, Anna Alice
The ride (Shelley)

Chapman, Arthur
For you (Smith)
Indian trail song (Loomis)
Until the day breaks (Gounod)

Chapman, E. W.
Flowers for the brave (Bellini)

Chapman, Thomas
"My Betsy is the blithest maid" (Kirshaw)

Chapt'm un bindt'm. See Oi, alas, a robber

"Chaque beau jour qui s'écoule." See Parfum de fleur (Blanc)

"Chaque chose a son temps" ("There's a time for all things") Bergerette. e.f. WB

"A charge to keep have I" (Dennis) H. G. Nägeli. FSS 5

Charity. See "Voici l'hiver et son triste cortège" (Faure)

Charki hidjaz. See "The sun hangs high"

Charles I, king of England
"Mark how the blushful morn"
"Why should'st thou swear I am forsworn"

Charles II, king of England
The phoenix (Humfrey) Authorship uncertain

Charles, Mrs Elizabeth (Rundle)
"Praise ye the Father! for his loving-kindness" (Flemming)

"Charles John, our brave King." See "Carl Johan"

Charles of Sweden. See "Come jolly Bacchus"

Charlie is my darling. See O, Charlie is my daring

Charlton, Maude Martin
"All hail to thee, fair Western"

The charm. See Le charme (Chausson)

"Charm me asleep." Suabian folk air. Words by R. Herrick. DSH

"Charmant oiseau" ("Delightful bird") F. David. e.f. KS 1—MC

"Charmant oiseau" ("Thou lovely bird") e.f. OPS 1

"Charmant papillon" ("Graceful butterfly") A. Campra. e.f. KS 1—MC

La charmante Marguerite (Charming Marguerite) Old French air. e.f. EF—KF 2

Charming Marguerite. e. BD

Le charme (The charm) E. Chausson. Words by A. Silvestre. e.f. SAM

Charmente Gabrielle (Charming Gabrielle) Attributed to Henri IV (music and words) e. BSE

Charming beauty bright.   Kentucky mountain song.   WT
Variant of: The lover's lament

"Charming Chloë."   Composer and author unknown.   PR 2

"Charming eyes so wary."   See "Vezzosette e care" (Falconieri)

Charming Gabrielle.   See Charmente Gabrielle (Henry IV?)

"Charming is your shape and air."   See The reproof

Charming Marguerite.   See La charmante Marguerite

Charming Mary Neill.   Donegal song. JOI

"Charming Molly, I do love thee."   See Constant Johnny

"Charming Phyllis."   Old English air. BE 1

"Charõ to 'keïn to stoma sou."   See "Upon thy lovely lips"

El **charro** (The kind hearted boss)   Spanish-American song.   e.s.   LSS

"Chassons de nos plaisirs."   J. P. Rameau.   e.f.   SOA 1

"Chaste enchantress."   See "Casta diva, che inargenti" (Bellini)

Chata cara de bule (Bells of the Rosário)   Spanish-American song.   e.s.   LSS

The **chatterbox.**   Words by J. Taylor. FSS 6

The **chattering** squaw.   Cree Indian air. e.   TFC 2

Chaucer, Geoffrey
"The busy lark" (Chadwick)

Chausson, Ernest
Butterflies.   See Les papillons
Chanson perpétuelle
The charm.   See Le charme
Le charme
The dead.   See Les morts
The eternal song.   See Chanson perpétuelle
Les morts
Les papillons

Chauvenet, W. M.
In my beloved's eyes (Chadwick)

"Che angoscia, che affanno" ("With torments overpowering")   M. Cesti.   e.i. FEI 1

"Che bel moffin la Peppinetta."   See La Peppinetta

"Che bella cosa 'na iurnata 'e sole."   See 'O sole mio (Capua)

Che bella notte che fa.   See Quattro cavai

"Che dissi."   Rossini.   e.i.   PP

"Che farò senza Euridice" ("Alas! why hast thou left me")   C. W. von Gluck. e.i.   SOA 2
Che farò (Have I lost thee)   e.i.   CS 1
Che farò senza Euridice (I have lost my Euridice)   e.i.   KS 3
"Che farò senza Euridice" ("What sad lot the stars prepare me")   e.i. OPS 2

"Che fiero costume" ("What strange whim pursuing")   G. Legrenzi.   e.i. FEI 1
"Che fiero costume" ("How void of compassion")   e.i.   PA 1
"Che fiero costume" ("With cunning conniving")   e.i.   NG—PG 3— PG 4

"Che mai t'ho fatt', amor" ("Why do you turn your eyes away")   Abruzzian folk song.   e.i.   MSI

"Che mai vegg' io."   See Infelice! e tu credevi (Verdi)

Che t'ho fatto (Wherein have I offended)   Neapolitan popular song.   e.i.   SMF

"Cheeks of rose, tiny toes."   See Our baby

"Cheer, boys, cheer."   H. Russell.   Words by C. Mackay.   BOS—DM 2—FSS 2 —JO—JSE—SSS—WBT

Cheer for the purple.   Northwestern university song.   Words by E. H. Eversz. CHS—MPC

"Cheer thee, my soul's treasure."   See "Il mio tesoro intanto" (Mozart)

"Cheer up my mates."   P. Humfreys. Words by A. Cowley.   JE

Cheerily, cheerily.   FSS 4

"Cheerily the bugle sounds."   See The mountain bugle (Hewitt)

"Cheerily the huntsman."   See Der schütz (Weber)

Cheer'ly, man ("Oh, Sally Racket, hi-oh") Halliard chantey.   CR
For variant see following song of same title; also "Sally Racket"

Cheerly man ("O-o-ly-i-o cheerly man") Pulling chantey.   SE

"Cheerly, my hearts of courage true."   Attributed to T. Linley.   ME

"Cheesemakers all of Colombette."   See Ranz des vaches ("Lè z'armaillis dei Colombettè")

"Chekahbay tebik ondandayahn."   See My bark canoe

Chello che tu me dice ("Quello che tu mi dici."—"What thou of me requirest") L. Biscardi.   e.i.   FE

Chelvey.   See "A few more years shall roll"; Glory begun below (Hayne)

Cheng Hao
Spring-time (Chinese air)

Chénier, André Marie de
Mourir pour la patrie (Varney)

Chénier, Marie Joseph Blaise de
Le chant du départ (Méhul)

A **chequer'd** career.   Air: Oh, dear! what can the matter be.   Words by D. Rorie. SSS

"Le cher anneau d'argent."   See L'anneau d'argent (Chaminade)

"Cher objet de ma pensée."   See Air de Nicolette (Grétry)

Chère nuit (Dearest night)   A. Bachelet. Words by E. Adenis.   e.f.   SAM

Cherepnin, Nikolaï Nikolaevich
Cradle song
"Dark are now the candles"
L'étoile indiscrète.   See The tell-tale
stars
A kiss
Menaeceus
"Quiet night of waning summer"
"Stars of radiant night"
The tell-tale stars
"**Cherish** faith in one another."   See Faith
in one another (Woodbury)
"**Cherish** kindly feelings."   FSS 3
Cherished names.   L. B. Marshall.
Words by S. F. Smith.   JS
Chernobrovyi, chernoglazyï.   See The
gay bachelor
"**Cherries** and plums."   C. Dibdin.   ME
"**Cherries** are ripe."   FSS 8
"**Cherries** ripe."   Kindergarten song.
FSS 1—WSC
Cherry, Andrew
The bay of Biscay (Davy)
"There's a dear little plant" (Irish air;
also music by J. W. Cherry)
Tom Starboard (Mazzinghi)
Cherry, John William
The dear little shamrock.   See
"There's a dear little plant"
I wandered by the sea-beat shore.   See
Shells of ocean
Monarch of the woods
Shells of ocean
"There's a dear little plant"
"**Cherry** blooms."   Japanese song.   e.j.
BF 2
"**Cherry-bloom**" (Sakura)   e.j.   BO
"**Cherry** ripe."   C. E. Horn.   Words by
R. Herrick.   BE 1—BOH—DM 1—
FSS 8—HSE 1—NG
The **cherry** tree carol.   Traditional song:
Yorkshire version.   BSC—HC—
MF—WCC
—Big Laurel, N.C. version.   CSE
—Hot Springs, N.C. version.   CSE
**Cherubini, Maria Luigi Zenobio Carlo Sal-
vatore**
"Ave Maria"
Commencement song
"Guide mes pas" (from Les deux jour-
nées)
"Guide thou my steps."   See "Guide
mes pas"
"Holy, holy, Lord God of Hosts."   See
"Ave Maria"
"Like as a father pitieth his children,
so the Lord hath mercy"
O salutaris
The **Chesapeke** and the Shannon.   Air:
Pretty girl of Derby, O.   BOS
The **Cheshire** chambermaid.   Arnold.
Words by G. Colman.   BE 3
The **Cheshire** cheese.   18th century song.
BE 6—DM 2
The Cheshire man.   BOH—MM
The **Cheshire** hunt.   See Bucks a-hunting
go

"A **Cheshire** man sail'd into Spain."   See
The Cheshire cheese
"A **Cheshire** man sailed unto Spain."   See
The Cheshire cheese
Chesson, Mrs Nora (Hopper)
May eve (Irish air)
My fair love leaving me (Irish air)
My yellow-haired lad (Irish air)
Over the hills and far away (Irish air)
Soontree (Irish air)
*Chesterfield, Philip Dormer Stanhope, 4th
earl of, and Pulteney,*
Molly Lepell (Old English air)
Chesterton, Gilbert Keith
"O God of earth and altar" (Smart)
Chevalet, Emilie
La fille aux oiseaux (Dancla)
Chevalier, Albert
The future Mrs 'Awkins
Knock'd 'em in the old Kent road
Our little nipper
Wot cher.   See Knock'd 'em in the old
Kent road
La **chevelure** (Her hair)   A. C. Debussy.
Words by P. Louÿs.   e.f.   CM 1—
SAM
Chevy chase ("God prosper long our noble
king")   Air: Flying fame, or,
Chevy chase.   DM 1—JE
Chevy chace.   BOH
Chevy chase ("God prosper long our noble
king")   Air: In pescod time.   MM
Chezy, Wilhelmine Christiane von
Romanze aus Rosamunde (Schubert)
"**Chi** m'arresta."   S. Mercadante.   e.i.
SOA 2
Chi mi frena in tal momento.   For English
translation see Sextet (Donizetti)
Chi sa (Who knows)   R. d'Atri.   Words
by L. Criscuolo.   e.i.   FE—MN
"**Chi** se-zh taîâ krinichen ka."   See "Is
this the same brook"
"**Chi** trovò una bella amante."   See "Wer
ein liebchen hat gefunden" (Mozart)
"**Chi** vuol comprar la bella calandrina"
(Who will buy the beautiful canary)
N. Jommelli.   e.i.   PA 1
"**Chi** vuol la zingarella" ("Who'll try the
gipsy pretty")   G. Paisiello.   e.i.
PA 1
"**Chi** vuole innamorarsi" ("The man who
would turn lover")   A. Scarlatti.   e.i.
FEI 2
Chiabrera, Gabriello
"Se bel rio" (Rontani)
"**Chiagnaro-rò** la la mia sventura."   See
La fata di Amalfi
Chicka-hanka.   Negro folk song from
Virginia.   BN 1
The **chickadee**.   German folk air.   Words
by M. Morgan.   DO
"**Chicken** crowing on Sourwood mountain."
See Sourwood mountain (Kentucky
version)
"**Chickens** a-crowing in Sourwood moun-
tain."   See Sourwood mountain
(Georgia version)
"**Chide** me, if thou wilt, Masetto."   See
"Batti, batti" (Mozart)

"Chide mildly the erring." W. B. Bradbury. FSS 1

"Chide, oh, chide me." See "Batti, batti" (Mozart)

"A chieftain to the Highlands bound." See Lord Ullin's daughter (Thomson)

Chīem tebīa īa orgorchila. See The reproach

Chilcot, Thomas
"On a day—alack the day"

Child and mother. Words by E. Field. LBR

The child and the star. WSC

Child divine. J. F. Bridge. Words by F. K. Harford. HC

"A child, I told you of my love, believing." See "Fanciullo appena ti parlai d'amore"

The Child is born. Giardini. MCS

"Child, is life bright alone." See None can tell (Allen)

"Child Jesus came to earth this day." N. W. Gade. Words by H. Andersen. Tr of Barn Jesus i en krybbe lad. e. HC

"Child Jesus in his garden fair." See The crown of roses (Tchaikovsky)

The Child Jesus in the garden. J. Stainer (music and words) BSC—HC

"Child Jesus lay on Mary's knee." C. M. Conant. HC

"Child of beauty rare." See The holy family (Randegger)

"Child of earth with golden hair." See Titania's song (Horn)

Child of the regiment. Donizetti. e. FSS 3—WBT

"A child sleeps under a rosebush fair." See The rose bush (Perkins)

"A Child this day is born." Traditional air. BSC—HC—WCC

"A Child was born in Bethlehem." See "Et Barn er fodt i Bethlehem"

"Child, with thee I saw another wander." See Come to me

Childe the hunter. Folk song. BSW

The children at the Manger. See Les enfants à la Crecho

"Children go, to and fro." See Follow me, full of glee

"Children, hail! hail! hail! I'm gwine jine saints above." See Hail! hail! hail

"Children here on earth who dwell." H. Knight (music and words) HC

"Children of Norway." See "Sönner af Norge" (Blom)

"Children of the heavenly King" (Hendon) Malan. Words by J. Cennick. FSS 4

"Children, vie with one another." See Ao menino Jesus

Children, we all shall be free. Negro spiritual. JP

"Children, you'll be called on." Negro spiritual. JP—NMP

The children's angel. WSC

The children's Easter offering. J. D. Herron. Words by C. C. Rollitt. HC

The children's home. F. H. Cowen. HSS 1

Children's hosanna. G. J. Webb. Words by J. King. FSS 6—MCS—WBT—WS—WSC

"The children's king." Old air. HC

The children's kingdom. J. Blumenthal. Words by J. J. Lonsdale. FSS 6

The children's voices. Alpine air. Words by R. E. Burton. MCS

Child's dreamland. O. Roeder. WA—WBT—WSC—WSW

Child's hymn. Old air. FSS 1—WBT—WSC

A child's song (Chanson d'enfant) M. Moussorgsky. Words by L. Mey. e.f. SC

Chilean national hymn. See Dulce patria (Carnicer y Batlle)

Chilian song. See "It was a dream, delusive dream"

Chilly water. Negro song. JP

Chime again, beautiful bells. H. R. Bishop. FSS 3—WBT—WSC

"Chime, chime, merrily chime." G. E. Oliver. HC

"Chime out, ye bells of beauty." G. E. Oliver. HC

"Chimes of gladness, chimes of sadness." See The cloister (Stravinskiï)

Chimes of Zurich. C. E. Horn. Words by H. S. Van Dyke. FSS 8

"The chimes rang on till all the air." See The heavenly Guest

The chimney sweep. Folk song. BSW

Chinese baby song ("Snail, snail") e. HSD—WBT

Chinese lullaby. e. WSC

Chinese song. See "Sore is my heart with yearning"

Ching-a-ling. JSE—MPC—SSS—WBT

Chiquita. Spanish folk song. J. R. de Gomis. e. BD

"Chirp, chirp, chirp! soon as fades the light." See The cricket

Chit chat. F. W. Southwell. ME

"Chitotzu to ya." See New Year song

Chittenden, Kate Sara
"Brightest and best"

"Chloris, yourself you so excel." H. Lawes. Words by E. Waller. DM 2

Chō-chō. See Butterfly (Ross)

"Choisir! et pourquoi." See À quoi bon l'économie (Massenet)

"Choki de, sesse yuku no wa." See Song of the pleasure seekers

Chomiakoff, A. See Khomīakov, A.

"Choose when you can an acre of land." See Then you shall be a truelover of mine

Chope, Richard Robert
"Christ is risen! lift the song" (Smith)
"Hark! bright angels sweetly sing" (Irons)
"Hark! the full-voiced choir is singing" (Gowman)
"In the wintry heaven" (Smith)

Chope, Richard Robert —*Continued*
 "Merrily the Easter bells" (music by Hodges; Lissant)
 "Stars all bright are beaming" (Holt)
 "Upon the snow-clad earth without" (music by Gauntlett; Sullivan)
 "The wise men saw a light afar" (Gauntlett)
Chopin, Frédéric François
 Bacchanal
 The birdling. See L'oiselet
 Funeral song of the nation
 Lithauisches lied. See Lithuanian song
 Lithuanian song
 The little ring
 Mädchen's wunsch. See The maiden's wish
 The maiden's wish
 Meine freuden. See My delight
 A melody
 The messenger
 My delight
 L'oiselet
 The parted lovers
 Spring song. See The maiden's wish
 Zwei leichen. See The parted lovers
 Zyczenie. See The maiden's wish
Choral ("Down through the ages vast") Omaha Indian song. e.in. FIS
Choral ("Out of our suff'ring") Polish national song. e.p. BF 1
Choral sanctus. A. R. Gaul. TFC 2
Chorale. See "Commit thy ways, O pilgrim" (Bach)
The **chorister.** A. S. Sullivan. Words by F. E. Weatherly. FSS 7
Chorley, Henry Fothergill
 The brave old oak (Loder)
 The enchantress (Hatton)
 "I am a ruler on the sea" (Sullivan)
 The three ages of love (Loder)
Choron, Alexandre Étienne
 Treuer tod
Ho **choros** tou Zalongou. See The dance of Zalongo
Chorus of mourners. Gluck. [Tr of Ah! se intorno a quest' urna funesta] e. TL
Chorus of pilgrims. See Pilgrims' chorus (Wagner)
The **chosen** one. See Die auserwählte
"The **chough** and crow to roost are gone." See The robbers (Parker)
"**Choumi** Maritza." See "Join, O Maritza"
Chow song. Sailors' chantey air. Words by S. Fay. BSS
Chrétien, Hedwige Louise Marie
 Could I forget. See Que je t'oublie
 Que je t'oublie
The **Christ-Child** ("Angels above on Advent morn") P. Cornelius (music and words) e. HC
The **Christ-Child** ("At Yuletide, so the story tells") German song. e. MCS
The **Christ-Child** ("What time in strife and woe") W. V. Wallace. MCS

"**Christ** hath arisen." Easter carol. HC
"**Christ**, hath Christ's Mother borne." See Hominum laudes (Shaw)
"**Christ** is born! Christ is born." G. Shaw. HC
Christ is born—His name praise ("Radujte se narodi") Croatian carol. e.se. BF 1
Christ is born in Bethlehem. Christmas anthem. FSS 4
"**Christ** is born of Maiden fair." H. J. Gauntlett. [Tr of Christo paremus canticam, excelsis gloria] e. FSS 3—HC
 Born of maiden fair. e. MCS
"**Christ** is born of Maiden fair" (In excelsis gloria) Thibaut. [Tr of Christo paremus canticam, excelsis gloria] e. FSS 7—MCS—WBT
"The **Christ** is coming" ("Khristos rozhdaetsîa") Russian carol. e.r. BF 1
"**Christ** is risen, all triumphant." A. Ulmann. HC
"**Christ** is risen! alleluia." F. C. Maker. Words by J. S. B. Monsell. HC
"**Christ** is risen! alleluia." G. C. Pearson. Words by J. S. B. Monsell. HC
"**Christ** is risen! alleluia." H. Wilson. Words by J. S. B. Monsell. HC
"**Christ** is risen! Christ is risen! conquered death and all His foes." Mrs L. E. Morehouse. HC
"**Christ** is risen! Christ is risen! He hath burst His bonds in twain." J. T. Field. Words by A. T. Gurney. HC
"**Christ** is risen! Christ is risen! He hath burst His bonds in twain." A. S. Sullivan. Words by A. T. Gurney. HC
"**Christ** is risen from the dead." HC
"**Christ** is risen! lift the song." R. F. Smith. Words by R. R. Chope. HC
Christ on the Mount of Olives. Beethoven. e. OS 3
"**Christ** our God and Lord is risen." J. S. B. Hodges. HC
"**Christ** our Sun on us arose." See Joy hath come to earth again
Christ the Lord has risen today. See "Christ the Lord is ris'n today, alleluia! Sons of men and angels say" (Worgan)
"**Christ** the Lord hath risen." 12th century carol. Tr of Christus ist erstanden. e. HC
"**Christ** the Lord is born to-day." See Bohemian Christmas carol
"**Christ** the Lord is risen again." J. S. B. Hodges. Words by M. Weisse. Tr of Christus ist erstanden. e. HC
"**Christ** the Lord is ris'n today, alleluia! Sons of men and angels say" (Worgan) J. Worgan. Words by C. Wesley. BD
 Christ the Lord has risen today. TFC 2
"Jesus Christ is risen to day." WBT —WS

"**Christ** the Lord is risen to-day; listen while the angels say." German air. HC

"**Christ** was born in Bethlehem." Kentucky song. BF 2

"**Christ** was born on Christmas day; wreathe the holly, twine the bay; Christus natus hodie." German air. HC

"**Christ** was born on Christmas day; wreathe the holly, twine the bay; Christus natus hodie." Composer unknown. HC

"**Christ** was born on Christmas day; wreathe the holly, twine the bay; Christus natus hodie." G. E. Oliver. HC

"**Christ** was born on Christmas day; wreathe the holly, twine the bay; Christus natus hodie." C. L. Williams. HC

"**Christ** was born on Christmas day, wreathe the holly, twine the bay, light and life and joy is He." See Christmas carol (Helmore)

"**Christ** was born on Christmas night." T. T. Noble. Words by C. W. Stubbs. HC

"**Christ** was born on Christmas night." T. Wardle. Words by C. W. Stubbs. HC

"**Christ**, we sing Thy saving passion." G. B. Lissant. Words by W. C. Dix. HC

Christbaum. For English translation see "The Christmas tree is sparkling with light" (Cornelius)

"**Christian** children, wake and listen." G. E. Oliver. HC

"**Christian!** dost thou see them." J. B. Dykes. Words by St Andrew of Crete. ɪTr of Oy gar Blepeis tarat-tontasɪ e. LA

"The **Christian** flag." R. H. Woodman. Words by F. J. Crosby. LA

Christian men, rejoice and sing. See Christmas carol (Helmore)

"**Christian** people, come and sing." J. C. Macy. HC

Christian victor. See "Joyfully, joyfully onward I move"

"**Christians**, awake." Old English air. Words by J. Byrom. HSD
Salute the happy morn. FSS 7—MCS

"**Christians**, awake." J. Wainwright. Words by J. Byrom. HC

"**Christians**, carol sweetly." H. S. Irons. Words by W. C. Dix. HC

"**Christians**, carol sweetly." W. Spinney. Words by W. C. Dix. HC

"**Christians**, listen while we sing." J. Martin. Words by F. H. Groome. HC

"**Christians**, listen while we sing." R. F. Smith. Words by F. H. Groome. HC

"**Christina** and her mother laid gold upon the bier." See Sorrow's might

Christison, Sir Robert Alexander, bart. Bread and butter

Christmas aftermath. Anderson. Words by M. E. Sangster. MCS

"**Christmas** again." Words by J. Selwyn. MCS

Christmas as it comes. Words by H. Mather. MCS

Christmas bells ("I heard the church bells ringing") S. Cross (music and words) HC

"The **Christmas** bells are ringing." Flemish air. Words by G. P. Grantham. HC

"The **Christmas** bells are ringing." C. H. Sunderland. Words by G. P. Grantham. HC

"**Christmas** bells are sounding clear." FSS 3—JSE—MCS

"**Christmas** bells are sweetly pealing." See Over land and sea

"**Christmas** brings joy to every heart." Danish carol. C. E. F. Weise. e. MF

Christmas carol ("All this night") See "All this night bright angels sing" (Sullivan)

Christmas carol ("Bethlehem calls you."—"Menyböl az angyal") Hungarian song. e.hu. BF 1

A **Christmas** carol ("Carol, but with gladness") See Carol, brothers, carol (Custance)

Christmas carol ("Christ was born on Christmas day") T. Helmore. Words by J. M. Neale. FSS 1—MCS

Christmas carol ("The earth is cold") A. Reichardt. MCS

Christmas carol ("It came upon the midnight") See "It came upon the midnight clear" (Willis)

A **Christmas** carol ("Kind Christmas comes but once a year") A. S. Gatty. WSC

Christmas carol ("Rise, rise, ye shepherds") Austrian song. e. KSE

Christmas carol ("When Christ was born") See "When Christ was born in Bethlehem" (Locke)

Christmas carolling song. Traditional English air. TFC 2

The **Christmas** celebration. E. Prout. Words by J. H. Gurney. BSC
"Now to God on high be glory." HC

Christmas chant ("Mîlâdek ayyûha-l-masikh ilâhuna") Syrian folk song. ar.e. BF 2

Christmas chimes ("What bells are those") B. Richards. WBT—WSC—WSW

"The **Christmas** chimes are pealing high." See Christmas day

Christmas come again ("'Tis the Christmastide") C. Pinsuti. Words by E. Douglas. MCS

Christmas comes again ("Noel, Noel, Noel") C. Darnton. HC

Christmas comes again, and the merry, merry church bells ring." J. H. Hopkins (music and words) DC—HC

"**Christmas** comes again, our glad Noëls shall ring." See Noël nouvelet

"The **Christmas** comes let praise abound." C. H. Sunderland. HC

Christmas dawn. Bellini. Words by C. Thaxter. MCS

Christmas day ("The Christmas chimes are pealing high") Words by S. Coolidge. FSS 8

Christmas day ("Oh, Christmas is coming") German folk air. Words by R. Compton. DO

Christmas day ("Wake all music's magic powers") See "Wake all music's magic powers" (Stainer)

Christmas day in the morning ("Dame, get up") WSC

Christmas day in the morning ("I saw three ships") See "I saw three ships"

Christmas day in the morning ("Now 'tis the merry") M. B. Foster. DC

Christmas eve ("On the ground the snowflakes glisten") English folk air. Words by C. B. Fenno. DO

Christmas eve ("Watching in the meadows") See "Watching in the meadows" (Foster)

Christmas fanfare and carol. See "Hark! I hear, sweet and clear" (Foster)

Christmas green. G. Coles. MCS

Christmas greeting ("Khodit Mĩesiãts") Song from Great Russia. e.r. BF 1

A **Christmas** hymn ("From ev'ry spire") See "From ev'ry spire on Christmas eve" (Coles)

Christmas hymn ("With glory lit") H. Dielman. Words by J. McCaffrey. FSS 6—MCS

"**Christmas** in lands of the fir tree and pine." See Everywhere, everywhere, Christmas to-night (Redner)

Christmas is coming. H. Phillips. FSS 4 —MCS

Christmas is here ("Sing we so merrily") MCS

"**Christmas** is here; winds whistle shrill." See The mahogany tree (Campana)

Christmas joy forever. C. C. Converse. Words by T. Miller. MCS

Christmas lullaby ("Dormi, dormi, O bel bambin") See Canzone di Natale

Christmas lullaby ("Twilight falling") A. F. Harrison. Words by S. Telford. MCS

The **Christmas** message. H. L. Bianco. HC

Christmas morning. See "In the early morning, early" (Oliver)

Christmas night. A. H. Brown. BSC "On Christmas night true Christians sing." HC

Christmas of old. See Christmasse of olde

Christmas once a year. Words by J. Miller. MCS

Christmas polka. See Jul polska

Christmas song ("Alle jahre wieder") See "Alle jahre wieder" (Silcher)

Christmas song ("Little song of Christmastide") S. Liapounoff. Words from the Russian of A. Korinfsky. e. NM 1

Christmas song ("Minuit, chrétien") See Cantique de Noël (Adam)

Christmas song ("Once again") See "Once again, O blessed time" (Dykes)

Christmas song ("The star of joy beams bright today") DCS

"**Christmas** songs are ringing now." HC

"The **Christmas** stars are shining." F. W. Dawkins. Words by J. Goddard. HC

The **Christmas** story. F. E. Keene. Words by F. C. Fisher. HC

"The **Christmas** time draws nigh." See The time draws nigh

"**Christmas** time has come again, time to us so dear." G. E. Oliver. Words by the Misses Latta. HC

"**Christmas** time is a-rolling on." See The cruel mother (Georgia version)

"**Christmas** time is come again, Christmas pleasures bringing." Carol. FSS 1 —JSE—LA—MCS

"**Christmas** time is near." See Merry joy bells ring (Molloy)

Christmas treasures. V. Bellini. Words by E. Field. MCS

The **Christmas** tree ("Hurrah! and hurrah") J. C. Lowry. Words by C. Wallace. FSS 6—JSE—MCS—NMS

The **Christmas** tree ("Let India boast") German air. MCS

The **Christmas** tree ("O tannenbaum, o tannenbaum") See Der tannenbaum

The **Christmas** tree ("This tree was grown") Old carol. DCS—LA

"The **Christmas** tree is sparkling with light." P. Cornelius (music and words) Tr of Christbaum. e. HC

Christmas vesper hymn. D. F. E. Auber. Words by J. Hughes. MCS

Christmas violets. S. Glover. Words by A. Lang. MCS

Christmas voices. A. S. Gatty. WSC

Christmas waits. Bellini. Words by J. Ingelow. MCS

Christmasse of olde. Swiss air. Words by E. Field. MCS

Christmas of old. WBT

Christo paremus canticam, excelsis gloria. For English translations see "Christ is born of Maiden fair" (Gauntlett); "Christ is born of Maiden fair" (Thibaut IV); "When Christ was born of Mary free" (16th century air); "When Christ was born of Mary free" (Brown); "When Christ was born of pure Marie" (Irons)

Christopulos, Athanasios
O moisikos. See The musician (attributed)
The musician (attributed)

Christós voskrés. See "The Lord is risen! His praise is ringing" (Rachmaninov)

Christus ist erstanden ("Christ the Lord hath risen") For English translation see "Christ the Lord hath risen" (12th century air)

Christus ist erstanden ("Christ the Lord is risen again") For English translation see "Christ the Lord is risen again" (Hodges)

Christus victor. See "Onward, Christian soldiers" (Sullivan)

Christy, Edwin Pearce
Carry me back to ole Virginny

"Chro-Challain would gie me." See Colin's cattle

An **chuifhionn.** For English translations see The coolin; The coolun

"Chula la mañana." Mexican folk song. e.s. HS

Church militant. See "The Son of God goes forth to war" (Cutler)

"De **church** of God." Negro spiritual. HR

"The **church's** one foundation." S. S. Wesley. Words by S. J. Stone. WBT —WS

"The church's one foundation" (Aurelia) FSS 4—LA

A' **churinneag** Ileach ("Och, och, mar tha mi."—The Islay maiden) Gaelic song. e. MMS

"Churl winter his flight has taken." See A song of sunshine (Thomas)

Chwatal, Franz Xaver
"Lovely night! O lovely night"

La **cianciosa** (La vezzosa.—The young beauty) Neapolitan air. e.i. FE

"Ciascun lo dice." Donizetti. e.i. PP

Cibber, Colley
The blind boy (Stanley)

"Cicely sweet." Folk song. BSW

Cicerenella. Neapolitan song. e.i. MSI

"Le **ciel** a visité la terre" (Adore and quiet be) C. Gounod. Words by J. Ahrem. e.f. HSS 1—HSS 2—HSS 4

"Le **ciel** est clair et l'air est doux." See L'oiselet (Chopin)

"Le **ciel,** par d'éclatants miracles." See De noirs pressentiments (Gluck)

"**Ciel** pietoso, ciel clemente." Rossini. e.i. PP

"Le **ciel** sourit au flot limpide." See "Ich wollt' meine lieb" (Mendelssohn)

"Cielo e mar" ("Heaven and ocean") A. Ponchielli. e.i. OPS 3

"Cielo e mar" ("Ocean and sky") e.i. KS 4—SOA 3

"Les **cieux** bleus s'ouvrent infinis." See Printemps nouveau (Vidal)

Cimarosa, Domenico
Die bekehrte schäferin
"Ere the morning light is breaking." See "Pria che spunti in ciel l'aurora"
"Misero Bernardone" (from Giannina e Bernardone)
"O wretched Bernardone." See "Misero Bernardone"
"Pria che spunti in ciel l'aurora" (from Il matrimonio segreto)

"Cine primeşte steaua frumoasă si luminossă." See Steaua

Cinquegrana, P.
Margarita (Fassone)

Cirbiribin. A. Pestalozza. e. WBT

Citronenfalter im april (Butterfly in April) H. Wolf. Words by Mörike. e.g. PG 1

"The **city** is deserted." See Jeremiah's lament (Hiller)

City lad and country lass. See Städterbua und âlmadirn (Koschat)

Ckitaltz. See Skitalets

"Clad in rags the Saviour wanders." See La parabole du mauvais riche

"Clad in verdure green thy branches." See Ombra mai fu (Händel)

Clair de lune ("Dans la forêt que crée un rêve."—Moonlight) C. Saint-Saëns. Words by C. Menès. e.f. CM 2—HM 2

Clair de lune ("Votre âme est un paysage choisi."—Moonlight) G. Fauré. Words by P. Verlaine. e.f. HM 1

The **clang** of the forge. P. Rodney. Words by H. Vaughan. SM 4

The **clang** of the hammer. T. Bonheur. Words by G. W. Southey. SM 4

The **clang** of the wooden shoon. J. L. Molloy. FSS 4

Clare's dragoons. Air: Vive là. Words by T. Davis. BOS

Claribel, pseud. See Barnard, Mrs Charlotte (Alington)

"Clarinda, mistress of my soul." Schetki. Words by R. Burns. BSR

Clark, James G.
Marion Moore
Rain on the roof

Clark, John
Scotland. See "The voice of free grace"
"The voice of free grace"

Clarke, Ednah Proctor. See Hayes, Mrs Ednah Proctor (Clarke)

Clarke, H. A.
March of the men of Columbia (Composer unknown)
"To the bravest" (Mohring)

Clarke, Hugh Archibald
"Love virtue"

Clarke, Jeremiah
"The bonny grey-eyed morn" (attributed. From the fond husband)
"Come sweet lass"
Greenwich park. See "Come sweet lass"
St George, our protector
"While shepherds watched their flocks"

Clarke, Samuel Childs
"All hail! all hail to the natal day" (Thorne)
"Carol we joyfully" (Brown)
"God is gone up" (Brown)
"Hail! all hail this brightest morning" (Brown)
"On the eve before the Sabbath" (Brown)
"A Virgin did come" (Gregory)

Clarke-Whitfeld, John
"Joy, joy for ever"
Claro Paschali gaudio. For English translation see "That Easter-tide with joy was bright"
"Clasp me close upon thy breast." See "Drücke mich an deine brust" (Farwell)
Claudine. J. L. Molloy. Words by R. Reece. FSS 6
Claudius, Matthias
Abendlied (Schulz)
Deutsches weihelied (Methfessel)
Goliath und David (Fink)
Phidile (Schulz)
Rheinweinlied (André)
"Der säemann säet den samen" (Schulz)
Täglich zu singen (Schulz)
Der tod und das mädchen (Schubert)
Urians reise um die welt (Zelter)
"We plough the fields, and scatter" (Schulz. Tr of Im anfang war's auf erden)
Claus, Hermann
Vision
Clavelitos. Zambra gitana. Valverde. Words by Estic. s. LCP
Claxton, Elizabeth
"Bravely chime, O Easter bells" (Higinbotham)
Clay, Frederic
Gipsy John
"I'll sing thee songs of Araby"
"She wandered down the mountain side"
The clear cavalier. J. Banister. Words attributed to S. Butler. CO 2
"He that is a clear cavalier." JE
"Clear rippling brooklet, so silvery bright." See Liebesbotschaft (Schubert)
"Clear the air and fraught with fragrance." See The skylark (Grechaninov)
Clear the track ("I wish I was") Capstan chantey. SE
Clear the track ("Oh, the smartest clipper") Capstan chantey. CR
Clear the way ("The stars are fading") FSS 2
"Clear the way, for the calf of gold." See "Le veau d'or" (Gounod)
Clear the way for U. S. C. University of Southern California song. P. S. Shanahan (music and words) CHS
"Clear upon the night air sounding." J. S. B. Hodges. HC
The clearing up. Omaha Indian air. e. FI
Clementine. See Oh, my darling Clementine (Montrose)
Clements, R. G.
Dawning. See "Still, still with Thee"
"Still, still with Thee"
Clephane, Elizabeth Cecilia
The ninety and nine (Sankey)

Cleveland, Rose Alice
Hymn of the toilers (German air)
"The client now his suit forbears." See Old Christmas cheer
"Cliff of that lofty mountain." See Peña Hueca
Clifford, G.
Rain on the roof
Clifford, W. K.
While you sleep (Hadley)
Clifton, Henry Robert
Paddle your own canoe (Hobson)
Clifton, John Charles
"If music be the food of love, play on"
The climate. Air: Wilkins and his Dinah. Words by D. Stevens. BSS—TFC 1
Climb up, ye chillun climb. Negro song. WBT
"Clime beneath whose genial sun." Old Scotch folk song. HSD—WBT
The clinical examination. Air: Last May a braw wooer. Words by J. Smith. SSS
Cloak, George W.
Blest symbol of blest name (Briggs)
La cloche (The bell) C. Saint-Saëns. Words by V. Hugo. e.g. CM 2—CMF 2—HM 2—KF 2—PG 2—PG 4—SAM
Les cloches (The bells) A. C. Debussy. Words by P. Bourget. e.f. HM 1
The bells. e. WBW
"Cloches tristes, cloches graves." See The cloister (Stravinskii)
Clochette. J. L. Molloy. Words by A. Sketchley. FSS 7—WBT—WL
"Clock upon the landing." See The tall clock
The clod. See Der tost (Koschat)
"Cloe proves false, but still she is charming." See The slighted swain
The cloister (La novice) Song of spring. I. Stravinsky. Words by S. Gorodetski. e.f. NM 2
Les cloques (The bells) Belgian song. e.f. BF 2
"Cloques, sonez, cloques, sonez." See Les cloques
"Cloris, farewell, I now must go." W. Webb. Words by E. Waller. DM 1
"Close by the ox and the ass so gray." See Entre le boeuf et l'âne gris
"Close by the walls of Sevilla." See Séguédille (Bizet)
"Close your bright eyes, my baby dear." See Sleepy time
"Close your eyes, Lena, my darling." See Go to sleep, Lena darling (Emmet)
The closed window. See "Fenesta vascia"
"Closely to my heart I press thee." See Wreath of carnations (Hopkins)
The cloud and the mountain (Notchevála tootchka zolotáya) N. Rimsky-Korsakoff. Words by M. Lermontoff. e. SMR 2

"The **cloud-capp'd** towers."   Arr from a
glee by R. J. Stevens.   Words by
Shakespeare. KSS

"The **cloudless** noontide's golden rays."
See The shadow of the cross (Barry)

"**Cloudlets**, ye heav'nly clouds."   See
Heavenly clouds (Dargomyzhskiï)

The **clouds**.   See Les nuages (Bouval)

"The **clouds** across the moorland fleet."
See Safe home at last (Pinsuti)

"The **clouds** are scudding across the moon."
See The storm song (Gluck)

"**Clouds** may rise."   See "Sorge infausta"
(Händel)

Clough-Leighter, Henry
"I drink the fragrance of the rose"
"It was a lover and his lass"

Clouston, J. Storer
Bread and butter (Christison)

Clouston, R. H., jr.
"The buds are bursting on the trees"
Easter bells

The **clover**.   E. MacDowell.   Words by
M. Deland. AA

"The **clover-blossoms** kiss thy feet."   M.
Vogrich. AB 1

Clover so white.   FSS 8—LA

Clown's song.   See "When that I was a
little boy" (Schumann)

"**Club** your firelocks."   18th century song.
MM

Clunie, John
"I lo'e na a laddie but ane" (Old air)

"**Co'** l'antri hai da discorre, e parli bene."
See Ritornelli romaneschi

Coal black Rose.   H. Russell.   NMP

Coast of Peru.   Forecastle song.   CR

The **coasts** of High Barbary.   Folk song.
FSF—SEF 1—SO

Coates, Mrs Florence (Earle)
I love, and the world is mine (Johns)
"If love were not" (Johns)

Cobb, Gerard Francis
Back to the army again
For to admire
Hark! the holy voices

Cobb, James
"All will hail the joyous day" (Storace)
"Our country is our ship" (music by
Reeve; Storace)
"Peaceful slumb'ring on the ocean"
(Storace)
Ramchoondra (Reeve)
The shepherd and the little bird (Stor-
ace)
"With lowly suit and plaintive ditty"
(Storace)

The **cobbler** laddie.   Folk song.   GO

Co-ca-che-lunk ("When we first came on
this campus") College air. HSD—
MPC—WBT—WC

Co-ca-che-lunk ("When we started in our
scouting") Boy scout song. College
air. Words by B. Braley. BSS

"**Cock-a-doodle-doo**."   English folk song.
DO

Cock Robin ("Who killed Cock Robin")
SSS

Cock Robin and Jenny Wren.   FSS 5—
WSC

Cock up your beaver.   Scottish air.
Words by Burns. PS 2
"When first my brave Johnie lad."
BSR

Cockburn, Sir Alexander, bart.
"I would I were a king" (Sullivan)

Cockburn, Mrs Alicia (Rutherford)
The flowers of the forest (Traditional
air)

Cockles and mussels.   J. Yorkston. BOS
—CST—SSS
"In Dublin's fair city."   PI

Code, Henry Brereton
A spring of Shillelah (Irish air)

Co-education.   R. G. Cole.   Words by R.
M. Haines. CHS

Coenen, Willem
"Come unto me, all ye that labor"
Frühlingslied. See "Wenn die frühling
auf die berge steigt"
Lovely spring. See "Wenn die früh-
ling auf die berge steigt"
"Wenn die frühling auf die berge
streigt"

Le **coeur** de ma bien-aimée (The heart of
my well-beloved) French Canadian
folk song. e.f. BFS

Coffin, Charles
Thy King cometh (Nägeli. Tr of Instantis adventum Dei)
"What star is this" (Composer unknown. Tr of Quae stella sole
pulchrior)

Coghill, Mrs Annie Louisa (Walker)
"Work, for the night is coming" (Mason)

An **coineachan** (A fairy lullaby.—"I left my
darling lying here") Scottish song.
e. HSSS

Coire cheathaich.   For English translation see My misty dell

La **cojita**.   Spanish American song.   s.
LCP

"**Col** mio sangue comprerei" ("I would
spend my blood unheeding")   A.
Stradella. e.i. FEI 2

Col raggio placido.   G. F. Händel. e.i.
SOA 5
Col raggio placido (Hope with her ray
serene) e.i. KS 5

Colasse, Pascal
"Tout cède à vos doux appas" (from
Les saisons)

Colburn, H. H.
"Shine, O sun, in splendour bright"

"**Cold** and raw the north did blow."   Air:
Stingo, or, Oil of barley. DM 1

Cold blows the wind, sweetheart.   Folk
song. BSW—GO

"**Cold** blows the wind to my true love."
See The unquiet grave

"**Cold** was the day when in a garden bare."
See The Child Jesus in the garden
(Stainer)

Cold water song. A. Lee. Words by J. Selwyn. FSS 4

"The cold wave my love lies under." T. Attwood. Words by Moore. HSE 3

"Coldly the day is ending." See Povero marinar (Mililotti)

"Coldly, the day is fading." See Povero marinar (Mililotti)

Cole, R. G.
    The bird of hope
    Co-education
    Longing
    "The new woman"
    Polly, my sweetheart

Cole, Mrs. R. G.
    The scarlet and black (Balfe)

"Colea 'n vale, ah! la fântănă." See Două fete spală lână

Coleman, Edward
    "Bring back my comfort"
    "The glories of our birth and state"

Coleridge, Samuel Taylor
    "The shepherds went their hasty way" (Barnett)
    Song of Illyrian peasants (Schnecker)

Coleridge-Taylor, Samuel
    "O mistress mine"

Coles, George
    Christmas green
    Duane street. See "From ev'ry spire on Christmas eve"; "Jesus, my all, to heaven is gone"; "A poor wayfaring man of grief"
    "From ev'ry spire on Christmas eve"
    Glad hope of the ages. See "From ev'ry spire on Christmas eve"
    "Jesus, my all, to heaven is gone" (same air as "From ev'ry spire on Christmas eve")
    "A poor wayfaring man of grief" (same air as "From ev'ry spire on Christmas eve")

Colin and Grissy parting ("With broken words") Scottish air: Wae's my heart. Words by A. Ramsay. PS 2

Colind (O flowers wondrous) Rumanian song. e.ru. BF 2

Colin's cattle ("Cro-Challain would gie me") Old Highland air. Words from the Gaelic. [Tr of Crodh Chailleann] e. HSSS

Colin's complaint. Old air: Grim king of the ghosts. Words by N. Rowe. MM
    "Despairing beside a clear stream." BE 8

Colin's request. G. Monro. Words by A. Bradley. BE 7

Colin's success. Old song. ME

Coll, Aloysius
    The American eagle (Foerster)

Collan, Karl
    "Du är min ro"
    Rose-Marie
    Savolaisen laulu
    "Thou art my rest." See "Du är min ro"

"Colle to me the rysshes grene." See "Cull to me the rushes green"

Colleen dhas cruthen na moe. For English translation see The pretty girl milking her cow

The colleen dhas rue. See An cailín deas ruadh

Colleen oge astore. See Calino casturame

The colleen rue. Irish folk song. JOI

The college gown. Air: Pope and sultan. Words by J. Campbell. SSS

A college medley. CHS—MPC

The college on the hill. St Olaf college song. Words by C. K. Solberg. CHS

"The college that I love the best." See Old Butler

"College ties can ne'er be broken." Moravian college song. Words by J. K. Pfohl. CHS

Collegium. Hope college song. J. B. Nykerk. Words by H. E. Dosker. l. CHS

Collett, John
    "Free from the bustle, care, and strife"

"The collier has a daughter and oh! she's wonder bonnie! A laird he was that sought her, rich baith in land and money; the tutors watch'd the motion." See The collier's bonnie lassie

"The collier has a dochter." Air: The collier's bonie lassie. Words by R. Burns. BSR

"The collier has a dochter, and O she's wonder bonie! A laird was he that sought her, rich baith in lands and money: she wadna hae a laird." See "The collier has a dochter"

The collier's bonnie lassie. Scottish air. Words by Ramsay. PS 2

The collier's rant. Northumbrian ditty. MM

Collin, Paul
    Ariette (Vidal)
    Déception (Tchaikovsky)

Collings,
    January (Hook)

Collins,
    Ben Block the veteran

Collins, Laura Sedgwick
    Salute to the flag
    "Sing ho! the merry autumn time"

Collins, William
    Golden days of good Queen Bess (Old English air)

Colly, my cow. Folk song. BSW

Colman, George, the younger
    Caleb Quotem (Shield)
    The Cheshire chambermaid (Arnold)
    Hark! when the trumpet now calls you to arms (Arnold)
    Jonathan (Arnold)
    Lira, lira, la (Arnold)
    Savourneen deelish (Old air)
    "When pensive I thought of my love" (Kelly)

Colombeau, Eugène Félix Adenis de
    Chère nuit (Bachelet)
    Sérénade (Pierné)

Colón, Branlio Dueño
    El planatar
    Los reyes magos
    La terruca
    Las vacaciones
Colorado college song ("Youths and
    maidens") CHS
Colorado's sons and daughters.   See Hail
    to Denver U (Cutler)
Colum, Padraic
    "I heard in the night the pigeons"
        (Irish air)
    The wife of Tone (Londonderry air)
Columbia forever.   Football song.   Air:
    The battle cry of freedom.   Words by
    W. B. Donnell.   CU
Columbia, God preserve thee free.   J.
    Haydn.   FSS 2—MP—WBT—WSW
Columbia, hail.   A. F. M. Custance.   MP
Columbia medley.   J. T. Walker.   CU
"Columbia, my land! all hail the glad day."
    See Song of Columbus day (Haydn)
"Columbia, our hearts and hands."   See
    A pledge to Columbia (Wilhelm)
Columbia, the gem of the ocean.   T. à
    Becket; wrongly attributed to D.
    T. Shaw.   Words by T. à Becket;
    wrongly attributed to D. T. Shaw
    and to T. Dwight.   BD—BSE—
    DSH—FSS 1—OH—SN—TFC 1
    Columbia, the gem of the ocean (The
        red, white, and blue)   HSC—WCP
    The red, white, and blue.   CST—FMB
        —HSD—JS— LA—LBR— MP—
        MS—NMH—NMS— WA—WBT—
        WSC—WSW
    Rojo, blanco y azul.   s.   LCP
"Columbia's fame let us loudly proclaim."
    See The glorious Sophomore class
Columbia's Y. M. C. A.   Air: Son of a
    gambolier.   Words adapted by C. E.
    Pellew.   CU
Columbus.   German air.   Words by J.
    Miller.   LBR
Columbus day.   Italian air.   Words by
    J. Erwin.   DO
"Com' è bello."   Donizetti.   e.i.   PP
"Com' è gentil."   G. Donizetti.   e.i.
    SOA 3
    Serenade of Don Pasquale.   e.   FSS 3
Le combat naval (The sea-fight)   Norman
    folk song.   e.f.   TF
    "Le trente et un du mois d'août" ("The
        thirty-first of the month of Au-
        gust")   e.f.   SMW
"Combien j'ai douce souvenance" ("Mem-
    ories tender")   Auvergne folk song.
    e.f.   CM 2
Come again ("We will take from our part-
    ing")   FSS 2
"Come again, sweet love."   J. Dowland.
    BOH—DM 1—DSH—PR 1
"Come again to your fatherland."   See
    Polish maiden song (Goria)
"Come aid yourselves, and God will aid."
    See The tithe
"Come, all friends, and keep the feast."   H.
    F. Sheppard.   HC

"Come, all who live in the U. S. A."   See
    The U. S. A. forever (Emmett)
"Come all who roam."   See A woman's
    work is never done
"Come all with singing."   See To-day in
    Bethlehem
"Come, all ye brave united men."   See
    Billy Byrne of Ballymanus
"Come, all ye California men."   See All
    for the sake of California (Tully)
"Come, all ye children."   See Venid,
    niños queridos
"Come all ye fair and tender ladies."   See
    "Come all you fair and tender ladies"
    (Carmen, N.C. version no. 2)
"Come, all ye fair maidens."   Irish folk
    song.   JOI
"Come, all ye faithful."   See "Adeste
    fideles"   (Reading?)
"Come all ye fox-hunters."   See Tally-ho!
    hark away
"Come, all ye jolly sailors bold."   See
    The Arethusa
"Come, all ye jolly shepherds."   See
    When the kye come hame
"Come, all ye loyal classmen now."   See
    The red and blue (Goeckel)
"Come all ye nice maids."   See The ped-
    lar
"Come all ye pretty maidens."   See The
    spinster's lament
"Come, all ye shepherds."   6th century
    Bohemian song.   e.   MF
"Come, all ye sons and daughters true."
    See In praise of dear old Greer
"Come, all ye wayward trav'lers."   See
    The downward road is crowded
"Come all ye young and handsome girls."
    See "Come all you young and hand-
    some girls" (Kentucky version no. 1)
"Come, all ye young fellows that follow the
    sea."   See Blow the man down
"Come all ye young people and listen to
    me."   See Married and single life
"Come, all ye young sailormen."   See The
    Boston come-all-ye
"Come all ye young tars who are cruising
    for sperm."   See Coast of Peru
"Come all ye youths."   Words by T. Ot-
    way.   DM 1
"Come all you brisk young sailors bold."
    See The wreck off Scilly
"Come all you fair and tender ladies."
    Folk song: Carmen, N.C. version
    no. 1.   CSE
    —Hot Springs, N.C. version.   CSE
    —Flag Pond, Tenn. version no. 1.
        CSE
    —Flag Pond, Tenn. version no. 2.
        CSE
    —Kentucky version.   CSE
"Come all ye fair and tender ladies."
    Carmen, N.C. version no. 2.   SA
    Little sparrow.   Kentucky version.
        WLT
    Variant: "Come all you young and
        handsome girls"

"Come all you fair and tender ladies, be careful how you court young men." See "Come all you fair and tender ladies" (Flag Pond, Tenn. version no. 1)

"Come all you fair and tender ladies, come listen to my story." See Katie Morey (North Carolina version)

"Come all you fair and tender ladies, take warning how you court young men." See "Come all you fair and tender ladies" (Kentucky version; Flag Pond, Tenn. version no. 2)

"Come all ye gallant seamen bold." See Ward the pirate

"Come, all you jolly ploughboys, and help me to sing; I will sing in the praise of you all." See The jolly ploughboy (Dorset version)

"Come, all you jolly ploughboys, come, listen to my lays, and join with me in chorus." See The ploughboy (Sussex version)

"Come, all you jolly watermen." 18th century song. MM

"Come, all you lads and lasses." See Flora's holiday

"Come all you poga girls, listen to my song." See Harm Link

"Come all you sailors bold, lend an ear, lend an ear." See Benbow, the brother tar

"Come all you seamen bold and draw near, and draw near." See Admiral Benbow

"Come all you sporting bachelors." See Sporting bachelors

"Come, all you wild, young people." See Edwin in the lowlands low (Hampshire version)

"Come all you worthy Christian men." Folk song. SEF 2—SO
Variant: "Come, all you worthy Christians"

"Come, all you worthy Christians." Folk song from Sussex. SF 5
Variant: "Come all you worthy Christian men"

"Come all you young and handsome girls." Folk song: Kentucky version no. 1. CSE
—Kentucky version no. 2. WT
Variant of: Come all you fair and tender ladies

"Come all you young and tender ladies." See Come all you fair and tender ladies (Kentucky version)

"Come all you young fellows that carry a gun." See At the setting of the sun

"Come, all you young fellows that follow the sea." See Blow the man down

"Come all you young females wherever you be." See Fanny Blair (English version)

"Come, all you young gallants." See Molly bawn

"Come, all you young men, in your merry ways." FSS 4—WBT

"Come all young men of learning good." See Botany bay

"Come along, boys, and listen to my tale." See The old Chisholm trail

"Come along, come along, and let's go home." See Ole ship of Zion

"Come along, get you ready." See A hot time in the old town (Metz)

"Come and dance." See "Vi ska' ställa te'en roliger dans"

"Come and embark." See "Embarquez-vous" (Godard)

"Come and hear the grand old story." S. B. Saxton. Words by H. Bonar. HC

"Come and I will sing to you. What will you sing to me? I will sing you one-e-ry." See The ten commandments (English version)

"Come and I will sing you. What will you sing me? I will sing you one." See The ten commandments (Georgia version)

"Come, and I will sing you. What will you sing me? I will sing you One O." See The dilly song

"Come and join in song together, shout with might and main." See Hail to old I. U.

"Come and join the dancing, prancing, glancing." See Mazurka

"Come, and listen to my ditty." See The sailor's complaint

"Come and see me." FSS 2—WBT

"Come and twine the slim boughs" (Zaplaitesya plaiten) Russian folk song. e.r. BO
Round-dance (Spring song.—Zapletisîa pleten') e. SSR 3

"Come and watch the daylight dawning." See The dawn of day (Reay)

Come and worship. See "Angels from the realms of glory" (Smart)

"Come, Anna May, and tell me your name." See Lock and bolts (Carmen, N.C. version no. 1)

"Come, arm ye! come arm ye." See Inno di guerra dei cacciatori delle Alpi (Olivieri)

"Come, arouse thee, arouse thee." See The merry Swiss boy

"Come as of old and with thy words so tender." See Chata cara de bule

"Come away, lads, to labor." See The vine-dressers' song (Weber)

"Come away, sang the river." See The journey of the leaves

Come away to the fields. D. F. E. Auber. FSS 6

"Come back, come back, sweet May." See "Komm', lieber mai, und mache" (Mozart)

Come back in dreams. See "Come to me in the silence of the night" (Marzials)

Come back, sweet May. See "Komm', lieber mai, und mache" (Mozart)

"Come back to Erin." C. Barnard. FSS 5
—HSC— HSD— WA— WBT— WL— WSW

Come back to Sorrento. See Torna a Surriento (Curtis)

"**Come**, behold." See La mamma de rosa

"**Come** boat me o'er, come row me o'er." Scottish air: O'er the water to Charlie. Words by Burns. PS 2 Over the water to Charlie. FSS 1

"**Come** boat me o'er, come row me o'er." Jacobite air: Over the water to Charlie. Words by Burns. BSR

"**Come**! boor, your little blue." See The scout (Campana)

"**Come**, bridle me my milk-white steed." See Geordie

"**Come**, brothers, fill your glasses." See "Herr bruder, nimm das gläschen"

"**Come**, bumpers high! express your joy." Air: Ye're welcome Charlie Stewart. Words by R. Burns. BSR

"**Come**, buy my nice fresh ivy." See The holly and ivy girl

"**Come**, buy of poor Mary, primroses I sell." See Come, who'll buy primroses (Moulds)

"**Come** buy, pretty maidens, ground ivy I sell." See Ground ivy (Moulds)

"**Come** buy! who'll buy." See Little Sally's wooden ware (Arnold)

"**Come**, cheer up, my lads, 'tis to glory we steer." See Heart of oak (Boyce)

"**Come**, cheer up your hearts." J. Sheeles. Words by M. Parker. BE 8

"**Come** cheerful and gay as the glad sun in May." See The star of His birth

"**Come**, cheerful companions." Air: Vive la compagnie. FSS 2—WBT

"**Come**, children, and join in our festival song, and hail the sweet joys Christmas day brings along." See Happy Christmas to all

"**Come**, children, and join in our festival song, and hail the sweet joys which this day brings along." See Happy greeting to all

"**Come**, children, lift your voices." G. C. E. Ryley. Words by Mrs C. F. Hernaman. HC

"**Come**, Chloris, hie we to thy bower." H. Lawes. Words by H. Reynolds. DM 1

"**Come**, come, come, come to the sunset tree." See Tyrolese evening hymn (Browne)

"**Come**, come, come, o'er the hills, free from care." See Mountain maid's invitation (Werner)

"**Come**, come handsome fellow." See "Kom, kom fager ungersven"

"**Come**, come here; join in our song." Round. FSS 7

"**Come**! come let's embark, while the tide's flowing." See "Embarquez-vous" (Godard)

"**Come**, come, my beloved." See Ma gazelle

"**Come**, come, my brave boys." See Drink old England dry

"**Come**, come, my good shepherds." Sheep-shearing ballad. M. Arne. Words by D. Garrick. ME

"**Come**, come, my jolly lads." See Sling the flowing bowl (Linley)

"**Come**, come, my lads." C. Dibdin. DM 2

Come, come, my love, how sad am I. See La cabaña

"**Come**, come, my lovers." W. Porter. MM

"**Come**, come quickly away." FSS 4

"**Come**, come, sweet Molly." Folk air. BE 2

"**Come** companions, join your voices." See Dulce domum (Reading?)

Come dal ciel precipita. G. Verdi. e.i. SOA 5

"**Come** dance in the orchard." See Dancing in the orchard

"**Come**, dear mother, hear me say." See Musical alphabet

"**Come**, dear son, and tell me." See The soldier's farewell

"**Come**, dear teacher, hear me say." See Musical alphabet

"**Come**! Don Fernand! in these passes I tarry." See Le muletier de Tarragone (Henrion)

Come down, angels. Negro spiritual. JP

"**Come** down, come down, come down, sinner." See Come down, sinner

"**Come** down, come down, my Lord, come down." See My Lord's writing all the time

"**Come** down, Gabriel, blow your horn." See Angels meet me at de cross-roads (Hays)

Come down, sinner. Plantation song from Virginia. HR

"**Come**, each gallant lad." 18th century song. DM 2—MM

"**Come** every shepherd with his love." Air: Hob y derri dando (version 1) MMW

"**Come**, fall in line to music fine." See Harvard's day (Smith)

"**Come**, fellows, let us pull together." See Towing-song

"**Come**, fellows, let us raise a song." See Dartmouth song (Segur)

"**Come** fill up a bumper before we depart." See Wanderlied (Schumann)

Come fill up my cup. See Bonnie Dundee

"**Come**, fill your glasses, fellows." See Benny Havens, oh

"**Come**, follow, follow, follow, follow, follow, follow me." See Come, follow me (Hilton)

"**Come**, follow, follow me, you fairy elves that be." See The Spanish gipsy

Come, follow me. Round. Hilton. BD

"**Come**, follow." TFC 2 Follow me. CST

"**Come** forth and bring your garlands." H. Kotzschmar. Words by J. W. Anderson. HC

"**Come** forth and bring your garlands." A. Ulmann. Words by J. W. Anderson. HC

Come forth and let us proudly crown thee. See A wreath for Princess Kaiulani (Hopkins)

"Come forth, come forth, brave reapers." G. B. Lissant. Words by G. Moultrie. HC

"Come forth, ye wond'ring children all." See Legends of the Infancy (Bridge)

"Come, fortune's a jade." See Three merry men be we

"Come from the prairies." G. Verdi. BD

"Come from the wintry town." See Winterlied (Koss)

"Come, gallant waterman, tell to me." See The Danube's whirlpool

Come gather round, my classmates. See The jolly sophomore

"Come, get my clothes in order." See Shallow Brown

"Come, gie's a sang." See Tullochgorum

"Come, girls, come, sing us a song." Round. FSS 8

"Come, happy people! oh come, let us tell." See Washington and Lincoln (Work)

Come, haste away. Neapolitan air. FSS 7

"Come, haste to the wedding." Attributed to T. Arne. DM 2—JO

Haste to the wedding. HSE 2

"Come haul the water and haul the wood." See "Aa kjöre vatten aa kjöre ve"

"Come, hear ye how God's priest of old." G. B. Lissant. Words by W. H. Jewitt. HC

"Come here, fellow servant." J. Battishill. Words by D. Garrick. BE 7

"Come here, youth and maidens." See Long live Stuart hall

"Come here's to Robin Hood." Air: Lady Frances Nevile's delight. Words by J. Oxenford. JE—MM

"Come hither! come hither, cow." See Norsk fjeldsang (Thrane)

"Come hither, my country squire." See The modern beau (Carey)

"Come hither, son Jan." See Jan's courtship

"Come hither thou beautiful rover." See The carrier pigeon

"Come, Holy Ghost" (St Martin's) W. Tansur. Words by C. Wesley. FSS 5

"Come, Holy Spirit, heavenly Dove." Dykes. Words by I. Watts. FSS 1— WBT—WS—WSW

"Come, Holy Spirit, heavenly Dove." G. W. Warren. Words by I. Watts. FSS 4

Come home, father. H. C. Work (music and words) HSD—WBT

"Come home with me, Mannan." See Come, Mannan

"Come, humble sinner." T. Hastings. FSS 8

"Come, hunters, come, young and old." See Foresters bold

"Come, if you dare." H. Purcell. Words by Dryden. BE 1

"Come in, come in, loving Henry, said she." See Young hunting (Georgia version)

"Come in, come in, my old true love, and chat a-while with me." See The false young man (Flag Pond, Tenn. version no. 1)

"Come in come in, my old true love, and sit you down by me." See The true lover's farewell (Black Mountain, N.C. version)

"Come in come in, my old true love, and stay all night with me." See Young hunting (Carmen, N.C. version)

"Come in, come in, my old true love, and take a chair by me." See The false young man (Virginia version)

"Come in, come in, my own true love, and stay all night with me." See Young hunting (Alleghany, N.C. version; Carmen, N.C. version)

"Come in, come in, my pretty little boy." See Young hunting (Hot Springs, N.C. version)

"Come in, come in, my two little babes." See The wife of Usher's well (Hot Springs, N.C. version)

"Come in the ev'ning, or come in the morning." See The welcome

"Come in the springtime, come in the fall." See Come when thou wilt (Lansdon)

"Come in thy joy, bountiful day." See Love, hope, happiness (Ransford)

"Come in, you naughty bird." See The sparrow on the tree (Scott-Gatty)

"Come into the garden, Maud." M. W. Balfe. Words by Tennyson. DM 1 —HSE 3—TS—WBW

"Come, join my humble ditty." See Son of a gambolier

"Come jolly Bacchus" (Charles of Sweden) 18th century song. CO 2

"Come lads and lassies, stir about." See Mowing the hay (Carmichael)

"Come, landlord, fill the flowing bowl." See Landlord, fill the flowing bowl

"Come, lasses and lads." 17th century song. BE 1—BO—BOS—CO 2— CST—HSE 1—WBT—WSC

"Come lasses and lads" (The country wake) DM 1

"Come, lasses and lads" (English Maypole song) BMC

"Come, lassie and lad, be blithe and glad." See Maypole dance

"Come, laugh and be happy and banish care." See We'll laugh and sing all cares away (Verdi)

"Come, let me take thee to my breast." Air: Cauld kail. Words by R. Burns. BSR

Come, let us all go down. See Down in the valley

"Come let us all sweet carols sing." F. Champneys. Words from a Besançon carol. e. BSC

"Come, let us away to the fields, all away." See Come away to the fields (Auber)

"Come, let us banish sorrow." Air: The minstrelsy of Chirk castle. Words by A. A. Watts. MMW

"Come, let us drink a bout." Old song. CO 2

"Come, let us haste away." See Come, haste away

"Come let us join in a song." See Our college home (Ruggles)

"Come, let us join in merry chorus." See In merry chorus (Offenbach)

"Come, let us join our cheerful songs" (St Martin's) W. Tansur. Words by I. Watts. FSS 5

"Come, let us laugh, ha! ha! ha! let us sing." See Winter and spring

"Come let us learn to sing." See The scale

"Come, let us make his pleasant grave." See Because he loved you so (Dempster)

"Come, let us prepare." See The free and accepted mason

"Come, let us raise our voices in one triumphant strain." See The yellow and the brown

"Come, let us sing a merry song." Campbell university song. Words by E. W. Brown. CHS

"Come, let us sing the story." H. W. Little. HC

Come, let us speed away. See Ti rapirei (Tosti)

"Come, let's enjoy ourselves, my fair one." See Chanson de berger

"Come, let's go to Santa Anita." See "Vámonos por Santa Anita"

"Come, let's join in songs together." See Hail to Denver U (Cutler)

"Come, listen all, both great and small." See Childe the hunter

"Come listen all unto my song." See La chanson des mensonges

"Come listen awhile, and a story you'll hear." See The mare and the foal

"Come listen awhile (tho' the weather be cold)." See Blanket fair

"Come listen, dear child, while I tell to thee." See The good angels (Gumbert)

"Come listen, little girls and boys." See Tommy and his gun (McMichael)

"Come listen to another song." See The old Scottish cavalier

"Come, listen to my story, Christus natus hodie." 16th century air. Words by G. R. Woodward. HC

"Come, listen to my story, you can't tell how I feel." See Lucy Neal

"Come, listen to the story." J. B. Powell. Words by H. Knight. HC

"Come, little folks hasten, I beg of you all." See The butterfly's ball

"Come, live with me and be my love." 16th century air. Words by C. Marlowe. BOH—CO 1—MM
    The passionate shepherd to his love ("Come live with me") DM 2—JE

"Come live with me and be my love." Air: Tros y garreg. Words by C. Marlowe. MMW

"Come live with me, and be my love." H. R. Bishop. [Words by C. Marlowe] HSE 2

"Come live with me and be my love" (The passionate shepherd to his love) R. Goldmark. Words by C. Marlowe. HST

"Come live with me, and be my love." J. L. Hatton. Words by C. Marlowe. HSE 2

Come, love, come, the boat lies low. See Nancy Till

"Come, love, let us join." See Roger and Cicely

"Come, love, let's walk in yonder spring." 17th century song. MM

"Come, love, with me and let us rest." See Dream, dear one

"Come, lovely May, and bring us." See "Komm', lieber mai, und mache" (Mozart)

"Come, lovely Phillis." H. Lawes. PR 1

"Come, ma love, an' go wid' me, li'l' 'Liza Jane." See 'Liza-Jane

"Come, maiden, come and sail with me." See Come to the sea (Roberti)

Come, Mannan ("Ari Manan") Armenian song. a.e. BF 2

"Come, May, thou lovely lingerer." See "Komm', lieber mai, und mache" (Mozart)

"Come, me lass, slip, slip, slip." See Die auserwählte

"Come mother, dear mother." See The dying volunteer (Muse)

"Come, my brothers, let us gather in my room." See The conscript's departure

"Come my Daphne." W. Lawes. Words by J. Shirley. JE

"Come, my dearest, come, my fairest." See The saucy sailor

"Come my dearest, to my breast" ("Tule koju") Esthonian folk song. e.es. BF 1

"Come, my dearest, why so sad this morning." See "O bright sun"

"Come my fairest, come my dearest." See The saucy sailor

"Come, my gallant soldier, come." H. R. Bishop. FSS 3—WBT

"Come, my good steeds, Palkó, Jankó." See Palkó, Jankó

"Come, my jolly brisk boys." See The hop-planters' song

"Come, my soul, thou must be waking." J. S. B. Hodges. Words by F. R. L. Canitz. [Tr of Seele du musst munter werden] e. FMB

"Come, no shrinking! keep on drinking." See Bacchanal (Chopin)

"Come now all ye social powers." DM 2

"Come now, and listen to my tale of woe." See Romeo and Juliet (Bayly)

"Come now to the campus." See Sons of Geneva

"Come, O come! castanets are gaily sounding." See La cachuca

"Come, oh! come with me, the moon is beaming." Italian air. Words by B. S. Barclay. FSS 2—HSD—WBT

"Come, oh, come with me where the sparkling fountain." See Come to the sparkling fountain

"Come, O come, you must depart." See Farewell to the warriors

"Come, oh fairest maiden." Swedish dancing song from Dalecarlia. e. KSN

"Come, O my brother." See Tu sul labbro de' veggenti (Verdi)

"Come, O nightingale" (Ororotsi yerk) Armenian song. Words by K. Katiba. a.e. BF 2

"Come, oh Setti, from thy cabin." Swiss song. e. KSE

"Come, O sword of pain, of pain." See Across the Niemen

"Come o'er the bourne, Bessy." Words by W. Birche. CO 1
"Come o'er the bourn." JE

"Come o'er the sea." Irish air: Cuishla ma chree, or, Pulse of my heart. Words by T. Moore. MI—MMI

"Come o'er the stream, Charlie." Air: MacLean's welcome. Words by J. Hogg. e. MMS—PS 1

"Come on brudder an' help me sing." See I know I would like to read

"Come on, sister, wid your ups an' downs." See Listen to de lambs

"Come, our sacred shore defending." See March of the victors (Verdi)

"Come out, come out, my dears." See Le retour des promis (Dessauer)

"Come out, dear Dolly and make a snow man." See The snow man (Scott-Gatty)

"Come out hyah an shuck dis co'n." See Corn-shuckin' song

"Come out, snow-white lambkin." See Farmyard song (Grieg)

"Come out, 'tis now September." See All among the barley (Stirling)

"Come out to the green, ye joyous throng." See May-day

"Come over the born Bessy." See "Come o'er the bourne, Bessy"

"Come per me sereno." Bellini. e.i. PP

"Come, play me that simple air." Labitzky. Words by T. Moore. JO—WBT

"Come raggio di sol" ("As a sunbeam at morn") A. Caldara. e.i. BAS 2 —CS 2—MSS 2
"Come raggio di sol" ("As on the swelling wave") e.i. PA 1
"Come raggio di sol" ("As rays of setting sun") e.i. NG—PG 2—PG 3 —PG 4
"Come raggio di sol" ("Like the sun's golden ray") e.i. FEI 2

"Come! raise our banner o'er us." See Beloved Columbia (Ries)

"Come raise the song." Wesleyan university song. W. B. Davis. Words by F. L. Knowles. CHS

"Come, rest in this bosom." Air: Lough Sheeling. Words by T. Moore. FSS 5—MI
"Come, rest on this bosom." MI—MMI

"Come rise up, Willie Reilly." See Willie Reilly

"Come, Roger and Nell." Galliard. BE 8

"Come, said Jesus' gentle voice." Schnyder. Words by A. L. Barbauld. FSS 4

"Come, Sandy, man, an' bear a han'." See A crab song

"Come, send round the wine." Air: We brought the summer with us. Words by T. Moore. MI

"Come, seniors, wise and learned." See Rah! for the black and blue (Peters)

"Come sereno è il dì." Rossini. e.i. PP

"Come, shepherds, come! shake off your sleep." Tyrolese air. Tr of Ihr hirten steket alle auf von eurem tiefen schlaf. e. HC

"Come, shepherds, deck your heads." 2 airs. CO 1

"Come, shipmates and brothers, ho yo." See English chanty

Come, show me the way. Words by E. Thomas. MCS

Come, sing me that sweet air again. Words by T. Moore. FSS 2

"Come sing of Flanders' glory." See Flanders (Hol)

"Come sing this round with me." See Laughing glee (Martini)

Come sing to me again. M. Hobson. Words by J. H. Eccles. FSS 8

"Come, soft skies of blue." Indian air. FI

"Come, sons of old Columbia." See Glory, glory for Columbia

"Come Sukky! come Bossy cow! Suk Bossy." See Norsk fjeldsang (Thrane)

"Come sweet lass." J. Clark. Words attributed to T. D'Urfey. BE 8— DM 1—JE—MM
"Come, sweet lass" (Greenwich park) CO 2

"Come sweet love, let sorrow cease." See The shepherd's joy

"Come swell the strain." See The good Three Bells (Jarvis)

"Come, take thy harp." J. L. Molloy. Words by T. Moore. MI

"Come take your glass." See The northern lass (Fisher)

"Come, tell me, blue-eyed stranger." See Blue-eyed Mary

"Come, the magic tree is laden with treasure." See The magic tree

"Come, Thou almighty King." Air: God save the king. Words by C. Wesley. FSS 4

"Come, Thou almighty King." F. Giardini. Words by C. Wesley. DO—HSC —HSD—MS— NMH— NMS— OH —TFC 1—WBT—WS
"Come, Thou almighty King" (Italian hymn) BD—FSS 2—JS—TL

"Come, Thou Fount of every blessing." J. Wyeth. Words by R. Robinson. FSS 3—HSD—WBT—WS

Come, thou gracious beauty. See Viens, gentille dame (Boieldieu)

"Come, thou lovely May." See "Wonnevoller mai" (Gluck)

"Come thou with me, and climb the moor." See New Year carol (Scott-Gatty)

Come to battle. See Dowch i'r ffrwydr

Come to me ("Child, with thee") Turkish song. e. KSE

Come to me ("'Neath the silver silence") L. Denza. Words by W. Boosey. CB

"Come to me in the silence of the night" (Come back in dreams) T. Marzials. Words by C. G. Rossetti. MSF 2

"Come to me in the silence of the night" (Echo) H. Somerset. Words by C. G. Rossetti. MSF 1—SM 1

"Come to my cabin so lonely." See La cabaña

"Come to my window." Folk song. BSW

"Come to the forest." S. Glover. FSS 8

"Come to the home of boyhood's love." V. Bellini. FSS 3—JSE

"Come to the manger in Bethlehem." S. Smith. HC

"Come to the meadows." FSS 5—JSE

"Come to the old oak-tree." English song. FSS 1—WBT

"Come to the plain and meet the Frankish host." See Turkish war song

Come to the realm of roses and wine ("Au royaume du vin et des roses") N. Rimsky-Korsakov. Words by A. Fet. e.f. NR 4

Come to the sea (Barcarolle) G. Roberti. FSS 4

"Come to the shady glade." See "Nous n'irons plus au bois"

Come to the sparkling fountain. FSS 3

Come to thy window. See Parais à ta fenêtre (Gregh)

"Come trembleing down." Negro folk song from Kentucky. KA

"Come, trembling sinner, in whose breast." Words by E. Jones. FSS 4

"Come, tune your heart." F. A. G. Ouseley. [Words by C. F. Gellert. Tr of Auf, schicke dich] e. BSC

"Come una volta il sonno soleami consolar." See "Wie nahte mir der schlummer" (Weber)

"Come under my plaidie." J. MacGill. Words by H. Macneill. MMS—PS 1

"Come unto Him, all ye that labor, come unto Him." G. F. Händel. SAS 1

"Come unto Him, all ye who labor! Your Lord will give you rest and peace." C. Gounod. FSS 8—WBT

"Come unto Him, come unto Him." H. Leslie. FSS 4—HSS 1—HSS 3— HSS 4

Come unto me ("By Galilee's calm waters") Lindsay. Words by W. H. Bellamy. HSS 1

Come unto me ("Ihr alle") Dvořák. e.g. HSS 1—HSS 2—HSS 3—HSS 4

Come unto me ("A wand'rer worn") O. Barri. Words by L. Lennox. HSS 1 —HSS 4

"Come unto me, all ye that labor." W. Coenen. Words by H. Bonar. HSS 1 —HSS 3

"Come unto these yellow sands." J. Banister. Words by Shakespeare. BSE —KSS—VFS

"Come unto these yellow sands." H. Purcell. Words by Shakespeare. KSS —VFS

"Come vorrei saper del giovin ch'ho incontrato." See "Je voudrais bien savoir quel était ce jeune homme" (Gounod)

"Come, we will sing together." See The red and gold

"Come well to me, dear mother, he says." See Lord Thomas and fair Ellinor (Hot Springs, N.C. version)

"Come, when the rosy morning." See "Vieni, che poi sereno" (Gluck)

"Come when the soft twilight falls." See When the soft twilight (Schumann)

Come when thou wilt. W. Lansdon. FSS 7

"Come where flowers are flinging." Flotow. e. FSS 3

"Come where my love lies dreaming." S. Foster (music and words) HSD— TFC 2—WL

"Come where the aspens quiver." A. Lee. Words by T. H. Bayly. BE 2— HSE 2

Where the aspens quiver. FSS 7

"Come where the sunlight." F. Campana. FSS 8

"Come where the viols are singing." See The dancers (Lacome d'Estalenx)

"Come, while the twilight closes." See "Vieni, che poi sereno" (Gluck)

Come, who'll buy primroses. J. Moulds. ME

"Come with joyous hearts to-day." See With joyous hearts

"Come with the gipsy bride." See Gipsy song (Balfe)

"Come, with thy lute." German air. FSS 2

"Come with us, sweet flowers." See Carol of the flowers

Come ye back to old Grinnell. Iowa college song. W. B. Olds (music and words) CHS

Come, ye blessed. Gaul. OS 2

"Come, ye brave British lads." See Balance a straw (Oswald)

"Come, ye children, and hearken unto me." A. S. Sullivan. SAS 3

"Come, ye Christians all." Old French air. Words by J. T. Lightwood. HC

"Come, ye disconsolate." [Composer unknown. Words by T. Moore] LA

"Come, ye disconsolate." S. Webbe. Words by T. Moore. FSS 1—HSD— WA—WBT—WS—WSW

"**Come,** ye faithful, raise the strain." Flemish air. Tr of Asōmen pantes laoi. e. HC

"**Come,** ye faithful, raise the strain." A. S. Sullivan. Tr of Asōmen pantes laoi. e. HC

"**Come,** ye, lift your joyous voices." B. Briggs. HC

"**Come,** ye lofty, come, ye lowly." A. F. M. Custance. Words by A. Gurney. HC

"**Come,** ye lofty, come, ye lowly." G. J. Elvey. Words by A. Gurney. BSC—HC

"**Come,** ye lofty, come, ye lowly." A. Gurney (music and words) HC

"**Come,** ye merry girls and boys." Croatian folk air. Words by G. D. Donaldson. WF

"**Come,** ye sinners, poor and needy." J. Ingalls. FSS 4

"**Come** ye thankful people, come" (St George's Windsor) G. J. Elvey. Words by H. Alford. CST

"**Come,** ye that love the Lord." See Glory begun below (Hayne)

"**Come** ye, with the angels sing." A. H. Brown. Words by W. T. Brooke. HC

"**Come,** ye young men, come along." See The May pole

Come you back to Mandalay. See On the road to Mandalay (Trevannion)

"**Come** you here, laddie" ("Pridi ty šuhajko") Slovak folk song. sl.e. BF 1

"**Come** you not from Newcastle." See Newcastle

"**Come** you people old and young." See The Suffolk miracle (Allanstand, N.C. version)

"**Come** young, come old." See Katie Morey (Tennessee version)

"**Comely** swain, why sitt'st thou so." J. Playford. MM

Comer, Thomas
    Echoes of olden times
    The pagoda bells

"**Comes** he not, my heart, tell me why." See Rosemonde (Chaminade)

"**Cometh** now from forest old." See Die nacht (Strauss)

Comfort ye my people. G. F. Händel. SAS 3

"**Comfort** ye." OS 3

The **comforter** ("Low her voice is, soft and kind") Modern Greek song. e. BMC

"**Comin'** thro' the craigs o' Kyle." See O'er the muir amang the heather

Comin' thro' the rye. Air: The miller's daughter. Words by R. Burns. BOS— BSB—BSE— EF—FSS 1— GO— HSC— HSD—JO— JSE— MSS 1 — NMH —SS 1 —TFC 1— WA—WBT—WL—WSW
    Comin' thro' the rye ("Gin a body meet a body") HSSS—SMF
    "Gin a body meet a body." MMS— PS 1

"**Comin** thro' the rye, poor body." Air: Miller's wedding. Words by R. Burns. BSR

"**Coming** from the winter." T. R. G. Jozé. HC

"**Comm'** a l'acqua che passa." See Chi sa (Atri)

"**Comme** des chevreaux piqués par un taon." See La brise (Saint-Saëns)

"**Comme** un rideau, sous la blancheur de leurs pétales rapprochées." See Crépuscule (Massenet)

A **commencement** hymn ("Great God high over all") CHS

Commencement song ("Roses are waking") Cherubini-Méhul. Words by M. Leaf. TL

Commencement song ("'Tis June, the month of roses") A. Murray. Words by M. S. Morison. OH

"**Comment** veux-tu que je t'oublie." See Que je t'oublie (Chrétien)

"**Commit** thou all thy griefs and ways into His hands." See "Wirf alle deine sorg'" (Molique)

"**Commit** thy ways, O pilgrim." J. S. Bach. e. FSS 7
    Chorale. e. CST

Commit thy ways unto the Lord. See "Wirf alle deine sorg'" (Molique)

"**Como** nací en la calle." See La calle de la paloma

"**Como** quieres." Mexican folk song. e.s. HS

"**Como** tórtola errante y sin nido." See La tórtola (Marquez)

"**Companions,** all sing loudly." Basque carol. Tr of Khanta zagun guzick ahalik gorena. e. MF

The **complaint** ("Ach Gott") See Herzensbeklemmung (Thümmel)

The **complaint** ("Maiden, how canst thou") Greek love song. e. KSE

La **complainte** du déserteur (The deserter's plaint) French folk song. e.f. TSF

Compton, L.
    "My grandfather had some very fine ducks"

Compton, Richard
    The apple-tree house (German air)
    Christmas day (German folk air)
    Dancing in the orchard (Austrian folk air)
    Evening on the river (German folk air)
    God, our loving Father (Finnish air)
    "If I were a bird" (German folk air)
    "In May, in May" (German air)
    Lullaby (Scotch folk air)
    Memorial day (Bohemian folk air)
    "Once, long ago" (Old Bohemian air)
    Planting a garden (Flemish air)
    Playing ball on the stairs (French folk air)
    The pony ride (Flemish folk air)
    Riding on the elevated (Flemish folk air)
    St Valentine's day (French folk air)
    Song of praise (Bayly)
    Sunset in the city (English folk air)
    Who are you (German air)

"Comrades, comrades, ever since we were boys." F. McGlennon. WBT—WSC
"Comrades, good night." J. F. Reichardt. Words by J. E. Rankin. JS
"Comrades, have you seen the banners." See The year of jubilo (Work)
"Con piacer una vecchia mia canzon." See Finita è pei frati (Meyerbeer)
"Con tenue velo tu faz hermosa." See Perjura (Lerdo de Tejada)
"Con voi ber." See Chanson du toréador (Bizet)
Conant, Clarence M.
  "Child Jesus lay on Mary's knee"
"Concealed from ev'ry eye, where Providence has led." See Oh, ne t'éveille pas (Godard)
"Concealed in this retreat." See Oh! ne t'éveille pas (Godard)
"Concealed within this glade." See Oh! ne t'éveille pas (Godard)
"Conceive me, if you can, a most intense young man." See The nice young man (Sullivan)
"Conceive me if you can, an odd, delightful man." See An odd old man (Sullivan)
Concerning I and non-I. Volkslied: 'Seit vater Noah. Words by J. S. Blackie. SSS
"Concerning of a soldier." See The lady and the dragoon (Tennessee version)
"Concinamus, O Sodales." See Dulce domum (Reading?)
Concinat orbis cunctis, alleluya. For English translation see "Let the whole world chant and sing" (Smart)
Concone, Giuseppe
  "In my swift boat"
  Judith (from Judith)
  'Tis God who ordains me (from Judith)
Concord hymn. L. van Beethoven. Words by R. W. Emerson. LBR
El conde de Cabra. Game song. s. LCP
"El conde del cruel Araño." Mexican folk song. e.s. HS
The confession ("With sorrow and repentance") DM 2
Confession ("You are my sweetheart") Ojibway Indian song. e.in. BA
"Confide ye aye in Providence." See Ilka blade of grass (Wilson)
"Confounded be." Costa. OS 1
"Confutatis maledictis" (From the accursed") Verdi. e.l. OS 4
Congaudeat turba fidelium. For English translations see "From church to church"; "O hark to the bells' glad song"
Congdon, C. H.
  Merry autumn days
Congreve, William
  "Ah! stay! ah! turn" (Eccles)
  "Awake, Saturnia" (Händel)
  Hence, Iris, hence away (Händel)
  "Let ambition fire" (Weldon)

O sleep, why dost thou leave me (Händel)
The silent lover (Boyce)
"Tell me no more I am deceived" (Boyce)
"Where'er you walk" (Händel) See Pope, A. "Where'er you walk" (Händel)
The conjurer's song. See "Ye twice ten hundred deities" (Purcell)
Conkey, Ithamar
  Gently lead us
  "God is love, His mercy brightens"
  "Hail, Thou long-expected Jesus" (same air as Gently lead us)
  Rathbun. See Gently lead us; "Hail Thou long-expected Jesus"
Conkling, Mrs Grace Walcott (Hazard)
  "The nightingales of Flanders" (Foster)
Connais-tu le pays. A. Thomas. [Words by Goethe. Tr of "Kennst du das land"] e.f. MSS 2—SOA 2
  "Connais-tu le pays" ("Dost thou know that fair land") e.f. KS 2
  "Connais-tu le pays" ("Knowest thou the land") e.f. OPS 1
  "Connais-tu le pays" (Mignon) e.f. CS 2—SS 2
  "Know'st thou yonder land." e. WA —WBW
Connel and Flora. Air: Good morrow, fair mistress. Words by A. Wilson. JO
Connelly, Michael
  Farewell forever
Connolly's ale. Irish folk song. JOI
Conolly, Erskine
  Mary Macneil (Scottish air)
The conscript's departure (Sobiraïtes', brattsy-rebiatushki) Russian folk song e. SSR 3
The conscript's lament (Ne kukushechka vo syrom boru kukovala) Russian folk song. e. SSR 3
The conscript's return (Akh, talan li moï, talan) Russian folk song. e. SSR 3
"Consider, O my soul." Bach. e. OS 4
Consider the lilies. R. Topliff. HSS 1
"Consolati e spera" ("Forget thy grief") D. Scarlatti. e.i. NG
  "Consolati e spera" ("Take heart again") e.i. PA 1
Consolation (Mendelssohn) See "Abide with me! fast falls the eventide"; As pants the hart; "Sleep, noble hearts"; "Still, still with Thee"
Constancy. See My lodging is on the cold ground
The constant fair. Composer and author unknown. PR 2
Constant Johnny. Folk song. BSW
Constantinople. College song. WC
The Constitution and Guerrière. Forecastle song. CR
"Consume them all." F. Mendelssohn. e. SAS 4

"Contented am I, and contented I'll be."
  See The contented fellow
The **contented** camel. F. Ames. Words
  by D. Stevens. BSS
The **contented** fellow. 18th century song.
  Air: Since love is the plan. ME
"**Contented** wi' little." Air: Lumps of
  pudding. Words by R. Burns. BSR
"**Contented** wi' little." Air: The wee, wee
  man. Words by R. Burns. BSB
Contentment. See Die zufriedenheit (Mo-
  zart)
The **contrabandista.** Spanish folk song. e.
  GO
Converse, Charles Crozat
  Christmas joy forever
  The death of Minnehaha
  Forever and forever
  "God for us"
  Remember the Maine
  "What a Friend we have in Jesus"
Converse, Frederick Shepherd
  Under the stars and stripes
"**Convien** partir." Donizetti. e.i. PP
The **convivials.** F. Remy. Words by J.
  Oakman. ME
The **convoy** (Le convoi) J. Bleichmann.
  Words by A. Tolstoi. e.f. NR 1
Conway, Hugh, pseud.
  Prince Charming (Roeckel)
  Some day (Wellings)
Conway castle ("The sinking sun is beam-
  ing") Air: Y gadlys, or, The camp.
  Words by A. Boswell. BMC
Cook, Edward John
  Hip Ho-bart (Rose)
Cook, Eliza
  The Englishman (Blockley)
  "I'm afloat! I'm afloat" (Russell)
  The Indian hunter (Russell)
  Norah McShane (Horn)
  The old arm chair (Russell)
  The star of Glengary (Sporle)
Cooke, E. H.
  "The shepherds were watching" (Wat-
  son)
Cooke, Edith
  "I dreamed a dream of an old, old
  love"
Cooke, James Francis
  The breath of Allah
Cooke, Matthew
  " 'Neath the stars that shone so bright"
Cooke, Thomas Simpson
  Love's ritornella (wrongly attributed)
  See Planché, J. R. Love's ritor-
  nella
  Our Christmas rose
  "Over hill, over dale, thro' bush, thro'
  brier"
  Safely follow him
  Summer is coming
  Sweet Robin (attributed)
Cool little fountains, good-bye. See The
  dance of Zalongo
Coolbrith, Ina Donna
  In blossom-time (Needham)
Coolidge, Susan, pseud. See Woolsey,
  Sarah Chauncey

The **coolin** ("Had you seen my sweet
  coolin") Irish air: Molly St George.
  Words from the Irish. Tr of An
  chuilfhionn. e. MMI
The **coolun** ("Had you seen my sweet
  coolun") Irish folk song. [Tr of An
  chuilfhionn] e. EF—KF 1—KF 3
Coombs, Charles Whitney
  Her rose
Cooper, doctor
  I have been a foster
Cooper, George
  "Beautiful bells! O beautiful bells"
  (Composer unknown)
  "Beautiful isle of the sea" (Thomas)
  Gentle words and kindly deeds (Com-
  poser unknown)
  Graduation song (Ancient air)
  The little leaves (Ganz)
  Sweet Genevieve (Tucker)
  Swing, cradle, swing (Composer un-
  known)
Cooper, H. C.
  Ode to Denison (Old air)
Cooper, Isaac
  "Fareweel, ye streams"
Cooper, James Fenimore
  "My brigantine" (Saar)
Cooper, John. See Coperario, Giovanni
"The **cooper** o' Cuddie came here awa."
  Air: Bab at the bowster. Words by
  R. Burns. BSR—PS 2
Cooper's song. Suppé. e. HSD
Coote, Charles
  The tarpaulin jacket
"**Cope** sent a letter frae Dunbar." See
  Johnnie Cope
Coperario, Giovanni
  "Forth from my sad and darksome
  cell." See Mad Tom
  Mad Tom
Coppée, François
  Mai (Hahn)
  Obstination (Fontenailles)
  Ritournelle (Chaminade)
  Sérénade du passant (Massenet)
  Sous les branches (Rhodes)
Coquard, Arthur
  Alack-a-day. See Haï luli
  Haï luli
The **coquette** ("Ko sem k njej pršov")
  Slovenian folk song. e.slo. BF 1
Le **cor** (The horn) A. Flégier. e.f. SM 4
Coraggio, ben mio (My darling, be brave)
  Romanesca song. e.i. MSI
Corbett, F. St J. C.
  "Hark! the song of choirs angelic"
  (Lancaster)
Corbett, Grace
  "O, Mary, ye's be clad in silk"
Corde natus ex parentis. For English
  translation see "Of the Father's love
  begotten"
Corfe, James
  "Fill me a bowl"
"**Cori,** curuzzu" ("Oh heart, my own heart")
  Sicilian song. e.i. MSI
Cork and sweet Munster. Irish folk song.
  JOI

The **cork** leg.   J. Blewitt.   JO

Cormac oge ("The pigeons coo—the spring's approaching now") Irish song. e.   MMI

"The **corn** is all ripe, and the reapings begin."   See All of a row

"The **corn** is ripe for reaping."   J. Farmer. Words by C. A. Goodhart.   HC

Corn rigs are bonnie ("It was upon a Lammas night")   Air: Corn rigs. Old song with additional words by R. Burns.   BSB—PS 1
"It was upon a Lammas night."   BSR— MMS

Corn rigs are bonnie ("It fell upon a Lammas night")   Air: Corn rigs. Old song with additional words by C. Mackay.   PS 1

Corn-shuckin' song.   Negro folk song from Virginia.   BN 3

The **corn** song ("Heap high the farmer's wintry hoard") German air.   Words by J. G. Whittier.   LBR

The **corn** song ("We sing the plant") G. Marks.   Words by M. Herbert. FSS 7 —LA

Corneille, Pierre
Psyché (Paladilhe)

Cornelius, Peter
Betrayal.   See Untreu
The Christ-Child
"The Christmas tree" (Tr of Christbaum)
The kings (Tr of Die könige)
The monotone.   See Ein ton
The shepherds (Tr of Die hirten)
Ein ton
Untreu
Veilchen
Violets.   See Veilchen
"What sound is that."   See Ein ton

Cornell.   Words by G. R. Birge.   CHS

Cornish, William.   See Cornysshe, William

The **Cornish** bells.   T. T. Noble.   Words by C. W. Stubbs.   HC

The **Cornish** May song ("Robin Hood and Little John") Air: The Helston furry dance.   Traditional words.   GO
The hal-an-tow (Helston furry dance) BSW
"Robin Hood and little John."   DM 2 —MM

Cornish May song ("Ye maids of Helston, gather dew") Air: The Helston furry dance.   Words by A. Boswell. BMC— JE—JSE

Cornwall, Barry, pseud.   See Procter, Bryan Waller

Cornysshe, William
"Ah the sighs"
"Blow thy horn, hunter" (words and music)
"Blow thy horn, hunter" (words with traditional air)

Coronae.   See "Crown the Saviour, angels crown Him" (Monk)

Coronation.   See "All hail the power of Jesus' name" (Old air); "All hail the power of Jesus' name" (Holden)

Les **corps** de métiers (The trades) French Canadian folk song.   e.f.   BFS

Corri, Domenico
"He was famed for deeds of arms"

La **Corsairienne.**   Chant pour ramer.   e.f. SMW

Cortigiani, vil razza.   G. Verdi.   e.i. SOA 4

Cory, Thomas
The smuggler (Davy)

Corydon's doleful knell.   See "My Phillida, adieu, love"

Corydon's farewell.   R. Jones.   BE 8
"Farewell, dear love."   VFS

"Così, amor, mi fai languir" ("I languish, love, thy weary slave")   A. Stradella. e.i.   FEI 2

The **Cossack** ("Not the snowy cov'ring") Old Russian song of Ukraine.   e. KSN—SN

The **Cossack** ("Young and green."—Kozak) S. Moniuszko.   e.p.   BF 1

Cossack's lament ("Oï kriâche, kriâche") Ukrainian folk song.   e.r.   BF 1

The **Cossack's** lullaby.   N. Bachmetieff; attributed also to I. Orluff.   e. CST—KSN
Russian lullaby.   e.   TL

The **Cossack's** song ("High the Cossack's heart is bounding") J. C. Grünbaum. e.   CST—KSN—SN—TL

Costa, Sir Michael
"Although my house be not with God" (from Eli)
"Arise, O Lord" (from Naaman)
"Confounded be" (from Naaman)
Damascus (from Naaman)
David's prayer
"Embrace me not" (from Naaman)
The evening prayer.   See I lift my heart to Thee
I dreamt I was in heaven (from Naaman)
I lift my heart to Thee (from Eli)
"I will extol Thee, O Lord" (from Eli)
"If Thou should'st mark iniquities" (from Eli)
"It is a good thing to give thanks" (from Eli)
The morning prayer (from Eli)
"My sons, my sons" (from Eli)
"No evil shall befall thee" (from Eli)
"Open unto me the gates of righteousness" (from Eli)
"They shall be turned back" (from Naaman)

Costa, P. Mario
Canzone marinaresca.   See Luna nova
Caruli.   See Oje Carulì
Fisherman's song.   See Luna nova
'A frangesa
"Joy and courage"
Let me be.   See Mena, me'
Luna nova
Mena, me'
The new moon.   See Luna nova
Oje Carulì

Costello,
"All praise to Thee" (Tr of Gelobet seis tu Jesu Christ) Leyden. See "All praise to Thee"

Coster, F. B.
"Hell dig, du höga Nord" (Crusell)

Cotgrave, John
"Wert thou much fairer" (Wilson)

Le cotillon racheté (The ransomed petticoat) French Canadian folk song. e.f. BFS

"Cottage fair." See Hüttelein (Beschnitt)

The cottage maid. L. Dillon. JOI

The cottage well thatched with straw. Devon folk song. BOS
The cottage thatched with straw. BSW

Cott'n-dance song, dating from the time of slavery. Negro folk song from Florida. BN 3

Cott'n-packin' song. Negro folk song from Savannah, Ga. BN 3

Cott'n-pickin' song. Negro folk song from Florida. BN 3

Cotton, Charles
"Bring back my comfort" (Coleman)

Couch, Sir Arthur Thomas Quiller-. See Quiller-Couch, Sir Arthur Thomas

"Le coucou et l'alouette." See Les noces du coucou et de l'alouette

Coucy, Regnault, châtelain de
"Mercy I cry, who all bewildered stand"
"Quant li rosignol jolis"
"When the nightingale shall sing." See "Quant li rosignol jolis"

"Could a man be secure." S. Goodwin. BE 5

"Could I but come to thee once." See Vorrei (Tosti)

Could I forget. See Que je t'oublie (Chrétien)

"Could I know all the world." See The red lips

"Could I like sunbeam lift me toward blue heaven." See The maiden's wish (Chopin)

"Could I speak thy praise in music." See Stille liebe (Schumann)

Could my songs their way be winging. See Si mes vers avaient des ailes (Hahn)

"Could ye come back to me, Douglas! Douglas." See Douglas, tender and true (Scott)

Couldn't hear nobody pray. See I couldn't hear nobody pray

Couldst thou but know (Si tu savais) M. W. Balfe. e.f. KF 1

"Could'st thou know my deep emotion." See "Vidste du hvor hjertet skjaelver" (Warmuth)

"Couldst thou see, my beloved." See "Si vieras, vida mia"

"The count of the cruel Araño." See "El conde del cruel Araño"

Counterpoint for Music in the air. See Music in the air, Counterpoint for (Loomis)

"Countess, in thy dancing." See "Vous dansez, marquise" (Lemaire)

Counting song. Japanese New Year's song. e.j. BF 2
Counting song (Kazoe-uta) e.j. YJ

Country dance ("O let us all begin") Swedish folk song. e. DSH

A country dance ("When lambkins skip") Folk air. Modern words by S. Baring-Gould. BSW

The country fair. J. Barrett. Words by T. D'Urfey. MM
"In the pleasant month of May." DM 2

The country farmer's son. Folk song. BSW—DO

The country feast (Peerooshka) M. P. Moussorgsky. Words by Koltzoff. e. SMR 1

The country garden. See The vicar of Bray

A country lass. Scottish song. PS 2

"A country life is sweet." J. Eccles. Words by M. Parker. BE 7

The country parson ("I am a country parson") Air: Linco found Damon lying. Modern words by F. Kidson. MM

The country parson's lament ("Give me back my gown and trencher") St Andrews university song. Words by H. M. B. Reid. SSS

A country sheep-shearing. Air: The watermen's dance. DM 2

The country wake. See "Come lasses and lads"

The country's call. M. T. Armitage. BSS

County Guy. H. R. Bishop. Words by W. Scott. HSE 2
"Ah! County Guy." DM 2

County Guy. Air: Drink to me only with thine eyes. Words by W. Scott. FSS 7—JO

Couper, Robert
Joy of my heart (Scottish air)
"Red gleams the sun" (Scottish air)
"Red, red is the path to glory" (Scottish air)

Courmont, L. de
Par le sentier (Dubois)

The courteous knight. DM 1
"Yonder comes a courteous knight." CO 1

"Courtiers, courtiers, think not in scorn." See The king of Poland

Courting. Lindblad. e. KSN

Courtney, J. M.
"My heart's in the Highlands"

Cousin Jedediah. H. S. Thompson. FSS 7

Le couvre-feu (The curfew) French Canadian folk song. e.f. BFS

The Coventry carol. Ancient air. BSC—HC

Covert, Bernard
"Gloomy winter's now awa'"
Jamie's on the stormy sea
The sword of Bunker hill

The cow. WBT—WSC

Cowan, Samuel K.
Anchored (Watson)
"Lo: a star, ye sages hoary" (Newport)
"Out on the deep" (Löhr)
Coward, J. M.
"Weary of earth"
The **cowboy.** Cowboy song. Music by the "Kid." LC
The **cowboy's** lament. BF 2
"A **cowboy's** life is a dreary, dreary life." See The dreary, dreary life
Cowell, A.
"Thy name was once the magic spell"
Cowen, Frederick Hymen
"Be of good comfort" (from Ruth)
The better land
Bloom on, my roses
Boat song
The children's home
A farewell
"How excellent is Thy loving kindness" (from Ruth)
In the chimney corner
It was a dream
Light in darkness
"Like as a father pitieth his children, so the Lord pitieth them that fear Him" (from Ruth)
Listening angels
The mission of a rose
"O peaceful night! O time of holy calm" (from St John's eve)
Old and young Marie
The pilgrims
"Say, what dost thou bear in the secret deep" (from St John's eve)
"Sweet love of mine"
Though lost to sight
"Three kings once lived"
The watchman and the child
"With Thee there is forgiveness"
Cowley, Abraham
"Cheer up my mates" (Humfrey)
Cowper, William
Glory gilds the sacred page (Rossini)
"God moves in a mysterious way" (Scotch air)
"John Gilpin" (Old English air)
"The rose had been wash'd" (Manx air; also music by Webbe)
"Toll for the brave" (Händel)
Cox, Robert
The May pole (Composer unknown)
Coxe, Arthur Cleveland
The bird song (Herron)
Carol, carol, Christians (music by Bliss; Smith; also unknown composer)
"The **coy,** blushing Sylvia." Plowden. PR 2
A **crab** song. Air: There is nae luck about the hoose. SMW
"**Crabbed** age and youth." C. E. Horn. Words by W. Shakespeare. FSS 8— HSE 2
"**Crabbed** age and youth." H. W. Loomis. Words by W. Shakespeare. VFS
The **crabfish.** Folk song. SEF 2—SO

The **Cracovian** maid. FSS 5
Cradle hymn ("Away in a manger") See "Away in a manger" (Herbert); "Away in a manger" (Spilman)
Cradle hymn ("Hush, my babe") J. J. Rousseau. Words by I. Watts. HSC—JS—WBT—WSC
Cradle hymn (Greenville) FSS 1
"Hush, my babe." HSD
Cradle song ("Der abend schaut") See Wiegenlied (Ries)
Cradle song ("Bye-lo, baby, by-lo, bye") Rimsky-Korsakoff. Words from the Russian of L. Mei. e. NM 2
Cradle song ("En over de weide") See Wiegeliedje (Rennes)
Cradle song ("Ere the moon") R. De Koven. Words by T. B. Aldrich. HST
Cradle song ("Guten abend") See Wiegenlied (Brahms)
Cradle song ("Light and rosy") See Swedish cradle song
Cradle song ("Low, plaintive moaning") M. Moussorgsky. Words from the Russian of A. Golenistcheff-Koutousoff. e. NM 1
Cradle song ("Rockaby, lullaby") Wellesley college song. C. H. Raymond. CHS
Cradle song ("Schlaf, herzenssöhnchen") See Wiegenlied (Weber)
Cradle song ("Schlaf' in guter ruh'") See Wiegenlied (Taubert)
Cradle song ("Schlaf, kindchen") See "Schlaf, kindchen, schlaf"
Cradle song ("Schlaf', mein sohn") See Wiegenlied (Grieg)
Cradle song ("Schlafe, schlafe") See Wiegenlied (Schubert)
Cradle song ("Schlummre! schlummre") See Bei der wiege (Mendelssohn)
Cradle song ("Sleep, my baby, sleep, my pretty") N. Tcherepnin. Words from the Russian of Lermontoff. e. NM 2
Cradle-song ("Sleep, my darling, sleep, my starling."—Koluibélnaya) A. T. Gretchaninoff. Words from the Russian of A. Lermontoff. e. SMR 2
Slumber song ("Sleep, my baby, close to mother."—Berceuse) e.f. GMF
Cradle song ("Sleep, O baby mine."—Wiegenlied) P. I. Tchaikovsky. Words by Maikow. e.g. FO 2
Cradle song ("Sleep thou, sleep thou") F. Schubert. Words by V. N. Pierpont. TFC 2
Cradle-song ("Slumra du lilla") See Slummersång (Hägg)
Cradle song ("Sweet and low") See "Sweet and low" (Wallace)
Cradle song ("There once lived."—Komoriuta) Old Japanese folk song. e.j. YJ
Cradle song ("Vyssa, vyssa") See Vaggvisa (Söderberg)
Cradle song of soldier's wife. Words by T. T. Barker. FSS 3

A **cradle-song** of the blessed Virgin. See "The Virgin stills the crying" (Barnby)

Cradle-song of the poor (La berceuse du pauvre.—Berceuse of Yerómushka) M. Moussorgsky. Words by Nekrassow. e.f. SC Jeremouschka's cradle song. e. NM 1

Cradle-song of Virgin. See "The Virgin stills the crying" (Barnby)

"Cradled all lowly." See Bethlehem (Gounod)

The **cradles.** See Les berceaux (Fauré)

Crafts, W. F.
Our wonderful house (Composer unknown)

Craigher, J. N.
Die junge nonne (Schubert)

Craigie-burn wood. Air: Craigieburn wood. Words by R. Burns. BSB —PS 1
"Sweet fa's the eve on Craigie-burn." BSR

Craik, Mrs Dinah Maria (Muloch)
Douglas, tender and true (Scott)
The faithful little bird (Composer unknown)
"God rest ye merry, gentlemen" (Old English air) Additional words
A farewell (Cowen)
Gentle Mary (Composer unknown)
Mine own (Composer unknown)
Row, row, cheerly row (Composer unknown)
"Stars trembling o'er us" (Composer unknown)

Crambambuli. See Krambambuli

Crament, John Maude
"Softly the night is sleeping"
"Sow ye beside all waters"

Cramer, K. G.
"Feinde ringsum" (Gläser)

The **cramp.** Ancient song. CO 1

"The cramp is in my purse full sore." See The cramp

Crampton, Thomas
The holly wreath
"O'er old Judea's hills"
When the leaves are turning brown (same air as The holly wreath)

Crandall, R. K.
"Fair Smith" (Blodgett)

Crane, Amasa
"Hail, bright Easter" (Gounod)

Cranston, B.
"There came three kings from far away" (Hayward)

Crawford, Mrs Ann Spranger (Street) Barry
"Kathleen mavourneen" (Crouch) See Crawford, L. M. J. M. "Kathleen mavourneen" (Crouch)

Crawford, Caroline
"Singing while you soar to heaven" (Polish air)

Crawford, Jack, captain. See Crawford, John Wallace

Crawford, John Wallace
The sunshine boomerang (Harvey)

Crawford, Mrs Louisa Matilda Jane (Montague)
Dublin bay (Barker)
Eiieen achora (Knight)
Kathleen aroon (Abt)
"Kathleen mavourneen" (Crouch)
"The midnight moon" (Glover)

Crawford, Robert
The bush aboon Traquair (Scottish air)
I'll never leave thee (Scottish air)
"What beauties doth Flora disclose" (Scottish air)
"When trees did bud" (Scottish air; also music by Maigh)

Crawford, W.
Heigh-ho, the holly

Crawford, W. C.
Alma mater—Colby

Crawford, William
The bush aboon Traquair (Scottish air) See Crawford, R. The bush aboon Traquair (Scottish air)

Crawfurd, Robert. See Crawford, Robert

Creation. See "The spacious firmament on high" (Haydn)

Creation's hymn. See Die ehre Gottes aus der natur (Beethoven)

Credo. See "Je crois au Dieu" (David)

Credo con fermo cuor (Firmly I do believe) G. Verdi. e.i. KS 5
"Vanne; la tua meta già vedo" ("Go then! well thy fate I descry") e.i. OPS 4

Cremazie, Octave
The flag of Carillon (Sabatier)

A **creole** love-song. Mrs L. Moncrieff. Words by T. Marzials. MSF 2

Crépuscule ("Comme un rideau."—Twilight) J. Massenet. Words by A. Silvestre. e.f. GMF

Crepúsculo ("No has visto niña") Mexican folk song. e.s. HS

Crew song. Wellesley college song. A. W. Kellogg. CHS

Crewdson, Mrs Jane (Fox)
Joy in sorrow (Sankey)
A little while (Herron)

The **crib** and the cross. Bertha C. Boulter. Words by Ben C. Boulter. HC

The **cricket.** Children's song. FSS 8

Crimson velvet. See "Shepherd, saw thou not"

Criole Candjo. Negro creole folk song. e.f. KA

Criscuolo, Luigi
Chi sa (Atri)

Crnogorac crnogorki. See Montenegro

Croatian national anthem (Hrvatska domovina) J. Runjamin. e.se. BF 1
Hrvatska domovina. se. SN

The **crocodile.** Students' song. SSS

Crodh Chaillean. For English translation see Colin's cattle

Croft, William
Musidora
"O God, our Help in ages past"
Saint Anne.   See "O God, our Help in ages past"
Croly, George
"Spirit of God" (Hopkins)
Croon of the dew.   H. F. Gilbert.   Words by G. T. Phelps.   HST
The **croppy** boy.   Irish folk song.   JOI
Cros, Charles
Chanson perpétuelle (Chausson)
Crosby, Fanny
"Carol, sweetly carol, a Saviour born today" (music by Bunnett; Perkins)
"The Christian flag" (Woodman)
Music in the air (Root)
Three cheers for the olden time (Composer unknown)
"'Tis evening brings my heart" (Tucker)
Crosby, L. V. H.
Dear Santa Claus
Dearest Mae
The flag (same air as Dearest Mae)
Grave of Washington
My last cigar (same air as Dearest Mae)
Oh, dearest Mae.   See Dearest Mae
Crosland, Newton
The Indian maid (Hatton)
Cross, H. W.
The huntsman's chorus (Weber)
Cross, J. C.
The tar's sheet anchor (Reeve)
Cross, Mrs Marian (Evans)   See Eliot, George, pseud.
Cross, Sydney
Christmas bells
Cross, William
"Bound prentice to a waterman" (Sanderson)
Cross and crown.   See Kors och krona (Stenhammar)
The **cross** in the valley.   See La cruz del valle
Cross purposes.   Air: Tom and Mary.   MM
"The **cross**, the cross of Jesus." See Blest symbol of blest name (Briggs)
Crossing the bar.   J. Barnby.   Words by A. Tennyson.   BD
Crossing the bar.   H. H. Huss.   Words by A. Tennyson.   TL
Crossley, W.
"Sweetly sang the angels"
Crosswell, William
No myrrh of Araby (Composer unknown)
Crouch, Frederick William Nicholls
Dermot astore
"Kathleen mavourneen"
A **Crow** maiden's prayer song.   T. Lieurance.   e.   LN

Crow song.   Air: When Johnny comes marching home.   MPC—NMH—WBT—WC
Billy Magee, Magaw.   BSS
"There were three crows."   HSD
The three crows ("There were three crows")   SSS
Variant of: The three ravens
Crowe, Alfred G.
The glad bells all say (same air as See-saw waltz song)
See-saw waltz song
"**Crown** Him with many crowns."   G. J. Elvey.   Words by M. Bridges.   FSS 2 —WBT—WS
"The **crown** is on the victor's brow."   J. T. Field.   Tr of Finita jam sunt praelia.   e.   HC
"The **crown** is on the victor's brow."   J. S. B. Hodges.   Tr of Finita jam sunt praelia.   e.   HC
The **crown** of roses ("When Jesus Christ was yet a child") P. Tschaikowskv. Words from the Russian after an English original.   e.   HC
A legend (Légende)   e.f.   SC
"**Crown** the Saviour, angels crown Him" (Coronae)   W. H. Monk.   Words by T. Kelly.   LA
Crowther-Benyon, V. B.
"Yule returns; come, Christian people"
The **crucifix** ("Dry ye your tears") J. B. Faure.   [Tr of Crucifixus]   e.   BD
Crucifixion.   Negro spiritual.   JB
Variant of: "Never said a mumblin' word"
Crucifixus.   For English translation see The crucifix (Faure)
"**Cruda,** funesta smania."   G. Donizetti.   e.i.   SOA 4
"**Crudel!** di che peccato a doler t'hai." See La Catanzarese
"**Crudele!** ah! no, mio bene."   Mozart.   e.i.   PP
"**Crudele** Irene, tu m'hai lasciato" ("Unkind Irene, why have you left me") Abruzzian folk song.   e.i.   MSI
The **cruel** brother.   Folk song from North Carolina.   CSE—SA
Cruel Caramba.   See Tirana del Caramba y como te quiero
"**Cruel** fate! must I suffer them longer." See Os tormentos de amor
The **cruel** mother.   Folk song: English version.   SEF 1—SO
—Georgia version.   CSE
—Alleghany, N.C. version.   CSE
—Carmen, N.C. version.   CSE
—Tennessee version.   CSE
—Virginia version.   CSE
The **cruel** ship's carpenter.   Folk song: Hindman, Ky. version.   CSE
—Alleghany, N.C. version.   CSE
—Big Laurel, N.C. version.   CSE
—Black Mountain, N.C. version.   CSE
—Tennessee version.   CSE
Pretty Polly.   Harlan county, Ky. version.   WLT
—Knott county, Ky. version.   WT
Variant of: Polly Oliver

Crüger, Johann
  "Now thank we all our God." See "Nun
    danket alle Gott"
  "Nun danket alle Gott"
The cruise of the Bigler. Forecastle song.
    CR
The cruiskeen lawn ("Let the farmer praise
    his grounds") Old Irish song.
    MMI
  The cruiskeen lawn (The little jug)
    PI
The crusaders. C. Pinsuti. Words by
    W. Duthie.   BD—TL
Crusader's hymn.   See "Fairest Lord
    Jesus"
Crusell, Bernhard Hendrik
  "Hail, Northland high, all hail." See
    "Hell dig, du höga Nord"
  "Hell dig, du höga Nord"
La cruz del valle (The cross in the valley)
    Latin American song. e.s.   BF 2
"A cry is heard like thunder sound." See
    Die wacht am Rhein (Wilhelm)
The crystal maiden. See "Kristallen den
    fina"
"A crystal pavement lies the lake." J.
    Haydn. e.   SAS 3
"The crystal so fine like the bright sun may
    shine." See "Kristallen den fina"
The crystal spring. Folk song. SEF 2—
    SO
"Csillag elég ragyog."   See "See, love,
    above the stars"
"Csinom Palkó, Csinom Jankó."   See
    Palkó, Jankó
"C't un voyageur rev'nant de guerre." See
    Le retour du voyageur
"Cuando al brillar la aurora." See El
    suspiro
"Cuando al pie de tu ventana." See Sere-
    nata de Pierrot
"Cuando los carpinteros cogen la sierra."
    See Ris, ras
"Cuando los matadores." See Bolero
"Cuando me veas, en la desierta playa."
    See Un adios
"Cuando sali de la Habana, valgame Dios."
    See La paloma (Yradier)
"Cuando taca la guitarra."   See La gi-
    tana
The cuckoo   ("A-walking, a-talking")
    Folk song from Dorset.   SF 1
Cuckoo ("Cuckoo! cuckoo") A. S. Gatty.
    WBT—WSC
The cuckoo ("The cuckoo is a saucy bird")
    German folk air. Words by H. H.
    Harbour. DO
The cuckoo ("A little boy went out") See
    The boy and the cuckoo
The cuckoo ("Now the sun") M. Casson.
    FSS 2—LA—ME
The cuckoo ("O the cuckoo she's a pretty
    bird") Folk song. SEF 1—SO
"Cuckoo, cuckoo, calls from the tree." See
    Spring's message
"Cuckoo! cuckoo! pretty bird say." See
    Cuckoo (Scott-Gatty)

"Cuckoo, cuckoo, welcome thy song." See
    Spring's message
"The cuckoo is a saucy bird."   See The
    cuckoo (German folk air)
"The cuckoo is calling" ("Kukuvitsa kuka")
    Bulgarian folk song. b.e.   BF 1
The cuckoo yodel. CHS
Cucuruz ("Stalk of maize") Rumanian
    song. e.ru.   BF 2
Cuddle doon.   Words by A. Anderson.
    FSS 5
Cueca or zamacueca. Chilean folk song.
    e.s.   HS
Cui, César
  "Ach, wenn mutter Wolga." See "Ah,
    if mother Volga"
  "Ah, if mother Volga"
  "Dusk fallen"
  Hunger song
  Das hungerlied.   See Hunger song
  Nachtigall und kukuk.   See Poet and
    critic
  Poet and critic
  Le semeur. See The sower
  Souhait. See The wish
  The sower
  The wish
"Cujus animam" ("Savior, breathe forgive-
    ness o'er me") Rossini.   e.l.
    OS 3
  Cujus animam ("Through His bleeding
    side") e.   WA
"Cull to me the rushes green."   16th cen-
    tury song.   CO 1
"Cummari Nina." See Canto de' contadini
    Etnei
Cummings, William Hayman
  "Mountains, bow your heads majestic"
Cunningham, Allan
  Aikendrum (Scottish air)
  "Hame, hame, hame" (Jacobite air)
  "A wet sheet and a flowing sea"
    (French air)
Cunningham, John
  I'd wed, if I were not too young (Irish
    air; also music by Wicks)
Cunningham, Thomas Mounsey
  "Fareweel, ye streams" (Cooper)
Cunninghame-Graham, Robert
  "If doughty deeds my lady please"
    (Welsh air; also music by Sulli-
    van)
The cup of joy.   FSS 7
"Cupid can never."   See "Ah! quanto è
    vero" (Cesti)
"Cupid, sleep."   See "Dormi, Amore"
    (Gagliano)
Cupid's courtesy.   16th century song.
    BE 2
  Cupid's courtesie (I am so deep in love)
    CO 2
Cupid's garden.   Old song.   HSE 2—
    MM
Cupid's trick.   Air: Once I had a sweet-
    heart. Modern words by K. Moffat.
    MM
Curfew ("Solemnly, mournfully, dealing
    its dole") Composer unknown. Words
    by H. W. Longfellow. LBR

The **curfew** ("Veillez, veillez") See Le couvre-feu
"**Curiosity** led a young native of Erin." See The green linnet
"A **curly-haired** gallant I was in my youth." See Stadinger's song (Lortzing)
"**Curly** locks." WSC
The **Curragh** of Kildare. See "The winter it is past"
Curran, John Philpot
    "Dear Erin, how sweetly" (Irish air)
Curschmann, Karl Friedrich
    "Hark, hark! the lark"
The **curse** of Mora. Irish airs: The blind beggar of the glen, and, The yellow blanket. Words by E. Carbery. FSI
Curtis, Ernesto de
    Come back to Sorrento. See Torna a Surriento
    Torna a Surriento
Curtis, G. B. de
    Composer
    Carmè
    Carmela. See Carmè
    Author
    Torna a Surriento (Curtis, E. de)
Curtiss, A. E.
    "From east and west" (Tufts)
Cusack, Mary F.
    "Hark! the angels bright are singing" (Button)
Cushing, William O.
    "When He cometh" (Root)
Cussans, Jack
    Robinson Crusoe (18th century air)
Custance, Arthur F. M.
    Carol, brothers, carol
    A Christmas carol. See Carol, brothers, carol
    Columbia, hail
    "Come, ye lofty, come, ye lowly"
    "Easter flowers are blooming bright"
    The flag of our union forever
    The glorious Fourth
    "God of the year"
    "Good morning, sweet April"
    Hurrah for our banner
    Lo, the winter is past
    Morning song
    "O little town of Bethlehem"
    October
    "Sing with all the sons of glory"
    "Sleep, holy Babe"
    "Sweet spring is returning"
    Washington
    "The winds of March are blowing"
Cutler, Henry Stephen
    All saints. See "As shadows cast by cloud and sun"; "The Son of God goes forth to war"
    "As shadows cast by cloud and sun"
    Church militant. See "The Son of God goes forth to war"
    "Let the merry church bells ring"
    "The Son of God goes forth to war" (same air as "As shadows cast by cloud and sun")
Cutler, I. E.
    Hail to Denver U

Cutter, George Washington
    E pluribus unum (Composer unknown)
    Y **Cymry** dedwydd (The happy Cambrians. —"Fam'd for our warmth, we now rejoice") Old Welsh air. Words from the Welsh of R. Jones. e. MMW
Czibulka, Alphons
    "Among the lilies"
"**Czy** ty ne znajesz gdemoja chatynka." See The woodland cabin

D

"**Da** barnet sov ind med haand under kind." See Sövnen (Kjerulf); Sövnen (Reissiger)
"**Da** droben auf jenem berge da steh ich tausendmal." See Schäfers klagelied (Reichardt); Schäfers klagelied (Zelter)
"**Da** droben auf jenem berge da steht ein hohes haus." See Das mühlrad
"**Da** er gestraft" ("He was oppress'd") Kiel. e.g. OS 2
    "He was oppress'd and afflicted sore." e. SAS 2
"**Da** nachts wir uns küssten, o mädchen." See Verrathene liebe (Schumann)
Da patria o grito. See Hymno nacional (Brazil)
Da pomîanet Gospodi. See The beggar's blessing
"**Da** streiten sich die leut' herum." See Hobellied (Kreutzer)
"**Daar** ging een patertje aan den dans." See 'T patertje
"**Daar** ging er een meisje langs den kant." See Moetje varen (Verhulst)
Daar kommt een engel ("Once came an angel") Dutch carol. e. MF
Dabbling in the dew. Folk song. FSF—SEF 1—SO
"**Dacă** nu a şi nu e." See Aoleo
Dach, Simon
    "Ännchen von Tharau" (Silcher)
    Im frühling (Albert)
Daddy. A. H. Behrend. Words by M. Mark-Lemon. FMB—FSS 7—MSF 2 —WA—WBT—WSC—WSW
"**Daddy** Neptune one day to Freedom did say." See The tight little island
Dadmun, J. W.
    Homeward bound
    Rest for the weary
    There is rest for the weary. See Rest for the weary
"**Dae** va eigöng en kung'e" ("In olden times a king") Norse folk song. e.n. MAN
The **daemon** lover. Folk song: Kentucky version no. 1. CSE
    —Kentucky version no. 2. WT
    —Allanstand, N.C. version. CSE
    —Alleghany, N.C. version. CSE
    —Black Mountain, N.C. version. CSE
    —Hot Springs, N.C. version no. 1. CSE
    —Hot Springs, N.C. version no. 2. CSE
    —Spillcorn, N.C. version. CSE
    —Flag Pond, Tenn. version. CSE

"Dagen er oppe." See God morgen (Grieg)

Dagli immortali vertici. G. Verdi. e.i. SOA 4

Dahlgren, Frederik August
"Å jänta å ja" (Swedish folk air)
"I villande skogen" (Randel)
"Jag sjunger och dansar" (Randel)

Dahn, Felix
"Ach lieb, ich muss nun scheiden" (Strauss)
"All' mein gedanken, mein herz und mein sinn" (Strauss)
"Du meines herzens krönelein" (Strauss)

"Dai campi" ("From the fields") Boito. e.i. OPS 3

Daily growing. Vermont song. SSH Variant of: "The trees they do grow high"

The daily question. See "Du fragst mich täglich" (Meyer-Helmund)

"Daily walked in peerless beauty." See Der Asra (Rubinstein)

"Daily walk'd the fairest, whitest sultan's daughter, going, coming." See Der Asra (Rubinstein)

Dainty Davie. Scottish air. Words by Burns. BSB—PS 1
"Now rosy May comes in wi' flowers." BSR

"Dainty Davy was a lad." Irish folk song. JOI

"Dainty meshes, net enticeful." See "Caro laccio, dolce nodo" (Gasparini)

"A dainty plant is the ivy green." See The ivy green (Russell)

"Dainty wee stockings." I. B. Woodbury. MCS

The dairymaid. Old air: Packington's pound. MM
"In praise of a dairy." BE 8

Daisies ("At ev'ning, when I go to bed") C. B. Hawley. Words by F. D. Sherman. MSF 1

The daisy ("I'm a pretty little thing") WSC

"The daisy is fair, the day-lily rare." See Auld Joe Nicolson's bonnie Nannie

Daisy's song. Ruthenian folk air. Words by J. Keats. WF

Dakota serenade ("Shicé shicé") Dakota Indian folk song. e.in. BO
Evening song ("Shice shice shante") in. SN

"Dal cor per iscacciar quel sovvenir amalo." See Ô jours heureux (Meyer-beer)

Dal più remoto esilio. G. Verdi. e.i. SOA 3

"Dal profondo dell' obblio" ("From the depths") F. Campana. e.i. HSS 2—PG 4

Dalayrac, Nicolas
"Jeunes fillettes"
"Maidens, remember." See "Jeunes fillettes"
Young lasses. See "Jeunes fillettes"

Dale, R. F.
"No room within the dwelling"

Dalebu Jonson. Norse folk song. e.n. MAN

Dalecarlian maiden's song ("Many miles have I been straying") A. F. Lindblad. e.g. EF

Dalecarlian song ("Jag vet ett land") See Dalkarlasång (Lindblad)

"Dalej bracia." See "Onward brothers"

Dalekaya i blezkaya. See "O'er the distant lonely mountains"

Dalkarlasång (Dalecarlian song) O. Lindblad. Words by G. Nyblaeus. e.sw. HSOS

"Damamenowah dahbedug." See War song ("Hear the call")

Damascus. M. Costa. Words by W. Bartholomew. BD

"Dame, get up and bake your pies." See Christmas day in the morning

The Dame of Honour. See "Since now the world's turn'd upside down"

Dame Tartine. French folk song. f. DO

"The dames of France are fond and free." See The girl I left behind me

Damiani, Peter, Saint
"On the fount of life eternal" (German air. Tr of Ad perennis vitae fontem)

"Dammi ch'io libi l'alito" (I live and love thee) F. Campana. e.i. FMB

"Dammi un ricciolo dei capelli" ("Give me only a curl, to wear it") Abruzzian folk song. e.i. MSI

Damon and Florella. T. A. Arne. PR 2
"Cast, my love, thine eyes around." BE 6—DM 2

"A damsel possessed of great beauty." Folk air. BE 1

Dana, Malcolm
"When slumbers sweet enfold thee" (Forsell)

Dana, Mrs Mary Stanley Bunce (Palmer)
"Flee as a bird" (Spanish air)
"I'm a pilgrim" (Composer unknown)
Soft music is stealing (German air)

Danby, Gertrude
There's nae room for twa (Satter)

"Dance a baby diddy." WSC

Dance and sing. See Carmeña (Wilson)

"Dance and song make glad the night." See Carmeña (Wilson)

Dance around the tree. Omaha Indian air. e. FI

"Dance, O dance." See Danza, danza, fanciulla gentile (Durante)

Dance of the fairies. German air. Words by G. G. Richardson. FSS 6—WSC

The dance of the flock. See La danse du troupeau

The dance of Zalongo (Ho choros tou Zalongou) Greek folk song. e.gr. BF 2

Dance on forever. H. Aïdé. FSS 5

"**Dance**, play, sing, sorrow disdain." See Carmeña (Wilson)

Dance song from Jutland. See "Go javten"

"**Dance** the kolo, dance the kolo." See In the kolo

"**Dance** the leaves in sunlight." See Dance around the tree

Dance thee, my darling Cecilia. See "Mon pèr' n'avait fille que moi" (Cécilia)

"**Dance** to your daddy." Folk song from Berkshire. FSF

"A **dance** we had at our village home." See Städterbua und âlmadirn (Koschat)

"**Dance** with me." K. P. Harrington. Words by A. Adams. CHS

The **dancers** ("Come where the viols are singing") Arr from P. Lacome. Words by F. Manley. TFC 2

The **dancers** ("Hark! the thunder, mark the lightning."—Oy szumyt i hude) Ruthenian folk song. e.r. SMF

Dancing in the orchard. Austrian folk air. Words by R. Compton. DO

The **dancing** lesson. ₍Humperdinck. Tr of Brüderchen, komm tanz' mit mir₎ e. WSC

Dancla, Jean Baptiste Charles
 The birdies' maiden-friend. See La fille aux oiseaux
 La fille aux oiseaux
 "I'll never see my lover more." See Loin de lui
 Loin de lui
 Love's first confession. See Les premiers aveux
 Les premiers aveux

"**Dandelions** gold and green." Icelandic folk song. e. CST

Dandy Jim ob Caroline. Negro song. NMP

Daniel Boone. Air: The girl I left behind me. Words by F. H. Martens. BSS

"**Daniel** saw the stone." Negro spiritual. HR

Danish Christmas song. See "Et Barn er fodt i Bethlehem"

Danish love song ("The bright red sun in ocean slept") Traditional air: Jeg gik mig i skoven. Words by P. A. Heiberg. e. BMC

Danish national hymn ("Kong Christian") See "Kong Christian stod ved høien mast"

Danish national hymn ("There is a lovely land") See Danish patriotic song of 1820 (Kroyer)

Danish patriotic song of 1820 ("There is a lovely land") H. E. Kroyer. Words by A. G. Oehlenschläger. e. BMC·

Danish national hymn. e. JS

Danko, Pisto
 Broken is my violin
 "Eltörött a hegedüm." See Broken is my violin

Danks, Hart Pease
 "God of our fathers, let Thy face"

"**Dankt** dem Herrn! dankt dem Herrn." See Abendlied (Rolle)

"**Danmark**, deiligst vang og vaenge." See Thyra Dannebod (Rasmussen)

The **Dannebrog**. Danish patriotic song. R. Bay. e. KSN—LA—SN

Dans cette étable ("Here in a stable") Old French Noël. e. MF

"**Dans** la forêt que crée un rêve." See Clair de lune (Saint-Saëns)

"**Dans** la nuit, il chante en cheminant." See Through the fields in winter (Sokolov)

"**Dans** la plaine blonde et sous les allées." See Ritournelle (Chaminade)

"**Dans** l'ardent soleil j'avais foi." See A poet's epitaph (Medtner)

"**Dans** le bois à ma voix" ("Softly rest in thy nest."—Berceuse) Massé. e.f. OPS 2

"**Dans** le bois ténébreux." See The sleeping princess (Borodin)

"**Dans** le val, ah! dans le vallon." See A child's song (Musorgskiï)

"**Dans** les bois l'amoureux Myrtil." See Vieille chanson (Bizet)

"**Dans** les cieux vallonnées." See A southern night (Rimskiï-Korsakov)

"**Dans** les jardins d'mon père." See Auprès de ma blonde

"**Dans** mon beau pays j'avais un ami." See Chanson slave (Chaminade)

"**Dans** notre village" ("In our happy village") Villanelle. Attributed to J. Lefebvre. e.f. BO

"**Dans** Paris il y a, dans Paris il y a, que diti, que diton." See La bergère de France et le roi d'Angleterre

"**Dans** Paris, y-a-₤ une brune." See Cette aimable tourterelle

"**Dans** ton coeur dort un clair de lune." See Chanson triste (Duparc)

"**Dans** un sommeil que charmait ton image." See Après un rêve (Fauré)

La **danse** du troupeau (The dance of the flock) Canadian folk song. e.f. TF

The **Danube** river. H. Aïdé (music and words) FSS 2—HSD—JSE—PO—WBT—WL

The **Danube's** whirlpool. Austrian song. e. KSE

The **Danville** chariot. Negro spiritual. HR
 I doan' want fu' t' stay hyeah no longah. Arr by H. T. Burleigh. Old song with additional words by R. E. Phillips. BP—SM 2

Danza, danza, fanciulla gentile ("Dance, O dance, gentle maiden") F. Durante. e.i. FEI 2
 Danza, danza, fanciulla gentile ("Dance, O dance, maiden gay") e.i. PA 2
 Danza, danza, fanciulla gentile (Lightly dance, O happy maiden) e.i. PG 2

Daphne ("Daphne, on her arm reclin'd") W. Defesch. Words by J. Lyly. PR 2

Daphne ("When Daphne from faire Phoebus") 17th century song. CO 1

Daphne am bach ("Ich hab' ein bächlein funden") L. Reichardt. Words by Friedrich Leopold graf zu Stolberg. e. ED 3

Daphne am bach ("Ich hab' ein bächlein funden") J. R. Zumsteeg. Words by Friedrich Leopold graf zu Stolberg. g. ED 2

Daphne and Corydon. See Willy and Cuddy

"Daphne, on her arm reclin'd." See Daphne (Defesch)

"A dapple-grey horse, and a bright shiny gun." See Soldier song (Schumann)

"Där sjöngen fågel på lindekvist." See Fågelns visa (Söderberg)

Darby and Joan. J. L. Molloy. Words by F. E. Weatherly. FSS 4—HSC—HSD—JSE—WA—WBT—WL

"Darby dear, we are old and gray." See Darby and Joan (Molloy)

Darby Kelly. J. Whitaker. Words by T. Dibdin. ME

Dardiman yaru. See O my love, my plane-tree

Dargomyzhskiĭ Aleksandr Sergieĭvich
Forsaken
Heavenly clouds
"Ihr flüchtigen stunden." See "Ye dear, fleeting hours"
"Knight-errant"
Nur lieben. See Only love
"O thou rose-maiden"
Only love
Le paladin. See "Knight-errant"
"Ye dear, fleeting hours"

"Dark are now the candles." N. Tcherepnin. Words from the Russian of Fofanoff. e. NM 2

"Dark are the clouds." See Oh! hear the wild wind blow (Mattei)

"Dark day of horror." G. Rossini. [Tr of Giorno d'orrore] e. FSS 6

"Dark ey'd belle of calm still midnight." See Adieu my love (Hopkins)

The dark fairy rath ("Long, long have I wandered in search of my love") Irish air: Nora of the amber hair: 1st version. Words from the Irish of G. Roberts. e. MMI

"Dark lowers the night." See Connel and Flora

"Dark thro' the forest come the shadows creeping." See An evening song

"Dark was the evening." See Serenata ("Era la noche")

"Dark was the night and cold the ground." See My soul wants something that's new

"Darker and darker are woodland and hill." See Von ewiger liebe (Brahms)

Darkey Christmas song ("See dat Christmas tree") DCS

Darkly gleaming the streams of Punalau. See Waters of Punalau (Nape)

"Darkness hath fallen on forest and stream." See Von ewiger liebe (Brahms)

Darley, George
The call (Welsh air)
"Farewell to Sliev Morna" (Irish air)
The queen of the May (Welsh air)

"D'Arlina mi rammenti." See "The heart bow'd down" (Balfe)

Darling, go to rest. Nursery song. FSS 8—WBT

"Darling, my own." See "Caro mio ben" (Giordani)

Darling Nelly Gray. B. R. Hanby (music and words) HSC—HSD—JSE—NMH—NMP— WA—WBT— WL—WSW

"Darling Savishna" (Savichna, ma lumière) M. Moussorgsky (music and words) e.f. NM 1

"Darling sweetheart, if you're there." See Vergebliche liebesmüh'

Darnton, Charles
Christmas comes again
"O ring ye bells"

"Dartmouth, our Dartmouth." Dartmouth college song. CHS

Dartmouth song ("Come, fellows, let us raise") W. B. Segur. CHS

Darwall, L. J. T.
"One winter's night"

The Darwinian theory. Air: The king of the Cannibal islands. Words by J. Young. SSS

"Das also, das ist der enge schrein." See Vor meiner wiege (Schubert)

"Das ist ein brausen und heulen" ("Tempest and storm-furies shrieking") R. Franz. Words by H. Heine. e.g. FO 1

"Das ist im leben hässlich eingerichtet." See Es hat nicht sollen sein (Nessler)

"Das ist der herr von Rodenstein." See Das wilde heer (Schmezer)

"Das waren mir selige tage." See Die schifffahrt (Hurka)

Dashing away with the smoothing iron. Folk song. SEF 2

"Dashing through the snow." See Jingle bells (Pierpont)

The dashing white sergeant. H. R. Bishop. Words by Burgoyne. BOH—DM 1—HSE 1—JO

Dass, Peder
Fjeldbyggen (Norse folk air)

"Dass du so krank geworden." See Alte laute, I (Schumann)

"Dat day when you'se weary fightin' wiv sin." See When de debble comes 'round

Dauernde liebe ("Als ich noch im flügelkleide") W. A. Mozart. g. ED 1

"Daughter of kings, homage I render." See "Fille des rois" (Meyerbeer)

"The daughter of Zion, in the house of learning." See Raisins and almonds

"Daughter, you're too young." H. Carey. BE 5

The daughters of Erin ("We may roam thro' this world") Air: Garryowen. Words by T. Moore. BMC—BO—WBT

"We may roam through this world." MI—MMI—PI—WBT

"Daughters of Jerusalem." A. Sullivan. SAS 4

"The daughters of the city." Barnby. OS 4—SAS 4

Daumer, Georg Friedrich
"Wenn du nur zuweilen lächelst" (Brahms)
"Wie bist du meine königin" (Brahms)

D'Avenant, Sir William
"The lark now leaves his wat'ry nest" (Hatton)

David ap Gwilym
Gwilym and Ellen (Welsh air)
May and November (Welsh air)

David, Eugene
Le mariage des roses (Franck)

David, Félicien César
"Charmant oiseau" (from La perle du Brésil)
Credo. See "Je crois au Dieu"
"Delightful bird." See "Charmant oiseau"
Les hirondelles
"Je crois au Dieu" (from Herculanum)
The swallows. See Les hirondelles
"Thou lovely bird." See "Charmant oiseau"

David chantant devant Saül (David singing before Saul) L. Bordèse. Words by E. Plouvier. e.f. BS 2

David singing before Saul. See David chantant devant Saül (Bordèse)

David's prayer. M. Costa. HSS 3—HSS 4

Davidson, Thomas
The Yang-tsi-kiang (Dunlop)

Davies, Henry Walford
"As with gladness men of old"
The blessed birth

Dávila, Virgilio
La terruca (Colón)
Las vacaciones (Colón)

Davis, E. A.
A song of March (Jones)

Davis, Katherine Wallace
Jingle all your bells

Davis, Thomas Osborne
Annie dear (Irish air)
The boatman of Kinsale (Irish air)
Clare's dragoons (Composer unkown)
The flower of Finae (Irish air)
The girl of Dunbwy (Irish air)
"In a valley far away" (Irish air)
The invocation (Irish air)
"Oh! proud were the chieftains of green Innis-Fail" (Irish air)
"Oh! the marriage" (Irish air)
The welcome (Irish air)

Davis, W. B.
"Come raise the song"

Davuidoff, D. See Davydov, D.

Davy, John
The bay of Biscay
"Just like love is yonder rose"
May we ne'er want a friend, nor a bottle to give him
The smuggler
Will Watch

Davydd ap Gwilym. See David ap Gwilym

Davydov, D.
"Ye dear, fleeting hours" (Dargomyzhskiĭ)

Dawkins, F. W.
"The Christmas stars are shining"
"Through the midnight air"

Dawn ("This is the day") J. Barnby. TL

Dawn ("When the pale moon drowns the wide world") H. Somerset. Words by C. Walker. FMB—MSF 2

"Dawn, gentle flower." S. Bennett. Words by B. Cornwall. MSS 1—SS 1

"The dawn is breaking." M. W. Balfe. Words by T. Moore. FSS 8

"Dawn may be early breaking." See "Oh mattutini albori" (Rossini)

The dawn of day ("Come and watch") S. Reay. FSS 7

"Dawn of the day once more has broken." See Daybreak

Dawning. See "Still, still with Thee" (Clements)

The dawning of morn ("When I in morning's gloaming") Air: Y bore glas. Words from the Welsh. e. MMW

"The dawning of morn, the daylight's sinking." Air: Then market stake. Words by T. Moore. MI

The dawning of the day ("At early dawn") Irish air. Words by E. Walsh. MMI

The dawning of the day ("One morning early") Irish air. Words from the Irish [Tr of Fainne geal an lae] e. FSI—PI

Dawson, Arthur
Bumpers, squire Jones (O'Carolan) Authorship uncertain

Dawson, E. Mabel
"Alleluia! sing the triumph" (Brown)
"Now, prithee, minstrel, tell to me" (Brown)

Day, Alfred
"Music, when soft voices die"

"A day, a day of glory." Old French carol. e. HC

"A day, a day of glory" (Glory of Christmas) F. Campana. e. MCS

"Day and all its joys are ending." See Evening bells

"Day dawns with freight to haul." African song. af.e. BF 2

"Day has departed, and Silva not returned." See Ernani, Ernani, involami (Verdi)

"Day has gone down on the Baltic's broad billow." See Rise, gentle moon (Barnett)

"Day is breakin', Jacob, let me go." See Raslin' Jacob

"The day is cold, and dark, and dreary." See The rainy day (Dempster)

"Day is done, gone the sun." See Taps

"Day is dying, cool sweet winds." J. L. Roeckel. Words by F. E. Weatherly. TL

"**Day** is dying in the west." W. F. Sherwin. Words by M. A. Lathbury. BSS —TFC 2

"The **day** is ending, the night is descending." See Afternoon in February (Hullah)

"The **day** is gently sinking to a close." J. Barnby. Words by C. Wordsworth. FMB

"**Day** is gone, night has come." Round. FSS 5

"Day is gone, night is come." FSS 8

"**Day** is passing." Hungarian folk air. Words by D. Radford. WF

"The **day** of resurrection." G. E. Oliver. Words by St John Damascene. Tr of Anastaseōs hemera. e. HC

"The **day** of resurrection." W. H. Vibbert. Words by St John Damascene. Tr of Anastaseōs hemera. e. HC

"**Day** of thanksgiving." A. Messager. e. BD

"**Day** of wonder, day of gladness." Composer unknown. Words by B. H. Hall. FSS 2

"**Day** of wonder, day of gladness." G. E. Oliver. Words by B. H. Hall. HC

"**Day** of wonder, day of gladness." W. W. Rousseau. Words by B. H. Hall. HC

"**Day** on the mountain, the beautiful day." See The beautiful day (Hime)

"The **day** returns, my bosom burns." R. Riddell. Words by R. Burns. CST— PS 2

"The **day** star has long been sunk under the billow." See Pretty star of the night

"The **day-star** is shining." F. Abt. Words by G. Linley, FSS 8

"The **day** that I left my home for the rolling sea." See La paloma (Yradier)

"The **day** was clos'd, the moon shone bright." See The garden gate (Parke)

"The **day** went down." See The last lay of the dying bard

"The **day** when first I met thee." See Dreaming (Smith)

"**Daylight** closes round us, round us." See Swiss shepherd's song

"**Daylight** is done, setteth the sun." Round. FSS 6

Daybreak (Arshalouise) Armenian song. a.e. BF 2

"**Daylight** fades, evening shades o'er the silent waters creep." See Neva boatman's song (Nelson)

"**Daylight** now dawns." Dalmatian song. e. KSE

"**Daylight** slowly fades from the west." See "Über allen gipfeln ist ruh" (Schubert)

"**Days** and days have I been singing." See "Nu jag sjungit har i dagar"

"The **days** are all sunshine." J. Massenet. e. SAS 4

"The **days** are gliding swiftly by." J. W. Tosh. Words by Mrs E. H. Leland. HC

"The **day's** bright roses have gone to rest." See Grüssen (Lassen)

"**Days** grow longer." Ancient air. Words by J. M. Neale. HC

"**Days** grow longer." G. W. Warren. Words by J. M. Neale. HC

"**Days** in the wood." See Finland's forest

"**Days** of absence." J. J. Rousseau (music and words) e. JO—WBT

"Days of absence" (Rousseau's dream) e. FSS 2

Days of forty-nine. Cowboy song. LC

"The **days** of my youth have all silently sped." See Old easy-chair by the fire (Beckel)

"**Days** of summer glory." C. M. von Weber. FSS 1—WSC

The **days** of youth. See "Aus der jugendzeit" (Radecke)

Dayton, J.
"All quiet along the Potomac"

"**De** cet affreux combat je sors l'âme brisée." See Pleurez! pleurez, mes yeux (Massenet)

"**De** cuantas hojas bordan el suelo." See El planatar (Colon)

"**De** gik langs det legende hav." See Rav (Sinding)

"**De** grand matin me suis levé." See Joli mois de mai

"**De** la patria." Costa Rican national song. M. M. Guttierrez. e.s. SN

"**De** la paz en la dicha suprema." See Saludemos le patria (Aberle)

"**De** le belle cercavo la più bella." See Donna Clara (Gastaldon)

"**De** ma Soleïma l'ombre m'a visité cette nuit." See Soleïma

"**De** ma Zohra l'âme bercée." See Zohra

"**De** matin, ai rescountra lou trin." See Marcho dei rei

De' miei bollenti spiriti (Calm'd by her gentle, tender sway) Verdi. e.i. OPS 3

"**De** mon amie, fleur endormie" ("Of my beloved, flower that dreams") G. Bizet. Words by M. Carré. e.f. CM 1
Sérénade. e.f. PG 4

De noirs pressentiments. C. W. von Gluck. e.f. SOA 5

"**De** que araña se sale a pasear." See La rana

"**De** que sirve à las Usias." See Cancion de maja

"**De** quoi puis-je avoir envie." See Sans toi (Hardelot)

"**De** sa dent soudaine et vorace." See Le manoir de Rosemonde (Duparc)

"**De** sara se voroveau." See Colind

"**De** son coeur j'ai calmé la fièvre" (Berceuse) A. Thomas. e.f. SOA 5

"De son coeur j'ai calmé la fièvre" (Mignon's slumber-song) e.f. BS 2

"**De** tierra lejana venimos a verte." See Los reyes de Oriente

"La **dea** di tutti i cor." See Bella, adorata incognita (Mercadante)

The **dead**. See Les morts (Chausson)

The **dead** horse ("A poor old man came a-riding") Pulling chantey. FSF —SE
For variants see following song of same title; also O Johnny come to Hilo; Poor old man

The **dead** horse ("Poor old man, your horse") Long drag chantey. KB

"**Dead** is my heart, slain by a woman's eyes." See Unshriven

The **dead** soldier. See Der todte soldat (Esser)

"The **deadly** cup." FSS 1

Dean, T. C.
"Ring the bells, the Christmas bells"

"**Dear** alma mater, when in song we celebrate thy care." See Alma mater—Ohio Wesleyan

"**Dear** Bucknell." Words by S. S. Merriman. CHS

"**Dear** child of bondage." Spohr. e. OS 1

The **dear** companion. Folk song from North Carolina. CSE—SA

"**Dear**, dear are the Highlands." See Is toigh leam a' Ghaidhealtachd

"**Dear** Denison, 'tis thee." See Ode to Denison

"**Dear**, do not your fair beauty wrong." R. Johnson. BOH
"**Dear**, your fair beauty do not wrong." DM 2

"**Dear** Erin, how sweetly." Irish air. Words by J. P. Curran. MMI

Dear Evelina, sweet Evelina. HSD—MPC —NMH—SSS—WC
Dear Evelina. WA—WBT—WSW

"**Dear** eventime! when on the trees." See Eventime (Smith)

"**Dear** eyes, love-lighted." See "Occhietti amati" (Falconieri)

"**Dear** father, drink no more." FSS 4

"**Dear** friends around me all smiling." See "Mercè, dilette amiche" (Verdi)

"**Dear** friends, farewell! companions gay and daring." See "Convien partir" (Donizetti)

"**Dear** hall of song." See "Dich theure halle grüss' ich wieder" (Wagner)

"**Dear** harp of my country." See The farewell to my harp (Irish air); Farewell to my harp (Philips)

Dear heart ("In the night so plainly seeming."—Poli pumehana) D. Nape. Words by J. Kaahiki. e.h. HA

Dear heart ("So long the day") T. Mattei. Words by G. C. Bingham. FMB—KF 3

"**Dear** heart, rememb'rest thou thy promise." See "Te souviens-tu" (Godard)

Dear home, where dwelt my father. See Asile héréditaire (Rossini)

The **dear** home-land. W. Slaughter. Words by C. Bingham. SM 3

"**Dear**, if you change." See An old English love song (Allitsen)

The **dear** Irish boy ("My Connor his cheeks are as ruddy as the morning." —The dear Irish maid) Irish folk song. JOI

The **dear** Irish boy ("Oh, weary's on money") Irish folk song. MMI

The **dear** Irish maid. See The dear Irish boy ("My Connor his cheeks")

"**Dear** is my little native vale." Words by S. Rogers. DM 2—JE

"**Dear** is thy home-stead glade and glen." See Hamilton's song

"**Dear** Kenyon." Kenyon college song. CHS

"**Dear** kind Santa Claus, you'll see." See Let old Santa Claus come in

"**Dear** land! where first in childhood." See The home land

"**Dear** little Robin perch'd up in a tree." See Robin! Robin (Scott-Gatty)

The **dear** little shamrock. See "There's a dear little plant" (Cherry)

"**Dear** Lizzie, pray lend me that lantern of thine." See Die latern

"**Dear** Lord above, Whose kindly hand." See Thanksgiving hymn (Olds)

"**Dear** Lord, I thank Thee, Who hast made" (Wentworth) F. C. Maker. Words by A. A. Procter. LA

"**Dear** love, adieu! ever be true." See Adieu

"**Dear** love, I now must leave thee." See "Ach lieb, ich muss nun scheiden" (Strauss)

"**Dear** love, place thy hand on this heart of mine." See "Lieb liebchen" (Medtner)

"**Dear** love, regard my grief." See Fair lady, pity me

Dear love! thine aid. See Amour! viens aider (Saint-Saëns)

"**Dear** love, thou'rt like a blossom." See "Du bist wie eine blume" (Liszt)

"**Dear** mother, in dreams I see her." See Lullaby (Jakobowski)

Dear native home. Words by W. Ball. FSS 6

"**Dear** old pals." NMS—WBT

Dear old Reserve. Western Reserve university song. Words by W. H. Alburn. CHS—MPC

Dear old Yale. See "Bright college years"

"**Dear** one, do not leave me." See "Che farò senza Euridice" (Gluck)

"**Dear** one, thou hast wept once more." See "Du har sörjit nu igen"

Dear Santa Claus ("Oh, Santa Claus, dear Santa") L. V. Crosby. Words by C. Wallace. MCS

Dear Santa Claus ("Old Santa Claus in Christmas dress") Nursery song. FSS 7

"**Dear** student days, of you will we sing." See Studentsång (Gustaf)

Dear summer morn. S. Glover. FSS 8

"**Dear**, thou knowst sorrows grieve me." See Zueignung (Wolf)

"**Dear** thoughts are in my mind." See The lark in clear air

"**Dear,** your fair beauty do not wrong." See "Dear, do not your fair beauty wrong" (Johnson)

"**Dear** youth, be advised by your pastor." See The priest and the rake

"**Dearest** child, sweet one." See L'invitation au voyage (Duparc)

"**Dearest** companions, and you friends." See "Care compagne" (Bellini)

"**Dearest** consort." See "Cara sposa" (Händel)

"**Dearest,** farewell." See Abschied ("Liebchen ade")

Dearest Fernando. See O mio Fernando (Donizetti)

"**Dearest** heart, I beg of thee." See Entreaty (Bohm)

Dearest homeland, our vow has been spoken. See Dulce patria (Carnicer y Batlle)

"**Dearest** Kitty." Old English air. BE 5

"**Dearest** love, be coy, shun each wooing boy." See The young lover (Koschat)

"**Dearest** love, do you remember." See When this cruel war is over (Tucker)

"**Dearest** love, oh come to me." See Liebeständelei (Fitzenhagen)

Dearest Mae. L. H. V. Crosby; attributed also to J. Power. Words by F. Lynch. HSD—NMP—WBT
Oh, dearest Mae. FSS 6

"**Dearest** maiden, hark, I pray thee" (Krakowiak) Polish dance song. e.p. BO—SMF

"**Dearest** maiden, hear my song." See "Liebes mädchen hör' mir zu" (Haydn)

"**Dearest** maiden, list to my singing." See Kau fra Hallingdalen

"**Dearest** maiden, thou with the crimson cheeks." See The gipsy's song (Lvov)

Dearest mother, I am ill. See "Cara mamma, io sono malata"

"**Dearest** mother, the rain in the night beat so wild." See Walpurgisnacht (Loewe)

"**Dearest** mother, why art thou toiling at yonder sarafan." See The scarlet sarafan (Varlamov)

"**Dearest** mother, with fever I'm burning." See "Cara mamma, io sono malata"

Dearest name. See Caro nome (Verdi)

Dearest native land. H. Proch. FSS 6

Dearest night. See Chère nuit (Bachelet)

"**Dearest** one, do you remember." See When this cruel war is over (Tucker)

"**Dearest** Santa Anna, why is baby crying." See Arrullo (Chilian version)

The **dearest** spot is home. W. T. Wrighton (music and words) HSC—MP —NMH—NMS
"The dearest spot on earth to me." FSS 1—HSD—JS— LA—WBT— WSW

"The **dearest** thing of all, dears." See Christmas aftermath (Anderson)

Dearie. H. A. Norris. Words by H. Randall. HST

Death. See Vom tode (Beethoven)

Death and the girl. See Der tod und das mädchen (Schubert)

Death and the lady ("As I walk'd out") Folk song. SEF 1—SO
—Devon version. BSW

Death and the lady ("Fair lady, lay") Ancient song. CO 2—DM 2

Death and the maiden. See Der tod und das mädchen (Schubert)

Death and the peasant. See Trepak (Musorgskii)

The **death** of lovers. La mort des amants (Debussy)

The **death** of Minnehaha. C. C. Converse. Words by H. W. Longfellow. LBR

The **death** of Nelson. J. Braham. Words by S. J. Arnold. BE 2—BOH—BOS —DM 1—HSE 1—JO

The **death** of Parker. Folk song. BSW

The **death** of Queen Jane. Folk song. SEF 2—SO

Death of Rodrigo. See Per me giunto (Verdi)

The **death** of the betrothed. See La mort de la fiancée

The **death** of Warren. W. R. Dempster. Words by E. Sargent. JO

Death, the commander (Polkovódyetz) M. P. Moussorgsky. Words by A. Golenishtcheff-Kutoozoff. e. SMR 1

The **deathless** voice (Song of the deathless voice) Dakota Indian song. in. FIS

Death's lullaby (Koluibélnaya) M. P. Moussorgsky. Words by A. Golenishtcheff-Kutoozoff. e. SMR 1

Death's serenade (Serenáda) M. P. Moussorgsky. Words by A. Golenishtcheff-Kutoozoff. e. SMR 1
Serenade. e. NM 2

Deballi, D. I.
Himno nacional de la republica oriental del Uruguay

Deberiot, Charles Auguste. See Bériot, Charles Auguste de

El-debkah. See "Across the bridge, O come"

Debussy, Claude Achille
Beau soir
The bells. See Les cloches
La chevelure
Les cloches
The death of lovers. See La mort des amants
Evening fair. See Beau soir
Evening harmony. See Harmonie du soir
Fantoches
Green
Harmonie du soir
Her hair. See La chevelure
"Il pleure dans mon coeur"
Mandoline
La mort des amants
"L'ombre des arbres"
Puppets. See Fantoches
Romance
"The shadow of trees." See "L'ombre des arbres"
"The tears fall in my soul." See "Il pleure dans mon coeur"

Deceiver. See Tradetore

"December's come." W. B. Olds. Words by F. D. Sherman. NMS

Déception (Disappointment) P. I. Tchaikovsky. Words by P. Collin. e.f. FF—FO 2

Dechez, Louis Alexandre Hippolyte. See Jenneval, Louis Alexandre Hippolyte Dechez, known as

Dechme daghi. Turkish song. t. SN

"Deck not with gems." W. Turnbull. Words by T. H. Bayly. HSE 3

"Deck the altar with blossoms fair." J. S. B. Hodges. HC

"Deck the hall with boughs of holly." Welsh air. FSS 1—MCS—TFC 1

Decoration day. J. A. Geyer. Words by H. W. Longfellow. LBR

"Decrepit winter limps away." See Ode to spring (Arne)

Dedication ("Du meine seele") See Widmung (Schumann)

Dedication ("O danke nicht") See Widmung (Franz)

Dee, M. "Speed on, my bark, speed on" (Leslie)

"Deem not my heart ungrateful." See "Ah, non chiamarmi" (Gluck)

Deems, James Harry Our country

"Deep amid the leafy branches." See Leaving the nest (Reddall)

"Deep and secret lies the treasure." Dalmatian folk air. Words by D. Radford. WF

"Deep are the wounds" (Louvan) V. C. Taylor. Words by A. Steele. FSS 4

The **deep,** deep sea. C. E. Horn. Words by Mrs G. Sharpe. BE 4—HSE 1

"Deep furrows in thy face I see." See To my mother (Bradsky)

"Deep glow'd in the soul of the bard." See The bard's love

"Deep hidden in my heart" ("In meinem herzchen") A. Arensky. Words from the Russian of A. Golenistscheff Kutusoff. e.g. FM—NM 1

"Deep in a cool green valley." See Das zerbrochene ringlein (Glück)

"Deep in forest shaded." See "Parmi les lianes" (Masse)

"Deep in love was I" ("Wohl zu eignem leid") S. Rachmaninoff. Words from the Russian of A. Plestcheff. e.g. GMF

"Deep in ocean's diamond halls reclining." See Neckens polska

"Deep is the pain I suffer." See El sufrimiento

"Deep river." Negro spiritual. CST—DF—GMF—JB—SMF—TFC 2

"Deep shadows veil the night." See Elegy (Musorgskii)

"Deep the gloom and still the night." G. P. Grantham (music and words) HC

"Deeper, and deeper still, thy goodness, child." Händel. OS 3—SAS 3—TS

"Deeper now the shades of night are growing." See Kväll och frid (Geijer)

"The deer feed in the mountain glades." See The mother deer

Deer-flower (Pa-pup-ooh) T. Lieurance. e. LN

Deeves, M. Stonewall Jackson's requiem

"Deews, swehti Latwiju." See National hymn—Latvia

Defesch, William Daphne

Deffell, C. E. "Shepherds night-watch keeping"

Degele, Eugen "Du bist wie eine blume" "Ich möchte sterben wie der schwan" "So would I die, as dies the swan." See "Ich möchte sterben wie der schwan" "Thou art to me a flower." See "Du bist wie eine blume"

"Deh calma, o ciel." Rossini. e.i. PP

Deh, contentatevi (Pray, let me, suffering) G. Carissimi. e.i. FEI 1

"Deh! non voler costringere** ("Ah! do not let thy face") G. Donizetti. e.i. SOA 2 "Deh! non voler costringere" ("Why, since thy heart in sadness weeps") e.i. KS 3

"Deh più a me non v'ascondete" ("Ah! why let me ever languish") G. M. Bononcini. e.i. PA 1 "Deh più a me non v'ascondete" ("Oh, those charming lights") e.i. FEI 1

"Deh, rendetemi" ("O restore to me") F. Provenzale. e.i. FEI 2

"Deh! se mai senti spirarti sul volto." See Se mai senti (Leo)

"Deh vieni alla finestra" (Serenade) W. A. Mozart. e.i. SOA 4

Deh vieni, non tardar. W. A. Mozart. e.i. PP—SOA 1 Deh vieni, non tardar (Delightful joy, O come) e.f. KS 2

Deign my voice to hear ("Guschi ki behakk") Persian folk song. e.pe. BO

"The de'il cam' fiddlin' thro' the toun." See The deil's awa' wi' the exciseman

"Deilig er den himmel blå" (Norwegian Christmas song) e.n. DCS

The **deil's** awa' wi' the exciseman ("The de'il cam' fiddlin' thro' the toun") Air: The hempdresser. Words by Burns. BAS 1—BSB—HSSS—MMS—PS 1 "The deil cam fiddlin thro' the town." BSR The deil's away wi' the exciseman. BOS

"Dein angesicht" (Thy lovely face) R. Schumann. e.g. BAS 2

Dein gedenk' ich, Margareta (I think of thee, sweet Margareta) E. Meyer-Helmund. e.g. KF 3

Dein gedenk' ich, Margaretha (Thou art near me, Margarita) e.g. CB

Thee I think of, Margherita. e. WBW

"Dein herz und mein herz" ("My heart and thy heart") Round. Swabian folk song. e.g. SMF

Schwäbisches tanzlied (Swabian dance-song) e.g. SSG

"Dein schwert wie ist's von blut so roth." See Edward (Loewe)

Deinhardstein, Johann Ludwig Franz
Dem vogel in der luft (Harder)

"Déjà la nuit s'avance." See Adieu, belle France (Niedermeyer)

"Deka si bila." See "Where were you Cveta"

Dekker, Thomas
"Golden slumbers kiss your eyes" (Folk air; also music by Foote)
Sweet content (Smith)

De Koven, Reginald
Cradle song
Norman cradle song
Past and future
A winter lullaby

"Del mezzo giorno il ragio d'or." See The shadow of the cross (Barry)

"Del minacciar del vento" ("When winds are fiercely raving") Händel. e.i. BAS 2

Del mio core. J. Haydn. e.i. SOA 1

"Del nostro sangue nata." See La benedizione (Gordigiani)

Deland, Mrs Margaret Wade (Campbell)
The clover (MacDowell)
"Like small curled feathers, white and soft" (Howard)

Delarue, A.
Sérénade à Juanita (Jouberti)

Delavigne, Casimir
La Parisienne (Auber)

Delbrück, Alfred
"Un doux lien"
A tender tie. See "Un doux lien"
Tender ties. See "Un doux lien"

De Leva, Enrico. See Leva, Enrico de

Delgado, Frederick Pearce
A pledge to Columbia (Wilhelm)

Delibes, Clément Philibert Léo
"As falls the moonlight gently." See "Où va la jeune Indoue"
"Bonjour, Suzon"
"Bygone days." See "Jours passés"
Eclogue. See Eglogue
Eglogue
"Enfold me! O sea." See "Ô mer, ouvre-toi"
Fantaisie aux divins mensonges (from Lakmé)
Les filles de Cadix
"Good-day, Susanne." See Bonjour, Suzon"
"Good-morning, Claire." See "Bonjour, Suzon"

"Good morning, Sue." See "Bonjour, Suzon"

Indian bell song. See "Où va la jeune Indoue"

"Jours passés"

"Just as the daylight is fading." See "Tant que le jour dure"

The maidens of Cadix. See Les filles de Cadix

The maids of Cadix. See Les filles de Cadix

"Now while the daylight still lingers." See "Tant que le jour dure"

"Ô mer, ouvre-toi"

"O sea, dreadful sea." See "Ô mer, ouvre-toi"

"Où va la jeune Indoue" (from Lakmé)

"Prendre le dessin d'un bijou." See Fantaisie aux divins mensonges

"Tant que le jour dure" (from Jean de Neville)

"To take the design of a jewel." See Fantaisie aux divins mensonges

Delight of melancholy. See Wonne der wehmuth (Franz)

"Delightful bird." See "Charmant oiseau" (David)

Delightful joy, O come. See Deh vieni, non tardar (Mozart)

"The **delights** of good living." See The delights of the bottle (Locke)

The **delights** of the bottle. M. Locke. Words by T. Shadwell. CO 2—DM 2

Delille,
Lou nouvè di pescaire (Borel)
Lou revestidon (Borel)

"Delizie contente, che l'alma beate" ("O exquisite pleasure") F. Cavalli. e.i. KS 2

"Delizie contente, che l'alma beate" ("Ye blisses, that ravish") e.i. PA 2

"Dell' antro magico" ("Gates of gloom") F. Cavalli. e.i. NG—PG 2

"Della rosa il bel vermiglio." Rossini. e.i. PP

Della vita in sull' aurora (In my spring of life) Beethoven. e.i. OPS 3

Dell' Acqua, Eva
A rural song. See Villanelle
Villanelle

Del Leuto, Francesco. See Leuto, Francesco Del

Del Rio, Manuel. See Rio, Manuel del

De Luca, S. See Luca, S. de

"Deluded swain, the pleasure." Air: The collier's bonie lassie. Words by R. Burns. BSR

"Dem, der von allen nächten der stern." See Hymnus (Bruch)

"Dem matten wandrer winkt die ruh." See Himmlische ruhe (Molique)

Dem vogel in der luft ("In dem goldnen strahl") A. Harder. Words by L. F. Deinhardstein. g. ED 3

"Demain, dis-tu, qui sait où nous serons demain." See "Connais-tu le pays" (Thomas)

Demarest, Mrs Mary Augusta (Lee)
My ain countrie (Composer unknown)
"El demonio en la oreja."   Cuban folk
    song.   s.   HS
A demonstration.   W. H. Jones.   CHS
Dempster, William Richardson
Because he loved you so
"Break, break, break"
Irish emigrant's lament
Jeanie Morrison
The lament of the Irish emigrant.   See
    Irish emigrant's lament
The May queen
The rainy day
"When the night-wind bewaileth"
Den away, away, for I can't wait any long-
    er.   See Ole Shady (Hanby)
Den farewell, den farewell, den farewell,
    Mary Blane.   See Mary Blane
Den gefallenen kriegern ("Ferne in die
    fremden erde")   P. Müller.   Words
    by W. Hauff.   g.   ED 2
Den I wish I was in Dixie.   See Dixie
    (Emmett)
"Den lieben langen tag."   See Des mäd-
    chens klage
"Den sonntag, den sonntag in aller fruh'."
    See Liebesschmerz
Dene, Alison
The priceless gift (Gray)
"Dengang jeg var kun saa stor som saa."
    See When that I was a little tiny boy
    (Heise)
Denham, David
The saints' sweet home (Composer un-
    known)
Denmark ("Der er et land")   See Sang for
    Danske (Weyse)
"Denmark, by whose verdant strand."
    Danish patriotic song.   R. Bay.   e.
    KSN—SN
"Denmark with thy verdant meadows."   See
    Thyra Dannebod (Rasmussen)
Denmark's verdant meadows.   See Thyra
    Dannebod (Rasmussen)
Dennis (Nägeli)   See "Blest be the tie that
    binds"; "A charge to keep have I";
    "How gentle God's commands"; "The
    spirit in our hearts"
Denny, Alice Rose
Lullaby
Densmore, John Hopkins
April
Denza, Luigi
Call me back
Come to me
Funiculì-funiculà (with words "Behold
    above the clear horizon"; "Some
    think the world"; "Stasera, Nina
    mia")
I fear me to love him.   See J'ai peur
    de l'aimer
If.   See Se
In shadowland
J'ai peur de l'aimer
A merry heart.   See Funiculì-funiculà
    ("Some think the world")

Sailing o'er a summer sea.   See Fu-
    niculì-funiculà ("Behold above the
    clear horizon")
Se
Star of my heart
Lo telefono
The telephone.   See Lo telefono
Deo gratias.   15th century English folk
    song.   EF
Battle of Agincourt.   DM 1
The song of Agincourt.   CO 1
Song on the victory of Agincourt.
    BOS
"Depart awhile, each thought of care."   See
    Christmas vesper hymn (Auber)
Le départ du soldat (The soldier's depar-
    ture)   French folk song.   e.f.   TSF
"Depart! enough, my treasure I retain."   J.
    S. Bach.   e.   SAS 3
The departed.   J. Hine.   FSS 3
Departed days ("Sweet voices from the
    spirit land")   G. F. Root.   FSS 6
Departed days ("Yes, dear departed, cher-
    ished days")   Portuguese air.   FSS 5
"The departed! the departed! they visit us
    in dreams."   See The departed (Hine)
Departure ("Muss i denn")   See Abschied
Departure ("So leb' denn wohl")   See Ab-
    schied (Müller)
Departure for Syria.   See Partant pour la
    Syrie (Hortense Eugénie de Beauhar-
    nais)
Departure for the Alps in spring.   Swiss
    song.   e.   KSE—SN
The departure of the king (Brave Llewelyn
    turn'd and sigh'd)   Air: Ymdawiad y
    Brenin.   Words by A. Hunter.   BMC
The departure of the patriots.   See Le
    chant du départ
"Depth of mercy."   J. Blumenthal.   Words
    by C. Wesley.   FSS 5
"Depth of mercy" (Seymour)   C. M. von
    Weber.   Words by C. Wesley.   JS
"Depuis dix jours, j'erre de ville en ville."
    See Temple ouvre-toi (Gounod)
"Depuis hier je cherche en vain mon
    maître" ("Since yesterday I've sought
    in vain my master")   Gounod.   e.f.
    OPS 2
"Depuis un mois, chère exilée."   See Mai
    (Hahn)
"Der aander en tindrende sommerluft."
    See Brudefaerden i Hardanger (Kjer-
    ulf)
"Der den himmel und die erden."   See
    Ständchen (Raff)
"Der du am sternenbogen."   See Mäd-
    chenlied (Raff)
"Der du von dem himmel bist."   See
    Wanderers nachtlied (Schubert)
"Der er et land."   See Sang for Danske
    (Weyse)
"Der holdseligen."   C. M. Weber.   Words
    by J. H. Voss.   g.   ED 1—ED 2
"Der kriegeslust ergeben" ("To lust of war
    devoted")   L. Spohr.   e.g.   KS 5

"Der lebt ein leben wonniglich." See Das glück der freundschaft (Beethoven)

"Der ligger et land" ("There lies a fair land") Air: Ola Glomstulen. Words by B. Björnson. e.n. MAN

"Der ligger et land" ("There lies a fair land") R. Nordraak. Words by B. Björnson. e.n. MAN

Der rose sendung ("An Alexis send ich dich") F. H. Himmel. Words by C. A. Tiedge. g. ED 1
The message of the rose. e. WBT —WL
Der rose sendung ("To Alexis I send thee") e.g. FSS 3

"Der sjöng en fågel på lindeqvist." See Fågelns visa (Söderberg)

"Der skreg en fugl" ("I heard the gull") C. Sinding. Words by V. Krag. e.n. EF—KF 1—KF 3—SSN

"Der sonne letzter strahl." See Love's sorrow (Shelley)

Der spinnerin nachtlied ("Es sang vor langen jahren") L. Reichardt. Words by C. Brentano. g. ED 2

"Der stander et slot i Oesterrige" (There stands in Austria a castle) Norse folk song. e.n. MAN

"Der sto tre skjelmer a maka paa raa." See Möllervisen

Der wirtin töchterlein ("Es zogen drei burschen") 18th century air. Words by L. Uhland. g. ED 1
Der wirthin töchterlein (The hostess' daughter) e.g. BO
Der wirthin töchterlein (The landlady's daughter) e.g. SSG—SSS
The landlady's daughter. e. BSE

Derby, Mary. See Robinson, Mrs Mary (Derby)

The Derby ram. Derbyshire county song. BOH
Variant: Derby ram (Forecastle song)

Derby ram. Forecastle song. CR
Variant of: The Derby ram (Derbyshire county song)

"Dere was an old nigga." See Uncle Ned (Foster)

"Dere's a little wheel a-turnin' in my heart." See Little wheel a-turnin' in my heart

"Dere's a star in de eas' on a Christmas morn." See Rise up, shepherd and foller

"Dere's fire in de eas' an' fire in de wes'." See My way's cloudy

"Dere's no hidin' place down dere." Negro spiritual. JB
Variant: No hidin' place

Derfeldt, A.
Friendship

Dermot astore. F. W. N. Crouch. FSS 4

"De'rnte greit" ("It's no easy thing to get a beau") Norse folk song. e.n. MAN

"Dérobez-moi vos pleurs." See Ah! malgré moi (Gluck)

"Derrièr' chez mon père, vole, mon coeur vole" (Les trois princesses.—The three lovely ladies) French folk song. e.f. TSF

"Derrièr' chez nous y-a-t-un étang, derrièr' chez nous y-a-t-un étang, trois beaux canards s'en vont baignant." See Le canard blanc

"Derrièr' chez nous y-a-t-un étang; roulite roulant ma boule roulant." See En roulant ma boule

"Derrièr' chez nous y-a-t-un étang, suivons le vent, gai gaiment." See Le canard blanc (Variant)

"Derrière chez mon père les lauriers sont fleuris." See Le prisonnier de Holland (Breton version)

"Derrière chez mon père, vive la rose." See La marchande d'oranges

"Derrière chez mon père, vole, mon coeur, vole" (Les trois filles d'un prince.—The prince's three daughters.——Vole, mon coeur, vole.—Fly, my heart, fly thither) Canadian song. [L. Streabbog] e.f. TF

Dervish song. See "There's no deity but God"

"Des abends rosen sind abgeblüht." See Grüssen (Lassen)

"Des bolets, des oronges." See Gathering mushrooms (Musorgskiï)

"Des bon vieux airs très connus." See Première danse (Massenet)

Des Deutschen vaterland ("Was ist des Deutschen vaterland") G. Reichardt. Words by E. M. Arndt. g. ED 1
Des Deutschen vaterland (The German's fatherland) e.g. SSG. e. only BSE
The German fatherland. e. FSS 8
"Was ist des Deutschen vaterland" ("What is the German fatherland") e.g. SN
"Was ist des Deutschen vaterland" ("Where is the German fatherland." —National song of Germany) e.g. WCP

"Des ersten sehens wonne ist wie der duft im walde." See Erstes begegnen (Grieg)

Des geistes gesang (The spirit's song) J. Haydn. e.g. KF 1
The spirit's song. e. KF 2
The spirit's song (Hark! what I tell to thee) e. CS 1—MSS 2

Des glockenthürmers töchterlein (The bellringer's daughter) C. Loewe. Words by F. Rückert. e.g. KF 1—KF 3

"Des jahres ganze blumenzeit." See Blumentag

"Des jahres letzte stunde." See Am Sylvester-abend (Schulz)

Des mädchens klage ("Den lieben langen tag") Steirische volksweise. Words by P. J. Düringer. g. ED 1

Des mädchens klage (The maiden's lament.—"Das lieben langen tag") e.g. SSG

Den lieben langen tag (The long weary day) e. FSS 2

"Long, long weary day." e.g. EF. e. only HSD

The long weary day. e. JSE

The maiden's lament. e. BSE

Des mädchens klage ("Der eichwald brauset") See "Der eichwald brauset" (Schubert)

Des mädchens klage ("Hinaus, ach hinaus") See The blue bells of Scotland (Jordan)

Des Magyaren heimweh ("Meiner heimat schöne auen") Volkslied. g. ED 3

"Des morgens, wann die hähne krähen." See Soldatenliebe

Des sängers fluch ("Es stand in alten zeiten") J. Gersbach. Words by L. Uhland. g. ED 3

Des trinkers testament ("Ihr brüder, wenn ich nicht mehr trinke") Trinklied. g. ED 2

Des trinkers testament. For English translation with a different air see Drinking song ("My comrades")

"Des violettes, des roses, des fleurs." See Chant de quête de l'Alsace

"Des winters als het reghent" ("In winter, when it's raining") 16th century Flemish song. d.e. BDF—BF 2

The gay fisherboy. e. KSN—WL

"Descend thou, sleep, with sweet calm." See "Deh calma, o ciel" (Rossini)

The desert (Le desert) M. Balakirev. Words by A. Jemchoujnikov. e.f. NR 2

"Deserted and lonely." Carinthian song. e. KSE

"Deserted by the waning moon." See All's well (Braham)

The deserter's plaint. See La complainte du déserteur

Des Essarts, Emmanuel
Les trois prières (Paladilhe)

"Desire, what has it to offer." See Sans toi (Hardelot)

Desmond's song ("By the feal's wave benighted") Old Irish air. Words by T. Moore. MI—MMI—PI

"Desolate, alone, in the dark I sigh." See The laborer's plaint (Kopylov)

Desolation ("I could not speak with him") Hindu song. Air: Kurna na päce bät. e. BMC

"Despairing beside a clear stream." See Colin's complaint

Despairing Mary. J. Wilson. Words by Tannahill. PS 2

La despedida. F. Gutiérrez (music and words) s. LCP

The despised lover. See Der verschmähte

"Despoiled is thy crown of honor." M. Blumner. e. SAS 4

"Desponding, lonely." See "Son tutta duolo" (Scarlatti)

"The despot's heel is on thy shore." See Maryland, My Maryland

Desprez, F.
Love, I will love you ever (Bucalossi)

Dessauer, Josef
"Come out, come out, my dears." See Le retour des promis
Enticement. See Lockung
Lockung
Le retour des promis

"Dessous le rosier blanc." See La belle au rosier blanc

"Det fins en gosse och han är min" ("There is a laddie, and he is mine") A. Hallén. Words by Gellerstedt. e.sw. WM 1

"Det stiger" ("It rises") P. Heise. Words by H. Drachmann. da.e. WM 1

Det var då (In days of yore) H. Kjerulf. Words by J. L. Runeberg. e.sw. SSN

"Det var en gång en jungfru." See Jungfrun i det gröna

"Det var slig en vakker solskins-dag." See En solskins dag (Nordraak)

The deuks dang ow're my daddie. Scottish air. Words by R. Burns. PS 1

"The bairns gat out wi' an unco shout." BSR

Deutsche mahnung ("Stehe fest, o vaterland") A. Methfessel. Words by K. Göttling. g. ED 2

Der deutsche Rhein ("Sie sollen ihn nicht haben") After G. Kunze. Words by N. Becker. g. ED 1

Rheinlied (Rhine song) e.g. BSP

The Rhine song ("They shall not ever win thee") e. BMC

Des Deutschen vaterland. See entry under Des

Deutscher ehrenpreis ("Von allen ländern") A. Methfessel. Words by Schmidt von Lübeck. g. ED 2

Deutscher freiheit schlachtruf. See Vaterlandslied (Methfessel)

Deutscher trost ("Deutsches herz, verzage nicht") F. W. Berner. Words by E. M. Arndt. g. ED 2

"Deutsches herz, verzage nicht." See Deutscher trost (Berner)

Deutsches weihelied ("Stommt an mit hellem hohem klang") A. Methfessel. Words by M. Claudius. g. ED 1

Deutschland über alles. J. Haydn. Words by Hoffmann von Fallersleben. g. ED 1

Les deux bergères (The two shepherdesses) French folk song. e.f. TSF

Les deux coeurs. For English transla- see Two hearts (Fontenailles)

Les deux grenadiers (The two grenadiers) R. Wagner. [Words by Heine. Tr of Die beiden grenadiere] e.f. KF 4

Les deux grenadiers. For words in the original with a different air see Die beiden grenadiere (Schumann)

De Vere, Aubrey Thomas
"They leave the land of gems and gold" (Old French carol)

Devere, Harry
My little valley home (Beckel)

De Vere, Sir Stephen Edward
The snowy-breasted pearl (Irish air)

Devereaux, E.
"I think of you in waking hours" (Composer unknown)
Love s greeting (Elgar)
Serenata (Moszkowski)

Devereaux, L.
Maltese boatman's song

"A **devil** came up from Demonland." See Les corps de métiers

The **devil's** progress. 17th century song. CO 2

"**Devoid** of mathematic brain." See A mathematic monody (Newton)

Devonshire, Georgiana Cavendish, duchess of
"I have a silent sorrow here"

Devotion ("Du meine seele") See Widmung (Schumann)

Devotion ("Ja, du weisst es") See Zueignung (Strauss)

Devotion ("Oh, could our thoughts") See "Oh, could our thoughts"

"Un **devoto** por ir al rosario." See Rosario de la aurora

"The **dew** each trembling leaf unwreath'd." Irish air: Nancy of the branching tresses. Words by M. Balfour. MMI

"The **dew** it shines." See "Es blinkt der thau" (Rubinstein)

"The **dew** lay glitt'ring o'er the grass." See Five o'clock in the morning (Barnard)

"The **dewdrops** glitter in grass beclad night. See "Es blinkt der thau" (Rubinstein)

"The **dewdrops** shine on the grasses at night." See "Es blinkt der thau" (Rubinstein)

Dewi Mon. See Rowlands, David

Dewy violets. See Le violette (Scarlatti)

Dh' fhalbh mo leannan fhein ("My own dear one's gone") Old Gaelic air. Words from the Gaelic of Fionn (H. Whyte) e. HSSS

"**Dha** ke-de hia u-dha ho-dha." See Choral (Omaha Indian song)

"**Di** piacer mi balza il cor." Rossini. e.i. PP

"**Di** Provenza il mar" ("From Provence, both land and wave") Verdi. e.i. OPS 4

Di tanti palpiti. G. Rossini. e.i. SOA 2
Di tanti palpiti (For all the pains I bear) e.i. KS 3

"El **día** renace y alegre la aurora." See The star-spangled banner (Smith)

"Un **diable** est sorti des enfers." See Les corps de métiers

"Les **diamants** chez nous sont innombrables." See A song of India (Rimskiï-Korsakov)

"**Diana**, cruel goddess." See "Diane impitoyable" (Gluck)

"**Diane** impitoyable" ("Diana, cruel goddess") C. W. von Gluck. e.f. KS 5

Dibdin, Charles, 1745-1814
"Adieu, adieu, my only life." See The soldier's adieu
"All who of Britons bear the name." See Freedom's contribution
All's one to Jack
The anchorsmiths
"Blow high, blow low, let tempests tear" (from The seraglio)
"Cherries and plums" (from The waterman)
"Come, come, my lads"
Fair Rosalie
The flowing bowl
Freedom's contribution (from The sphinx)
The high-mettled racer
"I locked up all my treasure"
"I sailed in the good ship, the Kitty." See Yo, yea
In every port a wife (from The wags)
"I've sailed round the world." See Jack's gratitude
Jack at Greenwich (from The cake house)
"Jack Rattlin"
Jack's gratitude
The jolly young waterman (same air as The north country lass)
The lass that loves a sailor (from The robin)
Lovely Nan
Mounseer Nong Tong Paw (from The general election)
Ned that died at sea (from Christmas gambols)
The north country lass
Poor Jack (from The whim of the moment)
Poor Tom (from The waterman)
Reasons for drinking
The sailor's journal
The soldier's adieu (from The wags)
Sweet Willy, O
"Then farewell, my trim-built wherry." See Poor Tom
The token (from Castles in the air)
Tom Bowling (from The oddities)
Tom Tough (from A tour to the land's end)
True courage
The true English sailor
"While the lads of the village"
The wily fox
The woodman
Yo heave ho. See Tom Tough
Yo, yea (from Friendly tars)

Dibdin, Charles, 1768-1833

Composer

The bee proffers honey but bears a sting
Tink a tink. See The bee proffers honey but bears a sting

Dibdin, Charles, 1768-1833—*Continued*

Author

The heart should be happy and merry (Reeve)

Love has eyes (Bishop)

"The rose of the valley" (Reeve)

The Whip club (Reeve)

Dibdin, Thomas John

All's well (Braham)

The cabin boy (Ware)

Darby Kelly (Whitaker)

Every bullet has its billet (Bishop)

The origin of gunpowder (Braham)

Ti, tum, ti (Reeve)

The tight little island (Old air)

The Yorkshire man (Reeve)

"Dicen que los ojos azules." See Los ojos mexicanos

"Dich priest, Allmächtiger, der sterne jubelklang." See Erbarmen (Nicodé)

"Dich, theure halle grüss' ich wieder" ("Oh hall of song") R. Wagner. e.g. SOA 1

"Dich theure halle grüss' ich wieder" ("Dear hall of song") e.g. SS 2

Dichmont, William

Such a li'l' fellow

Dick, Cotsford

The land beyond (Pinsuti)

Dickens, Charles

"Autumn leaves" (Composer unknown)

The ivy green (Russell)

Merry autumn days (Congdon)

Dickhaut, B. E.

Take my love to Rosalie

Dickinson, Grace

"Let music break on this blest morn" (Calkin)

"Dickory, dickory, dock." FMB—WA—WBT—WSC—WSW

Dickson, Caspar G. See Eno, J. N., jt. auth.

"Dicky said to Johnson one cold winter's day." See The three butchers (North Carolina version)

"Did ev' you see the like before." See I know the Lord's laid His hands on me

Did not old Pharaoh get lost. See Didn't old Pharaoh get lost

"Dïd rudiï, baba ruda." See Red-haired family

"Did you ever see the like before." See I know the Lord's laid His hands on me

"Did you hear how dey crucified my Lord." Negro spiritual. HR

Did you hear my Jesus. Negro spiritual. HR

"Did you hear of the widow Malone." See The widow Malone

"Did you never hear tell of that general." See The plains of Mexico

"Did you not hear of a gallant sailor." See The unconstant fair

Didiée, Julien

Hosanna (Granier)

Didn't he ramble. Old popular song. BSS

Didn't my Lord deliver Daniel. Negro spiritual. JB—JP

Variant: My Lord delivered Daniel

Didn't old Pharaoh get lost. Negro spiritual. JB

Did not old Pharaoh get lost. JP

Dido's lament. See When I am laid in earth (Purcell)

Dido's song. See When I am laid in earth (Purcell)

"Die du so gern in hiel'gen nachten feierst." See An die hoffnung (Beethoven)

"Die ihr felsen und bäume bewohnt." See Einsamkeit (Medtner)

Die in de fiel'. Negro spiritual. JB

Diehl, Louis

After

Going to market

The water mill

Dielman, Henry

Christmas hymn

"Dies bildniss ist bezaubernd schön." W. A. Mozart. e.g. SOA 3

"Dies ist der tag, den Gott gemacht." M. Luther. Words by C. F. Gellert. g. ED 1

Dietrich, Friedrich

Frühlingsfeier

Dietrich, R.

"Auf wiederseh'n! so sprachst du leise" (Nevin)

"Dieu puissant, notre père." See Er re goli

"Dieu s'avance à travers les champs." See La procession (Franck)

Dieupart,

True happiness (attributed)

The diffident lover. S. Howard. PR 2

"Dig my grave." Negro folk song from the Bahamas. KA

Dignum, Charles

The disabled seaman

The fight off Camperdown

En digters sidste sang (The poet's last song) E. Grieg. Words by H. C. Andersen. e.n. MAN

Dilley, Edgar M.

"Hail, Pennsylvania" (Old air)

Dillon, Larry

The cottage maid

Dilly dally, shilly shally. J. Hook. Words by Houlton. ME

The dilly song. Cornish folk song. BSW

Variant of: The ten commandments

"Dim is the path before me lying." See Doubt: a death song

"Dimanche à l'aube en me levant." See La fille et le chasseur

"Dime, mujer adorada." Folk song from Santa Barbara. e.s. HS

Dimme 'na vota sì (Ah, say but yes) Scalisi. Words by M. Paolella. e.i. MN

Dimmi na vota sì ("Dimmi una volta sì."—"Give me thy word") e.i. FE

"Dimmi, amor" ("Tell me, love") A. Del Leuto. e.i. PA 2

"**Dimmi** dimmi, apuzza nica." See Lu labbru

"**Dimmi** una volta sì." See Dimme 'na vota sì (Scalisi)

Dimond, pseud. See Opie, Mrs Amelia (Alderson)

"**Ding,** dong, bell, call the people." Irish folk song. JOI

"**Ding,** dong, bell, pussy's in the well." FSS 4—WBT—WSC

"**Ding** dong bell, pussy's in the well." Another air. FMB

"**Ding** dong ding dong ding dong ding dong ding dong bell." See Legend of the bell (Planquette)

"**Ding** dong, ding dong, ding dong, I love the song." See Yeoman's wedding song (Poniatowski)

"**Ding,** dong, ding, dong, ding, dong, listen to the bell." See Legend of the bell (Planquette)

"**Ding** dong, ding dong, ding dong, peal out the bells." See On Christmas morning (Poniatowski)

"**Ding** dong! ding dong! the old year will soon be gone." Nursery song. FSS 8

Dingelstedt, Franz, freiherr von
An der Weser (Pressel)

"**Dio** dell' or." See "Le veau d'or" (Gounod)

"**Dio** possente, dio d'amor." See "Avant de quitter ces lieux" (Gounod)

Dip, boys, dip the oar. FSS 4

"**Dir** ch'io t'ami" ("Words elude me") F. Mancini. e.i. FEI 2

"**Dir,** du quell von huld und segen." See Morgenlied (Reichardt)

"**Dir** folgen meine tränen, dir." See An die wankelmütige (Schulz)

"**Dire** was the hate at old Harlaw." Air: The dragon of Wantley. Words by R. Burns. BSR

Dirge for the year ("Orphan hours, the year is dead") S. S. Wesley. Words by Shelley. DM 2

Dirnböck, Jacob
"Hoch vom dachstein" (Styrian air)
Das Steierland (Seidel)

"**Dis** cott'n want a-pickin' so bad." See Cott'n-pickin' song

"**Dis-moi,** mon vieux, dis-moi pourquoi." See Les enfants de la mer

The **disabled** seaman. C. Dignum. Words by M. G. Lewis. ME

Disappointed expectation. Lindblad. e. KSN

The **disappointed** serenader. See Vergebliches ständchen (Brahms)

The **disappointed** suitors ("Sadla muška na konárik") Slovak folk song. sl.e. BF 1

Disappointment. See Déception (Tchaikovsky)

The **disconsolate** sailor. J. Hook. Words by G. S. Carey. ME

Disdain returned. See Unfading beauty (Lawes)

"**Dismal** care." See "Esser mesto" (Flotow)

Dispetto (Spite) Italian song. e.i. BF 2

Disselhoff, August
Lieb heimatland, ade (Volksweise)

A **dissonance.** A. Borodine (music and words) e. NM 1—SC
Dissonance (The false note) e.f. NR 4

The **distant** drum. FSS 4

The **distant** shore. A. Sullivan. Words by W. S. Gilbert. FSS 5

Distel, C.
Bonne nuit (Massenet)

"**Disturb** not his slumbers." See Grave of Washington (Crosby)

"**Ditemi,** buona gente, vedeste Dinorah" ("Tell me, ye friendly neighbors, have ye seen Dinorah") Meyerbeer. e.i. OPS 2

"**Dites,** la jeune belle" (L'île inconnue.— The undiscovered country) Berlioz. Words by T. Gautier. e.f. MSS 2

"**Dites,** la jeune belle" ("Tell me, beautiful maiden."—Barcarolle) C. Gounod ₁Words by T. Gautier₁ e.f. FSS 6

Dittersdorf, Carl Ditters von
Wenn's immer so wär

The **diver.** E. J. Loder. Words by G. D. Thompson. BAS 1—BE 6—HSE 3

Dives and Lazarus. Traditional air. BSC—WCC

Divination by water (La divination par l'eau) M. Moussorgsky. e.f. SC

La **divination** par l'eau. See Divination by water (Musorgskiï)

The **divine** Pilot. See "Jesus, Saviour, pilot me" (Redhead)

"**Divinest** fair." H. Carey. DM 2

"**Divinités** du Styx" ("Ye awful Stygian powers") C. W. Gluck. e.f. KS 1
"Divinités du Styx" ("Ye gods of night profound") e.f. OPS 2
"Divinités du Styx" ("Ye powers that dwell below") e.f. CS 1—SS 1

Dix, William Chatterton
"As those who seek that break of day" (Smith)
"As with gladness men of old" (music by Davies; Kocher; Monk; Russell)
"Beauteous are the flowers of earth" (Stainer)
"Christ, we sing Thy saving passion" (Lissant)
"Christians, carol sweetly" (music by Irons; Spinney)
"Joy fills our inmost heart to-day" (music by Gadsby; Smith; also unknown composer)
"Like silver lamps" (music by Barnby; Steggall)
"O Babe! in manger lying" (Barnby)
"Put on thy beautiful robes" (Lissant)
"Rejoice! to-day earth tells abroad" (Smith)
"Through the long hidden years'" (Lissant)
"What Child is this" (Old English air; also music by Field)

Dixie ("I wish I was") D. D. Emmett (music and words) BD—BO— BSE— BSS—CST—GO— HSD— MS—TFC 1

Dixie land. DSH—FMB—JSE—NMS —OH— WA—WBT— WSC— WSW

Dixie's land. EF—HSC—JS—MP— NMH—NMP

Dixie ("Southrons, hear your country call you") D. D. Emmett. Words by A. Pike. JO

"Dja de wi dje ha." See Squaw dance

"Djupt i hafvet på demantehällen." See Neckens polska

"Dnyéper, ho! Dnyéper, hark." See On the river Dnyéper (Musorgskïï)

"Do do l'enfant dor" (French cradle-song) e.f. FSS 4

"Do I see rightly." See Infelice! e tu credevi (Verdi)

Do let me go. Capstan chantey. SE

"Do my Johnny Bowker." See Johnny Boker

Do not go, Gregory ("Oï ne khody Grytsïï") Ukrainian song. e.r. BF 1

"Do not go, my son, to dances." See Do not go, Gregory

"Do not leave me beloved." See Arabian melody (Borodin)

"Do not mingle one human feeling." See "Ah! non giunge" (Bellini)

"Do not rustle, mother forest." See The robber's fate

"Do not smoke the cigarette." See Beautiful nose

"Do not, sweetest, ah, do not fly me." See "Tu lo sai" (Scarlatti)

"Do not think that the dead are dead." See Les morts (Chausson)

"Do, Rada, marry me." See Rada

"Do, re, mi, fa, I'm quite sick of this sol fa-ing." Round. FSS 6

"Do re mi fa sol." Spanish round. s. LCP

"Do they miss me at home." S. M. Grannis. Words by C. A. Mason. FSS 3 —HSC—JO— NMH— NMS— WBT— WSW

"Do they think of me at home." C. W. Glover. Words by J. E. Carpenter. FSS 2—HSC—HSD—JS—NMH— WA —WBT—WSW

"Do you happen to know of a maiden." Air: The crystal ground. Words by L. S. Jast. MMW

"Do you hear the children crying." See The children's Easter offering (Herron)

"Do you know how many little stars." See God knows all

"Do you recall that night in June." See The Danube river (Aïdé)

"Do you recall the day." See Roses d'hiver (Fontenailles)

Do you remember. See "Te souviens-tu de ta promesse" (Godard)

"Do you see the good old sister." See Go chain the lion down

"Do you still, O still remember." See Remembrance

"Do you still think of chestnut trees in flow'r." See Chanson d'amour (Hollmann)

"Do you think of the days" (Answers) J. Blumenthal. Words by D. Greenwell. FSS 6

"Do you think of the days." H. Smart. Words by D. Greenwell. FSS 8

"Do you think that I am now all forlorn." See "Tänker du att jag förlorader är"

Doane, George Washington
"Fling out the banner: let it float" (Calkin)
"Softly now the light of day" (music by Donizetti; Gottschalk; Kücken; Weber)
"Thou art the way: to Thee alone" (Franc)

Doane, William Croswell
"Ancient of days" (Jeffery)
Sleeper awake (Jeffery)

Döbelin, Karl
Freiheit und gleichheit. See "Im kreise froher, kluger zecher"
"Im kreise froher, kluger zecher"

"Dobre, from a cliff of marble." See The gray dove

Dobrynia bids his mother farewell (Pro Dobrynïï) Russian folk song. e. SSR 1

The **doctor.** E. Newton. Words by T. Hood. SSS

Doctor Eisenbart. See Doktor Eisenbart

Doctor Irongray. See Doktor Eisenbart

Doddridge, Philip
"Awake, my soul, stretch every nerve" (Händel)
"Hark! the glad sound" (music by Hermann; also unknown composer)
"How gentle God's commands" (music by Barnby; Nägeli)
"Oh, happy day, that fixed my choice" (Rimbault)
"Ye golden lamps of heaven" (Composer unknown)

Dodge, Mrs Mary Elizabeth (Mapes)
Blossom time (Irish folk air)
"Can a little child, like me" (Bassford)

Dodge, Ossian Euclid
Ossian's serenade

Dodo ("A la puerta del cielo") Pyrenean song. e.s. SSP

"Dodo, baby, do." Old French lullaby. e. WSC

"Dodo, dodo, dodo, dodo, bas, plus bas que l'humble fleur des champs." See Cradle-song of the poor (Musorgskïï)

"Dodo, dodo, mon bel et beau gas." See Peasant cradle-song (Musorgskïï)

"Does haughty Gaul invasion threat." Air: Push about the jorum. Words by R. Burns. BSR

The dog and cat. WSC

Dogelberg, J.
Skördemannen

Doktor Eisenbart ("Ich bin der Doktor Eisenbart") Volkslied. g. ED 1
Doctor Eisenbart (Doctor Irongray) e.g. SSG

Dolby, Mme Charlotte Helen Sainton-. See Sainton-Dolby, Mme Charlotte Helen

"Dolce amor, bendato dio" ("God of love, fair blindfold Cupid") F. Caletti-Bruni. e.i. FEI 1

"Il dolce suono" ("I hear the breathing."
—Mad scene) G. Donizetti. e.i. KS 1
Mad scene. e.i. OPS 1

Dolcy Jones. S. C. Foster (music and words) NMP—WBT

Dole, Nathan Haskell
Butterflies (French folk air)
The holiday (Old French air)
My pony (Hering)
Santa Claus (Old German air)
The tall clock (German folk air)
Winter (Bohemian folk air)

"A dollar a day is a sailor's pay." See Leave her Johnny

"A dollar and a half won't pay my way." See Lowlands away

A dollar or two. FSS 3

Dollard, James Bernard
When the west wind blows (Irish air)

The doll's cradle-song (S' kookloi) M. P. Moussorgsky. e. SMR 1

Dolly and her mamma. WSC

Dolly Day. S. C. Foster (music and words) NMP—WBT

"Dolly, you're a naughty girl." See Dolly and her mamma

Dol-orous ditty. Nonsense rhymes. FSS 8

Dolphin lullaby. W. W. Gilchrist. Words by F. Manley. TL

Dom Miguel (Cantata a Dom Miguel I) Portuguese folk song. e. GO

The Dom Pedro. Forecastle song. CR

Domani, o me felice. G. Lillo. e.i. SOA 1
To-morrow (Bolero) e.i. OPS 1

Domaredansen (The judge-dance) Swedish folk song. e.sw. HSOS

Dominus regit me. See "The King of love my Shepherd is" (Dykes)

Don Juan's serenade. P. Tschaikowsky Words by A. Tolstoi. e. BAS 1
Don Juan's serenade (Sérénade de Don Juan.—Ständchen des Don Juan) e.f.g. AB 4
Don Juan's serenade (Ständchen des Don Juan) e.g. FO 2

"Doña Ana no está aquí." Old song. s. LCP

Dona Lombarda. Folk song: Piedmontese version. e.i. MSI
Donna Lombarda. Istrian version. e.i. MSI

Donald ("When first you courted me") Scottish song. PS 2

"Donald Caird's come again." 18th century Scottish air. Words by W. Scott. PS 2

Donaldson, G. D.
"Come, ye merry girls and boys" (Croatian air)
Másha (Slavonian air)
"Shadows on the Neva" (Russian air)
"Where are the birds of May" (Croatian air)
"Will he come who loves me dear" (Russian air)

"Donde va, mi cojita." See La cojita

"Done foun' my los' sheep." Negro spiritual. JB

"Done wid driber's dribin'." Negro folk song. KA

Donizetti, Gaetano
A tanto amor (from La favorita)
Ah! non avea più lagrime (from Maria di Rudenz)
Ah! parea che per incanto (from Anna Bolena)
Brindisi. See "Il segreto per esser felici"
"Calmly on sombre wings." See "Regnava nel silenzio"
Child of the regiment
"Ciascun lo dice" (from La figlia del reggimento)
"Com' è bello" (from Lucrezia Borgia)
"Com' è gentil" (from Don Pasquale)
"Convien partir" (from La figlia del reggimento)
"Cruda, funesta smania" (from Lucia di Lammermoor)
Dearest Fernando. See O mio Fernando
"Deh! non voler costringere" (from Anna Bolena)
"Il dolce suono" (from Lucia di Lammermoor)
"Down her soft cheek a pearly tear." See "Una furtiva lagrima"
"Ensanguined and lurid" (from Lucia di Lammermoor. Tr of O sole più ratto)
Farewell, those happy hours
"Fia dunque vero" (from La favorita)
"Una furtiva lagrima" (from L'elisir d'amore)
"The future still shines brightly." See O luce di quest' anima
Gentle breezes sighing
"Hail to the happy bridal day" (from Lucia di Lammermoor. Tr of Per te d'immenso giubilo)
Hoe out your row
"Hope brightly gleams." See "Hail to the happy bridal day"
"I hear the breathing." See "Il dolce suono"
"It is better to laugh than be sighing." See "Il segreto per esser felici"
Mad scene. See "Il dolce suono"
"Make me no gaudy chaplet" (from Lucrezia Borgia)

Donizetti, Gaetano—*Continued*

My soul's delight and treasure. See O luce di quest' anima

"Oh, Italia, Italia, beloved" (from Lucrezia Borgia)

O Lisbona, alfin ti miro (from Don Sebastiano)

O luce di quest' anima (from Linda di Chamounix)

O mio Fernando (from La favorita)

O my Fernando. See O mio Fernando

"Oh! that I never more might see" (from Anna Bolena)

"Oh, the secret of bliss." See "Il segreto per esser felici"

"Par che mi dica ancora" (from Il castello di Kenilworth)

Peace on earth

"Per non istare in ozio" (from Maria di Rohan)

"Poor tho' my cot may be" (from Betly. Tr of In questo semplice modesto asilo)

Rataplan (from La figlia del reggimento)

"Regnava nel silenzio" (from Lucia di Lammermoor)

"Search thro' the wide world" (from La figlia del reggimento)

"Il segreto per esser felici" (from Lucrezia Borgia)

Serenade of Don Pasquale. See "Com' è gentil"

Sextet (from Lucia di Lammermoor. Tr of Chi mi frena in tal momento)

"Si voli il primo" (from Lucrezia Borgia)

"Softly now the light of day"

"The sound of harps." See "Il suon dell' arpa angeliche"

"Spirto gentil" (from La favorita)

"Il suon dell' arpa angeliche" (from I martiri)

"Sweet village bells"

Terra adorata de' padri miei (from Don Sebastiano)

"Thou hast spread thy wings to heaven" (from Lucia di Lammermoor. Tr of Tu che a Dio spiegasti l'ali)

"Ti riveggo, Fanny" (from Il castello di Kenilworth)

The tribute of the birds (same air as Sextet)

"Vieni! la mia vendetta" (from Lucrezia Borgia)

"When stealing down her pallid cheek." See "Una furtiva lagrima"

"When the summer rain is over" (from L'elisir d'amore)

"Why, since thy heart in sadness weeps." See "Deh! non voler costringere"

The world is full of beauty

Donna ("Ako se zhenish") Bulgarian folk dance. b.e.   BF 1

Donna Clara. S. Gastaldon. Words by L. Bevacqua Lombardo. e.i.   SM 3

"La **donna** è mobile" ("Woman's unfeeling heart') Verdi. e.i.   OPS 3

Donna è mobile ("Woman is fickle") e.   WA—WL—WSW

"Woman is fickle." e.   WBT

Donna Lombarda. See Dona Lombarda

Donne, John

Loth to depart (17th century air)

The reproach (music by Leveridge; Young)

Donnell, William Ballou

Columbia forever (Composer unknown)

The land of Yippi Ki-yi (Lecocq)

"Les **donneurs** de sérénades." See Mandoline (Debussy)

"**Donnez, donnez**." G. Meyerbeer. e.f. SOA 2

Don't be sorrowful, darling. J. P. Webster. Words by A. Cary. LBR

"**Don't** be weary, traveller." Negro spiritual. HR

Don't bet your money on de Shanghai. S. C. Foster (music and words) NMP

Don't call de roll ("Jacob's ladder slim an' tall") Negro spiritual. HR

"**Don't** call the roll." Negro spiritual. DF

Don't fight your pack. Air: Son of a gambolier. Words by D. Stevens. BSS

"**Don't** forget dar's a weddin' to-night." H. J. Ballou. Words by J. W. Wheeler. WC

Don't I though. Oberlin college song. C. A. Brand. CHS

"**Don't** kill the birds." E. L. White. FSS 8—WBT

"**Don't** leave me, Lord." Negro spiritual. HR

Don't leave your mother, Tom. E. J. Symons. Words by C. Osborne. FSS 5

Don't let nobody turn yer roun'. Negro song. BOM

"**Don't** tickle me I pray." See Laughing glee (Martini)

"**Don't** worry." D. Stevens (music and words) BSS

"**Don't** ye view dat ship a come a sailin'." Negro spiritual. HR

"**Don't** you hear those Christians a-praying." See Stars in the elements

"**Don't** you 'member, a liddle while ago." See Arguing the bargain

"**Don't** you remember a poor peasant's daughter." See Down in a valley

"**Don't** you remember last Friday night." See The lover's lament (Alleghany, N.C. version; Carmen, N.C. version)

"**Don't** you see de black clouds." See Babylon is fallen (Work)

"**Donzella** nata in sen." See "A lonely Arab maid" (Weber)

"**Donzelle**, fuggite" ("Oh, hasten, ye maidens") F. Caletti-Bruni. e.i.   FEI 1

Doomka parássi. See Parásha's revery and dance (Musorgskii)

Doomka párobka. See Revery of the young peasant (Musorgskii)

"Doos yá bellee." See Love-song

"Doos yá lellee." See Love-song

Der **doppelgänger (M**y phantom double) F. Schubert. Words by H. Heine. e.g. FF—FO 1

Der doppelgänger (The wraith) e.g. BAS 1

Doran, A. W.
Lake Forest university song (Composer unknown)

Der **dorfschulmeister** ("A B C D E F G") Volksweise nach L. von Call. g. ED 3

"A, B, C, D, F, F, G." e. FSS 5

The alphabet. e. JSE

"**Dormi,** Amore" ("Cupid, sleep") M. da Gagliano. e.i. FEI 1

Dormi, bella, dormi tu ("Art thou sleeping, fair one") G. B. Bassani. e.i. PA 2

"**Dormi,** dormi, bel bambino." Ricci. e.i. PP

"**Dormi,** dormi, O bel bambin." See Canzone di Natale

Dormirò sol nel manto mio regal. G. Verdi. e.i. SOA 5

"Ella giammai m'amò" ("Her love was never mine") e.i. OPS 4

Dorn, Alexander Julius Paul
Schneeglöckchen
Snowdrops. See Schneeglöckchen

"**Dors** entre mes bras." See Dors, mon enfant (Wagner)

"**Dors,** mignon, près de ta mère." See Cradle-song (Grechaninov)

Dors, mon enfant (Slumber song) Wagner. e.f. MSS 1

Dorset, Charles Sackville, 6th earl of
"To all you ladies now at land" (Old English air)

"**Dort** blühet im garten manch apfelbaum." See Der apfelgarten (Lindblad)

"**Dort** hoch auf der Alpe." See Der alpenhirt

Dosker, Henry E.
Collegium (Nykerk)

"**Dost** know the land where orange blossoms fair." See "Kennst du das land" (Wolf)

"**Dost** know the pow'r of noble wine." See The three glasses (Fischer)

"**Dost** not hear the martial hum." See The soldier's return

"**Dost** remember, dear, when last autumn home we went." See Liden Karen (Heise)

"**Dost** remember, oh maiden of Bayamo." See La Bayamesa

"**Dost** thou know that fair land." See "Connais-tu le pays" (Thomas)

"**Dost** thou love me, sister Ruth." See Sister Ruth (Haydn)

"**Dost** thou no longer love me." See Siciliana

Dost thou not know. See Le sais-tu bien (Pierné)

"**Dost** thou recall thy wistful promise." See "Te souviens-tu de ta promesse" (Godard)

Doten, Elizabeth
Ye sons of the nation (Barnard)

"**D'où** viens-tu, bergère" ("Shepherdess, whence com'st thou") Canadian Noël. e.f. TF

"**D'où** viens-tu, bergère" ("Shepherdess, whence come you") e.f. BF 2

Douǎ fete spalǎ lânǎ (Two maidens washing wool) Rumanian song. e.ru. BF 2

Doubt. Ojibway Indian death song. e. BA

"**Douce** dame jolie" ("Sweet-heart, gentle and pretty") Guillaume de Machault. e.f. NG—PG 3

Doudney, Sarah
When the boats come home (Moore)

Douglas, Archibald
Merry bells of long ago (Reichardt)

Douglas, Ellen M.
Christmas come again (Pinsuti)
The joy of the morrow (Composer unknown)
Lo! now he is come (Composer unknown)
Sweet bells are chiming (Genée)
"Sweet village bells" (Donizetti)
The voices in the sky (Composer unknown)
"We greet thee, old friend" (Scotch air)

Douglas, J. P.
"Simple carollers are we" (Bougher)

Douglas, Mary
Thy story bides for aye (Phelps)

Douglas, William
Annie Laurie (Scott)

Douglas, tender and true. Lady John Scott. Words by D. M. Muloch. FSS 2—HSD—NMH—NML—PO —WBT

Douglas. WL

Doun the burn, Davie. See "When trees did bud"

Douty, Nicholas
The bell-man
"Better music ne'er was known"

"**Doux** ange de ma vie." See "The heart bow'd down" (Balfe)

"Un **doux** lien" ("Tender ties") A. Delbrück. Words by V. Wilder. e.f. MSF 1

A tender tie. e. WBW

Dovaston, J. M. E.
I think on thee (Welsh air)
"Loth to depart, love" (Welsh air)
The rising of the lark (Welsh air)

Dovaston, John Freeman Milward
"Why should I sigh" (Welsh air)

The **dove.** See La paloma (Yradier)

"**Dov'è,** dov'è l'amato bene." See Del mio core (Haydn)

"The **dove** has two white feet." Old Serbian song. e. KSE

Dove sei (Where art thou) Handel. e.i. CS 2

"**Dove** si stà jersira." See L'avvelenato

"A **dove** sits on a lily bough." See The dove's song

"Dove sono." Mozart. e.i. PP

Dove veto, cossa feto. See Villotta

The dove's song ("A dove sits on a lily bough") Swedish folk song. e. BMC

Dowanna, George
Ayo po

Dowch i'r ffrwydr (Come to battle.—"Hark, the martial trumpet sounding") Welsh song. e. MMW

Dowland, John
"Awake, sweet love"
"Away with these self-loving lads"
"Come again, sweet love"
The frog galliard. See "Now, O now, I needs must part"
"Now cease my wand'ring eyes"
"Now, O now I needs must part"
"Weep you no more, sad fountains"

Dowling, M. M. G.
"I'll speak of thee" (Hawes)

Down among the banks of roses. Folk song. BE 5

"Down among the daisies white." See The sparrow's nest

Down among the dead men ("Here's a health to the king") 17th century English drinking song. Words by J. Dyer; wrongly attributed to R. Dyer. BAS 1—BE 1—BMC—BOH—BOS—BS 1—CO 2—CU—HSE 1—JE—MM—PR 2—SSS—WBT
"Here's a health to the queen." DM 1

"Down by a river side." Folk song. BSW

"Down by my mother's dwelling." See Le prisonnier de Hollande (Canadian version)

"Down by some crystal spring." See The crystal spring

Down by the river ("Oh, hallelujah to the Lamb") Negro spiritual. JP

Down by the river ("When Christ the Lord was here below") Negro spiritual. HR

Down by the riverside. Words by A. Nash. CHS

"Down by the sally gardens." Air: Far beyond yon mountain. Words by W. B. Yeats. MMI

"Down by the sally gardens." Air: The maids of Mourne shore. Words by W. B. Yeats. FSI

"Down by the side of Bedlam city." See Bedlam city

"Down by the stream where I first met Rebecca." See One, two, three, four (Alaw)

Down from the heav'ns He long ago descended. See "Manger all-glorious"

"Down from the hillsides." See An autumn lullaby (Fearis)

"Down her soft cheek a pearly tear." See "Una furtiva lagrima" (Donizetti)

Down in a coal mine. J. B. Geoghegan. FSS 6

"Down in a leafy dell." Air: Gathering peascods. JE

"Down in a shady valley." See "In einem kühlen grunde" (Glück)

Down in a valley. 18th century song. ME

Down in de cornfield. See Massa's in the cold, cold ground (Foster)

"Down in Mobile." Southern song. BSS —CHS—TFC 2

"Down in the cane-brake." See Nancy Till

"Down in the lowland." See Unterländers heimweh

"Down in the mead." See Young Robin

"Down in the meadow the sun is shining." See When the sun shines

"Down in the Neckar vale." See Unterländers heimweh

"Down in the north country." See The farmer's daughter of merry Wakefield

Down in the sunless retreats. See "As down in the sunless retreats" (Shaw)

"Down in the vale below how mild and fair." Unterländers heimweh

Down in the valley. Negro spiritual. NMP
Come, let us all go down. JP

"Down in the valley, come meet me." See The fortune teller

"Down on de Mississippi floating." See Nelly was a lady (Foster)

Down on mother Volga. See Mother Volga

Down on Smiley's farm. H. H. Lemmel (music and words) BSS

Down the burn, Davie. See "When trees did bud" (Maigh)

"Down the flow'ry meadow way." See Love and summer (West)

Down the hill. Harrow song. LA

"Down the mountain side." See The waterfall

"Down the river swiftly sailing." See The golden boat

"Down the stream of mother Volga, Volga." See Mother Volga

"Down the stream so cheerily." See The miller's daughter

"Down the street the wind is roaring." See The wind

Down the Volga. See Mother Volga

"Down the west has gone the sun." See A love song

"Down through the great ages vast." See Choral (Omaha Indian song)

"Down where the waving willows." See Annie Lisle (Thompson)

"Down yonder green valley." See Llwyn on

Downing, Ellen Mary
"The earth is fair around us" (Irish air)

Downs (Mason) See "God of our fathers, by Whose hand"; "How sweet the name of Jesus sounds"

The downward road is crowded. Negro spiritual. HR

"Downy jailbirds of a feather." See Birds of a feather (Jakobowski)

Doxology. See Old hundred (Franc)

Drachmann, Holger
  "Ak, hvem der havde en hue" (Heise)
  "Alle klokker bringer fjaernt" (Kjerulf)
  "Det stiger" (Heise)
  Rav (Sinding)
  "Saa du knøsen, som strøg forbi" (Grieg)
  Sildig (Backer-Gröndahl)
  "Vaer hilset, i damer" (Grieg)
Drahaareen-o mochree ("I am a young fellow."—Little brother of my heart) Air: Jemmy mo veela sthore. e. JOI
Draherin o machree ("I grieve when I think on the dear happy days") Air: Jemmy mo veela sthore. Words by M. Hogan (Bard of Thomond) MMI
Drake, John
  Loud strike the strings (Beethoven) Authorship uncertain
  An odd old man (Sullivan)
  Santa Claus is come to town (Composer unknown)
  The sleigh ride (Composer unknown)
  Welcome to Christmas (Composer unknown)
Drake, Joseph Rodman
  The American flag (Tufts)
Drake, Sam
  Volga boat song (Russian air)
Draoigheanán donn (The drynaun dhun) Irish folk song. · e. JOI
Drap o' capie, O. Scottish song. PS 2
"**Draw** near, all ye people." Mendelssohn. e. OS 4—SAS 4
"**Draw** the sword, Scotland." Scottish air. Words by J. R. Planché. FSS 4—LA —PS 2—TS
"**Draw** Thou my soul, O Christ" (St Edmund) A. S. Sullivan. Words by L. Larcom. TL
The **Dreadnaught**. Forecastle song. CR
The **dream** ("I dream'd I lay where flow'rs were springing") Scottish air. Words by Burns. MMS
  "I dreamed I lay where flowers were springing." BSB—BSR—PS 2
The **dream** ("Instant charmant") See Le rêve (Massenet)
A **dream** ("Mir träumte einst") See Ein traum (Grieg)
The **dream** ("'Twas in a meadow by the way."—Der traum) A. Rubinstein. Words by Schukowsky. e.g. KF 2—TS
  The **dream** ("'Twas in a meadow by the way") e. WBW
  The **dream** ("Upon a meadow slope I lay."—Der traum) e.g. FO 1
Dream, dear one. Old French song. e. CST
Dream faces. W. M. Hutchinson. FSS 5 —HSD—WL
"The **dream** is past." S. Glover. FSS 7
The **dream** of home. See Il bacio (Arditi)
A **dream** of paradise. H. Gray. Words by C. Lyttleton. HSS 1—HSS 2— SM 1—WA—WS

A **dream** of summer. German air. Words by J. G. Whittier LBR
"The **dream** of those days." Air: I love you above all. Words by T. Moore. MI
Dream on, dream on. German song. e. FSS 3
"**Dream** on, in life's bright rosy day." See Dream on, dream on
"**Dream** on my darling." See Serenae (Smart)
"**Dream** on, young hearts." Sporle. FSS 5
Dream song. E. Jakobowski. WBT
Dreaming ("The day when first I met thee") G. Smith (music and words) HST
Dreaming ("Once again I saw") M. Wellings. Words by E. Oxenford. HSC— WBW
Dreaming ("Sag', welch wunderbare träume") See Träume (Wagner)
Dreaming golden dreams. S. Scuderi. Words by R. Barnett. FSS 7
Dreaming of home and mother. J. P. Ordway (music and words) HSC— NMH—WBT
"**Dreaming** of Lucette fair." See Vieille chanson (Bizet)
Dreaming of you. Hawaiian folk song. e. WL
Dreamings. Bohemian song. e. KSE —WL
Dreamland. C. Barnard. FSS 5
Dreams ("Oh! I have had dreams") F. H. Hodges. FSS 6
Dreams ("Sag', welch wunderbare träume") See Träume (Wagner)
Dreams ("When twilight comes") A. Strelezki. Words by Baroness Porteous. FMB—MSF 1
"**Drearily** drift the shadows." See Drifting (Barnard)
The **dreary** black hills. Cowboy song. LC
"The **dreary** day is wearing to its close." See The wish (Cui)
The **dreary**, dreary life. Cowboy song. LC
Drechsler, Josef
  "Brother so fine." See "Brüderlein fein"
  "Brüderlein fein" (from Der bauer als millionär)
  "Eh! my dear lad." See "Brüderlein fein"
  Mariandel
Die **drei** grossen Christlichen feste ("O du fröhliche") Sicilian air: O sanctissima. Words by J. Falk. g. ED 1
  "O du fröhliche." g. MCS
  O du fröhliche ("O thou joyful day") e. MCS
  O santissima (O thou joyful day) e. MF
  "O thou joyful day." e. WBT—WS —WSC

"**Drei** laub auf einer linden" (Three leaves on the linden tree) German song. e.g. BF 2

"**Drei** lilien, drei lilien." Volkslied. g. ED 1

Die **drei** reiche der natur ("Ich trink, und trinkend fällt bei mir") Volksweise. Words by G. E. Lessing. g. ED 2

Drei reiter am tor ("Es ritten drei reiter zum tore") Volkslied. g. ED 1
Drei reiter am thore (Parting) e. GO
Drei reiter am thore (Three horsemen) e.g. SSG
Parting. e. TL
"Three horsemen." e. BSE

Drei röselein ("Jetzt geh i ans brünnele") Schwäbisches volkslied. g. ED 1
Drei röslein (Three roses) e.g. SSG

Drei schneider ("Three tailors") Folk air. Words by C. Herlosssohn. e.g. SSG

Die **drei** sterne ("Es blinken drei freundliche sterne") F. H. Himmel. Words by T. Körner. g. ED 1

Die **drei** zigeuner ("Gypsies three") F. Liszt. Words by Lenau. e.g. PG 2

Das **dreigespann.** See Three-in-hand

Drennan, William
Rory O'More (Irish air)

"**Dress** a bad boy." Round. FSS 2

Dresser, Paul
The blue and the gray

Dricol, Anna S.
"Under the stars one holy night" (Brown)

De **drie** koningen. Flemish Epiphany carol. fl. HC

"**Drift**, my bark." F. Kücken. [Tr of Treibe schifflein] e. FSS 6

Drifting ("Dearily drift the shadows") C. Barnard (Claribel) WBT

"**Drifting** and dreaming the golden morning thro'." See Vo' altre putele che se' de maridar

Drill song (Shōtai) I. Shiyi. e.j. BSP

Drimborn, E. G.
Kaiser Wenzel (Reichardt)

"**Drink** of this cup." Air: Paddy O'Rafferty. Words by T. Moore. MI

Drink old England dry. Folk song from Worcestershire. SF 4
Variant: He swore he'd drink old England dry

Drink, puppy, drink. Hunting song. G. J. Whyte-Melville (music and words) BOS—FMB—SSS

"**Drink** round, brave boys." See He swore he'd drink old England dry

"**Drink** to her." Air: Heigh-ho! my Jacky. Words by T. Moore. MI

"**Drink** to me only with thine eyes." Old setting. Words by B. Jonson. DM 2

"**Drink** to me only with thine eyes." Old English air, attributed to R. Mellish; wrongly attributed to Mozart. Words by B. Jonson. BD—BE 5 —BOH—BOS— BSE— CHS—CU —DM 1—DSH—EF—ES— HSC— HSD—HSE 1—JE—JO—KF 3— KF 4—MM— MP— MPC— MS— NMH—NML—OH—PR 2—SM 4 —SSS—TFC 1—WA—WBT—WC —WL—WSW
Only with thine eyes. FSS 7

Drinking ("Im tiefen keller") See Der Rheinweinzecher (Fischer)

Drinking song ("Ma bouteille") See "Ma bouteille m'est fidèle"

Drinking song ("My comrades, when I'm no more drinking") [Tr of Des trinkers testament] e. CHS—MPC— WBT

Drinking song ("See the wine is gaily flowing") P. Mascagni. WBT

Drinkwater, T. W.
A song of water

Drive the cold winter away. 17th century air. CO 2
"All hail to the days." HC
To drive the cold winter away. BE 7

Drive the cold winter away. Air: When Phoebus addrest. CO 2

Driving away at the smoothing iron. Folk song. FSF—SO

"**Droop** all the flowers in my garden." See My rose

"**Droop** not, young lover." Händel. Words by W. Hills. BAS 1

Drouet, Louis François Philippe
"Partant pour la Syrie" (attributed; attributed also to Hortense Eugénie de Beauharnais)

The **drover's** song. See La chanson du bouvier

The **drowned** lover. Folk song: Hampshire version. SEF 1—SO
—Devon version. BSW

The **drowned** sailor ("As a lady was walking") Folk song from Oxfordshire. SF 4

"**Drücke** mich an deine brust" (Meeting) A. Farwell. Words by J. Ambrosius. e.g. HST

The **drum-major** of Schneider's band. A. J. Murphy (music and words) WC

The **drum-major's** song. See Air du tambour major (Thomas)

The **drummer** and his wife. Folk song from North Carolina. CSE

"The **drummer** told his wife he could do more in one day." See The drummer and his wife

Drummond, Algernon
All pull together (same air as Eton boating song)
Boating song. See Eton boating song
Eton boating song
"Jolly boating weather, jolly sweet harvest breeze" (same air as Eton boating song)

Drummond, William
"Phoebus, arise" (Sternberg)
The drunken maidens. Folk song. BSW
Drunken sailor ("What shall we do")
Capstan chantey. SE
The **drunken** sailor ("What shall we do")
Halliard chantey. CR
"**Drunten** im unterland." See Unterländers heimweh
Drusina, Fernando Luna y. See Luna y
Drusina, Fernando
"Dry the tear for holy Eva." See Little
Eva (Emilio)
"Dry them not, dry them not.' See Wonne
der wehmuth (Beethoven)
"Dry ye not, dry ye not." See Wonne
der wehmuth (Beethoven)
"Dry ye your tears." See The crucifix
(Faure)
Dryden, John
"Celamina, of my heart" (Pepusch)
"Come, if you dare" (Purcell)
"Fairest isle" (Purcell)
Harvest home (Purcell)
"I attempt from love's sickness to fly"
(Purcell)
"Two daughters of this aged stream"
(Purcell)
"What shall I do to show how much I
love her" (Purcell) Authorship uncertain
"Du aabner halvt kun øiet." See Blicken
(Alfvén)
"Du alte mutter bist so arm." See Gamle
mor (Grieg)
"Du är min ro" ("Thou art my rest") K.
Collan. e.sw. SSN
"Du bach mit den silbernen wellen." See
Der böse bach
"Du bist das keusche mondenlicht." See
Du bist mein all' (Bradsky)
"Du bist die herrlichste von allen" ("Thou
art the noblest of them all") F. Ries.
Words by F. Dahn. e.g. CB
"Du bist die ruh" ("My peace thou art")
F. Schubert. Words by F. Rückert. CMF 2—FF—FO 1
"Du bist die ruh" ("My sweet repose")
e.g. KF 1—KF 2—KF 3—PG 1—
PG 2
"Du bist die ruh" (Peace) e.g. MSS 1
Peace. e. BSE
Du bist mein all' (Thou art mine all) T.
Bradsky. e.g. MSF 1
"Du bist Orplid, mein land." See Gesang
Weyla's (Wolf)
"Du bist wie eine blume" ("Thou art to
me a flower") E. Degele. Words by
Heine. e.g. SOS 2
"Du bist wie eine blume" ("Dear love,
thou'rt like a blossom") Liszt.
Words by Heine. e.g. CS 2—
MSS 2
"Du bist wie eine blume" ("A flower
thou resemblest") e. FTS
"Du bist wie eine blume" ("Thou'rt like
unto a flower") e.g. KF 3—
KF 4
"Thou'rt like a gentle flow'ret." e.
KSE

"Du bist wie eine blume" ("O fair, and
sweet, and holy") Rubinstein.
Words by Heine. e.g. MSS 1—
SS 1
"Du bist wie eine blume" ("Thou'rt
like unto a flower") e.g. KF 1
—KF 2—KF 3—MS
"Du bist wie eine blume" ("Thou'rt
lovely as a flower") e.g. FO 1
"Thou'rt like unto a flower." e.g.
FSS 4. e. only LA—WBT—WL
"Du bist wie eine blume ("Thou'rt like a
lovely flower") Schumann. Words
by Heine. e.g. MSS 1
"Du bist wie eine blume" ("Thou'rt
lovely as a flower") e.g. CMF 2
"Du bist wie eine blume." For English
translation with a different air see "Oh
fair, oh sweet" (Cantor)
"Du, du liegst mir im herzen." Volkslied.
g. ED 1
Am I not fondly thine own. e. CHS
—FSS 7—NMH—NML—WBT
"Du, du, liegst mir im herzen" (Am I
not fondly thine own) e.g. WL
—WSW
"Du, du liegst mir im herzen" ("Thou,
thou fillest my heart, dear") e.g.
SSG
"Thou, thou, fillest my heart, dear."
e. BSE
"Du er min mor, jeg elsker dig." See Til
Norge (Grieg)
"Du fragst mich täglich" (The daily question) E. Meyer-Helmund. e.g. FMB
"Du frommes bild, vor dem." See Der
moench (Meyerbeer)
"Du gamla, du fria, du fjällhoga nord"
(Song of the north) Swedish song.
Words by R. Dybeck. e.sw.
HSOS
"Du gamla, du friska, du fjellhoga nord"
(Swedish national air) e.sw. WCP
"Du gamla, du friska, du fjellhöga nord"
("Thou ancient, thou wholesome,
thou mountainous north") e.
BSE
Nordland ("Du nord, du mein hohes")
g. ED 3
"Du gamle mor! du sliter arm." See
Gamle mor (Grieg)
"Du gibst mir also nicht dein herz." See
Der herzenswechsel (Himmel); Der
herzenswechsel (Reichardt)
"Du har sörjit nu igen" ("Dear one, thou
hast wept once more") Swedish folk
song. e.sw. HSOS
"Du holde kunst, in wie viel grauen stunden." See An die musik (Schubert)
"Du jour décline la lumière." See Evening (Tchaikovsky)
"Du lieber heilger frommer Christ." See
Gebet an den heiligen Christ (Siegert)
"Du liebes auge" ("Thou lovely dreamer")
R. Franz. Words by O. Roquette.
e.g. MS
"Du matin j'ai rencontré le train." See
Marcho dei rei

"Du mein gedanke, du mein sein und werden." See Jeg elsker dig (Grieg)
"Du meine seele, du mein herz." See Widmung (Schumann)
"Du meines herzens krönelein" ("Thou of my heart the diadem") R. Strauss. Words by F. Dahn. e.g. FO 2—GM
"Du moment qu'on aime." A. E. M. Grétry. e.f. SOA 3
"Du nord, du mein hohes." See "Du gamla, du fria, du fjällhoga nord"
"Du pauvre seul ami" (Slumber song) D. F. E. Auber. e.f. SOA 3
"Du schönes fischermädchen" ("O lovely fishermaiden") G. Meyerbeer. Words by H. Heine. e.g. KF 3 "Guide au bord ta nacelle" (The fishermaiden) e.f. SM 1
"Du schönes fischermädchen" (Das fischermädchen.—The fisher-maiden) F. Schubert. Words by H. Heine. e.g. GM
"Du schwert an meiner linken." See Schwertlied (Weber)
"Du skog! som böygjer deg imot." See Langs en å (Grieg)
"Du taudis voisin partent trois chemins." See The three roads (Koeneman)
"Du trauter stern." See "Ah, kindly star" (Glinka)
"Du underskøna dal, o, säg." See Farväl (Gustaf)
"Du vårens milde, skjønne barn." See Med en primulaveris (Grieg)
"Du wald, der sich herüber biegt." See Langs en å (Grieg)
"Du wirst mir's ja nit übel nehma." See Zum letzten mal
Duane street (Coles)   See "From ev'ry spire on Christmas eve"; "Jesus, my all, to heaven is gone"; "A poor wayfaring man of grief"
Dubee, H. William
The gold and olive
Dubinushka ("Come, fellows, let us pull together")   See Towing-song
Dubinushka ("Many songs have I heard") See The little cudgel
Dublin bay. G. Barker. Words by Crawford. FSS 4
Dubois, Clément François Théodore
By the path.   See Par le sentier
"God my Father, God, my Father" (from Les sept paroles du Christ)
"Oui, c'est lui" (from Aben Hamet)
Par le sentier
"Yes, 'tis he."   See "Oui, c'est lui"
Du Bois, Lilian
The fair transgressor
Ducker ("See the summer sun is glowing") LA
The dude who couldn't dance. Words by A. R. Raymond. WC
Dudgeon, William
The maid that tends the goats (Scottish air)
Dudley, Chester H. C.
Long live Stuart hall (Composer unknown)

Dudley, Sir Henry Bate, bart.
A smile from the girl of my heart (Shield)
"Duerme pronto."   See El canto de la madre
"Duérmete, nene."   See Canción de cuna
Duff, John Wight
"Salve boreale lumen" (Aberdeen university song)
Dufferin, Helen Selina (Sheridan), lady
Irish emigrant's lament (Dempster)
Katey's letter (Sainton-Dolby)
"O bay of Dublin" (Limerick air; also old air)
Duffield, George
"Blessed Saviour, Thee I love" (Composer unknown)
"Stand up, stand up for Jesus" (Webb)
Duffield, H. G.
"Ring out, ring out a joyful peal" (Borrow)
Dufresny, Charles, sieur de la Rivière
"Philis plus avare que tendre"
Dugard, F. J.
"O'er the hill and o'er the vale"
"Once in Bethlehem of Judah"
Duke Marlborough.   See "Malbrough s'en va-t-en guerre"
The duke of Bedford.   Folk song. SEF 2 —SO
The duke of Berwick's march.   See "How stands the glass around"
The duke of Marlborough.   Folk song. SEF 2
Duke street (Hatton)   See Evening hymn; "From all that dwell"; God be with us; "Jesus shall reign"; "Thy kindness to our fathers shown"
The duke's hunt.   Folk song. BSW
"Dulce cum sodalibus."   See Trifolium (Flemming)
Dulce domum.   Winchester college song. Attributed to J. Reading. Words attributed to F. Turner. e.l. DM 1—JE e. only TL. l. only BE 8—BOS— HSE 2—LA—SSS
Dulce patria (National anthem of Chili) Carnicer. e.s. WCP
Causion nacional Chilena (Chilean national hymn) e.s. MP
Dulcina ("As att noone") 16th century song. CO 1
Dulcina ("From Oberon in fairyland") 16th century air. Words by B. Jonson. CO 1
"From Oberon in fairyland." HSE 2 —JE
Robin good-fellow ("From Oberon in fairyland") DM 1
Dumb, dumb, dumb. Irish folk song. JOI
The dumb shepherdess. See La bergère muette
The dumb wife. Air: Paul's steeple, or, I am the Duke of Norfolk. BE 2
The dumb wife cured. MM
Dumont, Frank
Angel Gabriel (Stewart)

"D'un grand mal j'ay l'âme dolente." See À Lucette (Pierné)
"D'un sventurato amante provo tutte le pene." See Pena tiranna (Händel)
Dunbar, Paul Laurence
An ante-bellum sermon (Negro air)
Duncan, Mary Lundie
"Jesus, tender Shepherd, hear me" (music by Barnard; Dykes)
"Duncan Gray cam here to woo." Air: Duncan Gray. Words by R. Burns. BSB—BSR—JO—MMS—PS 1
Dundee (Franc) See "O God, our help in ages past"; These see His wonders in the deep; "Thou art the way: to Thee alone"
Dunhill, T. F.
"Sweetly sang the angels"
"Dunkel, wie dunkel in wald und in feld." See Von ewiger liebe (Brahms)
Dunker, B. A.
Ein familiengemälde (Volksweise)
"Die dunkle nacht nun deckt die weite erde." See To sleep (Tchaikovsky)
Dunlop, Alison Hay
The Yang-tsi-kiang
Dunlop, John
The year that's awa (Composer unknown)
"Dunois, so young and fair, called forth to Syrian wars." See Partant pour la Syrie (Hortense Eugénie de Beauharnais)
Dunois the brave. See Partant pour la Syrie (Hortense Eugénie de Beauharnais)
Dunstable, John
"What tidings bringest thou"
Dunstan, R.
"Over hill, over dale, thro' bush, thro' brier"
A duologue between Meg and the laird." See "I'll ha'e my coat o' gude snuff-brown"
Duparc, Henri Fouque
Chanson triste
Ecstasy. See Extase
Extase
The former life. See La vie antérieure
L'invitation au voyage
Invitation to the journey. See L'invitation au voyage
Le manoir de Rosemonde
Rosamond's manor. See Le manoir de Rosemonde
A sigh. See Soupir
A song of sorrow. See Chanson triste
Soupir
La vie antérieure
Du Puy, Jean Baptiste Édouard
"Carl Johan"
"Charles John, our brave King." See "Carl Johan"
"Karl John." See "Carl Johan"
Swedish national song. See "Carl Johan"
Duran, Juan
Imanírta (Valderrama)

Durand, Henry Strong
"Bright college years" (Wilhelm)
Durant, Horace B.
Waiting for me (Hance)
Durante, Francesco
"Dance, O dance." See Danza, danza, fanciulla gentile
Danza, danza, fanciulla gentile
Lightly dance, O happy maiden. See Danza, danza, fanciulla gentile
"Vergin, tutto amor"
"Virgin, fount of love." See "Vergin, tutto amor"
"Virgin, full of grace." See "Vergin, tutto amor"
Durch dich musst' ich verlieren ('Tis thou whose spells) Wagner. e.g. OPS 4
Durch die wälder. C. M. von Weber. e.g. SOA 3
"Durch feld und wald zu schweifen." See Der musensohn (Schubert)
D'Urfey, Thomas
"All on a misty morning" (Old English air)
Brave men of Kent (Leveridge)
"Come, sweet lass" (Clark) Authorship uncertain
The country fair (Barrett)
"In January last" (17th century air)
The king's jig (Composer unknown)
"Lady, thee I love" (Old English air)
The lass of Lynn (Old English air)
The mouse-trap (Old English air)
"O Jenny, O Jenny, where hast thou been" (Old English air)
"Room, room for a rover" (Plaisable)
"Since now the world's turn'd upside down" (Old English air; also air: I am a lusty, lively lad)
"The sun had loosed" (Old English air)
"Tom Tinker's my true love" (Old air)
"We all to conqu'ring beauty bow" (Blow)
Within a mile of Edinboro' (Hook)
"Ye nymphs and sylvan gods" (16th century air; 18th century air)
Düringer, Philipp Jacob
Des mädchens klage (Volksweise)
Durwan's song (Rustic song) Persian folk song. e.p.e. BO
"Dusk fallen." C. Cui. Words from the Russian. e. NM 1
"A dusky maid with ebon hair." See The Indian maid (Hatton)
"The dusky night rides down the sky." See A-hunting we will go (Arne?)
"The dusky robes of ev'ning fell." See All hail, thou Bethlehem
Dust and ashes. Negro spiritual. JP
Dust an' ashes. HR
The dustman. J. L. Molloy. Words by F. E. Weatherly. WBT—WBW—WSC
The Dutch company. HSD—MPC—WBT—WC
Dutch dolls. M. Ostlere. Words by H. L. d'A. Jaxone. ES
Dutch national song. See "Wien Neêrlandsch bloed" (Wilms)

Dutch war song.   See Bergen op Zoom
Dutch warbler.   See Where has my little
   dog gone
The **Dutchwoman's** jigg.   See Bartholo-
   mew fair
Duthie, William
   The crusaders (Pinsuti)
Du Toit, St.
   The Transvaal flag (Composer un-
    known)
Dutton, D.
   The rosy crown (Weber)
"Duva che 't' ses, O bela vita d'or."   See
   T' ses tüta mia furtüna
Duval, Alexandre
   Joseph (Mehul.   Tr of À peine au sor-
    tir de l'enfance)
Dvořák, Anton
   "Als die alte mutter."   See "Songs my
    mother taught me"
   "As my dear old mother."   See "Songs
    my mother taught me"
   Come unto me
   "Give ear, ye people" (from Saint Lud-
    mila)
   "Good-night"
   Humoreske (with words "When de
    shadders spread aroun'"; "When
    the moon is shining")
   "I was not deceived" (from Saint Lud-
    mila)
   "Ihr alle."   See Come unto me
   "Long ago in childhood's days."   See
    "Songs my mother taught me"
   "Massa dear"
   O grant me in the dust to fall (from
    Saint Ludmila)
   "O guide me in the way" (from Saint
    Ludmila)
   "Songs my mother taught me"
   "Thy leading would I had not followed"
    (from Saint Ludmila)
   "When de shadders spread aroun'."
    See Humoreske
   "When the moon is shining."   See
    Humoreske
   "Within what gloomy depths of forest"
    (from Saint Ludmila)
"Dwell I on the lofty mount."   See "Boer
   jeg paa det hoje fjeld"
"Dwell on me, thou dark eye tender."   See
   Bitte (Franz)
Dwight, John Sullivan
   Noël (Adam)
   "O Lord! correct me" (Händel)
    See also Brooks, Charles Timothy, jt.
    auth.
Dwight, Timothy
   Columbia, the gem of the ocean (Beck-
    et)   See Becket, T. à (Composer
    and author)   Columbia, the gem
    of the ocean
   "I love Thy kingdom, Lord" (Händel)
Dybeck, Richard
   "Du gamla, du fria, du fjällhoga nord"
    (Swedish air)
   "Mandom, mod och morske män"
    (Swedish air)

"D'ye ken John Peel with his coat so gay."
   See John Peel
"D'ye ken Van Am with his snowy hair."
   See Van Am
Dyer, Sir Edward
   "My mind to me a kingdom is" (Byrd)
    Authorship uncertain
Dyer, John
   Down among the dead men (17th cen-
    tury air)
Dyer, Robert
   Down among the dead men (17th cen-
    tury air)   See Dyer, J.   Down
    among the dead men (17th century
    air)
Dyéva i' sólntze.   See The maid and the sun
   (Rimskiï-Korsakov)
The **dying** cowboy.   Cowboy song.   BF 2
   —LC
Dying Moon-Flower.   Indian song.   T.
   Lieurance.   LS
The **dying** ranger.   Cowboy song.   LC
The **dying** soldier.   See Brother Green
The **dying** volunteer.   A. E. A. Muse.
   HSD—WBT
Dykes, John Bacchus
   Alford.   See "Ten thousand times ten
    thousand"
   All the saints adore Thee.   See "Holy,
    holy, holy! Lord God Almighty"
   Aspiration.   See "Saviour, blessed
    Saviour! listen while we sing"
   "Calm on the listening ear of night"
   "Christian! dost thou see them" (Tr of
    Oy gar Blepeis tarattontas)
   Christmas song.   See "Once again, O
    blessed time"
   "Come, Holy Spirit, heavenly Dove"
   Dominus regit me.   See "The King of
    love my Shepherd is"
   "Father of love"
   "From far away"
   "God, my King, Thy might confessing"
   "Hark! hark! my soul"
   "Holy, holy, holy! Lord God Almighty"
   "I heard the voice of Jesus say"
   In terra pax
   "It came upon the midnight clear"
   "Jesus, tender Shepherd, hear me"
   "Jesus, Lover of my soul"
   "Jesus! the very thought of Thee"
   "The King of love my Shepherd is"
   "Lead, kindly light"
   "Let glory be to God on high"
   Lux benigna.   See "Lead, kindly light"
   Melita.   See "Let glory be to God on
    high"; The people's prayer
   Nicaea.   See "Holy, holy, holy! Lord
    God Almighty"
   Now all the bells are ringing
   "Now to Bethlehem haste we"
   "On the birthday of the Lord" (Tr of
    In natali Domini)
   "Once again, O blessed time"
   The people's prayer (same air as "Let
    glory be to God on high")
   Pilgrims.   See "Hark! hark! my soul"
   Prayer.   See "They who seek the
    throne of grace"

Dykes, John Bacchus—*Continued*
"Rock of ages, cleft for me"
St Oswald. See "God, my King, Thy might confessing'
"Saviour, blessed Saviour! listen while we sing"
"Sleep, holy Babe"
Song of the angels. See "It came upon the midnight clear"
"Ten thousand times ten thousand"
"They who seek the throne of grace"
Thou Bethlehem
Vox angelica. See "Hark! hark! my soul"
"While thee I seek"

E

"E a dha ah e he a ha." See Song to the spirit
E awaiaulu kealoha. See "The remembrance of our last meeting" (Hopkins)
"E c'eran tre sorelle." See O pescator dell' onda
"E dho he." See The mother's vow
"E dove t'aggiri" ("Oh, whither art roaming") M. Cesti. e.i. FEI 1
"E Ihowa, Atua." See God defend New Zealand (Woods).
"E ka wiliwili wai." See Surging waters (Hopkins)
"E kann so mangen ein vakker. sang." See Den Nordlandske bondestand
E ke aloha. See Flower of my heart (Hopkins)
E kii mai hoi e lei. See A wreath for Princess Kaiulani (Hopkins)
"E kuu belle oka po lailai." See Adieu my love (Hopkins)
E lei hoi. See "O budding flowers" (Nape)
"E lo mio amore è andato a soggiornare" ("My love has gone to live in lovely Lucca") L. Gordigiani. e.i. MSI
"È mezanotte e cu stu mandulino." See 'A serenata d' 'e rrose (Capua)
"È nata mmiezo mare." See Michelemmà
E non mi credevo trovarmi così. See Serenata ("Bella siccome un angelo")
"E oe Liliu I koinoa." See Haili crowned with lehua (Hopkins)
"E passu di notti e ti salutu strata." See Salitana
E pluribus unum. Words by G. W. Cutter. WBT—WCP
"È pronta la partenza." See Napole mio
"E puoi sì barbara." See Amore (Lucantoni)
"E quando ve n'andate" ("O when will ye e'er leave me") A. F. Tenaglia. e.i. PA 2
"E questo il loco." See Ah! se tu dormi, svegliati (Vaccai)
"È sgombro il loco." See Ah! parea che per incanto (Donizetti)

"È strano! è strano! in core scolpiti ho quegli accenti" ("Surprising! surprising! his words are all rooted in my bosom") Verdi. e.i. OPS 1 —PP
Also in Ah, fors' è lui (Verdi) KS 1— MC
È strano poter il viso suo veder. See "Ah! je ris de me voir" (Gounod)
"E Susanna non vien." Mozart. e.i. PP
"E ya-a he! ah he dhe he dhe." See Weton song
"E ya ha e ha e tha." See Hiding the disks
"Each day he proves anew." See Old dog Tray (Foster)
"Each night when I slumber." Irish folk song. JOI
The eagle (Der adler) A. Arensky. Words from the Russian of Golenistscheff-Kutusoff. e.g. NM 1
"An eagle poised on craggy peak." See The eagle (Arenski)
Earl Brand. Folk song: Georgia version. CSE
—Allanstand, N.C. version. CSE
—Hot Springs, N.C. version. CSE
—White Rock, N.C. version. CSE
Earle, Henry Edward
"All hail the gladsome Easter morn"
"Early at dawn I rose one day." See Joli mois de mai
"Early blowing, violets growing." See Le violette (Scarlatti)
Early, early in the spring. Folk song: Allanstand, N.C. version. CSE
—Alleghany, N.C. version. CSE
—Hot Springs, N.C. version no. 1. CSE
—Hot Springs, N.C. version no. 2. CSE
"Early ere the dawn of the morning." J. H. Hopkins (music and words) HC
The early horn. Galliard. PR 2
"Early one morning." English folk song: 1st verson. BE 2—BOH—BOS— DM 1—HSE 1—JE—MM
—2d version. DO
"Early strolling at my leisure." See "L'autrier par la matinée" (Thibaut IV)
"Early to bed." Round. TFC 1—WBT
"Earth below is teeming." Composer unknown. Words by J. S. B. Monsell. HC
"Earth below is teeming." A. W. Hamilton-Gell. Words by J. S. B. Monsell. HC
"Earth has many a noble city." See Thou Bethlehem (Dykes)
"The earth is clothed in cheerful green." See Celia's invitation
"The earth is cold and drear to-night." See Christmas carol (Reichardt)
"The earth is fair around us." Irish air: When she answered me her voice was low. Words by E. M. Downing. MMI

"The **earth,** parched at even." See Le soir (Thomas)

"**Earth's** hopes awaken, Christ life hath taken." See Die drei grossen Christlichen feste

East Indian song. See "Our sorrow is vain"

Eastburn, R. A.
Little brown jug

Easter ("There's a music up in the frozen hills") H. K. Hadley. Words by F. Manley. TL

Easter bells ("Hear the loving Easter bells") R. H. Clouston, jr. Words by H. G. Farmer. HC

Easter bells ("Let the merry") See "Let the merry church-bells ring" (Howard)

"The **Easter** bells are ringing." H. A. Farnsworth. Words by M. Ford. HC

"The **Easter** dawn is breaking." H. A. Farnsworth. Words by M. Ford. HC

"**Easter** day hath dawned again." C. A. Barry. HC

"**Easter** flowers and dressing." A. H. Brown. HC

"**Easter** flowers are blooming bright." A. H. Brown. HC

"**Easter** flowers are blooming bright." A. F. M. Custance. HC

"**Easter** flowers are blooming bright." J. T. Field. HC

"**Easter** flowers are blooming bright." F. A. G. Ouseley. HC

"**Easter** flowers, Easter carols." W. H. A. Hall. Words by W. J. Roberts. HC

Easter hymn. Words by R. I. Halsey. NMS

"**Easter** morn with gladness shine." A. Rubinstein. HC

Easter song. C. Johns. Words by F. Manley. TL

"The **Easter** sunshine breaks again." Composer unknown. HC

"The **Easter** sunshine breaks again." G. E. Oliver. HC

An **eastern** college boating song. E. W. Newton. CHS

"**Eastern** monarchs, sages three." 15th century words. Tr of Tres magi de gestibus. e. HC

Eastern romance (Vostótchnui románs.— "The rose has charmed the nightingale."—Plenívshis rósoi, salavyéi) N. Rimsky-Korsakoff. Words by A. Koltzoff. e. SMR 2

Eastman, Mrs Elaine (Goodale)
Ashes of roses (music by Mason; Woodman)

Easy and gay ("While Phillis refuses my love to requite") 18th century song. ME

"**Eat** your bread, Mary." See Morning

"Les **eaux** du Nil, toutes pâles, s'écoulent." See Le Nil (Leroux)

Eayrs, M. P.
Song of the sea

Ebeling, J. E.
"Would'st thou magnify the story" (Tr of Alle, die ihr Gott zu ehren)

Eberhard, A. G.
"Viel tausend sterne prangen" (Call)

Eberhart, Mrs Nelle Richmond (McCurdy)
"Far off I hear a lover's flute" (Cadman)
"From the land of the sky-blue water" (Cadman)
"The moon drops low" (Cadman)
"The white dawn is stealing" (Cadman)

Ebers, Karl Friedrich
Trinklied

Ebert, Karl Egon, ritter von
Das erste veilchen (Mendelssohn)

Eberwein, Max
Ergo bibamus
Punschlied
Table-song. See Tischlied
Tischlied

Ecce homo. M. Piccolomini. e. HSS 3 —HSS 4

"**Ecce** quam bonum." 1. CHS—WBT

Eccles, J. H.
Come sing to me again (Hobson)

Eccles, John
"Ah! stay; ah! turn"
Amyntor's well-a-day
The avowal
"A country life is sweet"
"Fly! fly! ye lazy hours"
"The jolly, jolly breeze" (from Rinaldo and Armida)
"To meet her Mars"

"**Ecco** il punto, o Vitellia." See Non più di fiori (Mozart)

"**Eccolo,** a voi l'affido." Rossini. e.i. PP

"**Eccolo,** il mio figliuol." See "Oui, c'est lui" (Dubois)

"**Eccomi** al fine, in Babilonia." See Ah! quel giorno (Rossini)

"**Eche** geia, kaymene kosme." See The dance of Zalongo

Echete geia, brysoules. See The dance of Zalongo

Echo ("Come to me") See "Come to me in the silence of the night" (Somerset)

Echo ("How sweet the answer Echo makes") Irish air. Words by T. Moore. MMI

Das **echo** ("Ich lausche dem echo") J. Greith. Words by A. Franz. g. ED 3

The **echo** ("O hark! O hear") FSS 2

Echo song ("Have you ever heard") German folk air. Words by J. Irwin. DO

Echoes ("Sweet echoes, floating on the breeze") H. W. Loomis (music and words) BSS

Echoes of olden times. T. Comer. Words by H. Martin. MCS

"**Echoing** bell-tones." See "Glöcklein im thale" (Weber)

"The **echoing** horn." T. A. Arne. Words by I. Bickerstaffe. DM 2—ME

Echtes glück ("Ach umsonst auf aller länder karten") F. A. Kempt. Words by Schiller. g. ED 2

Eckert, Karl
The rose

Eclogue. See Eglogue (Delibes)

"Écoute moi ma douce et tendre enfant." See Vigil (Glinka)

"Écoutez, brave jeunesse." See Le blasphemateur châtié

"Écoutez, je vais vous chanter." See La chanson des mensonges

"Écoutez la complainte, petits et grands." See La bergère muette

"Écoutez tous, petits et grands." See La Passion de Jésus-Christ

Ecstasy ("J'étais seul") See Extase (Gueroult)

Ecstasy ("Sur un lys pâle") See Extase (Duparc)

"Ed anche Beppe amò" ("Beppe then also loves") Mascagni. e.i. OPS 3

"Ed arzira caminandu caminai." See Strambotto

Eddy, R. J.
Beloit song (German airs)

Der edelfalk (The falcon) K. Loewe. Words by F. Freiligrath. e.g. FM

Der edelmann und der invalide. See Die tabakspfeife (Pilz)

The Eden of love. FSS 5

Edite, bibite. e.g. SSS. e. only BMC —WBT
Altes studentisches tafellied ("Ça ça geschmauset") g. ED 1

Edmeston, James
Evening prayer (Stebbins)
"Lead us, heavenly Father, lead us" (Gounod)

Edson, Lewis
"Arise, my soul"
Great joy we bring
Lenox. See "When little Samuel woke"
"When little Samuel woke"

Edward. Folk song: Carmen, N.C. version. CSE
—Hot Springs, N.C. version. CSE
—Tennessee version. SA

Edward. C. Loewe. Words by Herder from an old English folk ballad. e.g. KF 4—PG 3

Edwards, A.
"My love is as fair as the blossom" (Welsh air)
My own dear maid (Welsh air)
Waiting (Welsh air)

Edwards, A. M.
"Now the year is crowned with blessing"

Edwards, John
A wreath for Princess Kaiulani (Hopkins)

Edwin in the lowlands lòw. Folk song: Georgia version. CSE
—Black Mountain, N.C. version. CSE
—Hot Springs, N.C. version. CSE
—Tennessee version. CSE
Young Edwin in the lowlands low. Hampshire version. SF 3

"Een chick-ee-noo! long years ago there lived a squaw." See The chattering squaw

"E'en in slumber do I languish." See "Immer leiser wird mein schlummer" (Brahms)

"E'en little things." See "Auch kleine dinge" (Wolf)

"E'er since thine eyes returned my glances." See "Seitdem dein aug' in meines schaute" (Strauss)

"E'er will I sigh." See "Tanto sospirerò" (Bencini)

"Ef yo mother want to go." See Roll de ol' chariot along

"Ef you want to get to hebben." See Did you hear my Jesus

"Eg beislad min styvel eg sadlad mit sverd." See Den bakvende visa

"Eg gjaette Tulla" (My Tulla) Norse folk song. e.n. MAN

"Eg rodde meg ut paa Seiagrunden." See Strilevise

"Eg seer deg ut før gluggjin" ("I see you through the window") Norwegian song. e.n. BF 2
"Eg ser deg ut för gluggjin" ("I see your shadow yonder") e.n. MAN

Egar, John H.
"Sing, sing for Christmas" (Hodges)

Egeberg, Anna
The young birch. See Ungbirken
Ungbirken

"Egerāsa, mōre paidia." See Old Demos and his rifle

Eglantine, Philippe François Nazaire Fabre d'. See Fabre d'Eglantine, Philippe François Nazaire

Egli,
"The lark sings loud"

"Egli ancora non giunge." See Ah! non avea più lagrime (Donizetti)

Eglogue (Eclogue) L. Delibes. Words by V. Hugo. e.f. PG 1

Egyptian love song. See "The wind is playing 'mongst the reeds"

"Eh! lass! you've hurt me sadly, oh, sadly." See Mena, me' (Costa)

"Eh! my dear lad." See "Brüderlein fein"

"Eh, ughnyem." See Volga boat song

Die ehre Gottes aus der natur ("Die himmel rühmen") Beethoven. Words by C. F. Gellert. g. ED 1—ED 2
Creation's hymn. e. BC—BD
Die ehre Gottes aus der natur (Nature's adoration) e.g. PG 4
Die ehre Gottes aus der natur (The praise of God) e.g. CS 1
"The heavens declare His glory." e. WS
"The heavens resound." e. TFC 1—TL
Nature's adoration. e. HSS 4—KF 4

"Ehre sei Gott in der höhe." Air: Lobe den Herren. Words by A. H. Niemeyer. g. ED 1

Ehren on the Rhine. W. M. Hutchinson. FSS 4

"Ei-euch nyem." See Volga boat song

"Ei taivaan alla ja avaralla." See Song of my dear

"Eï ukhnem." See Volga boat song

"Eï véli e ni méti alem." See Hamidie (Nedjib Pacha)

"Eià meninos á porfia." See Ao menino Jesus

Eiapopeia. Bohemian folk song. e. FSS 3

Eichberg, Julius
　"To thee, O country"

Eichendorff, Joseph Karl Benedikt, freiherr von
　Frühlingsnacht (music by Jensen; Schumann)
　Gute nacht (Franz)
　Heimweh (Wolf)
　"In einem kühlen grunde" (German folk air; also music by Berger; Gluck)
　Der jäger abschied (Mendelssohn)
　Der letzte gruss (Levi)
　Mondnacht (Schumann)
　Morgengebet (Folk air)
　Nachtlied (Kugler)
　Sonntag (Franz)
　Waldesgespräch (music by Jensen; Schumann)
　Wanderlied der Prager studenten (Volksweise)
　Die zigeunerin (Wolf)

"Der eichwald brauset" (Des mädchens klage.—The maiden's lament) F. Schubert. Words by F. von Schiller. e.g. GMF

"Der eichwald brauset." J. R. Zumsteeg. Words by F. von Schiller. g. ED 2

Eidenbenz, Christian Gottlieb
　Kriegslied

"Eight little birds." A. S. Gatty. WSC

Eighty-eight. See Hanskin

"Eikur sa eg ad tvaer saman stodu." See Tölf synir

Eilean an Fhraoich ("I wish I were now in that isle of the sea") Scottish air. Words from the Gaelic of M. MacLeod. e. MMS

An-t-eilean Muileach (The isle of Mull) Scottish air. Words from the Gaelic of D. MacPhail. e. MMS

Eileen achora. J. P. Knight. Words by Crawford. FSS 2

Eileen aroon. Old air. Words by G. Griffin. JO—WBT

Eilidh bhàn ("Ailie bain o' the glen") Scottish air: Buain na rainich. Words from the Gaelic of E. MacColl. e. HSSS—MMS

"Eily mavourneen." Benedict. TS

Das eine lied ("Ich weiss der lieder viele und singe") J. Gersbach. Words by F. Rückert. g. ED 3

Einei, einei. See Surging waters (Hopkins)

Einkehr ("Bei einem wirte wundermild") J. Gersbach. Words by L. Uhland. g. ED 2

Einkehr ("Bei einem wirte wundermild") X. Schnyder von Wartensee. Words by L. Uhland. g. ED 3

"Einsam bin ich, nicht alleine." C. M. von Weber. Words by P. A. Wolf. g. ED 1

"Einsam? einsam? nein, das bin ich nicht." See In der ferne (Weber)

"Einsam in trüben tagen." See Elsa's traum (Wagner)

"Einsam wandelt dein freund." See Adelaïde (Beethoven); Adelaide (Pilz)

Der einsame (The solitary) F. Schubert. Words by C. Lappe. e.g. FM

Einsamkeit (Solitude) N. Medtner. Words by J. W. von Goethe. e.g. NM 1

"Einst hat mir mein leibarzt geboten." See Der leibarzt und der trinker

"Einst zum narren jemand spricht." See "Some one said unto the fool" (Tchaikovsky)

An Eirinn 'ní neósainncéhi. For English translation see For Ireland I'd not tell her name

The Eisteddfod ("Strike the harp, awake the lay") Air: The inspired bard (J. Parry's version) MMW

"Ekh polnym polna korobushka." See The peddler

Ekschlager, A.
　Maienblümlein (Weber)

"El taivaan alla ja avaralla." See Song of my dear

"The elder's scent is waxing." See "Was duftet doch der flieder" (Wagner)

Elderton, William
　York! York for my money (Old English air)

Eldred, C.
　Rose-time (Hadley)

Elegia. See Elegy (Musorgskiĭ)

Élégie. J. Massenet. Words by L. Gallet. e.f. SOS 1—SOS 2
　Élégie (Elegy) e.f. FF—PG 2
　Elegy. e. WBW
　Lost love. e. WL

Elegy ("Beyond the cloudy haze."—Elégia) M. P. Moussorgsky. Words by A. Golenishtcheff-Kutoozoff. e. SMR 1

Elegy ("Ô doux printemps d'autrefois") See Élégie (Massenet)

Elegy on the death of a mad dog. English air. Words by O. Goldsmith. TL

Elek, Erkel
　"None of the many stars"

The elephant battery. Traditional air. BOS

The elfin's song. See Die bekehrte (Wolf)

Elgar, Sir Edward William
　Love greetings
　"My love dwelt in a northern land"
　Salut d'amour. See Love greetings

Eli Yale. College song. LA

Elijah the prophet ("Eliyahu ha-nāvi") Jewish folk song. e.y. BF 2

Eliot, George, pseud.
　"Sweet evenings come and go" (Composer unknown)

Eliot, Samuel A.
　The songs we sang (Composer unknown)

"**Eliyahu** ha-nvāi." See Elijah the prophet

Eliza (When I landed in Glasgow) Irish folk song. JOI

Elizabeth ("Now peace to earth") Liszt. e. OS 1

Elizabeth's prayer. See Gebet der Elisabeth (Wagner)

"**Ella** giammai m'amò." See Dormirò sol nel manto mio regal (Verdi)

Ellacombe. See "To Thee, my God, my Saviour"; "With songs and honors sounding loud"

"**Elland** was tired, long the summer day." See Huldra aa en Elland

"**Elle** a fui le palais." See Salomé! Salomé (Massenet)

Elle danse! en cadence. For English translation see Waltz song (Offenbach)

"**Elle** ne croyait pas" ("Ne'er dreamed the tender maid") A. Thomas. e.f. KS 4
"**Elle** ne croyait pas" ("Never the maiden dream'd") e.f. SOA 3
"**Elle** ne croyait pas" ("Pure as a bud of spring") e.f. OPS 3

Ellen Bayne. S. C. Foster. WBT—WL

Ellerton, John
"Again the morn of gladness" (Stainer)
"O strength and stay" (Mendelssohn)
"Saviour, again to Thy dear name we raise" (music by Hopkins; also unknown composer)

Ellie Rhee. S. Winner (music and words) JSE—NMP—SSS—WBT

Elling, Catherinus
Fiskeren til sønnen
The fisherman to his son. See Fiskeren til sønnen

Elliot, Jane
Flowers of the forest (Old air)

Elliott, C. W.
Bonny Eloise (Thomas)

Elliott, Charlotte
Calm was the night (Sullivan)
God's will and love (Troyte)
Integer vitae (Flemming)
"Just as I am" (Bradbury)
Troyte's chant (Troyte)

Elliott, Ebenezer
"When wilt Thou save the people" (Booth)

Elliott, Emily Elizabeth Steele
"There came a little Child to earth" (Brown-Borthwick)
"Thou didst leave Thy throne" (Powell)

Elliott, James William
The feast of lanterns
"Fiddle-de-dee"
"Jack and Jill"
"The king of France"
"Little Bo-Peep"
"Little Jack Horner"
Lullaby
"Once more the liberal year laughs out"
Pussy

Ellis, G. M.
Star of the east (Composer unknown)

"**Eloigné** de Nanette." See Nanette

Elsa's dream. See Elsa's traum (Wagner)

Elsa's traum (Elsa's dream.—"Einsam in trüben tagen") R. Wagner. e.g. OPS 1—SOA 1

Elson, Louis Charles
More and more (Seifert)

"**Eltörött** a hegedüm." See Broken is my violin (Danko)

Elua maua me 'ke aloha. See United

The **elves'** dance. Portuguese folk air. Words by H. H. Harbour. DO

Elvey, Sir George Job
"Come, ye lofty, come, ye lowly"
"Come ye thankful people, come"
"Crown Him with many crowns"
"Let the whole creation cry" (same air as "Come ye thankful people, come")
"Praise to God and thanks we bring" (same air as "Come ye thankful people, come")
"Praise to God, immortal praise" (same air as "Come ye thankful people, come")
St George's chapel. See "Praise to God, immortal praise"
St George's Windsor. See "Come ye thankful people, come"; "Praise to God and thanks we bring"

Elwell, Nelly E.
Kind words are dear to all (Noorden)

Embark-away. See "Embarquez-vous" (Godard)

"**Embarquez-vous**" ("Come and embark") B. Godard. Words by U. Guttinguer. e.f. CM 1—HM 2
Come and embark. e. BD
"Embarquez-vous" (Embark-away) e.f. PG 3—PG 4

Embarrassment. See Verlegenheit (Abt)

"**Embrace** me not." Costa. OS 3

Emdin, J.
Who deeply drinks of wine

Emerson, Joseph M.
"The lead strikes English ground" (Gilholy)

Emerson, Luther Orlando
The reaper and the flowers
"Star of the twilight"
"We are coming, Father Abra'am"

Emerson, Ralph Waldo
Concord hymn (Beethoven)
The humble bee (German air; also music by Neidlinger)
The poet (Kücken)
"Thine eyes still shined" (Kreutzer)
Waldeinsamkeit (Mendelssohn)
Woodnotes (Müller)

Emerson, our Emerson. College song. Words by E. L. McIntosh. CHS

Emgann Sant-Kast (The battle of St Cast) Breton song. br.e. KA

The **emigrant's** complaint. See My ain countrie

Emilio, Manuel
  Little Eva
Emmanuel ("Joy fills") See "Joy fills our inmost heart to-day" (Composer unknown)
Emmanuel ("The night is dark") P. Rodney. Words by W. Stevens. HSS 3 —HSS 4
Emmanuel, God with us. See "Joy fills our inmost heart to-day" (Gadsby)
Emmet, Joseph Kline
  Emmet's lullaby. See Go to sleep, Lena darling
  Go to sleep, Lena darling
Emmet's lullaby. See Go to sleep, Lena darling (Emmet)
Emmett, Daniel Decatur
  Dixie (with words "I wish I was"; "Southrons, hear your country")
  The U. S. A. forever (same air as Dixie)
"Emporte ma folie." See Fleur jetée (Fauré)
"An empress am I in my way." See "Je marche sur tous les chemins" (Massenet)
Empty splendor. See La splendeur vide (Saint-Saëns)
Emra, W. H.
  None can tell (Allen)
"En chasse, en chasse, en chasse." See Chant du chasseur (Meyerbeer)
"En Cuba, la isla hermosa del ardiente sol." See Tú (Fuentes)
"En descendant du ciel." See The spirit of poesy (Arenski)
En dormant, c'est à moi. J. F. Halévy. e.f. SOA 1
"En el fondo del mar nació la perla." See La perla (Araya?)
En elespejo de tu mirada niña (The Spanish gipsy) e. GO
"En gång i bredd med mig" ("When thou stand'st up with me") Swedish folk song. e.sw. HSOS
"En, juventus Andreana." See Carmen seculare (Oakeley)
"En la mente de Dios nació el poeta." See El poeta
"En los montes más remotos." Folk song from the Andes mountains. e.s. HS
"En menant paître mon troupeau." See Lisette
"En m'y promenant à l'ombrage." See Les adieux des amants
"En noche lóbrega, galán incógnito, las calles céntricas atravesó, y al pié la clásica ventana dórica." See El galán incógnito (Spanish American version)
"En noche lóbrega galán incógnita las calles céntricas atravezó, y bajo clásica ventana gótica templo su cítara y asi cantó." See El galán incógnito (Mexican version)
"En noche lóbrega galán incógnito por calles céntricas atravesó, y bajo plácida ventana gótica cogió su cítara y así cantó." See Incógnito
"En nombre del cielo." See Los peregrinos

"En over de weide daar blonk er de zon." See Wiegeliedje (Rennes)
"En passant par la Lorraine." See Les trois capitaines
"En passant par un échalier" ("In passing by a hedgerow tall") French folk song. e.f. TSF
"En revenant d'Auvergne." f. FMB
"En revenant de la joli' Rochelle." Canadian rowing song. e.f. SMW
"En revenant de la joli' Rochelle" ("As I came back from beautiful Rochelle") e.f. TF
"En revenant de noces" ("Back from the wedding coming") French folk song. e.f. TSF
"En revenant de noces" ("Home from the wedding") Breton version. e.f. TF
  Variant: "À la claire fontaine"
"En revenant de Varennes." See Ils m'ont appelé' vilaine
En roulant ma boule (A-rolling my bowl) French Canadian folk song. e.f. BFS
"En un delicioso lago." See Un lago delicioso
"En un delicioso puerto." See La barquillera
"En una jaula de oro." See La jaula de oro
"Ena pali hauliuli." See United
"Encantadora María." Mexican folk song. e.s. HS
  "Encantadora Maria" ("Maria dear") e.s. HF
The enchanted isle. G. Verdi. e. FSS 6 —HSD
The enchanted white duck. Irish folk song. JOI
Enchanting is the landscape. See "Beautiful Waipio" (Likelike)
The enchantress ("By the lore of ages far") J. L. Hatton. Words by H. F. Chorley. CS 1
The enchantress ("Una linda y mágica mujer") See La mágica mujer
"Encompassed by an angel's frame." W. Jackson. BE 6
The encounter. See Begegnung (Wolf)
End this war. Negro song. JP
"Ended at last the strife." See Pleurez! pleurez, mes yeux (Massenet)
Enderssohn, G.
  Star of my heart (Denza)
Endless love ("Die thräne bebt") P. I. Tchaikovsky. Words from the Russian of A. Tolstoi. e.g. NM 2
The endless song. W. H. Neidlinger. Words by F. Manley. TL
"Endure! endure." Bach. e. OS 3
Endzweck der schöpfung ("Für wen schuf Gottes güte") Miehl. Words by J. W. L. Gleim. g. ED 2
"The enemy said." Händel. OS 1
"L'Enfant Jésus dans son jardin." See The crown of roses (Tchaikovsky)

Les **enfants** à la Crecho (The children at the Manger) Noël provençal. e. MF

"**Enfants**, c'est moi qui suis Lisette." See Souvenirs de Lisette (Bérat)

Les **enfants** de la mer. Chanson pour ramer. e.f. SMW

"**Enfin** nous te tenons, petite souris grise." See La petite souris grise

"**Enfold** me! O sea." See "Ô mer, ouvre-toi" (Delibes)

Engel, Carl
Go to it

Der **engel**. See The angel (Rubinstein)

Engelbrecht, J. C.
Good-bye

English, Thomas Dunn
Ben Bolt (German air)

English chanty ("Come, shipmates") HSD

English Maypole song. See "Come, lasses and lads"

The **Englishman**. J. Blockley. Words by E. Cook. DM 1

L'**enlèvement** en mer. See "Isabeau se promène"

The **enlisted** soldiers. Negro folk song. HR

Ennery, Adolphe d', pseud. See Philippe, Adolphe

The **Enniskillen** dragoon. Irish folk song. JOI

Eno, J. N., Thomas, Arthur, and Dickson, Caspar G.
On the chapel steps (Gow)

Enoch, Frederick
By the blue sea (Smart)
The land of dreams (Wilton)
My boat is waiting here for thee (Smart)
"When the swallow comes" (Pinsuti)

"**Enrolled** in our bright annals." See The fight off Camperdown (Dignum)

"**Ensam** i skogen sjöng den vackra Rose-Marie." See Rose-Marie (Collan)

"**Ensanguined** and lurid." G. Donizetti. [Tr of O sole più rotto] e. WBT

"**Entfernt** von gram und sorgen." See Die landlust (Haydn)

"**Enthroned** between two sparkling lakes." See Alma mater—Wisconsin

Enticement. See Lockung (Dessauer)

Entrance song. E. Millocker. e. WBT

Entre le boeuf et l'âne gris ("Close by the ox and the ass so gray") 17th century French Noël. e. MF

Entre le boeuf el l'âne gris. For another English translation with a different air see The sleep of the Infant Jesus (Gevaert)

"**Entré** un jardín." Folk song from San Juan Capistrano. e.s. HS

Entreaty ("Dearest heart, I beg of thee") C. Bohm. Words by H. Schmidt. [Tr of Bitte] e. WBW

Entreaty ("Last night I dreamed') Love song. W. G. Smith. Words by I. Allen, jr. AA

Entschluss ("Was soll ich in der fremde tun") P. von Lindpaintner. Words by J. V. Adrian. g. ED 2

Entschuldigung ("Wenn wir durch die strassen ziehen") F. Nestler. Words by W. Müller. g. ED 1

"**Eolus**, you must appear." Purcell. BS 2

Epilog (Last farewell) E. Grieg. e.g. PG 4

Epitaph on a parish clerk. Round. S. Webbe. TL

Epitaphe. See A poet's epitaph (Medtner)

"**Eppur** sento d'amarla." See Bella del tuo sorriso (Braga)

"**Er** blickt hinauf in himmelsau'n." See Die wacht am Rhein (Wilhelm)

"**Er**, der herrlichste von allen" ("He, more knightly than the noblest") R. Schumann. Words by A. von Chamisso. e.g. KF 2—PG 2

"**Er**, der herrlichste von allen" ("He, the noblest of the noble") e.g. FO 1

"He the best of all." e. BC

"**Er** gab mir eine rose." See Verwelkt (Proch)

Er hat ein rot gesichte ("Wo sind sie denn geblieben") Air: Ich stand auf hohem berge. g. ED 2

"**Er** is een kindetje geboren op d'aard'." See De nederige geboorte

"**Er** ist gekommen" (He came) R. Franz. Words by F. Rückert. e.g. KF 2—PG 1

"**Er** ist gekommen" (His coming) e.g. FO 1

Er ist's (A song of spring) R. Schumann. Words by E. Mörike. e.g. PG 1

Er ist's (Song to spring) H. Wolf. Words by E. Mörike. e.g. CMF 2—FO 2

Er liebte mich so sehr. See He truly loved me so (Tchaikovsky)

"Det **er** nat så vide over vei og vang." See Majnat (Sinding)

"**Er** was een maagdetje zuiver en net." See De boodschap van Maria

"**Era** la noche." See Serenata

Erbarmen (O Thou most compassionate) J. L. Nicodé. e.g. HSS 1—HSS 2

"**Erdő**, erdő, sürü erdő." See "In the forest, the deep forest"

"**Ere** around the huge oak." Shield. HSE 2—NG

"**Ere** the long roll of the ages end." See Fainne geal an lae

"**Ere** the moon begins to rise." See Cradle song (De Koven)

"**Ere** the morning light is breaking." See "Pria che spunti in ciel l'aurora" (Cimarosa)

"**Ere** the twilight bat was flitting." See Jamie's on the stormy sea (Covert)

Ergo bibamus ("Hier sind wir versammelt") M. Eberwein. Words by Goethe. g. ED 1—ED 2

"**Erhebe** dich, genossin meiner schmach." See Durch dich musst ich verlieren (Wagner)

Eri tu che macchiavi. G. Verdi. e.i. SOA 4
    Eri tu che macchiavi (And wouldst thou thus have sullied) e.i. OPS 4
    Eri tu che macchiavi (Is it thou who hast sullied) e.i. KS 5
Erin is my home. German air. Words by T. H. Bayly. JO—WBT
Erin! oh, Erin ("Like the bright lamp") Irish air: Thamma hulla, or, Thamama hulla. Words by T. Moore. MI—MMI
"Erin! the tear and the smile in thine eyes." Air: Eileen aroon. Words by T. Moore. JO—MI—MMI
Erin's lovely home. Folk song. SO
Erk, Ludwig Christian
    "Das alte jahr vergangen ist"
    "Aus der jugendzeit"
    Freude in ehren
    Froher mut
    "Gott grüsse dich"
    Lorelei
    Mancherlei boten
    "Mir ist leide"
    "Nur ein wandern ist das leben"
    "Die sonne sank"
    "Zu Bacharach am Rheine." See Lorelei
Erkel, Ferencz
    Hungarian national hymn
    Hymnusz. See Hungarian national hymn
Das **erkennen** (Recognition) H. Proch. Words by J. N. Vogl. e.g. AB 4
"Erkennet, erkennt, dass der Herr ist Gott" (Arioso from 100th psalm) S. Jadassohn. e.g. HSS 1—HSS 2
The **erl** king. See Erlkönig (Loewe); Erlkönig (Schubert)
Erlkönig (The erl king) C. Loewe. Words by J. W. von Goethe. e.g. PG 4
Erlkönig (The erl king) Schubert. Words by J. W. von Goethe. e.g. AB 1—BAS 1—BS 1—FF—FO 1—KF 4—PG 4. e. only FTS
Ernani, Ernani, involami. Verdi. e.i. OPS 1—PP
Erneuter schwur ("Wenn alle untreu werden") Air: Frisch auf zum fröhlichen jagen. Words by M. von Schenkendorf. g. ED 2
Eros. E. Grieg. Words by O. Benzon. e.g. CMF 2—FO 2
Die **erscheinung** ("Ich lag auf grünen matten") L. Berger. Words by L. T. Kosegarten. g. ED 3
Erskine, Andrew
    "How sweet this lone vale" (Gaelic air)
Erskine, C.
    "Ring the bells, the Christmas bells"
Erskine, Sir Henry, bart.
    "In the garb of old Gaul" (Reid)
Erskine, John
    To stand by thee, Columbia
Das **erste** veilchen (The first violet) Mendelssohn. Words by E. Ebert. e.g. KF 1—KF 2—PG 1—PG 2—SS 1

"Des ersten sehens wonne ist wie der duft im walde." See entry under Des
Erster verlust (First loss) N. Medtner. Words by J. W. von Goethe. e.g. NM 1
Erstes begegnen (First meeting) E. Grieg. Words from the Norwegian of B. Björnson. e.g. FM
"Erwacht zum neuen leben." See Frühlingsanfang (Mozart)
Erwin, John
    April vacation (English air)
    The bells (French folk air)
    Columbus day (Italian air)
    Evacuation day (German folk air)
    For Patriots' day (Dutch folk air)
    The light-house (English folk air)
    Slumber song (Brahms)
    A song for sailors and soldiers (English folk air)
    "Tirra-lirra-lirra" (German folk air)
    "Winter, good-bye! blue is the sky" (German folk air)
"Es blickt so hold der mond mich an." See Mutterseelenallein (German folk air)
"Es blickt so still der mond mich an." See Mutterseelenallein (Braun)
"Es blinken drei freundliche sterne." See Die drei sterne (Himmel)
"Es blinkt der thau" ("The dew it shines") A. Rubinstein. Words by G. von Boddien. e.g. SS 1
"Es blinkt der thau" ("The dewdrops glitter") e.g. KF 2—PG 4. e. only FTS
"Es blinkt der thau" ("Now shines the dew") e.g. FO 1—NM 2
"Es blüht ein blümchen irgendwo." See Das blümchen wunderhold (Beethoven)
"Es blüht eine schöne blume." See Die blume der blumen (Reichardt)
"Es braust ein ruf wie donnerhall." See Die wacht am Rhein (Wilhelm)
"Es el amor mariposa" (Butterfly love) Spanish-American song. e.s. LSS
"Es el móvil océano gran espejo." See La terruca (Colón)
"Es, es, es und es, es ist ein harter schluss." See Handwerksburschen-abschied
Es fällt ein stern herunter. For French and English translations see Lied (Mertens)
"Es fiel ein himmelstaue." See Der mai
"Es fiel ein reif in der frühlingsnacht." See Weder glück noch stern
Es führt drei könige Gottes hand. For English translations see "There came three kings by God's own hand" (Vincent); "There came three kings from eastern land"
"Es geht bei gedämpfter trommel klang." See Der soldat (Silcher)
"Es gingen drei jäger wohl auf die birsch." See Der weisse hirsch
"Es glänzt im abendsonnengolde." See Im frühling (Fesca)
"Es grünet ein nussbaum vor dem haus." See Der nussbaum (Schumann)

"Es hat die rose sich beklagt" ("The rose complained") R. Franz. Words by F. von Bodenstedt (Mirza Schaffy) e.g. FF—FO 1—MS. e. only FTS

Es hat nicht sollen sein. V. E. Nessler. Words by Scheffel. e.g. SOA 4 Behüt' dich Gott (My love, farewell) e.g. CB
Es hat nicht sollen sein (It was not so to be) e.g. AB 1—FMB—KF 4 —OPS 4. e. only WA
It was not so to be. e. WBT—WL

"Es hatten drei gesellen." See Fiducit (Briesewitz)

"Es herrscht ein heiliger friede." See Frühlingslied (Fesca)

"Es heult der sturm." See Lied deutscher männer (Schneider)

"Es ist bestimmt in Gottes rat." F. Mendelssohn-Bartholdy. Words by E. von Feuchtersleben. g. ED 1
Auf wiedersehn. e. NMS
Auf wiedersehn (From days of old) e. FSS 2
"Es ist bestimmt in Gottes rath" ("It is ordained by God's decree") e.g. SSG
"Es ist bestimmt" ("Mourn not") e.g. CS 2
"It is ordained by God's decree." e. BSE
Song of parting. e. LA

"Es ist ein reis entsprungen." 16th century air. g. ED 1
"Es ist ein ros' entsprungen" (Hail! Thou glorious Scion) e.g. FSS 3

"Es ist ein schnitter" ("There is a reaper") German folk song. e.g. BF 2
"Es ist ein schnitter" (Der schnitter Tod) L. Reichardt. Words from a folk song. g. ED 2

"Es ist ein schuss gefallen." See Schneiderschreck (Reichardt)

"Es ist kommen, es ist kommen." L. Reichardt. Words by J. Praetorius. g. ED 3

"Es ist schon spät." See Waldesgespräch (Jensen); Waldesgespräch (Schumann)

"Es kam von einer Neustadt her." See Die macht der tränen

"Es kamen drei schneider wohl an den Rhein." See Drei schneider

"Es kann ja nicht immer so bleiben." See Ewiger wechsel (André); Ewiger wechsel (Himmel)

Es klappert die mühle am rauschenden bach. For English translation see The mill-wheel

"Es klingt ein heller klang." See Das lied vom Rhein (Nägeli)

Es komt ein schiff geladen. For English translation see "There comes a galley, laden"

"Es la mar calma y tranquila." See Torna a Surriento (Curtis)

"Es lebe, was auf erden stolziert in grüner tracht." See Jägers lust (Nathusius)

"Es leben die alten." J. A. Naumann. Words by J. M. Müller. g. ED 2

"Es muss ein wunderbares sein" ("O wondrous mystery of love") F. Liszt. Words by O. von Redwitz. e.g. CS 2—MSS 2—SS 2
"Es muss ein wunderbares sein" ("The love that linketh soul to soul") e.g. KF 2—KF 3
"Es muss ein wunderbares sein" ("A wondrous rapture must it be") e.g. CMF 1
"Oh life must wondrous be, and fair." e. KSE

Es muss was wunderbares sein (Most wondrous it must be) F. Ries. Words by O. von Redwitz. e.g. KF 1

"Es reden und träumen die menschen." See Die hoffnung (Reichardt)

"Es ritt ein jäger wohlgemut." See Jäger (Reichardt)

"Es ritt ein jägersmann über die flur." See Der jäger (Reichardt)

"Es ritten drei reiter zum tore hinaus." See Drei reiter am tor

"Es sang vor langen jahren." See Der spinnerin nachtlied (Reichardt)

"Es sass die prinzessin im frauengemach." See "Prinsessen sad höjt i sit jomfrubur" (Grieg)

"Es schwebte ein engel den himmel entlang." See The angel (Rubinstein)

"Es sind einmal drei schneider gewesen." See Romanze von den schneidern (Himmel)

"Es singt der sänger dunkler nächte." See Poet and critic (Cui)

"Es stand in alten zeiten." See Des sängers fluch (Gersbach)

"Es steht ein baum im Odenwald." See Der baum im Odenwald (Reichardt)

"Es steht ein baum in jenem thal." See In der fremde (Taubert)

"Es steht ein' lind' in jenem thal." See Die linde im thal

"Es tanz ein Bibabutzemann." See Bibabutzemann

"Es war, als hätt' der himmel." See Mondnacht (Schumann)

"Es war ein alter könig" ("There was an aged monarch") A. Rubinstein. Words by H. Heine. e.g. FO 1

"Es war ein könig in Thule." See Der könig in Thule (Reichardt); Der könig in Thule (Zelter); Der könig von Thule (Liszt)

"Es war ein sonntag hell und klar." See O schöne zeit, o sel'ge zeit (Götze)

Es war ein traum (It was a dream) E. Lassen. Words by H. Heine. e.g. KF 1—KF 2—KF 3—KF 4
Ah! 'tis a dream. e. TFC 2—WBT —WBW—WSW
"Ich hatte einst schönes vaterland" (Ah! 'tis a dream) e.g. FMB
An idle dream. e. BD

"Es war einmal ein gärtner." See Der gärtner (Sievers)

"Es war einmal klein Käthchen."   See Liten Karin

"Es wâr grâd tânz, af ter sennerhuam." See Städterbua und âlmadirn (Koschat)

"Es waren zwei königskinder."   See Die königskinder

"Es wear'n die wies'n grüen."   See Das Seiser almlied

"Es wollt' ein jäger jagen."   See Der jäger und das mädchen

"Es wollt' ein mägdlein in der früh' aufstehn."   See Der verwundete knabe

"Es zogen drei burschen wohl über den Rhein."   See Der wirtin töchterlein

L'esclave (The bondmaid) E. Lalo. Words by T. Gautier.   e.f.   SAM—SM 2
L'esclave (The captive)   e.f.   CM 2—CMF 2—HM 2

Esenwein, Joseph Berg
Taps

Es führt drei könige Gottes hand.   For English translation see "There came three kings from eastern land"

"Esia Samoa."   Samoan war song.   pol. SN

Eskimo song.   See "Long I gaze across the snow"

Esmond, A.
"All my heart this night rejoices" (Tr of Fröhlich soll mein herze springen)
"L'esperto nocchiero" ("The wise sailor steering") G. B. Bononcini.   e.i. FEI 2—KS 2

Essarts, Emmanuel Adolphe Langlois des.
See Des Essarts, Emmanuel Adolphe Langlois

"Das essen, nicht das trinken."   See Die arche Noah (Schneider)

Esser, Heinrich
The dead soldier.   See Der todte soldat
"Farewell, O joyous, sunny grove" (Tr of Ade du lieber tannenwald)
Der todte soldat
"Esser mesto" ("Dismal care")   Flotow. [Tr of Bange trauer]   e.i.   KS 3—OPS 2

Essex' last good-night ("Sweet England's prize")   See Well-a-day

Essex's last good night ("All you that cry") Old song.   CO 1

"Est-ce un lutin, est-ce une femme."   See La fille aux oiseaux (Dancla)

"Estaba un charro sentado."   See El charro

"Estaba un payo sentado."   See El payo

"Estaba una pájara pinta."   See La pájara pinta

"Estaba una pastora."   See La pastora

Estabrooke, Horace Melvyn
O, dear loved Maine

Estalenx, Paul Jean Jacques Lacome d'.
See Lacome d'Estalenx, Paul Jean Jacques

"Esteialon de tsonoué Jesos ahatonhia." See Jesos ahatonhia

Estic,
Clavelitos (Valverde)

La estrella del norte.   Mexican folk song. e.s.   HS

"'Esu phile mousiké."   See The musician (Christopulos?)

"Esy poü serneis ton choro."   See The lute player and the dancing lass

"Et de jour et de nuit je vais."   See Martha's song (Musorgskiĭ)

Eternal love.   See Von ewiger liebe (Brahms)

The eternal song.   See Chanson perpétuelle (Chausson)

L'étoile indiscrète.   See The tell-tale stars (Cherepnin)

"Les étoffes au mur tendues."   See Brises d'autrefois (Hüe)

Eton boating song.   A. Drummond. CST —LA—WBT—WC
Boating song.   JS—SMW
Eton boat song.   OH

"Étrange regard."   See Elle ne croyait pas (Thomas)

The Ettrick shepherd.   See Hogg, James

Etzler, Karl Friedrich
Die sterne des lebens

Eulalie.   J. W. Hobbs.   Words by W. H. Bellamy.   BE 5

Evacuation day.   German folk air.   Words by J. Erwin.   DO

Evald, Johan.   See Ewald, Johannes

"Evanescent breath of the lily."   See Romance (Debussy)

Evangeline.   W. S. Hays.   FSS 2

Evans, Evan
Morva Rhuddlan (Welsh air)

Evans, J. G.
Belle ob Baltimore

Evans, Marian.   See Eliot, George, pseud.

Eveleen's bower.   Irish air.   Words by T. Moore.   MI

"Even bravest heart may swell."   See "Avant de quitter ces lieux" (Gounod)

Even me.   FSS 1

Even song.   See Abendlied (Wickede)

Evening ("The light of day is slowly fading."—Le soir) P. Tschaikowsky. Words after the Little-Russian of Shevtchenko.   e.f.   SC

Evening ("Shades of evening now descend") L. von Beethoven.   WBT

Evening ("Le soir ramène")   See Le soir (Gounod)

Evening ("La terre embrasée")   See Le soir (Thomas)

Evening ("Voici que les jardins")   See Soir (Fauré)

Evening and peace.   See Kväll och frid (Geijer)

The evening bell ("Hark! the pealing") FSS 4—NMS—WBT
Vesper bell.   FSS 2

Evening bells ("Day and all its joys are ending") BSS

The evening-bells ("See how the glorious sunset") C. S. von Seckendorf. FSS 8

Evening bells ("Those evening bells") See "Those evening bells"

"The **evening** bells sound clearly." See The quiet night (Abt)

Evening boat-song. See Auf dem wasser zu singen (Schubert)

Evening colors. See "Hail Columbia" (Phile)

Evening fair. See Beau soir (Debussy)

"**Evening** falls, the sun is sinking." See Queen of night (Meyer-Helmund)

Evening glow. See Im abendroth (Schubert)

The **evening** gun. Words by T. Moore. FSS 4

Evening harmony. See Harmonie du soir (Debussy)

"**Evening** how gentle, sunlight how red." See Vom Monte Pincio (Grieg)

"**Evening** how tender! sunset how red." See Vom Monte Pincio (Grieg)

Evening hymn ("Forgive me, Lord."— Ward) Scotch air. FSS 4

Evening hymn ("Glory to Thee") See "Glory to Thee, my God, this night" (Hatton)

Evening hymn ("Hail, thou most sacred one") FSS 1

Evening hymn ("Saviour, again") See "Saviour, again to Thy dear name we raise" (Composer unknown)

Evening hymn ("Sun of my soul") See "Sun of my soul" (Monk)

Evening hymn of the crusaders. N. W. Gade. e. TL

"The **evening** is coming, the sun sinks to rest." See Bed-time

Evening meditation. See "Ave Maria" (Gounod)

Evening on the campus. Words by G. W. Carryl. CHS—CU

Evening on the lake. C. S. Putnam. Words by C. W. Fisher. CHS

Evening on the river. German folk air. Words by R. Compton. DO

Evening prayer ("As I lay me, weary, down to rest") German song. e. WSC

The **evening** prayer ("Matthew, Mark and Luke") Folk song. BSW

Evening prayer ("Saviour, breathe an evening blessing") G. C. Stebbins. Words by J. Edmeston. JS

The **evening** prayer ("This night I lift") See I lift my heart to thee (Costa)

Evening prayer ("When I lay me down to sleep") E. Humperdinck. e. WBT —WSC—WSW

"**Evening** shades are falling." See Darling, go to rest

"The **ev'ning** softly is stealing." See An evening song (Abt)

An **evening** song ("Dark thro' the forest") Old Lithuanian air. Words by H. H. Harbour. DO

An **evening** song ("The ev'ning softly is stealing") F. Abt. FSS 8

An **evening** song ("Glory to Thee") See "Glory to Thee, my God, this night" (Gounod)

Evening song ("Hush the waves") See Gaelic lullaby

Evening song ("Leise, leise") See Gebet (Weber)

Evening song ("Now reigns deep silence") Schumann. e. BSE

Evening song ("O brother, brother mine") See Dakota serenade

Evening song at Cornell. CHS

Evening song to the Virgin. Words by Hemans. JO

"The **evening** star a watch doth keep." See Wiegenlied (Ries)

Evening thoughts. See Abendempfindung (Mozart)

"**Ev'ning's** crown'd with clouds entrancing." See Necken (Söderberg)

Eventide. See "Abide with me! fast falls the eventide" (Monk)

"**Eventide!** the sun's career is finish'd." See Abendempfindung (Mozart)

Eventime. M. Smith (music and words) BE 5

"**Ever** be happy and light as thou art." See Pirates' chorus (Balfe)

Ever near. See Nära (Lindblad)

"**Ever** of thee." F. Hall. Words by G. Linley. HSC—HSD— NML— WA— WBT—WL—WSW

Ever thine. J. W. Kalliwoda. e. KSE

"**Ever** to the right." FSS 8

Ever with thee. See Immer bei dir (Raff)

Everest, J.
"Faithful people, now rejoice" (Lissant)

Everhart, R. O.
Mamie's charms (Jones)

"**Evermore** thy sons shall be." See Hip Hobart (Rose)

Eversz, Ernest H.
Cheer for the purple (Old air)

"**Ev'ry** boy who'd be a soldier." See Der kleine rekrut (Kücken)

Every bullet has its billet. H. Bishop. Words by T. J. Dibdin. DM 1

"**Ev'ry** day in the early misty morning." See The voice of the bell

"**Ev'ry** day that passes lightly." See Parfum de fleur (Blanc)

"**Ev'ry** day the wondrous lovely sultan's daughter paced the garden." See Der Asra (Loewe); Der Azra (Rubinstein)

"**Ev'ry** flower is equally cherished." G. Verdi. [Tr of Questa o quella] e. WBT

"**Every** flower that blossoms." G. E. Oliver. HC

Every inch a sailor. J. Read. FSS 8

"**Every** man take a glass in his hand." See A health to all honest man

"**Every** man take his glass in his hand." See A health to all honest men

"**Every** one is gossiping." See Menina Rosa

"**Ev'ry** one lift up the branch." See Approach to the tree

Every Sabbath thine altar shall be lighted. See Ogni sabato avrete il lume acceso (Gordigiani)

"**Ev'ry** thought we have is grounded." See "Il pensier sta negli oggetti" (Haydn)

"**Ev'ry** time I feel the spirit." Negro spiritual.   HR
  "Ev'ry time I feel de spirit."   JB
  "O ev'ry time I feel de spirit."   BN 2

"**Ev'ry** time I think about Jesus." See Calvary

Ev'ry valley shall be exalted.   G. F. Händel.   SAS 3
  "Ev'ry valley."   OS 3

"**Ev'ry** year there comes to us the dear Christ-Child."   See "Alle jahre wieder" (Silcher)

Everything's gone.   See Alles ist hin

Ev'rywhere a welcome stranger. See "Old Santa Claus" (Read)

Everywhere, everywhere, Christmas tonight.   L. H. Redner.   Words by P. Brooks.   HC

Eve's lamentation.   M. P. King.   FSS 5—HSS 1

Ev'ning.   For entries beginning Ev'ning see Evening

"**Evoe!** laeta requies."   See Floreat Rugbeia (Moberly)

Ev'ry.   For entries beginning Ev'ry see Every

Ewald, Johannes
  "Kong Christian stod ved høien mast" (Old air)

The **ewe-bughts.**   Scottish song.   PS 1
  "Will ye go to the ewe-bughts, Marion."   MMS

Ewen, John
  The boatie rows (Scottish air) Authorship uncertain

The **ewie** wi' the crookit horn ("Were I but able to rehearse") Air: Carron's reel.   Words by J. Skinner.   MMS—PS 1

Ewiger wechsel ("Es kann ja nicht immer so bleiben")   A. André.   Words by A. von Kotzebue.   g.   ED 3

Ewiger wechsel ("Es kann ja nicht immer so bleiben")   F. H. Himmel. Words by A. von Kotzebue.   g. ED 1
  Ewiger wechsel (Tempora mutantur) e.g.   SSG

Ewing, Alexander
  Ewing.   See "Jerusalem the golden"
  "Jerusalem the golden" (Tr of Urbs Syon aurea)

Ewing college song.   Words by B. M. Godwin.   CHS

"**Exact** to appointment I went to the grove." See False Phillis

The **examiner's** song.   M. Lutz.   Words by R. J. A. Berry.   SSS

Exaudet, Antoine
  Menuet d'Exaudet
  Exaudet's minuet.   See Menuet d'Exaudet

Excelsis! gloria.   See Noël ("O qu'a-dj'oyou")

Execution song (Lamentation) Irish air: Na mná deasa Bhaile-Locha-Riabhach, or, The pretty lasses of Loughrea.   JOI

The **exile** of Erin ("There came to the beach")   Irish air: Savourneen deelish. Words by T. Campbell.   FSS 4—JO—MMI

Extase ("J'étais seul près des flots."—Ecstasy) A. Gueroult.   Words by V. Hugo.   e.f.   SOS 2

Extase ("Sur un lys pâle."—Ecstasy) H. Duparc.   Words by J. Lahor.   e.f. HM 1

The **exultant** lover ("What care I tho' 'tis snowing") Air: Prestych bells.   Words by K. R. Moffat.   MMW

"**Ey** veli yi niymeti alem chehinchahi djihan."   See Hamidie (Nedjib Pacha)

"**Eye** hath not seen."   A. R. Gaul.   OS 2—SAS 2—WS

Eyes blue and dreaming.   See "Mit deinen blauen augen" (Lassen)

Eyes of old Yale blue.   See Polly (Smith)

"The **eyes** of spring so azure."   See "Die blauen frühlingsaugen" (Ries)

"**Eyes** so alluring."   See "Luci vezzose" (Gaffi)

"**Eyes** so tender."   See "Per la gloria d'adorarvi" (Bononcini)

"**Ezekiel** saw de wheel."   Negro spiritual. HR

F

Faber, Frederick William
  "Faith of our fathers, living still" (Hemy and Walton)
  "Hark! hark! my soul" (music by Armstrong; Dykes; Roe; Smart)
  "O paradise, O paradise" (Barnby)
  "Sweet Savior, bless us ere we go" (Monk)
  Sweet will of God (Scotch air; also music by Methfessel)
  "There's a wideness in God's mercy" (Tourjee)

Fabre d'Eglantine, Philippe François Nazaire
  L'orage (French air)

"**Fac** ut portem" ("Lord, Thy glory fills the heaven") Rossini.   e.l.   MSS 1—OS 2

"**Fade,** fade each earthly joy."   See Jesus is mine (Perkins)

The **faded** coat of blue.   J. H. McNaughton.   HSD—WBT

Faded flowers.   J. Power.   Words by J. H. Brown.   FSS 6

"**Fades** the star of morning."   See Love song (Omaha Indian air); Love song (Lieurance)

"**Fading** light dims the sight."   See Taps (Esenwein)

"**Fading,** still fading."   Portuguese air. FSS 3—HSD

"**Fågel** du lilla, fast du är arm."   See Tiggargossen

Fågelns visa (The bird's song)   W. T. Söderberg.   Words by Z. Topelius. e.sw.   HSOS—SSN
  The little bird.   e.   JS

"Fåglen på grenen sjunger lika gällt." See Nära (Lindblad)

Die **fahnenwacht** ("Der sänger hält im feld") P. von Lindpaintner. Words by F. Löwe. g. ED 1

Die fahnenwacht ("The standard watch") e.g. AB 4

The standard bearer. e.g. FSS 8

"Fahr wohl! o goldne sonne." See Bei sonnenuntergang (Reichardt)

"Fahr' zu mein schiff." See Frische brise (Stange)

Fahy, Francis A.
Irish lullaby (Needman)
Little Mary Cassidy (Irish air)
The ould plaid shawl (Irish air)

"Fai tira, moun brave equipage." See Lou revestidon (Borel)

"Faiblesse de la race humaine." See Inspirez-moi (Gounod)

"Fain would I see other places." See The Swiss mountaineer

"Fain would you know it." See "Saper vorreste" (Verdi)

Fáinne geal an lae ("Ere the long roll of the ages end") Irish air. Words by A. Milligan. e. FSI

Fáinne geal an lae ("One morning early") For English translation see The dawning of the day

"Faint a lonely rose-tree stood." See Maiden and rose

"Faint and wearily." See The way-worn traveller (Arnold)

Faint heart ne'er won fair lady. R. T. Whitehouse (music and words) CHS

"**Fainter** and fainter may fall on my ear." See Faithful (Mozart)

"Faintly as tolls the evening chime." See Canadian boat song (Canadian air); A Canadian boat song (Arnold)

"Faintly flow, thou falling river." Spanish air. Words by J. G. Percival. FSS 3 —LA

"Faintly the child sighs." See Death's lullaby (Musorgskiï)

"**Fair** Aminta." See Aminte

Fair Annie. Folk song from North Carolina. CSE

"Fair as the morning." G. F. Root. FSS 1—WBT

"Fair Christmas comes." Labitzky. Words by H. Martin. MCS

"Fair damozel, wilt thou dance with me." See La Bastringue

A fair dove ("Měla sem holubka") Silesian folk song. bo.e. BF 1

Fair Ellen Pugh ("A young man I heard") Air: A' songster am I. Words by Ieuan Dhu. MMW

The fair garden. A. Borodine. Words from the Russian. e. NM 1

The **fair-haired** maiden ("Tho' the last glimpse of Erin") Air: The coolun, or, Coulin. Words by T. Moore. BMC
"Though the last glimpse of Erin." MI—MMI

"Fair Harvard." Air: My lodging is on the cold ground. CHS—HSD—LA—MPC— NMS— WA— WBT— WC—WSW

"Fair Hebe." Attributed to T. A. Arne. MM

Fair Helen of Kirkconnel. See "I wish I war where Eelin lies"

The **fair** hills of Eire O. See Bán-cnoic Éireann óg

The **fair** hills of holy Ireland ("Beautiful and wide are the green fields of Erin") Irish air. Words by E. Walsh. MMI

Fair in her grace so loving. See Bella del tuo sorriso (Braga)

Fair is the summer. See Schön ist der sommer

"Fair Isabeau was walking." See "Isabeau s'y promène"

"Fair Isabel was walking." See "Isabeau s'y promène"

Fair Julia. See "Giulia gentil"

"Fair lady in your virgin bower." See Le spectre de la rose (Berlioz)

"Fair lady, lay those costly robes aside." See Death and the lady

"Fair lady, lay your costly robes aside." See Death and the lady

Fair lady, pity me. Folk song. BSW
"Dear love, regard my grief." BE 4

"Fair land of hope." F. Schira. FSS 8

Fair land of Poland. M. W. Balfe. FSS 5

"A fair little girl sat under a tree." See Good night and good morning

"A fair little miss all in the garden." See The broken token (Allanstand, N.C. version no. 1)

"Fair Luna." J. Barnby. FSS 6

The **fair** maid of Sorrento. See La vera Sorrentina

The **fair** maid of the white-rose tree. See La belle au rosier blanc

The **fair** maid of Voghera. See "La biondina di Voghera"

The **fair** maiden ("Hast seen the fair-hair'd maiden") Greek love song. e. KSE

Fair maiden, come with me. See Nennella vienete

"Fair maiden, tell me why." See Nennella vienete

Fair maidens' beauty will soon fade away. Irish folk song. JOI
"My love she was born in the north countrie." MMI

Fair Margaret and sweet William. Folk song: English version no. 1. CO 2
—English version no. 2. SEF 2
—Dorset version. SF 1
—Kentucky version. CSE
—Allanstand, N.C. version. CSE
—Carmen, N.C. version no. 1. CSE
—Carmen, N.C. version no. 2. CSE
—Tennessee version. CSE
—Mount Fair, Va. version. CSE
—Woodridge, Va. version. CSE
Variant: Sweet William and Lady Margery

"Fair Marg'ret stood at her bow'r window." See Fair Margaret and sweet William (Dorset version)

Fair Nottiman town. Kentucky mountain song. WT

The fair of Mast' Andrea. See La fiera de Mast' Andrea

"Fair pearls hath the ocean." See A toi mon coeur (Gounod)

"Fair Radcliffe." Words by K. Fullerton. CHS

Fair Rosalie. C. Dibdin. Words by Richardson. ME

"Fair Rosalind." 18th century song. CO 2

"Fair Sally." M. Greene. BE 4—MM

"Fair Smith." College song. B. C. Blodgett. Words by R. K. Crandall. CHS

"Fair spring of days now gone by." See Élégie (Massenet)

"Fair Susan I left with my heart full of woe." Dorset folk song. SF 1

"Fair Susan slumbered in shady bower." Folk air. Modern words by H. F. Sheppard. BSW

"Fair the night in Bethl'hem land." See Bethlehem land (Noble)

"Fair thou, Lake Erie, standest all bright." See Alma mater—Lake Erie (Abt)

The fair transgressor. Smith college song. L. Du Bois (music and words) CHS

"Fair trees, that hang your heads and bow." See Langs en å (Grieg)

Fair Una. See Úna bán

"Fair waved the golden corn." T. H. Spinney. Words by J. H. Gurney. HC

"Fair Wells." College song. CHS

"A fair young birch tree is standing." See Ungbirken (Egeberg)

The fair young child. See Paisdin fionn

Fair young Mary. See Mairi bhàn òg

"Fairer far than poet's vision." See Memory song to Amherst

The fairest angel. See Der schönste engel (Graben-Hoffmann)

"Fairest grace our souls inherit." See Truth

"Fairest isle." H. Purcell. Words by J. Dryden. BE 2—JE—MM

"Fairest Lord Jesus." ₁Tr of Schönster Herr Jesu₎ e. WBT
   "Fairest Lord Jesus" (Crusaders' hymn) e. FSS 4—LA—WS

"Fairest night of starry ray." See "Belle nuit" (Offenbach)

"The fairest nymph the valleys." 17th century song. CO 1

"Fairest of the virgin train." See The fairy

"Fairest! put on awhile." Irish air: Cummilium. Words by T. Moore. MI—MMI

Fairfax, Charles H.
   "Speed up"

The fairies ("Mark the merry elves of fairyland") Glee. Callcott. MS

The fairies ("Now the hungry") See "Now the hungry lions roar" (Leveridge)

"The fairies are dancing by brake and by bow'r." Irish song. MMI

"The fairies are dancing, how nimbly they bound." See Dance of the fairies

The fairies' dance. C. W. Glover. FSS 7

The fairies' lullaby ("Sweet babe") See "Sweet babe, a golden cradle holds thee"

Fairies' song. See The noontide ray (Auber)

Fairlamb, James Remington
   "Across the Eastern hill-tops"
   Song of April

Fairmount, fond Fairmount. Fairmount college song. Words by C. C. Isely. CHS

Fairweather, Una
   "Blue waves are sparkling" (Verdi)
   The tribute of the birds (Donizetti)

The fairy (A midnight madrigal) 18th century song. ME

Fairy-belle. S. C. Foster. WBT

The fairy boy. Words by S. Lover. FSS 1

Fairy haunts ("My home's on the mountain") Jackson. Words by J. Fitzgerald. MMI

A fairy lullaby ("I left my darling") See An coineachan

The fairy of Amalfi. See La fata di Amalfi

The fairy ring. FSS 2—WBT—WSC

The fairy ship. WSC

"A fairy tale is thy mouth." See The singer

"Fairy visions melted away." See "O beaux rêves évanouis" (Saint-Saëns)

"Fais tirer, mon brave équipage." See Lou revestidon (Borel)

"Faites l'aumône, bonnes gens." See Beggar's song (Wihtol)

"Faites-lui mes aveux" ("Gentle flowers in the dew") C. Gounod. e.f. OPS 2
   "Faites-lui mes aveux" ("In the language of love."—Flower song) e.f. KS 2
   The flower song. e. BD
   "Lovely flowers, I pray." e. WA—WBT—WL—WSW

"Faites-moi un homm' sans tête." See Je n'veux pas me marier

Faith ("Faith, thou beacon ever bright") Three-part round. Mozart. Words by V. A. Pierpont. TFC 2

Faith ("O sometimes gleams upon our sight") Rossini. Words by Whittier. LA

"Faith be no longer coy." W. Lawes. DM 1

Faith in one another. I. B. Woodbury. FSS 6

Faith in spring. See Frühlingsglaube (Schubert)

"Faith of our fathers, living still." H. F. Hemy and J. G. Walton. Words by F. W. Faber. BSS—TFC 2

"Faith, thou beacon ever bright." See Faith (Mozart)

Faithfu' Johnnie. Scottish air: When will you come again, arr by Beethoven. FSS 3

Faithfu' Johnie. SM 2

Faithfull Johnie ("O, wann kehrst du zurück."—Der treue Johnie) g. ED 3

My faithful Johnny. CST

Faithful ("Fainter and fainter") Arr from W. A. Mozart. Words by P. Cary. LBR

"Faithful and true, we lead ye forth." See Bridal chorus (Wagner)

The faithful comrade. See Der gute kamerad

A faithful heart ("He who calls a heart his own") F. Abt. Words by J. E. Carpenter. JSE

Basseti. FSS 6

The faithful heart ("Je serai ta douceur profonde") See Le fidèle coeur (Vidal)

The faithful little bird. Words by D. M. Craik. FSS 1—JSE

The faithful lover. T. A. Arne. PR 2

"Faithful people, now rejoice." G. B. Lissant. Words by J. Everest. HC

Faithfull Johnie. See Faithfu' Johnnie

Faithless as fair. See "Tu lo sai" (Scarlatti)

The falcon ("Die fürstin zog zu walde") See Der edelfalk (Loewe)

The falcon ("I know a falcon swift and peerless") F. Silcher. Words by J. R. Lowell. LBR

Falconer, Edmund
"Her gentle voice" (Balfe)
Killarney (Balfe)

Falconieri, Andrea
"Bella porta di rubini"
"Charming eyes so wary." See "Vezzosette e care"
"Dear eyes, love-lighted." See "Occhietti amati"
"Locks so beautiful." See "O bellissimi capelli"
"Naked archer." See "Nudo arciero"
"No more love's yearning." See "Non più d'amore"
"Non più d'amore"
"Nudo arciero"
"O bellissimi capelli"
"Occhietti amati"
"Ruby portal, fair, beguiling." See "Bella porta di rubini"
"Vezzosette e care"

Falk, Johannes
Der arme Thoms (Zelter)
Die drei grossen christlichen feste (Sicilian air)

"Fall'n is my foe." See Il balen del suo sorriso (Verdi)

"Fallen is thy throne." Martini. Words by T. Moore. FSS 4

Fallersleben, Hoffmann von. See Hoffmann von Fallersleben, August Heinrich

"Falling leaf, and fading tree." See Goodbye (Tosti)

The false bride. Folk song. BSW

The false knight ("When summer's radiant months are come") Air: The lamb's-fold vale. Words by C. B. Wilson. MMW

The false knight upon the road. Folk song: North Carolina version. CSE
—Tennessee version. CSE—SA

False Lamkin. Folk song from Cambridgeshire. SEF 2—SF 4—SO
Variant: Lamkin

The false note. See A dissonance (Borodin)

False Philander. See "Farewell, thou false Philander"

False Phillis. 18th century song. ME

The false young man. Folk song: Kentucky version. CSE
—North Carolina version. CSE
—Flag Pond, Tenn. version no. 1. CSE—SA
—Flag Pond, Tenn. version no. 2. CSE
—Virginia version. CSE
Variant of: "As I walked out"

"Fam'd for our warmth, we now rejoice." See Y Cymry dedwydd

"The famed ship California, a ship of high renown." See The girls around Cape Horn

Ein familiengemälde ("Mein herr maler") Volksweise. Words by B. A. Dunker. g. ED 2

"A famous Scotch professor was walking by the Nile." See The crocodile

"Fanciulla, ma perchè." See Nennella vienete

"Fanciulla son io" ("I know not Lord Love") L. Rossi. e.i. NG

Fanciulla, vieni a me. See Nennella vienete

"Fanciullo appena ti parlai d'amore" (I told you of my love) Abruzzian folk song. e.i. BF 2
"Fanciullo appena, ti parlai d'amore" ("While yet a boy, I told you how I lov'd you") e.i. MSI

Fanfare and carol ("Hark! I hear") See "Hark! I hear, sweet and clear" (Foster)

Fanfare and carol ("Hark! the Christmas bells are ringing") DSC

Faning, Eaton
"I've something sweet to tell you"

Fanny ("Oh Fanny is more fair") Welsh song. e. WBT—WL

Fanny Blair. Folk song: English version. SEF 1—SO
—Kentucky version. WT

Fantaisie aux divins mensonges. L. Delibes. e.f. SOA 3
"Prendre le dessin d'un bijou" ("To take the design of a jewel") e.f. OPS 3

Fantoches (Puppets) A. C. Debussy. Words by P. Verlaine. e.f. GMF

"Far above Cayuga's waters." See Alma mater—Cornell

"Far above the deep blue sea." See The sea gulls

"Far above the earth he soars." See The gift of peace

Far away ("Where is now") Mrs J. W. Bliss (music and words) FSS 1—HSD —MCS—WBT

"Far away beyond three oceans." See The maid and the sun (Rimskiĭ-Korsakov)

"Far be sorrow, tears, and sighing." J. S. B. Hodges. Tr of Cedant justi signa luctus. e. HC

"Far beneath the crystal waters dreaming." See Neckens polska

"Far, far from me my lover flies." M. P. King. Words by J. T. Allingham. BE 5

"Far, far from Tawe's valley." See Nancy

"Far, far o'er hill and dell." See Far o'er hill and dell

"Far, far upon the sea." See Far upon the sea (Russell)

Far from home. See In der ferne (Silcher)

"Far from my birthplace." See Der wanderer (Fesca)

Far greater in his lowly state. See Plus grand dans son obscurité (Gounod)

"Far in a shaded valley." See "In einem kühlen grunde" (Glück)

"Far in the forest my cabin is standing." See Findland's forest

"Far in the mountains with you." Irish air. Words by R. D. Joyce. MMI

"Far in the North sea." See "Yderst mod norden"

Far o'er hill and dell. Words by J. R. Planché. FSS 8—WBT

Far o'er the sea. G. Kingsley. Words by F. Hemans. FSS 7

"Far o'er the stars there is rest." See "Über den sternen ist ruh" (Abt)

"Far o'er the valley sinks the day." See Fairmount, fond Fairmount

"Far o'er the wave." See Dear native home

"Far o'er the woods the moonlight is dying." See Laura to Filon

"Far off I hear a lover's flute." Omaha tribal air. C. W. Cadman. Words by N. R. Eberhart. CF

"Far on the road we two journeyed together." M. Ippolitoff-Ivanoff. Words from the Russian of D. U. Tsertelev. e. NM 1

"Far out at sea an island lies." See The isle (Rachmaninov)

"Far out on the desolate billow." See Never alone (Silcher)

"Far over yon hills of the heather sae green." See Flora Macdonald's lament (Gow)

"Far remov'd from noise and smoke." See The woodman (Dibdin)

"Far, so far." Hungarian folk air. Words by D. Radford. WF

"Far to the eastward in Kraakalund." See Kraakalund

Far upon the sea. H. Russell. Words by C. Mackay. FSS 3

"Far yonder, near Whyst." Old Serbian song. e. KSE

Fare thee well ("Schöne wiege") See "Schöne wiege meiner leiden" (Schumann)

Fare thee well, fare thee well, fare thee well, my fairy fay. See Polly-wolly-doodle

"Fare thee well, love, fare thee well." B. Briggs. Words by W. M. Praed. FSS 8

"Fare thee well, lovely year." C. B. Adams. NMS

"Fare-thee-well, my Flemish maiden." See The Flemish maiden and the Frenchman

"Fare thee well, my little village." See In der ferne (Silcher)

"Fare thee well, O earth's dear daughter." See Adieu (Mozart)

"Fare thee well, old world" (Bulgarian song) Air: Tri godini. Words by L. S. Jast. BMC

"Fare thee well, thou true and loving hearted." See The farewell (Beethoven)

"Fare ye on! and the blessing of God." See Moses' death (Lange)

"Fare you well green fields." See A prisoner for life

"Fare-you-well, my own Mary Anne." See My Mary Anne (Tyte)

Farebrother, Mrs C.
"Sing ye the songs of praise"

"Fareweel, O, fareweel." Scottish air. Words by Nairne. MMS

"Fareweel to a' our Scottish fame." Air: A parcel of rogues in a nation. Words by R. Burns. BSR

"Fareweel, ye streams." I. Cooper. Words by T. M. Cunningham. FSS 6

Farewell ("Du undershöna dal") See Farväl (Gustaf)

The farewell ("Fare thee well, thou true and loving hearted") L. von Beethoven. e. WBT

Farewell ("Die höh'n und wälder") See Gute nacht (Franz)

Farewell ("I have come, my dear Zeiserl") Carinthian song. e. KSE

Farewell ("Liebchen ade") See Abschied

A farewell ("Look in my face, dear") F. H. Cowen. Words by D. M. M. Craik. FSS 4

Farewell ("Morgen muss ich") See Lebewohl (Silcher)

Farewell ("Sad am I") See Soiridh

Farewell ("Tho' dark fate hath 'reft me") Irish air: Kitty O'Hara. Words by J. J. Callanan. MMI

Farewell ("The water lingers") H. K. Hadley. Words by F. W. Bourdillon. NML

"Farewell, and adieu to you, fair Spanish ladies." Sea song. KB
For variants see following song of similar title; also Farewell to you, ye fine Spanish ladies

"Farewell and adieu to you, Spanish ladies." Capstan chantey. BE 3
Spanish ladies. SEF 2—SO

"Farewell! but whenever you welcome the hour." Irish air: Moll Roone. Words by T. Moore. FSS 8—JO—MI —MMI—PI

"Farewell! but whenever you welcome the hour." A. F. Keene. Words by T. Moore. MI

Farewell, darling Maggie. N. W. Gade. e. KSN

"Farewell, dear love, since thou wilt needs be gone." See Corydon's farewell (Jones)

"Farewell, dearest Louisa." See "Adieu, chère Louise" (Monsigny)

"Farewell, farewell is a lonely sound." See Good-bye (Engelbrecht)

"Farewell! farewell, my peaceful vale." See The Cracovian maid

"Farewell! farewell, my Polly dear." See The sailor's farewell

"Farewell, farewell to my only child." See Rough and rolling sea

"Farewell, farewell to thee, Araby's daughter." See Araby's daughter (Kiallmark)

"Farewell! farewell, ye limpid springs and floods." See Farewell, ye limpid springs and floods (Händel)

Farewell! for I must leave thee. See The wearing of the green

Farewell forever. M. Connelly. Words by H. B. Farnie. FSS 5—HSC—MPC—NML—WBT—WC

Farewell, good night. Air: Robin Adair. FSS 8

"Farewell if ever fondest prayer." S. Wesley. Words by Lord Byron. JE

"Farewell, lads." Folk song from Sussex. SF 5

"Farewell, Manchester." W. Felton. DM 2

"Farewell, mother! tears are streaming." See The bride's farewell (Williams)

"Farewell, my brave and beautiful child." See Wotans abschied (Wagner)

"Farewell, my brother." Negro song. JP

"Farewell, my dearest Nancy." See Farewell, Nancy

Farewell, my Lilly dear. S. C. Foster (music and words) NMP—WBT

"Farewell, my love, I leave thee." See L'addio del volontario

"Farewell, my lovely Nancy." See Lovely Nancy

"Farewell, my own dear Napoli." See Addio a Napole

"Farewell, my own, light of my life." Sullivan. HSD

Farewell, Nancy. Folk song. SEF 1—SO

"Farewell, O joyous, sunny grove." H. Esser. ꜰTr of Ade du lieber tannenwaldꜰ e. FSS 1—JSE—LA—WBT

"Farewell, O love, forever." See "Adios, adios, amores"

Farewell song. Words from the German. e. HSD—LA—WBT

Farewell, those happy hours. G. Donizetti. FSS 5

"Farewell, thou fair day." See The song of death

"Farewell, thou false Philander" (False Philander) Traditional air. DM 2

"Farewell! thou false Philander." Gouge. BE 8

"Farewell, thou stream." Air: Alace yat I came owr the moor. Words by R. Burns. BSR

"Farewell, thou stream." Air: Nanny's to the greenwood gane. Words by R. Burns. PS 2

Farewell to Fiunary. See Soraidh slàn le Fionn-Airidh

Farewell to Llanberis. Welsh air. Words by S. Taylor. MMW

"Farewell to Lochaber." See Lochaber no more (Reilly?)

"Farewell to love! your country calls you." See "Lascia amor, e siegui Marte" (Händel)

The farewell to my harp ("Dear harp of my country") Air: New Langolee. Words by T. Moore. MI
"Dear harp of my country." MMI

Farewell to my harp ("Harp of my country") E. Philips. ꜰWords by T. Mooreꜰ FSS 8

Farewell to Naples ("Addio mia bella Napoli") See Addio a Napole ("Addio mia bella Napoli")

Farewell to Naples ("Nce simmo a la partenza") See Addio a Napole ("Nce simmo a la partenza")

"Farewell to pleasant Dilston hall." Air: Derwentwater's farewell. PS 2.

"Farewell to Sliev Morna." Irish air. Words by G. Darley. CMF 1—FSI

Farewell to the forest. Mendelssohn ꜰTr of Abschied vom waldeꜰ e. JS—JSE —LA—TFC 2

"Farewell to the Highlands." See My heart's in the Highlands

"Farewell to the home of my childhood." See In the land of my birth (Harroway)

Farewell to the Maig ("A long farewell I send to thee") Irish song. e. MMI

Farewell to the sweetheart. See Abschied vom dirndel

Farewell to the warriors ("Umbe animadjag") Chippewa Indian song. e.in. BF 2

"Farewell to the white house." See The wagoner's lad (Tennessee version)

Farewell to the woods. German air. e. FSS 1

Farewell to thee. See Aloha oe (Liliuokalani)

"Farewell to thee for ever." See Il lacerato spirito (Verdi)

"Farewell to thee, Llanberis." See Farewell to Llanberis

Farewell to you, ye fine Spanish ladies. Chantey. SMW
Variant: "Farewell, and adieu to you, fair Spanish ladies"

"Farewell, winding stream." See Queen Mary's farewell to Alloa

"Farewell, ye dungeons dark and strong." See McPherson's farewell

Farewell, ye limpid springs and floods. G. F. Händel. OS 1—SAS 1

Farewell! your country calls you. See "Lascia amor, e siegui Marte" (Händel)

Fargus, Frederick John. See Conway, Hugh, pseud.

Farlozn. See Forsaken

Farmer, H. G.
Easter bells (Clouston)

Farmer, Henry
Little Sunbeam

Farmer, John
"The corn is ripe for reaping"
Football song. See "Forty years on"
"Forty years on"
"In the field with their flocks abiding"
Onward

Farmer, Thomas
"The night her blackest sables wore"
"When busy fame"

The farmer ("The farmer on the lowland") French folk song. e. DO

The farmer ("I'm glad I am") Children's song. FSS 8

The farmer ("Sedlák, sedlák") Czech folk dance. bo.e. BF 1

The farmer ("Shall I show you") FSS 1 —NMS—WBT—WSC

"Farmer in the dell." Children's song. NMS—WSC

"The farmer on the lowland." See The farmer

The farmer's boy. Folk song. BE 1— FSS 8

The farmer's curst wife. Folk song: North Carolina version. CSE
—Virginia version. CSE

The farmer's daughter of merry Wakefield. Yorkshire song. DM 2

"A farmer's dog leap'd over the stile." See Little Bingo

"The farmer's heart with joy is filled." See The Jamestown homeward bound

The farmyard ("Had me a cat and the cat pleased me") Folk song from North Carolina. CSE
Variant of: The barnyard song

Farmyard song ("Come out, snow-white lambkin") E. Grieg. WBT—WSC

Farnie, Henry Brougham
"Among the lilies" (Czibulka)
Bethlehem (Gounod)
Farewell forever (Connelly)
The guardian angel (Gounod)
The old, old song (Lefort)

Ring on, sweet angelus (Gounod)
The scout (Campana)
The stirrup cup (Arditi)

Farnsforth, Mrs H. A.
"The Easter bells are ringing"
"The Easter dawn is breaking"
"The stars are brightly shining"
"We sing our Saviour's praises"

Farrar, Frederick William
"All jubilant with psalm and hymn" (Bridge)
"In sorrow and in want" (Bridge)
"In the field with their flocks abiding" (Farmer)

"The farrier's daughter stands at the door." See The clang of the hammer (Bonheur)

Farväl (Farewell) Prince Gustaf, duke of Upland. Words by H. Satherberg. e.sw. HSOS

Farwell, Arthur
"Build thee more stately mansions"
"Drücke mich an deine brust"
Meeting. See "Drücke mich an deine brust"

Fase, Henry
Keep a light heart

Fasolo, G. B.
"Cangia, cangia tue voglie"
"Change, O change thy fond wishes." See "Cangia, cangia tue voglie"

Fassone, Vittorio
Margarita

La fata di Amalfi (The fairy of Amalfi) e.i. SMW

"Fate gave the word—the arrow sped." Air: Finlayston house. Words by R. Burns. BSR

"Father a gard'ner made of me." See Ma mi', faites-moi-z-un bouquet

Father Abraham. Negro spiritual. JB
"Father Abraham" (Tell it) KA
"Oh, when I git t' heaven." HR

"Father and I went down to camp." See Yankee Doodle

"Father, dear father, come home with me now." See Come home, father (Work)

"Father eternal, Thou that dost number." See "Ave Maria" (Gounod)

"Father! from a distant land." See Evening hymn of the crusaders (Gade)

"Father, have mercy." See "Padre, perdona" (Hasse)

"Father! I bend to Thee." See Gebet während der schlacht (Himmel)

"Father, I call on Thee." See Gebet während der schlacht (Himmel)

"Father, I cry to Thee." See Gebet während der schlacht (Himmel)

"Father, I scarcely dare to pray." See A last prayer

"Father in heaven! may Thy name be hallow'd." See "Ave Maria" (Gounod)

"Father in heaven, Thy children hear." See Largo (Händel)

"Father in heaven, Thy name be hallowed." See "Ave Maria," no. 1 (Saint-Saëns); "Ave Maria," no. 2 (Saint-Saëns)

Father Joe. F. von Flotow. FSS 8

"Father! love is my only sin." See The hallelujah of love (Musorgskïï)

Father Murphy of the county Wexford. Irish folk song. JOI

Father of heav'n! from Thy eternal throne. G. F. Händel. SAS 2

"Father of love" (St Agnes) J. B. Dykes. Words by W. J. Ivors. JS

Father O'Flynn. Air: Top o' the Cork road. Words by A. P. Graves. GO—PI

"Father, on Thee I call." See Gebet während der schlacht (Himmel)

"Father, thine arms about me throw." C. Gounod. e. SAS 3

"Father, whate'er of earthly bliss." L. Mason. WBT

"Father, whate'er of earthly bliss" (Naomi) FSS 1

"Father, Whose blessing we entreat." J. Benedict. SAS 2

The fatherland. See "Where is the true man's fatherland" (Bellmann)

"Fatte la nonna" (Lullaby) Roman song. e.i. MSI. e. only BSE

Fauré, Gabriel Urbain
After a dream. See Après un rêve
Après un rêve
Les berceaux
The broken flower. See Fleur jetée
Clair de lune
The cradles. See Les berceaux
Evening. See Soir
Fleur jetée
Lydia
A meeting. See Rencontre
Moonlight. See Clair de lune
Nell
Rencontre
"The roses of Ispahan." See "Les roses d'Ispahan"
"Les roses d'Ispahan"
Soir

Faure, Jean Baptiste
Charity. See "Voici l'hiver et son triste cortège"
The crucifix (Tr of Crucifixus)
"Dry ye your tears." See The crucifix
"In dreams I've heard the angels." See Sancta Maria
Palm branches. See Les rameaux
The palms. See Les rameaux
Les rameaux
Sancta Maria
"Voici l'hiver et son triste cortège"
"The winter days so cold." See "Voici l'hiver et son triste cortège"

Favart, Charles Simon
Menuet d'Exaudet (Exaudet)

Favoring breeze. See Frische brise (Stange)

A favorite place. See Lieblingsplätzchen (Mendelssohn)

The favorite spot. See Lieblingsplätzchen (Mendelssohn)

Fawcett, John
"Blest be the tie that binds" (Nägeli)
"Lord, dismiss us with Thy blessing" (Composer unknown) Authorship uncertain

Fawkes, Francis
"When I drain the rosy bowl" (Baildon)

Fay, Stephen
Chow song (Sailors' chantey air)
Get away from dis co'nfiel' (American air)
Levee song (American air)
Poetry (Sullivan)
Red, white and blue (Bergh)

Faye, P. de
Tell her I love her so

Fayles, Philip. See Phile, Philip

La fe. Porto Rican song. s. LCP

Fear a bhàta. See Fhir a bhàta

"Fear no more the heat o' the sun." C. H. H. Parry. Words by W. Shakespeare. VFS

"Fear not, he sayeth, tho' far away." See Lonely

"Fear not, my love, nor deem me all unworthy." See Generoso chi sol brama (Händel)

"Fear not, my sweetheart." See The treasure

"Fear not, O sweetest one." See The treasure

"Fear was within the tossing bark." See Stilling the tempest (Watson)

Fearis, J. S.
An autumn lullaby

The feast of lanterns ("Lanterns lit a year ago") Chinese song. c.e. BF 2

The feast of lanterns ("Will you come into my parlor") J. W. Elliott. TFC 2

The feast of roses. Words by T. Moore. FSS 5

The feast of Vladímir (Kak vo gorodïe stol'no-Kïevskom) Russian folk song. e. SSR 1

"Feasting on milk and honey and wine." See Brothers, don't get weary

Feather bed song. BSS

February. W. B. Olds. Words by A. N. Gilmore. NMS

Fedeli, Ruggiero
"Il mio core non è con me"
My heart is no longer mine. See "Il mio core non è con me"

"Feed your horse we're able." See The trooper and the maid (North Carolina version)

"Feinde ringsum." K. L. T. Gläser. Words by K. G. Cramer. g. ED 2

Feld- und waldlied ("In frischer luft") F. L. A. Kunzen. Words by W. Wackernagel. g. ED 3

Feldeinsamkeit ("In summer fields") J. Brahms. Words by H. Almers. e.g. CMF 1—FO 2
Feldeinsamkeit (Summer dreams) e.g. PG 2

"Feldeinwärts flog ein vögelein." See Herbstlied (Berger)

Die feldflasche ("Helft, leutchen") C. Keller. Words by A. Veith. g. ED 2

Der feldmarschall (Song of the fieldmarshal) German folk song. e. GO

Felix. Irish folk song. JOI

Felton, William
"Farewell, Manchester"
"Give that wreath to me" (same air as "Farewell, Manchester")

La femme avare et le crucifix (The miserwoman and the crucifix) French Canadian folk song. e.f. BFS

"Femme sensible, entends-tu" ("O lady bright") E. N. Méhul. e.f. SOA 4
"Femme sensible, entends-tu" ("O lady fair") e.f. KS 5

"Fenesta che lucivi e mò non luci" ("Thou window that hast shone") Neapolitan song. e.i. MSI

"Fenesta vascia" ("The window low") Calascionata. Neapolitan song. e.i. MSI
"Fenesta vascia" (The closed window.—Water-carrier's song) e.i. SMW

Fenno, Cordelia Brooks
Christmas eve (English folk air)
The village dance (Hungarian air)
The vision (Netherlands air)

Fenollosa, Manuel
"Quien quisiera ser libre que a prendra"
Spanish national hymn. See "Quien quisiera ser libre que a prendra"

Feola, F.
Catarì! Catarì (Luca)
"Fere selvagge" ("Wild woodland creatures") G. Caccini. e.i. KS 1
"Fere selvaggie" ("Beasts of the forest") e.i. FEI 1

Ferguson, Robert
My ain kind dearie, O (Scottish air)

Ferguson, Sir Samuel
The lark in clear air (Irish air)

Ferme les yeux, ô belle maîtresse. J. Massenet. e.f. SOA 2

Fermoy, pseud. See Pigot, John Edward

Fernández Grilo, A.
El planatar (Colón)

Fernández Juncos, Manuel
Borinquen (Astol)
Canción de la mañana (Tavárez)
El huérfano (Campos)
Los reyes de Oriente (Porto Rican air)
Los reyes magos (Colón)

"Fernando, ei del suo cor la brama." See A tanto amor (Donizetti)

"Fernando with all his heart doth love thee." See A tanto amor (Donizetti)

"Ferne dir, o ferne." See Die trennung (Rousseau)

"Ferne in der fremden erde." See Den gefallenen kriegern (Müller)

Ferrari, Gabrielle
"I've such a host of things to tell you." See "J'ai tant de choses à vous dire"
"J'ai tant de choses à vous dire"

The ferret. See Le furet du bois joli (Onfroy de Bréville)

Ferruh ("Oh my Ferruh, so proud") Persian song. e. BMC

The ferry. Round. CST—TFC 2
"A boat, a boat to cross the ferry." FSS 8
Boat to cross the ferry. HSC

Ferryman John. P. Rodney. Words by H. Vaughan. MSF 2

Fesca, Alexander Ernst
"Far from my birthplace." See Der wanderer
Frühlingslied
Im frühling
In springtime. See Im frühling
Spring song. See Frühlingslied
Der wanderer

Fesca, Friedrich Ernst
An die glocke
Rudelsburg (same air as Soldatenabschied)
Soldaten-abschied
Soldier's farewell. See Soldatenabschied

Fesch, William de. See Defesch, William

La festa di Piedigrotta (The festival at Piedigrotta) Neapolitan song. e.i. MSI

Ein' feste burg ("A mighty fortress is our God") M. Luther (music and words) e. EF—FMB—FSS 2 —HSC—JS—TL
"A mighty fortress is our God." e. DSH—OH—WBT—WS
"A mighty fortress" (Luther's hymn) e. BD

Der feste mann ("Wer ist ein mann") H. G. Nägeli. Words by E. M. Arndt. g. ED 3

Festing, Michael Christian
The lass of the mill

The festival at Piedigrotta. See La festa di Piedigrotta

Fet, A.
Come to the realm of roses and wine (Rimskiï-Korsakov)
"I have come to say good morning" (music by Medtner; Rimskiï-Korsakov)
In the silence of the night (Rachmaninov)
"Slumber reigns" (Grechaninov)
Spring (Alferakiï)

Feuchtersleben, Ernst, freiherr von
"Es ist bestimmt in Gottes rat" (Mendelssohn)

Das feuerlied ("Aus feuer ist der geist geschaffen") E. M. Arndt (music and words) g. ED 3

"Les feuilles s'ouvraient sur le bord des branches." See Les cloches (Debussy)

A **few** more years ("Bretherin, a long time
I lived in sin") Negro spiritual. JP
"A **few** more years shall roll" (Chelvey)
Hayne. Words by H. Bonar. FSS 5
Fhir a bhàta (The boatman) Old Highland
air. Words from the Gaelic. e.
SSS
The boatman ("I climb the moun-
tains") e. BMC
Fear a bhata (The boatman) e.
SMW
Fear a bhàta ("I climb the mountains."
—The boatman) e. MMS
Fhir a bhàta ("I climb the mountains")
e. HSSS
"I climb the mountain." e. BF 2
"**Fia** dunque vero." See O mio Fernando
(Donizetti)
Der **fichtenbaum.** See The pine-tree (Ba-
lakirev)
Ein **fichtenbaum** steht einsam. For Nor-
wegian and English translations see
"Pa Norges kolde vidder" (Holter)
Fickle shepherdess. See "Bergère légère"
Fiddle and I. A. Goodeve. Words by
F. E. Weatherly. SOS 2—WA—WSC
Fiddle-de-dee. Nursery song. J. W. El-
liott. FSS 5—JSE—WBT—WSC
Le **fidèle** coeur (The faithful heart) P.
Vidal. Words by Blanchecotte. e.f.
SAM
Fiducit ("Es hatten drei gesellen") Briese-
witz. Words by E. Salomon. g.
ED 1
Field, Eugene
Child and mother (Voigtlaender)
Christmas treasures (Bellini)
Christmasse of olde (Swiss air)
Listen to my tale of woe (Smith)
Little Boy Blue (Smith)
"Wynken, Blynken, and Nod" (Paisiel-
lo)
Field, James T.
"All this night bright angels sing"
"Christ is risen! Christ is risen! He hath
burst His bonds in twain"
"The crown is on the victor's brow"
(Tr of Finita jam sunt praelia)
"Easter flowers are blooming bright"
"Sleep, holy Babe"
"What Child is this"
Field beloved (O, du wogendes feld) S.
Rachmaninoff. Words from the
Russian of A. Tolstoi. e.g. GMF
—NM 2
"O thou billowy harvest-field." e.
SC
The **field** of Monterey. M. D. Sullivan.
HSD
Fielding, Henry
A-hunting we will go (Arne?)
The roast beef of old England (Lever-
idge)
Fields, James Thomas
"We were crowded in the cabin" (mu-
sic by Barker; Woodbury)
"**Fields** and woods are crown'd with ver-
dure." See "Markje grönast"

"**Fields** are rich with golden grain." See
Harvest hymn
"The **fields** are white to harvest." H. F.
Sheppard. Words by S. Baring-Gould.
HC
"**Fields,** forests, meadows lie shrouded in
gloom." See Trepak (Musorgskiĭ)
"**Fields** of gold are glowing." A. H.
Brown. Words by I. J. Postgate. HC
"The **fields** were green." See He stole my
tender heart away
"The **fiend** of darkness each blessing shall
render." See Liebe ist die zarte blühte
(Spohr)
La **fiera** de Mast' Andrea (The fair of Mast'
Andrea) Neapolitan song. e.i. MSI
"A **fierce** flame burnt, at boyhood's dawn."
See For Ireland
"**Fierce** now the flames glow." See "Stride
la vampa" (Verdi)
"**Fiercely** this night the spring gale blus-
ter'd." See Begegnung (Wolf)
"The **fife** and drum sound merrily." T.
Linley. ME
Fifinella. See Punchinello (Tchaikovsky)
"The **fifteenth** day of July." See Lord
Willoughby (Byrd)
A **fig** for those by law protected. See
"See the smoking bowl before us"
The **fight** off Camperdown. C. Dignum.
ME
Fighting on! hallelujah. Negro spiritual.
JP
Fighting on. HR
Figueredo, Pedro
Himno Bayamés
"A **figure** so fair, with eyes of blue rare."
See Et syn (Grieg)
"**Fill** all your glasses full tonight." See
A toast to Dewey
"**Fill** away, fill away for the sea." See
Een liedje van de zee
"La **fill'** du roi d'Espagne." See "La fille
du roi d'Espagne"
"**Fill** high the blue Hirlas." See The Hir-
las horn
"**Fill** high, till with wine ev'ry goblet brim-
ming." See Libiamo ne' lieti calici
(Verdi)
"**Fill** me a bowl." J. Corfe. Words from
Anacreon. e. BE 5
"**Fill** the bumper fair." Air: Bob and
Joan. Words by T. Moore. JO—MI—
MMI
"**Fill** with sparkling wine your glasses."
See Toast to Lehigh
La **fille** à la fontaine (The maid at the
fountain) Folk song: Breton ver-
sion. e.f. TF
—Canadian version. e.f. TF
—Norman version. e.f. TF
La **fille** aux oiseaux (The birdies' maiden-
friend) C. Dancla. Words by E. Che-
valet. e.f. SOS 2
La **fille** de Parthenay (The lass of Mont
TSF
"**Fille** des rois." G. Meyerbeer. e.f.
SOA 4
Parnasse) French folk song. e.f.

La **fille** du coupeur de paille (The straw-cutter's daughter) French folk song. e.f.   TSF

"La **fille** du roi d'Espagne" (The king of Spain's daughter) French Canadian folk song. e.f.   BFS

La **fille** et le chasseur (L'occasion man-quée.—The maiden and the huntsman.—The lost opportunity) Breton song. e.f.   TSF

La **fille** matelot (The sailor-lass) Norman folk song. e.f.   TF

La **fille** vendue au diable (The maiden sold to the devil) French Canadian folk song. e.f.   BFS

Les **filles** de Cadix (The maids of Cadiz) L. Delibes.   Words by A. de Mus-set. e.f.   CM 1—HM 2
   The maidens of Cadiz.   e.   BC

"**Filli**, non t'amo più" ("Phyllis no more I love") G. Carissimi.   e.i.   FEI 1

"**Fin**' de eas', fin' de wes'."   See What yo' gwine to do when yo' lamp burn down

Finch, Francis Miles
   Smoking away (Taylor)

Fine flowers in the valley (Smile na sae sweet, my bonnie babe) Scottish air.   Words by R. Burns. HSSS—MMS—PS 2
   "She sat down below a thorn."   BSR

"**Fine** is the sea, when it calmly is throw-ing."   See Nordhavet (Lindeman)

The **fine** old English gentleman.   C. H. Purday.   BE 2—BOS—DM 2—FSS 5—JO—JSE—WBT
   The old English gentleman.   BS 1

"**Fine** Sally, fine Sally, fine Sally, said he." See The brown girl (Big Laurel, N.C. version)

Finita è pei frati (The monks and their con-vents) Meyerbeer.   e.i.   BS 2

Finita jam sunt praelia.   For English translations see "The crown is on the victor's brow" (Field); "The crown is on the victor's brow" (Hodges); The strife is o'er: the battle done (Palestri-na)

Fink, Gottfried Wilhelm
   Abendlied
   Der geheilte bursche
   Goliath und David
   "Gott mit uns auf allen wegen"
   Der leichtsinn
   Die verlassene
   "While humble shepherds watched their flocks."   See While shepherds watched their flocks
   While shepherds watched their flocks

Finland.   See Finnland (Jordan)

Finland's forest ("Days in the wood."—Suomen salossa) Finnish folk song. e.   BMC
   "Far in the forest" (Suomen salossa) e.fi.   BF 1

Finnish hymn ("O, hasten, hasten all."—"Nyt ylös, sieluni") e.fi.   BF 1

Finnish hymn ("Sons of a race that bled") See Björneborgarne's march

Finnish national air ("Vårt land, vårt land")   See Vårt land, vårt fosterland (Pacius)

Finnish rune ("Tho' from poets") e. KSN—SN

Finnland (Finland) S. Jordan.   Words by V. Stuckenberg.   da.e.   WM 1

Fionn, pseud.   See Whyte, Henry

"**Fiorin** d'argento."   See Stornelli

The **fir-tree.**   See Der tannenbaum

Fire down below.   Capstan chantey.   CR Variant: Fire! fire

Fire! fire.   Capstan chantey.   SE Variant of: Fire down below

"**Fire** in the east and fire in the west."   See Run, Mary, run

The **fire** of home.   G. Worster.   FSS 4—LA

Fireflies (Hotaru) G. Ross.   Words from the Japanese.   e.   RAS

Firefly.   Ojibway Indian song.   in.   BA

"**Firm** is the ice."   G. Verdi.   e.   BD

Firm, united, let us be.   See "Hail, Colum-bia" (Phile)

Firmly I do believe.   See Credo con fermo cuor (Verdi)

"**Firmly** stand, my native land."   Nägeli. HSD

"The **first** came in was a gay ladye."   See Lord Orland's wife

"The **first** came in was dress'd in red."   See Little Matthew Grove

"The **first** came in were lily white."   See Little Musgrave and Lady Barnard (Hindman, Ky. version)

First Christmas gifts.   C. Barnard.   Words by J. Selwyn.   MCS

The **first** Christmas night.   W. H. Sang-ster.   Words by E. Husband.   HC

"The **first** come down was a raven white." See Little Musgrave and Lady Barnard (Hot Springs, N.C. version)

"**First** comes January when the sun lies very low."   See The months of the year

The **first** dance.   See Première danse (Mas-senet)

"The **first** day of spring in the year ninety three."   See Reynard the fox

"The **first** evening in the new home."   See Första aftonen i det nya hemmet (Gei-jer)

"The **first** good joy that Mary had."   See The seven joys of Mary

The **first** kiss.   See Den första kyssen (Sibelius)

First loss.   See Erster verlust (Medtner)

First meeting.   See Erstes begegnen (Grieg)

"The **first** night I was married."   See The lowlands of Holland

The **first** Noel ("Noel! Noel! Noel! Noel! born is the King of Israel") H. J. Gauntlett.   HC

"The first Nowell." Traditional carol.
BD— BOS— BSC— BSS— CST—
DSH— HSD— MCS— MF—TFC 1
—WBT—WCC
"The first Noël." DO
"The first Nowel." DC—HC
"The first of my journeys is very well
known." See The rambler from Clare
The first primrose. See Med en primula-
veris (Grieg)
"The first time in my life." See "Den
första gång i världen"
The first violet ("Als ich das erste veil-
chen erblickt") See Das erste veil-
chen (Mendelssohn)
The first violets ("It's a beautiful day to be
glad in") Bellini. Words by A. H.
Branch. LA
"First violets of April." M. Hauptmann.
MS
"First when Maggie was my care." See
Whistle o'er the 'lave o't
Fischer, Karl Ludwig
Drinking. See Der rheinweinzecher
Grinding (same air as Der rheinwein-
zecher)
"Im kuhlen keller." See Der rhein-
weinzecher
"Im tiefen keller sitz' ich hier." See
Der rheinweinzecher
"In cellar cool." See Der rheinwein-
zecher
Der rheinweinzecher
The three glasses
Fischer, William Gustavus
"I love to tell the story"
Der fischer ("Das wasser rauscht") J. F.
Reichardt. Words by Goethe. g.
ED 2
Das fischermädchen. See "Du schönes
fischermädchen" (Schubert)
Fischleins lied. See The little fish's song
(Arenski)
Fisher, Clellan W.
Champlain (Putnam)
Evening on the lake (Putnam)
Fisher, F. C.
The Christmas story (Keene)
Fisher, William
The northern lass
Fisher, William Arms
"Blow, blow, thou winter wind"
Mammy's lullaby. See Swing low
"Sigh no more, ladies"
Swing low
When Allah spoke
The fisher by the stream. FSS 7
"Fisher in your bright bark rowing." See
O pescador
The fisher-maiden ("Du schönes fischer-
mädchen") See "Du schönes fischer-
mädchen" (Schubert)
The fishermaiden ("Du schönes fischermäd-
chen") See "Du schönes fischer-
mädchen" (Meyerbeer)
The fisherman ("The hush of noon is round
me") Song of the Fiji islands. Words
by L. S. Jast. BMC

The fisherman ("In the Alford's circle fish-
erman am I") Hungarian song. e.
KSE
The fisherman ("Pescador da barca bella")
See O pescador
The fisherman to his son. See Fiskeren
til sønnen (Elling)
Fisherman, thy bait now lower. See Pes-
cator, affonda l'esca (Ponchielli)
Fisherman with hook well baited. See
Pescator, affonda l'esca (Ponchielli)
The fisherman's song ("Eg ser deg ut för
gulggjin") See Strilevise
Fisherman's song ("La luna nova sù sù pel
mare") See Luna nova (Costa)
Fisherman's song ("Oki no kamome ni")
Japanese folk song. e.j. YJ
Fisherman's song ("Up wi' the carls")
See Hey, ca' thro'
The fishermen ("Hurrah! the seaward
breezes") H. Gilbert. Words by J. G.
Whittier. JSE
The fishermen ("Hurrah! the seaward
breezes") C. G. Neefe. Words by J.
G. Whittier. LBR
Fishermen's chorus. D. F. E. Auber. e.
FSS 6—LA
Fishermen's song ("È nata mmiezo mare")
See Michelemmà
"The fishers sat within their boat." H. E.
Button. HC
"The fishers sat within their boat." H.
E. Nichol. HC
The fishes. See The Boston come-all-ye
Fiskeren til sønnen (The fisherman to his
son) C. Elling. Words by K. Janson.
e.n. WM 1
Fitzball, Edward
"From rushy beds of silver Nile"
(Balfe)
"In this old chair my father sat" (Balfe)
Little gipsy Jane (Glover)
"The peace of the valley" (Balfe)
Revenge (Hatton)
Starlight is streaming (Balfe)
"There is a flower that bloometh"
(Wallace)
'Tis the harp in the air (Wallace)
When the bloom is on the rye (Bishop)
Fitzenhagen, W.
Liebeständelei
Love's pleading. See Liebeständelei
Fitzgerald, Lady Edward. See Fitzgerald,
Pamela, lady
Fitzgerald, Joseph
Fairy haunts (Jackson)
"This rock that overhangs the foam"
(Irish air)
Fitzgerald, Pamela, lady
How my childhood fleeted by. See
I remember how my childhood
I remember how my childhood
"I remember, I remember." See I re-
member how my childhood
Song of the maple
Fitzsimmons, C.
"Ring out the anthem, Jesus lives"
"Five hundred faces." Harrow school
song. LA

Five o'clock in the morning. C. Barnard (Claribel) FSS 7—WBT—WL
"Five of them were wise." See The ten virgins
"Fjäriln vingad syns på Haga" (A butterfly at Haga) C. M. Bellman. e.sw. HSOS
Fjeldbyggen (The mountaineer) Norse folk song. Words by P. Dass. n. MAN
"Fjerran i skog, långt fråndig skild." See Herdegossen (Berg)
"Fjorton år tror jag visst att jag va'." See När jag blef sjutton år
The flag ("Our flag, our flag") H. K. Hadley. Words by J. Lewis. TL
The flag ("That ocean-guarded flag of light") L. V. H. Crosby. Words by J. Riley. LBR
The flag goes by ("Hats off! hats off") A. Foote. Words by H. H. Bennett. BD
The flag going by ("O beautiful banner") German folk air. Words by H. H. Harbour. DO
The flag of Carillon. C. W. Sabatier. Words by O. Crémazie. e. BC
The flag of our country ("She's up there") M. S. Mercer. Words by F. Stanton. MP
The flag of our union forever. A. F. M. Custance. [Words by G. P. Morris] MP—NMS
The flag of our union forever. W. V. Wallace. Words by G. P. Morris. FSS 3—WBT
Flag of '76. O. S. Matteson. WBT
"Flag of the free." [R. Wagner] FSS 1— LA—WBT—WSC—WSW
　"Flag of the free" (Our country's flag) MP
"Flags flying ev'rywhere." See Red, white and blue (Bergh)
Flame of love. See Flamme vengeresse (Auber)
"Die flamme lodert, milder schein." See Opferlied (Beethoven)
Flamme vengeresse (Flame of love) D. F. E. Auber. e.f. KS 2
Flanders. Dutch patriotic song. R. Hol. e. KSN—SN
Flatman, Thomas
　"O the sad day" (Humfrey)
"A flaxen headed cowboy." See The ploughboy (Shield)
The flaxen tress. See La treccia bionda
"Flee as a bird." Spanish air. Words by M. S. B. Dana. FSS 2—HSC— HSD—PO—WBT—WSW
Fleeting vision. See Vision fugitive (Massenet)
Flégier, Ange
　Le cor
　The horn. See Le cor
　Love-song. See Stances
　Stances
Fleming, Paul
　Pilgerspruch (Mendelssohn)

The Flemish maiden and the Frenchman. Flemish song. e. KSN
Flemming, Friedrich Ferdinand
　Flemming. See "Praise ye the Father! for His loving-kindness"
　"Hier in des abends traulich ernster stille" (same air as "Integer vitae")
　"Integer vitae" (with original words; also words "O holy Saviour")
　The man of upright life. See "Integer vitae" (with original words)
　"Praise ye the Father! for His loving-kindness"
Flemming, J. J.
　Trifolium
Flemming, Paul. See Fleming, Paul
Flemming. See "Praise ye the Father! for His loving-kindness" (Flemming)
Fles, Anna
　Zonnelied (Rennes)
Fletcher, Alfred
　Indian spring bird (Lieurance)
Fletcher, John
　"Cast your caps and cares away" (Wilson)
　"Orpheus with his lute" (music by Busch; Greene; Manney; Sullivan) See Shakespeare, W. "Orpheus with his lute" (music by Busch; Greene; Manney; Sullivan)
　See also Beaumont, Francis, jt. auth.
Fletcher, T.
　"Hark! sweet angel voices singing" (Belcher)
Fleur jeté (The broken flower) G. Fauré. Words by A. Silvestre. e.f. PG 1
Fleur messagère (A flower message) J. Bouval. Words by H. Passerieu. e.f. HM 1
Une fleur pour réponse. French sea song. e.f. SMW
"La fleur que tu m'avais jetée" ("This flower that you threw to me") G. Bizet. e.f. SOA 3
　"La fleur que tu m'avais jetée" ("This flower you gave to me") e.f. KS 4
　"La fleur que tu m'avais jetée" ("This flower you threw to me") e.f. OPS 3
Fleurs d'amour. See Flowers of love (Borodin)
Fleury, Maria de
　"How tedious and tasteless the hours"
"Flickan gick på ängen" ("To the mead the maidie") Swedish folk song. e.sw. HSOS
"Flickorna de små uti dansen de gå" ("Lassies high and low") Swedish dance song. e.sw. HSOS
Fliehe hin, nachtigall. See Fly away, nightingale (Rubinstein)
The Fliggyboo bird. D. Macgregor. Words by A. A. Powers. CU
"Fling out the banner: let it float." J. B. Calkin. Words by G. W. Doane. BD

"Fling out the banner on the breeze." L. B. Marshall. Words by S. F. Smith. JS

The flitch of bacon. J. Hook. Words by Morris. ME

"Float away." German air. FSS 2

"Floating away like the fountains' spray." See Smoking away (Taylor)

Floating 'mid the lilies. R. W. Atkinson. NML

"Floating on the wind." S. Glover. FSS 3

"The floating scow of old Virginny." See Carry me back to ole Virginny (Christy)

"Flocks and herds all have ceased their browsing." See Noon at the village (Thomas)

"Flocks are sporting." Pastoral. H. Carey. DM 2
A pastoral. PR 2
Spring. MM

"The flocks were wrapt in slumber." R. F. Smith (music and words) HC

Floods of spring (Frühlingsfluthen) S. Rachmaninoff. Words from the Russian of Tiutchev. e.g. NM 2

"Flora gave me fairest flowers." J. Wilbye. BOH

Flora Macdonald's lament ("Far over yon hills") N. Gow. Words by J. Hogg. HSSS—MMS
The lament of Flora Macdonald. PS 1

Flora the lily of the west. Folk song: Lew Down version. BSW
—Yorkshire version. BSW

Flora's holiday. 18th century song. ME

Floreat Rugbeia. Rugby school song. C. E. Moberly (music and words) 1. BOS

Flores a María. Porto Rican song. Gonzales. s. LCP

Florian, Jean Pierre Claris de
"Ah! s'il est dans votre village" (music by Godard; Maria Charlotte Amelia)
"Plaisir d'amour" (Martini)

Florian's song. See "Ah s'il est dans votre village" (Godard)

Florile dalbe. See Colind

Flotow, Friedrich, freiherr von
"Ach! so fromm" (from Martha)
"Ah! so pure, ah! so bright." See "Ach! so fromm"
"Come where flowers are flinging" (from Martha)
"Dismal care." See "Esser mesto"
"Esser mesto" (from Martha. Tr of Bange trauer)
Father Joe
Good-night
"Guide me, O Thou great Jehovah"
"Heaven may to you grant pardon" (from Martha. Tr of Himmel euch vergeben)
Joyous anthem swelling
"Lasst mich euch fragen." See Porter lied
"Lord, with glowing heart I'd praise Thee"
Maidens, bright and fair (from Martha. Tr of Mädchen, brav und treu)
"M'appari tutt' amor." See "Ach! so fromm"
"My childhood's love" (from Leoline)
"O'er my head" (from Martha. Tr of Ja, seit früher kindheit tagen)
Porter lied (from Martha)

"Flow gently, sweet Afton." See Afton water (Old Scottish air); Afton water (Scottish air); Afton water (Hume); Afton water (Spilman)

"Flow, Rio Verde." FSS 8

"Flow, thou regal purple stream." Arnold. Words by J. O'Keefe. BE 3—HSE 1

The flower ("'Tis for all") Herzegovinian folk air. Words by S. H. Ward. WF

The flower among flowers. See Blomman bland blommorna

The flower girl's song ("Tender flowers") Air: Mwynen Dolgellau, or, The fair one of Dolgellau. Words by Miss Rascoe. MMW

"The flower it blaws, it fades, it fa's." See Lovely Polly Stewart

A flower message. See Fleur messagère (Bouval)

The flower of Finae ("Bright red is the sun on the waves of Lough Sheelin") Irish air: Do you remember that night. Words by T. Davis. MMI

The flower of liberty. C. Wilhelm. Words by O. W. Holmes. LBR

Flower of my heart (Ke aloha ihiki mai) C. K. Hopkins. Words by M. Kalaukoa. e.h. HA

Flower song ("Faites-lui mes aveux") See "Faites-lui mes aveux" (Gounod)

Flower song ("Pansies, lilies") See "Pansies, lilies, roses" (Oliver)

Flower song ("Sweet roses fair perfume the air") G. Lange. e. WBT

Flower song ("Ume wa saitaka") Japanese folk song of 19th century. e.j. YJ

"A flower thou resemblest." See "Du bist wie eine blume" (Liszt)

"The flower which you stooped to pick." See Das vergissmeinnicht (Suppé)

"The flow'rets all sleep soundly." See Sandmännchen

"Flow'rets blooming, winds perfuming." See Praise of tears (Schubert)

"The flow'rets close at eve, my love" (Serenade) F. Abt. Words by C. G. Rowe. NML

"Flowerlets grow so brightly." See Peasant-idyl

"The flowers all are sleeping." See Sandmännchen

"The flow'rs for sleep are sighing." See While you sleep (Hadley)

Flowers for the brave. Bellini. Words by E. W. Chapman. FSS 4—WBT

"Flow'rs from the shady greenwood dell." See In memoriam

"Flowers greet him, bird-songs meet him." See Morning song

"The **flow'rs** have gone to beddy." See Sandmännchen

"The **flowers** in garden, field and wood." H. F. Nicholls (music and words) HC

Flowers in the valley. Old English air. BOS

"The **flowers** of earth are blooming." H. E. Nichol (music and words) HC

"**Flowers** of joy." See "Glädjens blomster"

Flowers of love (Fleurs d'amour) A. Borodine. e.f. SC

The **flowers** of May. Arbor day song. FSS 7

Flowers of the forest ("I've heard the liltin'") Old air. Words by J. Elliot. JO

The **flowers** of the forest ("I've seen the smiling of fortune beguiling") Traditional air. Words by A. R. Cockburn. BMC—JO

The **flowers** o' the forest ("I've seen the smiling") MMS—PS 1

The **flowers** of the heath ("The violet and the primrose") Air: Blodau'r grug, or, The heath blossom. MMW

"**Flow'rs** on the meadow bloom." See Love song

"The **flow'rs** so fair have faded." See The birthday of a King (Guglielmo)

"The **flowers** that bloom in the spring." A. Sullivan. Words by W. S. Gilbert. FSS 5—HSD—JSE—OH—WBT

The **flowing** bowl. C. Dibdin. HSE 2

Flowing water ("Tečie voda z javora") Slovak folk song. sl.e. BF 1

Flow'r. For entries beginning Flow'r see Flower

"**Flüchtiger** als wind und welle flieht die zeit." See Lied des lebens

Floyd, A. E.
　　"O'er Bethlehem's hill in time of old"

"**Fly** around, gentle swallows." See Les hirondelles (David)

Fly away, nightingale (Fliehe hin, nachtigall) Rubinstein. Words by Kolzoff. e.g. TS

"**Fly** away, pretty moth." T. H. Bayly (music and words) BE 5—FSS 2—HSE 2—JSE

"**Fly** away to my native land, sweet dove." See The carrier dove (Johnson)

"**Fly,** bird, fly over Fura's waves a-sailing." See "Flyv, fugl, flyv" (Hartmann)

"**Fly,** birdie, fly." See "Flyv, fugl, flyv" (Hartmann)

"**Fly!** fly! ye lazy hours." J. Eccles. BE 4

Fly, my heart, fly hither. See "Derrière chez mon père, vole, mon coeur, vole" (Streabbog)

"**Fly** not yet." Air: Planxty Kelly. Words by T. Moore. JO—MI—MMI —PI

"A **fly** on the brink of a tankard was sipping." See Wine and glory

The **Flying** Cloud. Forecastle song. CR

The **Flying** Dutchman. J. Parry. Words by R. Ryan. BE 1—HSE 3

"**Flying** with flowing sail over the summer sea." See Anchored (Watson)

"**Flyv,** fugl, flyv" ("Fly, bird, fly") J. P. E. Hartmann. Words by G. Winther. da.e. BF 2

"**Fly,** birdie, fly." e. KSN

"The **foe** behind, the deep before." J. Naylor. Words by J. M. Neale. HC

Foerster, Adolph Martin
　　The American eagle
　　Tristram and Iseult

"**Fofae,** fofae." See Song of the Samoan islanders

Fofanov, K.
　　"Dark are now the candles" (Cherepnin)
　　"Stars ethereal" (Kalinnikov. For music by Cherepnin see "Stars of radiant night")
　　"Stars of radiant night" (Cherepnin)

Fogelberg, J.
　　The harvester. See Skördemannen
　　Skördemannen

The **foggy** dew ("Oh! a wan cloud") Old Irish air. Words by A. P. Graves. PI

The **foggy** dew ("One night as I lay") English folk song. FSF

The **foggy** dew ("When I was a bachelor") Irish folk song. JOI

Foix, Gaston, comte de, known as Gaston Phoebus
　　"Aquéros mountagnos" (attributed)
　　"High the craggy mountains." See "Aquéros mountagnos" (attributed)

Fol de rol. College song. CU

"**Fold** thy hands, little one." See Sleep, darling, sleep

Foli, Mme
　　Oh! hear the wild wind blow (Mattei)

"The **folk** of the Tyrol are jolly and gay." See Tyroler (Haibel)

"**Follow!** all who knew her." See Másha

"**Follow,** follow over mountain." S. T. Smith. HSE 2

"**Follow** him nor fearful deem." See Safely follow him (Cooke)

Follow me ("Come, follow, follow, follow") See Come, follow me (Hilton)

Follow me, full of glee. FSS 1—WA—WBT—WSC—WSW

"**Follow** Mother Corn, who breathes forth life." Indian processional air. FI

Follow my leader game song. Indian air. e. FI

Follow the drum. Old English air. Words by Hudson. BE 2—DM 2

Fond fancy. See Svärmeri (Arlberg)

"**Fond** regrets and tender longings." See Saudade

Fondest affections still cling to home. FSS 4

Fontenailles, H. de
　　Obstination
　　A resolve. See Obstination
　　Roses d'hiver
　　Steadfast love. See Obstination
　　Two hearts (Tr of Les deux coeurs)
　　Winter roses. See Roses d'hiver

The **foolish** boy. See The swapping song

"**Foolish** lovers, cease to languish." See Cancion de maja

"**Foolish** women who part with their treasure." See The maid's resolution (Leveridge)

A **foot** ball song ("Our boys are on the football field") Leland Stanford, jr., university song. Air: Marching through Georgia. CHS

The **foot**-traveler. German students' song. e. FSS 5
   The wanderer. e. LA

Football song ("Forty years on") See "Forty years on" (Farmer)

Foote, Arthur William
   The bells
   The flag goes by
   "Golden slumbers kiss your eyes" (from Patient Grisel)
   A lullaby. See "Golden slumbers kiss your eyes"
   "Over the land in glory"

For a' that, an' a' that ("I am a bard") See "I am a bard"

For a' that, an' a' that ("Is there for honest poverty") See A man's a man for a' that

For a' that, an' a' that ("Tho' women's minds") See "Tho' women's minds like winter winds"

For a' the joys that Gowd can gie. See "O Philly, happy be that day"

"**For** a toast, your own will avail me." See Chanson du toréador (Bizet)

For all the pains I bear. See Di tanti palpiti (Rossini)

For an autumn festival. J. André. Words by J. G. Whittier. LBR

"**For**, behold, darkness shall cover." G. F. Händel. SAS 4

For Christmas day. Traditional air. Words by Hall. BSC

"**For** England when with fav'ring gale." See The heaving of the lead (Shield)

For ever and a day. A. A. Mack. Words by T. B. Aldrich. AA

For ever mine (Auf ewig mein) O. Cantor. Words by A. Baker. e.g. SM 1

"**For** full five hundred years I've swung." See Song of the old bell (Barry)

For heaving the anchor. See Opsang

"**For** he's a jolly good fellow." Air: Chanson de Mambron. BSS—EF—TFC 1

"**For** I'm goin' to heav'n above." See O mother, don't you weep

For Ireland. Irish air. Words by S. MacManus. FSI

For Ireland I'd not tell her name ("One eve as I happen'd to stray") Irish song. [Tr of An Eirinn 'ní neósainncéhi] e. MMI

For it's always fair weather. See A stein song (Bullard)

For king and fatherland. See "Wien Neêrlandsch bloed" (Wilms)

"**For** know ye, for know that the Lord is God." See "Erkennet, erkennt, dass der Herr ist Gott" (Jadassohn)

"**For** know ye not." F. Mendelssohn. e. SAS 4

"**For** lack of gold." Scottish air. Words by Austin. PS 1

For liberty. H. Berlioz. BD

For Lincoln we will ever stand. Lincoln university song. A. S. Thompson (music and words) CHS

"**For** love of a brown maid." See La complainte du déserteur

For love of Wooster U. University of Wooster song. Words by H. R. Harington. CHS

"**For** love's sweet moment, wild and brief." See One moment

"**For** me my fair a wreath has wove." Giardini. Words by D. Garrick. DM 1

"**For** me the jasmine buds unfold." See I love, and the world is mine (Johns)

"**For** Midland let us cheer and sing." See Rah-rah-rah for Midland

For music. See Für musik (Franz)

For my love thus to die. See Non m'è grave morir per amore (Marcello)

For my ole massa told me so. See Dandy Jim ob Caroline

"**For** my soul is athirst for God." F. Kiel. e. SAS 2

"**For** Norge, kjaempers födeland" ("To Norway, mother of the brave") A. Grétry. Words by J. N. Brun. e.n. MAN

For once again (Akahi hoi) Kalakaua. e.h. HA

For Patriots' day. Dutch folk air. Words by J. Erwin. DO

"**For** sacred law from east to west." See Law and order (Sullivan)

"**For** seven long years I courted Sally." Windlass chantey. SMW

"**For** seven long years I've borne my care." See Archibald Douglas (Loewe)

"**For** seven years I fed my jay." See "J'ai bien nourri le geai sept ans"

"**For** tenderness formed." Paesiello. FSS 7

"**For** the birthday of a soldier." See Washington's birthday

"**For** the blessings that surround me." See My native land (Abt)

For the czar is making war. Dalmatian folk air. Words by R. R. Whitehead. WF

For the last time. See Zum letzten mal

"**For** the love my heart doth prize." See "Per la gloria d'adorarvi" (Bononcini)

"**For** the pirate who goes on board." See La Corsairienne

For the sake o' somebody. See "My heart is sair, I daurna tell"

For the sight of Van Am raised the hat from my head. See Van Am

"For the study of woman is hard."   See The study of woman (Lehar)

"For thee, dear home."   P. I. Tschaikowsky.   e.   BD

"For thee is laughing nature gay."   Air: Scots queen.   Words by R. Burns. BSR

"For thee, O dear, dear country."   J. D. Herron.   Words by Bernard of Cluny. [Tr of O bona patria, lumina sobria te speculantur]   e.   LA

"For thee, O dear, dear country."   G. E. Oliver.   Words by Bernard of Cluny. [Tr of O bona patria, lumina sobria te speculantur]   e.   LA

"For thus I tell you all."   See Jeremiah's lament (Hiller)

For to admire.   G. F. Cobb.   Words by R. Kipling.   SSS

"For to go and gather berries in the woods."   See Sylvan roundelay (Rimskiï-Korsakov)

For we are jolly good fellows.   See "It's a way we have at Columbia"

"For what could my soul be longing."   See Sans toi (Hardelot)

For you ("They say the years have swallows' wings")   S. Smith.   Words by A. Chapman.   HSD—WBT

"For you, all useless gluttons here."   See Canzone del rabbino (Mascagni)

Forbes, G.
    His love shines over all

Ford, Margaret
    "The Easter bells are ringing" (Farnsworth)
    "The Easter dawn is breaking" (Farnsworth)
    "The stars are brightly shining" (Farnsworth)
    "We sing our Saviour's praises" (Farnsworth)

Ford, Thomas
    Passing by
    "Since first I saw your face"

"Fore mura nce sta 'na picciotta."   See Carmè (Curtis)

The forecastle sailor.   T. A. Geary.   ME

The forest choir.   Ojibway Indian song. e.   BA

"Forest fair, what mighty hand."   See Der jäger abschied (Mendelssohn)

The forest glade.   J. Kreipl.   Words by B. Taylor.   JSE
    "Near in the forest."   LBR

Forest-song ("Auf dem rasen im walde") See Waldes-lied (Kreutzer)

Forest song ("In the forest")   See "In the forest, lonely"

Forest song ("A song for the beautiful trees")   W. H. Jones.   Words by W. H. Venable.   NMS

"Forest, thy green arbors."   See "Selve, voi che le speranze" (Rosa)

Forest voices.   See Waldesgespräch (Jensen)

Foresters bold.   Alpine air.   FSS 7

"La forêt frémit, la forêt qui bruit."   See Song of the dark forest (Borodin)

Forever and forever ("I think of all thou art to me")   F. P. Tosti.   FSS 4—WBT —WL

Forever and forever ("A maid reclined beside a stream")   C. C. Converse.   FSS 1

"Forever with the Lord."   Gounod. Words by J. Montgomery.   HSS 3— HSS 4

Forevermore.   M. Wellings.   Words by H. Mather.   MCS

"Förgäfves uppå stigen" ("In vain upon the pathway")   Swedish folk song.   Words by S. J. Hedborn.   e.sw.   HSOS

Le forgeron.   See The blacksmith (Koeneman)

The forget-me-not ("Die blume die an baches rand")   See Das vergissmeinnicht (Suppé)

The forget-me-not ("Freundlich glänzt an stiller")   See Das vergissmeinnicht (Himmel)

Forget-me-not ("I look on thee, thou little flow'r")   G. Graben-Hoffmann.   [Tr of Vergissmeinnicht]   e.   WBT—WBW

"Forget-me-not" ("Kék nefelejts")   L. Serly.   e.hu.   BF 1

Forget-me-not ("Thou sweetest bloom of evening hour")   C. K. Hopkins.   e.h. HA

"Forget-me-not, forget-me-not, blue-eyed flow'ret by the lake."   See "Forget-me-not" (Serly)

"Forget me not, forget me not, oh thou, Father and Lord."   See "Vergiss mein nicht, vergiss mein nicht" (Bach)

Forget-me-nots ("These fresh forget-me-nots")   H. Parker.   NML

"Forget not the field."   Air: The lamentation of Aughrim.   Words by T. Moore. MI—MMI

"Forget thy grief."   See "Consolati e spera" (Scarlatti)

"Forgive me, Lord, thro' Thy dear Son."   See Evening hymn

Forlorn.   Franz.   [Words from a folk song.   Tr of Herzeleid]   e.   TL

"Forlorn my love, no comfort near."   Air: Let me in this ae night.   Words by R. Burns.   BSR

Forma sublime, eterea.   A. C. Gomes.   e.i. SOA 3

The former life.   See La vie antérieure (Duparc)

"Förr, när min vän var här."   See Den långa dagen (Kjerulf)

Forsaken ("Forsaken, forsaken, forsaken am I")   Koschat.   [Tr of Verlassen bin i]   e.   HSC—HSD—LA— TFC 2—WA—WBT—WL—WSW
    Forsaken ("My love hath now left me")   e.   CHS—MPC—NMH—NML
    Forsaken am I.   e.   FSS 4

Forsaken ("How soon thou, alas")   Dargomijsky.   e.   KSN

Forsaken ("Nightingale, O nightingale") See "Nightingale, O nightingale" (Varlamov)

"**Forsaken**, forsaken, forsaken, standing here." See Petrus klage (Brandts-Buys)

A **forsaken** lover's complaint ("As I walked forth") R. Johnson. DM 1—JE
"As I walked forth one summer day." NG
"As I walked forth one summer's day." BOH—MM

Forsell, F. H.
"When slumbers sweet enfold thee"

"**Forsi** pirchi nun m'ami." See Siciliana

Första aftonen i det nya hemmet (The first evening in the new home) E. G. Geijer (music and words) e.sw. HSOS

"Den **första** gång i världen" ("The first time in my life") Swedish folk song. e.sw. HSOS

Den **första** kyssen (The first kiss) J. Sibelius. Words by J. L. Rimeberg. e.sw. FM

Det **förste** möde (Love's first meeting) E. Grieg. Words by B. Björnson. e.n. SSN

Forster, Adolf Martin
"I love thee." See "Ich liebe dich weil ich dich lieben muss"
"Ich liebe dich weil ich dich lieben muss"

"**Forth** from my sad and darksome cell." See Mad Tom (Coperario)

"**Forth** in Thy name, O Lord, I go" (Canonbury) R. Schumann. Words by C. Wesley. BD—CST

"**Forth** to the battle." See Rhyvelgyrch cadpen Morgan

Fortunatus, Venantius
"Sing the battle" (Monk. Tr of Pange lingua gloriosi proelium certaminis)
"Welcome, happy morning" (Arnold. Tr of Salve, festa dies)

The **fortune** in the daisy. W. G. Becker. Words by P. Cary. LBR

"**Fortune**, my foe." W. Byrd. DM 1— JE 1
Fortune. CO 1

The **fortune** teller ("Down in the valley, come meet me") Air: Open the door softly. Words by T. Moore. MI

"**Forty-nine** bottles." MPC—NMH—WA —WBT—WSW

"**Forty** years on." Harrow school song. J. Farmer. Words by E. E. Bowen. BOS
"Forty years on" (Football song) LA

"**Forward**! forward! forward, O weary feet." See Morning song and march (Gade)

"**Forward** through the ages." A. S. Sullivan. Words by W. C. Gannett. BSS

Fosdick, W. W.
The independent farmer (Root)

Foster, E. W.
My own shall come to me

Foster, Fay
"The nightingales of Flanders"

Foster, Myles Birket
Christmas day in the morning
Christmas eve
Fanfare and carol. See "Hark! I hear, sweet and clear"
Good-night! and Christmas prayer
"Hark! I hear, sweet and clear"
"O Christmas, merry Christmas"
"Seek ye first the kingdom of God" (from Seed-time and harvest)
"Watching in the meadows"
"Your heav'nly Father knoweth" (from Seed-time and harvest)

Foster, Stephen Collins
Alumni song (same air as My old Kentucky home)
Angelina Baker
Away down souf
"Beautiful dreamer"
De Camptown races
"Come where my love lies dreaming"
Dolcy Jones
Dolly Day
Don't bet your money on de Shanghai
Ellen Bayne
Fairy-belle
Farewell, my Lilly dear
Gentle Annie
The Glendy Burke
The good turns pay (same air as Old dog Tray)
Gwine to run all night. See De Camptown races
Hard times come again no more
I'm busy to-day (same air as De Camptown races)
Lou'siana belle
Maggie by my side
Massa's in de cold, cold ground
Melinda May
Music everywhere
My brudder Gum
My old dog Tray. See Old dog Tray
My old Kentucky home
"Nelly Bly"
Nelly was a lady
O, boys, carry me 'long
"Oh! Lemuel"
Oh! Susanna
Oh! Willie, we have miss'd you
Old black Joe
Old dog Tray
Old dog Tray: Boy scout verses
Old folks at home
The old Kentucky home. See My old Kentucky home
Poor old Joe. See Old black Joe
Ring, ring de banjo
Suwanee river. See Old folks at home
Swanee river. See Old folks at home
Uncle Ned
Under the willow she's sleeping
Way down in Ca-i-ro
Willie, we have missed you

Foster, William Prescott
"Beam from yonder star" (Bullard)

"**Found** in the garden, dead in his beauty."
See The burial of the robin (Scott-Gatty)

The **fountain** ("Into the sunshine") German air.   Words by J. R. Lowell.   JSE—LBR

The **fountain** ("Into the sunshine") H. K. Hadley.   Words by J. R. Lowell. TL

Four and twenty elders.   Negro spiritual. DF
    "See fo' an' twenty elders."   HR

Four horses.   See "Quattro cavai"

The **four-leaved** shamrock.   S. Lover (music and words)   JO

"**Four** maidens fair and comely."   See Schnödahöpfl

The **four** seasons in Kioto.   Japanese Koto song.   e.j.   BF 2

"**Four** sturdy horses trotting by."   See "Quattro cavai"

The **four** winds.   L. B. Marshall.   Words by F. D. Sherman.   JS

"**Fourfold** deep lie my roots within the land."   Omaha Indian ritual air.   e. FI

"**Fourteen** years I had seem'd just to be." See När jag blef sjutton år

"**Fourteen** years was I happy and free." See När jag blef sjutton år

The **Fourth** of July ("From dawn of day") German air.   Words by J. Irwin. DO

Fourth of July hymn ("To Thee our Father."—Ortonville)   T.   Hastings. FSS 7

"A **fowler** bold in me you see."   See Der vogelfänger (Mozart)

Fox, G. D.
    Over the garden wall

The **fox** ("The fox went out") Folk song. BSW

Fox and goose.   See Warnung

The **fox-chase**.   See "A southerly wind and a cloudy sky"

"De **fox** hab hole in de groun'."   See Hard trials

The **fox** jumped over the parson's gate. Old English air.   BOS

"The **fox** lay low 'neath the birch-tree root."   See Jngrids vise (Kjerulf)

"The **fox** once lay 'neath birch-tree's root." See Jngrids vise (Kjerulf)

"The **fox** went out one winter night."   See The fox

"**Fox**, you've stolen my gray gander." See Warnung

"The **foxes** have holes in the ground." See Hard trials

Foxwell, A. J.
    "Land of greatness! home of glory" (Haydn)
    "When the spring with magic finger" (Polish air)

"**Frae** the friends and land I love."   Air: Carron side.   Words by R. Burns. BSR

"**Frag'** ob die rose" ("Ask if yon damask rose be sweet")   G. F. Händel. e.g.   NG—PG 3
    "Ask if yon damask rose be sweet." e.   PR 2

"**Fragrant** air."   F. Abt.   FSS 6

Franc, Guillaume
    "All people that on earth do dwell." See Old hundred
    "Be Thou, O God, exalted high."   See Old hundred
    Doxology.   See Old hundred
    Dundee.   See "O God, our help in ages past";   These see His wonders in the deep;   "Thou art the way"
    "From all that dwell" (same air as Old hundred)
    "O God, our help in ages past"
    Old hundred (with words "All people that on earth do dwell"; "Be Thou, O God, exalted high"; "Praise God from Whom all blessings flow"; "With one consent let all the earth")
    Old hundred ("From all that dwell") See "From all that dwell"
    "Praise God from Whom all blessings flow."   See Old hundred
    These see His wonders in the deep (same air as "O God, our help in ages past")
    "Thou art the way: to thee alone" (same air as "O God, our help in ages past")
    "Thou Grace divine, encircling all"
    "With one consent let all the earth." See Old hundred

"**Francewards** returning were two grenadiers."   See Les deux grenadiers (Wagner)

Francillon, Robert Edward
    Bloom on, my roses (Cowen)
    It was a dream (Cowen)

Franck, César Auguste
    The gathered rose.   See Lied
    Lied
    Le mariage des roses
    Marriage of roses.   See Le mariage des roses
    The marriage of the roses.   See Le mariage des roses
    La procession
    Processional.   See La procession

Francke, Hermann
    "Ring on, ye bells" (Abt)

'A **frangesa**.   P. M. Costa.   e.i.   FE

Frank,
    A swain in despair

Franklin is fled away.   17th century song. CO 2

"**Franklin**, my loyal friend, O hone, O hone."   See Franklin is fled away

Franz, Agnes
    Das echo (Greith)
    Im frühling (Mozart)

Franz, Robert
"Ach wenn ich doch ein immchen wär'"
"Ah! were I but a little bee." See "Ach wenn ich doch ein immchen wär'"
Auf dem meere
"Aus meinen grossen schmerzen"
Bitte
"Born of a pain undying." See "Aus meinen grossen schmerzen"
"The butterfly's fallen in love with the rose." See "Der schmetterling ist in die rose verliebt"
"Das ist ein brausen und heulen"
Dedication. See Widmung
Delight of melancholy. See Wonne der wehmuth
"Du liebes auge"
"Er ist gekommen"
"Es hat die rose sich beklagt"
Farewell. See Gute nacht
For music. See Für musik
Forlorn (Tr of Herzeleid)
"From grief I cannot measure." See "Aus meinen grossen schmerzen"
Für musik
Gute nacht
"Hark! how still." See Stille sicherheit
He came. See "Er ist gekommen"
His coming. See "Er ist gekommen"
Im herbst
"Im wunderschönen monat mai"
In autumn. See Im herbst
"In the dreamy wood I wander." See "Wandl' ich in dem wald des abends"
"Lassie with the lips so rosy." See "Mädchen mit dem rothen mündchen"
Die lotosblume
The lotus flower. See Die lotosblume
The lovely month of May. See "Im wunderschönen monat mai"
Marie
"Das meer hat seine perlen"
"Mother, O sing me to rest"
"Mutter, o sing' mich zur ruh'." See "Mother, O sing me to rest"
"Now welcome, my wood." See "Willkommen, mein wald"
"On ocean's breast." See Auf dem meere
"Out of my soul's great sadness." See "Aus meinen grossen schmerzen"
Request. See Bitte
The rose complained. See "Es hat die rose sich beklagt"
"Ruhe süss, liebchen"
Schlummerlied. See "Ruhe süss, liebchen"
"Der schmetterling ist in die rose verliebt"
"The sea its pearls possesses." See "Das meer hat seine perlen"
Serenade. See Ständchen
Slumber song. See "Ruhe süss, liebchen"

Sonntag
Ständchen
Stille sicherheit
Sunday. See Sonntag
"Tempest and storm-furies shrieking." See "Das ist ein brausen und heulen"
"Thou lovely dreamer." See "Du liebes auge"
"Wandl' ich in dem wald des abends"
Widmung
"Willkommen, mein wald"
Wonne der wehmuth
Frau nachtigall ("Nachtigall, ich hör dich singen") Volkslied. g. ED 2
Fräulein Kunigund ("Als wir jüngst in Regensburg waren") Bayrische volksweise. g. ED 1
"Fray Martín." Round. Air: O how lovely is the evening. s. LCP
"Fredda sinistra e nera." See Povero marinar (Mililotti)
Free America. Air: The British grenadiers. Words by J. Warren. HSD—WBT
The **free** and accepted mason. See The freemason's health
"Free from noise, free from strife." See Rural life
"Free from slumber." Nursery song. FSS 6—JSE
"Free from the bustle, care, and strife." J. Collett. ME
Free grace and dying love. See Mary and Martha
Freedom's contribution ("All who of Britons bear the name") C. Dibdin (music and words) ME
Freedom's flag. A. Geibel. Words by J. J. Hood. FSS 1—LA
Freedom's laurel crown defending. See "Oid, mortales, el grito sagrado" (López y Planes)
"Freely go marching along." See Baptizing hymn
The **freemason** ("Come, let us prepare") Air: Saith nos olau, or, Seven light nights. [Words by M. Birkhead] MMW
The **freemason's** health ("Come let us prepare") 17th century air. Words by M. Birkhead. DM 2
"Come let us prepare." CO 2
The free and accepted mason. MM
"Fregt di welt än älte kashyeh." See The old, old questions
"Ein freies leben führnen wir." See Räuberlied
"Freiheit, die ich meine." C. Groos. Words by M. von Schenkendorf. g. ED 1
Freiheit und gleichheit. See "Im kreise froher, kluger zecher" (Döbelin)
Freiligrath, Ferdinand
Der edelfalk (Loewe)

French, Arthur W.
"Take me back to home and mother" (Huntley)
French Canadian song. See Le canard blanc
French Christmas song. e. DCS
French cradle-song. See "Do do l'enfant dor"
French patriotic song. e. FSS 8
French pins. See 'E spingole frangese (Leva)
The French shepherdess and the king of England. See La bergère de France et le roi d'Angleterre
"Frère Jacques." Round. f. FMB
"Are you sleeping." e. BSS—TFC 1
Friar John. e. CST
"Wake from slumber." e. BD
Frescobaldi, Girolamo
"Se l'aura spira"
"When soft the breezes." See "Se l'aura spira"
Fresenius, A.
Sehnsucht (Righini)
"Fresh and fresh and new and new" ("Taza b-taza") Song from India. e.ind. SMW
"Fresh and strong the breeze is blowing." Arne. FSS 7—HSE 2
"The fretted fires of Mora." See The curse of Mora
Die freude ("Komm, freude") D. G. Türk. Words by J. G. E. Maass. g. ED 3
Freude in ehren ("Ein lied in ehren") L. Erk. Words by J. P. Hebel. g. ED 3
Freude in unschuld ("Wonne schwebet") J. A. P. Schulz. Words by F. Brun. g. ED 2
"Freude, schöner Götterfunken." See An die freude
"Freudvoll und leidvoll" ("Joyful and mournful") L. van Beethoven. Words by Goethe. e.g. KF 1
"Freudvoll und leidvoll" (Klärchens lied im Egmont) J. F. Reichardt. Words by Goethe. g. ED 1
Der freund (The friend) H. Wolf. e.g. PG 3—PG 4
"Freunde, wählt euch einen talisman." See Der talisman
"Freundlich glänzt an stiller quelle." See Das vergissmeinnicht (Himmel)
"Freut euch des lebens." H. G. Nägeli. Words by M. Usteri. g. ED 1
"Freut euch des lebens" ("Life let us cherish") e.g. SSG
"Life let us cherish." e. FSS 1— WBT—WSC
"Sow not in sorrow." e. LA
"Friar Bacon walks again." See The devil's progress
Friar John. See "Frère Jacques"
The friar of orders gray. W. Reeve; also attributed to Shield. Words by J. O'Keeffe. AB 3—KF 4
"I am a friar of orders grey." BAS 1 —BE 1—HSE 1

Fricker, Anne
"I built a bridge of fancies"
"There's a sigh in the heart"
Fridenberg, Percy
Sans souci (Composer unknown)
Frieberg, F. A.
Sångarfanan
The singers' banner. See Sångarfanan
"Friedlich ist's, und wald und felder." See The skylark (Grechaninov)
Friedman, Alfred
Die rosen kommen (Cantor)
The friend. See Der freund (Wolf)
"A friend o' mine cam' here yestreen." See My wife has ta'en the gee
"Friend of the brave." Callcott. Words by T. Campbell. HSE 3
"Friend so unhappy, oh, well I know." See "Povero amico! oh! lo conosco il male che tu soffri" (Mascagni)
"Friendly forest, O fragrant shadows." See "Selve amiche, ombrose piante" (Caldara)
"Friends of freedom, swell the song." See Song of temperance (Naumann)
Friends that we never forget. A. Hawthorne (S. Winner) FSS 5
Friendship ("My true love") See "My true love hath my heart" (Marzials)
Friendship ("Why so hopeless and dim is thine eye") A. Derfeldt. e. KSN
Frimann, Claus
Den norske fisker (Norse air)
Frische brise (Favoring breeze) M. Stange. Words by E. Steiger. e.g. KF 3
"Die frist ist um." R. Wagner. e.g. SOA 4
Fritzsch, Martin
"Now, oh, prepare"
The frog galliard. See "Now, O now, I needs must part" (Dowland)
"A frog he went a-courting." Folk song: Big Laurel, N.C. version. CSE
—Hot Springs, N.C. version. CSE
Variant of: The wedding of the frog and mouse
"A frog he would a-wooing go." English folk song. DO—JO
Variant of: The wedding of the frog and mouse
The frog in the spring. Vermont song. SSH
Variant of: The wedding of the frog and mouse
The frog in the well. Folk song from Virginia. CSE
Variant of: The wedding of the frog and mouse
Frog round. BSS
"Frog went a-courting." Kentucky mountain song. WLT
Variant of: The wedding of the frog and mouse
Frohe botschaft ("Kommt a vogerl geflogen") W. Müller. g. ED 1
Frohe botschaft (Joyful message) e.g. SSG
The little bird. e. WBT—WSC

Froher mut ("Weiss nicht, was mir das morgen beut") L. Erk. Words by K. C. Tenner. g. ED 3

"Fröhlich schwebt die flinke lerche." See Sehnsucht (Righini)

Fröhlich soll mein herze springen. For English translations see "All my heart this night rejoices" (Booth); "All my heart this night rejoices" (Esmond); "All my heart this night rejoices" (Maker); "All my heart this night rejoices" (Parker)

"Fröhlich und frei bin ich, juchhei." See Jünglings weihe

"Fröhlich und wohlgemut, la, la, la, la." See Zitherbubens morgenlied (Bornhardt)

"From a dream to my heart thou'rt speaking." See Invocation (Widor)

"From afar returns my well-beloved." See Lullaby ("Sleep, my bonny blue-eyed little treasure")

"From all that dwell" (Old hundred) Guillaume Franc. Words by I. Watts. HSC—HSD—JS The old hundredth. FMB

"From all that dwell" (Duke street) J. Hatton. Words by I. Watts. FSS 7

"From aloft the sailor looks around." Storace. Words by P. Hoare. ME

From an Indian village. T. Lieurance. LS

"From beyond the forest green and dark." See The swan maiden

"From beyond the wooded island." See Sten'ka Razin

"From Boston harbor we set sail." See Boston

"From boyhood trained in battlefield." C. M. von Weber. KS 4

"From celestial seats descending." Händel. OS 3—SAS 3

"From church to church." Tr of Congaudeat turba fidelium. e. HC

"From dawn of day to set of sun." See The Fourth of July

"From day to day my wife doth scold." See Cooper's song (Suppé)

From days of old. See "Es ist bestimmt in Gottes rath" (Mendelssohn)

From depths of Swedish hearts. See "Ur svenska hjertans" (Lindblad)

"From Deutschland I came." See Buy a broom (Lee?)

"From earth's heart a spring there welled." See Källan (Lagercrantz)

"From east and west." J. W. Tufts. Words by A. E. Curtiss. HC

From every graveyard. Negro song. JP

"From ev'ry land and nation." See Our country

"From ev'ry spire on Christmas eve" (Glad hope of the ages) [G. Coles] Words by E. A. Hunter. MCS A Christmas hymn (Duane street) FSS 7

"From every stormy wind that blows." See The mercy seat (Hastings)

"From ev'ry village round." See La chanson de la mariée

"From far away." J. B. Dykes. Words by W. Morris. BSC—HC—MCS

"From far Pacific's Golden gate." See Emerson, our Emerson

"From forest wide and free" (Planting the tree) G. E. Oliver. [Words by E. Shaw] NMS

"From forest wide and free" (Song for Arbor day) J. W. Tufts. Words by E. Shaw. JS

"From forth my sad and darksome sell." See Gray's inn masque

From Ghost Dance canyon. Indian song. T. Lieurance. LS

"From Greenland's icy mountains." L. Mason. Words by R. Heber. FSS 2—WBT—WS Missionary hymn. HSD

"From Greenland's icy mountains." M. Vogrich. [Words by R. Heber] AB 3

"From grief I cannot measure." See "Aus meinen grossen schmerzen" (Franz)

"From heaven above to earth I come." See "Vom himmel hoch da komm' ich her" (Luther)

From heaven high come I here. See "Vom himmel hoch da komm' ich her" (Luther)

"From heav'nly heights to earth descended." See "Le ciel a visité la terre" (Gounod)

"From heavenly maid." W. Byrd. HC

"From heaven's dome above me." See Sorgen

"From heav'n's lofty arch." See "Der himmel hat eine thräne geweint" (Kücken)

"From her balcony green." See "Auf dem grünen balcon" (Wolf)

"From her heart the fever departed." See "De son coeur j'ai calmé la fièvre" (Thomas)

"From high Olympus." See "Vom hoh'n Olymp" (Schnoor)

"From highest heaven I come to tell." See Luther's carol (Higgs)

"From ill do Thou defend me." J. S. Bach. e. WBT

"From Lucerne to Weggis on." See Weggiser lied

From mighty kings. Händel. OS 1

From Monte Pincio. See Vom Monte Pincio (Grieg)

"From morning till night." See The chatterbox

"From my breast dropt a lovely flowret." See Soupir (Widor)

"From my soul's depths." See "Anger is welling" (Rubinstein)

"From my window height." See At the window (Varlamov)

"From my youthful days." See "Aus der jugendzeit" (Radecke)

"From Nippon bridge." Japanese song. e.j. BF 2

"From noise of scarefires rest ye free." See The bell-man (Douty)

"From Oberon in fairyland."   See Dulcina

"From our land we are driven."   See A song of captivity

"From our merry Swiss home we come, we come."   See Our merry Swiss home (Glover)

"From out the dark of night."   See From an Indian village (Lieurance)

"From out the heav'nly fields."   See The spirit of poesy (Arenski)

"From out the tomb the dead heroes are speaking."   See Inno di guerra dei cacciatori delle Alpi (Olivieri)

"From out their peaceful village."   See Jerusalem (Parker)

"From out thy casement glancing."   See "Deh vieni alla finestra" (Mozart)

"From Provence, both land and wave."   See "Di Provenza il mar" (Verdi)

"From realms of glory far away."   See Good news we bring and peace (Simper)

"From rushy beds of silver Nile."   Balfe. Words by E. Fitzball. BS 1

"From silent shades, and the Elysian groves."   See Mad Bess (Purcell)

"From silver gates of Ecbatoun."   See The quest of the three kings (Noble)

"From slumber awaken."   See "Und schläfst du, mein mädchen" (Jensen)

"From swarming highways I now have escaped."   G. Vierling.   e.   SAS 2

"From Swedish hearts."   See "Ur svenska hjertans"   (Lindblad)

"From tender childhood e'er united."   See "Unis dès la plus tendre enfance" (Gluck)

"From Teutschland I came."   See Buy a broom (Lee?)

"From the accursed."   See "Confutatis maledictis" (Verdi)

"From the boughs o'erhead."   See Autumn song

"From the branches dead leaves sever." See Autumn

"From the city gate at dawning grey."   See The children's kingdom (Blumenthal)

"From the cloud on the cliff."   See Aloha oe (Liliuokalani)

"From the coast of Massachusetts."   See The gold and olive (Dubee)

"From the dachstein high."   See Das Steierland (Seidel)

"From the depths."   See "Dal profondo dell' obblio" (Campana)

"From the desert I come to thee."   See Bedouin love-song (Pinsuti)

"From the distant Aar."   See Das Steierland (Seidel)

"From the east breaks the morn."   J. Baildon.   MM

"From the eastern mountains."   G. B. Lissant.   Words by G. Thring.   HC

"From the fair Lavinian shore."   J. Wilson.   Words attributed to Shakespeare.   JE

"From the fields."   See "Dai campi" (Boito)

"From the forest comes the night."   See Die nacht (Strauss)

"From the fort where soldiers are sleeping."   See Reveille

From the great deep, to the great deep we go.   Croatian folk air.   Words by J. Russell.   WF

"From the hagg and hungrie goblin."   See Tom a Bedlam

"From the hillside, from the hollow."   See March of the men of Columbia

"From the hovel door three roads stretch before."   See The three roads (Koeneman)

"From the land of the sky-blue water."   Omaha tribal air.   C. W. Cadman. Words by N. R. Eberhart.   CF

"From the mountain's height."   See "Hoch vom dachstein"

"From the palace she fled."   See Salomé! Salomé (Massenet)

From the Pincian hill.   See Vom Monte Pincio (Grieg)

"From the road I hear the post-horn ring." See Die post (Schubert)

"From the sea's deep hollow faintly pealing."   H. Smart.   Words from Schleswig-Holstein.   e.   SMW

"From the smiling fields of Rakosh."   See The Tiszian

"From the times of youth."   See "Aus der jugendzeit" (Radecke)

"From the Volga was he riding."   See Minka

"From the white blossom'd sloe."   See The thorn (Shield)

"From thee, Eliza, I must go."   Air: Donald.   Words by R. Burns.   BSB

"From thee Eliza, I must go."   Air: Gilderoy.   Words by R. Burns.   BSR

"From thee to me she turns her eyes."   Old English air.   Modern words by S. Baring-Gould.   BE 7

"From these dear mountains."   See Abschied vom dirndel

"From this hour the pledge is given."   Air: Renardine.   Words by T. Moore. MI

"From thy skies sad fate alas! now takes me."   See Patria (Mattei)

"From yonder dark forest what horsemen advance."   See Lützows wilde jagd (Weber)

"From yonder on the mountains."   See "Là-bas, sur ces montagnes"

From youth's happy day.   See "Aus der jugendzeit" (Radecke)

"Frondi tenere e belle."   See Ombra mai fu (Händel)

Le front dans la poussière.   V. de Joncières.   e.f.   SOA 5

"The frozen serpent in my breast."   See Revenge (Hatton)

"Früh, da im osten der morgen kaum tagte."   See Lithuanian song (Chopin)

Die frühen gräber ("Willkommen, o silberner mond")   C. von Gluck.   Words by F. G. Klopstock.   g.   ED 2

Der **frühling** ("Ja, noch einmal konnt'."—Springtide) E. Grieg. Words by A. O. Vinje. e.g. FO 2

Frühling ("Now melts the snow") See Springtime (Tchaikovsky)

"**Frühling** lässt sein blaues band." See Er ist's (Schumann); Er ist's (Wolf)

Frühlings-ankunft ("Nach diesen trüben tagen") F. W. Berner. Words by H. Hoffmann von Fallersleben. g. ED 3

Frühlingsanfang ("Erwacht zum neuen leben") W. A. Mozart. Words by C. C. Sturm. g. ED 2

Frühlingsblumen (Spring-flowers) C. Reinecke. e.g. SOS 1

Frühlingsempfindung ("Alles liebt und paart sich wieder") J. F. X. Sterkel. Words by W. G. Becker. g. ED 1

Frühlingsfeier ("O nimm mich auf in deine heil'gen hallen") F. Dietrich. Words by J. F. W. Steinhausen. g. ED 3

Frühlingsfluthen. See Floods of spring (Rachmaninov)

Frühlingsglaube (Spring faith) F. Ries. ⌈Words by Uhland⌉ e.g. KF 1

Frühlingsglaube (Faith in spring) F. Schubert. Words by Uhland. e.g. KF 2. e. only FTS

Frühlingsgruss an das vaterland ("Wir mir deine freuden") B. Klein. Words by M. von Schenkendorf. g. ED 2

Frühlingsliebe ("Wenn der frühling kommt") Composer unknown. Words by G. Keil. g. ED 1

Frühlingslied ("Es herrscht ein heiliger friede."—Spring song) A. Fesca. e.g. KF 2

Frühlingslied ("Wenn der frühling") See "Wenn der frühling auf die berge steigt" (Coenen)

Frühlingsnacht ("Ueber'm garten durch die lüfte."—Spring night) A. Jensen. ⌈Words by J. von Eichendorff⌉ e.g. KF 2—PG 1

Frühlingsnacht ("Ueber'm garten durch die lüfte."—Spring night) R. Schumann. Words by J. von Eichendorff. e.g. CMF 2—FO 1—GM—PG 1—PG 3

Frühlingszeit. See "Wenn der frühling auf die berge steigt" (Becker)

Fruttchey, F.
"All this night bright angels sing"

Fry, Herbert
As I'd nothing else to do (Hatton)

Fryxell, Anton
Vermeland (Swedish air)

Fu Dio che disse. G. Apolloni. e.i. SOA 5

"**Fu** ki to i u mo." See Fuki

Fuadach nan gàidheal ("I mourn for the Highlands") Air: Lord Lovat's lament. Words by H. Whyte. e. MMS

"**Fuchs,** du hast die gans gestohlen." See Warnung

Fuchslied ("Was kommt dort von der höh") 18th century folk song. Air: Bei hall' ist eine mühle. g. ED 1

Fuentes, Eduardo Sánchez de
La Borinquen
Tú
You. See Tú

Fugitive love. See "Plaisir d'amour" (Martini)

Fuji (Ode to the mountain Fujiyama) G. Ross. Words by Arikoto. e. RAS

Fuki. Koto song. j. SN

Fulkerson, Fannie
The ghost-dance (Bissell)

"**Full** and harmonious." See Hymn to music

"**Full** far away a city stands." See The land of memory

"**Full** fathom five." J. Banister. Words by W. Shakespeare. BSE—KSS

"**Full** fathom five." J. Ireland. Words by W. Shakespeare. KSS

"**Full** fathom five." R. Johnson. Words by W. Shakespeare. VFS

"**Full** fathom five." H. Purcell. Words by W. Shakespeare. KSS—SMW—VFS

"**Full** many fair and famous streams." See The Genesee

"The **full** moon beams on yonder peak." See Romanze aus Rosamunde (Schubert)

"**Full** of beautiful blossoms." See Pleasure-pain (Kjerulf)

Fuller, H. J.
Bonnie. See Bring back my Bonnie to me
Bring back my Bonnie to me
"My Bonnie." See Bring back my Bonnie to me

Fuller, H. N.
On the banks of the old Raritan (Composer unknown)

Fuller and Warren. Cowboy song. LC

Fullerton, Katharine. See Gerould, Mrs Katharine (Fullerton)

"**Füllest** wieder busch und tal." See An den mond (Gackstätter); An den mond (Zelter)

Fulmer, H. T.
Wait till the clouds roll by

Fum, fum, fum. Catalan carol. e. MF

Funeral dirge. G. F. Händel. Words by I. Watts. FSS 4—WBT

Funeral song of the nation. F. Chopin. WBT

Funicoli-funicola ("Behold above the clear horizon."—Sailing o'er a summer sea) L. Denza. Words by C. L. Burnham. EF

Funiculi, funicula ("Some think the world") L. Denza. Words by E. Oxenford. BD—DSH—SSS—WA WBT—WL—WSW
Funiculi-funicula (A merry heart) CST—FE—OH—WC
A merry life. TFC 1—TL

Funiculi-funiculà ("Stasera, Nina mia, io son montato") L. Denza. e.i. MN. i. only FE

"A **funny** old fellow." F. H. Brown. Words by H. Martin. MCS

"**Fuori** mura ci sta una picciotta." See Carmè

Für mädchen ("Jahre kommen, jahre schwinden") V. Righini. Words by K. Reinhard. g. ED 2

Für musik (For music) R. Franz. Words by E. von Geibel. e.g. FF—KF 3—KF 4—PG 2—PG 3

"**Für** wen schuf Gottes güte wohl diese welt so schön." See Endzweck der schöpfung (Miehl)

Le **furet** du bois joli. P. de Bréville. Words by J. Bénédict. f. DO

Le furet du bois joli (The ferret) e.f. HM 1

"The **furnace** fires are shining." See The clang of the forge (Rodney)

"Die **fürstin** zog zu walde." See Der edelfalk (Loewe)

"Una **furtiva** lagrima" ("Down her soft cheek a pearly tear") Donizetti. e.i. OPS 3

"Una furtiva lagrima" ("When stealing down her pallid cheek") e.i. KS 4

Furze bloom. Folk song. BSW

Fuss, Johann
"All's the same to me." See "'s ist mir alles eins" (attributed)
"Oh! to me't's all one." See "'s ist mir alles eins" (attributed)
"'s ist mir alles eins" (attributed)

Fussreise (Tramping) H. Wolf. Words by E. Mörike. e.g. FO 2

The **future** Mrs 'Awkins. Coster song. A. Chevalier (music and words) CU—WA—WBT—WSW

"The **future** still shines brightly." See O luce quest' anima (Donizetti)

"**Fy**, let us a' to Kirkcudbright." Air: Fy, let us a' to the bridal. Words by R. Burns. BSR

Fyles, Philip. See Phile, Philip

Fyllas sang (Fylla's song) F. Rung. Words by A. Oehlenschlager. da.e. SSN

G

"**Gaaer** jeg udi skoven" ("I wander through woodlands") Danish folk song. da.e. BO

The **Gaberlunzie** man ("The pawky auld carle cam' owre the lea") Air: Bung your eye. MMS

Gabriel, Virginia
The light in the window
"Only a face at the window"
Only her love I ask for
Weary
"Words vain words"

Gackstätter, Johann Gottlieb David
An den mond

An **Gadaighe** Grána (The Goddhee Grawna.—The ugly thief) Irish folk song. e. JOI

Gade, Niels Wilhelm
The birch-tree. See Birken
Birken
By the sea shore
"Child Jesus came to earth this day" (Tr of Barn Jesus i en krybbe lad)
Evening hymn of the crusaders (from Die Kreuzfahrer)
Farewell, darling Maggie
Knud Lavard
March violets. See Martsviolerne
Martsviolerne
Morning song and march (from Die Kreuzfahrer)
"O! with pure devotion" (from Die heilige nacht)
Olufs ballade
Polish patriotic song. See Polsk faedrelandssang
Polsk faedrelandssang
Serenade. See By the sea shore
"When onward I am gazing" (from Die heilige nacht)

Gadsby, Henry Robert
Emmanuel, God with us. See "Joy fills our inmost heart to-day"
"Joy fills our inmost heart to-day"

"**Gae** bring to me a pint o' wine." Scottish air. Words by R. Burns. BSB

"**Gae** bring to me a pint o' wine." J. Oswald. Words by R. Burns. PS 1

"Go, fetch to me a pint o' wine." BSR

Gae to the kye wi' me, Johnny. Scottish song. PS 2

Gaelic lullaby ("Hush! the waves are rolling in") Composer unknown. e. JSE
Evening song. e. LA
Old Gaelic lullaby. e. FSS 5

Gaellic lullaby ("Hush! hush! the waves are rolling in") V. Harris. e. TL

Gaffer Gray. Words by T. Holcroft. ME

Gaffi, Bernardo
"Eyes so alluring." See "Luci vezzose"
"Luci vezzose"

Gagliano, Marco da
"Cupid, sleep." See "Dormi, Amore"
"Dormi, Amore" (from La Flora)

Gai lon la. See Le prisonnier de Hollande

"**Gaiczek** zielony." See The green grove

"**Gaiety** here, ever is near." See The merry maidens

Gailhard, Pierre
Le géant
The giant. See Le géant

Gaillard, John Ernest
"After the pangs"
"Come, Roger and Nell" (from The harlequin sorcerer)
The early horn (from The royal chace)
The lover's message
"On a bank of flowers in a summer day"
"Take, oh! take those lips away"

Gaily beats the drum. German song. e. MCS
Marching song. e. FSS 2
Processional march song. e. LA

"Gaily, boys." Hungarian song. e. KSE

Gaily I take my way. G. Linley. HSE 3

"Gaily our boat glides." FSS 5

Gaily sings the lark. Mozart. FSS 5

"Gaily still the moments roll." See Who deeply drinks of wine (Emdin)

"Gaily the troubadour." T. H. Bayly (music and words) DM 1—FSS 1—HSC —HSD—HSE 1—JO—JSE—TFC 1— WBT—WL

Gaily thro' life wander. G. Verdi. e. FSS 4

Gaines, Samuel Richards
The mother-heart

" 'Gainst Thee alone I oft have been rebelling." See Busslied (Beethoven)

Gala water ("Braw, braw lads") Air: Galla water. Words by R. Burns. BSB—MMS
"Braw, braw lads on Yarrow braes." BSR—PS 1

El galán incógnito. Folk song: Spanish American version. e.s. HS
El galán incógnito (The incognito gallant) e.s. HF
—Mexican version. e.s. BF 2
Variant: Incógnito

"The gale whose breath such joy imparts." See The regrets of Bōkhāra (Page)

Galina, G.
"Before my window" (Rachmaninov)
"How sweet the place" (Rachmaninov)
Sorrow in spring (Rachmaninov)

Gall, Jan
"Mädchen mit dem rothen mündchen"
"Maid with lips like blooming roses." See "Mädchen mit dem rothen mündchen"

Gall, Richard
"Romantic Esk" (Scottish air)
"Thy cheek is o' the rose's hue" (Scottish air)

The gallant poacher. See The Lincolnshire poacher

The gallant sailor. Old English air. BE 4

The gallant ship. See Le beau vaisseau

"The gallant soldier." See "Le beau galant"

The gallant troubadour. French song. e. JO

"The gallant vessel is afloat." Air: The Mary Ann. Words from the Welsh. e. MMW

The gallant weaver. Air: The weaver's march. Words by R. Burns. BSB
"Where Cart rins rowin to the sea." BSR

Gallet, Louis
Élégie (Massenet)
Nuit d'Espagne (Massenet)
See also Philippe, Adolphe, jt. auth.

Galliard, John Ernest. See Gaillard, John Ernest

"Gallop, and gallop, and gallop away." See The ride (Shelley)

Galloping dreary dun. Arnold. Words by O'Keeffe. BE 1

Galuppi, Baldassare
"Son troppo vezzose" (from Enrico)
"Thy rose-lips beguiling." See "Son troppo vezzose"

Gamble, John
"A kiss I begged"

Gambling song. Ojibway Indian song. e.in. BA

Game song. Indian song of the plains tribes. in. BF 2

Gamle mor ("My dear old mother") E. Grieg. Words by A. O. Vinje. e.n. SSN
Die alte mutter (The old mother) e.g. FF

"Gane is the day, and mirk's the night." See Guidwife, count the lawin

Ganne, Louis Gaston
Marche lorraine

Gannett, William Channing
"Forward through the ages" (Sullivan)
"Praise to God and thanks we bring" (Elvey)

Ganz, Wilhelm
The little leaves
"Sing, sweet bird"
The story of a star

"Das ganze dorf versammelt sich." Volksweise. Words by J. M. Miller. g. ED 2

Die ganze welt, Herr Jesu Christ. For English translation see "The world itself is blithe and gay"

The gap in the hedge. Irish air. Words by C. Barnard. ES

Garborg, Arne
Das kind der berge (Grieg)

Garden. See When we arrive at home (Ingalls)

"Garden fair, shaded park." See The fair garden (Borodin)

The garden gate. W. T. Parke. Words by Upton. BE 1—HSE 2

The garden of Eden. Negro spiritual. DF

The garden of love. See Le jardin d'amour

The garden of sleep. I. de Lara. Words by C. Scott. FMB

"The gard'ner's pretty daughter." See La Luisella

The gardener's son. Irish folk song. JOI

Gardenia flower (Pua sadinia) D. Nape. e.h. HA

"The gardens of the night soon will bloom in the sky." See Soir (Fauré)

Gardner, of Aberdeenshire
Jenny dang the weaver
"At Willie's wedding on the green." See Jenny dang the weaver

Gardner, A. T.
"Softly the night is sleeping"

Gardons nos moutons (I'll tend my sheep) French folk song. e.f. TSF

The Garibaldi hymn. See Inno di guerra dei cacciatori delle Alpi (Olivieri)

Garibaldi's war hymn. See Inno di guerra dei cacciatori delle Alpi (Olivieri)

The **garland** ("Ah, far in the field."—Aĭ vo
polĭe lipen'ka) Russian Whitsuntide
song. e. SSR 1
The **garland** ("By Celia's arbor")   See
"By Celia's arbor" (Mendelssohn)
"Gar'n wunderlieb's dirndel hab' i heut
woanen g'sehn."   See Schaut's aussi
Garnett, J.
    Star of glory, brightly streaming
Garrett, George Mursell
    My luve is like a red, red rose
    "Oh, my luve's like a red, red rose."
        See My luve is like a red, red rose
Garrett, Louis J.
    "There came three sages from afar"
Garrick, David
    "Care flies from the lad that is merry"
        (Arne)
    "Come, come, my good shepherds"
        (Arne)
    "Come here, fellow servant" (Battishill)
    "For me my fair a wreath has wove"
        (Giardini)
    Heart of oak (Boyce)
    "How little do the landsmen know"
        (Composer unknown) Authorship
        uncertain
    Sweet passion of love (Arne)
Garth, John
    "Care, thou canker of our joys"
Der **gärtner** ("Es war einmal ein gärtner")
    After J. F. L. Sievers. Words by J.
    M. Miller. g. ED 3
Gascon carol. See "Infant so gentle"
The **Gascon** vespers. D. Lee. FSS 6
Gaskell, Mrs Anne
    "I hear the children's voices" (Lemare)
    "Ring out, ye merry bells" (Lemare)
    "Shepherds watching o'er the plain"
        (Lemare)
Gasparini, Carlo Francesco
    "Caro laccio, dolce nodo"
    "Dainty meshes, net enticeful."   See
        "Caro laccio, dolce nodo"
    "Lasciar d'amarti per non penar"
    "Love's bond to sever." See "Lasciar
        d'amarti per non penar"
    "Though pain and sorrow it bring to
        me." See "Lasciar d'amarti per
        non penar"
Gastaldon, Stanislas
    Donna Clara
Gaston Phébus. See Foix, Gaston, comte
    de, known as Gaston Phoebus
"Gat ye me, oh, gat ye me." See The lass
    of Ecclefechan
The **gate** of heaven. B. Tours. Words
    by H. L. D. Jaxone. HSS 2—HSS 3—
    HSS 4
Gates, Mrs Ellen (Huntington)
    Home of the soul (Phillips)
    Your mission (Grannis)
Gates, Jessie Rose
    Your mission (Grannis)   See Gates,
        E. H. Your mission (Grannis)
"Gates of gloom." See "Dell' antro
    magico" (Cavalli)
"Gather around the Christmas tree." J.
    H. Hopkins (music and words) HC

"Gather them in." H. Smith. HC
"Gather roses while they bloom."   See
    Time doth pass away
"Gather ye rosebuds while ye may." W.
    Lawes. Words by R. Herrick.
    BE 6—CO 1—DM 1—MM—PR 1
"Gather your rose-buds while you
    may." BOH—JE
"Gather, you lasses, roses while you may."
    See Advice
"Gathered in the house divine." M. S.
    Skeffington. Words by Moule. HC
The **gathered** rose. See Lied (Franck)
Gathering mushrooms (Aux champignons)
    M. Moussorgsky. Words from the
    Russian of L. Mey. e.f. NM 1
Gathering peascods. Old English air.
    BE 2
Gattie, Mrs J. B.
    "Through the forest"
Gatty, A. L.
    Twenty years ago
Gatty, Sir Alfred Scott-. See Scott-Gatty,
    Sir Alfred
Gatty, R. A.
    I wait, my love, for thee (Scott-Gatty)
"Gaudeamus igitur." Medieval students'
    song. e.l. HSD—LA. l. only
    BOS—CHS—CST—CU—ED 1—FSS 6
    —MPC—SSS—WBT
Gaul, Alfred Robert
    Ascribe unto the Lord worship and
        power (from The ten virgins)
    Choral sanctus (from The holy city)
    Come, ye blessed (from The holy city)
    "Eye hath not seen" (from The holy
        city)
    "Glory be to Thee, O Lord" (from
        Ruth)
    "My soul is athirst for God" (from The
        holy city)
    "No shadows yonder" (from The holy
        city)
    "Now go your ways, my daughters
        well-belov'd" (from Ruth)
    "O gracious Lord, cast down Thine
        eyes" (from Ruth)
    "Sun of my soul, Thou Saviour dear"
        (from The ten virgins)
    These are they which came out of great
        tribulation (from The holy city)
    "Thou art the guide of our youth"
        (from The ten virgins)
    To the Lord our God belong mercies
        (from The holy city)
Gauntlett, Henry John
    Born of Maiden fair. See "Christ is
        born of Maiden fair"
    "Christ is born of Maiden fair"
    The first Noel
    "Jesus lives! thy terrors now"
    "No room in the inn"
    "Once in royal David's city"
    "Upon the snow-clad earth without"
    "The wise men saw a light afar"
Gauthier-Villars, Henry
    A Lucette (Pierné)
    Brises d'autrefois (Hüe)

Gautier, Théophile
Absence (Berlioz)
"Dites, la jeune belle" (music by Berlioz; Gounod)
L'esclave (Lalo)
Les papillons (Chausson)
Soupir (Widor)
Le spectre de la rose (Berlioz)
Villanelle (Berlioz)
Gaveaux, Pierre
Le petit matelot
"Über die beschwerden dieses lebens." See Le petit matelot
Gavotte. See "Je marche sur tous les chemins" (Massenet)
Gavotte du masque (Gavotte of the masquerade) A. Georges. Words by Montjoyeux. e.f. HM 2
Gavotte of the masquerade. See Gavotte du masque (Georges)
Gay, John
Black-eyed Susan (Leveridge)
"Cease your funning" (Composer unknown)
"How happy could I be with either" (Old English air)
The melancholy nymph (Händel)
"My lodging is on the cold ground" (17th century air)
"Three children sliding" (Composer unknown)
"Through all the employments of life" (Old English air)
"'Twas when the seas were roaring" (Händel)
"Youth's the season made for joys" (Traditional air)
The gay bachelor (Chernobrovyĭ, chernoglazyĭ) Russian folk song. e. SSR 1
"Gay dances Bibabutzemann." See Bibabutzemann
The gay fisher boy. See "Des winters als het reghent"
The gay vagabond. See L'heureux vagabond (Bruneau)
The gay young bachelor (Kullan ylistys) Finnish folk song. e.fi. BF 1
"Gayget wahbahdod." See Gambling song
Gayley, Charles M.
The golden bear (Composer unknown)
The yellow and blue (Balfe)
"Gayly dawns the morning." See "Chula la mañana"
Gayman, Charles W.
The scarlet and gray forever
Gaynor, Mrs Jessie Lovel (Smith)
"Shepherd of tender youth"
Thanksgiving song
"Gazing around upon this fair assembly." See "Blick' ich umher" (Wagner)
"Gazing on the iron grating." See Blondel's lied (Schumann)
"Gdy człek w taniec polski stanie." See Polonaise ("Polonaise the dance of nobles")
"Gdy w czystem polu słoneczko świeci." See When the sun shines
"Gdybym ja była słonczkiem na niebie." See The maiden's wish (Chopin)

Gdye tui zvyózdotchka. See "Little star, where art thou" (Musorgskiĭ)
"Gdzież to jedziesz Jasiu." See "Jack, where are you going"
Le géant (The giant) P. Gailhard. Words by V. Hugo. e.f. AB 3
Geary, T. A.
The forecastle sailor
Gebet ("Herr, den ich tief."—Prayer.— "Lord of my inmost heart's recesses") F. Hiller. Words by Geibel. e.g. HSS 1 —HSS 2—HSS 3—HSS 4—KF 2— KF 4
Gebet ("Leise, leise, fromme weise") K. M. von Weber. Words by F. Kind. g. ED 3
Evening song. e. LA
Prayer. e. FSS 1—WBT—WSC
"Songs revealing." e. LA
Also in "Wie nahte mir der schlummer" (Weber) KS 1—PP
Gebet an den heiligen Christ ("Du lieber heil'ger frommer Christ") G. Siegert. Words by E. M. Arndt. g. ED 1
Gebet der Elisabeth (Elizabeth's prayer) R. Wagner. e.g. OPS 1
"Allmächt'ge Jungfrau." e.g. SOA 1
"Allmächt'ge Jungfrau" (Elizabeth's prayer) e.g. SS 2
Gebet des Amfortas. R. Wagner. e.g. SOA 4
Gebet vor der schlacht ("Hör' uns, Allmächtiger") Air: O sanctissima etc. Words by T. Körner. g. ED 2
Gebet vor der schlacht ("Hör' uns, Allmächtiger') K. M. von Weber. Words by T. Körner. g. ED 3
Gebet während der schlacht ("Vater, ich rufe dich") F. H. Himmel. Words by T. Körner. g. ED 1
The battle prayer. e.g. MP. e. only BSE—FSS 5—HSS 4—JO— JSE—KF 4—LA
Körner's battle prayer. e. HSD
Prayer. e. TL
Geboren ist uns ein Kinderlein. For English translation see "To us is born a little Child"
"Die gedanken sind frei" ("The thoughts are free") German song. e.g. BF 2
Geddes, Alexander
Lewie Gordon (Jacobite air)
Geddes, James
"O spirit of the nation, come" (Tufts)
Geddes, Sir William Duguid
Canticum in almam matrem (Aberdeen university song)
Geer, George Jarvis
"Hark! what mean those holy voices"
Den gefallenen kriegern. See entry under Den
Der gefangene admiral (The captive admiral) E. Lassen. e.g. AB 2
Die gefangenen sänger ("Vöglein, einsam in dem bauer") C. M. von Weber. Words by M. von Schenkendorf. g. ED 2
Gefunden ("Ich ging im walde") J. Gersbach. Words by Goethe. g. ED 2

Der **geheilte** bursche ("Ich hatt' mal einen schweren stand") G. W. Fink (music and words) g. ED 2

"Gei ich mir shpatsirn." See Forsaken ("Going out a-walking")

"Gei na gori ta zhentsï zhnut'." See Reapers on the mountain

Geibel, Adam
Freedom's flag

Geibel, Emanuel
"At Easter morn the lark ascending" (Knecht)
Burschenlust (Folk air; also music by Lyra)
Für musik (Franz)
Gebet (Hiller)
Der knabe mit dem wunderhorn (Schumann)
Lied des alten im bart (Löffler)
Lob der edlen musica (Volksweise)
Mädchenlied (Raff)
"Mein herz ist wie die dunkle nacht" (Mendelssohn)
O tempora! O mores (Student song)
Reue (Lachner)
"Wenn sich zwei herzen scheiden" (Mendelssohn)

Geijer, Erik Gustav
Evening and peace. See Kväll och frid
The first evening in the new home. See Första aftonen i det nya hemmet
Första aftonen i det nya hemmet
Kväll och frid

Geirionydd, Ieuan Glan. See Evans, Evan

"Geist der liebe, trage mich empor." See Vision (Claus)

Eine **geisterstimme.** See Schill

Des **geistes** gesang. See entry under Des

Gelähmter flug ("Wär' ich ein wilder falke") J. F. Reichardt. Words after a folk song. g. ED 3

"Gelb rollt mir zu füssen" ("Golden at my feet") A. Rubinstein. Words by F. von Bodenstedt. e.g. FF—FO 1
"Gelb rollt mir zu füssen" ("Gold rolls here beneath me") e.f.g. KF 4
"Yellow at my feet." e. BD

Gell, A. W. Hamilton-. See Hamilton-Gell, A. W.

Gellerstedt, Albert Teodor
"Det fins en gosse och han är min" (Hallén)
En liten visa (Hallström)

Gellert, Christian Fürchtegott
Busslied (Beethoven)
"Dies ist der tag, den Gott gemacht" (Luther)
Die ehre Gottes aus der natur (Beethoven)
"Gott, deine güte reicht" (Beethoven)
"Jesus lives! no longer now" (Composer unknown. Tr of Jesus lebt, mit ihm auch ich)
"Now, oh, prepare" (Fritzsch)

"Gelobet seis tu Jesu Christ." B. Gesius. ɾWords by M. Lutherɹ g. HC

"Gelobet seis tu Jesu Christ." For English translation with a different air see "All praise to thee" (Costello)

Gelübde ("Ich hab mich ergeben") Volksweise. Words by H. F. Massmann. g. ED 1

"Geluckig is het land." See Geluckig vaderland

Geluckig vaderland ("Oh, happy is the land") Dutch song. d.e. BDF

Das **gemälde** ("Maler, mal mir mein liebchen") g. ED 2

Gems and flowers of rich perfume. C. S. Baker. HC

Genée, Richard
Anna song. See "Was ist denn heut' wohl fuer ein tag"
As the wind blows
Sweet bells are chiming
"Was ist denn heut' wohl fuer ein tag" (from Nanon)

"General Florido! indeed, fo' true dey can't catch me." See Runaway's song of defiance

The **general** roll. Negro spiritual. NMP
Variant of: General roll call

General roll call. Negro spiritual. HR
Variants: The general roll; "I'll be there in the morning"

"General Taylor." Pulling chantey. SE

Generalbeichte ("Lasset heut im edeln kreis") Air: Gaudeamus igitur. Words by Goethe. g. ED 2

Generoso chi sol brama. G. F. Händel. e.i. SOA 2

The **Genesee.** University of Rochester song. Words by B. H. Wallace. CHS

"Geniesst den reiz des lebens." See Genuss des lebens

Genrebillede (Idyl) J. Backer-Lunde. Words by J. P. Jacobsen. da.e. WM 1

"Gentle airs, melodious strains." G. F. Händel. SAS 3

Gentle Annie. S. C. Foster (music and words) FSS 7—HSD—TFC 2—WBT—WL

The **gentle** bird ("O sing again, my gentle bird") Air: Y 'deryn pur. Words by Talhaiarn. MMW

Gentle birds above are sweetly singing. See Sailors' and soldiers' memorial day

Gentle breezes sighing. G. Donizetti. FSS 8

"Gentle flowers in the dew." See "Faites-lui mes aveux" (Gounod)

A **gentle** hint. F. Riker. Words by W. Packard. BD

"Gentle is the fair stream flowing." Air: I live not where I love. Words by G. Macfarren. DM 2

The **gentle** maiden ("There's one that is pure as an angel") Old Irish air. Words by H. Boulton. BOS

"Gentle maiden, those eyes remind me." V. Bellini. ɾTr of Tu non sai in quel begli occhiɹ e. WBT
Aria of Rudolph. e. FSS 7

Gentle Mary. Words by D. M. Muloch. FSS 4

"Gentle moon, that movest yonder." See An den mond

Gentle Nettie Moore. G. S. Pike. Words by M. S. Pike. NMP—WBT

"Gentle Saviour, day and night." French Flanders song. e. HC

"Gentle shade, well beloved." See "Ombra cara, amorosa" (Traetta)

"Gentle shepherd, will you love me." See "Se tu m'ami" (Pergolesi)

"Gentle spirit, well beloved." See "Ombra cara, amosa" (Traetta)

"Gentle tears, oh! say where are ye flown." See Tears (Varlamov)

"Gentle waves upon the deep." See All things love thee, so do I (Horn)

Gentle words and kindly deeds. Words by G. Cooper. FSS 1

"Gentle Zephyr." W. S. Bennett. BAS 2

"Gentle Zitella, whither away." See Love's ritornella (Planché)

"A gentleman came to our house." See Aunt Leah's song

"Gently blaw, ye eastern breezes." See Oh, she's bonnie

"Gently blow, oh, southern wind." See Take my love to Rosalie (Dickhaut)

"Gently falls the winter snow." H. S. Irons. Words by E. Caswall. HC

"Gently, gently sighs the breeze." See Gently sighs the breeze (Glover)

Gently, Johnny my Jingalo. Folk song. FSF—SEF 1—SO

Gently lead us (Rathbun) I. Conkey. Words by T. Hastings. FSS 2

"Gently rest" (The mother's song) Kücken. Words by W. Powell. FSS 4
Slumber song. LA

Gently sighs the breeze. S. Glover. Words by J. E. Carpenter. FSS 4—FSS 7

"Gently swaying, slowly rise." See Snake-charmer's song

"Gently the breezes blow thro' the forest." See Night song

"The gentry to the King's Head go." See The taverns' song (Young)

Genuss des lebens ("Geniesst den reiz des lebens") Composer unknown. Words by F. Jünger. g. ED 2

Geoghegan, J. B.
Down in a coal mine
Ten thousand miles away

Geography song. Words by M. B. C. Slade. FSS 1—WBT—WSC

Geordie. Folk song. SEF 1—SO
—Cambridgeshire version. SF 2
—Black Mountain, N.C. version. CSE
—Hot Springs, N.C. version. CSE
—Swannanoah, N.C. version. CSE

"George Collins." See Giles Collins

George Reilly. Folk song: Black Mountain, N.C. version. CSE
—Hot Springs, N.C. version. CSE
Variant: John Riley

George Ridler's oven. Gloucestershire folk song. BE 6

"George Washington was a very fine man." See The blue and the tan

Georges, Alexandre
Gavotte du masque
Gavotte of the masquerade. See Gavotte du masque

"Georgie Porgie." FMB—WSC

Georgieri, Giulio
Beautiful Istria. See Oll Istria
Oll Istria

Geraldine. W. C. Levey. Words by H. C. Hunter. FSS 6

Gérard, Rosemonde. See Rostand, Mme Rosemonde Gérard

"Gerechter Gott" ("Almighty powers") R. Wagner. e.g. OPS 2—SOA 2
"Gerechter Gott" ("Avenging God") e.g. KS 2

Gerhard, Wilhelm
Der kleine tambour (Pohlenz)
Liebes-A-B-C (Pohlenz)
Matrosenlied (Pohlenz)

Gerhardt, Paulus
"All my heart this night rejoices" (music by Booth; Esmond; Maker; Parker. Tr of Fröhlich soll mein herze springen)
"Give to the winds" (Composer unknown. Tr of Befiehl du deine wege)
"Holy Spirit, Source of gladness" (Naumann. Tr of O du allersüsste freude)
"Wake, my heart, while round thee swelling" (Kruger)
"Would'st thou magnify the story" (Ebeling. Tr of Alle, die ihr Gott zu ehren)

Gericke, J. L.
Die wahrsagerin (Seidel)

Germaine. French folk song. e.f. TSF

German, Edward
The yeomen of England

German cradle-song ("Lulul labeichen") See "Lulul labeichen, koch' mei'm kind ein breichen"

German cradle song ("Schlaf, kindchen") See "Schlaf, kindchen, schlaf"

The German fatherland. See Des Deutschen vaterland (Reichardt)

German grandfather dance. See Grossvaterlied

The German watchman's song. I. Heffernan. e. FSS 3—JO

The German's fatherland. See Des Deutschen vaterland (Reichardt)

Ho gerō-Demōs. See Old Demos and his rifle (Carreris)

Gerould, Mrs Katharine (Fullerton)
"Fair Radcliffe" (Composer unknown)

Gersbach, Joseph
Barbarossa
Des sängers fluch
Das eine lied
Einkehr
Gefunden
Morgenlied

Gerstenberg, Johann Daniel
Trinklied
Der **gesang** ("Wo man singet") Volks-
weise. Words by J. G. Seume. g.
ED 1
Gesang ausziehender krieger ("Hinaus in
die ferne") A. Methfessel (music and
words) g. ED 1
Gesang der mönche ("Rasch tritt der tod")
L. van Beethoven. Words by F. von
Schiller. g. ED 3
Der **gesang** Miriams. See "Sound the loud
timbrel" (Molique)
Gesang Weyla's (Weyla's song) H. Wolf.
Words by E. Mörike. e.g. FO 2—
GM—PG 4
Gesellschaftslied. See "Im kreise froher,
kluger zecher" (Folk air)
Gesius, Bartholomäus
"Gelobet seis tu Jesu Christ"
Das **geständnis** ("Wohl gibt es der mäd-
chen") A. André. Words by W. G.
Becker. g. ED 3
"**Gestern** abend in der stillen ruh'." See
Im wald bei der amsel
"**Gestern** abend war vetter Michel hier."
See Vetter Michel
"**Gestern** beim mondenschein ging ich spa-
zieren." See Beim mondenschein
"**Gestern,** brüder, könnt ihr's glauben."
See Der tod
"**Gesund** und frohen mutes geniessen wir
des gutes." See Tischlied (Schulz)
Get away from dis co'nfiel'. American
song. Words by S. Fay. BSS
"**Get** down, get down, get down, says he."
See Lady Isabel and the elf knight (Al-
lanstand, N.C. version)
Get on board. Negro spiritual. BSS
Git on board little children. HR
Git on board, little chillen. JB
"The gospel train." JP—NMP
"**Get** out de population an' raise yo' voices
high." See Poor mourner
"**Get** thee up! there, thy offspring I do per-
mit thee to behold." See Eri tu che
macchiavi (Verdi)
Get up and bar the door ("It fell about
the Mart'mas time") Scottish song.
MMS—PS 1
"**Get** up, get up, look behind you." See
Huldre-kvaee
"**Get** up, get up pretty Polly, he says."
See Six kings daughters
"**Get** up, lazy beauty." See "Levántese
niña"
Get you ready, there's a meeting here to-
night. See There's a meeting here to-
night
Getting ready to die. Negro spiritual.
FSS 5—JP
Gevaert, François Auguste
The sleep of the infant Jesus. (Tr of
Entre le boeuf et l'âne gris)
Geyer, Johann Aegidius
Decoration day
The **ghost-dance.** Pomona college song.
A. D. Bissell. Words by F. Fulker-
son. CHS

"**Ghost** dance up on Indian hill." See The
ghost-dance (Bissell)
"**Già** il sole dal Gange" ("O'er Ganges now
launches") A. Scarlatti. e.i. PA 2
Già l'ira m'abbandona. Meyerbeer. [Tr
of Ô toi qui m'abandonnes] e.i.
OPS 2
"**Già** son fuggiti ahi mè." See Tradetore
Giacomo, Salvatore di
Luna nova (Costa)
Marechiare (Tosti)
Mena, me' (Costa)
Oje Carulì (Costa)
"'E spingole frangese" (Leva)
The **giant.** See Le géant (Gailhard)
Giardini, Felice
The Child is born
"Come, Thou almighty King"
"For me my fair a wreath has wove"
"It came upon the midnight clear"
Italian hymn. See "Come, Thou al-
mighty King"; "Rise, glorious Con-
queror"; "Thou, Whose almighty
word"
"Rise, glorious Conqueror" (same air
as "Come, Thou almighty King")
Song of the angels. See "It came
upon the midnight clear"
"Thou Whose almighty word" (same
air as "Come, Thou almighty
King")
"**Gib,** blanke schwester, gib mir wein." See
Die wahrsagerin (Seidel)
Gib me dat water-million. T. P. Westen-
dorf. CHS
"**Gib** mir die blumen, gib mir den kranz."
Volksweise. Words by C. A. Vulpius.
g. ED 3
Gibbons, Orlando
"The silver swan"
Gibert, Mirra Lochwitzky-. See Lokhvit-
skaĩa, Mirra Aleksandrovna
Gideon's band ("I hail to my sister")
Negro spiritual. JP
De band o' Gideon. JB
Gideon's band (De milk-white horses)
HR
Gideon's band ("Oh, keep your hat upon
your head") Negro song. NMP—
WBT
"**Gif** akt! hvem där." See Lifdrabanten
och kung Erik (Lindblad)
The **gift** ("A mother was watching") A. H.
Behrend. Words by F. E. Weatherly.
WBW
The **gift** of peace. Otoe Indian song.
e.in. FIS
Gil, Constantino
Niña Pancha (Romea y Valverde)
Gilbert, Mrs Ann (Taylor) See Taylor,
Ann
Gilbert, Henry Franklin Belknap
Croon of the dew
Gilbert, Hermann
Beim rheinwein
The fishermen
Gilbert, Rosa (Mulholland), lady
"The silent bird is hid in the boughs"
(Irish air)

Gilbert, Samuel J.
"Hark! what mean those holy voices"
Gilbert, W.
"Sing we now of joy and gladness"
Gilbert, Sir William Schwenck
The distant shore (Sullivan)
"The flowers that bloom in the spring" (Sullivan)
"Henceforth, Strephon" (Sullivan)
"I hear the soft note" (Sullivan)
"Sorry her lot" (Sullivan)
Tit willow (Sullivan)
Gilchrist, William Wallace
Dolphin lullaby
"Home they brought her warrior"
The piper
"Prayers of love"
We two together
Whip-poor-will
Gilder, Richard Watson
A midsummer song (Abt)
Gilderoy ("O, Gilderoy was a bonnie boy") Scottish song. MSS—PS 1
Gile, and Remick,
Our honored Bates (Composer unknown)
Giles, Thomas
"Triumph now with joy and mirth"
Giles Collins. Folk song: Allanstand, N.C. version. CSE
—Big Laurel, N.C. version. CSE
—Henderson co., N.C. version. CSE
—Hot Springs, N.C. version. CSE
—Tennessee version. CSE
"Giles Scroggins." BE 1—DM 2
Gilfillan, Robert
The emigrant's complaint (Scottish air)
My ain countrie (Scottish air)
Gilfillan, William
The braes aboon Bonaw (Scottish air)
Gilholy, Barry M.
"The lead strikes English ground"
Gill, Edward J.
Madoline (Nelson)
Gill, J.
"When Lubin sings of youth's delight" (Hobbs)
Gill, William Henry
"Singing the reapers homeward come"
"Three kings from out the Orient"
An gille donn (The brown lad) Waulking song from the Hebrides. e.ga. BF 2
Na gillean mo rùin (Hogmanay night) New Year's song from the Hebrides. e.ga. BF 2
Gilm zu Rosenegg, Hermann von
All souls' day (Lassen. Tr of Aller-seelen)
Allerseelen (Strauss)
Die nacht (Strauss)
Zueignung (Wolf)
Gilman, Mrs Caroline (Howard)
Trancadillo (Brown)
Gilmore, Anna Neil
February (Olds)
Gilmore, H. G.
"Breaks the joyful Easter dawn"
Gilmore, Joseph Henry
"He leadeth me" (Bradbury)

Gilmore, Patrick Sarsfield
"When Johnny comes marching home"
"Gilt by the sun, like embers glowing." See Sonnet d'amour (Thomé)
Gimme dat ol'-time religion. See This old time religion
"Gin a body meet a body." See Comin' thro' the rye
"Gin I had a wee house." See Bide ye yet
"Gin Johnnie kent I was na weel." See I'm a' doun for lack o' Johnnie
"Gin living worth could win my heart." See The waefu' heart
Ginisty, Paul
Chanson slave (Chaminade)
"Gioite al canto mio." See Invocazione di Orfeo (Peri)
Giordani, Giuseppe
"Canst thou believe." See "Caro mio ben"
"Caro mio ben"
"Darling, my own." See "Caro mio ben"
"My dearest love." See "Caro mio ben"
Queen Mary's lament (attributed)
"Thou, all my bliss." See "Caro mio ben"
"Turn once again." See "Caro mio ben"
Giorno d'orrore. For English translation see "Dark day of horror" (Rossini)
"Gipsies three across the meadows once took their way." See A gipsy wooing
The gipsy ("Cuando taca la guitarra") See La gitana
The gipsy ("From the smiling fields") See The Tiszian
The gipsy countess: part 1 ("There came an earl a riding by") Folk song. BSW
The gipsy countess: part 2 ("Three gipsies stood at the castle gate") Folk song. BSW
"The gipsy fires are burning." See Gipsy John (Clay)
The gipsy hat. J. Hook. Words by Upton. ME
Gipsy John. F. Clay. Words by G. J. Whyte-Melville. KF 4—SM 4
The gipsy king. W. West. Words by Goethe. e. BE 3
The gipsy-maid. See Die zigeunerin (Wolf)
Gipsy song ("Come with the gipsy bride") M. W. Balfe. WBT
"Come with the gipsy bride." FSS 1 —JSE
Gipsy song ("'Tis of a young damsel") Sussex song. MM
A gipsy wooing (Die werbung: Zigeuner-lied) Russian folk song. e. GO
The gipsy's song ("Dearest maiden, thou with the crimson cheeks") A. Lvoff. e. KSN
The girl and the wherry. See La barquillera
The girl from Capua. See La Capuana

The **girl** I left behind me ("The dames of France are fond and free") 18th century air: Brighton camp. HSD—JO

The **girl** I left behind me ("The hour was sad I left the maid") 18th century air: Brighton camp. Words by S. Lover. EF—PI

The **girl** I left behind me ("I'm lonesome since I cross'd the hill") 18th century air: Brighton camp. American version of words. BE 4—BOS—BSE—HSE 1—JSE—ME —MP—NMH—WA— WBT—WL—WSW

The girl I left behind me (Brighton camp) CO 2—FSS 2

The girl I've left behind me. DM 1

The **girl** of Dunbwy ("'Tis pretty to see the girl of Dunbwy") Irish air: Oganaighe oig. Words by T. Davis. MMI

The **girl** of Sorrento. See La vera Sorrentina

The **girl** of the seasons. J. Sanderson. Words by E. Button. ME

The **girl** who would not dance (Kak u nashego shirokago dvora) Russian folk song. e. SSR 1

The **girl** with the golden hair. See "Me gustan todas"

"**Girls** and boys come out to play." WBT —WSC

The **girls** around Cape Horn. Forecastle song. CR

Girls at the river ("Mati zakliče") Slovenian folk song. e.slo. BF 1

"The **girls** scornful glances throw." See Der tost (Koschat)

Giroflé, girofla. French folk song. f. DO

Git on board, little children. See Get on board

La **gitana** (The gipsy) Pyrenean song. e.s. SSP

"**Giulia** gentil" (Fair Julia) Tuscan song. e.i. MSI

"**Giunse** alfin il momento." Mozart. e.i. PP
    Also in Deh vieni, non tardar (Mozart) SOA 1—KS 2

Give a fee. Song for young advocates. Air: Buy a broom. Words by J. S. Blackie. SSS

"**Give** a rouse, then, in the Maytime." See A stein song (Bullard)

"**Give** alms, give alms." See "Donnez, donnez" (Meyerbeer)

"**Give** back the heart you stole from me." See "Ah! rendimi" (Rossi)

"**Give** ear, give ear, good Christian men." Composer unknown. Words by J. M. Neale. HC

"**Give** ear, O Lord" ("Ana bekorenu") Hebrew song. e.he. BSP

"**Give** ear to me, both high and low." See Ned that died at sea (Dibdin)

"**Give** ear, ye people." A. Dvořák. e. SAS 4

"**Give** him a march with his old bones." Servian folk song. Words by J. Russell. WF

"**Give** me back my gown and trencher." See The country parson's lament

"**Give** me back my hope, my lov'd one." See "O rendete mi la speme" (Bellini)

"**Give** me but health and a day." Bohemian folk air. Words by J. Russell. WF

"**Give** me daylight's golden beauty." See Longing (Rubinstein)

"**Give** me days of golden glory." See Longing (Rubinstein)

"**Give** me heart's-ease and all things else deny." See Heart's-ease

Give me Jesus ("Oh, when I come to die") Negro spiritual. DF—FSS 3—JB—JP—JSE—NMP

"**Give** me Jesus, I implore ye." Bach. e. OS 4

"**Give** me noble ale of the right Burton, pale." See Burton ale (Barrett)

"**Give** me only a curl, to wear it." See "Dammi un ricciolo dei capelli"

Give me the waltz (Piper Heidsieck) C. E. Pratt. CHS—WC

"**Give** me thy word." See Dimme 'na vota sì (Scalisi)

"**Give** me your love." See Dona Lombarda

"**Give** that wreath to me." W. Felton. Words by T. H. Bayly. BE 6

"**Give** three long cheers for sailors on the sea." See A song for sailors and soldiers

"**Give** to the winds." Words by P. Gerhardt. [Tr of Befiehl du deine wege] e. FSS 7

"**Give** us boys of will and spirit." See The country's call (Armitage)

"**Give** us our daily bread." See Our daily bread (Hutchinson)

"**Give** ye, gay lords." See "Nobles seigneurs, salut" (Meyerbeer)

Gjeite lok (Norwegian goat-herd's call) n. BMC
    Gjeite lok (The goat-herd's call) n. MAN

"Ein **gjente** eg såg som gjorde meg fjag." See Et syn (Grieg)

Gjorgjévic, J.
    Serbian national anthem (Jenko)

Glad angel voices. F. R. Rickman. HC

The **glad** bells all say. A. G. Crowe. Words by C. Wallace. MCS

"**Glad** Christmas bells." Christmas hymn. FSS 1

Glad Christmas comes again. H. H. Sutcliffe (music and words) HC

Glad hope of the ages. See "From ev'ry spire on Christmas eve" (Coles)

"**Glad** light." Carol for Easter. A. L. Brown. LA

The **glad** new day. Words by T. Moore. MCS

"**Glad** news from Bethlehem, my comrade." See Mes esta dí (Ranquet)

"**Glad** news, glad news, a-near and far." Christmas carol. HC

Glad tidings ("This is the Christ") M. Luther. Words by J. Imlah. MCS

"**Glad** tidings, oh, Armenian bards" (Nor oghchioon) Armenian patriotic song. Bishop Minas (music and words) e. SN

"**Glad** with sound of children's laughter." See Joy must reign to-night (Campana)

Gladden, Washington
The mountains

"**Glädjens** blomster" ("Flowers of joy") Swedish folk song. e.sw. HSOS
Flowers of joy. e. CST

Gladly God exalt, rejoicing. See Jauchzet Gott in allen landen (Bach)

Gladness is taken away. A. C. Mackenzie. SAS 2

The **glancing** of her apron. Scottish song. PS 2

"**Glare** of the flames was all around." See The sacrifice

Glaser, Carl Gotthilf
Azmon. See "Oh, for a thousand tongues"; "Once more, my soul"
"Oh, for a thousand tongues"
"Once more, my soul" (same air as "Oh, for a thousand tongues")

Gläser, Karl Ludwig Traugott
"Feinde ringsum"

Glazunov, Aleksandr Constantinovich
The Nereid

"**Gleam**, gleam, O silver stream." See Tell her I love her so (Faye)

"**Gleaming** at morning." See "Morgenlich leuchtend" (Wagner)

Gleim, Johann Wilhelm Ludwig
Endzweck der schöpfung (Miehl)
Das hüttchen (Volksweise)
The invitation (Suabian folk air. Tr of Das hüttchen)
Meine wünsche (Mozart)

Glen, I. M.
Oh, Oregon! oh, Oregon (Strong)

Glen, William
Wae's me for Prince Charlie (Scottish air)

Glenara ("O, heard ye yon pibroch sound") Scottish air. Words by T. Campbell. MMS

The **Glendy** Burke. S. C. Foster (music and words) NMP—WBT

Glenlogie ("Three score o' nobles rade up the king's ha'") Aberdeenshire ballad. BMC—HSSS—MMS

"**Glide** onward, my bark canoe." See My bark canoe

"**Gliding** 'mid the poor and lowly." See Father Joe (Flotow)

Glière, Reinhold Moritzovich
"Ah, twine no blossoms"
"O, winde keine duft'ge blüte." See "Ah, twine no blossoms"

Glinka, Mikhail Ivanovich
"Ah, kindly star" (from Russlan and Ludmilla)
"Du trauter stern." See "Ah, kindly star"
"Die gluth des heissen tages." See "The shades of night the stifling heat have cooled"

"How sweet it is when I'm with you"
The journey
"The shades of night the stifling heat have cooled" (from Russlan and Ludmilla)
Star of the north
"The truth is suspected" (from A life for the czar)
Veillée. See Vigil
Vigil
"Wie süss ist's, kann bei dir ich sein." See "How sweet it is when I'm with you"

"**Glocke,** du klingst fröhlich." See An die glocke (Fesca)

Glockengeläute (Bell-tones) G. Hölzel. Words by L. Schreyer. e.g. AB 3

Des **glockenthürmers** töchterlein. See entry under Des

"**Glöcklein** im thale" ("Echoing bell-tones") C. M. von Weber. e.g. KS 1

La **gloire** et la fortune. G. Rossini. e.f. SOA 4

Gloire immortelle de nos aïeux. For English translation see Soldiers' chorus (Gounod)

"**Gloomy** night, how full of shadow" ("Tavna noći") Serbian and Herzegovenian folk song. e.se. BF 1

"The **gloomy** night is gath'ring fast." Air: Roslin castle. Words by R. Burns. BSB—BSR

"**Gloomy** winter's now awa'." Scottish air. Words by R. Tannahill. PS 1

"**Gloomy** winter's now awa'." B. Covert. Words by R. Tannahill. FSS 8—JSE

"**Gloomy** woods, in darkness receive me." See "Bois épais, redouble ton ombre" (Lully)

"**Gloria** al bravo pueblo" ("Glory to the brave people") Venezuelan national air. J. Sandaeta. Words by V. Sálias. e.s. SN
"Glory to the brave men." e.s. MP

Gloria in excelsis ("O blessed town of Bethlehem") T. T. Noble. Words by C. W. Stubbs. HC

Gloria in excelsis ("When Christ was born") See "When Christ was born of Mary free"

Gloria laus et honor. For English translation see Glory, laud, and honor (Teschner)

Gloria Patri. Composer unknown. FSS 5 —WBT

Gloria Patri. H. W. Greatorex. LA— NMS

"The **glories** of our birth and state." E. Coleman. Words by J. Shirley. DM 2

"A **glorious** angel from heaven came." See The Sussex mummers' carol

"**Glorious**, beauteous, golden-bright." M. Tiddeman. Words by A. M. E. Nichols. BSC—MCS

"**Glorious** forever." S. Rachmaninoff. Words from the Russian of N. A. Nekrásof. e. DSH

The **glorious** Fourth ("We'll march and shout hurrah") Old air. HSD—LA —WBT

The **glorious** Fourth ("We'll march and shout hurrah") A. F. M. Custance. NMS

Glorious song of old. See "It came upon the midnight clear"

The **glorious** Sophomore class. Irish air. Words by G. W. Carryl. CU

"The **glorious** star has fallen from its bright place above." See Lied (Mertens)

"**Glorious** things of Thee are spoken." F. J. Haydn. Words by J. Newton. TL—WBT—WS

Glorious things are spoken. FSS 6— JSE—LA

Glory and honor ("Live humble, humble") Negro spiritual. HR

"**Glory** and honor our bosoms fill." See Soldiers' chorus (Gounod)

"**Glory** and love to the men of old." See Soldiers' chorus (Gounod)

Glory be to God on high. See "Christmas time is come again"

"**Glory** be to the Father." See Gloria Patri (Composer unknown); Gloria Patri (Greatorex)

"**Glory** be to Thee, O Lord." A. R. Gaul. SAS 4

Glory begun below (Chalvey) Hayne. Words by I. Watts. FSS 8

Glory gilds the sacred page (Manoah) [Rossini] Words by W. Cowper. FSS 2

"What glory gilds the sacred page" (Manoah) JS

Glory, glory for Columbia. College song. Air: Battle hymn of the republic. CU

Glory, glory hallelujah. See "John Brown's body"

Glory, laud, and honor. M. Teschner. 9th century words. [Tr of Gloria laus et honor] e. FSS 6—MCS

"All glory, laud, and honor." e. WBT

"**Glory** now and forever to God in heaven." See The song of praise

Glory of Christmas. See "A day, a day of glory" (Campana)

"**Glory** to God in the highest is ringing." F. Mendelssohn. Words by W. J. Irons. HC

"**Glory** to God in the highest is ringing." R. F. Smith. Words by W. J. Irons. HC

"**Glory** to God in the highest, to God in the highest." See The angels' song (Pergolesi)

"**Glory** to the brave men." See "Gloria al bravo pueblo" (Sandaeta)

Glory to the Lord in Zion ("Kol' slaven") D. S. Bortniansky. e.r. BF 1

"**Glory** to Thee, my God, this night" (An evening song) C. Gounod. Words by Ken. HSS 1—HSS 3

"**Glory** to Thee, my God, this night" (Evening hymn.—Duke street) J. Hatton. Words by Ken. FSS 6 Evening hymn. WBT—WS—WSC

Glounthaun Araglin eeving (The beautiful little vale of Araglin) Irish folk song. e.ir. JOI

Glover, Charles William
"Do they think of me at home"
The fairies' dance
"I'm a merry laughing girl"
Jeannette and Jeannot
Kitty Tyrrell
Little children's day
Little gipsy Jane
"Loving voices"
Melodies of many lands
Moriar, Melpomene
"Mother, are there angels dwelling"
Music on the waves
The old familiar place
Our merry Swiss home
Song of the daisy
"Sunshine and cloud"

Glover, Jean
O'er the moor amang the heather (Scottish air)

Glover, Stephen Ralph
"Beside a green meadow"
Blanche Alpen
Christmas violets
"Come to the forest"
Dear summer morn
"The dream is past"
"Floating on the wind"
Gently sighs the breeze
The good-bye at the door
I love the merry sunshine
"In the starlight"
"Meek and lowly"
Mermaid's evening song
Merry Christmas
"The midnight moon"
The monks of old
The murmuring sea
"Over the waves we float"
Sleep, my child
Smiling faces
Song of Blanche Alpen. See Blanche Alpen
"Wandering in the May-time"
"We are fairies of the sea"
"What are the wild waves saying"

"**Glowing** with love, on fire for fame." See The gallant troubadour

Gluck, Christoph Willibald, ritter von
Ah! malgré moi (from Alceste)
"Ah, non chiamarmi" (from Telemacco)
"Author of all my joys." See "O del mio dolce ardor"
"Beside the mill"
"Blooming May." See "Blüten mai"
"Blüten mai"
"Che farò senza Euridice" (from Orfeo)
Chorus of mourners (from Orpheus. Tr of Ah! se intorno a quest' urna funesta)
"Come, thou lovely May." See "Wonnevoller mai"
"Come, when the rosy morning." See "Vieni, che poi sereno"
"Come, while the twilight closes." See "Vieni, che poi sereno"

Gluck, C. W., ritter von —*Continued*
De noirs pressentiments (from Iphigénie en Tauride)
"Deem not my heart ungrateful." See "Ah, non chiamarmi"
"Diana, cruel goddess." See "Diane impitoyable"
"Diane impitoyable" (from Iphigénie en Aulide)
"Divinités du Styx" (from Alceste)
"From tender childhood e'er united." See "Unis dès la plus tendre enfance"
Die frühen gräber
Have I lost thee. See "Che farò senza Euridice"
I have lost my Euridice. See "Che farò senza Euridice"
"O del mio dolce ardor" (from Paride ed Elena)
"Oh, from my tender love." See "O del mio dolce ardor"
"O my belov'd." See "O del mio dolce ardor"
"O thou belov'd." See "O del mio dolce ardor"
"Ô toi l'objet" (from Iphigénie en Aulide)
The proposal
The storm song
Summer-time
"To thee I kneel." See "Ô toi l'objet"
"Unis dès la plus tendre enfance" (from Iphigénie en Tauride)
"Vieni, che poi sereno" (from La Semiramide riconosciuta)
"What sad lot the stars prepare me." See "Che farò senza Euridice"
"Wonnevoller mai"
"Ye awful Stygian powers." See "Divinités du Styx"
"Ye gods of night profound." See "Divinités du Styx"
"Ye powers that dwell below." See "Divinités du Styx"

Glück, Friedrich
The broken ring. See "In einem kühlen grunde"
Homesickness for Switzerland. See Schweizer heimweh
In die ferne
"In einem kühlen grunde"
Schweizer heimweh
Das zerbrochene ringlein. See "In einem kühlen grunde"

"Glück auf, glück auf! der steiger kömmt." See Bergmannslied

Das **glück** der freundschaft (The happiness of friendship) Beethoven. e.g. NG

"Die **gluth** des heissen tages." See "The shades of night the stifling heat have cool'd" (Glinka)

"Go along, my children dear." See Briolage

"Go ask of the high stars gleaming." See "Pregúntale a las estrellas"

Go chain the lion down. Negro spiritual. NMP

Go, Chicago. College song. A. M. Hirsh. OH

Go down, Moses. Negro spiritual. BN 1 —DF—FSS 6—GO—HR— JB— JP— JSE—TFC 2—WBT—WC

Go down to de cotton field. See "Oh! Lemuel" (Foster)

"Go, fetch to me a pint o' wine." See "Gae bring to me a pint o' wine" (Oswald)

"Go, forget me." J. P. Knight. Words by C. Wolfe. BE 3

"Go! forget me." W. Mozart. Words by C. Wolfe. FSS 1—JO—WBT

"Go from my window." Folk ballad. Old words. CO 1

"Go from my window." Folk ballad air. Modern words by F. Kidson. MM

"Go, gentle gales, go bear my sighs away." See The faithful lover (Arne)

"Go, go, go, go! falsest of thy sex, begone." See The precautioned nymph (Ramonden)

"Go javten" ("Good evening") Danish folk song. da.e. BF 2
Go javten, go javten (Dance song from Jutland) e. GO

"Go hand me down my looking glass." See Giles Collins (Big Laurel, N.C. version)

"Go, lovely flowers." H. F. Nicholls. HC

Go, Mary, and toll the bell. Negro spiritual. DF
Go Mary, an' toll de bell. HR

Go, my faithful soldier, go. Händel. BAS 2

"Go, my heart, upon the breeze." See Beyond the wood

"Go now, my sighings, seek my beloved." See "Vuela suspiro"

"Go patter to lubbers and swabs, do ye see." See Poor Jack (Dibdin)

"Go, pretty rose." T. Marzials. Words by M. Beverly. FMB

Go tell it on de mountain. Christmas plantation song. HR

"Go ter sleep, baby chil'." See Lullaby (Virginia version)

"Go ter sleep, go ter sleep." See Lullaby

"Go then—'tis vain to hover" (Neapolitan song) Words by T. Moore. BMC

"Go then to the fate that awaits thee." See Credo con fermo cuor (Verdi)

"Go then! well thy fate I descry." See "Vanne; la tua meta già vedo" (Verdi)

"Go thou and dream." Words by T. Moore. FSS 6

"Go to Berwick, Johnny." Scottish song. PS 2

Go to it. C. Engel. Words by D. Stevens. BSS

Go to sleep, Lena darling. J. K. Emmet (music and words) FSS 4—HSD
Emmet's lullaby. JS—WBT—WC
Go to sleep, Lena darling (Emmet's lullaby) NMH—WA—WSC— WSW

"Go to sleep, my little darling." See Santa Claus to-night (Hatton)

Go 'way, old man. Louisiana slave song. HSD—WBT

"Go where glory waits thee." Irish air: Bean dubh an ohleanna, or, The dark maiden of the valley. Words by T. Moore. BMC—MI—MMI —PI

"Go where glory awaits thee." FSS 3

"Go ye to the forest." See Carol, carol, Christians (Coxe)

The goat-herd's call. See Gjeite lok

Gobble duet. E. Audran. e. WBT— WSC

Göckingk, Leopold Friedrich Günther von "Lasst die politker nur sprechen" (Volksweise)

"God advances across the fields." See La procession (Franck)

"God all powerful, our Father." See Er re goli

God be with us (Duke street) J. Hatton. Words by L. Bacon. TL

"God be with you." W. G. Tomer. Words by J. E. Rankin. HSD— JS—NMH—WBT—WS

"God be with you" (Mizpah) OH

"God bless our fatherland." See National hymn—Latvia

"God bless our native land! firm may she ever stand." Adapted from H. Carey. Words by C. T. Brooks and J. S. Dwight. LA—WBT

"God bless our native land, on this firm shore we stand." S. P. Tuckerman (music and words) JS

God bless the prince of Wales ("Among our ancient mountains") B. Richards. Words from the Welsh of J. C. Hughes. e. MMW

God bless us, every one. MCS

God defend New Zealand. National anthem. J. J. Woods. Words by T. Bracken. e.pol. MP—SN

"God ever glorious." Air: Russian national hymn. Words by S. F. Smith. WCP

God for Poland ("Boże coś Polske") Attributed to Kurpinski. e.p. BSP

"O, Thou Lord God" ("Boże! coś Polske") e.p. BF 1

"God for us." C. C. Converse. FSS 6— JS

"God girt her about with the surges" (New Zealand national song) Words by W. P. Reeves. BMC

New Zealand's national song. WBT

"God give ye merry Christmas tide." Traditional air. HC

"God hath sent His angels." J. C. D. Parker. Words by P. Brooks. FSS 5 —HC

"God is eternal." S. de Lange. e. SAS 4

"God is gone up." A. H. Brown. Words by S. C. Clarke. HC

"God is love; His mercy brightens" (Sardis) Arr from Beethoven. Words by J. Bowring. CST

"God is love, His mercy brightens." I. Conkey. Words by J. Bowring. HSD —WBT—WS

"God is moving across the fields." See La procession (Franck)

"God is my song, He is the King almighty." See The power of God (Beethoven)

God is present everywhere. See "They who seek the throne of grace" (Händel)

"God keep you safe, my little love." See My little love (Hawley)

God knows all. WSC

God morgen (Good morning) E. Grieg. Words by B. Björnson. e.n. MAN—SSN

Guten morgen (Good morning) e.g. PG 2

Sunrise. e. BD

"God moves in a mysterious way" (Avon) Scotch air. Words by W. Cowper. FSS 4

"God my Father, God, my Father." T. Dubois. e. SAS 4

"God, my Father, while I stray." See God's will and love (Troyte)

"God, my King, Thy might confessing" (St Oswald) J. B. Dykes. LA

"The God of Abrah'm praise" (Leoni) Jewish air. Words by T. Olivers. CST

"God of all nations, sov'reign Lord." See Army hymn (Lvov)

"God of justice! Thou who saved us." See Serbian national anthem (Jenko)

"God of love, fair blindfold Cupid." See "Dolce Amor, bendato dio" (Cavalli)

"God of nations! at Thy feet." See God defend New Zealand (Woods)

"God of our boyhood." G. F. Blanchard. BSS

"God of our fathers, by Whose hand" (Downs) L. Mason. FSS 2

"God of our fathers, known of old." G. F. Blanchard. Words by R. Kipling. BSS

"God of our fathers, let Thy face." H. P. Danks. Words by S. Wolcott. JS

"God of our fathers, let Thy face." G. B. Nevin. Words by S. Wolcott. MP— NMS

"God of our fathers, Whose almighty hand." See National hymn (Warren)

"God of the earth." H. F. Hemy and J. G. Walton. Words by S. Longfellow. BSS

"God of the nations." G. Verdi. LA Anvil chorus. OH—TFC 1

"God of the year." A. F. M. Custance. NMS

"God, our Father, made the daylight." See Song of praise (Bayly)

God, our loving Father. Finnish air. Words by R. Compton. DO

"God placed Adam in de garden." See Good Lord, shall I ever be de one

"God preserve our Franz." See "Gott erhalte Franz den kaiser" (Haydn)

"God preserve our gracious emp'ror." See "Gott erhalte Franz den kaiser" (Haydn)

"God preserve our noble emperor." See "Gott erhalte Franz den kaiser" (Haydn)

"God prosper long our noble king." See Chevy chase

God reigns. F. Mendelssohn. Words by F. S. Key. MP—NMS—WBT

"God rest ye merry, gentlemen." Old English song. FSS 8—MCS
"God rest ye merry, gentlemen." With additional words by D. M. Muloch. MCS
"God rest you merry, gentlemen." BMC— BSC— CST— DSH— MF —WBT—WCC
"God rest ye merry, gentlemen." Old English song. Another traditional setting. HC
"God rest ye merry, gentlemen." L. H. Redner. Old English words. HC

"God rest you, Chrysten gentil men." See Christmasse of olde

"God rest you, merry Chrysten gentil men." See Christmasse of olde

"God save America! bless the United States." Round. MP—WBT

"God save America! here may all races." Lvoff. Words by W. G. Ballatine. LA

"God save our glorious czar." See Russian national hymn (Lvov)

"God save our gracious king." See God save the king (Carey)

"God save our gracious queen." See God save the king (Carey)

"God save our lord the king." See God save the king (Air from the Harmonia Anglicana); God save the king (Bull?); God save the king (Carey)

"God save our noble king." See God save the king (Carey)

"God save our noble tsar." See Russian national hymn (Lvov)

"God save our president." S. Winner. WBT

God save the king ("God save our lord the king") Air from the Harmonia Anglicana. DM 1
"God save our lord the king." CO 2

God save the king ("God save our lord the king") Old version. Attributed to J. Bull. DM 1

God save the king ("God save our noble king") British national anthem. Attributed to H. Carey; also attributed to J. Oswald. BD— BMC— BOS— BSE— BSP—DM 1 — FMB— JE— JO— MM— MP— NA— NMH— NMS— PR 2—SN— SSS—WA—WBT—WSW
The British national anthem. LA
God save the queen. BE 1—WCP

God save the nation. H. C. Work. WBT

"God save the noble czar." See Russian national hymn (Lvov)

God save the queen. See God save the king (Carey)

God save the tsar. See Russian national hymn (Lvov)

"God shall charge His angel legions" (Trust) Mendelssohn. Words by J. Montgomery. FSS 3
Watch and ward. WBT

God speed the right. German air. Words by W. E. Hickson. HSD—LA—LBR

"God the All-terrible." See Russian national hymn (Lvov)

"God the Lord a King remaineth" (Regent square) H. Smart. Words by J. Keble. LA

"God told Moses, O Lord." See Little David, play on your harp

"God took from me my all" (Vsyo ótnyal ōō minyá) S. Rachmaninoff. Words by F. Tyutcheff. e. SMR 2

"God uphold thee, mighty emp'ror." See "Gott erhalte Franz den kaiser" (Haydn)

"God when He made this world." A. Redhead. HC

"God! Who in bygones hast saved us Thy people." See Serbian national anthem (Jenko)

"God, Who of Poland's mighty pow'r and splendor." See God for Poland (Kurpinski)

"God, Who once to bright Hungaria sorrow gave." See Hungaria's treasure

"God, Who rulest through the ages." A. Ulmann. HC

Godard, Benjamin Louis Paul
"Ah! s'il est dans votre village"
L'amour
Chanson de Florian. See "Ah! s'il est dans votre village"
Come and embark. See "Embarquez-vous"
Do you remember. See "Te souviens-tu de ta promesse"
Embark-away. See "Embarquez-vous"
"Embarquez-vous"
Florian's song. See "Ah! s'il est dans votre village"
Love. See L'amour
Lullaby ("Cachés dans cet asile") See Oh! ne t'éveille pas
Lullaby ("Sleep, so your tale") (same air as Oh! ne t'éveille pas)
Oh, may thy dream not soon be o'er. See Oh, ne t'éveille pas
Oh! ne t'éveille pas (from Jocelyn)
Remembrance. See "Te souviens-tu de ta promesse"
"Te souviens-tu de ta promesse"

Goddard, Julia
"The Christmas stars are shining" (Dawkins)
"Soft falls the snow" (Brown)
"Through the midnight air" (Dawkins)

"Goddess fairest, goddess fairest." See "Casta diva, che inargenti" (Bellini)

"The goddess of ev'ry heart." See Bella, adorata incognita (Mercadante)

"Goddess of those who grieve." See "Ô des infortunés" (Spontini)
"Goddesses three." Offenbach. Words from the French. e. BOS
The **Goddhee** Grawna. See An Gadaighe Grána
Godfrey, Daniel
　Happy days gone by
Godnat (Good night) P. Lasson. Words by H. Wergeland. e.n. SSN
"**God's** a-gwine ter move all de troubles away." Negro spiritual. BN 2
"**God's** dear Son." Traditional air. BSC
"**God's** great gift to man forlorn." See Christmas waits (Bellini)
"The **gods** have foreshewn me the future." See De noirs pressentiments (Gluck)
God's will and love. A. H. D. Troyte. Words by C. Elliott. LA
Godwin, B. M.
　Ewing college song (Composer unknown)
Goeckel, W. J.
　The red and blue
Goethe, Johann Wolfgang von
　Abendlied (Kuhlau. Words adapted; for music by Schubert with original words see "Über allen gipfeln ist ruh")
　An den mond (music by Gackstätter; Zelter)
　An Mignon (Zelter)
　Anakreon's grab (Wolf)
　Die bekehrte schäferin (Cimarosa)
　Bundeslied (Reichardt)
　Canzonette (Loewe)
　"Connais-tu le pays" (Tr of "Kennst du das land." Thomas, Ambroise)
　Einsamkeit (Medtner)
　Ergo bibamus (Eberwein)
　Erlkönig (music by Loewe; Schubert)
　Erster verlust (Medtner)
　Der fischer (Reichardt)
　"Freudvoll und leidvoll" (music by Beethoven; Reichardt)
　Gefunden (Gersbach)
　Generalbeichte (Composer unknown)
　The gipsy king (West)
　Heidenröslein (music by Schubert; Werner. For German folk air see The wild rose)
　"Die heiligen drei könig' mit ihrem stern" (Zelter)
　The holy family (Randegger)
　Jägers nachtlied (Reichardt)
　"Kennst du das land" (music by Beethoven; Himmel; Liszt; Reichardt; Romberg; Wolf. For music by Arthur Goring Thomas see Mignon; for music by Ambroise Thomas see "Connais-tu le pays")
　Der könig in Thule (music by Liszt; Reichardt; Zelter. For music by Gounod see Le roi de Thule)
　Die liebende schreibt (Mendelssohn)
　Mailied (Medtner)
　"Meine ruh ist hin" (music by Graben-Hoffmann; Schubert)
　Mignon (Thomas, Arthur Goring. Tr of "Kennst du das land")
　Mit einem gemalten band (Beethoven)

　Der musensohn (music by Schubert; Zelter)
　Marmotte (Beethoven)
　Nähe des geliebten (music by Beethoven; Lassen)
　"Nur wer die sehnsucht kennt" (Tchaikovsky)
　Peace (Liszt)
　"Purer yet and purer I would be in mind" (Composer unknown)
　Der rattenfänger (Volksweise)
　Le roi de Thule (Gounod. Tr of Der könig in Thule)
　Schäfters klagelied (music by Reichardt; Zelter)
　Schneiderschreck (Reichardt)
　Schweizerlied (Volksweise)
　Suleika (Mendelssohn)
　Tischlied (Eberwein)
　"Über allen gipfeln ist ruh" (Schubert. For music by Kuhlau with words adapted see Abendlied)
　Vanitas! vanitatum vanitas (Zelter)
　Das veilchen (music by Mozart; Reichardt)
　Wanderers nachtlied (music by Liszt; Schubert)
　"Was machst du mir vor liebchen's thür" (Lassen)
　The wild rose (German folk air. Tr of Heidenröslein)
　Wonne der wehmuth (music by Beethoven; Franz)
　Zum neuen jahr (Reichardt)
Goetschius, Percy
　"Ring out, O bells, ring silver-sweet"
　The new year. See "Ring out, O bells, ring silver-sweet"
Going home. Scotch air. FSS 3
"**Going** out a-walking." See Forsaken
Going to church. 16th century round. TFC 2
Going to heaven. Negro spiritual. HR
Going to market. L. Diehl. Words by H. Wynn. FSS 5
"**Going** to meet the brothers there." See From every graveyard
"**Going** to meet those happy Christians." See I ain't going to die no more
"**Going** to ride up in the chariot." Negro spiritual. JP—NMP
"**Going** to see my mother some of these mornings." See Some of these mornings
Going to shout all over God's heav'n. See All God's chillun got wings
"**Going** to write to Massa Jesus." See Turn back Pharaoh's army
Going up. See Gwine up
Gold and blue. Franklin college song. C. R. Parker. CHS
The **gold** and olive. Lombard university song. H. W. Dubee. Words by B. F. Stacey. CHS
The **gold**-beater. A. Randegger. AB 2
"The **gold** rain of eve was descending." See The cailin deas
"**Gold** rolls here beneath me." See "Gelb rollt mir zu füssen" (Rubinstein)

"Golden at my feet." See "Gelb rollt mir zu füssen" (Rubinstein)

The golden bear. University of California song. Words by C. M. Gayley. CHS—NMS

The golden boat. German air. Words by H. H. Harbour. DO

"A golden cage of sunbeams half down a rainbow hung." See The bird of hope (Cole)

The golden carol of Melchoir, Bathazer and Caspar. Old English song. MF
The golden carol. HC

Golden days ("Once in the days of golden weather") A. S. Sullivan. Words by L. H. Lewin. CS 1—FSS 4—HSE 3

Golden days of good Queen Bess. Old English air: Ally Croker. Words by W. Collins. BE 8—DM 2

"The golden evening sun is shining." See Im frühling (Fesca)

The golden glove. Folk song from North Carolina. CSE
Variant: The lady and the glove

"The golden glow of a summer's day." See Valedictory (King)

"Golden harps are sounding." E. P. Parker. Words by F. R. Havergal. HC

"Golden harps are sounding." A. Sullivan. Words by F. R. Havergal. HC

"Golden is my steed." Hungarian song. e. KSE—WL

"Golden on ev'ry hand." Indian air. e. FI

The golden pathway. H. Gray. Words by A. St Ives. HSS 3—HSS 4—SM 3

"The golden ray." J. Ingalls. MCS

The golden rule ("To do to others") School song. FSS 7—WBT—WSC

"The golden rule, the golden rule." FSS 1

The golden shore ("I remember, I remember") A. S. Gatty. FSS 2—JSE—WBT

The golden shore ("Lo! the seal of death is breaking") Jewish air. FSS 5

"Golden slumbers kiss your eyes." Air: May fair. Words by T. Dekker. DM 1—FSS 2—LA—MM—MSS 1 —PR 2—TFC 2—WBT
Mayfair. JE

"Golden slumbers kiss your eyes" (A lullaby) A. Foote. [Words by T. Dekker] TL

"Golden stars for me are shining." See Dearest native land (Proch)

"The golden sun is shining bright." See The merry haymakers

"The golden sun sinks in the west." J. Strauss. FSS 3—JSE—WSC

"Golden the sunlight, beaming brightly." See Sonnet d'amour (Thomé)

The Golden Vanity ("A ship I have got") Folk song. BSW—MM—SSS
The Golden Vanity ("It's I have got a ship") DM 2
The Golden Vanity ("O there was a ship") SEF 1—SO

The Golden Vanity ("Some were waving hats") Hot Springs, N.C. version no. 2. CSE
The Golden Vanity ("There was a little ship in the North Amerikee") Black Mountain, N.C. version. CSE
The Golden Vanity ("There was a little ship in the South Amerikee") Hot Springs, N.C. version no. 1. CSE
The Golden Vanity ("There was a ship") BOS
The Golden Vanity ("'Twas of a lofty ship") CR
Variants: The Mary Golden Tree; The Spanish Canoe

De golden wedding. J. A. Bland (music and words) WC

"Golden years ago in a mill beside the sea." See The maid of the mill (Maybrick)

"Goldenhorn and Rosey, and Lilly-white and Posey." See Huldre lokk

The goldfinch. See Lu cardillo (Labriola)

Goldmark, Rubin
The passionate shepherd to his love

"Goldne abendsonne, wie bist du so schön." See An die abendsonne (Nägeli)

Goldoni, Carlo
La pastorella (Schubert)

Goldsmith, Oliver
Elegy on the death of a mad dog (English air)

Goldthred's song. W. A. Barratt. Words by W. Scott. SSS

Golenishchev-Kutusov, A., graf
After the battle (Musorgskiï)
After years (Musorgskiï)
By the water (Musorgskiï)
Cradle song (Musorgskiï)
Death, the commander (Musorgskiï)
Death's lullaby (Musorgskiï)
Death's serenade (Musorgskiï)
"Deep hidden in my heart" (Arenski)
"Deep shadows veil the night" (Musorgskiï)
The eagle (Arenski)
In my attic (Musorgskiï)
Resignation (Musorgskiï)
Retrospect (Musorgskiï)
Trepak (Musorgskiï)

Goliath und David ("War einst ein riese Goliath") G. W. Fink. Words by M. Claudius. g. ED 2

Gollmick,
Hail! ever-blessed morn. See "See, amid the winter's snow"
"Pleasure climbs to every mountain"
"See, amid the winter's snow"

Gollomb, Joseph
Rah! rah! C. C. N. Y.

La golondrina. N. Serradell. s. LCP
The swallow. e. WL

Golova-l' ty moîá golovushka. See The lovesick maiden

Goltermann, Georg Eduard
The heart's tear. See Die thränen des herzens
Die thränen des herzens

Gomes, Antonio Carlos
    C'era una volta un principe (from Il
        Guarany)
    Forma sublime, eterea (from Salvator
        Rosa)
    "Senza tetto, senza cuna" (from Il
        Guarany)
    Without roof, without home. See
        "Senza tetto, senza cuna"
Gómez, R.
    Alma Andaluza
Gomis, J. R. de
    Chiquita
The **gondola** ("Quiet is the bright night")
    Venetian barcarolle. e. BMC
The **gondolier** ("How gaily rows the gon-
    dolier") A. Lee. FSS 7
"The **gondolier** at the closing of day." See
    "Le gondolier dans sa pauvre nacelle"
    (Halévy)
"Le **gondolier** dans sa pauvre nacelle." J.
    F. Halévy. e.f. SOA 2
Gondolier waltz. See On Venice waters
    (Roeder)
Gone ("Another hand is beck'ning us") T.
    Stein. Words by J. G. Whittier. LBR
Gone ("De sidste gaester") See Borte
    (Grieg)
Gone are the days ("Pour fuir son sou-
    venir") See Ô jours heureux (Mey-
    erbeer)
"**Gone** are the days when my heart was
    young and gay." See Old black Joe
    (Foster)
"**Gone** are the swallows from field and
    hill." See November
"**Gone** art thou, Marion, Marion Moore."
    See Marion Moore (Clark)
"**Gone** from me evermore." See "J'ai per-
    du celle" (Henry III)
"**Gone** is winter, and spring again." See
    Au printemps (Gounod)
Gone where the woodine twineth. A.
    Street. WBT
"The **gonesome** scenes of winter." Ken-
    tucky mountain song. WLT
Gongora y Argote, Luis de
    Story of the shepherd (Barnby)
"**Gönnt** mir goldne tageshelle." See
    Longing (Rubinstein)
Gontier, Adam Bois-. See Bois-Gontier,
    Adam
Gonzáles,
    Flores a María
Good advice ("By the window one youth
    now is standing") Carinthian song.
    e. KSE
Good advice ("Leave off this foolish prat-
    ing") Drinking song. R. Leveridge.
    (music and words) DM 1
Good advice ("Why all this sorrow."—
    Jilted) R. Leveridge. DM 2
The **good** angels. F. Gumbert. FSS 8
Good-bye ("Falling leaf") F. P. Tosti.
    Words by G. J. White-Melville.
    MSF 1—WA—WBW
Good-bye ("Farewell, farewell is a lonely
    sound") J. C. Engelbrecht. FSS 2
    —HSD—WBT

The **good-bye** at the door. S. Glover.
    Words by J. E. Carpenter. FSS 5—
    WBT
Good bye, brother. Negro song. NMP
Good-bye, fare ye well ("It's of a flash
    packet") Capstan song. SMW
    For variant see following song of simi-
    lar title
Good-bye, fare you well ("O fare you
    well") Capstan chantey. CR
"**Good-bye**, good-bye, lovely world of sor-
    row." See The dance of Zalongo
"**Good-bye**, good-bye, to summer." See
    Robin Redbreast
Good-bye, my little lady ("The boats are
    pushing from the shore") J. C. Macy
    (music and words) WC
Goodbye, my love, goodbye ("I'm bound
    away") Halliard chantey. CR
Good-bye, my lover, good-bye ("The ship
    goes sailing") T. H. Allen (music
    and words) MPC—WBT—WC—
    WSW
Good-bye, my lover, good-bye ("The ship
    is sailing") American air. [Words
    by T. H. Allen] TFC 1
"**Good-by**, old year! I can but say." See
    The old year and the new (Sayles)
Good-bye, sweetheart, good-bye. J. L.
    Hatton. Words by F. Williams.
    DM 1—HSD—HSE 1—NML—TS
    WBT—WL
    Good-bye, sweetheart. FSS 6—HSC
    —JS
Good cheer. Cracovienne, or Polish dance.
    FSS 1
"**Good** Christian men, rejoice." German
    song. [Tr of Wir Christenleut haben]
    e. BSC—HC—MCS—WCC
"**Good** Christian people all." H. G. Trem-
    bath. Words by E. Haskins. HC
"**Good** Christians, rise, this is the morn."
    N. B. Warren. HC
"**Good** evening, good evening to ev'ry one
    that's here." See "Go javten"
"**Good-day**, Susanne." See "Bonjour,
    Suzon" (Delibes)
"**Good** e'en, my sweetheart, oh my darling,
    good e'en." See Vergebliches ständ-
    chen (Brahms)
"**Good** ev'ning, good ev'ning, together we
    are come." See "Go javten"
"**Good** folk, your pity I implore." See
    Beggar's song (Wihtol)
"**Good** friend, for Jesus' sake forbear." L.
    van Beethoven. Words by Shakes-
    peare. KF 2—KF 4
"**Good** King Wenceslas." Traditional air.
    Words from the Latin. e. BOS—
    BSC—CST— DC—DO— DSH—HC—
    MCS—MF—TFC 2—WCC
"**Good** Lord, shall I ever be de one." Ne-
    gro spiritual. HR
"The **good** men all of Chastres." 16th
    century Arpajon carol. Tr of Les
    bourgeois de Chastres. e. HC
Good morning ("Dagen er oppe") See
    God morgen (Grieg)

"Good morning, Claire." See "Bonjour, Suzon" (Pessard)

"Good morning, good morning, my fair young lady." See The broken token (Black Mountain, N.C. version)

Good morning, ladies all. Capstan chantey. SE

"Good morning, little yellow bird." See Who are you

"Good morning, my pretty little miss." Folk song from North Carolina. CSE

"Good-morning, Sue." See "Bonjour, Suzon" (Delibes)

"Good morning, sweet April." A. F. M. Custance. NMS

"Good morrow, gossip Joan." 17th century song. CO 2—DM 2—JE—MM

"Good morrow, 'tis St Valentine's day." Traditional song. Words attributed to Shakespeare. DM 1—JE

"Good-morrow to thy sable beak." See The blackcock

The good-natured lad ("When I first com'd to Lunnon") Welsh air. Words by J. Parry. MMW

"Good news." Stirling. MCS

"Good news, de chariot's comin'." Negro spiritual. HR
"Good news, chariot's comin'." BN 1

"Good news from the hills of Judea." Sainton-Dolby. HC

"Good news, good news is sent." R. F. Smith. Words by W. H. Jewitt. HC

Good news, good news the angels bring. See Glad tidings (Luther)

"Good news on Christmas morn, good news, O children dear! No sweeter joy e'er born." See On Christmas morn (Philips)

"Good news on Christmas morning, good news, O children dear! For Christ, once born in Bethlehem." See "Good news" (Stirling)

"Good news we bring and peace." C. Simper. Words by G. W. Brindley. HC

Good night ("Ah, dear friends, these moments fair") Offenbach. FSS 4

Good night ("Godnat, godnat") See Godnat (Lasson)

"Good-night" ("Good-night, beloved") Bohemian folk song. e. CST

"Good night" ("Good night, dear little dreamers") Christmas carol. HC

"Good night" ("Good night! good night! and is it so."—"Gut' nacht") A. Rubinstein. Words by T. Moore. e.g. FO 1

"Good-night" ("Good-night, good-night, my sweet maiden fair") A. Dvořák. WBW

"Good-night" ("Good night, good night, time sounds the warning call") Round. LA

"Good-night" ("Good-night, ladies") See "Good-night, ladies"

Good-night ("Gray shadows are a-stealing)" Mount Holyoke college song. M. P. Pingree. CHS

Good night ("How soft the happy evening's close") German air. FSS 2

Good-night ("In the heaven earth reposes") J. Raff. e. TL

Good night ("In the west the sun declining") F. Abt. FSS 1—LA—WBT

Good-night ("Now good-night, now good-night") F. von Flotow. BD

Good night ("Now to all a kind good night") FSS 5—HSC—WBT
"Now to all a kind good night." FSS 7

Good-night ("The sweet west wind") Arr from W. O. Perkins. LA

Good-night! and Christmas prayer. M. B. Foster. DC—DCS

Good night and good morning. FSS 3—WSC

"Good night, and joy be wi' ye a'." Air: Johnny Armstrong's good night. Words by A. Boswell. JO—MMS—PS 1

Good night and pleasant dreams. W. V. Wallace. WBT

Good night beloved. See "Good night, good night beloved" (Moir)

"Good-night, beloved, good-night, good-night." See "Good-night" (Bohemian folk song)

"Good night, dear little dreamers." See "Good night" (Christmas carol)

"Good night, farewell." F. Kücken. e. FSS 7—HSC—HSD—LA

"Good night! good night! and is it so." See "Good night" (Rubinstein)

Good night, good night, beloved. M. W. Balfe. Words from H. W. Longfellow. DM 1—HSE 3—TS

"Good night, good night beloved" (Good night beloved) F. L. Moir. Words by H. W. Longfellow. CB

"Good-night! good-night, belovèd" (Serenade) E. W. Nevin. [Words by H. W. Longfellow] MSF 1—SM 2

"Good-night, good-night, beloved." C. Pinsuti. Words by H. W. Longfellow. TFC 2

"Good-night, good-night, my sweet maiden fair." See "Good-night" (Dvořák)

"Good-night, good-night! now blest be thy slumber." See Godnat (Lasson)

"Good night, good night, time sounds the warning call." See "Good-night" (Round)

"Good-night, ladies." CHS—FSS 6—MPC—NMH— NMS— OH—TFC 1—WA—WBT—WSW
"Good-night." HSD—JS—SSS—WC

Good-night, my love. Marschner. NML

"Good-night! our songs are sung." See Good-night! and Christmas prayer (Foster)

"Good night, slumber sound." Round. FSS 3

Good-night, sweet child. See Gute nacht, du mein herziges kind (Abt)

"Good night to you all." BSS

Good old blue and white will fix you. P. Barnes. CU

The good old college days.   MPC

Good old Jeff.   See The poor old slave

"Good old mother Fairie."   See To mother Fairie

"Good people all of ev'ry sort."   See Elegy on the death of a mad dog

"Good people attend and soon you shall hear."   See The Lincolnshire farmer

"Good people, give ear."   J. Swire. Words by J. Barmby.   HC

"Good Pierrot."   See "Au clair de la lune"

The good Rhein wine.   J. Gray.   Words by J. Reed.   SSS

The good Rhine wine.   WBT

"Good ringers be we that in Torrington dwell."   See The ringers of Torrington town

"Good Saint Anne, great Saint Anne." See "Bonne Sainte Anne, grande Sainte"

The good Shepherd.   O. Barri.   Words by G. C. Bingham.   FSS 5—HSS 2— HSS 4

"The good ship rode at anchor."   See Jack at sea (Roeckel)

"A good sword and trusty hand."   See Song of the western men

The good Three Bells.   C. Jarvis.   FSS 3 —WBT

"Good tidings, good tidings."   G. E. Oliver.   HC

The good time coming.   English air. Words by C. Mackay.   FSS 8—JO

"There's a good time coming."   JO

The good time coming is almost here. See Wake, Nicodemus (Work)

The good turns pay.   S. C. Foster. Words by S. E. Kiser.   BSS

"Good-will to men."   A. Lee.   MCS

Goodale, Elaine.   See Eastman, Mrs Elaine (Goodale)

Goodban, Thomas Goodhurst
"All who sing"

Goodbye.   For entries beginning Goodbye see Good-bye

Goodeve, Arthur
Fiddle and I

Goodgroome, John
"Will Cloris cast her sun-bright eye"

Goodhart, C. A.
"The corn is ripe for reaping" (Farmer)

Goodwin, F. D.   See Memmott, F. W., jt. auth.

Goodwin, Starling
"Could a man be secure"

"Goosey goosey gander."   WSC

Gopi's complaint ("Jala bharna chalī rī mā'ī jamanā ghāta") Song from India. e.ind.   BF 2

Gordigiani, Luigi
The benediction.   See La benedizione
La benedizione
La Bianchina
"E lo mio amore è andato a soggiornare"
Every Sabbath thine altar shall be lighted.   See Ogni sabato avrete il lume acceso

"My love has gone to live in lovely Lucca."   See "E lo mio amore è andato a soggiornare"
"O come hither, and hearken"
Ogni sabato avrete il lume acceso
Tempo passato perchè non retorni
Why are days we have lived lost for ever.   See Tempo passato perchè non retorni

Gordon, Alexander Gordon, 4th duke of
"There's cauld kail in Aberdeen" (Scottish air)

Goreh, Ellen Lakshmi
"In the secret of His presence how my soul delights to hide" (Stebbins)

Goria,
Polish maiden song

Górnimee tikho letyéla dooshá nyebesámi. See "Silently floated a spirit" (Musorgskiĭ)

Gorrin, Cipriano
The inquiry

Gorodetskiĭ, Sergeĭ
The cloister (Stravinskiĭ)
Tar (Vassilenko)

"The gospel train is comin'."   See Get on board

Goss, Sir John
Hymn for Christmas day.   See "See amid the winter's snow"
"See amid the winter's snow"

"Gott, deine güte reicht" ("To Thee, my God") Beethoven.   Words by Gellert. e.g.   HSS 3

"Der Gott der eisen wachsen liess."   See Vaterlandslied (Methfessel)

"Gott erhalte Franz den kaiser ("God preserve our noble emperor") F. J. Haydn.   Words by L. L. Haschka; wrongly attributed to J. C. von Zedlitz.   e.g.   BSP
Austrian hymn ("God uphold thee")   e. BSE
Austrian national anthem ("Gott erhalte Franz")   e.g.   SSS
Austrian national hymn ("God preserve our Franz, the kaiser")   e.   FSS 3 —KSE
Austrian national hymn ("God preserve our gracious emp'ror")   e.   BMC
Austrian national song ("Gott erhalte Franz")   e.g.   WCP
"God preserve our noble emperor." e.g.   SN
"Gott erhalte Franz, den kaiser" (Austrian national hymn)   e.g.   WA
Österreichisches nationallied.   g.   ED 1

"Gott grüss euch, alter."   See Die tabakspfeife (Pilz)

"Gott grüsse dich."   L. Erk.   Words by J. Sturm.   g.   ED 3

"Gott mit uns auf allen wegen."   G. W. Fink (music and words)   g.   ED 3

"Gott sei mir gnädig" ("Show me, Almighty")   F. Mendelssohn-Bartholdy. e.g.   AB 2

"Gott! welch' dunkel hier."   See In des lebens frühlingstagen (Beethoven)

Gottergebenheit ("Meine seel' ist stille")
Air: Eine hand voll erde. Words by
A. Mahlmann. g. ED 3

Göttling, Karl Wilhelm
Deutsche mahnung (Methfessel)
Rheinweinlied (Methfessel)

Gottschalk, Louis Moreau
"Holy Ghost, with light divine"
"Holy Spirit, truth divine"
O loving heart, trust on
"Softly now the light of day"

Gottschall, Rudolf von
Marie (music by Franz; Jensen)

Götze, Karl
"Calm as the night." See "Still wie
die nacht, tief wie das meer, o
mensch, muss deine liebe sein"
O happy day, O day so dear. See O
schöne zeit, o sel'ge zeit
O lovely day, O happy day. See
O schöne zeit, o sel'ge zeit
O schöne zeit, o sel'ge zeit
"Still wie die nacht, tief wie das meer,
o mensch, muss deine liebe sein"

Goudimel, Claude
O'er the grave victorious

Gouge,
"Farewell! thou false Philander"

Gould, John Edgar
"Jesus, Saviour, pilot me"
Pilot. See "Jesus, Saviour, pilot me"
Thoughts of home

Gould, Monk
"Who is Sylvia"

Gould, Sabine Baring-. See Baring-Gould,
Sabine

Gounod, Charles François
À toi mon coeur (Tr of "Das meer hat
seine perlen")
Adore and quiet be. See "Le ciel a
visité la terre"
Ah! fairest sun, arise. See Ah! lève-
toi, soleil
"Ah! je ris de me voir" (from Faust)
"Ah! je veux vivre" (from Roméo et
Juliette)
Ah! lève-toi, soleil (from Roméo et
Juliette)
"Ah! si je redevenais" (from Philé-
mon et Baucis)
"Ah! the joy past compare." See "Ah!
je ris de me voir"
All hail, thou dwelling. See Salut!
demeure chaste et pure
L'amour! oui, son ardeur a troublé.
See Ah! lève-toi, soleil
Anges du paradis (from Mireille)
Aprile. See Au printemps
At the smithy. See "Au bruit des
lourds marteaux d'airain"
"Au bruit des lourds marteaux d'airain"
(from Philémon et Baucis)
Au printemps
"Avant de quitter ces lieux" (from
Faust)
"Ave Maria"
Barcarolle ("Dites, la jeune belle")
See "Dites, la jeune belle"

Barcarolle ("Nymphes attentives") See
"Nymphes attentives"
Belén. See Bethlehem
Bethlehem
Le Calvaire. See "There is a green
hill far away"
Canti, ridi, dormi. See Chantez
riez et dormez
Ce que je suis sans toi
Chanson de la sorcière (from Mireille)
Chantez riez et dormez
"Le ciel a visité la terre"
"Clear the way for the calf of gold."
See "Le veau d'or"
"Come unto Him, all ye who labor!
Your Lord will give you rest and
peace"
"Cradled all lowly." See Bethlehem
"Depuis hier je cherche en vain mon
maître" (from Roméo et Juliette)
"Dio dell' or." See "Le veau d'or"
"Dio possente, dio d'amor." See
"Avant de quitter ces lieux"
"Dites, la jeune belle"
È strano poter il viso suo veder. See
"Ah! je ris de me voir"
"Even bravest heart may swell." See
"Avant de quitter ces lieux"
Evening. See Le soir
Evening meditation. See "Ave Maria"
An evening song. See "Glory to Thee,
my God, this night"
"Faites-lui mes aveux" (from Faust)
Far greater in his lowly state. See
Plus grand dans son obscurité
"Father eternal." See "Ave Maria"
"Father in heaven." See "Ave Maria"
"Father, thine arms about me throw"
(from Tobie)
The flower song. See "Faites-lui mes
aveux"
"Forever with the Lord"
"Gentle flowers in the dew." See
"Faites-lui mes aveux"
"Glory to Thee, my God, this night."
See An evening song
The guardian angel
"Hail, bright Easter"
"In the language of love." See
"Faites-lui mes aveux"
Inspirez-moi (from La reine de Saba)
Je veux vivre dans ce rêve. See "Ah!
je veux vivre"
"Je voudrais bien savoir quel était ce
jeune homme" (from Faust)
Jerusalem (from Gallia)
Jésus de Nazareth. See Nazareth
Jewel song ("Ah! je ris") See "Ah! je
ris de me voir"
Jewel song ("Je voudrais bien") See
"Je voudrais bien savoir quel était
ce jeune homme"
"The King of love my Shepherd is"
The king of Thule. See Le roi de
Thulé
"Lead us, heavenly Father, lead us"
Lend me your aid. See Inspirez-moi
"Let me gaze" (from Faust. Tr of
Laisse-moi, laisse-moi)

Gounod, Charles François —*Continued*

Like a vision. See "Ah! je veux vivre"
Love in spring. See Au printemps
"Lovely appear" (from La rédemption)
"Lovely flowers I pray." See "Faites-lui mes aveux"
Loving smile of sister kind. See "Avant de quitter ces lieux"
"Mab, la reine des mensonges" (from Roméo et Juliette)
"Mab, Queen Mab the fairies' midwife." See "Mab, la reine des mensonges"
"Maids may boast." See "Si les filles d'Arles"
Mandolin song
Margherita (from Faust)
Medjé
The message of love. See "Ô légère hirondelle"
Mon coeur ne peut changer (from Mireille)
The moonbeam. See Le soir
More grand is his humble estate. See Plus grand dans son obscurité
More royal in his humble state. See Plus grand dans son obscurité
My heart to thee. See À toi mon coeur
Nazareth
Night radiant in splendor. See Nuit resplendissante
Noël
"Now's the time to love." See Chanson de la sorcière
Nuit resplendissante (from Cinq-Mars)
"Nymphes attentives" (from Polyeucte)
O divine Redeemer. See Repentir
O harp immortal. See Ô ma lyre immortelle
Ô jours heureux (from Sapho)
"Ô légère hirondelle" (from Mireille)
Ô ma lyre immortelle (from Sapho)
O my lyre ever-living. See Ô ma lyre immortelle
"Ô riante nature" (from Philémon et Baucis)
"O tender moon" (from Faust. Tr of Ô nuit d'amour)
"O that we two were maying"
"O the smile of the spring-time." See "Ô riante nature"
O turn thee (from Gallia)
Open thy gates. See Temple ouvre-toi
Plus grand dans son obscurité (from La reine de Saba)
Power and love
"Praise ye the Father! let all the earth sing praises"
"Quand tu chantes." See Chantez riez et dormez
"Que les songes heureux" (from Philémon et Baucis)
Repentir
Ring forever
Ring on, sweet angelus
"Ring out, wild bells"
Le roi de Thulé (from Faust. Tr of Der könig von Thule)

Salut! demeure chaste et pure (from Faust)
Sappho's farewell. See Ô ma lyre immortelle
"Send out Thy light"
Serenade ("Quand tu chantes") See Chantez riez et dormez
Serenade ("Vous qui faites") See "Vous qui faites l'endormie"
She alone charmeth my sadness. See Sous les pieds d'une femme
The shepherds' nativity hymn. See Bethlehem
"Si le bonheur à sourire" (from Faust)
"Si les filles d'Arles"
"Since yesterday I've sought in vain my master." See "Depuis hier je cherche en vain mon maître"
Sing glad songs for him (same air as Soldiers' chorus)
Sing, smile and slumber. See Chantez riez et dormez
Le soir
Soldiers' chorus (from Faust. Tr of Gloire immortelle de nos aïeux)
Song, jest, perfume and dances. See "Ah! je veux vivre"
"Source délicieuse" (from Polyeucte)
Sous les pieds d'une femme (from La reine de Saba)
"The sparks fly thro' the smithy door." See "Au bruit des lourds marteaux d'airain"
"Tell me, beautiful maiden." See "Dites, la jeune belle"
Temple, ouvre-toi
"There is a green hill far away"
'Tis love, ah! 'tis love. See Ah! lève-toi, soleil
"To clang of brazen hammer's blow." See "Au bruit des lourds marteaux d'airain"
To spring. See Au printemps
Toast to Wisconsin
Unfold, ye portals (from La rédemption)
Until the day breaks
The valley. See Le vallon
Le vallon
"Le veau d'or" (from Faust)
"Virgin-born! we bow before Thee"
"Vous qui faites l'endormie" (from Faust)
Vulcan's song. See "Au bruit des lourds marteaux d'airain"
Waltz song. See "Ah! je veux vivre"
"When all was young." See "Si le bonheur à sourire"
"When to thy vision." See "Si le bonheur à sourire"
Without thee. See Ce que je suis sans toi

"**Goûtons** des plaisirs, ma bergère." See Chanson de berger

Gow, G. C.

Composer

On the chapel steps

Author

And then— (Hosmer)

Gow, Niel
Bonnie Charlie (attributed)
Caller herrin' (attributed)
"Far over yon hills." See Flora Macdonald's lament
Flora Macdonald's lament
The lament of Flora Macdonald. See Flora Macdonald's lament
"Out over the Forth, I look to the north"
"Roy's wife of Aldivalloch"
"There's a youth in this city"
"Tho' you leave me now"
"Where, braving angry winter's storms"
Will ye come back again. See Bonnie Charlie (attributed)
Will ye no more back again. See Bonnie Charlie (attributed)

Gowman, William
"Hark! the full-voiced choir is singing"
"The gown you wear is new, Antonià." See Antonià

Graben-Hoffmann, Gustav
The brightest angel. See Der schönste engel
Forget-me-not (Tr of Vergissmeinnicht)
"I at thy feet would fain be lying." See "Zu deinen füssen möcht' ich liegen'
"Meine ruh' ist hin"
"My peace is gone." See "Meine ruh' ist hin"
Der schönste engel
"Stars with golden feet are wandering." See "Sterne mit den goldnen füsschen"
"Sterne mit den goldnen füsschen"
"Zu deinen füssen möcht' ich liegen"

Grabgesang ("Selig die toten") J. A. Blüher. Words by A. Mahlmann. g. ED 2
Grace before meat at Hampton. Negro spiritual. HR
"**Graceful** butterfly." See "Charmant papillon" (Campra)
The **graceful** maiden ("One morn when mists did hover") Irish song. e. MMI
"The **Graces** and the wand'ring loves." See The wandering beauty (Pepusch)
"The **gracious** Father hears us when we call." C. M. von Weber. e. SAS 1
"**Gracious** Spirit, Love divine." I. Pleyel. WS
Pleyel's hymn. HSC
"**Grad** aus dem wirtshaus nun komm ich heraus." See Bedenklichkeiten
Gradinom cveće cvetalo. See Rose of yesteryear
The **graduates'** farewell. See "How sad mid the sunshine" (Old air)
Graduation song ("As the voyager turns") Air: My lodging is on the cold ground. Words by Davenant. LA
Graduation song no. 1. NMS
Graduation song ("Our school-days") Ancient air. Words by G. Cooper. LA

Graduation song no. 1 ("As the voyager turns") See Graduation song ("As the voyager turns")
Graduation song no. 2 ("How sad") See "How sad, 'mid the sunshine" (Pierce)
Graeff, Johann Georg
"Adieu to delight"
Graham, Robert Cunninghame-. See Cunninghame-Graham, Robert
"Le **grain** que ton ardeur par les labours sema." See The sower (Cui)
Lo **Granatiello** (Il Granatiello) Neapolitan air. e.i, FE
La **grande** et la petite (When the wine whirls) French Canadian folk song. e.f. BFS
Grandfather's clock. H. C. Work. WA —WBT—WSC—WSW
"**Grandma**, please tell me the way." See Come, show me the way
Grandmougin, Charles Jean
Chanson d'amour (Hollmann)
Loin de lui (Dancla)
Rencontre (Fauré)
Granier, Jules
Hosanna
Grannis, S. M.
"Do they miss me at home"
Your mission
"**Granny's** red-haired, granddad too." See Red-headed family
Grant, Mrs, of Carron. See Grant, Mrs Elizabeth
Grant, Rev. Dr
"Care, thou canker of our joys" (Garth)
Grant, Mrs Anne (Macvicar)
The blue bells of Scotland (Jordan)
Loth to depart (Welsh air)
The marsh of Rhuddlan (Welsh air)
The rising of the lark (Welsh air)
Grant, Mrs Elizabeth
Roy's wife of Aldivalloch (Scottish air)
Grant, Mrs James. See Grant, Mrs Anne (Macvicar)
Grant, Sir Robert
Litany (Composer unknown)
O come, let us worship (Haydn)
"**Grant** me but one single smile, love." See "Wenn du nur zuweilen lächelst" (Brahms)
"**Grant** me daylight's splendor." See Longing (Rubinstein)
Grantham, George P.
Composer and author
"Angel hosts in bright array"
"As Mary walked in the garden green"
"Deep the gloom and still the night"
"Moonbeams are streaming"
"Near the tomb where Jesus slept"
"Now sing we a strain of joy"
"Shine calm and bright, ye moonbeams bright"
"A song and a carol for Christmastide"

Grantham, George P.—*Continued*
Author
"As Mary walked in the garden green"
(Smith; also music by author)
"The Christmas bells are ringing"
(Flemish air; also music by Sun-
derland)
"In the star of morning" (Smith)
"The pearly gates aside are rolled"
(Irons)
"A rhyme, a rhyme, for Easter time"
(Lissant)
"When the crimson sun had set"
(Greatheed)
Graun, Karl Heinrich
Die auferstehung
"**Grausame** frühlingssonne." See Citro-
nenfalter im April (Wolf)
The **grave** of Bonaparte. H. S. Washburn.
Words by L. Heath. FSS 5—JO
Grave of Washington. L. V. H. Crosby.
Words by M. S. Pike. FSS 6—WBT
Graves, Alfred Perceval
The banks of the daisies (Old Irish air)
"By the lakes of Killarney" (Irish air)
Father O'Flynn (Old Irish air)
The foggy dew (Old Irish air)
If I were king of Ireland (Irish air)
The little red lark (Old Irish air)
"My love's an arbutus" (Irish air)
Spring song (Mackenzie)
"When she answered me her voice was
low" (Old Irish air)
Graves, John Woodcock
John Peel (Old Border air)
The **graves** of a household. N. Barker.
Words by F. Hemans. JO
Where are those dreamers now.
FSS 3
Gray, Charles
O Charlie is my darling (Jacobite air)
See also Pickering, George, jt.
auth.
Gray, Hamilton, pseud.
A dream of paradise
The golden pathway
The heavenly song
The priceless gift
Gray, J. B.
"Away! with loyal hearts"
Gray, John
The good Rhein wine
Gray, Louisa
Looking back (Sullivan)
Gray, Russell
"Words vain words" (Gabriel)
Gray, William
"The hunt is up" (16th century air) Au-
thorship uncertain
The **gray** dove ("Stapil Dobre") Bulgarian
folk song. b.e. BF 1
"**Gray** shadows are a-stealing." See Good-
night (Pingree)
Gray's Inn masque. See Mad Tom (Co-
perario)
Graziella. See Raziella
"**Great** Adamastor, the king of the ocean."
See "Adamastor, roi des vagues pro-
fondes" (Meyerbeer)

"**A great** and mighty wonder." See Our
Christmas festal
"**Great** and wonderful are all Thy works."
J. Raff. e. SAS 2
"**Great** Britain is the noblest land." At-
tributed to Shield. ME
A **great** camp meetin' ("There's a great
camp meetin'") Negro spiritual.
BOM
Variant of: A great camp-meeting in
the promised land
A **great** camp-meeting in the promised land
("Oh, walk together") Negro spir-
itual. JP
A great camp-meetin' in de promised
land ("Oh walk togedder") HR
A great campmeetin' ("Oh, walk to-
gedder") KA
Variant: A great camp meetin'
("There's a great camp meetin'")
"**Great** glory is the Lord's in Zion." See
Glory to the Lord in Zion (Bortniân-
skiĭ)
"**Great** God, high over all." See A com-
mencement hymn
"The **great** God of heaven" (The incarna-
tion) Traditional air no. 1. Words by
H. R. Bramley. BSC
"The **great** God of heaven." Traditional
air no. 2. Words by H. R. Bramley.
HC
"**Great** God of nations." Thanksgiving
song. J. H. Howe. MP—NMS
"**Great** happiness, gifts of gladness." See
Aya po (Dowanna)
"**Great** hearts that have battled in ages
behind us." See The vision
"**Great** is Jehovah, the Lord." See Die
Allmacht (Schubert)
"**Great** is the moon that looks at me." See
The moon
"**Great** Isis! great Osiris." See "O Isis
und Osiris" (Mozart)
Great joy we bring. L. Edson. MCS
"**Great** Leader went to fight." See
Pawnee war-song
"**Great** prince, thy resolution's just."
G. F. Händel. BS 2
"**Great** prophetess! my soul's on fire." See
In the battle, fame pursuing (Händel)
"**Great** queen! be calm." G. F. Händel.
SAS 3
Greatheed, Samuel Stephenson
"When the crimson sun had set"
Greatorex, Edward
"Put on, put on your best array"
Greatorex, Henry Wellington
Gloria Patri
Grechaninov, Aleksandr Tikhonovich
"Alles schläft." See "Slumber reigns"
"Another little hour I begged"
Berceuse. See Cradle-song
Le captif. See The captive
The captive
Cradle-song
"Hushed the song of the nightingale"
"Ich wollt' ein wenig mit dir plaudern."
See "Another little hour I begged"

Grechaninov, A. T.—*Continued*
"Il s'est tu, le charmant rossignol." See "Hushed the song of the nightingale"
Koluibélnaya. See Cradle-song
Kraï tui moï. See My native land
My native land
On the steppe. See Over the steppe
Óstroyu syekeeroi. See The wounded birch
Over the steppe
Palm branches
Schneeflöckchen. See Snowflakes
Das schneeglöckchen. See The snowdrop
The siren
Sirene. See The siren
The skylark
"Slumber reigns"
Slumber song. See Cradle-song
The snowdrop
Snowflakes
Styépyu idoo ya o͞onúiloyu. See Over the steppe
"Triste est le steppe." See Over the steppe
Vöglein. See The skylark
The wounded birch
The Greek huntsman. Old Dutch legend. e. KSN
Greek love song. See Love song ("Thousand times I've wandered here")
Greek national song. See "Sons of Greece, come, arise"
Green ("Voici des fruits") A. C. Debussy. Words by P. Verlaine. e.f. GMF
The green bed. Folk song: Devon version. BSW
—North Carolina version. CSE
Green broom. Folk song. SEF 1—SO
—Devon version. BSW
Variant: Broom, green broom
Green bushes. Folk song. SEF 1—SO
—Devon version. BSW
Green fields of America. FSS 5
The green grove ("Gaiczek zielony") Polish song. e.p. BF 1
Green grow the rashes, O ("There's nought but care on ev'ry hand") Scottish air. Words by Burns. BSB—FSS 4—JO—JSE— MMS— PS 1—SSS
"There's nought but care on ev'ry han'." BSR
"Green grows the holly." Henry VIII. DM 2
"Green in the valley and blue on the hill." See August (Olds)
The green linnet. Irish folk song. JOI
The green little shamrock. See "There's a dear little plant"
Green pastures. See "The Lord is my Shepherd" (Koschat)
Green-sleeves ("Alas! my love, you do me wrong") 16th century song. BOH —VFS

Green sleeves ("Oh! could we do") See "Oh! could we do with this world of ours"
"The green trees whispered low and mild." Balfe. Words by Longfellow. CS 1—HSE 3
The green wedding. Folk song. Air: The boatsman and the tailor. SEF 1 —SO
Greene, Albert Gorton
"Old Grimes" (Composer unknown)
Greene, Maurice
"Busy, curious, thirsty fly"
"Fair Sally"
"Das leben welkt wie gras"
"Like as a huntsman"
"The merry cuckoo, messenger of spring"
"The nymph that undoes me"
"Orpheus with his lute"
"Trust not the treason of those smiling lookes"
"With tuneful pipe and merry glee"
Greenhill, James
Autolycus' song. See "Lawn as white as driven snow"
"Lawn as white as driven snow"
Greenland fishery (The whale) Forecastle song. CR
Greenlee, C. E.
Hillsdale and the blue (Monroe)
"A greenness light and tender." German folk song. e. FSS 4
Greenville (Rousseau) See Cradle hymn; "Days of absence"; "Hark! 'tis the breeze"; "Thoughts of wonder"; "When the mists"; While to Bethl'em going
Greenwell, Dora
"Do you think of the days" (music by Blumenthal; Smart)
Greenwich park. See "Come, sweet lass" (Clark)
The greenwood tree. S. Nelson. FSS 4
"Greet we now the morning." See Morning serenade (Offenbach)
Greeting ("Des abends rosen sind abgeblüht") See Grüssen (Lassen)
Greeting ("Hello! Peter") TFC 2
Greetings. BSS
Greeting ("Leise zieht durch mein gemüth") See Gruss (Mendelssohn)
Greeting ("Sweetheart, when you walk") C. B. Hawley. Words by F. L. Stanton. MSF 1—SM 4
Greeting ("To thee and thine."—"Mnogaia ljeta") Serbian folk song. e.se. BF 1
"Greeting, O peaceful one." See Song of greeting
Greeting song. Air: Hanging Johnny. FSF
Greetings ("Hello! Peter") See Greeting ("Hello! Peter")
"Greetings to master and to mistress." See L'Aguignolé
Gregersen, Wilhelm
"Mine tanker" (Hartmann)

Gregh, Louis
  Come to thy window. See Parais à ta fenêtre
  Open thy lattice. See Parais à ta fenêtre
  Parais à ta fenêtre
Gregory, G. H.
  "A Virgin did come"
Greig, James
  "My lord a-hunting he is gane"
Greith, Johann
  Das echo
Gretchaninoff, Alexander Tichonovitch. See Grechaninov, Aleksandr Tikhonovich
Gretchen am spinnrade. See "Meine ruh' ist hin" (Schubert)
Gretchen at the spinning wheel. See "Meine ruh' ist hin" (Schubert)
"Gretchen lies in her gloomy bed in the wet, wet mold." See Moderen synger (Sinding)
"Gretchen lies in her gloomy couch in the dismal mold." See Moderen synger (Sinding)
"Gretchen ligger i kiste dybt i den sorte muld." See Moderen synger (Sinding)
Gretchens beichte ("Wieder ist es lange zehn") Schottische volksweise. Words by H. Hoffmann von Fallersleben. g. ED 3
Gretelein ("Schaust so freundlich aus") F. Kücken. Words by L. Hecker. g. ED 1
Grétry, André Ernest Modeste
  Air de Nicolette (from Aucassin et Nicolette)
  "Anguish of mind, sadness, too, leaves me." See "Plus de dépit, plus de tristesse"
  "Du moment qu'on aime" (from Zémire et Azor)
  "For Norge, kjaempers födeland"
  "Heart of hearts." See Air de Nicolette
  Naissantes fleurs (from Céphale et Procris)
  "Ô Richard, ô mon roi" (from Richard Coeur de Lion)
  "Plus de dépit, plus de tristesse" (from Les deux avares)
  "Tandis que tout sommeille" (from L'amant jaloux)
  "To Norway, mother of the brave." See "For Norge, kjaempers födeland"
  Ye budding flowers. See Naissantes fleurs
Greville, Sir Fulke. See Brooke, Fulke Greville, 1st baron
The **grey** cock. Folk song from North Carolina. CSE
The **grey** mare. Folk song. BSW
Grieg, Edvard Hagerup
  Afloat. See Im kahne
  Die alte mutter. See Gamle mor
  Am schönsten sommerabend war's
  An einem bache. See Langs en å
  At Monte Pincio. See Vom Monte Pincio
  At the brookside. See Langs en å
  Auf der reise zur heimath
  Autumnal gale. See Herbststurm
  "Be greeted, ye ladies." See "Vaer hilset, i damer"
  Borte
  Cradle song. See Wiegenlied
  En digters sidste sang
  A dream. See Ein traum
  Epilog
  Eros
  Erstes begegnen
  Farmyard song
  First meeting. See Erstes begegnen
  The first primrose. See Med en primulaveris
  Det förste möde
  From Monte Pincio. See Vom Monte Pincio
  From the Pincian hill. See Vom Monte Pincio
  Der frühling
  Gamle mor
  God morgen
  Gone. See Borte
  Good morning. See God morgen
  Guten morgen. See God morgen
  Herbststurm
  Humility. See Ungbirken
  "Hun er saa hvid"
  I love thee. See Jeg elsker dig
  Ich liebe dich. See Jeg elsker dig
  Im kahne
  In the boat. See Im kahne
  Jeg elsker dig
  Das kind der berge
  Land sighting. See Olaf Trygvason
  Landkjending. See Olaf Trygvason
  Langs en å
  Last farewell. See Epilog
  Lauf der welt
  Love's first meeting. See Det förste möde
  Margaretes vuggesang
  Margaret's cradle song. See Margaretes vuggesang
  Med en primulaveris
  Mit einer primula veris. See Med en primulaveris
  The mountain maid. See Das kind der berge
  "My dear old mother." See Gamle mor
  Oh, beware. See Sieh dich vor
  Olaf Trygvason
  The old mother. See Gamle mor
  On St John's eve. See Zur Johannisnacht
  On the journey home. See Auf der reise zur heimath
  On the way home. See Auf der reise zur heimath
  The poet's last song. See En digters sidste sang
  The primrose. See Med en primulaveris
  The princess. See "Prinsessen sad höjt i sit jomfrubur"
  Prinsessen. See "Prinsessen sad höjt i sit jomfrubur"

Grieg, Edvard Hagerup —*Continued*
"Prinsessen sad höjt i sit jomfrubur"
Die prinzessin. See "Prinsessen sad höjt i sit jomfrubur"
Rosebud
"Saa du knøsen, som strøg forbi"
Ein schwan. See En svane
"See the fellow that passed just now." See "Saa du knøsen, som strøg forbi"
Sieh dich vor
"So white is she." See "Hun er saa hvid"
Solveig's song. See Solvejgs sang
Solvejg's cradle-song. See Solvejgs wiegenlied
Solvejgs lied. See Solvejgs sang
Solvejgs sang (from Peer Gynt)
Solvejg's song. See Solvejgs sang
Solvejgs wiegenlied (from Peer Gynt)
Springtide. See Der frühling
Summer evening. See Am schönsten sommerabend war's
A summer evening in Norway. See Am schönsten sommerabend war's
Sunrise. See God morgen
Sunshine song. See Solvejgs sang
En svane
A swan. See En svane
Et syn
"Tak for dit råd"
"Thanks for thy counsel." See "Tak for dit råd"
Til Norge
To a primrose. See Med en primulaveris
To a swan. See En svane
To a violet. See Med en primulaveris
To Norway. See Til Norge
Ein traum
Ungbirken
"Vaer hilset, i damer"
Vandring i skoven
A vision. See Et syn
Vom Monte Pincio
Wandering in the woods. See Vandring i skoven
The way of the world. See Lauf der welt
Wiegenlied
With a primrose. See Med en primulaveris
With a violet. See Med en primulaveris
Woodland roving. See Vandring i skoven
Woodland wandering. See Vandring i skoven
The young birch. See Ungbirken
Zur Johannisnacht
"**Grieve** no longer, my beloved." See Parásha's revery and dance (Musorgskiï)
"**Grievous** my fate, dear." See "Vivo penando"
Griffin, Gerald
Eileen aroon (Celtic air)
"I love my love in the morning" (Irish air)
The wanderer's return (Irish air)

Griffiths, C.
"Pansies, lilies, roses" (music by Booth; Oliver)
Grilo, A. Fernández. See Fernández Grilo, A.
Grinding. L. Fischer. Words by H. M. B. Reid. SSS—WBT
Gröndahl, fru Agathe Ursula (Backer) See Backer-Gröndahl, fru Agathe Ursula
Groome, Francis Hindes
"Christians, listen while we sing" (music by Martin; Smith)
Groos, Karl
"Freiheit, die ich meine"
Groser, William Howse
"A joyous song once more we bring" (Maker)
"A song of spring once more we sing" (music by Benson; Booth)
Grosheim, Georg Christoph
Das mädchen aus der fremde
"**Gross** ist Jehova der Herr." See Die Allmacht (Schubert)
Das **grossvaterlied** ("Als der grossvater die grossmutter nahm") German folk air. Words by A. Langbein. g. ED 1
Grossvater tanz (German grandfather dance) e.g. BMC
Das grossvaterlied ("Als der grossvater die grossmutter nahm."--"When my grandfather my grandmother wed") e.g. SSG
Das grossvaterlied ("Back in the time when my grandfather wed") e. GO
Groth, Klaus
"Wie melodien zieht es mir" (Brahms)
The **ground** hog. Kentucky mountain song. WLT
"The **ground** is strewn" (Nu'a o ka palai) Leleiohoku. e.h. HA
Ground ivy. J. Moulds. ME
"The **ground** was all cover'd with snow one day." See The snowbird
"The **groves** of Blarney." Words by R. A. Millikin. FSS 4—JO—WBT
"**Grow** old along with me." See Rabbi Ben Ezra (Hadley)
Grübel, Johann Konrad
Der schlossergesell (Folk air)
Gruber, Franz
Die heilige nacht
"Holy night! peaceful night." See Die heilige nacht
"Noche de paz." See Die heilige nacht
"Silent night! holy night." See Die heilige nacht
"Stille nacht! heilige nacht." See Die heilige nacht
The gruel. See El atole
Grünbaum, J. C.
"High the Cossack's heart is bounding." See The Cossack's song
The Cossack's song
Gruppe,
Niemand hat's geseh'n (Loewe)

Gruss ("Leise zieht durch mein gemüth."—Greeting) F. Mendelssohn. Words by H. Heine. e.g. PG 4

Grüssen ("Des abends rosen sind abgeblüht."—Greeting) E. Lassen. e.g. AB 2

Guadalquiver. C. Nelson. Words by C. Jefferys. FSS 2

La **guajira** ("Yo soy guajira, nacíen Melena") Cuban folk song. e.s. HS

La **guajira** ("Yo vivo sola en el mundo."—The peasant girl) Mexican song. e.s. BF 2

"**Gualtier** Maldè." See Caro nome (Verdi)

The **guard** and King Eric. See Lifdrabanten och kung Erik (Lindblad)

"**Guarda** il mare com' è bello." See Torna a Surriento (Curtis)

"**Guarda** la luna" (See the moon) Italian song. e.i. BF 2

The **guardian** angel ("Last night") See "Last night, as I lay sleeping"

The **guardian** angel ("Still is the night") C. Gounod. Words by H. Farnie. FSS 8

Guardian angels ("When children lay them down to sleep") R. Schumann. [Tr of Wenn kleine kinder schlafen geh'n] e. WBT

"**Guardian** mother." F. Abt. FSS 7

Guatemala, around thy free banner. See Guatemala, en tu limpia bandera (Alvarez)

Guatemala, en tu limpia bandera (Guatemala, around thy free banner) National song. R. Alvarez. Words by R. P. Molina. e.s. SN

Guatemala, around thy free banner. e.s. MP

"**Guatemala** feliz!. . . ya tus aras." See Himno nacional de Guatemala (Alvarez)

"**Guatemala!** rejoice in thy freedom." See Himno nacional de Guatemala (Alvarez)

Guckkasten-lied ("Raritete sein ssu sehn") Volkslied. g. ED 3

"**Gude** e'en to ye, kimmer, and are ye alane." See We're a' noddin'

Guernsey, Wellington

Composer

"I'll hang my harp on a willow tree": old English air arranged

"Ye say they all have passed away" (same air as "I'll hang my harp on a willow tree": old English air arranged)

Author

Alice, where art thou (Ascher)

Gueroult, A.
Ecstasy. See Extase
Extase

The **guests** arrive (Ne bylo vîetru, vdrug povîanulo) Russian folk song. e. SSR 3

"The **guests** have left me in stillness unbroken." See Borte (Grieg)

Guglielmo, Pasquale D.
The birthday of a King
Night (Tr of La notte è bella)
"The night is fine." See Night

"**Guid** mwornin', bonny Leezie." See Die latern

"**Guide** au bord ta nacelle." See "Du schönes fishermädchen" (Meyerbeer)

"**Guide** me, O Thou Great Jehovah." Spanish air. [Words by W. Williams] LA

"**Guide** me, O Thou great Jehovah." F. von Flotow. Words by W. Williams. JS

"**Guide** me, O thou great Jehovah." T. Hastings. Words by W. Williams. FSS 4

"**Guide** me, O Thou great Jehovah." F. Hérold. [Words by W. Williams] FSS 1—WS

Guide me, great Jehovah. WBT

"**Guide** mes pas" ("Guide thou my steps") L. Cherubini. e.f. KS 5

"**Guide** thou my steps." See "Guide mes pas" (Cherubini)

"**Guided** by us, thrice happy pair." See Bridal chorus (Wagner)

"**Guide'en** to you, kimmer, and how do you do." Air: We're a' noddin'. Words by R. Burns. BSR

The **guiding** light. See "Vado ben spesso cangiando loco" (Rosa)

Guidwife, count the lawin. Scottish air. Words by R. Burns. PS 2
"Gane is the day." BSR

Guillaume de Machaut
"Douce dame jolie"
"Sweet-heart, gentle and pretty." See "Douce dame jolie"

Guillaume Franc. See Franc, Guillaume

Guiterman, Arthur
Bow! wow (Ames)

Guldterning. Norwegian song. e. KSN

Güll, Friedrich
Der kleine rekrut (Küchen)

The **gum-tree** canoe. See Tom-big-bee river

Gumbert, Ferdinand
The good angels
"The merry birds"
O bitt' euch liebe vögelein
The pirate. See Der seeräuber
The poet and the children
Der seeräuber
The tear. See Die thräne
Die thräne
Ye merry birds. See O bitt' euch liebe vögelein

Gumeneva, I.
The brook (Bleikhman)

Gummere, Francis B.
"It's a right little, tight little college" (Becket)

Gungl,
"The heart that knows no sorrow"

Die **gunst** des augenblicks ("Und so finden wir uns wieder") K. F. Zelter. Words by Schiller. g. ED 2

"Gur-a mis' tha fo mhulaid." See An gille donn

Gurney, Archer Thompson
Composer
"Come, ye lofty, come, ye lowly"
"Now we bring our Christmas treasures"
Author
"Christ is risen! Christ is risen! He hath burst His bonds in twain" (music by Field; Sullivan)
"Come, ye lofty, come, ye lowly" (music by Custance; Elvey; also music by author)

Gurney, John Hampden
The Christmas celebration (Prout)
"Fair waved the golden corn" (Spinney)
"Lord of the harvest! Thee we hail" (Lissant)

Gurney, R.
"Soft the autumn suns are shining" (Horner)

Gurnsey, Wellington. See Guernsey, Wellington

"Guschi ki behakk." See Deign my voice to hear

Gustaf, duke of Uppland
Farewell. See Farväl
Farväl
"I rosens doft"
"Im rosenduft." See "I rosens doft"
"If peace and content." See "När själen är nöjd"
"Midst roses sweet." See "I rosens doft"
"När själen är nöjd"
Student-song. See Studentsång
Studentsång
"Where roses fair." See "I rosens doft"
"Where roses grow." See "I rosens doft"

"Gut' nacht" ("Good night! good night") See "Good night" (Rubinstein)
Der **gute** kamerad ("Ich hatt' einen kameraden") Words by L. Uhland. **g.** ED 1
The faithful comrade. **e.** FSS 8—WSC
Der gute kamerad (My comrade) **e.g.** SSG
Gute nacht ("Die höh'n und wälder."—Farewell) R. Franz. Words by J. von Eichendorff. **e.g.** FM
Gute nacht, du mein herziges kind (Good-night, sweet child) F. Abt. **e.g.** MSF 2
Gute ruhe ("Im arm der liebe ruht sich's wohl") P. von Winter. Words by W. Ueltzen. **g.** ED 2
"**Guten** abend, gut' nacht." See Wiegenlied (Brahms)
"**Guten** abend, mein schatz." See Vergebliches ständchen (Brahms)
Guten morgen ("Dagen er oppe") See God morgen (Grieg)
"**Guten** morgen, liebes Lieserl." See Die latern

"**Guten** va tröit, somardagen heit." See Huldra aa en Elland
"**Guter** mond, du gehst so stille." See An den mond

Gutiérrez, Felipe
La despedida

Gutierrez, Mel. Ma.
"De la patria"

Guttinguer, Ulrich
"Embarquez-vous" (Godard)

Guy Fawkes. Air: The barking barker. Words by T. Hudson. DM 2
Guy Fawkes (It might have been) ME

Gwendoline ("There's a name which doth delight me") Air: Lili lon, or, Bright lily. Words by L. S. Jast. MMW

Gwenllian. Welsh folk song. **e.** GO

Gwilym, Davydd ap. See David ap Gwilym

Gwilym and Ellen ("Poor Ellen lov'd Gwilym") Air: Lady Owen's delight. Words by Gwilym Davydd. **e.** MMW

"**Gwine** to lay down my burden." See I ain't gwine study war no more

Gwine to live humble to de Lord. Negro spiritual. HR
Variant of: Humble yourself

Gwine to run all night. See De Camptown races (Foster)

"**Gwine** to see my mother some o' dese mornin's." See Some of these mornings

"**Gwine** to write to Massa Jesus." See Turn back Pharaoh's army

Gwine up. Negro spiritual. HR—JB
Going up. JP

Gwinter sing all along de way. Negro spiritual. JB
I'm going to sing all the way. JP

Gybson, Leonard
Light o' love (Ancient air)

"**Gypsies** three I saw one day." See Die drei zigeuner (Liszt)

The **gypsy** forge. Hungarian air: Csillag elég ragyog. Words by M. L. Baum. GO

The **gypsy** laddie. Folk song: Black Mountain, N.C. version. CSE
—Hot Springs, N.C. version. CSE
—Flag Pond, Tenn. version. CSE
—Rocky Fork, Tenn. version no. 1. CSE
—Rocky Fork, Tenn. version no. 2. CSE
—Virginia version. CSE

H

H_2SO_4. College song. M. E. Russell. CHS—MPC
"Ha a a ho e tha a." See Hand game song
"Ha du' kji hoppa" (Halling from Valders) **e.n.** MAN
"Ha! free a poacher's living." See The jolly poacher

"Ha, ha, ha ha ha! ha ha! hi hi! ha ha! hi." See The laugh

Ha, ha, ha, you and me. See Little brown jug (Eastburn)

"Ha hay hi! ha hay hi." See Game song

"Ha he ha ha he ha he ha we dhe ha dha." See The old man's love song

"Ha! my pretty brace of fellows." See "Ha! wie will ich triumphiren" (Mozart)

"Ha ni an bé." See Khedival hymn

"Ha! thy cheek now crimson grows." See Suspicion (Lindblad)

"Ha! what am I reading." See Parting sorrow

"Ha! what splendour unwonted." See O voi dell' Erebo (Händel)

"Ha! wie will ich triumphiren" (Ha! my pretty brace of fellows) Mozart. e.g.i. BS 2

"Ha! yet this hero all victorious." See Entrance song (Millocker)

"Haaheo e ka ua i na pali." See Aloha oe (Liliuokalani)

"Haalele ma kou ia Honolulu." See Hawaiian hula (Maunawili) (Hopkins)

Habanera ("L'amour est un oiseau rebelle."—"Love is like a wild bird rebelling") Bizet. e.f. CM 1
Habanera ("Ah! love, thou art a wilful wild bird") e. WA—WBT—WL
Habanera ("L'amour est un oiseau rebelle."—"Love is just like a tameless bird") e.f.i. OPS 2
Habanera ("L'amour est un oiseau rebelle."—"Love is like any woodbird wild") e.f. SOA 2

Haberban (Haperpan) Armenian song. a.e. BF 2

Habergham, Mrs Fleetwood
"I sow'd the seeds of love" (Folk air; Sussex air; also air: The willow tree) Authorship uncertain

"Hacesado la lucha sangrienta." See Dulce patria (Carnicer y Batlle)

Had fickle fortune, not betraying (Wenn mich für häuslichkeit) P. I. Tchaikovsky. e.g. KS 5

"Had I a cave." Air: Robin Adair, or, Aileen a roon. Words by R. Burns. BSR

"Had I a heart for falsehood framed." Old air: Grammachree. Words by R. B. Sheridan. JO

"Had I but love." H. Purcell. DM 2

"Had I Hanover, Bremen and Varding." See Molly Lepell

"Had I the wyte." Air: Come kiss with me. Words by R. Burns. BSR

Had I wings like a dove. Words by C. Jefferys. FSS 7

"Had me a cat and the cat pleased me." See The farmyard

"Had you seen my sweet coolin." See The coolin

"Had you seen my sweet coolun." See The coolun

Hadji, Emin
Hamidie (Nedjib Pacha)

Hadley, Henry Kimball
Easter
Farewell
The flag
The fountain
"How do I love thee"
"I plucked a quill from Cupid's wing"
Rabbi Ben Ezra
Rose-time
While you sleep

Haē Basilēs. See Saint Basil

Hāfiz, Muhammed Shams al-Dīn
The bouquet (Alferakiï)

Hägg, Gustaf
Cradle-song. See Slummersång
Slummersång (Tr of Wiegenlied)

"Hagios Basilēs erchetai." See Saint Basil

Hahn, Karl
Das steckenpferd (Hering)

Hahn, Reynaldo
Could my songs their way be winging. See Si mes vers avaient des ailes
L'heure exquise
The hour of dreaming. See L'heure exquise
Mai
May. See Mai
"My songs of love"
The perfect hour. See L'heure exquise
Rêverie
Si mes vers avaient des ailes
"With haste my song would be flying." See Si mes vers avaient des ailes

Haï luli. A. Coquard. Words by X. de Maistre. e.f. HM 1
Hai luli (Alack-a-day) e.f. SAM

"Hai-yo hai-yan." See Song of Chinese rowers

Haibel, Jakob
"The folk of the Tyrol are jolly and gay." See Tyroler
The Tyroleans. See Tyroler
Tyroler (from Der Tyroler wastl)
"Tyrolese are blithesome." See Tyroler

"Die haide ist braun." See Im herbst (Franz)

Haiden-röslein. See Heidenröslein (Schubert)

"Hail, all hail, each happy season." See Christmas as it comes

"Hail, all hail, our beautiful land." See Croatian national anthem (Runjamin)

"Hail! all hail the sons of 'Uni.'" See University, live for aye

"Hail! all hail this brightest morning." A. H. Brown. Words by S. C. Clarke. HC

"Hail, all hail, to our prince, the noble King Alfonso." See Marcha real

"Hail, alma mater, old Amherst the true." See Alma mater—Amherst

"Hail and farewell." See Parting graduation song (Barnard)

"Hail, beauteous stranger of the grove." See Spring-time once again (Sullivan)

Hail, Beloit. Beloit college song. W. B. Olds. CHS

"Hail, bright Easter." C. Gounod. Words by A. Crane. TFC 2

"Hail, Columbia." P. Phile (called also J. Fayles, Fyles, Phyla, Phylo and J. Vales) Words by J. Hopkinson. BD—BMC—BSE— BSP— CST— EF—FMB—FSS 1—FSS 5—HSC— HSD—JO— JS—JSE— LA— LBR —MP—MS— NMH—NMS— SSS —WA—WBT— WCP— WSC— WSW

"Hail Columbia" (Evening colors) SN

Hail Columbia, The new. ꞁP. Phileꞁ Words by O. W. Holmes. FSS 5— LA

"Hail, Columbia! happy land." See "Hail, Columbia" (Phile)

"Hail, Columbia! strong and free." See Hail Columbia, The new (Phile)

"Hail, David, our deliv'rer." F. Hiller. e. SAS 1

"Hail, Easter bright, in glory dight." 16th century air. Tr of Serena lux, amena lux. e. HC

Hail, evening bright. Marie Antoinette ꞁi.e. Maria Charlotte Ameliaꞁ FSS 3

Hail! ever-blessed morn. See "See, amid the winter's snow" (Gollmick)

"Hail-fellow-well-met, a soldier boy." See Le retour funeste

"Hail, gentle Jesus." Christmas carol. HC

Hail, gentle King. See Nowell (Maristow)

Hail! hail! hail. Negro spiritual. HR

"Hail, hail put John on de islan'." See Put John on de islan'

"Hail! hail! the gang's all here." BSS

"Hail! hail! Thou glorious Scion." See "Es ist ein ros' entsprungen"

"Hail him! hail him! all hail our noble King Alfonso." See Marcha real

Hail Lafayette. College song. Words by Sciple. CHS

"Hail, Mary, hail." See "Ave Maria" (Verdi)

"Hail, Northland high, all hail." See "Hell dig, du höga Nord" (Crusell)

"Hail! O North! thy wind send." See I-ou'-tin game song

"Hail, Pennsylvania." University of Pennsylvania song. Air: Russian national hymn. Words by E. M. Dilley. CHS—MPC—NMS

"Hail, poetry! thou heav'n-born maid." See Poetry (Sullivan)

"Hail, sacred isle! dear land." See Gesang Weyla's (Wolf)

Hail, Stanford, hail. Leland Stanford, jr, university song. Words by A. W. Smith. CHS—MPC

"Hail, sweet Babe, so pure and holy." G. E. Oliver. Words by E. Wiglesworth. HC

"Hail! sweet Babe, so pure and holy." E. Pettman. Words by E. Wiglesworth. HC

"Hail the blest morn." L. Mason. Words by R. Heber. MCS

"Hail the hero of our land." See Dom Miguel

"Hail the northern beacon." See "Salve boreale lumen"

"Hail the sun's bright morning rays" (Siamese song) Air: Cha Lok Lo-ang. e. BMC

"Hail thee, our Bethany." Bethany college song. CHS

Hail! Thou glorious Scion. See "Es ist ein ros' entsprungen"

"Hail! Thou long-expected Jesus" (Hope of the world) I. Conkey. Words by C. Wesley. MCS

"Hail, Thou long-expected" (Rathbun) FSS 7—LA

"Hail, Thou most sacred One." See Evening hymn

"Hail, Thou once despised Jesus." Spanish air. Words by J. Bakewell. FSS 5

"Hail thou, whose victor's crown." See "Heil dir im siegerkranz" (Carey)

Hail to Denver U. I. E. Cutler (music and words) MPC

Hail to Juniata. Juniata college song. CHS

Hail to old I. U. Indiana university song. CHS

Hail to our flag. See The American hymn (Keller)

"Hail to the birthday of freedom." See Independence day (Oehmler)

"Hail to the brightness." T. Hastings. FSS 2

"Hail to the chief." Scottish air. Words by W. Scott. PS 2

"Hail to the chief." H. R. Bishop. Words by W. Scott. JO

"Hail to the chief." J. Sanderson. Words by W. Scott. FSS 2—HSD—JSE—WBT

"Hail to the emperor, ruler and guide." See Russian national hymn (Lvov)

"Hail to the happy bridal day." G. Donizetti. ꞁTr of Per te d'immenso giubiloꞁ e. WBT

"Hope brightly gleams." e. FSS 8

"Hail to the Lord's anointed." L. Mason. Words by J. Montgomery. FSS 8 The Lord's anointed. MCS

"Hail to the Lord's anointed" (His reign on earth begun) G. 'J. Webb. Words by J. Montgomery. MCS

"Hail to thee, Mary, full of grace." See "Ave Maria" (Verdi)

"Hail to thee, O alma mater." See Alma mater—University of North Dakota

"Hail to thee, song of the careless collegians." See The student song (Maxfield)

Hail your birthland! hail its ruler. See Hymno nacional—Portugal (Pedro IV)

Haili crowned with lehua (Haili po ika lehua) C. K. Hopkins. e.h. HA

Haili po ika lehua. See Haili crowned with lehua (Hopkins)

Haines, R. M.
Co-education (Cole)
"The new woman" (Cole)

The **hal-an-tow.** See The Cornish May song

Hal-li, hal-lo. See "Herr bruder, nimm das gläschen"

Hâle, Adam de la. See Adam da la Halle

Hale, Mrs Sarah Josepha (Buell)
The Lord's prayer (Composer unknown)

Halem, G. A. von
Trinklied (Gerstenberg)

Halévy, Jacques François Fromental Élie
Bright star of hope. See "Call me thine own"
"Call me thine own" (from L'éclair. Tr of Quand de la nuit)
En dormant, c'est à moi (from La fée aux roses)
"Le gondolier dans sa pauvre nacelle" (from La reine de Chypre)
Humble fille des champs (from Charles VI)
"If harsh decree." See "Si la rigueur"
"Se il rigor." See "Si la rigueur"
"Si la rigueur" (from La Juive)
"Thou faithless men." See "Si la rigueur"
"Il va venir" (from La Juive)

"**Half** conceal'd by the ivied wall." See An eine Aeolsharfe (Brahms)

The **half-hitch.** Vermont song. SSH

Halka. S. Moniuszko. e.p. BF 1

Halket, George
Logie o' Buchan (Scottish air)

Hall, Benjamin H.
"Day of wonder, day of gladness" (music by Oliver; Rousseau; also unknown composer)

Hall, Charles Sprague
"John Brown's body" (Old air)

Hall, Foley
"Ever of thee"

Hall, Joseph
For Christmas day (Traditional air)

Hall, W. B.
"Joys that we've tasted"

Hall, W. H. A.
"Easter flowers, Easter carols"
"Silent stars were watching"

"The **hall** is empty—all absent on their duty." See Ah! parea che per incanto (Donizetti)

Halle, Adam de la. See Adam de la Halle

Halleck, Fitz-Greene
"Young thoughts have music" (Kroeger)

Hallelujah ("Hallelujah! an' a hallelujah") Negro spiritual. JB

Hallelujah ("Hallelujah! hallelujah! hallelujah! O sing the Lord in holy fear") O. Lob. BSS

Hallelujah chorus. G. F. Händel. FSS 5 —MCS

"**Hallelujah!** hallelujah! hallelujah! O sing the Lord in holy fear." See Hallelujah (Lob)

"**Hallelujah!** hallelujah! song of triumph." See Hallelujah! song of triumph (Smith)

The **hallelujah** of love (Allelúia lubvee) M. P. Moussorgsky. e. SMR 1

"**Hallelujah,** raise the song." J. W. Andrews. HC

"**Hallelujah!** raise the song." A. H. Brown. HC

Hallelujah! song of triumph. R. F. Smith. Words by G. Thring. HC

"**Hallelujah** to the Lamb, Jesus died for ev'ry man." See Fighting on! hallelujah

"**Hallelujah** to the Lamb, we are walking in the light." See We are walking in the light

Hallén, Johan Andreas
"And many thousand ducats." See "Och många tusen kronor"
"Det fins en gosse och han är min"
"Och många tusen kronor"
"There is a laddie, and he is mine." See "Det fins en gosse och han är min"

Halling from Valders ("Ha du' kji hoppa") See "Ha du' kji hoppa"

Halling from Valders ("Rötnam's Knut") See "Rötnam's Knut"

Halling from Valders ("Suttam sudelita luttam") See Kvaalins halling

Hallström, Ivar
"Black swans." See "Svarta svanor"
En liten visa
A little song. See En liten visa
"Svarta svanor"

Halsey, Rena Isabelle
Around the May-pole (Composer unknown)
Easter hymn (Composer unknown)
The king of night (Composer unknown)
The May-pole dance (Composer unknown)
St Valentine (Composer unknown)
The song of the months (Composer unknown)

"**Halt** there! who comes? the sea grows green." See Lifdrabanten och kung Erik (Lindblad)

Halvorsen, Leif
Hel mig mine strenge
Mend me my strings. See Hel mig mine strenge

La **hamaca** (The hammock) Spanish-American song. e.s. LSS

Hamburg (Mason) See "Kingdoms and thrones to God belong"; Whose sins have pardon gained

"**Hamburg** is a jolly city." See "Hamburg ist ein schönes städtchen"

"**Hamburg** ist ein schönes städtchen" ("Hamburg is a jolly city") e.g. SMW

Hame cam' our gudeman at e'en. Scottish song. PS 2

"Hame, hame, hame." Jacobite air. Words by A. Cunningham. HSSS—MMS—PS 2

Hamelberg, H. A. L.
"Heft, burgers, 't lied der vrijheid" (Nicolaï)

Hamerton, Samuel Collingwood
Composer and author
"Waken, Christian children"
Author
"O let us all, rejoicing" (Irons)

Hamidie. Turkish imperial air. Nedgib Pacha. Words by Hadji Emin Bey. e.f.t. SN
L'hamidié (Song to the sultan) e.t. BSP
Song of the sultan. e.t. MP

Hamilton, Elizabeth
My ain fireside (Scottish air)

Hamilton, Eugene Lee-. See Lee-Hamilton, Eugene

Hamilton, Henry
Private Tommy Atkins (Potter)

Hamilton, John
The braes of Yarrow (Scottish air)
The ploughman (Scottish air)
Up in the morning early (Scottish air)

Hamilton, Mary C. D.
Hymn for the airmen (Oliver)

Hamilton-Gell, A. E.
"Earth below is teeming"

Hamilton's song. Hamilton college song. CHS

"The hamlet lies a dreaming." See Sildig (Backer-Gröndahl)

"Hammer on the drum, pound it." See Carousal

Hammerin' song. Negro folk song from the mines of Virginia. BN 4

The hammock. See La hamaca

"Han anem ort e blümeli g'seh." See 's blümeli (Kuhn)

"Han Mass aa'en Lasse, der gingo paa raad" (Mass and Lasse) Norse folk song. e.n. MAN
Variants: Mass aa'en Lass ("Han Mass aa'n Lass skulde"); Mass aa'n Lasse ("Han Mass aa'en Lasse, dei gingo")

"Han Mass aa'en Lasse dei gingo paa raa." See Mass aa'n Lasse ("Han Mass aa'en Lasse dei gingo")

"Han Mass aa'n Lass skulde ut aa gaa." See Mass aa'n Lass ("Han Mass aa'n Lass skulde")

Hanby, Benjamin Russel
Darling Nelly Gray
Old Shady

Hance, Robert
Waiting for me

Hancke, Gottfried Benjamin
Jägerlied (French air)

Hand game song. Indian song. in. FI

"Eine hand voll erde." Attributed to C. B. Klein. Volkslied. g. ED 2

Händel, Georg Friedrich
"Affani del pensier" (from Ottone)
"Ah! mio cor" (from Alcina)

"Ah, poor heart." See "Ah! mio cor"
"Amaz'd to find the foe so near" (from Belshazzar)
Angels, ever bright and fair (from Theodora)
Antioch. See "Joy to the world"
Arm, arm, ye brave (from Judas Maccabaeus)
As when the dove laments her love (from Acis and Galatea)
"Ask if yon damask rose be sweet." See "Frag' ob die rose"
"Awake, my soul, stretch every nerve"
"Awake, Saturnia" (from Semele)
"Awful, pleasing being, say" (from Joshua)
"Banish thy sorrow" (from Rinaldo)
"Behold! a Virgin shall conceive" (from The Messiah)
"Behold, I tell you a mystery" (from The Messiah)
"Beneath the cypress' gloomy shade" (from Susanna)
"Born amid the rugged wildwood." See "Nasce al bosco"
"But oh! what art can teach" (from Ode for St Cecilia's day)
"But who is this? tremendous to behold" (from Joshua)
"But who may abide the day of His coming" (from The Messiah)
"Cangiò d'aspetto" (from Admeto)
"Cara sposa, amante cara" (from Rinaldo)
"Clouds may rise." See "Sorge infausta"
Col raggio placido (from Agrippina)
"Come unto Him, all ye that labor, come unto Him" (from The Messiah)
Comfort ye my people (from The Messiah)
"Dearest consort." See "Cara sposa"
"Deeper, and deeper still, thy goodness" (from Jephtha)
"Del minacciar del vento" (from Ottone)
Dove sei (from Rodelinda)
"Droop not, young lover"
"The enemy said" (from Israel in Egypt)
Ev'ry valley shall be exalted (from The Messiah)
Farewell, ye limpid springs and floods (from Jephtha)
Farewell! your country calls you. See "Lascia amor, e siegui Marte"
Father of heav'n! from Thy eternal throne (from Judas Maccabaeus)
"For, behold, darkness shall cover" (from The Messiah)
"Frag' ob die rose"
"From celestial seats descending" (from Hercules)
From mighty kings (from Judas Maccabaeus)
Funeral dirge
Generoso chi sol brama (from Scipione)

Händel, Georg Friedrich —*Continued*

"Gentle airs, melodious strains" (from Athalia)

Go, my faithful soldier, go (from Theodora)

God is present everywhere.   See "They who see the throne of grace"

"Great prince, thy resolution's just" (from Solomon)

"Great Prophetess! my soul's on fire" (from Deborah)

"Great queen! be calm" (from Athalia)

Hallelujah chorus (from The Messiah)

"Hark! 'tis the linnet" (from Joshua)

"He that dwelleth in heaven" (from The Messiah)

He was despised and rejected (from The Messiah)

Hence, Iris, hence away (from Semele)

"Heroes, when with glory burning" (from Joshua)

"Hide thou thy hated beams" (from Jephtha)

His sceptre is the rod of righteousness (from The occasional oratorio)

"Holy, holy, Lord God Almighty"

"Honour and arms" (from Samson)

Hope with her ray serene.   See Col raggio placido

"How beautiful are the feet of them" (from The Messiah)

"How changed the vision."   See "Cangiò d'aspetto"

"Humbled with fear" (from The occasional oratorio)

Hymen, haste! thy torch prepare (from Semele)

I feel the Deity within (from Judas Maccabaeus)

"I know that my Redeemer liveth" (from The Messiah)

"I know the pangs that cleave the bleeding heart" (from Susanna)

"I love Thy kingdom, Lord"

I rage, I melt, I burn (from Acis and Galatea)

"If torn from thee" (from Amadigi. Tr of Se estinto è l'idol mio)

"In gentle murmurs will I mourn" (from Jephtha)

In the battle, fame pursuing (from Deborah)

"It must be so"   (from Jephtha)

Jehovah! to my words give ear (from The occasional oratorio)

"Joy to the world"

Largo ("Frondi tenere") See Ombra mai fu

Largo (same air as Ombra mai fu; with words "Father in heav'n, Thy children hear"; "Lord in heav'n above, Who ruleth us")

"Lascia amor, e siegui Marte" (from Orlando)

Lascia ch'io pianga (from Rinaldo)

Leave me to languish.   See Lascia ch'io pianga

Let me wander not unseen (from L'allegro ed Il pensieroso)

"Let the bright Seraphim" (from Samson)

"Let their celestial concerts unite" (from Samson)

"Light as the night-moth."   See "Qual farfalletta giro a quel lume"

"Lord remember me in my trouble"

"Lord, to Thee, each night and day" (from Theodora)

"A love like mine, so faithful" (from Susanna)

"Love that's true will live forever." See "Sì, tra i ceppi"

The melancholy nymph (from What d'ye call it)

Messiah: selection

"My arms! against this Gorgias will I go" (from Judas Maccabaeus)

"My father! ah! methinks I see" (from Hercules)

My Father, look upon my anguish (from The Passion)

"My grief for this forbids mine eyes to close" (from Samson)

'Mid lures, 'mid pleasures.   See Lascia ch'io pianga

"Nasce al bosco" (from Ezio)

"Now give the army breath" (from Joshua)

"Now that the sun is beaming bright" (same air as "While shepherds watched their flocks")

"O agonies of thought."   See "Affanni del pensier"

Oh god-like youth (from Saul)

"Oh had I Jubal's lyre" (from Joshua)

"O Judah, Judah! chosen seed" (from Athalia)

"O Lord! correct me"

O Lord, Whom we adore (from Athalia)

"Oh Lord, Whose mercies numberless" (from Saul)

"Oh, loss of sight" (from Samson)

"O ruddier than the cherry" (from Acis and Galatea)

O sleep, why dost thou leave me (from Semele)

"O thou that tellest good tidings to Zion" (from The Messiah)

O voi dell' Erebo (from La Ressurrezione)

Ombra mai fu (from Serse)

Oppress'd with never-ceasing grief (from Belshazzar)

"The peasant tastes the sweets of life" (from Joseph)

"The people that walked in darkness" (from The Messiah)

Pena tiranna (from Amadigi)

"Pious orgies, pious airs" (from Judas Maccabaeus)

"Pour forth no more unheeded prayers" (from Jephtha)

"Qual farfalletta giro a quel lume" (from Partenope)

Rend' il sereno al ciglio (from Sosarme)

Händel, Georg Friedrich —*Continued*
Rejoice greatly, O daughter of Zion (from The Messiah)
Return, O God of hosts (from Samson)
Revenge, Timotheus cries (from Alexander's feast)
Sacred raptures cheer my breast (from Solomon)
St Thomas. See "I love Thy kingdom, Lord"
"See, she blushing turns her eyes" (from Semele)
"Sì, tra i ceppi" (from Berenice)
Slumber, dear maid. See Ombra mai fu
"The smiling hours, a joyful train" (from Hercules)
"The soft complaining flute" (from Ode for St Cecilia's day)
"Sorge infausta" (from Orlando)
"Sound an alarm" (from Judas Maccabaeus)
"Subtle love, with fancy viewing" (from Alexander Balus)
Sweet rose and lily (from Theodora)
Tears, such as tender fathers shed (from Deborah)
Theodora. See "They who seek the throne of grace"
"They who seek the throne of grace"
Thou shalt break them with a rod of iron (from The Messiah)
"Thou shalt bring them in" (from Israel in Egypt)
"Thrice blest that wise discerning king" (from Solomon)
"Thus saith the Lord" (from The Messiah)
"Thus when the sun" (from Samson)
To thy sad brow let joy return. See Rend' il sereno al ciglio
"Toll for the brave"
Torment unending. See Pena tiranna
"Total eclipse! no sun, no moon" (from Samson)
"The trumpet shall sound" (from The Messiah)
" 'Twas when the seas were roaring"
" 'Twill be a painful separation" (from Jephtha)
"Tyrannic love! I feel thy cruel dart" (from Susanna)
Up! lords of Erebus. See O voi dell' Erebo
"Verdant meadows." See "Verdi prati, selve amene"
"Verdi prati, selve amene" (from Alcina)
"Waft her, angels, through the skies" (from Jephtha)
Weeping for ever. See Lascia ch'io pianga
"What though I trace each herb and flower" (from Solomon)
"What's sweeter than a new-blown rose" (from Joseph)
"When all Thy mercies"

"When first I saw my lovely maid" (from Susanna)
"When war-like ensigns wave on high" (from The occasional oratorio)
"When winds are fiercely raving." See "Del minacciar del vento"
Where art thou. See Dove sei
"Where'er you walk" (from Semele)
"While shepherds watched their flocks"
"Why do the nations so furiously rage together" (from The Messiah)
"Why does the God of Israel sleep" (from Samson)
"Wide spread his name" (from Theodora)
"With pious hearts" (from Judas Maccabaeus)
"Ye pangs of anxious thought." See "Affani del pensier"
"Ye sacred priests" (from Jephtha)
"Ye verdant hills, ye balmy vales" (from Susanna)
"You see, my friends" (from Belshazzar)

Handley, Edward
"In low'ring gloom and cloudiness"
"The Lord is risen! risen, indeed"
"Morn of beauty"
"O haste, the blessed Babe is born"
" 'Twas at the matin hour" (Tr of Patris sapientia, veritas (bonitas) divina)

Handsome Sally. Folk song: Irish version. JOI
—North Carolina version. CSE

Handwerksburschen-abschied ("Es, es, es und es") Volkslied. g. ED 1

Handy, H. L.
"Jack and Gill"

Handy Jim. Long-rope hauling chantey. SMW

Hanging Johnnie ("They call me Hanging Johnnie") Long drag chantey. KB
For variants of this song see following songs of the same title

Hanging Johnny ("And they calls me Hanging Johnny") Pulling chantey. FSF—SE

Hanging Johnny ("Oh, they call me Hanging Johnny") Halliard chantey. CR

"Hangman, hangman, hold your rope." See The maid freed from the gallows (Woodridge, Va. version)

"Hangman, hangman, slack up your rope." See The hangman's song

"Hangman, hangman, spare my life." See The maid freed from the gallows (Mount Fair, Va. version)

The **hangman's** song. Kentucky mountain song. WLT
Variants: The briery bush; The maid freed from the gallows

Hanitsch, Georg Friedrich
Bundeslied

Hankey, Katherine
"I love to tell the story" (Fischer)

Hanlyn, M.
"Joy for the sturdy trees"
The night has a thousand eyes"
Song for Arbor day. See "Joy for the sturdy trees"

Le hanneton. See The beetle (Musorgskiï

"**Hanohano** launa ole." See "Wrapt in verdure" (Hopkins)

"**Hanohano** wale oe." See Kalakaua's serenade (Hopkins)

Hans and Lisa. See Hans und Liesel (Woyna)

Hans Sachs's monologue. See "Was duftet doch der flieder" (Wagner)

Hans und Liesel ("Und der Hans schleicht umher") F. von Woyna. Author of words unknown. g. ED 1
Hans und Liesel (Hans and Lisa) e.g. SSG

Hansell, John
All round my hat (Valentine)

Hansen, B. M.
"Blandt alle lande"
"Of all the lands." See "Blandt alle lande"

Hanskin ("Jog on."—Eighty-eight) 17th century song. Words from Shakespeare. CO 1
"Jog on, jog on." DM 1—MM

Hanson, H.
"Astri! mi Astri" (Norse air)

Haperpan. See Haberban

"**Hapless** one! my strength is failing." See Non m'è grave morir per amore (Marcello)

Hapless Silva, whilst thou believing. See Infelice! e tuo credevi (Verdi)

"**Happiness** is a thing of changes." See "La bonheur est chose légère" (Saint-Saëns)

The **happiness** of friendship. See Das glück der freundschaft (Beethoven)

"**Happy** and light." M. W. Balfe. FSS 8 —WBT

Happy and merry. See The heart should be happy and merry (Reeve)

"**Happy** are we to-night." M. S. Pike. FSS 4—MPC—NMH—WBT

Happy as a big sunflower. Old American song. BSS

Happy Bayadere. N. C. Bochsa. e. FSS 3

The **happy** beggars. Attributed to H. Carey (music and words) MM

Happy bells are ringing. G. E. Oliver. HC

The **happy** Cambrians. See Y Cymry dedwydd

Happy Christmas morning. C. Simper. Words by A. S. Woods. HC

Happy Christmas to all. MCS

"The **happy** day is coming." See Little children's day (Glover)

"**Happy** day, with hope beaming bright." See "Jour heureux" (Sacchini)

Happy days gone by. D. Godfrey. FSS 2 —JSE

"**Happy** enclosures where my belov'd is wand'ring." See "Mura felici" (Rossini)

The **happy** family. G. Jones. Words by W. Perkins. BSS

The **happy** farmer. R. Schumann. JSE

Happy greeting to all. FSS 3

"**Happy**, happy bells are ringing." See Happy bells are ringing (Oliver)

"**Happy** hours, all hours excelling." See The happy man (Holcombe)

The **happy** kitten. Nursery song. WSC "See the happy kitten." FSS 6

Happy land ("There is a happy land") See "There is a happy land"

"**Happy** land! happy land." E. F. Rimbault. Words by J. Bruton. BE 6—FSS 1

The **happy** man ("Happy hours, all hours excelling") H. Holcombe. ME

"**Happy** nation, still receiving." C. M. von Weber. e. SAS 3

Happy New Year. French folk air: Semons la salade. Words by J. Irwin. DO

The **happy** stranger. Folk song from Hampshire. SF 3
Variant of: I'm a poor stranger and far from my own

"**Happy** streams from woods afar flowing down." See Flowing water

Happy summer. Planquette. Words by H. S. Leigh. FSS 8

"**Happy** the time when free from love." DM 2

Happy three. J. L. Roeckel. Words by R. S. Hichens. AB 1

"**Här** är gudagodt att vara" ("Oh, how good it is to be here") G. Wennerberg (music and words) e.sw. HSOS

Harbour, Homer H.
Army of the Yankees (Lorraine folk air)
Bobbie Shaftoe (English air)
"Caterpillar! caterpillar" (Russian folk air)
The cuckoo (German folk air)
The elves' dance (Portuguese folk air)
An evening song (Lithuanian air)
The flag going by (German folk air)
The golden boat (German air)
If I were an elfin (Bohemian folk air)
In memoriam (Bohemian folk air)
In the firelight (English folk air)
It snows in the night (Slavonic folk air)
The journey of the leaves (German folk air)
The lamps of night (English air)
Lincoln's birthday (Dutch folk air)
Lords and ladies (Old French air)
The mail-box (German folk air)
The merry-go-round (French folk air)
Moon song (Bohemian folk air)
My garden of flowers (English folk air)
My playmate (Russian folk air)
New Year's day (French folk air)
A night in the woods (Dutch folk air)

Harbour, Homer H. —*Continued*
November (Bohemian folk air)
On a summer day (French folk air)
Our country (Old air)
A picnic on the grass (German folk air)
The pine tree swing (German folk air)
A sailing song (German folk air)
Shining wires (German folk air)
The sleigh-ride (Canadian folk air)
A song of bread (German folk air)
A song of ships (English air)
Song of the life-boat men (Russian folk air)
Song of the sea-gull (Irish air)
The sparrow's nest (Old French air)
The swallows (Onfroy de Bréville)
Swing song (German folk air)
Thanksgiving day (French folk air)
The trolley ride (French folk air)
Valentines (Old English air)
Washington's birthday (French folk air)
When fields are white (German folk air)
The wind (German folk air)
The winds and the shadows (Old French air)
Hard times, come again no more. S. C. Foster (music and words) CU—HSD —NMH—NMP— WA—WBT— WC— WSW
Hard trials ("Been a-lis'nin' all de night long") Negro spiritual. DF
Variant of: "I've been a-listening all de night long"
Hard trials ("The foxes have holes in the ground") Negro song. JP— NMP
Hard trials ("De fox hab hole in de groun'") HR
Hardelot, Guy d', pseud.
Beneath the branches. See Sous les branches
Invocation (Tr of Ich hab' ein traum geweinet)
Sans toi
Sous les branches
Without thee. See Sans toi
Hardenberg, Friedrich, freiherr von
"Wenn ich ihn nur habe" (Reichardt)
Harder, Augustin
Dem vogel in der luft
Das landmädchen
Die spinnerin
Winterlied
Harding, J. P.
"Brightest and best"
"There dwelt in old Judea"
"Hardly fifteen was I when mother took me." See La monacella
The hardy Norseman. Norse national song. e. HSD—WBT
Hardyknute. Air: The battle of Largs. PS 2
Hare and hounds (Oi za gaem, gaem) Russian folk song. e. GO
Hare and hunter ("As the moon shone") FSS 7
Harel, Rose
L'amour (Godard)

Hares in the old plantation. Folk song. BE 4
Hares on the mountains ("If all those young men") Folk song. FSF
For variant see following song of same title
Hares on the mountains ("Young women they'll run") Folk song. SEF 1—SO
Harford, F. K.
Child divine (Bridge)
"Joy, ye people, great and small" (Bridge)
Häring, Georg Wilhelm Heinrich. See Alexis, Wilibald, pseud.
Harington, Herbert Russell
For love of Wooster U. (Composer unknown)
"Hark! a burst of heavenly music." F. Schilling. Words by Mrs M. N. Meigs. HC
"Hark! a thrilling song." H. Proch. Words by T. G. La Moille. MCS
"Hark! a voice rings with clang appalling." See Mourir pour la patrie (Varney)
"Hark! as the twilight pale tenderly glows." See Thou art my rose
"Hark! bright angels sweetly sing." H. S. Irons. Words by R. R. Chope. HC
"Hark, ev'ry man, to the shout of rejoicing." See Himno nacional (Argentina)
"Hark, from mountain, hill, and valley." See Wake the echoes
"Hark, hark! his morning praise." See The rising of the lark
"Hark! hark! how sweetly sings the lark." See "Hark! hark! the lark" (Schubert)
"Hark! hark! my soul" (Angelic songs are swelling) J. M. Armstrong. Words by F. W. Faber. FSS 1—HSD
"Hark! hark! my soul." J. B. Dykes. Words by F. W. Faber. WBT— WS
"Hark! hark, my soul" (Pilgrims) BD
Vox angelica. CST
"Hark! hark, my soul." J. E. Roe. Words by F. W. Faber. LA
"Hark! hark! my soul" (Pilgrims) H. Smart. Words by F. W. Faber. TL
"Hark! hark! the dogs do bark." WSC
"Hark! hark! the joy-inspiring horn." See The joy-inspiring horn (Bride)
"Hark, hark! the lark." K. F. Curschmann. Words by W. Shakespeare. VFS
"Hark! hark! the lark." F. Schubert. Words by W. Shakespeare. BD— FSS 8—LA— VFS—WA— WBT —WL
"Hark! hark! the lark" ("Horch, horch, die lerch") e.g. FF—FO 1. e. only FTS
"Hark! hark! the lark" (Ständchen) e.g. MS—PG 3—TS. e. only KSS
"Hark! hark! what I tell to thee." See Des geistes gesang (Haydn)

"Hark! hark! when the trumpet now calls you to arms." See Hark! when the trumpet now calls you to arms (Arnold)

"Hark! hear ye not the angel-song." Traditional air. Words by G. Thring. HC

"Hark! how loud the storm blows" (Malagasy song) e. BMC

"Hark! how still the dusky wood has grown." See Stille sicherheit (Franz)

"Hark! how the bells." J. B. Powell (music and words) HC

"Hark! how the sleigh-bells ring." See Winter (Marshall)

"Hark! I hear a voice." CHS—HSD—MPC—NMH—WBT
'Way up on the mountain-top-tip-top. WC

"Hark! I hear an angel sing." R. G. Shrival. Words by W. C. Baker. FSS 7 —WBT

"Hark! I hear, sweet and clear." M. B. Foster. Words by R. S. Watson. HC
Christmas fanfare and carol. LA
Fanfare and carol. DCS

"Hark! I hear the foe advancing." See Rhyfelgyrch gwyr Harlech

"Hark! listen to the trumpeters." See The enlisted soldiers

"Hark! listen well! all the birds." See The forest choir

"Hark! my soul." L. von Beethoven. WBT

"Hark! o'er the stilly lake." D. F. E. Auber. e. FSS 4

"Hark! sweet angel voices singing." W. T. Belcher. Words by T. Fletcher. HC

"Hark! ten thousand." Words by T. Kelly. FSS 7

Hark! the angel choir. Words by P. Cary. MCS

Hark! the angel sound. MCS

"Hark! the angels bright are singing." H. E. Button. Words by M. F. Cusack. HC

"Hark! the bell is ringing." See The bell is ringing (Silcher)

"Hark! the Christmas bells are ringing; hear their chime so sweet and clear." See Joyous anthem swelling (Flotow)

"Hark! the Christmas bells are ringing, ringing thro' the frosty air." See Welcome Christmas cheer (Storace)

"Hark! the Christmas bells are ringing, through the midnight, loud and clear." See Fanfare and carol

"Hark! the Christmas songs are singing." G. J. Magill. HC

"Hark! the full-voiced choir is singing." W. Gowman. Words by R. R. Chope. HC

"Hark the glad sound." Composer unknown. Words by P. Doddridge. FSS 7

"Hark! the glad sound." N. Hermann. Words by P. Doddridge. FSS 7—MCS

"Hark! the herald angels sing." Mendelssohn. Words by C. Wesley. FSS 2—HC— JS—MCS— OH—TFC 1—WA—WBT—WS—WSC—WSW

"Hark! the herald angels sing" (Herald angels) DC

"Hark! the herald angels sing" (Mendelssohn) BD—LA

"Oíd un son en alta esfera." s. LCP

"Hark! the herald angels sing." W. Mozart. Words by C. Wesley. FSS 7—MCS

"Hark! the herald angels singing." Composer and author of words unknown. HC

"Hark! the herald-host is singing." E. Humperdinck. Tr of Leise weht's durch alle lande. e. HC

Hark! the holy voices. G. Cobb. Words by C. Wordsworth. MCS

"Hark! the joyful Christmas greeting." F. T. Southwick. HC

"Hark, the martial trumpet sounding." See Dowch i'r ffrwydr

"Hark, the mavis' ev'ning sang." See Ca' the yowes to the knowes

"Hark! the merry Christmas bells." M. A. Hofland (music and words) HC

"Hark! the merry peal is ringing." See The Gascon vespers (Lee)

"Hark! the pealing, softly stealing." See The evening bell

"Hark! the song of choirs angelic." E. Lancaster. Words by F. S. Corbett. HC

"Hark! the sound of holy voices." See Hark! the holy voices (Cobb)

"Hark! the summons." Old Welsh air. Traditional words. DO—DSH

"Hark! the thunder, mark the lightning." See The dancers

"Hark, the trumpets sound to arms." See A lover's complaint

"Hark! the vesper hymn is stealing." See Vesper hymn (Bortniansky)

Hark! those holy voices. See "Hark! what mean those holy voices" (Geer)

"Hark! 'tis the angelus! sweetly ringing." See Ring on, sweet angelus (Gounod)

"Hark! 'tis the breeze." J. Rousseau. Words by T. Moore. WBT—WS

"Hark! 'tis the linnet." Händel. OS 1

"Hark to nature's voice enchanting." See Suomi's song (Pacius)

"Hark to the castanets, O Carmencita." See La cachucha

"Hark! to the harps of gold." See With every golden string (Auber)

"Hark to the peasant gay." See The peasant gay

"Hark to the shrill trumpet calling." See The officer's funeral

"Hark to the sound of the distant drum." See The distant drum

"Hark! what celestial sounds." See Great joy we bring (Edson)

"Hark! what heavenly sounds are floating." H. T. Tiltman. HC

Hark! what I tell to thee. See Des geistes gesang (Haydn)

"Hark, what mean those holy voices." G. B. Arnold. Words by J. Cawood. HC

"Hark! what mean those holy voices" (Hark! those holy voices) G. J. Geer. Words by J. Cawood. FSS 6— MCS

"Hark! what mean those holy voices." S. J. Gilbert. Words by J. Cawood. MS

"Hark! what mean those holy voices." C. W. Pearce. Words by J. Cawood. HC

"Hark! what merry voices." J. Hecker. MCS

"Hark! what mystic sounds are those." See Mermaid's evening song (Glover)

"Hark! what sounds are sweetly stealing." Christmas carol. HC

Hark! when the trumpet now calls you to arms. S. Arnold. Words by G. Colman. ME

"Hark! ye neighbors, and hear me tell." See German watchman's song (Heffernan)

"Hark ye to the complaint, grown and little." See La bergère muette

"Harken all, both young and old." See La Passion de Jésus-Christ

"Harken, all ye good young men." See Le blasphemateur châtié

"Harlech, raise thy banner o'er us." See Rhyfelgyrch gwyr Harlech

"Harlequin and pallid Pierrot." See Fantoches (Debussy)

Harm Link. Folk song from Tennessee. CSE

Harmer, Samuel Young
Rest for the weary (music by Dadmun; McDonald)

Harmonie du soir (Evening harmony) A. C. Debussy. Words by C. Baudelaire. e.f. HM 1

"The harp, at nature's advent strung." German air. Words by J. G. Whittier. LBR

"The harp is now silent." See The Jewish maiden (Kücken)

"Harp of my country." See Farewell to my harp (Philips)

The harp song (Kannel) Esthonian folk song. e.es. BF 1

"The harp that once through Tara's halls." Air: Gramachree, or, Molly astore. Words by T. Moore. BAS 1—BOS— BS 1—BSE—DO—EF—FSI—FSS 1— GO—HSC—JO—JS—JSE— MI—MMI —MP—MS—NMH—NMS— OH—PI— SN—WA—WBT—WCP—WSW

Harper, Edmund B.
Truth in absence

"Harpist, that strain." See Lament

Harries, Heinrich
"Heil dir im siegerkranz" (Carey)

Harrigan, Ed.
Paddy Duffy's cart (Braham)

Harrington, C. S.
Homeward bound (attributed) See Dadmun, J. W. Homeward bound

Harrington, Henry
"How sweet in the woodlands"
"Three years a sailor's life"

Harrington, Karl P.
"Dance with me"
The song of the A. B.

Harris, Victor
April
Gaellic lullaby
The hills o' Skye
Just as it used to do

Harrison, Annie Fortesque
"Bonnie hills of heather"
Christmas lullaby (same air as "In the gloaming, oh, my darling")
"In the gloaming little children" (same air as "In the gloaming, oh, my darling")
"In the gloaming, oh, my darling"

"Harrow marches onward." School song. LA

Harroway, J.
In the land of my birth

Harry Gray. Folk song from North Carolina. CSE

Harry, the tailor. Air: The tailor. Folk song from Cambridgeshire. SF 2

"Harsh my singing sounds to you." See The blacksmith (Koeneman)

Hart, A.
A little more cider too

Hart, James
"Since Phillis swears inconstancy"

Hart, Mary Elizabeth
"All hail to thee, fair Western" (Charlton)

Harte, Bret
What the chimney sang (Hopkins)

Hartley, William F.
Where the eagle is king

Hartman, J. E.
Heidelberg (Power)

Hartmann, Johan Peter Emilius
Danish national hymn. See "Kong Christian stod ved høien mast": old air arranged
"King Christian." See "Kong Christian stod ved høien mast": old air arranged
"Kong Christian stod ved høien mast": old air arranged
"Mine tanker"
"My thoughts." See "Mine tanker"
"Flyv, fugl, flyv"
"Fly, bird, fly." See "Flyv, fugl, flyv"
"Fly, birdie, fly." See "Flyv, fugl, flyv"
"Jeg synge skal en vise"
"You'd have me sing." See "Jeg synge skal en vise"

Hartmann, Ludwig
"I dreamed of a pallid princess-maid." See "Mir träumte von einem königskind"
"Mir träumte von einem königskind"

Hartwell, H.
South African national song (Composer unknown)
Haru-no-uta. See New Year song
"Haru no yayoi no." See Buddhist chant
Harvard's day. C. L. Smith, jr. CHS
Harvest home ("Oh, come to the field") Old air. Words by P. Hastings. TFC 2
Harvest home ("Our oats they are hoed") H. Purcell. Words by J. Dryden. JE
Harvest home ("When the farmer") L. Atterbury. BE 5
Harvest home ("Your hay it is mow'd") DM 2—MM
Harvest home song ("The year has sped") W. B. Olds. Words by B. E. Bush. NMS
Harvest hymn ("Fields are rich with golden grain") Russian folk song. e. JSE
Russian harvest hymn ("Fields are rich with golden grain") e. BMC
"The harvest moon was beaming." See Winnie Wen (Owen)
Harvest song ("Again the fertile land") L. B. Marshall. Words by W. W. Caldwell. JS
The harvester. See Skördemannen (Fogelberg)
Harvey, David
Composer
The sunshine boomerang
Author
Li'l Liza Jane (Old southern air)
Harvey, W. B.
"No one to love"
"Has sorrow thy young days shaded." Irish air: Sly Patrick, arr by J. A. Stevenson. Words by T. Moore. FSI— HSC— MI— MMI— PI— WBT
I'll weep with thee. FSS 8
Haschka, Lorenz Leopold
"Gott erhalte Franz den kaiser" (Haydn)
Haskins, E.
"Good Christian people all" (Trembath)
"Hasngon gof dya." Marianna island song. pol. SN
Hasse, Johann Adolf
"Father, have mercy." See "Padre, perdona"
"Padre, perdona" (from Demofoonte)
Hassler, Hans Leo von
"In heavenly love abiding"
"Hast seen the fair-hair'd maiden." See The fair maiden
"'Hast Thou for me a look, a thought." Spohr. e. OS 1—SAS 1
"Hast thou not seen, darling." See Crepúsculo
"Hasta la mañana" (To-morrow) Pyrenean song. e.s. SSP
"Haste away, ye lovely breezes." See Botschaft (Brahms)

"Haste, nor be delaying." See Les deux bergères
"Haste over sea." Upper Austrian song. e. KSE
"Haste thee, nymph." Round. F. Arnold. Words by J. Milton. CST—TFC 2—TL
"Haste to the greenwood." Air: On a fair morning. Words by J. Thomas (Ieuan Dhu) MMW
Haste to the wedding. See "Come, haste to the wedding" (Arne?)
"Haste, ye shepherds." Bach. e. OS 3
"Hasten, sinner, to be wise." I. Pleyel. Words by T. Scott. FSS 2
Hastings, Horace Lorenzo
"Shall we meet beyond the river" (Rice)
Hastings, Paul
All pull together (Drummond)
Harvest home (Old air)
"I have a song to sing" (Sullivan)
Hastings, Thomas
Composer
"Come, humble sinner"
Fourth of July hymn
"Guide me, O Thou great Jehovah"
"Hail to the brightness"
The light hath shone
"A little word in kindness said" (same air as Fourth of July hymn)
"Majestic sweetness" (same air as Fourth of July hymn)
The mercy-seat. See Retreat
Ortonville. See Fourth of July hymn; "A little word in kindness said"; "Majestic sweetness"
Retreat
"Rock of ages, cleft for me"
Author
Gently lead us (Conkey)
A hasty vow. See Vorschneller schwur (Brahms)
Hatch, Edwin
"Breathe on me, breath of God" (Sweetser)
"Hâtez-vous, voisine." See Les deux bergères
"Hats off! hats off! along the street there comes." See The flag goes by (Foote)
Hatton, Christopher
The silver swan (Gibbons)
Hatton, John
Baker university hymn
Duke street. See "From all that dwell"; "Glory to Thee, my God, this night"; God be with us; "Jesus shall reign"; "Thy kindness to our fathers shown"
Evening hymn. See "Glory to Thee, my God, this night"
"From all that dwell"
"Glory to Thee, my God, this night" (same air as "From all that dwell")
God be with us (same air as "From all that dwell")

Hatton, John —*Continued*
"Jesus shall reign" (same air as "From all that dwell")
"Thy kindness to our fathers shown" (same air as "From all that dwell")
Hatton, John Liptrot
As I'd nothing else to do
The bells. See "I heard the bells on Christmas day"
Beware
"Bid me to live"
"Come live with me, and be my love"
The enchantress
Good-bye, sweetheart, good-bye
"I heard the bells on Christmas day"
"If my mistress hide her face"
The Indian maid
"It was fifty years ago"
"The lark now leaves his wat'ry nest"
Light of the world
Revenge
Santa Claus to-night
"See, amid the winter's snow"
Serenade. See "The lark now leaves his wat'ry nest"
The shepherd's winter song
Simon the cellarer
To Anthea. See "Bid me to live"
"Weep no more, thou sorry boy"
The wreck of the Hesperus
Hatuey. Cuban folk song. e.s. HS
Hauch, Johannes Carsten
Birken (Gade)
Knud Lavard (Gade)
Polsk faedrelandssang (Gade)
Hauchope, George
Missouri (Thompson)
Hauff, Wilhelm
Den gefallenen kriegern (Müller)
Reiters morgenlied (Folk air)
Soldatenmut (19th century air)
"Steh' ich in finstrer mitternacht" (Volksweise; also music by Wurda)
Haug, Johann Christoph Friedrich
Walzlied (Schwäbischer volkstanz)
Haul away ("Oh once I had a nigger girl") Short-rope pulling song. SMW
For variants of this song see following songs of similar title
Haul away, Joe ("Away, haul away") Short drag chantey. KB
Haul away, Joe ("Haul away, haul away") Short drag chantey. CR
Haul away, Joe ("O you talk about your Aver girls") Pulling chantey. SE
"Haul on the bow-line." Pulling chantey. SE
For variants see following songs of similar title
"Haul on the bowlin'." Short-haul chantey. HSD—WBT
"Haul on the bowline." Short drag chantey. CR
"Haul the bowline." Short drag chantey. KB
Haul the bowline ("We'll haul the bow-line") Capstan chantey. SMW
Haulin' the bowlin' ("Haul on the bow-lin'") Capstan chantey. SMW

Hauptmann, M.
"First violets of April"
"Live we singing"
"Haut, haut, Peyrot." Béarnais Christmas carol. f. HC
"Hav for bougen mersseil sat." See Tilsjös (Backer-Gröndahl)
Havalisava. See How fair is she
Havanaise (La islana.—L'isolana) E. Paladilhe. Words from the Spanish. e.f. HM 2
"Havde du hjerte, som du har öine." See Bestikkelse (Lie)
"Have compassion upon a soul departing." See "Ah! I have sighed to rest me" (Verdi)
Have I lost thee. See "Che farò senza Euridice" (Gluck)
"Have I then, have I then to be off from the town." See Abschied ("Muss i denn")
"Have mercy, dark eyes." See "Begli occhi, mercè" (Tenaglia)
"Have pity, my beloved." See "Pietà, mio caro bene" (Bononcini)
"Have you any bread and wine." See The Roman soldiers
"Have you been at Carrick." Irish air. Words by E. Walsh. [Tr of Am raib tú ag an g-Carraig] e. MMI
"Have you been at Carrick" (Munster love song) e. BMC
"Have you ever heard an echo clear." See Echo song
"Have you forgotten, love, so soon." See Une nuit de mai (Thomas)
"Have you gazed at Shane Glas." See Shane Glas
"Have you heard the wondrous story." H. W. Parker. HC
"Have you not hopp'd round before you now do so." See "Ha du' kji hoppa"
"Have you seen but a bright lily grow" (Love song) F. G. Cauffman. Words by B. Jonson. TL
"Have you seen but a white lily grow." English air. Words by B. Jonson. PR 1
"Have you seene but a whyte lillie grow" (So sweete is shee) CMF 1
Havergal, Frances Ridley

Composer

"O'er the plains the darkness deepens"

Author

But when morning dawneth (Randegger)
"Golden harps are sounding" (music by Parker; Sullivan)
"Now let us sing the angel's song" (Randegger)
"O Christmas, merry Christmas" (music by Foster; Lassen)
Havergal, William Henry
The Bethlehem shepherd-boy's tale
"Remember thy Creator now"
The Worcestershire Christmas carol
"Havet er skjönt naar det roligen hvael-ver." See Nordhavet (Lindeman)

"Hawaii ponoi." See Our native land (Berger)

"Hawaii! sea-girt land." See Our native land (Berger)

Hawaiian farewell song. See Aloha oe (Liliuokalani)

Hawaiian hula (Maunawili)   C. K. Hopkins. h. HA

Hawaiian hula (Moanalua)   h.   HA

Hawaiian hula (Paahana)   C. K. Hopkins. h.   HA

Hawaiian hula (Tomi! tomi)   D. Nape. h. HA

Hawaiian national song.   See Our native land (Berger)

Haweis, Hugh Reginald
"Arise, arise, the morning bells" (Moss)
"The homeland! O the homeland" (Sullivan)

Haweis, Thomas
"To Thee, my God, my Saviour" (Composer unknown)

Hawes, Maria Billington
"I'll speak of thee"

Hawes, William
Old Ringwood

Hawker, Robert Stephen
Song of the western men (Old Cornish air)

Hawkins, W. See Richards, Mrs Laura Elizabeth (Howe), jt. auth.

Hawks, Mrs Annie Sherwood
"I need thee every hour" (Lowry)

Hawley, C. B.
"Because I love you, dear"
Daisies
Greeting
My little love
The nightingale and the rose
"Were I a star"

Haworth, Lloyd B.
Technology

The hawthorn tree.   Air: Dargason, or, The Sedany.   BOH
"It was a maid of my countrie."   MM

A merry ballad of the hawthorn tree ("It was a maid of my country") DM 1

Hawthorne, Alice, pseud.   See Winner, Septimus

Hay, John. See Tweeddale, John Hay, 2d marquis of

"Hay ah o hah hay a hah."   See I-ou'-tin game song: Song for the north side

"Hay un marino."   Costa Rican folk song. e.s.   HS

Hayden, Arthur
Horse-shoe song (Composer unknown)

Hayden, George
"As I saw fair Clora walk"

Hayden, Joe
A hot time in the old town (Metz)

Haydn, Franz Joseph
"Ah, poor heart."   See "Il pensier stà negli oggetti"
An die freundschaft
"And God created man" (from Die schöpfung)

"And God said, let the earth bring forth grass" (from Die schöpfung)

"And God said: Let the waters bring forth abundantly" (from Die schöpfung)

"And God said, let the waters under the heaven" (from Die schöpfung)

"As down in the sunless retreats"

"At last the bounteous sun" (from Die jahreszeiten)

Austrian hymn.   See Columbia, God preserve thee free; Deutschland über alles; "Gott erhalte Franz den kaiser"; "Land of greatness! home of glory"; "Lord, with glowing heart I'd praise Thee"; Our country; "Praise the Lord! ye heavens, adore Him"; Stand, Columbia

"Behold, along the dewy grass" (from Die jahreszeiten)

"Bind' auf dein haar."   See "My mother bids me bind my hair"

"Brightly, brightly gleam the sparkling rills" (from Die jahreszeiten)

Columbia, God preserve thee free (same air as "Gott erhalte Franz den kaiser")

Creation.   See "The spacious firmament on high"

"A crystal pavement lies the lake" (from Die jahreszeiten)

"Dearest maiden, hear my song."   See "Liebes mädchen, hör' mir zu"

Del mio core (from Orfeo)

Des geistes gesang

Deutschland über alles (same air as "Gott erhalte Franz den kaiser")

"Dost thou love me, sister Ruth"

"Glorious things of Thee are spoken"

"God preserve our gracious emp'ror."   See "Gott erhalte Franz den kaiser"

"God preserve our noble emperor."   See "Gott erhalte Franz den kaiser"

"Gott erhalte Franz den kaiser"

"Hark! what I tell to thee."   See Des geistes gesang

"How wondrous and great"

"In native worth and honour clad" (from Die schöpfung)

"Land of greatness! home of glory" (same air as "Gott erhalte Franz den kaiser")

Die landlust

"Liebes mädchen, hör mir zu"

"Lo! where the plenteous harvest" (from Die jahreszeiten)

"Lord, with glowing heart I'd praise Thee" (same air as "Gott erhalte Franz den kaiser")

The mermaid's song.   See Die seejungfer

"My mother bids me bind my hair"

"Now heav'n in fullest glory" (from Die schöpfung)

"Now the dancing sunbeams play."   See Die seejungfer

"O how pleasing to the senses" (from Die jahreszeiten)

Haydn, Franz Joseph—*Continued*
"O Thou who dryst the mourner's tear"
"O welcome now, ye groves and bow'rs" (from Die jahreszeiten)
"On mighty pens uplifted soars" (from Die schöpfung)
"On thee each living soul awaits" (from Die schöpfung)
Östereichisches nationallied. See "Gott erhalte Franz den kaiser"
Our country (same air as "Gott erhalte Franz den kaiser")
"Il pensier stà negli oggetti" (from Orfeo)
"Praise the Lord! ye heavens, adore Him" (same air as "Gott erhalte Franz den kaiser")
"Rolling in foaming billows" (from Die schöpfung)
Die seejungfer
Serenade. See "Liebes mädchen, hör mir zu"
"She never told her love"
Singing in the rain
Sister Ruth
Soldiers' hymn
"The spacious firmament on high" (from Die schöpfung)
The spirit's song. See Des geistes gesang
Spring
Stand, Columbia (same air as "Gott erhalte Franz den kaiser")
"Stets barg die liebe sie." See "She never told her love"
"Three women went forth"
"The trav'ler stands perplex'd" (from Die jahreszeiten)
Verdure. See "We feel thy calm"
"We feel thy calm"
A wealthy lord
"When I think upon Thy goodness"
With joy the impatient husbandman (from Die jahreszeiten)
"With verdure clad the fields appear" (from Die schöpfung)
The woman of Canaan

Haydn, Johann Michael
"The angels sing around the stall"
"Holy night, silent night": old air arranged (Tr of Die heilige nacht)
In absence
Lyons. See O come, let us worship; Song of Columbus day
O come, let us worship
"Our land, O lord"
Song of Columbus day (same air as O come, let us worship)
"Stille nacht" (wrongly attributed) See Gruber, F. Die heilige nacht

Hayes, Clara L.
"O weary feet" (Beirly)

Hayes, Mrs Ednah Proctor (Clarke)
April weather (Rogers)

Hayes, William
The spring
"Wind, gentle evergreen"

Haylock,
Lack-a-day, O (Hook)
The **haymaker** ("'Twas in June, rosy June") W. Reeve. DM 2
Haymaking song ("Boys and girls come out to-day") WBT—WSC

Hayne, Leighton George
Chalvey. See Glory begun below
Chelvey. See "A few more years shall roll"
"A few more years shall roll"
Glory begun below (same air as "A few more years shall roll")

Hayne, Paul Hamilton
Will and I (Composer unknown)

Haynes, W.
The Priory chimes

Hays, Arthur Garfield
She is my Angelina (Penney)

Hays, William Shakespeare
Angels meet me at de cross-roads
Evangeline
"I went to see my Susie." See Susan Jane
Mollie darling
Nora O'Neal
Susan Jane

Hayward, G. F.
"There came three kings from far away"

The **hazel** dell. G. F. Root. HSD—WBT —WL
Nelly of the hazel dell. NML

"**He** ah e ya ha e tha." See Atá-a-kut game song
"**He-back**, she-back." Capstan chantey. FSF—SE
"**He** built a platform in the air." See He is King of kings
"**He** by whose mighty word." See Il est doux, il est bon (Massenet)
He came. See "Er ist gekommen" (Franz)
"**He** came from the north." See The man of the north countrie
"**He** can sing like a bird." See The wild boy
"**He** clench'd his pamphlets in his fist." Air: Killiecrankie. Words by R. Burns. BSR
"**He** comes from the wars." See Rest, warrior, rest (Kelly)
"**He** comes, he comes! oh god-like youth." See Oh god-like youth (Händel)
"**He** counteth all your sorrows." F. Mendelssohn. e. SAS 3
"**He** deliver'd Daniel from the lion's den." See Didn't my Lord deliver Daniel
"**He** eats the meat and gives us the bones." See "Ali! alo"
"**He** gave her a ring and a holly wreathe." See Three Christmas eves
"**He** gied us Scripter names to spell." See The maister
He giveth His beloved sleep ("Sleep is thine when work is done") J. Benedict. HSS 1—HSS 2—HSS 4

He giveth His beloved sleep ("Sorrow and care may meet") F. Abt. Words by T. C. Tildesley. FSS 2—JSE—LA—WBT

He giveth His beloved sleep ("Who are the Lord's beloved") J. L. Roeckel. Words by M. Mark-Lemon. HSS 1

"**He** has brought his fine guitar." Bosnian folk air. Words by D. Radford. WF

"**He** has come, the Christ of God." See The Prince of peace (Mozart)

"**He** is calling from the river." See The old lock (Wellings)

"**He** is dead, the child I cherish." H. Maréchal. e. SAS 2

"**He** is gone where the woodbine twineth." See Gone where the woodbine twineth (Street)

He is good, he is kind. See Il est doux, il est bon (Massenet)

"**He** is King of kings." Negro spiritual. HR

He is my love. See "Ah! s'il est dans votre village" (Maria Charlotte Amelia)

"**He** is risen from the dead." A. H. Brown. Words by C. F. Hernaman. HC

"**He** is risen, He is risen, tell it with a joyful voice." HC

"**He** is tardy in coming." See Ah! non avea più lagrime (Donizetti)

"**He** kicked her, he choked her, as we understand." See Poor Omie (Big Laurel, N.C. version)

"**He** killed the gentle Mudjekeewis." See Hiawatha's mittens (James)

"**He** lay upon his dying bed." See The sword of Bunker hill (Covert)

"**He** leadeth me." W. B. Bradbury. Words by J. H. Gilmore. HSD—OH—WBT

"**He** led her through hedges and mire so deep." See The cruel ship's carpenter (Alleghany, N.C. version)

"**He** lives a life of true delight." See Das glück der freundschaft (Beethoven)

"**He** loved the wild, a forest seer." See Woodnotes (Muller)

He loves, and rides away. C. Horn. HSE 2

He loves me well. Modern Bohemian song. J. R. Rozkošný. e. KSE

"**He** met his death in foreign land." See After the battle (Musorgskii)

"**He**, more knightly than the noblest." See "Er, der herrlichste von allen" (Schumann)

He never said he loved. G. A. Hodson. FSS 4

"**He** oft hath said that I was fair." See He never said he loved (Hodson)

He piped so sweet. J. Hook. ME

He raise a poor Lazarus. Negro spiritual. HR

"**He** rode up to her father's gate." See Earl Brand (Allanstand, N.C. version)

"**He** rode up to the old man's gate." See Earl Brand (Georgia version; Hot Springs, N.C. version)

"**He** sailed away o'er the ocean spray." See The robin redbreast (Levey)

"**He** sang of the sea." Ieuan Dhu (J. Thomas) (music and words) MMW

"**He** saw the wheat-fields waiting." H. E. Nichol (music and words) HC

"**He** shot it at that carrion crow." See The carrion crow

He stole my tender heart away. Old English song. DM 2

He swore he'd drink old England dry. Old Sussex song. DM 2—HSE 3 Variant: Drink old England dry

"**He** that dwelleth in heaven." G. F. Händel. SAS 3

"**He** that is a clear cavalier." See The clear cavalier (Banister)

"**He** that loves a rosy cheek." See Unfading beauty (Lawes)

"**He** that will not merry, merry be." See Three merry men of Kent

"**He** the best of all." See "Er, der herrlichste von allen" (Schumann)

"**He**, the noblest of the noble." See "Er, der herrlichste von allen" (Schumann)

He truly loved me so (Er liebte mich so sehr) P. I. Tchaïkovsky. Words from the Russian of Apukhtin. e.g. FM

"**He** was a jolly hunter and a sportsman gay." See L'occasion manquée (Canadian version)

"**He** was a little tin soldier." See The little tin soldier (Molloy)

"**He** was a Punchinello." See Punchinello (Molloy)

"**He** was born of high degree." See All that glitters (Roeckel)

He was despised and rejected. G. F. Händel. OS 2—SAS 2

"**He** was famed for deeds of arms." D. Corri. HSE 2

"**He** was nervous." A. S. Thompson. CHS

"**He** was oppress'd and afflicted sore." See "Da er gestraft" (Kiel)

"**He** went thro' the forest the whole day long." See Tonen (Nordraak)

"**He** who calls a heart his own." See A faithful heart (Abt)

"**He** who heav'n created, lully, lully, lu." See "Qui creavit coelum, lully, lully, lu"

"**He** who is upright, kind, and free from error." See "Integer vitae" (Flemming)

"**He** whose compelling word." See Il est doux, il est bon (Massenet)

"**He** whose words by their might." See Il est doux, il est bon (Massenet)

"**He** will be here! ev'ry nerve is a-thrill in fear." See "Il va venir" (Halévy)

"**He** will be our dearest Friend." See Run to Jesus

"**He** will ere long be here." See "Qui Radamés verrà" (Verdi)

He with his net there. See "Des winters als het reghent"

Headlam, Margaret Ann
"Holy is the seed-time" (Lowe)

"Heah e tha ae he thae thae." See Little papoose

Heale, H.
The three kings

A health to all good fellows. A. G. Chaffee. NMS

A health to all honest men. 18th century English song. BE 8
"Every man take a glass in his hand." DM 1
"Every man take his glass in his hand." MM
Here's a health to all honest men. CO 2

"Heap high the farmer's wintry hoard." See The corn song

Hear de angels singin'. Negro spiritual. HR

Hear de lambs a cryin'. See Hear the lambs a-crying

"Hear, hear you not, adown the steppe so dreary." See Cossack's lament

"Hear how the breakers angrily lash the sand." See Det var då (Kjerulf)

"Hear me but once." Irish air: Mountains of Wicklow. Words by T. Moore. MMI

"Hear me, ye northern-born hearts." See Eros (Grieg)

"Hear me, ye nymphs, and ev'ry swain." See The bush aboon Traquair

"Hear mosquito buzzing." See The mosquito

"Hear sweet music softly saying I love you." See Waltz song (Lehár)

"Hear the angels telling." F. Iliffe. HC

Hear the birds of summer sing. FSS 4

"Hear the call to war, warriors all." See War song

"Hear the children's voices rising clear and strong." See The children's voices

Hear the lambs a-crying. Negro spiritual. BF 2
Hear de lambs a cryin'. HR

"Hear the lively song of the frogs in yonder pond." See Frog round

"Hear the loving Easter bells." See Easter bells (Clouston)

"Hear the May-bells clearly ringing." See May-bells (Bargiel)

"Hear the postilion riding by." See The postilion (Abt)

"Hear the sledges with the bells, silver bells." See The bells (Foote)

"Hear ye Amorea's daughters." See Oriental chant (Musorgskiĭ)

"Hear! ye gods of Britain." Purcell. BS 2

"Hear ye, Israel! hear what the Lord speaketh." F. Mendelssohn. e. OS 1—SAS 1

"Hear ye! the Lord hath done great things for us." See Sound the loud timbrel (Reinecke)

"Heard ye his voice" ("Vernahmet ihr") A. Rubinstein. Words from the Russian of Puschkin. e.g. FO 1

"Hearken to the jubilee" ("Saut yūbīl isma'u innahu saut el-surūr") Syrian folk song. ar.e. BF 2

"Hearken to the thankful reapers." R. F. Smith. Words by J. Bownes. HC

"Hears not my Phyllis how the birds." See The knotting song (Purcell)

Heart-ache for home. Words by H. Morford. FSS 5—JSE

"The heart bowed down." M. W. Balfe. FSS 1—HSC—HSD— HSE 3—JS— JSE—WWA—WBT. e.f.g.i. PO

Heart-broken mariner. See Povero marinar (Mililotti)

Heart-broken sailor boy. See Povero marinar (Mililotti)

"The heart hath tears that differ." See Die thränen des herzens (Goltermann)

"The heart is the fortune of all womankind." See Loving Nancy

"The heart may be sad in its heyday." See Cakes and ale (Lowe)

"Heart, my heart, why art thou sorry." See Schweizer heimweh (Glück)

The heart of a sailor. S. Adams. HSD— WBT

"Heart of hearts." See Air de Nicolette (Grétry)

"Heart of my own heart." See "Alma del core" (Caldara)

The heart of my well-beloved. See Le coeur de ma bien-aimée

Heart of oak. W. Boyce. Words by D. Garrick. BAS 1—BE 4—BOS— BS 1—CO 2—HSE 1—JE—MM— PR 2—SSS
Hearts of oak. DM 1

The heart should be happy and merry. W. Reeve. Words by C. Dibdin. HSE 2
Happy and merry. FSS 7

"The heart that knows no sorrow." Gung'l. FSS 4

"The heart that thou didst give to me." See Two hearts (Fontenailles)

"The heart! the heart." German song. e. FSS 8

Heart throbs. See "Wie berührt mich wundersam" (Bendel)

Heartache. See Herzeleid

"The hearth is swept, the fire is bright." See The wife's welcome (Woodbury)

"Hearts and homes." J. Blockley. Words by C. Young. FSS 2—HSE 3—WBT

Heart's desire. Ruthenian folk air. Words anonymous. WF

Heart's-ease ("Give me heart's-ease") 16th century song. DM 2

Heart's-ease ("Singe care away") 16th century air. Words by T. Rychardes. CO 1—VFS
"Sing care away." DM 2

Hearts of oak ("Bold be your stroke") F. Campana. FSS 4

Hearts of oak ("Come cheer up my lads") See Heart of oak (Boyce)

The heart's tear. See Die thränen des herzens (Goltermann)

The hearty good fellow. Folk song. BSW

Heath, George
"My soul, be on thy guard" (Mason)

Heath, Lyman
The grave of Bonaparte (Washburn)
"The **heath** is all lonely." Serenade. FSS 6
"The **heath** this night." Attributed to J. Mazzinghi. Words by Scott. JO
The **heather** glen ("There blooms a bonnie flower") Irish air: An smachtaoin crón, or, The brown little mallet. Words by G. Sigerson. FS 1—MMI
"The **heather** is brown." See Im herbst (Franz)
"**Heather** Jock's noo awa'." Scottish song. PS 2
"The **heather** was blooming." Air: The tailor's march. Words by R. Burns. BSR
Heave away ("As I walked out") See We're all bound to go
"**Heave** away, heave away, heave away you ruler king." Chantey. SMW
Heave away, my bully, bully boys. See Cape Cod chantey
Heave away, my Johnny ("As I walked out one fine morning") Chantey. FSF For variants see following songs of same title; also We're all bound to go
Heave away, my Johnny ("As I walked out one morning fine") Chantey. TFC 2
Heave away, my Johnny ("As I was going") Capstan chantey. SMW
Heave away, my Johnny ("It's of a farmer's daughter") Capstan chantey. SE
"**Heaven** and ocean." See "Cielo e mar" (Ponchielli)
Heav'n boun' soldier. Negro spiritual. JB
"**Heav'n** be praised! here am I." See Flamme vengeresse (Auber)
Heaven hath shed a tear. See "Der himmel hat eine thräne geweint" (Kücken)
Heaven in the vale. See Der himmel im thal (Marschner)
Heaven is my home. A. S. Sullivan. Words by T. R. Taylor. FSS 4—HSD—WBT
"**Heaven** may to you grant pardon." F. von Flotow. [Tr of Himmel euch vergeben] e. WBT
"**Heaven** with rosy morn is glowing." J. R. Higinbotham. Tr of Aurora lucis rutilat. e. HC
Heavenly Aida. See Celeste Aida (Verdi)
Heavenly clouds. A. Dargomijsky. Words by M. Lermontov. e. SC
"**Heavenly** Father, God alone." G. B. Lissant. Words by G. Moultrie. HC
"**Heavenly** Father, send Thy blessing." F. Peel. Words by C. Wordsworth. HC
The **heavenly** Guest. Words by M. Sidney. MCS
Heavenly love abiding. See "In heav'nly love abiding" (Hassler)
The **heavenly** rest. See Himmlische ruhe (Molique)
The **heavenly** song. H. Gray. Words by C. Lyttleton. HSS 1—HSS 4—SM 2

"The **heav'ns** are telling Jehovah's glory." See Die ehre Gottes aus der natur (Beethoven)
"The **heavens** declare His glory." See Die ehre Gottes aus der natur (Beethoven)
"The **heav'ns** proclaim God's majestical glory." See Die ehre Gottes aus der der natur (Beethoven)
"The **heav'ns** proclaim Him with ceaseless devotion." See Die ehre Gottes aus der natur (Beethoven)
"The **heavens** resound." See Die ehre Gottes aus der natur (Beethoven)
"The **heav'ns** with praise to the Lord are abounding." See Die ehre Gottes aus der natur (Beethoven)
"**Heavily** wears the day." German air. FSS 3—WBT
The **heaving** of the lead. W. Shield. Words by W. Pearce. BE 7—DM 2—HSE 1—JO—ME
Heaving the anchor. See Ved ankerhion-ing
Heav'n. For entries beginning Heav'n see Heaven
"**Heavy** the beat of the weary waves." Old dirge from the isle of Mull. Air: An cronan Muillach. HSSS
"**Heavy** the beat of the weary waves" (Isle of Mull dirge) MMS
Hebbe, Wendela
"Klara stjärnor med de ögon snälle" (Swedish folk air)
"**Hebe**, sieh! in sanfter feier." F. H. Himmel. Words by G. A. E. von Nostiz und Jänkendorf. g. ED 2
Hebel, Johann Peter
Abendlied, wenn man aus dem wirtshaus geht (Methfessel)
Freude in ehren (Erk)
Musketierlied (Silcher)
Heber, Reginald
"As with gladness men of old" (Monk)
"Bread of the world" (Composer unknown)
"Brightest and best" (music by Monk; Chittenden; Harding; Kiallmark; Mendelssohn; Webbe)
"By cool Siloam's shady rill" (Composer unknown)
"From Greenland's icy mountains" (music by Mason; Vogrich)
"Hail the blest morn" (Mason)
"Holy, holy, holy! Lord God Almighty" (Dykes)
"I see them on their winding way" (Composer unknown)
"If thou wert by my side" (Nelson)
"The Son of God goes forth to war" (Cutler)
"Virgin-born! we bow before Thee" (Gounod)
Hebrew love-song (Chanson hebraïque) N. Rimsky-Korsakow. Words by L. Mey. e.f. SC
"**Hecher** besser." See My youngest one is wedded
Hecker, J.
"Hark! what merry voices"

Hecker, L.
Gretelein (Kücken)
Hedberg, Frans
Källan (Lagercrantz)
Hedborn, Samuel Johan
"Förgäfves uppå stigen" (Swedish folk air)
Hedge roses. See Heidenröslein (Schubert)
"Hee balou, my sweet wee Donald." Air: The highland balou. Words by R. Burns. BSR
Heel and toe stamping on the floor. See "Sul mare torbido"
Heffernan, I.
German watchman's song
"Heft, burgers, 't lied der vrijheid" (Sing, citizens, the song of freedom) National air of Orange Free State. W. F. G. Nicolaï. Words by H. A. L. Hamelberg. d.e. SN
The he-i blossom (Pua o ka he-i) C. K. Hopkins. e.h. HA
Heibel, Jakob. See Haibel, Jakob
Heiberg, Peter Andreas
Danish love song (Traditional air)
"Die heide ist braun." See Im herbst (Franz)
Heidelberg. Heidelberg university song. F. A. Power. Words by J. E. Hartman. e. CHS
Heidenröslein (The wild rose) Schubert. Words by W. von Goethe. e. FTS
Haiden-röslein (Hedge roses) e.g. PG 1
Haiden röslein (The wild rose) e.g. MS—MSS 1
The wild-rose. e. BSE
The wild rosebud. e. LA
Heidenröslein ("Sah ein knab ein röslein stehn") H. Werner. Words by W. von Goethe. g. ED 1—ED 2
Heidenröslein (Wild rose) e.g. SSG
Once I saw a rose. e. WSC
"Once I saw a sweet brier-rose." e. FSS 1—WBT
The two roses. e. CHS—HSD— MPC—NMH—NML— WBT—WC
The wild rose. e. LA
Heidenröslein. For English translation with a different air see The wild rose ("In the wood a boy one day")
Heigh-ho! for a husband. Ancient air. VFS
Heigh ho! maid of the mill ("Oh, come to the greenwood") Talhairn (music and words) e. MMW
Heigh-ho, the holly. W. Crawford. Words by E. M. Thomas. MCS
"Heigh-ho! what shall I do." T. Welsh. BE 3
"Heigho! how bracing the air." See Paa fjellet (Kjerulf)
"Heil dir im siegerkranz." German national song. H. Carey. Words by H. Harries. g. ED 1—SN
"Heil dir im siegerkranz" ("Hail thou, whose victor's crown") e.g. SSG

"Heil, unserm könig, heil." Bavarian national song. H. Carey. g. SN
Die heilige nacht ("Stille nacht") F. Gruber; wrongly attributed to M. Haydn. Words by J. Mohr. g. ED 1—FSS 6—MCS
Holy night. e. MCS—OH
"Holy night! peaceful night." e. NMS—WA—WBT—WS— WSC— WSW
"Noche de paz." s. LCP
"Silent night." e. BD—BSS—DC— DO— FSS 1—HC— HSD— LA— TFC 1
"Stille nacht." g. MS
Stille nacht ("Silent night") e. MF
"Stille nacht! heilige nacht" ("Silent night! holy night") e.g. SSG
Die heilige nacht. For English translations with different airs see "Holy night! peaceful night" (Barnby); "Holy night, silent night" (Arr by Haydn); "Silent night! hallow'd night" (Composer unknown)
"Die heiligen drei könig' mit ihrem stern." K. F. Zelter. Words by W. von Goethe. g. ED 3
Heim, Ignaz
Switzerland
"Heimgang! so the German people." See Going home
Die heimkehr ("Im Aagäu sind zweu liebi") See Die Aagauer lieben
Heimkehr ("Leiser schwanken die äste."— Homeward) R. Strauss. Words by A. F. von Schack. e.g. CMF 2
Heimliche liebe ("Kein feuer") Volkslied. g. ED 1
Heimliche liebe (Secret love) e.g. BF 2
Heimlicher liebe pein ("Mein schatz") C. M. von Weber. Volkslied. g. ED 2
Heimlicher liebe pein (Woes of hidden love) e.g. SSG
Heimweh ("Anders wird die welt."— Homesickness) H. Wolf. Words by E. Mörike. e.g. GM
Das heimweh ("Wenn in die ferne vom felsen") P. Müller (music and words) g. ED 3
Heimweh ("Wer in die fremde will wandern."—Longing) H. Wolf. Words by J. von Eichendorff. e.g. PG 2
Heine, Heinrich
À toi mon coeur (Gounod. Tr of Auf dem meere)
Der Asra (music by Loewe; Rubinstein)
Auf dem meere (Franz. For music by Gounod see À toi mon coeur)
"Auf flügeln des gesanges" (Mendelssohn)
"Aus meinen grossen schmerzen" (Franz)
Die beiden grenadiere (Schumann. For music by Wagner see Les deux grenadiers)

Heine, Heinrich —*Continued*
"Die blauen frühlinsaugen" (music by Ries; Rubinstein)
"Das ist ein brausen und heulen" (Franz)
Les deux grenadiers (Wagner. Tr of Die beiden grenadiere)
Der doppelgänger (Schubert)
"Du bist wie eine blume" (music by Degele; Liszt; Rubinstein; Schumann. For music by Cantor see "Oh fair, oh sweet")
"Du schönes fischermädchen" (music by Meyerbeer; Schubert)
"Es war ein alter könig" (Rubinstein)
Es war ein traum (Lassen)
Gruss (Mendelssohn)
"Ich grolle nicht" (Schumann)
"Ich wollt' meine lieb ergösse" (Mendelssohn)
Ihr bild (Schubert)
"Im wunderschönen monat mai" (music by Franz; Schumann)
Invocation (Rhodes. Tr of Ich hab' ein traum geweinet)
"Lehn' deine wang' an meine wang'" (Jensen)
Lied (Mertens. French tr of Es fällt ein stern herunter)
Die Lorelei (music by Liszt; Silcher)
Die lotosblume (music by Franz; Schumann)
"Mädchen mit dem rothen mündchen" (music by Franz; Gall)
"Mir träumte von einem königskind" (Hartmann)
"Mit deinen blauen augen" (Lassen. For music by Arlberg see Svärmeri)
"Mit myrthen und rosen" (Schumann)
"Morgens send' ich dir die veilchen" (Meyer-Helmund)
"My songs are envenomed and bitter" (Borodin. Tr of Vergiftet sind meine lieder)
"Oh fair, oh sweet" (Cantor. Tr of "Du bist wie eine blume")
"På Norges kolde vidder" (Holter. Tr of Ein fichtenbaum steht einsam)
Reiselied (Mendelssohn)
"Die rose, die lilie, die taube" (Schumann)
"Der schmetterling ist in die rose verliebt" (Franz)
"Schöne wiege meiner leiden" (Schumann)
"Sterne mit den goldnen füsschen" (Graben-Hoffmann)
Svärmeri (Arlberg. Tr of "Mit deinen blauen augen")
"Wandl' ich in dem wald des abends" (Franz)
Warum (Tchaikovsky)
"Wenn ich in deine augen seh'" (Bleichman)
"**Heirs** of unending life" (Dennis) H. G. Nägeli. Words by Beddome. FSS 1

Heise, Peder Arnold
"Ah, who once wore a fine bonnet." See "Ak, hvem der havde en hue"
"Ak, hvem der havde en hue"
Arnes sang
Arne's song. See Arnes sang
"Dengang jeg var kun saa stor som saa." See When that I was a little tiny boy
"Det stiger"
"It rises." See "Det stiger"
Liden Karen
Little Karen. See Liden Karen
When that I was a little tiny boy
"**Hej!** hej! from the mowing of the hill grass." See Reapers on the mountain
Hej onward. See Volga boat song
"**Hej, Slované.**" See "Ho, Slavonians"
"**Hej!** the young and handsome gay Jovo." See Sarajevo kolo
Hel mig mine strenge (Mend me my strings) L. Halvorsen. Words by V. Krag. e.n. WM 1
Hela'r 'sgyvarnog (Hunting the hare) Old Welsh folk song. e.w. BO
Hunting the hare. e. GO
"**Hélas,** que je suis à mon aise." See Le départ du soldat
"**Helft,** leutchen, mir vom wagen doch." See Die feldflasche (Keller)
"**Helil** faium valladac iarum." Nile river song. ar. SMW
Hell, Theodor, pseud. See Winkler, Karl Gottfried
"**Hell** dig, du höga Nord" ("Hail, Northland high, all hail") B. Crusell. Words by F. B. Coster. e.sw. HSOS
"**Hellig** Olaf" (St Olaf) Air: Stusle söndags kvellen. Words by J. S. Welhaven. e.n. MAN
"**Hello!** Peter! you're a friend of mine." See Greeting
Helmore, Thomas
Christmas carol
"Here is joy for every age"
Helmund, Erik Meyer-. See Meyer-Helmund, Erik
Help it on. Old air. Words by E. R. Sill. LA
"**Help** me, dearest mother." See The song of the bride (Rimskiï-Korsakov)
"**Help** me, each harmonious grove." See Colin's request (Monro)
Helston furry dance. See The Cornish May song
Hemans, Mrs Felicia Dorothea (Browne)
The better land (music by Bennett; Brown; Cowen)
Breathings of spring (Weber)
"Bring flowers" (French air)
The captive knight (Browne)
Evening song to the Virgin (Composer unknown)
Far o'er the sea (Kingsley)
The graves of a household (Barker)
The Hirlas horn (Welsh air)
The hour of prayer (Hérold)
"I come, I come! ye have called me long" (Bellini)

Hemans, Mrs F. D. B. —*Continued*
"I dream of all things free" (Weber)
"If thou hast crushed a flower" (Bellini)
Kindred hearts (German air)
Landing of the Pilgrims (Browne)
The messenger bird (Browne)
"Mother, O sing me to rest" (music by Franz; Hildach)
"Night sinks on the wave"(Auber)
"O lovely voices of the sky" (Traditional air; also old air; also music by King)
The rock of Cader Idris (Welsh air)
The songs your fathers loved (Welsh air)
Stilling the tempest (Watson)
Taliesin's prophecy (Welsh air)
Treasures of the deep (Browne)
Tyrolese evening hymn (Browne)
The **hemlock** tree ("O hemlock tree") German air: Der tannenbaum. Words adapted from Longfellow. GO
The **hemlock** tree ("O tannenbaum") See Der tannenbaum
Hemy, Henry F., and Walton, J. G.
"Faith of our fathers, living still"
"**Hence!** away with idle sorrow." See Hunting the hare
Hence, Iris, hence away. Händel. Words by Congreve. CS 2
Hence, hence with your trifling deity. H. Purcell. Words by Shadwell. PR 1
"**Henceforth**, Strephon." A. Sullivan. Words by W. S. Gilbert. DSH
Henderson, William James
"Look not upon me with thine eyes" (Bartlett)
Hendon (Malan) See "Children of the heavenly King"; "Lord! we come before Thee now"
Hendrickson, William D.
The Spanish cavalier
Henrion, Paul
The muleteer of Tarragona. See Le muletier de Tarragone
Le muletier de Tarragone
"This happy day" (from La Manola)
Henry VIII, king of England
"Green grows the holly"
The kynge's balade. See "Pastime with good company"
"Pastime with good company"
Whereto should I express
Henry III, king of France
"Gone from me evermore." See "J'ai perdu celle" (attributed)
"J'ai perdu celle" (attributed)
"Nun ach! verlor ich sie." See "J'ai perdu celle" (attributed)
Henry IV, king of France
Charmente Gabrielle (attributed)
Charming Gabrielle. See Charmente Gabrielle (attributed)
Henry Martin ("There were three brothers") Folk song. FSF—SEF 1—SO
Variant: Henry Martyn

Henry Martyn ("In merry Scotland") Folk song. BSW
Variant of: Henry Martin
"**Henry** our royal king, would ride a hunting." DM 2
Henschel, Georg
Morgen-hymne
Morning hymn. See Morgen-hymne
Her blanket. Navajo Indian song. T. Lieurance. e. BF 2—LN
"**Her** bright eyes whose radiant gleaming." See Il balen del suo sorriso (Verdi)
Her bright smile haunts me still. W. T. Wrighton. Words by J. E. Carpenter. HSD—WL
Her bright smile. CR—FSS 6—HSC —NML—WBT
"**Her** daddie forbad, her minnie forbad." Air: Jumpin' John. Words by R. Burns. BSR
"**Her** daddy forbade." PS 2
"**Her** eye so mildly beaming." See Ho-ro mo nighean donn, bhòidheach
"**Her** eyes are like the morning bright." Air: Yr eneth lan, or, The fair damsel. MMW
"**Her** eyes like clouded stars." See Spanish serenade (Lee)
"**Her** gentle hand for me did sever." See Lied (Franck)
"**Her** gentle voice." M. W. Balfe. Words by E. Falconer. FSS 8
Her hair ("Cette nuit, j'ai rêvé") See La chevelure (Debussy)
"**Her** hair was like the beaten gold." See Gentle Mary
Her hjemme (Home forever) Air: En liten gut ifraa Tistedal'n, or, A little lad down in Tistedale. Words by J. Olafsen. e.n. MAN. e. only GO
"**Her** love was never mine." See Dormirò sol nel manto mio regal (Verdi)
"**Her** né rutbé." See "The sun hangs high"
Her portrait. See Ihr bild (Schubert)
Her rosary. See The weaver (Lieurance)
Her rose. Love-song. C. W. Coombs. Words by J. G. Mottet. AA
Her shadow ("Ayquanahquog peah bedahgo jing") Ojibway Indian song. e.in. BA—BF 2
Herald angels. See "Hark! the herald angels sing" (Mendelssohn)
"**Herald** of evening tender." See Mädchenlied (Raff)
Herbert, Annie
"When the mists" (Rousseau)
Herbert, George
"Sweet day, so cool" (17th century air)
Herbert, J. B.
"Away in a manger"
Cradle hymn. See "Away in a manger"
Herbert, Mary
The corn song (Marks)
"Ripe are the apples" (Composer unknown)

Herbert, Victor
.Because you're you
Toyland
Herbstfrühlingslied ("In autumn") O. Weil.
e.g. SOS 1
Herbstgang (Autumn) S. Jordan. Words by P. Remer. e.g. WM 1
Herbstlied ("Bunt sind schön die wälder") J. F. Reichardt. Words by von Salis.
g. ED 2
Herbstlied ("Feldeinwärts flog ein vöge-lein") L. Berger. Words by L. Tieck.
g. ED 2
Herbststurm (Autumnal gale) E. Grieg.
e.g. KF 2
"Der **herbstwind** rüttelt die bäume." See Reiselied (Mendelssohn)
Herd of cattle. See Ranz des vaches ("Lè z'armaillis dei Colombettè")
Herdegossen (The herdsman's song) I. A. Berg. e.sw. SSN
Herder, Johann Gottfried von
Edward (Loewe)
Lied des lebens (Composer unknown)
The **herdgirl's** Sunday. See Saetergjen-tens söndag (Bull)
Herdsman's mountain home. See Der schweizerbue
The **herdman's** song ("Fjerran i skog") See Herdegossen (Berg)
Herdsman's song ("To Swiss in stranger's land") See Ranz des vaches ("To Swiss in stranger's land")
"**Here**, a sheer hulk, lies poor Tom Bowling." See Tom Bowling (Dibdin)
"**Here** alone waiting the hour." See Mid-night tryst
"**Here** am I, a merry Switzer boy." See The Switzer boy
"**Here** at school we gather daily." See Work and play
"**Here** at the pleasant twilight hour." See On the chapel steps (Gow)
"**Here** awa, there awa, wandering Willie." See Wandering Willie
"**Here**, by the gushing fountain." See Morning tryst
"**Here** comes on crutches Sally." See "Kjaerringa med' staven"
"**Here** comes the major, with his company." See Majoren og hans kompani
"**Here** cometh Rosalind, chasing the bee." See Rosalind
"**Here** hope's consoling ray." See "Bel raggio lusinghier" (Rossini)
"**Here** I go over the lea, tra-la-lee." See L'heureux vagabond (Bruneau)
"**Here** in a stable." See Dans cette étable
"**Here** in the wood, far, far from thee." See Herdegossen (Berg)
"**Here** is a staircase so steep and so tall." See Playing ball on the stairs
Here is a title. See "Thou art always the same to me, dear" (Hopkins)
"**Here** is joy for every age." Composer unknown. Words by J. M. Neale. HC
"**Here** is joy for every age." T. Helmore. Words by J. M. Neale. HC

"**Here** is the open trolley." See The trol-ley ride
"**Here** is the usual place for the smugglers to gather." See Je dis que rien ne m'épouvante (Bizet)
"**Here** let us rest awhile." See Vallons de l'Helvétie (Adam)
"**Here** lies, within this tomb so calm, old Giles." See Epitaph on a parish clerk (Webbe)
"**Here** lieth Sir John Guise." Round. FSS 7
"**Here** mark the poor desolate maid." See 'Tis but fancy's sketch (Braham)
"**Here** 'neath your balcony I'm waiting." See Serenata ("Son soto")
"**Here** the rose-buds in June." See The rose-buds in June
"**Here** the ruins I see." See Nonnes qui reposez (Meyerbeer)
"**Here** under the leafy greenwood tree." See The greenwood tree (Nelson)
"**Here** upon the mountain oft in dreamy rest I stay." See On the mountain (Lindblad)
"**Here** we come a-carolling." See Christ-mas carolling song
"**Here** we come a-wassailing" (The wassail song) Folk song. BSC—CST—MCS—WCC
"**Here** we come a-wassailing." York-shire version. HC
Variants: Somersetshire wassail; Was-sail song
"**Here** we come on our ponies." See The pony ride
"**Here** we dwell in holiest bowers." See Love and the novice
"**Here** we go round the mulberry bush." See The mulberry bush
"**Here** we stand, hand in hand." Move-ment song. Air: Smiling May comes in play. FSS 2
"**Here** we stand ready now to go on our way." Indian ritual air. e. FI
"**Here**, while dawn's brilliant rays enfold him." See Naissantes fleurs (Grétry)
"**Here** wi' lips foretok'ning kisses." See Eilidh bhàn
"**Here's** a bank with rich cowslips." See The queen of the May
"**Here's** a beautiful goldfinch I'm teaching." See Lu cardillo
"**Here's** a birdie come flying." See Frohe botschaft
"**Here's** a fair wind." See Le canard blanc
Here's a health to all honest men. See A health to all honest men
"**Here's** a health to all them that we love." See Here's to you
Here's a health to ane I lo'e dear. Old air: Here's a health to them that's awa', hiney. Words by R. Burns. BSB—JO—PS 1
"Altho' thou maun never be mine." BSR
Here's a health to the barley mow, my boys. See The barley mow

"Here's a health to the jolly blacksmith." See Twankydillo

"Here's a health to the king." See Down among the dead men

"Here's a health to the lass." Old English air. BE 6

"Here's a health to the queen." See Down among the dead men

"Here's a health to them that we love." Round. FSS 5

"Here's a health to them that's awa'." Scottish air. Words by Burns. BSR —MMS

"Here's a health to you all." See Wanderlied

"Here's a health to you, comrades." See Reiterlied (Zahn)

"Here's a health unto his majesty." J. Savile. BE 6—BOH—BOS—CO 2— DM 1—JE—MM—SSS

"Here's a health unto the jolly woodcutter." See The woodcutter

"Here's a toast, let's drink together." See Chanson du toréador (Bizet)

"Here's adieu to all judges and juries." Folk song from Sussex. SF 5

"Here's cakes and wines for you, young man." See The trooper and the maid (Tennessee version)

"Here's good wind." See Le canard blanc

"Here's the autumn come again." See L'hivernage

"Here's the bower." Old English song. FSS 8

"Here's the stone that is slippery." See Las mananitas

"Here's the tender coming." Scotch song. SMW

"Here's to B. S. A." See Bingo

"Here's to Columbia college." See Bingo

"Here's to good old Yale." See Bingo

"Here's to our alma mater." See Columbia medley (Walker)

"Here's to Rensselaer." See Bingo

"Here's to the fox." See Drink, puppy, drink (Whyte-Melville)

"Here's to the maiden of bashful fifteen." Air: Half Hanykin, arr by T. Linley. Words by Sheridan. BE 1 — BOH— BOS— DM 1—FMB— HSE 1—JE—MM—SSS—WBT
    Let the toast pass. BSE

"Here's to the prettiest." See Here's to you

"Here's to the rector come to see." See The profs' song

"Here's to the year that's awa'." See The year that's awa'

"Here's to thee, my boy." Drinking song. H. Carey. MM

"Here's to thy health, my bonie lass." Air: Laggan burn. Words by R. Burns. BSR

Here's to you ("Here's a health to all them that we love") Round. NML

Here's to you ("Here's to the prettiest") MP

"Here's to you! in faith 'tis delightful." See Chanson du toréador (Bizet)

"Here's where the smugglers." See Je dis que rien ne m'épouvante (Bizet)

"Here's your mother's cloak." See The Suffolk miracle (Big Laurel, N.C. version)

Hering, Karl Gottlieb
    The hobby horse. See Das steckenpferd
    My pony (same air as Das steckenpferd)
    Das steckenpferd
    Der wachtelschlag

The heritage. Arr from the German. Words by J. R. Lowell. LBR

Herloszsohn, Karl
    Abschied (Abt)
    Drei schneider (Folk air)

Hermann, N.
    "Hark! the glad sound"

Hermes, Johann Timotheus
    An die wankelmütige (Schulz)
    Wert der freundschaft (König)

"Hermit bird, whose melody." See The nightingale

"A hermit there was." Words by P. Parley. FSS 5

Hernaman, Mrs Claudia Frances (Ibotson)
    "Angels singing, church bells ringing" (German air)
    "Come, children, lift your voices"(Ryley)
    "He is risen from the dead" (Brown)
    "It is a day of gladness" (Barry)
    "Now to Bethlehem haste we" (Dykes)
    "Sing with joy, 'tis Christmas morn" (Stainer)

"Heroes do mar, nobre povo." See A Portuguesa (Keil)

"Heroes, when with glory turning." G. F. Händel. SAS 2

Hérold, Louis Joseph Ferdinand
    "Guide me, O Thou great Jehovah"
    The hour of prayer
    Hymn of the fishermen's children
    "Tell me, oh, ye stars" (same air as Hymn of the fishermen's children)

The hero's serenade. C. Jarvis. Words by H. Schmidt. FSS 3

"Herr bruder, nimm das gläschen." Volkslied. g. ED 1
    "Herr bruder, nimm das gläschen" ("Come, brothers, fill your glasses") e.g. SSS
    Hi-le, hi-lo. e. WBT

"Herr, den ich tief im herzen trage." See Gebet (Hiller)

"Herr Magnus han stir rer is vinter natten ud." See Knud Lavard (Gade)

Herr Ulrich ("Wer singet im walde") Hoffmann von Fallersleben (music and words) g. ED 2

Herrick, Robert
    "Amidst the myrtles" (music by Battishill; Lawes)
    The bell-man (Douty)
    "Bid me to live" (music by Hatton; Lawes)

Herrick, Robert—*Continued*
Carol for Christmas eve (Composer unknown)
"Charm me asleep" (Suabian folk air)
"Cherry ripe" (Horn)
"Gather ye rosebuds while ye may" (Lawes)
Passing by (music by Ford; Purcell)
The primrose (Lawes)
The **herring** fisher's song.   See Sildfiske vise
Herring the king ("Of all the fish that roam the sea") Irish song.   MMI
Herron, J. D.
The bird song
"Brief life is here our portion" (Tr of Hic breve vivitur)
The children's Easter offering
"For thee, O dear, dear country" (Tr of O bona patria, lumina sobria te speculantur)
A little while
"Nearer, my God, to Thee"
"The world is very evil" (Tr of Hora novissima)
Hervey, Arthur
Nirvana
Once
Hervey, D. E.
"The bells are ringing glad and sweet"
Hervey, E. L.
Legends of the Infancy (Bridge)
Hervey, Frederick Alfred John
"Make melody within your hearts"
Herwegh, Georg
Reiterlied (Lyra)
"Ein **herz**, das sich mit sorgen quält."   See Nur guten mut
"Das **herz** hat andre thränen."   See Die thränen des herzens (Goltermann)
"**Herz**, mein herz, warum so traurig."   See Schweizer heimweh (Glück)
"Das **herz**, vom kummer tief gebeugt."   See "The heart bow'd down" (Balfe)
"**Herzallerliebstes** schatzerl du."   F. W. Kücken.   g.   ED 1
Herzeleid (Heartache) Swabian folk song.   e.g.   SSG
Heartache.   e.   BSE
The mourner.   e.   FSS 1
Herzeleid.   For English translation with a different air see Forlorn (Franz)
Herzensbeklemmung ("Ach Gott")   After J. Thümmel.   Words by O. Roquette.   g.   ED 2
Herzensbeklemmung (The complaint) e.g.   SSG
Der **herzenswechsel** ("Du gibst mir also nicht dein herz") F. H. Himmel.   g.   ED 3
Der **herzenswechsel** ("Du gibst mir also nicht dein herz") J. F. Reichardt.   g.   ED 3
He's aye a kissing me ("I winna marry ony man") Scottish song.   MMS
"He's blest, whose sins have pardon gained."   See Whose sins have pardon gained (Mason)

He's dear to me tho' he's far frae me ("As I was walking by yon river-side") Gaelic air.   MMS
He's jus' de same today.   Negro spiritual.   JB
"He's owre the hills."   Scottish song.   PS 1
"He's run his little legs orff."   See The nipper's lullaby (Andrews)
"He's such a li'l' fellow."   See Such a li'l' fellow (Dichmont)
He's the lily of the valley.   Negro spiritual.   FSS 5—JP—JSE—WBT
He's the Lord of lords.   Negro spiritual.   HR
L'heure du rêve.   See The hour of dreams (Arenski)
L'heure exquise (The perfect hour) R. Hahn.   Words by P. Verlaine.   e.f.   CM 2—HM 2
L'heure exquise (The hour of dreaming)   e.f.   MSF 1
L'heureux vagabond (The gay vagabond) A. Bruneau.   Words by C. Mendès.   e.f.   SAM
"**Heus,** fratres, ecce Lalage."   See Carmen de Lalages agno (Winner)
"**Heute** fröhlichkeit."   See Heute und morgen (Nathusius)
Heute und morgen ("Heute fröhlichkeit") M. Nathusius.   Words by H. Hoffmann von Fallersleben.   g.   ED 3
"**Heute** scheid' ich, heute wandr' ich."   See Soldaten-abschied (Fesca)
Heutzutage ("In der liebe götterwelt")   A. André.   Words by A. Mahlmann.   g.   ED 3
Hewitt, D. C.
The wounded Hussar
Hewitt, James H.
The mountain bugle
Hewitt, Richard
"The music of thy voice" (Composer unknown)
Roslin castle (Old air)
Hey, Wilhelm
"Alle jahre wieder" (music by Rinck; Silcher)
"Die schönste zeit, die liebste zeit" (Nägeli)
Hey, ca' thro'.   Boat song.   Words by R. Burns.   BSB
The carles o' Dysart (Fisherman's song)   PS 2
"Up wi' the carls o' Dysart."   BSR
Hey! come hither, ye fancies.   See Su, venite a consiglio (Scarlatti)
"**Hey,** diddle, diddle."   Nursery song.   FMB—WA—WBT—WSC—WSW
"**Hey** diddle diddle."   Nursery song.   Another version.   CHS
Hey Donald, how Donald, hey Donald Couper.   See "O, Donald Couper and his man"
"**Hey,** git along, git along, Josey."   See Jim along, Josey
"**Hey,** hey, hey! come hither, ye fancies."   See Su, venite a consiglio (Scarlatti)

Hey, ho, my honey. See "I am a poor shepherd undone"

Hey! Johnie Cope, are ye wauking yet. See "Sir John Cope trode the north right far"

Hey, Johnnie Cope ("Cope sent a letter") See Johnnie Cope

"Hey! kimmer Nina." See Canto de' contadini Etnei

"Hey, my winsome Mary, Mary fondly free." See Mairi laghach

"Hey, pretty Marianna, now whither dost fare." See "Ma belle Marianne"

"Hey the bonny, how the bonny." See The bonnie breast-knots

"Hey the dusty miller." Air: Dusty miller. Words by R. Burns. BSR—PS 2

Hey, then up go we. Air from "Caricatures and ballads." Words by F. Quarles. CO 1

Hey, then up go we. Air from "Musica antiqua." Words by F. Quarles. CO 1

Hey tutti, taiti. See "Landlady, count the lawin"

Hey, 'twas in the May. See 'T patertje

"Heyah heyah heyah hey heyah ha." See A song of faith

"Heyah heyah heyah hey heyah hey ah." See Visiting song

"Heyah heyah heyah heyah heyah heyah ha ha." See A song of trust

Heyberg, Nils Pedersen
Bonden i bryllaupsgarden (Norse folk air)

Heyduk, Adolf
"Songs my mother taught me" (Dvořák)

Heyse, Paul Johann Ludwig
Abschied (Cavallo)
"Murmelndes lüftchen, blüthenwind" (Jensen)

Heywood, John
All a green willow (16th century air)

"Hi a ha ha ha a he a-we dho he e." See Mi-ka-thi

"Hi dha ho! sha a-ma wi un-don-be a-me dho he." See Trysting love song

"Hi dho ho hi." See The deathless voice

"Hi! ha! ha! the Hopak! I'm the wife of a Kosak." See Hopak (Musorgskiĭ)

Hi-le, hi-lo. See "Herr bruder, nimm das gläschen"

"Hi, says the blackbird sitting on a chair." See The bird song (Vermont version)

"Hi ya ho hi ya." See I-ou'-tin game song; Victory song

Hiawatha's death song. Ojibway Indian song. e.in. BA

Hiawatha's mittens. T. James. BSS

Hic breve vivitur. For English translation see "Brief life is here our portion" (Herron)

Hichens, Robert S.
The bird and the rose (Horrocks)
Happy three (Röckel)

Hick's farewell. Folk song from North Carolina. CSE

Hickson, William Edward
God speed the right (German air)
That day the world shall see (Callcott)

"Hide thou thy hated beams." Händel. OS 3

Hiding the disks. Indian game song. in. FI

Hie away home. Plantation song. BSS

"Hie to the fields." W. A. Mozart. e. BD

"Hie upon Hielands and laigh upon Tay." See Bonnie Georgie Campbell

Hiemer, Franz Karl
Kriegslied (Eidenbenz)
Slummersång (Hägg. Tr of Wiegenlied)
Wiegenlied (Weber)

"Hier hab' ich so manches liebe mal." See An der Weser (Pressel)

"Hier in des abends traulich ernster stille." F. F. Flemming. Words by C. Schulz. g. ED 2

"Hier sind wir versammelt." See Ergo bibamus (Eberwein)

"Hier sitz ich auf rasen." See Neuer vorsatz (Schmidt)

"Hier, sur le pont d'Avignon." See Sur le pont d'Avignon (Canadian version)

"Hier unten im schatte." See Aufgegebene liebe

Higanúyahí. Cherokee Indian song. e.in. SN

Higbee, Elnathan Elisha
O'er the grave victorious (Goudimel)
The water into wine (Composer unknown)

Higginson, Mrs Ella (Rhoads)
When the birds go north again (Warren)

Higgs, James
Luther's carol (Tr of "Vom himmel hoch da komm' ich her")

High Barbaree ("There was two lofty ships") Forecastle song. CR
For variant of this song see following song of same title

High Barbaree ("There were two lofty ships") Sea song. KB

High Germany ("Abroad as I was walking") Folk song: Dorset version. SF 1

High Germany ("O Polly") Somerset version. BOS—SEF 1—SO

"High is raised the singers' banner." See Sångarfanan (Frieberg)

"High, low, my old mare." See Moscow gypsy song

The **high-mettled** racer. Dibdin. HSE 2

A **high** mountain stands ("Stoït' gora visokaíà") Russian song. e.r. BF 1

"High on the crest." Air: Morva Rhuddlan, or, The marsh of Ruddlan. Words by C. M. Oliver. MMW

"High on the mountains of Kiso." See A song from Kiso

"High on the world did our fathers of old." See Under the stars and stripes (Converse)

"High row, de boatmen, row." See De boatmen's dance (Smith)

"High the Cossack's heart is bounding." See The Cossack's song (Grünbaum)

"High the craggy mountains." See "Aquéros mountagnos" (Foix?)

"High up in her bow'r sat a princess maid." See "Prinsessen sad höjt i sit jomfrubur" (Kjerulf)

"Higher still and higher." See The skylark

Highland cradle song ("The mirk is gathering in the glen") Air: Baba mo leanabh. Words by K. R. Moffat. MMS

Highland cradle song ("Slumber sweetly, little Donald") R. Schumann. Words by R. Burns. MS

"A Highland lad my love was born." Air: O, an ye were dead, guidman. Words by R. Burns. BSR

"A Highland lad my love was born." Air: The white cockade. Words by R. Burns. BSB—GO—MMS—PS 1

Highland Mary ("Ye banks and braes") Air: Katherine Ogie, or, Lady Catherine Ogle. Words by R. Burns. BSB—FSS 6—JO—JSE—MMS—PS 1—WBT

"Ye banks and braes and streams around." BSR

Highland Mary ("Ye banks and braes") H. N. Bartlett. Words by R. Burns. AA

The Highland watch. Scottish song. PS 1

The Highland widow's lament. Scottish air. Words by R. Burns. PS 2

"O, I am come to the low countrie." BSR

The highlander. See "Plecat-a motul la tara"

Higinbotham, Julia R.
"Bravely chime, O Easter bells"
"Heaven with rosy morn is glowing" (Tr of Aurora lucis rutilat)
"It came upon the midnight clear"

"Hija soy de una aislada madrépora." See El himno de Puerto Rico (Pericás)

"El hijo del conde caramba." See El conde de Cabra

"Hiki mai ana kealoha." See "The remembrance of our last meeting" (Hopkins)

Hildach, Eugen
Little fidget. See Strampelchen
"Mein liebster ist ein weber"
"Mother, oh sing me to rest"
"Mutter, o, sing' mich zur ruh'." See "Mother, oh sing me to rest"
"My lover is a weaver." See "Mein liebster ist ein weber"
Strampelchen

Hiles, Henry
"The shadows of the evening hours"

Hill, Aaron
Lotharia (Arne)
"Oh! forbear" (Whichello)

Hill, Junius W.
My college girl

Hillebrand, N. P.
Journeyman's song

Hiller, Ferdinand
"All my strength hath fled away" (from Die zerstörung Jerusalems) Gebet
"Hail, David, our deliv'rer" (from Saul)
Jeremiah's lament (from Die zerstörung Jerusalems)
"King of Israel" (from Saul)
"Lord, of my inmost heart's recesses." See Gebet
Obedience 'tis, the Lord of Hosts demandeth (from Saul)
Prayer. See Gebet
"They fled, the gloomy powers" (from Saul)
"Yes, Thou wilt yet remember" (from Die zerstörung Jerusalems)

Hiller, Johann Adam
"Als ich auf meiner bleiche" (from Die jagd)
Liebe und wein
"Woodman, spare that tree"

Hills, William
"Droop not, young lover" (Händel)

"The hills and forests are dark'ning." See Gute nacht (Franz)

The hills o' Skye. V. Harris. Words by W. McLennan. HST

Hillsdale and the blue. Hillsdale college song. G. D. Monroe. Words by C. E. Greenlee. CHS

Hilo verde. Old song. 2 airs. s. LCP

Hilton, John
Come, follow me
Follow me. See Come, follow me
Hunting song
"O, had not Venus been beguiled"

Hime, D.
The beautiful day

Hime, Edward Laurence
"I love to sing"

Himmel, Friedrich Heinrich
Battle prayer. See Gebet während der schlacht
The blessed country
Die drei sterne
Ewiger wechsel
Gebet während der schlacht
"Hebe, sieh! in sanfter feier"
Der herzenswechsel
Der himmel hängt voll geigen
"Kennst du das land"
Körner's battle prayer. See Gebet während der schlacht
The message of the rose. See Der rose sendung
Mignon. See "Kennst du das land"
Romanze von den schneidern
Der rose sendung (from Das echo, oder, Alexis und Ida)
Tempora mutantur. See Ewiger wechsel
Das veilchen
Das vergissmeinnicht
Die weihe (from Urania)
Die welt, ein orchester (from Fanchon)
Yarico to her lover

"Der himmel da oben, der freut mich sehr." See Der himmel im thale (Marschner)

Himmel euch vergeben. For English translation see "Heaven may to you grant pardon" (Flotow)

Der **himmel** hängt voll geigen ("Wir geniessen die himmlischen freuden") F. H. Himmel. Words after M. Sturm. g. ED 2

"Der **himmel** hat eine thräne geweint" (Heaven hath shed a tear) F. Kücken. e.g. SOS 2

Der **himmel** im thale (Heaven in the vale) H. Marschner. e.g. KF 4

"Die **himmel** rühmen des Ewigen ehre." See Die ehre Gottes aus der natur (Beethoven)

Himmlische ruhe (The heavenly rest) Molique. Words by Tappan. e.g. HSS 3

Himno Bayamés. Hymn of free Cuba. P. Figueredo (music and words) e.s. NA. s. only LCP

El **himno** de Puerto Rico. J. Pericás. Words by J. A. Negrón Sanjurjo. s. LCP

Himno de Riego. Huerta. s. LCP
El himno de Riego (Riego's hymn) e.s. BSP
Hymne de Riego. e.s. SN
Spanish hymn. e.s. NMH

Himno nacional ("Oid mortales."—National hymn) Argentine song. V. López. e.s. BSP
National hymn. e.s. MP
"Oid, mortales, el grito sagrado." s. SN

Himno nacional de Guatemala (National hymn of Guatemala) R. Alvarez. Words anonymous. e.s. WCP

Himno nacional de la republica oriental del Uruguay. D. I. Deballi (music and words) s. SN

Himno nacional de Mejico (Mexican national hymn) J. Nunó. e.s. WCP

"**Hinaus,** ach hinaus zog des Hochlands kühner sohn." See The blue bells of Scotland (Jordan)

"**Hinaus** in die ferne." See Gesang ausziehender krieger (Methfessel)

"**Hinden** over heide, so faa me ara fleire." See Hindraleiken

"The **Hindoo** girl." V. Bellini. FSS 8

Hindoo song ("Brahma, Dieu des croyants") See Chant hindou (Bemberg)

Hindraleiken (Hunting the hind) Words from an old Norse play. e.n. MAN

The **Hindu** child ("I go unto the fair") Hindu song. e. BMC

Hindu song ("Night doth on the river fall") See "Night doth on the river fall"

The **Hindustani** girl's lament. Biggs. Words by Mrs Opie. BE 5

Hine, Gertrude
"In the country nigh to Bethlehem"

Hine, James
The brookside
The departed

"Ann **hini** gouz" ("A ripe old dame do I woo") Breton song. br.e.f. TSF

Hinkel, Karl
Bundeslied (French air)

Hinkson, Mrs Katharine (Tynan)
All in the morning early, O (Irish air)
At dawning of the day (Irish air)
The red-hair'd man's wife (Irish air)
Song of an island fisherman (Irish air)
The wind that shakes the barley (Irish air)
"Would God I were the tender apple blossom" (Irish air: also another Irish air)

Hinson, Otis
The orange and the black—Albany (Shackelton)
The yellow and the brown (Composer unknown)

Hip Ho-bart. C. J. Rose. Words by E. J. Cook. CHS

The **Hirlas** horn ("Fill high the blue Hirlas") Air: Three hundred pounds. Words by F. Hemans. MMW

Hiromori, Hayashi
Japanese national hymn. See "Kimi ga yo"
"Kimi ga yo"
"May our lord for ever reign." See "Kimi ga yo"
"May our lord long reign." See "Kimi ga yo"
"May our lord reign long." See "Kimi ga yo"
National hymn of Japan. See "Kimi ga yo"
Reign of my king. See "Kimi ga yo"
Reign of my sovereign. See "Kimi ga yo"

L'hirondelle, messagère de l'amour (The swallow, messenger of love) French Canadian folk song. e.f. BFS

Les **hirondelles** (The swallows) F. David. e.f. CM 1

Hirsh, A. M.
Adelina, the Yale Boola girl. See Boola song
Boola song
Boola song: Yale athletic version (same air as Boola song)
Go, Chicago (same air as Boola song)
Yale Boola song. See Boola song

Der **hirt** ("Bin ich im wald ferne von dir") Berg. g. ED 3

Die **hirten.** For English translation see The shepherds (Cornelius)

"**His** Chloris, now thou'rt fled away." See Amyntor's well-a-day (Eccles)

His coming. See "Er ist gekommen" (Franz)

"**His** eye was on my bouquet." See "Il regardait mon bouquet" (Monsigny)

His favorite flower. W. W. Lowitz. Words by H. G. Canfield. ES

"**His** hair was black, his eye was blue." See Shule agra

"**His** kiss is sweet, his word is kind." See The boatman of Kinsale

His love shines over all. G. Forbes. WBT

"His mercy such as I receiving." See "Mir ist erbarmung widerfahren" (Pressel)

His reign on earth begun. See "Hail to the Lord's anointed" (Webb)

"His salvation is nigh them that fear Him." S. Bennett. OS 3—SAS 3

His sceptre is the rod of righteousness. Händel. OS 4—SAS 4

Hisel,
"Wenn der schnee von der alma weg- gageht"

Historia von Noah. See Noah

"Hither come, come to me, flowers." In- dian air. e. FI

Hither, Mary, hither come. See Love's call (Hook)

"Hitotsu to ya." See Counting song

L'hivernage (Wintering) Canadian folk song. e.f. TF

Hjemreise fra saetren (Home again) Norse folk song. Words by E. Storm. e.n. MAN
Hjemreise fra saeteren (Homeward from the mountains) e.n. BO
Hjemreise fra saeteren (The saeter song) e. GO

"Hla-chi dai-nin, hla-chi dai-nin." See Mocking bird song

"Hm. . . . .m! hurdy-gurdy, hurdy-gurdy." See The hurdy-gurdy

"Ho! broder Teague, dost hear de decree." See Lillibulero (Purcell)

"Ho! drain the bright wine cup." See Wanderlied ("Wohlauf noch getrunk- en")

"Ho! every sleeper, waken." Round. BSS —TFC 1

Ho! for Lou'siana! I'm bound to leave this town. See The Glendy Burke (Foster)

"Ho, for the slum." BSS

"Ho ha! Is-te wa-ta si wi-ta ha." See Look up

"Ho Hah-ars si-rah ti we-ra." See "Thy father is coming"

"Ho! ho! ho! ho! ho! high the Cossack's heart is bounding." See The Cos- sack's song (Grünbaum)

"Ho, ho, vacation days are here." See Va- cation days are here (Johnson)

"Ho il cor gonfio di lagrime." See Stella del marinar (Ponchielli)

"Ho-o ha-re ha-re re ha-re." See The bird's nest

"Ho-o! ho-o! dance we singing." Indian ritual air. FI

"Ho o Ka-was ta wha-kara-tsa we." See "Kawas, thy baby is crying"

"Ho Ragne va fattig" ("Poor Ragna") Air: Ifjor gaett'eg geitinn', or, Last year, I tended the goats. Words by H. A. Wergeland. e.n. MAN

Ho-ro mo nighean donn, bhòidheach (Ho- ro my nut-brown maiden) Old Highland song. e.ga. SSS
The brown-hair'd maiden ("Horo, my brown-hair'd maiden") e. BMC —WBT
Mo nighean donn, bhòidheach (My brown-haired maiden) e. HSSS

Ho-ro, my nut-brown maiden. See Ho-ro mo nighean donn, bhòidheach

"Ho, Slavonians" ("Hej, Slované") Slovak song. Air: Jeszcze Polska nie zginęła. c.e.   BF 1

"Ho sull' 'anima il tedio." See Nirvana (Hervey)

"Ho, the boating! lightly floating merrily away." FSS 8

"Ho! why dost thou shiver and shake, Gaffer Gray." See Gaffer Gray

"Ho! ye who at the anvil toil." See All who labor

Hoare, Prince
The Arethusa (Old air)
"Behold I am a village lass" (Storace)
"From aloft the sailor looks around" (Storace)
"Three years a sailor's life" (Harring- ton)
Well-a-day! lack-a-day (Storace)

Hobbs, John William
Eulalie
"Phillis is my only joy"
"When Lubin sings of youth's delight"

The hobby horse. See Das steckenpferd (Hering)

Hobellied ("Da streiten sich die leut herum") K. Kreutzer. Words by F. Raimund. g. ED 1
Hobellied (Song of the plane) e.g. SSG

Hobson, M.
Come sing to me again
Paddle your own canoe

"Hoch vom dachstein an." See Das Stei- erland (Seidel)

Hodges, Faustina Hasse
Dreams

Hodges, John Sebastian Bach
"Christ our God and Lord is risen"
"Christ the Lord is risen again" (Tr of Christus ist erstanden)
"Clear upon the night air sounding"
"Come, my soul, thou must be waking" (Tr of Seele du musst munter wer- den)
"The crown is on the victor's brow" (Tr of Finita jam sunt praelia)
"Deck the altar with blossoms fair"
"Far be sorrow, tears, and sighing" (Tr of Cedant justi signa luctus)
"Let the merry church bells ring"
"Let the song be begun"
"Merrily the Easter bells"
"O sons and daughters, let us sing" (Tr of O filii et filiae, Rex coelestis, Rex gloriae)
"Ring out the bells for Christmas"
"Sing, sing for Christmas"
"We've decked the church with ivy"
"The world itself keeps Easter day"
"Ye happy bells of Easter-day"

Hodson, George Alexander
He never said he loved
"O give me but my Arab steed"
The parting
"Tell me, Mary, how to woo thee"

Hoe out your row. Arr from Donizetti. FSS 2—JSE

Hoffman, Charles Fenno
"Sparkling and bright" (Taylor)

Hoffmann, Caroline
Forget-me-not (Graben-Hoffmann. Tr of Vergissmeinnicht)

Hoffmann, Gustav Graben-. See Graben-Hoffmann, Gustav

Hoffmann von Fallersleben, August Heinrich
Composer and author
Auf der wanderung. See Nur in Deutschland
Im frühlinge. See Jägerleben
Herr Ulrich
Jägerleben
Nur in Deutschland
Author
Abendlied (Folk air; also music by Rinck)
Der alpenhirt (Oesterreichische volksweise)
"Das alte jahr vergangen ist" (Erk)
Der böse bach (Volksweise)
Deutschland über alles (Haydn)
Frühlings-ankunft (Berner)
Gretchens beichte (Scottische volksweise)
Heute und morgen (Nathusius)
In der fremde (Taubert)
Liebesglück (Weber)
May-bells (Bargiel)
Morgenlied (Gersbach)
"Neues jahr, neues jahr" (Volksweise)
"Nur ein wandern ist das leben" (Erk)
Soldatenliebe (Volksweise)
"Die sonne sank" (Erk)
Trinklied (Composer unknown)
Veilchen (Nägeli)
"Was bringt der weihnachtsmann" (Schlesisches volksweise)
Der weihnachtsmann (Volksweise)

Hoffmeister, Franz Anton
"O wie lieblich ist's im kreis"

Die hoffnung ("Es reden und träumen") J. F. Reichardt. Words by Schiller. g. ED 2

Hoffnung ("Wenn die rosen blühen."—"In the time of roses") L. Reichardt. e.g. ES
"In the time of roses." e. WBT—WL

Hoffnung ("Hoffnung, hoffnung! mild wie frühlingsschimmer") Volkslied. g. ED 3

Hoffnung und erinnerung ("Mir blüht eine stelle") J. F. Reichardt. Words by C. A. Tiedge. g. ED 3

Hofland, M. A.
"Hark! the merry Christmas bells"

The hog eye man ("Oh, the hog-eye man") Capstan chantey. CR
For variant see following song of similar title

The hog-eyed man ("O who's been here") Capstan chantey. SE

"Höga berg och djupa dalar" ("Mountains high and valleys lowly") Swedish folk song. e.sw. HSOS
"Höga himmelen vet hvad som händer" ("O, 'tis heav'n only knows what will happen") Swedish folk song. e.sw. HSOS

Hogan, Michael
Draherin o machree (Irish air)
A summer love dream (Irish air)

Hogar, dulce hogar. See Home, sweet home (Bishop)
"Hogar, por ti suspiro." See Home, sweet home (Bishop)

Hogg, James
"Ae nicht i' the gloaming" (Scottish air)
Allister MacAllister (Scottish air)
Auld Joe Nicolson's bonnie Nannie (Scottish air)
"Bird of the wilderness" (Scottish air; also music by Blewitt; unknown composer)
"Cam' ye by Athol" (Scottish air)
"Come o'er the stream, Charlie" (Scottish air)
Flora Macdonald's lament (Gow)
The keel row (Border air)
"My love she's but a lassie yet" (Scottish air)
The Stuarts of Appin (Wilson)
Twa bonnie maidens (Scottish air)
When the kye come hame (Scottish air)

Hogmanay night. See Na gillean mo rùin
"Högre mot sanden svallar den vreda sjön." See Det var då (Kjerulf)
"Die höh'n und wälder schon steigen." See Gute nacht (Franz)
"Hoi! for the gay Hopak." See Hopak (Musorgskiĭ)
"Hoï! hop! hop! au Hopak." See Hopak (Musorgskiĭ)
"Hoi! hop, hop, hop, dansons." See Hopak (Musorgskiĭ)

Hol, Richard
Flanders
"Hola ta laphia boskoune." See The mother deer

Holcombe, Henry
"Happy hours, all hours excelling." See The happy man
The happy man

Holcroft, Thomas
Ah, well-a-day, my poor heart (Shield)
Gaffer Gray (18th century air)

"Hold fastere omkring mig." See Ångest (Alfvén)
"Hold, men, hold! we are very cold." See Mummers' song
Hold out yo' light you heav'n boun' soldier. See Heav'n boun' soldier
Hold the light. Negro spiritual. JP
"Hold thy peace." Catch. Old English air. Words by Shakespeare. TFC 2
"Hold up your hand, O Joshuay, she cried." See The maid freed from the gallows (North Carolina version)

"**Hold** up your hands and Joshua, he cries."
See The maid freed from the gallows
(Tennessee version)

"**Holde** nacht, dein dunkler schleier."
Volkslied. g. ED 2

Holden, Oliver
Composer
"All hail the power of Jesus' name"
Coronation. See "All hail the power
of Jesus' name"
Author
"They who seek the throne of grace"
(music by Dykes; Händel)

"**Holder** klingt der vogelsang." See Minnelied (Brahms)

"Der **holdseligen**" (Weber) See entry under Der

"**Holdvilágos** csillagos az éjszaka." See
Moonlight and starry night

"**Holi-**, holi-, holiday, on the very first day
of the year." See Little Musgrave
and Lady Barnard (Clay co., Ky. version)

The **holiday** ("One morning early") Old
French air. Words by N. H. Dole.
DO

"**Holl** amrantaur sêr ddywedant." See Ar
hyd y nos (Owen)

Holland, Josiah Gilbert
"There's a song in the air" (music by
Jones; Martin)

Holland's national hymn. See "Wien
Neêrlandsch bloed" (Wilms)

"Der **hölle** selbst will ich segen entringen."
See Liebe ist die zarte blüthe (Spohr)

Hollins, Alfred
"Holy was that night so fair"

Hollmann, Joseph
Chanson d'amour
Love-song. See Chanson d'amour

The **holly** ("What feeling heart") Welsh
air. Words by Ieuan Dhu. MMW

The **holly** and ivy girl ("Come, buy my
nice fresh ivy") Irish air: The fair maid
of Wicklow. Words by J. Keegan.
MMI

"The **holly** and the ivy." Old French carol
air. BSC—HC—MCS—MF—WCC

Holly crowns the green. G. Rossini.
Words by C. Wallace. MCS

Holly green with berries red. MCS

The **holly** twig. Folk song from Virginia.
CSE

The **holly** wreath. T. Crampton. FSS 4

Holmès, Augusta Mary Anne
L'appel du printemps
The call of spring. See L'appel du
printemps
An Irish Noël. See Noël d'Irlande
Noël d'Irlande
A threnody. See Thrînôdia
Thrînôdia

Holmes, Oliver Wendell
"Angel of peace" (Keller)
Army hymn ("God of all nations")
(Lvov)
Army hymn ("O Lord of hosts")
(Oliver)

A ballad of the Boston tea party
(Composer unknown)
"Build thee more stately mansions"
(Farwell)
The flower of liberty (Wilhelm)
Hail Columbia, The new (Phile)
The katydid (German air)
"Lord of all being" (music by Linley;
Taylor)
Ode for Washington's birthday (Bee-
thoven)
Old Ironsides (German air; also music
by Klein; Lardner)
The sweet little man (Scotch air)
The visions of morning (Harvard class
song)

Holstein. See "Ye golden lamps of heav-
en"

Holt, Mrs Eliza
Sunny Manoa (Hopkins)
Waters of Punalau (Nape)

Holt, W. R.
"Stars all bright are beaming"

Holtei, Karl von
Der altè reiter und sein mantel (Volksweise)
Auf die schlacht bei Torgau (Volksweise)
"In Berlin, sagt' er" (Composer unknown)

Holter, Iver Paul Fredrik
"On frost-cold Norway's moorlands."
See "På Norges kolde vidder"
"På Norges kolde vidder"

Hölty, H.
Minnelied (Brahms)

Hölty, Ludwig Heinrich Christoph
Aufmunterung zur freude (music by
Reichardt; also unknown compos-
er)
"Ich liebe dich, so wie du mich" (Bee-
thoven)
Lebenspflichten (Reichardt)
Mailied (Schulz)
Die mainacht (Brahms)
Minnelied (Brahms)
Das rheinwein-paradies (Composer un-
known)
Seligkeit der liebe (Schulz)

"**Holy** Bible, book divine." J. F. Barton.
FSS 2

The **holy** family. A. Randegger. Words
by Goethe. e. MCS

"**Holy** Ghost, with light divine." L. M.
Gottschalk. Words by A. Reed.
HSD—WBT—WS

"**Holy** God, we praise Thy name." BSS

"**Holy**, holy holy! Lord God almighty." J.
B. Dykes. Words by R. Heber.
HSD—MS—TFC 2—WBT—WSC
All the saints adore Thee (Nicaea)
FSS 1
"Holy, holy, holy! Lord God almighty"
(Nicaea) BD—LA—TL
Holy! holy! Lord God almighty. WA
—WS—WSW

"**Holy**, holy, holy Lord God of hosts! God
Almighty." See Holy, holy, Lord
(Spohr)

"Holy, holy, holy, Lord of hosts: holy, holy, holy, is the Lord of hosts." See Choral sanctus (Gaul)

Holy, holy, Lord. Spohr. e. LA

"Holy, holy, Lord God almighty." Händel. HSS 1—HSS 3

"Holy, holy, Lord God of hosts, bow we before Thee." See "Ave Maria" (Cherubini)

"Holy is the seed-time." A. Lowe. Words by M. A. Headlam. HC

Holy night. See Die heilige nacht (Gruber)

"Holy night! peaceful night." J. Barnby. ₁Words by J. Mohr. Tr of Die heilige nacht₁ e. DC—JS Silent night. e. LA

"Holy night! peaceful night." For words in the original with a different air see Die heilige nacht (Gruber)

"Holy night, silent night." Arr by M. Haydn. ₁Words by J. Mohr. Tr of Die heilige nacht₁ e. MS

"Holy one, dying for mortals." A. Klughardt. e. SAS 4

"Holy Sabbath, happy morning." See Sabbath morning bells

"Holy Spirit, Source of gladness." Naumann. ₁Words by P. Gerhardt. Tr of O du allersüsste freude₁ e. FSS 8

"Holy Spirit, truth divine." L. Gottschalk. Words by S. Longfellow. TL

"Holy was that night so fair." A. Hollins. Words by A. Campbell. HC

The holy well. Traditional air. BSC—WCC

Holyoke. Mount Holyoke college song. Words by S. Averhill. CHS

Hölzel, G. Bell-tones. See Glockengeläute Glockengeläute

Homage to Sweden. See Hyllning till Sverige (Sandberg)

Home, F. Wyville Sunshine and rain (Blumenthal)

Home again ("Os ha gjort") See Hjemreise fra saetren

"Home again, home again." M. S. Pike (music and words) FSS 5—HSC—HSD—JS— LBR— MCS—MP—NMH—WBT—WSW

Home, can I forget thee. See "Home, home, can I forget thee"

The home-coming. See Die Aargauer lieben

Home, dearie, home ("O Amble is a fine town") Sea song. DM 2 For variants see following songs of same title

Home, dearie, home ("Oh, Amble is a fine town") Chantey. SMW

Home, dearie, home ("Oh, Boston's a fine town") Forecastle song. CR

"Home, fare thee well." See Our way across the sea

Home forever. See Her hjemme

"Home from the war." See Joli tambour

"Home from the wedding." See "En revenant de noces"

"Home, home, can I forget thee." German air. FSS 1—FSS 6—HSC—NMH—WBT—WSC—WSW Home, can I forget thee. MP—NMS

Home is dear. Words by J. Selwyn. MCS

The home land ("Dear land! where first in childhood") LA

Home, love and liberty. H. Bishop. DM 2

"Home my sweetheart comes from roving" (Runo-laulu) Finnish rune song. e.fi. BO

Home of my childhood. FSS 5

Home of my heart ("Sweet vale of Llandovery") Air: Dynevor castle. Words by M. S. Laurence. MMW

"Home of our college days." See Dear old Reserve

"Home of the happy and free." F. H. Pease. Words by A. Berry. MP

Home of the soul. P. Phillips. Words by E. H. Gates. FSS 1—JS

Home on the range. Cowboy song. LC

"Home or shelter have we never." See "Senza tetto, senza cuna" (Gomez)

Home so blest. F. Abt. Words by B. S. Montgomery. FSS 8

Home, sweet home. H. R. Bishop. Words by J. H. Payne. BD—BE 2—BSE—BSP—CS 1—DM 1—DO— EF— FSS 1— HSC— HSD HSE 1—JO—JS—JSE—LA— LBR MCS—MP— MPC— NMH—NMS —OH—PO—SS 1—TFC 1—WA—WBT—WSC—WSW Hogar, dulce hogar. s. LCP

Home, sweet home, and Rubinstein's melody. Arranged. BD

"Home they brought her warrior." W. W. Gilchrist. Words by A. Tennyson. TL

Home they brought her warrior. G. A. Macfarren. Words adapted from A. Tennyson. LA Sweet my child. FSS 8

"Home to our mountains." G. Verdi. ₁Tr of Ai nostri monti ritorneremo₁ e. BD—HSD—WBT

"Homeland mine, my native land." See My native land (Grechaninov)

"The homeland! O the homeland." A. Sullivan. Words by H. R. Haweis. WBT

The homeland. HSD

"Homeland we love, dear fatherland." See Vårt land, vårt fosterland (Pacius)

Homer, Sidney Requiem Underwoods. See Requiem

"Home's not merely four square walls." G. Rossini. Words by C. Swain. FSS 2 —JSE—WBT

Homesickness ("Wer in die fremde") See Heimweh (Wolf)

Homesickness for Switzerland. See Schweizer heimweh (Glück)

Homeward ("Leiser schwanken die äste") See Heimkehr (Strauss)

Homeward bound ("Loose every sail") M. Arne. Words by Thompson. ME

Homeward bound ("Out on an ocean") J. W. Dadmun; also attributed to C. S. Harrington. Words by W. F. Warren. FSS 3—HSD—JS—WBT—WS

Homeward bound ("We're homeward bound to Boston town") Capstan chantey. KB

Homeward from the mountains. See Hjemreise fra saetren

The homeward way (Vse mine) Croatian song. e. GO

"Homeward we go, calling his name." Indian song. e. FI

Hominum laudes. M. Shaw. Words by L. Johnson. HC

Honesakala. See Honeysuckles (Nape)

"Honest lover." Arne. Words by J. Suckling. DM 2

The honest Yorkshireman. H. Carey (music and words) MM

Honeysuckles (Honesakala) D. Nape. Words by T. Lindsey. e.h. HA

"Honkaen keskellä mökkini seisoo." See Finland's forest

Honor His holy Name. FSS 5

"Honor to Lincoln the brave." See Lincoln's birthday

"Honored in song and story." See A marching song

"Honour and arms." Händel. BAS 1— OS 4—SAS 4

Honour'd be the soldier's grave. See The soldier's return ("Dost not hear")

Hood, Basil
The yeomen of England (German)

Hood, John J.
Freedom's flag (Geibel)

Hood, Thomas
The doctor (Newton)
"I remember, I remember the house where I was born" (Blockley)
'Tis all that I can say (Temple)

Hoodah-day. Capstan chantey. KB

"Hooheno keia no ka honesakala." See Honeysuckles (Nape)

Hoohihi ka manao. See Sweet violet (Hopkins)

Hook, James
Absence
The blackbird
The bonny sailor
"Bright Phoebus"
Bring me, boy, a bowl of wine
By and by
The captain with the smart cockade
Dilly dally, shilly shally
The disconsolate sailor
The flitch of bacon
The gipsy hat
He piped so sweet
Hither, Mary, hither come. See Love's call
I must try another
I'll be the squire's bride
January
Lack-a-day, O

Lashed to the helm
The lass of Richmond hill
Listen to the voice of love
The little waste
Love's call
"My friend is the man"
Never say No when you wish to say Yes
O listen to the voice of love
"On Entick's green meadows." See The captain with the smart cockade
"On Richmond hill there lives a lass." See The lass of Richmond hill
"Once, twice, thrice"
She lives in the valley below
"Softly waft, ye southern breezes"
Sweet lilies of the valley
Sweet Patty
Sweet Robinette
" 'Twas within a mile o' Edinboro' town." See Within a mile of Edinboro'
Two bunches a penny primroses
The wedding-day
"When the morning peeps forth"
The willow song
Within a mile of Edinboro'

Hoop de dooden do. A. Nish. HSD— NMP—WBT

Hooray you roller, bowler. See Roller, bowler

"Hop, hop, hop! nimble as a top." See Das steckenpferd (Hering)

"Hop, hop, hop! reins I will not drop." See My pony (Hering)

The hop-planters' song. Kentish song of 1759. BE 8

Hopak. M. Moussorgsky. Words from the Little-Russian of Shevtchenko. e.f. GMF—NM 1—SC

Hope ("Hope, when in thy youth's glad morning") J. Benedict. Words by Claribel. WS

The hope ("Not while a throb beats in Jewish hearts") National Hebrew hymn. H. A. Russotto. e. CST

"Hope brightly gleams." See "Hail to the happy bridal day" (Donizetti)

A hope carol. D. S. Smith. Words by C. G. Rossetti. TFC 2—TL

Hope of the world. See "Hail Thou long-expected Jesus" (Conkey)

Hope, the hermit. Air: Lady Frances Neville's delight. Words by J. Oxenford. BE 2

"Hope, thou nurse of young desire." Weldon. Words by I. Bickerstaffe. BE 2

"Hope told a flattering tale." Composer unknown. Words by P. Pindar. BE 6 —DM 1—HSE 1

"Hope, when in thy youth's glad morning." See Hope (Benedict)

Hope with her ray serene. See Col raggio placido (Händel)

Hopkins, Charles K.
Adieu my love
Adios ke aloha. See Adieu my love
Ke aloha ihiki mai. See Flower of my heart

Hopkins, Charles K. —*Continued*
Awaiaulu. See "The remembrance of our last meeting"
Flower of my heart
Forget-me-not
Haili crowned with lehua
Haili po ika lehua. See Haili crowned with lehua
Hawaiian hula (Maunawili)
Hawaiian hula (Paahana)
The he-i blossom
Kalakaua's serenade
He lei no Kaiulani. See A wreath for Princess Kaiulani
Lei poni moi. See Wreath of carnations
Maui. See "Wrapt in verdure"
Maunawili. See Hawaiian hula
Nuuanu waipuna. See "Oh, tempt me not, my darling"
"Oh, tempt me not, my darling"
Paahana. See Hawaiian hula
Pua o ka he-i. See The he-i blossom
Remember be sure and be there
"The remembrance of our last meeting"
Sunny Manoa
Surging waters
Sweet lei mamo
Sweet violet
"Thou art always the same to me, dear"
Violeta
Waipio. See "Thou art always the same to me, dear"
Wiliwili wai. See Surging waters
"Wrapt in verdure"
A wreath for Princess Kaiulani
Wreath of carnations
Hopkins, Edward Jerome
Benediction. See "Spirit of God"
"Calm on the listening ear of night"
"Spirit of God"
Hopkins, Edward L.
"Lift up, ye everlasting doors"
Hopkins, Edwin John
"At dead of night, when all is still"
"The joyful morn is breaking"
Parting hymn. See "Saviour, again to Thy dear name we raise"
"Saviour, again to Thy dear name we raise"
"To-day doth blossom Jesse's stem" (Tr of Jam radix)
What the chimney sang

Hopkins, John Henry
"Art thou weary, art thou languid" (Tr of Kopon te kai kamaton)
"Awake! awake! 'tis Easter morn"
"Christmas comes again"
"Early ere the dawn of the morning"
"Gather around the Christmas tree"
"Let every heart now dance with joy"
"Roman soldier, tell us true"
"Sadly in the gathering gloom"
"Thee we praise, O God of harvest"
Three kings of Orient
"We three kings of Orient are." See Three kings of Orient

Hopkinson, Joseph
"Hail, Columbia" (Phile)

"Hopp, hopp, hopp! pferdchen, lauf galopp." See Das steckenpferd (Hering)
Hopper, Edward
"Jesus, Saviour, pilot me" (music by Gould; Redhead)
Hopper, Nora. See Chesson, Mrs Nora (Hopper)
"Hopsa! Lisella" (Trip it! Lisella) Folk song from central Alsace. e.f. FTF
"Hör' uns, Allmächtiger." See Gebet vor der schlacht (Weber)
Hora. Rumanian dance song. e.ru. BF 2
Hora novissima. For English translation see "The world is very evil" (Herron)
Horace. See Horatius Flaccus, Quintus
Horae Andreanae. Air: Wohlauf noch getrunken. St Andrews university song. Words by G. Park. SSS
Horatius Flaccus, Quintus
"Integer vitae" (Flemming)
"Horch, horch, die lerch." See "Hark! hark! the lark" (Schubert)
"Horch! horch! was dein treuer spricht." See Des geistes gesang (Haydn)
"Horch, wie schallt's dorten." See Der wachtelschlag (Hering)
"Horch, wie still es wird im dunkeln hain." See Stille sicherheit (Franz)
Horn, Charles Edward
After many roving years
All things love thee, so do I
Allan water. See The banks of Allan water: traditional air arranged
The banks of Allan water: traditional air arranged
The breaking of the day
"Cherry ripe"
"Child of earth with golden hair." See Titania's song
Chimes of Zurich
"Crabbed age and youth"
The deep, deep sea
He loves, and rides away
"I know a bank whereon the wild thyme blows"
"I've been roaming"
Long time ago: negro air arranged
"Near the lake where drooped the willow." See Long time ago: negro air arranged
Norah McShane
"On the banks of Allan water." See The banks of Allan water: traditional air arranged
"The sun is on the mountain." See The breaking of the day
"Through the wood, through the wood"
Titania's song
The horn. See Le cor (Flégier)
Hornabrook, M.
"On Bethlehem's silent plain"
Horne, Abel
Laughing song (Old American air)
Old Dan Tucker (Old American air)
"Where is John" (Smetana)
Hornemann, Christian Frederik Emil
A soldier brave

Horner, W. F.
"Soft the autumn suns are shining"
"Horo, my brown-haired maiden." See Ho-
ro mo nighean donn, bhòidheach
Horrocks, Amy Elise
The bird and the rose
Horse-shoe song. Words by A. Hayden.
CHS
The horseman's morning song. See Reit-
ers morgenlied
Horsley, William
Carmen Carthusianum
"The rose that weeps"
Horspool, A.
Ora pro nobis (Piccolomini)
"Hörst du den vogel singen." See Alte
laute, II (Schumann)
"Hörst du nicht die bäume rauschen." See
Lockung (Dessauer)
"Hört die trommete von Egyptens meer."
See "Sound the loud timbrel" (Mo-
lique)
"Hört ihr den schwäbischen wirbeltanz."
See Walzlied
"Hört mich, ihr frostigen herzen im nord."
See Eros (Grieg)
"Hört, wie die wachtel im grünen schön
schlagt." See Wachtelschlag (Rei-
chardt)
Hortense Eugénie de Beauharnais, queen
of Holland
Departure for Syria. See "Partant
pour la Syrie" (attributed)
Dunois the brave. See "Partant pour
la Syrie" (attributed)
"It was Dunois the young and brave."
See "Partant pour la Syrie" (at-
tributed)
"Partant pour la Syrie" (attributed)
Romance of Dunois. See "Partant
pour la Syrie" (attributed)
Hosanna. Easter song. J. Granier.
Words by J. Didiée. e. WA—WS
Hosmer, E. A.
And then—
"O give me a home by the sea"
Hosmer, Frederick Lucian
"Over the land in glory" (Foote)
"Uplift the song of praise" (Traditional
air)
Höst (Autumn) F. Beyer. da.e. WM 1
The hostess' daughter ("Es zogen drei bur-
schen") See Der wirtin töchterlein
The hostess' daughter ("The hostess of the
Ring of Bells") Folk song. BSW
"The hostess of the Ring of Bells." See
The hostess' daughter
"Hot cross buns! hot cross buns." WBT
—WSC
"Hot cross buns, one a penny buns." FSS 5
A hot time in the old town. T. A. Metz.
Words by J. Hayden. MP
Hotaru. See Fireflies (Ross)
Hottentot song. See "The cattle from the
kraal have strayed"
Houghton, A. Styler
"O lowly, sacred stable"

Houghton, Richard Monckton Milnes, 1st
baron
The brookside (Hine)
Houis. See The sure hope
Houlton,
Dilly dally, shilly shally (Hook)
"The hounds are all out." H. Carey (mu-
sic and words) ME
"The hounds were by the river." Air:
Glyn tawy. Words by J. Lloyd.
MMW
"The hour is late." See Waldesgespräch
(Jensen)
The hour of dreaming. See L'heure ex-
quise (Hahn)
The hour of dreams (L'heure du rêve) A.
Arensky. Words by D. Rathaus. e.f.
NR 4
The hour of parting ("Sad hour of part-
ing") V. Bellini. WBT
"The hour of parting threatens." See Na-
pole mio
The hour of prayer. Hérold. Words by
F. Hemans. WBT
The hour of rest. J. L. Roeckel. Words
by F. E. Weatherly. FSS 7—JSE
"The hour swift is flying." See "Que
l'heure est donc brève" (Massenet)
"The hour was sad I left the maid." See
The girl I left behind me
"Houra hoi sano." See Japanese rowing
song
"Hours there were." J. Wade. Words
by T. Moore. FSS 6—WBT
Hovey, Richard
A stein song (Bullard)
How, William Walsham
"Behold a little Child" (Brown-Borth-
wick)
"On wings of living light" (French air)
"Summer suns are glowing" (music by
Marshall; Smith; also unknown
composer)
"How abundant and warm is the spring"
("Qu'il est doux le printemps") N. So-
koloff. Words from the Russian of
Lokhvitsky. e.f. NM 2
"How are Thy servants blessed, O Lord."
See These see His wonders in the deep
"How badly is the course of life adjusted."
See Es hat nicht sollen sein (Nessler)
"How beauteous are their feet." See Be-
hold thy King
"How beautiful are the feet of them." G.
F. Händel. SAS 1
How beautiful are Thy dwellings, O Lord.
S. de Lange. e. SAS 1
"How beautiful thy site." See Hymn to
College hill (Newton)
"How, beloved, did I grieve thee." See
The reproach
"How blest are we seamen." Sea song.
ME
"How blythe ilk morn was I to see." See
The brume o' the Cowdenknowes
"How blythe was I ilk morn to see." See
The brume o' the Cowdenknowes

How brief is the hour. See "Que l'heure est donc brève" (Massenet)

"How bright and fair." G. Rossini. FSS 5 —JSE

"How came this blood on your shirt sleeves." See Edward (Tennessee version)

"How can I bear to leave thee." See Soldier's farewell (Kinkel)

"How can I leave thee so." See Treue liebe (Kücken)

"How can I part from thee." See Treue liebe (Kücken)

"How can my poor heart be glad." Air: O'er the hills and far away. Words by R. Burns. BSR

"How can the tree but waste and wither away." 16th century song. CO 1— JE

"How changed the vision." See "Cangiò d'aspetto" (Händel)

"How charming is the lovely valley." See Sweet lei mamo (Hopkins)

"How clear were the skies the night that is gone." See Nocturne (Balakirev)

"How close the world round me doth meet." See In's freie (Schumann)

"How cold the wind doth blow." See The unquiet grave

"How come that blood on your shirt sleeve." See Edward (Hot Springs, N.C. version)

"How cruel are the parents." Air: John Anderson my jo. Words by R. Burns. BSR

"How dark and drear this world would be." See The star of hope

"How dear to all her loyal sons." See Our honored Bates

"How dear to me the hour when daylight dies." Air: The twisting of the rope. Words by T. Moore. MI—MMI

"How dear to my heart are the scenes of my childhood." See The old oaken bucket (Old air); The old oaken bucket (Kiallmark)

"How dearly are prized." See "Ragion sempre addita" (Stradella)

"How deep a sleep hath bound thee." See Winter (Pierce)

"How deep, how wonderful the silence." See Morgengebet

"How delightful this branch of fresh flowers." See Moo-lee-hwa

"How delightful to see, in those evenings in spring." See The sheep-shearing

"How dimm'd is the glory that circled the Gael." See Lament for Ireland

"How do I love thee." H. K. Hadley. Words by E. B. Browning. HST

How do I love thee. M. V. White. ₁Words by E. B. Browning₁ SM 4— WBW

"How do you do, oh, don't you know me." See The king of night

"How does the song come, whence upswell." See Source of song

"How doleful is this place." See Monstre affreux (Rameau)

"How excellent is Thy loving kindness." F. H. Cowen. SAS 3

How fair art thou ("Wie gerne dir") See Wie schön bist du (Weidt)

"How fair art thou, heavenly stillness." See The night (Schubert)

"How fair art thou, my lovely queen." See "Wie bist du, meine königin" (Brahms)

How fair is she (Havalisava) Serbian folk song. e.se. BF 1

"How firm a foundation." Attributed to J. Reading. Words attributed to R. Keene; wrongly attributed to G. Keith and to Kirkham. BSS— OH—TFC 1—WBT—WS

"How firm a foundation" (Portuguese hymn) FSS 4—HSC

"How folks will very often fight." See Hobellied (Kreutzer)

"How frail and weak a thing is man." See Inspirez-moi (Gounod)

"How friendly sleep was to me." See "Wie nahte mir der schlummer" (Weber)

"How full of charm the sky." See C'era una volta un principe (Gomes)

"How gaily rows the gondolier." See The gondolier (Lee)

"How gaily the linnet sings." See The heart should be happy and merry (Reeve)

"How gentle God's commands." J. Barnby. Words by P. Doddridge. MS

"How gentle God's commands." H. G. Nägeli. Words by P. Doddridge. HSC—HSD— NMH— NMS—TL —WBT—WS—WSC

"How gentle God's commands" (Dennis) FSS 1—LA

"How gentle was my Damon's air." See The maiden's complaint (Arne)

"How gladsome the sunlight that glistens and glows." See Sol (Alnaes)

How glorious the day. MCS

"How glorious was the blessed day." See How glorious the day

"How grand and how bright that wonderful night." See The Worcestershire Christmas carol (Havergal)

"How grand is my dear native land." See Mit födeland (Ibsen)

How great, O Lord, is Thy goodness. J. Benedict. OS 4—SAS 4

"How happy a state does the miller possess." 18th century song. ME

"How happy art thou." H. Lawes. PR 1

"How happy could I be with either." Old English air. Words by Gay. BE 7

"How happy is the child who hears." Words by Bruce. FSS 1—WBT— WSC

How happy we have been. T. Baker. FSS 7

"How, how do I love thee." See How do I love thee (White)

How I have loved thee. Composer unknown. Words by F. J. Price. NMH —NML

"How I love the mountains."   Styrian song.   e.   KSE

"How I love to gaze" (Lei ohaoha) D. Nape.   e.h.   HA

"How I love to look on the fresh green moss." Air: Cwyn yr alldud, or, The exile's complaint.   Words by M. A. Browne.   MMW

"How joyful, how joyful, how joyful for me."   See Que gusto me da

"How lang and dreary is the night." Air: Cauld kail in Aberdeen.   Words by R. Burns.   BSB—PS 2
"How long and dreary is the night." BSR

"How little do the landsmen know."   Sea song.   Words attributed to D. Garrick. ME

How long a day appears.   Words by J. Taylor.   FSS 3

"How long and dreary is the night."   See "How lang and dreary is the night"

"How long sometimes a day appears." See How long a day appears

"How lovely this sweet branch of flowers." See Moo-lee-hwa

"How lovely thy note."   See The lark (Mendelssohn)

"How many a time I sat and dreamed." See An der Weser (Pressel)

"How many hired servants."   A. Sullivan. TS

"How many miles to baby land."   See To Babyland

"How merrily, this summer morn."   See Dear summer morn (Glover)

How my childhood fleeted by.   See I remember how my childhood (Fitzgerald)

"How my heart aches."   See Sorrow in spring (Rachmaninov)

"How my heart with bitter pangs is raging."   See Ah! the torment (Paderewski)

"How neat the cot, and sweet the farms." See Ogwr valley

"How, now, shepherd, what means that." See Willy and Cuddy

"How oft at twilight, with lover's comprehension."   See Raziella

"How oft has the banshee cried."   Air: The dear black maid.   Words by T. Moore.   MI

"How oft, how oft to mind I call."   See Carmarthen bells

"How oft in life are met the saddest crosses."   See Es hat nicht sollen sein (Nessler)

How oft to mind I call.   See Carmarthen bells

"How often at midnight in days long since fled."   See To the children (Rachmaninov)

"How often haunting the highest hill-top." See Fhir a bhàta

"How pleasant is it in the blossom of the year."   See The blossom of the year

"How pleasant the banks."   Air: Bhannerach dhon na chrie.   Words by R. Burns.   BSR

"How pleasant the banks" (The banks of the Devon)   Air: The maids of Arrochar.   Words by R. Burns.   BSB

"How quiet is the moonrise."   See "Verstohlen geht der mond auf"

"How sad mid the sunshine" (The graduates' farewell) Old air.   Words by W. T. Adams [or W. L. Smith]   HSD

"How sad, 'mid the sunshine" (Graduation song no 2) E. H. Pierce.   Words by [W. T. Adams or] W. L. Smith.   NMS

"How shall I unhappy" ("Cóż ja nieboraczek") Polish folk song.   e.p.   SMF

"How should I your true love know."   16th century air.   Words by Shakespeare. DM 1—DO—MM

"How soft the happy evening's close."   See Good night

"How softly are glancing."   Mozart.   e. FSS 2

"How soon thou, alas, wilt forget me." See Forsaken (Dargomyzhskiï)

"How stands the glass around."   Air: Why, soldiers, why.   BE 8—DM 1—HSE 2—JO—ME
"How stands the glass around" (The duke of Berwick's march.—Why, soldiers, why)   CO 2

"How still the earth."   See La naissance du Christ

"How strange is life."   See Es hat nicht sollen sein (Nessler)

"How strange was his look."   See Elle ne croyait pas (Thomas)

"How sweet are the flowers."   See When the heart is at ease (Arne)

"How sweet in the woodlands."   Harrington.   BE 7

"How sweet is love's first meeting."   See Det förste möde (Grieg)

"How sweet is the horn."   See Bucks a-hunting go

"How sweet it is to be in the arms of new-found bliss."   See Qué bello es querer

"How sweet it is when I'm with you" ("Wie süss ist's, kann bei dir ich sein") M. I. Glinka.   e.g.   SC

"How sweet the cider smells tonight."   See "Was duftet doch der flieder" (Wagner)

"How sweet th' embraces of twilight's peace." See Til Ole Bull (Folk air); Til Ole Bull (Reissiger)

"How sweet the answer Echo makes."   See Echo

"How sweet the name of Jesus sounds" (Downs) L. Mason.   Words by J. Newton.   FSS 4

"How sweet the place."   S. Rachmaninoff. Words by G. Galina.   e.   SC

"How sweet this lone vale."   Gaelic air. Words by A. Erskine.   PS 2

"How sweet to reflect on the joys that await me."   See The Eden of love

"How sweetly falls on heart and ear."   See The old, old song (Lefort)

"How sweetly peal o'er hill and vale."   See The wood-horn

"How tedious and tasteless the hours." M. de Fleury. Words by J. Newton. FSS 5

How the wind blows. FSS 8

"How times have changed." See "Wie anders war es" (Brüll)

"How void of compassion." See "Che fiero costume" (Legrenzi)

"How well can I remember." See Don't leave your mother, Tom (Symons)

"How wondrous and great." J. Haydn. Words by H. U. Underdonk. DO

"How wondrous! how wondrous." See Ah! fors' è lui (Verdi)

"How wretched is the anguish." See Spanish national song (Huerta)

"How yé to sien hwaaa." See Moo-lee-hwa

Howard, Alonzo Potter
  Easter bells. See "Let the merry church-bells ring"
  "In the lonely midnight"
  "Let the merry church-bells ring"
  "Like small curled feathers, white and soft"
  The vision of the shepherds. See "While shepherds watched their flocks"
  "While shepherds watched their flocks"

Howard, C.
  Buy my strawberries

Howard, Sir Robert
  "I attempt from love's sickness to fly" (Purcell)
  "They tell us that you mighty powers" (Purcell)

Howard, Rowland
  You never miss the water

Howard, Samuel
  Ah, well-a-day (attributed)
  The diffident lover
  The lass of the hill
  Myrtilla
  "On the brow of a hill." See The lass of the hill

Howarth, Ellen Clementine
  "Thou wilt never grow old" (Linley)

Howdy. Negro spiritual. DF

Howe, James Hamilton
  "Great God of nations"

Howe, Mrs Julia (Ward)
  Battle hymn of the republic (Old plantation air)

Howells, William Dean
  Pleasure-pain (Kjerulf)
  The sea (MacDowell)

"However cold the showers." See The skylark

Howitt, Mrs Mary (Botham)
  Old Christmas (Mozart)
  The spider and the fly (Old English air)

Howland, George
  Around the hearth (Scotch air)

"Hoy a una doncella." See Repique el pandero

"Hoy que de nuevo un sol sonriente." See 'O sole mio (Capua)

Hoyt, May P.
  "Wise men from Egypt's ancient land" (Oliver)

"Hr. Sinklar" (The Sinclair brave) Norse folk song. Words by E. Storm. e.n. MAN

"Hrály dudy." See The bag-pipes

Hrvatska domovina. See Croatian national anthem (Runjamin)

Hryc. See The woodland cabin

"Hu hei! kor er det vel friskt og lett upp aa fjellet." See Paa fjellet (Kjerulf)

Hubi-Newcombe, G.
  In shadowland (Denza)

Hübsch, Eduard A.
  "Long live our noble king." See "Tracascâ regele"
  "Long live the king." See "Tracascâ regele"
  Rumania. See "Tracascâ regele"
  "Tracascâ regele"

Huckleberry hunting ("The boys and the girls went a-huckleberry hunting") Capstan chantey. SE
For variant of this song see following song of same title

Huckleberry hunting ("Oh, the boys and the girls went a-huckleberry hunting") Halliard chantey. CR

Hückstädt, Friederich
  Ubi bene, ibi patria (Composer unknown)

Hudson,
  Follow the drum (Old English air)

Hudson, Thomas
  Guy Fawkes (Old air)
  The spider and the fly (Composer unknown)

Hudson, W.
  The lass of Richmond hill (Hook) See MacNally, L. The lass of Richmond hill (Hook)

Hüe, Georges Adolphe
  Breezes of other days. See Brises d'autrefois
  Brises d'autrefois
  Memories of yore. See Brises d'autrefois

Huelani,
  Violeta (Hopkins)
  Wreath of carnations (Hopkins)

El huérfano. J. M. Campos. Words by M. Fernandez Juncos. s. LCP

Huerta,
  Himno de Riego
  Hymne de Riego. See Himno de Riego
  Riego's hymn. See Himno de Riego
  Spanish hymn. See Himno de Riego

Hughes, Henry
  Amyntor's well-a-day (Eccles)

Hughes, J.
  Christmas vesper hymn (Auber)

Hughes, John
  The wandering beauty (Pepusch)

Hughes, John Ceiriog
  God bless the prince of Wales (Richards)
  Winnie Wen (Owen)

Hughes, Mrs Mary Anne (Browne)   See
    Browne, Mary Anne
Hughie Graham.   Air: Drumion dubh.
    Ancient ballad, altered and added
    to by Burns.   PS 2
    "Our lords are to the mountains gane."
    BSR
Hugo, Victor Marie, comte
    Albaÿde (Widor)
    La captive (Berlioz)
    Chantez riez et dormez (Gounod)
    La cloche (Saint-Saëns)
    Eglogue (Delibes)
    Extase (Gueroult)
    Le géant (Gailhard)
    Invocation (Widor)
    "Je ne veux pas autre chose" (Widor)
    "My songs of love" (Hahn)
    "Oh, when I sleep" (Liszt)
    Les pas d'armes du roi Jean (Saint-
       Saëns)
    Rêverie (Hahn)
    Sans toi (Hardelot)
    Si mes vers avaient des ailes (Hahn)
    "Si vous n'avez rien à me dire" (Roths-
       child)
    "When you slept" (Kjerulf)
    "Ya brilla la aurora" (Tavarez)
Hukagawa.   See Song of the pleasure
    seekers
The **hulder** and Elland.   See Huldra aa en
    Elland
The **hulder's** call.   See Huldre lokk
The **hulder's** song.   See Huldre-kvaee
Huldra aa en Elland (The hulder and El-
    land) Norse folk song. e.n.   MAN
Huldre-kvaee (The hulder's song) Norse
    folk song. e.n.   MAN
Huldre lokk (The hulder's call) Norse folk
    song e.n.   MAN
Hullah, John Pyke
    Afternoon in February
    The hunter's song
    The kiss of a little child
    The storm
    "Three fishers went sailing"
Hüller, Johann Adam.   See Hiller, Johann
    Adam
"**Hum,** hum, goes my top."   See The hum-
    ming top
"**Hum,** hum, hum, my wheel keep whirling."
    See Spinning chorus (Wagner)
The **humble**-bee.   German air.   Words by
    R. W. Emerson.   LBR
The **humble** bee.   W. H. Neidlinger.
    Words by R. W. Emerson.   TL
The **humble** beggar.   Scottish song.   PS 2
Humble fille des champs.   J. F. Halévy.
    e.f.   SOA 2
Humble, humble, humble yourself.   See
    Humble yourself
Humble, humble, humble yourselves.   See
    Gwine to live humble to de Lord
Humble yourself.   Negro spiritual.   JP
    Variant: Gwine to live humble to de
    Lord

"**Humbled** with fear."   G. F. Händel.
    SAS 4
    Also in His sceptre is the rod of right-
       eousness (Händel)   OS 4
Hume, Alexander
    Afton water
Hume, David
    Old man Moses
Humfrey, Pelham
    "Cheer up my mates"
    "I pass all my hours in a shady old
       grove."   See The phoenix
    "O the sad day"
    The phoenix
    "Where the bee sucks"
    "Wherever I am or whatever I doe"
    The willow song
    Willow willow.   See The willow song
Humility.   See Ungbirken (Grieg)
Humming all the trade is.   W. Reeve.
    Words by E. Knight.   ME
The **humming** top.   Children's song.   WSC
Humoreske ("When de shadders spread
    aroun'")   A. Dvořák.   Words by F.
    H. Martens.   BSS
Humoreske ("When the moon is shining")
    A. Dvořák.   Author of words un-
    known.   WBT
A **humorous** lullaby.   See Baadn laatt
Humperdinck, Engelbert
    The dancing lesson (from Hansel und
       Gretel. Tr of Brüderchen, komm
       tanz' mit mir)
    Evening prayer (from Hansel und
       Gretel)
    "Hark! the herald-host is singing" (Tr
       of Leise weht's durch alle lande)
    A little man (from Hansel und Gretel)
Humphrey, Pelham.   See Humfrey, Pel-
    ham
"**Humpty** Dumpty."   Nursery song.
    FSS 4—WA—WBT—WSC—WSW
"**Humpty** Dumpty."   Nursery song. An-
    other air.   FMB
"**Hun** er saa hvid" ("So white is she") E.
    Grieg.   Words by H. C. Andersen.
    da.e.   WM 1
The **hundred** pipers ("Wi' a hundred pipers
    an' a', an' a'") Jacobite song.
    Words by Nairne.   BAS 1—BMC
    —BS 1—JSE—PS 2—WBT
    "Wi' a hundred pipers an' a'."   BOS—
       MMS
"A **hundred** years on the eastern shore."
    Pulling chantey.   SE
A **hundred** years to come.   W. C. Brown.
    FSS 3
Hungarian cradle-song ("Hush, my darling,
    hush") e.   FSS 3
Hungarian national hymn ("Bless our land
    with gladness") F. Erkel.   Words
    by F. Kosely. e.   BMC—NMS—
    WA
    Hymnusz (National hymn) e.hu.
       BSP
Hungarian national song ("Swear, Hunga-
    rian, by thy country") e.   KSE
    "Swear, Hungarian, by thy country."
       e.   SN

Hungaria's treasure ("Magasan repül a darù") Hungarian folk song. e.hu. BO

Hunger song (Das hungerlied) C. Cui. Words from the Russian of N. Nekrasoff. e.g. NM 1

Das **hungerlied.** See Hunger song (Cui)

Hunt, G. W.
The bold fisherman

Hunt, Geoffrey
"The starlight in thine eyes"

Hunt, Mrs Helen Maria (Fiske) See Jackson, Mrs Helen Maria (Fiske) Hunt

"The **hunt** is up." 16th century air. Words attributed to W. Gray. CO 1—HSE 2—JE—MM—PR 1
The king's hunt. BOH
The king's hunt's-up. DM 1

Hunt the wren. Manx folk song. BO

Hunter, Mrs Anne (Home)
The departure of the king (Welsh air)
Hunting the hare (Welsh air)
The Indian's death song (Composer unknown)
May-day (Welsh air)
"My mother bids me bind my hair" (Haydn)
Queen Mary's lament (Giordani)
The sailor's farewell (Welsh air)
The sylphs (Welsh air)

Hunter, Eleanor A.
"From ev'ry spire on Christmas eve" (Coles)

Hunter, H. C.
Geraldine (Levey)

Hunter, Harry
Over the garden wall (Fox)

Hunter, Mrs John. See Hunter, Mrs Anne (Home)

Hunter, William
"Joyfully, joyfully onward I move" (Composer unknown)

The **hunter** in his career ("Long ere the morn") Air: Bass's career. Words by W. Basse. DM 1
The hunter in his career (Basse's career) CO 1

"A **hunter** went a hunting, found nothing all the day." See The Greek huntsman

"A **hunter** went out a-hunting, a hunter went out a-hunting." See Ved balasthioning

The **hunter's** serenade. German air. Words by W. C. Bryant. LBR

The **hunter's** song ("'Mid woods and forest treasure") J. Hullah. FSS 6

Hunter's song ("Mit dem pfeil") See Der schütz (Weber)

A **hunter's** song ("Mit lust thät ich ausreiten") See Jagdlied (Mendelssohn)

The **hunter's** song ("See the sun's first gleam") Schaffer. e. FSS 2

"See the sun's first gleam." e. FSS 4

The **hunting** day. W. Williams (music and words) BOS

The **hunting** of Arscott of Tetcott. Folk song. BSW

Hunting song ("Away, away, away, away") Weber. e. FSS 1

Hunting song ("The first day of spring") See Reynard the fox

Hunting song ("Waken, lords and ladies gay") Welsh air. Words by W. Scott. MS

Hunting song ("What shall he have") See "What shall he have that killed the deer" (Hilton)

Hunting the hare ("Awn i hela'r ysgyfarnog") See Hela'r 'sgyvarnog

Hunting the hare ("Hence! away with idle sorrow") Air: Hela'r ysgyfarnog. Words by A. Hunter. MMW

Hunting the hare ("Sir, pray be so good") Round. BD

Hunting the hare ("Songs of shepherds") DM 2

Hunting the hare ("What sport can compare") 18th century song. ME

Hunting the hind. See Hindraleiken

Huntington, D. W. C.
Over there

Huntington, George
Carleton spelling song (Old air)
"Two empires" (Old air)

Huntingtower ("When ye gang awa, Jamie") Scottish song. PS 1

Huntley, William A.
"Take me back to home and mother"

A **hunt's-up.** 16th century song. DM 2

The **huntsman** ("In woods and on the heather") LA

The **huntsman** ("Sees the hunter far below") Tyrolese song. e. KSE

"The **huntsman** blows his horn in the morn." See The fox jumped over the parson's gate

Huntsman, rest. Mazzinghi. Words by W. Scott. HSE 2

Huntsman's chorus ("In health are the days") C. M. von Weber. [Tr of Was gleicht wohl auf erden dem jägervergnügen] e. BD

The **huntsman's** chorus ("The sunshine glows") C. M. von Weber. Words by H. W. Cross. LA

The **huntsman's** farewell. See Der jäger abschied (Mendelssohn)

Huntsman's song ("O waidmann du zu haus") See Waidmannslied (Slansky)

The **huntsman's** song ("What shall he have") See "What shall he have that killed the deer" (Traditional air)

The **huntsmen** ("A southerly wind") See "A southerly wind and a cloudy sky"

The **huntsmen's** farewell. See Der jäger abschied (Mendelssohn)

The **hurdy-gurdy.** Children's song. FSS 7 —JSE

Hurka, Friedrich Franz
Die schifffahrt
Sehnsucht

"**Hurra,** my boys, for lettet anker." See Ruffen

"**Hurrah!** and hurrah for the Christmas tree." See The Christmas tree (Lowry)

"Hurrah for ivied towers." See Un-
crowned kings (Loomis)
"Hurrah for Jonas Anton Hjelm." See
Opsang for Jonas Anton Hjelm
Hurrah for our banner. A. F. M. Cus-
tance.   MP
"Hurrah! jolly! says he." See "Juche,
lustig, seggt he"
"Hurrah! the seaward breezes sweep down
the bay amain." See The fishermen
(Gilbert); The fishermen (Neefe)
"Hurrah! the snow again is here." L.
Oehmler (music and words)   NMS
Hursley.   See "Sun of my soul"
Husarenliebe ("Wohlan, die zeit ist kom-
men") Volkslied. g.   ED 3
"Wohlan, die zeit ist kommen."   g.
ED 1
Husband, Edward
The first Christmas night (Sangster)
Husband, J. J.
Revive us again
"Husband, husband, cease your strife." See
My spouse, Nancy
The husbandman and servingman. Folk
song. FSF
Hush-a-by. For entries beginning Hush-a-
by see Hushaby
"Hush, baby mine, and weep no more."
See Lullaby
"Hush, hush, baby, go to sleep, go to
sleep." See Wallachian lullaby
"Hush! hush, my child, speak not that holy
Name." See Honor His holy Name
"Hush! hush! the waves are rolling in."
See Gaellic lullaby (Harris)
"Hush! hush! with lovely eyes." See The
sleeping princess (Borodin)
"Hush, little babe, go to sleep, little one."
See The naked bear
"Hush, my babe, lie still and slumber." See
Cradle hymn (Rousseau)
"Hush, my baby, sleep; soon my little child
will slumber." See "Do do l'enfant
dor"
"Hush, my darling, hush, my darling."
See Hungarian cradle-song
"Hush, my darling, repose thee."   J.
Plouvé. Words by C. J. Sprague.
FSS 8
"The hush of noon is round me." See
The fisherman
"Hush! the waves are rolling in." See
Gaelic lullaby (Composer unknown)
"Hush! thee, my wee flower." See Wi-um
(Lieurance)
"Hush ye, my bairnie." See Cagaranan
Gaolach
"Hushaby and good-night, in the sky stars
are bright." See Slumber song
(Brahms)
Hushaby, baby ("Hushaby, hushaby,
baby") Nursery song. FSS 6
"Hushaby, baby, the night winds are sigh-
ing." See Lullaby
"Hush-a-by, darling, and hush-a-by, dear
O." See Lullaby
"Hushaby, hushaby, baby, do not weep."
See Hushaby baby

"Hushaby, my little child." See Vaggvisa
(Söderberg)
"Hush-a-bye, baby on the tree-top." See
"Rock-a-bye, baby"
"Hushed in silence, evening closes." See
Hail, evening bright (Maria Charlotte
Amelia)
"Hushed the song of the nightingale" ("Il
s'est tu, le charmant rossignol") A.
Gretchaninoff. Words from the Rus-
sian of J. Nikitine. e.f.   FM
"Husička divoká." See Little wild goose
"Husker du i höst." See Liden Karen
(Heise)
Huss, Henry Holden
Crossing the bar
My world
The recessional
Hussey, Matthew
"If Phillis denies me relief"
Die hussiten vor Naumburg. Hungarian
folk air: 's ist mir auf der welt nichts
lieber. Words by C. Seyferth. g.
ED 1
Huston, N. W.
Long may our college stand (Composer
unknown)
Hutchinson, Abby
"Kind words can never die"
Hutchinson, Jesse
Old Granite state (Hutchinson)
Song of Arbor day (Pettings)
Hutchinson, Judson Joseph
The age of progress
Bingen on the Rhine
Mountaineer's farewell. See Old
Granite state
November (same air as Old Granite
state)
Old Granite state
The pauper's drive
Hutchinson, William M.
Dream faces
Ehren on the Rhine
Our daily bread
Pierrot
Summer studies (same air as Dream
faces)
"Sweet dreamland faces"
True love is sweet
"What said the shepherds"
Das hüttchen ("Ich hab ein kleines hütt-
chen") Volksweise. Words by J. W.
L. Gleim. g.   ED 2
Das hüttchen. For English translation
with a different air see The invitation
Hüttelein ("Cottage fair") J. Beschnitt.
e.g.   CHS
Hvad fattas dig (The light of the world)
O. Ahnfeldt (music and words) e.sw.
SSN
"Hvad jag har lofvat, det skall jag hålla"
("What I have promised, that will I
hold to") Swedish folk song. e.sw.
HSOS
"Hvad månd'det landet heta." See Mån
tro? jo, jo (Lindblad)

"Hvarför skall man tvinga mig att sjunga" ("Oh, why will you try to make me sing now") O. Lindblad (music and words) e.sw. HSOS

"Hvi längtar du åter till fäderne strand." See Norrländingens hemlängtan (Brooman)

"Hvi staaer du saa eensom, o birketrae." See Birken (Gade)

"Hvis du har varme tanker" ("If you have kindly feelings") H. Børresen. Words by H. Nyblom. da.e. WM 1

"Hvor herligt er mit födeland." See Mit födeland (Ibsen)

"Hvor södt at favnes af aftnens fred." See Til Ole Bull (Folk air); Til Ole Bull (Reissiger)

"Hvorfor svömmer dit öie tidt i en taareglands" ("Wherefore sparkle with dew drops") L. Rosenfeld. Words by J. Paulsen. e.n. SSN

"The hyacinth and daffodil." See The springtime (Scott-Gatty)

Hyah, rattler. Negro folk song. BN 4

Hyatt, Nathaniel Irving
The spring of love

Hyde, Lewis Henry
"Carolling, carolling all thro' the night" (Simper)

Hyde, T. D.
"O Christmas bells, ring far and near" (Simper)
"Sweet angels, ever bright and fair" (Simper)

Hyde Park. Air: The crossed couple. DM 2

Hyllning till Sverige (Homage to Sweden) H. Sandberg. Words by H. Wranér. e.sw. HSOS

Hymen, haste! thy torch prepare. Händel. CS 2

Hymn ("O none in all the world before") Sung at Christmas by the scholars of St. Helena's Island, S.C. A. G. Methfessel. Words by J. G. Whittier. LBR

Hymn for airmen. H. K. Oliver. Words by M. C. D. Hamilton. LA

Hymn for Christmas day. See "See amid the winter's snow" (Goss)

Hymn of praise. See Laoidh molaidh

Hymn of thanks. See "Wilt heden nu treden" (Kremser)

Hymn of the adoption. H. H. Lemmel (music and words) BSS

Hymn of the dying. Words by D. Wolder. e. FSS 6

Hymn of the fishermen's children. Hérold. Words by C. J. Rowe. LA

Hymn of the Marseillaise. See La Marseillaise (Rouget de Lisle)

Hymn of the proclamation of the republic. See Hymno da proclamacao da republica (Miguez)

Hymn of the toilers. Air: Ach, wie ist's möglich dann. Words by R. A. Cleveland. LA

Hymn to College hill. Tufts college song. E. W. Newton (music and words) CHS

Hymn to freedom ("Se gnori z'apo tin kopsi") Greek song. N. Manzaros. Words by Salomos. e.gr. BSP—MP

Hymn to music. Air: Glorious Apollo. LA
"Full and harmonious." FSS 3

Hymn to Saint Anne. See "Bonne Sainte Anne, grande Sainte"

Hymn to the sun (Air of the queen of Shemakhá.—Piésn Shemakhánskoi tzarítzui K'sólntzu) N. Rimsky-Korsakoff. e. SMR 2

Hymnas. See Lithuanian national hymn

Hymne an die Jungfrau. See Ave Maria (Schubert)

Hymne de Riego. See Himno de Riego (Huerta)

Hymne des Marseillaise. See La Marseillaise (Rouget de Lisle)

Hymno da proclamacao da republica (Hymn of the proclamation of the republic) Brazilian national air. L. Miguez. Words by Medeiros e Albuquerque. e.po. SN
National air of the United States of Brazil (Hymn of the proclamation of the republic) e.po. WCP

Hymno nacional ("Amanheceu finalmente." —National hymn) Brazilian song. e.po. BSP
National hymn. e.po. MP

Hymno nacional ("O' patria, o rei."—National hymn) Portuguese song. Dom Pedro IV (music and words) e.po. BSP
National hymn. e.po. MP

Hymnus (Thou only canst give peace) M. Bruch. e.g. HSS 1—HSS 2—HSS 3

Hymnusz. See Hungarian national hymn (Erkel)

I

"I a girl have seen." See La Carolina

I ain't going to die no more. Negro spiritual. NMP

I ain't got weary yet. Negro spiritual. JP

I ain't gwine study war no more. Negro spiritual. DF—TFC 2

"I am a bard." Air: For a' that, an' a' that. Words by R. Burns. BSR

"I am a bold undaunted youth." See Charming Mary Neill

"I am a brisk and bonny lass." See My mother did so before me

"I am a brisk and sprightly lad." Sea song. ME

"I am a brisk lad, but my fortune is bad." See The sheepstealer

"I am a cheerful fellow." See The little waste (Hook)

"I am a contrabandista." See The contrabandista

"I am a country parson." See The country parson

I am a fiddler to my trade. See "Let me ryke up to dight that tear"

"I am a friar of orders grey." See The friar of orders gray (Reeve)

"I am a gay young gentleman." See The Virginian lover

"I am a glad maiden." See Son vergin vezzosa (Bellini)

"I am a jolly bowler." See The Oxford bowlers (Vanbrugh)

I am a jolly miller. Air: Dull o'r triban. Words by Talhaiarn. MMW

"I am a jovial collier lad." See Down in a coal mine (Geoghegan)

"I am a jubilant rider." See Der knabe mit dem wunderhorn (Schumann)

"I am a poor girl and my fortune's been bad." See The wagoner's lad (Kentucky version)

"I am a poor man, heaven knows." See Ragged and torn and true

"I am a poor shepherd undone." 17th century English song. BE 6
"I am a poor shepherd undone" (Hey, ho, my honey) CO 2

"I am a Prussian." See Preussens vaterland (Neithardt)

"I am a roamer bold and gay." See "Ich bin ein vielgereister mann" (Mendelssohn)

"I am a ruler on the sea." A. Sullivan. Words by H. F. Chorley. BAS 2

"I am a shoemaker by my trade." See The shoemaker

"I am a sailor stout and bold." See The rambling sailor

"I am a shepherd boy." Air: Cerdinen, or, The fern. Words by Ieuan Dhu. MMW

"I am a son of Mars." Air: Soldier's joy. Words by R. Burns. BSR

"I am a Sunday-school scholar, lar, lar, lar." See The Sunday-school scholar

"I am a Texas cowboy." See The Texas cowboy (Thomson)

"I am a wand'ring minstrel man." See Brideen ban mo store (O'Carolan)

"I am a young damsel that flatters myself." See The lottery

"I am a young fellow that always loved rural sport." See Drahaareen-o mochree

"I am a young lass of Lynn." See The lass of Lynn

"I am a young maiden." Air: Cainc y medelwr, or, The reaper's strain. MMW

"I am a young pedlar." See An ceannuighe Sugach

I am alone ("Je suis seul") See "Je suis seul" (Massenet)

"I am alone at last." See Plus grand dans son obscurité (Gounod)

"I am alone here in the night." See "Me voilà seule dans le nuit" (Bizet)

"I am an honest miller." See I am a jolly miller

"I am at last alone." See Plus grand dans son obscurité (Gounod)

"I am bounden for to love thee." See El capotin

"I am content." C. H. Sainton. Words by C. Barnard. FSS 3—JS

I am dreaming of thee. A. Lee. FSS 7

"I am far frae my hame." See My ain countrie

"I am gloomy, I fret and worry." See Haï luli (Coquard)

"I am goin' to join in this army." Negro song. HR

"I am going far away." See The old cabin home (Paine)

I am here in her boudoir. See Me voici dans son boudoir (Thomas)

"I am in truth a country youth." See The honest Yorkshireman (Carey)

"I am leaving of Kilyonan." See When the west wind blows

"I am lonely here, and weary." See Nirvana (Hervey)

"I am mournful and I am lonely." See Haï luli (Coquard)

"I am mournful, darling father." See A bride's sorrow

"I am my mammie's ae bairn." See I'm owre young to marry yet

"I am Ormond the brave." See Ormond the brave

"I am Parisian, far fam'd as a singer." See 'A frangesa (Costa)

"I am ready to depart." See Addio a Napole

"I am seekin' for a city." See I don't feel no-ways tired

"I am seeking in every valley." See "Vo' cercande in queste valli" (Astorga)

I am so deep in love. See Cupid's courtesy

"I am the glad New Year." Nursery song. FSS 7

"I am the jolly prince of drinkers." Composer and author of words unknown. MM

"I am the monk Waltramus." See Vale carissima (Wallnöfer)

"I am the spirit who denieth." See "Son lo spirito che nega" (Boito)

I am thinking, love, of thee. R. W. Atkinson. NML

I am Titania. See Je suis Titania (Thomas)

"I am waiting here for you love." See Ciribiribin (Pestalozza)

"I ance was a wanter." See The married man's lament

"I arise from dreams of thee." Composer unknown. Words by Shelley. CHS —NML

"I arise from dreams of thee." C. Salaman. Words by Shelley. DM 2—KF 3

"I at thy feet would fain be lying." See "Zu deinen füssen möcht' ich liegen" (Graben-Hoffmann)

"I attempt from love's sickness to fly." H. Purcell. Words by Dryden. BE 7 —BOH—BS 2—HSE 1—JE—KF 3— KF 4—KS 4—PR 1—SM 1

"I await the morrow, Niña mia." See "Hasta la mañana"

I been wukkin' on de railroad. See Levee song

"I believe in God, by all in heav'n adored." See "Je crois au Dieu" (David)

"I, beneath her window height." Bohemian song. e. KSE

"I bless thee night and day, love." See Night and day, love (Abt)

"I bought my wife a stane o' lint." See The weary pund o' tow

"I breakfast on it daily." See A song of water (Drinkwater)

"I bridled my boots, and I saddled my sword." See Den bakvende visa

"I bridled my nag." Irish folk song. JOI

"I buckle on my armour when glory bids me start." See Charmente Gabrielle (Henry IV?)

"I built a bridge of fancies." A. Fricker. FSS 6

"I came from Alabama." See Oh! Susanna (Foster)

"I came to Alabama." See Oh! Susanna (Foster)

"I came to the cross in the valley." See La cruz del valle

"I came to this country in eighteen-forty-nine." See Pretty Saro (Georgia version; Carmen, N.C. version)

"I can hear them o'er the meadows." See At the ferry (Wellings)

"I can scarcely hear, she murmur'd." See Will he come (Sullivan)

"I cannot change as others do." See My lodging is on the cold ground

"I cannot discover the reason." See Die Lorelei (Silcher)

"I cannot eate but lytyll meate." Words from "Gammer Gurton's needle." SSS

"I cannot explain wherefore." See Die Lorelei (Liszt)

"I cannot get to my love if I would dee." See The water of Tyne

"I cannot help thinking I've oft been to blame." See Never say No when you wish to say Yes (Hook)

"I cannot sing the old songs." Claribel (C. Barnard) (music and words) FSS 3— HSC— HSD— NMH— PO— WA—WBT—WSW

"I chant my song to the fragrant honeysuckle." See Honeysuckles (Nape)

"I chose myself a sweetheart." See Les métamorphoses

"I climb the mountain." See Fhir a bhàta

"I cling to Thee." Old English song. WS

"I coft a stane o' haslock woo." Air: The cardin o't. Words by R. Burns. BSR

"I come from countries far from here." See Der wanderer (Schubert)

"I come from haunts of coot and hern." See The brook (Wilson)

"I come from heaven high above." See "Vom himmel hoch da komm' ich her" (Luther)

"I come from regions high and free." See Der wanderer (Schubert)

"I come here from my mountains lone." See Der wanderer (Schubert)

"I come, I come, if in that tide." See The cold wave my love lies under (Attwood)

"I come, I come! ye have called me long." V. Bellini. Words by F. Hemans. FSS 4

"I come this night for to sing and pray." See Oh, yes! oh, yes

"I come to the spring." See Drei röslein

"I come to town de udder night." See Old Dan Tucker (Russell)

"I come with a shout, and scatter about." See A song of March (Jones)

"I could not speak with him." See Desolation

I couldn't hear nobody pray. Negro spiritual. HR—JB

Couldn't hear nobody pray. BN 1

"I count my treasures o'er with care." See Christmas treasures (Bellini)

"I courted a maiden both buxom and gay." See The false bride

"I dance the bright bolero." See The Spanish gipsy

"I declare, to-morrow I'll have done with sorrow." See "Jag tror jag får börja öfverge att sörja"

"I devise to end my days in a tavern drinking." See "Mihi est propositum" (Pearsall)

"I do confess thou art sae fair." Air: The cuckoo. Words by R. Burns. BSR

"I do confess thou'rt smooth and fair." H. Lawes. Words attributed to R. Ayton. BE 7—MM—PR 1

"I do not ask for the heart of thy heart." See Bid me to love (Barnard)

"I do not count the hours I spend." See Waldeinsamkeit (Mendelssohn)

"I do not dare despond." See "Non posso disperar" (Luca)

I doan' want fu' t' stay hyeah no longah. See The Danville chariot

"I done been to heaven." See The Danville chariot

I done done what ya' tol' me to do. Negro spiritual. JB

I don't feel no-ways tired. Negro spiritual. HR

I doubt it. L. Adams. Words by A. Nash. CHS—MPC

"I dream, I dream of my fatherland." See I dream of my fatherland

"I dream of all things free." Weber. Words by F. Hemans. FSS 2

I dream of my fatherland. Alpine air. FSS 4

"I dream of thee, sweet Madoline." See Madoline (Nelson)

"I dream of you in the flowering time."
See A summer love dream

"I dreamed a dream of an old, old love."
E. Cooke. FSS 8

"I dreamed a dream the other night, Lowlands, Lowlands, away, my John." See
Lowlands

"I dream'd I lay where flow'rs were springing." See The dream

"I dreamed of a pallid princess-maid." See
"Mir träumte von einem königskind"
(Hartmann)

"I dreamed of my true love last night."
See Locks and bolts (Hot Springs,
N.C. version)

"I dreamt a dream the other night. Lowlands, Lowlands, hurrah! my John; I
dreamt a dream." See Lowlands a-ray

"I dreamt a dream the other night, Lowlands Lowlands, hurrah! my John, I
dreamt I saw." See Lowlands

I dreamt I was in heaven. M. Costa.
CS 2—OS 2

"I dreamt that I dwelt in marble halls."
M. W. Balfe. Words by A. Bunn.
BE 6—DM 1—HSD—HSE 3—PO
—WA—WSW
"I dreamt I dwelt in marble halls."
FSS 2—NML—WBT

"I dressed me all in feathers gay." See
"Je me suis habillé en plumes"

"I drink the fragrance of the rose." H.
Clough-Leighter. Words by C. H.
Towne. HST

"I ensomme stunde" (In lonely moments)
O. Bull. Words by M. J. Monrad.
e.n. MAN

"I fain a winning tale would tell thee."
See Verlegenheit (Abt)

"I fain would speak to thee, ah vainly."
See Verlegenheit (Abt)

I fear me to love him. See J'ai peur de
l'aimer (Denza)

"I fee'd a man at Martinmas." Air: O can
ye labour lea. Words by R. Burns.
BSR

"I feel, I feel the Deity within." See I
feel the Deity within (Händel)

"I feel just as happy as a big sunflow'r."
See Happy as a big sunflower

I feel the Deity within. G. F. Händel.
SAS 4
Also in Arm, arm, ye brave (Händel)
OS 4

"I feel thy breath blow around me." See
"Ich fühle deinen odem" (Rubinstein)

"I fling the night behind me with the
dawn." Air: Gyda'r wawr, or, With
the dawn. Words by L. S. Jast.
MMW

"I follow Thee also." Bach. e. OS 1

"I gaed a waefu' gate yestreen." See The
blue-eyed lassie (Riddell)

"I gaed up to Dunse." Air: Rob shear'd
in hairst. Words by R. Burns. BSR

"I gave her a rose in the golden days."
See In the golden eventide (Pinsuti)

"I gave my love a cherry that has no
stones." See The riddle song

"I gaze all day on the burning plain." See
A creole love-song (Moncrieff)

"I gaze on the sun, it mounts in the skies."
See Saetergjentens söndag (Bull)

"I give thee all, I can no more." See My
heart and lute (Bishop); My heart and
lute (Kjerulf)

"I go outside on my balcony." See Song
of the little bird

"I go unto the fair." See The Hindu child

"I got a home in-a dat rock." Negro spiritual. JB

"I got a mother in de heaven." Negro
spiritual. DF

"I got a mother in de heavenly lan'."
Negro spiritual. BOM

"I got a mother in heaven." See Stan'
still Jordan

"I got a robe, you got a robe." See All
God's chillun got wings

"I grieve when I think on the dear happy
days." See Draherin o machree

"I groan as I put my nets away." See
Song of an island fisherman

"I ha daheim e maidli g'ha." See Die
maidli im Schwizerland

"I had a bird, a little bird." See The
faithful little bird

"I had a cat and the cat pleased me." See
The barnyard song

"I had a faithful comrade." See Der gute
kamerad

"I had a first cousin call'd Arthur Mac-
Bride." See Arthur MacBride

"I had a little nut-tree." See The nut-tree

"I had a little sail-boat." French folk
air: La bergère. Words by J. Irwin.
DO

"I had a sister Sally." See The old maid's
song

"I had a trusty comrade." See Der gute
kamerad

"I had faith in dazzling sunlight." See A
poet's epitaph (Medtner)

"I had four brothers over the sea." See
Perri merri dictum, domine

"I had gold, I had gems." FSS 7

"I had sax owsen in a pleugh." Air: The
bottom of the punch bowl. Words by
R. Burns. BSR

"I hae a wife o' my ain." Scottish air.
Words by R. Burns. BSB—BSR

"I hae been at Crookieden." Air: The
old Highland laddie. Words by R.
Burns. BSR

"I hae laid a herrin' in saut." Scottish
air. Words by J. Tytler. MMS—
PS 1

"I hagen sat modri." See Millom rosor
(Beyer)

"I hail my mother in the morning coming
along." See Zion's children

"I hail to my sister." See Gideon's band

"I hammer, I hammer my gold." See The
gold-beater (Randegger)

"I have a cottage by the hill." See The
invitation

"I have a Father in the promised land."
See The promised land

"I have a silent sorrow here." Georgina,
duchess of Devonshire. Words by
R. B. Sheridan. BE 6

"I have a sister dear." See Rachella

"I have a song to sing." A. S. Sullivan.
Words by P. Hastings. BSS

I have been a foster. Cooper. CO 1

I have but a mark a year. 17th century
song. CO 2

"I have come from the mountains of the
Old Granite state." See Old Granite
state (Hutchinson)

"I have come, my dear Zeiserl." See
Farewell

"I have come to say good morning." N.
Medtner. Words from the Russian of
A. Fet. e. NM 1

"I have come to say good morning" ("Me
voici, je te salue") N. Rimsky-Korsakoff. Words from the Russian of A.
Fet. e.f. NM 2

"I have grown old, too old, my boys."
See Old Demos and his rifle

"I have heard sweet music stealing." See
Come sing to me again (Hobson)

"I have heard the mavis singing." See
Mary of Argyle (Nelson)

"I have here a little cake." See "J'ai encor
un tel paté" (Adam de la Halle)

"I have house and land in Kent." 16th
century song. CO 1—DM 2

"I have lifted my eyes by night to the
skies." See Stances (Flégier)

I have lost my Euridice. See Che farò
senza Euridice (Gluck)

"I have lost my senses." See A song of
sorrow (Nihad)

"I have loved thee." FSS 8

"I have loved your winsome face." See
Haberban

"I have my hammock a-swinging." See
La hamaca

"I have rambled, I own it." See In search
of a wife

I have received Thy mercy. See "Mir ist
erbarmung widerfahren" (Pressel)

"I have roamed over mountain." See My
own native land (Bradbury)

"I have run down with my wagon." See
'K heb mijn wagen volgeladen

"I have seen a maiden slender." See La
Carolina

"I have sought, ah! with earnest endeavor."
See "Jeg har sögt" (Nordraak)

"I have told you that I love you very
dearly." See T'aggio ditto

"I have waked the winter's nights." 17th
century song. JE

"I hear a tone so wondrous rare." See
Ein ton (Cornelius)

"I hear, I hear, I hear my lady, ha! ha! ha."
See My lady

I hear my true lub weep. See Way down
in Ca-i-ro (Foster)

"I hear not a footfall." See Music at
nightfall (Nelson)

"I hear people say." See Aye sure

"I hear the breathing." See "Il dolce
suono" (Donizetti)

"I hear the children's voices." E. Lemare.
Words by Gaskell. HC

I hear the mill. See "Mon père a fait
bâtir maison" (J'entends le moulin)

I hear the pibroch sounding. See March
o' the Cameron men

I hear the robin sing. See Rothkehlchen
(Abt)

"I hear the soft note." A. Sullivan.
Words by W. S. Gilbert. DSH

"I hear the streamlet splashing." See
Ständchen (Franz)

"I hear thee speak of the better land." See
The better land (Bennett); The better
land (Browne); The better land (Cow-
en)

"I hear them tell in far-off climes." See
The fire of home

"I hear tonight the old bells chime." See
Love's golden dream (Lennox)

"I hear you, little bird." S   joy of the
morning (Ware)

"I heard a brooklet gushing." E. J. Loder.
Words by Müller. [Tr of Wohin] e.
DM 1

"I heard a brooklet gushing." For words
in the original with a different air see
Wohin (Schubert)

"I heard a robin a-singing his song." See
O robin, red robin

"I heard a streamlet gushing." See Wohin
(Schubert)

"I heard a thousand blended notes." See
Lines written in early spring (Waller)

"I heard a voice long years ago." See
Looking back (Sullivan)

"I heard a wee bird singing." G. Linley.
JSE

"I heard the wee bird singing." FSS 3

"I heard an old farmer talk one day." See
Rainfall follows the plow

I heard from heaven to-day. See Peter,
go ring them bells

"I heard in the night the pigeons." Irish
air. Words by P. Colum. CMF 1—
FSI

"I heard it again, 'tis the harp." See 'Tis
the harp in the air (Wallace)

"I heard the bells on Christmas day." A.
H. Brewer. Words by H. W. Longfellow. HC

"I heard the bells on Christmas day" (The
bells) J. L. Hatton. Words by H. W.
Longfellow. HSE 3

"I heard the church bells ringing." See
Christmas bells (Cross)

"I heard the gay spring coming." See
Idle (Seidel)

"I heard the gull." See "Der skreg en
fugl" (Sinding)

"I heard the rippling brooklet sing." See
It was a dream (Cowen)

"I heard the voice of Jesus say." J. B.
Dykes. Words by H. Bonar. LA—
TL

"I heard the voice of Jesus say." A. A.
Wild. Words by H. Bonar. LA

"I heard the wee bird singing." See "I heard a wee bird singing" (Linley)

"I himlen" ("In heaven") J. Selmer. Words by H. C. Andersen. da.e. SSN

"I hold the distaff in my hand." See The weaver (Lieurance)

"I hope my mother will be there." Negro spiritual. HR

"I hope you'll all be ready." See When the Bridegroom comes

I implore thee, O, my brother. See Je t'implore, ô mon frère (Thomas)

"I jealous am, O Psyche." See Psyché (Paladilhe)

"I jist come out a-fore you." See Miss Lucy Long

"I joy once more now, O home to behold thee." See Pilgrims' chorus (Wagner)

"I knew by the smoke that so gracefully curl'd." See The woodpecker (Irish air); The woodpecker (Kelly)

"I know a bank whereon the wild thyme blows." C. E. Horn. Words by Shakespeare. FMB—FSS 6—LA

"I know a falcon swift and peerless." See The falcon (Silcher)

"I know a hail more sweet, I wis." See Första aftonen i det nya hemmet (Geijer)

"I know a home 'midst hills and valleys." See Min lilla vrå bland bergen (Sandstrom)

"I know a lad, and he's my own." See En liten visa (Hallström)

"I know a maiden fair to see." See Beware (Hatton)

"I know a pretty maiden named Luisella fair." See La Luisella

"I know a wondrous lovely land." See Switzerland (Heim)

"I know an eye, so softly bright." See "Ich kenn' ein aug', das so mild" (Reichardt)

"I know I would like to read." Negro song. HR

"I know my robes gwinter fit me well." See By an' by

"I know not from whence it so cometh." See Lind (Backer-Gröndahl)

"I know not how lovely your face is." See At the ball (Tchaikovsky)

"I know not if you love me." See "Yo no sé si me quieres"

"I know not Lord Love." See "Fanciulla son io" (Rossi)

"I know not what e'er hath befallen." See Die Lorelei (Silcher)

"I know not what is the meaning." See Die Lorelei (Silcher)

"I know not what it betokens." See Die Lorelei (Liszt)

"I know not what it meaneth." See Die Lorelei (Silcher)

"I know not what it presages." See Die Lorelei (Silcher)

"I know not what means the sad feeling." See Die Lorelei (Silcher)

"I know not what spell is enchanting." See Die Lorelei (Silcher)

"I know not what spell is o'er me." See Die Lorelei (Liszt)

"I know not what the future hath." W. Irmer. Words by J. G. Whittier. LBR

"I know not when the day shall be." See Some day (Wellings)

"I know not whence comes the power." See Lind (Backer-Gröndahl)

"I know not whence it cometh." See Die Lorelei (Silcher)

"I know not why, but my gladness." See Die Lorelei (Silcher)

"I know not why dreams o'ershadow." See Die Lorelei (Silcher)

"I know not why I love thee." WBT

"I know so many a pretty lay." See Den nordlandske bondestand

"I know that my Redeemer lives." See Sinner, please don't let this harvest pass

"I know that my Redeemer liveth." G. F. Händel. OS 1—SAS 1. g. also FMB

"I know that water is chilly and cold." See Chilly water

I know the Lord's laid His hands on me. Negro spiritual. DF—HR

"I know the pangs that cleave the bleeding heart." G. F. Händel. SAS 1

"I knows a gal that you don't know." See Li'l Liza Jane

"I knows a little doner." See The future Mrs 'Awkins (Chevalier)

I kvell eg gløymde no kubbin aa reise. See "Eg seer deg ut før gluggjin"

"I laid me down so softly." See "Jeg lagde mig saa sildig"

"I laid me down to rest." See "Jeg lagde mig saa sildig"

"I languish, love, thy weary slave." See "Così, amor, mi fai languir" (Stradella)

"I lay on that rock where the storms." See The rock of Cader Idris

"I left my darling lying here." See An coineachan

"I left my flock to stray upon the plain." See David chantant devant Saül (Bordèse)

"I let the dearest dream depart." See Matin song (Paine)

I lift my heart to Thee. M. Costa. CS 1 The evening prayer. OS 2—SAS 2

"I like them all, the pretty girls." See "Me gustan todas"

"I linger round the very spot." See Once again (Sullivan)

"I little know or care." See For ever and a day (Mack)

I live and love thee. See "Dammi ch'io libi l'alito" (Campana)

"I live for the good of my nation." See Old Rosin, the beau

"I live forever weeping the fate." See "Vivo llorando la suerte"

"I live, my heart is beating" (The resurrection) R. Pugno. e. SAS 3

I live not where I love ("Loyal lovers that are distant") 16th century song. BE 8—PR 1

I live not where I love ("With my love my life was nested") 16th century song. CO 1—PR 1

"I loathe that I did love." See "In youth when I did love" (Traditional air)

"I locked up all my treasure." Dibdin (music and words) HSE 1

"I lo'e na a laddie but ane." Air: My lodging is on the cold ground. Verse 1 by J. Clunie, verses 2-5 by H. Macneill. MMS
I lo'ed ne'er a laddie but ane. FSS 3—JO

"I long to climb the mountains high." See "Til fjelds over bygden" (Kjerulf)

"I look at the sun, it rises on high." See Saetergjentens söndag (Bull)

"I look from my window." See Waiting

"I look o'er yander, what I see." Negro folk song from the Bahamas. KA

"I look on thee, thou little flow'r." See Forget-me-not (Graben-Hoffmann)

"I look ovah yondah on Jericho's walls." See O, rocks don't fall on me

"I look over Jordan, and what do I see." See Swing low, sweet chariot

"I looked and I sighed." See The silent lover (Boyce)

"I looked and saw your eyes." See Three shadows (Bedford)

"I looked into the midnight deep." See In my beloved's eyes (Chadwick)

"I looked ober Jordan and what did I see." See Swing low, sweet chariot

"I looked over Jordan, what d'I see." See Swing low, sweet chariot

"I lov'd a maid, her name was Nell." See My dog and I

"I lov'd a lass, a fair one." Air: Y gofid glâs, or, The blue devils. Words by G. Wither. MMW

"I love a beauteous maid." See The lass of Grongar hill

"I love a pretty Maui girl." See Maui girl

I love, and the world is mine. C. Johns. Words by F. E. Coates. AA

I love but thee ("If after all") M. Vogrich. Words by T. Moore. AB 2

"I love but thee as thou dost me." See "Ich liebe dich, so wie du mich" (Beethoven)

I love dem shorten gals. See Jaybird

"I love, I know I love her." See Bella del suo sorriso (Braga)

"I love it, I love it." See The old arm chair (Russell)

"I love little pussy." See Pussy (Elliott)

I love my love ("What is the meaning of the song") C. Pinsuti. Words by C. Mackay. FSS 6—HSC—JS—NML—WBT—WL

I love my love in secret ("My Sandy gi'ed to me a ring") Scottish air. Words by R. Burns. MMS—PS 2
"My Sandy gied to me a ring." BSR

"I love my love in the morning." Irish air: The mountains high. Words by G. Griffin. FSI—MMI—PI

"I love Pepa and that's no story." See Mi Pepa

"I love the cheerful summer-time, with all its birds and flow'rs, its shining garments green and smooth." See Summer-time (Gluck)

"I love the cheerful summer time, with all its buds and flowers; its tender grass so green and smooth." See I love the summer time

"I love the din of beating drums." Limerick air. Words by S. Mac Cathmhaoil. FSI

I love the merry sunshine. S. Glover. Words by J. W. Lake. FSS 2—HSE 3

"I love the song of birds." See What I love and hate

"I love the sounding horn." See Le cor (Flégier)

"I love the spring, when slumb'ring buds." See The seasons (Mozart)

I love the summer time. FSS 3—WSC

"I love the white girl and the black." See A little more cider too (Hart)

I love thee ("Ich liebe dich") See "Ich liebe dich, so wie du mich" (Beethoven)

I love thee ("Min tankes tanke") See Jeg elsker dig (Grieg)

I love thee ("O sag' es noch einmal") See "O sag' es noch einmal" (Slansky)

"I love thee, darling." NML

"I love thee dear! said morning to the day." See Morning (Rachmaninov)

"I love thee, I love thee, 'tis all that I can say." See 'Tis all that I can say (Messager); 'Tis all that I can say (Temple)

"I love thee, my dear, what else can I do." See "Ich liebe dich weil ich dich lieben muss" (Förster)

"I love thee, my star in heaven brightly beaming." See Una stella (Mililotti)

I love thee, my wreath of peacock feathers. See Remember be sure and be there (Hopkins)

"I love thee violet, modest fragrant flow'r." See Violeta (Hopkins)

"I love this fierce and elemental strife." See Rage, thou angry storm (Benedict)

"I love Thy kingdom, Lord" (St Thomas) G. F. Händel. Words by T. Dwight. FSS 5—FSS 8

"I love to gaze on smiling faces." See Smiling faces (Glover)

"I love to see the Sepoy." See The elephant battery

"I love to shout, I love to sing." See Come down, angels

"I love to sing." E. L. Hime. FSS 6

"I love to sit and think and dream." See Alma mater—Muhlenberg (Kistler)

"I love to tell the story." W. G. Fischer. Words by K. Hankey. FSS 2—NMH—NMS—WBT—WS

"I love to wander when the day is o'er." Irish song. e. MMI

"I love you! your lips say, and seal it." See A dissonance (Borodin)

I loved. For entries beginning I lov'd see I lov'd

"I made love to Kate." 18th century air. MM

"I married me a wife, I got her home." See The wife wrapt in wether's skin (Kentucky version no. 1)

"I may sit in my wee croo house." See When the king comes owre the water

"I met a pilgrim on the way." See My Lord delivered Daniel

"I met ayont the cairnie." Air: Jenny Nettles. MMS

"I met four chaps yon birks amang." See Jenny's bawbee

"I met her at evening." See La Calavresella

"I met her in the morning." See Won't you go my way

"I met my love in a dream last night." See My love beyond the sea (Sullivan)

"I min ungdom så gladde mig att sjunga" ("In my youth I loved well") Swedish folk song. e.sw. HSOS

"I moanalua hai ke au." See Hawaiian hula (Moanalua)

"I mourn as a dove." J. Benedict. OS 1 —SAS 1

"I mourn for the Highlands." See Fuadach nan gàidheal

"I mourn no more my vanished years." See My psalm (Mozart)

"I mow by the Neckar." See Das ringlein

"I murmur not, although my heart is broke." See "Ich grolle nicht" (Schumann)

I must go. Negro song. JP

I must try another. J. Hook. ME

"I nebber see de like since I been born." See Johnny come down to Hilo

"I need thee every hour." R. Lowry. Words by A. S. Hawkes. TFC 1— TL

"I ne'er can know how it befell me." See Seligkeit (Meyer)

"I never lov'd but one fair maid." Air: Gogerddan. MMW

"I never saw a face till now." Welsh air: The little brown jug. MMW

"I never saw a face till now" (Phillis) Pack. MM

"I never saw a fairer." Air: My wife's a wanton wee thing. Words by R. Burns. BSR

"I never shall forget that day." See Reign, Massa Jesus

I never will forget you. See Gardenia flower (Nape)

"I often for my Jenny strove." 17th century song. CO 2

"I once did have a dear companion." See The dear companion

"I once did know a girl named Grace." See Levee song

"I once did love a yellow gal." See Mary Blane

"I once did lub a colored gal." See Stop that knocking at the door

"I once had a cousin called Arthur Le Bride." See Arthur Le Bride

"I once had a faithful comrade." See Der gute kamerad

"I once had a sweet little doll, dears." See The lost doll

"I once had houses, riches and lands." See The gypsy laddie (Rocky Fork, Tenn. version no. 2)

"I once knew a pretty girl and I loved her as my life." See The rejected lover (Virginia version)

"I once lov'd a bird." See The bonny bird

"I once lov'd a boy." Old Irish street ballad. MMI

"I once that was great." See In Limbo

"I once was a guest at a nobleman's wedding." Irish air: The nobleman's wedding. Modern words by W. Allingham. MMI

"I once was a maid tho' I cannot tell when." Air: Sodger laddie. Words by R. Burns. BSR

"I paid her a bet in mousquetaires." See She answered me nay (Jones)

"I pass all my hours in a shady old grove." See The phoenix (Humfrey)

"I passed by a garden." See The little Dutch garden (Mawson-Marks)

"I plac'd o'er my heart the portrait you gave me." See Letters from lovers (Offenbach)

"I pledge allegiance to my flag." See Salute to the flag (Collins)

"I plucked a quill from Cupid's wing." H. K. Hadley. Words by A. Boucicault. CMF 2—ES

"I pray thee, I pray thee, how do we best sing a scale." See The scale (Beethoven)

"I pray thee send me back my heart." See I prithee send me back my heart (Miller)

"I press on this flow'ret a fond kiss of rapture." See Fleur messagère (Bouval)

I prethee love, turn to me. See "My lodging it is on the cold ground" (Locke)

"I prithee, send me back my heart." H. Lawes. Words by J. Suckling. MM

"I prethee, send me back my heart." PR 1

[I prithee, send me back my heart] "I pray thee send me back my heart." E. Miller. Words by J. Suckling. BE 6

"I put my hand all in her own." See Gently, Johnny my Jingalo

I rage, I melt, I burn. Händel. BS 1 Also in O ruddier than the cherry (Händel) KS 5

"I reckon the days is departed." See The last of the singers

"I recollect it. Yes, that millstream." See Vi ravviso, O luoghi ameni (Bellini)

I rede you, beware at the hunting, young men. See "The heather was blooming"

"I remember how I lingered." See Remembrances

I remember how my childhood. Lady Edward Fitzgerald. Words by W. M. Praed. FSS 4

"I remember, I remember." BE 2—JO

"I remember, I remember" (How my childhood fleeted by) HSE 2

"I remember, I remember an old garden gay and trim." See An old garden (Temple)

"I remember, I remember, how my childhood fleeted by." See I remember how my childhood (Fitzgerald)

"I remember, I remember, in years long passed away." See The golden shore (Scott-Gatty)

"I remember, I remember the house where I was born." J. Blockley. Words by T. Hood. JO—WBT

"I remember well a sunny vale." See Farewell, those happy hours (Donizetti)

"I 'ribed into New York." See Jordan am a hard road to trabbel (Briggs)

"I ride a little trot." See My trusty trot (Arthur)

"I ride my pony ev'rywhere." See My pony

"I rjukande uvaer og fjkande vind." See Bonden i bryllaupsgarden

"I roam'd on the mountain." See Verbung

"I rode my little horse." Folk song. BSW

"I rode up to her uncle." See Locks and bolts (Carmen, N.C. version no. 2)

"I rosens doft" ("Where roses grow") Prince Gustaf, duke of Upland. Words by H. Sätherberg. e.sw. HSOS
"Midst roses sweet." e. KSN—WL
"Where roses fair" ("Im rosenduft") e.g. FSS 8

"I rowed my boat out on the billows." See Strilevise

"I saddled my horse, and away I did ride." See The hearty good fellow

"I said, I will forget thee." See "Nicht mehr zu dir zu gehen" (Brahms)

"I sail'd in the good ship, the Kitty." See Yo, yea (Dibdin)

"I sat beneath the maples old." See A spring song (Pinsuti)

"I sat on a bank in trifle and play." See The jolly goss-hawk

"I saunter out as evening creeps." See Lauf der welt (Grieg)

I saw a rosebud. See "Ich sah ein röschen am wege stehn" (Weber)

"I saw a ship a-sailing" (The little ship) English folk song. DO

"I saw a ship a-sailing." C. Reinecke. Words from an English folk song. FSS 5—JSE

"I saw a sweet maiden that weeping did go." See Schaut's aussi

"I saw a sweet maiden trip over the lea." See The blue kerchief

"I saw from the beach." Air: Miss Molly. Words by T. Moore. MI

"I saw that you were grown so high." H. Purcell. DM 2

"I saw the autumn nighing." See "Ich sah den wald sich färben" (Pressel)

"I saw thee 'midst the flowers." See Der schönste engel (Graben-Hoffmann)

"I saw three ships." Traditional song. DO
Christmas day in the morning. MCS —WCC
"I saw three ships." Derbyshire version. BSC—HC—MF

"I saw thy form in youthful prime." Air: Domhnall, or, Donald. Words by T. Moore. MI—MMI

"I say, old man, your horse will die." See Poor old man

I say that by fear I'm not haunted. See Je dis, que rien ne m'épouvante (Bizet)

"I scarce know what means this sorrow." See Die Lorelei (Liszt)

"I see a form, I see a face." See O this is no my ain lassie

"I see by your eyes." See "Jag ser uppå dina ögon"

"I see fair meadows green beside a rill." See Es war ein traum (Lassen)

"I see her in dreams." See Megan's fair daughter

"I see I am the first at this sad rendezvous." See Ô jours heureux (Gounod)

"I see my home in the twilight dim." See Dreamland (Barnard)

"I see the moon." Irish folk song. JOI

I see the ships. See "Vedo li bastimenti"

"I see them on their winding way." Words by Heber. JO

"I see you through the window." See "Eg seer deg ut før gluggjin"

"I see your shadow yonder." See "Eg seer deg ut før gluggjin"

"I seem to see my native land again." See Es war ein traum (Lassen)

I seen her at de window. Negro song. NMP—WBT

"I send a farewell from my heart to thee." See Glounthaun Araglin eeving

I seraljens lustgård (The seraglio garden) E. Sjögren. e.sw. SSN

I served down at Kjölstad. See "Je tjente paa Kjölstad ifjor"

"I served my time in the Black Ball line." See The Black Ball line

"I set the bell a-ringing." See The bell ringer (Wallace)

"I shipped on board of a Liverpool liner." See Sally Brown

"I shot an arrow into the air." See The arrow and the song (Balfe)

"I should like to have heard the angels sing." See The first Christmas night (Sangster)

"I sigh and lament me in vain." See Queen Mary's lament (Giordani)

"I sigh for a maid." See The gipsy hat (Hook)

"I sigh of love." See Chanson à danser

"I sing a doleful tragedy." See Guy Fawkes

"I sing and I dance." See "Jag sjunger och dansar" (Randel)

"I sing, I sing, of the love of Jeanne." See Chantons les amours de Jean

"I sing of a land." See The Stuarts of Appin (Wilson)

"I sing of a whistle." Attributed to R. Riddell. Words by R. Burns. BSR

I sing of the love of Jean. See Chantons les amours de Jean

"I sing the Birth was born tonight." G. C. Martin. Words by B. Johnson. BSC—HC

"I skogen smaagutten gik dagen lang." See Tonen (Nordraak)

"I sleep; my heart at break of day can never sleep." See Hebrew love-song (Rimskiï-Korsakov)

"I so lonely walked along." See Kattyglö visa

"I sow'd the seeds of love." Air: The willow tree. Words attributed to Mrs F. Habergham. DM 2
Variant: The sprig of thyme

"I sow'd the seeds of love" (The seeds of love) Folk air. Words attributed to Mrs F. Habergham. SEF 1—SO

"I sowed my seeds of love" (The seeds of love) Sussex air. Words attributed to Mrs F. Habergham. SF 5

"I spoke to a shoemaker." See El zapatero

"I spoke to Rémon." See Rémon, Rémon

"I stand upon my watch-tower." See Der thürmer (Matys)

"I stood before her portrait." See Ihr bild (Schubert)

"I stood on the bridge at midnight." See The bridge (Bliss)

"I stood where the summer tide, flowing." See By the blue sea (Smart)

"I sung my passion to the wind." See Rosalinda (Butler)

"I tell you now as I told you before." See Reign, Master Jesus

"I tell you what I mean to do." See Keep me from sinking down

"I think I heard the old man say." See Rio Grand

"I think it 'twas 'bout twelve o'clock." See Prayer is de key of heaven

"I think of all thou art to me." See Forever and forever (Tosti)

"I think of the morn when I sailed away from thee." See La paloma (Yradier)

"I think of thee at morn, my love." See Truth in absence (Harper)

I think of thee, sweet Margareta. See Dein gedenk' ich, Margareta (Meyer-Helmund)

"I think of thee, Teresita mia." See Teresita mia

"I think of thee when the bright sun." See Nähe des geliebten (Lassen)

"I think of thee with deepest devotion." See "Yo pienso en ti"

"I think of you by day, my love." See Acushla gal machree

"I think of you in waking hours." Words by E. Devereaux. WBT—WL

"I think of you, when the mists are falling." See Love thoughts

"I think of you when the world's at rest." See In shadowland (Denza)

I think on thee ("All the live-long night") Air: Ar hyd y nos. Words by J. M. E. Dovaston. MMW

"I think upon the lighted halls." See The bard's lament

"I think, when I read that sweet story." See That sweet story of old

"I thought I heard our captain say." See Good morning, ladies all

"I thought I heard the old man say." See Leave her, Johnny

"I thought that love had been a boy." W. Byrd. BOH

"I to-morrow, love, must go." See Lebewohl (Silcher)

I told you of my love. See "Fanciullo appena ti parlai d'amore"

"I took a pretty girl to ride." See Faint heart ne'er won fair lady

I took off my coat, and roll up my sleeve. See Jordan am a hard road to trabbel (Briggs)

"I took the charming Dolly to the Harvard assembly." See The dude who couldn't dance

"I toss my cap up into the air." See The rambling sailor

"I travelled this country round and round." See Cork and sweet Munster

"I triumph! I triumph." See "Vittoria! vittoria" (Carissimi)

"I used to have a sweetheart." See The rejected lover (Tennessee version)

"I villande skogen" ("All in the dim forest") A. Randel. Words by F. A. Dahlgren. e.sw. HSOS

I vow that nothing shall prevent me. See Je dis que rien ne m'épouvante (Bizet)

I wait, my love, for thee. A. Scott Gatty. Words by R. A. Gatty. NML

"I wait, my love, I wait for thee." See Jenny Lind's Good night (West)

"I waited for the Lord." F. Mendelssohn. [Tr of Ich harrete des Herrn] e. TFC 2

"I walked abroad at eventide." See "Jag gick mig ut en aftonstund"

"I walked and I walked." FSS 7

"I walked out one bright May morning to hear the birds sing sweet." See The false young man (Kentucky version)

"I walked out one May morning to hear the small birds sing." See The false young man (North Carolina version)

"I wander through woodlands." See "Gaaer jeg udi skoven"

"I wandered along the mountains" (Sāl dam'ī) Syrian folk song. ar.e. BF 2

"I wander'd by the brookside." See The brookside (Hine)

I wandered by the sea-beat shore. See Shells of ocean (Cherry)

"I wandered out one summer day a-roving." See Sommerdagen

"I wandered today to the hill, Maggie." See When you and I were young, Maggie (Butterfield)

"I want forty dozen of fine waxen dolls." See Christmas is coming

"I want no stars in heav'n to guide me." See Beauty's eyes (Tosti)

I want to be ready. Negro spiritual. HR
    I want to be ready (Walk in Jerusalem just like John) JP

I want to go across to see my Lord. See Oh, give way, Jordan

"I want to go to heaven when I die, do love the Lord." See Wake up Jacob

"I want to go to heaven when I die! view the land, view the land." See View de land

"I want ye wee again, laddie." See The mother-heart (Gaines)

"I was a wandering sheep." See The peaceful fold (Zundel)

"I was a young maiden truly." See The Sandgate lass's lament

"I was born of God, I know I am." See View de land

I was born to love thee. See "Nasci para te amar"

"I was brought up in Sheffield, but not of high degree." See The Sheffield apprentice (Norfolk version)

"I was brought up in Snowfield in such a low degree." See The Sheffield apprentice (Hot Springs, N.C. version)

"I was down at Piedigrotta." See La vera Sorrentina

"I was just aboot smoor'd wi' a kittlin' cough." See The clinical examination

"I was not deceived." Dvořák. e. OS 4

"I was sad and oppress'd." See Rencontre (Fauré)

"I was seated at thy feet." See Non è ver (Mattei)

I was seeing Nellie home. See The quilting party

"I was sleeping in the Tamba-tangane." See "Autiko mai na"

"I was still a child, alas! when my mother died." See När jag var ett litet

"I welcome thee with gladness." See Song of the May

"I went down to Sandy Hook de oder arternoon." See Turkey in the straw

"I went in de room, I didn't stay long." See I'm gwine see my friends agin

"I went into my stable to see what I might see." See Old Wichet

"I went off to the well, oh." See A la fontaine

"I went to see my Susan." See Susan Jane (Hays)

"I went to the fair." J. Whitaker. BE 1

"I went to town the other day." See Old Dan Tucker

"I went up on de mountain." See Tell Jesus

"I whipped my horse." Folk song from North Carolina. CSE

"I whisper'd my great sorrow." See The sedges

"I will arise." A. Sullivan. TS

I will be happy too. S. Nelson. Words by C. J. Jefferys. FSS 8

I will bear the indignation of God (The repentance of Manasseh) C. H. H. Parry. SAS 3

"I will buy a waist-coat of finest silk." See Zur Johannisnacht (Grieg)

"I will cry in quietness." See Lucyna

"I will extol Thee, my God, O King." B. Molique. OS 1—SAS 1

"I will extol Thee, O Lord." M. Costa. OS 1—SAS 1

"I will give you a paper of pins." See The keys of heaven (Virginia version)

"I will give you the keys of heav'n." See The keys of heaven (English version)

"I will lay me down." S. Neukomm. FSS 6

I will love Thee, O Lord. S. Bennett. OS 1

"I will not grieve." See "Ich grolle nicht" (Schumann)

I will not hurry. See Je n'veux pas me marier

"I will not let you go, my Lord." See He's the Lord of lords

I will sing of Thy great mercies. Mendelssohn. e. OS 1

"I will sing the first part." See We'll all go a-singing

"I will sing unto the Lord a new song." C. H. H. Parry. SAS 1

"I will sing willingly an old song." See Finita è pei frati (Meyerbeer)

"I will sing you a song of that beautiful land." See Home of the soul (Phillips)

"I winna marry ony man." See He's aye a kissing me

"I wish I could but know." See "Je voudrais bien savoir quel était ce jeune homme" (Gounod)

"I wish I had the shepherd's lamb." Irish folk song. e. JOI

"I wish I war where Eelin lies." Air: Fair Helen of Kirkconnel. Words by R. Burns. MMS—PS 2
    Fair Helen of Kirkconnel ("I wish I were where Helen lies") HSSS

[I wish I war where Eelin lies] "O, that I were where Helen lies." Air: Where Helen lies. Words by R. Burns. BSR

"I wish I was by that dim lake." Air: Shule aroon. Words by T. Moore. MI—PI

"I wish I was in Boston city." See Shool

"I wish I was in de land ob cotton." See Dixie (Emmett)

"I wish I was in London town; ha-hee, ha-oo, are you most done." See Clear the track

"I wish I was in the land ob cotton." See Dixie (Emmett)

"I wish I was old Stormey's son; to my way, yah, stormalong, I'd give those sailors lots of rum." See Old Stormey

"I wish I was old Stormy's son; to my way ay Stormalong John. I wish I was old Stormy's son." See Stormalong John

"I wish I were now in that isle of the sea." See Eilean an Fhraoich

"I wish I were on yonder hill." See Shule aroon

"I wish I were where Helen lies." See "I wish I war where Eelin lies"

"I wish naught but to survey thee." See "Non vogl' io se non vederti" (Scarlatti)

"I wisht I was in London town: oh, say, where are you bound to." See Across the western ocean

"I wonder where my mother is gone." See Peter, go ring dem bells

"I won't marry a man that's tall." See The old maid

"I worship Thee, sweet will of God." See Sweet will of God (Scotch air); Sweet will of God (Methfessel)

"I would be to thy heart its sweetness." See Le fidèle coeur (Vidal)

I would I were a boy again. F. Romer. Words by M. Lemon. FSS 4—FSS 7
  "O would I were a boy again." WBT
  Would I were a boy again ("Oh, would I were a boy again") JO

"I would I were a king." A. Sullivan. Words by A. Cockburn. BS 1

"I would indite this ditty." See Sherlock Holmes (Ralston)

"I would kiss thee, my beloved." See A kiss (Cherepnin)

"I would not be a monarch great." See The country farmer's son

"I would not die in springtime." M. Moore. FSS 7

"I would not give my Irish wife." Irish air: We'll all take coach and trip away. Words by T. D. McGee. MMI

"I would not live alway." G. Kingsley. Words by W. A. Muhlenberg. FSS 1

"I would now sing for and I might." See The three kings (Heale)

"I would spend my blood unheeding." See "Col mio sangue comprerei" (Stradella)

"I would that my love." See "Ich wollt' meine lieb' ergosse" (Mendelssohn)

I wrestle and pray. J. S. Bach. e. DSH

"I yielded without repenting." See "Begli occhi, io non mi pento" (Perti)

"I yince was a light-headed laddie." See Capped and doctored and a'

"Ia fǎ-te mai mǎricel." See Mugur, mugurel

"Ianthe the lovely." J. Barrett. BE 7

Ibby Damsel. Folk song from North Carolina. CSE

Ibsen, Henrik
  Borte (Grieg)
  Margaretes vuggesang (Grieg)
  En svane (Grieg)
  Solvejgs sang (Grieg)
  Solvejgs wiegenlied (Grieg)

Ibsen, Lars Möller
  Mit födeland
  My native land. See Mit födeland
  Det norske flag
  Norway's flag. See Det norske flag

Ice upon the river. See Bulgǎraş

Iceland ("Island, farsaeldsa frón") See Island

Iceland ("Yderst mod norden") See "Yderst mod norden"

Icelandic folk song. See Tölf synir

"Ich armes käuzlein kleine." See Käuzlein (Reichardt)

Ich auch war einst jüngling mit lockigem haar. For English translation see Stadinger's song (Lortzing)

"Ich bin der Doktor Eisenbart." See Doktor Eisenbart

"Ich bin der mönch Waltramus." See Vale carissima (Wallnöfer)

"Ich bin der schneider Kakadu." See Der schneider Kakadu (Müller)

"Ich bin der wohlbekannte sänger." See Der rattenfänger

"Ich bin ein lust'ger geselle." See Der knabe mit dem wunderhorn (Schumann)

"Ich bin ein Preusse." See Preussens vaterland (Neithardt)

Ich bin ein soldat. For English translation see Soldier song (Schumann)

"Ich bin ein vielgereister mann" ("I am a roamer bold and gay") F. Mendelssohn. e.g. KS 5
  "I am a roamer bold." e. AB 4—BAS 1—BS 1

Ich can sprech-a. College song. CHS

"Ich danke Gott und freue mich." See Täglich zu singen (Schulz)

"Ich denk an euch, ihr himmlisch schönen tage." See Sehnsucht (Bornhardt)

"Ich denke dein, wenn durch den hain" (Andenken.—Remembrance) L. van Beethoven. Words by Matthisson. e.g. KF 1

"Ich denke dein, wenn durch den hain." J. R. Zumsteeg. Words by Matthisson. g. ED 2

"Ich denke dein, wenn mir der sonne." See Nähe des geliebten (Beethoven); Nähe des geliebten (Lassen)

"Ich fühle deinen odem" ("I feel thy breath blow around me") A. Rubinstein. Words by F. Bodenstedt (Mirza-Schaffy) e.g. SC

"Ich fuhr über meer" ("I've journeyed o'er land") H. Kjerulf. e.g. WM 1

"Ich gei arois." See Song of the little bird

"Ich ging einst einen frühlingstag." See Die wiese (Reichardt)

"Ich ging im mondenschimmer." See Selige erinnerung (Schulz)

"Ich ging im walde so für mich hin." See Gefunden (Gersbach)

"Ich grolle nicht" ("I will not grieve") R. Schumann. Words by Heine. e.g. BS 1—KF 2—KF 4—PG 4
"Ich grolle nicht" ("I'll not complain") e.g. FF—FO 1—GM
"Ich grolle nicht" (The poet's love) e.g. AB 1

"Ich hab den ganzen vormittag." W. Müller. Author of words unknown. g. ED 1

"Ich hab' ein bächlein funden." See Daphne am bach (Reichardt)

"Ich hab' ein kleines hüttchen nur." See Das hüttchen

Ich hab' ein traum geweinet. For French and English translations see Invocation (Rhodes)

"Ich hab' es getragen sieben jahr." See Archibald Douglas (Loewe)

"Ich hab mein' sach auf nichts gestellt." See Vanitas! vanitatum vanitas (Zelter)

"Ich hab mich ergeben mit herz und mit hand." See Gelübde

"Ich hab' mir eines erwählet." See Liebeslied (Weber)

"Ich hab' mir mein kind'l fein schlafen gelegt." Schlesisches volkslied. g. ED 3

Ich harrete des Herrn. For English translation see "I waited for the Lord" (Mendelssohn)

"Ich hatt' einen kameraden." See Der gute kamerad

"Ich hatt' mal einen schweren stand." See Der geheilte bursche (Fink)

"Ich hatte einst ein schönes vaterland." See Es war ein traum (Lassen)

"Ich hör' meinen schatz." See Der schmied (Brahms)

"Ich hört' ein bächlein rauschen." See Wohin (Schubert)

"Ich kam vom walde hernieder." See Der letzte gruss (Levi)

Ich kann ja nicht spinnen. See Die spinnerin (Volkslied)

"Ich kenn' ein aug', das so mild" (Thou art so near, and yet so far) A. Reichardt. e.g. FSS 5

"Ich kenne einen klaren bach." See The brook (Bleikhman)

"Ich klage hier, o echo." See Klage

"Ich komme schon durch manches land." See Marmotte (Beethoven)

"Ich komme vom gebirge her." See Der wanderer (Schubert)

"Ich konnte heute nicht schlafen." See Laengsel (Kjerulf)

"Ich lag auf grünen matten." See Die erscheinung (Berger)

"Ich lausche dem echo so gerne." See Das echo (Greith)

Ich liebe dich ("Min tankes tanke") See Jeg elsker dig (Grieg)

"Ich liebe dich, so wie du mich" (I love thee) Beethoven. Words by Hölty. e.g. PG 3

"Ich liebe dich weil ich dich lieben muss" ("I love thee") A. Förster. Words by F. Rückert. e.g. KF 1—KF 3

"Ich möchte dir wohl etwas sagen." See Verlegenheit (Abt)

"Ich möchte sterben wie der schwan" ("So would I die, as dies the swan") E. Degele. e.g. SOS 2

"Ich möchte wohl der kaiser sein, der kaiser sein." See Meine wünsche (Mozart)

"Ich nehm mein gläschen in die hand." See Vive la compagneia

"Ich ruhe still im hohen grünen gras." See Feldeinsamkeit (Brahms)

"Ich sah den wald sich färben" (The woodlands all are turning) G. Pressel. e.g. KF 4
"Ich sah den wald sich färben" ("The woodlands all were turning") e.g. AB 4

"Ich sah dich unter blüthen." See Der schönste engel (Graben-Hoffmann)

"Ich sah ein röschen am wege stehn" (An junge spröde schönen) A. Methfessel. Words by K. Müchler. g. ED 3
"Ich sah ein röschen am wege stehn." C. M. von Weber. Words by K. Müchler. g. ED 2
I saw a rosebud. e. WBT—WL
Das röschen (The rose) e.g. SSG

"Ich sass und spann vor meiner tür." See Die spinnerin (Harder)

"Ich schiess den hirsch im wilden forst." See Jägers liebeslied

"Ich schnitt' es gern in alle rinden ein." See Ungeduld (Schubert)

"Ich spring an disem ringe." See Minnelied

"Ich stand in dunkeln träumen." See Ihr bild (Schubert)

"Ich steh' auf einem hohen berg." See Das lied von dem jungen grafen

"Ich steh' auf meinem thurme." See Der thürmer (Matys)

"Ich trage, wo ich gehe." See Die uhr (Loewe)

"Ich trink, und trinkend fällt mir bei." See Die drei reiche der natur

"Ich und mein fläschchen." Volksweise. Words by A. Langbein. g. ED 1

"Ich war bei Chloen ganz allein." See Der kuss (Beethoven)

"Ich war erst sechszehn sommer alt." See Phidile (Schulz)

"Ich war jüngling noch an jahren." See Joseph (Méhul)

"Ich war wohl recht ein springinsfeld." See Wilhelm (Schulz)

"Ich wäre wohl fröhlich so gerne." See Stille klage

"Ich weih' im tale den tiefsten hain." See Die weihe (Himmel)

"Ich weiss, dass mein Erlöser lebet." See "I know that my Redeemer liveth" (Händel)

"Ich weiss der lieder viele und singe, was ihr liebt." See Das eine lied (Gersbach)

"Ich weiss es nicht, wie es gekommen." See Seligkeit (Meyer)

"Ich weiss nicht was soll es bedeuten." See Die Lorelei (Silcher)

"Ich weiss nicht, was soll's bedeuten." See Die Lorelei (Liszt)

"Ich wollt ein sträusslein binden." L. Reichardt. Words by C. Brentano. g. ED 2

"Ich wollt' ein wenig mit dir plaudern." See "Another little hour I begged" (Grechaninov)

"Ich wollt' meine lieb' ergösse" (I would that my love) F. Mendelssohn. Words by Heine. e.f.g. FMB. e.g. MS
"I would that my love." e.g. WA. e. only FSS 7—HSC—HSD—LA—NML—TFC 2—WL

Ichabod. Tschaikowsky. e. TS

Ichibuzzhi. See Ish'-i-buz-zhi

"Ick bin ein Franzose, mes dames." See Die 'ölzerne bein

"I'd be a butterfly." Mrs T. H. Bayly. Words by T. H. Bayly. BE 2—JO

"I'd cut it deep on all the trees that grow." See Ungeduld (Schubert)

"I'd just as soon be a beggar as a king." See The beggar

"I'd like to die." See "Vorrei morire"

"I'd mourn the hopes that leave me." Irish air. Words by T. Moore. MI—MMI —PI

"I'd offer thee this hand of mine." FSS 5 —WBT

"I'd rather be a daisy." See Song of the daisy (Glover)

I'd wed, if I were not too young ("In holiday gown") Irish air: The road she went. Words by J. Cunningham. MMI

I'd wed if I were not too young ("In holiday gown") G. Wicks. Words by J. Cunningham. ME

"I'd weep with thee." C. M. von Weber. FSS 4

Idle ("I heard the gay spring") F. L. Seidel. Words by A. Cary. LBR

"Idle days in summertime." Welsh folk song. WL

An idle dream. See Es war ein traum (Lassen)

Idle hours. See Vo' altre putele che se'da maridar

"Idlest of dreams." H. Maréchal. e. SAS 4

Idyl. See Genrebillede (Backer-Lunde)

Ieuan Ddu. See Thomas, John

If—("If I were a cat") Words by G. E. Wood. CHS

If ("If love were what") See "If love were what the rose is" (Pinsuti)

If ("Se un tuo pictoso accento") See Se (Denza)

"If a body meet a body." See Comin' thro' the rye

"If after all you still will doubt and fear me." See I love but thee (Vogrich)

"If all the world were paper." WSC

"If all those young men were as hares on the mountains." See Hares on the mountains

"If an S and an I and an O." See The speller's fate

"If angels sung our Saviour's birth." A. H. Brown. HC

"If any of those children of hunger shall cry." Irish folk song. JOI

"If, as you wander where of old we met." See Call me back (Denza)

"If by some chance you e'er should meet him." See "Ah! s'il est dans votre village" (Godard)

"If doughty deeds my lady please" (Oh, tell me how to woo thee) Air: Per Alaw, or, Sweet Richard. Words by R. Cunninghame-Graham. BMC—WBT

"If doughty deeds my lady please." A. Sullivan. Words by R. Cunninghame-Graham. BAS 2

"If e'er my heart's best treasure." See The miller's daughter

"If ever I get married." See The banks of the roses

"If ever I see." FSS 4

"If Florindo be faithful." See "Se Florindo è fedele" (Scarlatti)

"If for me alone thou'rt longing." See Se tu m'ami, se sospiri (Pergolesi)

"If gloomy and forbidding the world may often seem." See Jul (Alnaes)

"If harsh decree." See "Si la rigueur" (Halévy)

"If I a bird could be." See "Wenn ich ein vöglein wär' "

"If I could play in a big brass band." See The little drummer

"If I do not love thee, love thee only." See "Que no te amo"

"If I give thee honour due." See Let me wander not unseen (Händel)

"If I go to the brook tonight." See The joyous meeting

"If I had a beau for a soldier who'd go." See The dashing white sergeant (Bishop)

"If I had a-known before I'd a-courted." See Come all you fair and tender ladies (Hot Springs, N.C. version)

"If I had but a thousand a year, Gaffer Green." See The better wish (Russell)

"If I had the art, dear." See "Si formas tuvieran mis pensamientos"

"If I should be that warrior." See Celeste Aida (Verdi)

"If I was a sinner tell yer what I would do." See Don't let nobody turn yer roun'

"If I were a bird." German folk air. Words by R. Compton. DO

"If I were a cat." See If—

"If I were a sunbeam." German air. Words by L. Larcom. LBR

"If I were a sunbeam." Composer unknown. [Words by L. Larcom] FSS 8

Were I a sunbeam. WBT

If I were an elfin. Bohemian folk air. Words by H. H. Harbour. DO

If I were king of Ireland. Irish air. Words by A. P. Graves. FSI

"If I were like you." See "Se come voi piccina io fossi" (Puccini)

"If in a state of exhilaration." See Bob up serenely (Audran)

"If in thy dreams thou hearest." See In thy dreams (Buck)

"If in your heart a corner lies." See Bid me good-bye (Tosti)

"If in your village you have dwelling." See "Ah! s'il est dans votre village" (Godard)

"If love my feet enchaineth." See Se amor m'annoda il piede (Stradella)

"If love were not." C. Johns. Words by F. E. Coates. HST

"If love were what the rose is." C. Pinsuti. Words by A. C. Swinburne. WBT—WL

If. FSS 8—NML

"If love's a sweet passion." H. Purcell. BE 3

"If music be the food of love, play on." J. C. Clifton. Words by W. Shakespeare. VFS

"If my lover starts, with his boat I'll sail." See "Si va el vapor"

"If my mistress hide her face." J. L. Hatton. Words by B. Abercrombie. HSE 3

"If my voice you can hear, O blossoms dear." See "Faites-lui mes aveux" (Gounod)

If papa knew. See "Mon pèr' n'avait fille que moi"

"If peace and content." See "När själen är nöjd" (Gustaf)

"If Phillis denies me relief." M. Hussey. DM 1

"If power divine for once were mine." See "Wenn ich einmal der Herrgott wär'" (Binder)

"If Ser Romeo thy son's life ended." See "Se Romeo tuccise un figlio" (Bellini)

"If she forsake me." P. Rosseter. Words by T. Campion. BOH

"If she were mine, and lov'd me well." See She must be mine

"If the Atlantic sea could only champagne be." See "Wenn das Atlantische meer lauter champagner wär"

"If the brook or breeze that passes." See "Se bel rio" (Rontani)

"If the quick spirit of your eye." H. Lawes. PR 1

"If the summer's long of coming." See Martha's spinning wheel

"If there's a shepherd in your parish." See "Ah! s'il est dans votre village" (Godard); "Ah! s'il est dans votre village" (Maria Charlotte Amelia)

"If there's anybody here like weeping Mary." See Weeping Mary

"If thou hast crushed a flower." V. Bellini. Words by F. Hemans. FSS 4

"If thou lov'st me." See Se tu m'ami, se sospiri (Pergolesi)

"If thou my death proclaiming." See "Se tu della mia morte" (Scarlatti)

"If thou should ask my love." Air: Jamie, come try me. Words by R. Burns. BSR

"If Thou should'st mark iniquities." Costa. OS 4

"If thou shouldst see me." See Un adios

"If thou shouldst tell me." See "Tu me dirais" (Chaminade)

"If thou wert by my side." S. Nelson. Words by R. Heber. FSS 2—JO—WBT

"If thou wilt not be heeding." See Se (Denza)

"If thou'lt be mine." Irish air: Caiteach roin, or, The winnowing sheet. Words by T. Moore. MI—MMI

If thou'rt not sincere. Bohemian song. e. KSE

"If Thy disciples." Bach. e. OS 2

If 'tis I alone thou lovest. See Se tu m'ami, se sospiri (Pergolesi)

"If 'tis sorrow so to love thee." See "Yo m'alegro do habèr sido"

"If to thy soul comes a gentle voice calling." See "Se mai senti" (Leo)

"If torn from thee." Händel. Tr of Se estinto è l'idol mio. BE 6

"If where a wound is." See "Se mai vien tocca" (Bononcini)

"If wings were mine now." See Mo rùn geal, dìleas

"If with all your hearts ye truly seek me." F. Mendelssohn. e. OS 3—SAS 3—TFC 2—TL—TS

"If ye love God, serve Him." See Love an' serve de Lord

"If ye want to see Jesus." Negro spiritual. HR

"If you are thinking of getting married." See Donna

"If you ask us why our mother." See The royal purple (Bartlett)

"If you be my May Margaret." See May Margaret (Marzials)

"If you can not on the ocean." See Your mission (Grannis)

"If you could have married the king's daughter dear." See The daemon lover (Allanstand, N.C. version)

"If you cross the hill by my father's mill." See Tit for tat (Pontet)

If you ever look on love. See "Se amor mai da vu se vede"

"If you have kindly feelings." See "Hvis du har varme tanker" (Børresen)

"If you love me.' G. Bizet. [Tr of Si tu m'aimes, Carmen] e. WBT

"If you to me be cold" (Just as it used to do) V. Harris. ES

"If you to me be cold" (One or two) W. T. Wrighton. FSS 5

"If you want to go a-courting." Folk song from North Carolina. CSE

"If you want to go through college." See The son of a trustee

"If you want to know where the tenderfoots are." See We saw them

If you want to see Jesus. Negro spiritual. JP
Ef ye want to see Jesus. HR

"If you want your souls converted." See Pharaoh's army

If you would, so would not I. Early 19th century song. ME

"If your lovers, maids, forsake you." See If you would, so would not I

"If your wife and my wife." See The pound of tow

"If you're a scout and I'm a scout, doodah! doodah." See I'm busy to-day (Foster)

"If you're on pursuit for your own true lover." See William Taylor (North Carolina version)

"If you're seeking refined education." See Oh, won't you come up to Columbia

"Ige ige." See War song

Igjennem nat og traengsel. For English translation see "Through the night of doubt and sorrow" (Paine)

"Igra kolo." See In the kolo

"Igrali su kolo u kolu lijepi Jovo." See Sarajevo kolo

Ihr ("Namen nennen dich nicht") A. Kretzschmer. Words by W. Ültzen. g. ED 2

"Ihr alle." See Come unto me (Dvořák)

Ihr bild (Her portrait) F. Schubert. Words by H. Heine. e.g. FO 1

"Ihr brüder, wenn ich nicht mehr trinke." See Des trinkers testament

"Ihr flüchtigen stunden." See "Ye dear, fleeting hours" (Dargomyzhskii)

Ihr hirten steket alle auf von eurem tiefen schlaf. For English translation see "Come, shepherds, come! shake off your sleep"

"Ihr kinderlein, kommet." See Die kinder bei der krippe (Schulz)

"Ihr Mägdelein, nehmt euch in acht." See Warnung (Meyer-Helmund)

"Ihren schäfer zu erwarten." See Phyllis und die mutter

"Ik heb mijn wagen volgeladen." See 'K heb mijn wagen volgeladen

"Il court, il court le furet." See Le furet du bois joli (Onfroy de Bréville)

"Il est au loin une colline." See "There is a green hill far away" (Gounod)

"Il est défendu de crier dans la rue." See Le couvre-feu

Il est doux, il est bon. J. Massenet. e.f. SOA 1
Air of Salomé. e.f. OPS 1
"Celui dont la parole" ("He whose compelling word") e.f. KS 2
He is good, he is kind. e. BC

"Il était trois petits enfants." See Le miracle de Saint-Nicolas

"Il était un' bergère" ("There was a little maiden") French folk song. e.f. BO—TSF
La bergère. f. DO—FMB
Variant: La bergère à confesse

"Il était un' bergère, et ron, ron, ron, petit patapon." See "Il était un' bergère"

"Il était un' bergère, pon pon pon, petit patapon." See La bergère à confesse

"Il était un' dame Tartine." See Dame Tartine

"Il était un petit homm'." See Le petit chasseur

"Il était un petit navire." See Le petit navire

"Il était un roi de Thulé." See Le roi de Thulé (Gounod)

"Il était un roi d'Yvetot." See Le roi d'Yvetot

"Il était une barque à trente matelots." See Chanson de matelots

"Il m'a dit: Cette nuit j'ai rêvé." See La chevelure (Debussy)

"Il mang' la viande et nous donn' les os." See "Ali! alo"

"Il pleure dans mon coeur" ("The tears fall in my soul") A. C. Debussy. Words by P. Verlaine. e.f. CMF 2 —HM 1

"Il regardait mon bouquet." P. A. Monsigny. e.f. SOA 1

"Il s'est tu, le charmant rossignol." See "Hushed the song of the nightingale" (Grechaninov)

"Il va venir." J. F. Halévy. e.f. SOA 1

L'île inconnue. See "Dites, la jeune belle" (Berlioz)

Iliffe, Frederick
"Hear the angels telling"

"Ilk care and fear, when thou art near." Air: Braes o' Balquhidder. Words by R. Burns. BSR

Ilka blade of grass. J. Wilson. Words by J. Ballantine. FSS 5

I'll ay ca' in by yon town. See "There's nane shall ken, there's nane can guess"

"I'll be no submissive wife." A. Lee. Words by T. H. Bayly. HSE 3

I'll be the squire's bride. J. Hook. ME

"I'll be there, I'll be there." See The general roll

"I'll be there in the morning." Negro spiritual. HR
Variant of: General roll call

"I'll bewail my misfortune." See La fata di Amalfi

"I'll bid my heart be still." Ancient Border air. Words by T. Pringle. MMS—PS 2

"I'll build myself a gallant ship." Folk song. BSW

"I'll buy a horse and steal a gig." See Push the business on

I'll do my duty. FSS 2

"I'll give to you a paper of pins, and that's the way our love begins." See The keys of heaven (Black Mountain, N.C. version; Hot Springs, N.C. version)

"I'll give to you a paper of pins, for that's the way that love begins." Children's song. WSC
Variants: The keys of Canterbury; The keys of heaven

"I'll go along this year." See La festa di Piedigrotta

"I'll ha'e my coat o' gude snuff-brown" (A duologue between Meg and the laird) Scottish air. Words by A. Boswell. PS 2

"I'll hang my harp on a willow tree." Old English air, arr by W. Guernsey. FSS 5—HSD—JO—WBT

"I'll have no other one" ("Já nechci žádného") Czech folk song. bo.e. BF 1

I'll hear the trumpet sound. Negro spiritual. DF—JP—NMP—WC
"You may bury me in de eas'." JB—KA

"I'll keep the freedom that I prize." See Gardons nos moutons

"I'll love thee if thou'lt love me." Hungarian song. e. KSE

I'll never leave thee ("One day I heard Mary say") Scottish air. Words by R. Crawford. MMS

I'll never love thee more. 17th century song. Air from Gamble's ms. CO 1
"My dear and only love." BE 8

I'll never love thee more. 17th century song. Air from "Pills to purge melancholy." CO 1

"I'll never see my lover more." See Loin de lui (Dancla)

"I'll not complain." See "Ich grolle nicht" (Schumann)

"I'll not reveal my true love's name." Irish Jacobite song. e. MMI

Ill omens ("When daylight was yet sleeping under the billow") Air: Kitty of Colleraine. Words by T. Moore. MI

Ill omens ("When daylight was yet sleeping under the billow") Air: Paddy's resource. Words by T. Moore. MI

"I'll put you myself, my baby! to slumber." See Irish lullaby

"I'll range around the shady bowers." Air: Dilyn serch, or, The pursuit of love. MMW

"I'll riddle to you, my younger son." See Lord Thomas and fair Ellinor (Allanstand, N.C. version)

"I'll sail upon the Dog-star." H. Purcell. BE 3—BOH—JE

"I'll seek a four-leav'd shamrock." See The four-leaved shamrock (Lover)

"I'll sing my children's death-song." Irish air: O thou of the beautiful hair. Words from the Irish. e. MMI

"I'll sing thee songs of Araby." F. Clay. Words by W. G. Wills. FMB—KF 3 —WBT—WL

"I'll sing you a good old song." See The fine old English gentlemen (Purday)

"I'll sing you a song of the fish of the sea." See Rio Grande

"I'll sing you an old ballad." See The fine old English gentleman (Purday)

"I'll speak of thee." M. B. Hawes. Words by M. M. G. Dowling. BE 4

"I'll take my gospel trumpet." See Weary traveler

I'll tell on thee. Bohemian song. e. KSE—WL

"I'll tell thee, Dick, where I have been." See A song of a wedding

"I'll tell you a tale now without any flam." See The cork leg (Blewitt)

"I'll tell you a tale of the olden time." See A tale of the olden time (Trevaldwyn)

"I'll tell you how I found the Lord." See I'm so glad

"I'll tell you of an awful wedding." See The awful wedding

I'll tend my sheep. See Gardons nos moutons

"I'll to some shady cool retreat." See The constant fair

"I'll weave my love a garland." See The loyal lover

The ill-wed wife. See La maumariée

I'll weep with thee. See "Has sorrow thy young days shaded"

Illinois. Air: Baby mine. Words by C. H. Chamberlain. OH

Illinois. W. H. Jones. [Words by C. H. Chamberlain] CHS

Ils m'ont appelé vilaine (They said I was not pretty) Canadian folk song. e.f. TF

"Iluna au o Wailana." See "Upon the crest of Wailana" (Nape)

I'm a' doun for lack o' Johnnie. Scottish song. PS 2

"I'm a jolly roving tar." W. Reeve. ME

"I'm a little chinaquita." See "Yo soy una chinaquita"

"I'm a little prairie flow'r." See I'm wild

I'm a man that's done wrong. Folk song. BE 8

"I'm a man that's in trouble and sorrow." See I'm a man that's done wrong

"I'm a meek and humble Freshman." See Columbia's Y. M. C. A.

"I'm a merry gipsy maid." See Little gipsy Jane (Glover)

"I'm a merry laughing girl." C. W. Glover. FSS 6

"I'm a nice guajira." See La guajira

"I'm a pilgrim." Italian air. Words by M. S. B. Dana Shindler. FSS 4—HSD —WBT—WS

I'm a poor stranger and far from my own ("As I went a-walking one morning in spring") Irish folk song. JOI—MMI

"As I went a-walking one morning in spring." PI
Variant: The happy stranger

"I'm a poor, wayfarin' stranger." See Pilgrim's song

"I'm a pretty little thing." See The daisy

I'm a rambling rake of poverty. See Son of a gambolier

"I'm a sailor, says he." See "In Berlin sagt' er"

"I'm a shepherd born to sorrow." Welsh air. TFC 2

"I'm a shepherd of the valley." F. G. Klauer. e. FSS 1

"I'm a Sunday-school scholar-ar-ar-ar." See Sunday-school scholar

"I'm a sweet Bohemian maid." See The Bohemian maid

"I'm a tough, true hearted sailor." See Every bullet has its billet (Bishop)

"I'm a true English sailor." See Blow the man down

"I'm a 'varsity examiner." See The examiner's song (Lutz)

Im abendroth (Evening glow) F. Schubert. Words by C. Lappe. e.g. CMF 2 —GM

"Im Aergäu sind zweu liebi." See Die Aargauer lieben

"I'm afloat! I'm afloat." H. Russell. Words by E. Cook. BE 1—FSS 8

"I'm a-going to tell you about the coming of the Saviour." See In that great getting-up morning

"I'm a gwine to tell you bout de comin' ob de Saviour." See In that great getting-up morning

"I'm alone, alone at last." See Ah! fuyez, douce image (Massenet)

"I'm alone! quite alone." See Ah! fuyez, douce image (Massenet)

Im anfang war's auf erden. For English translation see "We plough the fields, and scatter" (Schulz)

"Im antlitz dir schon furchen ruh'n." See To my mother (Bradsky)

"Im Ärgäu sind zweu liebi." See Die Aargauer lieben

"Im arm der liebe ruht sich's wohl." See Gute ruhe (Winter)

I'm a-rolling. Negro spiritual. HR—JP JSE
I'm a-rollin'. DF—JB

"I'm a-tellin' yo', mah bredren." See Oh, yes

I'm a-trav'ling to the grave. Negro spiritual. HR—NMP

"I'm bound away to leave you." See Goodbye, my love, goodbye

"I'm bound to Alabama." See Roll the cotton down

I'm busy to-day. S. C. Foster. Words by H. Snow. BSS

"I'm but a stranger here." See Heaven is my home (Sullivan)

"I'm called little Buttercup." A. Sullivan. WA—WBT—WSW

"I'm Captain Jinks, of the Horse Marines." See Captain Jinks

Im chinari yaru. See O my love, my plane-tree

"I'm dreaming now of Hallie." See Listen to the mocking-bird (Winner)

"I'm 'ere in a ticky ulster." See Back to the army again (Cobb)

"Im felde schleich ich still und wild." See Jägers nachtlied (Reichardt)

"Im finstern geh' ich suchen." See Blinde kuh (Brahms)

"Im föhrenwald alleine steht eine blume dort." See Die waldblume

Im frühling ("Es glänzt im abendsonnen golde."—In springtime) A. Fesca. Words by W. Viol. e.g. KF 1— KF 2

Im frühling ("Lieder gib mir") W. A. Mozart. Words by A. Franz. g. ED 3

Im frühling ("Die lust hat mich gezwungen") H. Albert. Words by S. Dach. g. ED 3

Im frühlinge ("O lieber, guter frühling") See Jägerleben (Hoffmann von Fallersleben)

"I'm glad I am a farmer." See The farmer

"I'm goin' lay down my sword an' shield." See Ain't goin' study war no more

"I'm going away to see the good old Daniel." See My ship is on the ocean

"I'm going to Georgia." Folk song from North Carolina. CSE

"I'm going to join the great 'sociation." See Oh, then my little soul's going to shine

"I'm going to live with Jesus." Negro spiritual. JP

I'm going to sing all the way. See Gwinter sing all along de way

"I'm going to sit at the welcome table." See Shine, shine

"I'm gwine away by the light of the moon." See In the morning by the bright light (Bland)

I'm gwine see my friends agin. Negro song. BOM

"I'm gwine to Alabamy." Negro folk song. KA

"I'm gwine to jine de great 'sociation." See Oh, then my little soul's gwine to shine

"I'm gwine to join the great 'sociation." See Oh, then my little soul's gwine to shine

Im haine (In the grove) F. Schubert. Words by Bruchmann. e.g. FM

Im halbschlaf. See Revery (Arenski)

"I'm Handy Jim from Caroline." See See Handy Jim

Im herbst (In autumn) R. Franz. Words by W. Müller. e.g. GM—KF 2— PG 4—SM 2

"I'm January, I bring good cheer." See The song of the months (Halsey)

"I'm just about the proudest man that walks." See Our little nipper (Chevalier)

Im kahne (In the boat) E. Grieg. Words by V. Krag. e.g. CMF 2—PG 1 In the boat. e. WBT—WBW

"Im kreise froher, kluger zecher" (Gesellschaftslied) Folk air. Words by Ludwig. g. ED 3

"Im kreise froher, kluger zecher" (Freiheit und gleichheit) K. Döbbelin. Words by Ludwig. g. ED 2

"Im krug zum grünen kranze." See Brüderschaft

"Im kühlen keller." See Der rheinweinzecher (Fischer)

Im lager von Akkon, 1190. See Biterolf (Wolf)

"I'm leaving thee." G. Barker. FSS 7

"I'm little Robin Redbreast." T. Marzials. FSS 7

"I'm lonesome since I crossed the hill." See The girl I left behind me

"I'm longing for Aooah." See Aooah (Lieurance)

I'm not myself at all. S. Lover (music and words) FSS 5
"Oh! I'm not myself at all." MMI—PI

I'm not quite of peasantry. See Je ne suis pas si vilaine

I'm o'er young, I'm o'er young. See I'm owre young to marry yet

"I'm oft at the sorry conclusion arriving." See The miller's man

"I'm often ask'd by plodding souls." See Reasons for drinking (Dibdin)

"Im Osterland kenn ich ein städtchen." See Das mädchen im Osterland

I'm owre young to marry yet. Scottish air. Words by R. Burns. BSB—MMS—PS 1
"I am my mammy's ae bairn." BSR

"I'm parish clerk and sexton here." See Caleb Quotem (Shield)

"I'm pass'd, I'm pass'd and capp'd at last." See Chancellor Inglis

"I'm Pierre de Bonton." See Rosalie (Knight)

"Im rosenduft." See "I rosens doft" (Gustaf)

I'm saddest when I sing. H. R. Bishop. Words by T. H. Bayly. FSS 6—JO—WBT

"Im schwarzen Walfisch zu Askalon." See Jonas

I'm seventeen come Sunday. Folk song. FSF—SEF 1—SO

"I'm sittin' on the stile, Mary." See Irish emigrant's lament (Dempster)

I'm so glad. Negro spiritual. JP—NMP

"Im sommer such' ein liebchen" ("In summer seek a sweetheart") C. Reinecke. e.g. MS

"Im sommer wie war da so grün der wald." See Herbststurm (Grieg)

"I'm sowing the rue, the mint and lily." See Sowing the rue

"I'm standing by the window sill." See When you and I were young (Allen)

"Im stillen, heitern glanze." See Der mond (Reichardt)

"I'm the girl of the seasons." See The girl of the seasons (Sanderson)

"I'm the man who can find it." See Gambling song

"I'm the pedlar! I'm the pedlar." See Autolycus' song (Greenhill)

"I'm the son of old Baciccia." See "Son figlio di Baciccia"

"I'm the spirit who denieth." See "Son lo spirito che nega" (Boito)

"Im tiefen keller sitz' ich hier." See Der rheinweinzecher (Fischer)

I'm troubled in mind. Negro spiritual. BMC—DF—JB—JP—WBT

"I'm very fond of a social song." FSS 4

I'm very fond of water. See A song of water (Drinkwater)

Im wald bei der amsel (At the nightingale's) Folk song. e.g. SSG

"Im wald, im wald." C. M. von Weber. Words by P. A. Wolff. g. ED 2

"Im wald und auf der heide." See Jägerleben

"I'm wearin' awa'." See The land o' the leal

I'm wild. Student song. BSS

"Im windsgeräusch in stiller nacht." See Lied der nacht (Reichardt)

I'm wukkin' on de levee. See Levee song

"Im wunderschönen monat mai" (The lovely month of May) R. Franz. Words by H. Heine. e.g. PG 1

"Im wunderschönen monat mai" (The month of May) R. Schumann. [Words by H. Heine] e.g. BS 2

"I'm your little dove, my darling." See La paloma blanca

Image, Selwyn
"The snow lies thick" (Shaw)
"Three kings in great glory" (Shaw)

Imanírta (Why, Creator) C. Valderrama, from Inca themes. Words by J. Duran. e.in.s. BF 2

Imayo. See Buddhist chant

"Imellem visne halmstraa." See Violen (Svendsen)

Imitation of a bagpipe. Student song. CHS

Imlah, John
Glad tidings (Luther)
Where Gadie rins (Scottish air)

Immer bei dir (Ever with thee) Raff. Words by Schleiden. e.g. PG 3
Immer bei dir ("In thy dear eyes") e.g. MSS 2

"Immer ging ich hin zum strande." Russian folk song. g. ED 3

"Immer langsam voran." See Der krähwinkler landsturm

"Immer leiser wird mein schlummer" ("E'en in slumber do I languish") J. Brahms. Words by H. Lingg. e.g.   PG 2

"Immer leiser wird mein schlummer" ("Lighter far is now my slumber") e.g.   FO 2—GM

"Immortal Babe, who this dear day." See For Christmas day

Impatience. See Ungeduld (Schubert)

"Imperial Solomon, thy pray'rs are heard." See Sacred raptures cheer my breast (Händel)

The impish little girl (Akh ty Khrist'ka, Khrist'ka chernen'kaîa) Russian folk song.   e.   SSR 3

"Improve the passing hours." See Merrily, merrily sing

The improvvisatore. See Er passagallo

"In a cavern, in a canyon." See Oh, my darling Clementine (Montrose)

"In a cavern in the forest." See Rinaldo Rinaldini

"In a cradle bright and golden." See Lullaby

"In a day that will be bye and bye." See N. S. U. so gay (Merrill)

In a foreign land. See In der fremde (Schumann)

"In a little white cottage." See Gentle Nettie Moore (Pike)

"In a manger He is lying." Polish carol. Tr of Wzlobia lezy ktoz po biezy.   e. MF

"In a manger lies the Child." See Ring the joyful Christmas bells (Peskett)

In a March-night. See In der märznacht (Taubert)

"In a shady forest, built two doves their nest." See The turtle dove

"In a shady nook one moonlight night." See The leprehaun

"In a simmer gloamin'." Gaelic air: Gu ma slan a chi mi. Words by W. Motherwell.   MMS

"In a small pleasant village by nature complete." See Sweet Nan of the vale (Arne)

In a strange land. See In der fremde (Taubert)

"In a valley far away." Irish air. Words by T. Davis.   MMI

"In a year, dearest maid, in a year." See "Ueber's jahr" (Bohm)

"In Aargau dwelt two sweethearts." See Die Aargauer lieben

In absence. M. Haydn. Words by P. Cary.   LBR

"In allen guten stunden." See Bundeslied (Reichardt)

"In Amsterdam there dwelt a maid." See A-roving

"In Amsterdam there lived a maid." See A-roving

"In armour bright rides forth a knight." See The red scarf (Bonheur)

"In Austria stands a noble castle." See "Der stander et slot i Oesterrige"

In autumn ("Die heide ist braun")   See Im herbst (Franz)

"In autumn when the roses fade." See Herbstfrühlingslied (Weil)

"In beautiful summer." See "Om sommaren sköna"

"In Berlin, sagt' er." Air: In Schönbrunn. Words by C. von Holtei.   g. ED 1

In Berlin sagt' er (The sailor)   e. GO

In Bethlehem geboren ("In Bethlehem, the lowly") 17th century Dutch carol.   e. MF

"In Bethl'hem of Judah."   C. Simper. Words by A. S. Woods.   HC

"In Bethlehem, that noble place."   F. A. G. Ouseley.   BSC—MCS

"In Bethlehem, the lowly." See In Bethlehem geboren

"In Bibberley town."   Folk air.   Modern words by H. F. Sheppard.   BSW

"In bloom was the meadow." See Millom rosor (Beyer)

In blossom-time.   A. A. Needham. Words by I. D. Coolbrith.   MSF 2

"In Boston town there lived a merchant." See "In Seaport town" (Carmen, N.C. version)

"In bright mansions above."   Negro spiritual.   HR

"In Brooklyn city there lived a maid." See Michael Roy

"In Bruton town there lived a farmer." See Bruton town

"In Car'lina's clime I spent a happy time." See My little valley home (Beckel)

"In cellar cool." See Der rheinweinzecher (Fischer)

"In childhood I dallied with sceptre and crown." See "Sonst spielt ich" (Lortzing)

"In childhood, with crown and with scepter I played." See "Sonst spielt ich" (Lortzing)

"In class-room cold I sit and con." See Grinding (Fischer)

"In coffins they were hurried." See Blaris moor

"In coming by the brig o' Dye." See Theniel Menzie's bonnie Mary

"In Concord and in Lexington." See For Patriots' day

"In Cuba, lovely isle." See Tú (Fuentes)

"In Cuba, the isle of the beautiful sun." See Tú (Fuentes)

In dat great gittin-up mornin'. See In that great getting-up morning

"In David's town was born a maid." See De boodschap van Maria

"In days gone by when I've heard tell." See Das pfäfflein (Schäffer)

"In days of grief and sorrow." See His love shines over all (Forbes)

"In days of old, when knights were bold." See A warrior bold (Maybrick)

In days of yore ("Högre mot sanden") See Det var då (Kjerulf)

"In days of yore, from Britain's shore." See The maple leaf forever (Muir)

"In days of yore the hero Wolfe." See The maple leaf forever (Muir)

In de mornin'. Negro forecastle song. CR

"In deine augen will ich schauen." See Immer bei dir (Raff)

"In deinen blicken sich's wie wellenschlag regt." See The siren (Grechaninov)

"In dem Beishamikdosh, in a vinkl cheider." See Raisins and almonds

"In dem goldnen strahl über berg und tal." See Dem vogel in der luft (Harder)

"In dem schatten meiner locken" ("In the shadow of my tresses") H. Wolf. Words from an anonymous Spanish poet. e.g. CMF 2

"In dem wilden kriegestanze." See Auf Scharnhorsts tod

In der ferne ("Einsam? einsam? nein, das bin ich nicht") C. M. von Weber. Words by T. Hell. g. ED 2

In der ferne ("Nun leb wohl du kleine gasse nun ade") F. Silcher. Words by Albert graf Schlippenbach. g. ED 1

In der ferne (Far from home) e.g. SSG

In der ferne ("Wehe dem fliehenden welt hinnaus ziehenden."—Afar) F. Schubert. Words by L. Rellstab. e.g. FM

In der ferne ("Will ruhen unter den bäumen hier") C. Kreutzer. Words by L. Uhland. g. ED 2

In der fremde ("Aus der heimath hinter den blitzen roth."—In a foreign land) R. Schumann. e.g. PG 2

In der fremde ("Es steht ein baum in jenem thal."—In a strange land) W. Taubert. Words by Hoffmann von Fallersleben. e.g. MSS 1

"Es steht ein baum in jenem thal" (In a strange land) e.g. CS 2—SS 2

In der fremde (My darling was so fair) e.g. KF 1

In der frühe (Morning) H. Wolfe. Words by E. Mörike. e.g. FO 2

"In der liebe Götterwelt." See Heutzutage (André)

In der märznacht (In a March-night) W. Taubert. e.g. KF 1

In des lebens frühlingstagen (In life's day of springtime beauty) L. van Beethoven. e.g. KS 4

"In des waldes finstern gründen." See Rinaldo Rinaldini

In die ferne ("Siehst du im abend") F. Glück. Words by H. Kletke. g. ED 2

"In diesen heil'gen hallen" ("Within this hallow'd dwelling") W. A. Mozart. e.g. SOA 5

"In diesen heil'gen hallen" ("Within this sacred dwelling") e.g. KS 5

"In diesen heil'gen hallen" ("Qui sdegno."—"Within these sacred bowers") e.g.i. BS 1

"In diesen heil'gen hallen" ("Qui sdegno non s'accende."—"To scenes of peace retiring") e.g.i. AB 1

"Qui sdegno non s'accende" ("Within these sacred bowers") e.i. OPS 4

"Within this sacred dwelling." e. FSS 5

"In dieser stunde" ("This very hour") M. Spicker. Words by R. Prutz. e.g. SM 3

"In distant land." See "In fernem land" (Wagner)

"In Doncaster there dwelt a lass." See Maid of Doncaster

"In dreams I had a vision fair." See Ein traum (Grieg)

"In dreams I saw thy face so fair." See "Dein angesicht" (Schumann)

"In dreams I've heard the angels." See Sancta Maria (Faure)

"In Dublin's fair city." See Cockles and mussels (Yorkston)

"In dulci jubilo." 14th century air, arr by R. L. de Pearsall. e. BOS—DC—HC

"In early youth to fear a stranger." See The tar's sheet anchor (Reeve)

"In eighteen hundred and fifty-three, I sailed away beyond the sea." See Railway

"In eighteen hundred and sixty-one the Yankee war it was begun." See John Brown

"In eighty-eight, ere I was born." See The Spanish Armada

"In einem kühlen grunde" (The broken ring.—Mill of the valley) German folk air. Words by J. von Eichendorff. e.g. KF 4

"In einem kühlen grunde" (Das zerbrochene ringlein) L. Berger. Words by J. von Eichendorff. g. ED 3

"In einem kühlen grunde" (Das zerbrochene ringlein) After F. Glück. Words by J. von Eichendorff. g. ED 1

The broken ring. e.g. EF. e. only BSE—WBT—WL

Das zerbrochene ringlein (The broken ring) e.g. BO—SSG—SSS. e. only FSS 2

"In einem tal bei armen hirten." See Das mädchen aus der fremde (Grosheim)

"In ev'ry land an angel." See The children's angel

In every port a wife. C. Dibdin (music and words) ME

In excelsis gloria ("Christ is born") See "Christ is born of Maiden fair" (Thibaut IV)

In excelsis gloria ("Not in halls of regal splendor") Welsh air. FSS 8—MCS

"In far-off land, to mortal feet forbidden." See "In fernem land" (Wagner)

"In father's lovely garden." See La marchande d'oranges

"In fernem land" ("In distant land") R. Wagner. e.g. KS 4—OPS 3

"In fernem land" ("In far-off land") e.g. SOA 3

"In flakes of a feathery white." See Silently falling snow

"In former days, which many praise." See Co-education (Cole)

"In frischer luft und sonnenschein." See Feld- und waldlied (Kunzen)

"In Frisco bay." Pulling chantey. SE

In front of old Pardee. Lafayette college song. W. C. Stier (music and words) CHS

"In gay Seville, long, long ago." See The bells of Seville (Jude)

"In gentle murmurs will I mourn." Händel. OS 2

"In good King Charles's golden days." See The vicar of Bray

In Gorensko ("Na Gorenskem je fletno") Carniolan folk song. e.sl. BF 1

"In grüner landschaft sommerflor." See Auf ein altes bild (Wolf)

"In happy moments day by day." W. V. Wallace. FSS 3—WA—WBT—WSC —WSW

"In health are the days of the hunter abounding." See Huntsman's chorus (Weber)

"In heaven a spirit doth dwell." See Israfel (King)

"In heav'n above, when the angels small." See "I himlen" (Selmer)

"In heavenly love abiding." Composer unknown. Words by A. L. Waring. LA

"In heavenly love abiding." J. Bensel. Words by A. L. Waring. LA

"In heavenly love abiding." H. L. von Hassler. Words by A. L. Waring. DO

Heavenly love abiding. DSH

"In heavenly love abiding." F. Mendelssohn. [Words by A. L. Waring] WBT—WS

"In heaven's vault above me." See Sorgen

"In her kitchen-garden wanders Masha fair and slender." See In the kitchen-garden

"In her youth went the maiden forth." See Martha's song (Musorgskiĭ)

"In hilly Silesia there grows a wine." See Der schlesische zecher und der teufel (Reissiger)

"In holiday gown." See I'd wed, if I were not too young (Irish air); I'd wed if I were not too young (Wicks)

"In hours of deep discouragement." See Prayer (Liszt)

"In infancy." Arne. BE 6

"In Ischia there are not so many fans." See "A Ischia no nce so tanta ventaglie"

"In January last." 17th century air. Words by D'Urfey. CO 2

"In jedes haus, wo liebe wohnt." See Liebesglück (Weber)

"In Klagenfurt's fair valley." See Our valley

In Kraakalund. See Kraakalund

"In Lauterbach hab' i mein'n strump verloren." See Zu Lauterbach

In life's day of springtime beauty. See In des lebens frühlingstagen (Beethoven)

"In life's hours of gloom and sadness." See Sing thou, sing (Järnefelt)

In Limbo. Old English air. BE 2

"In London far city a lady did dwell." See The cruel ship's carpenter (Harlan county, Ky. version)

"In London sweet city a fair damsel did dwell." See The cruel ship's carpenter (Tennessee version)

"In lonely cot, by Humberside." See The lass of Humberside (Blewitt)

In lonely moments. See "I ensomme stunde" (Bull)

"In lovely August last." See The glancing of her apron

"In low'ring gloom and cloudiness." E. Handley. HC

"In Mantua in fetters." See Andreas Hofer

"In Mauchline there dwells six proper young belles." Air: Bonie Dundee. Words by R. Burns. BSR

"In May fifteen hundred and eighty and eight." See The Spanish Armada (Arnold)

"In May, in May." German folk air. Words by R. Compton. DO

"In meadow and in garden." G. E. Oliver. LA

"In Meadville high upon a hill." See Old Allegheny

"In meinem herzchen." See "Deep hidden in my heart" (Arenski)

In memoriam ("Flow'rs from the shady greenwood dell") Bohemian folk air. Words by H. H. Harbour. DO

In memoriam ("Though from us thou sever") G. Rossini. Words by J. Troutbeck. HSS 2—HSS 4

In merry chorus. J. Offenbach. FSS 5— MCS

"In merry Scotland, in merry Scotland." See Henry Martyn

"In mia man alfin tu sei" ("Where are now the hopes I cherished") V. Bellini. e.i. FSS 4

In mirrored waters. Sioux Indian song. T. Lieurance. e.in. LS

In my attic (V' tchetuiryókh styenákh) M. P. Moussorgsky. Words by A. Golenishtcheff-Kutoozoff. e. SMR 1

In my beloved's eyes. G. W. Chadwick. Words by W. M. Chauvenet. AA

"In my breast I find no hope of assuaging." See "El tormento de amor"

In my dreams ("Noriu miego") Lithuanian folk dance. e.li. BF 1

"In my garden grew plenty of thyme." See The sprig of thyme (Devon version)

In my gondola I lie. See Quattro cavai

In my home, my fair home. See Princess Kaiulani's home (Likelike)

"In my native land a dear love had I." See Chanson slave (Chaminade)

"In my song no graces lie that know I." See The smith (Koreshchenko)

"In my soul's inner garden." See La splendeur vide (Saint-Saëns)

In my spring of life. See Della vita in sull' aurora (Beethoven)

"In my swift boat." J. Concone. FSS 6

"In my youth I loved well." See "I min ungdom så gladde mig att sjunga"

"In natali Domini." Traditional Christmas carol. 14th century air. 1. HC

In natali Domini. For English translation with a different air see "On the birthday of the Lord" (Dykes)

"In native worth and honour clad." J. Haydn. e. OS 3—SAS 3—TL—TS

"In northern zone a beauteous land is lying." See Sang for Danske (Weyse)

"In Nottingham there lives a jolly tanner." See Arthur-a-Bland

In old Madrid. H. Trotère. Words by C. Bingham. FMB—HSD—NML—WA—WBT—WSW

"In old North Carolina I was bred and was born." See The wagoner's lad (Hot Springs, N.C. version)

"In olden times a king." See "Dae va eigöng en kung'e"

"In our happy village." See "Dans notre village" (Lefebvre)

"In our little bark we glide." WBT

"In pantaloons and waistcoats." See The golden glove

"In Paris there are o'er." See La bergère de France et le roi d'Angleterre

"In Paris there's a little brunette." See Cette aimable tourterelle

"In Paris there's a maiden brown." See La brune et le brigand

"In passing by a hedgerow tall." See "En passant par un échalier"

"In Perth there lived a bonny lad." See The cobbler laddie

"In Plymouth town there lived a maid." See A-roving

"In praise of a dairy." See The dairymaid

In praise of ale. 17th century song. MM "When the chill charokoe blows." DM 2

In praise of dear old Greer. Greer college song. CHS

In praise of old De Pauw. De Pauw university song. C. Langlotz. CHS

"In praise of the useful plough." See The useful plough

"In pursuit of a lass." See Betty Brown

"In pursuit of some lambs." See Labour in vain

"In questa tomba oscura." L. van Beethoven. Words by G. Carpani. i. KF 2—KF 4

"In questa tomba oscura" ("In this sepulchral darkness") e.i. AB 1

"In questa tomba oscura" ("Mark yonder tomb") e.i. CS 1

In questo semplice modesto asilo. For English translation see "Poor tho' my cot may be" (Donizetti)

"In readiness of mind to the field we go." Indian ritual air. e. FI

"In returning from pretty Rochelle." See "En revenant de la joli' Rochelle"

"In runic measure, full and strong." See "Ur svenska hjertans" (Lindblad)

"In sad and ashy weeds." 16th century song. CO 1

"In safety! Heav'n, I thank thee." See Madre, pietosa Vergine (Verdi)

"In Scarlet town, where I was born." See Barbara Allen

"In Scotland I was born and bred." See Barbara Allen

"In Scotland there liv'd a humble beggar." See The humble beggar

"In Seaport town." Folk song: Allanstand, N.C. version. CSE
—Alleghany, N.C. version. CSE
—Carmen, N.C. version. CSE
—Hot Springs, N.C. version. CSE

In search of a wife. 18th century song. MM

In shadowland ("I think of you") L. Denza. Words by G. Hubi-Newcombe. SM 4

In shadowland ("She sits alone") C. Pinsuti. FSS 6

"In sì barbara." G. Rossini. e.i. SOA 2

"In silence fall the evening shadows." See Le soir (Gounod)

In silent woods (V' tiómnoi róshtchye zamólk salavyéi) N. Rimsky-Korsakoff. Words by Nikitin. e. SMR 2

"In simmer, when the hay was mawn." Air: The country lass. Words by R. Burns. BSR

In solitude. See La solitaire (Saint-Saëns)

"In somma il falso io sono." See Te voglio bene assaje

"In sorrow and anguish day and night." See Albaÿde (Widor)

"In sorrow and in want." J. F. Bridge. Words by Farrar. HC

"In South Car'lina de darkies go." See Kemo kimo

In springtime ("Es glänzt") See Im frühling (Fesca)

In springtime ("Ya viene la primavera") See La primavera

"In springtime one day." See Pastorale (Bizet)

"In stiller wehmut, in sehnsuchtstränen." See An die freundschaft (Haydn)

"In storms when clouds obscure the sky." See Lashed to the helm (Hook)

"In summer fields." See Feldeinsamkeit (Brahms)

"In summer seek a sweetheart." See "Im sommer such' ein liebchen" (Reinecke)

"In summer the woods are so green, so green." See Herbststurm (Grieg)

"In summer time when days are long." Air: A-roving. FSF

"In summer time when flow'rs do spring." Air: Sellenger's round. Traditional words. JE
Oh, how they frisk it (Leather apron.— Under the greenwood tree) CO 2

"In summer time when flow'rs do spring" (Under the greenwood tree) Old English air. Traditional words. BE 7

"In sunlit paths did we meet." See Le sais-tu bien (Pierné)

"In surprise all our army fled away like women." See Le front dans la poussière (Joncières)

"In Tapscott's line we're bound to shine." See The Black Ball line (Capstan chantey)

"In tempus old a hero lived." See The polyglot's wooing (Lozier)

In terra pax. J. B. Dykes. Words by Alderson. BSC

In that great getting-up morning. Negro spiritual. JP
In dat great gittin-up mornin'. HR

In that morning, my Lord. See I'll hear the trumpet sound

"In that pure flame." See "Nel puro ardor" (Peri)

"In the Alfold's circle fisherman am I." See The fisherman

In the battle, fame pursuing. Händel. e. OS 2—SAS 2

"In the bleak midwinter." T. B. Strong. Words by C. G. Rossetti. HC

In the boat. See Im kahne (Grieg)

"In the bright candle light." See Lords and ladies

In the camp of Akkon, 1190. See Biterolf (Wolf)

"In the caverns deep of the ocean cold." See The diver (Loder)

In the chimney corner. F. H. Cowen. Words by F. E. Weatherly. FMB— KF 2—SM 2

"In the Christian's home in glory." See Rest for the weary (Dadmun); Rest for the weary (McDonald)

"In the country nigh to Bethlehem." G. Hine. Words by K. Bartlett. BSC— HC

"In the dark of the winter." See Valentines

"In the days of old." Harrow song. Air: Trelawny. LA

"In the days of yore, there sat at his door." See The cottage well thatched with straw

"In the dreamy wood I wander." See "Wandl' ich in dem wald des abends" (Franz)

"In the dungeon have I languish'd." See The outlaw

"In the early morning, early." W. Borrow. Words by F. G. Lee. HC

"In the early morning early" (Christmas morning) G. E. Oliver. Words by F. G. Lee. HC

"In the evening by the moonlight." See Southern memories

"In the field with their flocks abiding." J. Farmer. Words by F. W. Farrar. HC

"In the fields, in the fields" (Vo luzíakh) Russian folk song. e. SSR 3

In the firelight. English folk air. Words by H. H. Harbour. DO

"In the flick'ring light." See The soldier's dream (Rodney)

"In the flow'ry month of May." See The cottage maid (Dillon)

In the foggy dew. H. W. Loomis. HST

In the forest ("Es ist schon spät") See Waldesgespräch (Schumann)

"In the forest, lonely." Ojibway Indian song. e. BA
Forest song. in. BA

"In the forest, the deep forest" ("Erdő, erdő, sürü erdő") Hungarian song. e.hu. BF 1

"In the garb of old Gaul." G. Reid. Words by Erskine. PS 1—SSS

"In the garden at early morning." See Volksliedchen (Schumann)

"In the gloaming little children." [A. F. Harrison;] wrongly attributed to J. L. Molloy. Words adapted. WSC

"In the gloaming, oh, my darling." A. F. Harrison. Words by M. Orred. FSS 4—HSC— HSD—JSE— NMH— NML— OH— WA— WBT— WL— WSW

In the golden eventide. C. Pinsuti. Words by M. Mark-Lemon. FSS 5

"In the green boughs on the tree-top." See Birdie in the cradle (Abt)

"In the green valley thou'rt lingering yonder." See Wilt thou soon return (Rocke)

In the grove. See Im haine (Schubert)

"In the hallowed manger." T. Adams. Words by R. E. Adderley. HC

"In the hazel dell my Nelly's sleeping." See The hazel dell (Root)

"In the heart of ev'ry scout." See Tramp, tramp, tramp (Root)

"In the heaven earth reposes." See Goodnight (Raff)

"In the hour of trial." Words by J. Montgomery. LA

"In the hush of the dreamy twilight." See Ferryman John (Rodney)

"In the hut you see, dear." See The tiny hut

In the kingdom. Negro spiritual. HR

In the kitchen-garden (Vo sadu li v ogordíe) Russian folk song. e. SSR 2
"In the orchard, in the garden" ("Vo sadu li, v ogorodíe") e.r. BF 1

In the kolo ("Igra kolo") Croatian dance. e.se. BF 1

In the land of my birth. J. Harroway. Words by C. Jefferys. FSS 8

"In the language of love." See "Faites-lui mes aveux" (Gounod)

"In the little village of Bethlehem." See The birthday of a King (Neidlinger)

"In the lonely midnight." A. P. Howard. Words by T. C. Williams. HC

In the Louisiana lowlands. Negro song. NMP

In the meadow ("Es wear'n die wies'n grüen") See Das Seiser almlied

"In the meadow wide and green beyond the lane." See The girl who would not dance

"In the meadows fair, thro' lanes so shady." See Ritournelle (Chaminade)

"In the merry month of May." See Phillida and Corydon (Wilson)

"In the midst of rolling prairies." See Alma mater—Greenville

"In the month of February." See A valentine

"In the month of hot July." See July song (Scott-Gatty)

"In the month of November." See The hunting of Arscott of Tetcott

In the morning by the bright light. J. A. Bland (music and words) WC

"In the morning of life." Air: The little harvest rose. Words by T. Moore. MI

"In the name of heaven." See Los peregrinos

In the night, a longing. See Dear heart (Nape)

"In the night my babe was taken." See "L'altra notte in fondo al mare" (Boito)

"In the night so plainly seeming." See Dear heart (Nape)

"In the North sea liv'd a whale." See The torpedo and the whale (Audran)

In the open. See In's freie (Schumann)

"In the orchard, in the garden." See In the kitchen-garden

"In the peaceful ev'ning time." See The bells of Aberdovey

"In the pleasant month of May." See The country fair

"In the prison cell I sit." See Tramp! tramp! tramp (Root)

"In the quarries should you toil." See Make your mark

"In the river of Jordan." Negro spiritual. JP

"In the sad month of October." See October song (Scott-Gatty)

"In the secret of His presence how my soul delights to hide." G. C. Stebbins. Words by E. L. Goreh. OH

"In the secret of His presence I am kept from strife of tongues." G. E. Oliver. Words by H. Burton. LA

"In the shade of the garden strolling." See The bridegroom's plea

"In the shadow of my tresses." See "In dem schatten meiner locken" (Wolf)

"In the shady woods." See "Aux échos des bois"

In the silence of the night (V' moltchányi nótchi táïnoi) S. Rachmaninoff. Words by Fet. e. SMR 2

"In the silent hours, the hour of midnight." See Media noche

"In the silver moonlight." See "Au clair de la lune"

"In the sky the bright stars glittered." See The quilting party

"In the sombre forest glade." See Near Krakow

"In the star of morning." R. F. Smith. Words by G. P. Grantham. HC

"In the starlight." S. Glover. Words by J. E. Carpenter. FSS 2

"In the still night, the long hours through." See My bark canoe

In the sugar camp. Ojibway Indian song. e.in. BA

In the sweet by and by. See Sweet by-and-by (Webster)

"In the tall boughs on the tree-top." See Birdie in the cradle (Abt)

"In the time of roses." See Hoffnung (Reichardt)

In the tomb. S. Vassilenko. Words from the Russian of V. Bruce. e. NM 2

"In the tower tolling." See The old college clock in the tower (Arthur)

"In the tow'r and spire were ringing." See Lincoln's birthday

"In the vale, oh! in the valley." See A child's song (Musorgskiĭ)

"In the valley, ah! in the fountain's pool." See Două fete spală lână

"In the west the sun declining." See Good night (Abt)

"In the wigwam with Nokomis." See The death of Minnehaha (Converse)

"In the wild chamois track." See The Alpine horn (Rimbault)

"In the wilderness untrammelled." See "En los montes más remotos"

"In the wintry heaven." R. F. Smith. Words by R. R. Chope. HC

"In the wood a boy one day." See The wild rose

"In the woods Myrtil when in love." See Vieille chanson (Bizet)

"In the woods the trees, the trees are gay." See Polka

"In the world live I all lonely." See La guajira

"In the world's, in the world's crooked path where I've been." See A smile from the girl of my heart (Shield)

"In thine ears my sorrow pouring." See "In sì barbara" (Rossini)

"In this calm sheltered villa." Irish air: The Irish hautboy. e. MMI

"In this old chair my father sat." M. W. Balfe. Words by E. Fitzball. BE 4 —HSE 3

"In this sepulchral darkness." See "In questa tomba oscura" (Beethoven)

"**In** this sheltered mossy dell." See The fairies' dance (Glover)

"**In** thorny woods in Buckinghamshire." See The poacher's song

"**In** those lonely moments." See "I en-somme stunde" (Bull)

"**In** thousand shaded valleys." See Sleep, comrades, sleep (Marshall)

"**In** thy dear eyes." See Immer bei dir (Raff)

In thy dreams. D. Buck. Words from the German. e. HST

"**In** Vaenor's peaceful glade, Mary dear." Air: Mentra Gwen. Words from the Welsh. e. MMW

"**In** vain I seek you blindfold." See Blinde kuh (Brahms)

"**In** vain upon the pathway." See "För-gäfves uppå stigen"

"**In** verdant landscape, summer's mead." See Auf ein altes bild (Wolf)

"**In** winter, when it's raining." See "Des winters als het reghent"

"**In** winter when the fields are white." See When fields are white

"**In** winter, when the rain rain'd cauld." See Tak' your auld cloak about ye

"**In** winter, when the wind I hear." See The four winds (Marshall)

"**In** woods and on the heather." See The huntsman

"**In** ye days when ye salvages lived in ye land." See Vive le capitaine John

"**In** yonder vale there stands a tree." See In der fremde (Taubert)

"**In** yonder valley, there dwelt alone." See The mountain sprite

"**In** yonders town where I was born." See Barbara Allen

"**In** youth when I did love" (The aged lover) Traditional air. Words by Lord de Vaux. DM 2
"I loathe that I did love." ɾWords modified₎ CO 1

"**In** youth when I did love." 16th century air. Words by Lord de Vaux. JE

"**In** zou' in zène criole Candjo." See Criole Candjo

"**Incarnate** Jesus Christ be praised." See Kyrie eleison

The **incarnation.** See "The great God of heaven"

Inching along. Negro spiritual. DF—NMP
Variant of: Keep a-inchin' along

Incógnito. Spanish American song. s. LCP
Variant of: El galan incógnito

The **incognito** gallant. See El galan in-cógnito

An **inconstant** lover. Kentucky mountain song. WT

"**Indeed,** I would not sorrow." See "Och inte vill jag sörja"

Independence day. L. Oehmler. Words by Veazie. NMS

The **independent** farmer. G. F. Root. Words by W. W. Fosdick. HSD

La **India.** Mexican folk song. s. HS

Indian bell song. See "Où va la jeune Indoue" (Delibes)

The **Indian** coquet (Song of the Indian co-quet) Omaha Indian song. in. FIS

"An **Indian** girl was sitting." See The Indian girl's lament (Mendelssohn)

The **Indian** girl's lament. Arr from F. Mendelssohn-Bartholdy. Words by L. H. Bryant. LBR

The **Indian** hunter. H. Russell. Words by E. Cook. FSS 7

Indian love. See Canoe song (Lieurance)

Indian lullaby. See Wi-um (Lieurance)

The **Indian** maid. J. L. Hatton. Words by N. Crosland. TL

Indian serenade. See "O come, my love, with me to-night"

Indian song ("A-ha! hi-a-ha") Song of the Dakota tribe. e. BSS—GO

Indian taffeta ("Tafta Hindī") Syrian folk song. ar.e. BF 2

Indian trail song. H. W. Loomis. Words by A. Chapman. BSS

Indy, Vincent d'
Lied maritime
Madrigal dans le style ancien
Madrigal in the old manner. See Madrigal dans le style ancien
A sea song. See Lied maritime

"**Infant** of days, yet Lord of life." See In terra pax (Dykes)

"**Infant** so gentle." Gascon carol. Tr of Qu'il est amiable. e. HC
Gascon carol. e. DC

Infelice ("Lone and joyless") Mendelssohn. e.i. SS 2

Infelice! e tu credevi. G. Verdi. e.i. SOA 5
Infelice! e tu credevi (Hapless Silva, whilst thou believing) e.i. OPS 4

"**Infelice!** già dal mio sguardo si deliguò." See Infelice (Mendelssohn)

Infelice sconsolata (Lonely, reft and bro-ken-hearted.—"Non paventar") W. A. Mozart. ɾTr of Zum leiden bin ich auserkohren₎ e.i. MC

"**Infida!** il dì che brami e questo" ("So, traitress! my fondest love thou art spurning") Verdi. e.i. OPS 3

Ingalls, Jeremiah
"Come, ye sinners, poor and needy"
Garden. See When we arrive at home
"The golden ray"
When we arrive at home

Ingelow, Jean
Christmas waits (Bellini)
O fair dove, O fond dove (Scott-Gatty)
"O night of nights" (Composer un-known)
"One morning, oh, so early" (Scott-Gatty)
"Over the green downs" (Composer unknown)
Song of seven ₍Composer unknown)
"When I remember" (Scott-Gatty)

Ingemann, Bernhard Severin
"Through the night of doubt and sorrow" (Paine. Tr of Igjennem nat og traengsel)
"**Ingemisco** tamquam reus" ("Sadly groaning") Verdi. e.l. OS 3
"**Ingerid** Sletten." A. Söderman. Words by B. Björnson. e.n. SSN
Ingham, John Hall
"Land of our hearts" (Chadwick)
Ingle, Charles
My old Dutch
The **ingle** side. T. V. Wiesenthal. Words by H. Ainslie. FSS 1—JO—WBT
Ingmire, Katharine
"Ring out, ring out, O Christmas bells" (Roper)
Ingraham, George
"The owl and the pussy cat"
L'**ingrat** ne vient pas encore (My faithless lover is forgetting) French Canadian folk song. e.f. BFS
Ingrid's song. See Jngrids vise (Kjerulf)
"The **Injian** ocean sets an' smiles." See For to admire (Cobb)
"**Inmitten** des balles." See At the ball (Tchaikovsky)
The **inn.** See Das wirtshaus (Schubert)
Innes, J. W. Brodie-. See Brodie-Innes, J. W.
Innisfail. E. C. Phelps. Words by T. C. Latto. FSS 4—LA—WBT
Inno di guerra dei cacciatori delle Alpi (Garibaldi's hymn) Attributed to A. Olivieri. Words by L. Mercantini. e.i. SN
The Garibaldi hymn. e.i. NA. e. only CST
Garibaldi's war hymn. e.i. BSP—MP—NMH. e. only BD—WBT
Italian national hymn. e. HSD
Italian national hymn (Inno di guerra dei cacciatori delle Alpi.—Garibaldi's hymn) e.i. WCP
National hymn of Italy. e. MP—NMS
War hymn of Garibaldi. e.i. WA. e. only BMC
"He **inoa** keia no Paahana." See Hawaiian hula (Paahana) (Hopkins)
He **inoa** keia no Waipio. See "Thou art always the same to me, dear" (Hopkins)
The **inquiry.** C. Gorrin. Words by C. Mackay. JO
The **inquisitive** lover. Kentucky mountain song. WT
In's freie (In the open) R. Schumann. Words by W. von der Neun. e.g. GM
L'**insana** parola. G. Verdi. e.i. SOA 1
"**Insensate!** to believe that I can love." See "Bethörte! die an meine liebe glaubt" (Weber)
The **insignia** of thunder (Putting on the insignia of the thunder god) Omaha Indian song. in. FIS

Inspirez-moi. C. Gounod. e.f. SOA 3
Inspirez-moi (Lend me your aid) e.f. KS 4—OPS 3
Lend me your aid. e.f. TS
"**Instant** charmant où la crainte fait trève." See Le rêve (Massenet)
Instantis adventum Dei. For English translation see Thy King cometh (Nägeli)
Institute song ("Now we'll celebrate") CHS
"**Integer** vitae." F. F. Flemming. Words by Q. Horatius Flaccus. l. BOS—CHS— CU—ED 1—ED 2—FSS 6—MPC—SSS—TFC 2—WBT—WC. e.l. HSD—LA
Integer vitae ("Night shadows falling."—The man of upright life) F. F. Flemming. Words by A. T. Russell. TFC 2
Integer vitae ("Night shadows falling") TL
Integer vitae ("O holy Saviour") F. F. Flemming. Words by C. Elliott. JS
The **interrupted** serenade. P. Stair (music and words) CHS
"**Into** the silent room the moon." See The river's message (Braun)
"**Into** the sunshine, full of the light." See The fountain (German air); The fountain (Hadley)
"**Into** the woods my Master went." See The trees and the Master (McCaskey)
"**Intorno** all' idol mio" ("About my beloved idol") M. Cesti. e.i. FEI 1
"Intorno all' idol mio" ("Caressing mine idol's pillow") e.i. PA 1
"Intorno all' idol mio" ('Round thee, my idol) e.i. PG 3
Ka **inu** wai. See Kohala's breezes (Nape)
"Un **invariable** tema se repite en mi arpa." See El arpa triste
The **invincible** Armado. Arnold. Words by J. O'Keefe. BE 5
The **invitation** ("I have a cottage by the hill") Swabian folk air. Words by J. W. L. Gleim. [Tr of Das hüttchen] e. BMC
The **invitation** ("Mon enfant, ma soeur") See L'invitation au voyage (Duparc)
L'**invitation** au voyage (The invitation) H. Duparc. Words by C. Baudelaire. e.f. CM 1
L'invitation au voyage (Invitation to the journey) e.f. SAM
Invitation to the journey. See L'invitation au voyage (Duparc)
Invocation ("All that springeth") Omaha Indian air. e. FI
The **invocation** ("Bright fairies by Glengariff's bay") Irish air: Planxty Power. Words by T. Davis. MMI
Invocation ("Mes yeux pleuraient en rêve") G. d'Hardelot. Words after Heine. [Tr of Ich hab' im traum geweinet] e.f. SOS 2
Invocation ("Now 'tis time") See To Russia (Balakirev)

Invocation ("Signor, cui sempre loda")
See Invocazione a Dio (Mariani)
Invocation ("Tu me parles") C. M. Widor.
Words by V. Hugo. e.f. AB 2—
PG 4
Invocation ("Voici donc les débris") See
Nonnes qui reposez (Meyerbeer)
Invocation of Orpheus. See Invocazione
di Orfeo (Peri)
Invocazione a Dio (Invocation) A. Mariani.
Words by D. Capellina. e.i. AB 3—
HSS 4
Invocazione di Orfeo (Invocation of Or-
pheus) J. Peri. e.i. FEI 1
"Io la vidi a Piedigrotta." See La vera
Sorrentina
"Io ti lascio, o cara, adio." See Adieu
(Mozart)
"Iomraibh, iomraibh, iomraibh, illean"
(Love boat song) Gaelic song. e.ga.
SMW
I-ou'-tin game song. Indian air. e. FI
I-ou'-tin game song: Song for the north
side. Indian air. in. FI
I-ou'-tin game song: Song for the south
side. Indian air. in. FI
I-ou'-tin game song: Victory song. Indian
song. in. FI
Ipiddinisca sutta li to' finestri ("Beneath
thy windows") Sicilian folk song. e.i.
BF 2
Ippolitov-Ivanov, Mikhail Mikhaïlovich
Adieu. See Parting
"Far on the road we two journeyed to-
gether"
"Once there lived a king"
Parting
Romance
Ireland, John
"Full fathom five"
Iris ("Schön sind rosen und jasmin")
Words by C. F. Weisse. g. ED 2
The **Irish** christening. D. Maguinnis.
WC
Irish emigrant's lament. W. R. Dempster.
Words by H. S. Sheridan (Lady
Dufferin) FSS 7—WBT
The lament of the Irish emigrant. JO
The **Irish** girl. Folk song: Irish version.
JOI
—Hampshire version. SF 3
Irish love song. See "Would God I were
the tender apple blossom"
Irish lullaby ("I'll put you myself, my
baby! to slumber") Irish song. e.
MMI
Irish lullaby ("Oh, to and fro on my bosom
of love") A. A. Needham. Words by
F. A. Fahy. MSF 2
Irish Molly-O. Irish folk song. JOI
An **Irish** Noël. See Noël d'Irlande
(Holmès)
The **Irish** peasant to his mistress ("Through
grief and through danger") Air: I once
had a true love. Words by T. Moore.
MI
Irish war song. See "Bright sun, before
whose glorious ray"

Irmer, W.
"I know not what the future hath"
Irons, Herbert Stephen
"Christians, carol sweetly"
"Gently falls the winter snow"
"Hark! bright angels sweetly sing"
"O let us all, rejoicing"
"The pearly gates aside are rolled"
"Sing the carol! raise your voices"
"When Christ was born of pure Marie"
(Tr of Christo paremus canticam,
excelsis gloria)
Irons, William Josiah
"Glory to God in the highest is ring-
ing" (music by Mendèlssohn;
Smith)
"Joy of joys! He lives, He lives"
(Sheppard)
"O sing we a carol" (Brown)
"Sing with all the sons of glory" (Cus-
tance)
Irwin, John
Autumn song (Bohemian folk air)
Echo song (German folk air)
The Fourth of July (German air)
Happy New Year (French folk air)
"I had a little sail-boat" (French folk
air)
On a frosty morning (French folk air)
"Is grád le m'anam mo páisdín fionn." See
Páisdín fionn
"Is it an elf, or is't a woman." See La fille
aux oiseaux (Dancla)
"Is it far beyond the mind's dreaming."
See Heart's desire
Is it thou who hast sullied. See Eri tu che
macchiavi (Verdi)
"Is it to try me." See The lovers' contro-
versy (Carey)
"Is it true, then." Hungarian song. e.
KSE—WL
Is master going to sell us to-morrow. See
Massa gwine to sell us to-morrow
"Is not His word like a fire." F. Mendels-
sohn. e. SAS 4
"Is not the life more than meat." See
Consider the lilies (Topliff)
"Is on earth another love like mine." Sla-
vonian song. e. KSE—SN
"Is that fair day no more by thee re-
member'd." See "Willst jenes tag's du
nicht dich mehr entsinnen" (Wagner)
"Is the swineherd now at home." Hun-
garian song. e. KSE
"Is there a heart that never lov'd." Bra-
ham. HSE 2
"Is there a heart which saucy love" (Mexi-
can song) e. BMC
"Is there for honest poverty." See A
man's a man for a' that
"Is there pity in heaven at last." See O
Lisbona, alfin ti miro (Donizetti)
"Is this a time to be cloudy and sad." See
An Arbor day song (Molloy)
"Is this the same brook" ("Chi se-zh tafà
krinichen'ka") Ukrainian folk song.
e.r. BF 1

"Is this thy plighted, fond regard." Air: Ruffian's rant.   Words by R. Burns. BSR

Is toigh leam a' Ghaidhealtachd ("Dear, dear are the Highlands") Gaelic song. Words by J. Campbell.   e.   MMS

"Is truagh nach robh mi's mo rogha cèile." See Mo rùn geal, dìleas

Is tusa mo rún, mo rún, mo rún.   See Páisdín fionn

"Isaac a ransom while he lay."   See Didn't old Pharaoh get lost

"Isabeau s'y promène" (L'enlèvement en mer.—Carried off to sea) French Canadian song.   e.f.   TF

"Isabeau s'y promène" ("Fair Isabeau was walking")   French   Canadian   song. Another air.   e.f.   BF 2

I'se arguin' a barg'in, my honey love.   See Arguing the bargain

"I'se gwine back to Dixie."   C. A. White. SSS

Isely, C. C.
Fairmount, fond Fairmount (Composer unknown)

Ish'-i-buz-zhi (Ichibuzzhi) Omaha Indian dance song.   in.   FIS

Iskhodila mladen'ka.   See The lonely waif

The island ("Daddy Neptune one day") See The tight little island

Island ("Island, farsaeldsa frón."—Iceland) Ancient Icelandic folk song.   e.ic. BSP

The Islay maiden.   See A' churinneag Ileach

The isle ("Far out at sea."—Ostrovók) S. Rachmaninoff.   Words after Shelley.   e.   SMR 2

Isle of beauty.   T. A. Rawlings.   Words by T. H. Bayly.   JO

Isle of beauty.   C. S. Whitmore.   Words by T. H. Bayly.   DM 1—FSS 3— HSE 2—LA—TFC 2—WBT

The isle of France.   Folk song from Sussex.   SF 5

The isle of Mull.   See An-t-eilean Muileach

Isle of Mull dirge ("Heavy the beat")   See "Heavy the beat of the weary waves"

"The isle of Mull is of isles the fairest." See An-t-eilean Muileach

La islena.   See Havanaise (Paladilhe)

L'isolana.   See Havanaise (Paladilhe)

Isolde's liebestod.   R. Wagner.   e.g. SOA 1

Isouard, Niccolò
"We have lived and loved together"

Israfel.   O. King.   Words by E. A. Poe. AB 2

"Ist denn lieben ein verbrechen." Volksweise.   Author of words unknown g.   ED 2

"Isten, àldd meg a Magyart."   See Hungarian national hymn (Erkel)

"Iszeit, pareit jaunasis bernytis."   See "From afar returns my well-beloved"

"It befell at Martynmas when wether waxed colde."   See Sick, sick

"It came upon the midnight clear" (Glorious song of old)   Old English air. Words by E. H. Sears.   MCS

"It came upon the midnight clear."   J. B. Dykes.   Words by E. H. Sears. MCS
Song of the angels.   FSS 6

"It came upon the midnight clear" (Song of the angels) Giardini.   Words by E. H. Sears.   MCS

"It came upon the midnight clear."   J. R. Higinbotham.   Words by E. H. Sears. HC

"It came upon the midnight clear."   M. F. Mac Connell.   Words by E. H. Sears.   MS

"It came upon the midnight clear."   R. S. Willis.   Words by E. H. Sears. DC— HC—WA— WBT— WS— WSW
Christmas carol.   OH
Willis.   LA

"It came with the merry May, love."   See Only a year ago (Tosti)

"It chanced when I was walking."   Irish air: This time twelve months I married. Words from an old broadside ballad. MMI

"It fell about the Martinmas time."   See Get up and bar the door

"It fell on a day."   See The bonnie house o' Airlie

"It fell upon a Lammas night."   See Corn rigs are bonnie

"It is a day of gladness."   C. A. Barry. Words by Mrs C. F. Hernaman.   HC

"It is a good thing to give thanks."   M. Costa.   OS 2—SAS 2

"It is all in vain to implore me."   See Obstination (Fontenailles)

"It is better to laugh, than be sighing." See "Il segreto per esser felici" (Donizetti)

"It is Christmas day."   Oyster Bay carol. HC

"It is done! clang of bells and roar of gun." See Laus Deo (Battishill)

"It is enough."   F. Mendelssohn.   e. OS 4—SAS 4

"It is finished."   J. S. Bach.   e.   OS 2

"It is good for the mourner."   See This old time religion

"It is granted at last then."   See Deh vieni, non tardar (Mozart)

"It is hard dissembling."   See "Du moment qu'on aime" (Grétry)

"It is late! all around not a sound."   See Viens, gentille dame (Boieldieu)

"It is na, Jean, thy bonie face."   J. Oswald.   Words by R. Burns.   BSR

"It si na, Jean, thy bonnie face."   Air: Pinkie house.   Words by R. Burns. BSB

"It is night, and darkness falls o'er land and lea."   See Majnat (Sinding)

"It is not for his gold, sir."   Air: The allurements of love.   Words by J. Parry.   MMW

"It is not that I love you less" (The self-banished) J. Blow. Words by E. Waller. BOH—BS 2—DM 1—HSE 3 —JE—PR 1

"It is not that I love you less." C. Young. Words by E. Waller. MM

"It is not that you're fair." See Geraldine (Levey)

"It is not the tear, at this moment shed." Air: The sixpence. Words by T. Moore. MI

"It is ordained by God's decree." See "Es ist bestimmt in Gottes rath" (Mendelssohn)

"It is said that eyes of azure." See Los ojos mexicanos

"It is so cold." See Waldesgespräch (Schumann)

It is spring. Japanese song. e.j. BF 2

It is the love of God in heaven. See "O what can you tell" (Lowry)

"It is the 'O, W, U,' of which we sing to you." See Song of the "O. W. U." (O'Kane)

"It is the pretty Fanny, lon gai." See La belle Françoise

"It is the truth, then." See O mio Fernando (Donizetti)

It might have been. See Guy Fawkes

"It must be so." Händel. BS 1

"It now lies on the shelf." See Mother's old red shawl (Mouland)

"It ofttimes has been told." See The Constitution and Guerrière

"It rains, it rains, dear maiden." See L'orage

"It rains, it rains in merry Lincoln." See Little Sir Hugh

"It rises, it rises, it rises so high." See "Det stiger" (Heise)

"It seem'd as tho' the heavens." See Mondnacht (Schumann)

It snows in the night. Slavonic folk air. Words by H. H. Harbour. DO

"It was a blind beggar." See The blind beggar of Bethnal green (Rogers)

"It was a Breton village." See Saved from the storm (Barry)

It was a dream ("I heard the rippling brooklet sing") F. H. Cowen. Words by R. E. Francillon. MSS 1—PO—SS 1

It was a dream ("Ich hatte einst") See Es war ein traum (Lassen)

"It was a dream, delusive dream" (Chilean song) e. BMC

"It was a' for our rightfu' king." Air: Mally Stuart. Words by R. Burns. BSR

"It was a frog in the well." See The wedding of the frog and mouse

"It was a jolly fiddler." See O tempora! O mores

"It was a knight was drunk with wine." See The baffled knight

"It was a lover and his lass." G. Barton. Words by W. Shakespeare. ES—VFS

"It was a lover and his lass." H. Clough-Leighter. Words by W. Shakespeare. VFS

"It was a lover and his lass." Attributed to T. Morley. Words by W. Shakespeare. BAS 2—BE 7—BOH—BSE—CO 1—DM 1—HSE 1—JE—KSS—MM —MS—PR 1—VFS—WBT—WL

"It was a maid of my countrie." See The hawthorn tree

"It was a Sunday bright and clear." See O schöne zeit, o sel'ge zeit (Götze)

"It was as though the heaven." See Mondnacht (Schumann)

"It was Dunois, the young and brave." See Partant pour la Syrie (Hortense Eugénie de Beauharnais?)

"It was early in the morning." C. J. Ridsdale. HC

"It was early that I woke." See "Ce matin me suis levé"

"It was fifty years ago." J. L. Hatton. Words by H. W. Longfellow. HSE 3

"It was good for de Hebrew children." See This old time religion

"It was in and about the Mart'mas time." See Barbara Allen (Scottish version)

"It was in May." Moniot d'Arras. e. DT

"It was in simmer time o' year." See There's nae room for twa (Satter)

"It was in sweet Senegal." Air: The slave's lament. Words by R. Burns. BSR

"It was late in the night." See The gypsy laddie (Flag Pond, Tenn. version)

"It was midnight in the city." See The story of a star (Ganz)

It was not so to be. See Es hat nicht sollen sein (Nessler)

"It was on a fine summer morning." See The pretty girl milking her cow

"It was one Sunday bright and clear." See O schöne zeit, o sel'ge zeit (Götze)

"It was such a pleasant, sunny day." See En solskins dag (Nordraak)

"It was summer, and softly the breezes were blowing." See The banks of the Dee

"It was the charming month of May." Air: Dainty Davie. Words by R. Burns. BSR

"It was the eve of Christmas." See The star of Bethlehem (Maybrick)

"It was the frog in the well." 16th century song. JE Variant of: The wedding of the frog and mouse

"It was the schooner Hesperus." See The wreck of the Hesperus (Hatton)

"It was the Stately Southerner." See The Stately Southerner

"It was the very noon of night." See The story of the shepherd (Barnby)

"It was upon a Lammas night." See Corn rigs are bonnie

Italian air ("O charming Napoli") e. BSE Variant of: Santa Lucia

Italian boatman's song. See Oh! hear the wild wind blow (Mattei)

Italian cradle-song ("Sleep, my baby, sleep") G. da Sandtis. e. FSS 3

Italian hymn (Giardini) See "Come, Thou almighty King"; "Rise, glorious conqueror"; "Thou, Whose almighty word"

Italian national hymn. See Inno di guerra dei cacciatori delle Alpi (Olivieri)

"Ithers seek they kenna what." See Let loove sparkle in her e'e

"Itiskit, itasket." Children's song. NMS —WSC

"It's a beautiful day to ge glad in." See The first violets (Bellini)

"It's a guid mony year sin' I cam' here." See The botany class

"It's a right little, tight little college." Haverford college song. Air: Columbia, the gem of the ocean. Words by B. Gummere. CHS

"It's a rosebud in June." Folk song. SEF 2—SO
  Sheep-shearing song. FSF

"It's a way we have at Columbia." College song. CU

"It's a way we have at old Harvard." College song. HSD—WBT—WC

It's a way we have at school. See Students' way

It's all around my hat that I twine the weeping willow. See All around my hat (Valentine)

"It's been decreed from days of old." See "Es ist bestimmt in Gottes rath" (Mendelssohn)

"It's come and eat and tell me your name." See Locks and bolts (Spillcorn, N.C. version)

"It's come go back, my pretty little miss." See The gypsy laddie (Black Mountain, N.C. version)

"It's here awa', there awa', how they did rin." See Loons, ye maun gae hame

"It's holi-, holi-, holiday." See Little Musgrave and Lady Barnard (Flag Pond, Tenn. version no. 1)

"It's I have got a ship in the north countrie." See The Golden Vanity

"It's in Connacht or in Munster." See My little Kerry cow

"It's Logie o' Buchan." See Logie o' Buchan

It's me, O, Lord. Negro spiritual. JB
  It's me. DF
  'Tis me. HR
  'Tis me, O Lord. BN 2

"It's Monday morning go to school." See The two brothers (Black Mountain, N.C. version)

It's my darlings, my boys. See Na gillean mo rùin

"It's Nancy of London." See Nancy of London

"It's no easy thing to get a beau." See "De'rnte greit"

"It's now the day is dawin." Air: Three gude fellows ayont the glen. Words by R. Burns. BSR

"It's of a blind beggar who'd lost his sight." See The blind beggar of Bethnal green (Somerset version)

"It's of a brisk young sailor lad." See The bonny lighter-boy

"It's of a famous American ship." See The Shenandoah

"It's of a famous highwayman." See Brennan on the moor (Irish version)

"It's of a farmer's daughter." See Heave away, my Johnny

"It's of a fearless highwayman." See Brennan on the moor (English version)

"It's of a flash packet, a packet I've seen." See Good-bye, fare ye well

"It's of a flash packet, a packet of fame." See The Dom Pedro

"It's of a merchant's daughter belonged to Callio." See Do let me go

"It's of a nobleman lit with a thresherman one day." See The thresherman and the squire

"It's of a pretty ploughboy." See The pretty ploughboy (Sussex version)

"It's of a pretty shepherdess." See The knight and the shepherd's daughter

"It's of a sailor bold." Folk song from Dorset. SF 1

"It's of a youth, a kind young youth." See See The bailiff's daughter of Islington (Somerset version)

"It's one day when I was a-rambling around." See Wild Bill Jones

"It's rare to see the morning bleeze." See The ingle side (Wiesenthal)

"It's rose-time, rose-time." See Rose-time (Hadley)

"It's up wi' the Souters o' Selkirk." Air: The Souters o' Selkirk. Words by R. Burns. BSR—PS 2

"It's what did you eat for your breakfast, Jimmy Randal my son." See Lord Randal (Carmen, N.C. version)

"It's where does your pain lie." See The brown girl (Alleghany, N.C. version)

"It's whisper'd in parlour." Air: The brown blooms bonie. BSR

"Iu partu e su' custrittu di partiri." See Canzuna di li carriteri

Ivan Skizavitzky Skivar. College song. BSS
  Variants: Abdul, the Bulbul Ameer; Abdulla Bul-Bul Ameer

Ivanov, Mikhail Mikhaïlovich Ippolitov-. See Ippolitov-Ivanov, Mikhail Mikhaïlovich

"I've a goldfinch that I have been training." See Lu cardillo (Labriola)

"I've a good old mother in the heaven." See Judgment day is rolling round

"I've a letter from thy sire." See Baby mine (Johnston)

"I've a secret to tell thee." Irish air: Oh, southern breeze. Words by T. Moore. MI—MMI

"I've a shadow for a playmate." See My playmate

"I've been a-list'ning all de night long." Negro spiritual. HR
Variants: Been a listening; Hard trials ("Been a-lis'nin' all de night long")

"I've been rambling all the night." Bedfordshire May day carol. WCC

"I've been roaming." C. E. Horn. Words by G. Soane. BC—BE 1—BOH —CMF 1—FSS 2—HSE 1—JSE—NG PO—WBT

"I've been thinking of home." See Thoughts of home (Gould)

"I've been thro' Carolina." See See Belle ob Baltimore (Evans)

"I've been toilin' at de hill." Negro song. HR

"I've been travelin' all de day." See Ride on, Moses

"I've been traveling all this day." See Ride on, Moses

"I've come across the sea." See Rose of Lucerne

"I've come unto my home again." See The wanderer's return

"I've found a joy in sorrow." See Joy in sorrow (Sankey)

"I've got a good ole mudder in de heaven, my Lord." See Judgment day is rolling round

"I've got a little farm." See Little Mary of the Dee (Parry)

"I've got a mother in de heaven." Negro spiritual. HR

"I've got a pal, a reg'lar out an' outer." See My old Dutch (Ingle)

"I've got a robe, you've got a robe." See All God's chillun got wings

"I've journeyed o'er land." See "Ich fuhr über meer" (Kjerulf)

"I've just arrived in town to-day." See Nicodemus Johnson (Murphy)

"I've just come down from the wild goose nation." See Tommy's gone to Hilo

"I've heard the liltin'." See Flowers of the forest

"I've just arrived in town to-day." See Nicodemus Johnson (Murphy)

"I've just come from the fountain." Negro song. NMP

"I've left Ballymornach a long way behind me." See Norah McShane (Horn)

"I've left the snow-clad hills." G. Linley. HSD

"I've lost my doggy." WC

"I've no sheep on the mountain." See The maid of Llanwellyn

"I've often heard it said ob late." See Dandy Jim ob Caroline

"I've often seen your pretty sheep, dear." See The gobble duet (Audran)

"I've reached the land of corn and wine." See Beulah land (Sweney)

"I've roamed by Tweed." See Where Gadie rins

"I've sailed round the world." See Jack's gratitude (Dibdin)

"I've seen a tiger roaming the gloomy forest." Se La Scillitana

"I've seen the smiling of fortune beguiling." See The flowers of the forest

"I've something sweet to tell you." E. Faning. FMB—KF 3—SM 1—WL

"I've such a host of things to tell you." See "J'ai tant de choses à vous dire" (Ferrari)

"I've told you 'bout de banjo." See Dolly Day (Foster)

"I've traveled about a bit in my time." See Paddle your own canoe (Hobson)

"I've travel'd the wide world over." See Old Rosin the bow

"I've wandered east, I've wandered west." See Jeanie Morrison (Dempster)

"I've wandered many a league, Mary." See Absent friends and you, Mary (Spicer)

"I've wander'd to the village, Tom." See Twenty years ago (Willing)

Ivors, W. J.
"Father of love" (Dykes)

The ivy green. H. Russell. Words by C. Dickens. DM 1—FSS 8—JO— WBT

"Iyayana tiyata uŋgni kte." See Marriage song

Iz pod duba, iz pod viâza. See The rabbit's story

Iz za lîesu, lîesu temnago. See The swan maiden

"Iz-za ostrova, na strîâzhen'." See Sten'ka Razin

J

"Ja, du weisst es, theure seele." See Zueignung (Wolf)

"Ja hjemme er det dog allerbedst." See Her hjemme

"Ja, lustig bin ich, das ist wahr." See Trinklied

"Já nechci žádného." See "I'll have no other one"

"Ja, noch einmal konnt' den winter ich seh'n." See Der frühling (Grieg)

Ja, seit früher kindheit tagen. For English translation see "O'er my head" (Flotow)

"Ja, vi elsker dette landet" ("Ay, this land her sons and daughters") R. Nordraak. Words by B. Björnson. e.n. BSP

"Ja vi elsker dette landet" (Yes, we love this land.—National hymn of Norway) e.n. WCP

"Ja vi elsker dette landet" ("Yes, we love with fond devotion") e.n. MAN—SSN

Norwegian national hymn. e.n. MP —WA. e. only JS—NMS—WBT

Norwegian national song ("Yes, we love this country") e. BMC

"Jack and Gill." H. L. Handy. Words adapted from Mother Goose. HSD

"Jack and Jill." J. W. Elliott. Words from Mother Goose. FMB—FSS 3 —JSE— WA—WBT— WSC— WSW

Jack at Greenwich. C. Dibdin. ME

Jack at sea. J. L. Roeckel. Words by G. C. Bingham. FSS 7

"Jack dances and sings." See The true English sailor (Dibdin)

Jack Frost. Children's song. WSC

Jack Hall. Folk song. SEF 2—SO

"Jack he went a-sailing." See Jack went a-sailing (Virginia version)

Jack-in-the-pulpit. German folk air. Words by M. Morgan. DO

"Jack met his mother all alone." 17th century song. Air: An old woman poor and blind. DM 1—MM

Jack o' diamonds. Cowboy song. LC

"Jack Rattlin." Dibdin. HSE 2

"Jack Spratt." Nursery song. WBT— WSC

Jack the jolly tar O. Folk song from Devonshire. SF 4

Jack the sailor. English song. DM 2

Jack went a-sailing. Folk song: Georgia version. CSE
—Kentucky version. CSE
—North Carolina version. CSE
—Virginia version. CSE
Variant: Jackaro

"Jack, where are you going" ("Gdzież to jedziesz Jasiu") Polish song. e.p. BF 1

Jackaro. Kentucky mountain song. WLT
Variant of: "Jack went a-sailing"

The jackdaw and the falcon (V syrom boru tropina) Russian folk song. e. SSR 1

The jacket blue. Irish folk song. JOI

Jack's gratitude ("I've sailed round the world") C. Dibdin. ME

Jackson, of Ballingarry
Fairy haunts
"My home's on the mountain." See Fairy haunts

Jackson, C. L.
"Sing sweet carols, night is past" (Whiteley)

Jackson, George
L'adieu

Jackson, Mrs Helen Maria (Fiske) Hunt
"The birds must know" (Composer unknown)
A last prayer (Composer unknown)

Jackson, Robert
"There dwelt in old Judea"

Jackson, Vincent
"Where be you going, you Devon maid"

Jackson, William
The bonnie lass o' Ballochmyle. See "'Twas even—the dewy fields were green"
"Encompassed by an angel's frame" (from The lord of the manor)
"Love in thine eyes for ever plays"
"Time has not thinn'd my flowing hair"

"To fairest Delia's grassy tomb" (from Settima)
"'Twas even—the dewy fields were green"
"What shepherd or nymph of the grove" (from Settima)
"Ye shepherds, give ear to my lay"

"Jacob dreamt he saw a ladder reachin' to de sky." See Climb up, ye chillun climb

"Jacob, drink" (Pije kuba) Polish song. e. BMC

Jacob's ladder ("As Jacob with travel") Traditional air. BSC—DC—HC

Jacob's ladder ("We are climbing Jacob's ladder") Negro spiritual. DF—HR

"We am clim'in' Jacob's ladder." JB

"Jacob's ladder slim an' tall." See Don't call de roll

Jacobsen, Jens Peter
Genrebillede (Backer-Lunde)
Landskab (Børresen)

Jacobson, Myron
"You brought me flowers"

Jacoby, Johann Georg
Litaney (Schubert)
"Sagt, wo sind die veilchen hin" (Schulz)

Jadassohn, Salomon
Arioso from 100th psalm. See "Erkennet, erkennt, dass der Herr ist Gott"
"Erkennet, erkennt, das der Herr ist Gott"

"Jag går i tusen tankar" ("A thousand things I ponder") Swedish folk song. e.sw. HSOS

"Jag gick mig ut en aftonstund" ("I walked abroad at eventide") Swedish folk song. e.sw. HSOS

"Jag ser uppå dina ögon" ("I see by your eyes") Swedish folk song. e.sw. HSOS

"Jag sjunger och dansar" ("I sing and I dance") A. Randel. Words by F. A. Dahlgren. e.sw. HSOS

"Jag tror jag får börja öfverge att sörja" ("I declare, to-morrow I'll have done with sorrow") Swedish folk song. HSOS

"Jag unnar dig ändå allt godt" ("Sweet angel, still I wish thee well") Swedish folk song. e.sw. HSOS

"Jag vet en gosse, och han är min." See En liten visa (Hallström)

"Jag vet en hälsning mera kär." See Första aftonen i det nya hemmet (Geijer)

"Jag vet en vrå emellan bergen." See Min lilla vrå bland bergen (Sandstrom)

"Jag vet ett land långt upp i höga nord." See Dalkarlasång (Lindblad)

Jagdlied (A hunter's song) F. Mendelssohn. e.g. KF 3

Jäger, Daniel
"O wie lieblich ist's im kreis" (Hoffmeister)

Jäger ("Es ritt ein jäger wohlgemut wohl in der morgenstunde") J. F. Reichardt. Volkslied. g.   ED 3

Der jäger ("Es ritt ein jägersmann über die flur") J. F. Reichardt.   Words by A. Mahlmann. g.   ED 2

Der jäger abschied ("Wer hat dich, du schöner wald") F. Mendelssohn-Bartholdy. Words by J. von Eichendorff. g.   ED 1
Der jäger abschied (The huntsmen's farewell) e.g.   SSG
Hunter's farewell. e.   FSS 2—LA
The huntsman's farewell. e.   BSE

Der jäger aus Kurpfalz. Volkslied. g. ED 1

"En jager gik ud at jage."   See Ved balasthioning

"Der jäger in dem grünen wald."   Volkslied. g.   ED 3

Der jäger und das mädchen ("Es wollt' ein jäger jagen") Volkslied. g.   ED 3

Jägerleben ("Im wald und auf der heide") Words by W. Bornemann. g. ED 1
The hunter's life. e.g.   SSS

Jägerleben ("O lieber, guter frühling."—Im frühlinge) H. Hoffmann von Fallersleben (music and words) g.   ED 3

Jägerlied ("Auf, auf! zum fröhlichen jagen") French hunting air: Pour aller à la chasse faut être matineux.   Words by G. B. Hancke. g.   ED 1

Jägers liebeslied ("Ich schiess den hirsch") Composer unknown. Words by F. von Schober. g.   ED 1

Jägers lust ("Es lebe, was auf erden stolziert")   After M. Nathusius.   Words by W. Müller. g.   ED 3

Jägers nachtlied ("Im felde schleich ich still") J. F. Reichardt.   Words by Goethe. g.   ED 1—ED 2

"Das jahr ist gut."   See Bayerisches bierlied

"Jahre kommen, jahre schwinden."   See Für mädchen (Righini)

"Des jahres."   See entry under Des

"J'ai bien nourri le geai sept ans" ("For seven years I fed my jay") Folk song. Canadian version. e.f.   TF

"J'ai construit dans mon âme."   See La splendeur vide (Saint-Saëns)

"J'ai encor un tel paté" ("I have here a little cake") Rondel.   Adam de la Hale. e.f.   NG

"J'ai fait une maîtresse, y-a pas longtemps, j'ai fait une maîtresse, y-a pas longtemps. J'irai la voir dimanche, ah oui, j'irai."   See Le coeur de ma bienaimée

"J'ai fait une maîtresse y-a pas longtemps, j'ai fait une maîtresse, y-a pas longtemps, j'irai la voir dimanche sans plus tarder."   See Les métamorphoses

"J'ai laissé de mon sein de neige."   See Soupir (Widor)

"J'ai longtemps habité sous de vastes portiques."   See La vie antérieure (Duparc)

"J'ai mis sur cette fleur."   See Fleur messagère (Bouval)

"J'ai perdu celle" ("Gone from me evermore."—"Nun ach! verlor ich sie") Attributed to Henry III.   Words by J. Ahrem. e.f.g.   EF—KF 1—KF 3
"J'ai perdu celle" ("Gone from me evermore") e.   BSE

J'ai peur de l'aimer (I fear me to love him) L. Denza.   Words by Jeneseki. e.f. SOS 1—SOS 2

"J'ai tant de choses à vous dire" ("I've such a host of things to tell you") G. Ferrari. e.f.   ES—HM 1

"J'ai vu les séraphins en songe."   See Sancta Maria (Faure)

"J'ai vu passer l'hirondelle."   See Villanelle (Dell' Acqua)

"J'aime le son du cor."   See Le cor (Flégier)

Jakobowski, Eduard
Birds of a feather (from Erminie)
Dream song (from Erminie)
Lullaby (from Erminie)

Jakšić, Gjuro
Montenegro (Composer unknown)

"Jala bharna chalī rī mā'ī jamanā ghāta." See Gopi's complaint

Jam radix.   For English translation see "To-day doth blossom Jesse's stem" (Hopkins)

"Jamais je n'oublierai."   See La fille du coupeur de paille

James, Evan
Land of my fathers (James, J.)

James, James
Land of my fathers

James, Theodore
Hiawatha's mittens

The Jamestown homeward bound.   Forecastle song.   CR

Jamie, come try me. See "If thou should ask my love"

"Jamie! Jamie."   J. L. Molloy.   FSS 8

Jamie's on the stormy sea.   B. Covert. FSS 6—HSD—JO—WBT

The Jamschick's complaint.   Bachmetieff. e.   KSN

Janoff, M.
Morning (Rachmaninov)

Jan's courtship.   Folk song.   BSW

Janson, Kristofer Nagel
Fiskeren til sønnen (Elling)
Millom rosor (Beyer)
Paa fjellet (Kjerulf)

"Jänteli, Jänteli, jänta mi."   See En låt i tri toner (Beckman)

January ("Janus am I") W. B. Olds. Words by H. W. Longfellow.   NMS

January ("See, my fair") J. Hook. Words by Collings.   ME

"Janus am I, oldest of potentates."   See January (Olds)

Japanese chorus used when scrubbing the decks. j.   SMW

Japanese Christmas song.   Words adapted to air of Japanese lullaby. e.   DCS

Japanese death song. S. C. Sharp. CMF 2

Japanese lullaby. Traditional air. e. BMC

Japanese national hymn. See "Kimi ga yo" (Hiromori)

Japanese rowing song. j. SMW

Japanese sailors' song (Matsumai) j. SMW

Jarabe ("Ya el pato se está cociendo") See El atole

Jarabe tapatio (To Jerez we will go) Mexican dance. e.s. BF 2

Le jardin d'amour (The garden of love) Folk song from Alsace. e.f. FTF

Järnefelt, Evard Armas
Kanteleelle. See To the harp
Laula, laula. See Sing thou, sing
Sing thou, sing
To the harp

"J'arrive le premier au triste rendez-vous." See Ô jours heureux (Gounod)

Jarvis, Charles
"Call me pet names"
The good Three Bells
The hero's serenade

The jasmine flower. See Moo-lee-hwa

Jast, Louis Stanley
As cold as the snows (Welsh air)
"Do you happen to know of a maiden" (Welsh air)
"Fare thee well, old world" (Bulgarian air)
The fisherman (Fiji air)
Gwendoline (Welsh air)
"I fling the night behind me with the dawn" (Welsh air)
"Lady with eyes so dreaming" (Welsh air)
"Our sorrow is vain" (East Indian air)
"Who's this coming this way" (Welsh air)
"The wind is playing 'mongst the reeds" (Egyptian air)

Jauchzet Gott in allen landen (Gladly God exalt, rejoicing) J. S. Bach. e.g. GMF

La jaula de oro. Mexican folk song. e.s. HS

Jausen, L.
"The kiss, dear maid"

Jaxone, H. L. d'Arcy
Dutch dolls (Ostlere)
The gate of heaven (Tours)
Laddie (Pinsuti)
"Peace, troubled heart" (Pinsuti)

Jaybird. Negro song. BF 2

"De jaybird jump from lim' to lim'." See Jaybird

"Je comprends que la belle aime le militaire." See Air du tambour major (Thomas)

"Je connais un berger discret" ("There's a shepherd, few more discreet") Bergerette. e.f. WB

"Je crois au Dieu" (Credo) F. David. e.f. SOA 5

Je dis que rien ne m'épouvante. G. Bizet. e.f. SOA 1

Je dis, que rien ne m'épouvante (I say that by fear I'm not haunted) e.f. KS 1

Je dis que rien ne m'épouvante (I vow that nothing shall prevent me) e.f. OPS 1

"Je dors; mon coeur, au point du jour, jamais ne dort." See Hebrew love-song (Rimskiï-Korsakov)

"Je l'attends depuis l'aurore." See L'ingrat ne vient pas encore

"Je les ai vus ces deux grenadiers." See Die beiden grenadiere (Schumann)

"Je marche sur tous les chemins" ("An empress am I in my way."—Gavotte) Massenet. e.f. OPS 1

"Je marche sur tous les chemins" ("Wherever I go I command") e.f. MC

"Je me suis engagé." See La complainte du déserteur

"Je me suis habillé en plumes" ("I dressed me all in feathers gay") French Canadian folk song. e.f. BFS

"Je m'en vais par les chemins, li-re-lin." See L'heureux vagabond (Bruneau)

Je ne suis pas si vilaine (I'm not quite of peasantry) French Canadian folk song. e.f. BFS

"Je ne veux pas autre chose" ("Nothing I ask thee to give me") C. M. Widor. Words by V. Hugo. e.f. SAM

Je n'veux pas me marier (I will not hurry) French Canadian folk song. e.f. BFS

"Je sais au bord du Rhin." See Le moulin

"Je serai ta douceur profonde." See Le fidèle coeur (Vidal)

"Je suis dans ma cage." See The captive (Grechaninov)

"Je suis jaloux, Psyché." See Psyché (Paladilhe)

"Je suis, je suis le cri de joie." See La chanson de l'alouette (Lalo)

"Je suis seul! seul enfin." See Ah! fuyez, douce image (Massenet)

Je suis Titania (Behold Titania) A. Thomas. Words by Carré and Barbier. e.f. KS 1—MSS 2—SS 2

Je suis Titania (I am Titania) e.f. MC

Je suis Titania (Polonaise) e.f. SOA 1

Polonaise. e.f. OPS 1

"Je suis triste, je m'inquiète." See Haï luli (Coquard)

"Je suis un petit ponpon de belle figure." See La bonne aventure

"Je t'ai rencontrée en la vie." See Le sais-tu bien (Pierné)

Je t'implore, ô mon frère (I implore thee, O, my brother) A. Thomas. e.f. OPS 4

"Je tjente paa Kjölstad ifjor" (I served down at Kjölstad) Norse folk song. e.n. MAN

"Je veille, et nuit et jour mon front." See Albaÿde (Widor)

"Je veux garder ma liberté." Gardons nos moutons

Je veux vivre dans ce rêve. See "Ah! je veux vivre" (Gounod)

"Je voudrais bien savoir quel était ce jeune homme" (Jewel song) Gounod. e.f.i. OPS 1

Jealousy (Vozlie riechki, vozlie mostu) Russian folk song. e. SSR 2

Jean Pauls lieblingslied. See Ihr

Jeanie Morrison. W. R. Dempster. Words by W. Motherwell. JO

Jeanie's black een. Scottish air. Words by H. Macneil. PS 2

Jeannette and Jeannot. C. W. Glover. Words by C. Jefferys. FSS 2—HSE 3 —JO

Jeffery, J. Albert
"Ancient of days"
Sleeper awake

Jefferys, Charles
Blanche Alpen (Glover)
Guadalquiver (Nelson)
Had I wings like a dove (Composer unknown)
I will be happy too (Nelson)
In the land of my birth (Harroway)
Jeannette and Jeannot (Glover)
Kitty Tyrrell (Glover)
Mary of Argyle (Nelson)
"Mother, are there angels dwelling" (Glover)
Music at nightfall (Nelson)
"Oh, take her, but be faithful still" (Nelson)
The rose of Allandale (Nelson)
Song of the daisy (Glover)
"The summer days are coming" (Composer unknown)
"We have lived and loved together" (Isouard)

Jeg elsker dig (I love thee) E. Grieg. Words by H. C. Andersen. da.e. SSN—WM 1
I love thee. e. WBT—WL
Ich liebe dich (I love thee) e.g. FO 2—KF 1—KF 2—KF 3—KF 4. e. only WA

"Jeg gik mig ud en sommerdag at høre." See Sommerdagen

"Jeg har sögt" ("I have sought") R. Nordraak. e.n. MAN

"Jeg kunde slet ikke sove for nattergalens röst." See Laengsel (Kjerulf)

"Jeg lagde mig saa sildig" ("I laid me down so softly") Norwegian folk song. e.n. BF 2
"Jeg lagde mig saa sildig" ("I laid me down to rest") e.n. MAN
"Jeg lagde mig saa silde" ("I laid me down to rest") e.n. BO

"Jeg lagde mit öre til kildens bred." See Nökken (Kjerulf)

"Jeg saa enlig gik engang." See Kattyglö visa

"Jeg synge skal en vise" ("You'd have me sing") J. P. E. Hartmann. Words by C. K. F. Molbech. da.e. SSN

"Jeg ved ei, hvoraf det kommer." See Lind (Backer-Gröndahl)

"Jehovah! Jehovah! to my words give ear." See Jehovah! to my words give ear (Händel)

"Jehovah, Thou, my Father." See Christ on the Mount of Olives (Beethoven)

Jehovah! to my words give ear. G. F. Händel. SAS 3

Jekharag. See The spool

Jemchoujnikov, A. See Zhemchuzhnikov, A.

Jemmy mo veela sthore (Jemmy, my thousand treasures) Irish folk song. e. JOI

Jemmy, my thousand treasures. See Jemmy mo veela sthore

Jeneseki, comte
J'ai peur de l'aimer (Denza)

Jenkins, Ruthven
Though lost to sight (Cowen)

Jenko, Davorin
Serbian national anthem
Srpska narodna himna. See Serbian national anthem

Jenner, Henry Lascelles
"The birds are singing on the trees"

Jenneval, Louis Alexandre Hippolyte Dechez, known as
La Brabançonne (Campenhout)

Jenny ("With laughing looks I once arose") Old Irish air. Words adapted by A. P. Graves. PI

"Jenny and Molly and Dolly." See A country sheep-shearing

Jenny dang the weaver ("At Willie's wedding on the green") Gardner. Words by A. Boswell. PS 2

Jenny Johnson. Old air. Words by S. Paul. BSS

Jenny Jones ("My name's Edward Morgan") J. Parry. Words by C. Mathews. MMW

Jenny Jones ("We come to see Miss Jenny Jones") WBT—WSC
"We come to see Miss Jenny Jones." FSS 4—NMS

Jenny Lind's Bird song. Swedish song. e. FSS 5

Jenny Lind's Good night. H. West. FSS 3

"Jenny, my own true loved one." See Wait till the clouds roll by (Fulmer)

Jenny's bawbee ("I met four chaps yon birks amang") Old Scottish dance air. Words by A. Boswell. MMS— PS 1

Jensen, Adolf
"Alt Heidelberg, du feine"
"Am ufer des flusses, des Manzanares"
"A breath of spring." See "Wie lenzeshauch"
By Manzanares. See "Am ufer des flusses, des Manzanares"
Forest voices. See Waldesgespräch

Jensen, Adolf—*Continued*
"From slumber awaken." See "Und schläfst du, mein mädchen"
Frühlingsnacht
"Lehn' deine wang' an meine wang'"
"Leis' rudern hier, mein gondolier." See "Row gently here, my gondolier"
The Loreley. See Waldesgespräch
Lullaby of an infant chief. See "O hush thee, my babie"
Margaretta. See Margreth am thore
Margreth am thore
Marie
"Mein herz ist im Hochland." See "My heart's in the Highlands"
"Murmelndes lüftchen, blüthenwind"
Murmuring breezes. See "Murmelndes lüftchen, blüthenwind"
"My heart's in the Highlands"
"O hush thee, my babie" (Tr of Caidil gu lo)
"O lass dich halten, gold'ne stunde"
"O let me press thy cheek to mine." See "Lehn' deine wang' an meine wang'"
"Oh press thy cheek against mine own." See "Lehn' deine wang' an meine wang'"
"O stay thy passing, golden moments." See "O lass dich halten, gold'ne stunde"
"Old Heidelberg, the splendid." See "Alt Heidelberg, du feine"
Press thy cheek against mine own. See "Lehn' deine wang' an meine wang'"
"Row gently here, my gondolier"
Serenade. See Ständchen
Spring night. See Frühlingsnacht
Ständchen
"Und schläfst du, mein mädchen"
Waldesgespräch
"Wenn durch die piazzetta." See "When through the piazzetta"
"When through the piazzetta"
"Where flows the bright river." See "Am ufer des flusses, des Manzanares"
"Wie lenzeshauch"
Wiegenlied. See "O hush thee, my babie"
J'entends le moulin. See "Mon père a fait bâtir maison"
Jephtha's daughter ("Since our country, our God—oh, my sire") Hebrew song. Words by Byron. BMC
Jeremiah's lament. F. Hiller. e. SAS 4
Jerusalem ("Behold thy King") H. Parker. Words by Nella [Parker] FMB—HSD—HSS 1—HSS 2—HSS 3—HSS 4—WA—WBT—WS
Jerusalem ("Viae Sion lugent") C. Gounod. e.l. HSS 3—HSS 4
Jerusalem above (Materna) S. A. Ward. TL
"Jerusalem, Jerusalem, Jerusalem, Jerusalem." See O turn thee (Gounod)
Jerusalem mornin'. See "Sweet turtle dove"

"Jerusalem, my happy home." Latin hymn. [Tr of Mater Hierusalem] e. FSS 1
"Jerusalem the golden." A. Ewing. Words by St Bernard of Cluny. [Tr of Urbs Syon aurea] e. BD—CST—FMB—FSS 1—HSC—HSD—JS—LA— NMH—TL— WA— WBT—WS—WSC—WSW
Jerusalem, thou that killest the prophets. Mendelssohn. e. OS 1
"Jerusalem! Jerusalem! thou that killest the prophets." e. SAS 1
"Jes' wait a little while." See The old ark a-moving along
Jesos ahatonhia. Cantique huron pour la Fête des rois (Huron chant for the King's festival) Canadian folk song. in. TF
"Jesse James." Cowboy song. LC
Jessie ("When with Jessie") 18th century song. ME
Jessie, the flower o' Dumblane. R. A. Smith. Words by R. Tannahill. JO—PS 1—WBT
Jessie, the flower of Dumblane. FSS 5
Jesu dulcis memoria. For English translations see "Jesus! the very thought of Thee" (Dykes); "Jesus, the very thought of Thee" (Rossini)
"Jesu, hail! O God most holy." J. Stainer. [Tr of Ave Jesu Deus] e. BSC
"Jesu, Lover of my soul." See "Jesus, Lover of my soul" (Dykes)
"Jesu, word of God incarnate." See Ave verum (Mozart)
"Jesus ain't comin' here t' die no mo'." Negro spiritual. HR
"Jesus answered." S. Bennett. OS 4
"Jesus carry the young lambs in his bosom, bosom." See Rise and shine
"Jesus Christ is born to-day." German air. HC
"Jesus Christ is risen to-day." See "Christ the Lord is ris'n today, alleluia! Sons of men and angels say" (Worgan)
"Jésus-Christ s'habille en pauvre." See La parabole du mauvais riche
Jésus de Nazareth. See Nazareth (Gounod)
"Jesús, divino del mundo salvador." See Bethlehem (Gounod)
"Jesus heal' de sick." Negro spiritual from the Bahamas. KA
Jesus in the manger. H. Smart. Words from the Latin. e. BSC
Jesus is mine. T. E. Perkins. Words by H. Bonar. FSS 6
"Jesus, Jesus is my frien'." See Don't leave me, Lord
Jesus lebt, mit ihm auch ich. For English translation see "Jesus lives! no longer now"
"Jesus lives! no longer now" (St Albinus) Words by C. F. Gellert. [Tr of Jesus lebt, mit ihm auch ich] e. MCS
"Jesus lives! thy terrors now." H. J. Gauntlett. WBT—WS

"Jesus, Lover of my soul." F. Abt. Words by C. Wesley. FSS 2

"Jesu[s], Lover of my soul." J. B. Dykes. Words by C. Wesley. FMB

"Jesus, Lover of my soul." S. B. Marsh. Words by C. Wesley. FSS 1—HSC— NMH— NMS—OH— WA— WBT— WS—WSC

"Jesus, Lover of my soul." B. Tours. Words by C. Wesley. HSS 1—HSS 3

"Jesus meek and gentle." See By Thy Christmas cheer

"Jesus, my all, to heaven is gone." G. Coles. Words by J. Cennick. WBT

"Jesus, my all, to heaven is gone" (Duane street) FSS 5

"Jesus, o'er the grave victorious." See O'er the grave victorious (Goudimel)

Jesus of Nazareth. See Nazareth (Gounod)

"Jesus, our Saviour, we welcome Thy rising." S. P. Warren. HC

"Jesus, Saviour, pilot me" (Pilot) J. E. Gould. Words by E. Hopper. TL

"Jesus, Saviour, pilot me" (The divine Pilot) R. Redhead. Words by E. Hopper. LA

"Jesus shall reign" (Duke street) J. Hatton. Words by I. Watts. HSC

"Jesus, tender Shepherd, hear me." C. Barnard (Claribel) [Words by M. L. Duncan] OH

"Jesus, tender Shepherd, hear me." J. B. Dykes. [Words by M. L. Duncan] FSS 4—NMS—WS

"Jesus! the very thought of Thee." J. B. Dykes. [Words by Bernard of Clairvaux. Tr of Jesu dulcis memoria] e. FSS 1—HSD—WBT—WS

"Jesus walked." Negro song. BOM

"Jeszcze Polska." See Polish national song (Oginski?)

"J'étais seul près des flots." See Extase (Gueroult)

"J'étais triste et pensif." See Rencontre (Fauré)

"Jetzt geh' i an's brünnele." See Drei röselein

"Jetzt schwingen wir den hut." See Abendlied, wenn man aus dem wirtshaus geht (Methfessel)

"Jeunes fillettes" ("Maidens, remember") N. Dalayrac. e.f. WB

"Jeune fillette" ("Maidens, remember") e.f. CM 1

"Jeunes fillettes" (Young lasses) e.f. PG 3

"A jewel is my lady fair." H. Purcell. BE 6

Jewel song ("Ah! je ris") See "Ah! je ris de me voir" (Gounod)

Jewel song ("Je voudrais bien") See "Je voudrais bien savoir quel était ce jeune homme" (Gounod)

Jewett (Weber) See "My Jesus, as Thou wilt; "One sweetly solemn thought"

The Jewish maiden. F. Kucken. [Tr of Das mädchen von Juda] e. FSS 8

Jewitt, William Henry
"Come, hear ye how God's priest of old" (Lissant)
"Good news, good news is sent" (Smith)
"O Lord, who shed'st the sunlight's gold" (Smith)

Jilted ("Oh, Junior! oh, Junior") WC

Jilted ("Why all this sorrow") See Good advice (Leveridge)

Jim along, Josey. Plantation song. BSS—WBT

Jim crack corn. Negro song. NMP

"Jimmy Dannels went a-hunting." See Shooting of his dear (North Carolina version)

Jingle all your bells. K. W. Davis. DCS

Jingle, bells ("Dashing thro' the snow") J. Pierpont. CHS—CU— HSD—JSE —MPC— NMH—OH— SSS—WA— WBT—WC—WSC—WSW

"Jingle bells, jingle bells, in the misty moonlight." See The sleigh ride

Jngrids vise (Ingrid's song) H. Kjerulf. Words by B. Bjørnson. e.n. WM 1
Ingrid's song. e. CS 2—MSS 2— SS 2
Ingrids vise (Ingrid's song) e.n. MAN

"Jo-ho-hoe! jo-ho-ho-hoe." See "Traft ihr das schiff" (Wagner)

"Joan, to the May-pole away let us on." See To the May-pole away

"Joan's placket is torn." Old English air. Modern words by S. Baring-Gould. BE 5

Jock o' Hazeldean ("Why weep ye by the tide, ladye") Air: Willie and Annet, or, In January last. Words by W. Scott. FSS 3—HSSS—JO—MMS— PS 1

Jockey ("When Jockey dances on the green") Composer unknown. Words by S. Arnold. PR 2

Jockey to the fair. 18th century song. HSE 1—MM
With Jockey to the fair. BE 3—BOH —DM 2—PR 2

"Jockie's taen the parting kiss." Air: Bonie lass tak a man. Words by R. Burns. BSR
"Jockey's ta'en the parting kiss." BSB

"Jog, jog, tramp, tramp, down the hill we run." See Down the hill

"Jog on, jog on." See Hanskin

Johanna's abschied ("Lebt wohl, ihr berge") J. R. Zumsteeg. Words by Schiller. g. ED 2

John, of Damascus, Saint
"The day of resurrection" (music by Oliver; Vibbert. Tr of Anastaseōs hemera)

John, of Fornsete
"Sumer is icumen in" (attributed)

"John Anderson my jo, John." J. Watson. Words by R. Burns. BSB—BSR— CS 1—EF— FSS 1—HSC— HSD— HSSS—JO— JSE—LA— MMS—NMH —PS 1—WBT—WL

John Barleycorn. Folk song. SEF 2— SO

—Hampshire version. SF 3

John Brown ("In eighteen hundred and sixty-one") Sea song. SMW

"John Brown had a little Indian." See John Brown's little Indian

"John Brown's body." Air: Say, brothers, will you meet us, arr by W. Steffe. Old song with additional words by C. S. Hall. BOS—FSS 6—HSD— JO— MP— NMH—NMP— NMS— SSS—WBT

Glory, glory hallelujah. HSC

John Brown's body ("Old John Brown") Air: Say, brothers, will you meet us, arr by W. Steffe. Words by H. H. Brownell. HSD—JO

John Brown's little Indian. Round. JSE

"John Bull for pastime took a prance." See Mounseer Nong Tong Paw (Dibdin)

"John Cherokee." Capstan chantey. CR

John D. Rockefeller. Chicago university song. Words by F. F. Steigmeyer. CHS

John Dory. 16th century song. Air: I cannot eat but lyttyl meat. CO 1

John Dory. 16th century song. Another air. CO 1—DM 1

The ballad of John Dory. SMW

"John Gilpin." Old English air. Words by W. Cowper. DM 2

"John Grumlie." Scottish song. MMS— PS 1

"John Hardy." Folk song from North Carolina. CSE

John Macananty's courtship. Irish folk song. JOI

John of Badenyon. Scottish air. Words by J. Skinner. PS 1

"John Owens." Air: Y fedwen las. Words by Ieuan Dhu. MMW

John Peel. Old hunting song. Words by J. W. Graves. BOH—BOS—DM 1— FMB—HSE 3—SSS

John Riley. Kentucky mountain song. WLT

Variant of: George Reilly

"John said that Jerusalem was four-square." See I want to be ready

"John said the city was just four-square." See I want to be ready

"John saw de angels." Negro spiritual. BOM

John saw the holy number. Negro spiritual. JB

John saw. HR—JP

Johnie Scot. Folk song from North Carolina. CSE

Johnnie Cope ("Cope sent a letter frae Dunbar") Air: Fly to the hills in the morning. HSSS—MMS

Hey, Johnnie Cope. PS 1

"Johnnie was a parlor scout." See The parlor scout

Johnny Boker. Short drag chantey. CR —KB

Johnny Bowker. SE

Johnny come down to Hilo. Negro capstan chantey. CR

Johnny Doyle. Folk song: Hot Springs, N.C. version. CSE

—Virginia version. CSE

Johnny, go get a scout. Air: When Johnny comes marching home. Words by J. Weston. BSS

"Johnny had a little dog." FSS 4—WSC

Johnny Harvard. College song. CHS

Johnny, Johnny, what! what." Round. FSS 4

Johnny Sands. J. Sinclair; attributed also to J. Simmonds. BD—FSS 2— HSD

"Johnny Schmoker." g. FSS 8

"Johnny's in the cellar sifting cinders." See The happy family (Jones)

Johns, captain
The white squall (Barker)

Johns, Clayton
The barefoot boy
Easter song
I love, and the world is mine
"If love were not"

Johnson, Arthur
"Massa dear"

Johnson, Charles William
Composer and author
Autumn's glory
"O, starry flag of union, hail"
Author
'Tis Easter time (Marshall)

Johnson, Daniel
The carrier dove

Johnson, Franklin
My Ottawa (Composer unknown)

Johnson, George W.
When you and I were young (Butterfield)

Johnson, J. C.
"Ho, ho, vacation days are here." See Vacation days
"Let others dream"
The sleigh ride
Vacation days

Johnson, James A.
"At the early Easter morn"

Johnson, John Rosamond
Yestereve

Johnson, Lionel
Hominum laudes (Shaw)

Johnson, Robert
"As I walked forth one summer's day." See A forsaken lover's complaint
"Dear, do not your fair beauty wrong"
A forsaken lover's complaint
"Full fathom five"
"Lawn as white as driven snow" (attributed; attributed also to J. Wilson)
"Where the bee sucks"
"With endless tears"

Johnson, Rosa V.
"Shed not a tear" (Bayly)
Johnson, Willis Fletcher
The violet (Wilhelm)
"Johnson said to Dicky one cold winter's day." See The three butchers (Tennessee version)
Johnston, Archibald
Baby mine
Johnston, H. F. H.
"O Lord, Thy love unbounded" (Bach)
"Join, O Maritza" ("Choumi Maritza") Bulgarian popular air. b.e. BSP
"Blood, O Maritza." b.e. MP
"Shumi Maritsa." b.e. BF 1
Joli mois de mai (Oh! merry month of May) French folk song. e.f. TSF
Joli tambour (The pretty drummer) French folk song. e.f. TSF
"Jolly boating weather, and a hay harvest breeze." See Eton boating song (Drummond)
"Jolly boating weather, jolly sweet harvest breeze." [A. Drummond] Words by A. Thomas. CHS—MPC
"Jolly boating weather, win the race today." See All pull together (Drummond)
"Jolly Captain Palisse was a lucky chap and funny." See Monsieur de la Palisse
Jolly fellows that follow the plough. Folk song. BSW
The jolly fiddler. See O tempora! O mores
The jolly friar. See Das pfäfflein (Schäfer)
"Jolly golfing weather." L. Adams. Words by C. Arthur. CHS
The jolly goss-hawk. Folk song. BSW
"The jolly huntsman." [German song] e. WSC
The jolly jester. Old ditty. FSS 3
"The jolly, jolly breeze." J. Eccles. BE 3
The jolly miller. See The miller of the Dee
"Jolly old Saint Nicholas." FSS 1
The jolly poacher. Tyrolese song. e. KSE
"A jolly old sow once lived in a sty." See Three little pigs (Scott-Gatty)
The jolly pedlar. See An ceannuighe Sugach
The jolly ploughboy. Folk song: Dorset version. SF 1
—Irish version. MMI
Variant of: The ploughboy
The jolly sophomore. Air: Son of a gambolier. Words by R. Waller. CU
The jolly young waterman. C. Dibdin (music and words) BOH—HSE 1—JO
Jommelli, Niccolò
"Chi vuol comprar la bella calandrina"
Who will buy the beautiful canary. See "Chi vuol comprar la bella calandrina"

Jonas ("Im schwarzen Walfisch zu Askalon") Volksweise. Words by J. V. Scheffel. g. ED 1
"At the sign of the Whale in Askalon." e. CU
Jonathan. Arnold. Words by G. Colman. BE 5
Joncières, Victorin de
Le front dans la poussière (from Sardanapale)
"Pâles étoiles" (from Dimitri)
Jones, Edmund
"Come, trembling sinner, in whose breast" (Composer unknown)
Jones, Gregory
The happy family
Jones, John, 1792-1852
The bard's visit (Welsh air)
Jones, John, 1810-1869
Composer and author
Heigh ho! maid of the mill
"Oh, come to the greenwood." See Heigh ho! maid of the mill
Author
"All hail to thee, Cambria" (Welsh air)
The bells of Aberdovey (Welsh air)
"Britons, raise your banners high" (Welsh air)
The gentle bird (Welsh air)
I am a jolly miller (Welsh air)
Merch Megan (Welsh air)
Music, love, and wine (Welsh air)
"My mother scolds me every day" (Welsh air)
St David's day (Welsh air)
Serenade (Welsh air)
The spirit of May (Welsh air)
Watching the wheat (Welsh air)
"Wilt thou love me, fairest maiden" (Welsh air)
Winnie dear (Welsh air)
Jones, Karl
My silver throated fawn (Lieurance)
The rose (Lieurance)
Jones, Mary
The lass of the hill (Howard)
Jones, Rice
Y Cymry dedwydd (Welsh air)
Jones, Robert
Corydon's farewell
"Farewell, dear love." See Corydon's farewell
Love wing'd my hope
"My love bound me with a kisse"
Jones, S. A.
Polly, my sweetheart (Cole)
Jones, Walter Howe
Arbor day
The bonds of love
"Broke! broke! broke"
The centipede and the frog
A demonstration
Forest song
Illinois
Mamie's charms
Mount Vernon bells
Nothing—but another girl
"Old Winter"
The return of spring

Jones, Walter Howe —*Continued*
She answered me nay
She shook her head
A song of March
Summer even-song
"There's a song in the air"
The untruthful daisy
The vacant stare
"When the year is new"
Jones, William
The monks of old (Glover)
Jones, William, fl. 1830
The mellow horn
Jones, William Price Hartwell
The heavenly song
Jonson, Ben
"Drink to me only with thine eyes"
(Old setting; also music attributed
to Mellish)
Dulcina (16th century air)
"Have you seen but a white lily grow"
(English air; also music by Cauff-
man)
"I sing the Birth was born tonight"
(Martin)
To Charis (Composer unknown)
Jordan, Mrs Dorothea (Bland)
The blue-bell of Scotland ("Of all
flowers") (same air as The blue
bells of Scotland)
The blue bells of Scotland ("O where,
tell me where")
Des mädchens klage. See The blue
bells of Scotland ("O where, tell
me where")
Jordan, Sverre
Autumn. See Herbstgang
Finnland
Herbstgang
Jordan am a hard road to trabbel. T. F.
Briggs. HSD—NMP—WBT
Jordan, O my soul. See Waiting all the
day
José, T. R. G.
"Coming from the winter"
Joseph ("Ich war jüngling") E. H. Méhul.
Words by Duval. [Tr of A peine au
sortir de l'enfance] g. ED 1
Joseph and the angel. See "As Joseph
was a walking" (Terry)
"Joseph Baxter is my name." See Not
for Joseph
"Joseph was an old man." See The cherry
tree carol (English version)
"Joseph were a young man." See The
cherry tree carol (Hot Springs, N.C.
version)
Josephson, Jacob Axel
"Ring out, thou wondrous song." See
"Sjung, sjung, du underbara sång"
"Sjung, sjung, du underbara sång"
"Joshua fit de battle ob Jericho." Negro
spiritual. JB
"Joshua fit de battl' ob Jerico" (Arr by
Burleigh) See An ante-bellum ser-
mon
"Jošt' ne sviti' bijela zora." See "White
dawn has not come stealing"
Jouberti, A.
Sérénade à Juanita

Joukovsky, Vasilii Andreevitch. See Zhu-
kovski, Vasili Andreevich
"Un jour de printemps." See Pastorale
(Bizet)
Le jour est levé. See Chant du chasseur
(Meyerbeer)
"Le jour fuit dans le sombre." See Po-
vero marinar (Mililotti)
"Jour heureux." A. Sacchini. e.f.
SOA 3
"Un jour, le prince Eugène." See Le
prince Eugene
"Le jour, lugubrement, touche à sa fin."
See The wish (Cui)
The journey. M. I. Glinka. e. NM 1
The journey of the leaves. German folk
air. Words by H. H. Harbour. DO
Journeyman's song. N. P. Hillebrand.
e. KSN
"Jours passés" ("Bygone days") L. Delibes.
Words by A. Silvestre. e.f. CM 1
—HM 1
The jovial beggar. See A begging we will
go
Jović, Spiridion
Remembrance (Croatian folk air)
Joy, W. A.
Alma mater—Greenville (Old air)
Joy ("Ye mortals, say") Lindblad. e.
KSN
"Joy and courage." P. M. Costa. Words
by D. Stevens. BSS
"Joy and gladness." G. B. Lissant.
Words by G. W. Bethune. HC
"The joy bells once again we hear." See
The joy of the morrow
"Joy bells ring through all the vale." See
Joy bells ring to-day
Joy bells ring to-day. Scotch air.
FSS 2
"Joy-bells ringing." C. Vincent. HC
"Joy fills our inmost heart to-day." H.
Gadsby. Words by W. C. Dix.
HC
Emmanuel, God with us. BSC
"Joy fills our inmost hearts today" (Em-
manuel) Composer unknown. Words
by W. C. Dix. MCS
"Joy fills our inmost hearts to-day." S.
Smith. Words by W. C. Dix. HC
"Joy for the sturdy trees" (Song for Arbor
day) M. Hanlyn. Words by S. F.
Smith. MS
"Joy for the sturdy trees" (Arbor day
song) G. E. Oliver. Words by S.
F. Smith. LA—NMS
Joy hath come to earth again. Air from
the Swiss. Words by R. F. Little-
dale. HC
Joy in sorrow. I. D. Sankey. Words by
J. Crewdson. FSS 3
The joy-inspiring horn. R. Bride. BE 7
"Hark! hark! the joy-inspiring horn."
MM
"Joy is now kindled, risen the day." See
God morgen (Grieg)
"Joy, joy for ever." J. Clark-Whitfeld.
Words by T. Moore. BE 7
"Joy! joy! freedom to-day." FSS 8—LA

Joy must reign to-night. F. Campana. Words by W. W. Campbell. MCS

"Joy of joys! He lives, He lives." H. F. Sheppard. Words by W. J. Irons. HC

Joy of my heart ("Red, red is the path to glory") North highland song. Air: 'Stu mo run. Words by R. Couper. BMC—MMS—PS 2

"Red, red is the path to glory" ('Stu mo run) HSSS

Joy of the morning ("I hear you, little bird") H. Ware. Words by E. Markham. AA

The joy of the morrow ("The joy bells once again") Words by E. Douglas. MCS

"Joy to see the stars above us." See "Deilig er den himmel blå"

"Joy to the person of my love." 17th century air. MM

"Joy to the world" (Antioch) G. F. Händel. Words by I. Watts. BD—DC—FSS 6—MCS—TFC 2—TL—WBT—WS

"Joy to the world." L. Mason. Words by I. Watts. HSD

"Joy to thee, my brave canoe." See Voyageur's song

"Joy wait on thy morrow." French air. FSS 2

"Joy, ye people, great and small." J. F. Bridge. Words by F. K. Harford. HC

Joyce, Patrick Weston
The leprehaun (Irish air)
Nelly, my love, and me (Irish air)

Joyce, Robert Dwyer
"Far in the mountains with you" (Irish air)

"Joyful and mournful." See "Freudvoll und leidvoll" (Beethoven)

Joyful is the morn. See "Once again the olden story" (Bunnett)

Joyful message. See Frohe botschaft

"The joyful morn is breaking." E. J. Hopkins. HC

"The joyful morn is breaking." G. E. Oliver. HC

Joyful tidings. G. Verdi. Words by C. Bede. MCS

"Joyful tidings of a Saviour." S. M. Nourse. Words by E. A. H. Besly. HC

"Joyfully, joyfully angels are singing." C. F Roper. HC

"Joyfully, joyfully onward I move" (Christian victor) Words by W. Hunter. FSS 7

Joyous anthem swelling. Von Flotow. Words by A. L. Pratt. MCS

The joyous meeting (Vyĭdu-l' ĭâ na rĭê-chen'ku) Russian folk song. e. SSR 2

Joyous song ("Were it not for joyous song") FSS 6

"A joyous song once more we bring." F. C. Maker. Words by W. H. Groser. HC

"Joyous you shall be to-day." See Christ is born—His name praise

"Joyous young lasses, profit by the time." See "Jeunes fillettes" (Dalayrac)

"Joyously, joyously, silvery clear." A. C. White. HC

"The joys of love." See "Plaisir d'amour" (Martini)

"Joy's sweet blossoms may never spring from the soil of earth." See "Gläd-jens blomster"

"Joys that we've tasted." W. B. Hall. FSS 1—WBT

Juanita. Spanish air. Words by C. Norton. CHS—FMB—FSS 2—HSC—HSD— JS—MPC— MS— NMH—NML— OH—SSS— TFC 1—WA—WBT—WC—WL—WSW

"Jučer si meni rekla." See Reproach

"Juche, lustig, seggt he." Air: In Berlin sagt' er. e.g. SMW

Judas. Massenet. e. OS 4
"Ah, Mary, give an ear." e. SAS 4

Jude, William Herbert
Behold! I stand at the door
The bells of Seville
The mighty deep

The judge-dance. See Domaredansen

Judgment day is rolling round. Negro spiritual. JP
Judgment day is a-rollin' around. HR

Judith. J. Concone. Words by Belanger. e. FSS 5

Jukovski, Vasili Andreyevich. See Zhukovski, Vasili Andreevich

Jul (Yuletide) E. Alnaes. Words by P. Sivle. e.n. WM 1

Jul polska (Christmas polka) Swedish song. e.sw. BF 2

Juley. Negro halliard chantey. CR

Julia to the wood-robin. Spofforth. HSE 2

Julian, John
"Sweetly sang the angels" (music by Crossley; Dunhill)

Jullien, Louis
"Ah! for wings to soar"

July ("When the scarlet cardinal") W. B. Olds. Words by S. H. Swett. NMS

July song ("In the month of hot July") A. S. Gatty. WSC

"July the first in Oldbridge town." See The Boyne water

Juncos, Manuel Fernández. See Fernández Juncos, Manuel

June ("O June! delicious month") W. B. Olds. Words by F. D. Sherman. NMS

June ("What is so rare") P. A. Schnecker. Words by J. R. Lowell. TL

"Jung, fröhlich und heiter enthüpf ich ins feld." See Der sorgenfreie (Schulz)

"Jung Hänschen." Volksweise. Words by W. von Zuccalmaglio. g. ED 3

Die junge nonne (The novice) Schubert. Words by J. N. Craigher. e.g. SS 1

Die junge nonne (The young nun) e.g. KF 2—PG 2

Jünger, Friedrich
Genuss des lebens (Composer unknown)

Jungfrun i det gröna (Maiden in the garden) Swedish folk song. Words by B. E. Malmström. e.sw. HSOS

Der jüngling am bache ("An der quelle sass der knabe") Volksweise. Words by F. von Schiller. g. ED 2

Jünglings weihe ("Fröhlich und frei") Studenten-melodie. Words by C. von Buri. g. ED 2

Jüngst, Hugo Richard
Spinn! spinn

"Jure plaudunt omnia." Christmas carol. 1. HC

"Jurie came to jebussalem." Air: Dulcina (before 1615) JE

Just a song at twilight. See Love's old sweet song (Molloy)

Just after the battle. G. F. Root. WBT

"Just as I am." W. B. Bradbury. Words by C. Elliott. FSS 3—HSD—NMS—WS

Just as it used to do. See "If you to me be cold" (Harris)

"Just as the daylight is fading." See "Tant que le jour dure" (Delibes)

"Just as the moon was fading." See Kriss Kringle

"Just as the star that shines above so clear." See "Som stjärnan uppå himmelen så klar"

Just as the tide was flowing. Yorkshire air. MM

"Just at the stroke of midnight." See Gli scarriolanti

"Just before the battle, mother." G. F. Root (music and words) HSD—MP —NMH—WBT

Just behold that number. See From every graveyard

Just in the height of her bloom. Irish folk song. JOI

"Just like love is yonder rose." J. Davy. BE 3—DM 2—HSE 2

"Just look upon me." See The song of Khívria (Musorgskii)

"Just touch the harp gently." C. Blamphin. Words by S. N. Mitchell. FSS 7

"Just wait a little while." See The old ark a-moving along

"Just wait, I'll tell on thee." See I'll tell on thee

"Just when the day is over." See When the lights are low (Lane)

"Just without our little window" ("Pod tím nášim okeneckem") Slovak song. bo.e. BF 1

"J'y ai planté rosier." See La ronde du rosier

K

'k heb mijn wagen volgeladen ("I have run down with my wagon") Dutch folk song. d.e. BDF

"Ka de la wats." See Pawnee war-song

"Ka diandle, dâs mâg mi net." See Der tost (Koschat)

Kaahiki, James
Dear heart (Nape)

"De kabels los" (Matrozenlied) Dutch chantey. d.e. SMW

Kabyle song ("Ah! Stamboul lève sa bannière") See Stamboul (Si Mohammed Said?)

Kabyle song ("De ma Zohra l'âme bercée") See Zohra

"Kaetha yah." See Wa-wan wa-an

"Kah ninahnebah aeneen." See Carousal

"Kahkeenah wahweengay." See Before the battle

"Kahne'tah we nenosee." See Caribou dance

"'O kairos adelphoi." See War song ("Brothers up, swift arise")

Kaiser Wenzel ("Was schiert mich reich und kaiserprunk") J. F. Reichardt. Words by E. G. Drimborn. g. ED 2

Kak nyebesá tvoi vzoi vzor blistáyet. See "Like to the sky serenely smiling" (Rimskii-Korsakov)

Kak po sadiku, sadiku. See The bridegroom's plea

Kak u nashego shirokago dvora. See The girl who would not dance

Kak u nashikh u vorot. See The angry father-in-law

Kak vo gorodîe stol' no-Kievskom. See The feast of Vladímir

Kalakaua, David, king of Hawaii
Composer
Akahi hoi. See For once again
For once again
Sweet lei Lehua
Author
Our native land (Berger)

Kalakaua's serenade. C. K. Hopkins. Words by M. Kalaukoa. e.h. HA

Kalama, S.
One, two, three, four (Alau)

Kalaukoa, Malie
Flower of my heart (Hopkins)
Kalakaua's serenade (Hopkins)

Kalina. See The barberry (Komorowski)

Kalinnikov, Vasilii Sergîeevich
A prayer
"Klare sternelein." See "Stars ethereal"
Prière. See A prayer
"Stars ethereal"

Källan (The spring) W. Lagercrantz. Words by F. Hedberg. e.sw. HSOS

Kalliwoda, Johann Wenzeslaus
Barcarolle
Ever thine
"Yes! the die is cast" (attributed also to P. Pestel)

"**Kampfmüd** und sonnverbrannt." See Biterolf (Wolf)

Der **kanarienvogel.** See The canary (Tchaikovsky)

"**Kanenetah** we nenosee." See Caribou dance

Kannel. See The harp song

"**Kanske** vil der gå både vinter og vår." See Solvejgs sang (Grieg)

Kanteleelle. See To the harp (Jarnefelt)

Kapilina. See United

Kapper, Siegfried
Vorschneller schwur (Brahms)

"**Kara** Mustafa." Serbia-Bosnia folk song. e.se. BF 1

Karamzin, Nikolaï Mikhaïlovich. See Pushkin, Aleksandr Sergïeevich, jt. auth.

"**Karl** John, our great king." See "Carl Johan" (Du Puy)

Kate Kearney. Air: The beardless boy. Words by Lady Morgan. JO— PI
"Oh! did you not hear of Kate Kearney." MMI

Kate Kearney, Answer to. Air: The beardless boy. PI

Kate of Aberdeen ("The silver moon's enamour'd beam") J. Battishill. DM 2

Katey's letter ("Och, girls, did you ever hear") C. H. Sainton-Dolby. Words by Lady Dufferin. HSD— MMI—PI—WBT—WL
Katy's letter. FSS 1—NML

Kathleen ("Oh! leave not your Kathleen") W. Williams. FSS 7

Kathleen aroon. F. Abt. Words by L. M. J. M. Crawford. FSS 3—HSD— NML—WBT—WL

"**Kathleen** mavourneen." F. N. Crouch. Words [by L. M. J. M. Crawford;] wrongly attributed to A. B. Crawford. BSE—CS 1—FSS 2—HSC— HSD—JO —JSE—PI—SS 1—WA— WBT—WL —WSW

Katiba, Kamar
"Come, O nightingale" (Armenian air)
The sure hope (Armenian air)

Katie Morey. Folk song: North Carolina version. CSE
—Tennessee version. CSE

Katinka ("A Russian maid was Katinka") Russian folk song. e. GO

Kattyglö visa (The owl's song) Norse folk song. e.n. MAN

Katy darling. English ballad. FSS 2

Katy Kearney. See Kate Kearney

The **katydid.** German air. Words by O. W. Holmes. LBR

Katy's letter. See Katey's letter (Sainton-Dolby)

"**Kau** ano mai ana ia'u la." See "The ground is strewn" (Leleiohoku)

Kau fra Hallingdalen (Dearest maiden) Norwegian shepherd's song. e.n. BO—SMF

Käuzlein ("Ich armes käuzlein kleine") L. Reichardt. Volkslied. g. ED 3

"**Kawas,** thy baby is crying." Pawnee Indian song. e.in. FIS

"**Kaygoomowekayn** ahbinogees." See The naked bear

"**Kaygoomowekayn** nenejahneses." See Sleepy time

Kayser-Langenhannes, A.
Wiegenlied (Ries)

Kazoe-uta. See Counting song

"**Kde** domov můj." See "Where is my home" (Škroup)

"**Kdyby** mně to Pán Bůh dal." See "O, that the dear Giver of life"

"**Když** jsem plela len." See "Weeding flaxfields blue"

"**Ke-chi** ra-ku-wa-ku." See The wren

Kealakai,
"Oh, tempt me not, my darling" (Hopkins)

Kean, Edmund
"Sweet Kitty Clover"

Keats, John
Daisy's song (Ruthenian air)
"A thing of beauty" (Page)
"Where be you going, you Devon maid" (Jackson)

Keble, John
"God the Lord a King remaineth" (Smart)
Morning hymn (Beethoven)
"Sun of my soul, Thou Saviour dear" (music by Gaul; Monk)

Keegan, John
The holly and ivy girl (Irish air)

The **keel** row ("As I came down the Canongate") Air: Smiling Polly. Words by J. Hogg. WBT—WL
Merry may the keel row. PS 1

The **keel** row ("As I cam' doon the Sandgate") Air: Smiling Polly. Words from a Tyneside ballad. BOS
The keel row (Smiling Polly) CO 2
O, weel may the keel row. DM 1
Weel may the keel row. SMW

[The **keel** row] Weel may the keel row ("Oh, who is like my Johnnie") Air: Smiling Polly. Words by Thompson. JO—PS 1
Weel may the keel row ("Oh, who sae like my Johnny") ME

"**Keen** blaws the wind o'er Donocht-head." See The minstrel

"**Keen** blaws the wind o'er the braes o' Gleniffer." See The braes o' Gleniffer

Keene, Arthur F.
"Farewell! but whenever you welcome the hour" (2 airs)

Keene, Frederick A.
The Christmas story

Keene, Robert
"How firm a foundation" (Reading?)
Authorship uncertain
The **keenly** lode. Folk song. BSW
Keep a-inchin' along. Negro spiritual.
HR—JB
Variant: Inching along
Keep a light heart. H. Fase. FSS 8
Keep awake, Marie Picard, keep awake,
awake. See Le couvre-feu
"**Keep** looking for the flowers of May."
See The flowers of May
Keep me from sinking down. Negro spiritual. DF—FSS 5—JP—NMP
Keep me f'om sinkin' down. JB
Keep me from sinkin' down. HR
Oh, Lord, oh, my Lord. WBT
"**Keep** on whirling." See My youngest
one is wedded
Keep our love unblemish'd dear for ever.
See "My wreath of lehua" (Nape)
"**Keep** working, 'tis wiser than sitting
aside." See Never say fail
"**Keep** your lamps trimmed." Negro spiritual. DF
The **keeper**. Folk song: Warwickshire
version. FSF—SEF 2—SO
—Cornish version. BSW
"The **keeper** did a-shooting go." See The
keeper
"**Keezhoyah** 'shquandaym." See Winter
"**Kehrst** du zurück, .o liebe, schnell entronnen." See Love (Bleikhman)
Keiffer, A. S.
Twilight is falling (Unseld)
Keil, A.
A Portuguesa
Keil, Georg
Frühlingsliebe (Composer unknown)
"**Kein** feuer, keine kohle." See Heimliche
liebe
"**Kein** graben so breit." See Keine sorg'
um den weg (Raff)
"**Kein** hälmlein wächst auf erden" ("Soft
dews from heaven falling") W. F.
Bach. e.g. NG
"**Kein** schlaf noch kühlt das auge mir." See
In der frähe (Wolf)
"**Kein** schönrer tod ist in der welt." See
Schlachtlied (Silcher)
Keine sorg' um den weg (Love finds out
the way) J. Raff. e.g. KF 1—
KF 2—KF 3
Keith,
When the king comes owre the water
(Scottish air)
Keith, George
"How firm a foundation" (Reading?)
See Keene, R. "How firm a foundation" (Reading?)
"**Kék** nefelejts." See Forget-me-not (Serly)
Keller, C.
Die feldflasche

Keller, Matthias
The American hymn
"Angel of peace" (same air as The
American hymn)
Hail to our flag. See The American
hymn
"Speed our republic." See The American hymn
Kelley, Edgar Stillman
"O captain! my captain"
Kellogg, Alice W.
Composer
Crew song
Author
My college girl (Hill)
Kelly, Michael
Oh, no! my love, no
Rest, warrior, rest (from The royal
oak)
"When pensive I thought of my love"
(from Blue beard)
The woodpecker
Kelly, Thomas
"Crown the Saviour, angels crown
Him" (Monk)
"Hark! ten thousand" (Composer unknown)
Kellyburnbraes. Scottish song. Words
by R. Burns. PS 2
"There livèd a carl in Kellyburn braes."
BSR
Kelvin grove ("Let us haste to Kelvin
grove") Air: O the shearin's no for
you. Words by T. Lyle. FSS 2—
MMS—PS 1
Kemble, John Philip
My heart and lute (Bishop) See
Moore, T. My heart and lute
(Bishop)
Kemo kimo. Old song. SSS—WBT
Variant of: The wedding of the frog
and mouse
Kempt, F. A.
Echtes glück
Ken, Thomas
"Glory to Thee, my God, this night"
(music by Gounod; Hatton)
Old hundred (Franc)
"**Ken** ye ought o' Captain Grose." Air:
Sir John Malcolm. Words by R.
Burns. BSR
"**Kenbahmahshay** non Quakahbahnoques."
See Confession
Kenney, James
"Why are you wandering here, I pray"
(Nathan)
"**Kennst** du das land" ("Know'st thou the
land") L. von Beethoven. Words
by J. W. von Goethe. e.g. KF 1
KF 2—MSS 1
"**Kennst** du das land" (Mignon) e.g.
PG 1
"**Kennst** du das land" (Mignon) F. H.
Himmel. Words by J. W. von
Goethe. g. ED 1
"**Kennst** du das land" (Mignons lied.—
Mignon's song) F. Liszt. Words by
J. W. von Goethe. e.g. CS 2—
MSS 2

"**Kennst** du das land" (Mignon) J. F. Reichardt. Words by J. W. von Goethe. g. ED 2

"**Kennst** du das land" (Mignon) A. Romberg. Words by J. W. von Goethe. g. ED 3

"**Kennst** du das land" (Mignon) H. Wolf. [Words by J. W. von Goethe] e.g. PG 1

"**Kennt** ihr das land." See Unser vaterland (Nägeli)

Kent, W. P.
Listen, my lady

"**Kent** gij dat volk vol heldenmoed" ("Know ye that race of hero mold") C. F. van Rees (music and words) d.e. BSP
Boer national volkslied ("Right nobly gave, voortrekkers brave") e. BMC

Keppel, Lady Caroline
Robin Adair (Celtic air: Irish and Scotch version; also English version)

Kerner, Justinus
Alte laute, I (Schumann)
Alte laute, II (Schumann)
Stille liebe (Schumann)
Wanderlied (Folk air; also music by Schumann)
"Zur ruh, zur ruh" (Wolf)

The **Kerry** dance. J. L. Molloy (music and words) FSS 4—HSD—MCS—PI

Kessler, J.
Die thränen des herzens (Goltermann)

Ketchum, Mrs Annie (Chambers)
The bonnie blue flag (Macarthy)

Kethe, William
Old hundred (Franc)

Kettle, Charles E.
"Once in Bethlehem of Judah"

Key, Francis Scott
God reigns (Mendelssohn)
"Lord, with glowing heart I'd praise thee" (Spanish air; also music by Flotow; Haydn)
The star-spangled banner (Smith)

The **keys** of Canterbury. Folk song. FSF—SEF 2—SO
Variants: "I'll give to you a paper of pins, for that's the way that love begins"; The keys of heaven

The **keys** of heaven. Folk song: English version. CST
—Black Mountain, N.C. version. CSE
—Hot springs, N.C. version. CSE
—Virginia version. CSE
Variants: "I'll give to you a paper of pins, for that's the way that love begins"; The keys of Canterbury

"**Kezhegukin** tebikukee." See The witch

"**Kezhegukin** wayashkun." See Song to the morning star

"**Kezhegung** baymosed." See A song of trust

"**Kezhoyah** 'shquandaym." See Winter

Khanta zagun guzick ahalik gorena. For English translation see "Companions, all sing loudly"

Khedival hymn ("Ha ni an bé") ar.e. BSP—MP

"**Khodit** Mĭesĭats." See Christmas greeting

Khomĭakov, A.
Nocturne (Liapunov)
To the children (Rachmaninov)

"**Khristos** rozhdaetsĭa." See "The Christ is coming"

Kiallmark, George
Araby's daughter
"Brightest and best" (same air as Araby's daughter)
"Come, rest in this bosom"
The old oaken bucket (same air as Araby's daughter)

Kidd's lament. Old song. JSE
Variant of: Captain Kidd

Kidson, Frank
The country parson (Traditional air)
"Go from my window" (Folk air)
The perils of the isle (Manx air)
"Tom Tinker's my true love" (Traditional air)
"While o'erhead the storm is howling" (Traditional air)

Kiel, Friedrich
"Da er gestraft" (from Christus)
"For my soul is athirst for God" (from Der stern von Bethlehem)
"He was oppress'd and afflicted sore." See "Da er gestraft"
"Turn again to thy rest" (from Der stern von Bethlehem)

Kilburn, George
Billy boy (Old American air)

"**Killa** Bukk, Killa Blakk." See Gjeite lok

Killarney. M. W. Balfe. Words by E. Falconer. CS 2—FSS 2—HSC—HSD—LA— PI—SS 2—WA—WBT— WSC —WSW

Killebukken ("O my pet lamb") R. Nordraak. Words by B. Björnson. e.n. MAN

Killinen, K.
Sing thou, sing (Järnefelt)
To the harp (Järnefelt)

"**Kimi** ga yo" ("May our Lord long reign") H. Hiromori. e.j. BSP
Japanese national hymn. e.j. WA—WBT—WSW
"Kimi ga yo" (Japanese national hymn) e.j. WCP. e. only CST
"Kimi-ga-yo" (Reign of my king.—National hymn of Japan.—"May our Lord for ever reign") e.j. BMC
Kimi-ga-yo (Reign of my sovereign) e. TL
Kimigayo. e.j. NA
"May our lord reign long." e.j. MP

Kind, Friedrich
Brautjungfernlied (Weber)
Gebet (Weber)
"Wie nahte mir der schlummer" (Weber)

"**Kind** Christmas comes but once a year."
See A Christmas carol (Scott-Gatty)
Das **kind** der berge (The mountain maid)
E. Grieg. Words by A. Garborg. e.g.
FF
"**Kind** friends, we meet again." See Fare-
well, good night
"**Kind** friends, you must pity my horrible
tale." See The dreary black hills
"**Kind** friends, your pity pray bestow." See
Constantinople
The **kind** hearted boss. See El charro
Kind Robin lo'es me. Scottish song. JO
—PS 1
Kind words are dear to all. P. E. van
Noorden. Words by N. E. Elwell.
HSD
"**Kind** words can never die." A. Hutchin-
son. Author of words unknown.
FSS 1—WBT
"**Kind** words can never die." Arr from E.
E. Whittemore. Author of words un-
known. LBR
Die **kinder** bei der krippe ("Ihr kinderlein,
kommet") J. A. P. Schulz. Words
by C. von Schmid. g. ED 1
Ihr **kinderlein**, kommet ("O come, little
children") e. MF
"**Kindly** forest." See Selve amiche, om-
brose piante (Caldara)
"**Kindly** youthful gods of springtime." See
Mit einem gemalten band (Beethoven)
Kindred hearts. German air. Words by
F. Hemans. FSS 2
King, C. M.
"A Yankee ship and a Yankee crew"
King, Horatio C.

Composer

One grand sweet song
Valedictory

Author

Noble Dickinsonia (Composer un-
know)
King, John
Children's hosanna (Webb)
King, Matthew Peter
Eve's lamentation
"Far, far from me my lover flies"
(from The weathercock)
The minute gun at sea
Tom Steady (from Up all night)
King, Oliver
Israfel
"O lovely voices of the sky"
King, Robert
Love for love. See "Shall I wasting
in despair"
"Shall I wasting in despair"
"**King** Adamastor, the ruler of ocean." See
"Adamastor, roi des vagues profondes"
(Meyerbeer)
"**King** Arthur." Folk song: Dorsetshire
version. BOS—SSS
—Lancashire version. BOH
King Charles XII. See Kung Carl XII
(Westermark)
"**King** Christian." See "Kong Christian
stod ved høien mast"

King Emanuel. Negro spiritual. HR—
JP
"**King** ever glorious! King ever glorious."
See The majesty of the divine humilia-
tion (Stainer)
"The **king** he wrote a long letter." See
Lord Dunwaters
"The **king** is sleeping." See Que ton âme
si noble (Rossini)
"**King** Jesus in His chariot rides." See
He's the lily of the valley
"**King** Jesus is a-listening." Negro spir-
itual. DF
"**King** Khristian." See "Kong Christian
stod ved høien mast"
"The **king** of France." Composer un-
known. NMH—NMS—WBT— WSC
"The **king** of France." J. W. Elliott.
TFC 2
"**King** of Israel." F. Hiller. e. SAS 4
"The **King** of love my Shepherd is." J. B.
Dykes. Words by H. W. Baker.
FSS 1—MCS—MS
Dominus regit me. CST
"The **King** of love my Shepherd is." C.
Gounod. Words by H. W. Baker.
HSS 2—HSS 3—HSS 4—WBT—WS
The **king** of night. Words by R. I. Hal-
sey. NMS
The **king** of Poland ("Courtiers, courtiers")
17th century song. CO 2
The **king** of seasons all. S. Adams.
MCS
The **king** of Spain's daughter. See "La
fille du roi d'Espagne"
"**King** of the shades." See "Re dell' abis-
so" (Verdi)
The **king** of Thule ("Es war ein könig")
See Der könig von Thule (Liszt)
The **king** of Thule ("Il était un roi") See
Le roi de Thulé (Gounod)
"The **king** of worms, and little wife." See
Solfager og ormekongen
The **king** of Yvetot. See Le roi d'Yvetot
"A **king** once did have two young daugh-
ters so fair." See De to kongedøttre
"A **king** once reigned in Thule." See Der
könig von Thule (Liszt)
King Pharaoh: The miracle of the cock.
Sussex gypsies' carol. WCC
King Pharaoh: The miraculous harvest.
Sussex gypsies' carol. WCC
"**King** Pharaoh sat a-musing." See King
Pharaoh: The miracle of the cock
"A **king**, yes, a king, each old man seems to
me." See Old age (Lindblad)
Kingdom coming. H. C. Work (music
and words) HSD—NMP—SSS—
WA—WSW
Kingdom come. WBT
"**Kingdoms** and thrones to God belong"
(Hamburg) L. Mason. Word by I.
Watts. JS
The **kings**. P. Cornelius (music and
words) Tr of Die könige. e. HC
"The **king's** daughter sat in her lofty
bow'r." See "Prinsessen sad höjt i sit
jomfrubur" (Kjerulf)

The king's highway. J. L. Molloy. Words by F. E. Weatherly. FSS 7—LA

The king's hunt. See "The hunt is up"

The king's jig ("At Winchester was a wedding") Words by T. D'Urfey. CO 2

King's prayer. R. Wagner. ₁Tr of Mein Herr und Gott₁ e. WBT

Kingsley, Charles
"O that we two were maying" (music by Gounod; White)
One grand sweet song (King)
The sands o' Dee (music by Boott; Macfarren)
"Three fishers went sailing" (music by Hullah; Macfarren)
"When all the world is young" (music by Barnard; Schenck)

Kingsley, George
"I would not live alway"
"Mortals, awake, with angels join"
"Only a baby fair"
"Only a gentle word"
"With joy we hail the sacred day"

Kinkel, Johanna
Soldier's farewell (Tr of Ritters abschied)

Kinney, Coates
Rain on the roof (music by Clark; Clifford; Naumann)

Kipling, Rudyard
Back to the army again (Cobb)
For to admire (Cobb)
"God of our fathers, known of old" (Blanchard)
On the road to Mandalay (Trevannion
The recessional (Huss)

Kirby, John
The sunniest season of life

Kirkham, Thomas
"How firm a foundation" (Reading?) See Keene, R. "How firm a foundation" (Reading?)

Kirnberger, Johann Philipp
Die liebe

Ny kirree fo-sniaghtey (The sheep in the snow) Manx folk song. Words from the Manx. e. GO

Kirshaw, George
"My Betsy is the blithest maid"

Kiser, Samuel Ellsworth
The good turns pay (Foster)

A kiss ("I would kiss thee") N. Tcherepnin. Words from the Russian of A. Maikoff. e. NM 2

The kiss ("Ich war bei Chloen") See Der kuss (Beethoven)

"The kiss, dear maid." L. Jausen. Words by Byron. HSE 2

"A kiss I begged." J. Gamble. MM

Kiss me quick and go. F. Buckley. HSD—WBT

"Kiss me, sweetheart." W. G. Smith. Words by J. Payne. HST

The kiss of a little child. J. Hullah. Words by C. J. Rowe. FSS 8

Kistler, E. H.
Alma mater—Muhlenberg

Kitchel, William L.
"O'er the lake" (Shepard)

Kittredge, Walter
Tenting on the old camp ground
Tenting to-night. See Tenting on the old camp ground
"We're tenting to-night." See Tenting on the old camp ground

Kitty Fell. 18th century song. ME

Kitty Neil. Irish air: Huish the cat from under the table. Words by J. F. Waller. JO

Kitty of Coleraine ("As beautiful Kitty") Irish air. Words attributed to E. Lysaght. MMI—PI

Kitty Tyrrell. C. W. Glover. Words by C. Jefferys. FSS 3—HSD

Kitty, will you marry me. Irish folk song. JOI

Kivi, Aleksis, pseud. See Stenvall, Aleksis

"Kjaerringa med staven" ("Here comes on crutches Sally") Norse folk song. e.n. MAN

Kjerulf, Charles
"All the bells bring far-off word." See "Alle klokker bringer fjaernt"
"Alle klokker bringer fjaernt"

Kjerulf, Halfdan
Aftenstemning. See "Prinsessen sad höjt i sit jomfrubur"
A bridal party on the Hardanger fjord. See Brudefaerden i Hardanger
Brudefaerden i Hardanger
"I long to climb the mountains high." See "Til fjelds over bygden"
"Ich fuhr über meer"
In days of yore. See Det var då
Ingrid's song. See Jngrids vise
Ingrids vise. See Jngrids vise
"I've journeyed o'er land." See "Ich fuhr über meer"
Jngrids vise
Laengsel
Den långa dagen
Last night, when all was still. See Laengsel
The long day. See Den långa dagen
Longing. See Laengsel
"A magic power." See "Min elskte, jeg er bunden"
"Min elskte, jeg er bunden"
Mit hjerte og min lyre. See My heart and lute
The mountains of Norway. See Norges fjelde
My heart and lute
The Neck. See Nökken
The nightingale. See Laengsel
Nökken
Norges fjelde
On the mountain. See Paa fjellet
Over de höje fjelde
Over the lofty mountains. See Over de höje fjelde
Paa fjellet
Pleasure-pain (same air as Laengsel)
"Prinsessen sad höjt i sit jomfrubur"

Kjerulf, Halfdan—*Continued*
Sehnsucht. See Laengsel
"Sing, sing! nightingale, sing." See "Syng, syng"
Slumber. See Sövnen
Sövnen
"Syng, syng"
Synnöves lied. See Synnöves sang
Synnöves sang
"Til fjelds over bygden"
Twilight musing. See "Prinsessen sad höjt i sit jomfrubur"
Det var då
"When you slept"

Kjerulf, Theodor
"Syng, syng" (Kjerulf, H.)
Klage ("Ich klage hier") Volksweise. g. ED 3
"Klaget nicht, dass ich gefallen." See Schill
"Klara stjärnor med de ögon snälle" ("Little stars, whose bright eyes shine above me") Swedish folk song. Words by W. Hebbe. e.sw. HSOS
Klärchens lied im Egmont. See "Freudvoll und leidvoll" (Reichardt)
"Klare sternelein." See "Stars ethereal" (Kalinnikov)
Klauer, F. G.
"I'm a shepherd of the valley"
Kleffel, Arno
Primula veris
The **kleftman** (Ho kelphtēs) Greek song. A. Seiller. e.gr. BF 2
Klein, B.
Frühlingsgruss an das vaterland
Klein, Bruno Oscar
My mother's memory
Old Ironsides
Klein, Christian Benjamin
"Eine hand voll erde" (attributed)
Klein Käthchen. See Liten Karin
"Kleine blumen, kleine blätter." See Mit einem gemalten band (Beethoven)
Das **kleine** fischermädchen. For English translation see The little fishermaiden (Waldmann)
"Kleine gäste, kleines haus." See Mausfallen-sprüchlein (Wolf)
Der **kleine** rekrut ("Wer will unter die soldaten") F. Kücken. Words by F. Güll. g. ED 1
The young recruit. e. WSC
Die **kleine** spinnerin ("Was spinnst du") W. A. Mozart. g. ED 2
Der **kleine** tambour ("Bin der kleine tambour veit") A. Pohlenz. Words by W. Gerhard. g. ED 1
The little drummer. e. SSS
Kleinschmidt, E. C.
"Wär ich ein muntres vögelein" (Zumsteeg)
Ho klephtēs. See The kleftman (Seiller)
Klesheim, Anton von
's mailüfterl (Kreipl)
Kletke, Gustav Hermann
In die ferne (Glück)
Der sandmann (Schumann)

"Kling! klang! with sound of anvils sharply clinking." See The gypsy forge
Klingemann, G.
Sonntagslied (Mendelssohn)
Klingemann, Karl
"Ach, wie so bald verhallet der reigen" (Mendelssohn)
Bei der wiege (Mendelssohn)
Klopstock, Friedrich Gottlieb
Die auferstehung (Graun)
Die frühen gräber (Gluck)
Klughardt, August Friedrich Martin
"Holy one, dying for mortals" (from Die grablegung Christi)
"Truly this man was the son of God" (from Die grablegung Christi)
Der **knabe** and das veilchen ("Blühe, liebes veilchen") J. A. P. Schulz. Words by C. A. Overbeck. g. ED 1
Der **knabe** mit dem wunderhorn (The boy with the magic horn) R. Schumann. Words by E. Giebel. e.g. FM
"Der **knabe** Robert." A. Methfessel. Words by E. M. Arndt. g. ED 2
Kneass, Nelson
Ben Bolt: German air arranged
Sweet Alice, Ben Bolt. See Ben Bolt: German air arranged
Knecht, Justin Heinrich
"At Easter morn the lark ascending"
"O Jesu, Thou art standing"
"Kneel down in silence, stir not a muscle." See "Sois immobile" (Rossini)
Knight, E.
The lad with the carroty poll
Knight, Edward
"Britannia's sons at sea" (Reeve)
Humming all the trade is (Reeve)
The lad with the carroty poll (Knight)
"Sweet Kitty Clover" (Kean)
Knight, Henry
Composer
"Children here on earth who dwell"
"O'er hill and dell the Christmas bell"

Author
"Come, listen to the story" (Powell)
Knight, Joseph Philip
"Beautiful Venice"
Eileen achora
"Go, forget me"
"Of what is the old man thinking"
"Rocked in the cradle of the deep"
"Say, what shall my song be to-night"
"She wore a wreath of roses"
Knight, Launce
Rosalie
The **knight** and shepherd's daughter ("It's of a pretty shepherdess") 17th century air. MM
The **knight** and the shepherd's daughter ("There was a shepherd's daughter") Folk song. SEF 1—SO
"Knight-errant" (Le paladin) A. Dargomijsky. Words by Joukovsky. e.f. NR 4
"The knight met a child in the road." See The false knight upon the road (Tennessee version)

"The **knight** must forth unto the field of blood." See Loyal death (Stainer)
"A **knight** of a gay and gallant mien." See The bee proffers honey but bears a sting (Dibdin)
"A **knight** young and handsome." See The knight's courtship
The **knight's** courtship. Old Danish song. e. KSN—WL
The **knights** of the golden O. Oberlin college song. J. P. Scott. Words by R. E. Brown. CHS
"**Knock** a man down." Pulling chantey. SE
Knock'd 'em in the old Kent road. A. Chevalier. WBT
Knock'd 'em in the old Kent road (Wot cher) WA—WSW
"**Knocks** like Jesus." See Somebody's knocking at your door
A **knot** of white and blue. Columbia university song. A. D. Woodruff. Words by G. W. Carryl. CHS—CU
The **knotting** song. H. Purcell. Words by C. Sedley. JE—PR 1
"**Know** I've vow'd and vow once more." See The avowal (Eccles)
"**Know** this my brethren heaven is clear." See Hey, then up go we
"**Know** ye that race of hero mold." See "Kent gij dat volk vol heldenmoed" (Rees)
"**Know** ye the land of birk and rowan." See The Scottish fatherland (Tschirch)
"**Know** ye where I love to dwell." See Lieblingsplätzchen (Mendelssohn)
"**Knowest** thou the land" ("Connais-tu le pays") See "Connais-tu le pays" (Thomas)
"**Knowest** thou the land" ("Kennst du das land") See "Kennst du das land" (Beethoven)
Knowles, F. L.
    "Come raise the song" (Davis)
"**Know'st** thou where I love to stray." See "Wisst ihr, wo ich gerne weil'" (Mendelssohn)
"**Knowst** thou yonder land." See "Connais-tu le pays" (Thomas)
Knud Lavard. N. W. Gade. Words by C. Hauch. da.e. SSN
Knyvett, William
    The bells of Saint Michael's tower
Ko aloha. See Kohala's breeses (Nape)
"**Ko** sem k njej pršov." See The coquette
Kocher, Conrad
    "As with gladness men of old"
Kocipinski, A.
    "O'er the distant lonely mountains" (Russian folk air)
Kock, Laurids Olufsen
    Thyra Dannebod (Rasmussen)
Koeneman, Th.
    The blacksmith
    Le forgeron. See The blacksmith
    The three roads
    Les trois chemins. See The three roads

Kohala's breezes (Ka inu wai) D. Nape. Words by W. Sheldon. e.h. HA
Kok, Laurids Olufsen. See Kock, Laurids Olufsen
"**Kol' slaven.**" See Glory to the Lord in Zion (Bortniånskiĭ)
Koliåda. See Yuletide
Kol'tsov, Aleksiĕi Vasil'evich
    The banks of the Don (Musorgskiĭ)
    The call of freedom (Balakirev)
    The country feast (Musorgskiĭ)
    Eastern romance (Rimskiĭ-Korsakov)
    Fly away, nightingale (Rubinstein)
    The laborer's plaint (Kopylov)
    The nightingale and the rose (Rimskiĭ-Korsakov)
    "Oh come to me when breezes stir" (Balakirev)
Koluibélnaya ("Faintly the child sighs") See Death's lullaby (Musorgskiĭ)
Koluibélnaya ("Sleep, my darling") See Cradle-song (Grechaninov)
Kolyada ("Yuletide wakes") See Yuletide
"**Kolyada, Kolyada.**" Russian carol. e. MF
    Variant: Yuletide
Kolzoff, Alexis Vasilievitch. See Kol'tsov, Aleksieĭ Vasil'evich
"**Kom** Kjyra." See Norsk fjeldsang (Thrane)
"**Kom,** kom fager ungersven" ("Come, come handsome fellow") Swedish folk song. e.sw. HSOS
    "Come, come thou handsome lad." e. CST
Komachi
    Old Samurai prayer (Ross)
"**Komm'** aus der engen stadt." See Winterlied (Koss)
"**Komm,** fein liebchen." See Ständchen (Weber)
"**Komm,** feins liebchen." See Ständchen (Folk air); Ständchen (another folk air)
"**Komm,** freude, sei gesegnet." See Die freude (Tuerk)
"**Komm',** lieber mai, und mache" (May song) Mozart. Words by C. A. Overbeck. e.g. MS
    Come back, sweet May. e. FSS 3—WSC
    "Come, May, thou lovely lingerer." e. HC
Kommen und scheiden (Meeting and parting) R. Schumann. Words by N. Lenau. e.g. FM
"**Kommt** a vogerl geflogen." See Frohe botschaft (Müller)
"**Kommt** hier al' bij, aanhoort dees klucht." See Pierlala
"**Kommt** lasst uns ausspazieren." See Der spaziergang (Berner)
Komori-uta. See Cradle song
Komorowski, J.
    The barberry
    Kalina. See The barberry

"**Kong** Christian stod ved høien mast" ("King Christian stood beside the mast") National song of Denmark. Old air, arr by J. Hartmann. Words by J. Ewald. da.e. BSP
Danish national hymn. e. HSD
Danish national song. da.e. WA
"King Christian" ("King Christian stood by lofty mast") e. BMC —MP—NMS—WBT
"King Christian stood beside the mast." da.e. SN. e. only KSN
"King Khristian" (Danish national hymn) da.e. WCP
"**Kongen** han stood paa höienloftsval." See Sigurd aa troll-brura
König, Karl Gottlob
Wert der freundschaft
Der **könig** in Thule ("Es war ein könig") J. F. Reichardt. Words by J. W. von Goethe. g. ED 3
Der **könig** in Thule ("Es war ein könig") K. F. Zelter. Words by J. W. von Goethe. g. ED 1
King of Thule. e. BSE
Der **könig** von Thule ("Es war ein könig." —The king of Thule) F. Liszt. Words by J. W. von Goethe. e.g. FF. e. only FTS
Der **könig** von Thule. For French and English translations with a different air see Le roi de Thulé (Gounod)
Die **könige.** For English translation see The kings (Cornelius)
Die **königskinder** ("Es waren zwei königskinder") Volkslied. g. ED 1
"**Konnt'** ich als sonne." See The maiden's wish (Chopin)
"**Könnt'** ich dich in liedern preisen." See Stille liebe (Schumann)
Konopnicka, Marya
The three roads (Koeneman)
Kopisch, August
Noah (Reissiger)
Der schlesische zecher und der teufel (Reissiger)
Kopken, Friedrich von
Beruf zur freude (Bergt)
Kopon te kai kamaton. For English translation see "Art thou weary, art thou languid" (Baker); "Art thou weary, art thou languid" (Bullinger); "Art thou weary, art thou languid" (Hopkins)
Kopylov, Aleksandr Aleksandrovich
The laborer's plaint
Méditation du laboureur. See The laborer's plaint
Koreshchenko, Arsenii Nikolaevich
Autumn melody
Chant d'automne. See Autumn melody
The smith
Korinfskii, A.
Christmas song (Liapunov)

Körner, Karl Theodor
Die drei sterne (Himmel)
Gebet vor der schlacht (Sicilian air; also music by Weber)
Gebet während der schlacht (Himmel)
Liebeständelei (Fitzenhagen)
Lützows wilde jagd (Weber)
Männer und buben (Volksweise)
Schwertlied (Weber)
Treuer tod (Choron)
Körner's battle prayer. See Gebet während der schlacht (Himmel)
Korobeïnik. See The peddler
Koromandel, Crescentius
Krambambuli (Folk air)
Kors och krona (Cross and crown) P. U. Stenhammar. Words by J. O. Wallin. e.sw. HSOS
Korsakov, Nikolaï Andreevich Rimskii-. See Rimskiï-Korsakov, Nikolaï Andreevich
Der **Kosak** und sein mädchen. See Beautiful Minka
Koschat, Thomas
City lad and country lass. See Städterbua und âlmadirn
The clod. See Der tost
Forsaken (Tr of Verlassen bin i)
Green pastures. See "The Lord is my Shepherd"
"The Lord is my Shepherd"
Städterbua und âlmadirn
Der tost
The young lover
Kosegarten, Ludwig Theobul
Alles um liebe (Zumsteeg)
Die erscheinung (Berger)
Koseley, Ferencz
Hungarian national hymn (Erkel)
Koss, H. von
Winter song. See Winterlied
Winterlied
"**Kossuth** Lajos azt üzente." See Louis Kossuth
"**Kossuth's** messenger came calling." See Louis Kossuth
Kotschonbey, L.
"Oh! tell it her"
Kotzebue, August Friedrich Ferdinand von
Ewiger wechsel (music by André; Himmel)
Ständchen (Folk air; another folk air; also music by Weber)
"Über die berge mit ungestüm" (Weber)
Die welt, ein orchester (Himmel)
Kotzschmar, Hermann
"Come forth and bring your garlands"
"Merry Christmas bells are ringing"
Koutouzoff, Arseny Arkad'yevitch Golenistcheff-, graf. See Golenishchev-Kutusov, Arseniï Arkadîeevich, graf
Kozak. See The Cossack (Moniuszko)
Kraakalund (In Kraakalund) Norwegian song. e.n. BF 2
Kraft von Toggenburg, graf
"Mir ist leide" (Erk)

Krag, Vilhelm
"Der skreg en fugl" (Sinding)
Hel mig mine strenge (Halvorsen)
Im kahne (Grieg)
Majnat (Sinding)
Moderen synger (Sinding)
Der **Krähwinkler** landsturm ("Immer lang-
sam voran") Volkslied. g. ED 1
Kraï tui moï.   See My native land (Gre-
chaninov)
Krakowiak. See "Dearest maiden, hark,
I pray thee"
Krambambuli. 18th century German folk
air. Words by C. Koromandel.
g. ED 1.   e. only LA
Crambambuli.   e.   CU—MPC—SSS
—WBT—WC
Kramer, Arthur Walter
A sigh.   See Soupir
Soupir
Krasni sarafan.   See The scarlet sarafan
(Varlamov)
Kreipl, Joseph
The forest glade
's mailüfterl
May breezes.   See 's mailüfterl
"Near in the forest."   See The forest
glade
Kremser, Eduard
Hymn of thanks.   See "Wilt heden nu
treden"
Prayer of thanksgiving.   See "Wilt
heden nu treden"
Thanksgiving prayer.   See "Wilt he-
den nu treden"
"Wilt heden nu treden"
Kretzschmer, Andreas
Ihr
Jean Pauls lieblingslied.   See Ihr
Kreutzer, Konradin
Abreise
The chapel
Forest-song.   See Waldes-lied
Hobellied
In der ferne
"Ein schütz' bin ich"
Song of the plane.   See Hobellied
"Thine eyes still shined"
"Trailing rose-tree."   See "Vaga rosa"
Trinklied
"Vaga rosa"
Waldes-lied
"What beams so bright."   See The
chapel
"What noble joys a hunter's life."   See
"Ein schütz' bin ich"
Kriegers abschied ("Leb wohl, mein bräut-
chen") A. Methfessel. g. ED 2
"Der **kriegeslust** ergeben." See entry under
Der
Kriegslied ("Auf, auf, wer deutsche freiheit
liebet") J. R. Zumsteeg. Words by
M. Opitz. g. ED 2
Kriegslied ("Schön ist's, unter freiem")
C. G. Eidenbenz. Words by F. K.
Hiemer. g. ED 2

Kriegslied des maies ("Wenn des frühlings
wachen ziehen")   L. Reichardt.
Words by L. A. von Arnim. g.
ED 3
Kriss Kringle. Air: Drink to me only with
thine eyes. Words by T. B. Aldrich.
LBR
Kriss Kringle's ride. Alpine air. MCS
Kristalle, die reinen. See "Kristallen den
fina"
"**Kristallen** den fina" ("Like crystal that's
gleaming") Swedish folk song.
e.sw. HSOS
Kristalle die reinen (The crystal maid-
en) e. BSE
"Kristallen den fina" ("O crystal the
finest") e.sw. BF 2
Kroeger, Ernest Richard
"Young thoughts have music"
Kroyer, Hans E.
Danish patriotic song of 1820
"There is a lovely land." See Dan-
ish patriotic song of 1820
Kruger, J.
"Wake, my heart, while round thee
swelling"
Krumbhaar, Mrs Harriet (Ware)   See
Ware, Harriet
Krummacher, Friedrich Adolf
Winterlied (Harder)
Kücken, Friedrich Wilhelm
"Alles still in süsser ruh"
"Away now, joyful riding"
"Drift, my bark" (Tr of Treibe schiff-
lein)
"Gently rest" (same air as "Alles still
in süsser ruh")
"Good night, farewell"
Gretelein
Heaven hath shed a tear.   See "Der
himmel hat eine thräne geweint"
"Herzallerliebstes schatzerl du"
"Der himmel hat eine thräne geweint"
How can I leave thee.   See Treue
liebe
The Jewish maiden (Tr of Das mäd-
chen von Juda)
Der kleine rekrut
Lizette (same air as Der kleine rekrut)
The mother's song.   See "Gently rest"
The poet
Slumber song.   See "Alles still in süs-
ser ruh"; "Gently rest"
"Softly now the light of day"
Treue liebe
The young recruit ("See these rib-
bons") See Lizette
The young recruit ("Wer will unter die
soldaten") See Der kleine rekrut
Kugler, Franz
Composer
Nachtlied
Author
Rudelsburg (Fesca)
Ständchen (Brahms)
"Wenn der lenz erwacht" (Norwe-
gian folk air)

Küherlied der Emmenthaler ("Was kann schöner sein") Schweizerisches volkslied. Air: Lieber weidersmann, edler jäger-g'spann. g. ED 3

Kuhi au ahe pono keia. See My sweet (Leleiohuko)

"**Kühl** und labend sinkt der tau auf die fluren nieder." See Abendlied froher landleute (Seidel)

Kuhlau, Friedrich
Abendlied

Kuhn, Gottlieb Jakob
's blümeli

Kui ia ko lei. See Sunny Manoa (Hopkins)

"**Kukuvitsa** kuka." See "The cuckoo is calling"

Kul'chinskii, V.
"Burning out is the sunset's red flame" (Balakirev)

Kullan ylistys. See The gay young bachelor

Kullberg, Henrik A.
"Carl Johan" (Du Puy)

"**Kun** mun kultani tulisi." See "Home my sweetheart comes from roving"

Kung Carl XII (King Charles XII) O. Westermark. Words by E. Tegnér. e.sw. HSOS

Kunze, G.
Der deutsche Rhein
Rheinlied. See Der deutsche Rhein
The Rhine song. See Der deutsche Rhein
"They shall not ever win thee." See Der deutsche Rhein

Kunzen, Friedrich Ludwig Aemilius
Feld- und waldlied

Kupernik, Tatiana Lvovna Shchepkina-. See Shchepkina-Kupernik, Tatiana Lvovna

"**Kur** tas šaltinēlis." See At the spring

"**Kur** tu augi." See Where did you grow

Kurpinski, Karl Kasimir
"Boże! coś Polske." See God for Poland (attributed)
God for Poland (attributed)
"O, Thou Lord God." See God for Poland (attributed)

Kurze,
Abendlied (Rolle)

Der kuss (The kiss) L. van Beethoven. Words by C. F. Weisse. e.g. GMF —PG 4

Kutoozoff, Arseny Arkad'yevitch Golenishtcheff-, graf. See Golenishchev-Kutuzov, Arseniĭ Arkadĭeevich, graf

Küttner,
An die freundschaft (Haydn)

Kutusov, Arseniĭ Arkadĭeevich Golenishchev-, graf. See Golenishchev-Kutusov, Arseniĭ Arkadĭeevich, graf

"**Kuu** kumab körgest ülewast." See Moan to the moon

"**Kuu** pua i omau a paa." See Flower of my heart (Hopkins)

"**Kuule** kuinka soitto kaikuu." See Suomi's song (Pacius)

Kvaalins halling (Halling from Valders) n. MAN

Kväll och frid (Evening and peace) E. G. Geijer. Words by C. W. Böttiger. e.sw. HSOS

"**Kwaeje** no makashot." See "Day dawns with freight to haul"

Het **kwezelken** (The little nun) Folk song. d.e. BDF

The **kynge's** balade. See "Pastime with good company" (Henry VIII)

Kyrie eleison ("Incarnate Jesus Christ") 15th century air. Words by M. Luther. e. MCS

L

"**Là-bas,** sur ces montagnes" ("From yonder on the mountains") Canadian folk song. e.f. TF

"**Lá** ilahá illalláh." See "There's no deity but God"

"**La,** lalerala la la la la la la la la." See Beer waltz

"**Laatst** waren er drie koningen." See De drie koningen

Lu **labbru** (The lips) Sicilian song. Words by G. Meli. e.i. MSI

Labitzky, Joseph
"Adieu, my native land, adieu"
"Come, play me that simple air"
"Fair Christmas comes"

Laborde, Alexandre Louis Joseph, comte de
"Partant pour la Syrie" (Hortense Eugénie de Beauharnais?) Authorship uncertain

The **laborer's** plaint (Méditation du laboureur) A. Kopyloff. Words from the Russian of Koltsoff. e.f. NM 1

Labour in vain. 18th century song. ME

Labriola, Pietro
Il cardello. See Lu cardillo
Lu cardillo
The goldfinch. See Lu cardillo
T'aggio visto
"There! I saw you." See T'aggio visto
"T'ho veduta." See T'aggio visto

Le **lac** (The lake) L. Niedermeyer. Words by A. de Lamartine. e.f. CM 1

Il **lacerato** spirito. G. Verdi. e.i. SOA 5

Lachner, Franz
Repentence. See Reue
Reue

Lack-a-day, O. J. Hook. Words by Haylock. ME

Lacome d'Estalenx, Paul Jean Jacques
The dancers

The **lad** with the carroty poll. E. Knight. Words by Edward Knight. ME

Laddie ("O! Laddie was somebody's darling") C. Pinsuti. Words by H. L. D. Jaxone. FSS 7

Laddie with the golden hair. See Oigfhear a chùil-dualaich

"The **laddies** by the banks o' Nith." Air: Up an' waur them a' Willie. Words by R. Burns. BSR

"**Ladies** of London." 17th century song. CO 2

"The **lads** now make their manners, bowing so politely." See Bourée du Mont Doré

"**Lads**, there is a crimson flag should mean a lot to you." See Lenox crimson

The **lady** and prentice. Folk song. BSW

The **lady** and the dragoon. Folk song: North Carolina version. CSE
—Tennessee version. CSE

The **lady** and the glove. Kentucky mountain song. WLT
Variant of: The golden glove

Lady Ann Bothwell's lament. See "Baloo, my boy"

Lady Beatrice's lament. D. Speranza. FSS 6

Lady Isabel and the elf knight. Folk song: Allanstand, N.C. version. CSE
—Carmen, N.C. version. CSE
—Georgia version. CSE
—Kentucky version. CSE
—Massachusetts version. CSE
Variant: Six kings daughters

Lady Maisry. Folk song. SEF 1—SO
—Dorset version. SF 1

"**Lady** Margaret was sitting in her dower room." See Fair Margaret and sweet William (Carmen, N.C. version no. 2)

"**Lady** Marg'ret was sitting in her bower one day." See Fair Margaret and sweet William (Dorset version)

"**Lady** Margret was sitting in the new church door." See Fair Margaret and sweet William (Kentucky version)

Lady Mary Ann. Scottish air: Craigston's growing, or, Lady Mary Ann. Words by Burns. PS 2
"O, Lady Mary Ann." BSR

"**Lady** mine, thy casement open." See Morning song (Barnby)

Lady Moon ("O Lady Moon, your horns") Canon. H. W. Loomis. Words by C. G. Rossetti. TFC 2

"**Lady** Moon, Lady Moon." Children's song. WSC

The **lady** of the lea. H. Smart. Words by W. H. Bellamy. CS 2

Lady Onlie, honest lucky. See "A' the lads o' Thornie-bank"

"**Lady**, thee I love." Old English air. Words after T. D'Urfey. BE 7

"**Lady**, unheeding, love lies a-bleeding." See Love lies a bleeding

"**Lady** with eyes so dreaming." Air: The wassail. Words by L. S. Jast. MMW

Ladybird. German folk song. e. DO

Laengsel ("Jeg kunde slet ikke sove."—Longing) H. Kjerulf. Words by C. Winther. da.e. SSN
"Last night." e. BSE—CHS—CU—HSC— HSD—MP—MPC— NMH —NML— OH— TFC 2— WA— WBT— WC—WL—WSC— WSW
Last night, when all was still. e. FSS 5
The nightingale. e. CS 2—MSS 2—SS 2
Sehnsucht (Last night) e.g. FMB—KF 1—KF 2—KF 3—KF 4—MSF 2

Laengsel ("Storm, hvem gav dig din aande."—Longing) J. Backer-Lunde. Words by A. Ritter. e.n. WM 1

"**Laeti** laudate Dominum." See Carmen Carthusianum (Horsley)

La Forge, Frank
Avec une rose. See Like the rose
Like the rosebud

Lagercrantz, W.
Ändå
"As yet." See Ändå
Källan
The spring. See Källan

Un **lago** delicioso. Costa Rica plantation song. e.s. HS

La Harpe, Jean François de
"Ô ma tendre musette" (Monsigny?)

Lahor, Jean, pseud. See Cazalis, Henri

Lahorsky,
Weariness

Laidlaw, William
Lucy's flittin' (Composer unknown)

Laing, Alexander
The braes of Mar (Scottish air)

"The **laird** o' Cockpen." Air: When she cam' ben she bobbit, or, Cockpen. Words by Nairne. BO—HSD—HSSS —JO—MMS—PS 1

Laisse-moi, laisse-moi. For English translation see "Let me gaze" (Gounod)

Lake, J. W.
I love the merry sunshine (Glover)
Shells of ocean (Cherry)

The **lake** ("Ainsi, toujours poussés") See Le lac (Niedermeyer)

The **lake** ("Slowly o'er the dark, dark waters") F. Abt. Words by W. Lewis. TL

Lake Forest university song. Words by A. W. Doran. CHS

The **lake** of Coolfinn (Willie Leonard) Irish folk song. JOI
"'Twas early one morning." MMI

The **lake** sheen ("Mang o doogwin") Ojibway Indian song. in. BA

The **lake** sheen ("Nenemoshayn newahneah") Ojibway Indian song. in. BA. e. only BA

"**Lala** sunev! lala mej, lala." See Kau fra Hallingdalen

Lalo, Édouard Victor Antoine
"All in vain, O my beloved." See "Vainement, ma bien-aimée"
Aubade. See "Vainement, ma bienaimée"
The bondmaid. See L'esclave

Lalo, Édouard Victor Antoine—*Continued*
The captive. See L'esclave
La chanson de l'alouette
L'esclave
The lark's song. See La chanson de l'alouette
"Vainement, ma bien-aimée" (from Le roi d'Ys)
Lamartine, Alphonse Marie Louis de
Le lac (Niedermeyer)
Le soir (Gounod)
Le vallon (Gounod)
The lamb. G. W. Chadwick. Words by W. Blake. TL
"Lamb of God, Thou that takest away the world's guilt." See "Agnus Dei" (Bizet)
Lambert, Louis, pseud. See Gilmore, Patrick Sarsfield
Lament ("Bedwas hills, the voice of sorrow") Air: Britain's lament. Words by J. Thomas (Ieuan Dhu) MMW
Lament ("Harpist, that strain") Air: Davydd Garrig Wen. MMW
A lament ("My song is so sad and so dreary") A. Borodin. e. BC
The lament ("Oft I've bent beneath the burden") Air: Y galon drom. Words by J. Thomas (Ieuan Dhu) MMW
Lament ("Sad is my empty life") See All joy is gone
Lament ("There is something in the moaning") Air: Come ye near. Words by J. Lloyd. MMW
Lament for Ireland ("How dimm'd is the glory that circled the Gael") Irish song. e. MMI
The lament of Flora Macdonald. See Flora Macdonald's lament (Gow)
The lament of the Irish emigrant. See Irish emigrant's lament (Dempster)
Lamentation ("Attend, you feeling Christians") See Execution song
Lamentation ("Hear ye Amorea's daughters") See Oriental chant (Musorgskiï)
Lamkin. Folk song from North Carolina. CSE
Variant of: False Lamkin
La Moille, T. G.
"Hark! a thrilling song" (Proch)
The lamps of night. English air. Words by H. H. Harbour. DO
Lancaster, E.
"Hark! the song of choirs angelic"
"Land ahead! its fruits are waving." See Safe within the vail
Land beloved! our vow now receive. See Dulce patria (Carnicer y Batlle)
The land beyond. C. Pinsuti. Words by C. Dick. HSS 1—HSS 4
"A land I know that in the north doth lie." See Dalkarlasång (Lindblad)
The land o' the leal ("I'm wearin' awa', Jean") Air: Hey, tuttie, tattie. Words by C. Nairne. HSD—HSSS—PS 1
The land o' the leal ("I'm wearin' awa', John") FSS 1—JO—MMS—WBT

The land of dreams. A. Wilton. Words by F. Enoch. FSS 5
Land of flood and fell. See Farewell to Llanberis
"Land of greatness! home of glory" (Austrian hymn) J. Haydn. Words by A. J. Foxwell. MS
"Land of high heroic glory." See Our country (Haydn)
The land of memory. Bowdoin song. Air: Auld lang syne. Words by F. Sewall. FSS 1—LA
Land of my fathers ("Oh! land of my fathers") J. James. Words by E. James. MMW
"The land of my home is flitting." See Maggie by my side (Foster)
"Land of our fathers." FSS 8
"Land of our hearts." G. W. Chadwick. Words by J. H. Ingham. DSH
"Land of the forest, lake, and sea." See O, dear loved Maine (Estabrooke)
The land of Yippi Ki-yi. C. Lecocq. Words by W. B. Donnell. CU
Land sighting. See Olaf Trygvason (Grieg)
"The land was sweet with sunshine." See The dear home-land (Slaughter)
A land without a storm. FSS 6
Der landesvater. See Weihelied
Landing of the Pilgrims. A. Browne. Words by F. D. Hemans. FSS 8 —TFC 2—WBT
"The breaking waves dashed high." JS
Landing of the Pilgrims (Plymouth rock) FSS 5
The Pilgrim fathers. JO
"Landlady, count the lawin." Air: Hey tutti, taiti. Words by R. Burns. BSR
The landlady's daughter. See Der wirtin töchterlein
Landlord, fill the flowing bowl. Old English convivial song. CU—HSD—MPC—WBT—WC
"Come, landlord, fill the flowing bowl." BOS—FMB—JO—SSS
"The landlord he looks very big." See O good ale, thou art my darling
Das landmädchen ("An meines vaters hügel") A. Harder. Words by J. H. Voss. g. ED 3
Die landlust ("Entfernt von gram und sorgen") J. Haydn. g. ED 3
Landscape. See Landskab (Børresen)
Landskab (Landscape) H. Børresen. Words by J. P. Jacobsen. da.e. WM 1
Lane, Mrs Annie (Eichberg) King
"To thee, O country" (Eichberg)
Lane, Gerald M.
When the lights are low
Lane, Mrs John. See Lane, Mrs Annie (Eichberg) King
Laneir, Nicholas. See Laniere, Nicholas

Lang, Andrew
Christmas violets (Glover)
"My love dwelt in a northern land" (music by Elgar; Pasmore)
Lang, Margaret Ruthven
To the fringed gentian
True freedom
"Lang hae we parted been." Air: Laddie lie near me. Words by R. Burns. BSR
The lang lad they ca' Jumpin John. See "Her daddie forbad, her minnie forbad"
Lang', lang' ist's her. See Long, long ago (Bayly)
Lang o' comin'. Scotch song. FSS 6
Den långa dagen (The long day) H. Kjerulf. Words by Runeberg. e.sw. WM 1
Le langage des marins. French sailors' song. f. SMW
Langbein, August Friedrich Ernst
Das grossvaterlied (Dance air)
"Ich und mein fläschchen" (Volksweise)
Langbridge, F.
"Polly and I" (Wakefield)
"When Jack is tall and twenty" (Composer unknown)
Lange, Friedrich
Lied deutscher männer (Schneider)
Schäfer im mai (Moritz)
Lange, Gustav
Flower song
Lange, Samuel de
"God is eternal" (from Moses)
How beautiful are thy dwellings, O Lord (from Moses)
Moses' death (from Moses)
Lange, Thor
"Lille röde rönnebaer" (Lange-Müller)
Lange-Müller, Peter Erasmus
"Lille röde rönnebaer"
Little mountain maid. See "Lille röde rönnebaer"
Langerhannes, A. Kayser-. See Kayser-Langerhannes, A.
Langlotz, Carl
In praise of old De Pauw (same air as Old Nassau)
Old Nassau
Langran, James
The life laid down. See "Weary of earth"
"Weary of earth"
Langs en å (At the brookside) E. Grieg. Words by A. O. Vinje. e.n. WM 1
An einem bache (At the brookside) e.g. FF
"Langt i auster i Kraakalund." See Kraakalund
Längtan (Longing) A. Söderman. Words by H. Sätherberg. e.sw. SSN
Längtan till landet (Longing for the country) O. Lindblad. Words by H. Sätherberg. e.sw. HSOS
Lanier, Nicholas. See Laniere, Nicholas

Lanier, Sidney
Baby Charley (Old college air)
"May the maiden" (music by Barnby; Carmichael)
The trees and the Master (McCaskey)
Laniere, Nicholas
"Neither sighs, nor tears"
"Silly heart forbear"
Lansdon, W.
Come when thou wilt
"The lanterns gleam, the yellow flames leap and play." See The village dance
"Lanterns lit a year ago." See The feast of lanterns
The lanthorn. See Die latern
Laoidh molaidh (Hymn of praise.— "O Lord, I sing Thy praises") Scotch Highland song. e. MMS
Hē laphina. See The mother deer
Lapland song. See Song of my dear
Lappe, Karl
Der einsame (Schubert)
Im abendroth (Schubert)
So oder so (Schultz)
Laprade, Victor de
La chanson de l'alouette (Lalo)
Lara, Isidore de
The garden of sleep
Larboard watch. T. Williams. FSS 3— HSD—WBT
Larcom, Lucy
"Breaks the joyful Easter dawn" (German air; also music by Gilmore)
"Draw Thou my soul, O Christ" (Sullivan)
"If I were a sunbeam" (German air; also music by unknown composer)
"Ring, happy bells of Easter time" (Pike)
Lardner, William
Old Ironsides
Larghetto. Arr from Beethoven's 2d symphony. TL
Largo ("Father in heav'n, Thy children hear") Händel. Words by T. Williams. BSS—TFC 1—TL
Largo ("Frondi tenere") See Ombra mai fu (Händel)
Largo ("Lord in heav'n above, Who ruleth us") G. F. Händel. WBT—WSW
"Largo al factotum della città." Rossini. e.i. OPS 4
"Largo tiempo el peruano oprimido." See Somos libres, seamoslo siempre
The lark ("Alouette, gentille alouette") See Alouette
The lark ("How lovely thy note") Mendelssohn. FSS 8
The lark ("Lerche steiget") See Die lerche (Rubinstein)
The lark in clear air. Irish air: Kathleen Nowlan. Words by S. Ferguson. FSI
The lark in the morn. Folk song. FSF —SEF 1—SO
Variant: The lark in the morning
The lark in the morning. Folk song from Essex. SF 2
Variant: The lark in the morn

"The **lark** now leaves his wat'ry nest" (Serenade) J. L. Hatton. Words by W. Davenant. BAS 2

"**Lark,** oh tell me, tell me why." See To the lark

"The **lark** sings loud." Egli. FSS 3

"The **larks** awake the drowsy morn." See The serenade (Pack)

The **lark's** song. See La chanson de l'alouette (Lalo)

"**Lascia** amor, e siegui Marte" (Farewell! your country calls you) Händel. e.i. BAS 2

Lascia ch'io pianga (Leave me to languish) G. F. Händel. e.i. KS 2
   Lascia ch'io pianga ('Mid lures, 'mid pleasures) e.i. OPS 2
   Lascia ch'io pianga (Weeping for ever) e.i. CS 1

"**Lasciali** dir, tu m'ami" ("Let say, who will: you love me") F. Quaranta. e.i. SM 2

"**Lasciar** d'amarti per non penar" ("Though pain and sorrow it bring to me") F. Gasparini. e.i. FEI 2
   "Lasciar d'amarti" ("Love's bond to sever") e.i. PA 2

"**Lasciatemi** morire" ("Let death now come") C. Monteverde. e.i. FEI 1
   "Lasciatemi morire" ("Let death resolve my sorrow") e.i. KS 2
   "Lasciatemi morire" ("No longer let me languish") e.i. PA 2

Lashed to the helm. J. Hook. BE 2— ME

"**Lass** dich nur nichts nicht tauern." See Pilgerspruch (Mendelssohn)

The **lass** o' Gowrie ("'Twas on a simmer's afternoon") Air: Loch Erroch Side. Words by Nairne. JO—PS 1

The **lass** o' Gowrie ("'Twas on a simmer's afternoon") Air: O'er young to marry yet. Words by Nairne. MMS

"The **lass** o' Patie's mill." 17th century Scottish air. Words by A. Ramsay. JO—MMS
   "The lass of Patie's mill." PS 1

"**Lass,** o welt, o lass mich sein." See Verborgenheit (Wolf)

The **lass** of Ecclefechan. Scottish air: Jacky Latin. Words by Burns. PS 2
   "Gat ye me, O, gat ye me." BSR

The **lass** of Grongar hill ("I love a beauteous maid") Air: Y garrey lwyd. Words by Ieuan Dhu. MMW

The **lass** of Humberside. J. Blewitt. ME

The **lass** of Lynn. Old English air. Words from T. D'Urfey. BE 8

The **lass** of Mont Parnasse. See La fille de Parthenay

"The **lass** of Patie's mill." See "The lass o' Patie's mill"

The **lass** of Richmond hill ("On Richmond hill there lives a lass") J. Hook. Words attributed to L. McNally; attributed also to W. Hudson and to W. Upton. BE 3—BOH—BOS—DM 1— HSE 1—JO—ME—NG— TL—WBT— WL

The **lass** of the hill ("On the brow of a hill") S. Howard. Words by M. Jones. DM 1

The **lass** of the mill. Festing. BE 4

The **lass** that loves a sailor. C. Dibdin (music and words) HSE 2—JO—ME —PR 2—WBT

The **lass** with the delicate air. M. Arne; wrongly attributed to T. A. Arne. BSS—DM 2—EF—GMF—KF 3—MM —PR 2—SM 3—WBT—WBW

The **lass** with the golden locks. T. A. Arne. Words by Smart. BE 8

Lassen, Eduard
   Ah! 'tis a dream. See Es war ein traum
   All souls' day (Tr of Allerseelen)
   "Avec tes yeux, Mignonne." See "Mit deinen blauen augen"
   Bells across the snow. See "O Christmas, merry Christmas"
   The captive admiral. See Der gefangene admiral
   Es war ein traum
   Eyes blue and dreaming. See "Mit deinen blauen augen"
   Der gefangene admiral
   Greeting. See Grüssen
   Grüssen
   "I think of thee." See Nähe des geliebten
   "Ich hatte einst ein schönes vaterland." See Es war ein traum
   An idle dream. See Es war ein traum
   It was a dream. See Es war ein traum
   "Mein herz ist wie die dunkle nacht"
   "Mit deinen blauen augen"
   "My heart is like a dreary night." See "Mein herz ist wie die dunkle nacht"
   Nähe des geliebten
   "O Christmas, merry Christmas" (same air as "Mit deinen blauen augen")
   Resolution
   "Thine eyes so blue." See "Mit deinen blauen augen"
   "Was machst du mir vor liebchen's thür"
   "Why art before thy lover's door." See "Was machst du mir vor liebchen's thür"

"**Lasses,** call your lads ashore." See Liberty for the sailors

Lasses of Scotland. Irish air. Words by J. W. Brodie-Innes. SSS

"**Lasset** heut im edlen kreis." See Generalbeichte

A **lassie** all alone was making her moan. See "As I stood by yon roofless tower"

"**Lassie,** lend me your braw hemp heckle." Air: The Bob o' Dumblane. Words by R. Burns. BSR

Lassie wi' the lint-white locks. Air: Rothiemurchus' rant. Words by R. Burns. BSB—PS 1
"Now nature cleeds the flowery lea." BSR

"**Lassie** O, lassie O, lassie mine." See En låt i tri toner (Beckman)

"**Lassie** with the lips so rosy." See "Mädchen mit dem rothen mündchen" (Franz)

"**Lassies** high and low." See "Flickorna de små uti dansen de gå"

Lasson, Per
Godnat
Good night. See Godnat

"**Lasst** die politiker nur sprechen." Volksweise. Words by L. F. Goeckingk. g. ED 2

"**Lasst** mich euch fragen." See Porter lied (Flotow)

"**Lasst** uns, ihr brüder." See Lob der freundschaft

Lassus, Orlandus
"Matona, lovely maiden"

Last farewell. See Epilog (Grieg)

"**Last** Friday evening it happened but late." See Johnny Doyle (North Carolina version)

"The **last** gleam o' sunset in ocean was sinkin'." See Mary Macneil

"A **last** good-bye! the parting hour draws nearer." See Farewell song

The **last** greeting ("Adieu! 'tis love's last greeting") F. Schubert. [Tr of Der letzte gruss] e. FSS 3—WBT
"Adieu! 'tis love's last greeting." e. HSD—WBT

The **last** greeting ("Ich kam vom walde") See Der letzte gruss (Levi)

The **last** lay of the dying bard ("Thy day went down") Air: The Arethusa. Words by D. Ryan. MMI

The **last** man. W. H. Callcott. Words by T. Campbell. HSE 3

"**Last** May a braw wooer." Air: The Lothian lassie. Words by R. Burns. BSB—BSR—MMS—PS 1

"**Last** New-Year's day as I've heard say." See Richard of Taunton Dean

"**Last** New Year's morn, as I've heard say." See Richard of Taunton Dean

"**Last** night." See Laengsel (Kjerulf)

"**Last** night, as I lay sleeping" (The guardian angel) Old carol. MCS

"**Last** night as I lay sleeping" (The angels' song) C. Vincent. Words from an old carol. HC

"**Last** night as I was laid and slept." See The boy's dream (Monk)

"**Last** night I dreamed your golden hair." See Entreaty (Smith)

"**Last** night I found the violets." See Christmas violets (Glover)

"**Last** night, in the crowd." See After years (Musorgskiĭ)

"**Last** night in the deep, deep sea." See "L'altra notte in fondo al mare" (Boito)

"**Last** night, last night in the dark o' the moon." See Over the hills and far away

"The **last** night of the year." See Na gillean mo rùin

"**Last** night the dogs." Old English air. BE 2

"**Last** night the nightingale woke me." See Laengsel (Kjerulf)

Last night, when all was still. See Laengsel (Kjerulf)

The **last** of the singers. Folk air. Modern words by S. Baring-Gould. BSW

A **last** prayer. Words by H. H. Jackson. FSS 8—LA

The **last** rose of summer ("'Tis the last rose of summer") Air: Groves of Blarney. Words by T. Moore. BD— BMC— BO— CS 1— FSI— FSS 1—HSC— HSD— JO—JSE— MP—MSS 1—NMH— OH— SMF —SS 1—WA—WBT—WL— WSC —WSW
Sommers letzte rose ("Letzte rose") g. ED 1
"'Tis the last rose of summer." JS— MI—MMI. e.i. EF

"The **last** saraband has been danced in the hall." See The stirrup cup (Arditi)

"The **last**, the fatal hour is come." See Gilderoy

"The **last** time I came o'er the muir." Scottish air. Words by A. Ramsay. PS 1

"**Last** time I met my wife." See Aunt Jemima's plaster

"**Last** Valentine day I so merry was a-walking." See The stammering lovers

"**Last** Valentine's day, when bright Phoebus shone clear." See Black sloven

"**Last** week down our alley come a toff." See Knock'd 'em in the old Kent road (Chevalier)

"The **last** words of parting." See The probationer's farewell to St Andrews

En **låt** i tri toner (A tune in three keys) B. Beckman. Words by H. Wallander. e.sw. WM 1

Late ("Nu da de alle sover") See Sildig (Backer-Gröndahl)

"**Late** at night sat Ivan sadly on the divan." See Vanya

"**Late**, late, so late! and dark the night and chill." See Too late, too late (Bliss)

Die **latern** (The lanthorn) Swabian folk song. e.g. SMF
Schwäbisches volkslied (The lantern) e.g. SSG

Lathbury, Mary Ann
"Day is daying in the west" (Sherwin)
"Snowdrops, lift your timid heads" (Oliver)

Latta, A. M., and Latta, J. H.
"Christmas time has come again, time to us so dear" (Oliver)

Latta, J. H. See Latta, A. M., jt. auth.

Latto, Thomas C.
Innisfail

Lauf der welt (The way of the world) E. Grieg. Words by L. Uhland. e.g. FO 2—PG 3—PG 4

The laugh (Song of the laugh) Ponka Indian song. e. FIS

Laughing glee. G. Martini. e. FSS 7 The tickling trio. e. BD

Laughing song. Old American song. Words by A. Horne. BSS

Laughing water (Be-thae wa-an) Pawnee Indian melody. e. SMF

Laula, laula. See Sing thou, sing (Järnefelt)

Laulu Lapista. See Song of my dear

"Laura betet, engelsharfen hallen." See Die betende (Zelter)

Laura to Filon. Polish song. e. KSN

Laura y Georgina. J. M. Campos. s. LCP

"Laurel-crown'd Horatius." See "Lauriger Horatius"

Laurence, Mary Sophia
Home of my heart (Welsh air)

"Lauriger Horatius." Song of the wandering students of the middle ages. e.l. LA—SSS. l. only CHS—HSD—MPC —WBT

Laurin, Carl Oscar Johan
Vågen
The wave. See Vågen

Laus Deo. Arr from J. Battishill. Words by J. G. Whittier. LBR

The Lauterbach maiden. See Zu Lauterbach

Lauterbach song. See Zu Lauterbach

Lauzières de Thémines, Achille de
Amore (Lucantoni)

Lavater, Johann Caspar
Morgenlied (Reichardt)

"Lavender's blue." Old air. Traditional words. TFC 2

"Lavender's blue." Another air. Traditional words. FSS 5—WBT—WSC

Law and order. A. Sullivan. Words by J. A. Wilder. BSS

Law, physic, and divinity ("Three rosy-faced topers") Popely. ME

Lawes, Henry
"About the sweet bag of a bee"
"Amarantha sweet and fair"
"Amidst the myrtles"
The angler's song
"Ask me why I send you here." See The primrose
"Bacchus, Iacchus"
"Beauty and Love"
"Bid me to live"
"Caelia thy bright angel's face." See The celestial mistress
"Careless of love." See The surprise
The celestial mistress
"Chloris, yourself you so excel"
"Come, Chloris, hie we to thy bower"
"Come, lovely Phillis"
Disdain returned. See Unfading beauty
"Faith be no longer coy"
"Gather ye rosebuds while ye may"

"He that loves a rosy cheek." · See Unfading beauty
"How happy art thou"
"I do confess thou'rt smooth and fair"
"I prithee, send me back my heart"
"If the quick spirit of your eye"
"Little love serves my turn"
Love's votary. See "Bid me to live"
"Phillis, why should we delay"
The primrose
The surprise
"'Tis Christmas now"
To a lady weeping
Unfading beauty
"While I listen to thy voice"

Lawes, William
Beauty in eclipse
"Come my Daphne"

"Lawn, as white as driven snow." Traditional air. Words by W. Shakespeare. KSS

"Lawn as white as driven snow" (Autolycus' song) J. Greenhill. Words by W. Shakespeare. VFS

"Lawn, as white as driven snow" (Autolycus' song) W. Linley. [Words by W. Shakespeare] NG

"Lawn as white as driven snow." J. Wilson or R. Johnson. Words by W. Shakespeare. VFS

Lawreen, J. B.
Who's that calling

Lawrence, M. S.
Adieu to Cambria (Welsh air)

"A lawyer he went out one day." See Mowing the barley

Lawyer Lee. Folk song from Warwickshire. SF 4

"A lawyer there was I will call Mister Clay." See The warranty deed

"Lay by your pleading." See Love lies a bleeding

"Lay down the axe." See Our country's call

"Lay his sword by his side." Irish air: If all the sea were ink. Words by T. Moore. MI—MMI

Lay of the imprisoned huntsman (Lied des gefangenen jägers) Schubert. Words by W. Scott. BS 2

"Lay that sullen garland by thee." See Love's bacchanal (Wynne)

Lay the bent to the bonny broom. 17th century song. CO 2

Layng, W.
"Sing ye the songs of praise" (Farebrother)

Lays of a minstrel. See "Oh! 'tis the melody" (Bayly)

Lazarus. Folk song from Tennessee. CSE

The lazy cat. Children's song. WBT— WSC

"Lazy Mary, will you get up." Children's song. WSC

"The lazy mist hangs from the brow of the hill." Air: The lazy mist. Words by R. Burns. BSR

"**Lazy** sheep, pray tell me why" (The little boy and the sheep) Old French air: La bonne aventure.   Words by J. Taylor.   DO

"**Lazy** sheep, pray tell me why" (The sheep and the boy) Composer unknown. ⌊Words by J. Taylor⌋ WSC

Le sais-tu bien (Dost thou not know) G. Pierné.   Words by Blanchecotte. e.f. PG 4

The **lea** rig ("When o'er the hill") Old Scottish air.   Words by R. Burns. JO—PS 1

The **lea** rig (My ain kind dearie, O) BSB

My ain kind dearie, O ("When o'er the hill the eastern star") MMS—PS 1

"When o'er the hill the e'ening star." BSR

The **lea** rig ("When o'er the hill") J. Reid.   Words by R. Burns. BSB

"**Lead**, kindly light." J. B. Dykes. Words by J. H. Newman. FSS 1—HSC—HSD— JS—MS— NMH— OH—TFC 1—TL— WA—WBT— WS—WSW

"**Lead**, kindly light" (Lux benigna) BD—CST—LA

"**Lead**, kindly light." A. L. Peace. Words by J. H. Newman. LA

"**Lead**, kindly light." C. Pinsuti. Words by J. H. Newman. HSS 3—HSS 4

"**Lead**, kindly light." A. S. Sullivan. Words by J. H. Newman. HSS 1—HSS 3—HSS 4

"**Lead** me, O Lord." B. Molique. OS 4—SAS 4

"The **lead** strikes English ground." B. M. Gilholy.   Words by J. M. Emerson. SSS

"**Lead** us, heavenly father, lead us." Gounod.   Words by J. Edmeston. LA

The **leader's** song (Song of the leader) Omaha Indian rest song. in. FIS

"**Leading** my flock, on pasture bent." See Lisette

Leaf, Maurice
Commencement song (Cherubini)

Leander, Henry
"By those eyes"

Leaning on the Lord.   See If you want to see Jesus

Lear, Edward
"The owl and the pussy cat" (Ingraham)

Learmont, of Dalkeith
My goddess, woman (Scottish air)

"**Learn** to live, and live to learn."   English air.   Words by B. Taylor. LBR

Leather apron.   See "In summer time, when flow'rs do spring"

The **leather** bottèl ("Now God above that made all things") Air from "Wit and mirth." CO 2—JE

The **leather** bottèl (" 'Twas God above that made all things") Air from "Wit and drollery." BOH

The **leather** bottèl ("When I survey the world around") Air from "Wit and drollery." BAS 1—BE 2—BOS—DM 1 —HSE 1—JE—MM

Leathery.   Columbia university song. CU

Leave her Johnny ("A dollar a day") Capstan chantey, pumping version. CR

For variants of this song see following songs of similar title

Leave her, Johnny ("I thought I heard") Capstan chantey.   CR

Leave her Johnny ("O the times are hard") Capstan chantey.   SE

Leave her Johnny ("Oh, the times are hard") Capstan chantey.   CR

Leave her Johnny ("The times are hard") Capstan chantey.   SE

Leave her, Johnny, leave her ("Oh, the times are hard") Long drag chantey. KB

"**Leave**, lassies, your work."   See The miller's wedding

Leave me to languish.   See Lascia ch'io pianga (Händel)

"**Leave** off this foolish prating."   See Good advice (Leveridge)

Leave yo' sheep an' leave yo' lambs.   See Rise up, shepherd, an' foller

"The **leaves** are fading and falling."   See November (Hutchinson)

"The **leaves** around me falling."   Greek air.   FSS 3

"The **leaves** be green" (Browning) Old English song.   CO 1

"The **leaves** on the green boughs gently are swinging."   See Les cloches (Debussy)

Leaving the nest.   F. Reddall.   Words by E. M. Rhodes.   LA

"**Leb'** wohl, du kühnes, herrliches kind." See Wotans abschied (Wagner)

"**Leb'** wohl, mein bräutchen schön."   See Kriegers abschied (Methfessel)

Lebanon.   See The peaceful fold (Zundel)

"Das **leben** gleichet der blume."   See Trinklied (Gerstenberg)

"Das **leben** welkt wie gras."   M. Green. Words by K. Straube. g.   ED 3

"Ein **leben** wie im paradies."   See Das rheinwein-paradies

Lebenspflichten ("Rosen auf der weg") J. F. Reichardt.   Words by L. H. C. Holty.   g.   ED 2

Lebewohl ("Morgen muss ich fort von hier") F. Silcher. Volkslied. g. ED 1

Farewell.   e.   HSD—LA—WBT— WL

Lebewohl (Farewell)   e.g.   BO—SMW—SSG—SSS

"**Lebt** wohl, ihr berge."   See Johanna's abschied (Zumsteeg)

Leconte de Lisle, Charles Marie
Lydia (Fauré)
Nell (Fauré)
"Les roses d'Ispahan" (Fauré)

Lecocq, Charles
The land of Yippi Ki-yi
Lee, David
The Gascon vespers
Our mother's way
Lee, Frederick George
"In the early morning, early" (music by Borrow; Oliver)
"Sing of Maiden Mary" (French Noël)
"Slowly fall the snow-flakes" (Borrow)
Lee, George Alexander
Away to the mountain's brow
Buy a broom (attributed)
Cold water song
"Come where the aspens quiver"
"From Teutschland I come." See Buy a broom (attributed)
The gondolier
"Good-will to men"
I am dreaming of thee
"I'll be no submissive wife"
Macgregors' gathering
Mistress Santa Claus
My Jamie o'er the sea
October's party
O'er the sea in my fairy boat
Oh, 'twas sweet to hear her
The soldier's tear
Spanish serenade
"What's a' the steer, kimmer"
"The Yankee boy"
Lee, H. S.
"Oh, Syracuse" (Composer unknown)
Lee, Harry S.
"Carol, carol, Easter morn" (Russell)
Lee, Mary Augusta. See Demarest, Mrs Mary Augusta (Lee)
Lee-Hamilton, Eugene
Wood song (Watts)
"Lee l'andava e mi vegneva" (The road to Moltras) Italian song. e.i. BF 2
Leeson, Jane Eliza
" 'Twas a starry night of old" (Naylor)
Leeves, William
Auld Robin Gray
"Young Jamie lo'ed me weel." See Auld Robin Gray
Leezie Lindsay. Scottish song. 1st verse by R. Burns. BOS—PS 1
"Will ye gang to the Hielands, Leezie Lindsay." HSSS—MMS
"Will ye go to the Highlands, Leezie Lindsay." BSR
Lefebvre, Jacques
"Dans notre village" (attributed)
"In our happy village." See "Dans notre village" (attributed)
Lefort, G.
The old, old song
The **legacy** ("When in death I shall calm recline") Air: The bard's legacy. Words by T. Moore. MI
"When in death I shall calm recline." BAS 1—MMI
A **legend** ("Child Jesus in His garden") See The crown of roses (Tchaikovsky)

Legend of the bell. R. Planquette. e. WBT
Song of the bells. Words adapted. e. WSC
The **legend** of the Venetian laces. See Nenia (Randegger)
The **legend** of Volgá (O Vol'gře i Mikulře) Russian folk song. e. SSR 1
The **legend** of young nightingale (Soloveĭ Budimirovich) Russian folk song. e. SSR 1
Legende ("Child Jesus in His garden") See The crown of roses (Tchaikovsky)
Legends of the Infancy. J. F. Bridge. Words by E. L. Hervey. BSC
Legrenzi, Giovanni
"Che fiero costume" (from Eteocle)
"How void of compassion." See "Che fiero costume"
"What strange whim pursuing." See "Che fiero costume"
"With cunning conniving." See "Che fiero costume"
L'Égru, Ch.
Aufträge (Schumann)
Lehar, Franz
The study of woman (from The merry widow)
Vilia song (from The merry widow)
Waltz song (from The merry widow)
Lehmann, Liza
At the making of the hay
"**Lehn'** deine wang' an meine wang' " ("O let me press thy cheek to mine") A. Jensen. Words by H. Heine. e.g. KF 1—KF 2—KF 3
"Lehn' deine wang' an meine wang' " ("Oh press thy cheek against mine own") e.g. CB
"Lehn' deine wang' an meine wang' " (Press thy cheek against mine own) e.g. FF—FO 1
He **lei** no Kaiulani. See A wreath for Princess Kaiulani (Hopkins)
Lei ohaoha. See "How I love to gaze" (Nape)
Lei poni moi. See Wreath of carnations (Hopkins)
Der **leibarzt** und der trinker ("Einst hat mir mein leibarzt geboten") German song. Words by Schubarth. g. ED 2
Der **leichtsinn** ("Was ist doch karlinchen") G. W. Fink (music and words) g. ED 2
Leigh, Henry S.
Happy summer (Planquette)
Leighter, Henry Clough-. See Clough-Leighter, Henry
Leis an Lurgainn ("With the Loorgeen O hee") Old Scottish boat song. e. HSSS
Boat song ("With the Loorgeen, O hee") e. MMS
"**Leis**', rudere, hier." See "Row gently here, my gondolier" (Schumann)
"**Leis**' rudern hier." See "Row gently here, my gondolier" (Jensen)

"Leis sinkt der dämm'rung schleier." See Ave Maria (Raff)

"Leise flehen meine lieder." See Ständchen (Schubert)

"Leise, leise, fromme weise." See Gebet (Weber)

Leise weht's durch alle lande. For English translation see "Hark! the herald-host is singing" (Humperdinck)

"Leise zieht durch mein gemüth." See Gruss (Mendelssohn)

"Leiser schwanken die äste." See Heimkehr (Strauss)

Leitner,
Vor meiner wiege (Schubert)

Le Jeune, George Fitz-Curwood
"Oh, the golden, glowing morning"

Lejoindre, R.
Thy face is always near me (Marriott)

Lekeu, Guillaume
On a tomb. See Sur une tombe
Sur une tombe

Leland, Mrs E. H.
"The days are gliding swiftly by" (Tosh)

Le Lasseur de Ranzay, Louis
Roses d'hiver (Fontenailles)

Leleiohoku, prince
"The ground is strewn"
Moani ke ala. See My sweet
My sweet
Nu'a o ka palai. See "The ground is strewn"

Lemaire, Gaston
"Countess, in thy dancing." See "Vous dansez, marquise"
"Marchioness, your dancing." See "Vous dansez, marquise"
"Vous dansez, marquise"

Lemare, Edwin
"I hear the children's voices"
"A meteor bright its wondrous light"
"Ring out, ye merry bells"
"Shepherds watching o'er the plain"

Lemmel, Helen Howarth
Down on Smiley's farm
Hymn of the adoption
My dear-o

Le Moigne, Lucas
"Now sing we all full sweetly" (Traditional carol. Tr of Chantons, je vous en prie)

Lemon, Mark
I would I were a boy again (Romer)

Lemon, Mary Mark-. See Mark-Lemon, Mary

Lenau, Nicolaus
Bitte (Franz)
Die drei zigeuner (Liszt)
Kommen und scheiden (Schumann)
Primula veris (Kleffel)
Stille sicherheit (Franz)

Lend me your aid. See Inspirez-moi (Gounod)

Lennox, Lindsay
Come unto me (Barry)
Love's golden dream (Composer unknown)
Pardoned (Piccolomini)

Lenox crimson. Lenox college song. Words by N. B. Turner. CHS

"Lentement baissa le jour." See "Slowly the daylight departs" (Borodin)

Leo, Leonardo
"If to thy soul." See "Se mai senti"
"Se mai senti" (from La clemenza di Tito)
When around thy dear face. See "Se mai senti"

Leoni. See "The God of Abrah'm praise"

Leonore. H. Trotère. Words by C. Bingham. WBW

The leprehaun ("In a shady nook one moonlight night") Irish air. Words by P. W. Joyce. FSI—MMI

Die lerche (The lark) A. Rubinstein. Words by T. von Sacken. e.g. FM—KF 1

"Lerche steiget im gesang." See Die lerche (Rubinstein)

Lerdo de Tejada, Miguel
Perjura

Lermontov, Mikhail Iur'evich
The cloud and the mountain (Rimskiï-Korsakov)
Cradle song (music by Cherepnin; Grechaninov)
Heavenly clouds (Dargomyzhskiï)
"Like to the sky serenely smiling" (Rimskiï-Korsakov)
The little fish's song (Arenski)
Longing (Rubinstein)
Les nuages (Bouval)
The pine-tree (Balakirev)

Leroux, A.
Mignonette (Weckerlin)

Leroux, Xavier Henri Napoléon
Le Nil
The Nile. See Le Nil

"Les go to de golden wedding." See De golden wedding (Bland)

"Lesbia hath a beaming eye." Irish air: Nora criónna, or, Wise Nora. Words by T. Moore. MI—MMI—PI

Leslie, Ernest
Rock me to sleep

Leslie, Henry David
"Come unto Him, come unto Him"
"Speed on, my bark, speed on"

Lessing, Gotthold Ephraim
Die drei reiche der natur (Volksweise)
Die liebe (Kirnberger)
Der tod (Volksweise)

"Lessons I gave a maiden." See A cantar a una niña

Le Strange, Eliza
Absence (Hook)

"Let all that are to mirth inclined." Christmas carol. WCC

"Let all with Dutch blood in their veins." See "Wien Neêrlandsch bloed" (Wilms)

"Let ambition fire." Weldon. Words by W. Congreve. BE 6

"Let Bacchus to Venus libations pour fast." See Vive la compagnie

"Let children that would fear the Lord." See Child's hymn

"Let Christians all with one accord rejoice." See The black decree

"Let de heaven light shine on me." Negro spiritual. HR

"Let death now come." See "Lasciatemi morire" (Monteverdi)

"Let death resolve my sorrow." See "Lasciatemi morire" (Monteverde)

"Let Erin remember the days of old." Air: The red fox. Words by T. Moore. BOS—FSS 1—JO—JSE— LA— MI— MMI—PI—SN

"Let every good fellow." See Vive l'amour

"Let every heart now dance with joy." J. H. Hopkins (music and words) HC

"Let fame sound the trumpet." Shield. HSE 2

"Let gay ones and great." Shooting song. J. Baildon; wrongly attributed to Arne. Words attributed to I. Bickerstaffe. ME My dog and my gun. DM 2—HSE 2

"Let glory be to God on high" (Melita) J. B. Dykes. LA

"Let go the ropes, unfurl the sails." See "De kabels los"

"Let heaven and earth rejoice and sing." Old Cornish song. HC

"Let heaven and earth rejoice and sing." J. W. Sidebotham. HC

"Let him in whom old Dutch blood flows." See "Wien Neêrlandsch bloed" (Wilms)

"Let him who sighs in sadness here." See The minute gun at sea (King)

"Let India boast her spicy trees." See The Christmas tree

"Let life be short, life be long." Welsh air. Words by J. Parry. MMW

Let loove sparkle in her e'e. Air: Jockey fou and Jenny fain. Words by R. Burns. BSR

Let me be. See Mena, me' (Costa)

Let me be buried in the cellar. See Que l'on m'enterre dans la cave

Let me dream again. A. Sullivan. Words by B. C. Stephenson. FSS 4—HSD—PO

"Let me gaze." C. Gounod. [Tr of Laisse-moi, laisse-moi) e. WBT

"Let me go where'er I will, where'er I will." See The poet (Kücken)

"Let me love thee." L. Arditi. Words by W. Maynard. WBW

"Let me ryke up to dight that tear." Air: Whistle owre the lave o't. Words by R. Burns. BSR

Let me wander not unseen. Händel. Words by Milton. BE 6—SS 1

Let Miss Lindy pass. W. L. Rogers. Words by F. L. Stanton. AA

'Let music break on this blest morn." J. B. Calkin. Words by G. Dickinson. BSC—HC

"Let my fair one." 18th century song. ME

"Let no one be proud of his luck or his gold." F. von Suppé. e. KSE

"Let no one make alarum in the street." See Le couvre-feu

"Let not grief or pain annoy." FSS 8

"Let not woman e'er complain." Air: Duncan Gray. Words by R. Burns. BSR

Let old Santa Claus come in. MCS

"Let others dream." J. C. Johnson. FSS 2

"Let others sing of days gone by." See Now (Bliss)

"Let our gladness know no end." Old Bohemian song. e. HC—MF

"Let our voices, dearest comrades." See Dulce domum (Reading?)

"Let our watch-word, boys, be Service." See The watchword (Armitage)

"Let poets and historians record the brave Gregorians." See The merry Gregorians" (Carey)

"Let rogues and cheats prognosticate." See When the king enjoys his own again

"Let sailors sing of ocean deep." See The independent farmer (Root)

"Let say, who will: you love me." See "Lasciali dir, tu m'ami" (Quaranta)

"Let Spring her fairest posies." See My heart's beloved is mine (Nicolaï)

"Let sweet hope in us awaken." See War-song of the Hussites

"Let the bright Seraphim." Händel. OS 1—SAS 1

Let the bullgine run. Capstan chantey. SE Run with the bullgine. Negro halliard chantey. CR

"Let the Catholic church be now arrayed." See Bishop Butler of Kilcash

"Let the choral anthem rise." See Hail to Juniata

"Let the dreadful engines." Purcell. BAS 2—HSE 3

"Let the farmer praise his grounds." See The cruiskeen lawn

"Let the Grecian dream of his sacred stream." See Song to old Union (Ludlow)

"Let the merry church bells ring." Composer unknown. Words by J. M. Neale. HC

"Let the merry church bells ring." J. Blaikie. Words by J. M. Neale. HC

"Let the merry church bells ring." H. S. Cutler. Words by J. M. Neale. HC

"Let the merry church bells ring." J. S. B. Hodges. Words by J. M. Neale. HC

"Let the merry church-bells ring" (Easter bells) A. P. Howard. Words by J. M. Neale. HC

"Let the merry church bells ring." L. H. Redner. Words by J. M. Neale. HC

"Let the merry church-bells ring." G. W. Warren. Words by J. M. Neale. HC

"Let the palms wave." See Les rameaux (Fauré)

"Let the song be begun." Composer unknown. Words by J. M. Neale. HC

"Let the song be begun." J. S. B. Hodges. Words by J. M. Neale. HC

"Let the song be begun." E. S. Medley. Words by J. M. Neale. HC

"Let the song be begun." G. W. Warren. Words by J. M. Neale. HC

Let the toast pass. See "Here's to the maiden of bashful fifteen" (Linley)

"Let the whole creation cry." G. J. Elvey. Words by S. Brooks. BSS

"Let the whole world chant and sing." H. Smart. Tr of Concinat orbis cunctus, alleluya. e. HC

"Let the wind blow cold." See The sure hope

"Let the wine mantle high to a toast." See Horae Andreanae

"Let their celestial concerts unite." G. F. Händel. DSH

"Let us all in concert sing alleluia." See Alleluia

"Let us away! blue waters flowing." See "Embarquez-vous" (Godard)

Let us cheer the weary traveler. See Weary traveler

"Let us dance, let us sing." H. Purcell. PR 1

"Let us drink and be merry." See The town gallant (Smith)

"Let us endeaver to show that whenever." Round. FSS 8

"Let us go home 'tis near the break of day." See Parting

"Let us go, lassie, go." See The braes of Balquhidder

"Let us go to the land." See Green fields of America

"Let us go together now to our home." See Marriage song

"Let us haste to Kelvin grove, bonnie lassie." See Kelvin grove

"Let us laugh and let us sing." See The fairy ring

Let us love then, let's be daring. See War-song of the Hussites

"Let us now in youth rejoice." See "Gaudeamus igitur"

"Let us pause in life's pleasures." See Hard times come again no more (Foster)

"Let us praise Him." Negro spiritual. HR

Let us sing ("All together let us sing") Round. LA

"Let us sing alleluia to-day." Easter carol. HC

"Let us sing merrily." FSS 3

"Let us sing to — — — —." See Greeting song

"Let us tell the story." Phrygian-mode air. Words by J. M. Neale. HC

"Let us the Infant greet." S. Smith. Words by R. F. Littledale. HC

"Let us walk along together." Action song. Air: Hanging Johnny. FSF

"Let us with a gladsome mind." Words by J. Milton. BSS

"Let worldly minds the world pursue" (Maitland) G. N. Allen. FSS 5

"Let your feet tramp! tramp." See Marching game

Le Tourneaux, Nicholas
Adeste, coelitum chori (13th century air)

"Let's be off to yonder mountain." See Hjemreise fra saetren

"Let's drink and sing, my brother soldiers bold." Drinking song. ME

"Let's seek the bower of Robin Hood." W. Shield. Words by L. MacNally. ME

"Let's sing, just the time to pass." See La fille matelot

"Let's sing! let's sing! our voices merrily ring." See Russian Christmas song

"Let's sing of stage-coaches." 17th century song. DM 2

"The letters come all day to the mail-box bright." See The mail-box

Letters from lovers. J. Offenbach. e. WBT

Letts, Winifred M.
My little Kerry cow (Irish air)

Der letzte abend ("Wenn ich an der letzten abend gedenk' ") Volkslied. g. ED 3

Der letzte gruss ("Adieu! 'tis love's last greeting") For English translation see The last greeting (Schubert)

Der letzte gruss ("Ich kam vom walde hernieder."—The last greeting) H. Levi. Words by J. von Eichendorff. e.g. SM 4

"Letzte rose, wie magst du so einsam hier blühn." See The last rose of summer

Leuto, Francesco Del
"Dimmi, amor"
"Tell me, love." See "Dimmi, amor"

Leva, Enrico de
French pins. See " 'E spingole frangese"
" 'E spingole frangese"

"Levántese niña." Folk song from California. e.s. HS

Levee song ("I once did know a girl nam'd Grace") Old American song. CHS —CU—NMP

Levee song ("Oh, I was bo'n in Mobile town") Old American air. Words by S. Fay. BSS—TFC 1

Lever, Charles James
The widow Malone (Irish air)

Le lever de la lune (Moonrise) C. Saint-Saëns. Words imitated from Ossian. e.f. SAM

Leveridge, Richard
Black-eyed Susan
Brave men of Kent
The fairies. See "Now the hungry lions roar"
Good advice ("Leave off this foolish prating")
Good advice ("Why all this sorrow")
Jilted. See Good advice ("Why all this sorrow")
"Love is a bauble"
The maid's resolution
The man of Kent. See Brave men of Kent

Leveridge, Richard—*Continued*
"Now the hungry lions roar"
"One Sunday after mass" (attributed)
The reproach
The roast beef of old England
"Send back my long-stray'd eyes to me." See The reproach
"Send home my long-stray'd eyes to me." See The reproach
"Sweet are the charms of her I love"
The sweet rosy morn
Sweet William's farewell to black-ey'd Susan. See Black-eyed Susan
"To all you ladies now at land"
"Who is Sylvia"

Levey, William Charles
Geraldine
The robin redbreast
White blossoms
The wonderful weaver

Levi, Hermann
The last greeting. See Der letzte gruss
Der letzte gruss

Lewie Gordon. Jacobite song. Words by Geddes. PS 1

Lewin, Lionel H.
"Birds in the night" (Sullivan)
Golden days (Sullivan)
A life that lives for you (Sullivan)
Once again (Sullivan)

Lewis, Edwin H.
Alma mater—Chicago (Composer unknown)

Lewis, Joel
The flag (Hadley)

Lewis, L. F.
"Oh, the land that we love" (Balfe)
Skaters' song (Schumann)

Lewis, Matthew Gregory
The banks of Allan water (Traditional air)
The disabled seaman (Dignum)
Oh, no! my love, no (Kelly)
The soldier's return (Welsh air)

Lewis, Virginia
September (Olds)

Lewis, William
The lake (Abt)

Leyden. See "All praise to Thee" (Costello)

Lia au ika. See Honeysuckles (Nape)

"**Lia** wau ika moe." See Dear heart (Nape)

Liapunov, Sergeĭ Mikhaĭlovich
Christmas song
Nocturne

Libbey, Anna M.
"What said the shepherds" (Hutchinson)

"**Libertad,** libertad, orientales." See Himno nacional de la republica oriental del Uruguay (Deballi)

Liberty for the sailors. Scotch song. SMW

Libiamo ne' lieti calici (Brindisi) Verdi. e.i. PP

Liden Karen (Little Karen) P. A. Heise. Words by C. Ploug. da.e. SSN
Little Karen. e. EF—KF 1—KF 3—KSN—WL

Lie, Sigurd
Bestikkelse
Captured. See Bestikkelse

"**Lie** still, my dear, why doth thou rise." See Loth to depart

Lieb heimatland, ade ("Nun ade") Volksweise. Words by A. Disselhoff. g. ED 2

"**Lieb** liebchen" ("Dear love") N. Medtner. Words from the German. e.g. NM 1

"**Die lieb'** und unser vogelfang." See Der vogelsteller (Sterkel)

"**Liebchen, ade.**" See Abschied

Die liebe ("Ohne liebe lebe") J. P. Kirnberger. Words by G. E. Lessing. g. ED 3

Liebe ("Wilt thou return") See Love (Bleikhman)

Liebe in allem ("O selig, wer liebt") J. A. P. Schultz. Words by F. Brun. g. ED 2

Liebe in nöten ("Sieh an") Volkslied. g. ED 3

Liebe ist die zarte blüthe (Love's a tender flow'ret shedding) L. Spohr. Words by W. Bartholomew. e.g. AB 4

"**Liebe** kinder, gebt doch acht." See Der dorfschulmeister

"**Liebe** mutter, heut nacht heulte regen und wind." See Walpurgisnacht (Loewe)

Der liebe seligkeit ("Ach, mädchen") Volkslied. g. ED 1

"**Liebe** und leide! arm ist die freude." See Die sterne des lebens (Etzler)

Liebe und wein ("Ohne lieb und ohne wein") J. A. Hiller. Words by C. F. Weisse. g. ED 2

Lieben bringt freud' ("Das lieben bringt gross freud") Schwäbisches volkslied. g. ED 3

"**Den lieben** langen tag." See entry under Den

Die liebende. See Vien qua Dorina bella (Bianchi)

Die liebende schreibt (The lover's message) F. Mendelssohn. Words by Goethe. e.g. PG 1
Die liebende schreibt (My sweetheart writes) e.g. GMF

Liebes-A-B-C ("A B C D, wenn ich dich seh") A. Pohlenz. Words by W. Gerhard. g. ED 1

"**Liebes** mädchen, hör mir zu." J. Haydn. g. ED 1—ED 2
"Liebes mädchen hör' mir zu" ("Dearest maiden, hear my song") e.g. PG 3—PG 4
"Liebes mädchen hör mir zu" (Serenade) e.g. MS

Liebesbotschaft (Love's message) F. Schubert. Words by L. Rellstab. e.g. CMF 2

Liebesglück ("In jedes haus") K. M. von Weber. Words by J. Hoffman von Fallersleben. g. ED 3

Liebeskummer (The sorrow of love) Austrian folk song. e.g. SMF

Liebesleid ("The sun's last ray") See Love's sorrow (Shelley)

Liebeslied ("Ich hab' mir eines erwählet") K. M. von Weber. Volkslied. g. ED 3

Liebesqual ("Und schau ich hin") Schwäbisches volkslied. g. ED 1

Liebesqual (Love's distress) e.g. SSG

Love's distress. e. BSE

Liebesscherz ("Wo a klein's hüttle") Schwäbisches volkslied. g. ED 1

Liebesschmerz ("Den sonntag, den sonntag") Volkslied. g. ED 3

Liebeständelei (Love's pleading) W. Fitzenhagen. Words by T. Körner. e.g. SM 3

Liebestraum. For English translation see A love dream (Liszt)

Liebeszauber ("Mädel, schau mir ins gesicht") J. A. Schultz. Words by G. A. Bürger. g. ED 1

"Liebliche blume, bist du so früh schon wieder gekommen." See Primula veris (Kleffel)

Lieblingsplätzchen (The favorite spot) F. Mendelssohn. e.g. PG 2

"Wisst ihr, wo ich gerne weil'" (A favorite place) e.g. MS

Lied ("La belle étoile tombe."—Song) J. Mertens. Words after Heine. [Tr of Es fällt ein stern herunter] e.f. SOS 1

Lied ("Pour moi sa main cueillait des roses."—The gathered rose) C. Franck. Words by L. Paté. e.f. CM 1—HM 1

Lied der braut (The bride's song) Schumann. Words by Rückert. e.g. MSS 1

Lied der nacht ("Im windsgerausch") J. F. Reichardt. Words by L. Tieck. g. ED 2

Lied des alten im bart ("Aus tiefer nacht") A. Löffler. Words by E. Geibel. g. ED 2

Lied des gefangenen jägers. See Lay of the imprisoned huntsman (Schubert)

Lied des lebens ("Flüchtiger als wind") Melodie: Auf, ihr meine deutschen brüder. Words by J. G. von Herder. g. ED 2

Lied deutscher männer ("Es heult der sturm") W. Schneider. Words by F. Lange. g. ED 2

Lied eines landmanns in der fremde ("Traute heimat meiner lieben") V. Righini. Words by J. G. von Salis-Seewis. g. ED 2

"Ein lied in ehren." See Freude in ehren (Erk)

Lied maritime (A sea song) V. d'Indy (music and words) e.f. CM 2—HM 2—SAM

Das lied vom feldmarschall ("Was blasen die trompeten") Volksweise. Words by E. M. Arndt. g. ED 1

Das lied vom Rhein ("Es klingt ein heller klang") H. G. Nägeli. Words by M. von Schenkendorf. g. ED 1—ED 2

's lied vom Wiener beddlmandl ("'s beddlweibl wollt kîarfirt'n gehn") Volkslied. g. ED 3

Das lied von dem jungen grafen ("Ich steh' auf einem hohen berg") Volkswiese. g. ED 3

Das lied von den zwei hasen ("Zwischen berg und tiefem, tiefem tal") Volkslied. g. ED 3

"Lieder gib mir, süsse lieder." See Im frühling (Mozart)

Een liedje van de zee (A seaman's ditty) Dutch folk song. d.e. BDF

"Liepa naša domovina,—o junačka zemljo." See Croatian national anthem (Runjamin)

"Lieti signor, salute." See "Nobles seigneurs, salut" (Meyerbeer)

"Lietuva, tēvyne mūsų." See Lithuanian national hymn

Lieurance, Thurlow
Aooah
By the waters of Minnetonka
By the weeping waters
Canoe song
A Crow maiden's prayer song
Deer-flower
Dying Moon-Flower
From an Indian village
From Ghost Dance canyon
Her blanket
Her rosary. See The weaver
In mirrored waters
Indian love. See Canoe song
Indian lullaby. See Wi-um
Indian spring bird
Love song
My silver throated fawn
Pakoble. See The rose
Pa-pup-ooh. See Deer-flower
The blanket. See The weaver
The rose
A rose on an Indian grave
Ski-bi-bi-la. See Indian spring bird
The weaver
Wi-um

Lifdrabanten och kung Erik (The bodyguardsman and King Eric) O. Lindblad. Words by K. A. Nicander. e.sw. HSOS

Lifdrabanten och kung Eric (The guard and King Eric) e.sw. SSN

Life ("Our life is like a narrow raft") J. Blumenthal. HSS 2—HSS 4—SM 4

Life ("Winter wind blew keenly") Hungarian folk air. Words by R. R. Whitehead. WF

"Life does but a moment last." See Cantique du Trappiste (Meyerbeer)

"Life is but a fleeting dream." See Make the best of it

"Life is passing fast away." Beethoven. HSS 2

The life laid down. See "Weary of earth" (Langran)

"Life let us cherish." See "Freut euch des lebens" (Nägeli)

The life of the shepherdess. See "Y-a rien de si charmant"

"A life on the ocean wave." H. Russell. Words by E. Sargent. FSS 3—HSC —HSD—JO—LBR—WBT

A life that lives for you. A. S. Sullivan. Words by L. H. Lewin. BAS 1

"Lift me away, thou mighty death." See En digters sidste sang (Grieg)

"Lift thine eyes, behold the light." See Song of hope (Russotto)

"Lift thine eyes, O lift thine eyes." F. Mendelssohn. e. BD—MS— TFC 2

"Lift thine eyes" (The angel trio) e. JS

"Lift thine eyes, 'tis the gods who come near." See Look up

"Lift up thy voice with singing." G. E. Oliver. Words by E. G. Selden. HC

"Lift up, ye everlasting doors." E. L. Hopkins. HC

"Lift up your eyes, desponding freemen." See Song of a thousand years (Work)

"Light and rosy be thy slumbers." See Swedish cradle song

"Light as the night-moth." See "Qual farfalletta giro a quel lume" (Händel)

"Light-flitting shadow." See "Ombre légère" (Meyerbeer)

"Light from my lowly bed." See The rising of the lark

"The light has vanished from the day." See Moan to the moon

The light hath shone. T. Hastings. Words by J. Morrison. MCS

The light-house. See entry under Light-house

Light in darkness. F. H. Cowen. HSS 2 —HSS 3

The light in the window. V. Gabriel. Words by Lonsdale. FSS 2

Light o' love ("By force I am fixed") 16th century air: Lightie love. Words by L. Gybson. CO 1—VFS

Light o' love ("Oh, how can I learn") 16th century air: Lightie love. Words by W. Ball. DM 1

"The light of day is slowly fading." See Evening (Tchaikovsky)

"Light of my life whose image my heart holdeth." See Jeg elsker dig (Grieg)

"The light of other days." M. W. Balfe. Words by A. Bunn. BE 2—FSS 2— HSE 3—HSS 1—HSS 3—JO—WBT

The light of the world. See Hvad fattas dig (Ahnfeldt)

"Light our hearts and gay." Indian ritual air. e. FI

"Light roundelays I'm singing." See Minnelied

The light that is felt. A. G. Methfessel. Words by J. G. Whittier. LBR

Light to my dark soul bringing. See "Voce di donna" (Ponchielli)

"Light you down, light you down." See Young hunting (Kentucky version)

"Lighter far is now my slumber." See "Immer leiser wird mein schlummer" (Brahms)

The lighthouse ("The scene was more beautiful") Words attributed to T. Moore. FSS 5

The light-house ("There stands an island") English folk air. Words by J. Erwin. DO

"Lightly dance." See Danza, danza, fanciulla gentile (Durante)

"Lightly o'er the heather." See Hindraleiken

"Lightly row." Spanish air. BSE—FSS 1 —FSS 4—HSD—JSE—WBT—WSC

"Lightly tread." J. Scotland. MS

"Lightning flashes, thunders roll." See Can't you live humble

"The lights fade out of calmed sea." See At evening-time (Sporle)

Lights far out at sea. A. S. Gatty. WBT

Lightwood, J. T.
  "Come, ye Christians all" (Old French air)

Lihuokalani, Lydia Kamekeha, queen of Hawaii. See Liliuokalani, Lydia Kamekeha, queen of Hawaii

"Like a beam from above." See "Ach! so fromm" (Flotow)

"Like a blossoming lilac." See "Meine liebe ist grün" (Brahms)

"Like a clear crystal runnel." See Chi sa (Atri)

"Like a queen enthroned." See Hail, Lafayette (Sciple)

"Like a startled fawn by gadfly arous'd." See La brise (Saint-Saëns)

Like a vision. See "Ah! je veux vivre" (Gounod)

"Like any foolish moth I fly." See "Qual farfalletta amante" (Scarlatti)

"Like as a father pitieth his children, so the Lord hath mercy." Canon. Cherubini. TFC 2—TL

"Like as a father pitieth his children, so the Lord pitieth them that fear Him." F. H. Cowen. OS 2—SAS 2

"Like as a huntsman." Greene. Words by Spenser. DM 2

"Like children turning at twilight from their play." See Alumni song (Foster)

"Like crystal that's gleaming." See "Kristallen den fina"

"Like death's dark shadow night her gloom extendeth." See O du mein holder abendstern (Wagner)

"Like death's grim shadow darkness round me hovers." See O du mein holder abendstern (Wagner)

"Like Etna's dread volcano." See The anchorsmiths (Dibdin)

"Like gathering thunder spreads a cry." See Die wacht am Rhein (Wilhelm)

"Like morning." L. von Beethoven. e. WBT

"Like mountains the waves." N. Rimsky-Korsakov. Words from the Russian of A. Tolstoi. e. NM 2

"**Like** silver lamps."   J. Barnby.   Words by W. C. Dix.   DC—HC

"**Like** silver lamps."   C. Steggall.   Words by W. C. Dix.   HC
    The manger throne.   BSC—DC

"**Like** small curled feathers, white and soft."   A. P. Howard.   Words by Mrs Deland.   JS

"**Like** the bright lamp."   See Erin! oh, Erin

"**Like** the first fresh scent of the violet mild."   See The kiss of a little child (Hullah)

Like the rosebud (Avec une rose) F. La Forge.   Words by A. Bard.   e.f. AA

"**Like** the sun's golden ray."   See "Come raggio di sol" (Caldara)

"**Like** the whispering of a spirit."   See Invocation (Widor)

"**Like** to the sky serenely smiling" (Kak nyebesá tvoi vzor blistáyet) N. Rimsky-Korsakoff.   Words by Lermontoff.   e.   SMR 2

Likelike, princess
    Ainahau.   See Princess Kaiulani's home
    "Beautiful Waipio"
    "Maikai Waipio."   See "Beautiful Waipio"
    Princess Kaiulani's home

"**Li'l** David was a shepherd boy."   See Little David

Li'l Liza Jane.   Old Southern air. Words by D. Harvey.   TFC 2

Lilacs.   S. Rachmaninoff.   Words by K. Beketoff.   e.g.   SC

Liliuokalani, Lydia Kamekeha, queen of Hawaii
    Aloha oe
    Hawaiian farewell song.   See Aloha oe
    Farewell to thee.   See Aloha oe

"**Lille** röde rönnebaer" (Little mountain maid) P. E. Lange-Müller.   Words by T. Lange.   da.e.   SSN

Lilliburlero.   H. Purcell.   Words attributed to Wharton.   BSE—BSP—CO 2—PR 1
    Lilli burlero.   JE

Lilljebjörn, Henrik
    När jag blef sjutton år (Swedish folk air)

Lillo, Giuseppe
    Bolero.   See Domani, o me felice
    Domani, o me felice (from Osteria)
    To-morrow.   See Domani, o me felice

Lilly Dale.   H. S. Thompson.   HSD
    Lily Dale.   WBT

The **lily** ("What a lovely lily grows") Chinese song.   c.e.   BF 2

"The **lily** of the vale is sweet."   Air: Miss Forbes' farewell.   Words by A. Ramsay.   MMS—PS 1

The **lime** tree.   See Der lindenbaum (Schubert)

Limericks.   Old air.   TFC 2

Lincoln's birthday ("Honor to Lincoln the brave") NMS

Lincoln's birthday ("In tow'r and spire were ringing") Dutch folk air.   Words by H. H. Harbour.   DO

The **Lincolnshire** farmer.   Folk song from Norfolk.   SF 2

The **Lincolnshire** poacher.   Lincolnshire county song.   BOH—BOS—DM 2 —JE
    The gallant poacher.   BE 3
    "When I was a bound apprentice." MM
    Variant: The poacher

Lind (When the linden's in flower) A. Backer-Gröndahl.   Words by W. Bergsøe.   e.n.   SSN

Lind (The linden)   e.n.   WM 1

Linda mia.   Pyrenean song.   e.s.   SSP

"Una **linda** y mágica mujer."   See La mágica mujer

Lindblad, Adolf Fredrik
    Ah! my sad song dies away
    Ah, why? ay, ay.   See Mån tro? jo, jo
    Der apfelgarten
    The apple orchard. See Der apfelgarten
    Courting
    Dalecarlian maiden's song
    Disappointed expectation
    Ever near.   See Nära
    Joy
    Mån tro? jo, jo
    Nära
    Old age
    On the mountain
    Silvio to Laura
    En sommarafton
    The sparrow
    Summer eve.   See En sommarafton
    A summer evening.   See En sommarafton
    Suspicion
    The young postillion

Lindblad, Otto
    The bodyguardsman and King Eric. See Lifdrabanten och kung Erik
    Dalecarlian song.   See Dalkarlasång
    Dalkarlasång
    From depths of Swedish hearts.   See "Ur svenska hjertans"
    "From Swedish hearts."   See "Ur svenska hjertans"
    The guard and King Eric.   See Lifdrabanten och kung Erik
    "Hvarför skall man tvinga mig att sjunga"
    Längtan till landet
    Lifdrabanten och kung Erik
    Longing for the country.   See Längtan till landet
    "Oh, why will you try to make me sing now."   See "Hvarför skall man tvinga mig att sjunga"
    Swedish hymn.   See "Ur svenska hjertans"
    To King Oscar.   See "Ur svenska hjertans"
    "Ur svenska hjertans"

"**Linde** erglühte hell im brand."   See The sacrifice

Die **linde** im thal (The linden in the dale)
Folk song. e.g. SSG
Lindeman, Ludvig Mathias
Nordhavet
The North sea. See Nordhavet
The **linden.** See Lind (Backer-Gröndahl)
The **linden** in the dale. See Die linde im thal
"Die **linden** lüfte sind erwacht." See Frühlingsglaube (Ries); Frühlingsglaube (Schubert)
The **linden** tree. See Der lindenbaum (Schubert)
Der **lindenbaum** ("Am brunnen vor dem tore") After F. Schubert. Words by W. Müller. g. ED 1—ED 2
The linden tree. e. BSE—FSS 6—WBT
Der lindenbaum (The lime tree) e.g. BS 2
Der lindenbaum (The linden-tree) e.g. SSG. e. only FTS
Lindpaintner, Peter Joseph von
Entschluss
Die fahnenwacht
The standard bearer. See Die fahnenwacht
"The standard watch." See Die fahnenwacht
Stille liebe
Lindsay, Lady Anne. See Barnard, Lady Anne (Lindsay)
Lindsay, Maria. See Bliss, Mrs Maria (Lindsay)
Lindsey, Thomas
Honeysuckles (Nape)
Lines written in early spring. H. Waller. Words by W. Wordsworth. TL
Ling, J. R.
"Yes! the die is cast" (Kalliwoda)
Linger, Carl
The song of Australia
Lingg, Hermann Ludwig Otto
"Immer leiser wird mein schlummer" (Brahms)
Link o' day. Negro song. BF 2
Linley, Francis
"Lord of all being"
Linley, George
Composer
Gaily I take my way
"I heard a wee bird singing"
"I've left the snow-clad hills"
"Oh! is it thus we part"
"Thou art gone from my gaze" (wrongly attributed) See Linley, T. "Thou art gone from my gaze"
"Thou wilt never grow old"
The vesper chime
"Well-a-day! ah, well-a-day"
Author
"Bird of the forest" (Verdi)
"The day-star is shining" (Abt)
"Ever of thee" (Hall)
Lizette (Kücken)
Rage, thou angry storm (Benedict)
The Swiss girl (Composer unknown)
"Why do I weep for thee" (Wallace)

Linley, Thomas, 1732-1795
"Ah! could you possibly know"
"Cheerly, my hearts of courage true" (attributed)
"The fife and drum sound merrily" (from The camp)
"Here's to the maiden of bashful fifteen": traditional air arranged
Let the toast pass. See "Here's to the maiden of bashful fifteen": traditional air arranged
"The live-long day forlorn I go"
The mid-watch
"No flower that blows" (from Selima and Azor)
"O, bid your faithful Ariel fly"
"Primroses deck the bank's green side"
Sling the flowing bowl
"Still the lark finds repose" (from The Spanish rivals)
"Thou art gone from my gaze"
"Young Lubin was a shepherd boy" (from The carnival of Venice)
Linley, Thomas, 1756-1778
"On every tree, in every plain"
"To heal the wound a bee had made"
Linley, William
Autolycus' song. See "Lawn, as white as driven snow"
"Lawn as white as driven snow"
"Now the hungry lion roars"
Linn, Harry
You never miss the water (Howard)
The **Lion** man-o'-war. Chantey. SMW
"**Lionheart!** O my king." See "O Richard, ô mon roi" (Gretry)
Lipolipo ko wai o Punalau. See Waters of Punalau (Nape)
The **lips.** See Lu labbru
"**Lips** alluring." See Pur dicesti, o bocca bella (Lotti)
"**Lips** of roses." See Pur dicesti, o bocca bella (Lotti)
Lira, lira, la ("Little thinks the townsman's wife") S. Arnold. Words by G. Coleman. ME
Lis'en to de lam's. See Listen to de lambs
Lisette. Bergerette. e.f. WB
Lisle, Claude Joseph Rouget de. See Rouget de Lisle, Claude Joseph
Lisle, Charles Marie Leconte de. See Leconte de Lisle, Charles Marie
Lissant, George B.
"Christ, we sing Thy saving passion"
"Come forth, come forth, brave reapers"
"Come, hear ye how God's priest of old"
"Faithful people, now rejoice"
"From the eastern mountains"
"Heavenly Father, God alone"
"Joy and gladness"
"Lord of the harvest! Thee we hail"
"Merrily the Easter bells"
"Put on thy beautiful robes"
"A rhyme, a rhyme, for Easter time"
"Through the long hidden years"
"Twine the Easter garland"

"List! afar! what angel voices." See Child divine (Bridge)

"List, I hear the angels singing." G. E. Oliver. HC

"List our merry carol." Christmas carol. HC

"List the chiming." Words by H. Martin. MCS

"List! 'tis music stealing." See List to the convent bells (Blockley)

"List to me all you fair young maids." See The sprig of thyme

List to the convent bells. J. Blockley. FSS 3

Listen at de angels shoutin'. See Listen to the angels

"Listen, children! bells are ringing." See Their sweetest song

"Listen how the branches rustle." See Lockung (Dessauer)

"Listen, I've a dream to tell you." See In my dreams

"Listen, kind friends, I own a small parrot." See El periquito

"Listen, lordlings, unto me." 16th century Gascon carol. [Tr of Seignors, ore entendez à nus] e. HC
Carol for Christmas eve. e. DC

"Listen, lordlings, unto me" (Carol for Christmas-eve) F. A. G. Ouseley. [Tr of Seignors, ore entendez à nus] e. BSC

"Listen, love, to me." See Nuit d'Espagne (Massenet)

Listen, my lady. W. P. Kent (music and words) BSS

"Listen, please, you pleasant people." See Jingle all your bells (Davis)

"Listen! the birds are singing." See Alte laute, II (Schumann)

Listen to de lambs. Negro spiritual. BN 2—DF—HR
Lis'en to de lam's. JB

Listen to my tale of woe. H. T. Smith. Words by E. Field. BOS—CHS—SSS

Listen to the angels. Negro spiritual. JP
Listen at de angels shoutin'. DF

"Listen to the joyous bells." See The bells of Aberdovey

Listen to the mocking bird. S. Winner (music and words) FSS 6—HSC—HSD— JSE— NMH—WA— WBT—WL—WSW

"Listen to the tecolote." See Tecolote

Listen to the voice of love. J. Hook. BE 1
O listen to the voice of love. DM 1

"Listen to the water-mill." See The water mill (Diehl)

Listening angels. F. H. Cowen. Words by A. Procter. HSS 2

Liszt, Franz
"Angel fair with golden hair." See "Angiolin dal biondo crin"
"Angiolin dal biondo crin"
Bist du

"Dear love, thou'rt like a blossom." See "Du bist wie eine blume"
Die drei zigeuner
"Du bist wie eine blume"
Elizabeth (from Die legende von der heilige Elisabeth)
"Es muss ein wunderbares sein"
"A flower thou resemblest." See "Du bist wie eine blume"
"Gypsies three." See Die drei zigeuner
"Kennst du das land"
The king of Thule. See Der könig von Thule
Der könig von Thule
"The Lord my Shepherd is." See "Mein Gott der ist mein Hirt"
Die Lorelei
A love dream (Tr of Liebestraum)
"The love that linketh soul to soul." See "Es muss ein wunderbares sein"
"Mein Gott der ist mein Hirt"
Mignons lied. See "Kennst du das land"
Mignon's song. See "Kennst du das land"
"Now peace to earth." See Elizabeth
"Oh life must wondrous be, and fair." See "Es muss ein wunderbares sein"
"Oh, when I sleep"
"O wondrous mystery of love." See "Es muss ein wunderbares sein"
Peace
Prayer
"Soft as the zephyr." See Bist du
"Thou'rt like a gentle flow'ret." See "Du bist wie eine blume"
"Thou'rt like unto a flower." See "Du bist wie eine blume"
"Through the mist of the valleys" (from Die legende von der heiligen Elisabeth)
Wanderers nachtlied
Wanderer's night song. See Wanderers nachtlied
"A wondrous rapture must it be." See "Es muss ein wunderbares sein"

Litaney ("Ruh'n in frieden."—Litany) F. Schubert. Words by Jacobi. e.g. BAS 1
Litany for the feast of all souls. e.g. HSS 1—HSS 2—HSS 3—HSS 4

Litany ("Saviour, when in dust") Words by R. Grant. LA

Litany for the feast of all souls. See Litaney (Schubert)

Liten Karin (Little Karin) Swedish folk song. e.sw. HSOS
Klein Käthchen ("Es war einmal klein Käthchen") g. ED 3
Liten Karin (Little Katie) e.sw. BO
Little Katie. e. KSN

En liten visa (A little song) I. Hallström. Words by A. T. Gellerstedt. e.sw. HSOS

Lithauisches lied. See Lithuanian song (Chopin)

"Lithuania, land of heroes." See Lithuanian national hymn

Lithuanian national hymn ("Lithuania, land of heroes."—Hymnas) e.li. BF 1

Lithuanian song ("Sweet was the morning." —Lithauisches lied) F. Chopin. e.g. KF 1

"Liti Kersti" ("Little Kersti") Norse folk song. e.n. MAN

Litler, J. B.
"There stood three Maries by the tomb"

Litoria ("Yale college is a jolly home") LA

Little, H. W.
"Come, let us sing the story"

Little Annie Rooney. M. Nolan. WBT

"Little baby, good-night." See Wiegenlied (Brahms)

The little bee. Children's song. FSS 8

Little Bennie. G. R. Poulton. FSS 2

Little Bess the ballad-singer. ME

Little Bingo. English gipsy song. GO

"Little birch tree growing in the meadow." See The birch in the meadow

"Little birchen brand in the corner of the room." See The birchen brand

The little bird ("Där sjöngen fågel") See Fågelns visa (Söderberg)

The little bird ("Kommt a vogerl geflogen") See Frohe botschaft (Müller)

The little bird ("Oh, do not frighten") Children's song. FSS 6

"A little bird I held." See Un pajarito

Little bird on the green tree. Claribel (C. Barnard) FSS 2

Little birdie in the tree. P. P. Bliss. FSS 1

"Little birds are singing." C. L. Naylor. Words by M. E. J. Appleby. HC

"A little blithesome merry lass." See By and by (Hook)

"Little blushing mountain maid." See "Lille röde rönnebaer" (Lange-Müller)

"Little Bo-Peep." Nursery song. Composer unknown. FSS 4

"Little Bo-Peep." Nursery song. J. W. Elliott. FMB—HSD—TFC 2—WA— WBT—WSC

The little boat ("La barchetta che scorre") See La barchetta

The little boat ("Vem, meu anjo") See A barquinha

The little boy and the sheep. See "Lazy sheep, pray tell me why"

Little Boy Blue ("The little toy dog") J. E. Smith. Words by E. Field. FSS 6

"Little Boy Blue, come blow your horn." Nursery song. WA—WBT— WSC— WSW

"A little boy went out to shoot one day." See The boy and the cuckoo

"Little brother, darling boy." FSS 1— WBT

Little brother of my heart. See Drahaareen-o mochree

The little brown church in the vale. W. S. Pitts TFC 1

Little brown jug. Eastburn (J. E. Winner) BOS—FMB— HSC— SSS— WBT

"The little busy bee abroad doth roam thro' all the day." See The little bee

"Little by little." C. Barnard. FSS 3

Little Celia Connellan ("My Celia! smiling gladness") Irish air: The peeler and the goat. Words from the Irish. e. MMI

"Little Cherry Blossom." FSS 7

"A little Child is born to-night." A. H. Brown. HC

"The little child of summers three." See Thy story bides for aye (Phelps)

"Little children, can you tell." FSS 7— MCS

Little children's day. C. W. Glover. FSS 4

"Little Christian children, say." C. Vincent. HC

The little cock sparrow. WSC

"Little cottage lowly." See The tiny hut

The little cudgel (Dubinushka) Russian song. e.r. BF 1
Variant of: Volga boat song

"Little David, play on your harp." Negro spiritual. HR
"Lit'le David play on yo' harp." JB
Little David ("Li'l David was a shepherd boy") DF

Little dove ("Vyletěla holubička") Czech folk song. bo.e. BF 1

"Little drops of water." See Little things

The little drummer ("Binder kleine tambour") See Der kleine tambour (Pohlenz)

The little drummer ("If I could play") WBT—WSC

"Little duckling" (Utenushka lugovaîa) Russian gooslee tune. e. SSR 2

The little Dunee. Folk song from Oxfordshire. SF 4

The little dustman. See Sandmännchen

The little Dutch garden. C. Mawson-Marks. Words by H. Whitney. ES

Little empty stocking. Spanish air. MCS

Little Eva. M. Emilio. Words by J. G. Whittier. FSS 7

"Little face with hair of brown." See Biondina (Löhr)

The little family. Kentucky song. BF 2

"A little farm well tilled." Catch. FSS 7 —HSC

"Little Fay, pretty Fay." J. Barnett. Words by W. H. Bellamy. CS 2

Little fidget. See Strampelchen (Hildach)

The little fishermaiden. L. Waldmann. [Tr of Das kleine fischermädchen] e. WA—WBT—WSC

The little fish's song (Fischleins lied) A. Arensky. Words from Lermontoff. e.g. SC

Song of the little fish (Fischleins lied) e.g. NM 1

"A little flower." W. F. G. Nicolaï. e. KSN—WL

"The little flowers came from the ground." C. L. Naylor. Words by L. E. Richards and W. Hawkins. HC

"The little flowers came thro' the ground." See At happy Easter time (Reinecke)

Little gipsy Jane. C. W. Glover. Words by E. Fitzball. FSS 6

Little girl, don't you cry. WBT

Little girl's good-night. A. S. Gatty. WSC

The little girls of Camacha. See "As meninas de Camacha"

The little gray mouse. See La petite souris grise

"A little green peach in an orchard grew." See Listen to my tale of woe (Smith)

"Little grove, green in spring." See The green grove

"Little guests in tiny house." See Mausfallen-sprüchlein (Wolf)

The little house on the hill. F. Schubert. Words by A. Cary. LBR

Little Jack ("There was one little Jack") Words by J. Taylor. FSS 6

"Little Jack Horner." Nursery song. Composer unknown. FMB—FSS 4—WBT

"Little Jack Horner." Nursery song. J. W. Elliott. TFC 2—WA—WSC—WSW

"Little Joe, the wrangler." Cowboy song. LC

"Little Johnny." Air: The last rose of summer.. CHS

The little jug. See The cruiskeen lawn

Little Karen ("Husker du i höst") See Liden Karen (Heise)

Little Karin ("Och liten Karin") See Liten Karin (Swedish folk song)

Little Katie. See Liten Karin (Swedish folk song)

"Little Kersti." See "Liti Kersti"

The little lamb ("On the grassy meadow") WBT—WSC

"Little lamb, who made thee." See The lamb (Chadwick)

The little leaves. W. Ganz. Words by G. Cooper. FSS 6

"Little lips." Nursery song. FSS 8—WBT

"Little Love is a mischievous boy." H. R. Bishop. HSE 2

"Little love serves my turn." H. Lawes. PR 1

Little Maggie May. C. Blamphin. Words by G. W. Moore. FSS 3—NML—WBT—WL

A little man ("A tiny little man") Humperdinck. e. WSC

"Little man and maiden with palms and tapers laden." See Palm branches (Grechaninov)

Little Mary Cassidy. Irish air: The little stalk of barley. Words by F. A. Fahy. FSI

Little Mary of the Dee. J. Parry (music and words) ME

Little Matthew Grew. See Lord Orland's wife

Little Matthew Grove (Lord Daniel's wife) Kentucky mountain song. WT
  Variants: Little Musgrave and Lady Barnard; Lord Orland's wife

"Little Miss Muffet." Nursery song. FMB—WBT—WSC

"Little Miss Muffitt." Nursery song. Another air. WA

The Little Mohee. Kentucky mountain song. BF 2—WLT

A little more cider too. A. Hart. HSD—NMP—WBT

A little more faith in Jesus. Negro spiritual. JP—NMP—WBT

"Little mother, do not scold me." See Mother, do not scold me

Little mountain maid. See "Lille röde rönnebaer" (Lange-Müller)

Little Musgrave and Lady Barnard. Folk song: Clay co., Ky. version. CSE
  —Hindman, Ky. version. CSE
  —Big Laurel, N.C. version. CSE
  —Black Mountain, N. C. version. CSE
  —Hot Springs, N.C. version. CSE
  —Flag Pond, Tenn. version no. 1. CSE
  —Flag Pond, Tenn. version no. 2. CSE
  —Rocky Fork, Tenn. version. CSE
  Variants: Little Matthew Grove; Lord Orland's wife

"A little nightingale, whose notes at twilight rang." See The nightingale (Molloy)

The little nun. See Het kwezelken

"A little of love." Styrian song. e. KSE

"The little old red shawl." BSS—CU—WC

"Little ones, if unsuspicious." See "Se amor mai da vu se vede"

Little orphant Annie. Words by J. W. Riley. FSS 6

Little papoose (Wae-ton wa-an) Omaha Indian air. e.in. SMF

The little patriot's salute. WSC
  The little patriot's song. WBT

"A little peach in an orchard grew." See Listen to my tale of woe (Smith)

The little pig. Vermont song. SSH

"The little pretty nightingale." 16th century song. DM 2

Little purple poppy. See "Amapolita morada"

The little quail (Przepióreczka) Polish folk song. e.p. BF 1

"Little red-bird in the tree." See Little birdie in the tree (Bliss)

The little red lark ("Oh, swan of slenderness") Old Irish air. Words by A. P. Graves. EF—FSI—PI

"The little red lark is shaking his wings." See All in the morning early, O

The little ring. Polish song. Chopin. e. KSE

"Little Robin Red-Breast." WBT—WSC

"Little Sally Waters." WSC

Little Sally's wooden ware. S. Arnold. Words by S. J. Arnold. ME

A little set of quills. Negro spiritual. DF

"The little sheep-girl." See La petite bergère

The little shepherd (Owczarek) Polish folk song. e.p. BF 1

"Little shepherd, to the meadow do not lead your sheep." See The little shepherd

"Little shepherds, come forth from the vale." See Villancico

The little ship. See "I saw a ship a-sailing"

"Little shoes are sold at the doorway of heaven." See Dodo

"The little silver ring that once you gave to me." See L'anneau d'argent (Chaminade)

Little Sir Hugh. Folk song. SEF 1— SO

"Little snowdrops ever sing." See Schneeglöckchen (Dorn)

Little Snowflake's arietta. N. Rimsky-Korsakow. Words after A. Ostrovsky. e. SC

Little soldier-man. See "Petit soldat de guerre"

A little song ("Jag vet en gosse") See En liten visa (Hallström)

"Little song of Christmastide." See Christmas song (Liapunov)

Little sparrow. See Come all you fair and tender ladies (Kentucky version)

"Little star so bright." See "Little star, where art thou" (Musorgskii)

"Little star that shines so bright." See The child and the star

"Little star, where art thou." M. Moussorgsky (music and words) e. FM—NM 2

"Little star so bright" (Gdye tui zvyózdotchka) e. SMR 1

"Little stars, whose bright eyes shine above me." See "Klara stjärnor med de ögon snälle"

"Little streamlet, wherefore hurry." See Aufträge (Schumann)

"A little sun, a little rain." See The spring of love (Hyatt)

Little Sunbeam. H. Farmer. Words by J. E. Carpenter. FSS 8

"Little thanks I give the abbot grim and old." See The novice

Little things. Kindergarten song. FSS 1 —WA—WBT—WSC

"Little thinks the townsman's wife." See Lira, lira, la (Arnold)

The little tin soldier. J. L. Molloy. Words by F. E. Weatherly. FSS 7— LA—WSC

"Little Tommy Tucker." Nursery song. WSC

"The little toy dog is covered with dust." See Little Boy Blue (Smith)

The little turtle dove. Folk song. FSF Variant of: The turtle-dove

The little voice. Tauwitz. Words by B. Cornwall. FSS 8

The little waste. J. Hook. ME

Little wheel a-turnin'. Negro spiritual. DF—HR

A little while. J. D. Herron. Words by J. Crewdson. LA

Little wild goose ("Husička divoká") Moravian folk song. c.e. BF 1

The little witch. W. F. G. Nicolaï. e. KSN

The little woman. Children's song. WSC

"A little word in kindness said" (Ortonville) T. Hastings. FSS 7

Little Yashka (Akh ulitsa, ulitsa shirokaîa) Russian folk song. e. SSR 1

Littledale, Richard Frederick
"The cedar of Lebanon" (Old air)
Joy hath come to earth again (Swiss air)
"Let us the Infant greet" (Smith)

Littleton, George Littleton, 1st baron. See Lyttelton, George Lyttelton, 1st baron

"Live humble, humble, humble yourselves." See Glory and honor

"Live, live, live." Croatian folk air. Words by J. Russell. WF

"The live-long day forlorn I go." T. Linley. ME

Live this day in memory shining. See Ah! quel giorno (Rossini)

"Live we singing." M. Hauptman. MS

"Lived the pearl in the deeps of ocean shadow." See La perla (Araya?)

"Living echo, living echo, bird of eve." See Pretty mocking bird (Bishop)

"Living fire in your eyes is flaming." See Cueca or zamacueca

'Liza-Jane (Stealin' partners) Negro dance-game song. BN 4

"Liza Lee." Negro halliard chantey. CR —SE

"Lizard on de fence rail." See Let Miss Lindy pass (Rogers)

Lizette ("See these ribbons") F. Kücken. Words by G. Linley. CHS—MP —MPC—WBT
The young recruit. SSS

"Lizette one morn arose." See "Par un matin"

"Ljubeznice moja mila." See At parting ("O my love's bright eyes")

"Llegan de noche con gran cautela." See Los reyes magos (Colón)

"Llewelyn brave turn'd and sigh'd." See The departure of the king

Llorando a mares yo la busco doquiera. See La paloma (Porto Rican song)

Lloyd, Arthur
Not for Joseph

Lloyd, John
"The hounds were by the river" (Welsh air)
Lament (Welsh air)
Soldier's departure for foreign service (Welsh air)

Llwyn on ("The ash grove") Old Welsh song. e.w. BO. e. only CST
The ash grove. e. BOS—CS 1—GO —MSS 1—SS 1—TFC 2

"**Lo!** a darkness here." See Della vita in sull' aurora (Beethoven)

Lo! a fair rose is blooming. M. Praetorius. Words from the German. e. HC
Lo, how a rose e'er blooming. e. DC

"**Lo!** a little quail fled through the millet." See The little quail

"**Lo,** a rosebud lifts its head." See Rose of yesteryear

"**Lo:** a star, ye sages hoary." W. Newport. Words by S. K. Cowan. HC

"**Lo,** as the sun from his ocean bed rising." See There she blows

"**Lo!** descending, the heavens rending." See Christ is born in Bethlehem

"**Lo!** here the gentle lark." H. R. Bishop. Words by Shakespeare. HSE 1
Lo, how a rose e'er blooming. See Lo! a fair rose is blooming (Praetorius)

"**Lo!** in Kiev, the old and mighty town." See The feast of Vladímir

"**Lo!** in the depths of the sky." See My world (Huss)

"**Lo!** my bold and black-eyed lover." See The gay bachelor

Lo! now he is come. Words by E. Douglas. MCS

"**Lo!** now I bid farewell to Ventadorn." Bernard de Ventadorn. e. DT

"**Lo!** on Mikane's heights." See Love-lay indited by the Mikado Temmu (Ross)

"**Lo,** one March morn, raised my eyes." See Buddhist chant

"**Lo,** St Andrews' youths before ye." See Carmen seculare (Oakeley)

"**Lo!** the happy morn o'er eastern hills." See Echoes of olden times (Comer)

"**Lo,** the harvest ripe we have winnow'd now." See The sowing of the millet

"**Lo,** the highlander's departing." See "Plecat-a motul la tara"

"**Lo!** the seal of death is breaking." See The golden shore

Lo, the winter is past. A. F. M. Custance (music and words) HC

"**Lo,** 'tis Saint John's day." See "Voici la Saint-Jean"

"**Lo,** 'tis the month of May." See "Voici le mois de mai"

"**Lo!** where the plenteous harvest." J. Haydn. e. SAS 4

"**Lo,** while the zephyr of nightfall." See Zephyr of nightfall

"**Lo,** with what glow do all go to the strife." See Bergen op Zoom

"**Lo,** you come, the sun is sparkling." See Hymn to freedom (Manzaros)

"**Loaded** with gallant soldiers." See Ready

Lob, Otto
Hallelujah

Lob der edlen musica ("Ein lustger musikante") Volksweise. Words by E. Geibel. g. ED 1

Lob der freundschaft ("Lasst uns, ihr brüder") Volksweise. Author of words unknown. g. ED 2

"**Lobt** den Herrn." J. H. Rolle. Words by J. S. Patzke. g. ED 3

Loch Lomond. Jacobite air. BSE—CST —CU—DO— DSH—GO— HSD— JSE—SM 2—WBT—WL
The bonnie banks o' Loch Lomon'. BAS 1—BOS—HSD—PS 2
"By yon bonnie banks." HSSS— MMS—MS
Loch Lomond (The bonnie banks o' Loch Lomon') EF—KF 1—KF 2 —KF 3
Loch Lomond (The bonnie banks of Loch Lomond) OH—TL

Lochaber no more ("Farewell to Lochaber") Attributed to M. Reilly. Words by A. Ramsay. FSS 3— HSSS—JO
"Farewell to Lochaber." PS 1

Lochwitzky-Gibert, Mirra Aleksandrovna.
See Lokhvitskaía, Mirra Aleksandrovna

Lock! lock! ahoy. See The old lock (Wellings)

Locke, Mary V.
Christmas carol. See "When Christ was born in Bethlehem"
"When Christ was born in Bethlehem"

Locke, Matthew
"Behold, my love, how green the groves" (same air as "My lodging it is on the cold ground")
"The delights of the bottle" (from Psyche)
I prethee love, turn to me. See "My lodging it is on the cold ground"
"My lodging it is on the cold ground" (from The rivals)
On the cold ground. See "My lodging it is on the cold ground"

Lockhart, John Gibson
The bridal of Andalla (Browne)

Locks and bolts. Folk song: Kentucky version. CSE
—Carmen, N.C. version no. 1. CSE
—Carmen, N.C. version no. 2. CSE
—Hot Springs, N.C. version. CSE
—Spillcorn, N.C. version. CSE

"**Locks** so beautiful." See "O bellissimi capelli" (Falconieri)

"A **locksmith** had a 'prentice lad." See Der schlossergesell

The **locksmith's** lad. See Der schlossergesell

Lockung (Enticement) J. Dessauer. e.g. SM 2

Loder, Edward James
The brave old oak
The diver
"I heard a brooklet gushing" (Tr of Wohin)
"Martin, the man-at-arms"
Old house at home
The outlaw
"The pearl that worldlings covet" (same air as "The rose that all are praising")
Philip the falconer
"The rose that all are praising"
The three ages of love
"Wake, my love"
Loéma tombé. Negro folk song from Martinique. e.f. KA
Loewe, Karl
Archibald Douglas
Der Asra
The bellringer's daughter. See Des glockenthürmers töchterlein
Canzonette
Des glockenthürmers töchterlein
Der edelfalk
Edward
The erlking. See Erlkönig
Erlkönig
The falcon. See Der edelfalk
"Mädchen sind wie der wind"
"Maidens are like the wind." See "Mädchen sind wie der wind"
Meeresleuchten
Niemand hat's geseh'n
Nobody saw. See Niemand hat's geseh'n
"O dearest mother." See "O süsse mutter"
"O süsse mutter"
Phosphorescence. See Meeresleuchten
Die uhr
Walpurgis night. See Walpurgisnacht
Walpurgisnacht
The watch. See Die uhr
Löffler, A.
Lied des alten im bart
"Löft mig kun bort, du staerke död." See En digters sidste sang (Grieg)
"The lofty mountains rich in ore." Styrian song. e. KSE—SN
Logan, John
Spring-time once again (Sullivan)
Logan braes ("O Logan, sweetly didst thou glide") Air: Logan water. Words by R. Burns. BSB
"O Logan, sweetly didst thou glide." BSR
Logan water ("By Logan's streams") Scottish air. Words by Mayne. PS 1
Logie o' Buchan. Scottish air. Words by G. Halket. PS 1
"O Logie o' Buchan." BO—MMS
Löhr, Frederic N.
Biondina
Love's proving
"Out on the deep"
Loin de lui ("I'll never see my lover more") C. Dancla. Words by C. Grandmougin. e.f. SOS 1

Loker, J.
Tapping at the garden gate (New)
Lokhvitskaĭa, Mirra Aleksandrovna
"How abundant and warm is the spring" (Sokolov)
Love (Bleikhman)
Lola's song. P. Mascagni. [Tr of Fior di giaggiolo] e. WBT
Lombard, J. K.
Alma mater—Yale (Shepard)
Lombardo, L. Bevacqua. See Bevacqua Lombardo, L.
London bridge ("Proud and lowly") J. L. Molloy. Words by F. E. Weatherly. FSS 6—LA
"**London** bridge is broken down, dance over, my Ladye Lea." Play-time song. FSS 5
"**London** bridge is broken down, gold is won, and bright renown." Old Danish song. e. SMW
"**London** bridge is falling down." Folk song: English version. FSF —American version. NMH—NMS—WA—WBT—WSC
London is a fine town (Watton town's end) 17th century song. CO 2
"**Lone** and joyless." See Infelice (Mendelssohn)
The **lone** fish-ball ("There was a man") 1st version. HSD—LA—MPC
The **lone** fish-ball ("There was a man") 2d version. LA
"**Lone** in thy dark old tow'r." See La cloche (Saint-Saëns)
"**Lone** in thy darkling tower." See La cloche (Saint-Saëns)
"**Lone** in thy sombre tow'r." See La cloche (Saint-Saëns)
"**Lone** is my little room." See In my attic (Musorgskiĭ)
Lone starry hours. J. Power. Words by M. S. Pike. FSS 8
Lonely ("Fear not, he sayeth") Ojibway Indian song. e. BA
Lonely ("Ô fier jeune homme") See La solitaire (Saint-Saëns)
"**Lonely** and still was the wood and hill." See Bunker hill (Tuckerman)
"A **lonely** Arab maid" ("Donzella nata in sen") Weber. e.i. OPS 2
"The **lonely** clouds blow across the sky." See "Så ödsligt molnen på fästet gå"
"A **lonely** cowpuncher was moping." See El charro
Lonely, reft and broken-hearted. See Infelice sconsolata (Mozart)
The **lonely** waif (Iskhodila mladen'ka) Russian folk song. e. SSR 3
"**Lonely** wanders thy friend in spring's green garden." See Adelaïde (Beethoven)
The **lonesome** low. See The Mary Golden Tree
Long ago ("Long, long ago, long, long ago") F. Musgrave. HSD
The **long** ago ("Tell me the tales") See Long, long ago (Bayly)

Long ago in Bethlehem.   H. D. Wetton. Words by E. Beale.   HC

"**Long** ago in childhood's days."   See "Songs my mother taught me" (Dvořák)

"**Long** ago she rose and stood."   See Holyoke

"**Long** be thy reign, O king."   See "Tracascâ regele" (Hübsch)

"Le **long** du quai, les grands vaisseaux." See Les berceaux (Fauré)

The **long** day.   See Den långa dagen (Kjerulf)

"**Long** ere the morn expects the return." See The hunter in his career

"A **long** farewell I send to thee."   See Farewell to the Maig

"**Long** had their watch been and dreary." See First Christmas gifts (Barnard)

"**Long** hours I've tramped."   See The desert (Balakirev)

"**Long** I dwelt 'neath the echoing portico's vastness."   See La vie antérieure (Duparc)

"**Long** I gaze across the snow" (Eskimo song)   e.   BMC

Long is the night.   See To Chloe in sickness (Bennett)

"**Long** is the road."   See Banished

"**Long** live Canadian lasses."   See "Vive la Canadienne" (Streabbog)

"**Long** live Canadian maidens."   See "Vive la Canadienne" (Streabbog)

Long live Harvard.   College song.   CHS

Long live, long live America.   W. H. Pontius.   Words by J. E. Rankin.   JS

Long live our college.   MPC

"**Long** live our noble king."   See "Tracascâ regele" (Hübsch)

Long live Stuart hall.   College of Emporia song.   Words by C. H. C. Dudley. CHS

"**Long** live the king."   See "Tracascâ regele" (Hübsch)

Long, long ago.   T. H. Bayly (music and words)   BD—BE 6—CMF 1— FSS 1— HSC— HSD— HSE 3— NML—OH—WA—WBT— WL— WSW

Lang', lang' ist's her ("Sag mir das wort")   g.   ED 1

The long ago.   JO

"**Long**, long ago in Bethlehem."   See Long ago in Bethlehem (Wetton)

"**Long**, long ago, long, long ago."   See Long ago (Musgrave)

"**Long**, long ago, the angel throng."   See The Christmas story (Keene)

"**Long**, long have I wandered."   See The dark fairy rath

"**Long**, long is the night, and heavy comes the morrow."   See To Chloe in sickness (Bennett)

Long, long the night, heavy comes the morrow.   See "Can I cease to care"

"**Long**, long weary day."   See Des mädchens klage

Long may our college stand.   Iowa Wesleyan university song.   Air: America. Words by N. W. Huston.   CHS

"**Long** may she live, our college fair."   See Long live our college

"**Long** may she live, our Harvard fair." See Long live Harvard

"**Long** moons have passed."   See Waubunosa's longing

A **long** time ago ("Away down south") Halliard chantey.   CR—SE

For variant see following song of same title

A **long** time ago ("A long time and a very")   Long drag chantey.   KB

Long time ago ("Near the lake")   Negro air: Way down in the raccoon hollow, arr by C. E. Horn.   Words by G. P. Morris.   LBR

"Near the lake where drooped the willow."   FSS 1—HSE 3—JO

"A **long** time and a very long time."   See A long time ago

"**Long** time I courted you, miss."   Irish folk song.   JOI

A **long** ways from home.   See "Sometimes I feel like a motherless child"

The **long** weary day.   See Des mädchens klage

The **long** years.   See The meeting

"**Long** years ago, in old Madrid."   See In old Madrid (Trotter)

Longfellow, Henry Wadsworth

Afternoon in February (Hullah)

"Alike are life and death" (Rinck)

America: fugitive stanza (Carey)

The arrow and the song (Balfe)

Bear a lily in thy hand (Composer unknown)

Beware (Hatton)

The bridge (Bliss)

Curfew (Composer unknown)

The death of Minnehaha (Converse)

Decoration day (Geyer)

"Good night, good night beloved" (music by Balfe; Moir; Nevin; Pinsuti)

"The green trees whispered low and mild" (Balfe)

The hemlock tree (German air)

"I heard the bells on Christmas day" (music by Brewer; Hatton)

"It was fifty years ago" (Hatton)

January (Olds)

The open window (Scott-Gatty)

A psalm of life (Smart)

The rainy day (Dempster)

The reaper and the flowers (Emerson)

The ship of state (German air; also music by unknown composer)

"Stars of the summer night" (music by Balfe; Pease; Woodbury; also unknown composer)

"The sun is bright" (Weber)

To stay at home is best (Cate)

Upidee (Composer unknown)

The village blacksmith (Weiss)

The wreck of the Hesperus (Hatton)

Longfellow, Samuel
"God of the earth" (Hemy and Walton)
"Holy Spirit, truth divine" (Gottschalk)
"Sing we now our hymns of gladness" (Atherton)
"The summer days are come again" (Traditional air)
Summer parting hymn (Adams)
"We feel thy calm" (Haydn)

Longing ("Ah, longing! my tears ebb and flow") Maori song. S. Vassilenko. Words from the Russian of K. Ballmont. e. NM 2

Longing ("Grant me daylight's golden splendor."—Sehnsucht) A. Rubinstein. e.f.g. KF 2—KF 3
Longings (Give me daylight's golden beauty") e. BC
Yearnings ("Give me days of golden glory."—Sehnsucht) e.g. FO 1

Longing ("Jeg kunde slet ikke sove") See Laengsel (Kjerulf)
Longing ("Of all the myriad moods") R. G. Cole. Words by J. R. Lowell. TL
Longing ("River, flow, river, flow") Chinese song. c.e. BF 2
Longing ("Ser jag stjernorna") See Längtan (Söderman)
Longing ("Storm, hvem gav dig din aande") See Laengsel (Backer-Lunde)
Longing ("Wer in die fremde") See Heimweh (Wolf)
Longing for spring. German air. FSS 1
Longing for the country. See Längtan till landet (Lindblad)
"Longtemps captifs chez le Russe lointain." See Les deux grenadiers (Wagner)

Lonsdale, J. J.
The children's kingdom (Blumenthal)

Lonsdale, Mark
The light in the window (Gabriel)
The old commodore (Reeve)
"Still the lark finds repose" (Linley)

Lontos, S. S.
"Mana tēn agapō." See Why does he haunt my door
Why does he haunt my door

Looby loo. Children's song. NMS—WBT—WSC

The look. See Blicken (Alfvén)

"Look ahead, look a-starn." See The coasts of High Barbary
"Look at me, my little dear." See A nurse song
"Look at that beautiful singing bird." See The nightingale
"Look at that darkey there, Mister Banjo." See Musieu Bainjo
"Look at the dandy there, Mister Banjo." See Musieu Bainjo
"Look how the fruitful land is smiling." C. M. von Weber. e. SAS 3
"Look in my face, dear, openly and free." See A farewell (Cowen)

"Look not upon me with thine eyes." H N. Bartlett. Words by W. J. Henderson. HST
"Look not upon the wine." R. S. Willis. FSS 4
"Look our ransomed shore around." See Hail Columbia, The new
Look out dar, now! we's a gwine to shoot. See Babylon is fallen (Work)
Look out, how it's raining. See Schaut's aussi
"Look thou in the sultan's garden, love." See The breath of Allah (Cooke)
Look up. Pawnee Indian song. e.in. FIS
"Look ye now, all ye good folk." See The three gifts
Looking back. A. Sullivan. Words by L. Gray. CS 1—HSD

Loomis, George B.
"Baby bye, here's a fly"

Loomis, Harvey Worthington
Composer
"And let me the canakin clink"
Counterpoint for Music in the air. See Music in the air, Counterpoint for
"Crabbed age and youth"
In the foggy dew
Indian trail song
Lady Moon
Music in the air, Counterpoint for
Uncrowned kings
Composer and author
Echoes
The mosquito's serenade
Author
Love greetings (Elgar)
A song for Christmas eve (Sicilian air)

Loons, ye maun gae hame ("It's here awa', there awa', how they did rin") Jacobite song. MMS
"Loose ev'ry sail to the breeze." See Homeward bound (Arne)

Lopez de Mendonça, Henriques
A Portuguesa (Keil)

López y Planes, Vincento
Himno nacional
National hymn. See Himno nacional
"Oid, mortales, el grito sagrado." See Himno nacional

"Lor, lor, my little Betty Anne." See Betty Anne
"Lord at all times I will bless Thee." See "Caro cibus, sanguis potus" (Mendelssohn)
"The Lord at first did Adam make." Traditional carol. HC—WCC
A carol for Christmas eve. BSC
"Lord Bacon was a nobleman." See Young Beichan (White Rock, N.C. version)
"Lord Bateman was a noble lord." Folk song. SEF 1—SO
Variant: Young Beichan
Lord Batesman. See Young Beichan
"Lord, can it be." Bach. e. OS 2
Lord Daniel's wife. See Little Matthew Grove

"**Lord,** dismiss us with Thy blessing." Sicilian air. Words attributed to J. Fawcett; also attributed to W. Shirley. WBT—WS

"Lord, dismiss us with Thy blessing" (Sicilian mariners' hymn) FSS 3

Lord Dunwaters. Folk song from Hampshire. SF 3

Lord, for whom my soul is burning. G. Vierling. e. SAS 2

"**Lord,** forever at Thy side." C. M. von Weber. Words by J. Montgomery. FSS 3
Seymour. CST

"**Lord,** from my bed again I rise." See The morning prayer (Costa)

"**Lord** God of Abraham." F. Mendelssohn. e. SAS 4

"**Lord** God of hosts, whose mighty hand." See The people's prayer (Dykes)

"**Lord** God of morning and of night." See Morning hymn (Beethoven)

"**Lord** God, protect the czar." See Russian national hymn (Lvov)

Lord Gregory ("O mirk, mirk is the midnight hour") Ancient Galloway air. Words by Burns. BSB—HSSS—MMS—PS 1

"O, mirk, mirk is this midnight hour." BSR

"**Lord,** guard and guide the men who fly." See Hymn for airmen (Oliver)

"**Lord,** hear my voice." J. Raff. e. SAS 4

"**Lord!** I married me a wife." See Rain and snow

"**Lord,** I want to be a Christian." Negro spiritual. HR

"**Lord** in heav'n above, who ruleth us." See Largo (Händel)

"**Lord,** in this thy mercy's day." W. H. Monk. FSS 1—LA

"**Lord,** in Thy great, Thy glorious name" Schumann. Words by A. Steele. TL

"**Lord** in Thy mercy, oh, hear my pray'r." See David's prayer (Costa)

"The **Lord** into His garden comes." See When we arrive at home (Ingalls)

"The **Lord** is long-suffering and merciful." C. H. H. Parry. SAS 2

"The **Lord** is my Shepherd." Chant. Composer unknown. [Words by J. Montgomery] MP—WBT

"The **Lord** is my Shepherd." T. Koschat. Words by J. Montgomery. JS—JSE

"The Lord is my Shepherd" (Green pastures) BD

"The **Lord** is risen, He will dwell with men." A. Sullivan. OS 2—SAS 2

"The **Lord** is risen! His praise is ringing" (Christós voskrés) S. Rachmaninoff. Words by D. S. Mereshkovsky. e. SMR 2

"The **Lord** is risen! risen, indeed." E. Handley. HC

"The **Lord** is very pitiful." Benedict. OS 3

"**Lord,** lead me in Thy righteousness." See O salutaris (Cherubini)

"**Lord,** let war's tempests cease." See America: fugitive stanza (Carey)

"**Lord,** Lord, for whom my soul is burning." See Lord, for whom my soul is burning (Vierling)

"**Lord** Lovel." Folk song: English version. SEF 2—SO

—North Carolina version. CSE

"The **Lord** my Shepherd is." See "Mein Gott der ist mein Hirt" (Liszt)

"**Lord** of all being." F. Linley. Words by O. W. Holmes. LBR

"**Lord** of all being" (Louvan) V. C. Taylor. Words by O. W. Holmes. CST

"**Lord** of ev'ry land and nation." See Alleluia (Lowe)

"**Lord** of heaven, bless our land." See Hungarian national hymn (Erkel)

"**Lord,** of my inmost heart's recesses." See Gebet (Hiller)

"**Lord** of our fathers, known of old." See The recessional (Huss)

"**Lord** of the harvest! Thee we hail." G. B. Lissant. Words by J. H. Gurney. HC

"**Lord** of the living harvest." Composer unknown. Words by J. S. B. Monsell. HC

Lord Orland's wife (Little Matthew Grew) Kentucky mountain song. WT
Variants: Little Matthew Grove; Little Musgrave and Lady Barnard

"**Lord,** preserve me uncomplaining." See "Pro peccatis" (Rossini)

Lord Randal. Folk song: Georgia version. CSE

—Allanstand, N.C. version no. 1. CSE

—Allanstand, N.C. version no. 2. CSE

—Carmen, N.C. version. CSE

—Swannanoah, N.C. version. CSE
Variants: Lord Rendal; Lord Ronald

"**Lord,** remember me in my trouble." Händel. HSS 2—HSS 4

Lord Rendal. Somersetshire county song. BOH—FSF—SEF 2—SO
Variants: Lord Randal; Lord Ronald

Lord Ronald. Scottish song. PS 1
Variants: Lord Randal; Lord Rendal

"The **lord** said to the lady." See False Lamkin

Lord Thomas and fair Ellinor. Folk song: English version. SEF 2—SO

—Georgia version. CSE

—Massachusetts version. CSE

—Allanstand, N.C. version. CSE

—Carmen, N.C. version. CSE

—Hot Springs, N.C. version. CSE

—Tennessee version. CSE

—Virginia version. CSE

Lord Thomas and fair Ellendor (The brown bride) Kentucky version. WT

Lord Thomas of Winesberry. Folk song. SEF 1—SO

"Lord, Thy glory fills the heaven." See "Fac ut portem" (Rossini)

"Lord, to Thee, each night and day." G. F. Händel. OS 2—SAS 2

Lord Ullin's daughter. G. Thomson. Words by T. Campbell. JO

"Lord, until I reach my home." Negro spiritual. HR

"Lord! vouchsafe Thy loving kindness." Rossini. HSS 1—HSS 3

"Lord! we come before Thee now" (Hendon) Malan. FSS 4

"Lord, we pray Thee, Lord, we pray Thee." Mozart. HSS 1

"Lord, we pray Thee to comfort Thy servants." F. Morlachi. HSS 1

"Lord, while for all mankind we pray." See Prayer for our country (Tufts)

"Lord! Who dost see our heavy grief." Beethoven. HSS 2

"Lord, Who hast spread." See "O Heer die daer"

"Lord, why hidest Thou Thy face." Sullivan. OS 1—SAS 1

"The Lord will not be ever wroth." C. Rheinthaler. e. SAS 2

Lord Willoughby (Lord Willoughby's march.—Lord Willoughby's welcome home) W. Byrd. CO 1
Brave Lord Willoughby. DM 2

"Lord, with glowing heart I'd praise Thee" (With glowing heart) Spanish air. Words by F. S. Key. MCS

"Lord, with glowing heart I'd praise Thee." Flotow. [Words by F. S. Key] FSS 1 —LA

"Lord, with glowing heart I'd praise Thee" (With glowing heart I'd praise Thee.— Austrian hymn) Haydn. Words by F. S. Key. FSS 2

Lords and ladies. Old French air: Le pont d'Avignon. Words by H. H. Harbour. DO

The Lord's anointed. See "Hail to the Lord's anointed" (Mason)

The Lord's prayer ("Our Father in Heaven, we hallow Thy name") Composer unknown. Words by S. J. Hale. FSS 1

The Lord's prayer ("Our Father Which art in heaven") Another air. JS

The Lord's prayer ("Our Father Who art in heaven") A third air. HSD—NMS

The Lord's prayer ("Our Father, Who art in heaven") A fourth air. JP—WBT

Die Lore am tore ("Von allen den mädchen") Composer unknown. Words after H. C. Boie. g. ED 1

Die Lorelei ("Ich weiss nicht."—The Loreley) F. Liszt. Words by H. Heine. e.g. FF
Die Loreley. e.g. KF 1—MSS 2— PG 1. e. only FTS
The Loreley. e.g. SS 1

Die Lorelei ("Ich weiss nicht") F. Silcher. Words by H. Heine. e.g. MS— SSG—SSS. g. only ED 1
Die Lorelei (The Loreley) e.g. BO
The Lorelei. e.g. SMW. e. only DO
The Loreley. e.g. CHS—CU—NMH. e. only BSE—FSS 1—HSC—HSD —JSE— LA—WA—WBT— WL— WSC—WSW

Lorelei ("Zu Bacharach am Rheine") L. Erk. Words by C. Brentano. g. ED 3

The Loreley ("Es ist schon spät") See Waldesgespräch (Jensen)

The Loreley ("Ich weiss nicht") See Die Lorelei (Liszt); Die Lorelei (Silcher)

Loreley in the forest. See Waldesgespräch (Schumann)

Lorena. J. P. Webster. Words by H. D. L. Webster. FSS 7—HSD

Lorna Doone's song. A. Nevin. BD

"Lorsque au soleil couchant les rivières sont roses." See Beau soir (Debussy)

Lortzing, Albert
"In childhood I dallied." See "Sonst spielt ich"
Song of the czar. See "Sonst spielt ich"
"Sonst spielt ich" (from Czar und zimmermann)
Stadinger's song (from Der waffenschmied. Tr of Ich auch war einst jüngling mit lockigem haar)
With crown and scepter. See "Sonst spielt ich"

The lost chance. See L'occasion manquée

The lost chord. A. Sullivan. Words by A. A. Procter. BD—FMB—HSD— KF 2—MS—TFC 1—WA—WS—WSW

The lost doll. Children's song. WBT— WSC

Lost happiness. See 'O bene antico (Nutile)

The lost lady found. Folk song from Essex. SF 2

Lost love. See Élégie (Massenet)

The lost opportunity ("Dimanche à l'aube") See La fille et le chasseur

The lost opportunity ("Nous étions trois filles") See Les trois filles

Loth to depart ("Lie still, my dear") 17th century air. Words by Donne. DM 2

Loth to depart ("Sing with thy mouth") 2 airs. CO 1

Loth to depart ("So mild was the evening") Air: Anhawdd yma dael, or, Loth to depart. Words by A. Grant. BMC

"Loth to depart, love." Air: Anhawdd yma dael, or, Loth to depart. Words by J. M. E. Dovaston. MMW

Lotharia. T. A. Arne. Words by A. Hill. ME

Lothrop, Mrs Harriet Mulford (Stone)
The heavenly Guest (Composer unknown)
The lotos flower. See Die lotosblume (Franz); Die lotosblume (Schumann)
Die lotosblume (The lotus flower) R. Franz. Words by H. Heine. e.g. FO 1—MSS 1
Die lotosblume (The lotus flower) R. Schumann. Words by H. Heine. e.g. FF—FO 1—KF 1—KF 3— PG 1. e. only FTS
The lotus flower. e.g. FSS 6—MS
The lottery. 18th century song. MM
Lotti, Antonio
"Lips alluring." See Pur dicesti, o bocca bella
"Lips of roses." See Pur dicesti, o bocca bella
"Mouth so charmful." See Pur dicesti, o bocca bella
Pur dicesti, o bocca bella
"Speak, I pray thee." See Pur dicesti, o bocca bella
The lotus flower. See Die lotosblume (Franz); Die lotosblume (Schumann)
"Loud blaw the frosty breezes." Air: Morag. Words by R. Burns. BSR
"Loud let the glasses clink." See Edite, bibite
"Loud roar'd the dreadful thunder." See The bay of Biscay (Davy)
"Loud roaring pines, storm-swollen flood." See Aufenthalt (Schubert)
"Loud strike the sounding strings." Beethoven. Words by T. Williams or J. Drake. FSS 3
Loud strike the strings. MCS
"Loud the winds howl, loud the waves roar." See Skye boat-song
"Loudon's bonnie woods and braes." Scottish air. Words by Tannahill. PS 1
Louis XIII, king of France
Amaryllis
Louis Kossuth ("Kossuth Lajos azt üzente") Hungarian song. e.hu. BF 1
"Louis, what reck I by thee." Air: Louis, what reck. Words by R. Burns. BSR
Louisella. See La Luisella
Loukianoff. See Luk'iânov,
Les loups. See The wolves (Arenski)
Lou'siana Belle. S. C. Foster (music and words) NMP—WBT
Louvan (Taylor) See "Deep are the wounds"; "Lord of all being"
Louÿs, Pierre
La chevelure (Debussy)
Lov'd by thee. O. Cantor. Words by Browning. SM 2
Love, James
"Abroad we must wander" (Composer unkown)
Love ("E puoi se barbara") See Amore (Lucantoni)
Love ("Oui, je t'aime") See L'amour (Godard)

Love ("T'amo perchè sei bella") See Amore (Muratori)
Love ("Wilt thou return."—Liebe) J. Bleichmann. Words from the Russian of M. Lochwitzky-Gibert. e.g. FM
Love an' serve de Lord. Negro spiritual. HR
"Love, and if there be one." See Lorna Doone's song (Nevin)
Love and mirth. J. Strauss. FSS 2— WBT
Love and music ("'Tis love that makes all nature gay") J. Wynne. ME
Love and summer. J. E. West. Words by M. Rowles. BD
Love and the novice ("Here we dwell in holiest bowers") Air: Cean dubh deelish. Words by T. Moore. MI— MMI
Love at home. J. H. McNaughton. FSS 3
Love boat song. See "Iomraibh, iomraibh, iomraibh, illean"
"Love came down at Christmas." J. E. Borland. Words by C. G. Rossetti. HC
"Love divine, all love excelling" (Weston) J. E. Roe. Words by C. Wesley. LA
"Love divine, all love excelling." J. Zundel. Words by C. Wesley. TL— WBT—WS
A love dream. F. Liszt. [Tr of Liebestraum] e. WBW
"Love, fear not if sad thy dreaming." See Ar hyd y nos (Owen)
A love-feast in heaven. Negro spiritual. DF
Love finds out the way. See Keine sorg' um den weg (Raff)
Love for love. See "Shall I wasting in despair" (King)
Love greetings (Salut d'amour) E. Elgar. Words by H. W. Loomis. TFC 2
Love has eyes. H. R. Bishop. Words by C. Dibdin. BOH—DM 1—HSE 1
"Love, have you quite forgotten." See Reproach
Love, hope, happiness. E. Ransford. JSE
"Love, I must die." See Mi sueño
Love, I will love you ever. P. Bucalossi. Words by F. Desprez. FSS 4—NML —WBT
Love in May. See Villanelle (Berlioz)
Love in spring ("Le printemps chasse les hivers") See Au printemps (Gounod)
Love in springtime ("When the spring's soft breezes") German folk song. e. WL
"Love in thine eyes for ever plays." Jackson. BE 3
"Love is a bauble." R. Leveridge. JE— MM
"Love is a butterfly ever." See "Es el amor mariposa"
"Love is a queer little elfin sprite." See Because you're you (Herbert)
"Love is cruel, love is sweet." Irish air. Words by T. MacDonagh. FSI

"Love is just like a tameless bird." See Habanera (Bizet)

"Love is like a wild bird rebelling." See Habanera (Bizet)

"Love is like any woodbird wild." See Habanera (Bizet)

Love-lay indited by the Mikado Temmu. G. Ross. Words from the Manyôshiu. e. RAS

"Love leads to battle." See "Pupille nere" (Bononcini)

Love lies a bleeding ("Lady, unheeding") Air: The Cyclops. Words rewritten. BE 4

Love lies a bleeding ("Lay by your pleading") Air: The Cyclops. Traditional words. DM 2

"A love like mine, so faithful." G. F. Händel. SAS 2

Love! love. See "Amuri, amuri"

"Love me little, love me long." 17th century air: Mad Robin. BOH—DM 1— HSE 2—MM—PR 2

"Love not! love not." J. Blockley. Words by C. Norton. FSS 2—HSD —JO—WBT

"Love not the world." A. Sullivan. CS 1 —SAS 2

The love signal ("Pahata nawajiŋ") Dakota Indian song. e.in. BF 2

Love sleeping. See Amor dormiglione (Strozzi)

"Love smiles no more." Ahlstrom. Words by D. Ryan. FSS 3—JSE— NML

"Love! so beautiful and true." See Lebewohl (Silcher)

A love song ("Down the west has gone the sun") Chinese song. c.e. BF 2

Love song ("Fade the stars") T. Lieurance. Words by E. D. Proctor. LN

Love song ("Fades the star") Omaha Indian air. Words by E. D. Proctor. FIS

Love song ("Flow'rs on the meadow") Polish song. e. KSE

Love song ("Have you seen") See "Have you seen but a bright lily grow" (Cauffman)

Love song ("Holder klingt der vogelsang") See Minnelied (Brahms)

Love-song ("Quelquefois en levant les yeux") See Stances (Flégier)

Love-song ("Te souvient-il") See Chanson d'amour (Hollmann)

Love song ("Thousand times I've wander'd here") Greek song. e. KSE Greek love song. e. WL

Love-song ("Tread, O my joy."—"Doos yá lellee") Egyptian song. ar.e. BO

"Doos yá bellee." ar. SMW

Love song ("Warbling nightingales") Bosnian song. e. KSE

Love-song of the idiot (Svyétik Sávishna) M. P. Moussorgsky (music and words) e. SMR 1

"A love song to thee." See The he-i blossom (Hopkins)

A love sonnet. See Sonnet d'amour (Thomé)

The love-spell (Bîelolitsa, kruglolitsa) Russian folk song. e. SSR 3

"The love that I hae chosen." See The lowlands o' Holland

"The love that linketh soul to soul." See "Es muss ein wunderbares sein" (Liszt)

"Love that's true will live forever." See "Si, tra i ceppi" (Händel)

Love thoughts. Hawaiian folk song. e. WBT—WL

"Love, thy dazzling beauty." See Sunny Manoa (Hopkins)

"Love, 'tis not day." See Romeo and Juliet (Tchaikovsky)

Love-token. See Simple aveu (Thomé)

Love triumphant. See Von ewiger liebe (Brahms)

"Love virtue." H. A. Clarke. Words by J. Milton. TL

"Love wakes and weeps." J. G. Callcott. Words by W. Scott. TL

"Love was once a little boy." J. A. Wade. HSE 3

"Love we well our storm-beaten land." See "Ja vi elsker dette landet" (Nordraak)

Love will find out the way. 17th century song. BE 6—BOH—CO 1—DM 1— HSE 2—JE—MM—PR 1

Love wing'd my hope. R. Jones. JE

"Love wove our hearts in one by tender ties." See "Un doux lien" (Delbrück)

Love wreaths. Hawaiian folk song. e. WL

Lovelace, Richard
"Amarantha sweet and fair" (Lawes) To Althea (Wilson)

"A lovelorn lad wooed a coy maid once." See The bonds of love (Jones)

"Lovely and sweet as the rose in the vale." C. Rheinthaler. e. SAS 2

"Lovely appear." C. Gounod (music and words) e. BD—TFC 2

Lovely evening. Round. [Tr of O wie wohl ist mir am abend] e. TFC 1

"Lovely flowers I pray." See "Faites-lui mes aveux" (Gounod)

Lovely Joan. Folk song from Sussex. SF 5

"The lovely lass of Inverness." J. Oswald. Words by R. Burns. BSR

"The lovely lass, the lovely lass that leads the dance." See The lute player and the dancing lass

"Lovely maid, why dost roam in the fields so far from home." See Lucas

Lovely Mary Donnelly. T. T. Barker. Words by W. Allingham. FSS 7—JO

"Lovely May." Spanish air. e. FSS 4 —WBT—WSC

"Lovely Minka, I must leave thee." See Beautiful Minka

The lovely month of May. See "Im wunderschönen monat mai" (Franz)

Lovely Nan ("Sweet is the ship") C. Dibdin (music and words) HSE 1

Lovely Nancy ("Farewell, my lovely Nancy") 18th century song.   CO 2—FSS 8

"**Lovely** night! O lovely night."   F. X. Chwatal.   HSD

"**Lovely** night, O night so calm."   See "Belle nuit" (Offenbach)

"**Lovely** night whose starry smile."   See "Belle nuit" (Offenbach)

Lovely Polly Stewart.   Scottish air: Ye're welcome Charlie Stewart.   Words by R. Burns.   BSB
   "The flower it blaws, it fades, it fa's."   BSR
   Polly Stewart.   PS 1

The **lovely** rose ("A lovely white rose near the forest grew."—Ruusa laaksossa) Finnish folk song.   e.fi.   BF 1

Lovely rose ("Oh, how sweetly, in life's morning")   Venetian air.   FSS 1

Lovely spring.   See "Wenn der frühling auf die berge steigt" (Coenen)

"A **lovely** summer evening 'twas."   See Am schönsten sommerabend war's (Grieg)

"The **lovely** sunshine coming after shower." See 'O sole mio (Capua)

"**Lovely** thou as an angel fair."   See Serenata ("Bella siccome")

Lovely was she by the dawn.   See "It was the charming month of May"

"A **lovely** white rose near the forest grew." See The lovely rose

Lover, Samuel
      Composer and author
   Barney O'Hea
   The bowld sojer boy
   The four-leaved shamrock
   I'm not myself at all
   Molly bawn
   My mother dear
   "Now let me alone, though I know you won't."   See Barney O'Hea
   "What will you do, love"
   "Widow machree, it's no wonder you frown"
      Author
   The angels' whisper (Irish air)
   The fairy boy (Irish air)
   The girl I left behind me (18th century air)
   The low-backed car (Irish air)
   Molly Carew (Irish air)
   "Oh, did you ne'er hear of the Blarney" (Old Irish air)
   Rory O'More (Irish air)
   "There is a gentle gleam" (Irish air)
   "True love can ne'er forget" (O'Carolan)

"**Lover** and friend."   Mackenzie.   OS 1

Lover's choice.   Hungarian song.   e. KSE

A **lover's** complaint ("Hark, the trumpets sound to arms")   DM 2

A **lover's** complaint ("A poor soul sat sighing")   See The willow song (16th century air)

The **lovers'** controversy.   G. S. Carey. HSE 3

Lovers' farewell.   See Les adieux des amants

The **lover's** ghost.   Irish folk song.   JOI

The **lover's** lament ("Don't you remember")   Folk song: Alleghany, N.C. version.   CSE

The **lover's** lament ("Don't you remember")   Carmen, N.C. version. CSE

The **lover's** lament ("Now once I courted")   Virginia version.   CSE

The **lover's** lament ("Now once I did court")   Tennessee version.   CSE

The **lover's** lament ("Off to the war") Hot Springs, N.C. version.   CSE

"Now once I did court."   Tennessee version.   SA

Variants: Charming beauty bright; The soldier's return

thou."—Poduĭ, nepogodushka) Russian

The **lover's** lament ("Stormwind, blow thou."—Poduĭ, nepogodushka)   Russian folk song.   e.   SSR 3

The **lover's** message ("Ein blick von deinen augen")   See Die liebende schreibt (Mendelssohn)

The **lover's** message ("Ye little loves") Galliard.   PR 2

The **lover's** prayer ("O sue not thou for fortune's dower")   Basque song.   e. BMC

The **lover's** sigh.   See "Nel cor più non mi sento" (Paisiello)

"**Lovers**, sweethearts, come follow."   See L'appel du printemps (Holmès)

The **lover's** tasks.   Folk song.   BSW

Love's a tender flow'ret shedding.   See Liebe ist die zarte blüthe (Spohr)

Love's bacchanal.   J. Wynne.   ME

"**Love's** blind, they say."   See Love has eyes (Bishop)

"**Love's** bond to sever."   See "Lasciar d'amarti" (Gasparini)

Love's call (Hither, Mary, hither come) J. Hook.   DM 2

Love's distress.   See Liebesqual

Love's first confession.   See Les premiers aveux (Dancla)

Love's first meeting.   See Det förste möde (Grieg)

Love's golden dream ("I hear to-night") Words by L. Lennox.   FSS 7—WBT —WL

Love's greeting ("E passu di notti")   See Salitana

Love's greeting ("Softly the zephyr in the trees")   E. Elgar.   Words by E. Devereaux.   WBW

Love's labor lost.   See Vergebliche liebesmüh'

Love's message.   See Liebesbotschaft (Schubert)

Love's old, sweet song.   J. L. Molloy. Words by G. C. Bingham.   FMB— HSD—MP—MPC— MSF 2—NMH —NML— OH— TFC 1—WA— WBT—WL—WSW
   "Sing a song at twilight."   Words adapted.   WSC

Love's parting. Song of Little Russia. e.r. EF

Love's pleading. See Liebeständelei (Fitzenhagen)

Love's prisoner. See Lu carcerato p'ammore (Biscardi)

Love's proving. F. N. Löhr. Words by F. E. Weatherly. CB—WBW

Love's ritournella ("Gentle Zitella") J. R. Planché; wrongly attributed to T. Cooke. Words by J. R. Planché. BE 2—FSS 3—HSE 2—JO—WBT

Love's secret lost. See Verrathene liebe (Schumann)

Love's sorrow ("Ah! gloomy the forest is") Upper Austrian song. e. KSE—WL

Love's sorrow ("The sun's last ray is gone."—Liebesleid) H. R. Shelley. e.g. AA

Love's sorrow ("Where in the vale the pathway's dividing") Polish song. e. KSE

Love's the tune. O. Straus. WBT

Love's votary. See "Bid me to live" (Lawes)

Love's young dream ("Oh! the days are gone when beauty bright") Irish air: An thseann bheann bhocht, or, The old woman. Words by T. Moore. FSI—FSS 2—HSD—JO—MI— MMI—PI—WBT

Lovesick. See Malatu p'amuri

The lovesick maiden (Golova-l' ty moîa golovushka) Russian folk song. e. SSR 1

"Loving, I borrow many a sorrow." See "Sento nel core" (Scarlatti)

Loving Nancy. Kentucky mountain song. WLT
Variant of: The wagoner's lad

"Loving Redeemer, Light of the world." See Hymnus (Bruch)

Loving Reilly. Folk song: Georgia version. CSE
—North Carolina version. CSE

Loving smile of sister kind. See "Avant de quitter ces lieux" (Gounod)

"Loving, speaking eyes, lids that fall and rise." See Claudine (Molloy)

"Loving voices." C. W. Glover. FSS 4 —WBT

Loviot, Ferdinand
Stances (Flégier)

"Lov'st thou for beauty." C. Schumann. Words by Rückert. e. BC

The low-backed car ("When first I saw sweet Peggy") Irish air: The jolly ploughboy, or, Jolly ploughman. Words by S. Lover. BC—BSE—CST —EF—FSI—FSS 4—HSD— JO—LA— MMI—PI—WBT—WL—WSW

Low down in the broom. Folk song from Sussex. SF 4

"Low her voice is, soft and kind." See The comforter

The low, low lands of Holland. Folk song. SEF 2—SO

"Low, plaintive moaning." See Cradle song (Musorgskiï)

"Low, ye hills, in ocean lie." Air: Hob y derri dando (2d version) Words from the Welsh. e. MMW

Lowe, Albert
Alleluia
"Holy is the seed-time"

Lowe, Alexander
Mary's dream (Scottish air) Authorship uncertain

Lowe, De Clive
Cakes and ale

Löwe, Feodor
Die fahnenwacht (Lindpaintner)

Lowe, G. T.
A medical medley

Lowe, John
Mary's dream (Scottish air) Authorship uncertain

Lowell, Frances
Such a li'l' fellow (Dichmont)

Lowell, James Russell
Aladdin (Bellini)
The falcon (Silcher)
The fountain (German air; also music by Hadley)
The heritage (German air)
June (Schnecker)
Longing (Cole)
Peace on earth (Donizetti)
She came and went (German air)
True freedom (music by Lang; Silcher)
"Where is the true man's fatherland (music by Bellmann; Reichardt)

"Lower your eyes, dear." See "Baja esos ojos"

Lowitz, W. W.
His favorite flower

Lowlander's longing. See Unterländers heimweh

Lowlands ("I dreamed a dream") Capstan chantey. CR—GO—SMW
For variants see following songs of similar title

Lowlands ("We're bound away") Capstan chantey. CR

Lowlands a-ray ("I dreamt a dream") Traditional halliard chantey. DM 2

Lowlands away ("Lowlands, lowlands away") Capstan chantey. SE

Lowlands low ("Lowlands, lowlands, lowlands") Pulling chantey. SE

The lowlands o' Holland ("The love that I hae chosen") Scottish folk song. MMS—PS 1

The lowlands of Holland ("The first night I was married") ' Irish folk song. JOI

Lowly though they be. See The uninvited aunt

Lowry, J. C.
The Christmas tree
"O what can you tell"

Lowry, Robert
"I need thee every hour"
"Shall we gather at the river"

Loyal death. J. Stainer. Words by P. S. Worsley. SM 4

The loyal lover. Folk song. BSW

"Loyal lovers that are distant." See I live not where I love

"Loyal sons and daughters join." See Gold and blue (Parker)

Lozier, Horace
The polyglot's wooing

Lubin's rural cot. Folk song. BE 1

Lubly Dine. J. Sanford (music and words) NMP—WBT

"Lubly Melinda, come now my dear." See Melinda May (Foster)

"Lubly Rosa, Sambo cum." See Coal black Rose (Russell)

Luca, L. de
Catarì! Catarì

Luca, Olmstead
"All hail, Liberia, hail"

Luca, S. de
"I do not dare despond." See "Non posso disperar"
"Non posso disperar"

Lucantoni, G.
Amore
Love. See Amore

Lucas, Hippolyte Julien Joseph
Berceuse (Ropartz)
Two hearts (Fontenailles. Tr of Les deux coeurs)

Lucas, Samuel
Carve dat possum

Lucas. Swiss song. e.f. BF 2

"Luchina, luchinushka berezovaîâ." See The birchen brand

Luchinushka. See The birchen brand

"Luci vezzose" ("Eyes so alluring") B. Gaffi. e.i. FEI 1

The lucky trapper. Ojibway Indian song. e.in. BA

"Lucy Locket." Children's song. WBT —WSC

Lucy Long ("Oh! I jist come out afore you") Negro song. NMP—WBT

Lucy Long ("Was you ever on the Brumalow") Capstan chantey. SE

Lucy Neal. Negro song. NMP—WBT

Lucyna. Polish folk air. Words by M. H. B. Mussey. WF

Lucy's flittin'. Words by W. Laidlaw. FSS 4

Ludlow, F. H.
Song to old Union

Ludwig, Fritz von
"Im kreise froher, kluger zecher" (Folk air; also music by Döbelin)
Sommer-abendlied (Becker)

"Lui l'aurait dit de l'arbitraire." See La Brabançonne (Campenhout)

La Luisella (Luisella) Neapolitan folk song. e.i. FE—MSI
Louisella. e. CST
La Luisella (Luisella's garden) e. GO

Luisella's garden. See La Luisella

Luke, Mrs Jemima (Thompson)
That sweet story of old (Composer unknown

Luk'íânov,
"You brought me flowers" (Jacobson)

"Lulajże Jezuniu." See Lullaby carol

Lull me beyond thee. DM 2

"Lulla lullaby, hush, my babe." See "Lulul labeichen, koch' mei'm kind ein breichen"

Lullaby ("Beneath the pines my dearie, O") Scottish song. MMS

Lullaby ("Birds in the night") See "Birds in the night" (Sullivan)

Lullaby ("Bissam, bissam baadne") See Baadn-laatt

Lullaby ("Cachés dans cet asile") See Oh! ne t'éveille pas (Godard)

Lullaby ("Dear mother, in dreams") E. Jakobowski. Words by C. Bellamy. FSS 5—HSD—WA— WBT— WSC— WSW

Lullaby ("Fatte la nonna") See "Fatte la nonna"

Lullaby ("Go ter sleep") Negro folk song. BN 4
—Virginia version. BN 4

A lullaby ("Golden slumbers") See "Golden slumbers kiss your eyes" (Foote)

Lullaby ("Guten abend") See Wiegenlied (Brahms)

Lullaby ("Hush, baby mine, and weep no more") Irish folk song. [Tr of Suantraidhe] MMI

Lullaby ("Hushaby, baby, the night winds are sighing") Scotch folk air. Words by R. Compton. DO

Lullaby ("Hush-a-by, darling") Ancient Lochaber cronan or lullaby. e. MMS
"Hush-a-by, darling." HSSS

Lullaby ("In a cradle bright and golden") Irish air. MMI

Lullaby ("Lullaby and goodnight") J. W. Elliott. WSC

Lullaby ("Lullaby, lullaby, do not wake and weep") Slumber song. FSS 6

A lullaby ("My joy and grief") See Soontree

Lullaby ("Night her starlit curtain") Bohemian folk air. Words by J. Russell. WF

Lullaby ("O hush thee, baby") African song. e.af. BF 2

Lullaby ("Ô petits enfants") See Berceuse (Ropartz)

Lullaby ("Peaceful slumb'ring") See "Peaceful slumb'ring on the ocean" (Storace)

Lullaby ("Peacefully, my baby, sleep") Irish air. Words by A. R. Denny. MMI

Lullaby ("Schlafe, mein prinzchen") See Wiegenlied (Mozart)

Lullaby ("Shoheen-sho, baby-boy") Air: Hai lwli. MMW

Lullaby ("Sleep baby sleep! Dad is not nigh") Folk song. BSW

Lullaby ("Sleep, baby, sleep; thy father is watching his sheep") H. B. Whitney. Words from the German. [Tr of "Schlaf, kindchen, schlaf"] e. BSE

Lullaby ("Sleep, my bonny blue-eyed little treasure") Lithuanian folk song. e. BMC

"From afar returns my well-beloved." e.li. BO

Lullaby ("Sleep, sleep; lie down, dear") Japanese song. e.j. BF 2

Lullaby ("Sleep, so your tale of dreams be told") B. Godard. Words by F. H. Martens. TFC 2

Lullaby ("Sweet babe") See "Sweet babe, a golden cradle holds thee"

"Lullaby, and goodnight." See Wiegenlied (Brahms)

"Lullaby, baby." A. Sullivan. WBT—WSC

Lullaby carol ("Lulajże Jezuniu") Polish song. e.p. BF 1

"Lullaby, little pearl, dear baby Jesu." See Lullaby carol

"Lullaby, lullaby, do not wake and weep." See Lullaby ("Lullaby, lullaby, do not wake and weep") .

Lullaby, my baby, darling, hush-a-by." See Arrullo (Argentine version)

"Lullaby, my dear one, the daylight is done." See Wiegenlied (Brahms)

Lullaby of an infant chief. See "O hush thee, my babie" (Jensen)

"Lullay, Thou little tiny Child." See The Coventry carol

Lully, Jean Baptiste de
Composer
"All your shades." See "Bois épais, redouble ton ombre"

"Amour, que veux-tu de moi" (from Amadis)

"Bois épais, redouble ton ombre" (from Amadis)

"Gloomy woods, in darkness receive me." See "Bois épais, redouble ton ombre"

Author
"Au clair de la lune" (Composer unknown)

Lully, lully, lu. See "Qui creavit coelum, lully, lully, lu"

"Lulu is our darling pride." HSD—WBT

"Lulul labeichen, koch' mei'm kind ein breichen" (German cradle-song) e.g. FSS 3

Luna nova (The new moon.—Canzone marinaresca.—Fisherman's song) P. M. Costa. Words by S. di Giacomo. e.i. FE

Luna y Drusina, Fernando
Perjura (Lerdo de Tejada)

Lundberg, Ellen
Svarta rosor (Alfvén)

Lunde, Johan Backer-. See Backer-Lunde, Johan

"La lune blanche luit dans les bois." See L'heure exquise (Hahn)

"Lungi da lei per me non v'ha diletto." See De' miei bollenti spiriti (Verdi)

"Lungi dal caro bene" ("Should I from thee be parted") G. Sarti. e.i. PG 4

"Lungi dal caro bene" ("When two that love are parted."—Parted) e.i. CS 1

"Lungi dal caro bene" ("When far from my dear treasure") A. Secchi. e.i. FEI 2

Lurlaline. Old Irish air. FSS 4

"Die lust hat mich gezwungen." See Im frühling (Albert)

"Ein lustger musikante marschierte am Nil." See Lob der edlen musica

The lute player and the dancing lass ("Esy poū serneis ton choro") Greek folk song. e.gr. BF 2

Luther, Martin
Composer
"Dies ist der tag, den Gott gemacht" (same air as "Vom himmel hoch da komm' ich her")

Glad tidings
Composer and author
"Ein' feste burg"

"From heaven above to earth I come." See "Vom himmel hoch da komm' ich her"

From heaven high come I here. See "Vom himmel hoch da komm' ich her"

"From heaven's sphere." See "Vom himmel hoch da komm' ich her"

Luther's hymn. See "Ein' feste burg"

"A mighty fortress is our God." See "Ein' feste burg"

"Vom himmel hoch da komm' ich her" (For music by Higgs see Luther's carol)

Author
"All praise to Thee" (Costello. Tr of Gelobet seis tu Jesu Christ)

"Away in a manger" (music by Herbert; Spilman; also unknown composer)

"Gelobet seis tu Jesu Christ" (Gesius. For music by Costello see "All praise to Thee")

Kyrie eleison ("Incarnate Jesus Christ") (15th century air)

Luther's carol (Higgs. Tr of "Vom himmel hoch da komm' ich her")

Luther's carol. J. Higgs. Words by M. Luther. [Tr of "Vom himmel hoch da komm' ich her"] e. BSC

Lutz, Meyer
The examiner's song

Lutzow's wild hunt. See Lützows wilde jagd (Weber)

Lützows wilde jagd ("Was glänzt dort vom walde") C. M. von Weber. Words by T. Körner. g. ED 1

Lutzow's wild hunt. e. HSD—LA

Lux benigna. See "Lead, kindly light" (Dykes)

Lux ecce surgit aurea. For English translation see "Now with creation's morning song"

Luzzi, Luigi
  "Ave Maria"
  "O blessed Savior." See "Ave Maria"
  "Sing hallelujah with glad rejoicing." See "Ave Maria"
Lvov, Alexis Feodorovich
  "Bojé tsaria khrani." See Russian national hymn
  "Bòshe zaria chrani." See Russian national hymn
  The gipsy's song
  "God save America! here may all races" (same air as Russian national hymn)
  God save the czar. See Russian national hymn
  "God the All-terrible." See Russian national hymn
  "Lord God, protect the czar." See Russian national hymn
  Prayer for peace. See Russian national hymn
  "Rise, crowned with light" (same air as Russian national hymn)
  Russian national hymn
Lydia. G. Fauré. Words by Leconte de Lisle. e.f. PG 3
"Lying here on the ivied wall of this ancient terrace." See An eine Aeolsharfe (Brahms)
Lyle, Thomas
  Kelvin grove (Scottish air)
Lyly, John
  Daphne (Defesch)
Lynch, Francis
  Dearest Mae (Crosby)
Lynch, Thomas Toke
  "A thousand years have come and gone"
Lyndhurst. See "Purer yet and purer I would be in mind"
Lyons (Haydn) See O come, let us worship; Song of Columbus day
Lyra, Justus Wilhelm
  Burschenlust
  Meine muse
  Reiterlied
Lysaght, Edward
  Kitty of Coleraine (Irish air) Authorship uncertain
Lyster, Fred
  Thy true heart (Vogrich)
Lyte, Eliphalet Oram
  Beautiful bells
  "Row, row, row your boat"
Lyte, Henry Francis
  "Abide with me! fast falls the eventide" (music by Mendelssohn; Monk)
Lyttelton, George Lyttelton, 1st baron
  "Adieu to the village delights" (Baildon)
  O tell me, my heart, if this be love (Welsh air)
Lyttleton, Claude
  A dream of paradise (Gray)
  The heavenly song (music by Gray; Jones)

Lytton, Edward George Earle Lytton Bulwer-Lytton, 1st baron
  "When stars are in the quiet skies" (Composer unknown)
Lytton, Edward Robert Bulwer-Lytton, 1st earl
  Yestereve (Johnson)

M

"Ma belle Marianne" (Pretty Marianna) Folk song from Alsace. e.f. FTF
"Ma bouteille m'est fidèle" ("Oh, my bottle's ever faithful."—Chanson à boire.—Drinking song) Canadian folk song. e.f. TF
"Ma, che insolita luce." See O voi dell' Erebo (Händel)
"Ma che saccio int' 'a 'st'uocchie che tiene." See Catarì! Catarì (Luca)
Ma gazelle (My beloved) Moorish song. e.f. BO
Ma la sola, ohimè! son io. Bellini. e.i. PP
Ma Lawd's a-writin' down time. Air: He sees all you do, an' hyeahs all you see, arr by H. T. Burleigh. Words by R. E. Phillips. BP
Ma mi', faites-moi-z-un bouquet ("Father a gard'ner made of me") Norman folk song. e.f. TF
Ma mourri. Negro creole folk song. e.f. KA
Ma Normandie (My Normandy.—"When gloomy winter takes his flight") F. Bérat (music and words) e. BMC
  My Normandy. e. FSS 2—JSE—WBT
"Ma vie a son secret" ("A secret tell I thee") G. Bizet. e.g. PG 2
"Maa isänmaamme, Suomenmaa." See Vårt land, vårt fosterland (Pacius)
Maamme. See Vårt land, vårt fosterland (Pacius)
Maass, Johann Gebhard Ehrenreich
  Die freude (Tuerk)
"Mab, la reine des mensonges" ("Mab, Queen Mab the fairies' midwife") Gounod. e.f. OPS 4
"Mab, Queen Mab the fairies' midwife." See "Mab, la reine des mensonges" (Gounod)
Mabrooka ("My hopes are dreams of night") Arabian song. e. BMC
Macarthy, Henry
  The bonnie blue flag
McCabe, James J.
  America
  "My country, 'tis of thee." See America
McCaffrey, John
  Christmas hymn (Dielman)
Maccarthy, Denis Florence
  "My countrymen, awake, arise" (Irish air)

McCarthy, Henry.   See Macarthy, Henry
McCaskey, John Piersol
  The blushing maple tree
  The trees and the Master
MacCathmhaoil, Seosamh.   See Campbell, Joseph
MacColl, Evan
  Eilidh bhàn (Scottish air)
MacConnell, Marie Florence
  "It came upon the midnight clear"
McCoy, William J.
  May
MacCrimmon's lament ("O'er Collin's face the night is creeping") Scottish song. Words from the Gaelic.   e.   HSSS
MacCuaraig, J.
  An uair bha gàilig aig na h-eòin (Scottish air)
MacDonagh, Thomas
  "Love is cruel, love is sweet" (Irish air)
MacDonald, Alexander
  Mòrag
MacDonald, J.
  Mairi laghach
M'Donald, John
  "Thou dark-winding Carron"
McDonald, William
  "In the Christian's home in glory."   See Rest for the weary
  Rest for the weary
  There is rest for the weary.   See Rest for the weary
MacDonough, Glen
  Toyland (Herbert)
MacDowell, Edward Alexander
  At parting
  The clover
  The sea
  "The swan bent low to the lily"
Macedonia (Makedonets) Macedonia-Bulgarian song.   b.e.   BF 1
MacFarlane, Malcolm
  My ain hoose (Scottish air. Tr of Mo dhachaidh)
MacFarran, Walter Cecil
  "You stole my love"
Macfarren, George
  "Gentle is the fair stream flowing" (Traditional air)
  "The spring is coming" (Composer unknown)
Macfarren, Sir George Alexander
  Home they brought her warrior
  Midsummer night's dream
  "The monk within his cell" (from Robin Hood)
  My own, my guiding star
  The sands of Dee
  Sweet my child.   See Home they brought her warrior
  "Three fishers went sailing"
  "When sweet music"
McGee, Thomas D'Arcy
  "I would not give my Irish wife" (Irish air)
  The man of the north countrie (Irish air)

McGill, John
  "Come under my plaidie"
  "O, wilt thou go wi' me, sweet Tibbie Dunbar" (attributed)
McGlennon, Felix
  Comrades
Macgregor, Donald
  The Fliggyboo bird (from Cleopatra)
  Maisie
  "'Twas two days out from Boston town" (from In Vanity fair)
Macgregors' gathering.   A. Lee. Words by W. Scott.   PS 2—TS
"Mach' auf, mach' auf, doch leise, mein kind."   See Ständchen (Strauss)
Machault, Guillaume de.   See Guillaume de Machaut
Die macht der tränen ("Es kam von einer neustadt her") Schlesisches volkslied.   g.   ED 3
"Macht man in's leben kaum den ersten schritt."   See Die thräne (Gumbert)
McIntosh, Emily L.
  Emerson, our Emerson (Composer unknown)
McIntyre, Duncan Bàn
  Mairi bhàn òg (Scottish air)
  My misty dell (Scottish air.   Tr of Coire cheathaich)
Mack, Albert A.
  For ever and a day
Mackay, Charles
  Baby mine (Johnston)
  "Cheer, boys, cheer" (Russell)
  Corn rigs are bonnie (Scottish air)
  Far upon the sea (Russell)
  The good time coming (Composer unknown)
  I love my love (Pinsuti)
  The inquiry (Gorrin)
  The miller of the Dee (Old air)
  "Some love to roam" (Russell)
  "There grew a brier-brush at our ha' door" (Scottish air)
  "There's a good time coming" (Composer unknown)
  Tubal Cain (Russell)
  Under the holly bough (Barnard)
  What I love and hate (Composer unknown)
  "Who shall be fairest" (Moir)
  Wine and glory (Composer unknown)
Mackay, William Paton
  Revive us again (Husband)
Mac Kenna's dream.   Irish folk song. Air: Captain Rock.   JOI
Mackenzie, Sir Alexander Campbell
  Gladness is taken away (from The rose of Sharon)
  "Lover and friend" (from The rose of Sharon)
  Spring song
  "Unto my charger" (from The rose of Sharon)
  "We will open our mouth in a parable" (from The rose of Sharon)
  "The wilderness shall be" (from The rose of Sharon)

Mackenzie, William Andrew
"Shon Campbell" (Barratt)
McKowen, James
"Oh! if I were yon gossamer" (Irish air)
Maclagan, Sir Douglas
"Alma mater" (Oakeley)
Chancellor Inglis (Edinburgh university song)
M'Laren, A. M.
Queen Mary's farewell to Alloa (Scottish air)
MacLean,
Mo run geal dileas (Scottish air)
McLennan, William
The hills o' Skye (Harris)
MacLeod, M.
Eilean an Fhraoich
MacLeod, Norman
Soraidh slàn le Fionn-Airidh (Scottish air)
McLeod, Peter
My ain countrie: Scottish air arranged
"Oh! why left I my hame." See My ain countrie: Scottish air arranged
MacManus, Mrs Anna (Johnston)
The curse of Mora (Irish air)
The passing of the Gael (Irish air)
"A sword of light hath pierced the dark" (Irish air)
MacManus, Seumas
Bright darling of my heart (Irish air)
For Ireland (Irish air)
McMichael, Clayton F.
Tommy and his gun
MacNally, Leonard
The lass of Richmond hill (Hook) Authorship uncertain
"Let's seek the bower of Robin Hood" (Shield)
McNaught, W. G.
The spider and the fly
McNaughton, J. H.
Belle Mahone
The faded coat of blue
Love at home
Macneill, Hector
"Come under my plaidie" (McGill)
"I lo'e na a laddie but ane" (Old air)
Jeanie's black een (Scottish air)
My boy Tammy (Scottish air)
"My luve's in Germanie" (Jacobite air)
Saw ye my wee thing (Composer unknown)
"When merry hearts were gay" (Scottish air)
Macnie, John
Alma mater—University of North Dakota (Old air)
MacPhail, Dugald
An-t-eilean Muileach (Scottish air)
McPherson's farewell. Scottish air: McPherson's rant. Words by R. Burns. PS 2
"Farewell, ye dungeons dark and strong." BSR
McSorley's twins. G. Phillips (Oofty Goofty) (music and words) WBT—WC

Macvicar, Anne. See Grant, Mrs Anne (Macvicar)
Macy, James Cartwright
"The boats are pushing from the shore." See Good-bye, my little lady
"Christian people, come and sing" Good-bye, my little lady
Mad Bess. H. Purcell. BOH
"Mad! mad! all the world's mad." See "Wahn! wahn" (Wagner)
Mad scene. See "Il dolce suono" (Donizetti)
Mad Tom ("Forth from my sad and darksome cell") J. Coperario. Words by W. Basse. DM 2
Mad Tom (Gray's inn masque.—New mad Tom of Bedlam) CO 1
"**Madam'** Veto avait promis." See La Carmagnole
"**Madame** Veto once gave her word." See La Carmagnole
"**Madamina!** il catalogo è questo." W. A. Mozart. e.i. SOA 5
Madamina ("Pretty lady") e.i. KS 5 —OPS 4
Das **mädchen** aus der fremde ("In einem tal") G. C. Grosheim. Words by Schiller. g. ED 2
Mädchen, brav und treu. For English translation see Maidens, bright and fair (Flotow)
Das **mädchen** im Osterland ("Im Osterland") Volkslied. g. ED 2
"**Mädchen** mit dem rothen mündchen" ("Lassie with the lips so rosy") R. Franz. Words by H. Heine. e.g. FO 1
"**Mädchen** mit dem rothen mündchen" ("Maid with lips like blooming roses") L. Gall. Words by H. Heine. e.g. SM 3
"**Mädchen** sind wie der wind" ("Maidens are like the wind") C. Loewe. e.g. CMF 1
Das **mädchen** von Juda. For English translation see The Jewish maiden (Kücken)
"**Mädchen,** wollt ihr werden." See In der märznacht (Taubert)
"**Mädchenaug'!** mädchenaug'" ("Maiden fair") M. Moszkowski. Words by J. Wolff. e.g. AB 4
Mädchenlied ("Der du am sternenbogen." —To the evening star) J. Raff. Words by Geibel. e.g. CS 2—MSS 2
Mädchenlied ("O my darling mother") For English translation see Maiden's song (Meyer-Helmund)
Des **mädchens** klage. See entry under Des
Mädchens wunsch. See The maiden's wish (Chopin)
"**Mädel,** schau mir ins gesicht." See Liebeszauber (Schulz)
"**Mädele,** ruck, ruck, ruck." See Die auserwählte
Madeleine. J. L. Roeckel. TL

"Mademoisell', voulez-vous danser." See La Bastringue

Madoline. S. Nelson. Words by E. J. Gill. HSE 3

"Madre a la puerta hay un niño." See El niño Jesús

"Madre, el niño se ha perdido." Villancico. s. LCP

Madre, pietosa Vergine. G. Verdi. e.i. SOA 1

Madrigal dans le style ancien (Madrigal in the old manner) V. d'Indy. Words by R. de Bonnières. e.f. CM 2—HM 2

Madrigal in the old manner. See Madrigal dans le style ancien (Indy)

Maemae ka pua. See "Beautiful Waipio" (Likelike)

"Mag dir, du zartes frühlingskind." See Med en primulaveris (Grieg)

Magali. Provençal song. Words by F. Mistral. e.f.pr. TSF. e. only LA

"Magasan repül a daru." See Hungaria's treasure

"Mägdlein hielt tag und nacht." See Spinn! spinn (Jüngst)

Maggea, N. The orphan

Maggie by my side. S. C. Foster. HSD —WBT

Maggie Lauder ("Wha wadna be in love wi' bonnie Maggie Lauder") 18th century air. Words by F. Semple. MMS —PS 1

Maggie's pet. Children's song. WSC

Maggie's secret. C. Barnard (Claribel) FSS 7

Maggie's welcome. C. Barnard (Claribel) WBT

"The magi came out of the Orient land." See Three kings' song

"A magic power." See "Min elskte, jeg er bunden" (Kjerulf)

The magic tree. Words by C. Morton. MCS

La mágica mujer (The enchantress) Spanish-American song. e.s. LSS

Magill, George J. "Hark! the Christmas songs are singing"

Maginnis, Dan The Irish christening

The magpie and the little gypsy dancer (Soróka) M. P. Moussorgsky. Words by Pushkin. e. SMR 1

Magyar song. See "Marie mine"

Des Magyaren heimweh. See entry under Des

"Mah moo yuh wuh mah dah mah buh." See Old hundred (American Indian version)

"Mahalo au oka nani." See Wreath of carnations (Hopkins)

Mahelona, Lala "The remembrance of our last meeting" (Hopkins)

"Mahjeahsin ahbequan." See Prince of Wales song

Mahlmann, August Gottergebenheit (Volksweise) Grabgesang (Blüher) Heutzutage (André) Der jäger (Reichardt) Das reich der freude (Volksweise) Sehnsucht (Bornhardt)

"Mahnoo nenah ningamahjah." See Hiawatha's death song

The mahogany tree. F. Campana. Words by W. M. Thackeray. FSS 4—MCS

Mahony, Francis Sylvester Bells of Shandon (Irish air)

Mai ("Depuis un mois, chère exilée."— May) R. Hahn. Words by F. Coppée. e.f. PG 2

Der mai ("Es fiel ein himmelstaue") Flandrisches volkslied. g. ED 3

"Mai hoohihi oe e ke onaona." See "Oh, tempt me not, my darling" (Hopkins)

"Der mai ist gekommen." See Burschenlust (Lyra)

"Mai kō mashma-lan." See A Talmudical student's lament

Mai poina oe ia'u. See Forget-me-not (Hopkins)

"Mai revient, tout brille aux cieux." See Chant de quête de l'Alsace

The maid and the sun. N. Rimsky-Korsakoff. Words from the Russian of Maikoff. e. NM 2

The maid and the sun (Dyéva i sólntze) e. SMR 2

The maid at the fountain. See La fille à la fontaine

"Maid Elsie roams by lane and lea." See The bride bells (Roeckel)

The maid freed from the gallows. Folk song: North Carolina version. CSE

—Tennessee version. CSE

—Mount Fair, Va. version. CSE

—Woodridge, Va. version. CSE

Variants: "The briery bush"; The hangman's song

"Maid of Athens." H. R. Allen. Words by Lord Byron. LA—MPC—NML— WBT—WL

"Maid of Athens." J. Barnett. Words by Lord Byron. DM 2

"Maid of Athens." I. Nathan. Words by Lord Byron. JO

The maid of Catanzaro. See La Cantanzarese

The maid of Dôl ("Why looks the maid of Dôl so sad") Air: Griffith ap Cynan's delight. Words from the Welsh. e. MMW

Maid of Doncaster. Old English air. BE 8

The maid of Glenconnel. Scottish song. PS 1

The maid of Islay. Scottish song. PS 1

The maid of Islington. Folk song from Sussex. SF 5

Variant of: The bailiff's daughter of Islington

Maid of Llangollen ("Tho' lowly my lot") Welsh song.   FSS 3

The **maid** of Llanwellyn ("I've no sheep on the mountain") Air: Ystwtfwl, or, The doorclapper.   Words by J. Baillie. MMW

The **maid** of the mill.   S. Adams.   Words by H. Aïdé.   FSS 6—NML

"A **maid** reclined beside a stream."   See Forever and forever (Converse)

The **maid** that tends the goats.   Scottish air.   Words by Dudgeon.   PS 2

"The **maid** to the dance has gone."   See Rödan guldband

"**Maid** with lips like blooming roses."   See "Mädchen mit dem rothen mündchen" (Gall)

"The **maiden** and I."   See "Å jänta å ja"

Maiden and rose.   FSS 7

"**Maiden,** by night and day, why so sadly spin away."   See Spinn! Spinn! (Jüngst)

The **maiden** and the huntsman.   See La fille et le chasseur

"**Maiden** fair."   See "Mädchenaug'! Mädchenaug'" (Moszkowski)

"A **maiden** had Dalebu, fair as the sun."   See Dalebu Jonson

"The **maiden** hied her to the well."   See "Och jungfrun gick åt killan"

"**Maiden,** how canst thou cruelly bid me."   See The complaint

Maiden in the garden.   See Jungfrun i det gröna

"A **maiden** listened to the distant playing."   See "Meu anjo"

The **maiden** of Scilla.   See La Scillitana

"**Maiden** of Slovenian race."   See A Slovenian girl

The **maiden** of the Fleur de Lys.   E. A. Sydenham.   WC

"A **maiden** one day was dancing."   See Rödan guldband

A **maiden** sang.   S. Vassilenko.   Words from the Russian of A. Block.   e. NM 2

"A **maiden** sat a-weeping."   Folk song. BSW

"A **maiden** sat at her door."   See The distant shore (Sullivan)

"The **maiden** she decked herself in holy church to pray."   See Den bergtagna

The **maiden** sold to the devil.   See La fille vendue au diable

"A **maiden,** through the forest twilight wand'ring."   See Den första kyssen (Sibelius)

"The **maiden** went to the meadow."   See Blomman bland blommorna

"**Maiden,** with the meek brown eyes."   See Bear a lily in thy hand

"**Maidens** are like the wind."   See "Mädchen sind wie der wind" (Loewe)

"**Maidens,** beware ye."   Old English air. BE 7

The **maiden's** complaint.   T. A. Arne. MM

Maidens, bright and fair.   F. von Flotow. [Tr of Mädchen, brav und treu]   e. WBT

The **maiden's** lament.   See Des mädchens klage

The **maidens** of Cadix.   See Les filles de Cadix (Delibes)

"**Maidens,** remember."   See "Jeunes fillettes" (Dalayrac)

A **maiden's** revenge (To ne fåstreb sovykalsîå) Russian folk song.   e.   SSR 2

Maiden's song.   E. Meyer-Helmund.   [Tr of Mädchenlied]   e.   WBW

The **maiden's** wish.   Chopin.   Words by Witwicki.   e.   FTS—MS—WBT
   The maiden's wish (Mädchens wunsch) e.g.   KF 1—KF 2—SM 1
   Spring song.   e.g.   EF
   Spring song (Zyczenie)   e.p.   BF 1

"**Maidens** would ye fain be as March violets fair."   See In der märznacht (Taubert)

Die **maidli** im Schwizerland ("I ha daheim e maidli g'ha") Schweizerisches volkslied.   g.   ED 2

"**Maids** are grown so coy of late."   Composer unknown.   MM

"**Maids** may boast."   See "Si les filles d'Arles" (Gounod)

The **maids** of Cadiz.   See Les filles de Cadix (Delibes)

The **maid's** resolution.   R. Leveridge. PR 2

Maienblümlein.   C. M. von Weber.   Words by A. Ekschlager.   g.   ED 2

Maienthau (May dew.—"O'er the woodlands") W. S. Bennett.   Words by Uhland.   e.   DM 1
   May dew.   e.   MSS 1—SS 1

Maigh, David
   Down the burn, Davie.   See "When trees did bud"
   "When trees did bud"

"**Maikai** ka makani o Kohala."   See Kohala's breezes (Nape)

"**Maikai** Waipio."   See "Beautiful Waipio" (Likelike)

Maikov, Apollon Nikolaevich
   Cradle song (Tchaikovsky)
   A kiss (Cherepnin)
   The maid and the sun (Rimskiĭ-Korsakov)
   Menaeceus (Cherepnin)
   The octave (Rimskiĭ-Korsakov)
   The singer (Rimskiĭ-Korsakov)
   The tell-tale stars (Cherepnin)

The **mail-box.**   German folk air.   Words by H. H. Harbour.   DO

Mailied ("Willkommen, lieber, schöner mai") J. A. P. Schulz.   Words by L. H. C. Hölty.   g.   ED 3

Mailied ("Zwischen waizen und korn." —May song) N. Medtner.   Words by J. W. von Goethe.   e.g.   NM 1

's **mailüfterl** ("Wenn's mailufterl weht") J. Kreipl.   Words by A. von Klesheim.   g.   ED 1
   's mailüfterl (May breezes)   e.g. SSG.   e. only GO

"Main to tore dāman wāh lagun mere rām." See To the hem of thy garment I cling

Die **mainacht** (A night in May) J. Brahms. Words by L. Hölty. e.g. CS 2—MSS 2—SS 2

"**Maintenant** observons, écoutons." See Viens, gentille dame (Boieldieu)

Máirghréad na Róiste (Margaret Roche) Irish folk song. e.ir. JOI

Màiri bhàn òg (Fair young Mary.—"My love to my bride") Scottish air. Words from the Gaelic of D. B. McIntyre. e. HSSS

Màiri bhòidheach ("My pretty Mary."— Pretty Mary) Ancient Hebridean air. Words by A. Stewart. e. MMS

Màiri bhòidheach ("My pretty Mary") e. HSSS

Mairi laghach (Winsome Mary) Scottish air. Words from the Gaelic of J. Macdonald. e. HSSS

"**Mais** je suis, grâce au ciel." See Flamme vengeresse (Auber)

"**Mais** quand la chopine ils ont bu'." See La grande et la petite

"**Mais** que dis-je? femme timide." See Ô des amants le plus fidèle (Méhul)

Maisie. D. Macgregor. Words by A. A. Powers. CU

The **maister.** Scottish song. FSS 3

Maistre, Xavier, comte de
Hai luli (Coquard)

Maitland, C.
"Ring out, ye wild and merry bells"

Maitland (Allen) See "Let worldly minds the world pursue"; "Must Jesus bear the cross alone"

"**Majestic** sweetness" (Ortonville) T. Hastings. Words by S. Stennett. FSS 5

The **majesty** of the divine humiliation. Stainer. OS 3
"King ever glorious." SAS 3

Majnat (A May night) C. Sinding. Words by V. Krag. e.n. SSN

The **major** and his company. See Majoren og hans kompani

"**Majoren** med sit hele kompani." See Majoren og hans kompani

Majoren og hans kompani (The major and his company) Norse folk song. e.n. MAN

Makalapua. See "O budding flowers" (Nape)

"**Make** a bargain, pretty sweetheart." Polish song. e. KSN—WL

"**Make** answer, Liliu." See Haili crowned with lehua (Hopkins)

"**Make** for me a headless man." See Je n'veux pas me marier

"**Make** me no gaudy chaplet." Donizetti. e. FSS 4—HSD

"**Make** melody within your hearts." F. A. J. Hervey. HC

Make the best of it. FSS 2
"Life is but a fleeting dream." WBT

Make your mark ("In the quarries should you toil") FSS 2

Makedonets. See Macedonia

Makemake ae ana. See Kalakaua's serenade (Hopkins)

Maker, Frederick Charles
"All my heart this night rejoices" (Tr of Fröhlich soll mein herze springen)
"Christ is risen! alleluia"
"Dear Lord, I thank Thee, Who hast made"
"A joyous song once more we bring" Wentworth. See "Dear Lord, I thank Thee, Who hast made"

Malagasy song. See "Hark! how loud the storm blows"

Malama kealoha waiho iloko. See "My wreath of lehua" (Nape)

Malan, Henri Abraham César
"Children of the heavenly King"
Hendon. See "Lord! we come before Thee now"
"Lord! we come before Thee now"

Malatu p'amuri (Lovesick) Sicilian song. e.i. MSI

Malay song. See "Painful is my heart"

"**Malbrough** s'en va-t-en guerre" (La chanson de Malbrough.—The song of Malbrough) French folk song. e.f. TSF

Malbrough ("Beau page! ah! mon beau page") f. FMB

"**Malbrouk** s'en va-t-en guerre" ("Malbrouk to war is going") e.f. BSP

"**Mambrú** se fué a la guerra." s. LCP

Marlbrough s'en va-t-en guerre (Duke Marlborough) e. GO

Marlbrouk. e. BSE

"**Malbrough** to war is going." See "Malbrough s'en va-t-en guerre"

Malbrouk. See "Malbrough s'en va-t-en guerre"

"**Maler,** mal mir mein liebchen." See Das gemälde

Malibran, Mme Maria Félicita (Garcia)
The Alpine horn (Rimbault)

"**Malihini** ko'u ike ana." See Waters of Punalau (Nape)

Mallary, Raymond De Witt
They falter not

Mallet, David
The birks of Invermay (Scottish air)
Peace, the fairest child of heaven (Oswald)
Rule, Britannia. See Thomson, J.
Rule Britannia (Arne)
See also Thomson, James, jt. auth.

Malloch, Douglas
When the drive goes down (Composer unknown)

Mally's meek, Mally's sweet. See "As I was walking up the street"

Malmström, Bernhard Elis
Jungfrun i det gröna (Swedish folk air)

Maltese boatman's song. L. Devereux. FSS 6

"**Malt's** come down." W. Byrd. Old words. CO 1

"**Malt's** come down." T. Ravenscroft. Old words. CO 1

"**Maman,** dites-moi" ("Mother, tell me, do") Bergerette. e.f. WB

"**Mambrú** se fué a la guerra." See "Malbrough s'en va-t-en guerre"

Mamie's charms. W. H. Jones. Words by R. O. Everhart. CHS

La **mamma** de rosa (La mamma di rosa.—"Come, behold") Neapolitan air. e.i. FE

"La **mamma** del mio ben l'ha nom Oliva." See Dispetto

La **mamma** di rosa. See La mamma de rosa

Mamma, lasciami andare (Mother, let me go) Italian song. e.i. BF 2

"**Mamma,** mamma, c'è un cavaliere." See Piuriuri, ti vo' sposà

"**Mamma,** mamma, lasciami andare." See Mamma, lasciami andare

"**Mamma,** nun mi mannari all' acqua sula." See Alla fontana

"**Mamma,** pray, do not send me to the spring alone." See Alla fontana

Mamma's love. Nursery song. FSS 8

"**Mammy's** baby, go ter sleep." See Negro lullaby (Burleigh)

Mammy's lullaby. See Swing low (Fisher)

"The **man** aglow with patriot blood." See "Wien Neêrlandsch bloed" (Wilms)

"A **man** and a maid went a-rowing." See Down by the riverside

"**Man,** by nature enterprising." See Warnung (Mozart)

"The **man** in the moon." Children's song. WSC

"A **man** is dead, yet he shall rise again." See Hosanna (Granier)

Man is for the woman made. 17th century song. DM 2

The **man** of his word. Beethoven. e. BSE

The **man** of Kent. See Brave men of Kent (Leveridge)

The **man** of the north countrie ("He came from the north") Irish air. Words by T. D. McGee. MMI

The **man** of upright life. See Integer vitae (Flemming)

"**Man** sagt wohl, in dem maien." See Trinklied (Reichardt)

Mân tro? jo, jo (Ah, why? ay, ay) A. F. Lindblad (music and words) e.sw. HSOS

"The **man** who has plenty of good peanuts." See Peanut song

"The **man** who would turn lover." See "Chi vuole innamorarsi" (Scarlatti)

"A **man** whose name was Johnny Sands." See Johnny Sands (Sinclair)

The **man** without tears. Bohemian song. K. Zahorsky. e. KSE

"**Mana** tēn agapō." See Why does he haunt my door (Lontos)

Manahan, Thomas
"Brother, tell me of the battle" (Root)

Las **mañanitas.** Mexican folk song. e.s. HS

"He **mana'o** he aloha." See What is love

Mancherlei boten ("Röslein, röslein") L. Erk. Words by K. Schneider. g. ED 3

Mancherlei freuden ("Mit tausendfacher schöne") Volksweise. Words by E. von der Recke. g. ED 2

Mancini, E.
Se (Denza)

Mancini, Francesco
"Dir ch'io t'ami"
"Words elude me." See "Dir ch'io t'ami"

Mandolin ("Les donneurs de sérénades") See Mandoline (Debussy)

The **mandolin** song ("O I'm a happy creature") See Mandolinata (Paladilhe)

Mandolin song ("With silver strings") C. Gounod. WBW

Mandolinata ("Away the night is balmy") E. Paladilhe. e. WL

Mandolinata ("O I'm a happy creature."—The mandolin song.) [E. Paladilhe] e. FSS 6
The mandolin song. e. WBT

Mandoline (The mandolin) A. C. Debussy. Words by P. Verlaine. e.f. CM 1—SAM

"**Mandom,** mod och morske män" ("Manhood, might, and men, as well") Swedish folk song. Words by R. Dybeck. e.sw. HSOS
Ancient march from Dalecarlia. e. GO
"Brave of heart and warriors bold." e. KSN—SN

"**Mang** o doogwin nind enendam." See The lake sheen

"**Manger** all-glorious." Words by J. Selwyn. MCS

The **manger** throne. See "Like silver lamps" (Steggall)

"**Manhood,** might, and men, as well." See "Mandom, mod och morske män"

"**Manhood** might and stalwart men." See "Mandom, mod och morske män"

"**Manir,** manir, im jekharag." See The spool

Manley, Frederic
The dancers (Lacome d'Estalenx)
Dolphin lullaby (Gilchrist)
Easter (Hadley)
Easter song (Johns)
The endless song (Neidlinger)
"Massa dear" (music by Dvořák; Johnson)
May song (Smith)
Night song (Rittmeyer)
On, O thou soul (Serbian folk air)

Manley, Frederic —*Continued*
"Sleep, noble hearts" (Mendelssohn)
Song of April (Fairlamb)
Song of greeting (Omaha Indian air)
Song of the ghost dance (Indian air)
"Sweet day is softly dying" (Old French air)
To America (Waller)
Uncrowned kings (Loomis)
Whip-poor-will (Gilchrist)

The **manly** heart. See "Shall I, wasting in despair" (Barker)

Der **mann** im keller. See Der rheinweinzecher (Fischer)

"**Männer** suchen stets zu naschen." See Warnung (Mozart)

Männer und buben ("Das volk steht auf") Volksweise. T. Körner. g. ED 1

Manney, Charles Fonteyn
"Orpheus with his lute"

Manoah (Rossini) See Glory gilds the sacred page; "Jesus, the very thought of Thee"

Le **manoir** de Rosemonde (Rosamond's manor) H. Duparc. Words by R. de Bonnières. e.f. CM 1

A **man's** a man for a' that. Words by R. Burns. BSB—FSS 6—JO— LA— PS 1
For a' that, an' a' that ("Is there, for honest poverty") MMS
"Is there for honest poverty." BSR

"**Man's** life is but vain." See The angler's song (Lawes)

"**Man's** life's a vapor." Round. BSS

Mant, Richard
"Round the Lord in glory seated" (Oliver)

The **mantle** so green. Irish folk song. JOI

"**Many** a time when it was moonlight." See La Rozina

"**Many** and sweet the raptures." See "Troppo soavi i gusti" (Cavalli)

"**Many** as the stars that yonder." See Treue leibe ("Soviel stern' am himmel")

"The **many** happy evenings I spent." See Paddy Duffy's cart (Braham)

"**Many** have told of the monks of old." See The monks of old (Glover)

"**Many** miles have I been straying." See Dalecarlian maiden's song (Lindblad)

"**Many** songs have I heard in my dear motherland." See The little cudgel

"**Many** sunbeams golden from the sunset free." See Meeresleuchten (Loewe)

Many thousand go ("No more peck o' corn") Negro spiritual. KA
Variant of: Many thousands gone

Many thousands gone ("No more auction-block") Negro spiritual. FSS 5 —HR—KA—JP—NMP
Variant: Many thousand go

Manzaros, N.
Hymn to freedom
"Se gnori z'apo tin kopsi." See Hymn to freedom

Map, Walter
"Mihi est propositum" (Pearsall)

"**Maple**, from the leafy wildwood." See Song of the maple (Streeter)

The **maple** leaf forever ("In days of yore, from Britain's shore") National song of Canada. A. Muir (music and words) BD—BMC—BSP— CST—JSE— LA—MP—NMS—SN —SSS—WA—WBT—WSW

The maple leaf forever ("In days of yore the hero Wolfe") JS

"**M'appari** tutt' amor." See "Ach! so fromm" (Flotow)

Marcel, Léo
Que je t'oublie (Chrétien)

Marcello, Benedetto
For my love thus to die. See Non m'è grave morir per amore
"Il mio bel foco"
"My ardent longing." See "Il mio bel foco"
"My joyful ardor." See "Il mio bel foco"
"When I am near thee." See "Il mio bel foco"
Non m'è grave morir per amore

March, Mrs Mary Ann Virginia (Gabriel)
See Gabriel, Virginia

"**March!** march! Ettrick and Teviotdale." See Blue bonnets over the border

"**March**, march, march, we'll gladly march along." Round. FSS 5

The **march** of the Cameron men. Old Scottish air. Words by M. M. Campbell. JO—PS 2
March o' the Cameron men. FSS 7— LA

March of the kings. See Marcho dei rei

March of the men of Columbia. Words by H. A. Clarke. JS

March of the men of Harlech. See Rhyfelgyrch gwyr Harlech

March of the victors. G. Verdi. Words adapted. e. BD

March on ("Way over in the Egypt land") Negro spiritual. JP—NMP

"**March** on! Liberty's host." Verdi. Words by S. Rowe. e. TFC 1

"**March** on, march on, our way along" See Gaily beats the drum

March snow. See Märzschnee (Reinecke)

March violets. See Martsviolerne (Gade)

Marcha real (Royal march) Traditional Spanish march. Words by Almendros. e.s. BSP
Royal march. e.s. MP

La **marchande** d'oranges (The orange vender) French folk song. e.f. TSF

La marchande d'oranges (The orange tree) e. GO

La **marche** des rois. See Marcho dei rei

Marche lorraine. L. Ganne. e. TFC 1

"**Marchemos**, hijos de la patria." See La Marseillaise (Rouget de Lisle)

Marching along. W. B. Bradbury. HSD —MP—WBT

Marching game. Children's song. WSC

"**Marching** proudly, marching proudly." See Memorial day

A marching song ("Honored in song") Columbia university song. CHS

Marching song ("March on, march on") See Gaily beats the drum

Marching through Georgia. H. C. Work (music and words) BOS—FMB— HSD— MP—NMH— SSS— WA— WBT—WSC—WSW

"**Marchioness**, your dancing." See "Vous dansez, marquise" (Lemaire)

Marcho dei rei (March of the kings) Provençal Noël. e. GO
La marche des rois (The march of the kings) e.f.pr. TSF

The mare and the foal. Folk song from Warwickshire. SF 4

"**Mare**, potente mare." See "Ocean! thou mighty monster" (Weber)

Maréchal, Henri
"He is dead, the child I cherish" (from Le miracle de Naim)
"Idles of dreams" (from La Nativité)
"O my home" (from La Nativité)
"One would say, he reposes" (from Le miracle de Naim)

Marechiare. Canto Napolitano. F. P. Tosti. Words after the Neapolitan of S. di Giacomo. e.i. MN

"**Les marenquins** nous piquent." See Acadian boatmen's song

Margaret at the spinning-wheel. See "Meine ruh' ist hin" (Schubert)

Margaret Roche. See Máirghréad na Róiste

Margaretes vuggesang (Margaret's cradle song) E. Grieg. Words by H. Ibsen. e.n. MAN—SSN

Margaret's cradle song. See Margaretes vuggesang (Grieg)

Margaretta. See Margreth am thore (Jensen)

"**Margari**, Parete's beauty." See Margarita (Fassone)

Margarita ("Margarita de Parete") V. Fassone. Words by P. Cinquegrana. e.i. FE—MN

"**Margarita** of Parete." See Margarita (Fassone)

Margherita ("When joyous tho'ts") C. Gounod. e. WBT—WL

Margreth am thore (Margaretta) A. Jensen. Words by O. Roquette. e.g. PG 3

"**Margueridette** au bord du bois." See L'occasion manquée (Norman version)

"**Marguerite** herself has garnished." See Que l'on m'enterre dans la cave

"**Marguerite** s'est coiffée." See Que l'on m'enterre dans la cave

Maria auf dem berge ("Uf'm berge da geht der wind") Oberschlesisches volkslied. g. ED 1

Maria Charlotte Amelia, herzogin von Sachsen-Gotha
"Ah! s'il est dans votre village"
C'est mon ami. See "Ah! s'il est dans votre village"
Hail, evening bright
He is my love. See "Ah! s'il est dans votre village"

"**Maria** dear." See "Encantadora Maria"

Maria, Marì (Ah! Marì! ah! Marì) E. di Capua. Words by V. Russo. e.i. FE
Maria, Mari. e. only WBT—WL. s. only LCP
Maria, Marì (Marie, ah, Marie) e.i. MN

"**María, María**." Folk song from California. e.s. HS

Le mariage des roses (Marriage of roses) C. Franck. Words by E. David. e.f. CMF 2—HM 1—PG 2
Le mariage des roses (The marriage of the roses) e.f. SAM

Mariandel. J. Drechsler. g. ED 2

Mariani, Angelo
Invocation. See Invocazione a Dio
Invocazione a Dio

Marianina (The sea breeze) Italian folk song. e. CST

Marianson. Canadian folk song. e.f. TF

Marie ("Marie, am fenster") R. Franz. Words by R. Gottschall. e.g. KF 1 —KF 3. e. only BD—FTS

Marie ("Thou sittest in thy bow'r") A. Jenson. [Words by R. Gottschall] e. KF 3

Marie, ah, Marie. See Maria, Marì (Capua)

"**Marie**, am fenster sitzest du." See Marie (Franz)

Marie Antoinette, queen. For songs wrongly attributed to Marie Antoinette see Maria Charlotte Amelia, herzogin von Sachsen-Gotha

Marie-Clémence. Negro folk song from Martinique. e.f. KA

"**Marie**, I see thee, darling one." See Marie (Franz)

"**Marie**, mine." Hungarian song. e. WBT—WL
Magyar song. e. KSE

"**Marie**, the window frames thy face." See Marie (Franz)

"**Mariez-moi**, ma petite maman" (Marry me, mother dear) French Canadian folk song. e.f. BFS

The marigold. Folk song. BSW

Marigold lane. Folk air. BE 1

Marin, F. Gonzalo
La Borinquen (Fuentes)

The mariner. HSD

Les marins de Groix ("Nous étions deux, nous étions trois."—The sailors of Lee) French folk song: 1st version. e.f. TSF
Les marins de Groix ("Nous étions trois marins de Groix."—The sailors of Groix) 2d version. e.f. SMW

Marion. See "Rejoice ye pure in heart" (Messiter)

La Marion et le bossu (May and the hunchback) Savoyard folk song. e.f. TSF

Marion Moore. J. G. Clark (music and words) JO

"La Marion sos on pomi." See La Marion et le bossu

"La Marion sous un pommier." See La Marion et le bossu

Maristow, Walter
Hail, gentle King. See Nowell Nowell

"Mark how the blushful morn." Charles I. Words by T. Carew. JE

"Mark the merry elves of fairyland." See The fairies (Callcott)

"Mark well my heavy doleful tale." See A carol for Twelfth day

"Mark yonder pomp of costly fashion." Air: Deil tak the wars. Words by R. Burns. BSR

"Mark yonder tomb." See "In questa tomba oscura" (Beethoven)

Markewitsch, A.
Oh pray

Markham, Edwin
Joy of the morning (Ware)

"Markje grönast" ("Fields and woods are crown'd with verdure") Folk song. Words by E. Storm. e.n. MAN

Mark-Lemon, Mary
Afterwards (Mullen)
Arise! He calleth thee (Roeckel)
"Cast thy bread on the waters" (Roeckel)
Daddy (Behrend)
He giveth His beloved sleep (Roeckel)
In the golden eventide (Pinsuti)
The new kingdom (Tours)
This is my dream (Wellings)
Thou art the way (Roeckel)
The watchman and the child (Cowen)

Marks, C. Mawson-. See Mawson-Marks, C.

Marks, Godfrey
Corn song (same air as Sailing)
Sailing

Marlborough. See "Still, still with Thee"

"Marlbrook, the prince of commanders." See Marlbrouk (English version)

Marlbrough s'en va-t-en guerre. See "Malbrough s'en va-t-en guerre"

Marlbrouk ("Marlbrook, the prince of commanders") English version. BSE

Marlbrouk ("Malbrough s'en va-t-en guerre") See "Malbrough s'en va-t-en guerre"

Marlowe, Christopher
"Come, live with me and be my love" (16th century air; Welsh air; also music by Bishop; Goldmark; Hatton)

"Marmar zamānī." See My day is bitter

Marmotte ("Ich komme schon") L. van Beethoven. Words by Goethe. g. ED 2

Marnix, Philippe de, seigneur de Saint-Aldegonde
"Prince William of old Nassau." See "Wilhelmus van Nassouwe"
"Wilhelmus van Nassouwe"
William of Nassau. See "Wilhelmus van Nassouwe"

Marot, Clément
"Now my lightsome youth is gone"

Márquez, R.
La tórtola

Marriage. See The mousetrap

The marriage day. J. Sanderson. ME

Marriage of roses. See Le mariage des roses (Franck)

Marriage song (Tiyata uŋgni kte) Dakota Indian song. e.in. BF 2

Married and single life. Folk song from North Carolina. CSE

The married man's lament ("I ance was a wanter") Scottish air. Words by R. Nicoll. PS 2

Married to a mermaid. Chantey. SMW

Marriott, C. H. R.
Thy face is always near me

Marriott, John
"Thou Whose almighty word" (Giardini)

Marry me, mother dear. See "Mariez-moi, ma petite maman"

Marschner, Heinrich August
"An jenem tag" (from Hans Heiling)
Good-night, my love
Heaven in the vale. See Der himmel im thale
Der himmel im thale
"Upon that day." See "An jenem tag"
"We bring sweet flowers"

La Marseillaise (The Marseillaise) French national anthem. C. J. Rouget de Lisle (music and words) e.f. BSP—FMB— MP—MS—NA— NMH NMS— SN—SSS—TFC 1—WA—WBT—WSW. e. only BD—BSE—JSE—OH. f. only BOS
Hymne des Marseillaise. e.f. CST
La Marseillaise (Hymn of the Marseillaise) e.f. LA
The Marseillaise hymn. e. BMC—EF—FSS 1—HSD—JS
The Marseilles hymn (National hymn of France) e.f. WCP
La Marsellesa. s. LCP

Marsh, Simeon Butler
"Jesus, lover of my soul"
The marsh of Rhuddlan ("Mild is the sun on this soft dewy morning") Welsh air: Morva Rhuddlan. Words by A. Grant. BMC

Marshall, John Patton
O maître de tout
"O mighty one." See O maître de tout

Marshall, Leonard B.
Brunonia
Cherished names
"Fling out the banner on the breeze"
The four winds
Harvest song
Memorial day
"My native land! what words can be"
Precious lives
Sleep, comrades, sleep
"Strew the fair garlands"
"Summer suns are glowing"
'Tis Easter time
The veterans
Washington
Winter

Marshall, William
"O' a' the airts the wind can blaw"
Marsk Stig's daughters. See Marsk Stigs døttre

Marsk Stigs døttre (Marstig's daughter) Danish heroic ballad. da.e. BO
Marsk Stigs døttre (Marsk Stig's daughters) da.e. BF 2
Marstig's daughter ("Oh, rede me, dear mother") e. BMC

Marstig's daughter. See Marsk Stigs døttre

Marston, George W.
"Bright Easter skies"

Martens, Frederic Herman
Daniel Boone (Composer unknown)
Humoreske (Dvořák)
Lullaby (Godard)

Martha's song (Chant de Marthe) M. Moussorgsky. Words from the Russian. e.f. NM 2—SC

Martha's spinning wheel ("If the summer's long of coming") Air: Y bachgen tawel. Words from the Welsh. e. MMW

Martin, Sir George Clement
"I sing the Birth was born to-night"

Martin, George Edward
"There's a song in the air"

Martin, Helen
The birthday of a King (Guglielmo)
Echoes of olden times (Comer)
"Fair Christmas comes" (Labitzky)
"A funny old fellow" (Brown)
"List the chiming" (Composer unknown)
"Only a baby fair" (Kingsley)

Martin, Jehu
"Christians, listen while we sing"

"Martin said to his man." 16th century song. CO 1

"Martin, the man-at-arms." E. J. Loder. Words by W. H. Bellamy. HSE 2

Martinez, J. C.
La Carolina (Pablo Andraca)

Martini, Giovanni Battista
"Fallen is thy throne"
"The joys of love" (wrongly attributed) See Martini, J. P. E. "Plaisir d'amour"
Laughing glee
"Plaisir d'amour" (wrongly attributed) See Martini, J. P. E. "Plaisir d'amour"
The tickling trio. See Laughing glee

Martini, Jean Paul Égide
Fugitive love. See "Plaisir d'amour"
"The joys of love." See "Plaisir d'amour"
"Plaisir d'amour" (from Célestine)

Martinique love-song. Negro folk song. e.f. KA

Martsviolerne (March violets) N. W. Gade. Words by H. C. Andersen. da.e. WM 1

"Marusya, the little dove." See Petrus

Marvin, F. O.
"Beyond the starry skies"

"Mary and a Martha's just gone along." See Mary and Martha

Mary and Martha. Negro spiritual. FSS 4—JP—JSE— NMP—WBT—WC

Mary at the tomb. J. Blumenthal. Words by J. Newton. FSS 7

Mary Blane. Negro song. NMP—WBT

"Mary had a little lamb." Nursery song. FMB—HSD— WA—WBT— WSC—WSW

"Mary had a little lamb." Nursery song. Hobart version. WC

The **Mary** Golden Tree (The lonesome low) Kentucky mountain song. WLT
Variant of: The Golden Vanity

Mary Macneil. Scottish air: Kinloch of Kinloch. Words by E. Conolly. PS 2

Mary Morison. See "O, Mary, at thy window be"

Mary of Argyle. S. Nelson. Words by C. Jefferys. DM 1—FSS 2—HSD— JO—PS 2—TS—WBT—WL

Mary of Limerick town ("One morning in July") Irish air: Nora of the amber hair: 2d version. MMI

Mary of the wild moor. Old English words and music. FSS 7—JO —Vermont version. SSH

"Mary, the last star trembling above thee." See Mattinata (Tosti)

"Mary to the Saviour's tomb." See Mary at the tomb (Blumenthal)

"Mary, tremando l'ultima stella." See Mattinata (Tosti)

"Mary, why thus waste thy youth-time in sorrow." See Despairing Mary (Wilson)

Maryland! my Maryland. German air: O
tannenbaum. Words by J. R.
Randall. BSE—EF—HSC—HSD
—JO— JS— MP— NMH— WA—
WBT—WSW
My Maryland. FSS 5—OH

Mary's dream ("The moon had climbed the
highest hill") Scottish air. Words
attributed to J. Lowe and to A. Lowe.
HSSS—JO—PS 1

Mary's little wise man. E. T. Carter.
CHS

Mary's quest (Son Presviatoĭ Bogoroditsy)
Russian folk song. e. SSR 2

Mary's tears. O. Shaw. Words by T.
Moore. FSS 7

Marzials, Théophile
Composer
Come back in dreams. See "Come
to me in the silence of the night"
"Come to me in the silence of the
night"
Friendship. See "My true love hath
my heart"
"Go, pretty rose"
"I'm little Robin Redbreast"
May Margaret
"My true love hath my heart"
"The stars are fading one by one"
The three sailor boys
Timothy's welcome
Twickenham ferry
Author
"Could I" (Tosti)
A creole love-song (Moncrieff)
Une nuit de mai (Thomas)
"O vision entrancing" (Thomas)

Märzschnee (March snow) C. Reinecke.
e.g. MS

Mascagni, Pietro
Alfio's entrance-song. See "Il cavallo
scalpita"
"Ave Maria" (from Cavalleria rusti-
cana)
"Beppe then also loves." See "Ed
anche Beppe amò"
Canzone del rabbino (from L'amico
Fritz)
"Il cavallo scalpita" (from Cavalleria
rusticana)
Drinking song
"Ed anche Beppe amò" (from L'amico
Fritz)
"Friend so unhappy, oh, well I know
the sorrow thou art bearing." See
"Povero amico! oh! lo conosco il
male che tu soffri"
Lola's song (from Cavalleria rusticana.
Tr of Fior di giaggiolo)
"O Lola, bianca come fior." See Sici-
liana
"O Lola, fair as flowers." See Sici-
liana
"Povero amico! oh! lo conosco il male
che tu soffri" (from L'amico Fritz)
Siciliana (from Cavalleria rusticana)

Song of the rabbi. See Canzone del
rabbino
"Surely you know, oh, mother." See
"Voi lo sapete, o mamma"
"Voi lo sapete, o mamma" (from Caval-
leria rusticana)

Másha. Slavonian folk air. Words by G.
D. Donaldson. WF

"A **mask** thy face concealing." See Gavotte du masque (Georges)

Masliânitsa. See Butter-week

Mason, Mrs Caroline Atherton (Briggs)
"Do they miss me at home" (Grannis)
"Whichever way the wind doth blow"
(Composer unknown)

Mason, Lowell
Antioch. See "Joy to the world"
Bethany. See "Nearer, my God, to
Thee"
Downs. See "God of our fathers, by
Whose hand"; "How sweet the
name of Jesus sounds"
"Father, whate'er of earthly bliss"
"From Greenland's icy mountains"
"God of our fathers, by Whose hand"
"Hail the blest morn"
"Hail to the Lord's anointed"
Hamburg. See "Kingdoms and
thrones to God belong"; Whose
sins have pardon gained
Happy land. See "There is a happy
land": Hindoo air arranged
"How sweet the name of Jesus sounds"
(same air as "God of our fathers,
by Whose hand")
"Joy to the world"
"Kingdoms and thrones to God belong"
The Lord's anointed. See "Hail to the
Lord's anointed"
Missionary hymn. See "From Green-
land's icy mountains"
"My faith looks up to Thee"
"My soul, be on thy guard"
Naomi. See "Father, whate'er of
earthly bliss"
"Nearer, my God, to Thee"
Olivet. See "My faith looks up to
Thee"
"Praise to God, immortal praise"
Sabbath morn. See "Praise to God,
immortal praise"
"Safely through another week"
"There is a happy land": Hindoo air
arranged
"Watchman, tell us of the night"
What of the night. See "Watchman,
tell us of the night"
"When I survey the wondrous cross"
"When shall we meet again"
Whose sins have pardon gained (same
air as "Kingdoms and thrones to
God belong")
"Work, for the night is coming"
Work song. See "Work, for the night
is coming"

Mason, Mrs Mary (Knight) Wood
Ashes of roses

Mass aa'n Lass ("Han Mass aa'n Lass skulde."—Mass and Lass) Norse folk song. e.n. MAN
Variants: "Han Mass aa'en Lasse der gingo paa raad"; Mass aa'n Lasse ("Han Mass aa'en Lasse, dei gingo")

Mass aa'n Lasse ("Han Mass aa'en Lasse, dei gingo."—Mass and Lass) Norse folk song. e.n. MAN
Variants: "Han Mass aa'en Lasse der gingo paa raad"; Mass aa'n Lass ("Han Mass aa'n Lass skulde")

"Massa dear." A. Dvořák. Words by by F. Manley. BSS—TFC 1

"Massa dear." A. Johnson. Words by F. Manley. TL

Massa gwine to sell us to-morrow. Negro song. HR
Is master going to sell us to-morrow. JP

"Massa lov'd his good old Jamaica." See Balm of Gilead (Bryant)

De **massa** run? ha, ha. See Kingdom coming (Work)

The **massacre** of Macpherson. Air: Bobbing Joan. BOS—SSS

"Massa's bin an' sol' yeh, O." See Link o' day

"Massa's gone de news to hear." See Sally come up (Sewell)

Massa's in de cold, cold ground. S. C. Foster (music and words) BOS —CU—HSC—JSE—OH—WC
Massa's in de col', col' ground. FMB
Massa's in de cold ground. HSD— MP—MPC—NMH—NMP— SSS— WA—WBT—WSW
Massa's in the cold, cold ground. JO —LA

Massé, Victor
Berceuse. See "Dans le bois à ma voix"
Brindisi. See "Sa couleur est blonde et vermeille"
"Dans le bois à ma voix" (from Paul et Virginie)
"Deep in forest shaded." See "Parmi les lianes"
"Parmi les lianes" (from Paul et Virginie)
"Rich and fair as roses blooming." See "Sa couleur est blonde et vermeille"
"Sa couleur est blonde et vermeille" (from Galathée)
"Softly rest in thy nest." See "Dans le bois à ma voix"

Massenet, Jules Émile Frédéric
À quoi bon l'économie (from Manon)
Ah! depart, image fair. See Ah! fuyez, douce image
Ah! fuyez, douce image (from Manon)
"Ah, Mary, give an ear." See Judas
Air of Salomé. See Il est doux, il est bon

Autumn thought. See Pensée d'automne
Bonne nuit
"Celui dont la parole." See Il est doux, il est bon
Chant provençal
Crépuscule
"The days are all sunshine" (from Marie-Magdeleine)
The dream. See Le rêve
Élégie
"An empress am I in my way." See "Je marche sur tous les chemins"
Ferme les yeux, ô belle maîtresse (from Le roi de Lahore)
The first dance. See Première danse
Fleeting vision. See Vision fugitive
Gavotte. See "Je marche sur tous les chemins"
He is good, he is kind. See Il est doux, il est bon
"He whose compelling word." See Il est doux, il est bon
How brief is the hour. See "Que l'heure est donc brève"
I am alone. See "Je suis seul"
Il est doux, il est bon (from Hérodiade)
"Je marche sur tous les chemins" (from Manon)
"Je suis seul" (from Manon)
Judas (from Marie-Magdeleine)
Lost love. See Élégie
"Ne pouvant réprimer" (from Hérodiade)
A night in Spain. See Nuit d'Espagne
Noël païen
Nuit d'Espagne
Ô souverain, ô juge, ô père
Oh, promise of a joy so sweet. See Promesse de mon avenir
Oh, weep! oh, weep, mine eyes. See Pleurez! pleurez, mes yeux
"Open thy blue eyes." See "Ouvre tes yeux bleus"
"Ouvre tes yeux bleus"
A pagan Noël. See Noël païen
Pensée d'automne
Pleurez! pleurez, mes yeux (from Le Cid)
"Plus de tournments et plus de peine" (from Le Cid)
Prayer. See Ô souverain, ô juge, ô père
Première danse
Promesse de mon avenir (from Le roi de Lahore)
Provence song. See Chant provençal
"Que l'heure est donc brève"
Le rêve (from Manon)
Salomé! Salomé (from Hérodiade)
Sérénade du passant
Sweet good-night. See Bonne nuit
"'Tis in vain that I seek a retreat" (from Marie-Magdeleine)
"'Twas even here those words were spoken" (from Marie-Magdeleine)
Twilight. See Crépuscule

Massenet, Jules Émile Frédéric—*Continued*
Vision fair.   See Vision fugitive
Vision fugitive (from Hérodiade)
"Wherever I go I command."   See "Je
  marche sur tous les chemins"
While there are such things as dice.
  See À quoi bon l'économie
Massmann, Hans Ferdinand
Gelübde (Volksweise)
"Måste ock af törnen vara."   See Kors
  och krona (Stenhammer)
"Master Charley of Holland was straying."
  See Il Sor Carlo l'armonico
"Master Cuckoo and Miss Skylark."   See
  Les noces du coucou et de l'alouette
"A master I have and I am his man."   See
  Galloping dreary dun (Arnold)
Masterton, Allan
"The Catrine woods were yellow seen"
"O Willie brew'd a peck o' maut"
"Thickest night, surround my dwelling"
"Ye gallants bright, I rede you right"
Matarile ("Ambos a dos") Game song.   s.
  LCP
"Matelots, les gens de terre."   See Le
  langage des marins
Mater Hierusalem.   For English transla-
  tion see "Jerusalem, my happy home"
Materna (Ward)   See America the beauti-
  ful; Jerusalem above; Peace hymn of
  the republic
A **mathematic** monody.   E. Newton.
  Words by J. M. Bulloch.   SSS
Mather, Helen
Christmas as it comes (Composer un-
  known)
Forevermore (Wellings)
Mathews, Charles
Jenny Jones (Parry)
"Mati zakliče."   See Girls at the river
Matin song.   J. K. Paine.   Words by
  B. Taylor.   HST
"Matona, lovely maiden."   Madrigal.   O.
  Lassus.   e.   TL
Matrosenlied ("Auf, matrosen, die anker")
  A. Pohlenz.   Words by W. Gerhard.
  g.   ED 1
Matrozenlied ("De kabels los")   See "De
  kabels los"
Matsumai.   See Japanese sailors' song
Matteaux, C. L.
"Over hills and over plains" (Saunders)
Mattei, Tito
Dear heart
Italian boatman's song.   See Oh! hear
  the wild wind blow
My native land.   See Patria
Non è ver
Odi tu
Oh! hear the wild wind blow
Patria
The sailor's prayer.   See Odi tu
Schlummerlied
Slumber-song.   See Schlummerlied
"'Tis not true."   See Non è ver
Matteson, O. S.
Flag of '76

"Matthew, Mark and Luke and John."   See
  The evening prayer
Matthisson, Friedrich von
Adelaide (music by Beethoven; Pilz)
Am sommerabend (Spazier)
Die betende (music by Rust; Zelter)
"Ich denke dein, wenn durch den hain"
  (music by Beethoven; Zumsteeg)
Opferlied (Beethoven)
Die vollendung (Schulz)
Mattinata.   F. P. Tosti.   Words by E.
  Panzacchi.   e.i.   SM 3
Matys, Karl
Der thürmer
The warder.   See Der thürmer
Mauberne, Jean
"Why, alas! in lowly stall"
Maui ("Wrapt in verdure")   See "Wrapt
  in verdure" (Hopkins)
Maui girl ("I love a pretty Maui girl")
  Hawaiian song.   e.   HA
Maulaya.   See "O mother mine, spread
  me the silken sheet"
"Mault's come downe."   See "Malt's come
  down" (Byrd); "Malt's come down"
  (Ravenscroft)
La **maumariée** (The ill-wed wife) Folk
  song: Breton version.   e.f.   TF
—Canadian version.   e.f.   TF
Maunawili.   See Hawaiian hula (Hopkins)
Maunder, J. H.
"Once in Bethlehem of Judah"
"Maur' ein' hē vykta sta bouna."   See
  The kleftman (Seiller)
"Maura dhu of Ballyshannon."   Irish air.
  Words by C. P. O'Conor.   FSI
Maurer, Ludwig Wilhelm
Praise of song
Mausfallen-sprüchlein (The mouse-trap) H.
  Wolf.   Words by E. Mörike.   e.g.
  CMF 2
Mavourneen.   F. Aylward.   Words by G.
  Weatherly.   BS 1
Mawson-Marks, C.
The little Dutch garden
Maxfield, W. Henry
The student song
**Maxwell, Caroline Elizabeth Sarah (Sheri-
  dan) Norton, lady.**   See Norton, Mrs
  Caroline Elizabeth Sarah (Sheridan)
"Maxwellton braes are bonnie."   See
  Annie Laurie (Scott)
"Maxwelton's braes are bonnie."   See
  Annie Laurie (Scott)
May, M.
Petites roses (Cesek)
May ("Depuis un mois")   See Mai (Hahn)
May ("The merry month") Round.   LA
May ("Now, who art thou")   W. J. Mc-
  Coy.   Words by M. V. G. Williams.
  BD
May and November ("Sweet May, ever
  welcome") Air: Rhegid.   Words from
  the Welsh of Davydd ap Gwilym.   e.
  MMW
May and the hunchback.   See La Marion
  et le bossu

May-bells. W. Bargiel. Words by Hoff-mann von Fallersleben. e. MS

May breezes. See 's mailüfterl (Kreipl)

"May comes singing." Round. LA

May-day ("Come out to the green") JSE

May-day ("Le premier jour de mai") See "Le premier jour de mai"

May-day ("Sweet, how sweet, the hawthorn blooming") North Wales air: Hob y derri dando. Words by A. Hunter. MMW

May-day carol ("Awake, ye pretty maids") Folk song. BSW

May-day song ("Under the May-pole gay") A. S. Gatty. WBT—WSC

"May de Lord—He will be glad of me." See Bright sparkles in de churchyard

May dew. See Maienthau (Bennett)

May eve. Irish air. Words by N. Chesson. FSI

"May ev'ry year but bring more near." See That day the world shall see (Callcott)

"May, fifteen hundred and eighty and eight." See The invincible Armado (Arnold)

The **May** fly. Callcott. MS

"May I kiss you dear." See She shook her head (Jones)

"May is here, the world rejoices." See Polish May song

"May laurels crown thy brow." See L'insana parola (Verdi)

May Margaret. T. Marzials. FSS 4

A **May** night. See Majnat (Sinding)

"May our emperor's reign endure." See "Kimi ga yo" (Hiromori)

"May our gracious emp'ror reign." See "Kimi ga yo" (Hiromori)

"May our lord for ever reign." See "Kimi ga yo" (Hiromori)

"May our lord long reign." See "Kimi ga yo" (Hiromori)

"May our lord's dominion last." See "Kimi ga yo" (Hiromori)

"May our sov'reign lord remain." See "Kimi ga yo" (Hiromori)

The **May-pole** ("Come, ye young men, come along") Air: Staines Morris. Words by R. Cox. DM 1—MM

To the Maypole haste away. HSE 2

The **May-pole** dance ("Now gaily round") Words by R. I. Halsey. NMS

The **May** queen. W. R. Dempster. Words by A. Tennyson. FSS 2

"May returns with skies serene." See Chant de quête de l'Alsace

May song ("De que sirve") See Cancion de maja

May song ("Komm', lieber mai") See "Komm', lieber mai, und mache" (Mozart)

May song ("May is here") See Polish May song

A **May** song ("May the maiden") See "May the maiden" (Carmichael)

May song ("Ye lads and lasses all") D. S. Smith. Words by F. Manley. TL

May song ("Zwischen waizen und korn") See Mailied (Medtner)

"May the glorious sun shed a flood of light." See Hymno da proclamacao da republica (Miguez)

"May the Lord be kind to you." See The beggar's blessing

"May the Lord, He will be glad of me." See Bright sparkles in de church yard

"May the springs purely flow." See Old Samurai prayer (Ross)

"May, the maiden." J. Barnby. Words by S. Lanier. LBR

"May the maiden" (A May song) M. Carmichael. [Words by S. Lanier] WBT —WBW

May we ne'er want a friend, nor a bottle to give him. J. Davy. HSE 2

Maybrick, Michael
　　The blue Alsatian mountains
　　The heart of a sailor
　　The king of seasons all
　　The maid of the mill
　　The midshipmite
　　Mona
　　Nancy Lee
　　The pilgrim
　　The Romany lass
　　The sailor's farewell. See The tar's farewell
　　The star of Bethlehem
　　The tar's farewell
　　They all love Jack
　　True blue
　　True hearts
　　A warrior bold
　　"What am I, love, without thee"

Mayfair. See "Golden slumbers kiss your eyes"

"Maygwah mahweod." See The omen

Maynard, Walter, pseud. See Beale, Thomas Willert

Mayne, John
　　Logan water (Scottish air)

Maypole dance ("Come, lassie and lad") 17th century song. TFC 2

"Maytime has come." See "Voici venir le mois de mai"

Mazurek ("Little cottage lowly") See The tiny hut

Mazurek ("See the sun yonder") Polish song. e. KSN—WL

Mazurka. Polish folk song. e. GO

Mazzaferrata, Giovanni Battista
　　"Presto, presto, io m'innamoro"
　　"Swift my heart surrenders." See "Presto, presto io m'innamoro"

Mazzinghi, Joseph
　　"The heath this night" (attributed) Huntsman, rest
　　"Once tired of life." See The wife in masquerade
　　"Tom Starboard" (from The turnpike gate)

Mazzinghi, Joseph—*Continued*
"When a little farm we keep" (from The free knights)
The wife in masquerade (from The exile)
"Ye shepherds, tell me"
Young Lobski's fishing tale (from The exile)

Mazzoni, P.
"Ave Maria" (Mascagni)
"**Me** gustan todas" (The girl with the golden hair) Pyrenean song. e.s. SSP
"**Me** puse a torear." Mexican folk song. e.s. HS
"**Me** thought the stars were blinking bright." See O fair dove, O fond dove (Scott-Gatty)
Me voici dans son boudoir. A. Thomas. e.f. SOA 2
Me voici dans son boudoir (I am here in her boudoir) e.f. KS 3
"C'est moi, j'ai tout brisé" ("'Tis I! somewhat disturbed") e.f. OPS 2
"**Me** voici, je te salue." See "I have come to say good morning" (Rimskiï-Korsakov)
"**Me** voilà seule dans la nuit." G. Bizet. e.f. SOA 1
"**Me** voilà seule enfin." See Plus grand dans son obscurité (Gounod)
"**Meanwhile,** go seek my darling." See "Il mio tesoro intanto" (Mozart)
Le **méchant** guillon (The wicked knight) French Canadian folk song. e.f. BFS
The **Med.** College song. CU
"**Med** dina blåa ögon." See Svärmeri (Arlberg)
Med en primulaveris (With a primrose) E. Grieg. Words by J. Paulsen. e.n. WM 1
Mit einer primula veris (The first primrose) e.g. FF—FO 2
Mit einer primula veris (The primrose) e. FTS
Mit einer primula veris (With a violet) e.g. KF 4—PG 2
To a primrose. e.g. MS
To a violet. e. BD

Medeiros e Albuquerque,
Hymno a proclamacao da republica (Miguez)
Media noche. Folk song from lower California. e.s. HS
A **medical** medley. G. T. Lowe. Words by R. J. A. Berry. SSS
Méditation du laboureur. See The laborer's plaint (Kopylov)
Medjé. Chanson arabe. C. Gounod. Words by J. Barbier. e.f. CM 2—HM 2. e. only WL
Medley, Edward S.
"Let the song be begun"
Medley, Samuel
Ariel (Composer unknown)
"Mortals, awake, with angels join" (Kingsley)

Medtner, Nikolaï
"Dear love." See "Lieb liebchen"
Einsamkeit
Epitaphe. See A poet's epitaph
Erster verlust
First loss. See Erster verlust
"I have come to say good morning"
"Lieb liebchen"
Mailied
May song. See Mailied
A poet's epitaph
Solitude. See Einsamkeit
Mee, William
Alice Gray (Millard)
"**Meek** and lowly." S. Glover. FSS 1—WS
"Das **meer** hat seine perlen." See Auf dem meere (Franz)
Meerschaum pipe. HSD—MPC—NMH—NMS—WA—WBT—WC—WSW
Meeresleuchten (Phosphorescence) C. Loewe. Words by C. Siebel. e.g. AB 1
"**Meet** me by moonlight alone." J. A. Wade (music and words) BE 4—BOH—FSS 5—HSE 1—JO—WBT
Meet me on the warlock knowe. See Dainty Davie
The **meeting** ("And doth not a meeting like this") Words by T. Moore. JO
"And doth not a meeting like this." MI
The long years. FSS 1
Meeting ("Drücke mich") See "Drücke mich an deine brust" (Farwell)
A **meeting** ("J'étais triste et pensif") See Rencontre (Fauré)
Meeting and parting. See Kommen und scheiden (Schumann)
The **meeting** of the waters ("There is not in the wide world") Irish air: The old head of Dennis. Words by T. Moore. DO—DSH—JO—MI—MMI—PI—TL—WBT
Mega kai paradoxon thagma. For English translation see Our Christmas festal
Megan's daughter ("Oh, have you e'er seen the daughter of Megan."—Merch Megan) Air: Merch Megan. Words by Talhaiarn. e. MMW
Megan's fair daughter ("I see her in dreams") Welsh folk song. Air: Merch Megan. e. WL
Méhul, Étienne Nicolas
Champs paternels (from Joseph en Égypte)
Le chant du départ
"Femme sensible, entends-tu" (from Ariodant)
Joseph (from Joseph. Tr of A peine au sortir de l'enfance)
Ô des amants le plus fidèle (from Ariodant)
"O lady fair." See "Femme sensible, entends-tu"

Méhul, Étienne Nicolas—*Continued*
O lover mine, most faithful-hearted. See Ô des amants le plus fidèle
Song of departure. See Le chant du départ
"Vainement Pharaon." See Champs paternels
"Vainly Pharaoh attempts." See Champs paternels

Meï, Lev Aleksandrovich
The canary (Tchaikovsky)
A child's song (Musorgskiĭ)
Cradle song (Rimskiĭ-Korsakov)
Gathering mushrooms (Musorgskiĭ)
Hebrew love-song (Rimskiĭ-Korsakov)
"Some one said unto the fool" (Tchaikovsky)
The song of Solomon (Musorgskiĭ)
To Russia (Balakirev)

"Mei dirndel is harb uf mi." See Der verschmähte

"Mei mutter mag mi nit." See Herzeleid

"Mei schatzerl." C. M. von Weber. Volkslied. g. ED 1
"Mei schatzerl" (My sweetheart) e.g. SSG

Meigs, Mrs M. N.
"Hark! a burst of heavenly music" (Schilling)
"There's a wonderful tree" (Schilling)

"Mein gläubiges herze frohlocke" ("My heart ever faithful, sing praises") J. S. Bach. e.g. HSS 1—PG 1
"My heart ever faithful." e. BD—SAS 1

"Mein Gott der ist mein Hirt" ("The Lord my Shepherd is") F. Liszt. e.g. HSS 3

"Mein herr maler, will er wohl uns abkonterfeien." See Ein familiengemälde

Mein Herr und Gott. For English translation see King's prayer (Wagner)

"Mein herz ist im Hochland." See "My heart's in the Highlands" (German folk air); "My heart's in the Highlands" (Jensen)

"Mein herz ist wie die dunkle nacht" ("My heart is like a dreary night") E. Lassen. ⌈Words by E. Geibel⌉ e.g. CS 2

"Mein herz ist wie die dunkle nacht" (Der mond.—The moon) F. Mendelssohn. Words by E. Geibel. e.g. CMF 1

"Mein herz schmückt sich mit dir" ("My heart all beauty takes from thee") A. Rubinstein. Words by F. Bodenstedt (Mirza-Schaffy) e.g. SC

"Mein hochgebor'nes schätzelein." See Des glockenthürmers töchterlein (Loewe)

"Mein, in des letzten sternes glanz." See For ever mine (Cantor)

"Mein lebenslauf ist lieb und lust." See Das reich der freude

"Mein liebster ist ein weber" ("My lover is a weaver") E. Hildach. e.g. SM 2

"Mein liebster wohnt' in fernem land." See "My love dwelt in a northern land" (Pasmore)

"Mein lied ist klein." See Untreu (Cornelius)

Mein pfeifchen ("Wenn mein pfeifchen dampft und glüht") Volksweise. Author of words unknown. g. ED 2

"Mein ross so müd' in dem stalle sich steht." See Lay of the imprisoned huntsman (Schubert)

"Mein schatz, der ist auf die wanderschaft hin." See Heimlicher liebe pein (Weber)

"Mein schatz ist a reiter." Volkslied. g. ED 1

"Mein schwan, mein stiller." See En svane (Grieg)

"Mein vater! hochgesegneter der helden." See Gebet des Amfortas (Wagner)

Meine freuden. See My delight (Chopin)

"Meine lebenszeit verstreicht." See Vom tode (Beethoven)

"Meine liebe ist grün" ("Like a blossoming lilac") J. Brahms. Words by F. Schumann. e.g. KF 2—KF 3—PG 3
"Meine liebe ist grün" (My heart is in bloom) e.g. FO 2

"Meine mus ist gegangen." See Meine muse (Lyra)

Meine muse. J. W. Lyra. Words by W. Müller. g. ED 1

"Meine ruh' ist hin" ("My peace is gone") Graben-Hoffmann. ⌈Words by Goethe⌉ e.g. KF 1—KF 2

"Meine ruh' ist hin" (Gretchen am spinnrade.—Gretchen at the spinning wheel) Schubert. Words by Goethe. e.g. MSS 1
Gretchen am spinnrade (Margaret at the spinning-wheel) e.g. PG 1
Margaret at the spinning-wheel. e. BC

"Meine seel' ist stille." See Gottergebenheit

Meine seele dürstet nach Gott. For English translation see As pants the hart (Mendelssohn)

Meine wünsche ("Ich möchte wohl der kaiser sein") W. A. Mozart. Words by J. W. L. Gleim. g. ED 2

"Meiner heimat schöne augen." See Des Magyaren heimweh

Meiner mutter. See To my mother (Bradsky)

Meixell, Granville H.
Rah-rah-rah for Midland (Composer unknown)

"Měla sem hołubka." See A fair dove

The melancholy nymph. Händel. Words by J. Gay. BE 8
"'Twas when the seas were roaring." JO

Meli, G.
Lu labbru

Melinda May. S. C. Foster (music and words) NMP

Melita (Dykes) See "Let glory be to God on high"; The people's prayer

Mellish, Miss
"My Phillida, adieu! love"

Mellish, R.
"Drink to me only with thine eyes" (attributed)
Only with thine eyes. See "Drink to me only with thine eyes" (attributed)

Mellon, Alfred
"Why linger, mourner memory"

The **mellow** horn. W. Jones. FSS 2—LA

Mellow notes of hunter's horn. FSS 7

Melodies of many lands. C. W. Glover. FSS 1—WBT

A **melody** ("They bore their cross") Chopin. e. KSE

Melville, A. P.
Re-united (Scottish air)

Melville, George John Whyte-. See Whyte-Melville, George John

Memmott, F. W., and Goodwin, F. D.
The royal purple (Bartlett)

Memorial day ("Marching proudly") Bohemian folk air. Words by R. Compton. DO

Memorial day ("Not costly domes") L. B. Marshall. Words by S. F. Smith. JS

Memorial day song ("Quiet our fallen heroes") W. B. Olds. Words by B. E. Bush. NMS

Memorial hymn ("Now all ye flow'rs") T. Allen. Words by D. Swing. TL

Memories of yore. See Brises d'autrefois (Hüe)

"Memories tender." See "Combien j'ai douce souvenance"

Memory song to Amherst. College song. CHS

Men of Harlech. See Rhyfelgyrch gwyr Harlech

"M'en vas à la fontaine." See À la fontaine

"Men! whose boast it is." See True freedom (Lang); True freedom (Silcher)

Mena, me' (Let me be) Canzone de Piedegrotta. P. M. Costa. Words by S. di Giacomo. e.i. MN

Menaeseus. N. Tcherepnin. Words by A. Maikov. e.f. NR 1

Menagerie. College song. MPC—WBT

Mend me my strings. See Hel mig mine strenge (Halvorsen)

Mendelssohn-Bartholdy, Felix
"Abide with me! fast falls the eventide"
"Ach, wie so bald verhallet der reigen"
Alone. See Sonntagslied
"And he journey'd with companions" (from Paulus)
The angel trio. See "Lift thine eyes"
As pants the hart (same air as "Abide with me! fast falls the eventide." Tr of Meine seele dürstet nach Gott)
"Auf flügeln des gesanges"
Auf wiedersehn. See "Es ist bestimmt in Gottes rath"

Autumn song. See "Ach, wie so bald verhallet der reigen"
"Be thou faithful unto death" (from Paulus)
Bei der wiege
Berlin. See "Abide with me! fast falls the eventide"; As pants the hart; "Sleep, noble hearts"; "Still, still with Thee"
Der blumenkranz. See "By Celia's arbor"
"Brightest and best"
But the Lord is mindful of his own (from Paulus)
"By Celia's arbor"
"Caro cibus, sanguis potus"
"Cast thy burden on the Lord" (from Elias)
Consolation. See "Abide with me! fast falls the hart; "Sleep, noble hearts"; "Still, still with Thee"
"Consume them all" (from Paulus)
Cradle song. See Bei der wiege
"Draw near, all ye people" (from Elias)
Das erste veilchen
"Es ist bestimmt in Gottes rath"
Farewell to the forest (Tr of Abschied vom walde)
A favorite place. See Lieblingsplätzchen
The favorite spot. See Lieblingsplätzchen
The first violet. See Das erste veilchen
"For know ye not" (from Paulus)
From days of old. See "Es ist bestimmt in Gottes rath"
The garland. See "By Celia's arbor"
"Glory to God in the highest is ringing"
God reigns (same air as "I waited for the Lord")
"God shall charge His angel legions"
"Gott sei mir gnädig" (from Paulus)
Greeting. See Gruss
Gruss
"Hark! the herald angels sing"
"He counteth all your sorrows" (from Lobgesang)
"Hear ye, Israel! hear what the Lord speaketh" (from Elias)
Herald angels. See "Hark! the herald angels sing"
Hunter's farewell. See Der jäger abschied
A hunter's song. See Jagdlied
The huntsmen's farewell. See Der jäger abschied
"I am a roamer bold and gay." See "Ich bin ein vielgereister mann"
"I waited for the Lord" (from Lobgesang. Tr of Ich harrete des Herrn)
I will sing of Thy great mercies (from Paulus)
I would that my love. See "Ich wollt' meine lieb' ergösse"

Mendelssohn-Bartholdy, Felix—*Continued*

"Ich bin ein vielgereister mann" (from Die heimkehr aus der fremde)
"Ich wollt' meine lieb' ergösse"
"If with all your hearts ye truly seek me" (from Elias)
"In heavenly love abiding"
The Indian girl's lament
Infelice
"Is not His word like a fire" (from Elias)
"It is enough" (from Elias)
"It is ordained by God's decree." See "Es ist bestimmt in Gottes rath"
Jagdlied
Der jäger abschied
"Jerusalem! Jerusalem! thou that killest the prophets" (from Paulus)
The lark
Die liebende schreibt
Lieblingsplätzchen
"Lift thine eyes, O lift thine eyes" (from Elias)
"Lone and joyless." See Infelice
"Lord at all times I will bless Thee." See "Caro cibus, sanguis potus"
"Lord God of Abraham" (from Elias)
The lover's message. See Die liebende schreibt
Der mond
The moon. See Der mond
"Mourn not." See "Es ist bestimmt in Gottes rath"
My sweetheart writes. See Die liebende schreibt
O for the wings of a dove. See "O könnt' ich fliegen wie tauben dahin"
"O God, have mercy" (from Paulus)
"O könnt' ich fliegen wie tauben dahin"
"O rest in the Lord" (from Elias)
"O strength and stay"
"O wert thou in the cauld blast"
"O wherefore do ye these things" (from Paulus)
"Oíd un son en alta esfera." See "Hark! the herald angels sing"
"On song's bright pinions." See "Auf flügeln des gesanges"
"On wings of song." See "Auf flügeln des gesanges"
Our song
Pilgerspruch
Reiselied
Resignation
Returning. See Reiselied
"Saviour, Source of every blessing" (same air as "God shall charge his angel legions")
"Show me, Almighty." See "Gott sei mir gnädig"
"Sing ye praise, all ye redeemed" (from Lobgesang)
"Sleep, gentle Babe"
"Sleep, noble hearts" (same air as "Abide with me! fast falls the eventide")
Song of parting. See "Es ist bestimmt in Gottes rath"

Sonntagslied
Spring song
"Still, still with Thee" (same air as "Abide with me! fast falls the eventide")
Suleika
Then shall the righteous shine forth (from Elias)
"There be none of beauty's daughters"
"This is the day." See Sonntagslied
Trust. See "God shall charge His angel legions"; "Saviour, Source of every blessing"
Venetianisches gondellied. See "When through the piazzetta"
Waldeinsamkeit (same air as Farewell to the forest)
Watch and ward. See "God shall charge His angel legions"
"Wenn sich zwei herzen scheiden"
"When through the piazzetta"
"Wisst ihr, wo ich gerne weil'." See Lieblingsplätzchen
Woe unto them who forsake Him (from Elias)
"Ye people, rend your hearts" (from Elias)
Zuleika. See Suleika

Mendès, Catulle
Clair de lune (Saint-Saëns)
L'heureux vagabond (Bruneau)

Mendonça, Henriques Lopez de. See Lopes de Mendonça, Henriques

"**Mene** nahgay nahgay." See In the forest

Menina Rosa (Miss Rosie) Portuguese song. e.po. BF 2

"As **meninas** de Camacha" (The little girls of Camacha) Song from Medeira. e.po. BF 2

"**Meninas**, vamos á dança." See Chamarrita

"**Mens** Nordhavet bruser mod fjeldbyg'd strand." See Det norske flag (Ibsen)

Mentra, Gwen (Venture, Gwen) Welsh song. e.w. BF 2

Menuet d'Exaudet (Exaudet's minuet) Words by Favart. e.f. CM 2—WB

Menyá tui v'tolpyé nye oöznála. See After years (Musorgskiï)

"**Menyböl** az angyal." See Christmas carol

La **mer.** See The sea (Borodin)

"La **mer** gronde et mugit." See The sea (Borodin)

"**Mer** jolie et bon vent." See Le brig black

Mercadante, Giuseppe Saverio Raffaele
"Ah! s'estinto ancor mi vuoi" (from Donna Caritea)
"Ah, since vainly I now implore thee." See "Ah! s'estinto ancor mi vuoi"
Bella, adorata incognita (from Il giuramento)
Blessed is He that cometh. See "Salve Maria"
"Brightly glows the morning star"
"Chi m'arresta" (from Medea)
La rosa

Mercadante, G. S. R.—*Continued*
The rose. See La rosa
"Salve Maria"
"Thousands of sins oppress me" (from Le sette parole di nostro Signore)
"Unto the hills"
"When to the lily fair" (from Le sette parole di nostro Signore)

Mercantini, Luigi
Inno di guerra dei cacciatori delle Alpi (Olivieri)
"**Mercè**, dilette amiche" ("Dear friends around me") G. Verdi. e.i. PP
"**Mercè**, dilette amiche" ("My thanks, beloved companions") e.i. MC

Mercer, Mary Speed
America for me
The flag of our country
United

Merch Megan ("I see her in dreams") See Megan's fair daughter

Merch Megan ("Oh, have you e'er seen") See Megan's daughter

"**Mercy** I cry, who all bewildered stand." Châtelain de Coucy. e. DT

The **mercy-seat**. See Retreat (Hastings)

"La **mère** Bontemps" ("Mother Bontemps") Bergerette. e.f. WB

Meredith, Owen, pseud. See Lytton, Edward Robert Bulwer-Lytton, 1st earl of

Merest, Mrs Maria Billington (Hawes) See Hawes, Maria Billington

Merezhkovskii, Dmitrii Sergieevich
"The Lord is risen! His praise is ringing" (Rachmaninov)
"Oh, no, I pray, do not depart" (Rachmaninov)

Merivale, Herman Charles
Venetian boat song (Blumenthal)

"**Merk**, toch hoe sterck." See Bergen op Zoom

The **mermaid** ("Oh, 'twas in the broad Atlantic") Arr by M. Watson. SSS
"Oh! 'twas in the broad Atlantic." BOS

The **mermaid** ("O were my men") Irish folk song. JOI

The **mermaid** ("On Friday morn") Folk song. BE 6—BOS—DM 1—MM
The mermaid ("'Twas Friday morn") CU— HSD—JSE— LA—MPC— NMH—NMS—SSS—WC
The stormy winds do blow. SMW

The **mermaid** ("Seht die sonnenstrahlen") See Die seejungfer (Haydn)

Mermaid's evening song. S. Glover. FSS 8

The **mermaid's** song ("Seht die sonnenstrahlen") See Die seejungfer (Haydn)

Merriam, Lillie Fuller
The mother-heart (Gaines)

Merrick, James
"To thy pastures fair and large" (Composer unknown)

Merrill, Lester R.
N. S. U. so gay

"**Merrily** every bosom boundeth." German air. FSS 2

"**Merrily**, merrily greet the morn." Round. BD—BSS—FSS 1—HSC—OH—TFC 1 —WBT

"**Merrily**, merrily rung the bells." See The bells of Saint Michael's tower (Knyvett)

Merrily, merrily sing. FSS 3—WSC

Merrily ring the bells. Air: Mandolinata. Words by C. Piersol. MCS

"**Merrily** the Easter bells." J. S. B. Hodges. Words by R. R. Chope. HC

"**Merrily** the Easter bells:" G. B. Lissant. Words by R. R. Chope. HC

Merrily we roll along. See "Good-night, ladies"

"**Merrily** we skip along." Children's song. WSC

Merriman, Samuel Sears
"Dear Bucknell"

"**Merry** all! merry all! and with holly deck the hall." See Welcome to Christmas

Merry autumn days. C. H. Congdon. Words by Dickens. JS

A **merry** ballad of the hawthorn tree. See The hawthorn tree

"The **merry** bells for us they ring." See Glad Christmas comes again (Sutcliffe)

Merry bells of long ago. A. Reichardt. Words by A. Douglas. MCS

"The **merry** birds." F. Gumbert. e. FSS 8

Merry Christmas ("Merry is December") S. Glover. Words by M. Ryan. MCS

"**Merry** Christmas bells are ringing." H. Kotzschmar. Words by M. E. Waite. HC

"The **merry** cuckoo, messenger of spring." M. Greene. Words by E. Spenser. MM

The **merry-go-round**. French folk air: Dame Tartine. Words by H. H. Harbour. DO

The **merry** Gregorians. H. Carey (music and words) MM

The **merry** haymakers. Folk air. Modern words by S. Baring-Gould. BSW

A **merry** heart. See Funiculì-funiculà (Denza)

"The **merry** hours of youth." G. Rossini. FSS 6

"**Merry** is December, merry as the May." See Merry Christmas (Glover)

Merry joy bells ring. J. L. Molloy. Words by R. Selden. MCS

A **merry** life. See Funiculì-funiculà (Denza)

The **merry** maidens. Dutch song. e. KSN

The **merry** May. Swiss air. FSS 7

Merry may the keel row. See The keel row

"A **merry**, merry Christmas! a merry Christmas, oh." See The best of holidays

"**Merry**, merry Christmas bells." G. E. Oliver. LA

The **merry** milkmaids. Air: The merry, merry milke maids. Words by M. Parker. JE

"The **merry** month begins today." See May

"**Merry** of heart, ye song-birds." See Sweet song-bird (Molloy)

The **merry** sportsman. German folk song. e. DO

The **merry** Swiss boy. e. FSS 3—WSC

Merry wives of Windsor. Old song. DM 2

Mertens, Joseph
Lied (French tr of Es fällt ein stern herunter)
Song. See Lied

Mes esta dí ("Glad news from Bethlehem, my comrade") Noël provençal. Ranquet. e. MF

"**Mes** larmes d'amour ont fait naître." See Flowers of love (Borodin)

"**Mes** vers fuiraient, doux et frêles." See Si mes vers avaient des ailes (Hahn)

"**Mes** yeux pleuraient en rêve." See Invocation (Rhodes)

Meshcherskiï,
Bist du (Liszt)

"**Mess** Parson Hogg shall now maintain." See Parson Hogg

The **message** ("Kommt a vogerl") See Botschaft (Brahms)

The **message** ("Whither, wee bird") Bohemian song. Moschelles. e. KSE

The **message** ("Ye birds that sing sweetly") H. Purcell. MM

"A **message** from our Father." See The Christmas message (Bianco)

The **message** of Christmas morn. See Lei pastorieu

The **message** of love. See "Ô légère hirondelle" (Gounod)

The **message** of Mary. See De boodschap van Maria

The **message** of the rose. See Der rose sendung (Himmel)

Messager, André Charles Prosper
"Day of thanksgiving" (from La Basoche)

Messager, Mme Hope (Temple) See Temple, Hope

Messages. See Aufträge (Schumann)

The **messenger.** Polish song. Chopin. e. KSE—WL

The **messenger** bird. Mrs Arkwright. Words by Mrs Hemans. JO

The **messenger** nightingale. See Le rossignol messager

Messiah: selection. Händel. TL

"**Messiah!** at Thy glad approach." See O Zion, hail thy King

Messiter, Arthur Henry
Marion. See "Rejoice ye pure in heart"
"Rejoice ye pure in heart"

Met sine rijfstoc, met sine strijcstoc. See "Des winters als het reghent"

Les **métamorphoses** (Metamorphosis) Old French folk song. e.f. TSF

Metamorphosis. See Les métamorphoses

"A **meteor** bright its wondrous light." E. Lemare. HC

Methfessel, Albert Gottlieb
Abendlied, wenn man aus dem wirtshaus geht
Abschied
An junge spröde schönen. See "Ich sah ein röschen am wege stehn"
Battle-cry of freedom. See Vaterlandslied
Deutsche mahnung
Deutscher ehrenpreis
Deutscher freiheit schlachtruf. See Vaterlandslied
Deutsches weihelied
Gesang ausziehender krieger
Hymn
"Ich sah ein röschen am wege stehn"
"Der knabe Robert"
Kriegers abschied
The light that is felt
Our native song
Rheinweinlied
Sweet will of God
Vaterlandslied
"While shepherds watched their flocks"

Metner, Nikolai. See Medtner, Nikolaï

"**Metsän** puita tuuli tuudittaa." See Polka

Metschersky. See Meshcherskiï,

Metz, Theodore A.
A hot time in the old town

Metzger, Anna
"When she is gone"

"**Meu** anjo" (My angel) Brazilian folk song. e.po. HF

Mexican national hymn. See Himno nacional de Mejico (Nunó)

Mexican song. See "Is there a heart which saucy love"

"**Mexicanos** al grito de guerra." See Himno nacional de Mejico (Nunó)

Mey, Lev Alexandrovitch. See Meï, Lev Aleksandrovich

Meyer, G.
Bliss. See Seligkeit
Seligkeit

Meyerbeer, Giacomo
"Adamastor, roi des vagues profondes" (from L'Africaine)
"Ah figliuol! mio figliuol." See "Ah! mon fils"
"Ah! mon fils" (from Le prophète)
"Ah! mon remords te venge" (from Dinorah)
"Ah! my son." See "Ah! mon fils"
"Ah! now I feel the burden." See "Ah! mon remords te venge"
Cantique du Trappiste
Chant du chasseur (from Dinorah)
"Ditemi, buona gente, vedeste Dinorah" (from Dinorah)
"Donnez, donnez" (from Le prophète)
"Du schönes fischermädchen"
"Fille des rois" (from L'Africaine)
Finita è pei frati (from Les Huguenots)

Meyerbeer, Giacomo —*Continued*
The fishermaiden.   See "Du schönes fischermädchen"
Già l'ira m'abbandona (from Le prophéte.   Tr of Ô toi qui m'abandonnes)
"Give ye, gay lords."   See "Nobles seigneurs, salut"
Gone are the days.   See Ô jours heureux
"Guide au bord ta nacelle."   See "Du schönes fischermädchen"
Invocation.   See Nonnes qui reposez
Le jour est levé.   See Chant du chasseur
"King Adamastor, the ruler of ocean."   See "Adamastor, roi des vagues profondes"
"Lieti signor, salute."   See "Nobles seigneurs, salut"
"Light-flitting shadow."   See "Ombre légère"
Der moench
Il monaco.   See Der moench
The monk.   See Der moench
The monks and their convents.   See Finita è pei frati
"Nel lasciar la Normandia" (from Roberto il diavolo)
No, caso egual giammai.   See Non, non, non, vous n'avez jamais
No, I'll engage that you have never.   See Non, non, non, vous n'avez jamais
"Nobil donna e`tanto onesta"
"Nobles seigneurs, salut" (from Les Huguenots)
Noblest of knights.   See "Nobles seigneurs, salut"
Non, non, non, vous n'avez jamais (from Les Huguenots)
Nonnes qui reposez (from Robert le diable)
Ô jours heureux (from L'étoile du nord)
O lieti di.   See Ô jours heureux
"O lovely fishermaiden."   See "Du schönes fischermädchen"
Ô paradis sorti de l'onde (from L'Africaine)
O paradise, from bright waves risen.   See Ô paradis sorti de l'onde
Oh, paradise to earth awarded.   See Ô paradis sorti de l'onde
"Ombra leggiera."   See "Ombre légère"
"Ombre légère" (from Dinorah)
Our songs of joy and gladness
Plus blanche que la blanche hermine (from Les Huguenots)
"Robert! Robert."   See "Roberto, o tu che adoro"
"Roberto, o tu che adoro" (from Robert le diable.   Tr of Robert, toi que j'aime)
"Sei vendicata assai."   See "Ah! mon remords te venge"
Shadow song.   See "Ombre légère"

Song of the Trappist.   See Cantique du Trappiste
"Sweeter than the breath of morning."   See "Nobil donna è tanto onesta"
"Tell me, ye friendly neighbors, have ye seen Dinorah."   See "Ditemi, buona gente, vedeste Dinorah"
"To you, my lords, a greeting."   See "Nobles seigneurs, salut"

Meyer-Helmund, Erik
The daily question.   See "Du fragst mich täglich"
Dein gedenk' ich, Margareta
"Du fragst mich täglich"
I think of thee, sweet Margareta.   See Dein gedenk' ich, Margareta
Maiden's song (Tr of Mädchenlied)
"Morgens send' ich dir die veilchen"
Queen of night
Thee I think of, Margherita.   See Dein gedenk' ich, Margareta
Thou art near me, Margarita.   See Dein gedenk' ich, Margareta
"Violets for thee I gather."   See "Morgens send' ich dir die veilchen"
The warning.   See Warnung
Warnung

Di **mezinke** ausgegeben.   See My youngest one is wedded
"**M'ha** preso alla sua ragna" ("'Tis love, that rogue so wily") P. D. Paradies.   e.i.   PA 2
A' **mhaighdean** àluinn (The peerless maiden. —"Sing the praises o' my dearie") Air: Slàn gu'n till na Gaidheil ghasda.   Words from the Gaelic of Fionn (H. Whyte) e.   HSSS
A' mhaighdean àluinn ("Sing the praises o' my dearie") e.   MMS
"A **Mháirghréad**, a Mháirghréad, a Mháirghréad na Róiste."   See Máirghréad na Róiste
A **mhuirnin** geal mo chroidhe.   See Bright darling of my heart
"**Mi** dicesti come lieta."   See Statt' attiente
"**Mi** gh'òo vuna sorella."   See Rachella
"**Mi** mamá me consejaba."   Costa Rican folk song.   e.s.   HS
Mi Pepa.   Spanish-American song.   e.s.   LSS
"**Mi** pizzica, mi muzzica."   See Tarantella
"**Mi** sono innamorato d'una stella."   See Una stella (Mililotti)
Mi sueño.   Mexican folk song.   e.s.   HS
Mi sueño (My dream) e.s.   HF
"La **mia** letizia infondere" ("So charming her voice") G. Verdi.   e.i.   OPS 3
"La **mia** letizia infondere" ("So sweet her voice")   e.i.   FSS 7
"La **mia** Linda es de Castilla."   See Linda mia
"**Mich** ergreift, ich weiss nicht wie."   See Tischlied (Eberwein)
"**Mich** fliehen alle freuden."   See "Nel cor piú non mi sento" (Paisiello)
Michael Roy.   Old song.   HSD—MPC—WBT—WC

Michelemmà (Fishermen's song) Neapolitan folk song. e.i. MSI
The fishermen's song. e. BSE

"Michié Préval." Negro creole folk song. e.f. KA

Mickiewicz, Adam
Ah! the torment (Paderewski)
My delight (Chopin)

Mickle, William Julius
There's nae luck about the house (Scottish air) Authorship uncertain; attributed also to J. Adam

"'Mid a wealth of roses." See Schlummerlied (Mattei)

"The mid-day sun is pouring his scorching beams along the sky." See The noontide ray (Auber)

"'Mid fair maidens longtime I sought the fairest." See Donna Clara (Gastaldon)

"'Mid fire and dense smoke." See Polish patriotic hymn

"'Mid grasses green, I dream the hours away." See Feldeinsamkeit (Brahms)

'Mid lures, 'mid pleasures. See Lascia ch'io pianga (Händel)

"'Mid pleasures and palaces though we may roam." See Home, sweet home (Bishop); Home, sweet home, and Rubinstein's melody (arranged)

"'Mid scenes of confusion and creature complaints." See The saints' sweet home

"'Mid the stress of dire misfortune." See Senza timore (Sieber)

"'Mid the winter storms we're sleeping." See Waking flowers (Reissman)

The mid-watch. T. Linley. Words by R. B. Sheridan. BE 3—ME

"Mid wither'd grass and mosses." See Violen (Svendsen)

"'Mid woods and forest treasure." See The hunter's song (Hullah)

Middleton, John C.
"The risen Lord to-day is King" (Redner)
"Sing your carols to-day" (Warren)

A midnight madrigal. See The fairy

"The midnight moon." S. Glover. Words by Crawford. FSS 8

"Midnight peace is resting on the mountain peaks." See Wanderers nachtlied (Rubinstein)

"Midnight, O Christian, 'tis the hour so solemn." See Cantique de Noël (Adam)

Midnight tryst. Ojibway Indian song of elopement. e.in. BA

The midshipmite. S. Adams. Words by F. E. Weatherly. CHS—CU—FSS 8 —HSC—HSD— MP—MPC— NMH— WBT—WSW

"Midst roses sweet." See "I rosens doft" (Gustaf)

"Midst the bright sheen of the mirror-like waters." See Auf dem wasser zu singen (Schubert)

Midsummer carol. Folk song. BE 3— BSW

Midsummer night's dream ("You spotted snakes") G. A. Macfarren. Words by W. Shakespeare. TL

A midsummer song. F. Abt. Words by R. W. Gilder. LBR

Miehl,
Endzweck der schöpfung

"Might I linger anear thee." See "Star vicino" (Rosa)

The mighty deep. W. H. Jude (music and words) AB 4—KF 4

"A mighty fortress is our God." See "Ein' feste burg" (Luther)

"Mighty Lord, and King all glorious." Bach. e. OS 4—SAS 4

Migliorato, A.
Lu carcerato p'ammore (Biscardi)

Mignon ("Connais-tu le pays") See "Connais-tu le pays" (Thomas, Ambroise)

Mignon ("Kennst du das land") See "Kennst du das land" (Beethoven); "Kennst du das land" (Himmel); "Kennst du das land" (Reichardt); "Kennst du das land" (Romberg); "Kennst du das land" (Wolf)

Mignon ("Know'st thou the land") Arthur Goring Thomas. Words by Goethe. [Tr of "Kennst du das land"] e. DM 1

Mignonette. J. B. Wekerlin. Words by A. Leroux. e.f. CMF 2

"Mignonne, ma mignonne." See La chanson des métamorphoses (Breton version)

"Mignonne, sais-tu comment." See Le mariage des roses (Franck)

"Mignonne, see, April is here." See Sérénade du passant (Massenet)

"Mignonne, tu dis que tu m'aimes." See A dissonance (Borodin)

"Mignonne, voici l'avril." See Sérénade du passant (Massenet)

Mignons lied. See "Kennst du das land" (Liszt)

Mignon's slumber-song. See "De son coeur j'ai calmé la fievre" (Thomas)

Mignon's song. See "Kennst du das land" (Liszt)

Miguez, Leopoldo
Hymn of the proclamation of the republic. See Hymno da proclamacao da republica
Hymno da proclamacao da republica National air of the United States of Brazil. See Hymno da proclamacao da republica

"Mihi est propositum." R. L. de Pearsall. Words attributed to W. Map. e.l. SSS

Mïjāna. See "Three maiden lovers"

Mi-ka-thi. Ponka Indian warrior's song. in. FIS

"Miks' riudut sa ihmisrinta." See Sing thou, sing (Järnefelt)

"Mīlādek ayyūha-l-masikh ilāhuna." See Christmas chant

"Mild and softly he is smiling." See Isolde's liebestod (Wagner)

"Mild is the sun on this soft dewy morning." See The marsh of Rhuddlan

Mild Mabel Kelly ("As when the softly blushing rose") Irish air: Donnel O'Graedh. Words from the Irish. e. MMI

"Mild und leise wie er lächelt." See Isolde's liebestod (Wagner)

"Mild wie ein lufthauch." See Bist du (Liszt)

"Mildes, warmes frühlingswetter." See Palmsonntag (Reichardt)

"A mile an' a bittock." W. A. Barratt. Words by R. L. Stevenson. SSS

Miles, Roger
  "Si j'étais jardinier" (Chaminade)

Mililotti, Leopoldo
  "Cade la sera"
  Heart-broken mariner. See Povero marinar
  Heart-broken sailor boy. See Povero marinar
  My star. See Una stella
  Povero marinar
  "Shadows of evening." See "Cade la sera"
  Una stella

De milk-white horses. See Gideon's band

The milking pail. See "Ye nymphs and sylvan gods"

Milkmaid's song. H. Parker. Words by Tennyson. AA

Mill May ("The strawberries grow") FSS 1

Mill of the valley. See "In einem kühlen grunde"

The mill wheel ("Da droben auf jenem berge") See Das mühlrad

The mill-wheel ("The mill-wheels are clapping") Kindergarten song. [Tr of Es klappert die mühle am rauschenden bach] e. FSS 1—WBT—WSC

"The mill-wheels are clapping." See The mill-wheel

Millard, Harrison
  Viva l'America

Millard, Mrs Philip. See Millard, Mrs Virtue

Millard, Mrs Virtue
  Alice Gray
  A thousand a year

Miller, Edward
  I prithee send me back my heart

Miller, Mrs Emily Clark (Huntington)
  New Year song (Oehmler)

Miller, James
  Bonnie Doon
  "Ye banks and braes o' bonnie Doon." See Bonnie Doon

Miller, Joaquin
  Christmas once a year (Composer unknown)
  Columbus (German air)

Miller, Johann Martin
  Abschiedsabend (Weiss)
  "Auf, ihr meine deutschen brüder" (18th century air)

"Das ganze dorf versammelt sich" (Volksweise)
  Der gärtner (Sievers)
  Zufriedenheit (music by Mozart; Neefe)

Miller, Thomas
  Christmas joy forever (Converse)

The miller and his sons. Folk song. BSW

The miller of the Dee ("There dwelt a miller, hale and bold") Words by C. Mackay. FSS 2—HSD—LA—WBT

The miller of the Dee ("There was a jolly miller once") 17th century air: The budgeon it is a delicate trade. BOS—MM
  The jolly miller. WSC
  The miller of Dee. BE 6
  "There was a jolly miller once." BAS 1—BOH—DM 1—HSE 1—JE

"The miller's big dog lay on the barn-floor." See Bingo (as sung at Brown)

The miller's daughter ("Der sto tre skjelmer") See Möllervisen

The miller's daughter ("Down the stream so cheerily") Bohemian air. FSS 3

The miller's daughter ("If e'er my heart's best treasure") Air: Merch y melinydd. Words from the Welsh. e. MMW

The miller's man. Salzburger song. e. KSE

The miller's tears. Hebrew air. Words by Warshavsky. e. CST

The miller's wedding. Old English air. Words by H. Woodward. BE 4

Millevoye, Charles Hubert
  Vieille chanson (Bizet)

Milligan, Alice
  Fainne geal an lae (Irish air)

Milliken, Richard Alfred
  "The groves of Blarney" (Composer unknown)

Millocker, E.
  Entrance song (from The beggar student)

"Millom bakkar og berg utmed havet" ("'Mong the rocks by the North sea's blue waters") Air: Dei vil altid klaga og kjyta. Words by I. Aasen. e.n. MAN

Millom rosor (Amid roses) F. Beyer. Words by K. Janson. e.n. WM 1

Mills, Mrs Elizabeth (King)
  The blessed country (Himmel)

Mills, John Proctor
  A moonlight song (Cadman)

The millwheel ("Da droben auf jenem berge") See Das mühlrad

Milnes, Richard Monckton. See Houghton, Richard Monckton Milnes, 1st baron

Milton, John
  "By dimpled brook" (Arne)
  "By the gaily circling glass" (Arne)
  "Haste thee, nymph" (Arnold)
  Let me wander not unseen (Händel)
  "Let us with a gladsome mind" (Composer unknown)

Milton, John—*Continued*
"Love virtue" (Clarke)
The Nativity, Stanzas from (Smith)
No war nor battle sound (Zundel)
"Now Phoebus sinketh in the west"
(Arne)
"**Min** elskte, jeg er bunden" ("A magic
power") H. Kjerulf. Words by J. S.
Welhaven.   e.n.   SSN
"**Min** fader han har sagt."   See Tre löften
(Beckman)
"**Min** hvide svane."   See En svane (Grieg)
Min lilla vrå bland bergen (My home 'midst
hills and valleys) J. Sandström.
Words by J. A. Wadman.   e.sw.
HSOS
"**Min** söde brud, min unge viv."   See Van-
dring i skoven (Grieg)
"**Min** tankes tanke ene du er vorden."   See
Jeg elsker dig (Grieg)
Min vän, min vän, och älskogsblomma.
See "Kristallen den fina"
Minas, bishop
"Glad tidings, oh, Armenian bards"
Nor oghchioon.   See "Glad tidings,
oh, Armenian bards"
"**Mind** my sister how you walk on de
cross."   See Oh, Jerusalem
"**Mine** eyes are turn'd to de hebbenly gate."
See Stay in de field
"**Mine** eyes have seen the glory."   See
Battle hymn of the republic
Mine own.   Words by D. M. Mulock.
FSS 6
"**Mine** tanker" ("My thoughts") J. P. E.
Hartmann.   Words by W. Gregersen.
da.e.   WM 1
"**Mine**, when the last star hangs on high."
See For ever mine (Cantor)
Mingled melodies.   Double round.   French
and English airs.   TFC 2
"**Ministri** dell' averno."   See Già l'ira
m'abbandona (Meyerbeer)
Minka ("From the Volga was he riding")
Cossack love song.   e.   BMC—WBT
"**Minka**, I must go to-morrow."   See Beau-
tiful Minka
Minnelied ("Holder klingt der vogelsang."
—Love song) J. Brahms.   Words
by H. Hölty.   e.g.   CMF 1—FF—
FO 2—PG 3.   e. only FTS
Love song.   e.   BD—WBW
Minnelied ("Ich spring an disem ringe."—
Minstrelsong)   Minnesingers' song.
e.g.   BO
Minskii, N.
"As fair is she as noonday-light"
(Rachmaninov)
"The **minster** bells have ceased to peal."
See Pardoned (Piccolomini)
The **minstrel** ("Durch feld und wald") See
Der musensohn (Schubert)
The **minstrel** ("Keen blaws the wind o'er
Donocht-head") Scottish air: Mary's
dream.   Words by G. Pickering and C.
Gray.   PS 2
"**Minstrel**, awaken."   See "Sönner af Nor-
ge" (Blom)

"The **minstrel** boy."   Air: The moreen.
Words by T. Moore.   BAS 1—BO—
BOS—BS 1—CS 1—CST—DSH—EF—
FSI—FSS 1—GO—HSC— JO—JSE—
MI—MMI—MP— MS—MSS 1—PI—
SN—SS 1—TFC 2—TS—WA—WBT—
WCP—WSW
"The **minstrel** guards the standard as
his right."   See Die fahnenwacht
(Lindpaintner)
"A **minstrel** wild, I wreath with flowers."
See The mountain minstrel
The **minstrel's** request.   Words by W.
Scott.   FSS 8—HSE 2
The **minstrel's** return.   Words by W.
Scott.   JO
Minstrelsong.   See Minnelied
Minuet ("Among the things that linger
yet") S. Taneieff.   Words after C.
d'Orias.   e.   NM 2
"**Minuit**, Chrétien, c'est l'heure solennelle."
See Cantique de Noël (Adam)
"**Minun** kultani kaunis on."   See The gay
young bachelor
The **minute** gun at sea.   M. P. King.
Words by R. S. Sharpe.   JO
"Il **mio** bel foco" ("My ardent longing")
B. Marcello.   e.i.   FEI 2
"Il **mio** bel foco" ("My joyful ardor")
e.i.   PA 1
"Il **mio** bel foco" ("When I am near
thee")   e.i.   PG 4
"Il **mio** ben quando verrà" ("When, my
love, wilt thou return") G. Paisiello.
e.i.   PA 1
"Il **mio** core non è con me" (My heart is
no longer mine) R. Fedeli.   e.i.   FEI 2
"Il **mio** tesoro intanto" ("Cheer thee, my
soul's treasure") W. A. Mozart.
e.i.   OPS 3
"Il **mio** tesoro intanto" ("Meanwhile,
go seek")   e.i.   SOA 3
"Il **mio** tesoro intanto" ("To my be-
loved hasten")   e.i.   KS 4
"**Mir** blühet kein frühling."   See Der trau-
ernde
"**Mir** blüht eine stelle."   See Hoffnung und
erinnerung (Reichardt)
"**Mir** ist, als müsst ich dir was sagen."   L.
Spohr.   Schottisches lied.   g.   ED 2
"**Mir** ist auf der welt nichts lieber."   See
Die schöne nachbarin (Winter)
"**Mir** ist erbarmung widerfahren" ("I have
received Thy mercy") G. Pressel.   e.g.
HSS 1—HSS 2—HSS 3
"**Mir** ist leide."   L. Erk.   Words by graf
Kraft von Toggenburg.   g.   ED 3
"**Mir** ist's so eng allüberall."   See In's
freie (Schumann)
"**Mir** klingt ein ton so wunderbar."   See
Ein ton (Cornelius)
"**Mir** träumte einst ein schöner traum."
See Ein traum (Grieg)
"**Mir** träumte von einem königskind" ("I
dreamed of a pallid princess-maid") L.
Hartmann.   Words by H. Heine.
e.g.   AB 3

"Mira el mar cuya belleza." See Torna a Surriento (Curtis)

Le miracle de Saint-Nicolas (The miracle of Saint Nicholas) French folk song. e.f. TSF

Le miracle du nouveau-né (The miracle of the new-born child) French Canadian folk song. e.f. BFS

The miracle of Saint Nicholas. See Le miracle de Saint-Nicolas

The miracle of the cock. See King Pharaoh: The miracle of the cock

The miracle of the new-born child. See Le miracle du nouveau-né

The miraculous harvest. See King Pharaoh: The miraculous harvest

"Mirella doth not know she holdeth." See Chant provençal (Massenet)

"Mirelle ne sait pas encore." See Chant provençal (Massenet)

Miriam's song. See Sound the loud timbrel (Reinecke)

Mirjam's siegsgesang. See Sound the loud timbrel (Reinecke)

"Mirk an' rainy is the nicht." See O! are ye sleepin', Maggie

"The mirk is gathering in the glen." See Highland cradle song

The mirk night o' December. See "O May, thy morn was ne'er so sweet"

Miruj, miruj, srce moje. See Be still my heart

Mirza Schaffy, pseud. See Bodenstedt, Friedrich Martin von

The miser-woman and the crucifix. See La femme avare et le crucifix

"Misero Bernardone" ("O wretched Bernardone") D. Cimarosa. e.i. KS 5

"Misero! io vengo meno." See Non m'è grave morir per amore (Marcello)

Miska and Panni (Sarga csizsmas Miska sárbran jar.—"Miska came clad in red") Hungarian folk song. Air: Magasan repül a daru szépen szól. e. BMC

"Miska came clad in red." See Miska and Panni

Miss Dawson's hornpipe. See Nancy Dawson

"Miss Em'ly was a maid so fair." See Edwin in the lowlands low (Tennessee version)

Miss Lucy Long. Negro song. HSD

Miss Rosie. See Menina Rosa

The mission of a rose. F. H. Cowen. Words by C. Bingham. MSF 1— WBW

"Missionaries us have told." See Japanese Christmas song

Missionary hymn. See "From Greenland's icy mountains" (Mason)

"A missive unto her I'll send." Swedish song. e. KSN—WL

Missouri. University of Missouri song. Words by G. Hauchope. CHS

Mister Banjo. See Musieu Bainjo

"Mr John Blunt." Composer and author of words unknown. BOS

The mistletoe bough. H. R. Bishop. Words by T. H. Bayly. BSE—HSE 3 —JO

"The mistletoe hung in the castle hall." See Mistletoe bough (Bishop)

Mistral, Frédéric
"La belle table est mise" (Provençal Noël)
Magali (Provençal air)

"Mistress Mary, quite contrary." Nursery song. FMB—WBT—WSC

Mistress Santa Claus. A. Lee. Words by A. S. Shelton. FSS 5—MCS

Mistress Shady. BSS—TFC 2

"The mists are hanging low." See On the Georgian hills (Rimskiĭ-Korsakov)

"Mit deinen blauen augen" ("Avec tes yeux, Mignonne."—"Thine eyes so blue and tender") E. Lassen. [Words by H. Heine] e.f.g. KF 3
Eyes blue and dreaming. e.g. FSS 6
"Mit deinen blauen augen" ("Thine eyes so blue and tender") e.g. FMB
"Thine eyes are blue and tender." e.g. NML
"Thine eyes so blue and dreaming." e. JS—JSE
"Thine eyes so blue and tender." e. WA—WBT—WL—WSW

"Mit deinen blauen augen." For Swedish and English translations with a different air see Svärmeri (Arlberg)

"Mit dem pfeil, dem bogen." See Der schütz (Weber)

Mit einem gemalten band (With a painted ribbon) L. van Beethoven. Words by J. W. von Goethe. e.g. FM

Mit einer primula veris. See Med en primulaveris (Grieg)

Mit födeland (My native land) L. M. Ibsen. Words by O. Wolf. e.n. MAN

Mit hjerte og min lyre. See My heart and lute (Kjerulf)

"Mit kein gebetene." See The uninvited aunt

"Mit lust thät ich ausreiten." See Jagdlied (Mendelssohn)

"Mit myrthen und rosen" ("With myrtle and roses") R. Schumann. Words by H. Heine. e.g. FO 1

"Mit rheinwein füllt den becher." See Am Rhein und beim wein (Ries)

"Mit tausendfacher schöne begrüsst der lenz die flur." See Mancherlei freuden

Mitchell, Clarence B.
The orange and the black—Princeton (Shackelton)

Mitchell, Humphrey
"Blessed are the pure in heart"

Mitchell, S. N.
"Just touch the harp gently" (Blamphin)

"Mitt lif är en våg." See Vågen (Laurin)

"Mitten im schimmer der spiegelnden wellen." See Auf dem wasser zu singen (Schubert)

Mizpah. See "God be with you" (Tomer)

"Mme voglio i a'nzo rare." See La ricciolella

"Mnogaia ljeta." See Greeting ("To thee and thine")

"Mnogo přesen slykhal na rodnoĭ storonĩe." See The little cudgel

Mnye li molodsú razoodálomu. See The call of freedom (Balakirev)

"Mo bouchaleen bwee." See My yellow-haired lad

Mo chraoibhin cno. See "A sword of light hath pierced the dark"

"Mo chreach a's mo dhíachairt" (My sorrow and trouble) Irish folk song. e.ir. JOI

"Mo connin, zins zens, ma mourri." See Ma mourri

Mo dhachaidh. For English translation see My ain hoose

Mo nighean chruinn, donn ("Since my loved one has gone") Old Gaelic song. e. HSSS—MMS

Mo nighean donn ("Singing ho, rova ho."— My brown maid) Old Gaelic song. e. HSSS

Mo nighean donn, bhòidheach ("Horo, my brown-haired maiden") See Ho-ro mo nighean donn, bhòidheach

"Mo parlé Rémon, Rémon." See Rémon, Rémon

Mo rùn geal dìleas (My faithful fair one.— "O, could I be, love, in form of seagull") Scottish air. Words by Maclean. e. MMS
Mo rùn geal, dìleas (My faithful fond one) e.ga. SSS

Moan to the moon (Waiksel ööl) Esthonian folk song. e.es. BF 1

Moanalua. See Hawaiian hula

Moani ke ala. See My sweet (Leleiohoku)

Moberly, C. E.
Floreat Rugbeia

Mobile bay. Negro capstan chantey. CR

Mochalov, P.
"O, thou sun, thou blessed, glowing sun" (Slonov)

"Moch's mi g eirdle sa Mhaduinn." Boat song. e.ga. SMW

"The mocking-bird is singing sweet." See Listen, my lady (Kent)

Mocking bird song ("Rain, people, rain") Tigua Indian song. e.in. FIS

A model college girl. CHS

Moderati, C.
Canto pel Natale

Moderen synger (The mother sings) C. Sinding. Words by V. Krag. e.n. EF—KF 1—SSN

The modern beau. H. Carey (music and words) ME

Modern patriotic war march. See Turkish patriotic song (Nedjib Pacha)

Modinha ("Wherefore have thy lips denied me") Portuguese folk song. e.po. BO

Modo delle lavandaie (Song of the washwoman near Palermo) Sicilian song. e.i. BF 2

Moe, Jørgen Engebretsen
Saetergjentens söndag (Bull)
Ungbirken (music by Egeberg; Grieg)

Møen paa baalet (Ole and Christine) Danish folk song. e. GO

Der moench (The monk.—Il monaco) G. Meyerbeer. e.g.i. KF 4

Moetje varen ("There lingered a lassie") J. J. H. Verhulst. d.e. BDF

Moffat, Alfred
"Carol, Christian children"

Moffat, Kate R.
Cupid's trick (Composer unknown)
The exultant lover (Welsh air)
Highland cradle song (Scottish air)
Noon and eve (Welsh air)
The old weaver (Welsh air)
Shadows at play (Welsh air)
"A welcome, sweet summer" (Welsh air)

Mohr, Josef
Die heilige nacht (Gruber)
"Holy night! peaceful night" (Barnby. Tr of Die heilige nacht)
"Holy night, silent night" (Arr by Haydn. Tr of Die heilige nacht)
"Silent night! hallow'd night" (Composer unknown. Tr of Die heilige nacht)

Mohring, F.
"To the bravest"

Moir, Frank Lewis
Best of all
"Good night, good night beloved"
Only once more
"Over the heather"
"Who shall be fairest"

Móirín ni Chealla (Moreen O'Kelly.—The pilgrimage to Skellig) Irish folk song. e. JOI

Le mois de mai (The month of May) Chant de quête de la Bresse. e.f. TSF

O moisikos. See The musician (Christopulos?)

Les moissonneurs. See The reapers (Vassilenko)

Moladh na landaidh (The praise of Islay.— "See afar yon hill Ardmore") Ancient Gaelic song. e. HSSS—MMS

Molbech, Christian Knud Frederik
"Jeg synge skal en vise" (Hartmann)

The mole-catcher. Folk song. BSW

Molina, Ramon P.
Guatemala, en tu limpia bandera (Alvarez)

Molique, Wilhelm Bernhard
"And the Lord looked down from heaven" (from Abraham)
Commit thy ways unto the Lord. See "Wirf alle deine sorg'"
Der gesang Miriams. See "Sound the loud timbrel"
The heavenly rest. See Himmlische ruhe
Himmlische ruhe
"I will extoll Thee, my God, O King" (from Abraham)

Molique, Wilhelm Bernhard—*Continued*
"Lead me, O Lord" (from Abraham)
"Pour out thy heart before the Lord" (from Abraham)
The song of Miriam. See "Sound the loud timbrel"
"Sound the loud timbrel"
"They kept not the law" (from Abraham)
"Wirf alle deine sorg' "

Möllervisen (The miller's daughter) Norse folk song. e.n. MAN. e. only GO

Mollie darling. W. S. Hays (music and words) HSC—WBT

Molloy, James Lyman
An Arbor day song
The boatswain's story
The clang of the wooden shoon
Claudine
Clochette
"Come, take thy harp"
Darby and Joan
The dustman
"In the gloaming little children" (wrongly attributed) See Harrison, A. F. "In the gloaming little children"
"Jamie! Jamie"
The Kerry dance
The king's highway
The little tin soldier
London bridge
Love's old sweet song
Merry joy bells ring
The nightingale
Punchinello
Rose-Marie
"Sing a song at twilight." See Love's old sweet song
Story of the nightingale. See The nightingale
Sweet song-bird
Thursday
"The wind may shout"

Molly bawn ("Come, all you young gallants") Irish folk song. JOI

Molly bawn ("O Molly bawn, why leave me pining") S. Lover (music and words) PI

Molly Carew ("Och hone! oh, what will I do") Air: Planxty Reilly. Words by S. Lover. JO—MMI

Molly Lepell. Old English air. Words by earl of Chesterfield and Mr Pulteney. BE 7

"Molly Van was a-walking." See Shooting of his dear (Tennessee version)

Molly's hoop. See O mother, a hoop

Momotaro (The peach boy) Japanese children's song. e.j. BF 2

"Mon amour, comme il me tarde." See The tell-tale stars (Cherepnin)

"Mon chant est amer et sauvage." See "My songs are envenomed and bitter" (Borodin)

"Mon coeur est plein d'un noir souci." See Anges du paradis (Gounod)

"Mon coeur lassé de tout." See Le vallon (Gounod)

Mon coeur ne peut changer. C. Gounod. e.f. SOA 1

"Mon coeur s'ouvre à ta voix" ("My heart at thy dear voice") C. Saint-Saëns. e.f. KS 2
"Mon coeur s'ouvre à ta voix" ("My heart at thy sweet voice") e.f. SM 2—SOA 2
"Mon coeur s'ouvre à ta voix" ("My heart to hear thy voice") e.f. OS 1
"My heart at thy sweet voice." e. WA—WBT—WL

"Mon enfant, ma soeur." See L'invitation au voyage (Duparc)

"Mon étoile bien aimée." See Sérénade basque

"Mon père a fait bâtir maison" ("My father built a house, did he."—Va, va, va, p'tit bonnet tout rond.—Ah, ha, ha, little cap so round) Canadian folk song. e.f. TF

"Mon père a fait bâtir maison" ("My father, O, a house built he."—J'entends le moulin.—I hear the mill) Canadian folk song. e.f. TF

"Mon père aussi m'a mariée." See La maumariée (Canadian version)

"Mon père m'a fait jardinier." See Ma mi', faites-moi-z-un bouquet

"Mon pèr' m'a mariée." See La maumariée (Breton version)

"Mon père m'envoie-t-à l'herbe" ("My father bade me pick herbs") French folk song. e.f. TSF
"Mon pèr' m'envoi-t-à l'herbe" ("Through fields my father sends me") Lorraine version. e.f. FTF

"Mon pèr' n'avait fille que moi" (Cécilia) Canadian folk song. e.f. BF 2

"Mon pèr' n'avait fille que moi" (Si mon papa le savait.—If papa knew) Canadian folk song. e.f. BFS

"Mon petit coeur à chaque instant soupire." See Mon petit coeur soupire

Mon petit coeur soupire (My little heart's a-sighing) e.f. SM 1

Mona. S. Adams. Words by F. E. Weatherly. NML—WA— WBT—WBW

La monacella ("Quanno mammà me fece monicella."—The young nun) Roman song. e.i. MSI

La monacella ("Zi monacella."—The young nun) Neapolitan song. e.i. MSI

Il monaco. See Der moench (Meyerbeer)

Monarch of the woods. J. W. Cherry. FSS 5—HSC

Moncrieff, Mrs L.
A creole love-song

Moncrieff, W. G. T.
Pretty star of the night (Composer unknown)
Der mond ("Im stillen, heitern glanze") J. F. Reichardt. Words by K. Rudolphi.   g.   ED 3
Der mond ("Mein herz ist wie die dunkle nacht")   See "Mein herz ist wie die dunkle nacht" (Mendelssohn)
"Der mond ist aufgegangen."   See Abendlied (Schulz)
"Der mond ist schlafen 'gangen."   See Ständchen (Franz)
"Der mond steht über dem berge."   See Ständchen (Brahms)
"Monday boys, I got me a wife."   See The holly twig
"Monday morning go to school."   See The two brothers (Hot Springs, N.C. version)
Mondnacht (Moonlight) R. Schumann. Words by J. von Eichendorff.   e.g. BAS 2—CMF 2—FO 1—GM.   e. only FTS
Mondschein ("Verstohlen geht der mond auf") Rheinische volksweise. Words by W. von Zuccalmaglio.   g. ED 2
"Verstohlen geht der mond auf" ("How quiet is the moonrise")   e.g.   BF 2
"Money makes the mare to go."   Song from India.   e.   SMW
" 'Mong the rocks by the North sea's blue waters."   See "Millom bakkar og berg utmed havet"
Moniot d'Arras, Pierre
"It was in May"
Moniuszko, Stanislaw
At the spinning wheel
The Cossack
Halka (from Halka)
Kozak.   See The Cossack
Prząśniczka.   See At the spinning wheel
Monk, Edwin George
"Sing the battle" (Tr of Pange lingua gloriosi proelium certaminis)
Monk, William Henry
"Abide with me! fast falls the eventide"
"As with gladness men of old"
The boy's dream
Coronae.   See "Crown the Saviour, angels crown Him"
"Crown the Saviour, angels crown Him"
Evening hymn.   See "Sun of my soul"
Eventide.   See "Abide with me! fast falls the eventide"
Hursley.   See "Sun of my soul"
"Lord, in this Thy mercy's day"
"Quiet, Lord, my froward heart"
Song of mercy
Sun of my soul, Thou Saviour dear"
"Sweet Savior, bless us ere we go"
With gladness men of old.   See "As with gladness men of old"

The monk.   See Der moench (Meyerbeer)
"The monk within his cell."   G. A. Macfarren.   Words by J. Oxenford. BS 1
"Monkey dress'd in soldier's clothes."   See Shine on (Schoolcraft)
"The monkey married the baboon's sister."   See The monkey's wedding
The monkey's wedding.   Traditional song. FSS 7
The monks and their convents.   See Finita è pei frati (Meyerbeer)
The monks' march.   See The monks of Bangor's march
The monks of Bangor's march ("When the heathen trumpets clang") Air: Ymdaith y mwnc.   Words by W. Scott.   BMC
The monks' march.   MMW
The monks of old.   S. Glover.   Words by W. Jones.   BE 1—HSE 3
Monlass, William
The vocal grove (Young)
The monotone.   See Ein ton (Cornelius)
Monrad, Marcus Jakob
"I ensomme stunde" (Bull)
Morning song and march.   N. W. Gade.   e.   TL
Monro, George
Colin's request
"My goddess Celia"
"Phillis, talk no more of passion"
The reproach.   See "Phillis, talk no more of passion"
Monroe, Grace D.
Hillsdale and the blue
Monsell, John Samuel Bewley
"Christ is risen! alleluia" (music by Maker; Pearson; Wilson)
"Earth below is teeming" (music by Hamilton-Gell; also by unknown composer)
"Lord of the living harvest" (Composer unknown)
"The spring-tide hour" (Booth)
Monsieur de la Palisse.   French folk song.   e.   GO
"Monsieur Préval gave a big ball."   See "Michié Préval"
Monsigny, Pierre Alexander
"Adieu, chère Louise" (from Le déserteur)
"Il regardait mon bouquet" (from Le roi et le fermier)
"Ô ma tendre musette" (attributed)
"Rustic flute, echo, sighing."   See "Ô ma tendre musette" (attributed)
"Sing to me, sweet musetta."   See "Ô ma tendre musette" (attributed)
Monstre affreux.   J. P. Rameau.   e.f. SOA 5
"Montagnes royales sont celles du Canigou."   See Le Canigou
Montenegro (Crnogorac crnogorki) National song.   Words by G. Jakšić. e.se.   BF 1

Monteverdi, Claudio
Ahi, troppo è duro (from Il balletto delle ingrate)
"Alas, all too harsh and ruthless." See Ahi, troppo è duro
"Lasciatemi morire" (from L'Arianna)
"Let death now come." See "Lasciatemi morire"
"Let death resolve my sorrow." See "Lasciatemi morire"
"No longer let me languish." See "Lasciatemi morire"
"Montez à Dieu, chants d'allégresse." See Noël (Gounod)
Montgomery, B. S.
Home so blest (Abt)
Montgomery, James
"Angels, from the realms of glory" (Smart)
"Forever with the Lord" (Gounod)
"God shall charge His angel legions" (Mendelssohn)
"Hail to the Lord's anointed" (music by Mason; Webb)
His reign on earth begun (Webb)
"In the hour of trial" (Composer unknown)
"Lord, forever at thy side" (Weber)
"The Lord is my Shepherd" (music by Koschat; also by unknown composer)
"A poor wayfaring man of grief" (Coles)
"Songs of praise" (Bach)
"A month has flown now, exiled dear one." See Mai (Hahn)
The month of May ("Im wunderschönen monat mai") See "Im wunderschönen monat mai" (Schumann)
The month of May ("Sweet, ah how sweet."—Muaj' i majit) Albanian song. al.e. BF 2
The month of May ("Voici venir le joli mois") See Le mois de mai
"The months are met, with their crownlets on." See October
The months of the year. Folk song. BSW
Montjoyeux, pseud. See Poignard, Jules
Montrose, Percy
Clementine. See Oh, my darling Clementine
Oh, my darling Clementine
Moo-lee-hwa (The jasmin-flower) Chinese folk song. c.e. BO—SMF
Moo-lee chwa (The moo-lee flower.— "How lovely this sweet branch of flowers") e. BMC
Moo-lee-wah (The jasmine flower) e. GO
Moo-lee-wha. e. SMW
The moon ("Great is the moon") Japanese children's song. e.j. BF 2
The moon ("Mein herz") See "Mein herz ist wie die dunkle nacht" (Mendelssohn)
"Moon Deer how near your soul divine." See By the waters of Minnetonka (Lieurance)

"The moon drops low." Omaha tribal air. C. W. Cadman. Words by N. R. Eberhart. CF
"Moon girl good bye." See In mirrored waters (Lieurance)
"The moon had climbed the highest hill." See Mary's dream
"The moon hangs over the hilltops." See Ständchen (Brahms)
"The moon is beaming clear and bright." See The interrupted serenade (Stair)
"The moon is beaming o'er the lake." J. Blockley. FSS 3—WBT
"The moon is beaming o'er the sparkling rill." See Who's that calling (Lawreen)
"The moon is blinking o'er the lea." See Smile again, my bonnie lassie
"The moon looks down so fair on me." See Mutterseelenallein
"The moon may shine with doubled splendor." See Vor dem fenster (Brahms)
"The moon on the ocean was dimmed by a ripple." See The lass that loves a sailor (Dibdin)
"De moon run down in a purple stream." See Didn't my Lord deliver Daniel
"The moon shines bright." Traditional New Year carol. BSC—HC
—Surrey and Sussex version. WCC
Moon song. Bohemian folk air. Words by H. H. Harbour. DO
"The moon walks in the fields of the sky." See Christmas greeting
"The moon was softly shining o'er mountain, sea, and shore." See Leonore (Trotter)
"The moon, with gleaming light." See Fyllas sang (Rung)
The moonbeam. See Le soir (Gounod)
"Moonbeams are streaming." G. P. Grantham (music and words) HC
"The moonbeams whiten boughs all around." See L'heure exquise (Hahn)
Moonlight ("Dans la forêt") See Clair de lune (Saint-Saëns)
Moonlight ("Es war, als hätt'") See Mondnacht (Schumann)
Moonlight ("Votre âme") See Clair de lune (Fauré)
"Moonlight and music." C. Pinsuti. Words by H. M. Burnside. BD
Moonlight and starry night ("Holdvilágos csillagos az éjszaka") Hungarian song. e.hu. BF 1
"Moonlight comes stealing." See En el espejo de tu mirada niña
"Moonlight fullness thy heart illuming." See Chanson triste (Duparc)
"The moonlight shimmers thro' the vine." See A moonlight song (Cadman)
"The moonlight silvers the valley." See Ständchen (Brahms)
A moonlight song. C. W. Cadman. Words by J. P. Mills. AA

Moonrise. See Le lever de la lune (Saint-Saëns)

The **moon's** lullaby. C. S. Burnham. ES

"The **moon's** on the lake." See Macgregors' gathering (Lee)

Moore, Edward
"Softly rise, O southern breeze" (Boyce)
"Tell me, lovely shepherd" (Boyce)

Moore, G. W.
Little Maggie May (Blamphin)

Moore, Milton
"I would not die in springtime"

Moore, Thomas

Composer

When the boats come home

Composer and author

Twilight dews

Author

After the battle (Irish air)
"Alone in crowds to wander on" (Irish air)
Araby's daughter (Kiallmark)
El arpa triste (German air. Tr of My harp has one unchanging theme)
"As a beam o'er the face of the waters" (Irish air)
"As down in the sunless retreats" (music by Haydn; Shaw)
"As slow our ship her foamy track" (Irish air)
"As vanquished Erin" (Irish air)
"At the mid hour of night" (Irish air)
"Avenging and bright" (Irish air)
The battle eve (Irish air)
Before the battle (Irish air)
"Believe me, if all those endearing young charms" (English air)
Bendemeer's stream (Irish air)
"The bird let loose" (German air; also music by Bruce)
Brien the brave (Irish air)
"By Celia's arbor" (Mendelssohn)
"By that lake, whose gloomy shore" (Irish air)
Canadian boat song (Canadian air; also music by Arnold)
Carnival of Venice (Neapolitan air)
The cold wave my love lies under (Attwood)
"Come o'er the sea" (Irish air)
"Come, play me that simple air" (Labitzky)
"Come, rest in this bosom" (Kiallmark)
"Come, send round the wine" (Irish air)
Come, sing me that sweet air again (Composer unknown)
"Come, take thy harp" (Molloy)
"Come, ye disconsolate" (music by Webbe; also unknown composer)
The daughters of Erin (Irish air)
"The dawn is breaking" (Balfe)
"The dawning of morn" (Irish air)
Desmond's song (Irish air)
"The dream of those days" (Irish air)

"Drink of this cup" (Irish air)
"Drink to her" (Irish air)
Echo (Irish air)
Erin! oh, Erin (Irish air)
"Erin! the tear and the smile in thine eyes" (Irish air)
Eveleen's bower (Irish air)
The evening gun (Irish air)
The fair-haired maiden (Irish air)
"Fairest, put on awhile" (Irish air)
"Fallen is thy throne" (Martini)
"Farewell! but whenever you welcome the hour" (Irish air; also music by Keene)
The farewell to my harp (Irish air; also music by Philips)
The feast of roses (Composer unknown)
"Fill the bumper fair" (Irish air)
"Fly not yet" (Irish air)
"Forget not the field" (Irish air)
The fortune teller (Irish air)
"From this hour the pledge is given" (Irish air)
The glad new day (Composer unknown)
"Go then—'tis vain to hover" (Neapolitan air)
"Go thou and dream" (Composer unknown)
"Go where glory waits thee" (Irish air)
"Good night" (Rubinstein)
"Hark! 'tis the breeze" (Rousseau)
"The harp that once thro' Tara's halls" (Irish air)
"Has sorrow thy young days shaded" (Irish air)
"Hear me but once" (Irish air)
"Hours there were" (Wade)
"How dear to me the hour when daylight dies" (Irish air)
"How oft has the banshee cried" (Irish air)
I love but thee (Vogrich)
"I saw from the beach" (Irish air)
"I saw thy form in youthful prime" (Irish air)
"I wish I was by that dim lake" (Irish air)
"I'd mourn the hopes that leave me" (Irish air)
"If thou'lt be mine" (Irish air)
Ill omens (Irish air)
"In the morning of life" (Irish air)
The Irish peasant to his mistress (Irish air)
"It is not the tear, at this moment shed" (Irish air)
"I've a secret to tell thee" (Irish air)
"Joy, joy for ever" (Clarke-Whitfeld)
The last rose of summer (Irish air)
"Lay his sword by his side" (Irish air)
The legacy (Irish air)
"Lesbia hath a beaming eye" (Irish air)
"Let Erin remember the days of old" (Irish air)
The lighthouse (Composer unknown) Authorship uncertain

Moore, Thomas—*Continued*

Love and the novice (Irish air)
Love's young dream (Irish air)
Mary's tears (Shaw)
The meeting (Composer unknown)
The meeting of the waters (Irish air)
"The minstrel boy" (Irish air)
The mountain sprite (Irish air)
"My gentle harp! once more I waken" (Celtic air; also Londonderry air)
My harp has one unchanging theme. For Spanish translation see El arpa triste (German air)
My heart and lute (music by Bishop; Kjerulf)
"Nay, tell me not, dear" (Irish air)
"Ne'er ask the hour" (Irish air)
The night-dance (Irish air)
"No, not more welcome" (Irish air)
"O Arranmore, loved Arranmore" (Irish air)
"Oh, banquet not in those shining bowers" (Irish air)
"Oh! blame not the bard" (Irish air)
"Oh! breathe not his name" (Irish air)
"Oh! could we do with this world of ours" (16th century English air; also Irish air)
"Oh! doubt me not" (Irish air)
"Oh, for the swords of former time" (Irish air)
"Oh! had we some bright little isle" (Irish air)
"Oh! love is a hunter boy" (Irish air)
Oh! the shamrock (Irish air)
"Oh, the sight entrancing" (Irish air)
"Oh! think not my spirits are always as light" (Irish air)
"O Thou who dryest the mourner's tear" (Haydn)
"Oh! 'tis sweet to think" (Irish air)
"Oh! where's the slave, so lowly" (Irish air)
"O ye dead" (Irish air)
"Oft in the stilly night" (Stevenson?)
On music (Irish air)
"One bumper at parting" (Irish air)
The parallel (Irish air)
"Poor wounded heart" (Vogrich)
The prince's day (Irish air)
"Quick! we have but a second" (Irish air)
"Remember the glories of Brien the brave" (Irish air)
"Remember thee" (Irish air)
"Rich and rare were the gems she **wore**" (Irish air)
"Row gently here, my gondolier" (music by Jensen; Schumann)
"Sail on, sail on, thou fearless bark" (Irish air)
St Senanus and the lady (Irish air)
"Shall the harp then be silent" (Irish air)
"She is far from the land" (Irish air)
"She sung of love" (Irish air)
"Silence is in our festal halls" (Irish air)

"Sing, sing, music was given" (Irish air)
The song of Fionnuala (Irish air)
The song of Innisfail (Irish air)
"Sing, sweet harp, oh, sing to me" (Irish air)
Song of O'Donahue's mistress (Irish air)
Song of O'Ruark, Prince of Breffni (Irish air)
"Sound the loud timbrel" (music by Molique; Reinecke)
Spring (Haydn)
"Sublime was the warning which liberty spoke" (Irish air)
"Sweet Innisfallen" (Irish air)
"Take back the virgin page" (Irish air)
"There are sounds of mirth" (Irish air)
"There's nothing bright, above, below" (Composer unknown)
There's nothing true but heaven (Shaw)
"They know not my heart" (Irish air)
"They may rail at this life" (Irish air)
"They tell me thou'rt the favour'd guest" (Balfe)
"This life is all chequer'd with pleasures and woes" (Irish air)
"Those evening bells" (music by Beethoven; Bellini; also unknown composer; also a round)
"Thou bidst me sing" (Irish air)
"Though humble the banquet" (Irish air)
"Though the last glimpse of Erin" (Irish air)
"The time I've lost in wooing" (Irish air)
"'Tis believed that this harp" (Irish air; also music by Tanieev)
"'Tis gone, and for ever" (Irish air)
"To Greece we give our shining blades" (Bishop)
"To ladies' eyes" (Irish air)
"'Twas one of those dreams" (Irish air)
Twilight dews (music by the author)
Vesper hymn (Bortnianski)
The wandering bard (Irish air)
"We may roam thro' this world" (Irish air)
"Weep on, weep on" (Irish air)
"What the bee is to the flow'ret" (Irish air)
"When cold in the earth" (Irish air)
"When first I met thee" (Irish air)
"When he, who adores thee" (Irish air)
"When love is kind" (Irish air)
"When thou art nigh" (Irish air)
"When thro' life unblest we rove" (Irish air)
"When through the piazzetta" (music by Jensen; Mendelssohn)
"Whene'er I see those smiling eyes" (Irish air)
"While gazing on the moon's light" (Irish air)
"While history's muse" (Irish air)
"The wine-cup is circling" (Irish air)

Moore, Thomas—*Continued*
The woodpecker (Irish air; also music by Kelly)
"Wreathe the bowl" (Irish air)
You and me (Irish air)
"You remember Ellen" (Irish air)
The young Indian maid (Composer unknown)
"The young May moon" (Irish air)
Moorehead, T.
"Thus when the mariner inclined to sleep"
Moorish song. See "Oh, Haidee"
Mòrag. Scottish air. Words by A. MacDonald. e. MMS
La Moraschina (The brunette) Lombardian folk song. e.i. MSI
Moravia ("Oh, land! 'mong the mountains") Moravian song. e. BMC
"O land 'mong the mountains." e. JSE
More and more. Seifert. Words by L. C. Elson. WC
More grand is his humble estate. See Plus grand dans son obscurité (Gounod)
More royal in his humble state. See Plus grand dans son obscurité (Gounod)
Moreen O'Kelly. See Móirín ni Chealla
Morehouse, Mrs L. E.
"Christ is risen! Christ is risen! conquered death and all His foes"
Morford, Henry
Heart-ache for home (Composer unknown)
Morgan, A. M.
"Now lift the carol, men and maids" (Brown)
Morgan, May
The chickadee (German folk air)
Jack-in-the-pulpit (German folk air)
The shadow (Old air)
The shower (German folk air)
Winter's past (German folk air)
Morgan, Sydney (Owenson), lady
Kate Kearney (Irish air)
"My love's the fairest creature" (Irish air)
Morgen-hymne (Morning hymn) G. Henschel. Words by R. Reinick. e.g. SM 2
Morning hymn. e. BC
"**Morgen**, kinder, wird's was geben." See Die weihnachtsfreude
"**Morgen** kommt der weihnachtsmann." See Der weihnachtsmann
"**Morgen** muss ich fort von hier." See Lebewohl (Silcher)
Morgengebet (Morning prayer) Folk air. Words by J. von Eichendorff. e.g. SSG
"**Morgenlich** leuchtend." See Walthers preislied (Wagner)
Morgenlied ("Dir, du quell") L. Reichardt. Words by J. K. Lavater. g. ED 3
Morgenlied ("Die sterne sind erblichen") J. Gersbach. Words by H. Hoffmann von Fallersleben. g. ED 3

"**Morgenrot**, morgenrot! leuchtest mir zum frühen tod." See Reiters morgenlied
"**Morgenrot** schon erglüht." See Lilacs (Rachmaninov)
"**Morgens** send' ich dir die veilchen" ("Violets for thee I gather") E. Meyer-Helmund. Words by H. Heine. e.g. SM 1
"Des **morgens**, wann die hähne krähen." See entry under Des
Morhof, Daniel Georg
Schlachtlied (Silcher)
Moriar, Melpomene. Glasgow university song. C. W. Glover. Words, by W. A. A. Armstrong. e. SSS
Mörike, Eduard
An eine Aeolsharfe (Brahms)
Auf ein altes bild (Wolf)
Begegnung (Wolf)
Citronenfalter im april (Wolf)
Er ist's (music by Schumann; Wolf)
Fussreise (Wolf)
Gesang Weyla's (Wolf)
Heimweh (Wolf)
In der frühe (Wolf)
Mausfallen-sprüchlein (Wolf)
Verborgenheit (Wolf)
"**Morir** vogl'io" ("O death, receive me") E. d'Astorga. e.i. FEI 2
"**Morir** vogl'io" ("That I might die") e.i. NG
Morison, John
The light hath shone (Hastings)
Morison, Mary Sanford
Composer and author
Boy scout march
Author
Commencement song (Murray)
Moritz, C. T.
Schäfer im mai
Morlacchi, Francesco
"Lord, we pray Thee to comfort Thy servants"
Morley, Thomas
"It was a lover and his lass" (attributed)
"Now is the month of Maying"
"O mistress mine"
"Sleep, O sleep, fond fancy"
"**Morn** hath woke the world again." See Sunday morning (Abt)
"The **morn** is fair, our hearts are light." See The enchanted isle (Verdi)
"**Morn** of beauty." E. Handley. HC
"The **morn** of life is past." See Old dog Tray (Foster)
"The **morn** was fair, the skies were clear." See The rose of Allandale (Nelson)
Morning ("Bright in the east") P. I. Tschaikowsky. e. BD
Morning ("Eat your bread, Mary") French folk air: Tremp' ton pain, Marie. Author of words unknown. DO
Morning ("I love thee, dear") S. Rachmaninoff. Words by M. L. Janoff. e. SC

Morning ("Kein schlaf noch kühlt") See In der frühe (Wolf)

"The morning air plays on my face." Air: The welcome of our hostess. Words by J. Baillie. MMW

"Morning bells I love to hear." Round. FSS 7

The morning-break ("Awake, ye drowsy maids") Air: May day carol. Words by A. Bradley. DM 2

The morning break ("Awake, ye drowsy swains") BE 8

"The morning breaks, the morning breaks." See Morning song (Custance)

"The morning breaks, those ruddy streaks." See The wily fox (Dibdin)

Morning colors. See The star-spangled banner (Smith)

Morning hymn ("Bald ist der nacht") See Morgen-hymne (Henschel)

Morning hymn ("Lord God of morning") L. van Beethoven. Words by J. Keble. JS—MS

"Morning is breaking." G. E. Oliver. HC

"Morning is dawning, risen the sun." See God morgen (Grieg)

"Morning is here, earth's flooded with light." See God morgen (Grieg)

"The morning light is breaking." G. J. Webb. Words by S. F. Smith. FSS 4

"Morning-light, morning-light." See Reiters morgenlied

"The morning of salvation." Composer unknown. Words by J. M. Neale. HC

Morning praise. Composer unknown. BSS

The morning prayer ("Lord, from my bed") M. Costa. OS 2—SAS 2

Morning prayer ("O wundersames") See Morgengebet

"The morning purples all the sky." Easter carol. Tr of Aurora coelum purpurat. e. HC

"Morning red." German air. Words by R. W. Raymond. e. FSS 1

Morning serenade. J. Offenbach. e. WBT

"Morning skies are aglow." See Lilacs (Rachmaninov)

"Morning so rosy and beautiful." See Zapateo cubano (Vilá)

Morning song ("Awake from sweetest slumber") WSC

Morning song ("Flowers greet him") Russian folk air. Words by R. R. Whitehead. WF

Morning song ("Lady mine, thy casement open") J. Barnby. Words by C. Bingham. TL

Morning song ("The morning breaks") A. F. M. Custance. NMS

Morning song ("Thou, true God alone") English folk song. DO

The morning star ("See! the morning") See "See! the morning is dwelling" (Bridge)

The morning star ("Through the long night") See Song to the morning star

"The morning sun has risen." See Le penitent et l'ivrogne

Morning tryst. Ojibway Indian song. e.in. BA

"Morning was gleaming with roseate light." See Walthers preislied (Wagner)

Morningside. Barnard college song. Words by A. Watterson. CHS

Morris, Charles
The flitch of bacon (Hook)
Reasons for drinking (Dibdin)

Morris, Eliza Fanny (Goffe)
The Priory chimes (Haynes)

Morris, George Pope
The flag of our union forever (music by Custance; Wallace)
Long time ago (Old air)
My mother's Bible (Russell)
"When other friends are round thee" (Composer unknown)
"Woodman, spare that tree" (music by Hiller; Russell)
Yankee Doodle (Old air)

Morris, William
"From far away" (Dykes)

Morrison, F.
"Tell me, Mary, how to woo thee" (Hodson)

Morrison, John. See Morison, John

Morrison, Lewis
Behold! I stand at the door (Jude)

La mort de la fiancée (The death of the betrothed) French folk song. e.f. TSF

La mort des amants (The death of lovers) A. C. Debussy. Words by C. Baudelaire. e.f. CM 1—HM 1

La mort du porte-enseigne (The banner-bearer's death) French folk song. e.f. TSF

La mort et le paysan. See Trepak (Musorgskiï)

"Mortals, awake, the morning is breaking." HC

"Mortals, awake, with angels join." G. Kingsley. Words by S. Medley. MCS

Morton, Clara
The magic tree (Composer unknown)
Sing glad songs for him (Gounod)

Morton, Thomas
Pretty mocking bird (Bishop)
"Tell me, my heart" (Bishop)

Les morts (The dead) E. Chausson. Words by J. Richepin. e.f. HM 1

Morva Rhuddlan. Old Welsh air. Words by I. G. Geirionnydd. e. BSE

"Mos e pi duhane, se t'sjell zavale moj und'e bukure." See Beautiful nose

Moscheles, Ignaz
The message
The Swiss girl
Switzer's song of home

Moscow gypsy song. Russian folk song. e. GO

Mosen, Julius
  Andreas Hofer (Swiss air)
  Der nussbaum (Schumann)
  Die waldblume (Volksweise)
Mosenthal, J.
  "Ring out the bells for Christmas"
Moses' death. S. de Lange. e. SAS 4
"Moses died in de days of old." See
  Where shall I be when de firs' trumpet
  soun'
The mosquito ("Hear mosquito buzzing")
  Iroquois Indian song. e. BA
The mosquito's serenade. H. W. Loomis
  (music and words) BSS—TFC 1
Moss, Edwin
  "Arise, arise, the morning bells"
Most done trabelling. Negro spiritual.
  HR
"Most noble my lov'd sovereign." See
  Kalakaua's serenade (Hopkins)
Most wondrous it must be. See Es muss
  was wunderbares sein (Ries)
Moszkowski, Moritz
  "Mädchenaug'! mädchenaug'"
  "Maiden fair." See "Mädchenaug'!
    mädchenaug'"
  Serenade
  Serenata. See Serenade
"Mother, are there angels dwelling." C.
  W. Glover. Words by C. Jeffreys.
  FSS 3—WBT
"Mother Bontemps." See "La mère Bon-
  temps"
"The mother calls them, her well-loved
  daughters." See Girls at the river
"A mother came, when stars were paling."
  See The fairy boy
"Mother, dear little mother." See Why,
  oh mother
The mother deer (Hē laphina) Greek folk
  song. e.gr. BF 2
Mother, do not scold me ("Ne brani menīā,
  rodnaīā") Russian song. e.r. BF 1
Mother! fair Columbia! where'er we chanc'd
  to roam. See Alumni song (Foster)
The mother-heart. S. R. Gaines. Words
  by L. F. Merriam. CMF 1
"Mother, I long to get married." See
  Whistle, daughter, whistle
"Mother, I love her so." See Why does
  he haunt my door
"Mother, is massa gwine to sell us to-mor-
  row." See Massa gwine to sell us to-
  morrow
"Mother, is master going to sell us to-mor-
  row." See Massa gwine to sell us to-
  morrow
Mother, let me go. See Mamma, lasciami
  andare
"Mother, may I go out to swim." WSC
"Mother, mother, a gay young gallant." See
  Piuriuri, ti vo' sposà
"Mother, mother, hear the news." Jaco-
  bite song. PS 2
"Mother, mother, let me be going." See
  Mamma, lasciami andare
"Mother, mother, ne'er believe." See Lied
  der braut (Schumann)

"Mother, O sing me to rest" ("Mutter, o
  sing' mich zur ruh'") R. Franz. Words
  by F. Hemans. e.g. CMF 1
"Mother, oh sing me to rest" ("Mutter, o,
  sing' mich zur ruh'") E. Hildach.
  Words by F. Hemans. e.g. SM 1
"The mother of my lover is so spiteful."
  See Dispetto
"Mother see my tears." See "Ave Maria"
  (Mascagni)
Mother sent me ("Siuntē mane") Lithu-
  anian folk song. e.li. BF 1
The mother sings. See Moderen synger
  (Sinding)
"Mother, stay'd on rock eternal." See
  Stand, Columbia (Haydn)
"Mother, tell me, do." See "Maman, dites-
  moi"
"Mother, tell me why must you finish that
  scarlet sarafan." See The scarlet
  sarafan (Varlamov)
Mother Volga (Vniz po matuschki po Vol-
  gi) Russian folk song. e. GO
  Down on mother Vólga (Vniz po ma-
    tushkīe po Volgīe) e. SSR 1
  Down the Volga ("Vniz po matushkīe
    po Volgīe") e.r. BF 1
"A mother was watching on Christmas
  night." See The gift (Behrend)
"A mother's gift to her country's cause."
  See The blue and the gray (Dresser)
Mother's old red shawl. C. Mouland.
  WA—WBT—WSC
"Mother's quite distracted." See Baby's
  ring
The mother's song. See "Gently rest"
  (Kücken)
The mother's vow. Dakota Indian song.
  e.in. FIS
Motherwell, William
  "In a simmer gloamin'" (Gaelic air)
  Jeanie Morrison (Dempster)
  "Oh! is it thus we part" (Linley)
Mottet, Jeanie Gallup
  Her rose (Coombs)
Mouland, C.
  Mother's old red shawl
Moulds, John
  Come, who'll buy primroses (from The
    sultan)
  Ground ivy
  "'Twas near a thicket's calm retreat"
Moule, George Evans
  "Gathered in the house divine" (Skef-
    fington)
Le moulin (The water-mill) Folk song
  from lower Alsace. e.f. FTF
Moultrie, Gerard
  "Come forth, come forth, brave reap-
    ers" (Lissant)
  "Heavenly Father, God alone" (Lis-
    sant)
  "Near the tomb where Christ hath
    been" (Skeffington)
  A tale of the olden time (Trevaldwyn)
  "There came three kings ere break of
    day" (Smith)
  "We march, we march" (music by
    Barnby; Oliver)

Mounseer Nong Tong Paw. C. Dibdin (music and words) ME

Mount Vernon bells. W. H. Jones. NMS

"**Mountagnas** regaladas." See Le Canigou

The **mountain** boy ("The mountain shepherd boy") FSS 5

The **mountain** bugle. J. H. Hewitt. FSS 3

The **mountain** captive. See Den bergtagna

The **mountain**-king. See Den bergtagna

The **mountain** maid ("Sie ist schmächtig") See Das kind der berge (Grieg)

"A **mountain** maid, both rich and fair." See Dilly dally, shilly shally (Hook)

"The **mountain** maid from her bow'r has hied." Sinclair. HSE 2

Mountain maid's invitation. H. Werner. e. FSS 1—JSE

The **mountain** minstrel ("A minstrel wild, I wreath with flowers") Air: The dairy house. Words by C. B. Wilson. MMW

"The **mountain** pines I had pass'd thro'." See Der letzte gruss (Levi)

"The **mountain** shepherd boy am I." See The mountain boy

The **mountain** sprite ("In yonder valley, there dwelt alone") Air: The mountain sprite. Words by T. Moore. MI

"A **mountain** tall against the sky." See A high mountain stands

The **mountaineer.** See Fjeldbyggen

Mountaineer's farewell. See Old Granite State (Hutchinson)

The **mountains** ("O, proudly rise") Williams college song. S. W. Gladden (music and words) CHS—LA

"The **mountains** are robed." See, As cold as the snows

"**Mountains** bath'd in morning light." See Shepherd's song

"**Mountains**, bow your heads majestic." W. H. Cummings. BSC—HC

"**Mountains** high and valleys lowly." See "Höga berg och djupa dalar"

"**Mountains** majestic, royal." See Le Canigou

The **mountains** of Norway. See Norges fjelde (Kjerulf)

Mourir pour la patrie (To die for home and country) French patriotic song. A. Varney. Words by A. Chenier. e.f. SN

Mourir pour la patrie (The chant of the Girondins) e.f. WCP

"**Mourn** not." See "Es ist bestimmt in Gottes rath" (Mendelssohn)

Mourn with temerity. See Seguita a piangere (Bassani)

"**Mourn** ye not o'er my departure." See Hiawatha's death song

"**Mourned** in de valley." Negro spiritual. NMP

The **mourner** ("Mei mutter mag mi nit") See Herzeleid

Mourner's Christmas. MCS

Mournful love (Z dvojenje) Slavonian song. e.se. BF 1

"The **mournful** one." See När jag var ett litet

The **mouse-trap** ("Kleine gäste") See Mausfallen-sprüchlein (Wolf)

The **mousetrap** ("Of all the simple things." —Marriage) Old English air. Words by T. D'Urfey. BE 8

The **mouse-trap** (Old Hob) CO 2

Moussorgsky, Modest Petrovitch. See Musorgskiï, Modest Petrovich

"**Mouth** so charmful." See Pur dicesti, o bocca bella (Lotti)

"**Move** now with measured sound." T. Campion (music and words) DM 2

"**Möven,** möven in weissen flocken." See Im kahne (Grieg)

"**Moving** o'er the troubled waters." A. Ulmann. HC

The **mowers'** song. German air. FSS 1 —JSE—WBT

Mowing the barley. Folk song. FSF— SEF 1—SO

Mowing the hay. M. Carmichael. WBT —WSC

Mozart, Wolfgang Amadeus
Abendempfindung
Abendruhe
Adieu
"Ah! lo so" (from Die zauberflöte. Tr of Ach ich fühls)
Ave verum
"Away with melancholy"
"Bald prangt, den morgen zu verkünden"
"Batti, batti" (from Don Giovanni)
The blacksmith
Bundeslied
"Cheer thee, my soul's treasure." See "Il mio tesoro intanto"
"Chide, oh, chide me." See "Batti, batti"
Come back, sweet May. See "Komm', lieber mai, und mache"
"Come, May, thou lovely lingerer." See "Komm', lieber mai, und mache"
Contentment. See Zufriedenheit
"Crudele! ah! no, mio bene" (from Don Giovanni)
Dauernde liebe
"Deh vieni alla finestra" (from Don Giovanni)
Deh vieni, non tardar (from Le nozze di Figaro)
Delightful joy, O come. See Deh vieni, non tardar
"Dies bildniss ist bezaubernd schön" (from Die zauberflöte)
"Dove sono" (from Le nozze di Figaro)
"Drink to me only with thine eyes" (wrongly attributed) See Mellish, R. "Drink to me only with thine eyes" (attributed)
"E Susanna non vien" (from Le nozze di Figaro)

Mozart, Wolfgang Amadeus —*Continued*

Evening thoughts. See Abendempfindung

Faith

Faithful

Frühlingsanfang

Gaily sings the lark

"Giunse alfin il momento" (from Le nozze di Figaro)

"Go, forget me"

"Great Isis! great Osiris." See "O Isis und Osiris"

"Ha! my pretty brace of fellows." See "Ha! wie will ich triumphiren"

"Ha! wie will ich triumphiren" (from Die entführung aus dem serail)

"Hark! the herald angels sing" (same air as The Prince of peace)

"Hie to the fields" (from Don Giovanni)

"How softly are glancing" (from Die zauberflöte)

Im frühling

"In diesen heil'gen hallen" (from Die zauberflöte)

Infelice sconsolata (from Die zauberflöte. Tr of Zum leiden bin ich auserkohren)

"Jesu, word of God incarnate." See Ave verum

Die kleine spinnerin

"Komm', lieber mai, und mache"

Lonely, reft and broken-hearted. See Infelice sconsolata

"Lord, we pray Thee, Lord, we pray Thee"

Lullaby. See Wiegenlied

"Madamina! il catalogo è questo" (from Don Giovanni)

May song. See "Komm', lieber mai, und mache"

Meine wünsche

"Il mio tesoro intanto" (from Don Giovanni)

My psalm (same air as "Komm', lieber mai, und mache")

"Non mi dir" (from Don Giovanni)

"Non paventar." See Infelice sconsolata

"Non più andrai" (from Le nozze di Figaro)

Non più di fiori (from La clemenza di Tito)

"O Isis und Osiris" (from Die zauberflöte)

Old Christmas

Only with thine eyes (wrongly attributed) See Mellish, R. "Drink to me only with thine eyes" (attributed)

"Porgi, amor" (from Le nozze di Figaro)

"Possenti Numi." See "O Isis und Osiris"

"Pretty lady." See "Madamina! il catalogo è questo"

The Prince of peace

"Quando miro quel bel ciglio"

"Qui sdegno non s'accende." See "In diesen heil'gen hallen"

"Rogues like you." See "Solche hergelauf' ne laffen"

Row, row, my boatie

"Saw ye never in the twilight"

"Se vuol ballare, signor contino" (from Le nozze di Figaro)

The seasons

Serenade. See "Deh vieni alla finestra"

Sleep and rest. See Wiegenlied

"So, Sir Page." See "Non più andrai"

"Solche hergelauf' ne laffen" (from Die entführung aus dem serail)

Song of the fowler. See Der vogelfänger

"Summer days once more are coming"

"Tell me, O fair ones." See "Voi, che sapete"

"To my beloved hasten." See "Il mio tesoro intanto"

"To scenes of peace retiring." See "In diesen heil'gen hallen"

"Vedrai, carino" (from Don Giovanni)

Das veilchen

The violet. See Das veilchen

Der vogelfänger (from Die zauberflöte)

"Voi, che sapete" (Le nozze di Figaro)

A warning. See Warnung

Warnung

"Wer ein liebchen hat gefunden" (from Die entführung aus dem serail)

"When a maiden takes your fancy." See "Wer ein liebchen hat gefunden"

Wiegenlied

"With a swanlike beauty gliding." See "Quando miro quel bel ciglio"

"Within this sacred dwelling." See "In diesen heil'gen hallen"

"Within these sacred bowers." See "In diesen heil'gen hallen"

Zufriedenheit

Muaj' i majit. See The month of May

"Much I loved a charming creature." Old English air. BE 3

Müchler, Karl

"Ich sah ein röschen am wege stehn" (music by Methfessel; Weber)

Der rheinweinzecher (Fischer)

Das veilchen (Himmel)

Das vergissmeinnicht (Himmel)

Wein, weib, gesang (Zelter)

Mud pies. A. S. Gatty. WSC

Mueller, Friedrich Konrad

Switzerland (Heim)

Mueller, J. Max

Rock me to sleep

"The muffled drum is beating." See Stonewall Jackson's requiem (Deeves)

"Muffled the drum, muffled the drum." See Funeral song of the nation (Chopin)

Mugur, mugurel ("Blossom, little bud") Rumanian song. e.ru. BF 2

Muhlenberg, William Augustus
Composer and author
Carol, brothers, carol
Shout the glad tidings
Author
Carol, brothers, carol (Custance; also
    music by author)
"I would not live alway" (Kingsley)
Mühler, Heinrich von
Bedenklichkeiten (Spanish air)
Das **mühlrad** ("Da droben auf jenem berge
    da steht") Volkslied. g. ED 1—
    ED 2
Das **mühlrad** (The mill wheel) e.g.
    SMF—SSG
"**Muh'voll** komm' ich und beladen" ("Sad
    I come and bending lowly") H. Wolf.
    Words from the Spanish of Don
    Manuel del Rio. e.g. FO 2
Muir, Alexander
The maple leaf forever
Muirland Willie ("O, hearken, and I will
    tell you how") Old Scottish song,
    with additional words by R. Burns.
    MMS—PS 1
Scottish wedding ("O hearken, and I
    will tell you how") HSSS
"**Mujer** de mis ensueños." See Maria,
    Mari (Capua)
"**Mujje** mukesin auyawaon." See Old
    shoes
La **mulata.** Folk song from Cuba and
    Mexico. s. HS
The **mulberry** bush. Old children's game
    song. WA—WBT—WSC—WSW
    "Here we go 'round the mulberry
    bush." NMH—NMS
The **muleteer** of Tarragona. See Le mule-
    tier de Tarragone (Henrion)
Le **muletier** de Tarragone (The muleteer
    of Tarragona) P. Henrion. e.f.
    AB 1
Mulholland, Rosa. See Gilbert, Rosa
    (Mulholland), lady
"**Mull** was a-stern, rum on the port." See
    Over the sea to Skye
Mullen, John W.
Afterwards
Müller, Friedrich
Soldaten-abschied (Fesca)
Müller, J. M.
"Es leben die alten" (Naumann)
Müller, Peter
Den gefallenen kriegern
Das heimweh
Müller, Peter Erasmus Lange-. See
    Lange-Müller, Peter Erasmus
Müller, Wenzel
Abschied (from Der Alpenkönig und
    der menschenfeind)
Departure. See Abschied
Frohe botschaft
"Ich hab den ganzen vormittag"
The little bird. See Frohe botschaft
Der schneider Kakadu
Song of the negro boatman
"Wer niemals einen rausch gehabt"
Woodnotes

Müller, Wilhelm
Die arche Noah (Schneider)
Brüderschaft (Folk air)
Entschuldigung (Nestler)
"I heard a brooklet gushing" (**Loder.**
    Tr of Wohin)
Jägers lust (Nathusius)
Der lindenbaum (Schubert)
Meine muse (Lyra)
Die post (Schubert)
Ungeduld (Schubert)
Das wandern (Schubert)
Das wirtshaus (Schubert)
Wohin (Schubert. For music by Lo-
    der see "I heard a brooklet gush-
    ing")
Müller, Wolfgang
Im herbst (Franz)
Widmung (Franz)
Mulock, Dinah Maria. See Craik, Mrs
    Dinah Maria (Mulock)
"**Multe** lacrämi am värsat." See Ardele-
    anca
Mummers' song. Old carol. BSS
"**Mun** muistuu mieleheni nyt." See Savo-
    laisen laulu (Collan)
Munch, Andreas
Brudefaerden i Hardanger (Kjerulf)
Wiegenlied (Grieg)
"Yderst mod norden" (Norse air)
Munday, Anthony
"You stole my love" (Macfarran)
Munjinger, U.
Under the trees
Munschtein, L.
Revery (Arenski)
Munster love song. See "Have you been
    at Carrick"
"**Mura** felici." G. Rossini. e.i. SOA 2
Muratori, G.
Amore
Love. See Amore
"**Murmelndes** lüftchen, blüthenwind" (Mur-
    muring breezes) A. Jensen. Words by
    Heyse. e.g. FO 1—KF 1—KF 2
"The **murm'ring** brooks, the fanning
    breeze." See Woman, love, and wine
"**Murmur,** gentle lyre." FSS 4
"**Murmuring** breeze of scented air." See
    "Murmelndes lüftchen, blüthenwind"
    (Jensen)
"**Murmuring** breezes, scented air." See
    "Murmelndes lüftchen, blüthenwind"
    (Jensen)
The **murmuring** sea. S. Glover. FSS 5
Murphy, Arthur J.
The drum-major of Schneider's band
Murphy, J. B.
Nicodemus Johnson
Murray, Alfred
Commencement song
Murray, Mrs Elizabeth Grant. See Grant,
    Mrs Elizabeth
Murray, John Chick
Washington (Custance)

Muse, A. E. A.
The dying volunteer
"The muse and the hero." J. Oswald. DM 2
Der musensohn ("Durch feld und wald."— The minstrel) F. Schubert. Words by Goethe. e.g. BS 2
Der musensohn ("Durch feld und wald") K. F. Zelter. Words by Goethe. g. ED 2
Musgrave, Frank
Long ago
Mush, mush. College song. SSS—WA— WBT—WC—WSW
"Mushrooms brown and tall, muster'd." See Gathering mushrooms (Musorgskiĭ)
Music at nightfall. S. Nelson. Words by C. Jefferys. FSS 5
"Music borne on Zephyr's wing." See Gruss (Mendelssohn)
Music everywhere. S. C. Foster. FSS 2
Music in the air. G. F. Root. Words by F. Crosby. TFC 2
"There's music in the air." CHS— FSS 1—HSC—HSD— LA—LBR— MPC—NMH— NMS—WBT— WC WSC—WSW
Music in the air, Counterpoint for. H. W. Loomis. TFC 2
"Music in the valley, music on the hill." See Music everywhere (Foster)
Music, love, and wine ("Why should we foolishly repine") Air: Divyrwch gwyr Carnarvon, or, The men of Carnarvon's pastime. Words by Talhaiarn. MMW
Music of labor. Kindergarten song. FSS 5
Work. NMS
"The music of thy voice." Words by R. Hewitt. WBT—WL
Music on the waves. C. W. Glover. FSS 1
"Music resoundeth ev'rywhere." See Sonntagslied (Mendelssohn)
"Music, when soft voices die." A. Day. Words by P. B. Shelley. DM 2
Musical alphabet. Children's song. FSS 3—WBT—WSC
The musical Master Charley. See Il Sor Carlo l'armonico
The musician (O moisikos) Attributed to A. Christopulos. e.gr. BO—SMF
Musidora. W. Croft. BE 4—DM 2
Musieu Bainjo. Negro creole folk song. e.f. KA
Mister Banjo. e. BSS
"Musing on the roaring ocean." Gaelic air: Druimionn dhu. Words by R. Burns. BSB—BSR—PS 2
Musketierlied ("Steh ich im feld") F. Silcher. Words by J. P. Hebel. g. ED 1
Musorgskiĭ, Modest Petrovich
After the battle
After years
"Ah, not with God's thunder"
Allelúia lubvee. See The hallelujah of love

Aux champignons. See Gathering mushrooms
The banks of the Don
The beetle
Berceuse de Yerómushka. See Cradle-song of the poor
La berceuse du pauvre. See Cradle-song of the poor
Berceuse du paysan. See Peasant cradle-song
The buxom matron. See The song of Khívria
By the water
Chanson d'enfant. See A child's song
Chant de Marthe. See Martha's song
A child's song
The country feast
Cradle song
Cradle-song of the poor
"Darling Savishna"
Death and the peasant. See Trepak
Death, the commander
Death's lullaby
Death's serenade
Divination by water (from Khovanshchina)
La divination par l'eau. See Divination by water
The doll's cradle-song
Doomka parássi. See Parásha's revery and dance
Doomka párobka. See Revery of the young peasant
Elégia. See Elegy
Elegy
Gathering mushrooms
Gdye tui zvyózdotchka. See "Little star, where art thou"
Górnimee tikho letyéla dooshá nyebesámi. See "Silently floated a spirit"
The hallelujah of love (from Khovanshchina)
Le hanneton. See The beetle
Hopak
In my attic
Jeremouschka's cradle song. See Cradle-song of the poor
Koluibélnaya. See Death's lullaby
Lamentation. See Oriental chant
"Little star so bright." See "Little star, where art thou"
"Little star, where art thou"
Love-song of the idiot
The magpie and the little gypsy dancer
Martha's song (from Khovanshchina)
Menyá tui v'tolpyé nye ooznála. See After years
La mort et le paysan. See Trepak
Na Dnyepryé. See .On the river Dnyéper
Night
Notch. See Night
Okóntchen prázdnui, schoomnui dyen. See Retrospect
On the river Dnyéper
Oriental chant (from Joshua Navin)
The orphan-girl
Parásha's revery and dance (from The fair at Sorochinsk)

Musorgskiĭ, Modest Petrovich—*Continued*
Parrot song (from Boris Godunov)
Peasant cradle-song
Peerooshka. See The country feast
Po nad Dónom sad tzvyetyót. See The banks of the Don
Polkovódyetz. See Death, the commander
Resignation
Retrospect
Revery of the young peasant (from The fair at Sorochinsk)
S' kookloi. See The doll's cradle-song
Savichna, ma lumière. See "Darling Savishna"
The seminarian
Seminaríst. See The seminarian
Serenade. See Death's serenade
The siege of Kazan (from Boris Godunov)
"Silently floated a spirit"
Sirótka. See The orphan-girl
Skootcháĭ. See Resignation
The song of Khívria (from The fair at Sorochinsk)
The song of Solomon
Soróka. See The magpie and the little gypsy dancer
Svyétik Sávishna. See Love-song of the idiot
Trepak
V' tchetuiryókh styenákh. See In my attic
Varlaám's ballad. See The siege of Kazan
Yevréiskaya pyésnya. See The song of Solomon

"**Muss** i denn, muss i denn." See Abschied

Musset, Alfred de
"Bonjour, Suzon" (music by Delibes; Pessard)
Les filles de Cadix (Delibes)
Ninon (Tosti)

Mussey, M. H. B.
Lucyna (Polish air)
The obliging moon (Ruthenian air)
The orphan (Ruthenian air)
The seagull (Russian air)

"**Must** I go." See Abschied ("Muss i denn")
"**Must** I go bound, must I go free." See The brisk young lover (North Carolina version)
"**Must** I go, must I go from my dear village home." See Abschied ("Muss i denn")
"**Must** I leave thee, must I leave thee." See Eve's lamentation (King)
"**Must** I then, must I then." See Abschied ("Muss i denn")
"**Must** Jesus bear the cross alone" (Maitland) G. N. Allen. Words by T. Shepherd. FSS 5
"**Must** the crown of thorns so cruel." See Kors och krona (Stenhammer)
"**Mutter**, mutter, glaube nicht." See Lied der braut (Schumann)

"**Mutter**, o sing' mich zur ruh'." See "Mother, O sing me to rest" (Franz); "Mother, oh sing me to rest" (Hildach)
Mutterseelenallein ("Es blickt so still."— All alone) German folk air. [Words by C. Tenner] e.g. SSG
Mutterseelenallein ("Es blickt so still") A. Braun. Words by C. Tenner. g. ED 1
My abode. See Aufenthalt (Schubert)
"**My** agitated heart is revealing." See Salut! demeure chaste et pure (Gounod)
My ain countrie ("I am far frae my hame") Words by M. L. Demarest. FSS 2— HSD
My ain countrie ("Oh! why left I my hame") Scottish air, arr by P. McLeod. Words by R. Gilfillan. JSE
The emigrant's complaint ("Oh! why left I my hame") BMC
"Oh! why left I my hame." FSS 3— HSSS—MMS—PS 2
My ain fireside ("O, I ha'e seen great anes") Scottish air. Words by E. Hamilton. JO—MMS—PS 1—WBT
My ain hoose ("Sing couthilie, couthilie, merrie an' free") Scottish air. Words from the Gaelic of M. MacFarlane. [Tr of Mo dhachaidh] e. MMS
My ain kind dearie, O ("When o'er the hill") See The lea rig
My ain kind dearie, O ("Will ye gang o'er the lea rig") Words by R. Ferguson. BO—PS 1
My angel. See "Meu anjo"
"**My** angel, come and stay with me." See A barquinha
"**My** ardent longing, whether near thee I tarry or distant wander." See "Il mio bel foco" (Marcello)
"**My** ardent lover in heav'n above." See Lola's song (Mascagni)
"**My** arms! against this Gorgias will I go." G. F. Händel. SAS 3
"**My** banks they are furnished with bees." T. A. Arne. Words by W. Shenstone. ME
My bark canoe ("Chekahbay tebik ondandayan") Ojibway Indian song. e.in. BA—BF 2. e. only BA
The bark canoe. e. TFC 2
My beloved. See Ma gazelle
"**My** Betsy is the blithest maid." G. Kirshaw. Words by T. Chapman. ME
My big lover. Ojibway Indian song. in. BA
"**My** bird, my bird, why go, my pet." See The bird song
My birthday. J. F. Reichardt. Words by J. G. Whittier. LBR
"**My** blessing rest on ye, O woods." See Benediction (Tchaikovsky)
"**My** boat is on the shore." H. R. Bishop. Words by Lord Byron. HSE 2
My boat is waiting here for thee. H. Smart. Words by F. Enoch. FMB

"My bonie lass, I work in brass." Air: Clout the caudron. Words by R. Burns. BSR

"My Bonnie." See Bring back my Bonnie to me

My bonnie boy. Folk song from Gloucestershire. SF 4
Variant of: My bonny, bonny boy

"My Bonnie lies over the ocean." See Bring back my Bonnie to me

"My bonnie Lizzie Baillie." See Bonnie Lizzie Baillie

My bonny, bonny boy. Folk song. SEF 1—SO
Variant: My bonnie boy

"My bonny cuckoo." Irish song. e. MMI

"My bonny keel laddie, my canny keel laddie." See The bonny keel laddie

"My bonny sailor won my mind." See The bonny sailor (Hook)

My boy Tammie ("Whar' ha'e ye been a' the day") 17th century Scottish air. Words by H. Macneill. MMS—PS 1

My boy Tammy ("Whar' ha'e ye been a' the day") HSSS

My boy Willie. Folk song: Worcestershire version. SEF 1—SF 4—SO
Billie boy. Kentucky version. WLT
Billy boy. FSS 3— HSC— JSE— TFC 2—WBT—WSC
My boy Billy. North Carolina version no. 1. CSE
—North Carolina version no. 2. CSE

"My brave lad sleeps in his faded coat of blue." See The faded coat of blue (McNaughton)

"My bretheren, don't get weary." Negro spiritual. HR

"My brigantine." L. V. Saar. Words by J. F. Cooper. TL

"My brother, de Lord has been here." See Seek and ye shall find

My brown-haired maiden. See Ho-ro mo nighean donn, bhòidheach

My brown maid. See Mo nighean donn

My brudder Gum. S. C. Foster (music and words) NMP—WBT

"My brudder sittin' on de tree ob life." See Roll, Jordan, roll

"My Celia! smiling gladness." See Little Celia Connellan

"My childhood's love." Von Flotow. e. FSS 8

"My children! O ye, my children." See Ah, la paterna mano (Verdi)

"My children, spare your tears." See Ah! malgré moi (Gluck)

"My choice! why should I choose." See À quoi bon l'économie (Massenet)

My coggie, sirs, my coggie, sirs. See "There's cauld kail in Aberdeen"

"My college days must have an end." Amherst college song. CHS

My college girl. J. W. Hill. Words by A. W. Kellogg. CHS

My comrade. See Der gute kamerad

"My comrades when I'm no more drinking." See Drinking song

"My Connor his cheeks are as ruddy as the morning." See The dear Irish boy

"My country! dear ungrateful country." See Di tanti palpiti (Rossini)

"My country dear, when soaring high." C. F. Price. Words by T. J. Sheppard. MP—NMS

"My country! 'tis of thee." See America (Carey); America (McCabe)

"My countrymen, awake, arise." Modern Irish air. Words by D. F. M'Carthy. MMI

"My daddie was a fiddler fine." Air: The reel o' Stumpie. Words by R. Burns. BSR

"My daddy was gone to the market." 18th century song. ME

My darling, be brave. See Coraggio, ben mio

"My darling love! my darling love." See The little witch (Nicolai)

"My darling, oh, my darling." See La chanson des métamorphoses (Breton version)

My darling was so fair. See In der fremde (Taubert)

My day is bitter ("Marmar zamānī") Syrian folk song. ar.e. BF 2

"My days are gliding swiftly by." See Shining shore (Root)

"My days were pass'd in idling." See "Per non istare in ozio" (Donizetti)

"My dear and only love." See I'll never love thee more

"My dear, if we were wandering." See "La bell' si nous étion' dadans"

"My dear mistress has a heart." Air: Y dydd cyntaf o Awst, or, The first of August. MMW

My dear-o. H. H. Lemmel (music and words) BSS

"My dear old mother." See Gamle mór (Grieg)

"My dear old mountains, I must leave you." See Abschied vom dirndel

"My dearest dear." Folk song from North Carolina. CSE

"My dearest love, true will I prove." See "Caro mio ben" (Giordani)

My delight (Meine freuden) F. Chopin. Words by A. Mickiewicz. e.g. FF

My dog and I. Old English air. BE 6

My dog and my gun. See "Let gay ones and great" (Baildon)

"My dolly." Old college air. WSC

My dream. See Mi sueño

"My ear to the brink of the stream I laid." See Nökken (Kjerulf)

"My eyes are closing in a drowsy, lazy slumber." See Revery (Arenski)

"My fair and rare one." See "Mo rùn geal, dìleas"

My fair love leaving me. Irish air. Words by N. Chesson. FSI

"**My** fairest child, I have no song to give you." See One grand sweet song (King)

"**My** faith looks up to Thee." L. Mason. Words by R. Palmer. HSD— NMH— NMS—WA— WBT—WS —WSW Olivet. LA

My faithful fair one. See "Mo rùn geal dìleas"

My faithful fond one. See "Mo rùn geal dìleas"

My faithless lover is forgetting. See L'ingrat ne vient pas encore

"**My** father! ah! methinks I see." G. F. Händel. SAS 1

"**My** father and mother were Irish." See The ninepenny fidil

"**My** father bade me pick herbs." See "Mon père m'envoie-t-à l'herbe"

"**My** father built a house, did he." See "Mon père a fait bâtir maison" (Va, va, va, p'tit bonnet tout rond)

"**My** father gave me an acre of land." See Sing ivy

"**My** father had no girl but me." See "Mon pèr' n'avait fille que moi" (Cécilia)

"**My** father has forty good shillings." Scottish song. PS 2

"**My** father he died, and I didn't know how." See Posey boy

"**My** father he has said." See Tre löften (Beckman)

"**My** father! highest venerated hero." See Gebet des Amfortas (Wagner)

"**My** father in leather was clad." See Adieu to old England

My Father, look upon my anguish. G. F. Händel. SAS 4

"**My** father made me marry." See La maumariée (Breton version)

"**My** Father, my Father, look upon my anguish." See My father, look upon my anguish (Händel)

"**My** father, O, a house built he." See "Mon père a fait bâtir maison" (J'entends le moulin)

"**My** father owns a fine house." See Young Edward

"**My** father owns a large estate." See Handsome Sally

"**My** father sent me to old Rutgers." See On the banks of the old Raritan

"**My** father, too, gave me away." See La maumariée (Canadian version)

"**My** father turn'd me out of doors." See Hares in the old plantation

"**My** father was a farmer." Air: The weaver and his shuttle. Words by R. Burns. BSR

My fatherland. J. Škroup. Words by **J. K. Tyl.** e. KSE "Where is my home" ("Kde domov můj") bo.e. BF 1

My friend and pitcher. Shield. BE 2— HSE 2

"**My** friend is the man." J. Hook. FSS 8

"**My** friend! my friend." A. H. Behrend. Words by F. E. Weatherly. BAS 1

"**My** garden I did plant." See My garden of flowers

My garden of flowers. English folk air. Words by H. H. Harbour. DO

"**My** gentle harp! once more I waken." Celtic air: The coina, or dirge. Words by T. Moore. MI—MMI

"**My** gentle harp, once more I waken." Londonderry air. [Words by T. Moore] DSH

My gentle village maid. C. Arthur (music and words) CHS

"**My** God and Father, while I stray." See Troyte's chant (Troyte)

"**My** goddess Celia." G. Monro. PR 2

My goddess, woman ("O' mighty nature's handiworks") Scottish air: The butcher boy. Words by Learmont. PS 2

My good Lord have been here. Negro spiritual. BOM

"**My** grandfather had some very fine ducks." L. Compton. CHS

"**My** grandfather's clock was too large for the shelf." See Grandfather's clock (Work)

"**My** grandma lives on yonder little green." See My grandma's advice

My grandma's advice. HSD

"**My** grandsire beat a drum so neat." See Darby Kelly (Whitaker)

"**My** grief for this forbids mine eyes to close." G. F. Händel. SAS 3

My harp has one unchanging theme. For Spanish translation see El arpa triste

"**My** Harry was a gallant gay." Scottish air: The Highlander's lament. Words by R. Burns. BSR—PS 2

"**My** hawk is tir'd of perch and of hood." See Lay of the imprisoned huntsman (Schubert)

"**My** head got wet with the midnight dew." See Don't be weary, traveller

"**My** head is solely forehead now." See Once too often

"**My** heart all beauty takes from thee." See "Mein herz schmückt sich mit dir" (Rubinstein)

My heart and lute. H. Bishop. Words by T. Moore; wrongly attributed to J. P. Kemble. DM 1—FSS 4

My heart and lute (Mit hjerte og min lyre) H. Kjerulf. Words by T. Moore. e.n. SSN—WM 1

"**My** heart and thy heart." See "Dein herz und mein herz"

"**My** heart at thy dear voice." See "Mon coeur s'ouvre à ta voix" (Saint-Saëns)

"**My** heart at thy sweet voice." See "Mon coeur s'ouvre à ta voix" (Saint-Saëns)

"**My** heart doth languish." See "Sento nel core" (Scarlatti)

"**My** heart doth long for rest." See Le vallon (Gounod)

"**My** heart ever faithful." See "Mein gläubiges herze frohlocke" (Bach)

"**My** heart for many a year was cheer'd." See "Eg gjaette Tulla"

"My heart found me a mistress long ago."
See Le coeur de ma bien-aimée

"My heart in need of rest."   See Le vallon
(Gounod)

"My heart is a-breaking, dear tittie."   Air:
Tam Glen.   Words by R. Burns.
BSR

"My heart is a-breakin', dear tittie" (Tam
Glen) Air: The muckin' o' Geordie's
byre.   Words by R. Burns.   BSB—
PS 1

"My heart is fill'd with gloomy fear."   See
Anges du paradis (Gounod)

"My heart is full of happy tears."   See
Stella del marinar (Ponchielli)

"My heart is heavy night and day."   See
My fair love leaving me

My heart is in bloom.   See "Meine liebe
ist grün" (Brahms)

"My heart is light."   Rossini.   FSS 6

"My heart is like a dreary night."   See
"Mein herz ist wie die dunkle nacht"
(Lassen)

"My heart is like the gloomy night."   See
"Mein herz ist wie die dunkle nacht"
(Mendelssohn)

My heart is no longer mine.   See "Il mio
core non è con me" (Fedeli)

"My heart is sair—I darena tell."   Air:
For the sake o' somebody.   Words by
R. Burns.   BSB—BSR

"My heart is sair, I daurna tell" (My heart
is sair for somebody) Scottish air.
Words by R. Burns.   FSS 8—JO—
MMS—PS 1

My heart is thine.   Proch.   e.   KSE

"My heart is wae, and unco wae."   Air:
Mary's dream.   Words by R. Burns.
BSR

My heart is weary.   A. G. Thomas.
Words by J. Sturgis.   e.g.
OPS 2—SOA 2

My heart is weary (Schwer liegt auf
dem herzen)   e.g.   KS 3

My heart, O sweet, is thine forever.   See
Sweet constancy

"My heart to hear thy voice."   See "Mon
coeur s'ouvre à ta voix" (Saint-Saëns)

My heart to thee.   See À toi mon coeur
(Gounod)

"My heart was ance as blythe and free."
Air: To the weaver's gin ye go.
Words by R. Burns.   BSR

"My heart, why weepest thou."   See Revery of the young peasant (Musorgskii)

"My heart with love is beating."   Attributed to Shield.   HSE 2—ME

My heart's belov'd is mine.   W. F. G.
Nicolaï.   e.   KSN

"My heart's in the Highlands."   Air: Cro
challin.   Words by R. Burns.   BSB—
MMS—PS 1

My heart's in the Highlands ("Farewell to
the Highlands") Air: The musket salute.   Words by R. Burns.   BSR

"My heart's in the Highlands."   Old air:
Portmore.   Words by R. Burns.
FSS 1—JO—JSE—LA—WBT

"My heart's in the Highlands" ("Mein
herz ist im Hochland") German
folk air.   Words by R. Burns.
e.g.   SSG
"Mein herz ist im Hochland."   g.
ED 1

"My heart's in the Highlands."   J. M.
Courtney.   Words by R. Burns.   OH
—TFC 2

"My heart's in the Highlands" ("Mein herz
ist im Hochland") A. Jensen.   Words
by R. Burns.   e.g.   FO 1.   e. only
FTS

"My heart's love to gain forever."   See
La seña

My home 'midst hills and valleys.   See
Min lilla vrå bland bergen (Sandstrom)

"My home to the east by Croatia is bound-
ed."   Carniolan song.   e.   KSE—
SN

My homeland. National song of Bohemia.
e.   CST

"My home's on the mountain."   See Fairy
haunts (Jackson)

"My hope is in the Everlasting."   J.
Stainer.   OS 3—SAS 3

"My hopes are dreams of night."   See
Mabrooka

"My! isn't this fine."   See At the hop
(Carter)

My Jamie o'er the sea.   A. Lee.   FSS 6

"My Jesus, as Thou wilt."   C. M. Weber.
Words by B. Schmolke.   [Tr of
Mein Jesu, wie du willt]   e.
HSD
"My Jesus, as Thou wilt" (Jewett)   e.
FSS 4—LA—MCS

"My Jesus Christ, a-walking down the
heavenly road."   See Zion, weep a-low

"My jewel, my joy."   Irish folk song.
JOI

My jo Janet ("Sweet sir, for your courtesie") Scottish song.   Words by R.
Burns.   MMS—PS 1

"My joy and grief, go sleep and gather."
See Soontree

"My joyful ardor."   See "Il mio bel foco"
(Marcello)

"My lad, be off, I warn you."   See La rosa
(Mercadante)

My laddie ("Oh, my laddie") Scotch love-
song.   W. A. Thayer.   Words by
Princess Troubetzkoy.   AA

My laddie far away.   Lindsay.   FSS 7

My lady ("I hear, I hear") College song.
WC

"My lady, your little parrot."   See "Señora, su periquito" (2d version)

My lady's bower.   H. Temple.   Words by
F. E. Weatherly.   CB

My lady's gown, there's gairs upon't.   See
"My lord a-hunting he is gane" (Greig)

My last abode.   See Aufenthalt (Schubert)

My last cigar.   [L. V. H. Crosby]   CHS—
CU—HSD—MPC— WBT—WC

"My life is a wave."   See Vågen (Laurin)

"My life is like the summer rose."   R.
Schumann.   Words by R. H. Wilde.
FSS 7

"My life is like the summer rose." C. Thibault. Words by R. H. Wilde. JO —WBT
"My little heart is all the time a-sighing." See Mon petit coeur soupire
My little heart's a-sighing. See Mon petit coeur soupire
My little Kerry cow. Irish air. Words by W. M. Letts. FSI
My little love. C. B. Hawley. MSF 2 —SM 1
"My little pretty one." 16th century song. CO 1—DM 1
My little valley home. G. W. Beckel. Words by H. Devere. FSS 8
My little woman. G. L. Osgood. CB
"My lodging is on the cold ground." 17th century air. Words by J. Gay (founded on an older song) BE 3 —HSE 1—PI
On the cold ground (I prethee love, turn to me) CO 2
"My lodging it is on the cold ground." M. Locke. Old words. BOH—DM 1
On the cold ground (I prethee love, turn to me) CO 2
My lodging is on the cold ground ("I cannot change as others do") 17th century air. Words by Rochester. WL
Constancy. DM 1
"My lodging is the cellar here." See Der rheinweinzecher(Fischer)
"My longing for thee never ceases." See Remember be sure and be there (Hopkins)
"My Lord a-hunting he is gane." J. Greig. Words by R. Burns. BSR
"My Lord calls me." See Steal away to Jesus
My Lord delivered Daniel. Negro spiritual. JP
My Lord delibered Daniel. HR
Variant of: Didn't my Lord deliver Daniel
"My Lord, He calls me." See Steal away to Jesus
"My Lord, what a morning." Negro spiritual. HR
"My Lord, what a mornin'." JB
"My Lord, what a mourning." JP
My Lord's writing all the time. Negro spiritual. JP
My Lord's a-writin' all de time. JB
My Lord's riding all the time. HR
My love beyond the sea. A. S. Sullivan. Words by J. P. Douglas. FSS 8
"My love bound me with a kisse." R. Jones. MM
"My love dwelt in a northern land." E. Elgar. Words by A. Lang. TL
"My love dwelt in a northern land" (A northern romance) H. B. Pasmore. Words by A. Lang. e.g. HST
My love, farewell. See Behüt' dich Gott (Nessler)

"My love has gone to live in lovely Lucca." See "E lo mio amore è andato a soggiornare" (Gordigiani)
"My love hath now left me." See Forsaken (Koschat)
"My love he built me a bonnie bower." See The border widow's lament
"My love he is fairer than a summer day." See Draoigheanán donn
"My love is as fair as the blossom." Air: The star of Llanedi. Words by A. Edwards. MMW
"My love is gone on his travels, poor lad." See Heimlicher liebe pein (Weber)
My love is like a red, red rose. See "My luve is like a red, red rose" (Scottish air)
"My love is slender, sweet, and fair." See My own dear maid
"My love is the flaming sword." See A song of Thanksgiving (Allitsen)
"My love is very distant." See Song of the shepherds
"My love, oh, know'st thou not how." See Le mariage des roses (Franck)
"My love she was born in the north counterie." See Fair maidens' beauty will soon fade away
"My love, she's but a lassie yet, a lightsome lovely lassie yet." Air: Put up your dagger, Jamie. Words by J. Hogg. HSSS—MMS—PS 1—WBT—WL
"My love she's but a lassie yet, my love she's but a lassie yet." Air: Put up your dagger, Jamie. Words by R. Burns. BSB—BSR
"My love, still I think that I see her." Irish air: Kathleen O'More. Words by G. Reynolds. MMI
"My love, thou'rt like a dew-gemm'd flower." Air: Craig y Ddinas, or, Dinas rock. Words by J. Thomas. MMW
"My love to my bride." See Mairi bhàn òg
"My love to thee" (Na Molokama) D. Nape. e.h. HA
My love to you ua hiki no. See Maui girl
"My love was born in Aberdeen." Air: The white cockade. Words by R. Burns. BSR—PS 2
"My lovely bretheren, how do you do." See Who'll jine de union
"My lovely bride, my dear young wife." See Vandring i skoven (Grieg)
My lovely Irish boy. Irish folk song. JOI
"My lover I hear." See Der schmied (Brahms)
"My lover is a weaver." See "Mein liebster ist ein weber" (Hildach)
"My love's a match in beauty." See If I were king of Ireland
"My love's an arbutus." Irish air: Coola Shore, arr by C. V. Stanford. Words by A. P. Graves. CST—EF—FSI—GO—KF 2—KF 3—PI—SM 4—WBT—WBW

"**My** love's in Germanie." See "My luve's in Germanie"

"**My** love's the blossom of the year." Air: Can y Lleissoniaid. Words from the Welsh. e. MMW

"**My** love's the fairest creature." Irish air: Shelah na Conolan. Words by Lady Morgan. MMI

My love's too highly born, I fear. See Des glockenthürmers töchterlein (Loewe)

"**My** luve is like a red, red rose." Air: Major Graham. Words by R. Burns. BSR

(**My** luve is like a red, red rose) "O my love is like a red, red rose." Air: Low down in the broom. Words by R. Burns. BSB

My love is like a red, red rose. PS 1—WBT

My luve's like a red, red rose. WL

"O, my love is like a red, red rose." MMS

"Oh, my love is like a red, red rose." HSSS

The red, red rose. FSS 2

(**My** luve is like a red, red rose) "Oh, my luve's like a red, red rose." G. M. Garrett. Words by R. Burns. TL

(**My** luve is like a red, red rose) O my love is like a red, red rose. R. Schumann. Words by R. Burns. MS

"**My** luve's in Germanie." Jacobite air. Words by H. Macniell. MMS

"My love's in Germanie." PS 1

My luve's like a red, red rose. See "My luve is like a red, red rose" (Air: Low down in the broom)

"**My** lytell prety one, my pretie boni one." See "My little pretty one"

"**My** maid's thrown me over." See Der verschmähete

"**My** mamma cut me and put me in the pot." See The enchanted white duck

"**My** man John." Somerset folk song. FSF—SEF 2—SO—TFC 2

"**My** mandolin is sighing." See 'A serenata d' 'e rrose (Capua)

My Mary Anne. M. Tyte. HSD—WBT

My Maryland. See Maryland, my Maryland

"**My** massa died a-shouting." See I'm a-trav'ling to the grave

My Merlindy Brown. Negro serenade. H. T. Burleigh. Words by J. E. Campbell. BF 2—BP—FMB—SM 3

"**My** mind being much inclined." See Captain Thompson

"**My** mind it is uneasy." Irish folk song. JOI

"**My** mind to me a kingdom is." W. Byrd. Words attributed to E. Dyer. DM 1—JE—MM

"**My** mistress is as fair as fine." J. Benet. DM 2

"**My** misty corrie, by deer frequented." See My misty dell

My misty dell. Scottish air. Words by D. B. MacIntyre. [Tr of Coire cheathaich] e. MMS

"**My** mither ment my auld breeks." See Robin Tamson's smiddy

"**My** mither's ay glowran owre me." Air: A health to Betty. Words by A. Ramsay. MMS

"My mither's aye glow'rin' owre me." PS 1

"**My** Moon-Flower, my Moon-Flower." See Dying Moon-Flower (Lieurance)

"**My** mother bid me." Folk song: Big Laurel, N.C. version. CSE

—Hot Springs, N.C. version. CSE

—Virginia version. CSE

"**My** mother bids me bind my hair." Haydn. Words by A. Hunter. BE 3—MSS 1—SS 1

"My mother bids me bind my hair" ("Bind' auf dein haar") e.g. KF 1—KF 2—PG 1

My mother dear. S. Lover. FSS 3—NMH—WBT

My mother did so before me. Folk song. BSW

"**My** mother has gone to journey away." See In the kingdom

"**My** mother loves me not." See Herzeleid

"**My** mother minds me not." See Forlorn (Franz)

"**My** mother scolds me every day." Air: Y teulu hynod, or, The noted family. Words by Talhaiarn. MMW

"**My** mother she told me to set him a chair." See My mother bid me (Hot Springs, N.C. version)

"**My** mother thou, belov'd and fair." See Til Norge (Grieg)

My mother's Bible. H. Russell. Words by G. P. Morris. FSS 2—HSD—JO—NMH—WBT

"**My** mother's gone to glory." See In bright mansions above

My mother's memory. B. O. Klein. Words by J. B. O'Reilly. TL

My mother's memory. W. Taubert. Words by J. B. O'Reilly. LBR

My mother's song. F. Schubert. FSS 4

"**My** moustache." Columbia university song. CHS—CU—HSD

"**My** name d'ye see's Tom Tough." See Tom Tough (Dibdin)

"**My** name is Captain Grant." See Captain Grant

"**My** name is Doctor Irongray." See Doktor Eisenbart

"**My** name is Edward Hollander." See The Flying Cloud

"**My** name is Paddy Leary." See Off to Philadelphia

"**My** name is Polly Hill." See The Yangtsi-kiang (Dunlop)

"**My** name is Solomon Levi." See Solomon Levi (Seaver)

"**My** name is Yankee Doodle and I am a good old scout." See Yankee Doodle-oodle

"My name is Yankee Doodle and my home's the U. S. A." See Yankee Doodle-oodle

"My name it is Hugh Reynolds." See She's the dear maid to me

"My name it is Jack." See The ploughman

"My name's, d'ye see, Tom Tough." See Tom Tough (Dibdin)

"My name's Edward Morgan." See Jenny Jones (Parry)

My Nannie, O. Scottish air. Words by Burns. BSB—PS 1
"Behind yon hills where Lugar flows." BSR

My Nannie's awa'. See "Now in her green mantle blythe nature arrays"

"My Nannie's gone to Pen-y-Vai." Air: O, let the wind blow as it may. Words from the Welsh. e. MMW

My Nanny ("Oh! when I think 'neath sorrow's smart") Air: Beth 'wedy di am fab i ffarmer, or, What sayest thou of a farmer's son. Words by Ieuan Dhu. MMW

My Naples. See Napole mio

My native land ("Al mio ciel") See Patria (Mattei)

My native land ("For the blessings that surround me") F. Abt. FSS 8—MP—NMS—WBT

My native land ("Homeland mine, my native land."—Kraï tui moï) A. T. Grechaninoff. Words by A. Tolstoi. e. SMR 2

My native land ("Hvor herligt er mit födeland") See Mit födeland (Ibsen)

My native land ("There is a land far o'er the mighty western sea") F. von Suppé. e. LA

"My native land again." See Es war ein traum (Lassen)

"My native land! what words can be." L. B. Marshall. Words by W. W. Caldwell. JS

My neighbor ("A susida") Ruthenian folk song. e.r. SMF

"My Nina still lies dreaming." See Nina (Pergolesi)

"My noble knights, I hail you." See "Nobles seigneurs, salut" (Meyerbeer)

My Normandy. See Ma Normandie (Bérat)

My old dog Tray. See Old dog Tray (Foster)

My old Dutch. C. Ingle. WA—WBT—WL—WSW

My old horse-blanket pin. F. Ames. Words by R. D. Ware. BSS

My old Kentucky home. S. C. Foster (music and words) BD—BSE—CHS—CST—DO— DSH—EF— FMB—GO—HSC—HSD— JO—JS—MP— MPC—NMH— NMP—NMS—OH—TFC 1—WA—WBT—WC—WSC—WSW

My only joe and dearie. 18th century Scottish air. Words by R. Gall. PS 1
"Thy cheek is o' the rose's hue." HSSS—MMS

My Ottawa. Ottawa university song. Words by F. Johnson. CHS

"My own America, land great and fair." See A prayer (Anderson)

My own dear maid ("My love is slender, sweet, and fair") Air: The vale of Clwyd. Words by A. Edwards. MMW

"My own dear one's gone." See Dh' fhalbh no leannan fhein

My own, my guiding star. G. A. Macfarren. Words by J. Oxenford. FSS 8—TS—WBT

My own native land. W. B. Bradbury. FSS 3—JS—WBT

My own shall come to me. E. W. Foster. Words by J. Burroughs. LBR

My parents treated me tenderly. Folk song: Allanstand, N.C. version. CSE
—Big Laurel, N.C. version. CSE
—Carmen, N.C. version. CSE
Variant: Peggy Walker

"My pastheen fionn is my soul's delight." See Páisdín fionn

"My peace is gone." See "Meine ruh' ist hin" (Graben-Hoffmann)

"My peace thou art." See "Du bist die ruh'" (Schubert)

"My Peggy's face, my Peggy's form." Air: My Peggy's face. Words by R. Burns. BSB—BSR

My phantom double. See Der doppelgänger (Schubert)

"My Phillida, adieu, love" (Corydon's doleful knell) Air: Babes in the wood. DM 1

"My Phillida, adieu! love." Miss Mellish. ME

My playmate. Russian folk air. Words by H. H. Harbour. DO

My pony ("Hop, hop, hop! reins I will not drop") [C. G. Hering] Words by N. H. Dole. DO

My pony ("I ride my pony ev'rywhere") WBT—WSC

"My poor Jacques." See "Pauvre Jacques" (Travanet)

"My pretty fishermaiden." See "Du schönes fischermädchen" (Meyerbeer)

"My pretty Jane." See When the bloom is on the rye (Bishop)

"My pretty Mary." See Màiri bhòidheach

My psalm. W. A. Mozart. Words by J. G. Whittier. LBR

My queen. See "Wie bist du meine königin" (Brahms)

"My red blanket I will put on." See Red blanket

"My Redeemer and my Lord." A. Sullivan. SAS 1

My rose ("Droop all the flowers in my garden") Irish air: Black-eyed Susan. Words by D. Sigerson. MMI

My rose of yester-e'en. M. Rich (music and words) ES

My Rosy. Modern Swiss ballad. T. Stauffer. e. KSE—WL

"**My** Sandy gi'ed to me a ring." See I love my love in secret

"**My** Savior spoke these words so sweet." See Hear the lambs a-crying

"**My** shadow's always with me." See The shadow

My ship is on the ocean. Negro song. JP

"**My** silks and fine array." Traditional air. Words by W. Blake. JE

My silver throated fawn. Sioux love song. T. Lieurance. Words by K. Jones. e. LN

"**My** sister dear, o'er this pale cheek." See "Pourquoi pleurer? pourquoi pleurer" (Auber)

"**My** sister, the Lord has been here." See Seek and you shall find

"**My** sister's took her flight and gone home." See Angels waiting at the door

"**My** son I reared as might the brooding partridge." See The wife of Tone

"**My** song is brief, a single line." See Untreu (Cornelius)

"**My** song is so sad and so dreary." See A lament (Borodin)

"**My** songs are envenomed and bitter" ("Mon chant est amer et sauvage") A. Borodine. Words after Heine. ⌈Tr of Vergiftet sind meine lieder⌉ e.g. NM 1

"**My** songs of love." R. Hahn. Words by V. Hugo. e. BC

"**My** songs to thee would be bringing." See Si mes vers avaient des ailes (Hahn)

"**My** sons, my sons." M. Costa. OS 4

My sorrow and trouble. See "Mo chreach a's mo dhíachairt"

"**My** soul, be on thy guard." L. Mason. Words by G. Heath. FSS 4

"**My** soul beseeches thy deepest blessing." See "Por ti respira"

"**My** soul is a witness for my Lord." See Who'll be a witness for my Lord

"**My** soul is athirst for God." A. R. Gaul. OS 3—SAS 3

"**My** soul is sad, my peace is o'er." See "Meine ruh' ist hin" (Schubert)

"**My** soul wants something that's new." Negro spiritual. HR

My soul's delight and treasure. See O luce di quest' anima (Donizetti)

My soul's gwine shine. See Oh, my little soul's gwine to shine

My spouse, Nancy. Air: My jo, Janet. Words by R. Burns. BSB
"Husband, husband, cease your strife." BSR

My star. See Una stella (Mililotti)

My sun. See 'O sole mio (Capua)

My sunshine. See 'O sole mio (Capua)

"**My** swan." See En svane (Grieg)

My sweet (Moani ke ala) Leleiohoku. e.h. HA

"**My** sweet repose." See "Du bist die ruh'" (Schubert)

"**My** sweetest bride, my dear young wife." See Vandring i skoven (Grieg)

"**My** sweetheart, come along." See Sweet nightingale

"**My** sweetheart is pretty." See "Mei schatzerl" (Weber)

My sweetheart writes. See Die liebende schreibt (Mendelssohn)

"**My** tears fell fast while dreaming." See Invocation (Rhodes)

"**My** thanks, beloved companions." See "Mercè dilette amiche" (Verdi)

"**My** thought of thoughts, my very inmost being." See Jeg elsker dig (Grieg)

"**My** thoughts are like ships outward sailing." See "Mine tanker" (Hartmann)

My title clear (Arlington). T. Arne. Words by I. Watts. FSS 7

My tocher's the jewel. Air: The muckin' o' Geordie's byre, or, The highway to Edinburgh. Words by R. Burns. BSB—PS 1
"O, meikle thinks my luve o' my beauty." BSR

"**My** Tom is gone, what shall I do." See Tom is gone to Hilo

"**My** true love hath my heart." Original setting. Words by P. Sidney. DM 2

"**My** true love hath my heart." Canon. T. Marzials. Words by P. Sydney. BD
"My true love hath my heart" (Friendship) FMB—WA

"**My** true love is there." See Der schmied (Brahms)

My trundle-bed. J. G. Baker. HSD

My trusty trot. C. Arthur (music and words) CHS

My Tulla. See "Eg gjaette Tulla"

"**My** Uncle Jack is what some people call a jolly tar." See Every inch a sailor (Read)

"**My** warning heed." M. Blummer. e. SAS 2

My way's cloudy. Negro spiritual. HR —JB—JP

"**My** wife and I lived all alone." See Little brown jug (Eastburn)

My wife has ta'en the gee ("A friend o' mine cam here yestreen") Air: The miller. MMS—PS 1

My wife's a wanton wee thing. See "She play'd the loon or she was married"

"**My** wife's a winsome wee thing." Air: My wife's a wanton wee thing. Words by R. Burns. BSB—JO—PS 1

My world. H. H. Huss. Words by K. Trask. HST

"**My** wreath of lehua" (Na'i aupuni) D. Nape. e.h. HA

"**My** years are barely twenty." See La cianciosa

My yellow-haired lad ("Mo bouchaleen bwee") Irish air: Coulin Dhas. Words by N. Hopper. FSI

My youngest one is wedded (Di mezinke ausgegeben) Jewish folk song. e.y. BF 2

Myrtilla. S. Howard. ME

"The **mysteries** divine of poetry harmonious." See The octave (Rimskiĭ-Korsakov)

N

N. S. U. so gay. Nevada state university song. L. R. Merrill. CHS

"**Na** cóżeś mnie pani matko." See Why, oh mother

Na Dnyeprýé. See On the river Dnyéper (Musorgskiĭ)

"**Na** Gorenskem je fletno." See In Gorensko

"**Na** ka wai lukini wai anuhea oka rose." See Princess Kaiulani's home (Likelike)

Na Molokama. See "My love to thee" (Nape)

Na ni wale kuu home. See Princess Kaiulani's home (Likelike)

"**Na** Ostland wil ik varen" ("To Araby will I wander") 13th century Netherland song. d.e. EF

"**Naar** solen falder bag top og tinde." See Solefaldssang (Olsen)

"**Nach** diesen trüben tagen." See Frühlings-ankunft (Berner)

"**Nach** Frankreich zogen zwei grenadier'." See Die beiden grenadiere (Schumann)

"**Nach** Sevilla." L. Reichardt. Words by C. Brentano. g. ED 1

"**Nach** süden nun sich lenken." See Wanderlied der Prager studenten

Die **nacht** ("Aus dem walde tritt die nacht." —Night) R. Strauss. Words by H. von Gilm. e.g. FO 2 The night. e. WBW

"Die **nacht** war kaum verblühet." See Sonntag (Franz)

"Die **nacht** war schwarz." See Reue (Lachner)

Die **nachtigall** ("Nightingale, oh nightingale") See "Nightingale, oh nightingale" (Alabiev)

Nachtigall ("O nachtigall, dein süsser schall."—Nightingale) J. Brahms. Words by C. Reinhold. e.g. GM

"**Nachtigall,** ich hör dich singen." See Frau nachtigall

"**Nachtigall,** o nachtigall." See The nightingale (Alabiev)

Nachtigall und kukuk. See Poet and critic (Cui)

"**Nächtlicher** duft weht durch die luft." See Ständchen (Jensen)

Nachtlied ("Vergangen ist der lichte tag") F. Kugler. Words by J. von Eichendorff. g. ED 3

Nachtstück. See Nocturne (Balakirev)

"**Nací** en la cumbra de una montaña." See Boanerges

"**Nacqui** all' affanno e al pianto." See Non più mesta accanto al fuoco (Rossini)

"**Nad** Tatrou sa blýská." See Slovak national anthem

"**Nadie** me quiere." Folk song from southern California. e.s. HS

Nadson, S.
By a new-made grave (Rachmaninov) The spirit of poesy (Arenski)

"**Nae** birdies sang the mirky hour." Air: Sweet Willy. Words by R. Burns. BSR

"**Nae** gentle dames, tho' ne'er sae fair." Air: McLauchlin's Scots-measure. Words by R. Burns. BSR

Nae luck about the house. See There's nae luck about the house

"**Nae** mair we'll meet again." Highland air: Robi donna Gorach. HSSS—MMS

Nagareymna. See Song sung during a calm at sea

Nägeli, Hans Georg
Die abenddämmerung
An die abendsonne
"Blest be the tie that binds"
"A charge to keep have I" (same air as "Blest be the tie that binds")
Dennis. See "Blest be the tie that binds"; "A charge to keep have I"; "How gentle God's commands"; "The spirit in our hearts"
Der feste mann
"Firmly stand, my native land"
"Freut euch des lebens"
"Heirs of unending life"
"How gentle God's commands" (same air as "Blest be the tie that binds")
Das lied vom Rhein
"Life let us cherish." See "Freut euch des lebens"
"Die schönste zeit, die liebste zeit"
"Sow not in sorrow." See "Freut euch des lebens"
"The spirit in our hearts" (same air as "Blest be the tie that binds")
Sunset song. See An die abendsonne
Thy King cometh (Tr of Instantis adventum Dei)
Unser vaterland
Veilchen

"**Näh** doch nicht, lieb mütterlein." See The scarlet sarafan (Varlamov)

"**Näh** nicht, liebes mütterlein." See The scarlet sarafan (Varlamov)

Nähe des geliebten ("Ich denke dein") L. von Beethoven. Words by Goethe. g. ED 2

Nähe des geliebten ("Ich denke dein."—"I think of thee") E. Lassen. [Words by Goethe] e.g. KF 2

"**Nähe,** mutter, nähe nicht." See The scarlet sarafan (Varlamov)

Na'i aupuni. See "My wreath of lehua" (Nape)

Nairne, Carolina (Oliphant) Nairne, baroness
  The auld hoose (Scottish air)
  "Balooloo, my lammie" (Scottish air)
  Bonnie Charlie (Gow)
  Caller herrin' (Gow?)
  Charlie is my darling (Jacobite air)
  "Fareweel, O, fareweel" (Scottish air)
  The hundred pipers (Jacobite air)
  "The laird o' Cockpen" (Scottish air)
  The land o' the leal (Scottish air)
  The lass o' Gowrie (Air: Loch Erroch Side; air: O'er young to marry yet)
  O Charlie is my darling (Old Scottish air)
  The rowan tree (German air; Scottish air)
  "There grows a bonnie brier-bush in oor kail-yard, and white are the blossoms on't" (Scottish air)
  Wha'll be king but Charlie (Scottish air)
La naissance du Christ (The birth of Christ) Noël. French folk song. e. GO
Naissantes fleurs (Ye budding flowers) A. E. M. Grétry. e.f. KS 2
"Naked archer." See "Nudo arciero" (Falconieri)
The naked bear. Ojibway Indian song. e.in. BA
"N'allume pas encore." See The hour of dreams (Arenski)
"Namen nennen dich nicht." See Ihr
Nan of Gloster green. 18th century song. ME
Nancy ("Far, far from Tawe's valley") Air: Pan o'wn i ar frig noswaith. Words by Ieuan Dhu. MMW
Nancy Dawson. 18th century English song. BE 8
  Nancy Dawson (Miss Dawson's hornpipe) CO 2
Nancy Gay. 18th century song. ME
Nancy Lee. S. Adams. Words by F. E. Weatherly. FMB—FSS 2—HSC—HSD—MP— OH—PO —TFC 1—WA —WBT—WL—WSW
Nancy of London. Folk song from Dorset. SF 1
Nancy the pride of the west. Irish folk song. JOI
Nancy Till. Negro song. NMP
Nanette. Bergerette. e.f. WB
"Nani wale au e ike nei." See "How I love to gaze" (Nape)
"Nani wale na hala." See Hawaiian hula (Tomi! tomi) (Nape)
"Nani wale no oe." See Sunny Manoa (Hopkins)
Nänny, J. C.
  "Wär ich ein brünnlein klar" (Volksweise)
Nanny of the hill. J. Worgan. ME
Naomi. See "Father, whate'er of earthly bliss" (Mason)

Nape, David
  Dear heart
  Gardenia flower
  Hawaiian hula
  Honesakala. See Honeysuckles
  Honeysuckles
  "How I love to gaze"
  Ka inu wai. See Kohala's breezes
  Kohala's breezes
  Lei ohaoha. See "How I love to gaze"
  Makalapua. See "O budding flowers"
  "My love to thee"
  "My wreath of lehua"
  Na Molokama. See "My love to thee"
  Na'i aupuni. See "My wreath of lehua"
  "O budding flowers"
  Oi hoi ha. See "Upon the crest of Wailana"
  Poli pumehana. See Dear heart
  Pua sadinia. See Gardenia flower
  Tomi! tomi. See Hawaiian hula
  "Upon the crest of Wailana"
  Wai o Punalau. See Waters of Punalau
  Waters of Punalau
Napole mio. See Addio a Napole
"Napolitaine, I am dreaming of thee." See I am dreaming of thee (Lee)
"Naqui all' affanno, al pianto." See Non più mesta accanto al fuoco (Rossini)
När jag blef sjutton år (When I was seventeen) Swedish folk song. Words by H. Lilljebjörn. e.sw. HSOS—SMF
När jag var ett litet (The mournful one.— "A very little child was I") Swedish folk song. e. BMC
  The orphan. e. KSN
"När själen är nöjd" ("If peace and content") Prince Gustaf, duke of Upland (music and words) e.sw. HSOS
"Når stormen ryger op fra nord." See Fiskeren til sønnen (Elling)
Nära (Ever near) A. F. Lindblad (music and words) e.sw. SSN
  Ever near. e. KSN
Nares, James
  "Rise, my soul, and stretch thy wings"
  "Since I've known a Saviour's name" (same air as "Rise, my soul, and stretch thy wings")
"Narodil se Kristus Pán." See Bohemian Christmas carol
"Nasce al bosco" ("Born amid the rugged wildwood") Händel. e.i. BS 1
"Nasci para te amar" (I was born to love thee) Brazilian folk song. e.po. HF
Nash, Arthur
  Down by the riverside (Composer unknown)
  I doubt it (Adams)
  Tarpaulin jacket (Composer unknown)
  "There were three books" (Composer unknown)
  We stand by our classes (Composer unknown)

"**Natale,** Natale, o giorno beato." See Canto pel Natale (Moderati)

Nathan, Isaac
"Maid of Athens"
"When a trembling lover dies" (from Alcaid)
"Where are you going, my pretty maid"
"Why are you wandering here, I pray" (from Sweethearts and wives)

Nathusius, frau Maria Karoline Elizabeth Luise (Scheele) von
Heute und morgen
Jägers lust

National air of the United States of Brazil. See Hymno da proclamacao da republica (Miguez)

National anthem of Chili. See Dulce patria (Carnicer y Batlle)

National hymn ("Amanheceu finalmente") See Hymno nacional (Brazilian song)

National hymn ("God of our fathers") G. W. Warren. Words by D. C. Roberts. CST—TFC 2

National hymn ("My country 'tis of thee") See America (Carey)

National hymn ("O' patria, o rei") See Hymno nacional—Portugal (Pedro IV)

National hymn ("Oid mortales") See Himno nacional—Argentina (López y Planes)

National hymn—Latvia ("Deews, swehti Latwiju") e.le. BF 1

National hymn of France. See La Marseillaise (Rouget de Lisle)

National hymn of Guatemala. See Himno nacional de Guatemala (Alvarez)

National hymn of Italy. See Inno di guerra dei cacciatori delle Alpi (Olivieri)

National hymn of Japan. See "Kimi ga yo" (Hiromori)

National hymn of Norway. See "Ja vi elsker dette landet" (Nordraak)

National praise ("Up to thee, almighty Father") WCP

National song of Bolivia ("O Bolivians, the angel of freedom") B. Vincenti. e. BMC

National song of Germany. See Des Deutschen vaterland (Reichardt)

National song of Holland. See "Wien Neêrlandsch bloed" (Wilms)

National song of Norway. See "Sönner af Norge" (Blom)

National song of Poland. See Polish national song (Ogiński?)

National song of Servia. See "Rise, O Servians"

National song of Switzerland. See Ranz des vaches

The **nation's** voice uplifted. See Hymno nacional (Brazilian song)

Native land ("There is a land") LA

The **Nativity,** Stanzas from. D. S. Smith. Words by J. Milton. TL

Natural history. Children's song. WSC

"La **nature** est endormie." See Parais à ta fenêtre (Gregh)

"**Nature** from her sleep is waking." See Lo, the winter is past (Custance)

"**Nature** is peacefully sleeping." See Parais à ta fenêtre (Gregh)

"**Nature** is quietly sleeping." See Parais à ta fenêtre (Gregh)

Nature's adoration. See Die ehre Gottes aus der natur (Beethoven)

"**Naught,** naught shall warn thee of thy doom." See Schweig'! damit dich niemand warnt (Weber)

"**Naught** of wealth and naught of power." See Softly slept the holy Child

Naumann, Johann Amadeus. See Naumann, Johann Gottlieb

Naumann, Johann Gottlieb
Chant of Breton peasants
"Es leben die alten"
"Holy Spirit, Source of gladness" (Tr of O du allersüsste freude)
Rain on the roof
Song of temperance

The **navy-blue** and white. Marietta college song. Words by D. F. Turner. CHS

"**Nay,** have no fear, my grievings." See Seguita a piangere (Bassani)

"**Nay,** I can't believe." See "Non, je ne crois pas"

"**Nay,** I'll to the woods no more." See "Non, je n'irai plus au bois"

"**Nay** na bána lá gigelo." See Durwan's song

"**Nay,** tell me not, dear." Irish air: Dennis, don't be threatening. Words by T. Moore. MI—MMI

"**Nay!** though my heart should break." Tschaikowsky. e. MSS 1

Naylor, C. L.
"Little birds are singing"
"The little flowers came from the ground"
"'Twas a starry night of old"

Naylor, John
"The foe behind, the deep before"

Nazareth. C. Gounod (music and words) e. AB 1—BAS 1—BD—BS 1—DC—HC— HSS 3—HSS 4—KF 4—LA—WA—WS
Jésus de Nazareth (Jesus of Nazareth) e.f. FMB

"**Nce** simmo a la partenza." See Addio a Napole

"**Nce** sta na giardenera." See La Luisella

"**Ndi-ndi** ndi-ndi ndi-ndi ndi-ndi ndi. . . pronti? gnorsi." See Le telefono (Denza)

Ne biêly sniêgi. See The white snow

"**Ne** brani menîa, rodnaîa." See Mother, do not scold me

Ne bylo viêtru, vdrug povîanulo. See The guests arrive

"**Ne** crois pas que les morts soient morts." See Les morts (Chausson)

"**Né** dans une crêche." See Nazareth (Gounod)

"**Ne** jamais la voir ni l'entendre." See Soupir (Duparc); Soupir (Kramer)

Ne kukushechka vo syrom boru kukovala. See The conscript's lament

"Ne m'abandonne point, espoir de la vengeance." See Asile héréditaire (Rossini)

"Ne pouvant réprimer." J. Massenet. e.f. SOA 3

Ne shumi, mati, zelenaĭa dubrovushka. See The robber's fate

Ne spasibo ĭa igumnu tomu. See The novice

Ne tesan terem. See The wedding-suit

Neale, John Mason
"All is bright and cheerful round us" (Walter)
"Around the throne of God" (Peel)
Christmas carol (Helmore)
"Days grow longer" (Ancient air; also music by Warren)
"The foe behind, the deep before" (Naylor)
"Give ear, give ear, good Christian men" (Composer unknown)
"Here is joy for every age" (music by Helmore; also unknown composer)
"Let the merry church bells ring" (music by Blaikie; Cutler; Hodges; Howard; Redner; Warren; also unknown composer)
"Let the song be begun" (music by Hodges; Medley; Warren; also unknown composer)
"Let us tell the story" (Composer unknown)
"The morning of salvation" (Composer unknown)
"O'er the hill and o'er the vale" (Old air; also music by Dugard)
"Sing alleluia, all ye lands" (Traditional air)
"There stood three Maries by the tomb" (Litler)
"The world itself keeps Easter day" (music by Hodges; Preston; Redner; Smith; Warren; also unknown composer)
"Young and old must raise the lay" (Old air; also music by unknown composer)

Neapolitan cradle song ("Sleep on, O baby dearest") e. WSC

Neapolitan song ("Go then") See "Go then—'tis vain to hover"

"Near an ancient hostelrie." See The maiden of the Fleur de Lys (Sydenham)

"Near Edinburgh was a young son born." Air: Hynde Horn. Words by R. Burns. BSR

"Near in the forest." See The forest glade (Kreipl)

Near Krakow ("Od Krakowa czarny las") Polish folk song. e.p. BF 1

Near me, near me, lassie, lie near me. See "Lang hae we parted been"

Near my own blonde sweetheart. See Auprès de ma blonde

"Near the bridge beside the river." See Jealousy

"Near the doorway of my father." See Advice to lovers

"Near the lake where drooped the willow." See Long time ago

"Near the tomb where Christ hath been." M. S. Skeffington. Words by G. Moultrie. HC

"Near the tomb where Jesus slept." G. P. Grantham (music and words) HC

"Near the village there lives a fair maiden." See Carmè (Curtis)

"Near Woodstock town." 17th century traditional air and words. CS 1— DM 1—HSE 1—MM
The Oxfordshire tragedy. CO 2

"Near thou com'st, I'll soon embrace thee." See "Eccolo, a voi l'affido" (Rossini)

"Near to the walls of Sevilla." See Séguédille (Bizet)

Nearer home. See "One sweetly solemn thought"

"Nearer, my God, to Thee." F. Abt. Words by S. F. Adams. FSS 4
"Nearer, my God, to Thee" (Nearer to Thee) LA

"Nearer, my God, to Thee." J. D. Herron. Words by S. F. Adams. LA

"Nearer, my God, to thee." L. Mason. Words by S. F. Adams. BSS—- FSS 1—HSD—JS—LBR— MP—- —NMH—NMS—OH—TFC 1—TL —WA— WBT—WS— WSC— WSW
"Nearer, my God, to thee" (Bethany) BD—FMB—HSC

"Nearer, my God, to Thee." A. S. Sullivan. [Words by S. F. Adams] LA

Nearer to Thee. See "Nearer, my God, to Thee" (Abt)

"A neat fair lady walking in the garden." See The sweetheart in the army

"'Neath a marvellous roof many mansions arise." See Star of the north (Glinka)

"'Neath an apple-tree sat May." See La Marion et le bossu

"'Neath skies of fair Spain I wander." See "Sotto il bel ciel delle Spagne" (Semet)

"'Neath the almond trees that blossom." See "Unter blüh'nden mandelbäumen" (Weber)

'Neath the elms ("Winds of night, around us sighing") LA

'Neath the elms of dear old Yale. College song. CHS

"'Neath the elms of our old Trinity." College song. CHS

"'Neath the shadow of a tree" (Chanson des rues) Russian folk song. e.f. BO

"'Neath the silver silence of the moon." See Come to me (Denza)

"'Neath the stars that shone so bright." M. Cooke. HC

"'Neath the waves on crystal rock reclining." See Neckens polska

"'Neath their sceptre of iron." See Humble fille des champs (Halévy)

" 'Neath thy window, love, I stand." See
Serenade (Moszkowski)

Neaves, Charles
"Adieu, Dundee" (Scottish air)

"Nebay denah geen." See In the sugar
camp

"Nebel brauen über den see." See Herbstgang (Jordan)

The neckan's polka. See Neckens polska

Necken (The sea king) W. T. Söderberg.
Words by E. J. Stagnelius. e.sw.
SSN

Neckens polska (On a crystal throne)
Swedish folk song. Words by A.
A. Afzelius. e.sw. BO—SMF
Necken polka. e. GO
Neckens polska (The neckan's polka)
e.sw. BF 2
Neckens polska (The watersprite)
e.sw. HSOS

Ned that died at sea. C. Dibdin (music
and words) ME

De nederige geboorte (The simple birth)
Dutch song. d.e. BF 2

Nedjib Pacha
Hamidie
Modern patriotic war march. See
Turkish patriotic song
Song of the sultan. See Hamidie
Turkish patriotic song

Needham, Alicia Adélaïde
In blossom-time
Irish lullaby

Neefe, Christian Gottlob
The fishermen
Zufriedenheit

"Ne'er ask the hour." Air: My husband's
a journey to Portugal gone. Words
by T. Moore. MI

Ne'er dreamed the tender maid. See Elle
ne croyait pas (Thomas)

"Una negra guachinanga." Cuban folk
song. e.s. HS

Negro lullaby. H. T. Burleigh. Words
by J. E. Campbell. BP

Negron Sanjurjo, J. A.
El himno de Puerto Rico (Pericás)
"Negros y tristes son los pensamientos."
See Los celos de Carolina

"Nehmt euch in acht." V. Righini. g.
ED 2

"Nei, sjaa, kor det lyser og gyller og
brenn." See Sol (Alnaes)

Neidhardt, August H. See Neithardt,
August H.

Neidhardt von Reuenthal
Sommerlied
Summertime. See Sommerlied

Neidlinger, William Harold
The birthday of a king
Blow, bugle, blow
The endless song
The humble bee
Serenade

"Neig', schöne knospe" ("Bend, lovely
bud") A. Rubinstein. Words by F.
Bodenstedt (Mirza-Schaffy) e.g. SC

Neilson, Frederick B.
Three cheers for the red and the blue
(Old air)

"Nein, holde liebe kleine." See Vien qua
Dorina bella (Bianchi)

"Nein, länger trag' ich nicht die qualen."
See Durch die wälder (Weber)

"Nein, nimmer liebte ich." See He truly
loved me so (Tchaikovsky)

Neithardt, August H.
"I am a Prussian." See Preussens va-
terland
Preussens vaterland

"Neither sighs, nor tears." N. Laneir.
DM 1

"Nek se hrusti." Croatian song. se.
SN

Nekrasov', Nikolaï Aleksïeevich
Cradle-song of the poor (Musorgskiï)
"Glorious forever" (Rachmaninov)
Hunger song (Cui)
The sower (Cui)

"Nel cor più non mi sento" ("No more my
heart is fervent") G. Paisiello. e.i.
FEI 2
The lover's sigh. e.g. FSS 8
"Mich fliehen alle freuden." g. ED 1
"Nel cor più non mi sento" ("Why
feels my heart so dormant") e.i.
PA 1

"Nel lasciar la Normandia." Meyerbeer.
e.i. PP

Nel Pugh ("By Ystwyth I number my
sheep") Air: Mae genyf fi fwthyn a
gardd. MMW

"Nel puro ardor" ("In that pure flame")
J. Peri. e.i. FEI 1

Nell. G. Fauré. Words by Leconte de
Lisle. e.f. CM 1—SAM

Nella. See Parker, Mrs Nella

"Nelly Bly." S. C. Foster (music and
words) BSE—NMP— WA—WBT—
WL—WSW

Nelly, my love, and me ("There's a beech-
tree grove by the river-side") Irish air.
Words by P. W. Joyce. FSI—MMI

Nelly of the hazel dell. See The hazel
dell (Root)

Nelly was a lady. S. C. Foster (music and
words) CHS— CST— MPC—
NMH— NMP—WA— WBT—WL
—WSW
Nellie was a lady. FMB—TFC 1—
WC

Nelson, C.
Guadalquiver

Nelson, Sydney
Around our blazing fires
The greenwood tree
I will be happy too
"If thou wert by my side"
Madoline
Mary of Argyle
Neva boatman's song
"Oh, take her, but be faithful still"
The pilot
" 'Twas Christmas eve"
"When night comes o'er the plain"

"Nemobeyon nemobeyon." See The beaver hunt

"Nenemoshayn newahneah." See The lake sheen

Nenia (The legend of the Venetian laces) G. A. Randegger. Words from E. F. Randegger. BD

"Nenneko oyama no." See Slumber song of Izumo (Ross)

Nennella vienete (Fanciulla, vieni a me.— Fair maiden, come with me) Neapolitan song. e.i. FE

"Nenni, Nenni, vattenne." See La rosa (Mercadante)

Neptune's raging fury. See "You gentlemen of England"

"Ner Maidagen lokka aa sole skjin so vart aa veent." See Vaarvise

The Nereid. A. Glazunoff. Words by A. Pushkin. e. SC

"Nesem vám noviny." Bohemian Christmas song. bo.e. DCS

Nesmüller, Josef Ferdinand
Der Tyroler und sein kind (from Die zillertaler)

Nessler, Victor Ernst
Behüt' dich Gott. See Es hat nicht sollen sein
Es hat nicht sollen sein (from Der trompeter von Säkkingen)
It was not so to be. See Es hat nicht sollen sein
My love, farewell. See Es hat nicht sollen sein

"Nesswe ahgoonay tahgo." See A song of absence and longing

Nestler, Friedrich
Entschuldigung

Nettleton, A.
While the days are going by (Wyeth)

Neuer vorsatz ("Hier sitz ich auf rasen") Volksweise. Words by K. Schmidt. g. ED 2

"Neues jahr, neues jahr." Volksweise. Words by H. Hoffmann von Fallersleben. g. ED 3

Neukomm, Sigismund, ritter von
"I will lay me down"
The sea
"Speed, my bark, O gently speed thee"

Neva boatman's song. S. Nelson. FSS 4

Neve' a man speak like this man ("O! look-a death") Negro folk song from the Bahamas. KA

"Never, ah, nevermore shall I be gay again." See Weeping for thee

Never alone. F. Silcher. Words by R. W. Raymond. FSS 6

"Never broke a regulation." See A model college girl

Never did I think I should e'er come to this. See Serenata ("Bella siccome un angelo")

"Never go gloomily, man with a mind." See Cheerily, cheerily

"Never is my heart so gay in the budding month of May, never does it beat a tune half so sweet in blooming June; never know such happiness as on such a day as this, when October dons her crown." See When the leaves are turning brown (Crampton)

"Never is my heart so gay in the budding month of May, never does it beat a tune half so sweet in blooming June; never know such happiness as on such a day as this, when the Christmas tree is seen." See The holly wreath (Crampton)

"Never more to see her or hear her." See Soupir (Duparc)

"Never said a mumblin' word." Negro spiritual. BOM
Variant: Crucifixion

Never say fail. FSS 2

Never say No when you wish to say Yes. J. Hook. ME

"Never the maiden dream'd." See "Elle ne croyait pas" (Thomas)

"Never till now knew I love's smart." 18th century song. ME

"Never weather-beaten sail." T. Campion (music and words) BOH

"Nevermore to see or to hear him." See Soupir (Kramer)

Nevin, Arthur Finley
"Auf wiederseh'n! so sprachst du leise" Lorna Doone's song

Nevin, Ethelbert Woodbridge
A bed-time song
"Good night! good night, beloved"
Serenade. See "Good night! good night, beloved"

Nevin, George Balch
"God of our fathers, let Thy face"

New, S. W.
Tapping at the garden gate

"A new co-ed has alighted in town." See Upidee

"New England, New England." WBT

The new (fresh) herring. See Die nieuwe haring

The new Hail Columbia. See Hail Columbia, The new (Phile)

The new kingdom. B. Tours. Words by M. Mark-Lemon. HSS 4—WS

New mad Tom of Bedlam. See Mad Tom (Coperario)

The new moon. See Luna nova (Costa)

"The new moon's crescent seaward descending." See Luna nova (Costa)

The new-mown hay. Folk song from Hampshire. SF 3
Variant: Among the new-mown hay

New Prince, new pomp. Scotch air. Words by R. Southwell. MCS

New Prince, new pomp. C. Steggall. Words by R. Southwell. BSC

"The new woman." R. G. Cole. Words by R. M. Haines. CHS

The new year. See "Ring out, O bells" (Goetschius)

New Year carol ("Come thou with me") A. S. Gatty. WSC

New Year song ("They say that the year") L. Oehmler. Words by E. H. Miller. NMS

New Year song ("Upon this first day of the year") A. S. Gatty. WSC

New Year song ("When night's shadows fly."—Haru-no uta) Japanese folk song. e.j. BO

New Year's day ("Bonsoir le maître") See L'Aguignolé

New Year's day ("When winter winds are blowing") French folk air. Words by H. H. Harbour. DO

New Zealand national song. See "God girt her about with the surges"

Newcastle. 17th century song. CO 1
"Came you not from Newcastle." BE 7
"Come you not from Newcastle." DM 1—HSE 2—MM

Newcombe, G. Hubi-. See Hubi-Newcombe, G.

Newman, John Henry
"Lead, kindly light" (music by Dykes; Peace; Pinsuti; Sullivan)
"Now that the sun is beaming bright" (Händel)

Newport, Walter
"Lo: a star, ye sages hoary"

Newry mountain. Irish folk song. JOI

"The news frae Moidart cam' yestre'en." See Wha'll be king but Charlie

Newton, Eddie
"Casey Jones"

Newton, Elbridge Ward
An eastern college boating song
Hymn to College hill

Newton, Ernest
The doctor
A mathematic monody
Our noble selves
The pocket Gray

Newton, James
"What's sweeter than the new-blown rose"

Newton, John
As when the traveler (Bradbury)
"Glorious things of Thee are spoken" (music by Haydn; Rossini)
"How sweet the name of Jesus sounds" (Mason)
"How tedious and tasteless the hours" (Fleury)
Mary at the tomb (Blumenthal)
"Quiet, Lord, my froward heart" (Monk)

Newton, William Wilberforce
"Awake! awake! glad voices make" (Arnold)

"The next come down was dressed in red." See Little Musgrave and Lady Barnard (Rocky Fork, Tenn. version)

"Next, winter comes slowly." H. Purcell. PR 1

"Ngreu moj Mahmude." See "Rise, my Mahmude"

"Ni-ka wi-ta wa-gun-dha ti-be-no." See Ish'-i-buz-zhi

Nicaea. See "Holy, holy holy! Lord God Almighty" (Dykes)

Nicander, Karl August
Lifdrabanten och kung Erik (Lindblad)
Vågen (Laurin)

The nice young girl. A. S. Sullivan. FSS 6—WBT
The nice young man. A. S. Sullivan. FSS 6

Nichol, Henry Ernest
"The fishers sat within their boat"
"The flowers of earth are blooming"
"He saw the wheat-fields waiting"
"Ring, happy bells of Christmas time"
"Sweet Mary lulled her blessed Child"
"Voices of children"
"With our songs we greet thee"

Nicholls, H. F.
"The flowers in garden, field and wood"
"Go, lovely flowers"

Nichols, Anna M. E.
"Glorious, beauteous, golden-bright" (Tiddeman)

"Nicht bloss für diese unterwelt." See Wert der freundschaft (König)

"Nicht fürchte, liebchen, dich." See The treasure

"Nicht mehr zu dir zu gehen" ("I said, I will forget thee") J. Brahms. e.g. BAS 2

"Nicht mit engeln" ("Not the angels") A. Rubinstein. Words by F. Bodenstedt (Mirza-Schaffy) e.g. NM 2
"Nicht mit engeln" ("Not with angels") e.g. SC

"Nicht so schnelle, nicht so schnelle." See Aufträge (Schumann)

Nicodé, Jean Louis
Erbarmen
O thou most compassionate. See Erbarmen

Nicodemus Johnson. J. B. Murphy. JSE —NMP—WBT

"Nicodemus, the slave, was of African birth." See Wake Nicodemus (Work)

Nicolai, Otto
"Als büblein klein an der mutter brust" (from Die lustigen weiber von Windsor. Tr of "When that I was a little tiny boy")
"A weanling small on my mother's breast." See "Als büblein klein an der mutter brust"

Nicolai, Philipp
Wachet auf (Composer unknown)

Nicolaï, Willem Frederik Gerard
"Heft, burgers, 't lied der vrijheid"
"A little flower"
The little witch
My heart's belov'd is mine
Sing, citizens, the song of freedom. See "Heft, burgers, 't lied der vrijheid"

Nicoll, Robert
"Bonnie Bessie Lee" (Scottish air)
The married man's lament (Scottish air)

Nicolò de Malte, pseud. See Isouard, Niccolò

Niebusch, Karl von. See Schneider, Karl

"Nie wyganiaj owczareczku." See The little shepherd

Niedermeyer, Louis
Adieu, belle France (from Marie Stuart)
Adieu, fair France. See Adieu, belle France
The lake. See Le lac
Le lac
"**Niels** Tallefjoren."   Norse folk song. e.n.   MAN
Niemand hat's geseh'n (Nobody saw) C. Loewe.   Words by Gruppe.   e.g. PG 1—PG 2
Niemann, August
Weihelied (Student song)
Niembsch, Nicolaus Franz, edler von Strehlenau. See Lenau, Nicholaus
Niemeyer, August Hermann
"Ehre sei Gott in der höhe" (Composer unknown)
Die **nieuwe** haring (The new (fresh) herring)   Dutch sea song. d.e. SMW
"**Nigh** to a grave that was newly made." See The old sexton (Russell)
"**Nigh** to the walls of Sevilla."   Séguédille (Bizet)
Night ("Aus dem walde") See Die nacht (Strauss)
The **night** ("How fair art thou") F. Schubert.   e.   LA
Night ("O thou silent."—"Akh ty nochka, nochen'ka") Russian song.   e.r.   BF 1
Night ("The stars in beauty shine") P. D. Guglielmo.   [Tr of La notte è bella]   e.   MS
"The night is fine."   e.   FSS 4
Night ("Thy gracious image."—Notch) A phantasy.   M. P. Moussorgsky.   e. SMR 1
Night and day, love.   F. Abt.   FSS 7
"**Night** closed around."   See After the battle
"The **night** comes over the hills, dear." See Night song (Rittmeyer)
The **night-dance** ("Strike the gay harp, see the moon is on high") Air: The night-cap.   Words by T. Moore.   MI
"**Night** doth on the river fall" (Hindu song) Bombay air.   e.   BMC
"**Night** fell around me."   See Emgann Sant-Kast
Night-gown chorus.   J. A. West.   DCS
"The **night** had faded scarcely."   See Sonntag (Franz)
"The **night** has a thousand eyes."   M. Hanlyn.   Words by F. W. Bourdillon. MS
"The **night** has a thousand eyes."   W. B. Olds.   Words by F. W. Bourdillon. NML
"**Night** has closed the gates."   French air. Words by J. B. Powell.   HC
"The **night** her blackest sables wore."   T. Farmer.   Modern words by S. Baring-Gould.   BE 8
"**Night** her starlit curtain draws."   See Lullaby
"**Night** her watch is keeping."   See Wanderer's night song (Varlamov)

"**Night,** I have often wish'd thy stay."   See To-morrow (Reeve)
A **night** in May.   See Die mainacht (Brahms)
"The **night** in solemn stillness hung."   J. G. Smith.   HC
A **night** in Spain.   See Nuit d'Espagne (Massenet)
A **night** in the woods.   Dutch folk air. Words by H. H. Harbour.   DO
"The **night** is dark, the storm is wild."   See Emmanuel (Rodney)
"**Night** is falling, soon the sounds of day will cease."   See Sunset
"The **night** is fine."   See Night (Guglielmo)
"**Night** of starlight."   See "Nuit d'étoiles" (Widor)
Night radiant in splendor.   See Nuit resplendissante (Gounod)
"**Night** shadows falling."   See Integer vitae (Flemming)
"**Night** sinks on the wave."   D. F. E. Auber.   Words by F. Hemans.   FSS 6
Night song ("Gently the breezes blow thro' the forest") Swedish folk song.   e. DSH
Night song ("The night comes over the hills, dear") W. Rittmeyer.   Words by F. Manley.   TL
"The **night** that I kiss'd you, dear maiden." See Verrathene liebe (Schumann)
"The **night** was black, the air seemed dead." See Reue (Lachner)
"The **night** was calm and peacefully."   See "Tacea la notte placida" (Verdi)
"The **night** was dark and fearful."   See The watcher
"A **night** was near, a day was near."   See A hope carol (Smith)
"The **night** was still."   Irish air: The lame yellow beggar.   Words by Callanan.   MMI
"The **night-wind** rustles the branches." See Reiselied (Mendelssohn)
The **nightingale** ("Allant m'y promener") See Au bois rossignolet
The **nightingale** ("Hermit bird, whose melody")   Air: Yr eos lais, or, The nightingale's song.   Words by Ieuan Dhu.   MMW
The **nightingale** ("Jeg kunde slet ikke sove")   See Laengsel (Kjerulf)
The **nightingale** ("A little nightingale, whose notes at twilight rang") J. L. Molloy.   Words by H. Andersen. e.   JSE
Story of the nightingale ("A little nightingale")   e.   FSS 8
The **nightingale** ("Look at that beautiful singing bird") German folk air.   DO
The **nightingale** ("Nightingale, oh nightingale") See "Nightingale, oh nightingale" (Alabiev)
Nightingale ("O nachtigall")   See Nachtigall (Brahms)
The **nightingale** ("One morning, one morning") Kentucky mountain song. WLT

"**Nightingale** amid the bushes." See Le rossignol messager

The **nightingale** and the rose ("A nightingale bent to a crimson rose") C. B. Hawley. Words by R. H. Beck. AA

The **nightingale** and the rose ("The nightingale sings to the rose") Oriental romance. N. Rimsky-Korsakoff. Words from the Russian of Koltzoff. e. NM 2

"A **nightingale** bent to a crimson rose." See The nightingale and the rose (Hawley)

"**Nightingale**, oh nightingale" (The nightingale) Alibieff. e. KSN
Die nachtigall. g. ED 1

"**Nightingale**, O nightingale." A. Varlamoff. e. WBT
"**Nightingale**, O nightingale" (Forsaken) e. BMC

"The **nightingale** sings to the rose." See The nightingale and the rose (Rimskiï-Korsakov)

Nightingale song ("Sing again") C. Zeller. e. WBT

"**Nightingale** sweetly singing." See "Roussignoulet qui cantos"

"The **nightingale**, who loves the flow'rs." See Song of Zuleika (Rimskiï-Korsakov)

"The **nightingales** of Flanders." F. Foster. Words by G. H. Conkling. BD

"**Nightingales** passion-stirred." See "Rossignols amoureux" (Rameau)

"**Night's** shadows, falling." See Integer vitae (Flemming)

"**Night's** wan veil of shadow falls upon the day." See The shadow

Nihad, Bey
A song of sorrow

Nikitin, Ivan Savvich
In silent woods (Rimskiï-Korsakov)
Through the fields in winter (Sokolov)

Nikitine, J.
"Hushed the song of the nightingale" (Grechaninov)

Le **Nil** (The Nile) X. Leroux. Words by A. Renaud. e.f. HM 2—SAM—SOS 1
The Nile. e. BC

The **Nile**. See Le Nil (Leroux)

"The **Nile's** pale waters are silently creeping." See Le Nil (Leroux)

Nina ("Tre giorni son che Nina") Pergolesi. e.i. BAS 2—KF 4—PG 3—PG 4
"Tre giorni" ("'Tis three long days") e.i. FEI 2

Niña Pancha. Guaracha. Romea y Valverde. Words by C. Gil. s. LCP

"La **niña** que á mi me quiera." See La seña

"**Nincsen** annyi tenger csillag." See Sea of stars

The **ninepenny** fidil. Irish air. Words by J. Campbell. FSI

"**Ninetta**, Ninetta, the world is a-dreaming." See Barcarola veneziana

The **ninety** and nine. I. D. Sankey. Words by E. C. Clephane. FSS 2—NMH—WBT

"**Ningitchenenemoshayn** dush." See My big lover

El **niño** Jesús. Porto Rican song. s. LCP

"**Niño** querido." Canción de cuna. s. LCP

Ninon. F. P. Tosti. Words by A. de Musset. e.f. KF 3

"**Ninon**, Ninon, que fais-tu de la vie." See Ninon (Tosti)

"**Ninon**, Ninon, sad indeed is thy lot." See Ninon (Tosti)

"Los **niños** en España cantan." s. LCP

The **nipper's** lullaby. B. Andrews. Words by M. B. Spurr. BSE
The toddler's lullaby. JSE

Nirvana. A. Hervey. Words by E. Panzacchi. e.i. SM 2

Nish, A.
Hoop de dooden do

"**Nit** kain gebetene." See The uninvited aunt

No, caso egual giammai. See Non, non, non, vous n'avez jamais (Meyerbeer)

"**No** chastening for the present seemeth to be joyous." A. S. Sullivan. SAS 3

"**No** churchman am I for to rail and to write." Air: Come let us prepare. Words by R. Burns. BSR

"**No** cold approach, no alter'd mien." J. Barrett. Words by R. Burns. BSR

"**No** daughter had father but only me." See "Mon pèr' n'avait fille que moi" (Si mon papa le savait)

"**No** evil shall befall thee." M. Costa. MS

"**No** figueiral figueiredo." See Canção do figueiral

"**No** fleeting dream so rapid." See Le roitelet (Paladilhe)

"**No** flower that blows." T. Linley. BE 6—PR 2

No hidin' place. Negro spiritual. BF 2
Variant of: "Dere's no hidin' place down dere"

"**No** has visto niña." See Crepúsculo

"**No** hay árbol." Costa Rican folk song. e.s. HS

"**No!** I can bear this pain no longer." See Durch die wälder (Weber)

"**No**, I never shall find a new lover." See Oxana's song (Rimskiï-Korsakov)

No! I shall go no more to the wood. See "Non, je n'irai plus au bois"

"**No**, I will not take my sheep up on the mountain." See Bartolillo

No, I'll engage that you have never. See Non, non, non, vous n'avez jamais (Meyerbeer)

"**No**; I'll not go to the wood." See "Non, je n'irai plus au bois"

"**No!** it cannot be so." See "No! possibil non è" (Puccini)

"No juorno jenno a spasso." See La Capuana

"No longer belong I 'mong children of this world." See Hel mig mine strenge (Halvorsen)

"No longer let me languish." See "Lasciatemi morire" (Monteverde)

"No longer spread the sail." See The voyagers (Silcher)

"No maiden I should e'er refuse." See "Alls ingen flicka lastar ja"

"No me mates." Costa Rican folk song. e.s. HS

"No more annoy, sorrowful meekness." See "Plus de depit, plus de tristesse" (Grétry)

"No more auction-block for me." See Many thousands gone

"No more by sorrow." Braham. HSE 2

"No more dams I'll make for fish." See Caliban's song (Smith)

"No more frosts and no more snows." See Summer is coming (Scott-Gatty)

No more lonely, hopeless waiting. See Non più mesta accanto al fuoco (Rossini)

"No more love's yearning." See "Non più d'amore" (Falconieri)

"No more my heart is fervent." See "Nel cor più non mi sento" (Paisiello)

No more of my Harriet." See The lass with the golden locks (Arne)

"No more peck o' corn for me." See Many thousand go

"No more the glowing sun." See "Die sonne scheint nicht mehr"

No myrrh of Araby. Words by W. Crosswell. MCS

No, never, no. Old ballad. HSD

"No, never shall they capture our free, our German Rhine." See Der deutsche Rhein (Kunze)

"No, no, hope has perished." See "No, no, non si speri" (Carissimi)

"No, no, mio core" ("Yield not, my heart") G. Carissimi. e.i. FEI 1

"No! no more with yearning." Swedish song. e. KSN

"No, no, no, no, no, no, caso egual giammai." See Non, non, non, vous n'avez jamais (Meyerbeer)

"No, no, no, no, no, no, I'll engage that you have never." See Non, non, non, vous n'avez jamais (Meyerbeer)

"No, no, no, no, no, no, ne'er hath page, I'll wager." See Non, non, non, vous n'avez jamais (Meyerbeer)

"No, no, non si speri" ("No, no, hope has perished") G. Carissimi. e.i. FEI 1

"No, non temete o piante." See Seguita a piangere (Bassani)

"No, not more welcome." Irish air: Luggelaw. Words by T. Moore. MI—MMI

"No one to love." W. B. Harvey. Words by A. H. G. Richardson. HSC—HSD—WBT

"No! possibil non è" ("No! it cannot be so") Puccini. e.i. OPS 4

"No room in the inn." H. J. Gauntlett. HC

"No room within the dwelling." R. F. Dale. HC

"No shadows yonder." A. R. Gaul. WBT

No sir ("Tell me one thing") A. M. Wakefield. WBT—WL

No, sir, no ("Yonder is a comely flower") Kentucky mountain song. WT Variant of: O no, John

"No sleep has cool'd my burning eyes." See In der frühe (Wolf)

"No sooner entered in my teens." See I'll be the squire's bride (Hook)

"No sound in the empty street." See The watchman and the child (Cowen)

"No te a cuerdas gentil Bayamesa." See La Bayamesa

"No tengo padre y mi madre." See El huérfano (Campos)

"No torments now and no more sorrow." See "Plus de tourments et plus de peine" (Massenet)

"No, 'twas not love I felt." See He truly loved me so (Tchaikovsky)

No use talkin' when de nigga wants to go. See Away down souf (Foster)

No war nor battle sound. J. Zundel. Words by J. Milton. MCS

"No wood-fire and no coal-flame so burningly glows." See Heimliche liebe

"No word shall e'er reveal it." See Resolution (Lassen)

Noah ("Als Noah aus dem osten war") C. G. Reissiger. Words by A. Kopisch. e.g. AB 3
Historia von Noah ("Als Noah") g. ED 1

Noah's ark ("Old Noah he built") JS—MPC—NMH—NMP—WBT—WC

Noah's ark ("Some say Noah was a foolish old man") Kentucky mountain song. WT

"Nobil donne è tanto onesta" ("Sweeter than the breath of morning") Meyerbeer. e.i. FSS 4

Noble, Thomas Tertius
Bethlehem land
"Christ was born on Christmas night"
The Cornish bells
Gloria in excelsis
"On yesternight I saw a sight, a star as bright as day, and heard among the heav'ns a song"
The quest of the three kings
The shepherds' song
"'Twas jolly, jolly Wat"

"Noble crown our patron bringing." See Canticum in almam matrem

Noble Dickinsonia. Words by H. C. King. CHS

"**Noble** knights I greet you." See "Nobles seigneurs, salut" (Meyerbeer)

"A **noble** lord once wooed a rustic maiden on the sly." See A wealthy lord (Haydn)

"The **noble** Maxwells and their powers." R. Riddell. Words by R. Burns. BSR

"**Noble** Poland, home of valor." See Polish national song (Ogiński?)

"**Noble** republic! happiest of lands." See Viva l'America (Millard)

"A **noble** rich man in Plymouth did dwell." See The half-hitch

"A **nobleman** liv'd in a village of late." Folk song: Scottish version. Air: The poor thresher. BSR
The squire and the thresher. Hampshire version. SF 3

The **nobleman's** wedding. Irish folk song. JOI

"**Nobles** seigneurs, salut" ("My noble knights") G. Meyerbeer. e.f. SOA 1
"Lieti signor" ("Give ye, gay lords") e.i. OPS 2
"Nobles seigneurs, salut" ("To you, my lords, a greeting") e.f. MC
"Nobles seigneurs, salut" ("To you my lords, a greeting."—"Lieti signor, salute") e.f.i. KS 2

Noblest of knights. e. BC

Nobody coming to marry me. Early 19th century song. ME

Nobody knows de trouble I see ("Brother, won't you pray") Negro spiritual: unusual version. DF—JB
Nobody knows the trouble I see. KA
Nobody knows the trouble I see, Lord. JP—NMP

Nobody knows the trouble I see ("Sometimes I'm up") Negro spiritual: familiar version. DF—TFC 2
Nobody knows de trouble I've seen. BF 2—HR—KA
Nobody knows the trouble I've seen. FSS 5—JP—JSE—LA—WBT

"**Nobody** loves me, I don't know why." See "Nadie me quiere"

Nobody saw. See Niemand hat's geseh'n (Loewe)

La **nocca** de tre colure (The tricolored banner) Neapolitan patriotic song. e.i. SN

Les **noces** du coucou et de l'alouette (The wedding of the cuckoo and the skylark) French folk song. e.f. TSF

"**Noch** ruh'n die felder schneebedeckt." See Floods of spring (Rachmaninov)

"**Noche** de paz." See Die heilige nacht (Gruber)

"**Noche** serena." Mexican folk song. e.s. HS
"Noche serena" (Serene night) e.s. HF

"La **noche** 'sta serena" (Serenade) Spanish-American song. e.s. LSS

Nochtenhofer,
Sun of Christmas-tide (Weidt)

Nocturne ("How clear were the skies."—Nachtstück) M. Balakireff. Words from the Russian. e.g. NM 1

Nocturne ("Twilight of evening") S. Liapounoff. Words from the Russian of A. Chomiakoff. e. NM 1

Noel, Thomas
The pauper's drive (Hutchinson)

Noël ("Minuit, Chrétien") See Cantique de Noël (Adam)

Noël ("Montez à Dieu, chants d'allégresse") Gounod. Words by J. Barbier. e.f. BS 2

Nöel ("O! qu'a-dj'oyou."—Excelsis! Gloria) Belgian song. e.f. BF 2

Noël d'Irlande (An Irish Noël) A. Holmès (music and words) e.f. HM 2

Noel! Noel ("'Tis the day") Ancient air. BSC

"**Noël!** Noël! 'neath the warm sky of morn." See Noël païen (Massenet)

"**Noel,** Noel, Noel, let us carols sing." See Christmas comes again (Darnton)

"**Noel!** Noel! Noel! Noel! born is the King of Israel." See The first Noel (Gauntlett)

"**Noël!** Noël! sous le ciel étonné." See Noël païen (Massenet)

"**Noël** nouvelet" ("Christmas comes again") French folk song. e.f. TSF

Noël païen (A pagan Noël) J. Massenet. Words by A. Silvestre. e.f. CM 2

Noite de natal ("All that wondrous Christmas night") Portuguese carol. e. MF

Nökken (The Neck) H. Kjerulf. Words by J. S. Welhaven. e.n. MAN

Nolan, Michael
Little Annie Rooney

Non è ver ('Tis not true) T. Mattei. e. FSS 8
"'Tis not true." WBW

"**Non-g'dhe** dhe-te hi-dha-ki-un te dhon-hi-de." See The insignia of thunder

"**Non,** je ne crois pas" ("Nay, I can't believe") Bergerette. e.f. WB

"**Non,** je n'irai plus au bois" ("Nay, I'll to the woods no more") Bergerette. e.f. WB
"Non, je n'irai plus au bois" (No! I shall go no more to the wood) e.f. PG 1

Non m'è grave morir per amore (For my love thus to die) B. Marcello. e.i. PA 2

"**Non** mi dir." Mozart. e.i. PP

Non, non, vous n'avez jamais (No, I'll engage that you have never) G. Meyerbeer. e.f. KS 3
No, caso egual giammai. e.i. OPS 2

"**Non** paventar." See Infelice sconsolata (Mozart)

"**Non** più andrai" ("Now your days") W. A. Mozart. e.i. SOA 5
"Non più andrai" ("So, Sir Page") e.i. BAS 2

"**Non** più d'amore" ("No more love's yearning") A. Falconieri. e.i. FEI 1

Non più di fiori. W. A. Mozart. e.i. SOA 1

Non più mesta accanto al fuoco. G. Rossini. e.i. SOA 2

Non più mesta accanto al fuoco (No more lonely, hopeless waiting) e.i. KS 3

"Non posso disperar" ("I do not dare despond") S. De Luca. e.i. PA 2

"Non t'accostar all' urna" ("Touch not the white urn hiding") F. Schubert. e.i. FM

"Non vogl' io se non vederti" ("I wish naught but to survey thee") A. Scarlatti. e.i. FEI 1

"None but the lonely heart." See "Nur wer die sehnsucht kennt" (Tchaikovsky)

"None can gainsay it, all must declare." See "Ciascun lo dice" (Donizetti)

None can tell. G. B. Allen. Words by W. H. Emra. FSS 2

"None of the many stars." Modern Hungarian ballad. E. Elek. e. KSE

"None so rare, none so fair." See "Ach! so fromm" (Flotow)

Nonnes qui reposez (Invocation) G. Meyerbeer. e.f. SOA 5

Noon and eve ("At noon we traversed together") Air: Pan deddwn ar ddydd yn cyd-rodio, or, When together we roam. Words by K. R. Moffat. MMW

Noon at the village. A. G. Thomas. WBW

The **noontide** ray (Fairies' song) Auber. FSS 3

Noorden, P. E. van
    Kind words are dear to all

Nor oghchioon. See "Glad tidings, oh, Armenian bards" (Minas)

Nora O'Neal. W. S. Hays. HSD—WBT

"Norah darling." M. W. Balfe. Words by J. Rankin. FSS 8

Norah McShane. C. E. Horn. Words by E. Cook. FSS 7

Norah, the pride of Kildare. J. Parry (music and words) PI

"Nord oder süd! wenn nur im warmen busen." See So oder so (Schulz)

Nordhavet (The North sea) L. M. Lindeman. Words by O. Wolf. e.n. MAN

Nordland. See "Du gamla, du fria, du fjällhoga nord"

The **Nordland** peasantry. See Den nordlandske bondestand

Den **nordlandske** bondestand (The Nordland peasantry) Norse folk song. e.n. MAN

Nordraak, Rikard
    "Ay, this land her sons and daughters." See "Ja vi elsker dette landet"
    "Der ligger et land"
    "I have sought." See "Jeg har sögt"
    "Ja vi elsker dette landet"
    "Jeg har sögt"
    Killebukken
    National hymn of Norway. See "Ja vi elsker dette landet"

Norwegian national song. See "Ja vi elsker dette landet"

"O my pet lamb." See Killebukken

Over de höje fjelde

Over the lofty mountains. See Over de höje fjelde

En solskins dag

The song. See Tonen

A sunny day. See En solskins dag

"There lies a fair land." See "Der ligger et land"

Tonen

Traeet

The tree. See Traeet

"Yes, we love this country." See "Ja vi elsker dette landet"

Yes, we love this land. See "Ja vi elsker dette landet"

"Yes, we love with fond devotion." See "Ja vi elsker dette landet"

"Norges bedste vaern og faeste." See Norges fjelde (Kjerulf)

Norges fjelde (The mountains of Norway) H. Kjerulf. Words by H. Wergeland. e.n. MAN

"Noriu miego." See In my dreams

Norman cradle song. R. de Koven. Words by V. O'Sullivan. AA

Normand, Jacques
    Première danse (Massenet)

Norris, Homer Albert
    Dearie

Norrländingens hemlängtan (The Northlander's longing for home) H. Brooman. Words by E. Sehlstedt. e.sw. HSOS

The **Norse** fisherman. See Den norske fisker

Norsk fjeldsang (The Norwegian echo song) W. Thrane. Words by H. A. Bjerregaard. e.n. SSN

"Kom Kjyra" (Norwegian echo song) e.n. SMF

Norsk sjomandssang. F. A. Reissiger. n. SMW

Den **norske** fisker (The Norse fisherman) Norse air: Aa Ole engang i sinde fik at beile til fader Mikkels datter. Words by C. Frimann. e.n. MAN

Det **norske** flag (Norway's flag) L. M. Ibsen. Words by C. N. Schwach. e.n. MAN

Den **norske** nationalsang. See "Sönner af Norge" (Blom)

"Den norske sjomand eret gjennem barket folkefaerd." See Norsk sjomandssang (Reissiger)

North, Christopher, pseud. See Wilson, John, 1785-1854

The **north** country lass ("There was a fair maiden") C. Dibdin. ME

"A north country lass up to London did pass." See The oak and the ash

"A north-country maid up to London had stray'd." See The oak and the ash

North German cradle-song. See "Schlaf, kindchen, schlaf"

The north of Amerikay. Irish folk song. JOI

The North sea ("Havet er skjönt") See Nordhavet (Lindeman)

"The North sea is lashing the rock-bound strand." See Det norske flag (Ibsen)

The north wind ("When the north wind") A. S. Gatty. WSC

"The north wind was blowing a terrible gale." See Bonden i bryllaupsgarden

The northern lass ("Come take your glass") W. Fisher (music and words) BE 1

The northern lass ("Tho' cruel fate") See "Tho' cruel fate should bid us part"

Northern Nancy. Old English air. BE 8

A northern romance. See "My love dwelt in a northern land" (Pasmore)

The Northlander's longing for home. See Norrländingens hemlängtan (Brooman)

The Northumberland bagpipes. 17th century song. CO 2

The Northumberland bagpiper. MM

Norton, Mrs Caroline Elizabeth Sarah (Sheridan)
Bingen on the Rhine (Hutchinson)
Juanita (Spanish air)
"Love not! love not" (Blockley)
O, take me back to Switzerland (Tyrolese air)
The officer's funeral (Composer unknown)
"On the mountains, when our toil is done" (Benedict)
"Thy name was once the magic spell" (Cowell)
"We have been friends together" (Russell)
"Would I were with thee" (Bossetti)

Norton, J. T.
Buy my roses

Norway's flag. See Det norske flag (Ibsen)

"Norway's oldest forts and boldest." See Norges fjelde (Kjerulf)

Norwegian Christmas song. See "Deilig er den himmel blå"

Norwegian echo song. See Norsk fjeldsang (Thrane)

Norwegian goat-herd's call. See Gjeite lok

Norwegian national song. See "Ja vi elsker dette landet" (Nordraak)

"Nor'western, star of brightest radiance." See Cheer for the purple

"Nos soldats étonnés ont fui comme des femmes." See Le front dans la poussière (Joncières)

Nostitz und Jänckendorf, Gottlob Adolf Ernst von
"Hebe, sieh! in sanfter feier" (Himmel)

"Not a drum was heard." See The burial of Sir John Moore (Barnett)

"Not a sparrow falleth." F. Abt. Words by W. S. Passmore. FSS 6—HSS 2

"Not a wind the branch is bending." See The bending branch

"Not costly domes, nor marble tow'rs." See Memorial day (Marshall)

"Not England's daughters, rosy cheek'd." See The Yankee girls

"Not far from old Kinvara." See The ould plaid shawl

Not for Joseph. A. Lloyd. FSS 3

"Not in halls of regal splendor." See In excelsis gloria

"Not my brother, but 'tis me, O Lord." See It's me, O Lord

"Not my mudder, but it's me, O Lord." See It's me, O, Lord

"Not only for thy beauty hast thou my soul's devotion." See Amore (Muratori)

"Not the angels." See "Nicht mit engeln" (Rubinstein)

"Not the snowy cov'ring of a bitter night." See The Cossack

"Not thy beauty." See "Sei sì caro" (Steffani)

"Not to those in soft apparel." See Shepherds in the field (Verdi)

"Not while a throb beats in Jewish hearts." See The hope (Russotto)

"Not with angels." See "Nicht mit engeln" (Rubinstein)

Notch. See Night (Musorgskiï)

Notchevála tootchka zolotáya. See The cloud and the mountain (Rimskiï-Korsakov)

Nothing—but another girl. W. H. Jones. CHS

"Nothing I ask thee to give me." See "Je ne veux pas autre chose" (Widor)

Nothing true but heaven. See There's nothing true but heaven (Shaw)

Notre Seigneur en pauvre (Our Lord in beggar's guise) French Canadian folk song. e.f. BFS

"Notre Seigneur s'habille en pauvre." See Notre Seigneur en pauvre

"Notre vaisseau va quitter cette plage." See Une fleur pour réponse

"Notre vie est un instant." See Cantique du Trappiste (Meyerbeer)

La notte è bella. For English translation see Night (Guglielmo)

"La notte xe bella fa presto Ninetta." See Barcarola veneziana

Nottingham ale. H. Purcell. BE 8

Nouèl de las flous. For English translation see Carol of the flowers

Nouèl des ausèls (Carol of the birds) 17th century carol from Bas-Quercy. e. DC
Carol of the birds ("Whence comes this rush of wings") e. HC—MF—TL

Nourse, Stanhope M.
"Joyful tidings of a Saviour"

"Nous aurons des lits pleins d'odeurs légères." See La mort des amants (Debussy)

"Nous avions pris le long chemin." See Sous les branches (Hardelot)

"**Nous** étions deux, nous étions trois." See Les marins de Groix

"**Nous** étions trois filles." See Les trois filles

"**Nous** étions trois marins de Groix." See Les marins de Groix

"**Nous** n'irons plus au bois" ("Come to the shady glade") French folk song. e.f. TSF

"**Nous** somm' venu' vous voir." See La chanson de la mariée

"**Nous** venions de voir le taureau." See Les filles de Cadix (Delibes)

Lou **nouvè** di pescaire. G. Borel. Words by Delille. pr. SMW

Novalis, pseud. See Hardenberg, Friedrich, freiherr von

November ("Gone are the swallows") Bohemian folk air. Words by H. H. Harbour. DO

November ("The leaves are fading and falling") J. Hutchinson. Words by A. Cary. LBR

November ("Who shall sing") W. B. Olds. Words by F. D. Sherman. NMS

La **novice** ("Chimes of gladness") See The cloister (Stravinskiĭ)

The **novice** ("Little thanks I give."—Ne spasibo ĭa igumnu tomu) Russian folk song. e. SSR 2

The **novice** ("Wie braust durch die wipfel") See Die junge nonne (Schubert)

Novikov, G.
Spring (Sakhnovskiĭ)

Now ("Let others sing") P. P. Bliss (music and words) LBR

"**Now** a ring of gold do I hide, do I hide." See Riddle-song

"**Now** a toast! your own I will make me." See Chanson du toréador (Bizet)

Now aint dat hard trials, great tribulation. See Hard trials

"**Now** all draw near and hear from me." See Pierlala

"**Now** all my friends are dead and gone." See I have but a mark a year

Now all the bells are ringing. J. B. Dykes. FSS 5—HC

"**Now** all the bells of Easter ring." F. R. Price. HC

"**Now** all ye flow'rs, make room." See Memorial hymn (Allen)

"**Now** are flown the shades of night" (Seymour) Arr from C. M. von Weber. Words by D. Bispham. BD

"**Now** arise, ye men, the clock strikes four." See Sildfiske vise

"**Now** at last comes the moment." See Deh vieni, non tardar (Mozart)

"**Now** at last winter's past." See Winter's past

"**Now** away, my brave boys." Attributed to H. Carey (music and words) DM 1 —MM

"**Now** blazing Yule logs." N. B. Warren. HC

"**Now** but little for my parent's bread I care." See The bold Hussar

"**Now** bylow, baby, and slumber sweet." See "Fatte la nonna"

"**Now** Cape Clear it is in sight." See Whip jamboree

"**Now** cease my wand'ring eyes." J. Dowland. JE

"**Now** comes in the flow'ry May." See A-maying

"**Now** cometh the springtime tender." See La primavera

"**Now,** courage take." J. Schopp. Words by J. Rest. e. MCS

"**Now** darkies, listen to me." See Dearest Mae (Crosby)

"**Now** darksome night the ample earth doth cover." See To sleep (Tchaikovsky)

"**Now** dawn is coming, clear glows the morning." See "Ya viene el alba"

"**Now** drink away, my boys." See The real Irish toper

"**Now** far, far eastward I'll hie me." See "Till Österland vill jag fara"

"**Now** fare thee well, my peaceful home." See Abschied (Müller)

"**Now** fare you well, sweet Cootehill town." See Sweet Cootehill town

"**Now** farewell to you, ye fine Spanish ladies." See Farewell to you, ye fine Spanish ladies

"**Now** gaily round the May-pole go." See The May-pole dance

"**Now** gaily will I dress my head." See The lucky trapper

"**Now** give the army breath." G. F. Händel. SAS 2

"**Now** go your ways, my daughters well-belov'd." A. R. Gaul. SAS 2

"**Now** God above that made all things." See The leather bottèl

"**Now** good-night, now good-night." See Good-night (Flotow)

"**Now** haply down yon gay green shaw." See O wat ye wha's in yon toun

"**Now** has come the hour sad of parting." See Aloha oe

"**Now** hath Flora robb'd her bow'rs." T. Campion (music and words) DM 2

"**Now** he said: In the night I dreamed." See La chevelure (Debussy)

"**Now** he who knows old Christmas." See Old Christmas (Mozart)

"**Now** hear, and mistake me not." See Pogner's anrede (Wagner)

"**Now** heav'n in fullest glory." J. Haydn. e. SAS 4

"**Now** I lay me down to sleep." WBT—WSC

"**Now** if you want me to sing a ditty." See "Aa vil du hava meg te aa kveda"

"**Now** I'll sing." See The ten commandments (Asheville, N.C. version)

"**Now** in her green mantle blythe nature arrays" ("My Nannie's awa') Air: My Nannie's awa'. Words by R. Burns. BSB—FSS 4—MMS—PS 1

"**Now** in her green mantle blythe nature arrays." Air: There are few good fellows when Jamie's awa. Words by R. Burns. BSR

"Now in joy or sorrow." T. Smetana. e. WL

"Now is our dancing ended." See The clearing up

"Now is the month of maying." T. Morley. BOH—DM 1—MM—PR 1—TFC 2

"Now I've left you, I feel so happy." See La smortina

"Now join we all with holy mirth." J. Stainer. Words by H. Blunt. HC

"Now let every tongue adore Thee." See Sleepers, wake (Bach)

"Now let me alone, tho' I know you won't." See Barney O'Hea (Lover)

"Now let us raise our harvest song." C. Simper. HC

"Now let us sing the angels' song." A. Randegger. Words by F. R. Havergal. HC

"Now lift the carol, men and maids." A. H. Brown. Words by A. M. Morgan. HC

"Now listen, little Dora." See "Och hör du unga Dora"

"Now Mass and Lass did together meet." See Mass aa'n Lass ("Han Mass aa'n Lass skulde")

"Now Mass and Lasse together did meet." See Mass aa'n Lasse ("Han Mass aa'en Lasse dei gingo")

"Now Mass, once, and Lasse, together did meet." See "Han Mass aa'en Lasse der gingo paa raad"

"Now may dreams of delight around your pillow tarry." See "Que les songes heureux" (Gounod)

"Now May has come back." See Burschenlust

"Now melts the snow, old winter whines." See Springtime (Tchaikovsky)

"Now my boys if you will listen." See The cruise of the Bigler

"Now my daddy's from home." See Sally Sweetbread (Carey)

"Now my lightsome youth is gone." C. Marot. e. DT

"Now nature cleeds the flow'ry lea." See Lassie wi' the lint-white locks

"Now nature hangs her mantle green." Air: Mary queen of Scots lament. Words by R. Burns. BSR

"Now 'neath the silver moon ocean is glowing." See Santa Lucia

"Now, niggers, listen to me." See Dearest Mae (Power)

"Now night's dark shades appear." See Song of night

"Now, O now I needs must part." J. Dowland. BE 4—BOH— JE—MM—PR 1
"Now, O now, I needs must part" (The frog galliard) DM 1

"Now, oh, prepare." M. Fritzsch. Words by C. F. Gellert. e. MCS

"Now old King Cole was a merry old soul." See Old King Cole

"Now on the first of May." See "Le premier jour de mai"

"Now once again have I seen spring at hand." See Der frühling (Grieg)

"Now once I did court a most charming beauty bright." See The lover's lament (Tennessee version)

"Now once I was courted by a bonny, bonny boy." See My bonny, bonny boy

"Now one last song before we part." See Summer parting hymn (Adams)

"Now open heart and window wide to greet the roses." See Die rosen kommen (Cantor)

"Now peace to earth." See Elizabeth (Liszt)

"Now Phoebus sinketh in the west." T. A. Arne. Words by Milton. DM 2 —HSE 1—PR 2

"Now, prithee, minstrel, tell to me." A. H. Brown. Words by E. M. Dawson. HC

"Now reigns deep silence over hill and plain." See Evening song (Schumann)

"Now Reynard sat in a hollow tree." See Jngrids vise (Kjerulf)

"Now rise up, ye shepherds." See The angel and the shepherds (Thorne)

"Now, Robin, lend to me thy bow." 16th century song. CO 1

"Now roof and rafters rise." See Margaretes vuggesang (Grieg)

"Now rosy May comes in wi' flow'rs." See Dainty Davie

"Now shines the dew." See "Es blinkt der thau" (Rubinstein)

"Now shut in the quiet fold." See Songs from the Pyrenees: 2

"Now silence all the world entrances." See Le soir (Gounod)

"Now simmer blinks on flow'ry braes." See The birks of Aberfeldy

"Now sing we a song for the harvest." S. Reay. Words by J. W. Chadwick. HC

"Now sing we a strain of joy." G. P. Grantham (music and words) HC

"Now sing we all full sweetly." Traditional carol. Words by Lucas Le Moigne. Tr of Chantons, je vous en prie. e. HC

"Now sleep and rest, lady fair." See Ferme les yeux, ô belle maîtresse (Massenet)

"Now sleeps the wave." See "Nu somnar vågen" (Backer-Gröndahl)

"Now sound, beloved harp." See To the harp (Järnefelt)

"Now spring has released." See Frühlingsblumen (Reinecke)

"Now spring is dressing in green once more." See Varvisa (Söderman)

"Now spring laughs again in blossoming hours." See Song of May (Saint-Saëns)

"Now stillness and dusk close around." See Berceuse (Arenski)

"**Now** sunlight dies and over the valley reigns delight." See The feast of roses

"**Now** that I seek no more." See "Or ch'io non seguo più" (Rontani)

"**Now** that the sapling has fallen." See El pavu rial

"**Now** that the sun is beaming bright" (Christmas) Arr from G. F. Händel. Words by J. H. Newman. BD

"**Now** the dancing sunbeams play." See Die seejungfer (Haydn)

"**Now** the day is over." J. Barnby. Words by S. Baring-Gould. BSS —HSD—JS—NMH—OH—TFC 2—TL —WBT—WS—WSC

"**Now** the day is slowly waning." See Bleib bei mir (Reichardt)

"**Now** the days are brief and drear." See The summers come and go (Schulz)

"**Now** the duck is in the stew-pot." See El atole

"**Now** the gander is a-boiling." See El atole

"**Now** the hungry lion roars." W. Linley. Words by W. Shakespeare. VFS

"**Now** the hungry lions roar" (The fairies) R. Leveridge. Words by W. Shakespeare. DM 2

"**Now** the merry spring." FSS 6

"**Now** the shadows darken." See Für musik (Franz)

"**Now** the silver moon arising." See Venetian boatmen's song (Bach)

"**Now** the spring is come." CO 1

"**Now** the sun has gone to rest." See Serenade (Bellini)

"**Now** the sun is in the west." See The cuckoo (Casson)

"**Now** the sun is low." See Japanese lullaby

"**Now** the vessel that flies o'er the billow." See La barchetta

"**Now** the winter no more is seen." See Au printemps (Gounod)

"**Now** the winter sun is sinking." See Merry bells of long ago (Reichardt)

"**Now** the year is crowned with blessing." A. M. Edwards. HC

"**Now** thunders forth the call once more." (Wilhelm)

"**Now** 'tis the hour to part." See Canzune di li carriteri

"**Now** 'tis the merry Christmas time." See Christmas day in the morning (Foster)

"**Now** 'tis time for thee to spread thy wings." See To Russia (Balakirev)

"**Now** to all a kind good night." See Good night

"**Now** to Bethlehem haste we." J. B. Dykes. Words by C. F. Hernaman. HC

"**Now** to conclude and to finish my song." See Eliza

"**Now** to God on high be glory." See The Christmas celebration (Prout)

"**Now** to heav'n our pray'r ascending." See God speed the right

"**Now** we are two, we once were three." See Les marins de Groix

"**Now** we bring our Christmas treasures." A. Gurney. Words by M. H. Bulfinch. HC

"**Now** we dance looby, looby, looby." See Looby loo

"**Now** we take this feeble body." Negro song. JP

"**Now** welcome, my wood." See "Willkommen, mein wald" (Franz)

"**Now** we'll celebrate the praises." See Institute song

"**Now** westlin winds and slaught'ring guns." Air: Port Gordon. Words by R. Burns. BSR

"**Now** what does Santa Claus bring Fränzchen, Santa Claus." See "Was bringt der weihnachtsmann"

"**Now** what have I done to that sweetheart of mine." See Untreue

"**Now** while the daylight still lingers." See "Tant que le jour dure" (Delibes)

"**Now** who art thou, my dainty maid." See May (McCoy)

"**Now** who's the man for a lass to wed." See The heart of a sailor (Maybrick)

"**Now** with creation's morning song." L. van Beethoven. Words by A. Clemens Prudentius. [Tr of Lux ecce surgit aurea] e. CST

"**Now,** woman, as thy wagging tongue." See Old Morgan and his wife

"**Now,** ye little folk." See Berceuse (Ropartz)

"**Now** your days of philand'ring are over." See "Non più andrai" (Mozart)

"**Now** your gallant serenaders." See Mandoline (Debussy)

Nowell ("Nowell, Nowell, Nowell. Hail gentle King."—Hail, gentle King) W. Maristow (music and words) HC

"**Nowell!** Nowell! good news I tell." Old German song. Tr of Weihnacht fliedlein. e. HC

"**Nowell,** Nowell, Nowell. Hail, gentle King." See Nowell (Maristow)

"**Nowell** nowell nowell nowell, this is the salutacyon of the angell Gabryell." 15th century English song. CO 1

"**Now's** the time to love." See Chanson de la sorcière (Gounod)

"'**Nta** sta vanedda cci abbita un scursuni." See Serenata

"**Nu** är det Jul igen, och nu är det Jul igen." See Jul polska

"**Nu** är det soligt och varmt på näset." See Skördemannen (Fogelberg)

"**Nu** da de alle sover." See Sildig (Backer-Gröndahl)

"**Nu** iuorno me ne iette da la casa." See "'E spingole frangese" (Leva)

"**Nu** jag sjungit har i dagar" ("Days and days have I been singing") Swedish folk song. e.sw. HSOS

"**Nu** klär sig våren igen så grön." See Vårvisa (Söderman)

"**Nu** löftes laft og lofte." See Margaretes vuggesang (Grieg)

"**Nu** maanen gjennem mulmet saa maegtigt bruder." See Fyllas sang (Rung)

"**Nu** somnar vågen" ("Now sleeps the wave") A. Backer-Gröndahl. Words by Z. Topelius. e.sw. WM 1

"**Nu** ştiu satul ce voeşte." See Tărăncuta

"**Nu** tak for alt, ifra vi var smaa." See Synnöves sang (Kjerulf)

"**Nu** vilja vi begynna en domaredans." See Domaredansen

Nu'a o ka palai. See "The ground is strewn" (Leleiohoku)

Les **nuages** (The clouds) J. Bouval. Words from the Russian of Lermontoff. e.f. HM 1

"**Nuages**, qui voguant." See Les nuages (Bouval)

"**Nudo** arciero" ("Naked archer") A. Falconieri. e.i. FEI 1

Une **nuit** de mai (A summer night) A. G. Thomas. Words by T. Marzials. e.f. CB—MSF 1

Nuit d'Espagne (A night in Spain) J. Massenet. Words by L. Gallet. e.f. CM 2—PG 4

"**Nuit** d'étoiles" (Starry night) C. M. Widor. Words by T. de Banville. e.f. PG 2—SAM

Nuit méridionale. See A southern night (Rimskiï-Korsakov)

Nuit resplendissante. Gounod. e.f.g. OPS 2. e.f.i. SOA 2
Nuit resplendissante (Night radiant in splendor) e.f. KS 3

"**Nulla** temer da un generoso core." See Generoso chi sol brama (Händel)

"**Nun** ach! verlor ich sie." See "J'ai perdu celle" (Henry III?)

"**Nun** ade, du mein lieb heimatland." See Lieb heimatland, ade

Nun danket alle Gott ("Now thank we all our God") J. Crager. Words by M. Rinkart. e. FSS 2
"Now thank we all our God." e. CST—DSH—WBT

"**Nun** die schatten dunkeln." See Für musik (Franz)

"**Nun** glänzen im lenzen die blümlein all'." See Frühlingsblumen (Reinecke)

"**Nun** hört, und versteht mich recht." See Pogner's anrede (Wagner)

"**Nun** leb' wohl, du kleine gasse." See In der ferne (Silcher)

"**Nun** macht die thor' and herzen weit, die rosen kommen." See Die rosen kommen (Cantor)

"**Nun** seh' ich hehre berg' und thäler wieder." See Auf der reise zur heimath (Grieg)

Nunó, Jaime
Himno nacional de Mejico
Mexican national hymn. See Himno nacional de Mejico

"**Nur** ein wandern ist das leben." L. Erk. Words by H. Hoffmann von Fallersleben. g. ED 3

Nur guten mut ("Ein herz, das sich mit sorgen quält") 18th century folk song. g. ED 2

"**Nur** immer langsam voran." See Der Krähwinkler landsturm

Nur in Deutschland ("Zwischen Frankreich und dem Böhmerland."—Auf der wanderung) Hoffmann von Fallersleben (music and words) g. ED 1

Nur lieben. See Only love (Dargomyzhskiï)

"**Nur** wer die sehnsucht kennt" ("Ah! sad indeed my heart") P. Tschaikowsky. Words by Goethe. e.g. KF 1—KF 2—KF 3
"Nur wer die sehnsucht kennt" ("None but the lonely heart") e.g. FF —FO 2—NM 2
"Only a yearning heart." e. BC
"Only the sad of heart." e. WBW

Nuremberg (Bach) See "Praise to God, immortal praise"; "Songs of praise"

A **nurse** song ("Look at me, my little dear") Air: Ar hyd y nos. MMW

A **nurse's** lullaby. See "O, can ye sew cushions"

"**Nursie**, listen to what has happen'd." See The beetle (Musorgskiï)

Der **nussbaum** (The almond tree) Schumann. Words by J. Mosen. e.g. FO 1—PG 1—SS 1

"The **nut-brown** maiden stood in the streamlet." See La Moraschina

"**Nut** brown maiden, thou hast a bright blue eye for love." CHS—HSD—MPC—WBT—WC

The **nut-tree** ("I had a little nut-tree") Old song. DO
"I had a little nut-tree." FMB

Nutile, E.
Lost happiness. See 'O bene antico
'O bene antico

Nuuanu waipuna. See "Oh, tempt me not, my darling" (Hopkins)

Ny kirree fo-sniaghtey. See entry under Kirree

Nyberg, Julia
"Vårvindar friska, leka och hviska" (Swedish folk air)

Nyblaeus, G.
Dalkarlasång (Lindblad)

Nyblom, Helene
"Hvis du har varme tanker" (Børresen)

Nye poi, krasávitza. See The songs of Grusia (Rachmaninov)

Nykerk, John B.
Collegium

"The **nymph** that undoes me." Greene. BE 7—DM 2

"**Nymphes** attentives" (Barcarolle) C. Gounod. e.f. OPS 3—SOA 3

"**Nymphs** and shepherds." H. Purcell. Words by T. Shadwell. BC—BOH—HSE 2—KF 1—MSS 1—PR 1

Nymphs of air and sea.   H. Smart.
    FSS 7
"Nyt kaiu kanteleeni ja mielein rauhoita."
    See To the harp (Järnefelt)
"Nyt ylös, sieluni."   See Finnish hymn

O

O.   Entries beginning O and Oh are ar-
    ranged in one alphabet under O
"O, a butterfly at Haga."   See "Fjäriln
    vingad syns på Haga" (Bellman)
"Oh, a dainty plant is the ivy green."   See
    The ivy green (Russell)
Oh! a helpmeet wise is his wife.   See Mis-
    tress Santa Claus (Lee)
"O a poor old man came a-riding by."
    See O Johnny come to Hilo
"O' a' the airts the wind can blaw."   See
    "Of a' the airts the wind can blaw"
    (Marshall)
"Oh! a wan cloud was drawn."   See The
    foggy dew
"O Adam was a ploughboy."   See The
    painful plough
"O Adam, where are you."   See The gar-
    den of Eden
"Oh! after many roving years."   See After
    many roving years (Horn)
"O Agnes, sweet little honey blossom."
    See "O Angenietje"
"O agonies of thought."   See "Affanni del
    pensier" (Händel)
"O! a-hunting we will go."   Singing game.
    FSF
Oh! ain't I glad.   See I ain't going to die
    no more
"O alien brothers, who have felt."   See
    French patriotic song
"Oh, Allister MacAllister."   See Allister
    MacAllister
"O alte burschenherrlichkeit."   See Rück-
    blick
"Oh! amber-hair'd Nora."   Irish song.
    e.   MMI
"O Amble is a fine town."   See Home,
    dearie, home
"O ammirabile, o bella gelosia d'alte glorie."
    See Al nome tuo temuto (Righini)
O, an ye were dead, gudeman.   See
    "There's sax eggs in the pan, gudeman"
"O Angenietje" (Agnes) Dutch song. d.e.
    BF 2
"O Araby! dear Araby."   Weber.   Words
    by Planché.   CS 1
O! are ye sleepin', Maggie ("Mirk an' rainy
    is the nicht")   Air: Sleepy Maggie.
    Words by R. Tannahill.   MMS
    "Mirk and rainy is the night."   PS 2
    Oh, are ye sleepin', Maggie.   FSS 5
"O are you weeping for my gold."   See
    The daemon lover (Flag Pond, Tenn.
    version)
"O around the corner we will go."   See
    Round the corner, Sally

"O Arranmore, loved Arranmore."   Air:
    Killdroughalt fair.   Words by T.
    Moore.   MI—MMI
"Oh, as I was out a-walking."   See The
    elves' dance
"Oh, as I went down to Dover."   See On
    a summer day
"Oh, as thro' Lorraine I took my way."
    See Les trois capitaines
"Oh, ask not, hope not thou too much."
    See Kindred hearts
"O, at thy feet how happy."   See "Wie
    schön bist du" (Weidt)
Oh, aye my wife she dang me.   Scottish
    air.   Words by Burns.   PS 2
    "On peace an' rest my mind was bent."
    BSR
"O Babe! in manger lying."   J. Barnby.
    Words by W. C. Dix.   HC
"O babes, O babes, if you was mine."   See
    The cruel mother (Tennessee version)
"O baby, O baby, if you were mine."   See
    The cruel mother (Virginia version)
"Oh, banquet not in those shining bowers."
    Air: Planxty Irwine.   Words by T.
    Moore.   MI
"O bay of Dublin."   Limerick air.   Words
    by H. S. Dufferin.   MMI
"O bay of Dublin" (Bay of Dublin) Old air.
    Words by H. S. Dufferin.   FSS 2—
    JO—WBT
Oh, be careful.   See Statt' attiente
"O be just, O be true."   Round.   FSS 8
"O beautiful banner all splendid with stars."
    See The flag going by
"O beautiful for spacious skies."   See
    America the beautiful (Ward)
"O beaux rêves évanouis."   C. Saint-Saëns.
    e.f.   SOA 1
Oh! Bell, don't you tell.   See Dolcy Jones
    (Foster)
"Oh bell' Istria, chi lungo il tuo lido."   See
    Oll Istria (Georgieri)
"O bellissimi capelli" ("Locks so beautiful")
    A. Falconieri.   e.i.   FEI 1
"O Beloit our alma mater."   See Beloit
    song
"Oh, Bessie Bell and Mary Gray."   See
    Bessie Bell and Mary Gray
"O Betsy be a lady fair."   See Betsy
"Oh! Betty, Betty, have you seen my ducks
    to-day."   See Betty and her ducks
"Oh, beware ere your pathway you go."
    See Sieh dich vor (Grieg)
"O, bid your faithful Ariel fly."   T. Linley.
    Words by Shakespeare.   HSE 1—SS 1
"O bienfaiteur universal."   See Hamidie
    (Nedjib Pacha)
ô bienheureuse nuit.   Basse-Normandy
    carol.   e.   CST—DC
    "O night, peaceful and blest."   e.
    HC
"O Billy Riley."   Pulling chantey.   SE
O bitt' euch liebe vögelein (Ye merry birds)
    F. Gumbert.   e.g.   KF 1
"Oh! blame not the bard."   Irish air: Kitty
    Tyrrell.   Words by T. Moore.   MI—
    MMI—PI

"O, bleib' bei mir." See The little fish's song (Arenski)

"O bless the happy Christmas morn." See God bless us, every one

"O blessed Savior, full of compassion." See "Ave Maria" (Luzzi)

"O blessed Savior, God of love." See "O salutaris" (Panofka)

"O blessed town of Bethlehem." See Gloria in excelsis (Noble)

"Oh blessed Virgin, hear my prayer." See Gebet der Elisabeth (Wagner)

"Oh! blest be the days when the green banner floated." See Saint Patrick's day

"Oh, blind eyes, be no more tearful." See Hark! the angel choir

"O Blodwen, my true love." J. Parry. WL

"Oh, blow the man down, bullies." See Blow the man down

"Oh, boatman, row me o'er." M. D. Sullivan. FSS 6

"O Bolivians, the angel of freedom." See National song of Bolivia (Vincenti)

O bona patria, lumina sobria speculantur. For English translations see "For thee, O dear, dear country" (Herron); "For thee, O dear, dear country" (Oliver)

"Oh, Boney was a warrior." Windlass chantey. SMW
Variants: Boney; "Boney was a warrior"; Bonny; "Bonny was a warrior"

"O, bonie was yon rosy brier." Air: I wish my love were in a mire. Words by R. Burns. BSR

"O bonnie was yon rosy brier." Air: Laggan burn. Words by R. Burns. BSB

"O, bonnie was yon rosy brier." Air: The wee, wee man. Words by R. Burns. MMS
"Oh, bonnie was yon rosy brier." PS 2

"Oh, Bonny was a warrior." See Bonny

"Oh, Boston's a fine town." See Home, dearie, home

"O Bothwell bank." Scottish song. PS 2

O, boys, carry me 'long. S. C. Foster (music and words) JO
Oh! boys, carry me 'long. NMP—WA—WBT—WSW

"Oh! breathe not his name." Irish air: Callin donn, or, The brown maid. Words by T. Moore. MI—MMI

O bretheren, my way, my way's cloudy. See My way's cloudy

"O brethren all, that mourn and weep." See The open door

"O bright blue eyes, long lashes under." See Mavourneen (Aylward)

"O bright sun" ("Sunce jarko") Serbian folk song. e.se. BF 1
"Come, my dearest" (Pjesma) e.se. BO—SMF

"O bring down some of your father's gold." See Lady Isabel and the elf knight (Massachusetts version)

"Oh, bring the wagon home, John." See Bring the wagon home, John

"Oh! bring to me the fragrant mignonette." See Allerseelen (Lassen)

"Oh, broad land." Children's song. FSS 8

"O brother, brother mine, sad my heart." See Dakota serenade

"O brother, can you play at ball." See The two brothers (Kentucky version)

"O, Brother Green, O come to me." See Brother Green

"O, brother how d'ye feel." See If you want to see Jesus

"O brother, say, is this the day." See Sabbath song

"O brother, you ought t'have been there." See Roll, Jordan, roll

O brothers, I love Jesus. See "I've just come from the fountain"

"O brothers, won't you help me." See I'm a-rolling

"Oh, brothers, you ought t'have been there." See Roll, Jordan, roll

"Oh, brothers you oughter been dere." See Roll, Jordan, roll

O brown Rosey, the rose of Alabama. See The rose of Alabama

"O budding flowers" (Makalapua) D. Nape. e.h. HA

"O bury me not on the lone prairie." See The dying cowboy

Oh, but to hear thy voice. Tschaikowsky. e. BS 1

Oh! but ye've been lang o' comin'. See Lang o' comin'

"O buy me, my lady, a cambric shirt." See The lover's tasks

O, by an' by. See By an' by

"Oh! call not to thy mind dark times of yore." See Oh pray (Markewitsch)

"O, cam ye here the fight to shun." Air: Cameronian rant. Words by R. Burns. BSR

O can ye labor lea, young man. See "I fee'd a man at Martinmas"

"O, can ye sew cushions" (A nurse's lullaby) Scottish song. MMS
"Oh, can ye sew cushions" (Old highland cradle song) PS 2

"O can't you see yon little turtle dove." See The little turtle dove

"O captain! my captain." E. S. Kelley. Words by W. Whitman. TL

"O captain! my captain." Arr from C. M. Wyman. Words by W. Whitman. LBR

"O! Carillon, my home in this new country." See The flag of Carillon (Sabatier)

"Oh, carry me 'long." See O, boys, carry me 'long (Foster)

"O cessate di piagarmi" (Cease my heart from wounding.—"O lasst ab, mich zu verwunden") V. A. Scarlatti. e.g.i.   KF 2—PG 2

"O cessate" ("Cease, oh maiden")   e.i. BAS 2

"O cessate di piagarmi" ("Cease to torment")   e.i.   FEI 2

"O cessate di piagarmi" ("O no longer seek to pain me")   e.i.   PA 1

ₜO Charlie is my darlingₜ " 'Twas on a Monday morning." Jacobite air. Old song with additional words by R. Burns. BSR

O, Charlie is my darling (" 'Twas on a Monday morning") Jacobite air. Old song with additional words by Nairne.   MMS
Charlie is my darling.   BOS—JO—PS 1
Oh, Charlie is my darling.   CST—HSSS

O Charlie is my darling ("When first his standard caught the eye") Jacobite air. Words by C. Gray.   WBT—WL

"O charming Napoli! O happy nation." See Italian air

"O children, do you think it's true." See Walk you in the light

"O Christmas bells, ring far and near."   C. Simper.   Words by T. D. Hyde.   HC

"Oh, Christmas bells, that, chiming clear." See Sweet bells are chiming (Genée)

"Oh, Christmas is coming, oh, Christmas is near."   See Christmas day

"O Christmas, merry Christmas."   M. B. Foster.   Words by F. R. Havergal. HC

"O Christmas, merry Christmas" (Bells across the snow) E. E. Lassen. Words by F. R. Havergal.   MCS

"Oh Christmas, oh Christmas, on this blessed day."   See Canto pel Natale (Moderati)

"O Christmas tree."   See Der tannenbaum

"Oh, Clavers and his Highland men."   See The battle of Killiecrankie

"Oh Columbia la joya del mundo."   See Columbia, the gem of the ocean (Becket)

"O Columbia, the gem of the ocean."   See Columbia, the gem of the ocean (Becket)

"O come, all my young lovyers."   See The unconstant lovyer

"O come, all ye faithful."   See "Adeste fideles" (Reading)

"Oh! come back, sinner, and don't go there."   See Oh! sinner man

"O come! castanets are gaily sounding." See La cachucha

"O come, come away."   FSS 1—HSD—WBT
"Oh, come, come away."   WSC

"Oh, come è bello il ciel."   See C'era una volta un principe (Gomes)

O come, Emmanuel.   See Veni Emmanuel

"O come hither, and hearken."   L. Gordigiani.   HSS 1—HSS 3

"O come, let links eternal."   See "Ah sì, ben mio; coll'essere io tuo" (Verdi)

O come, let us worship (Lyons) J. M. Haydn.   Words by R. Grant.   TL

"O come, little children."   See Die kinder bei der krippe (Schulz)

"Oh, come, maidens, come."   See Trancadillo (Brown)

"O come, my brethren, one an' all."   See General roll call

"O come, my love, with me to-night" (Indian serenade) Bengali air.   e.   BMC

"O come, my loving Riley."   See Loving Reilly (North Carolina version)

"O come, O come, Emmanuel."   See Veni Emmanuel

"O come on this bright Easter-day."   H. Smith.   HC

"Oh come to me when breezes stir" ("Viens près de moi") M. Balakirew. Words by A. Koltsow.   e.f.   SC

"Oh, come to me when daylight sets."   See Carnival of Venice

"Oh, come to the field."   See Harvest home

"Oh, come to the greenwood."   See Heigh ho! maid of the mill (Jones)

"O come with me in my little canoe."   See Ossian's serenade (Dodge)

"Oh come with me, my Irish girl."   Air: The Irish girl.   JOI

"Oh, come with me, my love."   See The deep, deep sea (Horn)

"O come you good people that go out a-tripping."   See The saucy bold robber

"O come you home, dear Johnny."   See The green bed (North Carolina version)

"O come you home, my own true love." See The daemon lover (Hot Springs, N.C. version no. 1)

"O, could I be, love, in form of sea-gull." See Mo rùn geal dìleas

"Oh! could I behold those glances."   See Il balen del suo sorriso (Verdi)

"O could I hide in your bosom."   See Vira do minho

"Oh, could I speak the matchless worth." See Ariel

"Oh, could our thoughts."   German air. Words by A. Steele.   FSS 2
Devotion.   LA

"Oh, could we do with this world of ours." Irish air: Basket of oysters.   Words by T. Moore.   MI

"Oh! could we do with this world of ours" (Green sleeves) 16th century English air.   Words by T. Moore.   DM 1

"O country, king and people."   See Hymno nacional—Portugal (Pedro IV)

"O County Guy, the hour is nigh."   See County Guy (Composer uncertain); County Guy (Bishop)

"O cruel cruel fate."   H. Purcell.   BE 3

"O cruel maid! what sin ever can torment you."   See La Catanzarese

"Oh cruel sun that's shining." See Citronenfalter im april (Wolf)

"O crystal the finest." See "Kristallen den fina"

"O curly locks, O curly locks, you wear no silk nor lace." See La ricciolella

"O danke nicht für diese lieder." See Widmung (Franz)

"Oh, dark, sweetest girl." See Peggy Browne

"O dark was the night." B. W. J. Trevaldwyn. HC

"O day that revealed the grand star of our glory." See Washington (Custance)

"O days of spring long ago." See Élégie (Massenet)

Oh, de band o' Gideon. See Gideon's band ("I hail to my sister")

"O, de blin' man stood on de road an' cried." See De blin' man stood on de road an' cried

"Oh, de downward road is crowded, crowded, crowded." See The downward road is crowded

"Oh de goosequill's a scratchin' in de 'countbook ob Gawd." See Ma Lawd's a-writin' down time

"Oh, de hebben is shinin'." Negro spiritual. HR

"Oh, de land I am bound for." See Sweet Canaan

"O de light-bugs glimmer down de lane." See My Merlindy Brown (Burleigh)

"Oh de ole sheep done know de road." See The ole sheep done know the road

"O, de river of Jordan is so wide." See Oh, wasn't that a wide river

Oh! de Shanghai, don't bet your money on de Shanghai. See Don't bet your money on de Shanghai (Foster)

"Oh de winter, de winter." See De winter'll soon be over

"O deacon can't yo' hold out yo' light." See Heav'n boun' soldier

"Oh! dear companions." See "Oh! mie fedeli" (Bellini)

"O dear, I think my heart will split." See Herzensbeklemmung (Thümmel)

"O, dear life." W. Byrde. Words by P. Sidney. DM 1

O, dear loved Maine. University of Maine song. H. M. Estabrooke. CHS

"Oh, dear me, with all its goodness." See Dol-orous ditty

"O dear minny, what shall I do." Air: O dear minny. Words by R. Burns. BSR

"O dear mother when we was there." See The cruel mother (Alleghany, N.C. version)

"Oh, dear! oh, dear! good gentle folks, it may be said." See The lad with the carroty poll (Knight)

"O dear! what can the matter be." 18th century song. HSD
    "Oh! dear, what can the matter be." BE 3—DM 2—GO—ME—TFC 2—WBT—WSC
    What can the matter be. FSS 1—JSE

"O dear sixpence, I've got sixpence." See The jolly jester

"Oh, dearest heart, as long as thou canst love." See A love dream (Liszt)

"O dearest love, now tell me, pray." See Che t'ho fatto

Oh, dearest Mae. See Dearest Mae (Crosby)

"O dearest mother." See "O süsse mutter" (Loewe)

"O death, receive me." See "Morir vogl'io" (Astorga)

O Death, rock me asleep. 16th century song. CO 1

"Oh, deep in my soul is my paistheen fion." Irish song. [Tr of Paisdin fionn] e. MMI

"O del ben che acquisterò" ("Soon I'll own riches divine") M. Cesti. e.i. FEI 1

"O del mio dolce ardor" ("Author of all my joys") C. W. Gluck. e.i. CS 2—MSS 2—SS 2
    "O del mio dolce ardor" ("Oh, from my tender love") e.i. KS 3
    "O del mio dolce ardor" ("O my belov'd") e.i. NG
    "O del mio dolce ardor" ("O thou belov'd") e.i. PA 1

"Oh delore! ed io vivea" ("Oh delusion! ah, what long season") Verdi. e.i. OPS 3

"Oh delusion! ah, what long season." See "Oh delore! ed io vivea" (Verdi)

Oh, dem golden slippers. J. A. Bland (music and words) NMP—WA—WBT—WC—WSW

"Oh! Dermot astore! between waking and sleeping." See Dermot astore (Crouch)

Ô des amants le plus fidèle (O lover mine, most faithful-hearted) E. N. Méhul. e.f. KS 3

"Ô des infortunés" ("Goddess of those who grieve") G. Spontini. e.f. KS 2

"Oh, did you ne'er hear of the Blarney." Irish air. Words by S. Lover. MMI—PI

"Oh! did you not hear of Kate Kearney." See Kate Kearney

"Oh, didn't you hear of the glorious news." See The orangeman

"Oh! didst thou know the pains of absent love." See As when the dove laments her love (Händel)

"Ô Dieu Brahma" ("Brahma divine") G. Bizet. e.f. SOA 1
    "Ô Dieu Brahma" ("O God of light") e.f. MC

"O, dinna think, bonnie lassie." Scottish song. PS 1

O divine Redeemer. See Repentir (Gounod)

"Oh, do, my Johnny Boker." See Johnny Boker

"Oh, do not frighten or destroy." See The little bird

"O don fatale" ("Oh, fatal dower") G. Verdi. e.i. KS 2—SOA 1

"O, Donald Couper and his man." Air: Donald Couper. Words attributed to R. Burns. BSR

"Oh, don't call de roll." See Don't call de roll

"O don't you remember on the rocky mountain top." See The rocky mountain top

"O don't you remember on yon green mountain." See Come all you fair and tender ladies (Carmen, N.C. version no. 1)

"Oh! don't you remember sweet Alice." See Ben Bolt

"Oh! don't you see the turtle-dove sitting under the yonder tree." See The turtle dove

"O don't you see yon turtle dove lamenting on yon vine." See The true lover's farewell (Tennessee version)

"Oh, don't you want to go to the gospel feast." See Deep river

"Oh! doubt me not." Air: Yellow Wat and the fox. Words by T. Moore. MI

"Ô doux printemps d'autrefois." See Élégie (Massenet)

"O down she threw her ivory comb." See Fair Margaret and sweet William (Mount Fair, Va. version)

"Oh, dream, oh, dream, children of Erin." See Noël d'Irlande (Holmès)

O du allersüsste freude. For English translation see "Holy Spirit, Source of gladness" (Naumann)

"O du Deutschland." Air: Soviel stern am himmel stehen. g. ED 1

"O du fröhliche." See Die drei grossen Christlichen feste

"O du lieber Augustin." See Alles ist hin

O du mein holder abendstern. R. Wagner. e.g. SOA 4
The evening star. e. OH—WBT—WSC—WSW
O du mein holder abendstern (O pure and tender star of eve) e.g. BAS 1—BS 1
O du mein holder abendstern (O star of eve) e.g. OPS 4
"O du mein holder abendstern" ("O thou sublime, sweet evening star") e.g. CB
To the evening star. e. HSD—WA

O, du wogendes feld. See Field beloved (Rachmaninov)

O dvukh Lazariakh. See The story of poor Lazarus

"O earth, on Easter morning." G. E. Oliver. HC

"Oh, Eileen achora! at last we have parted." See Eileen achora (Knight)

"O Elijah, prophet great." See Elijah the prophet

"O enchanted land! garden wondrous fair." See Ô paradis sorti de l'onde (Meyerbeer)

O esca viatorum. For English translation see "Bread to pilgrims given" (Barry)

"O evergreen." See Der tannenbaum

"O ev'ry time I feel de spirit." See "Ev'ry time I feel the spirit"

"Oh, ev'ry year hath its winter." See When the birds go north again (Warren)

"O exquisite pleasures." See "Delizie contente, che l'alma beate" (Cavalli)

"O fair, and sweet, and holy." See "Du bist wie eine blume" (Rubinstein)

O fair dove, O fond dove. A. S. Gatty. Words by J. Ingelow. FSS 4—HSC —NML—PO—WL

O fair, O fond love. See Flower of my heart (Hopkins)

"Oh fair, oh sweet." O. Cantor. Words by H. Heine. [Tr of "Du bist wie eine blume"] e. WBW

"Oh, fair sunshine." See An den sonnenschein (Schumann)

"Oh fairest maiden, when I behold thee." See Love's parting

"O faithful pine." See Der tannenbaum

"Oh Fanny is more fair than flow'rets sweet and rare." See Fanny

"Oh, far away in a tropic land." See The contented camel (Ames)

O fare thee well, O fare thee well. See Aloha oe

"Oh, fare-you-well, friends, I'm gwine to tell you all." See Oh, de hebben is shinin'

"O fare you well, I must be gone." See The true lover's farewell

"O fare-you-well my own Mary Anne." See My Mary Anne (Tyte)

"O fare you well, my own true love." See The true lover's farewell (Carmen, N.C. version)

"O fare you well, we're homeward bound." See Good-bye, fare you well

"O, farewell, my Frances." Air: Ffarwel Ffranses, or, Farewell Frances. MMW

"Oh fatal dower, oh cruel gift." See "O don fatale" (Verdi)

"O fate adverse and cruel." See Già l'ira m'abbandona (Meyerbeer)

"O fatherland, beloved country." See O, tu Palermo (Verdi)

"Oh father's gone to market-town he was up before the day." See A midsummer song (Abt)

"Oh, fath'r and I went down to camp." See Yankee Doodle

"Oh, Felix, my honey." See Felix

"O fetch the water." See "Aa kjøre vatten aa kjøre ve'"

"Oh! Fhairshon swore a feud." See The massacre of Macpherson

"Ô fier jeune homme." See La solitaire (Saint-Saëns)

"O figli, o figli miei." See Ah, la paterna mano (Verdi)

O filii et filiae, Rex coelestis, Rex gloriae. For English translations see "O sons and daughters, let us sing" (Hodges); "Ye sons and daughters of the King" (Warren)

"O fill the bowl with Rhine-wine." See Am Rhein und beim wein (Ries)

"O fir tree dark, O fir tree dear." Swedish carol. e. MF

"O fir-tree green! O fir-tree green." See Der tannenbaum

"Oh! firm as oak." H. R. Bishop. HSE 1

"Oh, fisher in the ocean." See "Oh, pescator dell' onda"

O fisherman on the waves. See O pescator dell' onda"

"O flower of silver." See Stornelli

O flowers wondrous. See Colind

"Oh, for a heart" (St Martin's) W. Tansur. Words by C. Wesley. FSS 7

"Oh, for a thousand tongues." C. G. Glaser. Words by C. Wesley. WBT

"Oh, for a thousand tongues" (Azmon) FSS 5

"O, for my ain king, quo' gude Wallace." Air: Gude Wallace. Words by R. Burns. BSR

"O, for the peace that floweth as a river." See A little while (Herron)

"Oh, for the swords of former time." Irish air. Words by T. Moore. MI—MMI—SN

O for the wings of a dove. See "O könnt' ich fliegen wie tauben dahin" (Mendelssohn)

"Oh! for those old familiar friends." J. Barnett. Words by J. E. Carpenter. BE 5

"Oh! forbear." A. Whichello. Words by A. Hill. BE 6

"Oh, freedom." Negro song. HR

"Oh, from my tender love." See "O del mio dolce ardor" (Gluck)

"O Gabrielle, my charmer." See Charmente Gabrielle (Henry IV?)

"Oh, gae to the kye wi' me, Johnny." See Gae to the kye wi' me, Johnny

"Oh! gaily, gaily through life wander." See Gaily thro' life wander (Verdi)

"Oh, gaily now I'm singing." See Happy Bayadere (Bochsa)

"O, Galloway Tam cam here to woo." Air: Galloway Tam. Words by R. Burns. BSR

"O, gambler, git up off yo' knees." Negro spiritual. JB

"O Genevieve, I'd give the world." See Sweet Genevieve (Tucker)

"O gentle springtimes of yore." See Élégie (Massenet)

"O gentle woman of the house." See An cailín deas ruadh

"Oh, gently, gently sighs the breeze." See Song of rest (Strauss)

"O, Gilderoy was a bonnie boy." See Gilderoy

"O! gin I were where Gadie rins." See Where Gadie rins

"O gin my love were yon red rose." Scottish air. 1st verse traditional, 2nd verse by Burns, 3rd verse by J. Richardson. MMS

"O girl who singest." Servian folk air. Words by D. Radford. WF

"O girls, come forward so sweetly." See Chamarrita

"O give me a home by the sea." E. A. Hosmer. HSD

"Oh, give me a home where the buffalo roam." See Home on the range

"O give me but my Arab steed." G. A. Hodson. FSS 7—HSE 2

"Oh, give me but my Arab steed" (At honor's glorious call) A. Sullivan. BD

Oh! give me the wings. Negro song. NMP

"Oh, give way, Jordan." Negro spiritual. HR

"Oh! gladly now we hail thee." V. Bellini. e. FSS 1—WBT

"O gladly now we hail ye." e. LA

"O glorious old mountain-crown'd land of the north." See "Du gamla, du fria, du fjällhoga nord"

"O glorious rose fair blooming." See Lo! a fair rose is blooming (Praetorius)

"O God! beneath Thy guiding hand." See God be with us (Hatton)

"O God, have mercy." Mendelssohn. e. OS 4—SAS 4

Oh god-like youth. Händel. OS 1

"O God, of all the Maker." See To-morrow (Wesley)

"O God of earth and altar." H. Smart. Words by F. K. Chesterton. LA

"O God of light." See "Ô Dieu Brahma" (Bizet)

"O God, our Help in ages past." W. Croft. Words by I. Watts. WBT—WS
Saint Anne. CST

"O God, our Help in ages past" (Dundee) G. Franc. Words by I. Watts. LA

"O, golden-beaked blackbird." Air: Y 'deryn du pigfelyn. Words from the Welsh. e. MMW

O good ale, thou art my darling. Old English song. BE 7—CO 2—ME
O, good ale. BOS

"O gracious Lord, cast down Thine eyes." A. R. Gaul. SAS 2

O grant me in the dust to fall. Dvořák. e. OS 1

"O graveyard." Negro song. KA

O gude ale comes, and gude ale goes. See "I had sax owsen in a pleugh"

"O guerriers! je suis né dans le pays des Gaules." See Le géant (Gailhard)

"O guide me in the way." Dvořák. e. OS 3

"O hab you heard de lates'." See De ballet of de boll weevil

"Oh had I Jubal's lyre." G. F. Händel. OS 1—SAS 1—SS 1

"Oh! had I wings like a dove." See Had I wings like a dove

"O, had not Venus been beguiled." J. Hilton. DM 1

"Oh! had we some bright little isle." Irish air: Chiling O'Guiry, or, Sheela na Guira. Words by T. Moore. MI—MMI

"Oh, Haidee" (Moorish song) e. BMC

"Oh, hall of song, I give thee greeting." See "Dich, theure halle grüss' ich wieder" (Wagner)

"Oh, hallelujah, oh, hallelujah." See Who'll jine de Union

"Oh, hallelujah to the Lamb, down by the river." See Down by the river

"Oh, hallelujah to the Lamb, the general roll is called." See The general roll

"Oh, hame cam' our gudeman at e'en." See Hame cam' our gudeman at e'en

"O hangman, stay thy hand." See The briery bush

O happy day, O day so dear. See O schöne zeit, o sel'ge zeit (Götze)

"Oh, happy day, that fixed my choice." E. F. Rimbault. Words by P. Doddridge. FSS 5—WBT—WS

"O happy days gone by." See Happy days gone by (Godfrey)

"Oh! happy, happy groves." See The pilgrim (Barrett)

"Oh, happy is the land." See Geluckig vaderland

"Oh, happy sons of bright Lorraine." See Marche lorraine (Ganne)

"O hark! O hear! how soft and clear." See The echo

"O hark to the bells' glad song." 11th century words. Tr of Congaudeat turba fidelium. e. HC

O harp immortal. See Ô ma lyre immortelle (Gounod)

"O, has she den fail'd in her truth." See Lubly Dine (Sanford)

"O haste and leave this sacred isle." See St Senanus and the lady

O haste now, O come now. See "Go javten"

"O haste, the blessed Babe is born." E. Handley. HC

"Oh, hasten, fair springtime." See "Venez, agréable printemps"

"O, hasten, hasten all." See Finnish hymn

"Oh, hasten, ye maidens." See "Donzelle, fuggite" (Cavalli)

"O haughty youth, of gazelles the proud slayer." See La solitaire (Saint-Saëns)

"O have pity." See "Per pietà" (Stradella)

"Oh, have you e'er seen the daughter of Megan." See Merch Megan

"Oh, have you heard geography sung." See Geography song

"Oh, have you heard the news, my Johnny." See One more day

"Oh! have you heard the news of late." See The Darwinian theory

"Oh, have you seen the heavens blue." See The golden bear

"Oh, He raise a poor Lazarus." See He raise a poor Lazarus

Oh, He sees all you do. See My Lord's writing all the time

"O hear me, pretty Swiss." See The Swiss girl

Oh! hear the wild wind blow. T. Mattei. Words by Madame Foli. KF 4

Oh! oh! hear the wild wind blow (Italian boatman's song) AB 3

"O heard ye of a silly harper." Air: The Lochmaben harper. Words by R. Burns. BSR

"O, heard ye yon pibroch sound." See Glenara

"O, hearken, and I will tell you how." See Muirland Willie

"Oh heart, my own heart." See "Cori, curuzzu"

"O heart sublime! O noble spirit." See Forma sublime, eterea (Gomes)

"O heart wherefore so light." See Waltz song (Audran)

"O heart's delight! when wilt thou hearken." See Absence (Berlioz)

"O heaven above how fair art thou." See Der himmel im thale (Marschner)

"O Heer die daer" ("Lord, who hast spread") Dutch song. d.e. BDF

"O hemlock tree! O hemlock tree." See The hemlock tree

"Oh, here come we jolly boys." See Pace-egging song

"Oh, here's to Johnny Harvard." See Johnny Harvard

O, he's a ranting, roving lad. See "My love was born in Aberdeen"

O ho ro, brown lad. See An gille donn

O ho ro, 'ille dhuinn. See An gille donn

"O-hoi-ye-ho, ho-ye-ho who's for the ferry." See Twickenham ferry (Marzials)

"O holy church, but yester-night." H. G. Batterson. HC

Oh! holy Lord. Negro spiritual. JP

"O, holy night." See Cantique de Noël (Adam)

"O holy Saviour! Friend unseen." See Integer vitae (Flemming)

Oh! home of my childhood. See Home of my childhood

"O, homeland mine, O, homeland mine." See My homeland

"Oh, hop-vine" ("Oj chmielu") Polish wedding song. e.p. SMF

"Oh, hope, delusive dream of bliss." See The pale white rose

"O house of Jacob." Benedict. OS 3

"O, how can I be blythe and glad." Air: The bonie lad that's far awa. Words by R. Burns. BSR

"Oh, how can I learn this deep sadness to bear." See Light o' love

"Oh, how cold the winter weather." See Longing for spring

"Oh! how familiar to mine ear." Spohr. e. OS 3—SAS 3

"Oh, how good it is to be here." See "Här är gudagodt att vara" (Wennerberg)

"Oh, how I wonder what I should see over the lofty mountains." See Over de höje fjelde (Kjerulf); Over de höje fjelde (Nordraak)

"O how kindly hast Thou led me." L. von Beethoven. WBT

"Oh, how lovely is the evening." See Lovely evening

"O how lovely is Thy world, Father." See Im abendroth (Schubert)

"Oh, how my heart is beating." See Mine own

"Oh how noble, oh how noble." See La nocca de tre colure

"O how pleasing to the senses." J. Haydn. e. OS 1—SAS 1

"O, how shall I, unskilfu', try." Air: Miss Muir. Words by R. Burns. BSR

"Oh, how sweet are the cooling breeze. and the blooming trees." See Musidora (Croft)

"Oh, how sweetly, in life's morning." See Gentle words and kindly deeds (Cooper)

Oh, how they frisk it. See "In summer time, when flow'rs do spring"

"O hush thee, baby, O hush thee." See Lullaby

"O hush thee, my babie" (Lullaby of an infant chief.—Wiegenlied) A. Jensen. Words tr by W. Scott ɪfrom Caidil gu loɪ e.g. FO 1

"O hush thee, my babie." A. Sullivan. Words tr by W. Scott ɪfrom Caidil gu loɪ e. BD—TFC 2

"Oh, hush thee, my babie." T. Whitaker. Words tr by W. Scott ɪfrom Caidil gu loɪ e. FSS 3

"Oh, hush thee, my baby." e. HSD —MS—NMH—PS 1—WBT

Oh! rest thee, babe. e. HSE 1

"O slumber, my darling." e. BSE—DM 1

Scotch lullaby. e. WSC

"O, I am come to the low countrie." See The Highland widow's lament

"O I am Jack and a jolly tar O." See Jack the jolly tar O

"Oh, I am lonely." See La monacella

"Oh! I am the child of the forest wild." See The outlaw (Loder)

"O I am wat, wat." See Ay wakin', O

Oh, I cannot now forget you. See Te voglio bene assaje

"O, I died one time." See Keep a-inchin' along

"Oh, I dont care where you bury my body." See Oh, my little soul's gwine to shine

"O, I forbid you maidens a'." Air: Tam Lin. Words by R. Burns. BSR

"O, O ha'e lost my silken snood." Air: Twine weel the plaiden. MMS

"O, I hae seen great anes." See My ain fireside

"Oh! I have had dreams." See Dreams (Hodges)

"Oh! I have roam'd in many lands." See Erin is my home

"Oh, I heard sweet music up above." See Oh, give way, Jordan

"Oh! I jist come out afore you." See Lucy Long

O, I know the Lord. See I know the Lord's laid His hands on me

"Oh, I love thee so." See Only love (Dargomyzhskiï)

Oh! I miss you, Nettie Moore. See Gentle Nettie Moore (Pike)

"O I say my mammy Dinah." See Sing, Sally O

"Oh, I was bo'n in Mobile town." See Levee song

"Oh, I went down south for to see my Sal." See Polly-wolly-doodle

"O I will drink out of the nipperkin, boys." See The barley-mow

"Oh, I wish I was in the land of cotton." See Dixie (Emmett)

"Oh! if I had a thousand a year, Gaffer Green." See A thousand a year (Millard)

"Oh! if I were yon gossamer." Irish air. Words by J. M'Kowen. FSI

"Oh, if my beloved were by me fast abiding." See The beloved

"O! if thou couldst desert me." Composer unknown. BE 2

"O if you wish, to Jerez we will go." See Jarabe tapatio

"Oh I'll build me a little hut." See Go 'way, old man

Oh, I'm a-going to sing. See Gwinter sing all along de way

"Oh, I'm a-gwine to leave you." See Shallo Brown

Oh, I'm a gwinter sing. See Gwinter sing all along de way

"O, I'm a happy creature." See Mandolinata

"Oh, I'm a scouting trooper." See One of a jolly crew

"O I'm going to leave her." See Shallow Brown

"Oh! I'm lonely to-night, love, without you." See Nora O'Neill (Hays)

"Oh, I'm not myself at all." See I'm not myself at all

"Oh, I'm the little drummer lad." See Der kleine tambour (Pohlenz)

"Oh, in eighteen hundred and sixty one." See Paddy works on the railway

"Oh, in the silent night." See In the silence of the night (Rachmaninov)

"Oh, in this world there's someone." See Das alte Guggisberger lied

"Oh! Irishmen! never forget." See Our own little isle

"Oh, is it not a pleasant thing." See The strawberry girl

"Oh! is it thus we part." G. Linley. Words by W. Motherwell. FSS 7

"O is there in your village dwelling." See "Ah! s'il est dans votre village" (Godard)

"Oh, is there such sorrow." See Mournful love

"Oh I'se from Lusianna, as you all know." See Jim along Josey

"O Isis und Osiris" ("O Isis and Osiris")
W. A. Mozart.   e.g.   KS 5
"Great Isis! great Osiris" ("Possenti
Numi")   e.i.   BS 2
"Oh! Isis and Osiris, guide them."
e.g.i.   AB 1
"O Israel, holy folk."   See Call to worship
"Oh, Italia, Italia, beloved."   Donizetti.
e.   TFC 2
"Oh, it's Sindbad the sailor and Robinson
Crusoe."   See Sindbad
"Oh, it's tackle hard and low, boys."   See
Columbia forever
"O, I've been to de sea."   See Hallelujah
"Oh, I've got a ship in the north countree."
See The Spanish canoe
"Oh! Jacob, get the cows home."   See
Cousin Jedediah (Thompson)
"O Jehovah, hear! oh hear me."   L. von
Beethoven.   e.   SAS 3
"O Jenny, O Jenny, where hast thou been."
Air: May fair.   Words by T. D'Urfey.
BE 8
O, Jenny's a' weet, poor body.   See "Com-
in' thro' the rye, poor body"
"Oh, Jerusalem."   Negro spiritual.   HR
"O Jesu, son of God."   See I wrestle and
pray (Bach)
"O Jesu, Thou art standing."   J. H.
Knecht.   Words by W. W. How.
FSS 1—LA
"O Jesus, Thou art standing."   WA—
WBT—WS—WSW
"O Jesus my Saviour, on Thee I'll depend."
See I'm troubled in mind
O Johnny come to Hilo.   Capstan chantey.
FSF—SE
Variant of: The dead horse
"Oh, Joseph, Mary, and Jesus were travel-
ling for the west."   See King Pharaoh:
The miraculous harvest
Ô jours heureux ("J'arrive le premier") C.
Gounod.   Words by E. Augier.   e.f.
SOA 3
Ô jours heureux ("Pour fuir son souvenir")
G. Meyerbeer.   e.f.   SOA 5
Gone are the days (O lieti di)   e.i.
BS 2
"O joyous Easter morning."   G. E. Oliver.
HC
"O Judah, Judah! chosen seed."   G. F.
Händel.   SAS 2
"Oh, Juley, you're a lady."   See Juley
"Oh, Julia fair, with brow of snow."   See
"Giulia gentil"
"O June! delicious month of June."   See
June (Olds)
"Oh, junior! oh, junior! poor old boy."
See Jilted
"O Katie dear, go ask your father."   See
Awake! awake (Black Mountain, N.C.
version)
"O kau hana mau no ia."   See "Thou art
always the same to me, dear" (Hop-
kins)
"Oh, keep your hat upon your head."   See
Gideon's band

"O, ken ye what Meg o' the mill has got-
ten."   Air: O bonie lass, will ye lie
in a barrack.   Words by R. Burns.
BSR
"O, ken ye what Meg o' the mill has got-
ten."   Air: O ken ye what Meg.
Words by R. Burns.   BSR
"O Kenmure's on and awa', Willie."   Scot-
tish air.   Words by R. Burns.
BSB—BSR—MMS
"Oh, Kenmure's on and awa', Willie."
PS 2
"Oh, King of kings, on Thee I call."   See
King's prayer (Wagner)
"Oh, Kitty, will you marry me."   See
Kitty, will you marry me
"Oh know you the maiden that robs my
repose."   See Gwenllian
"O könnt' ich fliegen wie tauben dahin"
(O for the wings of a dove) Men-
delssohn.   Words by W. Barthol-
omew.   e.g.   FMB
"O for the wings of a dove."   e.g.
HSS 1—HSS 2
"Oh! Laddie was somebody's darling."   See
Laddie (Pinsuti)
"Oh! laddie with the golden hair."   See
Oigfhear a chùil-dualaich
"Oh! ladies don't you blush."   See Way
down in Ca-i-ro (Foster)
"Oh! ladies don't you wonder when I again
appear."   See Dolcy Jones (Foster)
"O lady bright, hear the birds gaily sing-
ing."   See "Femme sensible, entends-tu"
(Méhul)
"O lady fair, hear the birds blithely sing-
ing."   See "Femme sensible entends-
tu" (Méhul)
"O, Lady Mary Ann looks o'er the castle
wa'."   See Lady Mary Ann
"O Lady Moon, your horns point toward
the east."   See Lady Moon (Loomis)
O lamb of God.   See "Agnus Dei" (Bizet)
"O land 'mong the mountains."   See
Moravia
"Oh! land of my fathers."   See Land of
my fathers (James)
"O lands of saints, of streams and song."
See Innisfail (Phelps)
"O lass dich halten, gold'ne stunde" ("O
stay thy passing, golden moments") A.
Jensen.   Words by O. Roquette.   e.g.
FO 1
"O lassie, are ye sleepin yet."   Air: Will
ye lend me your loom, lass.   Words
by R. Burns.   BSR
"O lassie, art thou sleeping yet."   Air: Let
me in this ae nicht.   Words by R.
Burns.   PS 2
O let me in this ae night.   BSB
"O lassie, art thou sleeping yet": Her
answer.   Air: Let me in this ae nicht.
Words by R. Burns.   PS 2
"O lasst ab, mich zu verwunden."   See "O
cessate di piagarmi" (Scarlatti)

O lay thy loof in mine, lass. Air: The cordwainer's march. Words by R. Burns. BSB—MMS
Oh, lay thy loof in mine, lass. PS 2
"A slave to love's unbounded sway." BSR
"O lay your cheek to mine, my dear." See Love's the tune (Straus)
"O lays of my land." Air: Hobed o hilion. Words from the Welsh of I. Vychan. e. MMW
"Oh! leave not your Kathleen." See Kathleen (Williams)
"O, leave novéls, ye Mauchline belles." Air: Ye Mauchline belles. Words by R. Burns. BSR
"O, leeze me on my spinnin-wheel." Air: Sweet's the lass that loves me. Words by R. Burns. BSR
"Ó légère hirondelle" (The message of love) C. Gounod. Words by M. Carré. e.f. SS
"Oh! Lemuel." S. C. Foster (music and words) NMP—WBT
"Oh let eternal honors crown his name." See From mighty kings (Händel)
"Oh! let me breathe the breath that plays." See "Dammi ch'io libi l'alito" (Campana)
"Oh! let me gaze awhile." See Winnie dear
O let me in this ae night. See "O lassie, art thou sleeping yet"
"O let me press thy cheek to mine." See "Lehn' deine wang' an meine wang'" (Jensen)
"O let me wander." Greek folk air. Words by R. R. Whitehead. WF
"Oh! let the kind minstrel." Air: Glan meddwdod mwyn, or, Good humoured, but fairly tipsy. Words by J. Parry. MMW
"O let us all begin with a merry, merry dance." See Country dance
"O let us all, rejoicing." H. S. Irons. Words by S. C. Hamerton. HC
"O, let us all start up with the dance of the judge." See Domaredansen
"O lieber, guter frühling." See Jägerleben (Hoffmann von Fallersleben)
O lieti di. See Ô jours heureux (Meyerbeer)
"Oh life must wondrous be, and fair." See "Es muss ein wunderbares sein" (Liszt)
"Oh, lilies sweet, oh, lilies fair." See Easter hymn
"Oh! Lilly dear it grieves me." See Farewell my Lilly dear (Foster)
O Lisbona, alfin ti miro. G. Donizetti. e.i. SOA 4
"Oh, list to my pleading, so true." See "Ich wollt' meine lieb' ergösse" (Mendelssohn)
"O list while the gentle waves murmur." See An eastern college boating song (Newton)
"O listen, I shall sing for you." See La chanson des mensonges

"O listen, listen to the voice of love." See Listen to the voice of love (Hook)
"Oh! listen, master goldsmith." See Farewell, darling Maggie (Gade)
"O listen, of Scotch and of civil law doctors all." See Give a fee
O listen to de lambs. See Listen to de lambs
O listen to the voice of love. See Listen to the voice of love (Hook)
"Oh! listen while we ask in common phraseology." See A medical medley (Lowe)
"O little Babe! in Bethl'hem born." A. F. Warner. HC
"O little bird of mine" ("Oi shlof main feigele") Jewish folk song. e.y. GF 1
"Oh, little bird upon the tree." See Autumn song (Scott-Gatty)
"Oh! little empty stocking." See Little empty stocking
"O, little Karin waited all in the young king's hall." See Liten Karin
"Oh, little soldier-man." See "Petit soldat de guerre"
"O little town of Bethlehem." J. Booth. Words by P. Brooks. HC
"O little town of Bethlehem." G. A. Burdett. Words by P. Brooks. JS
"O little town of Bethlehem." A. F. M. Custance. Words by P. Brooks. HC
"O little town of Bethlehem." L. H. Redner. Words by P. Brooks. DC—HC —MF—OH
Oh! Lizer! sweet Lizer! if yer die an old maid. See The future Mrs 'Awkins (Chevalier)
"O Logan, sweetly didst thou glide." See Logan braes
"O Lola." See Siciliana (Mascagni)
"Oh! London is a fine town." See London is a fine town
"O! look-a death." See Neve' a man speak like this man
"O Lord! correct me." Händel. Words by J. S. Dwight. BSE—HSS 2— WBT—WS
"O Lord, God of my master." J. Barnby. OS 4—SAS 4
"O Lord, have mercy, have mercy, O Lord, upon me." See O Lord have mercy upon me (Pergolesi)
O Lord have mercy on me. See "Going to ride up in the chariot."
O Lord, have mercy upon me. Pergolesi. HSS 4
"O Lord, have pity." See "Pietà, Signore" (Stradella)
"O Lord, I sing Thy praises." See Laoidh molaidh
"O Lord most holy, O God most mighty." See "Ave Maria" (Abt)
"O Lord, my darken'd heart enlighten." J. S. Bach. e. SAS 4
"O Lord, my God, I praise Thy name." See Larghetto (Beethoven)
"O Lord, my God, to Thee I turn." See A prayer (Kalinnikov)

"O Lord, oh Lord, Whom we adore." O Lord, whom we adore (Händel)

O Lord, O my Lord! O my good Lord. See Keep me from sinking down

"O Lord of all, with us abide." C. J. Wilson. Tr of Quaesumus, Auctor omnium. e. HC

"O Lord of Hosts! almighty King! behold the sacrifice we bring." See Army hymn (Oliver)

"O lord of the world, mighty king of kings." See Hamidie (Nedjib Pacha)

"O Lord our God, Thy mighty hand." See Peace hymn of the republic (Ward)

"O Lord, Thou hast searched me out." S. Bennett. CS 2—MSS 2—OS 2—SAS 2

"O Lord, Thy love unbounded." J. S. Bach. Words by H. F. H. Johnston. BD

"O Lord, to Whom for ever the choiring angels sing praises." See Invocazione a Dio (Mariani)

"O Lord to Whom in praises." See Invocazione a Dio (Mariani)

"O Lord, Who shed'st the sunlight's gold." R. F. Smith. Words by W. H. Jewitt. HC

O Lord, Whom we adore. G. F. Händel. SAS 2

"Oh Lord, Whose mercies numberless." G. F. Händel. SAS 2

"Oh, loss of sight." G. F. Händel. SAS 3

"Oh, Lou'siana's de same old state." See Lou'siana belle (Foster)

"O love, dear love, open thine eyes." See Amor dormiglione (Strozzi)

"Oh! love is a hunter boy." Irish air: As fada annso me, or, Long am I here, or, The gentle maiden. Words by T. Moore. MMI

"O, love is the soul of a neat Irishman." See A sprig of shillelah

"Oh, love it is a killing thing." Irish folk song. JOI

O love, lend thine aid. See Amour! viens aider (Saint-Saëns)

"O love! O love! ah, all my soul to thy ardor is waking." See Ah! lève-toi, soleil (Gounod)

"O love! O love! how have you led me astray, now." See "Amuri, amuri"

"Oh! love, this soul beguiling." See "Come per me serano" (Bellini)

"O love thou delight'st in man's ruin." Scottish song. Air: Miss Weir. PS 2

"O love, what wilt thou with me." See "Amour, que veux-tu de moi" (Lully)

"O, love will venture in." See "O luve will venture in"

"O loved Italia." See Parigi, o cara (Verdi)

"O lovely art." See An die musik (Schubert)

O lovely day, O happy day. See O schöne zeit, o sel'ge zeit (Götze)

"O lovely fisher-maiden, bring the boat now to land." See "Du schönes fischermädchen" (Schubert)

"O lovely fishermaiden! steer thy frail bark to shore." See "Guide au bord ta nacelle" (Meyerbeer)

"O lovely maiden mine with flaxen tresses." See La treccia bionda

"O lovely Mary Donnelly." See Lovely Mary Donnelly (Barker)

O lovely night. See "Belle nuit" (Offenbach)

"O lovely one! accept this fragrant rose bouquet." See The bouquet (Alferakiï)

O lovely Polly Stewart. See Lovely Polly Stewart

"O lovely star that shone so bright." C. Simper. HC

"O lovely voices of the sky." Traditional air. Words by F. Hemans. HC

"O lovely voices of the sky" (O voices of the sky) Air: Drink to me only with thine eyes.. Words by F. Hemans. MCS

"O lovely voices of the sky." O. King. Words by F. Hemans. HC

O lover mine, most faithful-hearted. See Ô des amants le plus fidèle (Méhul)

O loving heart, trust on. L. M. Gottschalk. Words by H. C. Watson. HSD

"O lowly, sacred stable." A. S. Houghton. Words by B. C. Roberts. HC

O luce di quest' anima. Donizetti. e.i. PP

"The future still shines brightly." e.i. FSS 4

O luce di quest' anima (My soul's delight and treasure) e.i. MC

"O luve will venture in." Air: The posie. Words by R. Burns. BSB—BSR

"O, love will venture in." MMS—PS 1

"Oh, love will venture in." HSSS

Ô ma lyre immortelle. C. Gounod. Words by E. Augier. e.f. SOA 2

Ô ma lyre immortelle (O harp immortal) e.f. OPS 2

Ô ma lyre immortelle (O my lyre everliving) e.f. CM 2—KS 2

Ô ma lyre immortelle (Sappho's farewell) e.i. CS 1—MSS 1

"Ô ma tendre musette" ("Rustic flute, echo, sighing") Attributed to Monsigny. Words by La Harpe. e.f. WB

"Ô ma tendre musette" ("Sing to me, sweet musetta") e.f. BO

"O madam, I will give to you the keys of Canterbury." See The keys of Canterbury

"Ô Magali." See Magali

Ô maitre de tout ("O mighty one") J. P. Marshall. Words by A. Silvestre. e.f. HST

"O Makalapua ulu mahiehie." See "O budding flowers" (Nape)

"Oh, many a time I am sad at heart." See Maggie's secret (Barnard)

"O, Margaret, Margaret, Margaret Roche." See Máirghréad na Róiste

O Mari, O Mari. See Maria, Marì (Capua)

"O marry, marry me, my mother dear." See "Mariez-moi, ma petite maman"

"O, Mary, at thy window be." Air: Duncan Davison. Words by R. Burns. BSR

"O, Mary, at thy window be" (Mary Morison) Air: The miller. Words by R. Burns. BSB—MMS—PS 1 Mary Morrison. FSS 5

"O Mary, don't you weep." Negro spiritual. TFC 1

"O Mary, go and call the cattle home." See The sands o' Dee (Boott); The sands of Dee (Macfarren)

"Oh, Mary had a little lamb, and he was wondrous wise." See Mary's little wise man (Carter)

"Oh, Mary had a little lamb,—the story is not new." See Feather bed song

"Oh! Mary, pure Virgin, all hail to Thee be." See The angel's greeting

"O, Mary, ye's be clad in silk." C. Corbett. MMS

"O massa said from firs' to las'." See Cott'n-dance song

"Oh mattutini albori." Rossini. e.i. PP

Oh, may thy dream not soon be o'er. See Oh, ne t'éveille pas (Godard)

"O May, thy morn was ne'er so sweet" (The mirk night o' December) Air: O May, thy morn. Words by R. Burns. PS 2

"O May, thy morn was ne'er so sweet." Air: The rashes. Words by R. Burns. BSR

"O Medjé." See Medjé (Gounod)

"O memory, be sweet to me." See The little house on the hill (Schubert)

"O memory, still bitter to my soul." See Oppress'd with never-ceasing grief (Händel)

"Ô mer, ouvre-toi" ("Enfold me! O sea") L. Delibes. Words by A. Silvestre. e.f. PG 2

"Ô mer, ouvre toi" ("O sea, dreadful sea") e.f. KF 1

"O, merry hae I been teethin a heckle." Air: Lord Breadalbine's march. Words by R. Burns. BSR

Oh! merry month of May. See Joli mois de mai

"O merry ring the Christmas bells." See The Cornish bells (Noble)

"Oh, Methodist it is my name." See Oh! give me the wings

"Oh! mie fedeli." Bellini. e.i. PP

"O' mighty nature's handiworks." See My goddess, woman

"O mighty one." See Ô maitre de tout (Marshall)

"Oh minha mãe" ("O mother mine") Song from Madeira. e.po. BF 2

O mio Fernando. G. Donizetti. e.i. PP—SOA 2

O mio Fernando (Dearest Fernando) e.i. OPS 2

O mio Fernando (O my Fernando) e.i. KS 2

"O mirk, mirk." See Lord Gregory

"Oh, Miss Jenny Johnson is de sweetes' girl in town." See Jenny Johnson

"Oh, mister, please be good." See The orphan-girl (Musorgskii)

"Oh, Mister Wing, we sing-a-ling-a-ling." See Sing-a-ling-a-ling

"O mistress mine." Traditional air, arr by W. Byrd. Words by W. Shakespeare. BOH—BSE—CO 1—DM 1—JE—MM —VFS

"O mistress mine." S. Coleridge-Taylor. Words by W. Shakespeare. VFS

"O mistress mine." Morley. Words by W. Shakespeare. KSS

"O mistress mine." A. Sullivan. Words by W. Shakespeare. BAS 2

"Oh, mistress mine." BC

"O Mistress Shady, she is a lady." See Mistress Shady

"O mistris mine where are you roming." See "O mistress mine" (Traditional air)

"O mój rozmarynie." See Rosemary (Polish song)

"O Mollie, O Mollie, it's for your sake alone." See Jack o' diamonds

"O Molly bawn, why leave me pining." See Molly bawn (Lover)

"O moment rare in this quiet Elysian." See Le rêve (Massenet)

"O monarch supreme of the universe." See Hamidie (Nedjib Pacha)

"O, moon, whose mystic veil." See Santa Lucia

O mother, a hoop. 18th century English song. BE 4 Molly's hoop. CO 2

"O mother dear, Jerusalem." See Jerusalem above (Ward)

"Oh! mother, dear mother." See Lady Maisry

O mother, don't you weep. Negro spiritual. DF

"O mother mine, mother mine." See "Oh minha mãe"

"O mother mine, spread me the silken sheet" (Maulaya) Syrian folk song. ar.e. BF 2

"O mother-my-love, if you'll give me your hand." See Child and mother (Voigtlaender)

"O mother, O mother." See Lord Thomas and fair Ellinor (Georgia version; Kentucky version; Virginia version)

"Oh, mother, take the wheel away." Claribel (C. Norton) WBT

O mount and go, mount and make ye ready. See The captain's lady

"O mountain pine, O mountain pine." See Der tannenbaum

"O music." Round. HSD

"O my belov'd, I sigh." See "O del mio dolce ardor" (Gluck)

"O my beloved one." S. Vassilenko. Words from the Russian of Balmont. e. NM 2

O my boatman, na hóro eile. See "I climb the mountain"

O, my bonie Highland lad. See "As I came o'er the Cairney mount"

"**Oh,** my bottle's ever faithful." See "Ma bouteille m'est fidèle"

"**Oh,** my bravest and best." V. Bellini. e. FSS 7

"**Oh,** my brother, did you come for to help me." See Sweet Canaan

"**Oh** my children, if you ever." See "Se amor mai du vu se vede"

"**O** my consort, Euridice." See "Che farò senza Euridice" (Gluck)

O my dark-eyed beauty, still unheeding. See "Guarda la luna"

Oh, my darling Clementine. P. Montrose (music and words) WA—WBT— WC—WSW
Clementine. BOS—SSS
O my darling Clementine. MPC

"**O** my darling mother, be not angry." See Maiden's song (Meyer-Helmund)

"**Oh,** my dear old Augustin." See Alles ist hin

O my Fernando. See O mio Fernando (Donizetti)

"**Oh** my Ferruh, so proud." See Ferruh

"**Oh,** my golden slippers." See Oh, dem golden slippers (Bland)

"**O** my harp, my harp beloved." See The harp song

"**Oh,** my heart is in bloom." See "Meine liebe ist grün" (Brahms)

"**Oh,** my heart is no longer mine." See "Il mio core non è con me" (Fedeli)

"**O** my heart is sad." See "Meine ruh' ist hin" (Schubert)

"**Oh!** my heart is sore within me." L. van Beethoven. e. SAS 3

"**O** my heart, my heart." See In blossom-time (Needham)

"**O** my home." H. Marechal. e. SAS 4

"**Oh,** my laddie, my laddie." See My laddie (Thayer)

Oh, my little soul's gwine to shine ("Oh, I don't care where you bury my body") Negro spiritual. DF

O my love is like a red, red rose. See "My luve is like a red, red rose" (Scottish air); My luve is like a red, red rose (Schumann)

O my love, my plane-tree (Im chinari yaru) Armenian dance song. a.e. BF 2

"**Oh,** my love stood under the walnut tree." See Over the garden wall (Fox)

"**O** my love's bright eyes whose radiant beams." See At parting

"**O** my love's like a red, red rose." See My luve is like a red, red rose (Schumann)

"**O,** my luve is like a red, red rose." See "My luve is like a red, red rose" (Scottish air)

O my lyre ever-living. See Ô ma lyre immortelle (Gounod)

"**Oh,** my mother counselled truly." See "Mi mamá me consejaba"

"**Oh,** my mudder's in de road." See Most done trabelling

"**O** my name it is Jack Hall." See Jack Hall

Oh, my painful sorrow. See "Och nan och, mo leir chradh"

"**Oh,** my peace is gone." See "Meine ruh' ist hin" (Schubert)

"**O** my pet lamb." See Killebukken (Nordraak)

"**Oh,** my poor little head so madly whirling." See The lovesick maiden

O my poor Nelly Gray. See Darling Nelly Gray (Hanby)

"**O** my Sávishna, bright-eyed falcon mine." See Love-song of the idiot (Musorgskii)

"**O** my son, still be wary." See Come dal ciel precipita (Verdi)

"**Oh!** my soul, my soul am a-gwine for to rest." See Angel Gabriel (Stewart)

"**Oh!** my sweet little rose." See Roisin dubh

"**O** nachtigall, dein süsser schall." See Nachtigall (Brahms)

"**O** name belov'd, name that is dear as heaven." See Caro nome (Verdi)

"**O** Nannie, wilt thou gang wi' me." T. Carter. Words by T. Percy. JO— PS 1

"**O** nation strong, awake." See Hymn of the toilers

"**O** native land." F. Reichardt. e. FSS 8

Oh! ne t'éveille pas (Lullaby) B. Godard. e.f. SOA 3
Lullaby. e.f. SOS 1—SOS 2. e. only BD—WA—WBT—WL— WSW
Oh, ne t'éveille pas encor (Oh, may thy dream not soon be o'er.—Lullaby) e.f. OPS 3

"**O** ne'er can I forget." See La fille du coupeur de paille

"**O** nein, ich fleh', geh' nicht von mir." See "Oh, no, I pray, do not depart" (Rachmaninov)

"**O** nenah nenahwendum." See Morning tryst

"**Oh!** n'enfermez pas mon coeur." See Canzonetta (Zolotarev)

"**O** never lay me down deep." See Canzonetta (Zolotarev)

"**O** night, mysterious goddess." See "O nuit, déesse du mystère" (Piccinni)

"**O** night, O night, who in gloom dost enfold me." See Ô nuit, qui me couvre (Barthe)

"**O** night of nights." Words by J. Ingelow. MCS

"**O** night, peaceful and blest." See Ô bienheureuse nuit

"**O** nightingale, thy plaintive lay." See Nachtigall (Brahms)

"**O** nimm mich auf in deine heil'gen hallen." See Frühlingsfeier (Dietrich)

"**Oh,** no, I pray, do not depart" ("O nein, ich fleh', geh' nicht von mir") S. Rachmaninoff. Words from the Russian of Mereschkovsky. e.g. NM 2

O no, John.   Somerset folk song.   BOS
—FSF—SEF 2—SO—TFC 2
Oh no, John.   DSH
Variants: No, sir, no; "Yonder sits a
fair young damsel"

"O no longer seek to pain me."   See "O
cessate di piagarmi" (Scarlatti)

Oh, no! my love, no.   M. Kelly.   Words
by M. G. Lewis.   BE 4

"Oh, no, we never mention her."   H. R.
Bishop.   Words by T. H. Bayly.   BE 4
—HSE 1—JO

"O none in all the world before."   See
Hymn (Methfessel)

"O notte, o dea del mistero."   See "Ô
nuit, déesse du mystère" (Piccinni)

"O now says the captain: Let's cast lots
and see."   See The silk merchant's
daughter (Big Laurel, N.C. version)

"O now the certain cause I know."   See
To a lady weeping (Lawes)

"O now you forbid us to bid you adieu."
See Tiddy I O

Ô nuit d'amour.   For English translation
see "O tender moon" (Gounod)

"Ô nuit, déesse du mystère" ("O notte, o
dea del mistero."—"O night, mysterious
goddess")   N. Piccinni.   e.f.i.   PA 1

Ô nuit, qui me couvre.   A. Barthe.   e.f.
SOA 1

Oh! oh! hear the wild wind blow.   See Oh!
hear the wild wind blow (Mattei)

"O-o-ly-i-o cheerly man, walk him up O."
See Cheerly man

"O, O, swing low, swing low, sweet chariot."
See Swing low   (Fisher)

"Oh, Ole, Ole, I loved you dearly."   See
"Aa Ola, Ola, min eigen onge"

"O once I bought me an old grey mare."
See The old grey mare (Flag Pond,
Tenn. version)

"O once I courted a pretty little girl."
See The rejected lover (North Carolina
version)

"Oh once I had a nigger girl."   See Haul
away

"O once I had thyme of my own."   See
The sprig of thyme

"O once I knew a pretty girl."   See The
rejected lover (Virginia version)

"O once I lay in stable."   See Poor old
horse

"O once I was courted by a bonny, bonny
boy."   See My bonnie boy

"O once mine eyes had seen you."   See
"Pill' ura chi ti vitti"

"Oh, once there was a maiden."   See
Jungfrun i det gröna

"Oh once there was a merchant wealthy."
See La fille vendue au diable

"Oh, once upon a time in Arkansaw."   See
The Arkansaw traveler

"Oh, once when lovely spring was young."
See 'Twas April (Tchaikovsky)

"O, open the door."   Irish air: Open the
door softly.   Words by R. Burns.
BSR

"Oh! open the door."   Scottish air: The
braes of Boyndlie.   Words by R.
Burns.   BSB—PS 1

Oh, Oregon! oh, Oregon.   University of
Oregon song.   F. Strong.   Words by
I. M. Glen.   CHS

"Oh, our college, the gem of the ocean."
See Three cheers for T. A. and P. U.

"O Paddy dear, and did you hear."   See
The wearing of the green

"Oh papa is out breaking rocks on the
street."   See Tourelay

Ô paradis sorti de l'onde.   G. Meyerbeer.
e.f.   SOA 3
Ô paradis sorti de l'onde (O paradise,
from bright waves risen)   e.f.
KS 4
Ô paradis sorti de l'onde (Oh, paradise
to earth awarded)   e.i.   OPS 3

O paradise, from bright waves risen.   See
Ô paradis sorti de l'onde (Meyerbeer)

"O paradise, O paradise."   J. Barnby.
Words by F. W. Faber.   HSD—
JS—MS—OH— TL— WA— WBT
—WS—WSW
Paradise.   LA

Oh, paradise to earth awarded.   See Ô
paradis sorti de l'onde (Meyerbeer)

"Oh patria! dolce e ingrata patria."   See
Di tanti palpiti (Rossini)

"Oh patria dolce, ingrata patria."   See
Di tanti palpiti (Rossini)

"Oh patria mia bendita tierra."   See America (Carey)

"O patria, o cara patria."   See O, tu Palermo (Verdi)

"O' patria, o rei, ó povo."   See Hymno
nacional—Portugal (Pedro IV)

"O peace, the fairest child of heaven."   See
Peace, the fairest child of heaven (Oswald)

"O peaceful night!   O time of holy calm."
F. H. Cowen.   SAS 1

"O peaceful night of the budding spring-
time."   See "Noche serena"

O pescator dell' onda ("E c'eran tre sorelle."—O fisherman on the waves)
Venetian folk song.   e.i.   BF 2

"Oh, pescator dell' onda" ("Oh, fisher in
the ocean") Venetian folk song.   e.i.
MSI

Oh, Peter, go ring dem bells.   See Peter,
go ring them bells

"Ô petits enfants, voici l'heure."   See
Berceuse (Ropartz)

"O Philly, happy be that day."   Air: The
sow's tail to Geordie.   Words by R.
Burns.   BSR

"Oh! pilot, 'tis a fearful night."   See The
pilot (Nelson)

"O pine-tree lonely standing."   See The
pine-tree (Salter)

"Oh, pity poor Reuben Ranzo."   See
Reuben Ranzo

O, po' sinner.   See What yo' gwine to do
when yo' lamp burn down

"O Polly dear, O Polly, the rout has now
begun."   See High Germany

"O Polly, love, O Polly, the rout has now begun." See High Germany

"O Polly, my sweetheart, so tender and true." See Polly, my sweetheart (Cole)

"O Polly, O Polly, if you will agree." See The cruel ship's carpenter (Big Laurel, N.C. version)

"O poor little flower, on fresh stem erect." See Lady Beatrice's lament (Speranza)

"Oh, poor old Reuben Ranzo." See Reuben Ranzo

"O poor Polly Oliver." See Polly Oliver

"O, poortith cauld." Air: Cauld kail. Words by R. Burns. BSB—BSR

[O poortith cauld] "O puirtith cauld." Air: I had a horse. Words by R. Burns. MMS—PS 1

"O, praise an' tanks! de Lord He come." See Song of the negro boatman (Muller)

Oh pray. A. Markewitsch. e. KSN

"Oh press thy cheek against mine own." See "Lehn' deine wang' an meine wang'" (Jensen)

"O pretty Polly, don't you cry." FSS 4 —WBT

"O pretty Polly Oliver." See Pretty Polly Oliver

Oh, promise of a joy so sweet. See Promesse de mon avenir (Massenet)

"Oh, promise to meet me." See Rose of Killarney (Thomas)

"Oh! proud were the chieftains of green Innis-Fail." Irish air: An bruach na carraige, or, The brink of the white rocks. Words by T. Davis. MMI

"O, proudly rise the monarchs of our mountain land." See The mountains (Gladden)

O pure and tender star of eve. See O du mein holder abendstern (Wagner)

"O! qu'a-dj'oyou e l'air." See Noël

"O quali mi risvegliano." See La serenata (Braga)

"Oh, raging fortune's withering blast." Scottish air: Tam Lin. Words by Burns. PS 2

O rare Turpin. Traditional air. DM 2 —MM

"O rattlin' roarin' Willie." See Rattlin' roarin' Willie

"O ray buttah ray." See "Old rags, bottles, rags"

"O re bho lá ma-n re." See Snake-charmer's song

"O re del ciel a te vengo tremante." See See Der moench (Meyerbeer)

"Oh! recall not." See "Ah! non giunge" (Bellini)

"Oh, rede me, dear mother, a sonsy rede." See Marsk Stigs døttre

O redeemed. Negro spiritual. JP— NMP

"O reign, O reign, O reign, my Saviour." See Reign, Massa Jesus

"Oh, religion is a fortune." See Religion is a fortune

O remembrance of scenes long vanished. See Vi ravviso, O luoghi ameni (Bellini)

"O rendete mi la speme." Bellini. e.i. PP

"O rest in the Lord." F. Mendelssohn. e. BD—CS 1—OS 2—SAS 2—TFC 2 —TL—WA—WS

Oh! rest thee, babe. See "Oh, hush thee, my babie" (Whitaker)

"O restore to me." See "Deh, rendetemi" (Provenzale)

"O riante nature" ("O the smile of the spring-time") C. Gounod. e.f. SS 2

"O Richard, ô mon roi." A. E. M. Grétry. e.f. SOA 4

"O, ride on, Jesus." Negro spiritual. BN 1

"Oh, ring the bells in the belfry high." See Ring the bells

"O ring ye bells." C. Darnton. HC

Oh, rise and shine, and give God the glory, glory. See Rise and shine

"Oh! rise up, children, get your crown." See Oh! holy Lord

"O rise you up, ye sev'n bretherens." See Earl Brand (White Rock, N.C. version)

"Oh Robert, oh my beloved." See "Roberto, o tu che adoro" (Meyerbeer)

"O, Robin-a-Thrush he married a wife." See Robin-a-Thrush

"O, Robin is my only joe." See Kind Robin lo'es me

O robin, red robin. FSS 7

"Oh! rock me, Julie." Negro song. KA

O, rocks don't fall on me. Negro spiritual. JB

"Oh, roll de ole chariot along." See Roll de ole chariot along

"Oh, roll the cotton, roll it down." See Roll the cotton down

"O rose of Ispahan." See "Les roses d'Ispahan" (Fauré)

"O rowan tree, O rowan tree." See The rowan tree

"O ruddier than the cherry." Händel. BS 1—KS 5

"O ruddy lover! O brave red clover." See The clover (MacDowell)

"O ruler, land and people." See Hymno nacional—Portugal (Pedro IV)

"Oh, run up, chillun, get your crown." See A love-feast in heaven

"Oh, sacred Head, once wounded." Greek air. Words by Bernard of Clairvaux. [Tr of Salve caput cruentatum] e. FSS 2

"O sacred Head! once wounded" (Passion chorale) S. Bach. [Words by Bernard of Clairvaux. Tr of Salve caput cruentatum] e. LA

"Oh, sad and heavy should I part." See Sae far awa'

"O sad were the homes." See Angus Macdonald (Roeckel)

"Oh, sadly pass the hours." See Las tristas horas

"O sadly the cuckoo is calling now." See The cuckoo yodel

"O sag' es noch einmal" (I love thee) L. Slansky. e.g. SM 3

"O säh ich auf der haide dort." See "O wert thou in the cauld blast" (Mendelssohn)

"Oh, St Patrick was a gentleman." See St Patrick was a gentleman

"Oh, saints and sinners, will-a you go." See Gwine up

"O Sally Brown she promised me." See Roll and go

"O Sally, my dear." Folk song. FSF—SEF 1—SO

"Oh, Sally Racket, hi-oh! cheerly man! pawned my best jacket." See Cheer'ly man

O salutaris ("Lord, lead me in Thy righteousness") Cherubini. e. HSS 2

"O salutaris" ("O blessed Savior, God of love") H. Panofka. e.l. HSS 1

"O sanctissima." Sicilian hymn. 1. MCS
Sicilian mariners' hymn. 1. SMW

"O, Sandy, why leaves thou my Nelly." See Thro' the wood, laddie

"Oh, Santa Claus, dear Santa." See Dear Santa Claus (Crosby)

"Oh, Santa Claus is coming." See Merrily ring the bells

O santissima (Old Sicilian air) See Die drei grossen Christlichen feste; "O sanctissima"

"O santissima Vergine Maria." See Ogni sabato avrete il lume acceso (Gordigiani)

"O Santy Anna gained the day." See Santy Anna

"O Savior, Lord of heaven." See "Ave Maria" (Arcadelt)

"O saw ye bonnie Lesley." Air: The collier's bonnie lassie. Words by R. Burns. BSB—BSR—PS 1

"O, saw ye my dear, my Philly." Air: When she cam ben she bobbit. Words by R. Burns. BSR

"O, saw ye my dearie, my Eppie McNab." Air: Eppie McNab. Words by R. Burns. BSB—BSR—PS 1

"O, saw ye my wee thing." See Saw ye my wee thing

"O say, can you see, by the dawn's early light." See The star-spangled banner (Smith)

"Oh, say, do you remember." FSS 7

"O say it again a thousand, thousand times." See "O sag' es noch einmal" (Slansky)

"O say not that my heart is cold." Irish air: Grammachree. Words by C. Wolfe. JO

"Oh! say not woman's heart is bought." J. Whitaker. Words by I. Pocock. HSE 1

"Oh, say, was you ever in Rio Grande." See Rio Grande

"O say what is that thing call'd light." See The blind boy (Stanley)

O schöne zeit, o sel'ge zeit (O happy day) K. Götze. e.g. CB—ES—KF 1 —KF 3—MSF 2
O lovely day, O happy day. e. WBT —WL

"Oh! se tu fossi meco." See Ti rapirei (Tosti)

"O sea, dreadful sea." See "Ô mer, ouvre-toi" (Delibes)

"O seagull, tell me is the flood-tide rising." See Fisherman's song

"Oh seda clu ja önne." See Wedding joy

"Oh, see dat water-million." See Gib me dat water-million (Westendorf)

"Oh, see the May-pole long and bare." See Around the May-pole

"Oh see, they come, the village children." See Les enfants à la Crecho

"Oh, see thou, dearest maid of spring." See Med en primulaveris (Grieg)

"O selig, wer liebt." See Liebe in allem (Schulz)

"O send Lewie Gordon hame." See Lewie Gordon

"O senora! your little parrot to the stream wants me to go." See Señora, su periquito (1st version)

"O Serbians rise." See "Rise, O Servians"

"Oh, shall we meet again in the distant When." See Brahmin love song (Blamphin)

"Oh, shame on thee, maiden." See Kau fra Hallingdalen

"O Shanadar I love your daughter." See Shanadar

"Oh! she is not like the rose." See The snowy-breasted pearl

"O she looked out of the window." See The two magicians

"O Shenandoah, I long to hear you." See Shenandoah

"Oh shepherdess fickle, I fear your bright eyes." See "Bergère légère"

"Oh, shepherdess smiling, your charms I must fear." See "Bergère légère"

Oh, she's bonnie. Old Scotch song. BC

"Oh! sing a merry carol." C. F. Roper. HC

"O sing a song of Bethlehem." J. Barnby. Words by L. F. Benson. HC

"O sing again, my gentle bird." See The gentle bird

"Oh, sing all de way, sing all de way." See Hear de angels singin'

"O sing, fair maid." See "Cante, cante, fiette"

"Oh! sing from thy spray." See My Jamie o'er the sea (Lee)

"O sing God's praise in winter too." WSC

"Oh! sing them on the sunny hills." See The songs your fathers loved

"O sing we a carol." A. H. Brown. Words by W. J. Irons. HC

"O sing with voices clear and strong." See Our native song (Methfessel)

Oh! sinner man ("Oh! come back, sinner") Negro spiritual. NMP

"O sinner man, you had better pray." See O sinner, you'd better get ready

O sinner, you'd better get ready. Negro spiritual. JP

Oh, sinner, you'd better get ready. HR

"Oh, siren, whose song from the thicket." See The blackbird

"O sister, can't you help me to sing." See Hold the light

Oh! sister dear. See "Pourquoi pleurer? qourquoi pleurer" (Auber)

"O sister, O sister, come go with me." See The two sisters (North Carolina version)

"O sleep, O sleep, why dost thou leave me." See O sleep, why dost thou leave me (Händel)

"Oh, sleep, sleep on, thou fair Child Jesus." Alsatian carol. e. MF

O sleep, why dost thou leave me. G. F. Händel. GMF

"O slumber, my darling." See "Oh, hush thee, my babie" (Whitaker)

"O smile as thou wert wont to smile." See We may be happy yet (Balfe)

'O sole mio. See entry under Sole

O sole più ratto. For English translation see "Ensanguined and lurid" (Donizetti)

"Oh, solemn hour when hearts were lowly bending." See Cantique de Noël (Adam)

"Oh! some may sing of Sweet Moselle." See Give me the waltz (Pratt)

"O some they do talk of bold Robin Hood." See Robin Hood and the bishop of Hereford

"O, some will court and compliment." Air: John, come kiss me now. Words by R. Burns. BSR
"Oh! some will court and compliment" (John, come kiss me now) PS 2

"O sometimes gleams upon our sight." See Faith (Rossini)

"O sonnenschein, o sonnenschein." See An den sonnenschein (Schumann)

"O sons and daughters, let us sing" J. S. B. Hodges. Tr of O filii et filiae, Rex coelestis, Rex gloriae. e. HC

"O sons of Norway." See "Sönner af Norge" (Blom)

"Oh, soon in my pow'r I shall hold him." See Amour! viens aider (Saint-Saëns)

"Oh, sooner in the mornin' when I rise." See The ole sheep done know the road

Ô souverain, ô juge, ô père (Prayer) J. Massenet. Words by d'Ennery, Gallet, and Blau. e.f. SOA 3

"O, speed, Lord Nithsdale." Scottish song. PS 1

"O spirit of the nation, come." J. W. Tufts. Word by J. Geddes. JS

"Oh! stand the storm, it won't be long." See We'll stand the storm

O star of eve. See O du mein holder abendstern (Wagner)

"O, star of mine high in the sky." See O du mein holder abendstern (Wagner)

Oh, star of wonder, star of might. See Three kings of Orient (Hopkins)

"O star-spangled banner! O red, white, and blue." See The stars and stripes

"O, starry flag of union, hail." C. W. Johnson (music and words) JS

"O stay, my child, and linger here by me." See The little fish's song (Arenski)

"O, stay, sweet warbling woodlark, stay." Air: Whare shall our gudeman lie. Words by R. Burns. BSR

"O stay thy passing, golden moments." See "O lass dich halten, gold'ne stunde" (Jensen)

"O, steer her up." Air: Steer her up. Words by R. Burns. BSR

"O Strassburg, o Strassburg." See Der unerbittliche hauptmann

"O strength and stay." F. Mendelssohn. Words by J. Ellerton. MS

"O sue not thou for fortune's dower." See The lover's prayer

"Oh, Sunday has come again today." See Sunday song

"O sunny beam." See An den sonnenschein (Schumann)

O sunshine. See An den sonnenschein (Schumann)

Oh! Susanna. S. C. Foster (music and words) CST—FSS 7—HSD—NMP—WBT

"O süsse mutter" ("O dearest mother") C. Loewe. Words by Rückert. e.g. PG 2

"O swallow dear, thou little wandering bird, sweet bird." See The prisoner to the swallow

"O swallow, swallow, you that fly about and around." See L'hirondelle, messagère de l'amour

"O swan of slenderness." See The little red lark

"Oh! sweep chimney, sweep." See The chimney sweep

"Oh, sweet and dim the light and shade." See The chorister (Sullivan)

"O sweet delight." 17th century air. Words by T. Campion. JE

"O sweet dream of days long ago." See Élégie (Massenet)

"O sweet is the vale where the Mohawk gently glides." See Bonny Eloise (Thomas)

"O, sweet sir, for your courtesie." See My jo Janet

"Oh, sweet were the voices heard in the sky." See The voices in the sky

"O swift goes my boat like a bird on the billow." See Mona (Maybrick)

"O swiftly glides the bonnie boat." Old Scottish air. Words by J. Baillie. JO

"Oh swing low, sweet chariot." See The Danville chariot

"Oh, swinging and swinging beneath our old tree." See Swing song

"Oh, Syracuse." College song. Words by H. S. Lee. CHS—NMS

"Oh, take her, but be faithful still." S. Nelson. Words by C. Jefferys. FSS 3—JO

O, take me back to Switzerland. Tyrolese air. Words by C. Norton. JO
   Oh, take me back to Switzerland. FSS 2

"O take me to your arms, love." See The willow tree

"O take me to your lovely child of spring." See Med en primulaveris (Grieg)

Oh! take your time, Miss Lucy. See Lucy Long

"O tannenbaum, du edles reis." F. Wollank. Words by L. Uhland. g. ED 3

"O tannenbaum, o tannenbaum." See Der tannenbaum

"Oh! tell it her." L. Kotschonbey. e. KSN—WL

Oh, tell me how to woo thee. See "If doughty deeds my lady please"

"O tell me, lovely vale, I pray." See Farväl (Gustaf)

O tell me, my heart, if this be love ("When Delia on the plain appears") Air: Mwynen Meirionydd, or, The delight of Meirionydd. Words by George, Lord Lyttelton. MMW

"O tell me what it meaneth." See Die Lorelei (Silcher)

"O tell me where did Katy live." See The katydid

"Oh, tell na me of wind and rain." See "O lassie, art thou sleeping yet": Her answer

O tempora! o mores. German air. Words from the German of E. Geibel. e. CST—TL
   The jolly fiddler. e. CU

"Oh, tempt me not, my darling" (Nuuanu waipuna) C. K. Hopkins. Words by Kealakai. e.h. HA

"Oh, ten to one when the game's begun." See Go, Chicago (Hirsh)

"O tender moon." C. Gounod. [Tr. of Ô nuit d'amour] e. WBT

"O tender shadow, that hover'st near." See "Ombre légère" (Meyerbeer)

"O thank me not for songs I sing thee." See Widmung (Franz)

"Oh, thank me not for what I sing thee." See Widmung (Franz)

"Oh, Thanksgiving morning is a time of glee." See Thanksgiving day

"O, that I had ne'er been married." Air: Crowdie. Words by R. Burns. BSR

"Oh! that I never more might see." Donizetti. e. FSS 4

"O, that I were where Helen lies." See I wish I war where Eelin lies

"Oh, that little old red shawl." See The little old red shawl

"O, that the dear Giver of life" ("Kdyby mně to Pán Bůh dal") Czech folk song. bo.e. BF 1

"O that thou had'st hearkened." A. Sullivan. SS 1

"O that we two were maying." C. Gounod. Words by C. Kingsley. BC

"O that we two were maying." A. M. Smith. Words by C. Kingsley. FMB

O that's the lassie o' my heart. See "O wha is she that lo'es me"

"Oh! the auld hoose, the auld hoose." See The auld hoose

Oh, the band of Gideon. See Gideon's band ("I hail to my sister")

"O the banks of the Lee." See The banks of the Lee (Arditi)

"O the beautiful old story." G. C. E. Ryley. Words by L. M. Alcott. HC

"Oh! the blacksmith's a fine sturdy fellow." See The blacksmith (Mozart)

"O! the bonny fisher lad." Scotch song. SMW

"Oh, the boys and the girls went a-huckleberry hunting." See Huckleberry hunting

"Oh! the boys of Kilkenny." Irish air: The head of old Dennis. MMI—PI

"Oh! the bull-dog on the bank." See The bull-dog on the bank

"Oh! the charming month of May." 18th century air. Words by J. Addison. DM 2—MM

"Oh, the clang of the wooden shoon." See The clang of the wooden shoon (Molloy)

"O the combat ensanguined has ended." See Dulce patria (Carnicer y Batlle)

"O the cuckoo she's a pretty bird." See The cuckoo

"O! the day it came at last." See On, on, on the boys came marching (Root)

"Oh, the days are gone when beauty bright." See Love's young dream

"O the days of the Kerry dancing." See The Kerry dance (Molloy)

"O the early time of love." See The three ages of love (Loder)

"O the fair town of Plymouth is by the sea-side." See Plymouth sound

"O the first time that I saw her." See Roller, bowler

"Oh, the flowers that I saw in the wildwood." See Faded flowers (Power)

"Oh, the gentle spring is coming bright and gay." See Spring song (Mendelssohn)

"Oh, the golden, glowing morning." G. F. Le Jeune. Words by G. T. Rider. HC

"Oh, the hog-eye man is the man for me." See The hog eye man

"Oh! the lady of the lea." See The lady of the lea (Smart)

Oh, the land I am bound for. See Sweet Canaan

"Oh, the land that we love." M. W. Balfe. Words by L. F. Lewis. MP —WBT

"Oh! the lone starry hours give me, love." See Lone starry hours (Power)

"Oh! the marriage." Irish air: The swaggering jig. Words by T. Davis. MMI

"O! the moments were sad when my love and I parted." See Savourneen deelish

"O, the moon and stars are shining." See Moonlight and starry night

"Oh, the moon shines bright." See The moon shines bright

"O the mouth of my Pepita." See La boca de Pepita

O the oak and the ash. See The oak and the ash

"Oh, the old house at home." See Old house at home (Loder); Old house at home (Woodbury)

Oh, the ole sheep done know the road. See The ole sheep done know the road

"O the ploughboy was a ploughing." See The simple ploughboy (Devon version)

"Oh, the river of Jordan is so wide." See Oh, wasn't that a wide river

"Oh, the rocks and the mountains." See The rocks and the mountains

"O the rose is dead." See My rose of yester-e'en (Rich)

"O the sad day." P. Humfrey. Words by T. Flatman. BOH—JE

Oh! the sailor shall sing. See La paloma (Yradier)

"Oh, the secret of bliss." See "Il segreto per esser felici" (Donizetti)

Oh! the shamrock ("Through Erin's isle") Air: Alley croker. Words by T. Moore. MI

"Oh, the sight entrancing." Air: Planxty Sudley. Words by T. Moore. MI

"Oh, the smartest clipper you can find." See Clear the track

"O the smile of the spring-time." See "Ô riante nature" (Gounod)

"Oh, the sports of childhood." See Swinging 'neath the old apple-tree (Barrows)

"O the stars in the elements are falling." See Stars in the elements

"Oh, the stillness that falls on the moor and the fen." See Stillness of night (Beach)

Oh, the stormy winds do blow. See The mermaid ("On a Friday morn")

"O the streams of Nantsian." See The streams of Nantsian

"Oh, the times are hard and the wages low, leave her, Johnny, leave her." See Leave her Johnny

"Oh, the times are hard and the wages low, you sailor, where you bound to." See Across the western ocean

"Oh, the wildest packet you can find." Chantey. SMW

Oh, then my little soul's gwine to shine ("I'm gwine to join the great 'sociation") Negro spiritual. JS

Oh, den my little soul's gwine to shine. HR

Oh, then my little soul's going to shine. JP

"O there was a keeper, a shooting did go." See The keeper

"O there was a ship in some foreign country." See The Golden Vanity

"O there was a woman, and she was a widow." See Flowers in the valley

"O, there's not a thrade that's going." See The bowld sojer boy (Lover)

"Oh, they call me Hanging Johnny." See Hanging Johnny

"Oh! they tell me thou art dead, Katy darling." See Katy darling

"Oh, they were clear and cloudless." See True hearts (Maybrick)

"Oh think how we, as moonlight shades were flitting." See My heart is thine (Proch)

"Oh! think not my spirits are always as light." Air: John O'Reilly the active. Words by T. Moore. JO—MI

"Oh, think of a home over there." See Over there (Huntington)

O this is no my ain lassie. Air: This is no my ain house. Words by R. Burns. BSB—MMS—PS 1

"I see a form, I see a face." BSR

"Oh! this old time religion." See This old time religion

"Oh, those charming lights." See "Deh più a me non v'ascondete" (Bononcini)

"O Thou afflicted." J. Benedict. OS 2—SAS 2

Oh, thou amid the angels bright. See Oh, tu che in seno agl'angioli (Verdi)

"Oh, thou ancient mountain" ("Stara planina") Bulgarian song. b.e. BF 1

"Oh! thou art all so tender." Scottish air: My love has forsaken me. Words by H. S. Riddell. PS 2

"O thou belov'd." See "O del mio dolce ardor" (Gluck)

"O thou, born of my people." See La benedizione (Gordigiani)

"O thou dearest maiden mine." See Alles ist hin

"O thou delicious fountain overflowing with evil." See "Source délicieuse" (Gounod)

"Oh! thou golden sunset." See An die abendsonne (Nägeli)

O thou joyful day, O thou blessed day, holy, peaceful Christmastide. See Die drei grossen Christlichen feste

"O Thou Lord God." See God for Poland (Kurpinski)

"O thou loveliest, if thou wilt take me." See "Belle mia" (Pergolesi)

"Oh, thou lovely land." See Ô paradis sorti de l'onde (Meyerbeer)

"O thou maiden, of maids most sweet and fair." See Vigil (Glinka)

"O thou mine own fair star of eve." See O du mein holder abendstern (Wagner)

O Thou most compassionate. See Erbarmen (Nicodé)

Oh! thou my Austria. F. von Suppé. e. KSE—SN

Oh thou, oh thou. See Surging waters (Hopkins)

"O thou pale orb that silent shines." Air: Scots queen. Words by R. Burns. BSR

"O thou rose-maiden." A. Dargomijsky. Words from the Russian of A. Pushkin. e. NM 1

"O thou silent autumn night." See Night

"O thou sublime sweet evening star." See O du mein holder abendstern (Wagner)

"O, thou sun, thou blessed, glowing sun" ("Soleil! ô clair soleil") M. Slonov. Words by P. Mochalov. e.f. NR 2

"O thou that rest in holy night revealest." See An die hoffnung (Beethoven)

"O thou that tellest good tidings to Zion." Händel. OS 2—SAS 2

"Oh! Thou, to whom this heart ne'er yet." See Sweet spirit, hear my prayer (Wallace)

"O Thou, who by a star." T. A. Arne. MCS

"O Thou who dryest the mourner's tear." Haydn. Words by T. Moore. HSS 2 —HSS 4

"Oh thou who in the wold dost dwell." See Waidmannslied (Slansky)

"O Thou whose presence went before." See Song of the free

"O Thou wonderful, thou lofty jealousy of olden glories." See Al nome tuo temuto (Righini)

"O thought of thoughts." See Jeg elsker dig

O Tibbie, I ha'e seen the day. Scottish air: Invercauld's reel. Words by R. Burns. PS 2
"Yestreen I met you on the moor." BSR

O 'tis a glorious sight to see. Weber. Words by J. R. Planché. TS

"O 'tis heav'n only knows what will happen." See "Höga himmelen vet hvad som händer"

"Oh, 'tis little Mary Cassidy's the cause of all my misery." See Little Mary Cassidy

"Oh! 'tis sweet to think." Irish air: Donall na greine, or, Daniel of the sun, or, Thady, you gander. Words by T. Moore. MI—MMI—PI

"Oh! 'tis the melody" (Lays of a minstrel) T. H. Bayly. HSE 2

"ô toi l'objet" ("To thee I kneel") Gluck. e.f. BAS 2

"Oh, to and fro on my bosom of love." See Irish lullaby (Needman)

"Oh! to me't's all one." See "'s ist mir alles eins" (Fuss)

"Oh! to remember the happy hours." See Synnöves lied (Kjerulf)

"Oh, Tommy's gone, what shall I do? Hilo, Hilo." See Tom's gone to Hilo

Oh, touch the harp. Old song. FSS 4— WBT

"Oh, touch those chords." FSS 4

"Oh tree of fir, oh tree of fir." See Der tannenbaum

"O, true love is a bonnie flower." Scottish song. PS 1

Oh, tu che in seno agl'angioli (Oh, thou amid the angels bright) Verdi. e.i. OPS 3

O, tu Palermo. G. Verdi. e.i. SOA 5

"O tula, mntwana, O tula." See Lullaby ("O hush thee, baby")

O turn thee. C. Gounod. e. TFC 2

"Oh, 'twas in the broad Atlantic." See The mermaid

Oh, 'twas sweet to hear her. A. Lee. FSS 6

"Oh, 'twas there I larned radin' an' writin'." See Mush, mush

"O Una Waun, thou blossom so wondrous fair." See Úna bán

"Oh! universal benefactor." See Hamidie (Nedjib Pacha)

"Oh, up aloft this yard must go." See So handy

"O vales with sunlight smiling." See Farewell to the forest (Mendelssohn)

"Oh venitele a vedere." See La mamma de rosa

"O Vermeland." See Vermeland

"ô vin, dissipe la tristesse." See Chanson bachique (Thomas)

"O vision entrancing." A. G. Thomas. Words by T. Marzials. KF 3—MSF 1 —OPS 3—SM 3

"Oh! vista, è dessa, l'adora to mio ben." See Ah! se tu dormi (Vaccai)

"O voi del mio poter ministri eletti." See "Sorge infausta" (Händel)

O voi dell' Erebo (Up! lords of Erebus) Händel. e.i. BAS 2

O voices of the sky. See "O lovely voices of the sky" (Mozart)

O Vol'ge i Mikulîe. See The legend of Volgá

"ô vous, esprits des eaux." See Divination by water (Musorgskiï)

"Oh, wae upon that fearfu' deed." Scottish air: Ochoin ochri, oh. PS 2

O, wae's me for Prince Charlie. See Wae's me for Prince Charlie

"O waidmann du zu haus im hain." See Waidmannslied (Slansky)

Oh, wait till I get on my robe. See Oh, yes! oh, yes ("I come this night")

Oh, wait till I put on my robe. See Oh, yes ("I'm a-tellin' yo'")

"Oh, wake, wake, my lady-love." Air: Mwynen Machno, or, The enjoyment of Machno. MMW

"Oh, walk together, children." See A great camp-meeting in the promised land

O waly, waly. English folk song. FSF —SEF 1—SO

"O waly, waly, up the bank." Scottish folk song. MMS—PS 1

"O, wann kehrst du zurück, mein treuer Johnie." See Faithfu' Johnie

Oh, wasn't that a wide river. Negro spiritual. JP—NMP
> O, wasn't dat a wide river. JB
> "Oh, wasn't dat a wide riber." HR

"O, wat ye wha that lo'es me." See "O wha is she that lo'es me"

O wat ye wha's in yon town. Air: I'll gae nae mair to yon toun. Words by R. Burns. BSB
> "Now haply down yon gay green shaw." BSR

Oh way over Jerdan. See View de land

Oh, way over Jordan. See View de land

"Oh, we are the students of the A. M. C." See The A. and M. college song (Scott)

"Oh, we can play on the big bass drum." See The orchestra

"Oh! we love the spring." See The king of seasons all (Maybrick)

"O we sail'd to Virginia." See Admiral Benbow

"Oh, we take him from the city or the plough." See Private Tommy Atkins (Potter)

"O, wearily, wearily lags the day." Old Irish peasant song. e. MMI

"O weary feet." A. Beirly. Words by C. L. Hayes. HSD

"Oh, weary, weary are our feet." See Orphan ballad singers (Russell)

"Oh, weary's on money." See The dear Irish boy

"O weel may the boatie row." See The boatie rows

O, weel may the keel row. See The keel row

"Oh! weep for the hour." See Eveleen's bower

Oh, weep! oh, weep, mine eyes. See Pleurez! pleurez, mes yeux (Massenet)

"O welcome bat and owlet gray." Air: Mantell Siani, or, Jane's mantle. Words by J. Baillie. MMW

"Oh! welcome, Charlie, o'er the main." See Lang o' comin'

"Oh, welcome, fair evening so blissful." See Sommer-abendlied (Becker)

"O welcome, happy day." H. Smith. HC

"O welcome now, ye groves and bow'rs." J. Haydn. e. OS 1—SAS 1

"Oh, well do I remember that serene and lovely hour." See The springtime of the year

"O we'll inch and inch and inch along." See Inching along

"O well may the boatie row." See The boatie rows

"Oh, we'll wait till Jesus comes." See Down by the river

"O, were I able to rehearse." See The ewie wi' the crooked horn

"Oh, were I just a flow'r." See Mignonette (Weckerlin)

"O were I on Parnassus hill." J. Oswald. Words by R. Burns. BSB—BSR
> "Oh! were I on Parnassus hill." PS 2

"O, were my love yon lilac fair." Air: Gin my love were yon red rose. Words by R. Burns. BSR

"O were my love yon lilac fair." Air: Hughie Graham. Words by R. Burns. BSB

"O were my men drunk or were my men mad." See The mermaid

"Oh, we're three jolly, jolly sailor boys." See The three sailor boys (Marzials)

"Oh! Wermeland, thou dearest." See Vermeland

"Oh wert thou in the cauld blast." Scottish air. Words by R. Burns. PS 1

"O, wert thou in the cauld blast." Air: Lenox love to Blantyre. Words by R. Burns. BSR

"O wert thou in the cauld blast." Mendelssohn. Words by R. Burns. BSB— FMB—MS— TFC 2—TL— WBT—WL
> "Oh, wert thou in the cauld blast." FSS 4—HSC—OH

O, wert thou, love, but near me. See "Forlorn my love, no comfort near"

"O wha is she that lo'es me." Air: Morag. Words by R. Burns. BSB—PS 1
> "O, wat ye wha that lo'es me." BSR

"O, wha my babie-clouts will buy." Air: Where wad bonie Annie lie. Words by R. Burns. BSR

"O, wha will to Saint Stephen's house." Air: Killiecrankie. Words by R. Burns. BSR

"O, whar gat ye that hauver-meal bannock." Air: Adew Dundee. Words by R. Burns. BSR

"O, wha's at the window, wha, wha." R. A. Smith. Words by A. Carlile. MMS—PS 2

"Oh, wha's for Scotland and Charlie." Jacobite song. PS 2

"O, what a plague is love." See Phillida flouts me

"O! what a thing it is to be." See Oh, you little darling

"Oh, what a you say, seekers." See Die in de fiel'

"O what can you tell." J. C. Lowry. Words by R. W. Raymond. FSS 5

"Oh! what can with our flow'ry plains compare." See The happy farmer (Schumann)

"O what do you say, seekers." See We'll die in the field

"O, what has caused this great commotion." See Tippecanoe and Tyler too (Ross)

"O what is man." Spohr. e. OS 4

"Oh, what is the matter with robin." FSS 4

"O what will you say when your father comes back." See Edward (Carmen, N.C. version)

"Oh, what's de use of workin' so hard." See In de mornin'

"Oh! what's so fine, dear." See 'O sole mio (Capua)

"Oh, when around thy dear face, gently sighing." See Se mai senti (Leo)

"Oh, when I come t' die I wan' t' be ready." See When I come t' die

"O when I come to die, O when I come to die." See Give me Jesus

"Oh, when I git t'heaven." See Father Abraham

"Oh, when I sleep." F. Liszt. Words by V. Hugo. e. BC

"Oh! when I think 'neath sorrow's smart." See My Nanny

"O, when she cam ben, she bobbed fu' law." Air: When she cam ben she bobbit. Words by R. Burns. BSR

"O when will ye e'er leave me." See "E quando ve n'andate" (Tenaglia)

"Oh! when you hear the roll of the big bass drum, then you may know that the Dutch have come." See The Dutch company

"Oh, when you hear the roll of the big bass drum, then you will know that the scouts have come." See The scouts company

"O where, and O where is your Highland laddie gone." See The blue bells of Scotland (Jordan)

"O, where are you going, my pretty fair maid." Donegal song. JOI

"Oh, where are you going, sweet Robin." See Sweet Robin (Composer unknown); Sweet Robin (Cooke?)

"O where are you going to, my pretty little dear." See Dabbling in the dew

"Oh, where art thou, my love, to-night." See Where sleepest thou, my dearie

"Oh, where can father be." See Pi-Pi-Pi-Pi-Pi

"Oh! where do fairies hide their heads." See When green leaves come again (Bishop)

"Oh where d'you think I found my soul." See Listen at de angels shoutin'

"O, where hae ye been, Lord Ronald, my son? O, where hae ye been, Lord Ronald, my son." Air: Lord Ronald, my son. Words by R. Burns. BSR

"O, where ha'e ye been, Lord Ronald, my son? O, where ha'e ye been, my handsome young man." See Lord Ronald

"O where have you been all the day, my boy Willie." See My boy Willie (Worcestershire version)

"Oh, where have you been, Billy boy, Billy boy." See My boy Willie (Billy boy; also North Carolina version no. 1)

"O where have you been, Lord Randal my son." See Lord Randal (Georgia version)

"O where is pretty Polly." See The cruel ship's carpenter (Hindman, Ky. version; Knott county, Ky. version)

"O where is the sphere like a student career." See The sunniest season of life (Kirby)

"Oh where, oh where is my little dog gone." See Where has my little dog gone (Winner)

"Oh! where, tell me where is your Highland laddie gone." See The blue bells of Scotland (Jordan)

"Oh where, where art thou, well-beloved." See Del mio core (Haydn)

"O wherefore do ye these things." F. Mendelssohn. e. SAS 4

"Oh! where's the slave, so lowly." Air: Sios agus sios liom. Words by T. Moore. MI

"Oh, whisky is the life of man." See Whisky for my Johnny

"Oh! whisper what thou feelest." See Whisper what thou feelest (Richards)

O whistle, and I'll come to you, my lad. Attributed to J. Bruce. Words by R. Burns. JO—MMS—PS 1—WBT

"But warily tent when ye come to court me." BSR

Oh! whistle and I'll come to you, my lad. BSB

"Oh, whither art roaming." See "E dove t'aggiri" (Cesti)

"Oh, who are the stuff." See We are the stuff

"O, who dat a-comin' ovah yondah." See Who dat a-comin' ovah yondah

"Oh, who do you call the King Emanuel." See King Emanuel

"Oh, who is like my Johnnie." See The keel row

"O who is that that raps at my window." Folk song from Sussex. SF 5 Variants: "Awake! awake"; The shining dagger

"Oh, who is this poor foreigner." See Irish Molly-O

"O who rides by night, thro' woodlands wild." See Erlkönig (Schubert)

"Oh, who sae like my Johnny." See The keel row

Oh, who so gay and free. FSS 5

"Oh who will buy the beautiful canary." See "Chi vuol comprar la bella calandrina" (Jommelli)

"O who will o'er the downs so free." See Who will o'er the downs (Pearsall)

"O who will smoke my meerschaum pipe." See Meerschaum pipe

"O who's been here since I've been gone." See The hog-eyed man

"Oh, why art thou not near me, O my love." See Good-night, my love (Marschner)

"Oh, why does the white man follow my path." See The Indian hunter (Russell)

"Oh! why left I my hame." See My ain countrie

O, why, should Fate sic pleasure have. See "O, poortith cauld and restless love"

"Oh, why so soon doth pass summer's pleasure." See "Ach, wie so bald verhallet der reigen" (Mendelssohn)

"Oh, why will you try to make me sing now." See "Hvarför skall man tvinga mig att sjunga" (Lindblad)

"O wie lieblich ist's im kreis." F. A. Hoffmeister. Words by D. Jäger. g. ED 2

"O, wie schön ist deine welt, Vater." See Im abendroth (Schubert)

O wie wohl ist mir am abend. See Lovely evening

"O wild is thy joy, my affectionate boy." Children's song. FSS 6

"O will you accept of the muselin so blue." See Blue muslin

"O! Willie brew'd a peck o' maut." A. Masterton. Words by R. Burns. BSB—BSR—MMS—PS 1

"O! Willie brew'd a peck o' maut." Shore. Words by R. Burns. BSB

"Oh! Willie, is it you, dear." See Willie, we have missed you (Foster)

"O, Willie was a wanton wag." Scottish song. MMS

Oh! Willie, we have miss'd you. See Willie, we have missed you (Foster)

"O, Willie's fair, and Willie's rare." Scottish song. MMS

O willo, willo, willo. See The willow song (16th century air)

O willo, willo, willo: parody. See The willow song: parody

O willow, willow. See The willow song (16th century air)

"O Willy was so blithe a lad." See Willy was so blithe a lad

"O, wilt thou go wi' me, sweet Tibbie Dunbar." Attributed to J. McGill. Words by R. Burns. BSR

"O wilt thou share an honored name." See Couldst thou but know (Balfe)

"O wind in the tree tops, you call us away." See Vom scheib'nschiessen

"O, winde keine duft'ge blüte." See "Ah, twine no blossoms" (Glière)

"Oh! wine it glads the heart of man." See Wein, weib, gesang (Zelter)

"O winter, dreary winter." See The shepherd's winter song (Hatton)

"O! with pure devotion." N. W. Gade. e. SAS 2

O wonderful moonlight. See A barquinha

"O wonderful the tidings." E. Bunnett. Words by E. Oxenford. HC

"O wondrous beauty past compare." See "Dies bildniss ist bezaubernd schön" (Mozart)

"O wondrous mystery of love." See "Es muss ein wunderbares sein" (Liszt)

Oh, won't you come up to Columbia. College song. CU

"O world, I now must leave thee." See Hymn of the dying

"O worse than death indeed." See Angels, ever bright and fair (Händel)

"O worship the King all glorious above." See O come, let us worship (Haydn)

"Oh would but heav'n in pity grant a boon to me." See Oh, but to hear thy voice (Tchaikovsky)

"O would I were a boy again." See I would I were a boy again (Romer)

"O wouldst thou quaff the finest beer." See Margreth am thore (Jensen)

"O wrap the flag around me, boys." R. S. Taylor. WBT

"O wretched Bernardone." See "Misero Bernardone" (Cimarosa)

"O wundersames, tiefes schweigen." See Morgengebet

"Oh! yah! yah! darkies, laugh wid me." See Old Shady (Hanby)

"O Yankee Doodle came to town." See Yankee Doodle

"O ye dead." Air: Plough tune. Words by T. Moore. MI

"O ye merry chorus gay." Greek folk air. Words by R. R. Whitehead. WF

"O ye, my spirits true." See "Sorge infausta" (Händel)

"O ye tears." F. Abt. [Tr of Rinnt, ihr thränen] e. FSS 2—HSD—WBT—WBW

"O ye that love the Lord." J. Barnby. OS 2

"O ye wide rolling plains." See The slain Cossack

"Oh, ye within whose burning veins." See "Wien Neêrlandsch bloed" (Wilms)

"Oh years so many in tears so many." See The miller's tears

Oh, yes ("I'm a-tellin' yo'") Negro spiritual. DF—HR

"Oh, yes, I have seen this Kate Kearney." See Kate Kearney, Answer to

Oh, yes, I'm gwine up. See Gwine up

Oh, yes! oh, yes ("I come this night") Negro spiritual. JP

"Oh yes, yonder comes my Lord." Negro spiritual. HR

"Oh, yet we trust that somehow good." See So runs my dream

"O! you are my dear, my dear, my dear O." See Páisdín fionn

"Oh, you got Jesus, hold him fast." See Oh, wasn't that a wide river

Oh, you little darling. Old popular song. WBT

O you Santy. Capstan chantey. Air: Larry Doolan. CR

"O you talk about your Aver girls." See Haul away, Joe

"O you tree, that so lovingly I've nurtured." See Canzonetta di campagnuolo

"Oh, you wicked little imp of a girl." See The impish little girl

Oh, you'll take the high road. See Loch Lomond

"Oh, your eyes, dear." See La estrella del norte

"Oh, you're welcome home again." See The lover's ghost

O Zion, hail thy King. MCS

O Zion, O Zion, O Zion, when the bridegroom came. See The ten virgins

O Zion, that bringest good tidings. J. Stainer. DC

Oh! Zion's children coming along. See Zion's children

The **oak** and the ash. 17th century air: The quodling's delight. BOH—JO—MM—WBT

O the oak and the ash ("A north country lass") BOS—DM 1

Oh! the oak and the ash. BE 8—CS 1 —HSE 1—MSS 1—SS 1

Oake, Alfred
"Ring the bells, the Christmas bells"

Oakeley, Sir Herbert Stanley
"Alma mater"
Carmen seculare
A song of centuries. See Carmen seculare

Oakman, J.
The convivials (Remy)

"**Oats** and beans and barley grow." Singing game. FSF
Variant: "Oats, peas, beans and barley grow"

"**Oats,** peas, beans and barley grow." NMS—WSC
Variant: "Oats and beans and barley grow"

"**Ob** heller tag." See "Whether day dawns" (Tchaikovsky)

Obedience 'tis, the Lord of hosts demandeth. F. Hiller. e. SAS 4

Oberek ("Podkóweczki dajcie ognia") Polish folk dance. e.p. BF 1

Oberschwäbischer ländler ("Rosestock, holderblüh'") Volkslied. g. ED 1

The **obliging** moon. Ruthenian folk air. Words by M. H. B. Mussey. WF

O'Brien, Basil
Sweet Kitty Magee (Irish air)

Obstination (Steadfast love) H. de Fontenailles. Words by F. Coppée, e.f. ES. e. only WL
Obstination (A resolve) e.f. MSF 1 —SM
Steadfast love. e. WBT

Ocampo, Armand
Chant hindou (Bemberg)

O'Carolan, Turlogh

Composer

The Arethusa (attributed; attributed also to W. Shield)
Brideen ban mo store (attributed)
Bumpers, Squire Jones
"I am a wand'ring minstrel man." See Brideen ban mo store (attributed)
"True love can ne'er forget"
"Ye good fellows all. " See Bumpers, Squire Jones

Author

Shane Glas (Irish air)

L'occasion manquée (The lost chance.—Ah! qui me passera le bois.—Ah, who will lead me thro' the wood) Folk song: Norman version. e.f. TF

L'occasion manquée (The lost chance. —"C'etait un chasseron, un chasseur de gibier."—"He was a jolly hunter and a sportsman gay") Canadian version. e.f. TF

L'occasion manquée ("Dimanche à l'aube") See La fille et le chasseur

L'occasion manquée ("Nous étions trois filles") See Les trois filles

"**Occhietti** amati" ("Dear eyes, love-lighted") A. Falconieri. e.i. FEI 1

The **ocean** ("The ocean has its silent caves") E. L. White. FSS 3

"**Ocean** and sky, radiant in splendor." See "Cielo e mar" (Ponchielli)

"**Ocean!** thou mighty monster." C. M. Weber. Words by Planché. OPS 1—SS 2
"Ozean! du ungeheuer." e.g. SOA 1

"The **ocean** winds are blowing." See A sailing song

"**Och** flickan hon går i dansen." See Rödan guldband

"**Och,** girls dear, did you ever hear." See Katey's letter (Sainton-Dolby)

"**Och** hey! Johnnie lad." Scottish air: The lasses of the ferry. Words by R. Tannahill. MMS—PS 2

"**Och** hone! oh, what will I do." See Molly Carew

"**Och** hör du unga Dora" ("Now listen, little Dora") Swedish folk song. e.sw. HSOS

"**Och** inte vill jag sörja" ("Indeed, I would not sorrow") Swedish folk song. e.sw. HSOS

"**Och** jungfrun gick åt killan" ("The maiden hied her to the well") Swedish folk song. e.sw. HSOS

"**Och** jungfrun gick sig åt ängen." See Blomman bland blommorna

"**Och** jungfrun hon skulle sig till ottesången gå." See Den bergtagna

"**Och** liten Karin tjänte på unga kungens gård." See Liten Karin

"**Och,** love is the soul of a neat Irishman." See Sprig of shillelah

"**Och** många tusen kronor" ("And many thousand ducats") A. Hallén. e.sw. WM 1

"**Och** mins du hvad du lofvade" ("Remember what you promised me") Swedish folk song. e.sw. HSOS

"**Och** nan och, mo leir chradh" ("Oh, my painful sorrow) Gaelic song. e.ga. SMW

"**Och** nan och, my painful sorrow." See "Och nan och, mo leir chradh"

"**Och,** never give your whole heart up." See The blatherskite

"**Och,** och, mar tha mi." See A' churinneag Ileach

"**Och,** when we lived in ould Glenann." See A song of Glenann

"**Och,** where am I from." See A broken song

O'Connor, John
"All the skies to-night sing o'er us" (German air)

O'Conor, Charles Patric
"Maura dhu of Ballyshannon" (Irish air)

The **octave.** N. Rimsky-Korsakoff. Words from the Russian of Maikoff. e. NM 2

October ("Birches now") A. F. M. Custance. NMS

October ("The months are met") Harrow school song. LA

"October gave a party." See October's party (Lee)

October song ("In the sad month of October") A. S. Gatty. WSC

October's party. G. A. Lee. FSS 5— JSE

"Od Krakowa czarny las." See Near Krakow

An odd old man. A. S. Sullivan. Words by J. Drake. MCS

"Odds bobs! what a time for a seaman to skulk." See The old commodore (Reeve)

Ode for Decoration day. FSS 8—WBT

Ode for Washington's birthday. L. van Beethoven. O. W. Holmes. LBR

Ode to Denison. Air: God save the king. Words by H. C. Cooper. CHS

Ode to spring ("Decrepit winter limps away") T. A. Arne. MM

Ode to the mountain Fujiyama. See Fuji (Ross)

Odi tu (The sailor's prayer) T. Mattei. e.i. CB

"Odna gora vesokaya." See "O'er the distant lonely mountains"

"Od's blood! what a time for a seaman to skulk." See The old commodore (Reeve)

"Od's, neighbour, ne'er blush for a trifle like this." See We all love a pretty girl under the rose (Arne)

Oehlenschläger, Adam Gottlob
Danish patriotic song of 1820 (Kroyer)
Fyllas sang (Rung)

Oehmler, Leo
"Hurrah! the snow again is here"
Independence day
New Year song

"O'er a thousand ancient trails." See Indian trail song (Loomis)

"O'er all our way." See Les rameaux (Faure)

"O'er all the way." See Les rameaux (Faure)

"O'er barren hills and flow'ry dales." See Sweet lilies of the valley (Hook)

"O'er Bethlehem's hill, in time of old." L. Carrott. Words by M. G. Pearse. HC

"O'er Bethlehem's hill in time of old." A. E. Floyd. Words by M. G. Pearse. HC

"O'er Collin's face the night is creeping." See MacCrimmon's lament

"O'er Ganges now launches." See "Già il sole dal Gange" (Scarlatti)

"O'er hill and dell the Christmas bell." H. Knight. HC

"O'er Kamenz the storm still hovers." Old Serbian song. e. KSE

"O'er me steal, I know not how." See Tischlied (Eberwein)

"O'er mountain, through woodland gay I wander." See Werbung

"O'er my distant home red lightnings glare." See In der fremde (Schumann)

"O'er my head." Flotow. [Tr of Ja, seit früher kindheit tagen] e. WBT

O'er my senses softly stealing. See Wreath of carnations (Hopkins)

"O'er Nelson's tomb, with silent grief opprest." See The death of Nelson (Braham)

"O'er old Judea's hills." T. Crampton. HC

"O'er peaks of the Sierra Nevada." See Romance (Ippolitov-Ivanov)

"O'er the blue wavelets dancing." See Ti rapirei (Tosti)

"O'er the branches all is at peace." See Wanderers nachtlied (Liszt)

O'er the crossing. Negro folk song from Virginia. KA

"O'er the distant lonely mountains" (Dalekaya i blezkaya) Russian folk song. Words by A. Kocipinski. e.r. BO—SMF

"O'er the eastern hills the morning." See Hela'r 'sgyvarnog

"O'er the garden thro' the ether." See Frühlingsnacht (Jensen)

"O'er the garden through blue ether." See Frühlingsnacht (Schumann)

"O'er the garden's scented bowers." See Frühlingsnacht (Schumann)

O'er the grave victorious. C. Goudimel. Words by E. E. Higbee. FSS 7

"O'er the hill and o'er the vale." Air: In vernali tempore. Words by J. M. Neale. HC

"O'er the hill and o'er the vale." F. J. Dugard. Words by J. M. Neale. HC

"O'er the lake." T. G. Shepard. Words by W. L. Kitchel. CHS

O'er the moor amang the heather. Air: O'er the moor amang the heather. Words by J. Glover. BSR
O'er the muir amang the heather. PS 1

O'er the mountains. M. M. Simpson. HC

"O'er the plain the soft cloud shadows." See For the czar is making war

"O'er the plains the darkness deepens." F. R. Havergal. Words by W. J. Vernon. HC

"O'er the ridge the sun now glides." See Aagots fjeldsang

"O'er the sea a gallant ship." See Le beau vaisseau

O'er the sea in my fairy boat. A. Lee. FSS 8

"O'er the sea in some far country." See The maid and the sun (Rimskiï-Korsakov)

"O'er the sea in Thule of old." See Le roi de Thulé (Gounod)

"O'er the tree-tops all is at rest." See Wanderers nachtlied (Liszt)

"O'er the white foam of the wild singing sea." See Dolphin lullaby (Gilchrist)

"O'er the woodlands, o'er the meadow." See May dew (Bennett)

"O'er waters blue, in canoe, with you." See Canoe song (Lieurance)

"O'er yon mountainous height." See A southern night (Rimskiǐ-Korsakov)

"Of a rose a boy caught sight." See Heidenröslein (Werner)

"Of a' the airts the wind can blaw." W. Marshall. Words by R. Burns. BSR—MMS
"O' a' the airts the wind can blaw." BSB—PS 1

"Of all flowers in Scotland." See The blue-bell of Scotland (Jordan)

"Of all heav'n gave to comfort man." See The flowing bowl (Dibdin)

"Of all the birds on bush or tree." See Goldthred's song (Barratt)

"Of all the birds that ever I see." See The owl

"Of all the busy people round." See Mistress Santa Claus (Lee)

"Of all the fair months, that round the sun." See Song of O'Donahue's mistress

"Of all the fish that roam the sea." See Herring the king

"Of all the girls I ever saw." See Nancy Gay

"Of all the girls in our town." See Nancy Dawson

"Of all the girls that are so smart." See Sally in our alley (Traditional air); Sally in our alley (Carey)

"Of all the lands in the east or west." See "Blandt alle lande" (Hansen)

"Of all the mem'ries of the past." See The good-bye at the door (Glover)

"Of all the myriad moods of mind." See Longing (Cole)

"Of all the religions I profess." See No hidin' place

"Of all the simple things we do." See The mouse trap

"Of all the trees in forest vast." See Holly green with berries red

"Of all the wives as e'er you know." See Nancy Lee (Maybrick)

"Of all things on earth." See The pipe

"Of all trades a-going." See An cailín deas ruadh

Of fair Navarre the princess royal. See C'est la princesse de Navarre (Boieldieu)

"Of her, my maiden, flow'r slumber-laden." See Sérénade (Bizet)

Of isles the fairest. See "Wrapt in verdure" (Hopkins)

"Of late so brightly glowing." See Lovely rose

"Of life's bright hopes how sternly fate disposes." See Es hat nicht sollen sein (Nessler)

"Of my beloved, flower that dreams." See "De mon amie, fleur endormie" (Bizet)

"Of my Soleïma came the shadow softly at midnight." See Soleïma

"Of Nassau, and Orania." See "Wilhelmus van Nassouwe" (Marnix)

"Of Nelson and the north." See Battle of the Baltic (Purday)

"Of our God ye are the champions." See Ancient chant of the Taborites

"Of passion unrequited I endure all the tortures." See Pena tiranna (Händel)

"Of priests we can offer a charmin' variety." See Father O'Flynn

"Of that dark scaffold." G. Verdi. [Tr of Di quella pira] e. WBT

"Of the father's love begotten." Flemish Noël. Words from Prudentius. Tr of Corde natus ex parentis. e. HC

"Of thy tongue to be the master." Round. FSS 7

"Of what are you thinking, my pretty maid." See The fortune in the daisy (Becker)

"Of what is the old man thinking." J. P. Knight. Words by T. H. Bayly. BE 5

Off to Philadelphia. Adapted from an old Irish air. PI

"Off to the dance goes the priest so blithe." See 'T patergje

Off to the war. See A la guerra

"Off to the war, to the war I did go." See The lover's lament (Hot Springs, N.C. version)

Offenbach, Jacques
Barcarolle ("Belle nuit") See "Belle nuit"
Barcarolle ("Silent now") See "Silent now the drowsy bird"
"Behold the sabre." See The sabre song
"Belle nuit" (from Les contes d'Hoffmann)
"Goddesses three"
Good night
In merry chorus
Letters from lovers (from La grande duchesse)
"Lovely night." See "Belle nuit"
Morning serenade (from Giroflè-Giroflà)
O lovely night. See "Belle nuit"
"Our home is on the sea"
The sabre song (from La grande duchesse. Tr of Le sabre de mon père)
"Silent now the drowsy bird" (same air as "Belle nuit")
Song of the sabre. See The sabre song
Waltz song (from Les contes d'Hoffmann. Tr of Elle danse! en cadence)
Welcome to morning

The officer's funeral. Words by C. Norton. FSS 6

"Offspring thou of heav'nly bliss." See Peace (Liszt)

"Oft hard is life for the fisherman." See Den norske fisker

"**Oft** in danger, oft in woe." Words by H. K. White. FSS 3—WBT

"**Oft** in the classic page I've read." See The college gown

"**Oft** in the stilly night." Attributed to J. Stevenson. Words by T. Moore. BSE—FSS 1—HSD—JO— MI— PI— MMI—TS—WBT

"**Oft** I've bent beneath the burden." See The lament

"**Oft** the blindfold boy." See "Spesso vibra per suo gioco" (Scarlatti)

"**Oft** when the hours were lonely." See Elsa's traum (Wagner)

"**Oft** within our little cottage." See Our mother's way (Lee)

"**Öfver** skogen, öfver sjön." See En sommarafton (Lindblad)

Og de fore vide om verden. See Marsk Stigs døttre

"**Og** eier jeg mere blandt menneskenes børn." See Hel mig mine strenge (Halvorsen)

"**Og** keiseren sad paasit nöje stot." See Ved ankerhioning

"**Og** raeven laa under birkerod." See Jngrids vise (Kjerulf)

Ogarev,
To sleep (Tchaikovsky)

Ogiński, Michał Kłeofas
"Jeszcze Polska nie zginęła." See Polish national song (attributed)
"Poland is not lost for ever." See Polish national song (attributed)
Poland still lives. See Polish national song (attributed)
"Poland's not yet dead in slavery." See Polish national song (attributed)
Polish national song (attributed)
Teszcze Polska. See Polish national song (attributed)

"**Ogitko** nemahdahbit." See Visiting song

"**Ogni** pena più spietata" ("All of anguish most unsparing") G. B. Pergolesi. e.i. PA 1
"Ogni pena più spietata" ("Though my day be dark with sorrow") e.i. CS 2—MSS 2—SS 2

Ogni sabato avrete il lume acceso (Every Sabbath thine altar shall be lighted) Gordigiani. e.i. MSS 1

Ogwr valley ("How neat the cot, and sweet the farms") Air: Beth wneir o'r llais ei afael, or, The slack of the hold. Words from the Welsh of Ieuan Dhu. e. MMW

Oh. For entries beginning Oh see O

"**Ohamo,** ohamo za ōpga oha." See Onward! onward

Ohaoha wale kuu lei. See "How I love to gaze" (Nape)

O'Hara, Kane
"Pray, Goody" (Old English air)

Ohé! mamma. F. P. Tosti. FSS 6

"**Ohne** dich, wie lange wird mir stund' und tag." See Que le jour me dure (Rousseau)

"**Ohne** lieb und ohne wein." See Liebe und wein (Hiller)

"**Ohne** liebe lebe, wer da kann." See Die liebe (Kirnberger)

"**Ohoiyeho,** hoyeho, who's for the ferry." See Twickenham ferry (Marzials)

Oi, alas, a robber (Oi gvalt, a ganef) Jewish folk song. e.y. GF 2

"**Oi** bruder, zog." See Sabbath song

"**Oi** dem tishtach fun dem tish." See Oi, alas, a robber

Oi, gvalt, a ganef. See Oi, alas, a robber

Oi hoi ha. See "Upon the crest of Wailana" (Nape)

"**Oï** krïache, krïache." See Cossack's lament

"**Oï** ne khody Grytsïu." See Do not go, Gregory

"**Oi** shlof main feigele." See "O little bird of mine"

"**Oi** the dish that held the fish." See Oi, alas, a robber

Oi za gaem, gaem. See Hare and hounds

"**Oiáooé!** goóa mów téoo felów." See Tongese water-song

"**Oid** mortales el grito sagrado." See Himno nacional—Argentina (López y Planes)

"**Oid** un son en alta esfera." See "Hark! the herald angels sing" (Mendelssohn)

"**Oienè,** mme daie na pena, na pena." See Mena, me' (Costa)

Oigfhear a chùil-dualaich ("Oh! laddie with the golden hair."—Laddie with the golden hair) Gaelic song. e. MMS

L'oiselet (The birdling) F. Chopin. e.f. KF 1

"**Oj** chmielu." See "Oh, hop-vine"

"**Oj** ty divčino, čarovničenkò." See Love's parting

Oje Carulì (Carulì) P. M. Costa. Words by Di Giacomo. e.i. MN
Caruli. e. WL

Los ojos mexicanos. Mexican folk song. e.s. HS

O'Kane, E. T.
Song of the "O. W. U."

O'Kane, Tullius Clinton
Over there (Huntington)

O'Keeffe, John
"Amo, amas, I love a lass" (Traditional air)
Ballinamona oro (Irish air)
"The billet-doux" (Shield)
"Flow, thou regal purple stream" (Arnold)
The friar of orders gray (Reeve)
Galloping dreary dun (Arnold)
The invincible Armado (Arnold)
"Old England's a lion" (Shield)
Old Towler (Shield)
The ploughboy (Shield)
The Spanish Armada (Arnold)
"Sweet Poll of Plymouth" (Arne)
The thorn (Shield)
The wolf (Shield)

O'Kelly, Patrick
The pearl of th' Irish nation (Irish air)
Okh ne buĭnyĭ vîeter zavyval. See The Tartar host
"**Oki** no kamome ni." See Fisherman's song
Okóntchen prázdnui, schoomnui dyen. See Retrospect (Musorgskiĭ)
"**Olaf** the viking sailed away." See Olaf Trygvason (Grieg)
Olaf Trygvason (Landkjending) E. Grieg. Words by B. Björnson. e.g. MS. e. only TFC 2
Land sighting. e. BD
Olaf Trygvason. F. A. Reissiger. Words by B. Björnson. e.n. MAN
Olafsen, J.
Her hjemme (Norse air)
Old Adam the poacher. Folk air. Modern words by S. Baring-Gould. BSW
"Old Adam." BE 4
Old age. Lindblad. e. KSN
Old Allegheny. Allegheny college song. Words by C. M. Snyder. CHS
Old and young Marie. F. H. Cowen. Words by F. E. Weatherly. FSS 7
The **old** ark a-moving along. Negro spiritual. CST—JP
De ole ark a-moverin' along. HR
The **old** arm chair. H. Russell. Words by E. Cooke. FSS 3—HSC—HSD— JO—NMH—WBT—WSW
Old black Joe. S. C. Foster (music and words) BD—DSH—FMB—HSC— HSD— JS— JSE— MP— MPC— NMH—NMP—NMS—OH—TFC 1 —WA—WBT—WC—WSW
Poor old Joe. BOS—SSS
Old Butler. Butler college song. Words by J. C. Brown. CHS
The **old** cabin home. T. Paine. FMB— HSC— HSD— NMH— NMP— SSS— WA—WBT—WSW
The **old** Chisholm trail. Cowboy song. LC
The Alamo trail. BSS
Old Christmas ("Now he who knows old Christmas") Mozart. Words by M. Howitt. MCS
Old Christmas ("Once more the rapid fleeting year") F. Romer. Words by J. Bridgeman. MCS
Old Christmas cheer. Words by G. Wither. MCS
Old college chum. Words by L. Adams. CHS—MPC—NMS
The **old** college clock in the tower. C. Arthur (music and words) CHS
Old college days. C. R. Smith. Words by E. M. Spencer. CHS—NMS
The **old** commodore. W. Reeve. Words by M. Lonsdale. HSE 2—ME
The **old** cottage clock. FSS 1
Old Dan Tucker ("I come to town de udder night") H. Russell. HSD
Ole Dan Tucker. NMP—WBT

Old Dan Tucker ("I went to town the other day") H. Russell. New words by A. Horne. BSS
"**Old** Daniel Boone, the pioneer." See Daniel Boone
Old Demos and his rifle (Ho gerō-Demōs) P. Carreris. e.gr. BF 2
Old dog Tray. S. C. Foster (music and words) BSE— BSS— JO—JSE— NMP— TFC 2— WA— WBT— WSW
My old dog Tray. HSD
Old dog Tray: Boy scout verses. S. C. Foster. Words by H. Snow. BSS
Old Dutch song ("Beside the stream") 15th century song. e. WL
Old Dutch ballad ("Beside the stream") e. KSN
Old easy-chair by the fire. J. C. Beckel. FSS 8—WBT
"**Old** Eli's sons may proudly boast." See Old college days (Smith)
"**Old** England's a lion." W. Shield. Words by J. O'Keeffe. DM 2—ME
The **old** English gentleman. See The fine old English gentleman (Purday)
An **old** English love song ("Dear, if you change") F. Allitsen. BAS 1
The **old** ewe with one horn. English folk song. DM 2
"The **old** familiar Christmas songs." See Mourner's Christmas
The **old** familiar place. C. W. Glover. Words by J. E. Carpenter. FSS 1— JSE—LA—MP—NMH—WBT
The **old** folks at home. S. C. Foster (music and words) BF 2—BMC— BO— BOS— CST— DO— DSH— EF—FMB— GO— HSC— HSD— JO—JS—JSE—MP—MPC— MS— NMH—NMP—NMS— OH— SM 2 —SSS—TFC 1—TL—WA—WBT— WC—WSC—WSW
Suwanee river. BD
Swanee river. CHS—LBR
Old friends and old times. J. R. Thomas. FSS 2
Old Gaelic lullaby. See Gaelic lullaby
An **old** garden. H. Temple. Words by H. M. Burnside. MSF 2
Old glory. G. E. Oliver. Words by W. H. Paddock. LA
Old Granite state (Mountaineer's farewell) [Judson Hutchinson;] wrongly attributed to J. C. Baker. Words by Jesse Hutchinson. FSS 3
The **old** grey mare. Folk song: Flag Pond, Tenn. version. CSE
—Rocky Fork, Tenn. version. CSE
"**Old** Grimes." Words by A. G. Greene. FSS 2
The **old** guard. P. Rodney. Words by H. Vaughan. AB 1
The **old** Guggisberg song. See Das alte Guggisberger lied
"**Old** Heidelberg, the splendid." See "Alt Heidelberg, du feine" (Jensen)

Old Highland cradle song. See "O, can ye sew cushions"

Old Hob. See The mouse-trap

Old house at home ("Oh, the old house at home") E. J. Loder. FSS 8

Old house at home ("Oh, the old house at home") I. B. Woodbury. FSS 3

"The **old** house by the lindens." See The open window (Scott-Gatty)

Old hundred ("All people that on earth do dwell") Attributed to Guillaume Franc. Words by W. Kethe. EF —NMH—NMS—WBT

The old hundredth. FMB

Old hundredth (Doxology.—"All people that on earth do dwell") BD—WA—WS—WSC—WSW

Old hundred ("Be thou, O God, exalted high") Attributed to Guillaume Franc. FSS 1

Old hundred ("From all that dwell") See "From all that dwell" (Franc)

Old hundred ("Praise God from Whom all blessings flow") Attributed to Guillaume Franc. Words by T. Ken. FSS 1—HSC—NMH—NMS—TL—WBT

Old hundred (Doxology.—"Praise God from Whom all blessings flow") JS —WA—WS—WSC—WSW

Old hundredth (Doxology.—"Praise God from Whom all blessings flow") BD

Old hundredth ("All people that on earth do dwell") See Old hundred ("All people that on earth do dwell") (Franc)

The **old** hundredth ("From all that dwell") See "From all that dwell" (Franc)

Old hundredth ("Praise God from Whom all blessings flow") See Old hundred ("Praise God from Whom all blessings flow") (Franc)

The **old** hundredth ("With one consent let all the earth") Attributed to Guillaume Franc. Words by Tate and Brady. FMB

Old Ironsides. Air: Andreas Hofer. Words by O. W. Holmes. LBR

Old Ironsides. B. O. Klein. Words by O. W. Holmes. TFC 2

Old Ironsides. W. Lardner. Words by O. W. Holmes. MP

"**Old** John Brown lies a-mouldering in the grave." See John Brown's body (Words by Brownell)

The **old** Kentucky home. See My old Kentucky home (Foster)

"**Old** King Alexander, 'way back in olden days." See Go to it (Engel)

"**Old** King Cole." Traditional song. DO —FMB—SSS
Variant: Auld King Coul

"**Old** King Cole." Traditional song. Another air. FSS 7—JO—WA—WBT—WSC—WSW

The **old** lock. M. Wellings. Words by F. E. Weatherly. FSS 7

The **old** lover and the new (Poïdu mlada po Dunaiū) Russian gooslee tune. e. SSR 3

"**Old** MacDonald had a farm." Old song. BSS

The **old** maid ("I won't marry a man that's tall") Kentucky mountain song. WT

"An **old** maid had a roguish eye." See Ramchoondra (Reeve)

The **old** maid's song ("I had a sister Sally") Kentucky mountain song. WLT

The **old** man ("Willy, Willy, Will") Old English song. DO

"The **old** man can't keep his wife at home." English folk song. BSW

"An **old** man he courted me." Irish folk song. JOI

Old man Moses. D. Hume (music and words) WC

The **old** man's love song. Omaha Indian song. in. FIS

"**Old** Missouri, fair Missouri, dear old 'varsity." See Missouri

Old Morgan and his wife ("Now, woman, as thy wagging tongue") Welsh song. e. MMW

"**Old** Moses kept a flower stand." See Old man Moses (Hume)·

The **old** mother. See Gamle mor (Grieg)

Old mother toad. Children's song. WSC

Old Nassau. Princeton song. C. Langlotz. Words by H. P. Peck. CHS—LA—MPC—NMS

"**Old** Noah he built himself an ark." See Noah's ark

The **old** oaken bucket. G. Kiallmark. Words by S. Woodworth. FSS 1—HSC— HSD— JO— JS— JSE— LBR — MP— NMH— NMS— OH— WA— WBT— WSC— WSW

The **old** oaken bucket. Air: Jessie, the flower of Dumblane. Words by S. Woodworth. FSS 4

The **old**, old questions (Di alte kashyeh) Jewish folk song. e.y. BF 2

The **old**, old song. G. Lefort. Words by H. B. Farnie. FSS 5

"**Old** rags, bottles, rags." Negro folk song. BN 4

Old Ringwood. W. Hawes. Words by R. Bloomfield. BE 6

Old Rosin the bow. Old English song. FSS 2—JSE—LA
Old Rosin, the beau. HSD—WBT

Old Samurai prayer. G. Ross. Words by Komachi. e. RAS

"**Old** Santa Claus in Christmas dress." See Dear Santa Claus

"**Old** Santa Claus sat all alone." See Santa Claus (Read)

"**Old** Satan am a mighty fool." See You must shun old Satan

"**Old** Satan's mighty busy." See Lord, until I reach my home

"Old Scotia, wake thy mountain strain."
See The Highland watch
The old Scottish cavalier. Old air.
Words by W. E. Aytoun. SSS
The old sexton. H. Russell. Words by
P. Benjamin. FSS 4—HSD—JO—
WA—WBT
Old Shady. B. R. Hanby. HSD
Ole Shady. NMP—WBT
Old ship of Zion. Negro spiritual. JP
Ole ship of Zion. HR
Old shoes. Ojibway Indian song. e.in.
BA
"Old Simon the cellarer." See Simon the
cellarer (Hatton)
Old Stormey. Pulling chantey. SE
Variants: Stormalong; Stormalong
John; Stormy
"Old Stormy he is dead and gone." See
Stormy
"Old Stormy was a fine old man." See
Stormalong
"Old Svyatosláv lived for ninety years."
See The legend of Volgá
The old time. J. R. Thomas. WBT
Old Towler. W. Shield. Words by J.
O'Keeffe. BOS—DM 1—HSE 2—ME
"Old Tubal Cain was a man of might."
See Tubal Cain (Russell)
"Old Uncle Pengerric a captain was." See
The keenly lode
"Old vineyard mine—go to." See The
vineyard and its master
"Old Washington and Jefferson forever."
See The red and the black
The old weaver ("Within a dark and low-
roofed room") Air: Y qwydd, or,
The weaver's song. Words by K. R.
Moffat. MMW
Old Wichet. English folk song. BSW
"Old Winter." W. H. Jones. Words by
J. G. Whittier. NMS
The old woman and the peddler. English
folk song. DO
The old year and the new. S. M. Sayles.
Words by J. G. Saxe. LBR
"The old year is dying." Welsh carol.
Words by W. Maynard. MS
"The old year now away is fled." See
Carol for New Year's day (Brown)
Old Zip Coon. Old American air. New
words by D. Stevens. BSS—TFC 1
Olds, W. B.
August
Come ye back to old Grinnell
December
February
Hail, Beloit
Harvest home song
January
July
June
Memorial day song
"The night has a thousand eyes"
November
September
Thanksgiving hymn
"Two little flies"
A western college boating song

Oldys, William
"Busy, curious, thirsty fly" (Greene)
Ole and Christine. See Møen paa baalet
The ole sheep done know the road. Negro
spiritual. JP
De ole sheep done know de road. HR
Oliphant, Carolina. See Nairne, Carolina
(Oliphant) Nairne, baroness
Oliver, Charles Mackay
The blackbird (Welsh air)
"High on the crest" (Welsh air)
Oliver, George Edgar
Arbor day song. See "Joy for the
sturdy trees"
"The bells are ringing joyfully"
"By the thorny way of sorrow"
"Chime, chime, merrily chime"
"Chime out, ye bells of beauty"
"Christ was born on Christmas day;
wreathe the holly, twine the bay;
Christus natus hodie"
"Christian children, wake and listen"
Christmas morning. See "In the early
morning early"
"Christmas time has come again, time
to us so dear"
"The day of resurrection" (Tr of
Anastaseōs hemera)
"Day of wonder, day of gladness"
"The Easter sunshine breaks again"
"Every flower that blossoms"
Flower song. See "Pansies, lilies,
roses"
"For thee, O dear, dear country" (Tr
of O bona patria, lumina sobria te
speculantur)
"From forest wide and free"
"Good tidings, good tidings"
"Hail, sweet Babe, so pure and holy"
Happy bells are ringing
"In meadow and in garden"
"In the early morning early"
"In the secret of His presence I am
kept from strife of tongues"
"Joy for the sturdy trees"
"The joyful morn is breaking"
"Lift up thy voice with singing"
"List, I hear the angels singing"
"Merry, merry Christmas bells"
"Morning is breaking"
"O earth, on Easter morning"
"O joyous Easter morning"
Old glory
"Once again the olden story"
"Once again with joyful voices"
"Pansies, lilies, roses"
Planting the tree. See "From forest
wide and free"
"Rejoice! the Christ is risen"
"Ring out, ye joyous Easter bells"
"Rise, crowned with light"
"Round the Lord in glory seated"
"The shepherds on fair Bethlehem's
plain"
"Snowdrops, lift your timid heads"
"Softly through the mellow starlight"
"'Twas on this Easter morning"
"We are little children"
"We march, we march to victory"
"Wise men from Egypt's ancient land"

Oliver, Henry Kemble
Army hymn
Hymn for airmen (same air as Army hymn)

Olivers, Thomas
"The God of Abrah'm praise" (Jewish air)

Olivet. See "My faith looks up to Thee" (Mason)

Olivieri, Alessio
The Garibaldi hymn. See Inno di guerra dei cacciatori delle Alpi
Inno di guerra dei cacciatori delle Alpi
Italian national hymn. See Inno di guerra dei cacciatori delle Alpi
War hymn of Garibaldi. See Inno di guerra dei cacciatori delle Alpi

Oll Istria (Beautiful Istria) Istrian national air. G. Georgieri. e.i. SN

Olsen, Ole
Solefaldssang
Sunset. See Solefaldssang

Olufs ballade (Oluf's ballad) N. W. Gade. da.e. SSN

Die **'ölzerne** bein ("Ich bin ein Franzose") Volkslied. g. ED 2

"**Om** dagen vid mitt arbete" ("By day, when I am working") Swedish folk song. e.sw. HSOS
"Om dagen vid mitt arbete" ("By day-time at my work") e.sw. BF 2

"**Om** sommaren sköna" ("In beautiful summer") Swedish folk song. Words by A. Wallenius. e.sw. HSOS

Omaha Indian "Wa-wan" ceremony (Song of approach) in. DCS

The **Omaha** tribal prayer. e.in. FIS

Omar Khayyām
"Yet ah, that spring should vanish" (Whiting)

"**Ombra** cara, amorosa" ("Gentle shade, well beloved") T. Traetta. e.i. PA 1
"Ombra cara, amorosa" ("Gentle spirit, well beloved") e.i. FEI 2

L'**ombra** della croce. See The shadow of the cross (Barry)

"**Ombra** leggiera." See "Ombre légère" (Meyerbeer)

Ombra mai fu. G. F. Händel. e.i. SOA 1
Ombra mai fu (Slumber, dear maid.—Händel's Largo) e.i. CS 1

"L'**ombre** des arbres" (The shadow of trees) A. C. Debussy. Words by P. Verlaine. e.f. HM 1

Ombre di mia prosapia. A. Ponchielli. e.i. SOA 5

"**Ombre** légère" ("Light-flitting shadow."—Shadow song) G. Meyerbeer. e.f. KS 1—MC
"Ombra leggiera." e.i. PP
"Ombra leggiera" (Shadow dance) e.i. OPS 1

The **omen.** Ojibway Indian song. in. BA

"**On** a bank of flowers in a summer day." J. Galliard. Words by R. Burns. BSR

"**On** a bank two roses fair." See Heiden-röslein (Werner)

"**On** a crystal throne." See Neckens polska

"**On** a day—alack the day." T. Chilcot. Words by Shakespeare. MM

"**On** a fair summer's morning of soft recreation." See The blackbird

"**On** a Friday morn, as we sent sail." See The mermaid

On a frosty morning. French folk air. Words by J. Irwin. DO

"**On** a holiday it is up, away." See The Boy scouts (Suppé)

"**On** a lake deliciously sparkling." See Un lago delicioso

"**On** a lone barren isle." See The grave of Bonaparte

"**On** a lovely bed of roses." See Blanche comme la neige

On a May morning so early. English folk song. Modern words by H. F. Sheppard. BSW

"**On** a Monday morning early." See The boys of Mullaghbawn

"**On** a pale lily is my rest." See Extase (Duparc)

On a summer day. French folk air: En passant par la Lorraine. Words by H. H. Harbour. DO

"**On** a sunny day in June." See The winds and the shadows

On a tomb. See Sur une tombe (Lekeu)

"**On** a tree by a river a little tomtit." See Tit willow (Sullivan)

"**On** Bethlehem's silent plain." M. Hornabrook. HC

"**On** billow rocking." R. Planquette. e. WBT

On board a ninety-eight. Folk song from Norfolk. SF 2

"**On,** by the spur of valour goaded." Shield. HSE 2

On Canaan shore. Negro spiritual. DF

"**On** Cessnock banks." Air: The butcher boy. Words by R. Burns. BSR

"**On** Cessnock banks." Air: The cardin' o't, or, Salt fish and dumplings. Words by R. Burns. BSB—PS 2

On Christmas morn ("Good news on Christmas morn") H. Philips. MCS

On Christmas morning ("Ding dong, ding dong") Poniatowski. MCS

"**On** Christmas night true Christians sing." See Christmas night (Brown)

"**On** December twenty-fifth, sing, fum, fum, fum." See Fum, fum, fum

"**On** dewy plain where shepherds were abiding." Glad angel voices (Rickman)

"**On** distant, foreign meadow." See Der todte soldat (Esser)

"**On** Dovre fjeld in Norway." See "Paa Dovrefjeld i Norge"

On Dovre mountain. See "Paa Dovrefjeld i Norge"

"**On** Easter day." Old air. Words by J. Erwin. DO

"**On** Easter morn Christ rose again." Flemish air. HC

"On Entick's green meadows." See The captain with the smart cockade (Hook)

"On Ettrick banks." Scottish song. MMS

"On every tree, in every plain." T. Linley. ME

"On foot I gaily take my way." See The foot-traveler

"On Friday morn, when we set sail." See The mermaid

"On frost-cold Norway's moorlands." See "Pä Norges kolde vidder" (Holter)

"On her finger Petko put a ring, dear." See Rada and Petko

"On his way a boy espied." See Heidenröslein (Schubert)

"On Hounslow heath as I rode o'er." See O rare Turpin

"On lonely Tauris' shore." See The Nereid (Glazunov)

"On me turn thy sparkling lustre." See Bitte (Franz)

"On mighty pens uplifted soars." J. Haydn. e. OS 1—SAS 1

"On Monday morn I married a wife." See A week's work well done

On music ("When thro' life unblest we rove") Irish air: The banks of Banna. Words by T. Moore. MMI
"When thro' life unblest we rove." MI

"On my ear softly falls his sweet voice beseeching." See "Il dolce suono" (Donizetti)

On, O thou soul. Serbian folk air. Words by F. Manley. e. TFC 1

"On ocean's breast many a pearl doth rest." See Auf dem meere (Franz)

"On old Long Island's sea-girt shore." See Rockaway (Russell)

"On, on! my boat, the winds awake." See Frische brise (Stange)

"On, on, O thou soul." See On, O thou soul

On, on, on the boys came marching. G. F. Root. WBT

"On one Friday mornin'." See My good Lord have been here

"On Richmond hill there lives a lass." See The lass of Richmond hill (Hook)

"On rising in the morning." See "Moch's mi g eirdle sa Mhaduinn"

On St John's eve. See Zur Johannisnacht (Grieg)

"On Saturday night you're as willing as I am." See Connolly's ale

"On Serpina think with pleasure." See "A Serpina penserete" (Pergolesi)

"On song's bright pinions." See "Auf flügeln des gesanges" (Mendelssohn)

"On steep Mount Carmel's height we stand." See The crusaders (Pinsuti)

"On that lone bank where Lubin died." See Fair Rosalie (Dibdin)

"On the alma." See Auf der alm (Poissl)

"On the Alpine radiant summits." See The Alpine rose

"On the banks of Allen water." See The banks of Allen water

On the banks of the old Raritan. Rutgers college song. Words by H. N. Fuller. CHS

"On the battle front we stand." See Tramp, tramp, tramp (Root)

"On the birthday of the Lord." J. B. Dykes. Tr of In natali Domini. e. BSC—HC

"On the breeze of ev'ning stealing." See Beautiful bells (Lyte)

"On the breeze, when the spring perfumes the leas." See Veilchen (Cornelius)

"On the bridge at Avignon." See "Sur le pont d'Avignon" (Canadian version)

"On the bridge of Avignon." See "Sur le pont d'Avignon" (French version)

"On the brow of a hill." See The lass of the hill (Howard)

"On the brow of Richmond hill." H. Purcell. MM

On the chapel steps. G. C. Gow. Words by J. N. Eno, A. Thomas, and C. G. Dickson. CHS—CU—MPS—NMS

On the cold ground. See "My lodging is on the cold ground" (17th century air); "My lodging it is on the cold ground" (Locke)

On the deep ("When ships afar are steering") Air: Mentra Gwen. MMW

"On the eve before the Sabbath." A. H. Brown. Words by S. C. Clarke. HC

"On the first bright Christmas day." C. J. Ridsdale. HC

"On the first day of May." See John Macananty's courtship

"On the floating scow of old Virginny." See Carry me back to old Virginny (Christy)

"On the fount of life eternal." German choral. Words by Damiani. [Tr of Ad perennis vitae fontem] e. FSS 3

"On the fourteenth of February." See The bold Princess Royal

"On the gay red sarafan, dear mother, work no more." See The scarlet sarafan (Varlamov)

On the Georgian hills (Sur les collines de Géorgie) N. Rimsky-Korsakow. Words by A. S. Pushkin. e.f. SC

"On the grass of the cliff." See The garden of sleep (Lara)

"On the grassy meadow, where the violet's seen." See The little lamb

"On the green hills of Ulster." See Rory O'More

"On the ground the snowflakes glisten." See Christmas eve

"On the hill I am standing." See The love signal

"On the hill stands a tower." See "Auf'm berg steht a schloss"

"On the hillside, with the birdies." See Schweizerlied

On the journey home. See Auf der reise zur heimath (Grieg)

On the mountain ("Here upon the mountain") Lindblad. e. KSN

On the mountain ("Hu hei! kor er det vel") See Paa fjellet (Kjerulf)

"On the mountain height." College song. Words adapted by S. Rowe. BSS

"On the mountain, steep and hoary." See Der schweizerbue

"On the mountain the wind blows wild." See "Auf dem berge da weht der wind"

"On the mountains, when our toil is done." J. Benedict. Words by C. Norton. FSS 5

"On the peaks the fir-trees weaving." See Halka (Moniusko)

On the river Dnyéper (Na Dnyepryé) M. P. Moussorgsky. Words by T. G. Shevtchenko. e. SMR 1

"On the road to Lim'rick." See An Gadaighe Grána

On the road to Mandalay. Barrack-room ballad. H. Trevannion. Words by R. Kipling. MP

"On the rocks by Aberdeen." A. Scott-Gatty. WBT

On the sea gray mists are spread. Russian folk air. Words by R. R. Whitehead. WF

"On the sea the sun is lying." See Dein gedenk' ich, Margareta (Meyer-Helmund)

On the seas and far away. See "How can my poor heart be glad"

"On the sea's rugged shore." See Thurmwächters lied (Weidt)

On the steppe. See Over the steppe (Grechaninov)

"On the sturdy wooden bridge." See The village Don Juan

"On the sward in the forest." See Waldeslied (Kreutzer)

"On the turret sits the page." See Genrebillede (Backer-Lunde)

"On the twelfth day of Christmas." See The twelve days of Christmas

"On the twenty-fourth of August last." See The little Dunee

"On the village green at sunset." See Yesterday evening

"On the wall, gems of ancient fabrics." See Brises d'autrefois (Hüe)

On the way home. See Auf der reise zur heimath (Grieg)

"On the way stands a tree" ("Af'n veg") Yiddish folk song. e.y. GF 2

"On thee each living soul awaits." F. J. Haydn. e. BD

"On this glorious Easter morning." Traditional air. HC

"On through the night's fearful darkness I roam." See Odi tu (Mattei)

"On to the field." V. Bellini. FSS 8—LA

"On Tom-big-bee river so bright I was born." See Tom-big-bee river

"On top of Old Smokey." See The wagoner's lad (Alleghany, N.C. version)

"On trembling limbs the peasant stands." See Hunger song (Cui)

On Venice waters ("Over the foam we glide") WBT

On Venice waters ("'Tis night on Venice waters.")—Gondolier waltz) O. Roeder. Words by H. Vaughan. WBW

"On walking out one summer's morning." See John Riley

"On we are floating in sunshine and shadow." See The boat song (Weber)

"On we rush to meet the foe." See For liberty (Berlioz)

"On wings of living light." French church air. Words by W. W. How. HC

"On wings of music." See "Auf flügeln des gesanges" (Mendelssohn)

"On wings of song." See "Auf flügeln des gesanges" (Mendelssohn)

"On winter nights when stormy winds." See In the firelight

"On yesternight I saw a sight, a star as bright as day; and all along, I heard a song." See The Virgin and Child (Steggall)

"On yesternight I saw a sight, a star as bright as day, and heard among the heav'ns a song." T. T. Noble. Words by C. W. Stubbs. HC

"On yonder fleeting river there turns a busy wheel." See "In einem kühlen grunde" (Volksweise); "In einem kühlen grunde" (Glück)

"On yonder hill there stands a creature." See O no, John

"On yonder rock reclining." D. F. Auber. [Tr of Voyez sur cette roche] e. FSS 6—WBT

Once ("Once, dear love") A. Hervey. Words by Mrs H. Webster. MSF 1—WBW

"Once a boy a rose espied." See Heidenröslein (Schubert)

"Once a boy a rosebud saw." See Heidenröslein (Schubert)

"Once a boy a wild rose found." See Heidenröslein (Schubert)

"Once a boy a wild rose spied." See Heidenröslein (Schubert)

"Once a Canadian lad." See "Un Canadien errant"

"Once a little titmouse lived far beyond the sea." See The wooing of the titmouse

Once again ("I linger round the very spot") A. S. Sullivan. Words by L. H. Lewin. FSS 5—HSE 3—TS—WBW

"Once again I saw the river." See Dreaming (Wellings)

"Once again, O blessed time." J. B. Dykes. Words by W. Bright. HC
Christmas song. BSC

"Once again, O blessed time." A. Sullivan. Words by W. Bright. FSS 2—MCS

"Once again the flowers we gather." See Flowers for the brave (Chapman)

"Once again the olden story" (Joyful is the morn) E. Bunnett. Words by E. Oxenford. HC

"Once again the olden story." G. E. Oliver. Words by E. Oxenford. HC

"Once again with joyful voices." G. E. Oliver. HC

"Once at the Green Wreath tavern." See Brüderschaft

"Once came an angel." See Daar kommt een engel

"Once, dear love, we went a-maying." See Once (Hervey)

"Once found I thee." See Silvio to Laura (Lindblad)

"Once from the depths of Sweden's heart." See "Ur svenska hjertans" (Lindblad)

"Once I caught a fair dove." See A fair dove

"Once I courted a charming beauty bright." See Charming beauty bright

"Once I courted a fair beauty bright." See The lover's lament (Virginia version)

"Once I had an old grey mare." See The old grey mare (Rocky Fork, Tenn. version)

"Once I loved a maiden fair." 17th century English song. BE 5—BOH—CO 1—MM—PR 1

"Once I saw a sweet brier-rose." See Heidenröslein (Werner)

"Once I was a brisk young bachelor." See The brisk young bachelor

"Once I was a shepherd boy." See The shepherd boy

"Once I was courting a lovely Irish boy." See My lovely Irish boy

"Once I was invited to a nobleman's wedding." See The nobleman's wedding

"Once in a blithe greenwood." See Hope, the hermit

"Once, in a sleep that thy beauty did fashion." See Après un rêve (Fauré)

"Once in Bethlehem of Judah." F. J. Dugard. Words by C. F. Alexander. HC

"Once in Bethlehem of Judah." C. E. Kettle. Words by C. F. Alexander. HC

"Once in Bethlehem of Judah." J. H. Maunder. Words by C. F. Alexander. HC

"Once in Bethlehem of Judah." C. V. Stanford. Words by C. F. Alexander. HC

"Once in royal David's city." H. J. Gauntlett. Words by C. F. Alexander. DC —HC—MCS

"Once, in the days of golden weather." See Golden days (Sullivan)

"Once in the dear dead days beyond recall." See Love's old sweet song (Molloy)

"Once in the ev'ning twilight." See A dream of paradise (Gray)

"Once, long ago." Old Bohemian Christmas carol. Words by R. Compton. DO

Once more across the land. Words by C. Scott. MCS

"Once more across the leafless land." See Once more across the land

"Once more alone, once more the land." See By a new-made grave (Rachmaninov)

"Once more, dear home." See Pilgrims' chorus (Wagner)

"Once more fill the cup." See Wanderlied (Schumann)

"Once more has heaven." See Song of an angel (Rubinstein)

"Once more I see thee, O Babylonia." See Ah! quel giorno (Rossini)

"Once more, my soul" (Azmon) C. G. Glaser. Words by I. Watts. FSS 7

"Once more o'er Transvaal hills and plains." See The Transvaal flag

"Once more the joy of harvest." HC

"Once more the liberal year laughs out." J. W. Elliott. Words by J. G. Whittier. HC

"Once more the rapid fleeting year." See Old Christmas (Romer)

"Once more we meet thee, all sadness apart." See Brightest of golden days (Balfe)

Once more we see the good by God provided. C. M. von Weber. e. SAS 1

"Once o'er the fields of Bethlehem." J. Booth. HC

"Once on a time in Thule of old." See Le roi de Thulé (Gounod)

"Once on a time old Johnny Bull." See Yankee Doodle

"Once on a time there was a man." See Peter Gray

"Once the sultan of the world, he spake." See Turkish patriotic song (Nedjib Pacha)

"Once there lived a king." Alsatian ballad. M. Ippolitoff-Ivanoff. e. NM 1

"Once there lived two brothers." See The story of poor Lazarus

"Once there was a little voice." See The little voice (Tauwitz)

"Once three little kittens they lost their mittens." See Three little kittens (Composer unknown)

"Once tired of life." See The wife in masquerade (Mazzinghi)

Once too often. FSS 5—MCS

"Once, twice, thrice." J. Hook. ME

"Once upon a midnight dreary." See The raven

Once upon a time (" 'Twas once upon a time") C. Barnard. Words by C. Wallace. MCS

"Once upon a time, there was a man." See Peter Gray

"Once upon a time there were three little kittens." See Three little kittens (Chant)

"Once was heard the song of children." See Song of the children

"Once we had a fragrant blossom." See Little Bennie (Poulton)

'Once we lived in peace." Polish song. e. KSE

Onderdonk, Henry Ustick
"How wondrous and great" (Haydn)
"The spirit in our hearts" (Nägeli)
"**Ondt** ofte lider den fiskermand." See Den norske fisker
"**One** arm stretched backward round his head." See Baby Charley
"**One** beautiful summer eve I strolled." See Am schönsten sommerabend war's (Grieg)
"**One** bumper at parting." Air: Moll Roe in the morning. Words by T. Moore. JO—MI—MMI
"**One** by one." V. Bellini. Words by A. A. Procter. FSS 4
"**One** clear summer morning, near blue Avonree." Irish song. e. MMI
"**One** cloudy ev'ning a gallant incognito." See El galán incógnito
"**One** cloudy night a gallant took his secret way." See El galán incógnito
"**One** cold and cloudy day in the month of May." See Barbara Allen (Chicopee co., Ga. version no. 2)
"**One** dainty badge we'll ever wear." See A knot of white and blue (Woodruff)
"**One** day a burning fever." See Blondel's song
"**One** day a poor boy to me was bound apprentice." See The captain's apprentice
"**One** day I heard Mary say." See I'll never leave thee
"**One** day I left my house to go a-peddling." See "'E spingole frangese" (Leva)
"**One** day I went a-walking." See La Capuana
"**One** day in October." See The bell ringing
"**One** day, one day, one high holiday." See Little Musgrave and Lady Barnard (Big Laurel, N.C. version)
"**One** day one young creole Candio." See Criole Candjo
"**One** day the soldier comes to town." See Le retour du mari soldat
"**One** day with Chloe left alone." See Der kuss (Beethoven)
"**One** eve as I happen'd to stray." See For Ireland I'd not tell her name
"**One** ev'ning a little before it was dark." See Hyde park
"**One** evening fair." Irish folk song. JOI
"**One** evening fresh and fair." See Sweet colleen rue
"**One** evening last week I walked down by yon bush." See Single and free
"**One** evening late I chanced to stray." See MacKenna's dream
"**One** evening of late as I happened to stray." See The spalpeen's complaint of the Cranbally farmer
"**One** evening, one evening, two brothers gone from school." See The two brothers (Mount Fair, Va. version no. 1)

"**One** evening young Lucy walked forth to the wood." See Sing hey ho, ne'er say no
"**One** fine day I left home to go a-trading." See "'E spingole frangese" (Leva)
"**One** for song and O." See Counting song
"**One** Friday morn when we set sail." See The mermaid
"**One** glance of thy dear eyes deep into mine, love." See Die liebende schreibt (Mendelssohn)
One grand sweet song. H. C. King. Words by C. Kingsley. LA
"**One** holiday, one righteous day." See Little Musgrave and Lady Barnard (Flag Pond, Tenn. version no. 2)
"**One** kind kiss before we part." See L'adieu (Jackson)
"**One** likes rosy apples well." See Lover's choice
"**One** little, two little, three little Indians." See Ten little Indians
"**One** long, last kiss at the shieling door." See The light at the window (Gabriel)
"**One** man shall mow my meadow." English folk song. SEF 2—SO
One moment ("Za jedan časak") Dalmatian folk song. e.se. BF 1
One more day ("Oh, have you heard") Capstan chantey. CR
For variants of this song see following songs of same title
One more day ("Only one more day") Pumping chantey. KB
One more day ("There is one thing") Capstan chantey. SE
"**One** morn when mists did hover." See The graceful maiden
"**One** morn when the wind." See Will Watch (Davy)
"**One** morning as I being free from care." See Bold Captain Freney
"**One** morning as I rambled." See We're all bound to go
"**One** morning early as I walked forth." See The dawning of the day
"**One** morning early, fragrant was the air." See The holiday
"**One** morning early, in the dawn pearly." See Tik, tak, tak
"**One** morning I chanced for to rove." See Nancy the pride of the west
"**One** morning in July." See Mary of Limerick town
"**One** morning in May." See Pastorale (Bizet)
"**One** morning in the month of May, as from my cot I stray'd." See The spotted cow
"**One** morning, in the month of May, down by a rolling river." See Just as the tide was flowing
"**One** morning in the summer time." See The party at the zoo (Winner)
"**One** morning, oh, so early." A. Scott-Gatty. Words by J. Ingelow. FSS 8 —WBW

"One morning, one morning in the spring."
See Early, early in the spring (Allan-stand, N.C. version)

"One morning, one morning, one morning in May, as I went a-walking to breathe the sweet air." See Fanny Blair (Kentucky version)

"One morning, one morning, one morning in May, I met a fair couple a-making their way." See The nightingale

"One morning so gay." See The spotted cow

"One night as I did wander." Air: John Anderson my jo. Words by R. Burns. BSR

"One night as I lay in my bed." See The foggy dew

"One night as I lay sleeping." See Loving Reilly (Georgia version)

"One night as the moon luminated the sky." See The trip we took over the mountain

"One night came on a hurricane." See Barney Buntline

"One night in my youth." Irish song. MMI

"One night when all the village slept." Air: Walpole, or, The happy clown. Words by C. Scroope. DM 2

"One night when the wind it blew cold." See Mary of the wild moor

"One noble knight it was indeed." See Lovely Joan

One of a jolly crew. Air: Son of a gambolier. Words by B. Braley. BSS

One or two. See "If you to me be cold" (Wrighton)

"One sails away to sea, to sea." See The sea (MacDowell)

"One sultry day a farmer's boy." See Hoe out your row (Donizetti)

One summer day. See Sommerdagen

"One summer eve, with pensive thought." See Shells of ocean (Cherry)

"One summer evening, a maiden fair." See The broken token (Devon version)

"One Sunday after mass." Attributed to Leveridge. MMI

"One Sunday fine all bright and clear." See O schöne zeit, o sel'ge zeit (Götze)

"One Sunday morn, as I've heard say." See Young Richard

"One sunny April morning." See Jack-in-the-pulpit

"One sweetly solemn thought" (Nearer home) Chant. Composer unknown. Words by P. Cary. LBR

"One sweetly solemn thought." R. S. Ambrose. Words by P. Cary. FMB—HSC—HSD—HSS 1—HSS 2—HSS 3——OH—WA—WBT—WS—WSW

"One sweetly solemn thought" (Jewett) K. M. Weber. Words by P. Cary. FSS 7

"One time a bumpkin was sitting." See El payo

One, two, three, four. J. Alau. Words by S. Kalama. HA

"One, two, three, our number is right." Catch. H. Purcell. MS

"One, two, three, that's the way, my dear." See Caroline

"One very keen winter and springtime of frost." See Ny kirree fo-sniaghtey

"One winter eve, lone in the waning light." See Ecce homo (Piccolomini)

"One winter's night." L. J. T. Darwall. Traditional words. HC

"One would say, he reposes." H. Maréchal. e. SAS 2

"One Zunday morn, as I've heerd zay." See Richard of Taunton Dean

O'Neill, Moira, pseud.
A broken song (Irish air)
A song of Glenann (Irish air)

Onfroy de Bréville, Pierre Eugene
The ferret. See Le furet du bois joli
Le furet du bois joli
The swallows (same air as Le furet du bois joli)

"Only a baby fair." G. Kingsley. Words by H. Martin. MCS

"Only a face at the window." See Only her love I ask for (Gabriel)

"Only a gentle word." G. Kingsley. FSS 4

Only a lock of her hair. W. T. Wrighton. WBT

"Only a rosebud, kissed by the dew." See The mission of a rose (Cowen)

Only a year ago. F. P. Tosti. Words by G. J. Whyte-Melville. FSS 6—MSF 2—WBW

"Only a yearning heart." See "Nur wer die sehnsucht kennt" (Tchaikovsky)

"Only bleed, tender heart." Bach. e. OS 1

Only her love I ask for. V. Gabriel (music and words) NML
"Only a face at the window." WBT—WL

Only love (Nur lieben) A. S. Dargomijsky. Words by D. Davuidoff. e.g. SC

Only once more. F. L. Moir. WBW

"Only one lock of her hair." See Only a lock of her hair (Wrighton)

"Only one more day of pumping." See One more day

"Only one more night." See Counting song

"Only the sad of heart." See "Nur wer die sehnsucht kennt" (Tchaikovsky)

"Only to see thee." F. Campana. FSS 8—WBT—WL

Only with thine eyes. See "Drink to me only with thine eyes" (Mellish?)

Onward ("Onward, ever onward") J. Farmer. LA

"Onward brothers" ("Dalej bracia") Polish song. e.p. BF 1

"**Onward**, Christian soldiers." A. S. Sullivan. Words by S. Baring-Gould. BSS— HSD— JS— MP— NMH— NMS— OH— TFC 1— TL— WA —WBT—WS—WSC—WSW
Christus Victor. LA
"**Onward**, Christian soldiers" (St Gertrude) BD—CST—FMB

"**Onward**, ever onward, front the noble fray." See Onward (Farmer)

Onward! onward ("Ohamo, ohamo za õpga oha") Montenegran national air. se. SN

"**Ooe** ka'u i haupu ae nei." See Forget-me-not (Hopkins)

Ooe no kau i upu ai. See Sweet constancy

The **open** door. Negro spiritual. DF

Open, Lord, my inward ear. L. van Beethoven. Words by C. Wesley. DSH

"**Open** thy blue eyes." See "Ouvre tes yeux bleus" (Massenet)

Open thy gates. See Temple ouvre-toi (Gounod)

Open thy lattice. See Parais à ta fenêtre (Gregh)

"**Open** unto me the gates of righteousness." M. Costa. OS 1—SAS 1

"**Open** wide thy blue eyes, my dearest." See "Ouvre tes yeux bleus" (Massenet)

The **open** window. A. Scott-Gatty. Words by H. W. Longfellow. LBR

"**Open** your hearts." See "Apra il suo verde seno" (Quagliati)

Operlied ("Die flamme lodert") L. van Beethoven. Words by F. von Matthisson. g. ED 2

Opie, Mrs Amelia (Alderson)
The Hindustani girl's lament (Biggs)
The pilgrim of love (Bishop)

Opitz von Boberfeld, Martin
Kriegslied (Zumsteeg)
Rechter sache gutes ende (Zelter)
Der spaziergang (Berner)

Opon de rock. Negro folk song. KA

Oppress'd with never-ceasing grief. Händel. BAS 2

Opsang (For heaving the anchor) Norwegian sea song. n. SMW

Opsang for Jonas Anton Hjelm. Norwegian chantey. n. SMW

"**Or** ch'io non seguo più" ("Now that I seek no more") R. Rontani. e.i. FEI 1

"**Or** lull'd with grief." See Sweet rose and lily (Händel)

Ora pro nobis. M. Piccolomini. Words by A. Horspool. HSS 1—HSS 2— WA

Ora vira, vira. See Vira do minho

L'**orage** (The storm) French folk song. Words adapted from Fabre d'Eglantine. e. GO

Oran an aiog. See The song of death

The **orange** and the black ("Although Yale has") Princeton university song. F. Shackelton. Words by C. B. Mitchell. CHS--LA

The **orange** and the black ("Though Eugene has") Albany college song. [F. Shackelton] Words by O. Hinson. CHS

The **orange** tree. See La marchande d'oranges

The **orange** vender. See La marchande d'oranges

The **orangeman.** Irish folk song. JOI

The **orchestra.** Old game song. TFC 2

Ordway, John P.
Dreaming of home and mother
"Twinkling stars are laughing, love"

O'Reilly, John Boyle
My mother's memory (music by Klein; Taubert)

Orias, Charles d'
Minuet (Tanieev)

Oriental chant (Lamentation) M. Moussorgskii. e. SC

Orientales, la patria o la tumba. See Himno nacional de la republica oriental del Uruguay (Deballi)

The **origin** of gunpowder ("When Vulcan forged the bolts of Jove") Braham. Words by T. Dibdin. HSE 1

The **origin** of the harp. See " 'Tis believed that this harp" (Irish air)

Orlov, I
Russian lullaby (attributed) See Bakhmetiev, N. I. The Cossack's lullaby

Ormond the brave. Folk song. BSW

Orne, Caroline Frances
All who labor (Composer unknown)

"**Örnen** löfter med staerke slag over de höie fjelde." See Arnes sang (Heise)

"**Oro**, sé do bheatha a bhaile" ("Oro, welcome home") Irish hauling-home song. e.ir. JOI

"**Oro**, welcome home." See "Oro, sé do bheatha a bhaile

Ororotsi yerk. See "Come, O nightingale"

O'Rourke, Edmund. See Falconer, Edmund

The **orphan** ("I was still a child") See När jag var ett litet

The **orphan** ("Sun bright in heaven") Ruthenian folk air. Words by M. H. R. Mussey. WF

The **orphan** ("Within your porch I'm standing") Greek song. N. Maggea. e. KSE

Orphan ballad singers. H. Russell. FSS 8

The **orphan** boys ("Our cot was shelter'd") HSD

The **orphan-girl** (Sirótka) M. P. Moussorgsky (music and words) e. SMR 1

"**Orphan** hours, the year is dead." See Dirge for the year (Wesley)

"**Orpheus** with his lute." C. Busch. Words attributed to W. Shakespeare; attributed also to J. Fletcher. VFS

"Orpheus with his lute." M. Greene. Words attributed to W. Shakespeare; attributed also to J. Fletcher. DM 2

Orpheus with his lute. C. F. Manney. Words attributed to W. Shakespeare; attributed also to J. Fletcher. HST— VFS

Orpheus with his lute. A. Sullivan. Words attributed to W. Shakespeare; attributed also to J. Fletcher. BC— CS 2—DM 2—KF 3—MSS 1—SM 3— SS 1

Orred, Meta
"In the gloaming, oh, my darling" (Harrison)

"Orthodox! orthodox! wha believe in John Knox." Air: Come, let us prepare. Words by R. Burns. BSR

Ortonville (Hastings) See Fourth of July hymn; "A little word in kindness said"; "Majestic sweetness"

"Orynthia, my beloved." See The pilgrim of love (Bishop)

"Os ha gjort." See Hjemreise fra saetren

Osborne, Charles
Don't leave your mother, Tom (Symons)

Osgood, Mrs
"Call me pet names" (Jarvis)

Osgood, George L.
My little woman

Osgood, Mabel G.
"The buds are bursting on the trees" (Clouston)

Ossian's serenade. O. E. Dodge. FSS 4

"Ostera! spirit of spring-time." J. I. Alexander. HC

Östereichisches nationallied. See "Gott erhalte Franz den kaiser" (Haydn)

Osterwald, Karl Wilhelm
"Ach wenn ich doch ein immchen wär'" (Franz)
Ständchen (Franz)

Ostlere, May
Dutch dolls

Ostrovók. See The isle (Rachmaninov)

Ostrovskiĭ, Aleksandr Nikolaevich
Little Snowflake's arietta (Rimskiĭ-Korsakov)
Peasant cradle-song (Musorgskiĭ)
Song of the shepherd Lehl (Rimskiĭ-Korsakov)
Sylvan roundelay (Rimskiĭ-Korsakov)

Óstroyu syekeeroi. See The wounded birch (Grechaninov)

O'Sullivan, Seumas, pseud. See Starkey, James

O'Sullivan, Vincent
Norman cradle song (De Koven)

Oswald, James
"Anna, thy charms my bosom fire"
Balance a straw
Gae bring to me a pint o' wine
"Go, fetch to me a pint o' wine." See Gae bring to me a pint o' wine
God save the king (attributed) See Carey, H. God save the king (attributed)

"It is na, Jean, thy bonie face"
"The lovely lass of Inverness"
"The muse and the hero"
"O, were I on Parnassus hill"
Peace, the fairest child of heaven
Roslin castle (attributed)
"'Twas in that season of the year." See Roslin castle (attributed)
"Yon wild mossy mountains"

Oswald, Mrs Lucy (Johnson)
"Thou ling'ring star with less'ning ray"

"T'other morning very early." See L'autr'ier par la matinée

"The other night, while I was sparking." See Kiss me quick and go (Buckley)

"Others they may tell you of bold Robin Hood." See Robin Hood and the bishop of Hereford

Otway, Thomas
"Come all ye youths" (17th century air)

"Où courez-vous masquée." See Gavotte du masque (Georges)

"Où dites-moi, beau cavalier." See Par le sentier (Dubois)

"Où est mon amant, a l'heur' de maintenant." See Le rosier d'argent

"Où suis-je? ah! oui je me rappelle." See Ô ma lyre immortelle (Gounod)

"Où va la jeune Indoue" ("As falls the moonlight gently."—Indian bell song) L. Delibes. e.f. KS 1— MC

"Où va la jeune Indoue" ("Why strays the Indian maiden."—Indian bell song) e.f. OPS 1

"Où vas-tu, souffle d'aurore." See Sérénade (Tchaikovsky)

"Oua mau pua lehua." See A wreath for Princess Kaiulani (Hopkins)

"Oui, c'est lui" ("Yes, 'tis he") T. Dubois. e.f.i. OPS 2

"Oui, depuis quatre jours." See Sous les pieds d'une femme (Gounod)

"Oui, Dieu le veut." See Adieu, forêts (Tchaikovsky)

"Oui, je t'aime, comme un bel ange." See L'amour (Godard)

"Oui, pour ce soir je suis reine des fées." See Je suis Titania (Thomas)

The ould plaid shawl. Irish air. Words by F. A. Fahy. FSI

"Our alma mater sits enthroned." See The purple and the white

"Our ancestors formerly great valour they have shown." See Ye natives of this nation

"Our auld King Coul was a jolly auld soul." See Auld King Coul

"Our auld Santa Claus is a saint so jolly." See Auld Santa Claus

Our baby. French folk song. e. HSD —WBT—WSC

Our banner. C. Wilhelm. Words by A. R. Robinson. MP

"Our bark was out far from the land." See The sailor's grave

"Our boat floats downstream." See Song of the pleasure seekers

"**Our** boys are on the football field." See A foot ball song

"**Our** boys will shine to-night." American air.   TFC 1
Variant: "Our troop will shine to-night"

"**Our** bright, starry flag." See Flag of '76 (Matteson)

"**Our** bugles sung truce." See The soldier's dream (Attwood)

"**Our** captain is a bully man." See Lowlands low

Our Christmas festal.   Words by Anatolius. ₍Tr of Mega kai paradoxon thagma₎ e.   MCS

Our Christmas rose.   T. Cooke.   FSS 8 —MCS

"**Our** college cheer."   CHS—MPC

Our college home.   Upper Iowa university song.   W. Ruggles (music and words) CHS

"**Our** college, 'tis of thee."   See Long may our college stand

"**Our** cot was shelter'd in a wood."   See The orphan boys

Our country ("From ev'ry land and nation") Old air.   Words by H. H. Harbour.   DO

Our country ("Land of high heroic glory") J. Haydn.   JSE

Our country ("We give thy natal day to hope")   Arr from F. Mendelssohn-Bartholdy.   Words by J. G. Whittier. LBR

Our country ("We'll thank thee for our country")   J. H. Deems.   JS

"**Our** country is our ship."   W. Reeve. ₍Words by J. Cobb₎ HSE 2

"**Our** country is our ship."   S. Storace. Words by J. Cobb.   ME

"**Our** country, 'tis so grand, you see." See The little patriot's salute

Our country's call.   Air: Der tannenbaum. Words by W. C. Bryant.   LBR

Our country's flag ("Flag of the free") See "Flag of the free" (Wagner)

"**Our** country's flag! O emblem dear." See Freedom's flag (Geibel)

Our daily bread.   W. M. Hutchinson. Words by A. A. Procter.   FSS 7

Our dear country bids us defend her.   See Le chant du départ

"**Our** Father in heaven, Creator of all." See A university hymn

"**Our** Father in heaven, we hallow Thy name."   See The Lord's prayer

"**Our** Father Which art in Heaven."   See The Lord's prayer

"**Our** Father, Who art in heaven."   See The Lord's prayer

Our fatherland.   F. Abt.   FSS 1
Our native land.   LA

"**Our** fathers' God, from out Whose hand." See Centennial hymn (Paine)

Our feast shall be without alloy.   See St David's day

"**Our** flag is there."   HSC—FSS 1—WBT —WCP—WSC

Our flag o'er us waving.   G. Verdi. FSS 5—WBT

"**Our** flag, our flag above the clouds."   See The flag (Hadley)

"**Our** God, our God, save to us our sultan." Turkish national air.   e.   SN

"**Our** God to us gave iron here."   See Vaterlandslied (Methfessel)

"**Our** gondola like bird is flying."   See Venetian song (Bemberg)

Our goodman.   Folk song: Big Laurel, N.C. version no. 1.   CSE
—Big Laurel, N.C. version no. 2.   CSE
—Hot Springs, N.C. version.   CSE

"**Our** harps were tun'd to sing Thy praise." See Babylon (Watson)

"**Our** hearts with joy are bounding."   See Boat song (Auber)

"**Our** home is on the sea."   J. Offenbach. FSS 5

Our honored Bates.   Bates college song. Words by Gile and Remick.   CHS

"**Our** king went forth to Normandy."   See Deo gratias

"**Our** land, O Lord."   M. Haydn.   MP— NMH—NMS—WBT—WSC—WSW

Our land, our fatherland.   See Vårt land, vårt fosterland (Pacius)

"**Our** life, our life is like a narrow raft." See Life (Blumenthal)

Our little nipper.   A. Chevalier.   WBT

"**Our** lofty elms so gently break."   See Steps song (Carter)

"**Our** Lord heal' de sick."   Negro spiritual. DF

Our Lord in beggar's guise.   See Notre Seigneur en pauvre

"**Our** lords are to the mountains gane." See Hughie Graham

Our merry Swiss home.   C. W. Glover. FSS 8

Our mother's way.   D. Lee.   FSS 8— WBT

"**Our** mountain brooks were rushing."   See Annie dear

Our native land ("Hawaii! sea-girt land."— "Hawaii ponoi") Hawaiian national air.   H. Berger.   Words by Kalakaua.   e.h.   SN
Hawaiian national song ("Hawaii ponoi") h.   BMC

Our native land ("The simple songs to thee") See Our fatherland (Abt)

Our native song ("O sing with voices clear") Methfessel.   HSD—LA

Our noble selves.   E. Newton.   Words by J. M. Bulloch.   SSS

"**Our** oats they are hoed."   See Harvest home (Purcell)

"**Our** own dear land."   LA

Our own little isle ("Oh! Irishmen! never forget") Irish air: The Carabhat jig. Words by Fermoy (J. E. Pigot) MMI —PI

"**Our** roof does arching rise."   See Margaretes vuggesang (Grieg)

"**Our** Saviour spoke these words so sweet." See Hear the lambs a-crying

"**Our** school-days now are past and gone." See Graduation song

"**Our** ship carried over nine hundred men." See Britons, strike home

"**Our** ship is about to sail." See Une fleur pour réponse

"**Our** ship she lies in harbour." Folk song from Hampshire. SF 3

Our songs of joy and gladness. Meyerbeer. FSS 8

"**Our** sorrow is vain" (East Indian song) Words by L. S. Jast. BMC

"**Our** souls are thine, dear fatherland." See To America (Waller)

"**Our** strong band can ne'er be broken." See Amici

"**Our** Swedish feelings." See "Ur svenska hjertans"

"**Our** thistles flourish'd fresh and fair." See Awa, Whigs, awa

"**Our** thrissles flourish'd fresh and fair." See Awa, Whigs, awa

"**Our** troop will shine to-night." American air. BSS
Variant of: "Our boys will shine tonight"

Our valley. Carinthian song. e. KSE —SN

Our way across the sea. FSS 5

"**Our** wonderful house. Words by W. F. Crafts. FSS 4

"**Our** young lady's a huntin gane." Air: The rowin't in her apron. Words by R. Burns. BSR

"**Our** youthful hearts for learning burn." See Away to school

Ouseley, Sir Frederick Arthur Gore
Carol for Christmas-eve. See "Listen, lordlings, unto me"
"Come, tune your heart" (Tr of Auf, schicke dich)
"Easter flowers are blooming bright"
"In Bethlehem, that noble place"
"Listen, lordlings, unto me" (Tr of Seignors, ore entendez à nus)

"**Out** among the cliffs a little dove did fly." See Little dove

"**Out** beyond the gray walls lives a maiden." See Carmè

"**Out** in a beautiful field." See Pretty pear tree

"**Out** in Pamerent in Holland." See Pumping chanty

"**Out** in the snow storm." See Our Christmas rose (Cooke)

"**Out** of my soul's great sadness." See "Aus meinen grossen schmerzen" (Franz)

"**Out** of our suff'ring, out of our sadness." See Choral

"**Out** of the dark and dreary street." See Ora pro nobis (Piccolomini)

"**Out** of the night-time into the light-time." See From the great deep, to the great deep we go

"**Out** of the window." Motion song. FSS 8—WBT

"**Out** on an ocean all boundless we ride." See Homeward bound (Dadmun)

"**Out** on the deep." F. N. Löhr. Words by S. K. Cowan. AB 1—CB—HSD— TFC 1

"**Out** on the lake my canoe is gliding." See Her shadow

"**Out** on the porch the king stood at dawn." See Sigurd aa troll-brura

"**Out** on the stormy sea." See "Sul mare torbido"

"**Out** over the Forth, I look to the north." N. Gow. Words by R. Burns. BSR —PS 2

The **outlandish** knight. Folk song. SEF 1—SO

The **outlaw** ("In the dungeon have I languish'd."—"Tri godini") Bulgarian folk song. b.e. BO—SMF

The **outlaw** ("Oh! I am the child of the forest wild") E. J. Loder. Words by H. C. Schiller. HSE 3

"**Ouvre** tes yeux bleus" ("Open thy blue eyes") J. Massenet. Words by P. Robiquet. e.f. HM 2—KF 3— PG 3
"Open thy blue eyes." e. BD— WBW

"**Ouvre-toi**, porte fatale." See Longing (Rubinstein)

"**Ouvrez**—ouvrez, c'est nous." See Le retour des promis (Dessauer)

"**Ov** dsidsernag." See The prisoner to the swallow

"**Ove** celare, oh Dio." See Terra adorata de' padri miei (Donizetti)

"**Over** all the land is glowing." A. H. Brown. Words by J. Brett. HC

"**Over** behind my aunt's." See La chanson des métamorphoses (Canadian version)

Over de höje fjelde (Over the lofty mountains) H. Kjerulf. Words by B. Björnson. e.n. MAN

Over de höje fjelde (Over the lofty mountains) R. Nordraak. Words by B. Björnson. e.n. MAN

"**Over** fields and over meadows" (Vo polé tuman zatumanelsya) Russian folk song. e.r. BO

"**Over** forest, over lake." See En sommarafton (Lindblad)

"**Over** hill and plain they're bounding." See Hela'r 'sgyvarnog

"**Over** hill and valley hear the footsteps patter." See Hare and hounds

"**Over** hill, over dale, as we hit the dusty trail." See Artillery song

"**Over** hill, over dale, thro' bush thro' brier." T. S. Cooke. Words by W. Shakespeare. HSE 3—VFS

"**Over** hill, over dale, thro' bush thro' brier." R. Dunstan. Words by W. Shakespeare. KSS

"**Over** hills and over plains." G. Saunders. Words by C. L. Matteaux. HC

"**Over** in the meadow, in the sand, in the sun." See Old mother toad

"**Over** in the meadows in the nest in the tree." See Sing, said the mother

Over land and sea. MCS

"Over marshes and meadows." See The lonely waif

"Over Tatra." See Slovak national anthem

"Over the banister." Student song. CHS —CU—MPC—NMH— NML— WBT— WC—WL—WSW

"Over the bay of azure." See Sailing at Napoli

"Over the bright blue sea." A. Sullivan. WBT

"Over the chimney the night-wind sang." See What the chimney sang (Hopkins)

Over the dark blue sea. Alpine air. FSS 3

"Over the foam we glide." See On Venice waters

Over the garden wall. G. D. Fox. Words by H. Hunter. HSD—WBT

"Over the green downs." Words by J. Ingelow. MCS

Over the happy town. D. F. E. Auber. MCS

"Over the heather." F. L. Moir. Words by W. Boosey. FMB

Over the hills and far away ("Last night, last night") Irish air. Words by N. Chesson. FSI

"Over the hills and far away, in a village by the sea." See Rose-Marie (Molloy)

"Over the land in glory." A. Foote. Words by F. L. Hosmer. HC

Over the lofty mountains. See Over de höje fjelde (Kjerulf); Over de höje fjelde (Nordraak)

"Over the mountain and over the moor." See The beggar girl (Piercy)

"Over the mountain wave." E. L. White. FSS 2—LA

"Over the mountains and over the waves." See Love will find out the way

"Over the mountains and under the caves." See Love will find out the way

"Over the mountains the evening star." See Song from the Pyrenees: 1

"Over the ocean Columbus came." See Columbus day

"Over the ocean night's star is beaming." See Santa Lucia

"Over the rippling sea." See Santa Lucia

"Over the sea, over the sea." FSS 7

Over the sea to Skye. Words by R. L. Stevenson. SSS

"Over the shining and mirror-like billows." See Auf dem wasser zu singen (Schubert)

"Over the snow-clad city." See The gate of heaven (Tours)

"Over the stars there is rest." See "Über den sternen ist ruh" (Abt)

Over the steppe (Styépyu idoo ya ōōnúi-loyu) A. T. Gretchaninoff. Words by A. Pleshtcheieff. e. SMR 2 On the steppe ("Triste est le steppe") e.f. NM 1

"Over the summer sea." Verdi. FSS 3 —JSE—OH—WBT—WSC

"Over the town of Novgorod." See The bells of Novgorod

Over the water to Charlie. See "Come, boat me o'er, come, row me o'er"

"Over the waves we float." S. Glover. Words by J. E. Carpenter. FSS 4

Over there ("Oh, think of a home") D. W. C. Huntington. Words by T. C. O'Kane. FSS 2

"Over there, over there, O hallelu." Modern negro song. JP

"Over there where my aunt lives." See Le prisonnier de Hollande (Canadian version)

"Over where the lake is dancing." See By the lake

Overbeck, Christian Adolf Der knabe an das veilchen (Schulz) "Komm' lieber mai, und mache" (Mozart) Die schifffahrt (Hurka) Der sorgenfreie (Schulz) Trost für mancherlei tränen (Schulz)

"Overhead the sun is riding." See The sun runs its course

Owain Alaw. See Owen, John

"Owass' nowatch shayngayshenoon." See Vanity

Owczarek. See The little shepherd

Owen, David All through the night. See Ar hyd y nos Ar hyd y nos Welsh lullaby. See Ar hyd y nos

Owen, John Winnie Wen

Owenson, Sydney. See Morgan, Sidney (Owenson), lady

The owl ("Of all the birds") 16th century song. BSW "Of all the birds." BOH—CO 1

The owl ("When icicles hang by the wall") T. A. Arne. Words by W. Shakespeare. VFS

"The owl and the pussy cat." G. Ingraham. Words by E. Lear. CST—WC

"The owl is abroad." Purcell. BAS 2—BS 2

The owlet. See Tecolotito

The owl's song. See Kattyglö visa

"Owre kynge went forth to Normandy." See Deo gratias

Oxana's song (Aria Oksánui) N. Rimsky-Korsakoff. e. SMR 2

The oxen ploughing. Folk song. BE 2 —BSW

Oxenford, Edward Boat song (Cowen) Dreaming (Wellings) Funiculì-funiculà (Denza) "O wonderful the tidings" (Bunnett) "Once again the olden story" (music by Bunnett; Oliver) "Thy sentinel am I" (Watson)

Oxenford, John
The bell ringer (Wallace)
"Come, here's to Robin Hood" (Composer unknown)
Hope, the hermit (Composer unknown)
"The monk within his cell" (Macfarren)
My own, my guiding star (Macfarren)
Oxenham, John
The people's prayer (Dykes)
The Oxford bowlers. Vanbrugh. DM 2
The Oxfordshire tragedy. See "Near Woodstock town"
Oy gar Blepeis tarattontas. For English translation see "Christian! dost thou see them" (Dykes)
Oy, Schmer'l take your fiddle out. See "Ten brothers"
"Oy szumyt." See The dancers
"Ozean! du ungeheuer." See "Ocean! thou mighty monster" (Weber)

P

"Pä Norges kolde vidder" ("On frost-cold Norway's moorlands") I. Holter. Words by H. Heine. [Tr of Ein fichtenbaum steht einsam] e.n. WM 1
"På silfvermolnets kant satt aftonstjernan." See Den första kyssen (Sibelius)
"Pa vann kousket." See Emgann Sant-Kast
Paa fjellet (On the mountain) H. Kjerulf. Words by K. Janson. e.n. MAN
"Paa solen jeg ser, det lider alt frem." See Saetergjentens söndag (Bull)
Paahana. See Hawaiian hula (Hopkins)
Paal paa hougje (Paul on the hill) Norwegian song. e.n. BF 2
Paal paa haugen (Paul on the hill-side) e.n.
Paal paa hougje (Paul on the hill-side) e.n. MAN
Pablo Andraca, M.
La Carolina
Pace-egging song. Westmorland Easter carol. WCC
Pace, pace, mio Dio. G. Verdi. e.i. SOA 1
Pacius, Friedrich
Finnish national air. See Vårt land, vårt fosterland
Maamme. See Vårt land, vårt fosterland
Our land, our fatherland. See Vårt land, vårt fosterland
Vårt land, vårt fosterland
Pacius, J.
Suomen laulu. See Suomi's song
Suomi's song
Pack, colonel
"I never saw a face till now"
Phillis. See "I never saw a face till now"
The serenade

Packard, Winthrop
A gentle hint (Riker)
Paddle your own canoe. M. Hobson. Words by H. Clifton. FSS 3—HSD
Paddling song. See Voyageur's song
Paddock, William Henry
Old glory (Oliver)
Paddy Doyle ("To me way-ay-ay-yah") Short drag chantey. CR
For variants of this song see following songs of same title; also We'll pay Paddy Doyle
Paddy Doyle ("To my way-ay-ay-ah") Short drag chantey. KB
Paddy Doyle ("To my way-ay ay-ay ay-yah") Pulling chantey. SE
Paddy Duffy's cart. D. Braham. Words by E. Harrigan. WC
Paddy works on the railway. Capstan chantey. CR
Paderewski, Ignacy Jan
"Ach! die qualen." See Ah! the torment
Ah! the torment
"Padezco, si, padezco por tu amor." See El sufrimiento
"Padre, perdona" ("Father, have mercy") J. A. Hasse. e.i. KS 3
A pagan Noël. See Noël païen (Massenet)
Page, Edgar
Beulah land (Sweney) Authorship uncertain
Page, Nathaniel Clifford
The regrets of Bŏkhära
"A thing of beauty"
"Pagen høit paa taarnet sad." See Genrebillede (Backer-Lunde)
The pagoda bells. T. Comer. FSS 4
"Pahata nawajiṇ." See The love signal
"Pahbahmahdaymowun wenemoshayn." See Apprehension
"Pain was childhood's sad dower." See Non più mesta accanto al fuoco (Rossini)
Paine, John Knowles
Centennial hymn
Matin song
"Through the night of doubt and sorrow" (Tr of Igjennem nat og traengsel)
Paine, Robert Treat
Adams and liberty (Arnold)
Paine, T.
The old cabin home
"Painful is my heart" (Malay song) Javanese air: Longkie. e. BMC
The painful plough. English folk song. BSW
Páisdín fionn (The air young child) Irish folk song. e.ir. BF 2
Páisdín fionn. For English translation with a different air see "Oh, deep in my soul is my paistheen fion"

Paisiello, Giovanni
"Chi vuol la zingarella"
"For tenderness formed"
The lover's sigh. See "Nel cor più non mi sento"
"Mich fliehen alle freuden." See "Nel cor più non mi sento"
"Il mio ben quando verrà"
"Nel cor più non mi sento" (from L'amor contrastato)
"No more my heart is fervent." See "Nel cor più non mi sento"
"When, my love, wilt thou return." See "Il mio ben quando verrà"
"Who'll try the gypsy pretty." See "Chi vuol la zingarella"
"Why feels my heart so dormant." See "Nel cor più non mi sento"
"Wynken, Blynken, and Nod"

La **pájara** pinta. Spanish American song. s. LCP

Un **pajarito**. Mexican folk song. e.s. HS

El **pájaro** errante. Porto Rican song. s. LCP

Pakoble. See The rose (Lieurance)

Paladilhe, Émile
Havanaise
La islena. See Havanaise
L'isolana. See Havanaise
Mandolinata (with words "Away the night is balmy"; "O I'm a happy creature")
Psyché
Le roitelet
Three prayers. See Les trois prières
Les trois prières
The wren. See Le roitelet

Le **paladin**. See "Knight-errant" (Dargomyzhskiï)

The **pale** girl. See La smortina

"**Pale** is the moon." See By the water (Musorgskiï)

The **pale** white rose. Words by R. W. Adams. FSS 6

"**Pâles** étoiles." V. Joncières. e.f. SOA 1

Palestrina, Giovanni Pierluigi da
The strife is o'er: the battle done (Tr of Finita jam sunt praelia)

Palkó, Jankó ("Csinom Palkó, Csinom Jankó") 17th century Hungarian folk song. e.hu. BF 1

Palm branches ("Little man and maiden") A. Gretchaninoff. Words from the Russian of A. Block. e. NM 1

Palm branches ("Sur nos chemins") See Les rameaux (Faure)

Palmer, Ray
"My faith looks up to Thee" (Mason)

The **palms**. See Les rameaux (Faure)

Palmsonntag ("Mildes, warmes frühlingswetter") L. Reichardt. Words by M. von Schenkendorf. g. ED 3

La **paloma** ("Cuando salí de la Habana, válgame Dios") S. Yradier. s. LCP. e. only WBT

La **paloma** (The dove) e. CST—WA—WL—WSW

La **paloma** (Oh! the sailor shall sing) e. FSS 6

La **paloma** ("Vi volar una blanca paloma") Porto Rican song. s. LCP

La **paloma** blanca. Folk song from Arizona and northern Mexico. e.s. HS

La **paloma** blanca (The white dove) e.s. HF

La **paloma** cuencana. Folk song from the Andes mountains. e.s. HS

"Una **palomma** ghianca." See Trippole trappole

Pange lingua gloriosi proelium certaminis. For English translation see "Sing the battle" (Monk)

"**Panis**, piscus, crinis, finis." See The seminarian (Musorgskiï)

Panofka, Heinrich
"O blessed Savior, God of love." See "O salutaris"
"O salutaris"

"**Pansies**, lilies, roses." J. Booth. Words by C. Griffiths. HC

"**Pansies**, lilies, roses" (Flower song) G. E. Oliver. [Words by C. Griffiths] LA

Panzacchi, Enrico
Mattinata (Tosti)
Nirvana (Hervey)

Paolella, Mariano
Dimme 'na vota sì (Scalisi)

"**Papa** Queléle has died, ay, ay, ay, ay, ay." See El Queléle

"Le **papillon** suit la chandelle" ("The butterfly the candle seeks") French Canadian folk song. e.f. BFS

Les **papillons** (Butterflies) E. Chausson. Words by T. Gautier. e.f. SAM

"Les **papillons** couleur de neige." See Les papillons (Chausson)

"Der **papst** lebt herrlich in der welt" (Pope and sultan) e.g. SSS
The pope. e. CHS—CU—MPC—WC

Pa-pup-ooh. See Deer-flower (Lieurance)

"**Par** che mi dica ancora." Donizetti. e.i. PP

"**Par** derrièr' chez ma tante il y a-t-un bois joli." See Le prisonnier de Hollande (Canadian version)

"**Par** derrièr' chez ma tante il y a-t-un étang." See La chanson des métamorphoses (Canadian version)

"**Par** la voix du canon d'alarme." See Mourir pour la patrie (Varney)

Par le sentier (By the path) T. Dubois. Words by L. de Courmont. e.f. PG 3

"**Par** quel trouble profond suis-je ici ramenée." See Nuit resplendissante (Gounod)

"Par Saint Gilles viens nous en." See Les pas d'armes du roi Jean (Saint-Saëns)

"Par un matin" ("Lizette one morn arose") Bergerette. e.f. WB

The parable of the sinful rich man. See La parabole du mauvais riche

La parabole du mauvais riche (The parable of the sinful rich man) French folk song. e.f. SMF—TSF

Paradies, Pietro Domenico
"M'ha preso alla sua ragna"
"'Tis love, that rogue so wily." See "M'ha preso alla sua ragna"

Paradise. See "O paradise" (Barnby)

Parais à ta fenêtre (Come to thy window) L. Gregh. e.f. KF 3
Parais à ta fenêtre (Open thy lattice) e.f. MSF 2

The parallel. Air: I would rather than Ireland. Words by T. Moore. MI

Parásha's revery and dance (Doomka Parássi) M. P. Moussorgsky. e. SMR 1

"Pardon, kind friends, I sing but ill, I fear me." See Modo delle lavandaie

Pardoned. M. Piccolomini. Words by L. Lennox. HSS 3—HSS 4

Parfum de fleur (Perfume of a flower) C. Blanc. Words by E. Blemont. e.f. HM 1

Parigi, o cara ("Oh, loved Italia") G. Verdi. e. FSS 5

La Parisienne (The Parisian) French patriotic song. Auber. Words by C. de la Vigne. e.f. SN

Park, George
Horae Andreanae (German air)

Parke, William Thomas
The garden gate

Parker, C. R.
Gold and blue

Parker, Edwin Pond
"Golden harps are sounding"

Parker, Henry
Jerusalem
Where the wicked cease from troubling

Parker, Horatio William
"All my heart this night rejoices" (Tr of Fröhlich soll mein herze springen)
Forget-me-nots
"Have you heard the wondrous story"
Milkmaid's song
The robbers

Parker, J. C. D.
"God hath sent His angels"

Parker, Martin
"Come, cheer up your hearts" (Sheeles)
"A country life is sweet" (Eccles)
The merry milkmaids (Composer unknown)
Ragged and torn and true (Old English air)
"What though I be a country lass" (Old English air)

When the king enjoys his own again (Traditional air)
"You gentlemen of England" (English air; Irish air)

Parker, Mrs Nella
Jerusalem (Parker, H.)

Parley, Peter, pseud.
"A hermit there was" (Composer unknown)

The parlor scout. College air. Words by B. Braley. BSS

"Parmi les lianes" ("Deep in forest shaded") V. Massé. e.f. KS 2

A parody song. Student song. Words by L. E. Baldwin. CHS

Parrot song. M. Moussorgsky. Words from the Russian. e. NM 2

Parry, Sir Charles Hubert Hastings, bart.
"Fear no more the heat o' the sun"
I will bear the indignation of God (from Judith)
"I will sing unto the Lord a new song" (from Judith)
"The Lord is long-suffering and merciful" (from Judith)
The repentance of Manasseh. See I will bear the indignation of God

Parry, John
Composer
Jenny Jones
Little Mary of the Dee
Norah, the pride of Kildare
"Smile again, my bonnie lassie"
Author
Aye sure (Welsh air)
"The bells were ringing merrily" (Welsh air)
The good-natured lad (Welsh air)
"It is not for his gold, sir" (Welsh air)
"Let life be short, let life be long" (Welsh air)
"Oh! let the kind minstrel" (Welsh air)
Peggy Wilkins (Welsh air)

Parry, John Orlando
The flying Dutchman

Parry, Joseph
"O Blodwen, my true love"
"Watchman, tell us of the night"

Parson Hogg. English folk song. BSW

Parsons, George Sanford
A toast to Columbia

"Partant pour la Syrie." Attributed to Hortense Eugénie de Beauharnais (music and words) Music attributed also to L. F. P. Drouet. Words attributed also to A. Laborde. e.f. LA—SN
Dunois the brave. e. JO
Partant pour la Syrie (Departure for Syria) e. BSE
Partant pour la Syrie (Dunois the brave) e. FSS 6
"Partant pour la Syrie" ("It was Dunois, the young and brave") e.f. BSP
Partant pour la Syrie (Romance of Dunois.—"It was Dunois, the young and brave") e. BMC

Parted. See "Lungi dal caro bene" (Sarti)

The **parted** lovers (Zwei leichen) F. Chopin. Words by B. Zaleski. e.g. FF

Parting ("Als wir beiden") See Abschied (Cavallo)

Parting ("Es ritten drei reiter") See Drei reiter am thore

Parting ("Let us go home") Ojibway Indian song. e.in. BA

Parting ("Muss i denn") See Abschied ("Muss i denn")

The **parting** ("Poor Bessy was a sailor's wife") G. A. Hodson. HSE 3

Parting ("We've trod one road."—Adieu) Ippolytov-Ivanov. Words by D. Tserteliev. e.f. NR 3

Parting graduation song. C. Barnard. WBT
"Hail and farewell." FSS 3—JS

Parting hymn. See "Saviour, again to Thy dear name we raise" (Hopkins)

Parting sorrow ("Ha! what am I reading") Old Russian song. e. KSN

Parting's sorrow ("Why, alas, bear I yet parting's sorrow") A. Warlamoff. e. KSN

Partridge, F. W.
"Sleep, holy Babe"

The **party** at the zoo. S. Winner. FSS 6

Parvum quando cerno Deum. For English translation see "When I view the Mother holding" (Barnby)

Les **pas** d'armes du roi Jean (The tourney of King John) C. Saint-Saëns. Words by V. Hugo. e.f. KF 3—KF 4—PG 3

"**Paseando** una mañana." See La mulata

Pasmore, Henry Bickford
"My love dwelt in a northern land" A northern romance. See "My love dwelt in a northern land"

"**Pass** me not, O God, my Father." See Even me

"**Pass** on! spoil not our tranquil pleasures." See "Chassons de nos plaisirs" (Rameau)

"**Pass** onward." See Der tod und das mädchen (Schubert)

Er **passagallo** (The improvvisatore) Romanesca song. e.i. MSI

"**Passed** is summer noontime." See Autumn's glory (Johnson)

Passerieu, Henri
Fleur messagère (Bouval)
Printemps nouveau (Vidal)

Passing by ("There is a lady") T. Ford. Words by R. Herrick. DM 2

Passing by ("There is a ladye") E. C. Purcell. Words by R. Herrick. CMF 1 —ES—SSS

The **passing** of the Gael. Irish air. Words by E. Carbery. CMF 1—FSI

"**Passing** thro' a town of fair Lorraine." See Les trois capitaines

Passion chorale. See "O sacred Head! once wounded" (Bach)

La **Passion** de Jésus-Christ (The Passion of Jesus Christ) French Canadian folk song. e.f. BFS

The **passionate** shepherd to his love. See "Come live with me and be my love" (16th century air); "Come live with me and be my love" (Goldmark)

Passmore, W. S.
"Not a sparrow falleth" (Abt)

Past and future. R. De Koven. Words by F. E. Weatherly. MSF 2

"**Past** eight o' clock, and it's bedtime for dolly." See Little girl's good-night (Scott-Gatty)

"**Past** is Lenten sadness." J. F. Bridge. HC

"**Past** is the combat now." See Pleurez! pleurez, mes yeux (Massenet)

"**Past** the gray walls a maiden is dwelling." See Carmè (Curtis)

"**Pastime** with good company." King Henry VIII (music and words) BE 1—CO 1—PR 1
The kynge's balade. JE

La **pastora** ("Estaba una pastora") s. LCP

A **pastoral** ("Flocks are sporting") See "Flocks are sporting" (Carey)

Pastoral ("Un jour de printemps") See Pastorale (Bizet)

Pastoral ("Peeping from his curtain'd pavilion") French air. TL

Pastorale ("Un jour de printemps."—Pastoral) G. Bizet. Words by J. F. Regnard. e.f. HM 1—PG 1

"**Pastorcitos** del valle, venid." See Villancico

La **pastorella** ("Ahi, meschina pastorella." —The shepherdess) Lombardian folk song. e.i. MSI

La **pastorella** ("La pastorella al prato contenta se ne va."—The shepherdess) F. Schubert. Words by Goldoni. e.i. FM

Lei **pastorieu** (The message of Christmas morn) Noël provençal. e. MF

"**Pat-a-cake.**" Nursery song. WSC

Pat Malloy. Irish air. Words by D. Boucicault. FSS 7—JO

Paté, Lucien
Lied (Franck)

'T **patertje** (Hey, 'twas in the May) Dutch song. d.e. BF 2

"The **path** lay by a babbling brook." See Wouldn't you (Shepard)

Patiently have I waited for the Lord. C. Saint-Saëns. e. SAS 2

Patria (My native land) T. Mattei. e.i. AB 2

La **patrie** amis nous appelle. See Le chant du départ (Méhul)

Patriotic song. See Cancion patriotica (Mexican song)

The **patriots.** Dutch song. e. KSN

Patris sapientia, veritas (bonitas) divina. For English translation see " 'Twas at the matin hour" (Handley)

"**Patter** go the nuts on a frosty morning."
See On a frosty morning

The **patteran**. F. Ames. Words by R.
D. Ware. BSS

Patten, Simon N.
To-morrow (Wesley)

Patzke, Johann Samuel
"Lobt den Herrn" (Rolle)

"**Pau** ole ko'u hoohihi." See Remember
be sure and be there (Hopkins)

Paul, Stuart
Jenny Johnson (Old air)
Ring the bells (Folk air)

Paul and I. Tauwitz. MCS

"**Paul** in the farm-yard his chickens collected." See Paal paa hougje

Paul Jones. Folk song. BSW

"**Paul** let his chickens run out on the hillside." See Paal paa hougje

Paul on the hill. See Paal paa hougje

Paulsen, John Olaf
Am schönsten sommerabend war's
(Grieg)
"Hvorfor svömmer dit öie tidt i en
taareglands" (Rosenfeld)
Med en primulaveris (Grieg)
Til Norge (Grieg)

Paun i kolo. See "Why so silent, tell me,
birdie"

"**Paun** pase, trava raste." See "Why so
silent, tell me, birdie"

The **pauper's** drive. J. J. Hutchinson.
Words by T. Noel. JO

"**Pauvre** Jacques" (Poor Jacques) De
Travanet. e.f. CM 2

Pauvre Pierre. French sea song. e.f.
SMW

"**Pauvre** soldat revient de guerre." See
Le retour du soldat

El **pavu** rial (The peacock) Mexican song.
e.s. BF 2

"The **pawky** auld carle cam' owre the lea."
See The Gaberlunzie man

Pawnee war-song ("Ka de la wats") American Indian folk song. e.in. BO

Payne,
"Kiss me, sweetheart" (Smith)

Payne, John Howard
Home, sweet home (Bishop)

El **payo** (The bumpkin) Mexican song.
e.s. BF 2

"**Pays** merveilleux, jardins fortunés." See
Ô paradis sorti de l'onde (Meyerbeer)

Peace, Albert Lister
"Lead, kindly light"

Peace ("Ah! all peace is lost unto me")
A. Warlamoff. e. KSN

Peace ("Du bist die ruh") See "Du bist
die ruh" (Schubert)

Peace ("Off-spring thou of heav'nly bliss")
F. Liszt. Words by Goethe. e.
HSS 4

Peace hymn of the republic. S. A. Ward.
Words by H. van Dyke. BSS

"The **peace** of the valley." Balfe.
Words by E. Fitzball. DM 2—HSE 3

Peace on earth. Donizetti. Words by
J. R. Lowell. FSS 5—LA—MCS

Peace, the fairest child of heaven. J. Oswald. Words by Mallet. PR 2

"**Peace** to the brave." W. T. Adams.
FSS 6—JSE

"**Peace,** troubled heart." C. Pinsuti.
Words by H. L. D. Jaxone. HSS 2
—HSS 3

"The **peaceful** day is ended." See Summer
even-song (Jones)

The **peaceful** fold (Lebanon) J. Zundel.
Words by H. Bonar. FSS 5
"I was a wandering sheep." WBT

"**Peaceful** slumb'ring on the ocean." S.
Storace. Words by J. Cobb.
BE 5—FSS 4—JE—ME—PR 2
Lullaby. DM 1

"**Peacefully,** my baby, sleep." See Lullaby

The **peach** boy. See Momotaro

The **peacock**. See El pavu rial

Peanut pickin' song. Negro folk song
from Suffolk county, Va. BN 4

Peanut song. Student song. WBT—WC
—WSW
"The man who has plenty of good pea-
nuts." CHS—MPC—NMH

Pearce, Charles William
"Hark! what mean those holy voices"

Pearce, William
The heaving of the lead (Shield)

The **pearl** ("En el fondo del mar") See La
perla (Araya?)

The **pearl** ("Pearl I seek of rarest worth")
Air: Sy je perdoys mon ami. 15th
century chanson. Words by R. Belleau. e. BMC

"**Pearl** I seek of rarest worth." See The
pearl

The **pearl** of th' Irish nation. Irish folk
song. Words by P. O'Kelly. JOI

"The **pearl** of the fountain." See The
maid of Glenconnel

"The **pearl** that worldlings covet." E. J.
Loder. FSS 2

Péarla an brollaig báin (The snowy-
breasted pearl) Irish folk song.
e.ir. BF 2
The snowy-breasted pearl. e. BOS
"There's a colleen fair as May." e.
MMI

"The **pearly** gates aside are rolled." H.
S. Irons. Words by G. P. Grantham.
HC

Pearsall, Robert Lucas de
"In dulci jubilo": 14th century air ar-
ranged
"Mihi est propositum"
Who will o'er the downs

Pearse, M. G.
"O'er Bethlehem's hill, in time of old"
(music by Carrott; Floyd)

Pearson, George C.
"Christ is risen! alleluia"
"Sing, O sing, ye children"

The **peasant** ("Hark to the peasant gay")
Bohemian song. e. KSE

The **peasant** at the wedding. See Bonden
i bryllaupsgarden

Peasant cradle-song (Berceuse du paysan) M. Moussorgsky. Words by Ostrowski. e.f. SC

The **peasant** girl ("Nu ştiu satul ce voeşte") See Tărăncuta

The **peasant** girl ("Yo vivo sola en el mundo") See La guajira

Peasant-idyl (U menîa-l' vo sadochîe) Russian folk song. e. SSR 2

"The **peasant** tastes the sweets of life." Händel. OS 2

Peasant's song. See Canzonetta di campagnuolo

Pease, Alfred Humphries
"Stars of the summer night"

Pease, Frederic H.
"Home of the happy and free"

"**Pease** porridge hot." Nursery song. WBT—WSC

Peck, H. P.
Old Nassau (Langlotz)

Peck, Samuel Minturn
At the making of the hay (Lehmann)

The **peddler** ("See! my pack is filled to over-flowing."—Korobeïnik) Russian song. e.r. BF 1

The **pedlar** ("Come all ye nice maids") Air: Y maelerwr. MMW

Pedro IV, king of Portugal
Hymno nacional
National hymn. See Hymno nacional

Peel, Frederick
"Around the throne of God"
"Heavenly father, send Thy blessing"

"**Peeping** from his curtain'd pavilion." See Pastoral

"**Peer** Swineherd." See "Per Svinaherde"

The **peerless** maiden. See A' mhaighdean àluinn

Peerooshka. See The country feast (Musorgskïi)

Peet, Ashton
Stillness of night (Beach)

"**Peg** Nicholson was a good bay mare." Air: Chevy chase. Words by R. Burns. BSR

Peg o' Ramsay. Ancient air. VFS

"**Peggie**, now the king's come." Scottish air: Carle, an the king come. Words by Ramsay. PS 2

Peggy ("Tho' Peggy's charms have oft been sung") T. A. Arne. PR 2

Peggy bawn ("As I gaed o'er the Highland hills") Irish folk song. MMI

Peggy Browne ("Oh, dark, sweetest girl") Irish air: Diarmid ua Duda, or, Dermot O'Dowd. Words from the Irish. e. MMI

Peggy Walker. Kentucky mountain song. WLT
Variant of: My parents treated me tenderly

Peggy Wynne. 18th century song. ME

Peggy Wilkins ("To London go with me") Welsh air. Words by J. Parry. MMW

"**Peña** de aquel cerro alto." See Peña Hueca

Peña Hueca (A teamster's song) Spanish-American song. e.s. LSS

Pena tiranna (Torment unending) G. F. Händel. e.i. KS 3

"**Penitence**, fearful pain." Bach. e. OS 2

The **penitent** and the drunkard. See Le penitent et l'ivrogne

Le **penitent** et l'ivrogne (The penitent and the drunkard) French Canadian folk song. e.f. BFS

Penney, Clarence John
She is my Angelina (from Her majesty's mischief-maker)

"**Pennsylvania**, the gem of creation." See Three cheers for the red and the blue

Pensée d'automne (Autumn thought) J. Massenet. Words by A. Silvestre. e.f. CM 2

"Il **pensier** stà negli oggetti" ("Ah, poor heart") J. Haydn. e.i. BAS 2

"Il **pensier** stà negli oggetti" ("Ev'ry thought we have") e.i. SOA 4

"The **people** that walked in darkness." G. F. Händel. SAS 4

The **people's** prayer (Melita) J. B. Dykes. Words by J. Oxenham. LA

Pepita's mouth. See La boca de Pepita

La **Peppinetta** (Peppinetta) Lombardian folk song. e.i. MSI

Pepusch, John Christopher
"Celamina, of my heart"
The wandering beauty

"**Per** la gloria d'adorarvi" ("Eyes so tender") G. B. Bononcini. e.i. PG 1

"**Per** la gloria" ("Proud and peerless") e.i. BAS 2—BS 2

"**Per** la gloria d'adorarvi" ("For the love my heart doth prize") e.i. PA 2

"**Per** la gloria d'adorarvi" ("Since 'tis glory to adore you") e.i. KS 1

"**Per** la gloria d'adorarvi" ("Though I only bow before you") e.i. FEI 1

Per me giunto (Death of Rodrigo) G. Verdi. e.i. SOA 4

"**Per** non istare in ozio." G. Donizetti. e.i. SOA 2

"**Per** pietà" ("O have pity") A. Stradella. e.i. FEI 2

"**Per** secale." Air: Comin' thro' the rye. Words by J. Smith. l. SSS

"**Per** Svinaherde" ("Peer Swineherd") Swedish folk song. e.sw. HSOS

Per te d'immenso giubilo. For English translation see "Hail to the happy bridal day" (Donizetti)

"**Per** voi, ghiottoni inutili." See Canzone del rabbino (Mascagni)

"The **perbadus** lady, the perbadus lady." See Pretty Nancy of Yarmouth

Percival, James Gates
The carrier pigeon (Irish air)
"Faintly flow, thou falling river" (Spanish air)

Percy, John
"Alas! for the days that are gone"
"Sweet smells the briar"
Wapping old stairs

Percy, Thomas
"O Nannie, wilt thou gang wi' me" (Carter)

"Perdí tu amor, perdí la dicha entera." See La fe

Los **peregrinos** (The pilgrims) Mexican song. e.s. BF 2

The **perfect** hour. See L'heure exquise (Hahn)

The **perfect** rose. See "Den yndigste rose"

"Perfidi! all' Anglo contro me v'unite." See Pietà, rispetto, onore (Verdi)

Perfume of a flower. See Parfum de fleur (Blanc)

Pergolesi, Giovanni Battista
"A Serpina penserete" (from La serva padrona)
"All of anguish most unsparing." See "Ogni pena più spietata"
The angels' song
"Bella mia" (from Il maestro di musica)
"Gentle shepherd." See "Se tu m'ami, se sospiri"
"Glory to God in the highest, to God in the highest." See The angels' song
"If thou lov'st me." See "Se tu m'ami, se sospiri"
If 'tis I alone thou lovest. See "Se tu m'ami, se sospiri"
Nina
O Lord, have mercy upon me
"O thou loveliest." See "Bella mia"
"Ogni pena più spietata"
"On Serpina think with pleasure." See "A Serpina penserete"
"Que ne suis-je la fougère"
"Se tu m'ami, se sospiri"
"Stizzoso, mio stizzoso"
"Though my day be dark with sorrow." See "Ogni pena più spietata"
"'Tis three long days." See Nina
"Tre giorni son che Nina." See Nina
"Unruly, sir, unruly." See "Stizzoso, mio stizzoso"
"Would I were the fern." See "Que ne suis-je la fougère"

Peri, Jacopo
"In that pure flame." See "Nel puro ardor"
Invocation of Orpheus. See Invocazione de Orfeo
Invocazione de Orfeo (from Euridice)
"Nel puro ardor" (from Euridice)

Pericás, Jaime
Así canto mis amores
El himno de Puerto Rico
Puesta de sol

El **perico.** See "Señora, su periquito"

The **perils** of the isle. Manx air: Ne kirree fo'n sniaghtey, or, The sheep under the snow. Modern words by F. Kidson. MM

Perinet, Joachim
Der schneider Kakadu (Müller)
"Wer niemals einen rausch gehabt" (Müller)

El **periquito.** Cuban folk song. e.s. HS

Perjura. M. Lerdo de Tejada. Words by F. Luna y Drusina. s. LCP

Perkins, Theodore Edson
"Carol, sweetly carol, a Saviour born today"
Jesus is mine
The rose bush

Perkins, William Oscar
Good-night

Perkins, Wilton
The happy family (Jones)

La **perla.** Attributed to J. Araya. Words by E. Blasco. s. LCP
La perla (The pearl) e.s. BF 2

"La **perle** est aux ondes." See À toi mon coeur (Gounod)

Pernette. French folk song. e.f. TSF

Perri merri dictum, domine. Old nursery ditty. FSS 1

Perronet, Edward
"All hail the power of Jesus' name" (Old air; also music by Holden)

Persian song. See "Sweet maid, come, if thou wouldst charm"

The **Persia's** crew. Forcastle song. CR

Perti, Giacomo Antonio
"Begli occhi, io non mi pento"
"I yielded without repenting." See "Begli occhi, io non mi pento"

O **pescador** (The fisherman) Portuguese folk song. e.po. BF 2

"**Pescador** da barca bella." See O pescador

Pescator, affonda l'esca (Fisherman, thy bait now lower) Ponchielli. e.i. OPS 4
"Ah! pescator." e.i. SOA 4
Pescator, affonda l'esca (Fisherman with hook well baited) e.i. KS 5

Peskett, Frank
Ring the joyful Christmas bells

Pessard, Émile Louis Fortuné
"Bonjour, Suzon"
"Good morning, Claire." See "Bonjour, Suzon"

Pestalozza, A.
Ciribiribin

Pestel, Paul
"Yes! the die is cast" (attributed also to J. W. Kalliwoda)

Peter Damiani, Saint. See Damiani, Peter, Saint

Peter, go ring them bells. Negro spiritual. JP
Peter, go ring dem bells. HR—JB

Peter Gray. College song. CHS—HSD —MPC

Peter on the sea. Negro spiritual. HR

Peters, J. Girvin
Rah! for the black and blue

Peterson, Frederick
  At parting (Rogers)
Le petit chasseur. Old French song. f.
  DO
Le petit matelot ("Über die beschwerden
  dieses lebens") P. Gaveaux. g.
  ED 1
Le petit navire. French sailors' song. e.f.
  SMW
"Petit soldat de guerre" (Little soldier-
  man) French folk song. e.f. TSF
La petite bergère ("The little sheep-girl")
  Belgian song. e.f. BF 2
La petite souris grise (The little gray
  mouse) French Canadian folk song.
  e.f. BFS
Petites roses (Sweet wild roses) H. A.
  Cesek. Words by M. May. e.f.
  SM 1
  Wild roses. e. WBW
"Petko Radi prŭsten dade, more." See
  Rada and Petko
Petri, Carl G.
  "When the shades of evening gather"
  (Composer unknown)
Petrus ("Bula sobĭ Marusĭã") Ukrainian
  song. e.r. BF 1
Petrus klage (The remorse of Peter)
  Brandts-Buys. e.g. HSS 4
Petrusia. See Winter
Pettings, S. J.
  Song of Arbor day
Pettman, Edgar
  "Hail! sweet Babe, so pure and holy"
"Un peu rude vous trouvez ma chanson."
  See The blacksmith (Koneman)
"Peuple français, peuple de braves." See
  La Parisienne (Auber)
Peyre, Louis de
  Ce que je suis sans toi (Gounod)
Das pfäfflein (The jolly friar) A. Schäffer.
  e.g. AB 2
Pfeffel, Gottlieb Conrad
  Die tabakspfeife (Pilz)
Pfeil, Heinrich
  Beim liebchen zu haus
  "Calm is the lake." See "Still ruht
  der see"
  "Still ruht der see"
  With my loved one at home. See
  Beim liebchen zu haus
Pfohl, J. K.
  "College ties can ne'er be broken"
Pharaoh's army. See Turn back Pharaoh's
  army
Phébus, Gaston. See Foix, Gaston, comte
  de, known as Gaston Phoebus
"A pheigidhonnnam blàthshul." See Ho-
  ro mo nighean donn, bhòidheach
Phelps, E. C.
  Innisfail
  Thy story bides for aye
  "When Jordan hushed"
Phelps, George Turner
  Croon of the dew (Gilbert)
Phidile ("Ich war erst sechszehn sommer
  alt") J. A. P. Schulz. Words by M.
  Claudius. g. ED 2

Phile, Philip
  Evening colors. See "Hail, Columbia"
  "Hail, Columbia"
  Hail Columbia, The new (same air as
  "Hail, Columbia")
Philip the falconer. E. J. Loder. Words
  by W. H. Bellamy. HSE 3
**Philippe, Adolphe, Gallet, Louis, and Blau,
Édouard**
  Ô souverain, ô juge, ô père (Massenet)
Philips, Elizabeth
  Farewell to my harp
"Philis plus avare que tendre" ("Phyllis,
  grasping, ne'er would philander")
  Words by Dufresny. e.f. WB
Phillida and Corydon ("In the merry month
  of May") J. Wilson. Words by
  N. Breton. BE 7—DM 1
  "In the merry month of May." MM
  Phillida and Coridon. PR 1
Phillida flouts me. 16th century song.
  BE 2—DM 1—HSE 2—MM
Phillips, Gus
  McSorley's twins
Phillips, Henry
  Christmas is coming
  On Christmas morn
  "Shall I, wasting in despair"
  Woman. See "Shall I, wasting in des-
  pair"
Phillips, Jonas B.
  Arms are strong and hearts are true
  (Composer unknown)
Phillips, Phillip
  Home of the soul
Phillips, R. E.
  De black-bird an' de crow (Negro air)
  I doan' want fu' t' stay hyeah no longah
  (Negro air)
  Ma Lawd's a-writin' down time (Ne-
  gro air)
  When de debble comes 'round (Negro
  air)
Phillis ("I never saw") See "I never saw
  a face till now" (Pack)
"Phillis, I can ne'er forgive it." H. Pur-
  cell. MM
"Phillis is my only joy." J. W. Hobbs.
  Words by C. Sedley. HSE 3
"Phillis, on the new-made hay." Air:
  Amarillis told her swain. Words re-
  written. PR 1
"Phillis on the new-mown hay." Air:
  Amarillis told her swain. Traditional
  words. BE 6
"Phillis, talk no more of passion" (The
  reproach) G. Monro. ME
"Phillis, talk not more of passion." D.
  Purcell. PR 1
Phillis the fair. Air: Robin Adair.
  Words by R. Burns. BSB
  "While larks with little wing." BSR
"Phillis, we don't grieve." T. A. Arne.
  PR 2
"Phillis, why should we delay." H.
  Lawes. PR 1
Philp, Elizabeth
  Song of the hop-pickers

Phoebus, Gaston. See Foix, Gaston, comte de, known as Gaston Phoebus
"Phoebus, arise." C. von Sternberg. Words by Drummond of Hawthornden. TL
The phoenix ("I pass all my hours") P. Humfrey. Words attributed to Charles II. BOH—JE
"I pass all my hours in a shady old grove." BE 3—NG—PR 1
Phosphorescence. See Meeresleuchten (Loewe)
Phyla, Philip. See Phile, Philip
"Phyllis, grasping, ne'er would philander." See "Philis plus avare que tendre"
"Phyllis no more I love." See "Filli, non t'amo più" (Carissimi)
Phyllis und die mutter ("Ihren schäfer zu erwarten") Composer and author of words unknown. g. ED 1—ED 2
Phylo, Philip. See Phile, Philip
Pi-Pi-Pi-Pi-Pi. Jewish lullaby. e.y. GF 1
"Piacer d'amor più che un dì sol non dura." See "Plaisir d'amour" (Martini)
Piano, piano, canto pio. See "Wie nahte mir der schlummer" (Weber)
"Pibroch of Donuil Dhu." Scottish air. Words by W. Scott. PS 1
"Pibroch of Donuil Dhu" (Piobaireach Donuil Duibh) MMS
Piccini, Niccolò
"O night, mysterious goddess." See "Ô nuit, déesse du mystère"
"O notte, o dea del mistero." See "Ô nuit, déesse du mystère"
"Ô nuit, déesse du mystère" (from Le faux lord)
Se il ciel mi divide (from Alessandro nell' Indie)
Since heaven has torn me. See Se il ciel mi divide
Piccolomini, Maria
Ecce homo
Ora pro nobis
Pardoned
Pickering, George, and Gray, Charles
The minstrel (Scottish air)
A picnic on the grass. German folk air. Words by H. H. Harbour. DO
"Pienso en ti, Teresita mia." See Teresita mia
Pierce, E. H.
Graduation song no. 2. See "How sad, 'mid the sunshine"
"How sad, 'mid the sunshine"
Winter
Piercy, H.
The beggar girl
"Over the mountain." See The beggar girl
Pierlala. Belgian song. e.fl. BF 2
Pierné, Gabriel
À Lucette
Dost thou not know. See Le sais-tu bien
Le sais-tu bien
Sérénade
To Lucette. See À Lucette

Pierpont, J. S.
Jingle, bells
Pierpont, John
Warren's address (Scottish air)
Pierpont, Victor N.
Cradle song (Schubert)
Faith (Mozart)
Pierrot. W. M. Hutchinson. Words by Weatherly. FSS 5
"Pierrot! Pierrot! Babette is calling sweet and low." See Pierrot (Hutchinson)
Piésn Shemakhánskoi tzarítzui K'sólntzu. See Hymn to the sun (Rimskiĭ-Korsakov)
Piésnia lubáshi. See The song of the bride (Rimskiĭ-Korsakov)
Piersol, Charlotte
Merrily ring the bells (Spanish air)
Sing, joyously sing (German air)
Pierson, Henry Hugo
"Ye mariners of England"
"Pietà, mio caro bene" ("Have pity, my beloved") G. M. Bononcini. e.i. FEI 1
Pietà, rispetto, onore. G. Verdi. e.i. SOA 4
"Pietà, Signore" ("O Lord, have pity") Attributed to A. Stradella. e.i. FEI 2
"Pietà Signore" ("Pity, O Saviour") e.i. HSS 2—KF 2
The pigeon ("Why tarries my love") 18th century song. ME
"The pigeons coo—the spring's approaching now." See Cormac oge
Pigot, John Edward
Our own little isle (Irish air)
The pigtail. F. F. Bullard. Words by A. von Chamisso. e. TL
Pije kuba. See "Jacob, drink"
Pike, Albert
Dixie (Emmett)
Pike, G. S.
Gentle Nettie Moore
Pike, Harry Hale
"Ring, happy bells of Easter time"
Pike, Marshall S.
Composer
"Happy are we to-night"
Composer and author
"Home again, home again"
Author
Gentle Nettie Moore (Pike, G. S.)
Grave of Washington (Crosby)
Lone starry hours (Power)
Pilgerspruch ("Lass dich nur nichts") F. Mendelssohn-Bartholdy. Words by P. Flemming. g. ED 3
The pilgrim ("Oh! happy, happy groves") J. Barrett. DM 2
The pilgrim ("The way had been long") S. Adams. Words by B. Abercrombie. HSS 3—HSS 4
The Pilgrim fathers. See Landing of the Pilgrims (Browne)
The pilgrim of love. H. R. Bishop. Words by Dimond (Mrs Opie) BE 4 —DM 1—HSE 1

"Pilgrim swallow, lightly winging." See La rondinella

The pilgrimage to Skellig. See Móirín ni Chealla

The pilgrims ("En nombre del cielo") See Los peregrinos

Pilgrims ("Hark! hark") See "Hark! hark, my soul" (Dykes); "Hark! hark! my soul" (Smart)

The pilgrims ("The way is long") F. H. Cowen. Words by A. Procter. HSS 3 —HSS 4

Pilgrims' chorus. R. Wagner. [Tr of Beglückt dorf nun dich] e. TFC 1 —TL

    Chorus of pilgrims. e. LA
    Pilgrim chorus. e. WBT
    Pilgrim's song. e. WSC

Pilgrim's song ("I joy once more now") See Pilgrims' chorus (Wagner)

Pilgrim's song ("I'm a poor, wayfarin' stranger") Negro spiritual. HR

"The pilgrims throng thro' the city gates." See Calvary (Rodney)

"Pill' ura chi ti vitti" ("O once mine eyes had seen you."—Siciliana) Italian folk song. e.i. SMF

Pilot ("Jesus, Saviour") See "Jesus, Saviour, pilot me" (Gould)

The pilot ("Oh! pilot, 'tis a fearful night") S. Nelson. Words by T. H. Bayly. BE 6—FSS 4—HSE 3—JO—WBT

Pilz, Karl Philipp Emanuel
    Adelaide
    Der edelmann und der invalide. See Die tabakspfeife
    Die tabakspfeife

Pindar, Peter, pseud. See Wolcot, John

The pine-tree ("By snow fields encompass'd."—Der fichtenbaum) M. Balakireff. Words from the Russian of Lermontoff. e.g. NM 1

The pine-tree ("O pine-tree lonely standing") M. T. Salter (music and words) AA

The pine tree ("O tannenbaum") See Der tannenbaum

The pine tree swing. German folk air. Words by H. H. Harbour. DO

Pingree, Maud Parepa
    Good-night

Pinkham, John E.
    "See! the morning star is dwelling"

Pinna, Joseph de
    "What fairy-like music"

Pinsuti, Ciro
    Bedouin love-song
    "The bugler pac'd thro' the driving snow"
    Christmas come again
    The crusaders
    "Good-night, good-night, beloved"
    I love my love
    "If love were what the rose is"
    In shadowland
    In the golden eventide
    Laddie
    The land beyond
    "Lead, kindly light"

    "Moonlight and music"
    "Peace, troubled heart"
    Safe home at last
    A spring song
    "Welcome, pretty primrose"
    "When the swallow comes"

Die Pinzgauer wallfahrt ("Die binschgauer wollten wallfahrten") Osterreichisches volkslied. g. ED 1

Piobaireach Donuil Duibh. See "Pibroch of Donuil Dhu"

"Pious orgies, pious airs." G. F. Händel. SAS 1

The pipe. Air: A wet sheet and a flowing sea. SSS

A piper ("A piper in the streets") Irish air. Words by S. O'Sullivan. FSI

The piper ("Piping down the valleys") W. W. Gilchrist. Words by W. Blake. TL

"The piper came to our town." See The piper of Dundee

Piper Heidsieck. See Give me the waltz (Pratt)

"A piper in the streets today." See A piper

The piper of Dundee. Scottish song. PS 1

"Piping down the valleys wild." See The piper (Gilchrist)

"Piper, pipe a tune, call the dancers out." See Wedding joy

The pirate. See Der seeräuber (Gumbert)

Pirates' chorus. Balfe. HSD
    "Ever be happy." FSS 4

Pitt, William
    Barney Buntline (Old English air)

"Pitter, patter, pitter, patter." See The shower (Scofield)

Pitts, William S.
    The little brown church in the vale

"Pity for one in childhood torn." See Pity one in childhood torn (Balfe)

Pity, kind gentlemen, friends of humanity. See The beggar girl (Piercy)

"Pity, O Savior." See "Pietà, Signore" (Stradella)

Pity one in childhood torn. M. W. Balfe. FSS 8

"Pity Reuben Ranzo." See Reuben Ranzo

Piuriuri, I'd marry you. See Piuriuri, ti vo' sposà

Piuriuri, ti vo' sposà (Piuriuri, I'd marry you) Romanesca song. e.i. MSI

Pjesma. See "Come, my dearest, why so sad"

"Place near to me the fragrant mignonette, dear." See Allerseelen (Lassen)

"Place on the board sweet mignonette before us." See Allerseelen (Strauss)

"Placid see on the lea." See Menuet d'Exaudet (Exaudet)

The plains of Mexico ("Did you never hear tell") Windlass chantey. SMW
    For variants of this song see following song of similiar title; also "Santy Anna"

The plains of Mexico ("Santa Anna gain'd the day") Capstan chantey. KB

Plaisable,
"Room, room for a rover"
"Plaisir d'amour" ("The joys of love")
J. Martini; wrongly attributed to
G. Martini. Words by Florian.
e.f.i. PA 1
"The joys of love." e. BC
"Plaisir d'amour" (Fugitive love) e.f.
MSS 1
El **planatar.** B. D. Colón. Words by
A. Fernández Grilo. s. LCP
Planché, James Robinson
Composer and author
"Gentle Zitella." See Love's ritornella
Love's ritornella (from The brigand)
Author
"Draw the sword, Scotland" (Scottish
air)
Far o'er hill and dell (Composer un-
known)
"O Araby! dear Araby" (Weber)
O 'tis a glorious sight to see (Weber)
"Ocean! thou mighty monster" (Web-
er)
Rise, gentle moon (Barnett)
Spring, gentle spring (Riviere)
The springtime of the year (Composer
unknown)
Planes, Vincento López y. See López y
Planes, Vincento
Planquette, Robert
Happy summer
Legend of the bell (from Les cloches
de Cornville) .
"On billow rocking" (from Les cloches
de Cornville)
"Silent horses" (from Les cloches de
Cornville)
Song of the bells. See Legend of the
bell
Waltz song (from Les cloches de Corn-
ville)
Planting a garden. Flemish air. Words
by R. Compton. DO
Planting the tree. See "From forest wide
and free" (Oliver)
Plaudite coeli. For English translation
see "Ye heav'ns, uplift your voice"
The **plausible** lover. H. Carey. PR 2
"**Play** a little tune." See A little set of
quills
Playford, John
"Comely swain, why sitt'st thou so"
Playing ball on the stairs. French folk
air. Words by R. Compton. DO
A **pleading.** Tschaikowsky. e. BS 1
"**Pleasant** journey." French folk song. e.
CST
Pleasant old age. J. Wynne. Words
from Anacreon. e. ME
"**Pleasure** climbs to every mountain." Goll-
mick. FSS 4
The **pleasure** of melancholy. See Wonne
der wehmuth (Beethoven)
Pleasure-pain. J. Kjerulf. Words by W.
D. Howells. LBR
"**Plecat-a** motul la tara" (The highlander)
Rumanian song. e.ru. BF 2

A **pledge** to Columbia. Columbia univer-
sity song. K. Wilhelm. Words by
F. P. Delgado. CU
Plenívshis rósoi, salavyéi. See Eastern
romance (Rimskiï-Korsakov)
Pleschtschejeff, A. See Pleshcheev, A.
Pleshcheev, A.
"Another little hour I begged" (Gre-
chaninov)
"Deep in love was I" (Rachmaninov)
Over the steppe (Grechaninov)
A prayer (Kalinnikov)
Springtime (Tchaikovsky)
Plestcheïev, A. See Pleshcheev, A.
Pleurez! pleurez, mes yeux. J. Massenet.
e.f. SOA 1
Pleurez! pleurez, mes yeux (Oh, weep!
oh, weep, mine eyes) e.f. OPS 1
Pleyel, Ignaz Josef
"Gracious Spirit, Love divine"
"Hasten, sinner, to be wise"
Pleyel's hymn. See "Gracious Spirit,
Love divine"
"Praise to God, immortal praise"
Thanksgiving. See "Praise to God,
immortal praise"
Ploug, Carl
Liden Karen (Heise)
The **ploughboy** ("Come, all you jolly
ploughboys") Folk song: Sussex
version. BOH—MM
The ploughboy ("As a jolly young
ploughboy") Irish version. JOI
Variants: The jolly ploughboy; The
simple ploughboy
The **ploughboy** ("A flaxen headed cow-
boy") Shield. Words by O'Keeffe.
BE 2—DM 1—HSE 1
The **ploughman** ("My name it is Jack")
Scottish air. Words by J. Hamilton.
MMS
"The **ploughman,** he's a bonie lad." Air:
The ploughman. Words by R. Burns.
BSR
The **ploughman's** ditty ("When Molly
smiles") 18th century English song.
BE 5—ME
Plouvé, J.
"Hush, my darling, repose thee"
Plouvier, Édouard
David chantant devant Saül (Bordèse)
Plowden, Mrs Dorothea
"The coy, blushing Sylvia"
Plowden, Mrs F.
"Adieu to delight" (Graeff)
"The **plumflow'r,** O has it bloomed." See
Flower song
Plumptre, Edward Hayes
"Rejoice, ye pure in heart" (Messiter)
"La **plus** aimable à mon gré." See Ramène
tes moutons
Plus blanche que la blanche hermine. G.
Meyerbeer. e.f. SOA 3
"**Plus** de dépit, plus de tristesse" ("An-
guish of mind, sadness, too, leaves
me") A. E. M. Grétry. e.f. MC
"Plus de dépit, plus de tristesse" ("No
more annoy, sorrowful meekness")
e.f. SOA 1

"**Plus** de tourments et plus de peine." J. Massenet. e.f. SOA 1

Plus grand dans son obscurité. C. Gounod. e.f. SOA 1

Plus grand dans son obscurité (Far greater in his lowly state) e.f. MSS 2—SS 2

Plus grand, dans son obscurité (More grand is his humble estate) e.f. OPS 1

Plus grand, dans son obscurité (More royal in his humble state) e.f. KS 2

Plus ne suis ce que j'ai été (The sun dial) e. GO

"**Plus** ne verrai mon doux ami." See Loin de lui (Dancla)

Plymouth rock. See Landing of the Pilgrims (Browne)

Plymouth sound. English folk air. Modern words by S. Baring-Gould. BSW

"**Po'** lil' Lolo." See "Pov' piti Lolotte"

Po nad Dónom sad tzvyetyót. See The banks of the Don (Musorgskïi)

The **poacher** ("When I was bound apprentice") Old Somersetshire song. HSE 2—SSS
Variant: The Lincolnshire poacher

The **poacher's** song ("In thorny woods") Ballad. MM

"**Pobre** mi madre querida." See A mi madre (Betinoti)

"**Pobrecita** de la Indita." See La India

The **pocket** Gray. E. Newton. Words by J. M. Bulloch. SSS

Pocock, Isaac
"Oh! say not woman's heart is bought" (Whitaker)

"**Pod** tím nášim okeneckem." See "Just without our little window"

"**Podkóweczki** dajcie ognia." See Oberek

Poduï, nepogodushka. See The lover's lament

Poe, Edgar Allan
The bells (Foote)
Israfel (King)
The raven (Composer unknown)

La **poésie**. See The spirit of poesy (Arenski)

The **poet** ("Let me go where'er I will") F. W. Kücken. Words by R. W. Emerson. LBR

Poet and critic (Nachtigall und kukuk) C. A. Cui. Words by A. S. Pushkin. e.g. SC

The **poet** and the children. F. Gumbert. Words by J. G. Whittier. LBR

"**Poet** of the laurel wreath." See "Lauriger Horatius"

El **poeta**. Air: La perla. s. LCP

Poetry. A. S. Sullivan. Words by S. Fay. TFC 2

A **poet's** epitaph (Epitaphe) N. Metner. Words by A. Biely. e.f. NR 3

"The **poets**, in conscience, have teased us too long." See Peggy Wynne

The **poet's** last song. See En digters sidste sang (Grieg)

The **poet's** love. See "Ich grolle nicht" (Schumann)

Pogner's address. See Pogner's anrede (Wagner)

Pogner's anrede (Address) Wagner. e.g. OPS 4
"'Nun hört, und versteht mich recht" (Pogner's address) e.g. BS 2— SOA 5

Pohlenz, August
Der kleine tambour
Liebes-A-B-C
The little drummer. See Der kleine tambour
Matrosenlied

Poïdu mlada po Dunaïu. See The old lover and the new

Poignard, Jules
Gavotte du masque (Georges)

The **poisoned** lover. See L'avvelenato

Poissl, J. N., freiherr von
Auf der alm

"**Poland** is not lost forever." See Polish national song (Oginski?)

Poland still lives. See Polish national song (Oginski?)

"**Poland's** glory is not vanished." See Polish national song (Oginski?)

"**Poland's** not yet dead in slavr'y." See Polish national song (Oginski?)

Poli pumehana. See Dear heart (Nape)

Polish maiden song. Goria. e. FSS 1

Polish May song. Polish song. e. FSS 1—JS—WBT—WSC
May song. e. LA—NMS

Polish national song ("Jeszcze Polska") Attributed to Oginski; attributed also to Sowinski. Words by Wybitski; attributed also to P. Soboieski. e.p. BSP—WA. e. only KSN—WCP
Jescze Polska (National song of Poland.—"Poland is not lost for ever") e. BMC
National song (Polish). e. GO
Poland still lives (Teszcze Polska) e. BD
Poland's national song. e. WBT
"Poland's not yet dead in slavery." e.p. SN
Polish hymn. e.p. MP—NMH— NMS
Polish national anthem ("Jeszcze Polska nie zginęla") e.p. BF 1

Polish patriotic hymn ("'Mid fire and dense smoke") Air: Z dymen pozaròw. e. BMC

Polish patriotic song ("Hvorfor svulmer weichselfloden") See Polsk faedrelandssang (Gade)

Politeness ("Politeness is to do and say") D. Stevens. BSS

Polka (Polska) Finnish folk song. e.fi. BF 1

Polkovódyetz. See Death, the commander (Musorgskiï)

The poll-parrot. See "Señora, su periquito"

Polly (Eyes of old Yale blue) D. S. Smith. Words by R. Watterson. CHS

"Polly and I." A. M. Wakefield. Words by F. Langbridge. WBW

"Polly and I" (A bunch of cowslips) MSF 2—SM 3

Polly, my sweetheart. R. G. Cole. Words by S. A. Jones. CHS

Polly Oliver. Folk song. Modern words by H. F. Sheppard. BE 7

Polly Oliver. Folk song: North Carolina version. CSE
Variants: The cruel ship's carpenter; Pretty Polly Oliver

"Polly, put the kettle on." Children's song. FMB—WBT—WSC

Polly Stewart. See Lovely Polly Stewart

"Polly was in the room with the nurses sitting." See Parrot song (Musorgskiï)

Polly-wolly-doodle. Old song. HSD—JSE—MPC—NMP—SSS—WA— WBT WC—WSW

Polonaise ("Oui, pour ce soir") See Je suis Titania (Thomas)

Polonaise ("Polonaise, the dance of nobles."—Polonez) Polish dance. e.p. BF 1

Polonez. See Polonaise

Polonski, J.
The reapers (Vassilenko)
The skylark (Grechaninov)

Poloobeela ya na petchál svayú. See The soldier's bride (Rachmaninov)

Polsk faedrelandssang (Polish patriotic song) N. W. Gade. Words by C. Hauch. da.e. SSN

Polska. See Polka

The polyglot's wooing. H. Lozier. CHS

"Pompe, vane di morte." See Dove sei (Händel)

Ponchielli, Amilcare
"Ah! pescator." See Pescator, affonda l'esca
The blind girl's song. See "Voce di donna o d'angelo"
"Cielo e mar" (from La Gioconda)
Fisherman, thy bait now lower. See Pescator, affonda l'esca
Fisherman with hook well baited. See Pescator, affonda l'esca
"Heaven and ocean." See "Cielo e mar"
Light to my dark soul bringing. See "Voce di donna o d'angelo"
"Ocean and sky." See "Cielo e mar"
Ombre di mia prosapia (from La Gioconda)
Pescator, affonda l'esca (from La Gioconda)
Stella del marinar (from La Gioconda)
"Thanks to thee, angelic voice." See "Voce di donna o d'angelo"
"Voce di donna o d'angelo" (from La Gioconda)

Poniatowski, Jozef Michal Franciszek Xaver Jan, prince
On Christmas morning (same air as Yeoman's wedding song)
Yeoman's wedding song

Le pont d'Avignon. See "Sur le pont d'Avignon" (French version)

Pontet, Henry
The broken pitcher
Tit for tat

Pontius, W. H.
Long live, long live America

The pony ride. Flemish folk air. Words by R. Compton. DO

"A poor beggar's daughter." 17th century song. DM 1

"Poor Bessy was a sailor's wife." See The parting (Hodson)

"Poor dog Bright." Children's song. WSC

"Poor Ellen lov'd Gwilym." See Gwilym and Ellen

"Poor insect, poor insect." See The May fly (Callcott)

Poor Jack. C. Dibdin (music and words) BE 1—HSE 2—JO

Poor Jacques. See "Pauvre Jacques" (Travanet)

"Poor Joe, the marine." J. Ashley. HSE 2

"Poor Johnny's dead, I hear his knell." Round. FSS 5

The poor little gipsy. Arnold. BE 2

"Poor Marguerite beside the wood." See L'occasion manquée (Norman version)

Poor mourner. Negro spiritual. DF

Poor old horse. English folk song. FSF —SO
—Devon version. BSW
—Warwickshire version. SEF 2—SF 4

Poor old Joe. See Old black Joe (Foster)

Poor old man ("I say, old man") Halliard chantey. CR
Variant of: The dead horse

"A poor old man came a-riding by." See The dead horse

"Poor old man, your horse is going to die." See The dead horse

Poor old Reuben Ranzo. Pulling chantey. FSF—SE
Variant of: Reuben Ranzo

The poor old slave. Negro song. NMP —WBT—WSW
Good old Jeff. SSS

"Poor old winter can't you be gay." See Winter

Poor Omie. Folk song: Kentucky version. CSE
—Alleghany, N.C. version. CSE
—Big Laurel, N.C. version. CSE

"Poor Ragna, her leave for the city is taking." See "Ho Ragne va fattig"

"Poor Sally sits a-weeping." Folk song from Dorset. SF 1

"The poor soul sat sighing." See The willow song (16th century air); The willow song (Hook); The willow song (Humfrey); The willow song (Rossini); The willow song (Sullivan)

"Poor tho' my cot may be." G. Donizetti. [Tr of In questo semplice modesto asilo] e. FSS 4

"Poor troubador am I." See El trobador

Poor Tom. C. Dibdin (music and words) JO
"Then farewell! my trim-built wherry." BE 2—BOH—HSE 1—JE—ME

The poor voter on election day. German air. Words by J. G. Whittier. LBR

"A poor wayfaring man of grief" (Duane) G. Coles. Words by J. Montgomery. FSS 3

"Poor wounded heart." M. Vogrich. Words by T. Moore. AB 2

"A poore foule sat sighing." See The willow song: parody

Pop! goes the weasel. Children's song. FMB—WSC

Pope, Alexander
"Rise, crowned with light" (music by Lvov; Oliver)
"Where'er you walk" (Händel)

The pope. See "Der papst lebt herrlich in der welt"

Pope and sultan. See "Der papst lebt herrlich in der welt"

Popely,
Law, physic, and divinity
"Three rosy-faced topers." See Law, physic, and divinity

"Poppy, little purple lady." See "Amapolita morada"

"Por ti respira." Mexican folk song. e.s. HS

"Porgi, amor." Mozart. e.i. PP

"Porqué, Creador del mundo." See Imanírta (Valderrama)

"Porque me dizes chorando." See Modinha

"Porro dunque morì." See Se il ciel mi divide (Piccinni)

Porteous, baroness
Dreams (Strelezki)

Porter, Mrs
"Thou hast wounded the spirit that loved thee"

Porter, Walter
"Come, come, my lovers"

Porter lied ("Lasst mich euch fragen") F. von Flotow. e.g. SOA 5

A Portuguesa. Portuguese national hymn. A. Keil. Words by H. Lopes de Mendonça. e.po. NA

Portuguese hymn (Reading?) See "Adeste fideles"; "How firm a foundation"

Portuguese song. See "The rose in the air"

"Pōs pot henéssetai." See Treue liebe (Kücken)

Posate, dormite (Sleep on, then) G. B. Bassani. e.i. PA 2

"Pošetala bela bula." See How fair is she

Posey boy. Vermont folk song. SSH
Variant of: The swapping song

Posmotrite-ka, dobrye liûdi. See The three gifts

"Possenti Numi." See "O Isis und Osiris" (Mozart)

"De possum meat am good to eat." See Carve dat possum (Lucas)

"Possum settin' on a hick'ry limb." See Hie away home

Die post (The post) F. Schubert. Words by W. Müller. e.g. GMF

The post captain. W. Shield. Words by Rannie. ME

"The post-house lamp had died away." See Three-in-hand

Postgate, I. J.
"Fields of gold are glowing" (Brown)

The postilion. F. Abt. e. FSS 3—MS

Postilion's song. See The village Don Juan

Pöthko,
Warnung vor dem Rhein

"Potrà lasciare il rio" ("Bid yonder rushing river") Attributed to F. Supriani. e.i. FEI 2

Pott, Francis
"Angel voices" (Sullivan)

Potter, S.
Private Tommy Atkins

Poulton, George R.
Little Bennie

The pound of tow. Irish folk song. JOI

"Pour forth no more unheeded prayers." Händel. BS 1

"Pour forth to God your songs of gladness." See Noël (Gounod)

"Pour fuir son souvenir." See Ô jours heureux (Meyerbeer)

"Pour moi sa main cueillait des roses." See Lied (Franck)

"Pour out rich perfume." See Thrinôdia (Holmès)

"Pour out the Rheinwine! let it flow." See The good Rhein wine (Gray)

"Pour out thy heart before the Lord." B. Molique. e. OS 3—SAS 3

"Pour ramener ton coeur à l'espoir, à la joie." See David chantant devant Saül (Bordèse)

"Pourquoi pleurer? pourquoi pleurer" (Oh! sister dear) D. F. E. Auber. e.f. FSS 5

"Pourquoi tardet-il à venir." See Rosemonde (Chaminade)

Poushkin, Aleksandr Sergieevich. See Pushkin, Aleksandr Sergîeevich

"Pov' piti Lolotte." Negro creole song. f. KA
"Pov' piti Lolotte" ("Po' lil Lolo") e.f. BF 2

"Povero amico! oh! lo conosco il male che tu soffri" ("Friend so unhappy, oh, well I know the sorrow thou art bearing") Mascagni. e.i. OPS 2

Povero marinar (Heart-broken mariner) L. Mililotti. e.f.i. KF 4—PG 4
Povero marinar (Heart-broken sailor boy) e.f.i. AB 4

Powell, James Baden
Composer
"Come, listen to the story"
"Thou didst leave Thy throne"
Composer and author
"Hark! how the bells"
Author
"Night has closed the gates" (French air)
Powell, W.
"Gently rest" (Kücken)
Power, F. A.
Heidelberg
Power, James
Dearest Mae. See Crosby, L. V. H. Dearest Mae
Faded flowers
Lone starry hours
Power, T.
Mountain maid's invitation (Werner)
Power and love ("By the glories of earth") C. Gounod. Words by J. Troutbeck. HSS 1—HSS 2—HSS 4
The power of God. L. von Beethoven. e. WBT
The power of love ("There's a pow'r whose sway") M. W. Balfe. FSS 7
"Powerless to repress such a frenzy of faith." See "Ne pouvant réprimer" (Massenet)
Powers, Arthur Augustus
The Fliggyboo bird (Macgregor)
Maisie (Macgregor)
"'Twas two days out from Boston town" (Macgregor)
"Powers celestial." Air: Macgilchrist's lament. Words by R. Burns. BSB
"Pow'rs eternal, pray, restore me." See "Ciel pietoso, ciel clemente" (Rossini)
"A practical, plain young girl." See The nice young girl (Sullivan)
Praed, Winthrop Mackworth
"Fare thee well, love, fare thee well" (Briggs)
I remember how my childhood (Fitzgerald)
Praetorius, Johann
"Es ist kommen, es ist kommen" (Reichardt)
Praetorius, Michael
Composer
Lo! a fair rose is blooming
"A shepherd band their flocks are keeping"
"This day is born Emmanuel"
"We will be merry, far and wide" (Tr of Wir wollen alle frölich seyn)
Author
"A shepherd band their flocks are keeping" (Tuckerman; also music by author)
Die **Prager** schlacht ("Als die Preussen marschierten") Volkslied. g. ED 2
"Praise God from Whom all blessings flow." See Old hundred (Franc)
"Praise not to me the new-born rose." See La charmante Marguerite

The **praise** of God. See Die ehre Gottes aus der natur (Beethoven)
The **praise** of Islay. See Moladh na landaidh
Praise of song. Maurer. LA
Praise of tears ("Flowerets blooming") F. Schubert. [Tr of Lob der thränen] e. FSS 5
"Praise, praise ye Jehovah's goodness." L. von Beethoven. e. SAS 1
"Praise the Grand Master." Round. FSS 7
"Praise the Lord! one accord, sound throughout creation." Traditional air. SSS
"Praise the Lord! ye heavens, adore Him" (Austrian hymn) Haydn. TL
"Praise to God and thanks we bring." G. J. Elvey. Words by W. C. Gannett. BSS
"Praise to God, immortal praise." S. Bach. Words by A. L. Barbauld. WBT
"Praise to God" (Nuremberg) FSS 2
"Praise to God, immortal praise" (Thanksgiving) Composer unknown. Words by A. L. Barbauld. CST
"Praise to God, immortal praise" (St George's chapel) G. J. Elvey. Words by A. L. Barbauld. LA
"Praise to God, immortal praise" (Sabbath morn) L. Mason. Words by A. L. Barbauld. FSS 8
"Praise to God, immortal praise" (Thanksgiving) I. Pleyel. Words by A. L. Barbauld. JS—MP—MS—NMS
"Praise ye Jehovah's name." Air: America. FSS 4
"Praise ye the Father! for His loving-kindness" (Flemming) Flemming. Words by E. Charles. LA
"Praise ye the Father! let all the earth sing praises." C. Gounod (music and words) e. BD
Pratt, Agnes Louise
Joyous anthem swelling (Flotow)
Pratt, Charles E.
Give me the waltz
Piper Heidsieck. See Give me the waltz
"Pray, Goody." Old English air. Words by K. O'Hara. BE 3—HSE 1
Pray, let me, suffering. See Deh, contentatevi (Carissimi)
"Pray on, keep a-prayin', sister." See Sun don't set in de mornin'
"Pray, pray, let me, suffering." See Deh, contentatevi (Carissimi)
Prayer ("Ah! tout est bien fini") See Ô souverain, ô juge, ô père (Massenet)
Prayer ("Alla mente confusa") See Preghiera (Tosti)
Prayer ("Allmächt'ger Vater") See "Allmächt'ger Vater" (Wagner)
Prayer ("Herr, den ich tief") See Gebet (Hiller)

Prayer ("In hours of deep discouragement") Liszt. HSS 1

A prayer ("My own America") Dedicated to the Boy scouts of America. J. Anderson (music and words) BSS

A prayer ("O Lord, my God."—Prière) V. Kalinnikov. Words by A. Plestcheiev. e.f. NR 2

Prayer ("Saviour, Source") See "Saviour, Source of every blessing" (Whitmore)

Prayer ("They who seek") See "They who seek the throne of grace" (Dykes)

Prayer ("Vater, ich rufe Dich") See Gebet während der schlacht (Himmel)

Prayer ("Vieni, o Levita") See Tu sul labbro de' veggenti (Verdi)

Prayer for our country. J. W. Tufts. Words by J. R. Wreford. JS

Prayer for peace. See Russian national hymn (Lvov)

"Prayer is de key of heaven." Negro spiritual. HR

Prayer of thanksgiving. See "Wilt heden nu treden" (Kremser)

Prayer of the warriors before smoking the pipe. See The warrior's prayer

"Prayers of love." W. W. Gilchrist. Words by Whittier. TL

The precautioned nymph. L. Ramonden. BE 5

Precious lives. L. B. Marshall. Words by S. F. Smith. JS

Preghiera (Prayer.—"When with doubting and dreading") F. P. Tosti. e.i. HSS 4
   "Alla mente confusa" (Prayer.—"When with doubting and dreading") e.i. HSS 1—HSS 2—HSS 3
   Preghiera ("When with doubting and dreading") e.i. PG 2

"Pregúntale a las estrellas." Mexican folk song. e.s. HS
   "Pregúntale a las estrellas" ("Go ask of the high stars gleaming") e.s. HF

"Le premier jour de mai" (May-day) Folk song from Champagne. e.f. FTF

Première danse (The first dance) J. Massenet. Words by J. Normand. e.f. SAM

Les premiers aveux (Love's first confession) C. Dancla. Words by A. Bois-Gontier. e.f. SOS 1

"Prendre le dessin d'un bijou." See Fantaisie aux divins mensonges (Delibes)

"A 'prentice-lad with his staff in his hand." See Das erkennen (Proch)

"Prepare thyself, Zion." J. S. Bach. e. OS 2—SAS 2

"Près des remparts de Séville." See Séguédille (Bizet)

The Presbyterian cat. Air: Auld lang syne. BOS

"Press on, press on." Scotch air. FSS 4

Press thy cheek against mine own. See "Lehn' deine wang' an meine wang'" (Jensen)

Pressel, Gustav Adolf
   An der Weser
   By the river. See An der Weser
   "I have received Thy mercy." See "Mir ist erbarmung widerfahren"
   "Ich sah den wald sich färben"
   "Mir ist erbarmung widerfahren"
   The woodlands all are turning. See "Ich sah den wald sich färben"
   "The woodlands all were turning." See "Ich sah den wald sich färben"

"Presto, presto io m'innamoro" ("Swift my heart surrenders") G. B. Mazzaferrata. e.i. FEI 1

Preston, John A.
   "The world itself keeps Easter day"

"The prettiest girl I ever saw." See Sucking cider through a straw

"Pretty am I" ("Shein bin ich") Jewish folk song. e.y. GF 1

"A pretty black-skinned maiden." See "Una negra guachinanga"

The pretty drummer. See Joli tambour

"A pretty fair maid all in her garden." See The broken token (Hot Springs, N.C. version)

Pretty Fanny. See La belle Françoise

The pretty girl milking her cow. Air: Cailin deas. [Tr of Colleen dhas cruthen na moe] e. BO—PI—WBT—WL

Pretty Kathrin. See "Catina bellina"

"Pretty lady! here's a list I would show you." See "Madamina! il catalogo è questo" (Mozart)

"Pretty little damsels, how they chat." See Chit chat (Southwell)

"Pretty little deer." Children's song. WBT—WSC

"Pretty little Madeleine." See Madeleine (Roeckel)

"Pretty little violets, waking from your sleep." See Song of the bobolink (Atkinson)

Pretty maidens come again. See The bells of Aberdovey

"Pretty maidens, pretty maidens." Catch. Atterbury. MS

Pretty Marianna. See "Ma belle Marianne"

Pretty Mary. See Mairi bhòidheach

Pretty mocking bird. H. R. Bishop. Words by T. Morton. HSE 1

Pretty Nancy of Yarmouth. Folk song from North Carolina. CSE

Pretty pear tree. Old song. FSS 6 Variant of: The tree in the wood

Pretty Peggy O. Folk song: Kentucky version. CSE
   —North Carolina version. CSE

The pretty ploughboy. Folk song: Sussex version. SF 5
   —Yorkshire version. MM

"Pretty Polly hadn't been married but a very short time." See The wife of Usher's well (Allanstand, N.C. version)

Pretty Polly Oliver ("As pretty Polly Oliver lay musing") 17th century song. BOH—BOS—DM 2—SMF
Variants: The cruel ship's carpenter; Polly Oliver

Pretty Polly Oliver ("O pretty Polly Oliver, the pride of her sex") Old English air. Modern words by H. Boulton. SM 4—MSF 1

The **pretty** red girl. See An cailín deas ruadh

Pretty Saro. Folk song: Georgia version. CSE
—Allanstand, N.C. version. CSE
—Carmen, N.C. version. CSE

"**Pretty** skylark, winging, singing skylark." See Alouette

Pretty star of the night. Composer unknown. Words by W. G. T. Moncrieff. BE 4

Preussens vaterland ("I am a Prussian") A. Neithardt. e.g. SN
"Ich bin ein Preusse" ("I am a Prussian") e.g. BSP

"**Pria** che spunti in ciel l'aurora" ("Ere the morning light is breaking") D. Cimarosa. e.i. KS 4

Price, Carl F.
"My country dear, when soaring high"

Price, F. R.
"Now all the bells of Easter ring"

Price, Frank Julian
How I have loved thee (Composer unknown)

The **priceless** gift. H. Gray. Words by A. Dene. HSS 3

Pridanyi udalyi, Ladu, Ladu. See Wedding-day song

"The **pride** of all nature was sweet Willy, O." See Sweet Willy, O (Dibdin)

"The **pride** of the village." See Fairy-belle (Foster)

"**Pridi** ty šuhajko." See "Come you here, laddie"

Prière. See A prayer (Kalinnikov)

The **priest** and the rake. Air: Sláinte righ Philip. JOI

La **primavera** (In springtime) Spanish-American song. e.s. LSS

The **primrose** ("Ask me why I send you here") H. Lawes. Words by R. Herrick. DM 2

The **primrose** ("Du vårens milde") See Med en primulaveris (Grieg)

"**Primroses** deck the bank's green side." T. Linley. HSE 1

Primula veris. A. Kleffel. Words by Lenau. e.g. AB 3

Prince Charming. J. L. Roeckel. Words by H. Conway. FSS 3

Le **prince** d'Orange (The prince of Orange) French Canadian folk song. e.f. BFS

Le **prince** Eugene (Prince Eugene) French Canadian folk song. e.f. BFS

The **prince** of Orange. See Le prince d'Orange

The **Prince** of peace. W. Mozart. MCS

Prince of Wales song. Ojibway Indian song. in. BA

"**Prince** William of old Nassau." See "Wilhelmus van Nassouwe" (Marnix)

The **prince's** day ("Tho' dark are our sorrows") Air: St Patrick's day. Words by T. Moore. MI—PI
Saint Patrick's day. BSP—WA—WSW
"Tho' dark are our sorrows." MMI

The **prince's** three daughters. See "Derrière chez mon père, vole, mon coeur, vole" (Streabbog)

The **princess.** See "Prinsessen sad höjt i sit jomfrubur" (Grieg)

The **princess** and the hangman. See La princesse et le bourreau

Princess Kaiulani's home (Ainahau) Likelike. e.h. HA

The **princess** of France married to an Englishman. See La princesse de France mariée à un Anglais

"The **princess** sat up in her lofty bower." See "Prinsessen sad höjt i sit jomfrubur" (Grieg)

"A **princess** there sits with her maidens gay." See "Prinsessen sad höjt i sit jomfrubur" (Kjerulf)

La **princesse** de France mariée à un Anglais (The princess of France married to an Englishman) Folk song: Norman version. e.f. TF

La **princesse** endormie. See The sleeping princess (Borodin)

La **princesse** et le bourreau (The princess and the hangman) French Canadian folk song. e.f. BFS

Pringle, Thomas
"I'll bid my heart be still" (Scottish air)

"**Prinsessen** sad höjt i sit jomfrubur" (Prinsessen.—The princess) E. Grieg. Words by B. Björnson. e.n. MAN
Die prinzessin (The princess) e.g. PG 3

"**Prinsessen** sad höjt i sit jomfrubur" (Aftenstemning.—Twilight musing) H. Kjerulf. Words by B. Björnson. e.n. SSN—WM 1

"La **printanière** et douce matinée." See Sur une tombe (Lekeu)

"Le **printemps** chasse les hivers." See Au printemps (Gounod)

Printemps nouveau (Returning spring) P. Vidal. Words by H. Passerieu. e.f. PG 1

"**Printemps** qui commence" ("The spring now has found us") Saint-Saëns. e.f. OPS 2
"Printemps qui commence" ("The spring, with her dower") e.f. SOA 2

"**Prinz** Eugen." Volkslied. g. ED 1

Die **prinzessin**. See "Prinsessen sad höjt i sit jomfrubur" (Grieg)

The **Priory** chimes. W. Haynes. Words by E. F. Morris. FSS 6

The **prisoner** and the gaoler's daughter. See Le prisonnier et la fille du geôlier

A **prisoner** for life. Cowboy song. LC

The **prisoner** of Holland. See Le prisonnier de Hollande (Breton version; Canadian version)

The **prisoner** to the swallow ("Ov dsidsernag") Armenian song. a.e. BF 2

Le **prisonnier** de Hollande (The prisoner of of Holland) Folk song: Breton version. e.f. TF
Gai lon la. Canadian version. e.f. SMF

Le **prisonnier** de Hollande (The prisoner of Holland) Folk song: Canadian version. Air: À la claire fontaine: 2d variant. e.f. TF

Le **prisonnier** et la fille du geôlier (The prisoner and the gaoler's daughter) French Canadian folk song. e.f. BFS

"**Prithee**, Celia." J. Weldon. PR 2

"**Prithee** lend your jocund voices." See The oxen ploughing

"**Prithee**, Sally, speak thy mind." See I must try another (Hook)

Private Tommy Atkins. S. Potter. Words by H. Hamilton. MP—WBT

Prize song. See "Morgenlich leuchtend" (Wagner)

Pro Dobrynii. See Dobrynia bids his mother farewell

"**Pro** peccatis" ("Lord, preserve me uncomplaining") Rossini. e.l. OS 4

The **probationer's** farewell to St Andrews. St Andrews university song. Air: Hunting the hare. Words by H. M. B. Reid. SSS

La **procession** (The procession) C. Franck. Words by C. Brizeux. e.f. PG 3
La procession (Processional) e.f. CM 1

Processional. See La procession (Franck)

Processional march song. See Gaily beats the drum

Proch, Heinrich
Dearest native land
Das erkennen
"Hark! a thrilling song"
My heart is thine
Recognition. See Das erkennen
Verwelkt
Withered rose. See Verwelkt

Procter, Adelaide Ann
"Dear Lord, I thank Thee, Who hast made" (Maker)
Listening angels (Cowen)
The lost chord (Sullivan)
"One by one" (Bellini)
Our daily bread (Hutchinson)
The pilgrims (Cowen)

A shadow (Sullivan)
"The shadows of the evening hours" (music by Bensel; Hiles)
The storm (Hullah)
Will he come (Sullivan)

Procter, Bryan Waller
"Dawn, gentle flower" (Bennett)
The little voice (Tauwitz)
The sea (Neukomm)
"Sing, maiden, sing" (Bennett)
The stormy petrel (Neukomm)
Touch us gently, Time (Composer unknown)

Proctor, Edna Dean
Love song (Omaha Indian air; also music by Lieurance)

The **profs'** song. Air founded on The Dutch company. St Andrews university song. SSS

Promesse de mon avenir. J. Massenet. e.f. SOA 4
Promesse de mon avenir (Oh, promise of a joy so sweet) e.f.i. OPS 3

Promise never to forget me. See Forget-me-not (Hopkins)

The **promised** land. Old song. HSD—WBT

"**Pronto** vendrá la manana." See Zapateo cubano (Vilá)

Proposal ("The violet loves the sunny bank") F. H. Brackett. Words by B. Taylor. ES

The **proposal** ("The violet loves a sunny bank") Arr from C. W. Gluck. Words by B. Taylor. LBR

"**Proud** and lowly, beggar and lord." See London bridge (Molloy)

"**Proud** and peerless." See "Per la gloria d'adorarvi" (Bononcini)

"**Proud** Dannebrog be flowing." See The Dannebrog (Bay)

"The **proudest** now is but my peer." See The poor voter on election day

"**Proudly** steps the sturdy steed." See "Il cavallo scalpita" (Mascagni)

"**Proudly** sweeps the rain-cloud o'er the cliff." See Aloha oe (Liliuokalani)

"**Proudly** swept the rain-cloud by the cliff." See Aloha oe (Liliuokalani)

Prout, Ebenezer
The Christmas celebration
"Now to God on high be glory." See The Christmas celebration

Prout, Father, pseud. See Mahony, Francis Sylvester

Provence song. See Chant provençal (Massenet)

Provenzale, Francesco
"Deh, rendetemi" (from La stellidaura vendicata)
"O restore to me." See "Deh, rendetemi"

Prudentius Clemens, Aurelius
"Now with creation's morning song" (Beethoven. Tr of Lux ecce surgit aurea)
"Of the Father's love begotten" (Flemish air. Tr of Corde natus ex parentis)

Prudhomme, René François Armand Sully-.
See Sully-Prudhomme, René François
Armand

Prutz, Robert
"In dieser stunde" (Spicker)

Prząśniczka. See At the spinning wheel
(Moniuszko)

Przepióreczka. See The little quail

A psalm of life. H. Smart. Words by
H. W Longfellow. LBR

Psyché. E. Paladilhe. Words by P.
Corneille. e.f. GMF—PG 1—SAM

"La p'tit' bergèr' s'en va aux champs." See
La petite bergère

Pua o ka he-i. See The he-i blossom
(Hopkins)

Pua sadinia. See Gardenia flower (Nape)

Puccini, Giacomo
"Back to a happy day." See "Torna
ai felici dì"
"If I were like you." See "Se come
voi piccina io fossi"
"No! it cannot be so." See "No!
possibil non è"
"No! possibil non è" (from Le Villi)
"Se come voi piccina io fossi" (from
Le Villi)
"Torna ai felici dì" (from Le Villi)

Puccitta, Vincenzo
"Strike the cymbal"

Puer natus in Bethlehem. For English
translations see "A Babe is born in
Bethlehem"; "A Boy is born in Bethlehem"

La puerta de Alcalá. Spanish game song.
s. LCP

Puesta de sol. Canción escolar. J. Pe-
ricas. Words by F. M. Bernier. s.
LCP

Puff. A. S. Gatty. WSC

Pugno, Raoul
"I live, my heart is beating" (from La
résurrection de Lazare)
The resurrection. See "I live, my
heart is beating"
"Thou, to whom Galilee kneeleth"
(from La résurrection de Lazare)
"Thy name I praise, O God" (from La
résurrection de Lazare)
"Yea, mystery supreme by the tomb is
concealed" (from La résurrection
de Lazare)

Pu-in game song. Indian song. e. FI

"The puir auld folk at hame, ye mind."
See We'd better bide a wee (Barnard)

"Puisqu'ici-bas toute âme donne à quel-
qu'un." See Rêverie (Hahn)

"Puisqu'on ne peut fléchir ces jalouses
gardiennes." See Vainement, ma bien-
aimée (Lalo)

Pujals, Eustaquio
La canción del soldado

Pull away, brave boys. Rossini. e.
FSS 2—JSE

"Pull, boys, pull! pull, boys, pull." See
Volga boat song

"Pull, brave boys, pull on together." See
Row, row, cheerly row

"Pull! my brave crew." See Lou revestidon (Borel)

"Pull off that silk, my pretty Polly." See
Lady Isabel and the elf knight (Kentucky version)

Pulma lust. See Wedding joy

Pulse of my heart ("Before the sun rose at
yester dawn") Irish song. (Tr of
Acuirle mo criode créad iau gruaim ort)
e. MMI

"The pulse of your glance is the pulse of
the waves." See The siren (Grechaninov)

Pulteney. See Chesterfield, Philip Dormer
Stanhope, 4th earl of, jt. auth.

Pumping chanty. Norwegian sea song.
e.n. SMW

Punchinello ("Blue is the sky") P. I.
Tschaikowsky (music and words)
e. BC

Punchinello (Fifinella) e. BD

Punchinello ("He was a Punchinello") J.
L. Molloy. Words after H. Andersen.
e. FSS 4—SM 4

Punschlied ("Vier elemente, innig gesellt")
M. Eberwein. Words by Schiller.
g. ED 2

"Pupille nere" ("Love leads to battle")
Buononcini. e.i. BAS 2—BS 1

Puppets. See Fantoches (Debussy)

Pur dicesti, o bocca bella ("Lips alluring")
A. Lotti. e.i. FEI 2
"Pur dicesti" ("Speak, I pray thee")
e.i. MSS 1
Pur dicesti, o bocca bella ("Lips of
roses") e.i. NG—PG 1—PG 3
—PG 4
Pur dicesti, o bocca bella ("Mouth so
charmful") e.i. PA 1

Purcell, Daniel
Alas! when charming Sylvia's gone
(from The Spanish wives)
"Phillis, talk not more of passion"

Purcell, Edward
Passing by

Purcell, Henry
"Ah, cruel, ruthless fate"
Ah me! too many deaths
Arise, ye subterranean winds (from
The tempest)
"Cease, O my sad soul"
"Celebrate this festival"
"Come, if you dare" (from King
Arthur)
"Come unto these yellow sands"
The conjurer's song. See "Ye twice
ten hundred deities"
Dido's lament. See When I am laid
in earth
Dido's song. See When I am laid in
earth
"Eolus, you must appear" (from The
tempest)
"Fairest isle" (from King Arthur)
"Full fathom five"
"Had I but love"
Harvest home

Purcell, Henry —*Continued*
"Hear! ye gods of Britain" (from Bonduca)
Hence, hence with your trifling deity
"I attempt from love's sickness to fly" (from The Indian queen)
"I saw that you were grown so high"
"If love's a sweet passion" (from The fairy-queen)
"I'll sail upon the Dog-star" (from A fool's preferment)
"A jewel is my lady fair"
The knotting song
"Let the dreadful engines"
"Let us dance, let us sing" (from Dioclesian)
Lilliburlero
Mad Bess
The message
"Next, winter comes slowly" (from The fairy-queen)
Nottingham ale (same air as Lilliburlero)
"Nymphs and shepherds" (from The libertine)
"O cruel cruel fate"
"On the brow of Richmond hill"
"One, two, three, our number is right"
"The owl is abroad"
"Phillis, I can ne'er forgive it"
"Return, return, revolting rebels" (from Timon of Athens)
"See, see the heavens smile" (from The tempest)
"Shepherd, shepherd, leave decoying"
Since from my dear Astrea's sight
"Strike the viol"
"They tell us that you mighty powers" (from The Indian queen)
"Two daughters of this aged stream" (from King Arthur)
"What shall I do to show how much I love her" (from Dioclesian)
When I am laid in earth (from Dido and Aeneas)
"When I have often heard" (from The fairy-queen)
"Ye twice ten hundred deities" (from The Indian queen)

Purday, Charles Henry
Battle of the Baltic
The fine old English gentleman
The old English gentleman. See the fine old English gentleman

"Pure as a bud of spring." See "Elle ne croyait pas" (Thomas)
"Pure city, Babylon's fallin'." See Babylon's fallin'
"Purer yet and purer I would be in mind" (Lyndhurst) Words by J. W. von Goethe. e. TL
"Purest Virgin, thou most holy Mother." See Mary's quest
The purple and gold ("She's circled by mountains") University of Washington song. J. L. Schultz. Words by S. E. Sprague. CHS

The purple and the gold ("Although Knox is") Knox college song. CHS

The purple and the gold ("'Tis ever sweetly") Elmira college song. Words by S. S. Boardman. CHS
The purple and the gold ("We know of a spot") Scio college song. Air: Columbia, the gem of the ocean. CHS
The purple and the white. Song of Pennsylvania college for women. CHS
The purple gold ribbon. See Rödan guldband
"Purtiest singin' ever I heard." See Singin' wid a sword in my han'
Push the business on. Singing game. FSF
Pushkin, Aleksandr Sergieevich
"Ah, kindly star" (Glinka)
The captive (Grechaninov)
"Heard ye his voice" (Rubinstein)
The magpie and the little gypsy dancer (Musorgskiĭ)
The Nereid (Glazunov)
"O thou rose-maiden" (Dargomyzhskiĭ)
On the Georgian hills (Rimskiĭ-Korsakov)
Poet and critic (Cui)
"The rainy day is past" (Rimskiĭ-Korsakov)
The songs of Grusia (Rachmaninov)
The wish (Cui)
Pushkin, Aleksandr Sergieevich, and Karamzin, Nikolaï Mikhaïlovich
The siege of Kazan (Musorgskiĭ)
Pussy ("I love little pussy") J. W. Elliot. Words by A. and J. Taylor. JSE
"I love little pussy." FMB—FSS 5—WSC
"Pussy-cat, pussy-cat, where have you been." Mother Goose song. FMB—FSS 4—WSC
"Pussy, where have you been today." See The lazy cat
Put John on de islan'. Negro song. HR
Put off, and row wi' speed. Highland boat song. Words by R. Allan. HSSS—MMS
"Put on, put on your best array." E. Greatorex. HC
"Put on thy beautiful robes." G. B. Lissant. Words by W. C. Dix. HC
"Put your right hands in." See Looby loo
Putman's hill. Folk song from Virginia. CSE
Putnam, C. S.
Champlain
Evening on the lake
Putting on the insignia of the thunder god. See The insignia of thunder
Pyrker, Johann Ladislav
Die Allmacht (Schubert)

Q

Q, pseud. See Quiller-Couch, Sir Arthur Thomas
"Qu'à ma voix la victoire s'arrête." See La gloire et la fortune (Rossini)

"**Qu'à** mes ordres ici tout le monde se rende." See C'est la princesse de Navarre (Boieldieu)

Quae stella sole pulchrior. For English translation see "What star is this"

Quaesumus, Auctor omnium. For English translation see "O Lord of all, with us abide" (Wilson)

Quaff with me the purple wine. Shield. BE 4

Quagliati, Paolo
"Apra il suo verde seno" (from Il carro di fedeltà d'amore)
"Open your hearts." See "Apra il suo verde seno"

The **Quaker's** song. See Ti, tum, ti (Reeve)

"**Qual** farfalletta amante" ("Like any foolish moth I fly") D. Scarlatti. e.i. CS 2—MSS 2—SS 2

"**Qual** farfalletta giro a quel lume" ("Light as the night-moth") G. F. Händel. e.i. MC

"**Quale** arcano poter qui di nuovo m'ha tratta." See "Nuit resplendissante" (Gounod)

"**Quand** aucun toit ne fume." See The wolves (Arenski)

Quand de la nuit. For English translation see "Call me thine own" (Halévy)

"**Quand** j'ai parti de mon pays." See Sept ans sur mer

"**Quand** je vais au jardin, jardin d'amour." See Le jardin d'amour

"**Quand** j'étais chez mon père, petite à la maison." See La fille à la fontaine (Breton version; Norman version)

"**Quand** j'étais chez mon pere, petite Jeanneton." See La fille à la fontaine (Canadian version)

"**Quand** j'étais de chez mon père, digue din din." See La danse du troupeau

"**Quand** la flamme de l'amour" ("When for aye") G. Bizet. e.f. SOA 5
"Quand la flamme de l'amour" ("When the flame of love") e.f. OPS 4
"Quand la flamme de l'amour" ("When the flame of love's desire") e.f. KS 5

"**Quand** le bouvier vient du labour." See La chanson du bouvier

"**Quand** le roi rentra dans Paris." See Les trois roses empoisonnées

"**Quand** le soldat arrive en ville." See Le retour du mari soldat

"**Quand** l'heure du soir le ramène." See J'ai peur de l'aimer (Denza)

"**Quand** nous suivions tous deux la même route." See Parting (Ippolitov-Ivanov)

"**Quand** ton sourire me surprit." See Le charme (Chausson)

"**Quand** tu chantes bercée." See Chantez riez et dormez (Gounod)

"**Quand** une voix bien tendre." See Then you'll remember me (Balfe)

"**Quand** viendra la saison nouvelle." See Villanelle (Berlioz)

"**Quando** miro quel bel ciglio" ("With a swanlike beauty gliding") Mozart. e.i. CS 1

"**Quando** sarà quel dì" ("When will the day e'er be") A. F. Tenaglia. e.i. PA 2

"**Quando** sorge la luna a Marechiare." See Marechiare (Tosti)

"**Quann'** 'o sole adderete 'a muntagna." See 'O bene antico (Nutile)

"**Quanno** mammà me fece monicella." See La monacella

"**Quanno** nascette Ninno a Bettelemme." See Canzone d'i zampognari

"**Quanno** Noene l'arca frabbicone." See Er passagallo

"**Quannt'** è bella, quannt' è bella la bannera verde." See La nocca de tre colure

"**Quant** li rosignol jolis" ("When the nightingale shall sing") Attributed to the châtelain de Coucy (music and words) e.f. BO

"**Quanti** volt al ciaar de luna." See La Rozina

Quaranta, Francesco
"Lasciali dir, tu m'ami"
"Let say, who will: you love me." See "Lasciali dir, tu m'ami"

Quarles, Francis
Hey, then up go we (Air from "Caricatures and ballads"; air from "Musica antiqua")

"**Quattro** cavai" (Four horses) Swiss song. e.i. BF 2

"**Qué** bello es estar en los brazos de otro amor." See Qué bello es querer

Qué bello es querer. Mexican folk song. e.s. HS

"**Que** fais-tu dans ces champs." See Lucas

Que gusto me da. Spanish-American folk song. e.s. HS

Que je t'oublie (Could I forget) H. Chrétien. Words by L. Marcel. e.f. HM 1

Que le jour me dure ("Wie der tag mir schleichet") J. J. Rousseau (music and words) g. ED 2—ED 3
Que le jour me dure ("Ohne dich."—Sehnsucht) g. ED 3

"**Que** les songes heureux." Slumber romance. C. Gounod. e.f. SOA 5

"**Que** l'heure est donc brève" (How brief is the hour) J. Massenet. Words by A. Silvestre. e.f. HM 2

Que l'on m'enterre dans la cave (Let me be buried in the cellar) Canadian folk song. e.f. TF

"**Que** ne suis-je la fougère" ("Would I were the fern") Pergolesi. Words by Riboutté. e.f. WB

"**Que** no te amo." Mexican folk song. e.s. HS

Que noite serena. See A barquinha

"**Qué** quieres, angel de mis amores." See Angel de mis amores

Que se pierdo el niño. See "Madre, el niño se ha perdido"

"**Que** t'as de belles filles." See Giroflé, girofla

Que ton âme si noble. G. Rossini. e.f. SOA 5

"Que tristes son las horas." See Las tristas horas

Queen Besses' Dame of Honour. See "Since now the world's turn'd upside down"

Queen Eleanor's confession. Ballad. MM

"Queen Jane was in labour." See The death of Queen Jane

Queen Mary's farewell to Alloa. Scottish air: Alloa house. Words by M'Laren. PS 2

Queen Mary's lament. Attributed to Giordani. Words by Mrs J. Hunter. PS 2

The Queen of Hearts. English folk song. BSW

Queen of May ("Upon a time I chanc'd") 17th century song. DM 2

The queen of May ("Upon a time I chanc'd") 17th century song. Another air. HSE 2

Queen of night. E. Meyer-Helmund. Words by D. K. Stevens. BD

The queen of the May ("Here's a bank with rich cowslips") Air: Troiad y droell, or, The whirling of the spinning-wheel. Words by G. Darley. MMW

"Queen of the night." J. S. Torry. FSS 8

The queen's Maries. Old Scotch song. FSS 6

"Quel dì che te go visto." See A Nina

"Quel trouble inconnu me pénètre." See Salut! demeure chaste et pure (Gounod)

El Queléle (The white hawk) Spanish-American song. e.s. LSS

"Quello che tu mi dici." See Chello che tu me dice (Biscardi)

"Quelquefois en levant les yeux." See Stances (Flégier)

Quem pastores laudavere. For English translation see "Whom of old the shepherds"

The quest ("Why are you standing") Bohemian folk song. e. CST

The quest of the three kings. T. T. Noble. Words by C. W. Stubbs. HC

Questa o quella. For English translation see "Ev'ry flower is equally cherished" (Verdi)

Questions and answers ("What's the life you love to lead") Hungarian folk song. e. GO

Questions and answers ("Where, O where") See The visions of morning

"Qui creavit coelum, lully, lully, lu." 15th century Latin carol. 1. HC Lully, lully, lu. e. MF

"Qui donc commande quand il aime." C. Saint-Saëns. e.f. SOA 4

"Qui jamais fut de plus charmant visage." See Madrigal dans le style ancien (Indy)

"Qui la voce." Bellini. e.i. PP

"Qui l'aurait dit de l'arbitraire." See La Brabançonne (Campenhout)

"Qui, pour ce soir je suis reine des fées." See Je suis Titania (Thomas)

"Qui Radamés verrà" ("He will ere long be here") Verdi. e.i. OPS 1

"Qui sdegno non s'accende." See "In diesen heil'gen hallen" (Mozart)

"Qui sola, vergin rosa." See The last rose of summer

"Qui veut ouïr chanson" ("Who now would hear a song") Folk song from Champagne. e.f. FTF

"Qui veut ouir, qui veut savoir." See La ronde de l'aveine

"Quick! we have but a second." Air: Paddy Snap. Words by T. Moore. MI—PI

"Quien quisiera ser libre que a prendra" (Spanish national hymn) M. Fenollosa. e.s. WA—WCP—WSW

"Quieres que te ponga." Folk song from southern California. s. HS

"Quiero á mi Pepa y no es broma." See Mi Pepa

"A quiet glade, deep in the shade." See And then— (Hosmer)

"Quiet is the bright night." See The gondola

"Quiet, Lord, my froward heart." W. H. Monk. Words by J. Newton. FSS 2

The quiet night ("The ev'ning bells sound clearly") F. Abt. FSS 8

"Quiet night of waning summer." N. Tcherepnin. Words from the Russian of Tiutcheff. e. NM 2

"Quiet our fallen heroes lie." See Memorial day song (Olds)

"Quiet was the day." See The guests arrive

Qu'il est amiable. For English translation see "Infant so gentle"

"Qu'il est doux le printemps." See "How abundant and warm is the spring" (Sokolov)

Quiller-Couch, Sir Arthur Thomas Tim, the dragoon (Stanford)

The quilting party. CHS —CU —HSD —MPC —NMH —WA —WBT —WC —WSW

"Quis gus ya nosvalientes." National air of San Domingo. J. Reyes. s. SN

"Quittez, pasteurs, vos brebis, vos houlettes" ("Ah, shepherds, leave your crooks") French Noël. e.f. TSF

"Qvällens guldmoln fästet kransa." See Necken (Soderberg)

R

Ra-ta-plan. See Rataplan (Donizetti)

Rab Roryson's bonnet. Scottish air. Words by Tannahill. PS 2

El rabada ("Wake, O wake, ye shepherds all") Catalan air. e. MF

Rabbi Ben Ezra. H. K. Hadley. Words by R. Browning. TL

The rabbit and the turtle. Japanese children's song. e.j. BF 2

The rabbit's story (Iz pod duba, iz pod viáza) Russian gooslee tune. e. SSR 3

"The race hath long in darkness pined." See The light hath shone (Hastings)

Rachella. Italian song. e.i. BF 2

Rachmaninov, Sergei Vassilievich
Aná, kak póldyen, kharashá. See "As fair is she as noonday-light"
"As fair is she as noonday-light"
"Before my window"
By a new-made grave
Christós voskrés. See "The Lord is risen! His praise is ringing"
"Deep in love was I"
Field beloved
Floods of spring
Frühlingsfluthen. See Floods of spring
"Glorious forever"
"God took from me my all"
"How sweet the place"
In the silence of the night
The isle
Lilacs
"The Lord is risen! His praise is ringing"
Morning
Nye poi, krasávitza. See The songs of Grusia
O, du wogendes feld. See Field beloved
"O nein, ich fleh', geh' nicht von mir." See "Oh, no, I pray, do not depart"
"Oh, no, I pray, do not depart"
"O thou billowy harvest field." See Field beloved
Ostrovók. See The isle
Poloobeela ya na petchál svayú. See The soldier's bride
The soldier's bride
The songs of Grusia
Sorrow in spring
To the children
V' moltchányi nótchi táïnoi. See In the silence of the night
Vsyo ótnyal ōō minyá. See "God took from me my all"
"Wohl zu eignem leid." See "Deep in love was I"

Rada ("Zemi ma, Rado") Bulgarian folk song. b.e. BF 1

Rada and Petko (Rada i Petko) Bulgarian folk song. b.e. BF 1

Rada i Petko. See Rada and Petko

Ráda song ("Ráda ráda") Czech song. bo.e. BF 1

Radcliffe, Mrs Ann (Ward)
"The rose that weeps" (Horsley)

Radecke, Robert
"Aus der jugendzeit"
The days of youth. See "Aus der jugendzeit"

From youth's happy day. See "Aus der jugendzeit"
The swallows' song. See "Aus der jugendzeit"

Radford, Dolly
"All my silver and gold" (Russian air)
"All the night and all the day" (Russian air)
"Day is passing" (Hungarian air)
"Deep and secret lies the treasure" (Dalmatian air)
"Far, so far" (Hungarian air)
"He has brought his fine guitar" (Bosnian air)
"O girl who singest" (Serbian air)

"Radujte se narodi." See Christ is born—His name praise

Raff, Joseph Joachim
Ave Maria
Be still. See Sei still
"Behold, the house of God is with men" (from Weltende)
Ever with thee. See Immer bei dir
Good-night
"Great and wonderful are all Thy works" (from Weltende)
Immer bei dir
"In thy dear eyes." See Immer bei dir
Keine sorg' um den weg
"Lord, hear my voice" (from Weltende)
Love finds out the way. See Keine sorg' um den weg
Mädchenlied
"See, now the dusk is falling." See Ave Maria
Sei still
Serenade. See Ständchen
Ständchen
"Thrust in thy sickle and reap" (from Weltende)
To the evening star. See Mädchenlied

Rage, thou angry storm. J. Benedict. Words by G. Linley. BAS 1

Ragged and torn and true. Air: Old Sir Simon the king. Words by M. Parker. BE 3

"Ragion sempre addita" ("How dearly are prized") A. Stradella. e.i. PA 2
"Ragion sempre addita" ("The soul taught by duty") e.i. KS 2

Rah! for the black and blue. Johns Hopkins university song. J. G. Peters (music and words) CHS—MPC

Rah! rah! C. C. N. Y. Song of the College of the city of New York. Words by J. J. Gollomb. CHS

"Rah! rah U of M." University of Michigan song. A. A. Stanley. CHS

Rah-rah-rah for Midland. Midland college song. Words by G. H. Meixell. CHS

An raib tú og an g-Carraig. For English translation see Munster love song

Railway. Sea song. SMW

Raimund, Ferdinand
　　Abschied (Müller)
　　"Brüderlein fein" (Drechsler)
　　Hobellied (Kreutzer)
Rain and snow.　Folk song from North
　　Carolina.　CSE
"The **rain** is on the river."　See Sunshine
　　and rain (Blumenthal)
Rain on the roof.　J. G. Clark.　Words
　　by C. Kinney.　JO
[**Rain** on the roof] Rain upon the roof.　G.
　　Clifford.　Words　by　C.　Kinney.
　　FSS 3
Rain on the roof.　J. G. Naumann.
　　Words by C. Kinney.　LBR
"**Rain,** people, rain! the rain is all about
　　us."　See Mocking bird song
The **rain** song.　See El capotin
Rain upon the roof.　See Rain on the roof
　　(Clifford)
Rainfall follows the plow.　FSS 8
The **rainy** day ("The day is cold") W. R.
　　Dempster.　Words by H. W. Long-
　　fellow.　HSD—JO—LBR
"The **rainy** day is past."　N. Rimsky-Kor-
　　sakoff.　Words from the Russian of
　　Pushkin.　e.　NM 2
"**Raise** loud, on high, your mingled voices."
　　See Praise of song (Maurer)
Raise the song for Easter.　B. E. Backus.
　　HC
"**Raise** your hands."　School song.　FSS 7
Raisins and almonds (Rozhinkes mit mand-
　　len) Jewish folk song.　e.y.　GF 1
The **rakes** of Mallow ("Beauing, belleing,
　　dancing, drinking") Irish song.　BMC
　　—MMI
Rakmaninov, Sergeï　Vasilievich.　See
　　Rachmaninov, Sergei Vassilievich
Ralegh, Sir Carew
　　The surprise (Lawes)
"**Rally,** Carletons, old and young."　See
　　Carleton spelling song (Root)
"**Rally** 'round the flag."　W. B. Bradbury.
　　MP—WBT—WSW
Ralston, Claude
　　Sherlock Holmes
The **rambler** from Clare.　Irish folk song.
　　JOI
The **rambling** comber.　English folk song.
　　SF 1
The **rambling** sailor ("I am a sailor stout
　　and bold") English folk song.　SEF 1
　　—SO
The **rambling** sailor ("I toss my cap up
　　into　the　air") English　folk　song.
　　BSW
Ramchoondra.　W. Reeve.　Words by J.
　　Cobb.　ME
Rameau, Jean Philippe
　　"Chassons　de　nos　plaisirs"　(from
　　　　Acanthe et Céphise)
　　Monstre affreux (from Dardanus)
　　"Nightingales　passion-stirred."　See
　　　　"Rossignols amoureux"
　　"Rossignols　amoureux"　(from　Hip-
　　　　polyte et Aricie)

Les **rameaux** (The palms) J. Faure.　e.f.
　　HSS 3—HSS 4—KF 4.　e. only
　　WA—WS—WSW
　　Palm branches.　e.　OH—TFC 1
　　The palms.　e.　BD—FSS 7—HSC—
　　　　LA—NMS—WBT—WSC
Ramène tes moutons (The　shepherdess)
　　Old French song.　e.f.　DO
Ramonden, Lewis
　　The precautioned nymph
Ramsay, Allan
　　"An thou wert mine ain thing" (Scot-
　　　　tish air)
　　"At Polwarth on the green" (Scottish
　　　　air)
　　Bessie Bell and Mary Gray (Scottish
　　　　air)
　　Bonny Bessy (Scottish air)
　　Colin and Grissy parting (Scottish air)
　　The collier's bonnie lassie (Scottish air)
　　"The lass o' Patie's mill" (Scottish air)
　　"The last time I came o'er the muir"
　　　　(Scottish air)
　　"The lily of the vale is sweet" (Scot-
　　　　tish air)
　　Lochaber no more (Reilly)
　　"My mither's ay glowran owre me"
　　　　(Scottish air)
　　"Peggie, now the king's come" (Scot-
　　　　tish air)
　　"Sweet youth's a blithe and heartsome
　　　　time" (Scottish air)
　　Thro' the wood, laddie (Scottish air)
　　"The　yellow-hair'd　laddie"　(Scottish
　　　　air)
La rana.　Mexican folk song.　e.s.　HS
Randall, Herbert
　　Dearie (Norris)
Randall, James Ryder
　　Maryland, my Maryland (German air)
Randegger, Alberto
　　Bid the day be born
　　But when morning dawneth
　　The gold-beater
　　The holy family
　　"Now let us sing the angel's song"
　　"Round the corner waiting"
　　"Sadly bend the flowers."　See But
　　　　when morning dawneth
Randegger, E. F.
　　Nenia (Randegger, G. A.)
Randegger, Giuseppe Aldo
　　The legend of the Venetian laces.　See
　　　　Nenia
　　Nenia
Randel, Andreas
　　"All in the dim forest."　See "I vil-
　　　　lande skogen"
　　"I sing and I dance."　See "Jag sjung-
　　　　er och dansar"
　　"I villande skogen"
　　"Jag sjunger och dansar"
"**Rane** moje ljuto tištu."　See Montenegro
Range of the buffalo.　Cowboy song.
　　LC
Rankin, J.
　　"Norah darling" (Balfe)

Rankin, Jeremiah Eames
"Comrades, good night" (Reichardt)
"God be with you" (Tomer)
Long live, long live America (Pontius)
They falter not (Mallary)
Rannie,
The post captain (Shield)
Ranquet,
"Glad news from Bethlehem, my comrade." See Mes esta dí
Mes esta dí
Ransford, Edwin
"Beautiful sea! beautiful sea! on thy calm bosom ever I'd be"
Love, hope, happiness
The **ransomed** petticoat. See Le cotillon racheté
Ranz des vaches ("Lè z'armaillis dei Colombettè."—Herd of cattle) Swiss song. e.f. BF 2
Ranz des vaches ("To Swiss in stranger's land") e. LA
Herdsman's song. e. KSE—SN
Herdsman's song (National song of Switzerland) e. WCP
Switzerland (Herdsman's song) e. MP—NMH—NMS
Ranzay, Louis le Lasseur de. See Le Lasseur de Ranzay, Louis
"**Ranzo,** boys, Ranzo, O poor old Reuben Ranzo." See Poor old Reuben Ranzo
"**Rapazes** e raparigas." See Sapateia
"**Rapide** comme un rêve." See Le roitelet (Paladilhe)
Rapture of melancholy. See Wonne der weymuth (Beethoven)
"A **rare,** red rose he brought me." See Verwelkt (Proch)
Rare the barley, rare the rye, rare the wheat ("Ritka buza, ritka árpa, ritka rozs") Hungarian song. e.hu. BF 1
"**Raritete** sein ssu sehn, schöne raritete." See Guckkasten-lied
"**Rasch** tritt der tod den menschen an." See Gesang der mönche (Beethoven)
Rascoe, Miss
The flower girl's song (Welsh air)
"**Rasker** och redlig är han" ("Vigorous and honest is he") Swedish folk song. e.sw. SMF
"**Raslin'** Jacob." Negro spiritual. HR
Rasmussen, Poul Edvard
Denmark's verdant meadows. See Thyra Dannebod
Thyra Dannebod
"**Rasserena,** O madre." See Rend' il sereno al ciglio (Händel)
Rastvoríl ya oknó. See By the window (Tchaikovsky)
Le **rat** de ville et le rat des champs. French folk song. f. FMB
Rataplan. Donizetti. e. FSS 4
Ra-ta-plan. e. BD
Rathaus, D.
"Ah, twine no blossoms" (Glière)
Autumn melody (Koreshchenko)
The hour of dreams (Arenski)
Rathbun (Conkey) See Gently lead us; "Hail, Thou long-expected Jesus"

Der **rattenfänger** ("Ich bin der wohlbekannte sänger") Volksweise. Words by W. von Goethe. g. ED 1
"A **rattler** went daown dat holler lawg." See Hyah, rattler
Rattlin' roarin' Willie. Scottish air. Words by R. Burns. PS 2
"O, rattlin, roarin Willie." BSR
Räuberlied ("Ein freies leben") Words by F. von Schiller. g. ED 1
"**Rauschender** strom, brausender wald." See Aufenthalt (Schubert)
"**Rauschendes** bächlein, so silbern und hell." See Liebesbotschaft (Schubert)
Rav (Amber) C. Sinding. Words by H. Drachmann. e.n. SSN
The **raven.** Composer unknown. Words by E. A. Poe. LBR
Ravenscroft, Thomas
"Malt's come down"
"Remember, O thou man"
Ravindranātha Thākura, Sir. See Tagore, Sir Rabindranath
"**Raving** winds around her blowing." Air: McGrigor of Rora's lament. Words by R. Burns. BSR
Rawlings, Thomas A.
Isle of beauty
Raymond,
"Take me home"
Raymond, Alfred R.
The dude who couldn't dance (Composer unknown)
Raymond, Clara Hovey
Cradle song
Raymond, D. R.
"There dwelt in old Judea" (music by Harding; Jackson)
Raymond, Rossiter Worthington
"Morning red" (German air)
Never alone (Silcher)
"O what can you tell" (Lowry)
Raziella (Graziella) Neapolitan air. e.i. FE—MN
Razstanak. See At parting
"**Re** dell' abisso" ("King of the shades") G. Verdi. e.i. KS 3
Er **re** goli (Breton sailors' litany) e.f. SMW
Read, John
Every inch a sailor
Santa Claus
Read, Thomas Buchanan
Where the eagle is king (Hartley)
Reading, John, d. 1692
Dulce domum (attributed)
Reading, John, 1677-1764
"Adeste fideles" (attributed)
"Come, all ye faithful." See "Adeste fideles" (attributed)
"How firm a foundation" (same air as "Adeste fideles"; attributed)
"O come, all ye faithful." See "Adeste fideles" (attributed)
Portugese hymn (attributed) See "Adeste fideles"; "How firm a foundation"
"**Reading** the stars on high." See "Volta la terrea fronte alle stelle" (Verdi)

Ready. Composer unknown. Words by P. Cary. LBR

The **real** Irish toper. Irish folk song. JOI

The **real** maid of Sorrento. See La vera Sorrentina

The **reaper** and the flowers. L. O. Emerson. Words by H. W. Longfellow. LBR

The **reapers** (Les moissonneurs) S. Vassilenko. Words by J. Polonski. e.f. NR 4

Reapers on the mountain ("Geĭ na gorĭ ta zhentsĭ zhnut' ") Ukrainian folk song. e.r. BF 1

Reasons for drinking. C. Dibdin. Words by C. Morris. JO

Reassured. See Die beruhigte

Reay, Samuel
　　The dawn of day
　　"Now sing we a song for the harvest"

The **rebbe** (Der rebi) Jewish folk song. e.y. GF 2

"Der **rebi**, der rebi, der heiliker man." See The rebbe

"**Receive** then my first and fondest kiss." See "Si voli il primo" (Donizetti)

The **recessional.** H. H. Huss. Words by R. Kipling. TL

Rechter sache gutes ende ("Wer Gott das herze gibet") K. F. Zelter. Words by M. Opitz. g. ED 3

Recke, Elisa von der
　　Mancherlei freuden (Volksweise)

Recognition. See Das erkennen (Proch)

Recordando mis pedres queridos. See La tórtola (Marquez)

The **red** and blue. University of Pennsylvania song. W. J. Goeckel. Words by H. E Westervelt. CHS

The **red** and gold. Simpson college song. CHS

The **red** and the black. Washington and Jefferson college song. Air: Columbia, the gem of the ocean. Words by O. Burroughs. CHS

"**Red** are thy waters, River Maritsa." See "Join, O Maritza"

Red blanket. Ojibway Indian song. e.in. BA

"**Red** gleams the sun." Scottish air. Words by Couper. PS 2

"**Red** glows the forge in Strighul's bounds." See The war-song of the men of Glamorgan

Red-haired family ("Dĭd rudiĭ, baba ruda") Ukrainian song. e.r. BF 1

The **red-hair'd** man's wife ("Though full as 'twill hold of gold") Irish air. Words by K. Tynan. MMI

The **red** herring. Folk song from Somerset. FSF

"The **red** light falls on castle walls." See True love is sweet (Hutchinson)

The **red** lips. Air: Coal black joke. BE 8

"The **red** moon is up o'er the moss-covered mountain." See The star of Glengary (Sporle)

"**Red**, red is the path to glory." See Joy of my heart

The **red**, red rose. See "My luve is like a red, red rose" (Scottish air)

The **red** sarafan. See The scarlet sarafan (Varlamov)

The **red** scarf. T. Bonheur. Words by G. W. Southey. CB

"The **red** sun floods the east." See My silver throated fawn (Lieurance)

The **red**, white and blue ("Britannia, the pride of the ocean") See "Britannia, the pride of the ocean" (Becket)

Red, white and blue ("Flags flying ev'rywhere") A. Bergh. Words by S. Fay. BSS

The **red**, white and blue ("O, Columbia the gem of the ocean") See Columbia, the gem of the ocean (Becket)

Redan, Karl, pseud. See Converse, Charles Crozat

Reddall, Frederic
　　Leaving the nest

Redden, Laura Catherine. See Searing, Mrs Laura Catherine (Redden)

Redding, Joseph Deighn
　　"Thou art my own love"

Redhead, Alfred
　　"The angels' songs this joyful day"
　　"Carol we high, carol we low"
　　"God when He made this world"
　　"Within a manger"

Redhead, Richard
　　The divine Pilot. See "Jesus, Saviour, pilot me"
　　"Jesus, Saviour, pilot me"

Redner, Lewis Henry
　　Everywhere, everywhere, Christmas tonight
　　"God rest ye merry, gentlemen"
　　"Let the merry church bells ring"
　　"O little town of Bethlehem"
　　"The risen Lord to-day is King"
　　"The world itself keeps Easter-day"

Redwitz, Oskar von
　　"Es muss ein wunderbares sein" (music by Liszt; Ries)

Reece, Robert
　　Claudine (Molloy)

Reed, Andrew
　　"Holy Ghost, with light divine" (Gottschalk)

Reed, James
　　The good Rhein wine (Gray)

Rees, Catherine F. van
　　Boer national volkslied. See "Kent gij dat volk vol heldenmoed"
　　"Kent gij dat volk vol heldenmoed"
　　"Know ye that race of hero mold." See "Kent gij dat volk vol heldenmoed"
　　"Right nobly gave, voortrekkers brave." See "Kent gij dat volk vol heldenmoed"

Reeve, William
"Britannia's sons at sea" (from The turnpike gate)
The friar of orders gray
Happy and merry. See The heart should be happy and merry
The haymaker
The heart should be happy and merry
Humming all the trade is (from The turnpike gate)
"I am a friar of orders grey." See The friar of orders gray
"I'm a jolly roving tar"
The old commodore (from The naval triumph)
"Our country is our ship"
The Quaker's song. See Ti, tum, ti
Ramchoondra (from Ramah Droog)
"The rose of the valley"
The tar's sheet anchor
Ti, tum, ti
To-morrow
The Whip club (from The aquatic Harlequin)
The Yorkshire man (from Family quarrels)

Reeves, William P.
"God girt her about with the surges" (Composer unknown)
Refrain of the washerwomen of Vomero. See Ritornello delle lavandare del Vomero
"Refrain thy voice from weeping." A. S. Sullivan. OS 3—SAS 3
Regent square (Smart) See "Angels, from the realms of glory"; "God the Lord a King remaineth"
Regnard, Jean François
Pastorale (Bizet)
Regnart, Jakob
Sehnsucht
"Regnava nel silenzio" ("Calmly on sombre wings") G. Donizetti. e.i. MC
"Regnava nel silenzio" ("Silent the sombre wings") e.i. PP
The **regrets** of Bŏkhăra. N. C. Page. Words from the Persian. e. HST
Das **reich** der freude ("Mein lebens lauf") Volksweise. Words by A. Mahlmann. g. ED 1
Reichardt, Alexander
The birth of Christ
Bleib bei mir
Christmas carol
"Ich kenn' ein aug', das so mild"
Merry bells of long ago
Stay, my darling, stay. See Bleib bei mir
Thou art so near, and yet so far. See "Ich kenn' ein aug', das so mild"
Reichardt, Gustav
Des Deutschen vaterland
The German's fatherland. See Des Deutschen vaterland
National song of Germany. See Des Deutschen vaterland
Thy land. See "Where is the true man's fatherland"
"Was ist des Deutschen vaterland." See Des Deutschen vaterland

"Where is the German fatherland." See Des Deutschen vaterland
"Where is the true man's fatherland" (same air as Des Deutschen vaterland)
Reichardt, Johann Friedrich
An den frühling
Aufmunterung zur freude
Der baum in Odenwald
Bei sonnenuntergang (same air as Der mond)
Bundeslied
"Comrades, good night"
Der fischer
"Freudvoll und leidvoll"
Gelähmter flug
Herbstlied
Der herzenswechsel
Die hoffnung ("Es reden")
Hoffnung und erinnerung ("Mir blüht eine stelle")
Jäger
Jägers nachtlied
Kaiser Wenzel
"Kennst du das land"
Klärchens lied im Egmont. See "Freudvoll und leidvoll"
Der könig in Thule
Lebenspflichten
Lied der nacht
Mignon. See "Kennst du das land"
Der mond
My birthday
"O native land"
Schneiderschreck
Trinklied
Das veilchen
"Der wächter mit dem silberhorn"
"Wie kommt's, dass du so traurig bist"
Zum neuen jahr
Reichardt, Luise
Die blume der blumen
Daphne am bach
Der spinnerin nachtlied
"Es ist ein schnitter"
"Es ist kommen, es ist kommen"
Hoffnung ("Wenn die rosen")
"Ich wollt ein sträusslein binden"
"In the time of roses." See Hoffnung
Käuzlein
Kriegslied des maies
Morgenlied
"Nach Sevilla"
Palmsonntag
Schäfers klagelied
Der schnitter Tod. See "Es ist ein schnitter"
Wachtelschlag
Wassersnot
Weihnachtslied
"Wenn ich ihn nur habe"
Die wiese
Reid, H. M. B.
The country parson's lament (St Andrews university song)
Grinding (Fischer)
The probationer's farewell to St Andrews (St Andrews university song)

Reid, James
The lea rig
Reid, John
"In the garb of old Gaul"
Reign, Massa Jesus. Negro spiritual. HR
Reign, Master Jesus. JP
Reign of my king. See "Kimi ga yo" (Hiromori)
Reign of my sovereign. See "Kimi ga yo" (Hiromori)
Reilly, Myles
"Farewell to Lochaber." See Lochaber no more (attributed)
Lochaber no more (attributed)
Reindeer song. Laplandish song. e. KSN
"Reindeer, galop fast." e. SN
La **reine** de la mer. See The sea-queen (Borodin)
Reinecke, Karl Heinrich Carsten
At happy Easter time
Frühlingsblumen
"I saw a ship a-sailing"
"Im sommer such' ein liebchen"
"In summer seek a sweetheart." See "Im sommer such' ein liebchen"
March snow. See Märzschnee
Märzschnee
Miriam's song. See Sound the loud timbrel
Mirjam's siegsgesang. See Sound the loud timbrel
Sound the loud timbrel
"Spinn, mägdlein, spinn! so wachsen dir die sinn"
Spinning song. See "Spinn, mägdlein, spinn! so wachsen dir die sinn"
Spring-flowers. See Frühlingsblumen
Reinhard, K.
Für mädchen (Righini)
Reinhold, C.
Nachtigall (Brahms)
Reinick, Robert
An den sonnenschein (Schumann)
Morgen-hymne (Henschel)
"Wie ist doch die erde so schön" (Steifensandt)
Reinthaler, Karl
"The Lord will not be ever wroth" (from Jephtha)
"Lovely and sweet as the rose in the vale" (from Jeptha)
"What! Miriam shall perish on sacrificial altar" (from Jephtha)
"Why art thou cast down, O my soul" (from Jephtha)
"**Reír** cuando se tiene el corazón herido." See Reír es necesario
Reír es necesario. Mexican folk song. e.s. HS
Os **reis** ("From the Orient they came a-riding") Portuguese carol. e. MF
Reiselied (Returning) F. Mendelssohn. Words by Heine. e.g. KF 4
"**Reiser** alle mand, det fire slaar." See Sildfiske vise

Reissiger, Friedrich August
Norsk sjomandssang
Olaf Trygvason
Der schlesische zecher und der teufel
The Silesian toper and the devil. See Der schlesische zecher und der teufel
Slumber. See Sövnen
Sövnen
Til Ole Bull
To Ole Bull. See Til Ole Bull
Reissiger, Karl Gottlieb
Noah
Historia von Noah. See Noah
Studentenleben
Reissman, A.
Waking flowers
Reiterlied ("Die bange nacht") J. W. Lyra. Words by G. Herwegh. g. ED 1
Reiterlied ("Wohlauf kameraden") C. J. Zahn. Words by F. von Schiller. g. ED 1
Reiterlied (Cavalry song) e.g. SSG. e. only GO
Reiters morgenlied ("Morgenrot, morgenrot") Volkslied. Words by W. Hauff. g. ED 1
"Morning red." e. WBT
Reiters morgenlied (The horseman's morning song) e.g. SSG
The **rejected** lover. Folk song: North Carolina version. CSE
—Tennessee version. CSE
—Virginia version. CSE—SA
Rejoice greatly, O daughter of Zion. Händel. OS 1—SAS 1
"**Rejoice!** rejoice! the summer months are coming." FSS 2
"**Rejoice,** rejoice, ye Christians." See Rejoice, ye Christians
"**Rejoice,** sons of Egypt." See Khedival hymn
"**Rejoice!** the Christ is risen." G. E. Oliver. HC
"**Rejoice!** to-day earth tells abroad." R. F. Smith. Words by W. C. Dix. HC
"**Rejoice** to-day with glad accord." F. T. Southwick. Words by H. R. Baldwin. LA
"**Rejoice** ye at my singing." See Invocazione di Orfeo (Peri)
Rejoice, ye Christians. Christmas song. MCS
"**Rejoice,** ye pure in heart." A. H. Messiter. Words by E. H. Plumptre. OH
Marion. CST
Religion is a fortune. Negro spiritual. DF—HR—JP
Rellstab, Ludwig
Aufenthalt (Schubert)
In der ferne (Schubert)
Liebesbotschaft (Schubert)
Ständchen (Schubert)
"**Remain,** love" (Algerian song) e. BMC

Remember be sure and be there. C. K. Hopkins. e.h. HA

Remember, Lord, what Thou hast laid upon us. L. Spohr. e. OS 3—SAS 3

"Remember, O thou man." T. Ravenscroft. CO 1—HC

"Remember the glories of Brien the brave." See Brien the brave

Remember the Maine. C. C. Converse. Words by R. B. Wilson. MP

"Remember thee." Irish air: Castle Tirowen. Words by T. Moore. MI— MMI

"Remember thy Creator now." W. H. Havergal. FSS 1—WBT—WSC

"Remember what you promised me." See "Och mins du hvad du lofvade"

"Rememb'rest thou that setting sun." See The evening gun

Remembrance ("Ich denke dein") See "Ich denke dein, wenn durch den hain" (Beethoven)

Remembrance ("Sejećaš li se onog sata") Croatian folk song. Words by S. Jović. e.se. BF 1

Remembrance ("Te souviens-tu") See "Te souviens-tu de ta promesse" (Godard)

"The remembrance of our last meeting" (Awaiaulu) C. K. Hopkins. Words by L. Mahelona. · e.h. HA

Remembrances ("I remember how I lingered") Air: Y ferch o'r Scêr. Words by D. Rowlands (Dewi Mon) MMW

Remer, Paul
Herbstgang (Jordan)

Remick. See Gile, jt. auth.

Rémon, Rémon. Negro creole folk song. e.f. KA

The remorse of Peter. See Petrus klage (Brandts-Buys)

Remy, F.
The convivials

Renaud, Armand
Le Nil (Leroux)
La solitaire (Saint-Saëns)
La splendeur vide (Saint-Saëns)

Rencontre (A meeting) G. Fauré. Words by C. Grandmougin. e.f. SAM

Rend' il sereno al ciglio (To thy sad brow let joy return) Händel. e.i. SS 2

Rennes, Catharina van
Cradle song. See Wiegeliedje
Sunshine song. See Zonnelied
Wiegeliedje
Zonnelied

Renshaw, Clarence
Technology (Haworth)

Repentance. See Reue (Lachner)

The repentance of Manasseh. See I will bear the indignation of God

The repentant shepherdess. See La bergère à confesse

Repentir (O divine Redeemer) C. Gounod. e.f. HSS 1—HSS 2

Repique el pandero. Porto Rican song. s. LCP

"Repose, ô belle amoureuse." See Ferme les yeux, ô belle maîtresse (Massenet)

The reproach ("How, beloved, did I grieve thee."— Chĭem tebĭa ĭa ogorchila) Russian folk song. e. SSR 2

Reproach ("Love, have you quite forgotten."—Ukor) Dalmatian folk song. e.se. BF 1

The reproach ("Phillis, talk no more") See "Phillis, talk no more of passion" (Monro)

The reproach ("Send back my long-stray'd eyes") R. Leveridge. Words by Donne. DM 2
"Send home my long-stray'd eyes to me." MM

The reproach ("Send back my long strayed eyes") A. Young. Words by Donne. BE 5

The reproof ("Charming is your shape and air") DM 2

Request. See Bitte (Franz)

Requiem (Underwoods) S. Homer. Words by R. L. Stevenson. AA

"Resign! thou art but born to weary." See Resignation (Musorgskiĭ)

Resignation ("No word shall e'er reveal it") F. Mendelssohn. WBT

Resignation ("Resign! thou art but born to weary."—Skootcháĭ) M. P. Moussorgsky. Words by A. Golenishtcheff-Kutoozoff. e. SMR 1

Resolution. E. Lassen. e. WBT— WBW

A resolve. See Obstination (Fontenailles)

Rest, Johann
"Now, courage take" (Schop)

Rest ("The sun goes down") Silesian song. e. BMC

"Rest all souls, all souls in peace rest." See Litaney (Schubert)

Rest for the weary. J. W. Dadmun. Words by S. Y. Harmer. HSD
There is rest for the weary. WS

Rest for the weary. W. McDonald. Words by S. Y. Harmer. FSS 3
"In the Christian's home in glory." WBT
There is rest for the weary. WBT

"Rest in peace, all souls departed." See Litaney (Schubert)

"Rest in peace, thou dear-lov'd creature." See "Com' è bello" (Donizetti)

"Rest, my child." H. Bishop. Words by S. J. Arnold. DM 2—HSE 3

"Rest, rest to the weary, peace, peace to the soul." See Calvary (Rodney)

"Rest thee, my sweet." See "Ruhe, süss-liebchen" (Brahms); "Ruhe süss, liebchen" (Franz)

"Rest thou, my pretty one, rest." See Wiegenlied (Mozart)

Rest, warrior, rest. M. Kelly. BE 6—HSE 2

The resurrection. See "I live, my heart is beating" (Pugno)

The retort. T. A. Arne. ME

Le retour des promis ("Come out, come out, my dears") Dessauer. Words by Bourges. e.f. SS 1

Le retour du mari soldat (The return of the soldier husband) French Canadian folk song. e.f. BFS

Le retour du soldat (The soldier's return) French folk song. e.f. TSF

Le retour du voyageur (The traveller's return) Canadian folk song. e.f. TF

Le retour funeste (The tragic home-coming) French Canadian folk song. e.f. BFS

Retreat. T. Hastings. Words by H. Stowell. HSD—WBT

Retreat (The mercy-seat) FSS 5

Retrospect (Okóntchen prázdnui, shoomnui dyen) M. P. Moussorgsky. Words by A. Golenishtcheff-Kutoozoff. e. SMR 1

"Return, my love, my soul reposing." See Absence (Berlioz)

Return, O God of hosts. G. F. Händel. SAS 2

Return, oh God of hosts. OS 2

The return of spring. W. H. Jones. Words by B. Taylor. NMS

The return of the soldier husband. See Le retour du mari soldat

"Return, return, O God of hosts." See Return, O God of hosts (Händel)

"Return, return, revolting rebels." H. Purcell. BS 2

Returning. See Reiselied (Mendelssohn)

"Returning home across the fields." See Lubin's rural cot

The returning hunter. Eskimo Indian song. es. SN

Returning spring. See Printemps nouveau (Vidal)

Reuben and Rachel. Old American song. TFC 1

Reuben Ranzo ("Oh, pity poor Reuben Ranzo") Halliard chantey. CR
For variants of this song see following songs of same title; also Poor old Reuben Ranzo

Reuben Ranzo ("Oh, poor old Rueben Ranzo") Long drag chantey. KB

Reuben Ranzo ("Pity Reuben Ranzo") Hauling chantey. GO—SMW

"Reuben, Reuben, I've been thinking." See Reuben and Rachel

Reue (Repentance) F. Lachner. Words by E. Geibel. e.g. AB 4

Reuenthal, Neidhart von. See Neidhardt von Reuenthal

Re-united. Air: Bonnie Dundee. Words by A. P. Melville. SSS

Le rêve (The dream) J. Massenet. e.f. CM 2

"Reve ta stogne." See "Rushes and roars the wide Dnieper"

Reveille. Dutch folk song. e. DO

"Réveillez-vous, belle endormie" ("Waken, my fair one, from thy slumber") French folk song. e.f. TSF

Revenge. J. L. Hatton. Words by E. Fitzball. BAS 2

Revenge, Timotheus cries. Händel. BAS 1

Rêverie ("Puisqu'ici-bas toute âme") R. Hahn. Words by V. Hugo. e.f. SM 2

Revery ("My eyes are closing."—Im halbschlaf) A. Arensky. Words from the Russian of L. Munschtein. e.g. NM 1

Revery of the young peasant (Doomka párobka) M. P. Moussorgsky. e. SMR 1

Lou revestidon. G. Borel. Words by Delille. e.f.pr. SMW

"Rêvez, rêvez, enfants d'Irlande." See Noël d'Irlande (Holmès)

"Reviens, reviens, ma bien-aimée." See Absence (Berlioz)

"Revive again, thou summer rain." See There is no end for souls like his (Sharland)

Revive us again. J. J. Husband. Words by W. P. Mackay. FSS 7

Reyes, Jose
"Quis gus ya nosvalientes"

Los reyes de Oriente. Porto Rican air. Words by M. Fernández Juncos. s. LCP

Los reyes magos. B. D. Colón. Words by M. Fernández Juncos. s. LCP

Reynard the fox ("The first day of spring in the year ninety three") Irish hunting song. JOI
Hunting song ("The first day of spring in the year ninety-three") MMI

Reynolds, Frederic
"When a little farm we keep" (Mazzinghi)
The wife in masquerade (Mazzinghi)
Young Lobski's fishing tale (Mazzinghi)

Reynolds, George Nugent
"My love, still I think that I see her" (Irish air)

Reynolds, Hans
Tilsjös (Backer-Gröndahl)

Reynolds, Henry
"Come, Chloris, hie we to thy bower" (Lawes)

Rheinlied. See Der deutsche Rhein (Kunze)

"Rheinwein nur aus römerbechern trink." See Rheinweinlied (Methfessel)

Das rheinwein-paradies ("Ein leben wie im paradies") Words by Hölty. g. ED 2

Rheinweinlied ("Bekränzt mit laub den lieben vollen") J. André. Words by M. Claudius. g. ED 1

Rheinweinlied ("Brüder, das ist deutscher wein") F. Silcher. Words by A. Schreiber. g. ED 3

Rheinweinlied ("Rheinwein nur aus römer-
bechern trink") A. Methfessel. Words
by K. Göttling. g. ED 2
Der rheinweinzecher ("Im kuhlen keller")
L. Fischer. Words by C. Müchler.
g. ED 1
Drinking. e. BOS
"Im kühlen keller" ("In cellar cool")
e.g. BO
"Im tiefen keller sitz' ich hier" ("In
cellar cool") e.g. AB 3—KF 4
"In cellar cool." e. WBT
Der mann im keller ("My lodging is the
cellar here") e.g. BS 1
Rheinweinzecher ("In cellar cool")
e.g. FMB—SSS
Rhine song. See Der deutsche Rhein
(Kunze)
Rhine-wine song. See Am Rhein und beim
wein (Ries)
Rhodes, Elizabeth Meserole
Leaving the nest (Reddall)
Rhodes, Mrs Helen (Guy) See Har-
delot, Guy d', pseud.
"**Rhwym** wrth dy wregys." See Rhyvel-
gyrch Cadpen Morgan
Rhyfelgyrch gwyr Harlech (Men of Har-
lech) Old Welsh patriotic song.
e.w. BSP—SN
The march of the men of Harlech
("Hark! I hear the foe advancing")
e. BMC—BOS
March of the men of Harlech ("Men
of Harlech") e.w. MP—NMH—
WBT—WSW. e. only DSH—
OH—TL
The men of Harlech. e.w. WA.
e. only BAS 1—CST—FSS 6—LA
—MS—SSS
Rhyfelgyrch gwyr Harlech (March of
the men of Harlech.—"Hark! I hear
the foe advancing") e. MMW
Rhyfelgyrch gwyr Harlech (March of
the men of Harlech.—"Men of Har-
lech! in the hollow") e.w. WCP
"A **rhyme**, a rhyme, for Easter time." G.
B. Lissant. Words by G. P. Grant-
ham. HC
Rhyme of the rail. Words by J. G. Saxe.
FSS 5
Rhyvelgyrch Cadpen Morgan (Captain
Morgan's march) Welsh folk song.
e.w. KA
"**Riberas** amenas de fértil llanura." See
La despedida (Gutiérrez)
Riboutté, Charles Henri
"Que ne suis-je la fougère" (Pergole-
si?)
Ricci, Federico
"Dormi, dormi bel bambino" (from La
prigione di Edimburgo)
La **ricciolella.** 18th century Neapolitan
folk song. i. BO
La ricciolella (Antonia) e. GO
Rice, E. S.
"Shall we meet beyond the river"
Rice, Lilian Dynevor
A bed-time song (Nevin)

Rich, Marie
My rose of yester-e'en
"**Rich** and fair as roses blooming." See
"Sa couleur est blonde et vermeille"
(Massé)
"**Rich** and rare were the gems she wore."
Air: The summer is coming. Words
by T. Moore. MI—MMI—PI—SS 1
"**Rich** in odours overflowing." See Le vio-
lette (Scarlatti)
"The **rich** man's son inherits lands." See
The heritage
The **rich** old lady. Folk song from North
Carolina. CSE
Richard of Taunton Dean ("Last New-
Year's day as I've heard say") Compos-
er unknown. MM
Richard of Taunton Dean ("One Zunday
morn, as I've heerd zay") Somerset-
shire folk song. BE 7—BOS—DM 2
Richards, Brinley
"Among our ancient mountains." See
God bless the prince of Wales
Christmas chimes
God bless the prince of Wales
"O whisper what thou feelest." See
Whisper what thou feelest
Where warbling waters
Whisper what thou feelest (from
Crown diamonds)
Richards, Mrs Laura Elizabeth (Howe)
At happy Easter time (Reinecke)
**Richards, Mrs Laura Elizabeth (Howe),
and Hawkins, W.**
"The little flowers came from the
ground" (Naylor)
Richardson,
Fair Rosalie (Dibdin)
Sweet lilies of the valley (Hook)
Richardson, A. H. G.
"No one to love" (Harvey)
Richardson, G. G.
Dance of the fairies (German air)
Richepin, Jean
Les morts (Chausson)
Rickman, F. R.
Glad angel voices
Riddell, Henry Scott
"Oh! thou art all so tender" (Scottish
air)
Riddell, Robert
The blue-eyed lassie
"The day returns, my bosom burns"
"I gaed a waefu' gate yestreen." See
The blue-eyed lassie
"I sing of a whistle" (attributed)
"The noble Maxwells and their pow-
ers"
The **riddle** song ("I gave my love a cher-
ry") Folk song from Kentucky. SA
Riddle-song ("Now a ring of gold do I
hide."—Uzh íã zoloto khoroníu) Rus-
sian folk song. e. SSR 1
The **ride.** H. R. Shelley. Words by A.
A. Chapin. HST
"**Ride** a cock-horse to Banbury Cross."
Nursery song. FMB—WSC
Ride on ("Some of dese mornin's") Negro
spiritual. HR

Ride on, Moses. Negro spiritual. JB—JP

Rider, George T.
"Oh, the golden, glowing morning" (Le Jeune)
"Sleep, my infant Saviour" (Rider)

Rider, H. de Koven
"Sleep, my infant Saviour"
"Riding down from Bangor." Student song. SSS

Riding on the elevated. Flemish folk air. Words by R. Compton. DO

Ridsdale, C. J.
"It was early in the morning"
"On the first bright Christmas day"

Riego's hymn. See Hymno de Riego (Huerta)

Riera, Deogracias
"Venid, pastorcillos" (Porto Rican air)

Ries, Franz
Am Rhein und beim wein
Beloved Columbia (same air as Am Rhein und beim wein)
"Die blauen frühlingsaugen"
Cradle song. See Wiegenlied
"Du bist die herrlichste von allen"
Es muss was wunderbares sein
"The eyes of spring so azure." See "Die blauen frühlingsaugen"
Frühlingsglaube
Most wondrous it must be. See Es muss was wunderbares sein
Rhine-wine song. See Am Rhein und beim wein
Spring faith. See Frühlingsglaube
"Thou art the noblest of them all." See "Du bist die herrlichste von allen"
Wiegenlied

Rig-a-jig. College song. HSD—MPC—WBT—WC

Righini, Vincenzo
Al nome tuo temuto (from La Selva incantata)
Für mädchen
Lied eines landmanns in der fremde
"Nehmt euch in acht"
Sehnsucht

"A right good sword, a constant mind." See Song of the western men
"Right noble gave, voortrekkers brave." See "Kent gij dat volk vol heldenmoed" (Rees)

Riker, Franklin Wing
A gentle hint

Riley, James
The flag (Crosby)

Riley, James Whitcomb
Little orphant Annie (Composer unknown)

Rimbault, Edward Francis
The Alpine horn
"Happy land! happy land"
"Oh, happy day, that fixed my choice"

Rimeberg, J. L.
Den första kyssen (Sibelius)

Rimskiĭ-Korsakov, Nikolaĭ Andreevich
Air of the queen of Shemakhá. See Hymn to the sun
Aira Óksánui. See Oxana's song
"Au royaume du vin et des roses." See Come to the realm of roses and wine
"Believe me not"
Chanson de Zuleika. See Song of Zuleika
Chanson hebraïque. See Hebrew love-song
Chanson indoue. See A song of India
The cloud and the mountain
Come to the realm of roses and wine
Cradle song (from The maid of Pskov)
Dyéva i sólntze. See The maid and the sun
Eastern romance
Hebrew love-song
Hymn to the sun (from The golden cockerel)
"I have come to say good morning"
In silent woods
Kak nyebesá tvoi vzor blistáyet. See "Like to the sky serenely smiling"
"Like mountains the waves"
"Like to the sky serenely smiling"
Little Snowflake's arietta (from The snow maiden)
The maid and the sun
"Me voici, je te salue." See "I have come to say good morning"
The nightingale and the rose
Notchevála tootchka zolotáya. See The cloud and the mountain
Nuit méridionale. See A southern night
The octave
On the Georgian hills
Oxana's song (from Christmas eve revels)
Piésn Shemakhánskoi tzarítzui K'sólntzu. See Hymn to the sun
Piésnia lubáshi. See The song of the bride
Plenívshis rósoi, salavyéi. See Eastern romance
"The rainy day is past"
"The rose has charmed the nightingale." See Eastern romance
Sadko's song of glorification (from Sadko)
The singer
A song of India (from Sadko)
The song of the bride (from The tzar's bride)
Song of the shepherd Lehl (from The snow maiden)
Song of Zuleika
A southern night
Sur les collines de Géorgie. See On the Georgian hills
Sylvan roundelay (from The snow maiden)
V' tiómnoi róshtchye zamólk salavyéi. See In silent woods

Rimskiï-Korsakov, N. A. —*Continued*
Velitchálnaya pyésnya. See Sadko's song of glorification
Vostótchnui romans. See Eastern romance
"Waves dashing and breaking"
Rinaldo Rinaldini ("In des waldes finstern gründen") German folk air. Words by A. Vulpius. e.g. SSG. g. only ED 1
Rinck, Johann Christian Heinrich
Abendlied
"Alike are life and death"
"Alle jahre wieder"
"As each happy Christmas." See "Alle jahre wieder"
Rinckart, Martin
Nun danket alle Gott (Crüger)
The **ring**. See Das ringlein
Ring again, ring again, beautiful bells. See Beautiful bells (Lyte)
"**Ring** around a rosy, sit upon a posy." Children's game song. FSS 4—WBT —WSC
"**Ring**, bells, ring." M. O. Brown (music and words) HC
Ring, bells! swing, bells. See The glad bells all say (Crowe)
Ring forever. C. Gounod. MCS
"**Ring**, happy bells of Christmas time." H. E. Nichol. Words by C. Sterne. HC
"**Ring**, happy bells of Easter time." H. P. Pike. Words by L. Larcom. HC
"**Ring** merrily." J. W. Treadwell. HC
Ring on, sweet angelus. C. Gounod. Words by H. B. Farnie. FSS 5
"**Ring** on, ye bells." F. Abt. Words by H. Francke. e. FSS 4
"**Ring** on, ye joyous Christmas bells." A. H. Brown. Words by H. G. Batterson. HC
"**Ring** on, ye joyous Christmas bells." H. Wilson. Words by H. G. Batterson. HC
"**Ring** out, O bells, ring silver-sweet." G. Barker. FSS 6
"**Ring** out, O bells, ring silver-sweet" (The new year) P. Goetschius. NMS
"**Ring** out, O bells! your peals to-day." Christmas carol. HC
"**Ring** out, ring out a joyful peal." W. Borrow. Words by H. G. Duffield. HC
"**Ring** out, ring out, O Christmas bells." C. F. Roper. Words by K. Ingmire. HC
"**Ring** out, song of the hills." See "Va loin"
"**Ring** out, sweet bells." W. J. Westbrook. HC
"**Ring** out, sweet Easter bells, ring out." J. Anketell (music and words) HC
"**Ring** out, sweet Easter bells, ring out." J. Blaikie. [Words by J. Anketell] HC
"**Ring** out the anthem, Jesus lives." C. Fitzsimmons. HC

"**Ring** out the bells for Christmas." Composer unknown. Words by E. A. Washburn. HC
"**Ring** out the bells for Christmas." J. S. B. Hodges. Words by E. A. Washburn. HC
"**Ring** out the bells for Christmas." J. Mosenthal. Words by E. A. Washburn. HC
"**Ring** out, thou wondrous song." See "Sjung, sjung, du underbara sång" (Josephson)
"**Ring** out, wild bells." C. Gounod. Words by A. Tennyson. BD
"**Ring** out, wild bells." F. P. Tosti. Words by A. Tennyson. MCS—TL
"**Ring** out, ye joyous Easter bells." G. E. Oliver. Words by E. J. Selden. HC
"**Ring** out, ye merry bells." E. Lemare. Words by A. Gaskell. HC
"**Ring** out, ye throbbing stars of night." Mrs J. H. Barbour. HC
"**Ring** out, ye wild and merry bells." C. Maitland. HC
Ring, ring de banjo. S. C. Foster (music and words) NMP—WBT
"**Ring**, ring the bells." F. A. Challinor. HC
Ring the bells ("Oh, ring the bells in the belfry high") Folk air. Words by S. Paul. TFC 2
"**Ring** the bells, the Christmas bells." A. H. Brown. Words by A. Burney. HC
"**Ring** the bells, the Christmas bells." T. C. Dean. Words by A. Burney. HC
"**Ring** the bells, the Christmas bells." C. Erskine. Words by A. Burney. HC
"**Ring** the bells, the Christmas bells." A. Oake. Words by A. Burney. HC
Ring the joyful Christmas bells. F. Peskett. HC
Ring ye bells merrily. See Welcome Christmas cheer (Storace)
The **ringers** of Torrington town. Folk song. BE 4
Das **ringlein** ("Bald gras ich am Neckar") Volkslied. g. ED 1
Das ringlein (The ring) e.g. SSG
"**Ringsum** erschallt in wald und flur." See Sonntagslied (Mendelssohn)
Rinkart, Martin. See Rinckart, Martin
Rinnt, ihr thränen. For English translation see "O ye tears" (Abt)
Rio, Manuel del
"Muh'voll komm' ich und beladen" (Wolf)
Rio Grand ("I think I heard") Capstan chantey. SE
For variants see following songs of similar title
Rio Grande ("I'll sing you a song") Chantey. SMW
Rio Grande ("Oh, say, was you ever") Capstan chantey. CR
"**Rio** Grande is no place for me." Capstan chantey. KB

"**Ripe** are the apples." Words by M. Herbert. FSS 6

"A **ripe** old dame do I woo." See "Ann hini gouz"

Riposa, o madre. For English translation see "Sleep, gentle mother" (Verdi)

Ripples touched by the moon. Words by A. Thompson. FSS 8

Ris, ras (El carpintero) Spanish American song. s. LCP

Rise and shine. Negro spiritual. DF——HR—JP

"**Rise**, arise, arise." See The sun worshippers

"**Rise** crowned with light." A. T. Lwoff. Words by A. Pope. CST—TL—WS
  "Rise, crowned with light" (Russian hymn) FSS 2—MCS

"**Rise**, crowned with light." G. E. Oliver. Words by A. Pope. LA

Rise from thy mourning. German air. FSS 6

Rise, gentle moon. J. Barnett. Words by J. R. Planché. BE 3

"**Rise**, glorious Conqueror" (Italian hymn) Giardini. Words by M. Bridges. FSS 8—MCS

"**Rise!** I say! ere departing." See Eri tu che macchia vi (Verdi)

"**Rise**, mourner, rise, an' don't be ashamed." Negro spiritual. BOM

"**Rise**, mourners, rise, mourners." Negro spiritual. JP—NMP

"**Rise**, my Mahmude" ("Ngreu moj Mahmude") Albanian wedding song. al.e. BF 2

"**Rise**, my soul, and stretch thy wings." Nares. Words by R. Seagrave. FSS 4

"**Rise**, O Servians" ("Ustaj, ustaj Srbine") Old Servian song. e.se. BSP
  O Serbians rise. e.se. MP
  "Rise, O Servians" (National song of Servia.—Ustay! Ustay! Serbine) e. BMC
  Servian national hymn. e.se. WA—WBT—WSW

"**Rise**, O sun; rise, thou glowing sun so red." See The captive maiden

"**Rise**, rise, free from thy mourning." See Rise from thy mourning

"**Rise**, rise, ye shepherds, still slumbering here." See Christmas carol

Rise, Servians ("Servia, peaceful land of flowers") Air: "Rise, O Servians." e. SN
  Rise, Servians (Servian hymn) e. KSE

"**Rise** up, rise up, Xarifa." See The bridal of Andalla (Browne)

Rise up, shepherd and foller. Negro spiritual. Christmas plantation song. DF
  Rise up, shepherd, an' foller. BF 2—HR

"The **risen** Lord to-day is King." L. H. Redner. Words by J. C. Middleton. HC

"**Rising** midst the golden cornfield." See Alma mater—Illinois

"The **rising** morn, the closing day." H. Townsend. HC

"**Rising** o'er the heaving billow." See The maid of Islay

The **rising** of the lark ("Hark, hark! his morning praise") Air: Codiad yr ehedydd. CST

The **rising** of the lark ("Light from my lowly bed") Air: Codiad yr ehedydd. Words by J. M. E. Dovaston. MMW

The **rising** of the lark ("See, oh see the breaking day") Air: Codiad yr hedydd. Words by A. Grant. BMC

"**Rita**, my beauty arise from thy pillow." See Lo Granatiello

"**Rita**, su svegliati, scendi bel bello." See Lo Granatiello

"**Ritka** buza, ritka árpa, ritka rozs." See Rare the barley, rare the rye, rare the wheat

"**Ritorna** vincitor." See L'insana parola (Verdi)

Ritornelli romaneschi (Ritornelli) Italian song. e.i. BF 2

Ritornello delle lavandare del Vomero (Refrain of the washerwomen of Vomero) Neapolitan song. e.i. MSI
  Refrain of the washerwomen of Vomero. e. BSE

Ritournelle. C. Chaminade. Words by Coppée. e.f. PG 1

Rittenhaus, Emil
  Am Rhein und beim wein (Ries)
  Beim rheinwein (Gilbert)

Ritter, Anna
  Laengsel (Backer-Lunde)

"Der **ritter** muss zum blutgen kampf hinaus." See Treuer tod (Choron)

Ritters abschied. For English translation see Soldier's farewell (Kinkel)

Rittmeyer, Wilhelm
  Night song

"**River**, flow, river, flow toward your ancient harbor-town." See Longing

"The **river** is clear as glass." See Evening on the river

The **River** Lee. See Bells of Shandon (Mahony)

River Shenandore. Windlass song. SMW
  Variants: Shanadar; Shenandoah

"A **river** with green and shady borders." See La casita

The **river's** message. A. Braun. FSS 8

Rives, Amélie. See Troubetzkoy, Amélie (Rives) Chanler

Riviere, J.
  Spring, gentle spring

The **road** to Moltras. See "Lee l'andava e mi vegneva"

"Roaming o'er the meadows far." Round. FSS 6

"A roar like thunder strikes the ear." See Die wacht am Rhein (Wilhelm)

The roast beef of old England. R. Leveridge. Verses 1-2 by H. Fielding, verses 3-6 by R. Leveridge. BE 4—BOH—BS 1—DM 1—HSE 1—JO—JSE—MM —WBT—WCP

"Rob Roy from the Highlands cam." Air: Mill, mill O. Words by R. Burns. BSR

"Rob Roy was my father ca'd." Air: Jenny dang the weaver. Words by R. Burns. BSR

Robaudi, V.
Alla stella confidente
"Bright star of love." See Alla stella confidente

The robber ("When I was eighteen") Folk song. SEF 2—SO

The robbers ("The chough and crow") H. Parker. Words by J. Baillie. TL

The robber's fate (Ne shumi, mati, zelenaîa dubrovushka) Russian folk song. e. SSR 2

"Robert! Robert." See "Roberto, o tu che adoro" (Meyerbeer)

Robert, toi que j'aime. For Italian and English translations see "Roberto, o tu che adoro" (Meyerbeer)

Roberti, G.
Barcarolle. See Come to the sea
Come to the sea

"Roberto, o tu che adoro." Meyerbeer. [Tr of Robert, toi que j'aime] e.i. OPS 1—PP
"Robert! Robert." e. FSS 7

Roberts, Brian C.
"O lowly, sacred stable" (Houghton)

Roberts, Daniel C.
National hymn (Warren)

Roberts, George
The dark fairy rath (Irish air)

Roberts, William J.
"Easter flowers, Easter carols" (Hall)

The robin ("There came to my window") Old song. DO

Robin-a-Thrush. English folk song. DO

Robin Adair ("What's this dull town to me") Celtic air: Eileen aroon. English version of air. Words by C. Keppel. BOS—BSE—EF—ES—FSS 1—HSC—HSD—HSSS— JO—JSE—LA— MMS—MS— MSS 1—NMH—NML—OH—PS 1—SMF—SS 1—WA—WBT—WL— WSW
—Irish and Scottish version of air. PS 1
Robin Adair ("Treu und herzinniglich") English version of air. g. ED 1

"The robin cam to the wren's nest." Air: The wren's nest. Words by R. Burns. BSR

Robin Good-fellow. See Dulcina

"Robin Hood and Little John." See The Cornish May song

Robin Hood and the bishop of Hereford. English folk song. MM
—Dorset version. SF 1

Robin Hood and the tanner. English folk song. SEF 1—SO

"Robin Hood, Robin Hood, said little John." 16th century song. DM 2 —JE

"Robin loves me." Adam de la Hale. e. DT

Robin Redbreast ("Good-bye, good-bye to summer") German air. Words by Allingham. FSS 1

The robin redbreast ("He sailed away o'er the ocean spray") W. C. Levey. Words by J. Thomson. FSS 7

Robin! Robin. A. S. Gatty. WSC

Robin Ruff. See The better wish (Russell)

Robin shure in hairst. See "I gaed up to Dunse"

The robin song. Old air. FSS 7

Robin Tamson's smiddy. Scottish song. Air: The taylor. PS 2

Robin was a rovin boy. See "There was a lad was born in Kyle"

Robinson, A. R.
Our banner (Wilhelm)

Robinson, John G.
"Wake! and tune your youthful voices" (Southwick)

Robinson, Mrs Mary (Derby)
"Bounding billows, cease your motion" (Composer unknown)

Robinson, Robert
Come, Thou Fount of every blessing" (Wyeth)
"Saviour, Source of every blessing" (music by Mendelssohn; Whitmore)

Robinson Crusoe. Air: Rogues' march. Words by J. Cussans. FSS 1—JO—JSE—MCS—WBT—WSC

Robiquet, Paul Pierre
"Ouvre tes yeux bleus" (Massenet)

Rochester, John Wilmot, 2d earl of
"All my pass'd life" (Blow)
My lodging is on the cold ground (Traditional air)

"Rock-a-bye, baby." Nursery song. Regular version of air. WA—WBT—WSC—WSW

"Rock-a-bye, baby." Nursery song. English version of air. WSC

"Rock-a-bye baby." Nursery song. 3d air. TFC 2

"Rock-a-bye, baby" (American cradle-song) Nursery song. 4th air. FSS 3

"Rock-a-bye, baby." Nursery song, with additional words by R. J. Burdette. 5th air. FSS 3

"Rock-a-bye, baby." Nursery song. A. S. Gatty. WSC

Rock me to sleep. E. Leslie. Words by E. A. Allen. BSE
Rock me to sleep, mother. FSS 4—HSC—HSD—NMH—WBT

Rock me to sleep. J. M. Mueller. Words by E. A. Allen. JO

"Rock of ages, cleft for me." J. B. Dykes. Words by A. M. Toplady. LA

"Rock of ages, cleft for me." T. Hastings. Words by A. M. Toplady. FMB— FSS 2—HSC— HSD— NMH— NMS— OH— WA— WBT— WS— WSC— WSW

"Rock of ages, let our song." Traditional air. BSS

The rock of Cader Idris ("I lay on that rock where the storms") Air: Llwyn on, or, The ash grove. Words by F. D. Hemans. BMC

"Rockaby, lullaby, bees in the clover." See Cradle song (Raymond)

Rockaway. H. Russell. Words by H. J. Sharpe. FSS 6—JO

Rocke, L.
Wilt thou soon return

"Rocked in the cradle of the deep." J. P. Knight. Words by E. Willard. BE 1 —DM 1—FSS 2—HSC—HSD—HSE 1 —JO—LA—NMH—OH—PO—TFC 1 —WA—WBT —WS—WSC—WSW

Röckel, Joseph Leopold. See Roeckel, Joseph Leopold

Rocks and storms I'll fear no more. See Safe within the vail

The rocks and the mountains. Negro spiritual. HR
Oh, the rocks and the mountains. NMP

"Rocks in de mountens." Negro forecastle song. CR

The rocky mountain top. Folk song from North Carolina. CSE

Rödan guldband (The purple gold ribbon) Swedish dance song. e.sw. BF 2
"Och flickan hon går i dansen" ("A maiden one day was dancing") e.sw. HSOS

Rodney, Paul
The brave sentinel
Calvary
The clang of the forge
Emmanuel
Ferryman John
The old guard
Sion
The soldier's dream

Rodwell, George Herbert Buonaparte
The banks of the blue Moselle

Roe, J. E.
"Hark! hark, my soul"
"Love divine, all love excelling"
Weston. See "Love divine, all love excelling"

Roeckel, Joseph Leopold
All that glitters
Angus Macdonald
Arise! He calleth thee
The bride bells
"Cast thy bread on the waters"
"Day is dying, cool sweet winds"
Happy three
He giveth His beloved sleep
The hour of rest

Jack at sea
Madeleine
Prince Charming
The skippers of St Ives
Thou art the way

Roeder, Otto
Child's dreamland
Gondolier waltz. See On Venice waters
On Venice waters

Roehlitz, Friedrich
Alinde (Schubert)

Rogé, Mme Charlotte Fiske (Bates)
Rose song (Smith)

Roger and Cicely. Old English air. BE 8

Rogers,
The blind beggar of Bethnal green

Rogers, James Hotchkiss
April weather
At parting

Rogers, Samuel
"Dear is my little native vale" (Composer unknown)

Rogers, Winthrop L.
Let Miss Lindy pass

Roger's courtship. H. Carey. BE 3

"Rogues like you." See "Solche hergelauf' ne laffen" (Mozart)

Le roi Dagobert. French folk song. f. FMB

Le roi de Thulé (The king of Thule) Gounod. Words by Goethe. Tr of Der könig von Thule e.f.i. OPS 1
The king of Thule. e. BD—BSE

Le roi d'Yvetot. French political song. Words by P. J. de Béranger. f. DO
The king of Yvetot ("There was a king of Yvetot once") e. BMC

"Le roi Renaud de guerre vint." See La chanson de Renaud

"Le roi sommeille." See Que ton âme si noble (Rossini)

Roisin dubh ("Oh! my sweet little rose") Irish air: Rois gael dubh, or, The fair black-hair'd little rose. Words from the Irish. e. MMI—PI

Le roitelet (The wren) E. Paladilhe. Words by A. Theuriet. e.f. GMF— SAM

Rojo, blanco y azul. See Columbia, the gem of the ocean (Becket)

Rolfsen, Nordahl
Solefaldssang (Olsen)

"Roll a river wide and strong." See A song of the flag

Roll and go. Capstan chantey. SE

Roll away. G. L. Tracy. Words by D. Stevens. BSS

Roll de ole chariot along. Negro spiritual. HR
Roll de ol' chariot along. JB

Roll, Jordan, roll ("Brothers, you oughter had a been there") Negro spiritual. DF

Roll, Jordan, roll ("O brother, you ought t'have been there") HR

Roll, Jordan, roll ("Oh, brothers, you ought t'have been there") BSE—FSS 4—JP—NMP—WC

Roll Jordan, roll ("Oh, brothers you oughter been dere") JB

Roll, Jordan, roll ("My brudder sittin' on de tree ob life") Negro spiritual. KA

Roll on, silver moon. Arr by J. W. Turner. FSS 2—JO—WBT—WL

"Roll onward, ever roll, deep surging ocean." See Block island song

Roll the cotton down ("I'm bound to Alabama") Negro halliard chantey. CR

For variant of this song see following song of same title

Roll the cotton down ("Oh roll the cotton, roll it down") Long drag chantey. KB

Roll the kaiser down. Air: Roll the cotton down. Long drag chantey. KB

Rolle, Johann Heinrich
Abendlied (same air as "Lobt den Herrn")
"Lobt den Herrn" (from Der tod Abels)

Roller, bowler. Capstan chantey. SE

Rolling home. Sea song. KB

"Rolling in foaming billows." Haydn. e. OS 4—SAS 4

Rolling king. Capstan chantey. CR

Rollitt, C. C.
The children's Easter offering (Herron)

"Roman soldier, tell us true." J. H. Hopkins (music and words) HC

The Roman soldiers. Singing game. FSF

Romance ("L'âme évaporée") A. C. Debussy. Words by P. Bourget. e.f. CMF 2—HM 1—SAM. e. only BC

Romance ("O'er peaks of the sierra Nevada") M. Ippolitoff-Ivanoff. Words from the Spanish. e. NM 1

Romance from Rosamunde. See Romanze aus Rosamunde (Schubert)

Romance of Dunois. See Partant pour la Syrie (Hortense Eugénie de Beauharnais?)

La Romanella. Neapolitan folk song. e.i. SMF

Romano, Giulio, pseud. See Caccini, Giulio

"Romantic Esk." Scottish air: Fy, gar rub her o'er wi' strae. Words by R. Gall. PS 2

The Romany lass. S. Adams. Words by F. E. Weatherly. FSS 8

"The Romany sat by his bright tent fire." See The Romany lass (Maybrick)

Romanze aus Rosamunde (Romance from Rosamunde) F. Schubert. Words by H. von Chezy. e.g. GM

Romanze von den schneidern ("Es sind einmal drei schneider") F. H. Himmel. Volkslied. g. ED 2

Romberg, Andreas
"Kennst du das land"
Mignon. See "Kennst du das land"

Romea y Valverde,
Niña Pancha

Romeo and Juliet ("Come now and listen") College song. [T. H. Bayly] CHS

Romeo and Juliet ("Love, 'tis not day."—Romeo i Julietta) Duet. P. I. Tchaikovsky. Words from Shakespeare. e. SMR 2

Romeo i Julietta. See Romeo and Juliet (Tchaikovsky)

Romer, Frank
I would I were a boy again
"O would I were a boy again." See I would I were a boy again
Old Christmas

La ronde de l'aveine (Round of the oats) French folk song. e.f. TSF

La ronde du rosier (Round of the rosetree) Folk song from Lorraine. e.f. FTF

La rondinella (The swallow) Tuscan song. e.i. MSI

"Rondinella pellegrina." See La rondinella

Rontani, Raffaello
"If the brook." See "Se bel rio"
"Now that I seek no more." See "Or ch'io non seguo più"
"Or ch'io non seguo più"
"Se bel rio"
"When the murm'ring." See "Se bel rio"

"Room for the city's factotum here." See "Largo al factotum della città" (Rossini)

"Room, room for a rover." Plaisable. Words by T. D'Urfey. BE 7

Root, Frederick Woodman
Beloved Columbia (Ries)

Root, George Frederick
"All together, all together"
The battle cry of freedom
"Brother, tell me of the battle"
Departed days
"Fair as the morning"
The hazel dell
The independent farmer
Just after the battle
"Just before the battle, mother"
On, on, on, the boys came marching
Shining shore
"There's music in the air"
Tramp! tramp! tramp
The vacant chair
"When He cometh"

Root hog or die. Cowboy song. LC

Ropartz, Joseph Guy Marie
Berceuse
Lullaby. See Berceuse

Roper, Charles F.
"Joyfully, joyfully angels are singing"
"Oh! sing a merry carol"
"Ring out, ring out, O Christmas bells"
"Sing, oh, sing this blessed morn"
"Sweetly the birds are singing"

Roquette, Otto
"Du liebes auge" (Franz)
Herzensbeklemmung (Thümmel)
Margreth am thore (Jensen)
"O lass dich halten, gold'ne stunde" (Jensen)
"Willkommen, mein wald" (Franz)

Rorie, David
A chequer'd career (Folk air)
The tounis colledge (Scottish air)

Rory O'More ("On the green hills of Ulster") Irish air. Words by Drennan. MMI

Rory O'More ("Young Rory O'More") Irish air. Words by S. Lover. JO—MMI—WBT
Rory O'Moore. HSD
"Young Rory O'More." PI

Rosa, Salvator
"Forest, thy green arbors." See "Selve, voi che le speranze"
The guiding light. See "Vado ben spesso cangiando loco"
"Might I linger anear thee." See "Star vicino"
"Selve, voi che le speranze"
"Star vicino"
"Though I go ranging." See "Vado ben spesso cangiando loco"
"To be near the fair idol." See "Star vicino"
"To be near thee." See "Star vicino"
"Vado ben spesso cangiando loco" (attributed; attributed also to G. B. Bononcini)

La **rosa** ("Nenni, Nenni, vattenne."—The rose) S. Mercadante. e.i. MN

Rosa ("Rosa, willen wy dansen") Flemish dance song. d.e. BO
Rosa ("Rosa, we'll go dancing") e. BMC

"**Rosa**, dear, shall we dance, then." See Rosa

Rosa Lee. HSD—JSE—NMP—WBT

"**Rosa**, we'll go dancing." See Rosa

"**Rosa**, willen wy dansen." See Rosa

Rosalie ("I'm Pierre de Bonton") L. Knight. CHS—HSD—MPC—SSS—WBT—WC

Rosalind ("Here cometh Rosalind") Children's song. FSS 8—WBT

Rosalinda ("I sung my passion to the wind") Butler. MM

Rosamond ("Sweet youthful charming ladies fair") 17th century song. Air from "Cambridge lute mss." CO 1

Rosamond ("Sweet youthful charming ladies fair") 17th century song. Air from "The dancing master." CO 1

Rosamond's manor. See Le manoir de Rosamonde (Duparc)

Rosario de la aurora (Serenata) Spanish folk song. s. LCP
Rosario (Serenade) e. GO

Das **röschen.** See "Ich sah ein röschen am wege stehn" (Weber)

Roscoe,
"Thy kindness to our fathers shown" (Hatton)

Rose, Charles John
Hip Ho-bart

Rose, George
Clochette

The **rose** ("Ich sah ein röschen") See "Ich sah ein röschen am wege stehn" (Weber)

The **rose** ("Nenni, Nenni, vattenne") See La rosa (Mercadante)

The **rose** ("The rose had been wash'd") See "The rose had been wash'd" (Manx air)

The **rose** ("Soft the eve'tide Sun God is sinking."—Pakoble) T. Lieurance. Words by K. Jones. e. LN

The **rose** ("A wild rose in the forest") K. Eckert. e. FSS 1—JSE—WBT

"The **rose** and the lily." See "Die rose, die lilie, die taube" (Schumann)

"The **rose** blooms so bright, sweet and perfect." See "Den yndigste rose"

"A **rose**-bud blossom'd in my bow'r." See To-day and to-morrow (Beethoven)

"A **rose**-bud by my early walk." See "A rosebud by my early walk"

The **rose**-buds in June. Folk song. MM

The **rose** bush. T. E. Perkins. Words from the German. e. FSS 6

"The **rose** complained." See "Es hat die rose sich beklagt" (Franz)

Rose de Provence. Pyrenean song. e.f. SSP

"Die **rose**, die lilie, die taube" ("The rose and the lily") Schumann. e.g. [Words by H. Heine] BS 2

"The **rose** had been wash'd" (The rose) Manx air: Mylecharaine. Words by W. Cowper. BMC

"The **rose** had been washed." Webbe. Words by W. Cowper. HSE 2

"The **rose** has charmed the nightingale." See Eastern romance (Rimskiï-Korsakov)

"The **rose** hath sadly, sadly moaned." See "Es hat die rose sich beklagt" (Franz)

"The **rose** in the air" (Portuguese song) e. BMC—WBT

"The **rose** lifts her head to thy royal sun." See Nell (Fauré)

Rose-Marie ("Ensam i skogen") K. Collan. Words by Z. Topelius. e.sw. SSN

Rose-Marie ("Over the hills and far away") J. L. Molloy. Words by F. E. Weatherly. FMB—FSS 7—PO—SM 4

The **rose** of Alabama. Words by S. S. Steele. HSD
The rose ob Alabama. NMP—WBT

The **rose** of Allandale. S. Nelson. Words by C. Jefferys. FSS 1—JO—TL—WBT—WL

"The **rose** of Ispahan." See "Les roses d'Ispahan" (Fauré)

Rose of Killarney. J. R. Thomas. WBT

Rose of Lucerne. Swiss air. FSS 5

"The rose of the valley." W. Reeve. Words by Dibdin. HSE 2

"Rose, of whiteness snowy." See Simple confession (Thomé)

Rose of yesteryear (Gradinom cveće cvetalo) Serbian folk song. e.se. BF 1

A rose on an Indian grave. T. Lieurance. LS

Der rose sendung. See entry under Der

"Rose softly blooming." See "Rose, wie bist du" (Spohr)

Rose song. D. S. Smith. Words by C. F. Bates. HST

"The rose that all are praising." E. J. Loder. Words by T. H. Bayly. FSS 3 —JO—WBT

"A rose that bloom'd in a desert land." See The bird and the rose (Horrocks)

"Rose that wast born with the morning." See Rose song (Smith)

"The rose that weeps." W. Horsley. Words by Radcliffe. BE 4

Rose-tide. See Die rosen kommen (Cantor)

Rose-time. H. Hadley. Words by C. Eldred. AA

"A rose-tree I did plant." See La ronde du rosier

"The rose, who is her sister." See Verrath (Zech)

"Rose, wie bist du" ("Rose softly blooming") L. Spohr. e.g. MSS 1 "Rose softly blooming." e. BC— GMF--KF 1—SS 1

Rosebud ("Rosebud, rosebud bright and fair") E. Grieg. e. BD

"A rosebud by my early walk." Air: The shepherd's wife. Words by R. Burns. BSB—PS 1—PS 2

"A rosebud, by my early walk." D. Sillar. Words by R. Burns. BSR

"Rosebud, rosebud bright and fair." See Rosebud (Grieg)

"Rosebud, you touched her." See Her rose (Coombs)

Rosedale, H. G. "All hail, ye merry folk to-day" (Terry)

"Roselil og hendes moder de sad over bord." See Roselille

Roselille. Danish song. da.e. BF 2

Rosemary ("Bloom, my little bud."—"O mój rozmarynie") Polish folk song. e.p. BF 1

Rosemary ("Rosemary, how dear."— "Rozmarin se je posušil") Slovenian folk song. e.slo. BF 1

"Rosemary, how dear to me thou art." See Rosemary (Slovenian song)

Rosemonde. C. Chaminade. e.f. SM 2. e. only WBW

Rosen, Egor Fedorovich, baron "The truth is suspected" (Glinka)

"Rosen auf den weg gestreut." See Lebenspflichten (Reichardt)

"Rosen brach ich nachts mir am dunklen hage." See Sapphische ode (Brahms)

"Die rosen, deine schwestern." See Verrath (Zech)

Die rosen kommen (Rose-tide) O. Cantor. Words by A. Friedman. e.g. SM 3

"Rosen sänker sitt hufvud." See I seraljens lustgard (Sjögren)

Rosenfeldt, Leopold "Hvorfor svömmer dit öie tidt i en taareglands" "Wherefore sparkle with dew drops." See "Hvorfor svömmer dit öie tidt i en taareglands"

"Rosenstock, holderblüh, wenn i mein dienderl sieh." See Oberschwäbischer ländler

"Roses are waking." See Commencement song (Cherubini)

"Roses bloom, fair roses flourish." See Plus ne suis ce que j'ai été

"Roses blossom for thee." See Anakreon's grab (Wolf)

"Roses blossom on the little hill above." Hungarian song. e. KSE

"Roses culled at night." See Sapphische ode (Brahms)

Roses d'hiver (Winter roses) H. de Fontenailles. Words by L. Le Lasseur de Ranzay. e.f. HM 1

"Les roses d'Ispahan" (The rose of Ispahan) G. Fauré. Words by Leconte de Lisle. e.f. PG 2—SAM "Les roses d'Ispahan" ("The roses of Ispahan") e.f. CM 1—HM 1

Rosewig, A. H. "All is quiet"

Le rosier d'argent (The silver rosebush) Folk song from Lorraine. e.f. FTF

Rosina. See La Rozina

"Rosła kalina z liściem szerokiem." See The barberry (Komorowski)

"Röslein, röslein, sag' mir fein." See Mancherlei boten (Erk)

Roslin castle ("'Twas in that season of the year") Air: House of Glams, attributed to J. Oswald. Words by R. Hewitt. JO—MMS—PR 2—PS 1

Ross, Alexander Coffman Tippecanoe and Tyler too (Composer unknown)

Ross, Gertrude Butterfly Chō-chō. See Butterfly Fireflies Fuji Hotaru. See Fireflies Love-lay indited by the Mikado Temmu Ode to the mountain Fujiyama. See Fuji Old Samurai prayer Slumber song of Izumo

Rosseter, Philip "If she forsake me"

Rossetti, Christina Georgina
"Come to me in the silence of the night" (music by Marzials; Somerset)
A hope carol (Smith)
"In the bleak midwinter" (Strong)
Lady Moon (Loomis)
"Love came down at Christmas" (Borland)
"The shepherds had an angel" (music by Bridge; Wiseman)
Rossetti, Dante Gabriel
Three shadows (Bedford)
Rossi, Francesco
"Ah! give me back thy heart."   See "Ah! rendimi"
"Ah! give to me."   See "Ah! rendemi"
"Ah! rendimi" (from Mitrane)
"Give back the heart you stole from me."   See "Ah! rendimi"
Rossi, Luigi
"Fanciulla son io"
"I know not Lord Love."   See "Fanciulla son io"
Rossignol, Féliz Ludger.   See Joncières, Victorin de
"Rossignol du vert bocage."   See Le rossignol messager
Le rossignol messager (The messenger nightingale) French folk song.   e.f. TSF
"Rossignolet qui chantes."   See "Roussignoulet qui cantos"
"Rossignols amoureux" ("Nightingales passion-stirred") J. P. Rameau.   e.f. KS 1
Rossini, Gioacchino Antonio
Ah! quel giorno (from Semiramide)
"All by the shady greenwood tree"
"As we row"
Asile héréditaire (from Guillaume Tell)
"Assisa a piè d'un salice" (from Otello)
"At last hope's cheering ray."   See "Bel raggio lusinghier"
"Bell raggio lusinghier" (from Semiramide)
"Che dissi" (from Otello)
"Ciel pietoso, ciel clemente" (from Zelmira)
"Come sereno è il dì" (from Bianca e Falliero)
Cujus animam (from Stabat Mater)
"Dark day of horror" (from Semiramide.   Tr of Giorno d'orrore)
Dear home, where dwelt my father.   See Asile héréditaire
"Deh calma, o ciel" (from Otello)
"Della rosa il bel vermiglio" (from Bianca e Falliero)
"Di piacer mi balza il cor" (from La gazza ladra)
Di tanti palpiti (from Tancredi)
"Eccolo, a voi l'affido" (from Zelmira)
"Fac ut portem" (from Stabat Mater)
Faith
For all the pains I bear.   See Di tanti palpiti
La gloire et la fortune (from Le siège de Corinthe)

Glorious things are spoken
Glory gilds the sacred page
Holly crowns the green
"Home's not merely four square walls"
"How bright and fair"
In memoriam
"In sì barbara" (from Semiramide)
"Jesus, the very thought of Thee" (same air as Glory gilds the sacred page)
"Largo al factotum della città" (from Il barbiere di Siviglia)
Live this day in memory shining.   See Ah! quel giorno
"Lord, preserve me uncomplaining."   See "Pro peccatis"
"Lord, Thy glory fills the heaven."   See "Fac ut portem"
"Lord! vouchsafe Thy loving kindness"
Manoah.   See Glory gilds the sacred page; "Jesus, the very thought of Thee"
"The merry hours of youth"
"Mura felici" (from La donna del lago)
"My heart is light"
No more lonely, hopeless waiting.   See Non più mesta accanto al fuoco
Non più mesta accanto al fuoco (from La Cenerentola)
"Oh mattutini albori" (from La donna del lago)
"Pro peccatis" (from Stabat Mater)
Pull away, brave boys (from Guillaume Tell)
Que ton âme si noble (from Robert Bruce)
"Saviour, breathe forgiveness o'er me."   See "Cujus animam"
"Serena i vaghi rai" (from Semiramide)
"Sois immobile" (from Guillaume Tell)
"There's a voice that I enshrine."   See "Una voce poco fà"
"Though his voice."   See "Una voce poco fà"
"To the tap of the drum"
"Up the hills"
"Una voce poco fà" (from Il barbiere di Siviglia)
"What glory gilds the sacred page."   See Glory gilds the sacred page
"When snow lies deep"
The willow song
Rostand, Mme Rosemonde (Gérard)
L'anneau d'argent (Chaminade)
"Tu me dirais" (Chaminade)
"Rostbruna, dunkelröda."   See Svarta rosor (Alfvén)
Rostopchina, Sophie.   See Ségur, Sophie (Rostopchine), comtesse de
The rosy crown.   C. M. von Weber.   Words by D. Dutton.   FSS 2
"The rosy morn, with golden tresses crown'd."   See The early horn (Galliard)
Der rote sarafan.   See The scarlet sarafan (Varlamov)
Rothkehlchen (I hear the robin sing) F. Abt.   e.g.   FSS 6

"Rothkehlchen singt im grünen grund."
See Rothkehlchen (Abt)
Rothschild, baroness Willy de
"Si vous n'avez rien à me dire"
"Why with your lovely presence haunt
me." See "Si vous n'avez rien à
me dire"
"Røtnam's Knut" ("Rötnam's Knut") Nor-
wegian song. e.n. BF 2
"Rötnam's Knut" (Halling from Val-
ders) e.n. MAN
Rouget de Lisle, Claude Joseph
Hymne des Marseillaise. See La Mar-
seillaise
La Marseillaise
La Marsellesa. See La Marseillaise
Rough and rolling sea. Negro song. HR
"Roun' de meadows am a-ringing." See
Massa's in de cold, cold ground (Fos-
ter)
"Round about the mountain." Negro song
from Kentucky. KA
"Round and pretty, young and witty."
See the love-spell
"Round and round on galloping horses."
See The merry-go-round
"Round and round the village." Chil-
dren's song. WSC
Round-dance. See "Come and twine the
slim boughs"
"Round de meadows am a ringing." See
Massa's in de cold, cold ground (Fos-
ter)
Round of the oats. See La ronde de
l'aveine
Round of the rose-tree. See La ronde du
rosier
"Round our beds shall sweetest odors be
breathing." See La mort des amants
(Debussy)
"Round the churchyard." Old Serbian
song. e. KSE
Round the corner, Sally. Pulling chantey.
SE
"Round the corner waiting." A. Randeg-
ger. FSS 5
"Round the Lord in glory seated." G. E.
Oliver. Words by R. Mant. LA
'Round the old camp fire. C. L. Smith, jr.
MP—NMH—NMS
'Round thee, my idol. See "Intorno all'
idol mio" (Cesti)
Rousseau, Jean Jacques
Cradle hymn
"Days of absence" (same air as Cradle
hymn)
Greenville. See Cradle hymn; "Days
of absence"; "Hark! 'tis the
breeze"; "Thoughts of wonder";
"When the mists"; While to Beth-
l'em going
"Hark! 'tis the breeze" (same air as
Cradle hymn)
"Hush, my babe." See Cradle hymn
Que le jour me dure
Rousseau's dream. See "Days of ab-
sence"
Rousseau's hymn. See "When the
mists"

"Thoughts of wonder" (same air as
Cradle hymn)
Sehnsucht. See Que le jour me dure
Die trennung (same air as Que le jour
me dure)
"When the mists" (same air as Cradle
hymn)
While to Bethl'em going (same air as
Cradle hymn)
"Wie der tag mir schleichet." See
Que le jour me dure
Rousseau, W. W.
"Day of wonder, day of gladness"
Rousseau's dream. See "Days of absence"
(Rousseau)
Rousseau's hymn. See "When the mists"
(Rousseau)
Roussel, G.
Venetian song (Bemberg. Tr of chant
vénitien)
"Roussignoulet qui cantos" ("Nightingale
sweetly singing") Béarnese song. e.f.
SMF—TSF
The **rover** ("When told by wandering
lovers") Air: Mi a âf tua glan yr afon.
Words from the Welsh. e. MMW
Roving Jack. Folk song. BSW
"Row gently here, my gondolier" ("Leis'
rudern hier, mein gondolier") A. Jen-
sen. Words by T. Moore. e.g. FF
—FO 1
"Row gently here, my gondolier" ("Leis',
rudere, hier") Schumann. Words by
T. Moore. e.g. TS
"Row, men, row! tho' the winds blow."
See Song of the life-boat men
"Row, boys, row." See Volga boat song
(Words by Drake)
"Row on, row on, my hearties." See
"Iomraibh, iomraibh, illean"
"Row, row, boatie, my boatie." See Row,
row, my boatie (Mozart)
Row, row, cheerly row. Words by D. M.
Muloch. FSS 2
"Row, row, gently row, on the water's
silv'ry flow." See Boat song (Cowen)
"Row! row! homeward we steer." See
Boatman's return (Sporle)
Row, row, my boatie. W. Mozart. FSS 7
"Row, row, row your boat." Round. E.
O. Lyte. BD—BSS—TFC 1
Row your boat. FSS 1—HSC
"Row thy boat lightly." I. B. Woodbury.
Words by H. T. Woodman. FSS 5
Row well ye mariners. Ballad air. JE
Row your boat. See "Row, row, row your
boat" (Lyte)
The **rowan** tree ("Oh! rowan tree, oh!
rowan tree") Scottish air. Words
by C. Nairne. MMS—PS 2
The **rowan** tree ("O rowan tree! O rowan
tree") ⌈Air: Der tannenbaum⌉ Words
by C. Nairne. FSS 6—WBT
Rowe, Ch. G.
"The flow'rets close at eve, my love"
(Abt)

Rowe, Charles J.
Hymn of the fishermen's children
(Hérold)
The kiss of a little child (Hullah)
"Still is the night, still is the night"
(Abt)
Rowe, Nicholas
Colin's complaint (Composer unknown)
Rowe, Sidney
A-scouting (Composer unknown)
"March on! Liberty's host" (Verdi)
Song of hope (Russotto)
Rowlands, David
Remembrances (Welsh air)
Shôn ap Evan (Welsh air)
The strolling fiddler (Welsh air)
The voice of one we love (Welsh air)
Rowles, Mary
Love and summer (West)
Royal march.   See Marcha real
The royal purple.   Williams college song.
B. T. Bartlett.   Words by F. W. Mem-
mott and F. D. Goodwin.   CHS

Rozhinkes mit mandlen.   See Raisins and
almonds
La Rozina (Rosina) Lombardian folk song.
e.i.   MSI
Rozkošný, Josef Richard
He loves me well
"Rozmarin se je posušil."   See Rosemary
(Slovenian song)
Rubinstein, Anton
The angel
"Anger is welling" (from Das verlorene
paradies)
Der Asra
"Be not so coy."   See "Thu' nicht
so spröde, schönes kind"
"Bend, lovely bud."   See "Neig',
schöne knospe"
"Die blauen frühlingsaugen"
"The dew it shines."   See "Es blinkt
der thau"
"The dewdrops glitter."   See "Es
blinkt der thau"
The dream
"Du bist wie eine blume"
"Easter morn with gladness shine"
Der engel.   See The angel
"Es blinkt der thau"
"Es war ein alter könig"
Fliehe hin, nachtigall.   See Fly away,
nightingale
Fly away, nightingale
"From my soul's depths."   See "Anger
is welling"
"Gelb rollt mir zu füssen"
"Gold rolls here beneath me."   See
"Gelb rollt mir zu füssen"
"Golden at my feet."   See "Gelb rollt
mir zu füssen"
"Good night"
"Gut' nacht."   See "Good night"
"Heard ye his voice"
"I feel thy breath blow around me."
See "Ich fühle deinen odem"
"Ich fühle deinen odem"
The lark.   See Die lerche
Die lerche

Longing
"Mein herz schmückt sich mit dir"
"My heart all beauty takes from thee."
See "Mein herz schmückt sich mit
dir"
"Neig', schöne knospe"
"Nicht mit engeln"
"Not the angels."   See "Nicht mit en-
geln"
"Not with angels."   See "Nicht mit en-
geln"
"Now shines the dew."   See "Es blinkt
der thau"
"O fair, and sweet, and holy."   See
"Du bist wie eine blume"
"Once more has heaven."   See Song
of an angel
"Seh' ich deine kleinen füsschen an"
Sehnsucht.   See Longing
Song of an angel (from Das verlorene
paradies)
"The spring's blue eyes."   See "Die
blauen frühlingsaugen"
"There was an aged monarch."   See
"Es war ein alter könig"
"Tho' all triumphant the heav'nly pow-
ers" (from Das verlorene paradies)
"Thou'rt like unto a flower."   See "Du
bist wie eine blume"
"Thou'rt lovely as a flower."   See "Du
bist wie eine blume"
"Thu' nicht so spröde, schönes kind"
"To me thou art a flower."   See "Du
bist wie eine blume"
Der traum.   See The dream
"Vernahmet ihr."   See "Heard ye his
voice"
Voices of the woods (same air as "Eas-
ter morn with gladness shine")
"Wake, ye spirits" (from Das verlorene
paradies)
Wanderers nachtlied
The wanderer's night song.   See Wan-
derers nachtlied
"Welcome, sweet springtime."   See
Voices of the woods
"When I see those little feet of thine."
See "Seh' ich deine kleinen füsschen
an"
Yearnings.   See Longing
"Yellow at my feet."   See "Gelb rollt
mir zu füssen"
"Roy's wife of Aldivalloch."   N. Gow.
Words by E. Grant.   FSS 4—HSD—
JO—MMS—PS 1
Rubinstein's melody.   See Home, sweet
home, and Rubinstein's melody (ar-
ranged)
"Ruby portal, fair, beguiling."   See "Bella
porta di rubini" (Falconieri)
Rückblick ("O alte burschenherrlichkeit")
Volksweise.   g.   ED 1
Rückert, Friedrich
"Aus der jugendzeit" (music by Erk;
Radecke)
Barbarossa (Gersbach)
Bei sonnenuntergang (Reichardt)
Des glockenthürmers töchterlein
(Loewe)

Rückert, Friedrich —*Continued*
"Du bist die ruh' " (music by Mozart; Schubert)
Das eine lied (Gersbach)
"Er ist gekommen" (Franz)
"Ich liebe dich weil ich dich lieben muss" (Förster)
Lied der braut (Schumann)
"Lov'st thou for beauty" (Schumann)
"O süsse mutter" (Loewe)
Schifffahrt (Witthauer)
Volksliedchen (Schumann)
Widmung (Schumann)
Rudelsburg ("An der saale") F. E. Fesca. Words by F. Kugler. g. ED 1
Rudolphi, Karoline Christiane Louise
"Ach, wie flieht das leben so geschwind" (André)
Der mond (Reichardt)
Ruel, E. H.
"Sing for joy"
Ruffen. Norwegian forecastle song. n. SMW
"**Rufst** du, mein vaterland" (Swiss national hymn) Air: God save the king. e.g. WA—WBT
Ruggles, W.
Our college home
Ruggleton's daughter of Iero. Folk song. SEF 2—SO
Variant: The wife wrapt in wether's skin
"**Rugiadose**, odorose." See Le violette (Scarlatti)
"**Ruhe** süss, liebchen" (Schlummerlied.— Slumber song) R. Franz. [Words by J. L. Tieck] e.g. KF 2
"**Ruhe**, süssliebchen" (Slumber-song) J. Brahms. Words by J. L. Tieck. e.g. FO 2—PG 4
"**Ruh'n** in frieden alle seelen." See Litaney (Schubert)
Rule, Britannia ("When Britain first, at heaven's command") British national song. T. A. Arne. Words probably by J. Thomson; attributed also to D. Mallet. BAS 1—BE 2—BMC—BOS —BSE—BSP—CO 2—CST— DM 1— FMB—FSS 7—HSE 1—JE—JO—JS— MM—MP—PR 2—SN—SSS—WBT— WCP
Rumania. See "Tracascâ regele" (Hübsch)
Rumsty-ho. Old English song. TFC 2 —WC
Run all de way, Lord. See Listen at de angels shoutin'
"**Run**, let the bull chimes run." Pumping chantey. SMW
Run, Mary, run. Negro spiritual. DF— HR—JP
Run to Jesus. Negro spiritual. JP— NMP
Run with the bullgine. See Let the bullgine run
Runaway's song of defiance. Creole negro water-song. e. SMW
"**Rundgesang** und rebenshaft lieben wir ja alle." See Rundum

Rundum ("Rundgesang und rebensaft") Volksweise. g. ED 2
Runeberg, Johan Ludvig
Den långa dagen (Kjerulf)
Det var då (Kjerulf)
Vårt land, vårt fosterland (Pacius)
Rung, Frederik
Fyllas sang
Fylla's song. See Fyllas sang
Runge, Philipp Otto
Die blume der blumen (Reichardt)
Runjamin, Josip
Croatian national anthem
Hrvatska domovina. See Croatian national anthem
Runo-laulu. See "Home my sweetheart comes from roving"
Rural life. 18th century song. ME
The rural queen. Gaelic air: Gu ma slan a chi mi. Words by A. Campbell. PS 2
A rural song. See Villanelle (Dell' Acqua)
"**Rushes** and roars the wide Dnieper" ("Reve ta stogne") Ukrainian song. e.r. BF 1
Russell, Alexander
"As with gladness men of old"
"Carol, carol, Easter morn" (same air as "As with gladness men of old")
Russell, Arthur T.
Integer vitae (Flemming)
Russell, George William
The voice of the sea (Irish air)
Russell, Henry
The better wish
"Cheer, boys, cheer"
Coal black Rose
Far upon the sea
"I'm afloat! I'm afloat"
The Indian hunter
The ivy green
"A life on the ocean wave"
My mother's Bible
The old arm chair
Old Dan Tucker
The old sexton
Ole Dan Tucker. See Old Dan Tucker
Orphan ballad singers
Robin Ruff. See The better wish
Rockaway
"Some love to roam"
Tubal Cain
"We have been friends together"
"Woodman, spare that tree"
Russell, John
"All the notes of all the earth make one great song" (Hungarian air)
From the great deep, to the great deep we go (Croatian air)
"Give him a march with his old bones" (Serbian air)
"Give me but health and a day" (Bohemian air)
"Live, live, live" (Croatian air)
Lullaby (Bohemian air)
The shadow (Russian air)

Russell, John —*Continued*
"Silent the happy songs" (Russian air)
A song of captivity (Russian air)
A song of the great adventure (Hungarian air)
Sunset (Hungarian air)
Unshriven (Ruthenian air)
Russell, Mary Eno
H_2SO_4
Russell's triumph. S. Akeroyde. MM
Russian Christmas song ("Let's sing") e. DCS
Russian driver's song. See Three in-hand
Russian harvest hymn. See Harvest hymn
Russian hymn. See Russian national hymn (Lvov)
Russian lullaby. See The Cossack's lullaby (Bakhmetiev)
"A **Russian** maid was Katinka." See Katinka
A **Russian** melody. See Beautiful Minka
Russian national hymn ("God the All-terrible") National anthem of imperial Russia. A. F. von Lvoff. Words by Joukovsky. e.r. WA—WSW. e. only BMC—MP—NMS
"Bòshe zaria chrani." e.r. NA
God save the czar ("Bojé tsaria khrani") e.r. BSP
"Lord God, protect the czar." e.r. SN
Prayer for peace ("God the All-powerful") e. LA
Russian hymn ("God save the noble czar") e.r. MP—NMH—NMS —WBT. e. only BSE
Russian hymn ("God, the All-terrible") e. BD
Russian national air ("God the All-terrible") e. JS—MS
Russian national anthem ("God save the noble czar") e. WCP
Russian national anthem ("God the All-terrible") e. FMB—SSS
The Russian national anthem ("Lord God, protect the czar") e. KSN
Russian national hymn ("Hail to the emperor") e. BOS
Russian national hymn ("Songs of praise") e. FSS 3
Russian song used for heaving the anchor. e. SMW
Russo, Ferd.
'O bene antico (Nutile)
Russo, Vincenzo
Maria, Marì (Capua)
'A serenata d' 'e rrose (Capua)
Russotto, Henry A.
The hope
Song of hope (same air as The hope)
Rust, Friedrich Wilhelm
Die betende
"**Rust-color'd**, carmined darkness." See Svarta rosor (Alfvén)
Rustic dance ("Up and down") Bohemian folk song. e. GO
"**Rustic** flute, echo, sighing." See "Ô ma tendre musette" (Monsigny?)

Rustic song. See Durwan's song
Rustige, H.
Der thürmer (Matys)
Ruth. See "Summer suns are glowing" (Smith)
Rutherford, Alison. See Cockburn, Mrs Alicia (Rutherford)
Ruusa laaksossa. See The lovely rose
Ryan, Mary
Merry Christmas (Glover)
Sweet harps, resound again (Sullivan)
Ryan, Michael Desmond
The last lay of the dying bard (Shield)
"Love smiles no more" (Ahlstrom)
Ryan, Richard
The flying Dutchman (Parry)
Rychardes, Thomas
Heart's ease (16th century air)
Ryley, G. C. E.
"Bring them to the Master"
"Come, children, lift your voices"
"O the beautiful old story"

S

'S e gillean mo rùin. See Na gillean mo rùin
"'s gibt kein schöner leben als studentenleben." See Studentenleben (Reissiger)
"'s isch äben e mönsch uf ärde." See Das alte Guggisberger lied
"'s ist gewiss und kein gedicht." See Von bösen frauen
"'s ist mir alles eins." Attributed to J. Fuss. g. ED 1
"'s ist mir alles eins" ("All's the same to me") e.g. BO
"'s ist mir alles eins" ("Oh! to me't's all one") e.g. SSG
S' kookloi. See The doll's cradle-song (Musorgskiï)
"**Sa** couleur est blonde et vermeille" ("Rich and fair as roses blooming."—Brindisi) Massé. e.f. OPS 2
"**Sa** i ëmbël ish muaj' i majit." See The month of May
"**Så** ödsligt molnen på fästet gå" ("The lonely clouds blow across the sky") Swedish folk song. e.sw. HSOS
"**S'a** sun tre culumbe bianche." See Le tre colombe
"**Saa** du knøsen, som strøg forbi" ("See the fellow that passed just now") E. Grieg. Words by H. Drachmann. da.e. WM 1
"**Saa** tidt jeg rider mig under ö ved dag." See Olufs ballade (Gade)
Saar, Louis Victor Franz
"My brigantine"
Sabatier, Ch. W.
The flag of Carillon
Sabbath morn. See "Praise to God, immortal praise" (Mason)
Sabbath morning bells. BSS

Sabbath song ("Oi bruder, zog") Jewish folk song. e.y. GF 2

Saboly, Nicolas
"Bring a torch, Jeannette, Isabella" (Old French carol) Authorship uncertain

Le **sabre** de mon père. For English translation see The sabre song (Offenbach)

The **sabre** song. [J. Offenbach. Tr of Le sabre de mon père] e. FSS 1
"Behold the sabre." e. LA
Song of the sabre. e. WBT

Sacchini, Antonio Maria Gasparo
"Jour heureux" (from Dardanus)
"Se mai più sarò geloso" (from Alessandro nell' Indie)
"Should I e'er again distrust thee." See "Se mai più sarò geloso"

Sachnofsky, G. See Sakhnovskiĭ, G.

Sacken, Theodor von
Die lerche (Rubinstein)

Sackville, Charles. See Dorset, Charles Sackville, 6th earl of

Sacramento. Capstan chantey. CR

Sacred raptures cheer my breast. Händel. OS 3

The **sacrifice** (Die verbrannte maid) Old Slavonic song. e.g. EF

"**Sad** am I and full sorry." See An gille donn

"**Sad** am I, and sorrow laden." See Soiridh

"**Sad** and dismal is the tale I will relate to you." See The Persia's crew

"**Sad,** but yet glad, our thoughts recall." See The veterans (Marshall)

"**Sad** hour of parting, too quickly here." See The hour of parting (Bellini)

"**Sad** I come and bending lowly." See "Muh'voll komm' ich und beladen" (Wolf)

"**Sad** is my empty life." See All joy is gone

"**Sad** lies the steppe." See Over the steppe (Grechaninov)

"**Sad** was the hour." H. Smart. FSS 7

Sadko's song of glorification (Velitchálnaya pyésnya) N. Rimsky-Korsakoff. e. SMR 2

"**Sadla** muška na konárik." See The disappointed suitors

"**Sadly** bend the flowers." See But when morning dawneth (Randegger)

"**Sadly** groaning." See "Ingemisco tamquam reus" (Verdi)

"**Sadly** in the gathering gloom." J. H. Hopkins (music and words) HC

Sadness. C. Saint-Saëns. WBW

Sae far awa'. Scottish air: Dalkeith Malden bridge. Words by R. Burns. PS 2

"**Sae** flaxen were her ringlets." Air: Oonagh's waterfall. Words by R. Burns. BSR

"Der **säemann** säet den samen." J. A. P. Schulz. Words by M. Claudius. g. ED 3

The **saeter** song. See Hjemreise fra saetren

Saetergjentens söndag (The chalet girl's Sunday) O. Bull. Words by J. Moe. e.n. MAN—SSN
Saetergjentens söndag (The herdgirl's Sunday) e.n. WM 1

Safe home at last. C. Pinsuti. FSS 5

Safe within the vail. FSS 1

Safely follow him. T. Cooke. Words by D. Terry. HSE 1

"**Safely** through another week." L. Mason. WBT

"**Sag** mir das wort, das so gern ich gehört." See Long, long ago (Bayly)

"**Sag',** welch wunderbare träume." See Träume (Wagner)

"**Sagt,** wo sind die veilchen hin." J. A. P. Schulz. Words by J. G. Jacobi. g. ED 2

"**Sah** ein knab' ein röslein steh'n." See Heidenröslein (Schubert); Heidenröslein (Werner)

"**Said** a smile to a tear." Braham. HSE 2

"**Said** my love, he'd come as soon." See Hora

"**Said** the thunder to the cloud passing by." See Song of the shepherd Lehl (Rimskiĭ-Korsakov)

The **sail-boat.** D. E. Auber. WSC

"**Sail** on afar, O ye heroes." See A Portuguesa (Keil)

Sail on, O ship of state. See The ship of state (German air)

"**Sail** on, sail on, O ship of state." See The ship of state (Composer unknown)

"**Sail** on, sail on, thou fearless bark." Air: The humming of the bars. Words by T. Moore. MI

Sailing ("Y'heave ho") G. Marks. FSS 5
—HSC— HSD— LA— MP— NMH— NMS— OH— WA— WBT— WSC —WSW

Sailing at Napoli. Italian air: Ti voglio bene assai. Words by A. F. Brown. GO

Sailing o'er a summer sea. See Funiculi-funicola (Denza)

Sailing, sailing, over the bounding main. See Sailing (Marks)

A **sailing** song ("The ocean winds are blowing") German folk air. Words by H. H. Harbour. DO

"**Sailing** was Olaf Trygvason." See Olaf Trygvason (Grieg)

The **sailor.** See "In Berlin sagt' er"

The **sailor-lass.** See La fille matelot

The **sailor** likes his bottle O. Pulling chantey. SE

Sailors' and soldiers' memorial day.   MP

"The sailors are all at the bar."   Scotch song.   SMW

The sailor's complaint.   Old sea song. CO 2
"Come and listen to my ditty."   MM

The sailor's farewell ("Farewell! farewell, my Polly dear")   Folk song.   BSW

The sailor's farewell ("To leave my dear girl")   Air: Ffarwel Ned Puw, or, Ned Pugh's farewell.   Words by A. Hunter.   MMW

The sailor's farewell ("When forced to bid farewell to Loo")   See The tar's farewell (Maybrick)

The sailor's grave ("Our bark was out far")   WBT

"A sailor's greatest pleasure."   See Bowline chanty

Sailor's home song.   F. Ames, with adaptation of two old chanties.   Words by D. Stevens.   BSS

The sailor's journal.   Dibdin (music and words)   HSE 1

"A sailor's life is a merry life."   See Sweet William

"A sailor's life is a roving life."   See A song of the sea

The sailors of Groix.   See Les marins de Groix

The sailors of Lee.   See Les marins de Groix

The sailor's prayer.   See Odi tu (Mattei)

"The sails are all swelling."   See The wanderer's farewell

"The sails are set of the gallant brig."   See Pauvre Pierre

Saineville, A. de
Sonnet d'amour (Thomé)

St Albinus.   See "Jesus lives! no longer now"

Saint-Aldegonde, Philippe de Marnix, seigneur de.   See Marnix, Philippe de, seigneur de Saint-Aldegonde

Saint Anne.   See "O God, our Help in ages past" (Croft)

"Saint Basil" (Haē Basilēs)   Greek New Year's song.   e.gr.   BF 2

St David's day ("St David was a Briton bold")   Air: Dydd gwyl dewi, or, St David's day.   Words by Talhaiarn. MMW

St Edmund.   See "Draw Thou my soul, O Christ" (Sullivan)

Saint George and the dragon.   See St George for England

St George for England.   17th century song.   CO 2
St George and the dragon.   JE

St George, our protector.   J. Clarke.   MM

St George's chapel.   See "Praise to God, immortal praise" (Elvey)

St George's Windsor.   See "Come ye thankful people, come" (Elvey)

St Gertrude.   See "Onward Christian soldiers" (Sullivan)

St Gregory.   See "Ye holy angels bright" (Barnby)

St Ives, Arthur
The golden pathway (Gray)

Saint Joles.   Harrow school song.   LA

St Martin's (Tans'ur)   See "Come, Holy Ghost"; "Come, let us join our cheerful songs"; "Oh, for a heart"

St Olaf.   See "Hellig Olaf"

St Oswald.   See "God, my King, Thy might confessing" (Dykes)

"Saint Patrick was a gentleman."   Irish air.   Words by H. Bennett and Mr Toleken, of Cork.   BOS—BSP—JO—WBT
"Saint Patrick was a gintleman." MMI

Saint Patrick's day ("Oh! blest be the days")   Irish folk song.   Words by M. J. Barry.   JSE—MP—NMS—PI—WBT—WCP

St Patrick's day ("Tho' dark are our sorrows")   See The prince's day

Saint-Saëns, Camille
Amour, viens aider (from Samson et Dalila)
"Ave Maria," no. 1
"Ave Maria," no. 2
The bell.   See La cloche
"Le bonheur est chose légère"
The breeze.   See La brise
La brise
Clair de lune
La cloche
Dear love! thine aid.   See Amour! viens aider
Empty splendor.   See La splendeur vide
"Father in heaven."   See "Ave Maria," no. 1; "Ave Maria," no. 2
"Happiness is a thing of changes."   See "Le bonheur est chose légère"
In solitude.   See La solitaire
Le lever de la lune
Lonely.   See La solitaire
"Mon coeur s'ouvre à ta voix" (from Samson et Dalila)
Moonlight.   See Clair de lune
Moonrise.   See Le lever de la lune
"My heart at thy dear voice."   See "Mon coeur s'ouvre à ta voix"
"My heart at thy sweet voice."   See "Mon coeur s'ouvre à ta voix"
"My heart to hear thy voice."   See "Mon coeur s'ouvre à ta voix"
"Ô beaux rêves évanouis" (from Étienne Marcel)
O love, lend thine aid.   See Amour! viens aider
Les pas d'armes du roi Jean
Patiently have I waited for the Lord (from Oratorio de Noël)
"Printemps qui commence" (from Samson et Dalila)
"Qui donc commande quand il aime" (from Henry VIII)
Sadness
La solitaire
Song of May (from Samson et Dalila. Tr of Voici le printemps nous portant des fleurs)

Saint-Saëns, Camille—*Continued*
La splendeur vide
"The spring now has found us." See "Printemps qui commence"
Thou, O Lord, art my protector (from Oratorio de Noël)
The tourney of King John. See Les pas d'armes du roi Jean
"When shepherds pipe their lay" (same air as "Mon coeur s'ouvre à ta voix")

St Senanus and the lady ("O haste and leave this sacred isle") Irish air: Droighneann donn, or, The brown thorn. Words by T. Moore. MI—MMI

St Thomas. See "I love Thy kingdom, Lord" (Händel)

St Valentine ("Who is that tapping on garden gate") Words by R. I. Halsey. NMS

St Valentine's day ("Among the winter's happy days") French folk air: Le roi d'Yvetot. Words by R. Compton. DO

"Sainted Olaf, while the flow'rs of mead and wood." See "Hellig Olaf"

Sainton-Dolby, Mme Charlotte Helen
Bonnie Dundee (attributed)
"Good news from the hills of Judea"
"I am content"
Katey's letter
"Och, girls, did you ever hear." See Katey's letter
"To the lords 'o' convention." See Bonnie Dundee (attributed)

The saints' sweet home. Words by D. Denham. FSS 5

Sakhnovskiĭ, G.
Spring

Sakura. See Cherry-bloom

Sāl dam'ī. See "I wandered among the mountains"

"Sal, mi bien, el lacho deja." See Ständchen (Schubert)

Salaman, Charles Kensington
"I arise from dreams of thee"

Sálias, Vicente
"Gloria al bravo pueblo" (Sandaeta)

Salis-Seewis, Johann Gaudenz, freiherr von
Herbstlied (Reichardt)
Lied eines landmanns in der fremde (Righini)

Salitana (Love's greeting) Sicilian song. e.i. BF 2

Sally ("Sure, Sally is the loveliest lass") T. A. Arne. PR 2
"Sure Sally is the loveliest lass." ME

Sally Brown ("I shipped on board") Pulling chantey. SE
For variants of this song see following songs of same title

"Sally Brown" ("Sally Brown is a bright mulatto") Capstan chantey. KB

"Sally Brown" ("Sally Brown she's a bright mulatter") Capstan chantey. CR

"Sally Brown" ("Sally Brown, she's a creole lady") Capstan chantey. TFC 2

"Sally Brown" ("Sally Brown was a bright mulatto") Capstan chantey. SMW

Sally come up. T. M. Sewell. HSD—NMP—WBT

Sally in our alley ("Of all the girls that are so smart") Old English air: The country lass. Words by H. Carey. BE 8—BMC— BO— BOS— DM 1— FSS 6—HSD—HSE 1—JE—JO—JS— MM—NML—PR 1—SSS—TS— WA— WBT—WSW

Sally in our alley ("Of all the girls that are so smart") H. Carey (music and words) CO 1—DM 1

Sally of the mill ("There lives a lass by yonder mill") Air: Banks of daisies. Words by Ieuan Dhu. MMW

"Sally Racket." Topsail-halyard song. SMW
Variant: Cheer'ly, man

Sally Sweetbread. H. Carey. BE 5

Salomé! Salomé. J. Massenet. SOA 4

Salomon, Elias
Fiducit (Briesewitz)

Salomos,
Hymn to freedom (Manzaros)

Salter, Mrs Mary Elizabeth (Turner)
The pine-tree

Saludemos la patria (Salute our country) National song of Salvador. J. Aberle. Words by J. J. Canas. e.s. SN

Salut d'amour. See Love greetings (Elgar)

Salut! demeure chaste et pure. C. Gounod. e.f. SOA 3. e. only WBT
Salut! demeure chaste et pure (All hail, thou dwelling chaste and lowly) e.f. OPS 3
Salut! demeure chaste et pure (All hail! thou dwelling pure and lowly) e.f. KS 4

Salute our country. See Saludemos la patria (Aberle)

Salute the happy morn. See "Christians, awake" (Wainwright)

Salute to the flag. L. S. Collins. BSS

"Salvador in her nobleness ever." See Saludemos la patria (Aberle)

"Salvation! oh, the joyful sound" (Arlington) T. Arne. Words by I. Watts. FSS 7

Salvator Rosa. See Rosa, Salvator

"Salve boreale lumen" ("Hail the northern beacon") Carmen Abredonense. Words by J. W. Duff. SSS

Salve caput cruentatum. For English translation see "Oh, sacred Head, once wounded" (Greek air); "O sacred Head! once wounded" (Bach)

Salve, festa dies. For English translation see "Welcome, happy morning" (Arnold)

"Salve Maria" (Blessed is He that cometh) S. Mercadante. e.i. HSS 1—HSS 3

"Salve, nobilis corona." See Canticum in almam matrem

"Salve, oh patria." National song of Ecuador. e.s. SN
"We salute thee." e.s. MP
"Salve, salve, o rupe de' monti regina." See La Sammarinese
"Sam Bass." Cowboy song. LC
Samain, Albert Victor
Soir (Fauré)
"Sam'el Sumph." Air: Duncan Gray. Words by J. S. Blackie. SSS
La **Sammarinese.** National air of San Marino. s. SN
"S'amor m'annoda il piede." See Se amor m'annoda il piéde (Stradella)
"Samson recherchant ma présence." See Amour! viens aider (Saint-Saëns)
"San Sereni de la buena, buena, buena vide." Game song. s. LCP
"San Serenín del monte." Game song. s. LCP
Sanchez, Fernan
Tú (Fuentes)
Sancta Maria ("J'ai vu les seraphins."—"In dreams I've heard the angels") J. Faure. e.f. HSS 1
"The sand is blowing" (Tunisian song) e. BMC
The **sand-man.** See Der sandmann (Schumann)
Sandaeta, Josiè
"Gloria al bravo pueblo"
"Glory to the brave men." See "Gloria al bravo pueblo"
"Glory to the brave people." See "Gloria al bravo pueblo"
Sandberg, Helge
Hyllning till Sverige
Homage to Sweden. See Hyllning till Sverige
Sanderson, James
"Bound prentice to a waterman" (from Sir Francis Drake)
The girl of the seasons
"Hail to the chief"
The marriage day
The **Sandgate** lass's lament. Scotch song. SMW
The **sandman.** See Sandmännchen
"The sandman comes." German song. e. WSC
Der **sandmann** (The sand-man) R. Schumann. Words by G. H. Kletka. e.g. GMF
Sandmännchen (The sandman) German folk song arr by J. Brahms. e.g. SMF—SSG. e. only GO
The little dustman. e.g. EF. e. only DO—DSH
The sandman. e. BSE
Sandmännchen (The little dustman) e.g. KF 1—SM 2
The **sands** o' Dee. F. Boott. Words by C. Kingsley. FSS 7—JO—JSE
The **sands** of Dee. G. Macfarren. Words by C. Kingsley. TL

"The sands o' life sae swiftly ran." See Dearie (Norris)
Sandström, J.
Min lilla vrå bland bergen
My home 'midst hills and valleys. See Min lilla vrå bland bergen
Sandtis, Guglielmo da
Italian cradle-song
Sandyman. See Sandmännchen
Sanford, J.
Lubly Dine
Sang for Danske (Song of Denmark) C. E. F. Weyse. Words by C. J. Boyse. da.e. BSP
Denmark. e. KSN
"Towards the north." e. SN
"Der sang ist verschollen." See Vagans scholasticus (Sommer)
Sångarfanan (The singers' banner) F. A. Frieberg (music and words) e.sw. HSOS
"Der sänger hält im feld die fahnenwacht." See Die fahnenwacht (Lindpaintner)
Des **sängers** fluch. See entry under Des
Sangster, Mrs Margaret Elizabeth (Munson)
Christmas aftermath (Anderson)
Sangster, Walter Hay
The first Christmas night
Sanjurjo, J. A. Negron. See Negron Sanjurjo, J. A.
Sankey, Ira David
Joy in sorrow
The ninety and nine
"Sans nul répit, j'ai marché dès l'aurore." See The desert (Balakirev)
Sans souci. Columbia university song. Words by P. Fridenberg. CHS—CU —MPC—NMS
Sans toi ("Without thee") G. d'Hardelot. Words by V. Hugo. e.f. KF 1— KF 2— KF 3— PG 1— MSF 1— SM 2
Without thee. e. WBW
"Santa Anna gain'd the day." See The plains of Mexico
Santa Claus ("Morgen kommt der weihnachtsmann") See Der weihnachtsmann
Santa Claus ("Old Santa Claus") J. Read. JSE—NMS
"Old Santa Claus." FSS 6—MCS— WSC
Santa Claus ("What clatters on the roofs") Old German air. Words by N. H. Dole. DO
Santa Claus is come to town. Words by J. Drake. MCS
"Santa Claus is coming." MCS
"Santa Claus, last Christmas eve." See Paul and I (Tauwitz)
"Santa Claus tomorrow comes." See Der weihnachtsmann
Santa Claus to-night. J. L. Hatton. MCS

Santa Lucia. Neapolitan fishermen's song. e.i. EF—MSI—SMW. e. only BSE —CST —GO —MS —HSD — OH —TFC 1—TL —WBT— WL —WSC

Santa Lucia (Barcarolle) e.i. BO

Santa Lucia ("Over the rippling sea") e.i. FE

Variant: Italian air

Santy Anna ("O Santy Anna gained the day") Capstan chantey. CR For variants of this song see following song of same title; also The plains of Mexico

"Santy Anna" ("Santy Anna run away") Capstan chantey. FSF—SE

Sapateia (The bootmaker) Dance song from The Azores. e.po. BF 2

"Saper vorreste ("Fain would you know it") G. Verdi. e.i. KS 2

"Saper vorreste" ("You'd fain be hearing") e.i. PP

"The sapling oak." Storace. HSE 2

Sapphische ode (Sapphic ode) J. Brahms. Words by H. Schmidt. e.g. FO 2—KF 2

Sappho's farewell. See Ô ma lyre immortelle (Gounod)

Sarajevo kolo. Dance from Herzegovina. e.se. BF 1

Sardis. See "God is love; His mercy brightens" (Beethoven)

Sarga csizsmas Miska sárbran jar. See Miska and Panni

Sargent, Epes
The death of Warren (Dempster)
"A life on the ocean wave" (Russell)
"When the night-wind bewaileth" (Dempster)

Sarjeant, J.
"Blow, blow, thou winter wind"

Sarro, Domenico
"As when a lamb confiding." See "Sen corre l'agnelletta"
"Sen corre l'agnelletta"

Sarti, Giuseppe
"Lungi dal caro bene" (from Giulio Sabino)
Parted. See "Lungi dal caro bene"
"Should I from thee be parted." See "Lungi dal caro bene"

Sätherberg, Carl Herman
Farväl (Gustaf)
"I rosens doft" (Gustaf)
Längtan (Soderman)
Längtan till landet (Lindblad)
Studentsång (Gustaf)

Satter, Gustav
There's nae room for twa

The saucy bold robber. Folk song from Norfolk. SF 2

The saucy sailor. Folk song. SEF 1—SO
—Devon version. BSW

Saudade ("Fond regrets") Song from the Azores. e.po. BF 2

"Saulit' tezej' tezedama." See The sun runs its course

Saunders, Gordon
"Over hills and over plains"
"Saut yūbīl isma'u innahu saut el-surūr." See "Hearken to the jubilee"

Sauter, Samuel Friedrich
Der wachtelschlag (Hering)

Sautez, mignonne Cécilia. See "Mon pèr' n'avait fille que moi" (Cécilia)

Saved from the storm. O. Barri. Words by F. E. Weatherly. e.g. FSS 6

"Savi saujaqdjuin tetetlirpavum." See Song of the tornit

Savichna, ma lumière. See "Darling Savishna" (Musorgskiĭ)

Savile, Jeremiah
"Here's a health unto his majesty"

"Saviour, again to Thy dear name we raise" (Evening hymn) Composer unknown. Words by J. Ellerton. FSS 3

"Saviour, again to Thy dear name we raise" (Parting hymn) E. J. Hopkins. ⌈Words by J. Ellerton⌉ LA

"Saviour, blessed Saviour! listen while we sing" (Aspiration) J. B. Dykes. Words by G. Thring. LA

"Saviour, breathe an evening blessing." See Evening prayer (Stebbins)

"Savior, breathe forgiveness o'er me." See "Cujus animam" (Rossini)

"Saviour, Source of every blessing" (Trust) Mendelssohn. Words by R. Robinson. FSS 3

"Saviour, Source of every blessing" (Prayer) ⌈C. S. Whitmore. Words by R. Robinson⌉ LA

"Saviour, when in dust to Thee." See Litany

Savolaisen laulu. Finnish patriotic song. K. Collan. e.fi. SN

Savourneen deelish. Old air. Words by G. Colman. JO
Savourneen dheelish. FSS 7

La Savoyarde (The Savoyarde) Piedmontese song. e.i. MSI—SMF
La Savoyarde ("Tell me, Giannetta") e.i. NG

"Saw a crow a-flying low." See The bedtime song

"Saw ye Johnnie comin'? quo' she." Scottish song. MMS—PS 1

"Saw ye my Saviour" (Bdellium) FSS 5

Saw ye my wee thing. Scottish air. Words by H. Macneill. JO
"O, saw ye my wee thing." PS 1

"Saw ye nae my Peggy." Scottish song. MMS

"Saw ye never in the twilight." Composer unknown. Words by C. F. Alexander. FSS 1—JSE
The stranger star. MCS

"Saw ye never in the twilight." Mozart. Words by C. F. Alexander. HC

"**Saw** ye never in the twilight." B. Tours. Words by C. F. Alexander. HC

"**Saw** you the nymph." H. Carey (music and words) DM 1

Sawyer, Charles Carroll
When this cruel war is over (Tucker)

Saxe, John Godfrey
The old year and the new (Sayles)
Rhyme of the rail (Composer unknown)

Saxton, S. B.
"Come and hear the grand old story"

"**Say**, ah! why dost thou unto me appear." See Ah! tell me why (Varlamov)

"**Say**, darkies, hab you seen de massa." Kingdom coming (Work)

"**Say**, dost thou know where the woodland cabin standeth." See The woodland cabin

"**Say**, nunnikin, won't you come dance, now." See Het kwezelken

"**Say**, what dost thou bear in the secret deep." Cowen. SAS 1

"**Say**, what dreams are these that hold me." See Träume (Wagner)

"**Say**, what shall my song be to-night." J. P. Knight. FSS 3—WBT

"**Say**, when our patriots march to battle." See The patriots

"**Say**, will you leave your village cot." See Nan of Gloster Green

Sayles, S. M.
"Beautiful star in heaven so bright"
The old year and the new (same air as "Beautiful star in heaven so bright")

"**Says** Damon to Phillis." See The arch denial (Arne)

"**Says** the fly, says he." See Fiddle-de-dee (Elliott)

"**Says** the robin as he flew." See The bird song (North Carolina version)

The **scale** ("Come let us learn to sing") Children's song. FSS 6—JSE

The **scale** ("I pray thee, I pray thee") L. van Beethoven (music and words) e. TFC 2

Scalisi,
Ah, say but yes. See Dimme 'na vota sì
Dimme 'na vota sì
"Give me thy word." See Dimme 'na vota sì

"**Scant** clouds just flake the noon sky." See spring-time

"**Scaramouche** et Pulcinella qu'un mauvais dessein rassembla." See Fantoches (Debussy)

Scarborough fair. Folk song. SEF 2—SO

Scarlatti, Alessandro
"All' acquisto di gloria" (from Tigrane)
Cease my heart from wounding. See "O cessate di piagarmi"
"Cease, oh maiden." See "O cessate di piagarmi"

"Cease to torment." See "O cessate di piagarmi"

"Chi vuole innamorarsi"

"Desponding, lonely." See "Son tutta duolo"

Dewy violets. See Le violette

"Early blowing, violets growing." See Le violette

Faithless as fair. See "Tu lo sai"

"Già il sole dal Gange"

Hey! come hither, ye fancies. See Su, venite a consiglio

"I wish naught but to survey thee." See "Non vogl' io se non verderti"

"If thou my death proclaiming." See "Se tu della mia morte"

"Loving, I borrow." See "Sento nel core"

"The man who would turn lover." See "Chi vuole innamorarsi"

"My heart doth languish." See "Sento nel core"

"Non vogl' io se non verderti"

"O cessate di piagarmi"

"O lasst ab, mich zu verwunden." See "O cessate di piagarmi"

"O no longer seek to pain me." See "O cessate di piagarmi"

"O'er Ganges now launches." See "Già il sole dal Gange"

"Oft the blindfold boy." See "Spesso vibra per suo gioco"

"Rugiadose, odorose." See Le violette

"Se Florindo è fedele"

"Se tu della mia morte"

"Sento nel core"

"Should Florindo be faithful." See "Se Florindo è fedele"

"Son tutta duolo"

"Spesso vibra per suo gioco"

Su, venite a consiglio

"To achieve all the glamor of glory." See "All' acquisto di gloria"

To Florindo. See "Se Florindo è fedele"

"To win glory." See "All' acquisto di gloria"

"Tu lo sai"

The violet. See Le violette

Le violette

"Would'st thou the boast of ending." See "Se tu della mia morte"

Scarlatti, Domenico
"Consolati e spera"
"Forget thy grief." See "Consolati e spera"
"Like any foolish moth I fly." See "Qual farfalletta amante"
"Qual farfalletta amante"
"Take heart again." See "Consolati e spera"

The **scarlet** and black. Iowa college song. Balfe. Words by Mrs R. G. Cole. CHS

Scarlet and cream. University of Nebraska song. Balfe. CHS—MPC

The scarlet and gray forever. Ohio state university song. C. W. Gayman (music and words) CHS—MPC—NMS

"A scarlet coat and smart cockade." See The volunteer

The scarlet sarafan. Russian song. Varlamov. Words by Ziganow. e. CST—GO—WSC

Krasni sarafan (The red sarafan) e.g. EF

The red sarafan. e. BSE

Der rote sarafan ("Näh nicht, liebes mütterlein") g. ED 1

The scarlet sarafan (Der rothe sarafan) e.g. FSS 2

Gli scarriolanti (The wheelbarrow loaders) Italian song. e.i. BF 2

"The scene was more beautiful far to my eye." See The lighthouse

"Scenes that are brightest." V. Wallace. Words by A. Bunn. DM 1—FSS 1—HSE 3—WA—WBT—WSC—WSW

"Scents rich and rare fill the night air." See Ständchen (Jensen)

Schack, Adolph Friedrich, graf von
"Breit über mein haupt dein schwarzes haar" (Strauss)
Heimkehr (Strauss)
"Seitdem dein aug' in meines schaute" (Strauss)
Ständchen (Strauss)
"Wie sollten wir geheim sie halten" (Strauss)

Schackburg, Richard. See Schuckburgh, Richard

Schäfer im mai ("Siehst du das vögelein") C. T. Moritz. Words by F. Lange. g. ED 3

"Der schäfer trägt sorgen." Schlesische volksweise. g. ED 3

Das schäfermädchen und der kuckuck ("Ein schäfermädchen weidete") Volkslied. Author of words unknown. g. ED 1

"Ein schäfermädchen weidete." See Das schäfermädchen und der kuckuck

Schäfers klagelied ("Da droben auf jenem berge") L. Reichardt. Words by W. von Goethe. g. ED 3

Schäfers klagelied ("Da droben auf jenem berge") C. F. Zelter. Words by W. von Goethe. g. ED 1

Schaffer,
The hunter's song
"See the sun's first gleam." See The hunter's song

Schäffer, August
The jolly friar. See Das pfäfflein
Das pfäfflein

Schaffy, Mirza, pseud. See Bodenstedt, Friedrich Martin von

Schamburg, Richard. See Schuckburgh, Richard

"Schatz, mein schatz, warum so traurig." See Treue liebe

"Schätzchen, reich' mir deine hand." See Zum abschied

"Schaust so freundlich aus, Gretelein." See Gretelein (Kücken)

Schaut's aussi (Look out, how it's raining) Austrian song. e.g. BF 2

Scheffel, Josef Viktor von
Biterolf (Wolf)
Es hat nicht sollen sein (Nessler)
Jonas (Volksweise)
Die Teutoburger schlacht (Composer unknown)
Das wilde heer (Schmezer)

Schenck, Elliott
"When all the world is young, lad"

Schenkendorf, Max von
Auf Scharnhorsts tod (Composer unknown)
Erneuter schwur (Volksweise)
"Freiheit, die ich meine" (Groos)
Frühlingsgruss an das vaterland (Klein)
Die gefangenen sänger (Weber)
Das lied vom Rhein (Nägeli)
Palmsonntag (Reichardt)
Schill (Composer unknown)

Schetky, Johann Georg Christoph
"Clarinda, mistress of my soul"

"Schier dreissig jahre bist du alt." See Der alte reiter und sein mantel

"Das schiff streicht durch die wellen, fidelin." See Schifferlied

Schifferlied ("Das schiff streicht durch die wellen") Italian air: Ô pescator dell' onde. Words by J. von Brassier. g. ED 1

Die schifffahrt ("Das waren mir selige tage") F. F. Hurka. Words by C. A. Overbeck. g. ED 1

Schifffahrt ("Wie ein schifflein auf dem meer") J. G. Witthauer. Words by F. Rückert. g. ED 3

Schikaneder, Emanuel
"Bald prangt, den morgen zu verkünden" (Mozart)
Tyroler (Haibel)
Der vogelfänger (Mozart)

Schill ("Klaget nicht."—Eine geisterstimme) Words by M. von Schenkendorf. g. ED 2

Schiller, H. Carl
The outlaw (Loder)

Schiller, Johann Christoph Friedrich von
An den frühling (Reichardt)
An die freude (Composer unknown)
An Emma (Zelter)
Echtes glück (Kempt)
"Der eichwald brauset" (music by Schubert; Zumsteeg)
Gesang der mönche (Beethoven)
Die gunst des augenblicks (Zelter)
Die hoffnung (Reichardt)
Johanna's abschied (Zumsteeg)
Der jüngling am bache (Volksweise)
Das mädchen aus der fremde (Grosheim)
Punschlied (Eberwein)
Räuberlied (18th century air)
Reiterlied (Zahn)
Der schütz (Weber)
Thekla, eine geisterstimme (Seidel)

Schilling, Frederick
"Awake, arise, good Christians"
"Hark! a burst of heavenly music"
"There's a wonderful tree"

Schira, F.
"Fair land of hope"

Schlachtlied ("Kein schönrer tod") F. Silcher. Words after D. G. Morhof. g. ED 1

"Schlaf', du theuerster knabe mein." See Solvejgs wiegenlied (Grieg)

"Schlaf', herzenssöhnchen." See Wiegenlied (Weber)

"Schlaf' holdes kind" ("Sleep, my dear child") R. Wagner. e.g. KF 1— KF 2—PG 2

"Schlaf' in guter ruh'." See Wiegenlied (Taubert)

"Schlaf, kindchen, schlaf" (North German cradle-song) Folk song. e.g. FSS 3
Cradle song. e. DO—HSD
German cradle song. e. WSC
"Sleep, baby, sleep." e. LA—OH

Schlaf', kindchen, schlaf' (Shepherd's cradle-song) A. Somervell. Words from the German. e. MSF 1

"Schlaf, kindchen, schlaf." For English translation with a different air see Lullaby (Whitney)

"Schlaf, lieb' kindlein, schlaf ein." See Wiegenlied (André)

"Schlaf', mein sohn, und schlumm're süss." See Wiegenlied (Grieg)

"Schlaf, söhnchen! dein vater war eisenumhüllt." See "O hush thee, my babie" (Jensen)

"Schlafe, kindchen, ein." See Cradle song (Tchaikovsky)

"Schlafe, mein prinzchen." See Wiegenlied (Mozart)

"Schlafe, schlafe, holder süsser knabe." See Wiegenlied (Schubert)

Schleiden,
Immer bei dir (Raff)

Der schlesische zecher und der teufel (The Silesian toper and the devil) F. A. Reissiger. Words by A. Kopisch. e.g. AB 2

Schlippenbach, Albert, graf
In der ferne (Silcher)

"A schlosser hot en g'sellen g'hot." See Der schlossergesell

Der schlossergesell ("A schlosser hot en g'sellen g'hot") Volksweise. Words by J. C. Grübel. g. ED 1
Der schlossergesell (The locksmith's lad) e.g. SSG

Schlummerlied ("Ruhe süss") See "Ruhe süss, liebchen" (Franz)

Schlummerlied ("Schlaf, herzenssöhnchen") See Wiegenlied (Weber)

Schlummerlied ("Wo der rosen fülle."— Slumber-song) T. Mattei. e.g. SOS 1—SOS 2

"Schlummre, liebe kleine." See Wiegenlied (Spazier)

"Schlummre, schlummre und träume von kommender zeit." See Bei der wiege (Mendelssohn)

Schmeril with his fiddle. See The uninvited aunt

Schmerl mit'n fidl. See The uninvited aunt

"Der schmetterling ist in die rose verliebt" ("The butterfly's fallen in love with the rose") R. Franz. Words by H. Heine. e.g. FM

Schmezer, Christoph
Das wilde heer

Schmid, Christoph von
Die kinder bei der krippe (Schulz)
Das waldhorn (Silcher)

Schmidt, Friedrich Wilhelm August
Stille klage (Volksweise)

Schmidt, Georg Philipp
Deutscher ehrenpreis (Methfessel)
Der wanderer (Schubert)
Zitherbubens morgenlied (Bornhardt)

Schmidt, H.
The hero's serenade (Jarvis)

Schmidt, Hans
Entreaty (Bohm. Tr of Bitte)
Sapphische ode (Brahms)

Schmidt, Klamer
Neuer vorsatz (Volksweise)

Schmidt von Lübeck. See Schmidt, Georg Philipp

Der schmied (At the forge) J. Brahms. Words by J. L. von Uhland. e.g. CMF 1—GM
Der schmied (The blacksmith) e.g. CS 2—MSS 2

Schmolke, Benjamin
"My Jesus, as Thou wilt" (Weber. Tr of Mein Jesu, wie du willt)

Schneckenberger, Max
Die wacht am Rhein (Wilhelm)

Schnecker, Peter August
June
Song of Illyrian peasants

"Schnee im märzen, schmerz im herzen." See Märzschnee (Reinecke)

"Der schnee zerrinnt: der winter weint." See Springtime (Tchaikovsky)

Schneeflöckchen ("Snowflakes flying") See Snowflakes (Grechaninov)

Schneeglöckchen ("Schneeglöckchen läuten immer zu."—Snowdrops) A. Dorn. e.g. AB 3

Das schneeglöckchen ("Where under the birches") See The snowdrop (Grechaninov)

Schneider, Friedrich
Die arche Noah

Schneider, Karl
Mancherlei boten (Erk)

Schneider, Wilhelm
Lied deutscher männer

Der schneider Kakadu ("Ich bin der schneider Kakadu") W. Müller. Words by J. Perinet. g. ED 1

Schneiderschreck ("Es ist ein schuss gefallen") J. F. Reichardt. Words by Goethe. g. ED 2
Der schnitter Tod. See "Es ist ein schnitter" (Reichardt)
Schnödahöpfl. Salzburger song. e. KSE—SN
Schnoor, Heinrich Christian
  "Vom hoh'n Olymp"
Schnyder von Wartensee, Xaver
  "Come, said Jesus' gentle voice"
  Einkehr
Schober, Franz von
  An die musik (Schubert)
  Jägers liebeslied (Composer unknown)
"Schön blinkt's aus allen sternen" (Arabian song) M. Vogrich. e.g. SOS 1)
Schön ist der sommer (Fair is the summer) German folk song. e. GO
"Schön ist's, unter freiem himmel." See Kriegslied (Eidenbenz)
"Schön sind rosen und jasmin." See Iris
"Schöne augen, schöne strahlen." See Die unbeständige
"Schöne Minka." See Beautiful Minka
Die schöne nachbarin ("Mir ist auf der welt nichts lieber") P. von Winter. Author of words unknown. g. ED 2
"Schöne wiege meiner leiden" (Fare thee well) R. Schumann. Words by Heine. e.g. PG 4
Der schönste engel (The fairest angel) G. Graben-Hoffmann. e.g. CB—SM 4
"Die schönste zeit, die liebste zeit." H. G. Nägeli. Words by W. Hey. g. ED 1
Schönster Herr Jesu. For English translation see "Fairest Lord Jesus"
"Schönstes schätzchen, liebstes mädchen." See Vergebliche liebesmüh'
Schop, Johann
  "Now, courage take"
Schubart, Christian Friedrich Daniel
        Composer and author
  Abschiedslied
  Schwäbisches bauernlied
        Author
  Der leibarzt und der trinker (Composer unknown)
  Schwäbisches bauernlied (Folk air; also music by author)
Schubert, Franz Peter
  Above the mountains. See "Über allen gipfeln ist ruh"
  "Adieu! 'tis love's last greeting." See The last greeting
  Afar. See In der ferne
  Alinde
  Die Allmacht
  The Almighty. See Die Allmacht
  An die musik
  At my cradle. See Vor meiner wiege
  Auf dem wasser zu singen
  Aufenthalt
  "Ave Maria"
  Cradle song. See Wiegenlied
  Death and the maiden. See Der tod und das mädchen

Des mädchens klage. See "Der eichwald brauset"
Der doppelgänger
"Du bist die ruh'"
"Du schönes fischermädchen"
"Der eichwald brauset"
Der einsame
The erl-king. See Erlkönig
Erlkönig
Evening boat-song. See Auf dem wasser zu singen
Evening glow. See Im abendroth
Faith in spring. See Frühlingsglaube
Das fischermädchen. See "Du schönes fischermädchen"
The fisher-maiden. See "Du schönes fischermädchen"
"Flowerets blooming." See Praise of tears
Frühlingsglaube
Gretchen am spinnrade. See "Meine ruh' ist hin"
Gretchen at the spinning wheel. See "Meine ruh' ist hin"
Haiden-röslein. See Heidenröslein
"Hark! hark! the lark"
Hedge roses. See Heidenröslein
Heidenröslein
Her portrait. See Ihr bild
"Horch, horch, die lerch." See "Hark! hark! the lark"
Hymne an die Jungfrau. See Ave Maria
Ihr bild
Im abendroth
Im haine
Impatience. See Ungeduld
In der ferne
In the grove. See Im haine
The inn. See Das wirtshaus
Die junge nonne
The last greeting (Tr of Der letzte gruss)
Lay of the imprisoned huntsman
Liebesbotschaft
Lied des gefangenen jägers. See Lay of the imprisoned huntsman
The lime tree. See Der lindenbaum
The linden tree. See Der lindenbaum
Der lindenbaum
Litaney
Litany for the feast of all souls. See Litaney
The little house on the hill
Love's message. See Liebesbotschaft
The maiden's lament. See "Der eichwald brauset"
Margaret at the spinning-wheel. See "Meine ruh' ist hin"
"Meine ruh' ist hin"
The minstrel. See Der musensohn
Der musensohn
My abode. See Aufenthalt
My last abode. See Aufenthalt
My mother's song
"My peace thou art." See "Du bist die ruh'"
My phantom double. See Der doppelgänger

Schubert, Franz Peter—*Continued*
"My sweet repose." See "Du bist die ruh' "
The night
"Non t'accostar all' urna"
The novice. See Die junge nonne
La pastorella
Peace. See "Du bist die ruh' "
Die post
Praise of tears (Tr of Lob der thränen)
Romance from Rosamunde. See Romanze aus Rosamunde
Romanze aus Rosamunde
Serenade. See Ständchen ("Leise flehen meine lieder")
La serenata de Schubert. See Ständchen ("Leise flehen meine lieder")
The shepherdess. See La pastorella
The sign-post. See Der wegweiser
The solitary. See Der einsame
Ständchen ("Hark! hark! the lark")
  See "Hark! hark! the lark"
Ständchen ("Leise flehen meine lieder")
"Through the leaves the night winds moving." See Ständchen ("Leise flehen meine lieder")
To be sung on the water. See Auf dem wasser zu singen
To music. See An die musik
Der tod und das mädchen
"Touch not the white urn hiding." See "Non t'accostar all' urna"
Traveler's evening song. See "Über allen gipfeln ist ruh"
"Über allen gipfeln ist ruh"
Ungeduld
Vor meiner wiege
Der wanderer
Wanderers nachtlied
The wanderer's night song. See Wanderers nachtlied
Wandering. See Das wandern
Das wandern
Wandrer's nacht-lied. See Wanderers nachtlied
"Was ist Sylvia." See "Who is Sylvia"
Der wegweiser
Whither. See Wohin
"Who is Sylvia"
Wiegenlied
The wild rose. See Heidenröslein
The wild rosebud. See Heidenröslein
Das wirtshaus
Wohin
The wraith. See Der doppelgänger
The young nun. See Die junge nonne

Schuckburgh, Richard
Yankee Doodle (Old air) Authorship uncertain

Schukowsky, Vassili Andreevitch. See Zhukovski, Vasili Andreevich

Schultz, Carl
"Awake from sleep and dreaming"

Schultz, Christian
So oder so

Schultz, Mrs Julia L.
The purple and gold

Schulz, Christian
"Hier in des abends traulich ernster stille" (Flemming)

Schulz, Johann Abraham Peter
Abendlied
Am Sylvester-abend
An die wankelmütige (from Fanny Wilkes)
Freude in unschuld
"Ihr kinderlein, kommet." See Die kinder bei der krippe
Die kinder bei der krippe
Der knabe an das veilchen
Liebe in allem
Liebeszauber
Mailied
"O come, little children." See Die kinder bei der krippe
Phidile
"Der säemann säet den samen"
"Sagt, wo sind die veilchen hin"
Selige erinnerung
Seligkeit der liebe
Der sorgenfreie
The summers come and go
Täglich zu singen
Tischlied
Trost für mancherlei tränen
Die vollendung
"We plough the fields, and scatter" (Tr of Im anfang war's auf erden)
Wilhelm
"Willkommen im grünen"
Wind and sea

Schumann, frau Clara Josephine (Wieck)
"Lov'st thou for beauty"

Schumann, Ferdinand
"Meine liebe ist grün" (Brahms)

Schumann, Robert Alexander
The almond tree. See Der nussbaum
Alte laute, I
Alte laute, II
An den sonnenschein
Aufträge
"Aus meinen tränen spriessen"
Die beiden grenadiere
Blondel's lied
Blondel's song. See Blondel's lied
The boy with the magic horn. See Der knabe mit dem wunderhorn
The bride's song. See Lied der braut
Bygone pleasures. See Alte laute, II
Canonbury. See "Forth in Thy name, O Lord, I go"
Clown's song. See "When that I was a little boy"
Dedication. See Widmung
"Dein angesicht"
Les deux grenadiers. See Die beiden grenadiere
Devotion. See Widmung
"Du bist wie eine blume"
"Er, der herrlichste von allen"
Er ist's
Evening song
Fare thee well. See "Schöne wiege meiner leiden"

Schumann, Robert Alexander—*Continued*
"Forth in thy name, O Lord I go"
Frühlingsnacht
Guardian angels (Tr of Wenn kleine kinder schlafen geh'n)
The happy farmer
"He, more knightly than the noblest." See "Er, der herrlichste von allen"
"He the best of all." See "Er, der herrlichste von allen"
"He, the noblest of the noble." See "Er, der herrlichste von allen"
Highland cradle song
"I will not grieve." See "Ich grolle nicht"
"Ich grolle nicht"
"I'll not complain." See "Ich grolle nicht"
"Im wunderschönen monat mai"
In a foreign land. See In der fremde
In der fremde
In the forest. See Waldesgespräch
In the garden. See Volksliedchen
In the open. See In's freie
In's freie
Der knabe mit dem wunderhorn
Kommen und scheiden
"Leis', rudere, hier." See "Row gently here, my gondolier"
Lied der braut
"Lord, in Thy great, Thy glorious name"
Loreley in the forest. See Waldesgespräch
Die lotosblume
The lotus flower. See Die lotosblume
Love's secret lost. See Verrathene liebe
Meeting and parting. See Kommen und scheiden
Messages. See Aufträge
"Mit myrthen und rosen"
Mondnacht
The month of May. See "Im wunderschönen monat mai"
Moonlight. See Mondnacht
"My life is like the summer rose" (same air as The happy farmer)
My luve is like a red, red rose
Der nussbaum
"Oh, fair sunshine." See An den sonnenschein
O my love is like a red, red rose. See My luve is like a red, red rose
"O sunny beam." See An den sonnenschein
O sunshine. See An den sonnenschein
The poet's love. See "Ich grolle nicht"
"The rose and the lily." See "Die rose, die lilie, die taube"
Die rose, die lilie, die taube"
"Row gently here, my gondolier"
The sand-man. See Der sandmann
Der sandmann
"Schöne wiege meiner leiden"
Silent love. See Stille liebe
Skaters' song (same air as The happy farmer)

Soldier song (Tr of Ich bin ein soldat)
A song of spring. See Er ist's
Spring night. See Frühlingsnacht
Stille liebe
Tears and sighs. See "Aus meinen tränen spriessen"
"Thou'rt like a lovely flower." See "Du bist wie eine blume"
"Thou'rt lovely as a flower." See "Du bist wie eine blume"
Thy lovely face. See "Dein angesicht"
The two grenadiers. See Die beiden grenadiere
Verrathene liebe
Volksliedchen
Waldesgespräch
The wanderer's song. See Wanderlied
Wanderlied
"We lay us calmly down to sleep"
"When gentle winds" (same air as The happy farmer)
"When that I was a little boy"
When the soft twilight
"Why are you ill and drooping." See Alte laute, I
Widmung
"With myrtle and roses." See "Mit myrthen und rosen"

Schutz ("Der abend sinkt."—Auf einer herbstreise) A. Bergt. Words by Friedrich Leopold graf zu Stolberg. g. ED 3
Der **schütz** ("Mit dem pfeil, dem bogen") B. A. Weber. Words by Schiller. g. ED 2
"Cheerily the huntsman." e. TFC 2
Hunter's song. e. WSC
"Ein **schütz**' bin ich" ("What noble joys a hunter's life") C. Kreutzer. e.g. AB 2
Schütze, Martin
Time is ever at June (Greek air)
The willow tree (Ruthenian air)
Schwab, Gustav Benjamin
Abschied (Methfessel)
Der **schwäbische** ritter an seinen sohn ("Sohn, da hast du meinen speer") Volksweise. Words by Friedrich Leopold graf zu Stolberg. g. ED 1
Schwäbisches bauernlied ("So herzig wie mein Liesel") Folk air. Words by C. F. D. Schubart. g. ED 2
Schwäbisches bauernlied ("So herzig, wie mein Liesel") C. F. D. Schubart (music and words) g. ED 3
Schwäbisches tanzlied ("Dein herz und mein herz") See "Dein herz und mein herz"
Schwäbisches volkslied ("Guten morgen, liebes Lieserl") See Die latern
Schwach, Conrad Nicolai
Det norske flag (Ibsen)
Die **schwälble** (The swallow) J. Brahms. e.g. CS 2
"Die **schwälble** ziehet fort." See Die schwälble (Brahms)
Ein **schwan**. See En svane (Grieg)

Schwartz, M. H., and Tully, Richard Walton
All for the sake of California (Tully)

Schwartzendorf, Johann Paul Egidius.
See Martini, Jean Paul Égide

"**Schwarz** wie ein flor hängen die wolken nieder." See Der seeräuber (Gumbert)

Schweig'! damit dich niemand warnt. C. M. von Weber. e.g. SOA 5

Der **Schweizer** ("Zu Strassburg auf der schanz") F. Silcher. Volkslied. g. ED 1

Schweizer heimweh ("Herz, mein herz") F. Glück. Words by J. R. Wyss der jüngere. g. ED 1
Schweizer heimweh (Homesickness for Switzerland) e.g. SSG

Der **schweizerbu** ("Steh nur auf") Volkslied. g. ED 1

Der **schweizerbue** ("On the mountain."— Herdsman's mountain home) e. FSS 2
Herdsman's mountain home. e. WBT

Schweizerlied ("Uf em bergli") Volksweise. Words by W. von Goethe. g. ED 1
Schweizerlied (Swiss song) e.g. SSG

Schwer liegt auf dem herzen. See My heart is weary (Thomas)

"**Schwerin** der hat uns kommandiert." See Auf die schlacht bei Torgau

Schwertlied ("Du schwert an meiner linken") C. M. von Weber. Words by T. Körner. g. ED 1
Sword song. e. LA

Schwesterlein, wann gehn wir nach haus. Volksweise. Words by W. von Zuccalmaglio. g. ED 3

"**Schwor** ein junges mädchen." See Vorschneller schwur (Brahms)

Sciple,
Hail, Lafayette (Composer unknown)

Scofield, R. Le Roy
The shower

The **scolding** wife ("Some men they do delight in hounds") Hampshire folk song. SF 3

The **scolding** wife ("Soon after I was married") Irish folk song. JOI

Scotch cradle-song ("Baloo, baloo, my wee, wee thing") Old lullaby. FSS 3

Scotch lullaby ("Oh, hush thee") See "Oh, hush thee, my babie" (Whitaker)

Scotch national hymn. See "Scots wha hae wi' Wallace bled"

Scotland, John
"Lightly tread"

Scotland ("The voice of free grace") See "The voice of free grace" (Clark)

"**Scotland's** burning." Round. BD—BSS —FSS 2—HSC— JSE—NMS— OH— TFC 1

"**Scots**, wha hae wi' Wallace bled." Air: Hey tuttie taitie, or, Now the day dawis. Words by R. Burns. BAS 1—BOS—BS 1—BSB—BSP— BSR— DSH— EF— FMB— GO— HSSS— JO— MMS— MS— PS 1— SN—SSS—WBT

"**Scots**, wha hae wi' Wallace bled" (Bruce to his men at Bannockburn) BMC

"**Scots** wha hae wi' Wallace bled" (Bruce's address) FSS 7—HSD— LA—WCP

"**Scots** wha hae" (Scotch national hymn) BSE

Scott, A. C.
The A. and M. college song

Scott, Alicia Anne (Spottiswoode), lady
Annie Laurie
Douglas, tender and true
"Maxwellton braes are bonnie." See Annie Laurie

Scott, Clement William
The garden of sleep (Lara)
Once more across the land (Composer unknown)

Scott, Lady John. See Scott, Alicia Anne (Spottiswoode), lady

Scott, John P.
The knights of the golden O

Scott, Thomas
"Hasten, sinner, to be wise" (Pleyel)

Scott, Sir Walter, bart.
"Ave Maria" (Schubert)
Blue bonnets over the border (Scottish air)
Bonnie Dundee (Sainton-Dolby)
County Guy (Old English air; also music by Bishop)
"Donald Caird's come again" (Scottish air)
Goldthred's song (Barratt)
"Hail to the chief" (Scottish air; also music by Bishop; Sanderson)
"The heath this night" (Mazzinghi)
Hunting song (Welsh air)
Huntsman, rest (Mazzinghi)
Jock o' Hazeldean (Scottish air)
Lay of the imprisoned huntsman (Schubert)
"Love wakes and weeps" (Callcott)
Macgregors' gathering (Lee)
The minstrel's request (Composer unknown)
The minstrel's return (Composer unknown)
The monks of Bangor's march (Welsh air)
"O hush thee, my babie" (music by Jensen; Sullivan; Whitaker. Tr from the old Gaelic song, Caidil gu lo)
The sun is low (Swiss air)
The war-song of the men of Glamorgan (Welsh air)
"A weary lot is thine, fair maid" (Sullivan)

Scott-Gatty, Sir Alfred
Action song
Autumn song
The burial of the robin
A Christmas carol
Christmas voices
Cuckoo
"Eight little birds"
The golden shore
I wait, my love, for thee
July song
Lights far out at sea
Little girl's good-night
May-day song
Mud pies
New Year carol
New Year song
The north wind
O fair dove, O fond dove
October song
"On the rocks by Aberdeen"
"One morning, oh, so early"
The open window
Puff
Robin! Robin
"Rock-a-bye, baby"
The snow man
The sparrow on the tree
The springtime
Summer is coming
Three little pigs
"When I remember"
The Scottish fatherland. W. Tschirch.
Paraphrased from the Deutsches lied
of E. Geibel. SSS
Scottish wedding. See Muirland Willie
The scout ("Come! boor, your little blue")
F. Campana. Words by H. B. Farnie.
FSS 5
The scout company. College air. Words
adapted by P. Hastings. BSS
Scout marching song. Old English air.
Words by B. Braley. BSS
The scouts international chorus. Bugle
calls. BSS
"Screw dis cott'n (heh)." See Cott'n-pack-
in' song
Scriven, Joseph
"What a Friend we have in Jesus"
(Converse)
Scrope, Sir Carr, bart.
"One night when all the village slept"
(Traditional air)
Scuderi, Salvatore
Dreaming golden dreams
"Scusati, amici, si nun cantu bonu." See
Modo delle lavandaie
Se (If) L. Denza. Words by E. Man-
cini. e.i. CB
"Se amor mai da vu se vede" (If you ever
look on love) Venetian folk song.
e.i. MSI
"Se amor mai da vu se vede" (Should
you chance on love at play) e.i.
SMF
Se amor m'annoda il pïède ("If love my
feet enchaineth") A. Stradella. e.i.
PA 2

"Se bel rio" ("If the brook") R. Rontani.
Words by G. Chiabrera. e.i.
FEI 1
"Se bel rio" ("When the murm'ring")
e.i. PA 2
"Se ben nemica sorte." See Col raggio
placido (Händel)
"Se come voi piccina io fossi ("If I were
like you") Puccini. e.i. OPS 1
Se estinto è l'idol mio. For English trans-
lation see "If torn from thee" (Hän-
del)
"Se eu entrara no teu peito." See Vira
do minho
"Se Florindo è fedele" ("Should Florindo
be faithful") A. Scarlatti. e.i.
PA 1
To Florindo. e. BC
"Se fossi una viola." See S'io fosse
"Se gnori z'apo tin kopsi." See Hymn to
freedom (Manzaros)
Se il ciel mi divide (Since heaven has torn
me) N. Piccinni. e.i. PA 2
"Se il rigor." See "Si la rigueur" (Halévy)
"Se l'aura spira" ("When soft the breez-
es") G. Frescobaldi. e.i. FEI 1
"Se mai più sarò geloso" ("Should I e'er
again distrust thee") A. Sacchini. e.i.
KS 4
"Se mai senti" ("If to thy soul") L. Leo.
e.i. FEI 2
Se mai senti (When around thy dear
face) e.i. KS 3
"Se mai vien tocca" ("If where a wound
is") G. B. Bononcini. e.i. FEI 2
"Se piensas engañarme." See Bolero cas-
tellano
"Se quel guerrier io fossi." Celeste Aida
(Verdi)
"Se Romeo tuccise un figlio" ("If Ser Ro-
meo thy son's life ended") V. Bellini.
e.i. KS 2
"Se tu della mia morte" ("If thou my death
proclaiming") A. Scarlatti. e.i.
PG 4
"Se tu della mia morte" ("Would'st
thou the boast of ending") e.i.
PA 1
Se tu m'ami, se sospiri ("If thou lov'st
me") G. B. Pergolesi. e.i. PA 1
"Se tu m'ami" ("Gentle shepherd")
e.i. CS 2—MSS 2—SS 2
"Se tu m'ami" ("If thou lov'st me")
e.i. FEI 2
"Se tu m'ami" (If 'tis I alone thou
lovest) e.i. PG 1—PG 2
"Se un tuo pietoso accento." See Se (Den-
za)
"Se vuol ballare, signor contino." W. A.
Mozart. e.i. SOA 5
The sea ("One sails away to sea, to sea")
E. A. MacDowell. Words by W. D.
Howells. FF
The sea ("The sea, the sea, the open sea")
S. Neukomm. Words by B. W. Proc-
ter. FSS 8—HSE 3—JO
The sea ("The sea tosses and raves."—La
mer) A. Borodine. e.f. NM 1

Sea-bird's song. Verdi. Words by J. Smith. FSS 2—JSE

The sea breeze. See Marianina

The sea-fight. See Le combat naval

The seagull. Russian folk air. Words by M. H. B. Mussey. WF

The sea gulls ("Far above the deep blue sea") FSS 6

"Seagulls flocking with feathers snowy." See Im kahne (Grieg)

"Sea gulls, sea gulls on white wings flying." See Im kahne (Grieg)

"Sea-gulls, sea-gulls with plumage snowy." See Im kahne (Grieg)

"The sea is a jovial comrade." See Wind and sea (Cauffmann); Wind and sea (Schulz)

"The sea its pearls possesses." See "Das meer hat seine perlen" (Franz)

The sea king. See Necken (Söderberg)

"Sea nymphs." See "Nymphes attentives" (Gounod)

Sea of stars ("Nincsen annyi tenger csillag") Hungarian song. e.hu. BF 1

The sea-queen (La reine de la mer) A. Borodine. e.f. SC

A sea scout chantey. J. A. Wilder (music and words) BSS

A sea song. See Lied maritime (Indy)

"The sea, the sea, the open sea." See The sea (Neukomm)

"The sea tosses and raves." See The sea (Borodin)

"The sea was bright and the bark rode well." See The white squall (Barker)

"The sea was hoary, hoary." See The voice of the sea

"The sea was rough, the clouds were dark." See The cabin boy (Ware)

Seagrave, Robert
   "Rise, my soul, and stretch thy wings" (Nares)

Seagull. For entries beginning Seagull and Seagulls, see Sea gull and Sea gulls

Seaman, Frederic Cromwell
   A toast to Columbia (Parsons)

A seaman's ditty. See Een liedje van de zee

Sean eternos los laureles. See Himno nacional—Argentina (López y Planes)

"Search the world over, can you discover." See Porter lied (Flotow)

"Search thro' the wide world." Donizetti. e. FSS 4

Searching for lambs ("As I went out") English folk song. SEF 1—SO

Searching for young lambs ("As young Johnny walked out") Irish folk song. JOI

Searing, Mrs Laura Catherine (Redden)
   Chant of Breton peasants (Naumann)

Sears, Edmund Hamilton
   "Calm on the listening ear of night" (Traditional air; also music by Dykes; Hopkins)
   "It came upon the midnight clear" (Old English air; also music by Dykes; Giardini; Higinbotham; MacConnell; Willis)

The seasons. W. Mozart. FSS 6

"Seated one day at the organ." See The lost chord (Sullivan)

"Seated upon the top-most stair." See The fair transgressor (Du Bois)

Seaver, Fred
   Solomon Levi

"Seaweed and sinking sands." See Japanese death song (Sharp)

"Sebben, crudele" ("Tho' not deserving") A. Caldara. e.i. PA 1

Secchi, Antonio
   "Lungi dal caro bene"
   "When far from my dear treasure." See "Lungi dal caro bene"

Seckendorff, Karl Siegmund, freiherr von
   The evening-bells

Secrecy. See Verborgenheit (Wolf)

"Secret fears oppress me." See "Nuit resplendissante" (Gounod)

Secret love. See Heimliche liebe

"A secret tell I thee." See "Ma vie a son secret" (Bizet)

The sedges. Donegal air. Words by S. O'Sullivan. FSI

"Sedlák, sedlák." See The farmer

Sedley, Sir Charles
   The knotting song (Purcell)
   "Phillis is my only joy" (Hobbs)

"See afar yon hill Ardmore." See Moladh na landaidh

"See amid the winter snow." R. A. Smith. Words by E. Caswall. HC

"See amid the winter's snow." French carol. Words by E. Caswall. HC

"See amid the winter's snow." J. Goss. Words by E. Caswall. FSS 8— HC
   Hymn for Christmas day. BSC—CST —DC
   See amid the snow. MCS

"See, amid the winters' snow" (Hail! ever-blessed morn) Gollmick. ₁Words by E. Caswall₁ MCS

"See, amid the winter's snow." J. L. Hatton. ₁Words by E. Caswall₁ TL

"See at your feet." M. W. Balfe. FSS 8 —HSD—WBT

"See, brothers, see, how the night comes on." See Maltese boatman's song (Devereux)

"See dat Christmas tree so fin'." See Darkey Christmas song

"See fo' an' twenty elders." See Four and twenty elders

"See heaven arching so pure and clear." See Martsviolerne (Gade)

"See how sad she leans there on her balcony." See Yoh-Wu-Mo

"See how the glorious sunlight." See Zonnelied (Rennes)

"See how the glorious sunset." See The evening-bells (Seckendorff)

"See, love, above the stars" ("Csillag elég ragyog") Hungarian folk song. e.hu. SMF

"See, my fair, the morning hazy." See January (Hook)

"See! my pack is filled to overflowing."
See The peddler

"See, my song, her fears allaying." See
"De son coeur j'ai calmé la fievre"
(Thomas)

"See now the bridegroom." Bach. e.
OS 2

"See, now the dusk is falling." See Ave
Maria (Raff)

"See, oh see the breaking day." See The
rising of the lark

"See! on the windows old Jack Frost has
come." See Jack Frost

"See, saw, Margery Daw." Nursery song.
WA—WBT—WSC—WSW

See-saw, see-saw, now we're up or down.
See See-saw waltz song (Crowe)

See-saw waltz song. A. G. Crowe. FSS 6
—HSD

See-saw. JSE—WA—WBT—WSC—
WSW

"See, see the heavens smile." Purcell.
BS 2

"See, she blushing turns her eyes." Händel. CS 2

"See, she is dancing." See Waltz song
(Offenbach)

"See the chariot at hand." See To Charis

"See the course throng'd with gazers."
See The high-mettled racer (Dibdin)

"See the fellow that passed just now."
See "Saa du knøsen, som strøg forbi"
(Grieg)

"See the happy kitten." See The happy
kitten

"See the little birch in the meadow." See
The birch in the meadow

"See the Maiden Mother mild." See Sleep,
my child (Glover)

See the moon. See "Guarda la luna"

"See the moonlight is steeping the vale
while thou'rt sleeping." See Rosario
de la aurora

"See, the morning fair and bright." A. H.
Brown. HC

"See! the morning star is dwelling" (The
morning star) J. F. Bridge. [Words
by W. Wood] BSC

"See! the morning star is dwelling." J.
E. Pinkham. Words by W. Wood.
HC

"See the pale moon passing." See "Guarda
la luna"

"See the proud banner of liberty streaming." See Our flag o'er us waving
(Verdi)

"See the rosy morn appearing." Round.
Shield. TL

"See the smoking bowl before us." Air:
Jolly mortals, fill your glasses. Words
by R. Burns. BSR

"See the summer sun is glowing." See
Ducker

"See the sun yonder shining in beauty."
See Mazurek

"See the sunbeams gaily dancing." See
Die seejungfer (Haydn)

"See the sun's first gleam." See The hunter's song (Schaffer)

"See the wine is gaily flowing." See
Drinking song (Mascagni)

"See these ribbons gaily streaming." See
Lizette (Kücken)

"See this branch of sweetest flow'rs." See
Moo-lee-hwa

"See, where my tears have fallen." See
"Aus meinen tränen spriessen" (Schumann)

"See where the rising sun." Words from
the German. e. FSS 2

"See where the star of eve beams gently
yonder." See Santa Lucia

"See yon chapel on the hill." See The
chapel

"See yonder! behold her." See Ah! se tu
dormi (Vaccai)

"See you the rover." Croatian folk air.
Words by S. H. Ward. WF

The seeds of love ("I sowed my seeds")
See "I sowed my seeds of love" (Sussex version)

The seeds of love ("I sow'd the seeds")
See "I sow'd the seeds of love" (Folk
song)

Die seejungfer (The mermaid) F. J.
Haydn. e.g. GMF
The mermaid's song ("Now the dancing
sunbeams play") e. MSS 1

"Seek and ye shall find." Negro spiritual. HR
Seek and you shall find. JP

"Seek ye first the kindom of God." M.
B. Foster. SAS 3

"Seeker, seeker, give up your heart to God."
See The rocks and the mountains

"Seeking the joys that my soul would cherish." See "Vado ben spesso cangiando
loco" (Rosa)

Seele du musst munter werden. For English translation see "Come, my soul,
thou must be waking" (Hodges)

"Seems to me the whole world's singing."
See The endless song (Neidlinger)

Der seeräuber (The pirate) F. Gumbert.
e.g. AB 2

"Sees the hunter, far below." See The
huntsman

*Seewis, Johann Gaudenz, freiherr von
Salis-.* See Salis-Seewis, Johann Gaudenz, freiherr von

"Il segreto per esser felici" ("It is better
to laugh than be sighing") e.i.
KS 3—SOA 2
"Il segreto per esser felici" ("Oh, the
secret of bliss."—Brindisi) e.i.
OPS 2
"It is better to laugh than be sighing."
e. BC—BD—FSS 3—WBT

Séguédille ("Près des remparts de Séville")
G. Bizet. e.f. SOA 2
"Près des remparts" ("Close by the
walls of Sevilla") e.f. KS 2
Seguidilla. e.f. OPS 2

Seguita a piangere (Mourn with temerity)
G. B. Bassani. e.i. PA 2

Ségur, Sophie (Rostopchine), comtesse de
Star of the north (Glinka)

Segur, W. B.
Dartmouth song (Composer unknown)
"**Seh**' ich deine kleinen füsschen an" ("When I see those little feet of thine") A. Rubinstein. Words by F. Bodenstedt (Mirza-Schaffy) e.g. SC

Sehlstedt, Elias
Norrländingens hemlängtan (Brooman)
Sehnsucht ("Fröhlich schwebt") V. Righini. Words by A. Fresenius. g. ED 3
Sehnsucht ("Grant me daylight's golden splendor") See Longing (Rubinstein)
Sehnsucht ("Ich denk an euch") J. H. C. Bornhardt. Words by A. Mahlmann. g. ED 1
Sehnsucht ("Jeg kunde slet ikke sove") See Laengsel (Kjerulf)
Sehnsucht ("Der stille schlaf") J. Regnart. g. ED 3
Sehnsucht ("Der wald, der dunkle wald") F. F. Hurka. g. ED 3
"**Seht**, die sonne sinkt ins meer." See Die abenddämmerung (Nägeli)
"**Seht** die sonnenstrahlen spielen." See Die seejungfer (Haydn)
"**Seht** ihr drei rosse vor dem wagen." See Three-in-hand
"**Sei** bella negli occhi." See Coraggio, ben mio
"**Sei** nun gedankt für der kindheit freud'." See Synnöves lied (Kjerulf)
"**Sei** sì caro" ("Not thy beauty") A. Steffani. e.i. FEI 2
Sei still (Be still) J. Raff. e.g. PG 2
"**Sei** vendicata assai." See "Ah! mon remords te venge" (Meyerbeer)
Seidel, Friedrich Ludwig
Abendlied froher landleute
Idle
Thekla, eine geisterstimme
Die wahrsagerin
Seidel, Karl
Das Steierland
Styrian song. See Das Steierland
Seidl, Johann Gabriel
Blondel's lied (Schumann)
Die uhr (Loewe)
Seifert,
More and more
"**Seigneur**, mon Dieu, protège-moi." See A prayer (Kalinnikov)
Seignors, ore entendez à nus. For English translations see "Listen, lordlings, unto me" (Gascon air); "Listen, lordlings, unto me" (Ouseley)
Seiller, A.
The kleftman
Ho klephtes. See The kleftman
Das **seiser** almlied (In the meadow) Austrian song. e.g. BF 2
"**Seit** vater Noah in becher goss." Volksweise: Ein niedliches mädchen, ein junges blut. Words by J. Baggesen. g. ED 2
"**Seitdem** dein aug' in meines schaute" ("E'er since thine eyes returned my glances") R. Strauss. Words by A. F. von Schack. e.g. FO 2

"**Seja** um pallio de luz desdobrado sob." See Hymno da proclamacao da republica (Miguez)
"**Sējan rūtą**." See Sowing the rue
"**Sejećaš** li se onog sata." See Remembrance
Selby, Helen W.
"Carol, Christian children" (Moffat)
Selden, Edward G.
"Lift up thy voice with singing" (Oliver)
"The shepherds on fair Bethlehem's plain" (Oliver)
Selden, Ella J.
"Ring out, ye joyous Easter bells" (Oliver)
Selden, Rowena
Merry joy bells ring (Molloy)
The **self-banished**. See "It is not that I love you less" (Blow)
"**Selig** die toten." See Grabgesang (Blüher)
Selige erinnerung ("Ich ging im mondenschimmer") J. A. P. Schulz. Words by Friedrich Leopold graf zu Stolberg. g. ED 2
Seligkeit (Bliss) G. Meyer. Words by A. Sonnemann. e.g. SM 1
Seligkeit der liebe ("Beglückt, beglückt") J. A. P. Schulz. Words by L. H. C. Hölty. g. ED 2
Selmer, Johan Peter
"I himlen"
"In heaven." See "I himlen"
Selve amiche, ombrose piante ("Friendly forest") A. Caldara. e.i. FEI 2
Selve amiche, ombrose piante ("Kindly forest") e.i. PA 1
"**Selve**, voi che le speranze ("Forest, thy green arbors") Salvator Rosa. e.i. FEI 1
Selwyn, John
"Bonnie hills of heather" (Harrison)
"Christmas again" (Composer unknown)
Cold water song (Lee)
First Christmas gifts (Barnard)
Home is dear (Composer unknown)
"Manger all-glorious" (Composer unknown)
What of Christmas day (Composer unknown)
"**Sem** slovenska deklica." See A Slovenian girl
Semet, Théophile Aimé Émile
"Sotto il bel ciel" (from Gil Blas)
Le **semeur**. See The sower (Cui)
The **seminarian** (Seminaríst) M. P. Moussorgsky (music and words) e. SMR 1
Semons la salade. French folk song. f. DO
Semple, Francis
Maggie Lauder (18th century air)
"**Sen** corre l'agnelletta" ("As when a lamb confiding") D. Sarri. e.i. PA 2

"Sen ta ska we chin cha la chan wasti ca gla." See In mirrored waters (Lieurance)

La seña (The signal) Mexican folk song. e.s. HF
Serenata. e.s. HS

"Send back my long-stray'd eyes." See The reproach (Leveridge); The reproach (Young)

"Send down Thy truth, O God." J. E. Sweetser. Words by E. R. Sill. LA

"Send out Thy light." C. Gounod. TFC 1—WBT

"Señora Santa Ana, porqué llora el niño." See Arrullo (Chilian version)

"Señora, su periquito." Mexican folk song. e.s. HS

"Señora, su periquito" (El perico.—The poll-parrot) Mexican folk song. Another air. e.s. BF 2

"Sensibility how charming." Air: Cornwallis's lament. Words by R. Burns. BSR

"Sente il cielo pietade alfin de' mali miei." See O Lisbona, alfin ti miro (Donizetti)

"Sento nel core" ("Loving, I borrow") A. Scarlatti. e.i. FEI 2
"Sento nel core" ("My heart doth languish") e.i. PA 2

"Senza tetto, senza cuna" ("Home or shelter") A. C. Gomez. e.i. SOA 4
"Senza tetto, senza cuna" (Without roof, without home) e.i. OPS 4

Senza timore (Undaunted) F. Sieber. e.i. AB 4

"Seprik a Váradi utczát." See Váradi's highways (Bartalus?)

Sept ans sur mer (Seven years at sea) French Canadian folk song. e.f. BFS

September. W. B. Olds. Words by V. Lewis. NMS

"Ser jag stjernorna sprida sitt flammande sken öfver skog." See Längtan (Söderman)

"Sera la viddi." See La Calavresella

The seraglio garden. See I seraljens lustgard (Sjögren)

Serbian national anthem (Srpska narodna himna) D. Jenko. Words by J. Gjorgjévič. e.se. BF 1—NA

"Serbians rise, your manhood find." See "Rise, O Servians"

"Serena i vaghi rai." Rossini. e.i. PP

Serena lux, amena lux. For English translation see "Hail, Easter bright, in glory dight"

Serenáda ("Sweet-scented breath of night") See Death's serenade (Musorgskiĭ)

Sérénade ("Au sein des nuits tout dort") G. Pierné. Words by E. Adenis. e.f. HM 2
Serenade. e. WBW

Sérénade ("De mon amie") See "De mon amie, fleur endormie" (Bizet)

Serenade ("Deh vieni") See "Deh vieni alla finestra" (Mozart)

Serenade ("Der den himmel") See Ständchen (Raff)

Serenade ("Un devoto por ir al rosario") See Rosario de la aurora

Serenade ("Dream on my darling") H. Smart. Words by B. Capes. DM 1

Serenade ("The flow'rets close") See "The flow'rets close at eve, my love" (Abt)

Serenade ("Good-night! good-night, beloved") See "Good-night! good-night, beloved" (Nevin)

The serenade ("The larks awake") Pack. DM 2

Serenade ("Leise flehen") See Ständchen (Schubert)

Serenade ("Liebes mädchen") See "Liebes mädchen hör mir zu" (Haydn)

Serenade ("Mach' auf") See Ständchen (Strauss)

Serenade ("Mignonne, voici l'avril") See Sérénade du passant (Massenet)

Serenade ("Der mond ist schlafen") See Ständchen (Franz)

Serenade ("Der mond steht") See Ständchen (Brahms)

Serenade ("Nächtlicher duft") See Ständchen (Jensen)

Serenade ("'Neath thy window, love") M. Moszkowski. Words by E. Devereux. WBT
Serenata ("'Neath thy window, love") WBW

Serenade ("La noche 'sta serena") See "La noche 'sta serena"

Serenade ("Now the sun has gone to rest") V. Bellini. FSS 7

Serenade ("'Nta sta vanedda") See Serenata ("'Nta sta vanedda")

Sérénade ("Où vas-tu, souffle d'aurore") P. I. Tchaikovsky. Words by E. Turquetiz. e.f. FM—FO 2
A serenade ("Sleep, the stars are on high") e. TS

Serenade ("Quand tu chantes") See Chantez riez et dormez (Gounod)

A serenade ("Sleep, the stars are on high") See Sérénade ("Où vas-tu, souffle d'aurore") (Tchaikovsky)

Serenade ("Stars of the summer night") See "Stars of the summer night" (Balfe); "Stars of the summer night" (Pease); "Stars of the summer night" (Woodbury)

Serenade ("Still is the moonlight") See By the sea shore (Gade)

Serenade ("Sweet and graceful") Air: Hedydd lon, or, Sweet Peggy. Words by Talhaiarn. MMW

Serenade ("Vous qui faites") See "Vous qui faites l'endormie" (Gounod)

Serenade ("Wenn die nacht") See "Wenn die nacht mit ihrem schleier" (Abt)

Serenade ("When oppress'd by soft slumber") WC

Serenade ("The wind is whisp'ring") W. H. Neidlinger. AA

Serenade ("Wondrous and soft the air") See Death's serenade (Musorgskiĭ)

Sérénade à Juanita (Serenade to Juanita) A. Jouberti. Words by A. Delarue. e.f. SM 1

Sérénade basque (Basque serenade) Folk song. e.f. TSF

Sérénade du passant (Serenade) J. Massenet. Words by F. Coppée. e.f. SM 3

Serenade of Don Pasquale. See "Com è gentil" (Donizetti)

Serenade of the roses. See 'A serenata d' 'e rrose (Capua)

Serenade to Juanita. See Sérénade á Juanita (Jouberti)

"Serenading beaux are courting." See Mandoline (Debussy)

Serenata ("Bella siccome."—Bound with chains) Italian song. e.i. BF 2

Serenata ("Un devoto por ir al rosario") See Rosario de la aurora

Serenata ("Era la noche") Folk song from southern California. e.s. HS

Serenata ("'Neath thy window, love") See Serenade (Moszkowski)

Serenata ("La niña que á mi me quiera") See La seña

Serenata ("'Nta sta vanedda."—Serenade) Sicilian song. e.i. MSI

La serenata ("O quali mi risvegliano."— Angel's serenade) G. Braga. e.i. SOS 1
Angel's serenade. e. WBT

Serenata ("Son soto i toi balconi."—Beneath your balcony) Italian song. e.i. BF 2

'A serenata d' 'e rrose (Serenade of the roses) E. di Capua. Words by V. Russo. e.i. MN
Serenade of the roses. e. WL

Serenata de Pierrot. Porto Rican song. Composer and author of words unknown. s. LCP

La serenata de Schubert. See Ständchen (Schubert)

"Serene I fold my hands and wait." See My own shall come to me (Foster)

Serene night. See "Noche serena"

"Serenely and with valor come raise your manly voices." See Hymno de Riego (Huerta)

"Serenos y alegres." See Himno de Riego (Huerta)

Serly, Lajos
Forget-me-not
"Kék nefelejts." See Forget-me-not

Serradell, Narciso
La golondrina
The swallow. See La golondrina

"Servia, peaceful land of flowers." See Rise, Servians

Servian hymn. See Rise, Servians

Servian national hymn. See "Rise, O Servians"

"Set is the sun so still is the gloaming." See Stay not, delay not

"Setzt euch, brüder, in die runde." Studentenlied. Words by C. F. Strakerjan. g. ED 2

"Seule en ta sombre tour." See La cloche (Saint-Saëns)

Seume, Johann Gottfried
Der gesang

The seven joys of Mary. Tinkers' carol from Ashdown forest. WCC

The seven joys of Mary. Traditional song. Another air. BSC—HC—MF

"Seven long years." Folk song from Georgia. CSE

Seven years at sea. See Sept ans sur mer

"Seven years has Annie." See Annie wept

"The seventeenth of June last by the dawning of the day." See The north of Amerikay

"Sew not, O my mother dear, on the red sarafan." See The scarlet sarafan (Varlamov)

Sewall, Frank
The land of memory (Scottish air)

Sewell, T. M.
Sally come up

Sextet. Donizetti. [Tr of Chi mi frena in tal momento] e. TFC 2

Seyferth, Karl
Die hussiten vor Naumburg (Hungarian folk air)

Seymour (Weber) See "As a little child"; "Depth of mercy! can there be"; "Lord, forever at Thy side"; "Now are flown the shades of night"; "Softly now the light of day"

Shackelton, Frances
The orange and the black—Albany (same air as The orange and the black—Princeton)
The orange and the black—Princeton

Shackley-hay. 17th century song. CO 2 —DM 2

"The shade of trees which o'er the river are bending." See "L'ombre des arbres" (Debussy)

"Shades of evening, close not o'er us." See Isle of beauty (Rawlings); Isle of beauty (Whitmore)

"Shades of evening now descend." See Evening (Beethoven)

"The shades of night the stifling heat have cool'd" ("Die gluth des heissen tages") M. I. Glinka. e.g. KS 3

"The shades of night were a-comin' down swift." See Upidee (Variation of Longfellow's words)

"The shades of night were falling fast." See Upidee (Words by Longfellow)

"Shades of silent night." C. H. Sunderland. HC

The shadow ("My shadow's always with me") Old air. Words by M. Morgan. DO

The shadow ("Night's wan veil") Russian folk air. Words by J. Russell. WF

A shadow ("What lack the valleys and mountains") A. Sullivan. Words by A. A. Procter. FSS 7

Shadow dance. See "Ombre légère" (Meyerbeer)

The **shadow** of the cross (L'ombra della croce) G. Barri. Words by F. E. Weatherly. e.i. HSS 3

The **shadow** of trees. See "L'ombre des arbres" (Debussy)

Shadow song. See "Ombre légère" (Meyerbeer)

Shadows at play ("When the sun sets") Air: The fall of the leaf. Words by K. R. Moffat. MMW

"The **shadows** lie across the dim old room." See Dream faces (Hutchinson)

"**Shadows** of ev'ning, o'er us are falling." See "Cade la sera" (Mililotti)

"The **shadows** of the evening hours." J. Bensel. Words by A. A. Procter. LA

"The **shadows** of the evening hours." H. Hiles. ₁Words by A. A. Procter₁ WBT

"**Shadows** on the Neva." Russian folk air. Words by G. D. Donaldson. WF

Shadwell, Thomas
    The delights of the bottle (Locke)
    Hence, hence with your trifling deity (Purcell)
    "Nymphs and shepherds" (Purcell)

"**Shaffat** thalāth banāt khaul-el-ma 'sarek." See "Three maiden lovers"

Shakespeare, William
    The songs are arranged alphabetically under the title of the play or poem in which they appear. A few miscellaneous songs precede this classified list
    No distinction has been made between Shakespeare's own songs and the traditional songs quoted in his plays
    "As it fell upon a day" (Bishop)
    "From the fair Lavinian shore" (Wilson)
    "Good friend, for Jesus' sake forbear" (Beethoven)
    "On a day—alack the day" (Chilcot)

          As you like it
    "Blow, blow, thou winter wind" (music by Arne; Fisher; Sarjeant; Whiting)
    "Crabbed age and youth" (music by Horn; Loomis)
    "It was a lover and his lass" (music by Barton; Clough-Leighter; Morley)
    "Under the greenwood tree, who loves to lie with me" (music by Arne; Busch)
    "What shall he have that killed the deer" (Traditional air; also music by Hilton)

          Cymbeline
    "Fear no more the heat o' the sun" (Parry)
    "Hark! hark! the lark" (music by Curschmann; Schubert)

          Hamlet
    "And will he not come again" (Traditional air)
    "Good morrow, 'tis St Valentine's day" (Traditional air)

"How should I your true love know" (16th century air; also English folk air)

          Henry VIII
"Orpheus with his lute" (music by Busch; Greene; Manney; Sullivan)

          Love's labour's lost
The owl (Arne)
"When daisies pied, and violets blue" (Arne)

          Measure for measure
"Take, oh! take those lips away" (music by Bishop; Gaillard; Wilson)

          The merchant of Venice
"Tell me where is fancy bred" (music by Arne; Stevenson)

          The midsummer night's dream
"By the simplicity of Venus' doves" (Bishop)
"I know a bank whereon the wild thyme blows" (Horn)
Midsummer night's dream (Macfarren)
"Now the hungry lion roars" (music by Leveridge; Linley)
"Over hill, over dale, thro' bush thro' brier" (music by Cooke; Dunstan)
"Through the forest" (Gattie)

          Much ado about nothing
"Sigh no more, ladies" (music by Arne; Fisher; Stevens; Sullivan)

          Othello
"And let me the canakin clink" (Loomis)
The willow song (16th century air; also music by Hook; Humfrey; Rossini; Sullivan)

          Romeo and Juliet
Romeo and Juliet (Tchaikovsky)

          The tempest
Caliban's song (Smith)
"The cloud-capp'd towers" (Stevens)
"Come unto these yellow sands" (music by Banister; Purcell)
"Full fathom five" (music by Banister; Ireland; Johnson; Purcell)
"O, bid your faithful Ariel fly" (Linley)
"Where the bee sucks" (music by Arne; Humfrey; Johnson; Sullivan)
"While you here do snoring lie" (Arne)

          Twelfth night
"Als büblein klein an der mutter brust" (Nicolai. Tr of "When that I was a little tiny boy")
"Hold thy peace" (Old English air)
"If music be the food of love, play on" (Clifton)
"O mistress mine" (Traditional air; also music by Coleridge-Taylor; Morley; Sullivan)
"She never told her love" (Haydn)
"When that I was a little tiny boy" (Traditional air; also music by Fielding; Heise; Schumann; Vernon. For music by Nicolai see "Als büblein klein an der mutter brust")

Shakespeare, William —Continued

The two gentlemen of Verona

"Should he upbraid" (Bishop)
"Who is Sylvia" (music by Gould; Leveridge; Schubert)

Venus and Adonis

"Bid me discourse" (Bishop)
"Lo! here the gentle lark" (Bishop)

The winter's tale

Hanskin (Traditional air)
"Lawn as white as driven snow" (Traditional air; also music by Greenhill; Linley; Wilson or Johnson)
"When daffodils begin to peer" (Composer unknown)

"**Shall** I come, sweete love, to thee." T. Campion (music and words) BOH
"Shall I come sweet love." JE
"**Shall** I go walk the woods so wild." See The woods so wild
"**Shall** I show you how the farmer." See The farmer
"**Shall** I wasting in despair." Old air. Words by G. Wither. CO 1
"**Shall** I, wasting in despair" (The manly heart) G. Barker. Words by G. Wither. SSS
"**Shall** I, wasting in despair." R. King. Words by G. Wither. MM
"Shall I wasting in despair" (Love for love) DM 2
"**Shall** I, wasting in despair" (Woman) H. Phillips. Words by G. Wither. HSE 3
"**Shall** old acquaintance be forgot, and mem'ry's garland fade." See Sing Augustana's praises
"**Shall** the harp then be silent." Air: McFarlane's lamentation. Words by T. Moore. MI
"**Shall** we gather at the river." R. Lowry. WA—WBT—WS—WSW
"**Shall** we meet beyond the river." E. S. Rice. Words by H. L. Hastings. FSS 2—HSD—WBT—WS
Shallo Brown ("Oh, I'm a-gwine") Negro halliard chantey. CR
For variants of this song see following songs of similar title
Shallow Brown ("Come, get my clothes") Pulling song. SMW
Shallow Brown ("O I'm going") Pulling chantey. SE
Shallow Brown ("A Yankee ship") Pulling chantey. SE
Shamburg, Richard. See Schuckburgh, Richard
Shame fa' the gear and the blathrie o't ("When I think on this world's pelf") Scottish song. MMS
"**Shame** upon you, Robin." See Milkmaid's song (Parker)
The **shamrock** shore. Irish folk song. JOI

Shanadar ("O Shanadar I love your daughter") Capstan chantey. SE
For variants of this song see following song of same title; also River Shenandore; Shenandoah
Shanadar ("Shanadar is a rolling river") Pulling chantey. SE
Shanahan, P. S.
Clear the way for U. S. C.
Shane Glas ("Have you gazed at Shane Glas") Irish air. Words from the Irish of O'Carolan. e. MMI
"De **Shanghai** chicken, when you put him in de pit." See Don't bet your money on de Shanghai (Foster)
Sharland, Joseph B.
There is no end for souls like his
Sharp, Earl Cranston
Japanese death song
Sharpe, Mrs George
The deep, deep sea (Horn)
Sharpe, Henry John
Rockaway (Russell)
Sharpe, R. S.
The minute gun at sea (King)
Sharrot, W.
"Carol, sweetly carol"
Shaw, Alfred C.
Somewhere (Campana)
Shaw, David T.
Columbia, the gem of the ocean (wrongly attributed) See Becket, T. à. Columbia, the gem of the ocean
Shaw, Emma
"From forest wide and free" (music by Oliver; Tufts)
Shaw, Geoffrey
"Christ is born! Christ is born"
"The snow lies thick"
Shaw, Martin
Hominum laudes
"Three kings in great glory"
Shaw, Oliver
"As down in the sunless retreats"
Down in the sunless retreats. See "As down in the sunless retreats"
Mary's tears
Nothing true but heaven. See There's nothing true but heaven
There's nothing true but heaven
Shchepkina-Kupernik, Tatíana Lvovna
Berceuse (Arenski)
Shcherbin, N.
A southern night (Rimskiĭ-Korsakov)
She alone charmeth my sadness. See Sous les pieds d'une femme (Gounod)
She answered me nay. W. H. Jones. CHS
"**She** beats me, she bangs me." See Our goodman (Hot Springs, N.C. version)
"**She** bloomed with the roses." FSS 4
"**She** called to her little page-boy." See Lady Maisry
She came and went. German air. Words by J. R. Lowell. LBR
"**She** had asked to have a caller." See Nothing—but another girl (Jones)

"She had shut the door." See The coquette

"She hadn't been married but a very short
time." See The wife of Usher's well
(Alleghany, N.C. version)

"She is a flower, flower of the prairie."
See Rose de Provence

She is a winsome wee thing. See "I
never saw a fairer"

"She is far from the land." Irish air: Open
the door. Words by T. Moore. JO—
MI—MMI

She is my Angelina. C. J. Penney.
Words by A. G. Hays. CU

"She is skilled in mathematics." See My
college girl (Hill)

"She is slender and young and fair." See
Das kind der berge (Grieg)

"She laid herself all against the oak." See
The cruel mother (Carmen, N.C. version)

She lives in the valley below. J. Hook.
ME

"She mounted on the milk white steed."
See Lady Isabel and the elf knight
(Carmen, N.C. version)

She must be mine. Welsh song. WBT—
WL

"She never told her love." J. Haydn.
Words by W. Shakespeare. SM 2
—VFS

"She never told her love" ("Stets barg
die liebe sie") e.g. NG—PG 3

"She paus'd, then blushing, led the lay."
See Huntsman, rest (Mazzinghi)

"She play'd the loon or she was married."
Air: My wife's a wanton wee thing.
Words by R. Burns. BSR

"She run her boat against the main." See
Sweet William (Carmen, N.C. version)

"She saddled up her milk-white steed."
See Geordie (Black Mountain, N.C. version)

"She sat down below a thorn." See Fine
flowers in the valley

"She sat on the steps at the eventide." See
The vacant stare (Jones)

She shook her head. W. H. Jones. CHS

"She sits alone all thro' the day." See In
shadowland (Pinsuti)

"She stands on the pier." See Old and
young Marie (Cowen)

"She sung of love." Air: The Munster
man. Words by T. Moore. MI

"She told me her love was undying." See
A dissonance (Borodin)

"She vow'd, she swore she wad be mine."
See Roy's wife of Aldivalloch

"She wandered down the mountain side."
F. Clay. Words by B. C. Stephenson.
HSE 3—MSS 1—SS 1

"She wandered where the daisies grew."
See The untruthful daisy (Jones)

"She was a dainty little miss." See His
favorite flower (Lowitz)

"She was going, I was coming." See "Lee
l'andava e mi vegneva"

"She was just as kind and good to me."
See Harry Gray

"She was standing by the wicket." See
Going to market (Diehl)

"She was the child of France's king." See
La princesse de France mariée à un
Anglais (Norman version)

"She was young and fair and handsome."
See My parents treated me tenderly
(Big Laurel, N.C. version)

"She who's fairest in my sight." See
Ramène tes moutons

"She wore a wreath of roses." J. P.
Knight. Words by T. H. Bayly. CS 1
—FSS 6—JO

"Shed not a tear." T. H. Bayly. Words
by R. V. Johnson. FSS 8

Sheela nee Guira. See Síghile ni Ghadhra

Sheeles, John
"Come, cheer up your hearts"

The sheep and the boy. See "Lazy sheep,
pray tell me why"

The sheep in the snow. See Ny kirree
fo-sniaghtey

The sheep-shearing ("How delightful to
see") English folk song. SO

Sheep-shearing song ("It's a rosebud")
See "It's a rosebud in June"

The sheepstealer. Folk song from Dorset. SF 1

"A sheer hulk here lies poor Tom Bowling."
See Tom Bowling (Dibdin)

The Sheffield apprentice. Folk song: Nor-
folk version. SF 2
—Allanstand, N.C. version. CSE
—Hot Springs, N.C. version. CSE

"Shein bin ich." See "Pretty am I"

"Shekogquean baydahbahnug." See The
lucky trapper

"Shekok quean baydahbahnug." See
Skunk song

Sheldon, William
Kohala's breezes (Nape)

Shelley, Harry Rowe
Liebesleid. See Love's sorrow
Love's sorrow
The ride

Shelley, Percy Bysshe
Dirge for the year (Wesley)
"I arise from dreams of thee" (music
by Salaman; also unknown com-
poser)
"Music, when soft voices die" (Day)
To night (Smith)

Shells of ocean. J. W. Cherry. Words
by J. W. Lake. BE 5—FSS 2—
HSE 2—WBT

I wandered by the sea-beat shore.
HSD

Shelton, Ada S.
Mistress Santa Claus (Lee)

The Shenandoah ("It's of a famous American ship") Forecastle song. Air:
The banks of Newfoundland. CR

For variants of this song see following
songs of same title; also River
Shenandore; Shanadar

Shenandoah ("O Shenandoah, I long to
hear you") Chantey. BSS

Shenandoah ("Oh Shenandoah, I long to
hear you") Capstan chantey. CR

Shenandoah ("Oh, Shenandoah I love your daughter."—The wide Missouri) Capstan chantey.　KB

Shenstone, William
　"My banks they are furnished with bees" (Arne)
　"When forced from dear Hebe to go" (Arne)

Shepard, Thomas G.
　Adelina, the Yale Boola girl.　See Boola song ("Well, here we are")
　Alma mater—Yale
　Boola song (with words "Away, way down"; "Well, here we are")
　"O'er the lake"
　Wouldn't you
　Yale Boola song.　See Boola song ("Well, here we are")

Shepherd, Thomas
　"Must Jesus bear the cross alone" (Allen)

The **shepherd** and the little bird.　S. Storace.　Words by Cobb.　BE 2

"A **shepherd** band their flocks are keeping."　M. Praetorius (music and words)　e.　HC

"A **shepherd** band their flocks are keeping."　S. P. Tuckerman.　Words by M. Praetorius.　e.　HC

The **shepherd** boy (To tsopanopoulo) Greek folk song.　e.gr.　BF 2

The **shepherd** girl.　See La zagala

"A **shepherd** kept sheep on a hill so high."　DM 2

"**Shepherd** of tender youth."　J. L. Gaynor.　TL

"A **shepherd** once a maid did love."　See The shepherd and the little bird (Storace)

"A **shepherd** sat him under a thorn."　See The Northumberland bagpipes

"**Shepherd** saw thou not."　Air: Crimson velvet.　JE—MM

"**Shepherd**, saw thou not" (Crimson velvet)　CO 1

"**Shepherd**, shepherd, leave decoying."　H. Purcell.　PR 1

Shepherd song.　See Chanson de berger

The **shepherdess** ("Ahi, meschina pastorella")　See La pastorella (Lombardian song)

The **shepherdess** ("La pastorella al prato") See La pastorella (Schubert)

The **shepherdess** ("La plus aimable")　See Ramène tes moutons

"A **shepherdess**, my sorrows pity."　See La pastorella (Lombardian folk song)

The **shepherdess** of the fields.　See "Y-a rien de si charmant"

"The **shepherdess** was straying."　See La pastorella (Schubert)

"**Shepherdess**, whence come you."　See "D'où viens-tu, bergère"

"**Shepherdess**, whence com'st thou."　See "D'où viens-tu, bergère"

The **shepherds** ("Shepherds watching their sheep") P. Cornelius.　Tr of Die hirten.　e.　HC

The **shepherds** ("The shepherds watch within the fields")　e.　CST

"The **shepherds** amazed."　A. H. Brown.　BSC

The **shepherd's** call ("As I rose on Sunday morning") Breton song.　Air: Ann aliké.　e.　BMC

Shepherd's cradle-song.　See Schlaf', kindchen, schlaf' (Somervell)

"**Shepherds** five in a ring."　See The shepherds' song (Noble)

"The **shepherds** had an angel."　J. C. Bridge.　Words by C. G. Rossetti.　HC

"The **shepherds** had an angel."　F. L. Wiseman.　Words by C. G. Rossetti.　HC

"**Shepherds**, have you seen my pastora."　Old English air.　BE 6

Shepherds in the field.　G. Verdi.　Words by C. Bede.　MCS

The **shepherd's** joy (Bara Fostus dream) 16th century song.　CO 1

The **shepherds'** nativity hymn.　See Bethlehem (Gounod)

"**Shepherds** night-watch keeping."　C. E. Deffell.　Words by M. E. Browne.　HC

"The **shepherds** on fair Bethlehem's plain."　G. E. Oliver.　Words by E. G. Selden.　HC

"**Shepherds**, rejoice, lift up your eyes."　Traditional air.　HC

"**Shepherds**, shake off your drowsy sleep."　See Chantons! bargiés, Noué, Noué

Shepherd's song ("Mountains bath'd in morning light") Bosnian song.　e.　KSE

"Mountains bath'd in morning light."　e.　SN

The **shepherds'** song ("Shepherds five in a ring") T. T. Noble.　Words by Stubbs.　HC

Shepherd's song ("Shepherds, while the lambkin grazes") Air: Nos galan, or, New Year's eve.　Words by Ieuan Dhu.　MMW

"The **shepherds** they had gathered on the hillside."　See Lei pastorieu

"The **shepherds** watch within the fields."　See The shepherds (Cornelius)

"**Shepherds** watching o'er the plain."　E. Lemare.　Words by A. Gaskell.　HC

"**Shepherds** watching their sheep."　See The shepherds (Cornelius)

"The **shepherds** went their hasty way."　J. F. Barnett.　Words by S. T. Coleridge.　BSC

"The **shepherds** were watching."　E. W. S. Watson.　Words by E. H. Cooke.　HC

"**Shepherds**, while the lambkin grazes."　See Shepherd's song

The **shepherd's** winter song.　J. L. Hatton.　e.　BE 7

Sheppard, Henry Fleetwood
Bonny Nell (Old English air)
"Come, all friends, and keep the feast" (Composer unknown)
"Fair Susan slumbered in shady bower" (Folk air)
"The fields are white to harvest" (Old air)
"In Bibberley town" (Folk air)
"Joy of joys! He lives, He lives" (Old air)
On a May morning so early (Folk air)
Polly Oliver (Folk air)
"Within a garden a maiden lingered" (Folk air)

Sheppard, T. J.
"My country dear, when soaring high" (Price)

Sheridan, Caroline Elizabeth Sarah. See Norton, Mrs Caroline Elizabeth Sarah (Sheridan)

Sheridan, Helen Selina. See Dufferin, Helen Selina (Sheridan), lady

Sheridan, Richard Brinsley Butler
"Had I a heart for falsehood framed" (Old air)
"Here's to the maiden of bashful fifteen" (Traditional air)
"I have a silent sorrow here" (Georgina)
The mid-watch (Linley)

Sherlock Holmes. C. Ralston (music and words) SSS

Sherman, Frank Dempster
Daisies (Hawley)
December (Olds)
The four winds (Marshall)
June (Olds)
November (Olds)

Sherwin, William Fisk
"Day is dying in the west"
Sing always

"She's a witch, the queen of witchery." See La mágica mujer

"She's all my fancy painted her." See Alice Gray (Millard)

"She's circled by mountain." See The purple and gold—University of Washington (Schultz)

"She's fair and fause." Air: The lads o' Leith. Words by R. Burns. BSB—BSR—MMS—PS 1

"She's fairer than the fairest morn." See Canzonette (Loewe)

She's gone, let her go. College song. WC

She's such a belle, a real dark swell. See Sally come up

She's the dear maid to me. Irish folk song. JOI

"She's up there—Old Glory." See The flag of our country (Mercer)

Shevchenko, Taras Grigorievich
Evening (Tchaikovsky)
Hopak (Musorgskiĭ)
On the river Dnyéper (Musorgskiĭ)
The soldier's bride (Rachmaninov)

"Shiba no orido no shizugaya ni." See Cradle song ("There once lived")

"Shicé shicé." See Dakota serenade

Shield, William
Ah, well-a-day, my poor heart (from The follies of a day)
The Arethusa (attributed; attributed also to T. O'Carolan)
"The billet-doux"
Caleb Quotem (from The review)
"Ere around the huge oak"
The friar of orders gray (attributed) See Reeve, W. The friar of orders gray
"Great Britain is the noblest land" (attributed)
The heaving of the lead (from Hartford bridge)
"Let fame sound the trumpet"
"Let's seek the bower of Robin Hood" (from Robin Hood)
My friend and pitcher (from The poor soldier)
"My heart with love is beating" (attributed)
"Old England's a lion" (from The farmer)
Old Towler (from The czar)
"On, by the spur of valour goaded"
The ploughboy (from The farmer)
The post captain (from Variety)
Quaff with me the purple wine
"See the rosy morn appearing"
A smile from the girl of my heart (from The woodman)
The thorn
The wolf (from The castle of Andalusia)

"Shimmering sun upon the lake." See The lake sheen

Shindler, Mrs Mary Stanley Bunce (Palmer) Dana. See Dana, Mrs Mary Stanley Bunce (Palmer)

"Shine calm and bright, ye moonbeams bright." G. P. Grantham (music and words) HC

"Shine, O Lady Moon, bright as day at noon." See The obliging moon

"Shine, O sun, in splendour bright." H. H. Colburn. HC

Shine on. Negro song. L. Schoolcraft. NMP

Shine, shine. Negro song. JP

"Shine! shine! shine! pour down your warmth, great sun." See We two together (Gilchrist)

The shining dagger. Vermont song. SSH
Variants: "Awake! awake"; "O who is that that raps at my window"

"Shining ones with drooping eyes." See Christmas dawn (Bellini)

Shining shore. G. F. Root. HSD—WBT

Shining wires. German folk air. Words by H. H. Harbour. DO

"A **ship**, a ship a sailing, a sailing on the sea." See The fairy ship

"A **ship** came sailing." English folk song. BSW

"The **ship** goes sailing down the bay." See Good-bye, my lover, good-bye (American air); Good-bye, my lover, good-bye (Allen)

"A **ship** have I got in the north country." See The Golden Vanity

"A **ship** I have got in the north country." See The Golden Vanity

The **ship** in distress. English folk song. SEF 2—SO

"**Ship** is at de landin'." Negro song. BOM

"The **ship** is sailing down the bay." See Good-bye, my lover, good-bye (American air)

"A **ship** is wood and metal." See A sea scout chantey (Wilder)

The **ship** of state. Composer unknown. Words by H. W. Longfellow. FSS 8 —LA—WBT

[The **ship** of state] Sail on, O ship of state. German air. Words by H. W. Longfellow. LBR

"A **ship** the restless ocean sweeps." See "Traft ihr das schiff" (Wagner)

"The **ship** went sailing out over the bar." See To Rio Grande we're bound away

"**Ships** in the harbor sailing, coming, going." See "Vedo li bastimenti"

"The **ships** sail the ocean." See A song of ships

Shipton, Mrs Anna
"Sow ye beside all waters" (Crament)

Shirley, James
"Come my Daphne" (Lawes)
"The glories of our birth and state" (Coleman)

Shirley, Walter
"Lord, dismiss us with Thy blessing" (Composer uncertain) Authorship uncertain

Shoals, A. F.
Valedictory (King)

The **shoemaker** ("I am a shoemaker by my trade") Folk song from North Carolina. CSE

The **shoemaker** ("Yo le dije á un zapatero") See El zapatero

"**Shoheen-sho**, baby-boy." See Lullaby

Shôn ap Evan ("Undaunted Shôn ap Evan") Air: Sion ap Ifan. Words by D. Rowlands (Dewi Môn) MMW

"**Shon** Campbell." W. A. Barratt. Words by W. A. Mackenzie. SSS

Shool. College song. MPC—WBT—WC

Shooting of his dear. Folk song: North Carolina version. CSE
—Tennessee version. CSE

Shore, William
"O! Willie brew'd a peck o' maut"

Short, Seymour S.
Arbor day (Jones)

Shorter, Mrs Dora (Sigerson)
My rose (Irish air)
Spring song—to Ireland (Irish air)
"When summer comes" (Irish air)

Shōtai. See Drill song (Shiyi)

"**Should** auld acquaintance be forgot, and never brought to mind." See Auld lang syne

"**Should** Florindo be faithful." See "Se Florindo è fedele" (Scarlatti)

"**Should** he upbraid." H. R. Bishop. Words from Shakespeare. BC—BE 1 —BOH—HSE 1—MSS 1—SS 1

"**Should** hot revenge or persecution." See "Si la rigueur" (Halévy)

"**Should** I e'er again distrust thee." See "Se mai più sarò geloso" (Sacchini)

"**Should** I from thee be parted." See "Lungi dal caro bene" (Sarti)

"**Should** old acquaintance be forgot, and days that come no more." See The songs we sang

Should you chance on love at play. See "Se amor mai da vu se vede"

"**Should** you see my love so true." German folk song. e. WBT—WL

"**Shoulder** to shoulder, firm and steady." See Boy scout march (Morison)

Shout the glad tidings. W. A. Muhlenberg. FSS 6—MCS

"**Show** me, Almighty." See "Gott sei mir gnädig" (Mendelssohn)

"**Show** me the way, O Lord." See Thou art the way (Roeckel)

The **shower** ("Pitter, patter, pitter") R. L. Scofield (music and words) CHS

The **shower** ("The thunder is growling") German folk air. Words by M. Morgan. DO

Shrine, Mrs Nesta (Higginson) See O'Neill, Moira, pseud.

Shrival, R. G.
"Hark! I hear an angel sing"

Shroy, John L.
August (Olds)

"**Shu-b'dhe** adhin-he on-don-ba i ga ho." See The leader's song

Shukowskij, Wassilij Andrejewitsch. See Zhukovski, Vasili Andreevich

Shule agra. Old Irish air. Old text adapted. e. FSI

Shule aroon ("I wish I were on yonder hill") Irish folk song. e. JOI
"I wish I were on yonder hill." e. PI

Shule arun ("I wish I were on yonder hill") e. MMI

"**Shumi** Maritsa." See "Join, O Maritza"

"**Si** formas tuvieran mis pensamientos." Folk song from Los Angeles. e.s. HS

"**Sì**, guerrieri, dell' idra saracena rintuzzato è l'orgoglio." See Fu Dio che disse (Apolloni)

"**Si** je n'étais captive." See La captive (Berlioz)

"**Si** j'étais fleur des bois." See Mignonette (Weckerlin)

"Si j'étais jardinier" ("Were I gardener") C. Chaminade. Words by R. Miles. e.f. HM 1—PG 3—SM 1

"Si j'étais rayon." See Ariette (Vidal)

"Sì, la mia figlia." See Cortigiani, vil razza (Verdi)

"Si la rigueur" ("If harsh decree") J. F. Halévy. e.f. KS 5
"Si la rigueur" ("Should hot revenge") e.f. SOA 5
"Se il rigor" ("Thou faithless men") e.i. BS 1

"Si le bonheur" ("When all was young") C. F. Gounod. e.f. KS 3—OPS 2
"Si le bonheur à sourire" ("When to thy vision") e.f. SOA 2
"When to thy vision." e. HSD

"Si les filles d'Arles" ("Maids may boast") C. F. Gounod. Words by M. Carré. e.f. BS 1

"Si me dan pasteles." See Aguinaldo

Si mes vers avaient des ailes (Could my songs their way be winging) R. Hahn. Words by V. Hugo. e.f. CM 2—ES—HM 2
Si mes vers avaient des ailes ("With haste my song would be flying" e.f. KF 3—PG 1

Si mon papa le savait. See "Mon pèr' n'avait fille que moi"

"Sì morir ella de'." See Ombre di mia prosapia (Ponchielli)

"Si quieres vámonos para Jerez." See Jarabe tapatio

"Si scopron le tombe, si levano i morti." See Inno di guerra dei cacciatori delle Alpi (Olivieri)

"Sì, tra i ceppi" ("Love that's true will live forever") Händel. e.i. BAS 2—BS 1

Si tu m'aimes, Carmen. For English translation see "If you love me" (Bizet)

Si tu savais. See Could'st thou but know (Balfe)

"Si va el vapor." Folk song from Mexico and Central America. e.s. HS

"Si vieras, vida mia." Mexican folk song. e.s. HS

"Si voli il primo." Donizetti. e.i. PP

"Si vous n'avez rien à me dire" ("Why with your lovely presence haunt me") Baroness Willy de Rothschild. Words by V. Hugo. e.f. HM 2

"Siałem proso na zagonie." See "Sown with millet was my garden"

"Siam salvi! han riso." See Pescator, affonda l'esca (Ponchielli)

Siamese song. See "Hail the sun's bright morning rays"

"Šiandien Betlėjuj." See To-day in Bethlehem

Sibelius, Jean
The first kiss. See Den första kyssen
Den första kyssen
Sydameni laulu. See Vale of shadow
Vale of shadow

Sic a wife as Willie had. Scottish air: The eight men of Moidart. Words by R. Burns. PS 2
"Willie Wastle dwalt on Tweed." BSR

Sicilian mariners' hymn. See Die drei grossen Christlichen feste; "Lord, dismiss us with Thy blessing"; "O sanctissima"; "While the morning bells are ringing"

Sicilian song ("Bright is the sun") See "Bright is the sun on the ocean"

Siciliana ("Forsi pirchi nun m'ami."—"Dost thou no longer love me") Italian folk song. e.i. EF
"Forsi pirchi nun m'ami" ("So this is sad love's ending") e.i. BO

Siciliana ("O Lola") P. Mascagni. e.i. OPS 3—SOA 3. e. only WA—WBT—WL
"O Lola, bianca come fior" ("O Lola, fair as flowers") e.i. KS 4

Siciliana ("Pill' ura chi ti vitti") See "Pill' ura chi ti vitti"

"Sick my heart and sorely in danger." See À Lucette (Pierné)

Sick, sick. 16th century song. Air from "Cittharn schoole." CO 1

Sick, sick. 16th century song. Air from "Lute book." CO 1

Sidebotham, Joseph W.
"Blessed night, when Bethlehem's plain"
"Let heaven and earth rejoice and sing"

Sidfel Vanîa. See Vanya

Sidney, Margaret, pseud. See Lothrop, Mrs Harriet Mulford (Stone)

Sidney, Sir Philip
"My true love hath my heart" (music by Marzials; also by unknown composer)
"O, dear life" (Byrd)

"De sidste gaester vi fulgte til grinden." See Borte (Grieg)

"Sie ahnen die wahrheit." See "The truth is suspected" (Glinka)

"Sie ging zum sonntagstanze." See Das verfehlte wort

"Sie ist schmächtig und zart und bleich." See Das kind der berge (Grieg)

"Sie schrieben mir, wozu es leugnen." See Had fickle fortune, not betraying (Tchaikovsky)

"Sie sollen ihn nicht haben." See Der deutsche Rhein (Kunze)

Siebel, C.
Meeresleuchten (Loewe)

Sieber, Ferdinand
Composer
Senza timore
Undaunted. See Senza timore
Author
"Wonnevoller mai" (Gluck)

The siege of Kazan (Varlaám's ballad) M. Moussorgsky. Words after Pushkin and Karamzin. e. SC

Siegert, Gottlob
Gebet an den heiligen Christ

Siegmunds liebeslied. R. Wagner. e.g. SOA 3
　"Winterstürme wichen dem wonne-mond" ("Winter storms have waned 'fore the month of May") e.g. KS 4

"**Sieh** an, mein schönstes kind." See Liebe in nöten

Sieh dich vor (Oh, beware) Grieg. Words by O. Benzon. e. FTS

"**Siehe,** der Herr hat grosses an uns ge-than." See Sound the loud timbrel (Reinecke)

"**Siehst** du das vögelein nisten im wald." See Schäfer im mai (Moritz)

"**Siehst** du im abend die wolken ziehn." See In die ferne (Glück)

"**Sietz-e-à-wā** sietz-e-à-wā like a cloud he comes." See A Crow maiden's prayer song (Lieurance)

Sievers, Johann Friedrich Ludwig
　Der gärtner

"**Sift** along, boys." Cowboy song. BF 2

"**Sig** himlen hvaelver saa reen og klar." See Martsviolerne (Gade)

Sigerson, Dora. See Shorter, Mrs Dora (Sigerson)

Sigerson, George
　The cailin deas (Irish air)
　The heather glen (Irish air)

The **sigh** ("J'ai laissé de mon sein") See Soupir (Widor)

A **sigh** ("Ne jamais la voir") See Soupir (Duparc); Soupir (Kramer)

"**Sigh** no more, ladies." Arne. Words by W. Shakespeare. DM 1

"**Sigh** no more, ladies." W. A. Fisher. Words by W. Shakespeare. VFS

"**Sigh** no more, ladies." R. J. S. Stevens. Words by W. Shakespeare. BOH—HSE 1—PR 2—TS—VFS

"**Sigh** no more, ladies." A. Sullivan. Words by W. Shakespeare. DM 2—VFS

"**Sigh** not o'er toil and trouble." See Gaily sings the lark (Mozart)

Síghile ni Ghadhra (Sheela nee Guira) Irish folk song. e. JOI

"**Sighing,** weeping, sorrow, need." J. S. Bach. e. SAS 1

Sighs from my heart. See "Suspiri di lu me core"

The **sign** of the Bonny Blue Bell. English folk song. SEF 1—SO

The **sign-post.** See Der wegweiser (Schubert)

The **signal.** See La seña

"**Signor,** cui sempre loda." See Invocazione a Dio (Mariani)

Sigourney, Mrs Lydia Howard (Huntley)
　"Ye say they all have passed away" (Old English air)

Sigurd aa troll-brura (Sigurd and the troll-bride) Norse folk song. e.n. MAN

Sigurd and the troll-bride. See Sigurd aa troll-brura

Silcher, Friedrich
　"Alle jahre wieder"
　"Ännchen von Tharau"
　"Annie of Tharau." See "Ännchen von Tharau"
　Battle-song
　The bell is ringing
　Christmas song. See "Alle jahre wieder"
　The falcon
　Far from home. See In der ferne
　Farewell. See Lebewohl
　In der ferne
　Lebewohl
　Die Lorelei
　Musketierlied
　Never alone (same air as Die Lorelei)
　Rheinweinlied
　Schlachtlied
　Der Schweizer
　Der soldat
　True freedom
　The voyagers (same air as Die Lorelei)
　Das waldhorn

Sildfiske vise (The herring fisher's song) Norse folk song. e.n. MAN

Sildig (Late) A. Backer-Gröndahl. Words by H. Drachmann. da.e SSN

"**Silence** is in our festal halls." Irish air: The green woods of Truigha. Words by T. Moore. MI—MMI

"**Silence!** silence." Old song. FSS 2

"**Silent** as night." See "Still wie die nacht" (Bohm)

"The **silent** bird is hid in the boughs." Irish air: The bastard. Words by R. Mulholland (Mrs Gilbert) MMI

"**Silent** horses." R. Planquette. e. WBT

Silent love. See Stille liebe (Schumann)

The **silent** lover. W. Boyce. Words by Congreve. ME

"**Silent** night! hallow'd night." Composer unknown. Words by J. Mohr. [Tr of Die heilige nacht] e. HC

"**Silent** night! holy night." See Die heilige nacht (Gruber)

"**Silent** night! peaceful night." See "Holy night! peaceful night" (Barnby); Die heilige nacht (Gruber)

"**Silent** now the drowsy bird" (Barcarolle) J. Offenbach. Words by I. L. Brown. TFC 1

"**Silent,** O Moyle, be the roar of thy water." See Song of Fionnuala

"**Silent** pine-nights, blackness shedding." See Finnland (Jordan)

"**Silent** stars were watching." W. H. A. Hall. HC

"**Silent** the happy songs." Russian folk air. Words by J. Russell. WF

"**Silent** the sombre wings of night." See "Regnava nel silenzio" (Donizetti)

"**Silently** blending night's shadows fall." See "Voi, che sapete" (Mozart)

The **silently** falling snow. Popular air. FSS 1—WBT—WSC

"Silently floated a spirit" (Górnimee tikho letyéla dooshá nyebesámi) M. P. Moussorgsky. Words by A. K. Tolstoi. e. SMR 1

"Silently, silently fades the day's light." S. S. Wesley. DM 1

"Silently! silently! ope and close the school room door." Spanish air. FSS 5

The Silesian toper and the devil. See Der schlesische zecher und der teufel (Reissiger)

The silk merchant's daughter. Folk song: Allanstand, N.C. version. CSE
—Big Laurel, N.C. version. CSE

"Silken curtains richly falling." See Brises d'autrefois (Hüe)

Sill, Edward Rowland
Help it on (Old air)
"Send down thy truth, O God" (Sweetser)
Students' way (Old air)
Truth (Composer unknown)

Sillar, David
"A rosebud, by my early walk"

"Silly heart forbear." N. Laneir. DM 1

The silly old man. English folk song. BSW

Silver, E. O.
Brunonia (Marshall)

Silver and gold. University of Colorado song. Balfe. CHS

Silver chimes. Claribel (C. Barnard) FSS 2—MCS

"The silver moon is shining." See Sandmännchen

"Silver moon sailing, thro' the sky sailing." See Moon song

"The silver moon's enamour'd beam." See Kate of Aberdeen (Battishill)

The silver ring. See L'anneau d'argent (Chaminade)

The silver rosebush. See Le rosier d'argent

"The silver swan." O. Gibbons. Words by C. Hatton. BOH

"Silver wires, high above us." See Shining wires

"The silv'ry moonlight streams on the wood." See L'heure exquise (Hahn)

"Silvery music is stealing." See Eglogue (Delibes)

Silvestre, Paul Armand
Le charme (Chausson)
Crépuscule (Massenet)
Fleur jetée (Fauré)
"Jours passés" (Delibes)
Noël païen (Massenet)
Ô maître de tout (Marshall)
"Ô mer; ouvre-toi" (Delibes)
Pensée d'automne (Massenet)
"Que l'heure est donc brève" (Massenet)

Silvio to Laura. Lindblad. e. KSN—WL

Silv'ry. For entry beginning Silv'ry see Silvery

Simmonds, John
Johnny Sands. See Sinclair, J. Johnny Sands

Simon the cellarer. J. L. Hatton. Words by W. H. Bellamy. AB 2—BAS 1— BE 1—BS 1— BOS—DM 2— FMB—HSD—HSE 1—SSS—WBT

Simper, Caleb
"Carol! carol joyfully"
"Carolling, carolling all thro' the night"
Good news we bring and peace
Happy Christmas morning
"In Bethl'hem of Judah"
"Now let us raise our harvest song"
"O Christmas bells, ring far and near"
"O lovely star that shone so bright"
"Softly the night is sleeping"
"Star of Bethlehem, sweetly shining"
"Sweet angels, ever bright and fair"
"Sweetest music, softly stealing"
"Waken, Christians! greet the morn"
"What do they say, these bells to me"
"Wheat and barley bright with sunshine"

Simple aveu (Love-token) F. Thomé. Words by S. Bordèse. e.f. SM 3
Simple confession. e. WBW

The simple birth. See De nederige geboorte

"Simple carollers are we." J. B. Boucher. Words by J. P. Douglas. HC

Simple confession. See Simple aveu (Thomé)

The simple ploughboy. Folk song: Devon version. BSW
—Virginia version. CSE
Variant of: The ploughboy

"Simple Simon." Nursery song. WSC

"The simple songs to thee we offer." See Our fatherland (Abt)

"A simple Yankee tar am I." See True blue (Maybrick)

Simpson, M. M.
O'er the mountains

Simrock, Karl Joseph
Warnung vor dem Rhein (Pöthko)
Wiegenlied (Brahms)

"Since all thy vows, false maid." Scottish air: Cromlock's lilt. MMS—PS 2

"Since break of day I've been a-waiting." See L'ingrat ne vient pas encore

"Since Dick and Nell were man and wife." See The flitch of bacon (Hook)

"Since fashion's all fiddle-de-dee." See The Whip club (Reeve)

"Since Father Noah first tapp'd the vine." See Concerning I and non-I

"Since first I saw your face." T. Ford. BOH—BOS—CO 1— DM 1— DSH—HSE 2—JE—MM

Since from my dear Astrea's sight. H. Purcell. MM

Since heaven has torn me. See Se il ciel mi divide (Piccinni)

"Since I saw her wander down the hill." See Aloha oe (Liliuokalani)

"Since I've known a Saviour's name." Nares. Words by C. Wesley. FSS 3

"Since mighty roast beef is an Englishman's food." See The roast beef of old England (Leveridge)

"Since my loved one has gone." See Mo nighean chruinn, donn

"Since now the world's turn'd upside down" (The Dame of Honour) Old English air. Words by T. D'Urfey. BE 7

"Since now the world's turn'd upside down" (Queen Besses' Dame of Honour) Air: I am a lusty, lively lad. [Words by T. D'Urfey] MM

"Since our country, our God—oh, my sire." See Jephtha's daughter

"Since Phillis swears inconstancy." J. Hart. MM

"Since the first dawn of reason." See May we ne'er want a friend, nor a bottle to give him (Davy)

"Since the spring comes on." J. Blow. DM 2

"Since 'tis glory to adore you." See "Per la gloria d'adorarvi" (Bononcini)

"Since we parted yestereve, yestereve." See Yestereve (Johnson)

"Since yesterday I've sought in vain my master." See "Depuis hier je cherche en vain mon maître" (Gounod)

Sinclair, John
    Johnny Sands
    "The mountain maid from her bow'r has hied"

The Sinclair brave. See "Hr. Sinklar"

"Sind heute drei und dreissig jahr." See Der gefangene admiral (Lassen)

"Sind wir vereint zur guten stunde." See Bundeslied (Hanitsch)

Sinbad. Negro forecastle song. CR

Sinding, Christian
    Amber. See Rav
    "Der skreg en fugl"
    "I heard the gull." See "Der skreg en fugl"
    Majnat
    A May night. See Majnat
    Moderen synger
    The mother sings. See Moderen synger
    Rav
    Sylvelin

Sing-a-ling-a-ling. Student song. TFC 2

"Sing a song, a rich refrain." See Champlain (Putnam)

"Sing a song at twilight." See Love's old sweet song (Molloy)

Sing a song o' the city. See Levee song

"Sing a song of golden wheat." See A song of bread

"Sing a song of sixpence." Nursery song. FMB

"Sing a song of sixpence." Nursery song. Another air. FSS 7

"Sing a song of sixpence." Nursery song. A third air. WA—WSC—WSW

"Sing a song together, boys." See Triangle song

"Sing again, sing again, sing again." See Nightingale song (Zeller)

"Sing alleluia, all ye lands." Traditional air. Words by J. M. Neale. HC

Sing always. W. F. Sherwin. FSS 1

Sing another song. D. Stevens (music and words) BSS

Sing Augustana's praises. Augustana college song. CHS

"Sing care away, with sport and play." See Heart's ease

Sing, citizens, the song of freedom. See "Heft, burgers, 't lied der vrijheid" (Nicolaï)

"Sing courting, courting, courting, cain." See The Suffolk miracle (Tennessee version)

"Sing couthilie, couthilie, merrie an' free." See My ain hoose

"Sing! ev'ry voice, in grateful morning praise." See Morning praise

"Sing for joy." E. H. Ruel. HC

"Sing, gaily sing." G. P. Weimar. FSS 1 —WSC

Sing glad songs for him. C. F. Gounod. Words by C. Morton. FSS 4

"Sing God praises." Ambrosius. Words by H. Weld. e. MCS

"Sing hallelujah with glad rejoicing." See "Ave Maria" (Luzzi)

Sing heedle liltie, teedle liltie. See "What merriment has taen the Whigs"

Sing hey ho, ne'er say no. 18th century song. ME

Sing hey my braw John Highlandman. See "A Highland lad my love was born"

"Sing ho! for a brave and a gallant ship." See Ten thousand miles away

"Sing ho! for a brave and a valiant bark." See Ten thousand miles away

"Sing ho! the merry autumn time." L. S. Collins (music and words) BD

"Sing it over with your might." Round. FSS 5

Sing ivy. Folk song from Hampshire. SF 3

Sing, joyously sing. Words by C. Piersol. MCS

"Sing, mädchen, sing." See "Sing, maiden, sing" (Bennett)

"Sing, maiden, sing" ("Sing, mädchen, sing") W. S. Bennett. Words by B. W. Procter. e.g. SS 2

Sing me a song of a lad that is gone. See Over the sea to Skye

Sing, my little Cecily. See "Mon pèr' n'avait fille que moi" (Si mon papa le savait)

"Sing no more at my window, sweet nightingale." See Fly away, nightingale (Rubinstein)

"Sing not, O fair Circassian maid." See The songs of Grusia (Rachmaninov)

"Sing not to me the rose new-born." See La charmante Marguerite

"Sing, O children, sing with gladness." Christmas carol. LA

"Sing, O heavens." B. Tours. DC

"Sing, oh, sing this blessed morn." C. F. Roper. Words by C. Wordsworth. HC

"Sing, O sing, thou merry bird." See Sing, thou merry bird

"Sing, O sing, ye children." G. C. Pearson. HC

"Sing of Maiden Mary." French Noël. Words by F. G. Lee. HC

Sing, said the mother. Folk song from North Carolina. CSE

Sing Sally O. Negro halliard chantey. CR—SE

"Sing, sing for Christmas." J. S. B. Hodges. Words by J. H. Egar. HC

"Sing, sing, music was given." Air: Humors of Ballymaguiry. Words by T. Moore. MI

"Sing, sing! nightingale, sing." See "Syng, syng" (Kjerulf)

Sing, smile and slumber. See Chantez riez et dormez (Gounod)

"Sing, sweet bird." W. Ganz. Words by L. M. Thornton. FSS 8

"Sing sweet carols, night is past." S. B. Whiteley. Words by C. L. Jackson. HC

"Sing, sweet harp, oh, sing to me." Words by T. Moore. MI

Sing tangent, co-tangent. Amherst song. Air: Villikins and his Dinah. Words by F. Browning. LA

"Sing the battle." E. G. Monk. Words by Fortunatus. Tr of Pange lingua gloriosi proelium certaminis. e. HC

"Sing the carol! raise your voices." H. S. Irons. Words by C. H. Wood. HC

"Sing the holly." Bellini. MCS

"Sing the praises o' my dearie." See A' mhaighdean àluinn

"Sing, then, of the heav'n-descended daughter of the starry realm." See Open, Lord, my inward ear (Beethoven)

Sing, thou merry bird. Kindergarten song. FSS 1

Sing thou, sing (Laula, laula) A. Järnefelt. Words by K. Killinen. e.fi. WM 1

"Sing to me, sweet musetta." See "Ô ma tendre musette" (Monsigny)

"Sing to the college with banner so bright." See The scarlet and black (Balfe)

"Sing to the colors that float in the light, hurrah for the scarlet and cream." See Scarlet and cream (Balfe)

"Sing to the colors that float in the light, hurrah for the silver and gold." See Silver and gold (Balfe)

"Sing to the colors that float in the light; hurrah for the yellow and blue." See The yellow and blue (Balfe)

"Sing we alleluia." G. H. Westbury. HC

"Sing we merry Christmas." C. T. Bowen (music and words) HC

Sing we Noël. 16th century French carol. e. DC

"Sing we now of joy and gladness." W. Gilbert (music and words) HC

"Sing we now our hymns of gladness." P. L. Atherton. Words by S. Longfellow. HC

"Sing we so merrily, lightly and cheerily." See Christmas is here

"Sing we the story of the Saviour's birth." See Sing we Noël

"Sing we to our alma mater, O. S. U." See Alma mater—Ohio state (Smith)

"Sing with a tuneful spirit." See Sing always (Sherwin)

"Sing with all the sons of glory." A. F. M. Custance. Words by W. J. Irons. HC

"Sing with joy, 'tis Christmas morn." J. Stainer. Words by C. F. Hernaman. HC

"Sing with thy mouth sing with thy heart." See Loth to depart

"Sing ye praise, all ye redeemed." F. Mendelssohn. e. SAS 3

"Sing ye the songs of praise." Mrs C. Farebrother. Words by W. Layng. HC

"Sing your carols to-day." G. W. Warren. Words by J. C. Middleton. HC

"Singe care away, with sport and playe." See Heart's ease

"Singe, nachtigall, nicht mir am fensterrand." See Fly away, nightingale (Rubinstein)

The singer ("A fairy tale is thy mouth") Armenian song. e. BMC

The singer ("Ugly am I, I know well") N. Rimsky-Korsakoff. Words by Maikov. e. NM 2

The singers' banner. See Sångarfanan (Frieberg)

Singin' wid a sword in my han'. Negro spiritual. JB

"Singing at their spinning." See At the spinning wheel (Moniuszko)

"Singing for Jesus." English carol. WBT—WS

"Singing ho, rova ho." See Mo nighean donn

Singing in the rain. F. J. Haydn. Words by E. A. Allen. FSS 1—JSE—WSC

"Singing, shouting, tramping half the night." See Through the fields in winter (Sokolov)

"Singing the reapers homeward come." W. H. Gill. HC

"Singing thro' the forests." See Rhyme of the rail

"Singing while you soar to heaven." Polish folk air. Words by C. Crawford. WF

Single and free. Irish folk song. JOI

The single girl. Folk song from North Carolina. CSE

"Sings the nightingale now his last note." See In silent woods (Rimskiï-Korsakov)

Sinico, C.
"All hail, San Giusto." See "Viva San Giusto"
"Viva San Giusto"

"The sinking sun is beaming." See Conway castle

Sinner, please don't let this harvest pass. Negro spiritual. DF

S'io fosse ("Se fossi."—"Were I a violet") Neapolitan folk song. e.i. FE
"Were I a violet." e. CST

Sion ("There is a city builded") P. Rodney. Words by G. C. Bingham. HSS 4— LA—WS

"Sion the marvelous story be telling." See Shout the glad tidings (Muhlenberg)

"Sir Eglamore that valiant knight." 17th century song. DM 2—MM

Sir Guy. Ancient English song. CO 2

"Sir Halwyn sang a little song." See "Sire Halewyn"

Sir Hugh. Folk song from North Carolina. CSE

Sir John Barleycorn. English folk song. BSW

"Sir John Cope trode the north right far." Air: Johnie Cope. Words by R. Burns. BSR

Sir Lionel. Folk song: North Carolina version. CSE
—Virginia version. CSE

"Sir Magnus looks out in the winter night so cold." See Knud Lavard (Gade)

"Sir Postilion, Sir Postilion, and whither now away." See The postilion (Abt)

"Sir, pray be so good." See Hunting the hare

"Sir Simon de Montfort." English folk song. DM 2

Sir Thomas, I cannot. Old English air. BE 2

"Sir Wisdom's a fool when he's fou." Air: Auld Sir Symon. Words by R. Burns. BSR

"Sire Halewyn." Flemish song. e.f.fl. TSF

"Sirel yem sern yeresin." See Haberban

The **siren** (Sirene) A. Gretchaninoff. Words from the Russian of Balmont. e.g. NM 1

Sirene. See The siren (Grechaninov)

Sirótka. See The orphan-girl (Musorgskii)

"Sister Cath'rine, hold your light." See On Canaan shore

Sister Ruth. J. Haydn. e. WBT— WSC
"Dost thou love me, sister Ruth." e. HSD

"Sitting round the old camp fire." See Round the old camp fire (Smith)

"Siuntē mane." See Mother sent me

Sivle, Per
Jul (Alnaes)
Sol (Alnaes)

Six kings daughters. Kentucky mountain song. WLT
Variant of: Lady Isabel and the elf knight

"Six little snails." Children's song. WBT—WSC

"Six lords went a-hunting." See The duke of Bedford

"Six weary days are past and over." See Sonntag (Brahms)

"Sixty seconds make a minute." See Calendar song

Sjögren, Johan Gustav Emil
The seraglio garden. See I seraljens lustgard
I seraljens lustgard

"Sjung om studentens lyckliga dag." See Studentsång (Gustaf)

"Sjung, sjung, du underbara sång" ("Ring out, thou wondrous song") J. A. Josephson (music and words) e.sw. HSOS

Skaters' song. Schumann. Words by L. F. Lewis. LA

Skeffington, M. S.
"Gathered in the house divine"
"Near the tomb where Christ hath been"
"The song of the heavenly harvest home"

Sketchley, Arthur, pseud. See Rose, George

Ski-bi-bi-la. See Indian spring bird (Lieurance)

"Skies proclaim a new day! we joyfully meet." Indian air. e. FI

Skinner, John
The ewie wi' the crookit horn (Scottish air)
John of Badenyon (Scottish air)
Tullochgorum (Scottish air)

The **skippers** of St Ives. Cornish song. J. L. Roeckel. Words by F. E. Weatherly. CB

Skitalets,
"All the bells, the little bells" (Bagrinovskii)
The blacksmith (Koeneman)

Skootchái. See Resignation (Musorgskii)

Skördemannen (The harvester) J. Fogelberg. Words by C. A. Wetterbergh. e.sw. HSOS

Škroup, Jan Nepomuk
"Kde domov můj." See My fatherland
My fatherland
"Where is my home." See My fatherland

Skunk song. Ojibway Indian song. in. BA

"The sky is bright, the breeze is fair." See To Greece we give our shining blades (Bishop)

Skye boat song. Jacobite song. Words by H. Boulton. CST—GO—OH—SMW

The **skylark** ("Clear the air and fraught with fragrance."—Vöglein) A. Gretchaninoff. Words from the Russian of L. Polonski. e.g. FM

The **sky-lark** ("Higher still and higher") Round. FSS 3—HSC

The **skylark** ("However cold the showers") Air: The tavern hath two doors. e. MMW

Slaap, mijn kindjelief ("Sleep, my little one") 17th century Dutch carol. e. MF

Slade, Mrs Mary B. C.
Geography song (Composer unknown)
Sleep, darling, sleep (Composer unknown)
Welcome to morning (Offenbach)

The **slain** Cossack (Akh ty pole moe) Russian folk song. e. SSR 1

"Slán do chuirim o'm chroidhe leat." See Glounthaun Araglin eeving

Slansky, Ludwig
Huntsman's song. See Waidmannslied
I love thee. See "O sag' es noch einmal"
"O sag' es noch einmal"
Waidmannslied

Slaughter, A. Walter
The dear home-land

Slav ho. Capstan chantey. CR

Slav song. See Chanson slave (Chaminade)

Slava. See The song of praise

"A slave to love's unbounded sway." See O lay thy loof in mine, lass

"Sleep, ah sleep, my darling baby, su su, lullaby." See The Cossack's lullaby (Bakhmetiev)

Sleep and rest. See Wiegenlied (Mozart)

Sleep, baby dear ("All is still and restful now") Tauwitz. FSS 5—WBT

"Sleep, baby dear, in my arms till the morrow." See Dors, mon enfant (Wagner)

"Sleep, baby sleep! Dad is not nigh." See Lullaby

"Sleep, baby sleep! on mountains steep." See Slumber song of Izumo (Ross)

"Sleep, baby, sleep, our cottage vale is deep." Old nursery song. DO—FSS 8

"Sleep, baby, sleep, thy father guards his sheep." See Schlaf', kindchen, schlaf' (Somervell)

"Sleep, baby, sleep! thy father guards the sheep." See "Schlaf, kindchen, schlaf" (German folk song)

"Sleep, baby, sleep; thy father is watching his sheep." See Lullaby (Whitney)

"Sleep, baby, sleep! thy father tends the sheep." See "Schlaf, kindchen, schlaf" (German folk song)

"Sleep, baby, sleep, thy father watches his sheep." See "Schlaf, kindchen, schlaf" (German folk song)

"Sleep, beloved, sleep, round thee watch we keep." See Wiegenlied (Taubert)

Sleep, comrades, sleep ("In thousand shaded valleys") L. B. Marshall. Words by S. F. Smith. JS

"Sleep, comrades, sleep, sleep and rest." See Decoration day (Geyer)

Sleep, darling, sleep. Words by M. B. C. Slade. FSS 8

"Sleep, deep in forest gloom." See The sleeping princess (Borodin)

"Sleep, gentle babe." Mendelssohn. e. TL

"Sleep, gentle mother." Verdi. [Tr of Riposa, o madre] e. FSS 3

"Sleep, holy Babe." Ancient air. Words by E. Caswall. HC

"Sleep, holy Babe." Composer unknown. Words by E. Caswall. HC

"Sleep, holy Babe." W. Austin. Words by E. Caswall. HC

Sleep, holy Babe. A. F. M. Custance. Words by E. Caswall. HC

"Sleep, holy Babe." J. B. Dykes. Words by E. Caswall. BSC—DC—HC

"Sleep, holy Babe." J. T. Field. Words by E. Caswall. HC

"Sleep, holy Babe." F. W. Partridge. Words by E. Caswall. HC

"Sleep is thine when work is done." See He giveth His beloved sleep (Benedict)

"Sleep little darling, those little eyes close." See Wiegenlied (Weber)

"Sleep, my babe, lie still and slumber." See Ar hyd y nos (Owen. Words adapted)

"Sleep, my baby, close to mother." See Cradle-song (Grechaninov)

"Sleep, my baby, sleep, my darling." See Italian cradle-song (Sandtis)

"Sleep, my baby, sleep, my pretty, hushaby by-low." See Cradle song (Cherepnin)

"Sleep, my bonny blue-eyed little treasure." See Lullaby

Sleep, my child ("See the Maiden Mother mild") S. Glover. MCS

"Sleep my child, and peace attend thee." See Ar hyd y nos (Owen)

"Sleep, my child, my pretty one" (Ainte) Syrian folk song. e.gr. BO—SMF

"Sleep, my darling baby, close thy dear eyes in slumber." See Baadn-laatt

"Sleep, my darling, my baby boy." See Solvejgs wiegenlied (Grieg)

"Sleep, my darling, sleep, my starling." See Cradle-song (Grechaninov)

"Sleep, my dear child, untouched by life's sorrow." See "Schlaf' holdes kind" (Wagner)

"Sleep, my heart's darling, in slumber repose." See Wiegenlied (Weber)

"Sleep, my heart's treasure, my blessing thou art." See Wiegenlied (Weber)

"Sleep, my infant Saviour." H. D. Rider. Words by G. T. Rider. HC

"Sleep my little one; see, the sun has gone." See Wiegenlied (Taubert)

"Sleep, my little one, sleep, my dearest one." See Slaap, mijn kindjelief
"Sleep, my own baby, my darling thou art." See Wiegenlied (Weber)
"Sleep, my Saviour, sleep." Bohemian air. Words by S. Baring-Gould. HC
"Sleep, my son, oh, slumber well." See Wiegenlied (Grieg)
"Sleep, my sweet baby." G. Verdi. WSC
"Sleep, noble hearts." Mendelssohn. Words by F. Manley. TFC 2
"Sleep, O baby mine." See Cradle song (Tchaikovsky)
"Sleep, oh, my darling, and rest." See Wiegenlied (Mozart)
"Sleep, O sleep, fond fancy." T. Morley. DM 1
"Sleep, O sleep! while breezes so softly are blowing." Slumber song. FSS 6
The sleep of the infant Jesus. F. A. Gevaert. Words from an old French Noël. ɪTr of Entre le boeuf et l'âne grisɪ e. HC
"Sleep on, for I know 'tis of me you are dreaming." Irish air. Words by F. Beamish. MMI
"Sleep on, O baby dearest." See Neapolitan cradle song
"Sleep on, sleep on, my beloved one." O. Cantor. Words by A. Baker. SM 4
Sleep on, then. See Posate, dormite (Bassani)
"Sleep, sleep; lie down, dear; go to sleep." See Lullaby
"Sleep, sleep, my darling, sleep tranquilly." See Slumber song
"Sleep, so your tale of dreams be told." See Lullaby (Godard)
"Sleep, the stars are on high and the moon." See A serenade (Tchaikovsky)
"Sleep thou, sleep thou, mother's arms enfold thee." See Cradle song (Schubert)
Sleeper awake ("Tell the story of the risen") J. A. Jeffery. Words by W. C. Doane. HC
Sleepers, wake ("Now let every tongue adore Thee") J. S. Bach. e. DSH
The sleeping beauty. See The sleeping princess (Borodin)
"The sleeping earth silent lies." See Bonne nuit (Massenet)
Sleeping for the flag. H. C. Work. WBT
"Sleeping I dream'd love." W. V. Wallace. WBT
The sleeping princess. A. Borodine (music and words) e. SC
    The sleeping beauty (La princesse endormie) e.f. NR 3
    The sleeping princess (La princesse endormie) e.f. NM 1
"Sleep'st thou or wak'st thou." Air: Deil tak the wars. Words by R. Burns. BSB—BSR
Sleepy time. Ojibway Indian song. e.in. BA

The sleigh ride ("Jingle bells, jingle bells, in the misty moonlight") Words by J. Drake. MCS
The sleigh ride ("Swiftly, swiftly o'er the snow") J. C. Johnson. FSS 7—MCS
The sleigh-ride ("Ting-a-ling-a-ling") Canadian folk air. Words by H. H. Harbour. DO
The slighted swain. Words by A. Bradley. ME
Sling the flowing bowl. T. Linley. MM
Slonov, Mikhail Akhimovich
    "O, thou sun, thou blessed, glowing sun"
    "Soleil! ô clair soleil." See "O, thou sun, thou blessed, glowing sun"
Slovak national anthem ("Over Tatra."— "Nad Tatrou sa blýská") sl.e. BF 1
A Slovenian girl ("Sem slovenska deklica") Slovenian folk song. e.slo. BF 1
"Slowly fall the snow-flakes." W. Borrow. Words by F. G. Lee. HC
"Slowly o'er the dark, dark waters." See The lake (Abt)
"Slowly the daylight departs" ("Lentement baissa le jour") A. Borodine. e.f. SC
"Slowly the snow comes floating down." See It snows in the night
Slumber ("Da barnet sov ind") See Sövnen (Kjerulf); Sövnen (Reissiger)
"Slumber, beloved, and take thy repose." J. Bach. e. OS 2—SAS 2
"Slumber, beloved, the shadows are falling." See "Ruhe, süssliebchen" (Brahms)
Slumber, dear maid. See Ombra mai fu (Händel)
"Slumber, my baby, my darling thou art." See Slummersång (Hägg)
"Slumber reigns" ("Alles schläft") A. Gretchaninoff. Words from the Russian of A. Fet. e.g. NM 1
"Slumber, slumber, dearest, sweetest treasure." See Wiegenlied (Schubert)
"Slumber, slumber, dreaming golden dreams." See Dreaming golden dreams (Scuderi)
"Slumber! slumber in dreams of the fast coming hours." See Bei der wiege (Mendelssohn)
"Slumber, slumber, lovely Babe, heavenly King, heavenly King." See Canzone di Natale
"Slumber, slumber, tender little flower." See Wiegenlied (Schubert)
The slumber song ("Alles still") See "Alles still in süsser ruh" (Kücken)
Slumber song ("Dors entre mes bras") See Dors, mon enfant (Wagner)
Slumber song ("Du pauvre seul ami") See "Du pauvre seul ami" (Auber)
Slumber song ("Gently rest") See "Gently rest" (Kücken)
Slumber song ("Hush-a-by, and goodnight") J. Brahms. Words by J. Erwin. DO
Slumber song ("Ruhe süss, liebchen") See "Ruhe süss, liebchen" (Franz)

Slumber-song ("Ruhe, süssliebchen") See "Ruhe, süssliebchen" (Brahms)

Slumber song ("Schlaf, herzenssöhnchen") See Wiegenlied (Weber)

Slumber song ("Sleep, my baby") See Cradle song (Grechaninov)

Slumber song ("Sleep, sleep my darling") French lullaby. e. WBT
"Sleep, sleep, my darling, sleep tranquilly." e. FSS 5—WSC

Slumber-song ("Wo der rosen fülle") See Schlummerlied (Mattei)

Slumber song of Izumo. G. Ross. Words from the Japanese. e.j. RAS

"Slumber sweetly, little Donald." See Highland cradle song (Schumann)

Slummersång (Cradle-song) G. Hägg. Words after F. C. Hiemer. [Tr of Wiegenlied] e.sw. HSOS

"Slumra du lilla, min älskling är du." See Slummersång (Hägg)

"Sly panenky silnicí." See "Tripping maidens"

"The small birds rejoice." Air: Captain O'Kane. Words by R. Burns. BSR

Smart, Christopher
The lass with the golden locks (Arne)

Smart, Henry Thomas
"Angels, from the realms of glory"
By the blue sea
Come and worship. See "Angels, from the realms of glory"
"Do you think of the days"
"From the sea's deep hollow faintly pealing"
"God the Lord a King remaineth" (same air as "Angels, from the realms of glory")
"Hark! hark! my soul"
Jesus in the manger
The lady of the lea
"Let the whole world chant and sing" (Tr of Concinat orbis cunctis, alleluya)
My boat is waiting here for thee
Nymphs of air and sea
"O God of earth and altar"
Pilgrims. See "Hark! hark! my soul"
A psalm of life
Regent square. See "Angels, from the realms of glory"; "God the Lord a King remaineth"
"Sad was the hour"
Serenade
"'Twas in the sunny Rhineland"

Smedley, R. C.
Tribute to Wesleyan

Smetana, Bedřich
"Now in joy or sorrow" (from The bartered bride)
"Where is John"

Smets, Wilhelm
Blumentag (Volksweise)

Smile again, my bonnie lassie ("The moon is blinking o'er the lea") Scottish song. PS 1

"Smile again, my bonnie lassie, lassie, smile again." J. Parry (music and words) BE 5

"Smile! and I'll teach thee what application." See "Vedrai, carino" (Mozart)

A smile from the girl of my heart. W. Shield. Words by B. Dudley. ME

Smile na sae sweet, my bonnie babe. See Fine flowers in the valley

"Smile, O sky, God's praises." See Raise the song for Easter (Backus)

"Smile praises, O sky." Easter carol. HC

Smiling faces. S. Glover. Words by E. M. Spencer. FSS 4

"Smiling heavens in azure drest." See Printemps nouveau (Vidal)

"The smiling hours, a joyful train." G. F. Händel. SAS 2

"Smiling May comes in play." FSS 2—JSE

"The smiling morn, the breathing spring." See The birks of Invermay

Smiling Polly. See The keel row

"The smiling spring comes in rejoicing." See Bonnie bell

Smith, A. E.
"We sing a song of Christmas-time" (Sullivan)

Smith, A. W.
Hail, Stanford, hail (Composer unknown)

Smith, Albert
"The wind may shout" (Molloy)

Smith, Alice Mary. See White, Mrs Alice Mary (Smith)

Smith, B. H.
Tribute to Wesleyan (Smedley)

Smith, C. Lawrence
Harvard's day
Round the old camp fire
A toast to Harvard

Smith, Clarence R.
Old college days

Smith, Dan D.
De boatmen's dance

Smith, David Stanley
Eyes of old Yale blue. See Polly
A hope carol
May song
The Nativity, Stanzas from
Polly
Rose song
To night

Smith, Eleanor
"We are little soldier men"

Smith, Ernest H.
"Whilst Bethlehem's shepherds kept their flocks"

Smith, Gerrit
Dreaming

Smith, Henry
"Gather them in"
"O come on this bright Easter-day"
"O welcome, happy day"

Smith, Hubbard T.
Listen to my tale of woe

Smith, J. E.
Little Boy Blue

Smith, J. G.
"The night in solemn stillness hung"

Smith, James
Sea-bird's song (Verdi)
Smith, John, 1825-1910
The clinical examination (Scottish air)
"Per secale" (Scottish air)
Smith, John Christopher
Caliban's song
"No more dams I'll make for fish."
See Caliban's song
Smith, John Stafford
The star-spangled banner (same air as
"To Anacreon in heaven")
"To Anacreon in heaven"
Smith, Montem
Eventime
Smith, R. F.
"As Mary walked in the garden green"
"As those who seek the break of day"
"Blithely from the moated churchyard"
Carol, carol, Christians
"Christ is risen! lift the song"
"Christians, listen, while we sing"
"The flocks were wrapt in slumber"
"Glory to God in the highest is ring-
ing"
"Good news, good news is sent"
Hallelujah! song of triumph
"Hearken to the thankful reapers"
"In the star of morning"
"In the wintry heaven"
"O Lord, who shed'st the sunlight's
gold"
"Rejoice! to-day earth tells abroad"
"There came three kings ere break of
day"
"The world itself keeps Easter day"
Smith, Ralph P.
Alma mater—Ohio state
Smith, Robert
The town gallant
Smith, Robert Archibald
The braes o' Balquhidder
Jessie, the flower o' Dumblane
"O, wha's at the window, wha, wha"
"See amid the winter snow"
Smith, S. T.
"Follow, follow over mountain"
Smith, Samuel
"Come to the manger in Bethlehem"
"Joy fills our inmost hearts to-day"
"Let us the Infant greet"
Ruth. See "Summer suns are glow-
ing"
"Summer suns are glowing"
Smith, Samuel Francis
America (music by Carey; McCabe)
Cherished names (Marshall)
"Fling out the banner on the breeze"
(Marshall)
"God ever glorious" (Old air)
"Joy for the sturdy trees" (music by
Hanlyn; Oliver)
Memorial day (Marshall)
"The morning light is breaking"
(Webb)
Precious lives (Marshall)
Sleep, comrades, sleep (Marshall)
"Strew the fair garlands" (Marshall)
The veterans (Marshall)

Smith, Sidney
For you
Smith, W.
Brutus (Beale)
Smith, W. A.
"Awake, glad soul! awake, awake"
Smith, W. Locke
"How sad, 'mid the sunshine" (Pierce)
Authorship uncertain
Smith, Wilson George
Entreaty
"Kiss me, sweetheart"
Sweet content
The **smith.** A. Korestschenko. Words
from the Russian. e. NM 1
Smits,
"Let all with Dutch blood in their
veins" (wrongly attributed) See
Wilms, J. W. "Wein Neêrlandsch
bloed"
"Wien Neêrlandsch bloed" (wrongly
attributed) See Wilms, J. W.
"Wien Neêrlandsch bloed"
"Smoke is rising as the steamer churns its
way." See The journey (Glinka)
Smoking away. J. B. Taylor. Words
by F. M. Finch. JO
La **smortina** (The pale girl) Lombardian
folk song. e.i. MSI
The **smuggler.** J. Davy. Words by T.
Cory. ME
Smythe, W.
"Sweet land of the mountain" (Welsh
air)
"Snail, snail, come out and be fed." See
Chinese baby song
Snake-charmer's song ("O re bho la ma-n
re") Song from India. e.ind. BO
Snoilsky, Carl
"Svarta svanor" (Hallström)
Snow, Henry
I'm busy to-day (Foster)
Old dog Tray: Boy scout verses (Fos-
ter)
We saw them (Composer unknown)
"The **snow** lay deep upon the ground." Tra-
ditional air. HC
"The **snow** lay on the ground." Christ-
mas carol. Italian air. HC
"The **snow** lay on the ground." Christ-
mas carol. Air of the Pifferari. HC
"The **snow** lies thick." G. Shaw. Words
by S. Image. HC
The **snow** man. A. S. Gatty. WSC
"Snow of March days, tears of heartaches."
See Märzschnee (Reinecke)
"Snow on the earth; tho' March is well
nigh over." See Spring song (Mac-
kenzie)
"Snow-white rose so winning." See
Simple aveu (Thomé)
The **snowbird.** Words by F. C. Wood-
worth. FSS 1
The **snowdrop** (Das schneeglöckchen) A.
Gretchaninoff. e.g. FM
Snowdrops ("Schneeglöckchen läuten im-
mer zu") See Schneeglöckchen
(Dorn)

"Snowdrops, lift your timid heads." G. E. Oliver. Words by M. A. Lathbury. HC

"Snowfields in silence." See Trepak (Musorgskiï)

Snowflakes (Schneeflöckchen) A. Gretchaninoff. Words from the Russian of W. Brüssoff. e.g. NM 1

"Snowflakes flying o'er our portals." See Snowflakes (Grechaninov)

The snowy-breasted pearl ("Atá cailín deas am cráð") See Péarla an brollaig báin

The snowy-breasted pearl ("Oh! she is not like the rose") Irish air: Pearl of the white breast. Words by S. E. De Vere. FSI—PI

Snyder, Charles McCoy
Old Allegheny (College song)

"So beware of those boarding-school lasses." See Just in the height of her bloom

"So charming her voice." See "La mia letizia infondere" (Verdi)

"So early, early in the spring." See Early, early in the spring (Hot Springs, N.C. versions no. 1-2)

So early in the morning ("South Carolina's a sultry clime") SSS—WBT

"So early in the morning the sailor likes his bottle O." See The sailor likes his bottle O

"So early one morning pretty Polly she rose." See Polly Oliver (North Carolina version)

"So fair and still the night is." See "La noche 'sta serena"

"So far away from friends and home." See The true lover's farewell (Hot Springs, N.C. version)

"So fare thee well, thou silent home." See Abschied (Müller)

So get out de way, ole Dan Tucker. See Old Dan Tucker (Russell)

"So glad I done done." See I done done what ya' tol' me to do

"So hab ich denn die stadt verlassen." See Abreise (Kreutzer)

"So hab' ich doch die ganze woche." See Sonntag (Brahms)

So handy ("Be handy in the morning") Pulling chantey. SE

So handy ("Oh, up aloft") Halliard chantey. CR

"So happy all the day." See The Bethlehem shepherd-boy's tale (Havergal)

"So help my bob I'm bully in the alley." See Bully in the alley

"So herzig wie mein Liesel." See Schwäbisches bauernlied (Folk air); Schwäbisches bauernlied (Schubart)

"So it fell upon a day." Lithuanian folk air. Words by R. R. Whitehead. WF

"So leb' den wohl, du stilles haus." See Abschied (Müller)

"So long the day, so dark the way." See Dear heart (Mattei)

So might it be, then. See "Upon the crest of Wailana" (Nape)

"So mild was the evening." See Loth to depart

So now is come our feast. Words by G. Wither. MCS

So oder so ("Nord oder süd") C. Schultz. Words by K. Lappe. g. ED 2

"So oft der herbst die rosen stahl." See Herbstfrühlingslied (Weil)

"So oft sie kam, erschien mir die gestalt." See Kommen und scheiden (Schumann)

"So poor Hans sidles round." See Hans und Liesel (Woyna)

So runs my dream. Words by A. Tennyson. FSS 7

"So sadly once the rose complained." See "Es hat die rose sich beklagt" (Franz)

"So, Sir Page." See "Non più andrai" (Mozart)

"So sweet the nightingale warbled." See Laengsel (Kjerulf)

So sweete is shee. See "Have you seen but a white lily grow"

"So they, being filled with the Holy Ghost." See I will sing of Thy great mercies (Mendelssohn)

"So this is sad love's ending." See "Forsi pirchi nun m'ami"

"So this is the casket straitly made." See Vor meiner wiege (Schubert)

"So 'tis we're onward driv'n." See Le lac (Niedermeyer)

"So traitress! my fondest love thou art spurning." See "Infida! il dì che brami e questo" (Verdi)

"So white is she." See "Hun er saa hvid" (Grieg)

"So will the Lord." See Adieu, forêts (Tchaikovsky)

"So would I die, as dies the swan." See "Ich möchte sterben wie der schwan" (Degele)

Soane, George
"I've been roaming" (Horn)
"Wake, my love" (Loder)

"Soaring in glee where the waters rave." See Sea-bird's song (Verdi)

"Soars the eagle, with strong wing-play." See Arnes sang (Heise)

Sobiraïtes', brattsy-rebiâtushki. See The conscript's departure

Soboieski, Paul
Polish national song (Oginski?) See Wybitski. Polish national song (Oginski?)

Söderberg, Wilhelm Theodor
The bird's song. See Fågelns visa
Cradle song. See Vaggvisa
Fågelns visa
The little bird. See Fågelns visa
Necken
The sea king. See Necken
Vaggvisa

Söderman, August Johan
"Ingerid Sletten"
Längtan
Longing. See Längtan
Spring song. See Vårvisa
Vårvisa

The sodger's return. See The soldier's return

"**Soft** as the zephyr." See Bist du (Liszt)

"**Soft** be thy slumbers, rude cares depart." See Ellen Bayne (Foster)

"**Soft** blew the air, and smooth flow'd the tide." See The mariner

"The **soft** complaining flute." G. F. Händel. SAS 1

"**Soft** dews from heaven falling." See "Kein hälmlein wächst auf erden" (Bach)

"**Soft** falls the snow." A. H. Brown. Words by J. Goddard. HC

"**Soft** hearts, pray still your flutter." See Bread and butter (Christison)

"**Soft** in the sun thy golden tresses." See Sonnet d'amour (Thomé)

Soft music is stealing. Words by M. S. B. Dana. WBT—WSC

"**Soft**, soft music is stealing." FSS 1— HSD—LA

"**Soft** o'er the fountain." See Juanita

"**Soft** on the sunset sky bright daylight closes." See Ashes of roses (Wood); Ashes of roses (Woodman)

"**Soft**, soft music is stealing." See Soft music is stealing

"The **soft** southern breeze plays around." J. Barnby. OS 3—SAS 3

"**Soft** the autumn suns are shining." W. F. Horner. Words by R. Gurney. HC

"**Soft** the breezes are sighing." See Heimkehr (Strauss)

"**Soft** the eve'tide sun god is sinking." See The rose (Lieurance)

"**Soft**, white snowflake, gently falling." See A song for Christmas eve

The **soft** winds kiss her robe. See "Across the bridge, O come"

"**Softest** pleadings shall my song bear." See Ständchen (Schubert)

"**Softly** blow the vernal breezes." See The wander-staff

"**Softly** evening shades descending." See Durwan's song

Softly flows the Niemen (Tykiai Nemunēlis teka) Lithuanian folk song e.li. BF 1

"**Softly** goes my song's entreaty." See Ständchen (Schubert)

"**Softly** glow the golden embers." See Rah! rah! C. C. N. Y.

"**Softly** now the light of day." Donizetti. [Words by G. W. Doane] FSS 1

"**Softly** now the light of day." L. M. Gottschalk. Words by G. W. Doane. FSS 3—JS

"**Softly** now the light of day." F. W. Kücken. Words by G. W. Doane. LBR

"**Softly** now the light of day." C. M. von Weber. Words by G. W. Doane. FMB—FSS 1—HSC—HSD—NMH —OH—WBT—WS Seymour. LA

"**Softly** rest in thy nest." See "Dans le bois à ma voix" (Massé)

"**Softly** rise, O southern breeze." W. Boyce. Words by E. Moore. BE 6

"**Softly** sighs the voice of evening." See Gebet (Weber)

"**Softly** sing when the hour of daylight fades away." See Chantez riez et dormez (Gounod)

Softly slept the holy Child. German song. e. MCS

"**Softly** slumber, my baby man." See Little papoose

"**Softly**, softly sing." See The sylphs

"**Softly** sways the oak her branches." See The rabbit's story

"**Softly** the gondola, glides o'er the broad lagoon." See Venetian barcarole

"**Softly** the night is sleeping." Christmas carol. J. M. Crament. HC

"**Softly** the night is sleeping." Christmas carol. A. T. Gardner. WBT

"**Softly** the night is sleeping." Christmas carol. C. Simper. HC

"**Softly** the zephyr in the trees is sighing." See Love's greeting (Elgar)

"**Softly** through the mellow starlight." G. E. Oliver. HC

"**Softly** waft, ye southern breezes." J. Hook. PR 2

"**Softly** Zohra's name ever breathing." See Zohra

"**Sogers** marchin' oop de street." See The drum-major of Schneider's band (Murphy)

"**Sohn**, da hast du meinen speer." See Der schwäbische ritter an seinen sohn

"**Söhne** von Norwegens uraltem reiche." See "Sönner af Norge" (Blom)

Le **soir** ("The light of day") See Evening (Tchaikovsky)

Le **soir** ("Le soir ramène le silence."—The moonbeam) C. Gounod. Words by A. de Lamartine. e.f. BS 2—CM 2— KF 2

Le **soir** ("La terre embrasée."—Evening) A. Thomas. Words by M. Carré. e.f. HM 2

Soir ("Voici que les jardins de la nuit vont fleurir."—Evening) G. Fauré. Words by A. Samain. e.f. SAM

"Le **soir** ramène le silence." See Le soir (Gounod)

Soiridh (Farewell.—"Sad am I, and sorrow laden") Old Hebridean song. e. MMS

Soiridh ("Sad am I, and sorrow-laden") e. HSSS

"**Sois** immobile." G. Rossini. e.f. SOA 4

Sokolov, Nikolaï Aleksīeevich
"How abundant and warm is the spring"
"Qu'il est doux le printemps." See "How abundant and warm is the spring"

Sokolov, Vladimir Timofeievich
À travers champs, l'hiver. See Through the fields in winter
Through the fields in winter

Sol (Sunlight) E. Alnaes. Words by P. Sivle. e.n. WM 1

Sol de mi vida, del corazón. See 'O sole mio (Capua)
Solberg, C. K.
The college on the hill (Composer unknown)
"Solche hergelauf' ne laffen" ("Rogues like you") Mozart. e.g.i. BS 2
Soldados, la patria. See Himno de Riego (Huerta)
Der soldat ("Es geht bei gedämpfter trommel") F. Silcher. Words after the Danish of H. C. Andersen. g. ED 1
Soldaten-abschied ("Heute scheid' ich") F. E. Fesca. Words by M. F. Müller. g. ED 2
Soldaten-abschied (The soldier's farewell) e.g. SSG
Soldatenliebe ("Des morgens, mann die hähne krähen") Air: Des morgens um halber viere. Words by H. Hoffmann von Fallersleben. g. ED 3
Soldatenliebe ("Steh' ich in finstrer mitternacht") See "Steh' ich in finstrer mitternacht" (Wurda)
Soldatenmut. Air: Mein lebenslauf ist lieb und lust. Words by W. Hauff. g. ED 1
"Soldier boy." Children's song. WSC
A soldier brave. Danish national song. Hornemann. e. KSN—SN
"The soldier loves his gen'ral's fame." See Cornell
Soldier of the cross (Arlington) T. A. Arne. Words by I. Watts. FSS 8
"A soldier of the legion." See Bingen on the Rhine (Hutchinson)
"Soldier, soldier, will you marry me." Game song. WSC
Variant: Soldier, won't you marry me
"Soldier, soldier, won't you marry me." See Soldier, won't you marry me
Soldier song. R. Schumann. ₍Tr of Ich bin ein soldat₎ e. WBT—WSC
"A soldier stood in the village street." See Ehren on the Rhine (Hutchinson)
"The soldier tired of war's alarms." T. Arne. HSE 1
Soldier, won't you marry me. Folk song from North Carolina. CSE
Variant: "Soldier, soldier, will you marry me"
The soldier's adieu ("Adieu, adieu, my only life") C. Dibdin. DM 2—HSE 2
"Soldiers! attention! right turn! one, two, three." See Drill song (Shiyi)
"Soldiers, awake! this is the festal hour." W. H. Walter. HC
"The soldier's back from war returning." See Le retour du soldat
The soldier's bride (Poloobeela ya na petchál svayú) S. Rachmaninoff. Words after the Little-Russian of Shevtchenko. e. SMR 2
Soldiers' chorus. C. Gounod. ₍Tr of Gloire immortelle de nos aïeux₎ e. BD—FSS 4—LA—OH—TFC 1—WBT
The soldier's departure. See Le départ du soldat

Soldier's departure for foreign service ("Borne on the breeze a martial strain") Air: White Snowdon. Words by J. Lloyd. MMW
The soldier's dream ("In the flick'ring light") P. Rodney. Words by H. Vaughan. AB 1
The soldier's dream ("Our bugles sung truce") T. Attwood. Words by T. Campbell. HSE 2—JO
The soldier's farewell ("Come, dear son, and tell me") Old Russian song. e. KSN
Soldier's farewell ("Heute scheid' ich") See Soldaten-abschied (Fesca)
Soldier's farewell ("How can I bear to leave thee") J. Kinkel. ₍Tr of Ritters abschied₎ e. CHS—CU—HSC —HSD—JS—JSE—LA—MP—MPC—NMH—NML—NMS—OH—WBT—WC—WL—WSW
"Soldier's glory 'tis ever on guard to stand." See A la guerra
Soldiers' hymn. J. Haydn. DSH
"A soldier's life has seen of strife." M. W. Balfe. FSS 2
"A soldier's life is a cruel life." See Sweet William (Alleghany, N.C. version no. 2)
Soldier's love. See "Steh' ich in finstrer mitternacht" (Wurda)
"Soldiers of France, the morn is breaking." See La Marseillaise (Rouget de Lisle)
The soldier's return ("Dost not hear the martial hum") Air: Rhyfelgyrch Cadpen Morgan, or, Captain Morgan's march. Words by M. G. Lewis. MMW
The soldier's return ("Pauvre soldat") See Le retour du soldat
The soldier's return ("'Twas once that I courted") Vermont song. SSH
Variant of: The lover's lament
The soldier's return ("When wild war's deadly blast") Air: The mill, mill O. Words by Burns. FSS 7—JO —MMS—PS 1
The sodger's return. BSB
"When wild war's deadly blast was blawn." BSR
Soldier's song ("There are not many so brave") G. Verdi. e. MS
The soldier's tear. A. Lee. Words by T. H. Bayly. FSS 3—HSD—HSE 1—JO—WBT
"A soldier's trade is a cruel life." See Sweet William (Alleghany, N.C. version no. 1; Swannanoa, N.C. version)
"Sole gaar bak Aase ne." See Aagots fjeldsang
'O sole mio. E. Di Capua. Words by G. Capurro. e. BD—WBT. s. only LCP
O sole mio (My sun) e. DSH—WA —WL
'O sole mio (My sunshine) e.i. FE—MN. e. only TFC 1

Sole survivor. Ojibway Indian song. in. BA

Solefaldssang (Sunset) O. Olsen. Words by N. Rolfsen. e.n. SSN

"Le soleil est levé." See Le penitent et l'ivrogne

"Soleil! ô clair soleil." See "O, thou sun, thou blessed, glowing sun" (Slonov)

"Le soleil rayonnait encore." See Déception (Tchaikovsky)

Soleïma (Chanson mauresque) Tunisian folk song. e.f. BO

"The solemn Nile." See Le Nil (Leroux)

Solfager and the king of worms. See Solfager og ormekongen

Solfager og ormekongen (Solfager and the king of worms) Norse folk song. e.n. MAN

La solitaire ("Ô fier jeune homme."— In solitude) C. Saint-Saëns. Words by A. Renaud. e.f. SAM

La solitaire (Lonely) e.f. CM 2

The solitary ("Wenn meine grillen schwirren") See Der einsame (Schubert)

"The solitary bird of night." Words by E. Carter. DM 1

Solitude. Se Einsamkeit (Medtner)

"Soll ich weren a rav." See A teamster's complaint

"Soll sich der mond nicht heller scheinen." See Vor dem fenster (Brahms)

Solomon Levi. F. Seaver (music and words) MPC—SSS—WA—WBT—WC—WSW

Soloveï Budimirovich. See The legend of young nightingale

En solskins dag (A sunny day) R. Nordraak. Words by B. Björnson. e.n. MAN

Solveig's song. See Solvejgs sang (Grieg)

Solvejg's cradle-song. See Solvejgs wiegenlied (Grieg)

Solvejgs lied. See Solvejgs sang (Grieg)

Solvejgs sang (Solveig's song) E. Grieg. Words by H. Ibsen. e.n. SSN
Solveig's song. e. SS 1
Solvejgs lied (Solvejg's song) e.g. FO 2
Solvejgs lied (Sunshine song) e.g. KF 2—PG 1

Solvejgs wiegenlied (Solvejg's cradle-song) E. Grieg. Words by H. Ibsen. e.g. SM 2

"Som stjärnan uppå himmelen så klar" ("The stars above me") Swedish folk song. e.sw. HSOS

"Som stjärnan" (As the star) e.sw. BF 2

"En sömands störete glade er." See Bowline chanty

"Somber and dreary are the thoughts tormenting." See Los celos de Carolina

"Some come cripple." Negro folk song from Kentucky. KA

Some day. M. Wellings. Words by H. Conway. FSS 4—HSC—HSD—NML—WBT—WL

"Some go to church fo' to sing an' shout." See Ezekiel saw de wheel

"Some hundred years ago or so." See Hoop de dooden do (Nish)

"Some love to roam." H. Russell. Words by C. Mackay. JO

"Some men they do delight in hounds." See The scolding wife

"Some of dese mornin's bright and fair." See Ride on

Some of these mornings ("Going to see my mother") Negro spiritual. JP
Some o' dese mornin's. HR

"Some old Robin Down they call me." See Ibsy Damsel

"Some one, I know not who." See "Un certo non so che" (Vivaldi)

"Some one said unto the fool" ("Einst zum narren jemand spricht") P. I. Tchaikovsky. Words by Mey. e.g. FO 2

"Some said that John, de Baptist." See I've been a-list'ning all de night long

"Some say it's naught but fancy." See The land of Yippi Ki-yi (Lecocq)

"Some say Noah was a foolish old man." See Noah's ark

"Some say that John the Baptist." See Been a listening

"Some seek de Lord, but doan seek Him right." See Come down, sinner

"Some talk of Alexander." See The British grenadiers

"Some think the world is made for fun and frolic." See Funiculi-funicula (Denza)

"Some were waving hats and some were waving caps." See The Golden Vanity (Hot Springs, N.C. version no. 2)

Somebody ("Were I oblig'd to beg my bread") Composer unknown. BE 6

Somebody's knocking at your door. Negro spiritual. DF—HR
Somebody's knockin' at yo' do'. JB

"Someone gave to me a flower." See To my little flower

Somerset, Lord Henry
"Come to me in the silence of the night"
Dawn
Echo. See "Come to me in the silence of the night"

Somersetshire wassail ("Wassail! wassail! all round the town") WCC
Variants: "Here we come a-wassailing"; Wassail song

Somervell, Arthur
Schlaf', kindchen, schlaf'
Shepherd's cradle-song. See Schlaf', kindchen, schlaf'

"Sometimes I dream that days of old are floating." See This is my dream (Wellings)

"Sometimes I feel discouraged." See Balm in Gilead

"Sometimes I feel like a moanin' dove." See "Sometimes I feel like a motherless child"

"Sometimes I feel like a motherless child." Negro spiritual. HR

"Sometimes I feel like a moanin' dove." DF

"Sometimes I'm up, and sometimes I'm down." See Nobody knows the trouble I see

"Sometimes we're bound for Liverpool." See Heave away

Somewhere. F. Campana. Words by A. C. Shaw. FSS 6

En sommarafton (Summer eve) A. F. Lindblad (music and words) e.sw. HSOS
A summer evening. e. KSN

Sommer, W.
Vagans scholasticus

Sommer-abendlied ("Willkommen, o seliger abend") W. G. Becker. Words by F. von Ludwig. g. ED 1
Welcome, fair evening. e.g. FSS 6

Sommerdagen (One summer day) Danish song. da.e. BF 2

Sommerlied (Summertime) Neidhardt von Reuenthal. e.g. BO

"Sommerlov og Sale, og Brandryg og Svale." See Huldre lokk

Sommers letzte rose. See The last rose of summer

Sommertag ("Trariro, der sommer der ist do") K. M. von Weber. Pfälzisches volkslied. g. ED 3

Somos independientes. See Cancion patriotica (Mexican song)

Somos libres, seámoslo siempre. Peruvian national air. s. SN

"Somrens dage svinder, nu kommer høstens vemodstid." See Höst (Beyer)

"Son figlio de Baciccia" ("I'm the son of old Baciccia") Lombardian folk song. e.i. MSI

"Son giovane gioconda felice." See La cianciosa

"Son giunta! grazie, o Dio." See Madre, pietosa Vergine (Verdi)

"Son io, mio Carlo." See Per me giunto (Verdi)

"Son lo spirito che nega" ("I am the spirit who denieth") A. Boito. e.i. KS 5 —OPS 4

Son of a gambolier. College song. MPC

The son of a trustee. Columbia university song. CU

"The Son of God goes forth to war." H. S. Cutler. Words by R. Heber. HSD—WBT—WS
All saints. CST
Church militant (All saints) FSS 6

Son Presvîatoĭ Bogoroditsy. See Mary's quest

"Son soto i toi balconi." See Serenata

"Son troppo vezzose" ("Thy rose-lips beguiling") B. Galuppi. e.i. KS 4

"Son tutta duolo" ("Desponding, lonely") A. Scarlatti. e.i. PA 1

Son vergin vezzosa ("Ah! with joy") Bellini. e.i. PP
"Son vergin vezzosa" ("I am a glad maiden") e.i. MC

"Sonent voces omnium." See Carmen Etonense (Barnby)

Song ("La belle étoile tombe") See Lied (Mertens)

The song ("I skogen smaagutten") See Tonen (Nordraak)

"A song, a song for the college in Wayne." See For love of Wooster U.

"A song and a carol for Christmas-tide." G. P. Grantham (music and words) HC

"Song-bird never sang so sweet." See Minnelied (Brahms)

"A song, boys! 'tis wrong, boys." See Bonny Nell

Song for Arbor day ("From forest wide") See "From forest wide and free" (Tufts)

Song for Arbor day ("Joy for the sturdy trees") See "Joy for the sturdy trees" (Hanlyn)

A song for Christmas eve. Sicilian air. Words by H. W. Loomis. DC

"A song for old Yale." See Alma mater—Yale (Shepard)

"A song for our banner." See The flag of our union forever (Custance); The flag of our union forever (Wallace)

A song for sailors and soldiers. English folk air. Words by J. Erwin. DO

"A song for the beautiful trees." See Forest song (Jones)

"A song for the oak." See The brave old oak (Loder)

A song from Kiso. Japanese song. e.j. BF 2

Song from Somma. See Canzone di Somma

Song, jest, perfume and dances. See "Ah! je veux vivre" (Gounod)

Song of a Burmese girl. See Amina's song

Song of a coward. See War song

Song of a thousand years. H. C. Work. HSD—WBT

A song of a wedding. 17th century air. Words by J. Suckling. MM
"I'll tell thee, Dick, where I have been." CO 2

A song of absence and longing. Ojibway Indian song. e.in. BA

The song of Agincourt. See Deo gratias

Song of an angel ("Once more has heaven") Rubinstein. OS 1

Song of an island fisherman (I groan as I put my nets away) Irish air. Words by K. Tynan. MMI

Song of approach. See Omaha Indian "Wa-wan" ceremony

Song of April. J. R. Fairlamb. Words by F. Manley. TL

Song of Arbor day. S. J. Pettings. Words by J. Hutchinson. FSS 3

The **song** of Australia. C. Linger. Words by Mrs C. J. Carleton. MP—SN

"A **song** of Boston sing today." See Evacuation day

A **song** of bread. German folk air. Words by H. H. Harbour. DO

A **song** of captivity. Russian folk air. Words by J. Russell. WF

A **song** of centuries. See Carmen seculare (Oakeley)

Song of Chinese rowers. c. SMW

Song of Columbus day. Haydn. Words by T. Brown. JS—NMS

The **song** of death ("Farewell, thou fair day") Air: Oran an aoig. Words by R. Burns. BSB
"Farewell, thou fair day." BSR—PS 1
The song of death (Oran an aoig.—"Farewell, thou fair day") MMS

Song of Denmark. See Sang for Danske (Weyse)

Song of departure. See Le chant du départ (Méhul)

A **song** of faith. Ojibway Indian song. in. BA

The **song** of Fionnuala ("Silent, O Moyle! be the roar of thy water") Irish air: Arah my dear Eveleen. Words by T. Moore. FSI—MI—MMI—PI

A **song** of Glenann. Irish air. Words by M. O'Neill. FSI

Song of greeting. Omaha Indian air. Words by F. Manley. TL

Song of hope. [H. A. Russotto] Words by S. Rowe. TFC 2

Song of Illyrian peasants. P. A. Schnecker. Words by S. T. Coleridge. TL

A **song** of India. N. Rimsky-Korsakow. e. BC
A song of India (Chanson indoue) e.f. GMF—NM 2

The **song** of Innisfail ("They came from a land beyond the sea") Air: Peggy bawn. Words by T. Moore. MI

"**Song** of joy, song of cheer." See Dream song (Jakobowski)

The **song** of Khívria (The buxom matron) Comic dance-song. M. P. Moussorgsky. e. SMR 1

The **song** of lies. See La chanson des mensonges

The **song** of Malbrough. See "Malbrough s'en va-t-en guerre"

A **song** of March. W. H. Jones. Words by E. A. Davis. NMS

Song of May. C. Saint-Saëns. [Tr of Voici le printemps nous portant des fleurs] e. BD

Song of mercy. W. H. Monk. WBT

The **song** of Miriam. See "Sound the loud timbrel" (Molique)

The **song** of Moses or Miriam. he. SMW
"Then did Moses sing" ("Az yshir Moshe") e.he. BSP

Song of my dear (Laulu Lapista) Lapp folk song. e.fi. BF 1
"Beneath the sky there does not blow" (Lapland song) e. BMC
"There's ne'er a blossom" (Laulu Lapista) e.fi. BO

A **song** of night ("Now night's dark shades appear") German song. e. FSS 4—JSE

Song of O'Donahue's mistress ("Of all the fair months, that round the sun") Air: The little and great mountain. Words by T. Moore. MI

Song of O'Ruark, Prince of Breffni ("The valley lay smiling before me") Air: Colleen dhas cruthen na moe, or, The pretty girl milking her cow. Words by T. Moore. MI—PI
"The valley lay smiling." EF

Song of parting. See "Es ist bestimmt in Gottes rath" (Mendelssohn)

A **song** of penitence. See Busslied (Beethoven)

The **song** of praise ("Glory now and forever to God."—Slava) Russian folk song. e. SSR 3

Song of praise ("God, our Father, made the daylight") [T. H. Bayly] Words by R. Compton. DO

The **song** of Renaud. See La chanson de Renaud

Song of rest. J. Strauss. FSS 8

Song of seven. Words by J. Ingelow. FSS 2

"**Songs** of shepherds." Old English air: Hunting the hare. BE 7

A **song** of ships. English air. Words by H. H. Harbour. DO

The **song** of Solomon (Yevréiskaya pyésnya) M. P. Moussorgsky. Words by L. Mey. e. SMR 1

The **song** of songs ("When nocturnal shadows gliding") A. Alpheraky. Words from the Song of Solomon. e. NM 1

A **song** of sorrow ("Dans ton coeur") See Chanson triste (Duparc)

A **song** of sorrow ("I have lost my senses") Turkish air. Nihad Bey. e. KSE

A **song** of spring ("Frühling lässt sein blaues band") See Er ist's (Schumann)

The **song** of spring ("Ner maidagen lokka") See Vaarvise

"A **song** of spring once more we sing." J. A. Benson. Words by W. H. Groser. HC

"A **song** of spring once more we sing." J. Booth. Words by W. H. Groser. HC

Song of sunshine ("Be content with what you have") FSS 7

A **song** of sunshine ("Churl winter his flight has taken") A. G. Thomas. SM 1

Song of temperance. Naumann. FSS 7

A song of Thanksgiving. F. Allitsen. Words by J. Thomson. WBW

The song of the A. B. University of North Carolina song. K. P. Harrington. Words by E. P. Willard. CHS

Song of the angels. See "It came upon the midnight clear" (Dykes); "It came upon the midnight clear" (Giardini)

Song of the bagpipers. See Canzone d'i zampognari

Song of the battle eve. See The battle eve

Song of the bells. See Legend of the bell (Planquette)

The song of the birds. See El cant des aucels

Song of the bird's nest. See The bird's nest

Song of the bobolink. R. H. Atkinson. NMS

The song of the bride ("Help me, dearest mother."—Piésnia lubáshi) N. Rimsky-Korsakoff. e. SMR 2

Song of the bride ("Nous somm' venu' vous voir") See La chanson de la mariée

Song of the brook. See The brook (Wilson)

Song of the children. English song. FSS 5

Song of the czar. See "Sonst spielt ich" (Lortzing)

Song of the daisies ("Up from the meadows free") Indian air. e. FI

Song of the daisy ("I'd rather be a daisy") C. W. Glover. Words by C. Jefferys. FSS 3

Song of the dark forest (Chanson de la forêt sombre) A. Borodine. e.f. SC

Song of the deathless voice. See The deathless voice

Song of the fieldmarshal. See Der feldmarschall

Song of the fig-tree orchard. See Canção do figueiral

Song of the fisher boy. FSS 8

A song of the flag. Air: Yankee Doodle. Words by M. W. Stryker. LBR

Song of the fowler. See Der vogelfänger (Mozart)

Song of the free. Words by J. G. Whittier. LA

Song of the ghost dance. Arapaho Indian air. Words by F. Manley. TL

Song of the giant. See La chanson du reuze

A song of the great adventure. Hungarian folk air. Words by J. Russell. WF

"The song of the heavenly harvest home." M. S. Skeffington. Words by S. Baring-Gould. HC

Song of the hop-pickers. E. Philp. Words by E. L. Blanchard. FSS 6— JSE

Song of the Indian coquet. See The Indian coquet

Song of the isle of Saint Kilda ("By the stream so pure and clear") Scottish song. HSSS

Song of the laborers of Berri. See Briolage

Song of the laugh. See The laugh

Song of the leader. See The leader's song

Song of the life-boat men. Russian folk air. Words by H. H. Harbour. DSH

Song of the little bird ("Ich gei arois") Jewish folk song. e.y. GF 1

Song of the little fish. See The little fish's song (Arenski)

Song of the maple. Mrs E. Fitzgerald. Words by R. M. Streeter. FSS 3

Song of the May. German song. e. FSS 5

The song of the months. Words by R. I. Halsey. NMS

Song of the moon. German song. e. WSC

The song of the moor. Folk air. Modern words by S. Baring-Gould. BSW

Song of the negro boatman. W. Müller. Words by J. G. Whittier. LBR

Song of the north. See "Du gamla, du fria, du fjällhoga nord"

Song of the "O. W. U." Ohio Wesleyan university song. E. T. O'Kane. Words by C. S. Anderson. CHS

Song of the old bell. O. Barri. FSS 7

Song of the peasants from Etna. See Canto de' contadini Etnei

Song of the plane. See Hobellied (Kreutzer)

Song of the pleasure seekers (Hukagawa) 18th century Japanese folk air. e.j. YJ

Song of the prisoner. See Canto del carcerato

Song of the rabbi. See Canzone del rabbino (Mascagni)

Song of the Samoan islanders ("Fofae, fofae") pol. SMW

Song of the Samoan islanders ("Tute tamai le fou ane") pol. SMW

Song of the sea ("Backward and forward, under the moon") M. P. Eayrs. CB

A song of the sea ("A sailor's life is a roving life") Old air. HSD

Song of the sea-gull. Irish air. Words by H. H. Harbour. DO—DSH

Song of the shepherd Lehl. N. Rimsky-Korsakoff. Words from the Russian of A. Ostrovsky. e. GMF—NM 2— SC

Song of the shepherds ("My love is very distant") Swiss song. e. KSE— SN

Song of the tornit. Eskimo Indian song. es. SN

Song of the Trappist. See Cantique du Trappiste (Meyerbeer)

Song of the violets. Indian air. e. FI

Song of the wagoners.   See Canzuna di li carriteri

Song of the washwoman near Palermo. See Modo delle lavandaie

Song of the western men.   Old Cornish song.   Words by R. S. Hawker.   BOS —DM 2

Song of the wild-roses.   Indian air.   e. FI

A song of the woods.   See Vieille chanson (Bizet)

Song of the wren.   See The wren

The song of transformations.   See La chanson des métamorphoses

A song of trust.   Ojibway Indian song. in.   BA

A song of water.   T. W. Drinkwater. Words adapted from the German by Neaves.   e.   SSS

Song of Zuleika (Chanson de Zuleika)   N. Rimsky-Korsakoff.   e.f.   NM 2

Song on the victory of Agincourt.   See Deo gratias

Song sung during a calm at sea (Nagareymna)   Japanese song.   j.   SMW

Song to old Union.   College song.   F. H. Ludlow.   CHS

Song to spring.   See Er ist's (Wolf)

Song to the chief (Fal il o ro, fal il o) Scottish song.   Words from the Gaelic.   e.   MMS

Song to the flag.   J. W. Tufts.   JS

Song to the morning star ("Through the long night")   Ojibway Indian song.   e.in.   BA
The morning star.   in.   BA

Song to the spirit.   Omaha Indian funeral song.   in.   FIS

Song to the sultan.   See Hamidie (Nedjib Pacha)

"Songo frangesa e vengo da Parigge."   See 'A frangesa   (Costa)

Songs from the Pyrenees: 1 ("Over the mountains")   Spanish folk song.   e. GO

Songs from the Pyrenees: 2 ("Now shut in")   Spanish folk song.   e.   GO

"Songs my mother taught me."   A. Dvořák.   e.g.   EF.   e. only WBT —WBW
    "As my dear old mother" ("Als die alte mutter")   e.g.   FF
    "Long ago in childhood's days."   e. BD
    "Songs my mother taught me" ("Als die alte mutter")   e.g.   KF 1— KF 2—KF 3—KF 4—SM 4

"Songs of gladness."   Easter carol.   HC

The songs of Grusia (Nye poi, krasávitza) S. Rachmaninoff.   Words by Pushkin. e.   SMR 2

"Songs of praise."   S. Bach.   Words by J. Montgomery.   MCS
    "Songs of praise" (Nuremberg)   FSS 3

"Songs of shepherds and rustical roundelays."   See Hunting the hare

"Songs, revealing sacred feeling."   See Gebet (Weber)

The songs we sang.   Words by S. A. Eliot.   CHS

The songs your fathers loved ("Oh! sing them on the sunny hills")   Air: Wyres Ned Puw, or, Ned Pugh's grand-daughter.   Words by F. Hemans.   MMW

"Die sonn erwacht."   See Wanderlied (Weber)

"Der sonne letzter strahl."   See entry under Der

Sonne, mond und sterne ("Und die sonne, sie machte")   Air: Es ritten drei reiter etc.   Words by E. M. Arndt.   g. ED 3

"Die sonne sank."   Volksweise.   Words by H. Hoffmann von Fallersleben.   g. ED 3

"Die sonne scheint nicht mehr" ("No more the glowing sun")   German folk song. e.g.   MS

"Die sonne sinkt in's tiefe meer."   See Alinde (Schubert)

"Sonne taucht in meeresfluthen."   See Dein gedenk' ich, Margareta (Meyer-Helmund)

Sonnemann, A.
    Seligkeit (Meyer)

"Sonnenstrahlen durch die tannen."   See Im haine (Schubert)

"Sönner af Norge" ("Children of Norway." —Den norske nationalsang)   C. Blom.   Words by H. A. Bjerregaard.   e.n.   FMB—SSS
    "Sönner af Norge" ("Minstrel, awaken")   e.n.   MAN
    Sönner af Norge (National song of Norway.—"Children of Norway") e.   BMC
    Sonner af Norge ("Sons of dear Norway")   e.g.   SN
    "Sønner af Norge" ("Sons of Norway") e.n.   BSP.   e.g.   WCP

Sonnet d'amour.   F. Thomé.   Words by A. de Saineville.   e.f.   SM 2
    Sonnet d'amour (A love sonnet)   e.f. ES—HM 2—PG 2

Sonntag ("Die nacht war kaum verblühet." —Sunday)   R. Franz.   Words by J. von Eichendorff.   e.g.   HSS 1— HSS 2

Sonntag ("So hab' ich die ganze."—Sunday)   J. Brahms.   Words by L. Uhland.   e.g.   GMF

"Den sonntag, den sonntag in aller fruh." See entry under Den

Sonntagslied ("This is the day")   Mendelssohn.   Words by G. Klingemann.   e.g.   HSS 1
    Sonntagslied (Alone)   e.   FTS

"Sons of a race that bled on Narva's heath." See Björneborgarne's march

"Sons of dear Norway."   See "Sönner af Norge" (Blom)

Sons of Geneva.   Geneva college song. CHS

The sons of Georgetown.   Georgetown university song.   CHS

"Sons of Greece, come, arise." Greek national air. e. KSE—SN—WCP
Greek national song ("Sons of Greece, rouse ye up") e. BMC
"Sons of Mars! by my birth I am of Gauls descended." See Le géant (Gailhard)
"Sons of men, behold." Thibaut. Words by C. Wesley. FSS 1—MCS—WBT
Sons of Norway. See "Sönner af Norge" (Blom)
"Sons of the nation to glory restored." See Ye sons of the nation (Barnard)
"The sons of the Prophet are hardy and bold." See Abdul, the Bulbul Ameer
"The sons of the Prophet are valiant and bold." See Abdulla Bul-Bul Ameer
"The sons of the Prophet were hardy and bold." See Ivan Skizavitzsky Skivar
"Sonst spielt ich" ("In childhood I dallied") A. Lortzing (music and words) e.g. AB 1
With crown and scepter (Song of the czar) e. FSS 6
"Sont trois faucheurs dedans les prés." See Le miracle du nouveau-né
"Sont trois jeunes garçons." See La mort de la fiancée
"Sont trois tambours s'en revenant de guerre." See Joli tambour
"Sontse nizen'ko." See The sun is low
"Soon after I was married a happy man to be." See The scolding wife
"Soon beyond the harbor bar." See Belle Mahone (McNaughton)
"Soon I'll own riches divine." See "O del ben che acquisterò" (Cesti)
"Soon night will pass." See Morgenhymne (Henschel)
"Soon, O soon wilt thou leave us, O butterweek." See Butter-week
"Soon will the meadows turn to lovely green." See Das Seiser almlied
Sooner in the morning. See "Going to ride up in the chariot"
Soontree (A lullaby) Irish air. Words by N. Hopper. FSI
"Soothing spells, ah, love, cast o'er me." See "Porgi, amor" (Mozart)
Il sor Carlo l'armonico (The musical Master Charley) Roman song. e.i. MSI
The musical Master Charley. e. BSE
Soraidh slàn le Fionn-Airidh (Farewell to Fiunary.—"The wind is fair") Scottish air. Words by McLeod. e. MMS
"Sore is my heart with yearning" (Chinese song) e. BMC
"Sorge infausta" ("Clouds may rise") Händel. e.i. BS 1
Sorgen (Sorrow) Swedish folk song. e.sw. SMF
"Allt under himmelens fäste" ("In heaven's vault above me") e.sw. HSOS
Der sorgenfreie ("Jung, fröhlich und heiter") J. A. P. Schulz. Words by C. A. Overbeck. g. ED 2

Soróka. See The magpie and the little gypsy dancer (Musorgskii)
Sorrow ("Allt under himmelens fäste") See Sorgen
"Sorrow and care may meet." See He giveth His beloved sleep (Abt)
Sorrow in spring. S. Rachmaninoff. Words from the Russian of Galina. e. NM 2
The sorrow of love. See Liebeskummer
"Sorrow with bitter tears." See Thee, St Stephens
Sorrow's might. Ancient Swedish song. e. KSN
"Sorry her lot." A. Sullivan. Words by W. S. Gilbert. FSS 5
"Sorta è la notte." See Ernani, Ernani, involami (Verdi)
"Sotto il bel ciel delle Spagne." T. A. E. Semet. e.i. OPS 2—SOA 2
Souhait. See The wish (Cui)
"Soul like rosy cloud, faintly living." See Romance (Debussy)
"Soul of lightest breath, softly sailing." See Romance (Debussy)
"Soul of love, O bear me up on high." See Vision (Claus)
"The soul taught by duty." See "Ragion sempre addita" (Stradella)
"Soulève ta paupière close." See Le spectre de la rose (Berlioz)
"Sound an alarm." G. F. Händel. SAS 3
"Sound, O bells! sound, O bells." See Les cloques
"The sound of harps." See "Il suon dell' arpa angeliche" (Donizetti)
"Sound our voices long and sweet." Bohemian air. FSS 2
"Sound, sound my pipe." See The reapers (Vassilenko)
"Sound the loud timbrel" (The song of Miriam.—Der gesang Miriams) Molique. Words by T. Moore. e.g. HSS 1
Sound the loud timbrel (Miriam's song.—Mirjam's siegsgesang) C. Reinecke. Words by T. Moore. e.g. HSS 1
Miriam's song of triumph (Mirjam's siegsgesang) e.g. HSS 2
"Sound ye the trumpet." V. Bellini. [Tr of Suoni la tromba] e. BD
"Sounds like Jesus, O hark." See Somebody's knocking at your door
Soupir ("J'ai laissé de mon sein de neige."—The sigh) C. Widor. Words by T. Gautier. e.f. HM 2
Soupir ("Ne jamais la voir ni l'entendre."—A sigh) H. Duparc. Words by A. Sully-Prudhomme. e.f. HM 1
Soupir ("Ne jamais la voir ni l'entendre."—A sigh) A. W. Kramer. Words by A. Sully-Prudhomme. e.f. CMF 1
"Source délicieuse." C. Gounod. e.f. SOA 3
"Source of life's too copious sorrow." See "Schöne wiege meiner leiden" (Schumann)

Source of song. Harrow school song. LA

Sourwood mountain. Folk song: Georgia version. CSE
—Kentucky version. WLT

"**Sous** le soleil, qui les irise." See Sonnet d'amour (Thomé)

Sous les branches (Beneath the branches) G. d'Hardelot. Words by F. Coppée. e.f. SOS 2

Sous les pieds d'une femme. C. Gounod. e.f. SOA 5
She alone charmeth my sadness. e. BS 1
Sous les pieds d'une femme (She alone charmeth my sadness) e.f. OPS 4

"**Sous** leur sceptre de fer ils ont tout comprimé." See Humble fille des champs (Halévy)

"**Sous** l'ombrage d'un pommier." See "'Neath the shadow of a tree"

South African national song ("The sunny hills of Africa") Words by H. Hartwell. BMC—JSE

"**South** Australia is my home." See Rolling king

"**South** Carolina's a sultry clime." See So early in the morning

"A **southerly** wind and a cloudy sky." Old English hunting song. JO
"A **southerly** wind and a cloudy sky" (The fox-chase) DM 2—HSE 2

"A **southerly** wind and a cloudy sky" (The huntsmen) Round. Old English words. LA—WBT

Southern memories. Plantation song. BSS—TFC 2

A **southern** night (Nuit méridionale) N. Rimsky-Korsakow. Words by N. Stcherbine. e.f. SC

Southey, G. W.
The clang of the hammer (Bonheur)
The red scarf (Bonheur)

Southey, Robert
The well of St Keyne (Cornish air)

"A **southland** Jenny." Popular Ayrshire song. PS 2

"**Southrons,** hear your country call you." See Dixie (Emmett)

Southwell, F. W.
Chit chat

Southwell, Robert
New Prince, new pomp (Scotch air; also music by Steggall)

Southwick, Frank Treat
"Hark! the joyful Christmas greeting"
"Rejoice to-day with glad accord"
The school-house and the flag
"Wake! and tune your youthful voices"

Souvenirs de Lisette (Béranger's Lisette) F. Bérat (music and words) e.f. CM 1

"**Soviel** stern' am himmel stehen." See Treue liebe

Sövnen (Slumber) H. Kjerulf. Words by B. Björnson. e.n. MAN—SSN

Sövnen (Slumber) F. A. Reissiger. Words by B. Björnson. e.n. MAN

"**Sovra** il sen." Bellini. e.i PP

"**Sow** not in sorrow." See "Freut euch des lebens" (Nägeli)

"**Sow** ye beside all waters." J. M. Crament. Words by A. Shipton. HC

The **sower** (Le semeur) C. Cui. Words by N. Nekrasov. e.f. NR 3

"**Sower** of wisdom, in fields where the peasants toil." See The sower (Cui)

"The **sower** went forth sowing." J. F. Bridge. Words by W. S. H. Bourne. HC

The **sowing** of the millet (A my proso sieiali, sieiali.—Spring song) Russian folk song. e. SSR 2

Sowing the rue ("Sejau rūtą") Lithuanian folk song. e.li. BF 1

Sowinski, Wojciech
"Poland's not yet dead in slavery" (attributed) See Ogiński, M. K. Polish national song
Polish hymn (attributed) See Ogiński, M. K. Polish national song

"**Sown** with millet was my garden" ("Sialem proso na zagonie") Folk song from Little Russia. e.r. SMF

"**Soy** cubanita, soy de la playa hermosa." See Niña Pancha (Romea y Valverde)

"**Soy** pajarillo errante." See El pájaro errante

"**Soyez** bénis ô vous! montagnes et bois." See Benediction (Tchaikovsky)

"The **spacious** firmament on high" (Addison) Composer unknown. [Words by J. Addison] LA

"The **spacious** firmament on high." J. Haydn. Words by J. Addison. DSH—WBT
"The spacious firmament on high" (Creation) BD—CST—FSS 3—TL

"**Spähend** nach dem eisengitter." See Blondel's lied (Schumann)

"**Spake** the angel, lo! to all men." See Joyful tidings (Verdi)

The **spalpeen's** complaint of the Cranbally farmer. Irish folk song. JOI

The **Spanish** Armada ("In eighty-eight ere I was born") Chantey. SMW

The **Spanish** Armada ("In May fifteen hundred and eighty eight") Arnold. Words by J. O'Keeffe. DM 2

The **Spanish** canoe. Chantey. SMW
Variant of: The Golden Vanity

The **Spanish** cavalier. W. D. Hendrickson (music and words) MPC—NMH—NML—OH—SSS—WC

The **Spanish** gipsy ("Come, follow, follow me") English folk song. Air: The Spanish gipsy. DM 2

The **Spanish** gipsy ("I dance the bright bolero") Spanish seguedilla bolero. e. BMC

The **Spanish** gipsy ("Moonlight comes stealing") See En elespejo de tu mirado niña

The **Spanish** guitar. Student song. SSS

Spanish hymn. See Himno de Riego (Huerta)

Spanish ladies. See "Farewell and adieu to you, Spanish ladies"

The Spanish lady. 16th century English song. CO 1—DM 1—JE
Ye Spanish lady. BE 7
The Spanish lady's love. MM

Spanish national hymn. See "Quien quisiera ser libre que a prendra" (Fenollosa)

Spanish national song ("How wretched is the anguish") [Huerta] e. BMC—MP—NMS—WBT

Spanish proverb. Student song. CHS

Spanish serenade. A. Lee. Words by T. H. Bayly. FSS 8—WBT

Sparabella's complaint. Old English air. BE 7

"Sparkling and bright, in its liquid light, is the water in our glasses." Temperance song. [J. B. Taylor. Author of words unknown] FSS 1—WBT

"Sparkling and bright in liquid light, does the wine our goblets gleam in." J. B. Taylor. Words by C. F. Hoffman. JO

"The sparks fly thro' the smithy-door." See "Au bruit des lourds marteaux d'airain" (Gounod)

The sparrow ("Sparrow rock'st in free air") Lindblad. e. KSN

The sparrow on the tree. A. S. Gatty. WSC

"Sparrow rock'st in free air." See The sparrow (Lindblad)

The sparrow's nest. Old French air: Ah! vous dirai-je. Words by H. H. Harbour. DO

"Sparve già l'aer gelido le colline già inverdano." See Au printemps (Gounod)

Spazier, Karl
Am sommerabend
Wiegenlied

Der spaziergang ("Kommt lasst uns ausspazieren") F. W. Berner. Words by M. Opitz von Boberfeld. g. ED 3

"Speak gently—it is better far." W. V. Wallace. Words by D. Bates. FSS 2—JSE

"Speak gently, there's enough of care." See Kind words are dear to all (Noorden)

"Speak, I pray thee." See Pur dicesti, o bocca bella (Lotti)

Speak to me. F. Campana. WBT

Le spectre de la rose (The spirit of the rose) Berlioz. Words by T. Gautier. e.f. MSS 2

"Speed away! speed away." I. B. Woodbury (music and words) FSS 1—HSD—LA—LBR—TFC 2

Speed, bonnie boat, like a bird on the wing. See Skye boat-song

"Speed, my bark, O gently speed thee." Neukomm. FSS 5

"Speed on, my bark, speed on." H. Leslie. Words by M. Dee. BAS 2

"Speed our republic." See American hymn (Keller)

"Speed thy flight." Irish air: The quern time. MMI

"Speed up." C. H. Fairfax. Words by E. Battell. TFC 2

The speller's fate. Student song. CHS

Spencer, E. M.
Old college days (Smith)
Smiling faces (Glover)

Spencer, William Robert
"Too late I stayed" (Irish air)
Wife, children, and friends (Old air)

Spenser, Edmund
"Like as a huntsman" (Greene)
"The merry cuckoo, messenger of spring" (Greene)
"Sweet smells the briar" (Percy)
"Trust not the treason of those smiling lookes" (Greene)

"Spento il rival." See Il balen del suo sorriso (Verdi)

Speranza, Domenico
Lady Beatrice's lament

"Speranza del mio cor eri una volta." See Tempo passato perchè non retorni (Gordigiani)

"Spesso vibra per suo gioco" ("Oft the blindfold boy") A. Scarlatti. e.i. PA 1

Spicer, commodore
Absent friends and you, Mary

Spicker, Max
"In dieser stunde"
"This very hour." See "In dieser stunde"

The spider and the fly ("Will you come into my parlor") Round. W. G. McNaught. Old words adapted. TFC 2

The spider and the fly ("Will you walk into my parlor") Old English air: Will you come to the bower. Old words by T. Hudson. BE 1—FSS 1—JO

The spider and the fly ("Will you walk into my parlor") Old English air: Will you come to the bower. Words by M. Howitt, based on an older song. JO

The spider and the scout. College song. BSS

Spilman, James E.
Afton water
"Away in a manger"
Cradle hymn. See "Away in a manger"
"Flow gently, sweet Afton." See Afton water

"Spin, maiden, spin! Be happy thoughts within." See "Spinn, mägdlein, spinn! so wachsen dir die sinn" (Reinecke)

Spin! spin. See Spinn! spinn (Jüngst)

"Spin, spin, O my darling daughter." See Die spinnerin (Volkslied)

"'E spingole frangese" (French pins) E. de Leva. Words by S. di Giacomo. e.i. FE—MN

"Spinn, mägdlein, spinn! so wachsen dir die
    sinn" (Spinning song)   C. Rei-
    necke.   Words from a folk song.
    e.g.   FSS 6
Spinning song.   e.   LA
Spinn! spinn (Spin! spin)   H. Jüngst.   e.g.
    MSF 2
Spin! spin.   e.   CST
"Spinn, spinn, meine liebe tochter."   See
    Die spinnerin (Volkslied)
"Spinne, mägdlein, spinne, so wachsen dir
    die sinne" (Spinnerlied)   J. R. Berls.
    Words from a folk song.   g.   ED 3
The spinner.   See Die spinnerin (Volks-
    lied)
Die spinnerin ("Ich sass und spann vor
    meiner tür")   A. Harder.   Words by
    J. H. Voss.   g.   ED 2
Die spinnerin ("Spinn, spinn, meine liebe
    tochter")   Volkslied.   g.   ED 3
Die spinnerin (The spinner)   e.g.
    BF 2
Spinnerliedchen (Spinning-song)   e.g.
    SSG
Der spinnerin nachtlied.   See entry under
    Der
Spinnerlied.   See "Spinne, mägdlein,
    spinne, so wachsen dir die sinne"
    (Berls)
Spinnerliedchen.   See Die spinnerin
    (Volkslied)
Spinney, Thomas Herbert
    Fair waved the golden corn"
    "This happy morn a King is born"
Spinney, Walter
    "Christians, carol sweetly"
"Spinning all night and day."   See Spinn!
    spinn (Jüngst)
Spinning chorus.   R. Wagner.   [Tr of
    Summ' und brumm', du gutes radchen]
    e.   MS
Spinning song ("Spinn, mägdlein")   See
    "Spinn, mägdlein, spinn! so wachsen
    dir die sinn" (Reinecke)
Spinning-song ("Spinn, spinn")   See Die
    spinnerin (Volkslied)
"Spinning was young Clochette."   See Clo-
    chette (Molloy)
The spinning-wheel ("To ease his heart and
    own his flame")   18th century song.
    ME
The spinning wheel ("Upon a sunshine
    summer's day")   18th century song.
    DM 2
The spinster's lament.   Vermont song.
    SSH
"The spirit in our hearts" (Dennis)   H.
    G. Nägeli.   Words by H. U. Onder-
    donk.   FSS 8
"A spirit of beauty walks the hills."   See
    The return of spring (Jones)
"Spirit of God" (Benediction)   E. J. Hop-
    kins.   Words by G. Croly.   TL
The spirit of May ("The summer is com-
    ing")   Air: Havod elwy.   Words by
    Talhaiarn.   MMW
The spirit of poesy (La poésie)   A. Aren-
    sky.   Words by S. Nadson.   e.f.
    NR 1

The spirit of the rose.   See Le spectre de
    la rose (Berlioz)
"Spirit so fair, brightly descending."   See
    "Spirto gentil" (Donizetti)
"Spirits of nether worlds."   See Divination
    by water (Musorgskiï)
The spirit's song.   See Des geistes gesang
    (Haydn)
"Spirto gentil."   Donizetti.   e.i.   OPS 3
    —SOA 3
Spite.   See Dispetto
Spla-foot Nance.   Irish folk song.   JOI
La splendeur vide (Empty splendor)   C.
    Saint-Saëns.   Words by A. Renaud.
    e.f.   CM 2
"A splendid place is London."   See In the
    foggy dew (Loomis)
"The splendor falls on castle walls."   See
    Blow, bugle, blow (Neidlinger)
Splittegarb, C. F.
    Die weihnachtsfreude (Volksweise)
Spofforth, Reginald
    Julia to the wood-robin
Spohr, Ludwig
    "Almighty God of Israel" (from Der
        fall Babylons)
    "Bright star of night"
    "Dear child of bondage" (from Der
        fall Babylons)
    "Der kriegeslust ergeben" (from Jes-
        sonda)
    "Hast Thou for me a look, a thought"
        (from Des heilands letzte stunden)
    Holy, Holy, Lord
    Liebe ist die zarte blüthe (from Faust)
    Love's a tender flow'ret shedding.   See
        Liebe ist die zarte blüthe
    "Mir ist, als müsst ich dir was sagen"
    "O! how familiar to mine ear" (from
        Der fall Babylons)
    "O what is man" (from Der fall Baby-
        lons)
    Remember, Lord, what Thou hast laid
        upon us (from Der fall Babylons)
    "Rose softly blooming."   See "Rose,
        wie bist du"
    "Rose, wie bist du" (from Zemire und
        Azor)
    "Tears of sorrow, shame and anguish"
        (from Des heilands letzte stunden)
    "To lust of war devoted."   See "Der
        kriegeslust ergeben"
    "When this scene of trouble closes"
        (from Des heilands letzte stunden)
"Spoke Zuleika thus to her canary."   See
    The canary (Tchaikovsky)
Spontini, Gasparo Luigi Pacifico
    "Goddess of those who grieve."   See
        "Ô des infortunés"
    "Ô des infortunés" (from La Vestale)
The spool (Jekharag)   Armenian song.
    a.e.   BF 2
Sporle, Nathan James
    At evening-time
    Boatman's return
    "Dream on, young hearts"
    The star of Glengary

Sporting bachelors. Kentucky mountain song. WT

"The sportsman hies him through the wood." See The merry sportsman

"Sposa! Euridice." See "Che farò senza Euridice" (Gluck)

The spotted cow. Folk song: Devon version. BSW

—Yorkshire version. MM

"Sprach die sultanin zum kanarienvogel." See The canary (Tchaikovsky)

Sprague, C. J.
"Hush, my darling, repose thee" (Plouvé)

Sprague, Sarah E.
The purple and gold (Schultz)

"Spread the tidings afar to the nations." See "Quien quisiera ser libre que a prendra" (Fenollosa)

"Spreading sail and swelling tide." See Tilsjös (Backer-Gröndahl)

"Spreading sails o'er the North sea speed." See Olaf Trygvason (Reissiger)

A sprig of shillelah ("O, love is the soul of a neat Irishman") Irish air. Words by H. B. Code. FSS 7—MMI

The sprig of thyme. Folk song. FSF—SEF 1—SO

—Devon version. BSW

—Dorset version. SF 1

—Version with modern words by A. F. Brown. GO

Variant: The seeds of love

Spring ("Again my heart beats time their measure") A. Alpheraky. Words from the Russian of A. Fet. e. NM 1

Spring ("Flocks are sporting") See "Flocks are sporting" (Carey)

The spring ("Källan sprang ur jordens barm") See Källan (Lagercrantz)

The spring ("The spring is come") Round. Hayes. HSD—OH

Spring ("Thou art, O God, the life and light") F. J. Haydn. Words by T. Moore. JS

Spring ("Thro' each rustle murmurs pass") G. Sachnofsky. Words from the Russian of G. Novikoff. e. NM 2

Spring ("When daisies pied") See "When daisies pied, and violets blue" (Arne)

Spring and winter. English folk song. BE 2

"Spring breezes crisp." See "Vårvindar friska, leka och hviska"

Spring faith. See Frühlingsglaube (Ries)

Spring-flowers. See Frühlingsblumen (Reinecke)

Spring, gentle spring. J. Riviere. Words by J. R. Planché. FSS 2—WBT

"Spring! spring! gentle spring." WSC

"The spring had come, the flow'rs in bloom." See Little Maggie May (Blamphin)

"The spring has come, the birds I hear." Round. FSS 8

"The spring has come, the flowrs in bloom." See Little Maggie May (Blamphin)

"Spring her azure banner flings." See Er ist's (Wolf)

"The spring is a-coming, all nature is blooming." See Spring is coming

"The spring is come, I hear the birds." See The spring (Hayes)

Spring is coming ("The spring is a-coming") Old English air: Bath medley. Words rewritten. BE 8

"The spring is coming resolved to banish." Air: Humours of the bath, or, Bath medley. Words by G. Macfarren. DM 2—JE

"Spring is on the way." See "Voici le printemps qui va-t-arriver"

"Spring is returning, she breathes on the plain." See Spring returning

Spring night ("Ueber'm garten") See Frühlingsnacht (Jensen); Frühlingsnacht (Schumann)

"The spring now has found us." See "Printemps qui commence" (Saint-Saëns)

The spring of love. N. I. Hyatt. Words by S. A. Brooke. HST

Spring returning. Round. FSS 7—HSC

Spring song ("Come and twine") See "Come and twine the slim boughs"

Spring song ("Es herrscht ein heiliger friede") See Frühlingslied (Fesca)

A spring song ("I sat beneath the maples old") C. Pinsuti. FSS 5

Spring song ("Lo, the harvest ripe") See The sowing of the millet

Spring song ("Nu klär sig våren") See Vårvisa (Söderman)

Spring song ("Oh, the gentle spring is coming") F. Mendelssohn. BD

Spring song ("Snow on the earth") A. C. Mackenzie. Words by A. P. Graves. SM 4

Spring song ("Thou calm-ray'd spring") 18th century song. MM

Spring song ("Were I a sunbeam") See The maiden's wish (Chopin)

Spring song ("When the spring has climb'd the mountain's height") O. Weil. Words by F. von Bodenstedt. [Tr of "Wenn der frühling auf die berge steigt"] e. WBW

Spring song ("The winter it is past") See "The winter it is past"

Spring song—To Ireland ("Weep no more") Irish air: Ballyvaughan. Words by D. Sigerson (Mrs C. Shorter) MMI

"Spring! spring! gentle spring." See Spring, gentle spring (Riviere)

Spring-tide. For entries beginning Spring-tide see Springtide

Spring-time. For entries beginning Spring-time see Springtime

"The spring, with her dower of bird and of flower." See "Printemps qui commence" (Saint-Saëns)

"Spring's a pleasant time." See Ay wakin' O

"The spring's blue eyes." See "Die blauen frühlingsaugen" (Rubinstein)

"**Spring's** bright sunlit time." See Castles in the air

Spring's message. German song. e. WBT—WSC
The cuckoo. e. FSS 1—FSS 8

Springtide ("Ja, noch einmal konnt'") See Der frühling (Grieg)

Springtide ("Wenn der frühling") See "Wenn der frühling auf die berge steigt" (Becker)

"The **spring-tide** hour." J. Booth. Words by J. S. B. Monsell. HC

The **springtime** ("The hyacinth and daffodil") A. S. Gatty. WSC

Springtime ("Now melts the snow."— Frühling) P. Tschaikowsky. Words by Pleshtcheyeff. e.g. SC

Spring-time ("Scant clouds just flake") Chinese reading air. Words by Cheng Hao. c.e. BF 2

Spring-time ("Wenn der frühling") See "Wenn der frühling auf die berge steigt" (Becker)

"The **springtime** is come, with a bright sun and shower." See Spring and winter

"The **springtime** is here, the heavens are clear." See Departure for the Alps in spring

"**Spring** time joys will soon be here." See Er ist's (Schumann)

The **springtime** of the year. Words by J. R. Planché. FSS 3

Spring-time once again. A. S. Sullivan. Words by J. Logan. FSS 4

Spurr, Mel. B.
The nipper's lullaby (Andrews)

Squaw dance. Iowa Indian song. in. SN

The **squire** and the thresher. See "A nobleman lived in a village of late"

"The **squire** he came home at night." See The gypsy laddie (Rock Fork, Tenn. version no. 1)

"The **squirrel** loves a pleasant chase." Children's song. WBT—WSC

Srpska narodna himna. See Serbian national anthem (Jenko)

Stacey, B. F.
The gold and olive (Dubee)

Stadinger's song. A. Lortzing. [Tr of Ich auch war einst jüngling mit lockigem haar] e. AB 4

Städterbua und âlmadirn (City lad and country lass) T. Koschat (music and words) e.g. EF

Stagnelius, Erik Johan
Necken (Söderberg)

Stainer, Sir John
"Again the morn of gladness"
"Beauteous are the flowers of earth"
The Child Jesus in the garden
Christmas day. See "Wake all music's magic powers"
"Jesu, hail! O God most holy" (Tr of Ave Jesu Deus)
"King ever glorious" (from The crucifixion)
Loyal death

The majesty of the divine humiliation (from The crucifixion)
"My hope is in the everlasting" (from The daughter of Jairus)
"Now join we all with holy mirth"
O Zion, that bringest good tidings
"Sing with joy, 'tis Christmas morn"
"Thus speaketh the Lord of hosts"
"Wake all music's magic powers"
"When the weary, seeking rest"

Stair, Patty
The interrupted serenade

"**Stalk** of maize with leaves that rise." See Cucuruz

Stamboul (Kabyle song) e.f. BO

Stamford, Heinrich Wilhelm von
Ständchen (Volksweise)

The **stammering** lovers. Ancient English folk song. BE 6

Stan' still Jordan. Negro spiritual. JB

Stances (Love-song) A. Flégier. Words by F. Loviot. e.f. SOS 2

Stand, Columbia. Columbia university song. J. Haydn. Words by G. O. Ward. CU

"**Stand** I alone at midnight deep." See "Steh' ich in finstrer mitternacht" (Wurda)

"**Stand!** the ground's your own, my braves." See Warren's address

"**Stand** to your guns." Carter. HSE 2

"**Stand** up, stand up for Jesus." G. J. Webb. Words by G. Duffield, jr. BD

"**Stand** up, ye sons of Harvard." See A toast to Harvard (Smith)

The **standard** bearer. See Die fahnenwacht (Lindpaintner)

"The **standard** on the braes o' Mar." See The braes of Mar

"The **standard** watch." See Die fahnenwacht (Lindpaintner)

Ständchen ("Der den himmel."—Serenade) J. Raff. e.g. KF 3—PG 4

Ständchen ("Hark! hark! the lark") See "Hark! hark! the lark" (Schubert)

Ständchen ("Komm, fein liebchen") B. A. Weber. Words by A. von Kotzebue. g. ED 2

Ständchen ("Komm, feins liebchen") Folk air. Words by A. von Kotzebue. g. ED 3

Ständchen ("Komm, feins liebchen") Another folk air. Words by A. von Kotzebue. g. ED 3

Ständchen ("Leise flehen meine lieder."— Serenade) F. Schubert. Words by L. Rellstab. e.g. CMF 2— FMB—TS. e. only WA—WL
Serenade. e. HSC—WBT—WSW
La serenata de Schubert. s. LCP
Ständchen ("Through the leaves the night winds moving") e.g. PG 3

Ständchen ("Mach' auf, mach' auf."—Serenade) R. Strauss. Words by A. F. von Schack. e.g. FF—FO 2—PG 3

Ständchen ("Der mond ist schlafen 'gangen."—Serenade) R. Franz. Words by W. Osterwald. e.g. KF 4

Ständchen ("Der mond steht."—Serenade) J. Brahms. Words by F. Kugler. e.g. CMF 1—PG 1

Ständchen ("Nächtlicher duft weht durch die luft."—Serenade) A. Jensen. e.g. KF 4

Ständchen ("Wenn die nacht mit süsser ruh") Volksweise. Words by H. W. von Stamford. g. ED 3

Ständchen des Don Juan. See Don Juan's serenade (Tchaikovsky)

Stanford, Sir Charles Villiers
"My love's an arbutus": Irish air arranged
"Once in Bethlehem of Judah"
Tim, the dragoon

Stange, Max
Favoring breeze. See Frische brise
Frische brise

Stanley, A. A.
"Rah! rah! U of M"

Stanley, Charles John
The blind boy

Stanley, Thornton
When the grand old flag goes by (Wilmarth)

"St'anno porz'io vogl'ì a la Maronna i Piedigrotta." See La festa di Piedigrotta

Stanton, Frank Lebby
The flag of our country (Mercer)
Greeting (Hawley)
Let Miss Lindy pass (Rogers)

Stanton, W. H.
"Because I love you, dear" (Hawley)

Stanzas from the Nativity. See The Nativity, Stanzas from (Smith)

"Stapil Dobre." See The gray dove

The star ("Cine primește") See Steaua

"Det står ett ljus i Österland" ("There is a light in Easterland") Swedish folk song. e.sw. HSOS

The star of Bethlehem ("It was the eve of Christmas") S. Adams. Words by F. E. Weatherly. WA—WS

The star of Bethlehem ("When marshalled on the nightly plain") Words by H. K. White. MCS

"Star of Bethlehem, sweetly shining." C. Simper. Words by A. S. Woods. HC

The star of Glengary. N. J. Sporle. Words by E. Cook. FSS 7

Star of glory, brightly streaming. J. Garnett. HC

The star of His birth. MCS

The star of hope. FSS 8

"The star of joy beams bright to-day." See Christmas song

"Star of mine, my dearest treasure." See Sérénade basque

Star of my heart. L. Denza. Words by G. Enderssohn. SM 3

Star of the east. Alfred university song. Words by G. M. Ellis. CHS

Star of the north. M. I. Glinka. Words from the Russian of Rostopchine. e. NM 1

"Star of the twilight." L. O. Emerson. HSD—WBT

The star-spangled banner ("O say, can you see by the dawn's early light") National song of the United States. Attributed to J. S. Smith; wrongly attributed to S. Arnold. Words by F. S. Key. BD— BMC— BOS — BSE— BSP— BSS— CST— DSH— EF— FMB— FSS 1— HSC — HSD— JO— JS— JSE— LA— — LBR— MP— MS— NA— NMH — NMS— OH— SSS— TFC 1— WA— WBT— WCP— WSC— WSW

La bandera de franjas y estrellas. s. LCP

The star-spangled banner (Morning colors) SN

"The star that bids the shepherd fold." See Now Phoebus sinketh in the west (Arne)

"Star vicino" ("Might I linger anear thee") Salvator Rosa. e.i. MSS 1
"Star vicino" ("To be near the fair idol") e.i. FEI 1
"Star vicino" ("To be near thee") e.i. NG—PG 4
"To be near the fair idol." e. BSE

"The star whose shining." MCS

"Stara planina." See "Oh, thou ancient mountain"

Starke, Gotthelf Wilhelm Christoph
Trinklied (Ebers)

Starkey, James
A piper (Irish air)
The sedges (Donegal air)

"The starlight in thine eyes." G. Hunt. WBT—WL

Starlight is streaming. [M. W. Balfe. Words by E. Fitzball] FSS 3

"Starlit spaces." See "Nuit d'étoiles" (Widor)

Starry night. See "Nuit d'étoiles" (Widor)

"The stars above me." See "Som stjärnan uppå himmelen så klar"

"Stars all bright are beaming." W. R. Holt. Words by R. R. Chope. HC

The stars and stripes ("O star-spangled banner") LA

"The stars are brightly shining." H. A. Farnsworth. Words by M. Ford. HC

"The stars are burning cheerily, cheerily." See Turn ye to me

"The stars are fading from the sky." See Clear the way

"The stars are fading one by one." T. Marzials. FSS 8—LA

"Stars are fewer in all the sky." See Sea of stars

"The stars are shining bright and clear." Christmas carol. E. W. Bullinger. HC

"The stars are shining bright and clear." Christmas carol. E. Bunnett. HC

"The stars are shining cheerily, cheerily." See Turn ye to me

"The stars brightly glancing." See Wake, freshman, wake

"Stars ethereal" ("Klare sternelein") B. Kalinnikoff. Words from the Russian of K. Fofanoff. e.g. NM 1

"Stars faintly gleaming, restful delight." See "Pâles étoiles" (Joncières)

"The stars in beauty shine." See Night (Guglielmo)

Stars in the elements. Negro song. HR

"Stars of radiant night." N. Tcherepnin. Words from the Russian of K. Fofanoff. e. NM 2

"Stars of the summer night" (Serenade) Balfe. Words by H. W. Longfellow. DM 2

"Stars of the summer night." A. H. Pease. Words by H. W. Longfellow. JO

"Stars of the summer night." I. B. Woodbury. Words by H. W. Longfellow. HSD—JS—JSE—LA—LBR—OH—TFC 1—WBT—WL

"Stars of the summer night" (Serenade) CHS— CU— HSC— MP— MPC—NMH—NML—WC

"Stars trembling o'er us." Words by D. M. Muloch. FSS 2—WBT

"Stars with golden feet are wandering." See "Sterne mit den goldnen füsschen" (Graben-Hoffmann)

"Stasera, Nina mia, io son montato." See Funiculì-funiculà (Denza)

"Stately, rolling, moves mother Volga." See Mother Volga

"The stately ships along the quay." See Les berceaux (Fauré)

The Stately Southerner. Forecastle song. CR

"Stately stept he east the wa'." See Hardyknute

"Stately wood, how didst thou spring." See Der jäger abschied (Mendelssohn)

Statt' attiente (Bada bene.—Oh, be careful) Neapolitan song. e.i. FE

"Statt up, statt up, sjaa atende." See Huldre-kvae

Stauffer, Theodore
My Rosy

"Staunch and gray thou stand'st before us." See Alma mater—Swarthmore

"Stay in de field." Negro song. HR

"Stay, my charmer, can you leave me." Air: An gille dubh ciar dubh, or, The black-haired lad. Words by R. Burns, BSB—BSR

Stay, my darling, stay. See Bleib bei mir (Reichardt)

Stay not, delay not. Ruthenian folk air. Words by R. R. Whitehead. WF

Stay! oh stay. A. Warlamoff. e. KSN—WL

"Stay, stay at home, my heart, and rest." See To stay at home is best (Cate)

"Stay, sweet enchanter of the grove." See Julia to the wood-robin (Spofforth)

Stcherbine, N. See Shcherbin, N.

Steadfast love. See Obstination (Fontenailles)

Steadman, C. M.
At evening-time (Sporle)

Steal away to Jesus. Negro spiritual. HR—JB

Steal away. BSE—DF—FSS 2—JP—JSE—NMP—TFC 1—WBT—WC

Stealin' partners. See 'Liza-Jane

Steaua (The star) Rumanian song. e.ru. BF 2

Stebbins, George Coles
Evening prayer
"In the secret of His presence how my soul delights to hide"

Das steckenpferd ("Hopp, hopp, hopp") C. G. Hering. Words by C. Hahn. g. ED 1
The hobby horse. e. FSS 1—WBT—WSC

Stedman, Edmund Clarence
"Thou art mine, thou art mine" (Baltzell)

Steel, Mark
Tally-ho! hark away (Traditional air)

"Steel-rimm'd boot-heels strike out fire." See Oberek

Steele, Anne
"Deep are the wounds" (Taylor)
"Lord, in Thy great, Thy glorious name" (Schumann)
"Oh, could our thoughts" (German air)

Steele, S. S.
The rose of Alabama (Composer unknown)
Tom-big-bee river (Composer unknown)

Steffani, Agostino
"Not thy beauty." See "Sei sì caro"
"Sei sì caro" (from Marco Aurelio)

Steffe, William
Battle hymn of the republic (same air as "John Brown's body": plantation air arranged)
"John Brown's body": plantation air arranged

Steggall, Charles
"Like silver lamps"
The manger throne. See "Like silver lamps"
New Prince, new pomp
The Virgin and Child

"Steh' ich im feld." See Musketierlied (Silcher)

"Steh' ich in finstrer mitternacht" (Treue liebe) Volksweise: Ich hab ein kleines hüttchen nur. Words by W. Hauff. g. ED 1
Treue liebe (True love) e.g. SSG
"When through the night my watch I keep." e. WL

"Steh' ich in finstrer mitternacht" (Soldatenliebe.—Soldier's love)   J. Wurda. ΓWords by W. Hauff]   e.g.   AB 3
"Steh nur auf, steh nur auf."   See Der schweizerbu
"Stehe fest, o vaterland."   See Deutsche mahnung (Methfessel)
Das Steierland ("Hoch vom dachstein an")   C. Seidel.   Words after J. Dirnböck.   g.   ED 1
"Hoch vom dachstein" ("From the mountain's height")   e.g.   BO
Das Steierland (The Styrian land)   e.g.   FSS 2
Das Steierland (Styrian song)   e.g. SSG
Steifensandt, Wilhelm
"Wie ist doch die erde so schön"
Steiger, Edward
Frische brise (Stange)
Steigmeyer, F. Frank
John D. Rockefeller (University of Chicago song)
Stein, Evaleen
Vive Purdue (Arthur)
Stein, K.
Der talisman (Volksweise)
Stein, Theodore
Gone
A stein song.   F. F. Bullard.   Words by R. Hovey.   CU—WC
Steinhausen, Johann Friedrich Wilhelm
Frühlingsfeier (Dietrich)
"Stell' auf den tisch die duftenden resenden."   See Allerseelen (Strauss)
Una stella (My star)   L. Mililotti.   e.i. PG 3
Stella del marinar.   Ponchielli.   e.i. OPS 1
Stenhammar, P. U.
Cross and crown.   See Kors och krona
Kors och krona
Sten'ka Razin.   Russian folk song.   e.r. BF 1
Stennett, Samuel
"Majestic sweetness" (Hastings)
Stenvall, Aleksis
Vale of shadow (Sibelius)
Stephanos ("Art thou weary")   See "Art thou weary, art thou languid" (Baker)
Stephenson, Benjamin Charles
Let me dream again (Sullivan)
"She wandered down the mountain side" (Clay)
"Le steppe inondé de lumière."   See The convoy (Bleikhman)
Steps song.   Princeton university song.   E. Carter (music and words)   CHS
Sterkel, Johann Franz Xaver
Frühlingsempfindung
Der vogelsteller
Sternberg, Constantin Ivanovich, edler von
"Phoebus, arise"
Sterne, Colin, pseud.   See Nichol, Henry Ernest
Die sterne des lebens ("Liebe und leide")   K. F. Etzler (music and words)   g. ED 3

"Sterne mit den goldnen füsschen" ("Stars with golden feet are wandering")   Graben-Hoffmann.   Words by H. Heine.   e.g.   KF 2
"Die sterne sind erblichen."   See Morgenlied (Gersbach)
Stesk.   See All joy is gone
"Stets barg die liebe sie."   See "She never told her love" (Haydn)
Stevens, David

Composer
Politeness
Composer and author
"Don't worry"
Sing another song
Author
The Arkansaw traveler (Old air)
The Boy scouts (Suppé)
The climate (Old air)
The contented camel (Ames)
Don't fight your pack (Composer unknown)
Go to it (Engel)
"Joy and courage" (Costa)
Old Zip Coon (Old American air)
Roll away (Tracy)
Sailor's home song (Ames)
Tramp, tramp, tramp (Root)
The year of jubilo (Work)
Stevens, David K.
Queen of night (Meyer-Helmund)
Stevens, George Alexander
The storm (Old English air)
Stevens, Junius W.
Alma mater—Syracuse (Old air)
Stevens, Richard John Samuel
"Sigh no more, ladies"
Stevens, Walter
Emmanuel (Rodney)
Stevenson, Sir John Andrew
"Believe me if all those endearing young charms": Irish air arranged
"Has sorrow thy young days shaded": Irish air arranged
I'll weep with thee.   See "Has sorrow thy young days shaded": Irish air arranged
"Oft in the stilly night" (attributed)
Tell me where is fancy bred
"This is the feast-day of our King"
Stevenson, R. T.
Alma mater—Ohio Wesleyan (Composer unknown)
Stevenson, Robert Louis
"A mile an' a bittock" (Barratt)
Over the sea to Skye (Composer unknown)
Requiem (Homer)
"The stormy evening" (Chadwick)
"Stevo in de l'orta a rancurar fenoci'."   See Villotta
Stewart, Alexander
Mairi bhòidheach (Hebridean air)
Stewart, James E.
Angel Gabriel
Stewart, W. J.
True hearts (Maybrick)

Steyrers heimweh ("Woni geh' und steh'")
Volkslied. g. ED 3

Stick to your mother, Tom. See Don't
leave your mother, Tom (Symons)

Stieler, C.
Vale carissima (Wallnöfer)

Stier, W. C.
In front of old Pardee

Stikh nishchikh. See The beggar's blessing

"**Still** as the night." See "Still wie die
nacht, tief wie das meer, soll deine liebe
sein" (Bohm)

"**Still,** how still the midnight's gloom."
See Strampelchen (Hildach)

"**Still** I see thee stand before me." See
The little ring (Chopin)

"**Still** is the moonlight, while silent I wander." See By the sea shore (Gade)

"**Still** is the night, low thro' the pine-tree."
See The guardian angel (Gounod)

"**Still** is the night o'er roof-tree and steeple."
See Der doppelgänger (Schubert)

"**Still** is the night, still is the night." F.
Abt. Words by C. J. Rowe. CB

"**Still** is the night, the streets are deserted."
See Der doppelgänger (Schubert)

"**Still** ist die nacht, es ruhen die gassen."
See Der doppelgänger (Schubert)

"**Still** ruht der see" ("Calm is the lake")
H. Pfeil (music and words) e.g.
AB 3

"**Still** so gently o'er me stealing." See
"Ah! perchè non posso odiarti" (Bellini)

"**Still,** still with Thee" (Marlborough)
Composer unknown. Words by H. B.
Stowe. CST—LA

"**Still,** still with Thee" (Windsor) J. Barnby. Words by H. B. Stowe. TL

"**Still,** still with Thee" (Dawning) R. G.
Clements. Words by H. B. Stowe.
FSS 1

"**Still,** still with Thee" (Consolation) F.
Mendelssohn. Words by H. B. Stowe.
BD

"**Still** Susanna delays." See "E Susanna
non vien" (Mozart)

"**Still** the lark finds repose." T. Linley.
Words by M. Lonsdale. DM 2—ME

"**Still** upon the field of battle." See Just
after the battle (Root)

"**Still** wie die nacht, tief wie das meer, o
mensch, muss deine liebe sein" ("Calm
as the night") C. Götze. e.g. FMB

"**Still** wie die nacht, tief wie das meer, soll
deine liebe sein" ("Calm as the
night") C. Bohm. e.g. FMB
"Still as the night." e. WA—WBT
—WL
"Still wie die nacht" ("Silent as night")
e.g. KF 1—KF 2—KF 3

"**Still,** wie still! 's ist mitternacht schon."
See Strampelchen (Hildach)

"**Stilla** skuggor breda sig i kvällen." See
Kväll och frid (Geijer)

Stille klage ("Ich wäre wohl fröhlich so
gerne") Volksweise. Words by F.
W. A. Schmidt. g. ED 2

Stille liebe ("Könnt' ich dich in liedern
preisen."—Silent love) R. Schumann.
Words by J. Kerner. e.g. FM

Stille liebe ("Treu geliebt und still geschwiegen") P. J. von Lindpaintner.
Words by J. F. Zehelein. g. ED 2

"**Stille** nacht." See Die heilige nacht
(Gruber)

"Der **stille** schlaf, der sonst stillt alles
wohl." See Sehnsucht (Regnart)

Stille sicherheit ("Hark! how still") R.
Franz. Words by N. Lenau. e.g.
FM

"**Stilled** my broken violin." See Broken
is my violin (Danko)

Stilling the tempest. M. Watson. Words
by F. Hemans. HSS 2

Stillness of night. J. Beach. Words by
A. Peet. BSS

"**Stimmt** an mit hellem hohem klang." See
Deutsches weihelied (Methfessel)

Stirling, Elizabeth
All among the barley
"Good news" (same air as All among
the barley)

**Stirling-Maxwell, Caroline Elizabeth Sarah
(Sheridan) Norton, lady.** See Norton,
Mrs Caroline Elizabeth Sarah (Sher-
idan)

The **stirrup** cup. L. Arditi. Words by
H. B. Farnie. BAS 2

Stites, E. P.
Beulah land (Sweney) Authorship
uncertain

"**Stizzoso,** mio stizzoso" ("Unruly, sir, unruly") G. B. Pergolesi. e.i. PA 1

"**Sto** crescenno no bello cardillo." See Lu
cardillo (Labriola)

"**Što** nisam davno." See Tik, tak, tak

Stockmann, A. C.
"Wie sie so sanft ruhn" (Beneken)

Stoddard, Richard Henry
Under the trees (Munjinger)

"Der **stode** tre skalke og taenkte paa et
raad." See De tre skalke

"**Stoïť** gora visokaĩa." See A high mountain stands

Stolberg, Friedrich Leopold, graf zu
Auf dem wasser zu singen (Schubert)
Daphne am bach (music by Reichardt;
Zumsteeg)
Schutz (Bergt)
Der schwäbische ritter an seinen sohn
(Volksweise)
Selige erinnerung (Schulz)
"Süsse, heilige natur" (André)
Weihnachtslied (Reichardt)

"**Stole** he beneath the window." Moravian
song. e. KSE

Stone, Samuel John
"The church's one foundation" (Wes-
ley)
"Weary of earth" (music by Langran;
Coward)

"The **stones** that built George Ridler's ov-
en." See George Ridler's oven

Stonewall Jackson's requiem. M. Deeves.
WBT

Stonewall's requiem. HSD

Stop that knocking at the door. Negro song. NMP

Storace, Stephen
"All will hail the joyous day" (from The siege of Belgrade)
"Behold I am a village lass" (from The three and the deuce)
"From aloft the sailor looks around" (from No song, no supper)
Lullaby. See "Peaceful slumb'ring on the ocean"
"Our country is our ship" (from The Cherokee)
"Peaceful slumb'ring on the ocean" (from The pirates)
"The sapling oak"
The shepherd and the little bird (from The Cherokee)
"The summer heats bestowing"
Welcome Christmas cheer
Well-a-day! lack-a-day (from My grandmother)
"With lowly suit and plaintive ditty" (from No song, no supper)

Storm, Edvard
"Hr. Sinklar" (Norse folk air)
Hjemreise fra saetren (Norse folk air)
"Markje grönast" (Norse folk air)

The storm ("Cease, rude Boreas, blust'ring railer") Old English air: Come and listen to my ditty, or, Welcome, brother debtor. Words by G. A. Stevens. BE 4—DM 1—HSE 2—JO
The storm ("It rains, it rains") See L'orage
The storm ("The tempest rages") J. Hullah. Words by A. Procter. CS 1—DM 2—FSS 5—LA
Storm-along. Pumping chantey. KB
For variants of this song see Old Stormey; Stormalong; Stormalong John; Stormy
"Storm, hvem gav dig din aande." See Laengsel (Backer-Lunde)
"The storm is wildly beating." See Fleur jetée (Fauré)
"The storm on the housetop in fury downpours." See Die junge nonne (Schubert)
The storm song. Arr from C. W. Gluck. Words by B. Taylor. LBR
"The storm through the forest is roaring amain." See Die junge nonne (Schubert)
"Storm-wind, blow thou." See The lover's lament
Stormalong. Capstan chantey. CR
For variants of this song see following songs of similar title; also Old Stormey; Storm-along
Stormalong John. Capstan chantey. SE
Stormy. Chantey. SMW
"The stormy evening." G. W. Chadwick. Words by R. L. Stevenson. TL
The stormy petrel. Neukomm. Words by B. W. Procter. JO
The stormy winds do blow. See The mermaid

"Stormy winds the trees are shaking." See The winds blow
"Stormy's gone, that good old man." See Storm-along
Stornelli. Italian song. e.i. BF 2
"A story, a story, I'll tell you just now." See Colly, my cow
The story of a star. W. Ganz. MCS
The story of poor Lazarus (O dvukh Lazariakh) Russian folk song. e. SSR 2
Story of the nightingale. See The nightingale (Molloy)
The story of the shepherd. J. Barnby. Words from the Spanish of Gongora. e. BSC—FSS 7—HC—MCS
"A story to you I will relate." See Sweet lovely Joan
"Stosst an! (Jena) soll leben." A. von Binzer (music and words) g. ED 1
Stowe, Mrs Harriet Elizabeth (Beecher)
"Still, still with Thee" (music by Barnby; Clements; Mendelssohn; also unknown composer)
Summer studies (Hutchinson)
Stowell, Hugh
Retreat (Hastings)
Strachwitz, Moritz, graf von
Wie schön bist du (Weidt)
Stradella, Alessandro
"Col mio sangue comprerei" (from Il Floridoro)
"Così, amor, mi fai languir"
"How dearly are prized." See "Ragion sempre addita"
"I languish, love, thy weary slave." See "Così, amor, mi fai languir"
"I would spend my blood unheeding." See "Col mio sangue comprerei"
"If love my feet enchaineth." See Se amor m'annoda il piede
"O have pity." See "Per pietà"
"O Lord, have pity." See "Pietà, Signore" (attributed)
"Per pietà"
"Pietà, Signore" (attributed)
"Pity, O Saviour." See "Pietà, Signore" (attributed)
"Ragion sempre addita"
Se amor m'annoda il piède
"The soul taught by duty." See "Ragion sempre addita"
"Straightway I come from the tavern." Bohemian song. W. H. Veit. e. KSE
Strakerjan, Christian Friedrich
"Setzt euch, brüder, in die runde" (Studentenlied)
Strambotto ("As I wandered") Italian song. e.i. BF 2
Strampelchen (Little fidget) Cradle-song. E. Hildach. Words by V. Blüthgen. e.g. MSF 2
Strandberg, Karl Vilhelm August
"Ur svenska hjertans" (Lindblad)
"Strange, how you talk so fast." See Ritornelli romaneschi
The stranger star. See "Saw ye never in the twilight"

"**Strangers** yet." C. Barnard (Claribel) FSS 4—WBT

Straube, Karl
"Das leben welkt wie gras" (Greene)

Straus, Oscar
Love's the tune (from Waltz dream)

Strauss, Johann
"The golden sun sinks in the west"
Love and mirth
Song of rest
The wild rose

Strauss, Richard
"Ach lieb, ich muss nun scheiden"
"All' mein gedanken, mein herz und mein sinn"
"All of the thoughts in my heart and my mind." See "All' mein gedanken, mein herz und mein sinn"
All souls' day. See Allerseelen
Allerseelen
"Breit über mein haupt dein schwarzes haar"
"Dear love, I now must leave thee." See "Ach lieb, ich muss nun scheiden"
Devotion. See Zueignung
"Du meines herzens krönelein"
"E'er since thine eyes returned my glances." See "Seitdem dein aug' in meines schaute"
Heimkehr
Homeward. See Heimkehr
Die nacht
Night. See Die nacht
"Seitdem dein aug' in meines schaute"
Serenade. See Ständchen
Ständchen
"Thou of my heart the diadem." See "Du meines herzens krönelein"
"Thy wonderful eyes my heart inspire." See "Breit über mein haupt dein schwarzes haar"
"Why should we keep our love a secret." See "Wie sollten wir geheim sie halten"
"Wie sollten wir geheim sie halten"
Zueignung

Stravinskiĭ, Igor Fedorovich
The cloister
La novice. See The cloister

The **straw-cutter's** daughter. See La fille du coupeur de paille

"The **strawberries** grow in the mowing." See Mill May

Strawberry fair. English folk song. BSW

The **strawberry** girl ("Oh is it not") Old English song. DO

The **strawberry** girl ("The sun was clear") A. Sullivan. FSS 5

Streabbog, L.
"Derrière chez mon père, vole, mon coeur, vole" (same air as "Vive la Canadienne")
Fly, my heart, fly thither. See "Derrière chez mon père, vole, mon coeur, vole"
"Long live Canadian lasses." See "Vive la Canadienne"
"Long live Canadian maidens." See "Vive la Canadienne"
The prince's three daughters. See "Derrière chez mon père, vole, mon coeur, vole"
Les trois filles d'un prince. See "Derrière chez mon père, vole, mon coeur, vole"
"Vive la Canadienne"
Vole, mon coeur, vole. See "Derrière chez mon père, vole, mon coeur, vole"

The **streams** of Nantsian. English folk song. BSW

Strebel, Valentine
"Über reisen kein vergnügen"

Street, Apsley
Gone where the woodbine twineth

The **street** called Dove street. See La calle de la paloma

Streeter, R. M.
Song of the maple (Fitzgerald)

Strehlenau, Nicolaus Franz Niembsch, edler von. See Lenau, Nicolaus

Strelezki, Anton
Dreams

Strephon of the hill. T. A. Arne. MM

"**Strew** the fair garlands." L. B. Marshall. Words by S. F. Smith. JS

"The **stricken** one may find a friend." See Heart-ache for home

"**Stride** la vampa" ("Fierce now the flames glow") Verdi. e.i. OPS 2

"The **strife** and the warfare is ended." See Dulce patria (Carnicer y Batlle)

The **strife** is o'er: the battle done. Arr from Palestrina. [Tr of Finita jam sunt praelia] e. TFC 2

"**Strike**, strike the harp." Air: Mwynen gwynedd. Words by Ieuan Dhu. MMW

"**Strike** the cymbal." Pucitta. FSS 3

"**Strike** the gay harp, see the moon is on high." See The night-dance

"**Strike** the harp, awake the lay." See The Eisteddfod

"**Strike** the harp gently." I. B. Woodbury. FSS 8—HSD—WBT

"**Strike** the viol." H. Purcell. MM

"**Strike** up, ye lusty gallants." Irish folk song. JOI

Strilevise (The fisherman's song) Norse folk song. e.n. MAN

Stringer, Arthur
The blatherskite (Irish air)
The time for love (Irish air)
"We're wearin' av the green" (Irish air)

"A **striped** apron they shall make." See "Ti faccio far'n' zinale"

The **strolling** fiddler ("Up and down the country side") Air: Cymro o b'le, or, A Welshman—whence. Words by D. Rowlands (Dewi Mon) MMW

Strong, Frank
Oh, Oregon! oh, Oregon

Strong, Thomas B.
"In the bleak midwinter"

Strozzi, Barbara
Amor dormiglione
Love sleeping. See Amor dormiglione
Stryker, Melancthon Woolsey
A song of the flag (Composer unknown)
'Stu mo run. See Joy of my heart
The Stuarts of Appin ("I sing of a land")
J. Wilson. Words by Hogg. PS 2
Stubbs, Charles William
Bethlehem land (Noble)
"Christ was born on Christmas night" (music by Noble; Wardle)
The Cornish bells (Noble)
Gloria in excelsis (Noble)
"On yesternight I saw a sight, a star as bright as day, and heard among the heav'ns a song" (Noble)
The quest of the three kings (Noble)
The shepherds' song (Noble)
"'Twas jolly, jolly Wat" (Noble)
Stuckenberg, Viggo
Finnland (Jordan)
The student and his bow-wow. J. Tabrar. Words by J. M. Bulloch. SSS
Student delight. See Burschenlust
The student song ("Hail to thee") W. H. Maxfield. Words by R. L. Bremner. SSS
Student-song ("Sjung om studentens") See Stundentsång (Gustaf)
Studentenleben ("'s gibt kein schöner leben") C. G. Reissiger. Author of words unknown. g. ED 1
Students' way (It's a way we have at school) Old air. Words by E. R. Sill. LA
Studentsång (Student-song) Prince Gustaf, duke of Upland. Words by H. Sätherberg. e.sw. HSOS
"Studia il passo, o mio figlio." See Come dal ciel precipita (Verdi)
Study, little ones. See "At the cosy hearth"
The study of woman. F. Lehar. e. WBT
Sturgis, Julian Russell
My heart is weary (Thomas)
Sturm, Christoph Christian
Frühlingsanfang (Mozart)
Sturm, Julius
"Gott grüsse dich" (Erk)
Sturm, Marcellin
Der himmel hängt voll geigen (Himmel)
Styépyu idoo ya ōōnúiloyu. See Over the steppe (Grechaninov)
Style all the while. Student song. BSS
The Styrian land. See Das Steierland (Seidel)
Styrian song. See Das Steierland (Seidel)
"Su l'odorante margine del rio cogliesti un fior." See Das vergissmeinnicht (Suppé)
Su, venite a consiglio (Hey! come hither, ye fancies) A. Scarlatti. e.i. PA 2
Suabian's song of home. See Unterländers heimweh

Suantraidhe. For English translation see Lullaby ("Hush, baby mine, and weep no more")
"Sublime cor! nobile spirto." See Forma sublime, eterea (Gomes)
"Sublime was the warning which liberty spoke." Air: The black joke. Words by T. Moore. MI
"Subtle love, with fancy viewing." G. F. Händel. SAS 1
Such a li'l' fellow. W. Dichmont. Words by F. Lowell. GMF
Sucking cider through a straw. College song. CHS
Suckling, Sir John
"Honest lover" (Arne)
"I prithee, send me back my heart" (music by Lawes; Miller)
A song of a wedding (17th century air)
"Why so pale and wan, fond lover" (Arne)
"Suena en la huerta dormida." See Así canto mis amores (Pericás)
The Suffolk miracle. Folk song: Allanstand, N.C. version. CSE
—Big Laurel, N.C. version. CSE
—Tennessee version. CSE
El sufrimiento. Mexican folk song. e.s. HS
"Sul mare luccica l'astro d'argento." See Santa Lucia
"Sul mare torbido" ("Out on the stormy sea") e.i. BF 2
Suleika. Mendelssohn. Words by Goethe. e.g. CS 2
Suleika (Zuleika) e.g. KF 1
"Sulle, sulle labbra." See Il bacio (Arditi)
Sullivan, Sir Arthur Seymour
"All this night bright angels sing"
"Angel voices"
At honor's glorious call. See "Oh, give me but my Arab steed"
"Birds in the night"
Calm was the night
Carol for Christmas day. See "All this night bright angels sing"
The chorister
"Christ is risen! Christ is risen! He hath burst His bonds in twain"
Christmas carol. See "All this night bright angels sing"
Christus victor. See "Onward, Christian soldiers"
"Come, ye children, and hearken unto me" (from The prodigal son)
"Come, ye faithful, raise the strain" (Tr of Asōmen pantes laoi)
"Daughters of Jerusalem" (from The light of the world)
The distant shore
"Draw Thou my soul, O Christ"
"Farewell, my own" (from H. M. S. Pinafore)
"The flowers that bloom in the spring" (from The mikado)
"Forward through the ages" (same air as "Onward, Christian soldiers")
Golden days

Sullivan, Sir Arthur Seymour—*Continued*
"Golden harps are sounding"
Heaven is my home
"Henceforth, Strephon" (from Io-
   lanthe)
"The homeland! O the homeland"
"How many hired servants" (from The
   prodigal son)
"I am a ruler on the sea" (from Kenil-
   worth)
"I have a song to sing"
"I hear the soft note" (from Patience)
"I will arise" (from The prodigal son)
"I would I were a king"
"If doughty deeds my lady please"
"I'm called little Buttercup" (from H.
   M. S. Pinafore)
Law and order (from Iolanthe)
"Lead, kindly light"
Let me dream again
A life that lives for you
Looking back
"The Lord is risen, He will dwell with
   men" (from The light of the world)
"Lord, why hidest Thou Thy face"
   (from The light of the world)
The lost chord
"Love not the world" (from The prod-
   igal son)
Lullaby. See "Birds in the night"
"Lullaby, baby"
My love beyond the sea
"My Redeemer and my Lord" (from
   The golden legend)
"Nearer, my God, to Thee"
The nice young girl (from Patience)
The nice young man (from Patience)
"No chastening for the present seemeth
   to be joyous" (from The prodigal
   son)
"Oh, give me but my Arab steed"
"O hush thee, my babie" (Tr of Caidil
   gu lo)
"O mistress mine"
"O that thou had'st hearkened" (from
   The prodigal son)
An odd old man (same air as The nice
   young man)
Once again ("I linger round")
"Once again, O blessed time"
"Onward, Christian soldiers"
"Orpheus with his lute"
"Over the bright blue sea" (from H.
   M. S. Pinafore)
Poetry
"Refrain thy voice from weeping" (from
   The light of the world)
St Edmund. See "Draw Thou my
   soul, O Christ"
St Gertrude. See "Onward, Christian
   soldiers"
A shadow
"Sigh no more, ladies"
"Sorry her lot" (from H. M. S. Pina-
   fore)

Spring-time once again
The strawberry girl
Sweet harps, resound again
Tit willow (from The mikado)
"Upon the snow-clad earth without"
"A wandering minstrel" (from The
   mikado)
"We sing a song of Christmas-time"
"A weary lot is thine, fair maid"
"When the Son of man" (from The
   light of the world)
"Where have they laid Him" (from The
   light of the world)
"Where is another sweet"
"Where the bee sucks"
Will he come
The willow song

Sullivan, M. Dix
The field of Monterey

Sullivan, Mrs Marion D.
The blue Juniata
"Oh, boatman, row me o'er"

Sully-Prudhomme, René François Armand
Les berceaux (Fauré)
Soupir (music by Duparc; Kramer)

"The **sultan's** barb'rous horde." See
   Promesse de mon avenir (Massenet)
"The **sultan's** troops so proud." See Pro-
   messe de mon avenir (Massenet)
"**Sumer** is icumen in" ("Summer is a-com-
   ing in") Attributed to John of Forn-
   sete. BOH—CO 1—DM 1—JE—PR 1
Summ' und brumm', du gutes radchen.
   For English translation see Spinning
   chorus (Wagner)
Summer ("Summer suns") See "Summer
   suns are glowing" (Marshall)
"**Summer** bird! swiftly roving." See "Ô
   légère hirondelle" (Gounod)
"The **summer** days are come again." Tra-
   ditional air. Words by S. Longfellow.
   HC
"The **summer** days are coming." Words
   by C. Jefferys. WBT
"**Summer** days once more are coming."
   Mozart. Words from the German. e.
   HC
Summer dreams. See Feldeinsamkeit
   (Brahms)
Summer eve ("Öfver skogen") See En
   sommarafton (Lindblad)
"**Summer** eve is gone and past." See The
   minstrel's request
Summer even-song ("The peaceful day")
   W. H. Jones. NMS
A **summer** evening in Norway. See Am
   schönsten sommerabend war's (Grieg)
"The **summer** heats bestowing." S. Sto-
   race. NG
"**Summer** is a-coming in." See "Sumer
   is icumen in" (John of Fornsete?)
"The **summer** is come and the grass is
   green." Irish folk song. JOI
Summer is coming ("Bees are all hum-
   ming") T. S. Cooke. FSS 3—JSE

Summer is coming ("No more frosts and no more snows") A. S. Gatty. WSC

"The **summer** is coming, let joy and mirth go hand in hand." See The spirit of May

A **summer** love dream ("I dream of you in the flowering time") Irish air: The little red lark. Words by M. Hogan (The Bard of Thomond) MMI

A **summer** night. See Une nuit de mai (Thomas)

Summer parting hymn ("Now one last song") C. B. Adams. Words by S. Longfellow. NMS

Summer song ("A-ja. A-ja-ja") Eskimo Indian song. es. SN

Summer song ("Tra, ri, ra all hail the summer months") FSS 7

Summer studies. W. M. Hutchinson. Words by H. B. Stowe. LBR

"**Summer** suns are glowing" (Summer) L. B. Marshall. Words by W. W. How. JS

"**Summer** suns are glowing" (Ruth) S. Smith. Words by W. W. How. CST

Summer suns glowing. FSS 7

The **summers** come and go. J. A. P. Schulz. Words by B. Taylor. LBR

Summer-time ("I love the cheerful summer-time") C. Gluck. JSE

Summertime ("Wohl dir, liebe sommerzeit") See Sommerlied (Neidhardt von Reuenthal)

"**Sun** bright in heav'n, be father mine." See The orphan

"The **sun** descends into the sea." See Alinde (Schubert)

Sun don't set in de mornin'. Negro spiritual. DF—HR

"The **sun** from the east." 18th century hunting song. MM

"The **sun** goes down." See Rest

"The **sun** had loosed." Old English air. Words after T. D'Urfey. BE 8

"The **sun** had set behind the hill." See The farmer's boy

"The **sun** had sunk behind the hill." See The farmer's boy

"The **sun** hangs high" (Charki hidjaz) Turkish folk song. e.t. BO—SMF

"The **sun** has gane down o'er the lofty Ben Lomond." See Jessie, the flower o' Dumblane (Smith)

"The **sun** he is sunk in the west." Air: Go from my window, love, do. Words by R. Burns. BSR

"The **sun** his parting ray had cast." See chimes of Zurich (Horn)

"The **sun** in the sky sinking down to his rest." See Sunset in the city

"The **sun** is bright." Weber. Words by H. W. Longfellow. LA

"The **sun** is gone behind the hill." See My boat is waiting here for thee (Smart)

The **sun** is low ("The sun upon the lake is low") Swiss air. Words by W. Scott. FSS 7

The **sun** is low ("When the day's shadows die."—"Sontse nizen'ko") Ukrainian folk song. e.r. BF 1

"The **sun** is o'er the mountain." See The sun o'er the mountain (Bishop)

"The **sun** is on the mountain." See The breaking of the day (Horn)

"The **sun** is rising o'er the ocean." See Welcome to morning (Offenbach)

"The **sun** is set, and the gold is gone." See Evening on the lake (Putnam)

"The **sun** is setting and the hour is late." See Let me dream again (Sullivan)

"The **sun** is shining upon the headlands." See Skördemannen (Fogelberg)

"The **sun** is up, the day is fair." See A-scouting

The **sun** o'er the mountain. H. R. Bishop. FSS 6

"The **sun** is o'er the mountain." HSE 2

"The **sun** o'er the wide steppe is sinking." See The convoy (Bleikhman)

Sun of Christmas-tide. H. Weidt. Words by Nochtenhofer. e. MCS

"The **sun** of earth is glowing." See 'Tis Easter time (Marshall)

"**Sun** of my soul, Thou Saviour dear." A. R. Gaul. [Words by J. Keble] SAS 1

"**Sun** of my soul, Thou Saviour dear." W. H. Monk. Words by J. Keble. HSD— MCS— WA— WBT— WS —WSC—WSW

"**Sun** of my soul" (Evening hymn) FSS 1

"**Sun** of my soul" (Hursley) BD—LA

"The **sun** rises bright in France." Scottish song. PS 2

"The **sun** rose sae rosy." See Jeanie's black een

The **sun** runs its course ("Saulit' tezej' tezedama") Latvian folk song. e.le. BF 1

"The **sun** sets at night." See The Indian's death song

"The **sun** sets brightly in the sea." See Carol for Christmas eve

"The **sun** shines bright in the old Kentucky home." See My old Kentucky home (Foster)

"The **sun** smiles in beauty." Welsh air: The ash grove. LA

"The **sun** that sets in yonder west." Air: Castell Nêdd. MMW

"The **sun** upon the lake is low." See The sun is low

"The **sun** was clear on the open lea." See The strawberry girl (Sullivan)

"The **sun** was fair and the clouds advanced." See The isle of France

"The **sun** was setting and vespers done." See Thursday (Molloy)

"The **sun** was sinking in the west." See The dying ranger

"The **sun** with his great eye." See Daisy's song

The **sun** worshippers. Zuni Indian song. e.in. TFC 1

"**Sunce** jarko." See "O bright sun"

"**Sunce** žarko." See "O bright sun"

Sunday ("Die nacht war kaum verblühet") See Sonntag (Franz)

Sunday ("So hab' ich die ganze") See Sonntag (Brahms)

Sunday morning. F. Abt. WBT

The **Sunday-school** scholar. Student song. CHS—MPC—WBT—WC

Sunday song ("Oh, Sunday has come") WSC

Sunderland, Charles H.
"The Christmas bells are ringing"
"The Christmas comes let praise abound"
"Shades of silent night"

Sunlight. See Sol (Alnaes)

The **sunniest** season of life. Aberdeen university song. J. Kirby. Words by J. M. Bulloch. SSS

A **sunny** day. See En solskins dag (Nordraak)

"The **sunny** hills of Africa." See South African national song

Sunny Manoa. C. K. Hopkins. Words by E. Holt. e.h. HA

Sunrise. See God morgen (Grieg)

"The **sun's** last ray is gone." See Love's sorrow (Shelley)

Sunset ("Naar solen falder") See Solefaldssang (Olsen)

Sunset ("Night is falling") Hungarian folk air. Words by J. Russell. WF

"**Sunset** and evening star." See Crossing the bar (Barnby); Crossing the bar (Huss)

"The **sunset** gates were open'd wide." See Lights far out at sea (Scott-Gatty)

Sunset in the city. English folk air. Words by R. Compton. DO

"**Sunset** o'er the sea is gleaming." See Dein gedenk' ich, Margareta (Meyer-Helmund)

Sunset song. See An die abendsonne (Nägeli)

"**Sunshine** and cloud." C. W. Glover. Words by J. E. Carpenter. FSS 5— JSE

Sunshine and rain. J. Blumenthal. Words by F. W. Home. MSF 1— SM 3

The **sunshine** boomerang. D. Harvey. Words by J. Crawford. BSS

"The **sunshine** glows on the lofty hills." See The huntsman's chorus (Weber)

Sunshine song ("Kanske vil der gå bŭde") See Solvejgs sang (Grieg)

Sunshine song ("Zie hoe het vriendlijke zonlicht") See Zonnelied (Rennes)

"**Sunshine's** warmer, flow'rs are in the meads appearing." See The messenger (Chopin)

Suomen laulu. See Suomi's song (Pacius)

Suomen salossa. See Finland's forest

Suomi's song (Suomen laulu) J. Pacius. e.fi. BF 1

"Il **suon** dell' arpa angeliche" ("The sound of harps") ₁G. Donizetti₁ e.i. FSS 4

Suoni la tromba. For English translation see "Sound ye the trumpet" (Bellini)

Suppé, Franz von
The Boy scouts
Cooper's song (from Boccaccio)
The forget-me-not. See Das vergissmeinnicht
"Let no one be proud of his luck or his gold"
My native land
Oh! thou my Austria
Das vergissmeinnicht

Supriani, Francesco
"Bid yonder rushing river." See "Potrà lasciare il rio" (attributed)
"Potrà lasciare il rio" (attributed)

"**Sur** la mer un beau vaisseau." See Le beau vaisseau

"**Sur** la promontoire." See Menaeceus (Cherepnin)

"**Sur** le pont d'Avignon" ("On the bridge of Avignon") Old French rondo. e.f. BO

Le pont d'Avignon. f. DO—FMB

Sur le pont d'Avignon ("Upon the bridge at Avignon") Canadian version. e.f. TF

Sur les collines de Géorgie. See On the Georgian hills (Rimskiĭ-Korsakov)

"**Sur** nos chemins les rameaux et les fleurs." See Les rameaux (Faure)

"**Sur** un lys pâle mon coeur dort." See Extase (Duparc)

Sur une tombe (On a tomb) G. Lekeu. e.f. SAM

The **sure** hope (Houis) Armenian song. Words by K. Katiba. a.e. BF 2

"**Sure,** Sally is the loveliest lass." See Sally (Arne)

"**Surely** you know, oh, mother." See "Voi lo sapete, o mamma" (Mascagni)

Surging waters (Wiliwili wai) C. K. Hopkins. e.h. HA

The **surprise** ("Careless of love") H. Lawes. Words by C. Raleigh. DM 1

"**Surprising!** surprising! his words are all rooted in my bosom." See "È strano! è strano! in core scolpiti ho quegli accenti" (Verdi)

"**Sus** le mar Cluro de Indèio." See Lou nouvè di pescaire

Susan Jane. W. S. Hays (music and words) NMP—WBT

"I went to see my Susie." Wesleyan university version. CHS

"**Suse,** lewe Suse, wat ruschelt in't stroh." See Wiegenlied

Suspicion. Lindblad. e. KSN

"**Suspiri** di lu me core" (Sighs from my heart) Sardinian folk song. e.i. BF 2

El **suspiro.** Mexican folk song. e.s. HS

"**Süsse,** heilige natur." J. André. Words by Friedrich Leopold graf zu Stolberg. g. ED 3

"Süsses liebchen! komm zu mir." See Liebeständelei (Fitzenhagen)

The Sussex mummers' carol. Christmas song. WCC

"Susy, little Susy." See Wiegenlied ("Suse, lewe Suse")

Sutcliffe, H. H.
Glad Christmas comes again

"A sutler's maids are fair and slim." See Le cotillon racheté

"Sutta li to' finestri sonu e cantu." See Ipiddinisca sutta li to' finestri

"Suttam sudelita luttam." See Kvaalins halling

Suwanee river. See Old folks at home (Foster)

Suzette. Negro creole folk song. e.f. BF 2

En svane (A swan) E. Grieg. Words by H. Ibsen. e.n. WM 1
A swan (Ein schwan) e.g. FF— FO 2—MS—PG 4

Svärmeri (Fond fancy) F. Arlberg. Words after H. Heine. [Tr of "Mit deinen blauen augen"] e.sw. HSOS

Svarta rosor (Black roses.—Tristi amori) H. Alfven. Words by E. Lundberg. e.sw. WM 1

"Svarta svanor" ("Black swans") I. Hallström. Words by C. Snoilsky. e.sw. WM 1

Sve veselo a ja tužan. See "White dawn has not come stealing"

Svendsen, Johan Severin
Violen
The violet. See Violen

"Sverige, frihets gamla fäste." See Hyllning till Sverige (Sandberg)

Svyétik Sávishna. See Love-song of the idiot (Musorgskiï)

Swabian dance-song. See "Dein herz und mein herz"

Swain, Charles
The bird of hope (Cole)
"Home's not merely four square walls" (Rossini)
"Tell me, oh, ye stars" (Hérold)

"A swain in despair." Frank. MM

The swallow ("Rondinella pellegrina") See La rondinella

The swallow ("Die schwälble ziehet fort") See Die schwälble (Brahms)

"The swallow leaves the young within her nest." See Home so blest (Abt)

The swallow, messenger of love. See L'hirondelle, messagère de l'amour

"The swallow says good-bye." See Die schwälble (Brahms)

The swallows ("The swallows fly in the sky") [Onfroy de Bréville] Words by H. H. Harbour. DO

The swallows ("Voltigez, hirondelles") See Les hirondelles (David)

"The swallows fly in the sky." See The swallows (Onfroy de Bréville)

The swallows' song. See "Aus der jugendzeit" (Radecke)

A swan ("Min hvide svane") See En svane (Grieg)

"The swan bent low to the lily." E. MacDowell (music and words) FTS

The swan maiden (Iz za líesu, líesu temnago) Russian folk song. e. SSR 3

Swanee river. See Old folks at home (Foster)

"Swannanoa town." Folk song from North Carolina. CSE

The swapping song. Kentucky mountain song. BF 2—WT
The foolish boy. CSE
Variant: Posey boy

"Sway to and from in the twilight gray." See A bed-time song (Nevin)

"Swear, Hungarian, by thy country." See Hungarian national song

"Sweden, freedom's ancient fastness." See Hyllning till Sverige (Sandberg)

Swedish cradle song. e. FSS 5—JSE
Cradle song. e. HSD

Swedish hymn ("Ur svenska hjertans") See "Ur svenska hjertans" (Lindblad)

Swedish national air ("Carl Johan") See "Carl Johan" (Du Puy)

Swedish national air ("Du gamla") See "Du gamla, du fria, du fjällhoga nord"

Swedish national hymn ("Ur svenska hjertans") See "Ur svenska hjertans" (Lindblad)

Swedish national song ("Carl Johan") See "Carl Johan" (Du Puy)

"Sweet, ah how sweet, the month of that May." See The month of May

Sweet Alice, Ben Bolt. See Ben Bolt

"Sweet alma home." See Heidelberg (Power)

"Sweet alma mater, as thou hast cherished me." See My Ottawa

"Sweet and clear the birds are singing." F. F. Bullard. HC

"Sweet and fair, a jasmin-flow'r." See Moo-lee-hwa

"Sweet and graceful." See Serenade

"Sweet and low." J. Barnby. Words by A. Tennyson. BD—CHS—FSS 2— HSC— HSD— JS— JSE— LA— MP— MPC— MS— NMH— NMS— OH— TFC 1—WA—WBT—WSC—WSW

"Sweet and low" (Cradle song) W. V. Wallace. Words by A. Tennyson. CS 2

"Sweet angel, still I wish thee well." See "Jag unnar dig ändå allt godt"

"Sweet angels, ever bright and fair." C. Simper. Words by T. D. Hyde. HC

"Sweet are the banks—the banks o' Doon." Air: Cambdelmore. Words by R. Burns. BSR

"Sweet are the charms of her I love." R. Leveridge. Words by B. Booth. BE 4—DM 2—MM

Sweet are thy waters. See Honeysuckles (Nape)

"Sweet babe, a golden cradle holds thee" (The fairies' lullaby) Irish song. e. MMI

"Sweet babe, a golden cradle holds thee" (Lullaby) Irish song. Another air. e. MMI
Ancient lullaby. e. BSE

Sweet bells are chiming. R. Genée. Words by E. M. Douglas. MCS

"Sweet bird, thy early note is gay." See The bluebird (Bériot)

"Sweet bird, whose heav'nly native strain." See To the nightingale (Worgan)

"The sweet birds are winging from arbor to spray." See The merry May

"Sweet breezes haunt yon mountain top." See Petites roses (Cesek)

The sweet by and by. J. P. Webster. Words by S. F. Bennett. FSS 5—HSD—JS
In the sweet by and by. HSC—NMH —NMS

Sweet Canaan. Negro spiritual. HR—JP

"Sweet Child divine." A. H. Brown. Words by J. Brett. HC

"Sweet Christmas month, the month that love was born." See When love was born (Wellings)

"The sweet church bells are pealing out." See The field of Monterey (Sullivan)

Sweet colleen rue. Irish folk song. JOI

"Sweet confessions of love." See Les premiers aveux (Dancla)

Sweet constancy ("Ua like no a like") Hawaiian song. e.h. HA

Sweet content. W. G. Smith. Words by T. Dekker. TL

Sweet Cootehill town. Irish folk song. JOI

"Sweet day is softly dying." Old French air. Words by F. Manley. BSS

"Sweet day, so cool." 17th century air. Words by G. Herbert. HSE 2

"Sweet dreamland faces." W. M. Hutchinson. WSC

"Sweet echoes, floating on the breeze." See Echoes (Loomis)

"Sweet Ellie Rhee, so dear to me." See Ellie Rhee (Winner)

"Sweet England's pride is gone." See Well-a-day

"Sweet England's prize is gone." See Well-a-day (Another air)

"Sweet Evangeline, my lost Evangeline." See Evangeline (Hays)

"Sweet evenings come and go." Words by G. Eliot. FSS 3

Sweet farewell. English folk song. BSW

"Sweet fa's the eve on Craigie-burn." See Craigie-burn wood

Sweet flow'rs, I'd be bringing. See Kalakaua's serenade (Hopkins)

Sweet Genevieve. H. Tucker. Words by G. Cooper. HSD—OH—TFC 2

Sweet good night. See Bonne nuit (Massenet)

Sweet harps resound again. A. S. Sullivan. Words by M. Ryan. MCS

Sweet-heart. For entries beginning Sweetheart see Sweetheart

"Sweet hour of prayer." W. B. Bradbury. Words by W. W. Walford. FSS 1—HSD—NMH—WA— WBT—WS—WSC—WSW

"Sweet, how sweet, the hawthorn blooming." See May-day

"Sweet Innisfallen." Air: The captivating youth. Words by T. Moore. MI

"Sweet is the morn." See Sur une tombe (Lekeu)

"Sweet is the ship that, under sail." See Lovely Nan (Dibdin)

Sweet Kitty ("As he was a-riding") English folk song. SEF 1—SO

"Sweet Kitty Clover." E. Kean. Words by Knight. BE 5

Sweet Kitty Magee ("With cheeks as bright as roses") Irish air: Kitty Magee. Words by B. O'Brien. MMI

"Sweet land of the mountain." Air: Ffarwel Jeuengetid. Words by W. Smythe. MMW

Sweet lei Lehua. Kalakaua. e. HA

Sweet lei mamo. C. K. Hopkins. Words by Huelani. e.h. HA

Sweet lilies of the valley. J. Hook. Words by Richardson. ME

"Sweet little ladybird, rest awhile." See Ladybird

The sweet little man. Air: Bonnie Dundee. Words by O. W. Holmes. LBR

"Sweet love of mine." F. Cowen. WBT

Sweet lovely Joan. English folk song. SO

"Sweet Maggie had a little bird." See Maggie's pet

"Sweet maid, come, if thou would'st charm" (Persian song) e. BMC

"Sweet Mary lulled her blessed Child." H. E. Nichol. Words by C. Sterne. HC

"Sweet May, ever welcome." See May and November

Sweet memories of thee. Italian air. FSS 4

"Sweet mignonette with leaflets interlacing." See Allerseelen (Strauss)

Sweet Mog the brunette. 18th century song. ME
Variant of: "Young Jockey he courted sweet Moggy"

Sweet my child. See "Home they brought her warrior, dead" (Macfarren)

Sweet Nan of the Vale. T. A. Arne. MM

"Sweet Nelly, my heart's delight." 18th century song. BE 1—CO 2—DM 2—MM

Sweet nightingale. Cornish air. BSW

Sweet passion of love. M. Arne. Words by D. Garrick. ME
"This cold flinty heart." DM 2

Sweet Patty. J. Hook. ME

"Sweet Poll of Plymouth." M. Arne. Words by J. O'Keeffe. ME

"A sweet pretty maiden sat under a tree." English folk song. BSW

The sweet priméroses. English folk song. SEF 1—SO

Sweet Robin ("Oh, where are you going") Composer unknown. FSS 8

Sweet Robin ("Oh, where are you going") Attributed to T. S. Cooke. ME

Sweet Robinette. J. Hook. ME

Sweet rose and lily. Händel. CS 2

Sweet rosebud of the fragrant mountains. See The he-i blossom (Hopkins)

Sweet rosebud oka uka onaona. See The he-i blossom (Hopkins)

"Sweet roses fair perfume the air." See Flower song (Lange)

"Sweet roses that wither." Scottish air. LA

The sweet rosy morn. R. Leveridge. MM

"Sweet Saviour, bless us ere we go." W. H. Monk. Words by F. W. Faber. FSS 1—WBT

"Sweet-scented breath of night." See Death's serenade (Musorgskiĭ)

"The sweet seductive arts that conquer maidens' hearts." See A life that lives for you (Sullivan)

"Sweet sir, for your courtesie." See My jo Janet

"Sweet smells the briar." J. Percy. Words by E. Spenser. BE 6

Sweet song-bird. J. L. Molloy. FSS 2— JSE—WSC

Sweet spirit, hear my prayer. W. V. Wallace. HSD

"Sweet spring is returning." A. F. M. Custance. NMS

"Sweet, sweet Robinette." See Sweet Robinette (Hook)

Sweet Tally-ho. 18th century song. ME Variant: Bucks a-hunting go

"Sweet the hour soon to come." See Chère nuit (Bachelet)

"Sweet thine eyes at Piedigrotta." See La vera Sorrentina

"Sweet turtle dove" (Jerusalem mornin') Negro spiritual. HR

"Sweet vale of Llandovery." See Home of my heart

"Sweet village bells." Donizetti. Words by E. Douglas. MCS

Sweet violet ("Ah I wonder where thou art dear") C. K. Hopkins. e.h. HA

"Sweet violet of sunny spring." See Med en primulaveris (Grieg)

"Sweet violet, thou child of spring." See Med en primulaveris (Grieg)

"Sweet voices from the spirit land I hear." See Departed days (Root)

"Sweet was the morning." See Lithuanian song (Chopin)

"The sweet west wind is flying." See Good-night (Perkins)

Sweet wild roses. See Petites roses (Cesek)

Sweet will of God (Avon) Scotch air. Words by F. W. Faber. FSS 7

Sweet will of God. Arr from Methfessel. Words by F. W. Faber. LA

Sweet William. Folk song: English version. SEF 2—SO
—Alleghany, N.C. version no. 1. CSE
—Alleghany, N.C. version no. 2. CSE
—Carmen, N.C. version. CSE
—Swannanoa, N.C. version. CSE

Sweet William and Lady Margery. Kentucky mountain song. WLT
Variant of: Fair Margaret and Sweet William

"Sweet William, don't cross that raging sea." See Early, early in the spring (Alleghany, N.C. version)

"Sweet William he rose in the month of May." See Fair Margaret and sweet William (Tennessee version)

"Sweet William he rose one morning in May." See Fair Margaret and sweet William (Carmen, N.C. version no. 1)

"Sweet William rose one early morning." See Sweet William and Lady Margery

"Sweet William was down to his dwell today." See Barbara Allen (Hot Springs, N.C. version)

"Sweet William went to Polly." See William and Polly

"Sweet William were taken with a pain in his breast." See William and Nancy

Sweet William's farewell to black ey'd Susan. See Black-eyed Susan (Leveridge)

Sweet Willy, O. C. Dibdin. ME

"Sweet youthful charming ladies fair." See Rosamond

"Sweet youth's a blithe and heartsome time." Air: Gin ye meet a bonnie lassie. Words by A. Ramsay. MMS

"Sweeter for the fragrance of night-pluck'd roses." See Sapphische ode (Brahms)

"Sweeter rings the thrush's song." See Minnelied (Brahms)

"Sweeter sounds the singing bird." See Minnelied (Brahms)

"Sweeter than the breath of morning." See "Nobil donna è tanto onesta"

"The sweetest flow'r that blows." See At parting (Rogers)

"Sweetest infant, all endearing." See "Dormi, dormi, bel bambino" (Ricci)

"Sweetest maiden, list, I pray." See "Liebes mädchen, hör mir zu" (Haydn)

"Sweetest music, softly stealing." C. Simper. Words by G. W. Brindley. HC

"Sweetest perfume fills the hours." See Le violette (Scarlatti)

Sweetest violet, never I'll forget. See violeta (Hopkins)

Sweetheart, come back to me. Student song. CHS—NML

"Sweetheart, farewell, the flutt'ring sail." See Though lost to sight (Cowen)

"Sweet-heart, gentle and pretty." See "Douce dame jolie" (Guillaume de Machaut)

"Sweetheart, I send you a red, red rosebud." See Love greetings (Elgar)

"Sweetheart, I wait for thee." T. D. Thomas (music and words) MPC— NML

"Sweetheart, if a hundred sheep were own'd by thee." See If thou'rt not sincere

The sweetheart in the army. Kentucky mountain song. WLT
Variant of: The broken token

"Sweetheart mine, I implore you." See A song of absence and longing

"Sweetheart mine, I long to kiss you." See The tell-tale stars (Cherepnin)

Sweetheart, sweetheart, love's own dear blossom. See "Kristallen den fina"

"Sweetheart, the day has no gladness." See Sweetheart, come back to me

"Sweetheart, when you walk my way." See Greeting (Hawley)

"Sweetly on the evening air." See The vesper chime (Linley)

"Sweetly sang the angels." W. T. Crossley. Words by J. Julian. HC

"Sweetly sang the angels." T. F. Dunhill. Words by J. Julian. HC

"Sweetly sleep." Beethoven. FSS 4

"Sweetly slumber, sweetest, dearest baby." See Wiegenlied (Schubert)

Sweetly, sweetly, fashioned meetly. See "Wie nahte mir der schlummer" (Weber)

"Sweetly the birds are singing." C. F. Roper. HC

Sweetser, Joseph Emerson
"Breathe on me, breath of God"
"Send down thy truth, O God"

"Swelling o'er the mountain." See O'er the mountains (Simpson)

Sweney, J. R.
Beulah land

Swett, Susan Hartley
July (Olds)

"Swift my heart surrenders." See "Presto, presto, io m'innamoro" (Mazzaferrata)

"Swift rushing stream." See Aufenthalt (Schubert)

"The swiftly driven troika dashes." See Three-in-hand

"Swiftly flying the breezes of Kohala." See Kohala's breezes (Nape)

"Swiftly passeth life away." See "Meine lebenszeit verstreicht" (Beethoven)

"Swiftly surging waters gliding." See Surging waters (Hopkins)

"Swiftly, swiftly o'er the snow." See The sleigh ride (Johnson)

"Swiftly the daylight is fading." See Carmela

"Swiftly the swallows are flying." See Villanelle (Dell' Acqua)

Swiftly they surge the waters ea. See "My love to thee" (Nape)

"Swiftly walk over the western wave." See To night (Smith)

Swinburne, Algernon Charles
Bid the day be born (Randegger)
"If love were what the rose is" (Pinsuti)

Swing, David
"Beautiful faces" (Composer unknown)
Memorial hymn (Allen)

"Swing, bells! Christmas is near." See Home is dear

Swing, cradle, swing. G. Cooper. FSS 6 —LA

Swing low ("I looked over Jordan") See Swing low, sweet chariot ("I looked over Jordan")

Swing low ("O, O, swing low."—Mammy's lullaby) W. A. Fisher. Words by H. Weeden. GMF

"Swing low, chariot." Negro spiritual. HR

Swing low, sweet chariot ("I looked over Jordan") Negro spiritual. BD— BSS— CST— DF— FSS 3—GO— HSC— HSD— JB— JP— JSE— NMP—OH—TFC 1—WBT—WC

Swing low. HR

Swing low, sweet chariot ("Oh de good ole chariot swing so low") Negro spiritual. HR

Swing song. German folk air. Words by H. H. Harbour. DO

"Swing the shining sickle." See Thanksgiving song (Gaynor)

Swinging 'neath the old apple-tree. O. R. Barrows. FSS 1

Swire, John
"Good people, give ear"

The Swiss girl ("O hear me") Words by G. Linley. FSS 5

The Swiss girl ("When the morn") I. Moscheles. FSS 3

Swiss hunter. Alpine air. FSS 6

The Swiss mountaineer ("Fain would I see other places") Swiss folk song. e. BMC

Swiss national hymn. See "Rufst du, mein vaterland"

Swiss shepherd's song. e. FSS 8

Swiss song. See Schweizerlied

The Switzer boy. Swiss air. FSS 3

Switzerland ("I know a wondrous lovely land") I. Heim. Words by F. K. Mueller. e. JS

Switzerland ("To Swiss in stranger's land") See Ranz des vaches

The Switzer's farewell. See Abschied vom dirndel

Switzer's song of home. I. Moscheles. FSS 2

The sword of Bunker hill. B. Covert. Words by W. R. Wallace. BSE— HSD—JO—LBR—MP—WBT

"A sword of light hath pierced the dark" (Mo chraoibhin cno) Irish air. Words by E. Carbery. FSI

Sydameni laulu. See Vale of shadow (Sibelius)

Sydenham, Edwin Augustus
The maiden of the Fleur de Lys

The sylphs ("Softly, softly sing") Air: The rising of the sun. Words by A. Hunter. MMW

Sylvan roundelay. N. Rimsky-Korsakow. Words after A. Ostrovsky. e. SC

Sylvelin. C. Sinding. e.g. FM

"Sylvia, thou art my dearest." See "Trop aimable Sylvie"

Symon, J. D.
Carmen de Lalages agno (Winner)

Symons, E. J.
Don't leave your mother, Tom

Et **syn** (A vision) E. Grieg. Words by A. O. Vinje. e.n. WM 1

"Syng, syng" ("Sing, sing! nightingale, sing") H. Kjerulf. Words by T. Kjerulf. e.n. SSN

Synnöves lied. See Synnöve's sang (Kjerulf)

Synnöve's sang (Synnöve's song) H. Kjerulf. Words by B. Björnson. e.n. SSN—WM 1
Synnöves lied (Synnöve's song) e.g. SM 2

"Szumią jodły na gór szczycie." See Halka (Moniusko)

T

T' ses tüta mia furtüna (You are all my treasure) Italian song. e.i. BF 2

"Ta rose de pourpre, à ton clair soleil." See Nell (Fauré)

"Ta won gdhon dhe-nun-ye de." See The Indian coquet

Die **tabakspfeife** (Der edelmann und der invalide.—"Gott grüss euch, alter") C. P. E. Pilz. Words by G. C. Pfeffel. g. ED 1

Table-song. See Tischlied (Eberwein)

Tabrar, Joseph
The student and his bow-wow

"Tacea la notte placida." Verdi. e.i. PP

"Taffy was a Welshman." Nursery song. WSC

"Tafta Hindī." See Indian taffeta

"Das tagewerk ist abgetan." See Abendlied (Zelter)

T'aggio ditto ("Te l'ho detto."—"I have told you") Neapolitan folk song. e.i. FE

T'aggio visto ("T'ho veduta."—"There! I saw you") P. Labriola. Words by M. Tancredi. e.i. FE

"Täglich ging die wunderschöne sultanstochter auf und nieder." See Der Asra (Loewe); Der Asra (Rubinstein)

Täglich zu singen ("Ich danke Gott") J. A. P. Schulz. Words by M. Claudius. g. ED 2

Tagore, Sir Rabindranath
Amina's song (East Indian air)

The **tailor** and the mouse. Folk song. GO

"Tain't my mother or my father." See It's me, O, Lord

"T'aje fatta la gonnella, Antonià." See Antonià

"Tak for dit råd" ("Thanks for thy counsel") E. Grieg. Words by B. Björnsen. e.n. WM 1

Tak' your auld cloak about ye ("In winter, when the rain rain'd cauld") Scottish song. MMS—PS 1

Tak' yer auld cloak about ye. JO

Take a bumper and try. See "The women all tell"

"Take back the heart." C. Barnard (music and words) FSS 5—HSC—HSD—NMH— NML— PO— WA— WBT—WL—WSW

"Take back the virgin page." Air: Dermott. Words by T. Moore. MI

"Take heart again." See "Consolati e spera" (Scarlatti)

"Take here, thou lovely child of spring." See Med en primulaveris (Grieg)

"Take in your flowing canvas." See The flying Dutchman (Parry)

"Take me back to home and mother." W. A. Huntley. Words by A. W. French. HSC

"Take me home." Raymond. HSD—WBT

"Take my head on your shoulder, daddy." See Daddy (Behrend)

Take my love to Rosalie. B. E. Dickhaut. Words by J. T. Bergen. CHS—NML

"Take my sword, my hands are tiring." See Montenegro

"Take, oh! take those lips away." H. R. Bishop. Words by W. Shakespeare; attributed also to Beaumont and Fletcher. HSE 3

"Take, oh! take those lips away." J. E. Galliard. Words by W. Shakespeare; attributed also to Beaumont and Fletcher. DM 1

"Take, O take those lips away." J. Wilson. Words by W. Shakespeare; attributed also to Beaumont and Fletcher. BSE—DM 1—JE—VFS

"Take thy choice, he gently whispered." See The priceless gift (Gray)

"Takes a humble soul to join." See I am goin' to join in this army

A **tale** of the olden time. B. W. J. Trevaldwyn. Words by G. Moultrie. HC

Talhaiarn, pseud. See Jones, John, 1810-1869

"Taliannuti a lu spissu." See Malatu p'amuri

Taliesin's prophecy ("A voice from time departed") Air: Toriad y dydd, or, The break of day. Words by F. Hemans. MMW

Der **talisman** ("Freunde, wählt euch einen talisman") Volksweise. Words by K. Stein. g. ED 2

The **talisman** ("When at night the rocks were shaking") Titoff. e. KSN

"Talk about the river, the river so wide." See Humble yourself

"Talk not so much to me of love." Webber. MM

The **tall** clock. German folk air. Words by N. H. Dole. DO

"**Tall** my neighbor's wheat is growing." See My neighbor

"A **tall** stalwart lancer lay dying." See The tarpaulin jacket (Coote)

Talley, Thomas Washington
Behold that star

Tally-ho! hark away. Words by M. Steel. DM 2

A **Talmudical** student's lament ("Mai kō mashma-lan") Jewish folk song. e.y. BF 2

Tam Glen. See "My heart is a-breakin', dear tittie"

"**Tam** na górze jawor stoi, jawor zeilonienki." See The Cossack (Moniuszko)

"**Tam** Pearce, Tam Pearce, lend me your grey mare." See Widdicombe fair

Tambourica (Tanburica) Slavonian folk song. e.se. BF 1

"**T'amo** perchè sei bella." See Amore (Muratori)

"**Tanburica** sitnim glasom udaraše." See Tambourica

Tancredi, Michel Angelo
T'aggio visto (Labriola)

"**Tandis** que tout sommeille." A. E. M. Grétry. e.f. SOA 3

Tanieev, Sergieĭ Ivanovich
The birth of the harp. See "'Tis believed that this harp"
Minuet
"'Tis believed that this harp"

"**Tänker** du att jag förlorader är" ("Do you think that I am now all forlorn") Swedish folk song. e.sw. HSOS

Tannahill, Robert
"Accuse me not" (Scottish air)
The braes o' Balquhidder (Smith)
The braes o' Gleniffer (Scottish air)
Despairing Mary (Wilson)
"Gloomy winter's now awa'" (Scottish air; also music by Covert)
Jessie, the flower o' Dumblane (Smith)
"Loudon's bonnie woods and braes" (Scottish air)
"Mirk and rainy is the night" (Scottish air)
O! are ye sleepin', Maggie (Scottish air)
"Och hey! Johnnie lad" (Scottish air)
Rab Roryson's bonnet (Scottish air)
"Thou bonnie wood of Craigielea" (Barr)
"Thou dark-winding Carron" (M'Donald)
"We'll meet beside the dusky glen" (Scottish air)

Der **tannenbaum** ("O tannenbaum") German folk song. g. ED 1
The fir-tree. e. BSE
"O evergreen." e. MCS
"O tannenbaum." e.g. DCS. e. only MCS
O tannenbaum ("O Christmas tree") e. MF

"O tannenbaum" ("O faithful pine") e.g. BO
The pine tree. e. DO
Der tannenbaum (The Christmas tree) e. WSC
Der tannenbaum (The fir-tree) e.g. SSG

Tans'ur William
"Come, Holy Ghost"
"Come, let us join our cheerful songs" (same air as "Come, Holy Ghost")
"Oh, for a heart" (same air as "Come, Holy Ghost")
St Martin's. See "Come, Holy Ghost"; "Come, let us join our cheerful songs"; "Oh, for a heart"
"While shepherds watched their flocks"

"**Tant** que le jour dure" ("Just as the daylight is fading") L. Delibes. e.f. OPS 2
"Tant que le jour dure" ("Now while the daylight still lingers") e.f. KS 3

"**Tant** sirop est doux." Negro creole song from Martinique. f. KA

"**Tanto** sospirerò" ("E'er will I sigh") P. P. Bencini. e.i. FEI 2

"**Tap,** tap, tap! who taps there." See Martinique love-song

Tappan,
Himmlische ruhe (Molique)

Tapping at the garden gate. S. W. New. Words by J. Loker. HSD—WBT

Taps ("Day is done, gone the sun") U.S. army bugle call. Words from Pennsylvania military college. BSS

Taps ("Fading light dims the sight") Pennsylvania military college song. B. Esenwein (music and words) CHS—MP

Tar. S. Vassilenko. Words from the Russian of S. Gorodetsky. e. NM 2

Tărăncuta (The peasant girl) Rumanian song. e.ru. BF 2

Tarantella. Sicilian song. e.i. BF 2

"La **tarde** declina ya se." See Puesta de sol (Bernier)

The **tarpaulin** jacket ("A tall stalwart lancer lay dying") C. Coote. Words by G. J. Whyte-Melville. BOS—SSS

Tarpaulin jacket ("Wrap me up in a tarpaulin jacket") Composer unknown. Words by A. Nash. CHS—MPC—WBT—WC

Tarry Trowsers. Folk song from Essex. SF 2

The **tar's** farewell. S. Adams. Words by F. C. Barnard. FSS 6—HSD—JSE
The sailor's farewell. PO

The **tar's** sheet anchor. W. Reeve. Words by J. C. Cross. PR 2

The **Tartar** host (Okh ne buĭnyĭ vĭeter zavyval) Russian folk song. e. SSR 3

Tate, Nahum
When I am laid in earth (Purcell)
"While shepherds watched their flocks" (Old English air; also music by Clarke; Fink; Händel; Howard; Methfessel; Tan'sur; also unknown composer)
"Who can resist my Celia's charms" (Trevers)

Tate, Nahum, and Brady, Nicholas
The old hundredth (Franc)

"Der tate nito hie'." See Pi-Pi-Pi-Pi-Pi

Taubert, Wilhelm
Cradle song. See Wiegenlied
"Es steht ein baum in jenem thal." See In der fremde
In a March-night. See In der märznacht
In a strange land. See In der fremde
In der fremde
In der märznacht
My darling was so fair. See In der fremde
My mother's memory
"Sleep, beloved, sleep" (same air as Wiegenlied)
Wiegenlied

Tauler, Johann
"There comes a galley, laden" (Composer unknown. Tr of Es komt ein schiff geladen)

Taunton Dean. See "There was an old fellow at Waltham Cross"

Tauwitz, Eduard
The little voice
Paul and I
Sleep, baby dear

Tavárez, M. G.
Canción de la mañana (same air as "Ya brilla la aurora")
Serenata. See "Ya brilla la aurora"
"Ya brilla la aurora"

The taverns' song ("The gentry to 'The King's Head' go") A. Young. ME
"The gentry to the King's Head go." DM 1

"Tavna noći." See "Gloomy night, how full of shadow"

"Tavse graner, sorte naetter." See Finnland (Jordan)

Taylor, Ann, and Taylor, Jane
Pussy (Elliott)

Taylor, Bayard
Autumn dreaming (Weiland)
Bedouin love-song (Pinsuti)
The forest glade (Kreipl)
"Learn to live, and live to learn" (English air)
Matin song (Paine)
The proposal (music by Brackett; Gluck)
The return of spring (Jones)
The storm song (Gluck)
The summers come and go (Schulz)
The voyagers (Silcher)
Wind and sea (music by Cauffman; Schulz)

Taylor, Ernest J.
Alma mater—Swarthmore (Old air)

Taylor, James B.
Bunker hill (Tuckerman)
Smoking away (same air as "Sparkling and bright in its liquid light, is the water in our glasses")
"Sparking and bright in liquid light, does the wine our goblets gleam in" (same air as "Sparkling and bright in its liquid light, is the water in our glasses")
"Sparkling and bright, in its liquid light, is the water in our glasses"

Taylor, Jane
"Ah, why will my dear little child be so cross" (Composer unknown)
The chatterbox (Composer unknown)
How long a day appears (Composer unknown)
"Lazy sheep, pray tell me why" (Old French air; also music by unknown composer)
Little Jack (Composer unknown)
"Twinkle, twinkle, little star" (French air; also music by unknown composer)
See also Taylor, Ann, jt. auth.

Taylor, M. A.
Cannibalee

Taylor, R. S.
"O wrap the flag around me, boys"

Taylor, S.
Farewell to Llanberis (Welsh air)

Taylor, Samuel Coleridge-. See Coleridge-Taylor, Samuel

Taylor, Thomas Rawson
Heaven is my home (Sullivan)

Taylor, Virgil Corydon
"Deep are the wounds"
"Lord of all being" (same air as "Deep are the wounds")
Louvan. See "Deep are the wounds"; "Lord of all being"

Taylor, W. F.
"When Christ was born in Bethlehem"
"The taylor fell thro' the bed." Air: I rede ye beware o' the ripells young man. Words by R. Burns. BSR
"The taylor he cam here to sew." Air: The drummer. Words by R. Burns. BSR

"Taza b-taza." See "Fresh and fresh and new and new"

Tchaikovsky, Peter Ilyich
Adieu, forêts (from The maid of Orleans)
"Ah! sad indeed my heart." See "Nur wer die sehnsucht kennt"
"Ah! weep no more"
An den schlaf. See To sleep
At the ball
Benediction
By the window
Le canari. See The canary
The canary
Cradle song
The crown of roses
Déception

Tchaikovsky, Peter Ilyich—*Continued*
Disappointment. See Déception
Don Juan's serenade
"Einst zum narren jemand spricht."
See "Some one said unto the fool"
Endless love
Er liebte mich so sehr. See He truly
loved me so
Evening
Fifinella. See Punchinello
"For thee, dear home"
Frühling. See Springtime
Had fickle fortune, not betraying (from
Eugene Onegin)
He truly loved me so
Ichabod
"Inmitten des balles." See At the ball
Der kanarienvogel. See The canary
A legend. See The crown of roses
Morning
"My blessing rest on thee, O woods."
See Benediction
"Nay! though my heart should break"
"None but the lonely heart." See
"Nur wer die sehnsucht kennt"
"Nur wer die sehnsucht kennt"
"Ob heller tag." See "Whether day
dawns"
Oh, but to hear thy voice
"Only a yearning heart." See "Nur
wer die sehnsucht kennt"
"Only the sad of heart." See "Nur
wer die sehnsucht kennt"
A pleading
Punchinello
Rastvoríl ya oknó. See By the win-
dow
Romeo and Juliet
Sérénade
Le soir. See Evening
"Some one said unto the fool"
Springtime
Ständchen des Don Juan. See Don
Juan's serenade
"Die thräne bebt." See Endless love
"'Tis evening, and the hues that made
the clouds so bright" (from Pique-
dame)
To sleep
To the forest
'Twas April
Warum
Wenn mich für häuslichkeit. See Had
fickle fortune, not betraying
"When Jesus Christ was yet a child."
See The crown of roses
"Whether day dawns"
Why. See Warum
Wiegenlied. See Cradle song
"Yes, I love you" (from Eugene One-
gin)
Tcherepnin, Nicolas Nicolaievitch. See
Cherepnin, Nikolaĭ Nikolaevich
"**Tching-a-ring-a-ring-tching,** feast of lan-
terns." See The feast of lanterns (El-
liott)
"**Te** l'ho detto." See T'aggio ditto

"**Te** souviens tu de ta promesse" (Remem-
brance) B. Godard (music and
words) e.f. CM 1—HM 2
Do you remember. e. WBT—WBW
"**Te** souviens-tu, mon bien-aimé." See
Une nuit de mai (Thomas)
"**Te** souvient-il des marronniers fleuris."
See Chanson d'amour (Hollmann)
Te voglio bene assaje (Ti voglio bene as-
sai.—Oh, I cannot now forget you)
Neapolitan folk song. e.i. FE
Tea in the arbor. J. Beuler. FSS 3
A **teamster's** complaint (A ba'al eglah
lied) Jewish folk song. e.y. BF 2
A **teamster's** song. See Peña Hueca
The **tear** ("Wohl war es") See "Wohl
Die thräne (Gumbert)
The **tear** ("Wohl war es") See "Wohl
war es eine seligkeit" (Witt)
"The **tear** fell gently from her eye." See
The anchor's weighed (Braham)
Tears ("Gentle tears, oh! say") A. War-
lamoff. e. KSN
Tears and sighs. See "Aus meinen tränen
spriessen" (Schumann)
"The **tears** fall in my soul." See "Il pleure
dans mon coeur" (Debussy)
"**Tears** for my heart." See Her blanket
(Lieurance)
"**Tears** of sorrow, shame and anguish."
Spohr. e. OS 4—SAS 4
Tears, such as tender fathers shed. G. F.
Händel. SAS 4
Technology. Song of Massachusetts in-
stitute of technology. L. B. Haworth.
Words by C. Renshaw. CHS
"**Tečie** voda z javora." See Flowing water
Tecolote. Central American folk song.
e.s. HS
Variant: Tecolotito
Tecolotito (The owlet) Mexican song.
e.s. BF 2
Variant of: Tecolote
Tegid, pseud. See Jones, John, 1792-1852
Tegnér, Esaias
Kung Carl XII (Westermark)
Tejada, Miguel Lerdo de. See Lerdo de
Tejada, Miguel
Lo **telefono** (The telephone) L. Denza.
Words by G. Turco. e.i. MN
The **telephone.** See Lo telefono (Denza)
Telford, Shirley
Christmas lullaby (Harrison)
Tell her I love her so. P. DeFaye.
Words by F. E. Weatherly. FSS 6—
KF 3
Tell it. See "Father Abraham"
"**Tell** Jesus." Negro spiritual. HR
"**Tell** me, adorable maiden, why thou
shouldst treat me thus coldly." See
"Dime, mujer adorada"
"**Tell** me, beautiful maiden, tell me, where
will you go." See "Dites, la jeune
belle" (Gounod)
"**Tell** me am I the faithless one." See Te
voglio bene assaje

"**Tell** me, fair Amarillis." See "Amarilli, mia bella" (Caccini)

"**Tell** me, fair maiden, whither away shall we go." See "Dites, la jeune belle" (Berlioz)

"**Tell** me, Giannetta." See La Savoyarde

"**Tell** me, have you seen my pretty Caruli." See Caruli (Costa)

"**Tell** me, little housewives." See Mud pies (Scott-Gatty)

"**Tell** me, love, tell me, I pray." See "Dimmi, amor" (Leuto)

"**Tell** me, lovely shepherd." Boyce. Words by E. Moore. BE 7

"**Tell** me, Mary, how to woo thee." G. A. Hodson. Words by F. Morrison. BE 4—HSE 1

"**Tell** me, my children." See Action song (Scott-Gatty)

"**Tell** me, my heart." H. R. Bishop. Words by T. Morton. BE 5—DM 2— HSE 1—SS 1

"**Tell** me, my old friend." See Les enfants de la mer

"**Tell** me no more her eyes are like." See Beauty in eclipse (Lawes)

"**Tell** me no more I am deceived." Boyce. Words by W. Congreve. DM 2

"**Tell** me no more, no more you love." J. Blow. BOH

"**Tell** me not in mournful numbers." See A psalm of life (Smart)

"**Tell** me not my heart's devotion." See "Non mi dir" (Mozart)

"**Tell** me now, my little darling." Polish song. e. KSN

"**Tell** me, O fair ones." See "Voi, che sapete" (Mozart)

"**Tell** me, O Lord, of thy reason." See Imanírta (Valderrama)

"**Tell** me, oh, ye stars." L. J. F. Hérold. Words by C. Swain. BD

"**Tell** me one thing, tell me truly." See No sir (Wakefield)

"**Tell** me pray." Austrian Silesian song. e. KSE—SN—WL

"**Tell** me, tell me, tell me where is fancy bred." See Tell me where is fancy bred (Stevenson)

"**Tell** me the tales that to me were so dear." See Long, long ago (Bayly)

"**Tell** me then what wondrous dreaming." See Träume (Wagner)

"**Tell** me, tiny bee, oh tell me." See Lu labbru

"**Tell** me what these dreams of wonder." See Träume (Wagner)

"**Tell** me where have you been, Billy boy, Billy Boy." See Billy boy

"**Tell** me where is fancy bred." T. A. Arne. Words by W. Shakespeare. BOH

Tell me where is fancy bred. J. Stevenson. Words by W. Shakespeare. BE 4

"**Tell** me why are the roses so pale." See Warum (Tchaikovsky)

"**Tell** me, who built the ark." See Who built the ark

"**Tell** me, ye friendly neighbors." See "Ditemi, buona gente, vedeste Dinorah" (Meyerbeer)

"**Tell** me, ye winged winds." See The inquiry (Gorrin)

The **tell-tale** stars (L'étoile indiscrète) N. Tcherepnin. Words by A. Maikov. e.f. NR 4

"**Tell** the story of the risen." See Sleeper awake (Jeffery)

"**Tell** us, rabbi, do." See What will happen when the Messiah comes

The **tempest** ("We were crowded") See "We were crowded in the cabin" (Barker)

"**Tempest** and storm-furies shrieking." See "Das ist ein brausen und heulen" (Franz)

Tempest of the heart. See Il balen del suo sorriso (Verdi)

"The **tempest** rages wild and high." See The storm (Hullah)

"The **tempest** rages wild on the hill" (Wendish song) e. BMC

Temple, Hope
  "I love thee." See 'Tis all that I can say
  My lady's bower
  An old garden
  'Tis all that I can say

Temple ouvre-toi (Open thy gates) C. Gounod. e.f. PG 1

Tempo passato perchè non retorni (Why are days we have lived lost for ever) L. Gordigiani. e.i. MSI

Tempora mutantur. See Ewiger wechsel (Himmel)

"**Tempt** me not, O world, again." See Verborgenheit (Wolf)

"**Ten** brothers" ("Tsen brider") Jewish folk song. e.y. GF 2
  "Ten brothers" ("Zehn brieder") e.y. BF 2

The **ten** commandments. Folk song: English version. SEF 2—SO
  —Georgia version. CSE
  —Asheville, N.C. version. CSE
  —Black Mountain, N.C. version. CSE
  Variant: The dilly song

Ten little Indians. Children's song. NMH —NMS—WSC

"**Ten** little niggers." Children's song. HSD

Ten thousand miles away ("Sing ho! for a brave and a valiant bark") J. B. Geoghegan (music and words) SSS

Ten thousand miles away ("Sing ho! for a brave and gallant ship") Forecastle song. CR

"**Ten** thousand times ten thousand" (Alford) J. B. Dykes. Words by H. Alford. CST—LA

The **ten** virgins. Negro spiritual. NMP

Tenaglia, Antonio Francesco
"Begli occhi, mercè"
"E quando ve n'andate"
"Have mercy, dark eyes." See "Begli occhi, mercè"
"O when will ye e'er leave me." See "E quando ve n'andate"
"Quando sarà quel dì"
"When will the day e'er be." See "Quando sarà quel dì"
"A **tender** child of summers three." See The light that is felt (Methfessel)
"**Tender** flowers." See The flower girl's song
A **tender** tie. See "Un doux lien" (Delbrück)
"**Tenderly** sleeping." Christmas carol. HC
"**Tengo** mi hamaca tendida." See La hamaca
"**Tengo**, señores, un periquito." See El periquito
"**Tengo** yo una cachuchita." See La cachucha
Tenner, Christian
Froher mut (Erk)
Mutterseelenallein (Folk air; also music by Braun)
Tennyson, Alfred Tennyson, 1st baron
The birth of Christ (Reichardt)
Blow, bugle, blow (Neidlinger)
"Break, break, break" (Dempster)
The brook (music by Wilson; also unknown composer)
"Come into the garden, Maud" (Balfe)
Crossing the bar (music by Barnby; Huss)
"Home they brought her warrior" (music by Gilchrist; Macfarren)
The May queen (Dempster)
Milkmaid's song (Parker)
"Ring out, wild bells" (music by Gounod; Tosti)
So runs my dream (Composer unknown)
"Sweet and low" (music by Barnby; Wallace)
Too late, too late (Bliss)
"Where is another sweet" (Sullivan)
Tenting on the old camp ground. W. Kittredge (music and words) BO—HSC—JO—JS—JSE—LBR
Tenting to-night. LA—MS—TFC 1
"We are tenting to-night." BD
"We're tenting tonight." BSE—FSS 6—HSD— MP—NMH—NMS —OH—WA—WBT—WSW
Teresita mia. Pyrenean song. e.s. SSP
"The **term** is past, and once again." See "Die frist ist um" (Wagner)
Terra adorata de' padri miei. G. Donizetti. e.i. SOA 2
"La **terre** dort au ciel pur." See Bonne nuit (Massenet)
"La **terre** embrasée attend la rosée qui tombe des cieux." See Le soir (Thomas)

La **terruca**. B. D. Colón. Words by V. Dávila. s. LCP
Terry, Daniel
Safely follow him (Cooke)
Terry, George F.
"All hail, ye merry folk to-day"
Terry, Richard Runciman
"As Joseph was a walking"
Joseph and the angel. See "As Joseph was a walking"
Teschner, Melchior
"All glory, laud, and honor." See Glory, laud, and honor
Glory, laud, and honor (Tr of Gloria, laus et honor)
Teszcze Polska. See Polish national song (Ogiński?)
Die **Teutoburger** schlacht ("Als die Römer frech geworden") Composer unknown. Words by J. V. Scheffel. g. ED 1
The **Texas** cowboy. Mrs R. Thomson. LC
Thackeray, William Makepeace
The mahogany tree (Campana)
"**Thae** nan ho dan." See Omaha Indian "Wa-wan" ceremony
Thalberg, Sigismund
"Amid the greenwood"
"The **Thames** flows proudly to the sea." Air: Robie donna gorach. Words by R. Burns. BSR
"**Thank** you, pretty cow." See The cow
"**Thankful** am I for the happy hours." See Synnöve's sang (Kjerulf)
"**Thanks** for thy counsel." See "Tak for dit råd" (Grieg)
"**Thanks** to thee, angelic voice." See "Voce di donna o d'angelo" (Ponchielli)
Thanksgiving ("Praise to God") See "Praise to God, immortal praise" (Composer unknown); "Praise to God, immortal praise" (Pleyel)
Thanksgiving day ("Oh, Thanksgiving morning") French folk air. Words by H. H. Harbour. DO
Thanksgiving hymn ("Dear Lord above") W. B. Olds. Words by B. E. Bush. NMS
Thanksgiving prayer ("Wilt heden") See "Wilt heden nu treden"
Thanksgiving song ("Swing the shining sickle") J. L. Gaynor. OH
That day the world shall see. J. W. Callcott. Words by W. E. Hickson. FSS 2
"**That** day when first I saw thee." See A Nina
"**That** Easter-tide with joy was bright." 15th century lowland carol. [Tr of Claro Paschali gaudio] e. HC
"**That** I might die." See "Morir vogl'io" (Astorga)
"**That** night I'll ne'er forget." See Waltz song (Planquette)
"**That** night we chose the longest road." See Sous les branches (Hardelot)

"That ocean-guarded flag of light." See The flag (Crosby)

"That old, old clock of the household stock." See The old cottage clock

"That old waltz by the linden trees." See Dance on forever (Aïdé)

"That seat of science, Athens." See Free America

"That so Thy blessed birth, O Christ." See The blessed birth (Davies)

That sweet story of old. Old air. Words by J. T. Luke. FSS 2
"I think, when I read that sweet story." OH—WBT

That Wilson chum of mine. Wilson college song. CHS

The thatcher ("All padded and muffled") Air: As I came home. Words by Ieuan Dhu. MMW

Thaxter, Mrs Celia (Laighton)
Christmas dawn (Bellini)

Thayer, William Armour
My laddie

Thee I think of, Margherita. See Dein gedenk' ich, Margareta (Meyer-Helmund)

Thee, St Stephens. College song. CHS

"Thee we praise, O God of harvest." J. H. Hopkins (music and words) HC

"Their groves o' sweet myrtle." Air: Humours of Glen. Words by R. Burns. BSR

Their sweetest song. MCS

Thekla, eine geisterstimme ("Wo ich sei") F. L. Seidel. Words by Schiller. g. ED 2

Thémines, Achille de Lauzières de. See Lauzières de Thémines, Achille de

Then carry me back to Tennessee. See Ellie Rhee (Winner)

"Then did Moses sing." See Song of Moses or Miriam

"Then does mem'ry turn to days." C. M. von Weber. e. SAS 1

"Then farewell! my trim-built wherry." See Poor Tom (Dibdin)

Then, gudewife, count the lawin. See "Gane is the day"

Then hail to the monarch high. See The corn song (Marks)

"Then he went unto the house." See The gypsy laddie (Virginia version)

"Then hear, and observe me well." See Pogner's anrede (Wagner)

Then hey for a lass wi' a tocher. See "Awa wi' your witchcraft o' beauty's alarms"

Then lay down the shovel and the hoe. See Uncle Ned (Foster)

Then love your neighbor as yourself. See Paddle your own canoe (Clifton)

"Then shall the King say, come, come." See Come, ye blessed (Gaul)

Then shall the righteous shine forth. Mendelssohn. e. OS 3—SAS 3—TS

Then soldiers patriotic, the nation looks to you. See Himno de Riego (Huerta)

"Then 'tis true, he is dead." See Se il ciel mi divide (Piccinni)

Then up wi't a', my ploughman lad. See "The ploughman, he's a bonie lad"

"Then while our hearts beat warm and true." See The good old college days

Then you shall be a truelover of mine. Irish folk song. JOI

Then you'll remember me ("When other lips") M. W. Balfe. Words by A. Bunn. e.f.i. PO. e. only DM 1—FSS 2—HSC—HSD—JS—MP— NMH— NML— NMS— TS —WA—WBT—WSW

"When other lips." BE 5—HSE 3

Theniel Menzie's bonnie Mary. Scottish air: The ruffians' rant. Words by R. Burns. PS 2
"In comin by the brig o' Dye." BSR

Theobald IV, king of Navarre. See Thibaut IV, king of Navarre

"There are flowers in the valley." See Young Kate of Kilcummer

"There are friends that we never forget." See Friends that we never forget (Winner)

"There are lonely hearts to cherish." See While the days are going by (Wyeth)

"There are not many so brave as we are." See Soldier's song (Verdi)

"There are sounds of mirth." Irish air: The priest in his boots. Words by T. Moore. MI—MMI

"There are tho'ts which seem to come from heav'n." See O loving heart, trust on (Gottschalk)

"There are three white doves a-flying." See Le tre colombe

"There are twa bonnie maidens." See Twa bonnie maidens

"There be none of beauty's daughters." F. Mendelssohn. Words by Lord Byron. BD

"There blooms a bonnie flower." See The heather glen

"There blossoms a tree before the door." See Der nussbaum (Schumann)

"There cam' a young man to my daddie's door." Scottish song. Air: The brisk young lad. PS 2

"There came a little Child to earth." R. Brown-Borthwick. Words by E. E. S. Elliott. HC

"There came a nymph dancing." See The young Indian maid

"There came an earl a-riding by." See The gypsy countess: part 1

"There came three kings by God's own hand." C. Vincent. Words from a German Christmas carol. [Tr of Es führt drei könige Gottes hand] e. HC

"There came three kings ere break of day." R. F. Smith. Words by G. Moultrie. HC

"There came three kings from eastern land." German Christmas carol. Tr of Es führt drei könige Gottes hand. e. HC

"There came three kings from far away." G. F, Hayward. Words by B. Cranston. HC

"There came three men from out the west." See Sir John Barleycorn

"There came three sages from afar." L. J. Garrett. HC

"There came to my window one morning in spring." See The robin

"There came to the beach." See The exile of Erin

"There comes a galley, laden." Composer unknown. Words by J. Tauler. Tr of Es komt ein schiff geladen. e. HC

"There dwells a maiden fair." See My gentle village maid (Arthur)

"There dwelt a miller, hale and bold." See The miller of the Dee

"There dwelt in old Judea." J. P. Harding. Words by D. R. Raymond. HC

"There dwelt in old Judea." R. Jackson. [Words by D. R. Raymond] HC

"There grew a bonnie brier-bush at our ha' door" (The bonnie brier-bush) Scottish air. Words by C. Mackay. PS 1

"There grew a fine fig-tree orchard." See Canção do figueiral

"There grows a bonie brier-bush in our kail-yard, there grows a bonie brier-bush in our kail-yard." Scottish air. Words by R. Burns. BSR

"There grows a bonnie brier-bush in oor kail-yard, and white are the blossoms on't." Scottish air. Old song with additional words by C. Nairne. HSSS—MMS
The bonnie brier-bush. PS 1

"There grows beneath the ocean." See Michelemmà

"There grows by the house an almond tree." See Der nussbaum (Schumann)

"There! I saw you." See T'aggio visto (Labriola)

There is a balm in Gilead. See Balm in Gilead

There is a bonny isle. Irish air. FSS 7

"There is a city builded upon a peaceful hill." See Sion (Rodney)

"There is a flash packet." See The Dreadnaught

"There is a flower that bloometh." V. Wallace. Words by E. Fitzball. BE 6—HSE 3

"There is a garden in her face." T. Campion (music and words) BOH

"There is a gard'ner's daughter." See La Luisella

"There is a gentle gleam." Irish air. Words by S. Lover. MMI

"There is a green hill far away." Gounod. Words by C. F. Alexander. HSS 2 —WA—WS—WSW
"There is a green hill far away" (Le Calvaire) e.f. FMB—HSS 1— PG 2—SM 3

"There is a green hill far away." R. S. Willis. Words by C. F. Alexander. FSS 5

"There is a happy land." Hindoo air, arr by L. Mason. FSS 1—WBT—WS —WSW
Happy land. HSD

"There is a laddie, and he is mine." See "Det fins en gosse och han är min" (Hallén)

"There is a lady grand." See My dear-o (Lemmel)

"There is a lady sweet and kind." See Passing by (Ford)

"There is a ladye sweet and kind." See Passing by (Purcell)

"There is a land far o'er the mighty western sea." See My native land (Suppé)

"There is a land where sunny skies." See The song of Australia (Linger)

"There is a light in Easterland." See "Det står ett ljus i Österland"

"There is a little perfumed flow'r." See Clover so white

"There is a lovely land." See Danish patriotic song of 1820 (Kroyer)

"There is a mill I know." See Le moulin

"There is a pathway in this vale of sorrow." See The Golden pathway (Gray)

"There is a reaper men call Death." See "Es ist ein schnitter" (German folk song)

"There is a reaper, whose name is Death." See The reaper and the flowers (Emerson)

"There is a school of jolly boys." See The school of jolly boys

"There is a snake that lives in yonder alley." See Serenata ("'Nta sta vanedda")

"There is a song we love to sing." See Ewing college song

"There is a tavern in the town." Cornish folk song. SSS—WC

"There is a time for ev'rything." See Aoleo

"There is a 'varsity out in the west." See John D. Rockefeller

"There is a wild boar in these woods." See Sir Lionel (Virginia version)

"There is an hour of peaceful rest." See Himmlische ruhe (Molique)

"There is an isle, a bonny isle." See There is a bonny isle

"There is beauty all around." See Love at home (McNaughton)

"There is beauty in the forest." See The world is full of beauty (Donizetti)

"There is dew for the flow'ret." See You and me

"There is fire in the galley." See Fire! fire

"There is fire in the lower hold." See Fire down below

"There is hovering about me." Arr from F. Abt. Words by A. Cary. LBR

"There is joy in ev'ry day." WBT—WSC

There is no end for souls like his. J. S. Sharland. Words by J. G. Whittier. LBR

"There is not in the wide world a valley so sweet." See The meeting of the waters

"There is one bright star in heaven." See My mother's memory (Klein); My mother's memory (Taubert)

"There is one thing more that grieves me." See One more day

There is rest for the weary. See Rest for the weary (Dadmun); Rest for the weary (McDonald)

"There is snow on the mountain." See The perils of the isle

"There is something in the moaning." See Lament

"There lies a fair land." See "Der ligger et land" (Nordraak)

"There lingered a lassie." See Moetje varen (Verhulst)

"There liv'd a man in yonder glen." Air: Johnie Blunt. Words by R. Burns. BSR

"There lived a sage in days of yore." See The pigtail (Bullard)

"There liv'd a wife in our gate end." See See Drap o' capie, O

"There lived a young maid on a cannibal isle." See Cannibalee (Taylor)

"There liv'd an old carl in Kellyburnbraes." See Kellyburnbraes

"There lived an old lady in the north country." See The two sisters (Albermarle county, Va. version)

"There lived an old lord by the northern sea." See The two sisters (Woodridge, Va. version)

"There lives a gard'ner's daughter." See La Luisella

"There lives a lass by yonder mill." See Sally of the mill

There lives a lass upon the green. 18th century song. CO 2

"There lives a lass upon the green." Air: Ffarwel Gwen. MMW

"There once liv'd a pretty young kitten call'd Puff." See Puff (Scott-Gatty)

"There once lived an old man." See Cradle song

"There once was a doctor (no foe to the proctor)." See The doctor (Newton)

"There once was a bold fisherman." See The bold fisherman (Hunt)

"There once were three students." See Der wirtin töchterlein

"There once were two royal children." See Zwei königskinder

"There over the meadows was shining the sun." See Wiegeliedje (Rennes)

"There quivers a glittering summer air." See Brudefaerden i Hardanger (Kjerulf)

"There reigns in holy calmness." See Frühlingslied (Fesca)

"There sang a bird on a linden-bough." See Fågelns visa (Söderberg)

There she blows. Whaling song. Air: Hail to the chief. CR

"There stands a lady." Singing game from Somerset. FSF

"There stands a tree in yonder glade." See In der fremde (Taubert)

"There stands hard by my father's." See "Derrière chez mon père, vole, mon coeur, vole" (Streabbog)

There stands in Austria a castle. See "Der stander et slot i Oesterrige"

"There stands on an island all rocky and bare." See The light-house

"There stood three Maries by the tomb." J. B. Litler. Words by J. M. Neale. HC

"There stood three rogues." See Möller-visen

"There was a battle in the north." Air: A country lass. Words by R. Burns. BSR

"There was a bee-i-ee-i-ee." See The bee and the pup

"There was a boat manned by thirty men." See Chanson de matelots

"There was a bonie lass." Air: A bonie lass. Words by R. Burns. BSR

"There was a bonny blade." See The dumb wife

"There was a crooked man." Nursery song. WSC

"There was a fair maiden." See The north country lass (Dibdin)

"There was a farmer had two sons." See Bohunkus

"There was a farmer had three sons." See The three sons

"There was a farmer's son kept sheep all on the hill." See Blow away the morning dew

"There was a frog in the spring, sing song Kitty can't you kimey O." See The frog in the well

"There was a frog lived in a spring, sing-song paddy woncha kymeo." See The frog in the spring

"There was a jolly blade that married a country maid." See Dumb, dumb, dumb

"There was a jolly farmer who lived a neighbor nigh." See Peggy Walker

"There was a jolly miller once lived on the river Dee." See The miller of the Dee

"There was a jovial beggar." See A begging we will go

"There was a king in Thule." See Der könig von Thule (Liszt)

"There was a king of Thule." See Der könig in Thule (Zelter)

"There was a king of Yvetot once." See Le roi d'Yvetot

"There was a lad was born in Kyle." Air: Dainty Davie. Words by R. Burns. BSR

"There was a lad was born in Kyle." Air: O gin ye were deid, guidman. Words by R. Burns. BSB—MMS—PS 1

"There was a lady all in the garden." See The broken token (Allanstand, N.C. version no. 2)

"There was a lady and gay was she." See The wife of Usher's well (Tennessee version)

"There was a lady dwelt in York." See The cruel mother

"There was a lady in the north country." See Lay the bent to the bonny broom

"There was a lady lived in New York." See The wife of Usher's well (Black Mountain, N.C. version)

"There was a lass and she was fair" (Bonnie Jean) Scottish air. Words by R. Burns. PS 1

"There was a lass and she was fair." Air: Willie was a wanton wag. Words by R. Burns. BSB—MMS—PS 2

"There was a lass, they ca'd her Meg." Air: Ye'll ay be welcome back again. Words by R. Burns. BSR

"There was a little boatsman." See The boatsman and the chest

"There was a little fam'ly lived up in Bethany." See The little family

"There was a little fishermaiden." See The little fishermaiden (Waldmann)

"There was a little maiden." See "Il était un' bergère"

"There was a little man." See The crab-fish

"There was a little ship and she sailed upon the sea." See The Mary Golden Tree

"There was a little ship in the North Amerikee she went by the name of the Golden Willow Tree." See The Golden Vanity (Black Mountain, N.C. version)

"There was a little ship in the South Amerikee that went by the name of the Weeping Willow Tree." See The Golden Vanity (Hot Springs, N.C. version no. 1)

"There was a little soldier boy who lately came from over." See The lady and the dragoon (North Carolina version)

"There was a little watersprite." See Lurlaline

"There was a little woman, as I've heard say." See The little woman

"There was a maid, and she went to the mill." See There was a maid went to the mill

"There was a maid the other day." See Heigh-ho! for a husband

There was a maid went to the mill ("There was a maid and she went to the mill") 17th or 18th century song. MM

There was an old woman liv'd under a hill ("There was a maid went to the mill") CO 2
Variant of: "There was an old woman liv'd under a hill"

"There was a man in ancient times." See Lazarus

"There was a man lived in the west, dan dù, dan dù." See The wife wrapt in wether's skin (Kentucky version no. 2)

"There was a man lived in the west; fal lal lal lal lido." See Ruggleton's daughter of Iero

"There was a man went up and down." See The lone fish-ball

"There was a man who lived in England." See Young Beichan (Kentucky version)

"There was a mason who lived by his trade." See The cruel ship's carpenter (Black Mountain, N.C. version)

"There was a Med from P. and S." See The Med

"There was a miller, as you shall hear." See The miller and his sons

"There was a place in childhood." See My mother dear (Lover)

"There was a Presbyterian cat." See The Presbyterian cat

"There was a professor in New York did dwell." See Sing tangent, co-tangent

"There was a proper tall young man." See Lady Isabel and the elf knight (Georgia version)

"There was a rich lady." See The brown girl (Allanstand, N.C. versions no. 1-2)

"There was a rich merchant in London did right." See The silk merchant's daughter (Allanstand, N.C. version)

"There was a rich old lady." See The rich old lady

"There was a rich young farmer." See Married to a mermaid

"There was a shepherd's daughter." See The knight and shepherd's daughter

"There was a ship came from the north country." See The Golden Vanity

"There was a silk merchant, in London he did dwell." See Jackaro

"There was a silk merchant in London town did dwell." See Jack went a-sailing (Georgia version)

"There was a squire lived in the east." See The green wedding

"There was a tailor had a mouse." See The tailor and the mouse

"There was a tree all in the woods." See The tree in the wood (North Carolina version)

"There was a tree in Odenwald." See The tree of Odenwald

"There was a wealthy merchant." See Jack went a-sailing (Kentucky version)

"There was a wife wonn'd in Cockpen." Air: Scroggam. Words by R. Burns. BSR

"There was a woman of the north." See The wife of Usher's well (Big Laurel, N.C. version)

"There was a young man who courted me." See The brisk young lover (Georgia version)

"There was a youth, and a well-beloved youth." See The bailiff's daughter of Islington

"There was a youth, and a well loved youth." See The maid of Islington

"There was an aged monarch." See "Es war ein alter könig" (Rubinstein)

"There was an old darkey and his name was Uncle Ned." See Uncle Ned (Foster)

"There was an old ewe with only one horn." See The old ewe with one horn

"There was an old fellow at Waltham Cross" (Taunton Dean) 17th century song. CO 2

"There was an old king in ancient days." See End this war

"There was an old man and he lived in a wood." See Broom, green broom

"There was an old man and he lived in the west." See Green broom

"There was an old man came over the sea." See My mother bid me (Virginia version)

"There was an old man he had a wife." See The wife wrapt in wether's skin (Virginia version)

"There was an old man lived out in the wood." See Green broom

"There was an old man lived under the hill." See The farmer's curst wife (Virginia version)

"There was an old man who followed the plough." See The farmer's curst wife (North Carolina version)

"There was an old nigger, and his name was Uncle Ned." See Uncle Ned (Foster)

"There was an old woman and she had a little pig." See The little pig

"There was an old woman, as I've heard tell." See The old woman and the peddler

"There was an old woman liv'd under a hill." Old English song. BE 7

There was an old woman liv'd under a hill ("There was a maid went to the mill") See There was a maid went to the mill

"There was anes a May." See Were na my heart licht I wad dee

"There was five carlins in the south." Air: Chevy chase. Words by R. Burns. BSR

"There was no room found in the inn." See Behold that star (Talley)

"There was on a time." Air: Caledonian hunt's delight. Words by R. Burns. BSR

"There was once a little ship." See Le petit navire

"There was once a man with a double chin." See Old Zip Coon

"There was once an old lady in the north country." See The two sisters (Mt Fair, Va. version)

"There was one little Jack." See Little Jack

"There was Spla-foot Nance." See Spla-foot Nance

"There was the Prince Eugene in Paris town one day." See Le prince Eugene

"There was three kings into the east." Air: Lull me beyond thee. Words by R. Burns. BSR

"There was two lofty ships." See High Barbaree

"There went a fiddler marching." See O tempora! O mores

"There were five jolly good fellows." See When Joan's ale was new

"There were lovers three." See Happy three (Roeckel)

"There were ninety and nine." See The ninety and nine (Sankey)

"There were shepherds abiding in the field." See Messiah: selection (Händel)

"There were shepherds watching." A. A. Wild. HC

"There were ten virgins." Negro spiritual. HR

"There were three books." Words by A. Nash. CHS

"There were three brothers in merry Scotland." See Henry Martin

"There were three crows sat on a tree, and they were black as crows could be." See Three crows

"There were three crows sat on a tree, O Billy Magee Magar." See Crow song

"There were three drunken maidens." See The drunken maidens

"There were three gipsies a-come to my door." See The wraggle taggle gipsies, O

"There were three jovial fellows." See When Joan's ale was new

"There were three jovial Welshmen." See Three jovial Welshmen

"There were three kings." See John Barleycorn

"There were three lads." See La mort de la fiancée

"There were three lovely sisters." See O pescator dell' onda

"There were three ravens." See The three ravens

"There were three rogues." See Möllervisen

"There were three travellers." See Three travellers

"There were two lofty ships from old England came." See High Barbaree

There'll never be peace till Jamie comes hame ("By yon castle wa'") Air: There are few good fellows when Jamie's awa'. Words by R. Burns. BSB—MMS—PS 1

"By yon castle wa' at the close of the day." BSR

"There's a beautiful flag." G. F. Wilson. Words by B. Webber. JS

"There's a beech-tree grove by the river side." See Nelly, my love, and me

"There's a bower of roses by Bendemeer's stream." See Bendemeer's stream

"There's a boy just over the garden fence." See Whistle and hoe

"There's a chantey song." See Sailor's home song (Ames)

"There's a chicken in the pot." Irish folk song. JOI

"There's a church in the valley by the wildwood." See The little brown church in the vale (Pitts)

"There's a colleen fair as May." See Péarla an brollaig báin

"There's a college in sunny southern land." See Clear the way for U. S. C. (Shanahan)

"There's a crying at my window." See May eve

"There's a dear little plant" (The green little shamrock) Irish air. Words by A. Cherry. MMI

"There's a dear little plant" (The dear little shamrock) J. W. Cherry. Words by A. Cherry. FSS 4—PI—WBT

"There's a fairy flying o'er the sea." See Marianina

"There's a gap in the hedge at Kilmare." See The gap in the hedge

"There's a girl whose parents have consented." See Wedding song

"There's a good time coming, boys, a good time coming." See The good time coming

"There's a good time coming, help it on, (help it on)." See Help it on

There's a good wind. See Le canard blanc

"There's a great camp meetin' over yonder." See A great camp meetin'

"There's a grim one-horse hearse." See The pauper's drive (Hutchinson)

"There's a haze that hides the meadows." See September (Olds)

"There's a land, a radiant land." See The land of dreams (Wilton)

"There's a land that bears a well-known name." See The Englishman (Blockley)

"There's a land that is fairer than day." See The sweet by and by (Webster)

"There's a limit to my patience." See "To-do tiene su hasta aquí"

"There's a little one lives by the city." See Carmè (Curtis)

"There's a lone green valley." See Darling Nelly Gray (Hanby)

There's a love-feast in the heavens by-an'-by. See A love-feast in heaven

"There's a low green valley." See Darling Nelly Gray (Hanby)

There's a meeting here to-night. Negro song. JP

"There's a music up in the frozen hills." See Easter (Hadley)

"There's a name which doth delight me." See Gwendoline

"There's a pow'r whose sway." See The power of love (Balfe)

"There's a pretty little village." See Oh, Oregon! oh, Oregon (Strong)

"There's a shepherd, few more discreet." See "Je connais un berger discret"

"There's a ship lies off Dunvegan." See The hills o' Skye (Harris)

"There's a sigh in the heart." A. Fricker. FSS 8

"There's a something, we're told." See Keep a light heart (Fase)

"There's a song in the air." W. H. Jones. Words by J. G. Holland. NMS

"There's a song in the air." G. E. Martin. Words by J. G. Holland. HC

"There's a spell on the face of the stream." See Ichabod (Tchaikovsky)

"There's a spot 'mid the hills of Alleghany." See Star of the east

"There's a time for all things." See "Chaque chose a son temps"

"There's a voice that I enshrine." See "Una voce poco fà" (Rossini)

"There's a wedding in the orchard, dear." See Blossom time

"There's a wideness in God's mercy." L. S. Tourjee. Words by F. W. Faber. BSS

"There's a wonderful tree." F. Schilling. Words by Mrs M. N. Meigs. HC

"There's a wonderful weaver." See The wonderful weaver (Levey)

"There's a youth in this city." N. Gow. Words by R. Burns. BSR

"There's always cheer to find." See The good turns pay (Foster)

"There's an old Spanish proverb." See Spanish proverb

"There's auld Rob Morris." See Auld Rob Morris

"There's cauld kail in Aberdeen." Air: Cauld kail. Old song with additional words by R. Burns. BSR

"There's cauld kail in Aberdeen" (Cauld kail in Aberdeen) Air: Cauld kail. Old song with additional words by the duke of Gordon. PS 1

"There's fire in the cook-tent." See Chow song

"There's fire in the east." See My way's cloudy

"There's folks that like the good dry land." See When the drive goes down

"There's, for flowers of spring, the hill Higashiyama." See The four seasons in Kioto

"There's light upon the sea today." See When the boats come home (Moore)

"There's many a man of the Cameron clan." See The march of the Cameron men

"There's melody, boys, in the splashing oar." See Arms are strong and hearts are true

"There's much good cheer in youthful days." See Good cheer

"There's music in my heart all day." See The wind that shakes the barley

"There's music in the air at morning and at noon." See Music in the air, Counterpoint for (Loomis)

"There's music in the air—when the infant morn is nigh." See Music in the air (Root)

There's nae luck about the house ("And are ye sure the news is true") Scottish song. Words attributed to J. Adam and to J. Mickle. BOS —MMS—PS 1

Nae luck about the house. JO

There's nae room for twa. G. Satter. Words by G. Danby. JO

"There's nane shall ken, there's nane can guess." Air: I'll gae nae mair to your town. Words by R. Burns. BSR

"There's naught but care on ev'ry han'." See Green grow the rashes, O

"There's ne'er a blossom." See Song of my dear

"There's news, lasses, news." Air: There's news, lasses. Words by R. Burns. BSR

"There's no deity but God" ("Lá ilahá il-lalláh."—Dervish song) ar.e. BO

"There's no dew left on the daisies and clover." See Song of seven

"There's no tree but casts its shadow during the summer." See "No hay arbol"

"There's not a cloud a-sailing by." See Furze bloom

"There's not a word." FSS 7

"There's nothing bright, above, below" (Avon) Words by T. Moore. LA

There's nothing true but heaven. O. Shaw. Words by T. Moore. JO
Nothing true but heaven. FSS 7

"There's nought but care on ev'ry han'." See Green grow the rashes, O

"There's one, I know him not." See "Un certo non so che" (Vivaldi)

"There's one that is pure as an angel." See The gentle maiden

There's one wide river. See Noah's ark

"There's Polly and Johnny and Kitty and Jane." See See-saw waltz song (Crowe)

There's room enough for all. Sunday school song. FSS 4

"There's sax eggs in the pan, gudeman." Air: O, an ye were dead guidman. Words by R. Burns. BSR

"There's three fair maids." See The cruel brother (North Carolina version)

There's three true gude fellows. See "It's now the day is dawin"

"There's Timothy left the wain." See Timothy's welcome (Marzials)

These are they which came out of great tribulation. A. R. Gaul. OS 1—SAS 1

"These fresh forget-me-nots so softly blue." See Forget-me-nots (Parker)

These see His wonders in the deep (Dundee) [Guillaume Franc] Words by J. Addison. TL

"These your words were." See Statt' attiente

Theuriet, André
Le roitelet (Paladilhe)

They all love Jack. S. Adams. Words by F. E. Weatherly. HSD—WBT

They are chiming gaily now. See Silver chimes (Barnard)

"They are going, going, going." See The passing of the Gael

"They are three mowers in the field." See Le miracle du nouveau-né

"They bore their cross in sorrow uncomplaining." See A melody (Chopin)

"They call me Hanging Johnnie." See Hanging Johnny

"They came from a land beyond the sea." See The song of Innisfail

They come with blissful song. W. T. Wrighton. MCS

"They crucified my Lord." See Crucifixion

They falter not. R. D. Mallary. Words by J. E. Rankin. JS

"They fled, the gloomy powers." F. Hiller. e. SAS 1

"They grew in beauty side by side." See The graves of a household (Barker)

"They had opened wide the mighty doors of oak." See The country feast (Musorgskiĭ)

"They hadn't been there but a very short time." See The wife of Usher's well (Carmen, N.C. version)

"They kept not the law." Molique. OS 2

"They know not my heart." Air: Coolon das. Words by T. Moore. MI

"They leave the land of gems and gold." Old French carol. Words by A. de Vere. HC

"They may rail at this life." Air: Noch bonin shin doe. Words by T. Moore. MI

"They play'd in their beautiful gardens." See The children's home (Cowen)

They said I was not pretty. See Ils m'ont appelé' vilaine

"They sailed away in a gallant bark." See Dublin bay (Barker)

"They sat by the fireside, his fair daughters three." See No, never, no

"They say Mister ** he ain't got no style." See Style all the while

"They say that the year is old and gray." See New Year song (Oehmler)

"They say the years have swallows' wings." See For you (Smith)

"They say true love is a blessing." See She's gone, let her go

"They shall be turned back." Costa. OS 1

"They shall not ever win thee." See Der deutsche Rhein (Kunze)

"They snool me sair an' haud me down." See An' O, for ane-an'-twenty, Tam

"They talk about arenas of the south." See Our noble selves (Newton)

"They tell me thou'rt the favour'd guest." Balfe. Words by T. Moore. DM 2

"They tell us that you mighty powers." H. Purcell. Words by R. Howard. BE 6

"They walk'd by the sea, in deep thought." See Rav (Sinding)

"They wanted me to go into the bull-fight." See "Me puse a torear"

"They whisper first of all." See Silver chimes (Barnard)

"They who seek the throne of grace" (Prayer) J. B. Dykes. Words by O. Holden. MS

"They who seek the throne of grace" (God is present everywhere) G. F. Händel. [Words by O. Holden] FSS 3

Thibault, Charles
"My life is like the summer rose"

Thibaut IV, king of Navarre
"L'autrier par la matinée"
"Christ is born of Maiden fair" (Tr of Christo paremus canticam, excelsis gloria)
"Early strolling at my leisure." See "L'autrier par la matinée"
In excelsis gloria. See "Christ is born of Maiden fair"
"T'other morning very early." See L'autrier par la matinée
"Sons of men, behold"

"**Thickest** night, surround my dwelling." A. Masterton. Words by R. Burns. BSR

Thiele, J. G. A.
"Beside the lake of Thun"

"**Thine** am I, my faithful fair." Air: The Quaker's wife. Words by R. Burns. BSR

Thine am I, my faithful fair. J. Whitaker. [Words by R. Burns] HSE 2

"**Thine** eyes are bright with fire." Arabian folk song. Words from the Arabic. e.f. BO

"**Thine** eyes are so lovely." See Coraggio, ben mio

"**Thine** eyes so blue." See "Mit deinen blauen augen" (Lassen)

"**Thine** eyes so gently open." See Blicken (Alfvén)

"**Thine** eyes still shined." K. Kreutzer. Words by R. W. Emerson. LBR

"**Thine** eyes they told me." See How I have loved thee

"**Thine** eyes with mine." See Die liebende schreibt (Mendelssohn)

"**Thine**, Lord, are the blessings of forest and field." C. Vincent. Words by Bickersteth. HC

Thine, O Saviour, is love unending. M. Blumner. e. SAS 2

"A **thing** of beauty." N. C. Page. Words by J. Keats. TL

"**Things** can not be this way for ever." See Ewiger wechsel (Himmel)

"**Think** not that any wrong I do thee." See Zum letzten mal

"**Think** not thou canst deceive me." See Bolero castellano

"**Thinking** of old times." See Old friends and old times (Thomas)

"The **third** day was the marriage feast." See The cup of joy

"The **thirty-first** of the month of August." See Le combat naval

"**This** bonnet that theekit his wonderfu' head." See Rab Roryson's bonnet

"**This** book is all that's left me now." See My mother's Bible (Russell)

"**This** cold flinty heart it is you who have warmed." See Sweet passion of love (Arne)

"**This** day is born Emmanuel." M. Praetorius. e. HC

"**This** evening, Nina dear, I rose above you." See Funiculì-funiculà ("Stasera, Nina mia") (Denza)

"**This** fair maid to the meadow's gone." Irish folk song. JOI

"**This** fair rose may tell." See "Della rosa il bel vermiglio" (Rossini)

"**This** flower you gave to me." See "La fleur que tu m'avais jetée" (Bizet)

"**This** flower you threw to me." See "La fleur que tu m'avais jetée" (Bizet)

"**This** happy day." P. Henrion. e. FSS 7

"**This** happy morn a King is born." T. H. Spinney. Words by Mrs H. Watson. HC

This is my dream. M. Wellings. Words by M. Mark-Lemon. FSS 5—JSE

This is no my ain lassie. See "I see a form, I see a face"

"**This** is the Christ, our God and Lord." See Glad tidings (Luther)

"**This** is the day of light." See Dawn (Barnby)

"**This** is the day the light was made." See Sonntagslied (Mendelssohn)

"**This** is the feast-day of our King." J. Stevenson. HC

"**This** is the month." See The Nativity, Stanzas from (Smith)

"**This** joyful Easter-tide." HC

"**This** life is all chequer'd with pleasures and woes." Air: The bunch of green bushes. Words by T. Moore. MI

This lovely turtle-dove. See Cette aimable tourterelle

"**This** merry month its greeting brings." See Le mois de mai

"**This** new Christmas carol." Traditional air. HC

"**This** night God's greatest kindness." See Sun of Christmas-tide (Weidt)

"**This** night I lift my heart to Thee." See I lift my heart to Thee (Costa)

This old time religion. Negro spiritual. JSE—NMP—WBT
Gimme dat ol'-time religion. JB

"**This** place is holy." See Ah! se tu dormi, svegliati (Vaccai)

"**This** rock that overhangs the foam." Irish air: The foggy dew. Words by J. Fitzgerald. MMI

"**This** song of mine is without an ending." See "Aa denne vise har ingen ende"

"**This** tree was grown on Christmas day." See The Christmas tree

"**This** very hour she thinks of me." See "In dieser stunde" (Spicker)

"**This** very night—can it be true." See Night-gown chorus (West)

"**This** way come, my gentle lasses." See Maidens, bright and fair (Flotow)

"**This** world is all a fleeting show." See There's nothing true but heaven (Shaw)

Tho'. For entries beginning Tho' see Though

"**T'ho** lasciato, e son contento." See La smortina

"T'ho veduta." See T'aggio visto (Labriola)

Thomas, Ambroise
Air du tambour major
Behold Titania. See Je suis Titania
Berceuse. See "De son coeur j'ai
calmé la fièvre"
"C'est moi, j'ai tout brisé." See Me
voici dans son boudoir
Chanson bachique (from Hamlet)
"Connais-tu le pays" (from Mignon.
Tr of "Kennst du das land")
"De son coeur j'ai calmé la fièvre"
(from Mignon)
"Dost thou know that fair land." See
"Connais-tu le pays"
The drum-major's song. See Air du
tambour major
"Elle ne croyait pas" (from Mignon)
Evening. See Le soir
I am here in her boudoir. See Me voici
dans son boudoir
I am Titania. See Je suis Titania
I implore thee, O, my brother. See
Je t'implore, ô mon frère
Je suis Titania (from Mignon)
Je t'implore, ô mon frère (from Ham-
let)
"Knowest thou the land." See "Con-
nais-tu le pays"
"Know'st thou yonder land." See
"Connais-tu le pays"
Me voici dans son boudoir (from
Mignon)
Mignon. See "Connais-tu le pays"
Mignon's slumber-song. See "De son
coeur j'ai calmé la fièvre"
Ne'er dreamed the tender maid. See
"Elle ne croyait pas"
"Ô vin, dissipe la tristesse." See Chan-
son bachique
Polonaise. See Je suis Titania
"Pure as a bud of spring." See "Elle
ne croyait pas"
Le soir
"'Tis I! somewhat disturbed." See
Me voici dans son boudoir

Thomas, Arthur
"Jolly boating weather, jolly sweet har-
vest breeze" (Drummond)
See also Eno, J. N., jt. auth.

Thomas, Arthur Goring
Mignon (Tr of "Kennst du das land")
My heart is weary (from Nadeschda)
Noon at the village
Une nuit de mai
O vision entrancing (from Esmeralda)
Schwer liegt auf dem herzen. See My
heart is weary
A song of sunshine
A summer night. See Une nuit de
mai
What would I do for my queen (from
Esmeralda)
"Winds in the trees"

Thomas, E.
"'Tis said that absence conquers love"

Thomas, Edith Matilda
Come, show me the way (Composer
unknown)
Heigh-ho, the holly (Crawford)

Thomas, Edwin
A warrior bold (Maybrick)

Thomas, Frederick William
"'Tis said the absence conquers love"
(Thomas)

Thomas, Helen
The bird's nest (Composer unknown)

Thomas, John
Composer and author
"He sang of the sea"
Author
Carmarthen bells (Welsh air)
Fair Ellen Pugh (Welsh air)
"Haste to the greenwood" (Welsh air)
The holly (Welsh air)
"I am a shepherd boy" (Welsh air)
"John Owens" (Welsh air)
Lament ("Bedwas hills") (Welsh air)
The lament ("Oft I've bent") (Welsh
air)
The lass of Grongar hill (Welsh air)
"My love, thou'rt like a dew-gemm'd
flower" (Welsh air)
My Nanny (Welsh air)
Nancy (Welsh air)
The nightingale (Welsh air)
Ogwr valley (Welsh air)
Sally of the mill (Welsh air)
Shepherd's song (Welsh air)
"Strike, strike the harp" (Welsh air)
The thatcher (Welsh air)
Young Robin (Welsh air)

Thomas, John Rogers
"Beautiful isle of the sea"
Bonny Eloise
Old friends and old times
Rose of Killarney
"'Tis but a little faded flower"
"'Twas when the hay was mown, Mag-
gie"

Thomas, T. Dillwyn
"Sweetheart, I wait for thee"

Thomé, François Luc Joseph
A love sonnet. See Sonnet d'amour
Love-token. See Simple aveu
Simple aveu
Simple confession. See Simple aveu
Sonnet d'amour

Thompson, of Newcastle
The keel row (18th century air)

Thompson, Alexander S.
For Lincoln we will ever stand
"He was nervous"

Thompson, Alfred
Ripples touched by the moon (Composer unknown)

Thompson, Edward
Homeward bound (Arne)
"The topsails shiver in the wind"
(Arne)

Thompson, G. Douglas
The diver (Loder)

Thompson, H. S.
Annie Lisle
Cousin Jedediah
Lilly Dale

"**Thoms** sass am hallenden see." See Der arme Thoms (Zelter)

Thomson, George
Lord Ullin's daughter

Thomson, James
Rule, Britannia (Arne) Authorship uncertain
A song of Thanksgiving (Allitsen)

Thomson, James, and Mallet, David
Arise, sweet messenger of morn (Arne)

Thomson, John
The robin redbreast (Levey)

Thomson, Mrs Robert
The Texas cowboy

The thorn. W. Shield. Words by J. O'Keeffe. DM 1—HSE 1—ME—PR 2

Thornby,
"The voice of free grace" (Clark)

Thorne, Edward Henry
"All hail! all hail to the natal day"
The angel and the shepherds

Thornton, L. M.
"Sing, sweet bird"

"**Those** bonny glades of Girvan woods." See Twenty years ago (Gatty)

"**Those** Christmas bells as sweetly chime as on the day when first they rung so merrily in the olden time, and far and wide their music flung." See Christmas once a year

"**Those** Christmas bells as sweetly chime as once when first they rang so joyous in the olden time, when conscious nature sang." See Christmas joy forever (Converse)

"**Those** days long vanish'd are to me regretful." See Tradetore

Those endearing young charms. See "Believe me, if all those endearing young charms"

"**Those** evening bells." Round. [Words by T. Moore] NMH—NMS

"**Those** evening bells." [Composer unknown. Words by T. Moore] FSS 1
Evening bells. LA

"**Those** evening bells." Attributed to Beethoven. Words by T. Moore. DM 1—HSD—HSE 1—JO—WBT

"**Those** evening bells." Bellini. Words by T. Moore. FSS 2

"**Thou**, all my bliss." See "Caro mio ben" (Giordani)

"**Thou** ancient, thou healthful, thou mountainous north." See "Du gamla, du fria, du fjällhoga nord"

"**Thou** ancient, thou wholesome, thou mountainous north." See "Du gamla, du fria, du fjällhoga nord"

"**Thou** art always the same to me, dear" (Waipio) C. K. Hopkins. e.h. HA

"**Thou** art come from the spirit's land." See The messenger bird (Browne)

"**Thou** art gane awa' frae me." Scottish song. PS 2

"**Thou** art gone from my gaze." T. Linley; wrongly attributed to G. Linley. BE 2—BSE—FSS 7—HSE 3

"**Thou** art great and Thou art good." See Grace before meat at Hampton

Thou art mine all. See Du bist mein all' (Bradsky)

"**Thou** art mine, thou art mine." W. J. Baltzell. Words by E. C. Stedman. HST

"**Thou** art more lovely than the flower blooming." See "Tu eres mas bella"

"**Thou** art my life, my soul and heart." See Widmung (Schumann)

"**Thou** art my only thought." See Jeg elsker dig (Grieg)

"**Thou** art my own love." J. D. Redding (music and words) CHS—CU—MPC—WC

"**Thou** art my rest, my hope, my stay." See "Du är min ro" (Collan)

Thou art my rose. Serenade. FSS 6—NML

"**Thou** art my soul, thou art my heart." See Widmung (Schumann)

Thou art near me, Margarita. See Dein gedenk' ich, Margareta (Meyer-Helmund)

"**Thou** art, O God, the life and light." See Spring (Haydn)

Thou art so near, and yet so far. See "Ich kenn' ein aug', das so mild" (Reichardt)

"**Thou** art sweet peace and tranquil rest." See "Du bist die ruh" (Schubert)

"**Thou** art the guide of our youth." A. R. Gaul. SAS 2

"**Thou** art the noblest of them all." See "Du bist die herrlichste von allen" (Ries)

"**Thou** art the pure and chaste moonlight." See Du bist mein all' (Bradsky)

Thou art the way ("Show me the way") J. L. Roeckel. Words by M. Mark-Lemon. HSS 4

"**Thou** art the way: to Thee alone" (Dundee) Guillaume Franc. Words by G. W. Doane. FSS 3

"**Thou** art to me a flower." See "Du bist wie eine blume" (Degele)

"**Thou** art welcome, O guest! Aman." See Welcome song

"**Thou** avaunt thee." See "Tu? indietro" (Verdi)

Thou Bethlehem. J. B. Dykes. MCS

"**Thou** bidst me sing." Irish air: I am a poor rambling boy. Words by T. Moore. MMI

"**Thou** blessed Virgin, hear my pleading." See "Allmächt'ge Jungfrau" (Wagner)

"**Thou** blooming Red Rose." See A rose on an Indian grave (Lieurance)

"**Thou** blossom bright with autumn dew." See To the fringed gentian (Lang)

"**Thou** bonnie wood of Craigielea." J. Barr. Words by Tannahill. PS 2

"**Thou** calm-ray'd spring, whose blooming face." See Spring song

"**Thou** canst not blame me if I sever." See The Tyrolese maiden's farewell

"**Thou** dark-winding Carron." J. M'Donald. Words by Tannahill. PS 2

"Thou didst leave Thy throne." J. B. Powell. Words by E. E. S. Elliott. HC

"Thou enchanted land, gardens of delight." See Ô paradis sorti de l'onde (Meyerbeer)

"Thou entomb'd art prostrate lying." See In the tomb (Vassilenko)

Thou fair pulse of my heart ("I think of you by day") See Acushla gal machree

Thou fair pulse of my heart ("When first into this town") See A chushla gal mochree

"Thou faithless men." See "Si la rigueur" (Halévy)

"Thou forest broad and weeping." See Farewell to the forest (Mendelssohn)

"Thou Grace divine, encircling all." G. Franc. LA

"Thou hast left me ever, Jamie." Air: Fee him, father. Words by R. Burns. BSB—BSR—PS 1

"Thou hast spread thy wings to heaven." G. Donizetti. [Tr of Tu che a Dio spiegasti l'ali] e. WBT

"Thou hast wounded the spirit that loved thee." Mrs Porter (music and words) JO—WBT

"Thou holy art, how oft in hours of sadness." See An die musik (Schubert)

"Thou holy form to thee in anguish turning." See Der moench (Meyerbeer)

"Thou know'st the land." See "Kennst du das land" (Liszt)

"Thou ling'ring star with less'ning ray" (To Mary in heaven) Air: Mary's dream (old setting) Words by R. Burns. BSB

"Thou ling'ring star with less'ning ray." L. J. Oswald. Words by R. Burns. BSR

"Thou lovely bird." See "Charmant oiseau" (David)

"Thou lovely child of early spring." See Med en primulaveris (Grieg)

"Thou lovely dreamer." See "Du liebes auge" (Franz)

"Thou lovely maiden, come and throw the golden dice with me." See Guldterning

"Thou monstrous fiend, whither dost haste." See "Abscheulicher! wo eilst du hin" (Beethoven)

Thou, O Lord, art my protector. C. Saint-Saëns. e. SAS 2

"Thou of my heart the diadem." See "Du meines herzens krönelein" (Strauss)

Thou only canst give peace. See Hymnus (Bruch)

"Thou only comfort of the lowly." See "Du pauvre seul ami" (Auber)

Thou shalt break them with a rod of iron. G. F. Händel. SAS 3

"Thou shalt bring them in." G. F. Händel. OS 2—SAS 2

"Thou sittest at thy window there." See Marie (Franz)

"Thou sittest in thy bow'r, Marie." See Marie (Jensen)

"Thou sittest on Thy judgment-seat." M. Blumner. e. SAS 1

"Thou soft-flowing Avon." T. A. Arne. HSE 2

"Thou speakest of the past, dear heart." See Past and future (De Koven)

"Thou, star resplendent, pure and bright." See O du mein holder abendstern (Wagner)

"Thou sweetest bloom of evening hour." See Forget-me-not (Hopkins)

"Thou sword so cheerly shining." See Schwertlied (Weber)

"Thou tall and e'er verdant mountains." See United

"Thou that hast wings for flying." See "Tu, ch'hai le penne, amore" (Caccini)

"Thou, thou fillest my heart, dear." See "Du, du liegst mir im herzen"

"Thou, thou, reign'st in this bosom." See "Du, du, liegst mir im herzen"

"Thou, to whom Galilee kneeleth." R. Pugno. e. SAS 1

"Thou, too, sail on, O ship of state." See The ship of state (Composer unknown)

"Thou, true God alone." See Morning song

"Thou wand'ring moon, whose soothing light." See "Com' è gentil" (Donizetti)

"Thou who grantest inspiration." See "Tu sul labbro de' veggenti" (Verdi)

"Thou Who holdest in Thy keeping." See Ständchen (Raff)

"Thou Who ordainest, for the land's salvation." See God save the nation (Work)

"Thou, Whose almighty word" (Italian hymn) F. Giardini. Words by J. Marriott. LA

"Thou Whose birth on earth angels sang to men." See Bid the day be born (Randegger)

"Thou wilt come no more, gentle Annie." See Gentle Annie (Foster)

"Thou wilt keep him in perfect peace." See Trust (Williams)

"Thou wilt never grow old." G. Linley. Words by E. C. Howarth. FSS 4

"Thou wilt not cower in the dust." See Maryland! my Maryland

"Thou window that hast shone." See "Fenesta che lucivi e mò non luci"

"Tho' all triumphant the heav'nly powers." A. Rubinstein. e. SAS 1

"Though beauty like the rose." H. Carey. DM 2

"Tho' begging is an honest trade." See The happy beggars (Carey)

"Tho' Chloe's out of fashion." W. Boyce. ME

"Tho' cruel fate should bid us part" (The northern lass) Air: The northern lass. [Words by R. Burns] PS 2

"Tho' cruel fate should bid us part." Air: She rose and let me in. Words by R. Burns. BSR

"Tho' dark are our sorrows." See The prince's day

"Tho' dark fate hath 'reft me." See Farewell

"Though Eugene has always favored the lemon color bright." See The orange and the black—Albany (Shackelton)

"Tho' far from thee roving o'er." See Home of my childhood

"Tho' from poets not descended." See Finnish rune

"Though from us thou sever." See In memoriam (Rossini)

"Though full as 'twill hold of gold." See The red-hair'd man's wife

"Though his voice was breath'd afar." See "Una voce poco fà" (Rossini)

"Though humble the banquet." Air: Farewell Eamon. Words by T. Moore. MI

"Though I blush, I love to hear." See He loves me well (Rozkošný)

"Tho' I go ranging the world over." See "Vado ben spesso cangiando loco" (Rosa)

"Though I only bow before you." See "Per la gloria d'adorarvi" (Bononcini)

Though lost to sight. F. H. Cowen. Words by R. Jenkins. FSS 8

"Tho' lowly my lot." See Maid of Llangollen

"Though many and bright are the stars that appear." See E pluribus unum

"Though many there be that daily I see." See The pearl of th' Irish nation

"Tho' mountains high the billows roll." See All's one to Jack (Dibdin)

"Though my day be dark with sorrow." See "Ogni pena più spietata" (Pergolesi)

"Tho' not deserving thy cruel scorn." See "Sebben, crudele" (Caldara)

"Though pain and sorrow it bring to me." See "Lasciar d'amarti per non penar" (Gasparini)

"Tho' Peggy's charms have oft been sung." See Peggy (Arne)

"Tho' polar snows are ever near." See Savolaisen laulu (Collan)

"Though poor be the chamber." See Nazareth (Gounod)

"Though the clouds are low'ring round me." See I'll do my duty

"Though the house be very small and quaint." See The wedding-suit

"Tho' the last glimpse of Erin." See The fair-haired maiden

"Tho' the storm is raging." See Stay! oh stay (Varlamov)

"Though wide be the moat." See Keine sorg' um den weg (Raff)

"Tho' winter depart and the springtime die." See Solvejgs sang (Grieg)

"Tho' women's minds like winter winds." Air: For a' that. Words by R. Burns. BSR

"Though you are young." 17th century air. Words by T. Campion. JE

"Tho' you leave me now." N. Gow. FSS 7

"Though your strangenesse fretts my heart." J. Wilson. MM

"A thought like music." See "Wie melodien zieht es mir" (Brahms)

"The thoughts are free." See "Die gedanken sind frei"

Thoughts of home. Chant. J. E. Gould. FSS 1

"Thoughts of wonder." J. J. Rousseau. FSS 4

"Thou'rt like a gentle flow'ret." See "Du bist wie eine blume" (Liszt)

"Thou'rt like a lovely flower." See "Du bist wie eine blume" (Schumann)

"Thou'rt like unto a flower." See "Du bist wie eine blume" (Liszt); "Du bist wie eine blume" (Rubinstein)

"Thou'rt lovely as a flower." See "Du bist wie eine blume" (Rubinstein); "Du bist wie eine blume" (Schumann)

A thousand a year. Mrs P. Millard. BE 2—HSE 1

A thousand leagues away. J. Barnby. Words by W. C. Bennett. FSS 6—HSD—MP—WBT

"A thousand miles from land are we." See The stormy petrel (Neukomm)

"A thousand things I ponder." See "Jag går i tusen tanker"

"A thousand, thousand birdlings gay." See O bitt' euch liebe vögelein (Gumbert)

"A thousand times I gaze upon thy form." See Fuji (Ross)

"Thousand times I've wandered here." See Love song

"A thousand years have come and gone." Traditional air. Words by T. T. Lynch. HC

"Thousands of sins oppress me." S. Mercadante. e. SAS 1

Thrane, Waldemar
"Kom Kjyra." See Norsk fjeldsang
Norsk fjeldsang
Norwegian echo song. See Norsk fjeldsang

Die thräne ("Macht man in's leben.")—The tear) F. Gumbert. e.g. FSS 5

"Die thräne bebt." See Endless love (Tchaikovsky)

Die thränen des herzens (The heart's tear) G. Goltermann. Words by J. Kessler. e.g. SOS 1

"Threat'ning death to traitor slave." See Vive le roi (Balfe)

The three ages of love. E. J. Loder. Words by H. F. Chorley. BE 7—HSE 3

"Three blind mice." Traditional round. BD— HSC— HSD— JSE— MPC— NMH— NMS— OH— TFC 1—WBT—WSC

"Three blind mice" (Double round) See Mingled melodies

The three butchers. Folk song: North Carolina version. CSE
—Tennessee version. CSE

The three captains. See Les trois capitaines

"Three centuries of bondage." See Cancion patriotica

"Three centuries oppression." See Cancion patriotica

Three cheers for K. S. U. University of Kansas song. CHS

Three cheers for T. A. and P. U. Pacific university song. Words by H. Brooks. CHS

Three cheers for the olden time. Air: Whichever way the wind doth blow. Words by F. Crosby. FSS 4—LA

Three cheers for the red and the blue. University of Pennsylvania song. Words by F. B. Neilson. CHS

"Three cheers, three cheers, for the olden time." See Three cheers for the olden time

"Three children sliding." 17th century song. Words by J. Gay. FSS 2—JSE

Three Christmas eves. MCS

Three crows ("There were three crows sat on a tree, and they were black as crows could be") Old English air. WC
For variants see following song of same title; also Crow song; The three ravens

The three crows ("There were three crows sat on a tree, O Billy Magee Magar") See Crow song

The three crows ("Three crows there were once who sat on a stone") WSC

The three doves. See Le tre colombe

"Three fair maidens a milking did go." See The blackbird in the bush

"Three fishers went sailing." J. Hullah. Words by C. Kingsley. CS 1—DM 2—FSS 4—HSC— HSD—HSE 1— JO—KF 2—KF 4—WA—WBT—WSW

"Three fishers went sailing" (The three fishers) G. A. Macfarren. Words by C. Kingsley. TL

The three gifts (Posmotrite-ka, dobrye lîudi) Russian spring song. e. SSR 1

"Three gipsies stood at the castle gate." See The gipsy countess: part 2

The three glasses. K. L. Fischer. CHS

Three good turns. Air: Polly-wolly-doodle. BSS

"Three horsemen went riding." See Drei reiter am thore

Three-in-hand. Russian folk song. Moscow air. e. KSN

Three-in-hand. Russian folk song. Petersburg air. e. KSN

Das dreigespann ("Seht ihr drei rosse") g. ED 1

Three-in-hand (Troika) e. EF—GO

Troika (Russian driver's song) e. FSS 2

The troika ("Vot mchitsîa troïka udalaîa") e.r. BF 1

"Three jolly good fellows came over the Rhine." See Der wirtin töchterlein

Three jovial Welshmen. English folk song. BSW

The three kings ("I would now sing for and I might") H. Heale. HC

"Three kings from out the Orient." W. H. Gill. Words by T. E. Brown. HC

"Three kings had journey'd from lands afar." See The kings (Cornelius)

"Three kings in great glory." M. Shaw. Words by S. Image. HC

Three kings of Orient. J. H. Hopkins (music and words) CST—FSS 7—LA—MCS—TFC 2

"We three kings of Orient are." BSC—DC—HC—MF—OH

"Three kings once lived." F. H. Cowen. Words by J. Bennett. HC

Three kings' song. French Flanders air. e. HC

"Three knights went riding away to the war, adè." See Drei reiter am thore

"Three lads and lassies we did go." See Les filles de Cadix (Delibes)

"Three lads journey'd merrily over the Rhine." See Der wirtin töchterlein

Three leaves on the linden tree. See "Drei laub auf einer linden"

"Three little children chanced to stray." See Le miracle de Saint-Nicolas

Three little kittens ("Once three little kittens") Composer unknown. WBT—WSC

Three little kittens ("Once upon a time") Chant. CHS—HSD—MPC

"Three little mice." Nursery song. WSC

The three little pigs. A. S. Gatty. HSD—WSC

The three lovely ladies. See "Derrièr' chez mon père, vole, mon coeur, vole"

"Three maiden lovers" (Mijāna) Syrian folk song. ar.e. BF 2

The three maids. See Les trois filles

"Three merry men, and three merry men, and three merry men be we." 16th century song. CO 1

Three merry men be we ("Come, fortune's a jade") Several old airs arranged. VFS

Three merry men of Kent ("He that will not merry, merry be") 17th century song. CO 2—DM 1

"He that will not merry, merry be." BE 8—MM

"Three old crows sat on a tree." See The three ravens (Virginia version)

The three poisoned roses. See Les trois roses empoisonnées

Three poor mariners. See "We be three poor mariners"

Three prayers. See Les trois prières (Paladilhe)

Three promises. See Tre löften (Beckman)

The three rascals. See De tre skalke

The three ravens. 16th century folk song. BOH—CS 1—DM 1—EF—HSE 1 —KF 1—MM—PR 1—SMF —Virginia version. CSE "There were three ravens." CO 1—JE Variants: Crow song; Three crows ("There were three crows sat on a tree"); The three crows ("Three crows there were once who sat on a stone")

The three roads (Les trois chemines) Élégie. T. Koeneman. Words by M. Konopnitzky. e.f. NR 2

Three roses ("Jetzt geh' i an's brünnele") See Drei röslein

"Three roses grew in a woodland vale." See Schön ist der sommer

"Three rosy-faced topers as ever was known." See Law, physic, and divinity (Popely)

The three sailor boys. T. Marzials. HSD —WBT

"Three schemers stood scheming together one fine day." See De tre skalke

"Three score o' nobles rade up the King's ha'." See Glenlogie

Three shadows. H. Bedford. Words by D. G. Rossetti. SOS 1

The three sons. Folk song from Somerset. FSF—SO

"Three tailors once came to the banks of the Rhine." See Drei schneider

Three travellers. 17th century song. e. CO 2 "There were three travellers." MM

"Three women went forth." Arr from Haydn. HC

"Three years a sailor's life." Harrington. Words by P. Hoare. DM 1

"Three youths and maidens, we did go." See Les filles de Cadix (Delibes)

A threnody. See Thrînôdia (Holmès)

The thresherman and the squire. Folk song from Sussex. SF 5

"Thrice blessed forest! with the town a-weary." See To the forest (Tchaikovsky)

"Thrice blest that wise discerning king." Händel. BS 2

Thring, Godfrey "From the eastern mountains" (Lissant) Hallelujah! song of triumph (Smith) "Hark! hear ye not the angel-song" (Traditional air) "Saviour, blessed Saviour! listen while we sing" (Dykes)

Thrînôdia (A threnody) A. Holmès (music and words) e.f. HM 2

"Through all the employments of life." Air: The old woman clothed in grey. Words by J. Gay. BE 6

"Through bushes and through briars." See Bushes and briars

"Thro' each rustle murmurs pass." See Spring (Sakhnovskii)

"Through Erin's isle." See Oh! the shamrock

"Through fields my father sends me." See "Mon père m'envoi-t-à l'herbe" (Lorraine version)

"Through grief and through danger." See The Irish peasant to his mistress

"Through His bleeding side retreating." See Cujus animam (Rossini)

"Thro' meadows, flowing swift and clear." See The brook (Bleikhman)

"Thro' my garden wicket hopping." See The magpie and the little gypsy dancer (Musorgskii)

"Through the cool and shady woods as I was ranging." See Cupid's courtesie

Through the fields in winter (A travers champs, l'hiver) V. Sokolov. Words by I. Nikitin. e.f. NR 1

"Through the forest." Mrs J. B. Gattie. Words by Shakespeare. KSS

"Thro' the forest's moan." See Song of the dark forest (Borodin)

"Through the garden of spring I freely wander." See Adelaïde (Beethoven)

"Through the leaves the night winds moving." See Ständchen (Schubert)

"Through the long hidden years." G. B. Lissant. Words by W. C. Dix. HC

"Through the long night all dark was the sky." See Song to the morning star

"Through the midnight air." F. W. Dawkins. Words by J. Goddard. HC

"Thro' the millet and corn." See Mailied (Medtner)

"Through the mist of the valleys." Liszt. e. OS 4

"Thro' the moated grange at twilight." See My lady's bower (Temple)

"Thro' the night a golden cloudlet rested." See The cloud and the mountain (Rimskii-Korsakov)

"Thro' the night, my songs entreating." See Ständchen (Schubert)

"Through the night of doubt and sorrow." J. K. Paine. Words by B. Ingemann. [Tr of Igjennem nat og traengsel] e. DSH

"Through the pine-trees light is sifting." See Im haine (Schubert)

"Thro' the rustling woods I wander." See Autumn dreaming (Weiland)

"Thro' the wood a pathway wound." See The jackdaw and the falcon

Thro' the wood, laddie ("O, Sandy, why leaves thou thy Nelly") Words by A. Ramsay. MMS

"Through the wood, through the wood." C. E. Horn. Words by W. H. Bellamy. BE 4—FSS 3—HSE 3

"Through toil I strove to gain." See Ô jours heureux (Meyerbeer)

"Through Váradi's dusty highways." See Váradi's highways (Bartalus?)

Through Vrenely's on the Guggisberg still. See Das alte Guggisberger lied

"Through winter stormy he came unshaken." See "Er ist gekommen" (Franz)

"Thro' woodlands lonely, wander'd pretty Rose-Marie." See Rose-Marie (Collan)

Throwing ballast. See Ved balasthioning

"Thrust in thy sickle and reap." J. Raff. e. SAS 2

"Thu' nicht so spröde, schönes kind" ("Be not so coy, my pretty maid") A. Rubinstein. Words by F. Bodenstedt (Mirza-Schaffy) e.g. SC "Thu nicht so spröde, schönes kind" ("Be not so coy, thou lovely child") e.g. FO 1

Thümmel, Julius
The complaint. See Herzensbeklemmung
Herzensbeklemmung

Thümmel, Moritz August von
Der vogelsteller (Sterkel)

"The thunder is growling." See The shower

Der thürmer (The warder) C. Matys. Words by H. Rustige. e.g. AB 3

Thurmwächters lied (Watchman's song) H. Weidt. e.g. AB 4

Thursday ("The sun was setting") J. L. Molloy. Words by F. E. Weatherly. CB

"Thursday in the morn, the nineteenth of May." See Russell's triumph (Akeroyde)

"Thus saith the Lord." G. F. Händel. OS 4—SAS 4

"Thus speaketh the Lord of hosts." J. Stainer. DC

"Thus when the mariner inclined to sleep." T. Moorehead. HSE 3

"Thus when the sun." G. F. Händel. OS 3

"Thus Zuleika spoke to her canary." See The canary (Tchaikovsky)

"Thy bow'r is finished, fairest." See The hunter's serenade

"Thy cheek is o' the rose's hue." See My only joe and dearie

"Thy daily question, love is Lov'st thou me." See "Du fragst mich täglich" (Meyer-Helmund)

"Thy dimpled cheek." Air: Twill yn ei boch, or, Y lana 'n fyw. MMW

"Thy ever-watchful guardians no ruse can vanquish." See Vainement, ma bien-aimée (Lalo)

Thy face is always near me. C. H. R. Marriott. Words by R. Lejoindre. NML
"Thy face is always near to me." WBT
Thy face is near. FSS 8

"Thy face is pale indeed as any flower." See Bianchina (Gordigiani)

"Thy father is coming." Pawnee Indian song. e.in. FIS

"Thy father is now far awa'." See Scotch cradle-song

"Thy gentle voice would lead me on." See My own, my guiding star (Macfarren)

"Thy glance, it makes me tremble." See "Tiemblo con tus miradas"

"Thy glowing earth with diamonds is teeming." See A song of India (Rimskiï-Korsakov)

"Thy gracious image spreads upon me its enchantment." See Night (Musorgskiï)

"Thy great blue eyes are gazing." See Svärmeri (Arlberg)

"Thy hand, Belinda, darkness shades me." See When I am laid in earth (Purcell)

"Thy heart with my heart." See "Dein herz und mein herz"

"Thy kindness to our fathers shown" (Duke street) J. Hatton. Words by Roscoe. FSS 7

Thy King cometh. H. G. Nägeli. ¡Words by C. Coffin. Tr of Instantis adventum Dei¡ e. MCS

Thy land. See "Where is the true man's fatherland" (Reichardt)

"Thy leading would I had not followed." A. Dvořák. e. SAS 2

"Thy lips say, I love thee, believe me." See A dissonance (Borodin)

Thy lovely bright eyes. Spanish folk song. e. WBT—WL

Thy lovely face. See "Dein angesicht" (Schumann)

"Thy name I praise, O God." R. Pugno. e. SAS 3

"Thy name was once the magic spell." A. Cowell. Words by C. Norton. FSS 2 —WBT

"Thy nativity, O Christ, our God." See Christmas chant

"Thy praise almighty One." See Erbarmen (Nicodé)

"Thy rare purple rose 'mid thy morning glows." See Nell (Fauré)

"Thy rose-lips beguiling." See "Son troppo vezzose" (Galuppi)

"Thy secret unto thy master tell." S Twang lango dillo day

"Thy sentinel am I." M. Watson. Word by E. Oxenford. AB 2

Thy story bides for aye. E. C. Phelps. Words by M. Douglas. MCS

"Thy throat is full of tune." See Time is ever at June

Thy true heart. M. Vogrich. Words by F. Lyster. AB 1

"Thy voice is near." W. T. Wrighton. FSS 5

"Thy way, not mine, O Lord" (Baxter) U. C. Burnap. Words by H. Bonar. FSS 3—LA

"Thy welcome, O'Leary." Irish air: Contented am I. MMI

Thy will be done. Barri. Words by A. Volkmer. HSS 3

"Thy wonderful eyes my heart inspire."
See "Breit über mein haupt dein
schwarzes haar" (Strauss)
Thyra Dannebod (Denmark's verdant
meadows) P. E. Rasmussen. Words
by L. O. Kok. da.e.   BSP
"Ti faccio far' n' zinale" ("A stripèd apron
they shall make") Roman song.
e.i.   MSI
"A striped apron they shall make."   e.
BSE
Ti rapirei (Come, let us speed away) Tos-
ti. e.i. PG 3
"Ti riveggo, Fanny." Donizetti. e.i.
PP
Ti, tum, ti (The Quaker's song) W. Reeve.
Words by T. Dibdin. ME
Ti voglio bene assai. See Te voglio bene
assaje
"Tiapa, bye-bye, Tiapa, sleep and dream."
See The doll's cradle-song (Musorg-
skiï)
"Tic-e-tic-e-toc." Italian folk song. e.
GO
Tickell, Richard
"Young Lubin was a shepherd boy"
(Linley)
The tickling trio. See Laughing glee (Mar-
tini)
Tiddeman, Maria
"Glorious, beauteous, golden-bright"
Tiddy I O. Pulling chantey. SE
"The tide is for the shore, boys." See
Row well ye mariners
Tiden görs mig lang. See Den bergtagna
Tidings glad that once the angels sang.
See With joyous hearts
"Tidings of great joy to you angels bring."
See "Nesem vám noviny"
"Tidings, people, take good heed." See
Welcome be our heavenly King
(Bridge)
Tieck, Johann Ludwig
Herbstlied (Berger)
Lied der nacht (Reichardt)
"Ruhe süss, liebchen" (music by
Brahms; Franz)
"Über reisen kein vergnügen" (Stre-
bel)
Tiedge, Christoph August
"Auf dem berge dort oben, da wehet der
wind" (Burgwedel)
Der rose sendung (Himmel)
Hoffnung und erinnerung (Reichardt)
Das verfehlte wort (Volksweise)
Die weihe (Himmel)
"Tiemblo con tus miradas." Folk song
from Sonora. e.s. HS
"La tierra de Borinquen." See Borinquen
(Astol)
Tiggargossen (The beggar-boy) Swedish
folk song. e.sw. HSOS
The beggar-boy. e. KSN
The tight little island. Air: The rogue's
march. Words by T. Dibdin.
BE 2—HSE 3—JO
The island. BOS

Tik, tak, tak. Serbian folk song. e.se.
BF 1
"Til fjelds over bygden" ("I long to climb
the mountains high") H. Kjerulf.
Words by J. S. Welhaven. e.n. MAN
Til Norge (To Norway) E. Grieg.
Words by J. Paulsen. e.n. SSN
Til Ole Bull (To Ole Bull) Scandinavian
folk air. Words by J. S. Welhaven.
e.n. MAN
Til Ole Bull (To Ole Bull) F. A. Reis-
siger. Words by J. S. Welhaven. e.n.
MAN
"Til til tara." Norse folk song. n.
MAN
"Til-til tove, tolv mann i skove, tolv mann
ere de, tolv svaer baere de" ("Til, til
torrest") Norse folk song. e.n.
MAN
"Til til tove, tolv mann i skove, tolv mann
voro de, tolv börso boro de" ("Til,
til torrest") Norse folk song. e.n.
MAN
Tildesley, T. C.
He giveth His beloved sleep (Abt)
"Tili, tili, tara." Norse folk song. n.
MAN
"Till Bethlehem" ("To Bethlehem") Swed-
ish folk song. e.sw. DCS
"Till Österland vill jag fara" ("Now far,
far eastward I'll hie me") Swedish
folk song. e.sw. HSOS
Tilsjös (At sea) A. Backer-Gröndahl.
Words by H. Reynolds. e.n. WM 1
Tiltman, Henry T.
"Hark! what heavenly sounds are float-
ing"
"While in peaceful slumbers lying"
Tilton, Theodore
"Baby bye, here's a fly" (Loomis)
Tim, the dragoon. C. V. Stanford.
Words by A. T. Quiller Couch ("Q")
SSS
"The time at last is drawing nigh." See
The time is drawing nigh
"Time by prophets told." See Sweet
harps, resound again (Sullivan)
Time doth pass away. Old song. FSS 2
"The time draws near the birth of Christ."
See The birth of Christ (Reichardt)
The time draws nigh. Christmas song.
MCS
"Time ever flowing bids us be going."
See Vale (Barnby)
The time for love. Irish air. Words
by A. Stringer. FSI
"Time has not thinn'd my flowing hair."
W. Jackson. BE 5
"Time-honored Marietta." See The navy-
blue and white
Time is a-coming that sinner must die.
See O sinner, you'd better get ready
The time is drawing nigh. Irish folk song.
JOI

Time is ever at June. Greek folk air. Words by M. Schutze. WF

"De time is nebber dreary." See Ring, ring de banjo (Foster)

"The time I've lost in wooing." Irish air: Pease upon a trencher. Words by T. Moore. MI—MMI—PI

"The time of the singing of birds." G. Barker. FSS 5

"Time was, when of my heart you were the treasure." See Tempo passato perchè non retorni (Gordigiani)

"The times are hard and the wages low." See Leave her Johnny

"The time's been sweet I've spent with you." See Hick's farewell

"The timid lotus flower." See Die lotosblume (Schumann)

Timothy. 18th century English song. ME

Timothy's welcome. T. Marzials. FSS 6

"Ting-a-ling-a-ling-a-ling-a-ling-a-ling! hello? that you." See Le telefono (Denza)

"Ting-a-ling-a-ling go the sleigh-bells sweet." See The sleigh-ride

Tiniakov, Aleksandr
At twilight

Tink a tink. See The bee proffers honey but bears a sting (Dibdin)

The tiny hut (Chałupeczka). 16th century Polish song. e.p. BF 1
"Little cottage lowly" (Mazurek) e.p. BO

"A tiny little man stands in forest dim." See A little man (Humperdinck)

Tioutchev, Fyodor. See Tiuchev, Feodor

Tippecanoe and Tyler too. Air: Little pigs. Words by A. C. Ross. FSS 6 —JO—LA

Tippling John. 18th century English song. MM

Tirana del Caramba y como te quiero (Cruel Caramba) Spanish folk song. e.s. SMF

Tired, so tired. M. Lindsay. Words by H. Burnside. FSS 7—WBT

Der Tiroler und sein kind. See Der Tyroler und sein kind (Nesmüller)

"Tirra-lirra-lirra." German folk air. Words by J. Erwin. DO

"'Tis a draught that alone such a dream could awaken." See Vision fugitive (Massenet)

"'Tis a draught which perchance such a dream might give to me." See Vision fugitive (Massenet)

"'Tis a hundred years." See The boatswain's story (Molloy)

"'Tis a lesson you should heed." See Try, try again

"'Tis a princess high-born." See La princesse et le bourreau

"'Tis advertised in Boston." See Blow, ye winds

'Tis all that I can say. H. Temple. Words by T. Hood. FMB—HSD —WBT—WL
"I love thee." NML

"'Tis all the world to have thee near." See Best of all (Moir)

"'Tis believed that this harp" (The origin of the harp) Air: Gage fane. Words by T. Moore. FSS 4—MI—MMI

"'Tis believed that this harp" (The birth of the harp) S. Tanieff. Words by T. Moore. NM 2

"'Tis but a little faded flower." H. R. Thomas. HSD

'Tis but fancy's sketch. Braham. HSE 2

"'Tis Christmas eve once more." See They come with blissful song (Wrighton)

"'Tis Christmas now." H. Lawes. HC

"'Tis Christmas time again." See Jul polska

"'Tis Dioclesian's natal day proclaims." See Go, my faithful soldier, go (Händel)

'Tis Easter time. L. B. Marshall. Words by C. W. Johnson. JS

"'Tis evening, and the hues that made the clouds so bright." P. Tschaikowsky. e. SC

"'Tis evening brings my heart." H. Tucker. Words by F. Crosby. FSS 7

"'Tis ever sweetly ringing." See The purple and the gold (Elmira college song)

"'Tis fine to see the old world." See America for me (Mercer)

"'Tis for all she blossoms and fragrance show'rs." See The flower

'Tis God who ordains me. J. Concone. Words by Belanger. e. FSS 5

"'Tis gone, and for ever." Air: Savournah deelish. Words by T. Moore. MI

"'Tis he whose gracious word doth banish ev'ry sorrow." See Il est doux, il est bon (Massenet)

"'Tis I! all gone to smash." See Me voici dans son boudoir (Thomas)

"'Tis I am the gipsy king." See The gipsy king (West)

"'Tis I, dear Carlos." See Per me giunto (Verdi)

"'Tis I! rules I defied." See Me voici dans son boudoir (Thomas)

"'Tis I! somewhat disturbed." See Me voici dans son boudoir (Thomas)

"'Tis I, 'tis I that am the cry." See La chanson de l'alouette (Lalo)

"'Tis in vain Pharaoh tries all gratitude can tender." See Champs paternels (Méhul)

"'Tis in vain that I seek a retreat." J. Massenet. e. OS 1—SAS 1

"'Tis in vain that I thought to escape from remorse." See Je t'implore, ô mon frère (Thomas)

"'Tis in vain your counsel beguiling." See Obstination (Fontenailles)

"'Tis June, the month of roses." See Commencement song (Murray)

"'Tis just a year ago today." See The poor old slave

"'Tis Lisette who offers you greeting." See Souvenirs de Lisette (Bérat)

" 'Tis lone on the waters." J. Blockley. FSS 2

'Tis love, ah! 'tis love. See Ah! lève-toi, soleil (Gounod)

" 'Tis love that makes all nature gay." Love and music (Wynne)

" 'Tis love, that rogue so wily." See "M'ha preso alla sua ragna" (Paradies)

" 'Tis love! 'tis love! ah! it is love." See Ah! lève-toi, soleil (Gounod)

'Tis me, O Lord. See It's me, O Lord

" 'Tis merry in the spring-time." See The song of the moor

" 'Tis midnight, and I'm standing 'neath your window." See 'A serenata d' 'e rrose (Capua)

" 'Tis midnight hour." Composer and author of words unknown. FSS 6—HSD—JO

" 'Tis moonlight on the sea, boys." See Dip, boys, dip the oar

" 'Tis night on Venice waters." See On Venice waters (Roeder)

" 'Tis night, 'tis night, 'tis night." See Starlight is streaming (Balfe)

" 'Tis not forbidden to change one's mind." See Le changement

" 'Tis not the valley, mountain and grove." See Fondest affections still cling to home

" 'Tis not the white birch." See Dobrynia bids his mother farewell

" 'Tis not to knights in armor clad." See The knights of the golden O (Scott)

'Tis not true. See Non è ver (Mattei)

" 'Tis now the hour of parting." See Addio a Napole

" 'Tis of a jolly ploughing-man." See A nutting we will go

" 'Tis of a young damsel." See Gipsy song

" 'Tis pretty to be in Ballinderry." Old Irish song. MMI—PI

" 'Tis pretty to see the girl of Dunbwy." See The girl of Dunbwy

" 'Tis said that absence conquers love." E. Thomas. Words by F. W. Thomas. JO—WBT

" 'Tis spring and ev'ry beating heart rejoices." See A pleading (Tchaikovsky)

" 'Tis sweet to wake in June." See The voice of one we love

" 'Tis the Christmastide." See Christmas come again (Pinsuti)

" 'Tis the daughter of a prison guard." Le prisonnier et la fille du geôlier

" 'Tis the day, the blessed day." See Noel! Noel

'Tis the harp in the air. W. V. Wallace. Words by E. Fitzball. HSE 3

" 'Tis the last rose of summer." See The last rose of summer

" 'Tis the moment, O Vitellia." See Non più di fiori (Mozart)

" 'Tis the prince of Orange blood." See Le prince d'Orange

'Tis the song, the sigh of the weary. See Hard times come again no more (Foster)

" 'Tis Thee I would be praising." Bach. e. OS 3

'Tis there on the ground. See "The ground is strewn" (Leleiohoku)

'Tis thou whose spells. See Durch dich musst' ich verlieren (Wagner)

" 'Tis three long days." See Nina (Pergolesi)

" 'Tis thy lovely bright eyes." See Thy lovely bright eyes

" 'Tis today that I must leave thee." See Soldaten-abschied (Fesca)

" 'Tis twilight, and the heat of day is slowly waning." See At twilight (Tiniākov)

" 'Tis when to sleep." H. R. Bishop. HSE 3

" 'Tis years since last we met." See Her bright smile haunts me still (Wrighton)

Tischlied ("Gesund und frohen") J. A. P. Schulz. Words by J. H. Voss. g. ED 3

Tischlied ("Mich ergreift") M. Eberwein. Words by W. von Goethe. g. ED 1

Table-song. e.g. SSS

"Tissa and Duna." Hungarian song. e. KSE

The Tiszian (The gipsy.—"From the smiling fields of Rakosh") Hungarian folk song. Air: Jártam kertben rózsák között. e. BMC

Tit for tat. H. Pontet. NML

Tit-willow. A. Sullivan. Words by W. S. Gilbert. FSS 5—WBT—WSW

Titania's song ("Child of earth with the golden hair") C. Horn. HSE 2

"Child of earth with the golden hair." BE 5—FSS 2

The tithe. 16th century Dutch patriotic song. e. KSN—SN

"The tither morn." Highland air. Words by Burns. PS 2

Titov, Nikolaï Aleksīeevich
    The talisman

Tiuchev, Feodor
    Canzonetta (Zolotarev)
    Floods of spring (Rachmaninov)
    "God took from me my all" (Rachmaninov)
    "Quiet night of waning summer" (Cherepnin)

Tiyata uṇgni kte. See Marriage song

"Tko je, srce, u te dirno,—da si tako sad." See Be still my heart

"To a good old well-known air." See Première danse (Massenet)

To a lady weeping. H. Lawes. Words by Cartwright. MM

To a primrose. See Med en primulaveris (Grieg)

To a swan. See En svane (Grieg)

To a thrush in autumn. See Trasten i höstkvällen (Wennerberg)

To a violet. See Med en primulaveris (Grieg)

"To achieve all the glamor of glory." See "All' acquisto di gloria" (Scarlatti)

"To Alexis." See Der rose sendung (Himmel)

"To all people in the world this day." See Happy New Year

"To all you ladies now at land." Old English air. Words by Lord Buckhurst, later earl of Dorset. CO 2 —DM 1

"To all you ladies now on land." BE 8 J. Wilson. Words by R. Lovelace. DM 2

To Althea. J. Wilson. Words by R. Lovelace. DM 2

To America. H. Waller. Words by F. Manley. TL

To an Aeolian harp. See An eine Aeolsharfe (Brahms)

To an ancient picture. See Auf ein altes bild (Wolf)

"To Anacreon in heav'n." [Attributed to J. S. Smith;] wrongly attributed to S. Arnold. Words by R. Tomlinson. EF —SN

To Anthea. See "Bid me to live" (Hatton)

"To Araby will I wander." See "Na Ostland wil ik varen"

"To arms, all! to arms, all." See Inno di guerra dei cacciatori delle Alpi (Olivieri)

To arms, jolly grenadiers. 18th century English song. MM

To arms, O patriots. See La Marseillaise (Rouget de Lisle)

"To arms! to arms! the tombs they are riven." See Inno di guerra dei cacciatori delle Alpi (Olivieri)

"To arms, to arms, to arms, my jolly grenadiers." See To arms, jolly grenadiers

To Babyland. Nursery song. WSC

"To be bold in her cause." See The army and navy of Britain

"To be lordly, whether he ride or run." See Be lordly, Willy, be lordly

"To be near the fair idol." See "Star vicino" (Rosa)

"To be near thee." See "Star vicino" (Rosa)

To be sung on the water. See Auf dem wasser zu singen (Schubert)

"To Bethlehem this night." See "Till Bethlehem"

To Charis ("See the chariot at hand") 17th century air. Words by B. Jonson. JE

To Chloe in sickness. W. S. Bennett. Words by R. Burns. BAS 2 Long is the night. DM 2

"To church one bright sunny morning." See Glockengeläute (Hölzel)

"To clang of brazen hammer's blow." See "Au bruit des lourds marteaux d'airain" (Gounod)

To daunton me, and me sae young. See "The blude red rose at Yule may blaw"

To-day. For entries beginning To-day see Today

"To dhrink wid the divil, though may be hilarious." Irish song. MMI

To die for home and country. See Mourir pour la patrie (Varney)

"To dig up Greek and Latin roots." See Chant of the "Short ags"

"To do to others as I would." See The golden rule

To drive the cold winter away. See Drive the cold winter away

"To earth there came this blessed night for us all." See De nederige geboorte

"To earth, while she reposes." See Mondnacht (Schumann)

"To ease his heart, and own his flame." See The spinning-wheel

"To fairest Delia's grassy tomb." W. Jackson. BOH

To Florindo. See "Se Florindo è fidele" (Scarlatti)

"To France, once were trav'ling two grenadiers." See Die beiden grenadiere (Schumann)

"To France there journey'd two grenadiers." See Die beiden grenadiere (Schumann)

"To France were returning two grenadiers." See Die beiden grenadiere (Schumann)

"To France were trav'ling two grenadiers." See Die beiden grenadiere (Schumann)

"To free my mind of her who appears to pursue me." See Ô jours heureux (Meyerbeer)

"To give me an answer." See Hymn to the sun (Rimskiï-Korsakov)

To Greece we give our shining blades. H. R. Bishop. Words by T. Moore. JO

"To Hans one day said Gretchen." See Der schwur (Bohm)

"To heal the smart a bee had made" (The bee) 18th century song. ME

"To heal the wound a bee had made." T. Linley, junr. 18th century words. ME

To hope. See An die hoffnung (Beethoven)

"To hug yourself in perfect ease." See True happiness (Dieupart)

To Jerez we will go. See Jarabe tapatio

To King Oscar. See "Ur svenska hjertans" (Lindblad)

De to kongedøttre (The two kings daughters) Danish folk song. e. GO

"To ladies' eyes." Irish air: Fág an bealach, or, Fague a ballagh, or, Clear the way. Words by T. Moore. MI —MMI

"To laugh though in one's bosom a wounded heart is hidden." See Reír es necesario

"To leave my dear girl." See The sailor's farewell

"To London go with me." See Peggy Wilkins

"To love thee I was born." See "Nasci para te amar"

To Lucette. See À Lucette (Pierné)

"To lust of war devoted." See "Der kriegeslust ergeben" (Spohr)

"To market, to market." Nursery song. WSC

To Mary in heaven. See "Thou ling'ring star with less'ning ray"

"To me thou art a flower." See "Du bist wie eine blume" (Rubinstein)

"To me way-ay-ay-yah." See Paddy Doyle

"To meet her Mars." J. Eccles. BE 5

"To meeting, to meeting, to meeting goes I." See An inconstant lover

To-morrow. For entries beginning To-morrow see Tomorrow

To mother Fairie. Air: What's a' the steer, kimmer. Words by A. Cary. LBR

To music. See An die musik (Schubert)

"To my beloved hasten." See "Il mio tesoro intanto" (Mozart)

"To my breast, fond flow'r." See Flower of my heart (Hopkins)

To my little flower. Children's song. WSC

To my mother (Meiner mutter) T. Bradsky. Words by Adamei. e.g. KF 2

"To my muse give attention." See Golden days of good Queen Bess

"To my native home I'm near." See "Di piacer mi balza il cor" (Rossini)

"To my sorrow I fell in love with him." See The soldier's bride (Rachmaninov)

To my way-ay-ay-ah! we'll hang Paddy Doyle for his boots. See Paddy Doyle

To my way-ay-ay-ay-ay-yah, we'll pay Paddy Doyle for his boots. See Paddy Doyle

"To myself, dear mother, deeply I vowed." See Vows

To ne fástreb sovykalsïá. See A maiden's revenge

"To ne vîeter vîetku klonit." See The bending branch

To night ("Swiftly walk") D. S. Smith. Words by P. B. Shelley. TL

To-night. For entries beginning To-night see Tonight

To Nina. See A Nina

To Norway ("Du er min mor") See Til Norge (Grieg)

"To Norway, mother of the brave." See "For Norge, kjaempers födeland" (Grétry)

To Ole Bull. See Til Ole Bull (Folk air); Til Ole Bull (Reissiger)

"To promenade went a Bula." See How fair is she

To rest I call ye lambkins all. Norwegian shepherd's song. e. KSN

"To rest, to rest! the toil is over." See "Zur ruh, zur ruh" (Wolf)

To Rio Grande we're bound away. Chantey. SMW

To Russia (Zapyévka.—Invocation) M. Balakireff. Words by L. Mey. e. SMR 2

"To Saint-Malo, port on the sea." See "À Saint-Malo, beau port de mer"

"To scenes of peace retiring." See "In diesen heil'gen hallen" (Mozart)

To sleep (An den schlaf) P. I. Tchaikovsky. Words by Ogarev. e.g. FO 2

To spring. See Au printemps (Gounod)

"To stand by thee, Columbia." J. Erskine. Words by M. H. Cane. CU

To stay at home is best. A. ten Cate. Words by H. W. Longfellow. LBR

"To Swiss, in stranger's land, sing ne'er." See Ranz des vaches

"To take the design of a jewel." See Fantaisie aux divins mensonges (Delibes)

"To tell thee something I am yearning." See Verlegenheit (Abt)

"To the bravest." F. Mohring. Words by H. A. Clarke. WC

To the child Jesus. See Ao menino Jesus

To the children. S. Rachmaninoff. Words by A. Khomiakov. e. NM 2

"To the combat away, Bayameses." See Himno Bayamés (Figueredo)

"To the doorway of my house." See The angry father-in-law

To the evening star. See Mädchenlied (Raff)

To the forest. Tschaikowsky. e. BAS 1

To the fringed gentian. M. R. Lang. Words by W. C. Bryant. TL

To the harp (Kanteleelle) A. Jarnefelt. Words by K. Killinen. e.fi. WM 1

To the hem of thy garment I cling ("Main to tore dāman wāh lagun mere rām") Song from India. e.ind. BF 2

To the lark. Lithuanian daina. e. KSN

To the Lord our God belong mercies. A. R. Gaul. SAS 3

"To the Lords o' convention." See Bonnie Dundee (Sainton-Dolby)

To the May-pole away ("Joan to the Maypole") 17th century song. HSE 2

"Joan to the Maypole." CO 2—DM 2

To the Maypole haste away ("Come, ye young men") See The May-pole

"To the mead the maidie." See "Flickan gick på ängen"

To the moon. See An den mond

To the nightingale ("Sweet bird, whose heav'nly native strain") J. Worgan. ME

"To the praise of truth." Round. FSS 2

"To the Queen of Hearts he's the Ace of Sorrow." See The Queen of Hearts

"To the realm of roses and wine, O come." See Come to the realm of roses and wine (Rimskïï-Korsakov)

"To the sea my mother sent me." See Mother sent me

"To the Spanish main we are bound away." See Slav ho

"To the tambourica's ringing." See Tambourica

"To the tap of the drum." Rossini. MS

"To the thunder called the flying cloud." See Song of the shepherd Lehl (Rimskiï-Korsakov)

"To the valley comes the herdsman." See Hjemreise fra saetren

"To the voice of a friend." See The convivials (Remy)

To the weaver's gin ye go, fair maids. See "My heart was ance as blythe and free"

"To the window I rushed." See By the window (Tchaikovsky)

"To the winds, to the waves." See Ah, well-a-day, my poor heart (Shield)

"To thee and thine long life." See Greeting

"To thee I kneel." See "Ô toi l'objet" (Gluck)

"To Thee, my God, my Saviour" (Ellacombe) Words by T. Haweis. LA

"To Thee, my God, Whose Presence." See "Gott, deine güte reicht" (Beethoven)

"To thee, O country." J. Eichberg. Words by Mrs J. Lane. TFC 2

"To Thee, our Father and our Friend." See Fourth of July hymn (Hastings)

"To this retreat we're led by God's protecting pow'r." See Oh! ne t'eveille pas (Godard)

"To those unhappy, life is torture." See Oh, tu che in seno agl'angioli (Verdi)

To Thy cradle throne. W. B. Bradbury. MCS

"To thy garment I cling, O Rama." See To the hem of thy garment I cling

"To thy pastures fair and large." Words by J. Merrick. FSS 2

To thy sad brow let joy return. See Rend' il sereno al ciglio (Händel)

"To, to, to! ça qui là." See Martinique love-song

"To us is born a little Child." 15th century air. Tr of Geborn ist uns ein Kinderlein. e. HC

"To wander is the miller's bliss." See Das wandern (Schubert)

"To war has gone Duke Marlborough." See "Malbrough s'en va-t-en guerre"

To where the sky is as clear. See The Jamestown homeward bound

"To win glory in far away regions." See "All' acquisto di gloria" (Scarlatti)

"To woo me and win me." See Colin's success

"To you, my lords, a greeting." See "Nobles seigneurs, salut" (Meyerbeer)

"Toad went a-courting and he did ride." See The toad's courtship

The toad's courtship. Kentucky mountain song. WT
Variant of: The wedding of the frog and mouse

A toast to Columbia. College song. G. S. Parsons. Words by F. C. Seaman. CU

A toast to Dewey ("Fill all your glasses") MP

A toast to Harvard. College song. C. L. Smith, jr. CHS

Toast to Lehigh. College song. CHS

Toast to Wisconsin. College song. Arr from Gounod. CHS

Tobacco is an Indian weed. 17th century air. Words by G. Wither. HSE 2
"Tobacco's but an Indian weed." CO 2 —DM 2—JE—MM—PR 1

"Tobacco is an Indian weed." Cornish air. Words by G. Wither. BSW

Der tod ("Gestern, brüder, könnt ihr's glauben") Volksweise. Words by G. E. Lessing. g. ED 1

Der tod und das mädchen (Death and the maiden) F. Schubert. Words by M. Claudius. e.g. FF—FO 1— KF 2—PG 4
Der tod und das mädchen (Death and the girl) e.g. PG 2

Der tod von Basel ("Als ich ein junggeselle war") Volkslied. g. ED 2

To-day and to-morrow. Beethoven. Words by L. Walter. LA

"To-day doth blossom Jesse's stem." E. J. Hopkins. Tr of Jam radix. e. HC

To-day in Bethlehem ("Šiandien Betlėjuj") Lithuanian Christmas carol. e.li. BF 1

"Today is Monday." U. S. army song. BSS—TFC 1

"Today the earth is dressed in green." See Ode for Decoration day

"To-day 'tis three and thirty years since I saw a sail." See Der gefangene admiral (Lassen)

The toddler's lullaby. See The nipper's lullaby (Andrews)

Todlen hame. Old bottle song. PS 2

"Todo tiene su hasta aquí." Folk song from southern California. e.s. HS

Der todte soldat (The dead soldier) H. Esser. e.g. AB 1

Toggenburg, graf Kraft von. See Kraft von Toggenburg, graf

"Togh pucheh kamin bagh bagh yeresis." See The sure hope

"Toi, qui as l'oeil du jeune faon." See "Thine eyes are bright with fire"

The token. C. Dibdin (music and words) HSE 1—ME

Toleken, of Cork. See Bennett, Henry, jt. auth.

Tólf synir ("Bravely sails my bark") Icelandic folk song. e.ic. BO
Tólf syner (Icelandic folk song) e. BMC

"Toll for the brave." G. F. Händel. Words by W. Cowper. BOS—SSS

Tollens, Hendrik
"Wien Neêrlandsch bloed" (Wilms)

Tolstoï, Aleksĭeĭ Konstantinovich, graf
"Ah, if mother Volga" (Cui)
"Ah, not with God's thunder" (Musorgskiï)
At the ball (Tchaikovsky)
At twilight (Tiniakov)
"Believe me not" (Rimskiï-Korsakov)
Benediction (Tchaikovsky)
The convoy (Bleikhman)
Don Juan's serenade (Tchaikovsky)

Tolstoĭ, A. K., graf —*Continued*
Endless love (Tchaikovsky)
Field beloved (Rachmaninov)
"Like mountains the waves" (Rimskiĭ-Korsakov)
My native land (Grechaninov)
"Silently floated a spirit" (Musorgskiĭ)
"Waves dashing and breaking" (Rimskiĭ-Korsakov)
The wolves (Arenski)
The wounded birch (Grechaninov)

Tom a Bedlam. 17th century song. CO 1

Tom-big-bee river. Words by S. S. Steele. CHS— HSD— MPC— NMH— NMP—WBT
The gum-tree canoe. FSS 5

Tom Bowling. C. Dibdin (music and words) BE 4—BOH—BOS—BSE— DM 1—HSD—HSE 1—JE—JO—ME— PR 2—TS

Tom is gone to Hilo. Pulling chantey. SE
For variants see songs of similar title, as Tommy's gone away; Tommy's gone to Hilo; Tom's gone to Hilo; Tom's gone to Ilo

"Tom loves Mary passing well." See Cross purposes

"Tom Pearce, Tom Pearce, lend me your grey mare." See Widdicombe fair

"Tom Pearse, Tom Pearse, lend me thy grey mare." See Widdicombe fair

"Tom Starboard." J. Mazzinghi. Words by A. Cherry. HSE 2—ME

"Tom Steady." M. P. King. Words by S. J. Arnold. ME

Tom, the piper's son. Nursery song. FMB

"Tom, Tom, the piper's son." WSC

"Tom Tinker's my true love." Old air. Old words by T. D'Urfey. DM 2

"Tom Tinker's my true love." Old air. Modern words by F. Kidson. MM

"Tom, Tom, the piper's son." See Tom, the piper's son

Tom Tough. C. Dibdin (music and words) DM 2—HSE 3
Tom Tough (Yo heave ho) JE
Yo, heave ho. BOH

Tomer, William Gould
"God be with you"
Mizpah. See "God be with you"

Tomi! tomi. See Hawaiian hula (Nape)

Tomlinson, Ralph
"To Anacreon in heav'n" (Smith)

"Tommy a' Lynn." English folk song. BSW

Tommy and his gun. C. F. McMichael (music and words) CHS

Tommy's gone away. Pulling chantey. SE
For variants see Tom is gone to Hilo; Tommy's gone to Hilo; Tom's gone to Hilo; Tom's gone to Ilo

Tommy's gone to Hilo ("I've just come down") Hauling chantey. SMW

Tommy's gone to Hilo ("Tommy's gone, what shall I do") Chantey. SMW

"Tommy's gone, what shall I do? heigh-yo to Ilo." See Tom's gone to Ilo

"Tommy's gone, what shall I do? hurrah, Hilo." See Tommy's gone to Hilo

"Tommy's gone, what shall I do? Tommy's gone." See Tommy's gone away

To-morrow ("Domani, domani o me felice") See Domani, o me felice (Lillo)

To-morrow ("Hasta la mañana") See "Hasta la mañana"

To-morrow ("Night, I have often wish'd thy stay") W. Reeve. HSE 2

To-morrow ("O God, of all the Maker") S. S. Wesley. Words by S. N. Patten. TFC 1

"Tomorrow, comrade, we." See The battle eve

"To-morrow morn? alas! who knows where we may be." See "Connais-tu le pays" (Thomas)

"Tomorrow, the fox will come to town." See Trenchmore (1st version)

"Tomorrow, tomorrow, O joy unspoken." See Domani, o me felice (Lillo)

"To-morrow! to-morrow! oh, my heart of gladness." See Domani, o me felice (Lillo)

Tom's gone to Hilo ("Oh, Tommy's gone") Halliard chantey. CR
For variants see following song of similar title; also Tom is gone to Hilo; Tommy's gone away; Tommy's gone to Hilo

Tom's gone to Ilo ("Tommy's gone, what shall I do") Long drag chantey. KB

Ein ton (The monotone) P. Cornelius (music and words) e.g. CMF 1 —FF
Ein ton ("What sound is that") e.g. KF 3—KF 4

Tonen (The song) R. Nordraak. Words by B. Björnson. e.n. MAN

Tongese water-song. pol. SMW

To-night I neglected to put out the signal. See "Eg seer deg ut før gluggjin"

"Tonight Samson comes to my presence." See Amour, veins aider (Saint-Saëns)

"Tonight! Samson makes his obeisance." See Amour, veins aider (Saint-Saëns)

"Tonight we gladly sing the praise." See Alma mater—Chicago

"Tonight what wonders fill the sky." See "Wås mehr muasz g'schêchäsei"

Too late. See Too late! too late (Bliss)

"Too late for redress." English song. DM 2

"Too iate I stayed." Irish air: The slender coat. Words by W. R. Spencer. JO

Too late, too late. M. Lindsay Bliss. Words by A. Tennyson. FSS 5— HSD—WBT
Too late. JO

"Too long hast thou been sleeping." See Nina (Pergolesi)

Topelius, Zakarias
Fågelns visa (Söderberg)
"Nu somnar vågen" (Backer-Gröndahl)
Rose-Marie (Collan)
Vårvisa (Söderman)

Toplady, Augustus Montague
"Rock of ages, cleft for me" (music by Dykes; Hastings)

Topliff, Robert
Consider the lilies
"The **topsails** shiver in the wind." M. Arne. Words by Capt. Thomson. MM

"**Toreador**, e'er watchful be. " See Chanson du toréador (Bizet)

Toreador song. See Chanson du toréador (Bizet)

Torelli, Giuseppe
"Tu lo sai"
"Well thou knowest." See "Tu lo sai"

"**Torkel** had, of all, the strongest arm, sir." See "Torkjell han va bygdis beste kar, san"

"**Torkjell** han va bygdis beste kar, san" ("Torkel had, of all, the strongest arm, sir") Norse folk song. e.n. MAN

Torment unending. See Pena tiranna (Händel)

"El **tormento** de amor." Folk song from southern California. e.s. HS

Os **tormentos** de amor (The torments of love) Brazilian folk song. e.po. HF

"Os **tormentos** que passa na vida." See Os tormentos de amor

"**Torments** of hate and vengeance." See "Cruda, funesta smania" (Donizetti)

The **torments** of love. See Os tormentos de amor

Torna a Surriento (Come back to Sorrento) E. de Curtis. Words by G. B. de Curtis. e.i. FE
Torna a Surriento. s. LCP

"**Torna** ai felici dì" ("Back to a happy day") Puccini. e.i. OPS 3

El **toro** y el ranchero (The bull and the cowboy) Mexican song. e.s. BF 2

The **torpedo** and the whale. E. Audran. e. WBT

Torry, Jane Sloman
"Queen of the night"

La **tórtola**. R. Márquez (music and words) s. LCP

Tosh, J. Westwood
"The days are gliding swiftly by"

Der **tost** (The clod) T. Koschat (music and words) e.g. EF

Tosti, Francesco Paolo
"Alla mente confusa." See Preghiera
Beauty's eyes
Bid me good-bye
Come, let us speed away. See Ti rapirei
"Could I." See Vorrei
Forever and forever
Good-bye
Marechiare
Mattinata
Ninon
Ohé! mamma
Only a year ago
Prayer. See Preghiera

Preghiera
"Ring out, wild bells"
Ti rapirei
Vorrei
"When with doubting and dreading." See Preghiera

"**Total** eclipse! no sun, no moon." G. F. Händel. SAS 3

"**T'other** morning very early." See entry under Other

"**Touch** not the cup." T. H. Bayly. Words by J. H. Aikman. FSS 3

"**Touch** not the white urn hiding." See "Non t'accostar all' urna" (Schubert)

Touch us gently, time. Words by B. W. Procter (B. Cornwall) FSS 6—JO

"**Touching** grace, we princes three." 16th century air. e. HC

The **tounis** colledge. Edinburgh university song. Air: Bonnie Dundee. Words by D. Rorie. SSS

Tounshend, Aurelian. See Townsend, Aurelian

Tourelay ("Oh papa is out breaking rocks") WBT

Tourjee, Lizzie S.
"There's a wideness in God's mercy"

The **tourney** of King John. See Les pas d'armes du roi Jean (Saint-Saëns)

Tours, Berthold
The gate of heaven
"Jesus, Lover of my soul"
The new kingdom
"Saw ye never in the twilight"
"Sing, O heavens"

"**Tous** ceux qui disent là: Le géant, il vient." See Le chanson du reuze

"**Tout** cède à vos doux appas." P. Colasse. e.f. SOA 1

"**Tout** sommeille dans Grenade." See Don Juan's serenade (Tchaikovsky)

"**Toward** ev'ning of the hunt they spake." See Colind

"**Toward** France were returning two grenadiers." See Die beiden grenadiere (Schumann)

"**Towards** a lonely graveyard." See Das wirtshaus (Schubert)

"**Towards** the north." See Sang for Danske (Weyse)

Towing-song (Dubinushka) Russian folk song. e. SSR 3
Variant of: Volga boat song

The **town** gallant. R. Smith. DM 1

Towne, Charles Hanson
"I drink the fragrance of the rose" (Clough-Leighter)

Townsend, Aurelian
"Bacchus, Iacchus" (Lawes)

Townsend, Herbert
"The rising morn, the closing day"

Toyland. V. Herbert. Words by G. MacDonough. HSD

"**Tra** la la la la la la, oh! summer night." See "Com' è gentil" (Donizetti)

"**Tra**, ri, ra, all hail, the summer months." See Summer song

"**Tra**, ri, ra, hear the birds of summer sing." See Hear the birds of summer sing

"Tracascâ regele" ("Long live our noble king") A. Hübsch. Words by V. Alexandri. e.ru. BSP
"Long live our noble king." e.ru. MP
Rumania. e.ru. NA
"Traeasca regele" ("Long live the king") e.ru. SN

Tracy, George Lowell
Roll away

Tradetore (Traditore.—Deceiver) Neapolitan folk song. e.i. FE

The trades. See Les corps de métiers

Traditore. See Tradetore

"Traeasca regele." See "Tracascâ regele" (Hübsch)

Traeet (The tree) R. Nordraak. Words by B. Bjørnson. e.n. MAN

Traeet. For English translation with a different air see The tree (Composer unknown)

Traeger, Albert
"Wie lenzeshauch" (Jensen)

Traetta, Tommaso
"Gentle shade, well beloved." See "Ombra cara, amorosa"
"Gentle spirit, well beloved." See "Ombra cara, amorosa"
"Ombra cara, amorosa" (from Antigone)

Traft ihr das schiff. R. Wagner. e.g. SOA 1
"Jo ho hoe! jo ho ho hoe! ho ho hoe! jo hoe." e.g. OPS 1

The tragic home-coming. See Le retour funeste

"Trahir Vincent! vraiment, ce serait être folle." See Mon coeur ne peut changer (Gounod)

"Trailing rose-tree." See "Vaga rosa" (Kreutzer)

Trainona. Irish folk song. Modern words by M. L. Baum. GO

"Traitors all! with England you combine against me." See Pietà, rispetto, onore (Verdi)

"Un traître a frappé le vaillant paladin." See "Knight-errant" (Dargomyzhskiĭ)

Trajetta, Tommaso. See Traetta, Tommaso

Tramp, tramp, tramp ("In the heart of ev'ry scout") [G. F. Root] Words by B. Braley. BSS

Tramp, tramp, tramp ("In the prison cell") G. F. Root (music and words) BSE—FSS 5—HSD—JSE— MP—NMH—OH—WA—WBT—WSW
Tramp! tramp! tramp! the boys are marching. FMB—SSS

Tramp, tramp, tramp ("On the battle front") G. F. Root. Words by D. Stevens. TFC 1

Tramping. See Fussreise (Wolf)

Trancadillo. F. H. Brown. Words by C. Gilman. FSS 4—JO—WBT

The Transvaal flag ("Once more o'er Transvaal hills and plains") Boer patriotic song. Words by S. Du Toit. e. BMC—WA
Boer national song. e. WBT

"Trariro, der sommer der ist do." See Sommertag (Weber)

Trask, Mrs Kate (Nichols)
My world (Huss)

Trask, Katrina, pseud. See Trask, Mrs Kate (Nichols)

Trasten i höstkvällen (To a thrush in autumn) G. Wennerberg (music and words) e.sw. HSOS

Der trauernde ("Mir blühet kein frühling") Volksweise. Author of words unknown. g. ED 2

Ein traum ("Mir träumte einst."—A dream) E. Grieg. Words by F. von Bodenstedt. e.g. FM—FO 2

Der traum ("'Twas in a meadow") See The dream (Rubinstein)

Träume (Dreaming) R. Wagner. Words by M. Wesendonck. e.g. PG 1 —PG 2
Dreams. e. BC
Träume (Dreams) e.g. CMF 2—FF

Träumelein ("Wohl heute noch und morgen") Volkslied. g. ED 3

"Traurig sehen wir uns an." See Abschiedsabend (Weiss)

"Traute heimat meiner lieben." See Lied eines landmanns in der fremde (Righini)

Travanet, Mme B. de
"Pauvre Jacques"
Poor Jacques. See "Pauvre Jacques"

Traveler's evening song. See "Über allen gipfeln ist ruh" (Schubert)

"Traveller, whither art thou going." See A land without a storm

The traveller's return. See Le retour du voyageur

"The trav'ler stands perplex'd." F. J. Haydn. e. OS 3—SAS 3

"Trav'ller was he, from war returning." See Le retour du voyageur

Le tre colombe (The three doves) Italian song. e.i. BF 2

"Tre giorni son che Nina." See Nina (Pergolesi)

Tre löften (Three promises) B. Beckman. e.sw. WM 1

De tre skalke (The three rascals) Danish song. da.e. BF 2

"Tread, O my joy." See Love-song

Treadwell, J. W.
"Ring merrily"

The treasure ("Wšak nám tak, nebude") Bohemian song and dance tune. bo.e.g. BO—SMF
The treasure ("Fear not, my sweetheart") e. BMC

Treasures of the deep. Mrs Arkwright. Words by F. Hemans. JO

Treat, Frances P.
Alma mater—Lake Erie (Abt)
La **treccia** bionda (The flaxen tress) Romanesca song. e.i. MSI
The **tree** ("The tree's early leaf-buds") Composer unknown. ₁Words by B. Bjørnson. Tr of Traeet₁ e. WSC
The **tree.** For words in the original with a different air see Traeet (Nordraak)
The **tree** in the wood. English folk song: 1st version. BSS—CST—FSF—TFC 2
—2d version. SEF 2—SO
—North Carolina version. CSE
Variant: Pretty pear tree
"**Tree** of mine, that so carefully I've tended." See Canzonetta di campagnuolo
The **tree** of Odenwald. German song. ₁Tr of Der baum in Odenwald₁ e. FSS 6
The **trees** and the Master. J. P. McCaskey. Words by S. Lanier. FSS 6—LA
"**Trees** are bare ev'rywhere." See The chickadee
"The **trees** are moaning." See Des mädchens klage (Schubert)
"The **tree's** early leaf-buds were bursting their brown." See Traeet (Nordraak); The tree (Composer unknown)
"The **trees** they are tall." See Daily growing
"The **trees** they do grow high." English folk song. SEF 2—SO
The **trees** they are so high. Devon version. BSW
Variant: Daily growing
"**Tregua** è cogl' Unni." See Dagli immortali vertici (Verdi)
Treibe schifflein. For English translation see "Drift, my bark" (Kücken)
Trembath, Henry Gough
"Good Christian people all"
"The **trembling** tears in thy dear eyes are shining." See Endless love (Tchaikovsky)
"**Tremp**' ton pain, Marie." French folk song. f. DO
"**Tremulant** wold, stars bright of ray." See Chanson perpétuelle (Chausson)
Trenchmore ("Tomorrow the fox") 16th century song. CO 1
Trenchmore ("Willy prethe goe to bed") 16th century song. CO 1
Trenchmore ("Willy, prithee go to bed") JE
"**Willy**, prythee go to bed." DM 1
Die **trennung** ("Ferne dir, o ferne") J. J. Rousseau. Words by G. A. Bürger. g. ED 3
"Le **trente** et un du mois d'août." See Le combat naval
Trepak. M. Moussorgsky. Words from the Russian of A. Golenistcheff-Koutouzoff. e. NM 2
Trepak (Death and the peasant.—La mort et le paysan) e.f. SC
"Die **trepp**' hinunter geschwungen." See Niemand hat's geseh'n (Loewe)

Tres magi de gestibus. For English translation see "Eastern monarchs, sages three"
"**Tres** siglos oprimidos." See Cancion patriotica (Mexican song)
"**Treu** geliebt und still geschwiegen." See Stille liebe (Lindpaintner)
"**Treu** und herzinniglich, Robin Adair." See Robin Adair
"Die **treue**, die uns brüder band." See Treuer kampf
Der **treue** Johnie. See Faithfu' Johnnie
Treue liebe ("Ach, wie ist's möglich dann") F. Kücken. Volkslied from the Thuringian forest. e.g.gr. SSS. g. only ED 1
"Ach, wie ist's möglich" ("How can I leave thee") e.g. KF 1—KF 2—KF 3
"How can I leave thee." e.g. EF. e. only CU—FSS 1—HSC—HSD—LA—NMH—OH—WBT
Treue liebe ("How can I leave thee") e. WA—WL—WSC—WSW
Treue liebe (True love) e.g. BO—SSG
True love ("Ah! it is hard to say") e. BMC
True love ("How can I leave thee") e. BSE
Treue liebe ("Schatz, mein schatz") Volkslied. g. ED 3
Treue liebe ("Soviel stern' am himmel") Volksweise. g. ED 1
Treue liebe (True love) e.g. SSG
True love. e. BSE
Treue liebe ("Steh' ich") See "Steh' ich in finstrer mitternacht"
Treuer kampf ("Die treue, die uns brüder") Composer unknown. g. ED 2
Treuer tod ("Der ritter muss zum blutgen kampf") A. E. Choron. Words by T. Körner. g. ED 1
Trevaldwyn, B. W. J.
"O dark was the night"
A tale of the olden time
Trevannion, Henry
On the road to Mandalay
Trevers,
"Who can resist my Celia's charms"
"**Tri** godini." See The outlaw
Triangle song. Air: Marching through Georgia. Words by H. J. Van Dyke. CHS
The **tribute** of the birds. G. Donizetti. Words by U. Fairweather. BD
Tribute to Wesleyan. Illinois Wesleyan university song. R. C. Smedley. Words by B. H. Smith. CHS
The **tricolored** banner. See La nocca de tre colure
Trifolium. J. J. Flemming. Song of the wandering students of the middle ages. l. SSS
Trinity Sunday. English folk song. BSW
Des **trinkers** testament. See entry under Des

Trinklied ("Bringt mir blut der edlen re-ben") E. M. Arndt (music and words) g. ED 2

Trinklied ("Ja, lustig bin ich") Words by H. Hoffmann von Fallersleben. g. ED 3

Trinklied ("Das leben gleichet der blume") I. D. Gerstenberg. Words by G. A. von Halem. g. ED 2

Trinklied ("Man sagt wohl") J. F. Reichardt. Volkslied. g. ED 3

Trinklied ("Der wein erfreut") See Wein, weib, gesang (Zelter)

Trinklied ("Wir sind die könige") K. F. Ebers. Words by G. W. C. Starke. g. ED 1

Trinklied ("Wir sind nicht mehr am ersten glas") C. Kreutzer. Words by L. Uhland. g. ED 2

"Triomf, de vreugde stij-ge in top." See Die nieuwe haring

"Trip it lightly." Old song. FSS 8

"Trip it! Lisella." See Hopsa! Lisella

"Trip, trip, over the grass." See The broken pitcher (Pontet)

The trip we took over the mountain. Irish folk song. JOI

"Tripping maidens" ("Šly panenky silnicí") Czech folk song. bo.e. BF 1

Trippole trappole. Neapolitan song of Spanish origin. e.i. MSI. e. only BSE

Las tristas horas. Folk song from Puebla. e.s. HS

"Triste est le steppe." See Over the steppe (Grechaninov)

Tristi amori. See Svarta rosor (Alfvén)

Tristram and Iseult. A. M. Foerster. Words by M. Arnold. HST

"Triumph! let gladness ascend on high." See Die nieuwe haring

"Triumph now with joy and mirth." T. Giles. Words by T. Campion. DM 2

El trobador. Folk song from southern California. e.s. HS

El trobador (The troubador) e.s. HF

"Trocknet nicht, trocknet nicht." See Wonne der wehmuth (Beethoven)

The trogger ("Wha will buy my troggin") Air: Buy broom besoms. Words by R. Burns. BSR

Troika. See Three-in-hand

Les trois capitaines (The three captains) Dance song. e.f. SMF—TSF "En passant par la Lorraine." f. DO The three captains. e. CST

Les trois chemins. See The three roads (Koeneman)

Les trois filles (L'occasion manquée.—The three maids.—The lost opportunity) French folk song. e.f. TSF

Les trois filles d'un prince. See "Derrière chez mon père, vole, mon coeur, vole" (Streabbog)

Les trois prières (Three prayers) E. Paladilhe. Words by E. des Essarts. e.f. SAM

Les trois princesses. See "Derrièr' chez mon père, vole, mon coeur, vole" (French folk song)

Les trois roses empoisonnées (The three poisoned roses) French Canadian folk song. e.f. BFS

The trolley ride. French folk air. Words by H. H. Harbour. DO

The trooper and the maid. Folk song: North Carolina version. CSE —Tennessee version. CSE

"Trop aimable Sylvie" ("Sylvia, thou art my dearest") Bergerette. e.f. WB

"Troppo soavi i gusti" ("Many and sweet the raptures") F. Cavalli. e.i. FEI 1

Trost für mancherlei tränen ("Warum sind der tränen") J. A. P. Schulz. Words by C. A. Overbeck. g. ED 3

"Trot, trot away, away." See The young postillion (Lindblad)

Trotère, H., pseud. See Trotter, Henry

Trotter, Henry
    In old Madrid
    Leonore

The troubador. See El trobador

Troubadour song ("Why should I be") e. WC

Troubetzkoy, Amélie (Rives) Chanler
    My laddie (Thayer)

Troutbeck, John
    In memoriam (Rossini)
    Power and love (Gounod)

Troy town. J. Wilson. CO 1

Troyte, Sir Arthur Henry Dyke
    God's will and love
    Troyte's chant

Troyte's chant. A. H. D. Troyte. Words by C. Elliott. TL

"Truce is proclaimèd." See Dagli immortali vertici (Verdi)

True blue. S. Adams. MP

True courage. Dibdin. HSE 2

The true English sailor. Dibdin. HSE 3

True freedom. M. R. Lang. Words by J. R. Lowell. TL

True freedom. F. Silcher. Words by J. R. Lowell. LBR

True happiness. Attributed to Dieupart. Words by W. Bedingfield. ME

"True-hearted was he, the sad swain o' the Yarrow." Air: Bonie Dundee. BSR —PS 2

True hearts. S. Adams. Words by W. J. Stewart. FSS 8

True love ("Ach, wie ist's möglich") See Treue liebe (Kücken)

True love ("Soviel stern'") See Treue liebe ("Soviel stern'")

True love ("Steh' ich") See "Steh' ich in finstrer mitternacht"

"True love can ne'er forget." T. O'Carolan. Words by S. Lover. FSS 2—JO—WBT

True love is sweet. W M. Hutchinson. FSS 5

The true lover's farewell. Folk song: English version. SEF 1—SO
—Black Mountain, N.C. version. CSE
—Carmen, N.C. version. CSE
—Hot Springs, N.C. version. CSE
—Tennessee version. CSE
Variant of: The turtle-dove

"Truly this man was the son of God." A. Klughardt. e. SAS 4

"The trumpet shall sound." G. F. Händel. SAS 4

"The trumpets all are sounding, hussars now to horse." See Der feldmarschall

Trust (Mendelssohn) See "God shall charge His angel legions"; "Saviour, Source of every blessing"

Trust ("Thou wilt keep him") C. L. Williams. TL

"Trust not the treason of those smiling lookes." M. Greene. Words by E. Spenser. MM

Truth ("Fairest grace") Words by E. R. Sill. LA

Truth in absence. E. B. Harper. Words by H. Brandreth. HSE 3

"The truth is suspected." M. I. Glinka. Words by Rosen. e.g. SC

Try, try again. School song. FSS 1—JSE—WBT—WSC

Trysting love song. Omaha Indian song. in. FIS

Tschaikovsky, Peter Ilyich. See Tchaikovsky, Peter Ilyich

Tschirch, Wilhelm
The Scottish fatherland

"Tsen brider." See "Ten brothers"

Tsepkinoi-Kupernik, Tatyana Lvovna. See Shchepkina-Kupernik, Tatîana Lvovna

Tsertelev, D. U.
"Far on the road we two journeyed together" (Ippolitov-Ivanov)
Parting (Ippolitov-Ivanov)

"Tsompanakos ēmouna." See The shepherd boy

To tsopanopoulo. See The shepherd boy

Tú ("En Cuba, la isla hermosa") Cuban habanera. E. S. de Fuentes. Words by F. Sanchez. s. LCP
Tú (You) e.s. GMF. e. only WL

Tu che a Dio spiegasti l'ali. For English translation see "Thou hast spread thy wings to heaven" (Donizetti)

"Tu, ch'hai le penne, amore" ("Thou that hast wings for flying") G. Caccini. e.i. FEI 1

"Tu ci sei nata con le rose in mano." See Dimme 'na vota sì (Scalisi)

"Tu crois ô beau soleil." See Amaryllis (Louis XIII)

"Tu eres mas bella." Costa Rican folk song. e.s. HS

"Tu? indietro" ("Thou avaunt thee") Verdi. e.i. OPS 3

"Tu lo sai" (Faithless as fair) A. Scarlatti. e.i. MSS 2

"Tu lo sai" ("Well thou knowest") G. Torelli. e.i. FEI 2

"Tu m'aje prommise quatto muccatora." See Ritornello delle lavandare del Vomero

"Tu m'ami ah si! bell' anima." See Then you'll remember me (Balfe)

"Tu mancavi a tormentarmi" ("Wilt no longer thou torment me") M. A. Cesti. e.i. PA 2

"Tu me dirais" ("If thou shouldst tell me") C. Chaminade. Words by R. Gérard. e.f. HM 1

"Tu me parles du fond d'un rêve." See Invocation (Widor)

"Tu nce si' nnata co le rose mmano." See Dimme 'na vota sì (Scalisi)

"Tu nel tuo letto a far de' sogni d'oro" ("Within, you are in bed and dreaming sweetly") Abruzzian folk song. e.i. MSI

Tu non sai in quel begli occhi. For English translation see "Gentle maiden those eyes remind me" (Bellini)

Tu sul labbro de' veggenti ("Come, O my brother."—Prayer) G. Verdi. e.i. SOA 5
"Tu sul labbro de' veggenti" ("Thou who grantest inspiration."—Prayer) e.i. OPS 4

Tubal Cain. H. Russell. Words by C. Mackay. BE 4
"Old Tubal Cain." FSS 4

Tucker, Henry
Sweet Genevieve
"'Tis evening brings my heart"
When this cruel war is over

Tuckerman, Henry L.
Bunker hill

Tuckerman, Samuel Parkman
"God bless our native land, on this firm shore we stand"
"A shepherd band their flocks are keeping"

Tuerk, Daniel Gottlob
Die freude

Tufts, John Wheeler
The American flag
"From east and west"
"From forest wide and free"
"O spirit of the nation, come"
Prayer for our country
Song for Arbor day. See "From forest wide and free"
Song to the flag

"Tula, tuulan, tuli, tuli tei." See Tuulan tei

"Tule koju." See "Come my dearest, to my breast"

Tule mulle, neitsikene. See Will you be mine

Tullochgorum ("Come, gie's a sang, the lady cried") Scottish air: Reel of Tullochgorum. Words by J. Skinner. JO—MMS—PS 1

Tully, Richard Walton
All for the sake of California

"Tune ev'ry harp and ev'ry voice, bid ev'ry care withdraw; let all with one accord rejoice in praise of old De Pauw." See In praise of old De Pauw (Langlotz)

"Tune ev'ry heart and ev'ry voice, bid ev'ry care withdraw; let all with one accord rejoice in praise of old Nassau." See Old Nassau (Langlotz)

"Tune ev'ry heart and ev'ry voice, let all with one accord rejoice; let music rule the fleeting hour." See We cheer for the "U of M" (Zintheo)

A tune in three keys. See En låt i tri toner (Beckman)

"Tune up your fiddle and rosin your bow." See The banks of Glenoe

Tunisian song. See "The sand is blowing"

"Tuonen lehto, öinen lehto." See Vale of shadow (Sibelius)

"Tuonne taakse metsämaan." See Beyond the wood

Turco, G.
Lo telefono (Denza)

Turkey in the straw. Old air. WBT

The Turkish lady ("Lord Bacon was a nobleman") See Young Beichan (Kentucky version)

The Turkish lady ("Young virgins all, I pray draw near") Folk song from Sussex. SF 5

Turkish patriotic song ("Once the sultan of the world") Nedjib Pacha. e. WCP
Modern patriotic war march. e. KSE—SN

Turkish war song ("Come to the plain and meet the Frankish host") e. BMC

Turkish war song ("We suffer that the fatherland") e. KSE

Turmut-hoeing. See The vly is on the turmut

Turn about the chamarrita. See Chamarrita

"Turn again, thou fair Eliza." Scottish air. Words by R. Burns. BSB—BSR—PS 1

"Turn again to thy rest." F. Kiel. e. SAS 2

Turn back Pharaoh's army. Negro spiritual. JP—NMP—WBT—WC
Pharaoh's army. DF—FSS 6

"Turn, lovely Gwen." Air: Y draeog, or, The hedgehog. Words from the Welsh. e. MMW

"Turn once again." See "Caro mio ben" (Giordani)

"Turn to me, dark eye so tender." See Bitte (Franz)

Turn ye to me ("The stars are burning cheerily, cheerily") Air: Horo mhairi dhu. Words by Christopher North (J. Wilson) HSSS—MMS—NG—PO

Turnbull, W.
"Deck not with gems"

Turner, D. F.
The navy-blue and white (Composer unknown)

Turner, Francis
Dulce domum (Reading) Authorship uncertain

Turner, Joseph W.
Roll on, silver moon: old air arranged

Turner, Nellie B.
Lenox crimson (Composer unknown)

Turnlied ("Wer gleichet uns turnern") Volksweise. Words by E. F. August. g. ED 2

Turquetiz, Édouard
Sérénade (Tchaikovsky)

The turtle dove ("In a shady forest") Old Russian song. e. KSN

The turtle-dove ("Oh! don't you see the turtle-dove") Folk song from Dorset. SF 1
Variants: The little turtle dove; The true lover's farewell

"Turtle, turtle, on your way." See The rabbit and the turtle

"Tus ojos son viva llama." See Cueca or zamacueca

"Tute tamai le fou ane." See Song of the Samoan islanders

"Tutto è deserto." See Il balen del suo sorriso (Verdi)

Tuulan tei. Finnish folk song. e.fi. BF 1

"Twa bonie lads were Sandy and Jockie." Air: Jenny's lamentation. Words by R. Burns. BSR

Twa bonnie maidens. Scottish air. Words by Hogg. PS 1

Twang lango dillo day. Old English air. BE 2

Twankydillo. Traditional air. BOS

"T'wards the garden bright with flow'rs." See Woe is me

"'Twas a beautiful night." See Moriar, Melpomene (Glover)

"'Twas a calm, still night." See Lilly Dale (Thompson)

"'Twas a-going of my rounds." See All round my hat (Valentine)

"'Twas a pleasant summer's morning." See As I'd nothing else to do (Hatton)

"'Twas a shepherdess to keep." See La bergère à confesse

"'Twas a starry night of old." C. L. Naylor. Words by J. E. Leeson. HC

"'Twas a trumpet's pealing sound." See The captive knight (Browne)

"'Twas about the dead of night." Easter carol. HC

'Twas April. Tchaikovsky. e. TS

"'Twas at morn I met the proud array." See Marcho dei rei

"'Twas at the matin hour." E. Handley. Tr of Patris sapientia, veritas (bonitas) divina. e. HC

"'Twas Christmas eve." S. Nelson. Words by F. E. Weatherly. MCS

"'Twas clear and cold." H. R. Bishop. MCS

"'Twas coat, vest and pantaloons." See The lady and the glove

" 'Twas down in a valley." See The lost lady found

" 'Twas down in Cupid's garden." See Cupid's garden

" 'Twas down in that place Tipperary." See The Irish christening (Maginnis)

'Twas down in the meadows. Irish folk song. JOI

" 'Twas early, early, all in the spring." See The croppy boy

" 'Twas early I walk'd on a midsummer morning." See Midsummer carol

" 'Twas early in the springtime of the year." See The sprig of thyme

" 'Twas early morn, when on the great highway." See Marcho dei rei

" 'Twas early one morning at breaking of day." See Jolly fellows that follow the plough

" 'Twas early one morning the ploughboy arose." See The simple ploughboy (Virginia version)

" 'Twas early one morning young Willie arose." See The lake of Coolfinn

" 'Twas east north east, so near the line." See The marigold

" 'Twas even here those words were spoken." J. Massenet. e. SAS 1

" 'Twas even—the dewy fields were green." Air: Ettrick banks. Words by R. Burns. BSR

" 'Twas even—the dewy fields were green" (The bonnie lass O' Ballochmyle) W. Jackson. Words by R. Burns. BSB

" 'Twas Friday morn when we set sail." See The mermaid

" 'Twas God above that made all things." See The leather bottèl

" 'Twas in a meadow by the way." See The dream (Rubinstein)

" 'Twas in a merry time." See Cock Robin and Jenny Wren

" 'Twas in eighteen hundred and fifty-three and of June the thirteenth day." See Greenland fishery

" 'Twas in fifty-five on a winter's night." See The midshipmite (Maybrick)

" 'Twas in June, rosy June." See The haymaker (Reeve)

" 'Twas in that season of the year." See Roslin castle

" 'Twas in the dark of a tavern door." See La femme avare et le crucifix

" 'Twas in the end of King James's street." Irish folk song. JOI

" 'Twas in the lovely month of May." See "Im wunderschönen monat mai" (Franz)

" 'Twas in the merry month of May, the green buds were swelling." See Barbara Allen (Kentucky version)

" 'Twas in the merry month of May, when all gay flowers were blooming." See Barbara Allen (Habersham co., Ga. version)

" 'Twas in the merry month of May, when bees from flow'r to flow'r did hum." See Follow the drum

" 'Twas in the month of May, when flowers spring." See Willy Coombe

" 'Twas in the prime of summer time." See The barley raking

" 'Twas in the season of the year." See Roslin castle

" 'Twas in the seventeen hunder year." Air: The children in the wood. Words by R. Burns. BSR

" 'Twas in the sunny Rhineland." H. Smart. FSS 7

" 'Twas in the town of Jacksboro." See Range of the buffalo

" 'Twas in the winter cold." J. Barnby. Words by J. C. Black. BSC—HC

" 'Twas in Trafalgar's bay." See The death of Nelson

" 'Twas inch by inch I sought the Lord." See Inching along

" 'Twas jolly, jolly Wat." T. T. Noble. Words by C. W. Stubbs. HC

" 'Twas just a horse-shoe." See Horse-shoe song

" 'Twas King Renaud rode home from war." See La chanson de Renaud

" 'Twas na her bonie blue e'e was my ruin." Air: Laddie, lie near me. Words by R. Burns. BSR—PS 2

" 'Twas near a thicket's calm retreat." J. Moulds. ME

" 'Twas not thy rank, nor pomp, nor state." See Thy true heart (Vogrich)

" 'Twas of a brisk young lady." See The lady and prentice

" 'Twas of a lofty ship, boys." See The Golden Vanity

" 'Twas off the blue Canary isles." See My last cigar (Crosby)

" 'Twas Ole and Christine were dancing away." See Møen paa baalet

" 'Twas on a bank of daisies sweet." See The blackbird (Hook)

" 'Twas on a bright mornin' in summer." See The pretty girl milking her cow

" 'Twas on a jolly summer's morn." See The vly is on the turmut

" 'Twas on a merry time." See Cock Robin and Jenny Wren

" 'Twas on a Monday morning as I came thro' Saint Ives." See The skippers of St Ives (Roeckel)

" 'Twas on a Monday morning, right early in the year." See O Charlie is my darling (Additional words by Burns); O, Charlie is my darling (Additional words by Nairne)

" 'Twas on a Monday morning when I beheld my darling." See Dashing away with the smoothing iron

" 'Twas on a pleasant summer's day." See Well-a-day

" 'Twas on a simmer's afternoon." See The lass o' Gowrie

" 'Twas on a summer evening, I heard a song so fair." See The heavenly song (Gray)

" 'Twas on a very stormy day." See The Flying Dutchman (Parry)

" 'Twas on a windy night." See Barney Brallaghan's courtship

" 'Twas on last Monday's morning." See Low down in the broom

" 'Twas on one Sunday bright and clear." See O schöne zeit, o sel'ge zeit (Götze)

" 'Twas on the morn of sweet May day." See Jockey to the fair

" 'Twas on the twenty-first of June." See The marriage day (Sanderson)

" 'Twas on this Easter morning." G. E. Oliver. HC

" 'Twas once that I courted a charming lady bright." See The soldier's return

" 'Twas once upon a time, dear." See Once upon a time (Barnard)

" 'Twas one morn when the wind from the northward blew keenly." See The smuggler (Davy)

" 'Twas one of those dreams." Irish air: The song of the woods. Words by T. Moore. MI—MMI

" 'Twas past one o'clock." Air: Cold frosty morning. Words by R. Burns. BSR

" 'Twas post meridian, half-past four." See The sailor's journal (Dibdin)

" 'Twas Sunday morn at break of day." See La fille et le chasseur

" 'Twas the beauty of Voghera." See "La biondina di Voghera"

" 'Twas two days out from Boston town." D. Macgregor. Words by A. A. Powers. CU

" 'Twas when the seas were roaring." See The melancholy nymph (Händel)

" 'Twas when the wan leaf frae the birk tree was fa'in'." See Lucy's flittin'

" 'Twas when I came to England." See Flora the lily of the west

" 'Twas when the hay was mown, Maggie." See The old time (Thomas)

" 'Twas within a mile of Edinboro' town." See Within a mile of Edinboro' (Hook)

Tweeddale, John Hay, 2d marquis of
"When Maggie and I was acquaint" (Scottish air)

" 'Tween ox and ass in humble shed." See Entre le boeuf et l'âne gris (Gevaert)

"12 are the 12 apostles." See The ten commandments (Black Mountain, N.C. version)

The twelve days of Christmas. English folk song. SEF 2—SO

"Twelve hundred years, at least." See St George, our protector (Clarke)

"The twenty-first of April, men." See La mort du porte-enseigne

Twenty years ago ("I've wander'd to the village, Tom") W. Willing. HSD

Twenty years ago ("Those bonny glades of Girvan woods") A. L. Gatty. WBT

" 'Twere vain to tell thee all I feel." Swiss air. Words by J. A. Wade. FSS 6—JO—WBT

Twickenham ferry. T. Marzials. FSS 2—WBT—WBW

Twilight ("Comme un rideau") See Crépuscule (Massenet)

Twilight dews. T. Moore (music and words) FSS 4—JO—WBT

"Twilight falling, baby weary." See Christmas lullaby (Harrison)

Twilight is falling ("Twilight is stealing") B. C. Unseld. Words by A. S. Keiffer. FSS 1—WBT

"Twilight is falling, crimson the sun." See Vom Monte Pincio (Grieg)

"Twilight is stealing over the sea." See Twilight is falling (Unseld)

Twilight musing. See "Prinsessen sad höjt i sit jomfrubur" (Kjerulf)

"Twilight o'er the woods around." See En sommarafton (Lindblad)

"Twilight of evening softly has spread." See Nocturne (Liapunov)

"The twilight shades, fast descending." See At twilight

" 'Twill be a painful separation." Händel. OS 2

"Twine the Easter garland." G. B. Lissant. Words by J. Bownes. HC

"Twinkle brightly, stars of light." See Baby's night

"Twinkle, twinkle, little star." French or German air. Words by J. Taylor. FSS 1— JSE— WA—WBT—WSC—WSW

"Twinkle, twinkle, little star." Composer unknown. [Words by J. Taylor] FMB

"Twinkling stars are laughing, love." J. P. Ordway (music and words) HSD—NML—WBT

The two brothers. Folk song: Kentucky version. SA
—Hot Springs, N.C. version. CSE
—Black Mountain, N.C. version. CSE
—Charlottesville, Va. version. CSE
—Mount Fair, Va. version no. 1. CSE
—Mount Fair, Va. version no. 2. CSE

"Two brothers they have just returned." See The two brothers (Charlottesville, Va. version)

Two bunches a penny primroses. J. Hook. Words by Upton. ME

"Two dainty little shoes I wear." See Der sandmann (Schumann)

"Two daughters of this aged stream." H. Purcell. Words by Dryden. BE 2

"Two empires." Air: God save the king. Words by G. Huntington. LA

"Two fond young lovers." See The parted lovers (Chopin)

The two grenadiers. See Die beiden grenadiere (Schumann); Les deux grenadiers (Wagner)

Two hearts. H. de Fontenailles. Words by H. Lucas. [Tr of Les deux coeurs] e. WBW

The two kings daughters. See De to kongedøttre

"Two little flies." W. B. Olds. CHS

"Two little friendless children." See The new kingdom (Tours)

The two magicians. English folk song. FSF—SEF 2—SO

Two maidens washing wool. See Două fete spală lână

"Two robin redbreasts, in a nest." See The robin song

Two royal children. See Zwei königskinder

The two shepherdesses. See Les deux bergères

The two sisters. Folk song: North Carolina version. CSE
—Albermarle county, Va. version. CSE
—Mt Fair, Va. version. CSE
—Woodridge, Va. version. CSE

"Ty sidish' odinoko i smotrish' s toskoĭ." See By the fireside

Ty vzoidi, solntse krasnoe. See The captive maiden

Tykiai Nemunēlis teka. See Softly flows the Niemen

Tyl, J. K.
My fatherland (Škroup)

Tynan, Katharine. See Hinkson, Mrs Katharine (Tynan)

"Tyrannic love! I feel thy cruel dart." G. F. Händel. BS 1—OS 3—SAS 3

The Tyroleans. See Tyroler (Haibel)

Tyroler. J. Haibel. Words by E. Schikaneder. g. ED 1
The Tyroleans ("Tyrolese, so happy and joyous") e. BMC—WBT
"Tyroler sind lustig" ("The folk of the Tyrol are jolly and gay") e.g. SSG
"Tyroler sind lustig" ("Tyrolese are blithesome") e.g. BO

"Tyroler sind lustig, so lustig und froh." See Tyroler (Haibel)

Der Tyroler und sein kind ("Wenn ich mich nach der heimat sehn'") J. F. Nesmüller (music and words) g. ED 1
Der Tiroler und sein kind (The Tyrolese and his child) e.g. EF
Der Tyroler und sein kind (The Tyrolese and his son) e.g. SSG

Tyrolerlied ("Wann i in der fruh aufsteh") Volkslied. g. ED 1

The Tyrolese and his child. See Der Tyroler und sein kind (Nesmüller)

The Tyrolese and his son. See Der Tyroler und sein kind (Nesmüller)

"Tyrolese are blithesome." See Tyroler (Haibel)

Tyrolese evening hymn. Mrs Hughes. Words by F. D. Browne. JO

The Tyrolese maiden ("All our laddies love shooting") Tyrolese song. e. KSE

The Tyrolese maiden's farewell ("Thou canst not blame me") Tyrolese song. e. KSE—WL

Tyrolese mountain song. See "We'll go to the mountains"

"Tyrolese, so happy and joyous." See Tyroler (Haibel)

Tyte, M.
My Mary Anne

The tythe pig. English folk song. BSW

Tytler, James
"I hae laid a herrin' in saut" (Scottish air)

Tyutcheff, Fyodor. See Tiuchev, Feodor

U

U d's Vreneli ab em Guggisberg. See Das alte Guggisberger lied

U kamina. See By the fireside

U menîâ-l' vo sadochîe. See Peasant-idyl

"U prząśniczki siedzą." See At the spinning wheel (Moniuszko)

The U. S. A. forever. D. Emmett. TFC 1

U vorot batîushkinykh. See Advice to lovers

"Ua like no a like." See Sweet constancy

An uair bha Gàilig aig na h-eòin ("When all the birds in Gaelic sang") Scottish air. Words from the Gaelic of J. MacCuaraig. e. MMS

"Über allen gipfeln ist ruh" (Traveler's evening song) F. Schubert. Words by Goethe. e.g. FSS 6
Above the mountains. e. LA

"Über den sternen ist ruh" ("Far o'er the stars there is rest") F. Abt. e.g. HSS 2—HSS 3—HSS 4
"Over the stars there is rest." e. FMB—FSS 3—JSE—WA—WBT—WS—WSC—WSW

"Über die berge mit ungestüm." C. M. von Weber. Words by A. von Kotzebue. g. ED 2

"Über die beschwerden dieses lebens." See Le petit matelot (Gaveaux)

"Über reisen kein vergnügen." V. Strebel. Words by L. Tieck. g. ED 3

"Über tal und fluss getragen." See An Mignon (Zelter)

"Überall bin ich zu hause." See Ubi bene, ibi patria

"Über's jahr." See "Ueber's jahr" (Bohm)

Ubi bene, ibi patria ("Überall bin ich zu hause") Composer unknown. Words after F. Hückstädt. g. ED 1. e. only LA

Ubi sunt, O, pocula. See "Lauriger Horatius"

"Uciekła mi przepiórecka w proso." See The little quail

"Ude Parmerent, i Holland." See Pumping chanty

"Ueber'm garten, durch die lüfte." See Frühlingsnacht (Jensen); Frühlingsnacht (Schumann)

"Ueber's jahr" ("In a year") C. Bohm. Words by D. Böttcher. e.g. SM 3

Ueltzen, W.
Gute ruhe (Winter)
Ihr (Volksweise)
"Uf em bergli bin i g'sässe." See Schweizerlied
"Uf'm berge da geht der wind." See Maria auf dem berge
"Ugly am I, I know well." See The singer (Rimskiï-Korsakov)
The ugly thief. See An Gadaighe Grána
Uhland, Ludwig
Abreise (Kreutzer)
Abschied (Volksweise)
The chapel (Composer unknown)
Der wirtin töchterlein (18th century air)
Des sängers fluch (Gersbach)
Einkehr (music by Gersbach; Schnyder von Wartensee)
Frühlingsglaube (music by Ries; Schubert)
Der gute kamerad (Composer unknown)
In der ferne (Kreutzer)
Lauf der welt (Grieg)
Maienthau (Bennett)
"O tannenbaum, du edles reis" (Wollank)
Der schmied (Brahms)
Sonntag (Brahms)
Trinklied (Kreutzer)
Der weisse hirsch (Volksweise)
Die uhr (The watch) C. Loewe. Words by G. Seidl. e.g. AB 4
Uina ka wai ona Molokama ea. See "My love to thee" (Nape)
"Uklad ze mna zrób, dzieweczko." See "Dearest maiden, hark, I pray thee"
Ukor. See Reproach
Ukranian song ("At Saratoff and Tzaritzine") East Russian folk song. e. BMC
Ulmann, Augustus
"Christ is risen, all triumphant"
"Come forth and bring your garlands"
"God, Who rulest through the ages"
"Moving o'er the troubled waters"
Ultzen, W. See Ueltzen, W.
Umanets, A.
"When leaves are falling sere" (Alferakiï)
"Umbe animadjag." See Farewell to the warriors
"Ume wa saitaka." See Flower song
Umlauf, S. C.
"Alleluia! King victorious"
Un di weib silt nid. See A teamster's complaint
Die unbeständige ("Schöne augen, schöne strahlen") Volkslied. g. ED 3
Úna bán (Fair Una) Irish folk song. e.ir. BF 2
"Uncle John is very sick." Children's song. WSC
Uncle Ned. S. C. Foster (music and words) BOS—FSS 5—NMP—SSS—WA—WBT—WSW

The unconstant fair. Old English song. DM 2
The unconstant lovyer ("O come, all my young lovyers") Middle western song. BF 2
Uncrowned kings. H. W. Loomis. Words by F. Manley. TL
"Und als der grossvater die grossmutter nahm." See Grossvaterlied
"Und das war Olaf Trygvason." See Olaf Trygvason (Grieg)
"Und der Hans schleicht umher." See Hans und Liesel (Woyna)
"Und die sonne, sie machte den weiten ritt um die welt." See Sonne, mond und sterne
"Und die Würzburger glöckli ha'n schönes geläut." See Die Würzburger glöckli
Und' e bukur. See Beautiful nose
"Und ob die wolke." C. M. von Weber. e.g. SOA 1
"Und schau' ich hin, so schaust du her." See Liebesqual
"Und schläfst du, mein mädchen" ("From slumber awaken") A. Jensen. Words from the Spanish of G. Vicente. e.g. FO 1
"Und so finden wir uns wieder." See Die gunst des augenblicks (Zelter)
Undaunted. See Senza timore (Sieber)
"Undaunted Shôn ap Evan." See Shôn ap Evan
"Under a spreading chestnut tree." See The village blacksmith (Weiss)
"Under our cottage window." Bohemian folk song. e. CST
"Under Spanish skies I'm lonely." See "Sotto il bel ciel delle Spagne" (Semet)
"Under the garden trees I picked finochi." See Villotta
Under the greenwood tree ("In summer time") See "In summer time, when flow'rs do spring"
"Under the greenwood tree, who loves to lie with me." T. A. Arne. Words by W. Shakespeare. BOH—DM 1—HSE 1—KSS—ME—PR 2
"Under the greenwood tree, who loves to lie with me." C. Busch. Words by W. Shakespeare. VFS
Under the holly bough. C. Barnard. Words by C. Mackay. MCS
"Under the May-pole gay." See May-day song (Scott-Gatty)
Under the stars and stripes. F. S. Converse. Words by M. Cawein. BSS
"Under the stars one holy night." M. C. Brown. Words by A. S. Dricol. DC
Under the trees. U. Munjinger. Words by R. H. Stoddard. LBR
"Under the wide and starry sky." See Requiem (Homer)
Under the willow she's sleeping. S. C. Foster. FSS 7—WBT—WL
"Under this ground lies Thomas Round." Round. FSS 8
"Underneath a shady tree." See The gay young bachelor

"Underneath the briny sea." Harrow school song. LA

"Underneath the May-tree's snow-white blossom." See White blossoms (Levey)

Underwoods. See Requiem (Homer)

The undiscovered country. See "Dites, la jeune belle" (Berlioz)

"Undrer mig paa, hvad jeg faar at se over de höje fjelde." See Over de höje fjelde (Kjerulf); Over de höje fjelde (Nordraak)

Der unerbittliche hauptmann ("O Strassburg") Volkslied. g. ED 1

Unfading beauty ("He that loves a rosy cheek") H. Lawes. Words by T. Carew. DM 2
Disdain returned ("He that loves a rosy cheek") JE

"Unfaithful heart." M. Blumner. e. SAS 1

Unfaithfulness. See Untreue

Unfold, ye portals. C. Gounod. e. BD

"En ungbirk stander ved fjorden." See Ungbirken (Egeberg); Ungbirken (Grieg)

Ungbirken (The young birch) A. Egeberg. Words by J. Moe. e.n. SSN

Ungbirken (The young birch) E. Grieg. Words by J. Moe. e.n. MAN
Humility. e. BD

Ungeduld (Impatience) F. Schubert. Words by W. Müller. e.g. KF 1—PG 2—PG 3

"Ungitchedah heyah heyah." See The bravest

The uninvited aunt ("Mit kein gebetene") Jewish folk song. e.y. BF 2
Uninvited ("Nit kain gebetene") e.y. GF 2

"Unis dès la plus tendre enfance" ("From tender childhood e'er united") C. W. Gluck. e.f. KS 4

United ("America, our mother fair") M. S. Mercer. MP

United ("Thou tall and e'er verdant mountains."—Kapilina) Hawaiian song. e.h. HA

United be our loving. See "The remembrance of our last meeting" (Hopkins)

A university hymn ("Our Father in heaven") Air: Adeste fideles. Words by T. Wistar. CHS

University, live for aye. Western university of Pennsylvania song. CHS

"Unjedu manito ninganomdog." See A song of faith

"Unkind Irene, why have you left me." See "Crudele Irene, tu m'hai lasciato"

"Unkind, love? ah! no, Ottavio." See "Crudele! ah! no, mio bene" (Mozart)

"Unlike the flowers so bright and gay." See Buy my roses (Norton)

"Unnumber'd diamonds lie within the caverns." See A song of India (Rimskiï-Korsakov)

The unquiet grave ("Cold blows the wind") English folk song. SEF 2—SO
The unquiet grave ("How cold the wind doth blow") Sussex version. SF 5

"Unruly, sir, unruly." See "Stizzoso, mio stizzoso" (Pergolesi)

Unseld, Benjamin Carl
Twilight is falling

Unser vaterland ("Kennt ihr das land") H. G. Nägeli. Words by L. Wächter. g. ED 2

Unshriven. Ruthenian folk air. Words by J. Russell. WF

"Unspoken words at parting." See At parting (MacDowell)

"Unsre freundschaft zu erneuen." See Alte freundschaft, alter wein (André)

"Unter allen wipfeln ist ruh." See Abendlied (Kuhlau)

"Unter blüh'nden mandelbäumen" ("'Neath the almond trees that blossom") C. M. von Weber. e.g. KS 4—SOA 3

"Unter Yankele's vigele." See "By the cradle of Yankele"

Unterländers heimweh ("Drunten im unterland") Schwabisches volkslied. Words by G. Weigle. g. ED 1
The lowland home. e. BSE—JSE
Suabian's song of home. e. FSS 8
Unterländers heimweh (Lowlander's longing) e.g. SSG

"Until I reach-a ma home." Negro spiritual. JB

Until the day breaks. Gounod. Words by A. Chapman. HSS 2

"Unto a poor blind lover." See "A un niño ciegocito"

"Unto my charger." Mackenzie. OS 4

"Unto the East Indies we were bound." Irish folk song. JOI

"Unto the hills." Mercadante. e. HSS 2

"Unto Thee, blest Trinity." See "Alla Trinità beata"

"Unto us is born a Son." Words from the Latin. e. HC

Untreu ("Mein lied ist klein."—Betrayal) P. Cornelius (music and words) e.g. CMF 1

Untreue ("Was hab ich denn") Volkslied. g. ED 1
Untreue (Unfaithfulness) e.g. SSG

The untruthful daisy. W. H. Jones. NML

"Unveil thy bosom, faithful tomb." See Funeral dirge (Händel)

"Up amang yon cliffy rocks." See The maid that tends the goats

"Up and down the country side." See The strolling fiddler

"Up and down, to and fro." See Rustic dance

Up, and warn a', Willie. See "When we gaed to the brae o' Mar"

Up and waur them a', Jamie. See "The laddies by the banks o' Nith"

"Up! arise! and thy son there." See Eri tu che macchiavi (Verdi)

"**Up** comrades and mount." See Reiterlied (Zahn)

"**Up** in the air the trains go flying." See Riding on the elevated

Up in the morning early ("Cauld blaws the wind frae east to west") Air: Cold and raw, or, Up in the morning early. Words by R. Burns. BSB

"Cauld blaws the wind frae east to west." BSR

Up in the morning early ("Cauld blaws the wind frae north to south") Air: Cold and raw, or, Up in the morning early. Words by J. Hamilton. MMS—PS 1

"**Up** comes the day in orange and gold." See God morgen (Grieg)

"**Up** from meadows free, coming full of glee." See Song of the daisies

"**Up** in a choir-loft a maid sang softly." See A maiden sang (Vassilenko)

Up! lords of Erebus. See O voi dell' Erebo (Händel)

Up on de mountain. Negro spiritual. JB

"**Up** the hills." Rossini. FSS 1—LA

"**Up** the sun rose like a dart." See O my love, my plane-tree

"**Up** to thee, almighty Father." See National praise (Martel)

"**Up!** up! ye dames, ye lasses gay." See Song of Illyrian peasants (Schnecker)

Up, warriors! 'tis your homeland. See Himno de Riego (Huerta)

"**Up** wi' the carls o' Dysart." See Hey, ca' thro'

"**Up** yonder at my father's." See La fille à la fontaine (Canadian version)

"**Up** yonder upon the mountain." See Das mühlrad

Upidee ("A new co-ed has alighted in town") College air. Words by C. Arthur. CHS

Upidee ("The shades of night were falling fast") College air. Words by H. W. Longfellow. FSS 1—HSD—JS—JSE — LA— MPC— NMH— SSS— WA— WBT—WC—WSW

Upidee ("The shades of night were a-comin' down swift") College air. Variation of Longfellow's words. JSE—LA

"**Uplift** the song of praise." Traditional air. Words by F. L. Hosmer. BSS

"**Upon** a lowly manger." M. Atwood. WBT—WSC

"**Upon** a meadow slope I lay." See The dream (Rubinstein)

"**Upon** a pond." See Le canard blanc

"**Upon** a Sunday morning." English folk song. BSW

"**Upon** a sunshine summer's day." See The spinning wheel

"**Upon** a time I chanced to walk along a green." See Queen of May; The queen of May (another air)

"**Upon** de mountain my Lord spoke." See Ev'ry time I feel the spirit

"**Upon** my endless wand'rings." See Das wirtshaus (Schubert)

"**Upon** our little lake." See The sail-boat (Auber)

"**Upon** that day." See "An jenem tag" (Marschner)

"**Upon** the breast of night." See Sérénade (Pierné)

"**Upon** the bridge at Avignon." See "Sur le pont d'Avignon" (Canadian version)

"**Upon** the crest of Wailana" (Oi hoi ha) D. Nape. e.h. HA

"**Upon** the day when thou didst vow to be mine." See "An jenem tag" (Marschner)

"**Upon** the height." German folk song. e. FSS 3

"**Upon** the hill he turned." See The soldier's tear (Lee)

"**Upon** the Lomonds I lay, I lay." See The Campbells are comin'

"**Upon** the mountain my Lord spoke." See Ev'ry time I feel the spirit

"**Upon** the snow-clad earth without." H. J. Gauntlett. Words by R. R. Chope. HC

"**Upon** the snow-clad earth without." A. Sullivan. Words by R. R. Chope. HC

"**Upon** this first day of the year." See New Year song (Scott-Gatty)

"**Upon** thy lovely lips" (Charõ) Syrian folk song. e.gr. BO

Upton, Robert
The blackbird (Hook)
Bring me, boy, a bowl of wine (Hook)
By and by (Hook)
The gipsy hat (Hook)
Two bunches a penny primroses (Hook)

Upton, W.
The garden gate (Parke)
The lass of Richmond hill (Hook) Authorship uncertain

"**Ur** svenska hjertans" (From depths of Swedish hearts) O. Lindblad. Words by C. W. A. Strandberg. e.sw. BSP
Swedish hymn. e. BSE
Swedish national hymn (To King Oscar) e. JS
To King Oscar. e. WCP
"Ur svenska hjärtans djup" ("From Swedish hearts") e.sw. HSOS
"Ur svenska hjertans" ("Our Swedish feelings") e.sw. SN
"Ur svenska hjertans" (Swedish national hymn) e.sw. WCP

Uralio. College song. WC

Urbs Syon aurea. For English translation see "Jerusalem the golden" (Ewing)

Urguhart, C. K.
Alma mater—Cornell (Old air)
Alma mater—Lehigh (Composer unknown)

Urians reise um die welt ("Wenn jemand eine reise tut") C. F. Zelter. Words by M. Claudius. g. ED 2

Urner, Frau Barbara (Welti)
An die abendsonne (Nägeli)

The **useful** plough.   Air: The merry milk-
maids.   DM 2
"Ustaj, ustaj Srbine."   See "Rise, O Ser-
vians"
"Ustay! Ustay! Serbine."   See "Rise, O
Servians"
Usteri, Martin
   "Freut euch des lebens" (Nägeli)
"Utenushka lugovaîa."   See "Little duck-
ling"
Uzh îâ zoloto khoronîu.   See Riddle-song

V

V' moltchányi nótchi táïnoi.   See In the
silence of the night (Rachmaninov)
V' syrom boru tropina.   See The jackdaw
and the falcon
V' tchetuiryókh styenákh.   See In my at-
tic (Musorgskiï)
V' tiómnoi róshtchye zamólk salavýei.
See In silent woods (Rimskiï-Korsa-
kov)
"Va loin" ("Ring out")   Auvergne folk
song.   Words by E. Calvé.   e.f.
CM 1
Va, va, va, p'tit bonnet tout rond.   See
"Mon père a fait bâtir maison"
Vaarvise (The song of spring)   Norse folk
song.   e.n.   MAN
Las **vacaciones.**   B. D. Colón.   Words by
V. Davila.   s.   LCP
The **vacant** chair.   G. F. Root.   Words
by H. S. Washburn.   FSS 3—HSC—
HSD— MP— NMH— WA— WBT—
WSW
The **vacant** stare.   W. H. Jones.   CHS
Vacation days are here.   J. C. Johnson.
WBT
   "Ho, ho, vacation days are here."
FSS 1
Vacation days.   WSC
"Vacation time has come with the warm
spring days."   See April vacation
Vaccai, Niccolò
   Ah! if thou sleepest, wake, my love.
See Ah! se tu dormi
   Ah! se tu dormi (from Giulietta e
Romeo)
"Vado ben spesso cangiando loco" (The
guiding light)   Salvator Rosa or
G. B. Bononcini.   e.i.   MSS 1
   "Vado ben spesso cangiando loco"
("Though I go ranging")   e.i.
FEI 2
"Vaer hilset, i damer" ("Be greeted, ye la-
dies")   E. Grieg.   Words by H.
Drachmann.   da.e.   WM 1
"Vaga rosa" ("Trailing rose-tree")   C.
Kreutzer.   e.i.   NG
Vagans scholasticus ("Der sang ist ver-
schollen")   W. Sommer.   Author of
words unknown.   g.   ED 1
Vågen (The wave)   C. J. O. Laurin.
Words by K. A. Nicander.   e.sw.
HSOS

Vaggvisa (Cradle song)   W. T. Söder-
berg.   e.sw.   SSN
"The vain and noisy day is done."   See
Retrospect (Musorgskiï)
The **vain** suit.   See Vergebliches ständ-
chen (Brahms)
"Vain the pomp of fun'ral splendour."   See
Dove sei (Händel)
"Vainement, ma bien-aimée" ("All in vain,
O my beloved")   E. Lalo.   e.f.
CM 2
   Vainement, ma bien-aimée (Aubade)
e.f.   SOA 3
"Vainement Pharaon."   See Champs pa-
ternels (Méhul)
"Vainly now ye strive to charm me."   See
Lotharia (Arne)
"Vainly Pharaoh attempts."   See Champs
paternels (Méhul)
Valderrama, Carlos
   Imanírta
   Why, Creator.   See Imanírta
Vale ("Time ever flowing")   Adelphi col-
lege song.   J. Barnby.   Words by A.
C. Ainger.   CHS—LA
Vale carissima.   A. Wallnöfer.   Words
by C. Stieler.   e.g.   AB 3
"The vale of Nuuanu was cloth'd in hazy
mist."   See Love wreaths
Vale of shadow (Sydameni laulu)   J. Sibe-
lius.   Words by A. Kivi.   e.fi.   BF 1
"Vale of Tuoni, vale of shadow."   See
Vale of shadow (Sibelius)
"The vale where my home lies."   See
Where my home lies
Valedictory.   H. C. King.   Words by A.
F. Shoals.   LA
Valentine, John
   All round my hat
A **valentine** ("In the month of February")
Old English air: Dulcina.   BE 8
Valentines ("In the dark of the winter")
Old English air.   Words by H. H.
Harbour.   DO
Vales, J.   See Phile, Philip
"The vales and mountains am I now sur-
veying."   See Auf der reise zur hei-
math (Grieg)
The **valley** ("Mon coeur lassé de tout")
See Le vallon (Gounod)
"The valley is going to sleep."   See A
winter lullaby (De Koven)
"The valley lay smiling before me."   See
Song of O'Ruark, Prince of Breffni
"The valley rings, the blackbird sings."
See The blackbird
Le **vallon** (The valley)   C. Gounod.
Words by A. de Lamartine.   e.f.
BAS 2—BS 2—CM 2—HM 2—KF 3—
KF 4—PG 4
Vallons de l'Helvétie.   A. Adam.   e.f.
SOA 5
Valverde,
   Clavelitos
Valverde, Romea y.   See Romea y Val-
verde
"Vámonos por Santa Anita."   Mexican
folk song.   e.s.   HS

Van Alstyne, Mrs Frances Jane (Crosby)
See Crosby, Fanny
Van Am.   Columbia university song.
English air: John Peel.   Words by
W. A. Bradley.   CU
"Van Amburgh is the man who goes to all
the shows."   See Menagerie
Vanbrugh, Sir John
The Oxford bowlers
Van der Stucken, Frank
Weave in, my hardy life
Vandring i skoven (Woodland roving)   E.
Grieg.   Words by H. C. Ander-
sen.   da.e.   MAN
Vandring i skoven (Woodland wander-
ing)   da.e.   SSN
Wandering in the woods.   e.   BD
Van Dyke, Harry Stoe
Chimes of Zurich (Horn)
Van Dyke, Henry
America for me (Mercer)
Peace hymn of the republic (Ward)
Triangle song (Old air)
"Vanish'd are ye, bright hours, for ever."
See "Dove sono" (Mozart)
"Vanishing is summer."   See Höst (Bey-
er)
Vanitas! vanitatum vanitas ("Ich hab mein'
sach auf nichts gestellt")   C. F. Zel-
ter.   Words by W. von Goethe.   g.
ED 1
Vanity.   Ojibway Indian song.   2 airs.
in.   BA
"Vanne, la tua meta già vedo."   See Credo
con fermo cuor (Verdi)
"The **vanquish'd** Brutus seiz'd the fatal
sword."   See Brutus (Beale)
Vanya (Sidîel Vanîa)   Russian folk song.
e.   SSR 1
"Var tyst, du trast."   See Trasten i höst-
kvällen (Wennerberg)
Váradi's highways ("Seprik a Váradi
utczát")   Attributed to S. Bartalus.
e.hu.   BO
Varlaám's ballad.   See The siege of Kazan
(Musorgskiï)
Varlamov, Aleksandr Igorovich
Ah! tell me why
At the window
Forsaken.   See "Nightingale, O night-
ingale"
Krasni sarafan.   See The scarlet sara-
fan
Die nachtigall.   See "Nightingale, O
nightingale"
"Nightingale, O nightingale"
Parting's sorrow
Peace
The red sarafan.   See The scarlet sara-
fan
Der rote sarafan.   See The scarlet
sarafan
The scarlet sarafan
Stay! oh stay
Tears
Wanderer's night song
"A **varmer** he lived in the west countree."
See The Barkshire tragedy

Varney, Pierre Joseph Alphonse
Mourir pour la patrie
To die for home and country.   See
Mourir pour la patrie
"**Varsity!** varsity! U-rah-rah! Wisconsin."
See Toast to Wisconsin (Gounod)
Vårt land, vårt fosterland (Our land, our
fatherland)   Finnish national song.
F. Pacius.   Words by J. L. Rune-
berg.   e.sw.   BSP
"Our land" (Maamme)   e.fi.   BF 1
Our land, our fatherland.   e.sw.   MP
"Vårt land" ("Our land."—Finnish na-
tional air)   e.sw.   SN—WCP
"**Vårvindar** friska, leka och hviska"
("Spring breezes crisp")   Swedish folk
air.   Words by J. Nyberg.   e.sw.
HSOS
Vårvisa (Spring song)   A. Söderman.
Words by Z. Topelius.   e.sw.   HSOS
A **Vassar** chant.   E. J. Biedermann.   CHS
"**Vassar,** we sing thy praises."   See Alma
mater—Vassar
Vassilenko, Sergei Nikiforovich
In the tomb
Longing
A maiden sang
Les moissonneurs.   See The reapers
"O my beloved one"
The reapers
Tar
"**Vater,** ich rufe Dich."   See Gebet wäh-
rend der schlacht (Himmel)
Vaterlandslied ("Der Gott, der eisen wach-
sen liess")   A. Methfessel.   Words
by E. M. Arndt.   g.   ED 1
Deutscher freiheit schlachtruf (Battle-
cry of freedom)   e.g.   SN
Vaughan, Henry
The brave sentinel (Rodney)
Calvary (Rodney)
The clang of the forge (Rodney)
Ferryman John (Rodney)
The old guard (Rodney)
On Venice waters (Roeder)
The soldier's dream (Rodney)
Vaux, Thomas Vaux, 2d baron
"In youth when I did love" (Tradi-
tional air; also 16th century air)
"**Ve'** che sorte m'è toccata."   See Lu car-
cerato p'ammore (Biscardi)
"**V'è** quà una giardiniera."   See La Luisella
"Le **veau** d'or" ("Clear the way, for the
calf of gold")   Gounod.   e.f.
OPS 4
"Clear the way for the calf of gold"
("Dio dell' or")   e.i.   BS 2
Veazie, George Augustus
Independence day (Oehmler)
Ved ankerhioning (Heaving the anchor)
Norwegian chantey.   n.   SMW
Ved balasthioning (Throwing ballast)
Norwegian chantey.   e.n.   SMW
"La **vedette** a Piedigrotta."   See La vera
Sorrentina
"**Vedo** li bastimenti" (I see the ships) Ital-
ian song.   e.i.   BF 2

"Vedrai, carino." Mozart. e.i. PP

Das **veilchen** ("Ein veilchen auf der wiese stand") W. A. Mozart. Words by W. von Goethe. g. ED 1

Das veilchen (The violet) e.g. FF— KF 1—PG 1—PG 2

The violet. e. BC—KSE

Das **veilchen** ("Ein veilchen auf der wiese stand") J. F. Reichardt. Words by W. von Goethe. g. ED 3

Veilchen ("Veilchen, wie so schweigend") H. G. Nägeli. Words by H. Hoffmann von Fallersleben. g. ED 3

Das **veilchen** ("Vom dunkeln laub umschlossen") F. H. Himmel. Words by K. Müchler. g. ED 2

Veilchen ("Zu dem duft, der da würzt die lenzesluft."—Violets) P. Cornelius (music and words) e.g. CMF 1

"Ein **veilchen** auf der wiese stand." See Das veilchen (Mozart)

"**Veilchen**, wie so schweigend." See Veilchen (Nägeli)

"**Veile**, rose, bliämälein." See Chant de quête de l'Alsace

"**Veiled** in purple gloom of midnight." See Don Juan's serenade (Tchaikovsky)

Veillée. See Vigil (Glinka)

Veillez, veillez, veillez, Mari' Picard. See Le couvre-feu

Veit, Wenzel Heinrich
"Straightway I come from the tavern"

Veith, Emanuel
Die feldflasche (Keller)

"**Vejo** tudo a embirrar." See Menina Rosa

Velitchálnaya pyésnya. See Sadko's song of glorification (Rimskiï-Korsakov)

Vellido, Oreste
Alma Andaluza (Gómez)

"**Vem**, meu anjo, que eu não posso." See A barquinha

"**Véme**, véme con esos tus ojos." See La estrella del norte

"**Ven** a mi pobre cabaña." See La cabaña

Ven, ven, mi amor, que triste estoy. See La cabaña

Venable, W. H.
Forest song (Jones)

Venetian barcarole ("La notte xe bella fa presto Ninetta") See Barcarola veneziana

Venetian barcarole ("Softly the gondola") Italian folk air. Words by A. F. Brown. GO

Venetian boat song ("The boatmen are calling") J. Blumenthal. Words by H. C. Merivale. BD

Venetian boatmen's song ("Now the silver moon") J. S. Bach. TL

Venetian song ("Oh, come to me") See "Oh, come to me when daylight sets"

Venetian song ("Our gondola like bird is flying") H. Bemberg. Words by G. Roussel. [Tr of Chant vénetien] e. WBW

Venetianisches gondellied. See "When through the piazzetta" (Mendelssohn)

"**Venez**, agréable printemps" ("Oh, hasten, fair springtime") Bergerette. e.f. WB

Veni Emmanuel. 12th century plain song. e. CST

O come, Emmanuel. e. FSS 6—LA —MCS

Venid, niños queridos ("Come, all ye children") Castillian song. e. MF

"**Venid**, pastorciilos." Porto Rican song. Words by D. Riera. s. LCP

"**Venid**, pastores." Porto Rican song. s. LCP

Venture, Gwen. See Mentra, Gwen

Venua, Frederico Marco Antonio
"Before Jehovah's awful throne"

La **vera** Sorrentina (The fair maid of Sorrento) Neapolitan folk song. e.i. BO

La vera Sorrentina (The girl of Sorrento) e.i. FE

La vera Sorrentina (The real maid of Sorrento) e.i. MSI

Verborgenheit (Secrecy) H. Wolf. Words by E. Mörike. e.g. FO 2— GM

Die **verbrannte** maid. See The sacrifice

"**Verdant** grove, farewell to thee." See Farewell to the woods

"**Verdant** meadows." See "Verdi prati, selve amene" (Händel)

Verdi, Guiseppe
"Ah, fors' è lui" (from La traviata)
"Ah! I have sighed to rest me" (from Il trovatore. Tr of Ah! che la morte ognora)
Ah, la paterna mano (from Macbeth)
"Ah sì, ben mio; coll' essere io tuo" (from Il trovatore)
Ah! was it he. See Ah, fors' è lui
And wouldst thou thus have sullied. See Eri tu che macchiavi
Anvil chorus. See "God of the nations"
Ave Maria (from Otello)
Il balen del suo sorriso (from Il trovatore)
"Beautiful spring-time" (same air as "Home to our mountains")
"Bird of the forest"
"Bird of the greenwood"
"Blue waves are sparkling" (same air as "La donna è mobile")
Bright her smiles. See Il balen del suo sorriso
Brindisi. See Libiamo ne' lieti calici
Calm'd by her gentle, tender sway. See De' miei bollenti spiriti
Caro nome (from Rigoletto)
Celeste Aida (from Aida)
Come dal ciel precipita (from Macbeth)
"Come from the prairies" (same air as "God of the nations")
"Confutatis maledictis" (from Messa da requiem)
Cortigiani, vil razza (from Rigoletto)
Credo con fermo cuor (from Otello)
Dagli immortali vertici (from Attila)

Verdi, Giuseppe —*Continued*

Dal più remoto esilio (from I due Foscari)

De' miei bollenti spiriti (from La traviata)

Dearest name. See Caro nome

Death of Rodrigo. See Per me giunto

"Di Provenza il mar" (from La traviata)

"La donna è mobile" (from Rigoletto)

Dormirò sol nel manto mio regal (from Don Carlo)

"È strano! è strano! in core scolpiti ho quegli accenti" (from La traviata)

"Ella giammai m'amò." See Dormirò sol nel manto mio regal

The enchanted isle (from Hernani)

Eri tu che macchiavi (from Un ballo in maschera)

Ernani, Ernani, involami (from Ernani)

"Ev'ry flower" (from Rigoletto. Tr of Questa o quella)

"Fain would you know it." See "Saper vorreste"

"Fierce now the flames glow." See "Stride la vampa"

"Firm is the ice" (from Il trovatore)

Firmly I do believe. See Credo con fermo cuor

"From Provence, both land and wave." See "Di Provenza il mar"

"From the accursed." See "Confutatis maledictis"

Gaily thro' life wander (from La traviata)

"Go then! well thy fate I descry." See "Vanne; la tua meta già vedo"

"God of the nations"

Hapless Silva, whilst thou believing. See Infelice! e tu credevi

"He will ere long be here." See "Qui Radamés verrà"

"Heav'nly Aida." See Celeste Aida

"Her love was never mine." See Dormirò sol nel manto mio regal

"Home to our mountains" (from Il trovatore. Tr of Ai nostri monti ritorneremo)

Infelice! e tu credevi (from Ernani)

"Infida! il dì che brami e questo" (from Attila)

"Ingemisco tamquam reus" (from Messa da requiem)

L'insana parola (from Aida)

Is it thou who hast sullied. See Eri tu che macchiavi

Joyful tidings

"King of the shades." See "Re dell' abisso"

Il lacerato spirito (from Simon Boccanegra)

Libiamo ne' lieti calici (from La traviata)

Madre, pietosa Vergine (from La forza del destino)

March of the victors (from Aida)

"March on! Liberty's host"

"Mercè, dilette amiche" (from I vespri Siciliani)

"La mia letizia infondere" (from I Lombardi)

"My thanks, beloved companions." See "Mercè, dilette amiche"

"Oh, beloved Italia." See Parigi, o cara

"O come, let links eternal." See "Ah sì, ben mio; coll' essere io tuo"

"Oh delore! ed io vivea" (from Attila)

"Oh delusion! ah, what long season." See "Oh delore! ed io vivea"

"O don fatale" (from Don Carlo)

"Oh, fatal dower." See "O don fatale"

Oh, thou amid the angels bright. See Oh, tu che in seno agl'angioli

Oh, tu che in seno agl'angioli (from La forza del destino)

O, tu Palermo (from I vespri Siciliani)

"Of that dark scaffold" (from Il trovatore. Tr of Di quella pira)

Our flag o'er us waving (same air as "God of the nations")

"Over the summer sea" (same air as "La donna è mobile")

Pace, pace, mio Dio (from La forza del destino)

Parigi, o cara (from La traviata)

Per me giunto (from Don Carlo)

Pietà, rispetto, onore (from Macbeth)

Prayer. See "Tu sul labbro de' veggenti"

"Qui Radamés verrà" (from Aida)

"Re dell' abisso" (from Un ballo in maschera)

"Sadly groaning." See "Ingemisco tamquam reus"

"Saper vorreste" (from Un ballo in maschera)

Sea-bird's song

Shepherds in the field

"Sleep, gentle mother" (From Il trovatore. Tr of Riposa, o madre)

"Sleep, my sweet baby" (same air as "Home to our mountains")

"So charming her voice." See "La mia letizia infondere"

"So sweet her voice." See "La mia letizia infondere"

"So traitress! my fondest love thou art spurning." See "Infida! il dì che brami e questo"

Soldier's song (from Rigoletto)

"Stride la vampa" (from Il trovatore)

"Surprising! surprising! his words are all rooted in my bosom." See "È strano! è strano! in core scolpiti ho quegli accenti"

"Tacea la notte placida" (from Il trovatore)

The tempest of the heart. See Il balen del suo sorriso

"Thou avaunt thee." See "Tu? indietro"

"Thou who grantest inspiration." See "Tu sul labbro de' veggenti"

"Tu? indietro" (from Otello)

"Tu sul labbro de' veggenti" (from Nabucodonosor)

Verdi, Giuseppe—*Continued*
"Vanne; la tua meta già vedo" (from Otello)
"Volta la terrea fronte alle stelle" (from Un ballo in maschera)
"Wear a bright smile"
We'll laugh and sing all cares away
"When o'er this earth of ours." See "Volta la terrea fronte alle stelle"
"Woman is fickle." See "La donna è mobile"
"Woman's unfeeling heart." See "La donna è mobile"
"**Verdi** prati, selve amene" ("Verdant meadows, forest spreading") G. F. Händel. e.i. CS 1—SOA 2
"Verdi prati, selve amene" ("Verdant meadows groves enchanting") e.i. KS 3
Verdure. See "We feel thy calm" (Haydn)
Das **verfehlte** wort ("Sie ging zum sonntagstanze") Volksweise. Words by C. A. Tiedge. g. ED 1
"**Vergangen** ist der lichte tag." See Nachtlied (Kugler)
Vergebliche liebesmüh' (Love's labor lost) Folk song. e.g. SSG
Vergebliches ständchen (The disappointed serenader) J. Brahms. Words from a folk-song. e.g. FO 2
Vergebliches ständchen (The vain suit) e.g. SM 1
Vergiftet sind meine lieder. For English and French translations see "My songs are envenomed and bitter" (Borodin)
"**Vergin,** tutto amor" ("Virgin, full of grace") F. Durante. e.i. FEI 2
"Vergin, tutto amor" ("Virgin, fount of love") e.i. PA 2
"**Vergiss** mein nicht, o teure." Composer and author of words unknown. g. ED 2
"**Vergiss** mein nicht, vergiss mein nicht" ("Forget-me-not") J. S. Bach. e.g. PG 2
Das **vergissmeinnicht** ("Die blume die an baches rand."—The forget-me-not) F. von Suppé. e.g.i. FMB
Das **vergissmeinnicht** ("Freundlich glänzt an stiller") F. H. Himmel. Words by K. Müchler. g. ED 3
The forget-me-not. e. FSS 4
Vergissmeinnicht ("I look on thee") For English translation see Forget-me-not (Graben-Hoffmann)
Verhulst, Johannes Josephus Herman
Moetje varen
"There lingered a lassie." See Moetje varen
Verlaine, Paul
Clair de lune (Fauré)
Fantoches (Debussy)
Green (Debussy)
L'heure exquise (Hahn)
"Il pleure dans mon coeur" (Debussy)
Mandoline (Debussy)
"L'ombre des arbres" (Debussy)

Verlassen bin i. For English translation see Forsaken (Koschat)
"**Verlassen,** verlassen, verlassen steh' ich da." See Petrus klage (Brandts-Buys)
Die **verlassene** ("Am heiligen abend") G. W. Fink (music and words) g. ED 2
Verlegenheit (Embarrassment) F. Abt. e.g. FMB
Embarrassment. e. FSS 8—HSD—WBT—WL
Vermeland. Swedish folk air. Words by A. Fryxell. e. CST—GO
"Ack, Värmeland, du sköna" ("O Vermeland, thou lovely") e.sw. HSOS
Vermeland (Wermeland) e.sw. BO
"**Vernahmet** ihr." See "Heard ye his voice" (Rubinstein)
Vernon, Joseph
"When that I was a little tiny boy"
Vernon, W. J.
"O'er the plains the darkness deepens" (Havergal)
Verrath (Betrayal) I. Zech. Words by P. J. Willatzen. e.g. SOS 2
Verrathene liebe (Love's secret lost) R. Schumann. Words by A. von Chamisso. e.g. FM
"**Vers** son sanctuaire depuis deux cents ans." Canadian voyageur's song. f. SMW
Der **verschmähte** ("Mei dirndel is harb uf mi") Volkslied. g. ED 1
The despised lover. e. BSE
Der verschmähete (The despised lover) e.g. SSG
"**Versez** les parfums." See Thrinôdia (Holmès)
"**Verstohlen** geht der mond auf." See Mondschein
Verwelkt (Withered rose) H. Proch. e.g. SM 2
Der **verwundete** knabe ("Es wollt' ein mägdlein in der früh' aufstehn") Volkslied. g. ED 3
"The **very** day I was married." See The low, low lands of Holland
Vesper bell ("Hark the pealing") See The evening bell
"The **vesper** bells were softly, softly ringing." See Oh, 'twas sweet to hear her (Lee)
The **vesper** chime ("Sweetly on the evening air") G. Linley. FSS 4
Vesper hymn ("Hark! the vesper hymn") Bortnianski. Words by T. Moore. FSS 2—LA—TFC 1
"Hark! the vesper hymn is stealing." WBT—WS
"The **vesper** sparrow now has sung." See Whip-poor-will (Gilchrist)
The **veterans.** L. B. Marshall. Words by S. F. Smith. JS
Vetter Michel ("Gestern abend") Volkslied. g. ED 1
"**Veux** tu mon nom? il est à toi." See Couldst thou but know (Balfe)
La **vezzosa.** See La cianciosa

"Vezzosette e care" ("Charming eyes so wary") A. Falconieri. e.i. PA 2

Vi ravviso, O luoghi ameni (O remembrance of scenes long vanished) V. Bellini. e.i. KS 5

"Vi ska' ställa te'en roliger dans" ("Come and dance") Swedish folk song. e.sw. HSOS

"Vi volar una blanca paloma." See La paloma

"Viae Sion lugent." See Jerusalem (Gounod)

Vibbert, William H.
"The day of resurrection" (Tr of Anastaseōs hemera)

The **vicar** of Bray. Old air: The country garden. Words by E. Ward. BAS 1—BE 1—BO—BOS—BSE—DM 1— GO—HSE 1—JE— MM—PR 2—SSS
The vicar of Bray (The country garden) CO 2

Vicente, Gil
"Und schläfst du, mein mädchen" (Jensen)

"La **Victoire** en chantant." See Le chant du départ (Méhul)

Victorious, my heart. See Vittoria, mio core (Carissimi)

"**Victorious,** victorious." See Vittoria, mio core (Carissimi)

"**Victory,** chanting firm." See Le chant du départ (Méhul)

"**Vict'ry** now chants her hymn." See Le chant du départ (Méhul)

Vidal, Paul Antonin
Ariette
The faithful heart. See Le fidèle coeur
Le fidèle coeur
Printemps nouveau
Returning spring. See Printemps nouveau
"Were I sunshine, I should come." See Ariette

"**Vidste** du hvor hjertet skjaelver" ("Could'st thou know") C. Warmuth. e.n. SSN

"En **vidtstrakt** hede med mossede sten." See Landskab (Børresen)

La **vie** antérieure (The former life) H. Duparc. Words by C. Baudelaire. e.f. CM 1

La **vie** de la bergère. See "Y-a rien de si charmant"

Vieille chanson ("In the woods") G. Bizet. Words by C. H. Millevoye. e.f. HM 1—SAM
Vieille chanson (A song of the woods) e.f. PG 3

"**Viel** tausend sterne prangen." L. von Call. Words by A. G. Eberhard. g. ED 2

"**Viele** meilen musst ich gehen." See Dalecarlian maiden's song (Lindblad)

Vien qua Dorina bella ("Nein, holde liebe kleine."—Der liebende) F. Bianchi. g. ED 2

"**Vieni,** che poi sereno" ("Come, when the rosy morning") C. W. Gluck. e.i. KS 2

"**Vieni,** che poi sereno" ("Come, while the twilight closes") e.i. MSS 1

"**Vieni!** la mia vendetta." G. Donizetti. e.i. SOA 5

"**Vieni,** o Levita." See Tu sul labbro de' veggenti (Verdi)

"**Viens** dans ce bocage, belle Aminte." See Aminte

"**Viens!** Don Fernand." See La muletier de Tarragone (Henrion)

Viens, gentille dame (Come, thou gracious beauty) F. A. Boieldieu. e.f. KS 4

"**Viens** près de moi." See "Oh come to me when breezes stir" (Balakirev)

"**Viens!** une flûte invisible." See Eglogue (Delibes)

"**Vier** elemente, innig gesellt." See Punschlied (Eberwein)

"Une **Vierge** féconde" ("A Virgin that conceivèd") Noël français. e.f. TF

Vierling, Georg
"From swarming highways I now have escaped" (from Constantin)
Lord, for whom my soul is burning (from Constantin)

Vieting,
Beggar's song (Wihtol)

View de land. Negro spiritual. HR
Way over Jordan. JP

"**View** my eyes, my lovely charmer." See The plausible lover (Carey)

Vig, Ole
"Blandt alle lande" (Hansen)

Vigil (Veillée) M. Glinka. e.f. NR 3

Vigne, Casimir de la. See Delavigne, Casimir

"**Vigorous** and honest is he." See "Rasker och redlig är han"

"**Viñut** vitri." See The winds blow

Vilá, Gabriel
Zapateo cubano

Vilia song. F. Lehar. e. WA—WBT—WSW

The **village** blacksmith. W. H. Weiss. Words by Longfellow. BAS 1—DM 1—HSE 1

The **village** dance. Hungarian dance air. Words by C. B. Fenno. TFC 2

The **village** Don Juan (Postilion's song.—Akh po mostu mostu) Russian folk song. e. SSR 1

Villancico ("Little shepherds") Latin American song. e.s. BF 2

Villanelle ("J'ai vu passer l'hirondelle."—A rural song) E. Dell' Acqua. e.f. KF 1—PG 1

Villanelle ("Quand viendra la saison nouvelle") H. Berlioz. Words by T. Gautier. e.f. HM 1—MSS 1

Villars, Henry Gauthier-. See Gauthier-Villars, Henry

Villotta ("Under the garden trees I picked finochi") Italian song. e.i. BF 2

Vincent, Charles John
The angel's song. See "Last night as I lay sleeping"
Benedicamus Domino
"Joy-bells ringing"
"Last night as I lay sleeping"
"Little Christian children, say"
"There came three kings by God's own hand" (Tr of Es führt drei könige Gottes hand)
"Thine, Lord, are the blessings of forest and field"

Vincenti, B.
National song of Bolivia
"O Bolivians, the angel of freedom." See National song of Bolivia
The **vine-dressers'** song. Weber. Words by W. Ball. FSS 6
The **vineyard** and its master ("Ampeli mou, paleampelo") Greek folk song. e.gr. BF 2
"Le **vingt-et-un** du mois d'avril." See La mort du porte-enseigne

Vinje, Aasmund Olafsen
Auf der reise zur heimath (Grieg)
Der frühling (Grieg)
Gamle mor (Grieg)
Langs en å (Grieg)
Et syn (Grieg)
"**Vintern** rasat ut bland våra fjällar." See Längtan till landet (Lindblad)

Vinton, James
Bingo ("Here's to B. S. A.") (College air)

Viol, W.
Im frühling (Fesca)
"**Viola**, bass und geigen." Student song. g. ED 1

Violen (The violet) J. S. Svendsen. e.n. MAN—SSN
The **violet** ("I mellem visne halmstraa") See Violen (Svendsen)
The **violet** ("Rugiadose, odorose") See Le violette (Scarlatti)
The **violet** ("Ein veilchen auf der wiese") See Das veilchen (Mozart)
The **violet** ("The violet blooms in springtime fair") New York university song. Air: Die wacht am Rhein. Words by W. F. Johnson. CHS—MPC
"The **violet** and the primrose." See The flowers of the heath
"The **violet** blooms in springtime fair." See The violet (New York university song)
"A **violet** blossomed in the grass." See Das veilchen (Mozart)
"A **violet** blossomed on the green." See Das veilchen (Mozart)
"The **violet** loves a mossy bank." See Mamma's love
"The **violet** loves a sunny bank." See The proposal (Gluck)
"The **violet** loves the sunny bank." See Proposal (Brackett)

"A **violet** on the meadow grew." See Das veilchen (Mozart)
Violeta ("I love thee violet") C. K. Hopkins. Words by Huelani. e.h. HA
Violets ("Zu dem duft") See Veilchen (Cornelius)
"**Violets** for thee I gather." See "Morgens send' ich dir die veilchen" (Meyer-Helmund)
"**Violets** have come in heav'nly hue." See Song of the violets
Violetta. See "La Violetta la va"
"La **Violetta** la va" (Violetta) Italian song. e.i. BF 2
Le **violette** (Dewy violets) A. Scarlatti. e.i. CS 2—MSS 2—SS 2
"Rugiadose, odorose" ("Early blowing, violets growing") A. Scarlatti. e.i. FEI 2
Le violette (The violet) e.i. KF 1—PG 1—PG 2
Vira do minho (The vira) Portuguese dance. e.po. BF 2
Vira volta a chamarrita. See Chamarrita
The **Virgin** and Child. C. Steggall. BSC
"**Virgin-born!** we bow before Thee." C. Gounod. Words by Heber. HC
"A **Virgin** did come." G. H. Gregory. Words by S. C. Clarke. HC
"**Virgin**, fount of love." See "Vergin, tutto amor" (Durante)
"**Virgin**, full of grace." See "Vergin, tutto amor" (Durante)
"**Virgin** Mary had one Son." See Jesus ain't comin' here t' die no mo'
"A **Virgin** most blessed." Traditional air. HC
"A **Virgin** most pure, as the prophet do tell, hath brought forth a Baby." Traditional air. HC
For variant see following song of similar title
"A **Virgin** most pure, as the prophet foretold, should bring forth a Savior." Composer unknown. WCC
"The **Virgin** stills the crying." J. Barnby. Words from the Latin. e. HC
A cradle-song of the blessed Virgin. e. BSC
Cradle-song of Virgin. e. MCS
"A **Virgin** that conceivèd." See "Une Vierge féconde"
"A **Virgin** unspotted." Traditional air. BSC
The **Virginian** lover. Folk song from North Carolina. CSE
A **vision** ("Ein gjente eg såg") See Et syn (Grieg)
Vision ("Geist der liebe") H. Claus. e.g. SOS 1
The **vision** ("Great hearts that have battled") Netherlands air. Words by C. B. Fenno. BSS
Vision fair. See Vision fugitive (Massenet)

Vision fugitive. J. Massenet. e.f. SOA 4

Vision fugitive (Fleeting vision) e.f. OPS 4

Vision fugitive (Vision fair) e.f. AB 3—KS 5

The **vision** of shepherds. See "While shepherds watched their flocks" (Howard)

The **visions** of morning. Harvard class song of 1829. Words by O. W. Holmes. FSS 1

Questions and answers. LA

Visiting song. Ojibway Indian song. in. BA

"La **vita** è inferno all' infelice." See Oh, tu che in seno agl'angioli (Verdi)

"**Vitti** na tigra dinta na silva scura." See La Scillitana

Vittoria, mio core (Victorious my heart is) G. Carissimi. e.i. AB 2—FEI 1 —PA 1

"Vittoria! vittoria" ("I triumph! I triumph") e.i. BAS 2—BS 1

"Vittoria, vittoria" ("Victorious, victorious") e.i. NG—PG 3—PG 4

La **viudita** del conde Laurel. Game song. s. LCP

"La **viudita**, la viudita, la viudita se quiere casar." See La viudita y el conde de Cabra

La **viudita** y el conde de Cabra. Game song. s. LCP

Viva l'America. H. Millard. FSS 2

"**Viva** San Giusto" ("All hail, San Giusto") National song of Trieste. C. Sinico. e.i. SN

"**Viva**! viva! magnanimo el rey Alfonso." See Marcha real

Viva, viva, viva o rei. See Hymno nacional—Portugal (Pedro IV)

Vivaldi, Antonio
"Un certo non so che"
"Some one, I know not who." See "Un certo non so che"
"There's one, I know him not." See "Un certo non so che"

"**Vivat** Bacchus." Composer unknown. Words by C. F. Bretzner. g. ED 1

"**Vive** la Canadienne." L. Streabbog. e.f. SN
"Vive la Canadienne" ("Long live Canadian lasses") e.f. TF
"Vive la Canadienne" ("Long live Canadian maidens") e.f. BSP

Vive la compagneia ("Ich nehm mein gläschen") Volkslied. g. ED 1

Vive la compagnie ("Let Bacchus to Venus") HSD

Vive l'amour ("Let ev'ry good fellow now fill up his glass") Composer and author of words unknown. BOS—MPC —SSS—WBT—WC

Vive l'amour ("Let ev'ry good fellow now join in a song") Old student song. TFC 2

Vive le capitaine John. Air: Vive l'amour. LA

Vive le roi ("Threat'ning death to traitor slave") M. W. Balfe. FSS 3

Vive le roy ("What though the zealots") 17th century song. CO 1—DM 2

Vive Purdue. Purdue university song. J. C. Arthur. Words by E. Stein. CHS

"**Vivo** llorando la suerte." Mexican folk song. e.s. HS

"**Vivo** penando." Folk song from Santa Barbara, Cal. e.s. HS

Vizzard, John
Wake the echoes (Composer unknown)

V'la l'bon vent. See Le canard blanc

The **vly** is on the turmut. Oxfordshire county song. BOH
Turmut-hoeing. BOS

"**Vniz** po matushkie po Volgie." See Mother Vólga

Vo' altre putele che se'da maridar (Idle hours) Italian folk song. e. GO

"**Vo'** cercando in queste valli" ("I am seeking in every valley") E. d'Astorga. e.i. FEI 2

"**Vo** Luzern uf Weggis zue." See Weggiser lied

Vo luziakh. See "In the fields, in the fields"

Vo polé tuman zatumanelsya. See "Over fields and over meadows"

Vo polie bereza stoiala. See The birch in the meadow

"**Vo** sadu li v ogorodie." See In the kitchen-garden

The **vocal** grove. C. Young. Words by W. Monlass. DM 2

"**Voce** di donna o d'angelo" ("Thanks to thee, angelic voice") A. Ponchielli. e.i. OPS 2
"Voce di donna" (The blind girl's song) e.i. SOA 2
"Voce di donna" (Light to my dark soul bringing) KS 3

"Una **voce** poco fà" ("There's a voice that I enshrine") G. Rossini. e.i. KS 2

"Una **voce** poco fà" ("Though his voice") e.i. OPS 2—PP

Der **vogelfänger**. W. A. Mozart. Words by E. Schikaneder. g. ED 1
Song of the fowler. e. FSS 6— HSD—WBT

Der **vogelsteller** ("Die lieb' und unser vogelfang") J. F. X. Sterkel. Words by M. A. von Thümmel. g. ED 3

Vogl, Johann Nepomuk
Das erkennen (Proch)

Vöglein ("Clear the air") See The skylark (Grechaninov)

"**Vöglein**, einsam in dem bauer." See Die gefangenen sänger (Weber)

"**Vöglein** im tannenwald." Schwäbisches volkslied. g. ED 1

Vogrich, Max
Arabian song. See "Schön blinkt's aus allen sternen"
"The clover-blossoms kiss thy feet"
"From Greenland's icy mountains"
I love but thee
"Poor wounded heart"
"Schön blinkt's aus allen sternen"
Thy true heart

"**Voi,** che sapete" ("Tell me, O fair ones") W. A. Mozart. e.i. KS 2—OPS 2— SOA 1

"**Voi** lo sapete, o mamma" ("Surely you know, oh, mother") Mascagni. e.i. OPS 1

"A **voice** from time departed." See Taliesin's prophecy

"A **voice** is heard like thunder loud." See Die wacht am Rhein (Wilhelm)

"The **voice** of free grace." J. Clark. Words by Thornby. FSS 3

The **voice** of one we love. Air: Dydd gwl dewi. Words by Rowlands. BSE

The **voice** of the bell. Harrow school song. LA

The **voice** of the nation sounding. See Hymno nacional (Brazil)

The **voice** of the sea. Irish air. Words by A. E. FSI

"A **voice** resounds like thunder peal." See Die wacht am Rhein (Wilhelm)

"**Voices** all merry, cheeks bright as a berry." See Song of the hop-pickers (Philp)

The **voices** in the sky. Words by E. Douglas. MCS

"**Voices** of children." H. E. Nichol (music and words) HC

"**Voices** of the belfry height." See Christmas voices (Scott-Gatty)

Voices of the woods. A. Rubinstein. WA —WBT—WSW

"Welcome, sweet springtime." TFC 1 —WSC

"**Voici** des fruits, des fleurs." See Green (Debussy)

"**Voici** donc les débris du monastère antique." See Nonnes qui reposez (Meyerbeer)

"**Voici** la Saint-Jean" ("Lo, 'tis Saint John's day") French folk song. e.f. TSF

"**Voici** la saison mignonne." See Chanson de la sorcière (Gounod)

"**Voici** l'automne arrivé." See L'hivernage

"**Voici** le mois de mai" ("Lo 'tis the month of May") French folk song. e.f. TSF

Voici le printemps nous portant des fleurs. For English translation see Song of May (Saint-Saëns)

"**Voici** le printemps qui va-t-arriver" ("Spring is on the way") Canadian folk song. e.f. TF

"**Voici** les tristes lieux." See Monstre affreux (Rameau)

"**Voici** l'heure bientôt." See Chère nuit (Bachelet)

"**Voici** l'hiver et son triste cortège" ("The winter days so cold."—Charity) J. Faure. e.f. HSS 1—HSS 2

"**Voici** qu'au loin traine et s'efface." See Berceuse (Arenski)

"**Voici** que les jardins de la nuit vont fleurir." See Soir (Fauré)

"**Voici** venir le joli mois." See Le mois de mai

"**Voici** venir le mois de mai" ("Maytime has come") Morning serenade from Dauphiny. e.f. TSF

"**Voici** venir le temps où vibrant sur sa tige." See Harmonie du soir (Debussy)

Voigt, Friedrich Abendlied froher landleute (Seidel)

Voigt, frau Johanna (Ambrosius) "Drücke mich an deine brust" (Farwell)

"**La** voile s'enfle, il va partir." See Pauvre Pierre

Vole, mon coeur, vole. See "Derrière chez mon père, vole, mon coeur, vole" (Streabbog)

Volga boat song. Russian folk song. e. CST

Hej onward ("Ėĭ ukhnem") e.r. BF 1

Song of the Volga boatman. New words by S. Drake. TFC 2

Volga boat-song (Ėĭ, ukhnem) e. SSR 2

Variants: The little cudgel; Towing song

"Das **volk** steht auf." See Männer und buben

Volkmer, Alois Thy will be done (Barry)

Volksliedchen (In the garden) R. Schumann. Words by F. Rückert. e.g. FM

Die **vollendung** ("Wann ich einst das ziel errungen") J. A. P. Schulz. Words by F. von Matthison. g. ED 3

"Der **vollmond** strahlt auf bergeshöhn." See Romanze aus Rosamunde (Schubert)

"**Volta** la terrea fronte alle stelle" ("Reading the stars on high") G. Verdi. e.i. PP

"**Volta** la terrea fronte alle stelle" ("When o'er this earth of ours") e.i. MC

"**Voltigez,** hirondelles." See Les hirondelles (David)

The **volunteer** ("A scarlet coat and smart cockade") 18th century song. DM 1

The **volunteer's** farewell. See L'addio del voluntario

"**Vom** dunkeln laub umschlossen." See Das veilchen (Himmel)

"**Vom** flaschenhaupt den pfropfen fort und vom humor den zügel." See Beim Rheinwein (Gilbert)

"**Vom** himmel hoch da komm' ich her." M. Luther (music and words) g. ED 1

"From heaven above to earth I come." e. HC

"From heaven's sphere." e. MCS

"Vom himmel hoch da komm' ich her" (From heaven high come I here) e.g. DCS

"**Vom** himmel hoch da komm' ich her." For English translation with a different air see Luther's carol (Higgs)

"Vom hoh'n Olymp." H. C. Schnoor. g. ED 1

"Vom hoh'n Olymp" ("From high Olympus") e.g. SSS

Vom Monte Pincio (At Monte Pincio) E. Grieg. Words by B. Björnson. e.g. PG 1
From the Pincian hill. e. BD
Vom Monte Pincio (From Monte Pincio) e.g. FF

Vom scheib'nschiessen (Bavarian song) German folk song. e. GO

Vom tode (Death) L. van Beethoven. e.g. NG

"Von allen den mädchen so blink und so blank." See Die Lore am tore

"Von allen ländern in der welt." See Deutscher ehrenpreis (Methfessel)

Von bösen frauen ("'s ist gewiss und kein gedicht") Volkslied. g. ED 3

"Von der strasse her ein posthorn klingt." See Die post (Schubert)

"Von dir geschieden, bin ich bei dir." Volksweise. g. ED 3

Von ewiger liebe (Love triumphant) J. Brahms. Words by J. Wentzig. e.g. CS 2—MSS 2—SS 2
Eternal love. e. BC

"Von meinem bergli muss i scheiden." See Abschied vom dirndel

Vor dem fenster (By the window) J. Brahms. Words from a folk song. e.g. CMF 1

"Vor liebchens fenster" (At my love's window) Folk song. e.g. SSG

Vor meiner wiege (At my cradle) F. Schubert. Words by Leitner. e.g. GM

"Vor verden er jo ofte saa skoddetung og sur." See Jul (Alnaes)

"Vor zeiten wie man noch so trank." See Das pfäfflein (Schäffer)

Vorrei ("Could I") F. P. Tosti. Words by T. Marzials. e.i. SM 1
"Could I." e. WBW

"Vorrei, allor che tu palido e muto." See Vorrei (Tosti)

"Vorrei morire" ("I'd like to die") Italian song. e.i. BF 2

Vorschneller schwur (A hasty vow) J. Brahms. Words by S. Kapper. e.g. GMF

"Vorüber, ach vorüber." See Der tod und das mädchen (Schubert)

"Vos-zhe vilstu." See "Will you marry"

Voss, Johann Heinrich
Abendlied (Zelter)
Am Sylvester-abend (Schulz)
"Der holdseligen" (Weber)
Das landmädchen (Harder)
Die spinnerin (Harder)
Tischlied (Schulz)
"Willkommen im grünen" (Schulz)

Vostótchnui románs. See Eastern romance (Rimskiĭ-Korsakov)

"Vot mchitsiâ troĭka udalaiâ." See Three-in-hand

"Votre âme est un paysage choisi." See Clair de lune (Fauré)

"Votre toast, je peux vous rendre." See Chanson du toréador (Bizet)

"Vous aurez beau faire et beau dire." See Obstination (Fontenailles)

"Vous dansez, marquise" ("Countess, in thy dancing") G. Lemaire. Words by E. Bazot. e.f. HM 2
"Vous dansez, marquise" ("Marchioness, your dancing") e.f. SM 1

"Vous qui faites l'endormie" (Serenade) C. Gounod. e.f. OPS 4—SOA 5

"Vous souvient-il du jour." See Roses d'hiver (Fontenailles)

The vow. See Der schwur (Bohm)

"Vow'd a tender maiden." See Vorschneller schwur (Brahms)

Vows ("Zarekokh se, mamo") Bulgarian song. b.e. BF 1

Vox angelica. See "Hark, hark, my soul" (Dykes)

"The voyage of life is often rough." Song from India. e. SMW

The voyagers. F. Silcher. Words by B. Taylor. LBR

Voyageur's song ("Joy to thee, my brave canoe") French-Canadian song. e. WBT
Paddling song ("Joy to thee, my brave canoe") e. BMC

"Voyez ce mulet-là, Musieu Bainjo." See Musieu Bainjo

Voyez sur cette roche. For English translation see "On yonder rock reclining" (Auber)

Vozliê riêchki, vozliê mostu. See Jealousy

Vse mine. See The homeward way

Vsyo ótnyal ōō minyá. See "God took from me my all" (Rachmaninov)

"Vuela suspiro." Argentine folk song. e.s. HS

"Vuelve otra vez con tus palabras tiernas." See Chata cara de bule

Vuelve, vuelve cariñosa. See La Carolina (Andraca)

Vulcan's song. See "Au bruit des lourds marteaux d'airain" (Gounod)

Vulpius, Christian August
"Gib mir die blumen, gib mir den kranz" (Volksweise)
Rinaldo Rinaldini (Folk air)
Wenn's immer so wär (Dittersdorf)

Vychan, Idris
"O lays of my land" (Welsh air)

Vyĭdu-l' iâ na riêchen'ku. See The joyous meeting

Vyletala golubina. See The blue dove

"Vyletěla holubička." See Little dove

"Vyssa, vyssa, liten kind." See Vaggvisa (Söderberg)

W

Wachet auf (Wake, for the night is flying) Words by P. Nicolai. e. FSS 2
Die wacht am Rhein ("Es braust ein ruf wie donnerhall") C. Wilhelm. Words by M. Schneckenburger. g. ED 1—SSS. e. only BSE
Die wacht am Rhein (The watch o'er the Rhine) e.g. SN
Die wacht am Rhein (The watch on the Rhine) e.g. BSP—MS—SSG—WCP. e. only BMC
The watch by the Rhine. e. BOS—EF
The watch on the Rhine. e.g. FSS 1 —WA
Der wachtelschlag ("Hörch wie schallt's dorten") K. G. Hering. Words by S. F. Sauter. g. ED 3
Wachtelschlag ("Hört, wie die wachtel") L. Reichardt. Volkslied. g. ED 3
Wächter, Leonhard
Unser vaterland (Nägeli)
"Der wächter mit dem silberhorn." J. F. Reichardt. g. ED 3
Wackernagel, Wilhelm
Feld- und waldlied (Kunzen)
Wade, J.
"Hours there were"
Wade, Joseph Augustine
Composer
"Love was once a little boy"
Composer and author
"Meet me by moonlight alone"
Author
The blossom of the year (Composer unknown)
"'Twere vain to tell thee all I feel" (Swiss air)
Wadman, Johan Anders
Min lilla vrå bland bergen (Sandstrom)
"Wae is my heart." Air: Wae is my heart, Words by R. Burns. BSR—PS 2
The waefu' heart. Scottish air. Words by S. Blamire. FSS 7—JO—PS 1
"Waer dat men sich" ("Where'er man ranges") Dutch battle song. d.e. BO
Wae's me for Prince Charlie ("A wee bird cam' to our ha' door") Air: Johnnie Faa, or, The gipsie laddie, or, Lady Cassilis lilt. Words by W. Glen. HSSS—MMS—PS 1
O, wae's me for Prince Charlie. PS 1
Wae-ton wa-an. See Little papoose
"Waft her, angels, through the skies." Händel. OS 3—SAS 4—TS
Wagenseil, Christian Jakob
"Auf, auf, ihr brüder, und seid froh" (Soldier's song)
Zufriedenheit (Wolf)
Wagner, Heinrich
Abschied (Volksweise)
Wagner, Richard
Address. See Pogner's anrede
"Allmächt'ge Jungfrau." See Gebet der Elisabeth
"Allmächt'ger Vater" (from Rienzi)

"Almighty Father." See "Allmächt'ger Vater"
"Almighty Powers." See "Gerechter Gott"
"Am stillen herd" (from Die meistersinger von Nürnberg)
"Avenging God." See "Gerechter Gott"
"Blick' ich umher" (from Tannhäuser)
Bridal chorus (from Lohengrin. Tr of Brautlied)
"By silent hearth." See "Am stillen herd"
Chorus of pilgrims. See Pilgrims' chorus
"Dear hall of song." See "Dich theure halle grüss' ich wieder"
Les deux grenadiers (Tr of Die beiden grenadiere)
"Dich theure halle grüss' ich wieder" (from Tannhäuser)
Dors, mon enfant
Dreaming. See Träume
Dreams. See Träume
Durch dich musst' ich verlieren (from Lohengrin)
"Einsam in trüben tagen." See Elsa's traum
Elizabeth's prayer. See Gebet der Elisabeth
Elsa's dream. See Elsa's traum
Elsa's traum (from Lohengrin)
Evening star. See O du mein holder abendstern
"Flag of the free" (same air as Bridal chorus)
"Die frist ist um" (from Der fliegende Holländer)
Gebet der Elisabeth (from Tannhäuser)
Gebet des Amfortas (from Parsifal)
"Gerechter Gott" (from Rienzi)
"Gleaming at morning." See "Morgenlich leuchtend"
Hans Sach's monologue. See "Was duftet doch der flieder"
"In distant land." See "In fernem land"
"In fernem land" (from Lohengrin)
"Is that fair day no more by thee remember'd." See "Willst jenes tag's du nicht dich mehr entsinnen"
Isolde's liebestod (from Tristan und Isolde)
"Jo hoe hoe! jo ho ho hoe! ho ho hoe! jo hoe." See Traft ihr das schiff
King's prayer (from Lohengrin. Tr of Mein Herr und Gott)
"Morgenlich leuchtend" (from Die meistersinger)
"Nun hört, und versteht mich recht." See Pogner's anrede
O du mein holder abendstern (from Tannhäuser)
O pure and tender star of eve. See O du mein holder abendstern
O star of eve. See O du mein holder abendstern
Our country's flag. See "Flag of the free"

Wagner, Richard—*Continued*
Pilgrims' chorus (from Tännhauser. Tr of Beglückt dorf nun dich)
Pogner's address. See Pogner's anrede
Pogner's anrede (from Die meistersinger von Nürnberg)
Prayer. See "Allmächt'ger Vater"
Prize song. See "Morgenlich leuchtend"
"Schlaf' holdes kind"
Siegmunds liebeslied (from Die Walküre)
"Sleep, my dear child." See "Schlaf' holdes kind"
Slumber song. See Dors, mon enfant
Spinning chorus (from Der fliegende Holländer. Tr of Summ' und brumm', du gutes radchen)
'Tis thou whose spells. See Durch dich musst' ich verlieren
To the evening star. See O du mein holder abendstern
Traft ihr das schiff (from Der fliegende Holländer)
Träume
The two grenadiers. See Les deux grenadiers
"Wahn! wahn" (from Die meistersinger von Nürnberg)
Walter's prize-song. See Walthers preislied
Walthers preislied (from Die meistersinger von Nürnberg)
"Was duftet doch der flieder" (from Die meistersinger von Nürnberg)
"Willst jenes tag's du nicht dich mehr entsinnen" (from Die fliegende Holländer)
"Winter storms have waned 'fore the month of May." See Siegmunds liebeslied
"Winterstürme wichen dem wonnemond." See Siegmunds liebeslied
Wolfram's address. See "Blick' ich umher"
Wotans abschied (from Die Walküre)
"Yo-ho-hoe! yo-ho-ho-hoe! yo-ho-hoe! yo-hoe." See Traft ihr das schiff
The **wagoner's** lad. Folk song: Kentucky version. CSE
—Alleghany, N.C. version. CSE
—Hot Springs, N.C. version. CSE
—Tennessee version. CSE
Variant: Loving Nancy
"**Wah**! tah-ho! tah-ho." See The sun worshippers
"**Wahn**! wahn." R. Wagner. e.g. SOA 5
Die **wahrsagerin** ("Gib, blanke schwester") F. L. Seidel. Words by J. L. Gericke. g. ED 2
"**Wahwahtaysee** wahwahtaysee e mow e shin." See Firefly
Wai o Punalau. See Waters of Punalau (Nape)
"**Wai**, wai, go home now." See Ways of the world
"**Waich** ee." Vancouver Indian song. in. SN

Waidmannslied (Huntsman's song) L. Slansky. e.g. AB 4
Waiksel ööl. See Moan to the moon
Wainwright, John
"Christians, awake"
Salute the happy morn. See "Christians, awake"
Waipio. See "Thou art always the same to me, dear" (Hopkins)
Wait for the wagon. R. B. Buckley (music and words) BSE—FSS 6—JO—LA—NMH—TFC 2—WBT—WL
Wait till the clouds roll by. H. T. Fulmer. WA—WBT—WL
Waite, M. E.
"Merry Christmas bells are ringing" (Kotzschmar)
Waiting ("Awaiting, awaiting you") Japanese song. e.j. BF 2
Waiting ("Bejeenug ningahbedugweshing") Ojibway Indian song. in. BA
Waiting ("I look from my window") Air: Blodeu'r gwinwydd, or, The blossom of the honeysuckle. Words from the Welsh of A. Edwards. e. MMW
Waiting all the day. Modern negro song. JP
Waiting for me. R. Hance. Words by H. B. Durant. FSS 8
"**Waiting** for the day to come." See Waiting all the day
"**Wake** all music's magic powers." J. Stainer. Words from the Latin. e. HC
Christmas day. e. BSC
"**Wake**! and tune your youthful voices." Christmas chorus. F. T. Southwick. Words by J. G. Robinson. LA
Wake, for the night is flying. See Wachet auf
Wake, freshmen, wake. Student song. LA
"**Wake** from slumber." See "Frère Jacques"
"**Wake**, happy children, in the dewy morn." See Waking or sleeping
"**Wake**, happy children, on the Christmas morn." See Waking or sleeping (Christmas version)
"**Wake**, my heart, while round thee swelling." J. Kruger. Words from P. Gerhardt. e. HC
"**Wake**, my love." E. J. Loder. Words by G. Soane. HSE 3
Wake Nicodemus. H. C. Work (music and words) FSS 3—JO—WBT
"**Wake**, O wake, ye shepherds all." See El rabada
Wake the echoes. Mt Union college song. Words by J. Vizzard. CHS
Wake up Jacob. Negro song. NMP—WBT
"**Wake**, wake, children." Words by C. Wallace. MCS
"**Wake**, wake the morning." FSS 1
"**Wake**, ye spirits." A. Rubinstein. e. SAS 4

Wakefield, Augusta Mary
A bunch of cowslips. See "Polly and I"
No sir
"Polly and I"

"Waken! Christian children." S. C. Hamerton (music and words) BSC—HC

"Waken, Christians! greet the morn." C. Simper. Words by A. S. Woods. HC

"Waken, lords and ladies gay." See Hunting song

"Waken, my fair one, from thy slumber." See "Réveillez-vous, belle endormie"

"Waking at early day, gaily I take my way." See Gaily I take my way (Linley)

Waking flowers. A. Reissman. FSS 7

Waking or sleeping ("Wake, happy children, in the dewy morn") Words by J. V. Blake. FSS 3

Waking or sleeping ("Wake, happy children, on the Christmas morn") Christmas version. Words by J. V. Blake. MCS

"Wa-kon-da dha-ni ga dhe ke." See The warrior's prayer

"Wa-kon-da dhe-dhu wa-pa dhin a-ton-he." See The Omaha tribal prayer

"Wakonda, hear us, hear us." See Song of the ghost dance

"Wa-kon'-da, here needy he stands." See The Omaha tribal prayer

"Der wald, der dunkle wald." See Sehnsucht (Hurka)

Die waldblume ("Im föhrenwald alleine steht eine blume dort") Volksweise: Es taget in dem osten. Words by J. Mosen. g. ED 3

Waldeinsamkeit. F. Mendelssohn-Bartholdy. Words by R. W. Emerson. LBR

Waldes-lied (Forest-song) C. Kreutzer. e.g. AB 1

Waldesgespräch (Forest voices) A. Jensen. Words by J. von Eichendorff. e.g. CMF 1
Waldesgespräch (The Loreley) e.g. PG 4

Waldesgespräch (In the forest) R. Schumann. Words by J. von Eichendorff. e.g. CMF 2—FF—FO 1
Waldesgespräch (Loreley in the forest) e. FTS

Das waldhorn ("Wie lieblich schallt durch busch") F. Silcher. Words by C. von Schmid. g. ED 3

Waldmann, Ludolf
The little fishermaiden (from Incognito. Tr of Das kleine fischermädchen)

Wales, Wales, home, sweet home is in Wales. See Land of my fathers (James)

Walford, William W.
"Sweet hour of prayer" (Bradbury)
Walk him along, Johnny, carry him along. See "General Taylor"
Walk in Jerusalem just like John. See I want to be ready
Walk you in the light. Negro spiritual. JP
Walk you in de light. HR
Variant: Walking in de light

Walker, Annie Louisa. See Coghill, Mrs Annie Louisa (Walker)

Walker, Archibald Stodart
Cakes and ale (Lowe)

Walker, Charles
Bonnie laddie, Highland laddie (Scottish air)

Walker, Clarence
Dawn (Somerset)

Walker, John Tempest
Columbia medley

Walking in a country town. 16th century song. CO 1

"Walking in a meadow greene." See Walking in a country town

Walking in de light. Negro spiritual. HR
We are walking in the light. JP
Variant of: Walk you in the light

Wallace, B. Holmes
The Genesee (Composer unknown)

Wallace, Clara
Brightest of golden days (Balfe)
The Christmas tree (Lowry)
Dear Santa Claus (Crosby)
The glad bells all say (Crowe)
Holly crowns the green (Rossini)
Once upon a time (Barnard)
"Wake, wake, children" (Composer unknown)

Wallace, William Ross
The sword of Bunker Hill (Covert)

Wallace, William Vincent
The bell ringer
The Christ-Child
Cradle song. See "Sweet and low"
The flag of our union forever
Good night and pleasant dreams
"In happy moments day by day" (from Maritana)
"Scenes that are brightest" (from Maritana)
"Sleeping I dream'd love"
"Speak gently—it is better far"
"Sweet and low"
Sweet spirit, hear my prayer (from Lurline)
"There is a flower that bloometh" (from Maritana)
'Tis the harp in the air
"Why do I weep for thee"
"Yes, let me like a soldier fall"

Wallachian lullaby ("Hush, hush, baby") Roumanian folk song. e. BMC

Wallander, Hjalmar
En låt i tri toner (Beckman)

Wallenius, A.
"Om sommaren sköna"

Waller, Edmund
"As I saw fair Clora walk" (Hayden)
"Chloris, yourself you so excel" (Lawes)
"Cloris, farewell, I now must go" (Webb)
"It is not that I love you less" (music by Blow; Young)

Waller, Henry
Lines written in early spring
To America

Waller, John Francis
Kitty Neil (Irish air)

Waller, Robert
The jolly sophomore (Composer unknown)

Wallin, Johan Olov
Kors och krona (Stenhammer)

Wallnöfer, Adolf
Vale carissima

Walpurgis night. See Walpurgisnacht (Loewe)

Walpurgisnacht (Walpurgis night) K. Loewe. Words by W. Alexis. e.g. FM

Walsh, Edward
Brideen ban mo store (O'Carolan?)
"Bright sun! before whose glorious ray" (Irish air)
The dawning of the day (Irish air. Tr of Fáinne geal an lae)
The fair hills of holy Ireland (Irish air)
"Have you been at Carrick" (Irish air)
"Ye dark-hair'd youths" (Irish air)

Walsingham. 16th century song. CO 1

Walter, Leslye
To-day and to-morrow (Beethoven)

Walter, William Henry
"All is bright and cheerful round us"
"Soldiers, awake! this is the festal hour"

Walter's prize-song. See Walthers preislied (Wagner)

Walthers preislied. R. Wagner. e.g. OPS 3
"Morgenlich leuchtend" ("Gleaming at morning."—Prize song) e.g. KS 4
Walthers preislied (Walter's prize-song) e.g. SOA 3

Walton, Ellis
Carmena (Wilson)

Walton, J. G. See Hemy, Henry F., jt. auth.

Waltz song ("Ah! je veux vivre") See "Ah! je veux vivre" (Gounod)

Waltz song ("Hear sweet music softly saying") F. Lehar. e. WA—WBT—WSW

Waltz song ("O heart wherefore so light") E. Audran. e. WBT

Waltz song ("See, she is dancing") J. Offenbach. [Tr of Elle danse! en cadence] e. WBT

Waltz song ("That night I'll ne'er forget") R. Planquette. e. WBT

Walzlied ("Hört ihr den schwäbischen wirbeltanz") Schwäbischer volkstanz. Words by J. C. F. Haug. e. ED 3

Wander song. See Wanderlied ("Wohlauf noch getrunken")

The **wander**-staff. German air. e. FSS 1

"Ein **wanderbursch** mit dem stab in der hand." See Das erkennen (Proch)

Der **wanderer** ("Ich komme vom gebirge her") F. Schubert. Words by G. F. Schmidt. e.g. FO 1
The wanderer. e. BC
Der wanderer (The wanderer) e.g. AB 3—BAS 1—BS 1—FF—KF 4—PG 4

The **wanderer** ("On foot I gaily") See The foot-traveler

Der **wanderer** ("Weit in der ferne."—"Far from my birthplace") A. Fesca. KF 3—KF 4

"A **wanderer**, alone upon the highway." See Temple ouvre-toi (Gounod)

"A **wand'rer** worn with worldly strife." See Come unto me (Barry)

The **wanderer's** farewell. German folk song. e. FSS 3

Wanderers nachtlied ("Aller berge gipfel." —The wanderer's night song) A. Rubinstein. e.g. FMB
Wanderer's night song. e.g. WA

Wanderers nachtlied ("Der du von dem himmel bist") F. Schubert. Words by Goethe. g. ED 2

Wanderers nachtlied ("Ueber allen gipfeln ist ruh."—Wanderer's night song) F. Liszt. Words by Goethe. e.g. FF—GM
Wanderer's nightsong. e. HSS 2

The **wanderer's** night song ("Aller berge gipfel") See Wanderers nachtlied (Rubinstein)

Wanderer's night song ("Night her watch is keeping") A. Warlamoff. e. KSN

Wanderer's night song ("Ueber allen") See Wanderers nachtlied (Liszt)

The **wanderer's** return ("I've come unto my home again") Irish air. Words by G. Griffin. MMI

Wanderer's song ("Wohlauf noch getrunken") See Wanderlied (Folk air); Wanderlied (Schumann)

Wandering. See Das wandern (Schubert)

The **wandering** bard ("What life like that of the bard can be") Air: Planxty O'Reilly. Words by T. Moore. MI

The **wandering** beauty. Pepusch. Words by J. Hughes. BE 7

A **wandering** Canadian. See "Un Canadien errant"

"**Wandering** in the May-time." S. Glover. FSS 5

Wandering in the woods. See Vandring i skoven (Grieg)

"A **wandering** minstrel." A. Sullivan. WBT

Wandering Willie. Air: Here awa', there awa'. Words by R. Burns. BSB —FSS 5—JO
"Here awa, there awa, wandering Willie." BSR—PS 1

Wanderlied ("Die sonn erwacht mit ihrer pracht") C. M. von Weber. Words by P. A. Wolff. g. ED 2

Wanderlied ("Wohlauf, noch getrunken") Air: Dort oben auf dem berge, da horstet der aar. Words by J. Kerner. g. ED 1. e. only BOS —SSS
Wander song. e. LA
Wanderlied (Wanderer's song) e.g. SSG

Wanderlied ("Wohlauf noch getrunken."—The wanderer's song) R. Schumann. Words by J. Kerner. e.g. BAS 1—PG 3

Wanderlied der Prager studenten ("Nach süden nun sich lenken") Volksweise. Words by J. von Eichendorff. g. ED 1

Das wandern (Wandering) F. Schubert. Words by W. Müller. e.g. MS
"Das wandern ist des müller's lust." See Das wandern (Schubert)

"Wandl' ich in dem wald des abends" ("In the dreamy wood I wander") R. Franz. Words by H. Heine. e.g. FO 1

Wand'rer. For entries beginning Wand'rer see Wanderer

"Wann der silberne mond." See Die mainacht (Brahms)

"Wann i häld frua afsteh." See Die beruhigte

"Wann i in der früh aufsteh." See Tyrolerlied

"Wann ich einst das ziel errungen habe." See Die vollendung (Schulz)

"Want to go to heaven when I die." Negro spiritual. HR

"Wantonness for evermair." Air: Wantonness. Words by R. Burns. BSR

Wap and rowe, wap and rowe. See "My daddie was a fiddler fine"

Wapping old stairs. J. Percy. DM 2—HSE 1—JO

"War einst ein riese Goliath." See Goliath und David (Fink)

War hymn of Garibaldi. See Inno di guerra dei cacciatori delle Alpi (Olivieri)

"Wär ich ein brünnlein klar." Volkslied. Words by J. C. Nänny. g. ED 2

"Wär ich ein muntres vögelein." J. R. Zumsteeg. Words by E. C. Kleinschmidt. g. ED 2

"Wär' ich ein wilder falke." See Gelähmter flug (Reichardt)

"War schöner als der schönste tag." See Canzonette (Loewe)

War song ("Brothers up, swift arise."—"'O kairos adelphoi") Greek song. e.gr. BSP

War song ("Hear the call to war") Ojibway Indian song. e.in. BA
Song of a coward. in. BA

War song ("Ige ige") Iroquois Indian song. in. SN

War-song of the Hussites. Bohemian national song. e. KSE—SN

The war-song of the men of Glamorgen (Cadlef gwyr Morganwg) Welsh air: Triban gwyr Morganwg. Words by W. Scott. MS
"Red glows the forge in Striguil's bounds." MMW

"The war was a-raging." See The warfare is raging (North Carolina version)

"War-worn and tropic-tann'd." See Biterolf (Wolf)

"Warbling nightingales now celebrate thy beauty." See Love song

Ward, Edward
The vicar of Bray (Old air)

Ward, Gilbert Oakley
The battle of Harlem heights (Composer unknown)
Stand, Columbia (Haydn)

Ward, S. H.
The flower (Herzegovinian air)
"See you the rover" (Croatian air)

Ward, Samuel Augustus
America the beautiful (same air as Jerusalem above)
Jerusalem above
Materna. See America the beautiful; Jerusalem above; Peace hymn of the republic
Peace hymn of the republic (same air as Jerusalem above)

Ward. See "Awake, my soul, and with the sun"; Evening hymn

Ward, the pirate. Norfolk county song. BOH—SF 2

The warder. See Der thürmer (Matys)

Wardle, Sir Thomas
"Christ was born on Christmas night"

Ware, Harriet
Joy of the morning

Ware, Richard D.
My old horse-blanket pin (Ames)
The patteran (Ames)
Yankee Doodle-oodle (College air)

Ware, William Henry
The cabin boy (from Harlequin and Mother Goose)

The warfare is raging. Folk song: North Carolina version. CSE
—Tennessee version. CSE

Waring, Anna Laetitia
"In heavenly love abiding" (music by Bensel; Hassler; Mendelssohn; also unknown composer)

Warmuth, Carl
"Could'st thou know." See "Vidste du hvor hjertet skjaelver"
"Vidste du hvor hjertet skjaelver"

Warner, Arthur F.
"O little Babe! in Bethl'hem born"

The warning ("Ihr Mägdelein") See Warnung (Meyer-Helmund)

A warning ("Männer suchen") See Warnung (Mozart)

Warnung ("Fuchs, du hast die gans gestohlen") Volksweise: Wer eine gans gestohlen hat. Words by E. Anschütz. g. ED 1
The fox and goose. e.g. FSS 5—WBT—WSC

Warnung ("Ihr Mägdelein, nehmt euch in acht."—The warning) E. Meyer-Helmund. e.g. CB

Warnung ("Männer suchen stets zu naschen."—A warning) W. A. Mozart. e.g. GMF

Warnung vor dem Rhein ("An den Rhein") Pöthko. Words by K. Simrock. g. ED 1—ED 3

The warranty deed. Vermont song. SSH

Warren, George William
"Come, Holy Spirit, heavenly Dove"
"Days grow longer"
"God of our fathers." See National hymn
"Let the merry church-bells ring"
"Let the song be begun"
National hymn
"Sing your carols to-day"
"The world itself keeps Easter day"
"Ye sons and daughters of the King" (Tr of O filii et filiae, Rex coelestis, Rex gloriae)

Warren, Joseph
Free America (16th century air)

Warren, N. B.
"Good Christians, rise, this is the morn"
"Now blazing Yule logs"

Warren, Richard Henry
When the birds go north again

Warren, S. P.
"Jesus, our Saviour, we welcome Thy rising"

Warren, W. F.
Homeward bound (Harrington)

Warren's address. Air: Scots wha hae. Words by J. Pierpont. FSS 2—LA

A warrior bold. S. Adams. Words by E. Thomas. FSS 7—HSC—HSD—MPC—NMH—NML—WA—WBT—WL

The warrior's prayer (Prayer of the warriors before smoking the pipe) Omaha Indian song. in. FIS

Warshawski,
The miller's tears (Hebrew air)

Warshawski, Mark
"Aufen pripatshak." See "At the cosy hearth"
"At the cosy hearth"

Wartensee, Xaver Schnyder von. See Schnyder von Wartensee, Xaver

Warum ("Warum sind denn die rosen."—Why) P. I. Tchaikovsky. Words by H. Heine. e.g. CMF 2—FF—FO 2

"Warum blickt doch so verstohlen mich des nachbars töffel an." See Blödigkeit

"Warum sind denn die rosen so blass." See Warum (Tchaikovsky)

"Warum sind der tränen unterm mond so viel." See Trost für mancherlei tränen (Schulz)

"Warum sollt im leben." See Bier, bier und wein

"Was bedeutet die bewegung." See Suleika (Mendelssohn)

"Was blasen die trompeten." See Das lied vom feldmarschall

"Was bringt der weihnachtsmann." Schlesisches volksweise. Words by Hoffmann von Fallersleben. e.g. DCS. g. only ED 1

"Was doch heut nacht ein sturm gewesen." See Begegnung (Wolf)

"Was duftet doch der flieder" (Hans Sachs's monologue) R. Wagner. e.g. BS 2—SOA 5

"Was eppä mehr muasz g'schêchäsei" (What wonders fill the sky) Austrian song. e.g. BF 2

"Was ever knight for lady's sake." See Sir Guy

"Was ever nymph like Rosamond." T. A. Arne. Words by J. Addison. ME

"Was frag ich viel nach geld und gut." See Zufriedenheit (Mozart); Zufriedenheit (Neefe)

"Was glänzt dort vom walde im sonnenschein." See Lützows wilde jagd (Weber)

Was gleicht wohl auf erden dem jägervergnügen. For English translation see Huntsman's chorus (Weber)

"Was hab' ich denn meinem feinsliebchen gethan." See Untreue

"Was I not thine when Allah spoke the word." See When Allah spoke (Fisher)

"Was ist denn heut' wohl fuer ein tag" (Anna song) R. Genée. e.g. FSS 5

"Was ist des Deutschen vaterland." See Des Deutschen vaterland (Reichardt)

"Was ist doch Karlinchen für ein hübsches mädel." See Der leichtsinn (Fink)

"Was ist es, das die seele füllt." See Alles um liebe (Zumsteeg)

"Was ist nun doch in mir erwacht." See Es muss was wunderbares sein (Ries)

"Was ist Sylvia." See "Who is Sylvia" (Schubert)

"Was kann schöner sein." See Küherlied der Emmenthaler

"Was klinget und singet." See Abschied

"Was kommt dort von der höh." See Fuchslied

"Was machst du mir vor liebchen's thür" ("Why art before thy lover's door") E. Lassen. Words by Goethe. e.g. AB 3

"Was schiert mich reich und kaiserprunk." See Kaiser Wenzel (Reichardt)

"Was schreibt er mir." See My heart is weary (Thomas)

"Was soll ich in der fremde tun." See Entschluss (Lindpaintner)

"Was spinnst du, fragte nachbars Fritz." See Die kleine spinnerin (Mozart)

"Was this the man my fancy saw." See "Ah, fors' è lui" (Verdi)

"Was vermeid ich denn die wege." See Der wegweise (Schubert)

"Was verwirrt mir das herz." See Nuit resplendissante (Gounod)

Was wet sain, az Meshiach wet kümmen. See What will happen when the Messiah comes

"Was you ever down in Mobile bay." See Mobile bay

"Was you ever on the Brumalow." See Lucy Long

Washburn, Edward A.
"Ring out the bells for Christmas" (music by Hodges; Mosenthal; also unknown composer)

Washburne, Henry S.
The grave of Bonaparte (Heath)
The vacant chair (Root)

Washed in the blood of the lamb. See O redeemed

Washington ("O day that revealed") A. F. M. Custance. Words by J. C. Murray. NMS

Washington ("What sacred memories") L. B. Marshall. Words by W. W. Caldwell. JS

Washington and Lincoln. H. C. Work. WBT

Washington's birthday. French folk air. Words by H. H. Harbour. DO

Wasn't that most cruel usage. See "Andrew Rose"

"Wassail and wassail all over the town." See Wassail song ("Wassail and wassail all over the town")

The wassail song ("Here we come a-wassailing") See "Here we come a-wassailing"

Wassail song ("Wassail and wassail all over the town") English folk song. SEF 2—SO
Variants: "Here we come a-wassailing"; Somersetshire wassail

"Wassail! wassail! all round the town." See Somersetshire wassail

"Das wasser rauscht, das wasser schwoll." See Der fischer (Reichardt)

Wassersnot ("Zu Koblenz auf der brücken") L. Reichardt. g. ED 2

Waste not, want not. See You never miss the water (Howard)

The watch. See Die uhr (Loewe)

Watch and ward. See "God shall charge His angel legions" (Mendelssohn)

The watch by the Rhine. See Die wacht am Rhein (Wilhelm)

"Watch her kindly, kindly, stars." See In absence (Haydn)

The watch on the Rhine. See Die wacht am Rhein (Wilhelm)

"Watch the sea so bright and lovely." See Torna a Surriento (Curtis)

The watcher. Spanish air. FSS 4

The Watchet sailor. English folk song. SEF 2—SO

"Watching in the meadows." M. B. Foster. Words by R. S. Watson. HC
Christmas eve. DC

Watching the wheat ("While I watch the yellow wheat") Air: Gwenith Gwyn. Words by Talhaiarn. MMW

The watchman and the child. F. H. Cowen. Words by M. Mark-Lemon. HSS 4

"Watchman, tell us of the night." L. Mason. Words by J. Bowring. FSS 3—LA
What of the night. MCS

"Watchman, tell us of the night." J. Parry. Words by J. Bowring. TFC 2

"The watchman's dog stood ten foot high." See Knock a man down

Watchman's song. See Thurmwächters lied (Weidt)

The watchword. M. T. Armitage. Words by C. T. Bryce. BSS

Water-carrier's song. See "Fenesta vascia"

The water into wine. Words by E. E. Higbee. FSS 7

"The water is wide, I cannot get o'er." See O waly, waly

"The water lingers where the leaves." See Farewell (Hadley)

The water-mill ("Je sais au bord du Rhin") See Le moulin

The water mill ("Listen to the water mill") L. Diehl. FSS 3—JSE

The water of Tyne. Scotch song. SMW

"Water parted from the sea." T. A. Arne (music and words) BE 3—DM 2—ME—PR 2

The waterfall (Bavarian yodle) e. WC

Waters of Punalau (Wai o Punalau) D. Nape. Words by E. Holt. e.h. HA

"The waters! the waters." Air: Cwyn y prydydd, or, The poet's complaint. Words by M. A. Browne. MMW

The watersprite. See Neckens polska

Watham, R.
"Yule returns; come, Christian people" (Crowther-Benyon)

"Watla't rās el-jebel fātish." See "I wandered among the mountains"

Watson, E. W. S.
"The shepherds were watching"

Watson, Henry C.
O loving heart, trust on (Gottschalk)

Watson, Mrs Howard
"This happy morn a king is born" (Spinney)

Watson, J.
"John Anderson my jo, John"

Watson, Michael
Anchored
Babylon
The mermaid: old air arranged
"Oh! 'twas in the broad Atlantic." See The mermaid: old air arranged
Stilling the tempest
"Thy sentinel am I"

Watson, R. S.
"Hark! I hear, sweet and clear" (Foster)
"Watching in the meadows" (Foster)

Watson, Sir William
April (music by Densmore; Harris)
Watterson, Ada
Morningside (Composer unknown)
Watterson, Roberta
Polly (Smith)
Watton town's end.   See London is a fine
town
Watts, A. A.
"Come, let us banish sorrow" (Welsh
air)
Watts, Isaac
"Before Jehovah's awful throne"
(Venua)
Behold thy King (Composer unknown)
"Come, Holy Spirit, heavenly Dove"
(music by Dykes; Warren)
"Come, let us join our cheerful songs"
(Tans'ur)
Cradle hymn (Rousseau)
"From all that dwell" (music by Franc;
Hatton)
Funeral dirge (Händel)
Glory begun below (Hayne)
"Hush, my babe" (Rousseau)
"Jesus shall reign" (Hatton)
"Joy to the world" (music by Händel;
Mason)
"Kingdoms and thrones to God belong"
(Mason)
My title clear (Arne)
"O God, our Help in ages past" (Franc)
"Once more, my soul" (Glaser)
"Salvation! oh, the joyful sound"
(Arne)
Soldier of the cross (Arne)
"When I survey the wondrous cross"
(music by Mason; also unknown
composer)
"With songs and honors sounding loud"
(German air)
Watts, Wintter
When I wake
Wood song
Waubunosa's longing.   Ojibway Indian
song. e.in.   BA
The **wave.**   See Vågen (Laurin)
"**Wave**, wave, wave, while over land and
sea."   See Song to the flag (Tufts)
"**Waves** dashing and breaking."   N. Rim-
sky-Korsakoff.   Words from the Rus-
sian of A. Tolstoi. e. NM 2
"**Waves**, oh! cease this wild caressing."
See Barcarole (Kalliwoda)
"**Waving** green palms, the throng goes on
its way."   See Les rameaux (Faure)
Wa-wan wa-an (Around the lodge)   in.
DCS
"**Way-ay-ay**, ah! we'll pay Paddy Doyle for
his boots."   See We'll pay Paddy
Doyle
"**Way-ay** roll and go."   See Roll and go
Way down in Ca-i-ro.   S. C. Foster (mu-
sic and words)   NMP
"**Way** down in Louisiana."   See In the
Louisiana lowlands
"**Way** down in the meadow."   See Dear
Evelina, sweet Evelina

"**Way** down on de old plantation."   See
Angelina Baker (Foster)
"**Way** down upon de Suwanee ribber."
See The old folks at home (Foster)
"**Way** down upon the Swanee river."   See
The old folks at home (Foster)
"**Way** down yonder in the wilderness."
See I must go
"The **way** had been long."   See The pil-
grim (Maybrick)
"The **way** is long and dreary."   See The
pilgrims (Cowen)
The **way** of the world.   See Lauf der welt
(Grieg)
"**Way** over in the Egypt land."   See
March on
Way over Jordan.   See View de land
The **way** to keep him ("Ye fair, possest of
ev'ry charm")   T. A. Arne.   ME
"'**Way** up on-a-de mountain top."   See
Father Abraham
"**Way** up on de mountain, Lord."   See Up
on de mountain
'**Way** up on the mountain-top-tip-top.   See
"Hark! I hear a voice"
The **way-worn** traveller ("Faint and wear-
ily")   Arnold.   HSE 2
"Faint and wearily."   FSS 8
Ways of the world.   Austrian song.   e.
KSE
We all love a pretty girl under the rose.
T. Arne.   HSE 1
"**We** all to conqu'ring beauty bow."   J.
Blow.   Words by T. D'Urfey.   MM
"**We** are a band of brothers."   See The
bonnie blue flag (Macarthy)
"**We** are all noddin'."   Old Scottish air.
FSS 4
"**We** are all good fellows."   See A health
to all good fellows (Chaffee)
"**We** are alone here."   See Il balen del
suo sorriso (Verdi)
"**We** are building on a rock."   Negro spir-
itual.   HR
"**We** are climbing Jacob's ladder, ladder."
See Jacob's ladder
"**We** are coming, Father Abra'am."   L. O.
Emerson.   MP—WBT
"**We** are fairies of the sea."   S. Glover.
FSS 8
"**We** are happy and free as a crew can be."
See Over the dark blue sea
"**We** are in word and action the champions
of our nation."   See Himno de Riego
(Huerta)
"**We** are little children."   G. E. Oliver.
HC
"**We** are little maids, you see."   See French
Christmas song
"**We** are little soldier men."   E. Smith.
OH
We are na fou, we're no that fou.   See
"O Willie brew'd a peck o' maut" (Mas-
terton); "O! Willie brew'd a peck o'
maut" (Shore)
"**We** are students by nature."   See Re-
united
"**We** are tenting to-night."   See Tenting
on the old camp ground (Kittredge)

We are the stuff. College song. CU

We are walking in de light. See Walking in the light

"We be soldiers three." Old song. CO 1 —DM 1—JE

"We be three poor mariners." 17th century English sea song. BMC— BOH—CO 1—DM 1—HSE 2—JE —MM—SMW—WBT
Three poor mariners. FSS 7

"We bring sweet flowers." Adapted from Marschner. HC

"We called her Little Sunbeam." See Little Sunbeam (Farmer)

We cheer for the "U of M." University of Minnesota song. C. J. Zintheo. CHS—MPC—NMS

"We come not with a costly store." See No myrrh of Araby

"We come to see Miss Jennie Jones." See Jenny Jones

"We feel thy calm" (Verdure) F. J. Haydn. Words by S. Longfellow. BD

"We from childhood play'd together." See Comrades (McGlennon)

"We gather together to ask the Lord's blessing." See "Wilt heden nu treden" (Kremser)

"We give thy natal day to hope." See Our country (Mendelssohn)

"We greet thee, old friend." Scotch air. Words by E. M. Douglas. MCS

We guard our independence. See Cancion patriotica (Mexican song)

"We had not sailed twenty or thirty miles from shore." See The Lion man-o'-war

"We hail the merry autumn days." See Merry autumn days (Congdon)

We hail thee, glad springtime. D. F. E. Auber. FSS 8

"We hail thee, harbinger of peace." See Hillsdale and the blue (Monroe)

"We have been friends together." H. Russell. Words by C. S. Norton. FSS 1 —JO—WBT

"We have come with joyful greeting." See Song of Arbor day (Pettings)

"We have done our bounden duty." See Hjemreise fra saetren

"We have heard our president and leader say." See Roll the kaiser down

"We have lived and loved together." Nicolo (N. Isouard) Words by C. Jefferys. FSS 2—JO—WBT

"We have you now at last." See La petite souris grise

We her children with fond adoration. See Saludemos la patria (Aberle)

"We know of a spot in Ohio." See The purple and the gold—Scio

"We lay us calmly down to sleep." Schumann. FSS 1—WBT

"We le goelcerth wen yn fflamio." See Rhyfelgyrch gwyr Harlech

"We lift up our voices." Dutch folk song. e. BD

"We look as if we could taste of good cheer." See In the sugar camp

"We love cold water." Round. FSS 4

"We love to go each day to school." See Brother and I

"We love to sing of O. S. U." See The scarlet and gray forever (Gayman)

"We march, we march." J. Barnby. Words by G. Moultrie. BD—LA

"We march, we march." G. E. Oliver. Words by G. Moultrie. LA

We may be happy yet. M. W. Balfe. Words by A. Bunn. FSS 5—HSE 3

"We may roam thro' this world." See The daughters of Erin

"We may rove the wide world o'er." See The old familiar place (Glover)

"We meet again to-night." College song. CHS—MPC—TFC 2

"We merry wives of Windsor." See Merry wives of Windsor

"We met, 'twas in a crowd." T. H. Bayly (music and words) BE 1—FSS 8 —HSE 1—JO

"We must go, sighed little Ruby." See The little leaves (Ganz)

"We must say farewell tonight." See Lebewohl (Silcher)

"We plough the fields, and scatter." J. A. P. Schulz. [Words by M. Claudius. Tr of Im anfang war's auf erden] e. HC—LA

"We praise Thee, O God." See Revive us again (Husband)

"We read in the story of old." See Arise! He calleth thee (Roeckel)

"We revel in song, in Spain we belong." See Ching-a-ling

"We roam the hills together." See Will and I

"We roam through forest shades." FSS 3

"We salute thee." See "Salve, oh patria"

"We sat by the river, you and I." See You and I (Barnard)

"We sat together as twilight gather'd round us." See Raziella

"We sate down and wept by the waters." S. S. Wesley. Words by Lord Byron. DM 1

"We saw a light shine out afar." See The golden carol of Melchoir, Bathazer and Caspar

We saw them. Words by H. Snow. BSS

"We shall meet, but we shall miss him." See The vacant chair (Root)

"We sing a song of Christmas-time." A. Sullivan. Words by A. E. Smith. HC

"We sing not thy praises in Latin or Greek." See The tounis colledge

"We sing of Billy the William goat." See Didn't he ramble

"We sing of the polar bear." See The climate

"We sing our Saviour's praises." H. A. Farnsworth. Words by M. Ford. HC

"We sing the plant of prairied west." See
The corn song (Marks)
"We sing to-day our Easter hymn." W.
D. Armstrong. Words by W. Austin.
HC
"We soldiers drink, we soldiers sing."
Drinking song. ME
"We speak of the realms of the blest."
See The blessed country (Himmel)
We stand by our classes. Student song.
Words by A. Nash. CHS—MPC
"We suffer that the fatherland may ever
mighty be." See Turkish war song
"We tars are all for fun and glee." See
Jack at Greenwich (Dibdin)
"We think it is the rule, sir." See Stu-
dents' way
"We three kings of Orient are." See
Three kings of Orient (Hopkins)
"We, thy soldiers, hail thee, hail thee."
See Soldiers' hymn (Haydn)
"We tuik wor keel up te the dyke." See
Weel may the keel row, that gets the
bairns their bread
We two have mingled our aloha's. See
United
We two together. W. W. Gilchrist.
Words by W. Whitman. TL
"We Vassar girls say." See A Vassar
chant (Biedermann)
"We want no cowards in our band." See
Children, we shall all be free
"We wear our colors, red and gold." Uni-
versity of Denver song. CHS
"We were crowded in the cabin" (The tem-
pest) N. Barker. [Words by J. T.
Fields] FSS 8
"We were crowded in the cabin" (The cap-
tain's daughter) I. B. Woodbury.
Words by J. T. Fields. LBR
"We were maidens three." See Les trois
filles
"We were three sailors of Groix." See
Les marins de Groix
"We will be merry, far and wide." M.
Praetorius. 14th century words. Tr
of Wir wollen alle frölich seyn. e.
HC
We will end this war, brethren. See End
this war
We will end this warfare. See Down by
the river
"We will open our mouth in a parable."
Mackenzie. OS 2
"We will take from our parting its bit-
terest word." See Come again
"We won't go home until morning." Air:
Chanson de Mambron. EF—TFC 1
"We wreathe with flowers the peaceful
graves." See Cherished names (Mar-
shall)
"The wealthy fool with gold in store." See
My friend and pitcher (Shield)
A wealthy lord. J. Haydn. Words by D.
Bispham. BC
The wean wants a cradle. See "There's
news, lasses, news"

"A weanling small on my mother's breast."
See "Als büblein klein an der mutter
brust" (Nicolai)
"Wear a bright smile." G. Verdi. FSS 6
Weariness. Bohemian song. Lahorsky.
e. KSE
The wearing of the green ("Oh, Paddy
dear, and did you hear") Irish
national song. Words from an
old ballad, with additional words
by D. Boucicault. BMC—BOS—
BSP— EF—FMB— FSI—FSS 5—
JO— MP— NMS— OH— SSS—
WA—WBT—WSW
The wearin' o' the green. BSE—PI
The wearing of the green (Farewell!
for I must leave thee) MMI
Weary ("Weary of living, so weary") V.
Gabriel. Words by F. L. Carter.
FSS 7
The weary are at rest. Ancient Irish
dirge. FSS 5—JSE
"Weary fa' you, Duncan Gray." Air: Dun-
can Gray. Words by R. Burns. BSR
"A weary lot is thine, fair maid." A.
Sullivan. Words by W. Scott. BAS 2
"Weary of earth." J. M. Coward. Words
by S. J. Stone. HSS 2—HSS 3—
HSS 4
"Weary of earth." J. Langran. Words
by S. J. Stone. LA
The life laid down. FSS 2
"Weary of living, so weary." See Weary
(Gabriel)
The weary pund o' tow. Scottish air.
Words by R. Burns. BSB—MMS
—PS 1
"I bought my wife a stane o' lint."
BSR
"Weary sighs from out my sad heart." See
"Suspiri di lu me core"
"Weary the way, heavy the cross we bear."
See Thy will be done (Barry)
Weary traveler. Negro spiritual. JB
Let us cheer the weary traveler. DF—
HR
"Weary winds are hushed to sleep." See
Song of the fisher boy

Weatherly, Frederick Edward
All that glitters (Roeckel)
Angus Macdonald (Roeckel)
At the ferry (Wellings)
Beauty's eyes (Tosti)
Bid me good-bye (Tosti)
Biondina (Löhr)
The boatswain's story (Molloy)
The bride bells (Roeckel)
Call me back (Denza)
The chorister (Sullivan)
Darby and Joan (Molloy)
"Day is dying, cool sweet winds"
(Roeckel)
The dustman (Molloy)
Fiddle and I (Goodeve)
The gift (Behrend)
The hour of rest (Roeckel)
In the chimney corner (Cowen)
The king's highway (Molloy)
The little tin soldier (Molloy)

Weatherly, Frederick Edward—*Continued*
London bridge (Molloy)
Love's proving (Löhr)
The midshipmite (Maybrick)
Mona (Maybrick)
"My friend! my friend" (Behrend)
My lady's bower (Temple)
Nancy Lee (Maybrick)
Old and young Marie (Cowen)
The old lock (Wellings)
Past and future (De Koven)
Pierrot (Hutchinson)
The Romany lass (Maybrick)
Rose-Marie (Molloy)
Saved from the storm (Barry)
The shadow of the cross (Barry)
The skippers of St Ives (Roeckel)
The star of Bethlehem (Maybrick)
Tell her I love her so (Faye)
They all love Jack (Maybrick)
Thursday (Molloy)
"'Twas Christmas eve" (Nelson)
"What am I, love, without thee" (May-brick)
Weatherly, George
Mavourneen (Aylward)
Weave in, my hardy life. F. Van der Stucken. Words by W. Whitman. TFC 2—TL
Weave then, darling, a garland. See Sunny Manoa (Hopkins)
The weaver (The blanket.—Her rosary) T. Lieurance. LN
Webb, George James
Children's Hosanna
"Hail to the Lord's anointed"
His reign on earth begun. See "Hail to the Lord's anointed"
"The morning light is breaking"
"Stand up, stand up for Jesus" (same air as "The morning light is breaking")
Webb, William
"Cloris, farewell, I now must go"
Webbe, Charles
"Cease, O my sad soul" (Purcell)
Webbe, Samuel
"Brightest and best"
"Come, ye disconsolate"
Epitaph on a parish clerk
"The rose had been washed"
Webber,
"Talk not so much to me of love"
Webber, Benjamin
"There's a beautiful flag" (Wilson)
Weber, Bernhard Anselm
"Cheerily the huntsman." See Der schütz
"Days of summer glory" (same air as Der schütz)
Hunter's song. See Der schütz
Der schütz
Ständchen
Weber, Karl Maria Friedrich Ernst, freiherr von
"As a little child"
"Bethörte! die an meine liebe glaubt" (from Euryanthe)
The boat song (from Oberon)

Brautjungfernlied (from Der frei-schütz)
Breathings of spring
Cradle-song. See Wiegenlied
"Depth of mercy" (same air as "As a little child")
"Donzella nata in sen." See "A lonely Arab maid"
Durch die wälder (from Der frei-schütz)
"Echoing bell-tones." See "Glöcklein im thale"
"Einsam bin ich, nicht alleine" (from Preciosa)
"From boyhood trained in battlefield" (from Oberon)
Gebet (from Der freischütz)
Gebet vor der schlacht
Die gefangenen sänger
"Glöcklein im thale" (from Euryanthe)
"The gracious Father hears us when we call" (from Jubel-cantata)
"Happy nation, still receiving" (from Jubel-cantata)
Heimlicher liebe pein
Der holdseligen
"How friendly sleep was to me." See "Wie nahte mir der schlummer"
Hunting song
Huntsman's chorus (from Der frei-schütz. Tr of Was gleicht wohl auf erden dem jägervergnügen")
The huntsman's chorus ("The sunshine glows")
"I dream of all things free"
I saw a rosebud. See "Ich sah ein röschen am wege stehn"
"Ich sah ein röschen am wege stehn"
"I'd weep with thee" (from Oberon)
"Im wald, im wald"
In der ferne
"Insensate! to believe that I can love." See "Bethörte! die an meine liebe glaubt"
Jewett. See "My Jesus, as Thou wilt"; "One sweetly solemn thought"
Liebesglück
Liebeslied
"A lonely Arab maid" (from Oberon)
"Look how the fruitful land is smiling" (from Jubel-cantata)
"Lord, forever at thy side" (same air as "As a little child")
Lutzow's wild hunt. See Lützows wilde jagd
Lützows wilde jagd
Maienblümlein
"Mei schatzerl"
"My Jesus, as Thou wilt" (Tr of Mein Jesu, wie du willt)
My sweetheart. See "Mei schatzerl"
"'Neath the almond trees that blossom." See "Unter blüh'nden mandelbäumen"
"Now are flown the shades of night" (same air as "As a little child")
"O Araby! dear Araby"
O 'tis a glorious sight to see (from Oberon)

Weber, Karl Maria F. E., freiherr von
　—Continued
　"Ocean! thou mighty monster" (from Oberon)
　Once more we see the good by God provided (from Jubel-cantata)
　"One sweetly solemn thought" (same air as "My Jesus, as Thou wilt")
　"Ozean! du ungeheuer." See "Ocean! thou mighty monster"
　Piano, piano, canto pio. See "Wie nahte mir der schlummer"
　Prayer. See Gebet
　Das röschen
　The rose. See Das röschen
　The rosy crown
　Schlummerlied. See Wiegenlied
　Schweig'! damit dich niemand warnt (from Der freischütz)
　Schwertlied
　Seymour. See "As a little child"; "Depth of mercy"; "Lord, forever at Thy side"; "Now are flown the shades of night"; "Softly now the light of day"
　Slumber song. See Wiegenlied
　"Softly now the light of day" (same air as "As a little child")
　Sommertag
　"The sun is bright"
　Sword song. See Schwertlied
　"Then does mem'ry turn to days" (from Jubel-cantata)
　"Über die berge mit ungestüm"
　"Und ob die wolke" (from Der freischütz)
　"Unter blüh'nden mandelbäumen" (from Euryanthe)
　The vine-dressers' song
　Wanderlied
　Weine nur nicht
　"Where hide myself." See "Wo berg' ich mich"
　"Wie nahte mir der schlummer" (from Der freischütz)
　Wiegenlied
　"Wo berg' ich mich" (from Euryanthe)
　Woes of hidden love. See Heimlicher liebe pein
　"Yet not alone of labor comes our plenty" (from Jubel-cantata)
Webster, H. D. L.
　Lorena (Webster)
Webster, Mrs Hume
　Once (Hervey)
Webster, Joseph Philbrick
　Don't be sorrowful, darling
　In the sweet by and by. See The sweet by and by
　Lorena
　The sweet by and by
Weckerlin, Jean Baptiste Théodore
　Mignonette
We'd better bide a wee. C. Barnard (music and words) FSS 2—HSD—NMH—NML—PO—WBT—WL
The **wedding** dance. Swiss song. e. KSE
The **wedding-day** ("What virgin or shepherd") J. Hook. PR 2

Wedding-day song ("Behold the gifts."—Pridanyi udalyi, Ladu, Ladu) Russian folk song. e. SSR 2
Wedding joy (Pulma lust) Estonian folk dance. e.es. BF 1
The **wedding** of the cuckoo and the skylark. See Les noces du coucou et de l'alouette
The **wedding** of the frog and mouse. Ancient English song. CO 1
　Variants: "A frog he went a-courting"; "A frog he would a wooing go"; The frog in the spring; The frog in the well; "Frog went a-courting"; "It was the frog in the well"; Kemo, kimo; The toad's courtship
Wedding song ("There's a girl") Ojibway Indian song. e.in. BA
The **wedding-suit** (Ne tesan terem) Russian folk song. e. SSR 1
Weder glück noch stern ("Es fiel ein reif in der frühlingsnacht") Folk air. g. ED 3
Weder glück noch stern ("Es fiel ein reif in der frühlingsnacht") Another older folk air. g. ED 3
The **wee** bird ("A wee bird sang") German song. e. FSS 7
"A **wee** bird cam' to our ha' door." See Wae's me for Prince Charlie
"A **wee** bird sang on the linden-bough." See The wee bird
"A **wee** goose, wild and shy." See Little wild goose
The **wee**, wee German lairdie ("Wha the de'il ha'e we gotten for a king") Jacobite song. MMS—PS 1
"**Wee** Willie Gray." Air: Wee Totum Fogg. Words by R. Burns. BSR
Weeden, Howard
　Swing low (Fisher)
"**Weeding** flax-fields blue" ("Když jsem plela len") Czech folk song. bo.e. BF 1
A **week's** work well done. English folk song. BSW
Weel may the keel row ("As I cam thro' Sandgate") See The keel row
Weel may the keel row, that gets the bairns their breed. Scotch song. Air: Smiling Polly. SMW
Weelkes, Thomas
　"Cease, sorrows, now"
"**Weep** for the fallen." Air: Portuguese hymn. FSS 1
"**Weep** no more, heart of my heart, no more." See Spring song—to Ireland
Weep no more, my lady. See My old Kentucky home (Foster)
"**Weep** no more, thou sorry boy." J. L. Hatton. BE 7
"**Weep** not, my mother." See I dreamt I was in heaven (Costa)
"**Weep**, O mine eyes." J. Benet. BOH
"**Weep** on, weep on." Air: The song of sorrow. Words by T. Moore. MI

"**Weep** you no more, sad fountains." J. Dowland. JE
Weeping for ever. See Lascia ch'io pianga (Händel)
Weeping for thee. Bohemian song. e. KSE
Weeping Mary. Negro song from Kentucky. KA
Weeping, sad and lonely. See When this cruel war is over (Tucker)
Weggiser lied (Weggis song) Swiss song. e.g. BF 2
Der **wegweiser** (The sign-post) Schubert. e.g. BS 2
"**Wehe** den fliehenden welt hinaus ziehenden." See In der ferne (Schubert)
"**Wehe**, lüftchen, lind und lieblich." See Botschaft (Brahms)
"**Wehet**, weht ihr flockensterne." See Snowflakes (Grechaninov)
"**Wehiwehi** ka ukai kanahele." See Sweet lei mamo (Hopkins)
Weidt, Heinrich
How fair art thou. See Wie schön bist du
Sun of Christmas-tide
Thurmwächters lied
Watchman's song. See Thurmwächters lied
Wie schön bist du
Weigle, Gottlieb
Unterländers heimweh (Volkslied)
Die **weihe** ("Ich weih' im tale den tiefsten hain") F. H. Himmel. Words by C. A. Tiedge. g. ED 3
Weihelied (Der landesvater.—"Alles schweige") Student song. Words by A. Niemann. g. ED 1
Weihnacht fliedlein. For English translation see "Nowell! Nowell! good news I tell"
Die **weihnachtsfreude** ("Morgen, kinder, wird's was geben") Volksweise. Words by C. F. Splittegarb. g. ED 1
Weihnachtslied ("Welche morgenröten wallen") L. Reichardt. Words by Friedrich Leopold, graf zu Stolberg. g. ED 3
Der **weihnachtsmann** ("Morgen kommt der weihnachtsmann") Volksweise. Words by Hoffmann von Fallersleben. g. ED 1
Der **weihnachtsmann** (Santa Claus) e.g. DCS
Weil, Oscar
Herbstfrühlingslied
"In autumn." See Herbstfrühlingslied
Spring song (Tr of Frühlingslied)
"**Weil'** auf mir, du dunkles auge." See Bitte (Franz)
Weiland, F.
Autumn dreaming
Will you love me then as now
Weimar, G. P.
"Sing, gaily sing"
"Der **wein** erfreut des menschen herz." See Wein, weib, gesang (Zelter)

Wein, weib, gesang (Wine, woman and song) C. F. Zelter. Words by C. Müchler. e.g. SSS
Trinklied ("Der wein erfreut") g. ED 1
Weine nur nicht. C. M. von Weber. Volkslied. g. ED 1
Weise, C. E. F.
"Christmas brings joy to every heart"
Weiss, Friedrich Wilhelm
Abschiedsabend
Weiss, Willoughby Hunter
The village blacksmith
"**Weiss** nicht, was mir das morgen beut." See Froher mut (Erk)
Weisse, Christian Felix
"Als ich auf meiner bleiche" (Hiller)
Iris (Composer unknown)
Der kuss (Beethoven)
Liebe und wein (Hiller)
Weisse, Michael
"Christ the Lord is risen again" (Hodges. Tr of Christus ist erstanden)
Der **weisse** hirsch ("Es gingen drei jäger") Volksweise: Es zogen drei bursche wohl über den Rhein. Words by Uhland. g. ED 2
"**Weit** in der ferne wandr' ich allein." See Der wanderer (Fesca)
"**Weit** in nebelgrauer ferne liegt mir das vergangne glück." See An Emma (Zelter)
"**Welche** morgenröten wallen." See Weihnachtslied (Reichardt)
The **welcome** ("Come in the evening") Irish air: Astoreen machree, or, O treasure of my heart. Words by T. O. Davis. JO—MMI
Welcome be our heavenly King. F. Bridge. HC
"**Welcome** be thou, heaven-King." See Welcome Yule
Welcome Christmas cheer. Storace. MCS
Welcome, fair evening. See Sommerabendlied (Becker)
"**Welcome**, happiest moment." See "Giunse alfin il momento" (Mozart)
"**Welcome**, happy morning." C. O. Arnold. Words from Fortunatus. Tr of Salve, festa dies. e. HC
"**Welcome**, lovely summertime." See Sommerlied (Neidhardt von Reuenthal)
"**Welcome**, pretty primrose." C. Pinsuti. e. FSS 8
Welcome, royal Charlie. Scottish song. PS 1
Welcome song ("Ahlan biman kad zār") Syrian folk song. ar.e. BF 2
"**Welcome** sweet springtime." See Voices of the woods (Rubinstein)
"A **welcome**, sweet summer, is waiting for thee." Air: Coroesaw'r wenynen. Words by K. R. Moffat MMW
"**Welcome**! the hour is nearing." See "Vieni! la mia vendetta" (Donizetti)
"**Welcome**, thou long'd-for day." See "Come sereno è il dì" (Rossini)

Welcome to Christmas. Words by J. Drake. MCS

Welcome to morning. Offenbach. Words by M. B. C. Slade. FSS 1

Welcome to spring ("All the birds so gaily sing") WBT—WSC

"Welcome to the day returning." See Ode for Washington's birthday (Beethoven)

Welcome Yule. 17th century air. HC

Weld, Heinrich
"Sing God praises" (Ambrosius)

Weldon, John
"Celia, let not pride undo you"
"Hope, thou nurse of young desire" (same air as "Let ambition fire")
"Let ambition fire" (from The judgment of Paris)
"Prithee, Celia"

"Wele goelcerth wen yn fflamio." See Rhyfelgyrch gwyr Harlech

Welhaven, Johann Sebastian Cammermeyer
"Hellig Olaf" (Norse air)
"Min elskte, jeg er bunden" (Kjerulf)
Nökken (Kjerulf)
"Til fjelds over bygden" (Kjerulf)
Til Ole Bull (Scandinavian folk air; also music by Reissiger)

Well-a-day ("Sweet England's pride is gone") 17th century song. CO 1

Well-a-day ("Sweet England's prize is gone."—Essex' last good-night) 17th century song. Old English air. DM 1

Well-a-day (" 'Twas on a pleasant summer's day") Old English air. BE 6

"Well-a-day! ah, well-a-day." G. Linley. FSS 4

Well-a-day! lack-a-day ("Ah me! I am lost and forlorn") S. Storace. Words by P. Hoare. ME

We'll all go a-singing. Children's song. WSC

We'll die in the field. Negro spiritual. JP—NMP

"We'll drink it out of the nut-brown bowl." See The barley-mow

"We'll gather by the twilight glow." See In front of old Pardee (Stier)

"We'll go to the mountains." Air: Bonnie Dundee. FSS 5

"We'll go to the mountains" (Tyrolese mountain song) Composer unknown. FSS 7—WBT

"Well, go your ways—I cannot choose but smile." See When I was a young one (Arne)

We'll hang Paddy Doyle for his boots. See Paddy Doyle

"We'll haul the bowline." See Haul the bowline

"Well, here we are; well, here we are." See Boola song: Yale athletic version (Hirsh)

We'll hide the cooper behint the door. See "The copper o' Cuddie came here awa"

"We'll hunt the wren." See Hunt the wren

"Well I know, young men, I must die." See Ma mourri

"Well, if I am Lord Dannel's wife." See Little Musgrave and Lady Barnard (Black Mountain, N.C. version)

"Well, if you won't, why then I will." See "Å vill int' du, så vill fäll ja"

We'll laugh and sing all cares away. Verdi. e. FSS 4

"We'll laugh at care and sorrow." See Oh, who so gay and free

"We'll march and shout hurrah! with flags and banners gay! for is it not the glorious Fourth we celebrate to-day? This day gave freedom birth." See The glorious Fourth (Old air)

"We'll march and shout hurrah with flags and banners gay; for is it not the glorious Fourth we celebrate to-day? This day gave freedom to the nation." See The glorious Fourth (Custance)

"We'll meet beside the dusky glen." Scottish air: Yon burn-side. Words by R. Tannahill. MMS—PS 2

"Well met, my brother friend." See The The husbandman and servingman

"Well met, well met, my old true love, well met, well met, says he." See The daemon lover

"Well met, well met, my own true love, it's well met." See The daemon lover

"Well met! well met, my own true love, long time am I seeking of thee." English folk song. BSW

We'll o'er the water, we'll o'er the sea. See "Come boat me o'er, come row me o'er"

The well of St Keyne. Old Cornish air. Words by R. Southey. BE 8
"A well there is in the west country." HSE 2

We'll pay Paddy Doyle ("Way-ay-ay, ah") Chantey. HSD
Variant of: Paddy Doyle

We'll pay Paddy Doyle for his boots. See Paddy Doyle

"We'll put for de souf." See Away down souf (Foster)

"We'll raise de Christians' banner." See Gwinter sing all along de way

"We'll raise the Christian banner." See Gwinter sing all along de way

"We'll raise the voice in joyful strain." See For Lincoln we will ever stand (Thompson)

"We'll run from night till morning." See Let the bullgine run

We'll stand the storm. Negro spiritual. JP

"We'll thank thee for our country." See Our country (Deems)

"A well there is in the west country." See The well of St Keyne

"Well thou knowest what love thou owest." See "Tu lo sai" (Torelli)

"Well, we've won, boys." See We stand by our classes

Wellings, Milton
 At the ferry
 Dreaming
 Forevermore
 The old lock
 Some day
 This is my dream
 When love was born
Welsh, Thomas
 "Heigh-ho! what shall I do"
Die **welt**, ein orchester.   F. H. Himmel.
 Words by A. von Kotzebue. g. ED 1
"Die **welt** ist nichts als ein orchester."   See
 Die welt, ein orchester (Himmel)
Wendish song.   See "The tempest rages
 wild on the hill"
"**Wenn** alle untreu werden."   See Erneu-
 ter schwur
"**Wenn** das Atlantische meer lauter cham-
 pagner wär."   German sea song. e.g.
 SMW
"**Wenn** der frühling auf die berge steigt"
 (Frühlingszeit.—Spring-time)   R.
 Becker.   ₁Words by F. von Boden-
 stedt₁ e.g. KF 1
 Frühlingszeit (Springtide) e.g. SM 1
"**Wenn** der frühling auf die berge steigt"
 (Frühlingslied.—Lovely spring)   W.
 Coenen.   ₁Words by F. von Boden-
 stedt₁ e.g. KF 1
"**Wenn** der frühling auf die berge steigt."
 For English translation with a different
 air see Spring song (Weil)
"**Wenn** der frühling kommt."   See Früh-
 lingsliebe
"**Wenn** der lenz erwacht."   Norwegische
 volksweise. Words by F. Kugler. g.
 ED 3
"**Wenn** der schnee von der alma wegga-
 geht."   Hisel. g. ED 1
"**Wenn** des frühlings wachen ziehen."   See
 Kriegslied des maies (Reichardt)
"**Wenn** die nacht mit ihren schleier"
 ("When the night in dusky shadows.")—
 Serenade)   F. Abt. e.g. CB
"**Wenn** die nacht mit süsser ruh'."   See
 Ständchen (Seckendorff)
"**Wenn** die rosen blühen."   See Hoffnung
 (Reichardt)
"**Wenn** die schwalben heimwärts ziehn."
 See Abschied (Abt)
"**Wenn** du, geliebte, nur beginnst zu reden."
 See My delight (Chopin)
"**Wenn** du nur zuweilen lächelst" ("Grant
 me but one single smile, love")   J.
 Brahms. Words by G. F. Daumer.
 e.g. CMF 1
"**Wenn** durch die piazzetta."   See "When
 through the piazzetta" (Jensen);
 "When through the piazzetta" (Men-
 delssohn)
"**Wenn** ich an den letzten abend gedenk'."
 See Der letzte abend
"**Wenn** ich ein vöglein wär."   Volkslied.
 g. ED 1
 "Wenn ich ein vöglein wär'" ("If I a
 bird could be") e.g. SSG
 "Were I a little bird." e. WSC

"**Wenn** ich einmal der Herrgott wär'" ("If
 power divine for once were mine")
 C. Binder. Words by E. Amthor. e.f.
 AB 3
"**Wenn** ich früh in den garten geh' in mein-
 em grünen hut."   See Volksliedchen
 (Schumann)
"**Wenn** ich ihn nur habe."   L. Reichardt.
 Words by F. von Hardenberg. g.
 ED 3
"**Wenn** ich in deine augen seh'" ("When
 gazing in thine eyes")   J. Bleichman.
 Words by H. Heine. e.g. NM 1
"**Wenn** ich mich nach der heimat sehn."
 See Der Tyroler und sein kind (Nes-
 müller)
"**Wenn** in die ferne vom felsen ich seh'."
 See Das heimweh (Müller)
"**Wenn** jemand eine reise tut."   See Urians
 reise um die welt (Zelter)
Wenn kleine kinder schlafen geh'n.   For
 English translation see Guardian angels
 (Schumann)
"**Wenn** mein pfeifchen dampft und glüht."
 See Mein pfeifchen
"**Wenn** meine grillen schwirren."   See Der
 einsame (Schubert)
Wenn mich für häuslichkeit.   See Had
 fickle fortune, not betraying (Tchai-
 kovsky)
"**Wenn** sich zwei herzen scheiden."   F.
 Mendelssohn-Bartholdy. Words by E.
 Geibel. g. ED 3
"**Wenn** wir durch die strassen ziehen."   See
 Entschuldigung (Nestler)
Wennerberg, Gunnar
 "Ack! i Arcadien äfven jag har varit"
 "Ah! in Arcadia I too once did wan-
  der."   See "Ack! i Arkadien äfven
  jag har varit"
 "Här är gudagodt att vara"
 "Oh, how good it is to be here."   See
  "Här är gudagodt att vara"
 To a thrush in autumn.   See Trasten
  i höstkvällen
 Trasten i höstkvällen
Wenn's immer so wär.   C. Ditters von
 Dittersdorf. Words by C. A. Vulpius.
 g. ED 1
"**Wenn's** mailüfterl weht."   See 's mai-
 lüfterl (Kreipl)
Wentworth.   See "Dear Lord, I thank
 Thee, Who hast made" (Maker)
Wenzig, Josef
 Von ewiger liebe (Brahms)
"**Wer** auf den wogen schliefe."   See Der
 freund (Wolf)
"**Wer** ein liebchen hat gefunden."   W. A.
 Mozart. Words by C. F. Bretzner.
 g. ED 2
 "Wer ein liebchen hat gefunden"
  ("When a maiden takes your fan-
  cy") e.g.i. BS 2
"**Wer** gleichet uns turnern, uns frohen."
 See Turnlied
"**Wer** Gott das herze gibet."   See Rechter
 sache gutes ende (Zelter)
"**Wer** hat dich, du schöner wald."   See
 Der jäger abschied (Mendelssohn)

"**Wer** in die fremde will wandern." See Heimweh (Wolf)

"**Wer** ist ein mann." See Der feste mann (Nägeli)

"**Wer** niemals einen rausch gehabt." W. Müller. Words by J. Perinet. g. ED 1

"**Wer** reitet so spät durch nacht und wind." See Erlkönig (Loewe); Erlkönig (Schubert)

"**Wer** singet im walde so heimlich allein." See Herr Ulrich (Hoffmann von Fallersleben)

"**Wer** will unter die soldaten." See Der kleine rekrut (Kücken)

"**Wer** wollte sich mit grillen plagen." See Aufmunterung zur freude (Composer unknown); Aufmunterung zur freude (Reichardt)

Werbung ("Z'nächst bin i halt gange."— Wooing) Austrian folk song. e.g. BO
Wooing. e. KSE—WL

Die **werbung**: Zigeunerlied ("Gipsies three across the meadows") See A gipsy wooing

"**We're** a lively troop of laughing boys." See Laughing song

We're a' noddin' ("Gude e'en to ye, kimmer, and are ye alane") Scottish song. JO—PS 1
And we're a' noddin'. MMS

We're a' noddin ("Guide'en to you, kimmer, and how do you do") See "Guide'en to you, kimmer, and how do you do"

"**We're** a scouting troop that's flown the coop." See Scout marching song

We're all bound to go ("As I walked out one morning."—Heave away) Capstan chantey. CR
For variants see following songs of same title; also Heave away, my Johnny

We're all bound to go ("One morning as I rambled") Capstan chantey. KB

We're all bound to go ("Sometimes we're bound for Liverpool."—Heave away) Capstan chantey. CR

"**We're** an army of the Yankees on the way to France." See Army of the Yankees

"**We're** bound away to Mobile bay." See Lowlands

"**We're** gathered now, my classmates." See Alma mater, O

"**We're** homeward bound to Boston town." See Homeward bound

"**Were** I a little bird." See "Wenn ich ein vöglein wär'"

"**Were** I a star." C. B. Hawley. SM 3

Were I a sunbeam ("If I were a sunbeam") See "If I were a sunbeam"

"**Were** I a sunbeam, high in heaven gleaming." See The maiden's wish (Chopin)

"**Were** I a violet." See S'io fosse

"**Were** I but able to rehearse." See The ewie wi' the crookit horn

"**Were** I gardener." See "Si j'étais jardinier" (Chaminade)

"**Were** I not here a captive." See La captive (Berlioz)

"**Were** I oblig'd to beg my bread." See Somebody

"**Were** I sunshine, I should come." See Ariette (Vidal)

"**Were** I the glorious sun in the heaven." See The maiden's wish (Chopin)

"**Were** I the sun so high in heaven soaring." See The maiden's wish (Chopin)

"**Were** I the sunlight." See The maiden's wish (Chopin)

"**Were** it not for joyous song." See Joyous song

"**We're** marchin' up to hebben." See Hear de angels singin'

Were na my heart licht I wad dee ("There was anes a May") Scottish air. Words by G. Baillie. MMS

"**Were** not the sinful Mary's tears." See Mary's tears (Shaw)

"**We're** safe now." See Pescator, affonda l'esca (Ponchielli)

"**We're** tenting to-night." See Tenting on the old camp ground (Kittredge)

"**We're** wearin' av the green." Irish air. Words by A. Stringer. FSI

"**Were** you ever in Rio Grand." Heave the anchor chantey-song. HSD— WBT

"**Were** you ever on a picnic." See A picnic on the grass

"**Were** you there." Negro spiritual. HR

Wergan, pseud. See Wagner, Heinrich

Wergeland, Henrik Arnold
Godnat (Lasson)
"Ho Ragne va fattig" (Norse air)
Norges fjelde (Kjerulf)

Wermeland. See Vermeland

Werner, Heinrich
Heidenröslein
Mountain maid's invitation
"Once I saw a sweet brier-rose." See Heidenröslein
The two roses. See Heidenröslein
Wild rose. See Heidenröslein

Wert der freundschaft ("Nicht bloss für diese unterwelt") K. G. König. Words by J. T. Hermes. g. ED 3

"**Wert** thou much fairer." J. Wilson. Words by Cotgrave. DM 2
"Wert thou more fairer than thou art." PR 1

"**Wert** thou true hearted as thou art wary." See Bestikkelse (Lie)

"**Wesahquodayweinini** ogeetahkobenung." See Sole survivor

Wesendonck, frau Mathilde (Luckemeyer)
Träume (Wagner)

Wesley, Charles
"Arise, my soul" (Edson)
"Christ the Lord is ris'n today, alleluia! Sons of men and angels say" (Worgan)
"Come, Holy Ghost" (Tans'ur)
"Come, Thou almighty King" (Old air; also music by Giardini)
"Depth of mercy" (music by Blumenthal; Weber)
"Forth in thy name, Lord I go" (Schumann)
"Hail, Thou long-expected Jesus" (Conkey)
"Hark! the herald angels sing" (music by Mendelssohn; Mozart)
"Jesus, Lover of my soul" (music by Abt; Dykes; Marsh; Tours)
"Love divine, all love excelling" (music by Roe; Zundel)
"Oh, for a heart" (Tans'ur)
"Oh, for a thousand tongues" (Glaser)
Open, Lord, my inward ear (Beethoven)
"Since I've known a Saviour's name" (Nares)
"Sons of men, behold" (Thibaut IV)

Wesley, Samuel Sebastian
Aurelia. See "The church's one foundation"
"The church's one foundation"
Dirge for the year
"Farewell if ever fondest prayer"
"Orphan hours, the year is dead." See Dirge for the year
"Silently, silently fades the day's light" To-morrow
"We sate down and wept by the waters"

West, H.
Jenny Lind's Good night

West, John A.
Night-gown chorus

West, John Ebenezer
Love and summer

West, William
The gipsy king

"West, thy breezes softly blowing." See Suleika (Mendelssohn)

Westbrook, William Joseph
"Ring out, sweet bells"

Westbury, G. H.
"Sing we alleluia"

"Eine weste wünsch' ich von seide mir." See Zur Johannisnacht (Grieg)

Westendorf, Thomas P.
Gib me dat water-million

Westermark, O.
King Charles XII. See Kung Carl XII
Kung Carl XII

A **western** college boating song ("With a shout") W. B. Olds. CHS

"**Western** wind." 16th century English song. CO 1
"Westron wynde." BOH—DM 1— JE

"**Western** wind." 16th century English song. Another air. CO 1

Westervelt, Harry E.
The red and blue (Goeckel)

Westlake, Frederick
"Alleluia! alleluia! hearts to heav'n and voices raise"

The **Westmorland** hunt. Traditional English song. DM 2

Weston, John
Johnny, go get a scout (Composer unknown)

Weston. See "Love divine, all love excelling" (Roe)

"**Westron** wynde when wyll thou blow." See "Western wind"

"**Westward** across the wave." See They falter not (Mallary)

"A **wet** sheet and a flowing sea." French military air: Le petit tambour. Words by A. Cunningham. FSS 5— JO—WBT

We-ton song. Dakota Indian song. in. FIS

Wetterbergh, Karl Anton
Skördemannen (Fogelberg)

Wetton, H. Davan
Long ago in Bethlehem

"**We've** come to see Miss Jenny Jones." See Jenny Jones

"**We've** decked the church with ivy." J. S. B. Hodges. HC

"**We've** met, we've met." See The daemon lover

"**We've** trod one road." See Parting (Ippolitov-Ivanov)

Weyla's song. See Gesang Weyla's (Wolf)

Weyse, Christoph Ernst Friedrich
Denmark. See Sang for Danske
Sang for Danske
Song of Denmark. See Sang for Danske
"Towards the north." See Sang for Danske

"**Wha** in a brulzie." See Bannocks o' bear meal

"**Wha** is that at my bower-door." Air: Lass, an I come near thee. Words by R. Burns. BSR

"**Wha** the de'il ha'e we gotten for a king." See The wee, wee German lairdie

"**Wha** wadna be in love wi bonnie Maggie Lauder." See Maggie Lauder

"**Wha** wadna fecht for Charlie." Air: Will ye go and marry Kettie. MMS— PS 1

"**Wha** will buy my troggin." See The trogger

"**Wha** will ride wi' gallant Murray." See The Athole gathering

The **whale.** See Greenland fishery

Wha'll be king but Charlie ("The news frae Moidart cam' yestre'en") Scottish air. Words by C. Nairne. HSSS —JO—MMS—PS 1

"**Wha'll** buy caller herrin'." See Caller herrin' (Gow?)

"**Wham** will we send to London town." Air: For a' that. Words by R. Burns. BSR

"Whar' ha'e ye been a' the day." See My boy Tammie

"Whare are you gaun, my bonie lass." Air: A waukrife minnie. Words by R. Burns. BSR

"Whare hae ye been sae braw, lad." Air: An ye had been where I hae been. Words by R. Burns. BSR

"Whare live ye, my bonie lass." Air: My collier laddie. Words by R. Burns. BSR

Wharton, Thomas Wharton, 1st marquis Lilliburlero (Purcell)

"What a charm has the drum." See Rataplan (Donizetti)

"What a fine horse I shall win." See Híganúyahí

"What a fine hunting day." See The hunting day (Williams)

"What a fine thing I have seen today." See O mother, a hoop

"What a Friend we have in Jesus." C. C. Converse. Words by J. Scriven. FSS 4—NMH—WBT—WS—WSC

"What a lovely lily grows." See The lily

"What a sorrowful ditty of poor Omie Wise." See Poor Omie (Alleghany, N.C. version)

"What a stupid fellow thou." See The musician (Christopulos?)

"What a sweet face has Peppinetta." See La Peppinetta

"What ails this heart o' mine." Air: My dearie, an' thou dee. Words by S. Blamire. JO—MMS—PS 1—WBT

"What am I, love, without thee." S. Adams. Words by F. E. Weatherly. BAS 1

"What are little boys made of." See Natural history

"What are the wild waves saying." S. Glover. Words by J. E. Carpenter. FSS 4—JO—WBT

"What beauties doth Flora disclose." Air: Tweedside. Words by Crawford. PS 2

"What bells are those, so soft and clear." See Christmas chimes (Richards)

"What booker can prognosticate." See When the king enjoys his own again

"What booker doth prognosticate." See When the king enjoys his own again

"What can a young lassie." Air: What shall I do with an auld man. Words by R. Burns. BSR

What can the matter be. See "Oh! dear, what can the matter be"

"What care I tho' 'tis snowing." See The exultant lover

"What care we for gold or silver." FSS 4 —WBT

"What Child is this." Old English air: Greensleeves. [Words by W. C. Dix] BSC—CST—DO—HC—MF

"What Child is this." J. T. Field. Words by W. C. Dix. HC

"What clatters on the roofs." See Santa Claus

"What comes on yonder height." See Leathery

"What could be lovelier than a day of sunshine." See 'O sole mio (Capua)

"What did you eat for your supper, Jimmy Randal my son." See Lord Randall (Allanstand, N.C. version no. 2)

"What do they say, these bells to me." C. Simper. Words by G. W. Brindley. HC

"What do you see in the fire, my darling." See In the chimney corner (Cowen)

"What d'ye think I have made with my red herring's head." See The red herring

"What fairy-like music." J. De Pinna. Words by Mrs C. B. Wilson. FSS 1— —HSD—WBT

"What feeling heart." See The holly

"What flow'r is this that greets the morn." See The flower of liberty (Wilhelm)

"What from vengeance yet restrains me." See Sextet (Donizetti)

"What gleams so bright." See The chapel (Kreutzer)

"What glory gilds the sacred page." See Glory gilds the sacred page (Rossini)

"What good news the angels bring." Traditional air from Rouen. HC

"What here behold I." See Infelice! e tu credevi (Verdi)

"What hid'st thou in thy treasure-caves and cells." See Treasures of the deep (Browne)

"What I have promised." See "Hvad jag har lofvat, det skall jag hålla"

What I love and hate. Words by C. Mackay. FSS 1

"What I would fain discover." See Mån tro? jo jo (Lindblad)

"What if a day, or a month, or a year." 17th century air. Words by T. Campion. CO 1—DM 1—JE—PR 1

"What if 'tis I am chosen." See Celeste Aida (Verdi)

"What if to-morrow bring sorrow or anything other than joy." See Sans souci

"What is home without a mother." A. Hawthorne (S. Winner) FSS 2— HSC—NMH—WBT—WSC

"What is it has awak'd in me." See Es muss was wunderbares sein (Ries)

"What is it that charms me." See Salut! demeure chaste et pure (Gounod)

"What is it the rain-dirge tells me." See A Talmudical student's lament

What is love ("He mana'o he aloha") Hawaiian song. e.h. BF 2

"What is new upon the earth." See Chant of Breton peasants (Naumann)

"What is so rare as a day in June." See June (Schnecker)

"What is the German's fatherland." See Des Deutschen vaterland (Reichardt)

"What is the meaning of the song." See I love my love (Pinsuti)

"What is this strange feeling coming." See What is love

"What joyful tidings, and true." See O mio Fernando (Donizetti)

"What kind of clothes does your William wear." See The jacket blue

"What kind of shoes are you going to wear." Negro song. JP

"What lack the valleys and mountains." See A shadow (Sullivan)

"What life like that of the bard can be." See The wandering bard

"What lovely sunshine! what a day of beauty." See 'O sole mio (Capua)

"What means Ivan." See My heart is weary (Thomas)

"What means this glory round our feet." See Peace on earth (Donizetti)

"What merriment has taen the Whigs." Air: The German lairdie. Words by R. Burns. BSR

"What! Miriam shall perish on sacrificial altar.' C. Rheinthaler. e. SAS 3

"What misfortune here has happened." See Lu carcerato p'ammore (Biscardi)

"What misfortune! I am a coward." See Ô des amants le plus fidèle (Méhul)

"What need have I." Old song. LA

"What noble joys a hunter's life." See "Ein schütz' bin ich" (Kreutzer)

What of Christmas day. Words by J. Selwyn. MCS

What of the night. See "Watchman, tell us of the night" (Mason)

"What pleasure folks feel." See Tea in the arbor (Beuler)

"What pretty wings you flutter." See Butterflies

"What sacred memories entwine." See Washington (Marshall)

"What sad lot the stars prepare me." See "Che farò senza Euridice" (Gluck)

"What said I? ah! 'tis not so, dear." See "Che dissi" (Rossini)

"What said the shepherds." W. M. Hutchinson. Words by A. M. Libbey. MCS

"What says the dog." See Down on Smiley's farm (Lemmel)

"What shall he have that killed the deer" (The huntsman's song) Traditional air. Words by W. Shakespeare. DM 2

"What shall he have that killed the deer" (Hunting song) J. Hilton. Words by W. Shakespeare. KSS

"What shall I do? I am undone." Willis. MM

"What shall I do to show how much I love her." H. Purcell. Words attributed to T. Betterton and to J. Dryden. BMC—BOH—HSE 1—MM
"What shall I do, to shew how much I love her." BE 8

"What shall I say to thee, heart of my heart." See Love's proving (Löhr)

"What shall we do with a drunken sailor." See Drunken sailor (Capstan chantey)

"What shall we do with the drunken sailor." See The drunken sailor (Halliard chantey)

"What shepherd or nymph of the grove." W. Jackson. BOH

"What ship is that a sailing, hallelujah." See Old ship of Zion

"What so high, what so bright as the firmament." See The legend of young nightingale

"What so whitely shineth." See The white snow

"What song doth the cricket sing." See Love and mirth (Strauss)

"What sorrow pierceth the righteous David's heart." L. von Beethoven. e. SAS 1

"What soul-inspiring music." Béarnese carol. e. BSC

"What sound is that." See Ein ton (Cornelius)

"What sounds are those that waken me." See La serenata (Braga)

"What sport can compare with the hunting of the hare." See Hunting the hare

"What star is this." Words by C. Coffin. [Tr of Quae stella sole pulchrior] e. MCS

"What strange whim pursuing." See "Che fiero costume" (Legrenzi)

"What the bee is to the flow'ret." Air: The yellow horse. Words by T. Moore. MI

What the chimney sang. E. G. Hopkins. Words by F. B. Harte. LBR

"What thou of me requirest." See Chello che tu me dice (Biscardi)

"What though I be a country lass." Old English air: Oil of barley. Words by M. Parker. BE 8

"What though I trace each herb and flower." G. F. Händel. SAS 2

"What though the ringlets of her hair." Air: Y Brython, or, The Britons. Words from the Welsh. e. MMW

"What though the zealots pull down the prelates." See Vive le roy

"What tidings bringest thou." J. Dunstable. HC

"What time I kept my sheep in fold." See Benedicamus Domino (Vincent)

"What time in strife and woe." See The Christ-Child (Wallace)

"What tones are those that are softly and sweetly playing." See Angel's serenade (Braga)

"What tongue can tell Thy greatness, Lord." J. S. Bach. e. DSH

"What virgin or shepherd in valley or grove." See The wedding day (Hook)

"What wakest thou, spring." See Breathings of spring (Weber)

What will happen when the Messiah comes (Was wet sain, àz Meshiach wet kümmen) Jewish folk song. e.y. BF 2

"What will I do gin my hoggie die." Air: What will I do, etc. Words by R. Burns. BSR

"What will you do, love." S. Lover (music and words) FSS 1—JO—WBT—WL

What wonders fill the sky. See "Wås eppä mehr muasz g'schĕchäsei"

What would I do for my queen. A. G. Thomas. KS 5—OPS 4

What yo' gwine to do when yo' lamp burn down. Negro spiritual. JB

What yo' gwine t' do when de lamp burn down. HR

"**What** you will to your father, Jimmy Randolph my son." See Lord Randall (Allanstand, N.C. version no. 1)

"**Whate'er** may vex or grieve thee." J. S. Bach. e. MS

"**Whatever** be our earthly lot." See Around the hearth

"**What's** a' the steer, kimmer." G. A. Lee. FSS 3—JO—MMS—PS 1

"**What's** sweeter than a new-blown rose." Händel. OS 1

"**What's** sweeter than the new-blown rose." J. Newton. ME

"**What's** the life you love to lead." See Questions and answers

"**What's** the use of your complaining." See The age of progress (Hutchinson)

"**What's** this dull town to me." See Robin Adair

"**Whaur'** hae ye been a' day." See My boy Tammie

"**Wheat** and barley bright with sunshine." C. Simper. Words by G. W. Brindley. HC

"A **wheel** in a wheel." Negro spiritual. DF—HR

The **wheelbarrow** loaders. See Gli scarriolanti

Wheeler, J. W.
"Don't forget dar's a weddin' to-night" (Ballou)

"**When** a bit of sunshine hits ye." See The sunshine boomerang (Harvey)

"**When** a child, I lived at Lincoln." See You never miss the water (Howard)

"**When** a little farm we keep." Mazzinghi. Words by F. Reynolds. BE 3

"**When** a maiden suggests a short stroll 'neath the moon." See I doubt it (Adams)

"**When** a maiden takes your fancy." See "Wer ein liebchen hat gefunden" (Mozart)

"**When** a trembling lover dies." Nathan. BE 2

"**When** absent from her." See The beautiful maid (Braham)

"**When** all the birds in Gaelic sang." See An uair bha gàilig aig na h-eòin

"**When** all the east is rosy." See El suspiro

"**When** all the sky is bright and clear." See L'oiselet (Chopin)

"**When** all the world is young." C. Barnard. Words by C. Kingsley. FSS 4 —LA

"**When** all the world is young." E. Schenck. Words by C. Kingsley. BD

"**When** all Thy mercies." G. F. Händel. Words by J. Addison. MS

"**When** all was young." See "Si le bonheur" (Gounod)

When Allah spoke. W. A. Fisher. Words by A. Bates. HST

When around thy dear face. See Se mai senti (Leo)

"**When** at night the rocks were shaking." See The talisman (Titov)

"**When** at night your street I pass." See Salitana

"**When** at nightfall so sweetly." See Ring forever (Gounod)

"**When** at the break of day." See Die beruhigte

"**When** at twilight so softly." See Chantez riez et dormez (Gounod)

"**When** baby's cheek press'd a soft hand, in rest." See Sövnen (Kjerulf)

"**When** bites the frost and winds are a-blowing." See Trinity Sunday

"**When** bright skies were o'er us and life lay before us." See Bowdoin beata

"**When** Britain first at heav'n's command." See Rule, Britannia (Arne)

"**When** busy fame." T. Farmer. CO 2

"**When** children lay them down to sleep." See Guardian angels (Schumann)

"**When** chill November's surly blast." Air: Peggy Bawn. Words by R. Burns. BSR

"**When** Chloë was by Damon seen." See The diffident lover (Howard)

"**When** Christ our Lord was born at Bethlehem afar." See Canzone d'i zampognari

"**When** Christ the Lord was here below." See Down by the river

"**When** Christ was born in Bethlehem" (Christmas carol) M. V. Locke. [Words from the Neapolitan] e. MCS

"**When** Christ was born in Bethlehem." W. P. Taylor. Words from the Neapolitan. e. HC

"**When** Christ was born of Mary free" (Gloria in excelsis) 16th century German carol. [Tr of Christo paremus canticam, excelsis gloria] e. MCS

"**When** Christ was born of Mary free." A. H. Brown. Tr of Christo paremus canticam, excelsis gloria. e. BSC—HC—MCS

"**When** Christ was born of pure Marie." H. S. Irons. Tr of Christo paremus canticam, excelsis gloria. e. HC

"**When** Christ was born on earth." See Canzone d'i zampognari

"**When** cold in the earth." Air: Limerick's lamentation. Words by T. Moore. MI—MMI

"**When** daffodils begin to peer." Composer unknown. Words by W. Shakespeare. BE 5

"When daisies pied and violets blue." T. A. Arne. Words by W. Shakespeare. BE 4—BOH—HSE 3——KSS—MM—PR 2

"When daisies pied and violets blue" (The cuckoo) VFS

"When daisies pied, and violets blue" (Spring) DM 1

"When Daisy's arms her poodle impris'n." See Don't I though (Brand)

"When Daphne from faire Phoebus did flie." See Daphne (17th century song)

"When dawned earth's greatest light." See El cant des aucels

"When day is done and by the fire we rest our weary feet." See Sing another song (Stevens)

"When daylight was yet sleeping under the billow." See Ill omens

"When de coons are gader'd." See She is my Angelina (Penney)

When de Debble comes 'round. Air: You shall have er new hidin'-place dat day, arr by H. T. Burleigh. Words by R. E. Phillips. BP

"When de shadders spread aroun'." See Humoreske (Dvořák)

"When deeds of fame, at honour's call." See Home, love and liberty (Bishop)

"When Delia on the plain appears." See O tell me, my heart, if this be love

"When dress as of old was intended for use." See Lack-a-day, O (Hook)

"When early morning's ruddy light." See The mowers' song

"When evening comes, and it's growing dark." See The lamps at night

"When eventide finds him before me." See J'ai peur de l'aimer (Denza)

"When fair Luna fills the skies." See Hymn of the fishermen's children (Hérold)

"When fairies are lighted by night's silver queen." Air: Ffarwel ednyfed fychan, or, Towyn castle. MMW

"When Fanny, blooming fair." Old English air. BE 7

"When far from my dear treasure." See "Lungi dal caro bene" (Secchi)

"When Father Noah built the ark aforetime." See Er passagallo

When fields are white. German folk air. Words by H. H. Harbour. DO

"When first a babe upon the knee." See Little Bess the ballad-singer

"When first his standard caught the eye." See O Charlie is my darling (Words by Gray)

"When first I came to be a man." See John of Badenyon

"When first I came to Stewart Kyle." Air: I had a horse, and I had nae mair. Words by R. Burns. BSR

"When first I came to the county Limerick." Irish folk song. JOI

"When first I kissed sweet Margaret." Student song. CHS

"When first I met thee." Air: O Patrick, fly from me. Words by T. Moore. MI

"When first I saw my lovely maid." G. F. Händel. SAS 2

"When first I saw sweet Peggy." See The low backed car

"When first I went to college." See The jolly sophomore

"When first into this town I came." See A chushla gal mochree

"When first my brave Johnnie lad." See Cock up your beaver

"When first the buds are blowing." See Der musensohn (Schubert)

"When first the magic of thy dear voice calls me." See My delight (Chopin)

"When first to college we were sent." See Fol de rol

"When first you courted me." See Donald

"When flowery May." Old English song. DM 2

"When flow'ry summer is at hand." See Sailors' and soldiers' memorial day

"When for aye for love you yearn." See "Quand la flamme de l'amour" (Bizet)

"When for my native land I sigh." See Der Tyroler und sein kind (Nesmüller)

"When forced from dear Hebe to go." T. A. Arne. Words by Shenstone. BE 7—HSE 1—JE—ME—PR 2

"When forced to bid farewell to Loo." See The tar's farewell (Maybrick)

"When France had her assistance lent." See Welcome, royal Charlie

"When Freedom from her mountain height." See The American flag (Tufts)

"When from the north the storm-winds come." See Fiskeren til sønnen (Elling)

"When gathered round the social board." See Alma mater—Colby (Crawford)

"When gazing in thine eyes." See "Wenn ich in deine augen seh'" (Bleikhman)

"When gentle winds." R. Schumann. Words by J. E. Carpenter. FSS 7—WBT

"When gloomy winter takes his flight." See Ma Normandie (Bérat)

When green leaves come again ("Oh! where do fairies hide their heads") H. R. Bishop. Words by T. H. Bayly. HSE 3

"When Guilford good our pilot stood." See The American war

"When, hand 'neath its cheek." See Sövnen (Kjerulf); Sövnen (Reissiger)

"When Harold was invaded." See Brave men of Kent (Leveridge)

"When Harry, the tailor was twenty years old." See Harry, the tailor

"When He cometh." G. F. Root. Words by W. O. Cushing. HSD—WBT

"When he dreams, when he dreams." See En dormant, c'est à moi (Halévy)

"When he who adores thee." Irish air: The foxes sleep. Words by T. Moore. MI—MMI

"When His salvation bringing." See Children's Hosanna (Webb)

"When Hope her cheering smile supplies." See Ma Normandie (Bérat)

When I am laid in earth. H. Purcell. Words by N. Tate. KS 3
Dido's lament. PR 1
Dido's song. BOH

"When I am near thee." See "Il mio bel foco" (Marcello)

"When I became a rover." See My parents treated me tenderly (Allanstand, N.C. version)

"When I beheld the first violet bloom." See Das erste veilchen (Mendelssohn)

"When I behold your manly form." See Gobble duet (Audran)

"When I can read my title clear." See My title clear (Arne)

When I come ("Muss i denn") See Abschied ("Muss i denn")

When I come t' die. Negro spiritual. HR

"When I did leave my own country." See Sept ans sur mer

"When I drain the rosy bowl." J. Baildon. Words by F. Fawkes. DM 1

"When I first came down to Rutgers." See Bow-wow-wow (Bragdon)

"When I first came to this country in eighteen and forty-nine." See Pretty Saro (Allanstand, N.C. version)

"When I first com'd to Lunnon." See The good-natured lad

"When I first was a civis I studied humanity." See A chequer'd career

"When I gaze at the stars." See Längtan (Söderman)

"When I get dere I will sit down an' tell." See When I come t' die

"When I go to draw the water, mother, at Jamna bank." See Gopi's complaint

"When I have often heard." H. Purcell. PR 1

"When I in morning's gloaming." See The dawning of morn

When I landed in Glasgow. See Eliza

"When I lay me down to sleep." See Evening prayer (Humperdinck)

"When I lib'd in Tennessee, u-li-a-li-o-la-e." See Rosa Lee

"When I look this way, you look that." See Liebesqual

"When I remember." A. Scott Gatty. Words by J. Ingelow. FSS 4

"When I see heav'n, gwine sing an' shout." See By-and-by

"When I see those little feet of thine." See "Seh' ich deine kleinen füsschen an" (Rubinstein)

"When I see water flowing." See Chi sa (Atri)

"When I set out I was but young." See Getting ready to die

"When I shall close my eyes for aye." See Weariness (Lahorsky)

"When I stopped at Kazan." See The siege of Kazan (Musorgskïi)

"When I survey the world around." See The leather bottél

"When I survey the wondrous cross." Air: Avon. Words by I. Watts. LA

"When I survey the wondrous cross." L. Mason. Words by I. Watts. WBT

"When I think on this warld's pelf." See Shame fa' the gear and the blathrie o't

"When I think upon Thy goodness." Haydn. e. HSS 1—HSS 3

"When I view the Mother holding." J. Barnby. [Tr of Parvum quando cerno Deum] e. BSC—HC—MCS

"When I view your comely grace." See Calino casturame

When I wake. W. Watts. Words anonymous. CMF 2

"When I was a bachelor airy and young." See The foggy dew

"When I was a beggar boy." See Aladdin (Bellini)

"When I was a beggarly boy." See Aladdin (Bellini)

"When I was a lad, I had cause to be sad." See Robinson Crusoe

"When I was a lady." Children's song. WSC

When I was a little boy. See "When that I was a little tiny boy" (Traditional air)

"When I was a little boy I lived by myself." See The swapping song

"When I was a little tiny boy." See When that I was a little tiny boy (Heise)

"When I was a maiden all crossed up in love." See Johnny Doyle (Virginia version)

"When I was a maiden fair and young." See The gardener's son

"When I was a seeker." See Go tell it on de mountain

"When I was a smart young lass." See Nobody coming to marry me

"When I was a student at Cadiz." See The Spanish guitar

"When I was a young girl." Singing game. FSF

"When I was a young man I lived upon the square." See Root hog or die

When I was a young one. T. A. Arne. Words by I. Bickerstaffe. ME

"When I was bound apprentice, in famous Lincolnshire." See The Lincolnshire poacher

"When I was bound apprentice, in famous Zummersetshire." See The poacher

"When I was down in Egypt's land." See My Lord's writing all the time

"When I was eighteen I took a wife." See The robber

"When I was gazing skyward." See Canzone di Somma

When I was seventeen. See När jag blef sjutton år

"When I was single, went dressed all so fine." See The single girl

"When I was young and in my prime and in my stable lay." See Poor old horse

"When I was young and in my prime, my age just twenty-one." See Erin's lovely home

"When I was young and scarce eighteen." See On board a ninety-eight

"When I was young Johnny I used to wait." See Jim crack corn

"When I went over Putman's hill." See Putman's hill

"When icicles hang by the wall." See The owl (Arne)

"When I'm an old alumnus." See The song of the A. B.

When I'm gone, when I'm gone. See O mother, don't you weep

"When in death I shall calm recline." See The legacy

"When in the setting sun ev'ry streamlet is gleaming." See Beau soir (Debussy)

"When in the street called Dove street." See La calle de la paloma

"When Israel was in Egypt's land." See Go down, Moses

"When I've a saxpence under my thumb." See Todlen hame

"When Jack is tall and twenty." Words by F. Langbridge. FSS 8

"When Januar' wind was blawin cauld." Air: The lass made the bed to me. Words by R. Burns. BSR

"When Jesus Christ was yet a child." See The crown of roses (Tchaikovsky)

When Joan's ale was new ("There were five jolly good fellows") Old English song. BOS
For variant see following song of same title

When Joan's ale was new ("There were three jovial fellows") Old English song. SSS

"When Jockey dances on the green." See Jockey

"When Johnie Scot saw this big, broad letter." See Johnie Scot

"When Johnny comes marching home." L. Lambert (music and words) BOS—HSD—MP—OH—SSS—TFC 1—WBT—WSW

"When Jordan hushed." E. C. Phelps. Words by T. Campbell. MCS

"When joyous tho'ts on thy sweet lips awaken." See Margherita (Gounod)

"When lambkins skip, and apples are growing." See A country lass

"When lawyer Lee went out one day." See Lawyer Lee

"When leaves are falling sere." A. Alpheraky. Words from the Russian of A. Umanetz. e. NM 1

"When life was gay." Gaelic tune: Robi donn gòrach. MMS

"When like the early rose, Eileen aroon." See Eileen aroon

"When little birdie bye-bye goes." See Lullaby (Elliott)

"When little Samuel woke." L. Edson. FSS 4

"When Lord Thomas he came home." See The gypsy laddie (Hot Springs, N.C. version)

"When love is kind." Old Irish air. Words by T. Moore. EF—ES—KF 2—PO—SM 3

When love was born. M. Wellings. MCS

"When love with unconfinèd wings." See To Althea (Wilson)

"When low the sun his latest ray." See Santa Claus is come to town

"When Lubin sings of youth's delight." J. W. Hobbs. Words by J. Gill. BE 6—HSE 3

"When Maggie and I was acquaint." Scottish air: Tweedside. Words by John, Lord Yester. PS 2

"When Mamie's glove her hand so tightly squeezes." See Mamie's charms (Jones)

"When marshalled on the nightly plain." See The star of Bethlehem

"When matadors are fighting." See Bolero

"When May breezes blow." See 's mailüfterl (Kreipl)

"When May-day makes tremble each leaf and flow'r in sunlit air." See Vaarvise

"When me fair dreams awaken." See "Par che mi dica ancora" (Donizetti)

"When merry hearts were gay." Scottish air: Donald and Flora. Words by H. Macneil. PS 2

"When midnight comes, and all are gone." See "Steh' ich in finstrer mitternacht" (Volksweise)

"When mighty roast beef was the Englishman's food." See The roast beef of old England (Leveridge)

"When Molly smiles beneath her cow." See The ploughman's ditty

"When Moses an' his soldiers." See He's jus' de same today

"When musing sorrow weeps the past." See Resignation (Mendelssohn)

"When my grandfather my grandmother wed." See Das grossvaterlied

"When my guitar I am playing." See La gitana

"When, my love, wilt thou return." See "Il mio ben quando verrà" (Paisiello)

"When my money was gone." See The disconsolate sailor (Hook)

"When my Normandy I quitted." See "Nel lasciar la Normandia" (Meyerbeer)

"When my radiant one is nigh." See Minnelied (Brahms)

"When nature first salutes the spring." See Two bunches a penny primroses (Hook)

"When night comes o'er the plain." S. Nelson. FSS 5

"When nightingales in pensive vales." See Andenken (Beethoven)

"**When** night's shadows fly." See New Year song

"**When** Noah left the ark for good." See Noah (Reissiger)

"**When** nocturnal shadows gliding." See The song of songs (Alferakiï)

"**When** o'er the hill the eastern star." See The lea rig (Scottish air)

"**When** o'er this earth of ours." See "Volta la terrea fronte alle stelle" (Verdi)

"**When** on its couch of rosy clouds." See Good night and pleasant dreams (Wallace)

"**When**, on Ramillies' bloody field." See Clare's dragoons

"**When** on the college campus." See Evening on the campus

"**When** on the world's first harvest day." See The blushing maple tree (McCaskey)

"**When** once I was a shepherd boy." English folk song. BE 1

"**When** once with Chloe quite alone." See Der kuss (Beethoven)

"**When** onward I am gazing." N. W. Gade. e. SAS 2

"**When** oppress'd by soft slumber." See Serenade

"**When** Orpheus went down." Boyce. Words from the Spanish. e. BE 5

"**When** other friends are round thee." Words by G. P. Morris. FSS 3—JO —WBT

"**When** other hands are clasp'd in thine." See Only once more (Moir)

"**When** other lips." See Then you'll remember me (Balfe)

"**When** our boys come home in triumph, brother." See Sleeping for the flag (Work)

"**When** ower the hill the eastern star." See The lea rig (Reid)

"**When** parting for the Holy land." See Partant pour la Syrie (Hortense Eugénie de Beauharnais)

"**When** Patty wanders far away." See Sweet Patty (Hook)

"**When** pensive I thought of my love." M. Kelly. Words by G. Colman. BE 3 —HSE 2

"**When** Phoebus addrest." 17th century song. CO 1—JE

"**When** Phoebus begins just to peep." Hunting song of the 18th century. ME

"**When** Phoebus bright." Attributed to Burn, a border minstrel (music and words) PS 2

"**When** plays my vagrant fancy." See Der einsame (Schubert)

"**When** returning from the city." See Ils m'ont appelé vilaine

"**When** rival lads and lasses gay." See He piped so sweet (Hook)

When roses bloom. German song. e. FSS 6

"**When** rosy May comes in wi' flowers." Air: The gardener's march. Words by R. Burns. BSR

"**When** sailing o'er time's restless sea." See The breeze from home

"**When** sev'nteen years old." See Abandoned

"**When** shall come spring's delightful weather." See Villanelle (Berlioz)

"**When** shall we meet again." L. Mason. FSS 1

"**When** shall we three meet again." HSD —JO—WBT

"**When** she answered me her voice was low." Irish air. Words by A. P. Graves. FSI—PI

"**When** she is gone." A. Metzger. CHS —NML

"**When** shepherds pipe their lay." C. Saint-Saëns. Words by U. Fairweather. BD

"**When** ships afar are steering." See On the deep

"**When** slumbers sweet enfold thee." F. H. Forsell. Words by M. Dana. NML

"**When** snow lies deep." Rossini. MCS

"**When** soft stars are peeping." See Sweet memories of thee

"**When** soft the breezes sweetly are blowing." See "Se l'aura spira" (Frescobaldi)

"**When** Sol drops down far behind the mountains." See Solefaldssang (Olsen)

"**When** spring arrays the earth with flowers." See I will be happy too (Nelson)

"**When** spring was young and leaves were green." See I wait, my love, for thee (Scott-Gatty)

"**When** spring's first violet dawn'd on my sight." See Das erste veilchen (Mendelssohn)

"**When** stars are in the quiet skies." Words by E. Bulwer, Lord Lytton. JO—WBT

"**When** stealing down her pallid cheek." See "Una furtiva lagrima" (Donizetti)

"**When** Steerwell heard me first impart." See The post captain (Shield)

"**When** summer comes." Irish air: Domnal og, or, Little Donnell. Words by D. Sigerson. MMI

"**When** summer's radiant months are come." See The false knight

"**When** sweet music." G. A. Macfarren. FSS 6

"**When** that I was a little boy" (Clown's song) R. Schumann. Words by W. Shakespeare. VFS

"**When** that I was a little tiny boy." Old English air. Words by W. Shakespeare. BE 1—DM 1—HSE 2—MM

"**When** [that] I was a little tiny boy" ("Dengang jag var kun saa stor som saa") P. Heise. Words by W. Shakespeare. da.e. WM 1

"**When** that I was a little tiny boy." J. Vernon. Words by W. Shakespeare. VFS

"When that I was a little tiny boy." For German translation with a different air see "Als büblein klein an der mutter brust" (Nicolai)

"When that I was and a tiny boy." See "Als büblein klein an der mutter brust" (Nicolai)

"When the Alabama's keel was laid." See Alabama

"When the autumn tiptoes softly." See Come ye back to old Grinnell (Olds)

When the birds go north again. R. H. Warren. Words by E. Higginson. HST

"When the black-letter'd list to the gods was presented." See Wife, children, and friends

When the bloom is on the rye ("My pretty Jane") H. R. Bishop. Words by E. Fitzball. EF—FSS 4—KF 3—NML

The bloom is on the rye ("My pretty Jane") DM 1—HSE 2—TS—WBT

"My pretty Jane." BE 3

When the boats come home. T. Moore. Words by S. Doudney. FSS 5

When the Bridegroom comes. Negro spiritual. DF—JP

"When the bright god of day." See The vocal grove (Young)

"When the chill charokoe blows." See In praise of ale

"When the chill sirocco blows." See In praise of ale

"When the corn is waving." C. Blamphin. FSS 6—HSC—WA—WBT—WL—WSW

"When the crimson sun had set." S. S. Greatheed. Words by G. P. Grantham. HC

"When the day with rosy light." FSS 1—WBT

"When the day's shadows die." See The sun is low

"When the dear Alps I climb." See Alpine peace

"When the dews of eve are falling." See Sweet constancy

When the drive goes down. Air: Song of a gambolier. Words by D. Malloch. BSS

"When the drum-beat charms, each bold British tar." Chantey. SMW

"When the drums do beat." See The captain's lady

"When the fair land of Poland was ploughed by the hoof." See Fair land of Poland (Balfe)

"When the farmer has fallowed and tilled all the land." See Harvest home (Atterbury)

"When the flame of love." See "Quand la flamme de l'amour" (Bizet)

"When the glow-worm gilds the elfin flow'r." See The banks of the blue Moselle (Rodwell)

"When the golden morn gilds Loo Lung hills." See The pagoda bells (Comer)

When the grand old flag goes by. W. G. Wilmarth. Words by T. Stanley. BSS

"When the green leaves." Old song. FSS 2

"When the gypsies want to show." See The patteran (Ames)

When the heart is at ease. T. A. Arne. ME

"When the heathen trumpets clang." See The monks of Bangor's march

"When the house of life is ringing." See Behold! I stand at the door (Jude)

"When the humid showers gather." See Rain on the roof (Clifford); Rain on the roof (Naumann)

"When the humid shadows hover." See Rain on the roof (Clark)

"When the king came in to Paris town." See Les trois roses empoisonnées

When the king comes owre the water. Scottish air. Words by Keith. PS 1

When the king enjoys his own again. 17th century air: The king's delight. Words by M. Parker. BOS—CO 1—DM 1—JE—MM—PR 1—SSS

When the kye come hame ("Come, all ye jolly shepherds") Old Border air: Shame fa' the gear and the blathrie o't. Words by J. Hogg. FSS 5 —HSSS—MMS—PS 1

When the kye comes hame. JO

When the leaves are turning brown. T. Crampton. FSS 3

"When the leaves from the trees are falling." See Happy summer (Planquette)

When the lights are low. G. M. Lane. HSD—WBT—WBW

"When the linden's in flower. See Lind (Backer-Gröndahl)

"When the little stars am peepin'." See Maisie (Macgregor)

"When the lovely spring comes o'er the hills." See "Wenn der frühling auf die berge steigt" (Becker)

"When the matin bell is ringing." See Uralio

"When the mists." J. J. Rousseau. Words by A. Herbert. FSS 7

Rousseau's hymn. LA

"When the moon is afloat." See Norman cradle song (De Koven)

"When the moon is beaming, o'er the waters gleaming." See Child's dreamland (Roeder)

"When the moon is shining and the little stars are pining." See Humoreske (Dvořák)

"When the moon rises over Marechiare." See Marechiare (Tosti)

"When the moon shone bright." See "Au clair de la lune"

"When the moon was the size av a cartwheel." See The time for love

"When the morn, when the morn o'er the mountain glows." See The Swiss girl (Moscheles)

"When the morning peeps forth." Hunting song. J. Hook. ME

"When the murm'ring brooklet gushes." See "Se bel rio" (Rontani)

"When the night in dusky shadows." See "Wenn die nacht mit ihrem schleier" (Abt)

"When the night was spent and the day coming in." See Fair Margaret and sweet William (Woodridge, Va. version)

"When the night-wind bewaileth." W. R. Dempster. Words by E. Sargent. FSS 6—JO

"When the nightingale shall sing." See "Quant li rosignol jolis" (Coucy)

"When the north wind keenly blows." See The north wind (Scott-Gatty)

"When the pale moon drowns the wide world." See Dawn (Somerset)

"When the people all are cheering." See When the grand old flag goes by (Wilmarth)

"When the plane-trees are glooming." See Havanaise (Paladilhe)

"When the red-coats all a-snorting." See The battle of Harlem heights

"When the roses bloom again, my love." See When roses bloom

"When the roses bloom in the gladsome days of summer." Ruthenian folk air. Words by R. R. Whitehead. WF

"When the scarlet cardinal tells." See July (Olds)

"When the shades of evening gather." Ursinus college song. Words by C. G. Petri. CHS

"When the shadows gently gather." See Chiquita (Gomis)

"When the sheep are in the fauld." See Auld Robin Gray (Scottish air); Auld Robin Gray (Leeves)

"When the ship is trim and ready." See They all love Jack (Maybrick)

"When the shepherds seek to woo." See Advice to the fair sex

"When the silvery moon gleams thro' the woven boughs." See Die mainacht (Brahms)

"When the sky blushes rose in the sunset." See 'O bene antico (Nutile)

"When the sky is low and leaden." See Polly (Smith)

When the soft twilight. R. Schumann. Words by J. E. Carpenter. FSS 5

"When the Son of man." Sullivan. OS 4

"When the spider goes out for a walk." See La rana

"When the spring has climb'd the mountain's height." See Spring song (Weil)

"When the spring laughs on winter's snow." See Au printemps (Gounod)

"When the spring with magic finger." Polish air. Words by A. J. Foxwell. TFC 2

"When the spring's soft breezes o'er the mountains blow." See Love in springtime

"When the springtide o'er the hills is seen." See "Wenn der frühling auf die berge steigt" (Becker); "Wenn der frühling auf die berge steigt" (Coenen)

"When the stars are in the quiet skies." Words by E. L. Bulwer. FSS 2

When the stormy winds do blow. See "You gentlemen of England"

"When the summer days are bright and long." See Under the trees (Munjinger)

"When the summer rain is over." Donizetti. e. FSS 4

"When the sun affords no light." See Bonnie lad and gentle lassie

"When the sun fades far away." See Evening song at Cornell

"When the sun in heaven rising." See The tribute of the birds (Donizetti)

"When the sun is just arising." See I am thinking, love, of thee (Atkinson)

"When the sun sets on the mountain so olden." See Shadows at play

When the sun shines ("Gdy w czystem polu słoneczko świeci") Polish folk song. e.p. BF 1

"When the swallow comes." C. Pinsuti. Words by F. Enoch. FSS 6

"When the swallows homeward fly." See Abschied (Abt)

"When the toil of day is ended." See That Wilson chum of mine

"When the toys are growing weary." See The dustman (Molloy)

"When the vengeance wakes." See Remember the Maine (Converse)

"When the village is sleeping." See The wolves (Arenski)

"When the war-cry of liberty rang through the land." See The death of Warren (Dempster)

"When the warm breezes whisper." See 's mailüfterl (Kreipl)

"When the waves are gently flowing." See Dein gedenk' ich, Margaretha (Meyer-Helmund)

"When the weary, seeking rest." J. Stainer. Words by H. Bonar. LA

When the west wind blows. Irish air. Words by J. B. Dollard. FSI

"When the whippoorwills are calling." See At the making of the hay (Lehmann)

When the wine whirls. See La grande et la petite

"When the year is new." W. H. Jones. NMS

When this cruel war is over. H. Tucker. Words by C. C. Sawyer. FSS 5—HSD—MP—WBT

"When this scene of trouble closes." Spohr. e. OS 1—SAS 1

When this warfare'll be ended. See "Children, you'll be called on"

"When thou art nigh." Irish air: 'Tis a pity I don't see my love. Words by T. Moore. MMI

"When thou dost see the dark flood below." See Ever thine (Kalliwoda)

"When thou stand'st up with me." See "En gång i bredd med mig"

"When thou'rt cradled at eve on my breast." See Chantez riez et dormez (Gounod)

"When thro' life unblest we rove." See On music

"When through love's garden at nightfall I glide." See Le jardin d'amour

"When through the night my watch I keep." See "Steh' ich in finstrer mitternacht" (Volksweise)

"When through the piazzetta" ("Wenn durch die piazzetta") A. Jensen. Words by T. Moore. e.g. FF—FO 1

"When through the piazzetta" (Venetianisches gondellied) F. Mendelssohn. Words by T. Moore. e.g. TS

"When through the woodland walking." Air: The noble sheriff. DM 2

"When thy song on the still ev'ning air soareth so high." See Chantez riez et dormez (Gounod)

"When time was young and the school was new." See Saint Joles

"When 'tis May, and the world is telling." See Villanelle (Berlioz)

"When 'tis night and the mid-watch is come." See The mid-watch (Linley)

"When to-morrow's sun shall rise." See Lebewohl (Silcher)

"When to the church unto service I go." See Dreamings

"When to the lily fair." S. Mercadante. e. SAS 3

"When to thy vision." See "Si le bonheur à sourire" (Gounod)

"When told by wandering lovers." See The rover

"When trees did bud" (Doun the burn, Davie) Scottish air. Words by R. Crawford. MMS

"When trees did bud" (Down the burn, Davie) D. Maigh. Words by R. Crawford. FSS 6—JO

"When Troy town for ten years wars." See Troy town (Wilson)

"When twilight comes with shadows drear." See Dreams (Strelezki)

"When twilight dews are falling fast." See Twilight dews (Moore)

"When twilight falls on the dim old walls." See When the lights are low (Lane)

"When twilight shades come stealing o'er thy pillow." See The hero's serenade (Jarvis)

"When two that love are parted." See "Lungi dal caro bene" (Sarti)

"When up the mountain climbing." Swiss air. FSS 3

"When Venus the goddess of beauty and love." See Nottingham ale (Purcell)

"When Vulcan forged the bolts of Jove." See The origin of gunpowder (Braham)

"When war-like ensigns wave on high." Händel. OS 3

"When we are gone, love." See Wood song (Watts)

"When we around our blazing fires." See Around our blazing fires (Nelson)

"When we arrive at home (Garden) J. Ingalls. FSS 5

"When we first came on this campus." See Co-ca-che-lunk

"When we gaed to the braes o' Mar." Air: Up, and warn a', Willie. Words by R. Burns. BSR

"When we met at Piedigrotta." See La vera Sorrentina

"When we started in our scouting." See Co-ca-che-lunk

"When wild the night." See The good shepherd (Barry)

"When wild war's deadly blast was blawn." See The soldier's return

"When will the day e'er be." See "Quando sarà quel dì" (Tenaglia)

"When will you come again, my faithfu' Johnnie." See Faithfu' Johnnie

"When wilt Thou save the people." J. Booth. Words by E. Elliott. TFC 1

"When winds are fiercely raving." See "Del minacciar del vento" (Händel)

"When winter winds are blowing." See New Year's day

"When with doubting and dreading." See Preghiera (Tosti)

"When with Jessie I spent the long days." See Jessie

"When woods are dark and late the hour." See Poet and critic (Cui)

"When ye gang awa, Jamie." See Huntingtower

"When ye were sleepin' on your pillows." See Caller herrin' (Gow?)

When you and I were young ("I'm standing by the window sill") G. B. Allen. FSS 2

When you and I were young, Maggie ("I wandered today to the hill") J. A. Butterfield. Words by G. W. Johnson. TFC 1—WA—WBT—WL

When you and I were young. HSC—HSD—NMH

"When you often meet my gazes." See Malatu p'amuri

"When you slept." H. Kjerulf. Words by V. Hugo. e. WBW

"When you start upon a hike." See Don't fight your pack

"When you surprised me with your smile." See Le charme (Chausson)

"When you're making up your pack." See My old horse-blanket pin (Ames)

"When you've grown up, my dears." See Toyland (Herbert)

"When you've hiked a half hundred miles." See "Ho, for the slum"

"Whence comes this rush of wings." See Nouèl des ausèls

"Whence comes this unwonted oppression." Salut! demeure chaste et pure (Gounod)

"Whence the last wind's agitation." See Suleika (Mendelssohn)

"Whene'er afar ye are roaming." See Heimweh (Wolf)

"Whene'er I ride thro' the charmed grove." See Olufs ballade (Gade)

"Whene'er I see those smiling eyes." Irish air: Father Quinn. Words by T. Moore. MI—MMI

"Whene'er my pride of spirit yields." See Les trois prières (Paladilhe)

"Whene'er she came her presence was to me." See Kommen und scheiden (Schumann)

"Whene'er the sailor sails o'er the ocean." See "Hay un marino"

"Whene'er we come into the halls." See Baker university hymn (Hatton)

"Whenever sore I long for home." See Der Tyroler und sein kind (Nesmüller)

"Whenever we meet you here we say." See A little more faith in Jesus

"Whenever you go to Liverpool." See Wo, Stormalong

"Whenever you have some time to spare." See Johnny, go get a scout

"Where am I." See Ô ma lyre immortelle (Gounod)

"Where are now the hopes I cherished." See "In mia man alfin tu sei" (Bellini)

"Where are the birds of May." Croatian folk air. Words by G. D. Donaldson. WF

"Where are the friends of my youth." G. Barker. FSS 2—WBT

"Where are the joys I hae met in the morning." Air: Saw ye my father. Words by R. Burns. BSB—BSR—MMS—PS 1

"Where are the vintage songs." See Far o'er the sea (Kingsley)

Where are those dreamers now. See The graves of a household (Barker)

"Where are you going, Billie boy, Billie boy." See My boy Willie

"Where are you going, my pretty maid." I. Nathan. FSS 3
"Where are you going to, my pretty maid." DO—WSC

"Where are you going? says the knight in the road." See The false knight upon the road (North Carolina version)

"Where are you going to, my pretty maid." See "Where are you going, my pretty maid" (Nathan)

"Where are you going? To Scarborough fair." See Scarborough fair

Where art thou. See Dove sei (Händel)

"Where art thou my darling, my sweet." See My sweet (Leleiohuko)

"Where be ye, my love, my love." 15th century song. DM 2

"Where be you going, you Devon maid." V. Jackson. Words by J. Keats. DM 1

"Where, braving angry winter's storms." N. Gow. Words by R. Burns. BSR

"Where can I hide, O heaven." See Terra adorata de' padri miei (Donizetti)

"Where can you find more charming face or fairer." See Madrigal dans le style ancien (Indy)

"Where, dear maid." Old English air. BE 7

Where did you grow ("Kur tu augi") Latvian folk song. e.le. BF 1

"Where do you think I found my soul." See Listen to the angels

"Where-e'er you walk." See "Where'er you walk" (Händel)

"Where flows the bright river." See "Am ufer des flusses, des Manzanares" (Jensen)

Where Gadie rins. Scottish air. Words by J. Imlah. FSS 5
"O! gin I were where Gadie rins." MMS—PS 2

"Where ha'e ye been a' the day." See Bonnie laddie, Highland laddie

"Where ha'e ye been sae braw, lad." Scottish song. PS 2

Where has my little dog gone. College song. S. Winner. CHS—JSE—MPC
Dutch warbler. WBT—WC—WSW
Where is my little dog gone. WSC

"Where hast thou hid thy sweet fragrance." See Gardenia flower (Nape)

"Where have they laid Him." A. Sullivan. OS 1—SAS 1

"Where have you been a-roving, Jimmy Randal my son." See Lord Randal (Swannanoah, N.C. version)

"Where have you been all the day, Rendal, my son." See Lord Rendel

"Where have you been, Billy boy, Billy." See My boy Willie (North Carolina version no. 2)

"Where have you been growing, my sweet." See Where did you grow

"Where hes ti' been, maw canny hinny." See Captain Bover

"Where hide myself." See "Wo berg' ich mich" (Weber)

"Where in the vale the pathway's dividing." See Love's sorrow

"Where is another sweet." A. Sullivan. Words by Tennyson. MSF 2

"Where is John." Smetana. Words by A. Horn. TFC 2

"Where is my home." See My fatherland (Škroup)

Where is my little dog gone. See Where has my little dog gone (Winner)

"Where is my Owen, where is my true love." Air: The red piper's melody. MMW

"Where is now the merry party." See Far away (Bliss)

"Where is the far land lying." See Ah! my sad song dies away (Lindblad)

"Where is the German fatherland." See Des Deutschen vaterland (Reichardt)

"Where is the true man's fatherland" (The fatherland) C. G. Bellmann. Words by J. R. Lowell. LBR

"Where is the true man's fatherland" (Thy land) Reichardt. Words by J. R. Lowell. LA

"Where juts yonder headland." See Menaeceus (Cherepnin)

"Where loud my heavy hammers sound." See "Au bruit des lourds marteaux d'airain" (Gounod)

"Where loud the mill-wheel roareth." See "In einem kühlen grunde" (Glück)

Where my home lies. Old song. FSS 7

"When night spreads her shadows around." See Yarico to her lover (Himmel)

"Where now the clear water." See At the spring

"Where, O where are the verdant freshmen." College song. CHS—MPC—NMS—WBT

"Where, O where are the visions of morning." See The visions of morning

"Where Potomac's stream is flowing Virginia's border through." See Mount Vernon bells (Jones)

"Where roses fair around our path are lying." See "I rosens doft" (Gustaf)

"Where roses grow, in bowr's of sweet seclusion." See "I rosens doft" (Gustaf)

"Where shall I be when de firs' trumpet soun'." Negro spiritual. HR—JB

"Where shall the Prince of peace be born." See The crib and the cross (Boulter)

Where sleepest thou, my dearie. Scottish song. Words from the Gaelic of Fionn. e. HSSS

"Where snow-crown'd mountains rear their summits t'wards the sky." See Oh! thou my Austria (Suppé)

"Where sweeps round the mountains the cloud on the gale." See Where the eagle is king (Hartley)

"Where tears of my passion have fallen." See Flowers of love (Borodin)

"Where, tell me, handsome cavalier." See Par le sentier (Dubois)

Where the aspens quiver. See "Come where the aspens quiver" (Lee)

"Where the bee sucks." T. A. Arne. Words by W. Shakespeare. BE 1—BOH—DM 1—HSE 1— KSS— MM—PR 2—SS 1—VFS

"Where the bee sucks." P. Humfrey. Words by W. Shakespeare. KSS—VFS

"Where the bee sucks." R. Johnson. Words by W. Shakespeare. BSE—KSS—VFS

"Where the bee sucks." A. Sullivan. Words by W. Shakespeare. KSS—MSS 2—SS 2

"Where the cliff looks o'er the valley." See The willow tree

Where the eagle is king. W. F. Hartley. Words by T. B. Read. LBR

"Where the elm-tree branches by the rain are stirred." See Singing in the rain (Haydn)

"Where the faded flower." Words by H. Bonar. FSS 7

"Where the Lehigh's rocky rapids." See Alma mater—Lehigh

"Where the lilacs threw their shade." See Prince Charming (Roeckel)

"Where the rolling foothills rise up t'wards mountains higher." See Hail, Stanford, hail

"Where the vale of Onondaga meets the eastern sky." See Alma mater—Syracuse

"Where the warbling waters flow." See Where warbling waters (Richards)

Where the wicked cease from troubling. H. Parker. HSS 3—HSS 4

"Where the wild rose sweetly doth blow." See The wild rose (Strauss)

"Where to find my lover can you tell me, pray." See Le rosier d'argent

"Where under birches the snow-cover lies." See The snowdrop (Grechaninov)

Where warbling waters. B. Richards. FSS 6

"Where were you all the day, my own pretty boy." Irish folk song. JOI

"Where were you Cveta" ("Deka si bila") Macedonia-Bulgarian song. b.e. BF 1

"Where wert thou yestereven." See L'avvelenato

"Where, where are you." See T' ses tüta mia furtüna

"Where, where will be the birds that sing." See A hundred years to come (Brown)

"Where wilt thou go, my agile little swallow." See La golondrina (Serradell)

"Where would I be." C. Zöllner. LA—WC

"Where'er I go, a time-piece I bear about with me." See Die uhr (Loewe)

"Where'er man ranges." See "Waer dat men sich"

"Where'er you walk." Händel. Words by Pope; wrongly attributed to W. Congreve. BC—BD—TS

"Wherefore have thy lips denied me." See Modinha

"Wherefore sparkle with dew drops." See "Hvorfor svömmer dit öie tidt i en taareglands" (Rosenfeld)

Wherein have I offended. See Che t'ho fatto

"Where's my dear love gone." Ruthenian folk air. Words by R. R. Whitehead. WF

"Whereto should I express." Henry VIII. CO 1—JE

"Wherever I am or whatever I doe." P. Humphrey. MM

"Wherever I go I command." See "Je marche sur tous les chemins" (Massenet)

"Wherto shuld I expresse." See "Whereto should I express" (Henry VIII)

"Whet up your knife, and whistle up your dog." See The ground hog

"Whether day dawns" ("Ob heller tag") P. I. Tchaikovsky. Words by A. Apuchtin. e.g. FO 2

"Whether you whisper low." Round. FSS 8

"Which way does the wind blow." Children's song. FSS 8—WBT—WSC

Whichello, Abiel
  "Oh! forbear"
"Whichever way the wind doth blow."
  Words by C. A. Mason. FSS 3—LA
"While angels thus, O Lord, rejoice." See
  The Child is born (Giardini)
"While beaux to please the ladies write."
  See Kitty Fell
"While ev'rything reposes." See "Tandis
  que tout sommeille" (Grétry)
"While gazing on the moon's light." Irish
  air: Oonagh. Words by T. Moore.
  MI—MMI
"While high the foaming surges rise." Sea
  song. ME
"While history's muse." Air: Paddy
  Whack. Words by T. Moore. JO—
  MI
"While humble shepherds watched their
  flocks." See While shepherds watched
  their flocks (Fink)
"While I hang on your bosom distracted
  to leave you." See Oh, no! my love,
  no (Kelly)
"While I listen to thy voice." H. Lawes.
  NG
"While I on earth abide." See Light of
  the world (Hatton)
"While I still lived at my father's, folderol-
  dee." See La danse du troupeau
"While I was out a-walking." See "A la
  claire fontaine"
"While I watch the yellow wheat." See
  Watching the wheat
"While in peaceful slumbers lying." H.
  T. Tiltman. HC
"While larks with little wing." See Phil-
  lis the fair
"While living with my father." See La
  fille à la fontaine (Breton version)
"While merrily once riding thro' cool and
  shady wood." See Jagdlied (Mendels-
  sohn)
"While o'erhead the storm is howling."
  Air: Of all the comforts I miscarried.
  Modern words by F. Kidson. MM
"While Phillis refuses my love to requite."
  See Easy and gay
"While shepherds watched their flocks."
  Old English air. Words by N. Tate.
  FSS 7—MCS
"While shepherds watched their flocks."
  Composer unknown. Words by N.
  Tate. HC
"While shepherds watched their flocks."
  J. Clarke. Words by N. Tate. MCS
[**While** shepherds watched their flocks]
  "While humble shepherds watched their
  flocks." G. W. Fink. Words from
  N. Tate. HC
"While shepherds watched their flocks."
  G. F. Händel. Words by N. Tate.
  WBT
"While shepherds watched their flocks"
  (The vision of the shepherds) A. P.
  Howard. Words by N. Tate. HC
"While shepherds watched their flocks."
  Arr from Methfessel. [Words by N.
  Tate] LA

"While shepherds watched their flocks."
  W. Tansur. [Words by N. Tate]
  WS
"While still I lived at home." See La
  fille à la fontaine (Norman version)
While the days are going by. [J. Wyeth]
  Words by A. Nettleton. FSS 2
"While the lads of the village." Dibdin
  (music and words) HSE 1
"While the morning bells are ringing" (Si-
  cilian hymn) FSS 2
While the stars of heaven shall burn. See
  Hail Columbia, The new (Phile)
"While the sun shines in wonted splendor."
  See Déception (Tchaikovsky)
"While thee I seek." J. B. Dykes. Words
  by H. M. Williams. BD
While there are such things as dice. See
  À quoi bon l'économie (Massenet)
"While there's a pearl in the depth of the
  sea." See Star of my heart (Den-
  za)
"While this heart its joy revealing." See
  "Sovra il sen" (Bellini)
While to Bethl'em going. J. J. Rousseau.
  Words by J. Bowring. MCS
"While we live she is still living." See
  Polish national song (Oginski?)
"While we shed a tear." Words by J.
  Addison. FSS 6
"While yet a boy, I told you how I lov'd
  you." See "Fanciullo appena, ti par-
  lai d'amore"
"While yet the fields are wrapp'd in snow."
  See Floods of spring (Rachmaninov)
"While you here do snoring lie." Attrib-
  uted to Arne. Words by W. Shakes-
  peare. KSS
While you sleep. H. K. Hadley. Words
  by W. K. Clifford. TL
"Whilst Bethlehem's shepherds kept their
  flocks." E. H. Smith. Words by L.
  Bainbridge. HC
The Whip club. W. Reeve. Words by
  C. Dibdin, jun. ME
Whip jamboree. Capstan chantey. SE
Whip-poor-will. W. W. Gilchrist. Words
  by F. Manley. TL
"Whirl, my spool; go whirling, whirling."
  See The spool
"Whiskey is the life of man." See Whis-
  key Johnny
Whiskey Johnny ("Whiskey is the life")
  Halliard chantey. CR
  For variants of this song see following
    songs of similar title
Whisky for my Johnnie ("Oh, whisky is
  the life") Long drag chantey. KB
Whisky for my Johnny ("Oh whisky is
  the life."—Whisky Johnny) Chantey.
  SMW
Whisky for my Johnny ("Whisky is the
  life") Pulling chantey. SE
Whisper what thou feelest. B. Richards.
  FSS 7
  "O whisper what thou feelest." WBT
"Whisper, whisper." Finnish folk air.
  Words anonymous. WF

Whistle and hoe ("There's a boy just over the garden fence") FSS 2
Whistle, daughter, whistle. English folk song. SEF 1—SO
Whistle o'er the lave o't. J. Bruce. Words by R. Burns. BSB—PS 1
  "First when Maggie was my care." BSR
Whitaker, John
  Darby Kelly
  "I went to the fair"
  "Oh, hush thee, my babie" (Tr of Caidil gu lo)
  Oh! rest thee, babe. See "Oh, hush thee, my babie"
  "Oh! say not woman's heart is bought"
  "O slumber, my darling." See "Oh, hush thee, my babie"
  Scotch lullaby. See "Oh, hush thee, my babie"
  Thine am I, my faithful fair
White, A. C.
  "Joyously, joyously, silvery clear"
White, Mrs Alice Mary (Smith)
  "O that we two were maying"
White, C. A.
  "I'se gwine back to Dixie"
White, Edward L.
  "Don't kill the birds"
  The ocean
  "Over the mountain wave"
White, Henry Kirke
  "Oft in danger, oft in woe" (Composer unknown)
  The star of Bethlehem (Composer unknown)
White, Maude Valerie
  How do I love thee
White as the snow. See Blanche comme la neige
White blossoms. W. C. Levey. FSS 7
The white cockade. English folk song. BSW
"White dawn has not come stealing" (Sve veselo a ja tužan) Serbian folk song. e.se. BF 1
"The white dawn is stealing." Iroquois tribal air. C. W. Cadman. Words by N. R. Eberhart. CF
The white dove. See La paloma blanca
The white duck. See Le canard blanc
"White folks, I'll sing for you." See My brudder Gum (Foster)
The white hawk. See El Queléle
"White-petalled blowers are born so lovely." See "Las blancas flores"
"White sand and gray sand." Round. FSS 3
The white snow (Ne bĭely snĭegi) Russian folk song. e. SSR 2
The white squall. G. A. Barker. Words by Captain Johns. HSE 3—JO
Whitehead, Ralph Radcliffe
  "All the night was dark and dreary" (Polish air)
  Autumn glory (Russian air)
  The beloved (Finnish air)
  Castles in the air (Greek air)

For the czar is making war (Dalmatian air)
Life (Hungarian air)
Morning song (Russian air)
"O let me wander" (Greek air)
"O ye merry chorus gay" (Greek air)
On the sea gray mists are spread (Russian air)
"So it fell upon a day" (Lithuanian air)
Stay not, delay not (Ruthenian air)
"When the roses bloom in the gladsome days of summer" (Ruthenian folk air)
"Where's my dear love gone" (Ruthenian air)
Whitehead, William
  "Ye belles, and ye flirts" (Composer unknown)
Whitehouse, R. T.
  Faint heart ne'er won fair lady
Whiteley, S. B.
  "Sing sweet carols, night is past"
Whitfeld, John Clarke-. See Clarke-Whitfeld, John
Whither ("Ich hört' ein bächlein") See Wohin (Schubert)
"Whither bound, O breeze of morning." See Sérénade (Tchaikovsky)
"Whither, wee bird, so fast." See The message (Moscheles)
Whiting, Arthur Battelle
  "Blow, blow, thou winter wind"
  "Yet ah, that spring should vanish"
Whitman, Walt
  "O captain! my captain" (music by Kelley; Wyman)
  We two together (Gilchrist)
  Weave in, my hardy life (Van der Stucken)
Whitmore, Charles Shapland
  Isle of beauty
  Prayer. See "Saviour, Source of every blessing"
  "Saviour, Source of every blessing" (same air as Isle of beauty)
Whitney, Hattie
  The little Dutch garden (Mawson-Marks)
Whitney, Hobart B.
  Lullaby (Tr of "Schlaf, kindchen, schlaf")
Whittaker, Thomas. See Whitaker, Thomas
Whittemore, Edward E.
  "Kind words can never die"
Whittier, John Greenleaf
  The barefoot boy (Johns)
  Centennial hymn (Paine)
  The corn song (German air)
  A dream of summer (German air)
  Faith (Rossini)
  The fishermen (music by Gilbert; Neefe)
  For an autumn festival (André)
  Gone (Stein)
  "The harp, at nature's advent strung" (German air)
  Hymn (Methfessel)

Whittier, John Greenleaf—*Continued*
"I know not what the future hath"
(Irmer)
Laus Deo (Battishill)
The light that is felt (Methfessel)
Little Eva (Emilio)
My birthday (Reichardt)
My psalm (Mozart)
"Old Winter" (Jones)
"Once more the liberal year laughs out"
(Elliott)
Our country (Mendelssohn)
The poet and the children (Gumbert)
The poor voter on election day (German air)
"Prayers of love" (Gilchrist)
Song of the free (Composer unknown)
Song of the negro boatman (Müller)
There is no end for souls like his (Sharland)
"Who aloft thy head did raise." See Der jäger abschied (Mendelssohn)
"Who are the Lord's beloved." See He giveth His beloved sleep (Roeckel)
Who are you ("Good morning, little yellow bird") German air. Words by R. Compton. DO
Who are you, what are you doing. See Villotta
"Who boasts of true Hollandish blood." See "Wien Neêrlandsch bloed" (Wilms)
Who built the ark. Negro spiritual. DF
"Who can resist my Celia's charms." Trevers. Words by N. Tate. MM
"Who comes along the upland ways." See Easter song (Johns)
"Who dashes on in sleet and snow." See Kriss Kringle's ride
Who dat a-comin' ovah yondah. Negro spiritual. JB
Who deeply drinks of wine. J. Emdin. HSE 2
"Who fears to meet a glorious death." See Battle-song (Silcher)
"Who goes there? halt! how green the sea." See Lifdrabanten och kung Erik (Lindblad)
"Who has a flock of stars up in the sky so high." See Song of the moon
"Who has e'er been at Baldock." See The lass of the mill (Festing)
"Who is he plants for the days to come." See Sing glad songs for him (Gounod)
"Who is Sylvia." M. Gould. Words by W. Shakespeare. VFS
"Who is Sylvia." R. Leveridge. Words by W. Shakespeare. DM 1—VFS
"Who is Sylvia." F. Schubert. Words by W. Shakespeare. BD—HSD—KSS—TFC 2—VFS—WL
"Who is Silvia." MS—TL
"Who is Silvia" (Was ist Silvia) FTS
"Who is Sylvia" ("Was ist Sylvia") e.g. FO 1—KF 2—KF 3—KF 4—PG 3—TS
"Who is that tapping on garden gate." See St Valentine (Halsey)

"Who kill'd Cock Robin." See Cock Robin
Who knows. See Chi sa (Atri)
"Who liveth so merry in all this land." 16th century song. CO 1—DM 1
"Who made ocean, earth, and sky." See God, our loving Father
"Who may give orders when he loves." See "Qui donc commande quand il aime" (Saint-Saëns)
"Who now will call the star in." See Steaua
"Who now would hear a song." See "Qui veut ouïr chanson"
"Who rides there so late." See Erlkönig (Schubert)
"Who rides yonder, proud and gay." See The king's highway (Molloy)
"Who rideth so late." See Erlkönig (Loewe); Erlkönig (Schubert)
"Who shall be fairest." F. Moir. Words by C. Mackay. FSS 4
"Who shall sing to bleak November." See November (Olds)
"Who sleeps upon life's ocean." See Der freund (Wolf)
"Who so sadly calls thro' the night." See The conscript's lament
"Who spurs on so late, thro' wood and waste." See Erlkönig (Schubert)
"Who wants to hear, who wants to know." See La ronde de l'aveine
"Who were the yeomen, the yeomen of England." See The yeomen of England (German)
Who will buy the beautiful canary. See "Chi vuol comprar la bella calandrina" (Jommelli)
Who will o'er the downs. R. L. de Pearsall. TFC 2
"Who withholds me." See "Chi m'arresta" (Mercadante)
"Who would not fight for freedom." Old Scotch air. DSH
"Who would not love thee, oh Mary." Bohemian song. e. KSE
"Who'd believe this arbitrary deed." See La Brabançonne (Campenhout)
"Who'd have believed such self-willed daring." See La Brabançonne (Campenhout)
Who'll be a witness for my Lord. Negro spiritual. JB
"Who'll buy caller herrin'." See Caller herrin' (Gow?)
"Who'll buy my posies." Round. FSS 3
"Who'll buy my roses." Catch. Three foreign airs arranged. BD
Who'll jine de Union. Negro spiritual. HR
"Who'll try the gipsy pretty." See "Chi vuol la zingarella" (Paisiello)
"Whom of old the shepherds." 14th century air. Tr of Quem pastores laudavere. e. HC
Whoopee ti yi yo, git along little dogies. Cowboy song. LC
"Who's all them come dressed in white." See Go, Mary, and toll the bell

"Who's seen Carulì, my pretty Carulì." See Oje Carulì (Costi)

Who's that calling. J. B. Lawreen. SSS —WBT

Who's that a-calling. TFC 2

"Who's that tapping at the garden gate." See Tapping at the garden gate (New)

"Who's this coming this way." Air: Plygiad y bedol, or, The bending horse shoe. Words by L. S. Jast. MMW

"Whose horse is that horse." See Our goodman (Big Laurel, N.C. version no. 1)

Whose sins have pardoned gained (Hamburg) L. Mason. FSS 3

"Whosoe'er on thy fair coast doth wander." See Oll Istria (Georgieri)

"Whosoever drinketh." S. Bennett. OS 4

Why ("Warum sind denn die rosen") See Warum (Tchaikovsky)

"Why, ah why, my heart, this sadness." See Switzer's song of home (Moscheles)

"Why, alas, bear I yet parting's sorrow." See Parting's sorrow (Varlamov)

"Why, alas! in lowly stall." J. Mauberne. Words from the Latin. e. MCS

"Why all this sorrow." See Good advice (Leveridge)

Why are days we have lived lost for ever. See Tempo passato perchè non retorni (Gordigiani)

"Why are you ill and drooping." See Alte laute, I (Schumann)

"Why are you standing outside, young man." See The quest

"Why are you wandering here, I pray." I. Nathan. Words by J. Kenney. HSE 3

"Why art before thy lover's door." See "Was machst du mir vor liebchen's thür" (Lassen)

"Why art thou cast down, O my soul." C. Reinthaler. e. SAS 1

"Why, by such a brittle stone." J. Wilson. DM 1

Why, Creator. See Imanírta (Valderrama)

"Why do I weep for thee." W. V. Wallace. Words by G. Linley. FSS 7—WBT

"Why do summer roses fade." G. Barker. FSS 2—WBT

"Why do the nations so furiously rage together." Händel. OS 4—SAS 4

"Why do you scratch me, Pussy." See The dog and cat

"Why do you turn your eyes away." See "Che mai t'ho fatt', amor"

Why does he haunt my door ("Mana tēn agapō") S. S. Lontos. Words from a Greek folk poem. e.gr. BF 2

"Why does the God of Israel sleep." G. F. Händel. SAS 3

"Why does the village always gossip." See Tărăncuta

"Why fear the pain that passes." FSS 5

"Why feels my heart so dormant." See "Nel cor più mi sento" (Paisiello)

"Why forsake the friendly highways." See Der wegweiser (Schubert)

"Why, He's the Lord of lords." See He's the Lord of lords

"Why is thy sword with blood so red." See Edward (Loewe)

"Why linger, mourner memory." A. Mellon. FSS 8

"Why, liquor of life, do I love you so." Irish song. e. MMI

"Why live, when life is sad." See Light in darkness (Cowen)

"Why long'st thou so deep for thy dear native land." See Norrländingens hemlängtan (Brooman)

"Why looks the maid of Dôl so sad." See The maid of Dôl

"Why, most Highest, art Thou lying in a manger poor and low." See Jesus in the manger (Smart)

"Why, my beauty, will you wound me." See Cantu di janna

"Why my little birchwood splinter." See The birchen brand

"Why, my mother, wilt thou sew the scarlet sarafan." See The scarlet sarafan (Varlamov)

Why, oh mother ("Na cóżeś mnie pani matko") Polish song. e.p. BF 1

"Why runs your sword so red wi' blood." See Edward (Loewe)

"Why seems this day so bright and gay." See "Was ist denn heut' wohl fuer ein tag" (Genée)

"Why should I be thus full of glee." See Troubadour song

"Why should I pray for land and wealth." See Die zufriedenheit (Mozart)

"Why should I sigh." Air: Peggy ban. Words by J. F. M. Dovaston. MMW

"Why should we boast of Arthur and his knights." See St George for England

"Why should we foolishly repine." See Music, love, and wine

"Why should we keep our love a secret." See "Wie sollten wir geheim sie halten" (Strauss)

"Why should we now boast of Arthur and his knights." See St George for England

"Why should we parted be, Kathleen aroon." See Kathleen aroon (Abt)

"Why should'st thou swear I am forsworn." Charles I. PR 1

"Why, since thy heart in sadness weeps." See "Deh! non voler costringere" (Donizetti)

"Why so hopeless and dim is thine eye." See Friendship (Derfeldt)

"Why so pale and wan, fond lover." T. A. Arne. Words by J. Suckling. BE 8—DM 2—PR 2

"Why so pale are the roses this year." See Warum (Tchaikovsky)

"Why so silent, tell me, birdie" (Paun i kolo) Bosnian folk song. e.se. BO—SMF

Why, soldiers, why. See "How stands the glass around"

"**Why** stand thou so lonely, O birch-tree, say." See Birken (Gade)

"**Why** still repel a love." See Amore (Lucantoni)

"**Why** strays the Indian maiden." See "Où va la jeune Indoue" (Delibes)

"**Why** tarries my love." See The pigeon

"**Why** the breath of the tempest." See Laengsel (Backer-Lunde)

"**Why** turn away when I draw near." See Speak to me (Campana)

"**Why** weep ye by the tide, ladye." See Jock o' Hazeldean

"**Why**, what's that to you." See True courage (Dibdin)

"**Why**, why tell thy lover." Air: Caledonian hunt's delight. Words by R. Burns. BSR

"**Why** with your lovely presence haunt me." See "Si vous n'avez rien à me dire" (Rothschild)

Why wound me. See Cantu di janna

Whyte, Henry
Dh' fhalbh mo leannan fhein (Old Gaelic air)
Fuadach nan gàidheal (Scottish air)
A' mhaighdean àluinn (Old Gaelic air)
Where sleepest thou, my dearie (Scottish air)

Whyte-Melville, George John
Composer and author
Drink, puppy, drink
Author
Gipsy John (Clay)
Good-bye (Tosti)
Only a year ago (Tosti)
The tarpaulin jacket (Coote)

"**Wi'** a hundred pipers an' a', an' a'." See The hundred pipers

"**Wi-de-wi-de-wen-ne.**" German song. e. JSE
"Wide-wide-wenne." e.g. FSS 5

The **wicked** knight. See Le méchant guillon

Wickede, Friedrich von
Abendlied
Even song. See Abendlied

Wicks, George
I'd wed if I were not too young

Widdicombe fair. Folk song: Devonshire version. BE 8—BOH—FSF
Widdecombe fair. BSW
Widdicombe fair. Somerset version. BOS

The **wide** Missouri. See Shenandoah

"**Wide,** open, wide, O window." See Maria, Marì (Capua)

"**Wide** spread his name." Händel. BS 2

"**Wide** thy window open." See Maria, Marì (Capua)

Wide-wide-wenne. See Wi-de-wi-de-wen-ne

"A **widespread** heath with moss-grown stone." See Landskab (Børresen)

Widmung ("Du meine seele, du mein herz."—Dedication) R. Schumann. Words by F. Rückert. e.g. BAS 1—FF—FO 1—KF 1—KF 2—PG 2
Dedication. e. WBW

Widmung ("O danke nicht fur diese lieder."—Dedication) R. Franz. Words by W. Müller. e.g. FF—FO 1—SM 4. e. only FTS
Dedication. e. WBT—WBW

Widor, Charles Marie
Albaÿde
Invocation
"Je ne veux pas autre chose"
"Nothing I ask thee to give me." See "Je ne veux pas autre chose"
"Nuit d'étoiles"
The sigh. See Soupir
Soupir
Starry night. See "Nuit d'étoiles"

"**Widow** machree, it's no wonder you frown." S. Lover (music and words) JO—MMI—PI—WBT—WL

The **widow** Malone ("Did you hear of the widow Malone") Irish air. Words by C. Lever. MMI

"**Wie** anders war es" ("How times have changed") I. Brüll. e.g. AB 2—SOA 4

"**Wie** berührt mich wundersam" (Heartthrobs) F. Bendel. e.g. MSF 1—SM 2
Heart throbs. e. WBT—WBW
"Wie berührt mich wundersam" ("Wondrous is the power") e.g. CB

"**Wie** bist du meine königin" ("Ah! sweet my love") J. Brahms. Words by G. F. Daumer. e.g. KF 3—KF 4—PG 3—PG 4
"Wie bist du, meine königin" ("How fair art thou, my lovely queen") e.g. BAS 2
"Wie bist du meine königin" (My queen) e.g. FF—FO 2

"**Wie** braust durch die wipfel der heulende sturm." See Die junge nonne (Schubert)

"**Wie** der tag mir schleichet." See Que le jour me dure (Rousseau)

"**Wie** die blumlein draussen zittern." See Bleib bei mir (Reichardt)

"**Wie** ein schifflein auf dem meer." See Schifffahrt (Witthauer)

"**Wie** gaat meê, wie gaat meê over zee." See Een liedje van de zee

"**Wie** gerne dir zu füssen." See Wie schön bist du (Weidt)

"**Wie** herrlich sind die abendstunden." See Abendruhe (Mozart)

"**Wie** ich liebe dich." See Only love (Dargomyzhskiï)

"**Wie** ist doch die erde so schön." W. Steifensandt. Words by R. Reinick. g. ED 3

"**Wie** kommt's, dass du so traurig bist." J. F. Reichardt. Volkslied. g. ED 3

"**Wie** lenzeshauch" ("A breath of spring") A. Jensen. Words by A. Traeger. e.g. FO 1

"**Wie** lieblich schallt durch busch und wald." See Das waldhorn (Silcher)

"**Wie** melodien zieht es mir" ("A thought like music") J. Brahms. Words by K. Groth. e.g. FF—FO 2

"**Wie** mir deine freuden winken." See Frühlingsgruss an das vaterland (Klein)

"**Wie** nahte mir der schlummer" ("How friendly sleep was to me") C. M. von Weber. ₁Words by F. Kind₁ e.g. KS 1
Piano, piano, canto pio. e.g.i. OPS 1 —PP

"**Wie** ruhest du so stille." See Winter-lied (Harder)

Wie schön bist du (How fair art thou) H. Weidt. Words by Moritz graf Strachwitz. e.g. AB 3—CB— KF 3—KF 4
How fair art thou. e.g. FSS 5
How fair thou art. e. HSC

"**Wie** sie so sanft ruhn." After F. B. Be-neken. Words by A. C. Stockmann. g. ED 1—ED 2

"**Wie** sollten wir geheim sie halten" ("Why should we keep our love a secret") R. Strauss. Words by A. F. von Schack. e.g. FO 2

"**Wie** süss ist's, kann bei dir ich sein." See "How sweet it is when I'm with you" (Glinka)

"**Wie** todesahnung dämm'rung deckt die lande." See O du mein holder abend-stern (Wagner)

"**Wie** viel sonnenstrahlen fielen golden schwer." See Meeresleuchen (Loewe)

"**Wie** war sie so klar die gestrige nacht." See Nocturne (Balakirev)

"**Wieder** ist es lange zehn." See Gretchens beichte

Wiegeliedje (Cradle song) C. van Ren-nes. Words by Antheunis. d.e. CMF 1

Wiegenlied ("Der abend schaut."—Cradle song) F. Ries. Words by A. Kay-ser-Langerhannes. e.g. KF 2

Wiegenlied ("Brother, thou and I") Ger-man lullaby. e. FSS 5

Wiegenlied ("Guten abend."—Cradle song) J. Brahms. Words by K. Simrock. e.g. CMF 1—CS 2—FO 2—KF 1. e. only FTS
Cradle song. e. DSH—WA—WBT —WBW—WSC—WSW
Lullaby. e.g. CHS. e. only TFC 2
"Lullaby, and good-night." e. WC
Wiegenlied (Lullaby) e.g. KF 2— MSS 2—SS 2

Wiegenlied ("O hush thee") See "O hush thee, my babie" (Jensen)

Wiegenlied ("Schlaf, herzenssöhnchen") C. M. von Weber. Words by F. C. Hiemer. g. ED 1
Cradle song. e. BSE—FSS 8— HSD—WBT—WSC

Schlummerlied (Slumber song) e.g. MS
Wiegenlied (Cradle song) e.g. KF 2 —SSG

Wiegenlied ("Schlaf, herzenssöhnchen") For Swedish and English translations with a different air see Slummersång (Hägg)

Wiegenlied ("Schlaf' in guter ruh'."— Cradle song) W. Taubert. e.g. KF 2
Cradle song. e. FSS 1—LA
"Sleep, beloved, sleep." e. HSD— WBT

Wiegenlied ("Schlaf, lieb' kindlein") A. André. Words by M. Wiesener. g. ED 3

Wiegenlied ("Schlaf, mein prinzchen") W. A. Mozart. Words by M. Brock. g. ED 3
Sleep and rest. e. WBT
Wiegenlied (Lullaby) e.g. CS 2

Wiegenlied ("Schlaf', mein sohn, und schlumm're süss."—Cradle song) E. Grieg. Words by A. Munch. e.g. FO 2

Wiegenlied ("Schlafe, schlafe, holder süs-ser knabe."—Cradle song) F. Schubert. e.g. MS—MSS 1
Cradle song. e. BSE—WBT

Wiegenlied ("Schlummre, liebe kleine") K. Spazier. Volkslied. g. ED 3

Wiegenlied ("Sleep, O baby mine") See Cradle song (Tchaikovsky)

Wiegenlied ("Suse, lewe Suse") Old Ger-man folk song. g. ED 3
"Susy, little Susy." e. WBT

"**Wien** Neêrlandsch bloed" ("Let all with Dutch blood in their veins") Dutch national song. J. W. Wilms; wrongly attributed to Smits. Words by H. van Tol-lens. d.e. BSP
Dutch national song. e. HSD— KSN
Holland's national hymn. d.e. MP —NMS—WA—WBT. e. only NMH
"Let him in whom old Dutch blood flows." e. JS
National song of Holland. e. LA —WCP
Wien Neêrlandsch bloed (For King and fatherland.—"Oh, ye within whose burning veins") e. BMC
Wien Nierlansch. e. SN

Die **wiese** ("Ich ging einst einen frühlings-tag") L. Reichardt. Words from the English. g. ED 3

Wiesener, M.
Wiegenlied (André)

Wiesenthal, T. V.
The ingle side

"**Wife** beloved, thou whom I cherish." See "Cara sposa, amante cara" (Händel)

Wife, children, and friends.　Old air. Words by W. R. Spencer.　JO

The **wife** in masquerade ("Once tired of life")　J. Mazzinghi.　Words by F. Reynolds.　ME

The **wife** of Tone.　Londonderry air. Words by P. Colum.　BF 2

The **wife** of Usher's well.　Folk song: Allanstand, N.C. version.　CSE
—Alleghany, N.C. version.　CSE
—Big Laurel, N.C. version.　CSE
—Black Mountain, N.C. version.　CSE
—Carmen, N.C. version.　CSE
—Hot Springs, N.C. version.　CSE
—Tennessee version.　CSE

The **wife** wrapt in wether's skin.　Folk song: Kentucky version no. 1.　SA
—Kentucky version no. 2.　CSE
—Virginia version.　CSE
Variant: Ruggleton's daughter of Iero

The **wife's** welcome.　I. B. Woodbury. FSS 7

Wiglesworth, Esther
"Hail, sweet Babe, so pure and holy" (music by Oliver; Pettman)

Wihtol, Josef Ivanovich
Beggar's song
Chant du mendiant.　See Beggar's song

Wilbye, John
"Flora gave me fairest flowers"

Wild, A. A.
"Bird and blossom"
"I heard the voice of Jesus say"
"There were shepherds watching"

Wild Bill Jones.　Folk song from North Carolina.　CSE

The **wild** boy.　Irish folk air.　Words by M. L. Baum.　GO

"A **wild** cry leaps like thunder roar."　See Die wacht am Rhein (Wilhelm)

The **wild** rose ("In the wood a boy one day")　German folk air.　[Words by Goethe.　Tr of Heidenröslein]　e. DO

The **wild** rose ("Sah ein knab'")　See Heidenröslein (Schubert); Heidenröslein (Werner)

The **wild** rose ("Where the wild rose sweetly doth blow")　J. Strauss.　WBT—WSC

"A **wild** rose in the forest."　See The rose (Eckert)

Wild roses ("La brise douce a caressé") See Petites roses (Cesek)

"**Wild-roses** come all bright and gay."　See Song of the wild-roses

"**Wild** roved an Indian girl, bright Alfarata."　See The blue Juniata (Sullivan)

"**Wild** was the day when he came with greeting."　See "Er ist gekommen" (Franz)

"**Wild** woodland creatures."　See "Fere selvagge" (Caccini)

Wilde, Richard Henry
"My life is like the summer rose" (music by Schumann; Thibault)

Das **wilde** heer ("Das war der herr von Rodenstein")　C. Schmezer.　Words by J. V. Scheffel.　g.　ED 1

Wilder, James A.

Composer and author
A sea scout chantey

Author
Law and order (Sullivan)

Wilder, Victor
"Un doux lien" (Delbrück)

"The **wilderness** shall be."　A. C. Mackenzie.　SAS 4

Wilhelm, Karl
"Bright college years" (same air as Die wacht am Rhein)
The flower of liberty (same air as Die wacht am Rhein)
Our banner (same air as Die wacht am Rhein)
A pledge to Columbia (same air as Die wacht am Rhein)
Die wacht am Rhein
The watch by the Rhine.　See Die wacht am Rhein
The watch on the Rhine.　See Die wacht am Rhein

Wilhelm ("Ich war wohl recht ein springinsfeld")　J. A. P. Schulz.　Words by G. A. Bürger.　g.　ED 2

"**Wilhelmus** van Nassouwe" ("Prince William of old Nassau")　Attributed to Marnix de Saint Aldegonde. d.e.　BSP
"Wilhelmus van Nassouwe" (William of Nassau)　d.e.　BDF
William of Nassau.　e.　KSN—SN

Wiliwili wai.　See Surging waters (Hopkins)

Will and I.　Composer unknown.　Words by P. H. Hayne.　LBR

"**Will** by Mary sad reposes."　See Sweet farewell

"**Will** Cloris cast her sun-bright eyes."　J. Goodgroome.　MM

Will he come ("I can scarcely hear")　A. Sullivan.　Words by A. A. Procter. CS 1—MSS 2

"**Will** he come who loves me dear."　Russian folk air.　Words by G. D. Donaldson.　WF

"**Will** ich in mein gärtlein gehn."　See Das bucklige männlein

"**Will** ruhen unter den bäumen hier."　See In der ferne (Kreutzer)

Will Watch.　J. Davy.　HSE 2

"**Will** ye gang o'er the lea-rig."　See My ain kind dearie, O

"**Will** ye gang to the Hielands, Leezie Lindsay."　See Leezie Lindsay

"**Will** ye go to the ewe-bughts, Marion." See The ewe-bughts

"Will ye go to the Indies, my Mary." Air: Ewe-bughts Marion. Words by R. Burns. BSR

Will ye no come back again. See Bonnie Charlie (Gow)

Will ye no more back again. See Bonnie Charlie (Gow)

Will you be mine (Tule mulle, neitsikene) Esthonian folk song. e.es. BF 1

"Will you come into my parlor? said the spider to the fly, 'tis the prettiest, snuggest little parlor that ever you did spy. Not today, thanks, Mister Longshanks." See The spider and the fly (McNaught)

"Will you come to Sabbath school." See There's room enough for all

"Will you come to the bow'r." Old song. WBT

"Will you come with me." See Wait for the wagon (Buckley)

"Will you hear a Spanish lady." See The Spanish lady

Will you love me then as now. F. Weiland (music and words) FSS 8—NML —WBT—WL

"Will you marry" ("Vos-zhe vilstu") Jewish folk song. e.y. GF 1

"Will you walk into my parlor? said a spider to a fly; 'tis the prettiest little parlor that ever you did spy. The way into my parlor is up a winding stair." See The spider and the fly (Words by Howitt)

"Will you walk into my parlour? said the spider to the fly, 'tis the prettiest little parlour that ever you did spy; you've only got to pop your head just inside of the door." See The spider and the fly (Words by Hudson)

Willard, E. Payson
The song of the A. B. (Harrington)

Willard, Mrs. Emma (Hart)
"Rocked in the cradle of the deep" (Knight)

Willatzen, P. J.
Verrath (Zech)

William and Nancy. Folk song from North Carolina. CSE

William and Polly. Folk song from North Carolina. CSE

William Hall. Kentucky mountain song. WLT

William of Nassau. See "Wilhelmus van Nassouwe" (Marnix)

"William Taylor." Folk song: English version. SEF 1—SO
—North Carolina version. CSE
Variant: Willie Taylor

Williams, Charles Lee
"As Thou wilt, Father" (from Gethsemane)
"Christ was born on Christmas day; wreathe the holly, twine the bay; Christus natus hodie"
Trust

Williams, Folkestone
Good-bye, sweetheart, good-bye (Hatton)

Williams, Helen Maria
"While thee I seek" (Dykes)

Williams, May V. Gibbons
May (McCoy)

Williams, Theodore Chickering
"In the lonely midnight" (Howard)

Williams, Thomas
Largo (Händel)
"Loud strike the sounding strings" (Beethoven) Authorship uncertain

Williams, Thomas E.
The bride's farewell
Larboard watch

Williams, W.
The hunting day

Williams, W. L.
Kathleen

Williams, William
"Guide me, O Thou great Jehovah" (Spanish air; also music by Flotow; Hastings: Hérold)

Willie Leonard. See The lake of Coolfinn

Willie Reilly. Irish folk song. JOI

Willie Taylor. Folk song: Irish version. JOI
Variant: "William Taylor"

"Willie was a youthful lover." See Willie Taylor (Irish version)

"Willie Wastle dwalt on Tweed." See Sic a wife as Willie had

Willie, we have missed you. S. C. Foster. WBT
Oh! Willie, we have miss'd you. HSD

Willing, William
Twenty years ago

Willis,
"What shall I do? I am undone"

Willis, B. R.
Alma mater—Colby (Crawford)

Willis, Richard Storrs
Christmas carol. See "It came upon the midnight clear"
"It came upon the midnight clear"
"Look not upon the wine"
"There is a green hill far away"
Willis. See "It came upon the midnight clear"

"Willkommen im grünen." J. A. P. Schulz. Words by J. H. Voss. g. ED 2

"Willkommen, lieber mondenschein." See An den mond (Auberlen)

"Willkommen, lieber schöner mai." See Mailied (Schulz)

"Willkommen, mein wald" ("Now welcome, my wood") R. Franz. Words by O. Roquette. e.g. FF—FO 1

"Willkommen, o seliger abend." See Sommer-abendlied (Becker)

"Willkommen, o silberner mond." See Die frühen gräber (Gluck)

"**Willkommen,** schöner jüngling." See An den frühling (Reichardt)

The **willow** song. 16th century air. Words by W. Shakespeare. PR 1 —VFS
   A lover's complaint (Willow, willow, willow) DM 1
   O willo, willo, willo. BSE
   O willow, willow. BO—HSE 1—MM
   Willow willow. CO 1

The **willow** [song] J. Hook. [Words by W. Shakespeare] ME

The **willow** song. P. Humfrey. Words by W. Shakespeare. VFS
   Willow willow. CO 1

The **willow** song. G. Rossini. Words by W. Shakespeare. VFS

The **willow** song. A. Sullivan. Words by W. Shakespeare. CS 2—DM 2—MSS 2

[The **willow** song] O willo, willo, willo: parody. 16th century air. BSE

"**Willow** the king." Harrow school song. LA

The **willow** tree ("O take me to your arms, love") Folk song from Hampshire. SF 3

The **willow** tree ("Where the cliff looks o'er the valley") Ruthenian folk air. Words by M. Schutze. WF

Wills, William Gorman
   "I'll sing thee songs of Araby" (Clay)
"**Willst** jenes tag's du nicht dich mehr entsinnen" ("Is that fair day no more by thee remember'd") Wagner. e.g. OPS 3

Willy and Cuddy ("How now, shepherd") 17th century song. Air: Daphne and Corydon. CO 1

Willy and Cuddy ("How now, shepherd") 17th century song. Air: Mayingtime. CO 1
   "How now, shepherd, what means that." DM 2

Willy Coombe. English folk song. BSW

"**Willy** prethe goe to bed." See Trenchmore

"**Willy,** prithee go to bed." See Trenchmore

Willy was so blithe a lad. Northern song. CO 2

"**Willy,** Willy, Will, the old man's coming." See The old man

Wilmarth, Walter G.
   When the grand old flag goes by

Wilmot, John. See Rochester, John Wilmot, 2d earl of

Wilms, Jan Willem
   Dutch national song. See "Wien Neêrlandsch bloed"
   For king and fatherland. See "Wien Neêrlandsch bloed"
   Holland's national hymn. See "Wien Neêrlandsch bloed"
   "Let him in whom old Dutch blood flows." See "Wien Neêrlandsch bloed"

   National song of Holland. See "Wien Neêrlandsch bloed"
   "Oh, ye within whose burning veins." See "Wien Neêrlandsch bloed"
   "Wien Neêrlandsch bloed"

Wilson, Alexander
   Connel and Flora (Composer unknown)

Wilson, C. B.
   The bard's lament (Welsh air)
   "The blithe birds are singing" (Welsh air)
   The false knight (Welsh air)
   The mountain minstrel (Welsh air)

Wilson, C. J.
   "O Lord of all, with us abide" (Tr of Quaesumus, Auctor omnium)

Wilson, Mrs Cornwell Baron. See Wilson, Mrs Margaret (Harris)

Wilson, G. F.
   "There's a beautiful flag"

Wilson, Grenville Dean
   The brook
   Song of the brook. See The brook

Wilson, H. Lane
   Carmeña (with words "Dance and song make glad the night"; "Dance, play, sing, sorrow disdain")
   Dance and sing. See Carmeña ("Dance, play, sing, sorrow disdain")

Wilson, Henry
   Alleluia! risen Lord
   "Christ is risen! alleluia"
   "Ring on, ye joyous Christmas bells"

Wilson, John
   Ilka blade of grass

Wilson, John, 1595-1674
   "Cast your caps and cares away"
   Despairing Mary
   "From the fair Lavinian shore"
   "I sing of a land." See The Stuarts of Appin
   "In the merry month of May." See Phillida and Corydon
   "Lawn as white as driven snow" (attributed; attributed also to R. Johnson)
   Phillida and Corydon
   The Stuarts of Appin
   "Take, O take those lips away"
   "Though your strangenesse fretts my heart"
   To Althea
   Troy town
   "Wert thou more fairer than thou art"
   "Why, by such a brittle stone"

Wilson, John, 1785-1854
   Turn ye to me (Scottish air)

Wilson, Mrs Margaret (Harris)
   "What fairy-like music" (Pinna)

Wilson, Robert Burns
   Remember the Maine (Converse)

"**Wilt** heden nu treden" (Prayer of thanksgiving) E. Kremser. d.e. BDF
   Hymn of thanks. e. CST
   Prayer of thanksgiving. e. DSH
   Thanksgiving prayer. e. TFC 2

"**Wilt** no longer thou torment me." See "Tu mancavi a tormentarmi" (Cesti)

"Wilt thou be my dearie." Air: The sutor's daughter, or, Nighean a ghreisich. Words by R. Burns. BSB— BSR—MMS—PS 1

"Wilt thou go, my bonnie lassie." See The braes aboon Bonaw

"Wilt thou love me, fairest maiden." Air: Marwnad Ivor Hael O'Geri, or, Elegy of Ivor the Liberal of Keri. Words by Talhaiarn. MMW

"Wilt thou return, O love so early ended." See Love (Bleikhman)

Wilt thou soon return. Finnish song. L. Rocke. e. KSN

"Wilt thou wander with me." Air: Snowy days of January. MMW

Wilton, Arthur
The land of dreams

The wily fox. C. Dibdin (music and words) DM 2

Winchilsea, Henry Stormont Finch-Hatton, earl of
The celestial mistress (Lawes)

The wind ("Down the street") German folk air. Words by H. H. Harbour. DO

Wind and sea. F. G. Cauffman. Words by B. Taylor. TL

Wind and sea. J. A. P. Schulz. Words by B. Taylor. LBR

"The wind blew a blast from the northward." See The forecastle sailor (Geary)

"The wind blows high, the wind blows low." See How the wind blows

"The wind blows north, the wind blows south." See As the wind blows (Genée)

"Wind! dost thou kiss my dear love o'er the sea." See Afar (Lindblad)

The wind from the west. Irish air. Words by E. Young. FSI

"Wind, gentle evergreen." Round. Hayes. TL

"The wind is blowing fresh, Kate." See A thousand leagues away (Barnby)

"The wind is fair, and the day is fine." See Soraidh slàn le Fionn-Airidh

"The wind is playing 'mongst the reeds" (Egyptian love song) Words by L. S. Jast. BMC

"The wind is whisp'ring low, my love." See Serenade (Neidlinger)

"The wind may shout." J. L. Molloy. Words by A. Smith. MCS

The wind that shakes the barley. Irish air. Words by K. T. Hinkson. FSI

"The window low." See "Fenesta vascia"

"Window, will you not open." See Maria, Marì (Capua)

The winds and the shadows. Old French air: Le petit chasseur. Words by H. H. Harbour. DO

The winds blow ("Vìnũt vitrï") Ukrainian song. e.r. BF 1

"Winds in the trees." A. G. Thomas. Words from the German. e. MSF 2

"The winds of March are blowing." A. F. M. Custance. NMS

"Winds of night, around us sighing." See 'Neath the elms of dear old Yale

"The winds softly sigh in their mystical caves." See Music on the waves (Glover)

"The winds were wailing." Words by Baring-Gould. HC

Wine and glory. Old air: The Bath medley. Words by C. Mackay. MM

"The wine-cup is circling." Air: Michael Hoy. Words by T. Moore. MI

Wine, woman and song. See Wein, weib, gesang (Zelter)

"Wine's in the head, merrily whirls." See La grande et la petite

Wing wong waddle, to my jack-straw straddle. See The swapping song

Winkler, Karl Gottfried Theodor
In der ferne (Weber)

"Winkum, Winkum, shut your eye." Children's song. FSS 8—WSC

Winner, J. E. See Eastburn, R. A.

Winner, Septimus
Carmen de Lalages agna (same air as Ellie Rhee)
Dutch warbler
Ellie Rhee
Friends that we never forget
"God save our president"
Listen to the mocking-bird
The party at the zoo
"What is home without a mother"

Winnie dear ("Oh! let me gaze awhile") Air: Mentra Gwen, or, Venture, Gwen. Words by Talhaiarn. MMW

Winnie Wen ("The harvest moon was beaming") Owain Alaw (J. Owen) Words by J. C. Hughes. MMW

"A winning way, a pleasant smile." See Little Annie Rooney

Winsome Mary. See Mairi laghach

Winter, Peter von
Gute ruhe
Die schöne nachbarin

Winter ("All the winter long") Bohemian folk air. Words by N. H. Dole. DO

Winter ("Blow, ye northern winds") Ojibway Indian song. e.in. BA

Winter ("Hark! how the sleigh bells ring") L. B. Marshall. Words by W. W. Caldwell. JS

Winter ("How deep a sleep") E. H. Pierce. NMS

Winter ("Poor old winter can't you be gay."—Petrusia) Russian folk song. e. GO

Winter and spring. Round. LA

"The winter days so cold." See "Voici l'hiver et son triste cortège" (Faure)

"Winter, good-bye! blue is the sky." German folk air. Words by J. Erwin. DO

"Winter, goodbye, we'll never sigh." German song. e. WSC

"The winter is over and gone at last." See The bird song (Herron)

"The winter it is past." Irish version. Old song. MMI

"The winter it is past" (The Curragh of Kildare) JOI

"The winter it is past." Scottish version. Old song with additional words by R. Burns. BSR—HSSS—MMS—PS 1

Spring song. DM 2

A winter lullaby. R. de Koven. MSF 1

"Der winter mag scheiden." See Solvejgs sang (Grieg)

"The winter may go and the spring disappear." See Solvejgs sang (Grieg)

"The winter may pass and the spring fade away." See Solvejgs sang (Grieg)

"The winter may wane and the springtime go by." See Solvejgs sang (Grieg)

Winter roses. See Roses d'hiver (Fontenailles)

Winter song. See Winterlied (Koss)

"Winter storms have ceased among our mountains." See Längtan till landet (Lindblad)

"Winter storms have wan'd." See Siegmunds liebeslied (Wagner)

"Winter-tide hath past away." Easter carol. 14th century words. Tr of Cedit hyems eminus. e. HC

"The winter was come, 'twas simmer nae mair." See Auld Robin Gray: sequel

"Winter wind blew keenly all the dreary dark day." See Life

"Winter yields to the wiles of spring." See Au printemps (Gounod)

Wintering. See L'hivernage

Winterlied ("Komm' aus der engen stadt."—Winter song) H. von Koss. e.g. SM 1

Winterlied ("Wie ruhest du") A. Harder. Words by F. A. Krummacher. g. ED 3

De winter'll soon be over. Negro song. HR

Winter's past. German folk air. Words by M. Morgan. DO

"Winterstürme wichen dem wonnemond." See Siegmunds liebeslied (Wagner)

Winther, Christian
"Flyv, fugl, flyv" (Hartmann)
Laengsel (Kjerulf)

"The wintry west extends his blast." Air: McPherson's rant. Words by R. Burns. BSR

Wir Christenleut haben. For English translation see "Good Christian men, rejoice"

"Wir geniessen die himmlischen freuden." See Der himmel hängt voll geigen (Himmel)

"Wir hatten gebauet ein stattliches haus." Thüringische volksweise. Words by A. von Binzer. g. ED 1

"Wir sind die könige der welt." See Trinklied (Ebers)

"Wir sind nicht mehr am ersten glas." See Trinklied (Kreutzer)

"Wir winden dir den jungfernkranz." See Brautjungfernlied (Weber)

Wir wollen alle frölich seyn. For English translation see "We will be merry, far and wide" (Praetorius)

"Wirf alle deine sorg'" (Commit thy ways unto the Lord) Molique. e.g. HSS 2—HSS 4

Das wirthshaus. See Das wirtshaus (Schubert)

Der wirtin töchterlein. See entry under Der

Das wirtshaus (The inn) F. Schubert. Words by W. Müller. e.g. BS 2—FF

"Wise men from Egypt's ancient land." G. E. Oliver. Words by M. P. Hoyt. HC

"The wise men saw a light afar." H. J. Gauntlett. Words by R. R. Chope. HC

"The wise men to Thy cradle throne." See To Thy cradle throne (Bradbury)

"The wise men were but seven." Catch. BD

"The wise sailor steering." See "L'esperto nocchiero" (Bononcini)

Wiseman, F. L.
"The shepherds had an angel"

The wish (Souhait) C. Cui. Words by Poushkin. e.f. NR 4

"Wishfully I look and languish." See Bonnie wee thing

"Wisst ihr wo ich gerne weil'." See Lieblingsplätzchen (Mendelssohn)

Wistar, Thomas
A university hymn (Old air)

"Wistfully I look and languish." See Bonnie wee thing

The witch. Ojibway Indian song. in. BA

"With a cheerful old friend." 18th century song. ME

With a down, hey, derry down. Catch. BD

"With a glory of winter sunshine." See The poet and the children (Gumbert)

"With a love for our glorious nation." See "De la patria" (Gutierrez)

"With a merry tale, sergeants beat the drum." See Humming all the trade is (Reeve)

With a painted ribbon. See Mit einem gemalten band (Beethoven)

With a primrose. See Med en primulaveris (Grieg)

"With a shout and a laugh and a song." See A western college boating song (Olds)

"With a swanlike beauty gliding." See "Quando miro quel bel ciglio" (Mozart)

With a violet. See Med en primulaveris (Grieg)

"With broken words." See Colin and Grissy parting

"With care I tend my rosebush gay." See "À ma main droite j'ai un rosier"

"With cautious steps as we tread our way thro'." See A dollar or two

"With cheeks as bright as roses." See Sweet Kitty Magee

"With crash of battle, armor gleaming." See Death, the commander (Musorgskii)

With crown and scepter. See "Sonst spielt ich" (Lortzing)

"With cunning conniving." See "Che fiero costume" (Legrenzi)

"With deep affection and recollection." See The bells of Shandon

"With endless tears." R. Johnson. DM 1

With every golden string. D. F. E. Auber. MCS

"With eyes so blue and dreaming." See "Mit deinen blauen augen" (Lassen)

"With features stern lies he, who ever." See The man without tears (Zahorsky)

"With flying hands the maiden weaves." See Nenia (Randegger)

"With fresh-cut staff, at break of day." See Fussreise (Wolf)

"With fruit and flow'rs I come." See Green (Debussy)

With gladness men of old. See "As with gladness men of old" (Monk)

"With glory lit the midnight air." See Christmas hymn (Dielman)

With glowing heart. See "Lord, with glowing heart I'd praise Thee" (Spanish air); "Lord, with glowing heart I'd praise Thee" (Haydn)

"With haste my song would be flying." See Si mes vers avaient des ailes (Hahn)

"With her no longer." See De' miei bollenti spiriti (Verdi)

"With his bow and arrow glist'ning in the sun." See Der schütz (Weber)

"With hounds and horn each rosy morn." See Sweet Tally-ho

"With its fang so sharp and voracious." See Le manoir de Rosemunde (Duparc)

With Jockey to the fair. See Jockey to the fair

With joy the impatient husbandman. J. Haydn. e. BAS 2—OS 4—SAS 4

"With joy we hail the sacred day." G. Kingsley. Words by H. Auber. FSS 5

With joyous hearts. Christmas song. MCS

"With laughing looks I once arose." See Jenny

"With love my heart is troubled." See "There's no deity but God"

"With lowly suit and plaintive ditty." Storace. Words by J. Cobb. BE 4 —HSE 1

"With many a curve my banks I fret." See The brook

"With meek uplifted eye." See The woman of Canaan (Haydn)

"With merry hounds and huntsmen." See Der edelfalk (Loewe)

"With my Ballinamona Oro, Ballinamona Oro." See Ballinamona Oro

"With my flock as walked I." Air: The faithful brothers. CO 1

"With my flock as walked I." Air: Northern Nancy. CO 1

"With my flock as walked I." Air from "Musica antiqua." CO 1

"With my flocks as once I wandered." 16th century folk song. EF

"With my love my life was nested." See I live not where I love

With my loved one at home. See Beim liebchen zu haus (Pfeil)

"With my tears that burn and swell." See Ardeleanca

"With myrtle and roses." See "Mit myrthen und rosen" (Schumann)

"With one consent let all the earth." See The old hundredth (Franc)

"With our songs we greet thee." H. E. Nichol (music and words) HC

"With overflowing heart, O Lord." J. Barnby. OS 3—SAS 3

"With parasol in hand, behold her passing." See My day is bitter

"With pious hearts." Händel. OS 4

"With roses at thy birth thou wert surrounded." See Dimme 'na vota sì (Scalisi)

"With sheathed swords and bows unstrung." See Damascus (Costa)

"With silver strings my mandoline adorning." See Mandolin song (Gounod)

"With song of freedom, citizens." See "Heft, burgers, 't lied der vrijheid" (Nicolaï)

"With song the air was filled." See Noël ("O! qu'a-dj'oyou")

"With songs and honors sounding loud" (Ellacombe) German air. Words by I. Watts. TL

"With sorrow and repentance true." See The confession

"With the golden truth of the days of youth." See "Aus der jugendzeit" (Radecke)

"With the Loorgeen, O hee." See Leis an Lurgainn

"With the moon's pale shimmer, little friend Pierrot." See "Au clair de la lune"

"With the rarest of perfumes." See Princess Kaiulani's home (Likelike)

"With the rattling roll of the drum." See Old glory (Oliver)

With thee dear beside love's flowing fountain. See "Oh, tempt me not, my darling" (Hopkins)

"With Thee there is forgiveness." F. H. Cowen. HSS 1—HSS 3—HSS 4

"With thunder shout the air is rent." See Die wacht am Rhein (Wilhelm)

"With this humble stock in store." See Buy my strawberries (Howard)

"With thy enticing glances." See Bolero castellano

"With torments overpowering." See "Che angoscia, che affanno" (Cesti)

"With trembling step, in life we scarce appear." See Die thräne (Gumbert)

"With tuneful pipe and merry glee." M. Greene. MM

"With verdure clad the fields appear." J. Haydn. e. MSS 2—OS 1—SAS 1

With whirling and turning. See Vira do minho

"With you, dear heart, when I journey." See It is spring

"With you to drink will be a pleasure." See Chanson du toréador (Bizet)

Wither, George
The blessed birth (Davies)
"I lov'd a lass, a fair one" (Welsh air)
Old Christmas cheer (Composer unknown)
"Shall I wasting in despair" (Old air; also music by Barker; King; Phillips)
So now is come our feast (Composer unknown)
"Tobacco is an Indian weed" (17th century air; also Cornish air)

Withered rose. See Verwelkt (Proch)

"Within a dark and low-roofed room." See The old weaver

"Within a garden a maiden lingered." Folk air. Modern words by H. F. Sheppard. BE 3—BSW

"Within a garden which held many a flower." See "Entré un jardin"

"Within a manger." A. Redhead. HC

Within a mile of Edinboro'. J. Hook. Words by T. D'Urfey. EF—FSS 3 —HSC—JO—JSE—WBT—WL
"'Twas within a mile o' Edinboro' town." ES
"'Twas within a mile o' Edinburgh town." MMS
Within a mile of Edinburgh town. MSS 1—PS 1—SS 1

"Within a veil as white as snow." See Crépuscule (Massenet)

"Within its cool enclosure." See "In einem kühlen grunde" (Glück)

"Within my father's garden, joy of the rose." See La marchande d'oranges

"Within my father's garden the laurels are in bloom." See Auprès de ma blonde

"Within my pathway a rosebud grew." See "Ich sah ein röschen am wege stehn" (Weber)

"Within the cellar's cool domain." See Der rheinweinzecher (Fischer)

"Within the forest deep." See The sleeping princess (Borodin)

Within the glen sae bushy, O. See "Nae gentle dames, tho' ne'er sae fair"

"Within the grove so dreamy wending." See Clair de lune (Saint-Saëns)

"Within these sacred bowers." See "In diesen heil'gen hallen" (Mozart)

"Within thine eyes will I behold me." See Immer bei dir (Raff)

"Within this hallow'd dwelling." See "In diesen heil'gen hallen" (Mozart)

"Within this sacred dwelling." See "In diesen heil'gen hallen" (Mozart)

"Within what gloomy depths of forest." A. Dvořák. e. OS 2—SAS 2

"Within, you are in bed and dreaming sweetly." See "Tu nel tuo letto a far de' sogni d'oro"

"Within your porch I'm standing." See The orphan (Maggea)

Without roof, without home. See "Senza tetto, senza cuna" (Gomes)

Without thee ("Ce qu'est le lierre") See Ce que je suis sans toi (Gounod)

"Without thee life has no charm, dear." See Sans toi (Hardelot)

Witt, Julius
The tear. See "Wohl was es eine seligkeit"
"Wohl war es eine seligkeit"

Witthauer, Johann Georg
Schifffahrt

Witwicki,
The maiden's wish (Chopin)

Wi-um (Indian lullaby) T. Lieurance. e. LN

"Wo a klein's hüttle steht." See Liebesscherz

"Wo berg' ich mich" ("Where hide myself") C. M. von Weber. e.g. KS 5 —SOA 4

"Wo der rosen fülle uns mit duft berauscht." See Schlummerlied (Mattei)

"Wo die rose hier blüht." See Anakreon's grab (Wolf)

"Wo ich sei, und wo mich hingewendet." See Thekla, eine geisterstimme (Seidel)

"Wo man singet, lass dich ruhig nieder." See Der gesang

"Wo mut und kraft in deutschen seelen flammen." See Bundeslied

"Wo sind sie denn geblieben." See Er hat ein rot gesichte

Wo, Stormalong. Pulling chantey. SE

"Wo unter den birken noch schnee zu hauf." See The snowdrop (Grechaninov)

"Wo zur frohen feierstunde." See Bundesfeier

Woe is me ("Birch tree white stood in the shady forest green") Russian folk song. e. GO

Woe is me ("T'wards the garden bright with flow'rs") Bohemian song. e. KSE

"Woe is me! where are ye." See The Jamschick's complaint (Bakhmetiev)

"Woe to the hapless wight." See In der ferne (Schubert)

"Woe to you, traitor." See La Romanella

Woe unto them who forsake Him. Mendelssohn. e. OS 2

Woes of hidden love. See Heimlicher liebe pein (Weber)

Wohin (Whither) F. Schubert. Words by W. Müller. e.g. KF 1—PG 4— SS 1

"Wohl dir, liebe sommerzeit." See Sommerlied (Neidhardt von Reuenthal)

"Wohl gibt es der mädchen so viele." See Das geständnis (André)

"**Wohl** heute noch und morgen." See Träumelein

"**Wohl** viele tausend vögelein." See O bitt' euch liebe vögelein (Gumbert)

"**Wohl** war es eine seligkeit" (The tear) Witt. e.g. NML

"**Wohl** zu eignem leid." See "Deep in love was I" (Rachmaninov)

"**Wohlan** die zeit ist kommen, mein pferd." See Husarenliebe

"**Wohlauf** kameraden, aufs pferd, aufs pferd." See Reiterlied (Zahn)

"**Wohlauf**, noch getrunken den funkelnden wein." See Wanderlied (Folk air); Wanderlied (Schumann)

"**Wol** dir, liebe summerzit." See Sommerlied (Neidhardt von Reuenthal)

Wolcot, John
"Hope told a flattering tale" (Composer unknown)
Yarico to her lover (Himmel)

Wolcott, Samuel
"God of our fathers, let Thy face" (music by Danks; Nevin)

Wolder, David
Hymn of the dying (Composer unknown)

Wolf, Ernst Wilhelm
Zufriedenheit (from Ehrlichkeit und liebe)

Wolf, Hugo
All at rest, my sweet, but thee. See "Alle gingen, herz, zur ruh"
"Alle gingen, herz, zur ruh"
Anacreon's grave. See Anakreon's grab
Anakreon's grab
"Auch kleine dinge"
"Auf dem grünen balcon"
Auf ein altes bild
Begegnung
Die bekehrte
"Benedeit die sel'ge mutter"
Biterolf
"Blessed be the tender mother." See "Benedeit die sel'ge mutter"
Butterfly in April. See Citronenfalter im april
Citronenfalter im april
"E'en little things." See "Auch kleine dinge"
The elfin's song. See Die bekehrte
The encounter. See Begegnung
Er ist's
The friend. See Der freund
Der freund
"From her balcony green." See "Auf dem grünen balcon"
Fussreise
Gesang Weyla's
The gipsy-maid. See Die zigeunerin
Heimweh
Homesickness. See Heimweh
Im lager von Akkon, 1190. See Biterolf
"In dem schatten meiner locken"
In der frühe
In the camp of Akkon, 1190. See Biterolf

"In the shadow of my tresses." See "In dem schatten meiner locken"
"Kennst du das land"
Longing. See Heimweh
Mausfallen-sprüchlein
Mignon. See "Kennst du das land"
Morning. See In der frühe
The mouse-trap. See Mausfallen-sprüchlein
"Muh'voll komm' ich und beladen"
"Sad I come and bending lowly." See "Muh'voll komm' ich und beladen"
Secrecy. See Verborgenheit
Song to spring. See Er ist's
To an ancient picture. See Auf ein altes bild
"To rest, to rest." See "Zur ruh, zur ruh"
Tramping. See Fussreise
Verborgenheit
Weyla's song. See Gesang Weyla's
Die zigeunerin
"Zur ruh, zur ruh"

Wolf, O.
Mit födeland (Ibsen)
Nordhavet (Lindeman)

The **wolf**. W. Shield. Words by J. O'Keeffe. BAS 1—BE 1—DM 1—HSE 1

Wolfe, Charles
The burial of Sir John Moore (Barnett)
"Go! forget me" (music by Knight; Mozart)
"O say not that my heart is cold" (Irish air)

Wolff, Julius
"Mädchenaug'! mädchenaug'" (Moszkowski)

Wolff, Pius Alexander
"Einsam bin ich, nicht alleine" (Weber)
"Im wald, im wald" (Weber)
Wanderlied (Weber)

Wolfram's address. See "Blick' ich umher" (Wagner)

Wollank, Friedrich
"O tannenbaum, du edles reis"

The **wolves** (Les loups) A. Arensky. Words by A. Tolstoi. e.f. NR 1

Woman. See "Shall I, wasting in despair" (Phillips)

"**Woman** is fickle." See "La donna è mobile" (Verdi)

Woman, love, and wine. 18th century song. MM

The **woman** of Canaan. J. Haydn. e. WBT—WS

"**Woman's** feeling heart." See "La donna è mobile" (Verdi)

A **woman's** work is never done. Folk song from Berkshire. SF 4

"The **women** all tell." 18th century song. Ancient air. CO 2

"The **women** all tell" (Take a bumper and try) 18th century song. Another air. BE 1

"The **women** are a' gane wud." Whig song. MMS—PS 2

"**Won** i geh' und steh'." See Steyrers heimweh

Won is our independence. See Cancion patriotica (Mexican song)

"**Wonder** where is good ol' Daniel." Negro spiritual. DF—HR

"A **wonderful** house have I." See Our wonderful house

"**Wonderful** night." J. F. Young. HC

"**Wonderful** the joy I feel." See Heart throbs (Bendel)

The **wonderful** weaver. W. C. Levey. FSS 6—JSE

"**Wondrous** and soft the air." See Serenade (Musorgskii)

"A **wondrous** change my spirit doth surprise." J. Benedict. SAS 3

"**Wondrous** is the power." See "Wie berührt mich wundersam" (Bendel)

"The **wondrous** lovely month of May." See "Im wunderschönen monat mai" (Schumann)

"A **wondrous** rapture must it be." See "Es muss ein wunderbares sein" (Liszt)

Wonne der wehmuth (Delight of melancholy) R. Franz. Words by J. W. von Goethe. e.g. FF

Wonne der wehmuth (The pleasure of melancholy) e.g. NG

Wonne der wehmuth (Rapture of melancholy) e.g. GM

"**Wonne** schwebet, lächelt überall." See Freude in unschuld (Schulz)

"**Wonnevoller** mai" ("Come, thou lovely May") C. W. Gluck. Words by F. Sieber. e.g. FM

Won't you go my way. Pulling chantey. FSF—SE

"**Won't** you tell me, Mollie darling." See Mollie darling (Hays)

Won't you tell me why, Robin. C. Barnard (music and words) FSS 2—NML

Wood, C. H.
"Sing the carol! raise your voices" (Irons)

Wood, George E.
If—

Wood, Mary (Knight) See Mason, Mrs Mary (Knight) Wood

Wood, W.
"See! the morning star is dwelling" (music by Bridge; Pinkham)

Woo'd and married and a'. Scottish air. Words by J. Baillie. PS 1

The **wood-horn** ("How sweetly peal o'er hill and vale") FSS 6

Wood song. W. Watts. Words by E. Lee-Hamilton. CMF 1

Woodbury, Isaac Baker
Be kind to the loved ones at home
The captain's daughter. See "We were crowded in the cabin"
"Dainty wee stockings"
Faith in one another
Old house at home
"Row thy boat lightly"
"Speed away! speed away"
"Stars of the summer night"
"Strike the harp gently"
"We were crowded in the cabin"
The wife's welcome

The **woodcutter**. Harvest home song. MM

The **woodland** cabin (Hryc) Ruthenian folk song. e.r. SMF

Woodland roving. See Vandring i skoven (Grieg)

Woodland wandering. See Vandring i skoven (Grieg)

"The **woodlands** all were turning." See "Ich sah den wald sich färben" (Pressel)

Woodman, H. T.
"Row thy boat lightly" (Woodbury)

Woodman, Raymond Huntington
Ashes of roses
"The Christian flag"

The **woodman** ("Far remov'd from noise") C. Dibdin. HSE 2

"**Woodman**, spare that tree." J. A. Hiller. Words by G. P. Morris. LBR

"**Woodman**, spare that tree." H. Russell. Words by G. P. Morris. DM 2 —FSS 3— HSC— JO—JSE—WBT—WSC

Woodnotes. W. Müller. Words by R. W. Emerson. LBR

The **woodpecker** ("I knew by the smoke that so gracefully curl'd") Irish air. Words by T. Moore. MMI

The **woodpecker** ("I knew by the smoke that so gracefully curl'd") M. Kelly. Words by T. Moore. BE 2—HSE 1—JO

Woodruff, Arthur D.
A knot of white and blue

Woods, Amy S.
"Carol! carol joyfully" (Simper)
Happy Christmas morning (Simper)
"In Bethl'hem of Judah" (Simper)
"Star of Bethlehem, sweetly shining" (Simper)
"Waken, Christians! greet the morn" (Simper)

Woods, John J.
God defend New Zealand

The **woods** so wild. Air: Greenwood. BOH—DM 2

Woodward, George Ratcliffe
"Come, listen to my story" (16th century air)

Woodward, Henry
The miller's wedding (Old English air)

Woodworth, Francis Channing
The snowbird (Composer unknown)

Woodworth, Samuel
The old oaken bucket (Old air; also music by Kiallmark)

"A **wooer** cam' to our town." See Aikendrum

Wooing ("Z'nächst bin i") See Werbung

The **wooing** of the titmouse (Za morem sinitsa) Russian folk song. e. SSR 3

Woolsey, Sarah Chauncey
Christmas day (Composer unknown)
The **Worcestershire** Christmas carol. W.
H. Havergal (music and words) HC
"Words elude me." See "Dir ch'io t'ami"
(Mancini)
"Words vain words." V. Gabriel. Words
by R. Gray. FSS 5
Wordsworth, Christopher
"Alleluia! alleluia! hearts to heav'n and
voices raise" (Westlake)
"The day is gently sinking to a close"
(Barnby)
Hark! the holy voices (Cobb)
"Heavenly father, send Thy blessing"
(Peel)
"Sing, oh, sing this blessed morn" (Ro-
per)
Wordsworth, William
Lines written in early spring (Waller)
Worgan, John
"Christ the Lord is ris'n today, alle-
luia! Sons of men and angels say"
"Jesus Christ is risen to-day." See
"Christ the Lord is risen today, al-
leluia! Sons of men and angels say"
Nanny of the hill
"Sweet bird, whose heav'nly native
strain." See To the nightingale
To the nightingale
Work, Henry Clay
Babylon is fallen
Come home, father
God save the nation
Grandfather's clock
Kingdom coming
Marching through Georgia
Sleeping for the flag
Song of a thousand years
Wake Nicodemus
Washington and Lincoln
The year of jubilo
Work ("Banging of the hammer") See
Music of labor
Work and play. French air. FSS 1—
WSC
"Work, for the night is coming." L. Ma-
son. Words by A. L. Coghill.
FSS 1—HSC—NMH—NMS— OH
— WA— WBT— WS— WSC—
WSW
"Work, for the night is coming" (Work
song) BSS
"The **world** is deep in sleep." See Sere-
nade (Pierné)
The **world** is full of beauty. G. Donizet-
ti. FSS 4
"The **world** is very evil." J. D. Herron.
Words by Bernard of Cluny. [Tr of
Hora novissima] e. LA
"The **world** itself is blithe and gay." 17th
century German Easter carol. Tr of
Die ganze welt, Herr Jesu Christ. e.
HC
"The **world** itself keeps Easter day." Com-
poser unknown. Words by J. M.
Neale. HC

"The **world** itself keeps Easter day." J.
S. B. Hodges. Words by J. M. Neale.
HC
"The **world** itself keeps Easter day." J. A.
Preston. Words by J. M. Neale. HC
"The **world** itself keeps Easter-day." L.
H. Redner. Words by J. M. Neale.
HC
"The **world** itself keeps Easter day." R.
F. Smith. Words by J. M. Neale.
HC
"The **world** itself keeps Easter day." G.
W. Warren. Words by J. M. Neale.
HC
"The **world** was made for men, to see."
See Roll away (Tracy)
"Worn out shoes I am a-wearing." See
Old shoes
Worsley, Philip Stanhope
Loyal death (Stainer)
Worster, George
The fire of home
"Worthy, worthy is the Lamb." See John
saw the holy number
Wot cher. See Knock'd 'em in the old
Kent road (Chevalier)
Wotans abschied. R. Wagner. e.g.
SOA 5
"Would God I were the tender apple blos-
som." Irish air from county Derry.
Words by K. T. Hinkson. FSI—PI
"Would God I were the tender apple blos-
som" (Irish love song) Another Irish
air. Words by K. T. Hinkson. MMI
"Would I be a rabbi." See A teamster's
complaint
Would I were a boy again. See I would
I were a boy again (Romer)
"Would I were the fern." See "Que ne
suis-je la fougère" (Pergolesi)
"Would I were with thee." C. Bossetti.
Words by C. E. S. Norton. HSD—
NML—WBT
"Would, love, I were the rosebud." See
Like the rosebud (La Forge)
"Would the diamond seem such a peer-
less gem." See My little woman (Os-
good)
"Would you know the baby's skies." Nurs-
ery song. FSS 8
Wouldn't you. T. G. Shepard. Words
by C. Arthur. CHS
"Would'st thou magnify the story." J.
E. Ebeling. Words by P. Gerhardt.
Tr of Alle, die ihr Gott zu ehren. e.
HC
"Would'st thou that my heart so soon,
dear." See "Cómo quieres"
"Would'st thou the boast of ending." See
"Se tu della mia morte" (Scarlatti)
The **wounded** birch (Óstroyu syekeeroi)
A. T. Gret\'aninoff. Words by A.
Tolstoi. e. SMR 2
The **wounded** hussar. D. C. Hewitt.
Words by T. Campbell. JO
"Wowiyúskiṇ tanka hca wan." See Aya
po (Dowanna)

Woyna, Franz von
Hans and Lisa. See Hans und Liesel
Hans und Liesel
Wozli ryczki wozli mosta. See "By the bridge"
The **wraggle** taggle gipsies, O. English folk song. CST—FSF—SEF 1—SO
The **wraith.** See Der doppelgänger (Schubert)
Wranér, H.
Hyllning till Sverige (Sandberg)
"**Wrap** me up in a tarpaulin jacket." See Tarpaulin jacket
"**Wrapt** in verdure" (Maui) C. K. Hopkins. e.h. HA
A **wreath** for Princess Kaiulani (He lei no Kaiulani) C. K. Hopkins. Words by J. Edwards. e.h. HA
Wreath of carnations (Lei poni moi) C. K. Hopkins. Words by Huelani. .e.h. HA
"**Wreathe** the bowl." Irish air: Nora kista. Words by T. Moore. MI—MMI
Wreathed with flowers. See "O budding flowers" (Nape)
The **wreck** of the Hesperus. J. L. Hatton. Words by Longfellow. BAS 1—HSE 1
The **wreck** off Scilly. English folk song. BSW
Wreford, John Reynell
Prayer for our country (Tufts)
The **wren** ("Ke-chi ra-ku-wa-ku."—Song of the wren) Pawnee Indian song. in. FIS
The **wren** ("Rapide comme un rêve") See Le roitelet (Paladilhe)
The **wren** ("The wren scho lyes") Old Scottish song. PS 2
The **wren-boys'** song ("The wren, the wren") Irish song. MMI
"The **wren** scho lyes in care's bed." See The wren (Old Scottish song)
"The **wren,** the wren." See The wren-boys' song
"**Wrestling** Jacob." Negro spiritual. JP
Wrighton, William Thomas
The dearest spot is home
Her bright smile haunts me still
"If you to me be cold" (same air as Her bright smile haunts me still)
One or two. See "If you to me be cold"
Only a lock of her hair
They come with blissful song
"Thy voice is near"
"**Wronge** not, deare empress of my hearte." Song of the time of Charles I. PR 1
"**Wšak** nám tak, nebude." See The treasure
"**Wśród** nocnej ciszy." See "Amid the silence"
Das **wunderblümchen** ("Ein blümchen schön") Volksweise. g. ED 3

Wurda, Josef
Soldatenliebe. See "Steh' ich in finstrer mitternacht"
Soldier's love. See "Steh' ich in finstrer mitternacht"
"Steh' ich in finstrer mitternacht"
Die **Würzburger** glöckli ("Und die Würzburger glöckli") Volkslied. g. ED 1
Wybitski,
Polish national song (Ogiński?)
Wyeth, John
"Come, Thou Fount of every blessing"
While the days are going by
Wyman, C. M.
"O captain! my captain"
"**Wynken,** Blynken, and Nod." G. Paisiello. Words by E. Field. LBR
Wynn, Harold
Going to market (Diehl)
Wynne, John
Love and music
Love's bacchanal
Pleasant old age
" 'Tis love that makes all nature gay." See Love and music
Wyss, Johann Rudolf
Schweizer heimweh (Glück)
Wzlobia lezy ktoz po biezy. For English translation see "In a manger He is lying"

Y

"**Y** a cantar a una niña yo le enseñaba." See A cantar a una niña
"**Y-a** rien de si charmant" (La bergère aux champs.—The shepherdess of the fields) French folk song. e.f. GMF
"**Y-a** rien de si charmant" (La vie de la bergère.—The life of the shepherdess) French folk song. Another air. e.f. TSF
Y tu dices que te alejas. See Torna a Surriento (Curtis)
"**Ya** brilla la aurora" (Serenata) M. G. Tavárez. Words by V. Hugo. s. LCP
"**Ya** el pato se está cociendo." See El atole
"**Ya** no voy almonte a ver mis carneros." See Bartolillo
"**Ya** pinta la aurora." See Canción de la mañana (Tavárez)
"**Yā** rā'ikheh ala-al-jisrī." See "Across the bridge, O come"
"**Ya** se cayo el arbolito." See El pavu rial
"**Ya** terminan las sabias explicaciones." See Las vacaciones (Colón)
"**Yā** ummī-frishī lī-lkharīr." See "O mother mine, spread me the silken sheet"
"**Ya** viene el alba." Folk song from California. e.s. HS
"**Ya** viene la primavera." See La primavera

"Yă, yă, yă, yă, yă, yă, yă." See Imitation of a bagpipe

Yale Boola song. See Boola song (Hirsh)

"Yale college is a jolly home." See Litoria

The Yang-tsi-kiang. A. H. Dunlop. Words by R. Davidson. SSS

"The Yankee boy." A. Lee. FSS 7

Yankee Doodle ("Father and I went down to camp") American Colonial song. Old air. Words attributed to R. Shuckburgh (wrongly called Schackburg, Schamburgh, and Shamburg) BMC— BOS— BSE— BSP— CST— FMB—FSS 3—GO—HSC—HSD— JO —JSE— MP— NMH— OH— SN— WA—WBT—WCP—WSC—WSW

Yankee Doodle ("O Yankee Doodle came to town") Old air. Words wrongly attributed to Shamburg. BD

"Yankee Doodle came to town." WSC

Yankee Doodle ("Once on a time old Johnny Bull") Old air. Words by G. P. Morris. BSE—SN

Yankee Doodle-oodle ("My name is Yankee Doodle and I am a good old scout") College air. Words by R. D. Ware. BSS

Yankee Doodle-oodle ("My name is Yankee Doodle and my home's the U. S. A.") College air. Words by R. D. Ware. TFC 1

The Yankee girls. American song. MP

"A Yankee ship." Chantey. SMW For variants of this song see Blow, boys, blow, and songs of similar title

"A Yankee ship, and a Yankee crew." C. M. King. HSD—MP—WBT

"A Yankee ship came down the river, blow, boys, blow! A Yankee ship and a Yankee skipper." See Blow, boys, blow (Long drag chantey)

"A Yankee ship came down the river, blow boys, blow. A Yankee ship came down the river." See "A Yankee ship"

"A Yankee ship came down the river, blow, boys, blow! Her masts and spars they shine like silver." See Blow, boys, blow (Halliard chantey)

"A Yankee ship came down the river; Shallow O, Shallow Brown." See Shallow Brown

Yarico to her lover. F. H. Himmel. Words by P. Pindar. HSE 2

"Yay te va el toro, muchacho." See El toro y el ranchero

"Yderst mod norden" (Iceland) Old Norse air: Rabna bryllupet i Kraakalund, or, The raven's wedding. Words by A. Munch. e.n. MAN

"Ye awful Stygian powers." See "Divinités du Styx" (Gluck)

"Ye banks and braes and streams around the castle o' Montgomery." See Highland Mary (Scottish air); Highland Mary (Bartlett)

"Ye banks and braes of bonnie Doon." See Bonnie Doon (Miller)

"Ye belles, and ye flirts." Words by W. Whitehead. DM 1

Ye bells of Christmas time. A. Berridge. HC

"Ye bells, ye bells, ye happy bells." See Ye bells of Christmas time (Berridge)

"Ye birds that sing sweetly." See The message (Purcell)

"Ye blisses, that ravish." See "Delizie contente, che l'alma beate" (Cavalli)

Ye budding flowers. See Naissantes fleurs (Grétry)

"Ye cheerful virgins, have ye seen." See Myrtilla (Howard)

"Ye cloudlets, wand'ring free." See Les nuages (Bouval)

"Ye colleges proud, with your charters old." See A toast to Columbia (Parsons)

"Ye country maidens gather dew." See Cornish May song

"Ye dark-hair'd youths." Irish air: I'll make my love a breast of glass. Words by E. Walsh. MMI

"Ye darksome woods, where echo dwells." See Old Ringwood (Hawes)

"Ye dear, fleeting hours" ("Ihr flüchtigen stunden") A. S. Dargomijsky. Words by D. Davuidoff. e.g. SC

"Ye fair, from man's insidious love." See The retort (Arne)

"Ye fair, possest of ev'ry charm." See The way to keep him (Arne)

"Ye fields of gaily tinted flowers." See Di tanti palpiti (Rossini)

"Ye flowery banks o' bonie Doon." Air: Ballendalloch's reel, or, Cambdelmore. Words by R. Burns. BSR

"Ye foes of man, your might is shaken." J. S. Bach. e. SAS 3

"Ye gallants bright, I rede you right." A. Masterton. Words by R. Burns. BSR

"Ye gods of night profound." See "Divinités du Styx" (Gluck)

"Ye golden lamps of heaven" (Holstein) Words by P. Doddridge. FSS 5

"Ye good fellows all." See Bumpers, Squire Jones (O'Carolan)

"Ye ha he ya e he dha." See Zon-zi-monde

"Ye happy bells of Easter-day." J. S. B. Hodges. HC

"Ye heav'ns, uplift your voice." Old Easter carol. 14th or 15th century words. Tr of Plaudite coeli. e. HC

"Ye holy angels bright" (St Gregory) J. Barnby. Words by R. Baxter. TL

"Ye Jacobites by name." Air: Ye Jacobites by name. Words by R. Burns. BSR

"Ye lads and lassies all, arise and speed." See May song (Smith)

"Ye little loves, that hourly wait." See The lover's message (Galliard)

"Ye maidens pretty." English folk song. BSW

"**Ye** maids of Helston, gather dew." See Cornish May song

"**Ye** mariners of England." J. W. Calcott. Words by T. Campbell. BOS—DM 1 —JE—JO

"**Ye** mariners of England." H. H. Pierson. Words by T. Campbell. SSS

"**Ye** maun gang to your father, Janet." Scottish song. Air: Fair Janet. PS 2

"**Ye** men of France, ye valiant people." See La Parisienne (Auber)

Ye merry birds. See O bitt' euch liebe vögelein (Gumbert)

"**Ye** Morrises." Air: The boatman. DM 2

"**Ye** mortals all hear the clamor exultant." See "Oid, mortales, el grito sagrado" (López y Planes)

"**Ye** mortals, say, know ye what joy is." See Joy (Lindblad)

"**Ye** muses nine, with me combine." See The shamrock shore

Ye natives of this nation. Irish folk song. JOI

"**Ye** nymphs and sylvan gods" (The milking pail) 16th century air. [Words by T. D'Urfey] HSE 2

"**Ye** nymphs and sylvan gods" (The bonny milkmaid) 18th century air. Words by T. D'Urfey. MM

"**Ye** pangs of anxious thought." See "Affani del pensier" (Händel)

"**Ye** parliament of England." Forecastle song. CR

"**Ye** people, rend your hearts." F. Mendelssohn. e. OS 3—SAS 3
Also in "If with all your hearts ye truly seek me" (Mendelssohn) TL— TS

"**Ye** powers above protect the widow." See The death of Parker

"**Ye** powers that dwell below." See "Divinités du Styx" (Gluck)

"**Ye** sacred priests." G. F. Händel. SAS 1
Also in Farewell, ye limpid springs and floods (Händel) OS 1

"**Ye** say they all have passed away." W. Guernsey. Words by L. H. Sigourney. LBR

"**Ye** seamen bold that plough the ocean." See The ship in distress

"**Ye** shepherds, give ear to my lay." W. Jackson. MM

"**Ye** shepherds, tell me." J. Mazzinghi. MS

"**Ye** sons and daughters of the King." G. W. Warren. Tr of O filii et filiae, Rex coelestis, Rex gloriae. e. HC

"**Ye** sons of Columbia, who bravely have fought." See Adams and liberty

"**Ye** sons of Columbia, your attention I do crave." See Fuller and Warren

"**Ye** sons of France, awake to glory." See La Marseillaise (Rouget de Lisle)

"**Ye** sons of freedom, wake to glory." See La Marseillaise (Rouget de Lisle)

"**Ye** sons of Norway." See "Sönner af Norge" (Blom)

"**Ye** sons of old Ireland." Air: Noch baineann sin dó. JOI

"**Ye** sons of old Killie." Air: Over the water to Charlie. Words by R. Burns. BSR

Ye sons of the nation. C. Barnard. Words by L. Doten. FSS 6

"**Ye** trees, that now so humbly bow." See Langs en å (Grieg)

"**Ye** twice ten hundred deities" (The conjurer's song) Purcell. BAS 2— HSE 1

"**Ye** verdant hills, ye balmy vales." G. F. Händel. BS 1—OS 3—SAS 3

"**Ye** who have scorned each other." See Under the holly bough (Barnard)

"**Ye** who love the republic." See The school-house and the flag (Southwick)

"**Ye** who love's power right well should know." See "Voi, che sapete" (Mozart)

"**Ye** whose care are the mountains and trees." See Einsamkeit (Medtner)

"**Yea,** for tonight am I queen of the fairies." See Je suis Titania (Thomas)

"**Yea,** I fell in the pit of love." See Ti, tum, ti (Reeve)

"**Yea,** mystery supreme by the tomb is concealed." R. Pugno. e. SAS 1

"The **year** has sped in joy and grief." See Harvest home song (Olds)

The **year** of jubilo. H. C. Work. Words by D. Stevens. TFC 2

"The **year** rolls round, the days return." See Three cheers for K. S. U.

The **year** that's awa. Air: 'Tis good to be aff wi' the old love. Words by J. Dunlop. CS 1—JO—PS 1

"The **year** toward its decline." See Pensée d'automne (Massenet)

Yearnings. See Longing (Rubinstein)

"The **years** creep slowly by, Lorena." See Lorena (Webster)

"The **years** of slavery are past." See La Brabançonne (Campenhout)

Yeats, William Butler
"Down by the sally gardens" (Air: Far beyond yon mountain; air: The maids of Mourne shore)

Ye'll a' hae heard tell o' Rab Roryson's bonnet. See Rab Roryson's bonnet

"**Ye'll** know him by his golden hair." See My laddie far away (Bliss)

The **yellow** and blue. University of Michigan song. Balfe. Words by C. Gayley. CHS—MPC—NMS

The **yellow** and the brown. Nebraska Wesleyan university song. Words by O. Hinson. CHS

"**Yellow** at my feet." See "Gelb rollt mir zu füssen" (Rubinstein)

"The **yellow-hair'd** laddie." Scottish air. Words by A. Ramsay. MMS—PS 1

Yeoman's wedding song. Poniatowski. e. FSS 6

The **yeomen** of England. E. German. Words by B. Hood. BOS

"**Yes,** dear departed, cherished days." See Departed days

"**Yes!** even love to fame must yield." See O 'tis a glorious sight to see (Weber)

"Yes, for this evening, I am queen of the revels." See Je suis Titania (Thomas)

"Yes, her doom is to die." See Ombre di mia prosapia (Ponchielli)

Yes, he's taken my feet out of the miry clay. See "Rise, mourner"

"Yes, I love thee as some bright angel." See L'amour (Godard)

"Yes, I love you." P. Tschaikowsky. e. WL

"Yes! let me like a soldier fall." V. Wallace. Words by E. Fitzball. BE 2—DM 1—HSE 3—TS

"Yes, now thou art my spouse by right." See "Ah si, ben mio; coll' essere io tuo" (Verdi)

"Yes, sad one of Sion, if closely resembling." See The parallel

"Yes! she flies from me still." See Sous les pieds d'une femme (Gounod)

"Yes, she's my daughter." See Cortigiani, vil razza (Verdi)

"Yes! the die is cast." J. W. Kalliwoda; attributed also to P. Pestel. Words by J. R. Ling. e. FSS 3—JO

"Yes, Thou wilt yet remember." F. Hiller. e. SAS 3

"Yes, time with fate e'er striving." See "Ah! non credea mirarti" (Bellini)

"Yes, 'tis he, it is my child." See "Oui, c'est lui" (Dubois)

"Yes, 'tis here, where once so brightly." See "Qui la voce" (Bellini)

"Yes, 'tis plain as the day." See Air du tambour major (Thomas)

"Yes, very many lovely flow'rs." See My Rosy (Stauffer)

"Yes, we love this country." See "Ja vi elsker dette landet" (Nordraak)

Yes, we love this land. See "Ja vi elsker dette landet" (Nordraak)

"Yes, we love with fond devotion." See "Ja vi elsker dette landet" (Nordraak)

"Yes, we'll rally round the flag, boys." See The battle cry of freedom (Root)

Yes, yes, my Lord, I'm going to join the heav'nly choir. See "What kind of shoes you going to wear"

Yester, John Hay, lord. See Tweeddale, John Hay, 2d marquis of

Yesterday ("And thou I lov'd art gone") J. Blockley. WBT

"Yesterday at evening in the wood." See Im wald bei der amsel

Yesterday evening. Istrian folk song. e. BF 1

"Yesterday you said to-day." See Cruel Caramba

Yestereve. J. R. Johnson. Words by Lord Lytton. BD

"Yestreen I had a pint o' wine." Air: Banks of Banna. Words by R. Burns. BSR

"Yestreen I met you on the moor." See O Tibbie, I hae seen the day

"Yestreen the queen had four Maries." See The queen's Maries

"Yet ah, that spring should vanish." A. Whiting. Words by Omar Khayyám. e. AA

"Yet not alone of labor comes our plenty." C. M. von Weber. e. SAS 1

Yevréiskaya pyésnya. See The song of Solomon (Musorgskiï)

"Y'heave ho! my lads, the wind blows free." See Sailing (Marks)

"Yield not, my heart." See "No, no, mio core" (Carissimi)

"Yisroel, am kdeishim." See Call to worship

"Yksi ruusu on kasvanut laaksossa." See The lovely rose

"Yn mhalas llwyn on gynt." See Llwyn on

"Den yndigste rose" (The perfect rose) Danish air. Words by E. Brorson. da.e. BF 2

"Yo he ah a tha-a he ah." See I-ou'-tin game song: Song for the south side

Yo heave ho ("My name") See Tom Tough (Dibdin)

"Yo, heave ho! round the capstan go." Capstan chantey. GO—SMW

"Yo-ho-hoey! yo-ho-ho-hoey." See "Traft ihr das schiff" (Wagner)

"Yo le dije á un zapatero." See El zapatero

"Yo m'alegro de habèr sido" ("If 'tis sorrow so to love thee") Seguidilla. e.s. BO

"Yo no sé si me quieres." Folk song from southern California or northern Mexico. e.s. HS

"Yo pienso en ti." Folk song from southern California. e.s. HS

"Yo soy el mejor torero." See Alma Andaluza (Gómez)

"Yo soy firme para amarte." See El capotin

"Yo soy guajira, nací en Melena." See La guajira

"Yo soy la viudita del conde Laurel." See La viudita del conde Laurel

"Yo soy tu paloma blanca." See La paloma blanca

"Yo soy una chinaquita." Mexican folk song. e.s. HS

"Yo te amo, idolatro." Costa Rican folk song. e.s. HS

"Yo trobador, yo pobre sin fortuna." See El trobador

"Yo vivo sola en el mundo." See La guajira

Yo, yea. C. Dibdin. DM 2
"I sailed in the good ship, the Kitty." ME

Yoh-Wu-Mo. Chinese song. c.e. BF 2

"Yoito korasamo." See Japanese chorus used when scrubbing the decks

"Yon wild mossy mountains." J. Oswald. Words by R. Burns. BSR

"Yonder comes a courteous knight." See The courteous knight

"Yonder, down on Mother Volga, Volga." See Mother Vólga

"**Yonder** fragrant marjoram is growing." See The bride's farewell

"**Yonder** is a comely flower." See No, sir, no

"**Yonder** sits a fair young damsel." Folk song from Hampshire. SF 3
Variant of: O no, John

York! York for my money. Air: Greensleeves. Words by W. Elderton. BE 8

The **Yorkshire** man. W. Reeve. Words by T. Dibdin. ME

Yorkston, James
Cockles and mussels
"In Dublin's fair city." See Cockles and mussels

You ("En Cuba, la isla hermosa") See Tú (Fuentes)

You and I. Claribel (C. Norton) FSS 8 —WBT—WL

You and I together, love. See Going to market (Diehl)

You and me. Words by T. Moore. FSS 5

You are all my treasure. See T' ses tüta mia furtüna

"**You** are gazing now on old Tom Moore." See Days of forty-nine

"**You** are going far away." See Jeannette and Jeannot (Glover)

You are my own. See T' ses tüta mia furtüna

"**You** are my sweetheart, you over yonder." See Confession

"**You** are not what you were, Robin." See Won't you tell me why, Robin (Barnard)

"**You** brought me flowers." M. Jacobson. Words from the Russian of Loukianoff. e. NM 1

"**You** captains bold and brave, hear my cries, hear my cries." See Kidd's lament

"**You** captains bold and brave, hear our cries, hear our cries." See Captain Kidd

"**You** combers all, both great and small." See The rambling comber

"**You** doubtless have heard of the Fliggyboo bird." See The Fliggyboo bird (Macgregor)

"**You** generals all and champions bold." See The duke of Marlborough

"**You** gentlemen of England." English air: The joviall cobbler. Words by M. Parker. BE 2—BOH— HSE 2—JE—JS—MM
When the stormy winds do blow. CO 2
"You gentlemen of England" (Neptune's raging fury) DM 1

"**You** gentlemen of England." Irish air. ⌊Words by M. Parker⌋ JOI

"**You** got a right." Negro spiritual. JB

"**You** got Jesus, hold Him fas'." See Put John on de islan'

"**You** have told me that you love me." See Will you love me then as now (Weiland)

You hear de lambs a cryin'. See Hear the lambs a-crying

"**You** kin do jes'-a what you please." See Peanut pickin' song

You know I'm your priest." See Ballinamona Oro

"**You** lasses and lads." See Come lasses and lads

"**You** little children there who live by the riverside." See Loéma tombé

"**You** maidens, now pity the sorrowful moan I make." See Jemmy mo veela sthore

"**You** may bury me in the east." See I'll hear the trumpet sound

"**You** may not kiss me, sir, she said." See A gentle hint (Riker)

"**You** may slight me, who's afraid." See The Cheshire chambermaid (Arnold)

You must shun old Satan. Negro spiritual. JP

"**You** must wake and call me early." See The May queen (Dempster)

You never miss the water. R. Howard. Words by H. Linn. FSS 6—HSD

"**You** old fool, you blind fool." See Our goodman (Big Laurel, N.C. version no. 2)

"**You** pinch me so, you bite me so." See Tarantella

"**You** promised, friend, I plainly heard." See The man of his word (Beethoven)

"**You** promis'd me four kerchiefs." See Ritornello delle lavandare del Vomero

"**You** promised to meet me at Adams's spring." See Poor Omie (Kentucky version)

"**You** rake and shovel and wheelbarrow bring." See Planting a garden

"**You** ramblin' boys of Liverpool." See The banks of Newfoundland

"**You** remember Ellen." Irish air: Were I a clerk. Words by T. Moore. MI —MMI

"**You** rural goddesses that woods and fields possess." See The merry milkmaids

"**You** see, my friends." Händel. MSS 2

"**You** Shanandore, I long to hear you." See River Shenandore

"**You** sit lonely today as the bright flames burn low." See By the fireside

"**You** speak of sunny skies to me." See Blanche Alpen (Glover)

"**You** spotted snakes with double tongue." See Midsummer night's dream (Macfarren)

"**You** stole my love." W. Macfarran. Words by A. Munday. MS

"**You** take a few pieces of zinc." See H_2SO_4 (Russell)

"**You** talk of your beauties of France and of Germany." See Lasses of Scotland

"**You** think I have a merry heart." See I'm saddest when I sing (Bishop)

"**You** think, oh sun so fair." See Amaryllis (Louis XIII)

"**You** who were born with beauty of the roses." See Dimme 'na vota sì (Scalisi)

"**You** wrote to me: so why deny it." See Had fickle fortune, not betraying (Tchaikovsky)

"**You'd** better be a-praying." See My bretheren, don't get weary

"**You'd** fain be hearing what dress he's wearing." See "Saper vorreste" (Verdi)

"**You'd** have me sing." See "Jeg synge skal en vise" (Hartmann)

Young, Anthony
  "The gentry to the King's Head go." See The taverns' song
  The reproach
  "Send back my long strayed eyes." See The reproach
  The taverns' song

Young, Charles
  "It is not that I love you less"
  The vocal grove

Young, Charlotte
  "Hearts and homes" (Blockley)

Young, Ella
  The wind from the west (Irish air)

Young, John
  The Darwinian theory (Composer unknown)

Young, John Freeman
  "Wonderful night"

"**Young** Agnes." D. F. E. Auber. e. FSS 8

"**Young** and bold am I." See The call of freedom (Balakirev)

"**Young** and green upon the mountain." See The Cossack (Moniuszko)

"**Young** and old must raise the lay." Old air. Words by J. M. Neale. HC

"**Young** and old must raise the lay." Composer unknown. Words by J. M. Neale. HC

The **young** beauty. See La cianciosa

Young Beichan. Folk song: Kentucky version. CSE
  Lord Batesman (The Turkish lady) WLT
  Young Beichan. Allanstand, N.C. version. CSE
  —Big Laurel, N.C. version. CSE
  —White Rock, N.C. version. CSE
  Variant of:"Lord Bateman"

"**Young** Bierlala was the only son." See Bierlala

The **young** birch. See Ungbirken (Egeberg); Ungbirken (Grieg)

Young Edward ("My father owns a fine house") Kentucky mountain song. WT

"**Young** Edward came to Emily." See Edwin in the lowlands low (Hot Springs, N.C. version)

Young Edwin in the lowlands low. See Edwin in the lowlands low (Hampshire version)

"**Young** Em'ly was a maid so fair." See Edwin in the lowlands low (Georgia version)

"**Young** Em'ly was a very nice girl." See Edwin in the lowlands low (Black Mountain, N.C. version)

Young hunting. Folk song: Georgia version. CSE
  —Kentucky version. SA
  —Alleghany, N.C. version. CSE
  —Carmen, N.C. version. CSE
  —Hot Springs, N.C. version. CSE
  —Virginia version. CSE

The **young** Indian maid. Words by T. Moore. FSS 7

"**Young** Jack he was a journeyman." See Roving Jack

"**Young** Jamie lo'ed me weel." See Auld Robin Gray (Old air); Auld Robin Gray (Leeves)

"**Young** Jamie, pride of a' the plain." Air: The carlin o' the glen. Words by R. Burns. BSR

"**Young** Jemmy." 17th century song. CO 2

"**Young** Jockey he courted sweet Mog the brunette." See Sweet Mog the brunette

"**Young** Jockey he courted sweet Moggy." 18th century song. ME
  Variant: Sweet Mog the brunette

"**Young** Jockie was the blythest lad." Air: Jockie was the blythest lad. Words by R. Burns. BSR

Young Kate of Kilcummer ("There are flowers in the valley") Irish air: My love has gone—my heart is sore. e. MMI

Young lasses. See "Jeunes fillettes" (Dalayrac)

Young Lobski's fishing tale. J. Mazzinghi. Words by F. Reynolds. ME

The **young** lover. T. Koschat. e. WC

"**Young** Lubin was a shepherd boy." T. Linley. Words by R. Tickell. ME

"A **young** man I heard." See Fair Ellen Pugh

"A **young** man sat sighing by a sycamore tree." See The willow song (Humfrey)

The **young** man's wish. See "Free from the bustle, care, and strife" (Collett)

"The **young** May moon." Air: The dandy O. Words by T. Moore. FSS 5—JO—MI—MMI—PI—WBT

"**Young** men and maidens, I pray draw near." See Handsome Sally

"**Young** men and maids on New Year's day." Air: Caper and firk it. DM 2

"**Young** men and maids, pray tell your age." See Locks and bolts (Kentucky version)

"**Young** Molly, who lives at the foot of the hill." See The lass with the delicate air (Arne)

"The **young** moon lies in the old moon's arms." See The moon's lullaby (Burnham)

The **young** nun ("Quanno mammà") See La monacella ("Quanno mammà")

The **young** nun ("Wie braust durch die wipfel") See Die junge nonne (Schubert)

The **young** nun ("Zi monacella") See La monacella ("Zi monacella")

"**Young** Palmus was a ferryman." See Shackley-hay

"**Young** Peggie blooms our bonniest lass." Scottish air: Peggie, I must love thee. [Words by R. Burns] PS 2

"**Young** Peggy blooms our boniest lass." Air: Loch Eroch Side. Words by R. Burns. BSR

"**Young** Philip the falconer's up with the day." See Philip the falconer (Loder)

The **young** postillion. Lindblad. e. KSN

Young ramble-away. See Brimbledon fair

The **young** recruit ("See these ribbons") See Lizette (Kücken)

The **young** recruit ("Wer will unter die soldaten") See Der kleine rekrut (Kücken)

"**Young** Reilly." Folk song from Hampshire. SF 3

Young Richard. Old English song from Somersetshire. BC

Young Robin ("Down in the mead") Air: Hud y bibell, or, The allurement of the pipe. Words from the Welsh. e. MMW

"**Young** Roger came tapping at Dolly's window." See Roger's courtship (Carey)

"**Young** Roger, the miller, went courting of late." See The grey mare

"**Young** Rory O'More." See Rory O'More

"**Young** sailor Dick, as he stepped on shore." See The green bed (Devon version)

"**Young** thoughts have music." E. R. Kroeger. Words by F. G. Halleck. TL

"**Young** Violetta, the fair, the gay." See "La Violetta la va"

"**Young** virgins all, I pray draw near." See The Turkish lady

"**Young** women they'll run like hares on the mountains." See Hares on the mountains

"**Your** friendship much can make me blest." Air: Banks of Spey. Words by R. Burns. BSR

"**Your** hand is cauld as snaw, Annie." See Annie's tryst

"**Your** hay it is mow'd." See Harvest home

"**Your** heav'nly Father knoweth." M. B. Foster. SAS 3

Your love dear, your love to me is grateful. See Kohala's breezes (Nape)

Your mission. S. M. Grannis. Words [by E. H. Gates;] wrongly attributed to J. R. Gates. FSS 1—HSD

"**Your** Molly has never been false, she declares." See Wapping old stairs (Percy)

"**Your** soul is a landscape wondrous and rare." See Clair de lune (Fauré)

"**You're** looking as fresh as the morn, darling." See Kitty Tyrrell (Glover)

"**You're** welcome to despots, Dumourier." Air: Robin Adair. Words by R. Burns. BSR

You're welcome, Willie Stewart. See "Come, bumpers high! express your joy"

"**Youths** and maidens, come and sing." See Colorado college song

"**Youth's** the season made for joys." Air: Cotillon. Words by J. Gay. DM 1 —MM

Yradier, Sebastian
The dove. See La paloma
Oh! the sailor shall sing. See La paloma
La paloma

"**Yule** returns; come, Christian people." V. B. Crowther-Benyon. Words by R. Waltham. HC

Yuletide ("Vor verden er") See Jul (Alnaes)

Yuletide ("Yuletide wakes."—Koliáda) Ukrainian song. e.r. BF 1
Variant of: "Kolyada, Kolyada"

"**Yulla** naily." Nile river song. ar. SMW

Z

Z dvojenje. See Mournful love

"**Z** dymem pożarów, z kurzem krwi bratniej." See Choral

"**Z** tamtej strony jezioreczka." See By the lake

"**Z**-z-z-z-z the mosquito is singing, O hark." See The mosquito's serenade (Loomis)

"**Za** jedan časak." See One moment

Za morem sinitsa. See The wooing of the titmouse

"**Za** Niemen." See Across the Niemen

La **zagala** (The shepherd girl) Latin American song. e.s. BF 2

Zahn, Christian Jacob
Cavalry song. See Reiterlied
Reiterlied

Zahorsky, Karel
The man without tears

Zaleski, Bohdan
The parted lovers (Chopin)

Zapateo cubano. Cuban song. G. Vilá. e.s. SN

El **zapatero** (The shoemaker) Spanish-American song. e.s. LSS

Zaplaitesya plaiten. See "Come and twine the slim boughs"

Zapletisîa pleten'. See "Come and twine the slim boughs"

Zapyévka. See To Russia (Balakirev)

"**Zarekokh** se, mamo." See Vows

Zech, J.
Betrayal. See Verrath
Verrath

Zedlitz, Joseph Christian, freiherr von
Austrian national hymn (Haydn) See Haschka, L. L. "Gott erhalte Franz den kaiser" (Haydn)

"**Zeg**, kwezelken, wildegy dansen." See Het kwezelken

Zehelein, Justus Friedrich
Stille liebe (Lindpaintner)
Zeller, Karl
Nightingale song (from The Tyrolean)
Zelter, Karl Friedrich
Abendlied
An den mond
An Emma
An Mignon
Der arme Thoms
Die betende
Die gunst des augenblicks
"Die heiligen drei könig' mit ihrem stern"
King of Thule. See Der könig in Thule
Der könig in Thule
Der musensohn
Rechter sache gutes ende
Schäfers klagelied
Trinklied. See Wein, weib, gesang
Urians reise um die welt
Vanitas! vanitatum vanitas
Wein, weib, gesang
Wine, woman and song. See Wein, weib, gesang
"Zehn brieder." See "Ten brothers"
"Zemi ma, Rado." See Rada
Zephyr of nightfall. Composer and author of words unknown. FSS 5—LA
Das **zerbrochene** ringlein. See "In einem kühlen grunde" (Berger); "In einem kühlen grunde" (Glück)
"**Zha-wa** i-ba i-ba e-he." Omaha Indian call. in. FI
Zhemchuzhnikov, A.
The desert (Balakirev)
"**Zhin-ga** dha-we dho dho we he ho-i." See The gift of peace
Zhukovskiĭ, Vasiliĭ Andreevich
The dream (Rubinstein)
"Knight-errant" (Dargomyzhskiĭ)
Russian national hymn (Lvov)
"**Zi** monacella." See La monacella
"**Zie** hoe het vriendlijke zonlicht." See Zonnelied (Rennes)
Ziganov,
The scarlet sarafan (Varlamov)
Die **zigeunerin** (The gipsy-maid) H. Wolf. Words by J. von Eichendorff. e.g. GM
Zintheo, C. J.
We cheer for the "U of M"
Zion, weep a-low. Negro spiritual. HR—JP
Zion's children. Negro spiritual. JP
"**Zion's** ways do languish." See Jerusalem (Gounod)
"**Zis-a** badea c'a veni." See Hora
Ziska, Jan
Ancient chant of the Taborites (Bohemian air)
Zitherbubens morgenlied ("Fröhlich und wohlgemut") J. H. C. Bornhardt. Words by G. P. Schmidt von Lübeck. g. ED 1

"**Z'Lauterbach** hab i mein'n strumpf verlorn." See Zu Lauterbach
"**Z'nächst** bin i halt gange." See Werbung
"**Z'nagst** bin i hald ganga." See Werbung
"**Zógt-she** rabbenov, was wet sain." See What will happen when the Messiah comes
Zohra (Kabyle song) Moroccan folk song. e.f. BO
Zöllner, Carl
"Where would I be"
Zolotarev, Vassiliĭ Andreevich
Canzonetta
Zonnelied (Sunshine song) C. van Rennes. Words by A. Fles. d.e. CMF 1
Zon-zi-mon-de. Omaha Indian song. in. FIS
"**Zu** Bacharach am Rheine." See Lorelei (Erk)
"**Zu** deinen füssen möcht' ich liegen" ("I at thy feet would fain be lying") Graben-Hoffmann. e.g. AB 2
"**Zu** dem duft, der da würzt die lenzesluft." See Veilchen (Cornelius)
"**Zu** des lebens freuden schuf uns die natur." See Beruf zur freude (Bergt)
Zu festgelagen ("Bruder, zu dem festlichen gelage") Volksweise. g. ED 1
"**Zu** Koblenz auf der brücken." See Wassersnot (Reichardt)
Zu Lauterbach. Süddeutsches volkslied. g. ED 1
The Lauterbach maiden. e.g. WC
Lauterbach song. e. WBT—WSW
"**Zu** Mantua in banden der treue Hofer war." See Andreas Hofer
"**Zu** Strassburg auf der schanz." See Der Schweizer (Silcher)
Zuccalmaglio, Wilhelm von
"Jung Hänschen" (Volksweise)
Mondschein (Volksweise)
Schwesterlein, wann gehn wir nach haus (Volksweise)
Zueignung (Devotion) R. Strauss. Words by H. von Gilm. e.g. FO 2
Zufriedenheit ("Arm und kleine ist meine hütte") E. W. Wolf. Words by C. J. Wagenseil. g. ED 1
Zufriedenheit ("Was frag ich viel nach geld und gut") W. A. Mozart. Words by J. M. Miller. g. ED 1
Die zufriedenheit (Contentment) e.g. HSS 3
Zufriedenheit ("Was frag ich viel nach geld und gut") C. G. Neefe. Words by J. M. Miller. g. ED 1
Zufriedenheit ("Zufriedenheit ist mein vergnügen") Volkslied. g. ED 2
Zuleika. See Suleika (Mendelssohn)
"**Zuleika** disait au canari." See The canary (Tchaikovsky)
Zum abschied ("Schätzchen, reich' mir deine hand") Volkslied. g. ED 3
"**Zum** Hänschen sprach das Gretchen." See Der schwur (Bohm)

Zum leiden bin ich auserkohren. For English and Italian translations see Infelice sconsolata (Mozart)

Zum letzten mal ("Du wirst mir's ja nit übel nehma") Air: Müssts ma nix übel aufnehma. Volkslied. **g.** ED 1

Zum letzten mal (For the last time) e.g. SSG

Zum neuen jahr ("Zwischen dem alten") J. F. Reichardt. Words by Goethe. **g.** ED 2

Zumsteeg, Johann Rudolph
Alles um liebe
Daphne am bach
"Der eichwald brauset"
"Ich denke dein, wenn durch den hain"
Johanna's abschied
Kriegslied
"Wär ich ein muntres vögelein"

Zundel, John
"I was a wandering sheep"
Lebanon. See The peaceful fold
"Love divine, all love excelling"
No war nor battle sound
The peaceful fold

Zur Johannisnacht (On St John's eve) E. Grieg. e.g. PG 3

"**Zur** ruh, zur ruh" ("To rest, to rest") H. Wolf. Words by J. Kerner. e.g. FO 2

Zvonili zvony v Novgorodîe. See The bells of Novgorod

"**Zwei** die sich liebten." See The parted lovers (Chopin)

"**Zwei** feine stieflein hab' ich an." See Der sandmann (Schumann)

Zwei königskinder (Two royal children) Folk song. e.g. SSG
Two royal children. e. BSE

Zwei leichen. See The parted lovers (Chopin)

"**Zwischen** berg und tiefem." See Das lied von den zwei hasen

"**Zwischen** dem alten, zwischen dem neuen." See Zum neuen jahr (Reichardt)

"**Zwischen** Frankreich und dem Böhmerland." See Nur in Deutschland (Hoffmann von Fallersleben)

"**Zwischen** waizen und korn." See Mailied (Medtner)

Zyczenie. See The maiden's wish (Chopin)

Zym, ti, toodledei. See The Fliggyboo bird (Macgregor)

SONG INDEX
SUPPLEMENT

AN INDEX TO MORE THAN 7000 SONGS
IN 104 SONG COLLECTIONS
COMPRISING 124 VOLUMES

PREFACE

So complained two writers of light verse in the days when the nineteenth century was still in its vigorous second half. Had they written at the present time they need not have lacked exact knowledge of either the words or of "how they go" for they could have used the Song Index and could have sung some 18,000 old songs if either their ambition or their voices had held out.

The basic volume of the Song Index, published in 1926, indexed more than 12,000 different songs in 262 volumes of 177 song collections. As many different versions as well as translations were included, the number which might perhaps have been counted as different songs was actually much greater. To this large total is now added the indexing of more than 7,000 songs in this first supplement to the Song Index, thus bringing the total number covered by the whole work to perhaps 18,000, even after allowance has been made for the possible 2,000 repeated, though with new references, from the basic work. Since each song is indexed under author and composer, when these are known, as well as under title, with cross references from all variant and translated titles, from first line and sometimes from refrain, the total number of entries in the two volumes can hardly be less than 100,000 and may well exceed that impressive total. Mere statistics do not give the real measure of the value of any reference book, but sometimes statistics such as these give a graphic picture of one side of the great task of making such an index, in that they show the huge amount of laborious and intricate detail which the editor of the work and her able and loyal assistant had to plan and carry through. The judgment and knowledge needed for the many editorial decisions, and the ability and experience in research required for the looking up of obscure points before such decisions could be made, are quite aside from statistics and can not be measured by any statistical yardstick.

Minnie Earl Sears, the principal editor of the Song Index, planned both volumes of the work, edited all of the basic volume and also edited nearly all of the Supplement, the last work that she did, only about five days before her death, being the editing of some of the later entries in this Supplement. Her death on November 28, 1933, left the writing of the prefatory material to two different hands. Phyllis Crawford, who did the actual indexing for the new volume and finished the editing which Miss Sears' death left incomplete, has written the explanatory introduction, and the writing of this present Preface has fallen to one who, while she has done none of the actual work on either volume, has had from the beginning a two-fold connection with the work, as a member of the Committee on the Song Index, of which Mr. Franklin F. Hopper was chairman, and as Miss Sears' close friend and associate who because of that friendship and association perhaps knew more about certain aspects of the work involved in making the Index than anyone else except Miss Sears' official collaborator and assistant.   Naturally this is a different kind of preface from the one which Miss Sears herself could, or would, have written.   The grasp of the detail of the work, the comprehension of some of its special problems and difficulties, and the wealth of interesting illustrations of such problems which the editor had in her special knowledge are all lacking to the present writer.   On the other hand, speaking from the standpoint of one who had no hand in the actual making of the work, she can say some things about it which its editor would not have said, and would not have wished to say, and she can speak of it from the standpoint of a reference librarian who has often made use of the Index with appreciation of its quality and gratitude for its existence.

What kinds of readers will use the Song Index and for what kinds of questions will it prove useful?   It is easy to answer the first question by saying that anyone who wants either the words or the music of a particular song or who wishes to know who wrote its words or composed its music, will use the Index. But such an answer merely changes the question to: Who will want such kinds of information?   To give a complete list of the classes of readers who might want it would be impossible, but some examples of its use and users may be recalled. In its early days, soon after the basic volume was published, one of the first reports of use which pleased its editor was that a public library in a small mining town had decided to buy two copies.   In moments of relaxation the editor sometimes speculated as to what the musical miners did with it, that they needed two copies:—Did they use it to find songs for community singing, or mining songs, or, more probably, songs that might furnish escape from daily drudgery?   They might have used it for any of these purposes, or teachers in the town might have used it to find songs for school singing, or children from miners' families of different nationalities might have found through it the national or folk songs, or the favorite old Christmas carols, of their parents' foreign homes.   A different type of use and user was indicated when the report came that moving picture concerns were buying and using the Index, in the days of the silent moving picture probably for the finding of appropriate accompanying music, but, with the advent of the talking picture, possibly to find songs that could be used in such productions.   Theatrical producers, either amateur or professional, may find through it songs which they want to use in some period play, or music for songs included in some older play—under Shakespeare, for example, is a list of the Shakespearean songs, grouped by plays to which they belong.   A new and very modern use is by a broadcasting company to find the songs which, over the radio, reach a larger number of persons than would ever ask about a given song in any one library.

The above are samples of uses where the music as well as the words of a song are needed, that is, where the approach is from the music point of view.

But the index meets other needs, especially in the fields of history, literature and literary biography. If there is truth in the old saying "Let me write the songs of a nation, I care not who writes its laws," then songs are a real part of social history, as those songs that voiced certain emotions or furnished certain war-cries are also part of political or military history. The student or reader of such history who wants the words of some old ballad or political song connected with his research may find his first aid in the Song Index. The new volume of the Index is particularly rich in its inclusion of American ballads and folk songs, either original songs of this type or older English ballads which were transplanted to this country and preserved here in popular use in certain regions. Another reader may want the words of a song because he thinks of it as poetry, rather than as music, as of course many songs are. Ballads belong in this group and many songs of other kinds are poems as well as songs, either because of their literary quality or because they were originally poems which were later set to music. For questions about such poems the Song Index is equally an index of poetry, including some poems, English or foreign, not findable through the Granger index, answering questions of authorship where the reader knows only the title or first line, throwing light on the popularity of some poems by showing the extent to which they have been translated or the number of collections in which they appear, showing the actual identity of poems which may have carried different titles in different places, and finally aiding the editor of a literary work by supplying help in the identification of songs mentioned only by title in the work that is being edited. Many questions of this last type come to libraries. Some-times they are about forgotten songs of a period, mentioned in some contem-porary book of that period, sometimes about older songs introduced into a later work of fiction as allusions to give local or period color. While some of these questions are easily answered others are difficult to run down without the aid of a comprehensive song index. As Miss Sears herself served a short but in-tensive apprenticeship in literary research of this kind which showed her both some of the difficulties of the subject and the need of such a general index, a few of her experiences may be of interest here.

In the work on their *George Eliot dictionary* (published 1924), one of the tasks which Miss Sears and her collaborator had set for themselves was the iden-tification of the many older songs which George Eliot used, often with consid-erable skill and always with historical exactness, to add touches of local and period color in her novels and short stories. This task was undertaken before the Song Index was even begun, but it had a certain connection with that index in that it made Miss Sears particularly interested, later, in undertaking the editor-ship of the index, and furnished some of the reference experience and knowledge upon which she built part of its structure.

One of the first song-titles looked up in this George Eliot work was one so easily findable that it is not worth mentioning here except as a possibly in-teresting example of the minor song sometimes more easily found through general aids than through the specialized reference works. This was "Hush, ye pretty warbling choir" which, as any lover of *Mill on the Floss* will remember, is the tune which Uncle Pullet's musical snuff-box plays. That it was a real tune, not one invented for the story, seemed probable, especially in view of the fact that

the original of the famous snuff-box was included in one of the exhibitions of
George Eliot relics held in England at the time of the George Eliot centenary
in 1919. Though not mentioned in any of the various indexes, histories of music
and other special music reference books consulted for this and other of the
George Eliot titles, it was easily identified through a *Notes and queries* index
which led to the information that the music was from Handel's pastoral opera
Acis and Galatea for which the poet Gay wrote most of the words, including the
words of "Hush, ye pretty warbling choir." Its interest here is not because of
any intricacy of reference method, but because it was one example of the kind of
question which made Miss Sears wonder, at one time, whether some general
sources of song information, such as *Notes and queries,* ought not to be indexed
in the Song Index.

A song question of greater difficulty which, before it could be answered,
was to take the George Eliot searchers through the principal music collections
of this country and, eventually, to a music manuscript in Paris, was the identification of "Ho perduto il bel sembiante," the song which Caterina sings for Sir
Christopher Cheverel in *Mr. Gilfil's love story,* one of the *Scenes of clerical life.*
In the text of the first edition of the *Scenes* this song, along with "Che farò
senza Euridice" is mentioned as being from Gluck's opera *Orfeo.* In an anno-
tated edition of the *Scenes* its editor disposes of the allusion, apparently to his
satisfaction, by stating that the song is in *Orfeo* and by supplying biographical
information about Gluck. Unfortunately, he had apparently not considered it
necessary to look in *Orfeo* itself, and when Miss Sears, with her characteristic
insistence on the use of original sources, looked there she found that that opera
did not contain the "Ho perduto." Did that mean that George Eliot's usual
accuracy in allusion had slipped for once? A comparison of the text of several
editions of the *Scenes* showed that George Eliot, who seldom made changes in
her text, had made one here, the revised edition reading "Sir Christopher's
favorite airs, by Gluck and Paisiello." As the "Che farò" was certainly by Gluck,
the search for "Ho perduto" shifted to Paisiello, for a time without success as
none of his works available in the several large music collections that were accessible contained the song, nor was any mention of it found in such books about
him as were searched. A letter to the Chief of the Music Division of the Library
of Congress, asking if the card index of that Division showed any copy of the
song, produced the information from Mr. Carl Engel, Chief of the Music Division, that though the library did not have the work in printed form it did have
a manuscript copy of the song which gave the words without, however, any in-
dication of the larger work of which they might form a part. He sent, however,
a copy of the words, in the hope, as he said, that they might furnish a clue for
further search. The hope was well founded. Short as the song was, it contained
two proper names, Dafne and Alceo, apparently the names of characters, and a
further search through comprehensive music bibliographies showed Paisiello listed
as the composer of a cantata, *Dafne ed Alceo,* which, as other information found
seemed to indicate, might be the same work as his cantata entitled *Amor vendicato,* first presented at Naples in 1786. The Paris *Conservatoire* was given as
possessing a manuscript of one of these and a Naples library as having the other.
As no copy of either *Dafne ed Alceo* or *Amor vendicato* could be found in any
accessible American library, Paris seemed indicated as the next port of call in
the long voyage of discovery, and a letter was sent to the American Library at

Paris asking if it would be possible to have some member of the staff of that library compare the copy of the song obtained from the Library of Congress with the manuscript of the cantata in the *Conservatoire*. Through the courtesy of the late W. Dawson Johnston, then librarian of the American Library, this was done, the comparison agreed exactly, and the long sought after "Ho perduto" was found to be a song from the cantata *Amor vendicato*. Before the answer could come from Paris another bit of information came to hand which, though not needed for the finding of the song, was of great interest for the light that it threw on George Eliot's care in making her allusions fit the setting and time of the tale. Mr. Engel, who had supplied the first copy of song, had kept the question in mind, and later he wrote that in going through some eighteenth century music programs he had found mention of the song as having been sung by the Italian singer, Anna Morichelli, in Belgium. With her name as clue, search started again. She had sung the song when the cantata was first presented in Naples, and she also made a trip to England some years later. The time of the beginning of *Mr. Gilfil's love story* is 1788. When Caterina sang "Ho perduto" for Sir Christopher, it was probably one of the popular operatic songs of the day, and George Eliot in putting it into the story was using one of her characteristically accurate touches of local and period color. A Paisiello specialist could probably have run the song down much more quickly than the two general reference workers who undertook it were able to do from the resources which they possessed. The story of the search is given here not as an ideal piece of reference work but as an instance of the difficulty a librarian may sometimes have in finding an unindexed song and as an example of the experience which Miss Sears later brought to the making of the Song Index.

In her preface to the basic volume of the Song Index Miss Sears was careful to insist that the work is an index merely, not a comprehensive dictionary of songs. That is, of course, true. Nevertheless so much reference work of a careful nature was necessary before her standards of indexing were satisfied, that the work, though merely an index in form, does supply some information of a dictionary or encyclopedic type. One example of this is the care with which different titles of the same song were traced and checked. In the making of the Index it was found that very frequently the same song, included in several different collections, was included there with different titles, and that translations of the same song often had different titles. Mere indexing might perhaps have been satisfied to index each under whatever title it had, with resultant confusion and decreased usefulness in the completed index. The comparison of the texts of such songs, and the checking and bringing together of the variant titles resulted in the accumulation of information which is really encyclopedic or dictionary in nature though index in form, and which has greatly increased both the use and the value of the Index. The incompleteness, or sometimes inaccuracy, with which authors' and composers' names were occasionally given in some of the song collections necessitated considerable work in looking up such names before they could be entered fully or accurately. A case which comes to the mind of the writer of this preface is the pursuit after Nella, the author of the words of "Jerusalem" for which Henry Parker composed the music. The song appears in nine collections, with the composer's name given fully but with the author represented by the single word Nella. In the first indexing of this piece it was assumed that the author was listed here by surname only, something that not infrequently happens. As search for the full name showed no song writer with this surname or pseudonym, the case began to look suspicious, and the editor decreed further search, along possibly different lines. Without rejecting the possibility that Nella might be a surname, she saw also its other possibility, that is, that it might be a feminine first name. Asking herself what circumstances might explain the use of the author's first name only when the composer's name was given in full, she saw that a possible explanation might be a family relationship, that is that Nella might be either wife, daughter or sister, of the composer. On that guess she started the hunt for Nella Parker, and soon found that there was such a person, of the right period, who had apparently written verse. For awhile nothing more definite appeared, but when the search shifted to Henry Parker, and biographical sketches of him in music periodicals were looked for, the needed information came to light. One such periodical article, supplied by information from the Boston Public Library, contained a statement by Henry Parker that his wife, Nella, herself a writer, had collaborated with him by writing words for some of his compositions. Mere indexing might have been content to list the author of the words of Jerusalem as "Nella," but cataloging research brought to light the fact that Nella was the wife of the composer, and listed her correctly in the Song Index as Parker, Mrs. Nella, with, of course, a cross reference from Nella. The total amount of such bits of supplied information in the Index probably mean a body of encyclopedic information which, in the aggregate, is very considerable.

No one reference book can cover every aspect of its subject and so sometimes a true compliment to a valued reference book is to show how other works, which may cover some part of the field not within the avowed scope of the work itself, may be used to supplement its information. In spite of the impressive total of nearly 18,000 songs included in the Song Index there are obviously many more than that number which some readers, somewhere, might be interested in tracing. Equally obviously, a reader's only clue to a wanted song might be something other than the four-fold approach (author, composer, title, first line, or sometimes refrain) of the Song Index—for example, he might remember only some one line, other than the first line or refrain, of the song. In such cases the sought-for song may not be in the Song Index at all, or it may be there but under some entry to which the reader or reference worker does not yet possess the clue. In the scope of this preface it would not be possible to give a comprehensive list of such supplementary aids, but it may not be without interest to point out a few of those, available in most fair-sized libraries, which might sometimes be used to advantage.

A very important general reference source for additional information about popular songs of an earlier period is that indispensable English periodical of question and answer, *Notes and queries*. Questions and notes about wanted songs started in the first volume of that periodical, in 1849, and, in varying numbers, have continued steadily to the present time, the number of titles asked about, or otherwise noted, from 1849 to 1932, reaching a total of nearly 2400. All of these notes and questions, and in many cases considerable information supplied in various answers to questions, are brought out in easily accessible reference form under the heading "Songs and Ballads" in the general indexes to the periodical. In many cases the information asked for, or given there, could now be found more quickly in the Song Index, but in other cases *Notes and queries* supplies information not available in the Song Index because the song was not included in any of the song collections indexed for that work. This supplementary material is of various kinds. Sometimes, as in the case of the George Eliot song already mentioned, "Hush, ye pretty warbling choir," it supplies a song not included in various printed or card indexes. Sometimes it gives historical information about the song or ballad, or about its author or composer, or in some cases points to its inclusion in song collections additional to those indexed in the Song Index. Not infrequently it identifies a song by some other line than its first line or refrain, and so supplies an additional approach to a song possibly included in the Song Index but listed there under a heading to which the searcher has not yet the clue. Because *Notes and queries* is a general reference work, which is naturally kept in the general library, not in the special music collection, its use in this respect may sometimes be overlooked.

Another general reference work sometimes overlooked as a source of information about songs, is the old but perennially useful French encyclopedia, Larousse *Grand dictionnaire universel* which includes separate articles, under French titles, on about 600 popular songs of various nationalities and languages. For each it gives usually some information about the song and its author when known, the words, in French, and the music of the air though not the full score. Some years ago the present writer was tracing some information about the song "The blue bells of Scotland," a song given in many song collections but of course in the original English. The Song Index lists a German translation, but in this particular case a French version was wanted which was found quickly in Larousse under the title: "Les campanules écossais." It may, of course, be given in many other places, but Larousse proved a quick first-aid. Like *Notes and queries,* Larousse is a general work which might be overlooked by a reader working only in the music collection.

Miss Sears was aware of the very considerable amount of information about songs given in *Notes and queries* and in Larousse, and at one time she considered the feasibility of including some indexing of this material in the Song Index. Since, however, these would have been only two out of many general sources, she wisely decided that the Song Index was best limited to its original and stated purpose, the indexing of songs included in the song-collections selected by libraries for such indexing, leaving the use of this borderland general material to the knowledge and resource of the individual librarian. Into this borderland group of aids fall also many anthologies of poems, songs and ballads of a particular region, such as an English county, which, while they may not give the music, will sometimes supply the words of a song the main interest or use of which is local. To another borderland source, the reference material on hymns, Miss Sears called attention in her original preface, where she said perhaps all that needs to be said about it when she quoted a librarian as saying for this subject "Let Julian do it." If the hymns indexed in the Song Index and in Julian are not enough for an enquiry, some specialist material may have to be added, naturally, such as, for Latin hymns, Chevalier's great Repertorium.

Title indexes of songs in musical reference books are of course known to reference workers in music collections but a few of these perhaps not known to the beginner in general reference work might be mentioned here. For some tracing of song titles, printed catalogs of some of the great music libraries are useful to the searcher who may be looking for a song not included in the song collections indexed by the Song Index. To mention only four of these: The catalog of the Allan A. Brown library not only catalogs separate songs but also analyzes many included in larger works. The catalog of printed music in the British Museum also analyzes many songs printed in magazines and may give some not included in the indexed collections, while the great catalog of manuscript music in the same library has two important indexes of titles and first lines of vocal music, the index of sacred vocal music in the first volume of the catalog and the index of secular vocal music in the second volume, the latter providing title or first line indexing to thousands of songs and similar compositions, including many foreign titles. Many songs thought of, or asked for, as separate things, may have originally been part of an opera, and the index of arias at the end of the Library of Congress catalog of opera librettos before 1800 furnishes a title index to these and shows the operas of which they are parts. All of the above works, and many not mentioned here, were known to Miss Sears and used by her in the editing of the Song Index. Not all of them will furnish the full indexing of words and music which the Song Index gives, but any one may be useful or indispensable for some piece of information outside the scope of the Song Index, which covers a large aggregate of both titles and references, and is, for ordinary purposes, the indispensable first aid.

The Preface, which began with one quotation, may perhaps be permitted to end with another, even though it be one so familiar and so frequently quoted that its essential truth may at times be overlooked. It is the firm belief of the present writer that the great and indispensable reference work in any field is not the special encyclopedia of that subject but the index of the subject, provided that index be carefully and accurately made and complete within its stated limits, and every year of added experience in using reference books only serves to strengthen that belief. The great reference work in medicine and medical history is not any one dictionary or encyclopedia, it is rather the index-catalog of the Surgeon-General's Library; the indispensable reference work for the modern research worker in chemistry is not an encyclopedia or dictionary, but is *Chemical abstracts*; for the worker in subjects connected with medieval and renaissance biography the basic aid is not any biographical dictionary of men of the middle ages but is Chevalier's great index to thousands of biographies of men and women of that period. The beginner in reference work is apt to rank highest the encyclopedia of the subject with its concise, or sometimes long and authoritative, articles on topics and names connected with that subject. In so doing he overlooks the fact that even the best special encyclopedia is necessarily selective within its subject—is, in fact doubly selective, first for the topics included and again for the facts given about those selected topics—and that not infrequently its most useful feature is its index feature, in other words its appended bibliographies referring the reader to other sources of information. The only type of reference work which can be anywhere near complete for its subject is the carefully made index which is inclusive for everything within the works which it indexes. Indexes of that type have a permanent value which lessens only slightly with the passage of time, and it is only as more such indexes as the Song Index are produced in other fields that we shall have the adequate reference aids for many of the types of questions which eager readers are asking and in the answering of which, from present inadequate aids, reference librarians are often spending much time. And so to the final quotation, to which these remarks of an enthusiast on good reference books have been leading. Alexander Pope may never before have been classed as an up-to-date reference librarian, but he showed a true understanding of the basic need of reference work when he wrote

> ". . . index learning turns no student pale
> Yet holds the eel of science by the tail."

If there is a special eel of song as well as of science the reference librarian who uses the Song Index has a good grip on at least the tip of its wriggling tail.

ISADORE GILBERT MUDGE

INTRODUCTION

This first Supplement to the Song Index was planned and supervised by Miss Sears, and she had almost completed the final editing at the time of her death. The greater part of the Supplement bears the stamp of her approval, and her suggestions have been faithfully carried out in the remainder.

The Supplement indexes 104 song collections in 124 volumes. These collections include over 7000 songs, of which nearly 5000 were not in the main volume. As in the Song Index, no attempt has been made to check the authorship of every song, but in some cases further information about the 2000 duplicated songs has been found. This new information has been designated in the Supplement by special brackets < > (e.g. "Drink to me only with thine eyes." Old English air <attributed to H. Harrington; wrongly attributed to R. Mellish and to Mozart>. See also entries for The quilting party, etc.)

Selection of Titles Included. The selection of the 104 collections in the Supplement is based on lists voted on by the following libraries: Public libraries of Brooklyn; Chicago; Cincinnati; Cleveland; Denver; Detroit; Evanston, Ill.; Haverhill, Mass.; Los Angeles; Louisville, Ky.; Milwaukee; Minneapolis; New York; Newark; Omaha, Neb.; Providence, R. I.; St. Louis; St. Paul; San Diego; San Francisco; Seattle; Springfield, Mass.; Tacoma, Wash.; Wilmington, Del.; other libraries: Enoch Pratt Free Library, Baltimore; Grosvenor Library, Buffalo, N.Y.; Sibley Musical Library, Eastman School of Music, Rochester, N.Y. Most of these libraries collaborated also on the main volume of the Song Index. With their advice 30 collections have been selected from the total number for first purchase in smaller libraries. These are marked with a star in the Classified List of Collections Indexed. By request, several new and enlarged editions of collections in the Song Index have been indexed in the Supplement. These are designated in the Classified List of Collections Indexed.

A full explanation of the principles of selection and arrangement is to be found in the main volume of the Song Index.

Entries. Entries are under *title* (the main entry), *composer,* and *author* of the words. *References from first line to title* are also included.

(1) TITLE ENTRY. This is the main entry, which gives: (a) title, followed by alternate titles or first line in parenthesis; (b) name of composer as given in the collections or supplied from outside information, or name of air, descriptive term, etc.; (c) name of author, when known; (d) language abbreviations for foreign songs; (e) location of song. All variations in title in different collections are indented under the main title entry.

Where the Supplement copy of a song has a different title from the Song Index copy, the original Song Index title has been supplied in brackets so that copies in both volumes may be found under the same main entry. The user of the Supplement will have to disregard the bracketed title in locating the song itself (e.g. ⌈The willow song⌉ O willow, willow. This song will be found in the indexed volume under the title O willow, willow. The negro spiritual, ₍My bretheren₎ don't get weary, will be found in the song volume under the title Don't get weary). When the Supplement title varies only slightly from the Song Index, the original title is not supplied but in all references and added entries the title is given as in the main entry in the Song Index (e.g. Blue bonnets over the border, in Song Index; Blue bonnets are over the border, in Supplement).

(2) COMPOSER. The composer entry contains the composer's name in roman type followed by a list of his songs. When the same air has been used for two songs, a note to this effect is added to the second. Occasionally the "Same air as" note in the Supplement refers to a song in the Song Index which is not found in the Supplement. If a song is known to be from an opera or oratorio this information is added. In cases where a composer is also author of words, that information is usually given only in title entry, but when he is composer of some songs and author or composer and author of others these titles are separated in the composer entry (e.g. Bayly, Thomas Haynes).

(3) AUTHOR. The author entry contains the author's name in italics, followed by a list of his songs. After the title of each poem is given composer's name or a descriptive phrase such as "French air."

(4) FIRST LINE REFERENCES. The first line is in quotation marks, even when used as title. When the title differs from first line, references have been made from first line in all translations as well as in the original. Reference from the first line of the chorus has been made in many cases.

Arrangement. Articles are always retained at the beginning of title and first line, but they are disregarded in filing, and the title is alphabeted by the following word in boldface. Abbreviations are filed as if spelled in full (e.g. Mr. is filed as Mister). Contractions and elisions are filed as one word (e.g. Who's is filed as Whos, C'est as Cest). In hyphenated words the hyphen is disregarded and the words are filed as separate words except when the hyphen is really part of the word (e.g. a-roving). Modified vowels in German, in the Scandinavian languages, etc., are filed as one letter unless written as two (e.g. Goethe). The many titles beginning O and Oh have been filed together, under O. This same rule has been applied in a few other cases (e.g. Flower and Flow'r).

Language of Entry. Foreign songs are entered under the title in the original language if given, with the exception of the languages noted below. When none of the collections indexed gives the original title or words, the entry is under the English title. In a few cases where the Song Index had only an English title and Supplement copies are in the original language, the main entry in the Supplement is under the original, with references from the Song Index translation (e.g. Lob der thränen).

Songs in the languages listed below, many of which do not use the Latin alphabet, are entered under the English title unless the original title is much better known (e.g. Aloha oe). If there is no English translation, the main entry is under whatever other translation is given (e.g. Junggesellenlied, a German translation of "Oï piïdu ia dolom") or, if there is no translation of any kind, under the original title transliterated into the Latin alphabet (e.g. A mädal in die johren). References are freely used to aid in finding such songs.

  (a) African languages
  (b) Albanian
  (c) American Indian languages
  (d) Finno-Ugrian languages, including Esthonian, Finnish, Hungarian
  (e) Greek, Modern
  (f) Oriental languages, including Hebrew
  (g) Russian and other Slavic languages and Lithuanian-Lettish, including Bohemian or Czech, Bulgarian, Lettish, Lithuanian, Polish, Russian, Serbo-Croatian, Slovak, Slovenian, Wendish
  (h) Yiddish

Language Abbreviations. The language is indicated in the main title entry by an abbreviation which precedes the location symbol. No language abbreviation is given for songs in English unless they are translations. The language abbreviations for Russian and other languages which do not use the Latin alphabet do not show whether the text is in the original characters or transliterated. No distinction is made between dialects and literary language (e.g. creole French is indicated by f., meaning French).

Transliteration. All titles and references are printed in the Latin alphabet. When transliteration was necessary, it was done according to the Library of Congress system.

Variants. In obvious cases variants have been noted as in the Song Index. Many folk songs indexed in the Supplement are variants of songs in the main volume of the Song Index. References are made to the versions in the main Index (e.g. Come down, angels (see Song Index). Variant: Let God's saints come in).

Acknowledgments. We are indebted to the libraries which cooperated in checking lists of titles to be included. The resources of the Music Division of the New York Public Library and of the Columbia University Library have been much used, and the cooperation of members of their staffs is appreciated. Special acknowledgement is made to Mr. William Ll. Davies, Librarian, the National Library of Wales; Miss Dorothy Lawton, Music Librarian of the Circulation Department, New York Public Library; Mrs. Margaret McNamara Mott, Music Librarian, The Grosvenor Library, Buffalo, N.Y.; Mr. Frank Megill, Music Division, Library of Congress; Miss Isadore G. Mudge, Reference Librarian, Columbia University; and Mr. David Stevens, C. C. Birchard and Company, for advice and for assistance in verifying disputed points. In the preparation of the Supplement all the typing and clerical work were done by Romaine Smith, and the proofreading was done by Rosetta Reisig, assisted by Miss Smith. Their interest and conscientious work is much appreciated. Thanks are due to the publishers who generously gave us copies of their books which are included in the Supplement.

PHYLLIS CRAWFORD

December, 1933

Contents

Classified List of Collections Indexed xxi

Collections Indexed in Song Index and Supplement xxix

Key to Symbols for Collections Indexed xxxv

Key to Language Abbreviations xxxix

Key to Miscellaneous Abbreviations xxxix

Directions for Use xl

Song Index 1-366

Classified List of Collections Indexed

Titles starred are recommended for first purchase
Unless otherwise indicated, collections contain piano accompaniment
When a collection is issued in two editions, high voice and low voice, this is specified
All prices are subject to change

Arrangement

General p. xxi
National and Folk Songs p. xxiii
  A. *General Collections p. xxiii*
  B. *Collections by Nationality p. xxiv*

American, including Negro p. xxiv
Canadian, French. See French
Creole. See French
Danish. See Scandinavian
English p. xxv
French, including Creole and French Canadian p. xxvi
German p. xxvi
Hebrew. See Jewish
Hungarian p. xxvi
Irish p. xxvi
Italian p. xxvi
Jewish p. xxvii

Jugoslav. See Yugoslav
Mexican and Spanish American p. xxvii
Norwegian. See Scandinavian
Russian p. xxvii
Scandinavian p. xxvii
Scottish p. xxvii
Spanish American. See Mexican and Spanish American
Swedish. See Scandinavian
Welsh p. xxvii
Yiddish. See Jewish
Yugoslav p. xxvii

Chanteys p. xxvii
Christmas Carols p. xxviii
Sacred Songs p. xxviii
School and College Songs p. xxviii

GENERAL COLLECTIONS

Album of twenty-five favorite encore songs. (Schirmer's library of musical classics v1364) G. Schirmer c1915 pa $1.25
  English; and French, German, Italian with English translations
  Contents: 6 traditional songs and 19 songs by Arne, Barnard, Bernard, Bohm, Brahms, Bungert, Delbruck, Eysler, Giordani, Hawley, Hildach, Lemaire, Loewe, Luckstone, Molloy, Mozart, Radecke, Raff

Baltzell, Winton James, comp. Something to sing; old and new masterpieces for the voice. (The Ditson music collections) Ditson c1916 pa $1.25
  English; and French, German, Italian with English translations
  Contents: 54 songs by Aldrich, Baltzell, Bartlett, Behrend, Bishop, Boott, Brackett, Brahms, Cadman, Chaminade, Clark, Cox, Fontenailles, Giordani, Godard, Händel, Holst, Horn, Jensen, Kern, Lacy, Lotti, Macy, Manney, Marshall, Mozart, Nevin, Reichardt, Richardson, Sawyer, Scarlatti, Scuderi, Sobeski, Somerset, Stange, Starnes, Strickland, Tosti, Webber, Weyts; 6 songs with traditional airs

*The blue book of favorite songs; the Golden book of favorite songs and the Gray book of favorite songs, combined with a supplement; comp. by John W. Beattie and others. 3 pts in 1 Hall & McCreary c1928 cl 75c
  Contents: 326 songs. Pt. 1, The golden book of favorite songs. rev. and enl. ed.; pt. 2, The gray book of favorite songs. rev. ed.; pt. 3, A supplement of spirituals, arr. by W. Goodell

The **Clarendon** song books; ed. by W. G. Whittaker, Herbert Wiseman and John Wishart. 6v C. Fischer c1929-30 staff ed pa ea 30c; piano ed pa ea $1.50
  English only
  Contents: v1, 5 nursery rhymes; 12 folk songs; 8 classical and modern songs by Brahms, Cornelius, Farjeon, Schubert, Schumann, Stanford, Whittaker; 6 rounds and canons by Caldara, Hauptmann, Tallis, Whittaker
  v2, 11 folk songs; 12 classical and modern songs by Bach, Bainton, Bennett, Brahms, Bridge, Campian, Cornelius, Händel, Judd, Mozart, Schubert, Whittaker; 4 rounds by Arnold, Mozart, Schubert, Whittaker
  v3, 5 folk and national songs; 11 classical and modern songs by Arne, Dowland, Mozart, Schubert, Schumann, Shield, Slater; 4 two-part songs by Demuth, Gluck, Händel, Work; 3 rounds by Beethoven, Haydn, Schubert
  v4, 5 folk songs; 8 classical and modern songs by Arne, Brahms, Mozart, Peerson, Piggott, Schubert, Schumann, Shield; 1 folk song with descant; 3 two-part songs by Bridge, Jones, Purcell; 3 rounds by Beethoven, Haydn, Hayes

v5, 4 folk songs; 7 classical and modern songs by Grace, Händel, Mozart, Nicholson, Schumann, Stanford, Vaughan Williams; old English song with descant; 3 two-part songs by Gluck, Purcell, Schubert; 2 rounds by Mozart, Salieri

v6, 3 folk songs; 5 classical and modern songs by Bach, Brahms, Byrd, Delius, Mozart; 5 two-part songs by Gluck, Peerson, Purcell, Slater; 3 rounds by Beethoven, Haydn, Mozart

Davison, Archibald Thompson; Surette, Thomas Whitney, and Zanzig, Augustus D. comps. A book of songs; with piano accompaniment. (The Concord series, no. 14) E. C. Schirmer c1924 teacher's ed cl $3

The students edition containing words and music without accompaniments is v4 in the Concord series (cl $1.25)

Contents: 143 songs of various kinds; 19 Christmas songs; 53 part-songs; 19 hymns; 23 rounds and catches

Dramatic concert arias, collected from sources other than operatic; twelve famous airs. G. Schirmer c1915 pa $3

French, German, Italian with English translations

Contents: 12 arias by Beethoven, Holstein, Joachim, Lachner, Liszt, Mendelssohn-Bartholdy, Nicodé, Raff, Rubinstein, Schubert, Volkmann

*****Girl** scout song book; ed. by George Newell. rev ed   Girl scouts c1929 cl $1

English only, except 2 songs in French only

Contents: 138 songs, including ballads, patriotic songs, chanteys, Christmas hymns, rounds, graces, part songs, spirituals, and special girl scout songs

Good old songs we used to sing; comp. by J. C. H. 2v Ditson c1887-95 v1 o.p. 1933; v2 pa $1.50

Contents: v1, 110 English and American songs; v2, 110 English and American songs

*****Goss,** John, ed. An anthology of song. C. Fischer c1929 pa $3.25

English; and French, German, Italian, with English translations

Contents: 3 anonymous songs, and songs by Arne, Bach, Beethoven, Berlioz, Blow, Borodin, Boyce, Caccini, Campion, Cavendish, Chopin, Ciampi, Cornelius, Danyel, Dowland, Edwardes, Ferrabosco, Franz, Gluck, Händel, Haydn, Liszt, Loder, Loewe, Marcello, Martini, Morley, Mozart, Musorgskiĭ, Orlando di Lasso, Purcell, Schubert, Schumann, Weber

Heinrich, Max, ed. Classic song album; fifty selected songs of old and modern masters. C. Fischer c1914 high, low pa ea $2.50; cl ea $3.75

English; and German, Italian, Latin with English translations

Contents: 50 songs by Barnby, Beethoven, Brahms, Brückler, Clay, Franz, Gounod, Grieg, Händel, Hatton, Haydn, Horrocks, Jensen, Liszt, Mackenzie, Mendelssohn, Molloy, Moór, Mozart, Scarlatti, Schubert, Schumann, Sieveking, Sullivan, Taubert, Tchaikovsky

Levermore, Charles Herbert, ed. The American song book; a collection of songs and hymns for use in schools and homes. Ginn c1917 cl $1

Contents: 38 familiar songs and folk songs; 25 college songs; 97 songs of devotion; 33 songs of loyalty and fraternity

McCaskey, John Piersol, ed. Favorite songs and hymns for school and home. American book company c1899 cl $1.20

Contains 450 songs and hymns in English, and a few songs in German, French, and Italian with English translations

*****MacMillan,** Ernest Campbell, ed. A book of songs; comp. for the entertainment and delight of English men and women everywhere, but especially for those at home and in Canada. Dutton c1929 cl $2.15; Dent 7s6d

English only, except 9 songs in French, generally with English translations, and several songs in Latin

Contents: 8 national and patriotic songs; 28 English songs; 13 Scottish songs; 10 Irish songs; 3 Welsh songs; 9 French and French Canadian songs; 7 American songs; 4 songs of other nations; 7 student songs; 18 hymns, chorales and carols

The **Oxford** song book; ed. by Thomas Wood. v2 C. Fischer c1927 piano ed cl $2.50

v1, edited by Buck (BOS) was indexed in the Song Index

A few of the songs have no accompaniments

Contents: 35 general songs; 20 sea songs and chanteys; 11 frivola; 34 rounds; 52 fiddle tunes and fragments of which 42 airs without words are omitted from this index

Pittmann, Josiah, ed. The baritone album. Boosey n.d. pa $5; cl $7.50

Italian with English translations

Contents: 45 songs from the operas Attila, Un ballo in maschera, Il barbiere di Siviglia, Beatrice di Tenda, La cenerentola, La contessa di Fertzen, Dinorah, Don Giovanni, Don Pasquale, Don Sebastiano, I due Foscari, Ernani, Faust, Il flauto magico, Il furioso, Gemma di Vergy, Gianni da Calais, L'elisire d'amore, I Lombardi, Lucrezia Borgia, Maometto secondo, Maria Padilla, Maria di Rohan, Maria di Rudenz, Marino Falliero, Marta, Nabucodonosor, I Normanni a Parigi, Le nozze di Figaro, La prigione di Edimburgo, Il reggente, Roberto Bruce, La sonnambula, Tannhäuser, Torquato Tasso, La traviata, Il trovatore, I vespri Siciliani

Pittmann, Josiah, ed. The contralto album; a collection of 50 celebrated songs, in their original keys for mezzo-soprano and contralto voices, extracted from the most famous operas, with Italian words and an English translation. Boosey n.d. pa $5; cl $7.50

50 songs in Italian and English, from the operas Abu Hassan, Andronico, Anna Bolena, L'assedio di Calais, Astarto, Il barbiere di Siviglia, Betly, I Capuleti ed i Montecchi, La cenerentola, Il crociato in Egitto, Dinorah, Donna Carità, La donna del lago, L'elisire d'amore, Faust, Gianni di Parigi, Giulietta e Romeo, Il giuramento, L'Italiana in Algeri, Linda di Chamounix, Lucrezia Borgia, Marco Visconti, Maria de Rohan, Marta, Nabucodonosor, Nitocri, Le nozze di Figaro, Oberto conte di S. Bonifacio, Orfeo, Il profeta, Il ratto di Proserpina, La regina di Golconda, Rinaldo, Saffo, Semiramide, Tancredi, Torquato Tasso, Il trovatore, Ugo conte di Parigi, Gli Ugonotti, La vestale

Spicker, Max, ed. Album of twenty-seven songs for contralto voice, with piano accompaniment. G. Schirmer c1893 pa $1

Cover title: Contralto album; 27 celebrated songs

English; and French, German, Italian with English translations

Contents: 3 folk songs, and 24 songs by Alary, Beethoven, Bizet, Brahms, Buononcini, Caldara, Cornelius, Fielitz, Franz, Godard, Hartmann, Haydn, Kahn, Leoncavallo, Marchesi, Massenet, Rosa, Saint-Saëns, Scarlatti, Scholz, Sullivan, Widor

Spicker, Max, comp. Favorite bass songs. (Schirmer's household music books) G. Schirmer c1909 pa 75c

English; and German, Italian with English translations

Contents: Songs by Allitsen, Behrend, Cowen, Davis, Elliot, Hawley, Haynes, Hiller, Hullah, Jude, Knight, Löhr, Marzials, Pinsuti, Rodney, Roeder, Somerset, Storch, Tosti, Trotère, Wellings

*Surette, Thomas Whitney, and Davison, Archibald Thompson, eds. The home and community song book. (The Concord series, no. 2) rev and enl ed E. C. Schirmer c1931 complete ed (voice and piano) bds $1

English only

The 1921 edition (DSH) was indexed in the Song Index. The vocal edition containing words and music without accompaniments is v19 in the Concord series (bds 50c). Sponsored by Better homes in America, Inc. and National recreation association

Contents: 10 patriotic and national songs; 64 folk songs; 24 choruses; 23 chorals, hymns and carols

*Treasury of modern song; 35 songs for soprano or tenor. G. Schirmer c1902 pa $1

French, German with English translations

Contents: 35 songs by Brahms, Bungert, Coquard, Delbruck, Dvořák, Faure, Fielitz, Franz, Grieg, Hahn, Haynes, Henschel, Hildach, Lalo, Lassen, Pomasanski, Rückauf, Sinding, Stange, Strauss, Sucher, Thomé, Tschaikowsky, Vidal

*Twice 55 community songs: the new green book; ed. by Peter W. Dykema and others. (No. 2) Birchard c1930 vocal ed pa 25c; cl 55c; complete ed (voice and piano) $2

The 1923 edition (TFC 2) was indexed in the Song Index

English only, except several songs in French and Latin. Contains 160 songs and choruses, and words only of 13 additional songs which are omitted from this index

Twice 55 part songs for boys: the orange book; comp. and ed. by Peter W. Dykema. (No. 6) Birchard c1927 pa 50c

Contents: 110 songs and choruses for men's voices, including "close harmony" numbers, in English only, except 1 song in Latin with English translation

*Twice 55 community songs for male voices: the blue book; comp. and ed. by Peter W. Dykema. (No. 4) Birchard c1926 pa 50c

Contents: 110 songs and choruses, in English only, except 2 Latin songs with English translations

*Twice 55 community songs for treble voices: the rose book; ed. by Peter W. Dykema. (No. 5) Birchard c1927 vocal ed pa 20c; complete ed (voice and piano) bds $1

Contents: 117 songs for girl's and women's voices, in English only, except 1 Latin song with English translation

*Twice 55 plus community songs: the new brown book; ed. by Peter W. Dykema and others. (No. 1) vocal ed Birchard c1930 pa 15c; cl 45c; complete ed (voice and piano) $1.50

The 1919 edition (TFC 1) was indexed in the Song Index

English only, except 1 song in French with English translation. Contains 176 songs, and words only of 9 additional songs which are omitted from this index

Wier, Albert Ernest, ed. Grand opera at home. (Whole world series, no. 3) rev ed Appleton-Century c1927 pa $1.25

The stories and the most popular music in Aida, Carmen, Cavalleria rusticana, Faust, Hansel and Gretel, Lohengrin, Lucia di Lammermoor, I pagliacci, Rigoletto, Tales of Hoffman, Tannhäuser, and Il trovatore

Wier, Albert Ernest, ed. Light opera at home. (Whole world series, no. 10) Appleton-Century c1917 pa $1.25

The stories and the most popular songs of the light operas The bartered bride, The beggar student, The chimes of Normandy, Erminie, Giroflé-Girofla, The grand duchess, Martha, The mascot, The merry widow, Olivette, The queen's lace handkerchief, and The waltz dream

NATIONAL AND FOLK SONGS

GENERAL

A **little** song book of the nations; ed. by A. E. W. Thomas; accompaniments by Hubert J. Foss, C. Fischer c1928 pa 75c

English only

Contents: 1 typical song from each of the following countries: Austria, Denmark, England, France, Germany, Holland, Ireland, Italy, Japan, Poland, Portugal, Russia, Scotland, Sweden, Switzerland, the United States, Wales

Möller, Heinrich, comp. Das lied der völker. (Edition Schott nr. 1700 A-C) 13v in 3 Schott n.d. v1-2 pa ea 20s; cl ea 22s; v3 pa 18s; cl 20s

Available also in 13v (pa bk 1 4s; bk 2-3, 5-6, 10-12, ea 5s; bk 4, 7-9, 13, ea 6s)

Words in the original languages with German translations. Songs in those languages not using the Latin alphabet are given in the original characters

Contents: v1, bk 1, 33 Russian songs; bk 2, 13 Swedish songs; 12 Norwegian songs; 3 Danish songs; 2 Icelandic songs; bk 3, 27 English songs; 4 American songs; bk 4, 7 Breton songs; 10 Welsh songs; 16 Scottish songs; 17 Irish songs; bk 5, 30 French songs

v2, bk 6, 10 Spanish songs; 2 Portuguese songs; 15 Catalonian songs; 8 Basque songs; bk 7, 43 Italian songs; bk 8, 6 Slovenian songs; 20 Croatian songs; 15 Serbian songs; 26 Bulgarian songs; bk 9, 12 Greek songs; 3 Albanian songs; 20 Rumanian songs
v3, bk 10, 22 Bohemian songs; 18 Slovak songs; bk 11, 26 Polish songs; 9 Wendish songs; bk 12, 44 Hungarian songs; bk 13, 12 Lithuanian songs; 5 Lettish songs; 5 Esthonian songs; 32 Finnish songs

Myers, Susanna, tr. Folk-songs of the four seasons; thirty-three traditional melodies associated with festivals and folkways; the harmonization by Harvey Officer. G. Schirmer c1929 pa $1.25; bds $1.75
33 folk songs in English only, classified by seasons. Includes American negro, Breton, Chinese, Czech, Dutch, English, Finnish, French, Hopi Indian, Irish, Italian, Japanese, Jewish, Mexican, Norwegian, Portuguese, Provençal, Russian, Suabian, Swiss, Yugoslav

AMERICAN

a. General

DeVore, Nicholas, ed. Fifty famous favorites; a collection of famous popular copyrighted songs, including many old favorites. Robbins music corporation [1930] pa 50c
Contents: 50 old popular songs, including 5 by Stephen C. Foster, 5 by George M. Cohan and 2 by Paul Dresser

*Dolph, Edward Arthur, comp. Sound off! soldier songs from Yankee Doodle to Parley voo; music arr. by Philip Egner; foreword by Peter B. Kyne. Farrar & Rinehart c1929 cl o.p. 1934
Over 300 army songs from all the American wars. Many fragments and songs without music and airs without words are included in the volume, but these are omitted from this index
Contents: Songs with hash-stripes: current section; Hinky-dinky, parley-voo?: World war section; In the days of the Empire: Spanish-American war section; The blue and the gray: Civil war section; On to Mexico: Mexican war section; From the Wabash to the Everglades: War of 1812 section; In the days of Yankee Doodle: Revolutionary war section; Songs from the regiments; West Point songs

*Geller, James J. Famous songs and their stories. Macaulay c1931 cl $3
Contents: 56 old American popular songs, and how they came to be written. Includes Silver threads among the gold, White wings, After the ball, The Bowery, Oh promise me, Asleep in the deep, Tell me, pretty maiden, etc.

*Howard, John Tasker, comp. A program of early and mid-nineteenth century American songs. (Fischer edition no. 6490) J. Fischer c1931 pa $1.25
Contents: 19 songs by Baker, Bristow, Clifton, Fry, Heinrich, Hewitt, Horn, Knight, McCarthy, Russell, Tucker, Winner, and an anonymous composer

Knowlton, Fanny Snow, comp. Songs of other days. Ditson c1922 pa 75c
Contents: Puritan days; Revolutionary days; Antebellum days
Suggests programs, costumes, etc., and includes 44 traditional and popular songs of the 3 periods

*Larkin, Margaret, comp. Singing cowboy; a book of western songs; arr. for the piano by Helen Black. Knopf c1931 cl $3.50
Contents: 42 songs, with notes and a glossary of cowboy lingo

*McGill, Josephine, comp. Folk-songs of the Kentucky mountains. Boosey c1917 pa $2
Contents: 20 traditional ballads and songs

Milligan, Harold Vincent, ed. Pioneer American composers; a collection of early American songs. (Schmidt's educational series 256a-b, 288a-b) 2v A. P. Schmidt co. c1921-23 high, low pa ea $1.25
Contents: v1, 7 songs by Carr, Pelissier, Reinagle, Swan, Taylor, von Hagen
v2, 7 songs by Hewitt, Pelissier, Reinagle, Taylor, von Hagen, Willson

Old time hits of the gay eighties and nineties. Marks [1931] pa 50c
Contents: 34 old popular songs, including The Boston burglar, The girl I loved in sunny Tennessee, My own Iona, The moth and the flame, Sweet Marie, Under the bamboo tree

Old-time song hits. Ditson c1909 pa $1
Contents: 20 songs by Baker, Bishop, Butterfield, Coard, Grannis, Hanby, Hays, Ordway, Pitts, Shattuck, Thomas, Webster, Work

Richardson, Mrs Ethel (Park) comp. American mountain songs; ed. and arr. by Sigmund Spaeth. Greenberg c1927 cl $3.50
Contents: 12 ballads; 14 lonesome and love tunes; 11 mountain spirituals; 24 nonsense songs
The songs are from the mountainous districts of Tennessee, the Carolinas, North Georgia, Kentucky, Virginia and Missouri

*Sandburg, Carl, comp. The American songbag. Harcourt c1927 $3.50
A few of the songs have no accompaniment
Contents: 280 songs and ballads from all sections of the United States, including 7 in Spanish with English translations

Sharp, Cecil James, comp. English folk songs from the southern Appalachians; ed. by Maud Karpeles. 2v C. Fischer c1932 cl ea $10
New edition of the Campbell and Sharp compilation in the Song Index (CSE). No accompaniments
Contents: 273 songs and ballads with 968 airs, including 39 airs contributed by Olive Dame Campbell. The book contains also fragments of songs; these are omitted from this index. An outstanding collection which should be acquired by every library that can afford it

Smith, Lee Orean, and Morse, Theodore, comps. Good old timers; 75 songs and choruses you can't forget. Feist c1922 pa 50c
Contents: 73 old popular songs, including The sidewalks of New York, The Darktown strutter's ball, Little Annie Rooney, That's how I need you, Where did you get that hat

*Spaeth, Sigmund Gottfried. Read 'em and weep; the songs you forgot to remember. Doubleday, Doran c1926 cl $4
Contains many old popular songs, mostly American, difficult to find elsewhere. Includes comments and directions for the singer, but no piano accompaniments. The volume contains also many fragments and songs without airs, which have been omitted from this index

*Spaeth, Sigmund Gottfried. Weep some more, my lady. Doubleday, Doran c1927 cl $4
Contains more old songs without piano accompaniment, similar in arrangement to the preceding collection. Fragments and words without music are not indexed

United States. Naval academy, Annapolis. Trident society. Book of navy songs; collected and ed. by the Trident society of the United States Naval academy at Annapolis, Maryland; music arr. and harmonized by Joseph W. Crosley. Doubleday, Doran c1926 cl $3.50
Contents: 7 historical songs and ballads; 29 wardroom songs; 34 forecastle songs and shanties; 17 songs of the landing parties; 24 Naval academy songs

b. Negro

Allen, William Francis; Ware, Charles Pickard, and Garrison, Lucy McKim, eds. Slave songs of the United States. P. Smith 1929 cl $2.50
First published in 1867. No accompaniments
Contents: 136 spirituals and folk songs from the slave states, including 6 negro creole songs in creole patois only

Burleigh, Henry Thacker, ed. Negro minstrel melodies. G. Schirmer c1910 pa $1
Contents: 21 songs, including 9 by Stephen C. Foster

*Fisher, William Arms, ed. Seventy negro spirituals. (The musicians library) Ditson c1926 high, low pa $2.50; cl $3.50
Contains also a discussion of spirituals and notes on the songs

Hampton, Va. Normal and agricultural institute. Religious folk-songs of the negro as sung at Hampton institute; ed. by R. Nathaniel Dett. Hampton institute press c1927 cl $2
Fourth edition of a collection first published in 1874. The 1909 edition edited by Fenner (HR) was indexed in the Song Index
Contents: 163 negro spirituals

Handy, William Christopher, ed. Blues; an anthology. Boni c1926 cl $3.50
Publisher reports indefinitely out of stock (1933)
Contents: 50 songs ranging from folk-blues to Gershwin. There are several selections for piano without words, which are omitted from this index

Johnson, Hall, ed. The Green Pastures spirituals; arranged for voice and piano. Farrar & Rinehart c1930 cl $2
21 of the spirituals sung in the play by Marc Connelly, and 4 choruses composed by Hall Johnson for use in the production

*Johnson, James Weldon, ed. The second book of negro spirituals; musical arrangements by J. Rosamond Johnson. Viking press c1926 cl $3.50
"The book of American negro spirituals" (JB) was indexed in the Song Index
Contents: 61 negro spirituals

*Paskman, Dailey, and Spaeth, Sigmund Gottfried. Gentlemen, be seated! a parade of the old-time minstrels. Doubleday, Doran c1928 cl $4
Fairly full historical sketch, material for amateur theatricals, and nearly 40 minstrel songs. The volume contains also several songs without music, which are omitted from this index

White, Clarence Cameron, comp. Forty negro spirituals; for solo voice with pianoforte accompaniment. Presser c1927 cl $2
Contains an index classified by subject matter and by song ranges

*Wier, Albert Ernest, comp. Songs of the sunny south. (Whole world series, no. 27) Appleton-Century c1929 pa $1.25
Contents: 87 plantation and minstrel ditties; 49 minstrel ballads; 50 negro spirituals; 39 of Stephen Foster's songs

ENGLISH

Broadwood, Lucy E., ed. English traditional songs and carols, with annotations and accompaniments. Boosey c1908 pa $3; cl $4.50
Contents: 50 English folk songs from Sussex and Surrey, and a few from Hampshire, Bedfordshire, Lincolnshire and Cumberland

Edwards, Edward, comp. A book of Shakespeare's songs; with musical settings by various composers. G. Schirmer c1903 bds $2.50
10 songs from Shakespeare, with 1 traditional air and settings by Arne, Bishop, l :ydn, Morley, Schubert

Gems of English song. Ditson c1875 pa $1.50
Contents: 75 songs by Abt, Adam, Adams, Allen, Ascher, Balfe, Boott, Campana, Lady Carew, Claribel, Cowen, Faure, Gabriel, Ganz, Gounod, Guglielmo, Harrison, Hatton, Howe, Levey, Lindsay, Linley, Lyle, Marzials, Mattei, Molloy, Osborne, Pinsuti, Ponlatowski, Randegger, Roeckel, Sainton-Dolby, Lady John Scott, Scott-Gatty, Smart, Sullivan, Topliff, Wallace, Weber, Wiegand

Spicker, Max, ed. Songs of the British Isles; a collection of forty popular English, Irish, Scotch and Welsh songs with piano accompaniment. G. Schirmer c1909 pa $1
    Contents: 13 old English songs; 12 Irish songs; 13 Scottish songs; 2 Welsh songs, of which one is in Welsh and English and the other is in English translation only

Wilson, H. Lane, ed. Old English melodies. Boosey c1899 pa $2
    Contents: 15 songs by Arne, Thomas Brown, Carey, Dibdin, Hook, Leveridge, Linley, Monro, Smart, Storace, Young; 6 traditional songs

FRENCH

Album of songs by composers of the Neo-French school, for medium voice and piano accompaniment. (No. 202) rev ed Boston music co. c1911 pa $1.25
    Cover title: Twelve songs by Neo-French composers
    Contents: 12 songs in French with English translations, by Auguin, Chausson, Coquard, Darcieux, Debussy, Fauré, Hüe, Leroux, Samuel-Rousseau

Croze, Austin de, comp. The beautiful folk-songs of France. 2v H. W. Gray 1925 v1 pa $1; v2 pa $2
    French with English translations. Book 1, Novello's school songs book 277, contains 12 songs. Book 2 has title "Twelve songs and dances of Flandre, Artois, Picardie, Normandie, Champagne, Lorraine, Alsace"

*****Gibbon**, John Murray, ed. Canadian folk songs (old and new); harmonizations by Geoffrey O'Hara and Oscar O'Brien. Dutton c1927 bds $2.50
    Thirty chansons of French or French-Canadian origin, with both English and French words set to old melodies

Grant-Schaefer, George Alfred, ed. French Canadian songs, with words in English and French. A. P. Schmidt co. c1921 pa $1.25
    Contents: 7 songs in French with English translations

Monroe, Mina, comp. Bayou ballads; twelve folk-songs from Louisiana; ed. with the collaboration of Kurt Schindler. G. Schirmer c1921 pa $2.50
    Contents: 12 songs in creole patois with French and English translations

GERMAN

Erk, Ludwig Christian, ed. Deutscher liederschatz; die schoensten weisen der alten sammlung Ludwig Erks neu bearbeitet—durch hundert lieder vermehrt und mit ausfuehrlichen anmerkungen herausgegeben von Max Friedlaender. Peters n.d. cl $3
    Former title: Volkslieder-album
    German only. Contents: 147 volks- und volkstümliche lieder; 11 Weihnachtslieder; 7 vaterlandslieder; 26 soldaten- und jägerlieder; 40 studentenlieder; 9 Rheinlieder

*****Gems** of German song. (The Ditson music collections) rev ed Ditson c1909 high, low pa $1.25
    German with English translations
    Contents: 47 songs by Becker, Beethoven, Bendel, Bohm, Brahms, Coenen, Fielitz, Franz, Götze, Jensen, Kjerulf, Lassen, Liszt, Mendelssohn, Meyer-Helmund, Mozart, Raff, Reichardt, Reimann, Rubinstein, Schaeffer, Schubert, Schumann, Strauss, Tchaikovsky

HUNGARIAN

Korbay, Francis, ed. Hungarian melodies. 2v Schott c1891-93 pa ea 6s
    Hungarian with English translations
    Contents: v1, 25 folk songs and songs by Bernáth, Egressi, Simonffy, Szerdahelyi
    v2, 9 songs by Szentirmay, and 16 folk songs and songs by Egressi, Füredi, Simonffy and Szerdahelyi

IRISH

*****Hatton**, John Liptrot, and Molloy, James Lyman, comps. The songs of Ireland, including the most favourite of Moore's Irish melodies, and a large collection of old songs and ballads, with new symphonies and accompaniments. Boosey n.d. pa $2.50; cl $4
    On cover, new and enlarged edition
    Contents: 78 settings of Thomas Moore's poems, and 30 songs which are traditional or of more recent composition. English words only

Hughes, Herbert, ed. Irish country songs. 2v Boosey c1909-15 high, medium, low pa ea $3
    Contents: v1, 22 Irish folk songs; v2, 20 Irish folk songs

The songs of Ireland; a collection of popular Irish airs. Ditson c1890 pa $1.25
    Contents: 66 songs, including 20 songs of Thomas Moore

ITALIAN

Krehbiel, Henry Edward, comp. Voices from the golden age of bel canto; a collection of twenty-six opera-songs of the seventeenth and eighteenth centuries from rare manuscripts and early prints collected by Henry Edward Krehbiel, with a preface and biographical notes; ed. by Max Spicker. G. Schirmer c1910 pa $2
    Italian with English translations

Contents: 26 songs from the operas Adriano (Bernasconi); Adriano in Siria (Galuppi); Alessandro nell' Indie (Schiassi); Catone (Pergolesi); Catone (Zamparelli); Dafne (Gagliano); Demetrio (Mazzoni); Euridice (Caccini); Euridice (Peri); Il podesta di chioggia (Orlandi); La Gerusalemme liberata (Righini); La Rosaura (Scarlatti); L'Olimpiade (Pergolesi); L'orfano della China (Bianchi); Orfeo (Monteverde); Siroë (Latilla); Temistocle (Orlandini); Vologeso (Rinaldo da Capua)

Zanon, Maffeo, ed. Twelve arias by old Italian masters; ed. from the original scores. (No. 214, 167) 2v Boston music co. c1915 pa ea $1
Italian with English translations
Contents: v1, songs by Amadori, d'Astorga, Ciampi, Galuppi, Marcello
v2, songs by Aniello, Bruni, Pergolesi, Piccinni, Sarti

JEWISH

Binder, Abraham Wolf, ed. New Palestinean folk songs. Bloch pub. co. c1926 pa $1
20 songs in transliterated Hebrew with English translations. Includes Yemenite songs, dance songs of the Chalutzim, national songs and love songs. Two additional songs without words are omitted from this index

Kremer, Isa, comp. Album of Jewish folk-songs (the Jewish life in song). Chappell-Harms co. c1930 pa $1.50
Contents: 24 songs in Yiddish only, transliterated into the Latin alphabet

Schack, Sarah Pitkowsky, comp. Yiddish folk songs; 50 songs for voice and piano; piano arrangements by Ethel Silberman Cohen. 2d ed rev Bloch pub. co. c1924 cl $2
Texts in Yiddish, with transliteration, and a paraphrase in English

MEXICAN AND SPANISH AMERICAN

Hague, Eleanor, comp. Early Spanish-Californian folk-songs; harmonized and set for voice and piano by Gertrude Ross. (No 5120-21) J. Fischer c1922 high, low pa ea $1.50
Contents: 5 songs, in Spanish with English translations

Manney, Charles Fonteyn, comp. Mexican and Spanish songs; the English texts by Frederick H. Martens. Ditson c1928 high, low pa $1
Contents: 11 songs with original Spanish words and English translations

Van Stone, Mrs Mary R., ed. Spanish folk songs of New Mexico; with a foreword by Alice Corbin. Seymour c1928 pa $1.50
Contents: 23 songs in Spanish with English translations

RUSSIAN

Album of ten songs by Russian composers. (No. 207, 161) Boston music co. c1914 high, low pa ea $1
Cover title: Russian composers; album of ten songs
English; and French, German, with English translations. Contents: 10 songs by Arenski, Borodin, Cui, Glière, Grechaninov, Ippolitov-Ivanov, Musorgskiĭ, Nikolaev, Rimskiĭ-Korsakov, Cherepnin

Newmarch, Rosa, ed. Russian folk-songs, with pianoforte accompaniment. c1915 Marks pa $1.50; Chester pa 3s
Contents: 10 folk songs and 17 songs in the folk style, in English only

Schindler, Kurt, ed. Songs of the Russian people. Ditson c1915 pa $1.50
Contents: 15 folk songs and songs by Bortnianskiĭ, Musorgskiĭ, Panchenko, Rimskiĭ-Korsakov, Zolotarev, in English only

SCANDINAVIAN

*****Werrenrath,** Reinald, ed. Modern Scandinavian songs. (The musicians library) v2 Ditson c1926 high, low pa $2.50; cl $3.50
The first volume (WM 1) was indexed in the Song Index
Contents: v2, 50 songs by Lange-Müller, Lie, Lund, Melartin, Merikanto, Neupert, Nielsen, Olsen, Palmgren, Peterson-Berger, Rangström, Sibelius, Sinding, Sjögren, Stenhammar, Svendsen, Winge

SCOTTISH

Gems of Scottish song; a collection of the most beautiful Scotch ballads, arranged and compiled from the very best sources and latest revivals of the authors' works. rev and enl ed Ditson c1894 pa $1.25
Contents: 213 songs in English only

WELSH

Williams, W. S. Gwynn, comp. Old Welsh folk-songs. Curwen c1927 vocal ed (Curwen edition 6341) 25c; piano ed (Curwen edition 2970) $1.50
Contents: 13 songs in Welsh with English translations

YUGOSLAV

Chatterton, Julia, ed. Jugo-Slav folk-songs. (Curwen edition 2976) Curwen c1930 pa $1.50
Contents: 6 songs in the original with English translations

CHANTEYS

Smith, Cicely Fox, ed. A book of shanties. Methuen c1927 cl 6s
> 31 chanteys with historical notes and a 9-page introduction. Only 8 of the chanteys have piano accompaniments

Terry, Sir Richard Runciman, ed. The shanty book. (Curwen edition 6321, 6340) 2v Curwen c1921-26 vocal ed pa ea 45c; pianoforte ed pa ea $1.80
> Contents: v1, 14 windlass and capstan chanteys; 12 halliard chanteys; 3 fore-sheet or sweating-up chanteys; 1 bunt chantey
> v2, 16 windlass and capstan chanteys; 18 halliard chanteys; 1 fore-sheet chantey

Whall, W. B., comp. Sea songs and shanties. 6th ed enl Brown, son & Ferguson c1927 cl 5s
> Earlier editions had title: Ships, sea songs and shanties. Contains notes about most of the songs
> Contents: 64 chanteys and forecastle songs

CHRISTMAS CAROLS

Dunstan, Ralph, ed. New book of Christmas carols. Reid bros. c1923 pa 2s; cl 3s6d
> Cover title: First book of Christmas carols
> In English only. Contents: 17 ancient English carols; 1 Welsh carol; 1 Scottish carol; 2 Irish carols; 4 Latin melodies with English words; 4 German melodies with English words; 3 French and Anglo-French carols; 2 Swedish melodies with English words; 9 local traditional and popular carols; 15 popular Christmas hymns and songs, 17th to 19th century

Dunstan, Ralph, ed. A second book of Christmas carols. Reid bros. c1925 pa 2s; cl 3s6d
> For first book of carols see "New book of Christmas carols" (above)
> English only. Contents: 3 ancient Christmas hymns; 19 ancient English and Tudor carols; 4 Irish carols; 1 Scottish carol; 9 Noëls; 5 German carols and Bach settings; 24 traditional carols; 1 modern Christmas carol

Finn, William Joseph. Father Finn's carol book; 60 Christmas songs and carols old and new, selected from the repertory of the Paulist choristers. Birchard c1917 melody ed 15c; complete ed (voice and piano) pa 75c
> 60 carols from many countries, in English only

*The **Oxford** book of carols; ed. by Percy Dearmer, R. Vaughan Williams, and Martin Shaw. J. Fischer c1928 music ed cl $2.50
> 197 carols in English only
> Contents: traditional English, Welsh and Irish carols; ancient carols set to similar old carol airs and traditional tunes; modern carols written for and adapted to traditional tunes; ancient carols set to tunes by modern composers; carols by modern writers and composers

SACRED SONGS

Album of sacred songs; a collection of twenty-two favorite songs suitable for use in the churches. (Schirmer's library of musical classics v1384-85) 2v G. Schirmer c1918 high, low pa ea $1.50
> English; and French, German and Latin with English translations
> Contents: 22 songs by Ambrose, Barri, Bizet, Coenen, Costa, Gounod, Hiller, Jadassohn, Krebs, Mendelssohn, Parker, Pinsuti, Randegger, Rodney, Saint-Saëns, Schlösser, Tours, Watson

Choice sacred solos. (The Ditson music collections) 2v Ditson c1883-1917 high, low pa ea $1.25
> English; and French, German, Italian, Latin with English translations
> Contents: v1, high voice, 34 songs; v2, low voice, 35 songs, of which 16 duplicate v1. The composers are Abt, Adams, Barri, Bendel, Blumenthal, Bohm, Cole, Costa, Cowen, Dana, Danks, Dubois, Faure, Gounod, Händel, Hargitt, Haydn, Henshaw, Hewitt, Hughes, Jordan, Jude, Keller, Lassen, Meyer-Helmund, Morsell, Moszkowski, Parker, Piatti, Piccolomini, Raff, Rodney, Roeckel, Saint-Saëns, Schloesser, Schulthes, Sullivan, Tosti, Tours, Winch

Sacred songs. (Imperial edition) 4v Boosey n.d. pa ea $2; cl ea $3.50
> Contents: v1, soprano, 32 songs; v2, contralto, 42 songs; v3, tenor, 34 songs; v4, baritone, 32 songs
> English, with original words for 2 songs, by Adam, Alberti, Bach, Beethoven, Caldara, Cherubini, Costa, Durante, Gounod, Graun, Händel, Hasse, Haydn, Hiller, Leo, Mendelssohn, Naumann, Pergolesi, Raff, Ricci, Rossini, Schubert, Serini, Stradella, Sullivan, Tchaikovsky and Winter

Treasury of sacred solos. (The Ditson music collections) 2v Ditson c1896-1904 high, low pa ea $1.25
> Cover title, v1: Treasury of sacred songs
> Contents: v1, high voice, 27 songs in English only, except 1 Latin with English translation; v2, low voice, 28 songs of which 13 duplicate v1, in English only, except a few songs in Latin and German with English translations. The composers are Abt, Balfe, Bartlett, Batchelder, Benedict, Bradsky, Cantor, Chenery, Coverley, Gaul, Geibel, Gounod, Hosmer, Howe, Howell, Jordan, Loud, Mascagni, Nevin, Perry, Peticolas, Piccolomini, Randegger, Reed, Roeder, Rupes, Schnecker, Sommers, Sutcliffe, Tosti, Van de Water, Watson

SCHOOL AND COLLEGE SONGS

Allen, Thornton Whitney, comp. Intercollegiate song book; alma mater and football songs of the American colleges. de luxe ed Intercollegiate song book, inc. c1927 cl $3
> Contents: 68 alma maters; 70 football songs; 6 songs from women's colleges

Allen, Thornton Whitney, comp. Intercollegiate song book; ed. by Carl F. Price.
popular ed Intercollegiate song book, inc. c1931 pa $1.50
Not the same as the preceding song collection, altho there is some duplication
Contents: 108 alma maters and football songs of 100 colleges and universities, including some of
the lesser known institutions

Hagen, John Milton, comp. Western college songs; songs of the universities and
colleges of the Far West. Sherman, Clay c1931 pa $1.25
Contents: Alma maters and football songs from 38 colleges and universities between the Rockies
and the Pacific coast

*ₜ**Kennedy,** Blanche B., and Kennedy, Herbert B., comps.ₗ University and college
song book; 119 songs of the prominent American universities and colleges.
University & college song book, inc. ₜpref. 1930ₗ pa $1
Contents: 119 alma maters and football songs, from 73 universities and colleges in all parts of the
United States

Kennedy, Blanche B., and Kennedy, Herbert B., comps. Varsity songs; 50 university
and college songs. University & college song book, inc. c1931 pa 50c
Contents: Alma maters and football songs from 50 colleges and universities

Collections Indexed in Song Index and Supplement

Abridged academy song-book. See Levermore, C. H. ed.
Afro-American folk songs. See Krehbiel, H. E. ed.
Album of bass songs. 4v AB 1-4 (Song Index)
Album of Jewish folk-songs. See Kremer, I. comp.
Album of sacred songs. 2v ASA (Sup.)
Album of songs by composers of the Neo-French school. ASN (Sup.)
Album of ten songs by Russian composers. ATS (Sup.)
Album of twenty-five favorite encore songs. AT (Sup.)
Album of twenty-seven songs for contralto voice. See Spicker, M. ed.
Allen, T. W. comp. Intercollegiate song book. de luxe ed AI (Sup.)
—Intercollegiate song book; ed. by C. F. Price. popular ed AIS (Sup.)
Allen, W. F., Ware, C. P. and Garrison, L. M. eds. Slave songs of the United States. AS (Sup.)
Aloha collection of Hawaiian songs. See Hopkins, C. A. K. ed.
American-English folk-songs. See Sharp, C. J. ed.
American home music album. See Wier, A. E. ed.
American mountain songs. See Richardson, E. P. comp.
American primitive music. See Burton, F. R. ed.
American song book. See Levermore, C. H. ed.
American songbag. See Sandburg, C. comp.
Anderson, R. B. See Moore, A. W. jt. ed.
Anthology of American song. AA (Song Index)
Anthology of Italian song. See Parisotti, A. ed.
Anthology of modern French song. See Spicker, M. ed.
Anthology of sacred song. See Spicker, M. ed.
Anthology of song. See Goss, J. ed.
Art songs of Japan. See Ross, G.

Bacon, M. S. H. ed. Songs every child should know. BSE (Song Index)
Ballads the whole world sings. See Wier, A. E. ed.
Baltzell, W. J. comp. Something to sing. BST (Sup.)
Bantock, G. R. ed. One hundred folk-songs of all nations. BO (Song Index)
—One hundred songs of England. BOH (Song Index)
—Sixty patriotic songs of all nations. BSP (Song Index)
Barbeau, M. and Sapir, E. eds. Folk songs of French Canada. BFS (Song Index)
Baring-Gould, S. ed. English minstrelsie. 8v BE 1-8 (Song Index)
—. Sheppard, H. F. and Bussell, F. W. eds. Songs of the west. BSW (Song Index)
Baritone album. See Pittmann, J. ed.
Baritone songs. 2v BAS 1-2 (Song Index)
Bass songs. 2v BS 1-2 (Song Index)
Bayou ballads. See Monroe, M. comp.

Beattie, J. W. jt. comp. See Blue book of favorite songs
Beautiful folk-songs of France. See Croze, A. de, comp.
Bentley, A. E. See Finck, H. T. jt. ed.
Bergerettes. See Wekerlin, J. B. ed.
Binder, A. W. ed. New Palestinean folk songs. BNP (Sup.)
Bispham, D. ed. Celebrated recital songs. BC (Song Index)
—David Bispham treasury of song. BD (Song Index)
Black, H. See Larkin, M. comp. Singing cowboy
Blackman, O. See Lawrence, W. M. jt. ed.
Blake, W. P. See Sturgis, M. H. jt. ed.
Blue book. See Twice 55 community songs for male voices: the blue book
Blue book of favorite songs; comp. by J. W. Beattie and others. 3 pts in 1 BB (Sup.)
Blues. See Handy, W. C. ed.
Bond, C. J. comp. Old melodies of the south; transcribed by M. Gillen and O. Chalifoux. BOM (Song Index)
Book of a thousand songs. See Wier, A. E. ed.
Book of American negro spirituals. See Johnson, J. W. ed.
Book of chanties. See King, S. H. ed.
Book of Christmas carols, New. See Dunstan, R. ed.
Book of Christmas carols, Second. See Dunstan, R. ed.
Book of navy songs. See U.S. Naval academy, Annapolis. Trident society
Book of Shakespeare's songs. See Edwards, E. comp.
Book of shanties. See Smith, C. F. ed.
Book of songs. See Davison, A. T., Surette, T. W. and Zanzig, A. D. comps.; MacMillan, E. C. ed.
Bos, C. ed. Dutch folk-songs. BDF (Song Index)
Botsford, F. H. ed. Folk songs of many peoples. 2v BF 1-2 (Song Index)
Boy scout song book. BSS (Song Index)
Bramley, H. R. and Stainer, J. eds. Christmas carols new and old. BSC (Song Index)
Broadwood, L. E. ed. English traditional songs and carols. BET (Sup.)
—See also Walter, L. E. ed. Christmas carols
Brockway, H. arr. See Wyman, L. ed.
Brown, C. See Pittmann, J. jt. ed.
Brown, J. D. and Moffat, A. eds. Characteristic songs and dances of all nations. BMC (Song Index)
Brown book. See Twice 55 community songs. v1
Brown book, New. See Twice 55 plus community songs: the new brown book
Buck, P. C. ed. Oxford song book. BOS (Song Index)
—same. v2. See Oxford song book. v2

Burleigh, H. T. ed. Negro minstrel melodies. BNM (Sup.)
—Plantation melodies old and new. BP (Song Index)
Burlin, N. C. ed. Negro folk-songs. 4v BN 1-4 (Song Index)
Burns, R. Songs of Burns. BSB (Song Index)
—Songs of Robert Burns; ed. by J. C. Dick. BSR (Song Index)
Burton, F. R. ed. American primitive music. BA (Song Index)
Bussell, F. W. See Baring-Gould, S. jt. ed.

Cadman, C. W. Four American Indian songs. CF (Song Index)
Calvé, E. comp. My favorite French songs. 2v CM 1-2 (Song Index)
Campbell, O. D. and Sharp, C. J. eds. English folk songs from the southern Appalachians. CSE (Song Index)
—same. For new edition see Sharp, C. J. comp.
Canadian folk song (old and new) See Gibbon, J. M. ed.
Canciones populares. See Luce, A. ed.
Carols old and carols new. See Hutchins, C. L. ed.
Cartwright, H. G. ed. Song treasury. CST (Song Index)
Celebrated recital songs. See Bispham, D. ed.
Century of Russian song from Glinka to Rachmaninoff. See Schindler, K. ed.
Chalifoux, O. See Bond, C. J. comp. Old melodies of the south
Chamberlain, D. B. and Harrington, K. P. eds. Songs of all the colleges. CHS (Song Index)
Chappell, W. ed. Old English popular music. 2v CO 1-2 (Song Index)
Characteristic songs and dances of all nations. See Brown, J. D. and Moffat, A. eds.
Chatterton, J. ed. Jugo-Slav folk-songs. CJ (Sup.)
Choice sacred solos. 2v CSS 1-2 (Sup.)
Christmas carols. See Walter, L. E. ed.
Christmas carols and hymns for school and choir. See Dann, H. ed.
Christmas carols new and old. See Bramley, H. R. and Stainer, J. eds.
Christmas in song, sketch, and story. See McCaskey, J. P. ed.
Christmas songs of many nations. See Davis, K. W. ed.
Clarendon song books; ed. by W. G. Whittaker, H. Wiseman and J. Wishart. 6v CSB 1-6 (Sup.)
Classic baritone and bass songs. CB (Song Index)
Classic song album. See Heinrich, M. ed.
Cohen, E. S. See Schack, S. P. comp. Yiddish folk songs
Colcord, J. C. ed. Roll and go. CR (Song Index)
College songs. See Waite, H. R. comp.
Coloratura album for soprano. See Marzo, E. ed.
Columbia university songs; comp. by W. B. Donnell, R. P. Hoyt, jr, L. G. McAneny, and G. O. Ward. CU (Song Index)
Contralto album. See Pittmann, J. ed.
Contralto album. See Spicker, M. ed. Album of twenty-seven songs for contralto voice
Contralto songs. 2v CS 1-2 (Song Index)
Cowboy songs. See Lomax, J. A. ed.
Crosley, J. W. See U.S. Naval academy, Annapolis. Trident society. Book of navy songs
Croze, A. de, comp. Beautiful folk-songs of France. 2v CBF 1-2 (Sup.)
Culp, J. comp. My favorite songs. 2v CMF 1-2 (Song Index)

Dann, H. ed. Christmas carols and hymns for school and choir. DC (Song Index)
—Fifty-eight spirituals for choral use; harmonized by H. W. Loomis. DF (Song Index)
David Bispham treasury of song. See Bispham, D. ed.
Davis, K. W. ed. Christmas songs of many nations. DCS (Song Index)
Davison, A. T. and Surette, T. W. eds. Home & community song-book. DSH (Song Index)
—same. For new edition see Surette, T. W. and Davison, A. T. eds.
—140 folk-songs. DO (Song Index)
—and Zanzig, A. D. comps. Book of songs. DSB (Sup.)
Dearmer, P., Williams, R. V. and Shaw, M. eds. See Oxford book of carols
De Croze, A. comp. See Croze, A. de, comp.

Dett, R. N. ed. See Hampton, Va. Normal and agricultural institute. Religious folk-songs of the negro
Deutscher liederschatz. See Erk, L. C. ed.
DeVore, N. ed. Fifty famous favorites. DFF (Sup.)
Dick, J. C. ed. See Burns, R. Songs of Robert Burns
Dickinson, D. and Dickinson, H. A. S. eds. Troubadour songs. DT (Song Index)
Dolph, E. A. comp. Sound off! music arr. by P. Egner. DSO (Sup.)
Donnell, W. B. jt. comp. See Columbia university songs
Dramatic concert arias. DCA (Sup.)
Duncan, E. ed. Minstrelsy of England. 2v DM 1-2 (Song Index)
Dunstan, R. ed. New book of Christmas carols. DN (Sup.)
—Second book of Christmas carols. DNS (Sup.)
Dutch folk-songs. See Bos, C. ed.
Dykema, P. W. See Twice 55 community songs for male voices
—See Twice 55 community songs for treble voices
—See Twice 55 part songs for boys
—and others, eds. See Twice 55 community songs
—See Twice 55 plus community songs

Early Italian songs and airs. See Floridia, P. ed.
Early Spanish-Californian folk-songs. See Hague, E. comp.
Echoes of Naples. See Favilli, M. ed.
Edwards, E. comp. Book of Shakespeare's songs. EB (Sup.)
Egner, P. See Dolph, E. A. comp. Sound off!
Elson, L. C. ed. Folk songs of many nations. EF (Song Index)
Encore songs. ES (Song Index)
Encore songs, Album of twenty-five favorite. AT (Sup.)
English folk-chanteys. See Sharp, C. J. ed.
English folk songs. See Sharp, C. J. ed.
English folk songs from the southern Appalachians. See Campbell, O. D. and Sharp, C. J. eds.
—same. For new edition see Sharp, C. J. comp.
English melodies from the 13th to the 18th century. See Jackson, V. ed.
English minstrelsie. See Baring-Gould, S. ed.
English songs of the Georgian period. See Moffat, A. and Kidson, F. eds.
English traditional songs and carols. See Broadwood, L. E. ed.
Erk, L. C. ed. Deutscher liederschatz. 3v ED 1-3 (Song Index)
Erk, L. C. ed. Deutscher liederschatz; ed. by M. Friedlaender. EDL (Sup.)

Family music book. FMB (Song Index)
Famous songs. See Krehbiel, H. E. ed.
Famous songs and their stories. See Geller, J. J.
Faning, E. See Hatton, J. L. jt. ed.
Farnsworth, C. H. and Sharp, C. J. eds. Folk-songs, chanteys and singing games. FSF (Song Index)
Farrar, G. comp. My favorite songs. FM (Song Index)
Farwell, A. See Lummis, C. F. ed. Spanish songs of old California
Father Finn's carol book. See Finn, W. J.
Favilli, M. ed. Echoes of Naples. FE (Song Index)
Favorite bass songs. See Spicker, M. comp.
Favorite songs and hymns for school and home. See McCaskey, J. P. ed.
Fenner, T. P. ed. See Hampton, Va. Normal and agricultural institute. Religious folk songs of the negro
Ferrari, G. ed. Ten folk-songs of Alsace, Lorraine and Champagne. FTF (Song Index)
Fifty Chistmas carols of all nations. See Marzo, E. ed.
Fifty famous favorites. See DeVore, N. ed.
Fifty master-songs by twenty composers. See Finck, H. T. ed.
Fifty Shakspere songs. See Vincent, C. J. ed.
Fifty-eight spirituals for choral use. See Dann, H. ed.
Finck, H. T. ed. Fifty master-songs by twenty composers. FF (Song Index)
—One hundred songs by ten masters. 2v FO 1-2 (Song Index)
—and Bentley, A. E. eds. Thirty sterling songs by the great masters. FTS (Song Index)
Finn, W. J. Father Finn's carol book. FC (Sup.)

First book of Christmas carols. See Dunstan, R. ed. New book of Christmas carols

Fisher, W. A. ed. Sixty Irish songs. FSI

—Seventy negro spirituals. FSN (Sup.)

Fletcher, A. C. ed. Indian games and dances with native songs. FI (Song Index)

—Indian story and song from North America. FIS (Song Index)

Floridia, P. ed. Early Italian songs and airs. 2v FEI 1-2 (Song Index)

Folk-songs, chanteys and singing games. See Farnsworth, C. H. and Sharp, C. J. eds.

Folk songs from Mexico and South America. See Hague, E. ed.

Folk-songs of Eastern Europe. See Whitehead, R. R. ed.

Folk-songs of England. See Sharp, C. J. ed.

Folk songs of French Canada. See Barbeau, M. and Sapir, E. eds.

Folk songs of many nations. See Elson, L. C. ed.

Folk songs of many peoples. See Botsford, F. H. ed.

Folk-songs of the four seasons. See Myers, S. tr.

Folk-songs of the Kentucky mountains. See McGill, J. comp.

Forty negro spirituals. See White, C. C. comp.

Forty-four French folk songs and variants from Canada, Normandy, and Brittany. See Tiersot, J. ed.

Foss, H. J. See Little song book of the nations

Four American Indian songs. See Cadman, C. W.

Franklin square song collection; selected by J. P. McCaskey. 8v FSS 1-8 (Song Index)

French Canadian songs. See Grant-Schaefer, G. A. ed.

Friedlaender, M. Deutscher liederschatz. See Erk, L. C. ed.

From the cradle to the chuppe. See Gideon, C. and Gideon, H. eds.

Garrison, L. M. See Allen, W. F. jt. ed.

Geller, J. J. Famous songs and their stories. GFS (Sup.)

Gems of antiquity. See Neitzel, O. ed.

Gems of English song. GE (Sup.)

Gems of German song. GG (Sup.)

Gems of Scottish song. GS (Sup.)

Gentlemen, be seated! See Paskman, D. and Spaeth, S. G.

Gerhardt, E. comp. My favorite German songs. GM (Song Index)

German, French and Italian song classics. See Parker, H. W. ed.

Gibbon, J. M. ed. Canadian folk songs (old and new); arr. by G. O'Hara and O. O'Brien. GC (Sup.)

Gideon, C. and Gideon, H. eds. From the cradle to the chuppe. 2v GF 1-2 (Song Index)

Gilbert, H. F. B. ed. One hundred folk-songs from many countries. GO (Song Index)

Gillen, M. See Bond, C. J. comp. Old melodies of the south

Girl scout song book; ed. by G. Newell. GSS (Sup.)

Gluck, A. comp. My favorite songs. GMF (Song Index)

Golden book of favorite songs. See Blue book of favorite songs. 3 pts in 1

Good old songs we used to sing; comp. by J. C. H. 2v GOS 1-2 (Sup.)

Good old timers. See Smith, L. O. and Morse, T. comps.

Goss, J. eds. Anthology of song. GA (Sup.)

Grand opera at home. See Wier, A. E. ed.

Grant-Schaefer, G. A. ed. French Canadian songs. GSF (Sup.)

Gray book of favorite songs. See Blue book of favorite songs. 3 pts in 1

Green book. See Twice 55 community songs. v2

Green book, New. See Twice 55 community songs: the new green book

Green Pastures spirituals. See Johnson, H. ed.

Hagen, J. M. comp. Western college songs. HW (Sup.)

Hägg, G. ed. Songs of Sweden. HSOS (Song Index)

Hague, E. comp. Early Spanish-Californian folk-songs; arr. by G. Ross. HE (Sup.)

—Folk songs from Mexico and South America. HF (Song Index)

—Spanish-American folk-songs. HS (Song Index)

Hale, P. ed. Modern French songs. 2v HM 1-2 (Song Index)

Hampton, Va. Normal and agricultural institute. Religious folk songs of the negro; arr. from the original edition by T. P. Fenner. HR (Song Index)

—same; ed. by R. N. Dett. HRD (Sup.)

Handy, W. C. ed. Blues. HB (Sup.)

Harrington, K. P. See Chamberlain, D. B. jt. ed.

Hatton, J. L. and Faning, E. eds. Songs of England. 3v HSE 1-3 (Song Index)

Hatton, J. L. and Molloy, J. L. comps. Songs of Ireland. HMI (Sup.)

Heart songs dear to the American people. HSD (Song Index)

Heinrich, M. ed. Classic song album. HCA (Sup.)

Henderson, W. J. ed. Sacred songs. 4v HSS 1-4 (Song Index)

Home & community song-book. See Davison, A. T. and Surette, T. W. eds.

—same. For new edition see Surette, T. W. and Davison, A. T. eds.

Home songs. HSC (Song Index)

Hopekirk, H. ed. Seventy Scottish songs. HSSS (Song Index)

Hopkins, C. A. K. ed. Aloha collection of Hawaiian songs. HA (Song Index)

Howard, J. T. comp. Program of early and mid-nineteenth century American songs. HP (Sup.)

Hoyt, R. P. jt. ed. See Columbia university songs

Hughes, H. ed. Irish country songs. 2v HI 1-2 (Sup.)

Hughes, Robert. See Sturgis, E. B. ed. Songs from the hills of Vermont

Hughes, Rupert, ed. Songs by thirty Americans. HST (Song Index)

Hungarian melodies. See Korbay, F. ed.

Hutchins, C. L. ed. Carols old and carols new. HC (Song Index)

Intercollegiate song book. See Allen, T. W. comp.

Irish country songs. See Hughes, H. ed.

Irish melodies. See Moore, T.

Irish songs. See Page, N. C. ed.

Indian games and dances with native songs. See Fletcher, A. C. ed.

Indian story and song from North America. See Fletcher, A. C. ed.

Jackson, V. ed. English melodies from the 13th to the 18th century. JE (Song Index)

Japanese folk songs for voice & piano. See Yamada, K.

Johnson, Charles W. ed. Songs of the nation. JS (Song Index)

Johnson, Clifton, ed. Songs every one should know. JSE (Song Index)

Johnson, Hall, ed. Green Pastures spirituals. JG (Sup.)

Johnson, Helen K. ed. Our familiar songs and those who made them. JO (Song Index)

Johnson, James W. ed. Book of American negro spirituals. JB (Song Index)

—Second book of negro spirituals. JB 2 (Sup.)

Joyce, P. W. ed. Old Irish folk music and songs. JOI (Song Index)

Jubilee and plantation songs. JP (Song Index)

Jugo-Slav folk-songs. See Chatterton, J. ed.

Kappey, J. A. ed. Songs of eastern Europe. KSE (Song Index)

—Songs of Scandinavia and Northern Europe. KSN (Song Index)

Karpeles, M. ed. See Sharp, C. J. comp. English folk songs from the southern Appalachians

Kennedy, B. B. and Kennedy, H. B. comps. University and college song book. KU (Sup.)

—Varsity songs. KV (Sup.)

Kidson, F. See Moffat, A. jt. ed.

Kimmins, G. T. H. ed. Songs from the plays of William Shakespeare; pianoforte accompaniments by R. Chanter. KSS (Song Index)

King, S. H. ed. King's book of chanties. KB (Song Index)

Knowlton, F. S. comp. Songs of other days. KSO (Sup.)

Korbay, F. ed. Hungarian melodies. 2v KH 1-2 (Sup.)

Krehbiel, H. E. ed. Afro-American folk songs. KA (Song Index)

—Famous songs. 4v KF 1-4 (Song Index)

—Songs from the operas. 5v KS 1-5 (Song Index)

—Voices from the golden age of bel canto; ed. by M. Spicker. KVG (Sup.)

Kremer, I. comp. Album of Jewish folk-songs. KAJ (Sup.)

Larkin, M. comp. Singing cowboy; arr. by H. Black. LSC (Sup.)

Laurel song book. See Tomlins, W. L. ed.

Lawrence, W. M. and Blackman, O. eds. Riverside song book. LBL (Song Index)

Levermore, C. H. ed. Abridged academy song-book. LA (Song Index)

—American song book. LAS (Sup.)

Lied der völker. See Möller, H. comp.

Lieurance, T. Nine Indian songs. LN (Song Index)

—Songs of the North American Indians. LS (Song Index)

Light opera at home. See Wier, A. E. ed.

Little song book of the nations; ed. by A. E. W. Thomas; arr. by H. J. Foss. LSB (Sup.)

Lomax, J. A. ed. Cowboy songs. LC (Song Index)

Lonesome tunes. See Wyman, L. ed.

Loomis, H. W. See Dann, H. ed. Fifty-eight spirituals for choral use

Love songs the whole world sings. See Wier, A. E. ed.

Luce, A. ed. Canciones populares. LCP (Song Index)

Lummis, C. F. ed. Spanish songs of old California; arr. by A. Farwell. LSS (Song Index)

McAneny, L. G. jt. comp. See Columbia university songs

McCaskey, J. P. ed. Christmas in song, sketch, and story. MCS (Song Index)

—Favorite songs and hymns for school and home. MFS (Sup.)

—See also Franklin square song collection

MacConnell, M. F. ed. Standard songs and choruses for high schools. MS (Song Index)

McGill, J. comp. Folk-songs of the Kentucky mountains. MK (Sup.)

MacMillan, E. C. ed. Book of songs. MBS (Sup.)

Manney, C. F. comp. Mexican and Spanish songs; the English texts by F. H. Martens. MSP (Sup.)

Martens, F. H. See Manney, C. F. comp. Mexican and Spanish songs

Marzo, E. ed. Coloratura album for soprano. MC (Song Index)

—Fifty Christmas carols of all nations. MF (Song Index)

—Neapolitan songs. MN (Song Index)

—Songs of Italy. MSI (Song Index)

Masters of Russian song. See Schindler, K. ed.

Mexican and Spanish songs. See Manney, C. F. comp.

Mezzo-soprano songs. 2v MSS 1-2 (Song Index)

Milligan, H. V. ed. Pioneer American composers. 2v MPA 1-2 (Sup.)

Minstrelsy of England. See Duncan, E. ed.; Moffat, A. and Kidson, F. eds.

Minstrelsy of Ireland. See Moffat, A. ed.

Minstrelsy of Scotland. See Moffat, A. ed.

Minstrelsy of Wales. See Moffat, A. ed.

Modern French songs. See Hale, P. ed.

Modern Russian songs. See Newman, E. ed.

Modern Scandinavian songs. See Werrenrath, R. ed.

Modern song favorites. 2v MSF 1-2 (Song Index)

Moffat, A. ed. Minstrelsy of Ireland. MMI (Song Index)

—Minstrelsy of Scotland. MMS (Song Index)

—Minstrelsy of Wales. MMW (Song Index)

—See also Brown, J. D. jt. ed.

—and Kidson, F. eds. English songs of the Georgian period. ME (Song Index)

—Minstrelsy of England. MME (Song Index)

Möller, H. comp. Lied der völker. 13v in 3 ML 1-3 (Sup.)

Molloy, J. L. See Hatton, J. L. jt. comp.

Monroe, M. comp. Bayou ballads; ed. with the collaboration of K. Schindler. MB (Sup.)

Moore, A. W. and Anderson, R. B. eds. Norway music album. MAN (Song Index)

Moore, T. Irish melodies. MI (Song Index)

Morse, T. See Smith, L. O. jt. comp.

Most popular college songs. MPC (Song Index)

Most popular home songs. See Noble, G. C. ed.

Most popular love songs. See Noble, G. C. ed.

Most popular plantation songs. See Noble, G. C. ed.

Most popular songs for every occasion. See Noble, G. C. ed.

Most popular songs of patriotism. MP (Song Index)

Music of the waters. See Smith, L. A.

My favorite folk songs. See Sembrich, M. comp.

My favorite French songs. See Calvé, E. comp.

My favorite German songs. See Gerhardt, E. comp.

My favorite songs. See Culp, J. comp.; Farrar, G. comp.; Gluck, A. comp.

Myers, S. tr. Folk-songs of the four seasons; harmonization by H. Officer. MFF (Sup.)

National anthems of the allies. NA (Song Index)

National, patriotic and typical airs of all lands. See Sousa, J. P. ed.

Neapolitan songs. See Marzo, E. ed.

Negro folk-songs. See Burlin, N. C. ed.

Negro minstrel melodies. See Burleigh, H. T. ed.

Neitzel, O. ed. Gems of antiquity. NG (Song Index)

New book of Christmas carols. See Dunstan, R. ed.

New Palestinean folk songs. See Binder, A. W. ed.

Newell, G. ed. See Girl scout song book

Newman, E. ed. Modern Russian songs. 2v NM 1-2 (Song Index)

Newmarch, R. ed. Russian folk-songs. NRF (Sup.)

—Russian song books. 4v NR 1-4 (Song Index)

Nine Indian songs. See Lieurance, T.

Noble, G. C. ed. Most popular home songs. NMH (Song Index)

—Most popular love songs. NML (Song Index)

—Most popular plantation songs. NMP (Song Index)

—Most popular songs for every occasion. NMS (Song Index)

Norway music album. See Moore, A. W. and Anderson, R. B. eds.

Obbligato-songs. See Spicker, M. ed.

O'Brien, O. See Gibbon, J. M. ed.

Officer, H. See Myers, S. tr. Folk-songs of the four seasons

O'Hara, G. See Gibbon, J. M. ed.

Old English melodies. See Wilson, H. L. ed.

Old English popular music. See Chappell, W. ed.

Old Irish folk music and songs. See Joyce, P. W. ed.

Old melodies of the south. See Bond, C. J. comp.

Old song favorites. See Potter, F. H. ed.

Old time hits of the gay eighties and nineties. OTG (Sup.)

Old-time song hits. OT (Sup.)

Old Welsh folk-songs. See Williams, W. S. G. comp.

One hundred English folksongs. See Sharp, C. J. ed.

One hundred folk-songs from many countries. See Gilbert, H. F. B. ed.

One hundred folk-songs of all nations. See Bantock, G. R. ed.

One hundred songs by ten masters. See Finck, H. T. ed.

One hundred songs of England. See Bantock, G. R. ed.

One hundred and one best songs. OH (Song Index)

140 folk-songs. See Davison, A. T. and Surette, T. W. eds.

Opera songs. 4v OPS 1-4 (Song Index)

Operatic anthology. See Spicker, M. ed.

Orange book. See Twice 55 part songs for boys: the orange book

Oratorio songs. 4v OS 1-4 (Song Index)

Our familiar songs and those who made them. See Johnson, H. K. ed.

Oxford book of carols; ed. by P. Dearmer, R. V. Williams, and M. Shaw. OB (Sup.)

Oxford song book. v1 See Buck, P. C. ed.

—same. v2; ed. by T. Wood. BOS 2 (Sup.)

Page, N. C. ed. Irish songs. PI (Song Index)

Parisotti, A. ed. Anthology of Italian song. 2v PA 1-2 (Song Index)

Parker, H. W. ed. German, French and Italian song classics. 4v PG 1-4 (Song Index)

Paskman, D. and Spaeth, S. G. Gentlemen, be seated! PSG (Sup.)

Pioneer American composers. See Milligan, H. V. ed.

Pittmann, J. ed. Baritone album. PB (Sup.)

—Contralto album. PC (Sup.)

—Prima donna's album. PP (Song Index)

—and Brown, C. eds. Songs of Scotland. 2v PS 1-2 (Song Index)

Plantation melodies old and new. See Burleigh, H. T.

Potter, F. H. ed. Old song favorites. PO (Song Index)
—Reliquary of English song. 2v PR 1-2 (Song Index)
Price, C. F. ed. See Allen, T. W. comp. Intercollegiate song book. popular ed.
Prima donna's album. See Pittmann, J. ed.
Program of early and mid-nineteenth century American songs. See Howard, J. T. comp.

Read 'em and weep. See Spaeth, S. G.
Religious folk songs of the negro. See Hampton, Va. Normal and agricultural institute
Reliquary of English song. See Potter, F. H. ed.
Richardson, E. P. comp. American mountain songs; ed. and arr. by S. Spaeth. RA (Sup.)
Riverside song book. See Lawrence, W. M. and Blackman, O. eds.
Roll and go. See Colcord, J. C. ed.
Rose book. See Twice 55 community songs for treble voices: the rose book
Ross, G. Art songs of Japan. RAS (Song Index)
—See also Hague, E. comp. Early Spanish-Californian folk-songs
Russian composers; album of ten songs. See Album of ten songs by Russian composers
Russian folk-songs. See Newmarch, R. ed.
Russian song books. See Newmarch, R. ed.

Sacred music the whole world loves. See Wier, A. E. ed.
Sacred songs. 4v SSO 1-4 (Sup.)
Sacred songs. See Henderson, W. J. ed.
Sandburg, C. comp. American songbag. SBA (Sup.)
Sapir, E. See Barbeau, M. jt. ed.
Schack, S. P. comp. Yiddish folk songs; piano arrangement by E. S. Cohen. SY (Sup.)
Schaefer, G. A. Grant-. See Grant-Schaefer, G. A.
Schindler, K. ed. Century of Russian song from Glinka to Rachmaninoff. SC (Song Index)
—Masters of Russian song. 2v SMR 1-2 (Song Index)
—Sixty Russian folk-songs for one voice. 3v SSR 1-3 (Song Index)
—Songs of the Russian people. SR (Sup.)
—See also Monroe, M. comp. Bayou ballads
Scottish students' song book. SSS (Song Index)
Sea songs and shanties. See Whall, W. B. comp.
Second book of Christmas carols. See Dunstan, R. ed.
Sembrich, M. comp. My favorite folk songs. SMF (Song Index)
Seventy negro spirituals. See Fisher, W. A. ed.
Seventy Scottish songs. See Hopekirk, H. ed.
Shakespeare, W. Book of Shakespeare's songs. See Edwards, E. comp.
—Fifty Shakspere songs. See Vincent, C. J. ed.
—Songs from the plays of William Shakespeare. See Kimmins, G. T. H. ed.
Shanty book. See Terry, Sir R. R. ed.
Sharp, C. J. ed. American-English folk-songs. SA (Song Index)
—English folk-chanteys. SE (Song Index)
—English folk songs. 2v SEF 1-2 (Song Index)
—English folk songs from the southern Appalachians; ed. by M. Karpeles. 2v SES 1-2 (Sup.)
—Folk-songs of England. 5v SF 1-5 (Song Index)
—One hundred English folk-songs. SO (Song Index)
—See also Campbell, O. D. jt. ed.; Farnsworth, C. H. jt. ed.
Shaw, M. jt. ed. See Oxford book of carols
Sheppard, H. F. See Baring-Gould, S. jt. ed.
Ships, sea songs and shanties. See Whall, W. B. comp.
Singing cowboy. See Larkin, M. comp.
Sixty folksongs of France. See Tiersot, J. ed.
Sixty Irish songs. See Fisher, W. A. ed.
Sixty patriotic songs of all nations. See Bantock, G. R. ed.
Sixty Russian folk-songs for one voice. See Schindler, K. ed.
Slave songs of the United States. See Allen, W. F., Ware, C. P. and Garrison, L. M. eds.
Smith, C. F. ed. Book of shanties. SBS (Sup.)
Smith, Laura A. Music of the waters. SMW (Song Index)
Smith, Lee O. and Morse, T. comps. Good old timers. SMG (Sup.)
Something to sing. See Baltzell, W. J. comp.
Song classics, German, French and Italian. See Parker, H. W. ed.

Song miscellany. 4v SM 1-4 (Song Index)
Song treasury. See Cartwright, H. G. ed.
Songs by thirty Americans. See Hughes, R. ed.
Songs every child should know. See Bacon, M. S. H. ed.
Songs every one should know. See Johnson, C. ed.
Songs from the hills of Vermont. See Sturgis, E. B. ed.
Songs from the north. See Stub, V. H. ed.
Songs from the operas. See Krehbiel, H. E. ed.
Songs from the plays of William Shakespeare. See Kimmins, G. T. H. ed.
Songs of all the colleges. See Chamberlain, D. B. and Harrington, K. P. eds.
Songs of Burns. See Burns, R.
Songs of eastern Europe. See Kappey, J. A. ed.
Songs of England. See Hatton, J. L. and Faning, E. eds.
Songs of Germany. See Spicker, M. ed.
Songs of Ireland. SI (Sup.)
Songs of Ireland. See Hatton, J. L. and Molloy, J. L. comps.
Songs of Italy. See Marzo, E. ed.
Songs of other days. See Knowlton, F. S. comp.
Songs of Robert Burns. See Burns, R.
Songs of Scandinavia and northern Europe. See Kappey, J. A. ed.
Songs of Scotland. See Pittmann, J. and Brown, C. eds.
Songs of Sweden. See Hägg, G. ed.
Songs of the British Isles. See Spicker, M. ed.
Songs of the nation. See Johnson, C. W. ed.
Songs of the North American Indians. See Lieurance, T.
Songs of the Pyrenees. See Sturgis, M. H. and Blake, W. P. eds.
Songs of the Russian people. See Schindler, K. ed.
Songs of the sunny south. See Wier, A. E. comp.
Songs of the west. See Baring-Gould, S., Sheppard, H. F. and Bussell, F. W. eds.
Songs the children love to sing. See Wier, A. E. ed.
Songs the whole world sings. See Wier, A. E. ed.
Soprano songs. 2v SS 1-2 (Song Index)
Sound off! See Dolph, E. A. comp.
Sousa, J. P. ed. National, patriotic and typical airs of all lands. SN (Song Index)
Spaeth, S. G. Read 'em and weep. SRW (Sup.)
—Weep some more, my lady. SW (Sup.)
—See also Paskman, D. jt. auth.; Richardson, E. P. comp.
Spanish American folk-songs. See Hague, E. ed.
Spanish folk songs of New Mexico. See Van Stone, M. R. ed.
Spanish songs of old California. See Lummis, C. F. ed.
Spicker, M. ed. Album of twenty-seven songs for contralto voice. SAT (Sup.)
—Anthology of modern French song. SAM (Song Index)
—Anthology of sacred song. 4v SAS 1-4 (Song Index)
—Favorite bass songs. SFB (Sup.)
—Obbligato-songs. 2v SOS 1-2 (Song Index)
—Operatic anthology. 5v SOA 1-5 (Song Index)
—Songs of Germany. SSG (Song Index)
—Songs of the British Isles. SSB (Sup.)
—See also Krehbiel, H. E. comp.
Stainer, J. See Bramley, H. R. jt. ed.
Standard songs and choruses for high schools. See MacConnell, M. F. ed.
Stub, V. H. ed. Songs from the north. SSN (Song Index)
Sturgis, E. B. ed. Songs from the hills of Vermont; music arr by R. Hughes. SSH (Song Index)
Sturgis, M. H. and Blake, W. P. eds. Songs of the Pyrenees. SSP (Song Index)
Surette, T. W. and Davison, A. T. eds. Home and community song book. rev and enl ed DSC (Sup.)
—See also Davison, A. T. jt. ed.

Ten folk-songs of Alsace, Lorraine and Champagne. See Ferrari, G. ed.
Tenor songs. TS (Song Index)
Terry, Sir R. R. ed. Shanty book. 2v TSB 1-2 (Sup.)
Thirty sterling songs by the great masters. See Finck, H. T. and Bentley, A. S. eds.
Thomas, A. E. W. ed. See Little song book of the nations
Tiersot, J. ed. Forty-four French folk songs and variants from Canada, Normandy, and Brittany. TF (Song Index)
—Sixty folksongs of France. TSF (Song Index)

Tomlins, W. L. ed. Laurel song book. TL (Song Index)

Treasury of modern song. TM (Sup.)

Treasury of sacred solos. 2v TSS 1-2 (Sup.)

Trident society. See U.S. Naval academy, Annapolis. Trident society

Troubadour songs. See Dickinson, C. and Dickinson, H. A. S. eds.

Twelve arias by old Italian masters. See Zanon, M. ed.

Twelve songs and dances of Flandre, Artois, Picardie, Normandie, Champagne, Lorraine, Alsace. See Croze, A. de, comp. Beautiful folk-songs of France. v2

Twelve songs by Neo-French composers. See Album of songs by composers of the Neo-French school

Twenty Kentucky mountain songs. See Wyman, L. ed.

Twice 55 community songs; the brown book; the green book. 2v TFC 1-2 (Song Index)

Twice 55 community songs: the new green book; ed. by P. W. Dykema and others. TFG (Sup.)

Twice 55 community songs for male voices: the blue book; ed. by P. W. Dykema. TFB (Sup.)

Twice 55 community songs for treble voices: the rose book; ed. by P. W. Dykema. TFR (Sup.)

Twice 55 part songs for boys: the orange book; ed. by P. W. Dykema. TFO (Sup.)

Twice 55 plus community songs: the new brown book; ed. by P. W. Dykema and others. TFP (Sup.)

U.S. Naval academy, Annapolis. Trident society. Book of navy songs; arr. by J. W. Crosley. US (Sup.)

University and college song book. See Kennedy, B. B. and Kennedy, H. B. comps.

Van Stone, M. R. ed. Spanish folk songs of New Mexico. VS (Sup.)

Varsity songs. See Kennedy, B. B. and Kennedy, H. B. comps.

Vaughan Williams, R. See Williams, R. V.

Vincent, C. J. ed. Fifty Shakspere songs. VFS (Song Index)

Voices from the golden age of bel canto. See Krehbiel, H. E. comp.

Volkslieder-album. See Erk, L. C. ed. Deutscher liederschatz; ed. by M. Friedlaender

Waite, H. R. comp. College songs. WC (Song Index)

Walter, L. E. ed. Christmas carols; harmonised by L. E. Broadwood. WCC (Song Index)

Ward, G. O. jt. comp. See Columbia university songs

Ware, C. P. See Allen, W. F. jt. ed.

Weep some more, my lady. See Spaeth, S. G.

Wekerlin, J. B. ed. Bergerettes. WB (Song Index)

Werrenrath, R. ed. Modern Scandinavian songs. v1 WM 1 (Song Index)

—same. v2 WM 2 (Sup.)

Western college songs. See Hagen, J. M. comp.

Whall, W. B. comp. Sea songs and shanties. WSE (Sup.)

White, C. C. comp. Forty negro spirituals. WFN (Sup.)

Whitehead, R. R. ed. Folk-songs of Eastern Europe. WF (Song Index)

Whittaker, W. G. jt. ed. See Clarendon song books

Wier, A. E. ed. American home music album. WA (Song Index)

—Ballads the whole world sings. WBW (Song Index)

—Book of a thousand songs. WBT (Song Index)

—Grand opera at home. WG (Sup.)

—Light opera at home. WLO (Sup.)

—Love songs the whole world sings. WL (Song Index)

—Sacred music the whole world loves. WS (Song Index)

—Songs of the sunny south. WSS (Sup.)

—Songs the children love to sing. WSC (Song Index)

—Songs the whole world sings. WSW (Song Index)

Williams, R. V. jt. ed. See Oxford book of carols

Williams, W. S. G. comp. Old Welsh folk-songs. WO (Sup.)

Wilson, H. L. ed. Old English melodies. WOE (Sup.)

Wiseman, H. jt. ed. See Clarendon song books

Wishart, J. jt. ed. See Clarendon song books

Wood, T. ed. See Oxford song book. v2

World's collection of patriotic songs and airs of the different nations. WCP (Song Index)

Wyman, L. ed. Lonesome tunes; pianoforte accompaniment by H. Brockway. WLT (Song Index)

—Twenty Kentucky mountain songs; piano accompaniments by H. Brockway. WT (Song Index)

Yamada, K. Japanese folk songs for voice & piano. YJ (Song Index)

Yiddish folk songs. See Schack, S. P. comp.

Zanon, M. ed. Twelve arias by old Italian masters. 2v ZT 1-2 (Sup.)

Zanzig, A. D. See Davison, A. T. jt. comp.

Key to Symbols for Collections Indexed

AI	Allen, T. W. Intercollegiate song book. de luxe ed Intercollegiate song book inc. c1927
AIS	Allen, T. W. Intercollegiate song book. popular ed Intercollegiate song book inc. c1931
AS	Allen, W. F., Ware, C. P., and Garrison, L. M. Slave songs of the United States. P. Smith 1929
ASA	Album of sacred songs. 2v G. Schirmer c1918
ASN	Album of songs by composers of the Neo-French school. Boston music co. c1911
AT	Album of twenty-five favorite encore songs. G. Schirmer c1915
ATS	Album of ten songs by Russian composers. Boston music co. c1914
BB	The blue book of favorite songs. Hall & McCreary c1928
BET	Broadwood, L. E. English traditional songs and carols. Boosey c1908
BNM	Burleigh, H. T. Negro minstrel melodies. G. Schirmer c1910
BNP	Binder, A. W. New Palestinean folk songs. Bloch pub. co. c1926
BOS 2	The Oxford song book; ed. by Thomas Wood. v2 C. Fischer c1927
BST	Baltzell, W. J. Something to sing. Ditson c1916
CBF 1-2	Croze, A. de. Beautiful folk-songs of France. 2v H. W. Gray 1925
CJ	Chatterton, J. Jugo-Slav folksongs. Curwen c1930
CSB 1-6	The Clarendon song books; ed. by W. G. Whittaker, Herbert Wiseman and John Wishart. 6v C. Fischer c1929-30
CSS 1-2	Choice sacred solos. 2v Ditson c1883-1917
DCA	Dramatic concert arias. G. Schirmer c1915
DFF	Devore, N. Fifty famous favorites. Robbins music corporation [1930]
DN	Dunstan, R. New book of Christmas carols. Reid bros. c1923
DNS	Dunstan, R. A second book of Christmas carols. Reid bros. c1925
DSB	Davison, A. T., Surette, T. W., and Zanzig, A. D. A book of songs. E. C. Schirmer c1924
DSC	Surette, T. W., and Davison, A. T. The home and community song book. rev and enl ed E. C. Schirmer c1931
DSO	Dolph, E. A. Sound off! Farrar & Rinehart c1929
EB	Edwards, E. Book of Shakespeare's songs. G. Schirmer c1903
EDL	Erk, L. C. Deutscher liederschatz; ed. by Max Friedlaender. Peters n.d.
FC	Finn, W. J. Father Finn's carol book. Birchard c1917
FSN	Fisher, W. A. Seventy negro spirituals. Ditson c1926
GA	Goss, J. An anthology of song. C. Fischer c1929
GC	Gibbon, J. M. Canadian folk songs (old and new) Dutton c1927
GE	Gems of English song. Ditson c1875
GFS	Geller, J. J. Famous songs and their stories. Macaulay c1931
GG	Gems of German song. rev ed Ditson c1909
GOS 1-2	Good old songs we used to sing; comp. by J. C. H. 2v Ditson c1887-95
GS	Gems of Scottish song. rev and enl ed Ditson c1894
GSF	Grant-Schaefer, G. A. French Canadian songs. A. P. Schmidt co. c1921
GSS	Girl scout song book; ed. by George Newell. rev ed Girl scouts c1929
HB	Handy, W. C. Blues; an anthology. Boni c1926
HCA	Heinrich, M. Classic song album. C. Fischer c1914
HE	Hague, E. Early Spanish-Californian folk-songs. J. Fischer c1922
HI 1-2	Hughes, H. Irish country songs. 2v Boosey c1909-15
HMI	Hatton, J. L., and Molloy, J. L. Songs of Ireland. Boosey n.d.

HP   Howard, J. T. Program of early and mid-nineteenth century American songs. J. Fischer c1931

HRD   Hampton, Va. Normal and agricultural institute. Religious folk-songs of the negro; ed. by R. N. Dett. Hampton institute press c1927

HW   Hagen, J. M. Western college songs. Sherman, Clay c1931

JB 2   Johnson, J. W. The second book of negro spirituals. Viking press c1926

JG   Johnson, H. The Green Pastures spirituals. Farrar & Rinehart c1930

KAJ   Kremer, I. Album of Jewish folk-songs. Chappell-Harms co. c1930

KH 1-2   Korbay, F. Hungarian melodies. 2v Schott c1891-93

KSO   Knowlton, F. S. Songs of other days. Ditson c1922

KU   Kennedy, B. B., and Kennedy, H. B. University and college song book. University and college song book, inc. [pref. 1930]

KV   Kennedy, B. B., and Kennedy, H. B. Varsity songs. University and college song book, inc. c1931

KVG   Krehbiel, H. E. Voices from the golden age of bel canto. G. Schirmer c1910

LAS   Levermore, C. H. The American song book. Ginn c1917

LSB   Little song book of the nations. C. Fischer c1928

LSC   Larkin, M. Singing cowboy. Knopf c1931

MB   Monroe, M. Bayou ballads. G. Schirmer c1921

MBS   MacMillan, E. C. A book of songs. Dutton c1929

MFF   Myers, S. Folk-songs of the four seasons. G. Schirmer c1929

MFS   McCaskey, J. P. Favorite songs and hymns for school and home. American book co. c1899

MK   McGill, J. Folk-songs of the Kentucky mountains. Boosey c1917

ML 1-3   Möller, H. Das lied der völker. 3v Schott n.d.

MPA 1-2   Milligan, H. V. Pioneer American composers. 2v A. P. Schmidt co. c1921-23

MSP   Manney, C. F. Mexican and Spanish songs. Ditson c1928

NRF   Newmarch, R. Russian folksongs, with pianoforte accompaniment. Chester c1915

OB   The Oxford book of carols; ed. by Percy Dearmer, Ralph Vaughan Williams, and Martin Shaw. J. Fischer c1928

OT   Old time song hits. Ditson c1909

OTG   Old time hits of the gay eighties and nineties. Marks [1931]

PB   Pittmann, J., ed. The baritone album. Boosey n.d.

PC   Pittmann, J., ed. The contralto album. Boosey n.d.

PSG   Paskman, D., and Spaeth, S. Gentlemen, be seated! Doubleday, Doran c1928

RA   Richardson, E. P. American mountain songs. Greenberg c1927

SAT   Spicker, M. Album of twenty-seven songs for contralto voice. G. Schirmer c1893

SBA   Sandburg, C. The American songbag. Harcourt c1927

SBS   Smith, C. F. A book of shanties. Methuen c1927

SES 1-2   Sharp, C. J. English folk songs from the southern Appalachians. 2v C. Fischer c1932

SFB   Spicker, M. Favorite bass songs. G. Schirmer c1909

SI   Songs of Ireland. Ditson c1890

SMG   Smith, L. O., and Morse, T. Good old timers. Feist c1922

SR   Schindler, K. Songs of the Russian people. Ditson c1915

SRW   Spaeth, S. G. Read 'em and weep. Doubleday, Doran c1926

SSB   Spicker, M. Songs of the British Isles. G. Schirmer c1909

SSO 1-4   Sacred songs. 4v Boosey n.d.

SW   Spaeth, S. G. Weep some more, my lady. Doubleday, Doran c1927

SY   Schack, S. P. Yiddish folk songs. Bloch pub. co. c1924

TFB   Twice 55 community songs for male voices: the blue book. Birchard c1926

TFG   Twice 55 community songs: the new green book. Birchard c1930

TFO   Twice 55 part songs for boys: the orange book. Birchard c1927

TFP   Twice 55 plus community songs: the new brown book. Birchard c1930

TFR	Twice 55 community songs for treble voices: the rose book. Birchard c1927	WG	Wier, A. E. Grand opera at home. rev ed Appleton-Century c1927
TM	Treasury of modern song. G. Schirmer c1902	WLO	Wier, A. E. Light opera at home. Appleton-Century c1917
TSB 1-2	Terry, R. R. The shanty book. 2v Curwen c1921-26	WM 2	Werrenrath, R. Modern Scandinavian songs. v2 Ditson c1926
TSS 1-2	Treasury of sacred solos. 2v Ditson c1896-1904	WO	Williams, W. S. G. Old Welsh folk-songs. Curwen c1927
US	U.S. Naval academy, Annapolis. Trident society. Book of navy songs. Doubleday, Doran 1926	WOE	Wilson, H. L. Old English melodies. Boosey c1899
		WSE	Whall, W. B. Sea songs and shanties. 6th ed enl Brown, son & Ferguson c1927
VS	Van Stone, M. R. Spanish folk songs of New Mexico. Seymour c1928	WSS	Wier, A. E. Songs of the sunny South. Appleton-Century c1929
WFN	White, C. C. Forty negro spirituals. Presser c1927	ZT 1-2	Zanon, M. Twelve arias by old Italian masters. 2v Boston music co. c1915

Key to Language Abbreviations

af.	African languages	in.	Indian, American, including **all** languages
al.	Albanian		
b.	Bulgarian	ir.	Irish
ba.	Basque	l.	Latin
bo.	Bohemian	le.	Lettish
br.	Breton	li.	Lithuanian
ca.	Catalan	n.	Norwegian
d.	Dutch	p.	Polish
da.	Danish	po.	Portuguese
e.	English (used only for English translations)	pr.	Provençal
		r.	Russian, including **Ruthenian**
		ru.	Rumanian
es.	Esthonian	s.	Spanish
f.	French, including dialects	se.	Serbo-Croatian, including the languages of Bosnia, Croatia, Dalmatia, Herzegovina Macedonia, Montenegro, Serbia, Slavonia, and some isles of the Adriatic
fi.	Finnish		
fl.	Flemish		
g.	German, including dialects		
ga.	Gaelic	sl.	Slovak
gr.	Greek, Modern	slo.	Slovenian
he.	Hebrew	sw.	Swedish
hu.	Hungarian	w.	Welsh
i.	Italian, including dialects	we.	Wendish
ic.	Icelandic, Modern	y.	Yiddish

Key to Miscellaneous Abbreviations

arr.	arranged	n.d.	no date
bds.	boards	o.p.	out of print
bp.	bishop	pa.	paper
cl.	cloth	pref.	preface
comp.	compiled, compiler	pseud.	pseudonym
ea.	each	rev.	revised
ed.	edited, edition, editor	sup.	supplement
enl.	enlarged	tr.	translated, -ion
jt. auth.	joint author	v.	volume, -s
jt. comp.	joint composer, compiler		

DIRECTIONS FOR USE

The *title entry* is the main entry and gives the fullest information, including name of composer, of author of words, abbreviation for language of song, symbols for collections in which the song is to be found. An example follows:

> La **chevelure** (Her hair) A. C. Debussy. Words by P. Louÿs. e.f. CM 1— SAM

If entry under composer, author, alternate title, or first line is consulted first, the title entry should then be consulted for fuller information.

Under the title entry, indented, are listed all variations of title in different collections. An example follows:

> **Auf** dem meere ("On ocean's breast") R. Franz. Words by Heine. e.g. PG 4
> "Das meer hat seine perlen" ("The sea its pearls possesses") e.g. GM

The symbols indicating the collections in which a song may be found are given in title entry only.

Foreign songs are entered under title in the original language, with the exception of some of the less well known languages. For list of these see the Introduction, p. xvii.

The language or languages of the text of a song are indicated for all songs where the original is not English by a language abbreviation in the title entry.

Entries for composers are printed in boldface roman (e.g. **Beethoven, Ludwig van**).

Entries for authors are printed in boldface italics (e.g. ***Burns, Robert***).

First lines are given in quotation marks, even when used as title.

Additional information about airs, composers and authors of songs in the Song Index is indicated in the Supplement by special brackets. An example follows:

> The **banks** of the blue Moselle. G. H. Rodwell. <Words by E. Fitzball> GOS 1

SONG INDEX SUPPLEMENT

"A, B, C, D, E, F, G, H, I, J, K, L, M, N, O, P, Q, R, S, and T, U, V, W (double-you), and X, Y, Z. Happy, happy shall we be." Nursery song. MFS

"A dios Granada, Granada mia." See Granadinas (Barrera y Calleja)

"A dormir va la rosa." See Nana (copla de cuna)

"A éigse Fodla dlúthaig." See An crúiscín lán

"A gdy będzie słońce i pogoda." See "Bei dem heitren frühlingssonnenscheine"

"À la claire fontaine" ("At the clear running fountain") Canadian folk song. e.f. GC—MBS
"À la claire fontaine" ("Down to the crystal streamlet") e.f. GSF

"À la vila de Tolosa, n'hi ha trés estudiants." See Los estudiants de Tolosa

"À l'abri sous la feuillée." See Pastourelle (Auguin)

"A las dos de la manana que le vengo a despertar." See Cancion de la luna

"A Mhàiri bhòidheach's a Mhàiri ghaolach." See Màiri bhòidheach

A moi les plaisirs. For English translation see "Be mine the delight" (Gounod)

"A ninna ninna, ccu la ninna ninna." See Ninna-nanna

"A patre unigenitus." See Make we joy

A. R. U. Railroad song. SBA

"A róisín na bíodh brón ort fá'r eirghidh dhuit." See Roisin dubh

A solis ortus cardine (From the region of the rising of the sun) 5th century Latin air. Words by Sedulius. e. DNS

A te riede, o caro figlio. Mercadante. e.i. PC

"A un niño ciequecito" (Bolero) g.s. ML 2

"A Úna bhán, a bhláith na ndlaoi ómrach." See Úna bán

"A vinticinc de Desembre." See Villancico-baile de Nadal

"Aa kungjen han sto paa högelofts svol." See Sjugur aa trollbrura

Aagots berglied. See Aagots fjeldsang (Thrane)

Aagots fjeldsang (Aagots berglied) Norse song. <W. Thrane> Words by H. A. Bjerregaard. g.n. ML 1

Aakjaer, Jeppe
Høgen (Nielsen)

Abalone. Song from Carmel, Cal. Words by G. Sterling. SBA

El abandonado. Mexican folk song. e.s. SBA

Abbietta zingara, fosca vegliarda. For English translation see "Sat there a gipsy hag" (Verdi)

Abdul Abulbul Amir. College song. SRW —US
Variant: Abdul, the Bulbul Ameer

Abdul, the Bulbul Ameer. College song. SBA
Variant: Abdul Abulbul Amir

[A begging we will go] The jovial beggar. 17th century song. [Words attributed to R. Brome] CSB 2

"Abend ist's, die sonne ist verschwunden." See Abendempfindung (Mozart)

Abendempfindung (Thoughts at eventide) W. A. Mozart. e.g. GA

Abendlied ("Der mond ist aufgegangen") J. A. P. Schulz. Words by M. Claudius. g. EDL

Abendlied ("Tarry with me") See "Tarry with me, O my Saviour" (Roeder)

"Abends ging ich noch vergnügt." See Der galgenstrick

Abends, will ich schlafen gehn. For English translation see Evening prayer (Humperdinck)

Der abendstern (To the evening star) R. Schumann. Words by Hoffman von Fallersleben. e. CSB 1

Aberystwith. See "Watchman, tell us of the night" (Parry)

"Abide with me! fast falls the eventide." W. H. Monk. Words by H. F. Lyte. BB—MFS—TFB—TFG

"Abide with me! fast falls the eventide." C. H. Reed. Words by H. F. Lyte. TSS 1

"Ablakomba, ablakomba besütött a holdvilág." See "Durch die fenster, durch die trüben"

"About the field they piped full right." See Tyrley, tyrlow (Heseltine)

"Above the edge of dark appear the lances of the sun." See A sunrise song (Baltzell)

Abraham's daughter (Raw recruit) Old air. Words by S. Winner. DSO

Abrede. Schlesische volksweise. g. EDL

"Abroad as I was walking, down by the river side." See The Irish girl (Surrey version)

Abschied ("Denke, denke mein geliebter."— Vspomnĭ, moĭ lîubeznyĭ) Russian folk song. g.r. ML 1

Abschied ("Liebchen ade") Folk air. Words after a folk song: Schätzchen, ade. g. EDL

Abschied ("Muss i denn") Suabian folk song. Words after an old folk song by H. Wagner (pseud. Wergan) g. EDL
When I come. e.g. MFS

Abschied ("So leb' denn wohl") W. Müller. Words by F. Raimund.   g.   EDL

ₜ**Abschied** ("Wenn die schwalben heimwärts zieh'n")₁   "When the swallows homeward fly."   F. Abt.   Words by C. Herlosssohn.   e.   BB—GOS 2—MFS

Abschied ("Wie scheinen die sternlein."—Parting)   R. Franz.   e.g.   HCA

Abschied vom walde.   For English translation see Farewell to the forest (Mendelssohn)

Abschied von der geliebten.   Volkslied.   g.   EDL

"**Abschiedstunde** schlägt dem feste."   See Dank der gäste

Absence ("Will ruhen unter den bäumen hier")   See In der ferne (Brahms)

Abt, Franz
    Abschied
    Dir nah' möcht' ich begraben sein
    Embarrassment.   See Verlegenheit
    Good night
    Home so blest
    Kathleen aroon
    King of glory, God of grace
    The last wish.   See Dir nah' möcht' ich begraben sein
    "Like the lark"
    Die lindenwirtin
    Night
    "Over the stars there is rest."   See "Über den sternen ist ruh"
    Song of parting
    "Über den sternen ist ruh"
    Verlegenheit
    "When the swallows homeward fly."   See Abschied

"**Ach!** ach! über berg und waldesgründe."   See Din Ploeşti pânä'n Gheboaia

"**Ach** Berta, wenn wir wären in dem walde hier."   See "La bell', si nous étiom' dedans"

"**Ach,** Bože môj, Pane môj."   See "Höre mich, mein herr und Gott"

"**Ach** denke, liebster, denke."   See Gute nacht

"**Ach** du ebne, weites blachgefild."   See Der rabe

"**Ach,** du liebe nacht."   See Night

"**Ach,** du mein kindel."   See In der spinnstub

"**Ach,** dybych já byla tú bílú holubičkú."   See "Wär' ich doch ein täubchen"

"**Ach,** ich soll nicht."   See "Is it true, then"

Ach jungfer, ich will ihr was aufzuraten geben.   See Rätsellied

"**Ach,** kein sturmwind ist's."   See The Tartar host

"**Ach,** keiner nimmt sich meiner an und achtet meiner klage."   See Santras lied

"**Ach** lieb, sie schlagen mich" ("Šuhajko, bijú mňa")   Slovak folk song.   g.sl.   ML 3

"**Ach,** mein faulbaum" ("Ai tu, iva")   Lettish folk song.   g.le.   ML 3

"**Ach,** mein leiden, ach, mein leiden schwer."   See The conscript's return

"**Ach,** není tu, není."   See All joy is gone

"**Ach,** nichts ist weit und breit."   See All joy is gone

"**Ach,** prší, prší rosička."   See "Still träufelt milder tau hernieder"

ₜ"**Ach!** so fromm"₁ Ah! so pure.   F. von Flotow.   e.   WLO

"**Ach,** wär' ich ein vöglein, ich flöge von hier."   See Layeta

"**Ach,** war wohl je eine liebe."   See Mournful love

"**Ach** weh, ach weh, mein leid."   See Caoineadh

Ach, weide, weide, weide.   See The willow song (16th century air)

"**Ach,** wenn mein mütterlein sähe."   See Malagueña

"**Ach,** wenn's nur der könig auch wüsst."   See Die soldatenbraut (Schumann)

"**Ach** wie die johren."   See Dem milner's thrären

"**Ach,** wie ist's möglich dann."   See Treue liebe (Volksweise); Treue liebe (Kücken)

Ach, wie war mir lang der winter (Koliko mī zīma duga bīla)   Serbian folk song.   g.se.   ML 2

"**Ach!** wo warst du den ganzen tag."   See Bonnie laddie, Highland laddie

"**Ach,** wozu die plage" ("Akh na chtozh bylo")   Russian folk song.   g.r.   ML 1

Achtzehn messingknöpfe.   See "Wasch in weisser milch"

"**Ack** Värmeland, du sköna."   See Vermeland

Across the field.   Ohio state university song.   W. A. Dougherty (music and words)   AI—AIS

"**Across** the hilltops comes the spring, blithe April's son."   See "Voici que le printemps, ce fils léger d'avril" (Debussy)

Across the Rockies ("Oh the times are hard")   See Across the western ocean

Across the Rockies ("Oh the young girl said to me one day") Pumping chantey.   SBS

Across the western ocean ("Oh, the times are hard")   Hauling chantey.   SBA—WSE
    For variants see following songs of same title

Across the western ocean ("O, tho' times are hard")   See Leave her, bullies, leave her

ₜ**Across** the western ocean₁ Across the Rockies ("Oh the times are hard")   Chantey.   SBS

Adagio.   T. Rangström.   Words by B. Bergman.   e.sw.   WM 2

Adair, my sweet Adair.   See My sweet Adair (Friedland)

Adam, Adolphe Charles
    Cantique de Noël
    Christmas song.   See Cantique de Noël
    Noël.   See Cantique de Noël
    "O holy night."   See Cantique de Noël

Adam, Jean
    There's nae luck about the house (Scottish air) Authorship uncertain; attributed also to W. J. Mickle
"**Adam** lay ybounden." P. Warlock. 15th century words. OB
Adam, where are you. See What a trying time
Adams, Frank R. See Hough, Will M., jt. auth.
Adams, Franklin Pierce
    Don't tell me what you dreamed last night (Hooker)
Adams, Jean. See Adam, Jean
Adams, Mrs Sarah (Flower)
    "Nearer, my God, to Thee" (Mason)
Adams, Stephen, pseud. See Maybrick, Michael
Adams and liberty. Air: To Anacreon in heaven <attributed to J. S. Smith> Words by R. T. Paine. SRW
Addison, Joseph
    "The spacious firmament on high" (Haydn)
"**Ade** zur guten nacht." Volkslied. g. EDL
Adelaïde ("Einsam wandelt dein freund") L. van Beethoven. Words by F. von Matthisson. e.g. GG—HCA
Adelita. Mexican folk song. e.s. SBA—VS
Adelphi field song ("We're from a school of great renown") W. A. Thayer (music and words) LAS
"**Adeste**, fideles" (Come, all ye faithful) Attributed to J. Reading. e.l. MFS
    "Adeste fideles" ("O come, all ye faithful") e.l. BB— TFB— TFR. e. only GSS
    "Adeste fideles" (Portuguese hymn) 1. FC
    "O come, all ye faithful." e. DN—DSB—DSC—TFP
"**Adieu**, adieu, fair Annie, he did say." See Fair Annie
L'**adieu** des bergers à la Sainte Famille. For English translation see The shepherds' farewell to the Holy Family (Berlioz)
Adieu to Maimuna. Forecastle song. Old German air: The mill wheel. WSE
"**Adios**, a tender el vuelo." See Las golondrinas
"**Adios**, ene maitia" ("Lebet wohl, teure freundin") Basque folk song. ba.g. ML 2
"**Adje** mori momčeto." See Come, dance the kolo
Admiral Benbow ("O we sailed to Virginia") 18th century song. BOS 2—WSE
Adolphus Morning Glory. D. Braham. WSS
"**Adon** olom." See "The Lord of all"
Adore and be still. See "Le ciel a visité la terre" (Gounod)
The **Advent** images carol. See The seven joys of Mary

Advertisement for a wife. Old English air. Words by "a middle-aged gentleman." SW
"**Af** bri." Jewish folk song. y. SY
Afsked (Farewell) E. Melartin. Words after Heine. [Tr of Der scheidende sommer] e.n. WM 2
After ("After showers, the tranquil sun") L. Diehl. MFS
After a dream. See Après un rêve (Fauré)
"**After** showers, the tranquil sun." See After (Diehl)
After the ball. C. K. Harris (music and words) GFS—SRW
[**After** the battle] "Night closed around." Air: The fair bosom, or, Thy fair bosom. Words by T. Moore. HMI
"**After** the din of the battle's roar." See Just as the sun went down (Udall)
The **afternoon** crawl. See The Broadway, opera and Bowery crawl (Operti)
"The **afternoon's** the time to see." See The Broadway, opera and Bowery crawl (Operti)
"**Aftnen** er stille, tonerne trille." See Längsel (Svendsen)
Afton water ("Flow gently, sweet Afton") Scottish air: Afton water. Words by R. Burns. GS
[**Afton** water] "Flow gently, sweet Afton." J. E. Spilman. Words by R. Burns. BB—DSB—DSC—GOS 1—GS—MFS—TFP
Aftonstämning (Twilight) W. Peterson-Berger. Words by D. Fallström. e.sw. WM 2
Afzelius, Arvid August
    Neckens polska (Swedish air)
"**Against** Thee have I sinn'd." See Busslied (Beethoven)
Agatha, Jane, and fair Marie. French air. Words by K. Davis. DSB
The **ages** of man. Sussex folk song. BET
The **aggie** pep song. Colorado state agricultural college song. D. E. Tefft. Words by W. Sweet, D. E. Tefft, and R. Williams. HW
The **Agincourt** song. See Deo gratias
"**Agnus** Dei" ("Lamb of God") G. Bizet. e.l. ASA
Ah! ah! ah! la bombe éclaté. For English translation see "Ha! ha! ha! the bomb is bursting" (Offenbach)
"**Ah**, beloved night." Russian folk song. e. NRF
"**Ah**, by the pow'r of love." See "Caro, son tua così" (Orlandini)
"**Ah!** ça ira" (Revolutionslied) Old dance: Carillon national de Bécourt. f.g. ML 1
Ah, c'est un fameux régiment. For English translation see "Ah! 'tis a famous regiment" (Offenbach)
Ah! che la morte ognora. For English translation see "Ah! I have sighed to rest me" (Verdi)
Ah! con lui mi fu rapita. Pacini. e.i. PC

"Ah, dearest Lord." German folk song. e. DSC

Ah, evenings we knew. See The mahogany tree (Campana)

"Ah! far in the field." See The garland

"Ah figliuol! mio figliuol." See "Ah! mon fils" (Meyerbeer)

"Ah! for wings to soar" (Prima donna waltz) Jullien. MFS

Ah! forgive me, forgive me, my daughter. See Ah! mia figlia, perdona all' affanno (Rossini)

"Ah, from my consort's bosom." See "Dal sen del caro sposo" (Rinaldo di Capua)

Ah! from that joyful day. See Ah! quel giorno (Rossini)

Ah! from thy vision wake thee, pray. See Ah! se tu dormi (Vaccai)

Ah! happy day. E. Audran. e. WLO

"Ah, how did that rover, the butterfly, discover." See Schmetterling (Cornelius)

"Ah! how I love the military." J. Offenbach. [Tr of Ah, que j'aime les militaires] e. WLO

Ah! how my heart beats with rapture anew. See Voices of the woods (Rubinstein)

Ah how oft in bliss enraptur'd prov'd I sweet. See Io l'udia ne' suoi bei carmi (Donizetti)

"Ah! I have sighed to rest me." G. Verdi. [Tr of Ah! che la morte ognora] e. MFS
Miserere. e. WG

"Ah! I love thee only." C. Gounod. [Tr of Oui, c'est toi, je t'aime] e. WG

[Ah, if mother Volga] "Oh, if mother Volga." S. W. Pantchenko. Words from the Russian of A. Tolstoi. e. SR

Ah! if thou could'st know. See Couldst thou but know (Balfe)

"Ah! je li gdje koja." See Mournful love

["Ah! je ris de me voir"] Jewel song. C. F. Gounod. e. WG

"Ah! la belle menotte" ("Ah! these pretty wee hands") Old colonial song. I. Luckstone. e.f. AT

Ah! le joli bois, mesdames (The pretty wood) Folk song from Flanders. e.f. CBF 2

"Ah! let the gay dancers." E. Audran. e. WLO

Ah! letters from lovers. See Letters from lovers (Offenbach)

"Ah, little girl, don't you cry." See Little girl, don't you cry

"Ah, love, how blind thou art." See "Amor, che cieco sei" (Righini)

"Ah, love, how can I leave thee." See "Weh' dasz wir scheiden müssen" (Kinkel)

"Ah! love, thou art a wilful wild bird." See Habanera (Bizet)

Ah! mia figlia, perdona all' affanno. Rossini. e.i. PB

Ah! mine fraulein! you ish so ferry unkind. See Corporal Schnaps (Work)

["Ah! mon fils"] "Ah figliuol! mio figliuol." G. Meyerbeer. e.i. PC

["Ah! mon remords te venge"] "Sei vendicata assai." G. Meyerbeer. e.i. PB

"Ah, my son." See "Ah! mon fils" (Meyerbeer)

"Ah! ne repousse pas." See Repentir (Gounod)

Ah! non avea più lagrime. G. Donizetti. e.i. PB

"Ah! nonsense 'tis." J. Strauss. e. WLO

"Ah! now I feel the burden." See "Ah! mon remords te venge" (Meyerbeer)

"Ah! perfido" ("With perfidy inhuman") L. van Beethoven. e.i. DCA

"Ah, poor bird." Four-part round. TFP

"Ah! pretty Giroflé, my timid gazelle." See O pretty Girofla (Lecocq)

Ah, que j'aime les militaires. For English translation see "Ah! how I love the military" (Offenbach)

Ah! quel giorno (Live this day) G. Rossini. e.i. PC

Ah! quello fu per me. Donizetti. e.i. PB

"Ah! qui me passera le bois." See L'occasion manquée (Canadian version)

Ah! se tu dormi, svegliati. N. Vaccai. e.i. PC

"Ah! s'estinto ancor mi vuoi" ("Ah, since vainly I now implore thee") G. S. Mercadante. e.i. PC

"Ah! si, mie care." See Or là sull' onda, col pensier mio (Mercadante)

"Ah! si mon moine voulait danser" ("If my old top were a dancing man") Canadian folk song. e.f. GC

"Ah! si no fos p'es carreto." See Cansó de sega

"Ah s'il est dans votre village" (Chanson de Florian.—Florian's song) B. Godard. Words by J. P. C. de Florian. e.f. BST

"Ah, since vainly I now implore thee." See "Ah! s'estinto ancor mi vuoi" (Mercadante)

Ah! so pure. See "Ach! so fromm" (Flotow)

"Ah, Suzette." See Suzette

"Ah! the birds are in the woodlands." J. Offenbach. [Tr of Les oiseaux dans la charmille] e. WG

"Ah! the joy past compare." See "Ah! je ris de me voir" (Gounod)

Ah, the love thy mother bears. See "Love thy mother, little one" (Himmel)

Ah there! stay there. Old song. SW

"Ah! these pretty wee hands." See "Ah! la belle menotte" (Luckstone)

Ah! thou my life, my all. See Wilt thou soon return (Rocke)

Ah till to lave a shameful stain. See Infelice! e tu credevi (Verdi)

"Ah! 'tis a dream. C. B. Hawley. Words by H. Heine. [Tr of Es war ein traum] e. SFB

Ah, 'tis a dream. For same words with a different air see Es war ein traum (Lassen)

"Ah! 'tis a famous regiment." J. Offenbach. [Tr of Ah, c'est un fameux régiment] e. WLO

Ah, 'tis the spirit's happy wingtime. See The dawn of Maytime (Flotow)

"Ah! Toucouyoute." See Vous t'é in morico

"Ah, trust him not, my dear." See Klage (Brahms)

"Ah! turn me not away." See Repentir (Gounod)

"Ah! wenn doch nicht der karren wäre." See Cansó de sega

"Ah! what can be her meaning." F. von Flotow. [Tr of Was soll ich dazu sagen] e. WLO

"Ah! when love is young." E. Jakobowski. WLO

"Ah! who will guide me thro' the wood." See L'occasion manquée (Canadian version)

"Ah! why recall." G. Verdi. [Tr of Deh non parlare al misero] e. WG

"Ah, why will my dear little child be so cross" (Nursery song) Words by J. Taylor. MFS

Ah! willow. Old English song. WOE

"Ah, with thee, dear." See Ah! con lui mi fu rapita (Pacini)

"Ah yah, tair um bam, boo wah." See Jungle mammy song

"Ah! yes, companions, for me bright days of full delight." See Or la sull' onda, col pensier mio (Mercadante)

"Ah'm goin' whah nobody knows my name." See Levee moan

"Ah'm gonna build mahself a raft." See De blues ain' nothin'

Ahrem, Jacques
"Le ciel a visité la terre" (Gounod)

"Ai! la le lo." See Alalá

Ai nostri fidi nunzio. See O, tu Palermo (Verdi)

Ai nostri monti ritorneremo. For English translation see "Home to our mountains" (Verdi)

"Ai tu, iva." See "Ach, mein faulbaum"

Aï! vo polïe lïpïn'ka. See The garland

Aïdé, Hamilton

Composer and author
The Danube river

Author
The blushing maple tree (McCaskey)
The maid of the mill (Maybrick)

"Aïde mori, kukni, kukni." See Rufe, kuckuck

Aiken, Walter H
Indian lullaby
The robin
The robin and chicken
Waiting to grow

Aikin Drum ("There liv'd a man in our town") Scottish folk song. CSB 2

Aikman, James H.
"Touch not the cup" (Bayly)

Aileen, aroon ("Girl of the forehead fair") C. C. Converse. GOS 2

Ain' go'n' to study war no mo'. See I ain't gwine study war no more

"Aine, dé, trois, Caroline." See Caroline

Ainñhara (Die schwalbe) Basque folk song. ba.g. ML 2

Ainslee, Hew
The ingle side (Wiesenthal)

"Ain't been to heav'n, but I' been tol'." See O Mary, don't you weep

Ain't goin' study war no more. See I ain't gwine study war no more

Ain't gonna rain. Old middlewestern dance song. SBA

Ain't got no style. See Style all the while (University of Texas version)

"Aïnte, aïnte, koimēsoy." See "Sleep, my child, my pretty one"

Air fal-al-al O. Gaelic folk song. e. CSB 3

The airy bachelor. Irish air from County Donegal. Traditional words. HI 2

Äiti ja tytär. See Mutter und tochter

Akers, Mrs Elizabeth (Chase) See Allen, Mrs Elizabeth (Chase) Akers

"Akh na chtozh bylo." See "Ach, wozu die plage"

"Akh, talan lï moï, talan." See The conscript's return

"Akh, ty nochen'ka." See Night

Akh ty pole chïstoe. See Der rabe

"Akkor szép a kis lány." See "Wisst ihr, wann mein kindchen"

"Al hostal de la Peyra (oleta)." See La criada del hostal

"Al mio core oggetti amati." Donizetti. e.i. PC

Al mos Trumpeldor. See Upon the death of Trumpeldor

"Al pla de Barcelona (ay! viva l'amor)." See La niña desenvuelta

The Alabama blossoms. Words by F. Dumont. WSS

"Alabama, listen, mother." See Alma mater—University of Alabama (Thompson)

Alack-a-day. See Haï luli (Coquard)

Aladdin (Castles in Spain) V. Bellini. Words by J. R. Lowell. MFS

Alalá (Lied) Galician folk song. s. ML 2

Alary, Giulio
"Quando avvolto"
"When the veil of night." See "Quando avvolto"

"Alas, my father he, your enemy." See Sin not, oh king (Händel)

"Albero, ti teneva tanto caro." See Canzonetta di campagnuolo

Alberti, Domenico
Hide not Thyself from me

Albertson, Ralph. See Ross, Malcolm, jt. auth.

Alburn, W. H.
Dear old Reserve (Kücken)

Aldrich, Henry
"Great Tom is cast"
"Hark! the bonny Christ church bells"

Aldrich, Perley Dunn
Good night
Aleichem, Shalom, pseud.   See Rabinowitz, Solomon J.
Alexander, Mrs Cecil Frances (Humphreys)
"Saw ye never in the twilight" (Composer unknown)
Alexander, Hartley Burr
Onward (Eames)
Alexander, John Paul
"Hail! hail! Nevonia"
Alexander.   H. Von Tilzer.   Words by A. B. Sterling.   SRW
Alexis, Wilibald, pseud.
"Fridericus Rex" (Loewe)
"Az alföldön halász legény vagyok én."
See The fisherman (Bernáth)
Alford, Henry
"Come, ye thankful people, come" (Elvey)
Ali Pascha (Kënga é Ali Pachës)   Albanian folk song.   al.g.   ML 2
Alice B.   Negro folk song.   SBA
Alice, where art thou.   J. Ascher. Words by W. Guernsey.   GE—MFS
"**Alïîâ,** more delïîâ."   See "Alija, du teufelskerl"
"**Alija,** du teufelskerl" ("Alïîâ, more delïîâ") Macedonian folk song.   b.g.   ML 2
All alone my watch I'm keeping.   See The hazel dell (Root)
All among the barley.   E. Stirling.   MFS
All and some.   15th century carol.   OB
"**All** are caught in love's fond snares." See Villagers' chorus (Smetana)
All bells in paradise.   English air: All among the leaves so green.   Traditional words.   DNS
Variant of: "Down in yon forest"
All bells in paradise.   M. Shaw.   Traditional words.   OB
All danger disdaining.   Handel.   SSO 2
"**All** day long on the prairies I ride." See The cowboy
"**All** de member better true believe." See My body rock 'long fever
All de world am sad and dreary.   See The old folks at home (Foster)
"**All** dem Mount Zion member."   See Hold out to the end
"**All** down the quay the ships so tall." See Les berceaux (Fauré)
"**All** ends well, so we're rejoicing."   Final chorus from The bartered bride.   B. Smetana.   e.   WLO
All for glory the soldier's life.   See A soldier's life (Jakobowski)
"**All** forward! all forward! all forward to battle."   See Inno di guerra dei cacciatori delle Alpi (Olivieri)
All God's chillun got wings.   Negro spiritual.   WSS
Goin' to shout.   FSN
Goin' to shout all over God's heav'n. HRD—WFN
Heav'n.   GSS
Heav'n, heav'n.   BB

"**All** hail, Arizona."   University of Arizona song.   D. H. Monroe.   Words by E. C. Monroe.   AI—HW—KU—KV
"**All** hail blue and gold."   University of California alma mater.   H. W. Bingham (music and words)   AI—HW—KU—KV
"**All** hail! hail! Wichita."   See Hail! Wichita (Lieurance)
All hail! O Washington.   See Alma mater—University of Washington (Hager)
"**All** hail the college that we love."   See The college song (Brigham Young university song)
"**All** hail the power of Jesus' name" (Coronation)   O. Holden.   Words by E. Perronet.   MFS
"**All** hail the power of Jesus' name" (Miles Lane)   Old air <by W. Shrubsole> Words by E. Perronet.   TFP
"**All** hail, thou dwelling."   See Salut! demeure chaste et pure (Gounod)
"**All** hail, thou lovely laughing May." Round.   F. Schubert.   CSB 3
"**All** hail to the days."   See Drive the cold winter away
"**All** hands on board! our boatswain cries." See Unmooring
"**All** hands on deck, there's a pretty little craft in sight."   U.S. navy song.   US
"**All** has ended happily."   See All is ended (Audran)
All I do, de church keep a-grumblin'. Negro spiritual.   JB 2
All I want, all I want.   See A little more faith in Jesus
"**All** in a misty morning."   See The Wiltshire wedding
"**All** in a stable cold and bare."   Old English carol air.   Words by Gaynor. FC
"**All** in a wood."   See The tree in the wood
All in accord ("Eilu vo-eilu modim") Palestinean folk song.   e.he.   BNP
"**All** in, all in the month of May."   See Barbara Allen (Barbourville, Ky. version no. 1)
"**All** in good order."   J. Offenbach. (Tr of En très bon ordre)   e.   WLO
"**All** in the merry month of May."   See Barbara Allen (Kentucky version no. 1; Carmen, N.C. version)
"**All** in the month, the month of May." See Barbara Allen (Tennessee version)
All in the morning ("It was on Christmas day") Traditional Christmas carol.   OB
All in the morning ("It was on holy Wednesday")   Traditional Easter carol. OB
"**All** into service let us sing merrily together."   See Going to church
All is ended.   E. Audran.   e.   WLO
All is not gold that glitters.   See All that glitters is not gold
"**All** is silent."   See Nightingale canon (Mozart)
"**All** is still in sweetest rest."   See "Alles still in süsser ruh" (Kücken)

ịAll joy is goneị "Ach, není tu, není" ("Ach, nichts ist weit und breit") Czech folk song. bo.g. ML 3

"All mein' gedanken, die ich hab, die sind bei dir." See Nur du

"All my friends fell out with me." See I love my love

"All my heart this night rejoices." Ebeling. Words by P. Gerhardt. ịTr of Fröhlich soll mein herze springenị e. DNS

All night long. Negro spiritual. SBA

All noddin'. American mountain song. RA
Variant of: We're a' noddin'

"All now is lonely." See Il balen del suo sorriso (Verdi)

"All on one summer's evening." See The grey cock

"All on one winter's morning." See "One cold winter's morning" (St Helen's, Ky. version)

"All on those Belfast mountains." See Belfast mountains

"All our grief." Rossini. e. SSO 4

"All people that on earth do dwell." See Old hundred (Franc?)

"All poor men and humble." See O deued pob Cristion

"All quiet along the Potomac tonight." J. H. Hewitt. Words by E. E. Beers <attributed also to L. Fontaine> DSO—HP

All saints. See "The Son of God goes forth to war" (Cutler)

"All soft through the twilight." See The shepherd of sleep

All souls' day. See Allerseelen (Lassen); Allerseelen (Strauss)

All that glitters is not gold ("Just an ivy covered cottage") Old song. SW

"All the birds are here again." See The birds' return

All the blue bonnets are over the border. See Blue bonnets over the border

"All the gay gems of day." See Gems of day

"All the golden stars are glowing." See The stars

"All the member better true believe." See My body rock 'long fever

"All the past we leave behind." See Pioneers (Grace)

All the saints adore Thee. See "Holy, holy, holy! Lord God Almighty" (Dykes)

"All the scholars in the school." See Sir Hugh (North Carolina version)

"All the winter long the trees are bare." See Winter

All the world is sad and dreary. See The old folks at home (Foster)

"All them Mount Zion member." See Hold out to the end

"All this night shrill chanticleer." See Chanticleer

"All those in favor of having a drink." U.S. navy song. US

All through the night ("Holl amrantau'r sêr, dywedant") See Ar hyd y ṇos (Owen)

All through the night ("Through the day I walked repining") ịD. Owenị Words by A. L. Salmon. GSS

"All together, all together." G. F. Root. MFS

"All under the leaves." See The seven virgins

"All who have sinned here." See Easter hymn (Gounod)

All ye mountains, praise the Lord. See Nos galan

All you little rookies, we wish the same to you. See "Today is Monday"

"All you southerners now draw near." See The battle of Shiloh

"All you that are to mirth inclined." See The sinners' redemption

"Alla mente confusa." See Preghiera (Tosti)

Allan, Robert
Put off, and row wi' speed (Highland boat air)

Allan Percy. Old song. GOS 1

"Alle jahre wieder." F. Silcher. Words by W. Hey. g. EDL

Allégresse à la naissance du Sauveur. Angevin Noël. e. DNS

Allein Gott in der höh sey ehr. For English translation see "To God on high be thanks and praise" (Decius)

Alleluia ("Let joyful praise to heaven ascend") German folk song. e. LSB

"Alleluia! alleluia! alleluia! now all the bells are ringing." See Now all the bells are ringing (Dykes)

"Alleluia! alleluia! alleluia! the strife is o'er, the battle done." See The strife is o'er: the battle done (Palestrina)

Alleluya to Jesus, who died on the tree. See Jacob's ladder ("As Jacob with travel")

Allen, Mrs Elizabeth (Chase) Akers
Rock me to sleep (Leslie)
Singing in the rain (Haydn)

Allen, George Benjamin
"I love my love in the morning"
None can tell

Allen, Henry Robinson
"Maid of Athens"
Now I lay me down to sleep

Allen, Lyman Whitney
"In the valley of Virginia" (Allen, T. W.)

Allen, Riley Harris
Alma mater—University of Washington (Hager)

Allen, T. H.
Good-bye, my lover, good-bye (words with old American air)

Allen, Thornton Whitney
"In the valley of Virginia"
Indian warriors' song
March of the fighting 'gators
Victory song
Wa-hoo. See Indian warriors' song

Allen, Thornton Whitney, and Holsclaw, Doug
Fight! wildcats, fight

Allen, Thornton Whitney, and Sheafe, M. W.
Colorado "C" men (same air as Washington and Lee swing)
Fight for Dickinson (same air as Washington and Lee swing)
Football song (same air as Washington and Lee swing)
Washington and Lee swing

Allen, W. N.
Driving saw-logs on the Plover (Old air)

Allerseelen ("Die die menschen hart verstiessen."—"Przez czyścowe upalenia") Polish folk song. g.p. ML 3

Allerseelen ("Stell auf den tisch."—All souls' day) E. Lassen. Words by H. von Gilm. e.g. GG

Allerseelen ("Stell auf den tisch."—All souls' day) R. Strauss. Words by H. von Gilm. e.g. TM

"Alles mit der zeit vergehet" ("Wszystko z czasem ulatuje") Polish folk song. g.p. ML 3

"Alles schweige, jeder neige ernsten tönen nur sein ohr." See Weihelied

"Alles still in süsser ruh" (The slumber song) F. Kücken. e.g. MFS

"Alleweil ein wenig lustig." See Bruder liederlich

Allez, jeunes filles, dansez et tournez vous. For English translation see "Come, ye pretty maidens" (Offenbach)

"Alli en el bosque" ("Here in the forest") Mexican folk song. e.s. VS

"Allie darling." H. P. Danks. Words by J. T. Rutledge. SRW

Allingham, William
"O spirit sweet of summer-time" (Irish air)
Robin Redbreast (music by Hubbard; Kücken)

Allison, Young Ewing
Derelict (Waller)

Allister MacAllister. Scottish air:<Jenny's bawbee> Words by J. Hogg. GS

Allitsen, Frances
"Since we parted." See Yestereve
Yestereve

ɾDie **Allmacht**ɿ Hymn to the Almighty. F. Schubert. ɾWords by J. L. Pyrkerɿ e. SSO 1

Allmers, Hermann

Composer and author
Rudelsburg

Author
Feldeinsamkeit (Brahms)

"Allons, enfants de la patrie." See La Marseillaise (Rouget de Lisle)

All's well. J. Braham. ɾWords by T. Dibdinɿ MFS

Allsop, Bass & co.—they each deserve a monument. See Bitter beer

Alma mater. Bates college song. H. P. Davis. Words by I. H. Blake. AI—KU—KV

"Alma mater." Brown university song. <G. Kiallmark. Words by J. A. De Wolf> AI—KU

Alma mater. Carnegie institute of technology song. J. V. O'Brien. Words by C. J. Taylor. AI—KU

Alma mater. Colgate university song. Spanish air: Juanita. Words by L. E. French. AI—KU

Alma mater. Cornell university song. Air: Annie Lisle <by H. S. Thompson> Words by C. K. Urguhart. AI—KU—KV

Alma mater. Drake university song. C. Bloom. Words by E. J. Scott. AI—KU

Alma mater. Franklin and Marshall college song. G. W. Thompson (music and words) AI

Alma mater. Furman university song. H. W. B. Barnes. AI

Alma mater. George Washington university song. ɾAttributed to H. Careyɿ Words by M. M. Davidson. AI—AIS

Alma mater. Georgia institute of technology song. F. Roman. Words by I. Granath. AI

Alma mater. Gettysburg college song. F. Reinartz. Words by P. S. Gilbert. AI

Alma mater. Howard college song. P. de Launay. Words by G. W. Macon. AIS

Alma mater—Lafayette college (Stier) See In front of old Pardee (Stier)

Alma mater. Lehigh university song. <H. S. Thompson. Words by J. J. Gibson> wrongly attributed to C. K. Urquhart. AI—KU

Alma mater. Loyola university song. N. W. Devereux. Words by J. W. Riordan. HW

Alma mater. Michigan state college song. ɾH. S. Thompsonɿ Words by A. M. Brown. KU—KV

Alma mater. North Carolina state college song. B. F. Norris. Words by A. M. Fountain. AI

Alma mater. Ohio Wesleyan university song. C. H. Cuppett. AI—KU

Alma mater. Pennsylvania state college song. C. C. Converse. Words by F. L. Pattee. KU

Alma mater. St Mary's college song. W. Stevens (music and words) AIS
"Hail! St Mary's hail." HW

Alma mater. Syracuse university song. Air: Annie Lisle <by H. S. Thompson> Words by J. W. Stevens. AI—KU

Alma mater. Tulane university song. Ruebush. Words by Williams. KU

Alma mater. U.S. military academy song. F. Kücken. Words by P. S. Reinecke. AI—DSO—KU—KV

Alma mater. University of Alabama song. ɾH. S. Thompsonɿ Words by H. Vickers. AI—KU

Alma mater. University of Arkansas song. H. D. Tovey. Words by B. Payne. KU—KV

Alma mater. University of Chicago song. Words by E. H. Lewis. AI—KU

Alma mater. University of Missouri song. J. T. Quarles. Words by T. T. Railey. AI—AIS—KU

Alma mater. University of New Mexico song. ₁H. S. Thompson₎ Words by S. Fay. HW

Alma mater. University of North Dakota song. Air: Austrian hymn <by F. J. Haydn> Words by J. Macnie. HW—KU

"Alma mater." University of Pittsburgh song. F. J. Haydn. Words by G. M. P. Baird. AI—KU

Alma mater—University of South Dakota. See Pioneer song (Colton)

"Alma mater." Song of the University of the South. N. Middleton (music and words) AI—AIS

Alma mater. University of Tennessee song. Mrs J. L. Meek (music and words) KU

Alma mater. University of Washington song. G. Hager. Words by R. H. Allen. AI

Alma mater. University of Wyoming song. J. E. Downey. AI—AIS—HW—KU—KV

Alma mater. Wabash college song. C. Ragan. AI

Alma mater. Washington university song. ₁F. W. Kücken₎ KU

Alma mater. Washington and Jefferson college song. ₁H. S. Thompson₎ Words by L. D. Hemingway. AIS—KU

Alma mater. Wittenberg college song. R. H. Hiller (music and words) AI

"Alma mater Fordham." Fordham university song. F. Joslyn. Words by H. A. Gaynor. KU—KV

Alma mater, Ohio. Ohio university song. K. S. Clark (music and words) KU—KV

"Alma mater Sewanee, my glorious mother ever be." See "Alma mater"—University of the South (Middleton)

Alma mater song. Oregon state agricultural college. W. H. Maris (music and words) HW

Alma mater song (Carry me back) KU

"Alma mater, we hail thee with loyal devotion." See "Alma mater"—Brown university (Kiallmark)

"Alma mater, wise and glorious." See "Alma mater"—University of Pittsburgh (Haydn)

"Alma mater's sons and daughters." See Fight 'em Washington (Lieber)

Alma Redemptoris Mater (Dear Mother of the Redeemer) 15th century carol, attributed to John of Dunstable. e. DNS

El alma si tu recordares. See "Alli en el bosque"

Almers, Hermann. See Allmers, Hermann

Almost over. Negro spiritual from Virginia. AS

Almost persuaded. See "Father in heaven, hear us today" (Bliss)

Almsgiving. See "O Lord of heaven, and earth, and sea" (Dykes)

Aloha ("The blue Pacific ocean") See Hail and farewell

Aloha oe. Hawaiian song. Liliuokalani. e. TFP—TFR
Aloha oe (Farewell to thee) e. DFF

Alone, all alone by the sea-side he left me. See The widow in the cottage by the sea-side (White)

"Along at evening as she returned." See "In Seaport town" (Hindman, Ky. version)

"Along the green lane in the Maytime." See Mabel Clare (Higgins)

Alouette. French-Canadian folk song. f. BB—MBS—TFG

The alphabet ("A b c d e f g") W. Mozart. BB

The Alpine horn. ₁Rimbault₎ Words by Malibran. MFS

"Als die grause schreckensnachricht unsres unglücks wir vernommen." See Lamento ("Quando junse la nuvella")

"Als die nachricht ich vernommen bei Ferrera von Orezza." See Lamento ("Quandu n'intesi la nova alle Ferrera d'Orezza")

"Als die Römer frech geworden." See Die Teutoburger schlacht

"Als dort das Kind zu Bettlehem geboren." See Canzone d'i zampognari

Als du die wachtel hieltest. See Quand tu tenais la caille

"Als ich ein junggeselle war." See Der tod von Basel

"Als ich in der jugend frühlicht." See Des sängers kindheit

"Als ich noch ein kleiner knabe" ("Kui mina alles noor veel olin") Esthonian folk song. es.g. ML 3

"Als ich zuletzt in Ballynure." See A Ballynure ballad

"Als mich mein mütterlein zum nönnchen macht'." See La monacella

"Als Noah aus dem kasten war." See Noah (Reissiger)

"Als Vater Noah die arche gemacht hatt'." See Er passagallo

"Als von Amerika wir aufbrachen." See Seemanns lied

"Als wir jüngst in Regensburg waren." See Fräulein Kunigund

Alt-Englands roast beef. See The roast beef of old England (Leveridge)

Die alte kasho. See The old, old questions

Der alte reiter und sein mantel ("Schier dreissig jahre bist du alt") Volksweise. Words by C. von Holtei. g. EDL

Der alte schäfer ("Ja som bača velmi starý") Slovak folk song. g.sl. ML 3

Alter Joe. See Old black Joe (Foster)

Alter tanz ("Grosse mädchen schlanke mädchen."—Vanha tanssi) Finnish folk song. fi.g. ML 3

Altes studentisches tafellied. See Edite, bibite

"**Altho'** thou maun never be mine." See Here's a health to ane I lo'e dear

Alvord, Jack W.
Look at the ears on him (Harrington)

Always in the way. C. K. Harris (music and words) SW

"**Always** keep a smile for mother." C. Baker. SW

"**Always** take mother's advice." J. Lindsay (music and words) OTG—SRW

"**Alzati!** là, tuo figlio a te concedo riveder." See Eri tu che macchiavi (Verdi)

"**Am** brunnen vor dem tore." See Der lindenbaum (Schubert)

"**Am** danat ti mae son." See Mentra, Gwen

"**Am** einunddreissigsten August." See Le combat naval

Am flüsschen. See Jealousy

"**Am** fünf-und-zwanzigsten Dezember." See Villancico-baile de Nadal

Am Harmiavesi (Harmiaveden rantaa) Finnish folk song. fi.g. ML 3

"**Am** himmel glänzen tausend sterne." See "See, love, above the stars"

Am I not fondly thine own. See "Du, du liegst mir im herzen"

Am Manzanares. See "Am ufer des flusses, des Manzanares" (Jensen)

Am meer. F. Schubert. Words by H. Heine. g. EDL

Am meer (By the sea) e.g. GG

Am morgen nach der hochzeit. See Wedding-day song

Am St Theodorsberg (St' agioy Thodōrhoy to boyno) Greek folk song. g.gr. ML 2

"**Am** schönsten sommerabend war's" (One summer night) Grieg. [Words by J. Paulsen] e.g. TM

"**Am** Sonntag morgen" ("On Sunday morning") J. Brahms. Words by P. Heyse. e.g. TM

Am strande (Rannalla istuja) Finnish folk song. fi.g. ML 3

Am strande des Saarijärvi (Saarijärven rantaan) Finnish folk song. fi.g. ML 3

Am Sylvester-abend ("Des jahres letzte stunde") J. A. P. Schulz. Words by J. H. Voss. g. EDL

"**Am** Theodor, am heilgen Theodor." See Am St Theodorsberg

"**Am** ufer des flusses, des Manzanares" (Am Manzanares.—By the Manzanares) A. Jensen. [Words from an anonymous Spanish poet] e.g. HCA

"**Am** un leu" (Trinklied) Rumanian song. g.ru. ML 2

"**Am** wiesenhügel schlummert' ich." See The dream (Rubinstein)

Amadori, Giuseppe
"E pur io"

"**Aman** ðevojko, uzun lepoto." See Erbarmen, schöne

Amang the rigs o' barley, O. See Corn rigs are bonnie

"**Amarilli**, mia bella" ("Amaryllis, now cruel") G. Romano (Caccini) e.i. GA

"**Amaryllis**, now cruel." See "Amarilli, mia bella" (Caccini)

Amber Lee. C. A. White. Words by T. Collier. SW

Ambrose, Robert Steele
"One sweetly solemn thought"

Ambrosius, Saint
"Creator alme siderum" (Old air)
Jesu Redemptor omnium (5th century air)

L'âme des fleurs (Souls of flowers) J. Massenet. Words by P. Délair. e.f. SAT

"**L'âme** d'une flûte soupire." See Arpège (Rousseau)

America ("America! America! thy name is in my heart") E. Bloch. TFP

America ("God bless our native land") Attributed to H. Carey. Words by C. T. Brooks and J. S. Dwight. BB—MFS

America ("My country, 'tis of thee") Attributed to H. Carey. Words by S. F. Smith. BB—DSB—DSC—LAS—TFP—TFR
National hymn. MFS

"**America!** America! thy name is in my heart." See America (Bloch)

"**America**, my country." W. J. Goodel. Words by N. H. Hall. BB

America, the beautiful. W. C. MacFarlane. Words by K. L. Bates. LAS

America, the beautiful. S. A. Ward. Words by K. L. Bates. DSC—GSS—TFP—TFR

America, the beautiful (Materna) BB

The **American** hymn ("Speed our republic") M. Keller (music and words) GOS 2
Keller's American hymn. BB

The **American** soldier (El soldado Americano) Song of the Spanish American war. Air: Son of a gambolier. DSO

Ames, Charles G.
"Father in heaven, hear us today" (Bliss)

Ames, Francis, pseud. See Stevens, David

"**Amici**, amici, chi'n Palermu jiti." See Canto del carcerato

"**Amid** a lowland valley." Russian folk song. e. NRF

"**Amid** the boughs of an old pine tree." See The pine tree swing

"**Amid** the greenwood." Thalberg. MFS

"**Amidst** the rock-bound highlands of the Hudson's shore." See Army, O army (Egner)

[**Aminte**] Tambourin. Bergerette. f.g. ML 1

"**Amo**, amas, I love a lass." [Air: The frog and the mouse, arr by S. Arnold. Words by J. O'Keeffe] KSO

"**Amol** is gefohren äuf'n yam." Jewish folk song. y. SY

"Amol is gewen a maaseh." See A maaseh

"Among the beauteous flow'rs I live." See The rose of the Alps (Linley)

"Among the Jewish nation." See Daniel in the lion's den

Among the leaves so green-o. See The keeper

"Amor, che cieco sei." V. Righini. e.i. KVG

Amor! quam dulcis est amor. See Een kint gheboren in Bethlehem

Amore, amore! gaudio tormento. For English translation see "O love immortal" (Verdi)

"L'amour de moi." 13th century French chanson. f. GA
"L'amour de moi" ("Mein herzensliebchen") f.g. ML 1

L'Amour interrogé par un berger. See Cupid and the shepherd (Taylor)

"Amours, amours, tant tu m'y faictz de mal." See Sarabande

Z'amours Marianne (Marianne's loves) Negro creole folk song. e.f. MB

Amsterdam. See A-roving

"Amul is gevein a maaseh." See A maaseh

"An' a howdy, howdy, sister." See Howdy

"An Alexis send ich dich." See Der rose sendung (Himmel)

An baches rande (Virran reunalla) Finnish folk song. fi.g. ML 3

"An dem bach am wiesenplan singt die drossel." See Aves, frutas y viento

"An dem flüsschen, an der brükke." See Jealousy

"An dem strom der mutter Wolga." See Mother Vólga

An den mond ("Guter mond, du gehst so stille") German folk song. g. EDL

"An den Rhein, an den Rhein." See Warnung vor dem Rhein (Pöthko)

An den sonnenschein. R. Schumann. Words by R. Reinick. g. EDL
An den sonnenschein ("O sunshine") e.g. CSB 5
"O sunny ray" ("O sonnenschein") e.g. HCA

An der mutter Wolga. See Mother Vólga

"An der Saale hellem strande." See Rudelsburg (Fesca)

An der Weser. G. Pressel. Words by F. Dingelstedt. g. EDL

An die freude ("Freude, schöner Götterfunken") Composer unknown. Words by F. Schiller. g. EDL

An die freude ("Freude, schöner Götterfunken") L. van Beethoven. Words by F. Schiller. g. EDL
Ode to joy. e. DSB

An die jungfrau Maria. See "O sanctissima"

An die musik (To music) F. Schubert. Words by Schober. e. CSB 4
An die musik. g. EDL

"An dir allein, an dir hab' ich gesündigt." See Busslied (Beethoven)

"An einem sommertage schön." See A forsaken lover's complaint (Johnson)

"An einem winterabend war's." See The Fanaid grove

An' he never said a mumbaling word. See Crucifixion

"An' I couldn't hear nobody pray." See I couldn't hear nobody pray

An junge spröde schönen. See "Ich sah ein röschen am wege stehn" (Weber)

[An'] O, for ane-and-twenty, Tam. Air: Up in the morning early, or, Cauld blows the wind. Words by R. Burns. GS

An' the pore little thing cried "Mammy." See The swapping song (American mountain version)

Anchor's aweigh. U.S. naval academy song. C. A. Zimmerman. Words by A. H. Miles. AI—AIS—US

The anchor's weighed. J. Braham. [Words by S. J. Arnold] GOS 1

And a hog-eye, railroad nigger. See The hog-eye man

"And a howdy, howdy, sister." See Howdy

And a' that e'er my Jenny had. See Jenny's bawbee

"And are ye sure the news is true." See There's nae luck about the house

And away, you santy, my dear honey. See Can't you dance the polka ("One day as I went walking")

"And de moon will turn to blood." See The day of judgment

And down from the mountains came the squadrons and platoons. See Slattery's mounted foot

And gladly singing to you always. See Oh! fairest alma mater (Sleeper)

"And God created man" (see Song Index) Also in "In native worth and honour clad" (Haydn) SSO 3

"And God said, let the earth bring forth grass" (see Song Index) Also in "With verdure clad the fields appear" (Haydn) SSO 1

"And God said, let the earth bring forth the living creature" (see Song Index) Also in "Now heaven in fullest glory" (Haydn) SSO 4

"And God said: Let the waters bring forth abundantly" (see Song Index) Also in "On mighty pens uplifted soars" (Haydn) SSO 1

"And God said, let the waters under the heaven" (see Song Index) Also in "Rolling in foaming billows" (Haydn) SSO 4

And God shall wipe away all tears. See "The Lord is risen, He will dwell with men" (Sullivan)

"And he journey'd with companions towards Damascus." See "But the Lord is mindful of His own" (Mendelssohn)

And he never said a mumbaling word. See Crucifixion

And her golden hair was hanging down her back. M. H. Rosenfeld. Words by F. McGlennon. SMG—SRW

And here we have Idaho. See Here we have Idaho

"And how do you like your pillow, said he." See Little Musgrave and Lady Barnard (Virginia version)

And how they titter'd. See The arm chair

"And I couldn't hear nobody pray." See I couldn't hear nobody pray

"And I mankind have not in mind." See My love that mourns for me (Giles)

And I would flee away. See Et moi je m'enfouiyais

"And I'll sink you in the Lowlands." See The Golden Vanity (Tennessee version)

And it's tidings of comfort and joy. See "God rest you merry, gentlemen"

And Mary bore Jesus Christ our Saviour for to be. See Sans Day carol

And O, for one-and-twenty, Tom. See An' O, for one-and-twenty, Tom

"And Ruth said: Entreat me not to leave thee." See Entreat me not to leave thee (Gounod)

And shall Trelawny die. See Song of the western men (Slater)

"And since my sweetie left me." See Harlem blues (Handy)

And sing blow away the morning dew. See Blow away the morning dew

And so our song we bring. See Alma mater—University of Wyoming (Downey)

"And so, since last I saw my darling." See Sonntag (Brahms)

And that is the navy of all Yankee sailor-men. See The countersigns

And the breezes still are sighing. See When the evening breeze is sighing "Home, sweet home" (Solman)

And the green leaves grew all around, around, around. See The tree in the wood

"And the moon will turn to blood." See The day of judgment

And the poor little thing cried "Mammy." See The swapping song (American mountain version)

And the stormy winds may blow, blow, blow. See The mermaid (North Carolina version)

"And then it's onward for Colorado." See Colorado "C" men (Allen and Sheafe)

"And then those pretty little babes." See The babes in the wood (Virginia version)

"And then we'll fight, fight, fight for U. of C." See Football song (Allen and Sheafe)

And therefore be merry, set sorrows aside. See "A Virgin most pure, as the prophets do tell, hath brought forth a Baby" (Air from Gilbert's "Some ancient Christmas carols")

"And they say that to the ladies." See Entrance song (Millöcker)

And was not this a joyful thing. See All in the morning (Christmas carol)

And was not this a woeful thing. See All in the morning (Easter carol)

And we're a' noddin', nid, nid, noddin'. See We're a' noddin'

"And when he had spent all." A. Sullivan. SSO 1

"And when old Trojan's men fall into line." See The cardinal and gold (Wesson)

"And when the song is sweetly sounding." K. Millöcker. e. WLO

"And will he not come again" ("Und kommt er nicht mehr zurück") [Traditional air] Words by Shakespeare. e.g. ML 1

And wouldst thou thus have sullied. See Eri tu che macchiavi (Verdi)

"And ye shall walk in silk attire." English air. Words by S. Blamire. GS

"And ye shall walk in silk attire." [Scottish air: The siller crown] Words by S. Blamire. GS

Andersen, Hans Christian
Jeg elsker dig (Grieg)
Punchinello (Molloy)
Der soldat (Silcher)
Vandring i skoven (Grieg)

André, Johann
Rheinweinlied

André, Pierre. See Montoya, G., jt. auth.

Andreas Hofer ("Zu Mantua in banden") Tyrolean national song. Words by J. Mosen. g. EDL. e. only MFS

Andrews, Addison Fletcher
Only a 'ittle dirly dirl

"Andy was the grand old man we loved so well." See Fight for the glory of Carnegie (Schmertz)

"Anfangs wollt' ich fast verzagen" ("Could I ever hope to endure it") F. Liszt. Words by H. Heine. e.g. GA

Angedenken (Memento) P. Cornelius (music and words) e.g. SAT

"The angel Gabriel." Traditional Devonshire air. OB

Angel Gabriel ("Oh! my soul") J. E. Stewart. <Words by F. Dumont> BNM—WSS

"Angel of peace." M. Keller. Words by O. W. Holmes. GOS 2

De **angel** roll de stone away. Negro spiritual. JB 2

"Angel voices ever singing their glad hymns up in the sky." French air. DSC

Angelic songs are swelling. See "Hark! hark! my soul" (Armstrong)

Angelina Baker. S. C. Foster (music and words) WSS

"Angelina gave a party to the dolls, last night." See The dolls' party (Macy)

The **angels** and the shepherds ("Hearken, shepherds") Bohemian carol air. Words by C. B. Fenno. FC

The **angels** and the shepherds ("Shepherds, we bring you tidings") Old Dutch folk song. e. MFF

"Angels came to us in dreams at night." See The angels spoke to us in dreams (Humperdinck)

"Angels, ever bright and fair." Händel. SSO 1

"Angels, from the realms of glory." Traditional air from the west of England. Words by J. Montgomery. DN

"Angels, from the realms of glory." French air: Les anges dans nos campagnes. Words by J. Montgomery. OB

"Angels holy." Flemish air: De dryvoudige geboorte. Words by J. S. Blackie. OB

De angels in heab'n gwineter write my name. Negro spiritual. JB 2

Angels, meet me at de cross-roads. W. S. Hays (music and words) BNM—WSS

Angels of Jesus, angels of light. See "Hark, hark, my soul" (Dykes)

The angels' song ("Thus angels sung") O. Gibbons. DN

The angels spoke to us in dreams. E. Humperdinck. ⌈Tr of Ihr englein, die uns so treu bewacht⌉ e. WG

"Angels we have heard on high." See Bergers, pour qui cette fête

The angels' whisper ("A baby was sleeping, its mother was weeping") Air: Mary, do you fancy me. Words by S. Lover. SI

The angel's whisper. HMI

Angels, whisper that our darling. See Where the little feet are waiting (Webster)

"Angelus ad Virginem." 13th century air. e.l. OB

Angelus emittitur. For English paraphrase see "Gabriel's message"

Anges purs, anges radieux. For English translation see "Holy angels" (Gounod)

The angler's song. H. Lawes. ⌈Words attributed to J. Chalkhill⌉ BOS 2

"Angry words." Childhood song. MFS

Aniello, Pancrazio
"Lo so che pria mi moro"

Animal fair. Minstrel song. SBA

"The animals went in one by one." See One more river

"Ännchen von Tharau." F. Silcher. Words by S. Dach. g. EDL

Annie Laurie. Lady John Scott. Words by W. Douglas of Fingland. BB—DFF—DSB—DSC—GS—GSS—MFS—SSB—TFP—TFR

Annie Lawrie. GOS 1

Annie Lisle. H. S. Thompson. WSS

Annie o' the banks o' Dee. S. Glover. Words by Crawford. GS

Annie Roonie. See Little Annie Rooney (Nolan)

Anon my 'venging sword shall seek thy worthless heart betraying. See Nuova ferita (Mercadante)

Anona. V. Grey (music and words) SMG

Añoranzas. See Deep river blues (Handy)

"Ans fensterlein schleich ich" ("Pod okonce pridem") Slovenian folk song. g.slo. ML 2

Anschütz, Ernst
Der tannenbaum (German folk air)
Warnung (Volksweise)

Answer to a child's question. C. V. Stanford. Words by S. T. Coleridge. CSB 1

Anthem. University of Santa Clara song. J. Riordan. HW

Antioch. See "Joy to the world" (Händel)

Anvil chorus ("God of the nations") See "God of the nations, in glory enthroned" (Verdi)

Anvil chorus ("See how the shadows of night are flying") G. Verdi. ⌈Tr of Vedi! le fosche⌉ e. WG

Anvil chorus ("See the proud banner") See Our flag o'er us waving (Verdi)

Anyhow, anyhow, anyhow my Lord. See I'm gwine up to heab'n anyhow

⌈Aoleo⌉ "Dacă nu e și nu e" (Klage) Rumanian song. g.ru. ML 2

"Der apfelbaum steht voll bluten weiss." See Brautlied

"Appear in all thy beauty." See "Deh vieni alla finestra" (Mozart)

Appearances. See the wedding-suit

Après avoir, tant bien que mal. For English translation see "Now having, not without defect" (Offenbach)

"Après la guerre fini." British army song. Air from Sur les ponts de Paris. DSO

Après un rêve (After a dream) G. Fauré. Words from the Tuscan of R. Bussine. e.f. TM

April ("Now April has come") Welsh traditional carol air: Hir oes i fair. Words by G. Dearmer. OB

Apsley Street, pseud. See Winner, Septimus

Ar hyd y nos (All through the night) D. Owen. Words from the Welsh. e. AT—SSB

All through the night. e. BB—BST—CSB 4—DSB—DSC—LSB—TFB—TFO—TFP

All through the night (Poor Mary Ann) e. TFO

Ar hyd y nos (In stiller nacht) g.w. ML 1

The night. e. SAT

"Ar mo ghabhailt dam tre Dhroichead na Tuaire." See Droichead na Tuaire

Araby's daughter. Kiallmark. Words by T. Moore. GOS 1

Araya, José
The pearl. See La perla (attributed)
La perla (attributed)

Archangel open the door. Negro spiritual from South Carolina. AS

⌈Ardeleanca⌉ "Multe lacrămi am vărsat" ("Viele tränen ich vergoss") Rumanian song. g.ru. ML 2

Ardell, Walter
Blaze away (Holzmann)

"Are you sleeping." See Frère Jacques; Mingled melodies

"Are you the doctor they sent for me here." See The brown girl (Woodridge, Va. version)

Are you the O'Reilly. P. Rooney. SMG—SRW

Arenski, Anton Stepanovich
"But lately in dance I embraced her"
"Sie schwebt' mir noch kürzlich im arme." See "But lately in dance I embraced her"
[The **Arethusa**] The saucy Arethusa. [Old air, attributed to W. Shield and to O'Carolan. Words by P. Hoare] WSE
"**Argizagi** ederra" ("Schöner mond, scheine mild") Basque folk song. ba.g. ML 2
Argwohn. Schwäbische volksweise. g. EDL
Ariadne's lament. See Plainte d'Ariane (Coquard)
Arietta ("O di che lode") B. Marcello. e.i. GA
Arioso from 100th psalm. See "Erkennet, erkennt, dass der Herr ist Gott" (Jadassohn)
Arise and hail the glorious star. West of England carol. DN
Arise, arise, awake to joy. See Cornish May song ("Ye maids of Helston")
Arise, arise the dawn of day. See Cornish May song ("Ye maids of Helston")
"**Arise,** arise ye slumbering sleepers." See "Awake! awake" (White Rock, Va. version)
"**Arise,** arise, you drowsy maiden" (see Song Index)
Variant of: "Awake! awake"
"**Arise,** arise, you slumbering sleepers." See "Awake! awake" (Beechgrove, Va. version)
"**Arise,** my love, my fair one." C. H. Graun. e. SSO 1
"**Arise** ye, arise ye." See Duce di tanti eroi (Rossini)
Arizona grid march. University of Arizona song. H. Keddie (music and words) AI
"**Ark** of freedom! glory's dwelling." See Columbia, God preserve thee free (Haydn)
The **Arkansaw** traveler. Old American air. Words by D. Stevens. TFG
Arkwright, Mrs. See Browne, Harriet Mary
"**Arm,** arm, sons of the Union." See The Union call
Arm, arm, ye brave. Händel. SSO 4
Arm! arm! your country bids you arm. See To arms
The **arm** chair. Old comic ballad. SW
Das **arme** mädchen (Köyhä tyttö) Finnish folk song. fi.g. ML 3
"**Armes** vöglein, bist du krank, bist du krank." See "Choriñua kaiolan"
Armida. See Lascia ch'io pianga (Händel)
Armitage, Marie Teresa
"Sleep, my dearie"
The **armored** cruiser squadron. U.S. navy song. US
"**Armseelchen** sass seufzend unterm maulbeerbaum früh." See The willow song (16th century air)

Armstrong, Catharine
Easter eve (Gounod)
Armstrong, Henry W.
Sweet Adeline
Armstrong, J. M.
"Hark! hark! my soul"
The **army** bean. Post-Civil war song. [J. P. Webster] DSO
Army blue. West Point song. [G. R. Poulton] DSO—US
Army blue of 1859. West Point song. [G. R. Poulton] DSO
"The **army** is gath'ring from near and from far." See Marching along (Bradbury)
"**Army** mule." U.S. Naval academy song. [G. Edwards] US
Army, O army. West Point football song. P. Egner. DSO
"The **army** team's the pride and dream." See On, brave old army team (Egner)
"The **army's** coming down the river." West Point football song. Air: Swing wide the golden gates. Words by L. E. Hibbs. DSO

Arndt, Ernst Moritz
Bundeslied (Hanitsch)
Des Deutschen vaterland (Reichardt)
Feuerlied (Hempel)
Gebet an den heiligen Christ (Siegert)
Vaterlandslied (Methfessel)
Arne, Michael
"Care flies from the lad that is merry" (from Cymon)
"Come, loose every sail to the breeze." See Homeward bound
Homeward bound
The lass with the delicate air
Arne, Thomas Augustine
"Blow, blow, thou winter wind"
Come away, death
"The echoing horn" (from Thomas & Sally)
The lass with the delicate air (wrongly attributed) See Arne, M. The lass with the delicate air
The plague of love
Rule Britannia (from Alfred)
Shakespeare's carol. See "Blow, blow, thou winter wind"
"Under the greenwood tree, who loves to lie with me"
"When daisies pied, and violets blue"
"Where the bee sucks"
Arnold, Henry
Denison marching song
Arnold, Oliver
The banks of the Dee, Parody on (Old air)
Arnold, Samuel
"Amo, amas, I love a lass": traditional air arranged (from The agreeable surprise)
"Haste thee, nymph"
The star-spangled banner (same air as "To Anacreon in heaven"; wrongly attributed) See Smith, J. S. The star-spangled banner
"To Anacreon in heaven" (wrongly attributed) See Smith, J. S. "To Anacreon in heaven"

Arnold, Samuel James
The anchor's weighed (Braham)
"Around a hop layout three dope-fiends lay." See Oh, in the morning
Around Cape Horn. Sea song. US
Around me, blessed image, ever soar. Old Irish air. Words by J. Oxenford. HMI
A-roving ("In Amsterdam there lived a maid") Capstan chantey. TSB 2 —WSE
Amsterdam. SBS
For variants see following songs of same title
A-roving₁ "In Amsterdam there lives a maid" (The maid of Amsterdam) Capstan chantey. US
A-roving ("In Plymouth town there lived a maid") Capstan chantey. TSB 2
Arpège (Arpeggios) M. Samuel-Rousseau. Words by A. Samain. e.f. ASN
Arpeggios. See Arpège (Rousseau)
"Art thou weary, art thou languid." J. H. Hopkins. [Tr of Kopon te kai kamaton] e. MFS
"The artilleree, the artilleree." See With the dirt behind their ears
Arvers, Félix
"Ma vie a son secret" (Bizet)
"As a beam o'er the face of the waters." Irish air: The young man's dream. Words by T. Moore. HMI
"As a bird in prison pining." See Be still my heart
"As a little child." C. M. Von Weber. MFS
"As beauteous as Flora." See Norah, the pride of Kildare (Parry)
"As beautiful Kitty one morning was tripping." See Kitty of Coleraine
"As der rebbe Elimelech is geworen sehr fröhlich." See Der rebbe Elimelech
"As Esther die gabbete hot derhört dem wunder." See Esther die gabbete
"As Georgie was a-walking up and down." See Geordie (Villamont, Va. version)
"As I about sunsetting." See Y gwŷdd
"As I came o'er the Glashy head." See The little rose of Gartan
"As I came over new London bridge." See Geordie (Dewey, Va. version)
"As I came thro' Sandgate." See The keel row
"As I come over we trip together." See Charlie's sweet (Virginia version)
"As I crossed over London's bridge." See Geordie (Swannanoah, N.C. version)
"As I gaed o'er the Highland hills." See Peggy bawn
"As I grew up in Boston." See The Sheffield apprentice (Allanstand, N.C. version)
"As I lay upon a night, my thought was on a berd so bright." See Alma Redemptoris Mater (Dunstable?)
"As I lie here adoring." See Je crois en vous (Berlioz)
"As I passed by a river-side." See The carnal and the crane

"As I roam'd the woods at leisure." See Die bekehrte (Stange)
"As I rode out a-hunting." See Sally Buck (Virginia version)
"As I rode out very early to view the green meadows in spring." See The maid with the bonny brown hair
"As I rode over Banstead downs." See Georgie
"As I roved out one morning down by a riverside, I heard a lovely maid lament." See John Riley (Sussex version)
"As I rummag'd thro' the attic." See My trundle-bed (Baker)
"As I sail home to Galveston." See Oleander time (Repper)
"As I sat at my spinning wheel." See The spinning-wheel
"As I sat in a lonesome grove." See The lonesome grove (Tennessee version)
"As I sat on a sunny bank." DN
"As I sat on a sunny bank" (Sunny bank) OB
Variant of: "I saw three ships"
"As I sit and dream at evening." University of Oregon song. R. H. Nelson. HW
"As I sit on my bunk arranging my junk." See The battle of Paris
"As I strayed from my cot at the close of the day." See Roll on, silver moon
"As I stroll'd out one evening when the silver moon was shining." See I love you
"As I view now these scenes so charming." See "Vi ravviso, o luoghi ameni" (Bellini)
As I walk along the Bois Boolong. See The man who broke the bank at Monte Carlo (Gilbert)
"As I walked down by the river." See Good morning, my pretty little miss (Kentucky version)
"As I walked down the Broadway one evening in July." See Can't you dance the polka
"As I walked down the new-cut road." See Charleston gals
"As I walk'd forth one summer's day to view the meadows sweet and gay." See A forsaken lover's complaint (Johnson)
"As I walk'd out by de light ob de moon." See Settin' on a rail
"As I walked out in the streets of Laredo." See The cowboy's lament
"As I walk'd out last Sunday night." See I seen her at de window
"As I walked out one cold winter's morning." See The true lover's farewell (Endicott, Va. version)
"As I walked out one cool summer morning." See George Reilly (Black Mountain, N.C. version)
"As I walked out one evening down by the riverside." See The Irish girl (North Carolina version)

"**As** I walked out one evening fair out of sight of land." See The mermaid (Hyden, Ky. version no. 2)

"**As** I walked out one evening late to hear the birds sing sweet." See The false young man (Knott or Letcher county version)

"**As** I walked out one evening's morning." See George Reilly (Micaville, N.C. version)

"**As** I walk'd out one fine morning, all in the month of May." See Heave away, my Johnny

"**As** I walked out one holiday some drops of rain did fall." See Sir Hugh (Bird's Creek, Tenn. version)

"**As** I walked out one holiday the drops of dew did fall." See Sir Hugh (Sevierville, Tenn. version)

"**As** I walked out one lonesome Sunday morning." See Tarry Trousers (Virginia version)

"**As** I walked out one May morning down by the riverside, I cast my eyes around me." See The Irish girl (Callaway, Va. version)

"**As** I walked out one May morning to hear the birds sing sweet." See The false young man (White Rock, Va. version)

"**As** I walked out one morning fair to view the meadows round." See Blow, ye winds of morning

"**As** I walked out one morning fine, all in the month of May." See Heave away, my Johnny

"**As** I walked out one morning in May for to hear the small birds sing sweet." See The false young man (Micaville, N.C. version)

"**As** I walked out one morning in May just as the day was dawning." See I'm seventeen come Sunday (Stuart, Va. version)

"**As** I walked out one morning in spring for to hear the little birds sing sweet." See The false young man (Flag Pond, Tenn. version no. 2)

"**As** I walked out one morning in spring, I saw a fair damsel." See I'm going to get married next Sunday

"**As** I walked out one morning, one morning in May." See Green bushes (Virginia version)

"**As** I walked out one summer's evening." See George Reilly (Manchester, Ky. version)

"**As** I walked out one summer's morning." See George Reilly (Hot Springs, N.C. version)

"**As** I walked out one sunny morn to view the meadows round." See Blow, ye winds, in the morning

"**As** I walk'd out one sweet summer's morning." See George Reilly (Tennessee version)

"**As** I was a-gwine down the road, tired team and a heavy load." See Turkey in the straw

"**As** I was a-walking down Paradise street." See Blow the man down

"**As** I was a-walking one morning by chance, I heard a maid making her moan." See I must live all alone

"**As** I was a walking, one morning for pleasure." See The dogie song; Git along little dogies; Whoopee, ti yi yo, git along little dogies

"**As** I was a-walking one morning in the spring, I met a young damsel, so sweetly she did sing." See The lark in the morn

"**As** I was goin' to Ballynure." See A Ballynure ballad

"**As** I was going to Strawberry fair." See Strawberry fair

"**As** I was lumb'ring down de street, down de street." See Buffalo gals

"**As** I was rambling down de street, down de street." See Buffalo gals

"**As** I was walkin' down Wexford street." Irish song: American version. SBA

"**As** I was walking out one day, along these —too-ra-loo-ra-loo." See Vous n'êtes pas mon berger

"**As** I was walking out one day, thinking of the weather." See Jockey hat and feather (Brockway)

"**As** I went down in de valley to pray." See The good old way

"**As** I went down to Derby town." See The Derby ram (Kentucky version; Virginia version)

As I went down to Dover. See On a summer day

"**As** I went forth to view the plain." See Bonnie Mary Gray (Lee)

"**As** I went over London's bridge." See Geordie (Hot Springs, N.C. version)

"**As** I went through the north country." See York! York for my money

"**As** I went up in town, sir." See The Derby ram (Tennessee version)

"**As** ich wolt gehat dem keisers oizres." See A wieglied

"**As** in the skies of the west are dying." See Carmela

"**As** it fell on a holiday, and upon a holy-tide-a." See John Dory

"**As** it fell out on a holy day, the drops of rain did fall." See The Withy carol

"**As** it fell out one May morning." See The holy well

"**As** it fell out upon one day, rich Dives made a feast." See Dives and Lazarus

"**As** Jack was walking thro' the square." See Doo me ama

"**As** Jacob with travel was weary one day." See Jacob's ladder

"**As** Joseph and Mary were a-walking the green." See The cherry tree carol (Big Laurel, N.C. version)

"**As** Joseph was a-walking." Air from an old Breton Noël. Traditional Somersetshire words. DNS
Variant of: The cherry tree carol

"**As** Lady Marg'ret was a-going to bed." See Young hunting (Mount Fair, Va. version)

"**As** me zopft fun mir dus blit arois." See Die piolische yuden

As Moshiach wet kummen. See What will happen when the Messiah comes

"Aš nueisiu sa sodelin." See "In den garten will ich gehen"

"As o'er the hills I wander'd in the merry month of May." See The locust tree

"As on the swelling wave." See "Come raggio di sol" (Caldara)

"As once in a fair garden fragrant." See That Viennese waltz (Straus)

"Aš paėmiau mergužele." See "Hab' ein liebes herzensliebchen"

"As pretty Polly Oliver." See Pretty Polly Oliver

"As she was sitting in her dower room." See Fair Margaret and sweet William (Allanstand, N.C. version)

"As she was sitting in her parlour door." See Young hunting (Burnsville, N.C. version no. 2)

"As slow our ship her foaming track." Air: The girl I left behind me, or, Brighton camp. Words by T. Moore. HMI

"As softly the evening shadows." See Alma mater—Gettysburg college (Reinartz)

"As the backs go tearing by." Dartmouth college song. C. W. Blaisdell. Words by J. T. Keady. AI—AIS

"As the blackbird in the spring." See Aura Lee (Poulton)

"As the corn we went a-shearing." See An gille ban

As the dew flies over the mulberry tree. Traditional song. KSO

"As the men of Fordham swing along." See Fordham marching song (Breslin)

"As the moon shone bright and fair." See Hare and hunter

As the sand flies at Boreas' blowing. See D'Egitto là sui lidi (Verdi)

As the wind blows. R. Genée. MFS

As through the park I go. Words by W. Lingard. SW

"As to your fortune you need not complain." See The horse's complaint

"As truag gan peata'n maoir." For English translation see "I wish I had the shepherd's lamb"

"As we marched down by the Ireo." See Pretty Peggy O (Hyden, Ky. version)

"As we marched down thro' Ivory." See Pretty Peggy O (North Carolina version)

"As we marched down to Fernario." See Pretty Peggy O (Knott county, Ky. version)

"As we rode down the steep hillside." See The merchants' carol

"As we sailed on the water blue." See Whisky Johnny

"As we're going down the road." See Seventy-sixth field artillery song (Ward)

"As with gladness men of old." Arr from C. Kocher. Words by W. C. Dix. DN

As your hair grows whiter. H. Dacre (music and words) OTG

A-sailing down all on the coasts of High Barbary. See The coasts of High Barbary

Ascher, Joseph
Alice, where art thou

"Ascolta! Se Romeo t'uccise un figlio." See "Se Romeo t'uccise un figlio" (Bellini)

The ash grove. See Llwyn on

Ashburn, Karl. See Chapman, Lamar, jt. auth.

Ashrenuh mah tov chelkenu. See All in accord

Ashworth, Iva, and Schaeffer, J. S.
"Play ball"

"Así cual mueren en occidente los tibios rayos del astro rey." See Carmela

"Ask me not why my heart with fond emotion." See Child of the regiment (Donizetti)

Asleep in the deep. H. W. Petrie. Words by A. J. Lamb. GFS

Asōmen pantes laoi. For English translation see "Come, ye faithful, raise the strain" (16th century German air)

Der Asra (The Asra) A. Rubinstein. Words by H. Heine. e.g. GG

"Assonna il re." See Ah! mia figlia, perdona all' affanno (Rossini)

"Astăzi beau și mâine beau." See Doïna Haiducului

Astin, Charlie
"Inez Rovina"

Astorga, Emanuele, barone d'
"Per non penar"
"Più non pensar"

A-swinging in the lane. See Rosie Nell

"At a gay reception given in a mansion grand and old." See The moth and the flame (Witt)

At a Georgia camp meeting. K. Mills (music and words) GFS

"At a port in France one morning." See Give my regards to Broadway (Cohan)

"At dawn Aurora gaily breaks." See The mellow horn (Jones)

"At dawn of day I saw a man stand by a grog saloon." See The drunkard's doom

"At daylight in the morning, when all hands are called." See The good ship Montezuma

"At eve I wander'd by the shore." Irish air. Words by W. Maynard. HMI

At evening-time. Sporle. Words by C. M. Steadman. MFS

At father's door. Little-Russian song. e. SR

"At last I'm thine, love." See "Il dolce suono" (Donizetti)

"At length, too soon, dear creature." See The soldier's farewell (Swan)

"At midnight on my pillow lying." See Dream song (Jakobowski)

"At my tears she is jeering." See These tears my bosom searing (Flotow)

"At Occidental's feet today." See Hail to Occidental (Thomson)

At Pierrot's door. See "Au clair de la lune"

"**At** summer morn." Old English round. DSB

At sunset. See När sol går ner (Stenhammar)

At the altar. See "Il dolce suono" (Donizetti)

"**At** the Blackwall docks we bid adieu." See Homeward bound

"**At** the clear running fountain." See "À la claire fontaine"

At the cradle. C. Franck. e. DSB

At the gym. Spanish air. Words by H. W. Loomis. TFO

"**At** the mid hour of night." Air: Molly, my dear. Words by T. Moore. HMI

"**At** the old concert hall on the Bowery." See She is more to be pitied than censured (Gray)

"**At** two o'clock in the morning I have come to wake you, dear." See Canción de la luna

Athens. See "'Twas about the dead of night"

Atlanta blues (Make me one pallet on your floor) W. C. Handy and D. Elman. HB

Atoh hu yodea. See Thou knowest

"**Attend,** you sons of high renown." See Boney's lamentation

"**Au** beau clair de la lun' m'en allant promener." See Nanette

"**Au** clair de la lune." Words by Lully. f. GSS. e. only LSB
    At Pierrot's door. e. BB
    "Au clair de la lune" ("Bei des mondes scheine") f.g. ML 1

Aubade ("Voici le matin, des feux de l'aurore") For English translation see Morning serenade (Lecocq)

Auber, Daniel François Esprit
    "Away! away! the moon and stars are shining"
    Fairies' song. See The noontide ray
    Fishermen's chorus (from La muette de Portici)
    The noontide ray
    "On yonder rock reclining" (from Fra Diavolo. Tr of Voyez sur cette roche)

Audran, Edmond
    Ah! happy day (from La mascotte)
    "Ah! let the gay dancers" (from La mascotte)
    All is ended (from Olivette)
    Bob up serenely (from Olivette)
    Coaching song (from La mascotte)
    "The convent slept" (from Olivette)
    The farandole (from Olivette)
    First love. See Waltz song
    Gobble duet (from La mascotte)
    "Ha! ha! ha! how melancholy his moan is" (from Olivette)
    I love my love so well (from Olivette)
    The legend of the mascots (from La mascotte)
    A loving kiss (from La mascotte)
    Marriage bells chorus (from Olivette)
    "The matron of an hour" (from Olivette)
    "Nearest and dearest" (from Olivette)
    "No more of drum or trumpet sounding" (from La mascotte)
    "Now the merry vintage closes" (from La mascotte)
    "Oh! give me back" (from La mascotte)
    Song of the drum (from La mascotte)
    The torpedo and the whale (from Olivette)
    Waltz song (from Olivette)
    "When I behold." See Gobble duet (from La mascotte)
    "Where balmy garlic scents the air" (from Olivette)

"**Auf!** auf! sonnenlicht." See Codiad yr haul

"**Auf** der wiese, auf der wiese" ("Széna széna széna terem a réten") Hungarian folk song. g.hu. ML 3

"**Auf** der Wolga breitem strome." See Sten'ka Razin

"**Auf** flügeln des gesanges." F. Mendelssohn. Words by Heine. g. EDL

"**Auf** flügeln des gesanges" ("On song's bright pinions."—"On wings of music") e.g. GG

"**Auf** flügeln des gesanges" (On wings of song) e.g. HCA

Auf hoher see. See "In mezo al mar"

"**Auf,** seele, zögre nicht." See Finnish hymn ("O, hasten, hasten all")

Aufforderung zum tanz ("Bin ich auch gleich ein taugenichts."—Tanssijatarjokas) Finnish folk song. fi.g. ML 3

Aufforderung zum tanze ("Dreh dich vor dem spielmann."—Napominanje k rejwanju) Wendish folk song. g.we. ML 3

Auguin, Louis
    Pastourelle
    The shepherdess. See Pastourelle

Auld Joe Nicolson's bonnie Nannie. Scottish air. Words by J. Hogg. GS

Auld lang syne ("Should auld acquaintance be forgot") Air: I fee'd a lad at Michaelmas. Words partly rewritten by R. Burns. BB—DFF—DSB—DSC—GOS 1—GS—GSS—KSO—MBS—MFS—SSB—TFP—TFR

Auld Robin Gray ("Young Jamie lo'ed me weel") Air: The bridegroom grat (greits). Words by A. L. Barnard. GS

Auld Robin Gray ("Young Jamie lo'ed me weel") W. Leeves. Words by A. L. Barnard. GE—GOS 1—GS

Aunt Dinah's quilting party. See The quilting party (Fletcher)

Aunt Jemina's plaster ("Aunt Jemima she was old") MFS

Auprès de ma blonde (Bei meiner blonden) French folk song. f.g. ML 1

Aura Lee. <G. R. Poulton. Words by W. W. Fosdick> LAS—PSG—TFO

Aurelia (Wesley) See Hymn of scouting; To-morrow

ᵣ**Aurore** Pradèreᵤ Aurore Bradaire. Negro creole folk song. f. AS

"**Aus** dem felsen" ("Zvira voda iz kamena") Croatian folk song. g.se. ML 2
"**Aus** dem Ungarland, dem schönen" ("Elindultam szép hazámbul") Hungarian folk song. g.hu. ML 3
"**Aus** dem walde tritt die nacht." See Die nacht (Strauss)
"**Aus** der jugendzeit" (From youth's happy day) R. Radecke. Words by F. Rückert. e.g. AT
Aus der rosenzeit (When roses bloom) A. von Fielitz. Words by G. Scherer. e.g. TM
Aus der Tajga. See "Von der insel dort"
"**Aus** feuer ist der geist geschaffen." See Feuerlied (Hempel)
"**Aus** meinen grossen schmerzen" ("Out of my bitter weeping") R. Franz. Words by H. Heine. e.g. HCA
"Aus meinen grossen schmerzen" ("Out of my soul's great sadness") e.g. GG
"Aus meinen grossen schmerzen" ("Where sorrows touch me nearest") e.g. GA
"**Aus** stankutzas hütte dringen." See "La bordei cu crucea naltă"
"**Aus** steinernem kerkerhof schwing dich." See Fussfesselmarsch der sträflinge
Die **auserwählte** ("Mädele, ruck") Swabian folk song. g. EDL
Die **ausgestossene.** See The lonely waif
"**Ausrufer** ruft, ruft von früh bis abends." See Die entlaufene sklavin
Austin, William
Chanticleer (English traditional air)
Australia. Chantey. GSS
"**Australia,** my lads, is a very fine place." See Australia
Austrian hymn (Haydn) See Alma mater—University of North Dakota; Alma mater—University of Pittsburgh; Columbia, God preserve thee free; Deutschland über alles; "Love divine, all loves excelling"; "Praise the Lord, ye heav'ns, adore Him"
Auswandererlied. See "Na Ostland wil ik varen"
"**L'autre** jour à la promenade." See Vous n'êtes pas mon berger
"**L'autrier** par la matinée" ("Morgens wandelnd in der auen") Count Thibaut of Champagne, king of Navarre. f.g. ML 1
Autumn ("Far, hvor flyver svanerne hen") See Efteraar (Lange-Müller)
Autumn ("Re'n trista höstregn strömma ner") See Höst (Palmgren)
"**Autumn** leaves." Words by C. Dickens. MFS
"The **autumn** rain falls sad and drear." See Höst (Palmgren)
Autumn song ("From the boughs o'erhead") Bohemian folk air. Words by J. Irwin. DSB
Autumn song ("The wither'd leaves are flying") German air. Words by R. Compton. DSB
An **autumn** tramp. Hungarian air. Words by J. L. Vandevere. TFO

Autumnal gale. See Herbststurm (Grieg)
["**Avant** de quitter ces lieux"] "Even bravest heart may swell" (Dio possente) C. Gounod. e. WG
"**Ave,** ave, verum corpus." See Ave verum (Mozart)
["**Ave** Maria"] Saviour of sinners. L. Cherubini. e. SSO 1—SSO 2
"**Ave** Maria" ("Father eternal") C. Gounod, arr from Bach. e. SSO 1
"**Ave** Maria" ("Father in heaven") e.l. HCA
Ave Maria ("Come all ye weary") See The cross of Calvary (Gounod)
"**Ave** Maria" ("Ave Maria, hear my pray'r") P. Mascagni. [Words by P. Mazzoni] e.l. TSS 2
"**Ave** Maria" ("O loving Father") e.l. TSS 1
Ave Maria ("See, now the dusk is falling") J. Raff. e. SSO 1—SSO 3
"**Ave** Maria" ("Ave Maria, Maiden mild."—Hymne an die Jungfrau) F. Schubert. Words by W. Scott. e.g.l. GG
Ave Maria! car voici l'heure sainte. See The Christmas angelus (Puget)
"**Ave** Maria sweet voices are singing." See The Christmas angelus (Puget)
"**Ave** sanctissima, we lift our souls to thee." See Evening song to the Virgin (Browne)
Ave verum (The voice of praise) W. A. Mozart. English words by J. L. Vandevere. e.l. TFO. e. only TFG
Avec la garde montante. For English translation see Street-boys' chorus (Bizet)
"**Avec** tes yeux mignonne." See "Mit deinen blauen augen" (Lassen)
"**Avenging** and bright." Irish air: [Cruachan na Feinne, Crooghan a Venee, or Mount of the Fenians] Words by T. Moore. DSC—HMI
Averill, Sara
Holyoke (Old air)
Aves, frutas y viento (Vögel, früchte und wind) Catalan folk song. ca.g. ML 2
The **aviator.** Hungarian folk air. Words by J. L. Vandevere. TFO
Avison, Charles
"Sound the loud timbrel"
L'**avvelenato** (Die liebste als schlangenköchin) Lombardian folk song. g.i. ML 2
Awake ("Awake from sleep") See "Awake from sleep and dreaming" (Schultz)
Awake and sing. Béarnais air. Words by E. Waugh. FC
"**Awake!** arise! ye men of might." See To arms
"**Awake!** awake." Folk song: Berea, Ky. version. SES 1
—Pineville, Ky. version. SES 1
—Allanstand, N.C. version. SES 1
—Alleghany, N.C. version. SES 1
—Black Mountain, N.C. version. SES 1

"Awake! awake."—*Continued*
—Beechgrove, Va. version. SES 1
—Callaway, Va. version. SES 1
—Montvale, Va. version no. 1. SES 1
—Montvale, Va. version no. 2. SES 1
—White Rock, Va. version. SES 1
Variant: "Arise, arise, you drowsy maiden"
"Awake! awake! and softly arise." See Ständchen (Strauss)
"Awake, awake, good people all." See May carol
"Awake, awake, ye drowsy souls, and hear what I shall tell." See The Lamb of God (Passion version)
"Awake! awake! you drowsy sleeper, awake! awake! it's almost day." See "Awake! awake" (Pineville, Ky. version; Allanstand, N.C. version; Alleghany, N.C. version; Callaway, Va. version)
"Awake from sleep and dreaming" (Awake) Round. [C. Schultz] GSS
"Awake, my love, from dreaming." See Recuerdas de amistad
"Awake, my soul, and with the sun" (Ward) Scottish air. [Words by T. Ken] MFS
"Awake, my soul, stretch every nerve." G. F. Händel. Words by P. Doddridge. DSC—TFP
"Awake, my soul, stretch every nerve" (Christmas) GSS
"Awake were they only." See Roedd yn y wiad honno
"Awake with joy, salute the morn." Praetorius. DN
"A-walking and a-talking, a-walking goes I." See The cuckoo (Hindman, Ky. version)
"A-walking and talking and talking goes I." See The cuckoo (Knott or Letcher county, Ky. versions no. 1-2)
"Away! away! the moon and stars are shining." Auber. MFS
Away, away, with sword and drum. See The armored cruiser squadron
Away down in Sunbury. Negro spiritual from Georgia. AS
[Away down souf] Way down souf. S. C. Foster (music and words) WSS
"Away down south in Alabama." See Way down south in Alabama
"Away down south in Dixie land, where sunsets burn in splendor grand." See Here's to the colors of crimson-white (Ludebuehl)
"Away down yonder in a cedar tree, sing song Kitty." See The opossum
"Away down yonder in the cedar swamp, where the water's deep and muddy." See Swing a lady
"Away from Mississippi's vale." See The rose of Alabama
"Away, haul away." See Haul away, Jo
"Away in a manger" (Luther's cradle hymn) J. B. Herbert. Words by M. Luther. e. BB
"Away in the manger." French Noël air. [Words by M. Luther] e. FC
"Away up high in the Sirey peaks." See Rusty Jiggs and Sandy Sam

"Away up yonder in the frozen north." See The frozen north
"Away with melancholy." W. Mozart. GOS 1—MFS
Away you rolling river. See Shenandoah
"Awful, pleasing being, say." G. F. Händel. SSO 2
The awful wedding. Folk song from Georgia. SES 2
Awfully clever. English music-hall song. G. W. Hunt (music and words) SW
Awjinula ('Ē Aygēnoyla) Greek folk song. g.gr. ML 2
"Ay au pena ren andia" (Klage) Basque folk song. ba.g. ML 2
Ay, ay, ay, ay. See Cielito lindo
"Ay, tear her tattered ensign down." See Old Ironsides (Composer unknown); Old Ironsides (Klein)
Aye and therefore be merry. See "A Virgin most pure, as the prophets do tell, hath brought forth a Baby"; "A Virgin unspotted"
"Aye for you my spirit yearneth." See "Ecco purch'a voi ritorno" (Monteverdi)
'Ē Aygēnoyla. See Awjinula
Azmon. See "Oh, for a thousand tongues" (Glaser)
"Azt mondjak nem adnak." See "Is it true then"

B

"B for Barney." Irish air from County Antrim. Words from a Belfast street song. HI 1
"Baa! baa! black sheep." Nursery song. BB
"Baa, baa, black sheep." Nursery song. W. G. Whittaker. CSB 1
Baadfart (Sailing) O. Olsen. da.e. WM 2
"The Babe in Bethlem's manger laid." See The Babe of Bethlehem
"A Babe is born all of a may." Ancient air. 15th century words. OB
"A Babe is born of high natúre." See What tidings bringest thou (Dunstable)
[The Babe of Bethlehem] The Saviour's work. Traditional song. OB
The babes in the wood. Folk song: Kentucky version. MK
—Virginia version. SES 1
"Babes, O babes, I wish you were mine." See The cruel mother (Nellysford, Va. version no. 2)
"Baby, born in Bethlehem." See De newborn baby
"Baby bye, here's a fly." G. B. Loomis. Words by T. Tilton. MFS
"Baby is a sailor boy." See Swing, cradle, swing (Cooper)
Baby mine (The sailor's wife) F. Boott. [Words by C. Mackay] GOS 2
Baby mine. [A. Johnston. Words by C. Mackay] SW

"Baby, O baby, if you were mine." See The cruel mother (Nellysford, Va. version no. 1)

"Baby, sleep! shadows creep." See Cradle song of soldier's wife

"A baby was sleeping." See The angels' whisper

Babylon ("Our harps were tun'd") M. Watson. ASA—TSS 1—TSS 2

Babylon's fallin'. Negro spiritual. HRD

Baby's night. <Christmas song> MFS

Bach, Johann Sebastian
"Ave Maria." See Gounod, C. F. "Ave Maria"
"Beside Thy cradle here I stand"
"Break forth, O beauteous, heavenly light" (from Weihnachts-oratorium. Tr of Brich an, o schönes morgenlicht)
"A Child is born in Bethlehem, alleluia." See Puer natus in Bethlehem: 15th century air arranged
Come let us to the bagpipe's sound
Cradle hymn
"Dir, dir, Jehovah"
Ein Kind geborn zu Bethlehem. See Puer natus in Bethlehem: 15th century air arranged
"Et exultavit" (from Magnificat)
"From ill do Thou defend me"
"Glory now to Thee be given." See Sleepers, wake
"Great God of nations"
Herz und mund und that und leben
"Hush, my dear." See Cradle hymn
"In dulci jubilo"
"In heavenly love abiding"
"Jesu, joy of man's desiring." See Herz und mund und that und leben
"Komm, süsser tod"
"Land of our birth"
"Lord Christ above." See Wo gehest du hin
"Mein gläubiges herze frohlocke"
"My heart ever faithful." See "Mein gläubiges herze frohlocke"
"My soul rejoices." See "Et exultavit"
"Now let every tongue adore Thee." See Sleepers, wake
Nuremberg. See "Praise to God, immortal praise"
Pfingstlied
"Praise to God, immortal praise"
Puer natus in Bethlehem: 15th century air arranged
Sleepers, wake (Tr of Wachet auf)
"Slumber, beloved, and take thy repose" (from Weihnachts-oratorium. Tr of Schlafe, mein liebster, geniesse der ruh')
"Slumber, my lov'd one." See "Slumber, beloved, and take thy repose"
"Sweet spring is advancing"
"These things shall be! a loftier race"
"To thee, Jehovah." See "Dir, dir, Jehovah"
"To us a Child is born from heav'n" (same air as Puer natus in Bethlehem: 15th century air arranged)

"What tongue can tell Thy greatness, Lord": old air arranged
"Willst du dein herz mir schenken"
"Wilt thou to me thy heart give." See "Willst du dein herz mir schenken"
Wo gehest du hin

Des baches wiegenlied. See entry under Des

Bachmetieff, Nikolas Ivanovitch. See Bakhmetiev, Nikolaï Ivanovich

Back in de cornfield. See Massa's in de cold, cold ground (Foster)

"Back of my auntie's cottage, there is a greenwood bright." See Le prisonnier de Hollande (Canadian version)

"Back of my auntie's house, there you will find a pond." See La chanson des métamorphoses

"Backward, turn backward, oh, time, in your flight." See Rock me to sleep (Leslie)

Bacon, Leonard
God be with us (Hatton)

Bacon and greens. Old song. SW

Bacon on the rind (A soldier's lament) Song of the Spanish American war. DSO

Baden polka. See Love and mirth (Strauss)

The badger ballad. University of Wisconsin song. Words by J. E. Olson. KU

"Bagolus m'um lo motsosi artso." See No matter, no matter

Bagpipers' carol. See Canzone d'i zampognari

Die Baike. Jewish folk song. y. KAJ

Bailey, Philip James
The rose and the nightingale (Barnby)

The bailiff's daughter of Islington. <English version> 17th century air: The jolly Pindar. GSS—SSB
—Berea, Ky. version. SES 1
—Hyden, Ky. version. SES 1
The bailiff's daughter. English version. MBS
The bailiff's daughter of Islington (Die vogtstochter aus Islington) English version. e.g. ML 1

Baillie, Joanna
"Saw ye Johnnie comin'? quo' she" (Scottish air)
Woo'd and married and a' (Scottish air) See Ross, A. Woo'd and married and a' (Scottish air)

Bainton, Edgar Leslie
"Ring out, wild bells"

Baird, George Mahaffey Patterson
"Alma mater"—University of Pittsburgh (Haydn)

"Bait a hook to catch a shad." See The shad

"Bake data batter bread good an' brown." See Mona

Baker, Charles
"Always keep a smile for mother"

Baker, Sir Henry Williams, bart.
"The King of love my Shepherd is" (music by Dykes; Gounod)

Baker, John C.
The inquiry
My trundle-bed
Where can the soul find rest.   See
The inquiry
Baker, John S.
Jem, the carter lad
Baker, Louise
"Where Goucher's far flung colors"
(Negro air)
Baker, W. C.
"Hark! I hear an angel sing" (Shrival)
Bakhmetiev, Nikolaï Ivanovich
The Cossack's lullaby
Le bal chez Boulé (Boulé's hop)   Canadian folk song.   e.f.   GC
"Bald gras' ich am Neckar."   See Das ringlein
"Bald ist der nacht ein end' gemacht."
See Morgen-hymne (Henschel)
Il balen del suo sorriso.   G. Verdi.   e.i.
PB
The tempest of the heart.   e.   WG
Balfe, Michael William
Ah! if thou could'st know.   See
Couldst thou but know
"Come with the gipsy bride."   See
Gipsy song
Couldst thou but know
"The day is done and the darkness falls
from the wings of night"
A dream (same air as "I dreamt that I
dwelt in marble halls")
The fair land of Texas (same air as
Fair land of Poland)
Gipsy song (from The Bohemian girl)
"Happy and light" (from The Bohemian girl)
"The heart bowed down" (from The
Bohemian girl)
"I dreamt that I dwelt in marble halls"
(from The Bohemian girl)
Killarney
"The light of other days"
The scarlet and cream (same air as
Pirates' chorus)
"See at your feet" (from The Bohemian girl)
The song of songs
Then you'll remember me
The yellow and blue (same air as Pirates' chorus)
Ball, Ernest R.
Love me and the world is mine
Will you love me in December as you
do in May
Ball, S. B.
Brother and I
The ball of Monsieur Préval.   See
"Michié Préval"
A ballad of a horse-race.   See The bonny
wee mare
A ballad of Napoleon.   See The bonny
bunch of roses
The ballad of the boll weevil.   See De
ballet of de boll weevil
A ballad of the famine.   See Skibbereen
Ballad of the Kremlin.   Siberian prison
song.   e.   SR

Ballad of the sinful rich man.   See Le
parabole du mauvais riche
Ballad of the Volga.   See Mother Volga
The ballad singer.   See Gaily I take my
way (Linley)
A ballad to Queen Elizabeth of the Spanish
Armada.   G. Slater.   Words by A.
Dobson.   CSB 6
Ballade de Jésus-Christ.   See La parabole du mauvais riche
Ballade von Jesus Christus.   See La parabole du mauvais riche
Ballantine, James
Castles in the air (Composer unknown)
Ballatella.   See High! high! aloft (Leoncavallo)
Ballet, William
Lute-book lullaby
De ballet of de boll weevil.   Texas song.
SBA
Variant of: Boll weevil song
A Ballynure ballad.   Irish air from
County Antrim.   Words from an
old ballad.   HI 1
A Ballynure ballad (Ballynurer lied)
e.g.   ML 1
Ballynurer lied.   See A Ballynure ballad
Balm in Gilead ("Sometimes I feel discouraged") Negro spiritual.   TFO
There is a balm in Gilead.   HRD
Balm of Gilead ("Massa lov'd his good old
jamaica") H. T. Bryant.   BNM—
WSS
"Balnoj' brolelis šyvą žirgelį."   See "Sein
weisses rosslein sattelt der bruder"
Baloo, baloo, my wee, wee thing.   See
Scotch cradle-song
Baltzell, Winton James
A sunrise song
Balulalow.   P. Warlock.   Words from
M. Luther.   [Tr of Vom himmel hoch
da komm' ich her]   e.   OB
Bamville croon.   See Mississippi delta
blues (Williams)
Band ob Gideon.   See Gideon's band
The band of children.   Old French air.
Words by F. Kendon.   OB
The band played on.   C. B. Ward.   Words
by J. F. Palmer.   GFS—SRW
"Die bange nacht ist nun herum."   See
Reiterlied (Lyra)
Bange trauer.   For English and Italian
translations see "Esser mesto" (Flotow)
"Bangry Rewey a-courting did ride."   See
Sir Lionel (North Carolina version)
Bangum and the boar.   See Sir Lionel
(Knott or Letcher county, Ky. version)
Banjo blues (Blue man Sam's lament)
S. Williams.   HB
Der bänkelsänger.   See Er passagallo
The banks of Allan water.   Traditional
air arr by C. E. Horn.   Words
by M. G. Lewis.   GOS 2—GS
"On the banks of Allan water."   MBS
The banks of Sacramento ("Boston city is
afire") Capstan chantey.   TSB 2
For variants see following songs of
same title

The **banks** of Sacramento ("The Camptown ladies sing this song") Negro chantey.   WSE
    Variant of: De Camptown races (Foster)
The **banks** of Sacramento ("Ho, boys, ho! for California, O") Fragment. SBA
    Variant: California
The **banks** of Sacramento ("In the Black Ball line I served my time") Capstan chantey.   SBS
The **banks** of sweet Dundee.   Folk song: Manchester, Ky. version.   SES 1
—Teges, Ky. version.   SES 1
—Tennessee version.   SES 1
The **banks** of the blue Moselle.   G. H. Rodwell.   <Words by E. Fitzball> GOS 2
The **banks** of the Dee, Parody on ("'Twas winter, and blue Tory noses were freezing")   Air: The banks of the Dee.   Words by O. Arnold.   DSO
[The **banks** of the Don] By the river Don. M. P. Moussorgsky.   [Words by A. V. Kol'tsov]   e.   GA
Bannocks o' bear-meal.   [Jacobite song. Air: The Killogie]   Words by R. Burns.   BOS 2
Banstead Downs.   See Georgie
"**Baptist**, Baptist is my name."   See Hard trials
Ar **baradoz** (Das paradies)   Breton folk song.   br.g.   ML 1
Barbara Allen ("In Scarlet town where I was born")   English folk song. KSO—MBS
    Barbara Allan ("It was in and about the Mart'mas time")   Scottish version.   GS
    Barbara Allen ("All in, all in the month of May") Barbourville, Ky. version no. 1.   SES 1
    Barbara Allen ("All in the merry month of May") Kentucky version no. 1. MK
    Barbara Allen ("All in the merry month of May") Carmen, N.C. version. SES 1
    Barbara Allen ("All in the month, the month of May") Tennessee version. SES 1
    Barbara Allen ("Down in London where I was raised") Pineville, Ky. version.   SES 1
    Barbara Allen ("Early, early in the spring")   Pine Mountain, Ky. version.   SES 1
    Barbara Allen ("In yonders town where I was born") Chicopee county, Ga. version no. 1.   SES 1
    Barbara Allen ("One cold and cloudy day") Chicopee county, Ga. version no. 3.   SES 1
    Barbara Allen ("One day, one day, in the month of May") Barbourville, Ky. version no. 2.   SES 1

    Barbara Allen ("One Monday morn in the month of May") Greenwood, Va. version.   SES 1
    Barbara Allen ("Sweet William died") Nellysford, Va. version.   SES 1
    Barbara Allen ("Sweet William was down") Hot Springs, N.C. version. SES 1
    Barbara Allen ("'Twas in the merry month of May") Habersham county, Ga. version.   SES 1
    Barbara Allen ("'Twas in the merry month of May") Kentucky version no. 2.   SES 1
    Barbra Allen ("In London City where I once did dwell") Georgia version. SBA
Barbara Buck.   Folk song from Virginia. SES 2
Barbauld, Mrs Anna Letitia (Aikin)
    "Praise to God, immortal praise" (Bach)
Barber, spare those hairs.   College parody.   H. Russell.   Words by J. Love.   SRW
Barber's cry.   Folk song from North Carolina.   SES 2
Barcarola ("Oh pescator dell' onda") See "Oh pescator dell' onda"
Barcarolle ("Dites, la jeune belle")   See "Dites, la jeune belle" (Gounod)
Barcarolle ("Silent now")   See "Silent now the drowsy bird" (Offenbach)
"Una **barchetta** in mar solcando va." Donizetti.   e.i.   PB
Barclay, B. S.
    "Come, O come with me, the moon is beaming" (Italian air)
"**Bárcsak** ez az éjszaka."   See "Wenn die nacht doch dauern möcht'"
Bard, Vivien
    A toast to De Pauw
The **bard** of Armagh.   Irish air from County Tyrone.   Traditional words. HI 2
Bard of Thomond, pseud.   See Hogan, Michael
Baring-Gould, Sabine
    "Now the day is over" (Barnby)
    "Onward, Christian soldiers" (Sullivan)
The **bark** canoe.   See My bark canoe
Barker, George A.
    Dublin bay
    Irish emigrant's lament
    "The time of the singing of birds" (same air as Dublin bay)
    "Why do summer roses fade"
Barker, T. T.
    Cradle song of soldier's wife (Composer unknown)
"**Barna** legény elbujdosott."   See "My brown boy is hiding away"
Barnard, Lady Ann (Lindsay)
    Auld Robin Gray (Scottish air; also music by Leeves)
Barnard, C.
    The first swallow (Irish air)
    The gap in the hedge (Irish air)
Barnard, Mrs Charles.   See Barnard, Mrs Charlotte (Alington)

Barnard, Mrs Charlotte (Alington)
Composer
"Hail and farewell." See Parting graduation song
"Jesus, tender Shepherd, hear me"
"Little by little"
Parting graduation song
Parting song. See Parting graduation song
Silver chimes
"When all the world is young"
Composer and author
"Come back to Erin"
"I cannot sing the old songs"
"Take back the heart"
We'd better bide a wee
You and I
Author
The blue Alsatian mountains (Maybrick)
"I am content" (Sainton-Dolby)

Barnard, F. C.
The tar's farewell (Maybrick) See Burnand, F. C. The tar's farewell (Maybrick)

Barnby, Sir Joseph
Cradle song of Virgin. See "The Virgin stills the crying"
Crossing the bar
"Fair Luna"
Holy Trinity. See "One holy church of God appears"
Merrial. See "Now the day is over"
'Neath our flag
"Now the day is over"
"One holy church of God appears"
The rose and the nightingale
"Sweet and low"
Twilight. See "Now the day is over"
"The Virgin stills the crying"
"When morning gilds the skies" (Tr of Beim frühen morgenlicht)

Barnes, H. W. B.
Alma mater—Furman university

Barnes, Manton M.
Hail C. I. T.

Barnes, Paul
Good-bye, Dolly Gray

Barnett, John
The Highland minstrel boy
"I once knew a Normandy maid"
Rose of Lucerne
The Swiss toy girl. See Rose of Lucerne

Barney, James A.
"Little footsteps"

Barney Buntline₁ A sailor's consolation. ₍Composer unknown. Words by W. Pitt₎ US

Barney O'Hea ("Now let me alone, tho' I know you won't") S. Lover (music and words) HMI—SI

The **barnyard** family. Old song. BB
Variant of: The barnyard song

The **barnyard** song. Kentucky mountain folk song. TFG
Variants: The barnyard family; Bought a cow

Barr, M. A.
Lethe (Boott)

Barrera y Calleja,
Granadinas

Barri, Odoardo, pseud. See Slater, Edward

Barrows, O. R.
Swinging 'neath the old apple-tree

Barry, Edward, pseud. See Slater, Edward

Barry, Michael Joseph
Saint Patrick's day (Irish folk air)

Bartholomew, William
"Hear my prayer" (Mendelssohn)

Bartlett, Charles D.
For Maine

Bartlett, Draper Cooke
"To the fairest college"

Bartlett, Homer Newton
"The wind is awake"

Bartlett, James Carroll
Grass and roses

Bas, William. See Basse, William

"**Base** traitors, for you my heart's peace." See Ella piangea la perfida (Mercadante)

The **bashful** young lady. C. W. Glover. SW

Baskette, Billy
Goodby Broadway, hello France

Basque lullaby ("Lullaby, twilight is spreading") Folk air. Words by F. Hoare. LAS

Basse, William
The hunter in his career (Composer unknown)

Batchelder, Frederick W.
"In heavenly love abiding"

Bates, David
"Speak gently—it is better far" (Wallace)

Bates, Katherine Lee
America, the beautiful (music by MacFarlane; Ward)

Battell, Edith
"Speed up" (Fairfax)

The **battle** call. Song of the Mexican war. Air: The boatmen's dance. DSO

The **battle** cry of freedom ("Yes, we'll rally round the flag") G. F. Root (music and words) BB—DSO—LAS—TFP

The **battle** hymn of the republic ("Mine eyes have seen the glory") Air: John Brown's body, arr by W. Steffe. Words by J. W. Howe. BB—DSB—DSC—DSO—GSS—LAS— LSB— MBS —MFS—TFP—TFR

The **battle** of Paris. Song of the European war. DSO

The **battle** of Shiloh. Folk song from Virginia. SES 2

The **battle** of Stonington. Words by P. Freneau. DSO

The **battle** of the kegs. Revolutionary song. Air: Yankee Doodle. Words by F. Hopkinson. DSO

The **battle** prayer. See Gebet während der schlacht (Himmel)

"**Ein** bauer einst war, der hatt' ein klein mädchen." See La filadora

"**Der** bauer hat ein taubenhaus." See Vom bauern und den tauben (Taubert)

Bauerle, Adolf
Frohe botschaft (Müller)
"Bäuerlein, bäuerlein." See The farmer

Baum, M. Louise
Carmeña (Wilson)
Goblet of youth (Lecocq)
"Baum, dich hab' ich gepflegt mit zarter liebe." See Canzonetta di campagnuolo
Der baum im Odenwald ("Es steht ein baum") Volksweise after J. F. Reichardt. g. EDL

Baumbach, Rudolf
Die lindenwirtin (Abt)
Der schwur (Bohm)

Bax, Clifford
"Come, see where golden-hearted spring" (Händel)
The bay of Biscay. J. Davy. Words by A. Cherry. MBS
Bay of Dublin. See "O bay of Dublin"

Bayly, Thomas Haynes
Composer
"Touch not the cup" (same air as Long, long ago)
Composer and author
"Gaily the troubadour"
Long, long ago
Author
Erin is my home (Bohemian or German air)
Isle of beauty (Whitmore)
The mistletoe' bough (Bishop)
"Oh! leave me to my sorrow" (Irish air)
"She wore a wreath of roses" (Knight)

Bazot, Eugène
"Vous dansez, marquise" (Lemaire)
"Be accurs'd, oh! world" ("Elátkozom ezt a cudar világot") Hungarian folk song. e.hu. KH 2
"Be comforted." See The Lord worketh wonders (Händel)
Be it ever so humble. See Home, sweet home (Bishop)
Be kind to the loved ones at home. [I. B. Woodbury (music and words)] GOS 1—SW
Be mention'd in the promis'd land. See "My brother, I wish you well"
Be merry, be merry. 15th century air and words. DNS
"Be mine the delight." C. F. Gounod. [Tr of À moi les plaisirs] e. WG
Be near me still. See Gebet (Hiller)
"Be sok falut, be sok várost." See "In full many a town"
Be still my heart] "As a bird in prison pining." Croatian folk song. Words adapted. e. DSB
"Be thou faithful unto death." Mendelssohn. [Tr of Sei getreu in den tod] e. SSO 3
"Be Thou my helper." G. A. Hasse. e. SSO 2
"Be Thou, O God, exalted high." See Old hundred (Franc?)
Be Thou with me. See Gebet (Hiller)

Beale, Thomas Willert
Composer
The last words of Emmet. See "When Erin shall stand 'mid the isles of the sea"
"When Erin shall stand 'mid the isles of the sea"
Author
"At eve I wander'd by the shore" (Irish air)
The bells of Aberdovey (Welsh air)
The emigrants (Irish air)
Forget not the angels (Irish air)
"I'm a poor Irish girl" (Irish air)
I'm a poor stranger (Irish air)
The lake of Coolfin (Irish air)
"Mourn not for me" (Irish air)
"The old year is dying" (Welsh carol)
"Though all bright flowers" (Irish air)

Beall, Thomas V.
Rally song
Bear de burden. Negro spiritual. WFN
"The bear went over the mountain." <Air: Chanson de Malbrouk> TFP
Beatrice. F. von Holstein. Scene from Schiller's "Bride of Messina." e.g. DCA
"Le beau galant" ("The gallant soldier") Folk song from Lorraine. e.f. CBF 1
"Beauing, belleing, dancing, drinking." See The rakes of Mallow

Beaumont, Francis, and Fletcher, John
Take, O take those lips away (Williams) See Shakespeare, W.
Take, O take those lips away (Williams)
The beauteous song. See Come unto me (Slater)
Beautiful bells ("On the·breeze") E. O. Lyte. MFS
"Beautiful bird, in the morning sing." See Beautiful bird, sing on (Howe)
Beautiful bird, sing on. T. H. Howe. GE
"Beautiful blue bells." W. H. Delehanty. SW
Beautiful Canaan nights ("Yofim hallelos") Palestinean folk song. e.he. BNP
The beautiful day. D. Hime. MFS
"Beautiful dreamer." S. C. Foster (music and words) WSS
"Beautiful Erin." S. Glover. Words by Mrs W. Boate. SI
"Beautiful faces." Words by D. Swing. MFS
"A beautiful maiden with heart so cold." O. Straus. e. WLO
"Beautiful sea, beautiful sea, oh, how I love on thy bosom to roam." Children's song. MFS
"Beautiful spring-time." Verdi. MFS
"Beautiful star in heaven so bright" (Star of the evening) J. M. Sayles (music and words) GOS 1
"Beauty lately." See Questo é il cielo (Händel)
Beauty's eyes. F. P. Tosti. Words by F. E. Weatherly. BST

Beaver creek.   American mountain song.
  RA
  Variant of: Kemo kimo
"**Because** I love you, dear."   C. B. Haw-
  ley.   Words by W. H. Stanton.
  AT
Because of you.   L. Strickland (music
  and words)   BST
Beckel, James Cox
  Old easy-chair by the fire
Becker, Niklas
  Der deutsche Rhein (Schumann)
Becker, Reinhold
  Frühlingszeit.   See "Wenn der früh-
    ling auf die berge steigt"
  Spring.   See "Wenn der frühling auf
    die berge steigt"
  "Wenn der frühling auf die berge
    steigt"
Becker, Valentin Eduard
  Lied fahrender schüler
Becket, Thomas à
  Columbia, the gem of the ocean
  The red white and blue.   See Colum-
    bia, the gem of the ocean
Beddome, Benjamin
  "Heirs of unending life" (Nägeli)
Bedenklichkeiten ("Grad aus dem wirts-
  haus")   Spanish air: La madrilena.
  Words by H. von Mühler.   g.   EDL
Bedfordshire May day carol.   See "I've
  been rambling all the night"
Bedouin love-song.   C. B. Hawley.
  ₁Words by B. Taylor₁   SFB
Bee, Barnard Elliott
  The infantry (German air)
The **bee** and the pup.   BB—TFB
Beecher (Zundel)   See "Light of ages
  and of nations"; "They who tread the
  path of light"
"**Been** here since de early morn."   See
  Get away from dis co'nfiel'
"**Been** in the pen so long."   Negro jail
  song.   SBA
"**Been** on the hummer since ninety-four."
  See A. R. U.
Beers, Mrs Ethelinda (Eliot)
  "All quiet along the Potomac tonight"
    (Hewitt)
Beethoven, Ludwig van
  Adelaïde
  "Ah! perfido"
  An die freude
  "Behold, my love, how green the
    groves"
  Busslied
  Constancy.   See "Ich liebe dich, so
    wie du mich"
  Contrition.   See Busslied
  Die ehre Gottes aus der natur
  "The heavens are telling."   See Die
    ehre Gottes aus der natur
  "The heavens resound."   See Die ehre
    Gottes aus der natur
  Homeland mine
  Hymn to joy.   See Open, Lord, my
    inward ear
  "Ich liebe dich, so wie du mich"
  "Keep us, O Lord"
  "Kennst du das land"
  The kiss.   See Der kuss

Der kuss
Metronome canon
Mignon.   See "Kennst du das land"
Morning song.   See "Now with cre-
  ation's morning song"
"Now with creation's morning song"
  (Tr of Lux ecce surgit aurea)
"O come, sweet slumber"
Ode to joy.   See An die freude
Open, Lord, my inward ear
Opferlied
Penitence.   See Busslied
The praise of God.   See Die ehre
  Gottes aus der natur
The scale
"To God eternal"
"With perfidy inhuman."   See "Ah!
  perfido"
"**Befo'** I'd stay in hell one day."   See
  My soul's been anchored in de Lord
"**Before** us spread the shining sea."   See
  Am meer (Schubert)
Begegnung im walde.   See Skogmöte has
  thorgjer skjelle
"A **beggar-man** laid himself down to sleep."
  See Rumsty-ho
The **beggar's** song ("How jolly are we beg-
  gars") R. Leveridge.   WOE
Beglückt darf nun dich.   For English
  translation see Pilgrims' chorus (Wag-
  ner)
"**Begone!** dull care."   17th century air:
  The queen's jig.   BOS 2—DSB—TFG
"**Behind** our house stands an old apple
  tree."   See "Derrièr' chez nous il
  pousse une ente"
Behind the times so they told him.   See
  Just behind the times (Harris)
"**Behind** yon hills where Lugar flows."
  See My Nannie, O
"**Behold** a noble hero."   See The bold
  militiaman
"**Behold,** a rose of beauty."   See Lo! a
  fair rose is blooming (Praetorius)
"**Behold** a simple tender Babe."   See New
  Prince, new pomp (Ireland)
"**Behold** a Virgin shall conceive" (see Song
  Index)
  Also in "O Thou that tellest good
    tidings to Zion" (Händel)   SSO 2
"**Behold** how brightly breaks the morning."
  See Fishermen's chorus (Auber)
Behold! I stand at the door.   W. H.
  Jude.   Words by L. Morrison.   CSS 2
"**Behold,** I tell you a mystery" (see Song
  Index)
  Also in "The trumpet shall sound"
    (Händel)   SSO 2—SSO 4
"**Behold,** my love, how green the groves."
  L. van Beethoven.   ₁Words by R.
  Burns₁   DSB
"**Behold** the brilliant sun in all its splen-
  dor."   See 'O sole mio (Capua)
"**Behold** the monarch of the woods."   See
  Monarch of the woods (Cherry)
"**Behold** the sabre of my father."   See
  The sabre song (Offenbach)
"**Behold,** thy King draws near the city
  gates."   See Jerusalem (Parker)
"**Behold,** 'tis May."   See "Voici venir le
  joli mai, qu'il est plaisant, qu'il est gai"

"Behold what splendour, hear that shout."
See The splendour
Behrend, Arthur Henry
Daddy
Behring sea song. ⌊J. R. Sweney⌋ US
"Bei dem glanz der abendröthe." See Die
bekehrte (Stange)
"Bei dem heitren frühlingssonnenscheine"
("A gdy będzie słońce i pogoda")
Polish folk song. g.p. ML 3
"Bei der schönen meisterin." See Küssen
ist keine sünd' (Eysler)
"Bei des mondes scheine." See "Au clair
de la lune"
"Bei mein rebben is gewesen." See A
ganevoh
Bei meiner blonden. See Auprès de ma
blonde
Die **beiden** grenadiere (The two grenadiers)
R. Schumann. Words by H. Heine.
e.f.g. GG
Beim frühen morgenlicht. For English
translation see "When morning gilds
the skies"
⌊Beim mondenschein⌋ "Gestern beim mon-
denschein" (Die kranzbinderin) Volks-
lied aus Österreich-Schlesien. g. EDL
Die **bekehrte** (Damon) M. Stange.
Words by J. W. von Goethe. e.g.
BST—TM
"**Bekränzt** mit laub den lieben vollen
becher." See Rheinweinlied (André)
Belfast mountains. Folk song from
Sussex. BET
Belgian rose, my drooping Belgian rose.
See My Belgian rose (Benoit, Leven-
son, and Garton)
Belief. See Je crois en vous (Berlioz)
"**Believe** me, if all those endearing young
charms." Air: My lodging is on
the cold ground, arr by J. A.
Stevenson. Words by T. Moore.
BB—DSB—DSC—GOS 1— HMI—
SI—TFP—TFR
Those endearing young charms. MFS
"**B'lieve** to my soul there's something goin'
on wrong." See Goin' down that
long long lonesome road (Nash)
"**Believer,** light the lamp." See The
white marble stone (South Carolina
version no. 1)
"**Believer,** O shall I die." See Shall I
die
Bell, Vincent Hardy
Here's to the colors of crimson-white
(Ludebuehl)
The **bell** ("The bell doth toll") See "The
bell doth toll"
Bell carol ("In every town and village")
French carol air: Je sais, Vierge Marie.
Words by S. Wilson. OB
The **bell-cow.** American mountain song.
RA
Bell da ring ("I know member") Negro
spiritual: South Carolina version
no. 1. AS
Bell da ring ("Do my brudder") South
Carolina version no. 2. AS

"The **bell** doth toll." Round. BB—
KSO—TFP
The bell. GSS
The **bell** goes a-ringing for Sai-rah. C. W.
Hunt (music and words) SW
The **bell** is ringing. Round. ⌊F. Silcher⌋
BB
The **bell** ringer. W. V. Wallace. Words
by J. Oxenford. GOS 2
"La **bell'**, si nous étiom' dedans" (Nique
nac no muse.—Knick knack, mein
·dudelsack) Normandy folk song. f.g.
ML 1
Bell song ("The bells ring out with a
solemn tone") Drinnenberg. Words
by J. L. Vandevere. TFO
"**Bella** e di sol vestita." Donizetti. e.i.
PB
Bella figlia dell' amore. For English
translation see "Fairest daughter of
the graces" (Verdi)
"**Bella** siccome un angelo in terra pelle-
grino." Donizetti. e.i. PB
Bellamy, Claxson
Lullaby (Jakobowski)
Belle Layotte. Negro creole folk song
from Louisiana. f. AS
⌊"**Belle** nuit"⌋ "Lovely night." J. Offen-
bach. e. WG
Belle ob Baltimore. J. G. Evans. BB—
WSS
Belle of Baltimore. SW
"**Belle** qui tiens ma vie captive dans tes
yeux." See Pavane
Bellini, Vincenzo
Aladdin
Castles in Spain. See Aladdin
Flowers for the brave
"Oh! divina Agnese" (from Beatrice di
Tenda)
"Oh! gladly now we hail thee"
"Oh, my bravest and best" (from I
Capuleti ed i Montecchi)
"One by one"
"Qui m'accolse oppresso, errante"
(from Beatrice di Tenda)
"Se Romeo t'uccise un figlio" (from
I Capuleti ed i Montecchi)
"Tu non sai con quei begli occhi" (from
La sonnambula)
"Vi ravviso, o luoghi ameni" (from La
sonnambula)
The **bellman's** song. See "The moon
shines bright"
The **bells** ("Les feuilles s'ouvraient")
See Les cloches (Debussy)
The **bells** of Aberdovey ("In the peaceful
evening time") Welsh air <attrib-
uted to C. Dibdin> Words by W.
Maynard. GE—LAS—MBS
⌊The **bells** of Novgorod⌋ "Zvonīli zvony v
Novgorodře" (Die glocken von Now-
gorod) Russian folk song. g.r.
ML 1
The **bells** of Osney. Three-part round.
TFP
The **bells** of paradise I heard them ring.
See "Down in yon forest"

The **bells** of Shandon ("With deep affection") Irish air: The groves of Blarney. Words by F. Mahony (Father Prout) HMI—SI

The **bells** of Shandon ("With deep affection") J. J. Daly. Words by F. Mahony (Father Prout) SI

"The **bells** ring out with a solemn tone." See Bell song (Drinnenberg)

"**Beloved** one, come." R. Wagner. ₁Tr of Geliebter, komm'! sieh' dort die grotte₁ e. WG

Beltzhoover-Dille, Lucie
"By the blue Monongahela"

Ben Bolt ("Oh! don't you remember sweet Alice") German air arr by N. Kneass. Words by T. D. English. DFF—GOS 1—KSO—MFS—WSS

Ben Jonson's carol. See "I sing the Birth was born to-night" (Boughton)

Bendall,
"Sweet Briar, Sweet Briar, flower fair"

Bendel, Franz
"See the light is fading"
"Wie berührt mich wundersam"
"Wondrous is the power." See "Wie berührt mich wundersam"

"**Bendin'** knees a-achin'." See O'er the crossing

"**Beneath** the silv'ry moon along the river way." See Nanette

Benedict, Sir Julius
"By the sad sea waves" (from The brides of Venice)
"The colleen bawn" (from The lily of Killarney)
"Eily mavourneen" (from The lily of Killarney)
Nel dolce incanto (from L'elisire d'amore)
"O Thou afflicted" (from St Peter)

Benjamin, Park
The old sexton (Russell)
To arms (Old air)

Bennett, Bertram
"Let's cheer again for Temple" (Zoob)

Bennett, G. J.
John Anderson's gane

Bennett, Henry, and Toleken, W., of Cork
"Saint Patrick was a gentleman" (Irish air)

Bennett, Sir William Sterndale
"Dawn, gentle flower"
"His salvation is nigh them that fear Him" (from The woman of Samaria)

Benny Havens, oh. West Point military academy song. <Air: The wearing of the green. Words by Lieutenant O'Brien> DSO—US

Benoit, George; Levenson, Robert, and Garton, Ted
My Belgian rose

Benson, Louis Fitzgerald
"O Thou Whose feet" (Franc)

Béranger, Pierre Jean de
Le roi d'Yvetot (French air)

Bérat, Frédéric
Ma Normandie
My Normandy. See Ma Normandie

Les **berceaux** (The cradles) G. Fauré. Words by A. Sully-Prudhomme. e.f. ASN

Berceuse ("Dors, dors, mon petit, dors."—Lullaby) Folk song from Alsace. e.f. CBF 1

Berceuse ("Gué-gué Solingaie") See "Gué-gué Solingaie"

Berceuse ("Sleep, my pretty one") See Cradle-song (Grechaninov)

Berdan, Harry B.
The girl I loved in sunny Tennessee (Redcliffe)
She was bred in old Kentucky (Redcliffe)
You're not the only pebble on the beach (Redcliffe)

Beresford, Curtis R.
"The red and black shall triumph" (Waterman)

Berger, Olof Vilhelm Peterson-. See Peterson-Berger, Olof Vilhelm

₁**Bergers,** pour qui cette fête₁ "Angels we have heard on high." Ancient Noël. e. FC—TFG

Bergh, Arthur
The gypsy king

Bergman, Bo
Adagio (Rangström)
Stjärnöga (Rangström)

Bergmannslied ("Glück auf") Volkslied aus dem Odenwald. g. EDL

Berkeley, George Charles Grantley Fitzhardinge
The clever woman (Blewitt)

Berlin, Irving
The schoolhouse blues

Berlioz, Hector
Belief. See Je crois en vous
Je crois en vous
"Nessun maggior piacere"
"No joy could be more thrilling." See "Nessun maggior piacere"
The shepherds' farewell to the Holy Family (from L'enfance du Christ. Tr of L'adieu des bergers à la Sainte Famille)

Bernard de Clairvaux, Saint
"Jesus, the very thought of Thee" (Rossini. Tr of Jesu dulcis memoria)

Bernard de Cluny
"Jerusalem the golden" (music by Ewing; Le Jeune. Tr of Urbs Syon aurea)

Bernard, Paul
Ça fait peur aux oiseaux
That frightens the birds. See Ça fait peur aux oiseaux

Bernasconi, Andrea
"Se non ti moro allato" (from Adriano in Siria)

Bernáth, Gáspár
"Az alföldön halász legény vagyok én." See The fisherman
The fisherman
"Where the Tisza's torrents through the prairies swell." See The fisherman

"**Bernytis** į karą jojo." See "Der jüngling zog aus in den krieg"

"Berries red and bright has the holly tree."
See Merry Yuletide (Rimskiï-Korsakov)

Berry, Romeyn
The big red team (Tourison)

Bertin, Fernand
Plainte d'Ariane (Coquard)

"Beside a Belgian 'staminet." See The
passing pilot

"Beside me set the ruddy glowing heather."
See Allerseelen (Strauss)

"Beside the old stone fountain." See
Der lindenbaum (Schubert)

"Beside the rushing water there stood an
ancient mill." See "In einem kühlen
grunde"

"Beside the stream a maiden fair." See
Old Dutch song

"Beside the window sittest thou, Marie."
See Marie (Jensen)

"Beside Thy cradle here I stand." J. S.
Bach. FC

The best thing in life. C. K. Harris (music and words) SW

Der besuch am grabe (Rów wopytanje)
Wendish folk song. g.we. ML 3

Bethany. See "Nearer, my God, to
Thee" (Mason)

Bethlehem ("Dans cette étable") See
"Dans cette étable"

Betrayal ("Die wasserlilie kichert leis'")
See Verrath (Brückler)

"Betsey was a maiden fair." Folk song.
KSO
Variant of: Betsy

Betsy. Folk song from North Carolina.
SES 2
Variant: "Betsey was a maiden fair"

ʟThe better wishɹ Robin Ruff. H. Russell.
GOS 1

Bettler-liebe (Pauper-love) A. Bungert.
Words by T. Storm. e.g. TM

Betty Anne. Folk song from North
Carolina. SES 2

"Between us twain were woven tender ties."
See "Un doux lien" (Delbrück)

Beulah land ("I've reached the land of
corn and wine") J. R. Sweney. Words
by E. Page ɟor E. P. Stitesɹ MFS

Beulah land ("A little while, O beautiful
land") M. M. Hughes. CSS 1—
CSS 2

Beuler, J.
Tea in the arbor

"Beware! dearest comrades all." Round.
J. Haydn. e. CSB 6

Beyond all earthly ken those joys divine
remain. See "Glory now to thee be
given" (Bach)

De bezem. Dutch round. d.e. BB

Bianchi, Francesco
La mia virtù non cede (from L'orfano
cinese)
Tu seconda i voti miei (from L'orfano
cinese)

Bibabutzemann. e.g. MFS

Bible stories. Old American song. US

Bickerstaffe, Isaac
"The echoing horn" (Arne)

A bicycle built for two. See Daisy Bell
(Dacre)

"Bid from thy soul, my love, all fears depart." See "Sgombra dall' anima"
(Latilla)

"Bid me discourse." H. R. Bishop. Words
by W. Shakespeare. EB

"Bid me to live" (To Anthea) J. L.
Hatton. Words by R. Herrick.
HCA

Big C. University of California song.
H. P. Williams. Words by N. S.
McLaren. AIS

Big-eye rabbit. American mountain song.
RA

"Big girl scouts walk slow." See Every
girl scout's round

The big red team. Cornell university
song. C. E. Tourison. Words by
R. Berry. AI—AIS

The big sunflower. See Happy as a big
sunflower (Emerson)

Bigerlow. Song of the Great Lakes.
SBA

Bile 'em cabbage down. American mountain song. RA
Variant of: The squirrel

Bill Bailey, won't you please come home.
H. Cannon (music and words) GFS

Billy boy. See My boy Willie

Billy Grimes. Folk song from Virginia.
SES 2

Billy Riley. Halliard chantey. SBS
Variant: "O Billy Riley"

Billy Venero. Cowboy song. LSC

Billy Vite and Molly Green. Old song.
SW

Bim ba bam, bam bim ba bam. See Der
philosoph

"Bin ein armer, kleiner bube." See I
maccheroni

"Bin ein schäfer, alt an jahren." See Der
alte schäfer

"Bin ich auch gleich ein taugenichts."
See Aufforderung zum tanz (Finnish
folk song)

"Bin ich auch nur'ne bauerndirn." See
"What though I be a country lass"

"Bin ich mir a kale." Jewish folk song.
y. KAJ

"Bin ich mir a schneider'l." Jewish folk
song. y. SY

Bin so traurig, matt und trübe. See The
old folks at home (Foster)

"Bind' auf dein haar." See "My mother
bids me bind my hair" (Haydn)

Bingham, G. Clifton
The good Shepherd (Slater)
In old Madrid (Trotter)
Love's old, sweet song (Molloy)
Sion (Rodney)

Bingham, Harold Woodworth
"All hail blue and gold"

Bingham, Seth Daniels
"Mother of men"

Bingo, Eli Yale ("Bingo, Bingo, Bingo")
C. Porter. LAS

"Die Binschgauer wollten wallfahrten
gehn." See Die Pinzgauer wallfahrt

Binyon, Laurence
  The shepherd (Austrian folk carol air)
Binzer, August, freiherr von
  Composer and author
  "Stosst an! (Jena) soll leben"
  Author
  "Wir hatten gebauet ein stattliches
    haus" (Thüringische volksweise)
[The birch in the meadow] "Vo polѐe bereza
  stoѝala" (Die birke)   Russian folk
  song.   g.r.   ML 1
[The birchen brand] "Luchīna, luchīnushka
  berezovaѝa" ("Du mein span") Russian
  folk song.   g.r.   ML 1
The bird and the rose.   A. E. Horrocks.
  Words by R. S. Hichens.   HCA
"Bird in a cage."   Folk song from Ken-
  tucky.   SBA
The bird song.   Folk song: North Caro-
  lina version.   SES 2
  —Virginia version.   SES 2
"Birdie sweet."   MFS
The birdies' ball.   A. Street.   GOS 2
The birds ("From out of a wood."—Žežulka
  z lesa vylitla, kuku)   Czech folk carol.
  e.   OB
"Birds are in the woodland."   Kinder-
  garten song.   MFS
The bird's nest ("A briery lane where wild-
  birds sing")   Words by H. Thomas.
  MFS
[Birds of a feather] Downy jailbirds.   E.
  Jakobowski.   WLO
The birds' return.   Bohemian folk air.
  Words by J. B. Walters.   BB
"The birds sleeping gently."   See Alice,
  where art thou (Ascher)
Birdseye, George W.
  I have sought, and I have found
    (Keller)
Die birke.   See The birch in the meadow
The birks of Aberfeldy.   Scottish air:
  <Birks of Abergeldy>   Words by
  R. Burns.   GS
Bishop, Sir Henry Rowley
  "Bid me discourse"
  The bloom is on the rye.   See When
    the bloom is on the rye
  Chime again, beautiful bells
  "Come, my gallant soldier, come"
  The dashing white sergeant
  Female volunteer for Mexico (same air
    as The dashing white sergeant)
  Home, sweet home
  The mistletoe bough
  My native Highland home
  When the bloom is on the rye
Bishop, Thomas Brigham
  The moon behind the hill
  Pretty as a picture
Bissell, A. D.
  The ghost-dance
"Bist du mit mir broigis."   Jewish folk
  song.   y.   KAJ
"Bist du treu, Garufalia, mir."   See Garu-
  faliá
Bitte ("Liebster schatz, i bitt' di schön."—
  Entreaty)   C. Bohm.   Words by H.
  Schmidt.   e.g.   AT

Bitte ("Weil' auf mir, du dunkles auge."—
  Request)   R. Franz.   Words by N.
  Lenau.   e.g.   GG
Die bitte ("Weil' auf mir, du dunkles auge."
  —The request)   E. Moór.   Words
  by N. Lenau.   e.g.   HCA
[Bitte] "Weil' auf mir, du dunkles auge"
  ("Turn to me, dark eye so tender") E.
  Sjögren.   Words by N. Lenau.   e.g.
  WM 2
Bitter beer.   Old song.   SW
Bivins, Nathan
  I ain't seen no messenger boy
Bizet, Georges
  "Agnus Dei"
  Castanet song (from Carmen)
  Chanson du toréador (from Carmen)
  "La fleur que tu m'avais jetée" (from
    Carmen)
  Habanera (from Carmen)
  "I am here, do thy will" (from Carmen.
    Tr of Vous pouver m'arrêter)
  "I try not to own that I tremble."
    See Je dis que rien ne m'épouvante
  "If you love me" (from Carmen. Tr of
    Si tu m'aimes, Carmen)
  Je dis que rien ne m'épouvante (from
    Carmen)
  "Lamb of God."   See "Agnus Dei"
  "Ma vie a son secret"
  Man of Alcala (from Carmen. Tr of
    Halte-là, qui va là)
  March of the toreadors (from Carmen.
    Tr of Voici, débouchant sur la
    place)
  "My home in yonder vale" (from Car-
    men. Tr of Ma mère je la vois)
  "My life a secret owns."   See "Ma
    vie a son secret"
  Séguédille (from Carmen)
  Street-boys' chorus (from Carmen. Tr
    of Avec la garde montante)
  "This flow'r that once to me you gave."
    See "La fleur que tu m'avais jetée"
  "'Tis all in vain" (from Carmen. Tr
    of En vain pour éviter les réponses
    amères)
  Toreador song.   See Chanson du
    toréador
Bjerregaard, Henrik Anker
  Aagots fjeldsang (Thrane)
  "Sönner af Norge" (Blom)
Bjørnson, Bjørnstjerne
  Längsel (Svendsen)
  Olaf Trygvason (Grieg)
  "Syng mig hjaem" (Neupert)
  Verborg'ne liebe (Grieg)
The black and the gold.   Colorado col-
  lege song.   E. W. Hille.   Words
  by A. T. French.   HW
The Black Ball line ("In the Black Ball
  line")   Capstan chantey.   TSB 2
  For variant see following song of same
  title
The Black Ball line ("In the Black Ball
  line") Windlass chantey.   WSE
[The black decree] "Let Christians all"
  (The decree)   Traditional song.
  OB

[The **black** decree] "Let Christians all"
(The decree) Traditional song.
2d air. OB
"**Black** girl." Folk song from Kentucky.
SES 2
Black is the colour. Folk song from
North Carolina. SES 2
Black sheep, where you left you' lamb.
Kentucky negro lullaby. FSN
The **Black** Tail range. Cowboy song.
LSC
"The **blackbird** sang unto our crew." See
Hilo somebody
Blackie, John Stuart
"Angels holy" (Flemish air)
Blackmar, A. E.
For bales (Gilmore)
The **blacksmith** ("Oh! the blacksmith's a
fine sturdy fellow") W. A. Mozart.
BB
"The **blacksmith** I hear." See Der
schmied (Brahms)
The **blacksmith's** sweetheart. See Der
schmied (Brahms)
Blackwood, Mrs Helen Selina (Sheridan)
See Dufferin, Helen Selina (Sheridan),
lady
Blaisdell, Carl W.
"As the backs go tearing by"
Blake, Irving H.
Alma mater—Bates college (Davis)
Blake, J. V.
Waking or sleeping (Composer un-
known)
Blake, James W.
The sidewalks of New York (Lawlor)
Blake, William
Night (French air)
Spring (Russian air)
"Sweet dreams, form a shade" (Wil-
liams)
Blake's cradle song. See "Sweet dreams,
form a shade" (Williams)
Blamire, Susanna
"And ye shall walk in silk attire" (Eng-
lish air; also Scottish air)
The waefu' heart (Scottish air)
Blamphin, Charles
Little Maggie May
"When the corn is waving"
Bland, Dora. See Jordan, Mrs Dorothea
(Bland)
Bland, Mrs Edith (Nesbit)
"Christmas is coming, the goose is
getting fat" (Composer unknown)
Bland, James A.
"Carry me back to old Virginny"
"In the evening by the moonlight"
Oh! dem golden slippers
Blasco, Eusebio
La perla (Araya?)
"The **blasted,** bloomin' spider." See The
spider and the spout
Blatchley, Louise
The rose and silver gray (Scottish air)
"**Blättlein,** röslein auf der aue." See Cu-
culeţ cu pana sură
"**Blau** leuchten die flut und der himmel
droben." See Fata morgana (Nicodé)
Blaze away. A. Holzmann. Words by
W. Ardell. SMG

"The **bleak** night of autumn with darkness
is rife." See Melancholy (Merikanto)
"**Bleibe** bei mir ganz in gnaden." See
"Tarry with me, O my Saviour" (Roe-
der)
Blessed Mary. See Mari lwyd
"**Blest** be the Lord, who look'd with gra-
cious eyes" (see Song Index)
Also in "What though I trace each
herb and flower" (Händel)
SSO 2
"**Blest** be the tie that binds." H. G.
Nägeli. Words by J. Fawcett. BB
Blewitt, Jonathan
The clever woman
The cork leg
The Lord Mayor's show
B'lieve. For entries beginning B'lieve
see Believe
"**Blif,** o blif i dina drommars rike." See
Dröm (Sjögren)
Blin'. For entries beginning Blin' see
Blind
The **blind** beggar of Bethnal green (see
Song Index)
Variant: The blind beggar's daughter
The **blind** beggar's daughter ("There was
a blind beggar") Folk song from
North Carolina. SES 1
Variant of: The blind beggar of Beth-
nal green
Blind man blues. B. McLaurin. Words
by E. Green. HB
"**Blind** man lay beside the way." Negro
spiritual. SBA
Variant of: De blin' man stood on de
road an' cried
De **blin'** man stood on de road an' cried.
Negro spiritual. JG
De blin' man. WFN
Variant: "Blind man lay beside the
way"
"The **blind** men held a meeting once."
See Blind man blues (McLaurin)
Bliss, Mrs Maria (Lindsay)
Far away
Bliss, Philip Paul
Almost persuaded. See "Father in
heaven, hear us today"
"Father in heaven, hear us today"
The Lord's prayer. See "Father in
heaven, hear us today"
The **blissful** strain is o'er. R. Wagner.
[Tr of Das süsse lied verhallt] e. WG
Bloch, Ernest
America
Blockley, John
"Hearts and homes"
"Love not, love not"
"The moon is beaming o'er the lake"
Blodau'r cwn (Flowers of the valley) Old
Welsh song. Modern words by Gwi-
li. e.w. WO
Blom, Christian
"Sönner af Norge"
"Sons of dear Norway." See "Sönner
af Norge"
"En **blomma** stod vid vägen" ("A floweret
by the wayside") J. Sibelius. Words
by E. Josephson. e.sw. WM 2

Blonde Paistin.   See Páisdín fionn

"Blondes mädel, heller morgen."   See Trinklied

"Blondlokkige Paistin, mein lieb bist du." See Páisdín fionn

Bloom, Clifford
Alma mater—Drake university

The bloom is on the rye.   See When the bloom is on the rye (Bishop)

Bloom on, my roses.   F. H. Cowen. Words by R. E. Francillon.   MFS

Blossom time.   ¡Irish folk song¡   Words by M. E. Dodge.   MFS

Blow, John
"It is not that I love you less"
The self banished.   See "It is not that I love you less"

Blow away the morning dew ("Upon the sweetest summer time")   Folk song. DSC

Blow away the morning dew ("A while before the gray of dawn")   Folk song.   DSB

"Blow! blow! the winds are so hoarse they cannot blow."   See The winter storms (Stanford)

"Blow, blow, thou winter wind."   T. A. Arne.   Words by W. Shakespeare. EB
"Blow, blow, thou winter wind" (Shakespeare's carol)   OB

"Blow, blow, thou winter wind" (Shakespeare's carol) R. J. S. Stevens.   Words by W. Shakespeare.   OB

Blow, boys, blow ("Oh! blow, my boys, I long to hear you")   Chantey.   WSE
For variant see following song of same title; also Blow, my bully boys

Blow, boys, blow ("A Yankee ship came down the river")   Halliard chantey. SBS—US

Blow, boys, blow for Californyeo.   See The banks of Sacramento

¡Blow, bugle, blow¡ Bugle song.   J. L. Hatton.   Words by A. Tennyson. LAS

Blow, Gabriel ("Heard somebody mournin'") Negro spiritual.   WFN

Blow high! blow low! and so sailed we. See The coasts of High Barbary

Blow, my bully boys ("A Yankee ship came down the river")   Halliard chantey. TSB 1
Variant of: Blow, boys, blow

Blow the man down ("As I was a-walkin'") Halliard chantey.   SBA
For variants see following songs of same title; also The Boston come-all-ye; The fishes; The song of the fishes

Blow the man down ("As I was a-walking") Hoisting chantey.   BB

Blow the man down ("As I was a-walking") Halliard chantey.   BOS 2—SBS

Blow the man down ("As I was a-walking") Long drag chantey.   GSS—SBS— WSE

Blow the man down ("As I was a-walking") Halliard chantey.   US

Blow the man down ("As I was a-walking") Halliard chantey.   WSE

Blow the man down ("Come all ye young fellows") Halliard chantey.   TFP— US—WSE

Blow the man down ("Oh a ship she was fitted out ready for sea") Halliard chantey.   WSE
Variant: The song of the fishes

Blow the man down ("Oh, over the bar on the thirteenth of May") Halliard chantey.   TSB 1

Blow the men down ("Well here comes the navy team")   Chantey.   U.S. Naval academy words.   US

Blow, ye winds, heigh-ho! a-roving I will go.   See "A capital ship"

Blow, ye winds, hi oh! a-roaming I will go. See Ten thousand miles away ("Sing I for a brave and a gallant barque")

Blow, ye winds, in the morning ("As I walked out one sunny morn") Sea song.   WSE
For variants see following songs of same or similar title

Blow, ye winds in the morning ("'Tis advertised")   Forecastle song.   US

Blow, ye winds of morning ("As I walked out one morning fair")   Capstan chantey.   TSB 2

Blow, ye winds of the morning ("Once on a time")   See Peter Gray

Blow ye winds westerly, gentle southwesterly.   See The fishes

Blow your trumpet, Gabriel ("Paul and Silas, bound in jail")   Negro spiritual: Charleston, S.C. version. AS
Blow your trumpet, Gabriel ("De talles' tree in Paradise")   Port Royal islands, S.C. version.   AS
Blow your trumpet, Gabriel ("De talles' tree in Paradise")   Virginia version.   FSN

The blue Alsatian mountains.   S. Adams. Words by Claribel.   GE—MFS
"By the blue Alsatian mountains." SW

The blue and the gray.   P. Dresser. (music and words)   DFF

Blue and white.   Duke university song. G. E. Leftwich.   AIS

The blue bells of Scotland ("O where, tell me where")   Jordan.   Words by A. M. Grant.   Original version of words.   SSB
The blue bells of Scotland (Where, tell me where)   GS
—Altered version of words.   BB— GOS 1
The blue bell of Scotland.   DSB— MBS—TFG—TFR

Blue bonnets are over the border.   Scottish patriotic song.   Words by W. Scott.   GS

The blue dove ("De tus encantos celestial") See La paloma azul

Blue eyed Ellen (The jealous lover of lone green valley)   American mountain ballad.   RA—SW

Blue-eyed Mary.   German air.   <Words by S. Woodworth>   GOS 1

Blue gummed blues. W. C. Handy. Words by D. Elman and W. C. Handy. HB

The blue Juniata. M. D. Sullivan (music and words) GOS 1—SW

Blue man Sam's lament. See Banjo blues (Williams)

"The blue Pacific ocean in constant cadenced motion." See Hail and farewell

"Blue shimmers the deep and the sky above it." See Fata morgana (Nicodé)

De blue tail fly. Minstrel song. PSG

"Bluebirds, linger here awhile." See Eulalie

De blues ain' nothin'. Negro folk blues. SBA

The blues I've got. N. E. Reed and E. Neal. HB

"Die blümelein sie schlafen." See Sandmännchen

Blumenthal, Jacques
   Christ the Pilgrim

"The blushing daughter of the thorn." See The pride of our plains (Hagen)

The blushing maple tree. ɪJ. P. Mc-Caskeyɪ Words by H. Aïdé. MFS

Blüthgen, Viktor
   Strampelchen (Hildach)

"Blutrot die sonne bei Arfon verglühet." See Morva Rhuddlan

"Blythe, blythe, and merry are we" (Trinklied) Scottish folk song. ɪAir: Andro and his cutty gunɪ e.g. ML 1

The boar's head carol. Traditional English air. DN—MBS—OB—TFB —TFG

"The boar's head." MFF

"The boar's head in hand bear I." See The boar's head carol

"The boar's head that we bring here." See Nowell, Nowell (Smert)

"A boat, a boat to cross the ferry." See The ferry (Jenkins)

"A boat, a boat, unto the ferry." See The ferry (Jenkins)

The boat song ("On we are floating") Weber. MFS

Boate, Mrs W.
   "Beautiful Erin" (Glover)

The boatie rows. Composer unknown. Words ɪattributed toɪ J. Ewen. GS

Boating song. Croatian air. Words by K. Davis. DSB

De boatman. Old river boat song. GSS
   Variant of: "De boatmen's dance"

"De boatman dance." See De boatmen's dance (Smith)

Boatman's return. N. J. Sporle. MFS

"The boatmen shout 'tis time to part." See Adieu to Maimuna

ɪDe boatmen's danceɪ "De boatman dance." ɪD. D. Smithɪ WSS
   Variant of: De boatman

The boatsman and the chest. Folk song: Kentucky version. SES 1
   —North Carolina version. SES 1

ɪThe boatswain's storyɪ The bo's'n. J. L. Molloy. Words by F. E. Weatherly. US

Bob up serenely. E. Audran. e. ɪWLO

Bobby Shafto ("Bobby Shafto's gone to sea") Traditional air. Words from Mother Goose. TFG—TFR

Bobby Shaftoe ("Bobby Shaftoe's gone to sea") Traditional Northumbrian air. Words from Mother Goose. BOS 2

The bobcat. Bates college song. H. D. Bradbury (music and words) KU

Boddien, G. von
   "Ich hab' ein kleines lied erdacht" (Bungert)

Bodenstedt, Friedrich Martin von
   "Es hat die rose sich beklagt" (Franz)
   "Wenn der frühling auf die berge steigt" (music by Becker; Coenen)

Bodley, Russ
   Hungry tigers

Boethius
   "O Thou Whose power" (16th century air)

"Bóg się rodzi, moc truchleje." See "Weltall bebt', als der herr geboren"

Bohemia, my fatherland. See My fatherland (Škroup)

Bohm, Karl
   Bitte
   "Calm as the night." See "Still wie die nacht, tief wie das meer, soll deine liebe sein"
   Entreaty. See Bitte
   "The Lord is my Shepherd, how blessed to know"
   Der schwur
   "Still as the night." See "Still wie die nacht, tief wie das meer, soll deine liebe sein"
   "Still wie die nacht, tief wie das meer, soll deine liebe sein"
   The vow. See Der schwur

Boie, Heinrich Christian
   Die Lore am tore (Composer unknown)

Boil 'em cabbage down. See Bile 'em cabbage down

"Bojé, tsarya khranee." See Russian national hymn (Lvov)

"Bold Dunkins was as fine a mason." See Lamkin (North Carolina version)

The bold fisherman ("Once there lived a bold fisherman") P. Greely. Words by M. Talbot. TFO

The bold lieutenant. Folk song: Berea, Ky. version. SES 1
   —Pine Mountain, Ky. version. SES 1
   —St Helen's, Ky. version. SES 1
   —Wasioto, Ky. version. SES 1

The bold militiaman. English music-hall song. SW

The bold pedlar and Robin Hood. Folk song from Sussex. BET

"Bold pilot unheeding." See "L'esperto nocchiero" (Bononcini)

The bold privateer. Folk song from Virginia. SES 2

Bolero ("A un niño ciequecito") See "A un niño ciequecito"

Boll weevil blues. Southern mountain song. RA
   Variant of: Boll weevil song

Boll weevil song. Negro folk song. SBA
Variants: De ballet of de boll weevil;
Boll weevil blues
Bolsum Brown. Railroad song. SBA
Bombed. Song of the European war.
Air: One keg of beer for the four of
us. DSO
"Bombed last night." See Bombed
Bonar, Horatius
"Come unto me, all ye that labor"
(Coenen)
"I heard the voice of Jesus say" (mu-
sic by DuBois; Perry)
Jesus is mine (Perkins)
Bond, J. D.
"Dear old elm-clad hill"
The bondmaid. See L'esclave (Lalo)
Boney. Short drag chantey. WSE
For variants see following song of sim-
ilar title; also Hilonday
"Boney was a warrior." Halliard chantey.
SBS—TSB 1
Boney's abdication. See Boney's lamen-
tation
Boney's defeat. Folk song from Ken-
tucky. SES 2
Boney's lamentation (Boney's abdication)
Folk song from Sussex. BET
Bonheur, Theodor
The red scarf
Bonne nuit, monsieur, bonne nuit. For
English translation see "Good-night"
(Offenbach)
The bonnets of Bonnie Dundee. See
Bonnie Dundee (Sainton-Dolby?)
The bonnie banks of Loch Lomond. See
Loch Lomond
Bonnie Bessie Gray. C. W. Glover.
Words by C. Jefferys. GS
The bonnie blue flag. H. McCarthy.
[Words by A. Chambers-Ketchum]
DSO—HP
"The bonnie, bonnie bairn sits in his hearth-
side place." See Castles in the air
"The bonnie, bonnie bairn sits pokin' in the
ase." See Castles in the air
Bonnie brave Scotland. N. Gow. GS
[The bonnie breast-knots] The briest-knots.
Scottish song. GS
[The bonnie breast-knots] Hey, the bonnie
breist-knots. Scottish song: another
version. GS
Bonnie Charlie ("Bonnie Charlie's now
awa'") Attributed to N. Gow.
Words by Nairne. MFS
"Bonnie Charlie's now awa'." DSB
Will ye no come back again. GS
Bonnie Charlie ("Oh! dearly do I love to
rove") Jacobite song. GS
Bonnie Doon. J. Miller. Words by
R. Burns. GOS 1—GS—MFS—
TFG
"Ye banks and braes." DSB—DSC—
LSB—MBS
Bonnie Dundee ("To the lords o' conven-
tion") <Air: The band at a dis-
tance> attributed to C. Sainton-
Dolby. Words by W. Scott.
DSC—GS

The bonnets of Bonnie Dundee.
BB—MBS
[Bonnie laddie, Highland laddie] The High-
land laddie (Der Hochlandbursche)
[Air: Highland laddie. Words by C.
Walker] e.g. ML 1
Bonnie lassie, artless lassie. See Lassie
wi' the lint-white locks
Bonnie lassie, will ye go. See The birks
of Aberfeldy
Bonnie Mary Gray. A. Lee. GS
Bonnie Prince Charlie ("Cam' ye by Athol,
Donald Macgillavry") See "Cam' ye
by Athol, Donald Macgillavry" (Gow)
Bonnie Prince Charlie ("Cam' ye by Athol,
lad wi' the philabeg") See "Cam' ye
by Athol, lad wi' the philabeg" (Gow)
The bonny bunch of roses ("By the margin
of the ocean."—A ballad of Napoleon)
Irish air from County Tyrone. Tra-
ditional words. HI 2
The bonny Earl o' Moray. Old Scottish
ballad. CSB 4
Bonny Eloise. J. R. Thomas. Words
by C. W. Elliott. TFP—WSS
The bonny wee mare (A ballad of a horse-
race) Irish air from County Donegal.
HI 1
Bononcini, Giovanni Battista
"L'esperto nocchiero" (from Astarto)
Hopeless 'tis. See "Per la gloria
d'adorarvi"
"Per la gloria d'adorarvi" (from
Griselda)
De boodschap van Maria (The message)
Dutch song. e. OB
"De book of revelation God to us revealed."
See Going to heaven
Booker, Charles H.
The West Texas blues
Boola [song] ("Well here we are") Yale
athletic version. A. M. Hirsh. LAS
Booth, Josiah
"When wilt Thou save the people"
Boott, Francis
Baby mine
"I am weary with rowing"
Lethe
The sailor's wife. See Baby mine
The sands o' Dee
"Born but to labour in sorrow." See
Non più mesta accanto al fuoco (Ros-
sini)
"Born is He, our Lord of grace." Old
French folk air. DSB
Bornemann, Wilhelm
Jägerleben (Folk air)
Borodin, Aleksandr Porfir'evich
The fair garden
The lovely garden. See The fair
garden
"My songs are envenomed and bitter"
(Tr of Vergiftet sind meine lieder)
Poisoned. See "My songs are en-
venomed and bitter"
Bortnîânskiĭ, Dmitrĭ Stepanovich
Divine praise. See Glory to the Lord
in Zion

Bortnîânskiï, Dmitriï Stepanovich—*Cont.*
　Glory to the Lord in Zion
　"Hark! the vesper hymn is stealing."
　　See Vesper hymn
　Kol slaven.　See Glory to the Lord
　　in Zion
　Vesper hymn
Das **bose** weib.　J. Haydn.　Words by
　G. E. Lessing.　g.　EDL
The **bo's'n.**　See The boatswain's story
　(Molloy)
Boston ("From Boston harbor we set sail")
　Forecastle song.　US—WSE
The **Boston** burglar.　M. J. Fitzpatrick.
　OTG—SRW
"**Boston** city is afire."　See The banks of
　Sacramento
The **Boston** come-all-ye (see Song Index)
　Variants: Blow the man down; The
　fishes; The song of the fishes
Boston university hymn.　Alma mater
　song.　J. P. Marshall.　Words by
　D. L. Marsh.　AIS—KU
Boswell, Sir Alexander, bart.
　Cornish May song (Old Cornish air)
Botany bay　("Oh! there's Glasgow")
　Chantey.　US
"A **bottle** o' rum and a bottle o' gin.　See
　The sailor likes his bottle, O
Bottomley, Joseph
　"My bonnie lass she smileth"
Boucicault, Dion
　The wearing of·the green (Irish air)
　　Additional words
Bought a cow.　American mountain
　song.　RA
　Variant of: The barnyard song
Boughton, Rutland
　Ben Jonson's carol.　See "I sing the
　　Birth was born to-night"
　"I sing the Birth was born to-night"
Boulé's hop.　See Le bal chez Boulé
Boulton, Harold
　Skye boat song (Scottish air)
Boum badiboum.　Canadian folk song.
　e.f.　GC
Bound for the Rio Grande.　See Rio
　Grande
Bound to California.　Capstan chantey.
　SBS
Bound to go.　Negro spiritual from South
　Carolina.　AS
Bound to the Rio Grande.　See Rio
　Grande
Bourget, Paul
　Les cloches (Debussy)
　"Voici que le printemps, ce fils léger
　　d'avril" (Debussy)
Bourne, William Oland
　Silently falling snow (German air)
Bovet, J.
　The Swiss chalet song.　See Le vieux
　　chalet
　Le vieux chalet
"**Bow** down to Washington."　University
　of Washington song.　L. J. Wilson
　(music and words)　AI—AIS
Bowdoin beata.　Bowdoin college song.
　<Air: Wake, freshmen, wake.　Words
　by H. H. Pierce>　AI—AIS

Bowed with guilt I kneel before Thee.　F.
　P. Ricci.　e.　SSO 3
Bowen, E. E.
　Foundation song (Farmer)
Bowering, Benjamin
　V.M.I. spirit
The **Bowery.**　P. Gaunt.　Words by
　C. H. Hoyt.　GFS—SRW
The **bowld** soger boy.　S. Lover (music
　and words)　DSO
Bowles, George H.
　　Composer and author
　I'm a jayhawk
　　Author
　Kansas City blues (Bowman)
Bowman, E. L.
　Kansas City blues
Bowring, Sir John
　Love divine (Howe)
　"Watchman, tell us of the night"
　　(Parry)
The **boy** and the sheep.　See "Lazy sheep,
　pray tell me why"
"A **boy** he had an auger."　Nonsense
　song.　SBA
The **boy** on the land.　Folk song from
　Kentucky.　SES 2
"A **boy** was born in Bethlehem."　See
　Puer natus in Bethlehem
Boyce, William
　"Come, swallow your bumpers, ye
　　Tories" (same air as Heart of oak)
　Heart of oak (from Harlequin's inva-
　　sion)
　The liberty song (same air as Heart of
　　oak)
　The liberty song: British soldiers' par-
　　ody (same air as Heart of oak)
　The Massachusetts liberty song.　See
　　"Come, swallow your bumpers, ye
　　Tories"
　Well judging Phyllis
Boyles, Bill
　We saw the damn thing through (Ha-
　　waiian air)
"**Boys** in brown and blue, we're right be-
　hind you."　See Fight, Tufts, fight
　(Hayes)
"The **boys** reap and sow."　See Chase the
　buffalo
"**Bože** môj, otče môj."　See Des leibeige-
　nen klagelied
Brackett, Frank Herbert
　Proposal
Bradbury, Hollis D.
　The bobcat
Bradbury, William Batchelder
　"Call John! John! John! louder, louder,
　　louder"
　"Chide mildly the erring"
　"Jesus loves me"
　Marching along
　My own native land
　Sound your A
Bradley, Arthur
　The slighted swain (Composer un-
　known)
Bradsky, Wenzel Theodor
　"O lamb of God that tak'st away"

Brady, Nicholas.   See Tate, Nahum, jt. auth.
Brady ("Down in St Louis at 12th and Carr")   American folk song. SBA
Brady ("Duncan and his brother was playing pool")   2d version.   SBA
The **braes** aboon Bonaw.   Scottish air. Words by W. Gilfillan.   GS
The **braes** o' Balquhither.   ₍R. A. Smith₎ Words by R. Tannahill.   GS

Braham, David
    Adolphus Morning Glory
    The gallant 69th
    Major Gilfeather
    Mulligan guards
    Paddy Duffy's cart
    The Skidmore fancy ball
Braham, John
    All's well (from The English fleet)
    The anchor's weighed
Brahms, Johannes
    Absence.   See In der ferne
    "Am Sonntag morgen"
    The blacksmith's sweetheart.   See Der schmied
    Cradle song ("Guten abend")   See Wiegenlied
    Cradle song ("Schlaf', kindchen, schlaf")   See "Schlaf', kindchen, schlaf'": folk song arranged
    Feldeinsamkeit
    "Good night, my dearest love."   See Ständchen
    "Hail, holy light! the world rejoices"
    "Immer leiser wird mein schlummer"
    In der ferne
    "In stiller nacht zur ersten wacht"
    In summer fields.   See Feldeinsamkeit
    Klage
    "Like melting tones it rises."   See "Wie melodien zieht es mir"
    The little dustman.   See Sandmännchen: folk air arranged
    The little sandman.   See Sandmännchen: folk air arranged
    Love song.   See Minnelied
    Lullaby.   See Wiegenlied
    "Lullaby and good-night."   See Wiegenlied
    Maria ging aus wandern.   See Maria's wallfahrt
    Maria's wallfahrt
    Minnelied
    "On Sunday morning."   See "Am Sonntag morgen"
    Parted.   See Sehnsucht
    Plaint.   See Klage
    Poland: folk air arranged
    The quest.   See Maria's wallfahrt
    The sandman.   See Sandmännchen: folk air arranged
    Sandmännchen: folk air arranged
    Sapphic ode.   See Sapphische ode
    Sapphische ode
    "Schlaf', kindchen, schlaf'": folk song arranged
    Der schmied
    Sehnsucht
    Serenade.   See Ständchen

"Sleep to me no rest is bringing."   See "Immer leiser wird mein schlummer"
The smith.   See Der schmied
"Soft strains of music drifting."   See "Wie melodien zieht es mir"
Sonntag
Ständchen
Sunday.   See Sonntag
"Wie melodien zieht es mir"
Wiegenlied
The wonderful inn.   See Poland: folk air arranged
Braisted, Harry, pseud.   See Berdan, Harry B.
Braley, Berton
    "Lord, we come with hearts aflame" (Kocher)
"Brannt' eine fichte" ("Pod borem sosna gorzała")   Polish folk song.   g.p. ML 3
Bratton, John Walter
    The sunshine of Paradise Alley
Das **braune** maidelein.   16th century German folk song.   g.   EDL
"Braune wirtin, bring mir wein."   See Trinklied
Brautjungfernlied ("Wir winden dir den jungfernkranz")   C. M. von Weber. Words by F. Kind.   g.   EDL
Brautlied ("Der apfelbaum steht voll blüten weiss."—"Pliot mola lülé") Albanian song.   al.g.   ML 2
Brautlied ("Faithful and true")   For English translation see Bridal chorus (Wagner)
Brautlied ("Nous sommes venus vous voir")   See La chanson de la mariée
"Brave men were ever faring where western skies were red."   See Our pioneers
The **brave** old oak.   E. J. Loder.   Words by H. F. Chorley.   MFS
"Braw, braw lads on Yarrow braes."   See Gala water
"Break forth, O beauteous, heavenly light."   J. S. Bach.   ₍Tr of Brich an, o schönes morgenlicht₎   e.   TFG
Break the news to mother.   C. K. Harris (music and words)   SRW
"Break thou, my heart."   See Sappho (Volkmann)
"The **breaking** waves dashed high."   See Landing of the Pilgrims (Browne)
The **breeze** ("Céfiro, que por la tarde")   See El céfiro
"Breeze, when at eve you are passing."   See El céfiro
Brennan, James A.
    The rose of No Man's Land
Brennan on the moor.   Folk song: Virginia version.   SES 2
Breslin, James F.
    Fordham marching song
Brewster, Louie
    The dying nun
Brewster, O. M.
    We girls never mean half we say
Brian, J. F.
    I'm dancing mad

Brich an, o schönes morgenlicht. For English translation see "Break forth, O beauteous, heavenly light" (Bach)

"The bridal ceremony's over." O. Straus. e. WLO

Bridal chorus. R. Wagner. [Tr of Brautlied] e. MFS—TFG—WG

The bride bells. J. L. Roeckel. [Words by F. E. Weatherly] GE—MFS

"The bride she cam' out o' the byre." See Woo'd and married and a'

Bridge, Mrs Elizabeth (Stirling) See Stirling, Elizabeth

Bridge, Frank
Pan's holiday
A spring song

The bridge. Carew. Words by H. W. Longfellow. GE

Bridges, Robert Seymour
Spring (Whittaker)

"The bridle and saddle." Folk song from North Carolina. SES 2

"A briery lane where wild-birds sing." See The bird's nest

Briesewitz, August Wilhelm Robert
Fiducit

The briest-knots. See The bonnie breast-knots (1st version)

Bright, William
"Once again, O blessed time" (Franck)

"Bright and joyful is the morn." Yorkshire air. DN

"Bright angels on the water." See The social band

"Bright are the flames beneath the cauldron leaping." See Sleeping princess

"Bright as a ray." J. Strauss. e. WLO

The bright beyond. T. H. Howe. GE

"Bright college years." Yale university song. C. Wilhelm. Words by H. S. Durand. AI—KU

Bright-eyed little Nell of Narragansett bay. Old American song. SW

Bright her smiles. See Il balen del suo sorriso (Verdi)

"The bright, rosy morning." GOS 1—MFS

"Bright shines the evening star on the clear water." See Santa Lucia

Bright spark of hope. See The letter in the candle

Bright sparkles in de churchyard. Negro spiritual. HRD

"Brightest and best." Composer unknown. Words by R. Heber. DN

"Brightest and best" (Morning star) J. P. Harding. Words by R. Heber. LAS

"Brightly, brightly gleam the sparkling rills." Haydn. e. MFS

"Brilliant more than meteors." See Song of the Moors (Lecocq)

Brindisi ("Il segreto per esser felici") See "Il segreto per esser felici" (Donizetti)

"Bring a torch, Jeannette, Isabella." Old French carol. [Words attributed to Saboly. Tr of Un flambeau, Jeannette, Isabelle] e. DSB—DSC—MBS—MFF

[Bring back my Bonnie to me] "My bonnie." [H. J. Fuller (music and words)] BB—DFF—MFS—TFP

Bring back my kitchen to me. [H. J. Fuller] Words by D. Root. DSO

Bring my harp to me again. See The old musician and his harp (Higgins)

"Bring peace on earth, holy, holy Lord." See A prayer (Wagner)

"Bring the good old bugle, boys." See Marching through Georgia (Work)

"Bring the poor old bugle, boys." See Marching through Georgia (Work)

Bring the wagon home, John. College song. TFB—TFG—TFO

"Bring to me my supper, boys." See I've been all around the world

"Bring us songs of cheer and joy." See "Kom med sange og helst af dem" (Sinding)

"Bringt ein hoch auf den könig und friedens bestand." See Down among the dead men

A brisk young lad he courted me. See The brisk young lover (North Lincolnshire version)

The brisk young lively lad. See The valiant lady

The brisk young lover. Folk song: Georgia version. SES 2
—Burnsville, N.C. version. SES 2
—Hot Springs, N.C. version. SES 2
—Virginia version. SES 2
Died of love (A brisk young lad he courted me) North Lincolnshire version. BET
"Go bring me back my blue-eyed boy." American version. SBA
Variant: "A brisk young sailor"

"A brisk young sailor" (see Song Index)
Variant of: The brisk young lover

"Briskly, briskly over the water." See Fringue, fringue sur l'aviron

Bristol town. Folk song from Sussex. BET
Variant of: "In Seaport town"

Bristow, George Frederick
Vivandière song (from Rip Van Winkle)

The British grenadiers. 16th century air: Sir Edward Nowell's delight. DSB—MBS

"Britons, raise your banners high." See Ymdawiad y brenin

"Bro' Joe, you ought to know my name—hallelujah." Negro spiritual from South Carolina. AS

The Broadway, opera and Bowery crawl. G. Operti. Words by P. Stoner. SW

The Broadway swell and Brooklyn belle. J. D. Kelly (music and words) SW

"Brock, Mad."
Wiegenlied (Mozart) See Gotter, F. W. Wiegenlied (Mozart)

Brockway, W. H.
Jockey hat and feather

The broken home. W. H. Fox. SW

The broken ring. See "In einem kühlen grunde" (Folk air)

The **broken** token.   Folk song: Allan-
     stand, N.C. version no. 1.   SES 2
—Allanstand, N.C. version no. 2.
     SES 2
—Black   Mountain,   N.C.   version.
     SES 2
—Hot Springs, N.C. version no. 1.
     SES 2
—Virginia version.   SES 2
"A pretty fair maid."   American
     version.   SBA
Brome, Richard
     A begging we will go (17th century
     English air) Authorship uncertain
Bromley, Harold V., pseud.   See Loomis,
     Harvey Worthington
The **brook** ("I come from haunts of coot
     and hern") J. Farmer.   Words by
     Tennyson.   GSS
Brooks, Charles Timothy, and Dwight,
     John Sullivan
     America (Carey?)
Brooks, Phillips, bp.
     "O little town of Bethlehem" (English
     folk air; air: The ploughboy's
     dream; also music by Redner; Ste-
     vens)
Brooks, Shelton
     The Darktown strutter's ball
The **brook's** lullaby.   See Das baches
     wiegenlied (Schubert)
The **broom** o' the Cowdenknowes.   See
     The brume o' the Cowdenknowes
"The **broom,** the broom, what do you with
     it."   See De bezem
Brother and I.   <S. B. Ball (music and
     words>   KSO
"**Brother** come and dance with me."   See
     The dancing lesson (Humperdinck)
"**Brother** George is a-gwine to glory."   See
     The sin-sick soul
Brother, guide me home.   Negro spiritual
     from Tennessee.   AS
"**Brother** Joe, you ought to know my name
     —hallelujah."   See "Bro' Joe, you
     ought to know my name—hallelujah"
Brother Moses gone.   Negro spiritual
     from South Carolina.   AS
Brougham, John
     The fine ould Irish gintleman (Old air)
Brown, A. M.
     Alma mater—Michigan state college
     (Thompson)
Brown, Arthur Henry
     In excelsis gloria.   See "When Christ
     was born of Mary free"
     "When Christ was born of Mary free"
     (Tr of Christo paremus canticam,
     in excelsis gloria)
Brown, Charles S.
     God save the people.   See "When
     wilt Thou save Thy people"
     "God's trumpet wakes the slumb'ring
     world"
     "When wilt Thou save Thy people"
Brown, Clarence Fayette, and Potter, Lars
     Sellstedt
     Yard by yard (Brown and Wood)
Brown, Clarence Fayette, and Wood, Ham-
     ilton Brooks
     Yard by yard

Brown, Herbert Lawyer
     Hip, hip, hip, for old Swarthmore
Brown, I. L.
     "Silent now the drowsy bird" (Offen-
     bach)
Brown, J. H.
     Faded flowers (Willing)
Brown, Thomas
     "Shepherd! thy demeanour vary"
Brown, W. C.
     A hundred years to come
Brown, Walter H.
     O little mother of mine (Nevin)
The **Brown** cheering song.   Brown uni-
     versity song.   H. S. Young.   Words
     by R. B. Jones.   AI—AIS—KU—KV
Brown-eyed Lee.   Cowboy song.   LSC
The **brown** girl.   Folk song: Berea, Ky.
     version.   SES 1
—Manchester, Ky. version.   SES 1
—Allanstand, N.C. version no. 1.
     SES 1
—Allanstand, N.C. version no. 2.
     SES 1
—Alleghany, N.C. version.   SES 1
—Big Laurel, N.C. version.   SES 1
—Burnsville, N.C. version.   SES 1
—Callaway, Va. version.   SES 1
—Meadows of Dan, Va. version.
     SES 1
—Woodridge, Va. version.   SES 1
Variant of: Lord Thomas and fair
     Ellinor
"The **brown** girl she has house and land."
     See Lord Thomas and fair Ellinor
     (Clay county, Ky. version; Blue Ridge
     Springs, Va. version; Dewey, Va.
     version)
"The **brown** girl she has houses and lands."
     See Lord Thomas and fair Ellinor
     (Alexander, N.C. version; Beechgrove,
     Va. version)
Browne, Felicia Dorothea.   See Hemans,
     Mrs Felicia Dorothea (Browne)
Browne, Harriet Mary
     Evening song to the Virgin
     Landing of the Pilgrims
     Tyrolese evening hymn
Browne, Mary Anne.   See Browne, Har-
     riet Mary
Browne, Raymond A.
     Little boy in blue (Morse)
Browning, Robert
     "The year's at the spring" (17th century
     air)
Bruce, John
     O whistle, and I'll come to you, my lad
     (attributed)
     Whistle o'er the lave o't
Bruce's address to his army.   See "Scots,
     wha hae wi' Wallace bled"
Brückler, Hugo
     Betrayal.   See Verrath
     The dreaming mere.   See Der
     träumende see
     Frühlingssegen
     Gebet
     Request.   See Gebet
     Spring's blessing.   See Frühlingssegen
     Der träumende see
     Verrath

"Brudder George is a-gwine to glory."
See The sin-sick soul
Brudder, guide me home an' I am glad.
See Brother, guide me home
"Brudder Moses gone to de promised land."
See Brother Moses gone
"Bruder, ich und du." See Wiegenlied
("Bruder, ich und du")
Bruder liederlich. Words by V. Rath-
geber. g. EDL
"Brüder, reicht die hand zum bunde." See
Bundeslied (Mozart)
Brüderchen, komm tanz' mit mir. For
English translation see The dancing
lesson (Humperdinck)
"Brüderlein fein." J. Drechsler. Words
by F. Raimund. g. EDL
Brüderschaft ("Im krug zum grünen
kranze") Volksweise: Ich stand auf
hohem berge. Words by W. Müller.
g. EDL
Brugghen, Jules van der
Fleur d'amour (Weyts)
[The **brume** o' the Cowdenknowes] "How
blythe ilk morn was I to see" (The
broom o' the Cowdenknowes) Scot-
tish song. GS
Bruni, Domenico
"Se meritar potessi"
"La vezzosa pastorella"
"Brünstige lohe." See Choral ("Out of
our suff'ring")
Bruton town (see Song Index)
Variant of: "In Seaport town"
Bryan, Alfred
Down in the old cherry orchard
(Henry)
I'm on my way to Mandalay (Fischer)
Peg o' my heart (Fischer)
Bryan, Robert
Suo-gân (Old Welsh song)
Bryan, Vincent P.
Down where the Wurzburger flows
(Von Tilzer)
Tammany (Edwards)
Bryant, H. T.
Balm of Gilead
"Buck Creek girl." See Cripple creek
Buckhurst, Charles Sackville, lord. See
Dorset, Charles Sackville, 6th earl of
Buckley, Frederick
"I'd chose to be a daisy"
Kiss me quick and go
Buckley, R. Bishop
Wait for the wagon
Buckner, Eva Fern
Where the sunset turns the ocean's
blue to gold (Petrie)
Buena Vista. Song of the Mexican war.
DSO
The **buff** and blue. George Washington
university song. E. Sweeney. AI—
AIS
The **buffalo** ("Come all you men and maid-
ens") Old buccaneer song. WSE
Buffalo gals. <Minstrel song> SW—
WSS
The **buffalo** skinners. See Range of the
buffalo
Bugail yr hafod (Einst hütet' ich herden)
Welsh song. g.w. ML 1

The **bugle** call ("O hear the bugle calling")
Westphalian air. Words by K. Davis.
DSB
"The **bugle** echoes are flying." See Bugle
song
Bugle song ("The bugle echoes are flying")
Air from a Prussian bugle call.
Words by H. Fitch. TFO
Bugle song ("The splendor falls") See
Blow, bugle, blow (Hatton)
Build a house in Paradise. Negro spir-
itual from South Carolina. AS
The **builders.** See Venez à Saint-Mau-
rice (Renard?)
The **bull-dog** on the bank. College song.
TFP
The **bull-dog.** BB
The **bull-frog** and the coon. J. S. Na-
than. Words by F. Feist. SMG
"**Bull-frog** dress'd in soldier clothes." See
Shine on (Schoolcraft)
Bullard, Frederic Field
The march of the people (same air as
Marching on)
Marching on
Bullet song. See Spirit of Gettysburg
(Saltzer)
Bullets of old Gettysburg. See Spirit of
Gettysburg (Saltzer)
The **bully** boat is coming. Halliard chan-
tey. TSB 2
The **bully** song (May Irwin's "bully" song)
C. E. Trevathan (music and words)
GFS
The new bully. SRW
*Bulwer-Lytton, Edward George Earle
Lytton.* See Lytton, Edward George
Earle Lytton Bulwer-Lytton, 1st baron
Bunch o' blackberries. A. Holzmann.
SMG
Bundeslied ("Brüder, reicht die hand") W.
A. Mozart. Author of words un-
known. g. EDL
Bundeslied ("In allen guten stunden") J. F.
Reichardt. Words by W. von Goethe.
g. EDL
Bundeslied ("Sind wir vereint") G. F.
Hanitsch. Words by E. M. Arndt.
g. EDL
Bungert, August
Bettler-liebe
"Ich hab' ein kleines lied erdacht"
Pauper-love. See Bettler-liebe
"Singend über die haide"
"Singing over the heather." See
"Singend über die haide"
"Within my heart a song I found."
See "Ich hab' ein kleines lied
erdacht"
Bunn, Alfred
"I dreamt that I dwelt in marble halls"
(Balfe)
"The light of other days" (Balfe)
"Scenes that are brightest" (Wallace)
Then you'll remember me (Balfe)
Buononcini, Giovanni Battista. See Bo-
noncini, Giovanni Battista
Bürger, Gottfried August
Liebeszauber (Schulz)
Burgoyne, John
The dashing white sergeant (Bishop)

Burikes. Jewish folk song. y. SY

Burkholder, Nadeen, and Fowler, Garnet
The tiger song

Burlatskaïa. See Volga boat song

Burnand, Sir Francis Cowley
The song of the Triton (Molloy)
The tar's farewell (Maybrick)

Burns, Robert
Afton water (Air: Afton water; also music by Spilman)
An' O, for ane-and-twenty, Tam (Air: Up in the morning early)
Auld lang syne (Air: I fee'd a lad at Michaelmas)
Bannocks o' bear-meal (Scottish air)
"Behold, my love, how green the groves" (Beethoven)
The birks of Aberfeldy (Scottish air)
Bonnie Doon (Miller)
Ca' the yowes to the knowes (Scottish air)
The Campbells are comin' (Old Scottish air)
Comin' thro' the rye (Old Scottish air)
"Coming through the rye, poor body" (Scottish air)
Corn rigs are bonnie (Scottish air)
Dainty Davie (Scottish air)
"Duncan Gray cam' here to woo" (Scottish air)
"Fairest maid on Devon banks" (Scottish air)
Gala water (Scottish air)
Green grow the rashes, O (Scottish air)
"Guide'en to you, kimmer, and how do you do" (Scottish air)
"Had I a cave" (Scottish air)
Here's a health to ane I lo'e dear (Scottish air)
"A Highland lad my love was born" (Air: The white cockade)
Highland Mary (Scottish air)
I'm owre young to marry yet (Scottish air)
"John Anderson, my jo, John" (Watson)
Lassie wi' the lint-white locks (Scottish air)
"Last May a braw wooer" (Scottish air)
The lea rig (Scottish air)
Leezie Lindsay (Scottish air)
"The lovely lass of Inverness" (Oswald)
A man's a man, for a' that (Scottish air)
"My heart is a breakin', dear tittie" (Air: The muckin' o' Geordie's byre)
"My heart is sair, I darena tell" (Air: The Highland watch's farewell; also music by Farmer)
"My heart's in the Highlands" (Scottish air; air: Cro challin; also music by Courtney)
"My love she's but a lassie yet, my love she's but a lassie yet" (Scottish air)

My luve is like a red, red rose (Air: Graham's strathspey; also music by Garrett)
My Nannie, O (Scottish air)
My wife's a winsome wee thing (Scottish air)
O Charlie is my darling (Jacobite air)
"O Kenmure's on and awa', Willie" (Scottish air)
"O Mary at thy window be" (Air: The Glasgow lasses; air: The miller)
"O, wert thou in the cauld blast" (Air: The lass o' Livingston; also music by Mendelssohn)
O whistle, and I'll come to you, my lad (Bruce?; also music by unknown composer)
"O Willie brew'd a peck o' maut" (Masterton)
"Of a' the airts the wind can blaw" (Marshall)
"A rosebud by my early walk" (Scottish air)
"Scots, wha hae wi' Wallace bled" (Scottish air)
"There was a lad was born in Kyle" (Air: O gin ye were daid, guidman)
"Thou hast left me ever, Jamie" (Scottish air)
"Thou ling'ring star, with less'ning ray" (Johnston)
Wandering Willie (Scottish air)
Wee Willie Gray (Scottish air)
Whistle o'er the lave o't (Bruce)
"Will ye go to the Indies, my Mary" (Scottish air)
"The winter it is past" (Scottish air)

Burrows,
Carol, carol Christians

"**Bursche** ging ins tal." See Junggesellenlied

"**Bursche** hatt' sich erwählt ein bräutchen." See Die verlobten

"**Bursche** war müd, sommersonne glüht." See Huldra aa en Elland

"**Burschen,** heraus." Composer and author of words unknown. g. EDL

ⵏBurschenlustⵏ "Der mai ist gekommen" (Wanderschaft) J. W. Lyra. Words by E. Geibel. g. EDL

Burt, Benjamin Hapgood
Ebenezer Frye. See Wal, I swan
Wal, I swan

Burt, Reynolds Johnston
The hiking song of the eighth infantry (Morales)

"**Bury** my bible at my head." See Sir Hugh (North Carolina version)

Bushby, Robert Brownell
Colgate invictus

Bussine, Romain
Après un rêve (Fauré)

Busslied (Penitence) Beethoven. ⵏWords by Gellertⵏ e.g. HCA
Contrition. e. SSO 3

The **busted** king of England. Old song. Revised words. DSO

"**But** black is the colour of my true love's hair." See Black is the colour

But fill the cup! where'er, boy, our choice may fall. See "To ladies' eyes"

But He ain't comin' here t' die no mo'. See Jesus ain't comin' here t' die no mo'

But hurrah for Lane county, the land of the free. See The Lane county bachelor

But I care not what others may say. See Rosalie (Knight)

But I love her, as you may suppose. See Roguish little beauty, Emeleen

"But lately in dance I embraced her" ("Sie schwebt' mir noch kürzlich im arme") A. Arensky. Words from the Russian of A. Fet. e.g. ATS

But oh, Jane doesn't look the same. See And her golden hair was hanging down her back (Rosenfeld)

But oh, the sunshine I dearly prize. See 'O sole mio (Capua)

But sweeter, dearer, yes. See Bonny Eloise (Thomas)

But the cat came back. See The cat came back (Miller)

"But the Lord is mindful of His own." F. Mendelssohn. ₁Tr of Doch der Herr vergisst der seiner nicht₁ e. BB—SSO 2—TFR

"But the springtime returneth, and new life doth bring." Air: The groves of Blarney. ₁Tr of Der lenz ist gekommen₁ e. WLO

"But when young Suse came to knew this." See The two brothers (Mount Fair, Va. version no. 2)

"But who is this? tremendous to behold" (see Song Index)
  Also in "Awful, pleasing being, say" (Händel) SSO 2

"But who may abide the day of His coming." Händel. SSO 4

The buttercup test. MFS

"Buttercups ev'ryone bright." See The buttercup test

Butterfield, James Austin
  When you and I were young, Maggie

The butterfly ("Ah, how did that rover, the butterfly, discover") See Schmetterling (Cornelius)

"Butterfly! butterfly! pretty yellow butterfly." Japanese song. e. LSB

"Butterfly, butterfly, whence do you come." Dutch folk song. e. DSB

Buy a broom. ₁Air: Lieber Augustin, attributed to A. Lee₁ GOS 1

Buy broom buzzems. Northumbrian folk song. BOS 2

Buy my caller herrin'. See Caller herrin' (Gow?)

Buy my roses ("Come buy my little roses red") G. A. Hudson. SW

Buy my strawberries. C. Howard. MFS

By an' by ("I know my robes") Negro spiritual. WSS
  By and by. HRD—WFN
  Bye an' bye. FSN

"By and by, by and by, stars shining." See "By'm by, by'm by, stahs shinin'"

By and by we will go and see him. See "Where O where is old Elijah"

"By Killarney's lakes and fells." See Killarney (Balfe)

By-low, my baby. See Good-bye, my lover, good-bye

"By that lake, whose gloomy shore." Air: The brown Irish girl. Words by T. Moore. HMI

"By the blue Alsatian mountains." See The blue Alsatian mountains (Maybrick)

"By the blue Monongahela." West Virginia university song. L. Beltzhoover-Dille. Words by E. D. Richards. AI—KU

By the blue sea. H. Smart. Words by F. Enoch. GE

"By the Don a garden fair." See The banks of the Don (Musorgskii)

By the Manzanares. See "Am ufer des flusses, des Manzanares" (Jensen)

"By the margin of the ocean." See The bonny bunch of roses

"By the old Pacific's rolling water." See Rally song (Beall)

By the river Don. See The banks of the Don (Musorgskii)

"By the rivers gently flowing." See Illinois (Jones)

"By the sad sea waves." J. Benedict. GOS 2

By the sea. See Am meer (Schubert)

By the watermelon vine. Negro song. BB

"By the waters of Babylon." C. T. Howell. TSS 1—TSS 2

"By thy rivers gently flowing." See Illinois (Jones)

"By yon bonnie banks." See Loch Lomond

Bye an' bye. See By an' by

"Bye, bye, baby." Lullaby from Virginia. SES 2

"Bye, bye, flannel-nightied." See Lullaby (Merikanto)

Bye-bye lullaby. See The Virgin and Child (15th century air)

Bye-bye, my darling! sleep to de rattle ob de bones. See Dolcy Jones (Foster)

Byers, S. H. M.
  When Sherman marched down to the sea (Rockwell)

Bŷlínka (A legend of Kieff) Ancient Russian folk song. e. SR

"By'm by, by'm by, stahs shinin'." Negro spiritual from Texas. SBA

Byrd, William
  Lord Willoughby
  "My little sweet darling"
  "My mind to me a kingdom is"
  "Non nobis, Domine"
  "O liebste mein." See "O mistress mine": traditional air arranged
  "O mistress mine": traditional air arranged

Byrom, John
  "Christians, awake" (Wainwright)

Byron, George Gordon Noel Byron, 6th baron
"Maid of Athens" (Allen)

C

"**C.** C. rider" ("C. C. rider, just see what you have done") Texas negro folk song: 2d version. SBA

C. C. rider ("Dat Sunshine Special comin' around de bend") Texas negro folk song: 1st version. SBA

"**C,** dat's de way to begin."   See Dat am de way to spell chicken

"**Ça** ça geschmauset."   See Edite, bibite

"**Ça** fait moin la peine, Clémentine."   See Clémentine

Ça fait peur aux oiseaux (That frightens the birds) P. Bernard.   e.f.   AT

"**Ça** me fait d'la peine, Clémentine."   See Clémentine

Ca' the yowes to the knowes.   Scottish air.   Words by R. Burns.   MBS
Ca' the yowes.   CSB 5

Caccini, Giulio
"Amarilli, mia bella"
"Amaryllis, now cruel."   See "Amarilli, mia bella"
"Non piango e non sospiro" (from L'Euridice)

Cachunk sang the little mister bull-frog. See The bull-frog and the coon (Nathan)

Cackle, cackle, cackle, cackle.   See The hen convention

Caddigan, Jack
The rose of No Man's Land (Brennan)

Cadets' graduating song for 1848.   West Point song.   Words attributed to Mrs W. Scott.   DSO

Cadman, Charles Wakefield
"The heart of her"
My lovely rose

"**Cælia,** in the shade reclining."   See The forsaken maid (Smart)

Cagaran Gaolach₁ "Hush ye, my bairnie." Old Gaelic (Lochaber) lullaby.   e. DSB—LAS

Cahill, P. J.
The Irish lullaby

Caidil gu lo.   For English translation see "O hush thee, my babie" (Sullivan); "Oh, hush thee, my babie" (Whitaker)

Caie, J. M.
Mo rùn geal dìleas (Gaelic air)

Cailín deás crúidhte na mbó (Die schöne kuhmagd) Irish folk song.   Old words.   g.ir.   ML 1
The pretty girl milking her cow.   e. GOS 2—HMI—SI
Who's the pretty girl milkin' the cow. Fragment.   e.   SBA

The **caisson** song ("Over hill, over dale") ₁T. A. Metz₁ Words by E. L. Gruber. DSC—DSO

Caisson song: coast artillery parody ("Di-dee di, di-dee di, can't you hear those babies cry") ₁T. A. Metz₁   DSO

Caisson song: infantry adaptation ("Over hill, over dale")   ₁T. A. Metz₁   DSO

Caisson song: variation ("In the storm, in the night")   ₁T. A. Metz₁   DSO

Caldara, Antonio
"As on the swelling wave."   See "Come raggio di sol"
"Come raggio di sol"
The incarnation
"Let us sing to-day"

Caldwell, Anne
Left all alone again blues (Kern)

Caldwell, James F., pseud.   See Loomis, Harvey Worthington

California ("When formed our band") Song of the Gold rush.   SBA
Variant of: The banks of Sacramento

California Joe.   Cowboy song.   Words by Captain J. Crawford.   LSC

Calinda.   See "Michié Préval"

Calkin, John Baptiste
Camden.   See "Press on! press on! ye sons of light"; "The wind ahead? the wind is free"
"I heard the bells on Christmas day"
"Press on! press on! ye sons of light"
"The wind ahead? the wind is free" (same air as "Press on! press on! ye sons of light")

"**Call** all hands to man the capstan."   See Rolling home

Call forth thy powers.   Handel.   SSO 3

"**Call** John! John, John, John! he don't hear."   Old song.   KSO

"**Call** John! John! John! louder, louder, louder."   W. B. Bradbury.   MFS

"**Call** me pet names."   ₁C. Jarvis. Words by Osgood₁   SRW

Callcott, John Wall
The cavaliers of Dixie (same air as "Ye mariners of England")
A sailing song

Calleja, Barrera y.   See Barrera y Calleja

Caller herrin'.   Attributed to N. Gow. Words by C. Nairne.   GS—GSS

Calliope.   Middlewestern song.   SBA

"**Calm** are the nights in Canaan."   See Beautiful Canaan nights

"**Calm** as the night, deep as the sea, thy love for me should be."   See "Still wie die nacht, tief wie das meer, soll deine liebe sein" (Bohm)

"**Calm** was the hallowed night."   See Calm was the night (Sullivan)

Calm was the night.   A. S. Sullivan. Words by C. Elliott.   MFS

Calomel.   Old song.   SW

"La **calunnia** è un venticello."   Rossini. e.i.   PB

Calvary ("Eb'ry time I think about Jesus") Negro spiritual.   WFN

Calvary ("Rest, rest to the weary")   P. Rodney.   Words by H. Vaughan. ASA—CSS 1—CSS 2

"**Cam'** ye by Athol, Donald Macgillavry" (Bonnie Prince Charlie)   <N. Gow> Words by D. Vedder.   GS

"Cam' ye by Athol, lad wi' the philabeg" (Bonnie Prince Charlie) <N. Gow> Words by J. Hogg. GS

Camden (Calkin) See "Press on! press on! ye sons of light"; "The wind ahead? the wind is free"

"Came three holy kings from the eastern land." See "Die heil'gen drei kön'ge aus morgenland" (Glière)

The camp fire. H. W. Loomis (music and words) TFO

"Camp-meeting down in the wilderness." See There's a meeting here to-night

"A camp meeting took place." See At a Georgia camp meeting (Mills)

The camp war song. See Co-ca-che-lunk

Campana, Fabio
  Come with me
  Do you remember
  The mahogany tree
  The scout
  Somewhere
  Speak to me

Campbell, Mrs
  Melvil Castle

Campbell, Frank
  Shew! fly, don't bother me

Campbell, Joseph
  The Gartan mother's lullaby (Irish air)
  The little rose of Gartan (Irish air)
  "Slow by the shadows" (Irish air)

Campbell, Mary Maxwell
  The march of the Cameron men (Old air)

Campbell, Thomas
  The exile of Erin (Irish air)

The Campbells are comin'. Scottish national song. Words by R. Burns. DSC—SSB

The Campbells are coming. GS

Campion, Thomas
  "Jack and Joan"
  "There is a garden in her face"

"The Camptown ladies sing this song." See The banks of Sacramento

De Camptown races. S. C. Foster (music and words) SRW
  De Camptown races (Gwine to run all night) BNM—GOS 2—WSS
  Variant: The banks of Sacramento ("The Camptown ladies")

Campus song ("When the shades of ev'ning gather") See "When the shades of ev'ning gather" (Shackelton)

Campus song ("You may talk of the halls of your college") University of Rochester song. N. Nairn. Words by J. L. O'Connor. KU—KV

Cân y melinydd (The miller's song) Old Welsh song. Words attributed to Rhuddenfab. e.w. WO

Cân yr alltud (Song of the exile) Old Welsh song. Modern words by R. W. Parry. e.w. WO

La caña (Das rohr) Andalusian folk song. g.s. ML 2

Canaan ("Together let us sweetly live") Mountain spiritual. RA

"Canaan land is the land for me." See Let God's saints come in

"Un Canadien errant" ("From his Canadian home") Canadian folk song. Air: La chanson des métamorphoses. e.f. GC

Le canard blanc (see Song Index)
  Variant: Les trois canards

Canção do figueiral (Das lied von den figueiredos) 13th century troubadour song. g.po. ML 2

Canción de cuna ("Que lla Virxen mas galana."—Wiegenlied) Asturian folk song. g.s. ML 2

Canción de la luna (A song of the moon) Mexican folk song. e.s. VS

La canción del olvido (Marinela) J. Serrano. Words by F. Romero and G. Fernandez Shaw. e.s. MSP

Candlemas eve. Old air. Words by R. Herrick. OB

Canitz, Friedrich Rudolf Ludwig, freiherr von
  "Come, my soul, thou must be waking" (Haydn. Tr of Seele du musst munter werden)

"A canner, exceedingly canny." See Limericks

Canning, Effie I.
  "Rock-a-bye baby"

Cannon, Hughie
  Bill Bailey, won't you please come home

Canonbury (Schumann) See "O God, Thy world is sweet with prayer"; "Out of the dark the circling sphere"

Cansó de Nadal (Weihnachtslied) Traditional Catalan Christmas song. ca.g. ML 2

Cansó de sega ("Ah! si no fos p'es carreto." —Kutscherruf.—Erntelied) Mallorcan folk song. ca.g. ML 2

Cansó de sega ("Sabs es segadós que fan." —Erntelied) Balearic folk song. ca.g. ML 2

"Canst thou bear the strong embraces." See Liv og salighed (Sinding)

"Canst thou believe love could deceive." See "Caro mio ben" (Giordani)

Can't you dance the polka ("As I walked down the Broadway") Capstan chantey. TSB 2—WSE
  For variant see following song of same title

Can't you dance the polka ("One day as I went walking") Capstan chantey. SBS

"Can't you hear the bugles blowing." See Keep them rolling

Can't you live humble. Negro spiritual. JB 2

Can't you see the rain and hail am fastly falling Alexander. See Alexander (Von Tilzer)

"Can't you stay one tiny moment." See The miller and the maid

"Cântă puiul cucului" (Der junge kuckuck) Rumanian song. g.ru. ML 2

Canti, ridi, dormi. See Chantez riez et dormez (Gounod)

"The cantie spring": sequel to Maggie Lauder. 18th century air: Maggie Lauder. Words by C. Gray. GS

Cantique de Noël. A. Adam. Words by M. Cappeau. e. TFP—TFR
    Cantique de Noël (Christmas song) e. MFS
    Cantique de Noël ("O holy night") e. BB
    Christmas song. e. GE
    Noël. e. SSO 3
    "O holy night." e. LAS

Canto dei gondolieri (Gesang der gondelführer) Venetian folk air. Words by T. Tasso. g.i. ML 2

Canto del carcerato (Gesang des sträflings) Sicilian song. g.i. ML 2

Canto del pastore (Hirtenweise) Tuscan folk song. g.i. ML 2

"Canto l'armi pietose e il capitano." See Canto dei gondolieri

Cantor, Otto
    Ever safe with God

Canzone dei zampognari (Weihnachtslied der schalmeibläser) Neapolitan carol. g.i. ML 2
    Bagpipers' carol. e. MFF

Canzonetta ("Star vicino") See "Star vicino" (Rosa)

Canzonetta di campagnuolo (Lied des landmanns) Italian folk song from the Romagna. g.i. ML 2

Canzuna di li carriteri (Kärrnerlied) Sicilian song. g.i. ML 2

Caoineadh (Totenklagen) Irish folk song. g.ir. ML 1

"A capital ship." Old English air. Words by C. E. Carryl. BB—GSS—TFB—TFP—US

"Cap'n, I believe." Negro work song. SBA

Cappeau, M.
    Cantique de Noël (Adam)

"Captain, captain, tell me true." See Sweet William (Tennessee version)

"Captain, I believe." See "Cap'n, I believe"

Captain Jinks. <Words by W. H. Lingard> BB—DSO—SW

"A captive, and perchance unremember'd." See L'esclave (Lalo)

"Captive, et peut-être oubliée." See L'esclave (Lalo)

Capua, Eduardo di
    My sun. See 'O sole mio
    My sunshine. See 'O sole mio
    'O sole mio

Capua, Rinaldo di. See Rinaldo di Capua

Capurro, G.
    'O sole mio (Capua)

Caput apri defero. See The boar's head carol

The **cardinal** and gold. University of Southern California song. A. Wesson (music and words) AI

"The cardinal is waving." Stanford university song. W. G. Paul (music and words) AI—AIS—KU—KV

"Care flies from the lad that is merry." M. Arne. Words by D. Garrick. CSB 4

Careless love ("Love, oh love, oh careless love") American folk song. SBA
    Careless love ("Love, oh love, oh keerless love") American mountain version. RA
    Careless love ("If I were a little bird") Negro version. HB

Carew, lady
    The bridge

Carey, Henry
Composer
    Alma mater—George Washington university (same air as God save the king; attributed)
    America (with words "God bless our native land"; "My country 'tis of thee"; same air as God save the king; attributed)
    "Christ the Lord is ris'n today, alleluia! Sons of men and angels say" (wrongly attributed) See Worgan, J. "Christ the Lord is ris'n today, alleluia! Sons of men and angels say"
    "Come, Thou almighty King" (same air as God save the king; attributed)
    "Flocks are sporting"
    "God bless our native land." See America (attributed)
    God save the king (attributed)
    Die Lore am tore. See Sally in our alley
    "My country 'tis of thee." See America (attributed)
    National hymn. See America (attributed)
    A pastoral. See "Flocks are sporting"
    "Praise ye Jehovah's name" (same air as God save the king; attributed)
    Sally in our alley
    "Two empires" (same air as God save the king; attributed)
    World-peace. See "Two empires"
Author
    Sally in our alley (Old English air; also music by author)

"Cari luoghi ov'io passai." Donizetti. e.i. PC

Carissima. See Hamilton's song

"Cariwch medd Dafydd fy nhelyn i mi." See Dafydd y garreg wen

Car'line, Car'line, can't you dance de beeline. See Old Aunt Jemima

Carmela ("Así cual mueren") Mexican folk song. e.s. HE—MSP

Carmelina ("Thro' the night shines a light") D. Stevens (music and words) TFO

Carmen Ohio. Ohio state university song. Air: Spanish chant. Words by F. A. Cornell. AI

Carmeña ("Dance, play, sing, sorrow disdain."—Dance and sing) H. L. Wilson. Words by M. L. Baum. TFG

The **carnal** and the crane. Traditional carol from Herefordshire. OB

Carnations. See Clavelitos (Valverde)

[“Caro cibus, sanguis potus”] “Lord, at all times I will bless Thee.” Mendelssohn. e. SSO 1

“Caro mio ben” (“Canst thou believe”) G. Giordani. e.i. BST

“Caro mio ben” (“Star of my heart”) e.i. AT

Caro nome (Carved upon my heart) Verdi. e. WG

“Caro, son tua cosi.” G. M. Orlandini. e.i. KVG

Carol (“Now every child that dwells on earth”) See Our brother is born (Farjeon)

Carol, brothers, carol. W. A. Muhlenberg (music and words) MFS

“Carol, but in gladness.” See Carol, brothers, carol (Muhlenberg)

Carol, carol Christians (“In the fields abiding”) Burrows. Author of words unknown. DN

A carol for everyman (“Let no man come into this hall”) P. W. Dykema. Old English words. TFB

[Carol for New Year’s day] Greensleeves (“The old year now away is fled”) Old English air: Greensleeves. OB

Carol for the Nativity. Air: The foggy dew. DN

Carol of beauty (“Praise we the Lord”) French carol air: Quelle est cette odeur agréable. Words by S. Wilson. OB

The carol of St Stephen. Ancient air. 15th century words. DN

Carol of service (“Up, my neighbour”) Old French air: C’est de nos moutons. Words by S. Wilson, based on an old carol, Promptement levez-vous, mon voisin. e. OB

Carol of the Advent. Besançon carol air. Words by E. Farjeon. OB

Carol of the birds. See Nouël des ausèls

Carol of the kingdom (“When Jesus was a baby”) Manx carol air: Ny drogh vraane. Words by S. Wilson. OB

Carol of the twelve days. Traditional song. DNS
Variant of: The ten commandments

Carolath, Emil, prinz von Schönaich-.
See Schönaich-Carolath, Emil, prinz von

Carolina coronata. University of South Carolina alma mater. [J. E. Spilman] Words by G. A. Wauchope. KU

A health to Carolina. AIS

“Carolina, here’s to you.” See Carolina’s day (Smith)

Carolina’s day. University of South Carolina song. R. Smith (music and words) AI—AIS

Caroline (“Aine, dé, trois, Caroline”) Negro creole folk song. f. AS

Caroline, Caroline, can’t you dance de beeline. See Old Aunt Jemima

Caroline of Edinboro’ town. Folk song from Kentucky. SES 1

Carpenter, Fanny R.
Fires of wisdom (Schneider)

Carpenter, John Alden
The home road

Carpenter, Joseph Edwards
“Do they think of me at home” (Glover)
The good-bye at the door (Glover)
Her bright smile haunts me still (Wrightson)
“In the starlight” (Glover)
Music on the waves (Glover)
The old familiar place (Glover)

Carr, Benjamin
Willow, willow. See The willow song
The willow song

The carrion crow. Folk song: Big Laurel, N.C. version. SES 2
—Marion, N.C. version. SES 2

Carry me back (“Within a vale of western mountains”) See Alma mater song
—Oregon state agricultural college (Maris)

“Carry me back to old Virginny.” J. Bland (music and words) BB—TFP —TFR

[Carry me back to old Virginny] “Floating scow of old Virginny.” E. P. Christy (music and words) WSS

Carryl, Charles Edward
“A capital ship” (Old English air)

Carryl, Charles Edward, and Newell, George
Robinson Crusoe’s story (Newell)

Carter, Florence L.
Weary (Gabriel)

Carter, Stanley, pseud. See Redcliffe, Frederick J.

Carter, Thomas
“Oh, Nannie, wilt thou gang wi’ me”

Carter’s song. See “Il cavallo scalpita” (Mascagni)

“Carv’d upon my inmost heart.” See Caro nome (Verdi)

Carve dat possum. S. Lucas (music and words) BB—WSS

Carved upon my heart. See Caro nome (Verdi)

Cary, Phoebe
“One sweetly solemn thought” (Ambrose)

Casasanta, Joseph J.
Hike, Notre Dame

Cases, Pablo
Granadinas (Barrera y Calleja)

Casey, Thomas F.
“Drill, ye engineers, drill” (same air as Drill, ye tarriers, drill)
Drill, ye tarriers, drill

Casey Jones. E. Newton. Words by T. L. Seibert. GFS—SBA—SRW
Variant: Mama have you heard the news

Casey would waltz with a strawberry blonde. See The band played on (Ward)

“Cast not away the flowers I have given.” See L’âme des fleurs (Massenet)

“Cast thy bread on the waters.” J. L. Roeckel. Words by M. Mark-Lemon. CSS 2

"**Cast** thy burden upon the Lord." F. Mendelssohn. ɪTr of Wirf dein anliegen auf den Herrnɪ e. BB

Castanet song. G. Bizet. WG

Castles in Spain. See Aladdin (Bellini)

Castles in the air ("The bonnie, bonnie bairn") Composer unknown. Words by J. Ballantine. GOS 2—GS—LAS

Caswall, Edward
"See amid the winter's snow" (music by Mendelssohn; Morris)

The **cat** and the catboat. Swedish folk air. Words by H. W. Loomis. TFO

The **cat** came back. H. S. Miller (music and words) SMG—SRW

"A **cat** stood on the shore one day." See The cat and the catboat

La **Catanzarese** (Das mädchen von Catanzaro) Calabrian song. g.i. ML 2

Catch round the table. S. Webbe. DSB

"**Caterpillar!** caterpillar." Russian folk air. Words by H. H. Harbour. DSB

"**Catina** bellina" ("Lieb Kätchen") Venetian folk song. g.i. ML 2

"**Cauld** blaws the wind." See Up in the morning early

The **cautious** cat. G. L. Tracy. Words by D. Stevens. TFO

The **cavaliers** of Dixie. Confederate army song. J. W. Callcott. Words by B. F. Porter. DSO

ɪIl **cavallo** scalpitaʺɪ Carter's song. P. Mascagni. e. WG

The **cavalry** remount. Song from the mounted service school at Fort Riley. DSO

The **cavalry** song ("Come, listen unto this my song") DSO

Cavendish, Michael
"Down in a valley, down in a valley"

Cawood, John
Hark, what mean those holy voices (French Noël air; Latin air)

Cawsand bay. Traditional British naval song. BOS 2

Cawsand bay. Traditional British naval song. 2d air. WSE

"**Cease,** oh, cease to wound and tease me." See "O cessate di piagarmi" (Scarlatti)

Cécilia. See "Mon pèr' n'avait fille que moi"

"**Céfiro,** que por la tarde." See El céfiro

El **céfiro** (The breeze) Mexican folk song. e.s. MSP

Ceiriog. See Hughes, John Ceiriog

Čekat ću ga. See Zwiegespräch

Célébrons le Seigneur (Glorify the Lord) G. Rupès. e.f. TSS 2

ɪCeleste Aidaɪ "Heav'nly Aida." Verdi. e. WG

The **'cello.** H. W. Loomis (music and words) TFO

Celui que j'aime (The one I love) Folk song from Champagne. e.f. CBF 1

"**Central** will shine." School song. BB
Variants: "Our boys will shine tonight"; "Our club will shine"; "Our troop will shine tonight"

Cert'n'y, Lord. Negro spiritual. JG

"**Červené** vínečko." See Rotes weinchen

Cesareo, Giovanni Alfredo
La serenata (Tosti)

"**C'est** dans tous les cantons." See Dans tous les cantons

C'est l'aviron qui nous mène en haut (It is the oar that impels us on) Canadian folk song. e.f. GC
Variant of: "En revenant de la joli' Rochelle"

C'est la salle de mes ancètres. For English translation see "Silent heroes" (Planquette)

C'est le vent qui va frivolant. See Les trois canards

"**C'est** une fille engagère." See La visite du jour de l'an

"**C'était** un vieux sauvage." See Tenaouich' tenaga, ouich'ka

Chadwick, George Whitefield
"The stormy evening"

Chahcoal man. Negro folk song. SBA

Chaikovskiĭ, Petr Il'ich. See Tchaikovsky, Peter Ilyich

Chaileans kühe. See "Crodh Chailean"

"**Chairs** to mend, old chairs to mend." Round. <W. Hayes> DSB—TFB—TFG
Oxford cries. BOS 2
Chairs to mend. Words adapted. GSS

Chalfant, Edward Chambers
"Way down in Easton" (Stier)

Chalkhill, John
The angler's song (Lawes) Authorship uncertain

Challis, H. W.
"The winds that waft my sighs to thee" (Wallace)

Challo Brown. Halliard chantey. WSE
Variants: Sally Brown; Shallow Brown

A **Chalutz** polka (Polka chalutsith) Palestinean folk song. e.he. BNP

Chamberlain, Charles H.
Illinois (Jones)

Chamberlain, Herbert Clayton
Victory (Waite)

Chamberlain, W. P.
Hurrah for old New England

Chambers-Ketchum, Mrs Annie. See Ketchum, Mrs Annie (Chambers)

Chaminade, Cécile Louise Stéphanie
Madrigal
"Thou little bird with pinions gay." See Madrigal

Chamisso, Adelbert von
The pigtail (Mozart)

Champagne Charlie ("Of gaiety I've seen a deal") A. Lee. Words by G. Leybourne. SRW

Champagne Charlie was my name. See Moet and Shandon for me

Champlain. University of Vermont song. C. S. Putnam. <Words by D. D. Fisher; wrongly attributed to C. W. Fisher> AI—KU

Chandos anthem. See "Righteousness and equity" (Händel)

Chanson à baller. See "Je vais entrer dans la danse"

Chanson d'Alsace (A song of Alsace) Alsatian folk song. e. CSB 1

Chanson de Florian. See "Ah! s'il est dans votre village" (Godard)

Chanson de la mariée (Brautlied) French folk song. f.g. ML 1

La chanson des beignets (The song of the pancakes) Folk song from Alsace. e.f.g. CBF 2

[La chanson des métamorphoses] "Par derrier' chez ma tant'" ("Back of my auntie's house") Folk song: Canadian version. GC

[Chanson du toréador] Toreador song. G. Bizet. e. WG

Chant d'exil (Song of exile) P. Vidal. Words by V. Hugo. e.f. TM

"Chante qui voudra les attraits." See La charmante Marguerite

Chantez, mignonne Cécilia. See "Mon pèr' n'avait fille que moi" (Cécilia)

[Chantez riez et dormez] Sing, smile, sleep. C. Gounod. Words by V. Hugo. e. GE

Sing, smile, slumber (Canti, ridi, dormi) e.f. MFS

Chanticleer. English traditional air. Words by W. Austin. OB

Chantons Noël. Traditional Anjevin Noël. e. DNS

The chapel ("See yon chapel on the hill") Words by Uhland. e. MFS

Chapman, E. W.
Flowers for the brave (Bellini)

Chapman, Lamar, and Ashburn, Karl
"Dear T. C. U."

Chappell, William
"Golden slumbers kiss your eyes" (Folk air) See Dekker, T.
"Golden slumbers kiss your eyes" (Folk air)

"Chapt im un bindt im." See Oi, alas, a robber

Charcoal man. See Chahcoal man

"Charge down the field and fight for Whittier." See Victory song (Tomlinson)

O charhos. See Der tod

"De chariot rode on de mountain top." See Great day

Charleston gals. Negro song from Arkansas. AS

Charlie Case song. Old song. SRW

"Charlie is a handsome man." See Charlie's sweet (North Carolina version)

Charlie is my darling. See O Charlie is my darling

"Charlie's neat and Charlie's sweet." See Charlie's sweet (Pine Mountain, Ky. version)

Charlie's sweet. Play-party game: Hindman, Ky. version. SES 2
—Pine Mountain, Ky. version. SES 2
—North Carolina version. SES 2
—Virginia version. SES 2
Variant: Weevily wheat

"Charlottie liv'd on a mountain top." See The frozen girl

La charmante Marguerite. Old French air. e.f. BST

"Charming, pleasing, unseen wand'rer." See Gentle zephyr (Hagen)

The charming young widow. Old song. SW

Chase the buffalo. Play-party game from Kentucky. SES 2

Chattaway, Thurland
I've grown so used to you
Little black me
Mandy Lee

The chatterbox. Words by J. Taylor. MFS

The chattering squaw. Cree Indian air. e. TFG

Chaucer, Geoffrey
Welcome, summer (Irish traditional air)

Chausson, Ernest
Le colibri
The hummingbird. See Le colibri

A chazan äuf Shabbos. Jewish folk song. y. SY

"Chazkele." Jewish folk song. y. KAJ

"Che farò senza Euridice" ("What sad lot the stars prepare me") C. W. von Gluck. e.i. PC
"Tho' the earth be bright." e. TFP

"Che mai vegg'io." See Infelice! e tu credevi (Verdi)

"Che val ricchezza e trono." Donizetti. e.i. PC

Cheapside. E. Farjeon. GSS

Cheder lied. Jewish folk song. y. SY

"Cheeks as red as a red, red rose." See Betty Anne

"Cheer, boys, cheer." H. Russell. Words by C. Mackay. MFS

"Cheer! cheer for old Notre Dame." See Victory march (Shea)

Cheer for Adelphi. See Adelphi field song (Thayer)

Cheer for alma mater. Boston university song. E. M. Nazarian. Words by G. S. Nies. KU—KV

Cheer for old Amherst. Amherst university song. J. N. Pierce (music and words) LAS

"Cheer for old Loyola." See Hail Loyola (Kowalski)

Cheer the weary traveller. See Weary traveler

Cheer till the sound wakes the blue hills around. See The big red team (Tourison)

"Cheer up, friends and neighbours." See Easter carol

Cheer up, Sam. S. C. Foster (music and words) WSS

Cheerily, my lads, yo ho. See The midshipmite (Maybrick)

"Cheerily the bugle sounds." See The mountain bugle (Hewitt)

"Cheerily the huntsman." See Der schütz (Weber)

Cheer'ly man ("O Nancy Dawson") Halliard chantey.   WSE
> For variants see following songs of similar title

Cheerly men ("Oh Nancy Dawson") Halliard chantey.   SBS

Cheer'ly men ("Oh, Nancy Dawson") Halliard chantey.   TSB 1

Chenery, Cornelius
> "There is an hour of hallowed peace"

Cheney, John Vance
> "The wind is awake" (Bartlett)

Chère enfant! que j'appelle comme autrefois.   For English translation see "Child of mine" (Offenbach)

Cherepnin, Nikolaï Nikolaevich
> To music

"Chernī ochī."   See "Schwarze äuglein"

Cherry, Andrew
> The bay of Biscay (Davy)
> "There's a dear little plant" (Cherry, J. W.)

Cherry, John William
> The dear little shamrock.   See "There's a dear little plant"
> Monarch of the woods
> Shells of ocean
> "There's a dear little plant"

"Cherry-bloom" (Sakura)   Japanese song. e.   MFF

Cherry blossoms ("Sweet blossoms, cherry blossoms") H. Hadley.   Words by S. Fay.   TFO

The **cherry** tree carol.   Traditional song: Yorkshire version.   OB
> —Barbourville, Ky. version.   SES 1
> —Hindman, Ky. version.   SES 1
> —Pineville, Ky. version.   SES 1
> —St Helen's, Ky. version.   SES 1
> —Big Laurel, N.C. version.   SES 1
> —Hot Springs, N.C. version.   SES 1
> The cherry tree.   Knott or Letcher county, Ky. version.   MK
> Variant: "As Joseph was a-walking"

The **cherry** tree carol.   Traditional song. 15th century air.   DN

The **cherry** tree carol.   Traditional song. Air from Fyfe.   OB

The **cherry** tree carol.   Traditional song. Air from Husk.   OB

Cherryman, Myrtle Koon
> Farewell to thee (Liliuokalani)
> My native land (Grieg)
> Night (Abt)
> "Sleep, soldier, sleep" (Davison)

Cherubini, Maria Luigi Zenobio Carlo Salvatore
> "Ave Maria"
> "Like as a father pitieth his children, so the Lord hath mercy"
> "Lord, lead me in Thy righteousness."   See O salutaris
> O salutaris
> Saviour of sinners.   See "Ave Maria"

₍The **Chesapeke** and the Shannon₎   Shannon and Chesapeake. ₍Air: The pretty girl of Derby, O₎   WSE

Chester, Anson G.
> Good night and pleasant dreams (Wallace)

The **Chester** carol.   See "Qui creavit coelum, lully, lully, lu"

Chesterton, Mrs Frances Alice (Blogg)
> Children's song of the Nativity (English traditional air)

Chesterton, Gilbert Keith
> The world's desire (Traditional air)

Chevrons.   West Point song.   P. Egner.   Words by J. C. Whitcomb. DSO

Chevy chase ("God prosper long our noble king")   Air: Flying fame, or, Chevy chase, or, The new Rogero, or, Now ponder well, you parents dear, or, The children in the wood.   BOS 2

"Chi da' lacci d'amor."   M. di Zanobi da Gagliano.   e.i.   KVG

"Chi mai sentì."   See Nell' orror di notte oscura (Rinaldo di Capua)

Chi mi frena in tal momento.   For English translation see Sextet (Donizetti)

The **Chicago** gouge.   W. C. Handy.   HB

Chicago is the city for stomps and struggles.   See The Chicago gouge (Handy)

The **Chickaleary** cove.   Words by A. G. Vance.   SW

"Chickens a-crowing in Sourwood mountain."   See Sourwood mountain (Georgia version)

"Chickens a-crowing on Sourwood mountain."   See Sourwood mountain (Lexington, Ky. version; Manchester, Ky. version)

"Chickens a-crowing on the Sourwood mountains."   See Sourwood mountain (Berea, Ky. version)

"The **chickens** they are crowing."   Playparty song: Kentucky version.   SES 2
> —Virginia version.   SES 2

"Chide mildly the erring."   W. B. Bradbury.   MFS

Le **chiffonnier** (The rag picker's bride) Breton air.   e.f.   ASN

The **child** and heaven.   Breton folk air. Words by L. Warner.   DSB

"Child in the manger."   See Leanabh an aigh

"A **Child** is born in Bethlehem, alleluia."   See Puer natus in Bethlehem

"A **Child** is born in Bethlehem, awaiteth Him all Jerusalem."   See Een Kint gheboren in Bethlehem

"Child, is life bright alone."   See None can tell (Allen)

"Child of earth with golden hair."   See Titania's song (Horn)

"Child of mine."   J. Offenbach.   ₍Tr of Chère enfant! que j'appelle comme autrefois₎   e.   WG

The **child** of the railroad engineer.   Old American song.   RA—SW

Child of the regiment.   Donizetti.   ₍Tr of Quando il destino in mezzo a strage ria₎   e.   MFS

"A **Child** this day is born."   Traditional air.   DN—OB

"A **Child** this day is born" (Good tidings) Gloucestershire air.   FC

"**Childhood's** days now pass before me."
See The cottage by the sea (Thomas)
"**Children** a-crying, crying for bread." See
The cuckoo (Dewey, Va. version)
Children do linger. Negro spiritual from
South Carolina. AS
"**Children** go, to and fro." See Follow
me, full of glee
"**Children** grumbled on de way." See I
can't stay away (Johnson)
Children, hail! hail! hail! I'm gwine jine
saints above. See Hail! hail! hail
"**Children** one and all be jolly." See
Christmas eve
Children, we all shall be free. Negro
spiritual. HRD
Children's play. See Piaceri fanciulleschi
(Mozart)
Children's song of the Nativity. English
traditional air: Stowey. Words by
F. Chesterton. OB
Chilly water. Negro song. BB—JB 2
Chime again, beautiful bells. H. R.
Bishop. MFS
Chiming bells of long ago. C. F. Shat-
tuck. OT
De **chimney's** falling down. See The
little old cabin in the lane (Hays)
"**Ching** Loo, China boy, flew his paper kite."
See Never mind
"**Chirp,** chirp, chirp! soon as fades the
light." See The cricket
The **Chisholm** trail ("Oh, come along,
boys") Cowboy song. 1st ver-
sion. LSC.
For variants see The Lone Star trail;
The old Chisholm trail; also fol-
lowing song of same title
The **Chisholm** trail ("Oh, come • along
boys") Cowboy song. 2d version.
LSC

Chitwood, Bill
Howdy, Bill

"**Chloe** proves false, but still she is charm-
ing." See The slighted swain
"**Choćbym** ja jeździł we dnie i w nocy."
See "Müsst' ich auch reiten tage und
nächte"
"**Chodzila** Mariška." See "Ging jung
Mariechen"
Choirs of angels. Old west of England
traditional air. DN
"**Choose** a partner, quickly choose her."
See The village dance

Chopin, Frédéric François
Lithauisches lied. See Lithuanian
song
Lithuanian song
The maiden's wish
"On to the morgue"
Spring song. See The maiden's wish
[Choral ("Out of our suff'ring")] "Z dymem
pożarów" ("Brünstige lohe") Po-
lish national song. g.p. ML 3
With smoke of fire (Z dymem pożarów)
e. LAS

Choral sanctus. A. R. Gaul. TFG
"**Chori** erresiñoula." See Errefusa

"**Chorietan** buruzagi" ("Unter des waldes
vöglein") Basque folk song. ba.g.
ML 2
"**Choriñua** kaiolan" (Vöglein im käfig)
Basque folk song. ba.g. ML 2

Chorley, Henry Fothergill
The brave old oak (Loder)
The long day closes (Sullivan)

Chorus of blessed spirits. C. W. Gluck.
[Tr of Vieni a' regni del riposo] e.
TFG
"**Chrétiens,** ouvrez vos volets." See Noël
des quêteurs bressans
"The **Christ-child** lay on Mary's lap." See
The world's desire
Christ est ressuscité. For English trans-
lation see Easter hymn (Gounod)
Christ is born in Bethlehem. Christmas
anthem. MFS
"**Christ** is born of Maiden fair." H. J.
Gauntlett. [Tr of Christo paremus
canticam, in excelsis gloria] e. FC
—MFS
Christ the Lord has risen today. See
"Christ the Lord is ris'n today, alleluia!
Sons of men and angels say" (Worgan)
"**Christ** the Lord in rags goes a-begging."
See Le parabole du mauvais riche
"**Christ** the Lord is born today, alleluia!
alleluia! Sons of men and angels say"
(Sing alleluia) French air. Words
adapted by S. Rowe. FC
Christ the Lord is risen ("Now is the hour
of darkness past") German air.
Words by I. Watts. OB
"**Christ** the Lord is ris'n today, alleluia!
Sons of men and angels say." J.
Worgan <wrongly attributed to H.
Carey> Words by C. Wesley.
BB—TFO
Christ the Lord has risen today. TFG
Christ the Pilgrim. J. Blumenthal. CSS 1
"**Christ** tol' the blin' man." See I'm so
glad trouble don't last alway
"**Christ** was born in Bethlehem." Moun-
tain spiritual from North Carolina.
SES 2
"**Christ** was born on Christmas day,
wreathe the holly, twine the bay;
Christus natus hodie." German air.
DN
"**Christ** was born on Christmas day,
wreathe the holly, twine the bay,
light and life and joy is He." See
Christmas carol (Helmore)
"**Christ,** when a child, a garden made."
See The crown of roses (Tchaikovsky)
Christbaum. For English translation see
The Christmas tree is sparkling with
light (Cornelius)
Christian men, rejoice and sing. See
Christmas carol (Helmore)
"**Christians** all, throw your shutters wide."
See Noël des quêteurs bressans
"**Christians,** awake." J. Wainwright.
Words by J. Byrom. DN
Christkindleins wiegenlied. 17th century
German folk song. g. EDL

Christmas ("Awake, my soul")   See "Awake, my soul, stretch every nerve" (Händel)

The **Christmas** angelus.   Puget (music and words)   ₍Tr of Ave Maria! car voici l'heure sainte₎   e.   DN

Christmas as it comes.   ₍Words by H. Mather₎   MFS

Christmas carol ("Christ was born on Christmas day")   T. Helmore.   Words by J. M. Neale.   MFS

Christmas carol ("Ye shepherds so drowsy")   See "Ye shepherds so drowsy"

Christmas carol of Strassburg.   See Noël de Strasbourg

Christmas carolling song.   Traditional English air.   TFG

Christmas day carol.   See "Christmas day is come, let us all prepare for mirth"

"**Christmas** day is come, let us all prepare for mirth" (Christmas day carol) Carol from County Wexford.   Air: The brown little mallet.   DNS Irish carol.   OB

Christmas eve ("Children one and all be jolly")   German air.   Words by H. H. Harbour.   DSB

Christmas eve ("The Lord at first")   See "The Lord at first did Adam make"

A **Christmas** hymn ("From ev'ry spire") See "From ev'ry spire on Christmas eve" (Coles)

Christmas is coming ("I want forty dozen of fine waxen dolls")   ₍H. Phillips₎ <Words by J. P. McCaskey>   MFS

"**Christmas** is coming, the goose is getting fat."   Three-part round.   Words by E. Nesbit.   TFP

Christmas is here ("Sing we all merrily, Christmas is here") English traditional song.   FC

"**Christmas** is here; winds whistle shrill." See The mahogany tree (Campana)

₍**Christmas** night₎ "On Christmas night all Christians sing" (Sussex carol)   Folk air.   OB

Christmas song ("Minuit, chrétien")   See Cantique de Noël (Adam)

"**Christmas**-time has come again, time to us so dear" (Ring on, Christmas bells) D. Stevens.   ₍Words by the Misses Latta₎   FC

"**Christmas** time is a rolling on."   See The cruel mother (Georgia version)

"**Christmas** time is come again, Christmas pleasures bringing."   Carol.   MFS

The **Christmas** tree ("Gather around the Christmas tree")   See "Gather around the Christmas tree" (Hopkins)

The **Christmas** tree ("The holly's up") See The Christmas tree is sparkling with light (Cornelius)

The **Christmas** tree ("O tannenbaum, o tannenbaum")   See Der tannenbaum

The **Christmas** tree ₍is sparkling with light₎ P. Cornelius (music and words)   e. OB

Christmasse of olde.   Swiss air.   Words by E. Field.   MFS

Christo paremus canticam, in excelsis gloria.   For English translations see "Christ is born of Maiden fair" (Gauntlett); "When Christ was born of Mary free" (French air); "When Christ was born of Mary free" (Brown); "When Christ was born of Mary free" (Shaw)

Christy, Edwin Pearce
Carry me back to old Virginny "Floating scow of old Virginny."   See Carry me back to ole Virginny

Chudíla se míla mama.   See Wen ich will zur ehe

An **chúil-fhionn** (Das mädchen mit dem goldhaar) Irish folk song.   ₍Air: The coolun₎   g.ir.   ML 1

Chunarska přesen'.   See Lied des kahnfahrers

"The **church** bells they were ringing." See The broken home (Fox)

Church militant.   See "The Son of God goes forth to war" (Cutler)

De **church** of God.   Negro spiritual. HRD

Chwatal, Francis Xaver
"Lovely night! O lovely night"

"**Cia** hé sin amuigh."   See Éamonn a' Chnuic

Ciampi, Francesco
"Quella barbara catena"
Fair Nina.   See Nina
Nina
"Tre giorni son che Nina."   See Nina

₍"**Ciascun** lo dice"₎ "Search thro' the wide world."   Donizetti.   e.   MFS

"**Čiaže** je to rolička nezoraná."   See "Wem soll dieses brachfeld wohl angehören"

Ciccuzza.   Neapolitan folk song.   g.i. ML 2

Cider song.   R. Planquette.   ₍Tr of La pomme est un fruit plein de sève₎   e. WLO

₍"Le **ciel** a visité la terre"₎ Adore and be still.   C. Gounod.   ₍Words by J. Ahrem₎   e.   TSS 2

Cielito lindo.   Mexican folk song.   s. SBA
Cielito lindo (Pretty creature)   e.s. VS

"**Cigarettes** will spoil yer life."   Old song. SBA

"**Cilia'r** haul draw dros ael bryniau hael Arfon."   See Morva Rhuddlan

Cill Mhuire.   See Cnocáinín aereach Chill-Mhuire

"**Cimentando** i venti e l'onde."   Rossini. e.i.   PC

Cine trece pe uliță (Wer geht draussen auf der strasse)   Rumanian song.   g.ru. ML 2

Ciobănaș dela miori (Der hirt)   Rumanian song.   g.ru.   ML 2

"**Circle** to the left, the old brass wagon." See Old brass wagon

"**Clad** in rags the Saviour wanders."   See La parabole du mauvais riche

The **clang** of the wooden shoon.   J. L. Molloy (music and words)   GE

Clapp, Mary Brennan
The warriors (Smith)

Clärchens lied. See "Freudvoll und leid-
voll" (Reichardt)
Clare de kitchen. Minstrel song. WSS
Clarendon, J. Hayden-. See Hayden-
Clarendon, J.
Claribel, pseud. See Barnard, Mrs Char-
lotte (Alington)
Clark, Edward
The voice of Jesus (Sutcliffe)
Clark, H. Qualli
You'll think of me
Clark, James Gowdy
The rover's grave
We've drunk from the same canteen
Clark, Kenneth Sherman
Alma mater, Ohio
Jungle march
Clark, Thomas Curtis
Somewhere
Clarke, H. Pitman
Swanee river moon
Clarke, Jeremiah
"Come, sweet lass"
Greenwich Park. See "Come, sweet
lass"
Komm, suss lieb. See "Come, sweet
lass"
Claudius, Matthias
Abendlied (Schulz)
Deutsches weihelied (Methfessel)
Rheinweinlied (André)
Der tod und das mädchen (Schubert)
Clauve, Lena Cecile
Hail to New Mexico
Clavelitos (Carnations) Zambra gitana.
Valverde. Words by Estic. e.s.
MSP
Clay, Frederic
Gipsy John
"I'll sing thee songs of Araby"
Clay Morgan. Folk song from North
Carolina. SES 2
Clear de track, let de bulgine run ("O de
worl' was made in six days")
Negro chantey. WSE
Variant of: Clear the track, let the
bullgine run
Clear the kitchen. See Clare de kitchen
Clear the track, let the bullgine run ("Oh,
the smartest clipper you can find")
Windlass and capstan chantey.
TSB 1
Variant: Clear de track, let de bulgine
run
Clémentine ("Ça fait moin la peine")
Negro creole folk song. e.f. MB
Clementine ("In a cavern, in a canyon")
See Oh, my darling Clementine (Mon-
trose)
Clephane, Elizabeth Cecilia
The ninety and nine (Sankey)
Clesi, N. J.
I'm sorry I made you cry
The clever woman. J. Blewitt. Words
by the Honourable G. F. Berkeley.
SW
Clifford, G.
Rain on the roof
Clifton, Harry
Shabby genteel

Clifton, William
"The last link is broken"
The climate. Air: Wilkins and his Dinah.
Words by D. Stevens. TFO—TFP—
TFR
Climb up, ye chillun, climb. Negro song.
<F. A. Kent> WSS
Clink, clink, drink, drink, drink. See
Bowdoin beata
Les cloches (The bells) A. C. Debussy.
Words by P. Bourget. e.f. ASN
Les cloches de Nantes. See "Dans les
prisons de Nantes"
The clock ("The clock is queer") German
folk air. Words by J. L. Vandevere.
TFO
"The clock is queer, you must admit."
See The clock
Clokey, Joseph Waddell
Kye song of Saint Bride
"Close beside the winding Cedar's sloping
banks of green." See Alma mater—
Michigan state college (Thompson)
"Close your eyes, Lena, my darling." See
Go to sleep, Lena darling (Emmet)
The clothier. Folk song from Kentucky.
SES 1
Cloud-ships. Tyrolese folk air. Words
by H. H. Harbour. DSB
Cloud song (Hevebe tawi) Hopi Indian
song of harvest time. e. MFF
Clunie, John
"I lo'e na a laddie but ane" (Old air)
Cnocáinín aereach Chill-Mhuire (Cill
Mhuire) Irish folk song. g.ir. ML 1
Cnochd a bheannichd (Feeenlied) Hebri-
dean song. ga.g. ML 1
Coaching song. E. Audran. e. WLO
Coad, J.
The Prince of life
Coal black Rose. [H. Russell] SW—
WSS
Coard, Henry A.
The gipsy's warning
Coast artillery marching song ("Roarious!
roarious") Air: One keg of beer for the
four of us. DSO
Coast artillery song ("Oh, they said the
coast artillery would never go to war")
DSO
The coast artilleryman ("I'm a man of ex-
perience") DSO
The coasts of High Barbary. Folk song.
DSB—DSC
Coates, Elmer Ruán
We have met, loved, and parted (East-
burn)
Cobb, Will D.
Good-bye, Dolly Gray (Barnes)
I can't tell why I love you, but I do
(Edwards)
I'll be with you when the roses bloom
again (Edwards)
The cobbler and the crow. Old song.
TFR
"The cobbler sang, for his heart was light."
See Paradise square (Löhr)
Co-ca-che-lunk ("Since our muskets we
have shouldered."—The camp war song)
Civil war song. DSO

Cocaine Lil.   American folk song.   Air: Willy the weeper.   SBA
Cock Robin (see Song Index)
Variant: Cocky Robin
Cockburn, Mrs Alicia (Rutherford)
The flowers of the forest (Traditional air)
The **cockroach.**   See La cucaracha
Cocky Robin.   Folk song: Kentucky version.   SES 2
—Burnsville, N.C. version.   SES 2
—Marion, N.C. version.   SES 2
—Micaville, N.C. version.   SES 2
Variant of: Cock Robin
Codiad yr haul (Sonnenaufgang)   Welsh song.   g.w.   ML 1
Codiad yr hedydd.   For English translation see "Rise, rise, thou merry lark"
Coenen, Willem
"Come unto me, all ye that labor"
Frühlingslied.   See "Wenn der frühling auf die berge steigt"
Lovely spring.   See "Wenn der frühling auf die berge steigt"
"Wenn der frühling auf die berge steigt"
Coerne, Louis Adolphe
To a rose
Coghill, Mrs Annie Louisa (Walker)
"Work, for the night is coming" (Mason)
Cohan, George Michael
Give my regards to Broadway
Mary's a grand old name
Over there, over there
So long Mary
The Yankee Doodle boy
You're a grand old flag
[An **coineachan**] "I left my baby lying here."   Scottish song.   e.   GSS
Colchester.   See "From age to age how grandly rise" (Purcell)
"**Cold** blows the wind o'er my true love."   See The unquiet grave (North Devonshire version)
"**Cold** sweat is on my brow."   R. Planquette.   [Tr of Ô ciel malheureux Grenicheux]   e.   WLO
Cole, Browne Greaton-.   See Greaton-Cole, Browne
Cole, C. E.
"Light of our way"
Cole, Florence V.
"On to victory"
Cole, Robert A.
Oh, didn't he ramble
Cole, Robert A., and Johnson, John Rosamond
The maiden with the dreamy eyes
Under the bamboo tree
Coleridge, Samuel Taylor
Answer to a child's question (Stanford)
Coles, George
A Christmas hymn.   See "From ev'ry spire on Christmas eve"
Duane street.   See "From ev'ry spire on Christmas eve"
"From ev'ry spire on Christmas eve"
Colgate, alma mater.   See Alma mater—Colgate university

Colgate invictus.   Colgate university song.   R. B. Bushby.   Words by G. M. Kelly.   AIS
Colgate marching song.   Colgate university song.   Words by F. M. Hubbard and G. M. Hubbard.   KU—KV
Le **colibri** (The hummingbird) E. Chausson.   Words by Leconte de Lisle.   e.f.   ASN
Colin's cattle.   See "Crodh Chailean"
"The **colleen** bawn."   J. Benedict.   SI
Colleen dhas cruthen na moe.   See Cailín deás crúidhte na mbó
College hymn.   Bryn Mawr college song.   [L. M. Ibsen]   Words by C. R. Foulke.   AI
College kick.   See Kollege kick (Hagen)
The **college** on the hill.   Union college song.   R. Knight (music and words)   AIS
The **college** song ("All hail the college that we love")   Brigham Young university song.   Old air.   Words by A. P. Greenwood.   HW
Collier, Robert Joseph
"Sons of Georgetown" (Welsh air)
Collier, Thomas
Amber Lee (White)
Colligan, John I.
Fight for old S. F.
"Hail San Francisco"
Collins, Herbert E.
Hail to dear old Whittier
Colman, George, the younger
Savourneen deelish (Old air)
Colombo.   Old song.   Revised words.   US
Colorado "C" men.   Colorado college song.   [T. W. Allen and M. W. Sheafe]   AI
Colorado halls.   University of Colorado song.   [Old English air, attributed to H. Harrington]   Words by R. E. Hieronymus.   KU
The **Colorado** trail.   Cowboy song.   SBA
"**Colorado** varsity comes marching on the field."   See Glory glory Colorado
Colorado's sons and daughters.   See Hail to Denver U (Thompson)
Colors of Washington.   University of Washington song.   C. M. Hatcher. Words by R. G. Phillips.   HW
Colton, Winfred R.
Alma mater—University of South Dakota.   See Pioneer song
Pioneer song
Colum, Padraic
Cruckhaun Finn (Irish air)
An island spinning song (Irish air)
She moved thro' the fair (Irish air)
Columbia, Columbia, we love thy honored name.   See Columbia quadrangle song (Kelley)
Columbia, gem of the ocean.   See Columbia, the gem of the ocean (Becket)
Columbia, God preserve thee free.   J. Haydn.   MFS
Columbia quadrangle song ("Come and lift your glasses")   W. E. Kelley (music and words)   LAS

Columbia, the gem of the ocean. T. à
Becket; wrongly attributed to D.
T. Shaw. Words by T. à Becket;
wrongly attributed to D. T. Shaw
and to T. Dwight. BB—DSC—
TFP
Columbia, gem of the ocean. MFS
Columbia, the gem of the ocean (The
red white and blue) GOS 1
Columbia's crew. Columbia university
song. W. E. Kelley (music and
words) KU
"Columbia's sons, rush forth in throngs."
See Strike for your rights! avenge your
wrongs
Columbus [day] Italian air. Words by
J. Erwin. DSB
Coma ti ya youpy, youpy ya, youpy ya.
See The Chisholm trail (1st version)
Coma ti yi youpy, youpy ya, youpy ya.
See The old Chisholm trail
Le combat naval; "Le trente-et-un du mois
d'août" ("Am einunddreibigsten au-
gust") Norman folk song. f.g.
ML 1
"Come! a song for Indiana, sing hurrah."
See Indiana, our Indiana (Harker and
King)
"Come again, sweet love." J. Dowland.
MBS—TFG
Sweet love doth now invite. TFG
"Come, all kind people, my story to hear."
See Ellen Smith (Degraph)
"Come all my young ladies, take warning
from me." See I'm going to Georgia
(Kentucky version)
"Come, all who live in the U.S.A." See
The U.S.A. forever (Emmett)
"Come all ye bold fishermen, listen to
me." See The song of the fishes
"Come all ye booze fighters ef you want to
hear." See Moonshine
"Come all ye fair and tender ladies." See
"Come all you fair and tender ladies"
(Barbourville, Ky. version; Berea, Ky.
version no. 1; Hindman, Ky. version
no. 2; Balsam, N.C. version)
Come, all ye faithful. See "Adeste,
fideles" (Reading?)
"Come all ye gallant volunteers who fear
not life to lose." See Join the Hick-
ory Blues
"Come, all ye jolly sailors bold." See
The Arethusa
"Come all ye jolly shepherds." See
When the kye come hame
"Come, all ye loyal classmen now." See
The red and blue (Goeckel)
"Come all ye railroad section men." See
Jerry, go an' ile that car
"Come all ye sons of Williams, sing."
See Yard by yard (Brown and Wood)
"Come all ye southern soldiers." Folk
song from North Carolina. SES 2
"Come all ye true-born shanty-boys."
See The jam on Gerry's Rock
"Come, all ye wayward trav'lers." See
The downward road is crowded

"Come all ye weary, cease from your
sighing." See The cross of Calvary
(Gounod)
"Come all ye weary wanderers beneath the
wint'ry sky." See Awake and sing
"Come all ye young and tender ladies."
See "Come all you fair and tender
ladies" (Hindman, Ky. version no. 1)
"Come all ye young fellows that follow
the sea." See Blow the man down
"Come all ye young people and listen to
me." See Married and single life
"Come all you airy bachelors." See The
airy bachelor
"Come all you Alabama girls." See "If
you want to go a-courting" (Burnsville,
N.C. version no. 1)
"Come, all you blades both high and low."
See Billy Vite and Molly Green
"Come all you bold sailors that follow
the Lakes." See Red iron ore
"Come all you brave young shanty-boys."
See James Whaland
"Come all you fair and tender ladies."
Folk song: Barbourville, Ky. ver-
sion. SES 2
—Berea, Ky. version no. 1. SES 2
—Berea, Ky. version no. 2. SES 2
—Berea, Ky. version no. 3. SES 2
—Berea, Ky. version no. 4. SES 2
—Hazard, Ky. version. SES 2
—Hindman, Ky. version no. 1. SES 2
—Hindman, Ky. version no. 2. SES 2
—Knott county, Ky. version. SES 2
—Balsam, N.C. version. SES 2
—Burnsville, N.C. version no. 1.
SES 2
—Burnsville, N.C. version no. 2.
SES 2
—Carmen, N.C. version. SES 2
—Hot Springs, N.C. version. SES 2
—Flag Pond, Tenn. version no. 1.
SES 2
—Flag Pond, Tenn. version no. 2.
SES 2
—Blue Ridge Springs, Va. version.
SES 2
—Franklin county, Va. version. SES 2
Little sparrow. Letcher county, Ky.
version. MK
Variant: "Come all you young and
handsome girls"
"Come all you fair and tender ladies, be
careful how you court young men."
See "Come all you fair and tender
ladies" (Hazard, Ky. version; Burns-
ville, N.C. version no. 1; Flag Pond,
Tenn. version no. 1)
"Come all you fair and tender ladies, be
careful how you love young men."
See "Come all you fair and tender
ladies" (Burnsville, N.C. version no. 2)
"Come all you fair and tender ladies, come
listen to my story." See Katie Morey
(Hot Springs, N.C. version)
"Come all you fair and tender ladies, take
warning by those false young men."
See "Come all you fair and tender
ladies" (Blue Ridge Springs, Va. version)

"**Come** all you fair and tender ladies, take warning how you court young men." See "Come all you fair and tender ladies" (Berea, Ky. versions no. 2-4; Letcher county, Ky. version)

"**Come** all you fair, young, tender ladies." See "Come all you fair and tender ladies" (Flag Pond, Tenn. version no. 2)

"**Come** all you faithful Christians that dwell here on earth" (Hereford carol) OB

"**Come** all you fine young fellows with hearts so warm and true." See Flat river girl

"**Come,** all you gallant poachers." See Van Diemen's land

"**Come,** all you gallant soldiers." See A helluva engineer

"**Come** all you good people the truth I'll relate." See Harding's defeat

"**Come** all you jolly cowboys." See The dreary life

"**Come** all you jolly driver boys." See Edwin in the lowlands low (Hyden, Ky. version)

"**Come,** all you jolly ploughboys." See The ploughboy

"**Come** all you men and maidens as wishes for to sail." See The buffalo

"**Come** all you people, old and young." See Samuel Young

"**Come** all you poga girls, listen to my song." See Harm Link

"**Come** all you pretty fair maids, and listen to my song." See The wealthy farmer's son

"**Come** all you rounders if you want to hear." See Casey Jones (Newton)

"**Come** all you sons of Britain." See Waterloo

"**Come** all you sons of Erin." See Morrissey and the Russian sailor

"**Come** all you unmarried men and set you down by me." See William and Nancy (Kentucky version)

"**Come** all you worthy Christian men" (Job) Folk song. <Somerset air> OB

"**Come** all you worthy Christian men" (Job) Folk song. Air from Westminster. OB

"**Come** all you worthy gentlemen that may be standing by" (Somerset carol) OB

"**Come** all you young and handsome girls." Folk song: Kentucky version no. 1. SES 2
  Variant of: "Come all you fair and tender ladies"

"**Come** all you young and tender ladies." See "Come all you fair and tender ladies" (Knott county, Ky. version)

"**Come** all you young companions." See Young companions

"**Come** all you young men and learn of me." See Harry Gray (Nash, Va. version; White Rock, Va. version)

"**Come,** all you young men, in your merry ways." Children's song. MFS

"**Come** all you young people take warning by me." See The rejected lover (Afton, Va. version)

"**Come** all you young people who handle the gun." See Shooting of his dear (Oneida, Ky. version)

"**Come,** all young girls, pay attention to my noise." See Kansas boys

"**Come** all young men and maidens, attend unto my rhyme." See Caroline of Edinboro' town

"**Come** all young men, both youth and beauty." See Loving Nancy (Virginia version)

"**Come** along, boys, and listen to my tale." See The old Chisholm trail

"**Come** along, come along, and let's go home." See Old ship of Zion (Virginia version)

"**Come** along get you ready." See A hot time in the old town (Metz)

"**Come** along, let us join in a song." See For the honor of old Purdue (Huston)

Come along, Moses. Negro spiritual from North Carolina. AS

"**Come** along, thro' autumn weather." An autumn tramp

"**Come** and get your quinine." See Sick call

"**Come** and hear me, sister darling." See Let me say my little prayer (Macey)

"**Come** and I will sing you. What will you sing me? I will sing you one." See The ten commandments (Georgia version)

"**Come** and I will sing you. What will you sing me? I will sing you one, O." See The dilly carol

"**Come** and I will sing you. What will you sing me? I will sing you twelve, O." See Carol of the twelve days; The ten commandments (Marion, N.C. version)

"**Come** and lift your glasses high, my lads." See Columbia quadrangle song (Kelley)

"**Come** and sing a good old song." See U of Colorado (Stevens)

"**Come** and sing, all ye loyal Amherst men." See Cheer for old Amherst (Pierce)

Come and sit by my side if you love me. See Red river valley

"**Come** and watch the daylight dawning." See The dawn of day (Reay)

"**Come,** Anna May, and tell me your name." See Locks and bolts (Carmen, N.C. version no. 1)

"**Come** a-runnin' boys." See The cornhusker (Stevens)

"**Come** away and join the dance." Bohemian air. Words by K. Davis. DSB

Come away, death. T. A. Arne. Words by Shakespeare. GA

"**Come** away then, away then my merry Swiss girl." See The merry Swiss girl

"**Come** back to Erin." C. Barnard (music and words) HMI—SI

"**Come** back with the south wind." See The first swallow

"**Come,** Basso, let's begin." See Sound your A (Bradbury)

"**Come** boat me owre, come row me owre" (Owre the water to Charlie) Old Jacobite song.   Words by J. Hogg. GS

"**Come!** boor, your little blue."   See The scout (Campana)

"**Come**, boys, and sound your A."   See Sound your A (Bradbury)

"**Come** buy my littles roses red."   See Buy my roses (Hudson)

"**Come** cheer for Washington and Lee." See Washington and Lee swing (Allen and Sheafe)

"**Come**, cheer up, my lads, 'tis to glory we steer."   See Heart of oak (Boyce)

"**Come**, cheerful companions."   Air: Vive la compagnie.   MFS

"**Come**, come, come away, death."   See Come, away, death (Arne)

"**Come**, come, come, come to the sunset tree."   See The Tyrolese evening hymn (Browne)

"**Come**, come, come, o'er the hills free from care."   See Mountain maid's invitation (Werner)

"**Come**, come, my jolly lads."   See Sling the flowing bowl (Forecastle song); Sling the flowing bowl (Linley)

"**Come**, come quickly away."   MFS

"**Come** dance Codaine."   See "Dansez Codaine"

"**Come** dance now, my neighbors."   See A dancing song

Come, dance the kolo ("Ajde mori momčeto") Yugoslav folk song.   e.se. CJ

"**Come** darkies to de river steal."   See De eel catcher's glee

"**Come**, dear mother, hear me say."   See Musical alphabet

"**Come**, dear teacher, hear me say."   See Musical alphabet

Come down, angel, and trouble the water. See Let God's saints come in

Come down, angels (see Song Index) Variant: Let God's saints come in

Come down, come down, come down, sinner.   See Come down, sinner

"**Come** down, Gabriel, blow your horn." See Angels, meet me at de cross-roads (Hays)

Come down ma evenin' star.   J. Stromberg.   Words by R. B. Smith. GFS

Come down, sinner.   Plantation song from Virginia.   HRD

"**Come**, Emily."   American ballad.   SW

"**Come**, ever smiling liberty."   Handel. SSO 1

"**Come**, ferry me o'er."   Jacobite song. Groom.   GS

Come fill up my cup.   See Bonnie Dundee

"**Come**, fill up your glasses, I'll give you a toast."   See The red guidon

"**Come**, fill your glasses, fellows, and stand up in a row."   See Benny Havens, oh

"**Come** fill your glasses, fellows, to the days of long ago."   See To the Carabao

"**Come**, follow, follow, follow, follow, follow, follow me."   See Come, follow me (Hilton)

Come, follow me.   Round.   J. Hilton. DSB

"**Come** follow."   GSS—TFB—TFG— TFR

"**Come** forward, ye brave sons of Neptune." See The mill-boy of the slashes

"**Come** gie's a sang."   See Tullochgorum

Come go with me.   Negro spiritual from Georgia.   AS

Come here Lord.   Negro spiritual.   JB 2

Come home ("Oh sinner hear thy Saviour calling thee.")   E. Lassen.   CSS 2

Come home, father.   H. C. Work (music and words)   SRW

"**Come** in, come in, loving Henry, said she."   See Young hunting (Georgia version)

"**Come** in, come in, my old true love, and chat awhile with me."   See The false young man (Flag Pond, Tenn. version no. 1)

"**Come** in, come in, my old true love, and sit you down by me."   See The true lover's farewell (Black Mountain, N.C. version)

"**Come** in, come in, my old true love, and stay all night with me."   See Young hunting (Burnsville, N.C. version no. 3; Carmen, N.C. version no. 1)

"**Come** in, come in, my old true love, and take a chair by me."   See The false young man (Woodridge, Va. version)

"**Come** in, come in, my own true love, and stay all night with me."   See Young hunting (Alleghany, N.C. version; Carmen, N.C. version no. 2)

"**Come** in, come in, my own true love, and stay awhile with me."   See The false young man (Burnsville, N.C. version)

"**Come** in, come in, my own true love, and take a chair by me."   See The false young man (Afton, Va. version)

"**Come** in, come in, my pretty little boy." See Young hunting (Hot Springs, N.C. version)

"**Come** in, come in, my two little babes." See The wife of Usher's well (Hot Springs, N.C. version)

"**Come** in, my rose, my rose come in" ("Gyere be rózsám, gyere be") Old Hungarian folk song.   e.hu. KH 1 "Gyere be rózsám, gyere be" ("Komm, du mein röschen, komm herein") g.hu.   ML 3

"**Come** in splendor, roses tender."   See Frühling liebster (Scholz)

"**Come**, join hand in hand, brave Americans all."   See The liberty song (Boyce)

Come, join our song to Lafayette, sir.   See "Way down in Easton" (Stier)

"**Come** join the band."   Stanford university song.   R. B. Hall.   Words by A. Ellerbeck.   HW

"Come, lasses and lads." 17th century song. <Air: Away to the Maypole> DSB—KSO—MBS
Maypole song (Maireigen) e.g. ML 1
    Variant: Maypole dance
"Come, lassie and lad, be blithe and glad." See Maypole dance
"Come, let us join in merry chorus." See In merry chorus (Offenbach)
"Come, let us learn to sing." See The scale
"Come, let us lift our hearts and voice." See The Prince of life (Coad)
"Come, let us sing the song of songs." See The song of songs (Balfe)
"Come let us sing. What shall we sing? We shall sing you 12." See The ten commandments (Kentucky version)
Come let us to the bagpipe's sound. J. S. Bach. e. TFP
"Come let's be merry." Old English song. WOE
"Come let's join in song together." See Hail to Denver U (Thompson)
"Come, listen, all you gals and boys." See Jim Crow (Rice)
"Come, listen! come, listen! ye rustics all." See "Udite! o rustici" (Donizetti)
"Come, listen to my story, you can't tell how I feel." See Lucy Neal
"Come, listen unto this my song, I'm as happy as can be." See The cavalry song
"Come, loose every sail to the breeze." See Homeward bound (Arne)
Come, love, come, the boat lies low. See Nancy Till
"Come, love we God." 15th century carol. R. Shann. DNS—OB
"Come, lovely May, and scatter." See "Komm', lieber mai, und mache" (Mozart)
"Come! lovely May is on the wing." See Rapsodia primaverile (Leoncavallo)
"Come, maiden, to thy window." See Lockruf (Rückauf)
"Come, messmates, pass the bottle 'round." See Farewell to grog
"Come, mountaineers and sing one song." See Farewell, W. V. U., farewell (Richards)
"Come, my gallant soldier, come." H. R. Bishop. MFS
"Come my little roving sailor." Folk song: Endicott, Va. version. SES 2
—Franklin county, Va. version no. 1. SES 2
—Franklin county, Va. version no. 2. SES 2
    Variant: "Kind miss"
Come, my love, the stars are shining. See In old Madrid (Trotter)
"Come, my loved one." See Come with me (Campana)
"Come, my soul, thou must be waking." F. J. Haydn. Words by F. R. L. von Canitz. [Tr of Seele du musst munter werden] e. TFP

"Come, my Way, my Truth, my Life." H. E. Piggott. Words by G. Herbert. CSB 4
Come notte a sol fulgente. See D'Egitto là sui lidi (Verdi)
"Come now, classmen, let us sing." See Victory (Leyden)
"Come now! for vengeance haste." See "Vieni! la mia vendetta" (Donizetti)
"Come, O come with me, the moon is beaming." Italian air. [Words by B. S. Barclay] MFS
"Come, oh, come with me where the sparkling fountain." See Come to the sparkling fountain
"Come o'er the sea." Irish air: Cuishla ma chree, or, Pulse of my heart. Words by T. Moore. HMI—SI
Come o'er the stream, Charlie. Air: McLean's welcome. Words by J. Hogg. GS
"Come off to the stable." See Stable call
"Come on, brudder, an' help me tell." See I know I would like to read
"Come on, Eph." Negro folk song. HB
Come on fellows fight for old Marquette. See Marquette fight song (Haukohl)
Come on, sinner. See "I'm all wore out a-toilin' fo' de Lawd"
"Come on, sister, wid yo' ups an' downs." See Listen to de lambs
"Come on you hungry tigers." See Hungry tigers (Bodley)
"Come out hyah an' shuck dis co'n." See Corn-shuckin' song
"Come out, 'tis now September." See All among the barley (Stirling)
"Come over the sea in my boat with me." See Over the sea in my boat with me
"Come, push about the jorum, boys." See Yankee Doodle Dandy, New
"Come raggio di sol" ("As on the swelling wave") A. Caldara. e.i. SAT
"Come, raise aloft the red, white, and blue." Song of the Mexican war. [C. M. King] DSO
"Come, raise the song." Wesleyan university song. W. B. Davis. Words by F. L. Knowles. AI
Come, Redeemer of the nations. See Veni Redemptor gentium
"Come, rest in this bosom." Air: Lough Sheeling. Words by T. Moore. HMI
"Come riddle, come riddle, dear mother, said he." See Lord Thomas and fair Ellinor (Montvale, Va. version)
"Come riddle, come riddle to me, dear mother." See Lord Thomas and fair Ellinor (Barbourville, Ky. version)
"Come riddle me down, my dear, old mother." See Lord Thomas and fair Ellinor (Hyden, Ky. version)
"Come riddle us all, our dear, good mother." See Lord Thomas and fair Ellinor (Wasioto, Ky. version)
"Come rise you up, my pretty Polly." See Lady Isabel and the elf knight (Berea, Ky. version)

"Come, see where golden-hearted spring." G. F. Händel. Words by C. Bax. CSB 2

"Come, send round the wine." Air: We brought the summer with us. Words by T. Moore. HMI

"Come, shake your dull noddles." See The liberty song (Boyce)

"Come, sheathe your swords! my gallant boys." See Sergeant Champe

"Come, sing about a band of Dutchmen." See The college on the hill (Knight)

"Come sing this round with me." See Laughing glee (Martini)

"Come sit thee down." J. Sinclair. GOS 1

"Come, stack arms, men, pile on the rails." See Stonewall Jackson's way

"Come, swallow your bumpers, ye Tories" (The Massachusetts liberty song) Revolutionary song. Boyce. DSO

"Come, sweet lass" (Greenwich park) ʲJ. Clarke. Words attributed to T. D'Urfeyʲ BOS 2

"Come sweet lass" (Komm, süss lieb) e.g. ML 1

"Come swell the strain." See The good Three Bells (Jarvis)

"Come, take thy harp." J. L. Molloy. Words by T. Moore. HMI

"Come, tell me, blue-eyed stranger." See Blue-eyed Mary

"Come the lords and ladies fine." See The minuet

"Come, Thou almighty King." Air: God save the king <attributed to H. Carey> Words by C. Wesley. MFS

"Come, Thou almighty King." F. Giardini. Words by C. Wesley. DSC

"Come, Thou almighty King" (Italian hymn) BB—TFP—TFR

Come thro' the heather. See Wha'll be king but Charlie

"Come tipping downstairs, pretty Peggy O." See Pretty Peggy O (St Helen's Ky. version)

"Come to dinner." Round. Air: Frère Jacques. BOS 2

Come to me each day. See The convict and the bird (Dresser)

Come to me sweet Marie. See Sweet Marie (Moore)

Come to the church in the wildwood. See The little brown church in the vale (Pitts)

"Come to the old oak-tree." English song. MFS

Come to the sparkling fountain. MFS

"Come under my plaidie." J. McGill. Words by H. Macneill. GS

Come unto Him ʲall ye that labor, come unto Himʲ G. F. Händel. CSS 1

Come unto me ("A wand'rer worn."—The beauteous song) O. Barri. Words by L. Lennox. CSS 1—CSS 2

"Come unto me, all ye that labor." W. Coenen. ʲWords by H. Bonarʲ ASA

Come unto me and rest. See "I heard the voice of Jesus say" (DuBois)

"Come unto me when the dark shadows gather." C. Gounod. TSS 1

"Come unto me, ye weary." Pinsuti. TSS 1

"Come well to me, dear mother, he says." See Lord Thomas and fair Ellinor (Hot Springs, N.C. version no. 2)

"Come, we'll wander together." See "Komm', wir wandeln zusammen" (Cornelius)

"Come where flowers are flinging." See Maidens, bright and fair (Flotow)

"Come where my love lies dreaming." S. Foster (music and words) BB—BNM—TFG—WSS

"Come where the viols are singing." See The dancers (Lacome d'Estalenx)

Come with me. F. Campana. Words by L. C. Elson. GE

"Come with the gipsy bride." See Gipsy song (Balfe)

"Come, with thy lute." ʲGerman airʲ BB

"Come, ye disconsolate." S. Webbe. Words by T. Moore. MFS

"Come, ye faithful, raise the strain." 16th century German air. <Words by St John Damascene> ʲTr of Asōmen pantes laoiʲ e. TFG

"Come, ye pretty maidens." J. Offenbach. ʲTr of Allez, jeunes filles, dansez et tournez vousʲ e. WLO

"Come ye thankful people, come." G. J. Elvey. Words by H. Alford. BB

"Come, ye thankful people, come" (St George's Windsor) TFP

"Come ye that weep, to Him bow down." See Crucifix (Faure)

"Come ye young men, come along." See The May-pole

ʲ"Come you here, laddie"ʲ "Prídi ty, šuhajko" ("Komme früh morgens") Slovak folk song. g.sl. ML 3

"Come you here, lassie, with eyes of blue." See Eyes of blue

"Come you not from Newcastle." See Newcastle

"Come you now and walk with me." Russian air. Words by K. Davis. DSB

"Come you people old and young." See The Suffolk miracle (Allanstand, N.C. version)

"Come young, come old." See Katie Morey (Tennessee version)

"Come young people with a rambling notion." See Loving Nancy (Kentucky version)

"Comes Kolyada, maid of light." See Russian carol (Rimskiï-Korsakov)

Comes the spring. See "Voici que le printemps, ce fils léger d'avril" (Debussy)

Comfort ye my people. G. F. Händel. SSO 3

"Coming along from pretty old Rochelle, ah." See C'est l'aviron qui nous mène en haut

"Coming down from Bangor on an eastern train." See The eastern train

Comin' thro' the rye.   Air: The miller's wedding, or, The miller's daughter. Words by R. Burns.   BB—DFF —GOS 1—GS—MBS—SSB—TFP "Gin a body, meet a body" ("Trifft ein jemand eine jemand")   e.g. ML 1

"Coming through the rye, poor body." Air: The miller's wedding, or, The miller's daughter. Words by R. Burns.   GS

Commencement song ("We sing of a milestone won") H. W. Loomis.   Words by J. L. Vandevere.   TFO

Common Bill.   American folk song. SBA

"Compatite, signor." B. Galuppi. Words by C. Goldoni.   e.i.   ZT 1

Compère et commère (The partners) Folk song from Normandy.   e.f.   CBF 2

Complainte de la reine Marie Stuart en prison (Mary Stuart's lament)   G. B. Martini.   Words by de Florian.   e.f. GA

Compton, Richard
Autumn song (German air)
God, our loving Father (Finnish air)
Lullaby (Scottish folk air)
"Once, long ago when the world lay asleep" (Old Bohemian air)

"Comrades, comrades ever since we were boys."   F. McGlennon.   DFF—SMG

"Concerning of a soldier."   See The lady and the dragoon (Tennessee version)

"Confounded, distracted, I fain would impart now."   See "Confusa, smarrita, spiegarti vorrei" (Pergolesi)

"Confusa, smarrita, spiegarti vorrei."   G. B. Pergolesi.   e.i.   KVG

Congaudeat turba fidelium.   Ancient carol. e.   OB

Congreve, William
O sleep, why dost thou leave me (Händel)
"Where'er you walk" (Händel)   See Pope, A.   "Where'er you walk" (Händel)

Conolly, Erskine
Mary Macneil (Scottish air)
ιThe **conscript's** returnι "Akh, talan lĭ moĭ, talan" (Des rekruten rückkehr)   Russian folk song.   g.r.   ML 1

Consecration.   See "Take my life and let it be consecrated, Lord, to Thee" (Jude)

Consider the lilies.   R. Topliff.   GE

Consolation.   See "Sleep, noble hearts" (Mendelssohn)

Constancy ("Ich liebe dich")   See "Ich liebe dich, so wie du mich" (Beethoven)

Constancy ("It is something sweet when the world goes ill")   C. F. Webber. Words by F. L. Stanton.   BST

The **constant** farmer's son.   See The merchant's daughter

The **Constitution** and the Guerrière. Forecastle song.   US

"Consume them all."   F. Mendelssohn. ιTr of Vertilge sie, Herr Zebaothι e.   SSO 4

Contemplez ces tristes apprêts.   For English translation see "O'er thy tomb" (Gluck)

Contentment.   See Zufriedenheit (Mozart)

Contrition.   See Busslied (Beethoven)

"The convent slept."   E. Audran.   e. WLO

Converse, C.
Toll the bell

Converse, Charles Crozat
Aileen, aroon
Alma mater—Pennsylvania state college
Forever and forever
"Only one more jungle season" (same air as "What a Friend we have in Jesus")
The rock beside the sea

The **convict** and the bird.   P. Dresser (music and words)   SRW

Convict eighty-four.   See Picture eighty-four

"A convict sat in a prison cell."   See The convict and the bird (Dresser)

"Coo, coo, coo, coo, how I love you." Four part round.   E. Farjeon and H. Farjeon.   GSS

"Coo-coo, coo-oo-oo" (Peacock song) South Carolina negro folk song.   SBA

Cook, Eliza
The old arm chair (Russell)
The piper's daughter (Composer unknown)
The star of Glengary (Sporle)

Cooke, Thomas Simpson
Love's ritornella (wrongly attributed) See Planché, J. R.   Love's ritornella

Coolidge, Mrs Mary Elizabeth Burroughs (Roberts) Smith
Hail, Stanford hail

The **coolun.**   See An chúil-fhionn

Coon can (Poor boy)   American folk song.   SBA

The **coon** republic.   U.S. navy song.   US

Cooper, George
Graduation song (Ancient air)
A jolly good laugh (Thomas)
"Light of our way" (Cole)
"Must we then meet as strangers" (Thomas)
Pretty as a picture (Bishop)
Rose of Killarney (Thomas)
"Softly o'er the rippling waters" (Thomas)
Strolling on the Brooklyn bridge (Skelly)
Sweet Genevieve (Tucker)
Swing, cradle, swing (Composer unknown)
Why did they dig ma's grave so deep (Skelly)

Coote, Charles
The dying aviator.   See The handsome young airman
The handsome young airman (same air as The tarpaulin jacket)
The tarpaulin jacket
"Wrap me up in my tarpaulin jacket." See The tarpaulin jacket

"Cope sent a challenge frae Dunbar." See Johnnie Cope

"Cope sent a letter frae Dunbar." See Johnnie Cope

Coppée, François
Obstination (Fontenailles)
Les trois oiseaux (Cui)

Coquard, Arthur
Alack-a-day. See Haï luli
Ariadne's lament. See Plainte d'Ariane
Haï luli
Plainte d'Ariane

"Un cor da voi ferito." A. Scarlatti. Words by G. B. Lucini. e.i. KVG

Corcoran, Frank J. See Lennon, Larry C., jt. comp.

Corde natus ex parentis. For English translation see "Of the Father's love begotten"

"Cori, curuzzu" ("O herz, mein herzlieb") Sicilian song. g.i. ML 2

"Corinna is divinely fair." H. Purcell. GA

The cork leg. ᵣJ. Blewittᵢ SW

The cork leg. Old song: Tyrone version. HI 2

Corn riggs ("My Patie is a love gay") Air: Corn rigs. Words by A. Ramsay. GS

Corn rigs ᵣare bonnieᵢ ("It was upon a Lammas night") Air: Corn rigs. Old song with additional words by R. Burns. GS

Corn-shuckin' song. Negro folk song from Virginia. MFF

The corn song ("We sing the plant") G. Marks. Words by M. Herbert. MFS

Cornelia Cob. Minstrel song. WSS

Cornelius, Peter
Angedenken
The butterfly. See Schmetterling
The Christmas tree is sparkling with light
"Come, we'll wander together." See "Komm', wir wandeln zusammen"
The kings (Tr of Die könige)
"Komm', wir wandeln zusammen"
Memento. See Angedenken
Schmetterling
Ein ton
Veilchen
The violet. See Veilchen
The voice. See Ein ton

Cornell, Fred A.
Carmen Ohio (Old air)

"Cornell may have her royal red." See Hip, hip, hip, for old Swarthmore (Brown)

Cornfield medley. Minstrel quartet. WSS

The cornhusker. Official field song of the University of Nebraska. R. W. Stevens. KU

Cornish, William. See Cornysshe, William

The **Cornish** May song ("Robin Hood and Little John."—Helston furry) Air: The Helston furry dance. Traditional words. BOS 2
Robin Hood and Little John. MFF

Cornish May song ("Ye maids of Helston gather dew") Air: The Helston furry dance. Words by A. Boswell. DSB—MBS
"Ye maids of Helston gather dew" (The Helston furry dance.—Mailied) e.g. ML 1

Cornwall, Barry, pseud. See Procter, Bryan Waller

Cornysshe, William
"Pleasure it is" (Waldis)

Coronation. See "All hail the power of Jesus' name" (Holden)

Corporal Schnaps. H. C. Work (music and words) DSO

Cory, Thomas
Will Watch (Davy)

"Una cosa me da risa." See La cucaracha

The **Cossack's** lullaby. N. Bachmetieff ᵣattributed also to I. Orluffᵢ e. DSB—LAS

The **Cossack's** song ("High the Cossack's heart is bounding") ᵣJ. C. Grünbaumᵢ e. TFB

Costa, Sir Michael
The evening prayer. See I lift my heart to Thee
I lift my heart to Thee (from Eli)
"I will extol Thee, O Lord" (from Eli)
"If Thou should'st mark iniquities" (from Eli)
Turn Thee unto me (from Eli)

The **cotillon.** See "Youth's the season made for joys"

The **cottage** by the sea. J. R. Thomas. GOS 2—OT

Cotten, Lyman Atkinson
The Philippine hombre (Old Spanish air)

Couchman, Bob
Hungry tigers (Bodley)

"Could I ever hope to endure it." See "Anfangs wollt' ich fast verzagen" (Liszt)

"Could ye come back to me, Douglas! Douglas." See Douglas, tender and true (Scott)

Couldn't hear nobody pray. See I couldn't hear nobody pray

ᵣCouldst thou but knowᵢ Ah! if thou could'st know. M. W. Balfe. GE

The **councillor's** daughter. Folk song from Tennessee. SES 1

The **counter-charm.** Czechoslovak folk air. Words by H. N. Parsons. TFG

Counterpoint for Music in the air. See Music in the air, Counterpoint for (Loomis)

The **countersigns.** U.S. navy song. US

Country dance ("O let us all begin") Swedish folk song. e. DSB

The country lass ("What though I be") See "What though I be a country lass"

Country lass and royal maid. O. Straus. e. WLO

The **county** of Mayo. Irish air: Billy
Byrne of Ballymanus. Words by T.
Luvelle. e. HI 2
The **courting** case. Folk song: Mont-
vale, Va. version. SES 2
—White Rock, Va. version. SES 2
Courtney, J. M.
"My heart's in the Highlands"
Cousin Jedediah. H. S. Thompson. BB
—GOS 2—MFS
Coveney, J. Ignatius
Fordham "ram"
The **Coventry** carol. Ancient air. DN
—OB
The **Coventry** carol. Modern version of
air. OB
Coverdale's carol. See Gelobet seist du
Jesu Christ
Coverley, Robert
Trusting in thee
Covert, Bernard
Jamie's on the stormy sea
Cowan, Samuel K.
"Out on the deep" (Löhr)
The **cowboy** ("All day long on the
prairies") Cowboy song. Old Eng-
lish air. LSC
The **cowboy's** heaven. Cowboy song.
LSC
[The **cowboy's** lament] "As I walked out
in the streets of Laredo." SBA
For variants see following song of same
title; also St James's hospital
The **cowboy's** lament ("My home's in
Montana") LSC
Cowen, Frederick Hymen
Bloom on, my roses
For a dream's sake
It was a dream
Light in darkness
Cox, Charles
"Return, O love" (Pelissier)
Cox, Robert
The May-pole (Composer unknown)
Cox, W. Ralph
Pansies
Crack, crack, goes my whip. See Jem,
the carter lad (Baker)
The **cradle** ("He smiles within his cradle")
See Ein kindlein in der wiegen
The **cradle** ("Piensa que por tus enojos")
See La cuna
Cradle hymn ("Hush, my babe") J. J.
Rousseau. Words by I. Watts.
MFS
[**Cradle** hymn] "Hush! my dear." Air:
Dismissal. Words by I. Watts.
DN
[**Cradle** hymn] "Hush! my dear" (Watts's
cradle song) Northumbrian air.
Words by I. Watts. OB
[**Cradle** hymn] "Hush, my dear." J. S.
Bach. Words by I. Watts. DSB
Cradle song ("Guten abend") See Wie-
genlied (Brahms)
Cradle song ("Schlaf', kindchen") See
"Schlaf', kindchen, schlaf'"
Cradle song ("Schlafe, mein prinzchen")
See Wiegenlied (Mozart)
Cradle song ("Schlafe, schlafe") See
Wiegenlied (Schubert)

Cradle-song] "Sleep, my pretty one, close
to mother" (Slumbersong.—Berceuse)
A. Gretchaninow. Words from the
Russian of A. Lermontoff. e.f. ATS
Cradle song ("Sleep thou, sleep thou")
F. Schubert. Words by V. N. Pier-
pont. TFG
Cradle song ("Su, su, come you not soon")
Swedish folk song. e. DSB
Cradle song ("Sweet and low") See
"Sweet and low" (Wallace)
Cradle song ("Sweet dreams") See
"Sweet dreams, form a shade" (Wil-
liams)
Cradle song of soldier's wife. Words by
T. T. Barker. MFS
Cradle song of Virgin. See "The Virgin
stills the crying" (Barnby)
The **cradles**. See Les berceaux (Fauré)
"A **craft** high on the waves one day did
sail." See "Una barchetta in mar
solcando va" (Donizetti)
Craik, Mrs Dinah Maria (Mulock)
Douglas, tender and true (Scott)
The faithful little bird (Composer un-
known)
Row, row, cheerly row (Composer un-
known)
"Stars trembling o'er us" (Composer
unknown)
Crane, Amasa
"Hail, bright Easter" (Gounod)
Crash through the line of blue. See
Princeton cannon song march (Hewitt
and Osborn)
Crashaw, Richard
Summer in winter (Alsatian air)
*Crawford, Mrs Ann Spranger (Street)
Barry*
"Kathleen mavourneen" (Crouch) See
Crawford, L. M. J. M. "Kath-
leen mavourneen" (Crouch)
Crawford, Jack, captain. See Crawford,
John Wallace
Crawford, John Wallace
California Joe (Cowboy song)
Crawford, Mrs Julia
"Kathleen mavourneen" (Crouch) See
Crawford, L. M. J. M. "Kath-
leen mavourneen" (Crouch)
*Crawford, Mrs Louisa Matilda Jane (Mon-
tague)*
Annie o' the banks o' Dee (Glover)
Dublin bay (Barker)
Kathleen aroon (Abt)
"Kathleen mavourneen" (Crouch)
Crawford, Robert.
"What beauties does Flora disclose"
(Scottish air)
"When trees did bud" (Maigh; also
music by unknown composer)
Crawfurd, Robert. See Crawford, Rob-
ert
Crazy song to the air of Dixie. [D. D.
Emmett] Words by W. W. Delaney.
SBA
Creation (Haydn) See "Oh realm of
light"; "The spacious firmament on
high"

"**Creator** alme siderum." Words by Saint Ambrose. 1. TFR

Une **crèche** de Noël. Old French Canadian Noël. e. DNS

Credo ("Je crois en Dieu") See O salutaris hostia (Faure)

La **criada** del hostal (Die herbergsmagd) Catalan folk song. ca.g. ML 2

The **cricket.** Children's song. MFS

The **cricket** and the ant. Italian folk song. e. MFF

Crimson and the blue. University of Kansas song. [H. S. Thompson] Words by G. B. Penny. AI—KU—KV

Cripple creek ("Buck Creek girl") Folk song: Oneida, Ky. version. SES 2
—Pineville, Ky. version. SES 2

"**Crodh** Chailean" [Colin's cattle] (Chaileans kuhe) Old Highland air. ga.g. ML 1

Croft, William
"O God, our Help in ages past"
St Anne. See "O God, our Help in ages past"

Cronan bleoghain (Melklied) Hebridean song. ga.g. ML 1

Croquet. J. R. Thomas. Words by C. H. Webb. SRW

Crosby, Fanny
Music in the air (Root)

Crosby, L. V. H.
Dearest Mae
My last cigar (same air as Dearest Mae)
'Twas off the blue Canaries. See My last cigar

Crosley, Joseph W.
Navy blue and gold

Cross and crown ("There is a cross") G. Dana. Words by W. D. Smith. CSS 2

The **cross** of calvary (Ave Maria) C. Gounod. Words by A. Phillips. ASA

Crossing the bar. J. Barnby. Words by A. Tennyson. TFG

Crouch, Frederick William Nicholls
Dermot astore
"Kathleen mavourneen"

The **crow** ("Eine krähe war mit mir") See Die krähe (Schubert)

The **crow-fish** man. Negro folk song. SES 2

"The **crow** is black." See The true lover's farewell (Kentucky version; Callaway, Va. version)

Crow song. Air: When Johnny comes marching home <by L. Lambert>
BB
The three crows. MBS
Variant of: The three ravens

Crowe, Alfred G.
See saw waltz song

The **crown** of roses ("When Jesus Christ was yet a child."—Legend) P. Tschaikovsky. [Words from the Russian after an English original] e. OB

A legend ("Christ when a child") e. DSC

A legend ("Once long ago") e. SSO 1—SSO 2—SSO 3—SSO 4

"**Crows** won't steal, I have heard folks say." See Down Mobile

The **crucified.** See "Were you there"

Crucifix ("Vous qui pleurez") J. B. Faure. [Tr of Crucifixus] e.f. CSS 2

Crucifixion. Negro spiritual. WSS
The crucifixion (He never said a mumblin' word) FSN
Variant of: "Never said a mumblin' word"

Crucifixus. For English and French translations see Crucifix (Faure)

Cruckhaun Finn. Irish air from County Derry. Words by P. Colum. HI 2

["**Cruda,** funesta smania"] "If thou plead'st for her." G. Donizetti. e. WG

"**Cruda** sorte! amor tiranno." Rossini. e.i. PC

"**Crudel!** di che peccato a doler t'hai." See La Catanzarese

"**Crudele** Irene, tu m'hai lasciato" ("Grausame schöne") Abruzzian folk song. g.i. ML 2

The **cruel** brother. Folk song: Hot Springs, N.C. version no. 1. SES 1
—Hot Springs, N.C. version no. 2. SES 1

"**Cruel** fate from us doth sever." See The shepherds' farewell to the Holy Family (Berlioz)

The **cruel** mother. Folk song: Georgia version. SES 1
—Berea, Ky. version no. 1. SES 1
—Berea, Ky. version no. 2. SES 1
—Hindman, Ky. version. SES 1
—Alleghany, N.C. version. SES 1
—Carmen, N.C. version. SES 1
—Marion, N.C. version no. 1. SES 1
—Marion, N.C. version no. 2. SES 1
—Micaville, N.C. version. SES 1
—Tennessee version. SES 1
—Nellysford, Va. version no. 1. SES 1
—Nellysford, Va. version no. 2. SES 1
—Woodridge, Va. version. SES 1
Variant: The greenwood side

The **cruel** ship's carpenter. Folk song: Barbourville, Ky. version. SES 1
—Berea, Ky. version no. 1. SES 1
—Berea, Ky. version no. 2. SES 1
—Berea, Ky. version no. 3. SES 1
—Berea, Ky. version no. 4. SES 1
—Hindman, Ky. version. SES 1
—Jackson, Ky. version. SES 1
—Manchester, Ky. version no. 1. SES 1
—Manchester, Ky. version no. 2. SES 1
—Manchester, Ky. version no. 3. SES 1
—Oneida, Ky. version. SES 1
—Pineville, Ky. version. SES 1
—Alleghany, N.C. version. SES 1
—Big Laurel, N.C. version. SES 1
—Black Mountain, N.C. version. SES 1
—Marion, N.C. version. SES 1

The **cruel** ship's carpenter.—*Continued*
—Tennessee version.   SES 1
—Afton, Va. version.   SES 1
—Callaway, Va. version no. 1.   SES 1
—Callaway, Va. version no. 2.   SES 1
—Dewey, Va. version.   SES 1
Variants: Polly Oliver; Pretty Polly Oliver

Crüger, Johann
"Now thank we all our God."   See Nun danket alle Gòtt
Nun danket alle Gott
"O sing a joyous carol unto the holy child"

An **crúiscín** lán (Trinklied) Old Irish song. g.ir.   ML 1
The cruiskeen lawn.   e.   HMI—SI
The cruiskeen lawn (The little jug) e.   HMI

The **cruising** boys of subdiv. nine.   U.S. navy song.   [G. F. Root]   US
The cruiskeen lawn.   See An crúiscín lán

Crum, John Macleod Campbell
Love is come again (French air)

Crusaders' hymn.   See "Fairest Lord Jesus"
Crush'd by the brunt.   See Duce di tanti eroi (Rossini)
Cry of vengeance that for ages in my bosom hid wert lying.   See "Sciagurata! hai tu creduto" (Verdi)
Cryin' oh, Lord, cryin' oh, my Lord.   See Death's gwinter lay his cold icy hands on me (Rare version)
"**Crystalline** fount of tears health-welling." See To music (Cherepnin)
"**Csak** akkor szép a lány."   See "What's the use of beauty" (Szentirmay)
"**Csak** egy szép lány van a világon."   See "There's on earth but one true precious pearl" (Szentirmay)
"A **csap-utczán** véges-végig, végig."   See "In der lauten strasse kann man sehen"
Csárdás.   Hungarian song.   Composer unknown.   e.hu.   KH 1
"**Csicseri** borsó."   See In der spinnstub ("Ach, du mein kindel")
"**Csikós** vagyok, tágas puszták királya." See "Reiter bin ich, herr der pussta"
"**Csillag** elég ragyog."   See "See, love, above the stars"
"**Csipke** bokor."   See "See the wild rose fadeth" (Szentirmay)
"**Cuando** no lleva lucero."   See Fandango
"**Cuando** uno quiere a una" ("When a lover loves a maiden")   Mexican folk song.   e.s.   VS
The **Cubanola** glide.   H. Von Tilzer. SRW

La **cucaracha** (The cockroach)   Mexican folk song.   e.s.   VS
La cucaracha (Mexican cockroach song)   e.s.   SBA
The **cuckoo** ("A-walking")   See The cuckoo (Hindman, Ky. version; Knott or Letcher county, Ky. versions no. 1-2)
Cuckoo ("Cuckoo, cuckoo, cuckoo, cuckoo") R. Nicholson.   CSB 5

The **cuckoo** ("Cuckoo, cuckoo, welcome thy song")   See Spring's message
The **cuckoo** ("The cuckoo is a pretty bird") Folk song: English version. DSB
The cuckoo ("A-walking and a-talking") Hindman, Ky. version. SES 2
The cuckoo ("A-walking and talking") Folk song: Knott or Letcher county, Ky. version no 1.   MK
The cuckoo ("A-walking and talking") Knott or Letcher county, Ky. version no. 2.   MK
The cuckoo ("Children a-crying, crying for bread") Dewey, Va. version. SES 2
The cuckoo ("The cuckoo is a pretty bird") Barbourville, Ky. version no. 1.   SES 2
The cuckoo ("The cuckoo is a pretty bird") Barbourville, Ky. version no. 2.   SES 2
The cuckoo ("The cuckoo is a pretty bird") Pineville,Ky. version no. 1. SES 2
The cuckoo ("The cuckoo is a pretty bird") Clyde, N.C. version. SES 2
The cuckoo ("The cuckoo is a pretty bird") Afton, Va. version no. 1. SES 2
The cuckoo ("The cuckoo is a pretty bird") Buena Vista, Va. version. SES 2
The cuckoo ("The cuckoo is a pretty bird")   White Rock, Va. version. SES 2
The cuckoo ("The cuckoo she's a pretty bird") Pineville, Ky. version no. 2.   SES 2
The cuckoo ("I'll build me a castle") Burnsville, N.C. version.   SES 2
The cuckoo ("Meeting's a pleasure") St Helen's, Ky. version.   SES 2
The cuckoo ("Pretty Bessy")   Afton, Va. version no. 2.   SES 2
The **cuckoo** ("Down yonder in the woodland")   Round.   GSS
The **cuckoo** ("I'll build me a castle")   See The cuckoo (Burnsville, N.C. version)
The **cuckoo** ("Meeting's a pleasure")   See The cuckoo (St Helen's Ky. version)
The **cuckoo** ("Pretty Bessy")   See The cuckoo (Afton, Va. version no. 2)
Cuckoo ("Then with reports most sprightly")   M. Peerson.   CSB 6
The **cuckoo** carol ("In Bethlehem I would be")   Czechoslovak folk song.   e.   MFF
"**Cuckoo,** cuckoo, cuckoo, cuckoo, cuckoo, cuckoo, cuckoo, cuckoo, so merrily sings the cuckoo."   See Cuckoo (Nicholson)
"**Cuckoo,** cuckoo, welcome thy song." See Spring's message
"The **cuckoo** is a pretty bird."   See The cuckoo (English version; Barbourville, Ky. version no. 1; Pineville, Ky. versions no. 1-2; Clyde, N.C. version; Afton, Va. version no. 1; Buena Vista, Va. version; White Rock, Va. version)

"The cuckoo she's a pretty bird." See The cuckoo (Pineville, Ky. version no. 2)

Cuckoo waltz ("Three times round the cuckoo waltz") Traditional dance song. SBA

Cuculeţ cu pana sură (Der kleine kuckuck) Rumanian song. g.ru. ML 2

Cui, César
Three birds. See Les trois oiseaux
Les trois oiseaux

"**Cujus** animam." Rossini. l. SSO 3

La **cuna** (The cradle) Mexican folk dance. e.s. VS

Cunningham, Allan
"Hame, hame, hame" (Jacobite air)
"A wet sheet and a flowing sea" (French air)

Cupid and the maiden. J. H. Richardson (music and words) BST

Cupid and the shepherd (L'amour interrogé par un berger) R. Taylor. e.f. MPA 1

"**Cupid** rambling once astray." See Cupid and the shepherd (Taylor)

Cuppett, Charles H.
Alma mater—Ohio Wesleyan university

The **curse** of an aching heart. A. Piantadosi. Words by H. Fink. SMG— SRW

Cussans, Jack
Robinson Crusoe (18th century air)

Cutler, Henry Stephen
All saints. See "The Son of God goes forth to war"
Church militant. See "The Son of God goes forth to war"
"The Son of God goes forth to war"

Cutler, Ira Eugene
Hail to Denver U (Thompson)

Cutter, George Washington
E pluribus unum (Composer unknown)

Le **cycle** du vin (Die weinrunde) French folk song. f.g. ML 1

D

D-rah. See Fairest of colleges

"**Dá** bhfeicfeasa an chuilfhionn 'gus i ag siubhal." See An chúil-fhionn

"**Da** droben auf jenem berge, da steht ein hohes haus." See Das mühlrad

"**Da** Luain, da Mairt" ("Monday, Tuesday") Irish air from the southern counties. Traditional words. HI 2

"**Da** mi je znati, Bozhe moj." See "Wenn ich doch wüsste, Herr, mein Gott"

Da quel dì che a lei narrata. See "Ditemi, buona gente, vedeste Dinorah" (Meyerbeer)

"**Da** streiten sich die leut' herum." See Hobellied (Kreutzer)

"**Da** vy, rebîata, derî druzhno." See Towing song ("Come, fellows, let us pull together")

"**Da** znaîsh' morî, mome." See Trauer um die jugend

Dabbling in the dew. Folk song. DSB
Variant: "Where be going to, dear little maiden"

"**Dacă** nu e şi nu e." See Aoleo

Dach, Simon
"Ännchen von Tharau" (Silcher)

Dacre, Harry
As your hair grows whiter
Daisy Bell
Elsie from Chelsea

Daddy ("Take my head on your shoulder, Daddy") A. H. Behrend. Words by M. Mark-Lemon. BST—SFB

Daddy wouldn't buy me a bow-wow. J. Tabrar. SW

Daddy's on the engine. Old American song. SW

The **daemon** lover. Folk song: Berea, Ky. version no. 1. SES 1
—Berea, Ky. version no. 2. SES 1
—Clay county, Ky. version. SES 1
—Hindman, Ky. version no. 1. SES 1
—Hindman, Ky. version no. 2. SES 1
—Proctor, Ky. version. SES 1
—Allanstand, N.C. version no. 1. SES 1
—Allanstand, N.C. version no. 2. SES 1
—Alleghany, N.C. version no. 1. SES 1
—Alleghany, N.C. version no. 2. SES 1
—Black Mountain, N.C. version. SES 1
—Burnsville, N.C. version no. 1. SES 1
—Burnsville, N.C. version no. 2. SES 1
—Hot Springs, N.C. version no. 1. SES 1
—Hot Springs, N.C. version no. 2. SES 1
—Micaville, N.C. version. SES 1
—Spillcorn, N.C. version. SES 1
—Flag Pond, Tenn. version no. 1. SES 1
—Flag Pond, Tenn. version no. 2. SES 1
—Harrogate, Tenn. version. SES 1
—Dewey, Va. version. SES 1
—Nellysford, Va. version. SES 1
Variant: The house carpenter

The **daffodils.** Finnish air. Words by W. Wordsworth. DSB

Dafinka ("Dafinka platno t"cheshe") Bulgarian folk song. b.g. ML 2

Dafydd y garreg wen (David vom weissen stein) Welsh folk air. Words by Ceiriog. g.w. ML 1

"**Dagli** immortali vertici." G. Verdi. e.i. PB

Daheim, daheim, daheim. See "Hame, hame, hame"

"**Daik,** mab gwenn Drouiz ore." See Ar rannou

Dainty Davie. Scottish air. Words by Burns. GS

"A **dainty** plant is the ivy green." See The ivy green (Russell)

Daisy Bell. H. Dacre (music and words) GFS

Daisy, Daisy, give me your answer do. See Daisy Bell (Dacre)

"The **daisy** is fair, the day-lily rare." See Auld Joe Nicolson's bonnie Nannie

Dakota land.   ₁J. R. Sweney₁   SBA

"**Dal** sen del caro sposo."   Rinaldo da Capua.   e.i.   KVG

Dalalin, dalalin, po yaichenku.   See "Easter eggs"

Dallas blues.   H. A. Wand.   Words by L. Garrett.   HB

Dalsheimer, A.
"A life on the Vicksburg bluff" (Russell)

Daly, John J.
The bells of Shandon

"**Damedade** za bakalche."   See Wen ich will zur ehe

"The **dames** of France are fond and free." See The girl I left behind me

Damn, damn, damn the Insurrectos.   See The soldiers' song (Root)

Damon.   See Die Bekehrte (Stange)

Dan McCarthy took a stick and made a smash at Dugan.   See Little Johnny Dugan (Mack)

Dana, George
Cross and crown

Dana, Mrs Mary Stanley Bunce (Palmer)
"Flee as a bird" (Spanish air)
Soft music is stealing (German air)

"**Dana** ging aus" ("Tr"gnala e Dana") Bulgarian folk song.   b.g.   ML 2

Danby, Gertrude
There's nae room for twa (Satter)

The **dance** ("Go javten")   See "Go javten"

"**Dance** a cachucha, fandango, bolero." Finale from The gondoliers.   A. S. Sullivan.   Words by W. S. Gilbert. DSC

"**Dance** all night with your bottle in your hand."   See Give the fiddler a dram

Dance and sing.   See Carmeña (Wilson)

Dance, dance my little pancakes.   See Pancakes

Dance de boatman dance.   See De boatmen's dance (Smith)

"**Dance,** play, sing, sorrow disdain."   See Carmeña (Wilson)

A **dance** song ("Floral off'rings let us bring")   Round.   W. G. Whittaker. CSB 2

Dance song ("O come, come along") Swedish air.   Words by K. Davis.   DSB

Dance the gay vira.   See Vira do Minho

Dance you, my bonny Cecilia.   See "Mon pèr' n'avait fille que moi" (Cécilia)

The **dancers** ("Come where the viols are singing")   Arr from   P. Lacome. Words by F. Manley.   TFG—TFR

"**Dancing** and music, laughter and song." See Goblet of youth (Lecocq)

₁The **dancing** lesson₁ "Brother come and dance with me."   Humperdinck.   ₁Tr of Brüderchen, komm tanz' mit mir₁ e.   WG

A **dancing** song ("Come dance now") Swabian folk song.   e.   DSB

Dancing song ("Je vais entrer dans la danse")   See "Je vais entrer dans la danse"

De **dandy** Broadway swell.   English music-hall song.   SW

Dandy Jim of Caroline.   Negro song. PSG—WSS

Daniel, John
"Eyes, look no more"

Daniel in the lion's den.   Folk song from Kentucky.   SES 2

Daniel saw the stone.   Negro spiritual. HRD
Daniel saw de stone.   JB 2

Daniels, Charles N.
Hiawatha
Song to Minnehaha.   See Hiawatha

Dank der gäste (Děkování hostů.—Hochzeitslied.—Svatební)   Moravian-Czech folk song.   bo.g.   ML 3

Danks, Hart Pease
"Allie darling"
"Darling, I am coming back" (same air as Silver threads among the gold)
"Little bright eyes, will you miss me"
"Remember me"
Silver threads among the gold

Dann werden die gerechten leuchten.   For English translation see Then shall the righteous shine forth (Mendelssohn)

"**Dans** cette étable" (Bethlehem)   Old French Noël.   <Traditional air arr by C. F. Gounod>   e.f.   OB

"**Dans** la maisonnette au pied de la lande." See Tra la la la

Dans les chantiers ("Now the winter's come to stay")   Canadian folk song. e.f.   GC

Dans les jardins de France."   See Les lauriers vont fleurir

"**Dans** les jardins d'mon père."   See Auprès de ma blonde

"**Dans** les prisons de Nantes" (Les cloches de Nantes.—Die glocken von Nantes)   French folk song.   f.g. ML 1
"Dans les prisons de Nantes" (Imprison'd once at Nantes")   Canadian version.   e.f.   GC

Dans tous les cantons ("In all the country round")   Canadian folk song.   e.f. GC

"**Dans** un sommeil que charmait ton image."   See Après un rêve (Fauré)

Dansé calinda, boudoum, boudoum.   See "Michié Préval"

"**Dansez** Codaine" ("Come dance Codaine") Negro creole folk song.   e.f.   MB

Dante Alighieri
"Nessun maggior piacere" (Berlioz. Words adapted)

The **Danube** river.   H. Aïdé (music and words)   GOS 2—WSS

The **Danville** chariot (I don't want to stay here no longer)   Negro spiritual. HRD

Danyel, John.   See Daniel, John

"**Dar** was ole Mister Johnson."   See The cat came back (Miller)

Darby, Samuel E.
The saltine warrior (Walsh)

Darby Kelly. J. Whitaker. [Words by T. Dibdin] BOS 2

Dargomyzhskiĭ, Aleksandr Sergieĭvich
It matters not

"Dark and dark some drizzling day." See Sir Hugh (Barbourville, Ky. version)

The dark girl dressed in blue. Old American song. SRW

The dark-haired girl. Irish air from County Dublin. Traditional words. HI 2

"Dark is the colour of my true love's hair." See Sweet William (Micaville, N.C. version)

"Dark the night." O. Jones. Words from the Welsh. e. OB

"Dark thro' the forest come the shadows creeping." See An evening song

"Dark was the ev'ning." See Serenata ("Era la noche")

"Dark was the night and cold the ground." See My soul wants something that's new

"The darkest midnight in December." See Carol for the Nativity

"Darkest the hour." E. Jakobowski. WLO

The Darktown strutter's ball. S. Brooks (music and words) SMG

Darley, George
Osme's song (East Indian air)

"Darling, I am coming back." Song of the European war. [H. P. Danks] DSO

"Darling, I am growing old." See Silver threads among the gold (Danks)

Darling Nelly Gray. B. R. Hanby (music and words) BB—GOS 2—OT—PSG—WSS

Darling Nellie Gray. BNM—TFP

"Darling vengeance! passion so dainty." See "La vendetta, oh, la vendetta" (Mozart)

"Dar's a better day a-comin'." See In that great getting-up morning

Dar's a meetin' here tonight. See There's a meeting here to-night

Dar's one more ribber. See Noah's ark

"Dartmouth, our Dartmouth." Dartmouth college song. LAS

Dashing away with the smoothing iron (see Song Index)
Variant of: Driving away at the smoothing iron

"Dashing thro' the snow." See Jingle, bells (Pierpont)

The dashing white sergeant. H. R. Bishop. Words by Burgoyne. DSO—KSO

Dat am de way to spell chicken. Negro song. BB

Dat ol'-time religion. See This old time religion

"Dat Sunshine Special comin' around de bend." See C. C. rider

[The daughters of Erin] "We may roam thro' this world." Air: Garryowen. Words by T. Moore. HMI

D'Avenant, Sir William
The winter storms (Stanford)

David, Lee
Sucking cider through a straw (Morgan)

David vom weissen stein. See Dafydd y garreg wen

Davidson, Maria Montejo
Alma mater—George Washington university (Carey?)

Davies, Vincent
Lardy dah (Page)

Davis, Benny. See Reisner, C. F., jt. auth.

Davis, Gussie L.
The fatal wedding
In the baggage coach ahead

Davis, Hubert P.
Alma mater—Bates college

Davis, Katherine Kennicott

Composer and author
Girl scout's goodbye round

Author
Agatha, Jane, and fair Marie (French air)
Boating song (Croatian air)
The bugle call (Westphalian air)
"Come away and join the dance" (Bohemian air)
"Come you now and walk with me" (Russian air)
Dance song (Swedish air)
The fairy dance (Swedish air)
Fairy music (French air)
"From the west the soldier came" (Slovak air)
A game of trades (Russian air)
"The golden day is dying" (Palmgren)
Here come three knights a-riding (Croatian air)
"In a shady garden walk'd a princess slender" (Silesian air)
In golden firelight dancing (Croatian air)
"In the poplars" (Dutch air)
"Land of beauty" (Hungarian air)
The locust tree (Swedish air)
Lovely May is coming (Polish air)
"Man in the moon, who may you be" (French air)
"A mighty ship was the Gundremar" (Norwegian air)
The minuet (Bohemian air)
"Morning comes early" (Slovakian air)
A mystery of the sea (Italian air)
Night song (Russian air)
October (Bohemian air)
"On a merry morn in May" (Lithuanian air)
Over the sea in my boat with me (English air)
The shepherd of sleep (Welsh air)
"The ship at her anchor is riding" (German air)
The singing bird (Netherlands air)
The singing river (Flemish air)
The song of the mermaid (German air)
Spinning song (Cashmere folk air)
Spring (French air)
A spring song (German air)
The stars (French air)

Davis, Katherine Kennicott—*Continued*
Sunny Spain (Spanish air)
The wanderer (Spanish air)
Weaving song (Russian air)
The willows (Dutch air)
Davis, L. S.
"A jolly fat friar"
Davis, William Butler
"Come, raise the song"
Davison, Alphens
"Sleep, soldier, sleep"
Davy, John
The bay of Biscay
The smuggler.   See Will Watch
Will Watch
Dawn ("When the pale moon drowns the wide world") H. Somerset. Words by C. Walker.   BST
"**Dawn,** gentle flower."   S. Bennett. Words by B. Cornwall.   CSB 2
The **dawn** of day ("Come and watch") S. Reay.   MFS
The **dawn** of Maytime.   F. von Flotow. Words by F. B. Merriam.   TFG
Dawn of night.   L. Nikolayef.   Words from the Russian of A. Struve.   e. ATS
"The **dawn**-wind now is waking."   See Summer carol
"**Day** is breakin', Jacob, let me go."   See 'Raslin' Jacob
"The **day** is cold, and dark and dreary." See The rainy day (Dempster)
"The **day** is done and the darkness falls from the wings of night."   M. W. Balfe.   Words by Longfellow.   GE
"**Day** is done, gone the sun."   See Taps
"The **day** is done, we seek our rest."   See Evening song (Mendelssohn)
"**Day** is dying in the west."   W. F. Sherwin.   Words by M. A. Lathbury. BB—TFG—TFR
"Day is dying in the west" (Evening praise)   LAS
"A **day** of joyful singing."   R. Jackson. Words from an old English Christmas song.   TFP
The **day** of judgment.   Negro spiritual from South Carolina.   AS
"**Day** of sorrow."   See Infelice (Mendelssohn)
"**Day** on the mountain, the beautiful day." See The beautiful day (Hime)
"The **day** that my dear came to us."   See Mañanitas
The **day** when you'll forget me.   J. R. Thomas.   Words by Morgan.   OT
"The **days** of my youth have all silently sped."   See Old easy-chair by the fire (Beckel)
Days so youthful, brightly beaming.   See "Questo sacro, augusto stemma" (Donizetti)
"**De** jó az a kis kutya."   See "Seht, wie gut der hund"
"**De** la Sierra Morena cielito lindo, vienen bajando."   See Cielito lindo
"**De** matin, ai rescountra lou trin."   See Marcho dei rei

"**De** palabras y amor incesante."   See El que a hierro mata
"**De** tus encantos celestial, paloma azul." See La paloma azul
The **dead** horse ("A poor old man came riding by")   Halliard chantey. TSB 1
For variants see following songs of same title; also Poor old man
The **dead** horse ("They say, old man") Halliard chantey.   SBA
The **dead** horse ("They say, old man") Pulling chantey.   WSE
The **deaf** woman's courtship.   Folk song from North Carolina.   SES 2
Dear alma mater.   Tufts college song. L. R. Lewis.   Words by D. L. Maulsby.   KU—LAS
"**Dear** alma mater at thy shrine."   See Alma mater—Wabash college (Ragan)
"**Dear** alma mater, ev'ry son and daughter." See Alma mater—University of Missouri (Quarles)
"**Dear** alma mater thy name is sweet to me."   See Alma mater—Washington university (Kücken)
"**Dear** Bucknell."   Bucknell university song.   Words by S. S. Merriman. AI—AIS
The **dear** companion.   Folk song from North Carolina.   SES 2
"**Dear** country, belov'd dear country." See O, tu Palermo (Verdi)
"**Dear** father, drink no more."   <Air: Auld lang syne>   MFS
"**Dear** friends of my youth, think not we are parted."   Final chorus.   R. Planquette.   [Tr of Si je suis vraiment dame et châtelaine]   e.   WLO
"**Dear** harp of my country."   See The farewell to my harp (Irish air); The farewell to my harp (Welsh air)
"**Dear** heart, this faded rose I hold."   See My lovely rose (Cadman)
"**Dear** is thy homestead glade and glen." See Hamilton's song
"**Dear,** kind sir! dear, kind sir."   See Love duet (Straus)
"**Dear** little One, how sweet Thou art." Old English carol air.   Words by Faber.   FC
"**Dear** little robin perch'd up in a tree." See Robin! robin (Aiken)
The **dear** little shamrock.   See "There's a dear little plant" (Cherry)
"**Dear** Lord and Father of mankind." F. C. Maker.   Words by J. G. Whittier.   TFO
"**Dear** mate, I see you're healthy now." See The drunkard's dream
"**Dear** mother, in dreams I see her."   See Lullaby (Jakobowski)
Dear Mother of the Redeemer.   See Alma Redemptoris Mater (Dunstable?)
"**Dear** old, dear old Mälzel."   See Metronome canon (Beethoven)
"**Dear** old elm-clad hill."   University of Tennessee song.   J. D. Bond (music and words)   AI

"Dear old Georgetown." See Georgetown's blue and gray (Lennon and Corcoran)

Dear old Reserve. Western Reserve university song. [F. W. Kücken. Words by W. H. Alburn] AI

"Dear T. C. U." Texas Christian university song. H. G. Elkins. Words by L. Chapman and K. Ashburn. AI

Dearest, for thee, thee only. See The mountain bugle (Hewitt)

"Dearest love, canst thou tell me the tale." See Warum (Tchaikovsky)

"Dearest love, do you remember." See When this cruel war is over (Tucker)

Dearest Mae. L. V. H. Crosby [attributed also to J. Power] Words by F. Lynch. BNM—GOS 2

Dearest native land. H. Proch. MFS

The dearest spot [is home] W. T. Wrighton (music and words) BB—GOS 2—MFS

Dearmer, Geoffrey
April (Welsh traditional carol air)
The Spirit (Angevin air)
Summer carol (Béarnais carol air)

Death and the lady ("Fair lady, throw those costly robes aside") Ancient song: Sussex version. BET

"Death come to my house, he didn't stay long." Negro spiritual. JB 2

"Death is gwineter lay his cold icy hands on me." See Death's gwineter lay his cold icy hands on me

The death of Crockett. Song of the Mexican war. [Air: To Anacreon in heav'n, attributed to J. S. Smith] DSO

The death of Queen Jane. St Helen's, Ky. version no. 1. SES 1
—St Helen's, Ky. version no. 2. SES 1

"Death then! on my name spotless is the dishonour stamp'd." See Nuova ferita (Mercadante)

"Death, what a solemn call." Mountain spiritual from Tennessee. RA

Death's gwineter lay his cold icy hands on me ("Death is gwineter lay his cold icy hands") Negro spiritual: familiar version. JB 2

Death's gwineter lay his cold icy hands on me ("O, sinner, sinner") Negro spiritual: rare version. JB 2

Death's go'n'ter lay his col', icy hands on me. JG

Debussy, Claude Achille
The bells. See Les cloches
Les cloches
Comes the spring. See "Voici que le printemps, ce fils léger d'avril"
"Voici que le printemps, ce fils léger d'avril"

"A débutante was sitting in the corner of her flat." See Don't tell me what you dreamed last night (Hooker)

Decius, Nikolaus
"To God on high be thanks and praise"

"Deck the hall with boughs of holly." Welsh air. BB—DN—DSB—FC—MFS—TFP—TFR

Deckt die Donau eis und schnee. See Înghețată-i Dunărea

Decollette. B. Fagan. SRW

The decree. See The black decree

"Dedans Paris, devinez ce qu'il y a." See Ah! le joli bois, mesdames

Dedication ("Du meine seele") See Widmung (Schumann)

Dedication ("O danke nicht") See Widmung (Franz)

Deed I ain't seen no messenger boy. See I ain't seen no messenger boy (Bivins)

Deem, Fred B.
Hail West Virginia (Miller and McWhorter)

"Deep blue sea, mamma, deep blue sea." American mountain song. RA

"Deep, deep within my heart." See Trusting I call (Jordan)

"Deep in the forest." See Finland's forest

Deep river. Negro spiritual. BB—FSN— GSS— HRD— TFG— TFR—WFN—WSS

Deep river blues (Añoranzas) L. M. Handy. Words by E. Green. e.s. HB

"Deep river, deep river, Mississippi river so deep and wide." See Deep river blues (Handy)

"Deeper, and deeper still, thy goodness, child." Händel. SSO 3

D'Egitto là sui lidi. Verdi. e.i. PB

"Degli augelletti al canto." F. Orlandi. e.i. KVG

Degraph, Peter
Ellen Smith

Deh non parlare al misero. For English translation see "Ah! why recall" (Verdi)

"Deh! non voler costringere" ("Why, since thy heart in sadness weeps") G. Donizetti. e.i. PC

"Deh vieni alla finestra." W. A. Mozart. e.i. PB

"Deign, pray, to cheer each heart." Final chorus from Erminie. E. Jakobowski. WLO

"Dein bildnis wunderselig." See Intermezzo (Schumann)

Dein gedenk' ich, Margaretha (Thou art near me, Margarita) E. Meyer-Helmund. e.g. GG

"Deiner harrte die familie." See Vocero

Dekker, Thomas
"Golden slumbers kiss your eyes" (Folk air)

Děkování hostů. See Dank der gäste

De Koven, Reginald
"Oh promise me" (from Robin Hood)

Delair, Paul
L'âme des fleurs (Massenet)

De La Mare, Walter John
The three traitors (English traditional air)

Delaney, William W.
Composer and author
Father was killed by the Pinkerton men
Author
Crazy song to the air of Dixie (Emmett)

De Launay, Paul de Valpincon. See Launay, Paul de Valpincon de

Delbrück, Alfred
"Un doux lien"
Tender ties. See "Un doux lien"

Delehanty, William H.
"Beautiful blue bells"

Delius, Frederick
Little birdie

Dem milner's thrären. Jewish folk song. y. SY

Dem Unendlichen (To the Eternal) F. Schubert. Words by Klopstock. e.g. GA
Dem unendlichen (To the Eternal One) e.g. HCA

Demar, John
Huntingtower: Scottish song arranged
"When ye gang awa, Jamie." See Huntingtower: Scottish song arranged

Dempster, William Richardson
I'm alone, all alone
"I'm sitting on the stile, Mary." See Irish emigrant's lament
Irish emigrant's lament
The lament of the Irish emigrant. See Irish emigrant's lament
The May queen
The rainy day

Demuth, Norman F.
"Weep you no more, sad fountains"

Den away, away, for I can't wait any longer. See Old Shady (Hanby)

Den carry me back to old Virginny. See Carry me back to old Virginny (Christy)

Den carry me back to Tennessee. See Ella Ree (Porter)

Den farewell, den farewell, den farewell, Mary Blane. See Mary Blane

Den I was gone. Minstrel song. WSS

"Den lieben langen tag." See Des mädchens klage

Den rise, chil'ren, sing around de door. See Early in de mornin'

Den up, and down, fast and slow. See Jim Crow's polka

Den walk in, den walk in I say. See walk in the parlour

Denison marching song. Denison university song. H. Arnold. Words by G. Long. AI—AIS

"Denke, denke mein geliebter unsrer alten liebe." See Abschied

Dennett, F. J.
The skipper (Jude)

Dennis (Nägeli) See "Blest be the tie that binds"; "Heirs of unending life"; "How gentle God's commands"

Denza, Luigi
Funiculì-funiculà (with words "Some think the world")
A merry life. See Funiculì-funiculà ("Some think the world")

[**Deo** gratias] The Agincourt song. 15th century English folk song. MBS

"Der den himmel und die erden." See Ständchen (Raff)

"Der du ruhm und glanz verleihst." See Rákóczi-marsch

"Der du sicher bist" ("Ty co w stałość") Polish folk song. g.p. ML 3

"Der du von dem himmel bist." See Wand'rers nachtlied (Jordan); Wand'rers nachtlied (Loewe)

"Der er ingenting i verden saa stillesom sne." See Sne (Lie)

"Der gives stjerner" ("I'll show thee stars") C. Sinding. Words by H. Drachmann. da.e. WM 2

"Der hat hingeben das ewig leben." See Von der edlen musik

Der rose sendung ("An Alexis send ich dich") F. H. Himmel. Words by C. A. Tiedge. g. EDL

Der schneider jahrstag. g. EDL

[**"Der** skreg en fugl"] "Es schrie ein vogel" ("There cried a bird") C. Sinding. Words by V. Krag. e.g. TM

Der wirtin töchterlein ("Es zogen drei bursche") 18th century air. Words by L. Uhland. g. EDL

The **Derby** ram. Folk song: Kentucky version. SES 2
—Tennessee version. SES 2
—Virginia version. SES 2

"Dere was an old nigga, dey call'd him Uncle Ned." See Uncle Ned (Foster)

Derelict. Waller. Words by Y. E. Allison. US

"Dere's a better day a-comin'." See In that great getting-up morning

"Dere's a han'writin' on de wall." Negro spiritual. JB 2

"Dere's a little wheel a-turnin' in my heart." See Little wheel a-turnin'

"Dere's a man goin' roun' takin' names." See "There's a man goin' 'roun' takin' names"

"Dere's a star in de eas' on Christmas morn." See Rise up, shepherd, and foller

Dere's no hidin' place down dere. Negro spiritual. JG

"Dere's no rain to wet you." See I want to go home (Negro spiritual)

"Dere's room enough, room enough." See I can't stay behind

Dermot astore. F. W. N. Crouch. SI

"Derrièr' chez mon père, vole, vole, mon coeur, vole" (Les trois princesses.— Die drei prinzessen) French folk song. f.g. ML 1

"Derrièr' chez nous il pousse une ente" ("Behind our house stands an old apple tree."—The haymakers' song) Folk song from Normandy. e.f. CBF 2

"Dèrrier', chez nous y-a-t-un étang, en roulant ma boule." See En roulant ma boule

Y deryn pur. For English translation see The gentle dove

Des baches wiegenlied (The brook's lullaby) F. Schubert. Words by W. Müller. e. CSB 3

Des beignets! des beignets. See La chanson des beignets

Des Deutschen vaterland ("Was ist des Deutschen vaterland") G. Reichardt. Words by E. M. Arndt. g. EDL

Des geistes gesang (The spirit's song) J. Haydn. e.g. SAT

"Des jahres letzte stunde." See Am Sylvester-abend (Schulz)

Des kindes vermächtnis. See Den lillas testamente

Des königs abschied. See Ymdawiad y brenin

"Des königs trommel rief zum ball." See "Le roy a fait battre tambour"

Des leibeigenen klagelied ("Bože môj, Otče môj") Slovak folk song. g.sl. ML 3

[Des mädchens klage] "Den lieben langen tag" (The long weary day) [Steirische volksweise. Words by P. J. Düringer] e. MFS

Des mädchens klage ("Der eichwald brauset") See "Der eichwald brauset" (Schubert)

Des rekruten rückkehr. See The conscript's return

Des sängers kindheit (Lauliku papsepõli) Esthonian folk song. es.g. ML 3

"Dese all my fader's children." See "These are all my father's children"

Dese bones gwine to rise again. Negro spiritual. SBA

"Lo desembre congelat, confus se retira." See Cansó de Nadal

Desengany (Der gefoppte) Catalan folk song. ca.g. ML 2

"Deserted by the waning moon." See All's well (Braham)

La desgracia (The misfortune) Mexican folk song. e.s. VS

"Despierta de ese sueño." See Recuerdas de amistad

Despo ('Ē Despō) Greek folk song. g.gr. ML 2

"The despot's heel is on thy shore." See Maryland! my Maryland

Der deutsche Rhein ("Sie sollen ihn nicht haben") R. Schumann. Words by N. Becker. g. EDL

Des Deutschen vaterland. See entry under Des

Deutsches weihelied ("Stimmt an mit hellem hohen klang") A. Methfessel. Words by M. Claudius. g. EDL

Deutschland über alles. J. Haydn. Words by Hoffmann von Fallersleben. g. EDL

"Deutu ganeme" ("Komm mit mir") Breton folk song. br.g. ML 1

De Vere, Sir Stephen Edward
The snowy-breasted pearl (Irish air)

Devereux, Nicholas W.
Alma mater—Loyola university

Devilish Mary. Folk song: Barbourville, Ky. version. SES 2
—St Helen's, Ky. version. SES 2

Devrient, Wilhelmine Schröder-. See Schröder-Devrient, Wilhelmine

De Wolf, James Andrews
"Alma mater"—Brown university

Dey never comes again. See Slavery days

"Dey tell me Joe Turner he done come." See Joe Turner

"Dh' fhalbh mo nighean chruinn, donn." See Mo nigheann chruinn, donn

"Di-dee di, di-dee di, can't you hear those babies cry." See Caisson song: coast artillery parody (Metz)

Di gioia il sen mi palpita. See "Rondinella pellegrina" (Petrella)

"Di Provenza il mar" ("From Provence, both land and wave") Verdi. e.i. PB

Di quella pira. For English translation see "Of that dark scaffold" (Verdi)

Di tanti palpiti. G. Rossini. e.i. PC

Di ye ken Elsie Marley, honey. See Elsie Marley

"El día en que tu naciste." See Mañanitas

Dibdin, Charles, 1745-1814
The bells of Aberdovey (attributed)
The tinker's song

Dibdin, Thomas John
All's well (Braham)
Darby Kelly (Whitaker)

"Dich preist man überall." See Mentra, Gwen

"Dichter Irlands, kommt herbei." See An cruiscín lán

Dickens, Charles
"Autumn leaves" (Composer unknown)
The ivy green (Russell)

Dickinson, Emily
The grass (Swiss air)

Dickinson, John
The liberty song (Boyce)

"Dickory, dickory, dock." BB

"Dicky said to Johnson one cold winter's day." See The three butchers (North Carolina version)

"Did ever you see the like before." See I know the Lord's laid His hands on me

Did she ever return? No, she never returned, and her fate is still unlearned. See The ship that never returned

Did she ever return? No, she never returned, tho' the train was due at one. See The train that never returned

Did she never return? No, she never returned, and her fate was yet unlearned. See The ship that never returned

"Did you ever hear about Cocaine Lil." See Cocaine Lil

"Did you ever hear tell about Willie the weeper." See Willie, the weeper

"Did you ever hear the story 'bout Willy, the weeper." See Willie the weeper

"**Did** you ever hear the story of long John Dean." See Long gone (Handy)

"**Did** you ever think as the hearse rolls by." See The hearse song

"**Did** you hear how dey crucified my Lord." Negro spiritual. HRD

[**Did** you hear my Jesus] "Ef you want to get to hebben." Negro spiritual. HRD

"**Did** you hear of the widow Malone." See The widow Malone (Irish air)

"**Did** you ne'er hear of widow Malone." See The widow Malone (2d Irish air)

Didn't my Lord deliver Daniel. Negro spiritual. WSS

Didn't old Pharaoh get lost. Negro spiritual. WSS

"**Die** die menschen hart verstiessen." See Allerseelen

"**Die** du über die sterne weg." See Gebet (Brückler)

Died of love. See The brisk young lover (North Lincolnshire version)

Diehl, Louis
After

Diese hand, die sich gewendet. For English translation see "That dread hand" (Flotow)

"**Digli**, ch'io son fedele." G. M. Schiassi. e.i. KVG

"**Digo**, Giannetta." See La Savoyarde

Digue dindaine (Ding-a-ding-dain-a) Canadian folk song. e.f. GC

Dille, Lucie Beltzhoover-.' See Beltzhoover-Dille, Lucie

Dilley, Edgar M.
"Hail, Pennsylvania" (Lvov)

Dillon, Harry
Do, do, my huckleberry, do (Dillon, J.)

Dillon, John
Do, do, my huckleberry, do

The **dilly** carol. Cornish folk song. DN
Variants: The dilly song; The ten commandments

The **dilly** song (see Song Index)
Variant of: The dilly carol

"**Dimanche**, après les vêpr's." See Le bal chez Boulé

Dime, artillerito, donde vas (Kriegerlied) Asturian folk song. g.s. ML 2

Din Ploeşti pânä'n Gheboaïa (Über berg und waldesgründe) Rumanian song. g.ru. ML 2

Ding-a-ding-dain-a. See Digue dindaine

Ding! ding! dong! 'twill pay, some day, for a dreadful crime. See The clock

"**Ding**, dong, bell, pussy's in the well." MFS

"**Ding** dong ding dong ding dong ding dong ding dong bell." See Legend of the bell (Planquette)

"**Ding** dong, ding dong, ding dong, I love the song." See Yeoman's wedding song (Poniatowski)

Dingelstedt, Franz, freiherr von
An der Weser (Pressel)

"**Dinna** forget." Millard. Words by J. Imlah. GS

Dio possente, dio d'amor. See "Avant de quitter ces lieux" (Gounod)

Dip, boys, dip the oar. <F. Sarona> BB—MFS

"**Dir**, dir, Jehovah" ("To thee, Jehovah") J. S. Bach. e.g. GA

Dir nah' möcht' ich begraben sein (The last wish) F. Abt. e.g. CSS 2

"**Ein dirndel** vom nord zog nach London fort." See The oak and the ash

Das **dirndl.** See "What though I be a country lass"

Dis mornin', dis evenin', so soon. Negro folk song. SBA

"**Dismal** care." See "Esser mesto" (Flotow)

Disselhoff, August
Lieb heimatland, ade (Volksweise)

The **distant** drum. MFS

Distyll y don (The ebb of the tide) Old Welsh song. e.w. WO

"**Disul** vintin aba zaviz." See Ann hollaika

"**Dite** ch'ogni momento." G. B. Pergolesi. e.i. ZT 2

"**Ditemi**, buona gente, vedeste Dinorah" ("Tell me, ye friendly neighbours, have ye seen Dinorah") Meyerbeer. e.i. PC

"**Dites**, la jeune belle" ("Tell me, beautiful maiden."—Barcarolle) C. Gounod. [Words by T. Gautier] e.f. MFS

Dites-lui qu'on l'a remarqué distingué. For English translation see "Say to him" (Offenbach)

"**Dívča**, dívča." See "Liebchen, schwälbchen"

Dives and Lazarus. Traditional carol: Herefordshire version. OB

Divine Lupita. See Lupita divina

Divine praise. See Glory to the Lord in Zion (Bortniänskiï)

"**Diw'** laiwiņas peld pa juhru." See "Zwei kleine boote fahren im meere"

Dix, William Chatterton
"As with gladness men of old" (Kocher)
"Joy fills our inmost heart to-day" (Composer unknown)
"What Child is this" (Old English air; also music by Engel)

Dixie ("I wish I was") D. D. Emmett (music and words) BB—DFF—DSO—LAS—TFP—WSE
Dixie. g. also ML 1
Dixie land. DSC—MBS—WSS
Dixie's land. GOS 2

Dixie ("O! Dixie's land is the land of glory") D. D. Emmett. Words by M. B. Wharton. LAS

"**Djupt** i hafvet på demantehällen." See Neckens polska

Do, do, my huckleberry, do. J. Dillon. Words by H. Dillon. SRW

"**Do** doan' yer weep for de baby." Negro spiritual from Georgia. FSN

"**Do** don't touch-a my garment, good Lord, I'm gwine home." Negro spiritual. JB 2

"**Do** I love thee." J. Wiegand. GE

Do let me go, girls. Capstan chantey. TSB 2

"Do my brudder, O yes, yes, member." See Bell da ring (South Carolina version no. 2)

Do not fear my little darling. See The little lost child (Stern)

Do not forget me! think sometimes of me still. See The maid of the mill (Maybrick)

Do not go ("Though the sun rests."—Ne menj el) E. Szentirmay (music and words) e.hu. KH 2

"Do not send me home." Russian folk song. e. NRF

"Do not think that just because you're angry." See La cuna

"Do not trust him, gentle lady." See The gipsy's warning (Coard)

Do not try to tempt me, miss. See Gold will buy 'most anything but a true girl's heart (Rosenfeld)

"Do they miss me at home." S. M. Grannis. Words by C. A. B. Mason. GOS 1—OT—SW

Do they miss me in the trenches. Confederate song. [S. M. Grannis] Words by J. W. Naff. DSO

"Do they think of me at home." C. W. Glover. Words by J. E. Carpenter. MFS—SW

Do ye ken Elsie Marley, honey. See Elsie Marley

"Do ye ken John Peel with his coat so gay." See John Peel

"Do you ask what the birds say." See Answer to a child's question (Stanford)

"Do you know what maroon and C crest mean." See Our Chicago (Reid)

"Do you recall that night in June." See The Danube river (Aïdé)

Do you remember ("Dost recall that summer night, love") Campana. e. GE

"Do you want a car, your honor." See The Irish jaunting car (Vousden)

Do your best for one another. See Pulling hard against the stream

Doane, George Washington
"Softly now the light of day" (music by Donizetti; Weber)

Dobbin's flowery vale. Irish air from County Armagh. Traditional words. HI 2

Dobra noc. See Gute nacht

Dobri. See The gray dove

"Dobry wečor mačerka." See Der besuch am grabe

Dobson, Austin
A ballad to Queen Elizabeth of the Spanish Armada (Slater)

Doch der Herr vergisst der seiner nicht. For English translation see "But the Lord is mindful of His own" (Mendelssohn)

Doddridge, Philip
"Awake, my soul, stretch every nerve" (Händel)
"Great God, we sing" (Oliver)
"Hark! the glad sound" (Jarman)
"High let us swell our tuneful notes" (Old Cornish air)
"How gentle God's commands" (Nägeli)

Dodge, Gilbert. See Pease, Harry, jt. comp. and auth.

Dodge, Henry Groff
Fight for Yale (Friedman)

Dodge, Mrs Mary Elizabeth (Mapes)
Blossom time (Irish folk air)

Dodge, Ossian Euclid
Ossian's serenade

Dodge, Russell M., pseud. See Loomis, Harvey Worthington

"Det doftar mull, och parkens blomster blunda." See Pionerna (Rangström)

The dogie song. Cowboy song. GSS —TFP
Variant of: Whoopee ti yi yo, git along, little dogies

Doheny, Michael
Shan Van Vocht (Irish air)

Doïna Haiducului (Haidukenlied) Rumanian song. g.ru. ML 2

Dolby, Mme Charlotte Helen Sainton-. See Sainton-Dolby, Mme Charlotte Helen

["Il dolce suono"] At the altar (Mad scene) G. Donizetti. e. WG

Dolcy Jones. S. C. Foster (music and words) WSS

Dole, Nathan Haskell
The fountain of knowledge (German air)
"Good-night" (German air)
May song (Netherlands air)
Summer (Scottish air)
Winter (Bohemian folk air)

"Dolina, dolina." See "Tal, du mein liebes tal"

The dolls' party. J. C. Macy. Words by K. Wells. BST

Dolly Day. S. C. Foster (music and words) WSS

[Domaredansen] The judge's dance. Swedish folk song. e. TFO

Dombrowski's march. See Polish national song (Ogiński?)

"Domine, Domine, adjutor meus." See Thou, O Lord, art my protector (Saint-Saëns)

Dominus regit me. See "The King of love my Shepherd is" (Dykes)

"Don' let yo' watch run down." Negro work song. SBA

Don Simon de mi vida ("Don Simon, dear old friend") Mexican folk song. e.s. VS

"Doncher let nobody turn you roun'." See Dont you let nobody turn you around

Done carry de key an' gone home. See "Too late, too late, sinnah"

"Done wid driber's dribin'." Negro folk song. AS

Donizetti, Gaetano

Ah! non avea più lagrime (from Maria di Rudenz)

Ah! quello fu per me (from Maria Padilla)

"Al mio core oggetti amati" (from L'assedio di Calais)

At the altar. See "Il dolce suono"

"Una barchetta in mar solcando va" (from Gianni da Calais)

"Bella e di sol vestita" (from Maria di Rohan)

"Bella siccome un angelo in terra pellegrino" (from Don Pasquale)

Brindisi. See "Il segreto per esser felici"

"Cari luoghi ov'io passai" (from Linda di Chamounix)

"Che val ricchezza e trono" (from La regina di Golconda)

Child of the regiment (from La figlia del reggimento. Tr of Quando il destino in mezzo a strage ria)

"Ciascun lo dice" (from La figlia del reggimento)

"Cruda, funesta smania" (from Lucia di Lammermoor)

"Deh! non voler costringere" (from Anna Bolena)

"Il dolce suono" (from Lucia di Lammermoor)

"Ensanguined and lurid" (from Lucia di Lammermoor. Tr of O sole più ratto)

Era anch' io di quella schiera (from Marino Falliero)

"Hail to the happy bridal day" (from Lucia di Lammermoor. Tr of Per te d'immenso giubilo)

"If thou plead'st for her." See "Cruda, funesta smania"

"Immortal Love, forever full"

"In questo semplice, modesto asilo" (from Betly)

Io l'udia ne' suoi bei carmi (from Torquato Tasso)

"It is better to laugh than be sighing." See "Il segreto per esser felici"

The lady in crepe (same air as "When twilight shadows lower")

Mad scene. See "Il dolce suono"

"Mira, o bella, il trovatore" (from Gianni di Parigi)

"Nella fatal di Rimini" (from Lucrezia Borgia)

"Oh, Italia, Italia beloved" (from Lucrezia Borgia)

O Lisbona, alfin ti miro (from Don Sebastiano)

"Oh! that I never more might see" (same air as "Deh! non voler costringere")

Peace on earth

"Per sua madre andò una figlia" (from Linda di Chamounix)

Perchè dell' aure in sen (from Torquato Tasso)

"Poor tho' my cot may be." See "In questo semplice, modesto asilo"

"Prova mi dai, lo sento" (from Ugo conte di Parigi)

"Questo sacro, augusto stemma" (from Gemma di Vergy)

"Raggio d'amor parea" (from Il furioso)

Raphael. See "Immortal Love, forever full"

"Regnava nel silenzio" (from Lucia di Lammermoor)

"Se crudele il cor mostrai" (from Betly)

"Search thro' the wide world." See "Ciascun lo dice"

"Il segreto per esser felici" (from Lucrezia Borgia)

Sextet (from Lucia di Lammermoor. Tr of Chi mi frena in tal momento)

"Softly now the light of day"

"Son leggero e ver d'amore" (from Maria de Rohan)

"Thou hast spread thy wings to heaven" (from Lucia di Lammermoor. Tr of Tu che a Dio spiegasti l'ali)

"Udite! o rustici" (from L'elisire d'amore)

"Vieni! la mia vendetta" (from Lucrezia Borgia)

"Were he but here." See "Regnava nel silenzio"

"What from vengeance now restrains me." See Sextet

"When twilight shadows lower" (from Lucia di Lammermoor. Tr of Verrano a me sull'aure)

The world is full of beauty

Donkey riding. Harbor work song. BOS 2

"La **donna** è mobile" ("Woman is fickle") Verdi. e. WG

Don't be lonely, sister darling. See Let me say my little prayer

Don't be weary, traveller. Negro spiritual. AS—FSN—HRD

Don't call de roll ("Jacob's ladder slim an' tall") Negro spiritual. HRD

Don't get weary. See My bretheren, don't get weary

Don't go away, stay at home if you can. See The dreary black hills

Don't leave me, Lord. Negro spiritual. HRD

Don't let it happen again. Old song. SW

Don't let nobody turn yer roun' (see Song Index)

Variant of: "Don't you let nobody turn you around"

"**Don't** let your watch run down." See "Don' let yo' watch run down"

Don't spit on the deck. See Transport song

Don't swat your mother. B. Hooker and P. Steele (music and words) SRW

Don't tell me what you dreamed last night (For I've been reading Freud) B. Hooker. Words by F. P. Adams. SRW

Don't that look like shortenin' bread. See Shortenin' bread

Don't wear your heart on your sleeve. Old song. SW

Don't ya heah Jerusalem moan. Mountain spiritual. RA

"Don't ye (you) view dat ship a-come a-sailin'." Negro spiritual. HRD

Don't you go, Tommy. Old song. SW

"Don't you hear the water rolling." See Niagara Falls

"Don't you hear those Christians a-praying." See Stars in the elements

"Don't you let nobody turn you around." Negro spiritual. WFN
Doncher let nobody turn you roun'. JG
Variant: Don't let nobody turn yer roun'

Don't you look behind. See The year of jubilo (Work)

"Don't you remember last Friday night." See The lover's lament (Alleghany, N.C. version; Carmen, N.C. version)

"Don't you see that ship a-sailin'." See Old ship of Zion (North Carolina version)

"Don't you view dat ship a-come a-sailin'." See "Don't ye view dat ship a-come a-sailin'"

Doo me ama. Forecastle song. WSE

Doodle, let me go, gels. See Do let me go, girls

Dor de ducă (Wandertrieb) Rumanian song. g.ru. ML 2

"Dormi, dormi, dormi, Nicola meu, dormi contentu." See Ninna di Borgia

"Dormi, Jesu! mater ridet" (The Virgin's cradle hymn) E. Rubbra. e.l. OB

"Dormi pure" (Slumber, my loved one) S. Scuderi. e.i. BST

"Dors, dors, mon petit, dors, les moutons sont là-dehors." See Berceuse

"Dors mignon près de ta mère." See Cradle-song (Grechaninov)

Dorset, Charles Sackville, 6th earl of
"To all you ladies now at land" (Old English air)

"Dort am schönen strand." See Loch Lomond

"Dort im felde liegt ein see" ("Hej tam w polu") Polish folk song. g.p. ML 3

"Dort in vaters garten fliege, fliege, herzchen, fliege." See "Derrièr' chez mon père, vole, vole, mon coeur, vole"

"Dort nied'n in jenem holze." Schlesische volksweise. g. EDL

"Dort oben, dort oben vor der himmlischen tür." See Maria und die arme seele vor der himmelstür

"Dort Saaleck, hier die Rudelsburg und unten tief im tale." See Rudelsburg (Allmers)

"Dort unten im tale läuft's wasser so trüb." See Argwohn

"Dort, wo der Rhein mit seinen grünen wellen." See Sehnsucht nach dem Rhein (Schmitt)

"Dost recall that summer night, love." See Do you remember (Campana)

"Dost thou love me, sister Ruth." See Sister Ruth (Haydn)

"Dost thou recall where lemon blossoms grow." See "Kennst du das land" (Schumann)

"Dosta smefâlî, fâlî î pîlî." See Wojewode manusch

"D'où viens-tu, bergère" ("Whence, O shepherd maiden") Canadian Noël. e.f. GC

Doughboys, cavalry, all you branches come. See Hike song of 1917

Dougherty, William Aldrew
Across the field

Douglas, William
Annie Laurie (Scott)

Douglas [tender and true] Lady John Scott. Words by D. M. Mulock. GE

Doun the burn, Davie. See "When trees did bud" (Composer unknown); "When trees did bud" (Maigh)

"Un doux lien" (Tender ties) A. Delbrück. Words by V. Wilder. e.f. AT—TM

"Dove si stà jersira." See L'avvelenato

Dowland, John
"Come again, sweet love"
"Fine knacks for ladies"
"I saw my lady weep"
Sweet love doth now invite. See "Come again, sweet love"

Down among the dead men ("Here's a health to the king") 17th century English drinking song. Words by J. Dyer; wrongly attributed to R. Dyer <and to E. Dyer> SSB
Down among the dead men (Trinklied) e.g. ML 1

"Down at a chittlin rag." See The Chicago gouge (Handy)

"Down at the races, keeping cases." See The handicap march (Rosey)

"Down beside our mother Volga, Volga." See Mother Volga

Down by mother Volga. See Mother Volga

Down by the old mill stream ("You must know that my uncle is a farmer") Minstrel song. WSS

Down by the river ("Oh, hallelujah to that Lamb") Negro spiritual. BB

Down by the river ("When Christ the Lord was here below") Negro spiritual. HRD

"Down by the river-side I stray." J. R. Thomas. Words by G. P. Morris. OT

"Down by the sally gardens." Air: The maids of Mourne shore. Words by W. B. Yeats. DSC—HI 1

Down, down derry down. Folk song: American version. SBA

Down in a coal mine. J. B. Geoghegan. MFS—SW

"Down in a valley, down in a valley." M. Cavendish. GA

"Down in Carlisle there lived a lady." See The bold lieutenant (Berea, Ky. version; Pine Mountain, Ky. version; St Helen's, Ky. version)

Down in Charleston jail. Colored soldiers' parody on When this cruel war is over. [H. Tucker] Words by Sergeant Johnson. DSO

Down in de cornfield.   See Massa's in de cold, cold ground (Foster)

Down in Dixie.   H. W. Loomis (music and words)   TFO

"**Down** in front of Casey's."   See The sidewalks of New York (Lawlor)

"**Down** in London where I was raised."   See Barbara Allen (Pineville, Ky. version)

"**Down** in Lones valley a damsel did dwell."   See Polly Oliver (Kentucky version)

"**Down** in Maryland."   West Point football song.   P. Egner.   DSO

Down in Mobile ("Some folks say that a crow won't steal") Southern song.   DFF—TFG
Variant: Down Mobile

"**Down** in my aunt's old orchard."   See Mon cri cra, tir' la lirette

Down in my old cabin home.   See The old cabin home (Paine)

"**Down** in St Louis at 12th and Carr."   See Brady

"**Down** in the cane-brake."   See Nancy Till

Down in the cornfield.   See Massa's in de cold, cold ground (Foster)

Down in the delta.   See Mississippi delta blues (Williams)

"**Down** in the glen where I live by the brook."   See Fairy mischief

"**Down** in the jail-yard beatin' on the old rock pile."   See Rock pile blues (Williams)

"**Down** in the jungles lived a maid."   See Under the bamboo tree (Cole and Johnson)

Down in the old cherry orchard.   S. R. Henry.   Words by A. Bryan.   OTG

Down in the valley (see Song Index)
Variant: The good old way

"**Down** in the valley, the valley so low."   Kentucky mountain song.   SBA

"**Down** in the valley where summer's laughing beam."   See The shepherd

"**Down** in yon forest."   Traditional carol from Derbyshire.   OB
Variant: All bells in paradise

Down Mobile ("Crows won't steal") Southern song.   TFB—TFO—TFR
Variant of: Down in Mobile

"**Down** (my honey baby lady) in my home in Kansas City."   See Kansas City blues (Bowman)

"**Down** on Armour avenue."   See The gouge of Armour avenue (Handy)

"**Down** on de Mississippi floating."   See Nelly was a lady (Foster)

"**Down** on little mother Volga."   See Mother Volga

"**Down** on the field they're fighting."   See Victory song (Allen)

"**Down** on the field where the team is fighting."   See Maroon victory (Stelljes)

"**Down** on the Mississippi floating."   See Nelly was a lady (Foster)

"**Down** paths fringed by fragrant flowers."   See "Ich wandle unter blumen" (Lassen)

"**Down** Saint Peter's road."   Russian folk song of the post-drivers in the province of Tver.   e.   SR

"**Down** stepped her old father dear."   See Lady Maisry (Teges, Ky. version)

Down the burn, Davie.   See "When trees did bud" (Composer unknown); "When trees did bud" (Maigh)

Down the dim river we float on forever.   See "Stars trembling o'er us"

Down the field.   Yale university song.   S. P. Friedman.   Words by C. W. O'Connor.   AI—AIS—LAS—KU—KV

"**Down** the runway, thundering swift."   See The aviator

"**Down** the stream so cheerily."   See The miller's daughter

"**Down** to the crystal streamlet."   See "À la claire fontaine"

Down went McGinty.   J. Flynn (music and words)   GFS—SRW

"**Down** where the waving willows."   See Annie Lisle (Thompson)

Down where the Wurzburger flows.   H. Von Tilzer.   Words by V. P. Bryan.   SRW

"**Down** with the rosemary and bays."   See Candlemas eve

"**Down** yonder in the woodland."   See The cuckoo

Downey, June Etta
Alma mater—University of Wyoming

Downing, John Hyatt
Field song (Woodworth)
"We're loyal to you U. S. D." (College airs arranged)

⌈The **downward** road is crowded⌋ Oh, de downward road is crowded.   Negro spiritual.   HRD

Downy jailbirds.   See Birds of a feather (Jakobowski)

Doxology ("May the grace of Christ")   See "May the grace of Christ, our Saviour"

Doxology ("Praise God")   See Old Hundred (Franc?)

Drachmann, Holger
"Der gives stjerner" (Sinding)
Perlen (Sinding)
Tro (Sinding)

Draherin o machree ("I grieve when I think on the dear happy days")   Air: Jemmy mo veela sthore, or, Draherin-o-machree.   Words by M. Hogan (Bard of Thomond)   HI 2

Draper, Bourne Hall
"Ye Christian heralds" (Zeuner)

Draper, George O.
A son of a musketeer (Old air)

"**Draussen** am garten führte mich mein weg vorbei."   See Mädchens klage

"**Draw** mae dyffryn uchel unig."   See Cân yr alltud

"**Draw** near, all ye people" (see Song Index)
Also in "Lord God of Abraham" (Mendelssohn)   SSO 4

"**Draw** near, young men, and learn of me."
See Harry Gray (Marion, N.C. version)
"**Draw** nigh young men and pay attention."
See The silver dagger (Virginia version)
Drayton, Frank
Won't you come along
The **Dreadnaught**. Forecastle song. US
A **dream** ("Blif, o blif i dina drömmars rike") See Dröm (Sjögren)
A **dream** ("I dreamed that I dwelt on an isle of cracked ice") Song of the Spanish-American war. [M. W. Balfe] DSO
The **dream** ("'Twas in a meadow by the way."—Der traum) A. Rubinstein. [Words by Schukowsky] e.g. GG
Dream, dream, ye lovers. See Midsummer dreams
Dream faces. W. M. Hutchinson. MFS
"**Dream** island, queen of the golden gloaming." See Mo rùn geal dìleas
The **dream** of the miner's child. Old American song. RA—SW
Dream so cherish'd, O dream of beauty. See A te riede, o caro figlio (Mercadante)
Dream song. E. Jakobowski. WLO
The **dreaming** mere. See Der träumende see (Brückler)
Dreaming of home and mother. J. P. Ordway (music and words) GOS 2 —OT
"**Dreaming**, to thee my heart I surrender." See Après un rêve (Fauré)
"**Dreamland** opens here." See "Gué-gué solingaie"
The **dreary** black hills. Cowboy song. LSC—SBA
The **dreary**, dreary life (see Song Index) Variant: The dreary life
The **dreary** life. Cowboy song. LSC Variant of: The dreary, dreary life
Drechsler, Josef
"Brüderlein fein" (from Der bauer als millionär)
"**Dreh** dich vor dem spielmann." See Aufforderung zum tanze (Wendish folk song)
Die **drei** grossen christlichen feste (O du fröhliche) Sicilian air: O sanctissima. Words by J. Falk. g. EDL
O thou joyful day (O du fröhliche) e. MFS
"**Drei** lilien, drei lilien." Volkslied. g. EDL
Die **drei** matrosen aus Groix. See Les trois matelots de Groix
Die **drei** prinzessen. See "Derrièr' chez mon père, vole, vole, mon coeur, vole"
Die **drei** raben. See The three ravens
Drei reiter am tor ("Es ritten drei reiter zum tore") Volkslied. g. EDL
Drei röselein ("Jetzt gang i ans brünnele") Schwabisches volkslied. g. EDL
"**Drei** tage sind's, dass ich vom krieg zurückgekehrt" ("Tri dni mi je, kak sam došel s tabora") Croatian folk song. g.se. ML 2

"**Drei** trommler jung, die kehrten aus dem kriege." See Le joli tambour
"**Drei** zichorienblätter fein." See Ciobănaş dela miori
Die **drei** zigeuner (The three gypsies) F. Liszt. Words by Lenau. e.g. HCA
"**Dreimal** in der früh traf ich" ("Trihs rihtiņu malti gahju") Lettish folk song. g.le. ML 3
Dresden China. See A twilight fancy (Molloy)
Dresser, Paul
The blue and the gray
The convict and the bird
Just tell them that you saw me
On the banks of the Wabash, far away
The pardon came too late
De **drie** koningen ("Three kings") Flemish Epiphany carol. e. OB
"**Drift**, my bark." F. Kücken. [Tr of Treibe schifflein] e. MFS
"**Drill**, ye engineers, drill." [T. F. Casey] DSO
Drill, ye tarriers, drill. T. F. Casey. GFS—SMG
"**Drink** to her." Air: Heigh-ho! my Jacky. Words by T. Moore. HMI
"**Drink** to me only with thine eyes." Old English air <attributed to H. Harrington; wrongly attributed to R. Mellish and to Mozart> Words by B. Jonson. BB—BST—DSC —GOS 2—LSB—MBS—SSB—TFB —TFP
"**Drink** to me only with thine eyes" ("Trinke mir nur mit blicken zu") e.g. ML 1
The **drinking** fusileers. British World war song. Revised words. DSO
Drinking song ("See how it glistens") C. Lecocq. [Tr of Le punch scintille] e. WLO
Drinking song ("See the wine is gaily flowing") P. Mascagni. [Tr of Viva il vino spumeggiante] e. WG
Drinnenberg,
Bell song
[**Drive** the cold winter away] The praise of Christmas. 17th century air. OB
Driven from home. W. S. Hays. GOS 2 —OT—SW
Driving away at the smoothing iron. Folk song. DSB
Variants: Dashing away with the smoothing iron; Hanging out the linen clothes
Driving saw-logs on the Plover. Old air. Words by W. N. Allen. SBA
Drivin' steel ("If I could drive steel like John Henry") Folk song from Tennessee. SBA
Variant of: "John Henry"
"**Drivin'** steel, drivin' steel, drivin' steel, boys, is hard work, I know." See Hammer man
Droichead na Tuaire (Entführung) Irish folk song. g.ir. ML 1
Dröm (A dream) E. Sjögren. Words by J. P. Jacobsen. e.sw. WM 2

"The **drooping** rose has made complaint."
See "Es hat die rose sich beklagt"
(Franz)
"**Drowsy** with sleep the moonlight gleaming." See Nächtlicher gruss (Storch)
The **drummer** and his wife. Folk song:
Kentucky version. SES 2
—North Carolina version. SES 2
The **drummer** and the cook. Capstan
chantey. TSB 2
"The **drummer** told his wife he could do
more in one day." See The drummer
and his wife (North Carolina version)
The **drunkard's** doom. Old American
song. SBA
The **drunkard's** dream. Old American
song. RA—SW
The **drunkard's** lone child. Old American song. SW
ɾThe **drunken** sailorɹ "What shall we do."
Halliard chantey. BOS 2—TSB 1
Early in the morning. WSE
Variant: "What are you going to do
with a drunken sailor"
"**Drunten** im unterland." See Unterländers heimweh
"**Dry** those eyes." V. Pelissier. Words
by Shakespeare. MPA 2
The **dryad** and the sunbeam. Russian
air. Words by E. H. Smith. DSB
Dryden, John
"Fairest isle" (Purcell)
Harvest home (Purcell)
"**Du** alter, du freier, du felsiger nord."
See "Du gamla, du fria, du fjällhoga
nord"
ɾ"**Du** bist die ruh"ɹ "O Thou my peace."
F. Schubert. ɾWords by F. Rückertɹ
e. LAS
"**Du** bist wie eine blume" ("Thou art lovely
as a flower") Liszt. Words by
Heine. e.g. GG
"**Du** bist wie eine blume" ("Thou'rt like
unto a flower") Rubinstein. Words
by Heine. e.g. GG—MFS
"**Du** bist wie eine blume" ("Thou'rt like a
flower—so winsome") Schumann. Words by Heine. e.g.
CSB 3
"Du bist wie eine blume" ("Thou'rt
lovely as a flower") e.g. GG
"**Du**, die mit süssen blikken sich stahl ins
herze mir." See Pavane
"**Du**, du liegst mir im herzen." Volkslied. g. EDL
Am I not fondly thine own. e.
GOS 2
"**Du** gamla, du fria, du fjellhöga nord" (Das
lied vom norden) Swedish song.
ɾWords by R. Dybeckɹ g.sw. ML 1
"**Du** harte maid, kann dich noch schmerzen
ein verbrechen."* See La Catanzarese
"**Du** hast versprochen mir vier taschentücher." See Ritornello delle lavandare del Vomero
"**Du** holde kunst, in wie viel grauen stunden." See An die musik (Schubert)
"**Du** hvita liljekonvalje." See Liljekonvalje (Palmgren)
"**Du** isst kein brot, und trinkst keinen
wein." See Ali Pascha

"**Du** lieber, heilger, frommer Christ." See
Gebet an den heiligen Christ (Siegert)
"**Du** mein gedanke, du mein sein und werden." See Jeg elsker dig (Grieg)
"**Du** mein liebling, äuglein lieblich" ("Kochaneczko, oczki moje") Polish folk
song. g.p. ML 3
"**Du** mein span." See The birchen brand
"**Du** meine seele, du mein herz." See
Widmung (Schumann)
"**Du** sänger zarter weisen, komm'." See
Errefusa
"**Du** schwert an meiner linken." See
Schwertlied (Weber)
"**Du** süsse braut, du holdes weib." See
Vandring i skoven (Grieg)
"**Du** traumst im warmen bett." See "Tu
nel tuo letto a far de' sogni d'oro"
"**Du** west sein a g'vir, mein Jamele." See
Jamele
Duane street. See "From ev'ry spire on
Christmas eve" (Coles)
Dubinushka ("Come, fellows, let us pull
together") See Towing-song
Dubinushka ("Many songs have I heard")
See The little cudgel
Dublin bay. G. Barker. ɾWords by
Crawfordɹ SI
Dubois, Archie A.
Come unto me and rest. See "I
heard the voice of Jesus say"
"I heard the voice of Jesus say"
Duce di tanti eroi. Rossini. e.i. PB
Dufferin, Helen Selina (Sheridan), lady
Irish emigrant's lament (music by
Barker; Dempster)
Katey's letter (Sainton-Dolby)
"O bay of Dublin" (Old air)
Dufresny, Charles, sieur de la Rivière
"Reveillez-vous, belle dormeuse"
(French folk air)
Duhamel, Maurice
Noël des quêteurs bressans (Bressan
air)
"Voici venir le joli mai, qu'il est
plaisant, qu'il est gai" (Bressan air)
The **duke** of Marlborough. Folk song:
Sussex version. BET
Duke street (Hatton) See God be with
us; "Lord of all being"; "These things
shall be! a loftier race"
"**Duke**, we thy anthems raise." See Blue
and white (Leftwich)
Dukke Lisse. U.S. Naval academy song.
E. Worsing. US
"**Dulce** bien, dulce bien." See Deep river
blues (Handy)
"**Dull** is the life of the soldier in peace."
See A soldier's life (Jakobowski)
Dumas, Alexandre
Jeanne d'Arc au bûcher (Liszt)
"**Dumattina** quest' è l' jornu di la virgine
Maria." See Lamento
Dumb, dumb, dumb (see Song Index)
Variant: The dumb wife
The **dumb** wife ("O, there was a jolly
blade") Traditional song. KSO
For variant see following song of same
title; also Dumb, dumb, dumb

The **dumb** wife ("There was a bonny blade") ₁Air: Paul's steeple, or, I am the Duke of Norfolk₁ BOS 2
The dumb wife cured. CSB 4
Dumbarton's bonny dell. J. Sinclair. Words by C. M. Westnacott. GOS 2 —GS
Dumont, Frank
 The Alabama blossoms (Composer unknown)
 Angel Gabriel (Stewart)
 Jennie, the flower of Kildare (Stewart)
Dunbar, William
 Rorate (Scottish traditional air)
Duncan, Mary Lundie
 "Jesus, tender Shepherd, hear me" (Barnard)
"**Duncan** and his brother was playing pool." See Brady
"**Duncan** Gray cam' here to woo." Air: Duncan Gray. Words by R. Burns. GS
Duncan-Rubbra, Edmund. See Rubbra, Edmund Duncan
Dundee. See "O Thou Whose feet" (Franc)
Dunderbeck. Air: Son of a gambolier. SRW
Dunkles röslein. See Roisin dubh
Dunlop, John
 The year that's awa' (Composer unknown)
Dunphy, C. J.
 Make the best of it
Dunstable, John
 Alma Redemptoris Mater (attributed)
 Dear Mother of the Redeemer. See Alma Redemptoris Mater (attributed)
 What tidings bringest thou
 Wonder tidings. See What tidings bringest thou
Dunstan, Ralph
 "I heard the bells on Christmas day"
 "I sing of a Maiden"
 "A little Child there is yborn." See Parvulus nobis nascitur
 Man, be merry as bird on berry
 Parvulus nobis nascitur
 Sir Christmas
 The three kings
Duorme (Wiegenlied) Neapolitan folk song. g.i. ML 2
Durand, Henry Strong
 "Bright college years" (Wilhelm)
Durante, Francesco
 "Hear my sighing"
"**Durch** das fenster späh ich" (Ia po svīetlītsīe mlada khozhu) Russian folk song. g.r. ML 1
"**Durch** den wald den dunkeln." See Frühlingslied (Mendelssohn)
"**Durch** die fenster, durch die trüben" ("Ablakomba, ablakomba besütött a holdvilág") Hungarian folk song. g.hu. ML 3
"**Durch** täler und fluren." See "I fjor gjæt' eg gjeitinn' "
"**Durchgebrannt** ist die popengattin." See Vor der abreise

D'Urfey, Thomas
 "Come, sweet lass" (Clarke) Authorship uncertain
 Within a mile of Edinboro' (Hook)
Düringer, Philipp Jacob
 Des mädchens klage (Volksweise)
Durriage, T. A.
 Remember the Alamo (Scottish air)
Dust an' ashes. Negro spiritual. HRD
Dutch carol ("A Child is born in Bethlehem") See Een Kint gheboren in Bethlehem
Dutton, D.
 The rosy crown (Weber)
Dvořák, Anton
 "I know that hope doth smile upon"
 "Ich weiss, dass meiner lieb' zu dir." See "I know that hope doth smile upon"
 "Massa dear"
 "Songs my mother taught me"
Dwight, John Sullivan
 "O Lord! correct me" (Händel)
 See also Brooks, Charles Timothy, jt. auth.
Dwight, Timothy
 Columbia, the gem of the ocean (Becket) See Becket, T. à (Composer and author) Columbia, the gem of the ocean
 "I love Thy kingdom, Lord" (Händel)
Dybeck, Richard
 "Du gamla, du fria, du fjällhoga nord" (Swedish air)
"**Dydd** da fo i ti, seren oleu." See Lliw gwyn rhosyn yr haf
"**D'ye** ken John Peel with his coat so gay." See John Peel
Dyer, Sir Edward
 Down among the dead men (17th century air) See Dyer, J. Down among the dead men (17th century air)
 "My mind to me a kingdom is" (Byrd) Authorship uncertain
Dyer, John
 Down among the dead men (17th century air)
Dyer, Robert
 Down among the dead men (17th century air) See Dyer, J. Down among the dead men (17th century air)
The **dying** aviator. See "A handsome young airman" (Coote)
₁The **dying** cowboy₁ The lone prairie. Cowboy song. LSC
 Variants: The lonesome prairie; "Oh, bury me not on the lone prairie, where the wild kiyotes will howl o'er me"
The **dying** hogger. Railroad song. SBA
The **dying** nun. L. Brewster. Words by Nathalie. GOS 2
Dykema, Peter William
 A carol for everyman
 "To shorten winter's sadness"

Dykes, John Bacchus
All the saints adore thee. See "Holy, holy, holy! Lord God Almighty"
Almsgiving. See "O Lord of heaven, and earth, and sea"
Dominus regit me. See "The King of love my Shepherd is"
"God of our fathers, known of old"
"God of the nations near and far"
"Hark! hark! my soul"
"Hark! ten thousand" (same air as "God, my King, Thy might confessing")
"Holy, holy, holy! Lord God almighty"
"The King of love my Shepherd is"
"Lead, kindly light"
Lest we forget. See "God of our fathers, known of old"
Nicaea. See "Holy, holy, holy! Lord God Almighty"
Now all the bells are ringing
"O Lord of heaven, and earth, and sea"
Pilgrims. See "Hark! hark! my soul"
St Oswald. See "Hark! ten thousand"
Salvator mundi. See "We may not climb the heav'nly steeps"
"Thy kingdom come—on bended knee" (same air as "God of the nations near and far")
"We may not climb the heav'nly steeps"

Dywyll, Dic. See Williams, Richard

"Džež ta swjetla woda bježi." See Trennung und wiedersehn

"Dži a khwataj holečo." See Der schlimme scherz

E

E allor perchè, di', tu m'hai stregato. For English translation see Love duet (Leoncavallo)

"È dunque ver." Scena ed aria. A. Rubinstein. e.i. DCA

È gettela la mia sorte. See "Dagli immortali vertici" (Verdi)

"È ingrato, lo veggio." B. Galuppi. e.i. KVG

E pluribus unum. Words by G. W. Cutter. GOS 1

"E pur io." G. Amadori. e.i. ZT 1

È quest' asilo ameno e grato. For English translation see Euridice and the happy spirits (Gluck)

"È questo il loco." See Ah! se tu dormi (Vaccai)

Each for all. Reissiger. Words by L. Larcom. LAS

"Each time you trill a song with Bill." See The half of it, dearie, blues (Gershwin)

The eagle ("Var hilset hog over granetop") See Høgen (Nielsen)

The eagle's whistle. See Fead an iolair

Eames, Henry Purmort
Onward

Eamonn a' Chnuic (Edmund vom Hügel) Irish folk song. g.ir. ML 1

Earl Brand. Folk song: Georgia version. SES 1
—Berea, Ky. version. SES 1
—Pine Mountain, Ky. version. SES 1
—St Helen's, Ky. version. SES 1
—Teges, Ky. version. SES 1
—Allanstand, N.C. version. SES 1
—Hot Springs, N.C. version. SES 1
—White Rock, N.C. version. SES 1
—Afton, Va. version. SES 1
—Beechgrove, Va. version. SES 1
—Crozet, Va. version. SES 1
—Nash, Va. version. SES 1

Early, early in the spring. Folk song: Allanstand, N.C. version. SES 2
—Alleghany, N.C. version. SES 2
—Hot Springs, N.C. version no. 1. SES 2
—Hot Springs, N.C. version no. 2. SES 2
—Virginia version. SES 2

"Early, early in the spring, the green buds they were swellin'." See Barbara Allen (Pine Mountain, Ky. version)

Early in de mornin' ("When de good ole Gabriel") Minstrel song. WSS

Early in the morning ("I meet little Rosa") Negro spiritual from South Carolina. AS

Early in the morning ("What shall we do") See The drunken sailor

Early mornings. See Mañanitas

"Early on a Monday morning." See Kevin Barry

"Early one morning." English folk song: 1st version. MBS—SSB
—2d version. DSB

"Early one morning." Girl scout song. English folk air. Words by B. O. Edey. GSS

"Early one morning, just as the sun was rising, I heard a bugle say." See "Early one morning" (Girl scout song)

"Early one morning, just as the sun was rising, I heard a maid sing." See "Early one morning" (English folk song)

Early Sunday morning. Play-party game from Virginia. SES 2
Variant of: The mulberry bush

"Early to bed." Round. <Words from Mother Goose> BB—DSB—GSS—TFP

"Early to bed." W. G. Whittaker. Words from Mother Goose. CSB 1

"Earth to-day rejoices." See January carol

"Earthly friends." 16th century German air: Omnis mundus jucundetur. Words by J. M. Neale. OB

"Earth's hopes awaken, Christ life has taken." See Die drei grossen Christlichen feste

East St Louis. Negro blues song. HB

East side, west side. See The sidewalks of New York (Lawlor)

"East, west or north or south." See New Year wishes

Eastburn, R. A.
Little brown jug
We have met, loved, and parted

Easter carol ("Cheer up, friends and neighbours") French carol air: Nous allons, ma mie. OB

"Easter eggs" (Dalalin, dalalin, po yaichenku) Russian folk song. e. OB

Easter eve. C. Gounod. Words by C. Armstrong. TSS 1—TSS 2

Easter hymn ("All who have sinned here") C. Gounod. ₁Tr of Christ est ressuscité₁ e. WG

The eastern train (The Pullman train) Old song. SRW

Eating goober peas. Confederate song. DSO

The ebb of the tide. See Distyll y don

Ebeling, Johann Georg
"All my heart this night rejoices" (Tr of Fröhlich soll mein herze springen)

Ebenezer Frye. See Wal, I swan (Burt)

Eberhart, Mrs Nelle Richmond (McCurdy)
"The heart of her" (Cadman)

Eberwein, Max
Ergo bibamus

"Eb'ry time I think about Jesus." See Calvary

Ebony song no. 2. See My Rose (Lacy)

"Ecco purch'a voi ritorno." C. Monteverdi. e.i. KVG

"Eccomi alfine in Babilonia." See Ah! quel giorno (Rossini)

"Eccomi solo alfine." See O vecchio cor, che batti (Verdi)

"Eche geia, chale moy mana." See "Lebe wohl, du gute mutter"

"Echer! besser." See "My youngest one is wedded"

The echo ("Oh-I-Ro! sing we upon the hill") Carinthian air. Words by H. H. Harbour. DSB

"The echoing horn." T. A. Arne. ₁Words by I. Bickerstaffe₁ CSB 3

"Écoutez donc la complainte de la mère de Rochel." See Lamento

Edey, Birdsall Otis
"Early one morning" (17th century air)
Girl scout's round (Hayes)
"Hail to the scouts" (Jeffery)

Edgar, Marjorie
"The trees they do grow high" (English air)

₁Edite, bibite₁ Altes studentisches tafellied ("Ça ça geschmauset") g. EDL

Edmeston, James
"Lead us, heavenly Father, lead us" (Sicilian air)

Edmund vom Hugel. See Eamonn a' Chnuic

Edmunds. C. B.
Nature's music

"Edna biekh moma u maika." See "Mutter so zärtlich mich liebte"

Edward. Folk song: Balsam, N.C. version. SES 1
—Carmen, N.C. version. SES 1
—Clyde, N.C. version. SES 1
—Hot Springs, N.C. version. SES 1
—Marion, N.C. version. SES 1
—Tennessee version. SES 1
—Callaway, Va. version. SES 1
—Endicott, Va. version. SES 1
—Villamont, Va. version. SES 1
—Woolwine, Va. version. SES 1

Edwardes, Richard. See Edwards, Richard

Edwards, Frank, pseud. See Loomis, Harvey Worthington

Edwards, Gus
"Army mule" (same air as Tammany)
I can't tell why I love you, but I do
I'll be with you when the roses bloom again
Tammany

Edwards, Richard
"When May is in his prime"

Edwin in the lowlands low. Folk song: Georgia version. SES 1
—Berea, Ky. version no. 1. SES 1
—Berea, Ky. version no. 2. SES 1
—Hyden, Ky. version. SES 1
—Black Mountain, N.C. version. SES 1
—Burnsville, N.C. version no. 1. SES 1
—Burnsville, N.C. version no. 2. SES 1
—Burnsville, N.C. version no. 3. SES 1
—Hot Springs, N.C. version. SES 1
—Tennessee version. SES 1
Variant: Young Edward

De eel catcher's glee. Minstrel song. PSG

"Een chick-ee-noo! long years ago there lived a squaw." See The chattering squaw

Ef ye want to see Jesus. See If you want to see Jesus

"Ef yo' see my mother." See Ride on, Jesus

"Ef you want to get to hebben, come along, come along." See Did you hear my Jesus

"Ef you want to git to heaven lemme tell yer how to do hit." See Jest talkin'

Efteraar (Autumn) P. E. Lange-Müller. Words by L. Holstein. da.e. WM 2

"Eg hev vand rat um verdi so mang ein veg." See Vandraren (Lund)

"Eg rodde meg ut paa Seiagrunden." See Strilevise

"Egli ancora non giunge." See Ah! non avea più lagrime (Donizetti)

Egner, Philip
Army, O army
Chevrons
"Down in Maryland"
Official West Point march
On, brave old army team

Ego. See Jag (Rangström)

Egressi, Béni
"Ereszkedik le a felhő." See "O'er the forest rainclouds lower"

Egressi, Béni—*Continued*

"Ez a vilag a milyen nagy." See "Oh! the earth is vast and spacious"

Hungaria's treasure (attributed; attributed also to J. Szerdahelyi)

"Juhász legény." See "Shepherd laddie"

"Kuhnen flugs steigt auf der kranich." See Hungaria's treasure (attributed)

"Ne menj rózsám a tarlóra." See "Rosebud, to the fields art going"

"Oh! the earth is vast and spacious"

"O'er the forest rainclouds lower"

"Rosebud, to the fields art going"

"Shepherd laddie"

"Eh! qui marierons-nous" (Who shall we marry) Folk song from Champagne. e.f.   CBF 2

Die **ehre** Gottes aus der natur ("Die himmel rühmen") Beethoven. Words by C. F. Gellert.   g.   EDL

Die ehre Gottes aus der natur (The praise of God) e.g.   SSO 2

"The heavens are telling."   e.   MFS

"The heavens resound."   e.   BB—TFP—TFR

Ehre sei Gott in der höh'.   See "It came upon the midnight clear" (Roeder)

Ehren on the Rhine.   W. M. Hutchinson. MFS

"Ei bübla, wennst mich so gern häst." See Verstehst

"Ei, du eintagsbaum, du lieber" ("Vai, tu diemed', diemedéli") Lithuanian folk song.   g.li.   ML 3

"Ei kukaan puhu puolestani, vaan jokahinen kaataa."   See Santras lied

"Eï, ukhnem."   See Volga boat song

Eia, Eia.   17th century German air. Words based on a folk carol, Zu Bethlehem geboren.   e.   OB

"Eia popeia, mein englein, schlaf ein." See Wiegenlied (Czech folk song)

"Der **eiberster** is der mechiten."   See Maseltof

Eibhlín a rúin (Eibhlin, mein lieb)   13th century Irish folk song.   g.ir.   ML 1

Eibhlin, mein lieb.   See Eibhlín a rúin

Eichberg, Julius
"To thee, O country"

Eiche und esche.   See The oak and the ash

"Eichen sah ich zwei zusammen stehen." See Tölf synir

Eichendorff, Joseph Karl Benedikt, freiherr von
Der frohe wandersmann (Fröhlich)
Gute nacht (Franz)
"In einem kühlen grunde" (German folk air; also music by Gluck)
Intermezzo (Schumann)
Wanderlied der Prager studenten (Volksweise)
Der jäger abschied (Mendelssohn)
"O taler weit, o höhen" (Mendelssohn)

"Der eichwald braust" (Des mädchens klage)   F. Schubert.   Words by F. von Schiller.   g.   EDL

Der **eifersüchtige** knabe.   Altes volkslied. g.   EDL

"Eikä ne haavan lehdet lakkaa."   See Die espenblätter

"Eikur sa eg ad tvaer saman stodu."   See Tölf synir

"Eilt hin, ihr meine seufzer."   See I sospiri

"Eilu vo-eilu modim."   See All in accord

"Eily mavourneen."   Benedict.   HMI

Ein dovor, ein dovor.   See No matter, no matter

"Einem bach, der fliesst."   C. W. Gluck. g.   EDL

"Einsam bin ich, nicht alleine."   C. M. von Weber.   Words by P. A. Wolf. g.   EDL

"Einsam wandelt dein freund."   See Adelaïde (Beethoven)

"Einst am sonntagabend wandert' ich und sann."   See Skogmöte has thorgjer skjelle

"Einst hatt' ich ein rösslein."   See "Had a horse, a finer no one ever saw"

"Einst hütet' ich herden."   See Bugail yr hafod

"Einst in Kieff, Kieffs altem herrschersitz sass Wladimir."   See The feast of Vladimir

"Einst kam ich durch Sandgate."   See The keel row

"Einst kam ich nach Tuaire geritten." See Droichead na Tuaire

"Einst stieg Dobri."   See The gray dove

"Ein einzig böses weib lebt höchstens in der welt."   See Das böse weib (Haydn)

"Eis toy kosmoy to taxeidi."   See Der wandrer (Smyrna folk song)

Der **eisenbahn.**   Jewish folk song.   y. SY

"Ej! ej! ej! uranila kosovka devojka." See Das mädchen vom Amselfeld

"Eju filaja la miò rocca."   See Vocero

El que a hierro mata (He who kills with the sword must die with the sword) Mexican folk song.   Words from an old Spanish proverb.   e.s.   VS

El-a-noy [Illinois]   American traditional song.   SBA

"Elátkozom ezt a cudar világot."   See "Be accurs'd, oh! world"

Elbel, Louis
The victors

Elderton, William
York! York for my money (Old English air)

Elek, Erkel
"Nie war hoch am himmel."   See Sea of stars
"None of all the many stars."   See Sea of stars
"Nincsen annyi tenger csillag."   See Sea of stars
Sea of stars

"Elena! oh tu ch'io chiamo."   Rossini. e.i.   PC

"Elenka, Elenka, komm zum kranken liebsten."   See Tanzlied

The **elfin** knight. Folk song: Kentucky version. SES 1
—North Carolina version. SES 1
Elgar, Sir Edward William
Love greetings
Salut d'amour. See Love greetings
"**Elindultam** szép hazámbul." See "Aus dem Ungarland, dem schönen"
Eliza Jane. Folk song: Hyden, Ky. version. SES 2
—Manchester, Ky. version. SES 2
—Pineville, Ky. version. SES 2
"Liza in the summer time" (She died on the train) North Carolina version. SBA
Liza Jane. SBA
Variants: Liza Anne; Mountain top; "Went up on the mountain"
Elkins, Henry Glasgow
"Dear T. C. U."
Ella piangea la perfida. Mercadante. e.i. PB
Ella Ree ("Oh! Ella Ree, so kind and true") J. W. Porter. [Words by C. E. Stewart] WSS
Elle danse! en cadence. For English translation see Waltz song (Offenbach)
Ellen Bayne. S. C. Foster (music and words) WSS
"**Ellen** mine! once more oh greet me." See "Elena! oh tu ch'io chiamo" (Rossini)
Ellen Smith. American mountain ballad. P. Degraph (music and words) RA
Ellerbeck, Aurania
"Come join the band" (Hall)
Ellie Rhee ("Sweet Ellie Rhee, so dear to me") S. Winner (music and words) WSS
Elliot, Jane
The flowers of the forest (Old air)
Elliott, C. W.
Bonny Eloise (Thomas)
Elliott, Charlotte
Calm was the night (Sullivan)
"My God, my Father, while I stray" (music by Moszkowski; Wagner. For music by Troyte see Troyte's chant, in Song Index)
Elliott, Ebenezer
"When wilt Thou save the people" (music by Booth; Brown)
Elliott, James William
The feast of lanterns
"The king of France"
"Little Bo-Peep"
"Little Jack Horner"
"The man in the moon came down too soon"
"Pussy cat, pussy cat, where have you been"
"Sing a song of sixpence"
Song of Hybrias the Cretan
"Three children sliding"
Elman, Dave. See Handy, William Christopher, jt. comp. and auth.
The **elopement.** J. H. Ross. Words by J. S. Freligh. SRW
[Elsa's traum] "I saw in splendor shining." R. Wagner. e. WG

Elsie from Chelsea. H. Dacre (music and words) SRW
Elsie Marley. Traditional song. GSS
Elson, Louis Charles
Come with me (Campana)
Elvey, Sir George Job
"Come, ye thankful people, come"
St George's Windsor. See "Come, ye thankful people, come"
The **emancipated** race. Song of the Spanish American war. DSO
There's many a man been murdered in Luzon. US
Embarrassment. See Verlegenheit (Abt)
Emerson, Billy
The big sunflower. See Happy as a big sunflower
Happy as a big sunflower
The **emigrants** ("Sad was the day we said farewell") Words by W. Maynard. HMI
Emigrants' song. See Row, row, cheerly row
Emmanuel ("Joy fills") See "Joy fills our inmost heart to-day" (Composer unknown)
Emmet, Joseph Kline
Emmet's lullaby. See Go to sleep, Lena darling
Go to sleep, Lena darling (from Fritz)
Emmet's lullaby. See Go to sleep, Lena darling (Emmet)
Emmett, Daniel Decatur
Crazy song to the air of Dixie (same air as Dixie)
Dixie (with words "I wish I was"; "O! Dixie's land")
The horse named Bill (same air as Dixie)
Kelly field air-service song (same air as Dixie)
Plantation walk around
The U.S.A. forever (same air as Dixie)
Emra, W. H.
None can tell (Allen)
"**En** avant, grénadiers" ("Forward march, grenadiers") Negro creole folk song. e.f. MB
"**En** Cuba, la isla hermosa del ardiente sol." See Tú (Fuentes)
"**En** el mil nueve cientos y diez." See Versos de Montalgo
"**En** gång i bredd med mig" ("Fragen wird feierlich") Swedish folk song. g.sw. ML 1
"**Én** istenem, add megérnem." See "Gott im himmel, mögst du geben"
"**En** passant par la Lorraine." See Les trois capitaines
"**En** passant près d'un moulin." See Et moi je m'enfouiyais
"**En** revenant de la joli' Rochelle" (see Song Index)
Variant: C'e ' l'aviron qui nous mène en haut
En roulant ma boule (On, roll on, my ball) French Canadian folk song. e.f. MBS
En roulant ma boule roulant (On, roll on, my ball I roll on) e.f. GC

En très bon ordre.   For English translation see "All in good order" (Offenbach)

"En vain de ma douleur affreuse."   See Complainte de la reine Marie Stuart en prison (Martini)

En vain pour éviter les réponses amères. For English translation see "'Tis all in vain" (Bizet)

"Th' enchanted woods and rivers say." See Schlummerlied (Schubert)

"Enchantress, farewell" (Kinloch)   Scottish air: Kinloch of Kinloch.   Words by W. Scott.   GS

"The enemy said."   Händel.   SSO 3

"Engedje mög édös anyám."   See Kätchen Kadar

Engel, Carl
  "What Child is this"

Engelbrecht, J. C.
  Farewell is a lonely sound.   See Good-bye
  Good-bye
  The separation

English, Thomas Dunn
  Ben Bolt (Kneass)

ıThe enlisted soldiersı They look like men of war (Negro battle hymn)   Negro folk song.   HRD

Enoch, Frederick
  By the blue sea (Smart)

"Ensanguined and lurid."   G. Donizetti. ıTr of O sole più rattoı   e.   WG

Entführing.   See Droichead na Tuaire

Die entlaufene sklavin ("Telal viče") Bosnian folk song.   g.se.   ML 2

ıEntrance songı Yes, this hero.   K. Millöcker.   e.   WLO

"Entre le boeuf et l'âne gris" ("Zwischen dem ochs und esulein") 17th century French Noël.   f.g.   ML 1

Entre le boeuf et l'âne gris.   For English translation with a different air see The sleep of the Infant Jesus (Gevaert)

"Entre Paris et Saint-Denis" ("From Paris to St Denis, see")   Canadian folk song.   e.f.   GC

Entreat me not to leave thee.   C. Gounod. e.   CSS 1

Entreaty.   See Bitte (Bohm)

Entschuldigung ("Wenn wir durch die strassen ziehen")   F. Nestler.   Words by W. Müller.   g.   EDL

L'envoi ("I'm a-going to travel")   Negro spiritual.   HRD

Envoyons d'l'avant, nos gens (Send her on along)   Canadian folk song.   e.f. GC

Epiphany.   See "There came three kings ere break of day" (Smith)

Er is een kindeken geboren op d'aard. See De nederige geboorte

"Er ist es nicht."   See Beatrice (Holstein)

"Er schlich sich die wände entlang."   See Verborg'ne liebe (Grieg)

"Er was een maagdetje zuiver en net." See De boodschap van Maria

Era anch' io di quella schiera.   Donizetti. e.i.   PB

"Era la noche."   See Serenata

"Era notte oscura, oscura."   Fioravanti. e.i.   PB

"Erbarmen! du schlanke, schöne."   See Erbarmen, schöne

Erbarmen, schöne ("Aman đevojko, uzun iepoto")   Serbian folk song.   g.se. ML 2

Erdbeeren (Mansikka)   Finnish folk song. fi.g.   ML 3

"Erdő, erdő, sűrű erdő."   See "In the forest, the deep forest"

"Ere departing to seek the stars."   See Gebet (Brückler)

"Ere the fair land of Texas."   See The fair land of Texas (Balfe)

"Ere the twilight bat was flitting."   See Jamie's on the stormy sea (Covert)

"Ereszkedik le a felhő."   See "O'er the forest rainclouds lower" (Egressi)

Ergo bibamus ("Hier sind wir versammelt")   M. Eberwein.   Words by Goethe.   g.   EDL

"Erhebt euch von der erde."   See Soldaten-morgenlied

Eri tu che macchiavi.   G. Verdi.   e.i. PB

Ericson, Gustaf H.
  The fifty-first coast artillery march-song (Composer unknown)

The E-ri-e.   Song of the Erie canal. SBA

The Erie canal.   Old song.   SBA— SRW

Erin is my home.   <German or Bohemian air>   ıWords by T. H. Baylyı GOS 1—SI

Erin! oh Erin ("Like the bright lamp") Irish air: Thamma hulla, or, Thamama hulla.   Words by T. Moore.   HMI

"Erin! the tear and the smile in thine eyes."   Air: Eileen aroon.   Words by T. Moore.   HMI

"Erkennet, erkennt, dass der Herr ist Gott" (Arioso from 100th psalm)   S. Jadassohn.   e.g.   ASA

The erl king.   See Erlkönig (Loewe); Erlkönig (Schubert)

Erlkönig (The erl-king)   C. Loewe. Words by J. W. von Goethe.   e.g. GA

Erlkönig (The erlking)   F. Schubert. Words by J. W. von Goethe.   e.g. GG

Erntelied ("Ah! si no fos p'es carreto") See Cansó de sega

Erntelied ("Sabs es segadós que fan") See Cansó de sega

Errefusa (Vergebliches ständchen) Basque folk song.   ba.g.   ML 2

Erskine, John
  Marching song (Pattberg)

Erwin, John,   pseud.   See Harbour, Homer H.

"Es braust ein ruf wie donnerhall."   See Die wacht am Rhein (Wilhelm)

"Es, es, es und es, es ist ein harter schluss." See Handwerksburschen-abschied

Es flien Yidalach.   See Maseltof

"Es freit ein wilder wassermann."   See Die schöne Lilofee

"Es geht bei gedämpfter trommel klang."
See Der soldat (Silcher)

"Es gibt kein schöner leben als studenten-leben." See Studentenleben (Reis-siger)

"Es ging'n drei kleine kinderlein." See Le miracle de Saint-Nicolas

"Es hat die rose sich beklagt" ("The rose complained") R. Franz. Words by F. von Bodenstedt (Mirza Schaffy) e.g. GG
The rose's complaint. e. TFR

"Es hatten drei gesellen." See Fiducit (Briesewitz)

"Es is gekummen amol." See A chazan äuf Shabbos

"Es ist alles dunkel, 's ist alles trube." See Woran ich meine freude hab

"Es ist bestimmt in Gottes rat." F. Men-delssohn-Bartholdy. Words by E. von Feuchtersleben. g. EDL

"Es ist ein reis entsprungen" (Das reis aus der wurzel Jesse) 16th century air. g. EDL
"Es ist ein' ros'." g. OB

"Es ist ein schnitter" (Der tod als schnit-ter) German folk song. g. EDL

Es ist genug. For English translation see "It is enough" (Mendelssohn)

"Es ist mein sohn, ich kann nicht daran zweifeln." J. Joachim. Scene from Schiller's unfinished drama "Demetri-us." e.g. DCA

"Es kann ja nicht immer so bleiben." See Ewiger wechsel (Himmel)

Es klappert die mühle am rauschenden bach. For English translation see The mill-wheel

"Es klingt ein heller klang." See Das lied vom Rhein (Nägeli)

Es komt ein schiff geladen. For English translation see "There comes a galley, laden"

"Es mahnt der wald, es ruft der strom." See Schlummerlied (Schubert)

"Es ritten drei reiter zum tore hinaus." See Drei reiter am tor

"Es schrie ein vogel." See Der skreg en fugl (Sinding)

"Es stehen drei sterne am himmel." See Der eifersüchtige knabe

"Es steht ein baum im Odenwald." See Der baum im Odenwald (Reichardt)

"Es steht, es steht gross Belgerad" ("Oj stoji, stoji Beligrad") Slovenian folk song. g.slo. ML 2

"Es tanzt ein Bibabutzemann." See Biba-butzemann

"Es war ein könig in Thule." See Der könig in Thule (Zelter)

"Es war ein sonntag hell und klar." See O schöne zeit, o sel'ge zeit (Götze)

[Es war ein traum] Ah, 'tis a dream. E. Lassen. Words by H. Heine. e. BB—MFS—TFG

Es war ein traum. For English transla-tion with a different air see Ah! 'tis a dream (Hawley)

"Es waren einmal drei reiter gefangn." See Die gefangenen reiter

"Es waren zwei königskinder." See Zwei königskinder

"Es wollt ein schneider wandern am Mon-tag in der fruh." See Schneiders hollenfahrt

"Es wollte sich einschleichen ein kühles lüftelein." See Vergissnichtmein

L'esclave (The bondmaid) E. Lalo. Words by T. Gautier. e.f. TM

Esenwein, Joseph Berg
Taps (U.S. army air)

Esmeralda. W. C. Levey. Words by A. Halliday. GE

Die espenblätter (Haavan lehdet) Finnish folk song. fi.g. ML 3

"L'esperto nocchiero" ("Bold pilot unheed-ing") G. B. Bononcini. e.i. PC

Esrom, D. A.
Hail! hail! the gang's all here (Sulli-van)

"Esser mesto" ("Dismal care") Flotow. [Tr of Bange trauer] e.i. PC

"Eště mě nemáš." See "Noch bin ich nicht dein"

Esther die gabbete. Jewish folk song. y. SY

Estic,
Clavelitos (Valverde)

Estrellita ("Little star") M. M. Ponce. e.s. MSP

Los estudiants de Tolosa (Die studenten von Tolosa) Catalan folk song. ca.g. ML 2

"Et exultavit" ("My soul rejoices") J. S. Bach. e.i. CSB 6

Et moi je m'enfouiyais (And I would flee away) Canadian folk song. e.f. GC

"Et tan patate-là tchuite." See Tan patate-là tchuite

"Eternal Father, strong to save." See For those in peril on the sea (Whiting)

Eternal rest (Requiem æternam) M. Piccolomini. Words by A. Horspool. e.i. CSS 1—TSS 2

Eternity, eternity. See Happy is eternity

"Étions trois belles filles, trois filles seule-ment." See Les trois jupons blancs

The Ettrick shepherd. See Hogg, James

Euch lüften, die mein klagen so traurig oft erfüllt. For English translation see "Ye wandering breezes" (Wagner)

Eulalie ("Bluebirds, linger") Minstrel bal-lad. WSS

Euridice and the happy spirits ("These fair meads") C. W. von Gluck. [Tr of È quest' asilo ameno e grato] e. CSB 3

Evans, Evan
Morva Rhuddlan (Welsh air)

Evans, George
In the good old summer time

Evans, Gordon W.
Trojan war song

Evans, J. G.
Belle ob Baltimore

Evans, John Stark
Oregon pledge song

Evans, William
"Pa bryd y deui eto" (Old Welsh air)
Eveleen's bower. Irish air. Words by T. Moore. HMI
"**Even** bravest heart may swell." See "Avant de quitter ces lieux" (Gounod)
"**Evening** comes, the sun has lost his glory." See Abendempfindung (Mozart)
Evening hymn ("Forgive me, Lord."— Ward) Scotch air. MFS
Evening hymn ("Hail, thou most gracious One") See Evening song to the Virgin (Browne)
Evening praise. See "Day is dying in the west" (Sherwin)
Evening prayer ("Leise, leise, fromme weise") See Gebet (Weber)
The **evening** prayer ("This night I lift") See I lift my heart to Thee (Costa)
Evening prayer ("When I lay me down to sleep") E. Humperdinck. [Tr of Abends, will ich schlafen gehn] e. WG
An **evening** song ("Dark thro' the forest") Old Lithuanian air. Words by H. H. Harbour. DSB
Evening song ("The day is done") Mendelssohn. e. SSO 2
An **evening** song ("Glory to Thee") See "Glory to Thee, my God, this night" (Gounod)
Evening song ("The sun upon the lake is low") See The sun is low
Evening song to the Virgin. <H. M. Browne> Words by F. Hemans. GOS 2
Evening hymn (Ave, Sanctissima) MFS
Ever after on (I'll love my baby till the sea runs dry) Negro folk blues. HB
Ever I'll praise thee. R. Wagner. [Tr of Stets soll nur dir] e. WG
"**Ever** of thee." F. Hall. Words by G. Linley. MFS
Ever safe with God. O. Cantor. TSS 1 —TSS 2
"**Ever** since Uncle John Henry been dead." Negro work song. SBA
"**Ever** to the right." MFS
Evermore and evermore, Christians, sing Alleluya. See Athens
"**Ev'ry** cloud has a silver lining." See Old cruise song
"**Every** college has a legend." See The Nittany lion (Leyden)
"**Ev'ry** day a pilgrim holy." See Christ the Pilgrim (Blumenthal)
"**Ev'ry** day the wondrous lovely sultan's daughter paced the garden." See Der Asra (Rubinstein)
[**Every** flower is equally cherished"] "In my heart." G. Verdi. [Tr of Questa o quella] e. WG
Every girl scout's round. Composer and author of words unknown. GSS
Every hour in the day. Negro spiritual from Georgia. AS
Ev'ry lassie has her laddie. See Comin' thro' the rye

"**Ev'ry** man must have a trade." See A game of trades
"**Ev'ry** morn at six o'clock I go straight to my work." See Everybody works but father (Lehman)
"**Every** night when the sun goes in." Folk song from North Carolina. SES 2
"**Ev'ry** person in the nation." See The Galway piper
"**Every** soldier leaves behind." See When the guns are rolling yonder
Ev'ry Sunday down to her home we go. See The sunshine of Paradise Alley (Bratton)
Ev'ry time I come to town. See They gotta quit kickin' my dawg aroun' (Perkins)
Every time I feel the spirit. Negro spiritual. FSN—HRD—WFN—WSS
"**Every** time I think about Jesus." See Calvary
Every valley [shall be exalted] G. F. Händel. SSO 3
"**Ev'rybody** has a sweetheart underneath the rose." See My sweetheart's the man in the moon (Thornton)
Everybody works but father. Old English air. Words by C. W. McClintock. SRW
Everybody works but father. S. Lehman. Words by C. W. McClintock. OTG
Ev'rywhere a welcome stranger. See Santa Claus (Read)
"**Ev'rywhere** the moorland is still." See Wand'rers nachtlied: I (Loewe)
Eve's lamentation. M. P. King. MFS
"**Evo**, jur me zove u daleki sviet." See Kriegers abschied von der mutter
Ev'ry. For entries beginning Ev'ry see Every

Ewald, Johannes
"Kong Christian stod ved høien mast" (Hartmann)
[The **ewe-bughts**] "Will ye gang to the ewe-bughts, Marion." Scottish song. GS
Ewen, John
The boatie rows (Scottish air) Authorship uncertain
Ewiger wechsel ("Es kann ja nicht immer so bleiben") F. H. Himmel. Words by A. von Kotzebue. g. EDL
Ewing, Alexander
"Jerusalem the golden"
"**Exact** to appointment I went to the grove." See False Phillis
The **exile** of Erin ("There came to the beach") Irish air: Savourneen deelish. Words by T. Campbell. HMI —SI
Explosions from a tropical language. U.S. navy song. [H. J. Sayers] US
"**Exult** now, ye faithful." See D'Egitto là sui lidi (Verdi)
"**Eye** hath not seen." A. R. Gaul. TSS 2
"**Eyes** like the morning star." See The Colorado trail
"**Eyes**, look no more." J. Danyel. GA
Eyes of blue. Slovakian folk air. S. Rowe. TFB

"The **eyes** of Texas." University of Texas song. Air: Levee song. Words by J. L. Sinclair. AI—AIS—KU—KV

"**Eyes** right! knapsacks tight." See The drinking fusileers

Eysler, Edmund S.
Kisses can do no harm. See Küssen ist keine sünd'
Küssen ist keine sünd' (from Bruder Straubinger)

Ez a kis lány hamis kis lány. See Pretty maid, how could you do so (Szerdahelyi)

"**Ez** a kis lány jaj be czifra." See "See the little pretty maiden"

"**Ez** a világ a milyen nagy." See "Oh! the earth is vast and spacious" (Egressi)

Ezekiel saw de wheel. Negro spiritual. HRD—WSS
"Ezekiel saw the wheel." WFN
Variants: "A wheel in a wheel"; "'Zekiel saw de wheel"

"**Ezek'l** saw de wheel." See Ezekiel, you and me

Ezekiel, you and me. Arrangement of five negro spirituals. SBA

"**Ezt** a kerek erdőt járom én." See "Through the darkling forest gay I roam" (Szerdahelyi)

F

Faber, Frederick William
"Dear little One, how sweet Thou art" (Old English air)
"Faith of our fathers, living still" (Hemy and Walton)
"Hark! hark! my soul" (music by Armstrong; Dykes)

"**Fade**, fade each earthly joy." See Jesus is mine (Perkins)

Faded flowers. W. Willing. [Words by J. H. Brown] GOS 2

"**Fading** light dims the sight." See Taps

"**Fading**, still fading." Portuguese air. GOS 1—MFS

Fagan, Barney
Decollette
My gal is a high born lady

Fagan, V. F.
Hike, Notre Dame (Casasanta)

Fahr' wohl, fahr' wohl, mein armes lieb. See Ritters abschied (Kinkel)

"**Fain** would I saddle." See "Jeg vilde sadle" (Lie)

Faint bells afar in the west are ringing. See Mo rùn geal dìleas

Fair Annie ("Adieu, adieu") Folk song from North Carolina. SES 1

Fair Annie of Lochyran ("O who will shoe my fair foot") Scottish folk song. SBA
Variants: The true lover's farewell; Who will shoe your pretty little foot

Fair are the flow'rs in the valley. See Flowers in the valley

"**Fair** are these fields." French air. Words by E. Smith. DSB

Fair as a lily, joyous and free. See Rosalie, the prairie flower (Root)

"**Fair** as an angel from above." See "Bella siccome un angelo in terra pellegrino" (Donizetti)

[A **fair** dove] "Měla sem holubka" ("Hatte einst ein täubchen") Silesian folk song. bo.g. ML 3

Fair Eleanor. See Lord Thomas and fair Ellinor (Alexander, N.C. version)

Fair, fair, with golden hair. See Under the willow she's sleeping (Foster)

[The **fair** garden] The lovely garden. A. Borodine. Words from the Russian. e. GA

"A **fair** good morrow, lovely maiden." See Lliw gwyn rhosyn yr haf

"A **fair-haired** boy in a foreign land." See The pardon came too late (Dresser)

The **fair-haired** lad. See An gille ban

[The **fair-haired** maiden] "Tho' the last glimpse of Erin." Air: The coolun, or, Coulin. Words by T. Moore. HMI—SSB

"**Fair** Harvard." Harvard university song. [Air: My lodging is on the cold ground] AI—KU

"**Fair** ladies, I being rather shy." See Advertisement for a wife

"A **fair** lady lived in Colchester." Traditional song. KSO

Fair lady of the plains. Cowboy song. LSC

"**Fair** lady, throw those costly robes aside." See Death and the lady

The **fair** land of Texas. Song of the Mexican war. [M. W. Balfe] DSO

"A **fair** little miss all in the garden." See The broken token (Allanstand, N.C. version no. 1)

"**Fair** Lucy sitting in her father's room." See Lizzie Wan

"**Fair** Luna." J. Barnby. MFS

Fair M. S. C. Montana state college song. Air: Der tannenbaum. Words by M. K. Hall. HW

"The **fair** maid who the first of May." Lithuanian air. Words from an old rhyme. DSB

Fair Margaret and sweet William. Folk song: Barbourville, Ky. version. SES 1
—Berea, Ky. version. SES 1
—Clay county, Ky. version. SES 1
—Allanstand. N.C. version. SES 1
—Burnsville, N.C. version. SES 1
—Carmen, N.C. version no. 1. SES 1
—Carmen, N.C. version no. 2. SES 1
—Micaville, N.C. version. SES 1
—Flag Pond, Tenn. version. SES 1
—Harrogate, Tenn. version. SES 1
—Beechgrove, Va. version. SES 1
—Blue Ridge Springs, Va. version. SES 1

Fair Margaret and sweet William.—*Cont.*
—Callaway, Va. version.   SES 1
—Crozet, Va. version.   SES 1
—Dewey, Va. version.   SES 1
—Mount Fair, Va. version.   SES 1
—Woodridge, Va. version.   SES 1
"Sweet William."   Knott or Letcher county, Ky. version.   MK
Fair Nina.   See Nina (Ciampi)
Fair Nottiman town (see Song Index)
Variant of: Nottamun town
"**Fair** spring-time beginning."   See "Printemps qui commence" (Saint-Saëns)
"The **fair** woodland bowers are peopled with flowers."   See Llwyn on
"**Fairest** daughter of the graces."   G. Verdi.   [Tr of Bella figlia dell' amore] e.   WG
"**Fairest** isle."   H. Purcell.   Words by J. Dryden.   MBS
"**Fairest** Lord Jesus" (Crusaders' hymn) [Tr of Schönster Herr Jesu] e.   BB
"**Fairest** maid on Devon banks."   Air: Rothmurche's rant.   Words by R. Burns.   GS
"**Fairest** of all in California."   See Hail to dear old Whittier (Collins)
Fairest of colleges (D-rah)   University of Denver song.   Words by D. Hickey.   HW
Fairfax, Charles H.
"Speed up"
Fairies' chorus.   See "When the cock begins to crow" (Purcell)
Fairies' song.   See The noontide ray (Auber)
Fairy-belle.   S. C. Foster (music and words)   BB—GOS 2—WSS
The **fairy** dance.   Swedish air.   Words by K. Davis.   DSB
Fairy gold.   Finnish folk song.   e.   MFF
Fairy mischief.   Norwegian folk song. e.   MFF
Fairy music.   French air.   Words by K. Davis.   DSB
["**Faites-lui** mes aveux] "Le parlate d'amor."   C. Gounod.   e.i.   PC
"Lovely flowers I pray."   e.   WG
Faith ("Faith, thou beacon ever bright") Three-part round.   Mozart.   Words by V. A. Pierpont.   TFB—TFG
Faith ("De klamres indenfor Islam")   See Tro (Sinding)
Faith of our fathers, born of noble mind. See Colgate invictus (Bushby)
"**Faith** of our fathers, living still."   H. F. Hemy and J. G. Walton.   Words by F. W. Faber.   BB—TFG
"**Faith,** thou beacon ever bright."   See Faith (Mozart)
"**Faithful** and true we lead you forth." See Bridal chorus (Wagner)
Faithful little bird.   Words by D. M. Craik.   MFS
Faithful, loyal, firm and true.   See Alma mater—University of Alabama (Thompson)
Faithless! those sad tears that wet thy brow.   See Ella piangea la perfida (Mercadante)

Falan-tiding.   See "Out of the orient crystal skies"
Falconer, Edmund
Killarney (Balfe)
Falk, Johannes
Die drei grossen christlichen feste (Sicilian air)
Fallen by the wayside.   C. K. Harris (music and words)   SW
Fallersleben, Hoffmann von.   See Hoffmann von Fallersleben, August Heinrich
Fallström, Karl Daniel
Aftonstämning (Peterson-Berger)
The **false** knight upon the road.   Folk song: North Carolina version.   SES 1
—Tennessee version.   SES 1
False Patricians, on you depending.   See Era anch' io di quella schiera (Donizetti)
False Phillis.   18th century song.   WOE
The **false** young man.   Folk song: Clay county, Ky. version.   SES 2
—St Helen's, Ky. version.   SES 2
—Alleghany, N.C. version.   SES 2
—Burnsville, N.C. version.   SES 2
—Micaville, N.C. version.   SES 2
—Flag Pond, Tenn. version no. 1. SES 2
—Flag Pond, Tenn. version no. 2. SES 2
—Afton, Va. version.   SES 2
—White Rock, Va. version.   SES 2
—Woodridge, Va. version.   SES 2
"As I walked out."   Knott or Letcher county version.   MK
"A **famous** hen convention."   See The hen convention
The **Fanaid** grove.   Irish folk song from County Donegal.   DSC—HI 1
The **Fanaid** grove (Der hain von Fanaid)   e.g.   ML 1
Fanciulle, che il core.   See "Ditemi, buona gente, vedeste Dinorah" (Meyerbeer)
Fandango.   Spanish folk song.   g.s. ML 2
"**Far** above Cayuga's waters."   See Alma mater—Cornell university (Thompson)
"**Far** above the deep blue sea."   See The sea gulls
"**Far** above the golden valley."   See Crimson and the blue (Thompson)
"**Far** above the Rio Grande."   See Alma mater—University of New Mexico (Thompson)
"**Far** and high the cranes give cry."   See Hungaria's treasure
Far away ("Where is now")   M. L. Bliss. (music and words)   GE—MFS
"**Far** away beyond the glamor of the city and its strife."   See The picture that is turned toward the wall (Graham)
Far away beyond the starlit skies.   See Twilight is falling (Unseld)
"**Far** away down south in Alabama."   See The Alabama blossoms
Far away! far way! oh, she wore it for her lover.   See For her lover who was far away

"Far away the nightingale now flieth." See The nightingale (Tchaikovsky)

"Far, hvor flyver svanerne hen." See Efteraar (Lange-Müller)

"Far off in Dixie land." See Down in Dixie (Loomis)

"Far across the country." See The first Christmas

"Far out on the desolate billow." See Never alone (Silcher)

'Far up upon the mountain, there stood an old chalet." See Le vieux chalet (Bovet)

The farandole. E. Audran. e. WLO

"Fare thee well, fare thee well, fare thee well, fare thee well." U.S. Naval academy song. US

Fare thee well, fare thee well, fare thee well, my fairy fay. See Polly-wolly-doodle

Fare thee well, for I must leave thee. See "There is a tavern in the town"

Fare ye well ("O fare you well, my brudder") Negro spiritual from South Carolina. AS

"Fare ye well, bright scenes and dearest." See "Cari luoghi ov'io passai" (Donizetti)

Fare you well ("I thought I heard the old man say") See Goodbye, fare ye well ("I thought I heard the old man say")

"Fare you well, I wish you well, hooraw." See Sing fare you well

Farewell ("Die höh'n and wälder") See Gute nacht (Franz)

Farewell ("Nu visner skoven atter") See Afsked (Melartin)

"Farewell and adieu to you, fine Spanish ladies" (Spanish ladies) Capstan chantey. BOS 2
For variants see following songs of similar title

"Farewell and adieu unto you Spanish ladies." Capstan chantey. WSE

"Farewell and adieu to you, Spanish ladies" (Spanish ladies) Capstan chantey. DSC

"Farewell and adieu to you, fine Spanish ladies" (Spanish ladies) BOS 2

"Farewell, as wings are spreading." See Las golondrinas

"Farewell! but whenever you welcome the hour." Irish air: Moll Roone. Words by T. Moore. HMI—SI

Farewell, darling Maggie. [N. W. Gade] e. LSB

"Farewell dear Rosanna." Folk song: Hindman, Ky. version. SES 2
—Pineville, Ky. version. SES 2

"Farewell, farewell is a lonely sound." See Good-bye (Engelbrecht)

Farewell, farewell, my own true love. See Ritters abschied (Kinkel)

"Farewell, farewell, my pretty maid." See The true lover's farewell

"Farewell, farewell, O earth." Finale from Aïda. G. Verdi. [Tr of O terra addio] e. WG

"Farewell, farewell to my only child." See Rough and rolling sea

"Farewell, farewell to thee, Araby's daughter." See Araby's daughter (Kiallmark)

"Farewell, farewell, ye limpid springs and floods." See Farewell, ye limpid springs and floods (Händel)

Farewell forever to old Tennessee. See Farewell, my Lilly dear (Foster)

"Farewell, Granada, from you I'm going." See Granadinas (Barrera y Calleja)

Farewell is a lonely sound. See Good-bye (Engelbrecht)

Farewell, mother! for you'll never see my name among the slain. See "Just before the battle, mother": Confederate parody (Root)

Farewell, mother, you may never press me to your heart again. See "Just before the battle, mother" (Root)

Farewell, my Lilly dear. S. C. Foster (music and words) WSS

Farewell to grog. U.S. navy song. Air: Come, landlord fill the flowing bowl. Words by C. Schenk. US

"Farewell to Lochaber." See Lochaber no more (Reilly?)

[The farewell to my harp] "Dear harp of my country." [Air: New Langolee] Words by T. Moore. HMI

[The farewell to my harp] "Dear harp of my country." Welsh air. Words by T. Moore. DSB

Farewell to summer. Swabian folk air. Words by J. B. Walters. BB

Farewell to the forest. Mendelssohn. [Tr of Abschied vom walde] e. TFG

"Farewell to the white house." See The wagoner's lad (Flag Pond, Tenn. version)

Farewell to the woods. German air. e. MFS

Farewell to thee ("Haaheo eka ua i na pali") See Aloha oe (Liliuokalani)

Farewell to thee ("Now our golden days") Liliuokalani. New words by M. K. Cherryman. BB

Farewell to whisky. See Neil Gow's farewell to whisky (Gow)

Farewell, W. V. U., farewell. West Virginia university song. E. D. Richards (music and words) KV

Farewell, ye limpid springs and floods. G. F. Händel. SSO 1

Farjeon, Eleanor
    Composer
Cheapside
Petticoat lane
    Author
Carol of the Advent (Besançon carol air)
Our brother is born (Farjeon, H.)
Thanksgiving carol (15th century German air)

Farjeon, Eleanor, and Farjeon, Harry
"Coo, coo, coo, coo, how I love you"

Farjeon, Harry
 Carol. See Our brother is born
 Our brother is born
 See also Farjeon, Eleanor, jt. comp.

Farmer, John
 The brook
 For the sake of somebody. See "My heart is sair, I dare na tell"
 Foundation song
 "My heart is sair, I dare na tell"

The **farmer** ("I'm glad I am") Children's song. MFS

[The **farmer**] "Sedlák, sedlák" ("Bäuerlein, bäuerlein") Czech folk dance. bo.g. ML 3

The **farmer** ("Shall I show you") BB—MFS

The **farmer** ("When the farmer comes to town") Old American song. SBA

"A **farmer** came to camp one day." See Here's your mule

"The **farmer** in the dell." Children's song. BB—SMG

The **farmer** is the man. See The farmer

"**Farmer** said to the boll weevil, I see you're on the square." See Boll weevil blues

"De **farmer** say to de weevil: What you doin' on de square." See De ballet of de boll weevil

The **farmer's** boy. Folk song. GOS 1

The **farmer's** curst wife. Folk song: Hindman, Ky. version. SES 1
 —Hyden, Ky. version no. 1. SES 1
 —Hyden, Ky. version no. 2. SES 1
 —Oneida, Ky. version. SES 1
 —North Carolina version. SES 1
 —Tennessee version. SES 1
 —Virginia version. SES 1

The **farmer's** old wife. H. Purcell. BOS 2

The **farmyard** ("Had me a cat and the cat pleased me") Folk song from North Carolina. SES 2

The **farmyard** ("Up was I on father's farm") Old London folk song. BB

Farnie, Henry Brougham
 Ring on, sweet angelus (Gounod)
 The scout (Campana)
 Speak to me (Campana)
 Up in a balloon (Composer unknown)
 "Who's at my window" (Osborne)

Fata morgana. J. L. Nicodé. e.g. DCA

"**Fatal** goffredo." See Io l'udia ne' suoi bei carmi (Donizetti)

La **fatal** pietra. For English translation see The fatal stone (Verdi)

The **fatal** stone. G. Verdi. [Tr of La fatal pietra] e. WG

The **fatal** wedding. G. L. Davis. Words by W. H. Windom. SRW

"**Fate**, if my woe thou hast decreed." See Io l'udia ne' suoi bei carmi (Donizetti)

The **fateful** blow. Folk song from Kentucky. SES 2

[**Father** Abraham] "Oh, when I get to heaven." Negro spiritual. FSN
 "Oh, when I git t' heaven." HRD

"**Father** and I went down to camp." See Yankee Doodle

"**Father**, dear, father, come home with me now." See Come home, father (Work)

"**Father** eternal, Thou that dost number." See "Ave Maria" (Gounod)

"**Father**, father, build me a boat." See Sweet William (Nellysford, Va. version no. 1)

"**Father**! I bend to Thee." See Gebet während der schlacht (Himmel)

"**Father** in heaven, gaze on Thy children." See "Ave Maria" (Gounod)

"**Father** in heaven, hear us today" (The Lord's prayer.—Almost persuaded) P. P. Bliss. Words by C. G. Ames. LAS

"**Father** in heaven, in Thy love abounding." See Praise for peace (Flemming)

"**Father** in heaven, O guide thy servant." See "Lascia ch'io pianga" (Händel)

"**Father** in heav'n, Thy children hear." See Largo (Händel)

Father, in our tribulation. See Guide us with Thy heavenly light (Tosti)

Father Joe. F. von Flotow. MFS

"**Father**, O father, I fear you have done wrong." See Still growing

Father of heav'n! [from Thy eternal throne] G. F. Händel. SSO 2

"The **Father** of Heaven His own Son He sent." See So blessed be the time

"**Father** of light, we sing in Thy praise." See "Gloria Patri" (Palestrina)

"**Father**, swans flying—where do they go." See Efteraar (Lange-Müller)

"A **father** to his only son said." See Do, do, my huckleberry, do (Dillon)

"**Father**, unto Thee we raise." See Foxlease vesper

"**Father** was a thrifty man" ("Nagy gazda volt az apám") Hungarian folk song. e.hu. KH 1

Father was killed by the Pinkerton men. W. Wildwave (music and words) SW

"**Father**, we thank Thee for the night." See Morning prayer (Wiggin)

Fatigue call. U.S. army bugle call. DSO

Fauré, Gabriel Urbain
 After a dream. See Après un rêve
 Après un rêve
 Les berceaux
 The cradles. See Les berceaux

Faure, Jean Baptiste
 Credo. See O salutaris Hostia
 Crucifix (Tr of Crucifixus)
 "I trust in God." See O salutaris Hostia
 O salutaris Hostia
 Palm-branches. See Les rameaux
 The palms. See Les rameaux
 Les rameaux

Fawcett, John
 "Blest be the tie that binds" (Nägeli)
 "Lord, dismiss us with Thy blessing" (Composer unknown) Authorship uncertain

Fay, Stephen, pseud. See Stevens, David

Fayles, Philip. See Phile, Philip

"**Fe** ddaw wythnos yn yr hâf." See Tros y garreg

Fead an iolair (The eagle's whistle) Irish Gaelic song. e. CSB 4

"Fear not, ye seek Jesus which was crucified." See The Lord is risen, He will dwell with men (Sullivan)

The **feast** of lanterns ("Tching-a-ring-a-ring-tching") J. W. Elliott. TFG —TFR

The **feast** of lights. See "Rock of ages, let our song"

The **feast** of song. See La festa di Piedigrotta

[The **feast** of Vladímir] "Kak vo Kievě stol'nom kievskom" (Wladímirs tafelrunde) Russian folk song. g.r. ML 1

Federal street (Oliver) See "Great God, we sing"; "Strong Son of God, immortal Love"

"Feed your horse we're able." See The trooper and the maid

Feeenlied. See Cnochd a bheannichd

Feel so low-down an' sad Lawd. See Friendless blues (Handy)

"Feel so sad and sorrowful." See Mountain top blues (Williams)

Feierlich schalle der jubelgesang. See "Vom hoh'n Olymp" (Schnoor)

"Fein's liebchen trau' du nicht." See Klage (Brahms)

Feist, Felix F.
The bull-frog and the coon (Nathan)

Feldeinsamkeit (In summer fields) J. Brahms. Words by H. Allmers. e.g. HCA

Felicella (Die sorglose) Neapolitan folk song. g.i. ML 2

"Der fels, an dem die wut der wogen sich zerschellt." See Fester sinn (Haydn)

"Female scions, female scions of my great tree." See "Miei rampolli femminini" (Rossini)

The **female** smuggler. Sea song. US —WSE

Female volunteer for Mexico. Song of the Mexican war. H. R. Bishop. DSO

Fenno, Cordelia Brooks
The angels and the shepherds (Bohemian air)
The first Christmas (Bohemian carol air)
The shepherd neighbors (Gevaert)
The sleeping shepherds (Old Béarnaise air)
"Star-beams light the countryside" (Bohemian carol air)
The village dance (Hungarian air)
The vision (Kremser)

Ferguson, Robert
My ain kind dearie, O (Scottish air)

"Ferme tes yeux" (Schlummerlied) Breton folk song. f.g. ML 1

Fernández Shaw, Guillermo. See Romero y Sarachaga, Federico, jt. auth.

"Fernher schnell kommen Husaren ins dörfchen." See Die Husaren kommen

Ferrabosco, Alfonso
"O eyes, O mortal stars"

The **ferry** ("A boat, a boat to cross the ferry") Round. <J. Jenkins> TFG

"A boat, a boat, unto the ferry." BOS 2

The **ferry** ("Ferry me across the water") J. Ireland. Words by C. Rossetti. GSS

"Ferry me across the water." See The ferry (Ireland)

The **ferryman's** slim, and the ferryman's young. See Twickenham ferry (Marzials)

Fesans raijouissance. For English paraphrase see So, brother

Fesca, Friedrich Ernst
Rudelsburg (same air as Soldatenabschied)
Soldaten-abschied

[La **festa** di Piedigrotta] The feast of song. Neapolitan song. e. MFF

[Ein' **feste** burg] "A mighty fortress is our God." M. Luther (music and words) e. DSC

"A safe stronghold our God is still." e. MBS

Fester sinn. J. Haydn. g. EDL

Festival carol ("How great the harvest is") Dutch air: De liefde voortgebracht. OB

Fet, A.
"But lately in dance I embraced her" (Arenski)

"Fetiţo din acel sat" ("Kleine maid vom dorfe") Rumanian song. g.ru. ML 2

"Feuchtersleben, Ernst, freiherr von
"Es ist bestimmt in Gottes rat" (Mendelssohn)

"Feuchtfroh und lustig sind wir." See "Blythe, blythe, and merry are we"

Feuerlied ("Aus feuer ist der geist geschaffen") L. Hempel. Words by E. M. Arndt. g. EDL

"Les feuilles s'ouvraient sur le bord des branches." See Les cloches (Debussy)

A **few** days, an' a few days. See There was an ole fish

"A few days more, a few days more." See Army blue of 1859 (Poulton)

Fhir a bhàta (Der schiffer) Old Highland air. ga.g. ML 1

"Ein fichtenbaum steht einsam" ("A pinetree standeth lonely") W. Stenhammar. Words by H. Heine. e.g. WM 2

"Fichtlein im walde, grüner fichtenbaum." See Kalinka

A **fickle** maiden. See Un pajarito

Fiddlers' green. Old U. S. cavalry song. DSO

Fiducit ("Es hatten drei gesellen") Briesewitz. Words by E. Salomon. g. EDL

"Fie, now, prithee John." Round. H. Purcell. BOS 2

Field, Eugene
  Christmasse of olde (Swiss air)
  Little Boy Blue (Smith)
  The singing in God's acre (Jordan)
Field song. University of South Dakota
  song. F. F. Woodworth. Words
  by J. H. Downing. AIS—KU—KV
Fielding, Henry
  The roast beef of old England (Lever-
  idge)
Fields, Arthur
  It's a long way to Berlin, but we'll get
  there (Flataw)
"Fields of corn, give up your ears." See
  Thanksgiving carol
Fielitz, Alexander von
  Aus der rosenzeit
  Frühlingslied
  "Grauer vogel über der haide"
  Heimliche grüsse
  "O Irmingard." See Heimliche grüsse
  "The silent waterlily." See "Die stille
  wasserrose"
  Song of spring. See Frühlingslied
  "Die stille wasserrose"
  "Thou gray birdling over the heather."
  See "Grauer vogel über der haide"
  When roses bloom. See Aus der
  rosenzeit
Fielitz, M. von
  Frühlingslied (Fielitz, A. von)
"Fier, my Saviour, fier." See Satan's
  camp a-fire
"Fier océan, vallons, vertes collines."
  See Célébrons le Seigneur (Rupès)
"Fierce now the flames glow." "Stride
  la vampa" (Verdi)
"Fifteen men on the Dead Man's Chest."
  See Derelict (Waller)
"The fifteenth day of July." See Lord
  Willoughby (Byrd)
The **fifty-first** coast artillery march-song.
  Words by G. H. Ericson. DSO
"A fig for your set of lancers." See See
  me dance the polka
"Fight, Alabama, never yield." See
  March of triumph (Jacoby)
"Fight away." West Point football song.
  AIS—DSO
"Fight, big blue team." U.S. Naval
  academy song. T. E. Klakring. US
Fight, Cincinnati. See "The red and
  black shall triumph" (Waterman)
Fight 'em Washington. Washington uni-
  versity song. C. A. Lieber (music
  and words) KU—KV
Fight, fight, fight for the blue and white.
  See Victory (Leyden)
"Fight, fight, fight for Washington state."
  See The fight song (Sayles)
Fight! fight! fight! till that last white line
  is made. See Fight, Tufts, fight
  (Hayes)
"Fight, fight for Yale." See Fight for
  Yale (Friedman)
Fight for California. University of Cali-
  fornia song. Air: Lights out.
  Words by R. N. Fitch. KU
  Fight for California (The golden bear)
  AI

Fight for California tech. California in-
  stitute of technology song. HW
Fight for Dickinson. Dickinson college
  song. [T. W. Allen and M. W.
  Sheafe] AI—AIS
Fight for Lawrence. See Viking song
  (Maesch)
Fight for old S. F. University of San
  Francisco song. Colligan. HW
Fight for the glory of Carnegie. Carnegie
  institute of technology song. R.
  Schmertz (music and words) AI—
  AIS—KU—KV
Fight for Yale. Yale university song.
  S. P. Friedman. Words by H. G.
  Dodge. LAS
"Fight men for California tech." See
  Fight for California tech
Fight on for old St Mary's. St Mary's
  college song. W. Stevens (music
  and words) HW
"Fight on Ignatians strong and bold."
  See Fight for old S. F. (Colligan)
Fight on, Pennsylvania. University of
  Pennsylvania song. D. Zoob. Words
  by B. S. McGiveran. AIS
The **fight** song ("Fight, fight, fight")
  State college of Washington song.
  P. Sayles. Words by Z. Melcher.
  AI—AIS—HW—KU—KV
Fight song ("On the banks of the Red
  Cedar") Michigan state college song.
  F. I. Lankey (music and words) KU
"Fight that team across the field." See
  Across the field (Dougherty)
Fight, Tufts, fight. Tufts college song.
  E. W. Hayes. KU
Fight! wildcats, fight. University of
  Arizona song. T. W. Allen and D.
  Holsclaw. Words by D. Holsclaw.
  AIS
Fighting on [hallelujah] Negro spiritual.
  HRD
La **filadora** (Die spinnerin) Catalan folk
  song. ca.g. ML 2
La **filatrice** (Spinning Jenny) W. A.
  Mozart. e. CSB 3
A **Filipino** hombre. See The Philippine
  hombre
"Fill the bumper fair." Air: Bob and
  Joan. Words by T. Moore. HMI
"La fill' du roi d'Espagne" ("The Princess
  Salamanca") French Canadian folk
  song: 2d version. e.f. GC
Filon is waiting. Polish folk song. e.
  LSB
"Fin ch'han dal vino." Mozart. e.i.
  PB
"Fine knacks for ladies." J. Dowland.
  CSB 3—MBS—TFG
The **fine** old colored gentleman. [Arr by
  C. H. Purday] PSG—WSS
The **fine** ould Irish gintleman. [Arr by
  C. H. Purday] Words by J. Brou-
  gham. GOS 1—SI
"Fine Sally, fine Sally, fine Sally, said he."
  See The brown girl (Big Laurel, N.C.
  version)

Finita jam sunt praelia. For English translation see The strife is o'er: the battle done (Palestrina)

Fink, Henry
The curse of an aching heart (Piantadosi)

[Finland's forest] "Deep in the forest." Finnish folk song. e. DSB

Finn, William Joseph
Tell Him a welcome

[Finnish hymn ("O, hasten, hasten all")] "Nyt ylös, sieluni" ("Auf, seele, zögre nicht") fi.g. ML 3

Fionn, pseud. See Whyte, Henry

Fior di giaggiolo. For English translation see Lola's song (Mascagni)

Fioravanti, Valentino
"Era notte oscura, oscura" (from La contessa di Fertzen)

"Fir-grove, my fir-grove." Russian folk song. e. NRF

Fire away (The song of Ringgold's artillery) Air: The Campbells are coming. DSO

Fire down below ("Fire in the galley") Pumping ship chantey. TSB 2
For variant see following song of same title

Fire down below ("There is fire in the lower hold") Capstan chantey. GSS

"Fire in de east, an' fire in de west." See Run, Mary, run

"Fire in the galley." See Fire down below

"Fire, my Saviour, fire." See Satan's camp a-fire

Fireflies ("When the purple evening shadows") Russian folk song. e. DSB

Fireman save my child. See No more booze

Fires of wisdom. Mills college song. E. F. Schneider. Words by F. R. Carpenter. HW

Firm, united, let us be. See "Hail Columbia" (Phile)

La firolera (The firolera) Mexican folk song. e.s. VS

"The first came in were lily white." See Little Musgrave and Lady Barnard (Hindman, Ky. version no. 1)

The first Christmas ("Far out across the country") Bohemian carol air. Words by C. B. Fenno. FC

"The first come down was a raven white." See Little Musgrave and Lady Barnard (Hot Springs, N.C. version)

"The first day of Christmas my true love sent to me." See The twelve days of Christmas

"The first good joy that Mary had." See The seven joys of Mary (Advent images carol); The seven joys of Mary (Traditional song)

"The first great joy Our Lady had." See The seven joys of Mary (Anglo Irish version)

"The first I saw was a young girl." See The three huntsmen

"The first landlord was dressed in white." See The cruel brother (Hot Springs, N.C. version no. 2)

First love. See Waltz song (Audran)

"The first Nowell." Traditional carol. DN —DSB—DSC—FC—GSS—MBS—OB—TFP

"The first Noël." BB

"The first on deck was the captain of the ship." See The mermaid (Hyden, Ky. version no. 1)

The first swallow. Old air. Words by C. Barnard. HMI

"First to come, as is the custom." See March of the toreadors (Bizet)

"First when Maggie was my care." See Whistle o'er the lave o't (Bruce)

Fischer, Frederick
I'm on my way to Mandalay
Ireland must be heaven for my mother came from there
Peg o' my heart
There's a little spark of love still burning

Fischer, Karl Ludwig
Der rheinweinzecher
Der trinker. See Der rheinweinzecher

Fischer, Thomas
"Spin, maiden, spin, the golden thread twirl in"
Spin, spin. See "Spin, maiden, spin, the golden thread twirl in"

Fischerlied. See Strilevise

Fisher, Clellan Waldo
Champlain (Putnam)

Fisher, D. David
Champlain (Putnam) See Fisher, C. W. Champlain (Putnam)

[The fisherman ("In the Alford's circle fisherman am I")] "Where the Tisza's torrents through the prairies swell" ("Az alföldön halász legény vagyok én") Hungarian song. <G. Bernáth (music and words> e.hu. KH 1

The fisherman's daughter. Sea song. US

Fishermen's chorus. D. F. E. Auber. e. MFS

The fishes ("Oh, a ship she was rigg'd") Sea song. WSE
Variants: Blow the man down; The Boston come-all-ye; The song of the fishes

Fitch, Helen, pseud. See Vandevere, J. Lilian

Fitch, Robert Newell
Fight for California (Old air)

Fitger, Artur
"Singend über die haide" (Bungert)

Fitzball, Edward
The banks of the blue Moselle (Rodwell)
When the bloom is on the rye (Bishop)

Fitzpatrick, M. J.
The Boston burglar

"Five can't ketch me." See Round the corn, Sally

Five times five are twenty-five. See Multiplication table

The **flag** going by ("O beautiful banner") German folk air. Words by H. H. Harbour.   DSB
"O beautiful banner."   GSS

Flag of maroon. University of Chicago song. D. Richberg (music and words)   AI—AIS

The **flag** of our union forever. W. V. Wallace. Words by G. P. Morris. MFS

"**Flag** of the free." R. Wagner. <Words by J. P. McCaskey>   BB— MFS

Flag we love, orange, float for aye.   See Alma mater — Syracuse university (Thompson)

Flaischlen, Cäsar
Höst (Palmgren)

Un **flambeau**, Jeannette, Isabelle. For English translation see "Bring a torch, Jeannette, Isabella"

"Die **flamme** lodert, milder schein."   See Opferlied (Beethoven)

Flat river girl. Lumberjack song.   SBA

Flataw, Leon
It's a long way to Berlin, but we'll get there

"A **flaxen-headed** cowboy."   See The ploughboy (Shield)

"**Flee** as a bird." Spanish air. Words by M. S. B. Dana.   GOS 1—MFS

"**Fleeting** love of this earth excelling." See "Le ciel a visité la terre" (Gounod)

Flemish carol ("Er is een kindeken geboren op d'aard")   See De nederige geboorte

Fleming, Friedrich Ferdinand
Freundschaft und liebe.   See "Hier in des abends traulich ernster stille"
"Hier in des abends traulich ernster stille" (same air as "Integer vitae")
"Integer vitae" (with original words; also words "Night shadows falling")
The man of upright life.   See "Integer vitae" (with original words)
Praise for peace (same air as "Integer vitae")

Fletcher, John, 19th century
Aunt Dinah's quilting party.   See The quilting party
The quilting party
When I saw sweet Nellie home.   See The quilting party

Fletcher, John, 1579-1625.   See Beaumont, Francis, jt. auth.

Fletcher, R. K
The gridiron king

Fleur d'amour (Flower of love)   H. Weyts. Words by J. V. Brugghen. e.f.   BST

t"La **fleur** que tu m'avais jetée"ı "This flow'r that once to me you gave."   G. Bizet.   e.   WG

"**Flickan** knyter" ("On Saint John's eve") W. Stenhammar. Words by J. L. Runeberg.   e.sw.   WM 2

Flies, Bernhard
Wiegenlied (attributed)   See Mozart, W. A.   Wiegenlied

"**Fliesse**, wasser, fliesse" ("Tečie voda, tečie") Slovak folk song.   g.sl. ML 3

The **flight** of summer. Bohemian folk air. Words by J. Landon.   TFO

"**Fling** wide our colors bright and true." See Fair M. S. C.

"**Floating** scow of old Virginny."   See Carry me back to old Virginny (Christy)

"**Flocks** are sporting" (A pastoral)   H. Carey.   WOE

"**Flog** daher die nachtigall" ("Preletel slavíček")   Moravian-Czech folk song. bo.g.   ML 3

"**Flog** ein falke" ("Sokol mi leti")   Macedonian folk song.   b.g.   ML 2

"**Flog** herbei ein junger falke" ("Ir atleke sakalelis")   Lithuanian folk song. g.li.   ML 3

Flora the lily of the west (see Song Index) Variant: The lily of the west

"**Floral** off'rings let us bring."   See A dance song (Whittaker)

Florian, Jean Pierre Claris de
"Ah! s'il est dans votre village" (Godard)
Complainte de la reine Marie Stuart en prison (Martini)

Florian's song.   See "Ah! s'il est dans votre village" (Godard)

Florida blues. W. K. Phillips.   Words by D. Hoffman and A. Neale.   HB

Flotow, Friedrich, freiherr von
"Ach! so fromm" (from Martha)
Ah! so pure.   See "Ach! so fromm"
"Ah! what can be her meaning" (from Martha.   Tr of Was soll ich dazu sagen)
"Come where flowers are flinging." See Maidens, bright and fair
The dawn of Maytime (same air as "Heaven may to you grant pardon")
"Esser mesto" (from Martha.   Tr of Bange trauer)
Father Joe
"Heaven may to you grant pardon" (from Martha.   Tr of Himmel euch vergeben)
Maid-servants' chorus (from Martha. Tr of Wohlgemuth, junges blut)
Maidens, bright and fair (from Martha. Tr of Mädchen, brav und treu)
"O'er my head" (from Martha.   Tr of Ja, seit früher kindheit tagen)
Porter lied (from Martha)
Porter song.   See Porter lied
Povero Lionello (from Martha)
"See what grace" (from Martha.   Tr of Nun fürwahr, fürwahr)
"Slumber, dearest"
"That dread hand" (from Martha.   Tr of Diese hand, die sich gewendet)
These tears my bosom searing (from Martha.   Tr of Sie lacht zu meinen leiden)

"Flow gently, sweet Afton." See Afton water (Scottish air); Afton water (Spilman)

"Flow, Rio Verde." Old song. MFS

Flower carol. See Tempus adest floridum

Flower of love. See Fleur d'amour (Weyts)

"A floweret by the wayside." See "En blomma stod vid vägen" (Sibelius)

"The flowers all are sleeping." See Sandmännchen

"The flow'rets all sleep soundly." See Sandmännchen

"Flow'rets blooming, winds perfuming." See Lob der thränen (Schubert)

Flowers for the brave. Bellini. Words by E. W. Chapman. MFS

"Flow'rs from the shady greenwood dell." See In memoriam

"The flow'rs have long been sleeping." See Sandmännchen

Flowers in the valley ("O there was a woman") Old English air. DSB—DSC

The flowers of the forest ("I've heard the lilting") Old air. Words by J. Elliot. GS

The flowers of the forest ("I've seen the smiling of fortune beguiling") Traditional air. Words by A. R. Cockburn. GS

Flowers of the valley ("Pan ddelo'r haf a'i flodau fyrdd") See Blodau'r cwm

"The flower's tender heart." See Pensée de printemps (Leroux)

"Flowers, wildwood flowers." See Wildwood flowers

Flowing river. Chilean folk song. e. TFP

Flow'r. For entries beginning Flow'r see Flower

Der flug der liebe. See "Wenn ich ein vöglein wär"

Fly forth, O gentle dove. C. Pinsuti. Words by F. E. Weatherly. GE

"Fly not yet." Air: Planxty Kelly. Words by T. Moore. HMI

Flyers' march. University of Dayton song. J. B. Meiler. AIS

"Flying, sweeping swallow" ("Szálldogál a fecske") E. Szentirmay (music and words) e.hu. KH 2

Flynn, Joseph
    Down went McGinty

"Foaie verde cimbrişor" ("Grünes blättlein, thymianblättlein") Rumanian song. g.ru. ML 2

"Foaie verde de şalbiţă." See Cine trece pe uliţa

"Foaie verde lămâiţă" ("Grünes blättchen der zitrone") Rumanian song. g.ru. ML 2

"Foaie verde şio răsură." See Cuculeţ cu pana sură

"Foaie verde trei alune" ("Grünes blatt, drei haselnüsse") Rumanian song. g.ru. ML 2

"Foaie verde trei cicori, măi." See Ciobănaş dela miori

"Foaie verde viorea, mai." See Îngheţată-i Dunărea

The foggy dew ("Oh, a wan cloud") Old Irish air. [Words by A. P. Graves] DSC

The foggy dew ("One night as I lay") Folk song: English version. DSC

The foggy dew ("I courted her all of the winter") Virginia version. SES 2

For variant see following song of similar title

Foggy, foggy dew ("When I was a bach'-lor") Folk song: American version. SBA

Variant: The weaver

"Fohrt der chossid'l." Jewish folk song. y. SY

"Furt a chussedl." y. KAJ

"Foicică de mohor." See Dor de ducă

Foley, James W.
    North Dakota hymn (Putnam)

Folks that put on airs. Minstrel song. WSS

Foller, foller, rise up, shepherd. See Rise up, shepherd, and foller

Follow me, full of glee. MFS

Follow thee, follow thee, wha wadna follow thee. See "Cam' ye by Athol, lad wi' the philabeg" (Gow)

"Follow thy mission." See "Pensa alla patria" (Rossini)

"Follow we the guard that's changing." See Street-boys' chorus (Bizet)

Fond hearts, entwining, cease all repining. See "Over the summer sea" (Verdi)

Fond hope redeeming, if thou'dst bereave me. See Se m'abbandoni, bella speranza (Mercadante)

"Fondest object whom I only cherish." See "Al mio core oggetti amati" (Donizetti)

Fontaine, Lamar
    "All quiet along the Potomac tonight" (Hewitt) See Beers, E. E. "All quiet along the Potomac tonight" (Hewitt)

Fontenailles, H. de
    Obstination
    Steadfast love. See Obstination

The foolish boy. See The swapping song

The fools are always sure to thrive. See "Ah! nonsense 'tis" (Strauss)

Football song ("And then we'll fight") University of Chattanooga song. [T. W. Allen and M. W. Sheafe] AI

For a dream's sake. F. H. Cowen. Words by C. Rossetti. SFB

"For a tender father." C. Lecocq. [Tr of Pour un tendre père] e. WLO

For bales. P. S. Gilmore. Words by A. E. Blackmar. DSO

"For, behold, darkness shall cover" (see Song Index) Also in "The people that walked in darkness" (Händel) SSO 4

"For Boston." Boston college song. T. J. Hurley. AIS

[For Christmas day] "Immortal Babe." Traditional air. Words by Hall. OB

For Colorado! our Colorado. See Our Colorado (Hille)

"**For** England when with fav'ring gale." See The heaving of the lead (Shield)

"**For** ever blessed." Handel. SSO 3

"**For** ever with the Lord." See "Forever with the Lord" (Gounod)

"**For** health and strength" (Grace) Round. GSS
Health and strength. TFP

For her lover who was far away. Old song. DSO

"**For** he's a jolly good fellow." College song. Air: Chanson de Mambron. DFF—TFP

For his heart is like the sea. See They all love Jack (Maybrick)

For His mercies still endure. See "Praise, O praise our God and King"

"**For** I often have heard." F. Lehar. e. WLO

For I will be dar. See I'll be dar

"**For** I'm a respectable wife." See I'm a respectable wife (Lehar)

For it is Mary, Mary. See Mary's a grand old name (Cohan)

For it is S. U. S. U. S. Q. U. E. H. A. N. N. A. our boon. See Old S. U. (Sheldon)

For it's a long stroke, and a strong stroke. See Columbia's crew (Kelley)

For it's boom! whiz! bang. See Caisson song: variation (Metz)

For it's your wassail, and it's our wassail. See "Wassail, and wassail, all over the town"

For I've been reading Freud. See Don't tell me what you dreamed last night (Hooker)

For I've worked eight hours this day. See I've worked eight hours this day (McGlennon)

"**For** Jack is gone a-sailing." See Jack went a-sailing (White Rock, Va. version)

"**For** know ye, for know that the Lord is God." See "Erkennet, erkennt, dass der Herr ist Gott" (Jadassohn)

For life goes a-fleeting along. See "Now, come to me, ye sirens" (Lehar)

For Maine. University of Maine song. C. D. Bartlett. AI

For men may come and men may go. See The brook (Farmer)

"**For** my heart's peace my love will never cease." See "Per non penar" (Astorga)

For my ole massa tole me so. See Dandy Jim ob Caroline

For Nebraska and the scarlet. See The cornhusker (Stevens)

For old time's sake. C. K. Harris (music and words) SW

For sale—a baby. C. K. Harris (music and words) SW

"**For** sev'n long years I courted Nancy." See The wide Missouri

For Texas now is free. See The song of Texas

"**For** the beauty of the earth." Arr from C. Kocher. Words by F. S. Pierpoint. TFP

For the girls they must love and adore us. See "I'll be a sergeant"

"**For** the glory of old State." See Alma mater — Pennsylvania state college (Converse)

For the honor of old Purdue. Purdue university song. F. C. Huston (music and words) AIS

For the long, long road to Tipperary is the road that leads me home. See The home road (Carpenter)

"**For** the love my heart doth prize." See "Per la gloria d'adorarvi" (Bononcini)

"**For** the mountains shall depart." Mendelssohn. [Tr of Ja es sollen wohl berge weichen] e. SSO 4

For the rain it raineth ev'ry day. See "When that I was a little tiny boy"

For the sake o' somebody. See "My heart is sair, I daurna tell" (Scottish air); "My heart is sair, I dare na tell" (Farmer)

"**For** the sake of you, my lassie." See I'm bound away

For the sound of his horn brought me from my bed. See John Peel

"**For** the study of woman is hard." See The study of woman (Lehar)

For the wind must blow, and the ship must go. See The tar's farewell (Maybrick)

"**For** these and all Thy mercies given." See Thanksgiving

For those in peril on the sea. U.S. Naval academy song. W. Whiting. US

For tonight we'll merry, merry be. See Farewell to grog

For when our line starts to weaken. See V. M. I. spirit (Bowering)

Ford, Corey
Roar, lion, roar (Webb and Watkins)

Ford, Lena Guilbert
Keep the home fires burning (Novello)

Ford, Thomas
Passing by
"Since first I saw your face"
"There is a lady sweet and kind." See Passing by

Ford, Walter H.
Only me (Bratton)
The sunshine of Paradise Alley (Bratton)

Fordham marching song. Fordham university song. J. F. Breslin. Words by J. H. McCabe. AI

Fordham "ram." Fordham university song. J. I. Coveney. AIS—KU

"**Foreign** land I'm bound to station." See In old Virginny (North Carolina version)

Foreman, Charles E.
Gold will buy 'most anything but a true girl's heart (Rosenfeld)

Forever and forever ("A maid reclined beside a stream") C. C. Converse. MFS

"Forever with the Lord." Gounod. Words by J. Montgomery. CSS 1—CSS 2

"Forget not that angels are hov'ring around." See Forget not the angels

Forget not the angels. Old air. Words by W. Maynard. HMI

"Forget not the field." Air: The lamentation of Aughrim. Words by T. Moore. HMI—SI

"Forgive me, Lord, thro' Thy dear Son." See Evening hymn

Forier di morte. See O du mein holder abendstern (Wagner)

Forsaken ("Forsaken, forsaken, forsaken am I") T. Koschat. [Tr of Verlassen bin i] e. TFB—TFG

[Forsaken ("Going out a-walking")] "Geh ich mir spazieren." Jewish folk song. y. SY
"Gei ich mir spatzieren." Jewish folk song. y. KAJ

"Forsaken, forsaken, forsaken am I." See Forsaken (Koschat)

[A forsaken lover's complaint] "As I walked forth" (Liebesklage) R. Johnson. e.g. ML 1

The forsaken maid. T. Smart. WOE

"Fort ist braunmägdlein schön." See Mo nigheann chruinn, donn

"Fort sind sie all, nach der andern bessern welt." See Old black Joe (Foster)

Fortenbaugh, Robert
Spirit of Gettysburg (Saltzer)

"Forward march, grenadiers." See "En avant, grenadiers"

Forward sons of Georgetown. See Georgetown's blue and gray (Lennon and Corcoran)

Forward the white. Bowdoin college song. G. Sumner. Words by K. A. Robinson. AI

Fosdick, William Whiteman
Aura Lee (Poulton)

Foster, Stephen Collins
Alter Joe. See Old black Joe
Angelina Baker
Away down souf
"Beautiful dreamer"
De Camptown races
Cheer up, Sam
"Come where my love lies dreaming"
Dolcy Jones
Dolly Day
Ellen Bayne
Fairy-belle
Farewell, my Lilly dear
Gentle Annie
"The Glendy Burke"
Gwine to run all night. See De Camptown races
Hard crackers (same air as Hard times, come again no more)
Hard times, come again no more
Jeanie with the light brown hair
"Lincoln hoss" and Stephen A. (same air as De Camptown races)
Lou'siana Belle
Massa's in de cold, cold ground
Mein alt Kentucky-heim. See My old Kentucky home
Melinda May
My brudder Gum
My old Kentucky home
Negers heimweh. See The old folks at home
Nell and I
"Nelly Bly"
Nelly was a lady
Oh! boys, carry me 'long
"Oh! Lemuel"
Oh! Susanna
Old black Joe
Old dog Tray
The old folks at home
"Open thy lattice, love"
Ring, ring de banjo
Some folks do
The song of the frog (same air as De Camptown races)
Swanee ribber. See The old folks at home
Uncle Ned
Under the willow she's sleeping
"Up from the sea" (same air as Old black Joe)
Way down in Ca-i-ro
Way down souf. See Away down souf
Where has Lulu gone
Willie, we have missed you

Foulke, Caroline Reeves
College hymn (Ibsen)

Found dead in the snow. Minstrel song. PSG

Foundation song. Harrow school song. J. Farmer. Words by E. E. Bowen. LAS

Fountain, Alvin M.
Alma mater—North Carolina state college (Norris)

The fountain of knowledge. German air. Words by N. H. Dole. DSB

[Four and twenty elders] "See fo' an' twenty elders." Negro spiritual. HRD

The four-leaved shamrock. S. Lover (music and words) SI

The four loves. Four part round. BOS 2
"The hart he loves the high wood." GSS

Four thousand years ago. American mountain song. RA
Variant of: "I was born almost ten thousand years ago"

Fourth of July hymn ("To Thee our Father."—Ortonville) T. Hastings. MFS

Fowler, Garnet
The tiger song (Burkholder and Fowler)
See also Burkholder, Nadeen, jt. comp.

Fox, G. D.
Over the garden wall

Fox, Will H.
The broken home
Twelve months ago to-night

The fox ("A fox went out") Folk song: Irish version. BOS 2
Variant: The old black duck

Fox and goose. See Warnung

"De **fox** hab hole in de ground." See Hard trials

"A **fox** went out on a moonlight night." See The fox

"**Fox** went out one bright moonlight." See The old black duck (Tennessee version)

"**Fox**, you've stolen my grey gander." See Warnung

Foxlease vesper. Composer and author of words unknown. GSS

Foxwell, A. J.
"When the spring with magic finger" (Polish air)

"**Fra** degno ed amore." G. Latilla. Words by Metastasio. e.i. KVG

"**Fragen** wird feierlich." See "En gång i bredd med mig"

"**Frägt** die welt an alte kasho." See The old, old questions

Fragte mich die liebe mutter. See Wen ich will zur ehe

Franc, Guillaume
"All people that on earth do dwell." See Old hundred
The doxology. See Old hundred
Dundee. See "O Thou Whose feet"
"O Thou Whose feet"
Old hundred (with words "All people that on earth do dwell"; "Be Thou, O God, exhalted high"; "Praise God from Whom all blessings flow")
"Praise God, from Whom all blessings flow." See Old hundred

Francillon, Robert Edward
Bloom on, my roses (Cowen)
It was a dream (Cowen)

Franck, César Auguste
At the cradle
The guardian angel

Franck, P.
"Once again, O blessed time."

"**Frankie** and Albert." American folk song. SBA
Variant of: "Frankie and Johnny"

"**Frankie** and Johnny." American folk song. SBA
"Frankie and Johnnie." SRW
Variants: "Frankie and Albert"; Frankie Baker; Frankie blues; Josie; Sadie

Frankie Baker. American mountain song. RA
Variant of: "Frankie and Johnny"

Frankie blues. American folk song. SBA
Variant of: "Frankie and Johnny"

"**Frankie** was a good woman." See Frankie blues

Franz, Robert
Abschied
"Aus meinen grossen schmerzen"
Bitte
Dedication. See Widmung
"Es hat die rose sich beklagt"
Farewell. See Gute nacht
"The gay butterfly lost his heart to the rose." See "Der schmetterling ist in die rose verliebt"
Gute nacht

"Ich hab' in deinem auge"
Lieber schatz, sei wieder gut mir
"Once in thine eyes." See "Ich hab' in deinem auge"
"Out of my bitter weeping." See "Aus meinen grossen schmerzen"
"Out of my soul's great sadness." See "Aus meinen grossen schmerzen"
Parting. See Abschied
Request. See Bitte
"The rose complained." See "Es hat die rose sich beklagt"
The rose's complaint. See "Es hat die rose sich beklagt"
"Der schmetterling ist in die rose verliebt"
Silent safety. See Stille sicherheit
Stille sicherheit
"Where sorrows touch me nearest." See "Aus meinen grossen schmerzen"
Widmung

Frary, Francelia. See Woodworth, Mrs Francelia (Frary)

Frau Holda und Elland. See Huldra aa en Elland

Frau Holdas lockruf. See Huldre lokk

Fräulein Kunigund ("Als wir jüngst in Regensburg waren") Bayrische volksweise. g. EDL

Free America. Air: The British grenadiers, or, Sir Edward Nowell's delight. Words by J. Warren. DSO—SRW

Free at las' free at las'. See I thank God I'm free at las'

Free grace and dying love. See Mary and Martha

Freed, Ralph J. See Kisco, Charles, jt. comp.

"**Freedom**, freedom once more enjoy 'mongst us." See Nel dolce incanto (Benedict)

Freedom's flag. A. Geibel. Words by J. J. Hood. MFS

Freeman, H. W.
Here's a health, bonnie Scotland, to thee (Lee)

"**Freiheit**, die ich meine." C. Groos. Words by M. von Schenkendorf. g. EDL

Freiligrath, Ferdinand
Prinz Eugen (Loewe)

Freligh, J. S.
The elopement (Ross)

"**Fremd** bin ich eingezogen." See Gute nacht (Schubert)

French, A. T.
The black and the gold (Hille)
Our Colorado (Hille)

French, Lindol Elmer
Alma mater—Colgate university (Spanish air)

Freneau, Philip Morin
The battle of Stonington (Composer unknown)

"**Frère** Jacques." Round. f. BOS 2
"Are you sleeping." e. BB—TFP
"Frère Jacque" ("Are you sleeping") e.f. DSB

"Fresh carnations! now for whom can I spare them." See Clavelitos (Valverde)

"Freude, schöner Götterfunken." See An die freude (Composer unknown); An die freude (Beethoven)

Freudig begrüssen wir die edle halle. For English translation see "Hail, bright abode, where song the heart rejoices" (Wagner)

"Freudvoll und leidvoll" (Clärchens lied) J. F. Reichardt. Words by Goethe. g.   EDL

Freundschaft und liebe. See "Hier in des abends traulich ernster stille" (Flemming)

"Freut euch des lebens." H. G. Nägeli. Words by M. Usteri. g.   EDL Life let us cherish. e.   MFS

Fridenberg, Percy Sans souci (Composer unknown)

"Fridericus Rex." C. Loewe. Words by W. Alexis (W. Häring) g.   EDL

Friedland, Anatole Lily of the valley My sweet Adair

Friedland, Anatole, and Morgan, Carey Moi-one-Ionae. See My own Iona My own Iona

"Friedlich sass ich jüngst am rokken." See Vocero

Friedman, Stanleigh Pohly Down the field Fight for Yale

Friendless blues. W. C. Handy. Words by M. Gilbert. HB

"Fringue, fringue sur la rivière." See Fringue, fringue sur l'aviron

Fringue, fringue sur l'aviron (St Lawrence boat song) French Canadian folk song. e.f.   GSF

Fröding, Gustaf Titania (Peterson-Berger)

The frog and the mouse. English folk song. DSB Variant of: The wedding of the frog and mouse

"A frog he went a-courting." Folk song: Barbourville, Ky. version. SES 2 —Berea, Ky. version. SES 2 —Harrogate, Ky. version. SES 2 —Hindman, Ky. version. SES 2 —St Helen's, Ky. version. SES 2 —Big Laurel, N.C. version. SES 2 —Burnsville, N.C. version. SES 2 —Hot Springs, N.C. version. SES 2 —Marion, N.C. version no. 1. SES 2 —Marion, N.C. version no. 2. SES 2 —Virginia version. SES 2 Frog went a-courtin'. Georgia version. RA "Frog went a-courting." Estill county, Ky. version. GSS "Mister frog went a-courting." Kentucky and Virginia version. SBA Variant of: The wedding of the frog and mouse

The frog in the well. Folk song: Berea, Ky. version. SES 2 —Pineville, Ky. version. SES 2 —Buena Vista, Va. version. SES 2 —Woodridge, Va. version. SES 2 Variant of: The wedding of the frog and mouse

Frog round. GSS—TFB The frogs. TFG

"Frog went a-courting." See "A frog he went a-courting" (Barbourville, Ky. version; Estill county, Ky. version; Hindman, Ky. version; St Helen's, Ky. version; Burnsville, N.C. version; Hot Springs, N.C. version; Marion, N.C. versions no. 1-2; Virginia version); The frog in the well (Buena Vista, Va. version)

The frogs. See Frog round

Frohe botschaft ("Kommt a vogerl geflogen") W. Müller. <Words by A. Bäuerle> g.   EDL

Der frohe wandersmann. F. T. Fröhlich. Words by J. von Eichendorff. g. EDL

Fröhlich, Friedrich Theodor Der frohe wandersmann

Fröhlich soll mein herze springen. For English translation see "All my heart this night rejoices" (Ebeling)

"From a village up the Hudson." See The dark girl dressed in blue

"From age to age how grandly rise" (Colchester) H. Purcell. Words by F. L. Hosmer. LAS

"From age to age they gather." See Marching on (Bullard)

"From all that dwell." 17th century German air. Words by I. Watts. MBS

"From Boston harbour we set sail." See Boston

"From church to Boulé's hop." See Le bal chez Boulé

"From church to church." See Congaudeat turba fidelium

"From Dan to Beersheba." See Upon the death of Trumpeldor

"From every spire on Christmas eve." G. Coles. Words by E. A. Hunter. BB A Christmas hymn (Duane street) MFS

"From far away" (Snow in the street) R. V. Williams. Words by W. Morris. OB

"From heav'n above to earth I come." See "Vom himmel hoch da komm' ich her" (Luther)

"From his Canadian home." See "Un Canadien errant"

"From ill do Thou defend me." J. S. Bach. e.   BB

"From Jerusalem to Metullah." See A Chalutz polka

From mighty kings. Händel. SSO 1

"From morning till night." See The chatterbox

"From my youthful days." See "Aus der jugendzeit" (Radecke)

"From o'er the rugged mountains standing high." See Hail! Pacific, hail (Warner)

"From out of a wood did a cuckoo fly." See The birds

"From Paris to St Denis, see." See "Entre Paris et Saint-Denis"

"From Provence, both land and wave." See "Di Provenza il mar" (Verdi)

"From silent woods, from shadow'd way." See Angedenken (Cornelius)

"From Teutschland I come." See Buy a broom (Lee?)

"From the boughs o'erhead." See Autumn song

"From the desert I come to thee." See Bedouin love-song (Hawley)

From the foothills to the bay. See Hail, Stanford hail (Coolidge)

"From the halls of Montezuma." See The marine's hymn

From the hills ("What will you take to town, lad") Basque air. Words by F. Hoare. LAS

"From the hills of Maine to the western plain." See Old Wabash (Ragan)

"From the Kremlin walls." See Ballad of the Kremlin

From the region of the rising of the sun. See A solis ortus cardine

"From the Sierra Morena, cielito lindo." See Cielito lindo

"From the west the soldier came." Slovak air. Words by K. Davis. DSB

"From the wood where she doth dwell." See Die nacht (Strauss)

"From this valley they say you are going." See Red river valley

"From woods around." Duet. E. Szentirmay. e. KH 2

"From yon far fam'd immortal hills." See "Dagli immortali vertici" (Verdi)

"From yonder dark forest what horsemen advance." See Lützows wilde jagd (Weber)

"From yonder sky." G. Verdi. [Tr of Lassù in cielo] e. WG

From youth's happy day. See "Aus der jugendzeit" (Radecke)

"Fromm und inniglich betend grüss ich dich." See Marienlied

The frozen girl. Folk song: Georgia version. SBA

The frozen north. American song. US

Frühling liebster (Springtide sweetheart) B. Scholz. Words by F. Rückert. e.g. SAT

Frühlingsglaube. F. Schubert. Words by Uhland. g. EDL

Frühlingslied ("Durch den wald den dunkeln."—Spring song) F. Mendelssohn-Bartholdy. Words by N. Lenau. e.g. HCA

Frühlingslied ("Und ein duften zieht über die erdenwelt."—Song of spring) A. von Fielitz. Words by M. von Fielitz. e.g. TM

Frühlingslied ("Wenn der fruhling") See "Wenn der frühling auf die berge steigt" (Coenen)

Frühlingssegen (Spring's blessing) H. Brückler. Words by H. Lingg. e.g. HCA

Frühlingszeit. See "Wenn der frühling auf die berge steigt" (Becker)

Fry, Joseph Reese
Romance (Fry, W. H.)

Fry, William Henry
Romance (from Leonora)

Fryxell, Anton
Vermeland (Swedish air)

Fuadach nan gàidheal (Der vertriebene gaele) Air: Lord Lovat's lament. Words by H. Whyte. ga.g. ML 1

"Fuchs, du hast die gans gestohlen." See Warnung

Fuchslied ("Was kommt dort von der höh") [18th century folk song. Air: Bei hall' ist eine mühle] g. EDL

Fuentes, Eduardo Sánchez de
Grant those glances. See Mirame así
Mirame así
"O Cuba." See Tú
Tú

Fulkerson, Frances
The ghost-dance (Bissell)

"Füll die täler aus" ("Porównaj boże góry z dołami") Polish folk song. g.p. ML 3

Full many a dream. See Viel träume (Henschel)

"Full many a flow'r has faded." See Viel träume (Henschel)

"Full many fair and famous streams." See The Genesee

"Full well do I remember my boyhood's happy hours." See Bright-eyed little Nell of Narragansett bay

Fuller, H. J.
Bring back my Bonnie to me
Bring back my kitchen to me (same air as Bring back my Bonnie to me)
"My Bonnie." See Bring back my Bonnie to me

Fuller, Howard Newton
On the banks of the old Raritan (Composer unknown)

Fuller and Warren. Cowboy song. LSC

Fulmer, H. T.
Wait till the clouds roll by

"Funeste piaggie." J. Peri. Words by Rinuccini. e.i. KVG

Fünf söhne. Ostfriesische volksweise. g. EDL

Funiculi, funicula ("Some think the world") L. Denza. Words by E. Oxenford. DSC
Funiculi, funicula (A merry life) BB
A merry life. LAS—TFP

"Für dich und für mich" ("Gia t'esena kai gia menane") Greek folk song. g.gr. ML 2

"Für solch derbe, kühne burschen taugt nur ein herrenleben." See Holzflösser

Füredi, Mihály
"Jaj be fényes csillag ragyog az égen." See "See the star that shines afar"
"See the star that shines afar"

Furlo' moon. West Point song. DSO

Furman, Allan Foster; Sharples, Harry P., and Killick, L. F.
Vermont victorious

Furry day carol. Traditional Cornish air: ʟThe Helston furry danceʟ OB

"**Furt** a chussedl." See "Fohrt der chossid'l"

Fussfesselmarsch der sträflinge ("Posredī palat kamennykh") Russian folk song. g.r. ML 1

Fyleman, Rose
Summer time (French air)

Fyles, Philip. See Phile, Philip

G

Gabriel, Virginia
Only her love I ask for
Ruby
Weary

"**Gabriel** from eyene King." See "Angelus ad Virginem"

"**Gabriel,** that angel bright." See Regina coeli, letare

"**Gabriel's** message." 16th century air. Words based on an old Easter carol, Angelus emittitur. e. OB

"**Gabst** die goldne kette mir." See Lisas lied

"**Gacsaj** pesta szép fiű vaut." See "War ein schöner junger bursche"

Gade, Niels Wilhelm
Farewell, darling Maggie

"**Gae** bring my gude auld harp ance mair." See Scotland yet (McLeod)

ʟ**Gaelic** lullabyʟ "Hush! the waves are rolling in" (Old Gaelic lullaby) Composer unknown. e. MFS

Gagliano, Marco da
"Chi da' lacci d'amor" (from Dafne)

Gai lon la, gai le rosier. See Le prisonnier de Hollande (Canadian version)

ʟ**Gaily** beats the drumʟ Marching song. German song. e. MFS

"**Gaily** bounds my gallant steed." See "Il cavallo scalpita" (Mascagni)

ʟ**Gaily** I take my wayʟ The ballad singer ("Waking at early day") G. Linley. GE

"**Gaily** singing runs the river." See The singing river

"**Gaily** the troubadour." T. H. Bayly (music and words) BB—GOS 1—SSB—TFP

ʟ**Gala** waterʟ "Braw, braw lads." Air: Galla water. Words by R. Burns. GS

Der **galgenstrick** ("Kapakasta kapakkahan") Finnish folk song. fi.g. ML 3

Galkin, Nikolaĭ Vladimirovich
The wind in the cherry trees

The **gallant** poachers. See Van Diemen's land

"A **gallant** ship was lab'ring." See The ship I love (McGlennon)

"The **gallant** soldier." See "Le beau galant"

The **gallant** 69th. D. Braham. Words by E. Harrigan. SW

The **gallant** Thunderbomb. Sea song. US

"**Gallants,** attend, and hear a friend." See The battle of the kegs

A **gallery** carol ("Rejoice and be merry") Christmas carol. OB

Galuppi, Baldassare
"Compatite, signor" (from Il filosofo di campagna)
"È ingrato, lo veggio" (from Adriano in Siria)
"Prigioniera, abbandonata" (from Adriano in Siria)

The **Galway** piper. Irish folk song. DSC

The **gambling** man ("The poor man gambled all the night alone") Folk song: Kentucky version. SES 2
The **gambling** man ("My pocket-book full of money") North Carolina version. SES 2

The **gamboling** man ("I am a roving traveler") Folk song. SBA
Variants: The roving gambler; "Yonder comes my pretty little girl"

A **game** of trades. Russian air. Words by K. Davis. DSB

A **ganevoh.** Jewish folk song. y. SY

"'**Gang** awa'' was Donald's cry." See The piper's daughter

"A **gang** of good fellows are we." See Hail! hail! the gang's all here (Sullivan)

"Y **gangen** fwyn lawen fain lân." See Mwynen merch

Ganne, Louis Gaston
Lorraine march. See Marche lorraine
Marche lorraine

Gannett, William Channing
"The morning hangs its signal" (Mason)

Ganz, Wilhelm
"Sing, birdie sing"
"Sing, sweet bird"

Die **ganze** welt ʟHerr Jesu Christʟ (Hilariter) 17th century German Easter carol. e. OB

The **gap** in the hedge. Irish air. Words by C. Barnard. AT—HMI

Gaping catch. Round. H. Harrington. BOS 2
"'Tis hum-drum." DSB

Garavuša. See Trinklied

"The **garden** breathes a sweet perfume." See Shine on, oh stars (Sawyer)

"**Garden** fair, shady groves." See The fair garden (Borodin)

A **garden** idyll. See "Ich wandle unter blumen" (Lassen)

The **garden** of Jesus. See Jesus' bloemhof

"**Gardez** les fleurs que je vous ai données." See L'âme des fleurs (Massenet)

"Gardez piti milatte-là."   See Musieu
   Bainjo
Gardner, William Henry
   Trusting in thee (Coverley)
'Ē Garhoyphalia.   See Garufaliá
Garibaldi's hymn.   See Inno di guerra
   dei cacciatori delle Alpi (Olivieri)
ₜThe garland ("Ah! far in the field")₁ Aï!
   vo polïe lipïn'ka (Pfingstreigen)   Rus-
   sian Whitsuntide song.   g.r.   ML 1
Garrett, George Mursell
   My luve is like a red, red rose
   "Oh, my luve's like a red, red rose."
   See My luve is like a red, red rose
Garrett, Lloyd
   Dallas blues (Wand)
Garrick, David
   "Care flies from the lad that is merry"
   (Arne)
   Heart of oak (Boyce)
Garryowen.   Old Irish air.   DSO
The Gartan mother's lullaby.   Irish air
   from County Donegal.   Words by S.
   MacCathmhaoil.   HI 1
Garton, Ted.   See Benoit, G., jt. comp.
   and auth.
Garufaliá ('Ē Garhoyphalia)   Greek folk
   song.   g.gr.   ML 2
Gaskell, William
   "Press on! press on! ye sons of light"
   (Calkin)
The gate of heaven.   B. Tours.   Words
   by H. L. D. Jaxone.   CSS 1—CSS 2
Gates, Mrs Ellen (Huntington)
   Home of the soul (Phillips)
"Gather around the Christmas tree" (The
   Christmas tree)   ₜJ. H. Hopkins (mu-
   sic and words)₁   FC
Gather'd them for sweet Mabel.   See
   Mabel Clare (Higgins)
ₜGathering mushrooms₁ Mushrooms.   M.
   Moussorgsky.   ₜWords from the Rus-
   sian of L. Mey₁   e.   GA
Gatty, Sir Alfred Scott-.   See Scott-
   Gatty, Sir Alfred
"Gaudeamus igitur."   Medieval students'
   song.   e.l.   BB—TFB—TFO.   l. on-
   ly EDL—MBS—MFS
Gaul, Alfred Robert
   Choral sanctus (from The holy city)
   "Eye hath not seen" (from The holy
   city)
Gaunt, Percy
   The Bowery
Gauntlett, Henry John
   "Christ is born of Maiden fair"
Gautier, Théophile
   "Dites, la jeune belle" (Gounod)
   L'esclave (Lalo)
Gavotte des Mathurins.   See "Vous dan-
   sez, marquise" (Lemaire)
Gay. John
   "How happy could I be with either"
   (Old English air)
   "My lodging is on the cold ground"
   (17th century air)
   "Three children sliding" (Elliott)
   "Youth's the season made for joys"
   (Traditional air)

"The gay butterfly lost his heart to the
   rose."   See "Der schmetterling ist in
   die rose verliebt" (Franz)
"Gay dances Bibabutzemann."   See Biba-
   butzemann
Gay, la, la, gay is the rose.   See Le
   prisonnier de Hollande (Canadian ver-
   sion)
ₜThe gay young bachelor₁ Kullan ylistys
   (Der liebsten preis)   Finnish folk
   song.   fi.g.   ML 3
Gayley, Charles Mills
   The yellow and blue (Balfe)
Gaynor,
   "All in a stable cold and bare" `(Old
   English air)
Gaynor, Hugo A.
   "Alma mater Fordham" (Joslyn)
"Gaze not on me, nor search for me, I
   pray you."   Se La desgracia
"Gazte tarsunac bainarabila."   See Aiñ-
   hara
"Gdi Fruška gora u Dunav silazi."   See
   ·Klage ("Wo saves fluten in die Donau
   münden")
"Gdzież to jedziesz Jasiu."   See "Jack,
   where are you going"
Gebet ("Die du über die sterne weg."—Re-
   quest)   H. Brückler.   Words by
   Hebbel.   e.g.   HCA
Gebet ("Herr, den ich tief."—Prayer.—Be
   near   me   still)   F.   Hiller.
   ₜWords by Geibel₁   e.g.   ASA
   "Herr, den ich tief" (Prayer.—Be Thou
   with me)   e.g.   SFB
   "Lord, on Thy tender love relying."
   e.   SSO 2
ₜGebet ("Leise, leise, fromme weise")₁
   Evening prayer.   K. M. von We-
   ber.   ₜWords by F. Kind₁   e.
   BB
   Prayer from Freischütz.   e.   MFS
Gebet an den heiligen Christ ("Du lieber
   heil'ger frommer Christ")   G. Sie-
   gert.   Words by E. M. Arndt.   g.
   EDL
Gebet während der schlacht ("Vater, ich
   rufe dich")   F. H. Himmel.
   Words by T. Körner.   g.   EDL
   The battle prayer.   e.   GOS 2
Geborn ist uns ein Kinderlein.   For Eng-
   lish paraphrase with a different air see
   The secret flower
Geddes, Alexander
   Lewie Gordon (Jacobite air)
Der gefangene ("Sonne wandert auf und
   nieder."—"Solntse vskhodït ï zakho-
   dït")   Russian   folk   song.   g.r.
   ML 1
Die gefangenen reiter.   Volkslied.   g.
   EDL
Der gefoppte.   See Desengany
"Geh ich mir spazieren."   See Forsaken
   (Jewish folk song)
"Geh ich zum grünen hain."   See Le
   jardin d'amour
"Geh nicht fort" ("Nechod tam")   Czech
   folk dance.   bo.g.   ML 3
"Geh und eile, mägdelein."   See Der
   schlimme scherz

"Geht a goy in schenck'l herein." Jewish folk song. y. SY

"Gei ich mir spatzieren." See Forsaken (Jewish folk song)

Geibel, Adam
Freedom's flag
"O Jesus, Thou art standing" (same air as "O salutaris Hostia")
"O salutaris Hostia"

Geibel, Emanuel
Burschenlust (Lyra)
Gebet (Hiller)
O tempora! O mores (Student song)
"O wie lieblich ist das mädchen" (Schumann)
"Die stille wasserrose" (Fielitz)

"Geiger kann im haus nicht walten." See Der musikant

Geirionydd, Ieuan Glan, pseud. See Evans, Evan

Des geistes gesang. See entry under Des

Geliebter, komm'! sieh' dort die grotte. For English translation see "Beloved one, come" (Wagner)

Gellert, Christian Fürchtegott
Busslied (Beethoven)
Die ehre Gottes aus der natur (Beethoven)
"Jesus lives! no longer now" (Composer unknown. Tr of Jesus lebt, mit ihm auch ich)

Gelobet seist du Jesu Christ ("Now blessèd be thou, Christ Jesu."—Coverdale's carol) English traditional air. [Words by M. Luther; tr by M. Coverdale] e. OB

Gelübde ("Ich hab mich ergeben") Volksweise. Words by H. F. Massmann. g. EDL

"Gemo in un punto e fremo." G. B. Pergolesi. e.i. KVG

Gems of day. 16th century French air. Words based on an old carol, Le vermeil du soleil. e. OB

Gen himmel aufgefahren ist ("God is ascended") 16th century German air. e. OB

Genée, Richard
As the wind blows

[General roll call] When the general roll is called. Negro spiritual. HRD
Variant: I'll be there in the morning

"Gen'ral Taylor" (Walk him along, Johnny) Pulling chantey. TSB 2

The Genesee. University of Rochester alma mater. <Words by T. T. Swinburne; wrongly attributed to B. H. Wallace> KU

Genns, Duncan McPherson
The grim grey Palisades. See The Palisades
"O grim, grey Palisades." See The Palisades
The Palisades

Gen'ral. For titles beginning Gen'ral see General

Gentle Annie. S. C. Foster (music and words) BB—GOS 2—MFS—TFG—WSS

The gentle dove. Welsh folk song. [Tr of Y deryn pur] e. CSB 3

"Gentle flow'rs, with your spell." See "Faites-lui mes aveux" (Gounod)

The gentle little mermaid, she bent her curly head. See A mystery of the sea

Gentle maiden, those eyes remind me. See "Tu non sai con quei begli occhi" (Bellini)

Gentle Nettie Moore. G. S. Pike. Words by M. S. Pike. WSS
Gentle Nettie Moore (Little white cottage) GOS 1

Gentle slumbers o'er thee glide. See Ellen Bayne (Foster)

Gentle zephyr ("Charming, pleasing unseen wand'rer") P. A. von Hagen. MPA 2

"Gentle Zitella, whither away." See Love's ritornella (Planché)

"Gentleman Frog lived in the well." See The frog in the well (Berea, Ky. version)

"A gentleman from the courts of England." See Young Beichan (Beattyville, Ky. version; Harrogate, Tenn. version)

Gentlemen sailors. U.S. Naval academy song. US

"Gently murmuring stream." See Der jüngling an der quelle (Schubert)

"Gently the breezes blow thro' the forest." See Night song

"Gently the waves rock my little boat." See I vassen (Palmgren)

Geoghegan, J. B.
Down in a coal mine

Geography ("State of Maine Augusta on the Kennebec river") Old song. KSO

Geordie. Folk song: Black Mountain, N.C. version. SES 1
—Hot Springs, N.C. version. SES 1
—Micaville, N.C. version. SES 1
—Swannanoah, N.C. version. SES 1
—Dewey, Va. version. SES 1
—Villamont, Va. version. SES 1
Variant: Georgie

"George Collins." See Giles Collins

George Reilly. Folk song: Beattyville, Ky. version. SES 2
—Manchester, Ky. version. SES 2
—Black Mountain, N.C. version. SES 2
—Burnsville, N.C. version. SES 2
—Hot Springs, N.C. version. SES 2
—Micaville, N.C. version. SES 2
—Tennessee version. SES 2
—Virginia version. SES 2

Georgetown's blue and gray. Georgetown university song. L. C. Lennon and F. J. Corcoran. KU

Georgian song. See Grusisches lied (Pomasanski)

Georgie (Banstead Downs) Folk song from Sussex. BET
Variant of: Geordie

Gerard, Richard H.
Sweet Adeline (Armstrong)

Gerhardt, Paulus
"All my heart this night rejoices" (Ebeling. Tr of Fröhlich soll mein herze springen)

German lullaby ("Bruder, ich und du") See Wiegenlied

Gershwin, George
The half of it, dearie, blues

Gershwin, Ira
The half of it, dearie, blues (Gershwin, G.)

Gesang ausziehender krieger ("Hinaus in die ferne") A. Methfessel (music and words) g. EDL

Gesang der flüchtlinge. See The Tartar host

Gesang der gondelführer. See Canto dei gondolieri

Gesang der hafenarbeiter. See Towing-song

Gesang der Wolgabootschlepper. See Volga boat song

Gesang des sträflings. See Canto del carcerato

"**Gestern** abend war vetter Michel hier." See Vetter Michel

"**Gestern** beim mondenschein ging ich spazieren." See Beim mondenschein

"**Gestern**, brüder, könnt ihr's glauben." See Der tod

"**Gestern** kam Janka heim ins dorf nieder." See Janka

Get along little dogies. See Git along little dogies

Get away from dis co'nfiel'. American song. Words by S. Fay. TFB—TFP

"**Get** down, get down, get down, says he." See Lady Isabel and the elf knight (Allanstand, N.C. version)

"**Get** down, get down, loving Henry, she said." See Young hunting (Burns-ville, N.C. version no. 1)

"**Get** in line! mark the time." See Spirit of Maine (O'Neil)

[**Get** on board] "De gospel train." Negro spiritual. FSN—WSS

Git on board, little children. HRD

"**Get** thee up! there." See Eri tu che macchiavi (Verdi)

Get up and bar the door ("It fell about the Mart'mas time") Scottish song. GS

Get you ready, there's a meeting here to-night. See There's a meeting here to-night

Gethsemane. See Thy will be done (Slater)

Getting ready to die. Negro spiritual. MFS

Gevaert, François Auguste
Lullaby of the Christ Child. See The sleep of the Infant Jesus
The shepherd neighbors (same air as The sleep of the Infant Jesus)
The sleep of the divine Infant. See The sleep of the Infant Jesus
The sleep of the Infant Jesus

The **ghost-dance.** Pomona college song. A. D. Bissell. Words by F. Fulkerson (Shaw). HW

"**Ghost** dance up on Indian hill." See The ghost-dance (Bissell)

Già i sacerdoti adunansi. For English translation see "See! to the hall the priests proceed" (Verdi)

Già l'ira m'abbandona. Meyerbeer. [Tr of Ô toi qui m'abandonnes] e.i. PC

Già scaglio il ferro. See Nuova ferita (Mercadante)

"**Gia** t'esena kai gia menane." See "Für dich und für mich"

"**Giammai** provai." N. Piccinni. e.i. ZT 2

Giardini, Felice
"Come, Thou almighty King"
Italian hymn. See "Come, Thou almighty King"

To **giasemi.** See Der jasmin

Gibbons, Orlando
The angels' song
"Let us with a gladsome mind"

Gibbs, Armstrong
Herrick's ode. See "In numbers, and but these few"
"In numbers, and but these few"

Gibson, John Jameson
Alma mater — Lehigh university (Thompson)

Gibson, Wilson and Johnson. See The three butchers (Sussex version)

[**Gideon's** band] "I hail to my sister" (Band ob Gideon) Negro spiritual. HRD

Gideon's band ("Oh, keep your hat upon your head") Negro song. WSS

Gilbert, De Witt
Mighty Oregon (Perfect)

Gilbert, Fred
The man who broke the bank at Monte Carlo

Gilbert, L. Wolfe
Lily of the valley (Friedland)
My own Iona (Friedland and Morgan)
My sweet Adair (Friedland)
Take me to that Swanee shore (Muir)
Waiting for the Robert E. Lee (Muir)

Gilbert, Mercedes
Friendless blues (Handy)

Gilbert, Paul S.
Alma mater—Gettysburg college (Rein-artz)

Gilbert, Sir William Schwenck
"Dance a cachucha, fandango, bolero" (Sullivan)
The judge's song (Sullivan)
"Little maid of Arcadee" (Sullivan)
The magnet and the churn (Sullivan)
Poetry (Sullivan)
"Prithee, pretty maiden" (Sullivan)
"Soon as we may, off and away" (Sulli-van)
Tit-willow (Sullivan)
"When Britain really rul'd the waves" (Sullivan)

Gilder, Richard Watson
"God of the strong, God of the weak" (Mason)

Giles, Nathaniel
My love that mourns for me

Giles Collins. Folk song: Allanstand, N.C. version.   SES 1
—Big Laurel, N.C. version.   SES 1
—Burnsville, N.C. version.   SES 1
—Henderson county, N.C. version. SES 1
—Hot Springs, N.C. version.   SES 1
—Tennessee version.   SES 1
Gilfillan, William
The braes aboon Bonaw (Scottish air)
An **gille** ban (The fair-haired lad)   Gaelic folk air.   e.   CSB 5
Gilligan, William
The picture that was drawn upon the floor
Gilm zu Rosenegg, Hermann von
Allerseelen (music by Lassen; Strauss)
Die nacht (Strauss)
Gilmore, Patrick Sarsfield
Crow song (same air as "When Johnny comes marching home")
For bales (same air as "When Johnny comes marching home")
The nautical almanac tale.   See Ponce Muir's "suns"
Ponce Muir's "suns" (same air as "When Johnny comes marching home")
The three crows.   See Crow song
"We are the boys of Potomac's ranks" (same air as "When Johnny comes marching home")
"When Johnny comes marching home"
Gimme dat ol'-time religion.   See This old time religion
Gimme yo' han'.   Negro spiritual.   JB 2
"**Gin** a body meet a body."   See Comin' thro' the rye
"**Gin** livin' worth could win my heart." See The waefu' heart
"**Ging** auf den jahrmarkt" ("Šel sedlák") Czech folk song.   bo.g.   ML 3
"**Ging** das nönnlein und sucht im garten." See La monachella e il demonio
Ging ein mädchen ("Kīnīsalo mome") Macedonian folk song.   b.g.   ML 2
"**Ging** ein schön mädchen jung."   See Ging ein mädchen
"**Ging** jung Mariechen" ("Chcdzila Mari-ška")   Slovak folk song.   g.sl. ML 3
"**Gioco** di rea fortuna."   See O Lisbona, alfin ti miro (Donizetti)
Giordani, Giuseppe
"Canst thou believe."   See "Caro mio ben"
"Caro mio ben"
"Star of my heart."   See "Caro mio ben"
The **gipsy** ("Hear the little bells")   See The magpie and the little gypsy dancer (Zolotarev)
The **gipsy** and his wife.   Jugoslav folk song.   e.   MFF
ıThe **gipsy** countess: part 2ı "Three gipsies stood at the castle gate" (The wraggle taggle gipsies, O)   Folk song. ıAir: The wraggle taggle gipsies, Oı GSS

Gipsy Davy.   See Gypsy Davy
"The **gipsy** fires are shining."   See Gipsy John (Clay)
Gipsy John.   F. Clay.   Words by G. J. White-Melville.   HCA
The **gipsy** king ("I roam the world")   See The gypsy king (Bergh)
The **gipsy** laddie.   See The gypsie laddie
ıGipsy songı "Come with the gipsy bride."   M. W. Balfe.   MFS
The **gipsy's** warning.   H. A. Coard.   OT
The **girl** I left behind me ("The dames of France are fond and free")   18th century air: Brighton camp.   Irish version of words.   DSO—HMI—SRW—SSB
The **girl** I left behind me ("The hour was sad I left the maid")   ı18th century air: Brighton camp.   Words by S. Loverı   DSO—GOS 1—SI
The **girl** I left behind me ("I'm lonesome since I cross'd the hill")   ı18th century air: Brighton camp.   American version of wordsı   BB—DFF—MBS
The **girl** I loved in sunny Tennessee.   S. Carter.   Words by H. Braisted. OTG
"**Girl** of the forehead fair, Aileen, aroon." See Aileen, aroon (Converse)
Girl of the laughing eye.   See Aileen, aroon (Converse)
"A **girl** scout wakes at dawn of day."   See Girl scout's round (Hayes)
Girl scout's goodbye round ("O come and sing a song")   Four part round. K. K. Davis (music and words)   GSS
Girl scout's round ("A girl scout wakes at dawn of day")   W. Hayes.   Words by B. O. Edey.   GSS
"**Girls,** if fair as violets you're anxious to grow."   See In der märznacht (Taubert)
A **girl's** love.   A. Guriliev.   e.   NRF
Git along little dogies.   Cowboy song: 1st version.   LSC
For 2d version see Whoopee ti yi yo, git along little dogies
Git along, you little dogies, git along there slow.   See "I ride an old paint"
Git on board, little children.   See Get on board
Giusti, Giuseppe
Preghiera (Tosti)
Give a cheer.   C. M. von Weber. Words by H. Fitch.   TFO
"**Give** me a fresh'ning breeze, my boys." See There's nothing like a fresh'ning breeze (Randegger)
"**Give** me alone every hour."   See "Je ne veux pas autre chose" (Widor)
Give me Jesus ("Oh, when I come to die") Negro spiritual.   FSN—MFS
Give me Jesus ("I heard my mother say")   WSS
Give me my home again.   See Das haidekind (Schaeffer)
Give me that old-time religion.   See This old time religion

"**Give** me the crow that is so black." See The true lover's farewell (Peaks of Otter, Va. version)

ₜ**Give** me the waltzₗ Sparkling Piper Heidsieck. ₜC. E. Prattₗ SW

"**Give** me three grains of corn, mother" (Three grains of corn) Old American song. SBA

Give me your hand. See Gimme yo' han'

Give my regards to Broadway. G. M. Cohan (music and words) DFF

"**Give** no more pain, ah, dearest." See "Non dar più pene, o caro" (Scarlatti)

Give the fiddler a dram. Folk song from Kentucky. SES 2

Give up the world. Negro spiritual from South Carolina. AS

"**Give** ye, gay lords." See "Nobles seigneurs, salut" (Meyerbeer)

Gjeite lok (Ziegen-lockruf) ₜNorwegian goat-herd's callₗ g.n. ML 1

"**Glad** Christmas bells." Christmas hymn. BB

Glad spring-time once again. See Spring-time once again (Sullivan)

"**Glad** that I live am I." G. Shaw. Words by L. W. Reese. GSS

Glad tidings ("Hark, hark, what news the angels bring") Cornish air. 17th century words. DN

Glad tidings ("Hark, hark, what news the angels bring") Northamptonshire air. 17th century words. DN

Gladden, Washington
The mountains

"**Glädjens** blomster" (Glücksblumen) Swedish folk song. g.sw. ML 1

Glascock, J. R.
"Nevada, my Nevada" (Haseman)

Glaser, Carl Gotthilf
Azmon. See "Oh, for a thousand tongues"
"Oh, for a thousand tongues"

Glen, William
Wae's me for Prince Charlie (Scottish air)

"The **Glendy** Burke." S. C. Foster (music and words) WSS

"**Glide**, glide, keep on a-glidin'." See The Cubanola glide (Von Tilzer)

"**Glide** on, glide on, thou snow-white swan." See The swans

"**Glide** onward, my bark canoe." See My bark canoe

"**Gliding** 'mid the poor and lowly." See Father Joe (Flotow)

Glière, Reinhold Moritzovich
"Die heil'gen drei kön'ge aus morgenland"
The three holy kings. See "Die heil'gen drei kön'ge aus morgenland"

Die **glocken** von Nantes. See "Dans les prisons de Nantes"

Die **glocken** von Nowgorod. See The bells of Novgorod

Gloire immortelle de nos aïeux. For English translation see Soldiers' chorus (Gounod)

"**Gloomy** night embraced the place." See Summer in winter

"**Gloomy** winter's now awa'." Scottish air: <Lord Balgonie's favorite> Words by R. Tannahill. GS

Gloria ("Gloria, gloria! the angels in heaven are singing gloria") Russian folk song for Easter. e. DSB

Gloria all' Egitto. For English translation see "Glory to Egypt" (Verdi)

"**Gloria,** gloria! the angels in heaven are singing gloria." See Gloria

Gloria Patri. Composer unknown. MFS

"**Gloria** Patri." G. P. da Palestrina. e.l. BB

"Glory to God." e. DSC

Gloria tibi, Domine. See Parvulus nobis nascitur (Dunstan)

Glorify the Lord. See Célébrons le Seigneur (Rupès)

ₜ**Glory** and honorₗ Live humble. Negro spiritual. HRD

"**Glory** and love to the men of old." See Soldiers' chorus (Gounod)

Glory be to God on high. See "Christmas time is come again, Christmas pleasures bringing"

"**Glory** be to the Father." See Gloria Patri (Composer unknown)

Glory, glory Colorado. University of Colorado song. ₜAir: John Brown's bodyₗ HW—KU—KV

Glory, glory, hallelujah! Glory, glory hallelujah! Glory, glory, hallelujah! His soul is marching on. See "John Brown's body"

Glory! glory! hallelujah! Glory! glory! hallelujah! Glory! glory! hallelujah! His truth is marching on. See The battle hymn of the republic

Glory, glory hallelujah! God's truth is marching on. See The world is marching on

Glory, glory, keep them rolling. See Keep them rolling

"**Glory** now and forever to God." See The song of praise (Russian folk song)

"**Glory** now to Thee be given." See Sleepers, wake (Bach)

"**Glory** to Egypt." G. Verdi. ₜTr of Gloria all' Egittoₗ e. WG

Glory to God. See "It came upon the midnight clear" (Roeder)

"**Glory** to God and unto His Son." See "Gloria Patri" (Palestrina)

Glory to heaven's eternal King. See "It came upon the midnight clear" (Meyer-Helmund)

"**Glory** to Him." S. Rachmaninov. Words by S. Fay. TFG

"**Glory** to old Reserve." Western Reserve university song. AI

ₜ**Glory** to the Lord in Zionₗ Divine praise (Kol slaven) D. S. Bortniansky. e. SR

"**Glory** to Thee, my God, this night" (An evening song) C. Gounod. Words by Ken. CSS 1—CSS 2

"**Glory** to Thee, my God, this night." T. Tallis. Words by Ken. MBS

Gloucestershire wassail. See "Wassail, wassail, all over the town"
Glover, Charles William
  The bashful young lady
  Bonnie Bessie Gray
  "Do they think of me at home"
  Jeannette and Jeannot
  Kitty Tyrrell
  "Loving voices"
  Melodies of many lands
  Music on the waves
  The old familiar place
Glover, Stephen Ralph
  Annie o' the banks o' Dee
  "Beautiful Erin"
  The good-bye at the door
  I love the merry sunshine
  "In the starlight"
  Mermaid's evening song
Gluck, Christoph Willibald, ritter von
  "Che farò senza Euridice" (from Orfeo)
  Chorus of blessed spirits (from Orfeo. Tr of Vieni a' regni del riposo)
  "Einem bach, der fliesst" (same air as "Holde frühlingszeit")
  Euridice and the happy spirits (from Orfeo. Tr of È quest' asilo ameno e grato)
  "Holde frühlingszeit" (from Die pilgrime von Mekka)
  "O, at my lady's feet." See "O del mio dolce ardor"
  "O del mio dolce ardor" (from Paride ed Elena)
  "O'er thy tomb" (from Iphigenia in Tauris. Tr of Contemplez ces tristes apprêts)
  Die sommernacht
  "There's an island"
  "These fair meads." See Euridice and the happy spirits
  "Tho' the earth be bright." See "Che farò senza Euridice"
Gluck, Elisabeth
  Gute nacht (Haynes)
Glück, Friedrich
  "In einem kühlen grunde"
  Das zerbrochene ringlein. See "In einem kühlen grunde"
Glück ("Das glücke kommt selten per posta zu pferde") G. P. Telemann. Words by D. Stoppe. g. EDL
"Glück auf! glück auf! der steiger kommt." See Bergmannslied
"Das **glücke** kommt selten per posta zu pferde." See Glück (Telemann)
Glücksblumen. See "Glädjens blomster"
"**Glükkes** blumen siehst du auf der erde grund." See "Glädjens blomster"
Der **gnade** heil ward dem blüsser beschieden. For English translation see "The Lord Himself now thy bondage hath riven" (Wagner)
A **gneive.** See Oi, alas, a robber
"**Go** and tell Aunty Nancy." See The old grey goose

"**Go** bring me back my blue-eyed boy." See The brisk young lover (American version)
"**Go** catch up my old grey horse." See The gypsy laddie (Hot Springs, N.C. version no. 1)
"**Go** down in de lonesome valley." See The lonesome valley
Go down, Moses. Negro spiritual. BB—HRD—JG—TFG—WFN—WSS
  Go down, Moses (Let my people go) FSN
Go down to de cotton field. See "Oh! Lemuel" (Foster)
"**Go** father, go father, go build me a boat." See Sweet William (Nellysford, Va. version no. 2)
"**Go** get me some of your father's gold." See Pretty Polly
Go get the ax. Nonsense song. SBA
"**Go** hand me down my looking glass." See Giles Collins (Big Laurel, N.C. version)
"**Go** home with me, little Matthy Groves." See Little Musgrave and Lady Barnard (Black Mountain, N.C. version)
"**Go** in and out the window." Nursery game song. SMG
Go in the wilderness. Negro spiritual from South Carolina. AS
["**Go** javten"] The dance. Danish folk song. e. DSB
Go, Mary, an' toll de bell. Negro spiritual. HRD
"**Go** tell him to clear me one acre of ground." See The elfin knight (Kentucky version)
Go tell it on de mountain. Christmas plantation song. HRD
  Go tell it on the mountains. FSN
"**Go** to Jane Glover." 17th century round. GSS
Go to sleep, Lena darling. J. K. Emmet (music and words) MFS
  Go to sleep, Lena darling (Emmet's lullaby) BB—WSS
"**Go** to sleep, my little pickaninny." See Little Alabama coon (Starr)
Go to sleep now, go to sleep now, birdeenee, birdeenee. See Fead an iolair
"**Go** to sleepy." Georgia negro lullaby. SBA
"**Go** 'way f'om mah window." Negro woodchopper's song from Arkansas. SBA
"**Go** where glory waits thee." Irish air: Bean dubh an ohleanna, or, The dark maiden of the valley. Words by T. Moore. HMI—SI
The **goat** ("There was a man") Air: And when I die. DFF—SRW
"The **goat** is old and gnarly." U.S. naval academy song. US
Gobble, Sam
  The spirit of the hill
[**Gobble** duet] "When I behold" (Gobble song) E. Audran. e. WLO
Goblet of youth. C. Lecocq. Words by M. L. Baum. TFR

[**God** be with us] "O God, beneath Thy guiding hand." J. Hatton. Words by L. Bacon. BB
"O God, beneath Thy guiding hand" (Duke street) GSS—LAS
"**God** be with you." W. G. Tomer. Words by J. E. Rankin. BB
"**God** bless our native land, firm may she ever stand." See America (Carey?)
"**God** bless Ricardo Primero, ero." See The governor of Guam
"**God** bless the master of this house, the mistress also." See Good-bye
"**God** bless the ruler of this house and send him long to reign." See The Lamb of God (New Year version)
"**God** bless you all, both great and small." See The host and his guests
"**God** don't want no coward soldiers." Negro spiritual from Virginia. SBA
"**God** ever glorious." Air: Russian national hymn <by A. T. Lwoff> Words by S. F. Smith. TFG
"**God** got plenty o' room." Negro spiritual from Virginia. AS
God help them tonight in their hour of affliction. See Father was killed by the Pinkerton men (Delaney)
"**God** is ascended." See Gen himmel aufgefahren ist
God is love. See "O salutaris Hostia" (Hargitt)
"**God** keep our Russian tsar." See The Russian national hymn (Lvov)
"**God** of our fathers, known of old" (Lest we forget) J. B. Dykes. Words by R. Kipling. LAS
"**God** of our fathers, known of old" (Recessional) E. C. MacMillan. Words by R. Kipling. MBS
"**God** of our fathers, Whose almighty hand." See National hymn (Warren)
"**God** of the earth." H. J. E. Holmes. Words by S. Longfellow. BB
"**God** of the nations, in glory enthroned" (Anvil chorus) G. Verdi. BB—TFB—TFP—TFR
"**God** of the nations near and far." J. B. Dykes. Words by J. H. Holmes. LAS
"**God** of the strong, God of the weak" (Hamburg) L. Mason. Words by R. W. Gilder. LAS
God, our loving Father. Finnish air. Words by R. Compton. DSB—GSS
"**God** placed Adam in de garden." See Good Lord, shall I ever be de one
"**God** prosper long our noble king." See Chevy chase
"**God** rest ye merry, gentlemen." Old English song. <London air> FC
"**God** rest you merry, gentlemen." DN—DSC—MBS—OB
"**God** rest you merry, gentlemen." Old English song. Another traditional setting. <Cornish air> OB
"**God** rest you, Chrysten gentil men." See Christmasse of olde
"**God** save our gracious king." See God save the king (Carey)

God save the king ("God save our noble king") British national anthem. [Attributed to H. Carey; attributed also to J. Oswald] MBS
God save the people. See "When wilt Thou save Thy people" (Brown)
"**God** shall charge His angel legions" (Watch and ward.—Trust) Mendelssohn. Words by J. Montgomery. MFS
God shall wipe away all tears from their eyes. See The Lord is risen, He will dwell with man (Sullivan)
"**God** told Moses, O Lord." See Little David, play on your harp
Godard, Benjamin Louis Paul
  "Ah! s'il est dans votre village"
  Chanson de Florian. See "Ah! s'il est dans votre village"
  Florian's song. See "Ah! s'il est dans votre village"
  Les larmes
  Lullaby ("Sleep, so your tale")
  Tears. See Les larmes
Goddard, Felix
  An old-time celebration (Newton)
God's a-gwineter trouble de water. Negro spiritual. JB 2
"**God's** dear Son." Traditional air. DNS—OB
"**God's** goin' to set this world on fire." Negro spiritual. SBA
"**God's** right hand doth wield the thunder." G. A. Hasse. e. SSO 2
"**God's** trumpet wakes the slumb'ring world." C. S. Brown. Words by S. Longfellow. LAS
Goeckel, William John
  The red and blue
Goethe, Johann Wolfgang von
  Die bekehrte (Stange)
  Bundeslied (Reichardt)
  Ergo bibamus (Eberwein)
  Erlkönig (music by Loewe; Schubert)
  "Freudvoll und leidvoll" (Reichardt)
  Heidenröslein (music by Schubert; Werner; for German folk air see The wild rose)
  Jägers nachtlied (Reichardt)
  "Kennst du das land" (music by Beethoven; Schumann)
  Der könig in Thule (Zelter)
  "Nur wer die sehnsucht kennt" (Tchaikovsky)
  Das veilchen (music by Mozart; Reichardt)
  Wand'rers nachtlied: I (music by Jordan; Loewe)
  Wand'rers nachtlied: II (Loewe)
  The wild rose (German folk air. Tr of Heidenröslein)
Goin'. For entries beginning Goin' see Going
"**Going** away to see my Jesus." See Heav'n bells a-ringin' in mah soul
Goin' down that long long lonesome road. Blues song. W. Nash (music and words) HB
Goin' down to town. Virginia folk song. SBA

Going home, going home, by the light of the silvery moon. See The drinking fusileers

"**Going** out a-walking." See Forsaken (Jewish folk song)

Going to Boston. Play-party game from Kentucky. SES 2

Going to church. 16th century round. DSB—TFG

"**Going** to fly to my Jesus' arms." See On the other side of Jordan

Going to follow. See Gwine follow

"**Going** to get up in de chariot." See Good news, de chariot's comin'

Going to heaven. Negro spiritual. HRD

"**Going** to lay down my sword and shield." See I ain't gwine study war no more

Goin' to leave ol' Texas. Cowboy song. GSS

Going to live humble to de Lord. See Gwine to live humble to de Lord

"**Going** to march away in de gold band." See The gold band

"**Going** to meet my brother there, yes." See Going to ride up in the chariot

ʟ**Going** to ride up in the chariotʟ Gwineter ride up in de chariot. Negro spiritual. JB 2—WSS

"**Going** to roll in my Jesus' arms." See On the other side of Jordan

"**Going** to see my mother some of these mornings." See Some of these mornings

"**Goin'** to see my Sarah." Negro work song. HB

"**Goin'** to set down an' rest awhile." Negro spiritual. FSN

Goin' to shout all over God's heaven. See All God's chillun got wings

"**Going** to study war no more." See I air.'t gwine study war no more

Going to the silver wedding. See The silver wedding

"**Going** to walk about Zion." See Sabbath has no end

"**Going** to write to Massa Jesus." See Turn back Pharaoh's army

Going up. See Gwine up

The **gold** band. Negro spiritual from Tennessee. AS

Gold will buy 'most anything but a true girl's heart. M. H. Rosenfeld. Words by C. E. Foreman. SRW

The **golden** altar. Negro spiritual from North Carolina. AS
Variant of: John, John, of the holy order

The **golden** bear ("Our sturdy golden bear") See Fight for California

The **golden** carol ("Now is Christemas y-come") R. V. Williams. 15th century words. OB

ʟThe **golden** carol of Melchoir, Bathazer, and Casparʟ "We saw a light" (The golden carol of the three kings of Cologne) Old English song. DN

The **golden** carol of the three kings of Cologne. See The golden carol of Melchoir, Bathazer, and Caspar

"The **golden** day is dying." S. Palmgren. Words by K. Davis. DSB—GSS

The **golden** glove. Folk song: North Carolina version. SES 1
—Virginia version. SES 1

Golden mornings. English traditional air. OB

The **golden** rule ("To do to others") School song. MFS

Golden sheaves. Basque air: Khanta zagun. Words by J. S. B. Monsell. OB

"**Golden** slumbers kiss your eyes." Air: May fair. Words by T. Dekker ˂wrongly attributed to W. Chappell˃ MBS—MFS—TFG—TFR
I will sing a lullaby. BB

The **golden** stair. See Where the little feet are waiting (Webster)

"**Golden** stars for me are shining." See Dearest native land (Proch)

"**Golden** sunlight, shine sweetly above me." See "Star vicino" (Rosa)

The **Golden** Vanity ("And I'll sink you in the Lowlands") Tennessee version. SES 1

The **Golden** Vanity ("I had a little ship") Hindman, Ky. version. SES 1

The **Golden** Vanity ("Some were waving hats") Hot Springs, N.C. version no. 2. SES 1

The **Golden** Vanity ("There was a little ship and she sailed upon the sea") Berea, Ky. version. SES 1

The **Golden** Vanity ("There was a little ship in the North Amerikee") Black Mountain, N.C. version. SES 1

The **Golden** Vanity ("There was a little ship in the South Amerikee") Hot Springs, N.C. version no. 1. SES 1

The **Golden** Vanity ("There was a little ship that sailed upon the sea") Pineville, Ky. version. SES 1

The **Golden** Vanity ("There was a ship a-sailing on the North Amerikee") Manchester, Ky. version. SES 1

The **Golden** Vanity ("There was a ship in the north") Virginia version. SES 1

The **Golden** Vanity ("There was a ship sailed from the North Amerikee") Lexington, Ky. version. SES 1
Variants: The Golden Willow Tree; The Mary Golden Tree

The **Golden** Willow Tree. Kentucky mountain song. MK
Variant of: The Golden Vanity

"**Golden** years ago in a mill beside the sea." See The maid of the mill (Maybrick)

"**Goldene** ohrring' an grindigen ohren." See Sylvesterlied

Goldoni, Carlo
"Compatite, signor" (Galuppi)

Goldstein, Walter. See Ten Hoor, Marten, jt. comp. and auth.

Lu **golio** de 'na figliola (Mädchensehnsucht) Neapolitan folk song. g.i. ML 2

Gollmick,
"Pleasure climbs to every mountain"

Las **golondrinas** ("Adios, a tender el vuelo."
—The swallows)　Mexican folk song.
e.s.　VS

"**Goń** tu rampu domoj."　See Der
schweinehirt

Gondellied ("Oh pescator dell' onda")
See "Oh pescator dell' onda"

Gondolier waltz.　See On Venice waters
(Roeder)

"**Gone** are the days when my heart was
young and gay."　See Old black Joe
(Foster)

"**Gone** to Cripple Creek."　Folk song
from Kentucky.　SES 2

The **good** boy.　See "I have led a good
life"

Good-bye ("Farewell, farewell is a lonely
sound")　J. C. Engelbrecht.
MFS
　Good-bye (Farewell is a lonely sound)
GOS 1

Good-bye ("God bless the master of this
house")　Christmas song.　Air: Wassail song: 1st air.　17th century
words.　OB

Good-bye ("God bless the master of this
house")　Christmas song.　Air: Wassail song: Yorkshire version.　17th
century words.　OB

Good-bye ("Good-bye, my brudder")
Negro spiritual from South Carolina.
AS

The **good-bye** at the door.　ιS. Glover.
Words by J. E. Carpenterι　SW

Goodby Broadway, hello France.　B.
Baskette.　Words by C. F. Reisner
and B. Davis.　SMG

"**Good-bye,** brother."　Negro song.　AS
—SBA

Good-bye, Dolly Gray.　P. Barnes.
Words by W. D. Cobb.　DFF—SMG

Goodbye, fare ye well ("I thought I heard
the old man say")　Capstan chan-
tey.　TSB 1
　Fare you well.　SBS
　For variant see following song of
similar title

Good-bye, fare you well ("O, fare you
well")　Capstan chantey.　BOS 2—
WSE

"**Good-bye,** girls, I'm going to Boston."
See Going to Boston

"**Good-bye,** good-bye to summer."　See
Robin Redbreast (Hubbard); Robin
Redbreast (Kücken)

"**Goodbye,** I'm goin' home."　See Somewhere around a throne

Good-by Liza Jane ("Our horse fell down
the well")　Minstrel song.　SBA

Good bye, Liza Jane ("The time has
come")　Minstrel song.　WSS

"**Good-bye,** my brudder, good-bye, hallelujah."　See Good-bye (Negro spiritual)

"**Good-bye,** my lads, good-bye, no one can
tell me why."　See Bound to California

Good-bye, my lover, good-bye ("The ship
is sailing")　American air.　ιWords
by T. H. Allenι　TFB—TFP—TFR

"**Goodbye,** old Paint."　Cowboy song.
LSC

Good cheer.　ιCracovienne, or Polish
danceι　MFS

"**Good** evening, good evening, to ev'ryone
who's here."　See "Go javten"

"**Good** evening to you everyone, I brought
the old banjo."　See P. T. Barnum's
show

"**Good** evening, white folks, lend your ears."
See Adolphus Morning Glory (Braham)

"**Good** King Wenceslas."　Traditional air:
<Tempus adest floridum>　Words
from the Latin.　e.　BB—DN—DSC
—FC—MBS—OB—TFB—TFG

"**Good** little Cricket was chirping in the
meadow."　See The cricket and the
ant

"**The** good lord he came trav'ling home."
See The gypsy laddie (Crozet, Va. version)

"**Good** Lord, in de manshans above."　See
in the mansions above

Good Lord, shall I ever be de one.
Negro spiritual.　HRD

"**Good** morning! good morning! and here is
come another day."　A. E. Johnstone.
Words by M. Talbot.　TFR

"**Good** morning, good morning, my fair
young lady."　See The broken token
(Black Mountain, N.C. version)

"**Good** morning, good morning, my pretty
little miss."　See Good morning, my
pretty little miss (North Carolina version)

Good morning, ladies all ("Now a long
goodbye to you, my dear")　Halliard
chantey.　TSB 1

"**Good** morning, Mr Zip-zip-zip."　R.
Lloyd (music and words) based on a
fragment attributed to Private Hogan.
DSO—SMG

Good morning, my pretty little miss.
Folk song: Kentucky version.
SES 2
—North Carolina version.　SES 2

"**Good** morning to you."　M. Hill.
Words by P. S. Hill.　BB

"**Good** morrow, gossip Joan."　17th century song.　BOS 2—DSB
　Gossip Joan.　CSB 1

Good news, de chariot's comin'.　Negro
spiritual.　HRD

"**Good** news from home."　Minstrel
song.　WSS

"**Good** news, member."　Negro spiritual
from South Carolina.　AS

Good night ("Fremd bin ich eingezogen")
See Gute nacht (Schubert)

"**Good-night**" ("Good-night, good-night,
companions all")　ιF. Silcherι
Words by N. H. Dole.　GSS

"**Good-night**" ("Good-night, good-night, my
lady fair")　F. Silcher.　e.　TFO

"**Good-night**" ("Good-night, good-night,
beloved mine")　e.　DSC

"Good-night" ("Good night, good night, time sends a warning call") Round. GSS

"Good-night" ("Good-night, monsieur, good-night") J. Offenbach. ⌐Tr of Bonne nuit, monsieur, bonne nuit⌐ e. WLO

"Good night" ("Good night to you all") See "Good night to you all"

Good night ("Im tiefsten innern") See Gute nacht (Haynes)

Good night ("In the west the sun declining") F. Abt. MFS

Good night ("Little boy sweetheart") P. D. Aldrich. BST

Good-night ("'Tis growing late") E. Jakobowski. WLO

Good night and pleasant dreams. W. V. Wallace. <Words by A. G. Chester> GOS 2

"Good-night, good-night, beloved! I come to watch o'er thee." C. Pinsuti. Words by H. W. Longfellow. TFG

"Good-night, good-night, beloved mine, good-night, sleep well, my dear." See "Good-night" (Silcher)

"Good-night, good-night, companions all." See "Good-night" (Silcher)

"Good-night, good-night, my lady fair." See "Good-night" (Silcher)

"Good-night, good-night, sleep soft and light." See Des baches wiegenlied (Schubert)

"Good night, good night, time sends a warning call." See "Good-night" (Round)

"Good-night, ladies." BB—DFF—DSC—MFS—TFP

Good night, little girl, good night. J. C. Macy. Words by J. M. Hays. BST

"Good-night, monsieur, good-night." See "Good-night" (Offenbach)

"Good night, my dearest love." See Ständchen (Brahms)

"Good night, slumber sound." Round. MFS

"Good night to you all." Round. BB—TFB

The good old man. Folk song: Hindman, Ky. version no. 1. SES 2 —Hindman, Ky. version no. 2. SES 2

The good old way. Negro spiritual from Tennessee. AS Variant: Down in the valley

"Good people all this Christmas time." 17th century Irish carol from County Wexford. DNS Wexford carol. OB

"A good roarin' fire." Irish air from County Derry. Words from an old song. HI 2

The good Shepherd ("The Lord is my Shepherd") See "The Lord is my Shepherd, I shall not want" (Van de Water)

The good Shepherd ("The night fell fast") O. Barri. Words by G. C. Bingham. ASA—CSS 1—CSS 2

The good ship Montezuma. U.S. navy song. US

Good sweet ham. Minstrel song. WSS

"A good sword and a trusty hand." See Song of the western men (Old Cornish air); Song of the western men (Slater)

The good Three Bells. C. Jarvis. MFS

Good tidings. See "A Child this day is born" (Gloucestershire air)

The good time coming is almost here. See Wake, Nicodemus (Work)

"The good we wish for often proves our bane." See Thy glorious deeds inspir'd my tongue (Händel)

"Good wine" ("Jó bor") Old Hungarian folk song. e. hu. KH 2

Goodbye. For entries beginning Goodbye see Good-bye

Goodel, Walter J. "America, my country"

Goodwin, Joe. See McCarthy, Joseph, jt. auth.

"Gorom jezdi Kraljeviću Marko." See Der königssohn Marko und seine geliebte Angjelia

"De gospel train is comin'." See Get on board

Gossip Joan. See "Good morrow, gossip Joan"

"Gossip monger, village gadder." R. Planquette. ⌐Tr of Oui, nous devons faire taire⌐ e. WLO

"Got dem blues." Negro folk song. SBA

"Got no mo' home dan a dog." Negro folk blues. HB

"Der Gott der eisen wachsen liess." See Vaterlandslied (Methfessel)

"Gott im himmel, mögst du geben" ("Én istenem, add megérnem") Hungarian folk song. g.hu. ML 3

⌐"Gott sei mir gnädig"⌐ "O God, have mercy." F. Mendelsohn-Bartholdy. e. SSO 4

Gotter, Friedrich Wilhelm
Wiegenlied (Mozart)

Gottschalk, Louis Moreau
"Holy Ghost! with light divine"

Gottschall, Rudolf von
Marie (Jensen)

Götze, Karl
O happy day. See O schöne zeit, o sel'ge zeit
O schöne zeit, o sel'ge zeit

The gouge of Armour avenue. W. C. Handy. HB

Gould, Jeanie T.
Tender and true, adieu (Knight)

Gould, John Edgar
"Land of our birth"

Gould, Sabine Baring-. See Baring-Gould, Sabine

Gounod, Charles François
Adore and be still. See "Le ciel a visité la terre"
"Ah! I love thee only" (from Faust. Tr of Oui, c'est toi, je t'aime)
"Ah! je ris de me voir" (from Faust)

Gounod, Charles François—*Continued*
"All hail, thou dwelling pure and lowly." See Salut! demeure chaste et pure
"Avant de quitter ces lieux" (from Faust)
"Ave Maria"
Ave Maria ("Come all ye weary") See The cross of Calvary
Barcarolle. See "Dites, la jeune belle"
"Be mine the delight" (from Faust. Tr of À moi les plaisirs)
Bethlehem. See "Dans cette étable": traditional air arranged
Canti, ridi, dormi. See Chantez riez et dormez
Chantez riez et dormez
"Le ciel a visité la terre"
"Come unto me when the dark shadows gather"
The cross of Calvary
"Dans cette étable": traditional air arranged
Dio possente. See "Avant de quitter ces lieux"
"Dites, la jeune belle"
Easter eve
Easter hymn (from Faust. Tr of Christ est ressuscité)
Entreat me not to leave thee
"Even bravest heart may swell." See "Avant de quitter ces lieux"
An evening song. See "Glory to Thee, my God, this night"
"Faites-lui mes aveux" (from Faust)
"Forever with the Lord"
"Glory to Thee, my God, this night"
The greeting (from Faust. Tr of Ne permettrez-vous pas, ma belle demoiselle)
"Hail, bright Easter"
"Holy angels" (from Faust. Tr of Anges purs, anges radieux)
Hymn to the night. See Hymne à la nuit
Hymne à la nuit
It is not always May. See "The sun is bright"
Jewel song. See "Ah! je ris de me voir"
"The King of love my Shepherd is"
"Let me gaze" (from Faust. Tr of Laisse-moi, laisse-moi)
"Lovely appear" (from La rédemption)
"Lovely flowers I pray." See "Faites-lui mes aveux"
Nazareth
O, divine Redeemer. See Repentir
"O tender moon" (from Faust. Tr of Ô nuit d'amour)
O turn thee (from Gallia. Tr of Convertere ad Dominum)
Parce Domine. See Repentir
"Le parlate d'amor." See "Faites-lui mes aveux"
The peace of God
Repentir
Ring on, sweet angelus
"Ring out, wild bells"

Salut! demeure chaste et pure (from Faust)
"Send out Thy light"
"Si le bonheur" (from Faust)
Sing glad songs for him (same air as Soldiers' chorus)
Sing, smile, sleep. See Chantez riez et dormez
Sing, smile, slumber. See Chantez riez et dormez
Soldiers' chorus (from Faust. Tr of Gloire immortelle de nos aïeux)
"The sun is bright"
"Tell me, beautiful maiden." See "Dites, la jeune belle"
Toast to Wisconsin
Unfold, ye portals (from La rédemption. Tr of Ouvrez vos portes éternelles)
Varsity toast. See Toast to Wisconsin
When all was young. See "Si le bonheur"
Worship

The **governor-general** or a hobo. Song of the Philippine insurrection. US
The **governor** of Guam. U.S. navy song. US

Gow, Niel
Bonnie brave Scotland (same air as "Cam' ye by Athol, lad wi' the philabeg")
Bonnie Charlie (attributed)
Bonnie Prince Charlie. See "Cam' ye by Athol, Donald Macgillavry"; "Cam' ye by Athol, lad wi' the philabeg"
Caller herrin' (attributed)
"Cam' ye by Athol, Donald Macgillavry" (same air as "Cam' ye by Athol, lad wi' the philabeg")
"Cam' ye by Athol, lad wi' the philabeg"
Farewell to whisky. See Neil Gow's farewell to whisky
Neil Gow's farewell to whisky
"Roy's wife, of Aldivalloch"
Will ye no come back again. See Bonnie Charlie (attributed)

"**Gozdič** je že zelen." See The woods will still be green

Grace, Harvey
Pioneers
Grace ("For health and strength") See "For health and strength"
Grace ("Hark to the chimes") See "Hark to the chimes"
Grace ("Oh, give thanks") See "Oh, give thanks"

Grace before meat at Hampton. Negro spiritual. HRD
"**Grad** aus dem wirtshaus nun komm ich heraus." See Bedenklichkeiten
"**Grádh** le m'anam mo phaistín fionn." See Páisdín fionn
Graduation song ("Our school-days") Ancient air. Words by G. Cooper. BB
Grafted into the army. Civil war song. H. C. Work. DSO

Graham, Charles
  The picture that is turned toward the wall
  Two little girls in blue
Graham, Robert Z., pseud. See Loomis, Harvey Worthington
Gramachree macruiskeen. See An crúiscín lán
Granadinas. Barrera y Calleja. Words by P. Cases. e.s. MSP
Granath, I.
  Alma mater—Georgia institute of technology (Roman)
Grand concours de peuples à Bethléem. 18th century Noël from Arpajon. e. DNS
Grandfather's clock. H. C. Work (music and words) OT
Grannis, S. M.
  "Do they miss me at home"
  Do they miss me in the trenches (same air as "Do they miss me at home")
Grant, Mrs, of Carron. See Grant, Mrs Elizabeth
Grant, Mrs, of Laggan. See Grant, Mrs Anne (Macvicar)
Grant, Mrs Anne (Macvicar)
  The blue bells of Scotland (Jordan)
Grant, Mrs Elizabeth
  "Roy's wife, of Aldivalloch" (Gow)
Grant, Mrs James. See Grant, Mrs Anne (Macvicar)
Grant, Sir Robert
  O come let us worship (Haydn)
Grant those glances. See Mirame así (Fuentes)
The grass ("The grass so little has to do") Swiss air. Words by E. Dickinson. DSB
Grass and roses. J. C. Bartlett. Words from the "Gulistan" of Saadi. e. TSS 1—TSS 2
"The grass so little has to do." See The grass
"Grau deckt der nebel den himmel zu." See Waisenkind
"Grauer vogel über der haide" ("Thou gray birdling over the heather") A. von Fielitz. Words by Prinz E. zu Schönaich-Carolath. e.g. SAT
Graun, Karl Heinrich
  "Arise, my love, my fair one"
  "Lord, hear my prayer"
  "Now rejoice in God thy Saviour"
"Grausame schöne." See "Crudele Irene, tu m'hai lasciato"
The grave of Bonaparte. L. Heath. [Words by H. S. Washburn] GOS 1
The gravedigger. See Todtengräbers heimweh (Schubert)
Graves, Alfred Perceval
  The foggy dew (Old Irish air)
  If I were king of Ireland (Irish air)
  The little red lark (Old Irish air)
  "My love's an arbutus" (Irish air)
  "O land of my fathers, O land of my love" (Ancient Welsh air)
  Spring song (Mackenzie)

Graves, John Woodcock
  John Peel (Old Border air)
The graveyard. Negro spiritual from South Carolina. AS
Gray, Charles
  "The cantie spring" (18th century air)
  O Charlie is my darling (Jacobite air)
Gray, Louisa
  Looking back (Sullivan)
Gray, Marian, pseud. See Loomis, Harvey Worthington
Gray, William
  "The hunt is up" (16th century air) Authorship uncertain
Gray, William B.
  She is more to be pitied than censured
[The gray dove] "Stúpíl Dobrî" (Dobri) Bulgarian folk song. b.g. ML 2
"Grazie, clementi dei." See A te riede, o caro figlio (Mercadante)
"The great bells of Osney." See The bells of Osney
[A great camp-meeting in the promised land] "Walk together, children." Negro spiritual. FSN—JB 2
  Walk togedder, children. HRD
"Great Creator, all compassion." See Ave verum (Mozart)
Great day. Negro spiritual. JB 2
"Great gawd, I'm feelin' bad." Negro folk song. SBA
"Great God of nations." Thanksgiving song. J. S. Bach. <Words by A. A. Woodhull> DSB
"Great God, we sing." H. K. Oliver. Words by P. Doddridge. DSC
"Great gods! what a disclosure." See Se m'abbandoni, bella speranza (Mercadante)
"Great grand-dad." Cowboy song. LSC
"Great hearts that have battled in ages behind us." See The vision (Kremser)
"Great is Jehovah and worthy to be praised." L. Leo. e. SSO 2
"Great is Jehovah, the Lord." See Die Allmacht (Schubert)
"The great Pacific railway for California hail." See The railroad cars are coming
"Great prophetess! my soul's on fire." See In the battle, fame pursuing (Händel)
"Great Tom is cast." Round. Aldrich; attributed also to H. Lawes. BOS 2 —DSB—GSS—TFP
"The greatness of God in his love has been shown." See Infinite light
Greaton-Cole, Browne
  Those pals of ours
Grechaninov, Aleksandr Tikhonovich
  Berceuse. See Cradle-song
  Cradle-song
  Slumbersong. See Cradle-song
Greely, Philip
  The bold fisherman
  "Happy are we tonight"
Green, Eddie
  Blind man blues (McLaurin)
  Deep river blues (Handy)

Green, F. W.
Nobody's child (Lee)
"Green are the woods to-day."   See The woods will still be green
The **green** bed.   Folk song: Barbourville, Ky. version no. 1.   SES 1
—Barbourville, Ky. version no. 2. SES 1
—North Carolina version.   SES 1
—Virginia version.   SES 1
Green bottles.   Traditional north country song: Yorkshire version.   BOS 2
The **green** brier shore.   Folk song from Kentucky.   SES 2
Green broom (see Song Index)
Variant: The jolly broom man
Green bushes.   Folk song: Virginia version.   SES 2
The **green** grass grew all around, my boys. See The tree on the hill
Green grow the rashes, O ("There's nought but care on ev'ry hand")   Scottish air.   Words by Burns.   GS
Green grow the rushes-ho ("I'll sing you one-ho")   English folk song. GSS
Variant of: The ten commandments
"**Green** grow'th the holly."   Henry VIII. OB
The holly and the ivy.   DNS
Green grows the laurel.   Folk song from Kentucky.   SES 2
"**Green** hills and vales, and mighty rolling ocean."   See Célébrons le Seigneur (Rupès)
Green sleeves ("The old year now away is fled")   See Carol for New Year's day (Old English air)
Greenland fishery (see Song Index)
Variants: Greenland's icy shores; The whale
Greenland's icy shores.   Forecastle song. US
Variant of: Greenland fishery
"A **greenness** light and tender."   German folk song.   e.   MFS
Greens.   Negro folk song.   SBA
"**Greens**, greens, good old culluhed greens." See Greens
Greensleeves ("The old year now away is fled")   See Carol for New Year's day (Old English air)
Greenwell, Dora
"If ye would hear" (16th century Dutch air)
Greenwich park.   See "Come, sweet lass" (Clarke)
Greenwood, Annie Pike
The college song (Old air)
Greenwood, George H.
Montana my Montana
The **greenwood** side.   Kentucky mountain song.   MK
Variant of: The cruel mother
The **greenwood** tree.   S. Nelson.   MFS
Greeting ("Hello! Peter")   TFG
The **greeting** ("High-born and lovely maid")   C. Gounod.   [Tr of Ne permettrez-vous pas, ma belle demoiselle]   e.   WG

Greeting at night.   See Nächtlicher gruss (Storch)
Gretchaninoff, Alexander Tichonovitch. See Grechaninov, Aleksandr Tikhonovich
Grey, Vivian
Anona
The **grey** cock.   Folk song from North Carolina.   SES 1
The **gridiron** king.   Harvard university song.   R. K. Fletcher.   LAS
Grieg, Edvard Hagerup
"Am schönsten sommerabend war's"
Autumnal gale.   See Herbststurm
Herbststurm
Hidden love.   See Verborg'ne liebe
I love thee.   See Jeg elsker dig
Ich liebe dich.   See Jeg elsker dig
Im kahne
In the boat.   See Im kahne
Jeg elsker dig
Landkjending.   See Olaf Trygvason
My native land
Olaf Trygvason
One summer night.   See "Am schönsten sommerabend war's"
Vandring i skoven
Verborg'ne liebe
Waldwanderung.   See Vandring i skoven
Wandering in the woods.   See Vandring i skoven
Griffin, Gerald
"I love my love in the morning" (Allen)
"Let others breathe in glowing words" (Irish air)
Griffin, Gerald E.
Composer and author
The red guidon
Author
Keep them rolling (Old air)
The mountain battery (Composer unknown)
O'Reilly's gone to hell (Old air)
The **grim** grey Palisades.   See The Palisades (Genns)
Groom, Mrs
"Come, ferry me o'er"
"Over the sea, over the sea"
Groos, Karl
"Freiheit, die ich meine"
Grosdanka und der häuptling Bogdan (Grozdanka i Bogdan voïvoda)   Bulgarian folk song.   b.g.   ML 2
"**Grosse** mädchen, schlanke mädchen gut zur liebe scheinen."   See Alter tanz
Die **grössten** sünden (Najveći grijesi) Slavonian folk song.   g.se.   ML 2
Groth, Klaus
"Wie melodien zieht es mir" (Brahms)
The **ground** hog.   Folk song: North Carolina version.   SES 2
Groun' hawg.   Another version.   RA
"The **ground** was all cover'd with snow one day."   See The snowbird
"A **group** of jolly cowboys, discussing plans at ease."   See When the work's all done this fall
Grove, Roxy Hariette
Round 'em up for dear old Baylor

"The **groves** of Blarney." ₁Words by R. A. Milliken₁ SI

Grozdanka i Bogdan voĭvoda. See Grosdanka und der häuptling Bogdan

Gruber, Edmond L.
The caisson song (Metz)

Gruber, Franz
Die heilige nacht
"Holy night! peaceful night." See Die heilige nacht
"Silent night." See Die heilige nacht

Grünbaum, J. C.
The Cossack's song

"**Grünes** blatt, drei haselnüsse." See "Foaie verde trei alune"

"**Grünes** blättchen der zitrone." See "Foaie verde lămâiţă"

"**Grünes** blättlein, thymianblättlein." See "Foaie verde cimbrişor"

"**Grünes** blättlein, veilchen klein." See Înghețată-i Dunărea

"**Grünes** hirseblättchen klein." See Dor de ducă

"**Grünes** salbeiblatt im grase." See Cine trece pe uliţă

Gruppe,
Niemand hat's geseh'n (Loewe)

Grusisches lied (Georgian song) N. Pomasanski. e.g. TM

"**Gu** ma slàn a chì mi mo chailin dìleas donn." See Mo chailin dìleas donn

The **guardian** angel ("Watch over me") C. Franck. e. DSB

"Un **guardo** volgi a me." B. Marcello. e.i. ZT 1

"**Guddeen** to you, kimmer." See "Guide'en to you, kimmer, and how do you do"

"**Gude** e'en to ye, kimmer, and are ye alane." See We're a' noddin'

"**Gué-gué,** balayez." See "Gué-gué Solingaie"

"**Gué-gué** Solingaie" (Berceuse) Creole negro folk song. e.f. MB

Guérin, Léon
Je crois en vous (Berlioz)

Guernsey, Wellington
Alice, where art thou (Ascher)

Guglielmo, Pasquale D.
The lover and the bird

"**Guide** me, O Thou great Jehovah" (Guide me, great Jehovah) F. Hérold. ₁Words by W. Williams₁ MFS

Guide us with Thy heavenly light (Help me to pray) F. P. Tosti. CSS 1

"**Guided** by us, thrice happy pair." See Bridal chorus (Wagner)

₁"**Guide'en** to you, kimmer, and how do you do"₁ We're a' noddin' ("Guddeen to you, kimmer") Air: We're a' noddin'. Words by R. Burns. GS

La **guignolée** (Mistletoe gifts) French-Canadian New Year's carol. e. MFF

Guild, Thacher Howland
Illinois loyalty. See "We're loyal to you, Illinois"
"We're loyal to you, Illinois"

Guillô, pran ton tamborin (Patapan) Burgundian carol. e. OB

Guldterning. Norwegian song. e. LAS

Güll, Friedrich
Der kleine rekrut (Kücken)
Vom bauern und den tauben (Taubert)

Gum-tree canoe. See Tom-big-bee river (Steele)

Gunboat sailors. U.S. navy song. US

"**Gura** mise 'tha tùrsach." See Fuadach nan gàidheal

Guriliev, Aleksandr Lvovich
A girl's love

"**Gusle** moje." See "Meine geige"

"**Gut'** nacht, gut' nacht, mein liebster schatz." See Ständchen (Brahms)

Der **gute** kamerad ("Ich hat einen kameraden") Words by L. Uhland. g. EDL

Gute nacht ("Ach denke, liebster, denke."—Dobra noc) Wendish folk song. g.we. ML 3

Gute nacht ("Fremd bin ich eingezogen."—Good night) F. Schubert. Words by W. Müller. e.g. HCA

Gute nacht ("Die höh'n und wälder."—Farewell) R. Franz. Words by J. von Eichendorff. e.g. GG

Gute nacht ("Im tiefsten innern."—Good night) B. Haynes. Words by B. Paoli. e.g. TM

"**Guten** abend, gut' nacht." See Wiegenlied (Brahms)

"**Guten** abend, mütterlein." See Der besuch am grabe

"**Guten** va tröytt, somardagen heit." See Huldra aa en Elland

"**Guter** mond, du gehst so stille." See An den mond

Guy Fawkes. ₁Air: The barking barber. Words by T. Hudson₁ BOS 2

Gwili. See Jenkins, John, 1872-

"**Gwine** away to see mah Jesus." See Heav'n bells a-ringin' in mah soul

Gwine follow. Negro spiritual from South Carolina. AS

"**Gwine** to fly to my Jesus' arms." See On the other side of Jordan

"**Gwine** to get up in de chariot." See Good news, de chariot's comin'

"**Gwine** to lay down my burden." See I ain't gwine study war no more

Gwine to live humble to de Lord. Negro spiritual. HRD

"**Gwine** to march away in de gold band." See The gold band

"**Gwine** to roll in my Jesus' arms." See On the other side of Jordan

Gwine to run all night. See De Camptown races (Foster)

"**Gwir** e to see my mother some o' dese mornin's." See Some of these mornings

"**Gwine** to walk about Zion." See Sabbath has no end

Gwine up. Negro spiritual. HRD

"**Gwine-a** lay down mah burden." See I ain't gwine study war no more

Gwine-a study war no mo'. See I ain't gwine study war no more

"**Gwineter** meet my brother dere, yes." See Going to ride up in the chariot

Gwineter ride up in de chariot. See Going to ride up in the chariot
Y **gwŷdd** (The loom)   Old Welsh song. e.w.   WO
   The loom (The weaver)   e.   CSB 5
Gwynneth, John
   My love that mourns for me (Giles)
"**Gyere** be rózsám, gyere be."   See "Come in my rose, my rose come in"
The **gypsy** ("Hear the little bells")   See The magpie and the little gipsy dancer (Zolotarev)
The **gypsy** and his wife.   See The gipsy and his wife
The **gypsy** countess: part 2.   See The gipsy countess: part 2
Gypsy Davy.   Old ballad.   Fragment. SBA
Gypsy John.   See Gipsy John (Clay)
The **gypsy** king ("I roam the world a gypsy king")   A. Bergh.   Words by J. Landon.   TFO
The **gypsy** laddie.   Folk song: Barbourville, Ky. version.   SES 1
   —Knott or Letcher county, Ky. version. MK
   —Black   Mountain,   N.C.   version. SES 1
   —Burnsville, N.C. version.   SES 1
   —Hot Springs, N.C. version no. 1. SES 1
   —Hot Springs, N.C. version no. 2. SES 1
   —Flag Pond, Tenn. version.   SES 1
   —Rocky Fork, Tenn. version no. 1. SES 1
   —Rocky Fork, Tenn. version no. 2. SES 1
   —Crozet, Va. version.   SES 1
   —Woodridge, Va. version.   SES 1
Gypsy song ("Come with the gipsy bride") See Gipsy song
The **gypsy's** warning.   See The gipsy's warning (Coard)

H

"**Ha** felülök, csuhaj, ha felülök."   See "Ich besteig', juchheissa, ich besteige"
Ha, ha, ha ("When the war is ended the boys will see their fun")   Folk song from Kentucky.   SES 2
Ha, ha, ha! don't you hear me now.   See Ha, ha, ha
"**Ha**! ha! ha! how melancholy his moan is." E. Audran.   e.   WLO
"**Ha**! ha! ha! the bomb is bursting."   J. Offenbach.   ɾTr of Ah! ah! ah! la bombe éclatéɿ   e.   WG
Ha, ha, ha! 'tis you and me.   See Little brown jug (Eastburn)
Ha! ha! ha! you and me.   See Little brown jug (Eastburn)
"**Ha**! ha! the neatest and completest, of all a pirate's artful dodges."   See Pirates' chorus (Lecocq)
"**Ha**, immer rauf."   See "Ah! ça ira"

Ha! yet this hero all victorious.   See Entrance song (Millöcker)
Haavan lehdet.   See Die espenblätter
"**Hab'** ein liebes herzensliebchen" ("Aš paėmiau mergužėle")   Lithuanian folk song.   g.li.   ML 3
"**Hab'** ein röslein dir gebrochen" ("See, for thee I've plucked a rosebud") E. Sjögren.   Words by J. Wolff. e.g.   WM 2
"**Hab** gesät auf meinem felde."   See "Sown with millet was my garden"
Habanera ("Ah! love, thou art a wilful wild bird")   G. Bizet.   e.   WG
Hache, Theodor von la.   See La Hache, Theodor von
"**Had** a horse, a finer no one ever saw" ("Volt nekem egy darú szőrű paripám")   Old Hungarian folk song.   e.hu.   KH 1
   "Volt nekem egy darú szőrü paripám" ("Einst hatt' ich ein rösslein") g.hu.   ML 3
"**Had** I a cave."   Air: Robin Adair, or, Eileen aroon.   Words by R. Burns. GS
"**Had** I but staid at home."   See Das haidekind (Schaeffer)
Had I the wings of a fairy gay.   Minstrel song.   PSG
ɾ**Had** I wings like a doveɿ The wings of a dove.   Words by C. Jefferys.   GOS 1
"**Had** me a cat and the cat pleased me." See The farmyard
Hadley, Henry Kimball
   Cherry blossoms
Hagar in der wüste (Hagar in the wilderness)   A. Rubinstein.   e.g.   DCA
Hagar in the wilderness.   See Hagar in der wüste (Rubinstein)
Hagen, John Milton
   Kollege kick
Hagen, Peter Albrecht von
   Gentle zephyr
   May morning
   Monody
   The pride of our plains
Hager, George
   Alma mater—University of Washington
Hahn, Karl
   Das steckenpferd (Hering)
Hahn, Reynaldo
   L'heure exquise
   The hour of dreaming.   See L'heure exquise
   Si mes vers avaient des ailes
   Were my song with wings provided. See Si mes vers avaient des ailes
"**Hai** già vinto la causa."   See Vedrò, mentr' io sospiro (Mozart)
Haï luli (Alack-a-day)   A. Coquard. ɾWords by X. de Maistreɿ   e.f.   TM
"**Hai**, salcâm, salcâm de vară" ("Linden grün, ihr blätterreichen")   Rumanian song.   g.ru.   ML 2
Das **haidekind** (Give me my home again) H. Schaeffer.   Words by Schröer. e.g.   GG
Haidukenlied.   See Doïna Haiducului

"Hail, all hail, each happy season." See Christmas as it comes

"Hail, alma mater, dear! to us be ever near." See Alma mater—United States military academy (Kücken)

"Hail alma mater, thy sons do call." See Marquette university anthem

Hail and farewell ("The blue Pacific ocean."—Aloha) Hawaiian folk air. Words by G. W. Pennington. TFO

"Hail and farewell, dear companions." See Parting graduation song (Barnard)

"Hail! Arizona wildcats." See Fight! wildcats, fight (Allen and Holsclaw)

"Hail, beauteous stranger of the grove." See Spring-time once again (Sullivan)

"Hail blue and gold." Song of the University of California at Los Angeles. B. Price (music and words) HW

"Hail, bright abode, where song the heart rejoices." Grand march and chorus, from Tannhäuser. R. Wagner. [Tr of Freudig begrüssen wir die edle halle] e. WG

"Hail, bright Easter." C. Gounod. Words by A. Crane. TFG

Hail C. I. T. California institute of technology song. M. M. Barnes. HW

"Hail Columbia." P. Phile (called also J. Fayles, Fyles, Phyla, Phylo and J. Vales) Words by J. Hopkinson. BB—GOS 1—MFS

Hail Columbia, The new. [P. Phile] Words by O. W. Holmes. MFS

"Hail, Columbia! happy land." See "Hail Columbia" (Phile)

"Hail, Columbia! strong and free." See Hail Columbia, The new (Phile)

"Hail! de King of Babylon." H. Johnson. JG

"Hail, glorious apostle." Irish song. SI

"Hail! hail! gamecocks, hail." University of South Carolina song. KU—KV

Hail! hail! hail. Negro spiritual. HRD

"Hail! hail! Nevonia." Franklin and Marshall college song. J. Alexander. AI—AIS

Hail, hail, put John on de islan'. See Put John on de islan'

"Hail! hail! the gang's all here." <A. Sullivan. Author of words unknown> TFO

Hail! hail! the gang's all here ("A gang of good fellows are we."—What the deuce do we care) A. Sullivan. Words by D. A. Esrom. SMG

Hail! hail! the gang's all here ("Oh, we're going to the Hamburg show") A. Sullivan. U.S. army version of words. DSO

"Hail, holy light! the world rejoices." J. Brahms. Words by E. P. Parker. TFP

Hail Loyola. Loyola university song. G. W. Kowalski (music and words) AIS

Hail, Mary ("I want some valiant soldier here") Negro spiritual from South Carolina. AS
Variant of: Some valiant soldier

"Hail, men of Fordham, hail." See Fordham "ram" (Coveney)

"Hail! mighty Phtha." G. Verdi. [Tr of Possente Ftha] e. WG

Hail! Minnesota. T. E. Rickard (music and words) AI—KU

Hail! Pacific, hail. Song of the College of the Pacific. L. Warner (music and words) HW

"Hail, Pennsylvania." University of Pennsylvania song. Air: Russian national hymn <by A. Lvov> Words by E. M. Dilley. AI

"Hail, poetry, thou heav'n-born maid! thou gildest even the pirate's trade." See Poetry (Sullivan. Words by Gilbert)

"Hail, poetry! thou heav'n-born maid! thy laurel crown shall never fade." See Poetry (Sullivan. Words by Stevens)

"Hail! Pomona! hail." Pomona college song. R. N. Loucks (music and words) HW

"Hail! proud Nevada." See The triumph hymn (Lvov)

"Hail, St Mary's hail." See Alma mater —St Mary's college (Stevens)

"Hail San Francisco." University of San Francisco song. Colligan. HW

Hail, Stanford, hail. Leland Stanford, jr, university song. <M. R. Coolidge> Words by A. W. Smith. AI—HW—KU

Hail sturdy men. University of Nevada song. HW

Hail the crown. See "Some come cripple"

"Hail thee, joy! all hail." See An die freude (Beethoven)

Hail, thou ever-blessed morn. See "See, amid the winter snow" (Mendelssohn); "See amid the winter's snow" (Morris)

"Hail, Thou long-expected Jesus." Mozart. [Words by C. Wesley] FC

"Hail, Thou most sacred One." See Evening song to the Virgin (Browne)

"Hail to California." University of California song. C. R. Morse (music and words) HW

Hail to dear old Whittier. Whittier college song. H. E. Collins (music and words) HW

Hail to Denver U. University of Denver song. <H. S. Thompson; wrongly attributed to I. E. Cutler> Words by I. E. Cutler. HW

"Hail to Georgia." University of Georgia song. AIS

"Hail to Him who dwells in might." See Worship (Gounod)

Hail to New Mexico. University of New Mexico song. L. C. Clauve. Words by G. St Clair. HW

Hail to Occidental. Occidental college song. W. Thomson. Words by D. S. Hammack. HW

Hail to old O. S. C.   Oregon state agricultural college song.   H. A. Wilkins (music and words)   HW
Hail to old O. S. C. (Rooter's song) KU—KV
"Hail to our sturdy men."   See Hail sturdy men
"Hail to the brightness."   T. Hastings. MFS
"Hail to the buff, hail to the blue."   See The buff and blue (Sweeney)
"Hail to the chief."   J. Sanderson.   Words by W. Scott.   BB—GS
"Hail to the glory of the morning."   See Onward (Eames)
"Hail to the happy bridal day."   G. Donizetti.   [Tr of Per te d'immenso giubilo]   e.   WG
Hail to the lion.   See The Nittany lion (Leyden)
"Hail to the Lord's anointed."   Mendelssohn.   [Words by J. Montgomery] FC
"Hail to the scouts."   J. A. Jeffery. Words by B. O. Edey.   GSS
"Hail to thee New Mexico."   See Hail to New Mexico (Clauve)
"Hail to thee O alma mater."   See Alma mater—University of North Dakota (Haydn)
"Hail to thee, our alma mater."   University of Redlands song.   W. B. Olds.   HW
Hail West Virginia.   West Virginia university song.   E. Miller and E. McWhorter.   Words by F. B. Deem. AI—AIS—KU
Hail! Wichita.   University of Wichita song.   T. Lieurance.   Words by S. A. Wofsy.   AIS
Der hain von Fanaid.   See The Fanaid grove
"Haj! Rákóczi Bercsényi! Bezerédi! Magyar vitézek nemes vezéri."   See Rákóczi-(Kurutzen-) lied II
"Hajej, můj andílku."   See Wiegenlied (Czech folk song)
Hajej, nynjej.   See Rocking
Hale, Mrs Sarah Josepha (Buell)
    The Lord's prayer (Composer unknown)
    The watcher (Lardner)
Haley, Ed
    "While strolling through the park"
Half horse and half alligator.   See The hunters of Kentucky
The half of it, dearie, blues.   G. Gershwin.   Words by I. Gershwin.   HB
"Halfway down the trail to hell."   See Fiddlers' green
Halket, George
    Logie o' Buchan (Scottish air)
Halkin, Nicholas Vladimirovich.   See Galkin, Nikolaï Vladimirovich
Hall, Charles Sprague
    "John Brown's body" (Old air)
Hall, Foley
    "Ever of thee"
Hall, J. Norman
    "Sons of old Grinnell"

Hall, Joseph
    For Christmas day (Traditional air)
Hall, Mabel Kinney
    Fair M. S. C. (German air)
Hall, Norman H.
    "America, my country" (Goodel)
Hall, R. B.
    "Come join the band"
Hall, W. B.
    "Joys that we've tasted"
Hallelu, hallelu ("Oh one day as anoder") Negro spiritual from South Carolina. AS
Hallelu, hallelu, O, my Lord.   See "Death come to my house he didn't stay long"
Hallelujah ("Hallelujah, an' a hallelujah") Negro spiritual.   JG
Hallelujah ("Hallelujah, hallelujah, hallelujah")   Round.   P. Hayes.   CSB 4
"Hallelujah, amen."   G. F. Händel. DSC
"Hallelujah, an' a hallelujah."   See Hallelujah (Negro spiritual)
Hallelujah chorus.   G. F. Händel. MFS
Hallelujah.   TFG
The hallelujah Christian.   Mountain spiritual from Tennessee.   RA
Hallelujah, I'm a bum.   Hobo song. [J. J. Husband]   SBA
"Hallelujah! King Jesus."   H. Johnson. JG
"Hallelujah to de Lamb, walking in de light."   See Walking in de light
"Hallelujah to the Lamb, Jesus died for eb'ry man."   See Fighting on! hallelujah
Halleluyah ("We are in tatters")   See Praised be the Lord
Halliday, Andrew
    Esmeralda (Levey)
Hällilaul.   See Wiegenlied (Esthonian folk song)
"Hallod e rózsám."   See "List to me, rosebud"
"Halloo, hello, and what do you know." See Round 'em up for dear old Baylor (Grove)
Halpine, Charles Graham
    We've drunk from the same canteen (Clark)
"Halt! there! who goes there."   See Man of Alcala (Bizet)
Halte-là, qui va là.   For English translation see Man of Alcala (Bizet)
"Hamavdil."   Jewish folk song.   y. SY
Hamburg (Mason)   See "God of the strong, God of the weak"; "O life that maketh all things new"
"Hame, hame, hame" (Daheim, daheim, daheim)   Jacobite air.   [Words by A. Cunningham]   e.g.   ML 1
Hamerling, Robert
    Viel träume (Henschel)
Hamilton, E. H.
    "O Davidson" (Shields)
Hamilton, Elizabeth
    My ain fireside (Scottish air)

Hamilton, James Shelley
Lord Geoffrey Amherst
"Oh, let us sing of Idaho" (same air as Lord Geoffrey Amherst)

Hamilton, John
Up in the morning early (Scottish air)
[Hamilton's song] Carissima. Hamilton college song. AI—AIS

Hamlet, prince of Denmark. College song. SRW

Hammack, Daniel Stewart
Hail to Occidental (Thomson)

"The hammer keeps a-ringin' on somebody's coffin." See Way over in the new buryin' groun'

Hammer man. Negro work song. SBA

The Hampshire mummers' Christmas carol. BET

"Han ser pa mig så spörgende." See Pigetanker (Winge)

Hanby, Benjamin Russel
Darling Nelly Gray
Old Shady

Händel, Georg Friedrich
All danger disdaining (from Deborah)
"Angels, ever bright and fair" (from Theodora)
Antioch. See "Joy to the world"
Arm, arm, ye brave (from Judas Maccabaeus)
"Awake, my soul, stretch every nerve" (same air as "While shepherds watched their flocks")
"Awful, pleasing being, say" (from Joshua)
"Beauty lately." See Questo é il cielo
"But who may abide the day of His coming" (from The Messiah)
Call forth thy powers (from Judas Maccabaeus)
Chandos anthem. See "Righteousness and equity"
Christmas. See "Awake, my soul, stretch every nerve"; "While shepherds watched their flocks"
"Come, ever smiling liberty" (from Judas Maccabaeus)
"Come, see where golden-hearted spring"
Come unto Him, all ye that labor, come unto Him (from The Messiah)
Comfort ye my people (from The Messiah)
"Deeper, and deeper still, thy goodness, child" (from Jephtha)
"The enemy said" (from Israel in Egypt)
Every valley shall be exalted (from The Messiah)
Farewell, ye limpid springs and floods (from Jephtha)
"Father in heaven, O guide Thy servant." See "Lascia ch'io pianga"
Father of heav'n! from Thy eternal throne (from Judas Maccabaeus)
"For ever blessed" (from Jephtha)
From mighty kings (from Judas Maccabaeus)

"Hallelujah, amen" (from Judas Maccabaeus)
Hallelujah chorus (from The Messiah)
He shall feed His flock (from The Messiah)
He was despised and rejected (from The Messiah)
"Heroes, when with glory burning" (from Joshua)
"Honour and arms" (from Samson)
"How beautiful are the feet of them" (from The Messiah)
How vain is man who boasts in fight (from Judas Maccabaeus)
"How willing my paternal love" (from Samson)
"I know that my Redeemer liveth" (from The Messiah)
"I love Thy kingdom, Lord"
"In gentle murmurs will I mourn" (from Jephtha)
In the battle, fame pursuing (from Deborah)
"It must be so" (from Jephtha)
"Joy to the world"
Largo (with words "Father in heav'n, Thy children hear")
Lascia ch'io pianga (from Rinaldo)
"Lass mich mit tränen" (from Rinaldo)
"Leave me to languish." See Lascia ch'io pianga
"Let the bright Seraphim" (from Samson)
"Let us take the road" (from Rinaldo)
"Lord, to Thee, each night and day" (from Theodora)
The Lord worketh wonders (from Judas Maccabaeus)
"O, had I Jubal's lyre" (from Joshua)
"O Lord! correct me"
"O Lord, Whose mercies numberless" (from Saul)
O sleep, why dost thou leave me (from Semele)
"O Thou that tellest good tidings to Zion" (from The Messiah)
"The people that walked in darkness" (from The Messiah)
"Pious orgies, pious airs" (from Judas Maccabaeus)
"Pour forth no more unheeded prayers" (from Jephtha)
Quando mai spietata sorte (from Radamisto)
Questo é il cielo
Rejoice greatly, O daughter of Zion (from The Messiah)
Return, oh God of hosts (from Samson)
"Righteousness and equity"
St Thomas. See "I love Thy kingdom, Lord"
"See, the conquering hero comes" (from Judas Maccabaeus)
See the raging flames arise (from Joshua)
"Shall I in Mamre's fertile plain" (from Joshua)
Sin not, oh king (from Saul)
Sing songs of praise (from Esther)

Händel, Georg Friedrich—*Continued*
So shall the lute and harp awake (from Judas Maccabaeus)
Tears, such as tender fathers shed (from Deborah)
Thou shalt break them with a rod of iron (from The Messiah)
"Thou shalt bring them in" (from Israel in Egypt)
"Thus saith the Lord, the Lord of hosts" (from the Messiah)
Thus saith the Lord to Cyrus (from Belshazzar)
"Thus when the sun" (from Samson)
Thy glorious deeds inspir'd my tongue (from Samson)
"Total eclipse! no sun, no moon" (from Samson)
"The trumpet shall sound" (from The Messiah)
"Trust in the Lord"
"Up the dreadful steep" (from Jephtha)
"Waft her, angels, through the skies" (from Jephtha)
"What though I trace each herb and flower" (from Solomon)
"When my eyes." See Quando mai spietata sorte
"When war-like ensigns wave on high" (from The occasional oratorio)
"Where'er you walk" (from Semele)
"While shepherds watched their flocks"
"Why do the nations so furiously rage together" (from The Messiah)
"Why does the God of Israel sleep" (from Samson)
Wise men flatt'ring may deceive you (from Judas Maccabaeus)
The **handicap** march.   G. Rosey.   Words by D. Reed.   OTG
"A **handsome** noble looking man came walking down the street."   See Fallen by the wayside (Harris)
Handsome Sally.   Folk song: North Carolina version.   SES 2
The **handsome** young airman.   British song of the European war.   [C. Coote]   SBA
"A handsome young airman" (The dying aviator)   DSO
Handwerksburschen-abschied ("Es, es, es und es") Volkslied.   g.   EDL
Handy, Lucile Marie
Añoranzas.   See Deep river blues
Deep river blues
Handy, Will, pseud.   See Cole, Robert A.
Handy, William Christopher
Blue gummed blues
The Chicago gouge
Friendless blues
The gouge of Armour avenue
Harlem blues
The hesitating blues
Joe Turner blues: folk air arranged
John Henry blues
Long gone
Loveless love

St Louis blues
Weary traveler: negro spiritual arranged
Handy, William Christopher, and Elman, Dave
Composers
Atlanta blues
Make me one pallet on your floor.   See Atlanta blues
Authors
Blue gummed blues (Handy)
Handy, my girls, so handy.   See "So handy, my girls"
Haney, Paul
Maroon and white (Wamsley)
Hang up de fiddle and de bow.   See Uncle Ned (Foster)
Hanging Johnnie ("They call me Hanging Johnnie")   Halliard   chantey.   SBS
For variants see following songs of same title; also Singin' Johnny
Hanging Johnny ("Oh they call me Hanging Johnny")   Halliard   chantey.   TSB 1
Hanging Johnny ("O! they call me Hanging Johnny")   Halliard   chantey.   WSE
Hanging out the linen clothes.   Folk song: California version.   SBA
Variant of: Driving away at the smoothing iron
Hangman ("Hangman, hangman, slack up on your rope")   Folk song.   SBA
Variants: The hangman's song; The maid freed from the gallows
"**Hangman**, hangman, hold your rope."   See The maid freed from the gallows (Barbourville, Ky. version; Woodridge, Va. version)
"**Hangman**, hangman, slack up on your rope."   See Hangman
"**Hangman**, hangman, spare my life."   See The maid freed from the gallows (Mount Fair, Va. version)
The **hangman's** song (see Song Index)
Variants: Hangman; The maid freed from the gallows
"**Hangsman**, hangsman, slack your rope."   See The maid freed from the gallows (Villamont, Va. version)
Hanitsch, Georg Friedrich
Bundeslied
"**Hanka**, du bist meine."   See Liebeseinigung
"**Hanka**, ty sy mója."   See Liebeseinigung
"**Hans** die rosse tränkte" ("Jasio konie poił")   Polish folk song.   g.p.   ML 3
Hans und Liesel ("Und der Hans schleicht umher")   F. von Woyna (music and words)   g.   EDL
"**Hänschen** sass im stübchen."   See Vanya
"**Hänschen**, willst du fliehen."   See "Jack, where are you going"
Hansen, Niels Ebbesen
The yellow and blue (Haynes)

The **hapless** bride. See Interrupted slumber

Hapless Silva, whilst thou believing. See Infelice! e tu credevi (Verdi)

"**Happy** and light." M. W. Balfe. MFS

Happy are we! good our portion. See All in accord

"**Happy** are we tonight." P. Greely. Author of words unknown. TFO

"**Happy** are we to-night." M. S. Pike. Author of words unknown. MFS

ɩ**Happy** as a big sunflowerɩ The big sunflower. Old American song. <B. Emerson> PSG—WSS

"**Happy** birds." Waltz song. E. Holst. Words by C. T. Steele. BST

"**Happy** Christmas morning, sing your sweetest song." French Noël. e. FC

"**Happy** girls are we." O. Straus. e. WLO

The **happy-go-lucky** one. See La realera (Rocha)

Happy in eternity. Mountain spiritual. RA

The **happy** lover. Old English song. WOE

Happy May, blithesome May. See Polish May song

Happy morning. Negro spiritual from South Carolina. AS

"**Happy** my life was shining." See "Bella e di sol vestita" (Donizetti)

Harbour, Homer H.
Autumn song (Bohemian folk air)
"Caterpillar! caterpillar" (Russian folk air)
Christmas eve (German air)
Cloud-ships (Tyrolese folk air)
Columbus day (Italian air)
The dryad and the sunbeam (Russian air)
The echo (Carinthian air)
An evening song (Lithuanian air)
"Fair are these fields" (French air)
The flag going by (German folk air)
In memoriam (Bohemian folk air)
It snows in the night (Slavonic folk air)
Lincoln's birthday (Dutch folk air)
The little goatherd (Swedish air)
Lullaby (Finnish Rune air)
On a summer day (French folk air)
"On Easter day" (Old air)
The pine tree swing (German folk air)
Valentines (Old English air)
When fields are white (German folk air)
"Winter, goodbye! blue is the sky" (German folk air)
See also entries in Song Index under pseuds. Erwin, John; Irwin, John; as well as under real name

Hard crackers. ɩS. C. Fosterɩ DSO

Hard times, come again no more. S. C. Foster (music and words) BB —PSG—WSS
Hard times. MFS

Hard trials ("De fox hab hole in de ground") Negro spiritual. HRD —WSS

Harding, John P.
"Brightest and best"
Morning star. See "Brightest and best"

Harding's defeat. Folk song from Virginia. SES 2

Hare and hunter ("As the moon shone") MFS

Harel, Paul
Les larmes (Godard)

Hargitt, Charles John
God is love. See "O salutaris Hostia"
"O salutaris Hostia"

Häring, Georg Wilhelm Heinrich. See Alexis, Wilibald, pseud.

Harington, Henry. See Harrington, Henry

"**Hark** from the clouds a joyful sound." Old carol. DNS

"**Hark**! hark! how all things in one sound rejoice." H. Purcell. GA

"**Hark**! hark! my soul" (Angelic songs are swelling) J. M. Armstrong. Words by F. W. Faber. MFS

"**Hark**! hark! my soul" (Pilgrims) J. B. Dykes. Words by F. W. Faber. LAS

Hark! hark! the angels whisper. See "Softly o'er the rippling waters" (Thomas)

"**Hark**! hark! the lark." F. Schubert. Words by W. Shakespeare. DSB— EB

"**Hark**, hark, the peal of clarions calling." C. J. Rouget de Lisle. Words by C. S. Smith. LAS

"**Hark**! hark! what I tell to thee." See Des geistes gesang (Haydn)

"**Hark**, hark, what news the angels bring." See Glad tidings

"**Hark**! hear the hosts of heaven sing." See "I heard the voice of Jesus say" (Perry)

"**Hark**, how still the darkling wood has grown." See Stille sicherheit (Franz)

Hark, how the sailor's cry joyously echoes nigh. See Santa Lucia

"**Hark**! I hear a voice." BB—TFR

"**Hark**! I hear an angel sing." R. G. Shrival. Words by W. C. Baker. GOS 1—MFS

"**Hark**! I hear the foe advancing." See Rhyfelgyrch gwyr Harlech

"**Hark**! listen to the trumpeters." See The enlisted soldiers

"**Hark**! now the drums beat up again." See Over the hills and far away

"**Hark**! ten thousand" (St Oswald) J. B. Dykes. Words by T. Kelly. BB

"**Hark**! the bell is ringing." See The bell is ringing (Silcher)

"**Hark**! the bells from the ivy'd tow'r." See Eternal rest (Piccolomini)

"**Hark**! the bonny Christ church bells." Round. Aldrich. BOS 2

Hark! the fiddle's merry sound. See "Come away and join the dance"

"Hark! the glad sound." T. Jarman. Words by P. Doddridge. DN

"Hark! the herald angels sing." Mendelssohn. Words by C. Wesley. BB—DN—GSS—MFS—TFP—TFR

"Hark the mavis' ev'nin' sang." See Ca' the yowes to the knowes

"Hark the merry bells thro' the valley ringing." See O star, lovely star

"Hark! the sound of Tar-Heel voices." University of North Carolina song. AI—KU

"Hark! the summons." Old Welsh air. Traditional words. DSB—DSC

"Hark, the tiny cowslip bell." 17th century English song. DSB

"Hark! the vesper hymn is stealing." See Vesper hymn (Bortniānskiĭ)

"Hark! 'tis the angelus! sweetly ringing." See Ring on, sweet angelus (Gounod)

"Hark to the chimes" (Grace) GSS

"Hark! to the sound of the distant drum." See The distant drum

[Hark, what mean those holy voices] "O hark! what mean those holy voices." French Noël air. [Words by J. Cawood] FC

"Hark! what mean those holy voices." Old Latin air: O sanctissima. Words by J. Cawood. DN

"Hark! what mystic sounds are those." See Mermaid's evening song (Glover)

Harker, Russell Pritchard
Indiana, our Indiana (Harker and King)

Harker, Russell Pritchard, and King, K. L.
Indiana, our Indiana

Harlem blues. W. C. Handy. HB

Harm Link. Folk song from Tennessee. SES 2

Harmiaveden rantaa. See Am Harmiavesi

"The harp that once through Tara's halls." Air: Gramachree, or, Molly astore. Words by T. Moore. BB—DSB—GOS 1—HMI—LAS—MBS—SSB
Tara's harp. MFS

Harrigan, Edward
The gallant 69th (Braham)
Major Gilfeather (Braham)
Mulligan guards (Braham)
Paddy Duffy's cart (Braham)
The Skidmore fancy ball (Braham)

Harrington, Henry
Colorado halls (same air as "Drink to me only with thine eyes"; attributed)
"Drink to me only with thine eyes" (attributed)
Gaping catch
"Look, neighbours, look"
"'Tis hum-drum." See Gaping catch
"Trinke mir nur mit blicken zu." See "Drink to me only with thine eyes" (attributed)

Harrington, Leigh W.
Look at the ears on him

Harris, C. S.
The panther

Harris, Charles Kassell
After the ball
Always in the way
The best thing in life
Break the news to mother
Fallen by the wayside
For old time's sake
For sale—a baby
Hello, central, give me heaven
In the city where nobody cares
Is life worth living
Just behind the times
There'll come a time
Why don't they play with me

Harris, Hazel Harper
Oleander time (Repper)

Harrison, Annie Fortesque
"In the gloaming, oh, my darling"

Harry Gray (Macafee's confession) Folk song: Alleghany, N.C. version. SES 2
—Marion, N.C. version. SES 2
—Nash, Va. version. SES 2
—White Rock, Va. version. SES 2

Hart, A.
A little more cider too

Hart, Joseph
Keep dem golden gates wide open
"The hart he loves the high wood." See The four loves

Harte, Bret
The jolly Switzer (Swiss air)

Hartman, J. E.
Heidelberg (Power)

Hartmann, Johan Peter Emilius
"King Christian." See "Kong Christian stod ved høien mast": old air arranged
"Kong Christian stod ved høien mast": old air arranged

Hartmann, Ludwig
Schwanenlied
Swan-song. See Schwanenlied

Harvardiana. Harvard university song. R. G. Williams and S. B. Steel (music and words) AI—AIS—LAS

Harvest home ("Oh, come to the field") Old air. Words by P. Hastings. TFG

Harvest home ("Our oats they are hoed") H. Purcell. Words by J. Dryden. BOS 2

Harvey, Charles
Twilight music (Loomis)

Harvey, David
Li'l Liza Jane (Old southern air)
"Spin, maiden, spin, the golden thread twine in" (Fischer)

Harvey, W. B.
"No one to love"

Has anybody here seen Kelly. C. W. Murphy and W. Letters. Words by W. J. McKenna. GFS

"Has anybody here seen my Lord." Negro spiritual from Tennessee. FSN

"Has sorrow thy young days shaded." Irish air: Sly Patrick, arr by J. A. Stevenson. Words by T. Moore. DSB—DSC—GOS 1—HMI—SI

Haseman, Charles
"Nevada, my Nevada"

Hasse, Johann Adolf
"Be Thou my helper"
"God's right hand doth wield the thunder"
Loving Jesu, Thou hast sought me
No sorrow like to His
Oh, mine offences cry to heaven
"Though the rocks in twain be riven"

Hassler, Hans Leo von
"In heavenly love abiding"

"Hast, hast, hast, bäuerlein" ("Máš, máš, máš, sedláčku") Czech folk song. bo.g. ML 3

Hast thou no feeling, to see me kneeling. See Love's chidings

"Haste and plunge in joy and pleasure." See "Va sbramando quegli ardori" (Spohr)

"Haste thee, nymph." Round. S. Arnold. Words by J. Milton. CSB 2 —DSB—TFG

Hastings, Horace Lorenzo
"Shall we meet beyond the river" (Rice)

Hastings, Paul, pseud. See Stevens, David

Hastings, Thomas
Fourth of July hymn
"Hail to the brightness"
"A little word in kindness said" (same air as Fourth of July hymn)
Ortonville. See Fourth of July hymn; "A little word in kindness said"

Hatcher, Charles M.
Colors of Washington

Hats off to the band. University of Maine song. J. A. McCusker (music and words) AIS

"Hatt' ein liebchen einst erwählt." See "Once I lov'd a maiden fair"

"Hatte einst ein täubchen." See A fair dove

"Hatten mich schon aufgegeben" ("Povedali, že som umrel") Slovak folk song. g.sl. ML 3

Hatton, John
Duke street. See God be with us; "Lord of all being"; "These things shall be! a loftier race"
God be with us
"Lord of all being" (same air as God be with us)
"O God, beneath Thy guiding hand." See God be with us
"These things shall be! a loftier race" (same air as God be with us)

Hatton, John Liptrot
"Bid me to live"
Blow, bugle, blow
Bugle song. See Blow, bugle, blow
The maiden's rose
So the story goes. See The maiden's rose
To Anthea. See "Bid me to live"
"When evening's twilight gathers round"

Hauff, Wilhelm
Reiters morgenlied (Folk air)
"Steh' ich in finstrer mitternacht" (Volksweise)

Haukohl, Robert G.
Marquette fight song

Haul away, Jo ("Away, haul away, O haul away together") Short drag chantey. WSE
For variants see following songs of same title

Haul away, Joe ("Way, haul away, we'll haul away the bowlin'") Fore-sheet or sweating-up chantey. TSB 2

Haul away, Joe ("Way, haul away, we'll haul away the bowlin'") Short drag chantey. BOS 2—TSB 1

"Haul! haul! araul ei rudd." See Codiad yr haul

"Haul on the bowlin'." Short-haul chantey. BB
For variants see following songs of similar title

"Haul the bowline." Short drag chantey. GSS

[**Haul** the bowline] "We'll haul the bowlin'." Capstan chantey. TSB 1

Hauptmann, Moritz
"Oh, how sweet, how sweet is our singing"
"Roses we bring"

"Have compassion upon a soul departing." See "Ah! I have sighed to rest me" (Verdi)

"Have you any work for the tinker, mistress." See The tinker

"Have you got good religion." See Cert'n'y, Lord

"Have yo' heard about dat bully." See The bully song (Trevathan)

Have you heard of a frolicsome ditty. See "How happy could I be with either"

"Have you heard the waters singing as they go." See Nature's music (Edmunds)

"Have you seen but a white lily grow." English air. [Words by B. Jonson] GA

Havergal, Frances Ridley
"Take my life and let it be consecrated, Lord, to Thee" (music by Jude; Schnecker)

Haweis, Thomas
"O Thou from Whom all goodness flows" (Rossini)

Hawg foot. American mountain song. RA

Hawker, Robert Stephen
Song of the western men (Old Cornish air; also music by Slater)

Hawks, Mrs Annie Sherwood
"I need Thee every hour" (Lowry)

Hawley, Charles Beach
Ah! 'tis a dream
"Because I love you, dear"
Bedouin love-song

Hawthorne, Alice, pseud. See Winner, Septimus

Hay diddy ump, diddy iddy um day. See Sourwood mountain (Georgia version)

"Hay en tu risa de cristal." See Mirame así (Fuentes)

"Hay recuerdas que el tiempo no ha borrado." See Recuerdas

Hayden, Joe
   A hot time in the old town (Metz)

Hayden-Clarendon, J.
   When the evening breeze is sighing
   "Home, sweet home" (Solman)

Haydn, Franz Joseph
   Alma mater—University of North Dakota (same air as "Gott erhalte Franz den kaiser")
   "Alma mater"—University of Pittsburgh (same air as "Gott erhalte Franz den kaiser")
   Austrian hymn.   See Alma mater—University of North Dakota; Alma mater—University of Pittsburgh; Columbia, God preserve thee free; Deutschland über alles; "Love divine, all loves excelling"; "Praise the Lord, ye heav'ns, adore Him"
   "Beware! dearest comrades all"
   "Bind' auf dein haar."   See "My mother bids me bind my hair"
   Das böse weib (same air as Fester sinn)
   "Brightly, brightly gleam the sparkling rills" (from Die jahreszeiten)
   Columbia, God preserve thee free (same air as "Gott erhalte Franz den kaiser")
   "Come, my soul, thou must be waking"
   Creation.   See "Oh realm of light"; "The spacious firmament on high"
   Des geistes gesang
   Deutschland über alles (same air as "Gott erhalte Franz den kaiser")
   "Dost thou love me, sister Ruth."   See Sister Ruth
   Fester sinn
   "The heavens are telling the glory of God" (from Die schöpfung. Tr of Die himmel erzählen die ehre Gottes)
   "How wondrous and great"
   "In native worth and honour clad" (from Die schöpfung)
   "The jolly month of May"
   "Liebes mädchen, hör mir zu"
   "Love divine, all loves excelling" (same air as "Gott erhalte Franz den kaiser")
   "My mother bids me bind my hair"
   "Now heaven in fullest glory" (from Die schöpfung)
   "Now the end of all things neareth"
   "O love divine"
   "Oh realm of light"
   "On mighty pens uplifted soars" (from Die schöpfung)
   "Praise Jehovah, every nation"
   "Praise the Lord, ye heav'ns, adore Him" (same air as "Gott erhalte Franz den kaiser")
   "Rolling in foaming billows" (from Die schöpfung)
   "She never told her love"
   Singing in the rain
   Sister Ruth
   Soldiers' hymn
   "The spacious firmament on high" (same air as "Oh realm of light")

   The spirit's song.   See Des geistes gesang
   "Still for sinners interceding"
   "Thou alone art holy"
   "When darkness falls around me"
   "With verdure clad the fields appear" (from Die schöpfung. Tr of Nun beut die flur das frische grün)
   Yes and no

Haydn, Johann Michael
   Die heilige nacht (wrongly attributed) See Gruber, F.   Die heilige nacht
   Lyons.   See O come let us worship
   O come let us worship
   "O worship the King."   See O come let us worship

Hayes, Elliott W.
   Fight, Tufts, fight

Hayes, Philip
   Hallelujah

Hayes, William
   "Chairs to mend, old chairs to mend"
   Girl scout's round
   Oxford cries.   See "Chairs to mend, old chairs to mend"
   "The rose's age is but a day"
   The spring
   "Wind, gentle evergreen"

The haymakers' song.   See "Derrièr' chez nous il pousse une ente"

Haynes, F. J.
   The yellow and blue

Haynes, Walter Battison
   Good night.   See Gute nacht
   Gute nacht

Hays, Julia M.
   Good night, little girl, good night (Macy)

Hays, William Shakespeare
   Angels, meet me at de cross-roads
   Driven from home
   The little old cabin in the lane
   Mollie darling
   Oh! Sam
   Susan Jane
   "Take this letter to my mother"
   "We parted by the river side"
   You've been a friend to me

Hayseed.   Minstrel song.   SBA

"A hayseed one day to himself did say." See Hayseed

The hazel dell.   G. F. Root. GOS 2— KSO—WSS

"He built a platform in the air."   See He is King of kings

He came among us at Christmas tide. See Weihnachtswiegenlied

"He cometh not! the restless wind I heard."   See Beatrice (Holstein)

"He crept all alone by the wall."   See Verborg'ne liebe (Grieg)

"He deliver'd Daniel from the lion's den." See Didn't my Lord deliver Daniel

He done, he done, he done, he done his level best.   See He done his level best

He done his level best.   Old West Point song.   Air: Son of a gamboleer. DSO

He flies through the air with the greatest of ease. See The man on the flying trapeze

"He followed her up and he followed her down." See Lady Isabel and the elf knight (Dewey, Va. version; Endicott, Va. version)

He found it. D. Stevens. Words from the San Francisco Bulletin. TFB

"He gave to her a beaver hat." See The two sisters (Berea, Ky. version no. 2)

"He! hei! der Ungar schlägt zusammen seine hakken." See Tanzlied

"He is gane fra' his hearth." See John Anderson's gane (Bennett)

He is King of kings. Negro spiritual. HRD

"He kicked her, he choked her, as we understand." See Poor Omie (Big Laurel, N.C. version)

"He knew the world was round-o." See Colombo

"He led her through hedges and mire so deep." See The cruel ship's carpenter (Alleghany, N.C. version)

"He looked over his left shoulder." See Earl Brand (St Helen's Ky. version; Beechgrove, Va. version)

"He mounted her on a milk-white steed." See Earl Brand (Pine Mountain, Ky. version)

He never cares to wander from his own fireside. F. McGlennon (music and words) SMG

He never said a mumbelin' word. See Crucifixion

"He picked the snake up in his hand." See Springfield mountain (Callaway, Va. version)

"He play'd a spring the laird to please." See The piper of Dundee

"He promised he'd bring me a fairing to please me." See O dear, what can the matter be

"He promised he'd buy me a beautiful fairing." See O dear, what can the matter be

[He raise a poor Lazarus] "Oh, He raise-a poor Lazarus." Negro spiritual. HRD

"He requires the tender maiden." See "Il vecchietto cerca moglie" (Rossini)

"He rode up to her father's gate." See Earl Brand (Allanstand, N.C. version)

"He rode up to the old man's gate." See Earl Brand (Georgia version; Clay county, Ky. version; Hot Springs, N.C. version)

He rose, He rose, He rose from de dead. See Dust and ashes

He shall feed His flock. Handel. DSB —SSO 2
　　Also in Come unto Him, all ye that labor, come unto Him (Händel) CSS 1

"He shot it at that carrion crow." See The carrion crow (Big Laurel, N.C. version)

"He smiles within his cradle." See Ein kindlein in der wiegen

"He stole from its nest in my golden hair." See Tender and true, adieu (Knight)

He stole McCarthy's wife. See Little Johnny Dugan (Mack)

"He that dwelleth in heaven" (see Song Index)
　　Also in Thou shalt break them with a rod of iron (Händel) SSO 3

"He that keepeth Israel." A. Schlösser. ASA—CSS 1

"He, uch-la." See Volga boat song

"He was a Punchinello." See Punchinello (Molloy)

He was despised [and rejected] G. F. Händel. SSO 2

He was her man, but he done her wrong. See "Frankie and Albert"; "Frankie and Johnny"

He wears a penny flower in his coat. See Lardy dah (Page)

"He went to his sister's house." See The miller's apprentice (Barbourville, Ky. version no. 1)

"He who bonds of love shall seek to sever." See "Chi da' lacci d'amor" (Gagliano)

"He who is noble, kind in thought and action." See "Integer vitae" (Flemming)

He who kills with the sword. See El que a hierro mata

"He who made both heav'n and earth." See "Qui creavit coelum, lully, lully, lu"

"He will be our dearest Friend." See Run to Jesus

"He, zigeuner" ("Hej te cigány") Hungarian folk song. g.hu. ML 3

Health and strength. See "For health and strength"

"A health to all who gather here." See A toast (Stevens)

A health to Carolina. See Carolina coronata (Spilman)

Hear de angels singin'. Negro spiritual. HRD

Hear de lambs a-cryin'. See Hear the lambs a-crying

Hear dem bells. D. S. McCosh (music and words) SMG

Hear from heaven to-day. Old Negro spiritual from South Carolina. AS

"Hear! hear! hear me, O God." See Hymn to God the Father (Piatti)

"Hear my prayer." F. Mendelssohn-Bartholdy. Words by W. Bartholomew. ASA

"Hear my sighing." F. Durante. e. SSO 2

"Hear, oh Lord! Father of all." See Preghiera (Marchesi)

"Hear our call." Round. Mozart. Words by A. G. Latham. CSB 5

Hear our cry ("Sh'ma kolenu") Palestinean folk song. e.he. BNP

"Hear our prayer, O Lord, our God." See Hear our cry

"Hear sweet music softly saying I love you." See Waltz song (Lehar)

Hear the angels singing. See Hear de angels singin'

Hear the (de) lambs a-cryin'.   Negro spiritual.   HRD

"Hear the little bells that tinkle."   See The magpie and the little gypsy dancer (Zolotarev)

"Hear the lively song of the frogs in yonder pond."   See Frog round

Hear the sweet voice of the child.   See Come home, father (Work)

Hear them bells.   See Hear dem bells (McCosh)

"Hear us, hear us, O Lord."   See Hear us, O Lord (Pergolesi)

Hear us, O Lord.   Pergolesi.   e. SSO 2

"Hear ye, Israel! hear what the Lord speaketh."   F. Mendelssohn.   [Tr of Höre, Israel, höre des Herrn stimme]   e.   SSO 1

"Heard somebody mournin'."   See Blow, Gabriel

"Hearken, ye shepherds, great news do we bring."   See The angels and the shepherds

The hearse song.   Old American song. SBA

"The old gray hearse."   DSO

"The heart bowed down."   M. W. Balfe. BB—GOS 1—MFS

"Heart, my heart, cease thy glowing and burning."   See Resignation (Tchaikovsky)

"The heart of her."   C. W. Cadman. Words by N. R. Eberhart.   BST

Heart of oak.   W. Boyce.   Words by D. Garrick.   MBS

Hearts of oak.   SSB

"A heart that thou hast wounded."   See "Un cor da voi ferito" (Scarlatti)

"Heartless woman! couldst e'er consider." See "Sciagurata! hai tu creduto" (Verdi)

"Hearts and homes."   J. Blockley. [Words by C. Young]   MFS

Heart's-ease ("My heart's-ease I set in my garden to blow")   Austrian folk song. e.   DSB

Hearts of oak ("Come cheer up my lads") See Heart of oak (Boyce)

Heath, Lyman
    The grave of Bonaparte

"Heave away, heave away! I'd rather court a yellow gal."   Negro chantey.   AS —SBA

Heave away [my Johnny] ("As I walk'd out one fine morning")   Chantey. DSC
    For variant see following song of same title; also We're all bound to go

Heave away, my Johnny ("As I walked out one morning fine")   Chantey. TFB—TFG

Heav'n ("I got a song")   See All God's chillun got wings

Heaven bell a-ring ("My Lord, my Lord") Negro spiritual from South Carolina. AS

"Heav'n bell a-ring, I know de road." See Jesus sittin' on de waterside

The heaven bells ("O mother I believe") Negro spiritual from North Carolina. AS

Heav'n bells a-ringin' in mah soul ("Gwine away to see mah Jesus")   Negro spiritual from Kentucky.   FSN

"Heav'n! disclos'd I now see thy portal." See "Oh dischiuso è il firmamento" (Verdi)

Heav'n, heav'n.   See All God's chillun got wings

Heaven help the foes of Washington. See "Bow down to Washington" (Wilson)

Heaven is my home.   A. S. Sullivan. Words by T. R. Taylor.   MFS

"Heaven may to you grant pardon."   F. von Flotow.   [Tr of Himmel euch vergeben]   e.   WLO

Heaven will protect the working girl. A. B. Sloane.   Words by E. Smith. SRW

"Heav'nly Aida."   See Celeste Aida (Verdi)

"Heav'nly Father, ever lead us."   See "Lead us, heavenly Father, lead us"

"The heavens are telling His praise with devotion."   See Die ehre Gottes aus der natur (Beethoven)

"The heavens are telling Jehovah's glory." See Die ehre Gottes aus der natur (Beethoven)

"The heavens are telling the glory of God." F. J. Haydn.   [Tr of Die himmel erzählen die ehre Gottes]   e.   DSC —TFG

"Heav'ns leap for joy."   See Allégresse à la naissance du Sauveur

"The heavens resound."   See Die ehre Gottes aus der natur (Beethoven)

"Heavily wears the day."   German air. MFS

The heaving of the lead.   W. Shield. Words by W. Pearce.   CSB 4

Heav'n.   For entries beginning Heav'n see Heaven

Hebbel, Friedrich
    Gebet (Bruckler)

Hebe deine augen auf zu den bergen. For English translation see "Lift thine eyes, O lift thine eyes" (Mendelssohn)

Heber, Reginald
    "Brightest and best" (music by Harding; also unknown composer)
    "Holy, holy, holy! Lord God almighty" (Dykes)
    "I see them on their winding way" (Hime)
    "The Son of God goes forth to war" (Cutler)

Hedberg, Tor Harald
    "Liten prins i vaggan" (Sjögren)

Hedge roses.   See Heidenröslein (Schubert)

"Hei! auf grüner flur."   See The garland

"Hei! hei! hei! morgens in der frühe ging das mädchen aus."   See Das mädchen vom Amselfeld

"Hei hier ein hain" ("Hej! hore háj, dole háj")   Slovak folk song.   g.sl. ML 3

"Hei, Rákóczi, Bercsényi! Bezerédi! edler Ungarnhelden führer ihr." See Rakoczi- (Kurutzen-) lied II

"Hei, Rákóczi! hei, Bercsényi! führer ihr der helden Ungarns." See Rakoczi- (Kurutzen-) lied I

Heidelberg. Heidelberg university song. F. A. Power. Words by J. E. Hartman. AI

Heidenröslein ("Sah ein knab ein röslein stehn") Schubert. Words by W. von Goethe. g. EDL
Hedge roses. e. DSB
Heiden-röslein (Hedge-roses) e.g. GG

Heidenröslein ("Sah ein knab ein röslein stehn") H. Werner. Words by W. von Goethe. g. EDL
The two roses. e. BB—TFB

Heidenröslein. For English translation with a different air see The wild rose ("In the wood a boy one day")

Heidenstam, Verner von
Till bruden (Peterson-Berger)

Heidsieck, yes, Piper Heidsieck. See Give me the waltz (Pratt)

Heigh-ho! sing, heigh-ho! unto the green holly. See "Blow, blow, thou winter wind" (Stevens)

Heigh, Nelly! ho, Nelly! See "Nelly Bly" (Foster)

Heigho ("I love to sing the birth of spring") C. Repper. Words by S. Fay. TFO

"Heigho! heigho! heigho! loud are October's songs." See October

"Heigho! now from the eaves no sound is dripping." See A song of seasons

Heil euch, heil zum neuen jahre. See Sylvesterlied

Die heilige nacht ("Stille nacht") F. Gruber; wrongly attributed to M. Haydn. Words by J. Mohr. g. EDL
"Holy night! peaceful night." e. GSS
"Silent night." e. BB—DSB—DSC —FC—MBS—MFS—TFO—TFP — TFR

"Die heil'gen drei kön'ge aus morgenland" (The three holy kings) R. Glière. Words by H. Heine. e.g. ATS

"Heim, heim, daheim." See "Hame, hame, hame"

Heimatlos (Kodista vieroitettu) Finnish folk song. fi.g. ML 3

Heimkehr von der alm. See Hjemreise fra saetren

Heimliche grüsse ("O Irmingard") A. von Fielitz. Words by K. Stieler. e.g. GG

Heimliche liebe ("Kein feuer") Volkslied. g. EDL

Heimlicher liebe pein ("Mein schatz") C. M. von Weber. Volkslied. g. EDL
Heimlicher liebe pein (The pain of love) e.g. GA

Heine, Heinrich
Afsked (Melartin. Tr of Der scheidende sommer)
Ah! 'tis a dream (Hawley. Tr of Es war ein traum)
Am meer (Schubert)
"Anfangs wollt' ich fast verzagen" (Liszt)
Der Asra (Rubinstein)
"Auf flügeln des gesanges" (Mendelssohn)
"Aus meinen grossen schmerzen" (Franz)
Die beiden grenadiere (Schumann)
"Du bist wie eine blume" (music by Liszt; Rubinstein; Schumann)
Es war ein traum (Lassen. For music by Hawley see Ah! 'tis a dream)
"Ein fichtenbaum steht einsam" (Stenhammar)
"Die heil'gen drei kön'ge aus morgenland" (Glière)
"Ich grolle nicht" (Schumann)
"Ich wollt' meine lieb' ergösse" (Mendelssohn)
"Im wunderschönen monat mai" (Schumann)
"J'ai pleuré en rêve" (Huë. Tr of Ich hab' im traum geweinet)
"Lehn' deine wang' an meine wang'" (music by Jensen; Sjögren)
Die Lorelei (music by Liszt; Silcher)
Die lotosblume (Schumann)
"Mit deinen blauen augen" (Lassen)
"My songs are envenomed and bitter" (Borodin. Tr of Vergiftet sind meine lieder)
"Der schmetterling ist in die rose verliebt" (Franz)
"Sie liebten sich beide" (Stenhammar)
Warum (Tchaikovsky)

Heinrich, Anton Philipp
The musical bachelor

Heinrich der vogler. C. Loewe. Words by J. N. Vogl. g. EDL

"Heinrich lieb, du söhnlein mein." See Der vergiftete knabe

"Heir nor ois, main taer kind." See Nein mame, nein mitter

"Heirs of unending life" (Dennis) H. G. Nägeli. Words by Beddome. MFS

"Hej! haj! Magyar ember." See Tanzlied

"Hej! hore háj, dole háj." See "Hei! hier ein hain"

"Hej Rákóczi! hej Bercsényi! régi vitéz magyaroknak." See Rákóczi- (Kurutzen-) lied I

"Hej tam w polu." See "Dort im felde liegt ein see"

"Hej te cigány." See "He, zigeuner"

[Hela'r 'sgyvarnog] Hunting the hare. Old Welsh folk song. e. DSC

Helf, J. Fred
A picture no artist can paint

Hell, or the vengeance of God. See Puritan hymn

Hello, central, give me heaven. C. K. Harris (music and words) SW

"Hello central, what's the matter with this line." See The hesitating blues (Handy)

"Hello, girls." Folk song: Kentucky version. SBA
Variant: Kansas boys

"Hello! hello." Greeting song. GSS

"Hello! Peter! you're a friend of mine." See Greeting

"Hello speaker." French or German air: Twinkle, twinkle little star, attributed to W. Mozart. BB

A helluva engineer. Air: Son of a gambolier. DSO

Helmore, Thomas
Christmas carol

Helmund, Erik Meyer-. See Meyer-Helmund, Erik

Help me to pray. See Guide us with Thy heavenly light (Tosti)

Helston furry. See The Cornish May song ("Robin Hood and Little John")

The Helston furry dance. See Cornish May song ("Ye maids of Helston")

"Heman dubh" (Walklied) Hebridean song. ga.g. ML 1

"Heman schwarz, lass mich gehen." See "Heman dubh"

Hemans, Mrs Felicia Dorothea (Browne)
Evening song to the Virgin (Browne)
Landing of the Pilgrims (Browne)
The songs your fathers loved (Irish air)
Tyrolese evening hymn (Browne)

Hemingway, L. D.
Alma mater—Washington and Jefferson college (Thompson)

Hempel, Ludwig
Feuerlied

Hemy, Henry Frederick, and Walton, James George
"Faith of our fathers, living still"

The hen convention. Minstrel song. WSS

"Hence, ye visions of glory." Serini. e. SSO 3

Hendrickson, William D.
The Spanish cavalier

Die henne (The pet chicken) German folk song. e. CSB 1

Henry VIII, king of England
"Green grows the holly"
The holly and the ivy. See "Green grows the holly"

Henry, S. R.
Down in the old cherry orchard

Henry Martin ("There were three brothers."—Salt seas) Folk song: Sussex version. BET

Henschel, Georg
Full many a dream. See Viel träume
Morgen-hymne
Morning hymn. See Morgen-hymne
Viel träume

Henshaw, Arthur
"When the mists have rolled in splendor"

"Her bright eyes whose radiant gleaming." See Il balen del suo sorriso (Verdi)

Her bright smile haunts me still. W. T. Wrightson. Words by J. E. Carpenter. GOS 2—SW

"Her cheek is like some blooming red rose." Kentucky mountain song. MK
Variant of: The true lover's farewell

"Her eye so mildly beaming." See Ho-ro mo nighean donn, bhòidheach

Her eyes don't shine like diamonds (Three little lads love-story) D. Marion. GFS

"Her glances 'Yes' do promise." See Yes and no (Haydn)

Her heart with truth teeming. See Norah, the pride of Kildare (Parry)

Her hjemme (In der heimat) [Air: En liten gut ifraa Tistedal'n, or, A little lad down in Tistedale] Words by J. Olafsen. g.n. ML 1

"Herauf, herauf, du morgensonn'. See Cornish May song ("Ye maids of Helston")

"Heraus, heraus die klingen." See Morgenlied der schwarzen freischar

Herbeck, J.
"O maiden bright"

Die herbergsmagd. See La criada del hostal

Herbert, Annie
"When the mists" (Henshaw)

Herbert, George
"Come, my Way, my Truth, my Life" (Piggott)

Herbert, J. B.
"Away in a manger"
Luther's cradle hymn. See "Away in a manger"

Herbert, Mary
The corn song (Marks)

Herbststurm (Autumnal gale) E. Grieg. e.g. HCA

Herdsman's mountain home. See Der schweizerbue

Here a boar's head now bear I. See The boar's head carol

Here and there. A. B. Winch. Words by L. Hunt. CSS 2

"Here awa', there awa', here awa', Willie." See Wandering Willie

"Here awa', there awa', wandering Willie." See Wandering Willie

Here come three knights a-riding. Croatian air. Words by K. Davis. DSB

"Here comes Carolina." University of North Carolina song. AI—AIS

"Here comes Jumbo thro' the window." See Jumbo

"Here comes the army with hopes so high." See Dukke Lisse (Worsing)

"Here comes the team, boys, rise up each man." See Victory (Waite)

"Here cometh Rosalind, chasing the bee." See Rosalind

"Here I'm alone for awhile now." See O vecchio cor, che batti (Verdi)

"Here in my modest home." See "In questo semplice, modesto asilo" (Donizetti)

"Here in the forest, alone I wander." See "Alli en el bosque"

Here is my old cabin home. See The old cabin home (Paine)

"Here is the sorrow, the sighing." See Here and there (Winch)
"Here on earth is no abiding city." Pergolesi. e. SSO 2
Here tyu, tyu, tyu. See "See the little pretty maiden"
"Here under the leafy greenwood tree." See The greenwood tree (Nelson)
"Here we come a-carolling." See Christmas carolling song
"Here we come a-wassailing." Folk song. DSB
　　"Here we come a-wassailing" (Wassail song) FC—OB
　　"Here we come a-wassailing" (Wassail song) Yorkshire version. OB
　　"Here we come a-wassailing" (The Yorkshire wassail song) Yorkshire version. DNS
　　For variants see following song; also "Wassail, and wassail, all over the town" and songs of similar title
"Here we come a-wesseling" (The vessel-cup carol.—The west riding Yorkshire wassail song) Folk song: Yorkshire version. DNS
"Here we come with a toast and song." See Hail to old O. S. C. (Wilkins)
"Here we dwell in holiest bowers." See Love and the novice
Here we have Idaho. University of Idaho song. HW
"Here we sit a-spinning, spinning." See Spinning song
"Here we stand, hand in hand." Movement song. Air: Smiling May comes in play. KSO
"Here where spangled wildernesses." See Alma mater—Carnegie institute of technology (O'Brien)
"Here while the oxen kneel in joy." See The sleep of the Infant Jesus (Gevaert)
Hereford carol ("Come all you faithful Christians") See "Come all you faithful Christians that dwell here on earth"
Here's a health, bonnie Scotland, to thee. A. Lee. Words by H. W. Freeman. GS
Here's a health to ane I lo'e dear. Old air: Here's a health to them that's awa, hiney. Words by R. Burns. GS
"Here's a health to fair Scotland." See Here's a health, bonnie Scotland, to thee (Lee)
"Here's a health to the jolly blacksmith." See Twankydillo
"Here's a health to the king." See Down among the dead men
"Here's a health unto his majesty." J. Savile. MBS
"Here's a leaf out." See "Manca un foglio" (Rossini)
"Here's a song for the olive and the blue." See The olive and blue (Ten Hoor and Goldstein)
"Here's adieu to old Kentucky." See The rebel soldier (St Helen's, Ky. version)

"Here's cakes and wines for you, young man." See The trooper and the maid (Tennessee version)
"Here's to Bates, our alma mater dear." See Alma mater—Bates college (Davis)
"Here's to De Pauw" (March on down the field) De Pauw university song. KU
"Here's to Southern California." See Song of Troy (Kisco and Freed)
Here's to the colors of crimson-white. University of Alabama song. J. P. Ludebuehl. Words by V. H. Bell. KU—KV
Here's to the cruiser days gone by. See The old destroyer squadron
"Here's to the cruisers of the fleet." See The armored cruiser squadron
"Here's to the golden avalanche." See Roll on old avalanche (Johnston)
"Here's to the maiden of bashful fifteen." Air: Half Hanykin, arr by T. Linley. Words by Sheridan. MBS—SSB
"Here's to the man who wears the 'D'." Drake university song. AI—AIS—KU—KV
"Here's to the third artillery." See Third coast artillery march (Woodward)
"Here's to the year that's awa'." See The year that's awa'
"Here's your mother's cloak." See The Suffolk miracle (Big Laurel, N.C. version)
Here's your mule. Confederate song. DSO
Hering, Karl Gottlieb
　　Hobby-horse. See Das steckenpferd Das steckenpferd
Herloszsohn, Karl
　　Abschied (Abt)
"Heroes, when with glory burning." G. F. Händel. SSO 2
Hérold, Louis Joseph Ferdinand
　　"Guide me, O Thou great Jehovah"
"Herr, den ich tief im herzen trage." See Gebet (Hiller)
Herr Gott Abrahams. For English translation see "Lord God of Abraham" (Mendelssohn)
"Herr Heinrich sitzt am vogelherd." See Heinrich der vogler (Loewe)
Herr Jesu Christ, ich weiss gar wohl. See Wo gehest du hin (Bach)
"Herr Malbrough zieht zum kampfe." See "Malbrough s'en va-t-en guerre"
Herr Ole (Ritter Ole) Faeroe islands song. da.g. ML 1
"Herrgott mein! Vater mein." See Des leibeigenen klagelied
Herrick, Robert
　　"Bid me to live" (Hatton)
　　Candlemas eve (Old air)
　　"In numbers, and but these few" (Gibbs)
　　Passing by (music by Ford; Purcell)
　　"What sweeter music can we bring" (German air)
Herrick's carol. See "What sweeter music can we bring"

Herrick's ode.   See "In numbers, and but these few" (Gibbs)

Herrosee,
"Ich liebe dich, so wie du mich" (Beethoven)

Herwegh, Georg
Reiterlied (Lyra)

"**Herz,** mein herz, werde still und entsage." See Resignation (Tchaikovsky)

Herz und mund und that und leben ("Jesu, joy of man's desiring")   J. S. Bach. e.   DSC

He's a helluva, helluva, helluva, helluva, helluva engineer.   See A helluva engineer

He's a-shoutin' hallelujah fo' me.   See "Mah brudder's died an' gone to hebben"

He's gone away.   Folk song: North Carolina version.   SBA
Variant of: The true lover's farewell

He's owre the hills.   Scottish song.   GS

He's the lily of the valley.   Negro spiritual.   FSN—HRD—MFS—WSS

[He's the Lord of lords] Why, He's the Lord of lords.   Negro spiritual. HRD

"**He's** wrong who imagines that sorrows and dangers."   See "S'inganna chi crede" (Sarti)

Heseltine, Peter
"Adam lay ybounden"
Balulalow
Tyrley, tyrlow

The **hesitating** blues.   W. C. Handy (music and words)   HB

Hess, Cliff
Homesickness blues

Hetsch, Gustav
"Kom med sange og helst af dem" (Sinding)

L'heure exquise (The hour of dreaming) R. Hahn.   [Words by P. Verlaine] e.f.   TM

"**Heut** war im kirchdorf ich zum tanze." See Tanz im kirchdorfe

"**Heute** scheid' ich, morgen wandr' ich." See Soldaten-abschied (Fesca)

"**Heute** zech ich, morgen zech ich."   See Doïna Haiducului

Hevebe tawi.   See Cloud song

Hewitt, Horatio D.
Suffer little children to come unto me

Hewitt, James
The twin roses

Hewitt, James H.   See Hewitt, John Hill

Hewitt, John Hill
"All quiet along the Potomac to-night"
The knight of the raven black plume
The minstrel
The mountain bugle

Hewitt, Joseph Frederick, and **Osborn, Arthur Herbert**
Princeton cannon song march

Hewitt, Mrs Mary Elizabeth (Moore)
"Sleeping I dream'd, love" (Wallace)

Hewitt, Richard
Roslin castle (Old air)

Hey, Wilhelm
"Alle jahre wieder" (Silcher)

Hey, Betty Martin, tip toe fine.   Song of the War of 1812.   DSO
Hey Betty Martin.   Fragment.   SBA

Hey day de ling dum day.   See Sourwood mountain (Berea, Ky. version)

Hey derry down dey, sweet youth is for pleasure.   See "Sweet spring is advancing" (Bach)

"**Hey,** diddle, diddle."   Nursery song. BB

Hey diddy ump diddy iddy um day.   See Sourwood mountain (Georgia version)

Hey for Somersetshire.   See "In summer time when flowers do spring"

Hey git along, git along, Josey.   See Jim along Josey

Hey! ho! away we go donkey riding, donkey riding.   See Donkey riding

Hey, Johnnie Cope ("Cope sent a challenge")   See Johnnie Cope

Hey Rube.   See Si Hubbard

Hey, the bonnie, ho, the bonnie.   See The bonnie breast-knots (2d version)

Hey, the bonnie, how the bonnie.   See The bonnie breast-knots (1st version)

Hey, willow waly O.   See "Prithee, pretty maiden" (Sullivan)

Heyse, Paul Johann Ludwig
"Am Sonntag morgen" (Brahms)
"Murmelndes lüftchen, blüthenwind" (Jensen)

Hi diddle unkum.   See The tailor and the mouse

Hi! my stave, will ye strike now.   See The little cudgel

Hi-o, de boatman row.   See De boatman

"**Hi,** with a whirl like a top."   See Spinning-top

Hi yi hi yi yi.   See The warriors (Smith)

Hiawatha (His song to Minnehaha)   N. Moret (C. N. Daniels)   Words by J. O'Dea.   GFS

"**Hiawatha** was an Indian."   See Tammany (Edwards)

Hibbard, Angus Smith
Praise for peace (Flemming)

Hibbs, Louis Emerson
"The army's coming down the river" (Old air)

Hichens, Robert S.
The bird and the rose (Horrocks)

Hickey, Dorothy
Fairest of colleges (Composer unknown)

Hickson, William Edward
"O come, come away" (Composer unknown)

Hicks's farewell.   Folk song: Burnsville, N.C. version.   SES 2
—Micaville, N.C. version.   SES 2
—Spillcorn, N.C. version.   SES 2
—Buena Vista, Va. version.   SES 2
—Dewey, Va. version.   SES 2
—Montvale, Va. version.   SES 2

Hidden love.   See Verborg'ne liebe (Grieg)

Hide not Thyself from me.   D. Alberti. e.   SSO 2

Hiemer, Franz Karl
Wiegenlied (Weber)
Hier bin ich, hier bin ich. See Old black Joe (Foster)
"Hier ein hain, dort einer." See "Hei! hier ein hain"
"Hier hab' ich so manches liebe mal." See An der Weser (Pressel)
"Hier in des abends traulich ernster stille" (Freundschaft und liebe) F. F. Flemming. Words by C. Schulz. g. EDL
"Hier, mein junge, lass uns bleiben" "Schità, sehni, mums dsihwoti") Lettish folk song. g.le. ML 3
"Hier sind wir versammelt." See Ergo bibamus (Eberwein)
"Hier, sur le pont d'Avignon." See "Sur le pont d'Avignon" (Canadian version)
Hieronymus, Rex E.
Colorado halls (Harrington?)
Higgins, A. J.
Mabel Clare
Higgins, H. M.
The old musician and his harp
"High aloft they fly." See High! high! aloft (Leoncavallo)
High Barbaree ("There were two lofty ships") Sea song. US—WSE
"High-born and lovely maid." See The greeting (Gounod)
High Germany ("O Polly") Folk song: Somerset version. DSB
"High heav'n hath stoop'd to earth so lowly." See "Le ciel a visité la terre" (Gounod)
High! high! aloft (Ballatella) R. Leoncavallo. ⌊Tr of Hui! hui! stridon lassù⌋ e. WG
High, high, up she rises. See "What are you going to do with a drunken sailor"
"High let us swell our tuneful notes." Old Cornish air. Words by Doddridge. DN
The high moon. Breton folk air. Words by L. Warner. DSB
"High o'er the waters of Lake Champlain." See Vermont victorious (Furman, Sharples and Killick)
"High the Cossack's heart is bounding." See The Cossack's song (Grünbaum)
"High upon a lonely hill." See The wanderer
High yaw for the Melican man. See The war junk Tennessee
"The higher the plum-tree." Round. W. Lawes. GSS
"The higher up the cherry tree." Play-party game from North Carolina. SES 2
The Highland fling. Scottish dance air. Words by D. Stevens. TFR
"A Highland lad my love was born" (John Highlandman) Air: The white cockade. Words by R. Burns. GS
The Highland laddie. See Bonnie laddie, Highland laddie
Highland Mary ("Ye banks and braes") Air: Katherine Ogie, or, Lady Catherine Ogle. Words by R. Burns. GS

The **Highland** minstrel boy. J. Barnett. Words by H. S. van Dyk. GS
Hike, Notre Dame. University of Notre Dame song. J. J. Casasanta. Words by V. F. Fagan. AI—AIS
Hike song ("Strap your pack") ⌊T. A. Metz⌋ Words by G. Sherwood. GSS
Hike song of 1917 ("Yea, the doughboys up at break of day") West Point song. DSO
Hiking song ("In a jolly crowd we tramp along") Dutch folk air. Words by J. L. Vandevere. TFO
Hiking song ("We're ten miles from home") See Ten miles from home
The hiking song of the eighth infantry. U.S. army song. T. Morales. Words by R. J. Burt. DSO
Hilariter. See Die ganze welt, Herr Jesu Christ
Hildach, Frau Anna (Schubert)
Im volkston (Hildach, E.)
Hildach, Eugen
Im volkston
Little fidget. See Strampelchen
Strampelchen
Hiljainen kaupunki. See The silent city (Sibelius)
Hill, Joe. See Hillstrom, Joseph
Hill, Mildred J.
"Good morning to you"
Hill, Patty Smith
"Good morning to you" (Hill, M. J.)
Hille, Earl Ward
The black and the gold
Our Colorado
Hiller, Ferdinand
Be near me still. See Gebet
Be Thou with me. See Gebet
Gebet
"Lord, on Thy tender love relying." See Gebet
Prayer. See Gebet
Hiller, R. H.
Alma mater—Wittenberg college
"The hill's a-gleam tonight." See An old-time celebration (Newton)
"The hills and forests are dark'ning." See Gute nacht (Franz)
Hillstrom, Joseph
The preacher and the slave (Webster)
Hilo, John Brown. See Stand to your ground
Hilo somebody. Halliard chantey. TSB 1
Hilonday. Halliard chantey. TSB 2
Variants: Boney; "Boney was a warrior"
Hilton, John
Come, follow me
Hime, B.
The beautiful day
"I see them on their winding way"
Himmel, Friedrich Heinrich
The battle prayer. See Gebet während der schlacht
Der rose sendung
Ewiger wechsel
Gebet während der schlacht
"Love thy mother, little one" (same air as Der rose sendung)

Die **himmel** erzählen die ehre Gottes. For English translation see "The heavens are telling the glory of God" (Haydn)

Himmel euch vergeben. For English translation see "Heaven may to you grant pardon" (Flotow)

"Die **himmel** rühmen des Ewigen ehre." See Die ehre Gottes aus der natur (Beethoven)

Hinaus auf die see. See Een liedje van der zee

"**Hinaus** in die ferne." See Gesang ausziehender krieger (Methfessel)

Hincke, John Ismert
Third coast artillery march (Woodward)

"**Hindraško**, ty synko mój." See Der vergiftete knabe

"**Hineh** mah tov." See "How good and beautiful"

The **hinges** are of leather. See The little old sod shanty

Hinkson, Mrs Katherine (Tynan)
"Would God I were the tender apple blossom" (Irish air)

Hinky dinky, parley-voo ("O mademoiselle") Song of the European war. DSO

Hinky dinky, parlee-voo. SBA

Hinky dinky, parley-voo ("The Pretoria passed a ship today") Post-war stanzas. DSO

Hip, hip, hip, for old Swarthmore. Swarthmore college song. H. L. Brown (music and words) AI—AIS

Hiraeth (Longing) Old Welsh song. e.w. WO

Hirsh, Allan Mortimer
Boola song

Der **hirt** ("Foaie verde trei cicori, măi") See Ciobănaş dela miori

Der **hirt** auf dem felsen (The shepherd on the rock) F. Schubert. Words after W. Müller. e.g. DCA

Hirten-lockruf ("Ptrui lemmikkin', ptrui ruskoni") Finnish folk song. fi.g. ML 3

Hirtenlied ("Disul vintin aba zaviz") See Ann hollaika

Hirtenweise ("Io de' sospiri te ne rimanno tanti") See Canto del pastroe

"**His** manly whisker swept her cheek." See Kissing on the sly (King)

"**His** salvation is nigh them that fear Him." S. Bennett. ASA

"**His** sword blade gleams and his eye-light beams." See Mad Anthony Wayne

Historia von Noah. See Noah (Reissiger)

De **history** ob de world. See Walk in the parlour

"**Hit** the line for Wittenberg." Wittenberg college song. AI

"**Hither!** hither! O come hither." See Osme's song

"**Hither** now, gather all." See Mid-servants' chorus (Flotow)

"**Hit's** the ole ship o' Zion." See The ole ship o' Zion

Hiyi, toho! hiyi, toho. See Round 'em up for dear old Baylor (Grove)

Hjemreise fra saeteren (Heimkehr von der alm) Norse folk song. Words by E. Storm. g.n. ML 1

"**Hm,** hm, my Lord! hm, po' mourner's got a home at las'." See Po' mourner's got a home at las'

Hm, mos' done toilin' here, O, bretheren. See Mos' done toilin' here

"**Ho!** a cheer for green and yellow." See Yellow and green (Putnam)

Ho a um day. See Sourwood mountain (Manchester, Ky. version)

"**Ho,** boys, ho! for California, O." See The banks of Sacramento

"**Ho!** broder Teague, dost hear de decree." See Lilliburlero (Purcell)

Ho-dee-ing-dong-doodle allay day. See Sourwood mountain (Kentucky version)

Ho-dee-ink-tum-diddle-ah-dee-day. See "I got a gal at the head of the holler"

"**Ho!** every sleeper waken." Round. TFP

Ho! for Lou'siana! I'm bound to leave this town. See "The Glendy Burke" (Foster)

"**Ho!** hey! here's another load." See Market song

"**Ho,** ho, ho! here come three knights a-riding." See Here come three knights a-riding

"**Ho!** ho! ho! ho! ho! high the Cossack's heart is bounding." See The Cossack's song (Grünbaum)

Ho! ho! ho! p'tit bonnet tout rond. See "Mon pèr' m'a fait bâtir maison"

Ho, ho, ho! who wouldn't go. See "Up on the house-top" (Christmas song)

"**Ho,** ho, vacation days are here." See Vacation days are here (Johnson)

Ho-la dri-jo-ri. See "In Gorensko"

"**Ho** la la! hear the voices 'neath the windows singing." See Sunny Spain

Ho-ro mo nighean donn, bhòidheach (Horo, my nut brown maiden) Old Highland song. e. CSB 1

Ho-ro, my island dear. See Moladh na landaidh

"**Ho,** sleepers arise! the sun's in the skies." See Sleepers, arise

Hoare, Florence
Basque lullaby (Folk air)
From the hills (Basque air)
"Pipe us the songs of freedom" (Basque air)

Hoare, Prince
The Arethusa (Old air)

Hob y derri dando. See "I'm a shepherd born to sorrow"

Hobby-horse. See Das steckenpferd (Hering)

Hobellied ("Da streiten sich die leut' herum") K. Kreutzer. Words by F. Raimund. g. EDL

The **hobo** blues. See I've been all around the world

The **hobo's** lament. See I've been all around the world

"Hoch dort im norden ein eiland."   See "Yderst mod norden"

"Höcher, besser."   See My youngest one is wedded

Der Hochlandbursche.   See Bonnie laddie, Highland laddie

Hochzeitslied ("Abschiedstunde schlägt dem feste")   See Dank der gäste

Hochzeitslied ("Der kuckuck auf dem zaune sass")   Westfälisches volkslied.   g. EDL

Hochzeitslied ("Sei nicht böse")   See "Sei nicht böse, mein lieb väterlein"

Hoffman, Dave, and Neale, Arthur
Florida blues

Hoffmann von Fallersleben, August Heinrich
Der abendstern (Schumann)
Deutschland über alles (Haydn)
Nur in Deutschland (Lyra)
Der weihnachtsmann (Volksweise)
Winters abschied (Volksweise)

Hoffnung ("Wenn die rosen blühen."—"In the time of roses")   Reichardt. e.g.   GG
"In the time of roses."   e.   BB—TFP
"In the time of roses" ("Wenn die rosen bluhen")   e.g.   BST

Hog-eye ("Hog-eye gal am a debbil of a gal")   South Carolina negro song. SBA
Variant: The hog-eye man

"Hog-eye gal am a debbil of a gal."   See Hog-eye

The hog-eye man ("Oh! go fetch me down my riding cane")   Capstan chantey.   WSE
For variants see following songs of same or similar title; also Hog-eye; Hog's-eye man

The hog-eye man ("O, the hog-eye men are all the go")   Capstan chantey.   SBA

The hog-eyed man ("Sal in the garden was sifting sand")   Folk song from Kentucky.   SES 2

Hog foot.   See Hawg foot

Hogan,
"Good morning, Mr Zip-zip-zip" (attributed)   See Lloyd, R.   "Good morning, Mr Zip-zip-zip"

Hogan, Michael
Draherin o machree (Irish air)

Høgen (The eagle)   C. Nielsen.   Words by J. Aakjaer.   da.e.   WM 2

Hogg, James
Allister MacAllister (Scottish air)
Auld Joe Nicolson's bonnie Nannie (Scottish air)
"Cam' ye by Athol, lad wi' the philabeg" (Gow)
"Come boat me o'er, come, row me o'er" (Jacobite air)
Come o'er the stream, Charlie (Scottish air)
"I downa laugh, I downa sing" (Scottish air)
"My love she's but a lassie yet, a lightsome, lovely lassie yet" (Scottish air)
When the kye come hame (Scottish air)

"A hogger on his death-bed lay."   See The dying hogger

The hog's-eye man ("Oh, the hog's-eye man is the man for me")   Windlass and capstan chantey.   TSB 1
Variant of: The hog-eye man

"Die höh'n und wälder schon steigen."   See Gute nacht (Franz)

"Hoi, hoi, yfe'fiyo."   See Oh, beauty, beauty

Hol' de win' don't let it blow.   Negro spiritual.   JB 2

Hold on.   Mountain spiritual from Kentucky.   SES 2

Hold out to the end.   Negro spiritual from Georgia.   AS

Hold the line, hold the line.   See Field song (Woodworth)

Hold the wind don't let it blow.   See Hol' de win' don't let it blow

"Hold thy peace."   Catch.   Old English air.   Words by Shakespeare.   BOS 2—DSB—TFB—TFG—TFR

"Hold up your hand, O Joshuay, she cried."   See The maid freed from the gallows (Black Mountain, N.C. version)

"Hold up your hands and Joshua, he cries."   See The maid freed from the gallows (Tennessee version)

Hold your light ("What make ole Satan")   Negro spiritual from South Carolina.   AS

"Holde frühlingszeit."   C. W. Gluck.   g.   EDL

Holde Mary.   See Màiri bhòidheach

Holden, Oliver
"All hail the power of Jesus' name"
Coronation.   See "All hail the power of Jesus' name"

"Holder klingt der vogelsang."   See Minnelied (Brahms)

"Holi-, holi-, holiday, on the very first day of the year."   See Little Musgrave and Lady Barnard (Clay county, Ky. version)

"Holiday, a holiday, the very first one of the year."   See Little Musgrave and Lady Barnard (Hindman, Ky. version no. 2)

"Holl amrantau'r sêr, dywedant."   See Ar hyd y nos (Owen)

Ann hollaika (Hirtenlied)   Breton folk song.   br.g.   ML 1

The holly and the ivy ("Green grow'th the holly")   See "Green grows the holly" (Henry VIII)

"The holly and the ivy now both are full well grown."   Old French carol air.   DN

"The holly and the ivy, when they are both full grown."   Traditional English air.   OB

The holly twig.   Folk song: Meadows of Dan, Va. version.   SES 1
—Montvale, Va. version.   SES 1
—Woodridge, Va. version.   SES 1
Variant: A week's work well done

"The holly's up, the house is all bright."   See The Christmas tree is sparkling with light (Cornelius)

Holmes, Henry James Ernest
"God of the earth"
Holmes, John Haynes
"God of the nations near and far"
(Dykes)
"The voice of God is calling" (Webb)
Holmes, Oliver Wendell
"Angel of peace" (Keller)
Hail Columbia, The new (Phile)
"Lord of all being" (music by Hatton;
Taylor)
"O Love divine" (Haydn)
Old Ironsides (music by Klein; also
unknown composer)
The young oysterman (Old air)
Holsclaw, Doug
Fight! wildcats, fight (Allen and Hols-
claw)
See also Allen, Thornton Whitney, jt.
comp.
Holst, Eduard
"Happy birds"
Holst, Gustav
"In the bleak mid-winter"
Lullay my liking
Mid-winter.   See "In the bleak mid-
winter"
Holstein, Franz von
Beatrice
Holstein, Ludvig Ditlef, greve
Efteraar (Lange-Müller)
Holt, Johan Sverdrup
Vandraren (Lund)
Holtei, Karl von
Der alte reiter und sein mantel (Volks-
weise)
"In Berlin, sagt er" (Composer un-
known)
Hölty, Ludwig Heinrich Christoph
"Ich liebe dich, so wie du mich" (Bee-
thoven)   See Herrosee. "Ich liebe
dich, so wie du mich" (Beethoven)
Minnelied (Brahms)
Winter song (Bohemian folk air)
"Holy angels."   C. Gounod. ₁Tr of Anges
purs, anges radieux₁   e.   WG
"Holy Ghost! with light divine."   L. M.
Gottschalk.   Words by A. Reed.
BB
"Holy, holy, holy! Lord God almighty."
J. B. Dykes.   Words by R. Heber.
BB—TFG—TFR
All the saints adore thee (Nicaea)
MFS
"Holy! holy! holy! Lord God Almighty!
holy! holy! holy! Lord God of
Sabaoth." Pergolesi.   e.   SSO 1
Holy, holy, holy, Lord, God of hosts!
Heav'n and earth are full of Thee.
See "Day is dying in the west"
(Sherwin)
"Holy, holy, holy, Lord of hosts: holy, holy,
holy, is the Lord of hosts."   See
Choral sanctus (Gaul)
"Holy Marguerite guard my little sweet."
See "Sainte Marguerite"
"Holy night! peaceful night."   See Die
heilige nacht (Gruber)
Holy Trinity.   See "One holy church of
God appears" (Barnby)

The **holy** well ("As it fell out one May
morning")   Traditional air.   OB
The **holy** well ("Sweet Jesus went down
to yonder town")   Old English or
Scottish air: The Withy carol.   DNS
Holyoke.   Mount Holyoke college song.
<Air: Lauriger Horatius>   Words
by S. Averill.   AI
Holystoning.   Chantey.   SBS
Holzflösser (Tukkipoika)   Finnish folk
song.   fi.g.   ML 3
Holzmann, Abe
Blaze away
Bunch o' blackberries
Hunky Dory
Smoky mokes
Uncle Sammy
"**Home** again, home again."   M. S. Pike
(music and words)   GOS 1—MFS
Home, boys, home ("Man, born of woman,
was a sailor for to be")   U.S. Naval
academy song.   Air: Son of a gam-
bolier.   US
Home, boys, home ("Man born of woman
was a soldier for to be")   See The
American soldier
Home, can I forget thee.   See "Home,
home, can I forget thee"
"**Home,** home, can I forget thee."   Ger-
man air: <Du du liegst mir im her-
zen>   DFF
Home, can I forget thee.   MFS
Home, home on the range.   See Home
on the range
₁"**Home** my sweetheart comes from roving"₁
Runo-laulu (Runengesang)   Finnish
rune song.   fi.g.   ML 3
"**Home** of our college days."   See Dear
old Reserve (Kücken)
Home of the soul.   P. Phillips.   Words
by E. H. Gates.   MFS
Home on the range.   Cowboy song.
GSS—LSC
The **home** road.   J. A. Carpenter (music
and words)   BB—TFO—TFP
Home so blest.   F. Abt.   Words by B.
S. Montgomery.   CSS 1
Home, sweet home.   H. R. Bishop.
Words by J. H. Payne.   BB—DFF—
DSB— DSC— GOS 1— GSS— MBS—
MFS—TFP
"**Home** to our mountains."   G. Verdi.
₁Tr of Ai nostri monti ritorneremo₁
e.   WG
Homeland mine ("When the night o'er
hills is creeping")   L. van Beethoven.
DSB
"**Homeless,** ragged and tann'd."   See The
vagabond (Molloy)
"**Home's** not merely four square walls"
(What is home)   Rossini.   Words
by C. Swain.   MFS
Homesickness blues.   C. Hess.   HB
Homeward bound ("At the Blackwell
docks we bid adieu")   Forecastle
song.   WSE
₁**Homeward** bound₁ "Come, loose every sail
to the breeze."   ₁M. Arne.   Words
by Thompson₁   WSE

"Homeward to their mother." See Don't swat your mother (Hooker and Steele)

The honest boy. Old song. KSO

"Honey won't you come and listen." See The West Texas blues (Booker)

"Honour and arms." Händel. SSO 4

Hood, John J.
Freedom's flag (Geibel)

Hood, Thomas
The Lord Mayor's show (Blewitt)

Hook, James
Mary of Allendale
The sweet little girl that I love
Within a mile of Edinboro'

Hooker, Brian
    Composer
Don't tell me what you dreamed last night
For I've been reading Freud. See Don't tell me what you dreamed last night

    Author
"Mother of men" (Bingham)

Hooker, Brian, and Steele, Porter
Don't swat your mother

"Hookey, hookey, oh how we love to play hookey, hookey." See The school-house blues (Berlin)

The hooking cow blues. D. Williams (music and words) HB

Hoop de dooden do. A. Nish. WSS

Hoorah! and up she rises. See The drunken sailor

Hooraw, we're seventy miles away. See Robinson Crusoe's story (Newell)

Hooray and up she rises. See The drunken sailor

Hoosen Johnny. Traditional Illinois song. SBA

"Hop, hop, hop! nimble as a top." See Das steckenpferd (Hering)

A hope carol. D. S. Smith. Words by C. G. Rossetti. TFB—TFG

"The hope I dream'd of was a dream." See For a dream's sake (Cowen)

Hopeless 'tis. See "Per la gloria d'adorarvi" (Bononcini)

Hoping, longing, and dreaming. See We have met, loved, and parted (Eastburn)

Hopkins, John Henry
"Art thou weary, art thou languid" (Tr of Kopon te kai kamaton)
The Christmas tree. See "Gather around the Christmas tree"
"Gather around the Christmas tree"
Kings of Orient. See Three kings of Orient
Three kings of Orient
"We three kings of Orient are." See Three kings of Orient

Hopkinson, Francis
The battle of the kegs (Old air)

Hopkinson, Joseph
"Hail Columbia" (Phile)

"Hopp, hopp, hopp! pferdchen, lauf galopp." See Das steckenpferd (Hering)

"Hopsa! Lisella." Folk song from central Alsace. e.f. CBF 1

"Hör, Ciccuzza, mach ein ende." See Ciccuzza

"Hör nor, du schön mädele." Jewish folk song. y. SY

"Hör nor reb Todros." Jewish folk song. y. SY

Horace. See Horatius Flaccus, Quintus

Horatius Flaccus, Quintus
"Integer vitae" (Flemming)

"Horch, ein wagen naht durch den dunklen wald" ("Oj grzmią wozy, grzmią po bukowinie") Polish folk song. g.p. ML 3

"Horch! horch! was dein treuer spricht." See Des geistes gesang (Haydn)

"Horch, was kommt von draussen rein." See Der verlassene liebhaber

"Horch, wie still es wird im dunkeln hain." See Stille sicherheit (Franz)

"Hore háj, dole háj." See "Hei! hier ein hain"

"Höre ich des kuckucks schlag." See "Unde aud cucu cântând"

"Höre, Israel, höre des Herrn stimme. For English translation see "Hear ye, Israel! hear what the Lord speaketh" (Mendelssohn)

"Höre, mein liebchen." See "List to me, rosebud"

"Höre mich, mein herr und Gott" ("Ach, Bože môj, Pane môj") Slovak folk song. g.sl. ML 3

"Höret an die bittre klage von der Mutter Rochel." See Lamento ("Écoutez donc la complainte")

Horn, Charles Edward
The banks of Allen water: traditional air arranged
"Child of earth with golden hair." See Titania's song
"I know a bank whereon the wild thyme blows"
"I've been roaming"
Long time ago: negro air arranged
"Near the lake where drooped the willow." See Long time ago: negro air arranged
A southern refrain. See Long time ago: negro air arranged
Titania's song
What can a poor maiden do

Horne, Abel, pseud. See Stevens, David

Horo, my nut brown maiden. See Ho-ro mo nighean donn, bhòidheach

Horrocks, Amy Elise
The bird and the rose

The horse named Bill. Nonsense song. [D. D. Emmett] SBA

The horse's complaint. Folk song from Virginia. SES 2

Horspool, A.
Eternal rest (Piccolomini)

"Hört die neue kunde an" ("Stała się nam novina") Polish folk song. 1st air. g.p. ML 3

"Hört die neue kunde an" ("Stała się nam novina") Polish folk song. 2d air. g.p. ML 3

"Hört, frau mütter, meine bitte." See Katchen Kadar

"Hört mich, Gottes tapfre streiter." See Hussitenlied

"Hört unsre botschaft, die wir euch gebracht." See "Nesem vam noviny"

Hosmer, Elmer Samuel
"There's a Friend for little children"

Hosmer, Frederick Lucian
"From age to age how grandly rise" (Purcell)
"Immortal by their deed and word" (Spohr)
Marching on (Bullard)
"One thought I have, my ample creed" (Wallace)
"Thy kingdom come—on bended knee" (Dykes)

Höst ("Re'n trista höstregn strömma ner." —Autumn) S. Palmgren. Words by C. Flaischlen. e.sw. WM 2

The host and his guests. Old English carol air. Words by S. Fay. FC

"Hot mutton pies." Three part round. J. F. Lampe. GSS

"Hot spice gingerbread." 18th century round. BOS 2

A hot time in the old town. T. A. Metz. Words by J. Hayden. GFS—OTG—SRW

Hough, Will M., and Adams, Frank R.
I wonder who's kissing her now (Howard)

The hour of dreaming. See L'heure exquise (Hahn)

Hour of sweet repose. T. H. Howe. GE

"The hour was sad I left the maid." See The girl I left behind me

"Hours there were." J. Wade. [Words by T. Moore] GOS 1

The house carpenter. Folk song. SBA Variant of: The daemon lover

"Hová csikós olyan szaporán." See "Shepherd, see thy horse's foaming mane"

Hovey, Richard
"Men of Dartmouth" (Wellman)

How, William Walsham
"O Jesus, Thou art standing" (Geibel)

"How beautiful are the feet of them." G. F. Händel. SSO 1

"How blest is a lover." See The happy lover

"How blithe, ilk morn, was I to see." See The brume o' the Cowdenknowes

"How brightly beams the morning star." See Wie schon leuchtet der morgenstern

"How came that blood on the point of your knife." See Edward (Balsam, N.C. version; Clyde, N.C. version)

"How can I bear to leave thee." See Ritters abschied (Kinkel)

"How can I leave thee." See Treue liebe (Kücken)

"How cold the winds do blow." See The unquiet grave (Surrey version)

"How come that blood on your shirt sleeve." See Edward (Hot Springs, N.C. version; Woolwine, Va. version)

"How dark the deep-flowing river." See Flowing river

"How dear to my heart are the scenes of my childhood." See The old oaken bucket (Kiallmark)

"How deserted, how lone and tearful." See "Se crudele il cor mostrai" (Donizetti)

"How do you like to go up in a swing." See The swing (Judd)

"How d'ye do." Student song. BB

"How far is it to Bethlehem." See Children's song of the Nativity

"How firm a foundation." Attributed to J. Reading. [Words attributed to R. Keene; wrongly atributed to G. Keith and to Kirkham] BB—TFP

"How firm a foundation, ye saints of the Lord" (Portuguese hymn) LAS

"How gentle God's commands" (Dennis) H. G. Nägeli. [Words by P. Doddridge] MFS

"How good and beautiful" ("Hineh mah tov") Palestinean folk song. e.he. BNP

"How grand and how bright, that wonderful night." See The Worcestershire Christmas carol (18th century air)

"How great in Sion Thou art praised." See Glory to the Lord in Zion (Bortniānskiĭ)

"How great the harvest is." See Festival carol

"How happy could I be with either" (Have you heard of a frolicsome ditty) Old English air. [Words by Gay] BOS 2

"How happy the soldier." British song of the Revolution. DSO

"How I long'd for peace and rest." See I have sought, and I have found (Keller)

"How jolly are we beggars." See The beggar's song (Leveridge)

"How long de train been gone." Negro spiritual. WFN

"How long did it rain." See I heard the preaching of the elder

"How lovely are the messengers." Mendelssohn. [Tr of Wie lieblich sind die boten] e. DSC—TFG

"How many hired servants." A. Sullivan. SSO 3

"How oft has the benshee cried." Air: The dear black maid. Words by T. Moore. HMI

"How oft I dream of childhood days." See Rosie Nell

"How oft in her fond arms." See Ah! quello fu per me (Donizetti)

"How old are you, my pretty little miss." See I'm seventeen come Sunday (Callaway, Va. version; Meadows of Dan, Va. version)

"How should I your true love know" ("Wie erkenn' ich dein treulieb") [16th century air] Words by Shakespeare. e.g. ML 1

"How stands the glass around" (Why, soldiers, why.—Wolfe's song)   Air: Why, soldiers, why.   DSO
"How sweet at the close of silent eve." See The voice of her I love
"How unkempt that scarf doth look on you, my dear" ("Jaj! de szennyes az a maga kendöje")   Hungarian folk song. e.hu.   KH 2
"How uplifted the heart."   See Dem Unendlichen (Schubert)
How vain is man who boasts in fight. G. F. Händel.   SSO 3
"How well I remember the ninth of November."   See The Lord Mayor's show (Blewitt)
"How well I remember there're 10 more days till June."   West Point song. DSO
"How willing my paternal love."   G. F. Händel.   SSO 4
"How wondrous and great."   J. Haydn. Words by H. U. Onderdonk.   DSB
Howard, C.
   Buy my strawberries
Howard, Frank, pseud.   See Martindale, Frank
Howard, Joseph E.
   I wonder who's kissing her now
   I'll be home to-morrow night
Howard, Rowland
   You never miss the water
Howdy ("An' a howdy, howdy, sister") Negro spiritual.   TFO—TFR
Howdy, Bill.   B. Chitwood (music and words)   RA
Howe, Mrs Julia (Ward)
   Battle hymn of the republic (Old plantation air)
Howe, T. H.
   Beautiful bird, sing on
   The bright beyond
   Hour of sweet repose
   Love divine (same air as Hour of sweet repose)
Howell, Charles T.
   "By the waters of Babylon"
Howitt, Mrs Mary (Botham)
   A spring song (Bridge)
Howliston, Mary H.
   "There are many flags in many lands" (Composer unknown)
Hoyt, Charles Hale
   The Bowery
Hubbard, Floyd Morse, and Hubbard, Giles Munro
   Colgate marching song (Composer unknown)
Hubbard, Giles Munro.   See Hubbard, Floyd Morse, jt. auth.
Hubbard, J. M.
   Robin Redbreast
[Huckleberry hunting] "O, the boys and the girls went a huckie berry hunting" (We'll ranzo way)   Halliard chantey.   WSE
   Variant: Tommy's gone to Hilo
Hudson, G. A.
   Buy my roses

Hudson, Thomas
   Guy Fawkes (Old air)
   The spider and the fly (Composer unknown)
Huë, Georges Adolphe
   "I wept, beloved, as I dreamed."   See "J'ai pleuré en rêve"
   "J'ai pleuré en rêve"
Hughes, Mrs Harriet Mary (Browne)   See Browne, Harriet Mary
Hughes, Jewell, and Walker, Catharine
   Razorback rootin' song (Paisley)
Hughes, John Ceiriog
   Dafydd y garreg wen (Welsh folk air)
   Tros y garreg (Welsh folk air)
Hughes, Mary M.
   Beulah land
Hugo, Victor Marie, comte
   Chant d'exil (Vidal)
   Chantez riez et dormez (Gounod)
   "Je ne veux pas autre chose" (Widor)
   Si mes vers avaient des ailes (Hahn)
Hui! hui! stridon lassù.   For English translation see High! high! aloft (Leoncavallo)
Huldra (Huldre) aa en Elland (Frau Holda und Elland)   Norse folk song. g.n. ML 1
Huldre lok (Frau Holdas lockruf)   Norse folk song. g.n.   ML 1
Hullah, John Pyke
   "Three fishers went sailing"
Humble, humble, humble yourselves.   See Gwine to live humble to de Lord
Humble yo'self de bell done ring.   Negro spiritual.   JB 2
The hummingbird.   See Le colibri (Chausson)
Humperdinck, Engelbert
   The angels spoke to us in dreams (from Hänsel und Gretel.   Tr of Ihr englein, die uns so treu bewacht)
   "Brother come and dance with me." See The dancing lesson
   The dancing lesson (from Hänsel und Gretel.   Tr of Brüderchen, komm tanz' mit mir)
   Evening prayer (from Hänsel und Gretel.   Tr of Abends, will ich schlafen gehn)
   A little man: folk song arranged (from Hänsel und Gretel)
   "O magic castle" (from Hänsel und Gretel.   Tr of O herrlich schlösschen)
   A riddle.   See A little man: folk song arranged
   "The sandman kind am I" (from Hänsel und Gretel.   Tr of Der kleine sandmann bin ich)
   "There stands a little man": folk song arranged
   "A tiny little man."   See A little man: folk song arranged
"Humpty Dumpty."   Nursery song. MFS
"Huna blentyn ar fy mynwes."   See Suogân

The **hundred** pipers ("Wi' a hundred pipers an' a', an' a'") Jacobite song. Words by Nairne.   DSC—GS
"Wi' a hundred pipers an' a'."   MBS
A **hundred** years ago.   Windlass song. SBA—WSE
Variant of: "A hundred years on the eastern shore"
"A **hundred** years is a very long time." See A hundred years ago
"A **hundred** years on the eastern shore." Halliard chantey.   TSB 2
Variant: A hundred years ago
A **hundred** years to come.   W. C. Brown. MFS
[**Hungaria's** treasure] "Magosan repül a darú szepen szol" ("Far and high the cranes give cry") Hungarian folk song <attributed to B. Egressi and to J. Szerdahelyi> e.hu.   KH 1
"Magasan repül a daru" ("Kühnen flugs steigt auf der kranich") g.hu.   ML 3
Hungary.   See "In heav'nly love abiding" (Iszlai)
Hungry tigers.   Song of the College of the Pacific.   R. Bodley.   Words by B. Couchman.   HW
Hunky dory.   A. Holzmann.   SMG
Hunt, Asa T., pseud.   See Loomis, Harvey Worthington
Hunt, C. W.
The bell goes a-ringing for Sai-rah
Hunt, G. W.
Awfully clever
Hunt, Miss L.
Here and there (Winch)
"The **hunt** is up."   16th century air. [Words attributed to W. Gray]   BOS 2 —DSB
"**Hunt** till you find him."   See Hunting for the Lord
Hunter, Mrs Anne (Home)
"My mother bids me bind my hair" (Haydn)
Hunter, Eleanor A.
"From ev'ry spire on Christmas eve" (Coles)
Hunter, Harry
Over the garden wall (Fox)
The **hunter** in his career ("Long ere the morn") [Air: Bass's career. Words by W. Basse]   BOS 2
The **hunter's** farewell.   See Der jäger abschied (Mendelssohn)
The **hunters** of Kentucky.   Song of the War of 1812.   Words by S. Woodworth.   DSO
The hunters of Kentucky (Half horse and half alligator)   SBA
[The **hunter's** song]   "See the sun's first gleam."   [Schaffer]   e.   MFS
Hunting for a city.   Negro spiritual from South Carolina.   AS
Hunting for the Lord.   Negro spiritual from South Carolina.   AS
Hunting the hare ("Awn i hela'r ysgyfarnog")   See Hela'r 'sgyvarnog

Huntington, D. W. C.
Over there
Huntington, George
"Two empires" (Carey?)
Huntingtower ("When ye gang awa, Jamie") Scottish song <arr by J. Demar>   GOS 2—GS
Hurley, T. J.
"For Boston"
Hurrah for Mary! hurrah for the lamb. See "Mary had a little lamb": Civil war version (Root)
Hurrah for old New England.   W. P. Chamberlain.   GOS 2
"**Hurrah** for the choice of the nation." See Lincoln and liberty
Hurrah for the flag.   See "There are many flags in many lands"
Hurrah! hurrah! for southern rights, hurrah.   See The bonnie blue flag (Macarthy)
Hurrah! hurrah! for the sunny south so dear.   See The southern girl (Macarthy)
Hurrah, hurrah for the terrible navy crew. See Why! oh why (Macarthy)
Hurrah, hurrah, Pennsylvania.   See The red and blue (Goeckel)
Hurrah, hurrah, we bring the jubilee. See Marching through Georgia (Work)
Hurrah, Lie.   American mountain song. RA
Hurry on, my weary soul.   See Hear from heaven to-day
Hursley.   See "Sun of my soul, Thou Saviour dear" (Monk)
Die **Husaren** kommen ("Iz daleke zemlje husari ideju")   Croatian folk song. g.se.   ML 2
[**Husarenliebe**] "Wohlan, die zeit ist kommen."   Volkslied.   g.   EDL
Husband, J. J.
Hallelujah, I'm a bum (same air as Revive us again)
"**Husband's** little father in the hall."   See Interrupted slumber
Hush-a-by.   For entries beginning Hush-a-by See Hushaby
"**Hush!** little Minnie and don't say a word." See The mocking bird (Virginia version)
"**Hush,** my babe, lie still and slumber." See Cradle hymn (Rousseau)
"**Hush!** my dear, lie still and slumber." See Cradle hymn (Northumbrian air); Cradle hymn (Composer unknown); Cradle hymn (Bach)
"**Hush!** the waves are rolling in."   See Gaelic lullaby (Composer unknown)
"**Hush** up, baby, don't say a word."   See The mocking bird (North Carolina version)
"**Hush** ye, my bairnie."   See Cagaran Gaolach
"**Hush-a-by,** baby, the night winds are sighing."   See Lullaby
Hush-a-bye, baby ("Now show me the lady")   Minstrel song.   WSS
Hussitenlied (Kdo jste Boží bojovníci) Czech folk song.   bo.g.   ML 3

Huston, Frank C.
    For the honor of old Purdue
Hüt du dich.   16th century German folk
    song.   g.   EDL
Hutchinson, Abby
    "Kind words can never die"
Hutchinson, Judson Joseph
    Mrs Lofty and I
Hutchinson, William M.
    Dream faces
    Ehren on the Rhine
Hutsell, Floyd M.
    The U. of M. rouser
"Huzzad czigány."   See "Play on, gipsy"
    (Szentirmay)
"Huzzadd, csak huzzadd."   See "Play,
    only play on"
"Hvar har du varit så länge, du Sven i
    rosengård."   See Sven i rosengård
"Hvar har du va't så lange, lilla dotter
    kind."   See Den lillas testamente
Hyatt, G. W.
    The mellow horn (Jones)
The hymn of praise ("I waited for the
    Lord")   See "I waited for the Lord"
    (Mendelssohn)
Hymn of St Francis.   See "Praise, O
    praise our God and King"
Hymn of scouting.   S. S. Wesley.
    Words by M. Prior.   GSS
Hymn to God the Father.   A. Piatti.
    Words by B. Jonson.   CSS 2
Hymn to joy.   See ·Open, Lord, my in-
    ward ear (Beethoven)
Hymn to St Raphael.   German folk song.
    e.   DSC
Hymn to the Almighty.   See Die All-
    macht (Schubert)
Hymn to the night.   See Hymne à la nuit
    (Gounod)
Hymne à la nuit (Hymn to the night)
    C. Gounod.   e.f.   TSS 1
Hymne an die Jungfrau.   See "Ave
    Maria" (Schubert)
"The hypocrite and the concubine."
    Negro spiritual from Virginia.   AS

I

"I ain't been long in this yer army."   See
    The raw recruit
"I ain't been to heav'n, but I' been tol'."
    See O Mary, don't you weep
I ain't gwine study war no more.   Negro
    spiritual.   BB—TFB—TFG—TFO
    —TFR
    Ain' go'n' to study war no mo'.   SBA
    Gwine-a study war no mo'.   FSN
    I ain't going t' study war no more.
    HRD
"I ain't gwine to work on de railroad."
    See Lazy song
I ain't seen no messenger boy.   N. Bivins.
    SMG
"I always wished to be laid when I die."
    See The lonesome prairie (Kentucky
    version)

"I am a brisk and sprightly lad" (Yeo, sir)
    Sea song.   Another air.   CSB 5
"I am a country lassie."   See Country
    lass and royal maid (Straus)
"I am a gay young gentleman."   See The
    Virginian lover (North Carolina ver-
    sion)
"I am a jovial collier lad."   See Down
    in a coal mine (Geoghegan)
"I am a jovial ranger."   See Travel the
    country round
"I am a lovely ladder."   See The green
    brier shore
"I am a man of constant sorrow."   See
    In old Virginny (Callaway, Va. version)
"I am a man of honour unto Blackwaters
    came."   See The Virginian lover
    (Kentucky version)
"I am a poor girl and my fortune's been
    bad."   See The wagoner's lad (Ken-
    tucky version)
"I am a poor innocent clown."   See
    Ralph's ramble to London
"I am a poor way-faring stranger."   See
    Poor pilgrim
"I am a rambling hero."   See The
    Slaney side
"I am a roving cowboy."   See The Black
    Tail range
"I am a roving gambler."   See The rov-
    ing gambler
"I am a roving traveler."   See The gam-
    boling man
"I am a sailor stout and bold."   See The
    rambling sailor
"I am a shoemaker by my trade."   See
    The shoemaker
"I am a Utah man, sir."   See Utah man
    (Seaver)
"I am, as you know, a Madison belle."
    See Up in a balloon
"I am content."   C. H. Sainton.   Words
    by C. Barnard.   GE
I am goin' to join in this army.   Negro
    song.   HRD
"I am going far away."   See The old
    cabin home (Paine)
"I am going to leave you to-morrow."
    See Meet me by the moonlight
"I am going to the dance."   See "Je vais
    entrer dans la danse"
"I am here, do thy will."   Finale from
    Carmen.   G. Bizet.   [Tr of Vous
    pouver m'arrêter]   e.   WG
"I am huntin' for a city, to stay awhile."
    See Hunting for a city
"I am looking rather seedy now."   See
    The little old sod shanty
"I am lost, and scarce know what I'm
    doing."   See "Non so più cosa son"
    (Mozart)
"I am mournful and I am lonely."   See
    Haï luli (Coquard)
"I am my mammy's ain bairn."   See I'm
    owre young to marry yet
"I am seekin' for a city, hallelujah."   See
    I don't feel no-ways tired
"I am so afraid, Clémentine."   See Clé-
    mentine
"I am stumpless quite since from the shot."
    See The leg I left behind me

"**I** am thinking today of dem years dat passed away." See Slavery days

"**I** am twice as happy as a millionaire." See Please go 'way and let me sleep (Von Tilzer)

"**I** am weary with rowing." F. Boott. Words by W. W. Story. GE—GOS 2

I am your own your Hiawatha brave. See Hiawatha (Daniels)

"**I** an' Satan had a race." Negro spiritual from South Carolina. AS

"**I** ax all dem brudder roun'." See Archangel open the door

"**I** ax fader Georgy for religion." See This is the trouble of the world

Ī az bi̇̆ekh edna na naĭka. See "Mutter so zärtlich mich liebte"

"**I** bought a cow an' my cow pleased me." See Bought a cow

"**I** brought my love a cherry." See The riddle song (Hyden, Ky. version)

"**I** build my house upon de rock." See Bound to go

"**I** came from Alabama." See Oh! Susanna (Foster)

"**I** came here strange and lonely." See Gute nacht (Schubert)

"**I** came to Alabama." See Oh! Susanna (Foster)

"**I** came to this country in eighteen-forty-nine." See Pretty Saro (Georgia version)

"**I** can always find a solace." See The songs my mammy sang to me

I canna leave the auld folk now. See We'd better bide a wee (Barnard)

"**I** cannot always trace the way." See Love divine (Howe)

"**I** cannot sing the old songs." Claribel (C. Barnard) (music and words) BB—GOS 2—WSS

"**I** can't get 'em up." See Reveille

"**I** can't stand the fire." Negro spiritual from South Carolina. AS

I can't stay away. Modern spiritual. H. Johnson. JG

I can't stay behind ("Dere's room enough") Negro spiritual from South Carolina. AS

I can't stay behind ("O, my mudder is gone") Negro spiritual from South Carolina. Another version of words. AS

I can't tell why I love you, but I do. G. Edwards. Words by W. D. Cobb. SMG

I care not what others may say. See Rosalie (Knight)

I catch-a da plenty of feesh. Song from San Francisco. SBA

"**I** come dis night to sing an' pray." See Oh, yes! oh, yes

"**I** come from Alabama." See Oh! Susanna (Foster)

"**I** come from haunts of coot and hern." See The brook (Farmer)

"**I** come here from my mountains lone." See Der wanderer (Schubert)

"**I** come this night to sing and pray." See Oh, yes! oh, yes! wait 'til I git on my robe

"**I** come to town de udder night." See Old Dan Tucker (Russell)

I couldn't hear nobody pray. Negro spiritual. HRD—WSS
Couldn't hear nobody pray. BB

"**I** courted fair Polly one livelong night." See The cruel ship's carpenter (Manchester, Ky. version no. 1)

"**I** courted her all of the winter." See The foggy dew (Virginia version)

"**I** done been to heaven." See The Danville chariot

I done done what ya' tol' me to do (See Song Index)
Variant: "O Lord, I done done"

ｌ**I** don't feel no-ways tiredｊ "I am seekin' for a city." Negro spiritual. HRD
Lord, I don't feel noways tired. JG
Variant: I don't feel weary

I don't feel weary. Negro spiritual from Virginia. AS
Variant of: I don't feel no-ways tired

"**I** don't like no railroad man." Kentucky mountain song. SBA

"**I** don't mind telling you, I took my girl to Kew." See Whoa, Emma

I don't want no more army. U.S. army song. DSO

I don't want to be a gambler. Negro spiritual. SBA

I don't want to play in your yard. H. W. Petrie. SW

I don't want to stay here no longer. See The Danville chariot

"**I** downa laugh, I downa sing." Scottish air. Words by J. Hogg (the Ettrick shepherd) GS

"**I** dream of Jeanie with the light brown hair." See Jeanie with the light brown hair (Foster)

"**I** dreamed a dream the other night—lowlands, lowlands, away my John." See Lowlands away

"**I** dreamed last night of my true love." Folk song: American mountain version. SBA
Variant of: Locks and bolts

"**I** dreamed of my true love last night." See Locks and bolts (Hot Springs, N.C. version)

"**I** dreamed that I dwelt on an isle of cracked ice." See A dream (Balfe)

"**I** dreamt that I dwelt in marble halls." M. W. Balfe. ｌWords by A. Bunnｊ GOS 1

"**I** fear no haughty nation." See The song of Texas

"**I** feel, I feel the Deity within" (see Song Index)
Also in Arm, arm, ye brave (Händel) SSO 4

I feel just as happy as a big sun flow'r. See Happy as a big sunflower (Emerson)

I feel like my time ain't long. Negro spiritual. JB 2

"I feel so sad today my man has gone away." See Stingaree blues (Kemp)

"I fjor gjætt' eg gjeitinn'" ("Durch täler und fluren") Norse folk song. g.n. ML 1

"I found a horseshoe." Old American song. SBA

"I found a red rose in a woodland glen." See Of the rose and you (Kern)

"I gave my love a cherry." See The riddle song (Pineville, Ky. version; St Helen's, Ky. version)

"I give thee thanks, my trusty swan." See Swan song (Wagner)

"I go where heav'n and duty call." See All danger disdaining (Händel)

"I got a gal at the head of the holler." Folk song from Kentucky. SBA Variant of: Sourwood mountain

"I got a home in that rock." Negro spiritual. WFN

"I got a letter from Jesus." Negro spiritual from South Carolina. SBA

"I got a robe, you got a robe." See All God's chillun got wings

"I got a song, you got a song." See All God's chillun got wings

"I got on old Smokey." See The wagoner's lad (Harrogate, Tenn. version)

"I greet thee, eagle, o'er pine-tree high." See Høgen (Nielsen)

"I grieve when I think on the dear happy days." See Draherin o machree

"I groan the while I tremble." See "Gemo in un punto e fremo" (Pergolesi)

"I guess you'll wonder to see me." See The Broadway swell and Brooklyn belle (Kelly)

"I had a bird, a little bird." See The faithful little bird

"I had a cat and the cat pleas'd me." See The barnyard song

"I had a dream, a happy dream." See The slave's dream

"I had a little ship, and I sailed her on the sea." See The Golden Willow Tree

"I had a little ship and I sailed on the sea." See The Golden Vanity (Hindman, Ky. version)

"I had a little singing bird." See The singing bird

"I had a little soldier no bigger than my thumb." See The little soldier (Vincent)

"I had a true love but she left me." See The Quaker's wooing

"I had four brothers over the sea." See Perri merri dictum, domine

"I ha'e laid a herrin' in saut" (Lass, gin ye lo'e me, tell me noo) Scottish air. Words by J. Tytler. GS

"I ha'e wander'd mony a night in June." See The Highland minstrel boy (Barnett)

"I hail to my mother, my mother hail to me." See I want God's heab'n to be mine

"I hail to my sister." See Gideon's band

"I hate to see de ev'nin' sun go down." See St Louis blues (Handy)

"I have a chestnut filly." See Cân y melinydd

"I have a little pony." Traditional nursery song. CSB 1

"I have a lovin' brother." See When de saints come marchin' in

"I have a silent sorrow here." A. Reinagle. Words by R. B. Sheridan. MPA 1

"I have a rooster, my rooster loves me." See The barnyard family

"I have a spiteful mother." See Boum badiboum

"I have been to sea and I have been to shore." See The green bed (Virginia version)

"I have brought poppies for thee, weary heart." See Lethe (Boott)

"I have come to say good-bye, Dolly Gray." See Good-bye Dolly Gray (Barnes)

"I have cull'd that lovely rosebud." See "J'ai cueilli la belle rose"

"I have fruit, I have flowers." J. A. Wade. MFS

"I have heard the mavis singing." See Mary of Argyle (Nelson)

"I have just come from the salt, salt sea." See The house carpenter

"I have led a good life." Air: Son of a gambolier. Words by M. Ross and R. Albertson. SRW The good boy. SBA

"I have liv'd long enough to be rarely mistaken." See Bacon and greens

"I have planted a rose-tree." See La ronde du rosier

"I have roamed over mountain." See My own native land (Bradbury)

I have sought, and I have found. M. Keller. Words by G. W. Birdseye. CSS 2

"I have the blues, ev'ry time my hubby leaves me I have the blues." See Left all alone again blues (Kern)

"I have this moment left a masqueradeing party." See Decollette (Fagan)

"I have travel'd the world over to and fro." See Vandraren (Lund)

"I hear dat bell a-ringing." See Roll out! heave dat cotton

I hear my true lub weep. See Way down in Ca-i-ro (Foster)

"I hear the millwheel." See "J'entends le moulin"

"I hear tonight the old bells chime." See Love's golden dream

"I heard a brooklet gushing." E. J. Loder. Words by Müller. [Tr of Wohin] e. GA

"I heard a voice in the morning." See The voice of Jesus (Sutcliffe)

"I heard a voice long years ago." See Looking back (Sullivan)

"I heard a wee bird singing." G. Linley. GS

I heard de preachin' of de word o' God. See I heard the preaching of the elder

I heard from heaven to-day. See Peter, go ring them bells

"I heard my mother say."   See Give me Jesus

I heard of a city called heaven.   Negro spiritual.   WFN

"I heard the bells on Christmas day." J. B. Calkin.   Words by H. W. Longfellow.   BB

"I heard the bells on Christmas day."   R. Dunstan.   Words by H. W. Longfellow.   DNS

I heard the preaching of the elder.   Negro spiritual.   HRD
  I heard de preachin' of de word o' God. JB 2

"I heard the rippling brooklet sing."   See It was a dream (Cowen)

"I heard the voice of Jesus say" (Come unto me and rest)   A. A. DuBois. [Words by H. Bonar]   CSS 1

"I heard the voice of Jesus say."   F. W. Perry.   [Words by H. Bonar]   Additional words for use at Christmas. TSS 1—TSS 2

"I heard they wanted men to fight."   See Look at the ears on him (Harrington)

"I held a little bird."   See Un pajarito

"I hold my brudder wid a tremblin' han'." See Wrestle on, Jacob

I hope I don't intrude.   Minstrel song. PSG—WSS

"I hope my mother will be there" (In that beautiful world on high.—The Mayo boys' song)   Negro spiritual.   HRD

I hoped, in my passion.   R. Leoncavallo. [Tr of Sperai, tanto il delirio accecato m'aveva]   e.   WG

"I implore thee, dearest heart."   See Bitte (Bohm)

"I implore you, I beseech you" ("Megkövetem a tens nemes")   Old Hungarian folk song.   e.hu.   KH 1

"I jes' arrive in town."   See Jordan is a hard road to trabel (Briggs)

"I joy once more now, O home to behold thee."   See Pilgrims' chorus (Wagner)

"I just come down from Louisville."   See The lily of the west

"I just received a telegram."   See This great war

"I knew a soldier by his horse."   See The trooper and the maid (Burnsville, N.C. version)

"I knew by the smoke that so gracefully curled."   See The woodpecker (Willson)

"I knew the little young soldier."   See The lady and the dragoon (Micaville, N.C. version)

"I know a bank whereon the wild thyme blows."   C. E. Horn.   Words by Shakespeare.   MFS

"I know a little dwelling."   See Le prisonnier de Hollande (Canadian version)

"I know a little pussy."   See Pussy willow

"I know a lovely angel-game."   See Ich weiss ein lieblich engelspiel

"I know a maiden, she's got the money." B. Smetana.   e.   WLO

"I know by the banks of the Rhine."   See Le moulin

I know de Lord's laid His hands on me. See I know the Lord's laid His hands on me

I know de udder worl' is not like dis.   See Run, Mary, run

"I know he is faithless."   See "È ingrato, lo veggio" (Galuppi)

"I know I have another building."   Negro spiritual.   WFN

[I know] I would like to read.   Negro spiritual.   HRD

I know it, 'deed I know it.   See Dese bones gwine to rise again

"I know member, know Lord."   See Bell da ring (South Carolina version no. 1)

"I know moonlight, I know starlight."   See Lay this body down

"I know my God's a mand o' war."   See Sinner, please don't let this harvest pass

"I know my love by his way o' walk." West Irish air.   Words from an old song.   HI 1

"I know my robe goin' to fit me well." See By an' by

"I know my robes gwine ter fit me well." See By an' by

"I know not if you love me."   See "Yo no sé si me quieres"

"I know not what it presages."   See Die Lorelei (Silcher)

"I know not what spell doth hold me." See Die Lorelei (Liszt)

"I know not what the future hath" (Lambeth)   [W. A. F. Schulthes] wrongly attributed to S. Webbe.   Words by J. G. Whittier.   LAS

"I know not why I love thee."   GOS 2

"I know sumpin' ain't gonna tell."   See Shortenin' bread

"I know that hope doth smile upon" ("Ich weiss, dass meiner lieb' zu dir")   A. Dvořák.   Words from the Bohemian of Pfleger-Moravsky.   e.g.   TM

"I know that my Redeemer lives."   See Sinner, please don't let this harvest pass

"I know that my Redeemer liveth."   G. F. Händel.   SSO 1

I know that she's waiting for me.   See Jennie, the flower of Kildare (Stewart)

"I know that water is chilly and cold." See Chilly water

I know the Lord's laid His hands on me. Negro spiritual.   HRD
  I know de Lord's laid His hands on me.   FSN—JB 2—WSS

I know the other world is not like this. See Run, Mary, run

I know when I'm going home.   Negro spiritual from South Carolina.   AS

"I know where I'm goin'."   Irish air from County Antrim.   HI 1

"I knows a gal that you don't know."   See Li'l Liza Jane

"I lay my head in a cottage door."   See The false young man (St Helen's, Ky. version)

"I lead a somewhat easy life." See Tommy Dodd

"I left my baby lying here." See An coineachan

"I lie at rest on waving, grassy lea." See Feldeinsamkeit (Brahms)

I lift my heart to Thee. M. Costa. SSO 2
The evening prayer. CSS 2

"I like a game at croquet." See Starry night for a ramble

"I linger round the very spot." See Once again (Sullivan)

"I live for the good of my nation." See Old Rosin, the beau

"I live in Vermont, and one morning last summer." See The charming young widow

"I lo'e na a laddie but ane." Air: My lodging is on the cold ground. Verse 1 by J. Clunie, verses 2-5 by H. Macneill. GS

"I long to be, long to see." See My own Iona (Friedland and Morgan)

I long to see the girl I left behind. J. T. Kelly (music and words) GFS

"I long to shout, I love to sing." See Mos' done toilin' here

"I looked ober Jordan and what did I see." See Swing low, sweet chariot

"I looked over Jordan and what did I see." See Swing low, sweet chariot

"I look'd where the roses were blooming." See Grass and roses (Bartlett)

I lost my equilibrium. See Decollette (Fagan)

"I love it, I love it." See The old arm chair (Russell)

"I love my little cat, I do." See Daddy wouldn't buy me a bow-wow (Tabrar)

I love my love ("All my friends") Folk song from North Carolina. SES 2

I love my love ("What is the meaning of the song") C. Pinsuti. Words by C. Mackay. GE

"I love my love in the morning." G. B. Allen. Words by G. Griffin. GE

I love my love so well. E. Audran. e. WLO

"I love na a laddie but one." See "I lo'e na a laddie but one"

I love the merry sunshine. S. Glover. Words by J. W. Lake. MFS

"I love the rest reflection brings." See The bright beyond (Howe)

"I love the white girl and the black." See A little more cider too (Hart)

I love thee ("Min tankes tanke") See Jeg elsker dig (Grieg)

I love thee darling, faithfully. See Verlegenheit (Abt)

"I love Thy kingdom, Lord" (St Thomas) G. F. Händel. Words by T. Dwight. MFS

"I love to roam in summer hours." See Blodau'r cwm

"I love to roam in the woodland." See The mocking bird (Winner)

"I love to sing the birth of spring." See Heigho (Repper)

"I love to sit upon the floor." See Only a 'ittle dirly dirl (Andrews)

I love you ("As I stroll'd out") Old song. SW

"I love you because I must love you." See "Te quiero porque te quiero"

"I love you, dear, as you love me." See "Ich liebe dich, so wie du mich" (Beethoven)

"I made up my mind in the early morn." See Trail to Mexico

"I married me a wife and took her home." See The wife wrapt in wether's skin (Hindman, Ky. version)

"I married me a wife, I got her home." See The wife wrapt in wether's skin (Kentucky version no. 1)

"I meet little Rosa early in de mornin'." See Early in the morning

"I met a little mermaid." See A mystery of the sea

"I met a man in my own home town." See Friendless blues (Handy)

"I met a pilgrim on the way." See My Lord delivered Daniel

I met her in the garden where the praties grow. Old American song. SBA

"I met her in the morning." See Won't you go my way

I must and I will get married. Folk song from Virginia. SES 2

"I must be sure to go, this year." See La festa di Piedigrotta

I must live all alone. Folk song from Sussex. BET

"I namn af hafvet det oändligt vida." See Till bruden (Peterson-Berger)

"I nebber see de like since I bin born." See Johnny come down to Hilo

"I need Thee every hour." R. Lowry. Words by A. S. Hawks. TFP

I never had a father. See Nobody's child

"I never saw a fairer." See My wife's a winsome wee thing

"I never see the like since I been born." See Johnny come down to Hilo

"I never shall forget that day, reign, Massa Jesus." See Reign, Massa Jesus

"I never will forget the day I left my home." See Homesickness blues (Hess)

"I once did have a dear companion." See The dear companion

"I once did love a yellow gal." See Mary Blane

"I once did lub a color'd gal." See Stop that knocking at the door

"I once had houses, riches and lands." See The gypsy laddie (Rocky Fork, Tenn. version no. 2)

"I once knew a Normandy maid." J. Barnett. GOS 2

"I once knew a pretty girl." See The rejected lover (Pineville, Ky. version; Mount Fair, Va. version)

"I once knew a young girl." See The rejected lover (Callaway, Va. version)

"I once loved a boy and a bold Irish boy." See I will walk with my love

"I opened the leaves of a book last night." See Ruby (Gabriel)

"I plac'd o'er my heart the portrait you gave me." See Letters from lovers (Offenbach)

"I pray for him, spare him." R. Wagner. ₁Tr of Ich fleh' für ihn₁ e. WG

"I pray thee, rise." R. Wagner. ₁Tr of O stehet auf! nicht sollet hier ihr knien₁ e. WG

"I pray you, I pray you." See The scale (Beethoven)

"I read the evening papers till my eyes got sore." See Old Arkansas

"I ride an old paint." Cowboy song. LSC—SBA

"I roam the world a gypsy king." See The gypsy king (Bergh)

"I rode up to her uncle." See Locks and bolts (Carmen, N.C. version no. 2)

"I run the old mill." See Wal, I swan (Burt)

"I. S. C." Iowa state college song. KU—KV

"I said it in the meadow path." See Each for all (Reissiger)

"I said to the dove: Spread thy wings above me." See Les trois oiseaux (Cui)

"I sail over the ocean blue." See I catch-a da plenty of feesh

"I sat beneath the maples old." See A spring song (Pinsuti)

"I sat down on a cold frozen stone." See Nottamun town (Hindman, Ky. version no. 2)

"I saw a fair maiden sitten and sing." See Lullay my liking (Holst)

"I saw a young lady a-walking all out." See The elfin knight (North Carolina version)

"I saw a youth and maiden on a lonely city street." See Take back your gold (Rosenfeld)

"I saw de light." Negro spiritual. WFN

I saw Esau. Old song. SW

"I saw from the beach." Air: Miss Molly. Words by T. Moore. HMI

"I saw her coming through the wood." See The wooing (Sieveking)

"I saw her—I loved her." See R'isiho

"I saw in splendor shining." See Elsa's traum (Wagner)

"I saw my lady weep." J. Dowland. GA

"I saw the beam in my sister's eye." Negro spiritual from South Carolina. AS

"I saw the wolf, the fox, the hare." 15th century French folk song. e. MFF

"I saw the light." See "I saw de light"

I saw them, I saw them. See Where they were

"I saw three ships." Traditional song: Cornish version. FC
—Derbyshire version. OB
—New Year's version. CSB 1—DSB
Variant: "As I sat on a sunny bank"

"I saw thy form in youthful prime." Air: Domhnall, or, Donald. Words by T. Moore. HMI

"I say, old man, your horse will die." See Poor old man

"I see brudder Moses yonder." See There's a meeting here to-night (Charleston, S.C. version)

"I see them on their winding way." <B. Hime> Words by Heber. GOS 1

"I see there, in the distance." See "Io veggio in lontananza" (Mazzoni)

"I seem to see my native land again." See Es war ein traum (Lassen)

I seen her at de window. Negro song. WSS

"I sent a letter to my love." See Fly forth, O gentle dove (Pinsuti)

"I sent my baby it's out one day." See The lost babe (Kentucky version)

"I set the bell a-ringing." See The bell ringer (Wallace)

"I sing a doleful tragedy." See Guy Fawkes

"I sing from hill tops high." See Peña

"I sing of a Maiden." R. Dunstan. 15th century words. DNS

"I sing of a Maiden." M. Shaw. 15th century words. OB

"I sing the Birth was born to-night" (Ben Jonson's carol) R. Boughton. Words by B. Jonson. OB

"I sing to you an honest song." See Taylor, the fine old Southern gentleman

"I sought my Lord in de wilderness." See I'm going home

"I stare into the silent night." See Nat (Lund)

"I started on the trail on June twenty-third." See The Lone Star trail

"I started out a-hunting." See Sally Buck (Kentucky version)

"I stood on the bridge at midnight." See The bridge (Carew)

"I stood where the summer tide, flowing." See By the blue sea (Smart)

"I take my text in Mattew." See There's a meeting here to-night (Port Royal, S.C. version)

I take off my coat and I roll up my sleeves. See The other side of Jordan

"I tell ye, bretheren, a mortal fac'." See Oh, yes

"I tell you of a brisk young farmer." See William Hall (North Carolina version)

"I tell you what I mean to do." See Keep me from sinking down

I thank God I'm free at las'. Negro spiritual. JB 2

"I think I hear my brother say." See Stars begin to fall

"I think I hear the angels sing." See Shew! fly, don't bother me (Campbell)

"I think it was 'bout twelve o'clock." See Prayer is de key of heaven

"I think, when I read that sweet story." See That sweet story of old

"I thought I heard the old man say good-bye, fare ye well." See Goodbye, fare ye well

"I tink I hear my brudder say." See Stars begin to fall

"I took her by the lily white hand." See The rejected lover (St Helen's, Ky. version)

"I trust in God." See O salutaris Hostia (Fauré)

"I trust in Thee, O Pow'r divine." See "O salutaris Hostia" (Hargitt)

"I try not to own that I tremble." See Je dis que rien ne m'épouvante (Bizet)

"I used to have a sweetheart." See The rejected lover (Tennessee version)

"I used to have an old grey horse." See Goin' down to town

"I used to live on mountain top." See Old Joe Clarke

I vassen (In the willows) S. Palmgren. Words by O. Sirén. e.sw. WM 2

"I vow my heart so troubled." See "Lo so che pria mi moro" (Aniello)

"I wait upon de Lord." See Go in the wilderness

"I waited for the Lord" (The hymn of praise) F. Mendelssohn. [Tr of Ich harrete des Herrn] e. TFG

"I walked out one bright May morning to hear the birds sing sweet." See The false young man (Clay county, Ky. version)

"I walked out one May morning to hear the small birds sing." See The false young man (Alleghany, N.C. version)

"I walked out one morning so early in spring." See The rebel soldier (Knott or Letcher county, Ky. version)

"I wander on as in a dream." See Love me and the world is mine (Ball)

"I wander'd lonely as a cloud." See The daffodils

"I wander'd, one lovely summer night." See "Am schönsten sommerabend war's" (Grieg)

"I wandered today to the hill, Maggie." See When you and I were young, Maggie (Butterfield)

"I want forty dozen of fine waxen dolls." See Christmas is coming (Phillips)

I want God's heab'n to be mine. Negro spiritual. JB 2

"I want no stars in heav'n to guide me." See Beauty's eyes (Tosti)

"I want some valiant soldier here." See Hail, Mary

"I want to be my Fader's chil'en." See The trouble of the world

I want to be ready. Negro spiritual. BB—HRD—JG—WFN—WSS Walk in Jerusalem jus' like John. JB 2

"I want to climb up Jacob's ladder." See Jacob's ladder (Florida version)

"I want to come into the dance." See "Je vais entrer dans la danse"

"I want to die easy when I die." Negro spiritual. JB 2

"I want to die like-a Lazarus die." Negro spiritual from South Carolina. AS

I want to go home ("Dere's no rain") Negro spiritual from South Carolina. AS

"I want to go home, I want to go home." Song of the European war. Words by Gitz Rice. DSO

"I want to go to heaven when I die, do love the Lord." See Wake up Jacob

I want to join the band. Negro spiritual from Florida. AS

I want to see the old home. J. E. Stewart. WSS

"I was a bachelor, I lived by myself." See The weaver

"I was a high-born gentleman." See Gypsy Davy

"I was born almost ten thousand years ago." Traditional song. SBA Variant: Four thousand years ago

"I was born in Boston, a city we all know well." See The Boston burglar (Fitzpatrick)

"I was born in old Virginny." See In old Virginny (Kentucky version)

"I was borned four thousand years ago." See Four thousand years ago

"I was brought up in Cornwall all in a high degree." See The Sheffield apprentice (Marion, N.C. version)

"I was brought up in Snowfield in such a low degree." See The Sheffield apprentice (Hot Springs, N.C. version)

"I was but a lad, you see." See Küssen ist keine sünd' (Eysler)

"I was but young when I began." See Ride on, King Jesus

"I was driving the famous Scotch express." See Daddy's on the engine

"I was goin' 'round the mountain one cold winter day." See The train that never returned

"I was lost, in a fever's mad dream." See When we parted (Ippolitov-Ivanov)

I was seeing Nellie home. See The quilting party (Fletcher)

"I was standing by the window yesterday morning." See The letter edged in black

"I watch'd last night the rising moon." See The moon behind the hill (Bishop)

"I went down by Saint James's hospital one morning." See St James's hospital (Dewey, Va. version)

"I went down to Sandy Hook de oder arternoon." See Turkey in the straw

"I went down to the depot." Jesse James ballad: negro version. SBA Variant of: "Jesse James"

"I went out a-hunting one day." See Sir Lionel (Barbourville, Ky. version)

"I went out one sweet summer morning." See George Reilly (Burnsville, N.C. version)

"I went to her father's house." See Katie Morey (Burnsville, N.C. version)

"I went to see my Susan." See Susan Jane (Hays)

"I went to the animal fair." See Animal fair

"I went up on de mountain, I didn't go dere for t' stay." See Tell Jesus

"I went up on the mountain to give my horn a blow." See "Went up on the mountain"

"I wept, beloved, as I dreamed." See "J'ai pleuré en rêve" (Hüe)

"I whipped my horse." Folk song from North Carolina. SES 2

"I will arise." A. Sullivan. SSO 3

"I will extol Thee, O Lord." M. Costa. ASA—SSO 1

"I will give you a paper of pins." See The keys of heaven (Burnsville, N.C. version; Virginia version)

"I will give you the keys of heaven." See The keys of heaven (Cheshire version)

I will go. See Theid mi g'ad' amharc

"I will not go, nor shall I not go." See Little Musgrave and Lady Barnard (Manchester, Ky. version)

"I will not let you go, my Lord." See He's the Lord of lords

"I will return, he said to me." See When the robins nest again (Martindale)

I will shout, and I'll dance. See Angel Gabriel (Stewart)

I will sing a lullaby. See "Golden slumbers kiss your eyes"

I will sing of Thy great mercies. Mendelssohn. [Tr of Lasst uns singen von der gnade des Herrn] e. SSO 1

"I will sing you a song of that beautiful land." See Home of the soul (Phillips)

"I will sing you a song, 'twill not take me long." See A rookie

"I will tell you of a fellow." See Common Bill

I will walk with my love. Irish air from County Dublin. Traditional words. HI 2

I wish I been dere. Negro spiritual from South Carolina. AS

I wish I had my old girl back again. P. Wallace. Words by B. MacDonald. OTG

"I wish I had someone to love me." See Moonlight

"I wish I had the shepherd's lamb." Irish folk song. Tr of As truag gan peata'n maoir. e. HI 1

I wish I was a child again. Play-party song from Virginia. SES 2

"I wish I was a little bird." American song. SBA

"I wish I was in de land ob cotton." See Dixie (Emmett)

I wish I was single again. Minstrel song. SBA

"I wish I were a little rock." See A little wish

"I wish I were a little sparrow." See "Come all you fair and tender ladies" (Franklin county, Va. version)

"I wish, I wish, I wish in vain." See I wish I was a child again

"I wish that I were back again." See Take me back to tech (Seaver)

"I wish to God I'd never been born." See Around Cape Horn

"I wish your breast was made of glass." See The lover's lament

"I woas nit, wie mir is." See Der sinnierende narr (Kain)

"I wonder where Maria's gone." See Maria's gone

"I wonder where my mother is gone." See Peter, go ring them bells

I wonder who's kissing her now. J. E. Howard. Words by Hough and Adams. GFS

I would like to read. See I know I would like to read

"I would not be a sinner." See Wade in de water

"I would not marry a blacksmith." See Soldier boy for me (Franklin county, Va. version)

"I would not wed the finest lass." See The musical bachelor (Heinrich)

"I would that my love." See "Ich wollt' meine lieb' ergösse" (Mendelssohn)

"I wuz standin' by the winder yest'day mornin'." See The letter edged in black

Ia po svietlitsie mlada khozhu. See "Durch das fenster späh ich"

Ianka. See Janka

Ibby Damsel. Folk song from North Carolina. SES 2

Ibsen, Lars Möller
College hymn (same air as Det norske flag)

"Ich besteig', juchheissa, ich besteige" ("Ha felülök, csuhaj, ha felülök") Hungarian folk song. g.hu. ML 3

"Ich bin a bal-agoleh." Jewish folk song. y. SY

"Ich bin a mädel in die johren." See A mädel in die johren

"Ich bin schoin a meidel in die yuren." See A mädel in die johren

"Ich bin zur hochzeit hier." See La chanson de la mariée

"Ich fahr dahin." 15th century German song. g. EDL

Ich fleh' für ihn. For English translation see "I pray for him, spare him" (Wagner)

"Ich gei arois." See Song of the little bird

"Ich gönne dir ja alles glück." See "Jag unnar dig ändå allt godt"

"Ich grolle nicht" ("I'll not complain") R. Schumann. Words by Heine. e.g. GG

"Ich hab die nacht geträumet." See Der schwere traum

"Ich hab' ein kleines lied erdacht" ("Within my heart a song I found") A. Bungert. Words by G. von Boddien. e.g. AT—TM

Ich hab' im traum geweinet. For French and English translations see "J'ai pleuré en rêve" (Hüe)

"Ich hab' in deinem auge" ("Once in thine eyes") R. Franz. Words by F. Rückert. e.g. SAT

"Ich hab mich ergeben mit herz und mit hand." See Gelübde

"Ich habe fünf liebe söhne gehabt." See Fünf söhne

Ich harrete des Herrn. For English translation see "I waited for the Lord" (Mendelssohn)

"Ich hatt' einen kameraden." See Der gute kamerad

"Ich hör' meinen schatz." See Der schmied (Brahms)

"Ich komme vom gebirge her." See Der wanderer (Schubert)

"Ich konnte heute nicht schlafen." See Laengsel (Kjerulf)

"Ich kumm jetzt vun mein zadik." Jewish folk song. y. SY

"Ich legte mich zur ruh." See "Jeg lagde mig saa sildig"

Ich liebe dich ("Min tankes tanke") See Jeg elsker dig (Grieg)

Ich liebe dich herzinniglich. See Verlegenheit (Abt)

"Ich liebe dich, so wie du mich." Beethoven. <Words by Herrosee; wrongly attributed to Hölty> g. EDL

"Ich liebe dich, so wie du mich" (Constancy) e.g. GA

"Ich möchte dir wohl etwas sagen." See Verlegenheit (Abt)

"Ich neh un neh a ganze woch." See Mit a nodel, ohn a nodel

"Ich nehm mein gläschen in die hand." See Vive la compagneia

"Ich rudert' eines morgens hinunter einen flub." See John Riley (Sussex version)

"Ich ruderte aus, und zu früher stund' an." See Strilevise

"Ich ruhe still im hohen grünen gras." See Feldeinsamkeit (Brahms)

"Ich sah ein röschen am wege stehn" (An junge spröde schönen) C. M. von Weber. Words by K. Müchler. g. EDL

"Ich schaue aus dem fenster." See "M'affaccio a la finestra"

"Ich schiess den hirsch im wilden forst." See Jägers liebeslied

"Ich schweift' umher und reiste weit." See Cnocáinín aereach Chill-Mhuire

"Ich spring an diesem ringe." See Minnelied

"Ich steh' auf einem hohen berg." See Das lied von dem jungen grafen

"Ich verlor mein jung rösslein" ("Man pasuda kumeliņis") Lettish folk song. g.le. ML 3

"Ich wandle unter blumen" (A garden idyll) E. Lassen. Words by V. Wilder. e.g. TM

"Ich war bei Chloen ganz allein." See Der kuss (Beethoven)

"Ich weiss, dass meiner lieb' zu dir." See "I know that hope doth smile upon" (Dvořák)

Ich weiss ein lieblich engelspiel. 14th century German carol. e. OB

"Ich weiss ein maidlein hübsch und fein." See Hüt du dich

"Ich weiss nicht, was soll es bedeuten." See Die Lorelei (Silcher)

"Ich weiss nicht, was soll's bedeuten." See Die Lorelei (Liszt)

"Ich weiss nicht, wie mir ist." See Der sinnierende narr (Kain)

"Ich will jauchzen, jauchzen." See Der sänger

"Ich wollt' ich wär' im Baumwollland." See Dixie (Emmett)

["Ich wollt' meine lieb' ergösse"] "I would that my love." F. Mendelssohn. Words by Heine. e. BB—MFS—TFG

Ich wünscht' ich wär' in Dixie. See Dixie (Emmett)

"Ick hebbe vyf leve söneken hat." See Fünf söhne

"I'd choose to be a daisy." F. Buckley. GOS 2

"I'd mourn the hopes that leave me." Irish air: <The rose tree> Words by T. Moore. HMI—SI

"I'd offer thee this hand of mine." GOS 1

"If a body meet a body." See Comin' thro' the rye

"If all the world were paper." BOS 2

"If at war's altar we should kneel." See To the eighteenth

"If by chance you look for me perhaps you'll not me find." See Reynardine

"If ever I see." MFS

"If he returns." R. Wagner. [Tr of Kommt er dann heim] e. WG

If her eyes are blue as skies. See Peggy O'Neil (Pease, Nelson and Dodge)

"If I but knew your heart, dear." See If I had a thousand lives to live (Solman)

"If I could I surely would." See Pharoah's army got drownded

"If I could drive steel like John Henry." See Drivin' steel

If I die a railroad man. Old American song. SBA Variant of: "John Henry"

"If I had a beau, for a soldier who'd go." See The dashing white sergeant (Bishop)

If I had a thousand lives to live. A. Solman. Words by S. Maguire. OTG

"If I had a-known before I'd a-courted." See "Come all you fair and tender ladies" (Hot Springs, N.C. version)

"If I had but a thousand a year, Gaffer Green." See The better wish (Russell)

"If I were a king I would make you my queen." See The magpie's nest

"If I were a little bird." See Careless love (Negro version)

"If I were a voice." I. B. Woodbury. GOS 2

If I were king of Ireland. Irish air. Words by A. P. Graves. TFO

"If in a state of exhilaration." See Bob up serenely (Audran)

If Jack were only here. See My mother was a lady (Stern)

"If my old top were a dancing man." See "Ah! si mon moine voulait danser"

"If, O massa, you love me so true." See Z'amours Marianne

"If only by deserving I might claim thy affection." See "Se meritar potessi" (Bruni)

"If Romeo thy son did slaughter." See "Se Romeo t'uccise un figlio" (Bellini)

"If the heart of a man is deprest with cares" ("Wenn das herz eines mannes die sorge drückt") Old English song. e.g. ML 1

"If the rose in the garden over the way." See Over the way (Marshall)

"If the wood is left unplaned what matter." See The wedding-suit

"If there's a shepherd in your parish." See "Ah! s'il est dans votre village" (Godard)

"If thou canst not be near me." See "Se non ti moro allato" (Bernasconi)

"If thou plead'st for her." See "Cruda, funesta smania" (Donizetti)

"If Thou should'st mark iniquities." Costa.   SSO 4

"If thou'lt be mine." Irish air: Caiteach roin, or, The winnowing sheet. Words by T. Moore.   HMI

"If to thy throne fond pray'rs ascend." See "Se fino al cielo ascendere" (Mercadante)

If we please you with our singing. See La guignolée

"If with all your hearts ye truly seek me." F. Mendelssohn-Bartholdy. [Tr of So ihr mich von ganzem herzen suchet] e.   SSO 3—TFG

"If words weigh not with thee, dear." See "Se al labro mio non credi" (Pergolesi)

"If ye would hear." 16th century Dutch air. Words by D. Greenwell. OB

"If yo' brudder talk about you." See I'm gwine up to heab'n anyhow

If you belong to Gideon's band. See Gideon's band

"If you could have married the king's daughter dear." See The daemon lover (Allanstand, N.C. version no. 1)

"If you evah go to Houston." See Midnight special (Negro jail song)

If you lak-a-me, lak I lak-a-you. See Under the bamboo tree (Cole and Johnson)

"If your look up de road you see fader Mosey." See Join the angel band (Port Royal islands version)

"If you love God, serve Him." See Love an' serve de Lord

"If you love me." G. Bizet. [Tr of Si tu m'aimes, Carmen] e. WG

"If you please, you see I'm a domestic." See The bell goes a-ringing for Sai-rah (Hunt)

"If you see my mother." See Ride on, Jesus

"If you should go to Aberdeen." See The Highland fling

"If you walk in the glen." See The song of the good little men

"If you want a buzzem." See Buy broom buzzems

"If you want to be a badger." See The badger ballad (Olson)

"If you want to go a-courting." Folk song: Allanstand, N.C. version. SES 2
—Burnsville, N.C. version no. 1. SES 2
—Burnsville, N.C. version no. 2. SES 2
—Virginia version.   SES 2

"If you want to get to heaven lemme tell yer how to do hit." See Jest talkin'

"If you want to get to hebben, come along." See Did you hear my Jesus

"If you want to go to heav'n you must be new-born again." See New-born again

If you want to have some fun. See P. T. Barnum's show

"If you want to know where the generals were." See Where they were

"If you want to know where the privates were." See Where they were

"If you want to know where the Super is." See Information

[If you want to see Jesus] Leanin' on de Lord. Negro spiritual. HRD

"If you'll listen a while, I'll sing you a song." See Jim Fisk

"If yo' brother done you wrong." See You fight on

"If your brother talk about you." See I'm gwine up to heab'n anyhow

"If you're on pursuit for your own true lover." See William Taylor (North Carolina version)

Ifan, Wil. See Evans, William

"Ihr, die ihr triebe." See "Voi, che sapete" (Mozart)

Ihr englein, die uns so treu bewacht. For English translation see The angels spoke to us in dreams (Humperdinck)

"Ihr freunde, die ihr nach Palermo gehhet." See Canto del carcerato

"Ihr kinderlein, kommet." See Die kinder bei der krippe (Schulz)

"Ihr lustigen Hannoveraner." Norddeutsches soldatenlied. g. EDL

"Ihr mädchen, sammelt wasser ein solang noch säumt der sonnenschein." See Cornish May song

"Ihren schäfer zu erwarten." See Phyllis und die mutter

Ikama zeema zeema rinktum. See The Swazi warrior

"Il a bholagain il bho m'aighean." See Cronan bleoghain

"Il était trois mat'lots de Groix." See Les trois matelots de Groix

"Il était trois petits enfants." See Le miracle de Saint-Nicolas

Il était un de mes aïeux. For English translation see The legend of the glass (Offenbach)

Il était une bergère ("A shepherdess was watching." — The shepherdess) French folk song. e. CSB 1
"There was a little maiden." e. DSC

"Il nous arrive un grand vaisseau." See Noël de Strasbourg

Ilka lassie has her laddie. See Comin' thro' the rye

"I'll be a sergeant." Civil war song. DSO

I'll be dar ("Tomorrow I am gwine away") Minstrel song. WSS

I'll be down to get you in a taxi, honey. See The Darktown strutter's ball (Brooks)

I'll be home to-morrow night. J. Howard. SRW

I'll be there ("Tomorrow I am gwine away") See I'll be dar

I'll be there in the morning. Negro spiritual. HRD
Variant of: General roll call

I'll be true to my love. See The two sisters

I'll be with you when the roses bloom again. Edwards. Words by Cobb. DFF

"I'll build me a castle on the mountain so high." See The cuckoo (Burnsville, N.C. version)

"I'll build me a castle on yonders mountain high." See The rebel soldier (Berea, Ky. version)

I'll drink a cup to Scotland yet. See Scotland yet (McLeod)

"I'll give to you a paper of pins, and that's the way our love begins." See The keys of heaven (American mountain version; Black Mountain, N.C. version; Hot Springs, N.C. version)

"I'll give to you a paper of pins to show the way that love begins." See The keys of heaven (Clinchfield, N.C. version)

"I'll go back to Maxim's." Finale of act II of The merry widow. F. Lehar. e. WLO

"I'll go up on the mountain top and grow me a patch of cane." See Mountain top

"I'll go up on the mountain top, and plant me a patch of cane." See Eliza Jane (Liza Jane)

I'll hear de trumpet soun'. Negro spiritual. FSN

I'll love my baby till the sea runs dry. See Ever after on

I'll love you true. See Waltz song (Lehar)

I'll ne'er forget where'er I roam. See You've been a friend to me (Hays)

"I'll not complain." See "Ich grolle nicht" (Schumann)

"I'll put on the golden shoes." See Way over yonder

"I'll put the case." K. Millöcker. e. WLO

"I'll rest where the green trees are whispering." See In der ferne (Brahms)

"I'll riddle to you, my younger son." See Lord Thomas and fair Ellinor (Allanstand, N.C. version)

"I'll seek a four-leav'd shamrock." See The four-leaved shamrock (Lover)

"I'll send a letter." Swedish folk song. e. LSB

"I'll show thee stars." See "Der gives stjerner" (Sinding)

"I'll sing thee songs of Araby." F. Clay. Words by W. G. Wills. HCA—TFG

"I'll sing you a fine ould song." See The fine ould Irish gintleman

"I'll sing you a song I am singing for ever." See The clever woman (Blewitt)

"I'll sing you a song of the fish of the sea." See Rio Grande

"I'll sing you one-ho! green grow the rushes-ho." See Green grow the rushes-ho

"I'll soon be home, mother. See I'll be home to-morrow night (Howard)

I'll stick to the ship, lads. See The ship I love (McGlennon)

"Ill sustaining." G. Verdi. ɪTr of Mal reggendo all' aspro assaltoɪ e. WG

I'll take another bottle of wizard oil. See Wizard oil

"I'll take my gospel trumpet." See Weary traveler

"I'll take you home again, Kathleen." T. P. Westendorf (music and words) GFS

I'll tell nobody. Old song. GOS 1

I'll tell the cock-eyed world they'd better let my man be. See Blue gummed blues (Handy)

"I'll tell you a sad story which happened in this land." See The banks of sweet Dundee (Teges, Ky. version)

"I'll tell you a story that is no sham." See The cork leg (Tyrone version)

"I'll tell you a story, there is one I know." See Plantonio

"I'll tell you a tale now without any flam." See The cork leg (Blewitt)

"I'll tell you of a brisk young farmer." See William Hall (St Helen's, Ky. version)

"I'll tell you of a soldier who lately come from sea." See The lady and the dragoon (Nellysford, Va. version)

"I'll tell you of a story of little Omie Wise." See Poor Omie (Burnsville, N.C. version no. 2)

"I'll tell you of an awful wedding." See The awful wedding

I'll tell you where they were. See Where they were

Illinois ("By thy rivers gently flowing") W. H. Jones. Words by C. H. Chamberlain. BB
"By the rivers gently flowing." AI

Illinois ("'Way down upon the Wabash") See El-a-noy

Illinois loyalty. See "We're loyal to you, Illinois" (Guild)

"I'm a Chickaleary bloke." See The Chickaleary cove

I'm a child of grace.   Negro spiritual.
WFN
"I'm a fella who doesn't like bothar."   See
Awfully clever (Hunt)
"I'm a flower of the field."   See The song
of Solomon (Musorgskiï)
"I'm a forester free."   E. Reyloff.   MFS
"I'm a gay tra, la, la."   See The jolly
Switzer
"I'm a hallelujah Christian."   See The
hallelujah Christian
I'm a jayhawk.   University of Kansas
song.   G. Bowles (music and words)
AI—AIS
I'm a little lone girl.   See The drunkard's
lone child
"I'm a maiden who never refuses."   See
Oysters and wine at 2 A.M.
"I'm a man of experience."   See The
coast artilleryman
"I'm a poor Irish girl."   Irish air.
Words by W. Maynard.   HMI
"I'm a poor lonesome cowboy."   See Poor
lonesome cowboy
I'm a poor stranger ("One cold winter
morning")   Old air.   Words by W.
Maynard.   HMI
"I'm a poor, wayfarin' stranger."   See
Pilgrim's song
I'm a rambling wreck from Georgia tech.
See Rambling wreck from Georgia tech
"I'm a rambling wretch of poverty."   See
Son of a gambolier
I'm a respectable wife.   F. Lehar.   e.
WLO
"I'm a shepherd born to sorrow."   <An-
cient Welsh pastoral song>   e.
TFG
    Hob y derri dando.   South Wales
    version.   Old verses adapted and
    revised.   e.   CSB 4
"I'm a shepherd of the valley."   F. G.
Klauer.   e.   MFS
"I'm a slim old pig."   See Razorback
rootin' song (Paisley)
I'm a son of the seventh.   See A son of
a musketeer
"I'm a stranger in your city."   See Port-
land county jail
I'm a Tar-Heel born.   See "Hark! the
sound of Tar-Heel voices"
I'm a Yankee Doodle Dandy.   See The
Yankee Doodle boy (Cohan)
I'm a-goin' down to town.   See Goin'
down to town
I'm a-goin' to tell you 'bout de comin' of
de Saviour.   See In that great getting-
up morning
"I'm a-going to travel."   See L'envoi
I'm a-gwine to tell you 'bout de comin' ob
de Saviour.   See In that great getting-
up morning
"I'm all wore out a-toilin' fo' de Lawd"
(Come on, sinner)   Negro spiritual
from Tennessee.   FSN
I'm alone, all alone ("I'm alone though I
rove")   W. R. Dempster.   Words
by L. F. Thomas.   GOS 2
"I'm alone, all alone, my friends all have
fled."   See The drunkard's lone child

"I'm alone though I rove through the city's
thronged street."   See I'm alone, all
alone (Dempster)
I'm always safe when I go in.   See
Tommy Dodd
"I'm an elegant swell, as you all can tell."
See Julius Cornelius Augustus Pompe-
lius Fredericus Plantaganet Brown
"I'm an old time Irish nabob."   See
Whiskers, five a bag
I'm a-rolling.   Negro spiritual.   FSN—
GSS—HRD—WSS
"I'm as happy as a bird in springtime."
See Roguish little beauty, Emeleen
"I'm as happy as the day is long."   See
I hope I don't intrude
I'm a-trav'ling to the grave.   Negro spiri-
tual.   HRD
"I'm a-trouble in de mind."   Negro spiri-
tual from South Carolina.   AS
    Variant of: I'm troubled in mind
"I'm born of God, I know I am."   See
View de land
I'm bound away ("For the sake of you,
my lassie")   Capstan chantey.   SBS
"I'm bound for Alabama."   See Roll the
cotton down
"I'm bound to follow the long horn cow."
Cowboy song.   LSC
"I'm but a stranger here."   See Heaven
is my home (Sullivan)
"I'm Captain Jinks of the Horse Marines."
See Captain Jinks
I'm chief cook and bottle-washer.   See
Root, hog, or die
I'm coming, I'm coming, for my head is
bending low.   See Old black Joe
(Foster)
I'm dancing mad.   J. F. Brian (music and
words)   SW
"I'm dreaming now of Hallie."   See
Listen to the mocking bird (Winner)
"I'm feeling lonesome, I'm feeling blue."
See Those pals of ours (Greaton-Cole)
"Im felde schleich ich still und wild."   See
Jägers nachtlied (Reichardt)
"I'm fond of life."   See Par excellence
"Im friedlichen haus, am rande der heide."
See Tra la la la
"I'm getting old and feeble now."   See
The little old cabin in the lane (Hays)
"I'm glad I am a farmer."   See The
farmer
I'm glad I live in Dixie.   See Dixie
(Emmett.   Words by Wharton)
"I'm goin' away for to stay a little while."
See He's gone away
"I'm goin' away to see de good ol' Daniel."
See My ship is on de ocean
"I'm goin' to leave ol' Texas now."   See
Goin' to leave ol' Texas
"I'm going back to Dixie."   See "I'se
gwine back to Dixie" (White)
"I'm going back to the Swannanoa town."
See "Swannanoa town" (Micaville, N.C.
version)
"I'm going down to the river of Jordan."
See Members, don't git weary
I'm going home.   Negro spiritual from
Tennessee.   AS

"I'm going to Alabamy." See "I'm gwine to Alabamy"

"I'm going to bear, Lord." See Bear de burden

"I'm going to build myself a raft." See De blues ain' nothin'

I'm going to Georgia. Folk song: Kentucky version. SES 2
—North Carolina version. SES 2

I'm going to get married next Sunday. Folk song from Tennessee. SES 2
Variant of: The sign of the Bonny Blue Bell

"I'm going to join the great 'sociation." See Oh, then my little soul's going to shine

"I'm going to lay down my sword and shield." See I ain't gwine study war no more

"I'm going to leave old Texas now." See Goin' to leave ol' Texas

"I'm going to set down at the welcome table, yes." See Some o' dese days

I'm going up to heaven anyhow. See I'm gwine up to heab'n anyhow

"I'm going where nobody knows my name." See Levee moan

"I'm go'n' to lay down my sword and shield." See I ain't gwine study war no more

"I'm go'n'ter set down at de welcome table, yes." See Some o' dese days

"I'm gwine down to de ribbuh ob Jordan." See Members, don't git weary

"I'm gwine to Alabamy." Negro folk song. AS

"I'm gwine to jine de great 'sociation." See Oh, then my little soul's gwine to shine

I'm gwine up to heab'n anyhow. Negro spiritual. JB 2

"I'm in love with a charming young lady." See Kathleen (Mora)

"I'm in love with a sweet little girlie." See Just one girl (Udall)

"I'm in trouble." Negro spiritual from Florida. AS

I'm just a young cowboy and I know I done wrong. See The cowboy's lament ("My home's in Montana")

"I'm just a-goin' over Jordan." Negro spiritual. FSN
Variant of: Pilgrim's song (Negro spiritual)

I'm just a-goin' over Jordan ("I'm a poor way-farin' stranger") See Pilgrim's song (Negro spiritual)

I'm just an old razorback. See Razorback rootin' song (Paisley)

Im kahne (In the boat) E. Grieg. Words by V. Krag. e.g. TM

"Im kerkerturm von Nantes." See "Dans les prisons de Nantes"

"Im krug zum grünen kranze." See Brüderschaft

"Im kühlen keller." See Der rheinwein-zecher (Fischer)

"I'm lazy Robin." See Lazy Robin

"I'm lonely to-night, love, without you." See Norah O'Neale

"I'm lonesome since I cross'd the hill." See The girl I left behind me

"Im meer könnt ihr das schifflein rauchen sehen." See "In mezo al mar"

"I'm not a free agent." See What the dickey birds say (Jakobowski)

I'm not myself at all. S. Lover (music and words) SI

"Im Oberland ist's lustig." See In Gorensko

I'm off to Charlestown. See Off to Charlestown

"I'm off to port." See "Voy a partir" (Ponce)

I'm on my way to Mandalay. F. Fischer. Words by A. Bryan. SMG

I'm owre young to marry yet. Scottish air. Words by R. Burns. GS

"I'm Paddy Whack from Ballynahack." See Since I've been in the army

"I'm Pierre de Bon Bon." See Rosalie (Knight)

"I'm Pierre de Bonton." See Rosalie (Knight)

"I'm right from old Virginny, wid my head so full of knarledge." See Walk in the parlour

"I'm right from old Virginny wid my pocket full ob news." See Root, hog, or die

"I'm sad and I'm lonely." Southern folk song. SBA

I'm satisfied. G. Tanner (music and words) RA

"Im schloss von llwyn onn einst." See Llwyn on

"Im schwarzen Walfisch zu Askalon." See Jonas

I'm seventeen come Sunday. Folk song: Callaway, Va. version. SES 2
—Endicott, Va. version. SES 2
—Meadows of Dan, Va. version. SES 2
—Stuart, Va. version. SES 2

"I'm sitting by the stile, Mary." See Irish emigrant's lament (Barker)

"I'm sitting on the stile, Mary." See Irish emigrant's lament (Dempster)

I'm so glad trouble don't last alway. Negro spiritual. HRD

"I'm so glad troubles don't last always." WFN

"I'm so sorry for old Adam." See Old Adam

"I'm sometimes up, I'm sometimes down." See Trouble will bury me down

"Im sommer wie war da so grün der wald." See Herbststurm (Grieg)

I'm sorry, dear, so sorry, dear. See I'm sorry I made you cry (Clesi)

I'm sorry I made you cry. N. J. Clesi. SMG

"Im tal von Barcelona (hoch lebe die lieb')." See La niña desenvuelta

"I'm the kid that's all the candy." See The Yankee Doodle boy (Cohan)

"I'm the shanty-man of the wild goose nation." See Tommy's gone to Hilo

"I'm thinking again of my childhood's happy hours." See The old cuckoo clock that hangs upon the wall (Wheeler)

"I'm thinking of Erin tonight." See Jennie, the flower of Kildare (Stewart)

"I'm thinking that no bootlegger ever should take him a wife." See La realera (Rocha)

"Im tiefsten innern ein süss erinnern." See Gute nacht (Haynes)

I'm to be queen o' the May, mother. See The May queen (Dempster)

"I'm trabling back to Georgia." See Trabling back to Georgia

"I'm troubled in de mind." See "I'm a-trouble in de mind"

I'm troubled in mind. Negro spiritual. FSN—HRD—WSS
    Variant: "I'm a-trouble in de mind"

"I'm unhappy, so unhappy, I feel so sad and blue." See Florida blues (Phillips)

Im volkston. E. Hildach. Words by A. Hildach. e.g.   TM

"Im wald und auf der heide." See Jägerleben

"I'm wearin' awa'." See The land o' the leal

"Im wirtshaus von La Peyra (holalla)." See La criada del hostal

["Im wunderschönen monat mai"] In lovely May. R. Schumann. Words by H. Heine. e.   DSB

Image, Selwyn
    "The snow lies thick" (Shaw)
    "Three kings in great glory" (Shaw)

The image of the rose. See "In einem thale friedlich stille" (Reichardt)

Imlah, John
    "Dinna forget" (Millard)

"Immer leiser wird mein schlummer" ("Sleep to me no rest is bringing") J. Brahms. Words by H. Lingg. e.g.   HCA

"Immortal Babe, who this dear day." See For Christmas day

"Immortal by their deed and word" (Spohr) Arr from L. Spohr. Words by F. L. Hosmer.   LAS

"Immortal Love, forever full" (Raphael) Arr from G. Donizetti. Words by J. G. Whittier.   LAS

"Imprison'd once at Nantes." See "Dans les prisons de Nantes"

"In a cavern, in a canyon." See Oh, my darling Clementine (Montrose)

"In a cheerless room there sits a sad young mother." See For sale— a baby (Harris)

"In a close town, where I did dwell." See The miller's apprentice (Barbourville, Ky. version no. 2)

In a garden. Folk song of Little Russia. e.   DSB

"In a jolly crowd we tramp along." See Hiking song

"In a little rosewood casket." See The little rosewood casket

"In a little white cottage." See Gentle Nettie Moore (Pike)

"In a rosebush I was born" ("Rózsabokorban jöttem") Hungarian folk song. e.hu.   KH 2

"In a shady forest, built two doves their nest." See The turtle dove

"In a shady garden walk'd a princess slender." Silesian air. Words by K. Davis.   DSB

"In a snug little field of a neighboring park." See The lark and the magpie

"In a well known club one evening." See The best thing in life (Harris)

"In Alabam' at Muscles Shoals dam." See John Henry blues (Handy)

In all my dreams, I dream of you. A. Piantadosi. Words by J. McCarthy. SMG

In all Nebraska's wide domain. See The Kinkaiders

"In all the country round." See Dans tous les cantons

"In all the ups and downs of life." See A motto for all

"In allen guten stunden." See Bundeslied (Reichardt)

"In Amsterdam there lived a maid." See A-roving

"In an Arizona town one day." See Billy Venero

"In an old old fashioned homestead." See I've grown so used to you (Chattaway)

"In ancient days there liv'd a Turk." See Kafoozalem

"In April, when primroses paint the sweet plain." See The yellow-haired laddie

"In armor bright rides forth a knight." See The red scarf (Bonheur)

"In Berlin, sagt er." Air: In Schönbrunn. Words by C. von Holtei. g.   EDL

"In Bethlehem I would be." See The cuckoo carol

"In Bethlehem, that fair city." 14th century air. 15th century words.   OB

"In Boston town there lived a merchant." See "In Seaport town" (Carmen, N.C. version)

In bright mansions above. Negro spiritual. HRD—JG

"In Bristol town, as I have heard tell." See Bristol town

"In Carmel bay the people say." See Abalone

"In Caroline, whar I was born." See Walk, jawbone

"In Cawsand bay lying." See Cawsand bay

"In Cusciones bergen friedlich sass die mutter vor der wiegen." See Nanna

In dat day. Negro spiritual from South Carolina.   FSN

In dat great gittin'-up mornin'. See In that great getting-up morning

"In days of old, when knights were bold." See A warrior bold (Maybrick)

"In days of yore, from Britain's shore." See The maple leaf forever (Muir)

"In days of yore the hero Wolfe." See The maple leaf forever (Muir)

"In de ebening by de moonlight." See "In the evening by the moonlight" (Bland)

In de Lord, in de Lord. See My soul's been anchored in de Lord

"In de mornin' when I rise." See Tell my Jesus morning

"In de vinter, in de vinter-time." See In de vinter time

In de vinter time. Traditional A.nerican song. SBA

"In dem dornbusch blüht ein röslein." See Lieber schatz, sei wieder gut mir (Franz)

"In dem grünen walde, auf dem weichen rasen." See Der Kosak

"In den garten will ich gehen" ("Aš nueisiu sa sodelin") Lithuanian folk song. g.li. ML 3

"In der erde trübem irrsal." See Der wandrer (Folk song from Smyrna)

In der ferne ("Nun leb wohl, du kleine gasse nun ade") F. Silcher. Words by Albert graf Schlippenbach. g. EDL

In der ferne ("Will ruhen unter den bäumen hier."—Absence) J. Brahms. Words by L. Uhland. e.g. CSB 6

In der heimat. See Her hjemme

"In der lauten strasse kann man sehen" ("A csap-utczán véges-végig, végig") Hungarian folk song. g.hu. ML 3

In der märznacht (A night in March) W. Taubert. e.g. HCA

In der spinnstub ("Ach, du mein kindel."—"Csicseri borsó") Hungarian folk song. g.hu. ML 3

In der spinnstub ("See, love, above the stars") See "See, love, above the stars"

"In deräussen is a zavieruche." See Yossel un Zlatte

"In des dorfes teiche dort" ("Na tom našem nátoni") Czech folk song. bo.g. ML 3

"In die weite fremde ruft mich fort von hier." See Kriegers abschied von der mutter

₁"In diesen heil'gen hallen"₁ "Qui sdegno non s'accende." W. A. Mozart. e.i. PB

"In distant land." See "In fernem land" (Wagner)

"In drunken sleep an old man lay." See Somebody's grandpa (Wood)

"In dulci jubilo." 14th century air arr by R. L. de Pearsall. <14th century words> e. DSC—MBS—OB

"In dulci jubilo." J. S. Bach. 14th century words. e. OB

"In eighteen hundred and forty one, my corduroy breeches I put on." See Paddy works on the railway

"In eighteen-hundred and sixty-one I did as plenty more have done." See Poor Paddy

"In 'eighty-eight, ere I was born." See The Spanish Armada

₁"In einem kühlen grunde"₁ The broken ring. German folk air. Words by J. von Eichendorff. e. TFB—TFO—TFP—TFR

"In einem kühlen grunde" (Das zerbrochene ringlein) After F. Glück. Words by J. von Eichendorff. g. EDL

"In einem thale friedlich stille" (The image of the rose) G. Reichardt. e.g. MFS

"In England lived a noble lord." See Young Beichan (Pine Mountain, Ky. version)

"In ev'ry faith are dissensions." See Tro (Sinding)

"In every town and village." See Bell carol

In excelsis gloria ("Not in halls of regal splendor") Welsh air. MFS

In excelsis gloria ("When Christ was born") See "When Christ was born of Mary free" (Brown); "When Christ was born of Mary free" (Shaw)

₁"In fernem land"₁ "In distant land." R. Wagner. e. WG

"In flakes of a feathery white." See Silently falling snow

"In fourteen-hundred ninety-two, a Dago from Italy." See Colombo

₁In front of Old Pardee₁ Alma mater. Lafayette college song. W. C. Stier (music and words) AI—AIS—KU—KV

"In full many a town" ("Be sok falut, be sok várost") Old Hungarian folk song. e.hu. KH 2

"In gentle murmurs will I mourn." Händel. SSO 2

In golden firelight dancing. Croatian air. Words by K. Davis. DSB

"In good King Charles's golden days." See The vicar of Bray

"In Gorensko" (Ho-la dri-jo-ri) Carniolan folk song. e. DSB

"Na Gorenjskem je fletno" ("Im Oberland ist's lustig") g.sl. ML 2

In Hawaii. Hawaiian folk air. Words by J. L. Vandevere. TFO

"In heavenly love abiding." J. S. Bach. Words by A. L. Waring. DSB

"In heavenly love abiding." F. W. Batchelder. Words by A. L. Waring. TSS 2

"In heavenly love abiding." H. L. von Hassler. Words by A. L. Waring. DSC

"In heav'nly love abiding" (Hungary) M. Iszlai. Words by A. L. Waring. LAS

"In heavenly love abiding." E. Lassen. Words by A. L. Waring. CSS 1

"In heavenly love abiding." F. Mendelssohn. Words by A. L. Waring. BB

"In his swaddling clothes all fresh and white." See At the cradle (Franck)

"In Jersey City." Old American song. SW

"In Karls, des guten, goldner zeit." See The vicar of Bray

"In London city where I once did dwell." See Barbara Allen (Georgia version)

"In London lived a worthy man." See Young Beichan (Webb's Creek, Tenn. version)

"In London sweet city a fair damsel did dwell." See The cruel ship's carpenter (Tennessee version)

"In Lorraine as we are dancing." See Les trois capitaines

In lovely May. See "Im wunderschönen monat mai" (Schumann)

"In Mantua in fetters." See Andreas Hofer

"In meiner liebsten garten." See Aus der rosenzeit (Fielitz)

"In meines vaters garten." See Auprès de ma blonde

In memoriam ("Flow'rs from the shady greenwood dell") Bohemian folk air. Words by H. H. Harbour. DSB

In merry chorus. J. Offenbach. MFS

"In mezo al mar" (Auf hoher see) Italian folk song. g.i. ML 2

In Mindanao. Song of the Spanish American war. Air: The girl I left behind me. DSO

In my Father's house. Negro spiritual from Texas. SBA

"In my heart all are equally cherish'd." See "Every flower is equally cherished" (Verdi)

"In native worth and honour clad." J. Haydn. e. SSO 3

"In Notamun town not a soul would look up." See Nottamun town (Hindman, Ky. version no. 1)

"In numbers, and but these few" (Herrick's ode) A. Gibbs. Words by R. Herrick. OB

"In ocean's name, of endless sweep and grandeur." See Till bruden (Peterson-Berger)

"In old Kentuck in de arternoon." See Clare de kitchen

In old Madrid. H. Trotère. Words by C. Bingham. SFB—TFP

"In old North Carolina I was bred and was born." See The wagoner's lad (Hot Springs, N.C. version)

In old Virginny. Folk song: Kentucky version. SES 2
—North Carolina version. SES 2
—Callaway, Va. version. SES 2
—Franklin county, Va. version. SES 2

"In olden time mankind was bred." See The world is marching on

"In pantaloons and waistcoats." See The golden glove (North Carolina version; Virginia version)

"In Paris town, guess what's to be found." See Ah! le joli bois, mesdames

"In Plymouth town there lived a maid." See A-roving

"In Poland there's an inn." See Poland

In Polen steht ein haus. For English translation see Poland

In praise of May. See Sommerlied (Neidhardt von Reuenthal)

In praise of old Nassau, my boys. See Old Nassau (Langlotz)

In praise of tears. See Lob der thränen (Schubert)

"In prime of years, when I was young." See The ages of man

In Princeton-town we've got a team. See Princeton cannon song march (Hewitt and Osborn)

"In questo semplice, modesto asilo." G. Donizetti. e.i. PC
"Poor tho' my cot may be." e. MFS

"In Scarlet town, where I was born." See Barbara Allen

"In Scotland's fair lands over mountains and rills." See Scotch lassie, Jean

"In seaport of late a fair damsel did dwell." See The cruel ship's carpenter (Afton, Va. version)

"In Seaport town." Folk song: Barbourville, Ky. version. SES 1
—Hindman, Ky. version. SES 1
—Hyden, Ky. version. SES 1
—Allanstand, N.C. version. SES 1
—Alleghany, N.C. version. SES 1
—Burnsville, N.C. version. SES 1
—Carmen, N.C. version. SES 1
—Hot Springs, N.C. version. SES 1
—Virginia version. SES 1
Variants: Bristol town; Bruton town

In shadowland ("She sits alone") C. Pinsuti. MFS

"In sì barbara." G. Rossini. e.i. PC

"In slumber rest." Old French Noël. Words adapted. DNS

"In South Carolina de darkies go." See Kemo kimo

"In southern California with grace and splendor bound." See Hail C. I. T. (Barnes)

In stiller nacht. See Ar hyd y nos (Owen)

"In stiller nacht zur ersten wacht." J. Brahms. Words after F. Spee. g. EDL

In summer fields. See Feldeinsamkeit (Brahms)

"In summer the forest was green and fair." See Herbststurm (Grieg)

"In summer time when flowers do spring" (Hey for Somersetshire) Air: Sellenger's round, or, The beginning of the world. Traditional words. BOS 2

"In summer time when flowers do spring" (Under the greenwood tree) Old English air. Traditional words. DSB
Under the greenwood tree (Unter der linde grun) e.g. ML 1

"In sunny May." German air. Words by A. Zahn. DSB

"In Tenn'see." See The fine old colored gentleman

In that beautiful world on high. See "I hope my mother will be there"

In that day. See In dat day

[In that great getting-up morning] In dat great gittin'-up mornin'. Negro spiritual. HRD—JB 2

"In that land of dopey dreams." See The soldiers' song (Root)

"In that poor stable." See "Dans cette étable"

"In the Alford's circle fisherman am I." See The fisherman (Bernáth)

In the baggage coach ahead. G. L. Davis (music and words) GFS—SRW

In the battle, fame pursuing. Händel. SSO 2

"In the Black Ball line I served my time, away-ay-ay, hooray, ah." See The Black Ball line

"In the Black Ball line I served my time—with a hoodah and a doodah." See The banks of Sacramento

"In the bleak mid-winter" (Mid-winter) G. Holst. Words by C. Rossetti. OB

In the boat. See Im kahne (Grieg)

In the camp, in the grave, on the field of war. See "Ciascun lo dice" (Donizetti)

In the campfire's light, ho! dance. See In golden firelight dancing

In the city where nobody cares. C. K. Harris (music and words) SW

"In the cool and dewy morning." See "La vezzosa pastorella" (Bruni)

"In the dark of the winter." See Valentines

"In the days of old Rameses." Whitechapel club song. SBA

"In the days of old when the knights were bold." See The saltine warrior (Walsh)

"In the evening by the moonlight." J. A. Bland (music and words) GFS

"In the evening by the moonlight." See Southern memories (Plantation songs arranged)

"In the evening when I sit alone a-dreaming." See Sweet Adeline (Armstrong)

"In the fields abiding." See Carol, carol Christians (Burrows)

"In the fields in frost and snows." Traditional song. BOS 2

["In the forest, the deep forest"] "Erdő, erdő, sürü erdő" ("Süsser sang ertönt") Hungarian song. g.hu. ML 3

   "In the forest's highest branches" ("Erdő, erdő, sürü erdő") e.hu. KH 1

"In the forest's highest branches." See "In the forest, the deep forest"

"In the Galuth I found nought." See No matter, no matter

"In the garden thy lover wanders lonely." See Adelaïde (Beethoven)

"In the gloaming, oh, my darling." A. F. Harrison. Words by M. Orred. BB—GE—TFP—TFR

In the good old summer time. G. Evans. Words by R. Shields. GFS

"In the green valley thou'rt lingering yonder." See Wilt thou soon return (Rocke)

In the halls of her home. See The badger ballad (Olson)

"In the hazel dell my Nelly's sleeping." See The hazel dell (Root)

"In the heart of Mississippi." See Maroon and white (Wamsley)

In the kingdom. Negro spiritual. HRD

In the Lord, in the Lord. See My soul's been anchored in de Lord

In the Louisiana lowlands. Negro song. WSS

In the mansions above. Negro spiritual from Georgia. AS

"In the merry green woods a-hunting." See Johnie Scot (Oneida, Ky. version)

"In the morning of life." Air: The little harvest rose. Words by T. Moore. HMI

"In the morning when I rise." See Tell my Jesus morning

"In the North sea liv'd a whale." See The torpedo and the whale (Audran)

"In the old romantic days poets sang the praise." See Columbia's crew (Kelley)

"In the peaceful ev'ning time." See The bells of Aberdovey

"In the poplars." Dutch air. Words by K. Davis. DSB

"In the prison cell I sit." See Tramp, tramp, tramp (Root)

"In the quarries should you toil." See Make your mark

"In the scent with the soft spring breezes blent." See Veilchen (Cornelius)

In the second cavalry. U.S. army song. DSO

"In the sky the bright stars glittered." See The quilting party (Fletcher)

"In the starlight." [S. R. Glover] Words by J. E. Carpenter. MFS

In the starry light of a summer night. See The banks of the blue Moselle (Rodwell)

"In the state of old Virginny." See The pardon of Sydna Allen

"In the storm, in the night." See Caisson song: variation (Metz)

"In the time of roses." See Hoffnung (Reichardt)

In the town. See Nous voici dans la ville

"In the town of Athol liv'd one Jimmy Lanigan." See Lanigan's ball

"In the twilight as I play." See A twilight fancy (Molloy)

"In the valley of Virginia." Washington and Lee university song. T. W. Allen. Words by L. W. Allen. AI

"In the west the sun declining." See Good night (Abt)

"In the wild chamois track." See The Alpine horn (Rimbault)

In the willows. See I vassen (Palmgren)

In the winter time. See In de vinter time

"In the wood a boy one day." See The wild rose

"In the world I've gain'd my knowledge."
See Pulling hard against the stream

"In the year 1910." See Versos de
Montalgo

"In thine ears my sorrow pouring." See
"In sì barbara" (Rossini)

"In this realm of souls departed." See
Chorus of blessed spirits (Gluck)

"In this time our God hath sent." Old
English air adapted. 16th century
words. DNS

"In Thorney woods in Buckinghamshire."
See The poacher's song

In those twelve days let us be glad. See
A new dial

"In tow'r and spire were ringing." See
Lincoln's birthday

"In Transport town there lived a merchant." See "In Seaport town" (Barbourville, Ky. version)

"In vain my griefs and woes oppress me."
See Complainte de la reine Marie Stuart
en prison (Martini)

In vernali tempore (Spring has come)
16th century spring carol. e. OB

"In wiesen und in auen ich froh und glück-
lich bin." See Felicella

"In winter when the fields are white."
See When fields are white

"In winter, when the rain rained cauld."
See Tak' your auld cloak about ye

"In wonderful and lovely May." See "Im
wunderschönen monat mai" (Schumann)

"In yonder cottage dwelling." See Ym
Mhont-y-pridd mae 'nghariad

"In yonder valley calmly blooming." See
"In einem thale friedlich stille" (Reichardt)

"In yonders town where I was born." See
Barbara Allen (Chicopee county, Ga.
version no. 1)

"In Yorkshire I was born and bred." See
Hey, Betty Martin, tip toe fine

The incarnation ("Their eyes are holden")
A. Caldara. e. SSO 2

Inchin' along. Negro spiritual. FSN
Variant of: Keep a-inchin' along

An inconstant lover (see Song Index)
Variant of: The wagoner's lad

Indian lullaby ("Rock-a-bye, my little
owlet") W. H. Aiken. Words by
H. W. Longfellow. BB

Indian war song. in. KSO

Indian warriors' song (Wa-hoo) William
and Mary college song. T. W. Allen.
Words by B. Roberts. AIS

Indiana, our Indiana. University of In-
diana song. R. P. Harker and K. L.
King. Words by R. P. Harker. AI
—AIS

"Inez Rovina." C. Astin (music and
words) SW

"Infami, ed io di loro." See Ella piangea
la perfida (Mercadante)

The infantry ("Our army is a motley
crew") Air: Der tannenbaum.
Words by B. E. Bee. DSO

The infantry song ("Now listen unto this
my song") Air: The cavalry song.
DSO

Infelice ("Day of sorrow") Mendelssohn.
e.i. DCA

Infelice! e tu credevi. G. Verdi. e.i.
PB

"Infelice! già dal mio sguardo si deliguò."
See Infelice (Mendelssohn)

Infin che un brando vindice. See Infelice!
e tu credevi (Verdi)

Infinite light. English traditional air.
OB

Information. School song adapted from
British army song: Where they were.
BB

Ingelow, Jean
O fair dove, O fond dove (Scott-Gatty)
"One morning, oh, so early" (Scott-
Gatty)

Înghețată-i Dunărea (Deckt die Donau eis
und schnee) Rumanian song. g.ru.
ML 2

The ingle side. T. V. Wiesenthal.
Words by H. Ainslie. GS—MFS

Ingle-side. GOS 1

Ingraham, George
"The owl and the pussy cat"

Inimiora mea (Mein armes herz) Rumanian song. g.ru. ML 2

Inneggiamo il Signor non è morto. For
English translation see "Let us sing of
Christ's resurrection" (Mascagni)

Innisfail. E. C. Phelps. Words by T.
C. Latto. MFS

[Inno di guerra dei cacciatori delle Alpi]
Italian national hymn (Garibaldi's
hymn) [Attributed to A. Olivieri.
Words by L. Mercantini] e. LAS

[The inquiry] Where can the soul find rest.
J. C. Baker. [Words by C. Mackay]
HP

[L'insana parola] "Pity, kind heaven." G.
Verdi. e. WG

Instead of spa we'll drink down ale. See
Garryowen

"Inta, inta, int just hear those trombones
blowing." See Trombone song (Saltman)

"Integer vitae." F. F. Flemming.
Words by Q. Horatius Flaccus. l.
EDL—MBS—MFS. e.l. BB—
DSB

"Integer vitae" (The man of upright
life) l. TFB—TFG

Integer vitae ("Night shadows falling")
F. F. Flemming. Words by A. T.
Russell. TFB—TFG

Intermezzo. R. Schumann. Words by
J. von Eichendorff. e.g. HCA

Interrupted slumber (The hapless bride)
Russian folk song from the province of
Tver. e. SR

"Into the woods my Master went." See
The trees and the Master (McCaskey)

"Into your hands I give my heart." See
"Mon coeur se recommande à vous"
(Lassus?)

Invocation ("Der du von dem himmel bist")
See Wand'rers nachtlied (Jordan)

"Io de' sospiri te ne rimanno tanti." See Canto del pastore

Io l'udia ne' suoi bei carmi. Donizetti. e.i. PC

"Io mi sono un poveretto senza oasa e senza letto." See I maccheroni

"Io veggio in lontananza." A. Mazzoni. e.i. KVG

Ippolitov-Ivanov, Mikhail Mikhaïlovich
When we parted

"Ir atléké sakalélis." See "Flog herbei ein junger falke"

Ireland, John
The ferry
New Prince, new pomp

Ireland must be heaven for my mother came from there. F. Fischer. Words by J. McCarthy and H. Johnson. SMG

Irish carol ("Christmas day is come") See "Christmas day is come; let's all prepare for mirth"

[Irish emigrant's lament] The Irish emigrant ("I'm sitting by the stile, Mary") G. Barker. Words by H. S. Sheridan (Lady Dufferin) HMI

[Irish emigrant's lament] The lament of the Irish emigrant ("I'm sitting on the stile, Mary") W. R. Dempster. Words by H. S. Sheridan (Lady Dufferin) GOS 1—SI

The Irish exile. Old air. HMI

The Irish girl. Folk song: North Carolina version. SES 2
—Callaway, Va. version. SES 2
—Peaks of Otter, Va. version. SES 2
The Irish girl (The new Irish girl) Surrey version. BET

The Irish jaunting car. V. Vousden. SI

The Irish jubilee. C. Lawlor. Words by J. Thornton. SW

An Irish love song. See "Would God I were the tender apple blossom"

The Irish lullaby ("Rock-a-bye baby on the tree top") P. J. Cahill. SMG

[The Irish peasant to his mistress] "Thro' grief and thro' danger." Air: I once had a true love. Words by T. Moore. HMI

Irmelin Rose. C. Nielsen. Words by J. P. Jacobsen. da.e. WM 2

Irwin, John, pseud. See Harbour, Homer H.

"Is buachaillín mise do shíubhlúigh a lán." See Cnocáinín aereach Chill-Mhuire

Is it strange when the band starts playing. See Little boy in blue (Morse)

"Is it then true." See "È dunque ver" (Rubinstein)

["Is it true, then"] "No, they say" ("Azt mondjak nem adnak") Hungarian song. e.hu. KH 1
"Azt mondják nem adnak" ("Ach, ich soll nicht") g.hu. ML 3

Is life worth living. C. K. Harris (music and words) SW

Is massa goin' to sell us tomorrow. See Massa gwine to sell us to-morrow

"Iš mažumélés be motinélés." See "Seit zarter kindheit"

"Is not His word like a fire." F. Mendelssohn. [Tr of Ist nicht des Herrn wort wie ein feuer] e. SSO 4

"Is not the life more than meat." See Consider the lilies (Topliff)

"Is there for honest poverty." See A man's a man, for a' that

"Isaac, a ransom while he lay." See Didn't old Pharaoh get lost

"I'se gwine back to Dixie." C. A. White. WSS
"I'm going back to Dixie. LAS

"I'se gwine to bear, Lord." See Bear de burden

"I'se gwine to leave old Dixie." Minstrel ballad. WSS

"I'se trabling back to Georgia." See Trabling back to Georgia

"Iskhodíla mladen'ka." See The lonely waif

Island ("Yderst mod norden") See "Yderst mod norden"

An island spinning song. Irish air from Innismurry. Words by P. Colum. HI 1

Isle of beauty. [C. S. Whitmore] Words by T. H. Bayly. BB—GOS 1—TFG

The isle of dreams. See Mo rùn geal dileas

Isle where romance is set in splendor. See In Hawaii

Ist nicht des Herrn wort wie ein feuer. For English translation see "Is not His word like a fire" (Mendelssohn)

Iszlai, Márton
Hungary. See "In heav'nly love abiding"
"In heav'nly love abiding"

"It ain't gonna rain." See Ain't gonna rain

"It bein' on the eighth of October last." See The bonny wee mare

It brings tidings of comfort and joy. See The seven joys of Mary

"It came upon the midnight clear." Traditional air. Words by E. H. Sears. DN

"It came upon the midnight clear" (Glory to heaven's eternal King) E. Meyer-Helmund. [Words by E. H. Sears] CSS 1—CSS 2

"It came upon the midnight clear" (Glory to God.—Ehre sei Gott in der höh') M. Roeder. [Words by E. H. Sears] e.g. TSS 1

"It came upon the midnight clear." R. S. Willis. Words by E. H. Sears. BB

"It fell about the Mart'mas time." See Get up and bar the door

"It is a legend old I tell." See The legend of the glass (Offenbach)

"It is better to laugh than be sighing." See "Il segreto per esser felici" (Donizetti)

"It is enough." F. Mendelssohn. [Tr of Es ist genug] e. SSO 4

"It is moonlight at the gate." See Only a rose (Wellings)

It is not always May. See "The sun is bright" (Gounod)

"It is not because your heart is mine." See Mine only, mine alone (Starnes)

"It is not that I love you less" (The self banished) J. Blow. Words by E. Waller. GA

"It is not the tear, at this moment shed." Air: The sixpence. Words by T. Moore. HMI

"It is something sweet when the world goes ill." See Constancy (Webber)

"It is the day of all the year." See Mothering Sunday

It is the oar that impels us on. See C'est l'aviron qui nous mène en haut

It is the spring so welcome. See "A greenness light and tender"

"It isn't any trouble just to s-m-i-l-e." See A laugh provoker

It matters not ("'Tis all the same to me") A. Dargomijsky. e. NRF

"It matters not, as I've been told." See The lonesome prairie (Burnsville, N.C. version no. 2)

"It may not be, it cannot be." See Annie o' the banks o' Dee (Glover)

"It must be so." Händel. SSO 4

"It must succeed." B. Smetana. e. WLO

"It ofttimes has been told." See The Constitution and Guerrière

"It rains and it hails." See Reap, boys, reap

It snows in the night. Slavonic folk air. Words by H. H. Harbour. DSB

"It was a beauteous lady, richly dress'd." See Allan Percy

It was a dream ("I heard the rippling brooklet sing") F. H. Cowen. Words by R. E. Francillon. GE

It was a fair and starry night. J. Strauss. e. WLO

"It was a lover and his lass." Attributed to T. Morley. Words by W. Shakespeare. DSB—EB—GA—MBS

"It was a Sunday bright and clear." See O schöne zeit, o sel'ge zeit (Götze)

"It was a wondrous fair and starry night." See It was a fair and starry night (Strauss)

"It was about the deep of night." See The three traitors

"It was down in old Joe's bar-room." See Those gambler's blues

"It was early in the morning that Mary did him seek." See The Lamb of God (Easter version)

"It was good for de Hebrew children." See This old time religion

"It was good for my ole father." See This old time religion

"It was Hankey the squièr." See The poor murdered woman

"It was in a concert garden." See Somebody's waiting for me (Von Tilzer)

"It was in and about the Mart'mas time." See Barbara Allan (Scottish version)

"It was in simmer time o' year." See There's nae room for twa (Satter)

"It was in the lovely month of May, I heard a poor soldier lamenting and say." See The troubled soldier

"It was in the merry month of May when I started for Texas far away." See The trail to Mexico

"It was late in the night." See The gypsy laddie (Flag Pond, Tenn. version)

"It was late one summer's evening when I bid L.A. adieu." See On the lake of the Poncho plains

"It was on a charming fine summer's weather." See The weaver's daughter

"It was on a cold winter's night." See When poor Mary came wandering home

"It was on a fine summer's morning." See Cailín deás crúidhte na mbó

"It was on a moonlight night." See The light of the moon

"It was on a summer morning, the weather being fair." See George Reilly (Virginia version)

"It was on a Wednesday night." See Jesse James

"It was on Christmas day." See All in the morning

"It was on holy Wednesday." See All in the morning

"It was on last Monday morning." See William and Polly (Kentucky version)

"It was on one Monday morning." See William and Polly (Virginia version)

"It was on one summer's evening." See Love among the roses

"It was one day, I believe in May." See Si Hubbard

"It was the eve of Christmas." See The star of Bethlehem (Maybrick)

"It was the frog in the well." 16th century song. BOS 2
Variant of: The wedding of the frog and mouse

"It was the hour of quiet night." Words from the Latin. e. DNS

"It was upon a Lammas night." See Corn rigs are bonnie

"It wuz one day, I believe in May." See Si Hubbard

Italian hymn. See "Come, Thou almighty King" (Giardini)

Italian national hymn. See Inno di guerra dei cacciatori delle Alpi (Olivieri)

It's a long way to Berlin, but we'll get there. L. Flataw. Words by A. Fields. SMG

It's a low and painted cottage. See Wandering cowboy

"It's a way we have in the army." [Air: Malbrough s'en va-t-en guerre] DSO

It's a-me, O Lord. See It's me, O Lord

"It's awf'ly nice of all you girls." See So long Mary (Cohan)

"It's come and eat and tell me your name." See Locks and bolts (Spillcorn, N.C. version)

"It's come go back, my pretty little miss." See The gypsy laddie (Black Mountain, N.C. version)

It's freedom forever. See Battle cry of freedom (Root)

"It's gay to ramble out at night." See Strolling on the Brooklyn bridge (Skelly)

"It's holi-, holi-, holiday." See Little Musgrave and Lady Barnard (Flag Pond, Tenn. version no. 1)

"It's how do you like my fine feather bed." See Little Musgrave and Lady Barnard (Burnsville, N.C. version)

"It's I could have married a queen's daughter." See The daemon lover (Berea, Ky. version no. 2)

It's me, O Lord. Negro spiritual. WFN—WSS
It's a-me, O Lord (Standin' in the need of prayer) BB—FSN
'Tis me. HRD

"It's Monday morning go to school." See The two brothers (Black mountain, N.C. version)

"It's not my brother but it's me, O Lord." See It's me, O Lord

It's not what you were, it's what you are today. D. Marion (music and words) OTG

"It's of a brisk young lively lad." See The valiant lady ·

"It's of a damsel both fair and handsome." See The young servant man

"It's of a merchant's daughter, belonged to Callao." See Do let me go, girls

"It's of a merchant's daughter in London town did dwell." See The merchant's daughter

"It's of a pretty sailor lad who ploughed the stormy sea." See The little lowland maid

"It's of a rich nobleman lately, we hear." See The rich nobleman and his daughter

"It's one day when I was a-rambling around." See Wild Bill Jones (North Carolina version)

"It's rare to see the morning bleeze." See The ingle side (Wiesenthal)

It's so easy to forget a little thing like a thought. See Philippinitis

"It's step her to your weev'ly wheat." See Weevily wheat

"It's the old ship of Zion." See The ole ship o' Zion (Mountain spiritual)

"It's the syme the whole world over." Old song. DSO—SBA

It's three o'clock in the morning. See Three o'clock in the morning

"It's true my waist is slender." See Jack went a-sailing (Villamont, Va. version)

It's West Virginia, it's West Virginia. See Hail West Virginia (Miller and Mc-Whorter)

"It's what did you eat for your breakfast, Jimmy Randal my son." See Lord Randal (Carmen, N.C. version)

"It's where does your pain lie." See The brown girl (Alleghany, N.C. version)

"Iu partu e su' custrittu di partiri." See Canzuna di li carriteri

Ivanov, Mikhail Mikhaïlovich Ippolitov-. See Ippolitov-Ivanov, Mikhail Mikhaïlovich

"I've a good ole mudder in de heaven." See Judgment day is rolling round

"I've a letter from thy sire." See Baby mine (Boott); Baby mine (Johnston)

"I've a letter that was written long ago." See A lock of my mother's hair

"I've a secret in my heart, sweet Marie." See Sweet Marie (Moore)

"I've been a moonshiner for sev'nteen long years." See Kentucky moonshiner

I've been a-list'ning all de night long. Negro spiritual. HRD

I've been all around the world (The hobo's lament.—The hobo blues) American folk song. SW

"I've been caught in a net by a dear little pet." See The fisherman's daughter

I've been in the storm so long. Negro spiritual. FSN

"I've been rambling all the night" (Bedfordshire May day carol) BET

"I've been roaming." C. E. Horn. [Words by G. Soane] BST—MFS

"I've been thro' Carolina." See Belle ob Baltimore (Evans)

I've been toilin' at de hill. Negro song. HRD

I've been wukkin' on de railroad. See Levee song

"I've brought thee an ivy leaf." D. Wood. Words by O. D. Martin. GOS 2

"I've brought you here a bunch of may." See May-day garland

"I've come across the sea." See Rose of Lucerne (Barnett)

"I've got a belly full o' whiskey." See Vesta and Mattie's blues

I've got a home up yonder. See There was an ole fish

"I've got a mother in de heaven." Negro spiritual. HRD

"I've got a mule, her name is Sal." See The Erie canal

"I've got a robe, you've got a robe." See All God's chillun got wings

"I've got the Dallas blues." See Dallas blues (Wand)

I've got the homesickness blues. See Homesickness blues (Hess)

I've got the you don't know the half of it, dearie, blues. See The half of it, dearie, blues (Gershwin)

I've grown so used to you. T. Chattaway (music and words) DFF

"I've heard the lilting at the ewe-milking." See The flowers of the forest

"I've just arrived in town today." See Nicodemus Johnson (Murphy)

"I've just come down from the wild goose nation." See Tommy's gone to Hilo

I've just come home, mother, don't feel bad. See I'll be home to-morrow night (Howard)

"I've just got here, thro' Paris."   See The man who broke the bank at Monte Carlo (Gilbert)

I've no time to be a-sighin'.   I. McCall (music and words)   TFO

"I've often heard it said ob late."   See Dandy Jim ob Caroline

"I've rambled and gambled all my money away."   See Rabble soldier

"I've reached the land of corn and wine." See Beulah land (Sweney)

"I've seen the smiling of fortune beguiling." See The flowers of the forest

"I've taken the nags as I've found them." See The cavalry remount

"I've told you 'bout de banjo."   See Dolly Day (Foster)

"I've told you the story you ask'd me to tell."   See Good night, little girl, good night (Macy)

"I've wandered sighing, weeping."   See El profeta

"I've wander'd to the village, Tom."   See Twenty years ago (Willing)

"I've wandered very far away."   See I want to see the old home (Stewart)

I've worked eight hours this day.   F. Mc-Glennon (music and words)   SMG

The ivy green.   H. Russell.   Words by C. Dickens.   GOS 1—MFS

"Iz daleke zemlje husari ideju."   See Die Husaren kommen

"Iž mažumėlės be motinėlės."   See "Seit zarter kindheit"

"Īz za ostrova na strezhen."   See Sten'ka Razīn

Izar ederra (Der schöne stern)   Basque folk song.   ba.g.   ML 2

J

Ja es sollen wohl berge weichen.   For English translation see "For the mountains shall depart" (Mendelssohn)

"Ja, hier gefällt mir's am besten noch." See Her hjemme

"Ja hjemme er det dog allerbedst."   See Her hjemme

Ja, seit früher kindheit tagen.   For English translation see "O'er my head" (Flotow)

"Ja som bača velmi starý."   See Der alte schäfer

Jack and Jean.   Scottish air.   Words by D. Stevens.   TFR

"Jack and Joan."   T. Campion.   CSB 2

Jack Hall (see Song Index) Variant: Samuel Hall

"Jack he went a-sailing."   See Jack went a-sailing (Burnsville, N.C. version no. 3; Woodridge, Va. version)

"Jack he's gone a-sailing."   See Jack went a-sailing (Burnsville, N.C. version no. 1)

Jack o' diamonds (see Song Index) Variant of: Rabble soldier

Jack went a-sailing.   Folk song: Georgia version.   SES 1
—Barbourville, Ky. version.   SES 1
—Berea, Ky. version.   SES 1
—Knott county, Ky. version.   SES 1
—Pine Mountain, Ky. version.   SES 1
—Burnsville, N.C. version no. 1. SES 1
—Burnsville, N.C. version no. 2. SES 1
—Burnsville, N.C. version no. 3. SES 1
—Hot Springs, N.C. version.   SES 1
—Harrogate, Tenn. version no. 1. SES 1
—Harrogate, Tenn. version no. 2. SES 1
—Blue Ridge Springs, Va. version. SES 1
—Buena Vista, Va. version.   SES 1
—Callaway, Va. version.   SES 1
—Dewey, Va. version.   SES 1
—Montvale, Va. version.   SES 1
—Nash, Va. version.   SES 1
—Villamont, Va. version.   SES 1
—White Rock, Va. version.   SES 1
—Woodridge, Va. version.   SES 1

["Jack, where are you going"] "Gdzież to jedziesz Jasiu" ("Hänschen, willst du fliehen")   Polish song.   g.p.   ML 3

The jackfish.   Folk song from Virginia. SES 2

"Jackie went a-sailing."   See Jack went a-sailing (Montvale, Va. version)

"Jackie's gone a-sailing."   See Jack went a-sailing (Buena Vista, Va. version; Dewey, Va. version)

Jackson, Robert
"A day of joyful singing" (same air as "There dwelt in old Judaea")

"Jackson is on sea."   Song of the war with Mexico.   SBA

"Jacob dreamt he saw a ladder reachin' to de sky."   See Climb up, ye chillun, climb (Kent)

["Jacob, drink"] Trinklied ("Jokkel stiess mit Jakob an."—Piosneczka pijacka) Polish song.   g.p.   ML 3

Jacobi, Johann Georg.   See Jacoby, Johann Georg

Jacob's ladder ("As Jacob with travel") Traditional air.   OB

Jacob's ladder ("We are climbing Jacob's ladder")   Negro spiritual.   TFR
"We are climbing Jacob's ladder." HRD

Jacob's ladder ("I want to climb up Jacob's ladder")   Florida version. AS

Jacob's ladder ("We'll climb up Jacob's ladder")   North Carolina mountain version.   SES 2

"Jacob's ladder deep an' long."   See To see God's bleedin 'lam'

"Jacob's ladder slim an' tall."   See Don't call de roll

Jacobsen, Jens Peter
Dröm (Sjögren)
Irmelin Rose (Nielsen)

Jacoby, Gabriel Dante
March of triumph
Jacoby, Johann Georg
Litaney (Schubert)
Jadassohn, Salomon
Arioso from 100th psalm. See "Erkennet, erkennt, dass der Herr ist Gott"
"Erkennet, erkennt, dass der Herr ist Gott"
Jag (Ego) T. Rangström. Words by E. Josephson. e.sw. WM 2
"Jag gråter blodiga tårar." See Jag (Rangström)
"Jag tror jag får börja öfverge att sörja" ("Nein, ich will von morgen") Swedish folk song. g.sw. ML 1
"Jag unnar dig ändå allt godt" ("Ich gönne dir ja alles glück") Swedish folk song. g.sw. ML 1
Der jäger abschied ("Wer hat dich, du schöner wald") F. Mendelssohn-Bartholdy. Words by J. von Eichendorff. g. EDL
The hunter's farewell. e. BB
Der jäger aus Kurpfalz. Volkslied. g. EDL
"Der jäger längs dem weiher ging." See Der jäger und die nixe
Der jäger und die nixe. Rheinische volksweise. Words by W. von Zuccalmaglio. g. EDL
Jägerleben ("Im wald und auf der heide") Words by W. Bornemann. g. EDL
Jägers abendlied. See Jägers nachtlied (Reichardt)
Jägers liebeslied ("Ich schiess den hirsch") Composer unknown. Words by F. von Schober. g. EDL
[Jägers nachtlied] "Im felde schleich ich still" (Jägers abendlied) J. F. Reichardt. Words by Goethe. g. EDL
"Ein jahr oder länger ich bange." See Cailín deás crúidhte na mbó
"Des jahres." See entry under Des
"J'ai cueilli la belle rose" ("I have cull'd that lovely rosebud") Canadian folk song. e.f. GC
"J'ai cueilli la belle rose" (The white rose tree) e.f. GSF
"J'ai dit au ramier: Pars et va quand-même." See Les trois oiseaux (Cui)
J'ai fait trois fois le tour du monde. For English translation see "With joy my heart" (Planquette)
J'ai le bonheur dans l'âme. For English translation see "My heart is full of joy" (Offenbach)
"J'ai pleuré en rêve" ("I wept, beloved, as I dreamed") G. Hüe. Words after H. Heine. [Tr of Ich hab' im traum geweinet] e.f. ASN
"J'ai un' méchante mère." See Boum badiboum
"Jaj be fenyes csillag ragyog az egen." See "See the star that shines afar" (Füredy)
"Jaj! de szennyes az a maga kendöje." See "How unkempt that scarf doth look on you, my dear"

Jakobowski, Eduard
"Ah! when love is young" (from Erminie)
Birds of a feather (from Erminie)
"Darkest the hour" (from Erminie)
"Deign, pray, to cheer each heart" (from Erminie)
Downy jailbirds. See Birds of a feather
Dream song (from Erminie)
Good-night (from Erminie)
"Join in pleasure" (from Erminie)
Lullaby (from Erminie)
A soldier's life (from Erminie)
What the dickey birds say (from Erminie)
"Jakŭ sem si frajírenku." See "Seht in anmut mein herzliebchen"
The jam on Gerry's Rock. Lumberjack song. SBA
Jamboree ("O it's now we're past o' the lizard lights") Chantey. London version of words. WSE
For variants see following song of same title; also Whip jamboree; Whoop jamboree
Jamboree ("The pilot he looks out ahead") Chantey. WSE
Jamele. Jewish folk song. y. SY
James V, king of Scotland
The jolly beggar (Scottish air) Authorship uncertain
James Whaland. Minnesota loggers' song. SBA
"Jamie! Jamie." J. L. Molloy (music and words) GE
Jamie's on the stormy sea. B. Covert. GOS 2—MFS
Jan Hinnerk up de Lammerstraat (De man, de sick wat maken kunn) Niederdeutsches volkslied. g. EDL
Janjas schatz kommt aus der schenke ("Kad se Jangīn īz mekhane pomoli") Serbian folk song. g.se. ML 2
Janka (Ianka) Bulgarian folk song. b.g. ML 2
Jannik Skolan. Breton folk song. br.g. ML 1
January and February. German folk air. Words by J. B. Walters. BB
January carol ("Earth to-day rejoices") Air: Ave maris stella lucens. Words by J. M. Neale. OB
[Le jardin d'amour] "Quand je vais au jardin" ("Geh ich zum grünen hain") Folk song from Alsace. f.g. ML 1
Jarman, T.
"Hark! the glad sound"
"Jártam kertben rózsák között." See "Roses in the garden knowing"
Jarvis, Charles
"Call me pet names"
The good Three Bells
"Jasio konie poił." See "Hans die rosse tränkte"
Der jasmin (To giasemi) 19th century Greek song. g.r. ML 2
"Jate sospire mieje." See I sospiri

Jaxone, H. L. d'Arcy
 The gate of heaven (Tours)
 Time and tide (Rodney)
"A **jay** came to the city once." See The little bunch of whiskers on his chin
Jay Gould's daughter. Railroad song. SBA
 Variant: On the Charlie so long
"**Je** crois en Dieu, le Roi du ciel et de la terre." See O salutaris Hostia (Faure)
Je crois en vous (Belief) H. Berlioz. Words by L. Guérin. e.f. GA
ᵣJe dis que rien ne m'épouvanteᵧ "I try not to own that I tremble." G. Bizet. e. WG
"**Je** fleuris dans les champs." See The song of Solomon (Musorgskiĭ)
"**Je** les ai vus ces deux grenadiers." See Die beiden grenadiere (Schumann)
"**Je** ne veux pas autre chose" ("Give me alone every hour") C. M. Widor. Words by V. Hugo. e.f. SAT
Je regardais en l'air. For English translation see Waltz song (Planquette)
"**Je** sais au bord du Rhin." See Le moulin
"**Je** suis triste, je m'inquiète." See Haï luli (Coquard)
Je t'ai sur mon coeur. For English translation see Letters from lovers (Offenbach)
"**Je** te plumerai la tête." See Alouette
"**Je** vais entrer dans la danse" ("I want to come into the dance") Folk song from Lorraine. e.f. CBF 2
 "Je vais entrer dans la danse" (Chanson à baller.—Dancing song) e.f. CBF 1
The **jealous** lover of lone green valley. See Blue eyed Ellen
Jealous suspicion that she betrays me. See Nuova ferita (Mercadante)
ᵣJealousyᵧ "Vozlĭe rĭechkĭ, vozlĭe mostu" (Am flüsschen) Russian folk song. g.r. ML 1
Jeanie with the light brown hair. S. C. Foster (music and words) TFB—TFP—WSS
Jeanne d'Arc au bûcher (Joan of Arc at the stake) F. Liszt. Words by A. Dumas. e.f. DCA
Jeannette and Jeannot. C. W. Glover. Words by C. Jefferys. MFS
"**Jede** mühsal hat ein ende" ("Sako delo konec ima") Croatian folk song. g.se. ML 2
Jeder eine hat die seine. See Comin' thro' the rye
Jeffery, J. Albert
 "Hail to the scouts" (same air as "Ancient of days")
Jefferys, Charles
 Bonnie Bessie Gray (Glover)
 Had I wings like a dove (Composer unknown)
 Jeannette and Jeannot (Glover)
 Kitty Tyrrell (Glover)
 Mary of Argyle (Nelson)

The rose of Allandale (Nelson)
"The summer days are coming" (Composer unknown)
ᵣJeg elsker digᵧ I love thee (Ich liebe dich) E. Grieg. ᵣWords by H. C. Andersenᵧ e.g. HCA
"**Jeg** lagde mig saa ᵣsildigᵧ" ("Ich legte mich zur ruh") Norwegian folk song. g.n. ML 1
"**Jeg** stirrer i den stille nat." See Nat (Lund)
"**Jeg** vilde sadle" ("Fain would I saddle") S. Lie. Words by V. Krag. e.n. WM 2
"**Jehovah,** hallelujah." Old negro spiritual from South Carolina. AS
Jem, the carter lad. J. S. Baker. MFS
Jenkins, John, 1592-1678
 "A boat, a boat, unto the ferry." See The ferry
 The ferry
Jenkins, John, 1872-
 Blodau'r cwm (Old Welsh air)
Jennie, the flower of Kildare. J. E. Stewart. Words by F. Dumont. GOS 2
Jennie's bawbee. See Jenny's bawbee
ᵣJenny Jonesᵧ "We come to see Miss Jennie Jones." MFS
 "We come to see Miss Jennie O'Jones." SMG
 Variant: Miss Jenny-o-Jones
"**Jenny,** my own true loved one." See Wait till the clouds roll by (Fulmer)
Jenny, the flower of Kildare. See Jennie, the flower of Kildare (Stewart)
Jenny's bawbee ("There's your plack, and my plack") Old Scottish dance song. CSB 3
 Jennie's bawbee. BOS 2
"**Jenom** ty mně, má panenko, povĕz." See "Sage mir, mein herzensliebchen"
"**Jenseits** von Etropole, mutter." See Die Lukowiterinnen
Jensen, Adolf
 Am Manzanares. See "Am ufer des flusses, des Manzanares"
 "Am ufer des flusses, des Manzanares"
 By the Manzanares. See "Am ufer des flusses, des Manzanares"
 "Lehn' deine wang' an meine wang'" Marie
 "Murmelndes lüftchen, blüthenwind"
 Murmuring zephyr. See "Murmelndes lüftchen, blüthenwind"
 Press thy cheek against mine own. See "Lehn' deine wang' an meine wang'"
"**J'entends** le moulin" ("I hear the millwheel") Canadian folk song. e.f. GSF
 Variant of: "Mon père a fait bâtir maison" (J'entends le moulin)
"**Jerdan's** mills a-grinding." See Jordan's mills
"**Jeresalem** my happie home" (The querister's song of Yorke) R. Shann. ᵣTr of Mater Hierusalemᵧ e. DNS
Jerry, go an' ile that car. Railroad song. SBA
Jerry's song. A. Reinagle. MPA 2

Jerusalem ("Behold, thy King") H. Parker. Words by Nella [Parker] ASA—CSS 1—CSS 2

Jerusalem! die du tödtest die propheten. For English translation see Jerusalem! thou that killest the prophets (Mendelssohn)

"Jerusalem, Jerusalem, Jerusalem, Jerusalem." See O turn thee (Gounod)

Jerusalem mornin'. See "Sweet turtle dove"

"Jerusalem, my happy home." Latin hymn. [Tr of Mater Hierusalem] e. MFS

"Jerusalem, my happy home." For the same hymn with a different air see "Jeresalem my happie home" (Shann)

"Jerusalem the golden." A. Ewing. Words by St Bernard of Cluny. [Tr of Urbs Syon aurea] e. MFS

"Jerusalem the golden." G. F. Le Jeune. Words by St Bernard of Cluny. [Tr of Urbs Syon aurea] e. BB

Jerusalem! thou that killest the prophets. Mendelssohn. [Tr of Jerusalem! die du tödtest die propheten] e. SSO 1

"Jes' moverin' 'long." See The old ark a-moving along

"Jes' wait a little while." See The old ark a-moving along

Jesse Cole. Folk song from Kentucky. SES 2

Jesse James ("It was on a Wednesday night") Cowboy song. SBA

"Jesse James was a lad." Cowboy song. LSC

For variants see "I went down to the depot"; Jesse James

Jessie, the belle at the bar. G. Ware (music and words) SW

Jessie, the flower o' Dumblane. R. A. Smith. Words by R. Tannahill. GS

"Jest let me in the kingdom." See I don't feel weary

Jest talkin'. Southern mountain song. RA

Jesu dulcis memoria. For English translation see "Jesus, the very thought of Thee" (Rossini)

"Jesu fili Virginis" (Jesus, Son of the Virgin) Ancient plainsong air: Jesu corona Virginum. e. DNS

"Jesu, joy of man's desiring." See Herz und mund und that und leben (Bach)

"Jesu, Lover of my soul." See "Jesus, Lover of my soul" (Tours)

"Jesu of Maid Thou would'st be born." See "Jesu fili Virginis"

Jesu Redemptor omnium. 5th century plainsong. Words by Saint Ambrose. e. DNS

[Jesus ain't comin' here t' die no mo'] But He ain't comin' here t' die no mo'. Negro spiritual. HRD

Jesus' bloemhof (The garden of Jesus) 17th century Dutch carol. e. OB

"Jesus carry de young lambs in his bosom, bosom." See Rise and shine

Jésus Christ en pauvre. See La parabole du mauvais riche

"Jésus-Christ s'habille en pauvre." See La parabole du mauvais riche

"Jesus Christus wandert als bettler." See La parabole du mauvais riche

"Jesus comes with all His grace." See Veni Redemptor gentium

Jesus in den stal. For English paraphrase see Jesus of the manger

Jesus is mine. T. E. Perkins. Words by H. Bonar. MFS

"Jesus, Jesus is my Frien'." See Don't leave me, Lord

Jesus lebt, mit ihm auch ich. For English translation see "Jesus lives! no longer now"

"Jesus lives! no longer now" (St Albinus) Words by C. F. Gellert. [Tr of Jesus lebt, mit ihm auch ich] e. MFS

"Jesus, Lover of my soul." S. B. Marsh. Words by C. Wesley. BB

"Jesus, Lover of my soul." J. Parry. Words by C. Wesley. LAS

"Jesus, Lover of my soul" ("Veni Creator spiritus") C. L. Peticolas. Words by C. Wesley. e.l. TSS 1

"Jesu[s], Lover of my soul." B. Tours. Words by C. Wesley. ASA—CSS 1 —CSS 2

"Jesus loves me." W. B. Bradbury. Words by A. B. Warner. BB

Jesus of the manger. Flemish carol. Words based on an old carol, Jesus in den stal. e. OB

Jesus on the water-side. See Jesus sittin' on de waterside

Jesus sittin' on de waterside. Negro spiritual. WFN

Jesus on the water-side. South Carolina version. AS

Jesus, Son of the Virgin. See "Jesu fili Virginis"

"Jesus, tender Shepherd, hear me." C. Barnard (Claribel) [Words by M. L. Duncan] BB

"Jesus, the very thought of Thee" (Manoah) Rossini. Words by Bernard of Clairvaux. [Tr of Jesu dulcis memoria] e. MFS

Jesus, won't you come by-and-bye. Negro spiritual from Georgia. AS

Jesus, won't you come b'm-by. SBA

"Jesuz! peger braz eo." See Ar baradoz

"Jetzt gang i ans brünnele." See Drei röselein

Jewel song ("Ah! je ris") See "Ah! je ris de me voir" (Gounod)

"Jewell'd humming bird, the king of the uplands." See Le colibri (Chausson)

"De Jews, dey took our Saviour." Negro spiritual. FSN

Jim along Josey. Plantation song. BNM—SW—WSS

Jim crack corn. Negro song. WSS

Jim Crow. T. D. Rice (music and words) PSG—WSS

Jim Crow's polka. Minstrel song. PSG —WSS

Jim Fisk. American folk song. SBA

Jim the roper.   Cowboy song.   LSC

"Jimmy Dannels went a-hunting."   See Shooting of his dear (North Carolina version)

"Jimmy Randal went hunting."   See Shooting of his dear (Virginia version)

"Jimmy Randles was a-hunting."   See Shooting of his dear (St Helen's, Ky. version)

Jine 'em.   Negro spiritual from South Carolina.   AS

Jingle, bells ("Dashing thro' the snow") J. Pierpont (music and words)   BB—TFP—TFR

"Jó bor."   See "Good wine"

Joachim, Joseph
     "Es ist mein sohn, ich kann nicht daran zweifeln"

Joan of Arc at the stake.   See Jeanne d'Arc au bûcher (Liszt)

Job.   See "Come all you worthy Christian men that dwell upon this land"

Jock o' Hazeldean ("Why weep ye by the tide, ladye")   Air: Willie and Annet, or, In January last.   Words by W. Scott.   GS—LAS

Jockey hat and feather.   W. H. Brockway.   Words by F. Wilson.   SW

Joe Bowers.   19th century song.   DSO

"Joe Jacobs."   Negro work song.   HB

Joe Turner ("Dey tell me Joe Turner he done come") Negro folk blues.   SBA

Joe Turner blues ("You'll never miss the water")   Folk air arr by W. C. Handy.   HB

John, of Damascus, Saint
     "Come, ye faithful, raise the strain" (German air)

John, of Dunstable.   See Dunstable, John

John, of Fornsete
     "Sommer kommt, die rosen glühn." See "Sumer is icumen in" (attributed)
     "Sumer is icumen in" (attributed)

John and William.   Kentucky mountain song.   MK
     Variant of: The two brothers

"John Anderson, my jo, John."   ⟨J. Watson⟩   Words by R. Burns.   GOS 2 —GS

John Anderson, my jo, John ("Tho' time, wi' nidderin' frost, John")   ⟨J. Watson⟩   Additional verses.   GS

John Anderson's gane.   G. J. Bennett. GS

The John B. sails.   Old sea song.   SBA

"John Brown's body."   Air: Say, brothers, will you meet us, arr by W. Steffe. ⟨Old song with additional words by C. S. Hall⟩   BB—DSO

"John Brown's body."   Capstan chantey version.   TSB 2

John Dory.   16th century song.   Another air.   BOS 2

"John Grumlie."   Scottish song.   GS

"John Hardy."   Folk song from North Carolina.   SES 2

"John Henry."   Negro folk song.   SBA
     Variants: Drivin' steel; If I die a railroad man; Swannanoa town

John Henry blues ("In Alabam' at Muscle Shoals dam")   W. C. Handy.   HB

"John Henry tol' his cap'n."   See "John Henry"

John Highlandman.   See "A Highland lad my love was born"

John, John, of the holy order.   Negro spiritual from South Carolina. AS
     Variant: The golden altar

"John, John, wid de holy order."   See John, John, of the holy order

John of Hazelgreen.   Folk song from Virginia.   SES 1

John Peel.   Old hunting song.   Words by J. W. Graves.   BB—GSS—MBS —SSB—TFB—TFP

John Riley.   Folk song: Sussex version. e.g.   ML 1

"John said dat city was jes' fo'square." See I want to be ready

"John said that Jerusalem was four-square." See I want to be ready

"John said the city was just four-square." See I want to be ready

John saw ⟨the holy number⟩   Negro spiritual.   HRD

"John sawr-O, John sawr-O."   See The golden altar

Johnie Scot.   Folk song: Oneida, Ky. version.   SES 1
     —St Helen's, Ky. version.   SES 1
     —North Carolina version.   SES 1

Johnnie Cope ("Cope sent a letter frae Dunbar") Jacobite song.   Air: Fly to the hills in the morning. ⟨Words by A. Skirving⟩   BOS 2 —MBS

     Hey, Johnnie Cope ("Cope sent a challenge frae Dunbar")   GS

Johnny Boker.   Short drag chantey. TSB 1—WSE

"Johnny Bull, beware! keep at your proper distance."   See Patriotic diggers

Johnny come down to Hilo.   Negro capstan chantey.   GSS—TSB 1

Johnny Doyle.   Folk song: North Carolina version.   SES 2
     —Virginia version.   SES 2

Johnny German.   Folk song from Kentucky.   SES 2

Johnny, get your gun.   Old song.   SW

"Johnny had a little dog."   MFS

Johnny Sands.   ⟨J. Sinclair; attributed also to J. Simmonds⟩   GOS 2

"Johnny Schmoker."   g.   MFS

John's gone to Hilo.   Pulling chantey. WSE
     Variants: My Tommy's gone away; Tom's gone to Hilo

Johnson, sergeant
     Down in Charleston jail (Tucker)

Johnson, George W.
     When you and I were young, Maggie (Butterfield)

Johnson, Hall
  "Hail! de King of Babylon"
  "Hallelujah! King Jesus"
  I can't stay away
Johnson, Howard
  M-o-t-h-e-r (Morse)
  See also McCarthy, Joseph, jt. auth.
Johnson, J. C.
  "Ho, ho, vacation days are here." See
    Vacation days are here
  Vacation days are here
Johnson, J. E.
  Katy avourneen
Johnson, John Rosamond. See Cole,
  Robert A., jt. comp. and auth.
Johnson, Robert
  "As I walked forth one summer's day."
    See A forsaken lover's complaint
  A forsaken lover's complaint
  Liebesklage. See A forsaken lover's
    complaint
Johnson, Walter R.
  Lavender, my lavender
"**Johnson** said to Dicky one cold winter's
  day." See The three butchers (Ten-
  nessee version)
"**Johnson** said to Jackson on one holiday."
  See The three butchers (Kentucky ver-
  sion)
Johnston, Archibald
  Baby mine
Johnston, Gene
  Trojan marching song
Johnston, Lucy
  "Thou ling'ring star, with less'ning ray"
  To Mary in heaven. See "Thou ling'-
    ring star, with less'ning ray"
Johnston, Stuart
  Roll on old avalanche
Johnstone, Arthur Edward
  "Good morning! good morning! and
    here is come another day"
Join all and sing His name, declare. See
  Les rameaux (Faure)
"**Join** in pleasure." Vocal gavotte. E.
  Jakobowski. WLO
Join the angel band ("If you look up de
  road") Negro spiritual: Port
  Royal islands, S.C. version. AS
Join the angel band ("O join 'em, all")
  Charleston, S.C. version. AS
"**Join** the chorus join the chorus." See
  Flag of maroon (Richberg)
Join the Hickory Blues. Song of 1846.
  Air: Lucy Neal. DSO
Join them. See Jine 'em
"**Jokkel** stiess mit Jakob an." See "Jacob,
  drink"
Le **joli** tambour (Der schone trommler)
  French folk song. f.g. ML 1
The **jolly** beggar. Words attributed to
  James V of Scotland. GS
The **jolly** broom man. English folk song.
  BOS 2
  Variant of: Green broom
"A **jolly** fat friar." Drinking song. L.
  S. Davis. SFB
A **jolly** good laugh. Thomas. Words
  by Cooper. TFO

The **jolly** miller. See The miller of the
  Dee
"The **jolly** month of May." Round. J.
  Haydn. CSB 4
"**Jolly** old Saint Nicholas." BB—MFS
The **jolly** raftsman. Minstrel song.
  WSS
The **jolly** Switzer. Swiss air. Words
  by B. Harte. TFO—TFR
The **jolly** waggoner. English folk song.
  BOS 2
Jonas ("Im schwarzen Walfisch zu Aska-
  lon") Volksweise. Words by J. V.
  Scheffel. g. EDL
Jones, John, 1810-1869
  Ymdawiad y brenin (Welsh air)
Jones, Lewis
  Cân y melinydd (Old Welsh song)
    Authorship uncertain
Jones, Owen
  "Dark the night"
Jones, Robert
  "Sweet Kate"
Jones, Robert Bradford
  The Brown cheering song (Young)
Jones, Walter Howe
  "By the rivers gently flowing." See
    Illinois
  Illinois
Jones, William, fl. 1830
  The mellow horn
Jonson, Ben
  "Drink to me only with thine eyes"
    (Harrington?)
  "Have you seen but a white lily grow"
    (English air)
  Hymn to God the Father (Piatti)
  "I sing the Birth was born to-night"
    (Boughton)
Jordan, Mrs Dorothea (Bland)
  The blue bells of Scotland ("O where,
    tell me where")
  Where, tell me where. See The blue
    bells of Scotland ("O where, tell
    me where")
Jordan, Jules
  Invocation
  The singing in God's acre
Jordan, Julian
  Trusting I call
Jordan is a hard road to trabel ("I jes'
  arrive in town") [T. F. Briggs]
  WSS
Jordan's mills. Negro song from Vir-
  ginia. AS
"**Jos** mie saisin." See "Wär' ich frei"
Joseph and Mary. English traditional
  carol. OB
"**Joseph** Baxter is my name." See Not
  for Joseph (Lloyd)
"**Joseph** dearest, Joseph mine." See
  Weihnachtswiegenlied
"**Joseph,** lieber Joseph mein." See Weih-
  nachtswiegenlied
"**Joseph** took Mary all on his right knee."
  See The cherry tree carol (Pineville,
  Ky. version)
"**Joseph** was a young man." See The
  cherry tree carol (Barbourville, Ky.
  version; St Helen's, Ky. version)

"Joseph was an old man." See The cherry tree carol (Air from Fyfe); The cherry tree carol (Air from Husk); The cherry tree carol (Yorkshire version)

"Joseph were a young man." See The cherry tree carol (Hot Springs, N.C. version)

Josephson, Ernst
"En blomma stod vid vägen" (Sibelius) Jag (Rangström)

"Josht' ne sviti bijela zora." See "White dawn has not come stealing"

"Joshua fit de battle of Jerico." Negro spiritual. JG

Josie. American folk song. SBA
Variant of: "Frankie and Johnny"

Josie dear. Traditional song. KSO

"Josie she's a good girl." See Josie

Josiphus Orange Blossom. Minstrel song. PSG—WSS

Joslyn, Frederic
"Alma mater Fordham"

Joukovsky, Vasilii Andreevitch. See Zhukovskiĭ, Vasiliĭ Andreevich

"Jovan bega stara majka." See Mutterfluch

The jovial beggar. See A begging we will go

"Joy fills our inmost heart to-day" (Emmanuel) Composer unknown. Words by W. C. Dix. MFS

"Joy forsakes me." See "Yn iach lawenydd"

"Joy! joy! freedom to-day." MFS

"Joy to the world." G. F. Händel. Words by I. Watts. BB—DSB—TFG
"Joy to the world" (Antioch) MFS

Joy to-day! joy, joy to-day. See "Joy! joy! freedom to-day"

Joy unspoken. See Liebesglück (Sucher)

Joys seven. See The seven joys of Mary

"Joys that we've tasted." ₍W. B. Hall₎ GOS 1

Juanita. Spanish air. Words by C. Norton. BB—DFF—DSC—GOS 1—MFS—TFP—TFR—WSS

Juba. Negro folk song. HB

"Juba dis an' Juba dat." See Juba

Jubalee ("What is de matter wid de mourners") Negro spiritual. JB 2

Jubilate. 7th century Gregorian chant. e. TFR

"Juchhe! will immer fröhlich sein" ("Juhe! zmiraj vesel, vesel") Slovenian folk song. g.slo. ML 2

Judd, Percy
The swing

Jude, William Herbert
Behold! I stand at the door
Consecration. See "Take my life and let it be consecrated, Lord, to Thee"
The skipper
"Take my life and let it be consecrated, Lord, to Thee"

"The judge is not at home." See Domaredansen

Judges in de gall'ry say oh, me oh my. See Smoky mokes (Holzmann)

The judge's dance. See Domaredansen

The judge's song. A. S. Sullivan. Words by W. S. Gilbert. DSC

Judgment ₍day is rolling round₎ Negro spiritual. HRD

"Jugend und kraft beflügelt den schritt mir." See Aiñhara

"Juhász legény." See "Shepherd laddie" (Egressi)

"Juhe! zmiraj vesel, vesel." See "Juchhe! will immer fröhlich sein"

Jukovski, Vasili Andreyevich. See Zhukovskiĭ, Vasiliĭ Andreevich

Julian Antecessor
"Stay in town" (Whittaker)

Juliana and her grand piana. English music-hall song. SW

Juliann, don't you heah me. See Hawg foot

Julius Cornelius Augustus Pompelius Fredericus Plantaganet Brown. English music-hall song. SW

Jullien, Louis
"Ah! for wings to soar"
Prima donna waltz. See "Ah! for wings to soar"

Jumbo. American mountain song. RA

Jung Wolga und Mikula. See The legend of Volgá

Der junge kuckuck. See "Cäntä puiul cucului"

Die Jungfrau von Covadonga. See "La Virgen de Covadonga"

Junggesellenlied ("Oï piïdu íà dolom") Ukrainian folk song. g.r. ML 1

Jungle mammy song. af. SBA

Jungle march. Princeton university song. K. S. Clark. LAS

Der jüngling an der quelle (The lad and the stream) F. Schubert. e.g. GA

"Ein jüngling einst von edler art." See The bailiff's daughter of Islington

"Der jüngling zog aus in den krieg" ("Bernytis į karą jojo") Lithuanian folk song. g.li. ML 3

Jüngst, Hugo Richard
Spin, spin. See Spinn! spinn
Spinn! spinn

Jusqu'au matin remplis. For English translation see The students' song (Offenbach)

Just a song at twilight. See Love's old sweet song (Molloy)

"Just an ivy covered cottage." See All that glitters is not gold

Just as the sun went down. L. Udall (music and words) SW

"Just before the battle, mother." G. F. Root (music and words) BB—DSO

"Just before the battle, mother." G. F. Root. Confederate parody of words. DSO

"Just before the doorway, hi." See At father's door

"Just behind the battle, mother." G. F. Root. DSO

Just behind the times. C. K. Harris (music and words) SW

Just break the news to mother. See Break the news to mother (Harris)

Just hang a light by my bed tonight. See The child of the railroad engineer

Just leave a light by my bed tonight. See The child of the railroad engineer

"Just let me in the kingdom." See I don't feel weary

"Just look at that." R. Planquette. ₁Tr of Voyez ceci, voyez celà₁ e. WLO

"Just moverin' 'long." See The old ark a-moving along

Just now. Negro spiritual from Maryland. AS

Just one girl. L. Udall (music and words) SW

"Just one year ago today love." See The widow in the cottage by the sea-side

Just plain folks. M. Stonehill (music and words) SMG

Just talking. See Jest talkin'

Just tell them that you saw me. P. Dresser (music and words) DFF—SRW

"Just think, old scout." Composer and author of words unknown. US

"Just wait a little while." See The old ark a-moving along

"Już spiéwasz skowroneszku." See Kleine lerche

"J'y ai planté rosier." See La ronde du rosier

K

K-K-K-Katy. G. O'Hara. SMG

"K večeri ću v selo pojti." See "Kehr ich abends heim"

"Kad se Jangīn īz mekhane pomolī." See Janjas schatz kommt aus der schenke

Kádár Kata. See Kätchen Kadar

Kafoozalem. Composer and author of words unknown. SRW

Kahn, Robert
"Ein obdach gegen sturm"
"A shelter from the storms." See "Ein obdach gegen sturm"

Kain, Johann
Der sinnierende narr

The kaiser ain't what he used to be. Song of the European war. Air: The old gray mare. DSO

"Kak īz ostrova." See "Von der insel dort"

"Kak pod lfesom." See Der Kosak

"Kak vo Kievīe stol' nom Kievskom." See The feast of Vladímir

"Kako može duša tvoja." See "Sag, wie kann nur deine seele"

Kalínka. Russian folk song. e. SR Kalīnka (Wacholder) g.r. ML ·1

Kaloper Pero i Jela. See Kriegerweihe

"Kam daher die reinste aller frauen." See Die taufe Christi

"Käm' mein liebster mir entgegen." See "Home my sweetheart comes from roving"

Kansas boys. American folk song. SBA
Variant of: "Hello, girls"

Kansas City blues. E. L. Bowman. Words by G. H. Bowles. HB

"Kapakasta kapakkahan." See Der galgenstrick

Kapitän und leutenant. 18th century German folk song. g. EDL

Kärrnerlied. See Canzuna di li carriteri

Kätchen Kadar (Kádár Kata) Hungarian folk song. g.hu. ML 3

Kate Kearney. ₁Air: The beardless boy₁ Words by Lady Morgan. HMI—SSB

Katey's (Katy's) letter ("Och, girls, did you ever hear") C. H. Sainton-Dolby. Words by Lady Dufferin. SI

Kathleen ("I'm in love with a charming young lady") H. Mora. OTG

Kathleen ("Oh! leave not your Kathleen") W. Williams. MFS

Kathleen aroon. F. Abt. Words by L. M. J. M. Crawford. SI

"Kathleen mavourneen." F. W. N. Crouch. Words by L. M. J. M. Crawford; wrongly attributed to A. B. Crawford <and to J. Crawford> BB —GOS 1—HMI—MFS—SI—SSB

Kathleen O'More. See "My love, still I think that I see her"

Katie Morey. Folk song: Burnsville, N.C. version. SES 2
—Hot Springs, N.C. version. SES 2
—Tennessee version. SES 2

Katy. See K-K-K-Katy (O'Hara)

Katy avourneen. J. E. Johnson. SI

Katy darling. <English or Irish ballad> GOS 1—SI

Katy's letter. See Katey's letter (Sainton-Dolby)

Kaufmann, Alexander
Verrath (Brückler)

"Kaupunki kattaa laakson." See The silent city (Sibelius)

Kdo jste Boží bojovníci. See Hussitenlied

"Když tě vidím, má panenko." See "Seh ich dich, mein herzensliebchen"

Keady, John Thomas
"As the backs go tearing by" (Blaisdell)

Keble, John
"Sun of my soul, Thou Saviour dear" (Monk)

Keddie, Hamilton
Arizona grid march

The keel row ("As I came thro' Sandgate") 18th century air: Smiling Polly. Words from a Tyneside ballad. DSB
O weel may the keel row (Ruderlied) e.g. ML 1
₁The keel row₁ Weel may the keel row ("O who is like my Johnnie") ₁18th century air: Smiling Polly. Words by Thompson₁ GS

Keene, Robert
"How firm a foundation" (Reading?) Authorship uncertain

Keep a-howling, oh way over yonder.
See Way over yonder

Keep a-inchin' along.   Negro spiritual.
HRD
Keep a-inching along.   WSS
Variant: Inching along

Keep dem golden gates wide open.   J.
Hart (music and words)   SMG

Keep me from sinkin' down.   Negro
spiritual.   HRD—WSS
Oh, Lord, keep me from sinking down.
MFS

Keep the home fires burning.   I. Novello.
Words by L. G. Ford.   BB

Keep them rolling.   [Air: John Brown's
body, arr by W. Steffe]   Words by
G. E. Griffin.   DSO

Keep up your spirits and try once more.
See Don't let it happen again

"Keep us, O Lord."   Response.   L. van
Beethoven.   TFO

"Keep working, 'tis wiser than sitting
aside."   See Never say fail

Keep your hand, keep your hand to the
plough.   See Hold on

The keeper.   English folk song.   DSB
—DSC—GSS

"The keeper did a-shooting go."   See
The keeper

"Keeping watch o'er my maiden."   See
La serenata (Tosti)

"Kehr ich abends heim" ("K večeri ću v
selo pojti")   Croatian folk song.
g.se.   ML 2

Keiffer, A. S.
Twilight is falling (Unseld)

"Kein feuer, keine kohle."   See Heimliche liebe

"Kein graben so breit."   See Keine sorg'
um den weg (Raff)

Un kein hey hob ich nit.   See A teamster's complaint

"Kein wort von dir, der freude oder klage."
See "No word from thee, in gladness
or in sorrow" (Tchaikovsky)

Keine sorg' um den weg (Love finds the
way)   J. Raff.   e.g.   AT

"Keinen tropfen im becher mehr."   See
Die lindenwirtin (Abt)

"Keiner, auch nicht einer in der weiten
welt" ("Nie to, nie to v širom svete
milšieho")   Slovak folk song.   g.sl.
ML 3

"Keino t'asterhii."   See Despo

Keith, George
"How firm a foundation" (Reading?)
See Keene, R.   "How firm a
foundation" (Reading?)

Keller, Matthias
The American hymn
'Angel of peace" (same air as The
American hymn)
I have sought, and I have found
Keller's American hymn.   See The
American hymn

Keller's American hymn.   See The American hymn (Keller)

Kelley, Walter Edward
Columbia quadrangle song
Columbia's crew

Kelly, Glenn Muirdun
Colgate invictus (Bushby)

Kelly, J. D.
The Broadway swell and Brooklyn belle

Kelly, John T.
I long to see the girl I left behind

Kelly, John W.
McCloskey's great fight.   See Throw
him down McCloskey
The songs my mammy sang to me:
medley arranged
Throw him down McCloskey

Kelly, Michael
"Last week I took a wife"   (from
The forty thieves)

Kelly, Thomas
"Hark! ten thousand" (Dykes)

Kelly field air-service song.   [D. D. Em-
mett]   DSO

Kelvin grove ("Let us haste to Kelvin
grove") Air: O the shearin's no' for
you.   Words by T. Lyle <attributed
also to J. Sim>   GS—MBS

Kemo kimo.   Old song.   WSS
Variant: Beaver creek

Kemo, kimo deero art.   See Beaver
creek

Kemp, Clinton A.
Stingaree blues

Ken, Thomas
"Awake, my soul, and with the sun"
(Scotch air)
"Glory to Thee, my God, this night"
(music by Gounod; Tallis)
Old hundred (Franc? For German air
and music by Tallis see "Praise
God, from Whom all blessings
flow")
"Praise God from Whom all blessings
flow" (17th century German air;
also music by Tallis. For music by
Franc see Old hundred)

Kendon, Frank
The band of children (Old French air)
The merchants' carol (English tradi-
tional air)

Kënga é Ali Pachës.   See Ali Pascha

Kennedy, Harry
"Say 'au revoir,' but not 'good-bye'"

Kenney, Charles Lamb
The vagabond (Molloy)

"Kennst du das land" (Mignon)   L. van
Beethoven.   Words by J. W. von
Goethe.   e.g.   SAT

"Kennst du das land" (Mignon)   R.
Schumann.   Words by J. W. von
Goethe.   e.g.   HCA

Kent, F. A.
Climb up, ye chillun, climb

Kentucky moonshiner.   American mountain song.   SBA

Keppel, Lady Caroline
Robin Adair (Celtic air: English version)

Kern, Carl Wilhelm
Of the rose and you

Kern, Jerome David
Left all alone again blues
You're here and I'm here

Kerner, Justinus
Wanderlied (Folk air)
The **Kerry** dance. J. L. Molloy (music and words) GE—LAS—SI—TFG
The **Kerry** recruit. Traditional south Irish song. BOS 2
Ketchum, Mrs Annie (Chambers)
The bonnie blue flag (Macarthy)
Kethe, William
Old hundred (Franc?)
Kevin Barry. Irish song: American version. SBA
Key, Francis Scott
The star-spangled banner (Smith)
The **keys** of Canterbury. Folk song: <Somerset version> DSB
Variant: The keys of heaven
The **keys** of heaven. Folk song: Cheshire version. TFR
—Kentucky version. SES 2
—Black Mountain, N.C. version. SES 2
—Burnsville, N.C. version. SES 2
—Clinchfield, N.C. version. SES 2
—Hot Springs, N.C. version. SES 2
—Virginia version. SES 2
"I wil give you the keys of heaven." Cheshire version. SSB
The keys to heaven. American mountain version. RA
Variants: The keys of Canterbury; "My man John"
Kiallmark, George
"Alma mater"—Brown university (same air as Araby's daughter)
Araby's daughter
The old oaken bucket (same air as Araby's daughter)
D'kièchla rüss! d'kièchla rüss. See La chanson des beignets
Kihlatut. See Die verlobten
"Killa Bukk, Killa Blakk." See Gjeite lok
Killarney. M. W. Balfe. Words by E. Falconer. BB—GE—HMI—MFS —SI—TFR
Killick, L. F. See Furman, A. F., jt. comp. and auth.
"Kimalio Kimalio war." See The Swazi warrior
Kimo kimeo, dairo way. See The opossum
Kind, Friedrich
Brautjungfernlied (Weber)
Gebet (Weber)
"Kind friends, if you will listen." See Brown-eyed Lee
"Kind friends you must listen to my pitiful tale." See The dreary black hills
Ein **Kind** geborn zu Bethlehem. See Puer natus in Bethlehem
"Kind miss." Kentucky folk song. SBA
Variant of: "Come my little roving sailor"
Kind Robin lo'es me. Scottish song. GS
"Kind words can never die." A. Hutchinson. Author of words unknown. MFS

Die **kinder** bei der krippe ("Ihr kinderlein, kommet") J. A. P. Schulz. Words by C. von Schmid. g. EDL
Des **kindes** vermächtnis. See entry under Des
Ein **kindlein** in der wiegen (The cradle) 17th century Austrian carol. e. OB
King, C. M.
"Come, raise aloft the red, white, and blue" (same air as "A Yankee ship and a Yankee crew")
King, H. F.
Kissing on the sly
King, K. L. See Harker, Russell Pritchard, jt. auth.
King, Matthew Peter
Eve's lamentation
"King Arthur." Folk song: Lancashire version. TFO
"King Christian." See "Kong Christian stod ved høien mast" (Hartmann)
"The king doth rest." See Ah! mia figlia, perdona all' affanno (Rossini)
King Emanuel ("O my King Emanuel") Negro spiritual from South Carolina. AS
King Emanuel ("Oh, who do you call de King Emanuel") Negro spiritual. HRD
King Henry, my son. Folk song from Cumberland. BET
Variants: The little wee croodin' doo; Lord Randal; Lord Ronald
"King Henry was sent for." See The death of Queen Jane (St Helen's, Ky. version no. 2)
King Herod and the cock. Traditional carol from Worcestershire. OB
Variant of: King Pharaoh: The miracle of the cock
"King Jesus in His chariot rides." See He's the lily of the valley
"The king of France." J. W. Elliott. TFG
King of glory, God of grace. F. Abt. TSS 1
"The King of love my Shepherd is" (Dominus regit me) J. B. Dykes. Words by H. W. Baker. LAS
"The King of love my Shepherd is." C. Gounod. Words by H. W. Baker. CSS 1—CSS 2
The king of Yvetot. See Le roi d'Yvetot
King Pharaoh: [The miracle of the cock] Sussex gypsies' carol. BET
Variant: King Herod and the cock
[King Pharaoh]: The miraculous harvest. Sussex gypsies' carol. OB
"King Pharaoh sat a-musing." See King Pharaoh: The miracle of the cock
"King Philip had vaunted his claims." See A ballad to Queen Elizabeth of the Spanish Armada (Slater)
The **kingdom.** Angevin folk air. Words based on an old Angevin carol, Quoi ma voisine. e. OB
Kingdom coming. H. C. Work (music and words) BNM—DSO—SW—WSS
The **kings** (Die könige) P. Cornelius (music and words) e. OB

The **king's** highway.   J. L. Molloy. Words by F. E. Weatherly.   GE

Kings in glory.   See "Three kings in great glory" (Shaw)

Kings of Orient.   See Three kings of Orient (Hopkins)

ɾ**King's** prayer₁ "Oh King of kings, on Thee I call."   R. Wagner.   ɾTr of Mein Herr und Gott₁   e.   WG

Kingsley, Charles
The sands o' Dee (Boott)
"Three fishers went sailing" (Hullah)
"When all the world is young" (Barnard)

"**Kīnīsalo** mome."   See Ging ein mädchen

The **Kinkaiders.**   Old American song. Air: Der tannenbaum.   SBA

Kinkel, Johanna
Ritters abschied
The soldier's farewell.   See Ritters abschied
"Weh' dasz wir scheiden müssen." See Ritters abschied

Kinloch.   See "Enchantress, farewell"

Kinney, Coates
Rain on the roof (Clifford)

Ɛen **Kint** gheboren in Bethlehem (Dutch carol)   e.   OB

Kipling, Rudyard
"God of our fathers, known of old" (music by Dykes; MacMillan)
"Land of our birth" (music by Bach; Gould; Mason)

Kirkham, Thomas
"How firm a foundation" (Reading?)
See Keene, R.   "How firm a foundation" (Reading?)

Kirkonkylantanssit.   See Tanz im kirchdorfe

"**Kirkonkyläss'** oli tanssit."   See Tanz im kirchdorfe

Kisco, Charles, and Freed, Ralph J.
Song of Troy

The **kiss** ("Ich war bei Chloen")   See Der kuss (Beethoven)

Kiss me quick and go.   ɾF. Buckley₁ SW—WSS

Kisses can do no harm.   See Küssen ist keine sünd' (Eysler)

Kissing on the sly.   H. F. King (music and words)   SW

"**Kitették** a holttestet az udvarra."   See "They have laid him dead upon the black draped bier"

Kittredge, Walter
Tenting on the old camp ground

Kitty of Coleraine ("As beautiful Kitty") Irish air.   ɾWords attributed to E. Lysaght₁   HMI—MBS—SI—SSB

Kitty Tyrrell.   C. W. Glover.   Words by C. Jefferys.   SI

Kjerulf, Halfdan
Laengsel
"Last night."   See Laengsel
Sehnsucht.   See Laengsel

Klage ("Ay au pena ren andia")   See "Ay au pena ren andia"

Klage ("Dacă nu e şi nu e")   See Aoleo

Klage ("Écoutez donc la complainte") See Lamento ("Écoutez donc la complainte")

Klage ("Fein's liebchen trau' du nicht."— Plaint)   J. Brahms.   e.g.   HCA

Klage ("White dawn has not come stealing")   See "White dawn has not come stealing"

Klage ("Wo saves fluten in die Donau münden."—Nezadovoljstvo)   Croatian folk song.   g.se.   ML 2

Klakring, Thomas Burton
"Fight, big blue team"
"Up and at 'em, navee"

"De **klamres** indenfor Islam."   See Tro (Sinding)

"En **klang** som af små violinar."   See Titania (Peterson-Berger)

"**Klar** und mild die sterne schimmern." See Ar hyd y nos (Owen)

Klauer, F. G.
"I'm a shepherd of the valley"

Klein, Bruno Oscar
Old Ironsides

Das **kleine** gurretäubchen.   See The little wee croodin' doo

Der **kleine** kuckuck.   See Cuculeţ cu pana surä

Kleine lerche (Skowronek)   Polish folk song.   g.p.   ML 3

"**Kleine** maid vom dorfe."   See "Fetiţo din acel sat"

Der **kleine** rekrut ("Wer will unter die soldaten")   F. Kücken.   Words by F. Güll.   g.   EDL

Der **kleine** sandmann bin ich.   For English translation see "The sandman kind am I" (Humperdinck)

"**Kleiner** kuckuck, auf und rufe laut."   See Rufe, kuckuck

Kletva s jabuka.   See Mutterfluch

"**Kling**, klang, kling, now loudly ringing." See Song of the forge

Klingemann, Karl
Sonntagslied (Mendelssohn)

Klopstock, Friedrich Gottlieb
Dem Unendlichen (Schubert)
Die sommernacht (Gluck)
"Ein **knäblein** ging spazieren ins rosengärtelein."   See Abrede

Knapp, Mrs Gertrude A.
Montana my Montana (Greenwood)

Kneass, Nelson
Ben Bolt: German air arranged

Knibbs, Henry Herbert
Walking John (Cowboy song)

Knick knack, mein dudelsack.   See "La bell', si nous étiom' dedans"

Knight, A. G.
Upi dei di (Old air)

Knight, Joseph Philip
The New Year's come
"Oh! Lord, I have wandered"
"Rocked in the cradle of the deep"
"She wore a wreath of roses"

Knight, J. S.
Tender and true, adieu

Knight, Launce
Pierre de Bon Bon.   See Rosalie Rosalie

Knight, Ralph
The college on the hill
"The **knight** met a child in the road." See
The false knight upon the road (Tennessee version)
The **knight** of the raven black plume. J.
H. Hewitt. HP
"**Knock**, knock, knock, we've come to see
Miss Jenny-o-Jones." See Miss Jenny-o-Jones
"**Knocks** like Jesus." See Somebody's
knocking at your door
"**Know** ye, dear friends, a drink more inspiring." See Porter lied (Flotow)
Knowles, Frederick Lawrence
"Come, raise the song" (Davis)
"**Know'st** thou the land." See "Kennst
du das land" (Beethoven)
"**Ko** jste Boží bojovníci." See Hussitenlied
"**Kochaneczko**, oczki moje." See "Du
mein liebling, äuglein lieblich"
Kocher, Conrad
"As with gladness men of old"
"For the beauty of the earth" (same
air as "As with gladness men of
old")
"Lord, we come with hearts aflame"
(same air as "As with gladness men
of old")
Kodista vieroitettu. See Heimatlos
"**Koivu** on metsässä yksinänsä." See
Heimatlos
"**Kol** jauns nevedęs buvau." See "Noch
jung und ledig war ich"
Kol slaven. See Glory to the Lord in
Zion (Bortníanskiĭ)
Kolar, Victor
March of the Titans
Koliko mí zíma duga bíla. See Ach, wie
war mir lang der winter
Kollege kick. J. M. Hagen. HW
Kol'tsov, Aleksieĭ Vasil'evich
The banks of the Don (Musorgskiĭ)
Kolyadka ("Berries red and bright") See
Merry Yuletide (Rimskiĭ-Korsakov)
Kolybel'naîa ("Schlaf, armer, schlaf zum
letzten mal") See Wiegenlied (Russian folk song)
Kolybel'naîa ("Susu, susu, sulcia") See
Wiegenlied (Ukrainian song)
"**Kom** med sange og helst af dem" ("Bring
us songs of cheer and joy") C. Sinding. Words by G. Hetsch. e.n.
WM 2
"**Komm**, Amyntha, komm mit mir zum
haine." See Aminte
"**Komm** blässlein mein, komm braune."
See Hirten-lockruf
"**Komm**, du kleine." See Will you be
mine
"**Komm**, du mein röschen, komm herein."
See "Come in, my rose, my rose come
in"
"**Komm** im glanze, komm und pflanze."
See Frühling liebster (Scholz)
"**Komm**, komm, komm, fischlein im teich"
("Som, som, som w stawie rybecki")
Polish folk song. g.p. ML 3

"**Komm**, lieber mai und mache" (Sehnsucht
nach dem frühlinge) Mozart.
Words by C. A. Overbeck. g.
EDL
Longing for spring. e. DSB
"**Komm**, mädchen, an dein fenster." See
Lockruf (Rückauf)
"**Komm** mit mir, des wonn'gen maien uns
zu freuen." See "Come sweet lass"
(Clarke)
"**Komm** mit mir, geliebte mein." See
"Deutu ganeme"
Komm, süss lieb. See "Come sweet lass"
(Clarke)
"**Komm**, süsser tod." J. S. Bach.
Author of words unknown. g. EDL
"**Komm'**, wir wandeln zusammen" ("Come,
we'll wander together") P. Cornelius.
e.g. SAT
"**Komme** früh morgens." See "Come you
here, laddie"
"**Kommt** a vogerl geflogen." See Frohe
botschaft (Müller)
"**Kommt** die sommerzeit herbei." See
Tros y garreg
Kommt er dann heim. For English
translation see "If he returns" (Wagner)
"**Kommt**, ihr burschen, kommt herbei."
See The May-pole
"**Kommt**, mädel heraus." See "Come,
lasses and lads"
"**Kommt**, seelen, dieser tag muss heilig sein
besungen." See Pfingstlied
Komu da me dade. See Wen ich will
zur ehe
["**Kong** Christian stod ved høien mast"]
"King Christian stood beside the mast."
National song of Denmark. Old air
arr by J. Hartman. Words by J.
Ewald. e. LAS
"**Kongen** spurgte datter sin." See Herr
Ole
"Der **könig** fragte die tochter sein." See
Herr Ole
Der **könig** in Thule ("Es war ein könig")
K. F. Zelter. Words by J. W. Goethe.
g. EDL
"Der **könig** stand auf hohem altan." See
Sjugur as trollbrura
Die **könige**. For English translation see
The kings (Cornelius)
Des **königs** abschied. See entry under
Des
"Des **königs** trommel rief zum ball." See
entry under Des
Die **königskinder** ("Es waren zwei konigskinder") See Zwei königskinder
Der **königssohn** Marko und seine geliebte
Angjelia (Kraljević Marko i Angjelija
ljuba) Slavonian folk song. g.se.
ML 2
Könntest du erfassen. For English
translation see "May he never leave
thee" (Wagner)
Kopisch, August
Noah (Reissiger)
Kopon te kai kamaton. For English
translation see "Art thou weary, art
thou languid" (Hopkins)

"Korcsmárosné, be barna."   See Trinklied (Hungarian folk song)

"Korn hab gesät ich" ("Zasial som žitko") Slovak folk song.   g.sl.   ML 3

Körner, Karl Theodor
Gebet während der schlacht (Himmel)
Lützows wilde jagd (Weber)
Schwertlied (Weber)

Koromandel, Crescentius
Krambambuli (Folk air)

Korsakov, Nikolaï Andreevich Rimskiï-. See Rimskiï-Korsakov, Nikolaï Andreevich

Der Kosak ("Kak pod lïesom")   Russian folk song.   g.r.   ML 1

Koschat, Thomas
Forsaken (Tr of Verlassen bin i)
"The Lord is my Shepherd; no want shall I know"

Kosovka ðevojka.   See Das mädchen vom Amselfeld

Kotzebue, August Friedrich Ferdinand von
Ewiger wechsel (Himmel)

Kowalski, George W.
Hail Loyola

Köyhä tyttö.   See Das arme mädchen

"Kradem ti se u vechere."   See Unterm fenster

Krag, Vilhelm
"Der skreg en fugl" (Sinding)
Im kahne (Grieg)
"Jeg vilde sadle" (Lie)
"O Herre" (Melartin)

Die krähe (The crow)   F. Schubert. e.g.   HCA

"Eine krähe war mit mir."   See Die krähe (Schubert)

Der Krakauer (Krakowiak)   Polish dance song.   g.p.   ML 3

Krakowiak ("Der Krakauer bin ich")   See Der Krakauer

Kraljević Marko i Angjelija ljuba.   See Der königssohn Marko und seine geliebte Angjelia

Krambambuli.   18th century German folk air.   Words by C. Koromandel.   g. EDL

Kramsu, Kaarlo
Melancholy (Merikanto)

Die kranzbinderin.   See Beim mondenschein

Krasnyï sarafan.   See The scarlet sarafan (Varlamov)

Krchtena Khrstovo.   See Die taufe Christi

Krebs, Karl August
The Lord's prayer
"Vater unser."   See The Lord's prayer

Kremser, Eduard
Prayer of thanksgiving.   See "Wilt heden nu treden"
Thanksgiving prayer.   See "Wilt heden nu treden"
The vision (same air as "Wilt heden nu treden")
"Wilt heden nu treden"
"Wir treten zum beten."   See "Wilt heden nu treden"

Kreutzer, Konradin
Hobellied

Kriegerlied.   See Dime, artilleriot, donde vas

Kriegers abschied von der mutter (Ljubav junaka prama svojoj majci)   Croatian folk song.   g.se.   ML 2

Kriegerweihe (Kaloper Pero i Jela)   Bosnian folk song.   g.se.   ML 2

Kriegslied der mannen von Harlech.   See Rhyfelgyrch gwyr Harlech

"Kristalle, die feinen."   See "Kristallen den fina"

"Kristallen den fina" ("Kristalle, die feinen")   Swedish folk song.   g.sw.   ML 1

"K'ruim onu b'luim onu."   See `Praised be the Lord

Kücken, Friedrich Wilhelm
"Alles still in süsser ruh"
Alma mater—United States military academy (same air as Treue liebe)
Alma mater—Washington university (same air as Treue liebe)
Dear old Reserve (same air as Treue liebe)
"Drift, my bark" (Tr of Treibe schifflein)
"How can I leave thee."   See Treue liebe
Der kleine rekrut
Robin Redbreast (same air as Der kleine rekrut)
The slumber song.   See "Alles still in süsser ruh"
Treue liebe

"Der kuckuck auf dem zaune sass."   See Hochzeitslied

Kugler, Franz
Rudelsburg (Fesca)

"Kühnen flugs steigt auf der kranich." See Hungaria's treasure

"Kui mina alles noor veel olin."   See "Als ich noch ein kleiner knabe"

"Kui mina olin wäiksekene."   See Des sängers kindheit

Kukni kukuvïtse.   See Rufe, kuckuck

Kullan ylistys.   See The gay young bachelor

Kulmann, Elisabeth Borisovna
"Pluck ye roses while they bloom" (Schumann. Tr of Pflücket rosen um, das haar)

"Kultani on kaukana."   See "Weit ist mein geliebter, weit"

"Kumm aher, du philosoph."   See Der philosoph

"Kun minä läksin Ameriikasta."   See Seemanns lied

"Kun mun kultani tulisi."   See "Home my sweetheart comes from roving"

"Kuresaare mõisa kubjas."   See Lied des hörigen

Der kuss (The kiss)   L. van Beethoven. [Words by C. F. Weisse]   e.g.   GA

Küssen ist keine sünd' (Kisses can do no harm)   E. S. Eysler.   e.g.   AT

Kutscherruf.   See Cansó de sega

"Kuules mun kulta eukkoni."   See Mutter und tochter

Kye song of Saint Bride. J. W. Clokey. Words by W. Sharp (Fiona MacLeod) TFG

Kyle, Frances
The quilting party (Fletcher)

L

"**Là-bas** sur ces montagnes" ("Out there on yonder mountains") Canadian folk song: 2d version. e.f. GC

"**La** bordei cu crucea naltă" ("Aus stankut-zas hütte dringen") Rumanian song. g.ru. ML 2

"**Là** ousqu'y sont, tous les raftsmen." See Les raftsmen

Lablache, Mrs Fanny Wyndham (Wilton)
'Tis I (Pinsuti)

Lachner, Vincenz
Vineta

Lacome d'Estalenx, Paul Jean Jacques
The dancers

Lacy, Caleb
Ebony song no. 2. See My Rose
My Rose

The **lad** and the stream. See Der jüng-ling an der quelle (Schubert)

"A **lad** set out one bright fall day." See Overwork (Stevens)

Laduvane. See Sylvesterlied

The **lady** and the dragoon. Folk song: Kentucky version. SES 1
—Allanstand, N.C. version. SES 1
—Burnsville, N.C. version. SES 1
—Micaville, N.C. version. SES 1
—Tennessee version. SES 1
—Afton, Va. version. SES 1
—Montvale, Va. version. SES 1
—Nellysford, Va. version. SES 1

Lady Gay. See The wife of Usher's well (Knott or Letcher county, Ky. version)

The **lady** in crêpe. Donizetti. SRW

Lady Isabel and the elf knight. Folk song: Georgia version. SES 1
—Barbourville, Ky. version. SES 1
—Berea, Ky. version. SES 1
—Clay county, Ky. version. SES 1
—Harrogate, Ky. version. SES 1
—Allanstand, N.C. version. SES 1
—Carmen, N.C. version. SES 1
—Buena Vista, Va. version. SES 1
—Dewey, Va. version. SES 1
—Endicott, Va. version. SES 1

Lady Leroy. See Sally and her lover

Lady Maisry. Folk song: Barbourville, Ky. version. SES 1
—Teges, Ky. version. SES 1

"**Lady** Margaret she mounted her milk-white steed." See Earl Brand (Afton, Va. version)

"**Lady** Margret was sitting in her dower room." See Fair Margaret and sweet William (Carmen, N.C. version no. 2)

"**Lady** Margret was sitting in the new church door." See Fair Margaret and sweet William (Clay county, Ky. version)

Lady Moon ("O Lady Moon, your horns") Canon. H. W. Loomis. Words by C. G. Rossetti. TFG—TFR

Lady Moon, leading your lambs. See The high moon

"A **lady** sat mute in her bow'r." See The knight of the raven black plume (Hewitt)

Ladybird ("Sweet little ladybird") German folk song. [Tr of Marien-würmchen] e. DSB

Ladybird. For another English transla-tion with a different air see Marien-würmchen (Schumann)

[**Laengsel**] "Last night." H. Kjerulf. Words by C. Winther. e. TFG

"**Last** night" (Sehnsucht) e.g. GG

"**Last** night the nightingale woke me." e. BB

La Hache, Theodor von
"Near the banks of that lone river"

La Harpe, Jean François de
"Ô ma tendre musette" (Monsigny?)

"The **laird** o' Cockpen." Air: When she cam' ben, she bobbit, or, Cockpen. Words by Nairne. GS

Laisse-moi, laisse-moi. For English translation see "Let me gaze" (Gounod)

Lake, J. W.
I love the merry sunshine (Glover)
Shells of ocean (Cherry)

The **lake** of Coolfin ("Oh! calm was the lake") Old air. Words by W. Maynard. HMI

"**Läksin** minä kesäyönä käymään." See "Wandelnd in dem sommernächtgen schweigen"

Lalo, Edouard Victor Antoine
The bondmaid. See L'esclave
L'esclave

Lamb, Arthur J.
Asleep in the deep (Petrie)

The **Lamb** of God ("Awake, awake") Traditional Shropshire air. Passion version of words. OB

The **Lamb** of God ("God bless the ruler of this house") Traditional Shropshire air. New Year version of words. OB

The **Lamb** of God ("It was early") Tra-ditional Shropshire air. Easter ver-sion of words. OB

"**Lamb** of God, Thou that takest away the world's guilt." See "Agnus Dei" (Bizet)

Lambert, Louis, pseud. See Gilmore, Patrick Sarsfield

Lambeth (Schulthes) See "I know not what the future hath"; "Prayer is the soul's sincere desire"

The **lame** crane. 17th century round. GSS

"My dame hath a lame tame crane." BOS 2

The **lament** of the Irish emigrant. See Irish emigrant's lament (Dempster)

Lamento ("Dumattina quest' è l' jornu di la virgine Maria."—Totenklage) Corsican folk song. g.i. ML 2

Lamento ("Écoutez donc la complainte."—Klage) Folk song from the Aosta valley. f.g. ML 2

Lamento ("Quando junse la nuvella."—Totenklage) Corsican folk song. g.i. ML 2

Lamento ("Quandu n'intesi la nova alle Ferrera d'Orezza."—Totenklage) Corsican folk song. g.i. ML 2

Lamkin. Folk song: Barbourville, Ky. version. SES 1
—Beattyville, Ky. version. SES 1
—Hindman, Ky. version. SES 1
—Manchester, Ky. version. SES 1
—North Carolina version. SES 1

Lampe, John Frederick
"Hot mutton pies"

"The land is free, united we." K. Millöcker. e. WLO

"Land of beauty." Hungarian air. Words by K. Davis. DSB

"Land of our birth." J. S. Bach. Words by R. Kipling. DSB

"Land of our birth." J. E. Gould. Words by R. Kipling. LAS

"Land of our birth." L. Mason. Words by R. Kipling. DSC

The land o' the leal ("I'm wearin' awa', Jean") [Air: Hey, tuttie, taitie] Words by C. Nairne. GS—SSB—TFP

Der landesvater. See Weihelied

Landing of the Pilgrims. A. [!] Browne. Words by F. D. Hemans. MFS—TFG

Landkjending. See Olaf Trygvason (Grieg)

"The landlord to his lady." See Lamkin (Manchester, Ky. version)

Landon, Jane, pseud. See Vandevere, J. Lilian

Landsknechtslied. See Lied der landsknechte

Lane, Mrs Annie (Eichberg) King
"To thee, O country" (Eichberg)

Lane, Mrs John. See Lane, Mrs Annie (Eichberg) King

The Lane county bachelor. Air: Irish washerwoman. SBA

Lange, Thor
"Skin ud, du klare solskin" (Lange-Müller)

Lange-Müller, Peter Erasmus
Autumn. See Efteraar
Efteraar
"Late in the night in frost cold." See "Silde ved nat hin kolde"
"The maples their leaves are shedding." See "Nu faelder sit løv den ahorn"
"Nu faelder sit løv den ahorn"
"Shine bright and clear, O sunshine." See "Skin ud, du klare solskin"
"Silde ved nat hin kolde"
"Skin ud, du klare solskin"

Langlotz, Carl A.
Old Nassau

Längsel ("Aftnen er stille."— Waiting) J. Svendsen. Words by B. Björnson. e.n. WM 2

Lanier, Sidney
The trees and the Master (McCaskey)

Lanigan's ball. Old song. SW

Lankey, F. I.
Fight song
"The lanterns gleam, the yellow flames leap and play." See The village dance

Larcom, Lucy
Each for all (Reissiger)
"O God, Thy world is sweet with prayer" (Schumann)

Lardner, William
The watcher

Lardy dah. Minstrel song. [E. V. Page. Words by V. Davies] WSS

"A large vessel has come to our shore." See Noël de Strasbourg

Largo ("Father in heav'n, Thy children hear") Händel. Words by T. Williams. BB—TFP

"Largo al factotum della città." Rossini. e.i. PB

The lark and the magpie. Round. GSS

The lark in the morn. Folk song. DSB

Les larmes (Tears) B. Godard. Words by P. Harel. e.f. SAT

Lascia ch'io pianga. G. F. Händel. e.i. PC
"Lascia ch'io pianga" ("Leave me to languish."—"Father in heaven") e.i. BST

Lass, gin ye lo'e me, tell me noo. See "I ha'e laid a herrin' in saut"

"Lass mich geleiten dich." See Eibhlín a rúin

"Lass mich mit tränen." G. F. Händel. g. EDL

The lass o' Gowrie ("Upon a simmer afternoon") Air: Loch Erroch Side. Modern words. GS

The lass o' Gowrie ("Upon a simmer afternoon") Air: Loch Erroch Side. Words by Nairne. GS

The lass o' Gowrie ("When Katie was scarce out nineteen") Air: Loch Erroch Side. Words by W. Reid. GS

The lass with the delicate air. M. Arne [wrongly attributed to T. A. Arne] AT

Lassen, Eduard
Ah, 'tis a dream. See Es war ein traum
All souls' day. See Allerseelen
Allerseelen
"Avec tes yeux mignonne." See "Mit deinen blauen augen"
Come home
Es war ein traum
A garden idyll. See "Ich wandle unter blumen"
"Ich wandle unter blumen"
"In heavenly love abiding"
"Mit deinen blauen augen"
"Thine eyes so blue." See "Mit deinen blauen augen"

Lassie wi' the lint-white locks. Air: Rothiemurchus' rant, or, Rothmurche's rant. Words by R. Burns. GS

Lasso, Orlando di. See Lassus, Orlandus

"Lasst mich euch fragen." See Porter lied (Flotow)

"Lässt sich amor bei euch schauen." See "Se amor mai da vu se vede"

Lasst uns singen von der gnade des Herrn. For English translation see I will sing of Thy great mercies (Mendelssohn)

Lassù in cielo. For English translation see "From yonder sky" (Verdi)

Lassus, Orlandus
"Into your hands I give my heart." See "Mon coeur se recommande à vous" (attributed)
"Matona, lovely maiden"
"Mon coeur se recommande à vous" (attributed)

The last carouse. Composer and author of words unknown. US

"Last Friday evening it happened but late." See Johnny Doyle (North Carolina version)

"Last Friday morning as we set sail." See The mermaid (Kentucky version)

"Last Friday night Lady Margret she lie." See Young hunting (Nellysford, Va. version)

"The last gleam o' sunset in ocean was sinkin'." See Mary Macneil

The last hour of the year. J. A. P. Schulz. ₍Words by J. H. Voss. Tr of Neujahrslied₎ e. LAS

"The last link is broken." W. Clifton. HP

"Last May a braw wooer." Air: The Lothian lassie, or, The queen o' the Lothians. Words by R. Burns. GS

The last mile. Danish folk air. Words by S. Fay. TFB

"Last night." See Laengsel (Kjerulf)

"Last night as I lay on the prairie." See The cowboy's heaven

"Last night I was a-married." See The lowlands of Holland (County Derry version)

"Last night, last night Lady Margret lay asleep." See Young hunting (Afton, Va. version)

"Last night the nightingale woke me." See Laengsel (Kjerulf)

The last rose of summer ("'Tis the last rose of summer") Air: Groves of Blarney. Words by T. Moore. BB—DFF—HMI—MFS—SSB
"'Tis the last rose of summer." GOS 1—SI—WLO

"Last Saturday night my wife taken sick." See A Monday was my courting day

"Last time I was in London." See Johnny German

"Last week I met a lady." See Ah there! stay there

"Last week I took a wife." Kelly. GOS 2

The last wish. See Dir nah' möcht' ich begraben sein (Abt)

The last words of Emmet. See "When Erin shall stand 'mid the isles of the sea" (Beale)

"Late in the night in frost cold." See "Silde ved nat hin kolde" (Lange-Müller)

"Late last night when my baby came home." See Ever after on

"Late one evening from the forest." Russian folk song. e. NRF

Latham, Albert G.
"Hear our call" (Mozart)
"The spendthrift spring" (Schubert)
"There's an island" (Gluck)
Vedrai, carino (Mozart)

Lathbury, Mary Ann
"Day is dying in the west" (Sherwin)

"Lather and shave." See Barber's cry

Latilla, Gaetano
"Fra degno ed amore" (from Siroë)
"Sgombra dall' anima" (from Siroë)

Latta, A. M., and Latta, J. H.
"Christmas-time has come again, time to us so dear" (Stevens)

Latta, J. H. See Latta, A. M., jt. auth.

Latto, Thomas C.
Innisfail (Phelps)

"Laue lüfte, blumendüfte." See Lob der thränen (Schubert)

Lauf, jäger, lauf. See Der jäger und die nixe

A laugh provoker. Air: The battle hymn of the republic, arr by W. Steffe. BB

Laugh, Punchinello. See Vesti la giubba (Leoncavallo)

Laughing glee. G. Martini. e. MFS

Laughing song ("De niggers from de souf") Minstrel song. WSS

Laulaja. See Der sänger

Lauliku papsepõli. See Des sängers kindheit

Launay, Paul de Valpincon de
Alma mater—Howard college

Les lauriers vont fleurir. French folk song. f. GSS

"Laut tönt's und dröhnt's von Nowgorods turm." See The bells of Novgorod

Lavallée, Calixa
"O Canada"

Lavender, my lavender. Song of the College of the city of New York. W. R. Johnson. Words by E. Lieberman. AI

"Lavender's blue." Old air. Traditional words. TFG—TFR

Lawes, Henry
The angler's song
"Great Tom is cast." See Aldrich, H. "Great Tom is cast"

Lawes, William
"The higher the plum-tree"

Lawlor, Charles B.
East side, west side. See The sidewalks of New York
The Irish jubilee
The sidewalks of New York

Lawreen, J. B.
 Who's that calling
"Laws-a-massey, what have you done."
 See Negro reel
"Lay him down, lay him down fine." See
 Giles Collins (Burnsville, N.C. version)
Lay this body down ("I know moonlight")
 Negro spiritual from South Caro-
 lina.   AS
 "I know moonlight."   SBA
 Variant: "O graveyard"
Lay this body down ("O graveyard")
 See "O graveyard"
Layeta.   Catalan folk song.   ca.g.
 ML 2
Lazarus.   Folk song: Tennessee version.
 SES 2
 —Virginia version.   SES 2
"Lazy Mary, will you get up."   Children's
 song.   SMG
Lazy Robin.   Welsh folk song.   CSB 2
"Lazy sheep, pray tell me why" (The boy
 and the sheep)   Old French air: La
 bonne aventure.   Words by J. Tay-
 lor.   DSB
Lazy song.   Old air.   Words by S.
 Rowe.   TFO
"L'chayim rebbe."   Jewish folk song.
 y.   SY
 "Lechaem, rebenu."   y.   KAJ
"Lèa! del sorriso suo gentil."   See
 Rapsodia primaverile (Leoncavallo)
[The lea rig]   "When o'er the hill"
 (My ain kind dearie, O)   Old Scot-
 tish air.   Words by R. Burns.   GS
"Lead, kindly light."   J. B. Dykes.
 Words by J. H. Newman.   BB—
 MFS—TFB—TFP
"Lead, kindly light."   C. Pinsuti.
 Words by J. H. Newman.   ASA
["Lead us, heavenly Father, lead us"]
 Sicilian mariners. Sicilian air. Words
 by J. Edmeston.   DSB
Lean on the Lord's side.   Negro spir-
 itual from South Carolina.   AS
Leanabh an aigh ("Child in the manger")
 Gaelic folk air.   Words by M. Mac-
 donald.   e.   CSB 1
Leanin' on de Lord.   See If you want to
 see Jesus
Lear, Edward
 "The owl and the pussy cat" (In-
 graham)
 "There was an old man, an old man
 who said" (Composer unknown)
The leather bottèl ("When I survey the
 world around")   [Air from "Wit and
 drollery"]   KSO
Leave her, bullies, leave her.   Hauling
 song.   SBA
 Across the western ocean.   WSE
 Variant of: Leave her, Johnnie
Leave her, Johnnie ("Oh the times are
 hard")   Capstan chantey.   SBS
 Variants: Leave her, bullies, leave her;
 Time for us to leave her
"Leave her Johnny and away we'll go."
 See Holystoning
"Leave me to languish."   See "Lascia
 ch'io pianga" (Händel)

Leave yo' sheep and leave yo' lambs.   See
 Rise up, shepherd, and foller
"The leaves around me falling."   Greek
 air.   MFS
Leavitt, John McDowell
 Our flag (Mersereau)
Leavitt, Michael Bennett
 "Little footsteps" (Barney)
"Lebe wohl, du gute mutter" ("Eche geia,
 chalē moy mana")   Greek folk song.
 g.gr.   ML 2
"Lebet wohl, teure freundin."   See "Adios,
 ene maitia"
Lebewohl ("Morgen muss ich fort von
 hier")   F. Silcher.   Volkslied.   g.
 EDL
"Lechaem, rebenu."   See "L'chayim rebbe"
Lecocq, Alexandre Charles
 Drinking song (from Giroflé-Girofla.
 Tr of Le punch scintille)
 "For a tender father" (from Giroflé-
 Girofla.   Tr of Pour un tendre
 père)
 Goblet of youth (same air as Drinking
 song)
 "Matamoras, our valiant captain great,
 hath all his captives brought in
 state" (from Giroflé-Girofla.   Tr
 of Matamoras, grande capitaine,
 enfin nous a tiré de peine)
 "Matamoras, the valiant captain, sails
 forth to rescue" (from Giroflé-
 Girofla.   Tr of Matamoras, grande
 capitaine, bientôt va vous tirer de
 peine)
 Morning serenade (from Giroflé-Girofla.
 Tr of Aubade)
 O pretty Girofla (from Giroflé-Girofla.
 Tr of Ma belle Girofla)
 "Pa, this same day" (from Giroflé-
 Girofla.   Tr of Père adoré, c'est
 Giroflé)
 Pirates' chorus (from Giroflé-Girofla.
 Tr of Parmi les choses délicates)
 "The scion of an ancient house" (from
 Giroflé-Girofla.   Tr of Mon père
 est un très gros banquier)
 Song of the Moors (from Giroflé-
 Girofla.   Tr of Plus brillants que
 des météores)
Leconte de Lisle, Charles Marie
 Le colibri (Chausson)
"Led her over mountains and valleys so
 deep."   See The cruel ship's carpenter
 (Callaway, Va. version no. 1)
Ledges troop song.   Girl scout song.
 Norwegian air.   GSS
Lee, Alfred
 Champagne Charlie
Lee, Andy, pseud.   See Delaney, William
 W.
Lee, George Alexander
 Bonnie Mary Gray
 Buy a broom (attributed)
 Here's a health, bonnie Scotland, to
 thee
 Macgregors' gathering
 Nobody's child
 "What's a' the steer, kimmer"
Leeves, William
 Auld Robin Gray

Leezie Lindsay.   Scottish song.   <Air:
    The ewe-bughts>   [1st verse by
    R. Burns]   BB—SSB
Lizzy Lindsay.   GS
"Will ye gang to the Hielands, Leezie
    Lindsay."   DSB
Lefébure-Wély, Louis James Alfred
    "Those evening bells"
Left all alone again blues.   J. Kern.
    Words by A. Caldwell.   HB
Leftwich, G. E.
    Blue and white
The **leg** I left behind me.   Song of the
    Mexican war.   [Air: Brighton camp]
    DSO
[The **legacy**] "When in death I shall calm
    recline."   Air: The bard's legacy, or,
    The legacy.   Words by T. Moore.
    HMI
A **legend** ("Christ, when a child")   See
    The crown of roses (Tchaikovsky)
A **legend** ("Once long ago")   See The
    crown of roses (Tchaikovsky)
Legend ("When Jesus Christ was yet a
    child")   See The crown of roses
    (Tchaikovsky)
A **legend** of Kieff.   See Bÿlínka
The **legend** of the bells.   R. Planquette.
    [Tr of Nous avons hélas! perdu d'excel-
    lents maitres]   e.   WLO
The **legend** of the glass.   J. Offenbach.
    [Tr of Il était un de mes aïeux]   e.
    WLO
The **legend** of the mascots.   E. Audran.
    e.   WLO
The **legend** of the pilgrims.   See Légende
    des pélerins
[The **legend** of Volgá]   O Vol'gře ĭ
    Mikulře (Jung Wolga und Mikula)
    Russian folk song.   g.r.   ML 1
Le **légende** de Saint-Nicolas.   See Le
    miracle de Saint-Nicolas
Légende des pélerins (The legend of the
    pilgrims.—The pilgrim legend)   Folk
    song from Champagne.   e.f.   CBF 1
Die **legende** vom Heiligen Nikolaus.   See
    Le miracle de Saint-Nicolas
"A **legény** egytöl egyig."   See "Trust
    them not" (Szentirmay)
Lehar, Franz
    "For I often have heard" (from The
        merry widow)
    "I'll go back to Maxim's" (from The
        merry widow)
    I'll love you true.   See Waltz song
    I'm a respectable wife (from The
        merry widow)
    "Now, come to me, ye sirens" (from
        The merry widow)
    "Ri-tan-tou-ri tan-ti-rette" (from The
        merry widow)
    Song of the silly horseman (from The
        merry widow)
    The study of woman (from The merry
        widow)
    "Then I go to Maxim's" (from The
        merry widow)
    Vilia song (from The merry widow)
    Waltz song (from The merry widow)

Lehman, Samuel
    Everybody works but father
"**Lehn'** deine wang' an meine wang'"
    (Press thy cheek against mine own)
    A. Jensen.   Words by H. Heine.
    e.g.   BST—GG
"**Lehn'** deine wang' an meine wang'"
    ("Oh, press thy cheek close to mine
    own")   E. Sjögren.   Words by H.
    Heine.   e.g.   WM 2
Der **lehrer.**   See Lo mestre
Des **leibeigenen** klagelied.   See entry un-
    der Des
"**Leinen** hatt' ich gezogen" ("Leniáles
    róvjau")   Lithuanian folk song.   g.li.
    ML 3
"Die **leineweber** haben eine saubere zunft."
    See Von den leinewebern
"**Leise** flehen meine lieder."   See Ständ-
    chen (Schubert)
"**Leise,** leise, fromme weise."   See Gebet
    (Weber)
"**Leise,** rieselnder quell."   See Der jüng-
    ling an der quelle (Schubert)
Le Jeune, George Fitz-Curwood
    "Jerusalem the golden"
    "Love divine, all loves excelling"
Le Mack, Thomas
    Little Johnny Dugan (Mack)
Le Mack, Will, pseud.   See Mack, An-
    drew
Lemaire, Gaston
    Gavotte des Mathurins.   See "Vous
        dansez, marquise"
    "Marchioness, your dancing."   See
        "Vous dansez, marquise"
    "Vous dansez, marquise"
Lemon, Mary Mark-.   See Mark-Lemon,
    Mary
Lenau, Nicolaus
    Bitte (music by Franz; Moór; Sjögren)
    Die drei zigeuner (Liszt)
    Frühlingslied (Mendelssohn)
    Stille sicherheit (Franz)
"**Leniáles** róvjau."   See "Leinen hatt'
    ich gezogen"
Lennon, Larry C., and Corcoran, Frank J.
    Georgetown's blue and gray
Lennox, Lindsay
    Come unto me (Slater)
    Love's golden dream (Composer un-
        known)
Der **lenz** ist gekommen.   For English
    translation see "But the springtime
    returneth, and new life doth bring"
Leo, Leonardo
    "Great is Jehovah and worthy to be
        praised"
    "O Jesu, my Saviour, who takest upon
        Thee"
Leonard, Eddie
    Roll them roly boly eyes
Leonard, George Hare
    Mothering Sunday (14th century Ger-
        man air)
Leoncavallo, Ruggiero
    Ballatella.   See High! high! aloft
    High! high! aloft (from I pagliacci.
        Tr of Hui! hui! stridon lassù)

Leoncavallo, Ruggiero—*Continued*
I hoped, in my passion (from I pagliacci. Tr of Sperai, tanto il delirio accecato m'aveva)
Love duet (from I pagliacci. Tr of E allor perchè, di', tu m'hai stregato)
"No, by my mother's soul" (from I pagliacci. Tr of No, per mia madre)
Prologue (from I pagliacci. Tr of Si puo? si puo)
Rapsodia primaverile
Serenade (from I pagliacci. Tr of O Columbina)
A spring rhapsody. See Rapsodia primaverile
"Such a game, believe me, friends" (from I pagliacci. Tr of Un tal gioco, credetemi)
Vesti la giubba (from I pagliacci)
"Lepa Jula, lepa Jula." See Reigen

Lermontov, Mikhail Iu'revich
Cradle-song (Grechaninov)
Leroux, Paul, pseud. See Loomis, Harvey Worthington
Leroux, Xavier Henri Napoléon
Pensée de printemps
Spring reverie. See Pensée de printemps
"Lesbia hath a beaming eye." Irish air: Nora criónna, or, Nora creina, or, Wise Nora. Words by T. Moore. HMI
Leslie, Ernest
Rock me to sleep
Lessing, Gotthold Ephraim
Das bose weib (Haydn)
Der tod (Volksweise)
Lest we forget. See "God of our fathers, known of old" (Dykes)
"Let all with gladsome voice." 17th century German air. e. DNS
"Let Bacchus' sons be not dismayed." See Garryowen
"Let but that spirit which first rush'd on me" (see Song Index)
Also in "Thus when the sun" (Händel) SSO 3
"Let Christians all with joyful mirth." See Yeoman's carol
"Let Christians all with one accord rejoice." See The black decree
Let de heaven light shine on me. Negro spiritual. HRD
Let de midnight special shine a light on me. See Midnight special (Negro song)
"Let Erin remember the days of old." Air: The red fox. Words by T. Moore. HMI—MFS—SI
"Let ev'ry good fellow." See Vive l'amour
Let God's saints come in. Negro spiritual from Virginia. AS
Variant of: Come down, angels
"Let joyful praise to heaven ascend." See Alleluia (German folk song)
Let me dream again. A. Sullivan. Words by B. C. Stephenson. GE

"Let me gaze." C. Gounod. [Tr of Laisse-moi, laisse-moi] e. WG
"Let me introduce a fellah." See Lardy dah (Page)
"Let me not be forgotten." See "Ne' giorni tuoi felici" (Pergolesi)
Let me say my little prayer. J. C. Macey (music and words) SW
"Let me tell you what is nat'rally de fac'." See Who is on the Lord's side
Let my people go. See Go down, Moses
"Let no man come into this hall." See A carol for everyman (Dykema)
"Let others breathe in glowing words." Irish air: Castle Hyde. Words by G. Griffin. HMI
"Let the air blow in upon me." See The dying nun (Brewster)
"Let the bridegroom rejoice" ("Yismach chathan") Yemenite wedding song. e.he. BNP
"Let the bright Seraphim." Händel. SSO 1
[Let the bullgine run] Oh run, let the bullgine run. Negro halliard chantey. BOS 2—TSB 1
Variants: Run, let the bulgine run; "Run, let the bull chimes run"
"Let the farmer praise his grounds." See An crúiscín lán
"Let the fifes and the clarions." H. Purcell. CSB 4
Let the heaven light shine on me. See Let de heaven light shine on me
Let the midnight special shine a light on me. See Midnight special
"Let the palms wave." See Les rameaux (Faure)
"Let the sinner sin right on." See You goin' to reap jus' what you sow
"Let the Swanee tiger scratch." See Yea Alabama (Sykes)
Let the toast pass. See "Here's to the maiden of bashful fifteen"
"Let thy glances rest upon me." See Die bitte (Moór)
"Let Tom or Dick or Harry get sick." See Calomel
Let us all unite in love. See "Hark! I hear a voice"
"Let us break bread togedder." See When I fall on my knees
Let us cheer the weary traveler. See Weary traveler
"Let us close our game of poker." See Hard crackers (Foster)
"Let us go, lassie, go." See The braes o' Balquhidder (Smith)
"Let us go up to our land rejoicing." See On to our land
"Let us haste to Kelvin grove, bonnie lassie." See Kelvin grove
"Let us live, then, and be glad." See "Gaudeamus igitur"
"Let us now in youth rejoice." See "Gaudeamus igitur"
"Let us pause in life's pleasures." See Hard times, come again no more (Foster)

"**Let** us praise Him." Negro spiritual. HRD

"**Let** us rejoice and sing." Old Scottish air: The broom of the Cowdenknowes. Words attributed to J. Wedderburn. DNS

"**Let** us sing of Christ's resurrection." P. Mascagni. ⌈Tr of Innéggiamo il Signor non è morto⌉ e. WG

"**Let** us sing to-day." Canon. A. Caldara. CSB 1

"**Let** us sow the lettuce." See Semons la salade

"**Let** us take the road." G. F. Handel. BOS 2

"**Let** us with a gladsome mind." O. Gibbons. Words by J. Milton. DSB

Lethe. F. Boott. Words by M. A. Barr. BST

"**Let's** cheer again for Temple." Temple university song. D. Zoob. Words by B. Bennett. KU

Let's fight for Vermont. See Vermont victorious (Furman, Sharples and Killick)

"**Let's** give a rah for West Virginia." See Hail West Virginia (Miller and McWhorter)

"**Let's** have a peal." 18th century English round. BOS 2—TFP

The **letter** edged in black. Old American song. RA—SW

"A **letter** here for me was the question that he ask'd." Old American song. SW

The **letter** in the candle. Old American song. SW

Letters, Will. See Murphy, C. W., jt. comp.

⌈**Letters** from lovers⌉ Ah! letters from lovers. J. Offenbach. ⌈Tr of Je t'ai sur mon coeur⌉ e. WLO

Der **letzte** tanz. See Schwesterlein, wann gehn wir nach haus

Levee moan ("Ah'm goin' whah nobody knows my name") Negro folk song. SBA

Levee moan ("O baby, where you been so long") Negro folk song. SBA

Levee song ("Oh, I was bo'n in Mobile town") Old American air. ⌈Words by S. Fay⌉ BB—TFB—TFP

Levenson, Robert. See Benoit, G., jt. comp. and auth.

Lever, Charles James
The widow Malone (Irish air; also 2d Irish air)

Leveridge, Richard
Alt-Englands roast beef. See The roast beef of old England
The beggar's song
The roast beef of old England
When dull care

Levey, William Charles
Esmeralda

Levy, Michael Bennett. See Leavitt, Michael Bennett

Lewie Gordon. Jacobite song. Words by Geddes. GS

Lewin, Lionel H.
Once again (Sullivan)

Lewis, Edwin Herbert
Alma mater—University of Chicago (Composer unknown)

Lewis, Leo Rich
Dear alma mater

Lewis, Matthew Gregory
The banks of Allan water (Traditional air)

Leybourne, G.
Champagne Charlie (Lee)

Leyden, James A.
The Nittany lion
Victory

"**Li** pas mandé robe mousseline." See Aurore Pradère

Li-tu-di-nu, Li-tu-di-nay. See Josie dear

The **liberty** song ("Come, join hand in hand") American Revolution song. Boyce. Words by J. Dickinson. DSO

The **liberty** song ("Come, shake your dull noddles") British soldiers' parody. Boyce. DSO

Lie, Sigurd
"Fain would I saddle." See "Jeg vilde sadle"
"Jeg vilde sadle"
Sne
Snow. See Sne

"**Lie** down lie down, little Matthy Groves." See Little Musgrave and Lady Barnard (Hindman, Ky. version no. 3)

Lieb heimatland, ade ("Nun ade") Volksweise. Words by A. Disselhoff. g. EDL

"**Lieb** Kätchen." See "Catina bellina"

"**Lieb** mutter mein, ich fleh zu dir." See Mutter und tochter

Lieb vaterland, magst ruhig sein. See Die wacht am Rhein (Wilhelm)

"**Liebchen,** ade." See Abschied

Liebchen, gute nacht (Mjej ty dobru nóc) Wendish folk song. g.we. ML 3

"**Liebchen,** schwälbchen" ("Dívča, dívča") Moravian-Czech folk song. bo.g. ML 3

"Der **liebe** weh ist wie leiblich schmerzen." See "Lo mal de l'amor"

"A **liebe** zu spielen." Jewish folk song. y. SY

⌈**Lieben** bringt freud'⌉ "Das lieben bringt gross freud" (Mein eigen soll sie sein) Schwäbisches volkslied. g. EDL

"Den **lieben** langen tag." See entry under Den

Lieber, Charles A.
Fight 'em Washington

Lieber schatz, sei wieder gut mir. R. Franz. Words by W. Osterwald. g. EDL

Lieberman, Elias
Lavender, my lavender (Johnson)

"**Liebes** mädchen, hör mir zu." J. Haydn. g. EDL

Liebeseinigung (Zgromadna lubość) Wendish folk song. g.we. ML 3

Liebesglück ("Wenn sti" mit seinen letzten flammen."—Joy unspoken) J. Sucher. e.g. TM

Liebesklage. See A forsaken lover's complaint (Johnson)

Liebeskrank. See Malatu p'amuri

Liebesscherz ("Wo a kleins hüttle") Schwäbisches volkslied. g. EDL

Das **liebesweh.** See "Lo mal de l'amor"

Liebeszauber ("Mädel, schau mir ins gesicht") J. A. P. Schulz. Words by G. A. Bürger. g. EDL

"**Lieblich** war der abend, die lenzluft labend." See The weaver's daughter

"**Liebliche** schläferin, erwachet." See "Reveillez-vous, belle dormeuse"

Lieblingsplätzchen. F. Mendelssohn-Bartholdy. <Words by F. Robert> g. EDL

Die **liebste** als schlangenköchin. See L'avvelenato

Der **liebsten** preis. See The gay young bachelor

"**Liebster** schatz, i bitt' di schön." See Bitte (Bohm)

Lied ("Ai! la le lo") See Alalá

Lied ("Dans la maisonnette au pied de la lande") See Tra la la la

Lied der landsknechte (Landsknechtslied) 16th century German air. Volksweise. g. EDL

Lied des hörigen (Wabadiku laul) Esthonian folk song. es.g. ML 3

Lied des kahnfahrers (Chunarska piěsen') Macedonian folk song. b.g. ML 2

Lied des landmanns. See Canzonetta di campagnuolo

Lied des ungarischen galeerensträflings (Magyar gályarabok éneke) 17th century Hungarian song. g.hu. ML 3

Lied fahrender schüler. V. E. Becker. Words by J. V. Scheffel. g. EDL

A **lied** fun a feigale. See Song of the little bird

Das **lied** vom jungen grafen ("Ich steh auf einem hohen berg") Volksweise. g. EDL

Das **lied** vom norden. See "Du gamla, du fria, du fjällhoga nord"

Das **lied** vom Rhein ("Es klingt ein heller klang") H. G. Nägeli. Words by M. von Schenkendorf. g. EDL

Das **lied** von dem jungen grafen. See Das lied vom jungen grafen

Das **lied** von den figueiredos. See Canção do figueiral

[Een **liedje** van der zee] Hinaus auf die see. Dutch folk song. g. EDL

"**Lieti** signor, salute." See "Nobles seigneurs, salut" (Meyerbeer)

Lieurance, Thurlow Hail! Wichita

Life and blessedness. See Liv og salighed (Sinding)

The **life** boat's crew. Sea song. US

"A **life** by de galley fire." Minstrel song. PSG

"A **life** in the soldiers' camp." Union song of the Civil war. [H. Russell] DSO

"**Life** is but a fleeting dream." See Make the best of it (Dunphy)

Life let us cherish. See "Freut euch des lebens" (Nägeli)

"A **life** on the ocean wave." H. Russell. Words by E. Sargent. GOS 1—MFS

"A **life** on the Vicksburg bluff." Confederate song of the Civil war. [H. Russell] Words by A. Dalsheimer. DSO

Lift the chorus ever onward, crimson and the blue. See Crimson and the blue (Thompson)

Lift the chorus, speed it onward, loud her praises tell. See Alma mater—Cornell university (Thompson)

"**Lift** thine eyes, behold the light." See Song of hope (Russotto)

"**Lift** thine eyes, O lift thine eyes." F. Mendelssohn. [Tr of Hebe deine augen auf zu den bergen] e. BB —TFG

"**Lift** your hidden faces." See Summer time

Light ("Og menniskja, ho sviv ikring") See Ljos (Sinding)

Light in darkness. F. H. Cowen. CSS 2

"The **light** is fading down the sky." See Hour of sweet repose (Howe)

"**Light**, light, light, my little Scotch-ee." See Little Scotch-ee

"**Light** of ages and of nations" (Beecher) J. Zundel. Words by S. Longfellow. LAS

"The **light** of other days." M. W. Balfe. Words by A. Bunn. GOS 2

"**Light** of our way." C. E. Cole. Words by G. Cooper. CSS 2

The **light** of the moon. Irish air from County Derry. Traditional words. HI 2

The **Light** of the world in the darkness has shone. See Infinite light

"**Light** off, light off, Lady Margaret." See Earl Brand (Nash, Va. version)

"**Light** you down, light you down." See Young hunting (Beattyville, Ky. version)

"**Lightly** row." <Spanish or German air> e. BB—MFS

"**Lightnin'** flashes, thunders roll." See Can't you live humble

"The **lights** along Broadway." See In the city where nobody cares (Harris)

"The **lights** fade out of calmed sea." See At evening-time (Sporle)

Lihuokalani, Lydia Kamekeha, queen of Hawaii. See Liliuokalani, Lydia Kamekeha, queen of Hawaii

Liisan laulu. See Lisas lied

"**Like** a beam from above." See "Ach! so fromm" (Flotow)

"**Like** a dream ye come to cheer me." See Chiming bells of long ago (Shattuck)

"**Like** a fountain clear and bright." See The fountain of knowledge

Like a rough and a rolling sea. See Rough and rolling sea

"Like as a father pitieth his children, so the Lord hath mercy." Canon. Cherubini. e. TFG

"Like melting tones it rises." See "Wie melodien zieht es mir" (Brahms)

"Like Peter when you said to him." See Oh, hear me prayin'

"Like snow white sailing boats on a blue sea." See Cloud-ships

"Like the bright lamp." See Erin! oh Erin

"Like the lark." F. Abt. Words by J. Oxenford. GE

Like the roses need their fragrance. See That's how I need you (Piantadosi)

Li'l Liza Jane. Old Southern air. Words by D. Harvey. TFG

Liliuokalani, Lydia Kamekeha, queen of Hawaii
Aloha oe
Farewell to thee (with original words) See Aloha oe
Farewell to thee (with words "Now our golden days")

Liljekonvalje (Lily of the valley) S. Palmgren. Words by O. Sirén. e.sw. WM 2

Den lillas testamente (Des kindes vermächtnis) Swedish folk song. g.sw. ML 1

Lilliburlero. H. Purcell. Words attributed to Wharton. MBS
Lilli Burlero. BOS 2

Lilly Dale. H. S. Thompson. KSO—WSS
Lily Dale. SW

Lily, Lily of the valley. See Lily of the valley (Friedland)

Lily of the valley ("Du hvita liljekonvalje") See Liljekonvalje (Palmgren)

Lily of the valley ("Lily, Lily of the valley") A. Friedland. Words by L. W. Gilbert. OTG

The lily of the west. Folk song from Kentucky. SES 2
Variant of: Flora the lily of the west

Limericks. Old air. TFG

Lincoln, Joe
Susan Van Doozen (Shepherd)

Lincoln and liberty. American political song of 1860. Air: Old Rosin, the beau. Words by F. A. Simpkins. SBA—SRW

"Lincoln hoss" and Stephen A. Republican political song of 1860. S. C. Foster. SRW

Lincoln's birthday ("In tow'r and spire were ringing") Dutch folk air. Words by H. H. Harbour. DSB

The Lincolnshire poacher. Lincolnshire county song. CSB 1—MBS

Lind, W. M.
Smoky mokes (Holzmann)

"Linden grün, ihr blätterreichen." See "Hai, salcâm, salcâm de varǎ"

"Linden im felde, grünende linden" ("W polu lipénka, w polu zielona") Polish folk song. g.p. ML 3

"Die linden lüfte sind erwacht." See Frühlingsglaube (Schubert)

The linden tree. See Der lindenbaum (Schubert)

Der lindenbaum ("Am brunnen vor dem tore") After F. Schubert. Words by W. Müller. g. EDL
The linden tree. e. BB—TFO

Die lindenwirtin. F. Abt. Words by R. Baumbach. g. EDL

Lindsay, Lady Ann. See Barnard, Lady Ann (Lindsay)

Lindsay, Jennie
"Always take mother's advice"

Lindsay, Maria. See Bliss, Mrs Maria (Lindsay)

"Lindy, Lindy, sweet as the sugar cane." See By the watermelon vine

Lingard, William Horace
As through the park I go (Composer unknown)
Captain Jinks (Composer unknown)
Par excellence (Composer unknown)
Walking down Broadway (Pratt)

Lingg, Hermann Ludwig Otto
Frühlingssegen (Bruckler)
"Immer leiser wird mein schlummer" (Brahms)

Linley, George
     Composer
The ballad singer. See Gaily I take my way
Gaily I take my way
"I heard a wee bird singing"
"Morning's ruddy beam"
The rose of the Alps
"Waking at early day." See Gaily I take my way
     Author
"Ever of thee" (Hall)

Linley, Thomas, 1732-1795
"Here's to the maiden of bashful fifteen": traditional air arranged
Sling the flowing bowl
While the foaming billows roll. See Sling the flowing bowl

Linn, Harry
You never miss the water (Howard)

Lioba. Swiss folk song. e. MFF

"Lionel's life sure will end." See Povero Lionello (Flotow)

"Lippe-Detmold." Westfälisches soldatenlied. g. EDL

Lisas lied (Liisan laulu) Finnish folk song. fi.g. ML 3

Lisle, Charles Marie Leconte de. See Leconte de Lisle, Charles Marie

Lisle, Claude Joseph Rouget de. See Rouget de Lisle, Claude Joseph

"List to me, rosebud" ("Hallod e rózsám") Old Hungarian folk song. e.hu. KH 2
"Hallod-e rózsám" ("Höre, mein liebchen") g.hu. ML 3

"Listen and I'll tell you 'bout Willie the weeper." See Willie the weeper

"Listen for a moment and I'll tell to ye a story." See Little Johnny Dugan (Mack)

"Listen, gentles, to the story." See The new born Child

"Listen in the moonlight." See Au clair de la lune

Listen! listen! echoes sound afar.   See Funicula, funicula (Denza)

"Listen, rose, thou sweet flower."   See La chanson des beignets

Listen Thou to these prayers of mine. See Tu seconda i voti miei (Bianchi)

Listen to de lambs.   Negro spiritual. FSN—HRD—WSS

Listen to that banjo man.   See Kansas City blues (Bowman)

Listen to the lambs.   See Listen to de lambs

Listen to the mocking bird.   S. Winner (A. Hawthorne)   (music and words) GOS 1— HP— KSO— MFS— SRW — WSS

Listen to the parrot shells.   See " 'Twas at the siege of Vicksburg" (Winner)

Liszt, Franz
"Anfangs wollt' ich fast verzagen"
"Could I ever hope to endure it."   See "Anfangs wollt' ich fast verzagen"
Die drei zigeuner
"Du bist wie eine blume"
Jeanne d'Arc au bûcher
Joan of Arc at the stake.   See Jeanne d'Arc au bûcher
Die Lorelei
"Thou art lovely as a flower."   See "Du bist wie eine blume"
The three gypsies.   See Die drei zigeuner

Litanei auf das fest "Aller seelen."   See Litaney (Schubert)

[Litaney] Litanei ("Ruh'n in frieden."— Litany)   F. Schubert.   Words by Jacobi.   e.g.   GA
Litanei auf das fest aller seelen.   g. EDL
Litany.   e.   SSO 4
Litany for the feast of all souls (Litanei auf das fest "Aller seelen")   e.g. GG

Litany for the feast of all souls.   See Litaney (Schubert)

Litchfield, Isaac White
Take me back to tech (Seaver)

"Liten prins i vaggan" ("Little prince a-cradled")   E. Sjögren.   Words by T. Hedberg.   e.sw.   WM 2

Lithauisches lied.   See Lithuanian song (Chopin)

[Lithuanian song] Lithuanian folk song (Lithauisches lied)   F. Chopin.   e.g. GA

"Líto je mně, můj tatíčku."   See "Sei nicht böse, mein lieb väterlein"

"Little Ah Sid."   Minstrel song: cowboy version.   SBA

Little Alabama coon.   [H. Starr]   PSG

Little Annie Rooney.   M. Nolan (music and words)   GFS—SMG
Annie Roonie.   DFF

Little barefoot.   Old song.   SW

The little bee.   Children's song.   MFS

The little bird ("Oh, do not frighten") Children's song.   MFS

Little birdie ("What does little birdie say") F. Delius.   Words by Tennyson. CSB 6

"De little black bull kem down de medder." See Hoosen Johnny

Little black me.   T. Chattaway (music and words)   SMG

"Little Bo-Peep."   Nursery song.   [J. W. Elliott]   BB—TFG—TFR

Little Boy Blue ("The little toy dog") J. E. Smith.   Words by E. Field. MFS

Little boy in blue.   T. Morse.   Words by R. A. Browne.   SMG

"Little boy sweetheart, with eyes that shine."   See Good night (Aldrich)

"Little bright eyes, will you miss me." H. P. Danks.   Words by J. T. Rutledge.   SW

The little brown church in the vale.   W. S. Pitts (music and words)   BB —TFP
The little brown church.   GOS 2— OT—TFR

A little brown cot, a shady green spot. See I long to see the girl I left behind (Kelly)

Little brown jug.   Eastburn (J. E. Winner)   GOS 2—SRW—WSS

The little bunch of whiskers on his chin. Old song.   SW

"The little busy bee abroad doth roam thro' all the day."   See The little bee

"Little by little."   C. Barnard.   MFS

"Little Cherry Blossom."   MFS

"Little chicken, hi, hi, hi."   See Die henne

"A little child on a sick-bed lay."   See The child of the railroad engineer

"A little Child on the earth has been born." See De nederige geboorte

"A little Child there is yborn."   See Parvulus nobis nascitur (Dunstan); Parvulus nobis nascitur (German air)

"Little children, then won't you be glad." Negro spiritual from Arkansas.   AS

Little Christ Jesus our brother is born. See Our brother is born (Farjeon)

[The little cudgel]   The song of the cudgel (Dubínushka)   Russian song.   e. SR
Variant of: Volga boat song

Little David, play on your harp.   Negro spiritual.   HRD—WSS
Little David, play on yo' harp.   WFN
"Little David was a shepherd boy."   See Little David, play on your harp

"A little doll with china eyes."   J. Offenbach.   [Tr of Une poupée aux yeux d'émail]   e.   WG

["Little duckling"]   Oh, duck of the meadows.   Russian gooslee air.   e. NRF

The little dustman.   See Sandmännchen

Little fidget.   See Strampelchen (Hildach)

"Little footsteps."   J. A. Barney.   Words by M. B. Leavitt.   SW

"Little Frankie went down to the barroom."   See Frankie Baker

Little girl, don't you cry.   <German song> e.   MFS

The little goatherd.   Swedish air.   Words by E. Smith.   DSB

Little Jack ("There was one little Jack") Words by J. Taylor. MFS

"Little Jack Horner." Nursery song. Composer unknown. MFS

"Little Jack Horner." Nursery song. ıJ. W. Elliottı BB—TFG

Little Jack Horner, et als. College song. Words from nursery rhymes (adapted). TFB

"Little Jesus, sweetly sleep, do not stir." See Rocking

"Little Joe, the wrangler." Cowboy song. <Words by N. H. Thorp> LSC

Little Johnny Dugan (He stole McCarthy's wife) A. Mack. Words by T. Le-Mack. SW

The little jug. See An crúiscin lán

The little lost child. J. W. Stern. Words by E. B. Marks. GFS—OTG—SRW

The little lowland maid. Folk song from Surrey. BET

Little Maggie May. C. Blamphin. Words by G. W. Moore. KSO—WSS

"Little maid of Arcadee." A. S. Sullivan. Words by W. S. Gilbert. GE

"A little maiden climbed an old man's knee." See After the ball (Harris)

A little man ("A tiny little man") <German folk song arr by Humperdinck> ıTr of Ein männlein steht im waldeı e. BB
A riddle. e. DSB
"A tiny little man." e. WG
"There stands a little man." e. MBS

A little more cider too. ıA. Hartı WSS

A little more faith in Jesus. Negro spiritual. WSS

Little Musgrave and Lady Barnard. Folk song: Barbourville, Ky. version no. 1. SES 1
—Barbourville, Ky. version no. 2. SES 1
—Clay county, Ky. version. SES 1
—Hindman, Ky. version no. 1. SES 1
—Hindman, Ky. version no. 2. SES 1
—Hindman, Ky. version no. 3. SES 1
—Manchester, Ky. version. SES 1
—Pine Mountain, Ky. version. SES 1
—Wasioto, Ky. version. SES 1
—Big Laurel, N.C. version. SES 1
—Black Mountain, N.C. version. SES 1
—Burnsville, N.C. version. SES 1
—Hot Springs, N.C. version. SES 1
—Flag Pond, Tenn. version no. 1. SES 1
—Flag Pond, Tenn. version no. 2. SES 1
—Rocky Fork, Tenn. version. SES 1
—Virginia version. SES 1

The little old cabin in the lane. W. S. Hays. WSS

The little old sod shanty. Old American song. SBA

"Little Omie, little Omie." See Poor Omie (Hindman, Ky. version no. 2; Pine Mountain, Ky. version)

Little owl. See Tecolotito

The little pig. Folk song: Vermont version. TFR

The old woman and the little pigee. Big Laurel, N.C. version. SES 2
—Burnsville, N.C. version. SES 2

"Little prince a-cradled." See "Liten prins i vaggan" (Sjögren)

"Little princess." See Princesita (Padilla)

The little red lark ("Oh, swan of slenderness") Old Irish air. Words by A. P. Graves. BST—SSB

The little rose of Gartan. Irish air from County Donegal. Words by S. MacCathmhaoil. HI 1

The little rosewood casket. Old American song. RA—SW

Little round cap. See "Mon pèr' m'a fait bâtir maison"

The little sandman. See Sandmännchen (Brahms)

Little Scotch-ee. Folk song: North Carolina version. SBA
Variant of: Young hunting

The little soldier. C. Vincent. Words adapted from a nursery rhyme. TFB

Little sparrow. See "Come all you fair and tender ladies" (Letcher county, Ky. version)

"Little star, far in the darkness burning." See Estrellita (Ponce)

"Little swallow, light and tender." See "Rondinella pellegrina" (Petrella)

A little talk wid Jesus makes it right. Negro spiritual. JB 2

"Little Tom Tinker." Round. BB

"The little toy dog is covered with dust." See Little Boy Blue (Smith)

"Little voices laughing free." See Where has Lulu gone (Foster)

The little wee croodin' doo (Das kleine gurretäubchen) Scottish folk song. e.g. ML 1
Variants: King Henry, my son; Lord Randal; Lord Ronald

Little wheel a-turnin'. Negro spiritual. FSN—WSS
"Dere's a little wheel a-turnin' in my heart." HRD

"A little while, O beautiful land." See Beulah land (Hughes)

Little white cottage. See Gentle Nettie Moore (Pike)

"Little white snowdrop, just waking up." See Waiting to grow (Aiken)

"Little Willie can you throw a ball." See The two brothers (Tennessee version)

A little wish. College song. TFB

"A little word in kindness said" (Ortonville) T. Hastings. MFS

"Liūli, liūli, liūliāta." See Wiegenlied (Ukrainian folk song)

Liv og salighed (Life and blessedness) C. Sinding. Words by I. Mortenson. e.n. WM 2

Live humble. See Glory and honor

"Live, live, live, our fields and woodlands need you." See Tree song

Live this day in memory shining. See Ah! quel giorno (Rossini)

"**Live-a** humble, humble, Lord." See Humble yo'self de bell done ring

Liza Anne. Folk song from Kentucky. SES 2
  Variant of: Eliza Jane

"**Liza** in the summer time." See Eliza Jane (North Carolina version)

Liza Jane. See Eliza Jane

"**Liza** Lee" (see Song Index)
  Variant: "Lizer Lee"

"**Lizer** Lee." Negro halliard chantey. TSB 2
  Variant of: "Liza Lee"

Lizzie Wan. Folk song from Kentucky. SES 1

Lizzy Lindsay. See Leezie Lindsay

Ljos (Light) C. Sinding. Words by P. Sivle. da.e. WM 2

Ljubav junaka prama svojoj majci. See Kriegers abschied von der mutter

Lliw gwyn rhosyn yr haf (White wild rose of my heart) Old Welsh song. Words by D. Dywyll. e.w. WO

Lloyd, Arthur
  Not for Joseph

Lloyd, Robert
  "Good morning, Mr Zip-Zip-Zip"

Llwyn on (Llwyn onn) Old Welsh song. g.w. ML 1
  The ash grove. e. DSC—MBS— TFG

[**Lo!** a fair rose is blooming] "Behold, a rose of beauty." M. Praetorius. Words from the German. e. FC
  "Lo, how a rose e'er blooming." e. DSB—DSC
  "Lo, what a branch of beauty." e. TFG
  The rose of Sharon. e. DN

"**Lo!** descending, the heavens rending." See Christ is born in Bethlehem

"**Lo,** how a rose e'er blooming." See Lo! a fair rose is blooming (Praetorius)

"**Lo** que digo." Mexican folk song from Jalisco. e.s. SBA

"**Lo** so che pria mi moro." P. Aniello. e.i. ZT 2

"**Lo!** the incarnate Lord." G. A. Naumann. e. SSO 3

"**Lo!** the walls of heaven star-lighted." See Bÿlínka

"**Lo,** what a branch of beauty." See Lo! a fair rose is blooming (Praetorius)

Lob der edlen musica. See O tempora! o mores

Lob der thränen (In praise of tears) F. Schubert. <Words by A. W. von Schlegel> e.g. GG
  Praise of tears. e. MFS

Lobgesang. See The song of praise

Loch Lomond. Jacobite air. AT—BB —BST—DSB— DSC— GSS— LAS —MBS—MFS—SSB—TFB— TFP. g. also ML 1
  Loch Lomond (The bonnie banks of Loch Lomond) GS

[**Lochaber** no more] "Farewell to Lochaber." [Attributed to M. Reilly] Words by A. Ramsay. GS—MBS— SAT

A **lock** of my mother's hair. Minstrel song. PSG

Lockruf (Lover's call) A. Rückauf. e.g. TM

Locks and bolts. Folk song: Kentucky version. SES 2
  —Carmen, N.C. version no. 1. SES 2
  —Carmen, N.C. version no. 2. SES 2
  —Hot Springs, N.C. version. SES 2
  —Spillcorn, N.C. version. SES 2
  Variant: "I dreamed last night of my true love"

The **locust** tree. Swedish air. Words by K. Davis. DSB

Loder, Edward James
  The brave old oak
  "I heard a brooklet gushing" (Tr of Wohin)

Loewe, Karl
  The erl-king. See Erlkönig
  Erlkönig
  "Fridericus Rex"
  Heinrich der vogler
  Niemand hat's geseh'n
  No one saw at all. See Niemand hat's geseh'n
  Prinz Eugen
  A song of the night: I. See Wand'rers nachtlied: I
  A song of the night: II. See Wand'rers nachtlied: II
  Wand'rers nachtlied: I
  Wand'rers nachtlied: II

Logan, John
  Spring-time once again (Sullivan)

[**Logie** o' Buchan] "O Logie o' Buchan." Scottish air. Words by G. Halket. GS

Löhr, Frederic N.
  "Out on the deep"
  Paradise square

Lola's song. P. Mascagni. [Tr of Fior di giaggiolo] e. WG

Lolotte. See Pov' piti Lolotte

"**Lomir** beide a liebe spielen." Jewish folk song. y. KAJ

"**Lomir** sich überbeten." Jewish folk song. y. SY

"**Lomir** sich iberbeten." y. KAJ

London bridge ("Proud and lowly") J. L. Molloy. Words by F. E. Weatherly. GE

"**London** bridge is broken down, dance over, my Lady Ley." Play-time song. BOS 2

"**London** bridge is falling down." Folk song: American version. SMG

"**London** city." Folk song: American version. SBA

London street cries ("Who'll buy my posies") Round. GSS

London waits. See Past three o'clock and a cold frosty morning

The **lone** fish-ball ("There was a man") 1st version. SRW

The **lone** prairie. See The dying cowboy

The **Lone** Star trail. Cowboy song. SBA
  Variant of: The Chisholm trail

Lone starry hours. J. Power <wrongly attributed to J. P. Ordway> Words by M. S. Pike. GOS 1

"**Lonely** in prison, sad and forsaken." See "Prigioniera, abbandonata" (Galuppi)

[The **lonely** waif] "Iskhodíla mladen'ka" (Die ausgestossene) Russian folk song. g.r. ML 1

"**Lonely** wanders thy friend in spring's green garden." See Adelaïde (Beethoven)

The **lonesome** grove. Folk song: Kentucky version. SES 2
—Tennessee version. SES 2
—Peaks of Otter, Va. version. SES 2
—Villamont, Va. version. SES 2

The **lonesome** prairie. Folk song: Kentucky version. SES 2
—Burnsville, N.C. version no. 1. SES 2
—Burnsville, N.C. version no. 2. SES 2
Variant of: The dying cowboy

Lonesome road. Folk song: Indiana version. SBA

The **lonesome** valley. Negro spiritual from South Carolina. AS

Long, Gordon
Denison marching song (Arnold)

Long ago in Kazan city. Russian folk song. e. NRF

"**Long** ago in the ancient city call'd Kazan." See Long ago in Kazan city

"**Long** ago she rose and stood." See Holyoke

"**Long** ago, when I was still free" ("Mikor én még legény voltam") J. Szerdahelyi (music and words) e.hu. KH 1

The **long** day closes. A. S. Sullivan. Words by H. F. Chorley. TFB

"Le **long** du quai, les grands vaisseaux." See Les berceaux (Fauré)

"**Long** ere the morn expects the return." See The hunter in his career

Long gone. W. C. Handy. Words by C. Smith. HB

"**Long** live King Henry." See Vive Henri quatre

Long live the merry, merry heart. See Some folks do (Foster)

Long, long ago. T. H. Bayly (music and words) BB—GOS 1—MFS—TFB—TFO—TFP—TFR

"A **long**, long time, and a very long time." See A long time ago

"The **long**, long weary day." See Des mädchens klage

A **long** time ago ("A long, long time, and a very long time") Halliard chantey. TSB 2

[**Long** time ago] "Near the lake" (A southern refrain) [Negro air: Way down in the raccoon hollow, arr by] C. E. Horn. Words by G. P. Morris. HP

A **long** time ago, a long time ago, oh I wish to God I'd never been born. See Around Cape Horn

Long time ago, long time ago, de little black bull kem down de medder. See Hoosen Johnny

"A **long** time ago since Tommy was dead." See Old Roger (Kentucky version)

The **long** weary day. See Des mädchens klage

A **long** white robe. Mountain spiritual from Virginia. RA

"**Long** years ago, in old Madrid." See In old Madrid (Trotter)

Longfellow, Henry Wadsworth
The bridge (Carew)
"The day is done and the darkness falls from the wings of night" (Balfe)
"Good-night, good-night, beloved! I come to watch o'er thee" (Pinsuti)
"I heard the bells on Christmas day" (music by Calkin; Dunstan)
Indian lullaby (Aiken)
The rainy day (Dempster)
The reaper and the flowers (Mendelssohn)
"Stars of the summer night" (Woodbury)
"The sun is bright" (Gounod)
Suspiria (Sjögren)
Upidee (Composer unknown)

Longfellow, Samuel
"God of the earth" (Holmes)
"God's trumpet wakes the slumb'ring world" (Brown)
"Light of ages and of nations" (Zundel)
"O Life that maketh all things new" (Mason)
"One holy church of God appears" (Barnby)
"Out of the dark the circling sphere" (Schumann)

"**Long-haired** preachers come out ev'ry night." See The preacher and the slave (Webster)

Longing ("Nid oes rhyngof ag ef heno") See Hiraeth

Longing for spring ("Komm', lieber mai") See "Komm', lieber mai, und mache" (Mozart)

Longing for spring ("Oh, how cold the winter weather") German air. MFS

Lonsdale, J. J.
Ruby (Gabriel)

"**Look** ahead, look a-stern." See The coasts of High Barbary

"**Look** at that mulatto, li'l Mister Banjo." See Musieu Bainjo

Look at the ears on him. L. W. Harrington. Words by J. W. Alvord. DSO

Look away. See Some of these mornings

"**Look** down, look down that lonesome road." See Lonesome road

"**Look** down the lone green valley." See Blue eyed Ellen

"**Look** here, Alexander, I was only fooling." See Alexander (Von Tilzer)

"**Look** into my eye, come near" ("Nézzél csak a szemembe") Old Hungarian folk song. e.hu. KH 1

"**Look**, neighbours, look." Round. Harrington. BOS 2

"**Look** not upon the wine." R. S. Willis. MFS

"**Look** our ransomed shores around." See Hail Columbia, The new (Phile)

"**Look** thee! O heav'n." Finale from Il trovatore. G. Verdi. ₁Tr of Vedi! cielo! è spento₁ e. WG

"**Look-a** how dey done my Lord." Negro spiritual. JB 2

Looking back. A. S. Sullivan. Words by L. Gray. GE

The **loom.** See Y gwŷdd

Loomis, George B.
"Baby bye, here's a fly"

Loomis, Harvey Worthington

Composer

Commencement song
Lady Moon
Music in the air, Counterpoint for
Second thoughts
The tree toads
Twilight music

Composer and author

The camp fire
The 'cello
Down in Dixie
The mosquito's serenade

Author

At the gym (Spanish air)
The cat and the catboat (Swedish folk air)
Cradle song (Schubert)
The dawn of Maytime (Flotow)
Faith (Mozart)
Hail and farewell (Hawaiian folk air)
Love greetings (Elgar)
The woodland brook (Ukrainian folk air)
See also entries in Song Index under pseud. Pierpont, Victor N., as well as under real name

"**Loose** ev'ry sail to the breeze." See Homeward bound (Arne)

Lor, lor, my little Betty Anne. See Betty Anne

"**Lord,** at all times I will bless Thee." See "Caro cibus, sanguis potus" (Mendelssohn)

"The **Lord** at first did Adam make" (Christmas eve) Traditional carol. <Air from Gilbert's "Some ancient Christmas carols"> OB

"The Lord at first had Adam made" (A Christmas eve carol) DNS

"The **Lord** at first did Adam make" (Christmas eve) Traditional carol. Air from Sandys's "Christmas carols." OB

"**Lord** Bacon was a nobleman." See Young Beichan (White Rock, N.C. version)

"**Lord** Batesman was a noble young man." See Young Beichan (Allanstand, N.C. version)

"**Lord** Batesman was a nobleman." See Young Beichan (Big Laurel, N.C. version no. 1)

"**Lord** Christ above." See Wo gehest du hin (Bach)

"**Lord,** dismiss us with Thy blessing" (Sicilian mariners' hymn) Sicilian air. ₁Words attributed to J. Fawcett; attributed also to₁ W. Shirley. MFS

Lord, feed my lam's. See Oh, hear me prayin'

Lord Geoffrey Amherst. Amherst college song. J. S. Hamilton. AI—AIS

"**Lord** God of Abraham." F. Mendelssohn. ₁Tr of Herr Gott Abrahams₁ e. SSO 4

The **Lord** hath arisen. Ancient carol. TFB—TFP

"**Lord,** have mercy, Lord, have mercy." Negro spiritual. HRD

"**Lord,** have mercy upon mine offences." See O Lamb of God (Naumann)

"**Lord,** he thought he'd make a man." See Dese bones gwine to rise again

"**Lord,** hear my prayer." C. H. Graun. e. SSO 3

"The **Lord** Himself now thy bondage hath riven." Final chorus from Tannhäuser. R. Wagner. ₁Tr of Der gnade heil ward dem blüsser beschei-den₁ e. WG

Lord, I can't stay away. See I can't stay away (Johnson)

Lord, I don't feel noways tired. · See I don't feel no-ways tired

"**Lord!** I married me a wife." See Rain and snow

"**Lord,** I want to be a Christian." Negro spiritual. HRD—JB 2

Lord, I'm a-climbing Jacob's ladder. See Sinner man (North Carolina version)

"The **Lord,** in His righteousness." Netherlands folk air. DSB

"**Lord!** in my heart's love deep I hide Thee." See Gebet (Hiller)

"**Lord,** in this Thy mercy's day." W. H. Monk. <Words by I. Williams> MFS

"The **Lord** is my Shepherd, how blessed to know." C. Bohm. Words by H. J. Lovejoy. CSS 2

"The **Lord** is my Shepherd, I shall not want" (The good Shepherd) B. Van de Water. TSS 1

"The **Lord** is my Shepherd; no want shall I know." T. Koschat. Words by J. Montgomery. BB

"The **Lord** is risen, He will dwell with men" (And God shall wipe away all tears) A. Sullivan. SAT

The **Lord** is risen (God shall wipe away all tears from their eyes) CSS 2

"**Lord** Jesus hath a garden." See Jesus' bloemhof

"**Lord** Joshuay, she cried." See The maid freed from the gallows (Burnsville, N.C. version no. 3)

"**Lord,** lead me in Thy righteousness." See O salutaris (Cherubini)

"**Lord** Lovel." Folk song: Berea, Ky. version. SES 1
—Knott or Letcher County, Ky. version. MK
—Allanstand, N.C. version. SES 1
—Burnsville, N.C. version. SES 1
—South Carolina version. SBA
—Nash, Va. version. SES 1
—Nellysford, Va. version. SES 1

"**Lord** Lover stands by his dest castle gate." See "Lord Lovel" (Burnsville, N.C. version)

"**Lord,** make me more patient." Negro spiritual from South Carolina. AS

The **Lord** Mayor's show. J. Blewitt. Words by T. Hood. SW

Lord, oh, hear me prayin', Lord. See Oh, hear me prayin'

"**Lord** of all being." J. Hatton. Words by O. W. Holmes. DSC

"**Lord** of all being." V. C. Taylor. Words by O. W. Holmes. BB

"The **Lord** of all did reign supreme" ("Adon olom") Palestinean folk song. e.he. BNP

Lord of all, to Thee we raise. See "For the beauty of the earth" (Kocher)

"**Lord,** on Thy tender love relying." See Gebet (Hiller)

Lord Randal. Folk song: Georgia version. SES 1
—Knott or Letcher county, Ky. version. MK
—St Helen's, Ky. version. SES 1
—Allanstand, N.C. version no. 1. SES 1
—Allanstand, N.C. version no. 2. SES 1
—Burnsville, N.C. version. SES 1
—Carmen, N.C. version. SES 1
—Swannanoah, N.C. version. SES 1
—Tennessee version. SES 1
—Buena Vista, Va. version no. 1. SES 1
—Buena Vista, Va. version no. 2. SES 1
—Buena Vista, Va. version no. 3. SES 1
—Callaway, Va. version. SES 1
—Nellysford, Va. version. SES 1
Variants: King Henry, my son; The little wee croodin' doo; Lord Ronald

Lord, remember me ("Oh Deat' he is a little man") Negro spiritual from South Carolina. AS

Lord Ronald. Scottish song. GS
Variants: King Henry, my son; The little wee croodin' doo; Lord Randal

Lord Thomas and fair Ellinor. Folk song: Rabun county, Ga. version no. 1. SES 1
—Rabun county, Ga. version no. 2. SES 1
—Barbourville, Ky. version. SES 1
—Berea, Ky. version. SES 1
—Hindman, Ky. version. SES 1
—Hyden, Ky. version. SES 1
—Manchester, Ky version. SES 1
—Wasioto, Ky. version. SES 1
—Massachusetts version. SES 1
—Allanstand, N.C. version. SES 1
—Burnsville, N.C. version no. 1. SES 1
—Burnsville, N.C. version no. 2. SES 1
—Burnsville, N.C. version no. 3. SES 1
—Carmen, N.C. version. SES 1

—Hot Springs, N.C. version no. 1. SES 1
—Hot Springs, N.C. version no. 2. SES 1
—Marion, N.C. version. SES 1
—Flag Pond, Tenn. version. SES 1
—Harrogate, Tenn. version. SES 1
—Bedford county, Va. version. SES 1
—Beechgrove, Va. version. SES 1
—Blue Ridge Springs, Va. version. SES 1
—Buena Vista, Va. version. SES 1
—Dewey, Va. version. SES 1
—Montvale, Va. version. SES 1
—Nellysford, Va. version. SES 1
—Woodridge, Va. version. SES 1
"The brown girl" (Fair Eleanor) Alexander county, N.C. version. SBA
Lord Thomas. Knott or Letcher county, Ky. version. MK
Variant: "The brown girl"

"**Lord** Thomas he was a bold forester." See Lord Thomas and fair Ellinor (Massachusetts version)

"**Lord** Thomas he was a brave young man." See Lord Thomas and fair Ellinor (Carmen, N.C. version; Hot Springs, N.C. version)

"**Lord** Thomas, Lord Thomas, is this your bride." See Lord Thomas and fair Ellinor (Flag Pond, Tenn. version)

"**Lord** Thomas, Lord Thomas, is this your wife." See Lord Thomas and fair Ellinor (Burnsville, N.C. version no. 3)

"**Lord** Thomas was a bold forester." See Lord Thomas and fair Ellinor (Marion, N.C. version)

Lord, Thou art our Shepherd. See The good Shepherd (Slater)

"**Lord,** to Thee, each night and day." G. F. Händel. SSO 2

Lord, until I reach my home. Negro spiritual. HRD

"**Lord,** we come with hearts aflame." Arr from C. Kocher. Words by B. Braley. TFP

"**Lord!** Whom my heart holds dear forever." See Gebet (Hiller)

Lord Willoughby. [W. Byrd] BOS 2

The **Lord** worketh wonders. Handel. SSO 4

"The **lords** of creation." Old song, by J. S. R. GOS 2

The **Lord's** prayer ("Father in heaven") See "Father in heaven, hear us today" (Bliss)

The **Lord's** prayer ("Our Father in Heaven, we hallow Thy name") Composer unknown. Words by S. J. Hale. MFS

The **Lord's** prayer ("Vater unser") C. Krebs. e.g. ASA

Die **Lore** am tore ("Of all the girls") See Sally in our alley (Old English air); Sally in our alley (Carey)

Die **Lore** am tore ("Von allen den mädchen") Composer unknown. Words after H. C. Boie. g. EDL

ɪDieɪ **Lorelei** ("Ich weiss nicht")   F. Silcher.   Words by H. Heine.   g. EDL
The Loreley.   e.   BB—TFP
ɪDie **Lorelei**ɪ "Ich weiss nicht" (Die Loreley.—Loreley)   F. Liszt.   ɪWords by H. Heineɪ.   e.g.   HCA
The **Loreley** ("Ich weiss nicht")   See Die Lorelei (Liszt); Die Lorelei (Silcher)
Lorena.   ɪJ. P. Webster.   Words by H. D. L. Websterɪ   DSO
Lorraine march.   See Marche lorraine (Ganne)
Löscher, Valentin Ernst
Pfingstlied (Bach)
The **lost** babe.   Folk song: Kentucky version.   SES 2
—North Carolina version.   SES 2
The **lost** chord.   A. Sullivan.   Words by A. A. Procter.   BB—GE—HCA—LAS—TFP—TFR
The **lost** lady found.   Folk song: Lincolnshire version.   BET
The **lost** lamb.   Romanze.   F. Schubert.   ɪTr of Die mutter sucht ihr liebes kindɪ   e.   CSB 2
Die **lotosblume** ("The lotus flower")   R. Schumann.   Words by H. Heine.   e.g.   GG
Die **lotosblume** ("The lotus blossom")   e.g.   CSB 4
Lotti, Antonio
Pur dicesti, o bocca bella
"Speak again, love."   See Pur dicesti, o bocca bella
"The **lotus** blossom."   See Die lotosblume (Schumann)
"The **lotus** flower."   See Die lotosblume (Schumann)
Loucks, R. N.
"Hail! Pomona! hail"
Loud, A. F.
"There is a city bright"
"**Loud** roar'd the dreadful thunder."   See The bay of Biscay (Davy)
"**Loud** the winds howl! loud the waves roar."   See Skye boat song
Loudly the bell in the old tower rings.   See Asleep in the deep (Petrie)
"**Loudon's** bonnie woods and braes."   ＜R. A. Smith＞   Words by Tannahill.   GS
Lou'siana Belle.   S. C. Foster (music and words)   SW—WSS
Love, John
Barber, spare those hairs (Russell)
Love all its pow'r now proveth.   See Già l'ira m'abbandona (Meyerbeer)
Love among the roses.   Minstrel song and dance.   SW—WSS
Love an' serve de Lordɪ "If you love God, serve Him."   Negro spiritual.   HRD
Love and battle.   Air: Yankee Doodle.   DSO
Love and joy come to you ("Here we come a-carolling")   See Christmas carolling song
Love and joy come to you ("Here we come a-wassailing")   See "Here we come a-wassailing"
Love and mirth (Baden polka)   J. Strauss.   MFS

Love and serve the Lord.   See Love an' serve de Lord
Love and the novice ("Here we dwell in holiest bowers")   Air: Cean dubh deelish.   Words by T. Moore.   HMI
Love divine ("I cannot always trace the way")   T. H. Howe.   Words by J. Bowring.   TSS 2
"**Love** divine! all love excelling."   Offertory solo.   F. S. Sommers.   ɪWords by C. Wesleyɪ   TSS 1
"**Love** divine, all loves excelling"   (Austrian hymn)   Haydn.   Words by C. Wesley.   DN
"**Love** divine, all loves excelling."   G. F. Le Jeune.   Words by C. Wesley.   LAS
Love duet ("Dear, kind sir")   O. Straus.   e.   WLO
Love duet ("Why hast thou taught me")   R. Leoncavallo.   ɪTr of E allor perchè, di', tu m'hai stregatoɪ   e.   WG
Love finds the way.   See Keine sorg' um den weg (Raff)
Love greetings (Salut d'amour)   E. Elgar.   Words by H. W. Loomis.   TFG
Love's greetings (Salut d'amour)   TFB
"**Love**, in your laughter crystal clear."   See Mirame así (Fuentes)
Love is come again.   French air: Noël nouvelet.   Words by J. M. C. Crum.   OB
"**Love** is like a gold brick in a bunco game."   See Loveless love (Handy)
Love letters.   B. Newcombe (music and words)   SW
Love me and the world is mine.   E. R. Ball.   Words by D. Reed.   GFS
"**Love** not, love not."   J. Blockley.   Words by C. Norton.   GOS 1
"**Love** not the world."   A. Sullivan.   SSO 2
"**Love**, oh love, oh careless love."   See Careless love (American folk song)
"**Love**, oh love, oh keerless love."   See Careless love (American mountain version)
"**Love**, oh love, oh loveless love."   See Loveless love (Handy)
"**Love** somebody, yes I do."   Kentucky mountain song.   SBA
Love song ("Holder klingt der vogelsang")   See Minnelied (Brahms)
A **love-sonnet**.   See Sonnet d'amour (Thomé)
"**Love** the Lord, oh, my heart."   See Sentence (Mendelssohn)
"**Love** thy mother, little one."   ɪF. H. Himmelɪ   MFS
Lovejoy, Helen J.
"The Lord is my Shepherd, how blessed to know" (Bohm)
Loveless love.   Blues song.   W. C. Handy.   HB
"**Lovely** appear."   C. Gounod (music and words)   e.   BB—TFG
Lovely Dine.   See Lubly Dine (Sanford)

Lovely evening. Round. ⌊Tr of O wie wohl ist mir am abend⌋ e. BB —GSS—TFB—TFP
"O how lovely is the evening." e. DSB

"Lovely flowers I pray." See "Faites-lui mes aveux" (Gounod)

The lovely garden. See The fair garden (Borodin)

Lovely lady. See Mwynen merch

"The lovely lass of Inverness." J. Oswald. Words by R. Burns. GS

"Lovely maiden, consuming passion not from thee my heart would crave." See "E pur io" (Amadori)

Lovely May is coming. Polish air. Words by K. Davis. DSB

"Lovely May, lovely May." <Spanish or German air: Lightly row> e. MFS

"Lovely Melinda, come, now my dear." See Melinda May (Foster)

"Lovely night! O lovely night." F. X. Chwatal. e. BB—TFB

"Lovely night whose starry smile." See "Belle nuit" (Offenbach)

"Lovely Rosa, Sambo come." See Coal black Rose (Russell)

Lovely spring. See "Wenn der frühling auf die berge steigt" (Coenen)

"Lovely summer comes again." See Sommerlied (Neidhardt von Reuenthal)

"The lovely sunshine coming after shower." See 'O sole mio (Capua)

Lover, Samuel

Composer and author

Barney O'Hea
The bowld sojer boy
The four-leaved shamrock
I'm not myself at all
Molly bawn
"What will you do, love"
"Widow machree, it's no wonder you frown"

Author

The angels' whisper (Irish air)
The girl I left behind me (18th century air)
The low-backed car (Irish air)
"Oh, did you ne'er hear of the Blarney" (Old Irish air)
Rory O'More (Irish air)

The lover and the bird. P. D. Guglielmo. GE

Lover's call. See Lockruf (Rückauf)

The lover's curse. Irish air from County Donegal. Words from an old ballad. HI 1

The lover's lament ("Don't you remember") Folk song: Alleghany, N.C. version. SES 2

The lover's lament ("Don't you remember") Carmen, N.C. version. SES 2

The lover's lament ("Now once I did court") Tennessee version. SES 2

The lover's lament ("Off to the war") Hot Springs, N.C. version. SES 2

The lover's lament ("Once I courted") Kentucky version. SES 2

The lover's lament ("Once I courted") Marion, N.C. version. SES 2

The lover's lament ("Once I courted") Dewey, Va. version. SES 2

The lover's lament ("Once I courted") Woodridge, Va. version. SES 2
Variant of: "My dearest dear"; The true lover's farewell

The lover's lament ("My dearest dear") American folk song: 1st version. SBA

The lover's lament ("I wish your breast was made of glass") 2d version. SBA

Love's chidings. Old song, by Nannie. GOS 2

"Love's flame, so fiercely burning." See "Giammai provai" (Piccinni)

Love's golden dream ("I hear to-night") Words by L. Lennox. MFS

Love's greetings ("Sweetheart, I send you a red, red rosebud") See Love greetings (Elgar)

Love's old, sweet song. J. L. Molloy. G. C. Bingham. BB—LAS—TFB—TFP—TFR

Love's ritornella ("Gentle Zitella") J. R. Planché; wrongly attributed to T. Cooke. Words by J. R. Planché. GOS 1—SRW

Love's the tune. O. Straus. e. WLO

Love's young dream ("Oh, the days are gone when beauty bright") Irish air: An thseann bheann bhocht, or, The old woman. Words by T. Moore. GOS 2
"Oh! the days are gone when beauty bright." HMI—SI

"Loving Hannah." Kentucky mountain song. MK

Loving Jesu, Thou hast sought me. G. A. Hasse. e. SSO 2

A loving kiss. E. Audran. e. WLO

Loving Nancy. Folk song: Kentucky version. SES 2
—Virginia version. SES 2

Loving Reilly. Folk song: Georgia version. SES 2
—North Carolina version. SES 2
Variant of: Willie Reilly

"Loving voices." C. W. Glover. MFS

"Low and low and low holiday." See Sir Hugh (Manchester, Ky. version)

The low-backed car ("When first I saw sweet Peggy") Irish air: ⌊The jolly ploughboy, or, Jolly ploughman⌋ Words by S. Lover. BB—GOS 2—TFR
The low back'd car. SI

Low bridge, ev'rybody down. See The Erie canal

Lowe, Alexander
Mary's dream (Scottish air) Authorship uncertain; attributed also to J. Lowe

Lowe, John
Mary's dream (Scottish air) Authorship uncertain; attributed also to A. Lowe

Lowell, Emily, pseud.   See Loomis, Harvey Worthington
Lowell, James Russell
Aladdin (Bellini)
Peace on earth (Donizetti)
Lowlands ("Lowlands, lowlands, away my John")   Windlass   chantey. WSE
For variants see following songs of similar title
Lowlands away ("I dreamed a dream") Halliard chantey.   SBS
Lowlands away ("Lowlands, lowlands, away")   Halliard chantey.   SBS
Lowlands away ("Lowlands, lowlands, away")   Windlass and capstan chantey.   TSB 1
The **lowlands** of Holland ("Last night I was a-married")   Folk song: County Derry version.   HI 2
The lowlands of Holland ("O the very first night I was married")   Virginia version.   SES 1
Lowry, J. C.
"O what can you tell"
Lowry, Robert
"I need Thee every hour"
"Loyola, Loyola we hail thee."   See Alma mater—Loyola university (Devereux)
Lubly Dine.   J. Sanford (music and words)   SW—WSS
"Lubly Melinda, come, now my dear." See Melinda May (Foster)
"Lubly Rosa, Sambo cum."   See Coal black Rose (Russell)
Lucas, Samuel
Carve dat possum
"Luchīna, luchīnushka berezovaîa."   See The birchen brand
Lucini, Giovanni Battista
"Un cor da voi ferito" (Scarlatti)
"Non dar più pene, o caro" (Scarlatti)
"Luck to the master and the mistress." See La guignolée
Luckstone, Isidore
"Ah! la belle menotte"
"Ah! these pretty wee hands."   See "Ah! la belle menotte"
Lucy Long ("Oh! I jist come out afore you")   Negro song.   WSS
ₜLucy Long₎   "Was you ever on the Brumalow" (Miss Lucy Long)   Capstan chantey.   TSB 2
Lucy Neal.   Negro song.   WSS
Ludebuehl, John Peter
Here's to the colors of crimson-white
Luke, Mrs Jemina (Thompson)
That sweet story of old (Composer unknown)
Lukovītskī momī.   See Die Lukowiterinnen
Die **Lukowiterinnen** (Lukovītskī momī) Bulgarian folk song.   b.g.   ML 2
"Lūĭala, ĭuĭala, majka sīnana."   See Wiegenlied (Serbian folk song)
Lulie.   Folk song from North Carolina. SES 2
Lulinke main sinenu.   See A maaseh
Lulinke, mein vögele.   See A maaseh

"Lulla, lullaby, all things now sleep 'neath the sky."   See Wiegenlied (Mozart)
Lullaby ("Dear mother, in dreams")   E. Jakobowski.   Words by C. Bellamy. WLO
Lullaby ("Dors, dors, mon petit, dors") See Berceuse
Lullaby ("Guten abend")   See Wiegenlied (Brahms)
Lullaby ("Huna blentyn ar fy mynwes") See Suo-gân
ₜLullabyₗ "Hush-a-by, baby, the night winds are sighing."   Scottish folk air. Words by R. Compton.   DSB
Lullaby ("Lullaby, lullaby, my lovely one") German folk song.   e.   DSB
Lullaby ("Pai, pai, paitaressu")   O. Merikanto.   Words by Mustakallio.   e.fi. WM 2
Lullaby ("Sleep, little baby")   Finnish rune air.   Words by E. Smith.   DSB
Lullaby ("Sleep, so your tale of dreams be told")   B. Godard.   Words by F. H. Martens.   TFG
"Lullaby and good night."   See Wiegenlied (Brahms)
"Lullaby, lullaby, my lovely one."   See Lullaby ("Lullaby, lullaby, my lovely one")
Lullaby of the Christ Child.   See The sleep of the Infant Jesus (Gevaert)
"Lullaby, twilight is spreading silver wings over the sky."   See Basque lullaby
Lullay, Jesu, lullay, lullay.   See "So blest a sight"
Lullay my liking.   G. Holst.   15th century words.   OB
Lullay, you little tiny child.   See The Coventry carol (Ancient air);   The Coventry carol (Modern version of air)
Lully, Jean Baptiste de
"Au clair de la lune" (Composer unknown)
Lully, lully, lu.   See "Qui creavit coelum, lully, lully, lu"
"Lulu is our darling pride."   Old song. SW
Lund, Signe
Nat
Night.   See Nat
Vandraren
The wanderer.   See Vandraren
"La lune blanche luit dans les bois."   See L'heure exquise (Hahn)
Lunt, Rosetta
Mabel Clare (Higgins)
Lupita divina (Divine Lupita)   Mexican folk song.   e.s.   VS
"Lupita, tu eres hermosa."   See Lupita divina
"Ein lust'ger musikante marschierte am Nil."   See O tempora! o mores
Lute-book lullaby ("Sweet was the song the Virgin sang")   W. Ballet (music and words)   OB
Luther, Martin
Composer and author
Ein' feste burg
Luther's carol.   See "Vom himmel hoch da komm' ich her"

Luther, Martin—Composer and author—
Continued
"A mighty fortress is our God." See
Ein' feste burg
"A safe stronghold our God is still."
See Ein' feste burg
"Vom himmel hoch da komm' ich her"
(For music by Heseltine see Balulalow)

Author

"Away in the manger" (French Noël
air; also music by Herbert)
Balulalow (Heseltine. Tr of "Vom
himmel hoch da komm' ich her")
Gelobet seist du Jesu Christ (English
traditional air)
Luther's carol. See "Vom himmel hoch
da komm' ich her" (Luther)
Luther's cradle hymn. See "Away in a
manger" (Herbert)
Lutzow's wild hunt. See Lützows wilde
jagd (Weber)
Lützows wilde jagd. C. M. von Weber.
Words by T. Körner. g. EDL
Lutzow's wild hunt. e. BB

Luvelle, Thomas
The county of Mayo (Irish air)
Lux ecce surgit aurea. For English
translation see Morning song (Beethoven)
Lvov, Alexis Feodorovich
"God ever glorious" (same air as Russian national hymn)
"Hail, Pennsylvania" (same air as Russian national hymn)
"Rise, crowned with light" (same air
as Russian national hymn)
Russian national hymn
The triumph hymn (same air as Russian national hymn)
Lydia Pinkham. Old American song.
SBA
Lyle, Gaston, pseud. See Knight, J. S.
Lyle, Thomas
Kelvin grove (Scottish air)
Lynch, Francis
Dearest Mae (Crosby)
Lyon, Mrs Agnes (L'Amy)
Neil Gow's farewell to whisky (Gow)
Lyons. See O come let us worship
(Haydn)
Lyra, Justus Wilhelm
Burschenlust
Meine muse
Nur in Deutschland
Reiterlied
Wanderschaft. See Burschenlust
Lysaght, Edward
Kitty of Coleraine (Irish air) Authorship uncertain
Lyte, Eliphalet Oram
Beautiful bells
"Row, row, row your boat"
Under the shade of the trees
Lyte, Henry Francis
"Abide with me fast falls the eventide"
(music by Monk; Reed)
Lytle, James T.
Texan rangers' song (Russell)

Lytton, Edward George Earle Lytton Bulwer-Lytton, 1st baron
"When stars are in the quiet skies"
(Composer unknown)
Lytton, Edward Robert Bulwer-Lytton, 1st earl of
Yestereve (Allitsen)

M

M is for the million things she gave me.
See M-o-t-h-e-r (Morse)
M-o-t-h-e-r. See entry under Mother
Ma belle Girofla. For English translation see O pretty Girofla (Lecocq)
Ma evenin' star I wonder who you are.
See Come down ma evenin' star
(Stromberg)
"Ma fille, veux-tu un bonnet" ("Töchterchen, willst ein häubchen du")
French folk song. f.g. ML 1
"Ma-ma-ma-ma-mi-ne-ga-ga." See Indian
war song
Ma mère je la vois. For English translation see "My home in yonder vale"
(Bizet)
[Ma Normandie] My Normandy. F.
Bérat (music and words) e. MFS
"Ma soul is a witness." See Who'll be a
witness for my Lord
"Ma vie a son secret" ("My life a secret
owns") G. Bizet. <Words by F.
Arvers> e.f. SAT
A maaseh. Jewish folk song. y. KAJ
—SY
Mabel Clare. A. J. Higgins. Words
by R. Lunt. GOS 2
Macafee's confession. See Harry Gray
McAloon, Thomas. See Le Mack, Thomas
McAloon, William Andrew. See Mack,
Andrew
Macarthy, Henry
The bonnie blue flag
The southern girl (same air as The
bonnie blue flag)
Why! oh why (same air as The bonnie
blue flag)
McCabe, James H.
Fordham marching song (Breslin)
McCall, Irene
I've no time to be a-sighin'
McCann, M. J.
O'Donnell aboo (Composer unknown)
McCarron, Charles R.
Oh Helen (Morgan)
McCarthy, Henry. See Macarthy, Henry
McCarthy, Joseph
In all my dreams, I dream of you
(Piantadosi)
There's a little spark of love still burning (Fischer)
McCarthy, Joseph, and Goodwin, Joe
That's how I need you (Piantadosi)
McCarthy, Joseph, and Johnson, Howard
Ireland must be heaven for my mother
came from there (Fischer)

McCaskey, John Piersol

Composer

The blushing maple tree
The trees and the Master

Author

Christmas is coming (Phillips)
"Flag of the free" (Wagner)

MacCathmhaoil, Seosamh.   See Campbell, Joseph

I maccheroni (Die nudeln)   Neapolitan tarantella.   g.i.   ML 2

McClintock, Charles W.
"Everybody works but father" (Old English air; also music by Lehman)

McCloskey's great fight.   See Throw him down McCloskey (Kelly)

McCosh, D. S.
Hear dem bells

MacCrimmon's lament ("Round Coolin's peak the mist is sailing")   Scottish song.   Words from the Gaelic.   e. CSB 6

McCusker, Joseph A.
Hats off to the band

McDermott, Leila
"We are Mills college girls"

MacDonald, Ballard
I wish I had my old girl back again (Wallace)

Macdonald, Mary
Leanabh an aigh (Gaelic folk air)

MacDonald's farm.   See "Old MacDonald had a farm"

Macey, J. C.
Let me say my little prayer

MacFarlane, Will Charles
America the beautiful

McGill, John
"Come under my plaidie"

McGiveran, Ben S.
Fight on, Pennsylvania (Zoob)

McGlennon, Felix

Composer

Comrades
The ship I love

Composer and author

He never cares to wander from his own fireside
I've worked eight hours this day

Author

And her golden hair was hanging down her back (Rosenfeld)

Macgregor, Donald
Twenty-seven bells by the Waterbury watch

Macgregors' gathering.   A. Lee.   Words by W. Scott.   GS

"Mach' auf, mach' auf, doch leise, mein kind."   See Ständchen (Strauss)

McHarrie, Lindsay
Victory for Washington

Mack, Andrew
He stole McCarthy's wife.   See Little Johnny Dugan
Little Johnny Dugan

Mackay, Charles
Baby mine (music by Boott; Johnston)
"Cheer, boys, cheer" (Russell)
I love my love (Pinsuti)
The inquiry (Baker)
The miller of the Dee (Old air)

McKenna, William J.
Has anybody here seen Kelly (Murphy and Letters)

Mackenzie, Sir Alexander Campbell
Spring song

"Mackerel, fresh mackerel."   See Chairs to mend

McKinley, Mabel.   See Grey, Vivien

McLaren, Norman Loyall
Big C (Williams)

McLaurin, Billie
Blind man blues

MacLeod, Fiona, pseud.   See Sharp, William

McLeod, Peter
Scotland yet

MacMillan, Ernest Campbell
"God of our fathers, known of old"
Recessional.   See "God of our fathers, known of old"

McNaught, W. G.
The spider and the fly

Macneill, Hector
"Come under my plaidie" (McGill)
"I lo'e na a laddie but ane" (Old air)
My boy Tammie (Scottish air)
Saw ye my wee thing (Composer unknown)

Macnie, John S.
Alma mater—University of North Dakota (Haydn)

Macon, George W.
Alma mater—Howard college (Launay)

McVicar, Anne.   See Grant, Mrs Anne (Macvicar)

McWhorter, Edward.   See Miller, Earl, jt. comp.

Macy, James Cartwright
The dolls' party
Good night, little girl, good night

Mad Anthony Wayne.   19th century air. Words from a Revolutionary song. DSO

Mad scene.   See "Il dolce suono" (Donizetti)

"Madam, I have gold and silver."   See The keys of heaven (Kentucky version)

"Madam, I've come to marry you."   See The wooing

Mädchen, brav und treu.   For English translation see Maidens, bright and fair (Flotow)

"Mädchen geht zum brunnen" ("Szőke kislány megy a kútra, hajaha")   Hungarian folk song.   g.hu.   ML 3

Das mädchen mit dem goldhaar.   See An chúil-fhionn

Mädchen und taube ("Podunushe Badīseva vetrove")   Serbian folk song.   g.se. ML 2

Das **mädchen** vom Amselfeld (Kosovka devojka) Serbian folk song. g.se. ML 2

Das **mädchen** von Catanzaro. See La Cantanzarese

Das **mädchen** von Scilla. See La Scillitana

"**Mädchen,** wollt ihr werden." See In der märznacht (Taubert)

Mädchenpreis. See Minnelied

Mädchens klage ("Draussen am garten führte mich mein weg vorbei."— "Sluchīlos'-to Mnfe, dobru molodtsu") Russian folk song. g.r. ML 1

Des **mädchens** klage. See entry under Des

Mädchens rache. See A maiden's revenge

Mädchensehnsucht. See Lu golio de 'na figliola

A **mädel** in die johren. Jewish folk song. y. SY

A **meidel** in die yuren. y. KAJ

"**Mädel,** schau mir ins gesicht." See Liebeszauber (Schulz)

"**Mädele,** ruck, ruck, ruck." See Die auserwählte

Madrigal ("Tes doux baisers sont des oiseaux."—"Thou little bird with pinions gay") C. Chaminade. e.f. BST

"**Mae** genni ebol melyn." See Cân y melinydd

"**Mae'n** chwith am lowri dafydd." See Distyll y don

Maesch, LaVahn Kenneth
Viking song

"**M'affaccio** a la finestra" ("Ich schaue aus dem fenster") Roman folk song. g.i. ML 2

"**M'agapas,** Garoyphalia moy." See Garufalia

"**Magasan** repül a daru." See Hungaria's treasure

Maggie Lauder ("Wha wadna be in love wi' bonnie Maggie Lauder") 18th century air. Words by F. Semple. GS

Maggill, John. See McGill, John

"The **magi** came out of the Orient land." See Three kings' song

The **magnet** and the churn. A. S. Sullivan. Words by W. S. Gilbert. DSC

"A **magnet** hung in a hardware shop." See The magnet and the churn (Sullivan)

"**Magosan** repül a darú." See Hungaria's treasure

[The **magpie** and the little gypsy dancer] The gipsy. W. Zolotarieff. Words by A. Pushkin. e. SR

The **magpie's** nest. Irish air from County Dublin. Traditional words. HI 2

Mag's song. Mountain folk song. SBA Variant: The orphan girl

Maguire, Sylvester
If I had a thousand lives to live (Solman)

Magyar gályarabok éneke. See Lied des ungarischen galeerensträflings

"**Mah** brudder's died an' gone to hebben." Negro spiritual from Tennessee. FSN

Mahlmann, August
Das reich der freude (Volksweise)

The **mahogany** tree. F. Campana. Words by W. M. Thackeray. MFS

Mahoney, Jack
When you wore a tulip and I wore a big red rose (Wenrich)

Mahony, Francis Sylvester
The bells of Shandon (Irish air; also music by Daly)

"**Der mai** ist gekommen." See Burschenlust (Lyra)

"**Mai** komashma lon." See A Talmudical student's lament

The **maid** and the mill. See "There was a maid went to the mill"

"**Maid** Elsie roams by lane and lea." See The bride bells (Roeckel)

The **maid** freed from the gallows. Folk song: Barbourville, Ky. version. SES 1

—Pine Mountain, Ky. version. SES 1

—Black Mountain, N.C. version. SES 1

—Burnsville, N.C. version no. 1. SES 1

—Burnsville, N.C. version no. 2. SES 1

—Burnsville, N.C. version no. 3. SES 1

—South Carolina version. SBA

—Tennessee version. SES 1

—Dewey, Va. version. SES 1

—Mount Fair, Va. version. SES 1

—Villamont, Va. version. SES 1

—Woodridge, Va. version. SES 1

Variants: Hangman; The hangman's song

"A **maid** goin' to Comber her markets to larn." See The next market day

The **maid** of Amsterdam. See A-roving

"**Maid** of Athens." H. R. Allen. Words by Lord Byron. GE—GOS 2

The **maid** of the mill. S. Adams. Words by H. Aïdé. MFS

"A **maid** reclined beside a stream." See Forever and forever (Converse)

Maid-servants' chorus. F. von Flotow. [Tr of Wohlgemuth, junges blut] e. WLO

"**Maid,** those bright eyes my heart impressing." See "Tu non sai con quei begli occhi" (Bellini)

The **maid** with the bonny brown hair. Irish air from County Donegal. Traditional words. HI 2

"**Maiden** in the garden, sweet and fair." See Cupid and the maiden (Richardson)

"**Maiden,** maiden, nut-brown maiden" ("Te vagy, te vagy barna kis lány") K. de Symonffy. Words by A. Petöfi. e.hu. KH 2

The **maiden** with the dreamy eyes. B. Cole and J. R. Johnson (music and words) SRW

"A **maiden** yonder sings" ("Tuol laulaa neitonen")   J. Sibelius.   Words by
M. Susman.   e.fi.   WM 2

Maidens, bright and fair.   F. von Flotow.
ₜTr of Mädchen, brav und treuₗ
e.   WLO

"Come where flowers are flinging."
e.   MFS

ₜA **maiden's** revengeₗ   "To ne ĩastreb
sovykalsiã" (Mädchens rache)   Russian folk song.   g.r.   ML 1

The **maiden's** rose (So the story goes)
J. L. Hatton.   Words by J. F.
Waller.   GE

A **maiden's** thoughts.   See Pigetanker
(Winge)

ₜThe **maiden's** wishₗ Spring song. Chopin.
ₜWords by Witwickiₗ   e.   DSB

Maigh, David
Doun the burn, Davie.   See "When
trees did bud"

"When trees did bud"

Mailied ("Ye maids of Helston")   See
Cornish May song

Máire ní ghríobhtha (Seemannslied) Irish
folk song.   g.ir.   ML 1

Maireigen.   See "Come, lasses and lads"

Màiri bhòidheach (Holde Mary)   Ancient
Hebridean air.   ₜWords by A.
Stewartₗ   ga.g.   ML 1

"**Mais** quand on pûre des chanquiers."
See Envoyons d'l'avant, nos gens

"**Mais** voici bien des jeunes gens."   See
Celui que j'aime

Maistre, Xavier, comte de
Haï luli (Coquard)

Maitanz.   See The May-pole

Maitland, Don, pseud.   See Loomis, Harvey Worthington

"Le **maître** a envoyé Jacquot secouer le
poirier."   See Le maître et Jacquot

Le **maître** et Jacquot (The master and
Jimmy) Folk song from Alsace.   e.f.
CBF 2

Major Gilfeather.   D. Braham.   Words
by E. Harrigan.   SRW

Make me one pallet on your floor.   See
Atlanta blues (Handy and Elman)

Make the best of it.   <C. J. Dunphy>
MFS

Make we joy.   15th century carol.   OB

"**Make** we merry."   M. Shaw.   15th
century words.   OB

Make your mark ("In the quarries should
you toil")   MFS

Maker, Frederick Charles
"Dear Lord and Father of mankind"

"Lo **mal** de l'amor" (Das liebesweh) Catalan folk song.   ca.g.   ML 2

Mal reggendo all' aspro assalto.   For
English translation see "Ill sustaining"
(Verdi)

Malagueña.   Spanish folk song.   g.s.
ML 2

Malatu p'amuri (Liebeskrank)   Sicilian
song.   g.i.   ML 2

"**Malbrouck** has gone a-fighting."   See
"Malbrough s'en va-t-en guerre"

"**Malbrough** s'en va-t-en guerre"   ("Herr
Malbrough zieht zum kampfe")
French folk song.   f.g.   ML 1

"**Malbrouk** s'en va-t-en guerre" ("Malbrouck has gone a-fighting")   e.f.
MBS

"**Malbrouk** s'en va-t-en guerre."   See
"Malbrough s'en va-t-en guerre"

Malibran, Mme Maria Félicita (Garcia)
The Alpine horn (Rimbault)

Mallet, David
Rule, Britannia (Arne)   See Thomson, J.   Rule, Britannia (Arne)

Malloch, Douglas
Michigan, my Michigan (Miessner)

Mally O.   Scottish folk song.   BOS 2

Mama, are there any angels black like me.
See Little black me (Chattaway)

Mama have you heard the news.   Railroad song.   SBA
Variant of: Casey Jones

"**Mama** mia, vuria, vuria" ("Mütterlein, ach
schenke mir")   Piedmontese folk song.
g.i.   ML 2

Mama's prison yard blues.   See Rock pile
blues (Williams)

"Die **mame** hot mich geschikt."   See A
yungele fun Poilen

"**Mamma**, mamma, ca moro, ca moro."   See
Lu golio de 'na figliola

"**Mamma** told me to open the gate."   See
My mother bid me (Barbourville, Ky.
version)

"**Mammani** maja on matala ja pieni."   See
Das arme mädchen

Mammie's li'l baby loves short'nin', short'-
nin'.   See Short'nin' bread

"**Mammy**, is massa goin' to sell us tomorrow."   See Massa gwine to sell us to-
morrow

"**Mammy** loves."   Lullaby from Virginia.
SES 2

"**Mammy** told me when a child."   See
Blue gummed blues (Handy)

Man, be merry as bird on berry.   R. Dunstan.   15th century words.   DNS

"**Man**, born of woman, was a sailor for to
be."   See Home, boys, home

"**Man** born of woman was a soldier for to
be."   See The American soldier

De **man**, de sick wat maken kunn.   See
Jan Hinnerk up de Lammerstraat

Man goin' roun'.   See "There's a man
goin' roun' takin' names"

"The **man** in the moon came down too
soon."   Children's song.   <J. W.
Elliott>   TFP

"**Man** in the moon, who may you be."
French air.   Words by K. Davis.   DSB
—GSS

The **man** o' Airlie.   Scottish song.   GS

Man of Alcala.   G. Bizet.   ₜTr of Halte-
là, qui va làₗ   e.   WG

The **man** of upright life.   See "Integer
vitae" (Flemming)

The **man** on the flying trapeze.   Old circus song.   SRW

"**Man** pasuda kumeliņis."   See "Ich verlor mein jung rösslein"

"Man schafft so gern sich sorg und müh."
See Freut euch des lebens (Nägeli)

The **man** who broke the bank at Monte
Carlo. F. Gilbert (music and
words) GFS

The man that broke the bank at Monte
Carlo. SRW

"A **man** whose name was Johnny Sands."
See Johnny Sands (Sinclair)

"A **man** will travel all about." See Ljos
(Sinding)

Mañanitas ("El día en que tu naciste."—
Early mornings) Mexican folk song.
e.s. SBA

"**Manca** un foglio." Rossini. e.i. PB

"**Manchmal** in des abends verschwiegen-
heit." See O little mother of mine
(Nevin)

The **mandolin** song ("O I'm a happy creature") See Mandolinata (Paladilhe)

Mandolinata ("O I'm a happy creature."—
The mandolin song) [E. Paladilhe]
e. MFS

Mandy Lee. T. Chattaway (music and
words) DFF—SMG

Manley, Frederic
The dancers (Lacome d'Estalenx)
"Massa dear" (Dvořák)
May song (Smith)
On, O thou soul (Serbian folk air)
"Sleep, noble hearts" (Mendelssohn)
"Sweet day is softly dying" (Old
French air)

"**Mann** von hundert mass getreide." See
Lied des hörigen

Manney, Charles Fonteyn
Night and day

Ein **männlein** steht im walde. For English translation see A little man

Manoah (Rossini) See "Jesus, the very
thought of Thee"; "O Thou from
Whom all goodness flows"

A **man's** a man, for a' that ("Is there for
honest poverty") <Air: For a' that
and a' that> Words by R. Burns.
GS

"**Man's** life is but vain." See The angler's song (Lawes)

"**Man's** life's a vapor." Round. GSS
—TFB

Mansikka. See Erdbeeren

"The **mansion** we builded." German song.
e. DSC

Manush Voïvoda. See Wojewode manusch

Many a harp's ecstatic sound. See Music in the air

Many are the fond notes. See Jeanie with
the light brown hair (Foster)

Many are the hearts that are weary tonight.
See Tenting on the old camp ground
(Kittredge)

"The **many** happy evenings I spent." See
Paddy Duffy's cart (Braham)

Many long years ago. See Old gray mare

"**Many** songs have I heard in my native
land." See The little cudgel

Many thousand go ("No more peck o'
corn") Negro spiritual: South
Carolina version. AS
Variant of: Many thousand gone

Many thousand gone ("No more auction
block") Negro spiritual. FSN—
MFS—WFN—WSS
"No more auction block." HRD
Variant: Many thousand go

"**Many** years ago today wedding bells were
ringing gay." See Mandy Lee (Chattaway)

The **maple** leaf forever ("In days of yore,
from Britain's shore") National song
of Canada. A. Muir (music and
words) BB—MBS

"The **maples** their leaves are shedding."
See "Nu faelder sit løv den ahorn"
(Lange-Müller)

Marcello, Benedetto
Arietta
"Un guardo volgi a me"

"**March,** all New York university men."
See N. Y. U. marching song

"The **march** is on, no brain or brawn."
See Hike, Notre Dame (Casasanta)

"**March!** march! Ettrick and Tiviotdale."
See Blue bonnets over the border

March, march, marching on to glory. See
Cheer for alma mater (Nazarian)

"**March,** march on down the field." See
Down the field (Friedman)

The **march** of the Cameron men. Old
Scottish air. [Words by M. M.
Campbell] GS

March of the fighting 'gators. University of Florida song. T. W. Allen.
AIS

March of the kings. See Marcho dei rei

March of the men of Harlech. See Rhyfelgyrch gwyr Harlech

The **march** of the people. F. F. Bullard.
Author of words unknown. LAS

March of the Titans. University of
Detroit song. V. Kolar. AIS

March of the toreadors. G. Bizet. [Tr
of Voici, débouchant sur la place]
e. WG

[**March** of the victors] "To the sacred
banks of the Nile." G. Verdi. [Tr
of Su! del Nilo al sacro lido accorrete]
e. WG

March of triumph. University of Alabama song. G. Jacoby (music and
words) AIS

March on ("Way over in de Egyp' lan'")
Negro spiritual. JG

March on as knights of old. See "Ring
out, then, your hoiah"

March on down the field ("Here's to De
Pauw") See "Here's to De Pauw"

"**March** on down the field and never yield."
Hobart college song. AI

"**March** on Florida." See March of the
fighting 'gators (Allen)

"**March** on! Liberty's host." Verdi.
Words by S. Rowe. TFP

"**March** on, march on, our way along."
See Gaily beats the drum

[**Marche** lorraine] Lorraine march. L.
Ganne. e. TFP

Marchesi, Salvatore, cavaliere de Castrone, marchese della Rajata
  Prayer. See Preghiera
  Preghiera
Marching along. W. B. Bradbury. DSO
Marching for Columbia. See Marching song (Pattberg)
Marching on ("From age to age they gather") F. F. Bullard. Words by F. L. Hosmer. LAS
Marching song ("March on, march on") See Gaily beats the drum
Marching song ("When you're marching for Columbia") Columbia university song. C. H. Pattberg. Words by J. Erskine. LAS
Marching through Georgia. H. C. Work (music and words) CSB 3—DSO— MBS
"Marching, we're marching to vict'ry." See For Maine (Bartlett)
"Marchioness, your dancing." See "Vous dansez, marquise" (Lemaire)
₁**Marcho** dei rei₁ March of the kings. Provençal Noël. e. DSB—DSC MFF
  The three kings. e. TFR
Margherita ("When joyous tho'ts") See "Si le bonheur" (Gounod)
Marguerite. C. A. White (music and words) GFS
"Marguerite! Marguerite! my star of hope." See Marguerite (White)
Mari lwyd (Blessed Mary) Old Welsh song. e.w. WO
Maria auf dem berge ("Uf'm berge, da geht der wind") Oberschlesisches volkslied. g. EDL
Maria die wollt' wandern gehn. See Marias wanderschaft
Maria ging aus wandern. See Maria's wallfahrt (Brahms)
Maria und die arme seele vor der himmelstür. Süddeutsches volkslied. g. EDL
"Maria wandelte unter uns" ("Marija se vzigne") Slovenian folk song. g.slo. ML 2
Marianina. Italian folk song. e. LAS—TFB—TFG—TFO—TFR
"Marianne s'en va-t-au moulin" ("Marianne wanders to the mill") Canadian folk song. e.f. GC
"Marianne wanders to the mill." See "Marianne s'en va-t-au moulin"
Marianne's loves. See Z'amours Marianne
Marianska. See Marienlied
Maria's gone. Play-party game from Kentucky. SES 2
Maria's wallfahrt (Maria ging aus wandern. —The quest) J. Brahms. Traditional words. e. OB
Marias wanderschaft (Maria die wollt' wandern gehn.—Mary's wandering) German folk song. e. OB
Marie ("Marie, am fenster") A. Jensen. Words by R. Gottschall. e.g. GG. e. only TFO
"Marie, am fenster sitzest du." See Marie (Jensen)

₁**"Marie** mine"₁ "Marishka! Marishka" (Mariskám) Hungarian song. <J. Szerdahelyi (music and words> e.hu. KH 2
Marienlied (Marianska) Wendish folk song. g.we. ML 3
Marienwürmchen (Ladybird) R. Schumann. Words from a German folk song. e. CSB 1
Marienwürmchen. For another English translation with a different air see Ladybird (German folk song)
"Marija se vzigne." See "Maria wandelte unter uns"
Marina girls. Folk song from Virginia. SES 2
Marinela. See La canción del olvido (Serrano)
"Mariner, mariner, on the dark foaming sea." See The song of the mermaid
The **marine's** hymn. U.S. marines song. US
Marion, Dave
  Her eyes don't shine like diamonds
  It's not what you were, it's what you are to-day
Marions ausflüchte. See Les répliques de Marion
Maris, W. Homer
  Alma mater song—Oregon state agricultural college
  Carry me back. See Alma mater song
"Marishka! Marishka." See "Marie mine" (Szerdahelyi)
Mariskám. See "Marie mine" (Szerdahelyi)
Market song. Czechoslovak folk song. e. MFF
Mark-Lemon, Mary
  "Cast thy bread on the waters" (Roeckel)
  Daddy (Behrend)
Marks, Edward B.
  The little lost child (Stern)
  My mother was a lady (Stern)
Marks, Godfrey
  The corn song (same air as Sailing)
  Sailing
Marmottenlied. See La Savoyarde
Maroon and white. Mississippi A & M college song. H. E. Wamsley. Words by P. Haney. KU—KV
Maroon victory. Roanoke college song. G. Stelljes (music and words) AI— AIS
Marquette fight song. Marquette university song. R. G. Haukohl (music and words) KU
Marquette university anthem. Composer and author of words unknown. KU
"Maros vize folyik csendesen." See "Ruhig fliesst die Maros"
Marriage bells ("Our marriage bells are ringing") M. O'Reardon. Words by W. J. O'Reardon. SMG
Marriage bells chorus ("Now my friends") E. Audran. e. WLO
Married and single life. Folk song from North Carolina. SES 2

A **married** woman's lament. 19th century American song. SRW

Marschall Stigs töchter. See Marsk Stigs døttre

La **Marseillaise.** French national anthem.
C. J. Rouget de Lisle (music and words) e.f. MBS
The Marseillaise. e.f. LAS—TFP
Marseillaise hymn. e. BB—MFS

Marsh, Charles H.
Onward, upward alma mater

Marsh, Daniel Lash
Boston university hymn (Marshall)

Marsh, Simeon Butler
"Jesus, Lover of my soul"

Marshall, John Patten
Boston university hymn
Over the way

Marshall, William
"Of a' the airts the wind can blaw"

Marsk Stigs døttre (Marschall Stigs töchter) Danish heroic ballad. da.g. ML 1

Martens, Frederic Herman
Lullaby (Godard)

Martin, O. D.
"I've brought thee an ivy leaf" (Wood)

Martindale, Frank
When the robins nest again

Martini, Giovanni Battista
Complainte de la reine Marie Stuart en prison
Laughing glee
Mary Stuart's lament. See Complainte de la reine Marie Stuart en prison

⌊**Martinique** love-song⌋ "Tap! tap! tap." Negro folk song. e. TFB—TFP

"**Mary** and a Martha's just gone 'long." See Mary and Martha

Mary and Martha. Negro spiritual. BB—WSS
"Mary an' Martha jes' gone 'long" (To ring dem charmin' bells) JB 2

Mary Blane. Negro song. WSS

"**Mary,** darling, must you leave me." Minstrel ballad. WSS

The **Mary** Golden Tree. American mountain song. RA
Variant of: The Golden Vanity

"**Mary** had a baby, yes, Lord." Negro spiritual. JB 2

"**Mary** had a little lamb." Civil war version. ⌊G. F. Root⌋ DSO

"**Mary** had a William goat." Old song. SBA

Mary Macneil. Scottish air: Kinloch of Kinloch. Words by E. Conolly. GS

Mary Morison. See "O Mary, at thy window be"

Mary of Allendale. J. Hook. WOE

Mary of Argyle. S. Nelson. Words by C. Jefferys. GOS 1—GS—MFS

Mary of Castle Cary. See Saw ye my wee thing

Mary of the wild moor. Old English words and music. GOS 2
Variant: When poor Mary came wandering home

Mary Stuart's lament. See Complainte de la reine Marie Stuart en prison (Martini)

"**Mary** wore three links of chain." Negro spiritual. SBA

Maryland! my Maryland. German air: O Tannenbaum. Words by J. R. Randall. DSO—KU—KV

Mary's a grand old name. G. M. Cohan. (music and words) DFF

Mary's dream ("The moon had climbed the highest hill") Scottish air. Words attributed to J. Lowe and to A. Lowe. GS

Mary's wandering. See Marias wanderschaft

Marzials, Théophile
The miller and the maid
The three sailor boys
Twickenham ferry

"**Máš,** máš, máš, sedláčku." See "Hast, hast, hast, bäuerlein"

Mascagni, Pietro
"Ave Maria" (from Cavalleria rusticana)
Carter's song. See "Il cavallo scalpita"
"Il cavallo scalpita" (from Cavalleria rusticana)
Drinking song (from Cavalleria rusticana. Tr of Viva il vino spumeggiante)
"Let us sing of Christ's resurrection" (from Cavalleria rusticana. Tr of Inneggiamo il Signor non è morto)
Lola's song (from Cavalleria rusticana. Tr of Fior di giaggiolo)
"No, no, Turiddu" (from Cavalleria rusticana)
"O Lola." See Siciliana
Siciliana (from Cavalleria rusticana)
The smith
"Voi lo sapete, o mamma" (from Cavalleria rusticana)
"You must know." See "Voi lo sapete, o mamma"

Maseltof. Jewish folk song. y. KAJ

Mason, Mrs Caroline Atherton (Briggs)
"Do they miss me at home" (Grannis)

Mason, Lowell
Bethany. See "Nearer, my God, to Thee"
"God of the strong, God of the weak" (same air as "Kingdoms and thrones to God belong")
Hamburg. See "God of the strong, God of the weak"; "Land of our birth"; "O Life that maketh all things new"
"Land of our birth" (same air as "Kingdoms and thrones to God belong")
"The morning hangs its signal"
"My faith looks up to Thee"
"Nearer, my God, to Thee"
"O Life that maketh all things new" (same air as "Kingdoms and thrones to God belong")
"Safely through another week"

Mason, Lowell—*Continued*
"There is a happy land": Hindoo air arranged
"When shall we meet again"
"Work, for the night is coming"
Mason, Mark, pseud.   See Winner, Septimus
"Massa dear."   A. Dvořák.   Words by F. Manley.   TFB—TFO
[**Massa** gwine to sell us to-morrow] Is massa goin' to sell us tomorrow. Negro song.   FSN
"Mother, is massa gwine to sell us." HRD
"Massa lov'd his good old jamaica."   See Balm of Gilead (Bryant)
De **massa** run? ha, ha.   See Kingdom coming (Work)
The **Massachusetts** liberty song.   See "Come, swallow your bumpers, ye Tories" (Boyce)
"Massa's gone the news to hear."   See Sally, come up (Sewell)
"Massa's gone to town de news to hear." See Sally, come up (Sewell)
Massa's in de cold cold ground.   S. C. Foster (music and words)   MBS
Massa's in de col', col' ground.   BNM
Massa's in de cold ground.   DFF—GOS 2—WSS
Massa's in the cold ground.   BB—MFS—TFP
Massenet, Jules Émile Frédéric
L'âme des fleurs
Souls of flowers.   See L'âme des fleurs
Massmann, Hans Ferdinand
Gelübde (Volksweise)
The **master** and Jimmy.   See Le maître et Jacquot
"The **master** has sent Jimmy to shake the pear tree."   See Le maître et Jacquot
"Masters in this hall."   Old French air. Words by W. Morris.   OB
Masterton, Allan
"O, Willie brew'd a peck o' maut"
Willie brew'd a peck o' maut.   See "O, Willie brew'd a peck o' maut"
"Matamoras, our valiant captain great, hath all his captives brought in state." Final chorus.   C. Lecocq.   [Tr of Matamoras, grande capitaine, enfin nous a tiré de peine]   e.   WLO
"Matamoras, the valiant captain, sails forth to rescue."   C. Lecocq.   [Tr of Matamoras, grande capitaine, bientôt va vous tirer de peine]   e.   WLO
Mater Hierusalem.   For English translations see "Jeresalem my happie home" (Shann); "Jerusalem, my happy home" (Latin hymn); Psalm of Sion (English air)
Mater Salutaris.   Ancient English Christmas carol.   13th century words.   e. DNS
Materna.   See America, the beautiful (Ward)
Mather, Helen
Christmas as it comes (Composer unknown)

"Matona, lovely maiden."   Madrigal.   O. Lassus.   e.   TFG
"The **matron** of an hour."   E. Audran. e.   WLO
"Matt Casey formed a social club."   See The band played on (Ward)
Mattei, Tito
Non è ver
'Tis not true.   See Non è ver
Matthisson, Friedrich von
Adelaïde (Beethoven)
Opferlied (Beethoven)
"Matula moja, śliczną coręˮ masz."   See "Mütterlein, gib acht"
Maulsby, David Lee
Dear alma mater (Lewis)
"Maxwellton braes are bonnie."   See Annie Laurie (Scott)
"Maxwelton's braes are bonnie."   See Annie Laurie (Scott)
May carol ("Awake, awake, good people all")   English traditional song.   OB
May day ("Le premier jour de mai")   See "Le premier jour de mai"
May-day garland ("I've brought you here a bunch of may")   Traditional carol from Northamptonshire.   OB
May-day song ("The moon shines bright") See "The moon shines bright"
"May de Lord—He will be glad of me." See Bright sparkles in de churchyard
"May he never leave thee."   R. Wagner. [Tr of Könntest du erfassen]   e. WG
May Irwin's "bully" song.   See The bully song (Trevathan)
"May is here, the world rejoices."   See Polish May song
May morning ("The mellow lustre of the morn")   P. A. von Hagen.   MPA 2
The **May** morning hymn ("Te Deum Patrem colimus")   B. Rogers.   1. BOS 2
[The **May-pole**] "Come, ye young men, come along" (Maypole song.—Maitanz) [Old air: Staines Morris.   Words by R. Cox]   e.g.   ML 1
The **May** queen.   W. R. Dempster. Words by A. Tennyson.   GOS 1—MFS
May song ("This is the gay time")   Netherlands air.   Words by N. H. Dole. DSB
May song ("Ye lads and lasses all")   D. S. Smith.   Words by F. Manley. TFP
"May the grace of Christ, our Saviour" (Doxology.—Sicilian [mariners'] hymn) MFS
"May the Lord—He will be glad of me." See Bright sparkles in de churchyard
May the temple be rebuilt (Yiboneh hamikdosh)   Palestinean folk song.   he. BNP
"May we be truthful and ever loyal be." See Scout chant
Maybrick, Michael
The blue Alsatian mountains
"By the Blue Alsatian mountains." See The blue Alsatian mountains

Maybrick, Michael—*Continued*
The maid of the mill
The midshipmite
Nancy Lee
The star of Bethlehem
The tar's farewell
They all love Jack
A warrior bold
Maynard, Walter, pseud. See Beale, Thomas Willert
The **Mayo** boys' song. See "I hope my mother will be there"
Maypole dance ("Come, lassie and lad") 17th century song. TFG
Variant of: "Come, lasses and lads"
Maypole song ("Come, lasses and lads") See "Come, lasses and lads"
Maypole song ("Come ye young men, come along") See The May-pole
Mazzinghi, Joseph
Young Lochinvar
Mazzoni, Antonio Maria
"Io veggio in lontananza" (from Demetrio)
Mazzoni, P.
"Ave Maria" (Mascagni)
M'chorotay (Shir shomrim) Palestinean watchman's song. e.he. BNP
"**Me** abandonastes, mujer, porque soy muy pobre." See El abandonado
"Die **mechetunem** gehen." Jewish folk song. y. KAJ
"**Medd** y brenin wrth y gâd." See Ymdawiad y brenin
Meek, Mrs John Lamar
Alma mater—University of Tennessee
Meen, George
O! Fred, tell them to stop
"Das **meer** erglänzte weit hinaus." See Am meer (Schubert)
Meet me by the moonlight ("I am going to leave you") American mountain song. RA
Meet me in St Louis, Louis. K. Mills. Words by A. B. Sterling. GFS
"**Meet** me tonight, comrades, gather around." See Practice cruise
Meet me to-night, lover, meet me. See Moonlight
"**Meet,** O Lord." Negro spiritual from Hilton Head island. AS
Meet you by an' by. See Get away from dis co'nfiel'
The **meeting** of the waters ("There is not in the wide world") Irish air: The old head of Dennis. Words by T. Moore. DSC— GOS 1— GSS— HMI —LAS—LSB—SI
"**Meeting's** a pleasure and parting's a grief." See The cuckoo (St Helen's, Ky. version)
"**Meg-követem** a tens nemes." See "I implore you, I beseech you"
"**Megelasane** tapoylia." See Der tod ("Mich hat belogen das vöglein")
Meï, Lev Aleksandrovich
Gathering mushrooms (Musorgskiĭ)
The song of Solomon (Musorgskiĭ)
A **meidel** in die yuren. See A madel in die johren

Meiler, J. B.
Flyers' march
Mein alt Kentucky-heim. See My old Kentucky home (Foster)
Mein armes herz. See Inimiora mea
Mein braunmägdlein schön. See Mo nigheann chruinn, donn
Mein eigen soll sie sein. See Lieben bringt freud'
["**Mein** gläubiges herze frohlocke"] "My heart ever faithful." J. S. Bach. e. SSO 1
Mein Herr und Gott. For English translation see King's prayer (Wagner)
"**Mein** herz, aus goldnen jugendtagen." See Frühlingssegen (Brückler)
"**Mein** herzenslieb, das Gott mir sandt'." See Máire ní ghríobhtha
"**Mein** herzensliebchen." See "L'amour de moi"
"**Mein** lebenslauf ist lieb und lust." See Das reich der freude
"**Mein** schatz, der ist auf die wanderschaft hin." See Heimlicher liebe pein (Weber)
"**Mein** schatz ist nicht da." See Sehnsucht (Brahms)
"**Mein** tagwerk war getan." See Quand tu tenais la caille
Mein treues braunmägdlein. See Mo chailin dileas donn
"**Meinasin** ottaa komeaan." See Aufforderung zum tanz (Finnish folk song)
"**Meine** geige" ("Gusle moje") Serbian folk song. g.se. ML 2
"**Meine** kühe und kälber weiden." See Cronan bleoghain
"**Meine** mus ist gegangen." See Meine muse (Lyra)
Meine muse. J. W. Lyra. Words by W. Müller. g. EDL
"**Meiner** mutter hütte ist eng und kahl und niedrig." See Das arme mädchen
"**Meirke** mein kind." Jewish folk song. y. SY
"**Meirke** mein suhn." Jewish folk song. y. SY
"**Měla** sem hołubka." See A fair dove
Melancholy ("The bleak night of autumn." —Onneton) O. Merikanto. Words by K. Kramsu. e.fi. WM 2
Melancholy ("Melancholy, folly! folly") Round. W. A. Mozart. CSB 6
Melartin, Erkki Gustav
Afsked (Tr of Der scheidende sommer)
Farewell. See Afsked
"O Herre"
"O Master." See "O Herre"
Melcher, Zella
The fight song (Sayles)
Melin, Karl Alfred
När sol går ner (Stenhammar)
Melinda May. S. C. Foster (music and words) WSS
Melklied. See Cronan bleoghain
Mellish, R.
"Drink to me only with thine eyes" (wrongly attributed) See Harrington, H. "Drink to me only with thine eyes" (attributed)

The **mellow** horn. W. Jones. <Words by G. W. Hyatt> GOS 1—MFS

"The **mellow** lustre of the morn." See May morning (Hagen)

Melodies of many lands. C. W. Glover. MFS

Melvil Castle. Campbell. Words from an old Scotch ballad. GS

Melville, George John Whyte-. See Whyte-Melville, George John

Members, don't git weary. Negro spiritual. JB 2

Memento. See Angedenken (Cornelius)

Memories ("Hay recuerdas que el tiempo no ha borrado") See Recuerdas

Memories of friendship. See Recuerdas de amistad

"**Men** of Dartmouth." Dartmouth college song. H. R. Wellman. Words by R. Hovey. AI

"**Men** of Harlech, in the hollow." See Rhyfelgyrch gwyr Harlech (Old Welsh patriotic song)

"**Men** of Harlech, lords of singing." See Rhyfelgyrch gwyr Harlech (Words by Vandevere)

"**M'en** revenant de la jolie Rochelle." See C'est l'aviron qui nous mène en haut

Menagerie. College song. SRW

Mendelssohn-Bartholdy, Felix
"Auf flügeln des gesanges"
"Be thou faithful unto death" (from Paulus. Tr of Sei getreu in den tod)
"But the Lord is mindful of His own" (from Paulus. Tr of Doch der Herr vergisst der seiner nicht)
"Caro cibus, sanguis potus" (from Lauda Sion)
"Cast thy burden upon the Lord" (from Elias. Tr of Wirf dein anliegen auf den Herrn)
Consolation. See "Sleep, noble hearts"
"Consume them all" (from Paulus. Tr of Vertilge sie, Herr Zebaoth)
"Day of sorrow." See Infelice
"Es ist bestimmt in Gottes rat"
Evening song
Farewell to the forest (Tr of Abschied vom walde)
"For the mountains shall depart" (from Elias. Tr of Ja es sollen wohl berge weichen)
Frühlingslied
"God shall charge His angel legions"
"Gott sei mir gnädig" (from Paulus)
"Hail to the Lord's anointed"
"Hark! the herald angels sing"
"Hear my prayer"
"Hear ye, Israel! hear what the Lord speaketh" (from Elias. Tr of Höre, Israel, höre des Herrn stimme)
"How lovely are the messengers" (from Paulus. Tr of Wie lieblich sind die boten)
The hunter's farewell. See Der jäger abschied
The hymn of praise. See "I waited for the Lord"

"I waited for the Lord" (from Lobgesang. Tr of Ich harrete des Herrn)
I will sing of Thy great mercies (from Paulus. Tr of Lasst uns singen von der gnade des Herrn)
"I would that my love." See "Ich wollt' meine lieb' ergösse"
"Ich wollt' meine lieb' ergösse"
"If with all your hearts ye truly seek me" (from Elias. Tr of So ihr mich von ganzem herzen suchet)
"In heavenly love abiding"
Infelice
"Is not His word like a fire" (from Elias. Tr of Ist nicht des Herrn wort wie ein feuer)
"It is enough" (from Elias. Tr of Es ist genug)
Der jäger abschied
Jerusalem! thou that killest the prophets (from Paulus. Tr of Jerusalem! die du tödtest die propheten)
Lieblingsplätzchen
"Lift thine eyes, O lift thine eyes" (from Elias. Tr of Hebe deine augen auf zu den bergen)
"Lord, at all times I will bless Thee." See "Caro cibus, sanguis potus"
"Lord God of Abraham" (from Elias. Tr of Herr Gott Abrahams)
"O God, have mercy." See "Gott sei mir gnädig"
"O rest in the Lord" (from Elias. Tr of Sei stille dem Herrn)
"O taler weit, o höhen"
"O wert thou in the cauld blast"
"On song's bright pinions." See "Auf flügeln des gesanges"
"On wings of music." See "Auf flügeln des gesanges"
On wings of song. See "Auf flügeln des gesanges"
The reaper and the flowers
"See, amid the winter snow"
Sentence
"Sleep, noble hearts"
Sonntagslied
Spring song ("Durch den wald") See Frühlingslied
Then shall the righteous shine forth (from Elias. Tr of Dann werden die gerechten leuchten)
Trust. See "God shall charge His angel legions"
Watch and ward. See "God shall charge His angel legions"
Woe unto them who forsake Him (from Elias. Tr of Weh ihnen, dass sie von mir weichen)

"**Mendian** zoinen eder epher zango gorri." See Izar ederra

Mentra, Gwen (Willkommen, Gwen) Welsh song. g.w. ML 1

Mercadante, Giuseppe Saverio Raffaele
A te riede, o caro figlio (from Il crociato in Egitto)
"Ah! s'estinto ancor mi vuoi" (from Donna Caritea)

Mercadante, Giuseppe Saverio R.—*Cont.*
Ella piangea la perfida (from I Normanni a Parigi)
Nuova ferita (from Il Reggente)
Or là sull' onda, col pensier mio (from Il giuramento)
"Se fino al cielo ascendere" (from La vestale)
Se m'abbandoni, bella speranza (from Nitocri)
"Soave immagine d'amore" (from Andronico)

Mercantini, Luigi
Inno di guerra dei cacciatori delle Alpi (Olivieri)
The **merchants'** carol ("As we rode down the steep hillside") English traditional air: Golden. Words by F. Kendon. OB
The **merchant's** daughter (The constant farmer's son) Folk song from Sussex. BET
"The **mere** lies dreaming in the wood." See Der träumende see (Brückler)
Meredith, Owen, pseud. See Lytton, Edward Robert Bulwer-Lytton, 1st earl of
Merikanto, Oskar
Lullaby
Melancholy
Onneton. See Melancholy
"Pai, pai, paitaressu." See Lullaby
Meripojan laulu. See Seemanns lied
The **mermaid** ("'Twas Friday morn") Folk song: <English version> DFF—GSS—SRW—US
The **mermaid** ("As I walked out") Hyden, Ky. version no. 2. SES 1
The **mermaid** ("The first on deck") Hyden, Ky. version no. 1. SES 1
The **mermaid** ("Last Friday morning as we set sail") Knott or Letcher county, Ky. version. MK
The **mermaid** ("O the raging sea") Virginia version. SES 1
The **mermaid** ("One Friday morning") North Carolina version. SES 1
Mermaid's evening song. S. Glover. MFS
Merrial. See "Now the day is over" (Barnby)
Merriam, Foster B., pseud. See Loomis, Harvey Worthington
"**Merrily** every bosom boundeth." German air. MFS
"**Merrily,** merrily, greet the morn." Round. BB—DSB—GSS—TFP—TFR
Merrily, merrily to welcome in the year, the year. See Spring
Merrily now we row along. See Over the dark blue sea
Merrily we roll along. See "Good-night, ladies"
Merriman, Samuel Sears
"Dear Bucknell" (Composer unknown)
"The **merry** bells of Hamburg." Three-part round. A. Moffat. TFP
Merry Christmas ("On Christmas eve the bells were rung") M. Shaw. Words adapted from W. Scott. OB

"A **merry** gath'ring all on a train." See Is life worth living (Harris)
A **merry** life. See Funiculi, funicula (Denza)
The **merry** Swiss girl. Swiss air arr by T. Valentine. Words by R. Ryan. SW
Merry widow waltz. See Waltz song (Lehar)
Merry Yuletide (Kolyadka) Christmas song from Little Russia. N. A. Rimsky-Korsakoff. e. SR
Mersereau, Mrs Nina P.
Our flag
"**Mes** parents m'ont mariée avec un sale chiffonnier." See Le chiffonnier
"**Mes** vers fuiraient, doux et frêles." See Si mes vers avaient des ailes (Hahn)
Die **mesinke.** See "My youngest one is wedded"
Mess call. U.S. army bugle call. DSO
The **message** ("A message came to a maiden young") See De boodschap van Maria
"A **message** came to a maiden young." See De boodschap van Maria
Lo **mestre** (Der lehrer) Catalan folk song. ca.g. ML 2
Metastasio, Pietro Antonio Domenico Bonaventura
"Fra degno ed amore" (Latilla)
"Sgombra dall' anima" (Latilla)
Methfessel, Albert Gottlieb
Deutsches weihelied
Gesang ausziehender krieger
Song of freedom. See Vaterlandslied
Vaterlandslied
"**Methought** the stars were blinking bright." See O fair dove, O fond dove (Scott-Gatty)
Metronome canon. L. von Beethoven. e. CSB 6
Metz, Theodore A.
The caisson song (same air as A hot time in the old town)
Caisson song: coast artillery parody (same air as A hot time in the old town)
Caisson song: infantry adaptation (same air as A hot time in the old town)
Caisson song: variation (same air as A hot time in the old town)
Hike song (same air as A hot time in the old town)
A hot time in the old town
"When you hear dem a bells go ding, ling, ling" (same air as A hot time in the old town)
"The **Mexican** bandits have crossed to our shore." See Fire away
Mexican cockroach song. See La cucaracha
"The **Mexicans** are doomed to fall." See We're the boys for Mexico
Mey, Lev Alexandrovitch. See Meĭ, Lev Aleksandrovich
Meyerbeer, Giacomo
"Ah figliuol! mio figliuol." See "Ah! mon fils"

Meyerbeer, Giacomo—*Continued*
"Ah! mon fils" (from Le prophète)
"Ah! mon remords te venge" (from Dinorah)
"Ditemi, buona gente, vedeste Dinorah" (from Dinorah)
Già l'ira m'abbandona (from Le prophète. Tr of Ô toi qui m'abandonnes)
"Lieti signor, salute." See "Nobles seigneurs, salut"
No, caso egual giammai. See Non, non, non, vous n'avez jamais
"Nobil donna è tanto onesta" (from Les Huguenots)
"Nobles seigneurs, salut" (from Les Huguenots)
Non, non, non, vous n'avez jamais (from Les Huguenots)
Our songs of joy and gladness
"Sei vendicata assai." See "Ah! mon remords te venge"
"Sweeter than the breath of morning." See "Nobil donna è tanto onesta"
Meyer-Helmund, Erik
Dein gedenk' ich, Margareta
Glory to heaven's eternal King. See "It came upon the midnight clear"
"It came upon the midnight clear"
Thou art near me Margarita. See Dein gedenk' ich, Margareta
Die **mezinke** äusgegeben. See My youngest one is wedded
A' **mhaighdean** àluinn (Das schöne mädchen) Old Gaelic air: Slàn gu'n till na Gaidheil ghasda. [Words by Fionn (H. Whyte)] ga.g. ML 1
"**Mi** marido esta en la cama." See La firolera
La **mia** virtù non cede. F. Bianchi. e.i. KVG
"**Mich** hat belogen das vöglein." See Der tod
Michael Finnigin. Old song. BOS 2
"**Michael** haul the boat ashore." Negro spiritual from South Carolina. AS
For variant see following song of similar title
"**Michael** row the boat ashore." Negro spiritual from South Carolina. AS
"**Michael** Kelly with his sweetheart came from County Cork." See Has anybody here seen Kelly (Murphy and Letters)
Michaelis, Sophus August Berthel
Nat (Lund)
"**Michié** Préval" (The ball of Monsieur Préval) Negro creole folk song. e.f. MB
Calinda. f. AS
Michigan, my Michigan. W. O. Miessner. Words by D. Malloch. BB
Mickle, William Julius
There's nae luck about the house (Scottish air) Authorship uncertain; attributed also to J. Adam
"The **mid-day** sun is pouring his scorching beams along the sky." See The noontide ray (Auber)

'**Mid** lures, 'mid pleasures. See Lascia ch'io pianga (Händel)
"'**Mid** musket fire and the boom of cannon." See Spirit of Gettysburg (Saltzer)
"'**Mid** pleasures and palaces though we may roam." See Home, sweet home (Bishop)
"'**Mid** smoking embers, reeking with slaughter." See Choral
"**Mid** the cornfields sings the sweet lark" ("Zöld vetés közt énekel a pacsirta") K. de Simonffy. e.hu. KH 1
Mid-winter. See "In the bleak midwinter" (Holst)
Middleton, Newton
"Alma mater"—University of the South
"**Midnight** is in the sky." See Starlight carol
"**Midnight,** O Christian, 'tis the hour so solemn." See Cantique de Noël (Adam)
Midnight special ("If you evah go to Houston") Negro jail song. SBA
Midnight special ("Yonder come Roberta") Negro song. SBA
"The **midnight** train." Negro folk song. SBA
The **midshipmite.** S. Adams. Words by F. E. Weatherly. BB—GE—MFS—US
Midsummer dance. Breton folk song. e. MFF
Midsummer day. Swiss folk song. e. LSB
Midsummer dreams. Portuguese folk song. e. MFF
"**Midsummer** eve is here." See Midsummer fires
Midsummer fires. Swiss folk song. e. MFF
"**Miei** rampolli femminini." Rossini. e.i. PB
Miessner, William Otto
Michigan, my Michigan
"**Miezo** a li campe io sola sto meglio de no rre." See Felicella
"A **mighty** fortress is our God." See Ein' feste burg (Luther)
"The **mighty** men of Washington are ready for the foe." See Victory for Washington (McHarrie)
Mighty Oregon. University of Oregon song. A. Perfect. Words by De W. Gilbert. AI—AIS—HW
"A **mighty** ship was the Gundremar." Norwegian air. Words by K. Davis. DSB—DSC
Mignon ("Kennst du das land") See "Kennst du das land" (Beethoven); "Kennst du das land" (Schumann)
"**Mikor** én még legény voltam." See "Long ago, when I was still free"
Mikor szép a kis lány. See "Wisst ihr, wann mein kindchen"
Miles, Alfred Hart
Anchor's aweigh (Zimmerman)
Miles Lane. See "All hail the power of Jesus' name" (Shrubsole)

The **mill-boy** of the slashes. American political song of 1844. Air: Old Rosin, the beau. SRW

Mill May ("The strawberries grow") MFS

The **mill-wheel** ("The mill-wheels are clapping") Kindergarten song. ₁Tr of Es klappert die mühle am rauschenden bach₁ e. MFS

"The **mill-wheels** are clapping." See The mill-wheel

Millard, Harrison
Whip-poor-will's song

Millard, Mrs Philip. See Millard, Mrs Virtue

Millard, Mrs Virtue
"Dinna forget"

Miller, Earl, and McWhorter, Edward
Hail West Virginia

Miller, Mrs Emily Clark (Huntington)
"Oh realm of light" (Haydn)

Miller, Henry S.
The cat came back

Miller, James
Bonnie Doon
"Ye banks and braes o' bonnie Doon." See Bonnie Doon

Miller, Johann Martin
Zufriedenheit (Mozart)

The **miller** and his sons (see Song Index) Variant: The miller's will

The **miller** and the maid. T. Marzials (music and words) SFB

The **miller** of the Dee ("There dwelt a miller, hale and bold") Words by C. Mackay. MFS

₁The **miller** of the Dee₁ "There was a jolly miller once" (The jolly miller) 17th century air: The budgeon it is a delicate trade. DSB—DSC

The miller of the Dee (Der müller an der Dee) e.g. ML 1

The **miller's** apprentice (The Oxford tragedy) Folk song: Barbourville, Ky. version no. 1. SES 1
—Barbourville, Ky. version no. 2. SES 1
—Pine Mountain, Ky. version. SES 1
—Pineville, Ky. version. SES 1
—Virginia version. SES 1

The **miller's** daughter ("Down the stream so cheerily") Bohemian air. MFS

The **miller's** song. See Cân y melinydd

The **miller's** will. Folk song: Kentucky version. SES 2
—North Carolina version. SES 2
Variant of: The miller and his sons

Milliken, Richard Alfred
"The groves of Blarney" (Composer unknown)

Millöcker, Karl
"And when the song is sweetly sounding" (from Der bettelstudent)
Entrance song (from Der bettelstudent)
"I'll put the case" (from Der bettelstudent)
"The land is free, united we" (from Der bettelstudent)

"One day I was perambulating" (from Der bettelstudent)
"Our husbands, alas" (from Der bettelstudent)
Swindler! liar (from Der bettelstudent)
"Why, he only a kiss" (from Der bettelstudent)
"When we have good rations" (from Der bettelstudent)
"With love's golden fetters" (from Der bettelstudent)
Yes, this hero. See Entrance song (from Der bettelstudent)

Mills, Frederick Allen
At a Georgia camp meeting
Meet me in St Louis, Louis

Mills, Kerry. See Mills, Frederick Allen

Milton, John
"Haste thee, nymph" (Arnold)
"Let us with a gladsome mind" (Gibbons)

Minard, Archibald Ellsworth
Yellow and green (Putnam)

"**Mind**, my sister, how you walk on de cross." See Oh, Jerusalem

"**Mine** eyes are turned to the hebbenly gate." See Stay in de field

"**Mine** eyes have seen the glory." See The battle hymn of the republic

"**Mine** heart ish proken into little pits." See Corporal Schnaps (Work)

Mine only, mine alone. P. Starnes. Words by A. Procter. BST

"A **miner** was leaving his home for his work." See The dream of the miner's child

"**Mingle** your cheers." Holy Cross college song. AI—AIS

Mingled melodies. Double round. French and English airs. TFG

"**Mini** Don v'ad B'er Sheva." See Upon the death of Trumpeldor

"**Ministri** dell' averno." See Già l'ira m'abbandona (Meyerbeer)

Minnelied ("All mein' gedanken") See Nur du

Minnelied ("Holder klingt der vogelsang." —Love song) J. Brahms. Words by H. Hölty. e.g. GG

₁**Minnelied**₁ "Ich spring an diesem ringe" (Mädchenpreis) Minnesingers' song. g. EDL

"**Minnesota** hail to thee." See Hail! Minnesota (Rickard)

"**Minnesota**, hats off to thee." See The U. of M. rouser (Hutsell)

The **minstrel** ("The minstrel's return'd from the war") J. H. Hewitt. HP

"The **minstrel** boy." Air: The moreen. Words by T. Moore. BB—DSC—GOS 1—MBS—MFS—SI—SSB—TFG

Minstrels and maids stand forth on the floor. See "From far away" (Williams)

"The **minstrel's** return'd from the war." See The minstrel (Hewitt)

The **minuet** ("Come the lords and ladies fine") Bohemian air. Words by K. Davis. DSB

Minuet ("Now winged hours") See "Now winged hours" (Mozart)

"**Minuit**, Chrétien, c'est l'heure solennelle."
  See Cantique de Noël (Adam)
"**Minun** kultani kaunis on."   See The gay
  young bachelor
"Il **mio** Lionel perira se amico il ciel non
  avra."   See Povero Lionello (Flotow)
"**Mir** ist ein schöns brauns maidelein gefalln
  in meinen sinn."   See Das braune
  maidelein
"**Mir** klingt ein ton so wunderbar."   See
  Ein ton (Cornelius)
"**Mira**, o bella, il trovatore."   Donizetti.
  e.i.   PC
[Le **miracle** de Saint-Nicolas] "Il était trois
  petits enfants" (Le légende de
  Saint-Nicolas.—Die legende vom
  Heiligen Nikolaus)   French folk
  song.   f.g.   ML 1
  The miracle of St Nicholas.   e.
  DSB—DSC
  Le miracle de Saint-Nicolas (The mira-
  cle of Santa Claus)   Lorraine
  version.   e.f.   CBF 1
The **miracle** of St Nicholas.   See Le mira-
  cle de Saint-Nicolas
The **miracle** of Santa Claus.   See Le mir-
  acle de Saint-Nicolas (Lorraine ver-
  sion)
The **miracle** of the cock.   See King
  Pharaoh: The miracle of the cock
The **miraculous** harvest.   See King
  Pharaoh: The miraculous harvest
Mirame así (Grant those glances)   Haba-
  nera.   E. S. de Fuentes (music and
  words)   e.s.   MSP
"**Mirusholayim** ad M'tuloh."   See A
  Chalutz polka
Miserere.   See "Ah! I have sighed to rest
  me" (Verdi)
The **misfortune**.   See La desgracia
"**Miss** Em'ly was a maid so fair."   See
  Edwin in the lowlands low (Tennessee
  version)
Miss Jenny-o-Jones.   Children's game
  song.   GSS
  Variant of: Jenny Jones
Miss Lucy Long.   See Lucy Long
Mississippi delta blues (Bamville croon)
  S. Williams.   HB
Missouri national.   West Point song.
  DSO
"**Missouri**, she's a mighty river."   See
  Shenandoah
"**Mistäs** piisaa, mistäs piisaa pitkii piikoi
  aina."   See Alter tanz
"**Mister** frog went a-courting."   See "A
  frog he went a-courting" (Kentucky
  and Virginia version)
"**Mister** froggie went a courtin'."   See
  "A frog he went a-courting" (Georgia
  version)
Mister Jefferson Lord play that barber shop
  chord.   See Play that barber shop
  chord (Muir)
"**Mr** Noah."   Old song.   US
The **mistletoe** bough.   H. R. Bishop.
  Words by T. H. Bayly.   DN—GOS 1
Mistletoe gifts.   See La guignolée
"The **mistletoe** hung in the castle hall."
  See The mistletoe bough (Bishop)

Mrs Lofty and I.   J. J. Hutchinson.
  GOS 2
Mistress Shady.   TFG—TFO—TFR
  "Oh, Mistress Shady."   BB
Mit a nodel, ohn a nodel.   Jewish folk
  song.   y.   SY
"**Mit** deinen blauen augen" ("Avec tes yeux
  mignonne."—"Thine eyes so blue
  and tender")   E. Lassen.   [Words
  by H. Heine]   e.f.g.   GG
  Thine eyes so blue and dreaming.   e.g.
  MFS
"**Mit** dem pfeil, dem bogen."   See Der
  schütz (Weber)
"**Mit** den kameraden allen" ("V Mikulášskej
  kompanii")   Slovak folk song.   g.sl.
  ML 3
"**Mit** einem blinden knaben hatt' ich er-
  barmen."   See "A un niño cieque-
  cito"
"**Mit** soviel seufzern muss ich dir treu ver-
  bleiben."   See Canto del pastore
Mitchell, John F.
  Twelve months ago to-night (Fox)
Mjej ty dobru nóc.   See Liebchen gute
  nacht
Mo chailin dìleas donn (Mein treues braun-
  mägdlein)   Old Gaelic song.   ga.g.
  ML 1
Mo déjà roulé tout la côte.   See Belle
  Layotte
"**Mo** grád, ón 'sí mo grád."   Se An searc
  'gá diúltugad
Mo nigheann chruinn, donn (Mein braun-
  mägdlein schön)   Old Gaelic song.
  ga.g.   ML 1
"**Mo** parlé Rémon, Rémon."   See Rémon,
  Rémon
"**Mo** roulé tout la côte."   See Belle
  Layotte
Mo rùn geal dìleas (The isle of dreams.—
  "Dream island, queen of the golden
  gloaming")   Scottish air.   Words
  by J. M. Caie.   e.   CSB 4
Moanish lady.   Negro spiritual.   SBA
  Variant of: Mona (You shall be free)
The **mocking** bird ("Hush up, baby, don't
  say a word")   Lullaby: North
  Carolina version.   SES 2
  The mocking bird ("Hush! Little
  Minnie and don't say a word")
  Virginia version.   SES 2
The **mocking** bird ("I love to roam in the
  woodland")   A. Hawthorne (S. Win-
  ner)   New words by P. Hastings.
  TFR
The **mocking** bird ("I'm dreaming now of
  Hallie")   For original words see
  Listen to the mocking bird (Winner)
A **moda** gallega (Volkstanz)   Portuguese
  folk song.   g.po.   ML 2
Moet and Shandon for me.   Old song.
  SW
Moffat, Alfred
  "The merry bells of Hamburg"
"**Mögst** du schlaf geniessen."   See Lieb-
  chen, gute nacht
Mohr, Josef
  Die heilige nacht (Gruber)
Moi-one-Ionae.   See My own Iona (Fried-
  land and Morgan)

Moladh na landaidh (The praise of Islay.—
"See afar yon hill Ardmore")
Ancient Gaelic song. e. CSB 2
The praise of Islay. e. DSB
Mollie darling. W. S. Hays (music and
words) GOS 2—OT
Mollie, fairest, sweetest, dearest. See
Mollie darling (Hays)
Molloy, James Lyman
The boatswain's story
The bo's'n. See The boatswain's
story
The clang of the wooden shoon
"Come, take thy harp"
Dresden China. See A twilight
fancy
"Jamie! Jamie"
The Kerry dance
The king's highway
London bridge
Love's old sweet song
"Oh! how delightful"
The old cottage clock
Punchinello
Rose-Marie
The song of the Triton
A twilight fancy
The vagabond
Molly bawn ("O Molly bawn, why leave
me pining") S. Lover (music and
words) SI
"Molly Van was a-walking." See Shoot-
ing of his dear (Tennessee version)
"Mon coeur se recommande à vous" ("Into
your hands I give my heart") At-
tributed to O. di Lasso. e.f. GA
"Mon compère, quand je danse." See
Compère et commère
Mon cri cra, tir' la lirette (Red river boat
song) Canadian folk song. e.f.
GSF
"Mon Dieu! j'étais une bergère." See
Jeanne d'Arc au bûcher (Liszt)
"Mon père a fait batir maison" (J'entends
le moulin) (see Song Index)
Variant: "J'entends le moulin"
"Mon père a fait bâtir maison" (Va, va,
va, p'tit bonnet tout rond) (see
Song Index)
Variant of: "Mon pèr' m'a fait bâtir
maison"
"Mon père a fait faire un étang." See
Les trois canards
Mon père est un très gros banquier. For
English translation see "The scion of
an ancient house" (Lecocq)
"Mon pèr' m'a fait bâtir maison" (Le p'tit
bonnet rond.—Little round cap)
Folk song from Champagne. e.f.
CBF 2
Variant: "Mon père a fait bâtir maison"
(Va, va, va, p'tit bonnet tout rond)
"Mon pèr' n'avait fille que moi" (Cécilia)
Canadian folk song. e.f. MBS
"Mon petit coeur à chaque instant soupire."
See Mon petit coeur soupire
Mon petit coeur soupire (My little heart's
a-sighing) e.f. AT
Mona (You shall be free) Negro spiri-
tual. SRW
Variant: Moanish lady

La monacella ("Quanno mammà me fece
monicella."—Das nönnchen) Roman
folk song. g.i. ML 2
La monachella e il demonio (Das nönnlein
und der teufel) Venetian folk song.
g.i. ML 2
"Monachella la va nell' orto." See La
monachella e il demonio
Monarch of the woods. J. W. Cherry.
MFS
"Der mond ist aufgegangen." See Abend-
lied (Schulz)
"Mond stieg herauf" ("Schadzka umówi-
ona") Polish folk song. g.p.
ML 3
"Monday morning go to school." See
The two brothers (Hot Springs, N.C.
version; Marion, N.C. version)
"Monday, Tuesday." See "Da Luain, da
Mairt"
A Monday was my courting day. Folk
song from North Carolina. SES 2
"Mondays, boys, I got me a wife." See
The holly twig (Woodridge, Va. ver-
sion)
[Mondschein] "Verstohlen geht der mond
auf" (Nachtgruss) Rheinische volks-
weise. Words by W. von Zuccalmag-
lio. g. EDL
Money ("O money is the meat in the cocoa-
nut") Old American song. SBA
"'Mong the beauteous flow'rs I live." See
The rose of the Alps (Linley)
Monk, William Henry
"Abide with me! fast falls the even-
tide"
Hursley. See "Sun of my soul, Thou
Saviour dear"
"Lord, in this Thy mercy's day"
"Sun of my soul, Thou Saviour dear"
"Monkey married the baboon's sister."
Old song. SRW
Variant of: The monkey's wedding
The monkeys have no tails in Zamboanga.
See Zamboanga
The monkey's wedding. Traditional song.
RA—SBA
"The monkey married the baboon's
sister." DSO
Variant: "Monkey married the baboon's
sister"
The monks' march. See The monks of
Bangor's march
[The monks of Bangor's march] "When the
heathen trumpets' clang" (The monks'
march) Air: Ymdaith y mwnc.
Words by W. Scott. DSC
Monody. P. A. von Hagen. MPA 1
Monro, George
"My goddess Celia"
"My lovely Celia." See "My goddess
Celia"
Monroe, Dorothy H.
"All hail, Arizona"
Monroe, E. C.
"All hail, Arizona" (Monroe, D. H.)
Monsell, John Samuel Bewley
Golden sheaves (Basque air)
"Monsieur Préval il donna grand bal."
See "Michié Préval"

Monsigny, Pierre Alexander
My tender musette. See "Ô ma tendre musette" (attributed)
"Ô ma tendre musette" (attributed)
Montana my Montana. University of Montana song. G. H. Greenwood. Words by G. A. Knapp. HW
Monteverdi, Claudio
"Ecco purch'a voi ritorno" (from Orfeo)
"Tu se' morta" (from Orfeo)
Montgomery, B. S.
Home so blest (Abt)
Montgomery, James
"Angels, from the realms of glory" (English air; French air)
"For ever with the Lord" (Gounod)
"God shall charge His angel legions" (Mendelssohn)
"Hail to the Lord's anointed" (Mendelssohn)
"The Lord is my Shepherd; no want shall I know" (Koschat)
"Prayer is the soul's sincere desire" (Schulthes)
Montoya, G., and André, Pierre
Pastourelle (Auguin)
Montrose, Percy
Clementine. See Oh, my darling Clementine
Oh, my darling Clementine
The **moon** behind the hill. T. B. Bishop. GOS 2
"De **moon** give a light in de heaven all round." See Give up the world
"The **moon** had climbed the highest hill." See Mary's dream
"The **moon** is beaming o'er the lake." J. Blockley. MFS
"The **moon** is beaming o'er the sparkling rill." See Who's that calling (Lawreen)
The **moon** reappears. H. Purcell. Words by C. Williams. CSB 5
"The **moon** shines bright" (The bellman's song) Traditional New Year carol. OB
The old "waits" carol. DN
"The moon shines bright." Surrey and Sussex version. BET
"The **moon** shines bright" (May-day song) Traditional carol: May day version. DSB
"The **moon** walks high." See The high moon
"The **moonbeams** whiten boughs all around." See L'heure exquise (Hahn)
Moonlight ("I wish I had someone to love me."—The prisoner's song) Kentucky mountain song. SBA
"The **moon's** on the lake." See Macgregors' gathering (Lee)
"The **moon's** pale beams are shining." Vopelius. DNS
Moonshine. Southern mountain song. RA
Moór, Emanuel
Die bitte
The request. See Die bitte

Das **moor** von Rhuddlan. See Morva Rhuddlan
Moore, G. W.
Little Maggie May (Blamphin)
Moore, Raymond
Sweet Marie
Moore, Thomas

Composer and author
Twilight dews

Author
After the battle (Irish air)
Araby's daughter (Kiallmark)
"As a beam o'er the face of the waters" (Irish air)
"As slow our ship her foaming track" (Irish air)
"At the mid hour of night" (Irish air)
"Avenging and bright" (Irish air)
"Believe me, if all those endearing young charms" (English air)
"By that lake, whose gloomy shore" (Irish air)
"Come o'er the sea" (Irish air)
"Come, rest in this bosom" (Irish air)
"Come, send round the wine" (Irish air)
"Come, take thy harp" (Molloy)
"Come, ye disconsolate" (Webbe)
The daughters of Erin (Irish air)
"Drink to her" (Irish air)
Erin! oh Erin (Irish air)
"Erin! the tear and the smile in thine eyes" (Irish air)
Eveleen's bower (Irish air)
The fair-haired maiden (Irish air)
"Farewell! but whenever you welcome the hour" (Irish air)
The farewell to my harp (Irish air; Welsh air)
"Fill the bumper fair" (Irish air)
"Fly not yet" (Irish air)
"Forget not the field" (Irish air)
"Go where glory waits thee" (Irish air)
"Has sorrow thy young days shaded" (Irish air)
"Hours there were" (Wade)
"How oft has the banshee cried" (Irish air)
"I saw from the beach" (Irish air)
I saw thy form in youthful prime (Irish air)
"I'd mourn the hopes that leave me" (Irish air)
"If thou'lt be mine" (Irish air)
"In the morning of life" (Irish air)
The Irish peasant to his mistress (Irish air)
"It is not the tear, at this moment shed" (Irish air)
The last rose of summer (Irish air)
The legacy (Irish air)
"Lesbia hath a beaming eye" (Irish air)
"Let Erin remember the days of old" (Irish air)
Love and the novice (Irish air)
Love's young dream (Irish air)
The meeting of the waters (Irish air)
"The minstrel boy" (Irish air)
"My gentle harp, once more I waken" (Londonderry air)

Moore, Thomas—Author—*Continued*
"Nay, tell me not, dear" (Irish air)
"No, not more welcome" (Irish air)
"Oh! blame not the bard" (Irish air)
"Oh! breathe not his name" (Irish air)
"Oh! doubt me not" (Irish air)
"Oh, for the swords of former time" (Irish air)
"Oh! had we some bright little isle" (Irish air)
Oh! the shamrock (Irish air)
"Oh! think not my spirits are always as light" (Irish air)
"Oh! 'tis sweet to think" (Irish air)
"Oft in the stilly night" (Stevenson?)
On music (Irish air)
"One bumper at parting" (Irish air)
The prince's day (Irish air)
"Remember thee" (Irish air)
"Rich and rare were the gems she wore" (Irish air)
St Senanus and the lady (Irish air)
The separation (Engelbrecht)
"She is far from the land" (Irish air)
Shule, agra (Irish air)
Song of Fionnuala (Irish air)
Song of O'Ruark, Prince of Breffni (Irish air)
"Sound the loud timbrel" (Avison)
"Sublime was the warning which liberty spoke" (Irish air)
"Take back the virgin page" (Irish air)
There's nothing true but heaven (Shaw)
"They may rail at this life" (Irish air)
"This life is all chequer'd with pleasures and woes" (Irish air)
"Those evening bells" (music by Lefébure-Wély; also unknown composer)
"The time I've lost in wooing" (Irish air)
"'Tis believed that this harp" (Irish air)
"To ladies' eyes" (Irish air)
Vesper hymn (Bortnianskii)
"When cold in the earth" (Irish air)
"When first I met thee" (Irish air)
"When he, who adores thee" (Irish air)
"When love is kind" (Irish air)
"Whene'er I see those smiling eyes" (Irish air)
"While gazing on the moon's light" (Irish air)
"While history's muse" (Irish air)
"Will you come to the bow'r" (Old air)
Authorship uncertain
The woodpecker (Willson)
"Wreath the bowl" (Irish air)
"You remember Ellen" (Irish air)
"The young May moon" (Irish air)
Mooztzur. See "Rock of ages, let our song"
Mora, Helene
Kathleen
Morales, Tomas
The hiking song of the eighth infantry
Moravský, Gustav Pfleger-. See Pfleger-Moravský, Gustav

Moret, Neil, pseud. See Daniels, Charles N.
Morfa Rhuddlan. See Morva Rhuddlan
Morgan,
The day when you'll forget me (Thomas)
Morgan, Carey
Oh Helen
Sipping cider thru a straw. See Sucking cider through a straw
Sucking cider through a straw
Thipping thider thru a thtraw. See Sucking cider through a straw
See also Friedland, A., jt. comp.
Morgan, Sydney (Owenson), lady
Kate Kearney (Irish air)
Morgen-hymne (Morning hymn) G. Henschel. Words by R. Reinick. e.g. TM
"Morgen, kinder, wirds was geben." See Die weihnachtsfreude
"Morgen kommt der weihnachtsmann." See Der weihnachtsmann
"Morgen muss ich fort von hier." See Lebewohl (Silcher)
Morgenlied der schwarzen freischar. Volksweise. Words by G. A. Salchow. g. EDL
"Morgenrot, morgenrot! leuchtest mir zum frühen tod." See Reiters morgenlied
"Morgenröte dämmernd schimmert." See "White dawn has not come stealing"
"Morgens in der ersten frühe stand ich auf und ging." See Die traurige braut
"Morgens in der frühe ging das mädchen aus." See Das mädchen vom Amselfeld
"Morgens wandelnd in der auen." See "L'autrier par la matinée" (Thibaut IV)
Morgenständchen. J. F. Reichardt. Volkslied. g. EDL
Mörike, Eduard
Die soldatenbraut (Schumann)
"Mörkgrön granskog skuggar öfver viken." See Aftonstämning (Peterson-Berger)
Morley, Thomas
"It was a lover and his lass" (attributed)
"Now is the month of Maying"
"Sleep, O sleep, fond fancy"
Zur ruh, mein wahn. See "Sleep, O sleep, fond fancy"
"The morn of life is past." See Old dog Tray (Foster)
"The morn was fair, the skies were clear." See The rose of Allandale (Nelson)
"Morning comes early." Slovakian folk air. English words by K. Davis. DSB—MBS
"The morning hangs its signal." L. Mason. Words by W. C. Gannett. LAS
Morning hymn ("Bald ist der nacht") See Morgen-hymne (Henschel)
Morning prayer ("Father, we thank Thee") K. D. Wiggin. BB

Morning serenade. A. C. Lecocq. [Tr of Aubade (Voici le matin, des feux de l'aurore)] e. WLO

Morning song ("Now with creation's morning song") See "Now with creation's morning song" (Beethoven)

Morning song ("The sun is rising out of bed") 18th century English song. DSB—GSS

Morning star. See "Brightest and best" (Harding)

"Morning's ruddy beam." G. Linley. MFS

Morris, George Pope
  "Down by the river-side I stray" (Thomas)
  The flag of our union forever (Wallace)
  Long time ago (Old air)
  "Near the banks of that lone river" (La Hache)
  "Woodman, spare that tree" (Russell)

Morris, Huw
  "Yn iach lawenydd" (Welsh air)

Morris, Reginald Owen
  "See amid the winter's snow"
  Winter's snow. See "See amid the winter's snow"

Morris, William
  "From far away" (Williams)
  "Masters in this hall" (Old French air)

Morrison, Lewis
  Behold! I stand at the door (Jude)

Morrissey and the Russian sailor. Lumberjack song. SBA

Morrow, John Albert
  Virginia, hail, all hail

Morse, Clinton Ralza
  "Hail to California"

Morse, Theodore F.
  Little boy in blue
  M-o-t-h-e-r

Morsell, Herndon
  "Now the shades of night are gone"

Mortenson, Ivar
  Liv og salighed (Sinding)

Morton, Clara
  Sing glad songs for him (Gounod)
  [Morva Rhuddlan] Morfa Rhuddlan (Das moor von Rhuddlan) Old Welsh air. Words by I. G. Geirionydd. g.w. ML 1

Morton, Thomas
  My native Highland home (Bishop)

Mos' done toilin' here. Negro spiritual. JB 2

Mosen, Julius
  Andreas Hofer (Swiss air)
  Der träumende see (Brückler)

"Moses died in de days of old." See Where shall I be when de firs' trumpet soun'

The mosquito's serenade. H. W. Loomis (music and words) TFP

Moss, Edwin
  "Still, still with Thee"

"Most chivalrous fish of the ocean." See The rhyme of the chivalrous shark

Most done toilin' here. See Mos' done toilin' here

Most done trabelling. Negro spiritual. HRD

"Most lovely of ladies is she." See Mwynen merch

Moszkowski, Moritz
  "My God, my Father, while I stray"

The moth and the flame. M. S. Witt. Words by G. Taggart. GFS—OTG —SRW

M-o-t-h-e-r (A word that means the world to me) T. Morse. Words by H. Johnson. SMG

"Mother dear come bathe my forehead." See Put my little shoes away

"Mother, is massa gwine to sell us to-morrow." See Massa gwine to sell us to-morrow

"A mother missed her darling child." See The lost lamb (Schubert)

"Mother, mother, do not scold me." See A girl's love (Guriliev)

"Mother, mother, do so no more." See The cruel mother (Marion, N.C. version no. 2)

"Mother, O mother." See Lord Thomas and fair Ellinor (Berea, Ky. version; Harrogate, Tenn. version)

"A mother of fashion was being array'd." See Only me (Bratton)

"Mother of men." Yale prize song, 1907. S. Bingham. Words by B. Hooker. LAS

"Mother off to the market goes." See Pancakes

Mother Volga. Russian folk song. e. DSB—DSC
  Ballad of the Volga. e. SR
  Down by mother Volga. e. NRF
  "Vnīz po matushkře po Volgře" (An der mutter Wolga) g.r. ML 1

Mothering Sunday. 14th century German air: Ich weiss ein lieblich engelspiel. Words by G. H. Leonard. OB

"A mother's gift to her country's cause." See The blue and the gray (Dresser)

The mother's lamentation. Old air. HMI

Motherwell, William
  "My heid is like to rend, Willie" (Swift)

A motto for all (Never trouble trouble, till trouble troubles you) Old song. SW

Le moulin (The water mill) Folk song from lower Alsace. e.f. CBF 1

Moultrie, Gerard
  "There came three kings ere break of day" (Smith)

"Mount! mount! and away o'er the green prairie ride." See Texan rangers' song (Russell)

The mountain battery. Words by G. E. Griffin. DSO

The mountain bugle. J. H. Hewitt. MFS

"The mountain city is her home." See Alma mater — Furman university (Barnes)

Mountain maid's invitation. H. Werner. <Words by T. Power> MFS

Mountain top ("I'll go up") Folk song. SBA
Variant of: Eliza Jane
Mountain top blues (Blue mama's suicide wail) S. Williams (music and words) HB
The mountains ("O, proudly rise") Williams college song. W. Gladden (music and words) AI—KU
"Mourn not for me." Irish air. Words by W. Maynard. HMI
Mourner, you shall be free. See Mona (A variant)
ʟMournful loveɪ Zdvojenje (Verzweiflung) Slavonian folk song. g.se. ML 2
"Mourning in the village dwells" ("Szilvás falu gyászban van") Old Hungarian folk song. e.hu. KH 1
"Szilvás falu gyászban van" ("Szilvás hallt von grabgeläut") g.hu. ML 3
Moussorgsky, Modest Petrovitch. See Musorgskiï, Modest Petrovich
"Möven, möven in weissen flocken." See Im kahne (Grieg)
"Moving waters, quav'ring breezes." See Adagio (Rangström)
The mowers' song. German air. MFS
Mozart, Wolfgang Amadeus
Abendempfindung
The alphabet
Ave verum
"Away with melancholy"
The blacksmith
Bundeslied
Children's play. See Piaceri fanciulleschi
Contentment. See Zufriedenheit
Cradle song. See Wiegenlied
"Deh vieni alla finestra" (from Don Giovanni)
"Drink to me only with thine eyes" (wrongly attributed) See Harrington, H. "Drink to me only with thine eyes" (attributed)
Faith
La filatrice
"Fin ch'han dal vino" (from Don Giovanni)
"Hail, Thou long-expected Jesus"
"Hear our call"
"Hello speaker" (same air as "Twinkle, twinkle, little star"; attributed)
"Ihr, die ihr triebe." See "Voi, che sapete"
"In diesen heil'gen hallen" (from Die zauberflöte)
"Komm', lieber mai, und mache"
Longing for spring. See "Komm', lieber mai, und mache"
Lullaby. See Wiegenlied
Melancholy
Minuet. See "Now winged hours"
Nightingale canon
Ninna-nanna. See Wiegenlied
"Non più andrai" (from Le nozze di Figaro)
"Non so più cosa son" (from Le nozze di Figaro)
"Now winged hours"

"O Isis und Osiris" (from Die zauberflöte)
Piaceri fanciulleschi
The pigtail
"Qui sdegno non s'accende." See "In diesen heil'gen hallen"
"Rose-leaves are falling." See Vedrai, carino
Sehnsucht nach dem frühlinge. See "Komm, lieber mai und mache"
"Silently blending." See "Voi, che sapete"
Spinning Jenny. See La filatrice
Thoughts at eventide. See Abendempfindung
A tragic story. See The pigtail
"Twinkle, twinkle, little star" (attributed)
Vedrai, carino (with words "Rose-leaves are falling")
Vedrò, mentr' io sospiro (from Le nozze di Figaro)
Das veilchen
"La vendetta, oh, la vendetta" (from Le nozze di Figaro)
The violet. See Das veilchen
"Voi, che sapete" (from Le nozze di Figaro)
The voice of praise. See Ave verum
"Who treads the path of duty"
Wiegenlied
Zufriedenheit
Müchler, Karl
"Ich sah ein röschen am wege stehn" (Weber)
Der rheinweinzecher (Fischer)
"Müde hier für und für farren schneid' ich." See Cnochd a bheannichd
Muhlenberg, William Augustus
Carol, brothers, carol
Shout the glad tidings
Mühler, Heinrich von
Bedenklichkeiten (Spanish air)
Das mühlrad ("Da droben auf jenem berge") Volkslied. g. EDL
Muir, Alexander
The maple leaf forever
Muir, Lewis F.
Play that barber shop chord
Take me to that Swanee shore
Waiting for the Robert E. Lee
"Muistatko tyttö, kun käveltiin sitä harmiaveden." See Am Harmiavesi
"Mujje mukesin auyawyon." See Old shoes
The mulberry bush (see Song Index)
Variant: Early Sunday morning
Mule skinner's song. Loggers' song. SBA
Mules ("On mules we find") Round. BB
Müller, Friedrich
Soldaten-abschied (Fesca)
Müller, Peter Erasmus Lange-. See Lange-Müller, Peter Erasmus
Müller, Wenzel
Abschied (from Der Alpenkönig und der menschfeind)
Frohe botschaft

Müller, Wilhelm
Brüderschaft (Folk air)
Des baches wiegenlied (Schubert)
Entschuldigung (Nestler)
Gute nacht (Schubert)
Der hirt auf dem felsen (Schubert)
"I heard a brooklet gushing" (Loder. Tr of Wohin)
Der lindenbaum (Schubert)
Meine muse (Lyra)
Das wandern (Schubert)

Müller, Wolfgang
Widmung (Franz)
Der müller an der Dee. See The miller of the Dee

Mulligan guards.   D. Braham.   Words by E. Harrigan.   GFS
The Mulligan guard.   SRW

Mulock, Dinah Maria.   See Craik, Mrs Dinah Maria (Mulock)

"Multe lacrămĭ am vărsat."   See Ardeleanca

Multiplication table ("Once two is two") Old song.   KSO

Munch, Andreas
"Yderst mod norden" (Norse air)
"Muoja! su questa fronte il disonor stampò." See Nuova ferita (Mercadante)
"Murmelndes lüftchen, blüthenwind" (Murmuring zephyr)   A. Jensen.   [Words by Heyse]   e.g.   HCA
"Murmur, gentle lyre."   GOS 2—MFS
Murmuring zephyr.   See "Murmelndes lüftchen, blüthenwind" (Jensen)

Murphy, C. W., and Letters, Will
Has anybody here seen Kelly

Murphy, J. B.
Nicodemus Johnson

Mushrooms.   See Gathering mushrooms (Musorgskiĭ)

Music in the air.   G. F. Root.   [Words by F. Crosby]   BB—GOS 2—TFG—TFO—TFR
Music in the air, Counterpoint for.   H. W. Loomis.   TFR
Music in the air, Optional accompaniment for.   TFG

Music on the waves.   C. W. Glover. <Words by J. E. Carpenter>   MFS

"**Music,** wild music the wintertime sings us." See A winter song

Musical alphabet.   Children's song. KSO—MFS

The **musical** bachelor.   A. P. Heinrich. Words by a gentlemen of Kentucky. HP

Musieu Bainjo.   Negro creole folk song. f.   AS
"Gardez piti milatte-là" ("Look at that mulatto")   e.f.   MB

Der **musikant** ("Tsĭgular' kúshcha ne khraní")   Bulgarian folk song.   b.g. ML 2

Musorgskiĭ, Modest Petrovich
The banks of the Don
By the river Don.   See The banks of the Don
Gathering mushrooms

Mushrooms.   See Gathering mushrooms

The **song** of Solomon
Song of the Hebrew maiden.   See The song of Solomon

"**Muss** i denn, muss i denn."   See Abschied

"**Müsst'** ich auch reiten tage und nächte" ("Choćbym ja jeździł we dnie i w nocy")   Polish folk song.   g.p. ML 3

"**Must** I go bound and you go free."   Irish air from County Derry.   Words from an old song.   HI 1

"**Must** I go bound, must I go free."   See The brisk young lover (Hot Springs, N.C. version)

"**Must** I go to Porto Rico."   See Porto Rico

"**Must** I leave thee, must I leave thee." See Eve's lamentation (King)

"**Must** I then, must I then."   See Abschied ("Muss i denn")

"**Must** we then meet as strangers."   J. R. Thomas.   Words by G. Cooper. OT

Mustakallio,
Lullaby (Merikanto)

"**Mutter,** mutter, ich schmacht', ich verschmachte."   See Lu golio de 'na figliola

"**Mutter** so zärtlich mich liebte" (Ĭ az břekh edna na maĭka)   Bulgarian folk song.   b.g.   ML 2

Die **mutter** sucht ihr liebes kind.   For English translation see The lost lamb (Schubert)

Mutter und tochter (Äiti ja tytär)   Finnish folk song.   fi.g.   ML 3

Mutterfluch (Kletva s jabuka)   Bosnian folk song.   g.se.   ML 2

"**Mütterlein,** ach schenke mir."   See "Mama mia, vuria, vuria"

"**Mütterlein,** gib acht" ("Matula moja, śliczną córę masz")   Polish folk song.   g.p.   ML 3

Mwynen merch (Lovely lady)   Old Welsh song.   Words by J. Thomas.   e.w. WO

My ain fireside ("O, I ha'e seen great anes")   Scottish air.   Words by E. Hamilton.   GS—LAS

My ain kind dearie, O ("When o'er the hill")   See The lea rig

My ain kind dearie, O ("Will ye gang o'er the lea rig")   <Old air: Lea rig> Words by R. Ferguson.   GS

"**My** ardent lover, in heav'n above."   See Lola's song (Mascagni)

My arms are reaching out into the west. See U of U trail (Rich)

"**My** army cross over."   Negro spiritual: Georgia version.   AS

My army cross over ("My brudder, tik keer Satan")   Negro spiritual: South Carolina version.   AS

My banjo.   Italian air.   DSB

[**My** bark canoe] The bark canoe.   Ojibway Indian song.   e.   TFG

"**My** bark of life was tossing."   See You've been a friend to me (Hays)

My Belgian rose.   G. Benoit, R. Levenson, and T. Garton (music and words) SMG

My best girl's a corker.   See My best girl's a New Yorker (Stromberg)

My best girl's a New Yorker.   J. Stromberg.   OTG

"**My** Bible leads to glory."   Mountain spiritual.   RA

My body rock 'long fever ("Wai', my brudder")   Negro spiritual: South Carolina version no. 1.   AS

My body rock 'long fever ("O my body's racked")   South Carolina version no. 2.   AS

"**My** Bonnie."   See Bring back my Bonnie to me (Fuller)

"**My** bonnie lass she smileth."   J. Bottomley.   TFG

"**My** Bonnie lies over the ocean."   See Bring back my Bonnie to me (Fuller)

"**My** bonny cuckoo."   Irish song.   e. CSB 2—HMI

My boy Billy.   See My boy Willie

My boy Tammie₁   "Whar hae ye been a' day" (My boy Tammy)   17th century Scottish air.   Words by H. Macneill.   GS

My boy Willie₁   Billy boy.   American version.   BB—GOS 2—KSO—TFG

Billy boy.   Northumbrian chantey version.   TSB 1

My boy Billy.   Black Mountain, N.C. version.   SES 2

—Hot Springs, N.C. version.   SES 2

—Virginia version.   SES 2

₁**My** bretheren₁ don't get weary.   Negro spiritual.   HRD

"**My** brother, de Lord has been here."   See Seek and ye shall find

My brother Gum.   See My brudder Gum (Foster)

"**My** brother, I wish you well."   Mountain spiritual.   RA

"**My** brother's died and gone to heaven."   See "Mah brudder's died an' gone to hebben"

"**My** brown boy is hiding away" ("Barna legény elbujdosott")   Hungarian folk song.   e.hu.   KH 2

"**My** brudder build a house in Paradise."   See Build a house in Paradise

My brudder Gum.   S. C. Foster (music and words)   WSS

"**My** brudder sittin' on de tree of life."   See Roll, Jordan, roll (South Carolina version)

"**My** brudder, tik keer Satan."   See My army cross over

My brudder, want to get religion.   See The lonesome valley

"**My** conscience's whippin' me."   See Mississippi delta blues (Williams)

"**My** country, 'tis of thee."   See America (Carey?)

"**My** dad has built a house for me."   See "Mon pèr' m'a fait bâtir maison"

"**My** daddy is an engineer."   See Wanderin'

"**My** daddy to my mammy said."   Air: Yankee Doodle.   DSO

"**My** dame had a lame tame crane."   See The lame crane

"**My** dame has in her hutch."   Old English catch.   DSB

"**My** dame hath a lame tame crane."   See The lame crane

My dancing day.   Traditional carol.   OB

My darling you will remember.   See "Alli en el bosque"

"**My** daughter has been absent, John."   See The green bed (Barbourville, Ky. version no. 2)

"**My** dear do you know a long time ago."   See Babes in the wood (Kentucky version)

"**My** dearest dear."   Folk song from North Carolina.   SES 2

Variant: The lover's lament

"**My** dearest dear, the time draws near that you and I must part, but it's little do you think of the grief and woe."   See The true lover's farewell (Dewey, Va. version)

"**My** dearest dear, the time draws near when I and you must part; and no one knows the inner grieves."   See "My dearest dear"

"**My** dearest dear, the time draws near when you and I must part; but little do you know the grief or woe."   See The lover's lament (1st version)

My evenin' star I wonder who you are.   See Come down ma evenin' star

"**My** faith looks up to Thee."   L. Mason.   Words by R. Palmer.   BB

My fame at stake lies in it.   See "Vieni! la mia vendetta" (Donizetti)

"**My** father had no girl but me."   See "Mon pèr' n'avait fille que moi"

"**My** father has had a pond made."   See Les trois canards

"**My** father hired me to a miller."   See The miller's apprentice (Virginia version)

"**My** father, how long."   Negro spiritual from Florida.   AS

"**My** father keeps a public house."   See Edwin in the lowlands low (Berea, Ky. version no. 2; Burnsville, N.C. version no. 2)

"**My** father owns a large estate."   See Handsome Sally

"**My** father sent me to old Rutgers."   See On the banks of the old Raritan

"**My** father took a light."   Negro spiritual from Georgia.   FSN

₁**My** fatherland₁ Bohemia, my fatherland.   ₁J. Škroup.   Words by J. K. Tyl₁ e.   LAS

"**My** fatherland! the place of my birth."   See M'chorotay

"**My** father's gane to fecht for him."   See He's owre the hills

"**My** friends all declare that my time is mis-spent."   See The sweet little girl that I love (Hook)

My gal is a high born lady.   B. Fagan (music and words)   GFS—SRW

"**My** gentle harp, once more I waken." Londonderry air. Words by T. Moore. DSB—DSC—GSS—HMI—MBS

"**My** girl's a hullabaloo." College song: De Pauw university version. KU

My God is so high. Negro spiritual. JG

"**My** God, my Father, while I stray." M. Moszkowski. ɩWords by C. Elliottɩ CSS 1

"**My** God, my Father, while I stray" (Resignation) R. Wagner. Words by C. Elliott. LAS

ɩ"**My** goddess Celia"ɩ "My lovely Celia." G. Monro. WOE

"**My** grandfather's clock was too large for the shelf." See Grandfather's clock (Work)

"**My** grandma lives on yonder little green." See My grandma's advice

My grandma's advice. GOS 1—KSO

"**My** grandmother lived on yonder little green." RA—SW

"**My** grandmother lived on yonder little green." See My grandma's advice

"**My** grandmother she, at the age of eighty-three." See The arm chair

"**My** grandsire beat a drum so neat." See Darby Kelly (Whitaker)

"**My** griefs for this forbid mine eye to close" (see Song Index)
Also in "Why does the God of Israel sleep" (Händel) SSO 3

My Hannah lady. Old popular song. OTG

"**My** head got wet with the midnight dew." See Don't be weary, traveller

"**My** head was wet with the midnight dew." See Don't be weary, traveller

"**My** heart am tender as de chick." See Cornelia Cob

"**My** heart as in my youth is beating." See Frühlingssegen (Brückler)

"**My** heart ever faithful." See "Mein gläubiges herze frohlocke" (Bach)

"**My** heart is a-breakin', dear tittie" (Tam Glen) Air: The muckin' o' Geordie's byre. Words by R. Burns. GS

"**My** heart is full of joy." J. Offenbach. ɩTr of J'ai le bonheur dans l'âmeɩ e. WG

"**My** heart is sad and I am weeping." See The weeping willow

"**My** heart is sair, I dare na tell" (For the sake of somebody) J. Farmer. Words by R. Burns. GSS

"**My** heart is sair, I daurna tell" (For the sake o' somebody.—My heart is sair for somebody) Scottish air: <The Highland watch's farewell> Words by R. Burns. GS

My heart is sair for somebody. SSB

"**My** heart is singing for joy of you." See Because of you (Strickland)

"**My** heart rejoices with mem'ry's voices." See Gute nacht (Haynes)

"**My** heart's-case I set in my garden to blow." See Heart's-ease

"**My** heart's in the Highlands." Scottish air. Words by R. Burns. GS

"**My** heart's in the Highlands." Air: Cro challin, or, Failte na miosg. Words by R. Burns. GS

"**My** heart's in the Highlands." J. M. Courtney. Words by R. Burns. TFG

"**My** heid is like to rend, Willie." H. Swift. Words by W. Motherwell. GS

"**My** Highland home, where tempests blow." See My native Highland home (Bishop)

"**My** home in yonder vale." G. Bizet. ɩTr of Ma mère je la voisɩ e. WG

"**My** home's in Montana." See The cowboy's lament

"**My** horses they are hungry." See The wagoner's lad (Virginia version)

"**My** Jesus Christ, a-walkin' down de hebbenly road." See Zion, weep a-low

My Johnny. Capstan chantey. TSB 2

My King of grace. F. P. Tosti. TSS 1

"**My** Lady Margaret sitting in her own chamber a-weeping." See Lady Maisry (Barbourville, Ky. version)

My last cigar. ɩL. V. H. Crosbyɩ US

My last cigar ('Twas off the blue Canaries) SRW

"**My** last old dollar." American mountain song. SW

"**My** last ole dollar." RA

"**My** life a secret owns." See "Ma vie a son secret" (Bizet)

My life is blissful since the happy day. See "Beautiful blue bells" (Delehanty)

"**My** Lilly dear is sleeping." See Toll the bell (Converse)

"**My** little dove, you're not alone." See The lonesome grove (Kentucky version)

"**My** little heart is all the time a-sighing." See Mon petit coeur soupire

My little heart's a-sighing. See Mon petit coeur soupire

"**My** little sweet darling." W. Byrd. CSB 6

My little, witching Maggie, Maggie. See Little Maggie May (Blamphin)

"**My** lodging is on the cold ground." 17th century air. Words by J. Gay (founded on an older song) SSB

"**My** Lord calls me." See Steal away to Jesus

My Lord delivered Daniel. Negro spiritual. BB

My Lord delibered Daniel. HRD

"**My** Lord, my Lord, my Lord says he's gwineter rain down fire." See My Lord says he's gwineter rain down fire

"**My** Lord, my Lord, what shall I do." See Heaven bell a-ring

My Lord says he's gwineter rain down fire. Negro spiritual. JB 2

My Lord sittin' in his Kingdom. See I don't want to be a gambler

My Lord, what a morning. Negro spiritual. HRD—WSS

"**My** Lord, what a mornin'." FSN—WFN

My Lord, what a mourning. BB

My Lord's a-riding all the time. See My Lord's writing all the time

[My Lord's writing all the time] My Lord's a-riding all the time. Negro spiritual. HRD

My Lord's a-writin' all de time. JG

"My love crossed the sea." See Sehnsucht (Brahms)

"My love is a rider." Cowboy song. B. Starr (music and words) LSC

"My love is gone on a journey afar." See Heimlicher liebe pein (Weber)

My love, oh, she is my love. See An searc 'gá diúltugad

"My love she's but a lassie yet, a lightsome, lovely lassie yet." Air: Put up your dagger, Jamie, or, Lady Badinscoth's reel. Words by J. Hogg. GS

"My love she's but a lassie yet, my love she's but a lassie yet." Air: Put up your dagger, Jamie, or, Lady Badinscoth's reel. [Words by R. Burns] GS

"My love, still I think that I see her" (Kathleen O'More) Irish air: Kathleen O'More. Words by G. Reynolds. HI 2—HMI

My love that mourns for me. N. Giles. Words by J. Gwynneth. DNS

"My loved wife has looked for me." See Hicks's farewell (Dewey, Va. version)

"My lovely bretheren, how ye do." See Who'll jine de Union

"My lovely bride, my dearest wife." See Vandring i skoven (Grieg)

"My lovely Celia." See "My goddess Celia" (Monro)

My lovely rose. C. W. Cadman. Words by F. W. Thomas. BST

"My love's a match in beauty." See If I were king of Ireland

"My love's an arbutus." Irish air: Coola Shore, arr by C. V. Stanford. Words by A. P. Graves. AT—MBS—SSB—TFP

"My loving wife, my bosom friend." See Hicks's farewell (Burnsville, N.C. version)

"My Lulu." Old American song. SBA

[My luve is like a red, red rose] My luve's like a red, red rose (The red, red rose) Air: Graham's strathspey. Words by R. Burns. GS

[My luve is like a red, red rose] "Oh, my luve's like a red, red rose." G. M. Garrett. Words by R. Burns. TFG

My luve's like a red, red rose. See My luve is like a red, rea rose (Air: Graham's strathspey)

"My mammy's in the cold, cold ground." See Po' boy

"My man John." Somerset folk song. TFG
Variant of: Keys of heaven

My Maria. Old song. SW

"My massa and my missis." See Off to Charlestown

"My massa died a-shouting." See I'm a-trav'ling to the grave

"My match is made since e'er last night." See The dark-haired girl

"My mind to me a kingdom is." W. Byrd. Words attributed to E. Dyer. BOS 2

My mother bid me. Folk song: Barbourville, Ky. version. SES 2
—Hindman, Ky. version. SES 2
—Big Laurel, N.C. version. SES 2
—Hot Springs, N.C. version. SES 2
—Virginia version. SES 2

"My mother bids me bind my hair" ("Bind' auf dein haar") Haydn. [Words by A. Hunter] e.g. HCA

"My mother called me to her deathbed side." See Coon can

"My mother has gone to journey away." See In the kingdom

"My mother has reached the bright glory." See I heard of a city called heaven

"My mother she told me to set him a chair." See My mother bid me (Hot Springs, N.C. version)

My mother was a lady. J. W. Stern. Words by E. B. Marks. OTG
My mother was a lady (If Jack were only here) SRW

"My mother, you follow Jesus." See I wish I been dere

"My mother's gone to glory." See In bright mansions above

"My mother's name was Mary." See Mary's a grand old name (Cohan)

"My mudder, you follow Jesus." See I wish I been dere

"My name is Frank Bolar." See The Lane county bachelor

"My name is Jem, the carter lad." See Jem, the carter lad (Baker)

"My name is Paddy Leary." See Off to Philadelphia

"My name is Sal a small town gal." See The blues I've got (Reed and Neal)

"My name is Yankee Doodle and my home's the U.S.A." See Yankee Doodle-oodle (Seaver)

"My name it is Clay Morgan." See Clay Morgan

"My name it is Joe Bowers." See Joe Bowers

"My name it is Josiphus Orange Blossom." See Josiphus Orange Blossom

My Nannie, O. Scottish air. Words by Burns. GS

My native Highland home. H. R. Bishop. Words by Morton. GS

My native land ("Oh, native land, how fair you seem") E. Grieg. Words by M. K. Cherryman. BB

"My native land, again it meets my eye." See Es war ein traum (Lassen)

"My native land again once meets my eye." See Ah! 'tis a dream (Hawley)

My Normandy. See Ma Normandie (Bérat)

"My old hammah." Negro convict song. SBA
Variant of: Swannanoa town

My old Kentucky home.   S. C. Foster
(music and words)   BB—BNM
—DFF—DSB— DSC— LAS— MFS
—TFP—TFR—WSS

My old Kentucky home (Mein alt Kentucky-heim)   e.g.   ML 1

"My old missus promised me."   See Oh!
dat watermelon

"My old sweetheart, now fare you well."
See True love from the eastern shore
(Montvale, Va. version)

"My old true love from the eastern shore."
See True love from the eastern shore
(Dewey, Va. version)

My own Iona (Moi-one-Ionae)   A. Friedland and C. Morgan.   Words by L.
W. Gilbert.   OTG

My own native land.   W. B. Bradbury.
MFS

My parents treated me tenderly.   Folk
song: Barbourville, Ky. version.
SES 2

—Pine Mountain, Ky. version.   SES 2
—St Helen's, Ky. version.   SES 2
—Allanstand, N.C. version.   SES 2
—Big Laurel, N.C. version.   SES 2
—Carmen, N.C. version.   SES 2

"My partners they come after me."   See
The fateful blow

"My Patie is a love gay."   See Corn
riggs

"My pocket-book full of money."   See
The gambling man (North Carolina
version)

"My poor husband's sick with a fever."
See La firolera

"My pretty Jane."   See When the bloom
is on the rye (Bishop)

"My pretty little pink."   Traditional
American dance song.   SBA

My raft is by the shore.   See The jolly
raftsman

My Rose ("Oh, my Rose ain't white."—
Ebony song no. 2)   C. Lacy.   Words
by R. M. Stuart.   BST

My ship is on de ocean ("I'm goin' away")
Negro song.   JB 2

"My ship is on the ocean, we'll anchor by
and by."   See We'll stand the storm

"My sin is forgiven and my soul set free."
See Hear from heaven to-day

"My sister she works in a laundry."
American folk song.   SBA

"My sister's gone to glory."   See In
bright mansions above

"My son is he, no longer can I doubt it."
See "Es ist mein sohn, ich kann nicht
daran zweifeln" (Joachim)

"My song would fly, all unaided."   See
Si mes vers avaient des ailes (Hahn)

ɪ"My songs are envenomed and bitter"ɪ
Poisoned.   A. Borodine.   Words
after Heine.   ɪTr of Vergiftet sind
meine liederɪ   e.   ATS

"My sons! my sons" (see Song Index)
Also in "If Thou should'st mark
iniquities" (Costa)   SSO 4

"My soul is a witness."   See Who'll be a
witness for my Lord

"My soul rejoices."   See "Et exultavit"
(Bach)

My soul wants something that's new.
Negro spiritual.   HRD

My soul's been anchored in de Lord.
Negro spiritual.   JB 2

My sun.   See 'O sole mio (Capua)

My sunshine.   See 'O sole mio (Capua)

My sweet Adair.   A. Friedland.   Words
by L. W. Gilbert.   OTG

My sweet Anona, in Arizona.   See Anona
(Grey)

My sweetheart's the man in the moon.   J.
Thornton (music and words)   GFS

"My tears like blood are falling."   See
Jag (Rangström)

My tender musette.   See "Ô ma tendre
musette" (Monsigny?)

My Tommy's gone away.   Halliard
chantey.   TSB 2
Variants: John's gone to Hilo; Tom's
gone to Hilo

My trundle-bed.   J. C. Baker.   GOS 2
—OT

"My uncle he sells old clo'."   See Ole clo'

"My waking thoughts to thee are ever
turning."   See Jeg elsker dig (Grieg)

My way's cloudy.   Negro spiritual.
HRD—WSS

"My wealth's a burly spear."   See Song
of Hybrias the Cretan (Elliott)

"My wife and I lived all alone."   See
Little brown jug (Eastburn)

My wife's a winsome wee thing.   Air:
My wife's a wanton wee thing.
Words by R. Burns.   GS

My William.   See Volksliedchen (Schumann)

"My wings of song uplifting."   See "Auf
flügeln des gesanges" (Mendelssohn)

"My young love said to me, my mother
wont mind."   See She moved thro'
the fair

ɪMy youngest one is weddedɪ   Die
mezinke äusgegeben.   Jewish folk
song.   y.   SY
Die mesinke.   y.   KAJ

"Myriads of stars! which is my star."
See Thou knowest

A mystery of the sea.   Italian air.
Words by K. Davis.   DSB

N

N. Y. U. marching song.   New York university song.   Words by D.
Schwartz.   KU

"Na-aleh l'artsenu."   See On to our land

"Na Gorenjskem je fletno."   See In
Gorensko

ɪ"Na Ostland wil ik varen"ɪ Auswandererlied.   15th century Netherland song.
g.   EDL

"Na tom našem nátoni."   See "In des
dorfes teiche dort"

Na utro poslíe svad'by.   See Wedding-
day song

"Naar vaaren leikad borti björkelid."   See
Ein vaartankje (Sinding)

"Nach der arbeit trüber tage folgt das fest."
See A moda gallega
"Nach Frankreich zogen zwei grenadier'."
See Die beiden grenadiere (Schumann)
"Nach Madrid zieht der eine." See Pasa-
calle o marcha-alborada
"Nach Ostland wollen wir fahren." See
"Na Ostland wil ik varen"
"Nach süden nun sich lenken." See
Wanderlied der Prager studenten
Nachbar Witan ("Vítane, bane") Bul-
garian folk song. b.g. ML 2
Die nacht ("Aus dem walde tritt die nacht."
—Night) R. Strauss. Words by H.
von Gilm. e.g. TM
Nachtgruss. See Mondschein
Die nachtigall im tannenwald. Badische
volksweise. g. EDL
Nächtlicher gruss (Greeting at night)
A. M. Storch. Words by J. N. Vogl.
e.g. SFB
"Nacqui all' affanno, al pianto." See Non
più mesta accanto al fuoco (Rossini)
"Nadie me quiere" (Old maid's song)
Folk song from southern California.
e.s. HE
"Nadie se fie en tener." See La caña
"Nae mair we'll meet again." [Highland
air: Robi donna Gorach] DSB
Naff, J. W.
Do they miss me in the trenches (Gran-
nis)
Nägeli, Hans Georg
"Blest be the tie that binds"
Dennis. See "Blest be the tie that
binds"; "Heirs of unending life";
"How gentle God's commands"
"Freut euch des lebens"
"Heirs of unending life" (same air as
"Blest be the tie that binds")
"How gentle God's commands" (same
air as "Blest be the tie that binds")
Das lied vom Rhein
Life let us cherish. See "Freut euch
des lebens"
"Nagy gazda volt az apám." See "Father
was a thrifty man"
"Näh nicht, liebes mütterlein." See The
scarlet sarafan (Varlamov)
Nairn, Norman
Campus song
Nairne, Carolina (Oliphant) Nairne, bar-
oness
Bonnie Charlie (Gow?)
Caller herrin' (Gow?)
The hundred pipers (Jacobite air)
"The laird o' Cockpen" (Scottish air)
The rowan tree (Scottish air)
The land o' the leal (Scottish air)
The lass o' Gowrie (Air: Loch Erroch
Side)
O Charlie is my darling (Old Scottish
air)
"There grows a bonnie brier-bush in
oor kail-yaird, and white are the
blossoms on't" (Scottish air)
Wha'll be king but Charlie (Scottish
air)
Najveći grijesi. See Die grössten sünden

Nana (copla de cuna) (Wiegenlied) An-
dalusian folk song. g.s. ML 2
Nancy Fat. Minstrel song. PSG—
WSS
Nancy Lee. S. Adams. Words by F.
E. Weatherly. BB—GE—LAS—TFP
—US
Nancy Till. Negro song. WSS
Nanette ("Au beau clair de la lun'")
Canadian folk song. e.f. GC
Nanna (Wiegenlied) Corsican folk song.
g.i. ML 2
Napominanje k rejwanju. See Auffor-
derung zum tanze (Wendish folk song)
När sol går ner (At sunset) W. Sten-
hammar. Words by K. A. Melin.
e.sw. WM 2
Nash, Thomas
Spring (Irish air)
Nash, Will
Goin' down that long long lonesome
road
Nat (Night) S. Lund. Words by S.
Michaëlis. e.n. WM 2
Nathan, Isaac
"Where are you going, my pretty maid"
Nathan, Joe S.
The bull-frog and the coon
National hymn ("God of our fathers")
G. W. Warren. Words by D. C.
Roberts. TFG
"God of our fathers." BB
National hymn ("My country, 'tis of thee")
See America (Carey?)
[Natural history] What are little boys
made of. Folk song: Barbour-
ville, Ky. version. SES 2
—Manchester, Ky. version. SES 2
Nature's music. C. B. Edmunds. LAS
Naumann, Giovanni Amadeo. See Nau-
mann, Johann Gottlieb
Naumann, Johann Gottlieb
"Lo! the incarnate Lord"
O Lamb of God
The nautical almanac tale. See Ponce
Muir's "suns" (Gilmore)
Navy blue and gold. U.S. Naval academy
song. J. W. Crosley. AI—US
Navy team. U.S. Naval academy song.
Air: Famous King of England. US
"Nay, tell me not, dear." Irish air: Den-
nis, don't be threatening. Words by
T. Moore. HMI
"Nay, tho' my grief delights thee." See
"So che godendo vai" (Zamperelli)
Nazareth. C. Gounod (music and words)
e. GE—SSO 4
Nazarian, Esther Marbel
Cheer for alma mater
"Ne' giorni tuoi felici." G. B. Pergolesi.
e.i. KVG
Ne menj el. See Do not go (Szentirmay)
"Ne menj rózsám a tarlóra." See "Rose-
bud, to the fields art going" (Egressi)
"Ne, ne búsulj rozsám, kincsem." See
Csárdás
"Ne parlez pas tant, Lisandre." See Ça
fait peur aux oiseaux (Bernard)

Ne permettrez-vous pas, ma belle demoiselle. For English translation see The greeting (Gounod)

"**Ne** sheï ty mnîe matushka." See The scarlet sarafan (Varlamov)

"**Ne** sirj Ninám, ne könyezz." See "Weine nicht, o Nina mein"

Neal, Ethel. See Reed, N. E., jt. comp.

Neale, Arthur. See Hoffman, Dave, jt. auth.

Neale, John Mason
Christmas carol (Helmore)
"Earthly friends" (16th century German air)
January carol (Old air)
" 'Twas about the dead of night" (Composer unknown)
"The world itself keeps Easter day" (Composer unknown)

Neander, Joachim
"Praise to the Lord, the Almighty" (17th century German air)

"**Near** Bridgewater a rich man lived." See "In Seaport town" (Hyden, Ky. version)

"**Near** Buena Vista's mountain chain." See Buena Vista

"**Near** by the ramparts of Sevilla." See Séguédille (Bizet)

"**Near** Thames' green banks." See Well judging Phyllis (Boyce)

"**Near** the banks of that lone river." T. Von La Hache. Words by G. P. Morris. GOS 2

"**Near** the campfire's flick'ring light." See Now I lay me down to sleep (Allen)

"**Near** where yon surges waste the shore." See Monody (Hagen)

"**Nearer**, my God, to thee." L. Mason. Words by S. F. Adams. BB—TFP
"Nearer, my God, to Thee" (Bethany) LAS—MFS

"**Nearest** and dearest." E. Audran. e. WLO

"**Neat** ha! ha." U.S. navy song. US

" '**Neath** a leafy shelter hiding." See Pastourelle (Auguin)

" '**Neath** Colorado's azure skies, before her mountain slopes." See Colorado halls (Harrington?)

'**Neath** our flag. J. Barnby. Words by J. L. Vandevere. TFO

" '**Neath** the deep blue waters of the ocean." See La perla (Araya?)

" '**Neath** the spreading forest trees." See Frühlingslied (Mendelssohn)

"**Nechod** tam." See "Geh nicht fort"

Neckens polska (Der Nöck) Swedish folk song. ｢Words by A. A. Afzelius」 g.sw. ML 1

｢De **nederige** geboorte」 Flemish carol. e. OB

Negers heimweh. See The old folks at home (Foster)

Negro battle hymn. See The enlisted soldiers

Negro reel ("Laws-a-massey") Kentucky and Tennessee folk song. SBA

Neht a schneider. Jewish folk song. y. SY

Neidhardt von Reuenthal
In praise of May. See Sommerlied
Sommerlied

"**Neighbour**, what was the sound, I pray." See Voisin, d'où venait ce grand bruit

Neil Gow's farewell to whisky. N. Gow. Words by A. Lyon. GS

"**Nein**, ich will von morgen." See "Jag tror jag får börja öfverge att sörja"

Nein mame, nein mitter. Jewish folk song. y. KAJ

Nein, mameschu, nein. See "Yome, Yome"

Nel dolce incanto. Benedict. e.i. PC

Nell and I. S. C. Foster (music and words) SW—WSS

Nell' orror di notte oscura. Rinaldo da Capua. e.i. KVG

Nella. See Parker, Mrs Nella

"**Nella** fatal di Rimini." Donizetti. e.i. PC

Nella stanza, che romita. See "Questo sacro, augusto stemma" (Donizetti)

"**Nelli** monti de Cuscioni v'era natu una zitedra." See Nanna

"**Nelly** Bly." S. C. Foster (music and words) BNM—WSS

Nelly was a lady. S. C. Foster (music and words) WSS
Nellie was a lady. BNM—TFB—TFO—TFP

Nelson, Ed G. See Pease, Harry, jt. comp. and auth.

Nelson, Robert H.
"As I sit and dream at evening"

Nelson, Sydney
The greenwood tree
Mary of Argyle
The rose of Allandale

"**Nem** volt párja a faluban." See "There was none to match Kerekes"

Németh, János. See Szentirmay, Elemér

"**Nennè**, guè guè frabotta." See Serenata di Pulcinello

"**Nenné**, see, see, look yonder." See Serenata di Pulcinello

Nesbit, Edith. See Bland, Mrs Edith (Nesbit)

"**Nesem** vám noviny" (Weihnachtslied) Bohemian Christmas song. bo.g. ML 3

"**Nessun** maggior piacere" ("No joy could be more thrilling") H. Berlioz. Words adapted from Dante. e.i. GA

Nestler, Friedrich
Entschuldigung

Neujahrslied. For English translation see The last hour of the year (Schulz)

Neupert, Edmund
"Sing me home." See "Syng mig hjaem"
"Syng mig hjaem"

"**Neutras** glocken läuten laut" ("Ty nitranské hodiny") Slovak folk song. g.sl. ML 3

"**Nevada**, my Nevada." University of Nevada song. C. Haseman. Words by J. R. Glascock. AI—AIS—KU

"**Nevadte** se." See "Seid nicht böse"

Never alone. F. Silcher. Words by R. W. Raymond. MFS

Never fear, give a cheer for Colgate. See Colgate marching song

Never mind. Chinese folk air. Words by T. Stanley. TFR

"Never said a mumblin' word" (see Song Index)
Variant: Crucifixion

"Never saw such a man before." See Daniel saw the stone

Never say fail. MFS

Never tell them what you were once upon a time. See It's not what you were, it's what you are to-day (Marion)

"Never to cry over what is past." See Don't let it happen again

Never trouble trouble, till trouble troubles you. See A motto for all

Neverni dragī. See "O bright sun"

Nevin, George Balch
O liebes mütterlein. See O little mother of mine
O little mother of mine

"The next come down was dressed in red." See Little Musgrave and Lady Barnard (Rocky Fork, Tenn. version)

"New-blown mushrooms, white and luscious." See Gathering mushrooms (Musorgskiĭ)

New-born again. Negro spiritual from South Carolina. FSN

De new-born baby. Christmas song of the negro fishermen of Charleston, S.C. FSN

The new born Child. Old French (Flanders) air. FC

The new bully. See The bully song (Trevathan)

A new dial. 16th century carol. OB

"New England, New England." <I. T. Stoddard> GOS 1

The new hail Columbia. See Hail Columbia, The new (Phile)

The new Irish girl. See The Irish girl

The new moon ("Se solen var splitrad") See Ny-måne (Sinding)

New Prince, new pomp. J. Ireland. Words by R. Southwell. OB

A New Year, a New Year, a Child was yborn. See So blessed be the time

New Year wishes ("East, west or north or south") Chinese folk song. e. MFF

The New Year's come. J. P. Knight. Words by J. B. Phillips. HP

The New Year's day visit. See La visite du jour de l'an

New Year's song ("The old year is dying") See "The old year is dying"

[Newcastle] "Come you not from Newcastle." 17th century song. CSB 2

Newcombe, Bobby
Love letters

Newell, George
Robinson Crusoe's story
See also Carryl, Charles Edward, jt. auth.

Newman, John Henry
"Lead, kindly light" (music by Dykes; Pinsuti)
"The news frae Moidart cam' yestreen." See Wha'll be king but Charlie

Newton, Eddie
Casey Jones

Newton, Elbridge Ward
An old-time celebration

Newton, John
"Safely through another week" (Mason)

The next market day. Irish air from Ulster county. Words from a Tyrone ballad. HI 1

Nezadovoljstvo. See Klage

"Nézzél csak a szemembe." See "Look into my eye, come near"

Niagara Falls. Folk song from Kentucky. SES 2

Nicaea. See "Holy, holy, holy! Lord God Almighty" (Dykes)

Nicholson, Richard
Cuckoo

Nicholson, Sydney Hugo
Welcome Yule

Nickernacks. Traditional song: Lancashire version. BOS 2

Nicodé, Jean Louis
Fata morgana

Nicodemus Johnson. [J. B. Murphy] SW—WSS

"Nicodemus, the slave, was of African birth." See Wake Nicodemus (Work)

Nicolai, Philipp
Sleepers, wake (Bach. Tr of Wachet auf)
"What tongue can tell Thy greatness, Lord" (Old air)
Wie schon leuchtet der morgenstern (16th century German air)

"Nid oes rhyngof ag ef heno." See Hiraeth

"Nie to, nie to v šírom svete milšieho." See "Keiner, auch nicht einer in der weiten welt"

"Nie war hoch am himmel." See Sea of stars (Elek)

Nielsen, August Carl
The eagle. See Høgen
Høgen
Irmelin Rose

Niemand hat's geseh'n (No one saw at all) C. Loewe. Words by Gruppe. e.g. AT

Niemann, August
Weihelied (Student song)

Niembsch, Nicolaus Franz, edler von Strehlenau. See Lenau, Nicolaus

Nies, Grace Sue
Cheer for alma mater (Nazarian)
"De niggers from de souf, ha, ha." See Laughing song

"Nigh to a grave that was newly made." See The old sexton (Russell)

Night ("Aus dem walde") See Die nacht (Strauss)

The night ("Holl amrantau'r sêr, dywedant") See Ar hyd y nos (Owen)

Night ("Jeg stirrer i den stille nat") See Nat (Lund)

₁Night ("O thou silent")₁ "Akh, ty no-chen'ka" ("Ach, du liebe nacht") Russian folk song. 2d air. g.r. ML 1

Night ("The sun descending in the west") French air. Words by W. Blake. DSB

Night ("The sunset glows") F. Abt. Words by M. K. Cherryman. BB

Night and day ("Silence inviting weary hearts to rest") C. F. Manney. Words by A. Westbrook. BST

"Night closed around." See After the battle

"Night comes and finds me, Lord." See Trusting in Thee (Coverley)

"The night fell fast upon the wold." See The good Shepherd (Slater)

Night herding song. Cowboy song. LSC

A night in March. See In der märznacht (Taubert)

"Night of nights." Christmas song. B. Van de Water (music and words) TSS 1—TSS 2

Night song ("Gently the breezes blow thro' the forest") Swedish folk song. e. DSC—GSS

Night song ("O'er the quiet meadow") Russian air: Vanya. Words by K. Davis. DSB

"The night was dark and fearful." See The watcher (Lardner)

"Night was hov'ring gloomy, gloomy." See "Era notte oscura, oscura" (Fioravanti)

"A night was near, a day was near." See A hope carol (Smith)

The nightingale ("Far away the nightingale now flieth") P. I. Tchaikovsky (music and words) e. SR

The nightingale ("One morning, one morning") Folk song: Berea, Ky. version. SES 2

—Pine Mountain, Ky. version no. 1. SES 2

—St Helen's, Ky. version no. 1. SES 2
—St Helen's, Ky. version no. 2. SES 2
—Tennessee version. SES 2
One morning in May. Pine Mountain, Ky. version no. 2. SBA

Nightingale canon. W. A. Mozart. CSB 2

"The nightingale is singing." French folk song. e. DSB

The nightingale's song ("Par derrièr' chez ma tante") See Le prisonnier de Hollande (Canadian version)

Night's shadows gloomy this lone vale now cover. See O du mein holder abendstern (Wagner)

"Niin musta niin synkkä yö syksyinen lie." See Melancholy (Merikanto)

Nikolaev, Leonid Vladimirovich
Dawn of night

"Nimm diesen abschiedsgruss, ich muss nun gehen." See Canzuna di li carriteri

"Nimm hin diesen schmuck." See Perlen (Sinding)

"Nimmer hören die espenblätter." See Die espenblätter

₁Nina₁ "Tre giorni son che Nina" (Fair Nina) <L. V. Ciampi; wrongly attributed to G. B. Pergolesi> e.i. GA

La niña desenvuelta (Der wildfang) Catalan folk song. ca.g. ML 2

"Nincsen annyi tenger csillag." See Sea of stars (Elek)

"Nincsen nekem jobb tanyám." See "Weiss kein bessres lager mir"

The ninety and nine. I. D. Sankey. Words by E. C. Clephane. MFS

Ninety years, without slumbering. See Grandfather's clock (Work)

Ninna di Borgia (Wiegenlied) Calabrian folk song. g.i. ML 2

Ninna-nanna ("A ninna ninna."—Wiegenlied) Calabrian folk song. g.i. ML 2

Ninna-nanna ("Schlafe, mein prinzchen") See Wiegenlied (Mozart)

Nique nac no muse. See "La bell', si nous étiom' dedans"

Nish, Anthony
Hoop de dooden do

"Nit kein gebetene." See The uninvited aunt

The Nittany lion. Pennsylvania state college song. J. A. Leyden. AI—AIS

No bread for the poor. See The orphan girl

"No, by my mother's soul." Finale from I pagliacci. R. Leoncavallo. ₁Tr of No, per mia madre₁ e. WG

No, caso egual giammai. See Non, non, non, vous n'avez jamais (Meyerbeer)

"No doubt you have heard of the great fancy fair." See O! Fred, tell them to stop (Meen)

No-e in the ark. See entry under Noe

"No figueiral figueiredo." See Canção do figueiral

"No heart can think, no tongue can tell." See 'Tis a wonder

"No home, no home, cried an orphan girl." See The orphan girl

"No joy could be more thrilling." See "Nessun maggior piacere" (Berlioz)

No man can hinder me. Negro spiritual from South Carolina. AS

No matter, no matter (Ein dovor, ein dovor) Palestinean folk song. e.he. BNP

"No me mireis ni mi busqueis os ruego." See La desgracia

No more a tear, alas. See Ah! non avea più lagrime (Donizetti)

"No more auction block for me." See Many thousand gone

No more booze (Fireman save my child) American song. SBA

"No more in Sion let the virgin throng." See Wise men flatt'ring may deceive you (Händel)

No more lonely, hopeless waiting. See Non più mesta accanto al fuoco (Rossini)

No more, no more, no more for ever. See MacCrimmon's lament

"No more of drum or trumpet sounding." Final chorus. E. Audran. e. WLO

"No more peck o' corn for me." See Many thousand go

"No more rain fall for wet you." Negro spiritual from South Carolina. AS

No more rivers ("We've got a hell of a way to go") U.S. Naval academy song. US

"No more weeping and a-wailing." See Soon I will be done

"No navy for mine." U.S. navy song. US

"No, no, no, no, no, no, caso egual giammai." See Non, non, non, vous n'avez jamais (Meyerbeer)

"No, no, no, no, no, no, ne'er hath page, I'll wager." See Non, non, non, vous n'avez jamais (Meyerbeer)

"No, no, Turiddu." P. Mascagni. e. WG

"No, not more welcome." Irish air: Luggelaw. Words by T. Moore. HMI

"No one e'er has seen or divin'd them." See Les larmes (Godard)

No one saw at all. See Niemand hat's geseh'n (Loewe)

No one to help me, no one to bless. See Driven from home (Hays)

"No one to love." W. B. Harvey. Words by A. H. G. Richardson. GOS 2

No, per mia madre. For English translation see "No, by my mother's soul" (Leoncavallo)

No room in the inn ("When Caesar Augustus had raised a taxation") Traditional carol. OB

No sir ("Tell me one thing") A. M. Wakefield. WSS

No sorrow like to His. G. A. Hasse. e. SSO 4

"No star is o'er the lake its pale watch keeping." See The long day closes (Sullivan)

"No, they say." See "Is it true, then"

No use talkin', no use talkin'. See Folks that put on airs

No use talkin' when de nigga wants to go. See Way down souf (Foster)

"No word from thee, in gladness or in sorrow" ("Kein wort von dir, der freude oder klage") P. Tschaikowsky. Words from the Russian of Tolstoi. e.g. TM

[Noah] "Als Noah aus dem kasten war" (Historia von Noah) C. G. Reissiger. Words by A. Kopisch. g. EDL

Noah's ark ("Old Noah he built") Negro spiritual. BB—WSS
There's one more river. GSS
Variant: One more river

Noah's ark ("Some say Noah was a foolish old man") (see Song Index)
Variant: No-e in the ark

"Nobil donna è tanto onesta" ("Sweeter than the breath of morning") Meyerbeer. e.i. MFS

"The noble man." Folk song from North Carolina. SES 2

["Nobles seigneurs, salut"] "Lieti signor, salute." G. Meyerbeer. e.i. PC

Nobody knows the trouble I see ("Sometimes I'm up") Negro spiritual: familiar version. FSN—GSS— TFG
Nobody knows. TFO
Nobody knows de trouble I see. JB 2 —WFN
Nobody knows de trouble I've seen. HRD—WSS
Nobody knows the trouble I've seen. BB—MFS
Variant: Nobody knows the trouble I've had

Nobody knows the trouble I've had ("One morning I was a-walking down") Negro spiritual from South Carolina. AS
Variant of: Nobody knows the trouble I see

Nobody knows who I am. See Heav'n bells a-ringin' in mah soul

"Nobody loves me, I don't know why." See "Nadie me quiere"

Nobody's child. A. Lee. Words by F. W. Green. SW

Nobody's darling. Old American song. SW

"Noch bin ich nicht dein" ("Ešte me nemáš") Czech folk song. bo.g. ML 3

"Noch jung und ledig war ich" ("Kol jauns nevedęs buvau") Lithuanian folk song. g.li. ML 3

"Noch shabbos im yirzoh 'Shem." See Der eisenbahn

Der Nöck. See Neckens polska

No-e in the ark. Kentucky mountain song. SES 2
Variant of: Noah's ark ("Some say Noah was a foolish old man")

Noël ("Minuit, chrétien") See Cantique de Noël (Adam)

Noël de Strasbourg (Christmas carol of Strassburg) Alsatian carol. e.f. CBF 1

Noël des quêteurs bressans (Noël of the Bressan waits) Bressan air. Words by M. Duhamel. e.f. ASN

Noël of the Bressan waits. See Noël des quêteurs bressans

Nolan, Michael
Annie Roonie. See Little Annie Rooney
Little Annie Rooney

"Non dar più pene, o caro." A. Scarlatti. Words by G. B. Lucini. e.i. KVG

[Non è ver] 'Tis not true. T. Mattei. e. GE

"Non nobis, Domine." Canon. W. Byrd. 1. MBS—TFG

[Non, non, non, vous n'avez jamais] No, caso egual giammai. G. Meyerbeer. e.i. PC

"Non piango e non sospiro." G. Caccini. Words by Rinuccini. e.i. KVG

"**Non** più andrai." A. Mozart. e.i. PB

Non più mesta accanto al fuoco. G. Rossini. e.i. PC

"**Non** so più cosa son." Mozart. e.i. PC

Non son io che la condanno. See "Qui m'accolse oppresso, errante" (Bellini)

"**None** but the lonely heart." See "Nur wer die sehnsucht kennt" (Tchaikovsky)

None can tell. G. B. Allen. Words by W. H. Emra. MFS

"**None** of all the many stars." See Sea of stars (Elek)

Das **nönnchen**. See La monacella

Das **nönnlein** und der teufel. See La monachella e il demonio

The **noontide** ray (Fairies' song) Auber. MFS

Norah O'Neale ("I'm lonely to-night, love, without you") Irish air from County Derry. Traditional words. HI 2

Norah, the pride of Kildare. J. Parry (music and words) SI

"**Normandy** pippin's good all over." See Cider song (Planquette)

Norris, Bonnie F.
Alma mater—North Carolina state college

North, Christopher, pseud. See Wilson, John, 1785-1854

"A **north** country lass up to London did pass." See The oak and the ash

North Dakota hymn. North Dakota agricultural college song. C. S. Putnam. Words by J. W. Foley. HW

"**North** Dakota, North Dakota, with thy prairies wide and free." See North Dakota hymn (Putnam)

North Dakota U. University of North Dakota song. F. Rickaby (music and words) HW

Northwestern push on song. Northwestern university song. D. G. Robertson (music and words) AI—AIS

Norton, Mrs Caroline Elizabeth Sarah (Sheridan)
Juanita (Spanish air)
"Love not! love not" (Blockley)

Norton, J.
"Out of the window"

Nos galan. Welsh New Year's eve carol. e. OB

"**Not** crying am I, nor sighing." See "Non piango e non sospiro" (Caccini)

"**Not** England's daughters rosy cheeked." See The Yankee girls

Not for Joe. See Not for Joseph (Lloyd)

Not for Joseph (Joe). A. Lloyd (music and words) SRW

"**Not** in halls of regal splendor." See In excelsis gloria

"**Not** ma brother, it's-a me, O Lord." See It's me, O, Lord

Not made with hands. See "I know I have another building"

"**Not** my brother, (no) it's a-me, O Lord." See It's me, O Lord

Not weary yet. Negro spiritual from South Carolina. AS

"**Nothing** now divides us lovers." See Hiraeth

Notre Seigneur en pauvre (see Song Index) Variant of: Le parabole du mauvais riche

Nottamun town. Folk song: Hindman, Ky. version no. 1. SES 2
—Hindman, Ky. version no. 2. SES 2
Variant: Fair Nottiman town

ιNouèl des ausèlsι Carol of the birds. 17th century carol from Bas-Quercy. e. FC

Nous avons hélas! perdu d'excellents maitres. For English translation see Legend of the bell (Planquette)

"**Nous** sommes venus vous voir." See La chanson de la mariée

Nous voici dans la ville (In the town) 15th century French carol. e. OB

Novello, Ivor
Keep the home fires burning

"**Now** a balmy air over the meadow sighs." See Frühlingslied (Fielitz)

"**Now** a long good-bye to you, my dear." See Good morning, ladies all

Now ain't dat hard trials, great tribulation. See Hard trials

Now all the bells ιare ringingι ιJ. B. Dykesι MFS

"**Now** April has come." See April

"**Now** before the dance is done." See Midsummer dance

"**Now** blessèd be thou, Christ Jesu." See Gelobet seist du Jesu Christ

"**Now** brothers lift your voices." See So, brother

"**Now** college men from sea to sea." See Navy blue and gold (Crosley)

"**Now,** come to me, ye sirens." F. Lehar. e. WLO

"**Now** comrades, fill your glasses." See Sweethearts and wives (Smith)

"**Now** darkies, listen to me." See Dearest Mae (Crosby)

"**Now** every child that dwells on earth." See Our brother is born (Farjeon)

"**Now** for a cheer, they are here, triumphant." See The victors (Elbel)

"**Now,** from the rising of the sun." See A solis ortus cardine

"**Now** give the army breath" (see Song Index)
Also in "Heroes, when the glory burning" (Händel) SSO 2

"**Now** glad of heart." See Wir wollen alle fröhlich sein (Praetorius)

"**Now** having, not without defect." Final chorus of La grande duchesse. J. Offenbach. ιTr of Après avoir, tant bien que malι e. WLO

"**Now** heaven in fullest glory." J. Haydn. e. SSO 4

"**Now** here I am, a-gwine to sing." See Piccayune Butler

"**Now** hope renew'd." G. Verdi. ιTr of Possente amor mi chiamaι e. WG

"**Now** how I came to get this hat." See Where did you get that hat (Sullivan)

Now I hate to tell. See Love among the roses

Now I lay me down to sleep ("Near the campfire's flick'ring light") H. R. Allen. MFS

"Now I'll sing." See The ten commandments (Asheville, N.C. version)

"Now in joy or sorrow." B. Smetana. e. WLO

"Now in the summer of life sweetheart." See Will you love me in December as you do in May (Ball)

"Now is Christemas y-come." See The golden carol (Williams)

"Now is the hour of darkness past." See Christ the Lord is risen

"Now is the month of Maying." T. Morley. DSB—MBS—TFG

Now, just try it nightly. See Kollege kick (Hagen)

"Now let every tongue adore Thee." See Sleepers, wake (Bach)

Now let good Christians all begin. See "The Lord at first did Adam make"

"Now let me alone, tho' I know you won't." See Barney O'Hea (Lover)

"Now let the trumpet." G. Verdi. [Tr of Squilli echeggi la tromba guerriera] e. WG

"Now listen unto this my song." See The infantry song

"Now listen what I'se gwan to say." See Jim Crow's polka

"Now melts the snow, the blossoms blow." Round. F. Schubert. CSB 2

"Now my friends we'll all be gay." See Marriage bells chorus (Audran)

"Now, my lad, we are married." See Will the weaver (Hyden, Ky. version)

"Now, my lads, be of good cheer." See Whoop jamboree

"Now nature cleeds the flow'ry lea." See Lassie wi' the lint-white locks

"Now 'neath the silver moon ocean is glowing." See Santa Lucia

"Now niggahs, listen to me." See Dearest Mae (Crosby)

"Now night's dark shades appear." See A song of night

"Now no more may we, lovesick philander, round the bowers of beauty meander." See "Non più andrai" (Mozart)

"Now, now, from the east, the east." See Cloud song

"Now, now, soldier, won't you marry me." See Soldier, won't you marry me (Kentucky version)

"Now on this good ship ——." See Transport song

"Now once I did court a most charming beauty bright." See The lover's lament (Tennessee version)

"Now our golden days are at an end." See Farewell to thee (Liliuokalani)

"Now poets may sing of the dear fatherland." See Down where the Wurzburger flows (Von Tilzer)

"Now quit your care and anxious fear and worry." See White Lent

"Now rejoice in God thy Saviour." C. H. Graun. e. SSO 1

"Now, Robin, laugh and sing." M. Peerson. CSB 4

"Now, Robin, lend to me thy bow." 16th century song. TFP

"Now rosy May comes in wi' flow'rs." See Dainty Davie

"Now show me the lady that never would roam." See Hush-a-bye, baby

"Now simmer blinks on flow'ry braes." See The birks of Aberfeldy

"Now sing we of the Paraclete." See Song of the spirit

"Now, soldier, soldier, will you marry me." See Soldier, won't you marry me (Tennessee version)

"Now thank we all our God." See Nun danket alle Gott (Crüger)

"Now the Chesapeake so bold sailed from Boston." See The Chesapeke and the Shannon

"Now the day is over." J. Barnby. Words by S. Baring-Gould. BB—TFB —TFG—TFR

"Now the day is over" (Merrial) TFO

"Now the day is over" (Twilight) GSS

"Now the end of all things neareth." Haydn. e. SSO 4

"Now the green blade riseth." See Love is come again

"Now the holly bears a berry." See Sans Day carol

"Now the joyful bells a-ringing." See Nos galan

"Now the king we hail." J. Strauss. e. WLO

"Now the merry vintage closes." E. Audran. e. WLO

"Now the shades of night are gone." H. Morsell. CSS 1

"Now the spring has come again." See In vernali tempore

"Now the winter's come to stay." See Dans les chantiers

"Now they were married, returning home again." See The lady and the dragoon (Burnsville, N.C. version)

"Now walking John was a big rope hoss." See Walking John

"Now we are met, let mirth abound." See Catch round the table (Webbe)

"Now welcome, summer, with thy sunne soft." See Welcome, summer

Now we're hunky dory. See Hunky dory (Holzmann)

"Now when the lumber camp is done." See Envoyons d'l'avant, nos gens

"Now where are all the gay raftmen." See Les raftsmen

"Now winged hours" (Minuet) W. A. Mozart. KSO

"Now with creation's morning song" (Morning song) L. van Beethoven. Words by A. Clemens Prudentius. [Tr of Lux ecce surgit aurea] e. DSB

Nowell, Nowell ("The boar's head that we bring here") R. Smert. DNS

Nowell, Nowell, now sing a Saviour's birth. See The Babe of Bethlehem

Nowell, Nowell, Nowell, Nowell, born is the King of Israel. See "The first Nowell"

Nowell, Nowell, Nowell, Nowell, sing all we may. See "A Child this day is born"

Nowell! Nowell! Nowell! Nowell sing we clear. See "Masters in this hall"

Nowell, Nowell, Nowell, Nowell! This is the salutacyon of the angel Gabriel (The salutation carol) 15th century English song. OB
The salutation of the angel Gabriel. DNS

Nowell, Nowell, Nowell, Nowell! Tidings good I think to tell. See Nowell, Nowell (Smert)

Nowell, Nowell, Nowell, sing we with mirth. See New Prince, new pomp (Ireland)

"Nowell sing we, both all and some." See All and some

"Now's the time when o'er the green grass." See Renouveau

"Nu faelder sit løv den ahorn" ("The maples their leaves are shedding") P. E. Lange-Müller. Words from a Slovak folk song. da.e. WM 2

"Nu visner skoven atter." See Afsked (Melartin)

Die nudeln. See I maccheroni

"Number one, number one, some likes cake and some likes bun." See Owd Joe Braddles

"Numi, che intesi mai." See Se m'abbandoni, bella speranza (Mercadante)

"Nun ade, du mein herzliebchen." See Nun ade, mein herzliebchen

"Nun ade, du mein lieb heimatland." See Lieb heimatland, ade

Nun ade, mein herzliebchen ("Srečno, srečno, ljub'ca moja") Slovenian folk song. g.slo. ML 2

Nun beut die flur das frische grün. For English translation see "With verdure clad the fields appear" (Haydn)

Nun danket alle Gott ("Now thank we all our God") J. Crüger. Words by M. Rinkart. e. MFS
"Now thank we all our God." e. BB—DSB—DSC—MBS

Nun fürwahr, fürwahr. For English translation see "See what grace" (Flotow)

"Nun genug geschmauset." See Wojewode manusch

"Nun leb' wohl, du kleine gasse." See In der ferne (Silcher)

"Nun, mein lieb Druidenkind." See Ar rannou

Nun sei bedankt, mein lieber schwan. For English translation see Swan song (Wagner)

"Nun so reis ich weg von hier." See Abschied von der geliebten

Nuori neito. See Die spröde

Nuova ferita. Mercadante. e.i. PB

Nur du. 15th century German folk song. g. EDL
Minnelied (Old love song) e.g. GG

Nur in Deutschland ("Zwischen Frankreich und dem Böhmerland") J. W. Lyra. Words by Hoffmann von Fallersleben. g. EDL

"Nur wer die sehnsucht kennt" ("None but the lonely heart") P. Tchaikovsky. Words by Goethe. e.g. GG

Nuremberg (Bach) See "Praise to God, immortal praise"

"Nut brown maiden, thou hast a bright blue eye for love." College song. BB—TFB—TFO

Ny-måne (The new moon) C. Sinding. From the Hindustani of Igbal. e.sw. WM 2

"Nyisd ki rózsám." See "Open, dearest"

Nymphs of air and sea. H. Smart. MFS

"Nyt ylös, sieluni." See Finnish hymn

"Nyugszik a nap." See Do not go (Szentirmay)

"Nyugtasd rajtam." See "Turn upon my worn and weary face" (Szentirmay)

O

"O a bulgine once was a heaving." See Run, let the bulgine run

"Oh, a hero's life I sing." See Hamlet, prince of Denmark

"O, a little talk wid Jesus, makes it right, all right." See A little talk wid Jesus makes it right

"Oh, a shantyman's life is a wearisome life." See The shanty-man's life

"Oh a ship she was fitted out ready for sea." See Blow the man down

"Oh, a ship she was rigg'd, and ready for sea." See The fishes

"Oh, a short time ago, boys." See The Irish jubilee (Lawlor)

"Oh, a wan cloud was drawn." See The foggy dew

"Oh a whisper is this same slander." See "La calunnia è un venticello" (Rossini)

"O Adam, where are you." See What a trying time

"O Ah drove three mules foh Gawge Mc-Vane." See Mule skinner's song

"Oh, Allister MacAllister." See Allister MacAllister

"O alte burschenherrlichkeit." See Rückblick

Oh, am I the boss. See The governor-general or a hobo

"O am I the doctor you sent for so shy." See The brown girl (Manchester, Ky. version)

Oh, Amherst, brave Amherst. See Lord Geoffrey Amherst (Hamilton)

Oh, Arabella. Old song. SW

"O are you weeping for my gold." See The daemon lover (Flag Pond, Tenn. version no. 2)

"O around the corner we will go." See Round the corner, Sally

"O as I walked down the landing stage." See We're all bound to go

"Oh, as I went down to Dover." See On a summer day

"O ask of the stars above you." See "Pregúntale a las estrellas"

"O, at my lady's feet." See "O del mio dolce ardor" (Gluck)

"O Awjinula, schönes kind." See Awjinula

"O babes, O babes, if you was mine." See The cruel mother (Tennessee version)

"O baby, O baby, if you were mine." See The cruel mother (Woodridge, Va. version)

"O baby, where you been so long." See Levee moan

"O Bangum would a-hunting ride." See Sir Lionel (Berea, Ky. version)

"Oh banner of our country." See To our flag

"O barber, spare those hairs." See Barber, spare those hairs (Russell)

"O Barb'ra Buck is my sweetheart's name." See Barbara Buck

"O bay of Dublin" (Bay of Dublin) Old air. Words by H. S. Dufferin. SI

"O beautiful banner all splendid with stars." See The flag going by

"O beautiful for spacious skies." See America, the beautiful (MacFarlane); America, the beautiful (Ward)

"Oh beautiful Major Gilfeather." See Major Gilfeather (Braham)

Oh, beauty, beauty ("Hoi, hoi, yfe'fiyo") Palestinean folk song. e.he. BNP

"O beauty, O daughter of the Galilee hills." See Oh, beauty, beauty

O Behring sea, bleak Behring sea. See Behring sea song (Sweney)

Oh! Belle, don't you tell. See Lou'siana Belle (Foster)

"O Betsy be a lady fair." See Betsy

Oh, Beulah land, sweet Beulah land. See Beulah land (Sweney)

Ô bienheureuse nuit ("A star, radiantly bright") Basse-Normandy carol. e. DN

"O night, peaceful and blest." e. FC

"O Billy Riley." Halliard chantey. TSB 2
Variant of: Billy Riley

"Oh! blame not the bard." Irish air: Kitty Tyrrell. Words by T. Moore. HMI

"Oh! blest be the days when the green banner floated." See Saint Patrick's day

"Oh! blow, my boys, I long to hear you." See Blow, boys, blow

Oh, blow the man down, bullies. See Blow the man down

"O Boney has gone to the wars of old fighting." See Boney's defeat

"Oh, Boney was a warrior, ah, hilonday." See Hilonday

"O, Boney was a warrior, away-ay-ah, a warrior, a terior." See Boney

"Oh Boney was a warrior, way-ay-oh! Oh Boney was a warrior." See "Boney was a warrior"

O bonnie, bonnie, Mary Gray. See Bonnie Mary Gray (Lee)

Oh, boys, Belle's a beauty. See Belle ob Baltimore (Evans)

Oh! boys, carry me 'long. S. Foster (music and words) MFS—WSS

"Oh! breathe not his name." Irish air: Callin down, or, The brown maid. Words by T. Moore. HMI

Oh! bretheren, my way, my way's cloudy. See My way's cloudy

["O bright sun"] "Sunce jarko" (Neverni dragī.—Der untreue) Serbian folk song. g.se. ML 2
Supplication to the sun ("Sunce jarko") e.se. CJ

"Oh, bring the wagon home, John." See Bring the wagon home, John

"Oh! bring to me the fragrant mignonette." See Allerseelen (Lassen)

"Oh, broad land." Children's song. MFS

"O brother, can you toss the stone." See The two brothers (St Helen's, Ky. version)

"Oh, brother how d'ye feel." See If you want to see Jesus

"O brother, O brother, play ball with me." See The two brothers (Barbourville, Ky. version no. 1)

"Oh, brother, you must bow so low." See Let de heaven light shine on me

"O brother, you ought t'have been there." See Roll, Jordan, roll

"O brothers, don't get weary." Negro spiritual from Florida. AS

"O brothers, won't you help me." See I'm a rolling

"Oh, brothers, you ought t'have been there." See Roll, Jordan, roll

"Oh! brothers you oughter been dere." See Roll, Jordan, roll

O brown Rosey, the rose ob Alabama. See The rose of Alabama

"Oh, brudder, you must bow so low." See Let de heaven light shine on me

"O bury me beneath the willow." Mountain folk song. SBA
Variant of: The weeping willow

"O bury me not in the lone prairie. These words came low and mournfully." See The lonesome prairie (Burnsville, N.C. version no. 1)

"Oh, bury me not on the lone prairie, these words came low and mournfully." See The dying cowboy

"Oh, bury me not on the lone prairie, where the wild kiyotes will howl o'er me." Cowboy song. SBA
Variant of: The dying cowboy

O, by an' by. See By an' by

"Oh! calm was the lake of Coolfin on that day." See The lake of Coolfin

"O, can ye sew cushions." Scottish folk song. CSB 2

Oh Canaan, bright Canaan. See Canaan

"O Canada." C. Lavallée. Words by A. B. Routhier. e.f. MBS. e. on-ly LAS

"Oh, captain! where are you boun' for." See Steamboat song

"Oh! carry me 'long." See Oh! boys, carry me 'long (Foster)

"O cessate di piagarmi" ("Cease, oh, cease") V. A. Scarlatti. e.i. BST

"O cessate di piagarmi" ("Oh, no longer seek to pain me") e.i. SAT

"O Challo, in the morning." See Challo Brown

O Charley he's a fine young man. See Weevily wheat

O Charlie is my darling ("'Twas on a Mon-day morning") Jacobite air. Old song with original words. GS

O Charlie is my darling ("'Twas on a Mon-day morning") Jacobite air. Old song [with additional words by R. Burns] GS

O Charlie is my darling ("'Twas on a Mon-day morning") Jacobite air. Old song with additional words by Nairne. DSB—GS
Charlie is my darlin'. TFB
Charlie is my darling. CSB 6—SSB

O Charlie is my darling ("When first his standard caught the eye") Jacobite air. Words by C. Gray. GS

"Oh, children, do you think it's true." See Walk you in the light

"Oh, Christ, He is the fountain." See My King of grace (Tosti)

ô ciel malheureux Grenicheux. For Eng-lish translation see "Cold sweat is on my brow" (Planquette)

"O clap your hands, mountains." See The Lord hath arisen

"Oh clear the way, V. M. I. is out to-day." See V. M. I. spirit (Bowering)

"O Columbia, the gem of the ocean." See Columbia, the gem of the ocean (Becket)

O Columbina. For English translation see Serenade (Leoncavallo)

"O Columbine, unbar to me, thy lattice high." See Serenade (Leoncavallo)

"O come, all ye faithful." See "Adeste fideles" (Reading?)

"Oh, come along boys, and listen to my tale." See The Chisholm trail

"Oh, come along, brothers, come along." See We are almost home

"O come and sing a song." See Girl scout's goodbye round (Davis)

"O come, come along, come, come along." See Dance song

"O come, come away." <Words by W. E. Hickson> MFS

O! come da quèl dì. See Ah! quel giorno (Rossini)

"O come, dear sister, and let's take a walk." See The two sisters (Burns-ville, N.C. version no. 3)

[O come let us worship] "O worship the King." J. M. Haydn. Words by R. Grant. BB
"O worship the King" (Lyons) LAS —TFP

"Oh! come let's sing Ohio's praise." See Carmen Ohio

"O come, list awhile, and you soon shall hear." See The female smuggler

"O come my brethren and sisters too." See On to glory

"O come, my brethren, one an' all." See General roll call

"O come my chillun, sing sweet an' low." See I've no time to be a-sighin' (Mc-Call)

"O come, my loving Riley." See Loving Reilly (North Carolina version)

"O come, O come, Emmanuel." See Veni Emmanuel

"Oh, come on mo'ners an' git you ready, ready." See Rise and shine

"O come, sweet slumber." Round. L. van Beethoven. CSB 4

"Oh, come to the field." See Harvest home

"Oh, come with me in my little canoe." See Ossian's serenade (Dodge)

"O come you home, dear Johnny." See The green bed (North Carolina ver-sion)

"O come you home, my own true love." See The daemon lover (Hot Springs, N.C. version no. 1)

"Oh! comrades, have you seen the ban-ners." See The year of jubilo (Work)

"Oh, could our thoughts." German air. Words by A. Steele. MFS

O could we ever dwell in social pleasure here. See "All together, all together" (Root)

"O Cuba." See Tú (Fuentes)

"Oh Cupid, oh Cupid, you use me severe." See A married woman's lament

"O cut me a stick both crooked and brown." See The holly twig (Mead-ows of Dan, Va. version)

Oh, Daddy, don't go to the mines to-day. See The dream of the miner's child

O Dakota land, sweet Dakota land. See Dakota land (Sweney)

"O, dance the vira of Minho, ai." See Vira do Minho

O Daniel. Negro spiritual from Florida. AS

"O danke nicht für diese lieder." See Widmung (Franz)

Oh! dat watermelon. Minstrel song. WSS

"O Davidson." Davidson college song. B. E. Shields. Words by E. H. Hamil-ton. AI—AIS

Oh, de band ob Gideon. See Gideon's band ("I hail to my sister")

"Oh, de blin' man stood on de road an' cried." See De blin' man stood on de road an' cried

"Oh, de blin' man stood on de way an' cried." See De blin' man stood on de road an' cried

"O de boatman dance." See De boat-man

"Oh, de boll weevil am a little black bug." See Boll weevil song

Oh, de downward road is crowded, crowded, crowded. See The downward road is crowded

"Oh, de good ole chariot swing so low." See Swing low, sweet chariot

Oh, de hebben is shinin'. Negro spiritual. HRD

"O de lamb done been down here an' died." See Sinner won't die no more

"Oh, de lamp burn down an' yo' cannot see." See What yo' gwine to do when yo' lamp burn down

Oh, de land I am bound for. See Sweet Canaan

O, de ol' ark's a-moverin'. See The old ark a-moving along

Oh, de ole sheep done know de road. See The ole sheep done know the road

O de vinter, O de vinter. See The winter (Negro spiritual)

Oh, de winter, winter. Se De winter'll soon be over

"O de worl' was made in six days." See Clear de track, let de bulgine run

Oh! dear, don't you wish that you were me. See I hope I don't intrude

"O dear land! tho' to me ungrateful." Se Di tanti palpiti (Rossini)

"O dear mother when we was there." See The cruel mother (Alleghany, N.C. version)

Oh! dear, what can the matter be. 18th century song. GSS—KSO—TFG

Oh! dearest Mae. See Dearest Mae (Crosby)

"Oh! dearly do I love to rove." See Bonnie Charlie

"Oh deat' he is a little man." See Lord, remember me

"Oh defenders of the white." See Forward the white (Sumner)

"O del mio dolce ardor" ("O, at my lady's feet") C. W. Gluck. e.i. GA

Oh delusion! she now betrays me. See "Qui m'accolse oppresso, errante" (Bellini)

Oh! dem golden slippers. J. A. Bland (music and words) BNM—DFF—WSS

"Oh dere's no hidin' place down dere." See Dere's no hidin' place down dere

"O Dermot astore! between waking and sleeping." See Dermot astore (Crouch)

O deued pob Cristion (Poverty) Welsh carol. e. OB

"O di che lode." See Arietta (Marcello)

"Oh, did you ne'er hear of the Blarney." Irish air. Words by S. Lover. LAS

"Oh, did you not hear of Kate Kearney." See Kate Kearney

Oh, didn't he ramble. W. Handy (B. Cole) OTG—SRW

Ô Dieu de quelle ivresse. For English translation see "O heav'n with sweetest joy" (Offenbach)

"Oh diletta." Weber. e.i. PC

Oh! Dine, Dine, Dine, I dearly love you Dine. See Lubly Dine (Sanford)

Oh! dis lub is like de sunshow'r. See Cornelia Cob

"Oh dischiuso è il firmamento." Verdi. e.i. PC

"Oh! divina Agnese." Bellini. e.i. PB

O, divine Redeemer. See Repentir (Gounod)

"O! Dixie's land is the land of glory." See Dixie (Emmett)

"Oh do, my Johnny Boker." See Johnny Boker

"Oh, do not frighten or destroy." See The little bird

"O do you know old Reuben Ranzo." See Reuben Ranzo (Treharne)

Oh, don't call de roll. See Don't call de roll

"O don't you remember on the rocky mountain top." See The rocky mountain top (Kentucky version; North Carolina version)

"O don't you remember on yon green mountain." See "Come all you fair and tender ladies" (Carmen, N.C. version)

"Oh! don't you remember, sweet Alice, Ben Bolt." See Ben Bolt

"Oh, don't you remember sweet Betsy from Pike." See Sweet Betsy from Pike

"O don't you see yon turtle dove, lamenting on yon vine." See The true lover's farewell (Tennessee version)

"Oh, don't you want to go to the gospel feast." See Deep river

"Oh! doubt me not." Air: Yellow Wat and the fox. Words by T. Moore. HMI

"Oh, down in Alabama, before I was set free." See Cheer up, Sam (Foster)

"O down she threw her ivory comb." See Fair Margaret and sweet William (Mount Fair, Va. version)

O du fröhliche. See Die drei grossen Christlichen feste

"O du heilige, hochbenedeiete." See "O sanctissima"

[O du mein holder abendstern] "Oh, star of eve." R. Wagner. e. WG
Oh! tu bell' astro incantator. e.i. PB

Oh, duck of the meadows. See Little duckling

Oh, Dunderbeck, oh, Dunderbeck, you was so very mean. See Dunderbeck

"Oh! Ella Ree, so kind and true." See Ella Ree (Porter)

"Oh ev'ry morn at seven o'clock." See Drill ye tarriers, drill (Casey)

"O eyes, O mortal stars." A. Ferrabosco. GA

"O fair and lovely homeland." See Chanson d'Alsace

O fair dove, O fond dove. A. S. Gatty. Words by J. Ingelow. GE—MFS

Oh! fairest alma mater. Smith college song. H. D. Sleeper. Words by H. Sperry. AI

"**Oh**, fare-you-well, friends, I'm gwine to tell you all." See Oh, de hebben is shinin'

"**O**, fare you well, I wish you well." See Good-bye, fare you well

"**O** fare-you-well, my bonny young girls." Hauling chantey. WSE
Variant of: Sing fare you well

"**O** fare you well, my brudder." See Fare ye well

"**O** fare you well, my own true love." See The true lover's farewell (Carmen, N.C. version)

"**O** fare you well, sweet Ireland." See The sons of liberty (Pineville, Ky. version)

"**Oh,** farewell to you, my Nancy." See Swansea town

"**O** fate adverse and cruel." See Già l'ira m'abbandona (Meyerbeer)

"**O** father dear, I ofttimes hear you talk of Erin's isle." See Skibbereen

"**O** father, father, go build me a boat." See Sweet William (White Rock, Va. version)

"**O** father, have you brought me any gold." See The maid freed from the gallows (Burnsville, N.C. version no. 2)

"**O** father, O father go build me a boat." See Sweet William (Burnsville, N.C. version no. 2)

"**O** Father, we would bring Thee." See Hymn of scouting (Wesley)

O femme Romulus, oh. See Rémon, Rémon

"**Oh!** fill our glasses with the sparkling wine." See The students' song (Offenbach)

"**Oh** fires of wisdom burning." See Fires of wisdom (Schneider)

"**O** fischer auf den fluten." See "Oh pescator dell' onda"

"**Oh,** for a thousand tongues" (Azmon) C. G. Glaser. Words by C. Wesley. MFS

O, for ane-and-twenty, Tam. See An' O, for ane-and-twenty, Tam

"**Oh,** for the swords of former time." Irish air. Words by T. Moore. HMI

O! Fred, tell them to stop. G. Meen (music and words) SRW

"**Oh,** freedom." Negro song. HRD

"**O** furlo' moon up in the sky." See Furlo' moon

"**O** Genevieve, I'd give the world." See Sweet Genevieve (Tucker)

O get you ready, dar's a meetin' here to-night. See There's a meeting here to-night

O, gimme yo' han'. See Gimme yo' han'

"**O** Giove onnipotente." Winter. e.i. PC

"**Oh,** give me a home where the buffalo roam." See Home on the range

"**Oh!** give me back." E. Audran. e. WLO

O, give me your hand. See Gimme yo' han'

"**O** give thanks." Old English round. DSB—TFR

"**Oh,** give thanks" (Grace) GSS

Oh, give way, Jordan. Negro spiritual. HRD

"**Oh!** gladly now we hail thee." V. Bellini. e. MFS

"**O** glorious the name and fame." See Boston university hymn (Marshall)

"**Oh!** go fetch me down my riding cane." See The hog-eye man

"**O** God, beneath Thy guiding hand." See God be with us (Hatton)

"**O** God have mercy." See "Gott sei mir gnädig" (Mendelssohn)

"**O** God, of all the Maker." See To-morrow (Wesley)

"**O** God, our Help in ages past." W. Croft. Words by I. Watts. BB—MBS

"O God, our Help in ages past" (St Anne) GSS

"O God, our Help in ages past" (St Anne's) TFP

"**O** God, Thy world is sweet with prayer" (Canonbury) R. Schumann. Words by L. Larcom. LAS

"**O** God! Who from the suckling's mouth." See Sing songs of praise (Händel)

"**Oh!** good gracious! I hope I'm not going to faint." See The bashful young lady (Glover)

"**Ó** grádh mo chroidhe le m'anam thú." See Máire ní ghríobhtha

"**O** grant it, heav'n, that our long woes shall cease." See So shall the lute and harp awake (Händel)

"**O** graveyard" (Lay this body down) Negro song. AS

"**O** grim, grey Palisades." See The Palisades (Genns)

"**O** grosses leid." See "Ay au pena ren andia"

"**Oh** gu ma slàn a chì mi mo chailin dìleas donn." See Mo chailin dìleas donn

O gur mis' tha sona dheth ("Though light my purse") Gaelic folk song. e. CSB 3

"**Oh!** had I a beau, who for Mexico would go." See Female volunteer for Mexico (Bishop)

"**Oh** had I Jubal's lyre." G. F. Händel. SSO 1—TFR

"**Oh!** had I the wings of a fairy gay." See Had I the wings of a fairy gay

"**Oh!** had I wings like a dove." See Had I wings like a dove

"**Oh!** had we some bright little isle." Irish air: Chiling O'Guiry, or, Sheela na Guira. Words by T. Moore. HMI

"**Oh,** halleluhay glory, oh, now balance down de middle." See The Skidmore fancy ball (Braham)

Oh, hallelujah, oh, hallelujah. See Who'll jine de Union

"**Oh,** hallelujah to that Lamb, down by the river." See Down by the river

"**O** hangman, hangman, slacken your rope." See The maid freed from the gallows (Dewey, Va. version)

O happy day, O day so dear. See O schöne zeit, o sel'ge zeit (Götze)

"Oh, happy sons of bright Lorraine." See Marche lorraine (Ganne)

"O hark! what mean those holy voices." See Hark, what mean those holy voices

"O, has she den failed in her troth." See Lubly Dine (Sanford)

"Oh, has she den fail'd in her truth." See Lubly Dine (Sanford)

"O haste and leave this sacred isle." See St Senanus and the lady

"O, hasten, hasten all." See Finnish hymn

"O, have ye been in love, me boys." See I met her in the garden where the praties grow

"Oh! have you seen the blushing rose." See Mary of Allendale (Hook)

"Oh, He raise a poor Lazarus." See He raise a poor Lazarus

O He sees all you do. See My Lord's writing all the time

"Oh! hear, heav'nly Agnes." See "Oh! divina Agnese"

Oh, hear me prayin' (Lord, feed my lam's) Negro spiritual. JB 2

"O hear the bugle calling." See The bugle call

"Oh, heart of mine no longer attempt that chain to sever." See "Più non pensar" (Astorga)

"O heart wherefore so light." See Waltz song (Audran)

"O heav'n! what dream I." See Perchè dell' aure in sen (Donizetti)

"O heav'n with sweetest joy." J. Offenbach. [Tr of Ô Dieu de quelle ivresse] e. WG

Oh Helen. C. Morgan. Words by C. R. McCarron. OTG

Oh here's to the fighting bob cat. See The bobcat (Bradbury)

"O Herre" ("O Master") E. Melartin. Words by V. Krag. e.n. WM 2

O herrlich schlösschen. For English translation see "O magic castle" (Humperdinck)

"O herz, mein herzlieb." See "Cori, curuzzu"

Oh H-H-Hel, oh H-H-Hel, oh Helen please be mine. See Oh Helen (Morgan)

"O hide not Thyself from me." See Hide not Thyself from me (Alberti)

Oh hog's-eye, oh, row the boat ashore for the hog's-eye. See The hog's-eye man

"O-hoi-ye-ho, ho-ye-ho who's for the ferry." See Twickenham ferry (Marzials)

"O holde Mary, du liebe kleine." See Màiri bhòideheach

"O holy night." See Cantique de Noël (Adam)

"Oh! how brightly, how brightly the sun moves along." Old song. GOS 2

"Oh, how cold the winter weather." See Longing for spring

"Oh! how delightful." Waltz song. J. L. Molloy. Words by A. Sketchley. GE

Oh, how is the Major Gilfeather. See Major Gilfeather (Braham)

"O how lovely is my darling." See "O wie lieblich ist das mädchen" (Schumann)

"Oh, how lovely is the evening." See Lovely evening

"O how old are you, my pretty little miss." See I'm seventeen come Sunday (Endicott, Va. version)

"Oh, how sweet, how sweet is our singing." Round. M. Hauptmann. CSB 1

"O Howard, alma mater true." See Alma mater—Howard college (Launay)

"O human existence! what end." See Todtengräbers heimweh (Schubert)

Oh hush, my love, you will break my heart. See The lover's lament (1st version)

"O hush thee, my babie." A. Sullivan. Words tr by W. Scott [from Caidil gu lo] e. TFB—TFG

["Oh, hush thee, my babie"] Oh! rest thee, babe. J. Whitaker. Words tr by W. Scott [from Caidil gu lo] e. GOS 1

"Oh, I am in love." See I'll tell nobody

"Oh, I been to de sea." See Hallelujah (Negro spiritual)

"O, I come from ole Virginny." See Walk in the parlour

"O, I died one time." See Keep a-inchin' along

"Oh, I don't want to be a gambler." See I don't want to be a gambler

"O I drove three mules foh Gawge McVane." See Mule skinner's song

"Oh, I had a horse and his name was Bill." See The horse named Bill (Emmett)

"O, I hae seen great anes." See My ain fireside

"O I have married a queen's daughter." See The daemon lover (Harrogate, Tenn. version)

"Oh! I have roam'd in many lands." See Erin is my home

"O I have seen a King's new baby." See The kingdom

"Oh, I have seen great ones." See My ain fireside

"Oh, I heard a-sweet music up above." See Oh, give way, Jordan

"Oh! I jist come out afore you." See Lucy Long

O, I know the Lord. See I know the Lord's laid His hands on me

"Oh, I love a good hearty laugh." See A jolly good laugh (Thomas)

O, I love the maiden fair. See Si mo leannan an

"Oh! I love to travel far and near." See Wizard oil

Oh, I miss you, Nettie Moore. See Gentle Nettie Moore (Pike)

"Oh-i-ro! sing we upon the hill." See The echo

"Oh, I was bo'n in Mobile town." See Levee song

"Oh, I was born in old Virginny." See The jolly raftsman

"Oh, I went down south for to see my Sal." See Polly-wolly-doodle

Oh, I will be there. See "I hope my mother will be there"

Oh! I wish I had my old girl back again. See I wish I had my old girl back again (Wallace)

"Oh, I wish I was a diamond upon my Lulu's hand." See She is a lulu

O I wonder if my clothes are out of pawn. See Jamboree

Oh, Idaho, my Idaho. See "Oh, let us sing of Idaho" (Hamilton)

"Oh, if I had a daughter, sir." See Rambling wreck from Georgia tech

"Oh, if mother Volga." See Ah, if mother Volga (Panchenko)

"O ihr herbstlich langen nächte, o." See Zwiegespräch

"Oh, I'll not sit on the grass." See The verdant braes of Skreen

"Oh! I'm a girl that's fond of life." See As through the park I go

"Oh, I'm a good old rebel." Song of Reconstruction days. DSO Variant: Rabble soldier

"O I'm a happy creature." See Mandolinata (Paladilhe)

"Oh, I'm a lone widdy." See The Widow Nolan's goat

Oh! I'm a swell, you all know well. See The Broadway swell and Brooklyn belle (Kelly)

"Oh, I'm a Texas cowboy." See The Texas cowboy

"Oh I'm goin' out west, down on the Rio Grande." See Alice B.

"Oh! I'm in love with such a dove." See Juliana and her grand piana

"Oh! I'm not myself at all." See I'm not myself at all

"Oh in eighteen hundred and forty-one." See Poor Paddy works on the railway

Oh, in the morning. Old song. SW Variant of: Willie the weeper

"O, Iowa, calm and secure on thy hill." See Old gold

"O Irmingard." See Heimliche grüsse (Fielitz)

"Oh I'se from Lusianna, as you all know." See Jim along Josey

Oh, I'se so wicked. Minstrel song. WSS

["O Isis und Osiris"] "O Isis and Osiris, guide them." W. A. Mozart. e. DSC

"Oh, Italia, Italia beloved." Donizetti. e. TFG

"O it's now we're past o' the Lizard lights." See Jamboree

"Oh, it's old Arizona again." See Old Arizona again

"O it's owre the borders, awa', awa'." See The hundred pipers

"Oh, I've been having a helluva time." See The governor-general or a hobo

"Oh, I've been to de sea." See Hallelujah (Negro spiritual)

O ivied walls! O storied halls. See "Come, raise the song" (Davis)

"O Jack he went a-sailing." See Jack went a-sailing (Burnsville, N.C. version no. 2)

"O Jack he went sailing." See Jack went a-sailing (Harrogate, Tenn. version no. 2)

"O Jack he's gone a-sailing." See Jack went a-sailing (Callaway, Va. version)

"O Jackie's gone a-sailing." See Jack went a-sailing (Nash, Va. version)

"Oh! Jacob, get the cows home." See Cousin Jedediah (Thompson)

"O jailor, won't you slack that rope." See The maid freed from the gallows (Burnsville, N.C. version no. 1)

Oh, Jean, my bonnie Jean. See Scotch lassie, Jean

O Jenny, get your oat-cake done. See Whoop jamboree

Oh, Jerusalem. Negro spiritual. HRD

"O jesenske duge noći, cj." See Zwiegespräch

"O Jesu, my Saviour, who takest upon Thee." L. Leo. e. SSO 2

"O Jesu, Saviour of mankind." See Jesu Redemptor omnium

O Jesulein süss, o Jesulein mild ("O little one") S. Scheidt (music and words) e. OB

O Jesulein süss, o Jesulein mild ("O little one") Air: Komm, heiliger Geist mit deiner Gnad, arr by J. S. Bach. Words by S. Scheidt. e. OB

"O Jesus my Saviour, on Thee I'll depend." See I'm troubled in mind

"Oh, Jesus tell you once before." See Babylon's fallin'

"O Jesus, Thou art standing." A. Geibel. Words by W. W. How. TSS 2

O Jimmy, farewell! your brothers fell. See Grafted into the army (Work)

"O John and William walked out one day." See John and William

"Oh, John, come and mow the lawn now." See The sudden cure

"Oh, Johnny was a rover." See We're all bound to go

"O Johnny's gone; what shall I do." See John's gone to Hilo

"O join 'em, all, join for Jesus." See Join the angel band (Charleston, S.C. version)

"O, Joseph being an old man truly." See Joseph and Mary

"O Katie dear, go ask your father." See "Awake! awake" (Black Mountain, N.C. version)

"Oh, keep your hat upon your head." See Gideon's band

"O Kenmure's on and awa', Willie." Scottish air. Words by R. Burns. GS

Oh, Kentucky, the hunters of Kentucky. See The hunters of Kentucky

"Oh, kind folks, listen to my song." See Abraham's daughter

"Oh, kind friend you may ask me." See Utah Carroll

"Oh King of kings, on Thee I call." See King's prayer (Wagner)

O! kiss me quick and go! my honey. See Kiss me quick and go (Buckley)

"Oh! ladies and gentlemen, please to draw near." See Down, down derry down

"Oh! ladies don't you blush." See Way down in Ca-i-ro (Foster)

"O ladies, don't you wonder when I again appear." See Dolcy Jones (Foster)

"O Lady Moon, your horns point toward the east." See Lady Moon (Loomis)

O Lamb of God ("Lord, have mercy upon mine offences") G. A. Naumann. e. SSO 2

"O Lamb of God that tak'st away." T. Bradsky. TSS 1—TSS 2

"O land of my fathers, O land of my love." Welsh national song. Ancient Welsh air. Words by A. P. Graves. LAS

"O land of saints, of streams and song." See Innisfail (Phelps)

O lang will his ladye look frae the Castle Doune. See The bonny earl o' Moray

"O lass' mich nur von ferne stehn." See Bettler-liebe (Bungert)

O, law, Ma, my toes are sore. See Weevily wheat

"O lay your cheek to mine, my dear." See Love's the tune (Straus)

"Oh! leave me to my sorrow." Irish air. Words by T. H. Bayly. HMI

"Oh! leave not your Kathleen." See Kathleen (Williams)

"Oh! Lemuel." S. C. Foster (music and words) WSS

"Oh let eternal honours crown his name." See From mighty kings (Händel)

"O let me only linger here." See Bettlerliebe (Bungert)

"Oh, let me tell my mother how I come along." See I've been in the storm so long

O let the Midnight special shine a light on me. See Midnight special (Negro jail song)

"O let us all begin with a merry, merry dance." See Country dance

"Oh, let us sing of Idaho." University of Idaho song. [J. S. Hamilton] AI

"O lieb, o lieb, wie grausam quälest du." See Sarabande

O liebes mütterlein. See O little mother of mine (Nevin)

"O liebste mein." See "O mistress mine" (Byrd)

"O Life that maketh all things new" (Hamburg) L. Mason. Words by S. Longfellow. LAS

"O-o-o-oh, lil' man, go get yo' pan." See Chahcoal man

"Oh! Lilly dear, it grieves me." See Farewell, my Lilly dear (Foster)

Oh, Lilly, sweet Lilly, dear Lilly Dale. See Lilly Dale (Thompson)

O Lisbona, alfin ti miro. G. Donizetti. e.i. PB

"O list to the strains of a poor Irish harper." See The bard of Armagh

"Oh! listen, master goldsmith." See Farewell, darling Maggie (Gade)

O listen to de lambs. See Listen to de lambs

"O little did I think He was so nigh." See Come here Lord

O little mother of mine (O liebes mütterlein) G. B. Nevin. Words by W. H. Brown. e.g. BST

"O little one." See O Jesulein süss, o Jesulein mild (Old air); O Jesulein süss, o Jesulein mild (Scheidt)

"O little rock." See "Petit rocher"

"O little town of Bethlehem." English folk air. Words by P. Brooks. DN

"O little town of Bethlehem." English traditional air: The ploughboy's dream. Words by P. Brooks. OB

"O little town of Bethlehem." L. H. Redner. Words by P. Brooks. BB —GSS—LAS—TFP

"O little town of Bethlehem." D. Stevens. Words by P. Brooks. FC

"O Logie o' Buchan." See Logie o' Buchan

"O Lola." See Siciliana (Mascagni)

"Oh, look up yander what I see, bright angels comin' arter me. Oh, look up yander what I see." See De church of God

"O look up yander, what I see, I'm on my journey home." See Hail! hail! hail

"Oh, look up yonder what I see, bright angels comin' arter me. Oh, two white angels walking down." See De winter'll soon be over

"O Lord! correct me." Händel. Words by J. S. Dwight. BST

"Oh Lord Geoffrey Amherst was a soldier of the king." See Lord Geoffrey Amherst (Hamilton)

"O Lord! have mercy, have mercy, O Lord, upon me." See O Lord, have mercy upon me (Pergolesi)

O Lord! have mercy on me. See Going to ride up in the chariot

O Lord, have mercy upon me. Pergolesi. e. SSO 2

"O Lord, I done done." Negro spiritual. FSN

Variant: I done done what ya' tol' me to do

"Oh! Lord, I have wandered." J. P. Knight. HP

"Oh Lord, I want some valiant soldier." See Some valiant soldier

Oh, Lord, keep me from sinking down. See Keep me from sinking down

"O Lord, my flock humbly I tended." See Jeanne d'Arc au bûcher (Liszt)

Oh! Lord, oh! my Lord! O my good Lord See Keep me from sinking down

"O Lord of heaven, and earth, and sea" (Almsgiving) J. B. Dykes. Words by C. Wordsworth. LAS

"O Lord, Whose mercies numberless." G. F. Händel. SSO 2

"Oh! loss of sight" (see Song Index) Also in "Total eclipse! no sun, no moon" (Händel) SSO 3

"**Oh**, Lou'siana's de same old state." See Lou'siana Belle (Foster)

Oh, love, dear love, be true.   See Ehren on the Rhine (Hutchinson)

"**O** Love divine."   F. J. Haydn.   Words by O. W. Holmes.   CSS 1

"**O** love immortal."   G. Verdi.   [Tr of Amore, amore! gaudio tormento]   e. WG

"**O** love is sweet, love is pleasant."   See William Hall (Tennessee version)

"**O** loving Father, hear my pray'r."   See "Ave Maria" (Mascagni)

Oh, M. S. C. right loyally, we offer songs of praise to thee.   See Fair M. S. C.

["**Ô** ma tendre musette"]   My tender musette.   [Attributed to Monsigny. Words by La Harpe]   e.   TFO

"**O** madam, I will give to you the keys of Canterbury."   See The keys of Canterbury (Somerset version)

"**O** madam, I'm a courting case."   See The courting case (White Rock, Va. version)

"**O** mademoiselle from gay Paree."   See Hinky dinky, parley-voo

"**O** magic castle."   E. Humperdinck.   [Tr of O herrlich schlösschen]   e.   WG

"**O** maiden bright."   J. Herbeck.   e.   TFB—TFO

O man, do never faint nor fear.   See "Saint Stephen"

"**O**, Mary, at thy window be."   Air: The Glasgow lasses.   Words by R. Burns.   GS

"**O**, Mary, at thy window be" (Mary Morison)   Air: The miller.   Words by R. Burns.   GS

O Mary, don't you weep.   Negro spiritual.   BB—TFB—TFP
Oh, Mary, doan' yer weep.   FSN
Oh, Mary, doncher weep.   JG
Variant: Pharaoh's army got drownded

"**O** Mary, go and call the cattle home."   See The sands o' Dee (Boott)

"**Oh**, Mary, thy laugh was sweet."   Irish song.   DSC

"**O** massa take dat new bran coat."   See Away down in Sunbury

"**O** Master, wearied sore am I."   See "O Herre" (Melartin)

"**O** me no weary yet."   See Not weary yet

"**Oh**, me! oh, my! that furlo' moon up in the sky."   West Point song.   DSO

"**O** me! O my! we'll get there by and by."   A toast.   BB

"**O** meer, du grausam bittres meer" ("Thalassa pikrhothalassa")   Greek folk song.   g.gr.   ML 2

"**Oh**, meet me when daylight is fading."   See Whip-poor-will's song (Millard)

"**O** mein hain" ("Oï gaïu moï")   Ukrainian folk song.   g.r.   ML 1

O mein lieber Augustin.   See Buy a broom (Lee?)

"**O** member, will you linger."   See Children do linger

"**O** menschheit, o leben! was soll's."   See Todtengräbers heimweh (Schubert)

"**Oh** merry young maiden, come and merrily dance."   See Air fal-al-al O

"**Oh** miei figli! è dolce il canto della nostra età primiera."   See Era anch' io di quella schiera (Donizetti)

Oh, mine offences cry to heaven.   G. A. Hasse.   e.   SSO 2

"**Oh** misfortune! oh fatal error."   See "Cruda sorte! amor tiranno" (Rossini)

"**O** Mister Wing, we sing-a-ling-a-ling."   See Sing-a-ling-a-ling

"**O** mistress, at your door our wassail begins."   See The wassail song

"**O** mistress mine."   Traditional air arr by W. Byrd.   Words by W. Shakespeare.   BOS 2
"O mistress mine" ("O liebste mein")   e.g.   ML 1

"**Oh**, Mistress Shady, she is a lady."   See Mistress Shady

"**O** Molly bawn, why leave me pining."   See Molly bawn (Lover)

"**O** money is the meat in the cocoanut."   See Money

"**O** moon, whose mystic veil."   See Santa Lucia

"**O** mortal man, remember well."   See The Sussex mummers' carol

"**Oh**, mother, ain't you glad."   See I've been toilin' at de hill

"**O** mother, dear, come rede your riddle."   See Lord Thomas and fair Ellinor (Burnsville, N.C. version no. 2)

"**O** mother dear, go dig my grave."   See Lord Thomas and fair Ellinor (Buena Vista, Va. version)

"**O** mother dear, Jerusalem."   See Psalm of Sion (English air)

"**O** mother, dear mother, for me do not weep."   See The sunny south (Nellysford, Va. version)

"**O** mother I believe."   See The heaven bells

"**O** mother, O mother, come dig my grave."   See Lord Thomas and fair Ellinor (Bedford county, Va. version)

"**O** mother, O mother, come riddle my sport."   See Lord Thomas and fair Ellinor (Knott or Letcher county, Ky. version)

"**O** mother, O mother, come roll us down."   See Lord Thomas and fair Ellinor (Burnsville, N.C. version no. 1)

"**O** mother, O mother, go dig my grave."   See The brisk young lover (Burnsville, N.C. version)

"**O** mother, O mother, go riddle my sport."   See Lord Thomas and fair Ellinor (Hindman, Ky. version)

"**O** mother, O mother, go roll a song."   See Lord Thomas and fair Ellinor (Rabun county, Ga. versions no. 1-2)

"**O** mother, O mother, O mother, says he."   See Lord Thomas and fair Ellinor (Woodridge, Va. version)

"**O** mother strong, our tasks are done."   See Valedictory

"**O** mountain pine, O mountain pine."   See Der tannenbaum

O mourner, let's go down.   See The good old way

"O music come and light my heart's dark places." See An die musik (Schubert)

"O my body's racked wid de fever." See My body rock 'long fever (South Carolina version no. 2)

Oh! my bonnie, bonnie boy. See Bonnie Charlie

"Oh, my bravest and best." V. Bellini. e. MFS

"Oh, my brother, did you come for to help me." See Sweet Canaan

"O my brothers have some pity." See The song of the blind beggar

"Oh my children! with pride recall I." See Era anch' io di quella schiera (Donizetti)

[Oh, my darling Clementine] Clementine. P. Montrose (music and words) MBS—SRW

"O my dear heart, young Jesus sweet." See Balulalow (Heseltine)

"O my dearest Molly." See The bold privateer

"Oh, my golden slippers." See Oh! dem golden slippers (Bland)

"Oh, my good Lord, show me de way." Negro spiritual. JB 2

"Oh, my heart is gone, and I'm forlorn." See Pretty as a picture (Bishop)

"O my honey, take me back." Negro folk song. SBA

"O my King Emanuel, my Emanuel above." See King Emanuel

Oh my Lisbon. See O Lisbona, alfin ti miro (Donizetti)

O my love I lov'd her so. See Looking back (Sullivan)

"O my love! lov'st thou me." 17th century round. TFP

"Oh, my love stood under the walnut tree." See Over the garden wall (Fox)

"O my love, will you wear red." See Will you wear red

"Oh, my luve's like a red, red rose." See My luve is like a red, red rose (Garrett)

Oh, my Maria's a fairy queen. See My Maria

"O, my mudder is gone! my mudder is gone." See I can't stay behind

"Oh, my mudder's in de road." See Most done trabelling

"Oh, my name is Samuel Hall." See Samuel Hall

O my poor Nelly Gray. See Darling Nelly Gray (Hanby)

"Oh, my Rose ain't white." See My Rose (Lacy)

Oh, my she look'd so sweet. See The yaller gal that winked at me

"Oh! my soul, my soul am a-gwine for to rest." See Angel Gabriel (Stewart)

"O my sister light de lamp." See The white marble stone (South Carolina version no. 2)

"Oh, my young Christians, I got lots for to tell you." See Glory and honor

"O Nancy Dawson." See Cheer'ly man; Cheerly men

"O Nancy Fat she was a gal." See Nancy Fat

"Oh, Nannie, wilt thou gang with me." T. Carter. Words by T. Percy. GS

"Oh, native land, how fair you seem." See My native land (Grieg)

Oh, naughty, naughty, naughty Cupid, I declare. See Cupid and the maiden (Richardson)

"O navy team, just sail a steady course." See The ocean waves may roll

"O neighbor, whence this wondrous strain." See The shepherd neighbors (Gevaert)

"O night, peaceful and blest." See Ô bienheureuse nuit

O no, John. Somerset folk song. BB —DSB—DSC—TFG—TFR

"Oh, no longer seek to pain me." See "O cessate di piagarmi" (Scarlatti)

"Oh noble poet." See Io l'udia ne' suoi bei carmi (Donizetti)

Oh, nobody knows the trouble I seen. See Nobody knows the trouble I see

"O now says the captain: Let's cast lots and see." See The silk merchant's daughter (Big Laurel, N.C. version)

Ô nuit d'amour. For English translation see "O tender moon" (Gounod)

Oh, oh, baby, hold your tongue. See The gouge of Armour avenue (Handy)

Oh, oh, oh! oh, oh, hone! come back to my bosom. See The Widow Nolan's goat

"Oh, ole Zip Coon he is a larned skolar." See Zip Coon

"O once I bought me an old grey mare." See The old grey mare (Flag Pond, Tenn. version)

"O once I courted a pretty little girl." See The rejected lover (Hot Springs, N.C. version)

"O once I knew a pretty girl." See The rejected lover (Endicott, Va. version)

"O once in my saddle I used to go dashing." See St James's hospital (Peaks of Otter, Va. version)

"O once there was a little boy." See The boy on the land

"O once there were three fishermen." See The three fishermen

"Oh, once upon a time in Arkansaw." See The Arkansaw traveler

"Oh one day as anoder, hallelu, hallelu." See Hallelu, hallelu

"Oh, outfits may come and outfits may go." See We lead the way

"Oh, over the bar on the thirteenth of May." See Blow the man down

"O Paddy, dear, and did you hear." See The wearing of the green

"Oh patria! dolce e ingrata patria." See Di tanti palpiti (Rossini)

"O patria, o cara patria." See O, tu Palermo (Verdi)

Oh! Patrizii. See Era anch' io di quella schiera (Donizetti)

"O pescator dell' onde" (Barcarola.—"O fischer auf den fluten."—Gondellied) Venetian folk song. g.i. ML 2

Oh, Peter, go ring dem bells.   See Peter, go ring them bells

"**Oh,** pity poor Reuben Ranzo."   See Reuben Ranzo

O po' Liza, po' gal.   See Liza Jane

Oh, po' sinner.   See What yo' gwine to do when yo' lamp burn down

"**O** Polly, love, O Polly, the rout has now begun."   See High Germany

"**O** Polly, O Polly, if you will agree."   See The cruel ship's carpenter (Big Laurel, N.C. version)

"**O** Polly, O Polly, it's for your sake alone." See The rebel soldier (Montvale, Va. version)

"**O** Polly, pretty Polly, come and go with me."   See The cruel ship's carpenter (Barbourville, Ky. version)

O poor Liza, poor gal.   See Liza Jane

O poor Miss Lucy Neal.   See Lucy Neal

"**Oh,** poor old Reuben Ranzo."   See Reuben Ranzo

"**Oh,** poor old Stormy's dead and gone." See Stormalong John

Oh, poor sinner.   See What yo' gwine to do when yo' lamp burn down

"**Oh,** potatoes they grow small."   See Over there

"**O** pray Thee, Great King of all creation." See "O Giove onnipotente" (Winter)

"**Oh,** press thy cheek against mine own." See "Lehn' deine wang' an meine wang'" (Jensen)

"**Oh,** press thy cheek close to mine own." See "Lehn' deine wang' an meine wang'" (Sjögren)

"**O** pretty fair miss all in the garden." See The broken token (Virginia version)

O pretty Girofla.   C. Lecocq.   [Tr of Ma belle Girofla]   e.   WLO

"**O** pretty Polly, don't you cry."   MFS

"**Oh** promise me."   R. De Koven. Words by C. Scott.   GFS

"**Oh,** promise to meet me."   See Rose of Killarney (Thomas)

"**O,** proudly rise the monarchs of our mountain land."   See The mountains (Gladden)

"**Oh,** put my clothes in order."   See Shallow Brown

O rare Turpin.   Traditional air.   CSB 2

"**Oh** realm of light" (Creation)   F. J. Haydn.   Words by E. H. Miller. BB

O reign, O reign, O reign, my Saviour. See Reign, Massa Jesus

"**Oh,** religion is a fortune."   See Religion is a fortune

"**O** rest in the Lord."   F. Mendelssohn. [Tr of Sei stille dem Herrn]   e. BB—TFG

Oh! rest thee, babe.   See "Oh, hush thee, my babie" (Whitaker)

O ride on, Jesus.   See Ride on, Jesus

"**Oh,** ring the bells in the belfry high." See Ring the bells

"**O** rišča ni, mila raćo."   See The song of the blind beggar

Oh, rise an' shine, an' give God de glory, glory.   See Rise and shine

"**O** rise you up, ye sev'n bretherens."   See Earl Brand (White Rock, N.C. version)

"**O** river, river, rolling on."   See Time and tide (Rodney)

"**Oh,** Robin Hood and Little John."   See The Cornish May song

"**O,** Robin is my only joe."   See Kind Robin lo'es me

"**O** rock o' jubilee, poor fallen soul."   See Rock o' jubilee

Oh, roll de ole chariot along.   See Roll de ole chariot along

"**Oh** roll the cotton down, my boys."   See Roll the cotton down

"**O** röslein, hänge nimmer deinem kummer nach."   See Roisin dubh

"**Oh,** row me cross the river."   See One more day

"**O** rowan tree! O rowan tree."   See The rowan tree

"**O** rududu, rududu" ("Oï ru-du-du, ru-du-du")   Russian   folk   song.   g.r. ML 1

Oh run, let the bullgine run.   See Let the bullgine run

"**O** run, Mary, run, hallelu, hallelu."   See The resurrection morn

O. S. C. our hats are off to you.   See Hail to old O. S. C. (Wilkins)

Oh S. D. S. C. hurrah for the yellow and blue.   See The yellow and blue (Haynes)

"**O** sag mir, mein kriegsmann, wohin willst du geh'n."   See Dime, artillerito, donde vas

"**O** säh ich auf der haide dort."   See "O wert thou in the cauld blast"   (Mendelssohn)

"**O** säh ich noch einmal mein treu braun-mägdelein."   See Mo chailin dileas donn

"**Oh,** saints an' sinners will-a you go."   See Gwine up

"**O** Sally Brown she's a bright mulatta." See Sally Brown

O salutaris ("Lord, lead me in Thy right-eousness")   Cherubini.   e.   SSO 2

O salutaris Hostia ("Je crois en Dieu."— "I trust in God."—Credo)   J. B. Faure.   e.f.l.   CSS 1—CSS 2

"**O** salutaris Hostia."   A. Geibel.   1. TSS 2

"**O** salutaris Hostia" (God is love)   C. J. Hargitt.   e.l.   CSS 2

"**O** salutaris, salutaris Hostia."   See O salutaris Hostia (Faure)

Oh! Sam.   W. S. Hays.   WSS

"**Oh!** Sammy put dat banjo down, O Sam." See Oh! Sam (Hays)

"**O** sanctissima" (An die jungfrau Maria) Sicilian hymn.   g.l.   ML 2

"**O** Santy Anna gained the day, hooray! Santy Anna."   See The plains of Mexico

"**Oh** Santy Anna won the day, way-ah, me Santy Anna."   See Santy Anna

"O Saro, Saro, I love you well." See The brisk young lover (Virginia version)

"Oh, saw ye my wee thing." See Saw ye my wee thing

"Oh, saw ye the lass wi' the bonny blue een." Scottish air. Words by R. Ryan. GS

"O say, can you see, by the dawn's early light." See The star-spangled banner (Smith)

Oh, say, darling, say, when I'm far away. See The Spanish cavalier (Hendrickson)

"Oh say, little dogies, why don't you slow down." See Night herding song

"Oh, say, was you ever in Rio Grande." See Rio Grande

"O say what glory." See Arietta (Marcello)

O schöne zeit, o sel'ge zeit (O happy day) K. Götze. e.g. GG

"Oh, send Lewie Gordon hame." See Lewie Gordon

O Shallow, O Shallow Brown. See Shallow Brown

"O Shannadore, I love your daughter." See The wide Mizzoura

"Oh! share my cottage, gentle maid." R. G. Shrival. GOS 1

Oh, she is a lulu. See She is a lulu

"Oh! she is not like the rose." See The snowy-breasted pearl

"O she tossed it high, she tossed it low." See Sir Hugh (Virginia version)

"O Shenandoah, I long to hear you." See Shenandoah

"Oh, shepherds awaken! arise from your sleep." See The sleeping shepherds

O shout away. Negro spiritual from Virginia. AS

"O shout, O shout, O shout away." See O shout away

"Oh! signor! padre del ciel." See Preghiera (Marchesi)

"O silver is a pretty thing." See The drummer and his wife (Kentucky version)

"O sing a joyous carol unto the holy Child." Crüger. FC

"Oh, sing a song of hikers on Datu Ali's trail." See On Datu Ali's trail

Oh, sing all de way, sing all de way. See Hear de angels singin'

O sing for He liveth. See The Lord hath arisen

O sing in cheerful measure. See Mandolinata (Paladilhe)

"Oh sing me not the tender song." See Grusisches lied (Pomasanski)

"Oh! sing, sing on, sweetly to cheer me." See The lover and the bird (Guglielmo)

"Oh! sing them on the sunny hills." See The songs your fathers loved

"O singe nicht das sanfte lied." See Grusisches lied (Pomasanski)

"Oh sinner hear thy Saviour calling thee." See Come home (Lassen)

O sinner-man, where are you going to run to. See Sinner man (Kentucky version)

"Oh, sinner-man, you had better pray." See Oh, sinner, you'd better get ready

"O, sinner, sinner, you better pray." See Death's gwineter lay his cold icy hands on me (Rare version)

Oh, sinner, you'd better get ready. Negro spiritual. HRD

"O Sion's daughter, where art thou." See Waer is die dochter van Syoen

"O sir, I see you come again." See The courting case (Montvale, Va. version)

"O sister, O sister, come go with me." See The two sisters (Hot Springs, N.C. version)

"O sister, O sister, there swims a swan." See The two sisters (Berea, Ky. version no. 1)

"O sisters too, how may we do." See The Coventry carol (Ancient air); The Coventry carol (Modern version of air)

O sleep, why dost thou leave me. G. F. Händel. <Words by Congreve> HCA

O sleep. GA

"Oh, slumber, my darling." See "Oh, hush thee, my babie" (Whitaker)

"O soldier, soldier." Old English folk song. TFP

"Oh, soldier, won't you marry, marry me." See Soldier, won't you marry me (American mountain version)

'O sole mio. See entry under Sole

O sole più ratto. For English translation see "Ensanguined and lurid" (Donizetti)

"Oh, solemn hour when hearts were lowly bending." See Cantique de Noël (Adam)

"Oh, some may sing of Sweet Moselle." See Give me the waltz (Pratt)

"O some tell me that a nigger won't steal." See Run, nigger, run (Arkansas version)

"Oh, someone buried in the graveyard." See I'm a child of grace

"Oh, someone sleepin' in the graveyard." See I'm a child of grace

"O sonnenschein, o sonnenschein." See An den sonnenschein (Schumann)

"Oh sons of tech arise behold." See Alma mater—Georgia institute of technology (Roman)

"Oh, soon-a in de mornin' when I ris." See The ole sheep done know the road

"Oh, sooner in de mornin' when I rise." See The ole sheep done know the road

O speranza di vendetta. See "Sciagurata! hai tu creduto" (Verdi)

"O spirit sweet of summer-time." Irish air. Words by W. Allingham. DSB

Oh, stand the storm, it won't be long. See We'll stand the storm

O star, lovely star. Old French air. Words by S. Fay. FC

"Oh, star of eve." See O du mein holder abendstern (Wagner)

Oh, star of wonder, star of might. See Three kings of Orient (Hopkins)

O star of wonder, star of night. See Three kings of Orient (Hopkins)

Oh! steer my bark to Erin's isle.   See Erin is my home

O stehet auf! nicht sollet hier ihr knien. For English translation see "I pray thee, rise" (Wagner)

"O Stormy, he is dead and gone."   See Stormalong

"O Strassburg, o Strassburg."   See Der unerbittliche hauptmann

"O sunny ray."   See An den sonnenschein (Schumann)

"O sunshine."   See An den sonnenschein (Schumann)

Oh! Susan Van Doozen, the girl of my choosin'.   See Susan Van Doozen (Shepherd)

Oh! Susanna.   S. C. Foster (music and words)   BNM—GOS 2—PSG—TFO —TFP—TFR—WSS

"O swan of slenderness."   See The little red lark

"O swan, thou singest never." See Schwanenlied (Hartmann)

"O sweet is the vale where the Mohawk gently glides."   See Bonny Eloise (Thomas)

"O sweetest Jesu! God and man."   See Sweetest Jesu

Oh, swing low, sweet chariot.   See The Danville chariot

Oh, sympathy deepens whenever we sing. See "Come, cheerful companions"

Oh! take your time Miss Lucy.   See Lucy Long

"O täler weit, o höhen."   F. Mendelssohn-Bartholdy.   Words by J. von Eichendorff.   g.   EDL

"O tannebaum, o tannebaum."   See Der tannenbaum (German folk song); Der tannenbaum (Words by Anschütz)

"Oh, tell me not the woods are fair."   See The rock beside the sea (Converse)

"O tell me, what is this sadness."   See Die Lorelei (Silcher)

O tempora! o mores.   German air.   Words by E. Geibel.   e.   TFB Lob der edlen musica.   g.   EDL

"O tender moon."   C. Gounod.   [Tr of Ô nuit d'amour]   e.   WG

O terra addio.   For English translation see "Farewell, farewell, O earth" (Verdi)

"O thank me not for songs I sing thee." See Widmung (Franz)

"Oh, thank me not for what I sing thee." See Widmung (Franz)

"Oh! that I never more might see."   Donizetti.   MFS

"O that thou had'st hearkened."   A. Sullivan.   SSO 1

Oh! that watermelon.   See Oh! dat watermelon

O, the army team may score.   See The ocean waves may roll

Oh, the band of Gideon.   See Gideon's band ("I hail to my sister")

"Oh! the blacksmith's a fine sturdy fellow." See The blacksmith (Mozart)

"Oh, the blind man stood on the road and cried."   See De blin' man stood on de road an' cried

"Oh, the boll weevil am a little black bug." See Boll weevil song

Oh! the booming of our guns is heard. See The sixth field artillery song

"O, the boys and the girls went a huckie berry hunting."   See Huckleberry hunting

O, the broom, the bonnie, bonnie broom. See The brume o' the Cowdenknowes

"Oh! the bull-dog on the bank."   See The bull-dog on the bank

"O the bully boat is coming."   See The bully boat is coming

"Oh! the clang of the wooden shoon." See The clang of the wooden shoon (Molloy)

"Oh the day of days is here."   See The bobcat (Bradbury)

"Oh! the days are gone when beauty bright."   See Love's young dream

"O, the days of the Kerry dancing."   See The Kerry dance (Molloy)

Oh, the downward road is crowded, crowded, crowded.   See The downward road is crowded

"Oh! the earth is vast and spacious" ("Ez a világ a milyen nagy")   B. Egressy.   Words by A. Petőfi.   e.hu. KH 1

Oh the E-ri-e was a-rising.   See The E-ri-e

"Oh, the flow'rs that I saw in the wildwood."   See Faded flowers (Willing)

"O the French are on the sea."   See The Shan Van Vocht (Irish air); The Shan Van Vocht (Air: Sean bhean bhocht)

"Oh, the good old chariot swing so low." See Swing low, sweet chariot

Oh, the good old days are past and gone. See I want to see the old home (Stewart)

Oh! the good ship, Three Bells.   See The good Three Bells (Jarvis)

Oh, the heaven is shining.   See Oh, de hebben is shinin'

"O, the hog-eye men are all the go."   See The hog-eye man

"Oh, the hog's-eye man is the man for me." See The hog's-eye man

"O the lamb done been down here and died."   See Sinner won't die no more

"Oh, the lamp burn down and you cannot see."   See What yo' gwine to do when yo' lamp burn down

Oh, the land I am bound for.   See Sweet Canaan

"Oh, the life boat's crew are we."   See The life boat's crew

"Oh! the lone starry hours give me, love." See Lone starry hours (Power)

"Oh the mate got drunk and he went below."   See Sailor likes his bottle

"Oh, the minstrels sing of an English king."   See The busted king of England

"Oh, the moment was sad when my love and I parted."   See Savourneen deelish

"Oh, the monkeys have no tails in Zamboanga."   See Zamboanga

"Oh the moon is all a-glow on the stream."
See Hiawatha (Daniels)

"Oh, the moon shines bright." See "The moon shines bright"

Oh the moonlight's fair tonight along the Wabash. See On the banks of the Wabash, far way (Dresser)

"Oh! the night that I struck New York." See The Bowery (Gaunt)

"O, the night was thick and hazy." See Robinson Crusoe's story (Newell)

Oh, the ocean waves may roll. See The mermaid

O, the old ark's a-moverin'. See The old ark a-moving along

Oh the old church-bells are ringing. See Where the sunset turns the ocean's blue to gold (Petrie)

"Oh, the old gray mare, she ain't what she used to be." See Old gray mare

Oh, the ole sheep done know the road. See The ole sheep done know the road

"Oh, the papers scream of a navy team." See Navy team

"Oh! the pretty, pretty creature." See The pretty creature (Storace)

"O the raging sea it rolls, rolls, rolls." See The mermaid (Virginia version)

"Oh, the river of Jordan is so wide." See Oh, wasn't that a wide river

Oh, the rocks and the mountains. See The rocks and the mountains

O the sea how it rolls. See The mermaid (Hyden, Ky. version no. 1)

"Oh, the secret of bliss." See "Il segreto per esser felici" (Donizetti)

Oh! the shamrock ("Thro' Erin's isle") Air: Alley croker. Words by T. Moore. HMI

"Oh, the smartest clipper you can find." See Clear the track, let the bullgine run

"Oh, the sports of childhood." See Swinging 'neath the old apple-tree (Barrows)

O the stars in the elements are falling. See Stars in the elements

Oh, the stormy winds, how they blow, blow, blow. See The mermaid

"Oh, the times are hard and the wages low —Amelia, whar you bound to." See Across the western ocean

"Oh the times are hard and the wages low, leave her, Johnnie, leave her." See Leave her, Johnnie

"Oh the times are hard and the wages low, oh leave her, bullies, leave her." See Leave her, bullies, leave her

"Oh, the trees are getting high." Folk song from Surrey. BET
Variant of: "The trees they do grow high" (English folk song)

"O the very first night I was married." See The lowlands of Holland (Virginia version)

O the winter, O the winter. See The winter (Negro spiritual)

Oh, the winter, winter. See De winter'll soon be over

"O the world was made in six days." See Clear de track, let de bulgine run

"Oh the young girl said to me one day." See Across the Rockies

[Oh, then my little soul's gwine to shine] "I'm gwine to jine de great 'sociation." Negro spiritual. HRD

Oh, then resign your ruby wine. See "Sparkling and bright, in its liquid light, is the water in our glasses" (Taylor)

"Oh! there above yon heather hill." See The man o' Airlie

"O, there was a jolly blade." See The dumb wife

"O there was a lady, gay." See The wife of Usher's well (Beechgrove, Va. version)

"Oh, there was a man call'd Willie the weeper." See Willie the weeper

"Oh! there was a moanish lady." See Moanish lady

"O there was a woman, and she was a widow." See Flowers in the valley

"O there was an old soldier and he had a wooden leg." See There was an old soldier

"Oh! there's Glasgow and Berwick and Penterville." See Botany bay

Oh, there's many a man been murdered in Luzon. See The emancipated race

"Oh, there's no hiding place down there." See Dere's no hidin' place down dere

"Oh, there's not a thrade that's going." See The bowld sojer boy (Lover)

"O Theseus! thou hast betray'd me." See Plainte d'Ariane (Coquard)

"Oh, they call me Hanging Johnny." See Hanging Johnny

"Oh, they said the coast artillery would never go to war." See Coast artillery song

"Oh, they tell me thou art dead, Katy darling." See Katy darling

"Oh! think not my spirits are always as light." Air: John O'Reilly the active. Words by T. Moore. HMI

"Oh, think of a home over there." See Over there (Huntington)

"O this door locked." Folk song from North Carolina. SES 2

Oh! this love is like the sunshow'r. See Cornelia Cob

Oh! this motto, to increase your joys. See A motto for all

Oh those days at Oregon. See "As I sit and dream at evening" (Nelson)

"O Thou afflicted." J. Benedict. TSS 2

"O, thou art divinest Lupita." See Lupita divina

"Oh, thou dearest, heav'nly treasure." See "Oh diletta" (Weber)

"Oh, thou duck, dear duck of the meadows." See "Little duckling"

"O Thou from Whom all goodness flows" (Manoah) Arr from Rossini. Words by T. Haweis. TFP

O thou joyful day, O thou blessed day, holy, peaceful Christmastide. See Die drei grossen Christlichen feste

"O Thou my peace." See "Du bist die ruh'" (Schubert)

O thou Palermo, my first affection.   See O, tu Palermo (Verdi)

"O thou silent autumn night."   See Night

"O Thou that tellest good tidings to Zion." Händel.   SSO 2

"Oh! Thou to Whom this heart ne'er yet." See Sweet spirit, hear my prayer (Wallace)

"O Thou Whose feet" (Dundee)   ⌈Guillaume Franc⌉   Words by L. F. Benson.   TFG

"O Thou Whose power."   16th century air.   Words by Boethius.   e.   DSC

O tidings of comfort and joy.   See "God rest you merry, gentlemen"

Oh tie t'buck t'bucky, tie bucky ru.   See The Chisholm trail (2d version)

"Oh, times is hard and wages low."   See Time for us to leave her

O 'tis my delight on a shining night.   See The Lincolnshire poacher

"Oh! 'tis sweet to think" ('Tis sweet to think)   Irish air: Donall na greine, or, Daniel of the sun, or, Thady, you gander.   Words by T. Moore.   HMI

Ô toi qui m'abandonnes.   For English and Italian translations see Già l'ira m'abbandona (Meyerbeer)

"Oh! Tommy's gone, what shall I do? Away to Hilo."   See Tom's gone to Hilo

Oh! tu bell' astro incantator.   See O du mein holder abendstern (Wagner)

"Oh tu oh tu cui mai finor."   See Sweet spirit, hear my prayer (Wallace)

O, tu Palermo.   G. Verdi.   e.i.   PB

O turn thee.   C. Gounod.   ⌈Tr of Convertere ad Dominum⌉   e.   TFG

"O, 'twas in the year of ninety-four."   See The whale

"O 'twas on a bright mornin' in summer." See Cailín deás crúidhte na mbó (Fragment)

"O Una bhan, mit lokken wie bernstein." See Úna bán

"Oh! Uncle Sammy, he needs the signal corps."   See Signal corps song

"Oh, Uncle Sammy, he pays the infantry." See Pay-day song

"O Värmeland."   See Vermeland

O vecchio cor, che batti.   Verdi.   e.i. PB

O Vol'gĩe ĩ Mĩkulĩe.   See The legend of Volgá

Oh, waillie, waillie, but love is bonnie. See Waillie, waillie

Oh, wait till I put on my robe.   See Oh, yes ("I tell ye, bretheren")

"O wake, O wake, you drowsy sleeper." See "Awake! awake" (Montvale, Va. version no. 2)

"O walk Jordan long road."   See Religion so sweet

"Oh, walk togedder, childron."   See A great camp-meeting in the promised land

O, walky-talky Jenny.   See Walky-talky Jenny

O waly, waly (see Song Index) Variant: Waillie, waillie

"O waly, waly up the bank."   Scottish folk song.   GS

"Oh, war now blows her ringing blast." See The battle call

"Oh, wasn't that a pity an' a shame."   See Crucifixion (Negro spiritual)

Oh, wasn't that a wide river.   Negro spiritual.   BB
    Oh, wasn't dat a wide riber.   HRD
    Oh, wasn't dat a wide river.   WSS

Oh, 'way over Jerdan.   See View de land

Oh, we ain't going home any more.   See Balm of Gilead (Bryant)

"Oh, we are the yearlings."   See The yearling

"Oh, we can play on the big bass drum." See The orchestra

"Oh, we come on the sloop John B."   See The John B. sails

"Oh, we don't have to hike like the infantry."   See We're in the Q. M. C.

"Oh, we sailed to Virginia."   See Admiral Benbow

Oh, we won't go back to Subic anymore. See Zamboanga

O weary heart that beatest.   See O vecchio cor, che batti (Verdi)

Oh, weary music the wind is making.   See An gille ban

"O weel may the boatie row."   See The boatie rows

O, weel may the keel row.   See The keel row

"Oh! weep for the hour."   See Eveleen's bower

"Oh we'll run all night till the morning." See Let the bullgine run

Oh, we'll wait till Jesus comes.   See Down by the river

"Oh, we're from dear old Wesley'n."   See Alma mater—Ohio Wesleyan university (Cuppett)

"Oh, we're going to the Hamburg show." See Hail! hail! the gang's all here (Sullivan)

"Oh! we're the old ninth infantry."   See The old ninth infantry

"Oh, we're three jolly, jolly sailor boys." See The three sailor boys (Marzials)

"O Wermeland, du schönes."   See Vermeland

"O, wert thou in the cauld blast."   Scottish air: ‹The lass o' Livingston› Words by R. Burns.   GS

"O wert thou in the cauld blast."   Mendelssohn.   Words by R. Burns. BB—GS—MFS—TFG—TFR

"O wert thou in the cauld blast."   Duet. Mendelssohn.   Words by R. Burns. GOS 2.   g. also GS

"Oh, what a thing it is to be."   See Oh, you little darling

"Oh! what a thrill."   See The spirit of the hill (Gobble)

"O what are you going to do when your father comes home."   See Edward (Villamont, Va. version)

"O what can you tell." J. C. Lowry. Words by R. W. Raymond. MFS

"O what did you have for your supper, my son." See Lord Randal (Callaway, Va. version)

"Oh, what is the matter with robin." MFS

"O what is this the blood of." See Edward (Endicott, Va. version)

"Oh, what was your name in the States." See What was your name in the States

"O what will you say when your father comes back." See Edward (Carmen, N.C. version)

"Oh, when I come to die, oh, when I come to die." See Give me Jesus

"Oh, when I git t' heaven." See Father Abraham

"O when I left the state of Georgia." See In old Virginny (Franklin county, Va. version)

"Oh! when I was a little piccaninny." See Poor old Uncle Rufe

"O when you come in summer time." See De blue tail fly

"O where, and O where is your Highland laddie gone." See The blue bells of Scotland (Jordan)

"O where are you going, my good old man." See The good old man (Hindman, Ky. version no. 1)

"O where are you going, Sally Anne." See Sally Anne

"O where are you going to, my pretty little dear." See Dabbling in the dew

"O where are you going to, my pretty maid." See The Rio Grande

"O where did you stay last night." See Lord Randal (St Helen's, Ky. version)

"Oh! where ha'e ye been a' the day." See Bonnie laddie, Highland laddie

"O where ha'e ye been, Lord Ronald, my son." See Lord Ronald

"Oh! where has the exile his home." See The Irish exile

"Oh, where have you been, Billy boy, Billy boy." See My boy Willie (American version; Hot Springs, N.C. version; Virginia version)

"O where have you been, Lord Randal my son." See Lord Randal (Georgia version)

"Oh where have you been this livelong day, my little wee croodin' doo." See The little wee croodin' doo

"Oh, where have you been wand'ring, King Henry, my son." See King Henry, my son

"O where is pretty Polly." See The cruel ship's carpenter (Berea, Ky. versions no. 1 and 3; Hindman, Ky. version; Jackson, Ky. version)

"Oh, where, tell me where is your Highland laddie gone." See The blue bells of Scotland (Jordan)

"O, whisky is the life of man, O Whisky Johnny." See Whisky

"Oh, whisky is the life of man, Whisky Johnny." See Whisky Johnny

"Oh! whisper what thou feelest." See Whisper what thou feelest (Richards)

Oh, whistle, and I'll come to you, my lad. Composer unknown. Words by R. Burns. GS

O whistle, and I'll come to you, my lad. [Attributed to J. Bruce] Words by R. Burns. GOS 2—GS

"Oh! white folks I was never born." See Oh, I'se so wicked

"Oh! white folks I will sing you a ditty." See Old Bob Ridley

"Oh white folks, listen, will you now." See Folks that put on airs

"O white robed maid." See I love my love so well (Audran)

"Oh, who do you call de King Emanuel." See King Emanuel

"O who is like my Johnnie." See The keel row

"O, who will drive the chariot when she comes." See When the chariot comes

"O who will o'er the downs so free." See Who will o'er the downs (Pearsall)

"O who will shoe my fair foot." See Fair Annie of Lochryan

"O, who will shoe your pretty little foot." See Who will shoe your pretty little foot

"Oh! whom shall we marry." See "Eh! qui marierons-nous"

"Oh, why camest thou before me." Welsh folk song. DSC

"Oh! why do you tease us." Old song. SW

"Oh, why don't you work like other men do." See Hallelujah, I'm a bum (Husband)

"O wie lieblich ist das mädchen" ("O how lovely is my darling") R. Schumann. Words by Geibel. e.g. GA

"O, wie so schön und gut ist doch ein freier mut." See Tanzlied

O wie wohl ist mir am abend. For English translation see Lovely evening

"O wild is thy joy, my affectionate boy." Children's song. MFS

"O William being a youthful lover." See William Taylor (Berea, Ky. version)

"O Willie brew'd a peck o' maut" (Willie brew'd a peck o' maut) A. Masterton. Words by R. Burns. GS

"Oh! Willie, is it you, dear." See Willie, we have missed you (Foster)

O willow, willow. See The willow song (16th century air)

O! willow, willow, willow. See The willow song (16th century air)

"O wilt thou share an honored name." See Couldst thou but know (Balfe)

"O wonderful sun, in your blaze of golden glory." See "O bright sun"

"Oh! won't you come along." See Won't you come along (Drayton)

Oh, won't you take me to that Swanee shore. See Take me to that Swanee shore (Muir)

"Oh, worse than death indeed." See "Angels ever bright and fair" (Händel)

"**O** worship the King all glorious above." See O come let us worship (Haydn)

O, write my name. See De angels in heab'n gwineter write my name

"**Oh!** yah! y'ah! darkies, laugh wid me." See Old Shady (Hanby)

"**O** Yankee Doodle went to town." See Yankee Doodle

"**Oh,** Yarmouth is a pretty town." Folk song from Sussex. BET

"**O** ye young, ye gay ye proud." See Happy in eternity

Oh! ye'll tak' the high road. See Loch Lomond

Oh, yes ("I tell ye, bretheren") Negro spiritual. HRD

"**Oh,** yes, I am a southern girl." See The southern girl (Macarthy)

Oh, yes, I'm gwine up. See Gwine up

Oh, yes! oh, yes. Negro spiritual. JB 2

"**Oh,** yes we'll fight, fight, fight for Dickinson." See Fight for Dickinson (Allen and Sheafe)

Oh! yes, yes, yes! she's all the world to me. See I love you

"**Oh,** yes, yonder comes my Lord." Negro spiritual. HRD

O yonder comes my true love. See Green bushes (Virginia version)

Oh, you better min'. See "You better min'"

"**Oh** you got Jesus, hold Him fast." See Oh, wasn't that a wide river

Oh you little darling. Old popular song. WSS

Oh, you men, oh, you men. See "Oh! why do you tease us"

"**O** you ought to be your Fader's chil'en." See The trouble of the world

Oh, you'll take the high road. See Loch Lomond

"**Oh** young Lochinvar is come out of the west." See Young Lochinvar (Mazzinghi)

"**Oh,** your cavalry and your infantry." See Why! oh why (Macarthy)

"**Oh,** you've heard of the navy." See The service boast

The **oak** and the ash (Eiche und esche) [17th century air: The quodling's delight] e.g. ML 1

"**Ob** ich einen krämer möchte." See Wen ich will zur ehe

"Ein **obdach** gegen sturm" ("A shelter from the storms") R. Kahn. Words by F. Rückert. e.g. SAT

Ober a malach is dos gewen. See Zie tut krawiec miescka

"**Oberlin** for ever! we will sing to you." See Oberlin pep song (Peery)

Oberlin, our alma mater. Oberlin college song. J. N. Pierce (music and words) AI—LAS

Oberlin pep song. Oberlin college song. R. R. Peery (music and words) AI —AIS

Oberschwäbischer ländler ("Rosestock, holderblüh'") Volkslied. g. EDL

O'Brien, J. Vick
Alma mater—Carnegie institute of technology

O'Brien, Lucius
Benny Havens, oh (Irish air)

Obstination (Steadfast love) H. de Fontenailles. Words by F. Coppée. e.f. BST

O'Carolan, Turlogh
The Arethusa (attributed; attributed also to W. Shield)
[L'occasion manquée] "Ah! qui me passera le bois" ("Ah! who will guide me thro' the wood") Folk song: Canadian version. e.f. GC

The **ocean** waves may roll. U.S. Naval academy song. Air: The mermaid. US

"**Och,** girls dear, did you ever hear." See Katey's letter (Sainton-Dolby)

O'Connor, John Lewis
Campus song (Nairn)

O'Connor, Caleb Wilson
Down the field (Friedman)

October ("Heigho! heigho! heigho! loud are October's songs") Bohemian air. Words by K. Davis. DSB

"**Oda** me tavane." See "Zimmer mit altan"

"**Odbegla** je popadija." See Vor der abreise

Ode to joy. See An die freude (Beethoven)

O'Dea, James
Hiawatha (Daniels)

O'Donnell aboo. Words by M. J. McCann. SI

"**O'er** all the way." See Les rameaux (Fauré)

"**O'er** my head." Flotow. [Tr of Ja, seit früher kindheit tagen] e. WLO

"**O'er** Pennsylvania's walls." See Fight on, Pennsylvania (Zoob)

O'er the crossing. Negro folk song from Virginia. AS

"**O'er** the forest rainclouds lower" ("Ereszkedik le a felhő") B. Egressy. Words by A. Petőfi. e.hu. KH 1

O'er the hills and o'er the main. See Over the hills and far away

"**O'er** the horizon's western plain." See När sol går ner (Stenhammar)

"**O'er** the lithe lily" ("Szomorú füzága") K. de Simonffy. e.hu. KH 2
"Szomorú fűz ága" ("Über die feldblume") g.hu. ML 3

"**O'er** the ocean flies a merry fay." See Marianina

"**O'er** the ocean, 'mid fearful dangers." See "Cimentando i venti e l'onde" (Rossini)

"**O'er** the quiet meadow who comes at close of day." See Night song

O'er the sea, o'er the sea, resounding. See Pull away, brave boys (Rossini)

"**O'er** thy tomb." Chorus of priestesses. C. W. von Gluck. [Tr of Contemplez ces tristes apprêts] e. CSB 6

"**O'er** thy waters darkly flowing." See Mother Volga

Of a Monday, ha, ha. See The song of the good little men

"**Of** a' the airts the wind can blaw." W. Marshall. Words by R. Burns. GS

"**Of** all the banjo songs that have been sung of late." See The other side of Jordan

"**Of** all the birds that ever I see." See The owl

"**Of** all the girls that are so smart." See Sally in our alley (Traditional air); Sally in our alley (Carey)

"**Of** all the mem'ries of the past." See The good-bye at the door (Glover)

"**Of** all the wives as e'er you know." See Nancy Lee (Maybrick)

"**Of** gaiety, I've seen a deal." See Champagne Charlie (Lee)

"**Of** love like this how vainly." See "Tacea la notte placida" (Verdi)

"**Of!** of; din Ploeşti până'n Gheboaïa." See Din Ploesti pana'n Gheboaia

"**Of** that dark scaffold." G. Verdi. [Tr of Di quella pira] e. WG

"**Of** the Father's love begotten." 13th century air. Words from Prudentius. [Tr of Corde natus ex parentis] e. DN

Of the place where we would be. See "In the valley of Virginia" (Allen)

Of the rose and you. C. W. Kern. Words by B. J. Wolf. BST

"**Off,** off we go, headlong, full speed." See Coaching song (Audran)

Off to Charleston. Minstrel song. WSS

Off to Philadelphia. Adapted from an old Irish air. SFB

"**Off** to the war, to the war I did go." See The lover's lament (Hot Springs, N.C. version)

Offenbach, Jacques
"Ah! how I love the military" (from La grande duchesse. Tr of Ah, que j'aime les militaires)
Ah! letters from lovers. See Letters from lovers
"Ah! the birds are in the woodlands" (from Les contes d'Hoffmann. Tr of Les oiseaux dans la charmille)
"Ah! 'tis a famous regiment" (from La grande duchesse. Tr of Ah, c'est un fameux régiment)
"All in good order" (from La grande duchesse. Tr of En très bon ordre)
Barcarolle. See "Silent now the drowsy bird"
"Behold the sabre." See The sabre song
"Belle nuit" (from Les contes d'Hoffmann)
"Child of mine" (from Les contes d'Hoffmann. Tr of Chère enfant! que j'appelle comme autrefois)
"Come, ye pretty maidens" (from La grande duchesse. Tr of Allez, jeunes filles, dansez et tournez vous)
"Good-night" (from La grande duchesse. Tr of Bonne nuit, monsieur, bonne nuit)

"Ha! ha! ha! the bomb is bursting" (from Les contes d'Hoffmann. Tr of Ah! ah! ah! la bombe éclaté)
In merry chorus
The legend of the glass (from La grande duchesse. Tr of Il était un de ·mes aïeux)
Letters from lovers (from La grande duchesse. Tr of Je t'ai sur mon coeur)
"A little doll with china eyes" (from Les contes d'Hoffmann. Tr of Une poupée aux yeux d'émail)
"Lovely night." See "Belle nuit"
"My heart is full of joy" (from Les contes d'Hoffmann. Tr of J'ai le bonheur dans l'âme)
"Now having, not without defect" (from La grande duchesse. Tr of Après avoir, tant bien que mal)
"O heav'n with sweetest joy" (from Les contes d'Hoffmann. Tr of Ô Dieu de quelle ivresse)
The sabre song (from La grande duchesse. Tr of Le sabre de mon père)
"Say to him" (from La grande duchesse. Tr of Dites-lui qu'on l'a remarqué distingué)
"Silent now the drowsy bird" (same air as "Belle nuit")
The students' song (from Les contes d'Hoffmann. Tr of Jusqu'au matin remplis)
Waltz song (from Les contes d'Hoffmann. Tr of Elle danse! en cadence)
Welcome to morning

L'**offeso** onor, signori. See Infelice! e tu credevi (Verdi)

"The **officers** live on top of the hill." See I don't want no more army

Official West Point march. P. Egner. Words by Parham. DSO

"**Oft** as Thee, my infant Saviour." Traditional carol. FC

"**Oft** I roam my garden bow'rs." See Shule, agra

"**Oft** in danger, oft in woe." Words by H. K. White. MFS

"**Oft** in the stilly night." [Attributed to] J. Stevenson. Words by T. Moore. GOS 1—HMI—MFS—SI—SSB—TFB

Oft still I wander. See Or là sull' onda, col pensier mio (Mercadante)

"**Og** menniskja, ho sviv ikring." See Ljos (Sinding)

Ogiński, Michał Kłeofas
Dombrowski's march. See Polish national song (attributed)
Polish national song (attributed)

Oh. For entries beginning Oh see O

O'Hara, Geoffrey
K-K-K-Katy

"**Ohe,** Ciccuzza, va guviernete." See Ciccuzza

Ohio, come cheer for Wesleyan. See Red and black (Wright)

"**Ohnegleichen** war Andreas Kerekes." See "There was none to match Kerekes"

"**Ohoiyeho**, hoyeho, who's for the ferry." See Twickenham ferry (Marzials)

Oi ahin, ahin, ahin.　See "Zu kennt ihr denn dos land"

ıOi, alas, a robberı A gneive.　Jewish folk song.　y.　KAJ

"**Oi** der rebbenu."　Jewish folk song.　y. SY

"**Oï** drěvoïche t"nko ta vīsoko."　See Lied des kahnfahrers

"**Oï** gaîu moï."　See "O mein hain"

Oi gewald, a ganef.　See Oi, alas, a robber

Oi hot er a pfeifer.　See Der eisenbahn

"**Oi**, ko žvengi, žirgeli."　See "Sag, was wieherst du, mein rösslein"

"**Oi** mein mann, wos wet sein m'koach burikes."　See Burikes

"**Oï** piïdu ïa dolom."　See Junggesel-lenlied

"**Oï** ru-du-du, ru-du-du."　See "O rududu, rududu"

Oisean is Malmhine (Ossian und Malwine) Old Gaelic folk song.　ga.g.　ML i

Les **oiseaux** dans la charmille.　For English translation see "Ah! the birds are in the woodlands" (Offenbach)

"**Oj** grzmią wozy, grzmią po bukowinie." See "Horch, ein wagen naht durch den dunklen wald"

"**Oj** stoji stoji Beligrad."　See "Es steht, es steht gross Belgerad"

O'Kane, Tullius Clinton
　　Over there (Huntington)

O'Keeffe, John
　　"Amo, amas, I love a lass" (Traditional air)
　　The ploughboy (Shield)

"**Okh**, ne buïnyï vïêter zavyval."　See The Tartar host

De **ol'** ark's a moverin'.　See The old ark a-moving along

De **ol'** sheep done know de road.　See The ole sheep done know the road

"**Olaf** the viking sailed away."　See Olaf Trygvason (Grieg)

Olaf Trygvason (Landkjending)　E. Grieg. Words by B. Björnson.　e.　TFG

Olafsen, J.
　　Her hjemme (Norse air)

"**Old** Abe Lincoln came out of the wilderness."　Air: Ol' gray mare come tearin' out de wilderness.　Campaign song of 1860.　SBA

Old Adam ("I'm so sorry for old Adam") Traditional song from Virginia.　SBA

Old Arizona again.　Old 4th cavalry song.　DSO

ıThe **old** ark a-moving alongı The old ark a-moverin along.　Negro spiritual. BB
　　De ole ark a-moverin' along.　HRD
　　De ol' ark's a moverin'.　JG
　　De ol' ark's a-moverin' an' I'm goin' home.　JB 2

Old Arkansas.　Folk song from Kentucky. SES 2

The **old** arm chair.　H. Russell.　Words by E. Cook.　GOS 1—HP

Old Aunt Jemima.　Plantation song. TFB—TFO—TFP

"**Old** bald eagle."　Play-party game from Kentucky.　SES 2

"**Old** Beebe had three full grown sons." See Oh, didn't he ramble (Cole)

"**Old** Billy Apple Tree he did die."　See Old Roger (North Carolina version)

"**Old** Billy Riley was a dancing master." See Billy Riley

The **old** black duck.　Folk song: North Carolina version.　SES 2
　　—Tennessee version.　SES 2
　　Variant of: The fox

Old black Joe.　S. C. Foster (music and words)　BB—BNM—DFF—DSC —LAS—TFP—TFR—WSS
　　Old black Joe (Alter Joe)　e.g. ML 1

Old Bob Ridley.　Minstrel song.　WSS

Old brass wagon.　Middle western dance song.　SBA

The **old** cabin home.　ıT. Paineı　BNM —LAS

Old Catholic hymn.　See Requiem (Schumann)

The **old** chariot.　Windlass chantey. BOS 2
　　Variant of: Roll de ole chariot along

The **old** Chisholm trail.　Cowboy song. TFP
　　Variant: The Chisholm trail (1st version)

Old clothes.　See Ole clo'

The **old** cottage clock.　<J. L. Molloy. Words by C. Swain>　MFS

Old cruise song.　U.S. Naval academy song.　US

The **old** cuckoo clock that hangs upon the wall.　J. W. Wheeler (music and words)　SW

Old Dan Tucker ("I come to town de udder night")　H. Russell.　PSG
　　Ole Dan Tucker.　BB—WSS

The **old** destroyer squadron.　U.S. navy song.　US

"**Old** Doc. Jones."　Play-party game from Kentucky.　SES 2

Old dog Tray.　S. C. Foster (music and words)　BB—TFG—WSS

ıOld Dutch songı "Beside the stream." 15th century song.　e.　LSB

Old easy-chair by the fire.　J. C. Beckel. MFS

The **old** familiar place.　C. W. Glover. ıWords by J. E. Carpenterı　MFS

The **old** folks at home.　S. C. Foster (music and words)　BB—BNM— DFF—DSB—DSC—GOS 1—LAS— MBS—MFS—TFP—TFR—WSS
　　Old folks at home (Swanee ribber.— Negers heimweh)　e.g.　ML 1

"**Old** folks, young folks, all you darkies come."　See Bible stories

Old Gaelic lullaby.　See Gaelic lullaby

Old gold.　State university of Iowa alma mater.　Irish air: My lodging is in the cold ground.　Words by J. C. Parish. KU—KV

"The old gray hearse." See The hearse song

Old gray mare ("Oh, the old gray mare, she ain't what she used to be") Air: The old gray mare came tearin' out the wilderness. SBA

The old grey goose. Folk song from North Carolina. SES 2

"The old grey hearse." See The hearse song

The old grey mare ("O once I bought me an old grey mare") Folk song: Flag Pond, Tenn. version. SES 2

The old grey mare ("Once I had an old grey mare") Rocky Fork, Tenn. version. SES 2

The old grey mare ("Once I had an old yellow mare") North Carolina version. SES 2

Old Hal o' the west. American political song of 1844. Air: Old Rosin, the beau. SRW

Old ham, it is the meat. See Good sweet ham

[Old hundred] "All people that on earth do dwell." [Attributed to Guillaume Franc] Words by W. Kethe. MBS

Old hundredth. DSB

Old hundred ("Be Thou, O God, exalted high") Attributed to Guillaume Franc. [Words by N. Tate and N. Brady] MFS

Old hundred ("Praise God, from Whom all blessings flow."—Doxology) Attributed to Guillaume Franc. [Words by T. Ken] MFS

"Praise God from Whom all blessings flow" (Old hundredth.—The doxology) BB

Old hundredth ("All people that on earth do dwell") See Old hundred ("All people that on earth do dwell") (Franc?)

Old hundredth ("Praise God from Whom all blessings flow") See Old hundred ("Praise God from Whom all blessings flow") (Franc?)

Old Ironsides. Composer unknown. Words by O. W. Holmes. US

Old Ironsides. B. O. Klein. Words by O. W. Holmes. TFG

"Old Jerry was sending them over." See Bring back my kitchen to me (Fuller)

Old Joe Braddles. See Owd Joe Braddles

Old Joe Clarke. Folk song from Virginia. SES 2

"Old King Cole." Traditional song. BOS 2—CSB 1

"Old King Cole." Traditional song. Old air arr by F. S. KSO

"Old King Cole." Modern air and words. BOS 2

"Old King Cole." British army version. DSO

"Old Lamkin was as good a mason." See Lamkin (Beattyville, Ky. version)

Old love song ("All' mein gedanken") See Nur du

"Old MacDonald had a farm" (MacDonald's farm) Old song. BB

The old maid's lament ("When I was young and fair and gay") Traditional song. KSO

The old maid's song ("I had a sister Sally") (see Song Index)

Variant: The spinster's lament

Old maid's song ("Nadie me quiere") See "Nadie me quiere"

"Old man come home at night." See Our goodman (Pineville, Ky. version)

"The old man he came home at night." See The poor couple

"The old man he came in from plough." See The wife wrapt in wether's skin (Hyden, Ky. version)

"An old man went to the field to plough." See The farmer's curst wife (Oneida, Ky. version)

Old massa, he was kind. See The Alabama blossoms

."The old Missouri tiger." See The tiger song (Burkholder and Fowler)

"An old mother, whose tears were flowing." See "Per sua madre andò una figlia" (Donizetti)

"Old Mother Wig Wag she jumped out of bed." See The old black duck (North Carolina version)

The old musician and his harp. H. M. Higgins. Words by W. S. Pitts. GOS 2

Old Nassau. Princeton song. C. Langlotz. Words by H. P. Peck. AI—KU—KV

The old ninth infantry. Regimental march. DSO

"Old Noah he built himself an ark." See Noah's ark

The old oaken bucket. G. Kiallmark. Words by S. Woodworth. BB—DFF—GOS 1—MFS—TFP

Old Oberlin for ever. See Oberlin, our alma mater (Pierce)

[The old, old question] Die alte kasho Jewish folk song. y. SY

"Old Oregon we pledge to thee." See Oregon pledge song (Evans)

"Old Ponce Muir he had three 'suns,' he did, he did." See Ponce Muir's "suns" (Gilmore)

Old Roger. Play-party game: Kentucky version. SES 2

—North Carolina version. SES 2

Old Rosin, the beau. Old English song. GOS 1—SRW

Old S. U. Susquehanna university song. E. E. Sheldon (music and words) AIS

"Old Santa Claus sat all alone." See Santa Claus (Read)

"Old Satan is a busy old man." See Come go with me

"Old Satan told me to my face." See I know when I'm going home

"Old Satan's mighty busy." See Lord, until I reach my home

The old sexton. H. Russell. Words by P. Benjamin. GOS 1

Old (Ole) Shady. ₁B. R. Hanby₁ WSS

The **old** sheep done know the road. See The ole sheep done know the road

₁**Old** ship of Zion₁ "Come along" ('Tis the ole ship of Zion) Negro spiritual: <Virginia version> HRD

Old ship of Zion ("Don't you see that ship") North Carolina version. AS

The old ship of Zion ("What ship is that") Maryland version. AS

The **old** ship of Zion ("Hit's the ole ship") See The ole ship o' Zion (Mountain spiritual)

Old shoes. Ojibway Indian song. e.in. GSS

The **old** time ("'Twas when the hay was mown, Maggie") J. R. Thomas. GOS 2

An **old-time** celebration. Tufts college song. E. W. Newton. Words adapted from Felix Goddard. LAS

Old-time religion. See This old time religion

Old Wabash. Wabash college song. C. Ragan. Words by E. M. Robinson. AI—AIS

The **old** "waits" carol. See "The moon shines bright"

The **old** woman and the little pigee. See The little pig

"**Old** woman, I'd go drown myself." See The rich old lady (Burnsville, N.C. version)

"**Old** woman, old woman, are you fond of smoking." See The deaf woman's courtship

"The **old** year is dying" (New Year's song) Welsh carol. Words by W. Maynard. DSB

"The **old** year now away is fled." See Carol for New Year's day (Old English air)

The **old** Yorkshire gooding carol. 16th century air: Well-a-day. DNS

Old Zip Coon. Old American air. New words by D. Stevens. TFP Variant of: Turkey in the straw; Zip Coon

Olds, W. B.
"Hail to thee, our alma mater"

De **ole** 'ark a-moverin' along. See The old ark a-moving along

Ole clo'. Round. GSS

Ole Dan Tucker. See Old Dan Tucker (Russell)

"**Ole** Noah he did built de ark." See Noah's ark

"**Ole** Satan is a busy ole man." See Come go with me

Ole Shady. See Old Shady (Hanby)

De **ole** sheep done know de road. Negro spiritual. HRD
De ol' sheep done know de road (De young lam's mus' fin' de way) JB 2

The **ole** ship o' Zion ("Hit's the ole ship") Mountain spiritual. RA Variant: When the chariot comes

Ole-time religion. See This old time religion

Oleander time. Sailor's song. C. Repper. Words by H. H. Harris. TFO

"**Olga** sits a-weaving, weaving." See Weaving song

The **olive** and blue. Tulane university song. M. Ten Hoor and W. Goldstein (music and words) AI—AIS—KU

Olive green and blue, we love thee. See Alma mater—Tulane university (Ruebush)

Oliver, Henry Kemble
Federal street. See "Great God, we sing"; "Strong Son of God, immortal Love"
"Great God, we sing" (same air as Army hymn)
"Strong Son of God, immortal Love" (same air as Army hymn)

Oliviere, Alessio
Garibaldi's hymn. See Inno di guerra dei cacciatori delle Alpi
Inno di guerra dei cacciatori delle Alpi
Italian national hymn. See Inno di guerra dei cacciatori delle Alpi

Olsen, Ole
Baadfart
Sailing. See Baadfart

Olson, Julius Emil
The badger ballad (Composer unknown)

"**Om** dagen vid mitt arbete" ("Was ich am tag auch tue") Swedish folk song. g.sw. ML 1

"**On** a bank two roses fair." See Heidenröslein (Werner)

"**On** a bright summer morning I pursued my way." See Love letters (Newcombe)

"**On** a dark stormy night." See In the baggage coach ahead (Davis)

"**On** a hallowed hill in Tennessee." See Alma mater—University of Tennessee (Meek)

"**On** a lone barren isle." See The grave of Bonaparte (Heath)

"**On** a merry morn in May." Lithuanian air. Words by K. Davis. DSB

"**On** a Monday mornin' it began to rain; aroun' the bend come a passenger train. On the bumpers was a hobo John." See Jay Gould's daughter

"**On** a Monday morning it began to rain, around the bend come a passenger train; on the bumpers was an old Jimmie Jones." See On the Charlie so long

"**On** a morning bright and clear." See The girl I loved in sunny Tennessee (Redcliffe)

"**On** a pleasant day in summer at the central station door." See Picture eighty-four

On a summer day ("Oh, as I went down to Dover") French folk air: En passant par la Lorraine. Words by H. H. Harbour. DSB
As I went down to Dover. MBS

"On a summer day, as the waves were rippling." See The ship that never returned (Old American song)

"On a summer's day while the waves were rippling." See The ship that never returned (Kentucky mountain version)

On a Sunday afternoon. H. Von Tilzer. SRW

"On a Sunday morn, sat a maid forlorn." See Wait 'till the sun shines, Nellie (Von Tilzer)

"On a tree by a river little tomtit." See Tit-willow (Sullivan)

"On April sixth in 'seventeen." See Sims's Flotilla

"On billow rocking." R. Planquette. [Tr of Va petit moussei] e. WLO

On, brave old army team. West Point song. P. Egner. AI—AIS

"On Christmas eve the bells were rung." See Merry Christmas (Shaw)

"On Christmas night all Christians sing." See Christmas night (Folk air)

On comrades bold, never failing. See The red scarf (Bonheur)

On Datu Ali's trail. Song of the Spanish-American war. Air: Levee song. DSO—US

"On Easter day." Old air. Words by J. Erwin. DSB

"On Hounslow Heath as I rode o'er." See O rare Turpin

"On last Friday morning just after break of day." See The cruel ship's carpenter (Dewey, Va. version)

"On me turn thy sparkling lustre." See Bitte (Franz)

"On mighty pens uplifted soars." J. Haydn. e. SSO 1

"On Monday morning going to school." See The two brothers (Burnsville, N.C. version)

"On mountains and in valleys." See Ever safe with God (Cantor)

"On mules we find two legs behind." See Mules

[On music] "When thro' life unblest we rove." Irish air: The banks of Banna. Words by T. Moore. HI 1—HMI

On my name spotless is the dishonour stamp'd. See Nuova ferita (Mercadante)

"On ne les a pas soupçonnées." See Les larmes (Godard)

On, O thou soul. Serbian folk air. Words by F. Manley. TFP

"On old Long Island's sea-girt shore." See Rockaway (Russell)

"On, on, O thou soul." See On, O thou soul

"On one parent stalk." See The twin roses (Hewitt)

"On one summer's day sun was shining fine." See Bill Bailey, won't you please come home (Cannon)

On, roll on, my ball. See En roulant ma boule

"On Saint John's eve every maiden twineth." See "Flickan knyter" (Stenhammar)

"On song's bright pinions." See "Auf flügeln des gesanges" (Mendelssohn)

"On Sunday morning, bravely in your best." See "Am Sonntag morgen" (Brahms)

"On Sunday mornin' I seek my Lord." See Jine 'em

"On the banks of Allan water." See The banks of Allan water

On the banks of the old Raritan. Rutgers university song. Words by H. N. Fuller. AI—AIS—KU—KV

"On the banks of the Red Cedar." See Fight song (Lankey)

On the banks of the Wabash, far away. P. Dresser (music and words) GFS

"On the battle front we stand." See Tramp, tramp, tramp (Root)

"On the beach at Cape May." E. N. Slocum (music and words) SW

"On the breeze of ev'ning stealing." See Beautiful bells (Lyte)

On the bridge of Avignon. See "Sur le pont d'Avignon"

"On the bridge, round and round." See "Sur le pont d'Avignon"

On the Charlie so long. Railroad song. Air: Jay Gould's daughter. SBA Variant of: Jay Gould's daughter

"On the deck of Patrick Lynch's boat." See The county of Mayo

"On the distant prairie where the heather wild." See Rosalie, the prairie flower (Root)

"On the fifteenth day of June, brave boys." See The sons of liberty (Hindman, Ky. version)

"On the first day of May, et lon lan la lire lire." See "Le premier jour de mai"

On the lake of the Poncho plains. Cowboy song. LSC

"On the mountain, steep and hoary." See Der schweizerbue

On the other side of Jordan. Negro spiritual. WFN

On the ramparts. See Sur les clanquarts

"On the rugged eastern foothills." See Big C (Williams)

"On the twelfth day of Christmas." See The twelve days of Christmas

"On the twenty-fourth November, boys, 'twas in the channel we lay." See Shakings

"On the twenty-fourth of February, the weather being clear." See The twenty-fourth of February

"On their way I met at break of day." See Marcho dei rei

On to glory. Negro spiritual from Maryland. AS

On to our land ("Na-aleh l'artsenu") Yemenite song. e.he. BNP

"On to the morgue." Air from Chopin's Funeral march. SBA

"On to victory." University of New Hampshire song. F. V. Cole. AIS

"On Tom-big-bee river so bright I was born." See Tom-big-bee river (Steele)

"**On** top of old Smokey." See The wagoner's lad (Alleghany, N.C. version)

On Venice waters (" 'Tis night on Venice waters."—Gondolier waltz) O. Roeder. Words by H. Vaughan. SFB

"**On** we are floating in sunshine and shadow." See The boat song (Weber)

"**On** wings of music." See "Auf flügeln des gesanges" (Mendelssohn)

On wings of song. See "Auf flügeln des gesanges" (Mendelssohn)

"**On** Wingsfield mountain there did dwell." See Springfield mountain (Peaks of Otter, Va. version)

"**On** yesternight I saw a sight, a star as bright as day, and all along I heard a song." See The Virgin and Child (15th century air)

"**On** yonder hill there stands a creature." See O no, John

"**On** yonder rock reclining." ιD. F. Auber. Tr of Voyez sur cette rocheι e. MFS

"**Once** a boy a rose espied." See Heidenröslein (Schubert)

"**Once** a king there was." See Irmelin Rose (Nielsen)

"**Once** a lass, all in her pride." See Le chiffonnier

"**Once** a little dryad dancing lightly." See The dryad and the sunbeam

Once again ("I linger round the very spot") A. S. Sullivan. Words by L. H. Lewin. GE

"**Once** again, O blessed time." P. Franck. ιWords by W. Brightι FC

"**Once** again the flowers we gather." See Flowers for the brave (Bellini)

Once by His bid supernal Moses was call'd to guide ye. See D'Egitto là sui lidi (Verdi)

"**Once** I courted a charming beauty bright." See The lover's lament (Dewey, Va. version)

"**Once** I courted a fair beauty bright." See The lover's lament (Kentucky version; Marion, N.C. version; Woodridge, Va. version)

"**Once** I found three wand'ring gypsies." See Die drei zigeuner (Liszt)

"**Once** I had a true love." See The rejected lover (Marion, N.C. version)

"**Once** I had an old grey mare." See The old grey mare (Rocky Fork, Tenn. version)

"**Once** I had an old yellow mare." See The old grey mare (North Carolina version)

"**Once** I knew a little girl." See The rejected lover (White Rock, Va. version)

"**Once** I knew of a brisk young farmer." See William Hall (Montvale, Va. version; Villamont, Va. version)

"**Once** I lov'd a maiden fair" ("Hatt' ein liebchen einst erwählt") 17th century English song. e.g. ML 1

"**Once** I was happy but now I'm forlorn." See The man on the flying trapeze

"**Once** in the dear dead days beyond recall." See Love's old sweet song (Molloy)

"**Once** in thine eyes." See "Ich hab' in deinem auge" (Franz)

"**Once** long ago, the legend saith." See The crown of roses (Tchaikovsky)

"**Once,** long ago when the world lay asleep." Old Bohemian Christmas carol. Words by R. Compton. DSB

"**Once** Mary would go wandering." See Marias wanderschaft

"**Once** me 'n' Lem Briggs." See They gotta quit kickin' my dawg aroun' (Perkins)

"**Once** more, dear home." See Pilgrims' chorus (Wagner)

"**Once** more I see thee, oh Babylonia." See Ah! quel giorno (Rossini)

"**Once** more the leaves are falling." See Afsked (Melartin)

"**Once** on a time, so I've been told." See The song of the Triton (Molloy)

"**Once** on a time there was a man." See Peter Gray

"**Once** there lived a bold fisherman." See The bold fisherman (Greely)

"**Once** there lived side by side two little maids." See I don't want to play in your yard (Petrie)

"**Once** there was a little boy." See The honest boy

"**Once** there was a little drummer." See The drummer and the cook

"**Once** there was a little tailor boy." See The miller's apprentice (Pineville, Ky. version)

"**Once** there was a man went to woods with gun." Old song. KSO

"**Once** three kings upon the break of day." See Marcho dei rei

"**Once** two is two." See Multiplication table

Onderdonk, Henry Ustick
"How wondrous and great" (Haydn)

"**One** bumper at parting." Air: Moll Roe in the morning. Words by T. Moore. HMI

"**One** by one." V. Bellini. Words by A. A. Procter. MFS

"**One** came before her and said." See An island spinning song

"**One** cold and cloudy day in the month of May." See Barbara Allen (Chicopee county, Ga. version no. 2)

"**One** cold freezing morning I lay dis body down." See Every hour in the day

"**One** cold winter morning, dejected and pale." See I'm a poor stranger

"**One** cold winter's morning." Folk song: Berea, Ky. version. SES 2
—St Helen's, Ky. version. SES 2

"**One** day a gnome, brimful of spite." See The legend of the mascots (Audran)

"**One** day as I was a walkin' along de heb'nly road." See My God is so high

"**One** day as I was walkin' along, gwine to live humble to de Lord." See Gwine to live humble to de Lord

"One day as I went walking down by the Clarence dock." See Can't you dance the polka

"One day down in some lonesome grove." See The lonesome grove (Villamont, Va. version)

"One day I thought I'd have some fun." See The tenderfoot

"One day I was perambulating." K. Millöcker. e. WLO

"One day in a lonesome grove." See The lonesome grove (Peaks of Otter, Va. version)

"One day on board rose a dreadful screaming." See William Taylor (Beattyville, Ky. version)

"One day, one day, in the month of May." See Barbara Allen (Barbourville, Ky. version no. 2)

"One day, one day, one high holiday." See Little Musgrave and Lady Barnard (Pine Mountain, Ky. version; Big Laurel, N.C. version)

"One day, one day, one holi, whole day." See Little Musgrave and Lady Barnard (Barbourville, Ky. version no. 2)

"One day, one day, one holiday." See Little Musgrave and Lady Barnard (Wasioto, Ky. version)

"One day when I was a-rambling around." See Wild Bill Jones

"One evenin' in de month of May." See Johnny, get your gun

"One evening, one evening, two brothers gone from school." See The two brothers (Mount Fair, Va. version no. 1)

"One fair day three kings in bright array." See Marcho dei rei

"One fine day me sittee in shop." See The war junk Tennessee

"One fine morning in May I was tilling the land." See The Kerry recruit

"One Friday morning we set sail." See The mermaid (North Carolina version)

"One glance, love, turn on me." See "Un guardo volgi a me" (Marcello)

"One holiday, one righteous day." See Little Musgrave and Lady Barnard (Flag Pond, Tenn. version no. 2)

"One holy church of God appears" (Holy Trinity) J. Barnby. Words by S. Longfellow. LAS

The one I love. See Celui que j'aime

One lies down near Appomattox. See The blue and the gray (Dresser)

One little, two little, three little, four little, five little nigger boys. See "Ten little niggers"

"One lone crow had follow'd me." See Die krähe (Schubert)

"One Monday morn in the month of May." See Barbara Allen (Greenwood, Va. version)

One more day ("Oh, row me cross the river") Chantey. TFO
For variants see following songs of same title

One more day ("Only one more day, my Johnny") Capstan chantey. TSB 2

One more day ("Only one more day my Johnny") Windlass chantey. WSE

One more river ("The animals went in one by one") Traditional song. BOS 2
Variant of: Noah's ark

"One morn when the wind from the northwest blew keenly." See The smuggler (Davy)

"One morning bright and early de news came safe to hand." See Song of the Memphis volunteers

"One morning fair as Phoebus bright his radiant charms display'd." See Dobbin's flowery vale

"One morning I was a-walking down." See Nobody knows the trouble I've had

One morning in May ("One morning, one morning") See The nightingale (Pine Mountain, Ky. version no. 2)

"One morning, oh, so early." A. Scott-Gatty. Words by J. Ingelow. GE

"One morning, one morning in the spring." See Early, early in the spring (Allanstand, N.C. version)

"One morning, one morning, one morning in May, all fields were in blossom." See Sally and her lover

"One morning, one morning, one morning in May, I heard a fair damsel lamenting and say." See The rebel soldier (Hyden, Ky. version)

"One morning, one morning, one morning in May, I heard a poor soldier." See The rebel soldier (Franklin county, Va. version; Meadows of Dan, Va. version)

"One morning, one morning, one morning in May I met a fair couple a-making their way." See The nightingale (Pine Mountain, Ky. versions no. 1-2; Tennessee version)

"One morning, one morning, one morning in May, I saw a fair couple a-making their way." See The nightingale (St Helen's, Ky. versions no. 1-2)

"One morning, one morning, one morning in May, I spied a fair couple a-making their way." See The nightingale (Berea, Ky. version)

"One morning, one morning, the weather being fine." See I must and I will get married (Beechgrove, Va. version)

"One night as I lay in my bed." See The foggy dew

"One night as I lay sleeping." See Loving Reilly (Georgia version)

"One night as I sat by my fireside so weary." See A pack of cards

"One night came on a hurricane." See Barney Buntline (Composer unknown)

"One night I had a pleasant dream." See Ring dat golden bell

"One night when I was weaving on the loom." See Y gwŷdd

"One night when the wind it blew cold." See Mary of the wild moor

"One summer eve, with pensive thought." See Shells of ocean (Cherry)

One summer night. See "Am schönsten sommerabend war's" (Grieg)

"One Sunday after dark, I went to take the air." See Youpe! youpe! sur la rivière

"One sweetly solemn thought." R. S. Ambrose. Words by P. Cary. ASA

"One thought I have, my ample creed" (Serenity) Arr from W. V. Wallace. Words by F. L. Hosmer. LAS

One thought of mother, at home alone. See Just as the sun went down (Udall)

"One, two, three, four, we don't need any more." See We saw the damn thing through

"One was a fair sea-captain." See The bold lieutenant (Wasioto, Ky. version)

"One wet night, upon the platform." See Somebody's child (Plimpton)

O'Neil, Harry D.
Spirit of Maine

Onivas, D., pseud. See Savino, Domenico

Only ("Only a face at the window") See Only her love I ask for (Gabriel)

"Only a face at the window." See Only her love I ask for (Gabriel)

Only a 'ittle dirly dirl. A. F. Andrews (music and words) SRW

Only a rose. M. Wellings. SFB

[Only her love I ask for] Only. V. Gabriel (music and words) GE

Only me. Bratton. Words by Ford. SRW

"Only one more day my Johnny." See One more day

"Only one more jungle season." Song from the 11th U.S. engineers. [C. C. Converse] DSO

Only smile. See "Star vicino" (Rosa)

"Only to see her face again." Minstrel ballad. J. E. Stewart. WSS

Onneton. See Melancholy (Merikanto)

"Onuh nih'yeh horishonim." See A song of the Chalutsim

Onward ("Hail to the glory of the morning") Scripps college alma mater. H. P. Eames. Words by H. B. Alexander. HW

"Onward, Christian soldiers." A. S. Sullivan. Words by S. Baring-Gould. BB—DSC—TFP

Onward, upward alma mater. University of Redlands song. C. H. Marsh. Words by E. B. Van Osdel. HW

"Open, dearest" ("Nyisd ki rózsám") Duet. Old Hungarian folk song. e.hu. KH 2

[Open, Lord, my inward ear] Hymn to joy. L. van Beethoven. [Words by C. Wesley] DSC

"Open thy lattice, love." S. C. Foster (music and words) WSS

"Open unto me the gates of righteousness" (see Song Index) Also in I will extol Thee, O Lord (Costa) SSO 1

Operti, Giuseppe
The Broadway, opera and Bowery crawl

Opferlied ("Die flamme lodert") L. van Beethoven. Words by F. von Matthisson. g. EDL

The opossum ("Away down yonder in a cedar tree") Folk song from Kentucky. SES 2

The opossum and the racoon. See Possum

"The opossum is a cunning thing." See The squirrel (Endicott, Va. version)

"Opossum up a gum-tree." See Possum

Oppenheimer, Mrs Helen Judith (Vickers) See Vickers, Helen Judith

Optional accompaniment for Music in the air. See Music in the air, Counterpoint for (Loomis)

Or là sull' onda, col pensier mio. Mercadante. e.i. PC

"Ora fatal giungesti." See Ah! quello fu per me (Donizetti)

The orchestra. Old game song. TFG —TFR

Orden, Oliver, pseud. See Loomis, Harvey Worthington

Ordway, John P.
Dreaming of home and mother
Lone starry hours (wrongly attributed) See Power, J. Lone starry hours
"Twinkling stars are laughing, love"

O'Reardon, M.
Marriage bells

O'Reardon, William J.
Marriage bells (O'Reardon, M.)

Oregon, our alma mater. See Mighty Oregon (Perfect)

Oregon pledge song. University of Oregon song. J. S. Evans. AI—KU —KV

O'Reilly, Miles, pseud. See Halpine, Charles Graham

"O'Reilly was a soldier, the pride of Battery B." See O'Reilly's gone to hell

O'Reilly's gone to hell. Air: When Reuben comes to town. Words by G. E. Griffin. DSO

Orem is nit gut. See The uninvited aunt

O'Riley, Miles, pseud. See Halpine, Charles Graham

Orlandi, Fernando
"Degli augelletti al canto" (from Il podestà di Chioggia)

Orlandini, Giuseppe Maria
"Caro, son tua così" (from Temistocle)

Orlov, I.
Russian lullaby (attributed) See Bakhmetiev, N. I. The Cossack's lullaby

O'Rourke, Edmund. See Falconer, Edmund

The orphan boys ("Our cot was shelter'd") SRW

The orphan girl ("No home, no home.")— No bread for the poor) Mountain folk song. SBA
Variant of: Mag's song

Orred, Meta
"In the gloaming, oh, my darling" (Harrison)

Ortonville (Hastings) See Fourth of July hymn; "A little word in kindness said"

"Os ha gjort." See Hjemreise fra saetren

Osborn, Arthur Herbert. See Hewitt, Joseph Frederick, jt. comp.

Osborne, George Alexander
"Who's at my window"

Osemnajset gumbov. See "Wasch in weisser milch"

Osgood, Mrs
"Call me pet names" (Jarvis)

Osme's song. East Indian air. Words by G. Darley. DSB

Ossian und Malwine. See Oisean is Malmhine

Ossian's serenade. O. E. Dodge. GOS 1

Österling, Anders
Pionerna (Rangström)

Osterwald, Karl Wilhelm
Lieber schatz, sei wieder gut mir (Franz)

O'Sullivan, Jane Beatrice
The triumph hymn (Lvov)

Oswald, James
God save the king (attributed) See Carey, H. God save the king (attributed)
"The lovely lass of Inverness"
Roslin Castle (attributed)

"Ot asoi neht a schneider." See Neht a schneider

"The other night, while I was sparking." See Kiss me quick and go (Buckley)

The other side of Jordan. Minstrel song. PSG

"Otvüd Etropole." See Die Lukowiterinnen

Où s'en vont ces gais bergers. 16th century French Canadian Noël. e. DNS

Oui, c'est toi, je t'aime. For English translation see "Ah! I love thee only" (Gounod)

Oui, nous devons faire taire. For English translation see "Gossip monger, village gadder" (Planquette)

Oungst, Webb M.
They gotta quit kickin' my dawg aroun' (Perkins)

Our alma mater. Utah state agricultural college song. Air: Der tannenbaum. HW

"Our alma mater fair through life, thy love, we bear." See Alma mater—George Washington university (Carey?)

"Our army is a motley crew." See The infantry

"Our boys will shine to-night." American air. TFP
Variants: "Central will shine"; "Our club will shine"; "Our troop will shine tonight"

Our brother is born. H. Farjeon. Words by E. Farjeon. OB
Carol ("Now every child that dwells on earth") CSB 1

"Our brothers, the doughboys, the highbrow engineers." See The hiking song of the eighth infantry (Morales)

"Our campfires shone bright on the mountain." See When Sherman marched down to the sea (Rockwell)

Our Chicago. University of Chicago song. N. Reid (music and words) KU—KV

"Our chosen state, all hail to thee." See Montana my Montana (Greenwood)

"Our club will shine." School song. TFR
Variants: "Central will shine"; "Our boys will shine tonight"; "Our troop will shine tonight"

Our Colorado. Colorado college song. E. W. Hille. Words by A. T. French. HW

"Our cot was shelter'd in a wood." See The orphan boys

"Our country's flag! O emblem dear." See Freedom's flag (Geibel)

"Our Father in Heaven, we hallow Thy name." See The Lord's prayer (Composer unknown)

"Our Father, Who art in heav'n." See The Lord's prayer (Krebs)

Our flag ("Wave, flag of beauty") N. P. Mersereau. Words by J. McD. Leavitt. LAS

Our flag o'er us waving (Anvil chorus) G. Verdi. MFS

"Our four-star admiral swore." See The cruising boys of subdiv. nine (Root)

"Our God to us gave iron here." See Vaterlandslied (Methfessel)

Our goodman. Folk song: Barbourville, Ky. version. SES 1
—Pineville, Ky. version. SES 1
—Big Laurel, N.C. version no. 1. SES 1
—Big Laurel, N.C. version no. 2. SES 1
—Hot Springs, N.C. version. SES 1

"Our harps were tun'd to sing Thy praise." See Babylon (Watson)

"Our horse fell down the well." See Good-by Liza Jane

"Our husbands, alas." K. Millöcker. e. WLO

"Our Jimmy has gone for to live in a tent." See Grafted into the army (Work)

"Our king went forth to Normandy." See Deo gratias

"Our land, our land, dear fatherland." See Vårt land, vårt fosterland (Pacius)

"Our marriage bells are ringing." See Marriage bells (O'Reardon)

"Our morning dawneth on the hills." The rose and silver gray

"Our oats they are hoed." See Harvest home (Purcell)

Our pioneers. French folk air. Words by J. L. Vandevere. TFO

Our pray'rs are always thine. See Old Wabash (Ragan)

"Our Saviour spoke dese words so sweet." See Hear the lambs a-crying

"Our school-days now are past and gone." See Graduation song

"Our sheep are folded in the pen." See Shearing time

"**Our** ship she lies in harbour." Folk song: Surrey version. BET

Our songs of joy and gladness. Meyerbeer. MFS

"**Our** sturdy golden bear." See Fight for California

"**Our** troop will shine tonight" (see Song Index)
Variants: "Central will shine"; "Our boys will shine tonight"; "Our club will shine"

"**Out** in a beautiful field." See Pretty pear tree

"**Out** in Texas with the hooking cows." See The hooking cow blues (Williams)

"**Out** in the forest-land deep." See The camp fire (Loomis)

"**Out** in this cold world alone." See Nobody's darling

"**Out** in this cold world, out in the street." See Driven from home (Hays)

"**Out** of my bitter weeping." See "Aus meinen grossen schmerzen" (Franz)

"**Out** of my soul's great sadness." See "Aus meinen grossen schmerzen" (Franz)

"**Out** of our suff'ring, out of our sadness." See Choral

"**Out** of the blossom sprang a thorn." Plainsong air. 15th century words. DNS

"**Out** of the dark the circling sphere" (Canonbury) R. Schumann. Words by S. Longfellow. LAS

"**Out** of the orient crystal skies." Air: A solis ortus cardine. 17th century words. DNS

"**Out** of the orient crystal skies" (Falantiding) Tyrolese air: Ihr hirten, stehet alle auf. 17th century words. OB

"**Out** of the window." Motion song. <J. Norton> MFS

"**Out** of your sleep." M. Shaw. 15th century words. OB

Out on dat ocean. See De Titanic

"**Out** on the deep." F. N. Löhr. Words by S. K. Cowan. TFP

"**Out** on the lawn in the evening gray." See Croquet (Thomas)

"**Out** there on yonder mountains." See "Là-bas sur ces montagnes"

"**Out** yonder in the moonlight." See The singing in God's acre (Jordan)

The **outlandish** knight (see Song Index) Variant: Pretty Polly

Ouvrez vos portes éternelles. For English translation see Unfold, ye portals (Gounod)

"**Over** hill and plain they're bounding." See Hela'r 'sgyvarnog

"**Over** hill, over dale, as we hit the dusty trail, and the caissons go rolling along." See The caisson song (Metz)

"**Over** hill, over dale, as we hit the dusty trail, it's the doughboys that still carry on." See Caisson song: infantry adaptation (Metz)

"**Over** hill, over dale, we have hit the dusty trail, and those caissons go rolling along." See The caisson song (Metz)

"**Over** the banister." Student song. DSC

Over the dark blue sea. Alpine air. MFS

"**Over** the foam we glide." See On Venice waters (Roeder)

Over the garden wall. ⌈G. D. Fox. Words by H. Hunter⌉ WSS

"**Over** the harden'd snow." See Sleighing-time

Over the hills and far away ("Hark! now the drums beat up again") Recruiting song of the Marlborough wars. BOS 2

Over the hills and far away ("Tom he was a piper's son") Traditional nursery song. CSB 1

"**Over** the hills and far away, in a village by the sea." See Rose-Marie (Molloy)

"**Over** the ocean Columbus came." See Columbus day

Over the sea in my boat with me. English air. Words by K. Davis. DSB

"**Over** the sea, over the sea." Jacobite song. <Groom> GOS 2—GS

"**Over** the snow-clad city." See The gate of heaven (Tours)

"**Over** the stars there is rest." See "Über den sternen ist ruh" (Abt)

"**Over** the summer sea." Verdi. MFS

"**Over** the tree-tops the moon has risen." See Filon is waiting

Over the way. J. P. Marshall. Words by K. E. Thomas. BST

Over there ⌈"Johnnie get your gun"⌉ G. M. Cohan. (music and words) SMG

Over there ("Oh, potatoes they grow small") 19th century American song. SRW

Over there ("Oh, think of a home") D. W. C. Huntington. Words by T. C. O'Kane. MFS

"**Over** yonder's a park, which is newly begun." See All bells in paradise (English air); All bells in paradise (Shaw)

Overbeck, Christian Adolf
"Komm', lieber mai, und mache" (Mozart)

Overwork. F. Ames. Words by J. L. Vandevere. TFO

Owd Joe Braddles. Old song. BOS 2

Owen, David
All through the night. See Ar hyd y nos
Ar hyd y nos (with words "Holl amrantau'r sêr"; "Through the day")
In stiller nacht. See Ar hyd y nos
Poor Mary Ann. See Ar hyd y nos

Owen, Mrs Harriet Mary (Browne) See Brown, Harriet Mary

⌈The **owl**⌉ "Of all the birds." 16th century song. BOS 2

"The **owl** and the pussy cat." G. Ingraham. Words by E. Lear. GSS

Owre the water to Charlie. See "Come boat me o'er, come row me o'er"

Oxenford, Edward
Funiculi, funicula (Denza)

Oxenford, John
Around me, blessed image, ever soar (Irish air)
The bell ringer (Wallace)
"Like the lark" (Abt)
Smile, my Kathleen, pray (Irish air)
"'Tis no time to take a wife" (Irish air)

Oxford cries. See "Chairs to mend, old chairs to mend" (Hayes)

The **Oxford** tragedy. See The miller's apprentice

"**Oy,** yiboneh yiboneh yiboneh yiboneh hamikdosh." See May the temple be rebuilt

Oysters and wine at 2 A.M. Old song. SW

P

P. T. Barnum's show. Air: Menagerie. SRW

"**Pa** bryd y deui eto" ("When will you come, my sweeting") Old Welsh song. Modern words by W. Ifan. e.w. WO

"**Pa,** this same day." C. Lecocq. ₁Tr of Père adoré, c'est Giroflé₁ e. WLO

Pacini, Giovanni
Ah! con lui mi fu rapita (from Saffo)

Pacius, Friedrich
"Our land." See Vårt land, vårt fosterland
Vårt land, vårt fosterland

A **pack** of cards. Old song. SW

Paddy Doyle ("To my way-a-y-ay ah") Short drag chantey. WSE
For variants see following songs of similar title

Paddy Doyle's boots ("To my way-ay-ay-ah") Bunt chantey. TSB 1

Paddy Doyle's boots ("To my way-ay-ay-yah") Bunt chantey. SBS

Paddy Duffy's cart. D. Braham. Words by E. Harrigan. SRW

Paddy works on the railway. Capstan chantey. TSB 2
Variant of: Poor Paddy works on the railway

Padilla, José
"Little Princess." See Princesita
Princesita

Page, E. V.
Lardy dah

Page, Edgar
Beulah land (Sweney) Authorship uncertain

"**Pai,** pai, paitaressu." See Lullaby (Merikanto)

The **pain** of love. See Heimlicher liebe pein (Weber)

Paine, Robert Treat
Adams and liberty (Smith?)

Paine, T.
The old cabin home

₁**Páisdín** fionn₁ An páistín fionn (Blonde Paistin) Irish folk song. g.ir. ML 1

Paisley, William M.
Razorback rootin' song

An **páistín** fionn. See Páisdín fionn

Un **pajarito** (A fickle maiden) Mexican folk song. e.s. HE

Paladilhe, Émile
The mandolin song. See Mandolinata
Mandolinata (with words "O I'm a happy creature")

Palestrina, Giovanni Pierluigi da
"Gloria Patri"
"Glory to God." See "Gloria Patri"
The strife is o'er: the battle done (Tr of Finita jam sunt praelia)

"**Pali** synephias' oyrhanos." See Waisenkind

The **Palisades.** New York university alma mater. D. M. Genns (music and words) AIS—KU—KV
The grim grey Palisades. AI
"O grim, grey Palisades." LAS

Palm branches ("Sur nos chemins") See Les rameaux (Faure)

Palmer, John F.
The band played on (Ward)

Palmer, John Williamson
Stonewall Jackson's way (Composer unknown) Authorship uncertain

Palmer, Ray
"My faith looks up to Thee" (Mason)

Palmgren, Selim
Autumn. See Höst
"The golden day is dying"
Höst
I vassen
In the willows. See I vassen
Liljekonvalje
Lily of the valley. See Liljekonvalje

The **palms.** See Les rameaux (Faure)

Die **palmweide** (Raita) Finnish folk song. fi.g. ML 3

La **paloma** azul (The blue dove) Mexican folk song. e.s. VS

Palomero, M. E.
Princesita (Padilla)

"**Pan** ddelo'r haf a'i flodau fyrdd." See Blodau'r cwm

"**Pan** oeddwn ar frig noswaith." See Y gwŷdd

"**Pan** oeddwn i'n fugail yn hafod y rhyd." See Bugail yr hafod

Pancakes ("Mother off to the market goes") Russian folk song. e. MFF

Pancakes! pancakes! joy and good luck to all at home. See La chanson des beignets

Panchenko, S. W.
Ah, if mother Volga
"Oh, if mother Volga." See Ah, if mother Volga

Pan's holiday. F. Bridge. Words by J. Shirley. CSB 4

Pansies. W. R. Cox. Words by J. W. Riley. BST

"Pansies! pansies! I love you, pansies."
See Pansies (Cox)

Pantchenko, S. W.   See Panchenko, S. W.

The panther.   University of Pittsburgh song.   C. S. Harris.   Words by H. C. Scott.   AI—AIS

Panxoliña de nadal (Spanish carol)   Galician folk song.   e.   OB

Paoli, Betty, pseud.   See Glück, Elisabeth

"Papa I'm so sad and lonely."   See Hello, central, give me heaven (Harris)

"Pappa lupas talon laittaa Saarijärven rantaan."   See Am strande des Saarijärvi

"Par derrièr' chez ma tante i' y'a-t-un bois joli."   See Le prisonnier de Hollande (Canadian version)

"Par derrièr' chez ma tant' il lui ya-t'un étang."   See La chanson des métamorphoses (Canadian version)

"Par derrièr' chez ma tante un oranger lui ya."   See Mon cri cra, tir' la lirette

Par excellence.   Old song.   Words by W. Lingard.   SW

"Par un dimanche au soir."   See Youpe! youpe! sur la rivière

The parable of the sinful rich man.   See Le parabole du mauvais riche

[Le parabole du mauvais riche]   The parable of the sinful rich man.   French folk song.   e.   DSC

Ballad of the sinful rich man.   e.   DSB

Ballade de Jésus-Christ (Ballade von Jesus Christus)   f.g.   ML 1

Jésus Christ en pauvre (Ballad of the sinful rich man)   e.f.   MBS

Variant: Notre Seigneur en p'auvre

Das paradies.   See Ar baradoz

Paradise square.   F. N. Löhr.   Words by F. E. Weatherly.   SFB

Parce Domine.   See Repentir (Gounod)

The pardon came too late.   P. Dresser (music and words)   SW

"Pardon now the bold outlaw."   See Rob Roy Macgregor

The pardon of Sydna Allen.   Modern American mountain ballad.   RA

"Lo pare y la mare no'm tenen sinó á mi."   See Lo mestre

Parham, Alfred Henry
Official West Point march (Egner)

Parish, John Carl
Old gold (Irish air)

Parker, Edwin Pond
"Hail, holy light! the world rejoices" (Brahms)

Parker, Henry
Jerusalem

Parker, Martin
"What though I be a country lass" (Old English air)

Parker, Mrs Nella
Jerusalem (Parker, H.)

"Le parlate d'amor."   See "Faites-lui mes aveux" (Gounod)

Parliament of England.   See Ye parliament of England

Parmi les choses délicates.   For English translation see Pirates' chorus (Lecocq)

Parody on The banks of the Dee.   See The banks of the Dee, Parody on

Parry, John
Norah, the pride of Kildare
Sister Ruth (wrongly attributed)   See Haydn, F. J.   Sister Ruth

Parry, John Orlando
Vilikins and his Dinah

Parry, Joseph
Aberystwith.   See "Watchman, tell us of the night"
"Jesus, Lover of my soul" (same air as "Watchman, tell us of the night")
"Watchman, tell us of the night"

Parry, Robert Williams
Cân yr alltud (Old Welsh air)

Parsons, H. N.
The counter-charm (Czechoslovak folk air)

Parted ("Mein schatz ist nicht da")   See Sehnsucht (Brahms)

Parting ("Wie scheinen die sternlein")   See Abschied (Franz)

Parting [graduation] song ("Hail and farewell")   C. Barnard.   MFS

Parting song.   See Parting graduation song (Barnard)

"Partner, when I dance."   See Compère et commère

The partners.   See Compère et commère

"Partridge in the pea-patch."   See The bell-cow

"A party of young village people."   See Just behind the times (Harris)

[Parvulus nobis nascitur]   "A little Child there is yborn" (Susanni)   German air.   15th century words.   e.   OB

[Parvulus nobis nascitur]   "A little Child there is yborn")   R. Dunstan.   15th century words.   e.   DNS

Parvum quando cerno Deum.   For English translation see "When I view the Mother holding" (15th century air)

Pasacalle o marcha-alborada (Wanderlied)   Galician folk song.   g.s.   ML 2

Er passagallo (Der bänkelsänger)   Romanesca song.   g.i.   ML 2

[Passing by]   "There is a lady."   T. Ford.   [Words by R. Herrick]   MBS

Passing by ("There is a lady")   E. C. Purcell.   Words by R. Herrick.   DSB—DSC

"Passing by along a mill."   See Et moi je m'enfouiyais

The passing pilot.   Song of the European war.   DSO

"A passing policeman found a little child."   See The little lost child (Stern)

Past three o'clock, and a cold frosty morning (Song of the watch)   Old English watchman's song.   DSB

Past three o'clock and a cold frosty morning (London waits)   Fragment.   BOS 2

A pastoral ("Flocks are sporting")   See "Flocks are sporting" (Carey)

Pastourelle (The shepherdess) L. Auguin. Words by G. Montoya and P. André. e.f. ASN

Patapan. See Guillô, pran ton tamborin

Patriotic diggers. Song of the war of 1812. Words by S. Woodworth. DSO

The **patriots** ("'Tis here we are pledging") Thüringian folk song. e. BB

Pattberg, Charles H. Marching song

Pattee, Fred Lewis Alma mater—Pennsylvania state college (Converse)

Patten, Simon N. To-morrow (Wesley)

"**Pattridge** in the pea-patch." See The bell-cow

Paul, Stuart, pseud. See Stevens, David

Paul, William Glae "The cardinal is waving"

"**Paul** and Silas, bound in jail, all night long." See All night long

"**Paul** and Silas, bound in jail, Christians pray both night and day." See Blow your trumpet, Gabriel (Charleston, S.C. version)

Paulsen, John Olaf "Am schönsten sommerabend war's" (Grieg)

Paun i kolo. See "Why so silent, tell me, birdie"

"**Paun** pase, trava raste." See "Why so silent, tell me, birdie"

Pauper-love. See Bettler-liebe (Bungert)

"**Pauv'** piti Mom'zelle Zizi" ("Pity poor Mam'zelle Zizi") Creole negro folk song. e.f. MB Variant of: "Pov' piti Lolotte"

"**Pauve** piti Lolotte." See "Pov' piti Lolotte"

"**Pauvre** petite Mam'zelle Zizi." See "Pauv' piti Mom'zelle Zizi"

Pavane. 16th century French song. f.g. ML 1

Pay-day song ("Oh, Uncle Sammy he pays the infantry") Song of the European war. Air: The old gray mare. DSO

Payne, Brodie Alma mater—University of Arkansas (Tovey)

Payne, John Howard Home, sweet home (Bishop)

"**Peace** be with all." Lithuanian air. Words by [D. Stevens] TFB—TFO

"**Peace** I leave with you." See The peace of God (Gounod)

The **peace** of God. C. Gounod. ASA

Peace on earth. Donizetti. Words by J. R. Lowell. MFS

"**Peaceful** rest all souls departed." See Litaney (Schubert)

Peacock song. See "Coo-coo"

Pealing, pealing come the laugh and shout. See "Brightly, brightly gleam the sparkling rills" (Haydn)

The **pear** tree. See Pretty pear tree

Pearce, William The heaving of the lead (Shield)

The **pearl** ("En el fondo del mar") See La perla (Araya?)

[**Péarla** an brollaig báin] The snowy-breasted pearl. Irish folk song. e. MBS

Pearls. See Perlen (Sinding)

Pearsall, Robert Lucas de "In dulci jubilo": 14th century air arranged Who will o'er the downs

Pease, Harry; Nelson, Ed G., and Dodge, Gilbert Peggy O'Neil

"**Pecchè** non duorme." See Duorme

Peck, Harlan Page Old Nassau (Langlotz)

Peck, Walter E. "We're here to win for Wooster" (Composer unknown)

"**Peepin'** through the knot-hole." See Go get the ax

Peerson, Martin Cuckoo "Now, Robin, laugh and sing"

Peery, Rob Roy Oberlin pep song

Peg o' my heart. F. Fischer. Words by A. Bryan. SMG

Peggy bawn ("As I gaed o'er the Highland hills") Irish folk song. HMI

Peggy O'Neil. H. Pease, E. G. Nelson and G. Dodge (music and words) SMG

Pelissier, Victor "Dry those eyes" "Return, O love"

"**Pellucid** the light." See Les cloches (Debussy)

Peña ("Peña, del cerro alto") Mexican folk song. e.s. VS

"**Peña,** del cerro alto." See Peña

Penitence ("An dir allein") See Buss-lied (Beethoven)

Pennington, George W., pseud. See Loomis, Harvey Worthington

Penny, George Barlow Crimson and the blue (Thompson)

"**Pensa** alla patria." Rossini. e.i. PC

Pensée de printemps (Spring reverie) X. Leroux. Words by A. Silvestre. e.f. ASN

The **peonies.** See Pionerna (Rangström)

People and tongues shall chant His praise. See Les rameaux (Faure)

"**People,** look East." See Carol of the Advent

"The **people** that walked in darkness." G. F. Händel. SSO 4

"**Per** aquet torrent avall cante la griva." See Aves, frutas y viento

"**Per** la gloria d'adorarvi" (Hopeless 'tis) G. B. Buononcini. e.i. SAT

"**Per** non penar." E. Astorga. e.i. ZT 1

"**Per** sua madre andò una figlia." Donizetti. e.i. PC

Per te d'immenso giubilo. For English translation see "Hail to the happy bridal day" (Donizetti)

"The **perbadus** lady, the perbadus lady."
   See Pretty Nancy of Yarmouth
Perchè dell' aure in sen.   Donizetti.
   e.i.   PB
Percy, Florence, pseud.   See Allen, Mrs
   Elizabeth (Chase) Akers
Percy, Thomas
   "O Nannie, wilt thou gang wi' me"
   (Carter)
Père adoré, c'est Giroflé.   For English
   translation see "Pa, the same day"
   (Lecocq)
Perfect, Albert
   Mighty Oregon
Pergolesi, Giovanni Battista
   "Confusa, smarrita, spiegarti vorrei"
   (from Catone)
   "Dite ch'ogni momento"
   "Gemo in un punto e fremo" (from
   L'Olimpiade)
   Hear us, O Lord
   "Here on earth is no abiding city"
   "Holy! holy! holy! Lord God Al-
   mighty! holy! holy! holy! Lord
   God of Sabaoth"
   "Ne' giorni tuoi felici" (from L'Olim-
   piade)
   Nina (wrongly attributed)   See
   Ciampi, L. V.   Nina
   O Lord, have mercy upon me
   "Se al labro mio non credi" (from
   L'Olimpiade)
Peri, Jacopo
   "Funeste piaggie" (from L'Euridice)
Perkins, Cy
   They gotta quit kickin' my dawg aroun'
Perkins, Leslie Crawford
   Tree song (Croatian folk air)
Perkins, Theodore Edson
   Jesus is mine
Perkins, Wilton, pseud.   See Stevens,
   David
[La **perla**] The pearl.   [Attributed to J.
   Araya.   Words by E. Blasco]   e.
   TFB—TFO
Perlen (Pearls)   C. Sinding.   Words by
   S. Trost.   e.g.   TM
[**Perri** merri dictum, domine]   "I had four
   brothers over the sea."   Old nursery
   ditty.   KSO
Perronet, Edward
   "All hail the power of Jesus' name"
   (music by Holden; Shrubsole)
Perry, Francis W.
   "I heard the voice of Jesus say"
"**Personent** hodie."   14th century carol.
   l.   OB
The **pet** chicken.   See Die henne
Peter, go ring dem bells.   Negro spiri-
   tual.   WFN—WSS
   I heard from heaven to-day.   HRD
   Oh, Peter, go ring dem bells.   BB
Peter Gray.   College song.   BB—LAS
Peter on the sea.   Negro spiritual.   HRD
   —WFN

Peterson-Berger, Olof Vilhelm
   Aftonstämning
   Till bruden
   Titania
   To the bride.   See Till bruden
   Twilight.   See Aftonstämning
Peticolas, C. L.
   "Jesus, Lover of my soul"
   "Veni Creator spiritus."   See "Jesus,
   Lover of my soul"
Le **petit** bonnet rond.   See "Mon pèr'
   m'a fait bâtir maison"
"**Petit** rocher" ("O little rock")   Canadian
   folk song.   e.f.   GC
Petöfi, Sándor
   "Maiden, maiden, nut-brown maiden"
   (Simonffy)
   "Oh! the earth is vast and spacious"
   (Egressi)
   "O'er the forest rainclouds lower"
   (Egressi)
   "Shepherd laddie" (Egressi)
Petrella, Errico
   "Rondinella pellegrina" (from Marco
   Visconti)
Petri, Carl G.
   "When the shades of ev'ning gather"
   (Shackelton)
Petrie, Henry W.
   Asleep in the deep
   I don't want to play in your yard
   Where the sunset turns the ocean's
   blue to gold
Petticoat lane.   E. Farjeon.   GSS
"**Pfaffe** liebt den starken kaffee" ("Szereti
   a pap a kávét")   Hungarian folk song.
   g.hu.   ML 3
"**Pfarrer** Magnus."   See "Sjera Magnus"
Der **pfarrer** von Bray.   See The vicar of
   Bray
Pfingstlied.   J. S. Bach.   Words by V.
   E. Löscher.   g.   EDL
Pfingstreigen.   See The garland
Pfleger-Moravský, Gustav
   "I know that hope doth smile upon"
   (Dvořák)
Pflücket rosen um, das haar.   For Eng-
   lish translation see "Pluck ye roses
   while they bloom" (Schumann)
Pharaoh's army got drownded.   Negro
   spiritual.   SBA
   Variant of: O Mary, don't you weep
Pharisee and Sadducee.   Old song.   SW
Pheil, Philip.   See Phile, Philip
Phelps, E. C.
   Innisfail
Phil the fluter's dancing.   See Rinnce
   Philib an cheoil
"**Philadelphia** is a handsome town."
   Play-party game from Kentucky.
   SES 2
Phile, Philip
   "Hail, Columbia"
   Hail Columbia, The new (same air as
   "Hail, Columbia")

The **Philippine** hombre. Song of the Spanish American war. Old Spanish air. Words by L. A. Cotten. US
A Filipino hombre. SBA
The Filipino hombre. DSO
Philippinitis. U.S. navy song. US
Phillips, Alfred
    The cross of Calvary (Gounod)
Phillips, Henry
    Christmas is coming
Phillips, Jonas B.
    The New Year's come (Knight)
Phillips, Philip
    Home of the soul
Phillips, Riemer Goldsmith
    Colors of Washington (Hatcher)
Phillips, William King
    Florida blues
"**Phillis** has such charming graces." A. Young. WOE
Der **philosoph.** Jewish folk song. y. KAJ—SY
"**Phoebe** in her petticoat." Folk song from North Carolina. SES 2
Phyla, Philip. See Phile, Philip
Phyllis und die mutter ("Ihren schäfer zu erwarten") Composer and author of words unknown. g. EDL
Phylo, Philip. See Phile, Philip
Piaceri fanciulleschi (Children's play) W. A. Mozart. e. CSB 2
Piantadosi, Al
    The curse of an aching heart
    In all my dreams, I dream of you
    That's how I need you
Piatti, Alfred
    Hymn to God the Father
"**Pibroch** of Donuil Dhu." Scottish air. Words by W. Scott. GS
Piccayune Butler. Minstrel song. WSS
Piccinni, Niccolò
    "Giammai provai" (from La donna vana)
Piccolomini, Maria
    Eternal rest
    Requiem æternam. See Eternal rest
Pick-axe, shovel, spade. See Patriotic diggers
Picture a home in New England town. See A picture no artist can paint (Helf)
Picture eighty-four (Convict eight-four) Old American song. SRW
A **picture** no artist can paint. J. F. Helf. SMG
The **picture** that is turned toward the wall. C. Graham (music and words) GFS —SRW
The **picture** that was drawn upon the floor. W. Gilligan (music and words) SW
Pie in the sky. See The preacher and the slave (Webster)
"**Piensa** que por tus enojos." See La cuna
"**Pienso** que los garroteros no pueden tener nada mujer." See La realera (Rocha)
Pierce, Henry H.
    Bowdoin beata (Old air)

Pierce, Jason Noble
    Cheer for old Amherst
    Oberlin, our alma mater
Pierce, W. H.
    Twilight dreams (Basque folk air)
Pierpoint, Folliott Sandford
    "For the beauty of the earth" (Kocher)
Pierpont, James S.
    Jingle, bells
Pierpont, Victor N., pseud. See Loomis, Harvey Worthington
Pierre de Bon Bon. See Rosalie (Knight)
Pigetanker (A maiden's thoughts) P. Winge. Words by K. Randers. e.n. WM 2
Piggott, H. E.
    "Come, my Way, my Truth, my Life"
[The **pigtail**] A tragic story. W. A. Mozart. [Words by A. von Chamisso] e. DSB
Pike, G. S.
    Gentle Nettie Moore
    Little white cottage. See Gentle Nettie Moore
Pike, Marshall S.

    Composer
    "Happy are we to-night"
    Composer and author
    "Home again, home again"
    Author
    Gentle Nettie Moore (Pike, G. S.)
    Lone starry hours (Power)
"**Pikkunen** lintu se etelästä lensi." See "Vöglein kam"
Pil-lie-a-i-oh! get along, little dogie. See Dogie song
"**Pile** pishchi." See "Vöglein singt"
Pilgrim chorus. See Pilgrims' chorus (Wagner)
The **pilgrim** legend. See Légende des pélerins
Pilgrims ("Hark! hark") See "Hark! hark! my soul" (Dykes)
The **pilgrims** ("Two weary pilgrims") Mexican folk carol. e. MFF
The **pilgrims** ("The way is long") W. Schulthes. Words by A. Procter. CSS 2
Pilgrims' chorus. R. Wagner. [Tr of Beglückt dorf nun dich] e. BB
    Pilgrim chorus. e. WG
Pilgrim's song ("I'm a poor wayfarin' stranger") Negro spiritual. HRD Variant: "I'm just a-goin' over Jordan"
"The **pilgrims** throng thro' the city gates." See Calvary (Rodney)
Pilly, willy winkum doo. See The cat and the catboat
"The **pilot** he looks out ahead." See Jamboree
"A **pine-tree** standeth lonely." See "Ein fichtenbaum steht einsam" (Stenhammar)
The **pine** tree swing. German folk air. Words by H. H. Harbour. DSB
Pinkerton, Mary
    "Sweet Briar, Sweet Briar, flower fair" (Bendall)

Pinna, Joseph de
"What fairy-like music"
Pinsuti, Ciro
"Come unto me, ye weary"
Fly forth, O gentle dove
"Good-night, good-night, beloved! I come to watch o'er thee"
I love my love
In shadowland
"Lead, kindly light"
A spring song
'Tis I
"Welcome, pretty primrose" (Tr of Salve, o rosa, amabile fior)
Die Pinzgauer wallfahrt ("Die binschgauer wollten wallfahrten") Osterreichisches volkslied. g. EDL
Piobair of Donuil Dhuidh. See "Pibroch of Donuil Dhu"
Die piolische yuden. Jewish folk song. y. KAJ
Pioneer song. University of South Dakota alma mater. W. R. Colton. Words by M. K. Richardson. KU
Alma mater. HW
"A pioneer state built a college to share." See Here we have Idaho
Pioneers. H. Grace. Words by W. Whitman. CSB 5
Pionerna (The peonies) T. Rangström. Words by A. Österling. e.sw. WM 2
Piosneczka pijacka. See "Jacob, drink"
"Pious orgies, pious airs." G. F. Händel. SSO 1
"Pipe us the songs of freedom." Basque air. Words by F. Hoare. LAS
"The piper came to our town." See The piper of Dundee
Piper Heidsieck. See Give me the waltz (Pratt)
The piper o' Dundee. Scottish song. GS
The piper's daughter. Words by E. Cook. GS
Pirates' chorus ("Ha! ha! the neatest and completest") C. Lecocq. [Tr of Parmi les choses délicates] e. WLO
"Piros, piros, piros." See "Rose-red, rose-red"
Pitt, William
Barney Buntline (Composer unknown)
Pitts, William S.
Composer and author
The little brown church in the vale
Author
The old musician and his harp (Higgins)
Pittsburgh's glory won't be trampled down to-day by any foe. See The panther (Harris)
"Pity, kind heaven." See L'insana parola (Verdi)
"Pity poor Mam'zelle Zizi." See "Pauv' piti Mom'zelle Zizi"
"Più non pensar." E. Astorga. e.i. ZT 1
"A place in thy memory, dearest." P. Smith. GOS 1
The plague of love. Arne. WOE

"A plague on melancholy." See Distyll y don
The plains of Mexico ("O Santy Anna gained the day") Chantey. WSE
Variant of: Santy Anna
Plaint. See Klage (Brahms)
Plainte d'Ariane (Ariadne's lament) A. Coquard. Words by F. Bertin. e.f. ASN
Planché, James Robinson
Composer and author
Love's ritornella (from The brigand)
Author
Spring, gentle spring (Riviere)
Planquette, Robert
Cider song (from Les cloches de Cornville. Tr of La pomme est un fruit plein de sève)
"Cold sweat is on my brow" (from Les cloches de Cornville. Tr of Ô ciel malheureux Grenicheux)
"Dear friends of my youth, think not we are parted" (from Les cloches de Cornville. Tr of Si je suis vraiment dame et châtelaine)
"Gossip monger, village gadder" (from Les cloches de Cornville. Tr of Oui, nous devons faire taire)
"Just look at that" (from Les cloches de Cornville. Tr of Voyez ceci, voyez celà)
Legend of the bell (from Les cloches de Cornville. Tr of Nous avons hélas! perdu d'excellents maitres)
"On billow rocking" (from Les cloches de Cornville. Tr of Va petit mousse)
"Silent heroes" (from Les cloches de Cornville. Tr of C'est la salle de mes ancètres)
"That night I'll ne'er forget." See Waltz song
Waltz song (from Les cloches de Cornville. Tr of Je regardais en l'air)
"With joy my heart" (from Les cloches de Cornville. Tr of J'ai fait trois fois le tour du monde)
Plantation walk around. D. Emmett. WSS
Plantonio. Cowboy song. LSC
"A plate of hot scouse wouldn't do us any harm." See The old chariot
"Plava moma, b'jeli danak." See Trinklied (Slavonian folk song)
"Play ball." V. P. I. fighting song. I. Ashworth and J. S. Schaeffer. Author of words unknown. KU
"Play on, gipsy" ("Huzzad czigány") E. Szentirmay (music and words) e.hu. KH 2
"Play, only play on" ("Huzzadd, csak huzzadd") Hungarian folk song. e.hu. KH 1
"Húzzadd, csak húzzadd" ("Spiel nur, o spiel") g.hu. ML 3
Play that barber shop chord. L. F. Muir. Words by W. Tracey. OTG
"Pleasant are Thy courts above." See King of glory, God of grace (Abt)

Please go 'way and let me sleep. H. Von Tilzer. SRW

"Please, mister, take me in your car." See Always in the way (Harris)

"Pleasure climbs to every mountain." Gollmick. MFS

"Pleasure it is." B. Waldis. Words by W. Cornish. OB

"Pledge the Canadian maiden." See "Vive la Canadienne"

Plimpton, A.
Somebody's child

"Pliot mola lüle." See Brautlied

La ploma de perdiu (Die rebhuhnfeder) Catalan folk song. ca.g. ML 2

The ploughboy ("Come, all you jolly ploughboys") Folk song: Sussex version. BOS 2

The ploughboy ("A flaxen-headed cowboy") Shield. ɪWords by O'Keeffeɪ CSB 3

"Pluck ye roses while they bloom." R. Schumann. Words by E. Kulmann. ɪTr of Pflücket rosen um, das haarɪ e. DSB

"A plump little robin flew down from a tree." See The robin and chicken (Aiken)

Plus brillants que des météores. For English translation see Song of the Moors (Lecocq)

Po' boy ("My mammy's in the cold, cold ground") Negro jail song. SBA

Po' li'l' Liza, po' gal. See "Liza in the summer time"

Po' mourner's got a home at las'. Negro spiritual. JB 2

ɪThe poacher's songɪ "In Thorney woods in Buckinghamshire." Ballad <from Sussex> BOS 2

"Un pobre pagés teniauna filla." See La filadora

"Pod borem sosna gorzała." See "Brannt' eine fichte"

"Pod okonce pridem." See "Ans fensterlein schleich ich"

Pod pendzheri. See Unterm fenster

"Podunushe Badiseva vetrove." See Mädchen und taube

ɪPoetryɪ "Hail, poetry, thou heav'n-born maid! thou gildest even the pirate's trade." A. S. Sullivan. Words by W. S. Gilbert. DSC

Poetry ("Hail, poetry! thou heav'n-born maid! thy laurel crown shall never fade") A. S. Sullivan. New words by S. Fay (D. Stevens) TFB—TFG

"Poijat kun raitilla laulelee." See "Wenn unsre burschen singen"

"Poika kihlasi morsiamen." See Die verlobten

Poisoned. See "My songs are envenomed and bitter" (Borodin)

Poland. German folk song arr by J. Brahms. Words from a folk song. ɪTr of In Polen steht ein hausɪ e. DSB
The wonderful inn. e. DSC

"Poland is not lost forever." See Polish national song (Ogiński?)

"Poling upstream a flat sampan." See Explosions from a tropical language

ɪPolish May songɪ Spring song. Polish song. e. DSB

Polish national song (Dombrowski's march) Attributed to Ogiński ɪattributed also to Sowinskiɪ Words by Wybitski ɪattributed also to P. Sobieskiɪ e. LAS

Polka chalutsith. See A Chalutz polka

Polly Oliver. Folk song: Kentucky version. SES 1
—North Carolina version. SES 1
—Virginia version. SES 1
Variants: The cruel ship's carpenter; Pretty Polly Oliver

"Polly, put the kettle on." Children's song. TFR

Polly-wolly-doodle. Old song. SRW
—WSS

Pomasanski, N.
Georgian song. See Grusisches lied
Grusisches lied

La pomme est un fruit plein de sève. For English translation see Cider song (Planquette)

"'Pon de mountain my Lord spoke." See Every time I feel the spirit

Ponce, Manuel M.
Estrellita .
"I'm off to port." See "Voy a partir"
"Little star." See Estrellita
"Voy a partir"

Ponce Muir's "suns" (The nautical almanac tale) U.S. navy song. ɪL. Lambertɪ US

Poniatowski, Józef Michał Franciszek Xaver Jan, prince
Yeoman's wedding song

Poor boy ("My mammy's in the cold, cold cold ground") See Po' boy

Poor boy ("My mother called me") See Coon can

The poor couple. Folk song from North Carolina. SES 2

"A poor girl stood one evening within her humble dwelling." See Gold will buy 'most anything but a true girl's heart (Rosenfeld)

Poor little Liza. See "Liza in the summer time"

"Poor little Nellie is weeping tonight." See Why did they dig ma's grave so deep (Skelly)

Poor lonesome cowboy. Cowboy song. LSC—SBA

"The poor man gambled all the night alone." See The gambling man (Kentucky version)

Poor Mary Ann. See Ar hyd y nos (Owen)

Poor mourner's got a home at last. See Po' mourner's got a home at las'

The poor murdered woman. Folk song: Surrey version. BET

"The poor old kaiser ain't what he used to be." See The kaiser ain't what he used to be

Poor old maid. Folk song from Kentucky. SES 2

Poor old man ("I say, old man") Halliard chantey. US
Variant of: The dead horse
"A poor old man came riding by." See The dead horse
The poor old slave. Negro song. WSS
"Poor old soldier, poor old soldier." See Rogue's march
Poor old Uncle Rufe. Minstrel song. WSS
Poor Omie. Folk song: Hindman, Ky. version no. 1. SES 2
—Hindman, Ky. version no. 2. SES 2
—Pine Mountain, Ky. version. SES 2
—Alleghany, N.C. version. SES 2
—Big Laurel, N.C. version. SES 2
—Burnsville, N.C. version no. 1. SES 2
—Burnsville, N.C. version no. 2. SES 2
Poor Paddy ("In eighteen-hundred and sixty-one") Capstan chantey. SBS
Variant of: Poor Paddy works on the railway
Poor Paddy works on the railway ("Oh in eighteen hundred and forty-one") Capstan chantey. SBA
Poor Paddy who works on the railway. WSE
Variants: Paddy works on the railway; Poor Paddy; Railway
Poor pilgrim. Negro spiritual. HRD
"Poor Rosy." Negro spiritual from Florida. AS
"Poor Sally was taken afflicted to her bed." See The brown girl (Callaway, Va. version)
"The poor soul sat sighing." See The willow song (16th century air); The willow song (Carr)
The poor stranger. See The rebel soldier
"Poor tho' my cot may be." See "In questo semplice, modesto asilo" (Donizetti)
"The poor working girl." American song. SBA
"Popa dice că nu bea" ("Pope sagt, er tränke nie") Rumanian song. g.ru. ML 2
Pope, Alexander
"Rise, crowned with light" (Lvov)
"Where'er you walk" (Händel)
"Pope sagt, er tränke nie." See "Popa dice că nu bea"
"Porównaj boże góry z dołami." See "Füll die täler aus"
Porter, Benjamin F.
The cavaliers of Dixie (Callcott)
Porter, Cole Albert
Bingo, Eli Yale
Porter, Mrs David
"Thou hast wounded the spirit that loved thee"
Porter, James W.
Ella Ree
[Porter lied ("Lasst mich euch fragen")]
Porter song. F. von Flotow. e. WLO
Porter song. See Porter lied (Flotow)
Portland county jail. American folk song. SBA

"A portly Roman senator was sipping his rock and rye." See A war bird's burlesque
Porto Rico. Folk song from Tennessee. SES 2
Portuguese hymn (Reading?) See "Adeste fideles"; "How firm a foundation, ye saints of the Lord"
"Poshetala prechista gospoja." See Die taufe Christi
"Posredi palat kamennykh." See Fussfesselmarsch der sträflinge
Possente amor mi chiama. For English translation see "Now hope renew'd" (Verdi)
Possente Ftha. For English translation see "Hail! mighty Phtha" (Verdi)
Possum (The opossum and the racoon) Negro song. BOS 2
"De possum meat am good to eat." See Carve dat possum (Lucas)
Possum, sweet potatoes, were sitting on the table. See The silver wedding
Possum up a gum-tree. See Possum
"De possum's meat am good to eat." See Carve dat possum (Lucas)
Post-rail song. Kentucky folk song. SBA
Pöthko, Gustav Ewald
Warnung vor dem Rhein
Potter, Lars Sellstedt. See Brown, Clarence Fayette, jt. auth.
Poulton, George R.
Army blue (same air as Aura Lee)
Army blue of 1859 (same air as Aura Lee)
Aura Lee
Une poupée aux yeux d'émail. For English translation see "A little doll with china eyes" (Offenbach)
"Pour forth no more unheeded prayers." Händel. SSO 4
Pour un tendre père. For English translation see "For a tender father" (Lecocq)
[Pov' piti Lolotte] Lolotte. Negro creole song. f. AS
Variant: "Pauv' piti Mom'zelle Zizi"
"Povedali, že som umrel." See "Hatten mich schon aufgegeben"
Povero Lionello. Flotow. e.i. PB
Poverty. See O deued pob Cristion
Power, F. A.
Heidelberg
Power, James
Dearest Mae. See Crosby, L. V. H.
Dearest Mae
Lone starry hours
Power, Thomas
Mountain maid's invitation (Werner)
Practice cruise. U.S. Naval academy song. US
Praetorius, Michael
"Awake with joy, salute the morn"
"Behold, a rose of beauty." See Lo! a fair rose is blooming
Lo! a fair rose is blooming
"Lo, how a rose e'er blooming." See Lo! a fair rose is blooming

Praetorius, Michael—*Continued*
"Lo, what a branch of beauty." See Lo! a fair rose is blooming
"Now glad of heart." See Wir wollen alle fröhlich sein
The rose of Sharon. See Lo! a fair rose is blooming
"While shepherds watched their flocks" Wir wollen alle fröhlich sein
Praise ("Praise Him, bless Him, Lord eternal") 7th century Gregorian chant. e. TFR
Praise for peace. F. F. Flemming. Words by A. S. Hibbard. BB
"Praise God, from Whom all blessings flow." 17th century German air. Words by T. Ken. MBS
"Praise God from Whom all blessings flow" (Tallis' canon) T. Tallis. ⌐Words by T. Ken⌐ CSB 1
"Praise God from Whom all blessings flow." For music attributed to Franc see Old hundred (Franc?)
"Praise Him, bless Him, Lord eternal." See Praise
"Praise Jehovah, every nation." Haydn. e. SSO 4
"Praise, member." Negro spiritual from South Carolina. AS
"Praise not to me the newborn rose." See La charmante Marguerite
"Praise, O praise our God and King" (Hymn of St Francis) Old English hymn air. DSB
The praise of Christmas. See Drive the cold winter away
The praise of God. See Die ehre Gottes aus der natur (Beethoven)
The praise of Islay. See Moladh na landaidh
Praise of tears. See Lob der thränen (Schubert)
"Praise the Lord, thou mighty sea." See Jubilate
"Praise the Lord, ye heav'ns, adore Him" (Austrian hymn) Haydn. DSB
"Praise to God, immortal praise" (Nuremberg) S. Bach. Words by A. L. Barbauld. MFS
"Praise to God in the highest." See The song of praise
"Praise to the king." J. Strauss. e. WLO
Praise to the Lord from Whom our deliverance has come. See "Bright as a ray" (Strauss)
"Praise to the Lord, the Almighty." 17th century German air. Words by J. Neander. e. MBS
"Praise we the Lord, Who made all beauty." See Carol of beauty
"Praise ye Jehovah's name." Air: America <attributed to H. Carey> MFS
Praised be the Lord (Halleluyah) Palestinean folk song. e.he. BNP
Pratt, Charles E.
Give me the waltz
Sparkling Piper Heidsieck. See Give me the waltz
Walking down Broadway

"Pray all de member." Negro spiritual from South Carolina. AS
"Pray forgive me, my friend." See "Compatite, signor" (Galuppi)
"Pray hear me! If Romeo thy son did slaughter." See "Se Romeo t'uccise un figlio" (Bellini)
"Pray on, pray on; pray on dem light us over." Negro spiritual from South Carolina. AS
"Pray on, prayin' sister." See Sun don't set in de mornin'
Prayer ("Alla mente confusa") See Preghiera (Tosti)
A prayer ("Bring peace on earth") R. Wagner. TFO
Prayer ("Herr, den ich tief") See Gebet (Hiller)
Prayer ("Oh! signor! padre del ciel") See Preghiera (Marchesi)
Prayer is de key of heaven. Negro spiritual. HRD
"Prayer is the soul's sincere desire" (Lambeth) ⌐W. A. F. Schulthes⌐ wrongly attributed to S. Webbe. Words by J. Montgomery. LAS
Prayer of thanksgiving. See "Wilt heden nu treden" (Kremser)
The preacher and the slave. ⌐J. P. Webster⌐ Words by J. Hill. SBA
A precious little picture, that made his heart feel sore. See The picture that was drawn upon the floor
Preghiera ("Alla mente confusa."—Prayer. —"To a mind worn and weary") F. P. Tosti. <Words by G. Giusti> e.i. CSS 1—CSS 2
Preghiera ("Oh! signor! padre del ciel."—Prayer) S. C. Marchesi. e.i. SAT
"Pregúntale a las estrellas" ("O ask of the stars above you") Mexican folk song. e.s. MSP
Preis der himmelskönigin. Composer and author of words unknown. g. EDL
Preis der schönen. See Tarantella de la bellona
"Preis und ruhm dem allmächtigen Gott in der höhe." See The song of praise
"Preletel slavíček." See "Flog daher die nachtigall"
"Le premier jour de m'ai" (May day) Folk song from Champagne. e.f. CBF 1
Prendi per me sei libero. See Nel dolce incanto (Benedict)
The Presbyterian cat. Air: Auld lang syne. MBS
Presents al niño Jesús (Weihegaben für das Jesuskind) Traditional Catalan Christmas song. ca.g. ML 2
"Press on! press on! ye songs of light" (Camden) J. B. Calkin. Words by W. Gaskell. LAS
Press thy cheek against mine own. See "Lehn' deine wang' an meine wang'" (Jensen)
Pressel, Gustav Adolf
An der Weser
Preston, Mrs M. J.
Under the shade of the trees (Lyte)

"The **Pretoria** passed a ship today." See Hinky dinky, parley-voo (Post-war stanzas)

"The **prettiest** girl that ever I saw." See Sucking cider through a straw (Morgan)

[**"Pretty** am I"] "Schein bin ich schein." Jewish folk song. y. KAJ

Pretty as a picture. T. B. Bishop. Words by G. Cooper. OT

"Pretty Bessy, pretty Bessy." See The cuckoo (Afton, Va. version no. 2)

Pretty creature ("De la Sierra Morena") See Cielito lindo

The **pretty** creature ("Oh! the pretty, pretty creature") S. Storace. WOE

"A **pretty** fair maid." See The broken token (American version; Hot Springs, N.C. version no. 1)

The **pretty** girl milking her cow. See Cailín deás crúidhte na mbó

Pretty maid, how could you do so (Ez a kis lány hamis kis lány) J. Szerdahelyi (music and words) e.hu. KH 1

"Pretty maiden, little maiden." See The saucy sailor (Kentucky version)

Pretty Nancy of Yarmouth. Folk song from North Carolina. SES 1

Pretty pear tree. Old song. MFS
The pear tree. TFR
Variant of: The tree in the wood

Pretty Peggy O. Folk song: Hyden, Ky. version. SES 2
—Knott county, Ky. version. SES 2
—St Helen's, Ky. version. SES 2
—North Carolina version. SES 2

Pretty Polly ("Go get me some of your father's gold") Folk song: American version. SBA
Variant of: The outlandish knight

"Pretty Polly hadn't been married but a very short time." See The wife of Usher's well (Allanstand, N.C. version)

Pretty Polly Oliver ("As pretty Polly Oliver") 17th century song. GSS
Variants: The cruel ship's carpenter; Polly Oliver

"Pretty Polly, pretty Polly." See The cruel ship's carpenter (Berea, Ky. versions no. 2 and 4; Manchester, Ky. version no. 2; Oneida, Ky. version)

Pretty, pretty, red, red rose. See The wild rose

Pretty Saro. Folk song: Georgia version. SES 2
—Allanstand, N.C. version. SES 2
—Carmen, N.C. version. SES 2
—Virginia version. SES 2

The **pretty** wood. See Ah! le joli bois, mesdames

"Préval in his hall gave a fancy ball." See "Michié Préval"

Pri odlazku. See Vor der abreise

Price, Bert
"Hail blue and gold"

"Prīdanyī udalyī, Ladu, Ladu." See Wedding-day song

The **pride** of our plains. P. A. von Hagen. MPA 1

The **pride** of the navy. U.S. Naval academy song. US

"The **pride** of the village." See Fairybelle (Foster)

"Prídi ty, šuhajko." See "Come you here, laddie"

"Prigioniera, abbandonata." B. Galuppi. e.i. KVG

Prima donna waltz. See "Ah! for wings to soar" (Jullien)

The **Prince** of life. J. Coad. DNS

[The **prince's** day] "Tho' dark are our sorrows." [Air: St Patrick's day] Words by T. Moore. HMI
Saint Patrick's day. MBS

Princesita ("Little princess") J. Padilla. Words by M. E. Palomero. e.s. MSP

"Princesita, princesita, la de ojos azules." See Princesita (Padilla)

"The **Princess** Salamanca." See "La fille du roi d'Espagne" (2d version)

Princeton cannon song march. Princeton university song. J. F. Hewitt and A. H. Osborn. AI—AIS—KU

"A **principal** point of charity is merry, merry e'er to be." See Be merry, be merry

"Printemps qui commence" ("Fair springtime beginning") Saint-Saëns. e.f. SAT

"Prinz Eugen." Volkslied. g. EDL

Prinz Eugen ("Zelte, posten, werdarufer") C. Loewe. Words by F. Freiligrath. g. EDL

Prior, Margaret
Hymn of scouting (Wesley)

The **prisoner's** song. See Moonlight

[Le **prisonnier** de Hollande] Gai lon la, gai le rosier (Gay, la, la, gay is the rose) Folk song: Canadian version. e.f. GC
Gai lon la, gai le rosier (The nightingale's song) Canadian version. e.f. GSF

"Prithee little maiden, working in a garden." See In a garden

"Prithee, pretty maiden." A. S. Sullivan. Words by W. S. Gilbert. DSC

Pritzkow, Louis W.
Take back your gold (Rosenfeld)

"Proč si k nám nepryšeu." See "Sag, warum bliebst du aus"

Proch, Heinrich
Dearest native land

Procrastination is the thief of time. See The hesitating blues (Handy)

Procter, Adelaide Anne
The lost chord (Sullivan)
Mine only, mine alone (Starnes)
"One by one" (Bellini)
The pilgrims (Schulthes)

Procter, Bryan Waller
"Dawn, gentle flower" (Bennett)
"Touch us gently, time" (Composer unknown)

El **profeta** (The prophet) Mexican folk song. e.s. VS

Prologue, from I pagliacci. R. Leoncavallo. [Tr of Si può? si può] e. WG

Promptement levez-vous, mon voisin. For English paraphrase see Carol of service

A prophecy. Creole folk air: Pauv' piti Mom'zelle Zizi. DSB

The prophet. See El profeta

Proposal ("The violet loves the sunny bank") F. H. Brackett. Words by B. Taylor. BST

"Proscrit, regarde les roses." See Chant d'exil (Vidal)

"Proud and lowly, beggar and lord." See London bridge (Molloy)

"Proud go the gypsy lads." See In golden firelight dancing

"Proudly as the eagle." L. Spohr. Words by A. Stone. BB—TFB—TFP

"Proudly sweeps the rain-cloud o'er the cliff." See Aloha oe (Liliuokalani)

"Proudly swept the rain-cloud by the cliff." See Aloha oe (Liliuokalani)

"Proudly the note of the trumpet is sounding." See O'Donnell aboo

Prout, Father, pseud. See Mahony, Francis Sylvester

"Prova mi dai, lo sento." Donizetti. e.i. PC

Prudentius Clemens, Aurelius
"Now with creation's morning song" (Beethoven. Tr of Lux ecce surgit aurea)
"Of the Father's love begotten" (13th century air. Tr of Corde natus ex parentis)

Prudhomme, René François Armand Sully-. See Sully-Prudhomme, René François Armand

"Przez czyścowe upalenia." See Allerseelen

Psalm of Sion. English traditional air. [Tr of Mater Hierusalem] e. OB

Psalme 100 ("Shout to Jehovah") See "Shout to Jehovah, all the earth"

"Psé sa boukë psé spi vérë." See Ali Pascha

Le p'tit bonnet rond. See "Mon pèr' m'a fait bâtir maison"

"Ptrui lemmikkin', ptrui ruskoni." See Hirten-lockruf

The publican. B. Van de Water. TSS 2

Puccitta, Vincenzo
"Strike the cymbal"

Puer natus in Bethlehem (Ein Kind geborn zu Bethlehem) 15th century German air arr by J. S. Bach. e. OB
"A Child is born in Bethlehem." e. FC

Puer nobis nascitur. 15th century German air. e. OB

Puget, Loïsa
The Christmas angelus (Tr of Ave Maria! car voici l'heure sainte)

"The puir auld folk at hame, ye mind." See We'd better bide a wee (Barnard)

Pull away, brave boys. Rossini. MFS

"Pull away lads, pull away lads." See Volga boat song

"Pull away, pull away, pull away, brave boys." See Pull away, brave boys (Rossini)

"Pull, brave boys, pull on together." See Row, row, cheerly row

"Pull off that silk, my pretty Polly." See Lady Isabel and the elf knight (Clay county. Ky. version)

Pulling hard against the stream. Old song. SW

The Pullman train. See The eastern train

Le punch scintille. For English translation see Drinking song (Lecocq)

Punchinello ("He was a Punchinello") J. L. Molloy. Words after H. Andersen. e. AT—HCA

Punchinello's serenade. See Serenata di Pulcinello

Pur dicesti, o bocca bella ("Speak again, love") A. Lotti. e.i. BST

Purcell, Edward C.
Passing by

Purcell, Henry
Colchester. See "From age to age how grandly rise"
"Corinna is divinely fair"
"Fairest isle" (from King Arthur)
Fairies' chorus. See "When the cock begins to crow"
The farmer's old wife (same air as Lilliburlero)
"Fie, now, prithee John"
"From age to age how grandly rise"
"Hark! hark! how all things in one sound rejoice"
Harvest home
"Let the fifes and the clarions" (from The fairy-queen)
Lilliburlero
The moon reappears (from The moon)
Passing by
"See those poor fellows"
"There was an old woman went up in a basket" (same air as Lilliburlero)
Trip it, trip it in a ring
"When the cock begins to crow"

Purday, Charles Henry
The fine old colored gentleman: old air arranged (same air as The fine ould Irish gintleman)
The fine ould Irish gintleman: old air arranged

"Pure as the dawn on the brow of thy beauty." See Alma mater—University of Arkansas (Tovey)

"Pure city, Babylon's fallin'." See Babylon's fallin'

Puritan hymn (Hell, or the vengeance of God) KSO

"Push on Northwestern and go in to win." See Northwestern push on song (Robertson)

Pushkin, Aleksandr Sergĕevich
The magpie and the little gypsy dancer (Zolotarev)

"Pussy cat, pussy cat, where have you been." Mother Goose song. <J. W. Elliott> TFR

Pussy willow. Traditional song. GSS

"Put away the little dresses." See Where the little feet are waiting (Webster)

"Put 'em up solid." See Post-rail song

Put John on de islan'. Negro song. HRD

Put my little shoes away. Old American song. SW

[**Put** off, and row wi' speed] Queen Mary's escape. Highland boat song. Words by R. Allan. GS

"**Put** them up solid." See Post-rail song

Putman's hill. Folk song from Virginia. SES 2

Putnam, Charles Symmons
Champlain

Putnam, Clarence Simeon
North Dakota hymn
Yellow and green

Pyrker, Johann Ladislav
Die Allmacht (Schubert)

Q

"A **quaint** New England homestead." See A picture no artist can paint (Helf)

The **Quaker's** wooing. Folk song. SBA

"**Qual** son? qual fui." See Perchè dell' aure in sen (Donizetti)

"**Qu'allais-tu** faire à la fontaine." See Les répliques de Marion

Qualunque sia l'evento. See "Vieni! la mia vendetta" (Donizetti)

"**Quan** un soldat ve de la guerra." See Desengany

"**Quand** je vais au jardin, jardin d'amour." See Le jardin d'amour

"**Quand** j'étais de chez mon père, digue dindaine." See Digue dindaine

"**Quand** la patate est cuite." See Tan patate-la tchuite

"**Quand** le marin revint de guerre." See Le retour du marin

"**Quand** mon âme ravie." See Je crois en vous (Berlioz)

"**Quand** tu chantes bercée." See Chantez riez et dormez (Gounod)

Quand tu tenais la caille (Als du die wachtel hieltest) French folk song. f.g. ML 1

"**Quando** avvolto" ("When the veil of night") G. Alary. e.i. SAT

Quando il destino in mezzo a strage ria. For English translation see Child of the regiment (Donizetti)

"**Quando** junse la nuvella." See Lamento

Quando mai spietata sorte ("When my eyes") G. F. Händel. e. CSB 5

"**Quando** nascette Ninno a Bettelemme." See Canzone d'i zampognari

"**Quandu** n'intesi la nova alle Ferrera d'Orezza." See Lamento

"**Quanno** mammà me fece monicella." See La monacella

"**Quanno** Noene l'arca frabbicone." See Er passagallo

Quarles, James Thomas
Alma mater—University of Missouri

"**Que** li darém a n'el noy de la mare." See Presents al niño Jesús

"**Que** lla Virxen galana ye que hay en esti pueblu." See Canción de cuna

"**Queen** Jane was in labour six weeks and some more." See The death of Queen Jane (St Helen's, Ky. version no. 1)

Queen Mary's escape. See Put off, and row wi' speed

Queen of heaven, rejoice. See Regina cœli, letare

"**Quell'** uzellin del bosc." See L'uzellin del bosc

"**Quella** barbara catena." F. Ciampi. e.i. ZT 1

"**Quem** pastores laudavere." 14th century air. 1. OB
"Quem pastores laudavere" (Rex gloriae) 1. FC

The **querister's** song of Yorke. See "Jerusalem my happie home" (Shann)

The **quest** ("Saint Mary goes a-seeking") See Maria's wallfahrt (Brahms)

"**Qu'est-c'** qui pass'ra sur les clanquarts." See Sur les clanquarts

Questa o quella. For English translation see "Every flower is equally cherished" (Verdi)

"**Queste** ch'io porgo umile più col cor." See Tu seconda i voti miei (Bianchi)

Questo é il cielo ("Beauty lately") G. F. Händel. English words by C. Williams. CSB 3

"**Questo** sacro, augusto stemma." Donizetti. e.i. PB

"**Qui** creavit coelum, lully, lully, lu" (The Chester carol) 15th century Latin carol. e.l. DNS
"Qui creavit coelum, lully, lully, lu" (Song of the nuns of Chester) 1. OB

"**Qui** m'accolse oppresso, errante." Bellini. e.i. PB

"**Qui** sdegno non s'accende." See "In diesen heil'gen hallen" (Mozart)

The **quilting** party. <J. Fletcher. Words by F. Kyle> BB—DFF—WSS
Aunt Dinah's quilting party. DSC—TFP
When I saw sweet Nellie home. GOS 2

Quittez, pasteurs, vos brebis, vos houlettes. For English paraphrase see White Lent

Quoi ma voisine. For English paraphrase see The kingdom

R

Rabbit in de briar patch. See Banjo blues (Williams)

"The **rabbit** is the kind of thing whut travels in the dark." See Big-eye rabbit

Rabble soldier. Cowboy song. SBA
Variants: Jack o' diamonds; "Oh, I'm a good old rebel"

"**Rabda** inima şi taci." See Inimioara mea

Der **rabe** (Akh ty pole chīstoe) Russian folk song. g.r. ML 1

Rabinowitz, Solomon J.
"Schlof mein kind, mein tröst" (Jewish song)
Rachmaninov, Sergeï Vassilievich
"Glory to Him"
"Triumph! thanksgiving"
Radecke, Robert
"Aus der jugendzeit"
From youth's happy day.   See "Aus der jugendzeit"
"Radiant with love's smile."   See "Raggio d'amor parea" (Donizetti)
Raff, Joseph Joachim
Ave Maria
Keine sorg' um den weg
Love finds the way.   See Keine sorg' um den weg
"See, now the dusk is falling."   See Ave Maria
Serenade.   See Ständchen
Ständchen
"Tarry with me, O my Saviour"
The raftmen.   See Les raftsmen
Les raftsmen (The raftmen)   Canadian folk song.   e.f.   GC
The rag picker's bride.   See Le chiffonnier
Ragan, Carroll
Alma mater—Wabash college
Old Wabash
"Raggio d'amor parea."   Donizetti.   e.i.
PB
"Rah! rah! rah! rah! rah! rah! for college, college."   See Kollege kick (Hagen)
Railey, Thomas Tarlton
Alma mater—University of Missouri (Quarles)
"Railroad an' de river."   See Den I was gone
"Railroad Bill."   Negro work song.
SBA
The railroad cars are coming.   19th century song.   SBA
Railroad chorus.   See Rhyme of the rail
Railway (see Song Index)
Variant of: Poor Paddy works on the railway
Raimund, Ferdinand
Abschied (Müller)
"Brüderlein fein" (Drechsler)
Hobellied (Kreutzer)
Rain and snow.   Folk song from North Carolina.   SES 2
"Rain fall and wet Becca Lawton."   Old negro spiritual from South Carolina.   AS
Rain on (upon) the roof.   G. Clifford.   [Words by C. Kinney]   MFS
Rain, rain, rain, rain, ev'ry time I pray for rain.   See Missouri national
Rain upon the roof.   See Rain on the roof (Clifford)
The rainy day ("The day is cold")   W. R. Dempster.   Words by H. W. Longfellow.   GOS 1
Rainy day round ("See the raindrops")   GSS
"Raise your hands."   School song.   MFS

Raisin, A.
A Talmudical student's lament (Jewish song)
Raita.   See Die palmweide
The rakes of Mallow ("Beauing, belleing, dancing, drinking")   Irish song.   HMI
Rakhmaninov, Sergeï Vasilievich.   See Rachmaninov, Sergeï Vassilievich
Rákóczi- (Kurutzen-)lied I ("Hei, Rákóczi! hei, Bercsényi! führer ihr der helden Ungarns."—Rákóczi ferencz dala)   17th century Hungarian song.   g.hu.   ML 3
Rákóczi- (Kurutzen-)lied II ("Hei, Rákóczi! Bercsényi! Bezeredi! edler Ungarnhelden führer ihr."—Rákóczi ferencz dala)   17th century Hungarian song.   g.hu.   ML 3
Rákóczi ferencz dala ("Hei, Rákóczi, Bercsényi! Bezerédi! edler Ungarnhelden führer ihr")   See Rákóczi- (Kurutzen-)lied II
Rákóczi ferencz dala ("Hei, Rákóczi! hei, Bercsényi! führer ihr der helden Ungarns")   See Rákóczi-(Kurutzen-)lied I
Rákóczi-induló.   See Rákóczi-marsch
Rákóczi-marsch (Rákóczi-induló)   g.hu.   ML 3
Rally song.   Song of the University of California at Los Angeles.   T. V. Beall.   HW
Ralph's ramble to London.   English song.   WOE
Ramble, ramble.   See Oh, didn't he ramble (Cole)
The rambling sailor ("I am a sailor stout and bold")   English folk song: sailors' version.   SBS
Rambling wreck from Georgia tech.   Georgia institute of technology song.   [Air: Song of a gambolier]   Words by F. Roman.   AI—AIS
[Les rameaux] The palms.   J. Faure.   e.   MFS
Palm branches.   e.   GE—TFP
Ramsay, Allan
Corn riggs (Scottish air)
Lochaber no more (Reilly?)
The yellow-haired laddie (Scottish air)
Randall, James Ryder
Maryland! my Maryland (German air)
Randegger, Alberto
"Save me, O God"
There's nothing like a fresh'ning breeze
Randers, Kristofer
Pigetanker (Winge)
Rando, Rando, hooray, hooray.   See The bully boat is coming
[Range of the buffalo] The buffalo skinners.   Cowboy song.   LSC—SBA
Rangström, Ture
Adagio
Ego.   See Jag
Jag
The peonies.   See Pionerna
Pionerna
Star-eyes.   See Stjärnöga
Stjärnöga

Rankin, Jeremiah Eames
"God be with you" (Tomer)
Rannalla istuja.   See Am strande
Ar rannou (Die reihe)   Breton folk song.
br.g.   ML 1
Rantin', rovin' Robin.   See "There was a
lad was born in Kyle"
Ranzo, boys, Ranzo.   See Reuben Ranzo
Raphael.   See "Immortal Love, forever
full" (Donizetti)
Rapsodia primaverile (A spring rhapsody)
R. Leoncavallo.   e.i.   SAT
[Rare the barley, rare the rye, rare the
wheat]   "Ritka buza, ritka árpa, ritka
rozs"   ("Seltner weizen, seltne gerste,
seltnes korn")   Hungarian song.
g.hu.   ML 3
'Raslin' Jacob.   Negro spiritual.   HRD
"Raslo drvo bademovo."   See "Stand ein
mandelbaum"
"Raslo drvo sred raja."   See Die grössten
sünden
Rathaus, D.
When we parted (Ippolitov-Ivanov)
Rathgeber, Valentin
Bruder liederlich (Composer unknown)
Von der edlen musik (Composer un-
known)
Rätsellied.   Schlesische volkslied.   g.
EDL
"Rattle, rattle, tell me water-chain."   See
The water chain
Ravenscroft, Thomas
"Remember, O thou man"
The raw recruit ("I ain't been long in this
yer army")   U.S. cavalry song.
Air: Reuben and Rachel.   DSO
The recruit.   US
Raw recruit ("Oh, kind folks, listen to my
song")   See Abraham's daughter
Raymond, Rossiter Worthington
Never alone (Silcher)
"O what can you tell" (Lowry)
Razorback rootin' song.   University of
Arkansas song.   W. M. Paisley.
Words by J. Hughes and C. Walker.
AIS
Read, John
Santa Claus
Reading, John, 1677-1764
"Adeste fideles" (attributed)
"How firm a foundation, ye saints of
the Lord" (same air as "Adeste
fideles"; attributed)
"O come, all ye faithful."   See
"Adeste fideles" (attributed)
Portuguese hymn.   See "Adeste fi-
deles"; "How firm a foundation, ye
saints of the Lord" (attributed)
La realera (The happy-go-lucky one)   J.
Rocha.   e.s.   VS
Reap, boys, reap.   Play-party song from
North Carolina.   SES 2
The reaper [and the flowers]   F. Mendels-
sohn.   Words by H. W. Longfellow.
HCA
Reay, Samuel
The dawn of day
Der rebbe Elimelech.   Jewish folk song.
y.   SY

"Rebbenu! wos is mein kind."   See Zie
tut krawiec miescka
"Der rebe mit die Chssidem."   See Scha
schtill
The rebel soldier (The poor stranger) Folk
song: Berea, Ky. version.   SES 2
—Hyden, Ky. version.   SES 2
—St Helen's, Ky. version.   SES 2
—Franklin county, Va. version.   SES 2
—Meadows of Dan, Va. version.   SES 2
—Montvale, Va. version.   SES 2
The forsaken girl.   Knott or Letcher
county, Ky. version.   MK
Die rebhuhnfeder.   See La ploma de
perdiu
Recessional ("God of our fathers")   See
"God of our fathers, known of old"
(MacMillan)
The recruit.   See The raw recruit
Recuerdas (Memories)   Mexican folk
song.   e.s.   VS
Recuerdas de amistad (Memories of friend-
ship)   Mexican folk song.   e.s.
VS
Red and black ("Wesleyan, let us all unite
and sing")   Ohio Wesleyan university
song.   R. W. Wright.   AI—KU—
KV
"The red and black shall triumph."   Uni-
versity of Cincinnati song.   A. T.
Waterman.   Words by C. R. Beres-
ford.   AIS
The red and blue.   University of Penn-
sylvania song.   W. J. Goeckel.
Words by H. E. Westervelt.   AI—
AIS
The red guidon.   G. E. Griffin (music
and words)   DSO
Red iron ore.   Song of the Great Lakes
region.   Old Irish air.   SBA
"The red moon is up o'er the moss-covered
mountain."   See The star of Glengary
(Sporle)
The red, red rose.   See "My luve is like
a red, red rose" (Scottish air)
Red river boat song.   See Mon cri cra,
tir' la lirette
Red river valley.   Traditional song from
Pine mountain.   SBA
The red sarafan.   See The scarlet sarafan
(Varlamov)
The red scarf.   T. Bonheur.   Words by G.
W. Southey.   TFO
The red white and blue ("O, Columbia the
gem of the ocean")   See Columbia,
the gem of the ocean (Becket)
Redan, Karl, pseud. See Converse, Charles
Crozat
Redcliffe, Frederick J.
The girl I loved in sunny Tennessee
She was bred in old Kentucky
You're not the only pebble on the
beach
Redmond, William Emerson.   See Emer-
son, Billy
Redner, Lewis Henry
"O little town of Bethlehem"
Reed, Andrew
"Holy Ghost! with light divine" (Gott-
schalk)

Reed, Carl Hempel
"Abide with me! fast falls the eventide"
Reed, David
The handicap march (Rosey)
Love me and the world is mine (Ball)
Reed, N. E., and Neal, Ethel
The blues I've got
"Reel away, Marina girls." See Marina girls
Reese, Lizette Woodworth
"Glad that I live am I" (Shaw)
Reeves, Billy
Shew! fly, don't bother me (Campbell)
"Regardez ce p'tit mulâtre." See Musieu Bainjo
Regina cœli, letare (Queen of heaven, rejoice) Plainsong air. 15th century words. e. DNS
["Regnava nel silenzio"] "Were he but here." G. Donizetti. e. WG
The regular army, oh. Old frontier song. DSO
[Das reich der freude] "Mein lebenslauf" (Weinlied) Volksweise. Words by A. Mahlmann. g. EDL
"Reich mir die harfe." See Dafydd y garreg wen
Reichardt, Gustav
Des Deutschen vaterland
The image of the rose. See "In einem thale friedlich stille"
"In einem thale friedlich stille"
Reichardt, Johann Friedrich
Der baum im Odenwald
Bundeslied
Clärchens lied. See "Freudvoll und leidvoll"
"Freudvoll und leidvoll"
Jägers abendlied. See Jägers nachtlied
Jägers nachtlied
Morgenständchen
Das veilchen
Reichardt, Luise
Hoffnung ("Wenn die rosen")
"In the time of roses." See Hoffnung
"Wenn die rosen blühen." See Hoffnung
Reid, Norman
Our Chicago
Reid, William
The lass o' Gowrie (Scottish air)
"There's cauld kail in Aberdeen" (Scottish air)
"Reif ist nun das schilf" ("Uccu bizony megérett a káka") Hungarian folk song. g.hu. ML 3
Reigen (Shīrvoña) Serbian folk song. g.se. ML 2
Reigenlied ("Why so silent, tell me, birdie") See "Why so silent, tell me, birdie"
Reign, Massa Jesus. Negro spiritual. HRD
Die reihe. See Ar rannou
Reilly, Myles
"Farewell to Lochaber." See Lochaber no more (attributed)
Lochaber no more (attributed)

Reinagle, Alexander
"I have a silent sorrow here"
Jerry's song (from The volunteer)
Reinartz, Frederick
Alma mater—Gettysburg college
Reinecke, Karl Heinrich Carstan
"When the little children sleep"
Reinecke, Paul S.
Alma mater—United States military academy (Kücken)
Reinick, Robert
An den sonnenschein (Schumann)
Morgen-hymne (Henschel)
Das reis aus der wurzel Jesse. See "Es ist ein reis entsprungen"
Reisner, C. F. and Davis, Benny
Goodby Broadway, hello France (Baskette)
Reissiger,
Each for all
Reissiger, Karl Gottlieb
Historia von Noah. See Noah
Noah
Studentenleben
"Reiter bin ich, herr der pussta" ("Csikós vagyok, tágas puszták királya") Hungarian song. g.hu. ML 3
Reiterlied ("Die bange nacht") J. W. Lyra. Words by G. Herwegh. g. EDL
Reiterlied ("Wohlauf, kameraden") C. J. Zahn. Words by F. Schiller. g. EDL
Reiters morgenlied ("Morgenrot, morgenrot") Volkslied. Words by W. Hauff. g. EDL
The rejected lover. Folk song: Pineville, Ky. version. SES 2
—St Helen's, Ky. version. SES 2
—Hot Springs, N.C. version. SES 2
—Marion, N.C. version. SES 2
—Tennessee version. SES 2
—Afton, Va. version. SES 2
—Callaway, Va. version. SES 2
—Endicott, Va. version. SES 2
—Mount Fair, Va. version. SES 2
—White Rock, Va. version. SES 2
"Rejoice and be merry in songs and in mirth." See A gallery carol
Rejoice and be merry, set sorrow aside. See "A Virgin most pure, as the prophets do tell, hath brought forth a Babe"; "A Virgin unspotted"
Rejoice greatly, O daughter of Zion. Händel. SSO 1
"Rejoice! my countrymen." See Thus saith the Lord to Cyrus (Händel)
"Rejoice, rejoice, rejoice greatly." See Rejoice greatly, O daughter of Zion (Händel)
Des rekruten rückkehr. See entry under Des
"Relieve Thy champion, image of Thy strength." See Return, O God of hosts (Händel)
Religion is a fortune. Negro spiritual. TFB—WSS
"Oh, religion is a fortune." HRD
Religion is a fortune, I really do believe. JB 2

Religion so sweet. Negro spiritual from South Carolina. AS

Rellstab, Ludwig
Ständchen (Schubert)

Remember ("Remember, O thou man") See "Remember, O thou man" (Ravenscroft)

"**Remember** me, my Saviour God." H. P. Danks. CSS 2

"**Remember,** O thou man" (Remember) T. Ravenscroft. OB

Remember the Alamo. Air: Scots, wha hae wi' Wallace bled. Words by T. A. Durriage. DSO

"**Remember** thee." Irish air: Castle Tirowen. Words by T. Moore. HMI

"**Remember** us poor Mayers all." See Furry day carol

"**Remember** what I promised you." See 'Way out in Idyho

Rémon ⌈Rémon⌉ Negro creole folk song. f. AS

"**Re'n** trista höstregn strömma ner." See Höst (Palmgren)

Renard, Urbain
The builders. See Venez à Saint-Maurice (attributed)
Venez à Saint-Maurice (attributed)

Renouveau (Spring's return) Breton folk song. e. CSB 1

Repentir (O divine Redeemer.—Parce Domine) C. Gounod. e.f.l. ASA

Les **répliques** de Marion (Marions ausflüchte) French folk song. f.g. ML 1

Repper, Charles Brashear
Heigho
Oleander time
Where is spring

"**Repül** a szán." See "Der schlitten eilt"

Request ("Die du über die sterne weg") See Gebet (Brückler)

Request ("Weil' auf mir") See Bitte (Franz); Die bitte (Moór)

Requiem ("Ruh' von schmerzensreichen mühen."—Old Catholic hymn) R. Schumann. e.g. GA

Requiem æternam. See Eternal rest (Piccolomini)

Resignation ("Heart, my heart."—Versöhnung) P. Tschaikowsky. Words by Schtscherbina. e.g. HCA

Resignation ("My God, my Father") See "My God, my Father, while I stray" (Wagner)

"**Rest** and peace to souls departed." See Litaney (Schubert)

"**Rest** at last, your labour over." See Requiem (Schumann)

"**Rest** in peace, all souls departed." See Litaney (Schubert)

"**Rest** in slumber deep, brave men." See We remember

"**Rest,** rest to the weary, peace, peace to the soul." See Calvary (Rodney)

The **resurrection** morn. Negro spiritual from South Carolina. AS

Le **retour** du marin (Seemanns heimkehr) French folk song. f.g. ML 1

Return, oh God of hosts. G. F. Händel. SSO 2

"**Return,** O love." V. Pelissier. Words by C. Cox. MPA 1

"**Return,** return, oh God of hosts." See Return, O God of hosts (Händel)

"**Return** to me, ah brother dear." See Romance (Fry)

Reuben and Rachel. Old American song. BB—TFP

Reuben Glue thought he knew a thing or two. See The little bunch of whiskers on his chin

Reuben Ranzo ("O do you know old Reuben Ranzo") B. Treharne. Words from a traditional chantey. TFB

Reuben Ranzo ("Oh, pity poor Reuben Ranzo") Halliard chantey. BOS 2—WSE
For variants see following songs of same title

Reuben Ranzo ("Oh, poor old Reuben Ranzo") Halliard chantey. US

Reuben Ranzo ("Oh, poor old Reuben Ranzo") Halliard chantey. TSB 1

Reuben Ranzo ("Oh poor old Reuben Ranzo") Halliard chantey. SBS

"**Reuben,** Reuben, I've been thinking." See Reuben and Rachel

Reuenthal, Neidhardt von. See Neidhardt von Reuenthal

Reveille ("I can't get 'em up") U.S. army bugle call. DSO

"**Reveillez-vous,** belle dormeuse" ("Liebliche schläferin, erwachet") French folk air: Reveillez-vous, belle endormie. Words by C. R. Dufresny. f.g. ML 1

Revolutionary tea. Old American song. BB

Revolutionslied. See "Ah! ça ira"

Rex gloriae. See "Quem pastores laudavere"

Rexford, Eben Eugene
Silver threads among the gold (Danks)

Reyloff, E.
"I'm a forester free"

Reynardine. Irish air from County Donegal. Words from an Ulster ballad. HI 1

Reynolds, George Nugent
"My love, still I think that I see her" (Irish air)

Rheinweinlied ("Bekränzt mit laub den lieben vollen") J. André. Words by M. Claudius. g. EDL

⌈Der **rheinweinzecher**⌉ "Im kühlen keller" (Der trinker) L. Fischer. Words by C. Müchler. g. EDL

Rhuddenfab. See Jones, Lewis

Rhyfelgyrch gwyr Harlech (Men of Harlech) Old Welsh patriotic song. e.w. SSB
March of the men of Harlech ("Hark! I hear the foe advancing") e. MBS
March of the men of Harlech ("Men of Harlech, in the hollow") e. BB

Rhyfelgyrch gwyr Harlech.—*Continued*
Men of Harlech ("Men of Harlech, in the hollow") e. TFP
Rhyfelgyrch gwyr Harlech (Kriegslied der mannen von Harlech) g.w. ML 1
[Rhyfelgyrch gwyr Harlech] Men of Harlech ("Men of Harlech, lords of singing") Old Welsh air. New words by J. L. Vandevere. TFP
The rhyme of the chivalrous shark. US
[Rhyme of the rail] Railroad chorus. 19th century air. [Words by J. G. Saxe] SW
"Ri-tan-tou-ri tan-ti-rette." F. Lehar. e. WLO
Ricci, F. P.
Bowed with guilt I kneel before Thee
Ricci, Federico
"Sulla poppa del mio brick" (from La prigione di Edimburgo)
Rice, Elihu S.
"Shall we meet beyond the river"
Rice, Gitz
"I want to go home, I want to go home"
Rice, Thomas Dartmouth
Jim Crow
Rich, Gladys
U of U trail
"Rich and rare were the gems she wore." Air: The summer is coming. Words by T. Moore. HMI—SI
"De rich folks 'cided to take a trip." See De Titanic
"The rich man lay on his velvet couch." See Mag's song
The rich nobleman and his daughter. Folk song from Surrey. BET
The rich old lady. Folk song: Allanstand, N.C. version. SES 1
—Burnsville, N.C. version. SES 1
—Virginia version. SES 1
Richards, Brinley
"Oh! whisper what thou feelest." See Whisper what thou feelest
Whisper what thou feelest (from Crown diamonds)
Richards, Elizabeth Davis
Composer and author
Farewell, W. V. U., farewell
Author
"By the blue Monongahela" (Beltzhoover-Dille)
Richardson, A. H. G.
"No one to love" (Harvey)
Richardson, J. Howard
Cupid and the maiden
Richardson, Mabel K.
Pioneer song (Colton)
Richberg, Donald Randall
Flag of maroon
Rickaby, Franz Lee
North Dakota U
Rickard, Truman Elwell
Hail! Minnesota
Riddell, Henry Scott
Scotland yet (McLeod)
The riddle song ("I brought my love a cherry") Folk song: Hyden, Ky. version. SES 2

The riddle song ("I gave my love a cherry") Pineville, Ky. version. SES 2
The riddle song ("I gave my love a cherry") St Helen's, Ky. version. SES 2
Ride around, little dogies. See "I ride an old paint"
Ride on ("Some of dese mornin's") Negro spiritual. HRD
Ride on, Jesus ("If yo' see my mother") Negro spiritual. HRD
Ride on, King Jesus ("I was but young when I began") Negro spiritual. FSN
"Riding in a street car." Old American song. SW
"Riding one morning, my fare I'd just paid." See Elsie from Chelsea (Dacre)
Righini, Vincenzo
"Amor, che cieco sei" (from La Gerusalemme liberata)
"Righteous art Thou, O Lord." Stradella. e. SSO 3
Righteous Joseph. Cornish air. Traditional words. DNS—OB
Righteous Joseph. Old English air. Traditional words. DNS
The righteous rejoice ("Uv'chen tsadikim") Palestinean folk song. e.he. BNP
"Righteousness and equity" (Chandos anthem) Handel. SSO 2
Riley, James Whitcomb
Pansies (Cox)
"There! little girl, don't cry" (Sobeski)
Riley, John Athelstan Laurie
"Ye watchers and ye holy ones" (German air)
Rimbault, Edward Francis
The Alpine horn
Rimskiĭ-Korsakov, Nikolaĭ Andreevich
Kolyadka. See Merry Yuletide
Merry Yuletide (from Christmas eve revels)
Russian carol (from Christmas eve revels)
A song of India (from Sadko)
Rinaldo di Capua
"Dal sen del caro sposo" (from Vologeso)
Nell' orror di notte oscura (from Vologeso)
Rinckart, Martin
Nun danket alle Gott (Crüger)
Ring again, ring again, beautiful bells. See Beautiful bells (Lyte)
"Ring around a rosy, sit upon a posy." Children's game song. MFS
Ring dat golden bell. Minstrel song. PSG—WSS
Ring her praises, never ceasing. See Alma mater—Washington and Jefferson college (Thompson)
Ring on, Christmas bells. See "Christmas-time has come again, time to us so dear" (Stevens)
Ring on, sweet angelus. C. Gounod. Words by H. B. Farnie. GE
"Ring out, O bells, your ancient chime." See Westminster chimes

"**Ring** out, then, your hoiah." Holy Cross college song. AI—AIS

"**Ring** out, wild bells." E. L. Bainton. Words by A. Tennyson. CSB 2

"**Ring** out, wild bells." C. Gounod. Words by A. Tennyson. CSS 1

Ring, ring de banjo. S. C. Foster (music and words) WSS

Ring, ring the banjo. BB

Ring, ring, ye silver chimes. See Ring the bells

Ring that golden bell. See Ring dat golden bell

Ring the bells ("Oh, ring the bells in the belfry high") Folk air: <Greensleeves> Words by S. Paul. TFG

Das **ringlein** ("Bald gras ich am Neckar") Volkslied. g. EDL

"**Ringsum** erschallt in wald und flur." See Sonntagslied (Mendelssohn)

Ringwaldt, Bartholomaus
Wo gehest du hin (Bach)

Rinkart, Martin. See Rinckart, Martin

Rinnce Philib an cheoil (Phil the fluter's dancing) Irish Gaelic song. e. CSB 5

Rinuccini, Ottavio
"Funeste piaggie" (Peri)
"Non piango e non sospiro" (Caccini)

[**Rio** Grande] "I'll sing you a song" (Bound for the Rio Grande) Chantey. TSB 1
We're bound for Rio. GSS
For variants see following songs of same title

Rio Grande ("Oh, say was you ever") Capstan chantey. SBS—US
Bound to the Rio Grande. WSE

The **Rio** Grande ("O where are you going to") Chantey. BOS 2

Riordan, Joseph W.
Composer
Anthem
Author
Alma mater—Loyola university (Devereux)

"**Rippling**, flashing, leaping, dashing." See The woodland brook

"**Rise** and hail the dawn of Maytime." See The dawn of Maytime (Flotow)

[**Rise** and shine] Oh, rise an' shine. Negro spiritual. JG
Rise an' shine. HRD

"**Rise**, arise, arise." See The sun worshippers

"**Rise**, crowned with light" (Russian hymn) A. T. Lvoff. Words by A. Pope. MFS

[**Rise** mourners, rise, mourners] "Rise, mourner, rise." Negro spiritual. JB 2

"**Rise** O sun, all wrapp'd in sadness." See "Questo sacro, augusto stemma" (Donizetti)

"**Rise**, rise, thou merry lark." Welsh folk song. [Tr of Codiad yr hedydd] e. CSB 2

"**Rise** up, rise up, you merry men all." See King Pharaoh: The miraculous harvest

Rise up, shepherd, an' foller. Negro spiritual. Christmas plantation song. HRD—JB 2

"**Rise** you up, rise you up, little Marget, he did say." See Earl Brand (Berea, Ky. version)

R'isiho ("I saw her—I loved her") Arabian love song. e.he. BNP

The **rising** of the sun and the running of the deer. See "The holly and the ivy"

"**Ritka** buza, ritka árpa, ritka rozs." See Rare the barley, rare the rye, rare the wheat

Ritornello ("Jate sospire mieje") See I sospiri

[**Ritornello** delle lavandare del Vomero] Ritornello di lavandaja (Waschfrauenlied) Neapolitan song. g.i. ML 2

Ritornello di lavandaja. See Ritornello delle lavandare del Vomero

Ritter Ole. See Herr Ole

[**Ritters** abschied] "Weh' dasz wir scheiden müssen" (Soldier's farewell) J. Kinkel (music and words) e.g. MFS
The soldier's farewell. e. BB—DFF—TFB—TFP—TFR

Riviere, J.
Spring, gentle spring

"**Riv'vos** kochovim eizeh hu kochovi." See Thou knowest

Roaming alone through this world's wilderness. See "No one to love" (Harvey)

Roanoke! let's go old Roanoke. See Maroon victory (Stelljes)

Roar, lion, roar. Columbia university song. R. Webb and M. W. Watkins. Words by C. Ford. AI—AIS—KU—KV

"**Roarious!** roarious; we'll make the coast artillery glorious." See Coast artillery marching song

The **roast** beef of old England (Alt-Englands roast beef) R. Leveridge. Verses 1-2 by H. Fielding [verses 3-4 by R. Leveridge] e.g. ML 1

Rob Roy Macgregor. Air: Duncan Gray. Author of words unknown. GS

Robert, Friederike
Lieblingsplätzchen (Mendelssohn)

Roberts, Barrett
Indian warriors' song (Allen)

Roberts, Daniel C.
National hymn (Warren)

Robertson, Donald G.
Northwestern push on song

The **robin** ("Dear little robin") See Robin! robin (Aiken)

Robin Adair ("What's this dull town to me") Celtic air: Eileen aroon. English version of air. Words by C. Keppel. BB—GOS 1—GS—GSS—SSB

The **robin** and chicken. Scale song. W. H. Aiken. BB

"**Robin** Hood and Little John." See The Cornish May song

"Robin Hood, Robin Hood, said Little John." 16th century song. DSB

Robin Redbreast ("Good-bye, good-bye to summer") J. M. Hubbard. [Words by Allingham] GOS 2

Robin Redbreast ("Good-bye, good-bye to summer") German air <by F. W. Kücken> Words by Allingham. BB

[Robin! robin] The robin. W. H. Aiken. BB

Robin Ruff. See The better wish (Russell)

Robinson, Clarence C.
Sing, Ohio

Robinson, Edwin Meade
Old Wabash (Ragan)

Robinson, Kenneth Allan
Forward the white (Sumner)

Robinson Crusoe. Air: Rogue's march. [Words by J. Cussans] BOS 2—MFS

Robinson Crusoe's story. G. Newell. Words by C. E. Carryl and G. Newell. GSS

Rocha, Jesus
The happy-go-lucky one. See La realera
La realera

"Rock-a-bye baby." Nursery song. 3d air <by E. I. Canning> TFG—TFR

"Rock-a-bye, my little owlet." See Indian lullaby (Aiken)

The rock beside the sea. C. C. Converse. GOS 1

Rock me to sleep. E. Leslie. [Words by E. A. Allen] GOS 2

Rock o' jubilee. Negro spiritual from South Carolina. AS

"Rock o' my soul." Negro spiritual from Virginia. AS

"Rock of ages, let our song" (The feast of lights.—Mooztzur) Traditional air. e. MFF

Rock pile blues (Mama's prison yard blues) S. Williams. HB

"Rock, rock, and breezes that blow." See Baadfart (Olsen)

Rockaway. H. Russell. Words by H. J. Sharpe. GOS 1

Rocke, L.
Wilt thou soon return

"Rocked in the cradle of the deep." J. P. Knight. Words by E. Willard. BB—GOS 1—SFB—TFP

Rocking (Hajej, nynjej) Czech carol. e. OB

Rocking hymn. See "Sweet baby, sleep! what ails my dear" (Williams)

[The rocks and the mountains] Oh, the rocks and the mountains. Negro spiritual. HRD

Rockwell, lieutenant
When Sherman marched down to the sea

The rocky mountain top. Folk song: Kentucky version. SES 2
—North Carolina version. SES 2

Rode, Helge
Sne (Lie)

Röder, Martin. See Roeder, Martin

Rodney, Paul
Calvary
Sion
Time and tide

Rodwell, George Herbert Buonaparte
The banks of the blue Moselle

Roeckel, Joseph Leopold
The bride bells
"Cast thy bread on the waters"

Roedd yn y wiad honno (Welsh carol) e. OB

Roeder, Martin
Abendlied. See "Tarry with me, O my Saviour"
Ehre sei Gott in der höh'. See "It came upon the midnight clear"
Glory to God. See "It came upon the midnight clear"
"It came upon the midnight clear"
"Tarry with me, O my Saviour"

Roeder, Otto
Gondolier waltz. See On Venice waters
On Venice waters

Rogers, Benjamin
The May morning hymn

Rogue's march. Old U.S. army song. DSO

Roguish little beauty, Emeleen. Old American song. SW

Das rohr. See La caña

"Le roi a fait battre tambour." See "Le roy a fait battre tambour"

[Le roi d'Yvetot] The king of Yvetot. French political song. Words by P. J. de Béranger. e. TFO

Roisin dubh (Dunkles röslein) [Irish air: Rois gael dubh, or, The fair black-hair'd little rose] g.ir. ML 1

Roll de ole chariot along ("We are travellin'") Negro spiritual. HRD
Variant: The old chariot

Roll dem bones. See Street urchins' medley

Roll, green wave. See The olive and blue (Ten Hoor and Goldstein)

Roll, Jordan, roll ("O brother, you ought t'have been there") Negro spiritual. HRD

Roll, Jordan, roll ("Oh! brothers, you ought t'have been there") BB

Roll, Jordan, roll ("Oh! brothers you oughter been dere") WSS

Roll, Jordan, roll ("My brudder sittin' on de tree of life") Negro spiritual: <South Carolina version> AS

Roll on old avalanche. Marquette university song. S. Johnston. KV

Roll on, roll on, roll on, little dogies. See The cowboy's heaven

Roll on, silver moon. Arr by J. W. Turner. WSS
The silver moon. GOS 1

"Roll on ye waves" ("Zirmu gallim") Palestinean folk song. e.he. BNP

Roll out! heave dat cotton. Minstrel song. WSS

Roll the chariot. Salvation army song. SBA

Roll the cotton down ("I'm bound for Alabama")   Negro halliard chantey.   TSB 2
For variant see following song of same title

Roll the cotton down ("Oh roll the cotton down, my boys")   Halliard chantey. SBS

Roll the old chariot along ("A plate of hot scouse")   See The old chariot (Chantey)

Roll the old chariot along ("We are travellin'")   See Roll de ole chariot along (Negro spiritual)

Roll them bones.   See Street urchins' medley

Roll them roly boly eyes.   E. Leonard (music and words)   OTG

Rolling home ("Call all hands")   Sea song.   WSE

Rolling home ("Call all hands")   Capstan chantey version.   SBS

"Rolling in foaming billows."   Haydn. e.   SSO 4

Rolling on, rolling on to glory children. See Johnny, get your gun

Roman, Frank
          Composer
Alma mater—Georgia institute of technology
          Author
Rambling wreck from Georgia tech (Old air)

Romanay.   Negro folk song.   GSS

"Romanay, Romanay, Romanay lady." See Romanay

Romance ("Return to me, ah brother dear")   W. H. Fry.   Words by J. R. Fry.   HP

Romano, Giulio, pseud.   See Caccini, Giulio

Romero y Saráchaga, Federico, and Fernández Shaw, Guillermo
La canción del olvido (Serrano)

"The Romish lady she had babes."   See The wife of Usher's well (Burnsville, N.C. version no. 1)

La ronde du rosier (The rose-tree)   Folk song from Lorraine.   e.f.   CBF 1

"Rondinella pellegrina."   Petrella.   e.i. PC

"Rongyos csárda."   See "Ruined stands the ancient tavern"

A rookie.   Song of the Spanish-American war.   DSO

"Room for the city's factotum here."   See "Largo al factotum della città" (Rossini)

Rooney, Pat
Are you the O'Reilly

Root, Dewey
Bring back my kitchen to me (Fuller)

Root, George Frederick
"All together, all together"
The battle cry of freedom
The cruising boys of subdiv. nine (same air as Tramp, tramp, tramp)
The hazel dell
"Just before the battle, mother"

"Just before the battle, mother": Confederate parody
"Just behind the battle, mother" (same air as "Just before the battle, mother")
"Mary had a little lamb": Civil war version (same air as The battle cry of freedom)
Rosalie, the prairie flower
The soldiers' song (same air as Tramp, tramp, tramp)
"There's music in the air"
Tramp, tramp, tramp (with words "In the prison cell"; "On the battle front")
The vacant chair

Root, hog, or die ("I'm right from old Virginny")   Minstrel song.   PSG—WSS

Rooter's song.   See Hail to old O. S. C. (Wilkins)

Rorate.   Scottish traditional air.   Words by W. Dunbar.   OB

Rory O'Moore ("Young Rory O'Moore")   Irish air.   Words by S. Lover.   SI

Rosa, Salvator
Canzonetta.   See "Star vicino"
Only smile."   See "Star vicino"
"Star vicino"

Rosa Lee.   WSS

Rosalie ("I'm Pierre de Bonton")   L. Knight (music and words)   BB
Pierre de Bon Bon.   SW

Rosalie, the prairie flower.   G. F. Root. KSO

Rosalind ("Here cometh Rosalind")   Children's song.   MFS

Rose, George
"Oh! how delightful" (Molloy)

The rose and silver gray.   Vassar college song.   Scottish air: Auld lang syne.   Words by L. Blatchley.   AI

The rose and the nightingale.   J. Barnby. Words by Baily.   HCA

"The rose complained."   See "Es hat die rose sich beklagt" (Franz)

"Rose, écoute douce fleur."   See La chanson des beignets

"The rose is weeping for her love."   See The rose and the nightingale (Barnby)

"Rose-leaves are falling."   See Vedrai, carino (Mozart)

"Rose, lovely rose, that blooms so sweetly." See To a rose (Coerne)

Rose-Marie ("Over the hills and far away") J. L. Molloy.   Words by F. E. Weatherly.   HCA

The rose ob Alabama.   Minstrel song. ⌐Words by S. S. Steele⌐   WSS

The rose of Allandale.   S. Nelson. Words by C. Jefferys.   BB—GOS 1 —GS—TFO

Rose of Killarney.   J. R. Thomas. <Words by G. Cooper>   GOS 2— OT

Rose of Lucerne (The Swiss toy girl) Swiss air <by J. Barnett>   GOS 1

The rose of No Man's land.   J. A. Brennan.   Words by J. Caddigan.   SMG

The rose of Sharon.   See Lo! a fair rose is blooming (Praetorius)

The **rose** of the Alps. G. Linley. GE
"**Rose**-red, rose-red" ("Piros, piros, piros")
Hungarian folk song. e.hu. KH 2
"**Rose**, rose, and up she rises." See Up
she rises
Der **rose** sendung. See entry under Der
The **rose**-tree. See La ronde du rosier
"The **rose** upon the brier will be him trouse
and doublet." See Wee Willie Gray
"A **rosebud** by my early walk." [Air:
The shepherd's wife] Words by R.
Burns. CSB 6
Rosebud, rosebud, rosebud red. See
Heidenröslein (Schubert)
"**Rosebud**, to the fields art going" ("Ne
menj rózsám a tarlóra") B. Egressy.
e.hu. KH 1
"**Rosen** brach ich nachts mir am dunkeln
hage." See Sapphische ode (Brahms)
Rosen im tal, mädel im saal. See Mond-
schein

Rosenfeld, Monroe H.

Composer
And her golden hair was hanging down
her back
Gold will buy 'most anything but a true
girl's heart
Take back your gold
Those wedding bells shall not ring out

Author
"With all her faults I love her still"
(Savino)

"The **rose's** age is but a day." W. Hayes.
Round. DSB
The **rose's** complaint. See "Es hat die
rose sich beklagt" (Franz)
"**Roses** culled at night." See Sapphische
ode (Brahms)
"**Roses** I have pluck'd, lovely roses." See
"J'ai cueilli la belle rose"
"**Roses** in the garden knowing" ("Jártam
kertben rózsák között") Hungarian
song. Composer unknown. e.hu.
KH 1
"**Roses** we bring." Round. Haupt-
mann. CSB 1
"**Rosestock**, holderblüh, wenn i mein
dirnderl sieh." See Oberschwäbischer
ländler
Rosetta and her gay ploughboy. Folk
song: Sussex version. BET
Rosey, George
The handicap march
Rosie Nell. 19th century song. SBA
Röslein auf der heiden. Volkslied. g.
EDL
Roslin castle ("'Twas in the season of the
year") Air: The house of Glams
[attributed to J. Oswald] Words by
R. Hewitt. GS
Ross, Alexander
Woo'd and married and a' (Scottish
air)
Ross, J. H.
The elopement
Ross, Malcolm, and Albertson, Ralph
"I have led a good life" (Old air)

Rossetti, Christina Georgina
The ferry (Ireland)
For a dream's sake (Cowen)
A hope carol (Smith)
"In the bleak mid-winter" (Holst)
Lady Moon (Loomis)
Rossini, Gioacchino Antonio
Ah! mia figlia, perdona all' affanno
(from Roberto Bruce)
Ah! quel giorno (from Semiramide)
"All our grief"
"La calunnia è un venticello" (from Il
barbiere di Siviglia)
"Cimentando i venti e l'onde" (from
L'Italiana in Algeri)
"Cruda sorte! amor tiranno" (from
L'Italiana in Algeri)
"Cujus animam" (from Stabat Mater)
Di tanti palpiti (from Tancredi)
Duce di tanti eroi (from Maometto
secondo)
"Elena! oh tu ch'io chiamo" (from La
donna del lago)
"Home's not merely four square walls"
"In sì barbara" (from Semiramide)
"Jesus, the very thought of Thee"
"Largo al factotum della città" (from
Il barbiere di Siviglia)
"Manca un foglio" (from Il barbiere
di Siviglia)
Manoah. See "Jesus, the very thought
of Thee"; "O Thou from Whom
all goodness flows"
"Miei rampolli femminini" (from La
cenerentola)
Non più mesta accanto al fuoco (from
La cenerentola)
"O Thou from Whom all goodness
flows" (same air as "Jesus, the very
thought of Thee")
"Pensa alla patria" (from L'Italiana in
Algeri)
Pull away, brave boys
"Il vecchietto cerca moglie" (from Il
barbiere di Siviglia)
"**Rösslein**, rösslein steht im stalle" ("Šeriau,
šeriau sau žirgeli") Lithuanian folk
song. g.li. ML 3
The **rosy** crown. C. M. Von Weber.
[Words by D. Dutton] MFS
Der **rote** sarafan. See The scarlet sara-
fan (Varlamov)
Rotes weinchen ("Červené vínečko")
Czech folk song. bo.g. ML 3
Rouget de Lisle, Claude Joseph
"Hark, hark, the peal of clarions call-
ing" (same air as La Marseillaise)
La Marseillaise
[**Rough** and rolling sea] Like a rough
and a rolling sea. Negro song.
HRD
"**Round** Colin's peak the mist is sailing."
See MacCrimmon's lament
"**Round** de meadows am a-ringing." See
Massa's in de cold, cold ground
(Foster)
Round 'em up for dear old Baylor. Baylor
university song. R. Grove (music
and words) KU

"**Round** her neck she wore a yellow ribbon."   See For her lover who was far away

"The **round-house** in Cheyenne is filled ev'ry night."   See The dreary black hills

" '**Round** my Indiana homestead wave the cornfields."   See On the banks of the Wabash, far away (Dresser)

Round the corn, Sally ("Five can't ketch me")   Negro corn-song from Virginia.   AS

Round the corner, Sally ("O around the corner we will go")   Pulling chantey.   TSB 2

"**Round** the meadows am a-ringing."   See Massa's in de cold, cold ground (Foster)

"**Rouse**, all ye brave lads of old '40."   See Old Hal o' the west

Rousseau, Jean Jacques
        Cradle hymn
        "Thoughts of wonder" (same air as Cradle hymn)

Rousseau, Marcel Auguste Louis
        Arpège
        Arpeggios.   See Arpège

Routhier, Sir Adolphe Basile
        "O Canada" (Lavallée)

Rouveyrol, Mrs Aurania (Ellerbeck)   See Ellerbeck, Aurania

The **rover's** grave.   J. G. Clark (music and words)   GOS 1

The **roving** gambler.   Folk song: American version.   SBA
        Variant: The gamboling man

"**Row**, boys, row."   See Volga boat song (Words by Drake)

"**Row**, men, row! tho' the winds blow! 'gainst the current, row, men, row."   See Volga boat song

Row, row, cheerly row (Emigrants' song) Words by D. M. Mulock.   MFS

"**Row**! row! homeward we steer."   See Boatman's return (Sporle)

"**Row**, row, row your boat."   Round. E. O. Lyte.   BB—TFP

"**Row** the boat, Whittington."   Round. TFO—TFR

Rów wopytanje.   See Der besuch am grabe

The **rowan** tree ("O rowan tree! O rowan tree")   Scottish air.   ₁Words by C. Nairne₁   GS

Rowe, Sidney, pseud.   See Stevens, David

"Le **roy** a fait battre tambour" ("Des königs trommel rief zum ball")   Old French folk song.   f.g.   ML 1

"**Roy's** wife of Aldivalloch."   N. Gow. Words by E. Grant.   GOS 1—GS

"**Rózsabokorban** jöttem."   See "In a rosebush I was born"

Rub-a-dub, rub-a-dub.   See The little soldier (Vincent)

Rubbra, Edmund Duncan
        "Dormi, Jesu! mater ridet"
        The Virgin's cradle hymn.   See "Dormi, Jesu! mater ridet"

Rubinstein, Anton
        Der Asra
        The dream
        "Du bist wie eine blume"
        "È dunque ver"
        Hagar in der wüste
        Hagar in the wilderness.   See Hagar in der wüste
        "Thou'rt like unto a flower."   See "Du bist wie eine blume"
        Der traum.   See The dream
        Voices of the woods
        "Welcome, sweet springtime."   See Voices of the woods

Ruby.   V. Gabriel.   Words by J. J. Lonsdale.   GE

Rückauf, Anton
        Lockruf
        Lover's call.   See Lockruf

Rückblick ("O alte burschenherrlichkeit") Volksweise.   g.   EDL

Rückert, Friedrich
        "Aus der jugendzeit" (Radecke)
        "Du bist die ruh'" (Schubert)
        Frühling liebster (Scholz)
        "Ich hab' in deinem auge" (Franz)
        "Ein obdach gegen sturm" (Kahn)
        Volksliedchen (Schumann)
        Widmung (Schumann)

Ruddenfab.   See Jones, Lewis

Rudelsburg ("An der Saale")   F. E. Fesca.   Words by F. Kugler.   g.   EDL

Rudelsburg ("Dort Saaleck")   H. Allmers (music and words)   g.   EDL

Ruderlied.   See The keel row

Ruebush, William H.
        Alma mater—Tulane university

Rufe, kuckuck (Kukní kukuvítse)   Macedonian folk song.   b.g.   ML 2

"**Rufus**, Rastus, Johnson Brown."   ₁H. Von Tilzer.   Words by A. B. Sterling₁ BB

"**Rugiadose**, odorose."   See Le violette (Scarlatti)

"**Ruh'** von schmerzensreichen mühen." See Requiem (Schumann)

"**Ruhe** in sanftem schlummer."   See Duorme

"**Ruhig** fliesst die Maros" ("Maros vize folyik csendesen")   Hungarian folk song.   g.hu.   ML 3

"**Ruh'n** in frieden alle seelen."   See Litaney (Schubert)

"**Ruined** stands the ancient tavern" ("Rongyos csárda")   Hungarian folk song.   e.hu.   KH 2

Rule Britannia ("When Britain first, at heaven's command")   British national song.   T. Arne.   Words probably by J. Thomson; attributed also to D. Mallet.   MBS

Rumsty-ho.   Old English song.   TFG

Run, let the bulgine run.   Negro chantey. WSE
        Variant of: Let the bullgine run

"**Run**, let the bull chimes run" (see Song Index)
        Variant of: Let the bullgine run

Run, Mary, run. Negro spiritual. HRD
Run, Mary, run (I know de udder worl'
  is not like dis) JB 2
Run, nigger, run. Folk song: Arkansas
  version. AS
—Kentucky version. SES 2
"Run, sinner, run." Negro spiritual.
  JG
Run to Jesus. Negro spiritual. FSN
  —HRD—WSS
"Run to the moon." See Sinner man
  (Kentucky version)
Runeberg, Johan Ludvig
  "Flickan knyter" (Stenhammar)
  "Våren flyktar hastigt" (Sibelius)
  Vårt land, vårt fosterland (Pacius)
Runengesang. See "Home my sweetheart
  comes from roving"
Runo-laulu. See "Home my sweetheart
  comes from roving"
Rupès, Georges
  Célébrons le Seigneur
  Glorify the Lord. See Célébrons le
    Seigneur
Russell, Arthur T.
  Integer vitae (Flemming)
Russell, Henry
  Barber, spare those hairs (same air as
    "Woodman, spare that tree")
  The better wish
  "Cheer, boys, cheer"
  Coal black rose
  The ivy green
  "A life in the soldiers' camp" (same
    air as "A life on the ocean wave")
  "A life on the ocean wave"
  "A life on the Vicksburg bluff" (same
    air as "A life on the ocean wave")
  The old arm chair
  Old Dan Tucker
  The old sexton
  Ole Dan Tucker. See Old Dan
    Tucker
  Robin Ruff. See The better wish
  Rockaway
  Texan rangers' song (same air as "I'm
    afloat! I'm afloat")
  Uncle Sam and Mexico (same air as
    Old Dan Tucker)
  War song of the Texan rangers. See
    Texan rangers' song
  "Woodman, spare that tree"
Russian carol ("Comes Kolyada, maid of
  light") N. Rimsky-Korsakoff (music
  and words) e. SR
The ᵣRussianᵣ national hymn. National
  anthem of imperial Russia. ᵣA. F.
  Lvoff. Words by Joukovskyᵣ e.r.
  NRF
Russotto, Henry A.
  Song of hope
Rusty Jiggs and Sandy Sam. Cowboy
  song. LSC
Ruter, A. L.
  "When Erin shall stand 'mid the isles
    of the sea"
Rutledge, John T.
  "Allie darling" (Danks)
  "Little bright eyes, will you miss me"
    (Danks)

Ryan, Richard
  The merry Swiss girl (Swiss air)
  "Oh, saw ye the lass wi' the bonny
    blue een" (Scottish air)

S

"'s gibt kein schöner leben als studenten-
  leben." See Studentenleben (Reis-
  siger)
"'s ist alles dunkel, 's ist alles trube."
  See Woran ich meine freude hab
Saadi Muslih-ud-din-Saadi. See Sa'dī
Saarijärven rantaan. See Am strande des
  Saarijärvi
Sabbath has no end. Negro spiritual
  from Virginia. AS
Saboly, Nicolas
  "Bring a torch, Jeannette, Isabella"
    (Old French carol. Tr of Un
    flambeau, Jeannette, Isabelle) Au-
    thorship uncertain
Le sabre de mon père. For English
  translation see The sabre song (Offen-
  bach)
ᵣThe sabre songᵣ "Behold the sabre of my
  father." J. Offenbach. ᵣTr of Le
  sabre de mon pèreᵣ e. WLO
"Sabs es segados que fan." See Cansó
  de sega
Sackville, Charles. See Dorset, Charles
  Sackville, 6th earl of
Sacred love my bosom firing. See O, tu
  Palermo (Verdi)
Sacrifice and faith ("Zivchu, zivche tse-
  dek") Palestinean folk song. e.he.
  BNP
Sad condition. Play-party game from
  Kentucky. SES 2
Sad, sad and lonely. See "Seven long
  years in state prison"
"Sad tales we hear of ev'ry day." See
  I'm dancing mad (Brian)
"Sad was the day we said farewell." See
  The emigrants
Sa'dī
  Grass and roses (Bartlett)
Sadie. American folk song. SBA
  Variant of: "Frankie and Johnny"
"Sadie went into the bar-room." See
  Sadie
Safe in the promised land. Mountain
  spiritual from Virginia. RA
  Variant: "Where O where is old Elijah"
"A safe stronghold our God is still." See
  Ein' feste burg (Luther)
"Safely through another week." L. Ma-
  son. <Words by J. Newton> BB
"Sag an, wie gross" ("Skazhī, moîā krasa-
  vītsa") Russian folk song. g.r.
  ML 1
"Sag mir, mein Hannchen." See La Sa-
  voyarde

"**Sag**, warum bliebst du aus" ("Proč si k nám nepryšeu") Slovak folk song. g.sl. ML 3

"**Sag**, was hör ich dort." See Die schwester prüft den bruder

"**Sag**', was tun die schnitter gleich." See Cansó de sega ("Sabs es segadós que fan")

"**Sag**, was wieherst du, mein rösslein" ("Oi, ko žvengi, žirgeli") Lithuanian folk song. g.li. ML 3

"**Sag**, wie kann nur deine seele" ("Kako može duša tvoja") Croatian folk song. g.se. ML 2

"**Sag**, wohin, du reiter, sage mir." See "Shepherd, see thy horse's foaming mane"

"**Sage** mir, mein herzensliebchen" ("Jenom ty mně, má panenko, povĕz") Moravian-Czech folk song. bo.g. ML 3

"**Sah** ein knab' ein röslein steh'n." See Heidenröslein (Schubert); Heidenröslein (Werner)

"**Sah** eine tig'rin tief im dunklen haine." See La Scillitana

"**Sahst** du nicht mein lokkenköpfchen." See An chúil-fhionn

"**Said** an aviator to a fighter." See Kelly field air-service song (Emmett)

"**Said** Robin, popping in his head." See La filatrice (Mozart)

"**Sail** away, ladies." Negro folk song. HB

"**Sail**! home, as straight as an arrow." See White wings (Winter)

"**Sail**, O believer." Negro spiritual from South Carolina. AS

"**Sail**, O sail! Sail, O brudder." See Sail over yonder

"**Sail** on, vikings, we'll get under way." See Viking song (Maesch)

Sail over yonder. Negro spiritual. FSN

Sailing ("Vug, vug, for vove og vind") See Baadfart (Olsen)

Sailing ("Y'heave ho") G. Marks. BB —TFB—TFP—TFR—US

Sailing, sailing, over the bounding main. See Sailing (Marks)

A **sailing** song ("When keen salt winds are blowing") J. W. Callcott. Words by H. Fitch. TFO

The **sailor** cut down in his prime. See St James's hospital

Sailor likes his bottle ("Oh the mate got drunk") Halliard chantey. SBS

The **sailor** likes his bottle, O ("A bottle o' rum") Chantey. TSB 2

"A **sailor** loved a lass." S. Storace. WOE

The **sailor's** life ("A sailor's life's the life I trow") Old English song. WOE

"A **sailor's** life's the life I trow." See The sailor's life

"A **sailor's** lot is a wearied life." See Sweet William (Kentucky version)

The **sailor's** wife. See Baby mine (Boott)

Saineville, A. de
Sonnet d'amour (Thomé)

St Albinus. See "Jesus lives! no longer now"

St Anne. See "O God, our Help in ages past" (Croft)

St Clair, George
Hail to New Mexico (Clauve)

Saint David's day ("When King Cadwallon fam'd of old") Air: Dydd gwyl dewi, or, St David's day. DSC

The St Day carol. See Sans Day carol

St George's Windsor. See "Come, ye thankful people, come" (Elvey)

St Helena soldier. Chantey. WSE

St James's hospital (The sailor cut down in his prime) Folk song: Dewey, Va. version. SES 2
—Peaks of Otter, Va. version. SES 2
Variants: The cowboy's lament; Those gambler's blues

St Joe's infirmary. See Those gambler's blues

St Lawrence boat song. See Fringue, fringue sur l'aviron

St Louis blues. W. C. Handy (music and words) HB

"**Saint** Mary goes a-seeking." See Maria's wallfahrt (Brahms)

"**Saint** Nicolas a trois clériaux." See Le miracle de Saint-Nicolas (Lorraine version)

St Oswald. See "Hark! ten thousand" (Dykes)

"**Saint** Patrick was a gentleman." Irish air. Words by H. Bennet and W. Tolekin, of Cork. MBS

Saint Patrick's day ("Oh! blest be the days") Irish folk song. Words by M. J. Barry. SI

Saint Patrick's day ("Tho' dark are our sorrows") See The prince's day

Saint-Saëns, Camille
"Fair spring-time beginning." See "Printemps qui commence"
"Printemps qui commence" (from Samson et Dalila)
Thou, O Lord, art my protector (from Oratorio de Noël)

St Senanus and the lady ("O haste and leave this sacred isle") Irish air: Droighneann donn, or, The brown thorn. Words by T. Moore. HM 1

"**Saint** Stephen was a clerk." See The carol of St Stephen

"**Saint** Stephen was a holy man." Traditional carol. OB

St Thomas. See "I love Thy kingdom, Lord" (Händel)

"**Sainte** Marguerite." French Canadian folk song. e.f. GSF

"The **sainted** isle of old." See Shan Van Vocht (Words by Doheny)

"**Sainted** Mary, Mother mild." See Mater Salutaris

Sainton-Dolby, Mme Charlotte Helen
The bonnets of Bonnie Dundee. See Bonnie Dundee (attributed)
Bonnie Dundee (attributed)
"I am content"
Katey's letter

"**Sako** delo konec ima." See "Jede mühsal hat ein ende"

Sakura. See "Cherry-bloom"

"**Sal** in the garden was sifting sand." See The hog-eyed man

Salchow, Gustav Adolf
Morgenlied der schwarzen freischar (Volksweise)

Salieri, Antonio
"Vivat, vivat, loving comrades"

Salley in our alley. See Sally in our alley (Carey)

"**Sally** am de gal dat I lub dearly." See Stand to your ground

Sally and her lover (Lady Leroy) Folk song from Kentucky. SES 2

Sally Anne. Folk song from North Carolina. SES 2

Sally Brown ("O Sally Brown she's a bright mulatta") Capstan chantey. WSE
For variants see following songs of same title; also Challo Brown; Shallow Brown

"**Sally** Brown" ("Sally Brown she's a bright mulatter") Windlass and capstan chantey. TSB 1

"**Sally** Brown" ("Sally Brown she's a bright mulatto") Capstan chantey. SBS

"**Sally** Brown" ("Sally Brown, she's a creole lady") Capstan chantey. TFG —US

Sally Buck. Folk song: Kentucky version. SES 2
—Virginia version. SES 2

Sally come up. [T. M. Sewell] PSG— WSS

Sally in our alley ("Of all the girls that are so smart") [Old English air: The country lass] Words by H. Carey. BB—SSB

Sally in our alley (Die Lore am tore) e.g. ML 1

Sally(Salley)in our alley ("Of all the girls that are so smart") H. Carey (music and words) KSO

Sally in our alley (Die Lore am tore) e.g. ML 1

Salmon, Arthur Leslie
All through the night (Welsh air)

Salomon, Elias
Fiducit (Briesewitz)

Sal's got a meat-skin. American mountain song. RA

Salt seas. See Henry Martin

The **saltine** warrior. Syracuse university song. D. R. Walsh. Words by S. E. Darby. AI—AIS—KU—KV

Saltman, Joseph C.
Trombone song

"A **salty** bunch of ensigns we." See Song of the officers' torpedo class

Saltzer, B. H.
Bullet song. See Spirit of Gettysburg
Spirit of Gettysburg

Salut d'amour. See Love greetings (Elgar)

[**Salut**! demeure chaste et pure] "All hail, thou dwelling pure and lowly." C. Gounod. e. WG

The **salutation** carol. See Nowell, Nowell, Nowell, Nowell! This is the salutacyon of the angell Gabryell

The **salutation** of the angel Gabriel. See Nowell, Nowell, Nowell, Nowell! This is the salutacyon of the angell Gabryell

Salvator mundi. See "We may not climb the heav'nly steeps" (Dykes)

Salvator Rosa. See Rosa, Salvator

Salve, o rosa, amabile fior. For English translation see "Welcome, pretty primrose" (Pinsuti)

"**Sam** Bass." Cowboy song. LSC— SBA

Samain, Albert Victor
Arpège (Rousseau)

"**Same** train." Negro spiritual. JB 2

Samuel Hall. Old folk song. US
Variant of: Jack Hall

Samuel-Rousseau, Marcel. See Rousseau, Marcel Auguste Louis

Samuel Young. Folk song from North Carolina. SES 2

Sánchez de Fuentes, Eduardo. See Fuentes, Eduardo Sánchez de

Sánchez, Fernan
Tú (Fuentes)

"**Sanctofy** me, sanctofy me." See Just now

Sanderson, James
"Hail to the chief"

The **sandman.** See Sandmännchen

"The **sandman** kind am I." E. Humperdinck. [Tr of Der kleine sandmann bin ich] e. WG

Sandmännchen. German folk song arr by J. Brahms. g. EDL
The little dustman. e. BB—DSB —GSS—MBS
The little sandman. e. LAS
The sandman. e. TFG
Sandmännchen (The little sandman) e.g. AT—BST

The **sands** o' Dee. F. Boott. Words by C. Kingsley. MFS

Sanford, J.
Lubly Dine

"Der **sang** ist verschollen." See Vagans scholasticus (Sommer)

"Le **sang** subtil des fleurs." See Pensée de printemps (Leroux)

Der **sänger** (Laulaja) Finnish folk song. fi.g. ML 3

Des **sängers** kindheit. See entry under Des

Sankey, Ira David
The ninety and nine

"**Sankt** Martin." See "Sankte Morten"

"**Sankte** Morten" ("Sankt Martin") Danish song. da.g. ML 1

Sans Day carol ("Now the holly bears a berry") Cornish folk song. OB
The St Day carol ("Now the holly bears a berry") DNS

Sans souci. Columbia university song. Words by P. Fridenberg. AI—LAS

"**Santa** Clara, alma mater." See Anthem (Riordan)

[**Santa** Claus] "Old Santa Claus sat all alone." J. Read. MFS

"**Santa** Claus had three little choir-boys." See Le miracle de Saint-Nicolas (Lorraine version)

Santa Lucia.   Neapolitan fishermen's song.   e.   BB—DSB—DSC—GSS—LSB—TFP—TFR

Santo amor che in me favelli.   See O, tu Palermo (Verdi)

Santran laulu.   See Santras lied

Santras lied (Santran laulu)   Finnish folk song.   fi.g.   ML 3

Santy Anna.   Windlass and capstan chantey.   TSB 1
Variant of: The plains of Mexico

"Šapaŕ ten paso pód gajkom."   See "Schäfer am haine"

Sapphische ode (Sapphic ode)   J. Brahms.   Words by H. Schmidt.   e.g.   GG—SAT

Sappho.   R. Volkmann.   e.g.   DCA

Sarabande.   Old French folk song.   f.g.   ML 1

Saráchaga, Federico Romero y.   See Romero y Saráchaga, Federico

Sargent, Epes
"A life on the ocean wave" (Russell)

Sarona, F.
Dip, boys, dip the oar

Sarti, Giuseppe
"S'inganna chi crede" (from Medoro)

"Sass einmal ein häslein an dem rain" ("Siedzi sobie zając pod miedzą")   Polish folk song.   g.p.   ML 3

"Sat there a gipsy hag."   G. Verdi.   [Tr of Abbietta zingara, fosca vegliarda]   e.   WG

"Satan's a liah."   Negro spiritual.   SBA

Satan's camp a-fire.   Negro spiritual from South Carolina.   AS

Satter, Gustav
There's nae room for twa

The saucy Arethusa.   See The Arethusa

The saucy sailor.   Folk song: Kentucky version.   SES 2

"Save me, O God."   A. Randegger.   ASA—TSS 1—TSS 2

Savile, Jeremiah
"Here's a health unto his majesty"

Savino, Domenico
"With all her faults I love her still"

Saviour of sinners.   See "Ave Maria" (Cherubini)

The Saviour's work.   See The Babe of Bethlehem

Savourneen deelish.   Old air.   Words by G. Colman.   HMI
Savourneen dheelish.   SI

[La Savoyarde]   "Digo, Giannetta" ("Sag mir, mein Hannchen."—Marmottenlied)   Piedmontese song.   g.i.   ML 2

"Saw ye Johnnie comin'? quo' she."   Scottish song.   <Air: Fee him, father.   Words by J. Baillie>   GS

[Saw ye my wee thing]   Mary of Castle Cary.   Scottish air: <Bonie Dundee>   Words by H. Macneill.   GS

"Saw ye never in the twilight" (The stranger star)   Composer unknown.   Words by C. F. Alexander.   MFS

Sawyer, Charles Carroll
When this cruel war is over (Tucker)

Sawyer, Frank E.
Shine on, oh stars

Saxe, John Godfrey
Rhyme of the rail (19th century air)

"Say 'au revoir,' but not 'good-bye.' "   H. Kennedy (music and words)   DFF GFS—SMG

"Say, darkies, hab you seen de massa."   See Kingdom coming (Work)

Say, darling, say, when I'm far away.   See The Spanish cavalier (Hendrickson)

"Say to him."   J. Offenbach.   [Tr of Dites-lui qu'on l'a remarqué distingué]   e.   WLO

Sayers, Henry J.
Explosions from a tropical language (same air as Ta-ra-ra boom-der-é)
Ta-ra-ra boom-der-é (from Tuxedo)

Saying goodbye, Pike county.   See Sweet Betsy from Pike

Sayles, James M.
"Beautiful star in heaven so bright"
Star of the evening.   See "Beautiful star in heaven so bright"

Sayles, Phyllis
The fight song

"Says the blackbird to the crow."   See The bird song (Virginia version)

"Says the robin as he flew."   See The bird song (North Carolina version)

The scale ("Come, let us learn to sing")   Children's song.   MFS

The scale ("I pray you, I pray you")   L. van Beethoven (music and words)   e.   CSB 3—TFG

"Scarce had the sun in our valley shone brightly."   See Lithuanian song (Chopin)

Scarlatti, Alessandro
"Cease, oh, cease."   See "O cessate di piagarmi"
"Un cor da voi ferito" (from La Rosaura)
"Non dar più pene, o caro" (from La Rosaura)
"O cessate di piagarmi"
"Oh, no longer seek to pain me."   See "O cessate di piagarmi"
The violet.   See Le violette
Le violette

The scarlet and cream.   University of Nebraska song.   Balfe.   AI—KU

[The scarlet sarafan]   The red sarafan.   Russian song.   Varlamov <wrongly attributed to N. A. Titoff>   [Words by Ziganov]   e.   NRF
Krasnyï sarafan (Der rote sarafan)   g.r.   ML 1
Der rote sarafan.   g.   EDL

"Scenes that are brightest."   W. V. Wallace.   Words by A. Bunn.   MFS

"The scent of earth, and dozing garden blossoms."   See Pionerna (Rangström)

Scha schtill.   Jewish folk song.   y.   KAJ

Schack, Adolf Friedrich, graf von
Ständchen (Strauss)

"Schadzka umówiona."   See "Mond stieg herauf"

Schaeffer, H.
Give me my home again. See Das haidekind
Das haidekind
Schaeffer, J. S. See Ashworth, Iva, jt. comp.
"Schäfer am haine" ("Šapaŕ ten paso pód gajkom") Wendish folk song. g.we. ML 3
Das **schäfermädchen** und der kuckuck ("Ein schäfermädchen weidete") Volkslied. Author of words unknown. g. EDL
"Ein **schäfermädchen** weidete." See Das schäfermädchen und der kuckuck
Schaffer,
The hunter's song
"See the sun's first gleam." See The hunter's song
Schaffy, Mirza, pseud. See Bodenstedt, Friedrich Martin von
"**Schaurig** in der dämmrung" ("Virradóra szóll a falu harangja") Hungarian folk song. g.hu. ML 3
Scheffel, Josef Viktor von
Jonas (Volksweise)
Lied fahrender schüler (Becker)
Die Teutoburger schlacht (Composer unknown)
Der **scheidende** sommer. For English and Norwegian translations see Afsked (Melartin)
Scheidt, Samuel
O Jesulein süss, o Jesulein mild (words and music)
O Jesulein süss, o Jesulein mild (words with old air)
"O little one." See O Jesulein süss, o Jesulein mild
"**Schein** bin ich schein." See "Pretty am I"
A **schein** meidale bin ich. See "Pretty am I"
Schenck, Caspar
Farewell to grog (Old English air)
Schenkendorf, Max von
"Freiheit, die ich meine" (Groos)
Das lied vom Rhein (Nägeli)
Soldaten-morgenlied (Volksweise)
Scherer, Georg
Aus der rosenzeit (Fielitz)
Schiassi, Gaetano Maria
"Digli, ch'io son fedele" (from Alessandro nell' Indie)
"**Schier** dreissig jahre bist du alt." See Der alte reiter und sein mantel
Der **schiffer.** See Fhir a bhàta
"Ein **schifflein** sah ich fahren." See Kapitän und leutenant
Schiller, Johann Christoph Friedrich von
An die freude (music by Beethoven; also unknown composer)
Beatrice (Holstein)
"Der eichwald brauset" (Schubert)
"Es ist mein sohn, ich kann nicht daran zweifeln" (Joachim)
Reiterlied (Zahn)
Der schütz (Weber)
"**Schità**, sehni, mums dsihwoti." See "Hier, mein junge, lass uns bleiben"

"**Schlaf**, armer, schlaf zum letzten mal." See Wiegenlied (Russian song)
"**Schlaf** ein, mein bübchen, schlaf, mein süsses liebchen." See Ninna-nanna
"**Schlaf**, herzenssöhnchen." See Wiegenlied (Weber)
["**Schlaf**', kindchen, schlaf'"] Cradle song. Folk song arr by J. Brahms. e. DSB
Schlaf', kindlein, schlaf' (Cradle song) e. CSB 1
Schlaf', kindlein, schlaf'. See "Schlaf', kindchen, schlaf'"
"**Schlaf**, mein kind, schlaf ein, mein töchterlein." See "Sleep, my child, my pretty one"
"**Schlaf**, schlaf ein, kindelein, mütterlein wiegt dich ein." See Wiegenlied (Serbian folk song)
Schlafe, mein liebster, geniesse der ruh'. For English translation see "Slumber, beloved, and take thy repose" (Bach)
"**Schlafe**, mein prinzchen." See Wiegenlied (Mozart)
"**Schlafe**, schlafe, holder süsser knabe." See Wiegenlied (Schubert)
Schlafe, schlafe, schlaf' du mein kindelein. See Sandmännchen
"**Schlafe**, schlafe, schlaf ein, mein kleiner Nikolaus." See Ninna di Borgia
"**Schlafen** geht die rose." See Nana (copla de cuna)
"**Schlaftrunken** hängt auf strauch und bäumen." See Nächtlicher gruss (Storch)
"**Schlag** zurück, Wela mädchen" ("Zapŕetnĭ, Velo mome") Bulgarian folk song. b.g. ML 2
"**Schlanke** maid, aus deinen tränen feuchten." See Lied des kahnfahrers
Schlegel, August Wilhelm von
Lob der thränen (Schubert)
"**Schliess** deine aeuglein zu." See "Ferme tes yeux"
Der **schlimme** scherz (Złe żorty) Wendish folk song. g.we. ML 3
Schlippenbach, Albert, graf
In der ferne (Silcher)
"Der **schlitten** eilt" ("Repül a szán") Hungarian folk song. g.hu. ML 3
Schloesser, Carl Wilhelm Adolph
"He that keepeth Israel"
Schlof main kind, schlof main kind. See A wieglied
"**Schlof** mein kind, mein tröst." Jewish song. Words by S. Aleichem. y. SY
"**Schlof** mein vögele." Jewish folk song y. SY
Schlummerlied ("Es mahnt der wald."—Slumber song) F. Schubert. e.g. GA
Schlummerlied ("Ferme tes yeux") See "Ferme tes yeux"
Schlummerlied ("Sleep, my child, my pretty one") See "Sleep, my child, my pretty one"
Schmertz, Robert
Fight for the glory of Carnegie

Schmetterling ("Ah, how did that rover, the butterfly, discover."—The butterfly) P. Cornelius (music and words)　e. CSB 1

"Der schmetterling ist in die rose verliebt" ("The gay butterfly lost his heart to the rose")　R. Franz.　Words by H. Heine.　e.g.　HCA

Schmid, Christoph von
Die kinder bei der krippe (Schulz)

Schmidt, Georg Filipp
Der wanderer (Schubert)

Schmidt, Hans
Bitte (Bohm)
Sapphische ode (Brahms)

Der schmied (The blacksmith's sweetheart) J. Brahms.　Words by J. L. von Uhland.　e.　CSB 1
The smith.　e.　DSB

Schmitt, Georg
Sehnsucht nach dem Rhein

Schneckenburger, Max
Die wacht am Rhein (Wilhelm)

Schnecker, Peter August
"Take my life, and let it be consecrated, Lord, to Thee"

Schneider, Edward F.
Fires of wisdom

Der schneider jahrstag.　See entry under Der

Schneiders höllenfahrt.　Volkslied.　g. EDL

Schnoor, Heinrich Christian
"Vom hoh'n Olymp"

Schober, Franz von
An die musik (Schubert)
Jägers liebeslied (Composer unknown)

Scholz, Bernhard
Frühling liebster
Springtide sweetheart.　See Frühling liebster

Schon drei jahre liege ich krank (Trī godīnī bolen lezham)　Macedonian folk song.　b.g.　ML 2

"Schon entflieht die winternacht."　See Cansó de Nadal

"Schon singst du, kleine lerche."　See Kleine lerche

Schönaich-Carolath, Emil, prinz von
"Grauer vogel über der haide" (Fielitz)

"Eine schöne gibt's nur auf der welt."　See "There's on earth but one true precious pearl" (Szentirmay)

"Schöne·Julie, schöne Julie."　See Reigen

Die schöne kuhmagd.　See Cailín deás crúidhte na mbó

Die schöne Lilofee.　Volkslied.　g. EDL

Das schöne mädchen.　See A' mhaighdean àluinn

Der schöne stern.　See Izar ederra

Der schöne trommler.　See Le joli tambour

"Schöner mond, scheine mild."　See "Argizagi ederra"

Schönster Herr Jesu.　For English translation see "Fairest Lord Jesus"

Schoolcraft, Luke
Shine on

The **schoolhouse** blues.　I. Berlin (music and words)　HB

Schröder-Devrient, Wilhelmine
Schwanenlied (Hartmann)

Schröer,
Das haidekind (Schaeffer)

Schtscherbina, N.　See Shcherbin, N.

Schubert, Franz Peter
"All hail, thou lovely laughing May"
Die Allmacht
Am meer
An die musik
"Ave Maria"
The brook's lullaby.　See Des baches wiegenlied
By the sea.　See Am meer
Cradle song ("Schlafe, schlafe")　See Wiegenlied
Cradle song ("Sleep thou") (same air as Wiegenlied)
The crow.　See Die krähe
Dem Unendlichen
Des baches wiegenlied (from Die schöne müllerin)
Des mädchens klage.　See "Der eichwald brauset"
"Du bist die ruh'"
"Der eichwald brauset"
The erlking.　See Erlkönig
Erlkönig
"Flowerets blooming."　See Lob der thränen
Frühlingsglaube
Good night.　See Gute nacht
The gravedigger.　See Todtengräbers heimweh
Gute nacht
"Hark! hark! the lark"
Hedge roses.　See Heidenröslein
Heidenröslein
Der hirt auf dem felsen
Hymn to the Almighty.　See Die Allmacht
Hymne an die Jungfrau.　See "Ave Maria"
In praise of tears.　See Lob der thränen
Der jüngling an der quelle
Die krähe
The lad and the stream.　See Der jüngling an der quelle
The linden tree.　See Der lindenbaum
Der lindenbaum
Litanei auf das fest "Aller seelen."　See Litaney
Litaney
Litany for the feast of all souls.　See Litaney
Lob der thränen
The lost lamb (from Die bürgschaft. Tr of Die mutter sucht ihr liebes kind)
"Now melts the snow, the blossoms blow"
"O Thou my peace."　See "Du bist die ruh'"
Praise of tears.　See Lob der thränen
Schlummerlied
Serenade.　See Ständchen ("Leise flehen meine lieder")

Schubert, Franz Peter—*Continued*
The shepherd on the rock. See Der hirt auf dem felsen
Slumber song ("Es mahnt der wald") See Schlummerlied
Slumber song ("Schlafe, schlafe") See Wiegenlied
"The spendthrift spring"
Ständchen ("Leise flehen meine lieder")
To music. See An die musik
To the Eternal. See Dem Unendlichen
Der tod und das mädchen
Todtengräbers heimweh
Der wanderer
The wanderer. See Der wanderer
Wandering. See Das wandern
Das wandern
"Was ist Sylvia." See "Who is Sylvia"
"Who is Sylvia"
Wiegenlied
Schuckburgh, Richard
Yankee Doodle (Old air) Authorship uncertain
Schukowsky, Vassili Andreevitch. See Zhukovskiĭ, Vasiliĭ Andreevich
Schulthes, Wilhelm August Ferdinand
"I know not what the future hath"
Lambeth. See "I know not what the future hath"; "Prayer is the soul's sincere desire"
The pilgrims
"Prayer is the soul's sincere desire" (same air as "I know not what the future hath")
Schultz, Carl
"Awake from sleep and dreaming"
Schulz, Christian
"Hier in des abends traulich ernster stille" (Flemming)
Schulz, Johann Abraham Peter
Abendlied
Am Sylvester-abend
Die kinder bei der krippe
The last hour of the year (Tr of Neujahrslied)
Liebeszauber
Schumann, Robert Alexander
Der abendstern
An den sonnenschein
Die beiden grenadiere
Canonbury. See "O God, Thy world is sweet with prayer"; "Out of the dark the circling sphere"
Dedication. See Widmung
Der deutsche Rhein
"Du bist wie eine blume"
"Ich grolle nicht"
"I'll not complain." See "Ich grolle nicht"
"Im wunderschönen monat mai"
In lovely May. See "Im wunderschönen monat mai"
Intermezzo
"Kennst du das land"
Ladybird. See Marienwürmchen
Die lotosblume
"The lotus blossom." See Die lotosblume

"The lotus flower." See Die lotosblume
Marienwürmchen
Mignon. See "Kennst du das land"
My William. See Volksliedchen
"O God, Thy world is sweet with prayer"
"O how lovely is my darling." See "O wie lieblich ist das mädchen"
"O sonnenschein." See An den sonnenschein
"O sunny ray." See An den sonnenschein
"O sunshine." See An den sonnenschein
"O wie lieblich ist das mädchen"
Old Catholic hymn. See Requiem
"Out of the dark the circling sphere" (same air as "O God, Thy world is sweet with prayer")
"Pluck ye roses while they bloom" (Tr of Pflücket rosen um, das haar)
Requiem
Die soldatenbraut
Spring morning. See Volksliedchen
"Thou'rt like a flower—so winsome." See "Du bist wie eine blume"
"Thou'rt lovely as a flower." See "Du bist wie eine blume"
To the evening star. See Der abendstern
The two grenadiers. See Die beiden grenadiere
Volksliedchen
Widmung
ᴛDer **schütz** ("Mit dem pfeil, dem bogen")ᴊ
"Cheerily the huntsman." ᴛB. A. Weber. Words by Schillerᴊ e. TFG
Schwäbische, bayrische dirndel, juchhe. See Fräulein Kunigund
Die **schwalbe.** See Aiñhara
"Ein **schwan** zieht auf dem see." See Schwanenlied (Hartmann)
Schwanenlied (Swan-song) L. Hartmann. Words by W. Schröder-Devrient. e.g. SAT
Schwartz, D.
N. Y. U. marching song (Composer unknown)
"**Schwarze** äuglein" ("Cherni ochi") Bulgarian folk song. b.g. ML 2
"**Schweige,** mein herz, leide still." See Inimiora mea
Der **schweinehirt** (Swinjacy pastyŕ) Wendish folk song. g.we. ML 3
Der **Schweizer** ("Zu Strassburg auf der schanz") F. Silcher. Volkslied. g. EDL
Der **schweizerbue** ("On the mountain."—Herdsman's mountain home) Volkslied. e. MFS
Der **schwere** traum. Volkslied. g. EDL
Schwertlied ("Du schwert an meiner linken") C. M. von Weber. Words by T. Körner. g. EDL
Die **schwester** prüft den bruder (Sestra kusha brata) Serbian folk song. g.se. ML 2

[Schwesterlein, wann gehn wir nach haus] Der letzte tanz. Volksweise. Words by W. von Zuccalmaglio. g. EDL

Der schwur (The vow) C. Bohm. Words by R. Baumbach. e.g. AT

"Sciagurata! hai tu creduto." Verdi. e.i. PB

La Scillitana (Das mädchen von Scilla) Calabrian folk song. g.i. ML 2

"The scion of an ancient house." C. Lecocq. [Tr of Mon père est un très gros banquier] e. WLO

Scollard, Walter F., pseud. See Loomis, Harvey Worthington

Scotch cradle-song ("Thy father now is far awa'") Old lullaby. MFS

Scotch lassie, Jean. Composer and author of words unknown. GOS 2—OT

Scotland yet. P. McLeod. Words by H. S. Riddell. GS

"Scotland's burning." Round. BB—DSB—KSO—TFP

"Scots wha ha'e wi' Wallace bled." Air: Hey, tuttie, taitie, or, Now the day dawis. Words by R. Burns. MBS—SSB

"Scots, wha hae wi' Wallace bled" (Bruce's address to his army) GS

Scott, Alicia Anne (Spottiswoode), lady
   Annie Laurie
   Douglas, tender and true

Scott, Clement William
   "Oh promise me" (De Koven)

Scott, Emma J.
   Alma mater—Drake university (Bloom)

Scott, H. C.
   The panther (Harris)

Scott, Lady John. See Scott, Alicia Anne (Spottiswoode), lady

Scott, Mrs Maria (Mayo)
   Cadets' graduating song for 1848 (Composer unknown) Authorship uncertain

Scott, Sir Walter, bart.
   "Ave Maria" (Schubert)
   Blue bonnets over the border (Scottish air)
   Bonnie Dundee (Sainton-Dolby?)
   "Enchantress, farewell" (Scottish air)
   "Hail to the chief" (Sanderson)
   Jock o' Hazeldean (Scottish air)
   Macgregors' gathering (Lee)
   Merry Christmas (Shaw)
   The monks of Bangor's march (Welsh air)
   "O hush thee, my babie" (music by Sullivan; Whitaker. Tr from the old Gaelic song, Caidil gu lo)
   "Pibroch of Donuil Dhu" (Scottish air)
   The sun is low (Irish air)
   Young Lochinvar (Mazzinghi)

Scott, Mrs Winfield. See Scott, Mrs Maria (Mayo)

Scott-Gatty, Sir Alfred
   O fair dove, O fond dove
   "One morning, oh, so early"

The scout ("Come! boor, your little blue") F. Campana. Words by H. B. Farnie. MFS

Scout chant ("May we be truthful") Girl scout song. GSS

Scuderi, Salvatore
   "Dormi pure"
   Slumber, my loved one. See "Dormi pure"

"Se al labro mio non credi." G. B. Pergolesi. e.i. KVG

"Se amor mai da vu se vede" ("Lässt sich amor bei euch schauen") Venetian folk song. g.i. ML 2

"Se crudele il cor mostrai." Donizetti. e.i. PC

"Se, der va en gang en konge." See Irmelin Rose (Nielsen)

"Se fino al cielo ascendere." Mercadante. e.i. PC

"'Se guth ciùin mo rùin a th' ann." See Oisean is Malmhine

Se m'abbandoni, bella speranza. Mercadante. e.i. PC

"Se meritar potessi." D. Bruni. e.i. ZT 2

"Se non ti moro allato." A. Bernasconi. e.i. KVG

"Se on tällä lailla." See Der sänger

"Se Romeo t'uccise un figlio" ("If Romeo thy son did slaughter") Bellini. e.i. PC

"Se solen var splitrad." See Ny-måne (Sinding)

The sea gulls ("Far above the deep blue sea") MFS

[Sea of stars] "Nincsen annyi tenger csillag" ("Nie war hoch am himmel") Hungarian song [by E. Elek] g.hu. ML 3

A sea picture. Russian folk air. Words by J. L. Vandevere. TFO

A sea scout chantey. J. A. Wilder (music and words) GSS

An searc 'gá diúltugad (My love, oh, she is my love) South Irish air. e.ir. HI 1

"Search thro' the wide world." See "Ciascun lo dice" (Donizetti)

Sears, Edwin Hamilton
   "It came upon the midnight clear" (Traditional air; also music by Meyer-Helmund; Roeder; Willis)

"Seated one day at the organ." See The lost chord (Sullivan)

Seaver, Fred
   Take me back to tech (same air as Solomon Levi)
   Utah man (same air as Solomon Levi)
   Yankee Doodle-oodle (same air as Solomon Levi)

Second thoughts. H. W. Loomis. Words by D. Stevens. TFO

The secret flower. 16th century air. Words based on an old German carol, Gebor'n ist uns ein Kindelein, e. OB

"Sedlák, sedlák." See The farmer

Sedulius, Coelius
   A solis ortus cardine (Latin air)

"See afar yon hill Ardmore." See Moladh na landaidh

"**See**, amid the winter snow." Mendelssohn. Words by E. Caswall. FC

"**See** amid the winter's snow" (Winter's snow) R. O. Morris. Words by E. Caswall. OB

"**See** at your feet." M. W. Balfe. MFS

"**See** dat host all dressed in white." See God's a-gwineter trouble de water

"**See** dat sister all dressed so fine." See The old ark a-moving along

"**See**, fair maid, thy bard." See "Mira, o bella, il trovatore" (Donizetti)

"**See** fo' an' twenty elders." See Four and twenty elders

"**See**, for thee I've plucked a rosebud." See "Hab' ein röslein dir gebrochen" (Sjögren)

"**See** from a root upspringing." See Lo! a fair rose is blooming (Praetorius)

"**See**, here be we coming." See Mari lwyd

"**See** how it glistens bright in the sun." See Drinking song (Lecocq)

"**See** how the shadows of night are flying." See Anvil chorus (Verdi)

["**See**, love, above the stars"] "Csillag elég ragyog" (In der spinnstub) Hungarian folk song. g.hu. ML 3

See me dance the polka. Old song. SW

"**See**, mother dear, look at Jack's picture." See Don't wear your heart on your sleeve

"**See**, now the dusk is falling." See Ave Maria (Raff)

"Der **see** ruht tief im· blauen traum." See Der träumende see (Brückler)

"**See-saw**, Margery Daw." Nursery song. BB

"**See-saw**, see-saw, down and up we go." See See-saw waltz song (Crowe)

See saw [waltz song] A. G. Crowe. TFP—TFR

"**See**, she is dancing." See Waltz song (Offenbach)

"**See** that host all dressed in white." See God's a-gwineter trouble de water

"**See** th'at sister all dressed so fine." See The old ark a-moving along

"**See**, the conquering hero comes." G. F. Händel. TFP

"**See** the light is fading." F. Bendel. CSS 2

"**See** the little pretty maiden" (Here tyu, tyu, tyu) Old Hungarian folk song. e.hu. KH 1

"**See** the proud banner of liberty streaming." See Our flag o'er us waving (Verdi)

See the raging flames arise. Händel. SSO 4

"**See** the raindrops now are gently falling." See Rainy day round

"**See** the star that shines afar" ("Jaj be fényes csillag ragyog az égen") M. Füredy. e.hu. KH 2

"**See** the sun's first gleam." See The hunter's song (Schaffer)

"**See** the wild rose fadeth" ("Csipke bokor") E. Szentirmay (music and words) e.h. KH 2

"**See** the wine is gaily flowing." See Drinking song (Mascagni)

"**See** the yellow catkins cover." See A spring song (Bridge)

"**See** them plunging down to the goal." See The big red team (Tourison)

"**See** those mokes, real colored folks." See Take me to that Swanee shore (Muir)

"**See** those poor fellows." Round. H. Purcell. TFO—TFR

"**See**! to the hall the priests proceed." G. Verdi. [Tr of Già i sacerdoti adunansi] e. WG

"**See** what grace." F. von Flotow. [Tr of Nun fürwahr, fürwahr] e. WLO

"**See** whence the rising sun" (Sunrise) Words from the German. e. GOS 2

"**See** yon chapel on the hill." See The chapel

"**Seed** a flea heave a tree." See Hurrah, Lie

Seek and ye shall find. Negro spiritual. HRD

"**Seeker**, seeker, give up your heart to God." See The rocks and the mountains

Seele du musst munter werden. For English translation see "Come, my soul, thou must be waking" (Haydn)

"Der **seemann** kommt vom krieg zurück." See Le retour du marin

Seemanns heimkehr. See Le retour du marin

Seemanns lied ("Als von Amerika wir aufbrachen."—Meripojan laulu) Finnish folk song. fi.g. ML 3

Seemannslied ("A Mhàiri bhoidheach's a Mhàiri ghaolach") See Máire ní ghríoghtha

"Il **segreto** per esser felici" ("Oh the secret of bliss."—Brindisi) Donizetti. e.i. PC

"It is better to laugh than be sighing." e. MFS

[**Séguédille** ("Près des remparts de Séville")] Seguidilla. G. Bizet. e. WG

"**Seh** ich dich, mein herzensliebchen" ("Když tě vidím, má panenko") Czech folk song. bo.g. ML 3

Sehnsucht ("Jeg kunde slet ikke sove") See Laengsel (Kjerulf)

Sehnsucht ("Mein schatz ist nicht da."—Parted) J. Brahms. Words from a German folk song. e.g. CSB 4

Sehnsucht nach dem frühlinge. See "Komm, lieber mai und mache" (Mozart)

Sehnsucht nach dem Rhein. G. Schmitt. Author of words unknown. g. EDL

"**Seht**, es leuchten die fanale." See Rhyfelgyrch gwyr Harlech

"**Seht** in anmut mein herzliebchen" ("Jaků sem si frajírenku") Slovak folk song. g.sl. ML 3

"**Seht**, wie gut der hund" ("De jó az a kis kutya") Hungarian folk song. g.hu. ML 3

"**Seht**, wie lieblich ist mein lieb." See The gay young bachelor

Sei getreu in den tod. For English translation see "Be thou faithful unto death" (Mendelssohn)

"Sei nicht böse, mein lieb väterlein" (Hochzeitslied.—"Líto je mně, můj tatíčku."—Svatebni) Czech folk song. bo.g. ML 3

Sei stille dem Herrn. For English translation see "O rest in the Lord" (Mendelssohn)

"Sei vendicata assai." See "Ah! mon remords te venge" (Meyerbeer)

Seibert, T. Lawrence
Casey Jones (Newton)

"Seid nicht böse" ("Nevadte se") Czech folk song. bo.g. ML 3

"Seid ruhig, mutter, zaget nicht." See Jannik Skolan

"Sein weisses rösslein sattelt der bruder" ("Balnoj brolelis šyvą žirgelį") Lithuanian folk song. g.li. ML 3

"Seinen ruf vernimmt mein ohr." See Oisean is Malmhine

"Seinneam duan a nis do'n mhaighdinn a tha aoibheil." See A' mhaighdean àluinn

"Seit zarter kindheit" ("Iš mažumėlės be motinėlės") Lithuanian folk song. g.li. ML 3

"Šel sedlák." See "Ging auf den jahrmarkt"

The self-banished. See "It is not that I love you less" (Blow)

"Seltner weizen, seltne gerste, seltnes korn." See Rare the barley, rare the rye, rare the wheat

Semons la salade ("Let us sow the lettuce") French folk song. e.f. CBF 2

Semple, Francis
Maggie Lauder (18th century air)

"Sen ihanaisen virran reunall' hausk' ol' ennen ollaksen'." See An baches rande

Send her on along. See Envoyons d'l'avant, nos gens

"Send out Thy light." C. Gounod. TFB—TFP

Sentence. F. Mendelssohn-Bartholdy. e. TFG

"Seoithín, seó, is tú mo leánabh." See Suantraidhe

The separation. J. C. Engelbrecht. Words by T. Moore. GOS 2

Serenade ("Der den himmel") See Ständchen (Raff)

Serenade ("Gut' nacht, gut' nacht") See Ständchen (Brahms)

Serenade ("Leise flehen") See Ständchen (Schubert)

Serenade ("Mach' auf") See Ständchen (Strauss)

Serenade ("O Columbine") R. Leoncavallo. [Tr of O Columbina] e. WG

Serenade ("Vola, o serenata") See La serenata (Tosti)

Serenata ("Era la noche."—Under Gothic arches) Folk song from southern California. e.s. HE

La serenata ("Vola, o serenata."—Serenade) F. P. Tosti. Words by G. A. Cesareo. e.i. SFB

Serenata di Pulcinello (Punchinello's serenade) Neapolitan folk song. e.i. SAT

Serenity. See "One thought I have, my ample creed" (Wallace)

Sergeant Champe. Song of the American revolution. Air: Barbara Allen. DSO

The sergeant, he is the worst of all. American song. SBA

"Šeriau, šeriau sau žirgelį." See "Rösslein, rösslein steht im stalle"

Serini, Giuseppe
"Hence, ye visions of glory"
"Tossed on seas of fierce temptation"

Serrano, J.
La canción del olvido
Marinela. See La canción del olvido

The service boast. U.S. Naval academy song. US

Sestra kusha brata. See Die schwester prüft den bruder

Settin' down side of the Holy Lamb. See "Oh, when I get to heaven"

Settin' on a rail. Minstrel song. WSS

Die seufzer. See I sospiri

The seven good joys. See The seven joys of Mary (Another air)

"Seven great towns." Three part round. GSS

The seven joys of Mary. Traditional song: Anglo Irish version. DNS

[The seven joys of Mary] The Advent images carol. Traditional song. Air: God rest ye merry, gentlemen. DNS

[The seven joys of Mary] Joys seven. Traditional song. Another air. OB

The seven good joys. DN

"Seven long years." Folk song from Georgia. SES 2

"Seven long years in state prison." Convict song. SBA

"Seven long years I've been bound to my trade." See "Seven long years"

The seven virgins. Traditional carol. DN

—Herefordshire version. OB

"Seventeen years had just passed." J. Strauss. e. WLO

"A seventh son of a seventh son." See A son of a musketeer

Seventy-sixth field artillery song. U.S. army song. E. H. Ward (music and words) DSO

Sewell, T. M.
Sally come up

Sextet. Donizetti. [Tr of Chi mi frena in tal momento] e. TFG
"What from vengeance now restrains me." e. WG

"A sexton stood one Sabbath eve." See Those wedding bells shall not ring out (Rosenfeld)

Seymour. See "Softly now the light of day" (Weber)

"Sgombra dall' anima." G. Latilla. Words by Metastasio. e.i. KVG
"Sh-ta-ra-dah-dey." Irish lullaby: American version. SBA
Shabby genteel. English music-hall song. H. Clifton. SW
Schackburg, Dr. See Schuckburgh, Richard
Shackelton, Frances
Campus song. See "When the shades of ev'ning gather"
"When the shades of ev'ning gather" (same air as The orange and the black)
The shad. Folk song from Virginia. SES 2
"Shades of evening, close not o'er us." See Isle of beauty (Whitmore)
"The shades of night were falling fast." See Upi dei di (Words by Knight); Upidee (Words by Longfellow)
"The shades of twilight gather o'er." See This wedding ring of mine
"The shadows lie across the dim old room." See Dream faces (Hutchinson)
Shakespeare, William
The songs are arranged alphabetically under the title of the play or poem in which they appear
No distinction has been made between Shakespeare's own songs and the traditional songs quoted in his plays
As you like it
"Blow, blow, thou winter wind" (music by Arne; Stevens)
"It was a lover and his lass" (Morley?)
"Under the greenwood tree, who loves to lie with me" (Arne)
Cymbeline
"Hark! hark! the lark" (Schubert)
Hamlet
"And will he not come again" (Traditional air)
"How should I your true love know" (16th century air)
Love's labour's lost
"When daisies pied, and violets blue" (Arne)
Measure for measure
"Take, O take those lips away" (Williams)
The midsummer night's dream
"I know a bank whereon the wild thyme blows" (Horn)
Othello
The willow song (16th century air; also music by Carr)
The tempest
"Dry those eyes" (Pelissier)
"Where the bee sucks" (Arne)
Twelfth night
Come away, death (Arne)
"Hold thy peace" (Old English air)
"O mistress mine" (Traditional air)
"She never told her love" (Haydn)
"When that I was a little tiny boy" (Traditional air)

Two gentlemen of Verona
"Who is Sylvia" (Schubert)
Venus and Adonis
"Bid me discourse" (Bishop)
Shakespeare's carol. See "Blow, blow, thou winter wind" (Arne); "Blow, blow, thou winter wind" (Stevens)
Shakings. Chantey. WSE
Shall I die. Old Negro spiritual from South Carolina. AS
"Shall I in Mamre's fertile plain." Handel. SSO 4
"Shall I show you how the farmer." See The farmer
Shall I so choice a blessing behold my slave possessing. See Vedrò, mentr' io sospiro (Mozart)
"Shall we meet beyond the river." E. S. Rice. Words by H. L. Hastings. MFS
Shall we never more behold thee. See Gentle Annie (Foster)
Shallow Brown ("Oh, put my clothes in order") Halliard chantey. TSB 2
Variants: Challo Brown; Sally Brown
The Shan Van Vocht ("O the French are on the sea") Irish air. Traditional words. BOS 2—SI
The Shan Van Voght ("O the French are on the sea") Air: Sean bhean bhocht, or, The poor old woman. Traditional words. MBS
Shan Van Vocht ("The sainted isle of old") Irish air. Words by M. Doheny. SI
Shann, Richard
"Come, love we God"
"Jeresalem my happie home"
The querister's song of Yorke. See "Jeresalem my happie home"
Shannon and Chesapeake. See The Chesapeke and the Shannon
The shanty-man's life. Minnesota lumberjack song. SBA
Sharp, William
Kye song of Saint Bride (Clokey)
Sharpe, Henry John
Rockaway (Russell)
Sharples, Harry P. See Furman, A. F., jt. comp. and auth.
Shattuck, Charles F.
Chiming bells of long ago.
The shaver. Capstan chantey. TSB 2
Shaw, Alfred C.
Somewhere (Campana)
Shaw, David T.
Columbia, the gem of the ocean (wrongly attributed) See Becket, T. à. Columbia, the gem of the ocean
Shaw, Mrs Frances (Fulkerson) See Fulkerson, Frances
Shaw, Geoffrey
"Glad that I live am I"
"The snow lies thick"
Shaw, Guillermo Fernández. See Fernández Shaw, Guillermo

Shaw, Martin
All bells in paradise
Christo paremus cantica, in excelsis gloria.   See "When Christ was born of Mary free"
"I sing of a Maiden"
In excelsis gloria.   See "When Christ was born of Mary free"
Kings in glory.   See "Three kings in great glory"
"Make we merry"
Merry Christmas
"Out of your sleep"
"Three kings in great glory"
"When Christ was born of Mary free"
Shaw, Oliver
There's nothing true but heaven
Shcherbin, N.
Resignation (Tchaikovsky)
"Shcho se, Leno, na golîemo."   See Warum Lena, so stolz
"She beats me, she bangs me."   See Our goodman (Hot Springs, N.C. version)
"She called for a silver basin."   See The silk merchant's daughter (Virginia version)
She came to the city where nobody cares. See In the city where nobody cares (Harris)
"She can swim like a duck."   See The gallant Thunderbomb
"She casts a spell, oh, casts a spell."   See An searc 'gá diúltugad
She died on the train.   See Eliza Jane (North Carolina version)
"She fixed them a table in the dining room."   See the wife of Usher's well (Burnsville, N.C. version no. 2)
"She had three babes, three pretty, little babes."   See The cruel mother (Berea, Ky. version no. 2)
"She hadn't been married but a very short time."   See The wife of Usher's well (Alleghany, N.C. version)
She has fallen by the wayside.   See Fallen by the wayside (Harris)
She is a lulu.   U.S. army song.   DSO
"She is far from the land."   Irish air: Open the door.   Words by T. Moore. HMI—SI
She is more to be pitied than censured. W. B. Gray (music and words) SRW
"She is small our alma mater."   See Mighty Oregon (Perfect)
"She laid down her iv'ry comb."   See Fair Margaret and sweet William (Dewey, Va. version)
"She laid herself all against the oak." See The cruel mother (Carmen, N.C. version)
She may have seen better days.   J. Thornton.   SRW
"She mounted on the milk-white steed." See Lady Isabel and the elf knight (Carmen, N.C. version)
She moved thro' the fair.   Irish air from County Donegal.   Words by P. Colum.   HI 1

"She never told her love."   J. Haydn. Words by W. Shakespeare.   EB—GA
"She picked him up all in her arms."   See Sir Hugh (Pine Mountain, Ky. version)
"She picked up her sweet little babe." See The daemon lover (Micaville, N.C. version)
"She promised she'd meet me."   American folk song.   SBA
She ran away with another man, po' boy. See Po' boy
"She rode up in the courthouse yard." See Geordie (Micaville, N.C. version)
"She run her boat against the main." See Sweet William (Carmen, N.C. version)
"She saddled up her milk-white steed." See Geordie (Black Mountain, N.C. version)
She said the same to me.   Irish song: American version.   SBA
"She sharpened her knife both sharp and keen."   See Young hunting (St Helen's, Ky. version)
"She sits alone all thro' the day."   See In shadowland (Pinsuti)
"She threw her arms around him."   See The cruel ship's carpenter (Pineville, Ky. version; Callaway, Va. version no. 2)
"She travelled over hills and mountains." See "In Seaport town" (Virginia version)
"She was a Stately Southerner."   See The Stately Southerner
She was bred in old Kentucky.   S. Carter. Words by H. Braisted.   GFS—OTG
"She was just as kind and good to me." See Harry Gray (Alleghany, N.C. version)
"She was mild as the summer air."   See The mother's lamentation
"She was young and fair and handsome." See My parents treated me tenderly (Big Laurel, N.C. version)
"She wears a gold ring on all of her fingers."   See Young Beichan (Virginia version)
"She wore a wreath of roses."   J. P. Knight.   Words by T. H. Bayly. GOS 1—MFS
Shea, John F.
Victory march (Shea, M. J.)
Shea, Michael J.
Victory march
Sheafe, M. W.   See Allen, Thorton Whitney, jt. comp.
Shearing time.   Welsh dance.   Air: Pant corlan yr wyn.   CSB 6
Sheepskin and beeswax made this awful plaster.   See Aunt Jemima's plaster
The **Sheffield** apprentice.   Folk song: Allanstand, N.C. version.   SES 2
—Hot Springs, N.C. version.   SES 2
—Marion, N.C. version.   SES 2
Sheldon, E. Edwin
Old S. U.
"She'll be comin' round the mountain." Railroad work song.   Old air. SBA
Variant of: When the chariot comes

Shelley, Percy Bysshe
  To music (Cherepnin)
Shells of ocean.   J. W. Cherry.   [Words by J. W. Lake]   GOS 1—MFS
"A **shelter** from the storms."   See "Ein obdach gegen sturm" (Kahn)
Shenandoah ("Missouri, she's a mighty river")   Chantey.   US—WSE
  For variants see following songs of same title; also The wide Mizzoura
Shenandoah ("O Shenandoah, I long to hear you")   Chantey.   DSC—GSS
Shenandoah ("Oh Shenandoah, I long to hear you")   Windlass and capstan chantey.   BOS 2—TSB 1
  The wide Missouri.   SBS
Shenshin, Afanasi Afanasievich.   See Fet, A.
Shepherd, Henry
  Susan Van Doozen
The **shepherd** ("Down in the valley") Austrian folk carol air: Hirtenlied. Words by L. Binyon.   OB
"**Shepherd** laddie" ("Juhász legény")   B. Egressi.   Words by A. Petöfi.   e.hu. KH 2
The **shepherd** neighbors.   F. A. Gevaert. Words by C. B. Fenno.   FC
The **shepherd** of sleep.   Welsh air. Words by K. Davis.   DSB
The **shepherd** on the rock.   See Der hirt auf dem felsen (Schubert)
"**Shepherd**, see thy horse's foaming mane" ("Hová csikós olyan szaporán") Old Hungarian folk song.   e.hu. KH 1
  "Hová csikós olyan szaporán" ("Sag, wohin, du reiter, sage mir")   g.hu. ML 3
"**Shepherd**! thy demeanour vary."   T. Brown.   WOE
The **shepherdess** ("À l'abri sous la feuillée") See Pastourelle (Auguin)
The **shepherdess** ("Il était un' bergère") See "Il était un' bergère"
"A **shepherdess** was watching."   See "Il était un' bergère"
The **shepherds'** farewell to the Holy Family.   H. Berlioz.   [Tr of L'adieu des bergers à la Sainte Famille]   e. DSC
"**Shepherds**, rejoice! lift up your eyes." West of England air.   DN
"**Shepherds**, we bring you tidings."   See The angels and the shepherds
Sheridan, Helen Selina.   See Dufferin, Helen Selina (Sheridan), lady
Sheridan, Richard Brinsley Butler
  "Here's to the maiden of bashful fifteen" (Traditional air)
  "I have a silent sorrow here" (Reinagle)
Sherwin, William Fisk
  "Day is dying in the west"
  Evening praise.   See "Day is dying in the west"
Sherwood, Grace
  Hike song (Metz)
"**She's** a girl that worked for others."   See La visite du jour de l'an

She's as pretty as a picture all the while. See Pretty as a picture (Bishop)
She's my sweetheart, I'm her beau.   See Little Annie Rooney (Nolan)
She's not the only pebble on the beach. See You're not the only pebble on the beach (Redcliffe)
She's such a belle, a real dark swell.   See Sally come up (Sewell)
Shew! fly, don't bother me.   F. Campbell. Words by B. Reeves.   DFF— WSS
  "Shoo, fly, don't bother me."   SRW
Shield, William
  The Arethusa (attributed; attributed also to T. O'Carolan)
  The heaving of the lead (from Hartford bridge)
  The ploughboy (from The farmer)
  "When e'er you make a promise"
Shields, B. Ernest
  "O Davidson"
Shields, Ren
  In the good old summer time (Evans)
"**Shine** bright and clear, O sunshine." See "Skin ud, du klare solskin" (Lange-Müller)
Shine on.   Negro song.   L. Schoolcraft (music and words)   BNM—WSS
Shine on, oh stars.   F. E. Sawyer.   BST
Shine on, shine on, all cross over Jordan. See Shine on (Schoolcraft)
Shine, shine, who wants a shine.   See Street urchins' medley
"The **ship** at her anchor is riding."   German air.   Words by K. Davis.   DSB
The **ship** I love.   F. McGlennon.   SMG
"The **ship** is sailing down the bay."   See Good-bye, my lover, good-bye (American air)
"A **ship** is wood and metal."   See A sea scout chantey (Wilder)
"A **ship** it was sailing on the full flowing tide."   See The cruel ship's carpenter (Manchester, Ky. version no. 3)
The **ship** that never returned.   Old American song.   SW
  —Kentucky mountain version.   SBA
Shir ha-Chalutsim.   See A song of the Chalutsim
Shir shomrim.   See M'chorotay
Shirley, James
  Pan's holdiay (Bridge)
Shirley, Walter
  "Lord, dismiss us with Thy blessing" (Composer unknown)   Authorship uncertain
Shirvoña.   See Reigen
"'**Shiúbhailfainn** féin a gcómhnuídheleat." See Eibhlín a rúin
"**Sh'ma** kolenu."   See Hear our cry
"**Shock** along, John."   Negro corn-song from Maryland.   AS
The **shoemaker.**   Folk song from North Carolina.   SES 2
"**Shoo**, fly, don't bother me."   See Shew! fly, don't bother me (Campbell)
"**Shoot** your dice and have your fun."   See Sugar babe

Shooting of his dear.   Folk song: Hyden, Ky. version.   SES 1
—Oneida, Ky. version.   SES 1
—St Helen's, Ky. version.   SES 1
—North Carolina version.   SES 1
—Tennessee version.   SES 1
—Virginia version.   SES 1

Shortenin' bread.   Negro folk song.   RA

"**Should** auld acquaintance be forgot, and never brought to mind."   See Auld lang syne

"**Shoulder** up your gun and call your dog." See The ground hog (North Carolina version)

"**Shout** on, children."   Negro spiritual from Georgia.   AS

Shout the glad tidings.   W. A. Muhlenburg (music and words)   MFS

"**Shout** to Jehovah, all the earth" (Psalme 100)   17th century air.   KSO

"**Shove** that hawg-foot furder under the bed."   See Hawg foot

Shovellin' iron ore.   Hobo song.   SBA

Shrival, R. G.
"Hark! I hear an angel sing"
"Oh! share my cottage, gentle maid"

Shrubsole, William
"All hail the power of Jesus' name"
Miles Lane.   See "All hail the power of Jesus' name"

"**Shta** s'ono chuje."   See Die schwester prüft den bruder

Shuckburgh, Richard.   See Schuckburg, Richard

Shukowskij, Wassilij Andrejewitsch.   See Zhukovskiï, Vasiliï Andreevich

Shule, agra ("Oft I roam my garden bow'rs") Air: Come, my love.   Words by T. Moore.   HMI

"**Si** fos ocellet 'niria volant."   See Layeta

Si: fuggian da queste mura.   For English translation see "Yes, we'll fly these walls" (Verdi)

Si Hubbard (Hey Rube)   Old circus song.   SBA

Si je suis vraiment dame et châtelaine. For English translation see "Dear friends of my youth, think not we are parted" (Planquette)

"**Si** la madrecita mia."   See Malagueña

"**Si** l'amour est si fort, cher monsieur." See Z'amours Marianne

"**Si** l'amour vous si fort, michié-là."   See Z'amours Marianne

["**Si** le bonheur"]   When all was young ("When joyous tho'ts")   C. F. Gounod.   e.   WG

"**Si** le roy m'avait donné" ("Wenn der könig Heinrich mir")   Old French folk song.   f.g.   ML 1

Si mes vers avaient des ailes (Were my song with wings provided)   R Hahn.   Words by V. Hugo.   e.f. TM

Si mo leannan an (O, I love the maiden fair)   Gaelic folk air.   Words by H. Whyte (Fionn)   e.   CSB 1

"**Si** n'hi habian trés ninetas."   See La ploma de perdiu

Si puo?   si puo.   For English translation see Prologue, from I pagliacci (Leoncavallo)

Si tu m'aimes, Carmen.   For English translation see "If you love me" (Bizet)

"**Siałem** proso na zagonie."   See "Sown with millet was my garden"

Sibelius, Jean
"En blomma stod vid vägen"
"A floweret by the wayside."   See "En blomma stod vid vägen"
Hiljainen kaupunki.   See The silent city
"A maiden yonder sings"
The silent city
"Swift the springtime passes."   See "Våren flyktar hastigt"
"Tuol laulaa neitonen."   See "A maiden yonder sings"
"Våren flyktar hastigt"

Sicilian mariners' hymn.   See Die drei grossen Christlichen feste; "Lead us, heavenly Father, lead us"; "Lord, dismiss us with Thy blessing"; "May the grace of Christ, our Saviour"; "O sanctissima"; "While the morning bells are ringing"

Siciliana ("O Lola")   P. Mascagni.   e. WG

Sick call.   U.S. army bugle call.   DSO

The **sidewalks** of New York (East side, west side)   C. B. Lawlor.
Words by J. W. Blake.   DFF
The side walks of New York.   SMG

"**Sidîel** Vanîa."   See Vanya

"**Sie** gleicht wohl einem rosenstock."   See Röslein auf der heiden

Sie lacht zu meinen leiden.   For English translation see These tears my bosom searing (Flotow)

"**Sie** liebten sich beide" ("They loved one another")   W. Stenhammar.   Words by H. Heine.   e.g.   WM 2

"**Sie** schwebt' mir noch kürzlich im arme." See "But lately in dance I embraced her" (Arenski)

"**Sie** sollen ihn nicht haben."   See Der deutsche Rhein (Schumann)

"**Siedzi** sobie zając pod miedzą."   See "Sass einmal ein häslein an dem rain"

Siegert, Gottlob
Gebet an den heiligen Christ

"**Sieh,** die schöne mutter Gottes unsres lieben dorfes schaut herein."   See Canción de cuna

Sieveking, Martinus
The wooing

Sigh for thee, die for thee.   See Bonnie brave Scotland (Gow)

"**Sighing** on the wings of the air."   See Arpège (Rousseau)

The **sign** of the Bonny Blue Bell (see Song Index)
Variant: I'm going to get married next **Sunday**

Signal corps song ("Oh! Uncle Sammy, he needs the signal corps")   Song of the European war.   Air: The old gray mare.   DSO

Silcher, Friedrich
"Alle jahre wieder"
"Ännchen von Tharau"
The bell is ringing
"Good-night" (with words "Good-night, good-night, companions all"; "Good-night, good-night, my lady fair")
In der ferne
Lebewohl
Die Lorelei
Never alone (same air as Die Lorelei)
Der Schweizer
Der soldat

"**Silde** vid nat hin kolde" ("Late in the night in frost cold")   P. E. Lange-Müller.   Words from a Flemish folk song.   da.e.   WM 2

"**Silence** inviting weary hearts to rest."   See Night and day (Manney)

The **silent** city (Hiljainen kaupunki)   J. Sibelius.   e.fi.   WM 2

"**Silent** heroes."   R. Planquette.   [Tr of C'est la salle de mes ancêtres]   e.   WLO

"**Silent** night! holy night."   See Die heilige nacht (Gruber)

"**Silent** now the drowsy bird" (Barcarolle)   J. Offenbach.   Words by I. L. Brown.   TFP—TFR

"**Silent**, oh Moyle, be the roar of thy water."   See Song of Fionnuala

Silent safety.   See Stille sicherheit (Franz)

"The **silent** waterlily."   See "Die stille wasserrose" (Fielitz)

Silently.   See "Silently! silently! ope and close the schoolroom door"

"**Silently** blending night's shadows fall."   See "Voi, che sapete" (Mozart)

Silently falling snow.   Popular air.   <Words by W. O. Bourne>   MFS

"**Silently**! silently! open and close the schoolroom door" (Silently)   <Spanish or German air: Lightly row>   KSO

The **silk** merchant's daughter.   Folk song: Kentucky version.   SES 1
—Allanstand, N.C. version.   SES 1
—Big Laurel, N.C. version.   SES 1
—Virginia version.   SES 1

"**Silly** soldier onward speed."   See Song of the silly horseman (Lehar)

Silver chimes.   Claribel (C. Barnard)   MFS

The **silver** dagger.   Folk song: Kentucky version.   SES 2
—Virginia version.   SES 2

The **silver** moon ("As I strayed from my cot")   See Roll on, silver moon

Silver threads among the gold.   H. P. Danks.   Words by E. E. Rexford.   DFF—GFS—WSS

The **silver** wedding.   Minstrel song.   WSS
Going to the silver wedding.   PSG

Silvestre, Paul Armand
Pensée de printemps (Leroux)

Sim, John
Kelvin grove (Scottish air)   See Lyle, T.   Kelvin grove (Scottish air)

Simmonds, John
Johnny Sands.   See Sinclair, J.   Johnny Sands

Simonffy, Kálmán
"Maiden, maiden, nut-brown maiden"
"'Mid the cornfields sings the sweet lark"
"O'er the lithe lily"
"Szomorú füzága."   See "O'er the lithe lily"
"Te vagy, te vagy barna kis lány."   See "Maiden, maiden, nut-brown maiden"
"Über die feldblume."   See "O'er the lithe lily"
"Zöld vetés közt énekel a pacsirta."   See "'Mid the cornfields sings the sweet lark"

Simpkins, F. A.
Lincoln and liberty (English air)

The **simple** ploughboy.   Folk song: Virginia version.   SES 1

Simrock, Karl Joseph
Warnung vor dem Rhein (Pöthko)
Wiegenlied (Brahms)

Sims's Flotilla.   U.S. navy song.   [Air: Son of a gambolier]   US

Sin ("I know my God's a mand o' war")   See Sinner, please don't let this harvest pass

Sin not, oh king.   Handel.   SSO 3

The **sin-sick** soul.   Negro spiritual from South Carolina.   AS

"**Since** first I saw your face."   T. Ford.   DSC—MBS

Since I've been in the army.   Civil war song.   Scottish air: Wha'll be king but Charlie.   DSO

"**Since**, Lysander, I'm so near you."   See Ça fait peur aux oiseaux (Bernard)

"**Since** our muskets we have shouldered."   See Co-ca-che-lunk

"**Since** the days of old the lure of gold."   See Chevrons (Egner)

"**Since** we parted yestereve, yestereve."   See Yestereve (Allitsen)

Sinclair, John
"Come sit thee down"
Dumbarton's bonny dell
Johnny Sands

Sinclair, John Lang
"The eyes of Texas" (Old air)

"**Sind** wir vereint zur guten stunde."   See Bundeslied (Hanitsch)

Sinding, Christian
"Bring us songs of cheer and joy."   See "Kom med sange og helst af dem"
"Der gives stjerner"
"Der skreg en fugl"
"Es schrie ein vogel."   See Der skreg en fugl
Faith.   See Tro
"I'll show thee stars."   See "Der gives stjerner"

Sinding, Christian—*Continued*
"Kom med sange og helst af dem"
Life and blessedness. See Liv og salighed
Light. See Ljos
Liv og salighed
Ljos
The new moon. See Ny-måne
Ny-måne
Pearls. See Perlen
Perlen
"There cried a bird." See Der skreg en fugl
A thought of spring. See Ein vaartankje
Tro
Ein vaartankje
Sinful to flirt. American mountain song. RA
Sing ("What as gay as cheery song") German folk air. Words by J. Landon. TFO
Sing a-ho that I had the wings of a dove. Negro spiritual from Tennessee. FSN
"**Sing** a hymn of freedom." See The home road (Carpenter)
Sing-a-ling-a-ling. Student song. TFG —TFR
"**Sing** a song, a rich refrain." See Champlain (Putnam)
"**Sing** a song of cities, cities great and small." See Street urchins' medley
"**Sing** a song of sixpence." Nursery song. 3d air <by J. W. Elliott> TFP
"**Sing** a song to our fighting men." See Indian warriors' song (Allen)
"**Sing** all good people gathered." See Venez à Saint-Maurice (Renard?)
Sing alleluia ("Christ the Lord") See "Christ the Lord is born today, alleluia! alleluia! Sons of men and angels say" (French air)
Sing alma mater, Heidelberg. See Heidelberg (Power)
Sing! and rejoice! all people, sing. See Palm branches (Faure)
"**Sing**, birdie sing." W. Ganz. Words by Zeila. GE
"**Sing** courting, courting, courting cain." See The Suffolk miracle (Tennessee version)
Sing fare you well. Halliard chantey. TSB 2
Variant: "O fare-you-well, my bonny young girls"
"**Sing** for the fame of Ohio." See Sing, Ohio (Robinson)
Sing glad songs for him. C. F. Gounod. Words by C. Morton. MFS
"**Sing**, good company, frank and free." See Jesus of the manger
Sing hey for braw John Highlandman. See "A Highland lad my love was born"
"**Sing** I for a brave and a gallant barque." See Ten thousand miles away
"**Sing** me home." See "Syng mig hjaem" (Neupert)

Sing Noël, sing Noël, and merry be alway. See "A day of joyful singing" (Jackson)
Sing O my love. See My dancing day
Sing, O-hi-o. Marching song of Ohio university. C. C. Robinson (music and words) KU
Sing on, pray on, ye followers of Immanuel. See "My Bible leads to glory"
"**Sing**, sing, darkies, sing." Minstrel song. WSS
Sing, smile, sleep. See Chantez riez et dormez (Gounod)
Sing, smile, slumber. See Chantez riez et dormez (Gounod)
Sing song Kitty can't you kimey O. See The frog in the well (Woodridge, Va. version)
Sing, song Kitty cayn't ya kimeo. See Beaver creek
Sing song Kitty won't you kimey O. See The opossum
Sing songs of praise. Handel. SSO 3
"**Sing**, sweet bird." W. Ganz. Words by L. M. Thornton. GE
"**Sing**, then, of the heav'n-descended daughter of the starry realm." See Open, Lord, my inward ear (Beethoven)
"**Sing** to me, sweet musetta." See "O ma tendre musette" (Monsigny?)
"**Sing** to the colors that float in the light, hurrah for the scarlet and cream." See The scarlet and cream (Balfe)
"**Sing** to the colors that float in the light, hurrah for the yellow and blue." See The yellow and blue (Balfe)
"**Sing** to the Lord of harvest." See Golden sheaves
"**Sing** we all merrily, Christmas is here." See Christmas is here
Sing we Noël ("Sing we the story of the Savior's birth") 16th century French carol. e. FC
"**Sing** we Noël! now to the earth comes Jesus our Saviour." See Chantons Noël
"**Sing** we the story of the Savior's birth." See Sing we Noël
Sing wo, my lads, gee wo. See The jolly waggoner
Sing your sweetest songs to me. See Eulalie (Minstrel ballad)
"**S'inganna** chi crede." G. Sarti. e.i. ZT 2
"**Singen** will ich den feldherrn und die waffen." See Canto dei gondolieri
"**Singend** über die haide" ("Singing over the heather") A. Bungert. Words by A. Fitger. e.g. TM
Singin' Johnny. Chantey. Words adapted. TFR
Variant of: Hanging Johnny
Singin' ki yi yippi yappi yay, yappi yay. See The Lone Star trail
The **singing** bird. Netherlands air. Words by K. Davis. DSB
The **singing** in God's acre. J. Jordan. Words by E. Field. TSS 2
Singing in the rain. F. J. Haydn. Words by E. A. Allen. BB

Singing la-e, lo-e, hush-a-bye baby. See Hush-a-bye, baby (Minstrel song)
Singing merrily, merrily, merrily. See Follow me, full of glee
"Singing over the heather." See "Singend über die haide" (Bungert)
The singing river. Flemish air. Words by K. Davis. DSB
Singing, row away, row. See Tom-big-bee river (Steele)
"Singing thro' the forests." See Rhyme of the rail
Singing tooroolie ooroolie ooroolay. See Botany bay
The single girl. Folk song: Barbourville, Ky. version. SES 2
—Berea, Ky. version. SES 2
—North Carolina version. SES 2
—Tennessee version. SES 2
—Virginia version. SES 2
"Singt das junge kukkucklein." See "Cântă puiul cucului"
"Singt der maid ein lied zum preise." See A' mhaighdean àluinn
Sinner man. Mountain spiritual: Kentucky version. SES 2
—North Carolina version. SES 2
"Sinner, O, see dat cruel tree." See Sinner, please don't let this harves' pass
Sinner, please don't let this harvest pass. Negro spiritual. WFN
Sin. FSN
Sinner, please don't let dis harves' pass. JB 2
"Sinner, to-day you' better repent." See Tomorrow you may die
Sinner won't die no more. Negro spiritual from Tennessee. AS
The sinners' redemption. 17th century carol. OB
Der sinnierende narr. J. Kain. Author of words unknown. g. EDL
Sion ("There is a city builded") P. Rodney. Words by G. C. Bingham. ASA—CSS 1—CSS 2
"Sion the marvelous story be telling." See Shout the glad tidings (Muhlenburg)
Sion's daughter. See Waer is die dochter van Syoen
Sipping cider thru a straw. See Sucking cider through a straw (Morgan)
Sir Christmas. 15th century carol. OB
Sir Christmas. R. Dunstan. 15th century words. DN
"Sir Eglamore that valiant knight." 17th century song. BOS 2—CSB 2—GSS
Sir Francis Drake. See The Spanish Armada
Sir Hugh. Folk song: Barbourville, Ky. version. SES 1
—Manchester, Ky. version. SES 1
—Oneida, Ky. version no. 1. SES 1
—Oneida, Ky. version no. 2. SES 1
—Pine Mountain, Ky. version. SES 1
—Teges, Ky. version. SES 1
—North Carolina version. SES 1
—Bird's Creek, Tenn. version. SES 1
—Sevierville, Tenn. version. SES 1
—Virginia version. SES 1

Sir Lionel. Folk song: Barbourville, Ky. version. SES 1
—Berea, Ky. version. SES 1
—North Carolina version. SES 1
—Virginia version. SES 1
Bangum and the boar. Knott or Letcher county, Ky. version. MK
Sirén, Oswald
I vassen (Palmgren)
Liljekonvalje (Palmgren)
"Sister Dolly light the lamp." See The white marble stone (South Carolina version no. 1)
"Sister Katy, want to get religion." See The lonesome valley
"Sister Mary came a-runnin'." See De angel roll de stone away
"Sister Rosy, you get to heaven before I go." See Travel on
[Sister Ruth] "Dost thou love me, sister Ruth." J. Haydn <wrongly attributed to J. Parry> GOS 2
"Sitting by the road side on a summer day." See Eating goober peas
"Sitting in a corner, on a Sunday eve." See Sparking on a Sunday night
Sitting on a rail. See Settin' on a rail
"Sitzend einsam am öden strande." See Am strande
"Sitzt e klois vogerl im tannewald." See Die nachtigall im tannenwald
Sivle, Per
Ljos (Sinding)
"Six little children all for to retain." See The single girl (Barbourville, Ky. version)
Six pretty maids, come gang along o' me. See The farmyard ("Up was I")
"Sixteen battleships all in a line." See The old destroyer squadron
The sixth field artillery song. U.S. army song of the European war. DSO
"Sjera Magnus" ("Pfarrer Magnus") Icelandic folk song. g.ic. ML 1
Sjögren, Johan Gustav Emil
Bitte
A dream. See Dröm
Dröm
"Hab' ein röslein dir gebrochen"
"Lehn' deine wang' an meine wang'"
"Liten prins i vaggan"
"Little prince a-cradled." See "Liten prins i vaggan"
"Oh, press thy cheek close to mine own." See "Lehn' deine wang' an meine wang'"
"See, for thee I've plucked a rosebud." See "Hab' ein röslein dir gebrochen"
"Sleepest thou, my soul." See "Sover du, min sjael"
"Sover du, min sjael"
Suckarna. See Suspiria
Suspiria
"Turn to me, dark eyes so tender." See Bitte
"Weil' auf mir, du dunkles auge." See Bitte

Sjugur aa trollbrura (Wie Sigurd seine braut gewann) Norwegian folk song. g.n. ML 1

"**Skazhĭ**, moĭa krasavĭtsa." See "Sag an, wie gross"

Skelly, Joseph P.
Strolling on the Brooklyn bridge
Why did they dig ma's grave so deep

Sketchley, Arthur, pseud. See Rose, George

Skibbereen (A ballad of the famine) Irish air from County Tyrone. Traditional words. HI 2

The **Skidmore** fancy ball. D. Braham. Words by E. Harrigan. SRW

"**Skin** ud, du klare solskin" ("Shine bright and clear, O sunshine") P. E. Lange-Müller. Words by T. Lange. da.e. WM 2

Skinner, John
Tullochgorum (Scottish air)

"**Skip** to my Lou." Game song. RA

The **skipper.** W. H. Jude. Words by F. J. Dennett. SFB

"A **skipper** am I." See The skipper (Jude)

Skirving, Adam
Johnnie Cope (Scottish air)

Skogmöte has thorgjer skjelle (Begegnung im walde) Norse air. Words by E. Storm. g.n. ML 1

Skowronek. See Kleine lerche

"**Škripi** djeram." See The water chain

Škroup, Jan Nepomuk
Bohemia, my fatherland. See My fatherland
My fatherland

Skye boat song. Jacobite song. Words by H. Boulton. DSB—GSS—MBS

"**Slack,** man, slack, man, slack up your rope." See The maid freed from the gallows (Pine Mountain, Ky. version)

"**Slack** your rope, hangs-a-man." See The maid freed from the gallows (South Carolina version)

Slade, Charles
"Thou hast learned to love another"

Slade, Mrs Mary B. C.
Welcome to morning (Offenbach)

The **Slaney** side. Irish air from County Kerry. Traditional words. HI 2

Slater, Edward
The beauteous song. See Come unto me
Come unto me
Gethsemane. See Thy will be done
The good Shepherd
Thy will be done

Slater, Gordon
And shall Trelawny die. See Song of the western men
A ballad to Queen Elizabeth of the Spanish Armada
Song of the western men

Slattery's mounted foot. Composer and author of words unknown. US

Slava. See The song of praise

Slav'ry chain. Negro spiritual. HRD

Slavery days. Minstrel song. SW

The **slave's** dream. Minstrel ballad. WSS

"**Sleep,** ah, sleep, my darling baby, su, su, lullaby." See The Cossack's lullaby (Bakhmetiev)

"**Sleep,** baby, sleep, our cottage vale is deep." Old nursery song. DSB

"**Sleep,** baby, sleep, thy father minds the sheep." See "Schlaf', kindchen, schlaf'" (German folk song)

"**Sleep,** baby, sleep, thy father tends the sheep." See "Schlaf', kindchen, schlaf'" (German folk song)

"**Sleep,** darling, sleep, the daylight dies down in the crimson west." See A song of sleep (Somerset)

"**Sleep,** little baby, comes the sandman." See Lullaby (Finnish air)

"**Sleep,** my baby, on my bosom." See Suo-gân

"**Sleep,** my child, and peace attend thee." See Ar hyd y nos (Owen)

["**Sleep,** my child, my pretty one"] "Aïnte, aïnte, koimēsoy" (Schlummerlied) Syrian folk song. g.gr. ML 2

"**Sleep,** my dearie." M. T. Armitage (music and words) TFR

"**Sleep,** my love, and peace attend thee." See Ar hyd y nos (Owen)

"**Sleep** my pretty one close to mother." See Cradle-song (Grechaninov)

"**Sleep,** noble hearts" (Consolation) Mendelssohn. Words by F. Manley. TFG

"**Sleep** now, my little one, sleep." See Wiegenlied (Mozart)

"**Sleep,** O babe, for the red bee hums." See The Gartan mother's lullaby

"**Sleep,** oh my darling, now sleep." See Wiegenlied (Mozart)

"**Sleep,** O sleep, fond fancy" (Zur ruh, mein wahn) T. Morley. e.g. ML 1

The **sleep** of the divine Infant. See The sleep of the Infant Jesus (Gevaert)

[The **sleep** of the Infant Jesus] The sleep of the divine Infant. [F. A. Gavaert. Words from an old French Noël. Tr of Entre le boeuf et l'âne gris] e. FC
Lullaby of the Christ Child. e. DSB

Sleep on! sleep on, sleep on, my little one. See Sandmännchen

"**Sleep,** sleep, my darling, sleep tranquilly." See Slumber song (French lullaby)

"**Sleep,** sleep, my little one, sleep." See Berceuse ("Dors, dors, mon petit, dors")

"**Sleep,** so your tale of dreams be told." See Lullaby (Godard)

"**Sleep,** soldier, sleep." Memorial day song. A. Davison. Words by M. K. Cherryman. BB

"**Sleep,** sweet babe! my cares beguiling." See "Dormi, Jesu! mater ridet" (Rubbra)

"**Sleep** thou, sleep thou, mother's arms enfold thee." See Cradle song (Schubert)

"Sleep to me no rest is bringing." See "Immer leiser wird mein schlummer" (Brahms)

Sleeper, H. D.
Oh! fairest alma mater

Sleeping princess ("Bright are the flames") Lithuanian air. GSS

Sleepers, arise. Three-part song. GSS

[Sleepers, wake] "Now let every tongue adore Thee." J. S. Bach. <Words by P. Nicolai. Tr of Wachet auf> e. DSB—DSC "Glory now to Thee be given." e. TFP

"Sleepest thou, my soul." See "Sover du, min sjael" (Sjögren)

"Sleeping I dream'd, love." W. V. Wallace. <Words by M. E. Hewitt> GOS 1

The sleeping shepherds. Old Béarnaise air. Words by C. B. Fenno. FC

Sleepy little maiden, I cannot lift my head. See Interrupted slumber

Sleighing-time. Canadian folk song. DSB

Slepačka pesma. See The song of the blind beggar

The slighted soldier. Folk song from Tennessee. SES 2

The slighted swain. [Words by A. Bradley] WOE

Sling the flowing bowl. Forecastle song. WSE

[Sling the flowing bowl] While the foaming billows roll. T. Linley. WOE

Sloane, Alfred Baldwin
Heaven will protect the working girl

Slocum, E. N.
"On the beach at Cape May"

"Slow by the shadows." Irish air from County Donegal. Words by S. Mac-Cathmh'aoil. HI 1

"Slowly the snow comes floating down." See It snows in the night

"Sluchilos'-to Mnře, dobru molodtsu." See Mädchens klage

["Slumber, beloved, and take thy repose"] "Slumber, my lov'd one." J. Bach. [Tr of Schlafe, mein liebster, geniesse der ruh'] e. SSO 2

"Slumber, dearest." F. von Flotow. e. MFS

Slumber, loved one, sweetly in thy tomb. See Amber Lee (White)

Slumber, my loved one ("Dormi pure") See "Dormi pure" (Scuderi)

"Slumber, my lov'd one, enjoy thy repose." See "Slumber, beloved, and take thy repose" (Bach)

"Slumber, slumber, sweet my joy and treasure." See Wiegenlied (Schubert)

"Slumber, slumber, tender little flower." See Wiegenlied (Schubert)

The slumber song ("Alles still") See "Alles still in süsser ruh" (Kücken)

Slumber song ("Es mahnt der wald") See Schlummerlied (Schubert)

Slumber song ("Schlafe, schlafe, holder süsser knabe") See Wiegenlied (Schubert)

Slumbersong ("Sleep, my pretty one") See Cradle-song (Grechaninov)

Slumber song ("Sleep, sleep, my darling") French lullaby. · e. MFS

"Slumber sweetly, slumber, O my baby." See Wiegenlied (Schubert)

Smart, Henry Thomas
By the blue sea
Nymphs of air and sea

Smart, Richard. See Smert, Richard

Smart, Thomas
The forsaken maid

Smash right thru that line of blue. See Fight song (Lankey)

Smert, Richard
Nowell, Nowell

Smetana, Bedřich
"All ends well, so we're rejoicing" (from The bartered bride)
"I know a maiden, she's got the money" (from The bartered bride)
"It must succeed" (from The bartered bride)
"Now in joy or sorrow" (from The bartered bride)
Villagers' chorus (from The bartered bride)
"Where is John"
"You are an awful stubborn case" (from The bartered bride)

Smile, my Kathleen, pray. Irish air. Words by J. Oxenford. HMI

Smith, Albert William
Hail, Stanford, hail (Coolidge)

Smith, Mrs Carolina Louisa (Sprague)
"Tarry with me, O my Saviour" (music by Raff; Roeder)

Smith, Charles S.
"Hark, hark, the peal of clarions calling" (Rouget de Lisle)

Smith, Chris
Long gone (Handy)

Smith, Dan D.
De boatmen's dance

Smith, David Stanley
A hope carol
May song

Smith, Deloss
The warriors

Smith, Dexter
Where the little feet are waiting (Webster)

Smith, Edgar
Heaven will protect the working girl (Sloane)

Smith, Everett H., pseud. See Harbour, Homer H.

Smith, Harry Bache
You're here and I'm here (Kern)

Smith, Harry D.
Victory song (Tomlinson)

Smith, Hubbard P.
Sweethearts and wives

Smith, J. E.
Little Boy Blue

Smith, John Stafford
Adams and liberty (same air as "To Anacreon in heaven"; attributed)
The death of Crockett (same air as "To Anacreon in heaven"; attributed)

Smith, John Stafford—*Continued*
　　The star-spangled banner (same air as
　　　"To Anacreon in heaven"; at-
　　　tributed)
　　"To Anacreon in heaven" (attributed)
Smith, Penelope
　　"A place in thy memory, dearest"
Smith, R. F.
　　Epiphany.　See "There came three
　　　kings ere break of day"
　　"There came three kings ere break of
　　　day"
Smith, Reed
　　Carolina's day
Smith, Robert Archibald
　　The braes o' Balquhidder
　　Jessie, the flower o' Dumblane
　　"Loudon's bonnie woods and braes"
Smith, Robert B.
　　Come down ma evenin' star (Strom-
　　　berg)
Smith, Samuel Francis
　　America (Carey?)
　　"God ever glorious" (Lvov)
Smith, William Dexter
　　Cross and crown (Dana)
The **smith** ("Ich hör' mein schatz")　See
　　Der schmied (Brahms)
The **smith** ("Winds of eve are freshly
　　blowing")　P. Mascagni.　Words by
　　S. Fay.　TFO
Smoky mokes.　A. Holzmann.　Words
　　by W. M. Lind.　SMG
The **smuggler**.　See Will Watch (Davy)
"**Snake** baked a hoe-cake."　See "Wake,
　　snakes" (Virginia version)
Sne (Snow)　S. Lie.　Words by H.
　　Rode.　e.n.　WM 2
"**Snoshchi** e Ianka v"v" sedo."　See Janka
Snow, Henry, pseud.　See Stevens, David
Snow ("Der er ingenting i verden saa
　　stillesom sne")　See Sne (Lie)
The **snow-bird**.　See The snowbird
"The **snow** had been falling."　See Found
　　dead in the snow
Snow in the street.　See "From far
　　away" (Williams)
"The **snow** lay on the ground."　Christ-
　　mas carol.　Anglo-Irish air.　DN
"The **snow** lay on the ground."　Christ-
　　mas carol.　Young.　FC
"The **snow** lies thick."　G. Shaw.　Words
　　by S. Image.　OB
"De **snow-man** in de cloud."　See Planta-
　　tion walk around (Emmett)
"**Snow** on the earth; tho' March is well
　　nigh over."　See Spring song (Mac-
　　kenzie)
The **snowbird**.　Words by F. C. Wood-
　　worth.　MFS
The **snowy-breasted** pearl ("Atá cailín deas
　　am cráд")　See Péarla an brollaig
　　báin
The **snowy-breasted** pearl ("Oh! she is not
　　like the rose")　Irish air: Pearl of
　　the white breast.　Words by S. E.
　　De Vere.　BST
"**Snowy**, snowy the sea-gulls flocking."
　　See Im kahne (Grieg)

So, behold, all the gates of heaven unfold.
　　See "Gabriel's message"
So blessed be the time.　Old air.　15th
　　century words.　DNS
"**So** blest a sight."　16th or 17th century
　　English air.　16th century words.
　　DNS
So, brother.　Besançon folk air.　Words
　　based on an old Besançon carol, Fesans
　　raijouissance.　e.　OB
"**So** che godendo vai."　D. Zamperelli.
　　e.i.　KVG
"**So** early, early in the spring."　See
　　Early, early in the spring (Hot Springs,
　　N.C. versions no. 1-2)
So early in the morning ("A bottle o'
　　rum")　See The sailor likes his bottle,
　　O
So early in the morning ("Oh the mate
　　got drunk")　See Sailor likes his
　　bottle
So early in the morning ("South Caro-
　　lina's a sultry clime")　WSS
"**So** early one morning pretty Polly she
　　rose."　See Polly Oliver (North
　　Carolina version)
So faithful in love and so dauntless in war.
　　See Young Lochinvar (Mazzinghi)
"**So** far away from friends and home."
　　See The true lover's farewell (Hot
　　Springs, N.C. version)
"**So** fare you well, fathers, and fare you
　　well, mothers."　See Green grows
　　the laurel
So fill your glasses to the brim.　See
　　The cavalry song
So fill your glasses with cold beer.　See
　　The infantry song
So get out de way, ole Dan Tucker.　See
　　Old Dan Tucker (Russell)
"**So** grün als ist die heiden."　Volkslied.
　　g.　EDL
"**So** hab' ich doch die ganze woche."　See
　　Sonntag (Brahms)
"**So** handy, my girls."　Halliard chantey.
　　WSE
"**So** handy, me gels."　TSB 2
So here's to you old Tennessee.　See
　　Alma mater—University of Tennessee
　　(Meek)
So hike along, comrades.　See At the
　　gym
So hoist up the John B. sails.　See The
　　John B. sails
So ihr mich von ganzem herzen suchet.
　　For English translation see "If with
　　all your hearts ye truly seek me"
　　(Mendelssohn)
So it's rip up the army team.　See The
　　pride of the navy
"**So** lately one morning down by the river-
　　side."　See The Irish girl (Peaks of
　　Otter, Va. version)
"**So** leb' denn wohl, du stilles haus."　See
　　Abschied (Müller)
So let us cheer, cheer, cheer for Denison.
　　See Denison marching song (Arnold)
So long Mary.　G. M. Cohan (music and
　　words)　DFF

So look a lookey there. See A Monday was my courting day

So muffle up de banjo. See Poor old Uncle Rufe

"So often on me rests his glance." See Pigetanker (Winge)

So shall the lute and harp awake. Handel. SSO 1

So sing, men, and swing, men. See Fordham marching song (Breslin)

So success attend Saint Patrick's fist. See "Saint Patrick was a gentleman"

So take off your coat, boys. See Jordan is a hard road to trabel

So the story goes. See The maiden's rose (Hatton)

"So they, being filled with the Holy Ghost." See I will sing of Thy great mercies (Mendelssohn)

"So traditore! t'inganni." See La mia virtù non cede (Bianchi)

So what care I, though death be nigh. See A warrior bold (Maybrick)

"So you tell me man right to my face." See You'll think of me (Clark)

"So you're going to leave the old home, Jim." See There's a mother always waiting you at home, sweet home (Thornton)

Soane, George
"I've been roaming" (Horn)

"Soave immagine d'amore." Mercadante. e.i. PC

Sobeski, Carl
"There! little girl, don't cry"

Soboieski, Paul
Polish national song (Ogiński?) See Wybitski, J. Polish national song (Ogiński?)

The social band. Negro spiritual from North Carolina. AS

Soda and b——. Old song. SW

"Soft as the voice of an angel." See Whispering hope (Winner)

"Soft be thy slumbers, rude cares depart." See Ellen Bayne (Foster)

Soft music is stealing. <German air: Du, du liegst mir im herzen> Words by M. S. B. Dana. MFS

"Soft o'er the fountain." See Juanita

"Soft, soft music is stealing." See Soft music is stealing

"The soft stars are shining." See The fairy dance

"Soft strains of music drifting." See "Wie melodien zieht es mir" (Brahms)

"The soft wind stirs the wild cherry trees." See The wind in the cherry trees (Galkin)

"Softly a trilling, all the air filling." See Längsel (Svendsen)

"Softly now the light of day." Donizetti. [Words by G. W. Doane] MFS

"Softly now the light of day." C. M. von Weber. Words by G. W. Doane. BB

"Softly now the light of day" (Seymour) TFO

"Softly o'er the rippling waters." J. R. Thomas. Words by G. Cooper. OT

"Softly sighs the breath of evening." See Gebet (Weber)

"Softly, so softly, floating in air." Finale from Ein walzertraum. O. Straus. e. WLO

"Softly, softly slumber, my loved one." See "Dormi pure" (Scuderi)

"Softly the wind is blowing." See Twilight dreams

"Sog-tze rebbenu, wos wet sein." See What will happen when the Messiah comes

"Sokol mī letī." See "Flog ein falke"

El soldado Americano. See The American soldier

Der soldat ("Es geht bei gedämpfter trommel") F. Silcher. Words after the Danish of H. C. Andersen. g. EDL

Soldaten-abschied ("Heute scheid' ich") F. E. Fesca. Words by F. Müller. g. EDL

Soldaten-morgenlied. Volksweise. Words by M. von Schenkendorf. g. EDL

Die soldatenbraut. R. Schumann. Words by E. Mörike. g. EDL

"Soldier boy." Children's song. BB

Soldier boy for me. Play-party song: Callaway, Va. version. SES 2
—Franklin county, Va. version. SES 2

"Soldier boy, soldier boy, where are you going." See "Soldier boy"

"A soldier he comply made." See The slighted soldier

"A soldier in the cavalry lay on a canvas bunk." See Bacon on the rind

"Soldier, soldier, won't you marry me." See Soldier, won't you marry me (North Carolina version)

"A soldier stood in the village street." See Ehren on the Rhine (Hutchinson)

Soldier, won't you marry me. Folk song: American mountain version. RA
—Kentucky version. SES 2
—North Carolina version. SES 2
—Tennessee version. SES 2

"A soldier wooed a peerless maid." See Love and battle

Soldiers' chorus. C. Gounod. [Tr of Gloire immortelle de nos aïeux] e. MFS—TFB—TFP—WG

The soldier's farewell ("At length, too soon, dear creature") T. Swan. MPA 1

Soldier's farewell ("How can I bear to leave thee") See Ritters abschied (Kinkel)

Soldier's farewell ("Weh' dasz wir scheiden müssen") See Ritters abschied (Kinkel)

Soldiers' hymn. J. Haydn. DSB

A soldier's lament ("A soldier in the cavalry") See Bacon on the rind

A soldier's life ("Dull is the life") E. Jakobowski. WLO

"A **soldier's** life is a cruel life." See Sweet William (Alleghany, N.C. version no. 2)

The **soldiers'** song ("In that land of dopey dreams")   Song of the Spanish-American war. [G. F. Root] DSO

"A **soldier's** trade is a cruel life." See Sweet William (Alleghany, N.C. version no. 1; Burnsville, N.C. version no. 1; Swannanoa, N.C. version)

"**Soldiers,** yes your vivandière." See Vivandière song (Bristow)

"**Sole** gaar bak Aasen ne." See Aagots fjeldsang (Thrane)

O **sole** mio (My sun)   E. di Capua. [Words by G. Capurro] e. GSS—LAS

O sole mio (My sunshine) e.i. TFR. e. only TFB—TFP

"**Soll** ich sein a rov." See A teamster's complaint

Solman, Alfred
If I had a thousand lives to live
When the evening breeze is sighing
"Home, sweet home"

"**Solntse** vskhodit i zakhodit." See Der gefangene

Solomon Levi and The Spanish cavalier, arranged. See A vocal encounter

"A **solution** to this vexing Chinese question." See The coon republic

"**Som,** som, som w stawie rybecki." See "Komm, komm, komm, fischlein im teich"

"**Som** stjärnan uppå himmelen så klar" ("Wie der stern in der höh") Swedish folk song. g.sw. ML 1

"**Sombre** pines still waters are enhancing." See Aftonstämning (Peterson-Berger)

"**Some** come cripple" (Hail the crown) Negro spiritual [from Kentucky] FSN

"**Some** fellahs sing about champagne." See Soda and b——

Some folks do. S. C. Foster (music and words) WSS

"**Some** folks like to sigh." See Some folks do (Foster)

"**Some** folks say that a crow won't steal." See Down in Mobile

"**Some** folks say that a nigger won't steal." See Down in Mobile

"**Some** go to church fo' to sing an' shout." See Ezekiel saw de wheel

"**Some** hundred years ago or so." See Hoop de dooden do (Nish)

Some love coffee. Play-party song from North Carolina. SES 2

Some o' dese days ("I'm go'n'ter set down") Negro spiritual. JG

"**Some** o' dese mornin's 'bout nine o'clock." See O Mary, don't you weep

"**Some** of dese mornin's bright an' fair." See Ride on

[**Some** of these mornings] "Gwine to see my mother" (Look away) Negro spiritual. HRD

"**Some** of these days about four o'clock." See Hold on

Some old fireman, some old engineer. See Goin' down that long long lonesome road (Nash)

"**Some** old Robin Down they call me." See Ibby Damsel

"**Some** rival has stolen my true love away." Folk song from Surrey. BET

"**Some** say No-e is a good old man." See No-e in the ark

"**Some** say that John de Baptist." See I've been a-list'ning all de night long

"**Some** seek de Lord and they don't seek Him right, pray all day and sleep all night." See Almost over

"**Some** seek de Lord, but doan seek Him right, come down, sinner, yo' none too late." See Come down, sinner

"**Some** talk of Alexander." See The British grenadiers

"**Some** tell us that women are delicate things." See Jerry's song (Reinagle)

"**Some** think the world is made for fun and frolic." See Funiculi, funicula (Denza)

Some valiant soldier. Negro spiritual from South Carolina. AS
Variant: Hail Mary

"**Some** were waving hats and some were waving caps." See The Golden Vanity (Hot Springs, N.C. version no. 2)

Somebody ("Somebody's tall and handsome") Old American song. SBA

"**Somebody** got lost in de storm." Negro spiritual. FSN

Somebody loves me. H. Starr (music and words) GFS—OTG

Somebody's child. A. Plimpton. Words by W. F. Vandervell. SW

"**Somebody's** eyes are my only light." See Somebody loves me (Starr)

Somebody's grandpa. C. F. Wood (music and words) SRW

Somebody's knocking at your door. Negro spiritual. HRD
Somebody knockin' at yo' door. WFN
Somebody's knockin' at your door. FSN—WSS

"**Somebody's** tall and handsome." See Somebody

Somebody's waiting for me. H. Von Tilzer. Words by A. B. Sterling. SMG

"**Somebody's** wrong about dis Bible." Negro spiritual. HB

Somerset, Lord Henry
Dawn
A song of sleep

Somerset carol ("Come all you worthy gentlemen") See "Come all you worthy gentlemen that may be standing by"

Somerset wassail ("Wassail, and wassail") See "Wassail, and wassail, all over the town"

Somersetshire wassail ("Wassail! wassail! all round the town") (see Song Index)
Variants: "Here we come a-wassailing"; "Wassail, and wassail, all over the town"; and songs of similar title

"Something happened the other day." See Shovellin' iron ore

"Something makes me now to laugh." See La cucaracha

"Sometimes I feel discouraged, and think my work's in vain." See Balm in Gilead

"Sometimes I feel discouraged, I think my work in vain." See Weary traveler (Arr by Handy)

"Sometimes I feel like a motherless child." Negro spiritual. FSN—HRD—JB 2—WSS

"Sometimes I feel like a motherless chile." WFN
Variant: "Sometimes I feel like I wanna go home"

"Sometimes I feel like I wanna go home." Negro spiritual from Kentucky. FSN
Variant of: "Sometimes I feel like a motherless child"

"Sometimes I'm up, sometimes I'm down." See Nobody knows the trouble I see

"Sometimes in the hush of the evening hour." See O little mother of mine (Nevin)

Somewhere ("Somewhere the wind is blowing") F. Campana. Words by A. C. Shaw. MFS

Somewhere ("'Twas years ago when last we parted") T. C. Clark (music and words) BST ·

Somewhere around a throne. Negro spiritual. WFN

Somewhere in this land of ours. See Those pals of ours (Greaton-Cole)

"Somewhere the wind is blowing." See Somewhere (Campana)

Somewhere, where sweeter flow'rs are springing. See Somewhere (Clark)

Sommer, W.
Vagans scholasticus

"Sommer kommt, die rosen glühn." See "Sumer is icumen in" (John of Fornsete?)

"Sommerlaub und Falbe und Rotrück und Schwalbe." See Huldre lokk

[Sommerlied] In praise of May. [Neidhardt von Reuenthal] e. MFF

"Sommerlöv og Sale, og Branderyg og Svale." See Huldre lokk

Die sommernacht. C. W. Gluck. Words by F. G. Klopstock. g. EDL

Sommers, Frederick S.
"Love divine! all love excelling"

"Sommers arbeit ist beendet." See Hjemreise fra saetren

"Son leggero e ver d'amore." Donizetti. e.i. PC

Son of a gambolier. College song. SBA—SRW

A son of a musketeer. Song from the 7th New York regiment. Air: A son of a gambolier. Words by G. O. Draper. DSO

"The Son of God goes forth to war" (Church militant.—All saints) H. S. Cutler. Words by R. Heber. MFS

"A song for our banner." See The flag of our union forever (Wallace)

"A song for the oak." See The brave old oak (Loder)

A song of Alsace. See Chanson d'Alsace

Song of exile. See Chant d'exil (Vidal)

[Song of Fionnuala] "Silent, oh Moyle, be the roar of thy water." Irish air: Arah, my dear Eveleen. Words by T. Moore. HMI

Song of freedom. See Vaterlandslied (Methfessel)

Song of glorification. See The song of praise

Song of hope. [H. A. Russotto] Words by S. Rowe. TFG

Song of Hybrias the Cretan. J. W. Elliott. SFB

A song of India. N. Rimsky-Korsakow. e. ATS

Song of joy, song of cheer. See Dream song (Jakobowski)

Song of Lorraine. See Les trois capitaines

A song of night ("Now night's dark shades appear") German song. e. MFS

[Song of O'Ruark, Prince of Breffni] "The valley lay smiling before me." Air: Colleen dhas cruthen na moe, or, The pretty girl milking her cow. Words by T. Moore. HMI—SI

Song of parting ("Sweet songs our voices blending") Graduation day song. F. Abt. MFS

[The song of praise ("Glory now and forever to God")] Slava (Lobgesang) Russian folk song. g.r. ML 1
"Praise to God" (Slava bogu na nebye) e. OB
Song of glorification. e. NRF

The song of Ringgold's artillery. See Fire away

A song of seasons. Hungarian air. Words by L. d'O. Warner. DSB

A song of sleep. H. Somerset (music and words) SFB

[The song of Solomon] Song of the Hebrew maiden. M. P. Musorgsky. Words by L. Mey. e.f. ATS

The song of songs ("Come, let us sing the song of songs") M. W. Balfe. TSS 2

Song of spring ("Und ein duften zieht über die erdenwelt") See Frühlingslied (Fielitz)

The song of Texas ("I fear no haughty nation") Patriotic song of 1845. Air: Lucy Neal. DSO

The song of the blind beggar (Slepačka pesma) Yugoslav folk song. e.se. CJ

A song of the Chalutsim (Shir ha-Chalutsim) Palestinean folk song. e.he. BNP

Song of the crib. See "Joseph lieber, Joseph mein"

The song of the cudgel. See The little cudgel

Song of the drum. E. Audran. e. WLO

Song of the exile. See Cân yr alltud

The song of the fishes. Sea song. US Variant of: Blow the man down ("Oh a ship she was fitted out ready for sea")

Song of the forge. Serbian folk air. Words by H. Snow. TFB

The **song** of the frog. S. C. Foster. Words by W. Perkins. TFR

The **song** of the good little men. Irish folk song. MFF

Song of the haulers on the Volga. See Volga boat song

Song of the Hebrew maiden. See The song of Solomon (Musorgskiĭ)

₍**Song** of the little bird₎ "Ich gei arois" (A lied fun ¹a feigale) Jewish folk song. y. KAJ

Song of the Memphis volunteers. Song of the Mexican war. Air: Lucy Neal. DSO

The **song** of the mermaid. German air. Words by K. Davis. DSB

A **song** of the moon ("A las dos de la mañana") See Canción de la luna

Song of the Moors. C. Lecocq. ₍Tr of Plus brillants que des météores₎ e. WLO

A **song** of the night: I ("Über allen") See Wand'rers nachtlied: I (Loewe)

A **song** of the night: II ("Der du von dem himmel bist") See Wand'rers nachtlied: II (Loewe)

Song of the nuns of Chester. See "Qui creavit coelum, lully, lully, lu"

Song of the officers' torpedo class. U.S. navy song of the World war. Air: Famous king of England. US

The **song** of the pancakes. See La chanson des beignets

Song of the ship. See "There comes a galley, laden"

Song of the silly horseman. F. Lehar. e. WLO

Song of the spirit. Old Dutch air. OB

The **song** of the Triton. J. L. Molloy. Words by F. C. Burnand. TFG

Song of the Volga boatmen. See Volga boat song

Song of the watch. See Past three o'clock, and a cold frosty morning

Song of the western men. Old Cornish song. Words by R. S. Hawker. MBS

Trelawny. LAS

₍**Song** of the western men₎ And shall Trelawny die. G. Slater. Words by R. S. Hawker. CSB 3

Song of Troy. University of Southern California song. C. Kisco and R. J. Freed. HW—KU

Song to Minnehaha. See Hiawatha (Daniels)

"A **song** to thee, fair state of mine." See Michigan, my Michigan (Miessner)

"A **song** we're gladly raising." See Give a cheer (Weber)

The **songs** my mammy sang to me. Medley arr by J. W. Kelly. SMG

"**Songs** my mother taught me." A. Dvořák. e. TFP

The **songs** our fathers loved. See The songs your fathers loved

"**Songs**, revealing sacred feeling." See Gebet (Weber)

₍The **songs** your fathers loved₎ The songs our fathers loved. Irish air: The lament of Gerald. Words by F. Hemans. LAS

"**Sonne**, strahlst so ungleich ʼauf uns nieder." See "O bright sun"

"Die **sonne** strahlt in das alte heimattal." See My old Kentucky home (Foster)

"**Sonne** taucht in meeresfluthen." See Dein gedenk' ich, Margareta (Meyer-Helmund)

"**Sonne** wandert auf und nieder." See Der gefangene

Sonnenaufgang. See Codiad yr haul

₍"**Sönner** ʼaf Norge"₎ "Sons of dear Norway." C. Blom. ₍Words by H. A. Bjerregaard₎ e. LAS

Sonnet d'amour (A love-sonnet) F. Thomé. Words by A. de Saineville. e.f. TM

Sonntag ("So hab' ich doche die ganze."— Sunday) J. Brahms. Words by L. Uhland. e.g. SAT

"**Sonntag** morgens, als ich aufstand." See Ann hollaika

Sonntagslied ("Ringsum erschallt in wald und flur") Mendelssohn. Words by C. Klingemann. g. EDL

"**Sons** of dear Norway." See "Sönner af Norge" (Blom)

"**Sons** of Georgetown." Georgetown university song. ⟨Welsh air: March of the Men of Harlech. Words by R. J. Collier⟩ AI—AIS—KU—KV

"**Sons** of Ireland." Old song. SI

The **sons** of liberty. Folk song: Hindman, Ky. version. SES 2
—Pineville, Ky. version. SES 2

"**Sons** of men, behold." Thibaut. Words by C. Wesley. MFS

"**Sons** of old Grinnell." Grinnell college song. J. N. Hall (music and words) AIS

"The **sons** of the Prophet are brave men and bold." See Abdul Abulbul Amir

"The **sons** of the Prophet are hardy and bold." See Abdul, the Bulbul Ameer

"**Sons** of the red and blue." See Fight on for old St Mary's (Stevens)

"**Soon** as we may, off and away." Finale from Iolanthe. A. S. Sullivan. Words by W. S. Gilbert. DSC

"**Soon** ez we-all cook swee' petatehs." See Sweet potatoes

Soon I will be done. Negro spiritual. HRD

"**Soon** night will pass." See Morgenhymne (Henschel)

Soon, oh, soon, I will be sleeping. See "Mary, darling, must you leave me"

Sorgete: in sì bel giorno. See Duce di tanti eroi (Rossini)

Die **sorglose.** See Felicella

"**Sosenushka** ty zelënafâ." See Kalīnka

I **sospiri** (Ritornello.—Die seufzer) Neapolitan folk song. g.i. ML 2

"Sotto il paterno tetto." Verdi. e.i. PC

Souls of flowers. See L'âme des fleurs (Massenet)

"A sound as of tiniest violins." See Titania (Peterson-Berger)

"A sound of music fills my mind." See Ein ton (Cornelius)

"Sound our voices long and sweet." Bohemian air. MFS

"Sound, sound your instruments of joy." West of England carol. DNS

"Sound the flute! now 'tis mute." See Spring

"Sound the loud timbrel." C. Avison. ₁Words by T. Moore₁ BB

Sound your A. W. B. Bradbury. Words by W. J. Wetmore. MFS

Soup song. See "Today is Monday"

"Soupy, soupy, soupy, without a single bean." See Mess call

Sourwood mountain. Folk song: Georgia version. RA—SES 2
—Berea, Ky. version. SES 2
—Lexington, Ky. version. SBA
—Manchester, Ky. version. SES 2
Variant: "I got a gal at the head of the holler"

"Sous le soleil, qui les irise." See Sonnet d'amour (Thomé)

"South Carolina's a sultry clime." See So early in the morning

"South Dakota! how dear to thy children thy name." See Pioneer song (Colton)

"South Dakota, land of empire." See Field song (Woodworth)

"A southerly wind and a cloudy sky" (The huntsmen) Round. Old English words. BB

The southern girl. H. Macarthy. HP

Southern memories. Plantation songs <arranged> TFB—TFG—TFO—TFR

A southern refrain. See Long time ago (Horn)

"Southern wind blowing on silver streams flowing." See Lovely May is coming

Southey, G. W.
The red scarf (Bonheur)

"Southward now fair summer goes." See The flight of summer

Southwell, Robert
New Prince, new pomp (Ireland)

"Sover du, min sjael" ("Sleepest thou, my soul") E. Sjögren. e.n. WM 2

"Soviel stern' am himmel stehen." See Treue liebe

Sowinski, Wojciech
Polish national song (attributed) See Ogiński, M. K. Polish national song

₁"Sown with millet was my garden"₁ "Siałem proso na zagonie" ("Hab gesät auf meinem felde") Folk song from Little Russia. g.p. ML 3

"The spacious firmament on high." J. Haydn. Words by J. Addison. DSB—TFP

"The spacious firmament on high" (Creation) BB

₁The Spanish Armada₁ "In 'eighty-eight, ere I was born" (Sir Francis Drake) Chantey. <Air: Hanskin, or, Jog on the footpath way, or, Eighty eight> BOS 2

Spanish carol. See Panxoliña de nadal

The Spanish cavalier. W. D. Hendrickson (music and words) BB—DFF—WSS

The Spanish cavalier and Solomon Levi, arranged. See A vocal encounter

Spanish ladies. See "Farewell and adieu to you, Spanish ladies"

Sparking on a Sunday night. Old American song. SW

"Sparkling and bright, in its liquid light, is the water in our glasses." Temperance song. ₁J. B. Taylor. Author of words unknown₁ MFS

Sparkling Piper Heidsieck. See Give me the waltz (Pratt)

Spaulding, Hector, pseud. See Loomis, Harvey Worthington

"Speak again, love." See Pur dicesti, o bocca bella (Lotti)

"Speak gently—it is better far." W. V. Wallace. Words by D. Bates. MFS

Speak to me. F. Campana. <Words by H. B. Farnie> GE

"Speak to me, my own beloved." Welsh folk song. e. TFB

Spee, Friedrich von
"In stiller nacht zur ersten wacht" (Brahms)

"Speed away! speed away." I. B. Woodbury (music and words) GOS 1—MFS—TFG

Speed, bonnie boat, like a bird on the wing. See Skye boat song

"Speed our republic." See The American hymn (Keller)

"Speed up." C. H. Fairfax. Words by E. Battell. TFG

"The spell is past, the dream is o'er." See We never speak as we pass by

Spencer, William Robert
Wife, children, and friends (Old air)

"The spendthrift spring." F. Schubert. Words by A. G. Latham. CSB 5

Sperai, tanto il delirio accecato m'aveva. For English translation see I hoped, in my passion (Leoncavallo)

"Sperate, o figli." See D'Egitto là sui lidi (Verdi)

Sperry, Henrietta
Oh! fairest alma mater (Sleeper)

"Spī bŕedniaga spī rodnoĭ." See Wiegenlied (Russian folk song)

The spider and the fly ("Will you come into my parlor") Round. W. G. McNaught. Old words adapted. TFG—TFR

The spider and the fly ("Will you walk into my parlor") ₁Old English air: Will you come to the bower. Old words by T. Hudson₁ MFS

The spider and the spout. College song. <Air: Son of a gambolier> BB

"Spied a boy a rosebud rare." See Heidenröslein (Schubert)

"Spiel nur, o spiel." See "Play, only play on"

Spilman, James E.
Afton water
Carolina coronata (same air as Afton water)
"Flow gently, sweet Afton." See Afton water
A health to Carolina. See Carolina coronata

"Spin, maiden, spin, the golden thread twine in." T. Fischer. Words by D. Harvey. TFO

Spin, spin. TFP

Spin, spin ("Mägdlein hielt tag und nacht") See Spinn! spinn (Jüngst)

Spin, spin ("Spin, maiden, spin") See "Spin, maiden, spin, the golden thread twirl in" (Fischer)

[Spinn! spinn] Spin, spin. H. Jüngst. e. TFB

"Spinn, spinn, meine liebe tochter." See Die spinnerin (Volkslied)

Die **spinnerin** ("Un pobre pagés teniauna filla") See La filadora

Die **spinnerin** ("Spinn, spinn, meine liebe tochter") Volkslied. g. EDL

Spinning Jenny. See La filatrice (Mozart)

Spinning song ("Here we sit a-spinning, spinning") Cashmere folk air. Words by K. Davis. DSB

Spinning-top. Russian folk dance. e. SR

The **spinning-wheel** ("As I sat at my spinning wheel") Scottish song. GS

The **spinster's** lament (see Song Index) Variant of: The old maid's song

The **spirit** ("Winds of God unfailing") Angevin air: Courons à la fête. Words by G. Dearmer. OB

Spirit of Gettysburg (Bullet song) Gettysburg college song. B. H. Saltzer. Words by R. Fortenbaugh. AI—AIS

Spirit of Maine. University of Maine song. H. D. O'Neil (music and words) AIS

The **spirit** of the hill. University of Tennessee song. S. Gobble (music and words) KU

The **spirit's** song. See Des geistes gesang (Haydn)

"The **splendor** falls on castle walls." See Blow, bugle, blow (Hatton)

The **splendour** ("Behold what splendour") West of England carol. DNS

Splittegarb, Karl Friedrich
Die weihnachtsfreude (Volksweise)

Spohr, Ludwig
"Immortal by their deed and word"
"Proudly as the eagle"
Spohr. See "Immortal by their deed and word"
"Va sbramando quegli ardori" (from Faust)

Sporle, Nathan James
At evening-time
Boatman's return
The star of Glengary

"Sprach der könig vor dem heer." See Ymdawiad y brenin

Sprague, Carolina Louisa. See Smith, Mrs Carolina Louisa (Sprague)

Spring ("Sound the flute") Russian air. Words by W. Blake. DSB

Spring ("Spring goeth all in white") W. G. Whittaker. Words by R. Bridges. CSB 1

The **spring** ("The spring is come") Round. Hayes. BB

Spring ("The sweet spring is the year's pleasant king") Irish air. Words by T. Nash. GSS

Spring ("Wenn der frühling auf die berge steigt") See "Wenn der frühling auf die berge steigt" (Becker)

Spring ("Who is she who cometh") French air. Words by K. Davis. DSB

Spring, gentle spring. J. Riviere. Words by J. R. Planché. MFS

"**Spring** goeth all in white." See Spring (Whittaker)

"The **spring** had come, the flow'rs in bloom." See Little Maggie May (Blamphin)

Spring has come ("Now the spring has come again") See In vernali tempore

"The **spring** has come, the flow'rs in bloom." See Little Maggie May (Blamphin)

"**Spring** has now unwrapped the flowers." See Tempus adest floridum

"The **spring** is come, I hear the birds." See The spring (Hayes)

The **spring** is waning fast, my love. See When the bloom is on the rye (Bishop)

"**Spring** like a maiden comes over the hill." See A spring song (German air)

Spring morning. See Volksliedchen (Schumann)

"**Spring** once said to the nightingale." See The birdies' ball (Winner)

Spring reverie. See Pensée de printemps (Leroux)

A **spring** rhapsody. See Rapsodia primaverile (Leoncavallo)

Spring song ("Durch den wald den dunkeln") See Frühlingslied (Mendelssohn)

A **spring** song ("I sat beneath the maples old") C. Pinsuti. MFS

Spring song ("May is here") See Polish May song

A **spring** song ("See the yellow catkins cover") F. Bridge. Words by M. Howitt. CSB 2

Spring song ("Snow on the earth") A. C. Mackenzie. [Words by A. P. Graves] HCA

A **spring** song ("Spring like a maiden") German air. Words by K. Davis. DSB

Spring song ("Were I a sunbeam") See The maiden's wish (Chopin)

"**Spring!** spring! gentle spring." See Spring, gentle spring (Riviere)

Spring-time. For entries beginning Spring-time see Springtime

Springfield mountain. Folk song: Callaway, Va. version. SES 2
—Peaks of Otter, Va. version. SES 2
Spring's blessing. See Frühlingssegen (Brückler)
[Spring's message] The cuckoo. German song. e. BB
Spring's return. See Renouveau
Springtide sweetheart. See Frühling liebster (Scholz)
Spring-time once again. A. S. Sullivan. Words by J. Logan. MFS
Die spröde (Nuori neito) Finnish folk song. fi.g. ML 3
Squilli echeggi la tromba guerriera. For English translation see "Now let the trumpet" (Verdi)
"The squire come home late in the night." See The gypsy laddie (Burnsville, N.C. version)
"The squire he came home at night." See The gypsy laddie (Rocky Fork, Tenn. version no. 1)
"The squirlie 'tis a pretty thing." See Bile 'em cabbage down
The squirrel. Folk song: Kentucky version. SES 2
—Callaway, Va. version. SES 2
—Endicott, Va. version. SES 2
Variant: Bile 'em cabbage down
"The squirrel is a pretty little thing." See The squirrel (Callaway, Va. version)
"The squirrel is a pretty thing." See The squirrel (Kentucky version)
"Srečno, srečno, ljub'ca moja." See Nun ade, mein herzliebchen
St' agioy Thodōrhoy to boyno. See Am St Theodorsberg
Stable call. U.S. army bugle call. DSO
"The stairway downward sweeping." See Niemand hat's geseh'n (Loewe)
"Stała się nam novina." See "Hört die neue kunde an" (1st air); "Hört die neue kunde an" (2d air)
Stan' by me. Negro spiritual. FSN
Stand back, villain, go your way. See Heaven will protect the working girl (Sloane)
Stand by me. See Stan' by me
"Stand ein baum in lenzblüte" ("Stoi jawor zielony") Polish folk song. g.p. ML 3
"Stand ein birkenbaum in dem felde." See The birch in the meadow
"Stand ein mandelbaum" ("Raslo drvo bademovo") Serbian folk song. g.se. ML 2
Stand fast! Chicago will win. See Flag of maroon (Richberg)
"Stand navy down the field." See Anchor's aweigh (Zimmerman)
Stand to your ground. Negro halliard chantey. WSE
Hilo, John Brown. TSB 2
"Stand up and cheer." University of Kansas song. KU
"Stand up! stand up! attention." See The mountain battery
Ständchen ("Der den himmel."—Serenade) J. Raff. e.g. GG

Ständchen [("Gut' nacht, gut' nacht, mein liebster schatz"] ("Good night, my dearest love."—Serenade) J. Brahms. e. CSB 2
Ständchen ("Leise flehen meine lieder."—Serenade) F. Schubert. Words by L. Rellstab. e.g. GG
Schubert's serenade. e. BB
Serenade. e. TFB
Ständchen ("Mach' auf, mach' auf."—Serenade) R. Strauss. Words by A. F. von Schack. e.g. GG
Standin'. For entries beginning Standin' see Standing
"Standing by the mizen mast." See "Sulla poppa del mio brick" (Ricci)
Standin' in the need of prayer. See It's me, O Lord
"Standing on the platform." See Eliza Jane (Hyden, Ky. version)
Standin' on the walls of Zion. Mountain spiritual. SBA
"Standing where the bleak winds whistled." See Little barefoot
Stanford, Sir Charles Villiers
Answer to a child's question
"My love's an arbutus": Irish air arranged
The winter storms
Stange, Max
Die bekehrte
Damon. See Die bekehrte
Stanley, Thornton, pseud. See Stevens, David
Stanton, Frank Lebby
Constancy (Webber)
Stanton, W. H.
"Because I love you, dear" (Hawley)
"Star-beams light the countryside." Bohemian carol air. Words by C. B. Fenno. FC
Star-eyes. See Stjärnöga (Rangström)
The star of Bethlehem ("It was the eve of Christmas") S. Adams. Words by F. E. Weatherly. CSS 1
The star of Glengary. N. J. Sporle. Words by E. Cook. GOS 2—TFB
"Star of my heart, my love thou art." See "Caro mio ben" (Giordani)
Star of the evening. See "Beautiful star in heaven so bright" (Sayles)
"A star, radiantly bright." See Ô bienheureuse nuit
The star-spangled banner ("O say, can you see by the dawn's early light") National song of the United States. Attributed to J. S. Smith; wrongly attributed to S. Arnold. Words by F. S. Key. BB—DFF—DSB—DSC—DSO—GOS 1—GSS—LAS—MBS—MFS—TFP—TFR—US
"Star vicino" ("Golden sunlight."—Canzonetta.—Only smile) Salvator Rosa. e.i. SAT
Starlight carol. Czechoslovak folk song. e. MFF
"The starlight was beaming on all the land." See Abschied (Franz)
Starnes, Percy
Mine only, mine alone

Starr, Mrs Belle (Shirley)
"My love is a rider"
Starr, Hattie
Little Alabama coon
Somebody loves me
"De **starry** crown in de heaven all round."
See Give up the world
Starry night for a ramble. Old American song. SW
The **stars** ("All the golden stars are glowing") French air. Words by K. Davis. DSB
"The **stars** are burning cheerily, cheerily." See Turn ye to me
Stars begin to fall. Negro spiritual from South Carolina. AS
Stars in the elements. Negro song. HRD
"**Stars** of the summer night." I. B. Woodbury. Words by H. W. Longfellow. BB—GSS—TFB—TFO—TFP—TFR
The **stars** shall light your journey. See The band of children
"**Stars** trembling o'er us." Words by D. M. Muloch. MFS
"**State** college of Iowa." Iowa state college song. Irish air: My lodging is in the cold ground. Words by E. N. Wentworth. AI—AIS—KU
"**State** of Maine Augusta on the Kennebec river." See Geography
The **Stately** Southerner. Forecastle song. SBS
Stay in de field. Negro song. HRD
"**Stay** in town." W. G. Whittaker. Words by Julian Antecessor, from the Greek anthology. e. CSB 2
"**Stay**, ladybird." See Marienwürmchen (Schumann)
"**Stay**, oh, stay, safe in thy dreamland kingdom." See Dröm (Sjögren)
"**Stay**, stay, don't be angry." See We girls never mean half we say (Brewster)
Stcherbine, N. See Shcherbin, N.
Steadfast love. See Obstination (Fontenailles)
Steadman, C. M.
At evening-time (Sporle)
Steal away to Jesus. Negro spiritual. HRD
Steal away. BB—FSN—MFS—TFB—TFO—TFP—WFN—WSS
Steamboat song ("Oh, captain! where are you boun' for") Negro work song. FSN
Stebbins, Mrs Mary Elizabeth (Moore) Hewitt. See Hewitt, Mrs Mary Elizabeth (Moore)
Das **steckenpferd** ("Hopp, hopp, hopp") C. G. Hering. Words by C. Hahn. g. EDL
Hobby-horse. e. MFS
Hop, hop, hop. e. BB
Steel, Sanger Bright. See Williams, Raymond George, jt. comp. and auth.
Steele, Anne
"Oh, could our thoughts" (German air)

Steele, Clarence T.
"Happy birds" (Holst)
Steele, Porter. See Hooker, Brian, jt. comp. and auth.
Steele, S. S.

Composer and author
Gum-tree canoe. See Tom-big-bee river
Tom-big-bee river

Author
The rose of Alabama (Composer unknown)
"**Steersman**, leave the watch." Sailor's chorus. R. Wagner. [Tr of Steuermann! lass die wacht] e. TFB
Steffe, William
The battle hymn of the republic (same air as "John Brown's body": plantation air arranged)
"John Brown's body": plantation air arranged
Keep them rolling (same air as "John Brown's body": plantation air arranged)
A laugh provoker (same air as "John Brown's body": plantation air arranged)
The world is marching on (same air as "John Brown's body": plantation air arranged)
"**Steh**' ich in finstrer mitternacht" (Treue liebe) Volksweise: Ich hab ein kleines hüttchen nur. Words by W. Hauff. g. EDL
"**Stell**' auf den tisch die duftenden reseden." See Allerseelen (Lassen); Allerseelen (Strauss)
Stelljes, George
Maroon victory
Stenhammar, Vilhelm
At sunset. See När sol går ner
"Ein fichtenbaum steht einsam"
"Flickan knyter"
När sol går ner
"On Saint John's eve." See "Flickan knyter"
"A pine-tree standeth lonely." See "Ein fichtenbaum steht einsam"
"Sie liebten sich beide"
"They loved one another." See "Sie liebten sich beide"
Sten'ka Razīn (Stjenjka Rasin und die fürstin) Russian folk song. g.r. ML 1
"**Stenka** Rasin." e. LSB
Stephenson, Benjamin Charles
Let me dream again (Sullivan)
"**Stepped** up on the railroad." See Eliza Jane (Pineville, Ky. version)
"**Sterben** muss ich" ("Umrem, umrem") Slovak folk song. g.sl. ML 3
Sterling, Andrew B.
Alexander (Von Tilzer)
Meet me in St Louis, Louis (Mills)
"Rufus, Rastus, Johnson Brown" (Von Tilzer)
Somebody's waiting for me (Von Tilzer)

Sterling, Andrew B.—*Continued*
Wait 'till the sun shines, Nellie (Von Tilzer)
You'll get all that's coming to you (Von Tilzer)
Sterling, Elizabeth. See Stirling, Elizabeth
Sterling, George
Abalone (Composer unknown)
Stern, Joseph W.
If Jack were only here. See My mother was a lady
The little lost child
My mother was a lady
"**Stern, du heller stern.**" See Despo
Stets soll nur dir. For English translation see Ever I'll praise thee (Wagner)
Steuermann! lass die wacht. For English translation see "Steersman, leave the watch" (Wagner)
Stevens, Mrs Cordelia Brooks (Fenno) See Fenno, Cordelia Brooks
Stevens, David

Composer

"Christmas-time has come again, time to us so dear"
He found it
"O little town of Bethlehem"
Overwork
Peace be with all
Ring on, Christmas bells. See "Christmas-time has come again, time to us so dear"

Composer and author

Carmelina
A toast

Author

Alma mater—University of New Mexico (Thompson)
The Arkansaw traveler (Old air)
The bold fisherman (Greely)
The cautious cat (Tracy)
Cherry blossoms (Hadley)
"Christ the Lord is born today, alleluia! alleluia! Sons of men and angels say" (French air)
The climate (Old air)
Eyes of blue (Slovakian folk air)
Get away from dis co'nfiel' (American air)
"Glory to Him" (Rachmaninov)
"Good morning! good morning! and here is come another day" (Johnstone)
Harvest home (Old air)
Heigho (Repper)
The Highland fling (Scottish air)
The host and his guests (Old English air)
Jack and Jean (Scottish air)
The last mile (Danish folk air)
Lazy song (Old air)
Levee song (American air)
"March on! Liberty's host" (Verdi)
The mocking bird (Winner)
Never mind (Chinese air)
O star, lovely star (Old French air)
Old Zip Coon (Old American air)

Poetry (Sullivan)
Ring the bells (Folk air)
Second thoughts (Loomis)
The smith (Mascagni)
Song of hope (Russotto)
Song of the forge (Serbian folk air)
The song of the frog (Foster)
To a rose (Coerne)
Tramp, tramp, tramp (Root)
The wearing of the green (Old Irish air)
"Where is John" (Smetana)
Where is spring (Repper)
The year of jubilo (Work)
See also entries in Song Index under pseuds. Ames, Francis; Fay, Stephen; Hastings, Paul; Horne, Abel; Paul, Stuart; Perkins, Wilton; Rowe, Sidney; Snow, Henry; Stanley, Thornton; as well as under real name
Stevens, Junius Wood
Alma mater — Syracuse university (Thompson)
Stevens, Richard John Samuel
"Blow, blow, thou winter wind"
Shakespeare's carol. See "Blow, blow, thou winter wind"
Stevens, Robert W.
The cornhusker
U of Colorado
Stevens, Will
Alma mater—St Mary's college
Fight on for old St Mary's
Stevenson, Sir John Andrew
"Believe me, if all those endearing young charms": Irish air arranged
"Has sorrow thy young days shaded": Irish air arranged
"Oft in the stilly night" (attributed)
Those endearing young charms. See "Believe me, if all those endearing young charms": Irish air arranged
Stevenson, Robert John
"Yoh Washington"
Stevenson, Robert Louis
"The stormy evening" (Chadwick)
The swing (Judd)
Stewart, Alexander
Màiri bhòidheach (Hebridean air)
Stewart, Charles E.
Ella Ree (Porter)
Stewart, James E.
Angel Gabriel
I want to see the old home
Jennie, the flower of Kildare
"Only to see her face again"
Stick to it, boys. See Victory (Waite)
Stieler, Karl
Heimliche grüsse (Fielitz)
Stier, Walter Crittenden
Alma mater—Lafayette college. See In front of old Pardee
In front of old Pardee
"Way down in Easton"
"**Still** as the night." See "Still wie die nacht, tief wie das meer, soll deine liebe sein" (Bohm)
"**Still** for sinners interceding." Haydn.
e, SSO 3

Still growing.   Folk song from Kentucky.   SES 1
    Variant of: "The trees they do grow high" (English folk song)
"**Still**, how still the midnight's gloom." See Strämpelchen (Hildach)
"**Still** smile, my dear."   See Smile, my Kathleen, pray
"**Still**, still with Thee."   E. Moss. Words by H. B. Stowe.   BB
"**Still** träufelt milder tau hernieder" ("Ach, prší, prší rosička")   Czech folk song. bo.g.   ML 3
"**Still** wie die nacht, tief wie das meer, soll deine liebe sein" ("Still as the night")   C. Bohm.   e.g.   GG
"Calm as the night."   e.   BB—TFP
"**Still**, wie still! 's ist mitternacht schon." See Strämpelchen (Hildach)
"**Stille** nacht."   See Die heilige nacht (Gruber)
Stille sicherheit (Silent safety)   R. Franz.   Words by N. Lenau.   e.g. TM
"Die **stille** wasserrose" ("The silent waterlily")   A. von Fielitz.   Words by E. Geibel.   e.g.   TM
"**Stimmt** an mit hellem hohen klang."   See Deutsches weihelied (Methfessel)
Stingaree blues.   A down home blues. C. A. Kemp (music and words)   HB
Stirling, Elizabeth
    All among the barley
Stirling-Maxwell, Caroline Elizabeth Sarah (Sheridan) Norton, lady.   See Norton, Mrs Caroline Elizabeth Sarah (Sheridan)
"**Stitch** no longer, mother dear."   See The scarlet sarafan (Varlamov)
Stites, E. P.
    Beulah land (Sweney)   Authorship uncertain
Stjärnöga (Star-eyes)   T. Rangström. Words by B. Bergman.   e.sw.   WM 2
Stjenjka Rasin und die fürstin. See Sten'ka Razin
Stoddard, I. T.
    "New England, New England"
"**Stoi** jawor zielony."   See "Stand ein baum in lenzblüte"
Stone, Alfred
    "Proudly as the eagle" (Spohr)
Stonehill, Maurice J.
    Just plain folks
Stoner, Philip
    The Broadway, opera and Bowery crawl (Operti)
Stonewall Jackson's way.   Words attributed to J. W. Palmer.   DSO
Stop that knocking at my door.   Negro song.   <A. F. Winnemore (music and words)>   WSS
    Stop dat knocking at my door.   PSG
Stoppe, Daniel
    Glück (Telemann)
Storace, Stephen
    The pretty creature
    "A sailor loved a lass"

Storch, Anton M.
    Greeting at night.   See Nächtlicher gruss
    Nächtlicher gruss
Storm, Edvard
    Hjemreise fra saetren (Norse folk air)
    Skogmöte has thorgjer skjelle (Norse air)
Storm, Theodor
    Bettler-liebe (Bungert)
Stormalong ("O Stormy, he is dead and gone")   Capstan chantey.   BOS 2 —WSE
    For variants see following songs of same or similar title
Stormalong ("Oh, Stormy he is dead and gone")   Halliard chantey.   TSB 2
Stormalong ("Stormey's dead that good old man")   Pumping and capstan chantey. SBS
Stormalong ("Stormie's gone, the good old man")   Chantey.   US
Stormalong John ("Oh, poor old Stormy's dead and gone")   Windlass and capstan chantey.   TSB 1
"**Stormey's** dead that good old man."   See Stormalong
"**Stormie's** gone, the good old man."   See Stormalong
"The **stormy** evening."   G. W. Chadwick. Words by R. L. Stevenson.   TFB
"**Stormy** the night and the waves roll high." See Asleep in the deep (Petrie)
The **stormy** winds do blow, blow, blow. See The mermaid (Kentucky version)
Story, William Wetmore
    "I am weary with rowing" (Boott)
"A **story** I will tell to you, it is of butchers three."   See The three butchers (Sussex version)
"A **story** I'm going to tell of a mother old and gray."   See I'll be home tomorrow night (Howard)
"A **story** to you I'll tell of little Omie Wise."   See Poor Omie (Burnsville, N.C. version no. 1)
"**Stosst** an! (Jena) soll leben."   A. von Binzer (music and words)   g.   EDL
Stowe, Mrs Harriet Elizabeth (Beecher)
    "Still, still with thee" (Moss)
Stradella, Alessandro
    "Righteous art Thou, O Lord" (from San Giovanni Battista)
Straight-out Democrat.   American political song of 1872.   Air: Rosin, the beau.   SRW
Strampedemi! ala mi presente.   See Lied der landsknechte
Strampelchen (Little fidget)   Cradle-song.   E. Hildach.   Words by V. Blüthgen.   e.g.   AT
The **stranger** star.   See "Saw ye never in the twilight"
"**Strap** your pack, to your back."   See Hike song (Metz)
Straus, Oskar
    "A beautiful maiden with heart so cold" (from Ein walzertraum)
    "The bridal ceremony's over" (from Ein walzertraum)

Straus, Oskar—*Continued*
Country lass and royal maid (from Ein walzertraum)
"Happy girls are we" (from Ein walzertraum)
Love duet (from Ein walzertraum)
Love's the tune (from Ein walzertraum)
"Softly, so softly, floating in air" (from Ein walzertraum)
That Viennese waltz (from Ein walzertraum)

Strauss, Johann
"Ah! nonsense 'tis" (from Der spitzentuch der königen)
Baden polka. See Love and mirth
"Bright as a ray" (from Der spitzentuch der königen)
It was a fair and starry night (from Der spitzentuch der königen)
Love and mirth
"Now the king we hail" (from Der spitzentuch der königen)
"Praise to the king" (from Der spitzentuch der königen)
"Seventeen years had just passed" (from Der spitzentuch der königen)
The truffle song (from Der spitzentuch der königen)
The wild rose (from Der spitzentuch der königen)

Strauss, Richard
All souls' day. See Allerseelen
Allerseelen
Die nacht
Night. See Die nacht
Serenade. See Ständchen
Ständchen

"The **strawberries** grow in the mowing." See Mill May
Strawberry fair. English folk song. DSB

Streabbog, L.
"Vive la Canadienne": old air arranged

Streeper, Caddie R.
U of U trail (Rich)

Street, Apsley, pseud. See Winner, Septimus

Street-boys' chorus. G. Bizet. ⌐Tr of Avec la garde montante⌐ e. WG

Street urchins' medley. Old songs arranged. BB

Strehlenau, Nicolaus Franz Niembsch, edler von. See Lenau, Nicolaus

"'**Stric** mi sealltuinn o'n chnoc a's àirde." See Fhir a bhàta

Strickland, Lily Teresa
Because of you

"**Stride** la vampa" ("Fierce now the flames glow") Verdi. e.i. PC

The **strife** is o'er: the battle done. Arr from Palestrina. ⌐Tr of Finita jam sunt praelia⌐ e. TFG

Strike for your rights! avenge your wrongs. Song of the Mexican war. Air: The rose of Alabama. DSO

"**Strike** the cymbal." Pucitta. MFS

Strilevise (Fischerlied) Norse folk song. g.n. ML 1

Strolling on the Brooklyn bridge. J. P. Skelly. Words by G. Cooper. SRW
Strolling through Norfolk. U.S. navy song. US

Stromberg, John
Come down ma evenin' star
My best girl's a New Yorker

"**Strong** Son of God, immortal Love" (Federal street) H. K. Oliver. Words by A. Tennyson. LAS

Struve, A.
Dawn of night (Nikolaev)

Stuart, Leslie
"Tell me, pretty maiden"

Stuart, Mrs Ruth (McEnery)
My Rose (Lacy)

Die **studenten** von Tolosa. See Los estudiants de Tolosa

Studentenleben ("'s gibt kein schöner leben") C. G. Reissiger. Author of words unknown. g. EDL

The **students'** song ("Oh! fill our glasses") J. Offenbach. ⌐Tr of Jusqu'au matin remplis⌐ e. WG

The **study** of woman. F. Lehar. e. WLO

"**Stúpil Dobrí.**" See The gray dove

"**Sturdy** sons of City college." See Lavender, my lavender (Johnson)

"**Stusle** sundagskvellen eingang för me va." See Skogmöte has thorgjer skjelle

Style all the while. Student song. BB
Aint got no style. University of Texas version. Quartet. AI

Su! del Nilo al sacro lido accorrete. For English translation see March of the victors (Verdi)

Su questa fronte il disonor stampò. See Nuova ferita (Mercadante)

"**Su,** su, come you not soon." See Cradle song

"**Su-su-su,** mein kind, schlaf ein." See Suantraidhe

Suantraidhe ("Seoithín, seó."—Wiegenlied) Old Irish folk song. g.ir. ML 1

"The **subject** of my little song." See Bitter beer

"**Sublime** was the warning that liberty spoke." Air: The black joke. Words by T. Moore. HMI

"**Such** a game, believe me, friends." R. Leoncavallo. ⌐Tr of Un tal gioco, credetemi⌐ e. WG

"**Such** dish by man not oft is seen." See The truffle song (Strauss)

Sucher, Josef
Joy unspoken. See Liebesglück
Liebesglück

Suckarna. See Suspiria (Sjögren)

Sucking cider through a straw. <C. Morgan. Words by L. David> SBA
Sipping cider thru a straw (Thipping thider thru a thtraw) OTG

The **sudden** cure. German folk air. Words by J. Landon. TFO

Suffer little children to come unto me. H. D. Hewitt. CSS 1

The **Suffolk** miracle.   Folk song: Allan-
    stand, N.C. version.   SES 1
—Big Laurel, N.C. version.   SES 1
—Tennessee version.   SES 1
—Callaway, Va. version.   SES 1
—Nellysford, Va. version.   SES 1
"**Sug** mir, du schein meidele."   Jewish
    folk song.   y.   KAJ
Sugar babe.   Folk song from Kentucky.
    SES 2
"**Šuhajko**, bijú mňa."   See "Ach lieb, sie
    schlagen mich"
"**Sulla** poppa del mio brick."   Ricci.   e.i.
    PB
"**Sullen** waves are moaning."   See A sea
    picture
Sullivan, Sir Arthur Seymour
    And God shall wipe away all tears.
        See "The Lord is risen, He will
        dwell with men"
    "And when he had spent all" (from
        The prodigal son)
    Calm was the night
    "Dance a cachucha, fandango, bolero"
        (from The gondoliers)
    God shall wipe away all tears from
        their eyes.   See "The Lord is
        risen, He will dwell with men"
    Hail! hail! the gang's all here (with
        usual words and with words "A
        gang of good fellows are we";
        "Oh, we're going to the Hamburg
        show")
    "Hail, poetry, thou heav'n-born maid."
        See Poetry
    Heaven is my home
    "How many hired servants" (from The
        prodigal son)
    "I will arise" (from The prodigal son)
    The judge's song (from Trial by jury)
    Let me dream again
    "Little maid of Arcadee"
    The long day closes
    Looking back
    "The Lord is risen, He will dwell with
        men" (from The light of the
        world)
    The lost chord
    "Love not the world" (from The prod-
        igal son)
    The magnet and the churn (from Pa-
        tience)
    "O hush thee, my babie" (Tr of Caidil
        gu lo)
    "O that thou had'st hearkened" (from
        The prodigal son)
    Once again ("I linger round")
    "Onward, Christian soldiers"
    Poetry (from The pirates of Penzance)
    Poetry (with words rewritten by
        Stevens)
    "Prithee, pretty maiden" (from Pa-
        tience)
    "Soon as we may, off and away" (from
        Iolanthe)
    Spring-time once again
    Tit-willow (from The mikado)
    What the deuce do we care.   See
        "Hail! hail! the gang's all here"
    "When Britain really rul'd the waves"
        (from Iolanthe)

Sullivan, Joseph J.
    Where did you get that hat
Sullivan, Mrs Marion D.
    The blue Juniata
Sully-Prudhomme, René François Armand
    Les berceaux (Faure)
"**Sumer** is icumen in" ("Summer is a-com-
    ing in")   Attributed to John of
    Fornsete.   BOS 2—MBS—TFG
"Sumer is a cumen in" ("Summer is a
    coming in")   DSB—GSS
"Summer is a coming in" ("Sommer
    kommt, die rosen glühn")   e.g.
    ML 1
Summer ("The winter now is past") Scotch
    air.   Words by N. H. Dole.   DSB
Summer carol ("The dawn-wind now is
    waking")   Béarnais carol air: Haut!
    haut! Pierrot.   Words by G. Dear-
    mer.   OB
"The **summer** days are coming."   Words
    by C. Jefferys.   MFS
Summer in winter.   Alsatian air.   Words
    by R. Crashaw.   OB
"**Summer** is a-coming in."   See "Sumer
    is icumen in" (John of Fornsete?)
"**Summer** joys are o'er, flow'rs bloom no
    more."   See Winter song (Bohemian
    folk air)
Summer time ("Lift your hidden faces")
    French air.   Words by R. Fyleman,
    based on the French carol, Une vaine
    crainte.   OB
"**Summer's** gone and winter's near."   See
    The gipsy and his wife
Sumner, George
    Forward the white
"**Sun** come and dry Becca Lawton."   See
    "Rain fall and wet Becca Lawton"
"The **sun** descending in the west."   See
    Night (French air)
Sun don't set in de mornin'.   Negro
    spiritual.   HRD
"De **sun** give a light in de heaven all
    round."   See Give up the world
"The **sun** had sunk behind the hill."   See
    The farmer's boy
"The **sun** has gane down o'er the lofty Ben
    Lomond."   See Jessie, the flower of
    Dumblane (Smith)
A **sun** I know of, that's brighter yet.   See
    'O sole mio (Capua)
"The **sun** is bright" (It is not always May)
    C. Gounod.   Words by H. W. Long-
    fellow.   HCA
[The **sun** is low]   "The sun upon the lake
    is low" (Evening song)   Irish air.
    Words by W. Scott.   DSB
"The **sun** is rising o'er the ocean."   See
    Welcome to morning (Offenbach)
"The **sun** is rising out of bed."   See
    Morning song (18th century English
    song)
"The **sun** is setting and the hour is late."
    See Let me dream again (Sullivan)
"**Sun** of my soul, Thou Saviour dear"
    (Hursley)   W. H. Monk.   Words
    by J. Keble.   TFP
"The **sun** shines bright in the old Kentucky
    home."   See My old Kentucky home
    (Foster)

"The sun upon the lake is low." See The sun is low (Irish air)

The sun worshippers. Zuni Indian song. e.in. TFP—TFR

"Sunce jarko." See "O bright sun"

Sunday ("So hab' ich doch die ganze woche") See Sonntag (Brahms)

"Sunday morning just at nine." See Down went McGinty (Flynn)

Sunny bank. See "As I sat on a sunny bank"

"Sunny showers, fragrant flowers." See Lob der thränen (Schubert)

The sunny south. Folk song: Endicott, Va. version. SES 2
—Nellysford, Va. version. SES 2
—West Virginia version. SES 2

Sunny Spain. Spanish air. Words by K. Davis. DSB

Sunrise ("See whence the rising sun") See "See where the rising sun"

Sunrise is coming, is coming. See Mañanitas

A sunrise song ("Above the edge of dark") W. J. Baltzell. Words by H. Van Dyke. BST

"The sun's bark was shatter'd." See Nymåne (Sinding)

"Sunset and evening star." See Crossing the bar (Barnby)

"The sunset glows in splendor." See Night (Abt)

The sunshine of Paradise Alley. J. W. Bratton. Words by W. H. Ford. GFS

"Suntag bin ich nit gewen in cheder." See Cheder lied

"Suntse zharko." See "O bright sun"

Suo-gân (Lullaby) Old Welsh song. Words by R. Bryan. e.w. WO

Supplication to the sun. See "O bright sun"

"Sur le pont d'Avignon"] On the bridge of Avignon. Old French rondo. e. MFF

"Hier, sur le pont d'Avignon" ("There on the bridge at Avignon") Canadian version. e.f. GC

Sur les clanquarts (On the ramparts) French folk song. e.f. CBF 2

Susan Jane. W. S. Hays (music and words) WSS

Susan Van Doozen. H. Shepherd. Words by J. Lincoln. SMG

Susannah Clargy. Folk song from Virginia. SES 2

Susanni. See Parvulus nobis nascitur

"Suse, lewe Suse, wat ruschelt in't stroh." See Wiegenlied

Susman, Margarete
"A maiden yonder sings" (Sibelius)

Suspiria (Suckarna) E. Sjögren. Words by H. W. Longfellow. e.sw. WM 2

Das süsse lied verhallt. For English translation see The blissful strain is o'er (Wagner)

"Süsser sang ertönt." See "In the forest, the deep forest"

Sussex carol ("On Christmas night") See Christmas night

The Sussex mummers' carol ("O mortal man") Christmas song. OB

The Sussex mummers' Christmas carol ("When righteous Joseph") BET

Süssmayr, Franz Xaver
"'Tis springtime"

"Susu, eia, eia, susu." See Wiegenlied (Esthonian folk song)

"Susu, susu, suleia, der hirte treibt die lämmlein." See Wiegenlied (Ukrainian folk song)

"Susy, little Susy." See Wiegenlied ("Suse, lewe Suse")

Sutcliffe, C. T.
The voice of Jesus

Suydan, Ralph, pseud. See Loomis, Harvey Worthington

"Suzanne, Suzanne, jolie femme" ("Suzanne, Suzanne, pretty one") Negro creole folk song. e.f. MB

"Suzanne, Suzanne, pretty one." See "Suzanne, Suzanne, jolie femme"

[Suzette] "Ah, Suzette, chère" ("Ah, Suzette, dear") Negro creole folk song. e.f. MB

Svatebni ("Abschiedstunde schlägt dem feste") See Dank der gäste

Svatebni ("Sei nicht böse") See "Sei nicht böse, mein lieb väterlein"

Sve veselo a ja tuzhan. See "White dawn has not come stealing"

Sven i rosengård (Sven im rosenhain) Swedish folk song. g.sw. ML 1

Sven im rosenhain. See Sven i rosengård

Svendsen, Johan Severin
Längsel
Waiting. See Längsel

Swain, Charles
"Home's not merely four square walls" (Rossini)
The old cottage clock (Molloy)

"The swallow leaves the young within her nest." See Home so blest (Abt)

The swallows ("Adios, a tender el vuelo") See Las golondrinas

Swan, Timothy
The soldier's farewell

Swan song ("I give thee thanks") R. Wagner. [Tr of Nun sei bedankt, mein lieber schwan] e. WG

Swan-song ("Ein schwan zieht auf dem see") See Schwanenlied (Hartmann)

Swanee ribber. See The old folks at home (Foster)

Swanee river moon. H. P. Clarke. SMG

"Swannanoa town." Folk song: Black Mountain, N.C. version. SES 2
—Micaville, N.C. version. SES 2
Variants: "John Henry"; "My old hammah"

The swans. Russian folk song. e. NRF
Variant: Wedding-day song

Swansea town. English folk song. DSC

[The swapping song] The foolish boy. Folk song: American mountain version. RA

The **swapping** song.—*Continued*
—Berea, Ky. version. SES 2
—Hindman, Ky. version. SES 2
—Tennessee version. SES 2
The **Swazi** warrior. British army song.
BOS 2
Sweeney, Eugene
The buff and blue
Sweeney, John R. See Sweney, John R.
Sweet, Walden; Tefft, Dorothy E., and Williams, Roy A.
The aggie pep song (Tefft)
Sweet Adeline. H. Armstrong. Words by R. H. Gerard. GFS
"**Sweet** alma home." See Heidelberg (Power)
"**Sweet** and low." J. Barnby. Words by A. Tennyson. BB—GSS—MFS TFB—TFP—TFR
"**Sweet** and low" (Cradle song) W. V. Wallace. Words by A. Tennyson. GOS 2
"**Sweet** baby, sleep! what ails my dear" (Wither's rocking hymn) R. V. Williams. Words by G. Wither. OB
Sweet Betsy from Pike. Old American song. SBA
"**Sweet** blossoms, cherry blossoms." See Cherry blossoms (Hadley)
"**Sweet** Briar, Sweet Briar, flower fair." Sweet Briar college song. Bendall. [Words by M. Pinkerton] AI
Sweet Canaan. Negro spiritual. HRD
Sweet chiming bells. See Chiming bells of long ago (Shattuck)
"**Sweet** day is softly dying." Old French air. Words by F. Manley. TFB—TFG—TFO
Sweet dreamland faces. See Dream faces (Hutchinson)
"**Sweet** dreams, form a shade" (Blake's cradle song) R. V. Williams. Words by W. Blake. OB
"**Sweet** Ellie Rhee, so dear to me." See Ellie Rhee (Winner)
"A **sweet** faced little girl of eight." See Why don't they play with me (Harris)
Sweet Genevieve. H. Tucker. Words by G. Cooper. BB—DFF—GFS— TFG—TFP—WSS
Sweet gentle breezes that fly. See Perchè dell' aure in sen (Donizetti)
"**Sweet** Jesus went down to yonder town." See The holy well
"**Sweet** Kate." R. Jones. CSB 4
The **sweet** little girl that I love. Hook. WOE
"**Sweet** little ladybird, rest awhile." See Ladybird
Sweet love doth now invite. See "Come again, sweet love" (Dowland)
Sweet Marie. R. Moore. Words by C. Warman. GFS—OTG
"**Sweet** Nelly, my heart's delight." 18th century song. KSO
Sweet potatoes. Creole folk song. e. TFO—TFP—TFR
"**Sweet** Saint Bride of the yellow hair." See Kye song of Saint Bride (Clokey)

"**Sweet** songs our voices blending." See Song of parting (Abt)
Sweet spirit, hear my prayer. W. V. Wallace. GOS 2. i. also GE
"**Sweet** spring is advancing." J. S. Bach. TFO
"The **sweet** spring is the year's pleasant king." See Spring
Sweet the crawflow'r's early bell. See "Gloomy winter's now awa"
"**Sweet** turtle dove" (Jerusalem mornin') Negro spiritual. HRD
"A **sweet** Tuxedo girl you see." See Ta-ra-ra boom-der-é (Sayers)
"**Sweet** was the song the Virgin sang." See Lute-book lullaby (Ballet)
Sweet William. Folk song: Kentucky version. SES 2
—Alleghany, N.C. version no. 1. SES 2
—Alleghany, N.C. version no. 2. SES 2
—Burnsville, N.C. version no. 1. SES 2
—Burnsville, N.C. version no. 2. SES 2
—Carmen, N.C. version. SES 2
—Micaville, N.C. version. SES 2
—Swannanoa, N.C. version. SES 2
—Tennessee version. SES 2
—Nellysford, Va. version no. 1. SES 2
—Nellysford, Va. version no. 2. SES 2
—White Rock, Va. version. SES 2
"**Sweet** William arose, and he put on his clothes." See Fair Margaret and sweet William (Micaville, N.C. version)
"**Sweet** William arose one May morning." See Fair Margaret and sweet William (Barbourville, Ky. version; Harrogate, Tenn. version; Blue Ridge Springs, Va. version; Callaway, Va. version)
"**Sweet** William arose one morning in May." See Fair Margaret and sweet William (Burnsville, N.C. version)
"**Sweet** William died choked up in love." See Barbara Allen (Nellysford, Va. version)
"**Sweet** William, don't you cross that raging sea." See Early, early in the spring (Alleghany, N.C. version)
"**Sweet** William arose one merry morning." See Fair Margaret and sweet William (Crozet, Va. version)
"**Sweet** William he rose in the month of May." See Fair Margaret and sweet William (Flag Pond, Tenn. version)
"**Sweet** William he rose on last May morning." See Fair Margaret and sweet William (Knott or Letcher county, Ky. version)
"**Sweet** William he rose one morning in May." See Fair Margaret and sweet William (Carmen, N.C. version no. 1)
"**Sweet** William rose one morning in May." See Fair Margaret and sweet William (Berea, Ky. version)
"**Sweet** William was down to his dwell to-day." See Barbara Allen (Hot Springs, N.C. version)
"**Sweet** William went to Polly." See William and Polly (North Carolina version)
"**Sweet** William were taken with a pain in his breast." See William and Nancy (North Carolina version)

"Sweet William's bride rose one merry morning." See Fair Margaret and sweet William (Beechgrove, Va. version)

"Sweeter sounds the song of birds." See Minnelied (Brahms)

"Sweeter than the breath of morning." See "Nobil donna è tanto onesta" (Meyerbeer)

"Sweetest girl I ever saw." See Sucking cider through a straw (Morgan)

Sweetest Jesu. Old French (Flanders) carol. e. FC

"The sweetest thing in life." See Walking down Broadway (Pratt)

"Sweetheart, I send you a red, red rosebud." See Love greetings (Elgar)

Sweethearts and wives. Drinking song. H. P. Smith. US

Swell the chorus! let it echo. See Alma mater—Michigan state college (Thompson)

Swell the chorus speed it onward. See Alma mater—University of New Mexico (Thompson)

Sweney, John R.
Behring sea song (same air as Beulah land)
Beulah land
Dakota land (same air as Beulah land)

Swift, H.
"My heid is like to rend, Willie"

"Swift the springtime passes." See "Våren flyktar hastigt" (Sibelius)

"Swiftly the daylight is fading." See Carmela

Swinburne, Thomas Thackeray
The Genesee (Composer unknown)

Swindler! liar. K. Millöcker. e. WLO

Swing, David
"Beautiful faces" (Composer unknown)
The swing ("How do you like to go up in a swing") P. Judd. Words by R. L. Stevenson. CSB 2

Swing a lady. Play-party song from Kentucky. SES 2

Swing, cradle, swing. Words by G. Cooper. MFS

"Swing low, chariot." Negro spiritual. HRD

Swing low, sweet chariot ("I looked over Jordan") Negro spiritual. BB— FSN— HRD— MFS— TFB— TFP— WFN—WSS

Swing low, sweet chariot ("Oh, de good ole chariot swing so low") Negro spiritual. HRD

Swinging 'neath the old apple-tree. O. R. Barrows. MFS

Swinjacy pastyŕ. See Der schweinehirt

Swish, swish, swish, the craft is diving. See The cruising boys of subdiv. nine (Root)

The Swiss chalet song. See Le vieux chalet (Bovet)

The Swiss toy girl. See Rose of Lucerne (Barnett)

"Swjatoslaw hatt' neunzig jahr' gelebt." See The legend of Volgá

Sykes, Ethelred Lundy
Yea Alabama

Sylvesterlied (Laduvane) Macedonian folk song. b.g. ML 2

Symonds, John Addington
"These things shall be! a loftier race" (music by Bach; Hatton)

Symonffy, Kálmán de. See Simonffy, Kálmán

"Syng mig hjaem" ("Sing me home") E. Neupert. Words by B. Björnson. e.n. WM 2

"Szálldogál a fecske." See "Flying, sweeping swallow" (Szentirmay)

"Széna széna széna terem a réten." See "Auf der wiese, auf der wiese"

Szentirmay, Elemér
"Csak akkor szép a lány." See "What's the use of beauty"
"Csak egy szép lány van a világon." See "There's on earth but one true precious pearl"
"Csipke bokor." See "See the wild rose fadeth"
Do not go
"Flying, sweeping swallow"
"From woods around"
"Huzzad czigány." See "Play on, gipsy"
"A legény egytöl egyig." See "Trust them not"
Ne menj el. See Do not go
"Nyugtasd rajtam." See "Turn upon my worn and weary face"
"Play on, gipsy"
"Eine schöne gibt's nur auf der welt." See "There's on earth but one true precious pearl"
"See the wild rose fadeth"
"Szálldogál a fecske." See "Flying, sweeping swallow"
"There's on earth but one true precious pearl"
"Trust them not"
"Turn upon my worn and weary face"
"What's the use of beauty"

Szerdahelyi, József
Ez a kis lány hamis kis lány. See Pretty maid, how could you do so
"Ezt a kerek erdőt járom én." See "Through the darkling forest gay I roam"
Hungaria's treasure (attributed; attributed also to B. Egressi)
"Long ago, when I was still free"
"Marie mine"
"Marishka! Marishka." See "Marie mine"
Mariskám. See "Marie mine"
"Mikor én még legény voltam." See "Long ago, when I was still free"
Pretty maid, how could you do so
"Through the darkling forest gay I roam"

"Szereti a pap a kávét." See "Pfaffe liebt den starken kaffee"

"Szilvás falu gyászban van." See "Mourning in the village dwells"

"Szilvás hallt von grabgeläut." See "Mourning in the village dwells"

"Szőke kis ιány megy a kútra, hajaha."
See "Mädchen geht zum brunnen"
"Szomorú füzága." See "O'er the lithe
lily" (Simonffy)

T

"Tá bliain nú níos mó 'gam ag eisteacht."
See Cailín deás crúidhte na mbó
"Ta bouche est comme une cerise." See
Fleur d'amour (Weyts)
Ta-ra-ra boom-der-é. H. J. Sayers (mu-
sic and words) SRW
Tabrar, Joseph
Daddy wouldn't buy me a bow-wow
["Tacea la notte placida"] "Of love like
this how vainly." Verdi. e. WG
"Tag dem, o död! och för dit mer." See
Suspiria (Sjögren)
Taggart, George
The moth and the flame (Witt)
"Tagliannuti a lu spisu." See Malatu
p'amuri
"Täglich ging die wunderschöne sultans-
tochter auf und nieder." See Der
Asra (Rubinstein)
The tailor and the mouse. Folk song.
DSB
The tailor's mouse. Folk song: American
version. GSS
" 'Tain't my mother or my father." See
It's me, O Lord
" 'Tain't my sister or my brother." See
It's me, O Lord
Tak' your auld cloak about ye ("In winter,
when the rain rain'd cauld") Scot-
tish song. GS
"Take back the heart." C. Barnard
(music and words) SRW
"Take back the virgin page." Air: Der-
mott. Words by T. Moore. HMI
Take back your gold. M. H. Rosenfeld.
Words by L. W. Pritzkow. GFS—
OTG—SRW
"Take heart, the journey's ended." See
Nous voici dans la ville
Take me back on a special train. See
Take me back to tech (Seaver)
Take me back to tech. Massachusetts
institute of technology song. F.
Seaver. Words by I. W. Litchfield.
AI—AIS
Take me down, down, down where the
Wurzburger flows. See Down where
the Wurzburger flows (Von Tilzer)
"Take me home to the place where I first
saw the light." See The sunny south
(Endicott, Va. version; West Virginia
version)
Take me to that Swanee shore. L. F.
Muir. Words by L. W. Gilbert.
DFF
"Take my head on your shoulder, daddy."
See Daddy (Behrend)

"Take my life and let it be consecrated,
Lord, to Thee" (Consecration) W.
H. Jude. Words by F. R. Havergal.
DN
"Take my life, and let it be consecrated,
Lord, to Thee." P. A. Schnecker.
Words by F. R. Havergal. TSS 1—
TSS 2
Take, O take the rosy, the rosy crown.
See The rosy crown (Weber)
"Take, O take those lips away." R. V.
Williams. Words by W. Shakespeare
[attributed also to Beaumont and
Fletcher] CSB 5
"Take the most of your father's gold."
See Lady Isabel and the elf knight
(Buena Vista, Va. version)
"Take them, O death! and bear away."
See Suspiria (Sjögren)
"Take this letter to my mother." W. S.
Hays (music and words) GOS 2
"Take thou our sorrow." See Hymn to
St Raphael
Take your auld cloak about ye. See Tak'
your auld cloak about ye
"Takes a humble soul to join." See I am
goin' to join in this army
"Tal, du mein liebes tal" ("Dolina, dolina")
Slovak folk song. g.sl. ML 3
Un tal gioco, credetemi. For English
translation see "Such a game, believe
me, friends" (Leoncavallo)
Talbot, Maurice, pseud. See Stevens,
David
"Täler du de stærke favntag." See Liv
og salighed (Sinding)
Talhaiarn, pseud. See Jones, John, 1810-
1869
"Talk about me jes' as much as you please."
See Hol' de win' don't let it blow
"Talk about the sooners, the Aggies and
the braves." See I'm a jayhawk
(Bowles)
"A tall stalwart seaman lay dying." See
The tarpaulin jacket (Coote)
"Tällaisille pojillehan ne herrain päivät
passaa." See Holzflösser
"De talles' tree in Paradise." See Blow
your trumpet, Gabriel (Port Royal
islands, S.C. version); Blow your trum-
pet, Gabriel (Virginia version)
Tallis, Thomas
"Glory to Thee, my God, this night"
"Praise God from Whom all blessings
flow"
Tallis' canon. See "Praise God from
Whom all blessings flow"
[A Talmudical student's lament] "Mai
komashma lon." Jewish song.
<Words by A. Raisin> y. SY
Tam Glen. See "My heart is a breakin',
dear tittie"
"Tämän kylän tytöt ovat." See "Unsres
dorfes dirnen"
Tambourin. See Aminte
Tammany. G. Edwards. Words by V.
P. Bryan. GFS—SRW
Tan patate-là tchuite ("When your potato's
done") Negro creole folk song.
e.f. MB

Tannahill, Robert
The braes o' Balquhidder (Smith)
"Gloomy winter's now awa'" (Scottish air)
Jessie, the flower o' Dumblane (Smith)
"Loudon's bonnie woods and braes" (Smith)
ₜDer **tannenbaum**ⱼ "O tannebaum." German folk song. g. EDL
The Christmas tree. e. DSB
ₜDer **tannenbaum**ⱼ "O tannebaum." New words by E. Anschütz. g. EDL
Tanner, Gid
I'm satisfied
Tanssijatarjokas. See Aufforderung zum tanz (Finnish folk song)
Tanz im kirchdorfe (Kirkonkylantanssit) Finnish folk song. fi.g. ML 3
Tanzlied ("Elenka, Elenka, komm zum kranken liebsten."—Elenke) Bulgarian. folk song. b.g. ML 2
Tanzlied ("He! hei! der Ungar schlägt zusammen seine hakken."—"Hej! haj! Magyar ember") Hungarian folk song. g.hu. ML 3
Tanzlied ("O, wie so schön") Composer and author of words unknown. g. EDL
Tanzlied ("Vi ska' ställa te' en roliger dans") See "Vi ska' ställa te' en roliger dans"
"**Tap!** tap! tap! who's tapping there." See Martinique love-song
Taps ("Day is done, gone the sun") U.S. army bugle call. Words from Pennsylvania military college. BB—GSS KU—TFR
Taps ("Fading light dims the sight") U.S. army bugle call. Pennsylvania military college song. ₜWords by J. B. Esenweinⱼ DSO—TFP
Tarantella de la bellona (Preis der schönen) Italian folk song. g.i. ML 2
"**Tarantella** de li Dei vo cantare." See Tarantella de la bellona
"**Tarantella** von schönen dingen." See Tarantella de la bellona
Tara's harp. See "The harp that once thro' Tara's halls"
The **tarpaulin** jacket ("A tall stalwart seaman lay dying") ₜC. Coote. Words by G. J. Whyte-Melvilleⱼ US
"Wrap me up in my tarpaulin jacket." SBA
Tarry Trousers. Folk song: Virginia version. SES 2
"**Tarry** with me, O my Saviour." Evensong. J. Raff. ₜWords by C. L. S. Smithⱼ CSS 1
"**Tarry** with me, O my Saviour" (Abendlied) M. Roeder. ₜWords by C. L. S. Smithⱼ e.g. TSS 2
The **tar's** farewell. S. Adams. Words by F. C. Burnand (wrongly called F. C. Barnard) GE
ₜThe **Tartar** hostⱼ "Okh, ne buĭnyĭ vĭeter zavyval" (Tatareneinfall.—Gesang der flüchtlinge) Russian folk song. g.r. ML 1

Tassels on the boots. Old American song. SW
Tasso, Torquato
Canto dei gondolieri (Venetian air)
Tatareneinfall. See The Tartar host
Tate, Nahum
"While shepherds watch'd their flocks" (Air from Webber's MS book; 16th century air; old English air; old Hampshire air; Sheffield air; old West of England air; also music by Händel; Praetorius)
Tate, Nahum, and Brady, Nicholas
Old hundred (Franc?)
"Der **tate** is gefuren kain balte." See Die Baike
"**Tatulu**, matulu." See "Väterlein, mütterlein"
Taubert, Wilhelm
In der märznacht
A night in March. See In der märznacht
Vom bauern und den tauben
Die **taufe** Christi (Krchtena Khrstovo) Serbian folk song. g.se. ML 2
Tauler, Johann
"There comes a galley, laden" (Composer unknown. Tr of Es komt ein schiff geladen)
Taylor, Bayard
Bedouin love-song (Hawley)
Proposal (Brackett)
Taylor, Charles J.
Alma mater—Carnegie institute of technology (O'Brien)
Taylor, James B.
"Sparkling and bright, in its liquid light, is the water in our glasses"
Taylor, Jane
"Ah, why will my dear little child be so cross" (Composer unknown)
The chatterbox (Composer unknown)
"Lazy sheep, pray tell me why" (Old French air)
Little Jack (Composer unknown)
"Twinkle, twinkle, little star" (French or German air)
Taylor, Raynor
L'amour interrogé par un berger. See Cupid and the shepherd
Cupid and the shepherd
The wounded soldier
Taylor, Thomas Rawson
Heaven is my home (Sullivan)
Taylor, Virgil Corydon
"Lord of all being"
Taylor, the fine old Southern gentleman. Old song. ₜAir: The fine old English gentlemanⱼ DSO
Tchaikovsky, Peter Ilyich
The crown of roses
"Kein wort von dir, der freude oder klage." See "No word from thee, in gladness or in sorrow"
A legend. See The crown of roses
The nightingale
"No word from thee, in gladness or in sorrow"
"None but the lonely heart." See "Nur wer die sehnsucht kennt"

Tchaikovsky, Peter Ilyich—*Continued*
"Nur wer die sehnsucht kennt"
Resignation
Versohnung. See Resignation
Warum
Why. See Warum
Tcherepnin, Nicholas Nicholaevitch. See Cherepnin, Nikolaï Nikolaevich
"Tching-a-ring-a-ring-tching, feast of lanterns." See The feast of lanterns (Elliott)
"Te Deum Patrem colimus." See The May morning hymn (Rogers)
"Te quiero porque te quiero" ("I love you") Mexican folk song. e.s. VS
"Te vagy, te vagy barna kis lány." See "Maiden, maiden, nut-brown maiden" (Simonffy)
Tea in the arbor. J. Beuler. MFS
[A teamster's complaint] "Soll ich sein a rov." Jewish folk song. y. SY
"The tear fell gently from her eye." See The anchor's weighed (Braham)
Tears ("On ne les a pas soupçonnées") See Les larmes (Godard)
Tears, such as tender fathers shed. G. F. Händel. SSO 4
"Tečie voda, tečie." See "Fliesse, wasser, fliesse"
Tecolote ("Tecolote donde viene") Folk song: New Mexican version. e.s. VS
Variant: Tecolotito
Tecolotito ("Tecolotito, orgulloso tecolotito."—Little owl) Folk song: New Mexican version. e.s. VS
Variant of: Tecolote
Tefft, Dorothy E.
The aggie pep song
See also Sweet, Walden, jt. auth.
Tei dei dei dam. See "Hör nor reb Todros"
Tei dei dei di dam. See "Wos wet sein vun dem rebben"
"Telal viče." See Die entlaufene sklavin
Telemann, Georg Philipp
Glück
Tell Him a welcome. W. J. Finn (music and words) FC
"Tell him that I am faithful." See "Digli, ch'io son fedele" (Schiassi)
Tell Jesus. Negro spiritual. HRD
"Tell me as time goes flying." See "Dite ch'ogni momento" (Pergolesi)
"Tell me, beautiful maiden, tell me, where will you go." See "Dites, la jeune belle" (Gounod)
"Tell me, O my darling" ("Vidim draga moja") Yugoslav folk song. e.se. CJ
"Tell me one thing, tell me truly." See No sir (Wakefield)
"Tell me, pretty maiden." L. Stuart. GFS
Tell me that you love me yet. See "We parted by the river side" (Hays)
"Tell me the tales that to me were so dear." See Long, long ago (Bayly)

"Tell me, ye friendly neighbours." See "Ditemi, buona gente, vedeste Dinorah" (Meyerbeer)
"Tell me, ye winged winds." See The inquiry (Baker)
Tell my Jesus morning. Negro spiritual from South Carolina. AS
"Tell old Bill, when he leaves home dis mornin'." See Dis mornin', dis evenin', so soon
"Tempest adest floridum." See Tempus adest floridum
The tempest of the heart. See Il balen del suo sorriso (Verdi)
Tempus adest floridum (Flower carol) Ancient spring song. e. OB
"Tempest adest floridum." 1. MBS
The ten commandments. Folk song:
Georgia version. SES 2
—Kentucky version. SES 2
—Asheville, N.C. version. SES 2
—Black Mountain, N.C. version. SES 2
—Marion, N.C. version. SES 2
Variants: Carol of the twelve days; The dilly carol; Green grow the rushes-ho
"Ten little niggers." Children's song. RA
Ten miles from home (Hiking song) Old English folk air: The farmer in the dell. TFO—TFR
"Ten thousand cattle." Cowboy song. LSC
Ten thousand miles away ("Sing I for a brave and a gallant barque") Old song. SBA
"Ten thousand miles away from home." Old American folk song. SBA
"Ten thousand strong sing we a song." See Oberlin, our alma mater (Pierce)
"Ten thousand voices sing thy acclaim." See Virginia, hail, all hail (Morrow)
Tenaouich' tenaga, ouich'ka ("There came an ancient Huron") Canadian folk song. e.f. GC
Tender and true, adieu. G. Lyle. [Words by J. T. Gould] GE
Tender ties. See "Un doux lien" (Delbrück)
The tenderfoot. Cowboy song. SBA
Ten Hoor, Marten, and Goldstein, Walter
The olive and blue
Tennyson, Alfred Tennyson, 1st baron
Blow, bugle, blow (Hatton)
The brook (Farmer)
Crossing the bar (Barnby)
Little birdie (Delius)
The May queen (Dempster)
"Ring out, wild bells" (music by Bainton; Gounod)
"Strong Son of God, immortal Love" (Oliver)
"Sweet and low" (music by Barnby; Wallace)
Tenth U.S. infantry song. Air: The tenth Illinois march. DSO
Tenting on the old camp ground. W. Kittredge (music and words) BB—DSO—GOS 2—TFP

Terebimbombom, terebimbombom. See Der philosoph

"**Térj** magadhoz drága Sion." See Lied des ungarischen galeerensträflings

"**Terrible** hour thou nearest." See Ah! quello fu per me (Donizetti)

"**Tes** doux baisers sont des oiseaux." See Madrigal (Chaminade)

Tessie. American song. SW

"**Tessie,** you make me feel so badly." See Tessie

Die **Teutoburger** schlacht ("Als die Römer frech geworden") Composer unknown. Words by J. V. Scheffel. g. EDL

"**Tevet,** va mamm, na spontet ket." See Jannik Skolan

Texan rangers' song. H. Russell. Words by J. T. Lytle. DSO

War song of the Texan rangers. SW

The **Texas** cowboy. Composer unknown. LSC

"**Tha** mi sgith s'mi leam fhin buain a rainich." See Cnochd a bheannichd

Thackeray, William Makepeace
The mahogany tree (Campana)

"**Thalassa** pikrhothalassa." See "O meer, du grausam bittres meer"

Thalberg, Sigismund
"Amid the greenwood"

"**Thank** ye, great gods eternal." See A te riede, o caro figlio (Mercadante)

"**Thanks** to my brethren." See How vain is man who boasts in fight (Händel)

Thanksgiving ("For these and all Thy mercies given") English folk song. MFF

Thanksgiving carol ("Fields of corn, give up your ears") 15th century German air. Words by E. Farjeon, based on Der tag der ist so freudenreich. OB

Thanksgiving prayer ("Wilt heden") See "Wilt heden nu treden" (Kremser)

"**Thar'** is gwine to be a festival this evenin'." See My gal is a high born lady (Fagan)

"**Thar's** a Meth'dist preacher." See Don't ya heah Jerusalem moan

That am the way to spell chicken. See Dat am de way to spell chicken

That bugler. See Upi dei di

"**That** dread hand." F. von Flotow. ¡Tr of Diese hand, die sich gewendet¡ e. WLO

That frightens the birds. See Ça fait peur aux oiseaux (Bernard)

"**That** night I'll ne'er forget." See Waltz song (Planquette)

"**That** old jack fish swimming up the stream." See The jackfish

"**That** old, old clock of the household stock." See The old cottage clock (Molloy)

That old-time religion. See This old time religion

"**That** seat of science, Athens." See Free America

"**That** Sunshine Special coming around the bend." See C. C. rider

¡**That** sweet story of old¡ "I think, when I read that sweet story." Old air. Words by J. T. Luke. BB

That Viennese waltz. O. Straus. e. WLO

"**That's** George that I hear." See Der schmied (Brahms)

That's how I need you. A. Piantadosi. Words by J. McCarthy and J. Goodwin. SMG

Thayer, William Armour
Adelphi field song

Theid mi g'ad' amharc (I will go) Gaelic folk song. e. CSB 2

"**Their** eyes are holden by earth-born fancies." See The incarnation (Caldara)

Then away, away, for I can't wait any longer. See Old Shady (Hanby)

Then blow, ye winds, heigh-ho. See "A capital ship"

Then blow ye winds westerly, westerly blow. See The song of the fishes

Then carry me back to old Virginny. See Carry me back to old Virginny (Christy)

Then carry me back to Tennessee, back where I long to be. See Ellie Rhee (Winner)

Then carry me back to Tennessee, dar let me live and die. See Ella Ree (Porter)

Then cheer anew for the B. Y. U. See The college song (Brigham Young university song)

Then combine your humble ditties. See Son of a gambolier

Then drill, ye tarriers, drill. See Drill, ye tarriers, drill (Casey)

Then drink to the holly berry. See Merry Christmas (Shaw)

Then farewell, then farewell, then farewell, Mary Blane. See Mary Blane

Then hail! all hail to old Purdue. See For the honor of old Purdue (Huston)

Then hail to the monarch high. See The corn song (Marks)

"**Then** he went unto the house." See The gypsy laddie (Woodridge, Va. version)

Then here's to cross cannon. See The red guidon (Griffin)

Then here's to the sailor. See Sailing (Marks)

Then here's to thy colors of crimson-white. See Here's to the colors of crimson-white (Ludebuehl)

"**Then** hit the line for Harvard." See The gridiron king (Fletcher)

"**Then** hit the line for old S. C." See Trojan war song (Evans)

Then ho, boys, ho! to California go. See California

Then hurrah for the flag, our country's flag. See "There are many flags in many lands"

Then hurrah, hurrah, for freedom's flag See Freedom's flag (Geibel)

"**Then** I go to Maxim's." F. Lehar. e. WLO

Then I was gone. See Den I was gone

"Then it's a hooraw, and a hooraw." See Standin' on the walls of Zion

Then it's hi! hi! hee! in the field artillery. See The caisson song (Metz)

Then it's hi! hi! hee! the coast artillery. See Caisson song: coast artillery parody (Metz)

Then it's hi! hi! hee! the good old infantree. See Caisson song: infantry adaptation (Metz)

Then it's home, boys, home. See Coast artillery song

Then lay down the shovel and the hoe. See Uncle Ned (Foster)

Then lift your voices! loudly sing our alma mater's praise. See Alma mater—North Carolina state college (Norris)

Then march, freemen, march. See The battle call

Then move your family westward. See El-a-noy

Then off to chase the buck and doe. See The Cornish May song

Then on the calmness cool and bright. See Beautiful Canaan nights

Then praise the Lord both high and low. See Wondrous works

Then rise, children, sing around the door. See Early in de mornin'

"Then shall the eyes of the blind be open'd." See He shall feed his flock (Händel)

"Then shall the just also see and be glad." See The righteous rejoice

Then shall the righteous shine forth. Mendelssohn. [Tr of Dann werden die gerechten leuchten] e. SSO 3

Then shout hurrah, shout hurrah. See The bold militiaman

Then sing a song for West Virginia. See Farewell, W. V. U., farewell (Richards)

Then sing to the oak. See The brave old oak (Loder)

Then sing we all, both great and small. See "The angel Gabriel"

Then sing you all, both great and small. See Righteous Joseph

"Then, then shall the righteous shine forth." See Then shall the righteous shine forth (Mendelssohn)

Then up, and down, fast and slow. See Jim Crow's polka

"Then we'll sing of Lydia Pinkham." See Lydia Pinkham

"Then were there brought unto him little children." See Suffer little children to come unto me (Hewitt)

Then where are the boys who vow'd eternal friendship. See Twelve months ago to-night (Fox)

"Then with reports most sprightly." See Cuckoo (Peerson)

Then you'll remember me ("When other lips") M. W. Balfe. [Words by A. Bunn] GOS 1—MFS

Theobald IV, king of Navarre. See Thibaut IV, king of Navarre

"There ain' no liars there." See In my Father's house

There angels sing in jubilant ring. See Jesus' bloemhof

"There are bonds of all sorts." See We've drunk from the same canteen (Clark)

"There are eyes of blue." See The maiden with the dreamy eyes (Cole and Johnson)

"There are many flags in many lands." Composer unknown. Words by M. H. Howliston. BB

"There are many young people here." See Celui que j'aime

"There are mem'ries, my dear." See Recuerdas

"There came a rain, a heavy frost." See The lost babe (North Carolina version)

"There came a young man over the sea." See My mother bid me (Hindman, Ky. version)

"There came an ancient Huron." See Tenaouich' tenaga, ouich'ka

"There came three kings ere break of day" (Epiphany) R. F. Smith. [Words by G. Moultrie] LAS

"There came three kings from Galilee." See The three kings (Dunstan)

"There came to the beach." See The exile of Erin

"There came to the cape a lady in crêpe." See The lady in crêpe (Donizetti)

"There came two gypsies from the north." See The gypsie laddie (Knott or Letcher county, Ky. version)

"There chanced to be a pedlar bold." See The bold pedlar and Robin Hood

[There comes a galley, laden"] Song of the ship. Composer unknown. Words attributed to J. Tauler. Tr of Es komt ein schiff geladen, or, Uns kompt ein schiff gefahren. e. OB

"There comes a ship a-sailing with angels flying fast." See "There comes a galley, laden"

"There cried a bird." See "Der skreg en fugl" (Sinding)

"There dwelt a miller, hale and bold." See The miller of the Dee

"There grows a bonnie brier-bush in oor kail-yaird, and white are the blossoms on't." Scottish air. Old song with additional words by C. Nairne. DSB

There is a balm in Gilead. See Balm in Gilead

"There is a charm I can't explain." See Happy as a big sunflower (Emerson)

"There is a city bright." A. F. Loud. TSS 1—TSS 2

"There is a city builded upon a peaceful hill." See Sion (Rodney)

"There is a cross of heavy weight." See Cross and crown (Dana)

"There is a flower within my heart." See Daisy Bell (Dacre)

"There is a garden in her face." T. Campion (music and words) GA

"There is a happy land." Hindoo air arr by L. Mason. <Words by A. Young> MFS

"There is a lady sweet and kind." See Passing by (Ford); Passing by (Purcell)

There is a mystery. See Somebody's child (Plimpton)

"There is a reaper, whose name is Death." See The reaper and the flowers (Mendelssohn)

"There is a tavern in the town." Cornish folk song. DSC—MBS—SRW—TFB

"There is a wild boar in these woods." See Sir Lionel (Knott or Letcher county, Ky. version; Virginia version)

"There is an hour of hallowed peace." C. Chenery. TSS 1—TSS 2

"There is beauty in the forest." See The world is full of beauty (Donizetti)

"There is fire in the lower hold." See Fire down below

"There is going to be a festival this evening." See My gal is a high born lady (Fagan)

There is no work in the army. 19th century song. DSO

"There is not in the wide world a valley so sweet." See The meeting of the waters

"There is nought on earth so still as the snow." See Sne (Lie)

"There is six good days all in the week." See The Hampshire mummers' Christmas carol

"There! little girl, don't cry." C. Sobeski. Words by J. W. Riley. BST

"There lived a lady, a lady gay." See The wife of Usher's well (Meadows of Dan, Va. version)

"There lived a lord in the old country." See The two sisters (Hindman, Ky. version)

"There liv'd a man in our town." See Aikin Drum

"There lived a mason who lived by trade." See The cruel ship's carpenter (Marion, N.C. version)

"There lived a rich old merchant." See The banks of sweet Dundee (Tennessee version)

"There liv'd a sage in days of yore." See The pigtail (Mozart)

"There lived an old lady in the north country." See The two sisters (Mount Fair, version no. 1)

"There lived an old lord by the northern sea." See The two sisters (American mountain version; Woodridge, Va. version)

"There on the bridge at Avignon." See "Sur le pont d'Avignon" (Canadian version)

"There stands a little man." See A little man

"There stands by the river, the Manzanares." See "Am ufer des flusses, des Manzanares" (Jensen)

"There walked on Plover's shady banks." See Driving saw-logs on the Plover

"There was a bee-i-ee-i-ee." See The bee and the pup

"There was a blind beggar, he lost his sight." See The blind beggar's daughter (North Carolina version)

"There was a bonny blade." See The dumb wife

"There was a bridal in our town, for ilka lass there was a loon." See The bonnie breast-knots (2d version)

"There was a bridal in this town, and till't the lasses a' were boun'." See The bonnie breast-knots (1st version)

"There was a councillor afright." See The councillor's daughter

"There was a fair damsel in Carlchester." See The clothier

"There was a fair lady who lived on the plains." See Fair lady of the plains

"There was a fair young lady so lately I've been told." See The banks of sweet Dundee (Manchester, Ky. version)

"There was a frog lived in a pool, doo-dah! doo-dah." See The song of the frog (Foster)

"There was a frog liv'd in a well." See The frog and the mouse

"There was a frog lived in the spring." See The frog in the well (Woodridge, Va. version)

"There was a frog lived in the well." See The frog in the well (Pineville, Ky. version)

"There was a gallant soldier just lately come from Spain." See The lady and the dragoon (Montvale, Va. version)

"There was a gypsy came to this country." See The gypsy laddie (Barbourville, Ky. version)

"There was a jolly beggar." See The jolly beggar

"There was a jolly boatsman." See The boatsman and the chest (Kentucky version)

"There was a jolly miller once lived on the river Dee." See The miller of the Dee

"There was a jolly old farmer who lived the neighbours nigh." See My parents treated me tenderly (Pine Mountain, Ky. version)

"There was a jovial beggar." See A begging we will go

"There was a king in Yvetot." See Le roi d'Yvetot

"There was a lad was born in Kyle" (Rantin', rovin' Robin) [Air: O gin ye were deid, guidman] Words by R Burns. GS

"There was a lady, a lady gay." See The wife of Usher's well (Knott or Letcher county, Ky. version; Wasioto, Ky. version)

"There was a lady all in the garden." See The broken token (Allanstand, N.C. version no. 2)

"There was a lady, and a lady gay." See The wife of Usher's well (Berea, Ky. version; Oneida, Ky. version; Pineville, Ky version)

"There was a lady and gay was she." See The wife of Usher's well (Flag Pond, Tenn. version)

"There was a lady in New York, all along little Omy." See The cruel mother (Marion, N.C. version no. 1)

"There was a lady in yonder town." See The greenwood side

"There was a lady lived in Cain." See Susannah Clargy

"There was a lady lived in York." See The wife of Usher's well (Black Mountain, N.C. version)

"There was a lady near the town." See The cruel mother (Berea, Ky. version no. 1)

"There was a little boatsman." See The boatsman and the chest (North Carolina version)

"There was a little hen." Drinking song. [Air: Turkey in the straw] US

"There was a little maiden." See "Il était un' bergère"

"There was a little man and he had a little can." See No more booze

"There was a little oak in yonders field." See The tree in the wood (St Peter's School, Va. version)

"There was a little ship and she sailed upon the sea." See The Golden Vanity (Berea, Ky. version)

"There was a little ship in the North Amerikee, she went by the name of the Golden Willow Tree." See The Golden Vanity (Black Mountain, N.C. version)

"There was a little ship in the South Amerikee that went by the name of the Weeping Willow Tree." See The Golden Vanity (Hot Springs, N.C. version no. 1)

"There was a litle ship that sail'd out on the sea." See The Mary Golden Tree

"There was a little ship that sailed upon the sea." See The Golden Vanity (Pineville, Ky. version)

"There was a little soldier boy who lately came from over." See The lady and the dragoon (Allanstand, N.C. version)

"There was a little soldier, just lately come from war." See The lady and the dragoon (Kentucky version)

"There was a maid went to the mill" (The maid and the mill) 17th or 18th century song. KSO

"There was a man in ancient times." See Lazarus (Tennessee version; Virginia version)

"There was a man lived in the west, dan du, dan du." See The wife wrapt in wether's skin (Kentucky version no. 2)

"There was a man named Dunderbeck." See Dunderbeck

"There was a man, now please take note." See The goat

"There was a man of pleasure." See The Virginian lover (Tennessee version)

"There was a man went up and down." See The lone fish-ball

"There was a man who lived in England." See Young Beichen (Hindman, Ky. version)

"There was a mason who lived by his trade." See The cruel ship's carpenter (Black Mountain, N.C. version)

"There was a merry cobbler." See The cobbler and the crow

"There was a noble lord." See Young Beichan (Manchester, Ky. version no. 1)

"There was a noble old gentleman." See My parents treated me tenderly (Barbourville, Ky. version)

"There was a Presbyterian cat." See The Presbyterian cat

"There was a proper tall young man." See Lady Isabel and the elf knight (Georgia version)

"There was a rich lady." See The brown girl (Berea, Ky. version; Allanstand, N.C. versions no. 1-2)

"There was a rich merchant in London did right." See The silk merchant's daughter (Allanstand, N.C. version)

"There was a rich old lady." See The rich old lady (Allanstand, N.C. version)

"There was a rich old merchant in London he did dwell." See Jack went a-sailing (Harrogate, Tenn. version no. 1)

"There was a ship a-sailing on the North Amerikee." See The Golden Vanity (Manchester, Ky. version)

"There was a ship in the north, in the north country." See The Golden Vanity (Virginia version)

"There was a ship sailed from the North Amerikee." See The Golden Vanity (Lexington, Ky. version)

"There was a silk-merchant in London did dwell, he had one only daughter none could excel." See The silk merchant's daughter (Kentucky version)

"There was a silk-merchant, in London he did dwell, he had one only daughter, the truth to you I'll tell." See Jack went a-sailing (Berea, Ky. version)

"There was a silk merchant in London town did dwell, he had one only daughter, and the truth to you I'll tell." See Jack went a-sailing (Georgia version)

"There was a star in David's land." See King Herod and the cock

"There was a tailor fine, lived down by the cowcumber vine." See The tailor's mouse

"There was a tailor had a mouse." See The tailor and the mouse

"There was a tall young oysterman." See The young oysterman

"There was a tree all in the woods." See The tree in the wood (North Carolina version)

"There was a tree upon a hill." See The tree on the hill

"There was a wealthy merchant, in London he did dwell. He had an only daughter." See Jack went a-sailing (Blue Ridge Springs, Va. version)

"There was a wealthy merchant, in London he did dwell, he had one lovely daughter." See Jack went a-sailing (Knott county, Ky. version)

"There was a wealthy merchant, in London he dwelled; he built a fine castle." See Lamkin (Hindman, Ky. version)

"There was a wee cooper wha liv'd in Fife." See The wee cooper of Fife

"There was a woman of the north." See The wife of Usher's well (Big Laurel, N.C. version)

"There was a young lady from London she came." See The brown girl (Meadows of Dan, Va. version)

"There was a young lady so fair." See The cruel mother (Hindman, Ky version)

"There was a young man who courted me." See The brisk young lover (Georgia version)

"There was a youth and a comely youth." See The bailiff's daughter of Islington (Berea, Ky. version; Hyden, Ky. version)

"There was a youth, and a well-beloved youth." See The bailiff's daughter of Islington (English version)

"There was an auld man and he lived in the west." See The jolly broom man

"There was an old and wealthy man." See The Suffolk miracle (Nellysford, Va. version)

"There was an old bachelor bold and brave." See The holly twig (Montvale, Va. version)

"There was an old chap called Michael Finnigin." See Michael Finnigin

"There was an old darkey and his name was Uncle Ned." See Uncle Ned (Foster)

"There was an old farmer in Sussex did dwell." See The farmer's old wife (Purcell)

"There was an old fellow lived under the hill." See The farmer's curst wife (Hyden, Ky. version no. 1)

There was an old fish. See There was an ole fish

"There was an old lady lived over the sea." See Revolutionary tea

"There was an old man, an old man who said." Four-part round. Composer unknown. Words from E. Lear. TFP

"There was an old man and he lived all alone." See The miller's will (Kentucky version)

"There was an old man and he lived in the west, and his trade was the cutting of broom, green broom." See The jolly broom man

"There was an old man came over the sea." See My mother bid me (Virginia version)

"There was an old man he had a wife." See The wife wrapt in wether's skin (Virginia version)

"There was an old man in the north countree." See The two sisters (Afton, Va. version)

"There was an old man lived in the west, bow down, bow down." See The two sisters (Burnsville, N.C. version no. 2)

"There was an old man lived under the hill." See The farmer's curst wife (Hyden, Ky. version no. 2; Virginia version)

"There was an old man who followed the plough." See The farmer's curst wife (North Carolina version)

"There was an old man who lived near hell." See The farmer's curst wife (Hindman, Ky. version)

"There was an old man who lived under the hill." See The farmer's curst wife (Tennessee version)

"There was an old miller by ev'ry one known." See The miller's will (North Carolina version)

"There was an old nigger, and his name was Uncle Ned." See Uncle Ned (Foster)

There was an old soldier. Civil war song. SBA

"There was an old woman and she had a little pig." See The little pig (Vermont version)

"There was an old woman in our town." See The rich old lady (Virginia version)

"There was an old woman lived on the seashore." See The two sisters (Barbourville, Ky. version no. 2)

"There was an old woman went up in a basket." H. Purcell. BOS 2

"There was an old woman who had a little pig." See The little pig (Big Laurel, N.C. version)

"There was an old woman who lived by the sea." See The two sisters (Meadows of Dan, Va. version)

"There was an old woman who owned a little pig." See The little pig (Burnsville, N.C. version)

There was an ole fish. Mountain spiritual. RA

"There was four and twenty ladies there." See Little Musgrave and Lady Barnard (Barbourville, Ky. version no. 1)

"There was none to match Kerekes" ("Nem volt párja a faluban") Hungarian folk song. e.hu. KH 1 "Nem volt párja a faluban" ("Ohnegleichen war Andreas Kerekes") g.hu. ML 3

"There was old Mister Johnson." See The cat came back (Miller)

"There was once a Filipino hombre." See The Philippine hombre

"There was once a man with a double chin." See Old Zip Coon

"There was once a poor young man." See Charlie Case song

"There was once a simple maiden." See And her golden hair was hanging down her back (McGlennon)

"There was once an old lady in the north country." See The two sisters (Mount Fair, Va. version no. 2)

"There was one little Jack." See Little Jack

"There went a fiddler marching." See O tempora! o mores

"There were a young and a lady bright." See The wife of Usher's well (Bird's Creek, Tenn. version)

"There were ninety and nine." See The ninety and nine (Sankey)

"There were ten green bottles hanging on the wall." See Green bottles

"There were ten virgins." Negro spiritual. HRD

"There were thirty four on board all told." See Greenland's icy shores

"There were three brothers in merry Scotland." See Henry Martin (Sussex version)

"There were three crows sat on a tree, lordy foldy ip fie oddy io." See The three ravens (Buena Vista, Va. version no. 2)

"There were three crows sat on a tree, O Billy Magee Magar." See Crow song (Gilmore)

"There were three gypsies a-come to my door." See The wraggle taggle gipsies, O

"There were three jovial Welshmen, as I have heard men say." See The three huntsmen

"There were three ra'ens." See The three ravens

"There were three young and gallant chafers." See The three chafers (Truhn)

"There were two brothers a-going to school." See The two brothers (Afton, Va. version)

"There were two crows sat on a tree." See The three ravens (Buena Vista, Va. version no. 1)

"There were whisperings in the heavens." English carol. FC

"There where the field of Rimini swam with the blood of legions." See "Nella fatal di Rimini" (Donizetti)

"There were two lofty ships from old England came." See High Barbaree

There'll come a time. C. K. Harris (music and words) SRW

"There's a better day a-comin'." See In that great getting-up morning

"There's a church in the valley by the wildwood." See The little brown church in the vale (Pitts)

"There's a colleen fair as May." See Péarla an brollaig báin

"There's a college down in Orono." See Hats off to the band (McCusker)

"There's a day, we feel gay." See On a Sunday afternoon (Von Tilzer)

"There's a dear little plant" (The dear little shamrock) J. W. Cherry. Words by A. Cherry. LAS

"There's a feeling come a stealing." See You're a grand old flag (Cohan)

"There's a Friend for little children." E. S. Hosmer. TSS 1

"There's a gap in the hedge at Kilmare." See The gap in the hedge

"There's a handwriting on the wall." See "Dere's a han'writin' on de wall"

"There's a letter in the candle." See The letter in the candle

"There's a little side street." See The sunshine of Paradise Alley (Bratton)

There's a little spark of love still burning. F. Fischer. Words by J. McCarthy. SMG

"There's a little wheel a-turnin' in my heart." See Little wheel a-turnin'

"There's a low green valley." See Darling Nelly Gray (Hanby)

"There's a malady terrific." See Philippinitis

"There's a man goin' 'roun' takin' names." Negro spiritual. WFN
"Dere's a man goin' roun' takin' names." FSN
"There's a man goin' roun' takin' names" (Man goin' roun') South Carolina version. SBA

"There's a meeting here to-night ("Campmeeting down in the wilderness") Negro spiritual. HRD
Dar's a meetin' here tonight. FSN
For variants see following songs of same title

There's a meeting here to-night ("I see brudder Moses yonder") Negro spiritual: Charleston, S.C. version. AS

There's a meeting here to-night ("I take my text in Mattew") Negro spiritual: Port Royal islands, S.C. version. AS

"There's a Methodist preacher." See Don't ya heah Jerusalem moan

There's a mother always waiting you at home, sweet home. J. Thornton (music and words) DFF—SMG

There's a name that's never spoken. See The picture that is turned toward the wall (Graham)

"There's a noise oh! boy! just hear it." See The aggie pep song (Tefft)

"There's a pretty spot in Ireland." See I long to see the girl I left behind (Kelly)

"There's a red light on the track for Bolsum Brown." See Bolsum Brown

There's a rose that grows on No Man's Land. See The rose of No Man's Land (Brennan)

"There's a saucy wild packet and a packet of fame." See The Dreadnaught

"There's a shining little island." See The wearing of the green

"There's a spot that the soldiers all love." See The army bean (Webster)

"There's a star in the east on Christmas morn." See Rise up, shepherd, and foller

"There's a time in each year." See In the good old summer time (Evans)

"There's a valley high and lonely." See Cân yr alltud

"There's a wedding in the orchard, dear." See Blossom time

"There's an aggregation." U.S. Naval academy song. US

"There's an island." C. W. von Gluck. Words by A. G. Latham. CSB 5

"There's an old plow 'hoss' whose name is 'Dug.'" See "Lincoln hoss" and Stephen A. (Foster)

"There's cauld kail in Aberdeen." Air: Cauld kail. Old song with additional words by W. Reid. GS

"There's fire in the east." See My way's cloudy

"There's going to be a silver wedding." See The silver wedding

There's her picture on the table. See The broken home (Fox)

There's many a man been murdered in Luzon. See The emancipated race

"There's many a man killed on the railroad." American song. SBA

"There's many a man of the Cameron clan." See The march of the Cameron men

"There's much good cheer in youthful days." See Good cheer

"There's music in the air at morning and at noon." See Music in the air, Counterpoint for (Loomis)

"There's music in the air, when the infant morn is nigh." See Music in the air (Root)

There's nae luck about the house ("And are ye sure the news is true") Scottish song. Words attributed to J. Adam and to J. Mickle. GS

There's nae luck about the house ("And are ye sure the news is true") Scottish song. Another version of words. GS

"There's nae room for twa." ₁G. Satter. Words by G. Danby₁ GS

"There's ne'er a nook in a' the land." See Dumbarton's bonny dell (Sinclair)

"There's no rain to wet you." See I want to go home (Negro spiritual)

There's nothing like a fresh'ning breeze. A. Randegger. GE

There's nothing true but heaven. O. Shaw. ₁Words by T. Moore₁ GOS 1

There's nought but care on ev'ry han'." See Green grow the rashes, O

"There's on earth but one true precious pearl" ("Csak egy szép lány van a világon") E. Szentirmay. e.hu. KH 2

"Eine schöne gibt's nur auf der welt" ("Csak egy szép lány van a világon") g.hu. ML 3

"There's one I am going this morning to meet." See Theid mi g'ad' amharc

There's one more river ("Ole Noah he did built de ark") See Noah's ark

There's one more river to cross ("The animals went in") See One more river

"There's one night in all the year." See Fairy gold

There's one wide river. See Noah's ark

"There's room enough, room enough." See I can't stay behind

There's Sergeant John McCafferty and Corporal Donahue. See The regular army, oh

"There's snakes on the mountain." See Wanderin'

"There's the nicest little club house down my way." See My sweet Adair (Friedland)

"There's the prettiest little thing as ever you did see." See The tree in the wood (Blue Ridge Springs, Va. version)

"There's three fair maids." See The cruel brother (Hot Springs, N.C. version no. 1)

"There's two little brothers going to school." See The two brothers (Berea, Ky. version)

"There's your plack, and my plack." See Jenny's bawbee

"These and those agree." See All in accord

"These are all my father's children." Negro spiritual from North Carolina. AS

These bones gwine to rise again. See Dese bones gwine to rise again

"These fair meads." See Euridice and the happy spirits (Gluck)

"These prayers I humbly raise." See Tu seconda i voti miei (Bianchi)

These tears my bosom searing. ₁Tr of Sie lacht zu meinen leiden₁ F. von Flotow. e. WLO

"These things shall be! a loftier race." J. S. Bach. Words by J. A. Symonds. DSB

"These things shall be! a loftier race" (Duke street) J. Hatton. Words by J. A. Symonds. LAS

"Thésée! il m'a trahie." See Plainte d'Ariane (Coquard)

They all love Jack. S. Adams. Words by F. E. Weatherly. BB—TFB

They always look so fine when in the line. See Hats off to the band (McCusker)

They are chiming gaily now. See Silver chimes (Barnard)

"They are roaming in the gloaming." See I'll be with you when the roses bloom again (Edwards)

"They bore him away when day had fled." See The rover's grave (Clark)

"They bored a hole in his left shoulder." See Young Beichan (Big Laurel, N.C. version no. 2)

"They call me Hanging Johnnie." See Hanging Johnnie

"They call me Singin' Johnny." See Singin' Johnny

"They crucified my Lord." See Crucifixion

"They dug him a grave at the set of the sun." See Jim the roper

They gotta quit kickin' my dawg aroun'. C. Perkins. Words by W. M. Oungst. RA

"They had not gone but nine miles." See The three butchers (Virginia version)

"They hadn't been gone but a very short time." See The wife of Usher's well (Burnsville, N.C. version no. 3)

"They hadn't been there but a very short time." See The wife of Usher's well (Carmen, N.C. version)

"They have laid him dead upon the black draped bier" ("Kitették a holttestet az udvarra") 19th century Hungarian folk song. e.hu. KH 1

"They lock'd me in an upper room." See The elopement (Ross)

They look like men of war. See The enlisted soldiers

"They loved one another." See "Sie liebten sich beide" (Stenhammar)

"They may rail at this life." Air: Noch bonin shin doe. Words by T. Moore. HMI

"They nail'd Him to the cross." See Weepin' Mary

They never comes again. See Slavery days

"They sailed away in a gallant bark." See Dublin bay (Barker)

"They saw the light shine out afar." See Golden mornings

"They say a little child." See The child and heaven

"They say I am a charming girl." See Oh, Arabella

"They say it is sinful to flirt." See Sinful to flirt

"They say, old man, your horse will die." See The dead horse

"They say that —— he ain't got no style." See Style all the while

"They say that old Texas she aint got no style." See Style all the while (University of Texas version)

"They snool me sair, and haud me down." See An' O, for ane-an'-twenty, Tam

They tell me Joe Turner he done come. See Joe Turner

"They took John Henry to the steep hill-side." See If I die a railroad man

"They were summon'd from the hillside." See Keep the home fires burning (Novello)

"They whisper first of all." See Silver chimes (Barnard)

"They who tread the path of labor" (Beecher) J. Zundel. Words by H. Van Dyke. LAS

They're over us, over us. See Bombed

Thibaut IV, king of Navarre
"L'autrier par la matinée"
"Morgens wandelnd in der auen." See "L'autrier par la matinée"
"Sons of men, behold"

"Thine eyes so blue." See "Mit deinen blauen augen" (Lassen)

"Thine image so beguiling." See Intermezzo (Schumann)

"Things are cheap on this side." See Cheapside (Farjeon)

"Things I used to do." Texas camp meeting spiritual. SBA

Think na lang, lassie. See Logie o' Buchan

Thipping thider thru a thtraw. See Sucking cider through a straw (Morgan)

Third coast artillery march. J. A. Woodward. Words by J. I. Hincke. DSO

"This blossom I name for my lover." See Midsummer dreams

"This chain is thine own." See Perlen (Sinding)

"This Child was born to men of God." See The secret flower

"This couple they got married." See Jack went a-sailing (Barbourville, Ky. version)

This day did Christ man's soul from death remove. See Yeoman's carol

"This endris night." 15th century carol. OB

"This flow'r that once to me you gave." See "La fleur que tu m'avais jetée" (Bizet)

This great war. U.S. navy song. US

"This great world is a trouble." See When dull care (Leveridge)

"This hard bondage that enchains me." See "Quella barbara catena" (Ciampi)

"This house is haunted." See Calliope

"This is Midsummer day." See Midsummer day

"This is our own, our native home." See Hurrah for old New England (Chamberlain)

"This is the gay time." See May song

This is the trouble of the world. Negro spiritual from South Carolina. AS

"This is the truth sent from above." See The truth from above

"This is the way we go to church." See Early Sunday morning

"This life is all chequer'd with pleasures and woes." Air: The bunch of green rushes. Words by T. Moore. HMI

"This may be my las' time." Negro spiritual. FSN

This mornin', this evenin', so soon. See Dis mornin', dis evenin', so soon

"This new Christmas carol." Traditional air. OB

"This night I lift my heart to Thee." See I lift my heart to Thee (Costa)

"This old man, he plays one." See Nickernacks

[This old time religion] Dat ol'-time religion. Negro spiritual. WSS
Ole-time religion. HRD

"This one and that one will court him." See The lover's curse

This outrage to my name, sirs. See Infelice! e tu credevi (Verdi)

This sun, my dearest. See 'O sole mio (Capua)

This the mission bells are telling. See Anthem (Riordan)

"This time is born a child full good." See Man, be merry as bird on berry (Dunstan)

"This way come, my gentle lasses." See Maidens, bright and fair (Flotow)

This wedding ring of mine. Old American song. SW

"This world is all a fleeting show." See There's nothing true but heaven (Shaw)

"This world seems filled with many schools." See Old S. U. (Sheldon)

"This world we may find a rough, hard world." See Cadets' graduating song for 1848

Tho'. For entries beginning Tho' see Though

Thomas, Edwin
A warrior bold (Maybrick)

Thomas, Flora W.
My lovely rose (Cadman)

Thomas, Helen
The bird's nest (Composer unknown)

Thomas, John, 1760?-1825?
Mwynen merch (Old Welsh song)

Thomas, John Rogers
Bonny Eloise
The cottage by the sea
Croquet
The day when you'll forget me
"Down by the river-side I stray"
A jolly good laugh
"Must we then meet as strangers"
The old time
Rose of Killarney
"Softly o'er the rippling waters"
"'Twas when the hay was mown, Maggie." See The old time

Thomas, Katherine Elwes
Over the way (Marshall)

Thomas, L. F.
I'm alone, all alone (Dempster)

Thomé, François Luc Joseph
A love-sonnet. See Sonnet d'amour
Sonnet d'amour

Thompson, of Newcastle
The keel row (18th century air)

Thompson, Edward
Homeward bound (Arne)

Thompson, G. W.
Alma mater—Franklin and Marshall college

Thompson, H. S.
Alma mater—Cornell university (same air as Annie Lisle)
Alma mater—Lehigh university (same air as Annie Lisle)
Alma mater—Michigan state college (same air as Annie Lisle)
Alma mater—Syracuse university (same air as Annie Lisle)
Alma mater—University of Alabama (same air as Annie Lisle)
Alma mater—University of New Mexico (same air as Annie Lisle)
Alma mater—Washington and Jefferson college (same air as Annie Lisle)
Annie Lisle
Cousin Jedediah
Crimson and the blue (same air as Annie Lisle)
Hail to Denver U (same air as Annie Lisle)
Lilly Dale

Thomson, James
Rule Britannia (Arne) Authorship uncertain

Thomson, Williel
Hail to Occidental

Thornton, James
Composer and author
My sweetheart's the man in the moon
She may have seen better days
There's a mother always waiting you at home, sweet home
Author
The Irish jubilee (Lawlor)

Thornton, L. M.
"Sing, sweet bird" (Ganz)

Thorp, N. Howard
"Little Joe, the wrangler" (Cowboy song)

"Those cows is to milk." See The single girl (Tennessee version)

Those endearing young charms. See "Believe me, if all those endearing young charms"

"Those evening bells." [Composer unknown] Words by T. Moore. BB

"Those evening bells." L. Lefébure-Wély. Words by T. Moore. TFO

Those gambler's blues ("It was down in old Joe's bar-room") Folk song. SBA
For variants see following song of same title; also St James' hospital

Those gambler's blues ("Went down to St Joe's infirmary") Folk song. SBA

"Thou art dead, ah, art dead, my beloved." See "Tu se' morta" (Monteverdi)

Those pals of ours. B. Greaton-Cole (music and words) TFB—TFO

Those wedding bells shall not ring out. M. H. Rosenfeld. SW

"Thou alone art holy." Haydn. e. SSO 1

"Thou art great and Thou art good." See Grace before meat at Hampton

"Thou art like the sun in the heav'ns at midday." See The song of praise

"Thou art lovely as a flower." See "Du bist wie eine blume" (Liszt)

"Thou art mistaken, thou tyrant." See La mia virtù non cede (Bianchi)

"Thou art my life, my soul and heart." See Widmung (Schumann)

Thou art near me, Margarita. See Dein gedenk' ich, Margareta (Meyer-Helmund)

"Thou art so like a flower." See "Du bist wie eine blume" (Rubinstein)

"Thou exile, see these fair roses." See Chant d'exil (Vidal)

"Thou forest broad and sweeping." See Farewell to the forest (Mendelssohn)

"Thou gentle dove with pinions blue." See The gentle dove

"Thou gracious inspiration, our guiding star." See College hymn (Ibsen)

"Thou gray birdling over the heather." See "Grauer vogel über der haide" (Fielitz)

"Thou hast learned to love another." C. Slade. GOS 1

"Thou hast left me ever, Jamie" (Thou hast left me Jamie) Air: Fee him, father. Words by R. Burns. GS

"Thou hast passed unto the grave." See Amber Lee (White)

"Thou hast spread thy wings to heaven." G. Donizetti. ₁Tr of Tu che a Dio spiegasti l'ali₁ e. WG

"Thou hast wounded the spirit that loved thee." ₁Mrs Porter (music and words)₁ GOS 2

Thou knowest (Atoh hu yodea) Palestinean folk song. e.he. BNP

"Thou lily white of the valley." See Liljekonvalje (Palmgren)

"Thou ling'ring star, with less'ning ray" (To Mary in heaven) L. Johnston. Words by R. Burns. GS

"Thou little bird with pinions gay." See Madrigal (Chaminade)

"Thou lovely image dear, so calmly resting." See "Soave immagine d'amore" (Mercadante)

"Thou lovely maiden, come and throw the golden dice with me." See Guldterning

Thou, O Lord, art my protector. C. Saint-Saens. e.l. ASA—CSS 1

"Thou, poor bird." Round. DSB—GSS

Thou shalt break them ₁with a rod of iron₁ G. F. Händel. SSO 3

"Thou shalt bring them in." G. F. Händel. SSO 2

Thou star resplendent, pure and bright. See O du mein holder abendstern (Wagner)

Thou sublime love, who didst guard me. See Di tanti palpiti (Rossini)

"Thou sweet evening star." See Der abendstern (Schumann)

"Thou, thou reign'st in this bosom." See "Du, du liegst mir im herzen"

"Thou who from heaven art." See Wand'rers nachtlied (Jordan)

"Thou who from thy heav'nly home." See Wand'rers nachtlied: II (Loewe)

"Thou who grantest inspiration." See "Tu sul labbro de' veggenti" (Verdi)

"Thou who watchest earth and heaven." See Ständchen (Raff)

"Thou wilt come no more, gentle Annie." See Gentle Annie (Foster)

"Thou wilt not cower in the dust." See Maryland! my Maryland

"Though all bright flowers." Air: The green bushes. Words by W. Maynard. HMI

"Tho' dark are our sorrows." See The prince's day

"Though dark the night, and rough the way before thee." See The peace of God (Gounod)

"Tho' Donald has nae mickle fraise." See The braes aboon Bonaw

"Though I have but little gear." See Si mo leannan an

"Though I'm not a gallant." Duet. Air from old Hungarian folk songs. e. KH 2

"Though light my purse." See O gur mis' tha sona dheth

"Though many and bright are the stars that appear." See E pluribus unum

"Though poor be the chamber." See Nazareth (Gounod)

"Tho' the earth be bright." See "Che farò senza Euridice" (Gluck)

"Tho' the last glimpse of Erin." See The fair-haired maiden

"Though the rocks in twain be riven." G. A. Hasse. e. SSO 4

"Tho' the rosebud her vigil keeping." See A loving kiss (Audran)

"Though the sun rests." See Do not go (Szentirmay)

"Tho' they sing of Eli Yale." See Colgate marching song

"Tho' time, wi' nidderin' frost, John." See John Anderson, my jo, John (Watson)

"Though wide be the moat." See Keine sorg' um den weg (Raff)

A thought of spring. See Ein vaartankje (Sinding)

Thoughts at eventide. See Abendempfindung (Mozart)

"The thoughts I think, the dreams I dream." See Nur du

"Thoughts of wonder." J. J. Rousseau. MFS

"Thou'rt like a flower—so winsome." See "Du bist wie eine blume" (Schumann)

"Thou'rt like unto a flower." See "Du bist wie eine blume" (Rubinstein)

"Thou'rt lovely as a flower." See "Du bist wie eine blume" (Schumann)

Thrane, Waldemar
  Aagots berglied. See Aagots fjeldsang
  Aagots fjeldsang

Three birds. See Les trois oiseaux (Cui)

"Three blind mice." Traditional round. BB—DSB—KSO—TFP

The three butchers. Folk song: Kentucky version. SES 1
  —North Carolina version. SES 1
  —Tennessee version. SES 1
  —Virginia version. SES 1
  The three butchers (Gibson, Wilson and Johnson) Sussex version. BET

The three chafers. F. H. Truhn. BB—TFB

"Three children sliding." <J. W. Elliott> ₁17th century song. Words by J. Gay₁ MFS—TFP

The three crows ("There were three crows sat on a tree, O Billy Magee Magar") See Crow song (Gilmore)

"Three days and nights fair Nina." See Nina (Ciampi)

The three fishermen ("O once there were three fishermen") College song. BB

"Three fishers went sailing" (The three fishers) J. Hullah. Words by C. Kingsley. MFS—SFB

"Three gallant ships from England came." See The battle of Stonington

"Three gipsies stood at the castle gate." See The gipsy countess: part 2

Three grains of corn. See "Give me three grains of corn, mother"

The three gypsies. See Die drei zigeuner (Liszt)

The three holy kings. See "Die heil'gen drei kön'ge aus morgenland" (Glière)

The **three** huntsmen ("The first I saw") Folk song from Virginia. SES 2

The **three** huntsmen ("There were three jovial Welshmen") Welsh song. DSB

The **three** kings ("De matin, ai rescountra lou trin") See Marcho dei rei

The **three** kings ("There came three kings from Galilee") R. Dunstan. Ancient words. DN

"**Three** kings are here, both wealthy and wise." See De drie koningen

"**Three** kings from Persian lands afar." See The kings (Cornelius)

"**Three** kings in great glory" (Kings in glory) M. Shaw. Words by S. Image. OB

Three kings of Orient. J. H. Hopkins (music and words) MFS—TFG

Kings of Orient. OB

"We three kings of Orient are." BB —DN—FC—TFO

Three kings' song. French Flanders air. e. FC

"**Three** ladies in a cambric." See Shooting of his dear (Hyden, Ky. version)

Three little lads love-story. See Her eyes don't shine like diamonds (Marion)

"**Three** little lads, one sunny day." See Le miracle de Saint-Nicolas

"**Three** little lads went out to play." See Le miracle de Saint-Nicolas

"**Three** little lads were seated one day." See Her eyes don't shine like diamonds (Marion)

"**Three** long nights, an' three long days." See Walk, Mary, down de lane

Three o'clock in the morning. Modern popular song. SMG

"**Three** old crows sat on a tree." See The three ravens (Charlottesville, Va. version)

The **three** petticoats. See Les trois jupons blancs

"**Three** pilgrims of God set out for St James." See Légende des pélerins

The **three** ravens. 16th century folk song. MBS

The three ravens (Die drei raben) e.g. ML 1

—Buena Vista, Va. version no. 1. SES 1

—Buena Vista, Va. version no. 2. SES 1

—Charlottesville, Va. version. SES 1 Variant: Crow song (Lambert)

The **three** sailor boys. T. Marzials (music and words) BB—TFO

"**Three** times round the cuckoo waltz." See Cuckoo waltz

The **three** traitors. English traditional air. Words by W. de la Mare. OB

Three white petticoats. See Les trois jupons blancs

"**Three** years ago this very day." See The regular army, oh

"**Three** years have passed." See "Tres años hace"

"**Three** young ladies was a-taking of a walk." See The cruel mother (Micaville, N.C. version)

"**Thro'** Erin's isle." See Oh! the shamrock

"**Thro'** grief and thro' danger." See The Irish peasant to his mistress

"**Through** Moorfields." Folk song from Sussex. BET

"**Thro'** night and weary day sadly Hilda spins away." See Spinn! spinn (Jüngst)

"**Through** the darkling forest gay I roam" ("Ezt a kerek erdőt járom én") J. Szerdahely. e.hu. KH 1

"**Through** the day I walked repining." See All through the night (Owen)

"**Thro'** the day, thro' the night." See The 'cello (Loomis)

"**Thro'** the leaves the night winds moving." See Ständchen (Schubert)

"**Thro'** the night, my songs entreating." See Ständchen (Schubert)

"**Thro'** the night shines a light." See Carmelina (Stevens)

"**Thro'** the night, with gentle sighing." See Ständchen (Schubert)

"**Thro'** the silence of the night." French Noël air. Words by H. Woodville. FC

"**Thro'** the tinted twilight calling." See Twilight music (Loomis)

Thro' this night so dark, so fearful. See Nell' orror di notte oscura (Rinaldo di Capua)

"**Throughout** the land dar is a cry." See Uncle Sam and Mexico (Russell)

Throw him down, McCloskey. J. W. Kelly. SRW

Throw him down, McCloskey (McCloskey's great fight) GFS

Thunder rolling, lightning bright. See The gipsy and his wife

"**Thus** angels sung, and thus sing we." See The angels' song (Gibbons)

"**Thus** saith the Lord, the Lord of hosts." G. F. Händel. SSO 4

Thus saith the Lord to Cyrus. G. F. Händel. SSO 2

"**Thus** when the sun." G. F. Händel. SSO 3

"**Thy** father now is far awa'." See Scotch cradle-song

Thy glorious deeds inspir'd my tongue. G. F. Händel. SSO 4

"**Thy** kingdom come—on bended knee." J. B. Dykes. Words by F. L. Hosmer. LAS

"**Thy** mouth is like a cherry gleaming." See Fleur d'amour (Weyts)

Thy praise we raise with loud acclaim. See Hail to Occidental (Thomson)

Thy vows, my treasure, are such possession. See Nel dolce incanto (Benedict)

Thy will be done (Gethsemane) Barri. Words by A. Volkmer. CSS 1—CSS 2

Ti di um dum dum dum. See "My grandmother lived on yonder little green"

Tibby hey rig a jig in a jaunting car. See Clear the track, let the bullgine run

Tick, tick! it said. See The old cottage clock (Molloy)

The **ticket** that's honest we'll honor. See Straight-out Democrat

Tidings true there be come new. See "Nowell, Nowell, Nowell, Nowell! This is the salutacyon of the angell Gabryell"

Tiedge, Christoph August
Der rose sendung (Himmel)

"Tief in meeres grünen felsenhallen." See Neckens polska

The **tiger** song. University of Missouri song. N. Burkholder and G. Fowler. Words by G. Fowler. KU

Till bruden (To the bride) W. Peterson-Berger. Words by W. von Heidenstam. e.sw. WM 2

Tilton, Theodore
"Baby bye, here's a fly" (Loomis)

Tilzer, Harry Von. See Von Tilzer, Harry

Tim Finigan's wake. Old song. US

Timber. Negro work song. SBA

Time and tide. P. Rodney. Words by H. L. D. Jaxone. SFB

Time for us to leave her. Halliard chantey. TSB 2
Variant of: Leave her, Johnnie

"The **time** has come, an' I must go." See Good bye, Liza Jane

"**Time** is flying on slow wing." See Ah! non avea più lagrime (Donizetti)

"De **time** is nebber dreary." See Ring, ring de banjo (Foster)

"The **time** is never dreary." See Ring, ring, de banjo (Foster)

"The **time** is sweetly rolling on." See Hicks's farewell (Montvale, Va. version)

"The **time** is swiftly passing by." See Hicks's farewell (Buena Vista, Va. version)

"The **time** is swiftly rolling on." See Hicks's farewell (Micaville, N.C. version)

"The **time** I've lost in wooing." Irish air: Pease upon a trencher. Words by T. Moore. HMI

"The **time** of the singing of birds." G. Barker. MFS

"The **time's** been sweet I've spent with you." See Hicks's farewell (Spillcorn, N.C. version)

"**Times** gettin' hard, boys." Negro folk song. SBA

The **tinker** ("Have you any work for the tinker") Round. GSS

A **tinker** and a tailor. See Jessie, the belle at the bar (Ware)

"A **tinker** I am, my name's Natty Dan." See The tinker's song (Dibdin)

The **tinker's** song. C. Dibdin. WOE

"A **tiny** little man stands in forest dim." See A little man

"**'Tis** a garden, that fair Hawaiian island." See In Hawaii

"**'Tis** a hundred years." See The boatswain's story (Molloy)

"**'Tis** a sight entrancing." See Rinnce Philib an cheoil

'Tis a wonder. Mountain spiritual from North Carolina. SES 2

"**'Tis** advertised in Boston." See Blow, ye winds in the morning

"**'Tis** all in vain." G. Bizet. [Tr of En vain pour éviter les réponses amères] e. WG

"**'Tis** all the same to me." See It matters not (Dargomyzhskiĭ)

"**'Tis** believed that this harp." Air: Gage fane. Words by T. Moore. HMI—SI

"**'Tis** break of day, the herds are lowing." See Lioba

"**'Tis** dawn of night! the calm brook flows." See Dawn of night (Nikolaev)

"**'Tis** growing late." See Good-night (Jakobowski)

"**'Tis** here we are pledging with heart and with hand." See The patriots

"**'Tis** hum-drum, 'tis mum, mum." See Gaping catch (Harrington)

'Tis I ("When the dark green waves") C. Pinsuti. Words by F. Lablache. SFB

"**'Tis** in vain your counsel beguiling." See Obstination (Fontenailles)

"**'Tis** just a year ago today." See The poor old slave

'Tis me, O Lord. See It's me, O Lord

"**'Tis** midnight hour." Composer and author of words unknown. GOS 1

"**'Tis** moonlight on the sea, boys." See Dip, boys, dip the oar (Sarona)

"**'Tis** night on Venice waters." See On Venice waters (Roeder)

"**'Tis** no time to take a wife." Irish air. Words by J. Oxenford. HMI

'Tis not true. See Non è ver (Mattei)

"**'Tis** of a fearless Irishman a story I will tell." See Brennan on the moor (Virginia version)

"**'Tis** of a rich merchant who in London did dwell." See Vilikins and his Dinah (Parry)

"**'Tis** Paul and Silas bound in chains, chains." See The winter

"**'Tis** springtime." Süssmayer. Words by J. B. Walters. BB

'Tis sweet to think. See "Oh! 'tis sweet to think"

'Tis the bean that we mean. See The army bean (Webster)

"**'Tis** the last rose of summer." See The last rose of summer

'Tis the ole ship of Zion. See Old ship of Zion (Virginia version)

'Tis the song and the sigh of the hungry. See Hard crackers (Foster)

'Tis the song, the sigh of the weary. See Hard times, come again no more (Foster)

"**'Tis** well, my friends." See Call forth thy powers (Händel)

"'Tis years since last we met." See Her bright smile haunts me still (Wrightson)

Tit-willow. A. Sullivan. Words by W. S. Gilbert. DSC

Titania ("En klang som af små violinar") V. Peterson-Berger. Words by G. Fröding. e.sw. WM 2

[Titania's song] "Child of earth with the golden hair." C. Horn. MFS

De Titanic. Negro ballad. SBA

"Titans on the red and white." See March of the Titans (Kolar)

Titov, Nikolaï Aleksïeevich
The scarlet sarafan (wrongly attributed) See Varlamov, A. I. The scarlet sarafan

"Titty Mary, you know I gwine follow." See Gwine follow

"Titty 'Ritta die like-a Lazarus die." See "I want to die like-a Lazarus die"

"To a mansion in the city came a couple old and gray." See Just plain folks (Stonehill)

"To a mind worn and weary." See Preghiera (Tosti)

To a rose. L. A. Coerne. Words by D. Stevens. TFB—TFO

"To act! with my heart madden'd with sorrow." See Vesti la giubba (Leoncavallo)

To all my faithful comrades be known soon my arrival. See O, tu Palermo (Verdi)

"To all the world our flag unfurl'd." See 'Neath our flag (Barnby)

"To all you ladies now at land." Old English air. Words by Lord Buckhurst, later Earl of Dorset. BOS 2

"To Anacreon in heav'n." Attributed to J. S. Smith [wrongly attributed to S. Arnold] Words by R. Tomlinson. DSO—SRW

To Anthea. See "Bid me to live" (Hatton)

To arms ("Awake! arise") Air: A wet sheet and a flowing sea. Words by P. Benjamin. DSO

To arms, to arms, ye brave. See La Marseillaise (Rouget de Lisle)

"To die, so pure and lovely." See The fatal stone (Verdi)

"To do to others as I would." See The golden rule

"To France were returning two grenadiers." See Die beiden grenadiere (Schumann)

"To God eternal." L. van Beethoven. e. LAS

"To God on high be thanks and praise." N. Decius (music and words) [Tr of Allein Gott in der höh sey ehr] e. DSC

"To Hans one day said Gretchen." See Der schwur (Bohm)

"To her we sing who keeps the ward." See Alma mater—University of Washington (Hager)

"La to jente t'aspettava tutt' allegra a lu balcone." See Vocero

"To keep us awake we have done our best." See All noddin'

"To ladies' eyes." Irish air: Fág an bealach, or, Fague a ballagh, or, Clear the way. Words by T. Moore. HMI

To Mary in heaven. See "Thou ling'ring star, with less'ning ray" (Johnston)

To-morrow. For entries beginning Tomorrow see Tomorrow

To music ("Crystalline fount of tears health-welling") N. Tscherepnin. Words from a Russian translation of Shelley. ATS

To music ("Du holde kunst") See An die musik (Schubert)

To my hi-rig-a-jig and a low-back car. See Clear de track, let de bulgine run

"To my way-a-y-ay ah! we'll pay Paddy Doyle for his boots." See Paddy Doyle

"To my way-ay-ay-ah, we'll pay Paddy Doyle for his boots." See Paddy Doyle's boots

"To my way-ay-ay-ah-yah, we'll pay Paddy Doyle for his boots." See Paddy Doyle's boots

"To ne îastreb sovykalsïa." See A maiden's revenge

"To old De Pauw we toast to-day." See A toast to De Pauw (Bard)

"To one and all both great and small." See Jesse Cole

To our flag. Flemish folk air. Words by J. L. Vandevere. TFO

To ring dem charmin' bells. See Mary and Martha

To see God's bleedin' lam'. Negro spiritual. JB 2

"To shorten winter's sadness." P. W. Dykema. Old English words. TFB —TFP

"To tell thee something I am yearning." See Verlegenheit (Abt)

To the bride. See Till bruden (Peterson-Berger)

"To the brook and the willow." See Ah! willow

To the Carabao. Air: Wearing of the green. US

To the eighteenth. Old 18th U.S. infantry song. Air: Old Heidelberg. DSO

To the Eternal One. See Dem unendlichen (Schubert)

To the evening star ("Thou sweet ev'ning star") See Der abendstern (Schumann)

"To the fairest college." Amherst college song. D. C. Bartlett (music and words) AI

"To the lords of convention." See Bonnie Dundee (Sainton-Dolby?)

"To the memory of Crockett." See The death of Crockett (Smith?)

"To the sacred banks of the Nile." See March of the victors (Verdi)

"To Thee a pray'r for mercy I am sending." See Busslied (Beethoven)

To thee I will not yield me. See La mia virtù non cede (Bianchi)

"To thee, Jehovah."   See "Dir, dir, Jehovah" (Bach)

"To thee, O country."   J. Eichberg. Words by Mrs J. Lane.   BB—TFB—TFG

"To Thee, our Father and our Friend." See Fourth of July hymn (Hastings)

"To think that once you held the plough." See Ah! happy day (Audran)

"To us a Child is born from heav'n."   15th century air: Puer natus in Bethlehem, arr by J. S. Bach.   DNS

"To us in Bethlem city."   See Eia, Eia

"To wander is the miller's joy."   See Das wandern (Schubert)

"To you I come from heav'n."   Scottish carol. Air: Hee balaw.   17th century words.   DN

"To you, oh! alma mater."   See Oh! fairest alma mater (Sleeper)

"Toad goes a-courting."   See "A frog he went a-courting" (Berea, Ky. version)

A toast ("A health to all who gather here") F. Ames (D. Stevens)   Words by D. Stevens.   TFB—TFO

A toast to De Pauw.   De Pauw university alma mater.   V. Bard.   AIS—KU

Toast to Wisconsin.   College song.   Arr from Gounod.   AI—AIS

Varsity toast.   KU—KV

"Töchterchen, willst ein häubchen du." See "Ma fille, veux-tu un bonnet"

Der tod ("Gestern, brüder, könnt ihr's glauben") Volksweise.   Words by G. E. Lessing.   g.   EDL

Der tod ("Mich hat belogen das vöglein."— O charhos) Greek folk song.   g.gr. ML 2

Der tod als schnitter.   See "Es ist ein schnitter"

Der tod und das mädchen.   F. Schubert. Words by M. Claudius.   g.   EDL

Der tod von Basel ("Als ich ein junggeselle war") Volkslied.   g.   EDL

"Today is Monday."   U.S. army song. TFP

Soup song (All you little rookies, we wish the same to you)   SMG

"Today we gladly sing the praise."   See Alma mater—University of Chicago

"Today you're all invited to our gymnasium."   See At the gym

Todtengräbers heimweh (The gravedigger) F. Schubert.   e.g.   GA

"Together let us sweetly live."   See Canaan

"Together to the cradle."   See Grand concours de peuples à Bethléem

Toleken, W., of Cork.   See Bennett, Henry, jt. auth.

Tölf synir (Zwölf söhne)   Icelandic folk song.   g.ic.   ML 1

Toll the bell.   C. Converse.   WSS

Toll, toll the bell at early dawn of day. See Bright-eyed little Nell of Narragansett bay

Toll, toll the bell, for gentle Lilly Dale. See Toll the bell (Converse)

Tolstoĭ, Aleksĭeĭ Konstantinovich, graf Ah, if mother Volga (Panchenko) "No word from thee, in gladness or in sorrow" (Tchaikovsky)

Tom-big-bee river (Gum-tree canoe)   S. S. Steele (music and words)   BNM —WSS

"Tom Bolynn."   Folk song: Hyden, Ky. version no. 1.   SES 2 —Hyden, Ky. version no. 2.   SES 2 Variant of: "Tommy a' Lynn"

"Tom he was a piper's son."   See Over the hills and far away

"Tom Pearce, Tom Pearce, lend me your grey mare."   See Widdicombe fair (Devonshire version)

Tomb that enshrin'st the lifeless heart. See Perchè dell' aure in sen (Donizetti)

Tomba che chiudi esanime.   See Perchè dell' aure in sen (Donizetti)

Tombigbee river.   See Tom-big-bee river (Steele)

Tomer, William Gould "God be with you"

Tomlinson, Bob Victory song

Tomlinson, Ralph "To Anacreon in heav'n" (Smith?)

"Tommy a' Lynn" (see Song Index) Variant: "Tom Bolynn"

Tommy Dodd.   English music-hall song. SW

"Tommy's gone, and I'll go too."   See Tom's gone to Hilo

[Tommy's gone to Hilo ("I've just come down")]   The wild goose shanty. Hauling chantey.   TSB 1 Variants: Huckleberry hunting; Tom's gone to Hilo

"Tommy's gone, what shall I do."   See My Tommy's gone away

To-morrow ("O God, of all the Maker."— Aurelia)   S. S. Wesley.   Words by S. N. Patten.   TFP

"Tomorrow I am gwine away."   See I'll be dar

"Tomorrow morning I'm sweet sixteen." See Billy Grimes

"Tomorrow shall be my dancing day." See My dancing day

"Tomorrow, the fox will come to town." See Trenchmore

Tomorrow you may die.   Negro spiritual. FSN

Tom's gone to Hilo ("Oh! Tommy's gone, what shall I do")   Halliard chantey.   SBS For variants see following song of same title; also John's gone to Hilo; My Tommy's gone away; Tommy's gone to Hilo

Tom's gone to Hilo ("Tommy's gone, and I'll go too")   Halliard chantey. TSB 1

Ein ton (The voice)   P. Cornelius (music and words)   e.g.   GA

"Tonight you see my face."   See Cruckhaun Finn

"**Too** late, too late, sinnah" (Done carry de key an' gone home) Negro spiritual. JB 2

"**Too** late you have come back to me." Old American song. SW

Too proud to beg, too honest to steal. See Shabby genteel (Clifton)

Topliff, Robert
Consider the lilies

"**Torches,** torches, run with torches." See Villancico de Navidad

"**Toreador,** e'er watchful be." See Chanson du toréador (Bizet)

Toreador song. See Chanson du toréador (Bizet)

The **torpedo** and the whale. E. Audran. e. WLO

"**Tortured** and torn by cruel scourges." See No sorrow like to His (Hasse)

"**Tossed** on seas of fierce temptation." Serini. e. SSO 1

Tosti, Francesco Paolo
Beauty's eyes
Guide us with Thy heavenly light
Help me to pray. See Guide us with Thy heavenly light
My King of grace
Prayer. See Preghiera
Preghiera
Serenade. See La serenata
La serenata
"To a mind worn and weary." See Preghiera

"**Total** eclipse! no sun, no moon." G. F. Händel. SSO 3

Totenklage ("Dumattina quest' è l' jornu di la virgine Maria") See Lamento ("Dumattina quest' è l' jornu di la virgine Maria")

Totenklage ("Eju filaja la miò rocca") See Vocero ("Eju filaja la miò rocca")

Totenklage ("Quando junse la nuvella") See Lamento ("Quando junse la nuvella")

Totenklage ("Quandu n'intesi la nova alle Ferrera d'Orezza") See Lamento ("Quandu n'intesi la nova alle Ferrera d'Orezza")

Totenklage ("La to jente t'aspettava tutt' allegra a lu balcone") See Vocero ("La to jente t'aspettava tutt' allegra a lu balcone")

Totenklagen ("Uch ón, uch ón") See Caoineadh

"The **Tottenham** toad." Folk song from Virginia. SES 2

"**Touch** not the cup." T. H. Bayly. Words by J. H. Aikman. MFS

Touch the elbow. Song of the 7th regiment of New York. DSO

"**Touch** us gently, time." Words by B. W. Procter (B. Cornwall) MFS

Touchdown song ("Touchdown, we want a touchdown") Lehigh university song. AIS

Touchdown song ("We want a touchdown") U.S. Naval academy song. D. Wilkerson. US

Tourison, Charles Edward
The big red team

Tours, Berthold
The gate of heaven
"Jesus, Lover of my soul"

Tovey, Henry Doughty
Alma mater—University of Arkansas

[**Towing-song**] Dubīnushka (Gesang der hafenarbeiter) Russian folk song. g.r. ML 1
Variant of: Volga boat song

"A **town** lies in the valley." See The silent city (Sibelius)

"**Tra** ballade repaces e niñas." See A moda gallega

Tra la la la ("Dans la maisonnette au pied de la lande."—Lied) Breton folk song. f.g. ML 1

"**Tra** la la la la, my banjo is saying." See My banjo

Trabling back to Georgia. Minstrel song. WSS

Tracey, William
Play that barber shop chord (Muir)

Tracy, George Lowell
The cautious cat

A **tragic** story. See The pigtail (Mozart)

The **trail** to Mexico. Cowboy song. LSC—SBA

The **train** that never returned. American mountain song. Air: The ship that never returned. RA—SW

"**Train's** a-comin'." Negro spiritual. HB

Tramp, tramp, tramp ("In the prison cell") G. F. Root (music and words) BB—DSO

Tramp, tramp, tramp ("On the battle front") G. F. Root. Words by D. Stevens. TFP

"A **tramp** whose hopes were shattered wander'd aimlessly along." See The picture that was drawn upon the floor (Gilligan)

Transport song (Don't spit on the deck) Song of the Spanish-American war. Air: Son of a gambolier. DSO

"**Traue** nimmer deinem glücke." See La caña

Trauer um die jugend (Zhal'ba za mladost') Macedonian folk song. b.g. ML 2

Der **traum** ("'Twas in a meadow") See The dream (Rubinstein)

Der **träumende** see (The dreaming mere) H. Brückler. Words by J. Mosen. e.g. HCA

"**Traurig** wiegt sich die birke" ("Vai, liūdnas, baltas berželis") Lithuanian folk song. g.li. ML 3

Die **traurige** braut (Žalostna zaručnica) Croatian folk song. g.se. ML 2

Travel on ("Sister Rosy, you get to heaven") Negro spiritual from South Carolina. AS

Travel on, my weary soul. See Hear from heaven to-day

Travel the country round. Folk song from Sussex. BET

Traveling back to Georgia. See Trabling back to Georgia

"**Tre** giorni son che Nina." See Nina (Ciampi)

The **tree** in the wood.   English folk song:
1st version.   BB—DSB—GSS—
TFG
—North Carolina version.   SES 2
—Blue Ridge Springs, Va. version.
SES 2
—St Peter's school, Va. version.
SES 2
Variants: Pretty pear tree; The tree
on the hill
The **tree** on the hill.   English folk song.
BOS 2
Variant of: The tree in the wood
Tree song ("Live, live, live")   Croatian
folk air.   Words by L. C. Perkins.
GSS
"A **tree** toad loved a wee toad."   See
The tree toads (Loomis)
The **tree** toads.   H. W. Loomis.   TFR
The **trees** and the Master.   ⌊J. P. Mc-
Caskey⌋ Words by S. Lanier.   MFS
"The **trees** they do grow high" (English
folk song) (see Song Index)
Variants: "Oh, the trees are getting
high"; Still growing
"The **trees** they do grow high."   English
folk air.   Girl scout words by M.
Edgar.   GSS
Treharne, Bryceson
Reuben Ranzo
"**Treib** die sau nach hause."   See Der
schweinehirt
Treibe schifflein.   For English translation
see "Drift, my bark" (Kücken)
Trelawny.   See Song of the western men
La **tremenda,** ultrice spada.   See "Se
Romeo t'uccise un figlio" (Bellini)
⌊**Trenchmore**⌋ "Tomorrow the fox."   ⌊16th
century song⌋   BOS 2
Trennung und wiedersehn (Wotsalenje a
zasowidženje)   Wendish folk song.
g.we.   ML 3
"Le **trente-et-un** du mois d'août."   See
Le combat naval
"Die **trepp'** hinunter geschwungen."   See
Niemand hat's geseh'n (Loewe)
"**Tres** años hace" ("Three years have
passed")   Mexican folk song.   e.s.
VS
Treue liebe ("Ach, wie ist's möglich dann")
Volksweise.   Volkslied from the
Thuringian forest.   g.   EDL
Treue liebe ("Ach, wie ist's möglich dann")
F. Kücken.   Volkslied from the
Thuringian forest.   g.   EDL
"How can I leave thee."   e.   BB—
DFF—TFB— TFO— TFP— TFR—
WSS
Treue liebe ("Soviel stern' am himmel")
Volksweise.   g.   EDL
Treue liebe ("Steh' ich")   See "Steh' ich
in finstrer mitternacht"
Trevathan, Charles E.
The bully song
May Irwin's "bully" song.   See The
bully song
The new bully.   See The bully song
Trezise, Frederick William
Viking song (Maesch)
"**Tr**″gnala e Dana."   See "Dana ging aus"

"**Tri** dni mi je, kak sam došel s tabora."
See "Drei tage sind's, dass ich vom
krieg zurückgekehrt"
Tri godīnī bolen lezham.   See Schon drei
jahre liege ich krank
"**Trifft** ein jemand eine jemand."   See
Comin' thro' the rye
"**Trihs** rihtiṇu malti gahju."   See "Dreimal
in der früh traf ich"
"**Trinke** mir nur mit blicken zu."   See
"Drink to me only with thine eyes"
(Harrington?)
Der **trinker.**   See Der rheinweinzecher
(Fischer)
Trinklied ("A éigse Fodla dlúthaig")   See
An crúiscín lán
Trinklied ("Am un leu")   See "Am un
leu"
Trinklied ("Blondes mädel, ḧeller morgen."
—Garavuša)   Slavonian folk song.
g.se.   ML 2
Trinklied ("Blythe, blythe")   See "Blythe,
blythe, and merry are we"
Trinklied ("Braune wirtin, bring mir wein."
—"Korcsmárosné, be barna")   Hun-
garian folk song.   g.hu.   ML 3
Trinklied ("Here's a health to the king")
See Down among the dead men
Trinklied ("Jokkel stiess mit Jakob an")
See "Jacob, drink"
Trip it, trip it in a ring.   H. Purcell.
DSB
Tritt zu.   Volkslied.   g.   EDL
The **triumph** hymn.   University of Ne-
vada song.   ⌊Air: Russian national
hymn, by A. F. Lvov⌋   Words by J.
O'Sullivan.   HW
"**Triumph!** thanksgiving."   S.   Rach-
maninoff.   e.   DSC
Tro (Faith)   C. Sinding.   Words by H.
Drachmann.   da.e.   WM 2
Les **trois** canards ("My father has had a
pond made")   French folk song.
e.f.   CBF 2
Variant of: Le canard blanc
⌊Les **trois** capitaines⌋   "En passant par
la Lorraine."   Dance song.   f.
DSB—MBS
"En passant par la Lorraine" ("Wollt'
durch Lothringen marschieren")
f.g.   ML 1
Song of Lorraine.   e.   DSC
"**Trois** jeun' tambours s'en rev'nant de la
guerre."   See Le joli tambour
Les **trois** jupons blancs (The three petti-
coats.—Three white petticoats)   Folk
song from upper Champagne.   e.f.
CBF 1
Les **trois** matelots de Groix (Die drei ma-
trosen aus Groix)   French folk song.
f.g.   ML 1
Les **trois** oiseaux (Three birds)   C. Cui.
Words by F. Coppée.   e.f.   ATS
"**Trois** pélerins de Dieu."   See Légende
des pélerins
Les **trois** princesses.   See "Derrièr' chez
mon père, vole, vole, mon coeur, vole"
(French folk song)
Trojan marching song.   University of
Southern California song.   G. John-
ston.   HW—KU—KV

Trojan war song. University of Southern California song. G. W. Evans (music and words) AI—AIS

"Trojans! march on! march on." See Trojan marching song (Johnston)

"Troll and goblin, come not here." See The counter-charm

Trombone song. Song of the College of the city of New York. J. C. Saltman (music and words) AI—AIS

Trono e corona. See Io l'udia ne' suoi bei carmi (Donizetti)

The trooper and the maid. Folk song: Big Laurel, N.C. version. SES 1
—Burnsville, N.C. version. SES 1
—Tennessee version. SES 1

Tros y garreg (Über den stein) Welsh folk air. Words by Ceiriog. g.w. ML 1

Trøst, Svend. See Drachmann, Holger

Trot, trot, trot, is the soldier's lot. See In the second cavalry

Trotère, H., pseud. See Trotter, Henry

Trotter, Henry
In old Madrid

The trouble of the world. Negro spiritual from South Carolina. AS

Trouble will bury me down. Negro spiritual. WFN

The troubled soldier. Folk song. Kentucky mountain air: One morning in May. SBA

"Trouble's gwine ter weigh me down." Negro spiritual from South Carolina. FSN

"True, I'm like the bee that flieth." See "Son leggero e ver d'amore" (Donizetti)

True love from the eastern shore. Folk song: Dewey, Va. version. SES 2
—Montvale, Va. version. SES 2

The true lover's farewell. Folk song: American version. SBA
—Kentucky version. SES 2
—Black Mountain, N.C. version. SES 2
—Carmen, N.C. version. SES 2
—Hot Springs, N.C. version. SES 2
—Tennessee version. SES 2
—Callaway, Va. version. SES 2
—Dewey, Va. version. SES 2
—Endicott, Va. version. SES 2
—Peaks of Otter, Va. version. SES 2
Variants: Fair Annie of Lochyran; "Her check is like some blooming red rose"; He's gone away; The lover's lament; Who will shoe your pretty little foot

The truffle song. J. Strauss. e. WLO

Truhn, Friedrich Hieronymus
The three chafers

"The trumpet shall sound." G. F. Händel. SSO 4

Trust. See "God shall charge His angel legions" (Mendelssohn)

"Trust in the Lord." G. F. Händel. LAS

"Trust them not" ("A legény egytöl egyig") E. Szentirmay (music and words) e.hu. KH 2

Trusting I call. J. Jordan (music and words) TSS 1—TSS 2

Trusting in Thee. R. Coverley. Words by W. H. Gardner. TSS 1—TSS 2

The truth from above. Traditional carol from Herefordshire. OB

"Try my bes' for to serve my Master." See All I do, de church keep a-grumblin'

Tsar' Murad i Mara. See Zar Murat und Mara

Tschaikovsky, Peter Ilyich. See Tchaikovsky, Peter Ilyich

Tscherepnin, Nikolas Nicolaievitch. See Cherepnin, Nikolaï Nikolaevich

"Tsïgular' küshcha ne khranï." See Der musikant

"Tsu, tsu, äiu, äiu, tsu, tsu." See Wiegenlied (Esthonian folk song)

Tú ("En Cuba, la isla hermosa."—"O Cuba") Cuban habanera. E. Sánchez de Fuentes. Words by F. Sánchez. MSP

Tu che a Dio spiegasti l'ali. For English translation see "Thou hast spread thy wings to heaven" (Donizetti)

Tu che accendi questo core. See Di tanti palpiti (Rossini)

"Tu m'aje prommise quatto muccatora." See Ritornello delle lavandare del Vomero

"Tu nel tuo letto a far de' sogni d'oro" ("Du traumst im warmen bett") Abruzzian folk song. g.i. ML 2

"Tu non sai con quei begli occhi." V. Bellini. e.i. PB

"Tu se' morta." C. Monteverdi. e.i. KVG

Tu seconda i voti miei. Prayer. F. Bianchi. e.i. KVG

"Tu sul labbro de' veggenti" ("Thou who grantest inspiration") G. Verdi. e.i. PB

Tucker, Henry
Down in Charleston jail (same air as When this cruel war is over)
Sweet Genevieve
Weeping, sad and lonely. See When this cruel war is over
When this cruel war is over

Tukkipoika. See Holzflösser

Tule mulle, neitsikene. See Will you be mine

Tullochgorum ("Come, gie's a sang, the lady cried") Scottish air: Reel of Tullochgorum. Words by J. Skinner. GS

"Tune ev'ry heart and ev'ry voice, let all with one accord rejoice in praise of old Nassau." See Old Nassau (Langlotz)

Tuney, Lemuel J. See Leonard, Eddie

"Tuol laulaa neitonen." See "A maiden yonder sings" (Sibelius)

Turkey in the straw ("As I was a-gwine down the road") Old air. SBA
For variants see following songs of same title; also Old Zip Coon; Zip Coon

Turkey in the straw ["I went down the levee"] Old air. Words by L. Wood. Chorus only. SMG

Turkey in the straw ("I went down to Sandy Hook."—Zip Coon) Old air. WSS

Turkey in the straw ("Went down to New Orleans") Old air. SBA

"The Turks they had a lovely daughter." See Young Beichan (Manchester, Ky. version no. 2)

"Turn again, Whittington." Old round. DSB—TFP

Turn back Pharaoh's army. Negro spiritual. BB—WSS

"Turn, sinner, turn today." See Turn, sinner, turn O

Turn, sinner, turn O. Negro spiritual from South Carolina. AS

Turn Thee unto me. M. Costa. CSS 1

"Turn to me, dark eye so tender." See Bitte (Franz); Bitte (Sjögren)

"Turn, turn, turn your eyes." See The moon reappears (Purcell)

"Turn upon my worn and weary face" ("Nyugtasd rajtam") E. Szentirmay (music and words) e.hu. KH 2

Turn ye to me ("The stars are burning cheerily, cheerily") [Air: Horo mhairi dhu] Words by Christopher North (J. Wilson) DSC

Turner, Joseph W.
Roll on, silver moon: old air arranged

The turtle dove ("In a shady forest") Old Russian song. e. DSB

"Tutto è deserto." See Il balen del suo sorriso (Verdi)

"Tuulen tuimuudesta puiden." See Die spröde

Twankydillo. <Sussex county song> Traditional air. SSB

"'Twas a calm still night." See Lilly Dale (Thompson)

"'Twas a cold winter night." See Katy avourneen (Johnson)

'Twas a false and cruel story. See "Ditemi, buona gente, vedeste Dinorah" (Meyerbeer)

"'Twas a inch by inch I sought the Lord." See Inching along

"'Twas about the dead of night" (Athens) Easter carol. <Words by J. M. Neale> OB

'Twas, ah, there, you beauty. See Ah there! stay there

"'Twas at a fancy ball." See Tassels on the boots

"'Twas at the Moorgate station." See Jessie, the belle at the bar (Ware)

"'Twas at the siege of Vicksburg." Confederate song. [S. Winner] DSO

"'Twas down at Dan McDevitt's." See Throw him down, McCloskey (Kelly)

"'Twas down in a valley." See The lost lady found

"'Twas early, early in the spring." See Early, early in the spring (Virginia version)

"'Twas early one morning the ploughboy arose." See The simple ploughboy (Virginia version)

"'Twas Easter eve, and to the house of prayer my steps I bent." See Easter eve (Gounod)

"'Twas Friday morn when we set sail." See The mermaid

"'Twas in a meadow by the way." See The dream (Rubinstein)

"'Twas in a Pennsylvania town not very long ago." See Father was killed by the Pinkerton men (Delaney)

"'Twas in eighteen hundred and thirty-six that we fought in the Everglades." See In the second cavalry

"'Twas in 'fifty-five on a winter's night." See The midshipmite (Maybrick)

"'Twas in the merry month of May." See Barbara Allen (Habersham county, Ga. version; Kentucky version no. 2)

"'Twas in the month of August, or the middle of July." See She said the same to me

"'Twas in the season of the year." See Roslin castle (Oswald?)

"'Twas in the town of Jacksboro." See Range of the buffalo

"'Twas Josie dear, and he did go." See Josie dear

"'Twas just about a year ago." See I saw Esau

"'Twas late one Sunday evening." See The lady and the dragoon (Afton, Va. version)

"'Twas off the blue Canary Isles." See My last cigar (Crosby)

"'Twas on a bright mornin' in summer." See Cailín deas cruídhte na mbó

"'Twas on a dark and holiday." See Sir Hugh (Teges, Ky. version)

"'Twas on a Monday morning, right early in the year." See O Charlie is my darling (Additional words by Burns); O Charlie is my darling (Additional words by Nairne)

"'Twas on a Monday morning, the first I saw my darling a-hanging out the linen clothes." See Hanging out the linen clothes

"'Twas on a Monday morning, when birds were singing clear." See O Charlie is my darling (Original words)

"'Twas on a Monday morning when I beheld my darling; O she was fair and she was free." See Driving away at the smoothing iron

"'Twas on a winter's evening when first came down the snow." See The Fanaid grove

"'Twas once upon a summer day." See The maiden's rose (Hatton)

"'Twas one morn when the wind from the nor'rard blew keenly." See Will Watch (Davy)

"'Twas one October mornin' that I seen a wond'rous sight." See Bigerlow

"'Twas the emancipated race." See The emancipated race

'Twas the picture of her father. See Picture eighty-four

'Twas the sound of his horn brought me from my bed. See John Peel
" 'Twas twenty-seven bells by the Waterbury watch." See Twenty-seven bells by the Waterbury watch (Macgregor)
" 'Twas when the hay was mown, Maggie." See The old time (Thomas)
" 'Twas winter, and blue Tory noses were freezing." See The banks of the Dee, Parody on
" 'Twas within a mile of Edinboro' town." See Within a mile of Edinboro' (Hook)
" 'Twas years ago when last we parted." See Somewhere (Clark)
Tweed side ("What beauties") See "What beauties does Flora disclose"
Tweed side ("When Maggie and I") See "When Maggie and I was acquaint"
Tweeddale, John Hay, 2d marquis of "When Maggie and I was acquaint" (Scottish air)
"12 are the 12 apostles." See The ten commandments (Black Mountain, N.C. version)
The twelve days of Christmas ("The first day of Christmas") Old English folk song. TFP
For variant see following song of same title
The twelve days of Christmas ("On the twelfth day of Christmas") English folk song. MFF
"Twelve months ago this very night." See Twelve months ago to-night (Fox)
Twelve months ago to-night. W. H. Fox. Words by J. F. Mitchell. GFS
"Twelve months he rose, put on his clothes." See The Suffolk miracle (Callaway, Va. version)
The twenty-fourth of February. Forecastle song. WSE
Twenty-seven bells by the Waterbury watch. D. Macgregor. US
Twenty years ago ("I've wander'd to the village, Tom") W. Willing. GOS 1
" 'Twere vain to tell thee all I feel." Swiss air. [Words by J. A. Wade] GOS 2
Twickenham ferry. T. Marzials. GE —MFS
Twilight ("Mörkgrön granskog skuggar öfver viken") See Aftonstämning (Peterson-Berger)
Twilight ("Now the day is over") See "Now the day is over" (Barnby)
Twilight dews. T. Moore (music and words) GOS 1
Twilight dreams. Basque folk air. Words by W. H. Pierce. TFO
A twilight fancy (Dresden China) J. L. Molloy. Words by F. E. Weatherly. GE
Twilight is falling ("Twilight is stealing") B. C. Unseld. Words by A. S. Keiffer. MFS
"Twilight is stealing over the sea." See Twilight is falling (Unseld)
Twilight music. W. F. Scollard. Words by C. Harvey. TFG

" 'Twill be a painful separation" (see Song Index)
Also in "In gentle murmurs will I mourn" (Händel) SSO 2
The twin roses. J. Hewitt. MPA 2
"Twinkle brightly, stars of light." See Baby's night
"Twinkle, twinkle, little star" (Twinkle, little star) French or German air <attributed to W. Mozart> Words by J. Taylor. BB
"Twinkling stars are laughing, love." J. P. Ordway (music and words) GOS 2—WSS
" 'Twixt honor and affection." See "Fra degno ed amore" (Latilla)
" 'Twixt ox and ass, O heav'nly Child." See The sleep of the Infant Jesus (Gevaert)
The two affectionate lovers. See The young servant man
The two brothers. Folk song: Barbourville, Ky. version no. 1. SES 1
—Barbourville, Ky. version no. 2. SES 1
—Berea, Ky. version. SES 1
—St Helen's, Ky. version. SES 1
—Black Mountain, N.C. version. SES 1
—Burnsville, N.C. version. SES 1
—Hot Springs, N.C. version. SES 1
—Marion, N.C. version. SES 1
—Tennessee version. SES 1
—Afton, Va. version. SES 1
—Charlottesville, Va. version. SES 1
—Mount Fair, Va. version no. 1. SES 1
—Mount Fair, Va. version no. 2. SES 1
Variant: John and William
"Two brothers they have just returned." See The two brothers (Charlottesville, Va. version)
"Two drummers sat at dinner." See My mother was a lady (Stern)
"Two empires" (World-peace) Air: God save the king <attributed to H. Carey> Words by G. Huntington. LAS
"Two German officers crossed the Rhine." See Hinky dinky, parley-voo
The two grenadiers. See Die beiden grenadiere (Schumann)
"Two little boys were going to school." See The two brothers (Barbourville, Ky. version no. 2)
Two little girls in blue. C. Graham (music and words) SMG—SRW
"Two little sisters side by side." See The two sisters (Barbourville, Ky. version no. 1; Burnsville, N.C. version no. 1)
"Two men went up into the temple to pray." See The publican (Van de Water)
The two roses. See Heidenröslein (Werner)
The two sisters. Folk song: American mountain version. RA
—Barbourville, Ky. version no. 1. SES 1

The **two** sisters.—*Continued*
  —Barbourville, Ky. version no. 2. SES 1
  —Berea, Ky. version no. 1.   SES 1
  —Berea, Ky. version no. 2.   SES 1
  —Hindman, Ky. version. SES 1
  —Burnsville, N.C. version no. 1. SES 1
  —Burnsville, N.C. version no. 2. SES 1
  —Burnsville, N.C. version no. 3. SES 1
  —Hot Springs, N.C. version. SES 1
  —Afton, Va. version. SES 1
  —Meadows of Dan, Va. version. SES 1
  —Mount Fair, Va. version no. 1. SES 1
  —Mount Fair, Va. version no. 2. SES 1
  —Woodridge, Va. version. SES 1
"**Two** stars shine in heaven." Austrian folk song. e. LSB
"The **two** to church together went." See Pharisee and Sadducee
"**Two** weary pilgrims, we come to your door." See The pilgrims
"**Two** white horses." Negro spiritual from Missouri. SBA
"**Ty** co w stałość." See "Der du sicher bist"
"**Ty** nitranské hodiny." See "Neutras glocken läuten laut"
Tyl, J. K.
  My fatherland (Škroup)
Tyrley, tyrlow. P. Warlock. 16th century words. OB
Tyrolese evening hymn. Browne (Mrs Hughes) Words by F. D. Browne. GOS 1
Tytler, James
  "I hae laid a herrin' in saut" (Scottish air)
Tytöt. See "Unsres dorfes dirnen"

U

U of Colorado. University of Colorado song. R. W. Stevens (music and words) AI—AIS—HW
The **U.** of M. rouser. University of Minnesota song. F. M. Hutsell (music and words) AI—AIS—KU
U of U trail. University of Utah song. G. Rich. Words by C. R. Streeper. HW—KU
The **U. S. A.** forever. D. Emmett. TFP
"**Über** allen gipfeln ist ruh." See Wand'rers nachtlied: I (Loewe)
Über berg und waldesgründe. See Din Ploeşti până'n Gheboaïa
Über den stein. See Tros y garreg
["**Über** den sternen ist ruh"] "Over the stars there is rest." F. Abt. e. MFS
"**Über** die feldblume." See "O'er the lithe lily" (Simonffy)

"**Über** waldge berge reitet Marko." See Der königssohn Marko und seine geliebte Angjelia
"**Über** weiden und wiesen weit irrt' ich einsame waise." See The lonely waif
Der **überläufer.** Volkslied. g. EDL
"**Uccu** bizony megérett a káka." See "Reif ist nun das schilf"
"**Uch** ón, uch ón, mo bhrón." See Caoineadh
Udall, Lyn
  Just as the sun went down
  Just one girl
"**Udite!** o rustici." Donizetti. e.i. PB
"**Üdv** hazánkon égi fény." See Rákóczimarsch
"**Uf'm** berge da geht der wind." See Maria auf dem berge
Uhland, Ludwig
  The chapel (Composer unknown)
  Der wirtin töchterlein (18th century air)
  Frühlingsglaube (Schubert)
  Der gute kamerad (Composer unknown)
  In der ferne (Brahms)
  Der schmied (Brahms)
  Sonntag (Brahms)
"**Um** mitternacht schallt's aus den höh'n." See "It came upon the midnight clear" (Roeder)
Um, tum, tum, tum, tum, tum, there they go. See Trombone song (Saltman)
"**Umrem,** umrem." See "Sterben muss ich"
Úna bán (bhán) Irish folk song. g.ir. ML 1
"**Uncle** Bill an' Missis Jane." See Old Aunt Jemima
Uncle Ned. S. C. Foster (music and words) BB—WSS
Uncle Sam and Mexico. Air: Old Dan Tucker [by H. Russell] DSO
Uncle Sammy. A. Holzmann. SMG
"**Uncounted** diamonds glitter in our stonecaves." See A song of India (Rimskiï-Korsakov)
"**Und** als die schneider jahrstag hattn." See Der schneider jahrstag
"**Und** der Hans schleicht umher." See Hans und Liesel (Woyna)
"**Und** ein duften zieht über die erdenwelt." See Frühlingslied (Fielitz)
"**Und** kommt er nicht mehr zurück." See "And will he not come again"
"**Unde** aud cucu cântând" ("Höre ich des kuckucks schlag") Rumanian song. g.ru. ML 2
Under Gothic arches. See Serenata ("Era la noche")
Under the bamboo tree. B. Cole and J. R. Johnson (music and words) GFS—OTG
Under the greenwood tree ("In summer time") See "In summer time, when flow'rs do spring"
"**Under** the greenwood tree, who loves to lie with me." T. A. Arne. Words by W. Shakespeare. EB

Under the shade of the trees. E. O. Lyte. Words by M. J. Preston. MFS

Under the willow she's sleeping. S. C. Foster (music and words) WSS

"Underneath the skies of blue." See U of U trail (Rich)

Der unerbittliche hauptmann ("O Strassburg") Volkslied. g. EDL

Unfold, ye portals. C. Gounod. [Tr of Ouvrez vos portes éternelles] e. BB

[The uninvited aunt] "Nit kein gebetene" (Orem is nit gut) Jewish folk song. y. SY

The Union call. Song of the Mexican war. Air: Blue bonnets over the border. DSO

The Union forever, hurrah, boys. See The battle cry of freedom (Root)

The union of lakes, the union of lands. See The flag of our union forever (Wallace)

Union was a mighty name in far off days of yore. See The college on the hill (Knight)

Unmooring. Forecastle song. WSE

The unquiet grave ("Cold blows the wind") English folk song: North Devonshire version. BET

The unquiet grave ("How cold the winds do blow") Surrey version. 1st air. BET

The unquiet grave ("How cold the winds do blow") Surrey version. 2d air. BET

"Uns corren para Castilla." See Pasacalle o marcha-alborada

Uns kompt ein schiff gefahren. For English translation see "There comes a galley, laden"

Unseld, Benjamin Carl
Twilight is falling

"Unser rebbenu." Jewish folk song. y. SY

"Unsrer heil'gen Gottesmutter hoher festestag ist heute." See Lamento ("Dumattina quest' è l' jornu di la virgine Maria")

"Unsrer heil'gen Jungfrau." See "La Virgen de Covadonga"

"Unsres dorfes dirnen" (Tytöt) Finnish folk song. fi.g. ML 3

"Unter dein fenster stehl' ich mich des abends spät." See Unterm fenster

Unter der linde grün. See "In summer time when flow'rs do spring"

"Unter des waldes vöglein." See "Chorietan buruzagi"

"Unter geht die sonne sacht." See Aagots fjeldsang (Thrane)

Unterländers heimweh ("Drunten im unterland") Schwäbisches volkslied. Words by G. Weigle. g. EDL

Unterm fenster (Pod pendzheri) Serbian folk song. g.se. ML 2

"Unto Thee, O Lord, do I lift up my soul." See Turn thee unto me (Costa)

"Unto us a Boy is born." See Puer nobis nascitur

"Unto us is born a Son." See Puer nobis nascitur

Der untreue ("O bright sun") See "O bright sun"

Untreue ("Was hab ich denn") Volkslied. g. EDL

"Up and at 'em, navee." U.S. Naval academy song. P. B. Klakring. US

Up and get us gone. See Carol of service

"Up at Five Points talking, Daddy an' me." See Atlanta blues (Handy and Elman)

"Up Eliza, poor girl." See Eliza Jane (Manchester, Ky. version)

"Up from the sea." U.S. Naval academy song. [S. C. Foster] US

Up in a balloon. Words by H. B. Farnie. SRW

"Up in a dark hollow." See Sir Hugh (Oneida, Ky. versions no. 1-2)

Up in the morning early ("Cauld blaws the wind frae north to south") Air: Cold and raw, or, Up in the morning early, or, Cauld blows the wind. Words by J. Hamilton. BOS 2—GS

"Up, my neighbour, come away." See Carol of service

"Up now, laggardly lasses." See Panxoliña de nadal

"Up on the house-top." Christmas song. BB

Up she rises. Play-party game from Kentucky. SES 2

"Up the dreadful steep." Händel. SSO 2

"Up the lane and down the lane." See Petticoat lane (Farjeon)

"Up was I on father's farm." See The farmyard

Upi dei di (That bugler) College air: Upidee. Words by A. G. Knight. DSO

Upidee ("The shades of night were falling fast") College air. [Words by H. W. Longfellow] DSC

"Upon a meadow stile, singing heigh, sing ho." See The last mile

"Upon a simmer afternoon." See The lass o' Gowrie

Upon the death of Trumpeldor (Al mos Trumpeldor) Palestinean folk song. e.he. BNP

"Upon the height." German folk song. e. MFS

"Upon the Lomonds I lay, I lay." See The Campbells are comin'

"Upon the mountain my Lord spoke." See Every time I feel the spirit

"Upon the sweetest summer time." See Blow away the morning dew

"Uranila kosovka devojka." See Das mädchen vom Anselfeld

Urbs Syon aurea. For English translation see "Jerusalem the golden" (Ewing); "Jerusalem the golden" (Le Jeune)

Urguhart, C. K. See Urquhart, Colin Keith

Urim is nit git. See "Chazkele"

Urquhart, Colin Keith
Alma mater — Cornell university (Thompson)
Alma mater — Lehigh university (Thompson) See Gibson, J. J.
Alma mater—Lehigh university (Thompson)
Uspavanka. See Wiegenlied (Serbian folk song)
Usteri, Martin
"Freut euch des lebens" (Nägeli)
Utah Carroll. Cowboy song. LSC
Utah man. University of Utah song. [F. Seaver] AI—HW—KU—KV
Utbö, Hans
Ein vaartankje (Sinding)
"Uuden kullan kellon käljyt ne jäi mun käteheni." See Lisas lied
"Uv'chen tsadikim." See The righteous rejoice
"Už sa svadba dokonává." See Dank der gäste
L**'uzellin** del bosc ("Das vöglein aus dem wald") Venetian folk song. g.i. ML 2
"Uzh kak Slava tebîê Bozhe na nebesī." See The song of praise

V

"**V** jutro rano se ja vstanem malo pred zorom." See Die traurige braut
V. M. I. spirit. Virginia military institute alma mater. B. Bowering (music and words) AIS—KU
"**V** Mikulášskej kompanii." See "Mit den kameraden allen"
V Taïgîê. See "Von der insel dort"
Va petit mousse. For English translation see "On billow rocking" (Planquette)
"**Va** sbramando quegli ardori." Spohr. e.i. PB
Ein **vaartankje** (A thought of spring) C. Sinding. Words by H. Utbö. da.e. WM 2
The **vacant** chair. G. F. Root. Words by H. S. Washburn. BB
[**Vacation** days are here] "Ho, ho, vacation days are here." J. C. Johnson. MFS
Vaccai, Niccolò
Ah! se tu dormi (from Giulietta e Romeo)
The **vagabond.** J. L. Molloy. Words by C. L. Kenney. GE
Vagans scholasticus ("Der sang ist verschollen") W. Sommer. Author of words unknown. g. EDL
"**Vågorna** vagga min hvita båt." See I vassen (Palmgren)
"**Vai,** liūdnas, baltas berželis." See "Traurig wiegt sich die birke"
"**Vai,** tu diemed', diemedėli." See "Ei, du eintagsbaum, du lieber"
"The **vainly** ambitious may proudly recite." See The wounded soldier (Taylor)

Valedictory ("O mother strong") Air: Stein song (Heidelberg) from Prince of Pilsen. LAS
Valentine, Thomas
The merry Swiss girl: Swiss air arranged
Valentines ("In the dark of the winter") Old English air. Words by H. H. Harbour. DSB
Vales, J. See Phile, Philip
The **valiant** lady (The brisk young lively lad) Folk song from Surrey. BET
"The **valley** lay smiling before me." See Song of O'Ruark, Prince of Breffni
Valverde, Joaquín
Carnations. See Clavelitos
Clavelitos
"**Van** e bor a korsóba." See "Were the pitcher full alway"
"**Van Amburgh** is the man who goes to all the shows." See Menagerie
Vance, A. G.
The Chickaleary cove (Composer unknown)
Van der Stucken, Frank
Weave in, my hardy life
Vandervell, W. F.
Somebody's child (Plimpton)
Vandevere, J. Lilian
An autumn tramp (Hungarian air)
Ave verum (Mozart)
The aviator (Hungarian folk air)
Bell song (Drinnenberg)
Bugle song (Prussian bugle call)
The clock (German folk air)
Commencement song (Loomis)
The flight of summer (Bohemian folk air)
Give a cheer (Weber)
The gypsy king (Bergh)
Hiking song (Dutch folk air)
In Hawaii (Hawaiian folk air)
'Neath our flag (Barnby)
Our pioneers (French folk air)
Overwork (Stevens)
Rhyfelgyrch gwyr Harlech (Old Welsh air)
A sailing song (Callcott)
A sea picture (Russian folk air)
Sing (German folk air)
The sudden cure (German folk air)
To our flag (Flemish folk air)
The village dance (Czech air)
We remember (Russian air)
A winter song (Hungarian air)
Van de Water, Beardsley
The good Shepherd. See "The Lord is my Shepherd, I shall not want"
"The Lord is my Shepherd, I shall not want"
"Night of nights"
The publican
Van Diemen's land (The gallant poachers) Folk song from Sussex. BET
Vandraren (The wanderer) S. Lund. Words by J. S. Holt. da.e. WM 2
[**Vandring** i skoven] Wandering in the woods (Waldwanderung) E. Grieg. [Words by H. C. Andersen] e.g. HCA

Van Dyke, Harry Stoe
The Highland minstrel boy (Barnett)
Van Dyke, Henry
A sunrise song (Baltzell)
"They who tread the path of labor" (Zundel)
Vanha tanssi. See Alter tanz
Van Osdel, E. B.
Onward, upward alma mater (Marsh)
ɪVanyaɪ "Sĭdĭel Vanĭa" (Hänschen.—Wanja) Russian folk song. g.r. ML 1
"Var hilset høg over granetop." See Høgen (Nielsen)
"Våren flyktar hastigt" ("Swift the springtime passes") J. Sibelius. Words by J. L. Runeberg. e.sw. WM 2
"Various men have various natures." See He never cares to wander from his own fireside (McGlennon)
Varlamov, Aleksandr Igorovich
Krasnyĭ sarafan. See The scarlet sarafan
The red sarafan. See The scarlet sarafan
Der rote sarafan. See The scarlet sarafan
The scarlet sarafan
Värmeland. See Vermeland
Värmland's visa. See Vermeland
Varsity toast. See Toast to Wisconsin (Gounod)
"Varsity! varsity! U-rah-rah! Wisconsin." See Toast to Wisconsin (Gounod)
ɪVårt land, vårt fosterlandɪ "Our land." Finnish national song. ɪF. Pacius. Words by J. L. Runebergɪ e. LAS
"Vater, ich rufe Dich." See Gebet während der schlacht (Himmel)
"Vater und mutter beide wollen mich gut erzieh'n." See Lo mestre
"Vater unser." See The Lord's prayer (Krebs)
"Vater will ein haus uns bauen an Saarijärvis strande." See Am strande des Saarijärvi
Vaterlandslied ("Der Gott, der eisen wachsen liess") A. Methfessel. Words by E. M. Arndt. g. EDL
Song of freedom. e. LAS
"Väterlein, mütterlein" ("Tatulu, matulu") Polish folk song. g.p. ML 3
"Vattnet rörs och vinden spelar." See Adagio (Rangström)
Vaughan, Henry
Calvary (Rodney)
On Venice waters (Roeder)
Vaughan Williams, Ralph. See Williams, Ralph Vaughan
"Vaults sacred, solemn." See Ah! se tu dormi (Vaccai)
"Il vecchietto cerca moglie." Rossini. e.i. PC
Vedder, David
"Cam' ye by Athol, Donald Macgillavry" (Gow)
Vedi! cielo! è spento. For English translation see "Look thee! O heav'n" (Verdi)

Vedi! le fosche. For English translation see Anvil chorus ("See how the shadows of night are flying") (Verdi)
Vedrai, carino ("Rose-leaves are falling") Mozart. New words by A. G. Latham. CSB 6
Vedrò, mentr' io sospiro. Mozart. e.i. PB
"Végig mentem az ormódi temetőn." See "War am Ormoder friedhof"
Das **veilchen** ("Ein veilchen auf der wiese stand") W. A. Mozart. Words by W. von Goethe. g. EDL
Das **veilchen** (The violet) e.g. CSB 5—GG—HCA
Das **veilchen** ("Ein veilchen auf der wiese stand") J. F. Reichardt. Words by W. von Goethe. g. EDL
Veilchen ɪ"Zu dem duft, der da würzt die lenzesluft"ɪ (The violet) P. Cornelius (music and words) e. CSB 2
"Ein **veilchen** auf der wiese stand." See Das veilchen (Mozart); Das veilchen (Reichardt)
"La **vendetta,** oh, la vendetta." Mozart. e.i. PB
Venez à Saint-Maurice (The builders) Angevin carol. Attributed to Urbain Renard. e. OB
Veni Emmanuel ("O come, O come, Emmanuel") 12th century plain song. e. TFG
"O come, O come Emmanuel." e. DN—FC
Veni Redemptor gentium (Come, Redeemer of the nations) 4th century Latin air. English words by C. Wesley. e. DNS
Veni Redemptor gentium. For English translation from the original words see Jesu Redemptor omnium
Venite adoremus Dominum. See "The snow lay on the ground"
Verborg'ne liebe (Hidden love) E. Grieg. Words from the Norwegian of B. Björnson. e.g. TM
Verbum lumen. Folk air of Amiens. e. FC
The **verdant** braes of Skreen. Irish air from County Derry. Words from an old ballad. HI 1
"**Verdant** grove, farewell to thee." See Farewell to the woods
Verdi, Giuseppe
"Ah! I have sighed to rest me" (from Il trovatore. Tr of Ah! che la morte ognora)
"Ah! why recall" (from Rigoletto. Tr of Deh non parlare al misero)
Anvil chorus (from Il trovatore. Tr of Vedi! le fosche)
Anvil chorus ("God of the nations") See "God of the nations, in glory enthroned"
Anvil chorus ("See the proud banner") See Our flag o'er us waving
Il balen del suo sorriso (from Il trovatore)
"Beautiful spring-time" (same air as "Home to our mountains")
Caro nome (from Rigoletto)

Verdi, Giuseppe—*Continued*

Carved upon my heart.   See Caro nome

Celeste Aida (from Aida)

"Dagli immortali vertici" (from Attila)

D'Egitto là sui lidi (from Nabucodonosor)

"Di Provenza il mar" (from La traviata)

"La donna è mobile" (from Rigoletto)

Eri tu che macchiavi (from Un ballo in maschera)

"Every flower is equally cherished" (from Rigoletto.   Tr of Questa o quella)

"Fairest daughter of the graces" (from Rigoletto.   Tr of Bella figlia dell' amore)

"Farewell, farewell, O earth" (from Aïda.   Tr of O terra addio)

The fatal stone (from Aida.   Tr of La fatal pietra)

"From yonder sky" (from Rigoletto. Tr of Lassù in cielo)

"Glory to Egypt" (from Aida.   Tr of Gloria all' Egitto)

"God of the nations, in glory enthroned"

"Hail! mighty Phtha" (from Aida. Tr of Possente Ftha)

"Heav'nly Aida."   See Celeste Aida

"Home to our mountains" (from Il trovatore.   Tr of Ai nostri monti ritorneremo)

"Ill sustaining" (from Il trovatore. Tr of Mal reggendo all' aspro assalto)

"In my heart."   See "Every flower is equally cherished"

Infelice! e tu credevi (from Ernani)

L'insana parola (from Aida)

"Look thee! O heav'n" (from Il trovatore.   Tr of Vedi! cielo! è spento)

March of the victors (from Aida.   Tr of Su! del Nilo al sacro lido accorrete)

"March on! Liberty's host"

Miserere.   See "Ah! I have sighed to rest me"

"Now hope renew'd" (from Rigoletto. Tr of Possente amor mi chiama)

"Now let the trumpet" (from Il trovatore.   Tr of Squilli echeggi la tromba guerriera)

"O love immortal" (from Aida.   Tr of Amore, amore! gaudio tormento)

"Oh dischiuso è il firmamento" (from Nabucodonosor)

O, tu Palermo (from I vespri Siciliani)

O vecchio cor, che batti (from I due Foscari)

"Of love like this how vainly."   See Tacea la notte placida

"Of that dark scaffold" (from Il trovatore.   Tr of Di quella pira)

Our flag o'er us waving (same air as "God of the nations, in glory enthroned")

"Over the summer sea" (same air as "La donna è mobile")

"Pity, kind heaven."   See L'insana parola

"Sat there a gipsy hag" (from Il trovatore.   Tr of Abbietta zingara, fosca vegliarda)

"Sciagurata! hai tu creduto" (from I Lombardi)

"See! to the hall the priests proceed" (from Aïda.   Tr of Già i sacerdoti adunansi)

"Sotto il paterno tetto" (from Oberto conte di S. Bonifacio)

"Stride la vampa" (from Il trovatore)

"Tacea la notte placida" (from Il trovatore)

The tempest of the heart.   See Il balen del suo sorriso

"To the sacred banks of the Nile." See March of the victors

"Tu sul labbro de' veggenti" (from Nabucodonosor)

"Wear a bright smile"

"Woman is fickle."   See "La donna è mobile"

"Yes, we'll fly these walls" (from Aida. Tr of Sì: fuggian da queste mura)

Vergebliches ständchen ("Chori erresiñoula")   See Errefusa

Vergiftet sind meine lieder.   For English translation see "My songs are envenomed and bitter" (Borodin)

Der **vergiftete** knabe (Z jjedom zawdaty Hindrašk)   Wendish folk song. g.we.   ML 3

Vergissnichtmein ("Es wollte sich einschleichen ein kühles lüftelein")   Volkslied. g.   EDL

Verlaine, Paul

L'heure exquise (Hahn)

Verlassen bin i.   For English translation see Forsaken (Koschat)

Der **verlassene** liebhaber.   Volkslied. g. EDL

Verlegenheit (Embarrassment)   F. Abt. e.g.   GE

Die **verlobten** (Kihlatut)   Finnish folk song. fi.g.   ML 3

Le **vermeil** du soleil.   For English paraphrase see Gems of day

₁**Vermeland**₁ Värmeland.   Swedish folk air. ₁Words by A. Fryxell₁ e.   TFB Värmland's visa (Das Wermländer lied) g.sw.   ML 1

Vermont victorious.   University of Vermont song.   Furman, Sharples and Killick (music and words) AIS—KU

Vermont victory.   AI

Verrano a me sull'aure.   For English translation see "When twilight shadows lower" (Donizetti)

Verrath ("Die wasserlilie kichert leis'."— Betrayal)   H. Brückler.   Words by A. Kaufmann.   e.g.   HCA

Versöhnung.   See Resignation (Tchaikovsky)

Versos de Montalgo.   Mexican folk song. e.s.   SBA

Verstehst.   Fränkisches volkslied.   g. EDL

"Verstohlen geht der mond auf." See Mondschein

"Le vert colibri, le roi des collines." See Le colibri (Chausson)

Vertilge sie, Herr Zebaoth. For English translation see "Consume them all" (Mendelssohn)

Der vertriebene gaele. See Fuadach nan gàidheal

"Vertrunken sei der batzen hier." See "Am un leu"

"The very first down to the table was set." See Lord Thomas and fair Ellinor (Nellysford, Va. version)

Verzweiflung. See Mournful love

Vesper hymn ("Hark! the vesper hymn") [Bortnianski] Words by T. Moore. TFO—TFP
"Hark! the vesper hymn is stealing." BB—MFS

The vessel-cup carol. See "Here we come a-wesseling"

Vesta and Mattie's blues. Negro folk song. HB

Vesti la giubba. R. Leoncavallo. e. WG

Vetter Michel ("Gestern abend") Volkslied. g. EDL

"La vezzosa pastorella." D. Bruni. e.i. ZT 2

"Vi ravviso, o luoghi ameni." V. Bellini. e.i. PB

"Vi ska' ställa te' en roliger dans" (Tanzlied) Swedish folk song. g.sw. ML 1

The vicar of Bray. Old air: Country garden. [Words by E. Ward] MBS—SSB
The vicar of Bray (Der pfarrer von Bray) e.g. ML 1

Vickers, Helen Judith
Alma mater—University of Alabama (Thompson)

"Victim of fortune's frowning." See O Lisbona, alfin ti miro (Donizetti)

The victors. University of Michigan march song. L. Elbel. AI—AIS

Victory ("Come now, classmen") Pennsylvania state college song. J. A. Leyden (music and words) KU—KV

Victory ("Here comes the team, boys") Wesleyan university song. C. L. Waite. Words by H. C. Chamberlain. AI—AIS

Victory for Washington. University of Washington song. L. McHarrie (music and words) KU

Victory march ("Cheer! cheer") University of Notre Dame song. M. J. Shea. Words by J. F. Shea. AIS

Victory song ("Charge down the field") Whittier college song. B. Tomlinson. Words by H. D. Smith. HW

Victory song ("Down on the field") University of Maryland song. T. W. Allen (music and words) AIS

"Vid horisontens vestra rand." See När sol går ner (Stenhammar)

Vidal, Paul Antonin
Chant d'exil
Song of exile. See Chant d'exil

"Vidim draga moja." See "Tell me, O my darling"

Viel träume (Full many a dream) G. Henschel. Words by Hamerling. e.g. TM

"Viel vögel sind geflogen." See Viel träume (Henschel)

"Viele tränen ich vergoss." See Ardeleanca

Vieni a' regni del riposo. For English translation see Chorus of blessed spirits (Gluck)

"Vieni! la mia vendetta." G. Donizetti. e.i. PB

"Viens dans ce bocage, belle Aminte." See Aminte

"Viens, lorsque dans l'azur les astres radieux." See Hymne à la nuit (Gounod)

Le vieux chalet (The Swiss chalet song) J. Bovet. e. GSS

View de land. Negro spiritual. HRD

"Le vigneron va planter sa vigne." See Le cycle du vin

Viking song. Lawrence college song. L. Maesch. Words by F. Trezise. AIS

[Vilia song] Vilia, fair wood-nymph. F. Lehar. e. WLO

Vilikins and his Dinah. J. Parry. SRW

The village dance ("Choose a partner") Czech air. Words by J. Landon. TFO

The village dance ("The lanterns gleam") Hungarian dance air. Words by C. B. Fenno. TFG

"A village maid was leaving home." See Heaven will protect the working girl (Sloane)

Villagers' chorus. B. Smetana. e. WLO

Villancico-baile de Nadal (Weihnachtstanz) Catalan folk song. ca.g. ML 2

Villancico de Navidad (Torches) Spanish carol from Galicia. e. OB

Vincent, Charles John
The little soldier

Vineta. V. Lachner. e.g. DCA

"The vintage over, then maid and lover." See The farandole (Audran)

"Viola, bass und geigen." Student song. g. EDL

The violet ("Rugiadose, odorose") See Le violette (Scarlatti)

The violet ("Ein veilchen auf der wiese") See Das veilchen (Mozart)

The violet ("Zu dem duft") See Veilchen (Cornelius)

"A violet blossomed on the green." See Das veilchen (Mozart)

"A violet in the meadow grew." See Das veilchen (Mozart)

"The violet loves the sunny bank." See Proposal (Brackett)

La violette (The violet) A. Scarlatti. e.i. HCA

[Vira do Minho] Dance the gay vira (The vira of Minho) Portuguese dance. e. LSB

"La Virgen de Covadonga" (Die Jungfrau von Covadonga) Galician folk song. g.s. ML 2

[The Virgin and Child] Bye-bye lullay. 15th century air. DN

"Virgin Mary had one Son, I'd fly away and be at rest." See Sing a-ho that I had the wings of a dove

"Virgin Mary had one Son, the cruel Jews had him hung." See Jesus ain't comin' here t' die no mo'

"A Virgin most pure, as the prophets do tell, hath brought forth a Babe." County Galway air. Traditional words. DNS

"A Virgin most pure, as the prophets do tell, hath brought forth a Baby." Air from Sharp's "English folk carols." Traditional words. OB

"A Virgin most pure, as the prophets do tell, hath brought forth a Baby." <Traditional air from Gilbert's "Some ancient Christmas carols." Traditional words> DNS—OB Variant: "A Virgin unspotted"

"The Virgin stills the crying" (Cradle song of Virgin) J. Barnby. Words from the Latin. e. MFS

"A Virgin unspotted." Traditional air. BOS 2—MBS Variant of: "A Virgin most pure, as the prophets do tell, hath brought forth a Baby"

Virginia, hail, all hail. University of Virginia song. J. A. Morrow. AIS

The Virginian lover. Folk song: Kentucky version. SES 2 —North Carolina version. SES 2 —Tennessee version. SES 2

The Virgin's cradle hymn. See "Dormi, Jesu! mater ridet" (Rubbra)

"Virradóra szóll a falu harangja." See "Schaurig in der dämmrung"

Virran reunalla. See An baches rande

The vision ("Great hearts that have battled") Netherlands air <by E. Kremser> Words by C. B. Fenno. TFB

La visite du jour de l'an (The New Year's day visit) Canadian folk song. e.f. GC

"Vītane, bane." See Nachbar Witan

"Vitti na tigra dinta na silva 'scura." See La Scillitana

Viva il vino spumeggiante. For English translation see Drinking song (Mascagni)

Vivandière song. G. F. Bristow. Words by J. H. Wainwright. HP

"Vivat, vivat, loving comrades." Round. A. Salieri. e. CSB 5

Vive Henri quatre ("Long live King Henry") French folk song. e. DSB

"Vive la Canadienne" ("Pledge the Canadian maiden") French Canadian folk song. <Air: Par derrièr' chez mon père, arr by L. Streabbog> e.f. GC —MBS

Vive la compagneia ("Ich nehm mein gläschen") Volkslied. g. EDL

Vive la compagnie ("Let ev'ry good fellow") See Vive l'amour

Vive l'amour ("Let ev'ry good fellow now fill up his glass") Composer and author of words unknown. MBS

Vive l'amour ("Let ev'ry good fellow now join in a song") Old student song. TFB—TFG—TFO—TFR

"Vnīz po matushkřè po Volgřè." See Mother Vólga

"Vo polřè bereza stořála." See The birch in the meadow

A vocal encounter: [The Spanish càvalier and Solomon Levi, arranged] TFR

Vocero ("Eju filaja la miò rocca."—Totenklage) Corsican folk song. g.i. ML 2

Vocero ("La to jente t'aspettava tutt' allegra a lu balcone."—Totenklage) Corsican folk song. g.i. ML 2

"Voděnka studená jako led." See "Wässerlein, kalt wie eis"

Vögel, früchte und wind. See Aves, frutas y viento

"Ein vogel wollte hochzeit machen in dem grünen walde." See Vogelhochzeit

"Vögelein im tannenwald." See "Vöglein im tannenwald"

Vogelhochzeit. Volkslied. g. EDL

Vogl, Johann Nepomuk
Heinrich der vogler (Loewe)
Nächtlicher gruss (Storch)

"Das vöglein aus dem wald." See L'uzellin del bosc

"Vöglein frisst und gräslein spriesset." See "Why so silent, tell me, birdie"

Vöglein im käfig. See "Choriñua kaiolan"

"Vöglein (Vögelein) im tannenwald." Schwäbisches volkslied. g. EDL

"Vöglein kam" (Voi, voi, voi) Finnish folk song. fi.g. ML 3

"Vöglein singt" ("Pīle pīshchi") Bulgarian folk song. b.g. ML 2

Die vogtstochter aus Islington. See The bailiff's daughter of Islington

"Voi, che sapete" ("Ye who love's power") W. A. Mozart. e.i. PC

"Voi, che sapete" ("Ihr, die ihr triebe." —"Silently blending") e.g.i. BST

"Voi että olen outo." See "Wie bin ich, ach, so fremd hier"

[Voi lo sapete, o mamma] "You must know." Mascagni. e. WG

Voi, voi, voi. See "Vöglein kam"

The voice ("Mir klingt ein ton") See Ein ton (Cornelius)

"The voice of God is calling" (Webb) G. J. Webb. Words by J. H. Holmes. LAS

The voice of her I love. Old song. WSE

The voice of Jesus. C. T. Sutcliffe. Words by E. Clark. TSS 1—TSS 2

The voice of praise. See Ave verum (Mozart)

Voices of the woods₁ "Welcome, sweet springtime." A. Rubinstein. BB—TFP—TFR
Welcome, sweet spring.   LAS
Voici, débouchant sur la place.   For English translation see March of the toreadors (Bizet)
"**Voici** la Noël" ("Weihnacht ist da") French Christmas song.   f.g.   ML 1
Voici le matin, des feux de l'aurore.   For English translation see Morning serenade (Lecocq)
"**Voici** l'hiver arrivé."   See Dans les **chantiers**
"**Voici** que le printemps, ce fils léger d'avril" (Comes the spring) C. Debussy.   Words by P. Bourget. e.f.   ASN
"**Voici** venir le joli mai, qu'il est plaisant, qu'il est gai" ("Behold, 'tis May")₁ Bressan air.   Words by M. Duhamel. e.f.   ASN
"**Voilà** ma journé' fait'."   See Quand tu tenais la caille
Voisin, d'où venait ce grand bruit (Wakingtime)   French carol.   e.   OB
"**Vola**, o serenata."   See La serenata (Tosti)
Volga boat song.   Russian folk song. e.   GSS
   "Ĕĭ, ukhnem" (Burlatskaïâ.—"He, uchla."—Gesang der Wolgabootschlepper)   g.r.   ML 1
Song of the haulers on the Volga.   e. NRF
Song of the Volga boatman.   e. TFG
Song of the Volga boatmen.   e. DSB—DSC—MBS
The Volga boatmen.   e.   TFB—TFO
Variants: The little cudgel; Towing song ("Come, fellows, let us pull together")
The **Volga** boatmen.   See Volga boat song
Volkmann, Friedrich Robert
   Sappho
Volkmer, Alois
   Thy will be done (Slater)
Volksliedchen (My William)   R. Schumann.   Words by F. Rückert. e.g.   GA
   Spring morning.   e.   DSB
Volkstanz.   See A moda gallega
The **volley** was fired at sunrise.   See The pardon came too late (Dresser)
"**Volt** nekem egy darú szőrű paripám." See "Had a horse, a finer no one ever saw"
Vom bauern und den tauben.   W. Taubert. Words by F. Güll.   g.   EDL
"**Vom** himmel hoch da komm' ich her"₁ Luther's carol.   M. Luther (music and words)   e.   DN
"**Vom** himmel hoch da komm' ich her." For English translation with a different air see Balulalow (Heseltine)
"**Vom** himmel hoch, ihr engel kommt." See Christkindleins wiegenlied

"**Vom** hoh'n Olymp."   H. C. Schnoor. g.   EDL
"**Von** all den mädchen so flink und fein." See Sally in our alley (Old English air); Sally in our alley (Carey)
"**Von** allen den mädchen so blink und so blank."   See Die Lore am tore
"**Von** Badiška wehten linde winde her." See Mädchen und taube
Von den leinewebern.   Volkslied.   g. EDL
Von der edlen musik.   Words by V. Rathgeber.   g.   EDL
"**Von** der felsküste steiler höhe."   See Fhir a bhàta
"**Von** der insel dort" ("Kak ĭz ostrova."— Aus der Tajga.—V Taĭgîe)   Russian folk song.   g.r.   ML 1
Von Hagen, Peter Albrecht.   See Hagen, Peter Albrecht von
"**Von** stillem ort, von kühler statt."   See Angedenken (Cornelius)
Von Tilzer, Harry
   Alexander
   The Cubanola glide
   Down where the Wurzburger flows
   On a Sunday afternoon
   Please go 'way and let me sleep
   "Rufus, Rastus, Johnson Brown"
   Somebody's waiting for me
   Wait 'till the sun shines, Nellie
   You'll get all that's coming to you
Vopelius, Gottfried
   "The moon's pale beams are shining"
"**Vor** deiner tür wie duftet süss der jasminstrauch."   See Der jasmin
"**Vor** dem bett sitzt Ganka."   See Wiegenlied
Vor der abreise (Pri odlazku)   Croatian folk song.   g.se.   ML 2
"**Vor** des windes wildem wehen."   See Die spröde
"**Vorüber**, ach, vorüber."   See Der tod und das mädchen (Schubert)
Voss, Johann Heinrich
   Am Sylvester-abend (Schulz)
   The last hour of the year (Schulz. Tr of Neujahrslied)
"**Vous** aurez beau faire et beau dire."   See Obstination (Fontenailles)
"**Vous** dansez, marquise" ("Marchioness, your dancing."—Gavotte des Mathurins)   G. Lemaire.   Words by E. Bazot.   e.f.   AT
Vous êtes un moricaud.   See Vous t'é in morico
Vous n'êtes pas mon berger (You're not my shepherd boy)   Folk song from Lorraine.   e.f.   CBF 2
Vous pouver m'arrêter.   For English translation see "I am here, do thy will" (Bizet)
"**Vous** qui pleurez, venez à ce Dieu."   See Crucifix (Faure)
Vous t'é in morico (You are a blackamoor) Negro creole folk song.   e.f.   MB
Vousden, Valentine
   The Irish jaunting car
The **vow**.   See Der schwur (Bohm)

"**Voy** a partir" ("I'm off to port") M. M. Ponce. e.s. MSP

"**Voyez** ce mulet là, Musieu Bainjo." See Musieu Bainjo

Voyez ceci, voyez celà. For English translation see "Just look at that" (Planquette)

Voyez sur cette roche. For English translation see "On yonder rock reclining" (Auber)

"**Vozlĭe** rĭechkĭ, vozlĭe mostu." See Jealousy

Vspomni, moĭ lĭubeznyĭ. See Abschied ("Denke, denke mein geliebter")

"**Vu** mleki se hmivam." See "Wasch in weisser milch"

"**Vug**, vug, for vove of vind." See Baadfart (Olsen)

W

"**W** polu lipeńka, w polu zielona." See "Linden im felde, grünende linden"

Wa-hoo. See Indian warriors' song (Allen)

Wabadiku laul. See Lied des hörigen

"**Wach** auf, meins herzens schöne." See Morgenständchen (Reichardt)

Wachet auf. For English translation see Sleepers, wake (Bach)

Wacholder, wacholder, wacholder mein. See Kalĭnka

Die **wacht** am Rhein ("Es braust ein ruf wie donnerhall") C. Wilhelm. Words by M. Schneckenburger. g. EDL

Wade, J.
"Hours there were"

Wade, Joseph Augustine

Composer
"I have fruit, I have flowers"

Author
" 'Twere vain to tell thee all I feel" (Swiss air)

Wade in de water ("I would not be a sinner") Negro spiritual from Arkansas. FSN

Wade in de water, children ("See dat host") See God's a-gwineter trouble de water

The **waefu'** heart. Scottish air. Words by S. Blamire. GS

Waer is de dochter van Syoen (Sion's daughter) Old Netherland carol. e. OB

Wae's me for Prince Charlie ("A wee bird cam' to our ha' door") Air: Johnnie Faa, or, The gipsie laddie, or, Lady Cassilis lilt. Words by W. Glen. GS

"**Waft** her, angels, through the skies." Händel. SSO 3

"**Wafting** fragrance o'er the meadow." See Le violette (Scarlatti)

Wagner, Heinrich
Abschied (Volksweise)

Wagner, Richard
"Beloved one, come" (from Tannhäuser. Tr of Geliebter, komm'! sieh' dort die grotte)

The blissful strain is o'er (from Lohengrin. Tr of Das süsse lied verhallt)

Bridal chorus (from Lohengrin. Tr of Brautlied)

Elsa's traum (from Lohengrin)

Ever I'll praise thee (from Tannhäuser. Tr of Stets soll nur dir)

"Flag of the free" (same air as Bridal chorus)

"Hail, bright abode, where song the heart rejoices" (from Tannhäuser. Tr of Freudig begrüssen wir die edle halle)

"I pray for him, spare him" (from Tannhäuser. Tr of Ich fleh' für ihn)

"I pray thee, rise" (from Tannhäuser. Tr of O stehet auf! nicht sollet hier ihr knien)

"I saw in splendor shining." See Elsa's traum

"If he returns" (from Lohengrin. Tr of Kommt er dann heim)

"In distant land." See "In fernem land"

"In fernem land" (from Lohengrin)

King's prayer (from Lohengrin. Tr of Mein Herr und Gott)

"The Lord Himself now thy bondage hath riven" (from Tannhäuser. Tr of Der gnade heil ward dem blüsser bescheiden)

"May he never leave thee" (from Lohengrin. Tr of Könntest du erfassen)

"My God, my Father, while I stray" (same air as O du mein holder abendstern)

O du mein holder abendstern (from Tannhäuser)

"Oh King of kings, on Thee I call." See King's prayer

"Oh, star of eve." See O du mein holder abendstern

Pilgrims' chorus (from Tannhäuser. Tr of Beglückt dorf nun dich)

A prayer

Resignation. See "My God, my Father, while I stray"

"Steersman, leave the watch" (from Die fliegende Holländer. Tr of Steuermann! lass die wacht)

Swan song (from Lohengrin. Tr of Nun sei bedankt, mein lieber schwan)

"Was't magic or a power divine" (from Tannhäuser. Tr of War's zauber, war es reine macht)

"Ye wandering breezes" (from Lohengrin. Tr of Euch lüften, die mein klagen so traurig oft erfüllt)

The **wagoner's** lad. Folk song: Kentucky version. SES 2

—Alleghany, N.C. version. SES 2

—Hot Springs, N.C. version. SES 2

The **wagoner's** lad.—*Continued*
—Flag Pond, Tenn. version.   SES 2
—Harrogate, Tenn. version.   SES 2
—Virginia version.   SES 2
Variant: An inconstant lover
"**Wah!** tah-ho! tah-ho."   See The sun worshippers
"**Wahn,** zur ruh, mein wahn."   See "Sleep, O sleep, fond fancy" (Morley)
Wai'.   For entries beginning Wai' see Wait
Waillie, waillie.   Folk song: American version.   SBA
Variant of: O waly, waly
Wainwright, John
"Christians, awake"
Wainwright, John Howard
Vivandière song (Bristow)
Waisenkind ("Pali synephias' oyrhanos") Greek folk song.   g.gr.   ML 2
Wait for the wagon.   R. B. Buckley (music and words)   KSO—TFG—WSS
"**Wait,** Mr Mackright."   Negro spiritual from South Carolina.   AS
"**Wai',** my brudder, better true believe." See My body rock 'long fever (South Carolina version no. 1)
"**Wai',** poor Daniel, he lean on de Lord's side."   See Lean on the Lord's side
Wait till the clouds roll by.   H. T. Fulmer.   WSS
Wait 'till the sun shines, Nellie.   H. Von Tilzer.   Words by A. B. Sterling. GFS—SRW
Waite, Clifford LeGrand
Victory
Waiting ("Aftnen er stille, tonerne trille") See Längsel (Svendsen)
Waiting for the Robert E. Lee.   L. F. Muir.   Words by L. W. Gilbert. DFF—GFS
Waiting to grow.   W. H. Aiken.   BB
"**Wake,** happy children, in the dewy morn." See Waking or sleeping
Wake Nicodemus.   H. C. Work (music and words)   BNM—MFS—PSG
"**Wake,** snakes."   Southern mountain song.   RA
"Snake baked a hoe-cake."   Virginia version.   SES 2
"**Wake** up, darling, don't sleep too late." See The crow-fish man
Wake up Jacob.   Negro song.   AS—WFN
"**Wake** up, wake up, you drowsy sleeper." See "Awake! awake" (Berea, Ky. version; Montvale, Va. version no. 1)
"**Wake** you up, wake you up, you seven sleepers."   See Earl Brand (Crozet, Va. version)
Wakefield, Augusta Mary
No sir
"**Waking** at early day, gaily I take my way." See Gaily I take my way (Linley)
Waking or sleeping ("Wake, happy children, in the dewy morn")   Words by J. V. Blake.   MFS
Waking-time.   See Voisin, d'où venait ce grand bruit

Wal, I swan (Ebenezer Frye)   B. H. Burt.   SRW
Waldis, Burkhard
"Pleasure it is"
Waldwanderung.   See Vandring i skoven (Grieg)
Wales! Wales! O but my heart is with you. See "O land of my fathers, O land of my love"
Walk, Dad Lew, oh, Mister Lew.   See Good bye, Liza Jane
Walk him along, Johnny, carry him along. See "Gen'ral Taylor"
Walk in Jerusalem jus' like John.   See I want to be ready
"**Walk** in, kind Saviour."   See No man can hinder me
Walk in the parlour.   Minstrel song. PSG
De history ob de world (Walk in de parlor)   WSS
Walk, jawbone.   Minstrel song.   WSS
Walk, Mary, down de lane.   Negro spiritual.   JB 2
"**Walk** together, children."   See A great camp-meeting in the promised land
Walk you in de light.   Negro spiritual. HRD
Variant: Walking in de light
"**Walked** all the way from East Saint Louis."   See East St Louis
Walker, Annie Louisa.   See Coghill, Mrs Annie Louisa (Walker)
Walker, Catharine.   See Hughes, Jewell, jt. auth.
Walker, Charles
Bonnie laddie, Highland laddie (Scottish air)
Walker, Clarence
Dawn (Somerset)
Walker, James John
Will you love me in December as you do in May (Ball)
Walking down Broadway.   C. E. Pratt. Words by W. Lingard.   SRW
[**Walking** in de light] We are walking in de light.   Negro spiritual.   HRD
Variant of: Walk you in the light
Walking John.   Cowboy song.   Words by H. H. Knibbs.   LSC
Walklied.   See "Heman dubh"
Walky-talky Jenny.   Minstrel song. SBA
Wallace, Bertrand Holmes
The Genesee (Composer unknown) See Swinburne, T. T.   The Genesee (Composer unknown)
Wallace, Paul
I wish I had my old girl back again
Wallace, William Vincent
The bell ringer
Cradle song.   See "Sweet and low"
The flag of our union forever
Good night and pleasant dreams
"One thought I have, my ample creed"
"Scenes that are brightest" (from Maritana)
Serenity.   See "One thought I have, my ample creed"
"Sleeping I dream'd, love"

Wallace, William Vincent—*Continued*
"Speak gently—it is better far"
"Sweet and low"
Sweet spirit, hear my prayer (from Lurline)
"The winds that waft my sighs to thee"
Waller, Edmund
"It is not that I love you less" (Blow)
Waller, Henry
Derelict
Waller, John Francis
The maiden's rose (Hatton)
"The **walls** are levell'd." See See the raging flames arise (Händel)
Walsh, David R.
The saltine warrior
Walters, Jane B.
The birds' return (Bohemian folk air)
Farewell to summer (Swabian folk air)
January and February (German folk air)
" 'Tis springtime" (Süssmayer)
Walton, James George. See Hemy, Henry Frederick, jt. comp.
ₜWaltz song ("Hear sweet music softly saying")ᵢ I'll love you true. F. Lehar. e. WLO
ₜWaltz songᵢ "O heart wherefore so light" (First love) E. Audran. e. WLO
Waltz song ("See she is dancing") J. Offenbach. ₜTr of Elle danse! en cadenceᵢ e. WG
ₜWaltz songᵢ "That night I'll ne'er forget." R. Planquette. ₜTr of Je regardais en l'airᵢ e. WLO
Waltz song ("Words are vain") See Waltz song (Lehar)
Wamsley, Henry E.
Maroon and white
Wand, Hart A.
Dallas blues
"**Wandelnd** in dem sommernächtgen schweigen" ("Läksin minä kesäyönä käymään") Finnish folk song. fi.g. ML 3
The **wanderer** ("Eg hev vand rat um verdi") See Vandraren (Lund)
The **wanderer** ("High upon a lonely hill") Spanish air. Words by K. Davis. DSB
Der **wanderer** ("Ich komme vom gebirge her."—The wanderer) F. Schubert. Words by G. F. Schmidt. e.g. GG
Der **wandrer** ("In der erde trübem irrsal." —"Eis toy kosmoy to taxeidi") Folk song from Smyrna. g.gr. ML 2
"A **wand'rer** worn with worldly strife." See Come unto me (Slater)
ₜWand'rers nachtliedᵢ "Der du von dem himmel bist" (Invocation) J. Jordan. ₜWords by Goetheᵢ e.g. CSS 2
Wand'rers nachtlied: II ("Der du von dem himmel bist."—A song of the night: II) C. Loewe. Words by Goethe. e.g. GA
Wand'rers nachtlied: I ("Über allen gipfeln ist ruh."—A song of the night: I) C. Loewe. Words by Goethe. e.g. GA

Wanderin' ("My daddy is an engineer") American song. SBA
Wanderin' ("There's snakes on the mountain") American song. SBA
Wandering ("Das wandern ist des müller's lust") See Das wandern (Schubert)
Wandering cowboy. Cowboy song. LSC
Wandering in the woods. See Vandring i skoven (Grieg)
ₜ**Wandering** Willieᵢ "Here awa', there awa'." Scottish song. Old version of words. GS
ₜ**Wandering** Willieᵢ "Here awa', there awa'." Air: Here awa', there awa'. Words by R. Burns. GS
Wandering Willie. Air: Here awa', there awa', from Oswald's collection. Words by R. Burns. GS
Wanderlied ("Uns corren para Castilla") See Pasacalle o marcha-alborada
Wanderlied ("Wohlauf, noch getrunken") ₜAir: Dort oben auf dem berge da horstet der aarᵢ Words by J. Kerner. g. EDL
Wanderlied der Prager studenten ("Nach süden nun sich lenken") Volksweise. Words by J. von Eichendorff. g. EDL
ₜDas **wandern**ᵢ Wandering. F. Schubert. ₜWords by W. Müllerᵢ e. DSB
Wanderschaft. See Burschenlust (Lyra)
Wandertrieb. See Dor de ducă
Wand'rer. For entries beginning Wand'rer see Wanderer
Wanja. See Vanya
Want to go to heab'n, when I die, when I die. See To see God's bleedin' lam'
"**Want** to go to heaven when I die." Negro spiritual. HRD—WSS
"**War** am Ormoder friedhof" ("Végig mentem az ormódi temetőn") Hungarian folk song. g.hu. ML 3
A **war** bird's burlesque. Song of the European war. SBA
"**War** ein schöner junger bursche" ("Gacsaj pesta szép fiu vaut") Hungarian folk song. g.hu. ML 3
"**War** einst ein lust'ger müllersmann." See The miller of the Dee
"**Wär'** ich doch ein täubchen" ("Ach, dybych já byla tú bílú holubičkú") Moravian-Czech folk song. bo.g. ML 3
"**Wär'** ich frei" ("Jos mie saisin") Finnish folk song. fi.g. ML 3
"**Wär'** ich geblieben doch." See Das haidekind (Schaeffer)
The **war** junk Tennessee. U.S. navy song. US
"**War** schon frühmorgens ganz heimlich im thale." See Lithuanian song (Chopin)
War song of the Texan rangers. See Texan rangers' song (Russell)
"The **war** was a-raging." See The warfare is raging (North Carolina version)
Ward, Charles B.
The band played on
Ward, Mrs Edith (Hanington)
Seventy-sixth field artillery song

Ward, Edward
The vicar of Bray (Old air)
Ward, Samuel Augustus
America, the beautiful
Materna. See America, the beautiful
Ward. See "Awake, my soul, and with
the sun"; Evening hymn
Ware, G.
Jessie, the belle at the bar
Ware, Richard D.
Yankee Doodle-oodle (Seaver)
"Waren drei schöne mägdelein." See La
ploma de perdiu
"Waren einstens drei studenten zu Tolosa."
See Los estudiants de Tolosa
"Waren matrosen drei aus Groix." See
Les trois matelots de Groix
The warfare is raging. Folk song: North
Carolina version. SES 2
—Tennessee version. SES 2
Waring, Anna Laetitia
"In heavenly love abiding" (music by
Bach; Batchelder; Hassler; Iszlai;
Lassen; Mendelssohn)
Warlamoff, Alexander. See Varlamov,
Aleksandr Igorovich
Warlock, Peter, pseud. See Heseltine,
Philip
Warman, Cy
Sweet Marie (Moore)
Warner, Anna Bartlett
"Jesus loves me" (Bradbury)
Warner, Langdon
The child and heaven (Breton folk air)
The high moon (Breton folk air)
Warner, Lois
Hail! Pacific, hail
Warner, Lorraine d'Oremieulx
A song of seasons (Hungarian air)
Warnung ("Fuchs, du hast die gans
gestohlen") Volksweise: Wer
eine gans gestohlen hat. Words
by E. Anschütz. g. EDL
Fox and goose. e.g. MFS
Warnung vor dem Rhein ("An den Rhein")
Pöthko. Words by K. Simrock. g.
EDL
Warren, George William
"God of our fathers." See National
hymn
National hymn
Warren, Joseph
Free America (16th century air)
A warrior bold. S. Adams. Words by
E. Thomas. BB—GE—TFP
The warriors. University of Montana
song. D. Smith. Words by M. B.
Clapp. HW
War's zauber, war es reine macht. For
English translation see "Was't magic
or a power divine" (Wagner)
Warum ("Warum sind denn die rosen."—
Why) P. I. Tchaikovsky. Words
by H. Heine. e.g. HCA
"Warum ist so stolz, o Lena, dein gemüt."
See Warum, Lena, so stolz
Warum, Lena, so stolz ("Shcho se, Leno,
na golïēmo") Macedonian folk song.
b.g. ML 2

"Warum sind denn die rosen so blass."
See Warum (Tchaikovsky)
"Was frag ich viel nach geld und gut."
See Zufriedenheit (Mozart)
"Was für eine strasse ist ohne staub."
See Rätsellied
"Was glänzt dort vom walde im sonnen-
schein." See Lützows wilde jagd
(Weber)
"Was he a-bookin' of his Phil." See He
done his level best
"Was hab ich denn meinem feinsliebchen
getan." See Untreue
"Was ich am tag auch tue." See "Om
dagen vid mitt arbete"
"Was ist aus der heimat der gaelen
geworden." See Fuadach nan gàidheal
"Was ist des Deutschen vaterland." See
Des Deutschen vaterland (Reichardt)
"Was ist Sylvia." See "Who is Sylvia"
(Schubert)
Was it from a grey hair'd mother. See
"A letter here for me was the question
that he ask'd"
"Was it magic or a power divine." See
"Was't magic or a power divine" (Wag-
ner)
"Was kommt dort von der höh." See
Fuchslied
"Was leuchtet ihr sterne." See Im volks-
ton (Hildach)
"Was 'nold fish an's name was whale."
See There was an ole fish
Was soll ich dazu sagen. For English
translation see "Ah! what can be her
meaning" (Flotow)
"Was soll ich geben dem sohne der mutter."
See Presents al niño Jesús
"Was tatest du am brunnen draussen."
See Les répliques de Marion
"Was you ever on the Brumalow." See
Lucy Long
"Wasch in weisser milch" ("Vu mleki se
hmivam") Croatian folk song. g.se.
ML 2
Waschfrauenlied. See Ritornello delle
lavandare del Vomero
Washburn, Henry S.
The grave of Bonaparte (Heath)
The vacant chair (Root)
Washington and Lee swing. Washington
and Lee university song. T. W. Allen
and M. W. Sheafe. Words by T. W.
Allen and C. A. Robbins. AI—AIS
Washington my Washington. State col-
lege of Washington alma mater. KU
"Wassail, and wassail, all over the town"
(Somerset wassail) Traditional
song. OB
For variants see following songs of
similar title; also "Here we come
a-wassailing"; Somersetshire wassail
Wassail song ("Here we come a-wassailing") See "Here we come a-wassailing"
The wassail song ("O mistress, at your
door our wassail begins") Cornish
carol. DN

Wassail song ("Wassail, wassail, all over the town")   See "Wassail, wassail, all over the town"
"Wassail, wassail, all over the town" (Gloucestershire wassail)   Traditional song.   OB
Wassail song.   BOS 2
"Wasser! wasser."   See Hagar in der wüste (Rubinstein)
"Wässerlein, kalt wie eis" ("Voděnka studená jako led")   Moravian-Czech folk song.   bo.g.   ML 3
"Die wasserlilie kichert leis'."   See Verrath (Brückler)
Wassersnot ("Zu Koblenz auf der brücken")   Volksweise: Der schwere traum.   g.   EDL
Wasson, David Atwood
    "The wind ahead? the wind is free" (Calkin)
"Was't magic or a power divine."   R. Wagner.   ₍Tr of War's zauber, war es reine macht₎   e.   WG
Waste·not, want not.   See You never miss the water (Howard)
Watch and ward.   See "God shall charge His angel legions" (Mendelssohn)
"Watch over me when I am waking."   See The guardian angel (Franck)
Watch them shufflin' along.   See Waiting for the Robert E. Lee (Muir)
Watch us as we climb to fame.   See Spirit of Maine (O'Neil)
The watcher.   <W. Lardner.   Words by S. J. Hale>   GOS 1
"Watchman, tell us of the night" (Aberystwith)   J. Parry.   Words by J. Bowring.   TFG
The water chain ("Škripi djeram")   Yugoslav folk song.   e.se.   CJ
The water mill ("Je sais au bord du Rhin")   See Le moulin
"Water! water."   See Hagar in der wüste (Rubinstein)
"The waterlily softly laughed."   See Verrath (Brückler)
Waterloo.   Folk song from Virginia.   SES 2
Waterman, Alan T.
    "The red and black shall triumph"
Watkins, Morris Wynn.   See Webb, Roy Denslow, jt. auth.
Watson, J.
    "John Anderson, my jo, John" (with words by Burns; also additional words)
Watson, Michael
    Babylon
Watts, Isaac
    Christ the Lord is risen   (German air)
    Cradle hymn (Northumbrian air; music by Bach; Rousseau; also unknown composer)
    "From all that dwell"   (German air)
    "Joy to the world"   (Händel)
    "O God, our Help in ages past" (Croft)
Watts's cradle song.   See Cradle hymn (Northumbrian air)
Wauchope, George Armstrong
    Carolina coronata (Spilman)

Waugh, Edwin
    Awake and sing (Béarnais air)
"Wave, flag of beauty! starred on high."   See Our flag (Mersereau)
Wave her colors ever.   See "Sons of Georgetown"
Wave, willows, murmur, waters.   See Annie Lisle (Thompson)
"'Way back at home there is a pond."   See En roulant ma boule
Way down in Ca-i-ro.   S. C. Foster (music and words)   WSS
"Way down in Easton."   Lafayette college song.   W. C. Stier.   Words by E. C. Chalfant.   KU
"Way down in green Arbee fair damsel did dwell."   See Polly Oliver (Virginia version)
"Way down in Louisiana, not many years ago."   See In the Louisiana lowlands
"'Way down in old New Jersey."   See Jungle march (Clark)
"Way down in the lone valley."   See Pretty Saro (Virginia version)
"Way down on de old plantation."   See Angelina Baker (Foster)
"Way down on the levee in old Alabamy."   See Waiting for the Robert E. Lee (Muir)
Way down souf.   See Away down souf (Foster)
Way down south in Alabama.   Minstrel song.   SW
"Way down south in Dixieland in Alabam with a banjo in his hand."   See Banjo blues (Williams)
"Way down south in the land of cotton, I wrote this song and wrote it rotten."   See Crazy song to the air of Dixie (Emmett)
"Way down the Ohio."   Folk song from Virginia.   SES 2
"Way down upon the Swanee river."   See The old folks at home (Foster)
"'Way down upon the Wabash."   See El-a-noy
"'Way down yond' on Beaver creek."   See Beaver creek
"Way down yonder in de graveyard walk."   See I thank God I'm free at las'
Way down yonder in the cornfield.   See Cornfield medley
"Way, haul away, we'll haul away the bowlin'."   See Haul away, Joe
"The way is long and dreary."   See The pilgrims (Schulthes)
"The way of evil doing is a-wide and fair."   See O Mary, don't you weep
'Way out in Idyho.   Cowboy song.   LSC
"Way over in de Egyp' lan'."   See March on
Way over in de promise' land.   See "Wonder where is good ole Daniel"
Way over in the new buryin' groun'.   Negro spiritual from Georgia.   SBA
Way over yonder ("I'll put on the golden shoes")   Minstrel song.   WSS
"Way over yonder in de harves' field."   See Who built de ark

Way, sing Sally. See Stand to your ground

"'Way up in-a dat valley, prayin' on my knees." See Slav'ry chain

"Way up on Clinch mountain, I wander alone." Folk song: American version. SBA

"Way up on Clinch mountain where the wild geese fly high." Folk song: 2d American version. SBA

"We all went down to New Orleans." See For bales (Gilmore)

"We are a band of brothers." See The bonnie blue flag (Macarthy)

"We are all noddin', nid nid noddin'." See All noddin'

We are almost home. Negro spiritual. HRD

"We are building on a rock." Negro spiritual. HRD

We are Chicago. See Our Chicago (Reid)

"We are climbing Jacob's ladder, ladder." See Jacob's ladder

We are coming back, coming back. See "Where Goucher's far flung colors"

"We are four bums." Hobo song. SBA

"We are from Crabtown." U.S. Naval academy song. US

"We are happy and free as a crew can be." See Over the dark blue sea

"We are in tatters." See Praised be the Lord

We are just plain folks. See Just plain folks (Stonehill)

"We are Mills college girls." Mills college song. L. McDermott. HW

We are na fou, we're no that fou. See "O Willie brew'd a peck o' maut" (Masterton)

"We are only gunboat sailors." See Gunboat sailors

"We are privates in the sixty-ninth." See The gallant 69th (Braham)

"We are the boys of Potomac's ranks." Civil war song. P. S. Gilmore. DSO

"We are the vanguard." See A song of the Chalutsim

"We are travellin' from mansions to mansions." See Roll de ole chariot along

"We are trying to carry this timber to the building." See Timber

We are walking in de light. See Walking in the light

"We be soldiers three." Old song <of the Netherland wars> BOS 2

"We be three poor mariners." 17th century English sea song. BOS 2

"We children, we gambol, we dance in a ring." See Piaceri fanciulleschi (Mozart)

"We come from the Sioux and Missouri." See The yellow and blue (Haynes)

"We come to see Miss Jennie Jones." See Jenny Jones

"We con, beside thy knee." See Dear alma mater (Lewis)

We could hear the darkies singing. See The girl I loved in sunny Tennessee (Redcliffe)

"We crave your condescension." See Mulligan guards (Braham)

"We dwell on Granite Ledges." See Ledges troop song

"We firmly stand pledged hand and hand." See North Dakota U (Rickaby)

"We gather together to ask the Lord's blessing." See "Wilt heden nu treden" (Kremser)

We girls never mean half we say. O. M. Brewster. GOS 2

We give Thee thanks, Thy name we sing. See "God of the earth, the sky, the sea" (Holmes)

"We go walking on the green grass." See Soldier boy for me (Callaway, Va. version)

"We growl but never grumble." See Arizona grid march (Keddie)

"We hail thee alma mater." See Alma mater—Franklin and Marshall college (Thompson)

"We hail thee Carolina." See Carolina coronata (Spilman)

"We happie herdsmen." 17th century carol. DN

"We have a just God to plead-a our cause." See Come along, Moses

"We have heard it asserted a dozen times o'er." See Shabby genteel (Clifton)

We have met, loved, and parted. Eastburn (J. E. Winner) Words by E. R. Coates. GOS 2

"We have studied navigation." See Gentlemen sailors

"We le goelcerth wen yn fflamio." See Rhyfelgyrch gwyr Harlech

We lead the way. 29th U.S. infantry song. DSO

"We love to go each day to school." See Brother and I (Ball)

We march behind the band. See The gallant 69th (Braham)

"We may not climb the heav'nly steeps" (Salvator mundi) J. B. Dykes. Words by J. G. Whittier. LAS

"We may roam thro' this world." See The daughters of Erin

"We may rove the wide world o'er." See The old familiar place (Glover)

"We meet again to-night." College song. LAS—TFB—TFG

"We meet 'neath the sounding rafter." See The last carouse

We never speak as we pass by. [F. Egerton (music and words)] SRW—WSS

"We never took stock in H. Greeley." See Straight-out Democrat

"We organized in 'seventeen." See The fifty-first coast artillery march-song

"We parted by the river side." W. S. Hays (music and words) GOS 2

"We parted in the springtime of life." See Nell and I (Foster)

"We praise thee for thy past, O alma mater." See Alma mater—Tulane university (Ruebush)

We remember. Armistice day and Memorial day song. Russian air. Words by J. L. Vandevere. TFO

"We said good-by to the brown babaye."
See In Mindanao

"We sat by the river, you and I." See
You and I (Barnard)

"We saw a light shine out afar." See
The golden carol of Melchoir, Bathazer,
and Caspar

We saw the damn thing through. Song
of the European war. [Hawaiian air:
One, two, three four] Words by B.
Boyles. DSO

We see him come, and know him ours.
See "What sweeter music can we
bring"

"We shall meet, but we shall miss him."
See The vacant chair (Root)

"We shouldered arms and marched and
marched away. See Mulligan guards
(Braham)

"We shoulder'd guns and march'd and
march'd away. See Mulligan guards
(Braham)

We sing a little, and laugh a little. See
The sailor's life

"We sing of a milestone won." See Commencement song (Loomis)

"We sing of the polar bear." See The
climate

"We sing the plant of prairied west." See
The corn song (Marks)

"We three kings of Orient are." See
Three kings of Orient (Hopkins)

"We, thy soldiers, hail thee, hail thee."
See Soldiers' hymn (Haydn)

"We want a touchdown." See Touchdown song (Wilkerson)

"We want no cowards in our band." See
Children, we all shall be free

"We was camped on the plains at the head
of the Cimarron." See Zebra Dun

"We was laying on the prairie at French
Ranch one night." See Wandering
cowboy

"We were forty miles from Albany." See
The E-ri-e

"We were three beautiful daughters." See
Les trois jupons blancs

"We will be merry far and wide." See
Wir wollen alle fröhlich sein

"We will march through the valley."
Negro spiritual from Virginia. AS

We will rant and we'll roar like true British
sailors. See "Farewell and adieu to
you, Spanish ladies"

"We will sing a song of glory." See
Tenth U.S. infantry song

The wealthy farmer's son. Folk song
from Sussex. BET

"Wear a bright smile." G. Verdi. MFS

The wearing of the green ("O Paddy dear,
and did you hear") Irish national
song. Words from an old ballad,
with additional words by D. Boucicault. BB—SI
The wearin' of the green. MBS

The wearing of the green ("There's a
shining little island") Old Irish air.
New words by S. Fay (D. Stevens)
TFP—TFR

Weary ("Weary of living, so weary") V.
Gabriel. Words by F. L. Carter.
GE

"Weary of living, so weary." See Weary
(Gabriel)

"Weary the way, heavy the cross we bear."
See Thy will be done (Slater)

[Weary traveler] Let us cheer the weary
traveler. Negro spiritual. HRD
—WSS
Let us cheer the weary traveller
(Cheer the weary traveller) Arr
by W. C. Handy. HB

Weatherly, Frederick Edward
Beauty's eyes (Tosti)
The boatswain's story (Molloy)
The bride bells (Roeckel)
Fly forth, O gentle dove (Pinsuti)
The king's highway (Molloy)
London bridge (Molloy)
The midshipmite (Maybrick)
Nancy Lee (Maybrick)
Paradise square (Löhr)
Rose-Marie (Molloy)
The star of Bethlehem (Maybrick)
They all love Jack (Maybrick)
A twilight fancy (Molloy)

Weave in, my hardy life. F. Van der
Stucken. Words by W. Whitman.
TFB—TFG

Weave them all together. See Spinning
song

The weaver ("I was a bachelor") Folk
song: American version. SBA
Variant of: Foggy foggy dew ("When
I was a bachelor")

The weaver ("One night when I was
weaving") See Y gwŷdd

The weaver's daughter. Irish air from
County Donegal. Words from
an Ulster ballad. HI 1
The weaver's daughter (Die weberstochter) e.g. ML 1

Weaving song ("Olga sits a-weaving,
weaving") Russian air. Words
by K. Davis. DSB

Webb, C. H.
Croquet (Thomas)

Webb, George James
"The voice of God is calling" (same
air as "The morning light is breaking")
Webb. See "The voice of God is
calling"

**Webb, Roy Denslow, and Watkins, Mor-
ris Wynn**
Roar, lion, roar

Webbe, Samuel
Catch round the table
"Come, ye disconsolate"
"I know not what the future hath"
(wrongly attributed) See Schulthes, W. A. F. "I know not
what the future hath"
Lambeth (wrongly attributed) See
Schulthes, W. A. F. "I know
not what the future hath"; "Prayer
is the soul's sincere desire"

Webbe, Samuel—*Continued*
"Prayer is the soul's sincere desire" (wrongly attributed) See Schulthes, W. A. F. "Prayer is the soul's sincere desire"

Webber, Charles F.
Constancy

Weber, Bernhard Anselm
"Cheerily the huntsman." See Der schütz
Der schütz

Weber, Karl Maria Friedrich Ernst, freiherr von
An junge spröde schönen. See "Ich sah ein röschen am wege stehn"
"As a little child"
The boat song (from Oberon)
Brautjungfernlied (from Der freischütz)
"Einsam bin ich, nicht alleine" (from Preciosa)
Evening prayer. See Gebet
Gebet (from Der freischütz)
Give a cheer
Heimlicher liebe pein
"Ich sah ein röschen am wege stehn"
Lutzow's wild hunt. See Lützows wilde jagd
Lützows wilde jagd
"Oh diletta" (from Abu Hassan)
The pain of love. See Heimlicher liebe pein
Prayer. See Gebet
The rosy crown
Schwertlied
Seymour. See "As a little child"; "Softly now the light of day"
"Softly now the light of day" (same air as "As a little child")
"When the thorn is white with blossom"
Wiegenlied

Die **weberstochter.** See The weaver's daughter

Webster, H. D. L.
Lorena (Webster, J. P.)

Webster, Joseph Philbrick
The army bean (same air as The sweet by and by)
The golden stair. See Where the little feet are waiting
Lorena
The preacher and the slave (same air as The sweet by and by)
Where the little feet are waiting

We'd better bide a wee. C. Barnard (Claribel) (music and words) GE—MFS

Wedderburn, John
"Let us rejoice and sing" (Old Scottish air) Authorship uncertain

"The **wedding** bells were ringing." See The fatal wedding (Davis)

[**Wedding-day** song ("Behold the gifts")]
Na utro poslïe svad'by (Am morgen nach der hochzeit) Russian folk song. g.r. ML 1
Variant: The swans

The **wedding** of the frog and mouse (see Song Index)
Variants: The frog and the mouse; "A frog he went a-courting"; The frog in the well; "Frog went a-courting"; "It was the frog in the well"; Kemo, kimo

[The **wedding-suit**] Appearances. Russian folk song. e. NRF

"A **wee** bird cam' to our ha' door." See Wae's me for Prince Charlie

The **wee** cooper of Fife. Old Scot's ballad. GSS

"A **wee** man all alone in the deep, dark wood." See A little man

Wee Willie Gray. Scottish folk air. Words by R. Burns. CSB 1

A **week's** work well done (see Song Index)
Variant of: The holly twig

Weel about and turn about and do jis' so. See Jim Crow (Rice)

Weel I wad my true love ken. See Lewie Gordon

Weel may the keel row ("O who is like my Johnnie") See The keel row

"**Weep** no more, Marta." See Happy morning

Weep no more, my lady. See My old Kentucky home (Foster)

"**Weep** not, O my rose, why sigh so." See Csárdás

"**Weep** you no more, sad fountains." N. F. Demuth. Author of words unknown. CSB 3

Weepin' Mary ("They nailed Him to the cross") Negro spiritual. FSN

Weeping, sad and lonely, hopes and fears, how vain. See When this cruel war is over (Tucker)

Weeping, sad and lonely, oh, how bad I feel. See Down in Charleston jail (Tucker)

The **weeping** willow. American mountain song. RA
Variant: "O bury me beneath the willow"

Weevily wheat ("It's step her to your weev'ly wheat") Traditional dance song. SBA
For variants see following song of same title; also Charlie's sweet

Weevily wheat ("Yore weevily wheat ain't fit to eat") Traditional dance song. RA

"**Weh'** dasz wir scheiden müssen." See Ritters abschied (Kinkel)

Weh ihnen, dass sie von mir weichen. For English translation see Woe unto them who forsake Him (Mendelssohn)

"**Weh** mir! nun brich, o herz." See Sappho (Volkmann)

Weigle, Gottlieb
Unterländers heimweh (Volkslied)

Weihegaben für das Jesuskind. See Presents al niño Jesús

Weihelied (Der landesvater.—"Alles schweige") Student song. Words by A. Niemann. g. EDL

"**Weihnacht** ist da." See "Voici la Noël"

Die **weihnachtsfreude** ("Morgen, kinder, wird's was geben") Volksweise. Words by C. F. Splittegarb. g. EDL

Weihnachtslied ("Lo Desembre congelat, confus se retira") See Cansó de Nadal

Weihnachtslied ("Hört unsre botschaft") See "Nesem vám noviny"

Weihtnachtslied der schalmeibläser. See Canzone d'i zampognari

Der **weihnachtsmann** ("Morgen kommt der weihnachtsmann") Volksweise. Words by Hoffmann von Fallersleben. g. EDL

Weihnachtstanz ("A vinticinc de Desembre") See Villancico-baile de Nadal

Weihnachtswiegenlied ("Joseph, lieber Joseph mein") 15th century carol. g. EDL
"Joseph lieber, Joseph mein" (Song of the crib) e. OB

"**Weil'** auf mir, du dunkles auge." See Bitte (Franz); Die bitte (Moór); Bitte (Sjögren)

"**Weil** ich denn scheiden muss." See Abschied

"**Weile**, rose, bliemla." See La chanson des beignets

"**Weinchen**, sollst mir aus dem trinkglas dich ergiessen." See Rotes weinchen

Weine nicht, mein liebchen. See My old Kentucky home (Foster)

"**Weine** nicht, o Nina mein" ("Ne sirj Ninám, ne könyezz") Hungarian folk song. g.hu. ML 3

Weinlied. See Das reich der freude

Die **weinrunde.** See Le cycle du vin

"**Weiss** kein bessres lager mir" ("Nincsen nekem jobb tanyám") Hungarian folk song. g.hu. ML 3

Weisse, Christian Felix
Der kuss (Beethoven)

"**Weisst** du noch, wie wir gingen einst an Harmiavesis." See Am Harmiavesi

"**Weit** ist mein geliebter, weit" ("Kultani on kaukana") Finnish folk song. fi.g. ML 3

"**Weit** nach dem schönen Schwanenfluss." See The old folks at home (Foster)

"**Wel**, dyma ni'n dwad." See Mari lwyd

"**Welcome** be Thou, heav'nly King." See Welcome Yule (West of England air); Welcome Yule (Nicholson)

Welcome, May! lovely May. See "When the spring with magic finger"

"**Welcome**, neighbor." Air: Twinkle, twinkle little star. BB

"**Welcome**, pretty primrose." ⌈Tr of Salve, o rosa, amabile fior⌉ C. Pinsuti. e. GE—MFS

Welcome, summer. Irish traditional air. Words by G. Chaucer. OB

"**Welcome**, sweet springtime." See Voices of the woods (Rubinstein)

Welcome to morning. Offenbach. ⌈Words by M. B. C. Slade⌉ MFS

Welcome Yule. Old West of England air. 15th century words. DNS

Welcome Yule. S. H. Nicholson. 15th century words. OB

"**Wele** goelcerth wen yn fflamio." See Rhyfelgyrch gwyr Harlech

"**Well-a-day!** well-a-day! Christmas too soon goes away." See The old Yorkshire gooding carol

"**We'll** bring down the red deer." See Come o'er the stream, Charlie

"**We'll** climb up Jacob's ladder." See Jacob's ladder (North Carolina mountain version)

"**We'll** gather by the twilight's glow." See In front of old Pardee (Stier)

"**We'll** haul the bowlin'." See Haul the bowline

"**Well** here comes the navy team." See Blow the men down (U.S. Naval academy version)

"**Well**, here we are; well, here we are." See Boola song: Yale athletic version (Hirsh)

"**Well**, howdy, Bill git down a minute." See Howdy, Bill (Chitwood)

"**Well**, I heard a mighty rumblin'." See Cornfield medley

Well, I swan. See Wal, I swan (Burt⌉

"**Well**, if I am Lord Dannel's wife." See Little Musgrave and Lady Barnard (Black Mountain, N.C. version)

Well judging Phyllis. W. Boyce. GA

"A **well-known** Indiana man." See He found it (Stevens)

We'll laugh and sing and merry be. See "We meet again to-night"

"**Well**, mates, you don't like stories." See California Joe

"**Well** met, well met, my old true love, well met, well met, says he." See The daemon lover (Hindman, Ky. version; Black Mountain, N.C. version; Nellysford, Va. version)

"**Well** met, well met, my own true love, it's well met, said he." See The daemon lover (Flag Pond, Tenn. version no. 1)

"**Well** met, well met, my own true love, well met, well met, says he." See The daemon lover (Clay county, Ky. version; Hindman, Ky. version; Proctor, Ky. version; Burnsville, N.C. versions no. 1-2; Hot Springs, N.C. version no. 2)

"**Well** met, well met, says an old true love." See The daemon lover (Berea, Ky. version no. 1)

"**We'll** pay Paddy Doyle for his boots." See Paddy Doyle's boots

"**We'll** put for de souf." See Away down souf (Foster)

"**We'll** raise the song." Kansas state teachers' college song. AI

We'll ranzo way. See Huckleberry hunting

"**We'll** roll, we'll roll the chariot along." See Roll the chariot

⌈**We'll** stand the storm⌉ Oh, stand the storm. Negro spiritual. HRD

Wellings, Milton
Only a rose

Wellman, Harry Richmond
"Men of Dartmouth"
Wells, Kathryn
The dolls' party (Macy)
Welsh carol ("Awake were they only")
See Roedd yn y wiad honno
"Weltall bebt', als der herr geboren" ("Bóg
się rodzi, moc truchleje") Polish
folk song. g.p. ML 3
Wély, Louis James Alfred Lefébure-. See
Lefébure-Wély, Louis James Alfred
"Wem Gott will rechte gunst erweisen."
See Der frohe wandersmann (Fröhlich)
"Wem soll dieses brachfeld wohl ange-
hören" ("Čiaže je to rolička nezoraná")
Slovak folk song. g.sl. ML 3
Wen ich will zur ehe (Komu da me dade)
Macedonian folk song. b.g. ML 2
"Wenn alle brünnlein fliessen." See
Tritt zu
"Wenn auf dem höchsten fels ich steh'."
See Der hirt auf dem felsen (Schubert)
"Wenn das herz eines mannes die sorge
drückt." See "If the heart of a man
is deprest with cares"
"Wenn der frühling auf die berge steigt"
(Frühlingszeit.—Spring) R. Becker.
[Words by F. M. von Bodenstadt]
e.g. GG
"Wenn der frühling auf die berge steigt"
(Frühlingslied.—Lovely spring) W.
Coenen. [Words by F. von Boden-
stedt] e.g. GG
"Wenn der könig Heinrich mir." See
"Si le roy m'avait donné"
"Wenn der schimmer von dem monde nun
herab in die wälder sich ergiesst." See
Die sommernacht (Gluck)
"Wenn die nacht doch dauern möcht'"
("Bárcsak ez az éjszaka") Hungarian
folk song. g.hu. ML 3
"Wenn die rosen blühen." See Hoffnung
(Reichardt)
"Wenn du wüsstest, mein lieb." See
Trauer um die jugend
"Wenn einsam ohne stern." See Fan-
dango
"Wenn ich doch wüsste, Herr mein Gott"
("Da mî je znatî, Bozhe moj") Ser-
bian folk song. g.se. ML 2
"Wenn ich ein vöglein wär" (Der flug der
liebe) Volkslied. g. EDL
"Wenn ich früh in den garten geh' in
meinem grünen hut." See Volkslied-
chen (Schumann)
"Wenn ich in stiller abendstund'." See
Dir nah' möcht' ich begraben sein (Abt)
"Wenn mich deine blikke streifen." See
Malatu p'amuri
"Wenn sie einmal ward verschmäht." See
Aoleo
"Wenn still mit seinen letzten flammen."
See Liebesglück (Sucher)
"Wenn unsre burschen singen" ("Poijat
kun raitilla laulelee") Finnish folk
song. fi.g. ML 3
"Wenn vun alle teichen." Jewish folk
song. y. SY
"Wenn wir durch die strassen ziehen."
See Entschuldigung (Nestler)

Wenrich, Percy
When you wore a tulip and I wore a
big red rose
Where do we go from here boys
"Went down to New Orleans, got on a
fence." See Turkey in the straw
"Went down to St Joe's infirmary." See
Those gambler's blues
"Went to de graveyard de other day."
See I feel like my time ain't long
"Went to the rocks, the rocks can't you
hide me." See Sinner man (North
Carolina version)
"Went up on the mountain." American
mountain song. RA
Variant of: Eliza Jane
Wentworth, E. N.
"State college of Iowa" (Irish air)
Wer geht draussen auf der strasse. See
Cine trece pe uliţă
"Wer geht mit, juchhe! über see." See
Een liedje van der zee
"Wer hat dich, du schöner wald." See
Der jäger abschied (Mendelssohn)
"Wer reitet so spät durch nacht und wind."
See Erlkönig (Loewe); Erlkönig (Schu-
bert)
"Wer steht vor der tür und ruft." See
Eamonn a' Chnuic
"Wer will unter die soldaten." See Der
kleine rekrut (Kücken)
"Werc me pola herca." See Aufforderung
zum tanze (Wendish folk song)
"We're a lonely dismal crew." See Poor
old maid
We're a' noddin' ("Guddeen to you, kim-
mer, and how do you do") See
"Guide'en to you, kimmer, and how do
you do"
We're a' noddin' ("Gude e'en to ye, kimmer,
and are ye alane") Scottish
song. GS
Variant: All noddin'
"We're a philanthropic couple be it known."
See Birds of a feather (Jakobowski)
We're all bound to go ("O as I walked
down the landing stage") Wind-
lass chantey. WSE
For variants see following song of
same title; also Heave away, my
Johnny
We're all bound to go ("Oh, Johnny was
a rover") Windlass and capstan
chantey. TSB 1
"We're all for the navy." See The pride
of the navy
"We're all together again." Scout greet-
ing song. GSS
We're bound for Rio. See Rio Grande
We're bound to work all night. See
"Lincoln hoss" and Stephen A. (Fos-
ter)
"We're from a school of great renown."
See Adelphi field song (Thayer)
"Were he but here." See "Regnava nel
silenzio" (Donizetti)
"We're here to win for Wooster." Woos-
ter college song. Air: Frat. Words
by W. E. Peck. AIS

"We're here to win the day for Washington." See Colors of Washington (Hatcher)

"We're homeward bound today, but where is my Johnny." See My Johnny

"Were I a sunbeam, in the heavens gleaming." See The maiden's wish (Chopin)

We're in the Q. M. C. Song of the European war. Air: The old gray mare. DSO

"Were it not for these men we could not do amiss." See What can a poor maiden do (Horn)

"We're loyal to you, Illinois" (Illinois loyalty) University of Illinois song. T. H. Guild (music and words) AI—AIS

"We're loyal to you U. S. D." University of South Dakota song. College airs arranged. Words by J. H. Downing. HW

"We're marchin' up to hebben." See Hear de angels singin'

Were my song with wings provided. See Si mes vers avaient des ailes (Hahn)

We're on our way to Berlin. See Kelly field air-service song (Emmett)

"We're only a rookie regiment." See The sixth field artillery song

We're poor little mids who have lost our way. See Gentlemen sailors

"We're ten miles from home." See Ten miles from home

"We're tenting to-night." See Tenting on the old camp ground (Kittredge)

We're the boys for Mexico. Song of the Mexican war. Air: Yankee Doodle DSO

"We're the boys of the thirsty-first." 31st U.S. infantry song. DSO

We're the fight, fight, fighting tigers from down at old Mizzou. See The tiger song (Burkholder and Fowler)

"Were the pitcher full alway" ("Van e bor a korsóba") Old Hungarian song. Composer unknown. e.hu. KH 1

"Were you ever in Quebec." See Donkey riding

"Were you there." Negro spiritual. WFN—WSS

"Were you there" (The crucified) FSN

"Were you there when they crucified my Lord." HRD—JB 2

Wergan, pseud. See Wagner, Heinrich

Das Wermländer lied. See Vermeland

Werner, Heinrich
Heidenröslein
Mountain maid's invitation
The two roses. See Heidenröslein

Wesley, Charles
"Christ the Lord is ris'n today, alleluia! Sons of men and angels say" (Worgan)
"Come, Thou almighty King" (Carey?; Giardini)
"Hail, Thou long-expected Jesus" (Mozart)

"Hark! the herald angels sing" (Mendelssohn)
"Jesus, Lover of my soul" (music by Marsh; Parry; Peticolas; Tours)
"Love divine, all loves excelling" (music by Haydn; Le Jeune; Sommers)
"Oh, for a thousand tongues" (Glaser)
Open, Lord, my inward ear (Beethoven)
"Sons of men, behold" (Thibaut IV)
Veni Redemptor gentium (4th century Latin air)

Wesley, Samuel Sebastian
Aurelia. See Hymn of scouting; To-morrow
Hymn of scouting (same air as "The church's one foundation")
To-morrow (same air as "The church's one foundation")

"Wesleyan, let us all unite and sing." See Red and black (Wright)

Wesson, Al
The cardinal and gold

"West Point, at thy call." See Official West Point march (Egner)

The west riding Yorkshire wassail song. See "Here we come a-wesseling"

The West Texas blues. C. H. Booker. HB

Westbrook, Arthur
Night and day (Manney)

Westendorf, Thomas P.
"I'll take you home again, Kathleen"

Westervelt, Harry Clarkson
The red and blue (Goeckel)

Westminster chimes. Composer and author of words unknown. TFP

Westnacott, C. M.
Dumbarton's bonny dell (Sinclair)

"A wet sheet and a flowing sea." [French military air: Le petit tambour. Words by A. Cunningham] US

Wetmore, William J.
Sound your A (Bradbury)

"We've come to see Miss Jenny-o-Jones." See Miss Jenny-o-Jones

We've drunk from the same canteen. Civil war song. J. G. Clark. Words by Private Miles O'Riley (C. G. Halpine) DSO

"We've got a hell of a way to go." See No more rivers

"We've met, we've met." See The daemon lover (Allanstand, N.C. version no. 2; Alleghany, N.C. versions no. 1-2; Spillcorn, N.C. version; Dewey, Va. version)

"We've not much longer here to stay." See Army blue (Poulton)

"We've reached the land of Arctic fame." See Behring sea song (Sweney)

"We've reached the land of desert sweet." See Dakota land (Sweney)

Wexford carol ("Good people all") See "Good people all, this Christmas-time"

Weyts, Henry
Fleur d'amour
Flower of love. See Fleur d'amour

"Wha in a brulzie." See Bannocks o' bear-meal

"**Wha** wadna be in love wi' bonnie Maggie Lauder." See Maggie Lauder

ɪ"**Wha** wadna fecht for Charlie"ɪ "Who wadna fight for Charlie." ɪAir: Will ye go and marry Kettieɪ LAS

Whach, hurrah! blood an' 'ounds. See Tim Finigan's wake

Whack fol tiddy fol lura ladee. See The good ship Montezuma

The **whale** ("O, 'twas in the year of ninety-four") Forecastle song. US—WSE
Variant of: Greenland fishery

Wha'll be king but Charlie ("The news frae Moidart cam' yestre'en") Scottish air. Words by C. Nairne. GS

"**Wha'll** buy caller herrin'." See Caller herrin' (Gow?)

"**Whar** hae ye been a' day." See My boy Tammie

"**Whar** now is good ole Noeh." See Safe in the promised land

"**Whar** you gwine po' sinnah." See You mus' hab dat true religion

Wharton, Morton Bryan
Dixie (Emmett)

Wharton, Thomas Wharton, 1st marquis
Lilliburlero (Purcell) Authorship uncertain

"**What** a happy time, chil'n." See Brother, guide me home

"**What** a sorrowful ditty of poor Omie Wise." See Poor Omie (Alleghany, N.C. version)

What a trying time. Negro spiritual from Virginia. AS
What a tryin' time (Adam, where are you) FSN

What are little boys made of. See Natural history

"**What** are the thoughts that are stirring his breast." See Under the shade of the trees (Lyte)

"**What** are they that are but one." See A new dial

"**What** are you going to do with a drunken sailor." Chantey. US
Variant of: The drunken sailor

"**What** as gay as cheery song." See Sing

"**What** beauties does Flora disclose" (Tweed side) Air: Tweedside. Words by Crawfurd. GS

"**What** blood is that all on your shirt." See Edward (Marion, N.C. version)

What can a poor maiden do. C. E. Horn. HP

"**What** care I if the world's turn'd 'round." See Moet and Shandon for me

"**What** care we for gold or silver." MFS

"**What** Child is this." C. Engel. ɪWords by W. C. Dixɪ FC

"**What** Child is this." Old English air: Greensleeves. ɪWords by W. C. Dixɪ DSB

"**What** did you eat for your supper, Jimmy Randal my son." See Lord Randal (Allanstand, N. C. version no. 2)

"**What** did you have for supper, Jimmy Randolph, my son." See Lord Randall (Burnsville, N.C. version; Nellysford, Va. version)

"**What** does little birdie say." See Little birdie (Delius)

"**What** fairy-like music." J. De Pinna. Words by Mrs C. B. Wilson. GOS 1 —MFS

"**What** for your supper, John Randolph, my son." See Lord Randal (Buena Vista, Va. versions no. 1-2)

"**What** from vengeance now restrains me." See Sextet (Donizetti)

"**What** from vengeance yet restrains me." See Sextet (Donizetti)

"**What** has come this blood on your shirt sleeve." See Edward (Tennessee version)

"**What** here behold I." See Infelice! e tu credevi (Verdi)

"**What** I will say today." See "Lo que digo"

"**What** if to-morrow bring sorrow or anything other than joy." See Sans souci

"**What** is de matter wid de mourners." See Jubalee

What is home ("Home's not merely four square walls") See "Home's not merely four square walls" (Rossini)

"**What** is home without a mother." A. Hawthorne (S. Winner) GOS 1

"**What** is that up yonder I see." See I want to join the band

"**What** is the matter with the mourners." See Jubalee

"**What** is the meaning of the song." See I love my love (Pinsuti)

"**What** is the sound and rumor." See The march of the people (Bullard)

"**What** joy, what bliss my bosom fills." See "Rondinella pellegrina" (Petrella)

What kin' o' pants does the gambler wear. Negro folk song. SBA

"**What** kind of shoes you going to wear." Negro spiritual. BB

"**What** lovely Infant can this be." Austrian folk carol. FC

"**What** make ole Satan da follow me so." See Hold your light

"**What** means this glory round our feet." See Peace on earth (Donizetti)

"**What** of the night, O heart, my heart." See Guide us with Thy heavenly light (Tosti)

"**What** pleasure folks feel." See Tea in the arbor (Beuler)

"**What** sad lot the stars prepare me." See "Che farò senza Euridice" (Gluck)

"**What** said John Paul Jones." See The countersigns

"**What** shall we do with a drunken sailor." See The drunken sailor

"**What** ship is that you're enlisted upon." See The old ship of Zion (Maryland version)

"**What** song doth the cricket sing." See Love and mirth (Strauss)

"What songs are these, faint heard and far."   See The band of children

"What sweeter music can we bring" (Herrick's carol)   German air: Als ich bei meinen schafen wacht.   Words by R. Herrick.   OB

What the deuce do we care.   See Hail! hail! the gang's all here (Sullivan)

What the dickey birds say.   E. Jakobowski.   WLO

"What though I be a country lass" (The country lass.—Das dirndl)   ₁Old English air: Oil of barley.   Words by M. Parker₎   e.g.   ML 1

"What though I trace each herb and flower."   G. F. Händel.   SSO 2

"What tidings bringest thou" (Wonder tidings)   J. Dunstable.   OB

"What tongue can tell Thy greatness, Lord."   <Old air arr by J. S. Bach>   Words by P. Nicolai.   e.   DSB— MBS

What was your name in the States.   Old American song.   SBA

What will happen when the Messiah comes₎   As Moshiach wet kummen.   Jewish folk song.   y.   SY

"What will you do, love."   S. Lover (music and words)   GOS 2—HMI—MFS

"What will you take to town, lad."   See From the hills

"What wordly pleasures canst proffer without thy sun."   See "Che val ricchezza e trono" (Donizetti)

What yo' gwine t' do when de lamp burn down.   Negro spiritual.   HRD

"What you gwain to do when the meat gives out, my baby."   See What kin' o' pants does the gambler wear

"What you will to your father, Jimmy Randal, my son."   See Lord Randal (Buena Vista, Va. version no. 3)

"What you will to your father, Jimmy Randolph my son."   See Lord Randal (Allanstand, N.C. version no. 1)

"What you will to your mother, my rambling young son."   See Lord Randal (Tennessee version)

"What'll we do with the baby."   Folk song from Kentucky.   SES 2

"What's a' the steer, kimmer."   Jacobite song.   Old air.   GS

"What's a' the steer, kimmer."   <Jacobite song>   G. A. Lee.   GOS 1—GS

"What's little babies made of."   See Natural history (Manchester, Ky. version)

"What's old women made of."   See Natural history (Barbourville, Ky. version)

"What's the use of beauty" ("Csak akkor szép a lány")   E. Szentirmay (music and words)   e.hu.   KH 2

"What's this dull town to me."   See Robin Adair

"What's this man's horse a-doing here."   See Our goodman (Barbourville, Ky. version)

Wheel about and turn about and do jis' so.   See Jim Crow (Rice)

"A wheel in a wheel."   Negro spiritual.   HRD
    Variants: "Ezekiel saw de wheel"; " 'Zekiel saw de wheel"

Wheel, oh, wheel, wheel in de middle of a wheel.   See " 'Zekiel saw de wheel"

Wheeler, J. W.
    The old cuckoo clock that hangs upon the wall

"When a fellow loves a maiden."   See La cucaracha

"When a lad, I stood one day."   See She was bred in old Kentucky (Redcliffe)

"When a lover loves a maiden."   See "Cuando uno quiere a una"

"When a woman blue."   Negro folk blues.   SBA

"When Adam was created."   Folk song from North Carolina.   SES 2

"When all the world is young."   C. Barnard.   Words by C. Kingsley.   MFS

"When all was young."   See "Si le bonheur" (Gounod)

"When at morn in the merry spring."   See Volksliedchen (Schumann)

"When at twilight so softly."   See Chantez riez et dormez (Gounod)

"When battle music greets our ear."   See Touch the elbow

"When beside thee I reclined."   See Non è ver (Mattei)

"When Bibo went down to the regions below."   Old American song.   SW

When boys go a-courting.   Folk song: Kentucky version.   SES 2
    —Callaway, Va. version.   SES 2
    —White Rock, Va. version.   SES 2

"When boys go a-courting, a-courting, a-courting."   See "The chickens they are crowing" (Virginia version)

"When boys goes a-courting they dress up so fine."   See When boys go a-courting (Kentucky version)

"When bright skies were o'er us and life lay before us."   See Bowdoin beata

"When brightly to his rest descending."   See Liebesglück (Sucher)

"When Britain first at heav'n's command."   See Rule, Britannia (Arne)

"When Britain really rul'd the waves."   A. S. Sullivan.   Words by W. S. Gilbert.   DSC

"When Brunonia's big brown team is in the game."   See The Brown cheering song (Young)

"When but a child I used to go to bed at eight each night."   See Where was Moses when the light went out

"When Caesar Augustus had raised a taxation."   See No room in the inn

"When Christ a Babe was born."   See Canzone d'i zampognari

"When Christ blessed his disciples."   See Song of the spirit

"When Christ the Lord was here below."   See Down by the river

"When Christ was born of Mary free."   Old French air.   15th century words. ₁Tr of Christo paremus canticam, in excelsis gloria₎   e.   FC

"When Christ was born of Mary free" (Christo paremus cantica, in excelsis gloria.—In excelsis gloria) A. H. Brown. <15th century words> e. OB

"When Christ was born of Mary free" (Christo paremus cantica, in excelsis gloria.—In excelsis gloria) M. Shaw. 15th century words. e. OB

"When cockle shells turn silver bells." See Waillie, waillie

"When cold in the earth." Air: Limerick's lamentation. Words by T. Moore. HMI

When Colorado "C" men fall in line. See Colorado "C" men (Allen and Sheafe)

"When 'cross the campus you can hear a mighty cheer." See The panther (Harris)

"When daisies pied, and violets blue." T. A. Arne. Words by W. Shakespeare. EB

"When darkness falls around me." Haydn. e. SSO 3

"When de good ole Gabriel gwine to blow de horn." See Early in de mornin'

When de saints come marchin' in. Negro spiritual. JG

"When de storm of life is ragin'." See Stan' by me

When dull care. R. Leveridge. WOE

"When early morning's ruddy light." See The mowers' song

"When e'er you make a promise." Four part round. W. W. Shield. GSS

"When Erin shall stand 'mid the isles of the sea" (The last words of Emmet) W. Maynard. Words by A. L. Ruter. SI

"When evening's quiet hour draws nigh." See Dir nah' möcht' ich begraben sein (Abt)

"When evening's twilight gathers round." J. L. Hatton. Author of words unknown. TFB

When fields are white. German folk air. Words by H. H. Harbour. DSB

"When first his standard caught the eye." See O Charlie is my darling (Words by Gray)

"When first I met thee." Air: O, Patrick, fly from me. Words by T. Moore. HMI

"When first I saw sweet Peggy." See The low-backed car

"When first I went a-waggoning." See The jolly waggoner

"When forced to bid farewell to Loo." See The tar's farewell (Maybrick)

"When formed our band, we are all well manned." See California

"When from out de shades ob night." See Come down ma evenin' star (Stromberg)

"When he, who adores thee." Irish air: The foxes sleep, or, The fox's sleep. Words by T. Moore. HMI

"When Hope her cheering smile supplies." See Ma Normandie (Bérat)

"When I became a rover." See My parents treated me tenderly (Allanstand, N.C. version)

"When I behold your manly form." See Gobble duet (Audran)

When I come ("Muss i denn") See Abschied ("Muss i denn")

"When I enlisted in the army." See Down in Charleston jail (Tucker)

When I fall on my knees wid my face to de risin' sun. Negro spiritual. JB 2

"When I first came to this country in eighteen and forty-nine." See Pretty Saro (Allanstand, N.C. version)

"When I, good friends, was call'd to the bar." See The judge's song (Sullivan)

"When I lay me down to sleep." See Evening prayer (Humperdinck)

"When I lib'd in Tennessee, u-li-a-li-o-la-e." See Rosa Lee

"When I lived at home with father." See Digue dindaine

When I saw sweet Nellie home. See The quilting party (Fletcher)

"When I set out I was but young." See Getting ready to die

"When I survey the world around." See The leather bottèl

"When I view the Mother holding." 15th century air. [Tr of Parvum quando cerno Deum] e. FC

"When I wait in the garden early." See Volksliedchen (Schumann)

When I walk dat levee round. See The bully song (Trevathan)

"When I wander'd, poor exile, dejected." See "Qui m'accolse oppresso, errante" (Bellini)

"When I was a bachelor bold and brave." See The holly twig (Woodridge, Va. version)

"When I was a bach'lor, I liv'd by myself." See Foggy, foggy dew

"When I was a beggarly boy." See Aladdin (Bellini)

"When I was a lad, I had cause to be sad." See Robinson Crusoe

"When I was a lady." Children's song. <Air: Alles ist hin> BB

"When I was a learner." See Go tell it on de mountain

"When I was a little boy I lived by myself." See The swapping song (American mountain version; Berea, Ky. version; Hindman, Ky. version; Tennessee version)

"When I was a little tiny boy, I went to sea in Stormy's employ." See The shaver

"When I was a maiden all crossed up in love." See Johnny Doyle (Virginia version)

"When I was a seeker." See Go tell it on de mountain

"When I was a single girl go dressed so neat and fine." See The single girl (Berea, Ky. version)

"When I was bound apprentice in famous Lincolnshire." See The Lincolnshire poacher

"When I was down in Egypt land." See My Lord's writing all the time

"When I was single I dressed neat and fine." See The single girl (Virginia version)

"When I was single I primpted and shined." See I'm satisfied (Tanner)

"When I was single, O then, O then." See I wish I was single again

"When I was single, went dressed all so fine." See The single girl (North Carolina version)

"When I was the prettiest boy." See The miller's apprentice (Pine Mountain, Ky. version)

"When I was wicked an'-a prone to sin." See You must be pure and holy

"When I was young and fair and gay." See The old maid's lament

"When I was young and foolish." American jail song.   SBA

"When I was young and full of love." See Devilish Mary (Barbourville, Ky. version)

"When I was young and in my youth." See Devilish Mary (St Helen's, Ky. version)

"When I was young I used to wait." See Jim crack corn

"When I went over Putman's hill." See Putman's hill

"When I with Chloe sat alone." See Der kuss (Beethoven)

"When I'm gone, doan' yer grieve after me." Negro spiritual.   FSN

"When in death I shall calm recline." See The legacy

"When in the azure dome, the stars, radiantly bright." See Hymne à la nuit (Gounod)

"When Israel was in Egypt's land." See Go down, Moses

"When January days are here." See January and February

"When Jesus Christ was twelve years old." See Wondrous works

"When Jesus Christ was yet a child." See The crown of roses (Tchaikovsky)

"When Jesus was a baby and born of mortal men." See Carol of the kingdom

"When Johnie Scot saw this big, broad letter." See Johnie Scot (North Carolina version)

"When Johnny comes marching home." L. Lambert (music and words)   BB —DSO—TFB—TFP—TFR

"When Joseph was a young man." See The cherry tree carol (Hindman, Ky. version)

"When Joseph was an old man." See The cherry tree carol (15th century air); The cherry tree carol (Knott or Letcher county version)

"When joyous tho'ts on thy sweet lips awaken." See "Si le bonheur" (Gounod)

"When Katie was scarce out nineteen." See The lass o' Gowrie

"When keen salt winds are blowing." See A sailing song (Callcott)

"When King Cadwallon fam'd of old." See Saint David's day

"When leaving dear old Ioway." See There is no work in the army

"When Lord Thomas he came home." See The gypsy laddie (Hot Springs, N.C. version no. 2)

"When Louis came home to the flat." See Meet me in St Louis, Louis (Mills)

"When love is kind." Old Irish air. Words by T. Moore.   AT—BST

"When Maggie and I were acquaint" (Tweed side)   Scottish air: Tweedside.   Words by John, Lord Yester, marquis of Tweeddale.   GS

"When May is in his prime." R. Edwardes (music and words)   GA

"When mighty roast beef was the Englishman's food." See The roast beef of old England (Leveridge)

"When morning gilds the skies." J. Barnby.   [Tr of Beim frühen morgenlicht]   e.   TFO

"When my eyes behold perfection." See Quando mai spietata sorte (Händel)

"When o'er the hill the eastern star." See The lea rig (Scottish air)

"When on its couch of rosy clouds." See Good night and pleasant dreams (Wallace)

"When on march, footsore and weary." See Song of the drum (Audran)

"When on the mountain top I stand." See Der hirt auf dem felsen (Schubert)

"When on the widespread battle plain." See Remember the Alamo

"When on the world's first harvest day." See The blushing maple tree (McCaskey)

"When other lips." See Then you'll remember me (Balfe)

When poor Mary came wandering home. American song.   SBA Variant of: Mary of The wild moor

"When Raleigh rose to fight the foes." See Foundation song (Farmer)

"When righteous Joseph wedded was to Israel's fairest maid." See Righteous Joseph (Old English air)

"When righteous Joseph wedded was to Israel's Hebrew maid." See Righteous Joseph (Cornish air)

"When righteous Joseph wedded was unto a virtuous maid." See The Sussex mummers' carol

When roses bloom ("In meiner liebsten garten")   See Aus der rosenzeit (Fielitz)

"When shall we meet again." L. Mason. MFS

When Sherman marched down to the sea. Lieutenant Rockwell.   Words by S. H. M. Byers.   DSO

When sickness overtake you.   See There's a mother always waiting you at home, sweet home (Thornton)

"When spring is whisp'ring in the birches green." See Ein vaartankje (Sinding)

"When stars are in the quiet skies." Words by E. Bulwer, Lord Lytton. GOS 1

"When still my life was youthful." See "Sotto il paterno tetto" (Verdi)

When that band of darkies began to play. See At a Georgia camp meeting (Mills)

"When that I was a little tiny boy." Old English air. Words by W. Shakespeare. BOS 2

"When the bell in the lighthouse rings ding dong." Minstrel song. PSG

"When the black letter'd list to the gods was presented." See Wife, children, and friends

When the bloom is on the rye] "My pretty Jane" (The bloom is on the rye) H. R. Bishop. Words by E. Fitzball. BST—GOS 1

"When the bold teams of old." See Roar, lion, roar (Webb and Watkins)

When the chariot comes. Mountain spiritual. SBA
Variants: The ole ship o' Zion; "She'll be comin 'round the mountain"

"When the cock begins to crow" (Fairies' chorus) H. Purcell. CSB 6

"When the corn is waving." C. Blamphin (music and words) BB—TFB —WSS

"When the curtains of night are pinned back." Cowboy song. SBA

"When the dark green waves are lying." See 'Tis I (Pinsuti)

"When the day with rosy light." <Swiss air> GOS 1

When the evening breeze is sighing "Home, sweet home." A. Solman. Words by J. Hayden-Clarendon. OTG

"When the farmer comes to town." See The farmer

When the general roll is called ("O come, my brethren") See General roll call

"When the gen'ral roll is called, yes, I'll be there." See I'll be there in the morning

"When the glow-worm gilds the elfin flow'r." See The banks of the blue Moselle (Rodwell)

"When the good ole Gabriel gwine to blow the horn." See Early in de mornin'

"When the green leaves." Old song. MFS

When the guns are rolling yonder. Air: When the roll is called up yonder. DSO

"When the heathen trumpets' clang." See The monks of Bangor's march

"When the house of life is ringing." See Behold! I stand at the door (Jude)

"When the humid showers gather." See Rain on the roof (Clifford)

"When the iceman rings the bell." See Second thoughts (Loomis)

When the kye comes hame ("Come, all ye jolly shepherds") Old Border air: Shame fa' the gear and the blathrie o't, or, The blathrie o't. Words by J. Hogg. GOS 2—GS

"When the little children sleep." C. Reinecke. e. LAS

"When the Lord called Moses." Negro spiritual from Tennessee. FSN

"When the mists have roll'd in splendor" (When the mists have cleared away) A. Henshaw. [Words by A. Herbert] CSS 1—CSS 2

"When the night o'er hills is creeping." See Homeland mine (Beethoven)

"When the night was spent and the day coming in." See Fair Margaret and sweet William (Woodridge, Va. version)

"When the nights grow cold." See Farewell to summer

"When the pale moon drowns the wide world." See Dawn (Somerset)

"When the purple evening shadows." See Fireflies

When the robins nest again. F. Howard (music and words) GFS

When the roses bloom again beside the river. See I'll be with you when the roses bloom again (Edwards)

"When the rosy morn appearing." Old English round. DSB

When the saints come marchin' in. See When de saints come marchin' in

"When the shades of ev'ning gather" (Campus song) Ursinus college song. <F. Shackelton. Words by C. G. Petri> AI

When the sheep are in the fauld. See Auld Robin Gray (Scottish air); Auld Robin Gray (Leeves)

"When the ship is trim and ready." See They all love Jack (Maybrick)

"When the silver dew is falling." See Fairy music

"When the spring has clim'b the mountain's height." See "Wenn der frühling auf die berge steigt" (Coenen)

"When the spring is climbing up the height." See "Wenn der frühling auf die berge steigt" (Becker)

"When the spring with magic finger." Polish air. Words by A. J. Foxwell. TFG

"When the storm of life is raging." See Stan' by me

"When the thorn is white with blossom." C. M. von Weber. GE

"When the veil of night." See "Quando avvolto" (Alary)

"When the war is ended the boys will see their fun." See Ha, ha, ha

"When the waves are gently flowing." See Dein gedenk' ich, Margareta (Meyer-Helmund)

"When the wind is in the east." See A prophecy

When the work's all done this fall. Cowboy song. SBA

"When their parents came to know." See William Hall (Barbourville, Ky. version)

When these three long years are over. See "Only one more jungle season" (Converse)

When this cruel war is over. H. Tucker. Words by C. C. Sawyer. DSO

When this cruel war is over (Weeping, sad and lonely) HP

When this cruel war is over, Parody on. See Down in Charleston jail (Tucker)

"When thou dost bend o'er me thy glance of splendor." See The blissful strain is o'er (Wagner)

"When thro' life unblest we rove." See On music

"When through thy valley, fair Chenango, twilight falls." See Alma mater—Colgate university

"When thy voice 'neath the moon's bright beams I do hear." See Chantez riez et dormez (Gounod)

"When trees did bud" (Doun the burn, Davie love) Composer unknown. Words by R. Crawford, with additional words. GS

"When trees did bud" (Doun the burn, Davie, love) D. Maigh. Words by R. Crawford. GS

"When twilight dews are falling soft." See Twilight dews (Moore)

"When twilight shadows lower." G. Donizetti. ₍Tr of Verrano a me sull'aure₎ e. WG

When Uncle Sammy rises in his might. See Uncle Sammy (Holzmann)

"When underneath a winter sky." See Agatha, Jane, and fair Marie

"When war-like ensigns wave on high." Händel. SSO 3

When Washington and Lee's men fall in line. See Washington and Lee swing (Allen and Sheafe)

"When we do meet again." Negro spiritual from South Carolina. AS

"When we have good rations." K. Millöcker. e. WLO

When we parted. M. Ippolitof-Ivanof. Words from the Russian of D. Rathaus. e. ATS

When we start the coon republic out in China. See The coon republic

When wild the night. See The good Shepherd (Slater)

"When will you come, my sweeting." See "Pa bryd y deui eto"

"When wilt Thou save the people." J. Booth. Words by E. Elliott. TFP

"When wilt Thou save Thy people" (God save the people) C. S. Brown. Words by E. Elliott. LAS

When with drawn sword like lightning flashing. See "Se Romeo t'uccise un figlio" (Bellini)

"When with sweet words of love without ending." See El que a hierro mata

"When ye gang awa, Jamie." See Huntingtower

"When ye were sleeping on your pillows." See Caller herrin' (Gow?)

When you and I were young, Maggie ("I wandered today to the hill") J. A. Butterfield. Words by G. W. Johnson. BB—GOS 2—OT—PSG—TFB—TFP—WSS

"When you come to my house come on your toes." See Lulie

"When you git a good thing, save it, save it." See Sal's got a meat-skin

"When you hear dem a bells go ding, ling, ling." Minstrel song. ₍T. A. Metz₎ PSG

"When you hear the thunder rollin'." See In dat day

"When you see a pretty maiden who has just turn'd seventeen." See You're not the only pebble on the beach (Redcliffe)

When you wore a tulip and I wore a big red rose. P. Wenrich. Words by J. Mahoney. SMG

"When young men go a-courting." See When boys go a-courting (White Rock, Va. version)

"When young men goes courting." See When boys go a-courting (Callaway, Va. version)

When your eyes so bright have lost their light. See I've grown so used to you (Chattaway)

"When your potato's done." See Tan patate-là tchuite

"When you're marching for Columbia." See Marching song (Pattberg)

"Whence appear these shepherds gay." See Où s'en vont ces gais bergers

"Whence art thou, my maiden." See Une crèche de Noël

"Whence comes this rush of wings." See Nouël des ausèls

"Whence, O shepherd maiden." See "D'où viens-tu, bergère"

"Whene'er I see those smiling eyes." Irish air: Father Quinn. Words by T. Moore. HMI

"Whene'er we take our book of mem'ries." See Alma mater, Ohio (Clark)

"Whene'er you make a promise." See "When e'er you make a promise" (Shield)

"Whenever we meet you here we say." See A little more faith in Jesus

"Where are you going, Lord Lovel, she said." See "Lord Lovel" (Nellysford, Va. version)

"Where are you going, my good old man." See The good old man (Hindman, Ky. version no. 2)

"Where are you going, my pretty maid." ₍I. Nathan₎ GOS 2

"Where are you going to, my pretty maid." CSB 1

"Where are you going? says the knight in the road." See The false knight upon the road (North Carolina version)

"Where are you going poor sinner." See You mus' hab dat true religion

"Where balmy garlic scents the air." E. Audran. e. WLO

"Where be going to, dear little maiden." Old Cornish air. AT
Variant of: Dabbling in the dew

Where did you get that hat. J. J. Sullivan (music and words) DFF—GFS —SMG—SRW

"Where did you get your little blood red." See Edward (Callaway, Va. version)

Where do the fellows as twilight falls. See Campus song (Nairn)

Where do we go from here boys. P. Wenrich. SMG

"Where Goucher's far flung colors." Goucher college song. Negro air. Words by L. Baker. AI

"Where ha'e ye been a' the day." See Bonnie laddie, Highland laddie

Where has Lulu gone. S. C. Foster (music and words) WSS

"Where have you been a-roving, Jimmy Randal my son." See Lord Randal (Swannanoah, N.C. version)

"Where have you been, Billy boy, Billy." See My boy Willie (Black Mountain, N.C. version)

"Where have you been Randal, it's Randal my son." See Lord Randal (Knott or Letcher county, Ky. version)

"Where hev ye been äal the day, Billy boy, Billy boy." See My boy Willie (Northumbrian chantey version)

Where is He, this little newly born. See Où s'en vont ces gais bergers

"Where is John." Smetana. Words by A. Horne. TFB—TFG

"Where is my home? where is my home." See My fatherland (Škroup)

"Where is now the merry party." See Far away (Bliss)

Where is spring. C. Repper. Words by D. Stevens. TFO

"Where is the land which Scotland surpasses." See Bonnie brave Scotland (Gow)

"Where is the landlord." See Lamkin (Barbourville, Ky. version)

"Where is the little gipsy's home." See Esmeralda (Levey)

"Where little birds are singing." See "Degli augelletti al canto" (Orlandi)

"Where now is good old Noah." See Safe in the promised land

"Where, O where are the verdant freshmen." College song. <Air: Safe in the promised land> BB

"Where, oh, where is bright spring." See Where is spring (Repper)

"Where O where is old Elijah." American folk song. SBA
Variant: Safe in the promised land

Where shall I be when de firs' trumpet soun'. Negro spiritual. HRD

"Where sorrows touch me nearest." See "Aus meinen grossen schmerzen" (Franz)

Where, tell me where. See The blue bells of Scotland (Jordan)

"Where the bee sucks." T. A. Arne. Words by W. Shakespeare. EB

"Where the elm-tree branches by the rain are stirr'd." See Singing in the rain (Haydn)

"Where the gay sunshine's airy caresses." See Sonnet d'amour (Thomé)

"Where the highlands meet the skylands." See Onward, upward alma mater (Marsh)

"Where the hills of Pennsylvania." See Alma mater—Washington and Jefferson college (Thompson)

"Where the Lehigh's rocky rapids." See Alma mater — Lehigh university (Thompson)

Where the little feet are waiting (The golden stair) J. P. Webster. Words by D. Smith. OT

"Where the Monument is flowing." See Our Colorado (Hille)

"Where the peaceful calm Chenango starts its journey thro' the vale." See Colgate invictus (Bushby)

"Where the pine-tree groweth." See Kalínka

Where the raging tempests blow. See The cavaliers of Dixie (Callcott)

"Where the rolling foothills rise." See Hail, Stanford, hail (Coolidge)

Where the sunset turns the ocean's blue to gold. H. W. Petrie. Words by E. F. Buckner. OTG

"Where the Tisza's torrents through the prairies swell." See The fisherman (Bernáth)

"Where the Tuscan sun is warm and bright." See Marianina

"Where the vale of Onondaga meets the eastern sky." See Alma mater—Syracuse university (Thompson)

"Where the western lights' long shadows." See Alma mater—University of Wyoming (Downey)

"Where the wild rose sweetly doth blow." See The wild rose (Strauss)

"Where the winds of Dixie softly blow." See Alma mater—North Carolina state college (Norris)

Where they were. British army song of the European war. SBA—US
I'll tell you where they were. DSO

Where thou wert fairest of the fair. See "Oh, Nannie, wilt thou gang wi' me" (Carter)

Where was Moses when the light went out. Old song. SW

"Where we go drifting." See Boating song

"Where, where, alas, is he, my heart's beloved." See Vineta (Lachner)

"Where, where will be the birds that sing." See A hundred years to come (Brown)

"Where'er you walk." Händel. Words by Pope; wrongly attributed to W. Congreve. BST—DSC—HCA—TFG

"Wherever I was born and bred." See Nobody's child (Lee)

"Whet up yer knife an' whistle up yer dawg." See The ground hog

Which makes my bright hammer to rise and to fall. See Twankydillo

"Which way does the wind blow." Children's song. MFS

"A while before the gray of dawn." See Blow away the morning dew

"While choirs of angels in the sky." See Choirs of angels

"While gazing on the moon's light." Irish air: Oonagh. Words by T. Moore. HMI

"While history's muse." Air: Paddy Whack. Words by T. Moore. HMI

"While I have life, alone my harps shall praise thee." See Ever I'll praise thee (Wagner)

"While in your beds you're peacefully sleeping." See Past three o'clock, and a cold frosty morning

"While riding down that greenwood road." See John of Hazelgreen

"While shepherds watched their flocks." Old English air. Words by N. Tate. DNS—OB

"While shepherds watch'd their flocks." Old air from Edward V. Webber's MS book. Words by N. Tate. DNS

"While shepherds watched their flocks." 16th century air: Winchester old. Words by N. Tate. DN

"While shepherds watch'd their flocks." Old Hampshire air. ₁Words by N. Tate₁ FC

"While shepherds watch'd their flocks." Traditional Sheffield air. Words by N. Tate. DNS

"While shepherds watch'd their flocks." Old West of England air. Words by N. Tate. DNS

"While shepherds watched their flocks." G. F. Händel. Words by N. Tate. BB

"While shepherds watched their flocks." M. Praetorius. Words by N. Tate. DSB ▸

"While strolling along with the city's vast throng." See She may have seen better days (Thornton)

"While strolling down the street one eve upon mere pleasure bent." See Just tell them that you saw me (Dresser)

"While strolling through Norfolk one day on a spree." See Strolling through Norfolk

"While strolling through the park." E. Haley. SRW

While the foaming billows roll. See Sling the flowing bowl (Linley)

While the merry, merry, merry horn calls, come, come away. See "The bright rosy morning"

"While the moon her watch is keeping." See Ar hyd y nos

"While the morning bells are ringing" (Sicilian hymn) MFS

"While the shot and shell were screaming." See Break the news to mother (Harris)

While the stars of heaven shall burn. See Hail Columbia, The new (Phile)

While the train rolled onward. See In the baggage coach ahead (Davis)

While the wedding bells were ringing. See The fatal wedding (Davis)

"While we are sitting 'round the blazing fire." See Washington my Washington

While we beg for those with plenty. See Little barefoot

Whip jamboree (see Song Index) Variant of: Jamboree

Whip-poor-will's song. H. Millard. GOS 2

Whipsee diddledee dandy. See The frog and the mouse

Whiskers, five a bag. Old song. SW

Whiskers, whiskers, here they go. See Whiskers, five a bag

"Whiskey is the life of man." See Whiskey Johnnie

Whiskey Johnnie ("Whiskey is the life") Halliard chantey. SBS
For variants see following songs of same or similar title

Whiskey, Johnny ("Whiskey is the life") Halliard chantey. US

Whisky ("O, whisky is the life of man") Halliard chantey. WSE

Whisky Johnny ("As we sailed on the water blue") Chantey. SBA

Whisky Johnny ("Oh, whisky is the life of man") Halliard chantey. TSB 1

₁Whisper what thou feelest₁ "Oh! whisper what thou feelest." B. Richards. GOS 2

Whispering hope. A. Hawthorne (S. Winner) GOS 2

"The whistle blows, the tiger knows." See The black and the gold (Hille)

Whistle, daughter, whistle. Folk song: Virginia version. SES 2

Whistle o'er the lave o't. J. Bruce. Words by R. Burns. GS

"Whistle, whistle, daughter." See Whistle, daughter, whistle (Virginia version)

Whitaker, John
    Darby Kelly
    "Oh, hush thee, my babie" (Tr of Caidil gu lo)
    Oh! rest thee, babe. See "Oh, hush thee, my babie"

Whitcomb, John C.
    Chevrons (Egner)

White, Charles Albert
    Amber Lee
    "I'm going back to Dixie." See "I'se gwine back to Dixie"
    "I'se gwine back to Dixie"
    Marguerite
    The widow in the cottage by the seaside

White, Henry Kirke
    "Oft in danger, oft in woe" (Composer unknown)

₁"White dawn has not come stealing"₁ Sve veselo a ja tuzhan (Klage) Serbian folk song. g.se. ML 2

"White folks, I'll sing for you." See My brudder Gum (Foster)

White Lent. Angevin air. Words based on a French Noël, Quittez, pasteurs, vos brebis, vos houlettes. e. OB

The white marble stone ("Sister Dolly light the lamp") Negro spiritual: South Carolina version no. 1. AS

The white marble stone ("O my sister") South Carolina version no. 2. AS

The white rose tree. See "J'ai cueilli la belle rose"

"White sand and grey sand." Round. BOS 2—TFP—TFR

White wings. B. Winter (music and words) GFS—OTG

White wild rose of my heart. See Lliw gwyn rhosyn yr haf

Whiting, William
For those in peril on the sea

Whitman, Walt
Pioneers (Grace)
Weave in, my hardy life (Van der Stucken)

Whitmore, Catharine, pseud. See Loomis, Harvey Worthington

Whitmore, Charles Shapland
Isle of beauty

Whittaker, William Gillies
"Baa, baa, black sheep"
A dance song
"Early to bed"
Spring
"Stay in town"

Whittier, John Greenleaf
"Dear Lord and Father of mankind" (Maker)
"I know not what the future hath" (Schulthes)
"Immortal Love, forever full" (Donizetti)
"We may not climb the heav'nly steeps" (Dykes)

"Who aloft thy head did raise." See Der jäger abschied (Mendelssohn)

Who am I, sir. See Utah man (Seaver)

"Who are the three there in yon lowly stall." See Tell Him a welcome (Finn)

Who built de ark ("Way over yonder in de harves' field") Negro spiritual. FSN

"Who ever saw or heard of woman more wretched than am I." See Nell' orror di notte oscura (Rinaldo di Capua)

"Who gwine to lay dis body." See The graveyard

"Who is going along the ramparts." See Sur les clanquarts

"Who is he plants for the days to come." See Sing glad songs for him (Gounod)

Who is on the Lord's side. Negro spiritual from Georgia. AS

"Who is she who cometh on a morn in May." See Spring

"Who is Sylvia." F. Schubert. Words by W. Shakespeare. MFS—TFG
Who is Silvia. EB—TFB
"Who is Sylvia" ("Was ist Sylvia") e.g. GG

"Who is there, that singest so." See Sir Christmas (Dunstan)

"Who is there that singeth so." See Sir Christmas (15th century carol)

"Who killed Cock Robin." See Cocky Robin (Marion, N.C. version)

"Who killed Cocky Robin." See Cocky Robin (Kentucky version)

"Who killed little Tommy Robin." See Cocky Robin (Burnsville, N.C. version)

"Who killed the golden robin." See Cocky Robin (Micaville, N.C. version)

"Who made ocean, earth and sky." See God, our loving Father

Who makes the gipsy's a life with pleasure laden. See Anvil chorus ("See how the shadows of night are flying") (Verdi)

"Who rides thro' the night." See Erlkönig (Loewe)

"Who rides yonder proud and gay." See The king's highway (Molloy)

"Who rideth so late." See Erlkönig (Schubert)

Who shall we marry. See "Eh! qui marierons-nous"

"Who treads the path of duty." W. A. Mozart. e. LAS

"Who wadna fight for Charlie." See "Wha wadna fecht for Charlie"

Who will o'er the downs. R. L. de Pearsall. TFB—TFG

Who will shoe your pretty little foot. Folk song. SBA
Variants: Fair Annie of Lochyran; The true lover's farewell

"Who would have forethought ever." See "Prova mi dai, lo sento" (Donizetti)

Whoa, Emma. Old song. SW

"The whole bright world rejoices now." See Die ganze welt, Herr Jesu Christ

[Who'll be a witness for my Lord] "My soul is a witness." Negro spiritual. WFN
Witness. JG

"Who'll buy my posies, who'll buy my roses." See London street cries

Who'll jine de Union. Negro spiritual. HRD

"Whom of old the shepherds." See "Quem pastores laudavere"

Whoop jamboree. Capstan chantey. TSB 2
Variant of: Jamboree

Whoopee, ti yi yo, git along, little dogies. Cowboy song. SBA
Git along little dogies. 2d version. LSC
Variants: The dogie song; Git along little dogies (1st version)

Whoop-tee ti yi yo get along, little dogie. See The dogie song

"Who's all dem come dressed in white." See Go, Mary, and toll de bell

"Who's at my window." G. A. Osborne. Words by H. B. Farnie. GE

Who's that calling. J. B. Lawreen (music and words) WSS

Who's that a-calling. TFB—TFG—TFO—TFR

Who's the pretty girl milkin' the cow. See Cailín deás crúidhte na mbó

Whose dat foot a-burning. See Plantation walk around (Emmett)

"Whose horse is that horse." See Our goodman (Big Laurel, N.C. version no. 1)

Why ("Warum sind denn die rosen") See Warum (Tchaikovsky)

"Why are we fond of toil and care." See Freut euch des lebens (Nägeli)

"Why are you sad, papa, my darling." See There'll come a time (Harris)

"Why are you sighing old schoolmate o' mine." See You're an aggie and you're my friend (Williams)

"Why chime the bells so merrily." See The New Year's come (Knight)

Why did they dig ma's grave so deep. J. P. Skelly. Words by G. Cooper. SRW

"Why do summer roses fade." G. Barker. MFS

"Why do the nations so furiously rage together." Händel. SSO 4

"Why does the God of Israel sleep." G. F. Händel. SSO 3

Why don't they play with me. C. K. Harris (music and words) SW

"Why hast thou taught me love's magic story." See Love duet (Leoncavallo)

"Why, he only a kiss." K. Millöcker. e. WLO

Why, He's the Lord of lords. See He's the Lord of lords

"Why live, when life is sad." See Light in darkness (Cowen)

Why! oh why. U.S. Naval academy song. [H. Macarthy] US

"Why should I pine for lack of gold." See Zufriedenheit (Mozart)

"Why should we parted be, Kathleen aroon." See Kathleen aroon (Abt)

"Why, since thy heart in sadness weeps." See "Deh! non voler costringere" (Donizetti)

"Why so silent, tell me, birdie"₁ Paun i kolo (Reigenlied) Bosnian folk song. g.se. ML 2

Why, soldiers, why. See "How stands the glass around"

"Why thus do you try me." See Love's chidings

"Why turn away when I draw near." See Speak to me (Campana)

"Why unhappy, little goatherd." See The little goatherd

"Why weep ye by the tide, ladye." See Jock o' Hazeldean

Whyte, Henry
Fuadach nan gàidheal (Scottish air)
A' mhaighdean àluinn (Old Gaelic air)
Si mo leannan an (Gaelic folk air)

Whyte-Melville, George John
Gipsy John (Clay)
The tarpaulin jacket (Coote)
"Wi' a hundred pipers an' a', an' a'." See The hundred pipers

Wi-de-wi-de-witt dem ziegenbock. See Der schneider jahrstag

Wid a who dar? who dar? who dar. See Stop that knocking at the door (Winnemore)

Wid my rub-a-dub-dub-dub. See Since I've been in the army

Widdecombe fair. Folk song: Devonshire version. DSB

The wide Missouri ("For sev'n long years I courted Nancy") Old cavalry song. DSO

The wide Missouri ("Oh Shenandoah, I long to hear you") See Shenandoah

The wide Mizzoura ("O Shannadore, I love your daughter") Capstan chantey. SBA Variant of: Shenandoah

Widmung ("Du meine seele, du mein herz." —Dedication) R. Schumann. Words by F. Rückert. e.g. GG

Widmung ("O danke nicht für diese lieder."—Dedication) R. Franz. Words by W. Müller. e.g. GG

Dedication. e. TFO

Widor, Charles Marie
"Give me alone every hour." See "Je ne veux pas autre chose"
"Je ne veux pas autre chose"

The widow in the cottage by the sea-side. C. A. White. GOS 2

"Widow machree, 'tis no wonder you frown." S. Lover (music and words) SI

The widow Malone ("Did you hear of the widow Malone") Irish air. Words by C. Lever. SSB

The widow Malone ("Did you ne'er hear of widow Malone") 2d Irish air. Words by C. Lever. SI

The widow Nolan's goat. Old song. SRW

"Wie berührt mich wundersam" ("Wondrous is the power") F. Bendel. e.g. GG

"Wie bin ich, ach, so fremd hier" ("Voi että olen outo") Finnish folk song. fi.g. ML 3

"Wie der glanz der sterne strahlet des adlers blick." See Izar ederra

"Wie der habicht auf die wachtel niederschiesst zum todesstoss." See A maiden's revenge

"Wie der stern in der höh." See "Som stjärnan uppå himmelen så klar"

"Wie erhebt sich das herz." See Dem Unendlichen (Schubert)

"Wie erkenn' ich dein treulieb." See "How should I your true love know"

"Wie gross wird, heiland mein." See Ar baradoz

Wie herrlich strahlt der morgenstern. See Wie schon leuchtet der morgenstern

Wie lieblich sind die boten. For English translation see "How lovely are the messengers" (Mendelssohn)

"Wie melodien zieht es mir" ("Like melting tones it rises") J. Brahms. Words by K. Groth. e.g. TM

"Wie melodien zieht es mir" ("Soft strains of music drifting") e.g. HCA

"Wie scheinen die sternlein so hell, so hell." See Abschied (Franz)

Wie schon leuchtet der morgenstern ("How brightly beams the morning star") 16th century German air. Words by P. Nicolai. e. OB

"How brightly beams the morning star." e. DNS

"How brightly shines the morning star." e. DN

Wie Sigurd seine braut gewann. See Sjugur aa trollbrura

"Wie tat doch roast beef einst dem Engländer gut." See The roast beef of old England (Leveridge)

"Wie vergessen steht eine birk' im walde." See Heimatlos

Wiegand, John
"Do I love thee"

Wiegenlied ("A dormir va la rosa") See Nana (copla de cuna)

Wiegenlied ("A ninna ninna, ccu la ninna ninna") See Ninna-nanna

Wiegenlied ("Bruder, ich und du."—"Brother, thou and I."—German lullaby) e.g. MFS

Wiegenlied ("Dormi, dormi, dormi, Nicola meu") See Ninna di Borgia

Wiegenlied ("Eia popeia, mein englein, schlaf ein."—"Hajej, můj andílku") Czech folk song. bo.g. ML 3

Wiegenlied ("Guten abend") J. Brahms. Words by K. Simrock. g. EDL
Cradle song. e. BB—GSS
Lullaby. e. LAS—TFG—TFR
"Lullaby and good-night." e. DSB
Wiegenlied (Cradle song) e.g. GG

Wiegenleid ("Nelli monti de Cuscioni v'era natu una zitedra") See Nanna

Wiegenlied ("Pecchè non duorme") See Duorme

Wiegenlied ("Que lla Virxen mas galana") See Canción de cuna

Wiegenlied ("Schlaf, armer, schlaf zum letzten mal."—Kolybel'naia) Russian folk song. g.r. ML 1

Wiegenlied ("Schlaf, herzenssöhnchen") C. M. von Weber. Words by F. C. Hiemer. g. EDL

Wiegenlied ("Schlaf, schlaf ein, kindelein, mütterlein wiegt dich ein."—Uspavanka) Serbian folk song. g.se. ML 2

Wiegenlied ("Schlafe, mein prinzchen") <W. A. Mozart; attributed also to B. Flies. Words by F. W. Gotter; wrongly attributed to "M. Brock"> g. **EDL**

Cradle song. e. DSB
Lullaby (Ninna-nanna) e. CSB 4

Wiegenlied ("Schlafe, mein prinzchen."—Lullaby) e.g. AT

:Wiegenlied ("Schlafe, schlafe, holder süsser knabe")₁ Cradle song. F. Schubert. e. DSB
Wiegenlied (Cradle song) e. CSB 1
Slumber song. e. BB

Wiegenlied ("Seoithín, seó") See Suantraidhe

[Wiegenlied ("Suse, lewe Suse")₁ "Susy, little Susy." Old German folk song. e. BB—WG

Wiegenlied ("Susu, eia, eia, susu."—Hällilaul) Estonian folk song. es.g. ML 3

Wiegenlied ("Susu, susu, suleia."—"Liuli, liuli, liuliata."—Kolybel'naia) Ukrainian folk song. g.r. ML 1

Wiegenlied ("Vor dem bett sitzt Ganka."—"Zaliuliálaĭ Ganka") Bulgarian folk song. b.g. ML 2

A **wieglied** ("As ich wolt gehat dem keisers oizres") Yiddish folk song. y. KAJ

Wiesenthal, T. V.
The ingle side

Wife, children, and friends. Old air. Words by W. R. Spencer. SRW

The **wife** of Usher's well. Folk song:
Berea, Ky. version. SES 1
—Oneida, Ky. version. SES 1
—Pineville, Ky. version. SES 1
—Wasioto, Ky. version. SES 1
—Allanstand, N.C. version. SES 1
—Alleghany, N.C. version. SES 1
—Black Mountain, N.C. version. SES 1
—Big Laurel, N.C. version. SES 1
—Burnsville, N.C. version no. 1. SES 1
—Burnsville, N.C. version no. 2. SES 1
—Burnsville, N.C. version no. 3. SES 1
—Carmen, N.C. version. SES 1
—Hot Springs, N.C. version. SES 1
—Bird's Creek, Tenn. version. SES 1
—Flag Pond, Tenn. version. SES 1
—Beechgrove, Va. version. SES 1
—Meadows of Dan, Va. version. SES 1
Lady Gay. Knott or Letcher county version. MK

The **wife** wrapt in wether's skin. Folk song: Kentucky version no. 1, from St Helen's. SES 1
—Kentucky version no. 2, from Lee county. SES 1
—Hindman, Ky. version. SES 1
—Hyden, Ky. version. SES 1
—Virginia version. SES 1

Wiggin, Mrs Kate Douglas (Smith)
Morning prayer

Wild Bill Jones. Folk song from the southern mountains. RA—SW
—North Carolina version. SES 2

The **wild** goose shanty. See Tommy's gone to Hilo

The **wild** rose ("In the wood a boy one day") German folk air.   ₁Words by Goethe.   Tr of Heidenröslein₁ e.   DSB

₁The **wild** rose₁ "Where the wild rose sweetly doth blow" (Wild rose song) J. Strauss.   e.   WLO

Wild rose song.   See The wild rose (Strauss)

"**Wild** roved an Indian girl, bright Alfarata."   See The blue Juniata (Sullivan)

Wilder, James Austin
A sea scout chantey

Wilder, Victor
"Un doux lien" (Delbrück)
"Ich wandle unter blumen" (Lassen)

Der **wildfang.**   See La niña desenvuelta

Wildwave, Willie, pseud.   See Delaney, William W.

Wildwood flowers.   Old song.   GOS 2

Wilhelm, Karl
"Bright college years" (same air as Die wacht am Rhein)
Die wacht am Rhein

Wilkerson, D.
Touchdown song

Wilkins, Harold A.
Hail to old O. S. C.
Rooter's song.   See Hail to old O. S. C.

"**Will** ruhen unter den bäumen hier."   See In der ferne (Brahms)

Will the weaver.   Folk song: Hyden, Ky. version.   SES 2
—St Helen's, Ky. version.   SES 2

Will Watch ₁The smuggler₁   J. Davy. ₁Words by T. Cory₁   BOS 2—WSE

"**Will** ye gang o'er the lea-rig."   See My ain kind dearie, O

"**Will** ye gang to the ewe-bughts, Marion." See The ewe-bughts

"**Will** ye gang to the Hielands, Leezie Lindsay."   See Leezie Lindsay

"**Will** ye gang wi' me, Lizzy Lindsay." See Leezie Lindsay

"**Will** ye go to Flanders, my Mally O." See Mally O

"**Will** ye go to the Indies, my Mary." Air: Ewe-bughts ₁Marion₁   Words by R. Burns.   GS

Will ye no come back again.   See Bonnie Charlie (Gow?)

₁**Will** you be mine₁   Tule mulle, neitsikene ("Komm, du kleine")   Esthonian folk song.   e.es.   ML 3

"**Will** you come into my parlor? said the spider to the fly, 'tis the prettiest, snuggest little parlor that ever you did spy. Not today, thanks, Mister Long-shanks."   See The spider and the fly (McNaught)

"**Will** you come to the bow'r."   Old song. <Words attributed to T. Moore> DSO—GOS 1

"**Will** you come with me."   See Wait for the wagon (Buckley)

Will you love me in December as you do in May.   E. R. Ball.   Words by J. J. Walker.   GFS

₁"**Will** you marry"₁   "Wos-ze willstu." Jewish folk song.   y.   SY

"**Will** you walk into my parlour? said the spider to the fly, 'tis the prettiest little parlour that ever you did spy; you've only got to pop your head just inside of the door."   See The spider and the fly (Words by Hudson)

Will you wear red.   Play-party game from North Carolina.   SES 2

Willard, Mrs Emma (Hart)
"Rocked in the cradle of the deep" (Knight)

William and Nancy.   Folk song: Kentucky version.   SES 2
—North Carolina version.   SES 2

William and Polly.   Folk song: Kentucky version.   SES 2
—North Carolina version.   SES 2
—Virginia version.   SES 2

"**William** courted him a wife."   See As the dew flies over the mulberry tree

William Hall.   Folk song: Barbourville, Ky. version.   SES 2
—St Helen's, Ky. version.   SES 2
—North Carolina version.   SES 2
—Tennessee version.   SES 2
—Montvale, Va. version.   SES 2
—Villamont, Va. version.   SES 2

William Taylor.   Folk song: Beattyville, Ky. version.   SES 1
—Berea, Ky. version.   SES 1
—North Carolina version.   SES 1

Williams, Charles
The moon reappears (Purcell)
Questo é il cielo (Händel)

Williams, Douglass
The hooking cow blues

Williams, Mrs Eva Joor
Alma mater—Tulane university (Rue-bush)

Williams, Harold Parish
Big C

Williams, Isaac
"Lord, in this Thy mercy's day" (Monk)

Williams, Ralph Vaughan
Blake's cradle song.   See "Sweet dreams, form a shade"
Cradle song.   See "Sweet dreams, form a shade"
"From far away"
The golden carol
Rocking hymn.   See "Sweet baby, sleep! what ails my dear"
Snow in the street.   See "From far away"
"Sweet baby, sleep! what ails my dear"
"Sweet dreams, form a shade"
"Take, O take those lips away"
Wither's rocking hymn.   See "Sweet baby, sleep! what ails my dear"

Williams, Raymond George, and Steel, Sanger Bright
Harvardiana

Williams, Richard
Lliw gwyn (Old Welsh air)

Williams, Roy A.
You're an aggie and you're my friend
See also Sweet, Walden, jt. auth.

Williams, Spencer
Bamville croon. See Mississippi delta blues
Banjo blues
Blue mama's suicide wail. See Mountain top blues
Blue man Sam's lament. See Banjo blues
Mama's prison yard blues. See Rock pile blues
Mississippi delta blues
Mountain top blues
Rock pile blues

Williams, Thomas
Largo (Händel)

Williams, W. L.
Kathleen

Williams, William
"Guide me, O Thou great Jehovah" (Hérold)

Willie brew'd a peck o' maut. See "O, Willie brew'd a peck o' maut" (Masterton)

"Willie Meek tho' good at grammar." See Oh Helen (Morgan)

Willie Reilly (see Song Index)
Variant: Loving Reilly

"Willie, take your little drum." See Guillô, pran ton tamborin

Willie, the weeper ("Did you ever hear tell about Willie the weeper") American folk song. SRW
For variants see following songs of same title; also Oh, in the morning

Willie the weeper ("Listen and I'll tell you 'bout Willie the weeper") American folk song. SW

Willie the weeper ("Oh, there was a man call'd Willie the weeper") American folk song. SW

Willie (Willy) the weeper ("Did you ever hear the story 'bout Willy the weeper") American folk song. SBA

Willie, we have missed you. S. C. Foster (music and words) MFS—SW—WSS

"Willie's gane to Melvil Castle." See Melvil Castle (Campbell)

Willing, William
Faded flowers
Twenty years ago

Willis, Richard Storrs
"It came upon the midnight clear"
"Look not upon the wine"

Willkommen, Gwen. See Mentra, Gwen

ɾThe **willow** songɹ O willow, willow. 16th century air. Words by W. Shakespeare. CSB 3
O! willow, willow, willow (Ach, weide, weide, weide) e.g. ML 1
"The poor soul sat sighing by a sycamore tree." EB
Willow, willow. GA

ɾThe **willow** songɹ Willow, willow. B. Carr. Words by W. Shakespeare. MPA 1

Willow, tit-willow, tit-willow. See Tit-willow (Sullivan)

Willow, willow. See The willow song (16th century air); The willow song (Carr)

The **willows** ("The willows are waving their silvery scarves") Dutch air. Words by K. Davis. DSB

"The **willows** are waving their silvery scarves." See The willows

Wills, William Gorman
"I'll sing thee songs of Araby" (Clay)

Willson, James
"I knew by the smoke that so gracefully curled." See The woodpecker
The woodpecker

"**Willst** du dein herz mir schenken" ("Wilt thou to me thy heart give") J. S. Bach. e.g. GA

Willy the weeper. See Willie the weeper

Wilson, Fred
Jockey hat and feather (Brockway)

Wilson, H. Lane
Carmeña (with words "Dance and song make glad the night")
Dance and sing. See Carmeña ("Dance and song make glad the night")

Wilson, John, 1785-1854
Turn ye to me (Scottish air)

Wilson, Lester J.
"Bow down to Washington"

Wilson, Mrs Margaret (Harris)
"What fairy-like music" (Pinna)

Wilson, Steuart
Bell carol (French carol air)
Carol of beauty (French carol air)
Carol of service (Old French air)
Carol of the kingdom (Manx carol air)

ɾ"**Wilt** heden nu treden"ɹ Prayer of thanksgiving. E. Kremser. e. DSC—TFB
Thanksgiving prayer. e. TFG
"Wir treten zum beten." g. EDL

Wilt thou be my dearie, O ("Now nature cleeds the flow'ry lea") See Lassie wi' the lint-white locks

"**Wilt** thou go, my bonnie lassie." See The braes aboon Bonaw

Wilt thou soon return. Finnish song. L. Rocke. e. LAS

"**Wilt** thou to me thy heart give." See "Willst du dein herz mir schenken" (Bach)

The **Wiltshire** wedding. Traditional English song. BOS 2

Winch, A. B.
Here and there

"The **wind** ahead? the wind is free" (Camden) J. B. Calkin. Words by D. A. Wasson. LAS

"The **wind** blows north, the wind blows south." See As the wind blows (Genée)

"**Wind,** gentle evergreen." Round. W. Hayes. DSB

The **wind** in the cherry trees. N. V. Halkin. e. NRF

"The **wind** is awake." H. N. Bartlett. Words by J. V. Cheney. BST

"The **wind** it blew up the railroad track." Old American song. SBA

Windom, W. H.
The fatal wedding (Davis)

"**Winds** of eve are freshly blowing." See The smith (Mascagni)

"**Winds** of God unfailing fill the sunlit sails." See The Spirit

"The **winds** softly sigh in their mystical caves." See Music on the waves (Glover)

"The **winds** that waft my sighs to thee." W. V. Wallace. Words by H. W. Challis. GOS 2

"**Windy** Bill." Cowboy song. LSC

Windy weather! stormy weather. See The fishes

"**Wine,** flow a fountain." See "Fin ch'han dal vino" (Mozart)

Wine of Spain in the Moorish gardens. See Drinking song (Lecocq)

Winge, Per
A maiden's thoughts. See Pigetanker Pigetanker

The **wings** of a dove. See Had I wings like a dove

"**Winkum,** Winkum, shut your eye." Children's song. MFS

Winner, J. E. See Eastburn, R. A.

Winner, Septimus
Composer
The birdies' ball
The mocking bird (same air as Listen to the mocking bird)
"'Twas at the siege of Vicksburg" (same air as Listen to the mocking bird)
Whispering hope
"What is home without a mother"
Composer and author
Ellie Rhee
Listen to the mocking bird
Author
Abraham's daughter (Old air)
See also entry in Song Index under pseud. Street, Apsley, as well as under real name

"A **winning** way, a pleasant smile." See Little Annie Rooney (Nolan)

Winter, Banks
White wings

Winter, Peter von
"O Giove onnipotente" (from Il ratto di Proserpina)
Wretched sinner, what availeth

Winter ("All the winter long") Bohemian air. Words by N. H. Dole. DSB

The **winter** ("'Tis Paul and Silas") Negro spiritual from North Carolina. AS
Variant of: De winter'll soon be ober

"**Winter** ade! scheiden tut weh." See Winters abschied

"**Winter,** goodbye! blue is the sky." German folk air: ⌈Winters abschied⌉ Words by J. Erwin. DSB

"The **winter** it is past." Scottish version. ⌈Old song, with additional words by R. Burns⌉ DSC

"The **winter** now is past; ling'ring summer's here at last." See Summer

A **winter** song ("Music, wild music the winter-time sings us") Hungarian air. Words by J. L. Vandevere. TFO

Winter song ("Summer joys are o'er") Bohemian folk air. Words by L. Hölty. e. GSS

The **winter** storms ("Blow! blow") C. V. Stanford. Words by W. D'Avenant. CSB 5

De **winter'll** soon be ober ("Oh, look up yonder") Negro spiritual. HRD
Variant: The winter ("'Tis Paul and Silas")

Winters abschied. Volksweise. Words by Hoffmann von Fallersleben. g. EDL

Winter's snow. See "See amid the winter's snow" (Morris)

Winther, Christian
Laengsel (Kjerulf)

Winthrop, Frederick A., pseud. See Loomis, Harvey Worthington

"Der **winzersmann** pflanzt ein seine rebe." See Le cycle du vin

"**Wir** beginnen einen lustigen tanz." See "Vi ska' ställa te' en roliger dans"

"**Wir** hatten gebauet ein stattliches haus." Thüringische volksweise. Words by A. von Binzer. g. EDL

"**Wir** treten zum beten." See "Wilt heden nu treden" (Kremser)

"**Wir** winden dir den jungfernkranz." See Brautjungfernlied (Weber)

Wir wollen alle fröhlich sein ("Now glad of heart") M. Praetorius. 14th century words. e. OB

"**Wir** zogen in das feld." See Lied der landsknechte

Wirf dein anliegen auf den Herrn. For English translation see "Cast thy burden upon the Lord" (Mendelssohn)

Der **wirtin** töchterlein. See entry under Der

Wise men flatt'ring may deceive you. Handel. SSO 1

"**Wisst** ihr, wann mein kindchen" (Mikor szép a kis lány) Hungarian folk song. g.hu. ML 3

"**Wisst** ihr wo ich gerne weil." See Lieblingsplätzchen (Mendelssohn)

"**Witan,** du kühner, hei, du mein lieber." See Nachbar Witan

With a ha-rum sca-rum diddle dum da-rum. See The frog and the mouse

With a hey ho! the wind and the rain. See "When that I was a little tiny boy"

With a long, long pull and a strong, strong pull. See The midshipmite (Adams)

"**With** a pick and with a shovel." See Fatigue call

With a row, dow, dow, with a row, dow, dow. See Darby Kelly (Whitaker)

"**With** all her faults I love her still." D. Onivas (D. Savino) Words by M. H. Rosenfeld. OTG—SRW

"**With** all my soul then let us part." See The separation (Engelbrecht)

With ardor true our band. See Song of parting (Abt)

With breezes vying, soft as they sigh. See That Viennese waltz (Straus)

"With broad and firm foundation." See Alma mater—Drake university (Bloom)

"With crimson in triumph flashing." See Harvardiana (Williams and Steel)

"With deep affection and recollection." See The bells of Shandon (Irish air); The bells of Shandon (Daly)

"With eyes so blue and dreaming." See "Mit deinen blauen augen" (Lassen)

With hal-an-tow sing merry, O. See The Cornish May song

With holan-to, sing merry, O. See Furry day carol

"With holy fear and humble song." See Puritan hymn

With how d'ye do, and how d'ye do. See The Wiltshire wedding

"With joy my heart." R. Planquette. [Tr of J'ai fait trois fois le tour du monde] e. WLO

"With love's golden fetters." K. Millöcker. e. WLO

"With merry heart let all rejoice in one." See Congaudeat turba fidelium

With my right fol leatherol. See The twenty-fourth of February

With my rub-a-dub-dub-dub. See Since I've been in the army

"With perfidy inhuman." See "Ah! perfido" (Beethoven)

"With poison my songs are all laden." See "My songs are envenomed and bitter" (Borodin)

"With right foot first and left foot then." See Come let us to the bagpipe's sound (Bach)

With smoke of fire. See Choral

"With sound of pipes." Breton May day song. e. MFF

With the dirt behind their ears. Air: Son of a gambolier. DSO

"With the moon's pale shimmer, little friend Pierrot." See "Au clair de la lune"

"With the throbbing drums, like a chief Montana comes." See The warriors (Smith)

"With thee to drink will be a pleasure." See Chanson du toréador (Bizet)

"With this humble stock in store." See Buy my strawberries (Howard)

"With verdure clad the fields appear." J. Haydn. [Tr of Nun beut die flur das frische grün] e. SSO 1

"With your charms my little dove of heav'nly blue." See La paloma azul

"With youth's white armor flashing." See Cheer for alma mater (Nazarian)

Wither, George
"Sweet baby, sleep! what ails my dear" (Williams)

"The wither'd leaves are flying." See Autumn song

Wither's rocking hymn. See "Sweet baby, sleep! what ails my dear" (Williams)

Within a mile of Edinboro'. J. Hook. Words by T. D'Urfey. GOS 1

Within a mile o' Edinboro. GS

Within a mile of Edinburgh town. SSB

"Within a vale of western mountains." See Alma mater song—Oregon state agricultural college (Maris)

"Within my heart a song I found." See "Ich hab' ein kleines lied erdacht" (Bungert)

"Within my sweetheart's garden." See Aus der rosenzeit (Fielitz)

"Within these sacred bowers." See "In diesen heil'gen hallen" (Mozart)

"Within thy casement bow'r enshrined." See Marie (Jensen)

The **Withy** carol. Old English or Scottish air. DNS

Witness. See Who'll be a witness for my Lord

Witt, Max S.
The moth and the flame

"**Wittenberg**, dear Wittenberg." See Alma mater—Wittenberg college (Hiller)

Witwicki, Stefan
The maiden's wish (Chopin)

Wizard oil. Minstrel song. SBA

Wladímirs tafelrunde. See The feast of Vladímir

"**Wo** a kleins hüttle steht." See Liebesscherz

"**Wo**, ach, wo find' ich ihn, den treugeliebten." See Vineta (Lachner)

"**Wo** bist du denn gewesen, geliebter sohn." See L'avvelenato

"**Wo** das klare wasser fliesset." See Trennung und wiedersehn

Wo gehest du hin ("Lord Christ above") Chorale. J. S. Bach. Words by B. Ringwaldt. e. CSB 2

"**Wo** saves fluten in die Donau münden." See Klage

"**Wo** seid ih ben geblieben? Ladu, Ladu." See Wedding-day song

"**Wo** warst du den ganzen langen tag." See The little wee croodin' doo

"**Wo** warst du denn am tag." See Bonnie laddie, Highland laddie

"**Wo** warst du denn so lange, du Sven im rosenhain." See Sven i rosengård

"**Wo** warst du denn so lange, mein lieb töchterlein." See Den lillas testamente

Woe unto them [who forsake Him] Mendelssohn. [Tr of Weh ihnen, dass sie von mir weichen] e. SSO 2

Wofsy, Samuel A.
Hail! Wichita (Lieurance)

Wohin. For English translation see "I heard a brooklet gushing" (Loder)

"**Wohlan**, die zeit ist kommen, mein pferd." See Husarenliebe

"**Wohlan**, genossen, zieht die last hoch." See Towing song ("Come, fellows, let us pull together")

"**Wohlauf**, die luft geht frisch und rein." See Lied fahrender schüler (Becker)

"**Wohlauf**, kameraden, aufs pferd, aufs pferd." See Reiterlied (Zahn)

"**Wohlauf**, noch getrunken den funkelnden wein." See Wanderlied (Folk air)

Wohlgemuth, junges blut. For English translation see Maid-servants' chorus (Flotow)

Wojewode manusch (Manush Voïvoda) Bulgarian folk song. b.g. ML 2

Woke up this mornin', woke up this mornin'. See Stingaree blues (Kemp)

Wolf, Benjamin J.
Of the rose and you (Kern)

Wolf, Pius Alexander. See Wolff, Pius Alexander

Wolfe's song. See "How stands the glass around"

Wolff, Julius
"Hab' ein röslein dir gebrochen" (Sjögren)

Wolff, Pius Alexander
"Einsam bin ich, nicht alleine" (Weber)

"**Wollt'** durch Lothringen marschieren." See Les trois capitaines

"**Wollt'** ein soldat nach hause gehen." See Desengany

"**Woman** is fickle." See "La donna è mobile" (Verdi)

Wonder tidings. See What tidings bringest thou (Dunstable)

"**Wonder** where is good ole Daniel." Negro spiritual. HRD
"Wonder where is good ole Daniel" (Way over in de promise' land) WFN

The **wonderful** inn. See Poland

"**Wondrous** is the power." See "Wie berührt mich wundersam" (Bendel)

Wondrous works. Traditional carol. OB

Won't you come along. F. Drayton. SW

Won't you come home, Bill Bailey. See Bill Bailey, won't you please come home (Cannon)

Won't you go my way. Pulling chantey. TSB 2

"**Won't** you tell me, Mollie darling." See Mollie darling (Hays)

Wood, C. F.
Somebody's grandpa

Wood, David
"I've brought thee an ivy leaf"

Wood, Hamilton Brooks. See Brown, Clarence Fayette, jt. comp.

Wood, Leo
Turkey in the straw (Old air)

Woo'd and married and a'. Scottish air. ⟨Words by A. Ross; wrongly attributed to J. Baillie⟩ GS

Woodbury, Isaac Baker
Be kind to the loved ones at home
"If I were a voice"
"Speed away! speed away"
"Stars of the summer night"

Woodhull, Alfred Alexander
"Great God of nations" (Bach)

The **woodland** brook. Ukrainian folk air. Words by H. W. Loomis. TFO

"**Woodman**, spare that tree." H. Russell. Words by G. P. Morris. BB— GOS 1—HP—SRW

"**Woodmen**, shepherds come away." See Pan's holiday (Bridge)

ᵣThe **woodpecker**ᵢ "I knew by the smoke that so gracefully curled." J. Willson. Words by T. Moore. MPA 2

The **woods** will still be green ("Gozdič je že zelen") Yugoslav folk song. e.se. CJ

Woodville, H.
"Thro' the silence of the night" (French Noël air)

Woodward, J. A.
Third coast artillery march

Woodworth, Mrs Francelia (Frary)
Field song

Woodworth, Francis Channing
The snowbird (Composer unknown)

Woodworth, Samuel
Blue-eyed Mary (German air)
The hunters of Kentucky (Old air)
The old oaken bucket (Kiallmark)
Patriotic diggers (Composer unknown)

The **wooing** ("I saw her coming through the wood") M. Sieveking. HCA

The **wooing** ("Madam, I've come to marry you") Traditional song. KSO

Woran ich meine freude hab. Volkslied. g. EDL

The **Worcestershire** ᵣChristmasᵢ carol. 18th century air. Words from an 18th century broadsheet. DNS

"A **word**, allow me." See Prologue, from I pagliacci (Leoncavallo)

"The **Word** made Flesh right rev'rently." See Verbum lumen

"**Words** are vain when music's strain says love me, do." See Waltz song (Lehar)

Wordsworth, Christopher
"O Lord of heaven, and earth, and sea" (Dykes)

Wordsworth, William
The daffodils (Finnish air)

Worgan, John
"Christ the Lord is ris'n today, alleluia! Sons of men and angels say"

Work, Henry Clay
Come home, father
Corporal Schnaps
Grafted into the army
Grandfather's clock
Kingdom coming
Marching through Georgia
Wake, Nicodemus
The year of jubilo

"**Work**, for the night is coming." L. Mason. Words by A. L. Coghill. BB—GOS 2

"**Works** my horses in my team." See Liza Anne

The **world** is full of beauty. G. Donizetti. MFS

The **world** is marching on. ᵣAir: Say, brothers, will you meet us, arr by W. Steffeᵢ Author of words unknown. LAS

"The **world** itself is blithe and gay." See Die ganze welt, Herr Jesu Christ

"The world itself keeps Easter day." Composer unknown. <Air: Hosanna in excelsis> Words by J. M. Neale. OB

World-peace. See "Two empires" (Carey?)

The world's desire. Traditional air. Words by G. K. Chesterton. OB

"Worn out shoes I am a-wearing." See Old shoes

Worship ("Hail to Him") C. Gounod. TFO

"Worship in righteousness." See Sacrifice and faith

Worsing, Elith
Dukke Lisse

"Worthy, worthy is the Lamb." See John saw the holy number

"Wos lernt a klein jüngele." Jewish folk song. y. SY

Wos wet sein as Moshiach wet kummen. See What will happen when the Messiah comes

"Wos wet sein vun dem rebben." Jewish folk song. y. SY

"Wos-ze willstu." See "Will you marry"

Wotsalenje a zasowidženje. See Trennung und wiedersehn

["Would God I were the tender apple blossom"] An Irish love song. Londonderry air. Words by K. T. Hinkson. TFP

"Would God that I might be an apple blossom." See "Would God I were the tender apple blossom"

"Would you be a soldier, laddy." Civil war song. DSO

The wounded soldier. R. Taylor. MPA 2

Woyna, Franz von
Hans und Liesel

The wraggle-taggle gypsies, O ("There were three gypsies") English folk song. DSB—TFR

The wraggle taggle gipsies, O ("Three gipsies stood at the castle gate") See The gipsy countess: part 2

"Wrap me up in my tarpaulin jacket." See The tarpaulin jacket (Coote)

"Wreath the bowl." Irish air: Nora kista, or, Noran kista. Words by T. Moore. HMI

Wrestle on, Jacob. Negro spiritual from South Carolina. AS

Wretched and half heart-broken. See Povero Lionello (Flotow)

Wretched sinner, what availeth. P. Winter. e. SSO 3

Wright, R. W.
Red and black

Wrighton, William Thomas
The dearest spot is home
Her bright smile haunts me still

"Write my name when-a you get home." See De angels in heab'n gwineter write my name

"Wszystko z czasem ulatuje." See "Alles mit der zeit vergehet"

"Wuchs ein baum im paradiese." See Die grössten sünden

"Wunderschön prächtige, grosse und mächtige." See Preis der himmelskönigin

"Wunst me 'n' Lem Briggs." See They gotta quit kickin' my dawg aroun' (Perkins)

"Wus farschteisti, philosoph." See Der philosoph

Wybitski, Josef
Polish national song (Ogiński?)

"Wypił Kuba do Jakuba." See "Jacob, drink"

Y

Ya viene a maneciendo. See Mañanitas

The yaller gal that winked at me. Minstrel song. WSS

Yankee Doodle ("Father and I went down to camp") American Colonial song. Words attributed to R. Schuckburgh (wrongly called Schackburgh, Schamburgh, Shackburg, Shamburg, and Shuckburgh) BB—DSO—GOS 1—MBS—MFS—TFP

Yankee Doodle ("O Yankee Doodle went to town") [Old air. Words wrongly attributed to Shamburg] DSC

The Yankee Doodle boy. G. M. Cohan (music and words) DFF

Yankee Doodle Dandy, New ("Come, push about the jorum, boys") Air: Yankee Doodle. DSO

Yankee Doodle is the tune, it comes so nation handy. See Yankee Doodle Dandy, New

Yankee Doodle-oodle ("My name is Yankee Doodle and my home's the U.S.A.") College air <by F. Seaver> Words by R. D. Ware. TFP

The Yankee girls. <American song of the War of 1812. Air: Auld lang syne> DSO

"A Yankee ship came down the river, blow, boys, blow. Her masts and yards they shine like silver." See Blow, boys, blow; Blow, my bully boys

Yard by yard. Williams college song. C. F. Brown and H. B. Wood. Words by C. F. Brown and L. S. Potter. AI—AIS—KU

"Yderst mod norden" (Island) [Old Norse air: Rabna bryllupet i Kraakalund, or, The raven's wedding] Words by A. Munch. g.n. ML 1

"Ye banks and braes, and streams around the castle o' Montgomery." See Highland Mary (Scottish air)

"Ye banks and braes o' bonnie Doon." See Bonnie Doon (Miller)

"Ye cavaliers of Dixie." See The cavaliers of Dixie (Callcott)

"Ye Christian heralds." H. C. Zeuner. Words by B. H. Draper. DSC

"Ye dismal hillsides." See "Funeste piaggie" (Peri)

"Ye gentlemen and ladies fair, who grace this famous city." See The hunters of Kentucky

"Ye Hielands and ye Lowlands." See The bonny Earl o' Moray

"Ye islands of the northern seas." Early 18th century air. DN

"Ye lads and lasses all, arise and speed." See May song (Smith)

Ye maidens, in springtime. See "Ditemi, buona gente, vedeste Dinorah" (Meyerbeer)

"Ye maids of Helston gather dew." See Cornish May song

"Ye parliament of England." Forecastle song. US
Parliament of England. DSO

"Ye people, rend· your hearts" (see Song Index)
Also in "If with all your hearts ye truly seek Me" (Mendelssohn) SSO 3

"Ye sacred priests" (see Song Index)
Also in Farewell, ye limpid springs and floods (Händel) SSO 1

Ye sailors, I'm bound to my love. See Homeward bound (Arne)

"Ye shepherds so drowsy" (Christmas carol) Austrian folk air. CSB 1

"Ye sons of Columbia, who bravely have fought." See Adams and liberty (Smith?)

"Ye sons of Columbia, your attention I crave." See Fuller and Warren

"Ye sons of France, awake to glory." See La Marseillaise (Rouget de Lisle)

"Ye stars in the gloaming." See Im volkston (Hildach)

"Ye wandering breezes." R. Wagner. [Tr of Euch lüften, die mein klagen so traurig oft erfüllt] e. WG

"Ye watchers and ye holy ones." 17th century German air. Words by J. A. L. Riley. DSB—DSC—GSS—TFG

"Ye who love's power right well should know." See "Voi, che sapete" (Mozart)

Yea Alabama. University of Alabama song. E. L. Sykes (music and words) AI—AIS

"Yea, the doughboys up at break of day." See Hike song of 1917

The year of jubilo. H. C. Work. Words by D. Stevens. TFB—TFG

The year that's awa'. [Air: 'Tis good to be aff wi' the old love] Words by J. Dunlop. GS

The yearling. West Point song. DSO

"Years are coming, speed them onward." See Years of peace

"The year's at the spring." 17th century air. Words by R. Browning. GSS

"The years creep slowly by, Lorena." See Lorena (Webster)

"Years have come and pass'd away." See The old musician and his harp (Higgins)

"The year's last hour is sounding." See The last hour of the year (Schulz)

Years of peace. Sicilian mariners' air. BB

Yeats, William Butler
"Down by the sally gardens" (Air: The maids of Mourne shore)

The yellow and blue. South Dakota state college song. F. J. Haynes. Words by N. E. Hansen. HW

The yellow and blue. University of Michigan song. Balfe. Words by C. M. Gayley. AI—KU—LAS

Yellow and green. North Dakota agricultural college song. C. S. Putnam. Words by A. E. Minard. HW

The yellow girl that winked at me. See The yaller gal that winked at me

The yellow-haired laddie ("In April, when primroses paint the sweet plain") Scottish air. Words by A. Ramsay. GS

"The yellow-haired laddie" ("The yellowhaired laddie sat down on yon brae") Scottish air. <Old version of words, wrongly attributed to A. Ramsay> GS

"Yeo, heave ho! yeo, heave ho." See Volga boat song

Yeo, sir. See "I am a brisk and sprightly lad"

Yeoman's carol ("Let Christians all with joyful mirth") OB

Yeoman's wedding song. Poniatowski. e. GE—MFS

Yes and no. Round. J. Haydn. e. CSB 3

Yes, come, the ripe clusters among the thick grass. See Mill May

"Yes, I am grief-worn and fain would rest me." See Home to our mountains (Verdi)

Yes, I hear now honour's calling. See "Dagli immortali vertici" (Verdi)

"Yes, I really do believe." See A long white robe

Yes, I want God's heab'n to be mine. See I want God's heab'n to be mine

"Yes, I'm in love, I feel it now." See The plague of love (Arne)

Yes, I've there been of th' host victorious. See Era anch' io di quella schiera (Donizetti)

"Yes! march, march, march, on down the field." See Denison marching song (Arnold)

"Yes, my lord, I'll tell you soon." See Will the weaver (St Helen's, Ky. version)

"Yes! that castle old by wizard is enchanted." See Legend of the bell (Planquette)

Yes, this hero. See Entrance song (Millöcker)

Yes, upon my finger there's a ring. See This wedding ring of mine

"Yes, we'll fly these walls." G. Verdi. [Tr of Si: fuggian da queste mura] e. WG

"Yes, we'll rally round the flag boys." See The battle cry of freedom (Root)

Yes, yes, my Lord, I'm going to join the heav'nly choir. See "What kind of shoes you going to wear"

Yes! yes! thou art he who knowest. See Thou knowest

Yester, John Hay, lord. See Tweeddale, John Hay, 2d marquis of

[**Yestereve**] "Since we parted." F. Allitsen. Words by Lord Lytton. SFB

"**Yestreen** I met a winsome lass." See Bonnie Bessie Gray (Glover)

"**Y'heave** ho! my lads, the wind blows free." See Sailing (Marks)

Yiboneh hamikdosh. See May the temple be rebuilt

Yillat tanim nugoh. See Beautiful Canaan nights

"**Yismach** chathan." See "'Let the bridegroom rejoice"

"**Yksin** istun ja lauleskelen." See Am strande

Ym Mhont-y-pridd mae 'nghariad ("In yonder cottage dwelling") Old Welsh song. e.w. WO

Ymdawiad y brenin (Des königs abschied) Welsh folk air. Words by Talhaiarn. g.w. ML 1

"**Yn** iach lawenydd" ("Joy forsakes me") Air: Diniweidrwydd. Words by H. Morris. e.w. WO

"**Yn** Mhalas llwyn onn gynt." See Llwyn on

"**Yo** andaba suspirando." See El profeta

"**Yo!** heave ho! yo! heave ho! toil on, toil on, yo! heave ho." See Volga boat song

Yo ho! yo ho! then give me a right good craft and crew. See The skipper (Jude)

"**Yo** no sé si me quieres" ("I know not if you love me") Folk song from southern California or northern Mexico. e.s. HE

"**Yofim** hallelos." See Beautiful Canaan nights

"**Yoh** Washington." University of Washington song. R. Stevenson. HW—KU—KV

"**Yome,** Yome." Jewish folk song. y. SY

"**Yonder** come Roberta." See Midnight special

"**Yonder** comes dat ole Joe Brown." See Walky-talky Jenny

"**Yonder** comes my pretty little girl." Folk song: southern version. SBA Variant of: The gamboling man

"**Yonder** comes sister Mary." Negro spiritual. FSN

"**Yonder** comes the high sheriff." Kentucky convict song. SBA

"**Yonder** stands young couple." Play-party game from Kentucky. SES 2

Yore an ole blind drunkard. See Hurrah, Lie

"**Yore** weevily wheat ain't fit to eat." See Weevily wheat

York! York for my money (York for my money) Air: Greensleeves. Words by W. Elderton. BOS 2

The **Yorkshire** wassail song. See "Here we come a-wassailing"

"**Yoshke,** Yoshke." Jewish folk song. y. SY

Yossel un Zlatte. Jewish folk song. y. SY

"**You** abandon me, woman, because I am very poor." See El abandonado

You and I ("We sat by the river") Claribel (C. Norton) (music and words) GE

You are a blackamoor. See Vous t'é in morico

"**You** are an awful stubborn case." B. Smetana. e. WLO

"**You** are going far away." See Jeannette and Jeannot (Glover)

"**You** ask me why upon my breast." See For old time's sake (Harris)

"**You** ask what place I like the best." See The Kinkaiders

"**You** ask what school we love the best." See Our alma mater

"**You** better min'." Negro spiritual. JG

"**You** call me sweet and tender names." See The day when you'll forget me (Thomas)

"**You** call yourself church-member." See O Daniel

You can talk about your battleships. See Sims's flotilla

"**You** constant lovers give attention while a tale to you I tell." See Rosetta and her gay ploughboy

You couldn't stop a lover. Irish air from County Donegal. HI 1

You don't know the half of it, dearie, blues. See The half of it, dearie, blues (Gershwin)

You fight on. Negro folk song. SBA

"**You** generals all, and champions bold." See The duke of Marlborough

"**You** go and get your father's gold." See Lady Isabel and the elf knight (Harrogate, Ky. version)

"**You** go, I'll go wid you." Negro spiritual. JB 2

You goin' to reap jus' what you sow. Negro spiritual. HRD

"**You** got Jesus, hold Him fas'." See Put John on de islan'

You got to cross it foh yohself. Negro spiritual from Texas. SBA

"**You** got to cross that river Jordan." See You got to cross it foh yohself

"**You** have loved lots of girls." See I wonder who's kissing her now (Howard)

You hear de lambs a-cryin'. See Hear the lambs a-cryin'

You made me what I am today. See The curse of an aching heart (Piantadosi)

"**You** may bury me in de eas'." See I'll hear the trumpet sound

"**You** may talk about good eating." See Good sweet ham

"**You** may talk about your home sweet home." See My Maria

"**You** may talk of the halls of your college." See Campus song (Nairn)

"**You** might well cause an eagle to come down from his nest." See You couldn't stop a lover

You mus' hab dat true religion. Negro spiritual. JB 2

You must be pure and holy. Negro spiritual from Auburn, N.Y. AS

"**You** must know, dear m'amma." See "Voi lo sapete, o mamma" (Mascagni)

"**You** must know that my uncle is a farmer." See Down by the old mill stream

"**You** must wake and call me early." See The May queen (Dempster)

"**You** needn't ride east, you needn't ride west." See Young hunting (Callaway, Va. version)

You never can tell what's in a woman's mind. See Harlem blues (Handy)

You never miss the water. R. Howard. Words by H. Linn. SRW

"**You** old fool, you blind fool." See Our goodman (Big Laurel, N.C. version no. 2)

"**You** parliament of England." See Ye parliament of England

"**You** promised to meet me at Adams's spring." See Poor Omie (Hindman, Ky. version no. 1)

"**You** promised to take me to the seashore." See Lady Isabel and the elf knight (Barbourville, Ky. version)

"**You** remember Ellen." Irish air: Were I a clerk. Words by T. Moore. HMI

"**You** ride dat horse, you call him Macadoni." See Jesus, won't you come by-and-bye

"**You** say you're aimin' for de skies." See Gimme yo' han'

You shall be free. See Mona

"**You** stole my boots." See St Helena soldier

You will be sorry, be sorry from your heart. See Joe Turner blues

You will eat, bye and bye. See The preacher and the slave (Webster)

"**You** your lawsuit have won, sir." See Vedrò, mentr' io sospiro (Mozart)

"**You'd** better be a-praying." See My brethren, don't get weary

You'll get all that's coming to you. H. Von Tilzer. Words by A. B. Sterling. SMG

"**You'll** hear the trumpet sound." See My Lord, what a morning

"**You'll** never miss the water." See Joe Turner blues

"**You'll** rue it, my boy, now mind what I say." See Don't you go, Tommy

You'll think of me. Blues song. H. Q. Clark. HB

Young, father
"The snow lay on the ground"

Young, Andrew
"There is a happy land" (Hindoo air)

Young, Anthony
"Phillis has such charming graces"

Young, Charlotte
"Hearts and homes" (Blockley)

Young, Howard Seth
The Brown cheering song

Young comp'anions. Cowboy song. LSC

The **young** girl goes a-weeping. See Across the Rockies

Young Beichan. Folk song: Beattyville, Ky. version. SES 1
—Hindman, Ky. version. SES 1
—Manchester, Ky. version no. 1. SES 1
—Manchester, Ky. version no. 2. SES 1
—Pine Mountain, Ky. version. SES 1
—Allanstand, N.C. version. SES 1
—Big Laurel, N.C. version no. 1. SES 1
—Big Laurel, N.C. version no. 2. SES 1
—White Rock, N.C. version. SES 1
—Harrogate, Tenn. version. SES 1
—Webb's Creek, Tenn. version. SES 1
—Virginia version. SES 1

Young Edward (see Song Index)
Variant of: Edwin in the lowlands low

"**Young** Edward came to Emily." See Edwin in the lowlands low (Hot Springs, N.C. version)

"**Young** Em'ly w'as a maid so fair." See Edwin in the lowlands low (Georgia version; Berea, Ky. version no. 1)

"**Young** Emily was a pretty fair maid." See Edwin in the lowlands low (Burnsville, N.C. version no. 3)

"**Young** Em'ly was a very nice girl." See Edwin in the lowlands low (Black Mountain, N.C. version)

"**Young** Emma she's a pretty fair maid." See Edwin in the lowlands low (Burnsville, N.C. version no. 1)

Young hunting. Folk song: Georgia version. SES 1
—Beattyville, Ky. version. SES 1
—St Helen's, Ky. version. SES 1
—Alleghany, N.C. version. SES 1
—Burnsville, N.C. version no. 1. SES 1
—Burnsville, N.C. version no. 2. SES 1
—Burnsville, N.C. version no. 3. SES 1
—Carmen, N.C. version no. 1. SES 1
—Carmen, N.C. version no. 2. SES 1
—Hot Springs, N.C. version. SES 1
—Afton, Va. version. SES 1
—Callaway, Va. version. SES 1
—Mount Fair, Va. version. SES 1
—Nellysford, Va. version. SES 1
Variant: Little Scotch-ee

"A **young** Irish lady from London she came." See The brown girl (Burnsville, N.C. version)

"**Young** Jack was a hardy Highlander free." See Jack and Jean

"**Young** Jamie loe'd me weel." See Auld Robin Gray (Old air); Auld Robin Gray (Leeves)

"**Young** Johnie, young Johnie, in the green woods." See Johnie Scot (St Helen's, Ky. version)

"**Young** Johnny's been on sea." See The green bed (Barbourville, Ky. version no. 1)

"Young ladies, beware, take excellent care." Old song. SW
"A young lady sat down in a sad condition." See Sad condition
De young lam's mus' fin' de way. See The ole sheep done know the road
Young Lochinvar. J. Mazzinghi. Words by W. Scott. GS
"A young man walked out one pleasant evening." See George Reilly (Beattyville, Ky. version)
"The young May moon." Air: The dandy O. Words by T. Moore. HMI—SI
"Young men and maids, pray lend attention." See The silver dagger (Kentucky version)
"Young men and maids, pray tell your age." See Locks and bolts (Kentucky version)
"Young Molly, who liv'd at the foot of the hill." See The lass with the delicate air (Arne)
The young oysterman. Air: Son of a gambolier. Words by O. W. Holmes. SRW
"Young Rory O'Moore." See Rory O'More
The young servant man (The two affectionate lovers) Folk song from Sussex. BET
Youpe! youpe! river along. See Youpe! youpe! sur la rivière
Youpe! youpe! sur la rivière (Youpe! youpe! river along) Canadian folk song. e.f. GC
"Your attention I ask for a while." See The yaller gal that winked at me
"Your name, kind sir, I'd like to know." See Jack went a-sailing (Pine Mountain, Ky. version)
Your symbol high we raise. See Flyers' march (Meiler)
"Your weevily wheat ain't fit to eat." See Weevily wheat
You're a grand old flag. G. M. Cohan (music and words) DFF
You're an aggie and you're my friend. Colorado state agricultural college song. R. A. Williams. HW
You're an ole blind drunkard. See Hurrah, Lie
You're here and I'm here. J. D. Kern. Words by H. B. Smith. SMG
"You're in the army now." Bugle-corps march. Traditional words. DSO
"You're looking as fresh as the morn, darling." See Kitty Tyrrell (Glover)
You're not my shepherd boy. See Vous n'êtes pas mon berger
You're not the only pebble on the beach. S. Carter. Words by H. Braisted. SW
"Youth is meant for dancing and for singing." See Come, dance the kolo
"Youth's the season made for joys" (The cotillon) Air: The cotillon. [Words by J. Gay] BOS 2
You've been a friend to me. W. S. Hays (music and words) GOS 2

"You've heard ob dandy niggers." See De dandy broadway swell
"You've heard of Julius Caesar." See Slattery's mounted foot
"You've surely heard o' famous Neil." See Neil Gow's farewell to whisky (Gow)
A yungele fun Poilen. Jewish folk song. y. KAJ

Z

"Z cyłej nutnoscú ja će witam tu." See Marienlied
"Z dymen pożarów, z kurzem krwi bratniej." See Choral
Z jjedom zawdaty Hindrašk. See Der vergiftete knabe
"Z-z-z-z the mosquito is singing, O hark." See The mosquito's serenade (Loomis)
"Za to nócne spańe." See Liebchen, gute nacht
Zahn, Anita
"In sunny May" (German air)
Zahn, Christian Jacob
Reiterlied
"Zalûlâlaï Ganka." See Wiegenlied
Žalostna zaručnica. See Die traurige braut
Zamboanga. U.S. army and navy song. Old Spanish air. US
The monkeys have no tails in Zamboanga. DSO
Z'amours Marianne. See entry under Amours
Zamperelli, Dionigi
"So che godendo vai" (from Catone)
"Zaprïetnï, Velo mome." See "Schlag zurück, Wela mädchen"
Zar Murad und Mara (Tsar' Murad ï Mara) Bulgarian folk song. b.g. ML 2
"Zasial som žitko." See "Korn hab gesät ich"
Zdrava, zdrava nora godïna. See Sylvesterlied
Zdvojenje. See Mournful love
Zebra Dun. Cowboy song. LSC
"'Zekiel saw de wheel." Negro spiritual. JB 2
Variants: "Ezekeil saw de wheel"; "A wheel in a wheel"
"Zek'l weep." Negro spiritual. SBA
"Zelte, posten, werdarufer." See Prinz Eugen (Loewe)
Zelter, Karl Friedrich
Der könig in Thule
Das zerbrochene ringlein. See "In einem kühlen grunde" (Glück)
Zeuner, Heinrich Christoph
"Ye Christian heralds"
Žežulka z lesa vylitla, kuku. See The birds
Zgromadna lubosć. See Liebeseinigung
Zhal'ba za mladost'. See Trauer um die jugend
"Zhïl Svïatoslav." See The legend of Volgá

Zhukovskii, Vasilii Andreevich
The dream (Rubinstein)
Russian national hymn (Lvov)
Zie tut krawiec miescka.   Jewish folk song.   y.   SY
Ziegen-lockruf.   See Gjeite lok
"Ziegenbock, ziege hell."   See Gjeite lok
Ziganov,
The scarlet sarafan (Varlamov)
Zimmerman, Charles A.
Anchor's aweigh
"Zimmer mit altan" ("Oda me tavane") Albanian song.   al.g.   ML 2
"Zion, nun bezwinge den schmerz."   See Lied des ungarischen galeerensträflings
Zion, weep a-low.   Negro spiritual. HRD
Zip Coon ("I went down to Sandy Hook") See Turkey in the straw
Zip Coon ("Oh, ole Zip Coon he is a larned skolar")   Old American air.   SRW
Variants: Old Zip Coon; Turkey in the straw
"Zirmu gallim."   See "Roll on ye waves"
"Zivchu, zivche tsedek."   See Sacrifice and faith
"Zlatni tsuraki na keliavi ushi."   See Sylvesterlied
Złe żorty.   See Der schlimme scherz
"Zöld vetés közt énekel a pacsirta."   See "'Mid the cornfields sings the sweet lark" (Simonffy)
Zolotarev, Vassilii Andreevich
The gipsy.   See The magpie and the little gypsy dancer
The magpie and the little gypsy dancer
Zoob, David
Fight on, Pennsylvania
"Let's cheer again for Temple"
Zu Bethlehem geboren.   For English paraphrase see Eia, Eia
"Zu dem duft, der da würzt die lenzesluft." See Veilchen (Cornelius)
"Zu Johann sprach die alte mutter."   See Mutterfluch
"Zu kennt ihr denn dos land."   Jewish folk song.   y.   SY
"Zu Koblenz auf der brücken."   See Wassersnot (Volksweise)
"Zu Lauterbach."   Süddeutsches volkslied. g.   EDL
"Zu Mantua in banden der treue Hofer war."   See Andreas Hofer

"Zu Strassburg auf der schanz, da ging mein trauern an.   Da wollt ich den Franzosen desertiern."   See Der überläufer
"Zu Strassburg auf der schanz, da ging mein trauren an: das Alphorn hört ich drüben wohl anstimmen."   See Der Schweizer (Silcher)
Zuccalmaglio, Wilhelm von
Der jäger und die nixe (Volksweise)
Mondschein (Volksweise)
Schwesterlein, wann gehn wir nach haus (Volksweise)
[Zufriedenheit ("Was frag ich viel nach geld und gut")]   Contentment.   W. A. Mozart.   [Words by J. M. Miller] e.   DSB
"Zum feigenwald figueiredo."   See Canção do figueiral
"Zum Hänschen sprach das Gretchen." See Der schwur (Bohm)
"Zum rebben well ich fohren."   Jewish folk song.   y.   SY
Zundel, John
Beecher.   See "Light of ages and of nations"; "They who tread the path of labor"
"Light of ages and of nations" (same air as "Love divine, all love excelling")
"They who tread the path of labor" (same air as "Love divine, all love excelling")
Zur ruh, mein wahn.   See "Sleep, O sleep, fond fancy" (Morley)
"Zur sommerzeit, wenn blumen blühn." See "In summer time when flow'rs do spring"
"Zvira voda iz kamena."   See "Aus dem felsen"
"Zvonili zvony v Novgorodie."   See The bells of Novgorod
"Zwei kleine boote fahren im meere" ("Diw' laiwiņas peld pa juhru")   Lettish folk song.   g.le.   ML 3
Zwei königskinder.   Folk song.   g. EDL
"Zwei töchter hatte Marschall Stig."   See Marsk Stigs døttre
Zwiegespräch (Čekat ću ga)   Croatian folk song.   g.se.   ML 2
"Zwischen dem ochs und esulein."   See "Entre le boeuf et l'âne gris"
"Zwischen Frankreich und dem Böhmerland."   See Nur in Deutschland (Lyra)
Zwölf söhne.   See Tölf synir